S90

DICTIONARY OF CANADIAN BIOGRAPHY

DICTIONARY OF CANADIAN BIOGRAPHY

DICTIONNAIRE BIOGRAPHIQUE DU CANADA

GENERAL EDITORS

GEORGE W. BROWN
1959–1963

DAVID M. HAYNE
1965–1969

FRANCESS G. HALPENNY
1969–

DIRECTEURS GÉNÉRAUX ADJOINTS

MARCEL TRUDEL
1961–1965

ANDRÉ VACHON
1965–1971

JEAN HAMELIN
1973–

UNIVERSITY OF TORONTO PRESS

LES PRESSES DE L'UNIVERSITÉ LAVAL

DICTIONARY
OF CANADIAN
BIOGRAPHY

VOLUME IX

1861 TO 1870

UNIVERSITY OF TORONTO PRESS
Toronto and Buffalo

STAFF OF THE DICTIONARY

TORONTO

MARY McD. MAUDE executive editor

HENRI PILON supervisory editor

DIANE M. BARKER, CRAIG HERON, ALAN STILLAR manuscript editors

PHYLLIS CREIGHTON translations editor

QUEBEC

GASTON TISDEL directeur des recherches

HUGUETTE FILTEAU adjoint au directeur des recherches

MARCEL BELLAVANCE, GÉRARD GOYER chargés de recherche

JEAN-PIERRE ASSELIN assistant à l'édition

TRANSLATOR J. S. WOOD

© University of Toronto Press and
Les Presses de l'université Laval, 1976
Printed in Canada

Library of Congress Catalog Card Number: 66-31909

Dictionary of Canadian biography. v. 1–
1000–1700 –

Toronto, University of Toronto Press 1966–
/ v. 26 cm.
1. Canada – Biog.
F1005.D49   920.07103   66-31909
ISBN 0-8020-3319-9 (Regular edition)
ISBN 0-8020-3320-2 (Laurentian edition)
ISSN 0070-4717

CONTENTS

INTRODUCTION

VOLUME IX is the fifth volume of the *Dictionary of Canadian Biography/Dictionnaire biographique du Canada* to be published. The programme of publication began in 1966 with volume I, devoted to persons of Canadian interest who died between the years 1000 and 1700. The years 1701–40 were examined in volume II (published in 1969) and 1741–70 in volume III (published in 1974). The last 30 years of the 18th century are the subject of volume IV, to be published in 1978. From 1967 the DCB/DBC has also been preparing volumes for the 19th century, beginning with volume X, death dates 1871–80, published in 1972. Working on both the 18th and 19th centuries results in publication dates not determined by the numerical or chronological sequence of volumes; the historical and practical reasons for the continuing and simultaneous attention to the 19th century are fully explained in the introduction to volume X. We should like to note here in addition that our present concern for the 19th century – the decision to follow volume X with volume IX, death dates 1861–70, being an example – is to gain the value of concentration by preparing volumes which relate most closely to those already completed and published. Thus our current programme has us working next on volume XI (1881–90) and on volumes V, VI, VII, VIII (1801–60). Our contributors and our editorial staff benefit from this schedule which allows an overview from several perspectives of some 100 years of Canadian history and concentrated study of the interrelations of persons living within this period. Our readers will, we hope, share this benefit as we gradually complete volumes for the 19th century. They should of course take note of the date of publication for each volume in order to appreciate the historical resources available to the contributors when they were writing for it.

Like volume X, volume IX has death dates covering a decade. The short scope of the volume reflects the size and spread of population; all areas of present-day Canada appear in it. Thus readers will be aware of the flourishing activities in timber, shipbuilding, and trade giving vigour and prosperity to the Maritimes, as well as of the area's lively concern with religion, education, and politics. They will follow the eventful years in which Lower and Upper Canada expanded settlement, built up trade and merchandising, acquired new modes of transportation, took cultural initiatives in education, religion, and literature, and at the same time were absorbed with developments towards responsible government, complicated and often embittered by conflicts, leading in 1837, 1838, and 1849 to civil strife, and with the debates preceding and following the union of 1841 and confederation in 1867. In the west the empire of the Hudson's Bay Company is the dominant force across the prairies and over the fur trade routes of the mountains, but the future which will bring many changes is already evident in the push of explorers north and west and the development of settlement at Red River and on the Pacific coast.

Volume IX does not contain any introductory essay after the style of volumes I, II, and III. For the 19th century it has been decided regretfully, after full discussion, that circumstances do not make such essays any longer possible. The early volumes of the DCB/DBC, covering longer periods of time and a relatively circumscribed space, offered suitable occasions for provision of general background or analysis of social organization. With the shorter time span and the sea-to-sea setting for 19th century volumes, it becomes impossible to mark out a general background or to isolate themes for a particular volume. An effort of synthesis for the 19th century as a whole will, we hope, be the eventual result of the work of our many contributors, but it must come when that work is done. At present the DCB/DBC's task is clear: to complete the volumes up to 1900 – including biographies, bibliographies, and indexes – with all deliberate speed.

The 311 contributors to volume IX, writing in either English or French, have provided 524 biographies ranging in length from 400 to 12,000 words. They were invited to contribute because of their special knowledge of the period of the volume and the persons who figured in it, and all have been asked to write in accordance with the DCB/DBC's *Directives to Contributors*. It sets out a general aim for articles:

> Each biography should be an informative and stimulating treatment of its subject, presented in readable form. All factual information should be precise and accurate, and be based upon reliable (preferably primary) sources. Biographies should not, however, be mere catalogues of dates and events, or compilations of previous studies of the same subject. The biographer should try to give the reader an orderly account of the personality and achievements of the subject, *against the background of the period in which the person lived and the events in which he or she participated.*

As always, the biographies of certain figures can be used as an indication of the times and places and themes of the volume. We may mention, for instance, a group of religious figures significant in the life of the several future provinces, Baillargeon, Robert Burns, Casault, Cockran, Cooke, Fulford, Mountain, Mullock, Strachan, and Turgeon, and contrast with them the homely figure of David Willson. Educators include Leitch, Lillie, Machar, Porter, and Robb. There is the first Canadian novelist in English, Julia Beckwith, but also two of our most important writers, F.-X. Garneau and T. C. Haliburton; a significant painter, Théophile Hamel, has his biography near that of a pioneer scientist, Abraham Gesner. Represented are family names well known to history – Baby, Boulton, Dorion, Jarvis, Ridout, Salaberry, Strickland, Taschereau, Uniacke. There are also a large number of entrepreneurs great and small, with many names familiar still in the 20th century: Cunard, Dow, Forsyth, Merritt, Moffatt, Molson, Price, Redpath, Sparks, Yeo. There are soldiers such as James FitzGibbon, Gore, Suzor, and Wetherall, and governors serving terms of office in British North America: Bannerman, Colborne, Colebrooke, Sir Howard Douglas, Elgin, Head, Huntley, Seymour. Politicians and public figures noteworthy in the events of the mid century display a wide range of opinion and activity: Baillie, Blake, Daly, J.-B.-É. Dorion, Duncombe, Gourlay, La Fontaine, McGee, Mackenzie, MacNab, Dominique Mondelet, Morin, Wolfred Nelson, Robinson, Rolph, Taché, D.-B. Viger, Wakefield, Whelan. Explorers appear for all parts of the country: Cormack, Finlayson, Franchère, Fraser, Richardson, Ross. A variety of men are significant in different ways in the lands dominated by the fur trade: Ellice, Hargrave of York Factory, Larocque, Mactavish, Riel père, Thomas Scott, Work. Among the women are a legendary heroine, Laura Secord; a pioneer of settlement, Susan Sibbald; and the Ojibwa spokeswoman, Nahnebahwequay (Catherine Sutton). The Indian figures range from Copway to Klatsassin, Assiginack and his son, Maskepetoon, and Peguis, representing the uneasy associations with the expanding white society. There is a place for the eccentric and the unusual: Barry, George Hunter Cary, McAskill, Montferrand, O'Beirne (Mr O'B), John Scott, Vattemare.

The DCB/DBC has over time maintained the principles and standards of operation and selection set out in the preliminary pages of its first volumes, but has, as might be expected, made certain minor procedural adjustments. We remain conscious of the generosity that has made steady continuation of our work possible: the bequest of James Nicholson, the participation of the Université Laval through the DBC, the assistance of the Centennial Commission (which supported our early years of research in the 19th century), and the grants of the Canada Council which in 1973 increased its assistance in order that the project might be carried forward in the future in the same spirit and manner but more quickly. The members of the DCB/DBC staff, who work in close association with the contributors, are listed on page iv. It is fitting that their care and concern in fulfilling their responsibilities for overseeing the contents of the volume and in leading the complex text through all stages of editorial preparation be acknowledged.

FRANCESS G. HALPENNY

JEAN HAMELIN

ACKNOWLEDGEMENTS

THE *Dictionary of Canadian Biography/Dictionnaire biographique du Canada* receives assistance, advice, and encouragement from many institutions and individuals. They cannot all be named nor can their kindness and support be adequately acknowledged.

The DCB/DBC, which owes its founding to the generosity of the late James Nicholson, has been sustained over the years by its parent institutions, the University of Toronto and the University of Toronto Press and the Université Laval and Les Presses de l'université Laval. Since 1973 the Canada Council has provided generous grants to the two university presses which have made possible the continuation and acceleration of the *Dictionary*'s publication programme.

Of the numerous individuals who assisted in the preparation of volume IX, we owe particular thanks to our contributors who made this work truly a community effort. We also have had the benefit of special consultation with a number of persons, some of them also contributors. We should like to thank: Pinhas Abrisor, F. H. Armstrong, Louis-Philippe Audet, Zilda Barker, J. Murray Beck, Phyllis R. Blakeley, Aurélien Boivin, J. M. S. Careless, Joseph P. Cossette, G. M. Craig, Michael Cross, David J. Davis, Nicholas De Jong, Andrée Désilets, C. Bruce Fergusson, Edith Firth, Jean Fleury, Micheline Fortin, G. S. French, Armand Gagné, Serge Gagnon, Ruth Gariépy-Smale, André Garon, John P. Greene, Frances Gundry, Marcel Hamelin, Clive Holland, J. K. Johnson, Frederick Jones, Kenneth Landry, Marc La Terreur, George MacBeath, Donald C. Mackay, Charles MacKinnon, Monique Mailloux, T. R. Millman, John Moir, Jacques Monet, Agnes O'Dea, Margaret A. Ormsby, Fernand Ouellet, Graeme Patterson, Honorius Provost, K. G. Pryke, Richard Ramsay, J. E. Rea, R. C. B. Risk, Ian Ross Robertson, Monica Robertson, Yves Roby, William R. Sampson, Pierre Savard, Elinor Senior, Denis Simard, Shirlee Smith, John W. Spurr, C. P. Stacey, G. M. Story, Norah Story, David Sutherland, Donald Swainson, Philippe Sylvain, Gerald Tulchinsky, Nive Voisine, Carl M. Wallace, Alan Wilson, and S. F. Wise. We should also like to mention the assistance of the late Jean Boone and M. L. Magill.

Throughout the preparation of volume IX we have enjoyed willing cooperation from libraries and archives in Canada and elsewhere. We are particularly grateful to the administrators and staffs of those institutions to which we have most frequently appealed: in Ottawa, the Public Archives of Canada; in Toronto, the University of Toronto Library, the Metropolitan Toronto Central Library, the United Church Archives, and the Archives of Ontario; in Quebec, the Archives nationales du

Québec, the Bibliothèque générale de l'université Laval, the Bibliothèque and Archives du séminaire de Québec, the Bibliothèque de l'Assemblée nationale, and the Archives de l'archidiocèse de Québec; in Montreal, the Archives nationales du Québec, and the McCord Museum. In addition, essential help was given by the Provincial Archives of Newfoundland and Labrador, the Public Archives of Nova Scotia, the Public Archives of Prince Edward Island, the New Brunswick Museum, the Provincial Archives of New Brunswick, the University of New Brunswick Library, Queen's University Archives, the Hamilton Public Library, the Provincial Archives of Manitoba, the Hudson's Bay Company Archives, and the Provincial Archives of British Columbia. We should like also to thank the staff of the *archives départementales* of France and of the Archives judiciaires du Québec, who answered our numerous requests for information so kindly.

The editors of volume IX were also assisted in the preparation of the volume by colleagues in both offices. In Toronto, editorial and research assistance has been given by Mary P. Bentley, Robert J. Burns, Jane E. Graham, Christopher F. Headon, Joan Mitchell, and Stuart Sutherland; Paula Reynolds, the administrative assistant, was in charge of secretarial services and was assisted by Sharon Barker, Susan Dick, Deborah Marshall, and Anita Noel. Robert Brown, Ruth Kazdan, and Deborah Marshall assisted in the reading of the proofs of the volume. In Quebec, Michel Paquin was a constant help in the final stages of the volume; Pierrette Desrosiers was in charge of the secretariat, assisted by Danielle Bourassa and Monique Baron; Lucie Bouffard, Frances Caissie, Marika Cancelier, Pierrette Desnoyers, Marcelle Duquet, Bertrand Juneau, Gérald Kamp, Johane La Rochelle, Richard Ouellet, Thérèse Pelletier-Lemay, and Jean Provencher provided assistance to the editors at one stage or other of the volume. Translation into French of biographies written in English was done with the collaboration of Jacques Poulin and of Ethel C. de Léry, Marie-Claire Lemaire, Marie-Agnès Séchet, Louis Tardivel, André Vachon, and Claire Wells.

We should also like to recognize the guidance and encouragement we have received from the two presses with which the DCB/DBC is associated, and in particular Marsh Jeanneret, Harald Bohne, H. Van Ierssel, and John Ecclestone at University of Toronto Press; Claude Frémont, J.-Arthur Bédard, and Jacques Boivin at Les Presses de l'université Laval.

DICTIONNAIRE BIOGRAPHIQUE DU CANADA   DICTIONARY OF CANADIAN BIOGRAPHY

Editorial Notes

PROPER NAMES

Persons have been entered under family name rather than title, pseudonym, popular name, nickname, or name in religion. Where possible the form of the surname is based on the signature. Commonly used variant spellings are included in parentheses. Occasionally, research for a volume has suggested a change in spelling in a family name from that used in volumes previously published: for example, Thomas BOUTILLIER was given in volume X as Bouthillier. In the case of French names, "La," "Le," "Du," and "Des" (but not "de") are considered as part of the name and are capitalized. When both parts of the name are capitalized in the signature, French style treats the family name as two words, e.g. Louis-Hippolyte LA FONTAINE. Some compound French names occur in this period: Léonard GODEFROY de Tonnancour; cross-reference is made in the text from the compound to the main entry, under the family name: from Tonnancour to Godefroy.

Married women and *religieuses* have been entered under their maiden names, with cross-references from their married names or names in religion: Julia Catherine BECKWITH (Hart); Rosanna MCCANN, named Mary Basilia.

Indian names have presented a particular problem, since an Indian might be known by his Indian name (spelled in a variety of ways by those unfamiliar with Indian languages), by a French or English nickname, and often by a French or English baptismal name. Because it is impossible to establish an original spelling for an Indian name the form chosen is the one found in standard sources or the one linguists now regard as correct. An effort has been made to include major variants of the original name, as well as nicknames, with appropriate cross-references: e.g. KAHGEGAGAHBOWH (Kahkakakahbowh, Kakikekapo) (known as George Copway).

CROSS-REFERENCES WITHIN VOLUME IX

The first time the name of a person who has a biography in volume IX appears in another biography, his or her family name is printed in capitals and level small capitals: e.g. Augustin-Norbert MORIN; Lord Elgin [BRUCE].

CROSS-REFERENCES TO OTHER VOLUMES

An asterisk following a name indicates either that the person has a biography in a volume already published – James William Johnston*; Louis-Joseph Papineau*– or that he will probably receive a biography in a volume to be published: Robert Baldwin*; Pierre-Joseph-Olivier Chauveau*. Birth and death (or *floruit*) dates for such persons are given in the index as an indication of the volume in which the biography will be found.

PLACE-NAMES

Place-names are generally given in the form used by contemporaries at the time of reference, with the modern name included in parenthesis. The modern name is based whenever possible on the gazetteers of Canada issued by the Canadian Board of Geographical Names, Ottawa, and on the *Répertoire géographique du Québec*, published by the Ministère des Terres et Forêts du Québec, Québec, 1969. European place-names are identified by county or department if not found in *The Canadian Oxford desk atlas of the world* (3rd ed., Toronto, 1972) and the *Atlas Larousse canadien* (Québec, Montréal, 1971).

Many sources have been found useful as guides in establishing 19th century place-names: G. P. V. and H. B. Akrigg, *1001 British Columbia place names* (2nd ed., Vancouver, 1970); *Lovell's gazetteer of British North America . . .* , ed. P. A. Crossby (Montreal, 1881); Hormidas Magnan, *Dictionnaire historique et géographique des paroisses, missions et municipalités de la province de Québec* (Arthabaska, Qué., 1925); *Manitoba historical atlas . . .* , ed. John Warkentin and R. I. Ruggles (HSSM pub., Winnipeg, 1970); *Municipalités et paroisses dans la province du Québec*, C.-E. Deschamps, compil. (Québec, 1896); *Place names of N.S.*; W. H. Smith, *Smith's Canadian gazetteer comprising statistical and general information respecting all parts of the upper province, or Canada West . . .* (Toronto, 1846; repr. Toronto, 1970); Walbran, *B.C. coast names*.

In the period of the union, from 10 Feb. 1841 to 1 July 1867, the former provinces of Lower and Upper Canada are generally referred to in English as Canada East and West, respectively.

QUOTATIONS

Quotations have been translated when the language of the original passage is different from that of the text of the biography. All passages quoted from government documents and works published in both languages are given in the accepted translations of these works. The wording, spelling, and punctuation in quotations are not altered unless necessary for meaning, in which case the changes are made within square brackets. A name appearing within square brackets has been added or substituted for the original in order to provide a cross-reference to a biography within the volume or in another volume.

BIBLIOGRAPHIES

Each biography is followed by a bibliography. Sources frequently used by authors and editors are cited in shortened form in individual bibliographies, and the general bibliography (pp. 861–903) gives these sources in full. Many abbreviations are used in the individual bibliographies, especially for archival sources; a list of these can be found on p. 2.

The individual bibliographies are generally arranged alphabetically according to the five sections of the general bibliography – manuscript sources, primary printed sources (including a section on contemporary newspapers), reference works, studies, and journals. Wherever possible, references to manuscript material give the location of the original documents rather than copies. In general the items in individual bibliographies are the sources as listed by the contributors, but these items have been supplemented by bibliographical research by the DCB/DBC staff. Any special bibliographical comments by contributors appear within square brackets.

BIOGRAPHIES

List of Abbreviations

AAQ	Archives de l'archidiocèse de Québec
ACAM	Archives de la chancellerie de l'archevêché de Montréal
ACFAS	Association canadienne-française pour l'avancement des sciences
ADB	*Australian Dictionary of Biography*
AHO	Archives historiques oblates
AJM	Archives judiciaires de Montréal
AJQ	Archives judiciaires de Québec
AJTR	Archives judiciaires de Trois-Rivières
ANQ	Archives nationales du Québec
ANQ-M	Archives nationales du Québec, dépôt de Montréal
ANQ-Q	Archives nationales du Québec, dépôt de Québec
ANQ-TR	Archives nationales du Québec, dépôt de Trois-Rivières
ASJCF	Archives de la Compagnie de Jésus, province du Canada français
ASQ	Archives du séminaire de Québec
ASSH	Archives du séminaire de Saint-Hyacinthe
ASSM	Archives du séminaire de Saint-Sulpice, Montréal
ASTR	Archives du séminaire de Trois-Rivières
AVM	Archives de la ville de Montréal
AVQ	Archives de la ville de Québec
BCHQ	*British Columbia Historical Quarterly*
BCHS	Brome County Historical Society
BNQ	Bibliothèque nationale du Québec
BRH	*Bulletin des recherches historiques*
BUM	Bibliothèques de l'université de Montréal
CCHA	Canadian Catholic Historical Association
CHA	Canadian Historical Association
CHR	*Canadian Historical Review*
CMS	Church Missionary Society
CPC	*Canadian parliamentary companion*
DAB	*Dictionary of American Biography*

DCB	*Dictionary of Canadian Biography*
DNB	*Dictionary of National Biography*
HBC	Hudson's Bay Company
HBRS	*Hudson's Bay Record Society*
HPL	Hamilton Public Library
HSSM	Historical and Scientific Society of Manitoba
IBC	Inventaire des biens culturels
JIP	*Journal de l'Instruction publique*
MTCL	Metropolitan Toronto Central Library
NWC	North West Company
OH	*Ontario History*
PABC	Provincial Archives of British Columbia
PAC	Public Archives of Canada
PAM	Provincial Archives of Manitoba
PANB	Provincial Archives of New Brunswick
PANL	Provincial Archives of Newfoundland and Labrador
PANS	Public Archives of Nova Scotia
PAO	Archives of Ontario
PAPEI	Public Archives of Prince Edward Island
PRO	Public Record Office
QDA	Quebec Diocesan Archives
QUA	Queen's University Archives
RHAF	*Revue d'histoire de l'Amérique française*
RSC	Royal Society of Canada
SCHÉC	Société canadienne d'histoire de l'Église catholique
SGCF	Société généalogique canadienne-française
UCA	United Church Archives
UNBL	University of New Brunswick Library
USPG	United Society for the Propagation of the Gospel
UTL-TF	University of Toronto, Thomas Fisher Rare Book Library
UWO	University of Western Ontario Library

BIOGRAPHIES

A

ABBOTT, JOSEPH, Church of England clergyman, educator, and author; baptized 10 June 1790 at Little Strickland, Westmorland, England, son of Joseph and Isabella Abbott; d. 10 Jan. 1862 in Montreal.

Born into an old Yorkshire family of modest means, Joseph Abbott first attended Bampton School, Bampton, Westmorland, and from 1808 to 1812 Marischal College, Aberdeen, Scotland, a college designed largely for sons of the upper classes. After graduation with an MA, he received ordination into the Church of England and accepted a curacy in Long Stratton, Norfolk, a populous parish where he immediately assumed large responsibilities. Although "not without a fair and reasonable prospect of preferment at home," Abbott, adventurous and ambitious with a romantic interest in North America, sought missionary employment with the Society for the Propagation of the Gospel. In 1818, at the age of 28, he left Britain with his younger brother William to take up a post at St Andrews (Saint-André-Est), Argenteuil seigneury, Lower Canada.

Abbott, unlike his latitudinarian predecessor, the Reverend Richard Bradford, was a high churchman who disdained dissenters, their camp meetings, and itinerant evangelists. A determined, energetic, and intelligent man with a flair for management, he began at once organizing the Anglican community, creating a parish structure, building churches, schools, a parsonage and glebe. He opened Anglican missions at Lachute, Hawkesbury, and Gore Township and provided Protestant service to the British troops at Grenville Settlement, thus augmenting his modest annual stipend of £200 from the SPG. In June 1822 Bishop Jacob Mountain* erected the parish of St Andrews and appointed Joseph Abbott its first rector. Three years later strife, poor health, and the desire "to break up fallow ground" persuaded him to exchange churches with his brother William, and he moved to the recently created Anglican mission near Yamaska Mountain, later named Abbottsford in the brothers' memory. In 1830 he returned to Argenteuil

County to take charge of a new Anglican mission at Grenville. Although he remained there until his retirement on pension from the SPG in 1847 he had in effect ceased to serve the congregation by 1845. In Grenville Abbott had built, at his own expense, the church and the parsonage, which he sold in 1848 to the SPG and the Society for the Propagation of Christian Knowledge. He also organized the Ottawa District Association of the Quebec Church Society, becoming its first chairman in 1844.

At Grenville, Abbott became absorbed in the Royal Institution for the Advancement of Learning's attempts to create a network of parish schools throughout Lower Canada, an interest he had acquired while at St Andrews. He was commissioner for Argenteuil County and visitor to the schools at Chatham, Côte Saint-Charles, Rigaud, Gore, Grenville, and New Scotland, endeavours which required extensive travelling, time, and attention. He and his brother became "the real backbone" of the institution's educational work in these communities.

Joseph Abbott also took a lively interest in the Royal Institution's attempt to establish McGill University. He attended the first meeting of the university's board of governors in 1829, and later accepted a wide range of duties: registrar and bursar (1843–52), librarian (1845–52), chaplain and vice-principal (1845–46), lecturer in history and geography (1846–52), and acting secretary to the board of governors (1843–52), all for an annual sum of £100. His administrative duties, however, were largely a sinecure which he owed to his friendship with the acting principal, John Bethune*, and for which he employed a deputy, his eldest son, John Joseph Caldwell Abbott*. A visitor's report for 1844 criticized their bookkeeping as irregular and incorrect. Abbott, closely associated with Bethune's policy of turning the college into an Anglican institution, lost much of his influence with Bethune's dismissal in 1846.

Abbott also achieved a modest literary reputation in Canada and Britain. His two major works, *Memoranda of a settler in Lower Canada; or, the emigrant in North America* and *Philip Musgrave*, won immediate acclaim. *The emigrant*, first published as a series of articles in January 1842 by the *Quebec Mercury*, went through three editions in Canada and one in Britain, and was used by the Canadian government as promotional literature in Great Britain. Announced as a practical, judicious compendium for prospective agricultural immigrants to Canada, based on 20 years' experience, this brochure offered a more subtle moral message, the superiority of Canada to the United States, by contrasting the morality, orderliness, and institutional amenities of church and state in Canada with the demoralized, riotous life of the American frontier, "the grave of Europeans." Abbott continued this theme in *Philip Musgrave*, a scarcely fictional account of an Anglican missionary's life drawn from his daily journal, comparing "true" religion's prosperity in a monarchical system to its fate in the "neighbouring republic." First printed in 1846 by a British publisher, it went through at least one other edition and like its predecessor was used to attract English immigrants to Canada. A third major work, "The halls of the north," a 400-page manuscript, was reputedly lost in transmission to the publisher. In 1828 the Society for the Encouragement of Arts and Science in Canada, founded the previous year, had awarded him a silver medal for an essay, "A brief view of the advantages and defects of the present system of agriculture in Canada, and the means of improving it in all its departments." He also contributed numerous short stories, based on Scottish border adventures, to the *Literary Garland*, under the pseudonym, "A Monk of G[renville] Abbey" (the title of his country house).

Joseph Abbott married Harriet, the daughter of the Reverend Richard Bradford, on 10 Aug. 1820. They had seven children, of whom the eldest, John Joseph Caldwell, became prime minister of Canada and the fifth, Henry Braithwaite, a distinguished engineer.

The career of Joseph Abbott, an intelligent, talented, articulate Tory and a dedicated, energetic missionary of Anglicanism, convinced of the need to buttress throne and altar in a colonial society, suggests the nature of the Anglican design in early 19th century Canada.

CARMAN MILLER

[In addition to the stories published in the *Literary Garland* (Montreal) from 1839 to 1850, Abbott wrote, as has been mentioned, the two works that follow, the first under the pseudonym "An immigrant farmer": *Memoranda of a settler in Lower Canada; or, the emigrant to North America, being a compendium of useful practical hints to emigrants . . . together with an account of every day's doings upon a farm for a year* (Montreal, 1842; 3rd ed., Edinburgh and London, 1844); *Philip Musgrave; or memoirs of a Church of England missionary in the North American colonies* (London, 1846). C.M.]

ANQ-M, État civil, Anglicans, Christ Church, 10 Aug. 1820, 10 Jan. 1862. McCord Museum, Library file, Joseph Abbott to Thomas Kains, 14 Feb. 1853, 11 Feb. 1855. McGill University Archives (Montreal), Minutes of the board of governors, 29 June 1829, 14 July 1843. Can., Prov. of, Legislative Assembly, *Journals*, 1849, III, app.G.G.G.G. Church of England, Church Soc. of the Diocese of Quebec, *Annual report* (Quebec), 1844. *Montreal Gazette*, 13 Nov. 1861–30 April 1862. *Montreal Transcript*, 1 Oct. 1844–1 March 1845. *Pilot* (Montreal), 15 Aug.–15 Nov. 1861. *Quebec Gazette*, 17 April 1828. *Cyclopaedia of Canadian biog.* (Rose, 1888), 740. A. R. Kelley, "The Quebec Diocesan Archives; a description of the collection of historical records of the Church of England in the diocese of Quebec," ANQ *Rapport*, 1946–47, 71, 189, 192. L.-P. Audet, *Le système scolaire*, IV. R. G. Boulianne, "The Royal Institution for the Advancement of Learning; the correspondence, 1820–1829, a historical and analytical study" (unpublished PHD thesis, McGill University, Montreal, 1970). H. E. MacDermot. *Maude Abbott; a memoir* (Toronto, 1941). G. D. McGibbon, *Glimpses of the life and work of the Reverend Richard Bradford as scholar, school principal, chaplain priest of the Church of England and S.P.G. missionary* ([Calgary], 1970). E. G. May, *A hundred years of Christ Church, St. Andrews, P.Q., an historical sketch of the pioneer church of the Ottawa valley* (Saint-Jean, Que., 1919). T. R. Millman, *Jacob Mountain, first lord bishop of Quebec, a study in church and state, 1793–1825* (Toronto, 1947), 238; *Life of Charles James Stewart*, 186. V. B. Rhodenizer, *Canadian literature in English* ([Montreal], 1965]). Cyrus Thomas, *History of the counties of Argenteuil, Que., and Prescott, Ont., from the earliest settlement to the present* (Montreal, 1896). B. N. Wales, *Memories of old St. Andrews and historical sketches of the seignory of Argenteuil* ([Lachute, Que., 1934]). M. [E.S.] Abbott, "A social history of the parish of Christ Church, St. Andrews, Que., from 1818 to 1875," *Montreal Churchman*, June–December 1934, 8.

ABRAHAM. *See* MASKEPETOON

ADAMSON, WILLIAM AGAR, Church of England clergyman and author; b. 21 Nov. 1800 in Dublin (Republic of Ireland), son of James Agar Adamson of Ballinalack, County Westmeath; m. in 1824 Sarah Walsh of Walsh Park, County Tipperary, and they had nine children; d. 7 Aug. 1868 at Ottawa, Ont.

William Agar Adamson matriculated at Trinity College, Dublin, in 1817 and graduated BA in 1821. He became a priest of the Church of Ireland and in 1824 curate of Lockeen and Parsonstown (Birr), County Offaly. He was vicar of Clonlen and of Ennis from 1833 to 1838, both in County Clare. It was in these parishes of western Ireland that he cultivated the love of angling, especially salmon fishing, which was to be a principal feature of his career in Canada. In 1838 he became rector of Kilcooly parish, counties Kilkenny and Tipperary, and chaplain to the Marquis of Normanby, then Whig lord lieutenant of Ireland. The growing weakness of the Whig ministry after 1838, and Normanby's consequent decline in influence, soon dampened his hopes of preferment. In 1840, however, Normanby's influence obtained for him the incumbency of Amherst Island, Upper Canada. He was introduced to Lord Sydenham [Thomson*], probably through Normanby, a former colleague of Sydenham, and became his personal chaplain, attending him when he died in 1841.

Adamson became chaplain and librarian to the Legislative Council of the Province of Canada in 1841. He performed the duties of librarian competently; in 1851 the post was made a sinecure and he held it until 1867 when he became librarian to the Senate. He resigned shortly before his death. He was in no sense the parliamentary librarian his younger colleague Alpheus Todd* would be. He received DCL degrees from McGill University and the University of Bishop's College. As a Canadian commissioner with Thomas D'Arcy McGee, he visited the Dublin Exposition in 1865.

Adamson won esteem as a powerful preacher, "one of the most eloquent in North America," and as a sportsman and author. He was assistant to Christ Church Cathedral, Montreal (1844–50), Holy Trinity Cathedral, Quebec (1851–55 and 1861–66), St George's, Toronto, and St Paul's, Yorkville (1856–60), and Christ Church, Ottawa (1867–68). He also served as secretary of the Church Society of the Diocese of Quebec, and was an evening lecturer at the cathedral in Quebec. Several of his sermons were printed.

He wrote on sports and nature themes in the Dublin *University Magazine*, *Blackwood's*, and other British periodicals, as well as in most Canadian magazines. Typical of his writings is one on "The decrease, restoration, and preservation of salmon in Canada," in the *Canadian Journal* (1857). His articles arising out of the pursuit of his hobby on the Saguenay and the Moisie rivers were collected and published in 1860 by Sir James Edward Alexander under the title *Salmon-fishing in Canada*. The book is pleasantly descriptive and hearty in tone; Adamson has been called the Izaak Walton of Canada though his work lacks the meditative quality of *The compleat angler*. The *Literary Gazette* of London wrote of it: "The author is evidently, as all anglers should be, a true lover of nature, and some of his descriptions of Canadian scenery are given with considerable effect." Its biographical interest lies in its revelation of the kind of clergyman Adamson was, an eloquent, kindly, sporting parson.

W. L. MORTON

W. A. Adamson's published works include *Things to be remembered; a sermon* (Montreal, 1846); *The churching of women* (Montreal, 1848); "The decrease, restoration, and preservation of salmon in Canada," *Canadian Journal*, new ser., II (1857), 1–7; and [ ], *Salmon-fishing in Canada*, ed. J. E. Alexander (London, 1860). *Letters and addresses, presented to the Rev. W. Agar Adamson, D.C.L., chaplain and librarian to the Honorable the Legislative Council of Canada* (Toronto, 1856). *Monck letters and journals, 1863–1868: Canada from Government House at confederation*, ed. W. L. Morton (Toronto and Montreal, 1970). Boase, *Modern English biog.*, IV. Morgan, *Bibliotheca Canadensis*. Notman and Taylor, *Portraits of British Americans*, III.

AIDANT, LOUIS ROBLOT, known as **Brother**. *See* ROBLOT

ANDERSON, JAMES, HBC chief factor and explorer; b. 15 Jan. 1812 in Calcutta (India), son of Robert Anderson and Eliza Charlotte Simpson; d. 16 Oct. 1867 at Sutton West, Ont.

James Anderson's father was first a military officer, then ran a plantation in India; he returned to England in 1817 and immigrated to Upper Canada in 1831. Relatives of the family included General Sir James Outram, who won renown in India, and Lieutenant-Colonel Alexander Seton, one of the heroes in the sinking of the *Birkenhead*.

Anderson joined the Hudson's Bay Company the year his father immigrated; his brother Alexander Caulfield* also served the company, becoming chief factor. James was first posted to Moose Factory, and soon after played a leading role in efficiently apprehending and summarily executing Indians who had murdered a white family at Hannah Bay in 1832. He was promoted chief trader in 1847 while serving at Nipigon post. In 1850 he was transferred to the Northern Department, and put in charge of the Athabasca District for one year. For the next eight he headed the more distant Mackenzie River District, and at Fort Simpson, its headquarters, tightened up the chaotic accounting he found there. Concluding that his principal subordinate, Robert Campbell*, was "almost a monomaniac" on the subject of the Yukon River, which he had helped to explore, Anderson secured approval for retrenchment there and on the upper Liard River. Profits for the district were significantly increased during his management, rising from an annual average of £19,291 in 1844–50 to £24,756 in 1851–57. He was promoted chief factor on 12 March 1855.

At this time the continuing search for the Arctic expedition of Sir John Franklin* was being hindered by the need for ships in the Crimean War, just when Dr John Rae* had turned up evidence that its members had perished near the estuary of the Great Fish (Back) River. The Admiralty asked the HBC to send an expedition down this river in the summer of 1855 to verify the report, and Anderson was appointed to lead it. Rae recommended employing shortened north canoes and an inflatable raft rather than the heavy boat used by George Back* in 1834. Anderson, delayed by a late spring and by the vain expectation of obtaining Inuit (Eskimo) interpreters, saved time by taking a difficult "mountain portage" route north from Great Slave Lake. Until he reached Lake Aylmer and could use Back's maps, he was exploring new country. With James G. Stewart*, whom he found "utterly useless," and 14 voyageurs in two canoes, he attained the sea on 31 July. They searched the shoreline "as if we were looking for pins," and on Montreal Island and elsewhere found scattered tools and wood fragments, one bearing the name *Terror*; Rae's report was thus confirmed. The deterioration of his canoes prompted Anderson to start up Great Fish River on 14 August. Its 84 rapids and falls were renegotiated safely before real winter set in. However, the exposure caused Anderson permanent loss of voice, and later his death from tuberculosis. Sir George Simpson* informed him that his expedition had "quite fulfilled all that was expected from it by reasonable people," the Admiralty awarded him £400 and the polar medal, and extracts from his pithy journal were published at Sir John RICHARDSON's urging in the Royal Geographical Society's *Journal*.

Simpson was anxious to open trade with the Inuit at Liverpool Bay. Anderson thought the Mackenzie delta more suitable, but in 1857 sent Roderick MacFarlane and a small party down the Beghula (Anderson) River northeast of Fort Good Hope; a post, Fort Anderson, eventually operated in the western Arctic but only from 1861 to 1866. By 1858 Anderson had had to seek an easier, less isolated district, and Simpson sent him to the north shore of the St Lawrence at Mingan seigneury. The HBC lease there was soon to expire and Anderson's proven skill in effecting economies was useful. In 1863 he re-

tired to Sutton West, and died there in October 1867, survived by his wife Margaret, daughter of Roderick McKenzie, a chief factor in the HBC, and six sons and one daughter.

James Anderson was a highly capable fur trade officer who also deserves an honourable mention in the annals of the search for Franklin.

C. S. MACKINNON

[James Anderson], "Chief Factor James Anderson's Back River journal of 1855," ed. C. H. D. Clarke, *Canadian Field-Naturalist* (Ottawa), LIV (1940), 63–67, 84–89, 107–9, 125–26, 134–36; LV (1941), 9–11, 21–26, 38–44; "Extracts from Chief-Factor James Anderson's Arctic journal," Royal Geographical Soc., *Journal* (London), 27 (1857), 321–28. PAC, MG 19, A29. HBC Arch. D.4/55, 10 Feb., 4 April 1859; D.4/71, 13 Dec. 1850; D.4/74, 26 Dec. 1853; D.4/75, 18 Nov. 1854; D.4/76a, 20 April, 14 June, 12 Dec. 1856, 24 June 1857. PABC, James Anderson papers.

ANDERSON, JOHN (originally named **Jack Burton**), fugitive slave; b. *c.* 1831; fl. 1862.

Jack Burton was a slave of Moses Burton of Fayette, Mo. Jack's father escaped from slavery shortly after Jack was born and his mother was sold to a slave trader when he was seven. On 25 Dec. 1850 he married Marie Tomlin, a slave who lived near the Burton property. Marie had two children from a previous marriage, and she and Jack were to have at least one child. In 1853 Jack Burton was sold to a farmer in Glasgow, Mo. Soon after, he illegally visited his wife; discovered and pursued by a local farmer, Seneca T. P. Diggs, Burton slew Diggs and escaped. With the aid of abolitionists, Burton made his way to Canada West and settled at Windsor in the home of the mother of Henry Bibb* in about September 1853. At this time he took the name John Anderson. He later worked as a plasterer and labourer in Hamilton and Caledonia.

In 1854 the United States government requested Anderson's extradition but the governor general of British North America, Lord Elgin [BRUCE], refused to issue the warrant; however, in April 1860 William Mathews, a Brantford magistrate, jailed Anderson on a charge of murder. Samuel B. Freeman, a Hamilton attorney, secured Anderson's freedom. Formal charges were then made by James A. Gunning, a Detroit detective, and affidavits were received from witnesses in Missouri which led to Anderson's reimprisonment in October 1860 on a warrant issued by a three-man magistrate's court in Brantford charging that he did "wilfully, maliciously and feloniously stab and kill" the Missouri farmer. Freeman, supported by Canadian abolitionists, secured a writ of *habeas corpus* on 20 Nov. 1860 from the Court of Queen's Bench in Toronto presided over by John Beverley ROBINSON [*see* Archibald MCLEAN]. On 15 December the court ruled by two to one that Anderson had committed murder by Missouri law, and that he could be extradited under terms of the Webster-Ashburton Treaty of 1842. Anderson was, however, momentarily protected by a statement by the court that it would offer no opposition to an appeal to the Court of Error and Appeal.

Canadian and British opinion was almost universally hostile toward the decision of 15 December. Thomas Henning, secretary of the Anti-Slavery Society of Canada, appealed to the British and Foreign Anti-Slavery Society in London and it applied to the Court of Queen's Bench at Westminster in January 1861 for a writ of *habeas corpus*. The court granted this after accepting the applicant's argument that the court's writ could, on the basis of precedents, be made to extend to Canada. In Canada news of the writ was denounced by most elements of public opinion as interference in the constitutional powers of Canadian courts. Before the British writ could be served in Canada, however, Anderson's attorneys appealed directly to the Court of Common Pleas in Toronto; in his decision on 16 Feb. 1861 Chief Justice William Henry Draper* discharged Anderson principally on the grounds that the warrant from the Brantford magistrate's court did not actually accuse Anderson of murder. The case led directly to the British Habeas Corpus Act of 1862, which stated that a writ could not be sent to any dominion or possession where a concurrent legal jurisdiction existed. A Canadian act in 1861 took away from magistrates' courts jurisdiction in extradition cases.

Anderson went to England in June 1861 at the invitation of a British anti-slavery organization. Between July and September 1861, he spoke to at least 25 anti-slavery meetings in London and southeastern England. After a short period of private instruction Anderson enrolled in December 1861 in the British Training Institution at Corby, Northhamptonshire. He remained there for one year; on 24 Dec. 1862 he sailed for Liberia and nothing more is known about him.

ROBERT C. REINDERS

Can., Prov. of, *Sessional papers*, 1861, IV, no.22. G.B., Parl., Command paper, 1861, LXIV, [2813], pp.293–345, *Correspondence respecting the case of the fugitive slave, Anderson. The story of the life of John Anderson, the fugitive slave*, ed. Harper Twelvetrees (London, 1863). *Weekly Globe*, 22 Feb. 1861. Fred Landon, "The Anderson fugitive case," *Journal of Negro History* (Lancaster, Pa., and Washington), VII (1922), 233–42.

ARCHIBALD, CHARLES DICKSON, lawyer and businessman; b. 31 Oct. 1802 at Truro, N. S., eldest son of Samuel George William Archibald* and Elizabeth Dickson; d. 12 Sept. 1868 at London, England.

Like his brothers Edward Mortimer* and Thomas Dickson, Charles Dickson Archibald attended Pictou Academy, graduating about 1822. His mentor there was Thomas McCulloch*, whom he was to support in the 1820s through the political controversies surrounding the repeated vetoing by the Legislative Council of the Nova Scotia assembly's attempts to grant financial aid to the school. Archibald studied law in his father's office in Truro, and was elected in 1826 to the assembly representing Truro Township. Although his four-vote victory was challenged by William Flemming, his nearest rival, the election was subsequently upheld by a select committee of the assembly. At age 24, one of the youngest members of the house, Archibald was under the shadow of his father, then speaker and solicitor general. Unlike many other members of the Archibald-Dickson family, Charles Dickson tired of political life and did not contest the election of 1830; instead he accepted an appointment as chief clerk and registrar of the Supreme Court of Newfoundland. He resigned from this post a year later to be succeeded by his brother Edward Mortimer Archibald.

On 18 Sept. 1832 Archibald married Bridget Walker, daughter of Myles Walker and heiress to Rusland Hall, a large estate in the parish of Colton, Lancashire, England. They had four daughters and one son, Charles William, who inherited this family property.

Throughout the remainder of his life, spent in England, Archibald maintained close ties with Nova Scotia and frequently visited the province. Between 1836 and 1838 he actively encouraged Thomas McCulloch to accept the presidency of Dalhousie College, and advised the latter on the political manœuvring necessary to win this post. In 1840 he was admitted a fellow of the Royal Society of London, the first Nova Scotian to be accorded that honour. Archibald had a wide range of business interests: from helping to raise funds in the 1850s for the development of iron ore extraction at Acadia Mines (Londonderry), N.S., not far from his former home, to acting as lobbyist for Peto, Brassey, Jackson, and Betts, British railway promoters.

In 1851, when hopes for an intercolonial railway linking the Canadas and the Maritimes were

Askin

revived, Archibald attended a conference in Toronto on the question with Joseph Howe* and Edward Barron Chandler*. On 21 June 1851, he addressed an open letter to Lord Elgin [BRUCE], the governor general, pleading for a transcontinental railway from Halifax to the Pacific as part of a world-wide transportation network binding the British Empire together. In florid prose he argued: "on the one side are the countless millions of the Indian archipelago, China, India and Hindustan . . . on the other the overcrowded busy marts of Europe. The British possessions in North America lie midway and I believe that the day is not far distant when this great highway of nations will traverse our neglected territory as surely as a straight line is the shortest distance between two points."

Archibald's next foray in imperial affairs was in June 1854 when he directed two letters to the Earl of Clarendon, then foreign secretary. These were later published under the title *A look toward the future of the British colonies*. Fearing a breakup of the empire and the "territorial aggrandizement" of the United States, Archibald called for the creation of "indissoluble ties" with the mother country. These could be best achieved, he believed, by the crowning of "a prince of the blood royal" as viceroy of British North America. Unlike his close friend Joseph Howe, Archibald was opposed to any form of colonial representation in the British parliament. Instead, he urged the development of a loose form of imperial federation.

WILLIAM B. HAMILTON

[There are scattered references to Charles Dickson Archibald in PAC, MG 24, B29; MG 27, I, H1; and in PANS, MG 1, 88 (Archibald family papers); 550–58 (Thomas McCulloch papers). Thomas Miller, *Historical and genealogical record of the first settlers of Colchester County* (Halifax, 1873), 34–108, contains a complete genealogy of the Archibald family. C. D. Archibald, *A look toward the future of the British colonies: two letters addressed to the Rt. Hon. the Earl of Clarendon* (London, 1854), may be found in the Legislative Library of Nova Scotia. W.B.H.]

E. J. Archibald, *Life and letters of Sir Edward Mortimer Archibald, K.C.M.G., C.B.: a memoir of fifty years of service* (Toronto, 1924). G. P. de T. Glazebrook, *A history of transportation in Canada* (Toronto, 1938). W. B. Hamilton, "Education, politics and reform in Nova Scotia, 1800–1848" (unpublished PHD thesis, University of Western Ontario, London, Ont., 1970). D. C. Harvey, *An introduction to the history of Dalhousie University* (Halifax, 1938). R. S. Longley, *Sir Francis Hincks; a study of Canadian politics, railways, and finance in the nineteenth century* (Toronto, 1943). William McCulloch, *Life of Thomas McCulloch, D. D. Pictou* ([Truro, N.S., 1920]).

ASKIN, JOHN BAPTIST (also known as **Jean-Baptiste**), militia officer, and office-holder; b. 10 April 1788 at Detroit, son of John Askin* Jr; m. 17 Oct. 1814 Elisa Van Allen of Haldimand County, Upper Canada, and they had eight children; d. 14 Nov. 1869 at London, Ont.

The maternal ancestry of John Baptist Askin is uncertain. His mother was a woman living in the Indian country west of Detroit, whose identity is not recorded. The London *Daily Advertiser*, in its obituary of Askin, stated that his mother was a full-blooded Indian and added that he took "great pride in his descent from the original lords of the forest." Actually, however, she may have been a white captive. His grandmother, the consort of John Askin*, was presumably an Indian woman named Manette.

In 1810 John Baptist Askin went with his father to St Joseph Island (near Sault Ste Marie, Ont.) and spent two winters trading in the St Croix River and Lac du Flambeau regions of northern Wisconsin. Following the outbreak of the War of 1812, they served under Captain Charles Roberts* in the capture of Michilimackinac from the Americans on 17 July 1812. In August John Baptist led a band of Indians to aid Major-General Isaac Brock* at Detroit but arrived after Brigadier-General William Hull, the American commander, had surrendered. Askin later served as an interpreter under Colonel Henry Procter* at the battle of Frenchtown (near Monroe, Mich.) on 22 Jan. 1813.

According to the London *Free Press*, Askin worked after the war as an assistant commissary officer until 1819. Settling in Vittoria, Norfolk County, Upper Canada, he was appointed clerk of the peace in 1819 and clerk of the district court in 1820, holding both offices until 1849. He was also a deputy clerk of the crown until 1859 and issuer of licences.

In 1831 Askin was appointed to the board of education for the London District along with John ROLPH and others, and in 1832 he moved to London, after the district court was transferred from Vittoria. Here he established himself as a prominent resident, living on a large estate in Westminster Township, now part of London. He issued certificates of settlement for Colonel Thomas Talbot*, and in 1833 took a leading part in the establishment of a mechanics' institute in the town. Askin was the first president of the Middlesex Agricultural Society, and held the position for 30 years until he stepped down in 1867.

As early as 12 Dec. 1837 Askin had started raising volunteers and taking part in actions to suppress the rebellion led by William Lyon MACKENZIE. Given command of a militia battalion on active service for a limited period, he was promoted colonel on 3 Feb. 1838. His military activities were not notable, consisting largely of destroying the press and type of the St Thomas *Liberal*, a paper published by John Talbot*, who fled to avoid arrest. Askin also took part in Sir Allan Napier MacNab's action against Dr Charles Duncombe at Scotland, Upper Canada.

Askin's Indian ancestry apparently proved to be no handicap and his paternal family connections, in a society in which connections were important, aided his career. Askin and his family were welcome in the best houses in London.

J. J. TALMAN

PAC, MG 24, G33; I26, 7. UWO, Westminster Township (Middlesex County, Ont.), assessment roll, 1869 (mfm. copies in PAO, RG 21, A). *Daily Advertiser* (London), 15 Nov. 1869. *The John Askin papers*, ed. M. M. Quaife (2v., Detroit, 1928–31), I, 68–69. *London Free Press*, 16 Nov. 1869. L. H. Irving, *Officers of the British forces in Canada during the war of 1812–15* (Welland, Ont., 1908), 211. *Ontario Register* (Madison, N.J.), I (1968), 46.

ASSIGINACK (Assikinock, Assekinack), JEAN-BAPTISTE (also known as **Blackbird**), Ottawa chief and public servant; b. probably in 1768, perhaps at Arbre Croche (Harbor Springs, Mich.); d. 3 Nov. 1866 at Manitowaning on Manitoulin Island, Canada West. His second wife was Theresa Catherine Kebeshkamokwe and one of their sons was Francis ASSIKINACK.

Jean-Baptiste Assiginack had apparently been a pupil at the Sulpician school at Lac-des-Deux-Montagnes (Oka) in Lower Canada and was converted there to Catholicism. He first comes to notice during the War of 1812. He may have taken part in the British capture of Michilimackinac in 1812 and of Prairie du Chien (Wis.) in 1814. In July 1813 Assiginack, as a chief of an Ottawa band, and Captain Matthew Elliott* led a number of Ottawas to the Niagara peninsula where they bolstered British strength after the battle of Beaver Dams and participated in a number of skirmishes. Assiginack may have received medals and a silk flag bearing the British coat of arms for his part in the war.

Following the war Assiginack was named in 1815 interpreter for the Indian Department at Drummond Island where he began a long friendship with Captain Thomas Gummersall Anderson*. "Sober, inoffensive and active," according to Anderson, Assiginack became an indispensable part of the Indian Department's operations in the northern Great Lakes area. Fluent in several Indian dialects, though apparently never comfortable in either English or French, he was the department's chief interpreter in the Manitoulin Island region and an influential voice in the councils of his people.

In 1827 Assiginack heard that a Catholic mission was to be established at Arbre Croche. He resigned as interpreter at Drummond Island and went to Arbre Croche to assist at the mission. To his disappointment there was no priest there but he himself catechized and preached. In 1830 he led a group of Ottawas to Penetanguishene, where the British garrison had relocated after the transfer of Drummond Island to the United States in 1828, and returned to the employ of the Indian Department as interpreter. In 1832 he moved to Coldwater which he intended making his permanent residence. He had continued to preach at Penetanguishene and over the years had been successful in leading many bands of the northern lakes area to Catholicism. At Coldwater he was instrumental in the conversion of the prominent Ojibwa chief, John Aisance*, from Methodism to Catholicism. Assiginack impressed Methodist missionary Kahkewaquonaby* (Peter Jones) as "a very intelligent man, open & pleasant in his manner." In January 1833 several chiefs at Coldwater petitioned Bishop Alexander Macdonell* that Assiginack "be appointed to perform service and to instruct us because he is a good man."

The Indian settlement at Coldwater was the result of the determination of the British authorities after 1830 to "civilize" the Indians by placing them in agricultural settlements. Coldwater was not successful, however, and in 1836 a bolder policy of encouraging the separation of the Indians from the white population was instigated by Lieutenant Governor Sir Francis Bond Head*. In that year Manitoulin Island was ceded to the Indians by a treaty, of which Assiginack was a signatory, and it was hoped that the village of Manitowaning (established the previous year) would become the focal point for the Indians on the island who were to adopt white ways and a mode of existence based on agriculture. Anderson was appointed northern superintendent of the Indian Department with headquarters at Manitowaning in 1837, and it was probably in the years that followed, until Anderson's retirement in 1845, that Assiginack's influence reached its height. Even after his own retirement from the Indian Department as interpreter in 1849, Assiginack remained an important link between his people and the government of the Province of Canada. He was active in the negotiations between the Indians of the upper lakes area and William Benjamin Robinson* which resulted in two treaties of 1850, and his help was also much

Assikinack

valued by Superintendent George IRONSIDE who succeeded Anderson.

On Manitoulin Island Assiginack bent all his efforts in the direction of Indian-white cooperation and of supporting plans to make the island a model Indian community. But as the decade of the 1850s passed, it became obvious that the original hopes for the island could not be met. It had not attracted as many Indians from central and northern Upper Canada as had been expected and the Ojibwa, who made up the bulk of the population of Manitowaning, continued to follow the traditional life based on hunting and fishing. Various tribes were represented in the island's Indian population and the old tribal distinctions proved strong deterrents to communal efforts. Christianity itself was a divisive factor; the predominantly Ottawa and Roman Catholic village of Wikwemikong, established before Manitowaning and 18 miles to the east of it, continued to flourish in the 1850s while Manitowaning, which had been established by the government and was supported by the Church of England, gradually lost its Indian population.

With the failure of Manitowaning and of the Manitoulin Island experiment the decision was taken by the government in 1861 to open the island to white settlers. However, strong opposition to the surrender of the island was expressed in Wikwemikong. At a council meeting held at Manitowaning in October 1861 Assiginack made a powerful but unsuccessful appeal in favour of the acceptance of a treaty proposed by the government. Negotiations lapsed for a year until William McDougall*, the commissioner of crown lands, came to the island prepared to grant better terms than those previously proposed to the Indian population in return for the island's surrender. Assiginack again supported the government position; at one council meeting he had to be protected by some of his sons from those opposing it. A treaty was signed in 1862 but it reflected the divisions among the Indians of the island: only two chiefs from Wikwemikong were among the signatories. The terms followed those of the Robinson treaties for the upper lakes: Manitoulin and adjacent islands were surrendered to the crown in return for a land grant (100 acres per family) and annuities drawn from the interest upon the capital accumulated from sales of land to white settlers. Indian fishing rights were guaranteed and the Crown Lands Department promised to survey the lands as quickly as possible. However, because of the opposition of the Wikwemikong chiefs the eastern end of Manitoulin Island was excluded from the provisions of the treaty until a majority of the chiefs and princi-

pal men of that area agreed to sign. Within a year of the signing of the treaty violence broke out between the Indians from Wikwemikong and government authorities over the rights of whites on Manitoulin Island and over the fishing privileges retained by those Indians who had not signed the 1862 treaty.

Assiginack signed the 1862 treaty, but the opposition of his coreligionists to the stand he took and the divisions between the two Indian communities on Manitoulin Island must have caused him much anguish. A large number of his own people questioned the wisdom of cooperating as he had with a society which seemed determined to force the disappearance of Indian cultural values. One of Assiginack's own sons, Edowish-cosh, was a spokesman for those opposing the 1862 treaty. Assiginack died in 1865 at Manitowaning, but was buried among his coreligionists at Wikwemikong.

DOUGLAS LEIGHTON

Archives of the Archdiocese of Toronto, Macdonell papers, AC07/02–04, AC14/05. PAC, RG 10, vols. 116–17, 124–28, 130–39, 273–76, 502–9, 612–15, 621, 691, 792. *Canada, Indian treaties and surrenders . . .* [from 1680 to 1906] (3v., Ottawa, 1891–1912; repr. Toronto, 1971). Can., Prov. of, *Sessional papers*, 1863, V, nos.41, 63. *Canadian Freeman* (Toronto), 20 Nov. 1862. *Loyalist narratives from Upper Canada*, ed. J. J. Talman (Toronto, 1946). J. G. Shea, *History of the Catholic missions among the Indian tribes of the United States, 1529–1854* (New York, 1855). D. B. Smith, "The Mississauga, Peter Jones, and the white man: the Algonkians' adjustment to the Europeans on the north shore of Lake Ontario to 1860" (unpublished PHD thesis, University of Toronto, 1975). Ruth Bleasdale, "Manitowaning: an experiment in Indian settlement," *OH*, LXVI (1974), 147–57.

ASSIKINACK (Assiginack), FRANCIS, public servant and school teacher; b. 1824 on Manitoulin Island, Upper Canada, son of Jean-Baptiste ASSIGINACK and his second wife, Theresa Catherine Kebeshkamokwe; d. 3 Nov. 1863 at Manitowaning, Manitoulin Island.

Jean-Baptiste Assiginack was for a long time prominent in the Ottawa band on Manitoulin Island, acting as a bridge between his people and the officials of the Indian Department. Jean-Baptiste's close relations with whites were reflected in his decision to send his son, Francis, a young man of some promise, to Upper Canada College in Toronto. In 1848, his education at the college complete, Francis asked the Indian Department for support to study medicine in France; his request was denied. The young Ottawa next proposed he be allowed to study medicine in Canada; this request too was denied, on the grounds that the Indians, whose funds would be used, would not receive benefits proportionate to the cost of such a project. In June 1849 the civil secretary, Thomas Edmund Campbell*, offered Francis the post of clerk and interpreter to Thomas Gummersall Anderson*, superintendent of the Indian Department in Toronto, at a salary of £100 per year, suggesting it was time he showed some results for all his education. When the young Ottawa replied that he wished to stay in school, Campbell brusquely urged him to take the departmental job. Assikinack was not happy as a clerk. Anderson commented that while he was of good disposition he did not seem to be well qualified for the post. When the school at the Roman Catholic settlement of Wikwemikong on Manitoulin Island asked for a master in 1850, the governor general, Lord Elgin [BRUCE], suggested that Assikinack, himself a Catholic, take the position, for he could be of great value to his people in disseminating the knowledge he had acquired partly at public expense. After one year as clerk Francis Assikinack left Toronto.

His father, recently retired, was living on Manitoulin Island, but nearness to his family did not make the young man happy as a schoolmaster. After three and a half years of frustration his temper broke. It was against Frederick O'Meara*, the strong-minded Church of England missionary at Manitowaning, that Assikinack directed his hostility, damaging some of the missionary's property and swearing at him. As a consequence of this uproar Assikinack was reposted to work under Anderson in the Indian Department at Toronto as chief clerk in 1854. Assikinack had been present as interpreter at Owen Sound in 1851 when lands along the Saugeen River were surrendered by Indians, and in the years following 1854 he frequently participated in treaty negotiations, such as that of Manitoulin Island in 1862. He retained the position of chief clerk in Toronto until September 1863 when he became seriously ill with consumption; he returned that month to Manitoulin Island to die before the end of the year.

The careers of the Assikinacks, father and son, indicate that the conduct of Indian-white relations would never run as smoothly as hoped by certain humanitarian reformers. The educational process favoured by whites might seem to succeed in its goals, as in Francis' case, but the dispensers of it could not assume that it would produce an individual who was quite content to return to his own people in a preordained role. That the 19th century failed to perceive this possibility was tragic.

DOUGLAS LEIGHTON

[Francis Assikinack wrote three essays for the *Canadian Journal* at the request of Daniel Wilson* while he was chief clerk for the Indian Department in the office of the central Indian superintendent. The first, "Legends and traditions of the Odahwah Indians," new ser., III (1858), 115–25, presented some legends and discussed symbolism and mythology. It is valuable mainly for the background note on Assikinack provided by the editor. The second essay, "Social and warlike customs of the Odahwah Indians," new ser., III (1858), 297–309, described such matters as methods of child discipline, tribal secret societies, and customs of war and treatment of prisoners. "The Odahwah Indian language," new ser., III (1858), 481–85, dealt with semantics and linguistic development of the Ottawa language. The three papers demonstrated Assikinack's direct style and his desire to reconcile, where possible, the traditions of his Indian background with those of his Christian faith.   D.L.]

MTCL, Samuel Peters Jarvis papers, vols.B58–B60. PAC, RG 10, vols.118, 129–39, 511–12, 532–35, 572–74. *Canada, Indian treaties and surrenders* [from 1680 to 1906] (3v., Ottawa, 1891–1912; repr. Toronto, 1971). *The roll of pupils of Upper Canada College, Toronto, January, 1830, to June, 1916*, ed. A. H. Young (Kingston, Ont., 1917). H. G. Tucker, "A warrior of the Odahwahs," *OH*, XVIII (1920), 32–36.

AUSTIN, Sir HORATIO THOMAS, naval officer and Arctic explorer; b. 1801 in England, son of an official in the Chatham Dockyard; d. 16 Nov. 1865 in London, England.

Horatio Thomas Austin joined the Royal Navy on 8 April 1813 as a second class volunteer. In April 1814 he joined the *Ramillies*, which was engaged in the attacks on Washington, Baltimore, and New Orleans in the War of 1812–14. For the next nine years, until January 1824, he served off the coast of Africa, in the English Channel, and on the South American station. He was promoted lieutenant on 9 Sept. 1822. In May 1824 he set out on *Fury* in William Edward Parry*'s third northwest passage expedition, which sailed by way of Lancaster Sound and wintered in Prince Regent Inlet. In August 1825 *Fury* was wrecked off the coast of Somerset Island, and Parry was obliged to return home on his other ship, *Hecla*.

In December 1827 Austin was appointed to another scientific exploring expedition, under Captain Henry Foster on *Chanticleer*, bound for the Caribbean, the South Atlantic, and the Antarctic. When Foster drowned in February 1831, Austin became acting commander. His promotion to commander was confirmed on 26 May 1831, soon after the ship's return to England. On 8 Nov. 1831 he married Ann Eliza Rawlinson (*née* Hawkins); it appears that they had children, but nothing is known of them.

Austin

From November 1832 to November 1837 Austin commanded in European waters, then for the next two years undertook research on the use of steam vessels in the navy. On 28 June 1838 he was promoted captain. From 1840 to 1843 he commanded *Cyclops* during the Syrian War (he was nominated a CB for his conduct), and off the Irish coast. He was involved in further work connected with steamers until he took charge of Woolwich Dockyard in December 1849.

At about this time, England's interest was focused on the Canadian Arctic, where Sir John Franklin*'s northwest passage expedition had been missing since 1845. When James Clark Ross' searching expedition returned unsuccessful in autumn 1849, the Admiralty planned an ambitious new expedition, with two sailing vessels, *Resolute* and *Assistance*, and two screw steamers, *Pioneer* and *Intrepid*. The use of steamers in ice was an experiment, and Austin's extensive experience with such vessels is perhaps an important reason why he was appointed on 28 Feb. 1850 to lead the expedition. Austin took command of *Resolute*, Captain Erasmus Ommanney of *Assistance*, and Lieutenants Sherard Osborn* and John Bertie Cator of *Pioneer* and *Intrepid*.

The fleet sailed on 3 May 1850 with orders to search Wellington Channel and in the region of Cape Walker. *Resolute* was detained by ice off Lancaster Sound, but Ommanney took *Assistance* and *Intrepid* into the sound and on 23 August discovered the first traces of Franklin's expedition at Cape Riley and Beechey Island. Austin joined him on 28 August, and they resumed their journey westward. However, they were soon beset by ice and had to winter in Barrow Strait. Three other ships sent out that year, *Lady Franklin* and *Sophia*, commanded by William Penny*, and *Felix*, by Sir John Ross*, wintered close by. They maintained communications with Austin's ships, and the three expeditions shared the search by sledge in spring 1851: Austin undertook to search to the west and south, Penny to examine Wellington Channel.

These sledging expeditions were undoubtedly the greatest triumph of Austin's voyage. They were extremely well planned, and they confirmed the practicability of man-hauling as a means of exploring the Arctic and of covering great distances in comparative safety. Austin did not himself take part, but must be given some credit for organization. His men undertook six major journeys and many smaller ones; they made extensive discoveries along the coasts of Bathurst, Byam Martin, Melville, and Prince of Wales islands, and surveyed the smaller islands in Barrow

Strait, but they found no further trace of Franklin.

The ships were released on 8 Aug. 1851 and, soon after, all three expeditions headed back to England. There was widespread disappointment at the early and unsuccessful return in September of both Austin's and Penny's expeditions. The Admiralty appointed an Arctic Committee of five naval veterans to report on the conduct of the two commanders. Their inquiry revealed a quarrelsome relationship between Austin and Penny for much of the voyage, leading to a foolish misunderstanding on 11 Aug. 1851 during discussion of further search up Wellington Channel; after it they had departed for home without further ado. Austin maintained afterwards that they had agreed to return home; Penny claimed that he had wanted to search beyond Wellington Channel with one of Austin's steamers but that Austin had refused. The Arctic Committee cleared both men and found their return justified, but neither escaped with his reputation unscathed. The committee clearly considered Penny more to blame for their dispute; yet many formed a poor impression of Austin's leadership and of his treatment of Penny. One of his senior officers, Sherard Osborn, sided openly with Penny, as did Lady Franklin [Jane Griffin*]. Moreover, George McDougall, second master of *Resolute*, spoke of Austin's many mistakes during the voyage and mentioned that because Austin talked of individual officers with others few of the officers were willing to serve under him again.

Austin at least considered continuing in Arctic service, but he took no further part in the search. In 1852 he was made superintendent of the packet service at Southampton and in October 1854 superintendent of Deptford Dockyard, a position he held until he was promoted rear-admiral on 28 Nov. 1857. He was superintendent of Malta Dockyard from 6 April 1863 to 26 Nov. 1864. He was promoted vice-admiral on 20 Oct. 1864, and was made a KCB on 28 March 1865, eight months before his death.

For most of his life, Austin followed an unblemished career as a capable and well-respected officer, but he made many enemies during the Franklin search. He was not the only officer who came under fire during those frenzied years of the search; nor can he be entirely blamed for clashing with such tempestuous characters as Penny and Osborn. But if many officers undoubtedly disliked him, he had his admirers, too. Sir Clements Markham, midshipman on *Assistance* in 1850–51, has provided the most sympathetic and, perhaps, the fairest assessment that is known. He gave him full credit for the brilliant organization of what was, in many ways, one of the most successful Arctic expeditions to that date: "there never was so good an organizer, as regards the work and the internal economy of the ships. His was not a personality that would be easily forgotten. . . . He was not without faults, perhaps a little inclined to fuss. But he was kindhearted and full of sympathy for those under his command."

CLIVE A. HOLLAND

Scott Polar Research Institute (Cambridge, Eng.), MS 116/57/1–9 (nine letters from Sherard Osborn to William Penny, 1850–52); MS 248/241 (journal of Sophia Cracroft, 12 Sept. 1851–28 Feb. 1852). G. B., Parl., Command paper, 1852, L, [1435], pp.1–261, *Arctic expeditions: report of the committee appointed by the lords commissioners of the Admiralty to inquire into and report on the recent Arctic expeditions in search of Sir John Franklin . . .* ; L, [1436], pp.269–670, *Additional papers relative to the Arctic expedition under the orders of Captain Austin and Mr. William Penny.* Sherard Osborn, *Stray leaves from an Arctic journal; or, eighteen months in the polar regions, in search of Sir John Franklin's expedition, in the years 1850–51* (London, 1852). O'Byrne, *Naval biographical dictionary* (1859–62), I, 30–31. C. R. Markham, *Life of Admiral Sir Leopold McClintock* (London, 1909), 71–77.

AYLEN (Vallely), PETER, timberer; b. 1799 in Liverpool, England; d. probably October 1868 in Aylmer, Que.

Peter Aylen, the "King of the Shiners," had a brief and bloody period of fame in the mid 1830s when he dominated the Ottawa valley by violence. He came to Canada about 1815, according to legend a runaway sailor. The story is given credence by his change of name: when selling land in 1837 he used what was apparently his legal surname, Vallely. Little is known of his life before the 1830s although it is clear he worked his way up to a significant position in the Ottawa valley timber trade. In 1832, by then a resident of Nepean Township, Carleton County, Upper Canada, Aylen was prominent enough to be a partner in the "Gatineau Privilege." He joined with the leading timberers on the Upper Ottawa – Ruggles, Tiberius, and Christopher Wright, Thomas McGoey, George Hamilton*, and C. A. Low – to obtain a monopoly on exploitation of timber on the Gatineau River. This profitable partnership, in which each participant took out 2,000 sticks of red pine per annum, continued until 1843. Aylen's connections in the timber trade were strengthened by his marriage to Eleanor, sister of William and John Thomson, two major Nepean timberers. Her sister married another leading Ottawa timberer, Peter White.

Aylen was a man of insatiable ambition and was prepared to take any measures necessary to advance his interests. The increasingly competitive situation in the Ottawa valley timber trade of the 1830s led Aylen to adopt violence as a business tactic. He was the most vigorous of a number of timberers who raided the limits of competitors, destroyed rivals' booms and rafts, and attacked and dispersed competitors' timber crews. Aylen also capitalized on the large pool of Irish labourers left unemployed by the completion of the Rideau Canal in 1832. Setting himself up as a champion of the Irish in their struggle to obtain jobs in the French Canadian-dominated timber camps, he employed only Irishmen, thereby winning their fighting support for his violent business tactics.

In virtual control of the river by 1835, Aylen moved the struggle into the community of Bytown (Ottawa), in an apparent attempt to seize political and economic control of the town. From 1835 to 1837 Aylen and a band of perhaps 200 Irishmen remained in Bytown after winter operations and terrorized the village. The "Shiners," as his followers were known, virtually controlled the working class Lower Town, and engaged freely in physical assaults and petty larceny. The lack of a professional police force allowed the Shiners to act with impunity. The pattern was set in July 1835 when Aylen was arrested for assault; the enraged Shiners went on a rampage which ended when they destroyed a canal steamer in Bytown harbour. The local magistrates soon learned that Aylen was untouchable.

Aylen's hegemony over Bytown lasted for two years, and was strengthened by his disruption of local institutions, including the Nepean Township Council, whose annual election meeting was broken up in January 1837 so that municipal officers could not be elected. Peace was re-established on the river, however. In March 1836 the Ottawa Lumber Association was created to stop violence in the trade. Aylen was one of its first officers, apparently feeling he had gained all he could from the use of force on the river. Indeed the association provided him with early advantages. Its first cooperative venture was improvement of the Madawaska River to ease the passage of timber. Aylen's timber operations were on the Madawaska and he was placed in charge of the improvements.

In Bytown, Aylen's hold was broken in the spring of 1837. Shiner rioting reached a peak in March of that year. As a prominent Bytown merchant, James Johnston*, wrote to the lieutenant governor, Sir Francis Bond Head*: "Mr. Peter Aylen . . . has already proved to all Bytown, that he neither respects himself, nor fears God, or Man. The laws are like cobwebs to him. There are now several warrants out for his apprehension, but there is not a constable in Bytown, who will undertake to arrest him." It was Aylen's attempt to have Johnston murdered on 25 March 1837 which shocked the community into action. The magistrates, supported by a citizen organization, formed armed night patrols and swore in special constables to arrest lawbreakers. With determined community action, the Shiners were brought under control in April and May 1837.

Aylen realized that his career in Bytown was over. In 1836 he had leased out most of his property in the area when he came to reside in the town. The transactions tell something of his wealth. He rented out a property of 150 acres on the Richmond Road, three miles from Bytown, containing a two-storey house, barns, and stables, a blacksmith shop, and a store; he also let a 300-acre lot and house in Horton Township and 12 ten-acre woodlots near Bytown. After his defeat in the spring of 1837, he leased his Bytown home and store and sold his wife's dower land, 250 acres in Nepean Township. Aylen moved to a farm on the north side of the Ottawa River, near Symmes' Landing, from which he continued his timber business.

In his new life, Aylen became a virtual pillar of respectability. The year following his move, he was one of four trustees elected to build a church in the settlement. He was a member of the Hull Township Council in 1846, an assessor of the new town when Symmes' Landing was incorporated as Aylmer in 1847, and superintendent of roads in the Ottawa County Council in 1855–56. In 1848 he had been appointed a justice of the peace. His new-found respectability was handed on to his sons, one of whom became a lawyer, one a doctor, and still another both a doctor and a lawyer.

Aylen's business grew apace; he added a saw mill at the Chats Falls on the Ottawa to his interests in the mid 1850s. His family, along with those of most major timber firms on the Ottawa, was represented on the 1849 Annexation Manifesto by the signature of his son, Peter. Aylen had not given over his old ways altogether, however. In 1851 his timber limits on the Madawaska River were confiscated by the Crown Lands Office because of his "illegal proceedings" and failure to pay the required dues. The leopard, leader of Aylmer society that he might be, had not entirely changed his Shiner spots.

MICHAEL S. CROSS

PAC, MG 24, B2, 3, p.3757; D8, 13, pp.4507–8; 21, pp.8120–21; 23, pp.8837, 8850–51, 8866; 30, pp.12601–2, 12831; 32, pp.14359–60; 36, pp.16559–60; 37, p.17544; I9, 11, pp.3240–42; 22, pp.5830–31; I40, 1, pp.219–21 (mfm.); RG 1, E1, 76, pp.485–86; L1, 31, p.679; 45, p.111; RG 5, A1, 152, 15 June 1835; 155, 13 July 1835; 156, 5 Aug. 1835; 158, 20 Oct. 1835; 159, 17 Nov. 1835; 174, 10 Jan., 16 Feb. 1837; 175; 176, 6 May 1837. PAO, RG 1, C-IV, Nepean Township, Ottawa front concessions 1 and 2.

Bathurst Courier (Perth, [Ont.]), 1835–37. *Bytown Gazette* ([Ottawa]), 1836–45. *Bytown Independent and Farmers' Advocate* ([Ottawa]), 1836. *Globe*, 25 Dec. 1856. *Packet* (Bytown [Ottawa]), 1846–51. Lucien Brault, *Hull, 1800–1950* ([Ottawa], 1950), 41; *Ottawa old & new* (Ottawa, 1946), 67–70, 127–28. A. A. Gard, *Pioneers of the upper Ottawa and the humors of the valley . . .* (4 pts. in 1v., Ottawa, [1906]), pt.II, 7, 12, 22, 33–34, 39–40; pt.IV, 8. J. L. Gourlay, *History of the Ottawa valley: a collection of facts, events and reminiscences for over half a century* (Ottawa, 1896), 52–53, 174. M. S. Cross, "The Shiners' war: social violence in the Ottawa valley in the 1830s," *CHR*, LIV (1973), 1–26. Miller Stewart, "King of the Shiners," *Flamboyant Canadians*, ed. Ellen Stafford (Toronto, 1964), 63–81.

B

BABY, CHARLES-FRANÇOIS-XAVIER (he signed F. Baby), seigneur, businessman, and legislative councillor; b. 19 June 1794 at Quebec, son of François Baby*, a seigneur and politician, and Marie-Anne Tarieu de Lanaudière; d. 6 Aug. 1864 at Quebec.

Charles-François-Xavier Baby, the eldest of a family of 12 children, studied at the Séminaire de Québec before going into business. In 1817 he was running a general store and became interested in the timber trade at Saint-Pierre-les-Becquets (Les Becquets), where he acquired some land in April of that year. He was already seigneur of the fief of Bruyères, and on 9 June 1819 he bought the holdings of Pierre-Michel Cressé*, which included two-thirds of the Nicolet seigneury, the farm attached to it, another farm of seven *arpents* by 40, the seigneurial buildings, the manor-house and outhouses, and the communal mills. The transaction totalled £12,000 to be paid as an annuity redeemable by payment of the capital. The young seigneur had barely settled in his new manor when he ran into serious financial difficulties. In January 1820, following an action brought by Quebec merchant Peter Sheppard, Baby lost a property on Rue Sainte-Anne in Quebec. Unable to meet the obligations incurred in purchasing the Nicolet seigneury, François Baby had to face the heirs of Cressé, who had died in October 1819. The Nicolet seigneury was seized in July 1820 and sold a few months later for £6,500.

After returning to Saint-Pierre-les-Becquets, François Baby lived through a difficult period, but he resumed his commercial activities and during the 1830s apparently became more involved in the timber trade. In 1837, as a result of his own imprudence and of the Anglo-American economic crisis, he found himself once again in a disastrous situation and had to seek refuge in Albany, N.Y.; from there, with the assistance of his brother Joseph who was his Montreal agent, he attempted to unravel the financial and legal tangle in which he was embroiled. After making over his assets to Robert Hunter Gairdner, a commissioner in bankruptcy, Baby was finally freed of all debts and claims in April 1844. (That year too his widowed mother died and the lengthy process of settling her estate – still going on in the early 1870s – was begun.) Baby returned to Saint-Pierre-les-Becquets and his lumber business. On 8 Nov. 1845 he signed an agreement with Charles A. Holt of Quebec which lasted until the end of the 1840s. The partners shared equally in the profits, and while Holt attended to financing the operations, supplied the lumber camps and Baby's store, and regularly informed him of price fluctuations, Baby supervised the felling, purchase, and shipping of lumber. Business seemed to go fairly well, particularly during 1846 when low water levels throughout Canada East gave the lumber camps near Quebec a distinct advantage. But Baby had not yet recovered from his last bankruptcy, and after the policy of imperial protection was abandoned, he suffered the difficulties that beset the whole Canadian lumber industry. He wrote to his brother Joseph in March 1847 to say that he could barely feed his family, and in November, that for weeks he had not seen even £5. In May 1850 he complained of the "great competition for contracts." Up to this time, then, he seems to have been more an impecunious, small-time contractor than the prominent businessman he was to become in succeeding years.

From 1851 on Baby received a series of contracts for building and maintaining lighthouses from the government and Trinity House in Quebec. In 1852 and 1853 he completed contracts at La Malbaie and Les Éboulements, and in 1856 on Anticosti Island and at Rivière-du-Loup. In April 1854 he obtained a contract from the North Shore Railway Company to construct its line between Quebec and Montreal and the company's buildings. However, the tightness of the English financial market delayed the contract's execution. Because he held the construction contract and was obligated to fulfil its terms, Baby found himself for several years involved in the monetary difficulties of the company, which soon was forced virtually to abandon its project. In September 1856 Baby seemed about to lose his influence with the company, but his interests were already deeply engaged elsewhere.

In September 1854, some months after he had become involved in the north shore railway venture, the government had granted Baby a seven-year contract for the towing service between Le Bic and Quebec. By this agreement, Baby was to receive an annual subsidy of £7,965, in addition to the limited fares he was authorized to charge users, and he undertook to build two tugs to replace the three steam vessels with which he would begin this service. A few months later the contract was revised to conform with the recommendations of the Board of Trade of Quebec: the duration was increased to ten years starting from February 1855, the service was extended to Anticosti Island, and the annual subsidy was raised to £11,300. The small number of users led Baby and the government to reduce the fares in June 1857, and the reduction was compensated by a supplementary subsidy of up to £7,500 in the first year and £5,000 in each of the following years. This decision followed an unsuccessful attempt by Baby to persuade the London insurance companies to lower the premiums required in cases where boats called upon the towing service, and the reduced fares apparently did not have the results anticipated. In fact, in August 1859 Baby claimed he had lost considerable sums of money in this affair and proposed that the government of united Canada cancel the contract, as well as the one he had just signed on 6 May 1859 for the mail service between Quebec and New Brunswick. Two other contracts which bound him to Trinity House in Quebec, one for laying and removing buoys, the other for transporting supplies, men, and material to lighthouses downstream from Quebec, were also to be annulled. For all of these contracts Baby received more than £20,000 annually from the public treasury. On 8 Aug. 1860 the government agreed to terminate them, and purchased for £56,386 Baby's five steam vessels, *Queen Victoria, Napoléon III, Lady Head,*

Badgley

Admiral, and *Advance*, on the following conditions: that Baby discharge his personal debt to the Bank of Upper Canada (£23,386), pay the sum he owed the government (£18,000) and pay an additional debt of £15,000, in all a total of £56,386.

Thus disencumbered, François Baby went into politics in June 1861, and, running as a Conservative, was elected legislative councillor for the division of Stadacona, a seat he held until his death. Baby's influence in the region of Quebec and the Gulf of St Lawrence was unquestionable and for some years he had been so important behind the scenes in Canadian politics that he was reputed to make and break ministries.

On 15 Aug. 1831, at Saint-Philippe-de-Laprairie, he had married Clothilde Pinsoneaut, sister of Pierre-Adolphe Pinsoneaut*, the first Catholic bishop of London (Ont.). Their son Michel-Guillaume, called Francis, represented Laprairie in the Legislative Assembly from 1857 to 1863, and their daughter Alice married Sir Joseph-Philippe-René-Adolphe Caron*.

ANDRÉ GARON

[Documents concerning the Baby family are found in ANQ-Q, AP-G-336/1-2. These are primarily business correspondence, accounts, receipts, and contracts that give some idea of Baby's business involvements but shed little light on his family. A part of his correspondence is deposited at BUM, Coll. Baby, Corr. générale, boîte 110. Three letters Baby wrote from exile in Albany (2, 5, and 14 Aug. 1838) and several others he wrote to his brother Joseph between March 1847 and July 1850 provide information on the state of his business. A.G.]

Can., *Doc. de la session*, 1867–68, V, no.8, 125–27. *Quebec Gazette*, 17 Aug. 1809; 27 Nov., 18 Dec. 1817; 20 Jan., 11 May 1820. J.-E. Bellemare, *Histoire de Nicolet, 1669–1924* (Arthabaska, Qué., 1924), 194–202, 206, 208–13. P.-B. Casgrain, *Mémorial des familles Casgrain, Baby et Perrault du Canada* (Québec, 1898). É.-Z. Massicotte, "Paul-Théophile Pinsonnault, ses ascendants et descendants," *BRH*, XXXIV (1928), 207–20.

BADGLEY, FRANCIS, doctor and professor; b. 14 June 1807 at Montreal, son of Francis Badgley*, merchant and member of the House of Assembly of Lower Canada, and Elizabeth Lilly; brother of William*, judge and attorney general for Canada East; d. 24 Dec. 1863 at Great Malvern, England.

Francis Badgley came from a London family of fur dealers who had set up in business at Montreal around 1785. He received his early education at Montreal, and then spent three years training in medicine under the famous Dr William Robertson*. He obtained his license to practise on 19 May 1826. A year later Badgley received his diploma from the Royal College of Physicians and Surgeons in Edinburgh, and went to Belfast and Paris to complete his studies. He carried on his profession first in Kensington (now a district of London), then in London, before coming back to Montreal in 1843.

On his return Badgley concentrated on teaching medicine, giving close scrutiny to what was being done at the Montreal General Hospital and the Faculty of Medicine of McGill University. These institutions, fearful of competition, excluded a number of doctors, including Badgley, François-Cornélius-Thomas Arnoldi, son of the celebrated Dr Daniel Arnoldi*, William Sutherland, Pierre-Antoine-Conefroy Munro, and Horace Henry Nelson, son of Wolfred NELSON. This group joined to found the Montreal School of Medicine and Surgery. The school, incorporated two years after its founding in 1843, sought to teach the medical sciences in French and English. Badgley was its secretary from 1843 to 1845, and from 1843 to 1849 he taught materia medica (the art of treatment by medicaments) and forensic medicine.

In 1844 Badgley and his colleague William Sutherland started the first medical journal in Montreal published in English, the *Montreal Medical Gazette*. It was replaced on 1 April 1845 by the *British American Journal of Medical and Physical Science*. This second periodical was begun and edited by Drs Archibald HALL and Robert Lea MacDonnell*; Dr Badgley was one of its regular contributors. He loved controversies and contributed his share to those current in hospital and university circles. In his editorials he campaigned against those in charge of McGill University and the Montreal General Hospital, and against the Montreal Board of Medical Examiners, since in his opinion they all gave proof of chauvinism and discrimination.

As secretary of the Montreal Medico-Chirurgical Society (founded in 1843) from 23 Sept. 1843 to 1 Feb. 1845, Dr Badgley recommended that an association comprising all the doctors in the united Province of Canada be formed to bring together the existing medical societies of Montreal, Quebec, the Eastern Townships, and Toronto. This plan was put forward again by Badgley in 1849, but it was not realized until 1867, when the Canadian Medical Association was founded at Quebec [*see* Joseph Painchaud*].

Dr Badgley also took an active part in setting up the College of Physicians and Surgeons of Lower Canada, and in securing official recognition for it by the legislature in 1847. The bill was not passed without argument. Drs Badgley and Joseph Émery-Coderre* worked with the members of the Frontier Medical Society of Clarenceville, Canada East, to ensure that future governors of the college would be elected on a basis of representation in proportion to the number of doctors in each region, and not be nominated by the medical societies. They maintained, with reason, that doctors in the towns, who did not know what a rural practice was like, were ill equipped to establish a law and regulations to conform with the aspirations, rights, and privileges of non-university doctors and country practitioners. Badgley and Émery-Coderre succeeded in getting the bill amended before it became law.

In 1849 Drs Badgley, Arnoldi, Sutherland, and Nelson broke with their Francophone colleagues of the Montreal School of Medicine and Surgery, which had been affiliated with the Faculty of Medicine of McGill since 1847. These colleagues were dissatisfied with the agreement concluded with the Anglophone Montreal university, and proposed in fact to bring before the legislature a bill which would give them university privileges so that they could grant to their students licences to practise. Badgley, Arnoldi, and Sutherland then accepted chairs at McGill. Badgley taught forensic medicine there for a year before going to Toronto, where he both practised his profession and gave some courses in internal medicine at the Upper Canada School of Medicine which became the faculty of medicine of Trinity College. In 1860 he left Toronto for England because of his wife's ill health. He practised at Cheltenham Spa, then at Great Malvern, where he died in December 1863.

ÉDOUARD DESJARDINS

Founder of and contributor to the *Montreal Medical Gazette*, which was published from 1844 to 1845, Francis Badgley also published several articles in the *British American Journal of Medical and Physical Science* (Montreal) between 1845 and 1850. ANQ-M, État civil, Anglicans, Christ Church, 26 June 1807. Can., prov. du, *Statuts*, 1844–45, c.81; 1847, c.26. Abbott, *History of medicine*, 56, 63–65, 67–70. E. A. Collard, *Montreal yesterdays* (2nd ed., Toronto, 1963). H. W. Cushing, *The life of Sir William Osler* (2v., Oxford, 1925). Heagerty, *Four centuries of medical history in Can.* D. S. Lewis, *The Royal College of Physicians and Surgeons of Canada, 1920–1960* (Montreal, 1962); *Royal Victoria Hospital, 1887–1947* (Montreal, 1969). H. E. MacDermot, *History of the Canadian Medical Association, 1867–1921* (Toronto, 1935), 18–25, 116, 140, 154–56; *A history of the Montreal General Hospital* (Montreal, 1950), 64.

BAILLARGEON, CHARLES-FRANÇOIS, Roman Catholic priest, archbishop of Quebec; b. 26 April 1798 on Île aux Grues, Lower Canada (although his parents lived on Île aux Oies), son of François Baillargeon, a farmer, and Marie-Louise Langlois, *dit* Saint-Jean; d. 13 Oct. 1870 at Quebec.

Young Charles-François studied under Pierre Viau, the parish priest of Cap-Saint-Ignace, then in 1813 entered the Collège de Saint-Pierre-de-la-Rivière-du-Sud (Saint-Pierre-Montmagny), and the following year went to the Collège de Nicolet. His choice of the priesthood was confirmed during four years of theology at Quebec, where he taught at the college of Saint-Roch parish and then at the seminary. He was ordained priest on 1 June 1822, and appointed chaplain of the church of Saint-Roch and director of the college. This double responsibility affected his already delicate health, but after a rest cure at Saint-François, on Île d'Orléans, in 1826 he recovered his strength. The following year he became parish priest of Château-Richer, serving also L'Ange-Gardien. Four years later, in 1831, Bishop Bernard-Claude Panet* appointed him to the cathedral as a parish priest.

This appointment occurred when some members of the seminary had been planning to have the Quebec parish of Notre-Dame served by an association of priests. The experience of living and working together that had been tested over time at the seminary and among the Sulpicians of Montreal was to be the model. A group of 18 priests in the city, backed by the churchwardens and parishioners, favoured this undertaking, which would provide permanent confessors, a large number of preachers, and pastoral services based on a better knowledge of the parishioners. Bishop Panet was well disposed towards the plan, but foresaw numerous difficulties, in particular the opposition of his Coadjutor Bishop Joseph Signay*. In 1832 Bishop Signay became administrator of the diocese and had to come to a decision, as the plan had reappeared with the arrival of the new parish priest, Baillargeon. Indeed, the latter was prepared to set up the Société de la cure de Québec, which would enjoy the irremovability until then accorded only to the parish priest. After consulting Bishop Jean-Jacques Lartigue*, assistant to the bishop of Quebec at Montreal, Bishop Signay did not consider he had the right to make such a change. Baillargeon attributed this setback primarily to "the stubbornness of our dear bishop."

The parish of Quebec imposed a heavy burden on its incumbent: about 900 baptisms and as many burials took place annually between 1831

Baillargeon

and 1835; in 1834 there were 10,291 French and 6,270 English speaking Roman Catholics to be ministered to in a population of 23,343 persons. The tragic cholera years of 1832, 1834, and 1849 taxed Baillargeon's missionary fervour to the full. Night and day he tended large numbers of dying persons at home or in hospitals. He took care of destitute families particularly among recent immigrants. He found homes for many orphans at Rivière-Ouelle, Sainte-Anne-de-la-Pocatière, L'Islet, and elsewhere. At the time of the disastrous fire in the district of Saint-Roch in 1845, his practical good sense and energy were of great help.

In these years Baillargeon was completing a project of Bishop Joseph-Octave Plessis*. This project, a French translation of the New Testament, was deemed important because the circulation of numerous Protestant versions encouraged unreliable interpretations. Bishop Lartigue had made a start but had never received the permission from Rome he believed necessary. In 1842 Baillargeon decided to proceed without bothering about the possible agreement of Rome. "Why such authorizations?" he wrote. "We assume a prohibitory law which I am sure does not exist." For 15 months he worked at the project, four and a half hours a day. He wanted to produce a work accessible to all, but at the same time aimed at a faithful and exact translation of the Vulgate. He believed he was closer to the original than Louis de Carrières, Henri-François de Vence, Isaac Lemaistre de Sacy, Denis Amelote, Antoine-Eugène de Genoude, Jacques-Bénigne Bossuet, and François de Ligny. In the 1,469 notes he refuted the Protestants' objections by literal, moral, and dogmatic explanations. He insisted, however, that Bishop Signay should assume sole responsibility for the publication: it was for him "to feed the sheep on the Word." Baillargeon's work appeared in 1846, was recommended by all bishops in 1850, and was still in print in 1861. The author himself proposed that it be bought for all private and public libraries. In 1865 he published a revised and corrected edition, and Pius IX expressed his praise and congratulations in a brief.

In 1850 Charles-François Baillargeon had resigned from his parish, for he had just been chosen agent, procurator, and vicar general of the Canadian bishops in Rome. He was well acquainted with their concerns, since he had presided over the deliberations of their councillors during a meeting in early May at Montreal preceding the council of the ecclesiastical province. Before the end of the year he had already settled a number of problems: the definition of the powers of the administrator of an ecclesiastical province, the re-establishment of the Quebec chapter, the annexation of the suffragan diocese of Newfoundland, obtaining the pallium for Pierre-Flavien TURGEON (he had become archbishop on 3 Oct. 1850 following Bishop Signay's death), and securing clear instructions about various religious ceremonies. Above all he realized the futility of consulting Rome about everything; nobody there knew anything about the problems currently preoccupying the Canadian clergy – for instance, the secret society of Oddfellows and the moral seriousness of dancing the waltz or the polka. Matters to be dealt with by the first provincial council, planned for Montreal in August 1851, included the decree *Tametsi*, against clandestine marriages in parishes not officially constituted, and a general list drawn up by the bishops of special powers and indults to be requested of Rome.

Baillargeon considered his presence in Rome really superfluous. To mail reports or deliver them personally came to the same thing. If an agent was absolutely necessary, as Bishop Ignace Bourget* seemed to hold, it would be cheaper to choose one on the spot. In Rome, Bishop Bourget was regarded as a hasty man who made frequent bothersome requests for indults, and had compromised the Propaganda and the pope from whom he demanded the retirement of Bishop Signay. The bishop of Montreal, however, found Baillargeon's own judgements "a little too precipitate and somewhat hasty." These concerned, for example, Roman liturgy: "What a sorry affair their church services are!"; the mentality of the eternal city: "It is indeed at Rome that the law is made; but it is elsewhere that it is observed"; and the policy of the Vatican, which to Baillargeon seemed reactionary because the pope's reforms were blocked by his entourage. In short, Baillargeon was not as fervent an ultramontane as Bishop Bourget.

Baillargeon was obliged to remain at Rome following his appointment as coadjutor to Bishop Turgeon, with the title of bishop of Tloa, a suffragan see of Myre, in Asia Minor (an appointment he did not in fact want). Rome could not fail to endorse the choice of the Canadian bishops who had extolled his virtues and his personal qualities: his profound knowledge in ecclesiastical matters, great zeal for discipline, firmness of character, judicious understanding of mankind, prudence and skill in business, all of which gave him the confidence of bishops, clergy, laity, and Protestants. He was consecrated in the church of the Lazarists on 23 Feb. 1851 by Cardinal Giacomo Filippo Fransoni, prefect of the Propaganda, assisted by John Hughes, archbishop of New York, and Charles-Joseph-Eugène de Mazenod, bishop of Marseille and founder of the Oblates of Mary Immaculate. A 43-year-old prediction was being fulfilled. "Now, I believe in it," Bishop Baillargeon wrote to his brother Étienne, the parish priest of Saint-Nicolas. One night in 1808 his mother, alone with her children and bewailing their sad future while praying to the Virgin Mary, had heard a voice: "Take comfort, two of thy children will be priests, and one will be a bishop."

After saying goodbye to the pope in person, Bishop Baillargeon left Rome without regret. Great demonstrations of joy greeted his return to Quebec on 1 June 1851. The new bishop became superior of the Ursulines, the Hôtel-Dieu, and the Hôpital Général. In 1852 he replaced Bishop Turgeon in the pastoral visit to the Gaspé, Baie des Chaleurs, and Labrador. When the archbishop was stricken with paralysis, he became administrator of the diocese on 11 April 1855; he valued annual contact with the diocese, and in June and July regularly visited some 30 parishes. Bishop Baillargeon had always been firmly determined to foster education. Under his administration, 110 schools were opened in the 30 parishes and 40 missions had been founded. He also encouraged the coming of the Frères de la Doctrine Chrétienne and the Sisters of Jesus and Mary, as well as the founding of the Congrégation des Sœurs Servantes du Cœur Immaculé de Marie (Sisters of the Good Shepherd). He considered parish libraries a necessary complement to the schools, and he extended the Œuvre des Bons Livres, as constituted by the bishops of united Canada in 1850. In 1857 he inaugurated the École Normale Laval. A few years later he supported the founders of Université Laval in their struggle against certain followers of Bishop Jean-Joseph Gaume. This group included a visiting professor, the Lorraine priest Jacques-Michel Stremler, and his Canadian follower, Abbé Alexis Pelletier*, professor at the Séminaire de Québec, who wanted to give a Christian emphasis to classical studies by eliminating pagan authors. Strengthened by Rome's approval, Bishop Baillargeon condemned the Gaumist ideas, which were being disseminated in articles and pamphlets. Stremler was relieved of his position in 1865, Pelletier resigned the following year and was welcomed at Sainte-Anne-de-la-Pocatière. Despite Bishop Gaume's protests, the bishop of Quebec held out, and condemned two more pamphlets published in the same spirit.

Bishop Baillargeon supported the first two rectors of Université Laval, Louis-Jacques CASAULT and Elzéar-Alexandre Taschereau*, in their opposition to the establishment of a rival university at Montreal; in their opinion this plan would lead to unfair and ruinous competition. Bishop Bourget, however, intervened three times at Rome, having adopted the conclusions of those responsible for higher learning (theology, law, medicine, and arts) at Montreal and Saint-Hyacinthe. The latter deplored the "inability" of Université Laval "to attract students . . . of the district of Montreal after their classical studies, and thereby to remove them from the dangers to faith and morals that they were exposed to at the Protestant university of the metropolis [McGill]." But Rome continued to support the delegates of Quebec. In 1870 Abbé Taschereau, now rector for a second time, proposed to Bishop Bourget that he set up a branch of Université Laval at Montreal for the chairs of law and medicine; this step was taken six years later.

Bishop Baillargeon also gave his attention to the intellectual training of priests. He set the same academic requirements as the university for the admission of candidates to the priesthood, and made young priests undergo an annual examination. He also made sure all priests were aware of the topics of the four annual ecclesiastical conferences. Concerned with spiritual renewal as well, he invited his colleagues each year to an eight-day retreat. He encouraged the founding of a hospice for old and infirm priests in the parish of Notre-Dame-des-Victoires at Quebec.

Bishop Baillargeon was president of the third and fourth provincial councils, and published the decrees enacted. The 1863 council dealt with a number of questions: faith and the principal obstacles to it – ungodly men, secret societies, bad books, mixed marriages; moral life and common failings such as cupidity, luxury, love of pleasure, drunkenness; the need for charitable works: poor relief, settlement, the collection of Peter's pence (introduced in 1862), the Propagation of the Faith, and the Holy Childhood. His encouragement of the last three undertakings shows the universality of the bishop's pastoral concerns. In 1868 the council fathers condemned intemperance and usury; they further proclaimed the temporal sovereignty of the pope and the Christian dimension in politics and elections.

Bishop Baillargeon had already intervened in 1858 and 1861 to improve the electoral climate. The advent of confederation led him to give his opinion on the constitutional evolution of Canada. Although he admitted that he was only the administrator of the metropolitan see, and had an "absolute incapacity for political affairs," Bishop Baillargeon nonetheless had foreseen by June 1864 the best position to adopt, and he held

Baillargeon

it until 1867. The stand taken by his principal collaborators and councillors, Elzéar-Alexandre Taschereau, rector of Université Laval, and Charles-Félix Cazeau*, vicar general, was a deciding factor. The bishop resigned himself to confederation, without enthusiasm, for several reasons: the threat of representation by population in the parliament of the Province of Canada (which would mean an Anglophone Protestant majority); the impossibility of dissolving the union of the two Canadas because of problems of debt, tariff, and canals; the threat of annexation to the United States as the only other possibility; and finally, the participation of able French Canadian statesmen in the negotiations for a federal Canada. On the request of Bishop Louis-François Laflèche* of Trois-Rivières, Bishop Baillargeon urged all suffragan bishops to issue a special pastoral letter on the occasion of confederation. His own pastoral communication of 12 June 1867, including both a pastoral letter on confederation and a memorandum on the next elections, did more than simply remind people about obedience to the established order; the bishop discreetly stressed the advantages of the new constitution.

Baillargeon, who had yet to succeed the archbishop, often found himself in tricky situations. In 1864, for example, he had to warn Bishop Bourget to refrain, in the absence of the other bishops' consent, from the revision of the 10-year-old provincial shorter catechism which he had announced. Until there was agreement, unity and uniformity had to be safeguarded in religious teaching. Besides, Baillargeon added, "we have made enough changes in discipline in recent years. People do not like reform in religious things. They are surprised, disturbed . . . and often scandalized." In a report to Rome on 28 Oct. 1864 Bishop Baillargeon denounced the poor administration of Bishop Pierre-Adolphe Pinsoneault*, who had transferred his episcopal see from London to Windsor in 1859, and thereby greatly displeased his people. Bishop Baillargeon had gently admonished him at the time of the third provincial council in 1863; the poor bishop had appeared hurt and had rejected the accusations, but in the mean time the administration of his diocese had worsened.

Bishop Baillargeon became archbishop on 28 Aug. 1867, following Bishop Turgeon's death, but he did not change his modest way of life in the slightest. On 2 Feb. 1868 he received the pallium from the hands of Charles La Rocque*, bishop of Saint-Hyacinthe. The diocese of Quebec had decreased in size after the formation of the diocese of Rimouski the preceding year. Bishop Baillargeon, who had thought of resigning as early as 1854 because of his health and had written to the pope in this regard, particularly in 1865, was to remain in office until his death, as the pope had advised.

He had gone to Rome in 1862 to settle an "important affair" on behalf of the Canadian bishops, and to respond to the pope's invitation to take part in canonizing 26 Japanese martyrs. He had come back with the title of assistant to the pontifical throne and Roman count. Seven years later he returned to Rome to take part in the ecumenical council Vatican I, feeling "very small and very puny" among the giants of intelligence and knowledge. He would have liked to vote in favour of the dogma of papal infallibility, but the discussion proved longer than anticipated, and he had to return to Canada because of poor health. On the way he stopped at Vichy, France, to enjoy the waters.

Bishop Baillargeon was in Quebec by May 1870 and undertook his pastoral visit, but had to interrupt it because his health was deteriorating. His illness ended in death at Quebec, on 13 October. As he had not appointed a coadjutor, two priests, Charles-Félix Cazeau and Elzéar-Alexandre Taschereau, served as administrators. Expressions of sympathy poured in from all sides. In his will, Bishop Baillargeon had asked for a simple, unpretentious funeral, "expressly forbidding any distribution of gloves, black bands, or other tokens of mourning" to those present. Bishop Bourget performed the funeral service, assisted by four other bishops. The body of the deceased was buried in the cathedral on the same day, 18 October. The epitaph, which he had prepared himself, recalls in simple language the principal stages of his life.

Baillargeon, always obliged to pay attention to his health, passed away when he was still fully involved in pastoral work. An active priest and bishop, he constantly sought fresh inspiration for his mind and spirit. He was simple and sober in manner, and drew people to him. The stature of his successor, Bishop Elzéar-Alexandre Taschereau, has left Bishop Baillargeon's pastoral work in the shadow; it was no less varied, realistic, enlightened, and wise.

LUCIEN LEMIEUX

AAQ, 20 A, VI, 64, 220; VII, 81, 83, 85, 177a, 177c, 179a, 220, 210 A, XIV, XXVIII, XXIX; CD, Diocèse de Québec, I, 146, 232; IV, 147–49, VI, 42f., 46, 48f., 51, 57f., 59; VII, 1786; IX, 43, 86, 118; 61 CD, Château-Richer, I; 61 CD, Notre-Dame de Québec, I, 90–92, 94, 99f., 114b, 121, 135. ACAM, RLL, 3, pp.228f.; RLB, 6, p.218; 295.099, 833–6, 833–7, 833–8, 833–9; 295.101,

823–13, 823–24, 833–42; 465.101. Archivio della Propaganda Fide (Rome), Scritture riferite nei Congressi: America Settentrionale, 6 (1849–57), ff.608f. ASQ, Évêques de Québec, 217E. *Mandements des évêques de Québec* (Têtu et Gagnon), IV, 223, 224–25, 245–46, 249–53, 264–65, 273–77, 293–94, 311, 321–23, 363–69, 381–82, 383–90, 409–19, 425–27, 431–33, 446, 457, 571–75, 579–82, 587–91, 615–48, 695, 730–31. *Monseigneur Baillargeon, archevêque de Québec: sa vie, son oraison funèbre prononcée à la cathédrale, son éloge dans les églises de Québec et ses funérailles, etc.*, [C.-E. Légaré, édit.] (2ᵉ éd., Québec, 1870). *Le Canadien*, 4 janv. 1836. Henri Têtu, *Notices biographiques: les évêques de Québec* (Québec, 1889), 617–43. Carrière, *Hist. des O.M.I.*, I, III, IV. Jacques Grisé, "Le premier concile provincial de Québec, 1851" (mémoire de DES, université de Montréal, 1969), 30, 46–47, 51. Lemieux, *L'établissement de la première prov. eccl.* Honorius Provost, "Historique de la faculté des Arts de l'université Laval, 1852–1902" (thèse de MA, université Laval, Québec, 1952). T. [-M.] Charland, "Un gaumiste canadien: l'abbé Alexis Pelletier," *RHAF*, I (1947–48), 195–236. Armand Gagné, "Le siège métropolitain de Québec et la naissance de la confédération," SCHÉC *Rapport*, 34 (1967), 41–54. Léon Roy, "Où Mgr Baillargeon est-il né ?," *BRH*, LI (1945), 127–32.

BAILLIE, THOMAS, colonial administrator and office-holder; b. 4 Oct. 1796 at Hanwell, Middlesex, England, son of Captain William Baillie of the 51st Light Infantry and magistrate at Hanwell; d. 20 May 1863 during a holiday at Boulogne, France.

Thomas Baillie joined the army in April 1815 as a lieutenant in the Royal Welsh Fusiliers. He reached the field of Waterloo with his regiment a few months later, just as Napoleon commenced his flight. For a year following he was stationed at Versailles with the British troops of occupation. He then served at Limerick (Republic of Ireland), where in 1824 he married Elizabeth Hall.

In the same year he entered the Colonial Office where his elder brother, George, was well established as first clerk in the North American Department. Soon after, however, Thomas was appointed commissioner of crown lands and surveyor general of New Brunswick. The appointment of a young, relatively inexperienced man to a post that was second in importance only to that of the lieutenant governor was criticized at the time, and many years later Sir James Stephen, the colonial under-secretary, described it as having been repayment for "the services of his father in elections in England." Members of Lord Liverpool's ministry, especially Lord Bathurst, the colonial secretary, were under obligations to Captain Baillie, and on a great many occasions in the future Thomas was to rest his authority in

New Brunswick on these bonds. According to his own testimony he was first offered a consulship in Tunis but took the New Brunswick appointment because he preferred a temperate climate.

New Brunswick had enjoyed nearly 20 years of prosperity when Baillie arrived at Fredericton late in 1824. During these years the timber trade had developed at a rapid rate and the whole well-being of the province now depended on its fortunes. Most of the timber exported to Britain was cut on crown lands, whose extent could be estimated only approximately at 14 to 16 million acres because of the uncertain boundary with the United States. Attempts to administer this domain in an orderly way and to extract a revenue from merchants who ignored regulations dated only from 1819. Baillie's purpose, as defined by the Colonial Office, was to bring efficient control to the timber trade and larger revenues to the crown. These revenues, known as "casual and territorial," were already enabling the province to facilitate settlement and subsidize schools.

Politically Baillie's position was a difficult one. Revenues collected by the imperial government from the crown lands were expended within the province but were beyond the control of the legislature. A tax of 1s. per ton was placed on timber without sanction of popular assent. Furthermore, the commissioner of crown lands boasted that his authority came from England and he appeared to enjoy the prospect of humiliating the official community as well as taxing the men of commerce. To the official families of Fredericton the arrival of an outsider in a place of great power was a serious affront. Indeed "the address and manner" in which Baillie settled upon his task at once made his presence almost unbearable. Though approving of the policy of forest management, the lieutenant governor, Sir Howard DOUGLAS, was continually embarrassed by Baillie's untactful and loquacious declarations of authority. "For to say truth your brother displayed and talked too much," he wrote to George Baillie.

Self-styled an estate-keeper, Baillie immediately commenced a series of reforms which, to the community at large, seemed tyrannical. A force of forest rangers closely supervised the operations of the timber merchants, keeping them to the limits of their "berths" and ensuring that every "stick" was taxed. Prosecutions for trespassing became numerous. The rivers, Baillie claimed, also came within his keeping; merchants who had erected wharves and booms along river banks were asked to pay rentals on water-lots. As the sale of New Brunswick's timber increased in Britain new policies for developing "the estate"

Baillie

presented themselves as realistic. In Baillie's view it would be more profitable and efficient to deal only with a few wealthy capitalists, such as Joseph CUNARD of the Miramichi, rather than with the large number of small contractors who sold their produce in Saint John, Chatham, or Bathurst for shipment overseas.

This possibility of a reorganization of the timber trade became imminent in 1829 when the British government accepted the economic philosophy that sale of crown lands would not only increase revenues but would enable the suffering poor of their own islands to settle advantageously in the North American colonies. Unlike his colleagues in similar offices in other colonies, Baillie accepted the plan for selling crown lands with avidity, prophesying the accumulation of an enormous capital sum, the interest on which could pay for the entire costs of government. Throughout the province the prospect alarmed all men of trade for it seemed that a few wealthy outsiders would gain complete control of the economy. Baillie himself set a pattern for this kind of development in 1831 by taking the lead in forming the London-based New Brunswick and Nova Scotia Land Company which purchased 350,000 acres in York County. Superficially the policy of selling land was at first a great success. During eight months in 1835 lands valued at £153,000 passed into private hands, a spectacular indication of complete triumph for the economic thinking behind the policy. Though many sales proved to be spurious when purchasers, after paying first instalments and stripping the land of its timber, defaulted on the balance of the payment, there was enough evidence to show that the sale of crown lands, discredited in other provinces, was working in New Brunswick.

What must be described as Baillie's arrogant exercise of power was made the more difficult for local inhabitants to accept by an unnecessary display of wealth. There is a Fredericton tradition that Baillie drove from his home, the Hermitage, on the outskirts of the town, in a coach and four with outriders, and that he outraged local egalitarian pride by attempting to dress the clerks of his office in uniforms with brass buttons. His scorn for the colonial aristocracy resulted in successful attacks upon his fees and salary, which at first had been so high that Governor Douglas intervened with the Colonial Office to secure a downward adjustment, though the reduction was not sufficient to gratify Baillie's enemies. When Charles Simonds*, speaker of the assembly, was fined by Baillie's officials for trespass in Saint John in 1827 he became Baillie's leading adversary. Political and commercial opin-

ion was mobilized to the point of view that, although immense sums were accruing in the treasury, most of the proceeds were absorbed by Baillie's increasing office establishment and by salaries for his "harpies," as the deputy-surveyors were called. The Crown Lands Office became so all-engrossing that other public offices were secondary to it, especially that of the receiver general, George Pidgeon Bliss*, whose numerous family connections now formed the nucleus of a popular party opposed to Baillie. To the commissioner the receiver general's office was unnecessary and in 1832 he succeeded in convincing the Colonial Office that it should be abolished, along with that of the auditor general, a triumph that proved fleeting when in face of an enraged public opinion Lieutenant Governor Sir Archibald Campbell* persuaded the Colonial Office to reverse its decision. Within the safety of the assembly chamber it was alleged that Baillie was embezzling funds from the casual revenue.

The Colonial Office was impressed by Baillie's bold planning and pleased with the prospect that the province would soon relieve the mother country of the parliamentary grant that paid for the civil list. But the times would no longer tolerate the authoritarian practice of which Baillie was such a zealous proponent. New Brunswickers were not eloquent in abstract expression of discontents, but control of a huge revenue by a single individual immune to criticism in the legislature was galling. Encouraged by Reform activity in the Canadas, a legislative delegation consisting of Edward Barron Chandler* and Charles Simonds carried a brief to London in 1833 exclusively directed against Baillie. Newspapers, especially the *New Brunswick Courier* where Robert Gowan*, under the *nom de plume* of John Gape, conducted witty and vindictive propaganda, depicted him as "a fourth branch of government," more powerful than the lieutenant governor, and as the architect of a Siberian tyranny. His promotion to the senior position in the newly constructed Executive Council was an additional insult to natives of the province who had given long service to government.

Spirited action of the assembly in 1833 almost resulted in a British decision to turn the crown lands over to control of the assembly, but negotiations with Colonial Secretary Lord Stanley broke down on detail. Baillie was now a source of embarrassment to both the British government and the lieutenant governors at Fredericton; they were compelled not only to support his policies but also to apologize for his eccentricities. Stanley attempted to meet the difficulty by offering Baillie the position of postmaster general of

Jamaica in 1833. Characteristically, Baillie refused, holding to a faith in his labours and to an appreciation of a healthy and invigorating climate where his sons were growing to sturdy manhood. Though Baillie was ever compelled by the envy of his neighbours to regard himself as "a stranger," he was an ardent champion of the province and its prospects. His *An account of the province of New Brunswick*, published when he was at the height of his influence, lauded the climate and natural resources of New Brunswick and proclaimed it a good country for grain and grazing.

But a posture such as that taken by Baillie could no longer be maintained in British North America. While the British Liberals grappled with problems of the Canadas, they could not afford to contemplate a discontented New Brunswick. A new colonial secretary, Lord Glenelg, was eager to make great concessions to bring tranquillity to the province. In 1836 he readily reached agreement with a second delegation from the assembly for the surrender of the crown lands, with all their accumulated and potential revenues, to the custody of the assembly. By reason of this bargain, put into effect in 1837, Baillie lost his seat in the Executive Council and his entire power, though he continued as surveyor general. His second marriage in 1833 to Elizabeth Odell, daughter of William Franklin Odell*, the provincial secretary, had improved his local stature, but the surrender of 1837 reduced him from the most important executive functionary in the province to a simple instrument of legislative decision. His triumphant adversaries would have deprived him of his office, but he was protected by the Civil List Act of the same year, part of the bargain with Lord Glenelg.

Over the next 14 years Baillie's tenacity can be a cause for wonder. The vengefulness of his enemies, Charles Simonds, William Henry Robinson, the Bliss family connections, young Lemuel Allan Wilmot*, everyone involved in the New Brunswick timber trade whom he had allegedly persecuted, never relented. In the legislature his accounts were rigidly scrutinized and there is ample reason to suspect that, however imposing his plans had been, the details of his administration were untidily managed. His subordinates in the Crown Lands Office apparently enjoyed freedom to take commissions on their own and to make use of privileged information in private investment. Baillie had to take responsibility for a great many alleged irregularities and to face charges of dishonest practices by himself. He invariably retorted by challenging his critics to take him to court. This they never ventured to do, and, in reports to the Colonial Office, successive lieutenant governors, Campbell, Sir John Harvey*, and Sir William COLEBROOKE, gave the opinion that the charges could not be sustained.

The fall from grace was the more abject when, late in 1839, Baillie's private affairs dissolved into ruin. All his resources, including his real property and that of his wife, and all the credit he could muster had been pledged to the fortunes of Duncan Barbour and Company, a private firm for the development of the peat moss industry. When it became bankrupt his enemies rejoiced for it appeared inevitable that the man they regarded as a public enemy would be driven from the province. While the case was reviewed, he was suspended from office, his place being filled by John Simcoe Saunders*. Nearly two years later he was restored but half his salary was impounded to satisfy his creditors.

In vastly reduced financial circumstances and public stature, Baillie remained a man of big ideas, still declaring his support for strong management of the public domain and protesting that "the humble squatter was the chief engineer of the Province." But he was powerless: the legislature renounced the sale of crown lands except for purposes of settlement and the forests he had once ruled as an emperor were opened to exploitation by the timber trade which made small return to the treasury. It seemed that public policy had become that of encouraging industry by depriving the province of revenue. Baillie's autocratic administration appears in a much better light when contrasted with the first four years of legislative control of the crown lands. In 1837 the province was financially prosperous, without debt and with an overflowing treasury. In spite of general prosperity, by 1841 the provincial coffers were bare with a deep and permanent debt in sight.

Not only tenacity but resiliency marked Baillie's last years in New Brunswick. He at last learned that political power must rest on public support. In 1846 he won election to the assembly for York County and became a member of Sir William Colebrooke's last government. Sir Edmund Walker HEAD's introduction of responsible government early in 1848, however, compelled his resignation from the Executive Council. Moreover, the lieutenant governor wanted the surveyor generalship for a salaried member of his new government. Yet Baillie was not compelled to relinquish his office until 1851 when the assembly complied with British terms and agreed to a pension of £500. After he retired in that year to reside at Budleigh Salterton in Devonshire, England, the British government granted an addi-

Baldwin

tional £250. Ironically the same kind of influence which had secured Baillie's appointment in 1824 was employed with the British Liberals in 1851: in supporting his brother's plea for a higher pension, George Baillie reminded Earl Grey that his father, Captain William Baillie, had supplied the first Earl Grey with the plan of battle at Minden (Federal Republic of Germany) in 1759 which the first earl had published.

When he died in 1863, Baillie left two sons by his first marriage and three children by his second.

W. S. MacNutt

Thomas Baillie wrote *An account of the province of New Brunswick including a description of the settlements, institutions, soil and climate of that important province, with advice to emigrants* (London, 1832). His *Case of Thomas Baillie, esquire, late commissioner of crown lands and forests, and surveyor-general of New Brunswick* (n.p., n.d.), *The memorial of Thomas Baillie . . .* (n.p., n.d.), and *Summary of the case of Mr. Thomas Baillie, late chief commissioner of crown lands and forests, and surveyor general of New Brunswick* (London, n.d.), may be found at the Foreign and Commonwealth Office (London). N.B. Museum, Ganong MS coll., Memoranda. PRO, CO 188/30–116; 188/123; 193/3. Fenety, *Political notes and observations*, 53–55. Hannay, *History of N.B.*, II, 34–35, 61–62. MacNutt, *New Brunswick*, 193–314.

BALDWIN, AUGUSTUS WARREN, naval officer and politician; b. 1 Oct. 1776 at Russell Hill farm, near Lisnegatt (County Cork, Republic of Ireland), sixth of the 16 children of Robert Baldwin Sr and Barbara Spread; d. 5 Jan. 1866 at Russell Hill, his estate near Toronto, Canada West.

Augustus Warren Baldwin entered the merchant navy as an apprentice in January 1792 but in May 1794 was able to join the crew of the sloop *La Trompeuse*. The captain, J. Erskine Douglas, a family friend, soon obtained a midshipman's commission for him. Baldwin served under Douglas for several years, mostly sailing on the Home and Halifax stations; from 1798 to 1804 he was on the *Boston*, which in 1799 ironically chased the ship carrying his family to America, mistaking it for a French vessel. He was commissioned lieutenant in 1800. He participated in the bombardment of Copenhagen in 1807, and in 1808 received a gold medal and a commander's commission for his part in the capture of the Russian ship *Sewolod*. After four years' inactivity he took command in February 1812 of the brig *Tyrian* operating largely in the English Channel. His activities were apparently profitable: after one engagement off Spithead he received £100 for recapturing a ship from a French privateer.

Posted captain in January 1817 and retired from his command, Baldwin decided to settle in Upper Canada. He purchased a 200-acre estate from Elizabeth Russell, half-sister of Peter Russell*, located to the east of Spadina, home of his brother, William Warren Baldwin*. Here Augustus built his own Russell Hill and established himself as a landed gentleman. He was appointed a magistrate of the Home District in 1822 and in 1823 a commissioner to hear claims arising from the War of 1812. On 4 Oct. 1827 he married Augusta Mary Melissa Jackson, daughter of the Reformer John Mills Jackson*; a son and two daughters died in their teens.

Baldwin soon played an active role in the financial life of the community. Probably under the aegis of his brothers, William Warren and John Spread Baldwin*, he invested heavily in the Bank of Upper Canada and in the Desjardins Canal Company. He also made a £1,000 loan to the firm of the merchant Quetton* de Saint-Georges, in which John S. became a partner, and in 1824–25 joined other members of his family in a shipbuilding operation.

Unlike his brother William Warren, Augustus was a Tory, and when Sir John COLBORNE was broadening the Legislative Council membership in 1831 he was appointed to that body. During the constitutional crisis of March 1836, when his nephew Robert Baldwin* and the rest of the Executive Council resigned in a dispute with Lieutenant Governor Sir Francis Bond Head*, Augustus, probably out of a sense of duty, was one of those who accepted appointment to replace them. He remained on both councils until June 1841, when he was appointed to the new Legislative Council of the united Province of Canada. He resigned almost immediately, however, probably because attendance would have involved travelling to Kingston. His ornamental role in politics was summed up in Head's *A narrative*: "his loyalty and his mild amiable disposition formed the conspicuous features of a character which was by all parties esteemed."

In his declining years Baldwin was one of the patriarchs of Toronto. Between 1832 and 1856 he was frequently a director of the Bank of Upper Canada and he was also a director of the British America Assurance Company. He sold part of his land between 1850 and 1857. A member of the Church of England, he was a founder and first rector's warden of St Paul's Church in 1842–44. On 1 Oct. 1846 he formally retired from the navy, but was promoted rear-admiral in 1851, vice-admiral in 1857, and admiral-of-the-white in 1862.

Although retaining his faculties to the last, he unfortunately remained too loyal to his early investments. When he died in January 1866 his estate, aside from land, was valued at $16,512, but some $10,500 was in stock and deposit in the Bank of Upper Canada which failed shortly afterward; also his stock in the Desjardins Canal Company was by then a rather limited asset. The remaining land, however, rapidly became valuable; it was left to Robert Baldwin's heirs and to Augustus' nephew William Augustus Baldwin, subject to the life interest of his wife. Baldwin's career demonstrates two points often forgotten: that not all Baldwins were Reformers, and that they were active in fields other than politics.

FREDERICK H. ARMSTRONG

MTCL, Robert Baldwin papers; William Warren Baldwin papers. PAC, RG 68, 1, General index, 1651–1841, pp.138, 192, 445, 450, 670–71. PRO, Adm. 196/3. York County Surrogate Court (Toronto), will of Augustus Warren Baldwin, 14 Aug. 1850, and inventory of the estate, 17 Jan. 1866. *Globe*, 6, 10 Jan. 1866. F. B. Head, *A narrative* (London, 1839), 454, 456–57. Armstrong, *Handbook of Upper Canadian chronology*, 14, 35. John Marshall, *Royal naval biography* . . . (4v. in 6 and 2v. supp., London, 1823–35). Morgan, *Sketches of celebrated Canadians*, 155–56. O'Byrne, *Naval biographical dictionary* (1849), 42. Wallace, *Macmillan dictionary*, 30, 343. R. M. and Joyce Baldwin, *The Baldwins and the great experiment* (Don Mills, Ont., 1969). T. W. Acheson, "John Baldwin: portrait of a colonial entrepreneur," *OH*, LXI (1969), 153–66.

BALDWIN, CONNELL JAMES, soldier and public servant; b. 1777 at Clogheneagh (County Cork, Republic of Ireland), son of Dr James Baldwin, MP, and Mary O'Connell; m. in 1830 Mary Sprague of Albany, N.Y., by whom he had one son and six daughters; d. 14 Dec. 1861 at Toronto, Canada West.

Connell James Baldwin was a member of a distinguished Irish family which included such military men as General Count Daniel O'Connell of the Irish Brigade of the French army. Baldwin's brother Herbert became MP for Dublin, and Daniel O'Connell, "the Liberator," was his cousin; the Upper Canadian Reform leader, Robert Baldwin*, was also a distant relative. After an education at a Jesuit college, probably either Saint-Omer in Brittany or Stonyhurst School in England, Connell Baldwin joined the Royal Navy at 14. Invalided out at 16, he joined the army and took a course at Farnham Military College. He fought with distinction in many of the major battles of the Peninsular War, gaining a medal and ten clasps, the position of aide-de-camp to General Thomas Picton, the rank of captain, and a pension because of four wounds.

After the war Baldwin did garrison duty as brigade-major in Britain and in the West Indies from 1820 until 1826, when he retired on half pay. From 1826 to 1828 he was involved in raising and commanding a regiment, composed largely of troops he had commanded in the Peninsular War, to serve under Emperor Dom Pedro I in Brazil. When his troops were used as common labourers Baldwin demanded a discharge for the men and passage home to Ireland.

In 1828 Baldwin immigrated to Canada and was joined by some of the men he had commanded in Brazil, including Father William John O'Grady*. Baldwin was granted 400 acres near Peterborough, where he lived briefly, and 400 acres in Toronto Gore Township where in 1830 he built a school and church for his neighbours, followers, and dependents, and established himself as a country squire. He served as a justice of the peace and had a reputation for great fairmindedness in his decisions in the minor civil suits with which he dealt. A commissioner of roads, he was also a militia colonel from 1835 to 1851. Politically he was a moderate Reformer strongly identified with Irish Catholic interests. In the mid 1830s he corresponded publicly with William Lyon MACKENZIE over the activities of the Orange Order and Tory indifference to what he saw as the Orange menace.

When rebellion broke out in 1837, however, Baldwin remained loyal to the government. He raised a corps of 1,200 men at his own expense for the defence of the Niagara frontier. This operation caused him much difficulty later: because of their poor quality Baldwin had refused uniforms he had ordered, and the supplier successfully sued for payment. Baldwin refused to petition for compensation because he felt the government would of itself grant aid, and he was forced to commute his half pay to discharge his debts. Left with only his wound pension, Baldwin had to reduce the scale of his activities. He closed his school but served on the board of trustees of the local separate school district when it was organized in 1841. He continued as a JP, but as a matter of pride never accepted a fee.

In the 1841 election he was a Reform candidate in the Orange stronghold of the 2nd York riding. Running against a rabid Orangeman, George Duggan* Jr, Baldwin withdrew to avoid bloodshed, but was not renominated when a new election was ordered in 1842, probably as a result of the disadvantage posed by his religion. In 1847, when cholera swept Toronto, Baldwin turned his home into a private hospital and cared for many of the destitute and diseased immigrants. He knew intimately and worked closely in the cause of Catholicism with bishops Alexander Mac-

Bangs

donell*, Michael Power*, and Armand-François-Marie de Charbonnel*. In 1859–60 he was a leader in the successful struggle of Toronto-area Catholics to stop the visiting Prince of Wales from recognizing the Orange Order by walking through its welcoming arch.

Baldwin died in 1861 while visiting Toronto. He had served in many capacities, particularly for the Reform party, the Catholic Church, and the underprivileged. Yet when he died, and after the death of his son some months later, his wife and daughters were left with heavy debts. Only a strong campaign by his nephew, Moore A. Higgins, and some of his friends secured Mrs Baldwin a tiny pension.

RONALD J. STAGG

PAO, Mackenzie-Lindsey papers, clippings, box 22A. *Arthur papers* (Sanderson). Can., Prov. of, Legislative Assembly, *Journals*, 1841. *Canadian Freeman* (Toronto), 28 Dec. 1871. *Church*, October–December 1841. *Examiner* (Toronto), 24 Feb., 24 March 1841. *Irish Canadian* (Toronto), 13 Dec. 1871. *Leader*, 16, 18 Dec. 1861. *Mirror* (Toronto), October–December 1841. Chadwick, *Ontarian families*. W. P. Bull, *From Brock to Currie, the military developments and exploits of Canadians in general and of the men of Peel in particular, 1791 to 1930* (Toronto, [1936]); *From Macdonell to McGuigan, the history of the Roman Catholic Church in Upper Canada* (Toronto, 1939); *From the Boyne to Brampton, or John the Orangeman at home and abroad* (Toronto, 1936). G. S. Tavender, *From this year hence, a history of the township of Toronto Gore, 1818–1967* (Brampton, Ont., 1967). J. R. Teefy *et al.*, *Jubilee volume, 1842–1892: the archdiocese of Toronto and Archbishop Walsh* (Toronto, 1892).

BANGS, NATHAN, Methodist minister and author; b. 2 May 1778 in Stratford, Conn., son of Lemuel Bangs and Rebecca Keeler; m. 23 April 1806 Mary Bolton of Edwardsburgh Township, Upper Canada, and they had 11 children; d. 3 May 1862 in New York City.

Nathan Bangs, a member of one of Massachusetts' oldest families, was raised in humble but purposeful surroundings. His father, a well-read blacksmith and an Episcopalian, encouraged him to acquire an education and stimulated his theological interests. Nathan became a teacher and surveyor, skills he practised near Niagara after he came to Upper Canada in 1799. There he met many Methodists, and through their guidance found the religious assurances he had long sought. To the Reverend Joseph Sawyer*, in particular, he "fully disclosed" his spiritual turmoil. In August 1800 God opened "the path of life and peace to [his] troubled soul," and received him "into the household of his saints."

The Methodist itinerants, always anxious to recruit men of ability and character, promptly pressed Bangs to join their ranks. He was admitted on trial by the New York conference in 1802 and stationed on the Bay of Quinte and Home District circuit. In 1804 he volunteered to become a missionary to the settlements along the lower Thames River, then separated by miles of wilderness from the townships around Niagara and York (Toronto). Leaving New York City in June after being ordained deacon and presbyter, he reached the vicinity of modern Chatham in August 1804. At his first meeting he announced: "I am bound for the heavenly city and my errand among you is to persuade as many as I can to go with me."

Bangs remained three months in the Thames region and spent the rest of 1804 in the Niagara area. In 1805 and part of 1806 he was on the Oswegatchie circuit in eastern Upper Canada. There he helped organize the first camp meeting in Upper Canada, at Adolphustown. The camp meeting for a time accelerated the diffusion of evangelical teaching and served as a corrective to the frustration and isolation experienced by the settlers. Bangs was sent to Quebec City in 1806, but in his three months there he met strong opposition from the established churches and sometimes held services with only one person present. He moved to Montreal and remained there during 1807, although his congregation numbered only 20. In 1808 he transferred to a circuit in New York State, and in 1812 was appointed presiding elder of the Lower Canada district. The outbreak of war prevented him from moving to Montreal. In his years as a missionary in Canada he had expounded the Methodist gospel from Detroit to Quebec City and had provided an enduring example of that self-sacrificing zeal on which Methodism's success largely rested. Moreover, Bangs acquired a lasting reputation in Upper Canadian Methodism, a position that was strengthened by the nature of his subsequent career.

Bangs' transfer to the United States coincided with a massive expansion of American Methodism, a development to which he would make significant contributions. He was a highly effective preacher, a skilful administrator and legislator, and on several occasions a reluctant candidate for episcopal office. More important, as "book agent" from 1820 to 1828 he was the effective founder of the Methodist publishing enterprise. He raised the standard of Methodist journalism as editor of the *Christian Advocate* and the *Methodist Magazine and Quarterly Review*, published in New York. One of the original sponsors of the Missionary Society and its first paid secretary, he helped expand domestic missions and begin Methodist foreign missions. In addition, he was a tireless writer, especially of Methodist Episcopal history, and in 1841–42 president of Wesleyan University in Middleton, Conn.

As publisher, journalist, historian, and ecclesiastical statesman Bangs helped to shape directly and indirectly the development of Methodism in Upper Canada. His presence and advice helped William Case*, Thomas Madden, and others to establish the autonomous Upper Canadian conference of the American church. In 1828 he was involved with John* and William Ryerson*, James Richardson*, and Philander SMITH in the formation of the independent Methodist Episcopal Church of Canada. His services were recognized by the offer of appointment as its first general superintendent or bishop, which he declined. Throughout the next troubled decade, his counsel strengthened the position of those who sought to promote the growth of a genuine Canadian Methodism in the face of a determined effort by English Wesleyans to assimilate Canadian Methodists to their polity and conservative attitudes. Similarly, the appointment in 1833 by the Canada Conference of Egerton Ryerson* as book agent (later steward), the establishment in 1829 of the *Christian Guardian* and in 1836 of Upper Canada Academy, and the careful organization of the Canadian missions reflected the intellectual, literary, and religious concerns that Bangs sought to foster in American Methodism. One of his last official functions before retiring in 1852 was to represent his American brethren at the 1848 session of the Canada Conference, where he met among others, William Case, one of the few survivors of the original American mission to Canada, and where he reminded his colleagues that the "doctrine of entire sanctification" had been "the distinguishing characteristic of Methodism." Bangs' retirement symbolized the end of the heroic phase of Methodist history in the United States and in British North America. By his example and influence he contributed to the widening and deepening of the Methodist impact on Upper Canada.

G. S. FRENCH

Nathan Bangs was the author of *The life of the Rev. Freeborn Garrettson . . .* (New York, 1829), *An authentic history of the missions under the care of the Missionary Society of the Methodist Episcopal Church* (New York, 1832), and *A history of the Methodist Episcopal Church* (4v., New York, 1838–41). For other works by Bangs see *National union catalog. Memorial of the golden wedding of the Rev. Nathan and Mrs. Mary Bangs, April 23, 1856* (New York, 1856). *Christian Advocate* (New York), 1826–36. *Christian Guardian*, 14 May 1862. *Methodist* (New York), 10 May 1862. *Methodist Magazine and Quarterly Rev.* (New York), 1820–28, 1832–36. *DAB.* Carroll, *Case and his cotemporaries.* French, *Parsons & politics.* Abel Stevens, *Life and times of Nathan Bangs, D.D.* (New York, 1863). A. H. Tuttle, *Nathan Bangs* (New York, 1909).

BANNERMAN, Sir ALEXANDER, merchant, banker, manufacturer, politician, and colonial administrator; b. 7 Oct. 1788 in Aberdeen, Scotland, eldest son of Thomas Bannerman; d. 30 Dec. 1864 in London, England.

Born into the family of a well-to-do Scottish wine merchant, Alexander Bannerman received a grammar school education and proceeded to Marischal College, Aberdeen, where he spent two sessions. In his early years he appears to have been noted for his outspoken Reform views and a penchant for practical jokes, which he never fully abandoned. After his father died in 1820 he and his brother Thomas took over the family wine business. As a result of his involvement in this and such other enterprises as banking, whaling, an iron foundry, and a cotton mill, Alexander became well known in Aberdeen. In 1832 he was acclaimed as the city's member in the reformed House of Commons. He continued to sit as a Whig until he retired in early 1847, never having faced a serious challenger.

On 14 Jan. 1825 in London Bannerman had married Margaret Gordon, later identified as "Carlyle's first love." This remarkable woman was born in Charlottetown, P.E.I., a granddaughter of Margaret Hyde and Walter Patterson*, the Island's first lieutenant governor. At school in Kirkcaldy, Scotland, Margaret Gordon had come to know the young schoolmaster Thomas Carlyle, who was attracted by her intelligence and wit. Yet she chose to marry her distant relative "Sandy" Bannerman, whom her biographer, Raymond Clare Archibald, described as "a young man of means and prominence, intellectually her inferior." To Carlyle he was a "rich insignificant Aberdeen Mr. Somebody." Noting Margaret's intellectual gifts and social ambitions, Archibald suggested that possibly Bannerman's "whole public career was largely shaped by his wife." This may well be an accurate assessment, for the disparity between his capacities and those of Margaret was marked. His dispatches give no evidence of literary attainments or particular acumen, and in his business ventures he almost always failed.

Bannerman accepted appointment as lieutenant governor of his wife's native colony late in

1850, after having declined previous offers of posts in the West Indies for fear of her health. He was knighted in February 1851 prior to his departure for Prince Edward Island. The colonial secretary, Lord Grey, instructed him to institute responsible government, which by this time had the overwhelming support of the Island population. Bannerman did this, and, aided by his Whiggish proclivities and jocular manner, quickly established warm personal relationships with members of the new Reform government led by George Coles*. When evidence of Orangeism appeared in the colony, in the form of the Orange oath published in the *Islander* in 1852, Bannerman, mindful of the sensitivities of the Irish Roman Catholic tenantry who supported the Reformers, issued a proclamation condemning the Orange Order. He also quarrelled with several of his Tory former executive councillors, including Edward Palmer*, John Myrie HOLL, Thomas Heath HAVILAND, and Daniel Brenan*, over the rank and precedence due to them. Hence he became identified as a Reform partisan, a great favourite with one section of the populace, and roundly condemned by another.

It was in this context that Bannerman gave the Colonial Office cause to doubt his political wisdom and continued usefulness in Prince Edward Island. The Reform government was defeated at the polls in mid 1853 by the Conservatives under Holl and Palmer, but it did not resign. When the successful Tory candidates petitioned for an early session Bannerman declined to act on their request. The new government, finally installed in office in February 1854, was soon involved in a bitter dispute with Bannerman. Since the Franchise Act of 1853 had only received royal assent after the election, he argued that the assembly no longer represented the electorate; and if any by-elections were held, the new members chosen by the enlarged electorate would be seated beside men elected under the old, restricted franchise. For these and other reasons Bannerman insisted that another dissolution was necessary, and, defying the unanimous opinion of his Executive Council, called an election for June 1854. The Liberals, who had petitioned for another election even before leaving office, reaped the benefits of the enlarged franchise and won handily.

The Colonial Office had already decided to transfer Bannerman to the Bahamas, where responsible government had not been instituted. He wished to stay in Prince Edward Island until September but his superiors recognized that he had abandoned viceregal detachment and become partisan in his actions. He was not allowed to remain to greet Coles upon his return to office in

1854. He was, nevertheless, permitted to sojourn in the Boston area until the autumn in order that his wife would not have to face the full rigours of the tropical climate immediately upon her arrival. She proved able to withstand it for two years before returning to England.

In mid 1857, Bannerman returned as governor to a more northerly region, Newfoundland, where Margaret rejoined him. A few months earlier Newfoundland had induced Britain to abrogate a draft convention extending French fishing privileges in the colony and to promise that "the consent of the Community of Newfoundland is . . . the essential preliminary to any modification of their territorial or maritime rights." Political leaders in a colony heavily dependent on the fishery considered this pledge a logical extension of the system of responsible government granted two years earlier. So confident was the political mood that Bannerman's installation attracted little public fanfare. The appointment of a new governor, noted the pro-government *Newfoundlander*, no longer caused the fear which it had "under the defunct irresponsible system" when the governor was all-powerful, and it mentioned Bannerman's positive role in the establishment of responsible government in Prince Edward Island.

Bannerman, however, maintained that "Responsible Government . . . increases rather than diminishes the Governor's responsibility." A governor could be impeached, but "his ministers cannot be . . . nor have they a particle of responsibility . . . excepting to their own constituencies." He agreed that a governor must select his council from those who had the confidence of the people and consult them, but he was "by no means obliged to follow their advice if he considers that advice to be wrong." Bannerman was appalled to find that his predecessor, Governor Sir Charles Henry DARLING, even on an imperial issue like the fishery convention, had admitted he was powerless to impose the views of the imperial government. As early as August 1858 Bannerman forcefully explained his view on the governor's prerogative to Liberal leader John Kent*.

Bannerman's term began on a personally vexatious note. Soon after his arrival in St John's his oath of office was "attacked" as offensive to Roman Catholics, who formed nearly half the colony's population and dominated the governing Liberal party. More serious was a dispute over his salary. In 1855 the assembly had reduced the governor's salary from £3,000 to £2,000 annually. The legislation, about which Bannerman evidently had no prior warning, came into effect only at his appointment. The government also began paying the salary in Newfoundland currency, which was worth slightly less than British sterling. Bannerman considered this action "not only irregular but illegal," and appealed to law officers of the Colonial Office. They decided in his favour, and the Newfoundland government accepted the verdict.

The souring influence of the currency issue, coupled with Bannerman's exaggerated views of his prerogative, was bound to create trouble between the governor and his independent-minded Executive Council. The prospect of conflict increased when Premier Philip Francis Little*, an experienced and astute political leader, resigned in 1858, and was succeeded by the fiery, intemperate John Kent. With evident distaste for colonial politics and little faith in the democratic process in Newfoundland's sectarian, class-divided, and semi-illiterate society, Bannerman soon became convinced that Kent and his ministers were unfit to govern.

Bannerman was annoyed that the Newfoundland government refused the British request for positive proposals to settle the vexed issue of French fishing rights on the western shore, while still insisting on a virtual veto over any decision of the imperial authorities. He was convinced that the Executive Council was exploiting the issue for narrow political gain and warned Kent that he would never follow Darling's precedent of informing his Executive Council of confidential dispatches from London on the French fishery question. Newfoundland politicians became alarmed when they learned in mid 1860 that negotiations were underway between Britain and France. Kent, who had been dropped from the Anglo-French commission on the fisheries in the spring of that year, complained bitterly at being excluded, though in reality the governor himself had little information on the subject.

Although diplomatically inept Bannerman was on sound constitutional ground in protecting the crown's prerogative on a matter of such direct imperial interest as the fisheries. But he also frequently took issue with his ministers on domestic matters. On one occasion in 1858 Bannerman had insisted on conducting his own inquiry before acting on a council resolution to dismiss Financial Secretary James Tobin* for his criticisms of clerical influence on the Supreme Court. Kent angrily threatened to resign. On another occasion in 1860 Bannerman dismissed a magistrate at Trinity Bay recently appointed by the Executive Council, which then threatened resignation. Instead the council formally censured Bannerman for not giving the magistrate opportunity to answer charges. The Colonial Office concurred and criticized Bannerman's procedure, though also supporting him in this situation. Bannerman, however, was not to be deterred by such criticism.

He again showed his resolve to be at the helm in late 1859 when the Executive Council failed to inform him about election riots which had occurred a few days earlier at Harbour Grace. When he received a report directly from the local magistrate, he charged that his council had deliberately "suppressed and withheld" documents intended for him. In the event of a recurrence of such an incident, he warned the council, he would "dispense with their services." Reports from Harbour Grace convinced Bannerman that the riots were caused by attempts of Roman Catholic priests to control the election. Since the governing Liberal party was overwhelmingly Roman Catholic, Bannerman undoubtedly suspected his council of political motives. He was anxious to keep the political influence of the Roman Catholic clergy in check as well as maintain law and order. He had not dismissed the Liberal council realizing that the Liberals would not have been defeated in an ensuing election.

To Bannerman's delight the political situation soon changed dramatically. In the spring of 1860 John Thomas MULLOCK, the influential Roman Catholic bishop of St John's and until then a strong supporter of the Liberals, publicly criticized the government for reneging on a pledge to establish a steamship service around the island and for its allegedly corrupt administration of poor relief. Bannerman heartily concurred and was pleased that Mullock at last saw the incompetence and corruption of the Kent government.

With Bishop Mullock now realigned against the government and the Liberal party seriously divided over regulations to control poor relief, Bannerman was free to act more decisively against his ministers. During an assembly debate on 25 Feb. 1861 the receiver general, Thomas Glen*, announced the withdrawal of a bill to legalize the use of Newfoundland currency for all official transactions except the payment of salaries to the governor and chief justice. The bill was withdrawn because Bannerman insisted that it could only be operative when formally sanctioned by the British government. The bill would also have nullified a pending court case by two assistant judges to have their salaries paid in British sterling. Hugh William Hoyles*, leader of the Tory Protestant opposition, informed the house that the two judges, on his advice, had petitioned the governor against the bill. Kent, who had not been informed of the petition,

Bannerman

charged that the bill had been defeated "by the minority in concert with the Judges and the Governor."

When Bannerman read reports of Kent's statement he immediately demanded to know whether the premier was accurately quoted. Kent curtly replied that the governor had no constitutional right to query him about his statements in the assembly. Bannerman now had the pretext he wanted and, after taking legal advice from Hoyles, he immediately dismissed the government and invited Hoyles to form the new government. Bannerman, as Kent and his colleagues were quick to charge, acted hastily and despotically. As a result the island was plunged into its worst political crisis since the introduction of representative institutions in 1832.

On Bannerman's advice Hoyles reserved three positions in the council for Roman Catholics in order to avoid sectarian violence, but managed to convince only Laurence O'BRIEN, the president of the Legislative Council, to join his ministry. With standings in the assembly unchanged, Hoyles' minority government was quickly defeated in a Liberal non-confidence motion. Bannerman obviously realized the importance for himself of a Tory victory in the general election, but the stakes were higher than he knew. The Duke of Newcastle, the colonial secretary, declared that "nothing can justify this extreme step except . . . success." If a Conservative majority was elected, Bannerman would be vindicated but, if Kent and the Liberals won, the governor "must probably resign or be recalled."

Bannerman probably expected Bishop Mullock's support but after several weeks' silence Mullock spoke forcefully against the reassertion in Newfoundland of Protestant Tory rule. To make matters worse the Anglican bishop, Edward Feild*, publicly took Bannerman's side. Contests were held in only four constituencies (the remaining seats were filled by acclamation) and despite Bannerman's military precautions, there was extensive violence in Carbonear, Harbour Grace, St John's, and Harbour Main [see Mullock, HOGSETT]. The overall result, pending the outcome of the two disputed districts of Harbour Grace and Harbour Main, gave the Tories 14 seats and Liberals 12. For the interim Bannerman had met Newcastle's criterion of success. But it was a precarious victory, threatened by the further crowd violence in St John's at the opening of the new assembly. Bannerman was convinced that the basic issue in Newfoundland was whether the colony was to be governed by the queen's representative or by what Hoyles described as a "purely Romish despotism,

marked by nominally free institutions." Consequently it was imperative to control at least one of the disfranchised districts and thus maintain a Protestant Tory majority. In the case of Harbour Main a Tory-dominated committee of the assembly studied the election results and ruled in favour of the more independent Liberal candidates who had no clerical backing. In Harbour Grace a peaceful by-election in November returned two Protestant Tories, giving the Hoyles government an absolute and dependable majority.

The Colonial Office declined to take any action on a petition of some 8,000 Catholics, including Bishop Mullock, indicting Bannerman for constitutional despotism before the elections and responsibility for the ensuing riots, but it criticized some of his actions, although stressing the difficulty of his position had the Liberals been elected. This imperial disapproval, the personal strain of 1861, and Bannerman's respect for Hoyles may have led the governor to be more cautious in the use of prerogative powers. When he retired in September 1864 he proudly emphasized that there had never been any disagreement between him and the Conservative government. A decade earlier he had written the same about his relationship with the Prince Edward Island Liberals as they were leaving office.

Bannerman planned to wind up his affairs at the Colonial Office and spend the remainder of his life in Aberdeen. But in London he contracted a bad cold, and, enfeebled, fell down a flight of stairs. Paralysis set in and he died on 30 Dec. 1864, predeceasing his wife by almost 14 years. They had had no children, and as Bannerman had never been careful with his personal finances, his widow passed her final years in considerably reduced circumstances. The influence of this strong-willed and capable woman over him in the exercise of his duties as governor must remain a matter for speculation. Certainly the least that can be said is that Bannerman, a former Whig MP, became a colonial governor with a strong belief in the prerogative of his office, and that in his political interventions he displayed remarkable obstinacy. In both Prince Edward Island and Newfoundland he came to be regarded as by almost half the population as unacceptably partisan.

EDWARD C. MOULTON AND
IAN ROSS ROBERTSON

PANL, GN 1/3A, 1856–62; GN 1/3B, 1855–58; GN 9/1, 1861–69. PRO, CO 194/150–65; CO 226/79–83, especially 226/79, 28–35, 42, 76–77, 84–85, 89–90; 226/80, 172–74, 213–60, 387, 620–23; 226/81, 14, 47, 138–39, 142–43, 270–71; 226/82, 45–49, 68–69, 222–31; 226/83,

18, 41–43, 78–79, 87–93, 99–103, 119, 123–29, 141–42, 148–55, 182–83, 186, 189–94. Grand Orange Lodge of P.E.I., *Annual report*, 1867, 11–12. P.E.I., House of Assembly, *Journal*, 1854, 8; app.L. *Examiner* (Charlottetown), 14, 18 Dec. 1850; 4 Jan. 1851; 30 Jan. 1865. *Islander*, 8, 15 Aug. 1851; 30 April, 14 May, 4 June, 10, 17, 24 Sept., 1, 15 Oct. 1852; 10 Feb., 26 May, 9, 16, 23 June 1854; 27 Jan. 1865. *Newfoundlander*, 1857–61. *Patriot* (St John's), 1860–61. *Protestant and Evangelical Witness*, 28 Jan. 1865. *Public Ledger* (St John's), 1861. *Royal Gazette* (Charlottetown), 17 Dec. 1850, 21 July 1851, 24 Oct. 1853, 30 May 1854. *Royal Gazette* (St John's), 1861. *St. John's Daily News and Newfoundland Journal of Commerce*, 1861.

R. C. Archibald, *Carlyle's first love, Margaret Gordon, Lady Bannerman; an account of her life, ancestry, and homes, her family, and friends* (London, 1910). W. R. Livingston, *Responsible government in Prince Edward Island: a triumph of self-government under the crown* (University of Iowa studies in the social sciences, IX, no.4, Iowa City, 1931). Prowse, *History of Nfld.* (1895). Robertson, "Religion, politics, and education in P.E.I.," 92–93. George Sutherland, *A manual of the geography and natural and civil history of Prince Edward Island, for the use of schools, families and emigrants* (Charlottetown, 1861), 132–34. Thompson, *French shore problem in Nfld.* D. C. Harvey, "Dishing the Reformers," *RSC Trans.*, 3rd ser., XXV (1931), sect.II, 37–44. W. S. MacNutt, "Political advance and social reform, 1842–1861," *Canada's smallest province* (Bolger), 124–27. E. C. Moulton, "Constitutional crisis and civil strife in Newfoundland, February to November 1861," *CHR*, XLVIII (1967), 251–72.

BARAGA, FREDERIC (Irenaeus Fridericus, Irenej Friderik, Friedrich), Roman Catholic priest, missionary, and bishop; b. 29 June 1797 near Dobrnič (Yugoslavia) at the castle of Malavas where his father was overseer, son of Maria Katharina Josefa Jenčič and Johann Nepomuc Baraga; d. 19 Jan. 1868 at Marquette, Mich.

Frederic Baraga was born into a prosperous Slovenian family, but not into the nobility as has sometimes been stated. He received his early education from tutors and at Laibach (Ljubljana, Yugoslavia) before studying law at the University of Vienna and entering the seminary at Laibach. He was ordained a priest on 21 Sept. 1823 and surrendered all rights to the family estates in order to take up pastoral work in the diocese of Laibach. He was soon attracted to foreign missions and in 1829, when the Leopoldine Society was established in Vienna to encourage missionary activity, he applied to be sent to the diocese of Cincinnati in the United States. Baraga was the first missionary sponsored by the society and arrived in New York City on 31 Dec. 1830. He was already fluent in several European languages including English and French.

After studying Ojibwa at Cincinnati, where he also preached to German congregations, Baraga set out in 1831 for Arbre Croche (Harbor Springs), a settlement of some 650 people in Michigan. In 1833 he went to Grand River (Grand Rapids, Mich.), in 1835 to La Pointe (Wis.), and in 1843 to L'Anse on Keweenaw Bay, where he established a mission. In 1848 he was named a vicar general of the diocese of Detroit and in 1853 bishop of Amyzonia responsible for the diocese of Upper Michigan. His episcopal seat was Sault Ste Marie (Mich.) until 1865 when he transferred to Marquette.

Baraga's first missions in the United States were among mixed populations which included Indians and fur-traders, many of them retired and many of them French Canadians or Métis. Because there were few Catholic missionaries in much of the territory north of lakes Huron and Superior Baraga soon made occasional missionary trips in the 1840s to settlements in this area, where he again served fur-traders and Indians. He depended at first on the bishop of Quebec, then after 1837 on the bishop of Kingston, to provide him with a share in the Leopoldine grants to carry on his work in Canadian territory. As a bishop himself after 1853 he was delegated jurisdiction by the bishop of Toronto for the missions on the north shore of Lake Superior from Bruce Mines to Fort William (Thunder Bay, Ont.), including the Jesuit missions at Fort William (where Father Dominique Duranquet served) and Garden River (under the care of Father Auguste Kohler), as well as the Indian missions at Michipicoton, Lake Nipigon, and Pic. In October 1854 he confirmed 44 persons at Garden River, the first confirmation to be held there. In 1856 the missions were transferred to the charge of Bishop John Farrell* of Hamilton, but responsibility for them continued to be delegated to Baraga. However, he himself served only the area around the Canadian Sault Ste Marie where, he said, "there are many Indians . . . who cannot speak but Indian" and he could provide better service to them. He visited the Sault regularly, and in 1862 celebrated the first Mass at Goulais Bay, some 20 miles to the north, in a church which he had begun.

Baraga's services as a missionary to the Indians in what became northern Ontario were extensive and pioneering, but his influence on both contemporary and later missionaries working among the Indians in Canada is the most significant aspect of his career. Before coming to North America he had published prayer books in Slovenian, and as early as 1832 he published one in Ojibwa. He published numerous prayer books,

books of meditation, and other devotional works in Indian languages, several of which went through many editions. He also published a volume in German on the customs of the Indians. His most significant works, however, were a grammar of the Ojibwa language, first published in Detroit in 1850, and an Ojibwa dictionary, in 1853. Both volumes were indispensable to missionaries wishing to learn the language, and were printed numerous times. Father Albert Lacombe* published editions of the two works in Montreal in 1878–80.

Bishop Baraga died at Marquette in 1868. His cultural and linguistic influence on later missionaries and on the study of the Ojibwa language and its dialects was felt well into the 20th century and his works continue to be republished and studied.

J. S. McGivern

Frederic Baraga's principal works were the following: *A theoretical and practical grammar of the Otchipwe language, the language spoken by the Chippewa Indians* . . . (Detroit, 1850; 2nd ed., [ed. Albert Lacombe], Montreal, 1878); and *A dictionary of the Otchipwe language, explained in English* . . . (Cincinnati, Ohio, 1853; new ed., [ed. Albert Lacombe], 2v., Montreal, 1878–80). References to other editions of these works and to other works by Baraga can be found in R. P. Čuješ, *Ninidjanissidog saiagiinagog; contribution of the Slovenes to the socio-cultural development of the Canadian Indians* (Antigonish, N.S., 1968), and *National union catalog. Appleton's cyclopædia of American biography*, ed. J. G. Wilson *et al.* (10v., New York, 1887–1924), I. *DAB.* Lorenzo Cadieux et Ernest Comte, *Un héros du Lac Supérieur, Frédéric Baraga* (Soc. historique du Nouvel-Ontario, *Documents historiques*, no.27, Sudbury, Ont., 1954). Chrysostom Verwyst, *Life and labors of Rt. Rev. Frederic Baraga, first bishop of Marquette, Mich.* . . . (Milwaukee, Wis., 1900).

BARDY, PIERRE-MARTIAL, teacher, doctor, and politician; b. 30 Nov. 1797 at Quebec, son of Pierre Bardy, a wig maker, and Louise Cochy, *dit* Lacouture; d. 7 Nov. 1869 at Quebec.

Mathieu Bardy, Pierre Martial's grandfather, was descended from a family of Italian origin that settled at Brest, France, and he came to Canada early in the 18th century. In 1811 Pierre-Martial entered the Petit Séminaire de Québec, where he received a classical education. He was a brilliant pupil, and with his friend Elzéar Bédard* was considered the best student in the philosophy class. Both began theological studies and were admitted to holy orders at the same time by Bishop Joseph-Octave Plessis*. While continuing to study theology at the Grand Séminaire de Québec, Bardy taught the *belles-lettres* and

rhetoric classes at the Petit Séminaire for two years. In 1821 he renounced his orders, and on 5 Feb. 1822 married Marie-Marguerite Archambault, of the parish of La Présentation, near Saint-Hyacinthe. Of their seven children only one reached adult age.

After leaving the Séminaire de Québec, Bardy turned to teaching: in 1825 he taught the basic elements of classics at Boucherville. He also tried his hand at poetry, and composed songs, such as one which has turned up, saying farewell to his friend Dr John Dies Nelson, brother of Robert* and Wolfred. Bardy kept his interest in education, holding the office of school inspector from 1842 to 1868.

By 1824 he had also become interested in medicine: he studied with Dr William Robertson* of Montreal and received his diploma on 13 Nov. 1829. He practised first in Saint-Jacques, then in Saint-Athanase-d'Iberville, and finally settled in the *faubourg* Saint-Roch in Quebec in 1839. He practised with his colleague Édouard Rousseau among the working class, and was known for his great devotion and charity. From 1848 to 1854 Bardy was secretary of the École de Médecine de Québec which he, Joseph Morrin, Charles-Jacques Frémont, and others founded. He gave courses there on the institutes of medicine and surgery, in medical jurisprudence, and botany. When the faculty of medicine of Université Laval was created [*see* Louis-Jacques Casault], he did not become a member of the professorial body. Around 1854 he became a supporter of homeopathy, a system popularized by Samuel Hahnemann, a German who practised medicine in Paris from 1835 to 1843. Bardy had heated exchanges with Dr Joseph Painchaud* on the subject in the Quebec press, and his ideas seem to have discredited him somewhat in the medical profession.

A close friend of Louis-Joseph Papineau* and an ardent Patriote, Bardy ran in the 1834 election in the county of Rouville. He easily defeated the Bureaucrat party's candidate, and sat in the assembly from 1834 to 1838. He then lost interest in politics for a time. On 9 Oct. 1840 he took as his second wife Marie-Soulange Lefebvre. They had two daughters; Marie-Virginie-Célina, the sole survivor of this family, was an occasional writer, and the wife of Pierre-Vincent Valin*, a Quebec businessman.

On 19 June 1842, following the Act of Union, conceived as a measure designed to destroy the French Canadian nationality, a large meeting was held at Saint-Roch. The Société Saint-Jean-Baptiste of Quebec was founded on that occasion, modelled on the society at Montreal, which dated from 1834 [see Jean-François-Marie-Joseph MacDonell]. Bardy, one of the most enthusiastic advocates of the project, was elected president. Napoléon Aubin* became vice-president, and James Huston* and Jacques-Philippe Rhéaume secretaries. On 24 June, in his presidential address on Saint-Jean-Baptiste day, Bardy stressed the importance of industrial development, "a necessary objective towards which we must direct all our energy. . . . Our products," he declared, "will be able in part to meet our pressing needs; let us safeguard them, let us manufacture them." As president of the society from 1859 to 1861, his name was associated with the erection of the Monument des Braves for the heroes of 1760. When there were insufficient funds to complete the monument in 1860, Bardy launched repeated appeals in the press and throughout the province. His wife organized a fair with the ladies of Saint-Roch and Saint-Jean. It was not until 19 Oct. 1863 that the governor general of Canada, Charles Stanley Monck*, unveiled the column. The monument, still not paid for, was declared public property in 1864; the promoters thus escaped their debts. This difficult affair, which compromised the society's finances, somewhat tarnished Bardy's reputation as an administrator. Later, in 1880, his daughter claimed that the society had unjustly forgotten her father, and she endeavoured to ensure that his memory was honoured.

In 1843 Bardy was among those who sought Papineau's return. In 1849, with Napoléon Aubin, Jacques-Philippe Rhéaume, Joseph Légaré*, Antoine Plamondon*, and other aggressive anti-unionists, he committed himself to annexationism. He chaired the meeting of 27 Oct. 1849 in Quebec and assumed the leadership of an annexation movement which gathered 600 signatures; he soon withdrew to give his full attention to his "professional affairs," although he did not change his opinion.

Contemporaries of Bardy praised his literary gifts and talent as a speaker. He died on 7 Nov. 1869 at Saint-Roch, and received the honour of being buried in the crypt of the Quebec Basilica. A street in Quebec commemorates his name, as does the house where the offices of the Société Saint-Jean-Baptiste of Quebec are located.

PIERRE SAVARD

PAC, MG 30, D62, 3, pp.253–57. *Daily Evening Mercury* (Quebec), 21 Jan. 1880. *L'Opinion publique* (Montréal), 13 mai 1880. P.-G. Roy, *Fils de Québec*, III, 89–91. H.-J.-J.-B. Chouinard, *Fête nationale des canadiens-français . . .* (4v., Québec, 1881–1903), IV, 315–16. *Le docteur Pierre Martial Bardy; sa vie, ses œuvres et sa mémoire*, F.-X. Burque, compil. (Québec, 1907). Sylvio Leblond, "Le Dr Pierre-Martial Bardy (1797–1869)," *Trois siècles de médecine québécoise* (Québec, 1970), 75–82. Monet, *Last cannon shot*. P.-G. Roy, *Les petites choses de notre histoire* (7 sér., Lévis, Qué., 1919–44), 6e sér. Benjamin Sulte, *Histoire des Canadiens-français, 1608–1880 . . .* (8v., Montréal, 1882–84), VIII, 130. Victor Morin, "Une chanson du Dr Bardy," *BRH*, XLVI (1940), 332–37. Damase Potvin, "Un petit roman d'amour a valu à Québec le fondateur de la Société St-Jean-Baptiste . . . ," *L'Information médicale et paramédicale* (Montréal), 19 janv. 1954, 8–9.

BARRY, JAMES, military surgeon; b. 1795, birthplace and parentage unknown, perhaps a nephew of James Barry, RA; d. 25 July 1865 in London, England.

James Barry, who early began to acquire aristocratic patrons, was a literary and medical student at the University of Edinburgh, receiving a diploma in medicine in 1812; after further medical studies in London, he joined the Army Medical Department as a hospital assistant in 1813. In 1816 he was posted to the garrison at Cape Town, Cape Colony (South Africa), as assistant surgeon.

In the Cape Colony he soon took on civil responsibilities, including the inspection of the sale of drugs and of government institutions such as jails. His undoubted ability and determination in his duties, in the Cape Colony as elsewhere, were accompanied by strong independence and often violent outbursts so that his career, while distinguished, was also turbulent. He lost his civil role in the colony after an incident in 1825. In the late 1820s he went to Mauritius as staff surgeon to the garrison, in 1831 to Jamaica with the same appointment, and later in the decade to St Helena Island as principal medical officer. His conflicts with his military colleagues and superiors resulted in his being sent home under arrest in 1838. Barry somehow survived his irregular actions, as he had done before and would do later, seemingly aided by friends in high places. In the 1840s he served in Trinidad and in Malta, as principal medical officer. These southern postings gave him much experience in dealing with epidemics and fever. While stationed on Corfu in the 1850s he had to provide facilities for casualties of the Crimean War.

In 1857 Barry was posted to Canada as inspector general of military hospitals. He worked to improve the diet, ample but monotonous, of the soldiers and also their lodgings, promoting particularly the innovation of providing means for housing married couples away from the single men's barracks. He drew attention to the unsatisfactory water and drainage systems in the Quebec barracks. During his service in Canada Barry was troubled with bronchitis and was treated by Dr George William Campbell*, later dean of the Medical Faculty of McGill University; following a serious attack of influenza in the spring of 1859, Barry was sent to England and put on half pay by the army.

After the physician's death in 1865 rumours, apparently begun by his charwoman, circulated in London that James Barry was a woman, and the story, reinforced by undoubted physical peculiarities in size and voice, was disseminated widely in the press. It has been believed then and since, but recent research shows room for doubt. More likely seems the suggestion, elaborating one made 80 years ago in the medical journal *Lancet*, that Barry was a male hermaphrodite who had feminine breast development and external genitalia. Barry's personal life must have been difficult in any case, though he accomplished much in his medical career.

CHARLES G. ROLAND

Bibliotheca Osleriana; a catalogue of books illustrating the history of medicine and science . . . , comp. William Osler (Montreal and London, 1969), no.5394. *DNB.* E. H. Burrows, *A history of medicine in South Africa up to the end of the nineteenth century* (Cape Town and Amsterdam, 1958), 80–85. Isobel Rae, *The strange story of Dr. James Barry, army surgeon, inspector-general of hospitals, discovered on death to be a woman* (London and New York [1958]). George Thomas, *Fifty years of my life* (2v., London, 1876). "A female medical combatant," *Medical Times and Gazette: a Journal of Medical Science, Literature, Criticism and News* (London), July–December 1865, 227–28. P. R. Kirby, "Dr James Barry, controversial South African medical figure; a recent evaluation of his life and sex," *South African Medical Journal* (Cape Town), 44 (1970), 506–16. E. Rogers, "A female member of the army medical staff," *Lancet* (London), July–December 1895, 1086–87.

BAVEUX, JEAN-CLAUDE-LÉONARD (known in Canada under the name of **Jean-Claude Léonard**), priest, Sulpician, Oblate of Mary Immaculate; b. 6 Nov. 1796 at Montier-en-Der (dept of Haute-Marne, France), son of Jean-Claude Baveux, farmer, and Marie-Catherine Lefranc; d. 21 Nov. 1865 at Montreal.

After serving in Napoleon's army, Jean-Claude-Léonard Baveux entered the Petit Séminaire de Monistrol-sur-Loire (dept of Haute-Loire), where he completed his studies, including theology. He prepared for his future vocation by accompanying various preachers,

whom he assisted by teaching the catechism. Because he wished to work in America, he joined the Sulpicians in 1827. On 31 May 1828 Baveux, already a deacon, was ordained a priest at Rouen, and shortly after he left for Montreal. The new priest was first sent to the Indian reserve at Lac-des-Deux-Montagnes (Oka), where he remained until 1834; in 1834–35 he was a teacher at the Collège de Montréal. Then after five years as curate of the parish of Notre-Dame de Montréal, he became the secretary of Charles-Auguste-Marie-Joseph de Forbin-Janson*, bishop of Nancy, during the latter's preaching tour in Canada (1840–42).

Baveux was attracted by missionary life and decided to enter the noviciate of the Oblates at Longueuil in 1842; on 2 Aug. 1843 he made his profession of perpetual vows. After his noviciate he remained for three years at Longueuil, where he gave his attention to the practical organization of the house and preaching in the parishes of Montreal diocese. In October 1846, with the encouragement of Joseph-Bruno Guigues*, the future bishop of Bytown (Ottawa), Father Baveux undertook a recruiting campaign in France, Belgium, and Savoy, and is said to have attracted more than 70 individuals to noviciates in France. Upon his return to Canada in 1848, Father Baveux was appointed founding director of the Saint-Pierre-Apôtre residence, in the *faubourg* Québec in the eastern part of Montreal and served there from 1848 to 1850. From 1850 to 1863 he was in charge of the church there. The *faubourg* Québec, under his prompting, became a fervent religious centre; his zeal and popularity in this poor district earned him the title of "father of the *faubourg*."

In 1864 ill health obliged Father Baveux to leave Montreal for Caughnawaga, where he was appointed director of the residence on the Indian reserve. Thus he ended his career, as he had begun some 30 years before, among the Indians. He entered the Hôtel-Dieu of Montreal on 28 July 1865, and died there after an illness of some months.

GASTON CARRIÈRE

Archives provinciales O.M.I. (Montréal), *Codex historicus*, Saint-Hilaire ; Longueuil ; Saint-Pierre de Montréal (copies at AHO). *Notices nécrologiques des O.M.I.*, I, 217–40. Carrière, *Hist. des O.M.I.*, I, III, IV, V, VI. Fernand Lepage, "Aux origines de la province belge; les vocations belges," *Missions de la Congrégation des Missionnaires Oblats de Marie-Immaculée* (Rome), 81 (1954), 294–305. Henri Verkin, "La tournée de propagande du père Léonard," *Études oblates* (Ottawa), 26 (1967), 55–88.

BAYARD, ROBERT, doctor and writer; b. in 1788 at Wilmot, N.S., son of Colonel Samuel Vetch Bayard of the King's Orange Rangers; m. 31 Dec. 1812 Frances Catherine Robertson of Halifax, and they had at least three children; d. 4 June 1868 at Welsford, N.B.

Descended from the Chevalier de Bayard of 16th century France, Robert Bayard's family was prominent in New York before the American War of Independence. His father settled at Wilmot at the conclusion of the war and was appointed lieutenant-colonel of the Royal Nova Scotia Regiment. Robert Bayard became a lieutenant in the British army at age 13, but was permitted to study at King's Collegiate School, Windsor, N.S. He eventually gave up his commission, and after reading medicine for a short time entered the University of Edinburgh from which he graduated with a medical degree in 1809. His graduate thesis was on complicated labour, anaesthesia in obstetrics, and blood-letting. In 1811 the degree of DCL was conferred on him by King's College, Windsor.

Bayard then became professor of obstetrics at the College of Physicians and Surgeons in the University of the State of New York, but during the War of 1812 chose to leave the country rather than take the oath of allegiance. He made his way to Portland, Maine, then, sailing in an open boat, to Saint John, N.B., in May 1813. After moving to Halifax, N.S., he settled with his wife in Kentville, N.S., where a son was born in 1814 and where Bayard practised until 1823.

That year they moved to Saint John where Bayard took a front place in the medical profession. He wrote at least two medical works, *Exposition of facts relative to a case of croup* and *Evidences of the delusions of homoeopathy*. A versatile person, he interested himself in the advancement of agriculture by speaking and writing and showed a taste for controversy. In August 1846 his writing in the press ended a movement for a public hospital, planned as a memorial to the loyalists. Excluded from the founding meeting of the project, Bayard criticized the private deliberations of the organizers, who included Judge Robert PARKER, John William Dering GRAY, Robert Leonard Hazen*, and Charles Simonds*, and suggested instead that a public infirmary be added to the Marine Hospital. In 1849 he spoke out strongly for the route of the proposed European and North American Railway from Saint John to Shediac, which became a reality in 1857.

In 1849 he also became involved in the controversies within the Church of England which reached the public through the press and pamphlets. Bayard was evangelical in his beliefs and opposed to Tractarian influences emanating from Bishop John Medley*. He supported the Reverend J. W. D. Gray, rector of Trinity Church, Saint John, and others in denouncing the Tractarians in *A statement of facts, as they occurred at the late annual meeting of the Diocesan Church Society* in 1849.

In 1837 Bayard was joined in medical practice by his eldest son, William, who promoted the establishment of the Saint John General Hospital in 1860 and served on its board of commissioners from 1863 to 1903. Another son, Edwin, also practised in Saint John.

In his later years Robert Bayard spent his summers on his farm in the Annapolis valley in Nova Scotia. For the last years of his life he resided on another farm on the Nerepis River in New Brunswick near Welsford, where he died in 1868. The railway station at this location was called "Bayard" for many years.

A. D. GIBBON

Robert Bayard was the author of *Evidences of the delusions of homoeopathy* (Saint John, N.B., 1857); *Exposition of facts relative to a case of croup, in a letter to Henry Cook, surgeon* (Saint John, N.B., 1826); *A statement of facts, as they occurred at the late annual meeting of the Diocesan Church Society: with a reply to some misstatements and expositions in the Rev'd. F. Coster's defence of the "Companion to the Prayer Book"* (Saint John, N.B., 1849; 1875). N.B. Museum, Trinity Anglican Church (Saint John, N.B.), Papers, 1790–1860. *Biographical review: this volume contains biographical sketches of leading citizens of the province of New Brunswick*, ed. I. A. Jack (Boston, 1900), 37–40. A. V. Hanscome, *History of the Saint John General Hospital and School of Nursing* (Saint John, N.B., 1955). J. W. Lawrence, "The medical men of St. John in its first half century," N.B. Hist. Soc., *Coll.*, I (1894), 298–99.

BAYNES, Sir ROBERT LAMBERT, naval officer; b. 1796, youngest son of Thomas Baynes, commander in the Royal Navy, and his wife Edith; m. in 1846 Frances, daughter of Thomas Denman, lord chief justice of England; d. 7 Sept. 1869 at Upper Norwood (now in London), England.

Robert Lambert Baynes entered the Royal Navy on 19 April 1810 and was promoted lieutenant on 8 April 1818. He served on *Asia* at the battle of Navarino in 1827, during the Greek War of Independence, and received a CB, three foreign decorations, and a captaincy. He was promoted rear-admiral on 7 Feb. 1855, serving in the Baltic, and was appointed commander-in-chief of the Pacific station at Valparaiso, Chile, on 8 July 1857, in *Ganges*, an 84-gun ship of the line.

Bazalgette

On 28 June 1858 the Admiralty instructed Baynes to ascertain that a sufficient naval force was on the northwest coast of North America to maintain law and order in the gold mining districts of British Columbia, then being invaded by Californian adventurers, and thus to uphold British sovereignty. Baynes arrived in *Ganges* at Esquimault on 17 Oct. 1858 and was among the official party at Fort Langley when the new colony of British Columbia was proclaimed on 19 Nov. 1858. He was responsible for ensuring that naval vessels were available for maintaining order and also for implementing Governor James Douglas*' regulations on mining. With winter approaching, however, the miners were leaving for California and Baynes was able to report to the Admiralty that all was quiet.

Baynes and the *Ganges* were absent from Esquimault between 22 Dec. 1858 and 5 Aug. 1859, attending to other station duties at Callao in Peru, and Valparaiso. Meanwhile the Anglo-American dispute over control of San Juan Island in lower Puget Sound had developed. On 27 July 1859 American soldiers under the orders of Brigadier-General William Selby Harney landed on the island to protect Americans against the alleged hostility of British colonial officials. Douglas wished the Royal Navy to land marines and oust them but Captain Geoffrey Thomas Phipps Hornby of *Tribune*, who replaced Baynes in his absence, refused. So too did Baynes on his return to Esquimault. As John T. Walbran* put it, "Neither the provocation of his enemies nor the rashness of his friends would allow him to hurry into ill-considered action, though he had an ample force to have prevented them landing or to effect their capture afterwards." Douglas' policy, Baynes said, would have resulted in war. As a compromise, Baynes urged a joint Anglo-American civil occupation of the island, but the American suggestion of a joint military occupation was adopted by the two governments towards the end of 1859. Both nations continued to maintain a military presence on San Juan until 1872 when Kaiser Wilhelm I offered his services as arbitrator and awarded the entire San Juan archipelago to the United States.

Both the Fraser River gold rush and the San Juan boundary dispute strengthened Baynes' conviction that the protection of British interests would be best served by the transfer of naval station headquarters from Valparaiso to the North Pacific. After Captain George H. Richards* in *Plumper* had completed surveys of possible sites, Baynes strongly recommended Esquimault to the Admiralty in November 1859 as the most suitable harbour. Although cabinet changes in Britain caused delays, the Admiralty adopted Esquimault as the Pacific station headquarters in 1862.

Baynes received a KCB on 18 April 1860, for what the Duke of Somerset, first lord of the Admiralty, termed the "good sense and prudence" he exhibited during the "intemperate proceedings" of General Harney. Criticism by Douglas, the colonial legislature, and the Victoria press of his policy of non-intervention died down by the time Baynes left Esquimault on 10 Sept. 1860. He left in *Ganges* for England which he reached on 27 April 1861, having completed 60,100 sea-miles during his four years as commander-in-chief. He was not employed again by the Royal Navy but, as was customary, advanced on the active list to vice-admiral in 1861 and admiral in 1865. During his visits to British Columbia he had painted water-colour landscapes, some of which are in the Provincial Archives in Victoria.

BARRY M. GOUGH

Maritime Museum of B.C. (Victoria), "H.M.S. *Ganges*, 1821–1929," [comp. P. W. Brock] (typescript). National Maritime Museum (London), Baynes coll., BAY/1–3. PABC, Colonial correspondence, Navy, H.M.S. *Ganges* correspondence. PRO, Adm. 1/5694, Y108, Y132, Y135, Y156; 1/5713, Y146; 1/5720, Y30; 1/5736, Y1, Y71; CO 60/1, 60/5–6, 305/12. B. M. Gough, *The Royal Navy and the northwest coast of North America, 1810–1914: a study of British maritime ascendancy* (Vancouver, 1971), 134–43, 161–66; "British policy in the San Juan boundary dispute, 1854–72," *Pacific Northwest Quarterly* (Seattle, Wash.), 62 (1971), 59–68; "'Turbulent frontiers' and British expansion: Governor James Douglas, the Royal Navy, and the British Columbia gold rushes," *Pacific Hist. Rev.* (Berkeley, Calif.), XLI (1972), 15–32.

BAZALGETTE, JOHN, army officer and colonial administrator; b. *c.* 1784 in London, England, son of Louis Bazalgette; m. Sarah Crawford Magdalen (her surname is not known), and they had at least 15 children; d. 28 March 1868 in London.

Descended from a French noble family which settled in England in the mid 18th century, John Bazalgette had already served with the British army in India, Egypt, Jersey, and Bermuda before arriving in Nova Scotia with the 99th Regiment in 1811. From aide-de-camp to Sir John Coape Sherbrooke*, Bazalgette advanced to a variety of staff appointments of which the principal were major of brigade at Halifax (1816–41) and deputy quartermaster-general and acting deputy adjutant general of Nova Scotia (1841–54). He became a major in 1819, a lieutenant-colonel in 1837, and a colonel in 1851. His seven youngest sons also entered the British army, introduced by clerkships in the brigade office or by purchased commissions, and two of his daughters took officers as husbands.

Bazalgette made only one six-month visit to England during 43 years of residence in Nova Scotia. His two eldest sons, Herbert Sawyer and John Van Norden, played brief but active roles in the Halifax business community in the 1830s and 1840s, where Bazalgette himself was a small investor in property and insurance and a director of the Bank of Nova Scotia. A nominal supporter of mainly Anglican-sponsored charities, he was also an initiator of such local organizations as the Halifax Athenaeum. Improvements at his residence, Belvedere, reflected his interest in agriculture and horticulture.

As senior military officer, Bazalgette acted as commander of the forces and administrator of the provincial government for Lieutenant Governor Sir John Harvey* from 30 May to 30 Sept. 1851 and from 22 March to 5 Aug. 1852. In 1851 Bazalgette dissolved the assembly, enabling the Liberal government to seek an electoral mandate to pursue Joseph Howe*'s railway policy. In 1852, in correspondence with the Colonial Office, Bazalgette firmly supported Nova Scotian views on the question of the controversial coastal fisheries. Conservative in outlook, he strove to advance provincial interests while fulfilling his first responsibility to the imperial government. In 1854, pressed by "weighty and irresistable claims," he returned to London where he retired from the army in 1858.

John Bazalgette's life depicts an unusual attachment by a British army officer to the military establishment and to a colonial city which it garrisoned.

S. BUGGEY

PAC, MG 24, A17, 4, pp.744–47, 1076–79; RG 8, I (C series), 1009, pp.97, 124. PANS, MG 12, HQ, 24–43; Vertical mss file, Societies, Athenaeum of Halifax, Prospectus, December 1834. PRO, CO 217/206, 217/208–9; RG 9/32, f.103, pp.9–10; WO 17/2358–401. St Paul's Anglican Church (Halifax), registers of baptisms and burials (mfm. at PANS). Somerset House (London), Probate Dept., will of John Bazalgette. *Acadian Recorder*, 13 Feb. 1819, 10 Nov. 1832, 6 Feb. 1841, 16 Aug. 1856. *British Colonist* (Halifax), 1851–52. *Morning Journal* (Halifax), 26 May, 10 Nov. 1854. *Novascotian*, 24 Jan. 1832; 10 Jan. 1833; 10 Aug., 14 Sept. 1836; 1851–52; 11 Jan. 1858. *Times* (London), 7 April 1868. G.B., WO, *Army list*, 1806–58. *Hart's army list*, 1846, 64, 87; 1869.

BEAUJEU, GEORGES-RENÉ SAVEUSE DE BEAUJEU, COMTE DE. *See* SAVEUSE

BECKWITH, JOHN CHARLES, British army officer and missionary; b. 2 Oct. 1789 at Halifax, N.S., the son of John Beckwith and Mary (Polly) Halliburton, sister of Brenton Halliburton*; d. 19 July 1862 at his home, La Torre, near Turin (Italy).

John Charles Beckwith's father had been an officer in the British army but he resigned his commission and settled in Nova Scotia where he served as adjutant-general and lieutenant-colonel in the provincial militia. On 2 June 1803 in England John Charles entered the British army as an ensign in the 50th or West Kent Regiment of Foot; on 29 Aug. 1804 he became a lieutenant in the 95th or Rifle Regiment of which his uncle, Sir Thomas Beckwith, was lieutenant-colonel. He rose to 1st lieutenant (13 June 1805) and captain (28 July 1808), and served in Hanover (1805–6), Denmark (1807), Sweden (1808), and in Portugal (1808–9) where he participated in Sir John Moore's retreat to Corunna, Spain. The regiment was in Walcheren (Netherlands) in 1809, but returned, in the winter of 1810, to Portugal where Beckwith took part in engagements against Masséna's retiring French army in the spring of 1811. In 1812 Beckwith became brigade-major to the 1st brigade of the light division and deputy assistant quartermaster-general. He received the Toulouse medal and rose to major (3 March 1814). In 1815 he served with Sir Thomas Picton's division at the battles of Quatre-Bras and Waterloo, where he lost his leg after it was shattered by a cannonball. He was rewarded with the Waterloo medal, promotion to lieutenant-colonel on 18 June 1815, and nomination as CB on 22 June. John Charles Beckwith was 25 years old and he had been in the army for 12 years fighting against Napoleon.

On 27 Jan. 1820 Beckwith was placed on half-pay as a member of the Rifle Brigade which had replaced the 95th; on 10 Jan. 1837 he was raised to colonel and on 7 Nov. 1846 to major-general.

After his injury Beckwith had returned to his parents in Halifax where he became a founder and patron of the town's first Sunday school established in connection with St George's Church. After 1825 this Sunday school continued under the direction of the rector Robert Fitzgerald UNIACKE. Beckwith also took an interest in the Royal Acadian School founded by Captain Walter Bromley* for poor children.

In 1826 Beckwith was invited to visit the Duke of Wellington at Apsley House in London; there he read Dr William Stephen Gilly's *Narrative of an excursion to the mountains of Piemont . . .* (London, 1824). This book led him to become concerned with the plight of a small group of

Beckwith

Protestants known as Waldensians or Vaudois who lived in the Piedmont valleys near Pinerolo. Beckwith visited the Waldensians for several years, then decided to make his headquarters near Turin and devote the rest of his life to assisting them. Drawing on his experience in Halifax, he worked to improve Waldensian schools some of which were as "ill-built as barns, as dirty as stables." He collected money from friends in England, visited the schools, urged building of new schools by the community, sent teachers to Lausanne and Florence for training, and encouraged the education of women. In all he opened or restored 120 district schools. When King Charles Albert of Sardinia adopted a more liberal policy and allowed Italian to be spoken, Beckwith sent young pastors and teachers to Florence to facilitate the process of substituting Italian for French. In 1848, in recognition of his labours with the Waldensians, Beckwith received the cross of St Maurice and St Lazarius from the king. In 1850 he married a Waldensian, Anne Susanne Caroline Valle.

PHYLLIS R. BLAKELEY

Somerset House (London), Probate Dept., will of John Charles Beckwith proved at London, 17 Sept. 1862. St Paul's Anglican Church (Halifax), registers of burials, baptisms, and marriages, 1785–92 (mfm. at PANS). *Church Times* (Halifax), 31 Dec. 1853. *Colonial Standard* (Pictou, N.S.), 16 Sept. 1862. *Illustrated London News*, 11 Oct. 1862. *DNB*. G.B., WO, *Army list*, 1804–39. *Hart's army list*, 1840–64. G. W. Hill, *Nova Scotia and Nova Scotians . . .* (Halifax, 1858), 36–38. F. E. Crowell, "Halliburton family," *Yarmouth Herald* (Yarmouth, N.S.), 12 Jan. 1932. A. W. H. Eaton, "Chapters in the history of Halifax, Nova Scotia," *Americana* (New York and Somerville, N.J.), XIII (1919), 37–38.

BECKWITH, JULIA CATHERINE (Hart), author; b. 10 March 1796 in Fredericton, N.B., daughter of Nehemiah Beckwith and his second wife, Julie-Louise Lebrun de Duplessis; d. 28 Nov. 1867 at Fredericton.

Julia Catherine Beckwith's mother, whose apparently well-to-do forebears had immigrated to Canada from France in the 17th and 18th centuries, may have been working as governess in the Fredericton household of Thomas Carleton*, lieutenant governor of New Brunswick, about the time she married Nehemiah Beckwith, a loyalist of old Connecticut stock. About 1780 he had taken up land at Maugerville, N.B., and he ultimately became prosperous in shipping and shipbuilding. Julie-Louise forswore Roman Catholicism and adopted her husband's Wesleyan Methodist faith, but no bitterness marred her relations with her family. Julia Beckwith had a cousin who left Methodism to become a nun of the Hôtel-Dieu in Montreal; she corresponded with another cousin at the Collège de Nicolet who was later to be well known as a historian, Jean-Baptiste-Antoine FERLAND, and she visited her French cousins during her girlhood, making the difficult journey to Quebec by canoe. It was the social and religious background of her mother's people that provided the subject-matter of her first novel, *St. Ursula's convent, or the nun of Canada*. With that world she was emotionally identified but because of her double heritage she could see it with a more detached vision. Written in Cornwallis and Fredericton when she was 17, the novel is filled with romance, suspense, complicated plots, and daring escapades, and resembles the picaresque and romantic literature of the time. It was not to be published for some ten years.

After her father's death by drowning in 1815, and probably in order to lessen the burden on her mother, Julia Beckwith went in 1820 to visit her aunt in Kingston, Upper Canada. There on 3 Jan. 1822 she married George Henry Hart, a bookbinder from England, and for two years ran a boarding school for girls. No doubt through her husband's connection with the book trade, in 1824 she found a publisher, Hugh C. Thomson*, for her novel, the first work of fiction written by a native-born Canadian and the first to be published in what is now Canada. She published it anonymously, with a dedication to the Countess of Dalhousie. Subscriptions were obtained from well-known persons in Upper Canada, New Brunswick, England, and the United States. In her preface she alludes to the "slow progress of improvement in British America, where until lately genius has slept . . . [and] scarcely a dawn of literary illumination is yet discerned." Two Montreal literary journals found her mode of expression elegant but repetitious and her plot sometimes too complicated to follow with ease, but were indulgent to the work of a young girl who had undertaken to do what had not been done before.

Mrs Hart's second novel, *Tonnewonte; or, the adopted son of America*, described as having been "written by an American," was published after she and her husband had moved, probably in 1824, to Rochester, N.Y. It exhibited a greater mastery of suspense, more depth of feeling, less resort to coincidence, but the same stilted expression and moral overtones of *St. Ursula's convent*. Mrs Hart wrote not just for entertainment but to express attitudes toward nature and society. In the beauties of the North American forest she saw God's beneficent hand; more significant was her view of the western frontier of settlement as a source of a spirit of freedom and independence. *St. Ursula's convent* had assumed the superiority of the aristocratic classes of the old world; her second novel contained some of the ideas that were to reappear with the frontier school of historiography of later times. Her conception of the simple and virtuous life of the American west no doubt stemmed from the 18th century ideas of the "noble savage" and "noble peasant" and reflected an obsession of the revolutionary age with the evils of social inequality, which she contrasted effectively with the character of life in the new settlements.

By 1831 Mrs Hart was back in Fredericton where her husband secured employment in the New Brunswick Crown Lands Office. There they continued to reside with their six children. Mrs Hart carried on her literary work, contributing to James Hogg's weekly paper, the *New Brunswick Reporter*. Among her later writings was a third novel, "Edith, or the doom," which received the qualified praise of certain local persons of prominence but which was never published.

ALFRED G. BAILEY

UNBL, [J. C. Beckwith (Hart)], "Edith, or the doom." [J. C. Beckwith (Hart)], *St. Ursula's convent, or the nun of Canada, containing scenes from real life* (2v., Kingston, [Ont.], 1824); *Tonnewonte; or, the adopted son of America: a tale containing scenes from real life, by an American* (2v. in 1, Watertown, N.Y., 1824–25; 2v. in 1, Albany, N.Y., 1825; 1v., Exeter, N.H., 1831). W. G. MacFarlane, *New Brunswick bibliography: the books and writers of the province* (Saint John, N.B., 1895). D. A. Loughlin, "The development of social and intellectual attitudes as revealed in the literature of New Brunswick" (unpublished MA thesis, University of New Brunswick, Fredericton, 1948). C. L. Bennet, "An unpublished manuscript of the first Canadian novelist," *Dal. Rev.*, XLIII (1963–64), 317–32. "The collector," *Canadian Bookman* (Toronto), XII (1930), 194–95. D. G. French, "Who's who in Canadian literature: some early writers," *Canadian Bookman* (Toronto), VIII (1926), 75–77. Philéas Gagnon, "Le premier roman canadien de sujet par un auteur canadien et imprimé au Canada," *RSC Trans.*, 2nd ser., VI (1900), sect.I, 121–32. "Julia-Catharine Beckwith," *BRH*, VII (1901), 369–72. L. M. B. Maxwell, "The first Canadian born novelist," *Dal. Rev.*, XXXI (1951–52), 59–64.

BE-GOU-AIS (Be-gwa-is). *See* PEGUIS

BÉLANGER, ALEXIS, priest and missionary; b. 18 Jan. 1808 at Saint-Roch-des-Aulnaies, Lower Canada, son of Pierre Bélanger and Marie-

Marthe Talbot; d. 7 Sept. 1868 at Sandy Point, Nfld.

The youngest of a family of 16 children, Alexis Bélanger was not considered healthy enough for heavy work on the land, and was early guided towards study. When the Collège de Sainte-Anne-de-la-Pocatière was opened on 1 Oct. 1829, he took up the humanities. He finished these studies in 1832, then spent three years at the Grand Séminaire de Québec, and was ordained priest by Bishop Joseph Signay* on 19 Sept. 1835. In 1836, after a brief period at Baie-du-Febvre (Baieville), Abbé Bélanger was appointed parish priest of Sainte-Marie-de-la-Nouvelle-Beauce (Sainte-Marie) with the flattering comment, an "interesting priest" and an "excellent student."

In 1839 Abbé Bélanger was sent as a missionary to the Îles-de-la-Madeleine, which at that period had a Catholic population of 1,380; he arrived in October by schooner. He served among these people of Acadian origin in peace and "the spirit of brotherhood as described in the Gospel" until 1845. However, the increasingly burdensome dues exacted by the heirs of Isaac Coffin*, the seigneur of the islands from 1798 to 1839, and the excessive fishing expeditions by Americans, who had overrun the ports and wharves to such an extent that the islanders had to pay to preserve their fishing rights, brought about a fresh exodus of Acadians in the late 1840s. Wishing to share the fate of his flock, Bélanger offered to minister to them in their new location and spent the winter of 1849–50 at Rustico, P.E.I., and Caraquet, N.B. At Caraquet he received authorization from the archbishop of Quebec to go to Labrador and the west coast of Newfoundland.

On 7 Sept. 1850 Bélanger arrived at St George's Bay with credentials as vicar general of John Thomas MULLOCK, bishop of Newfoundland. He took up residence at Sandy Point, the principal hamlet on the bay, in a log presbytery near a chapel in the same style. He set to work directly, ministering to the fishermen along the west coast. In 1850, 1852, and 1853 he even undertook missionary rounds, each of two months' duration, in the lower region of the north shore of the Gulf of St Lawrence, an area attached to the diocese of Newfoundland until February 1853.

Cut off and deprived even of necessities, the missionary found solace in visits to his *confrères* on Prince Edward Island, Cape Breton Island, and the islands of Saint-Pierre and Miquelon. They wrote to him regularly and occasionally sent him books from France, which he called his "dear comrades in exile." Bélanger proved to be

Belcher

a remarkable letter-writer, gifted with a limpid style, great sensitivity, solid judgement, and truly apostolic zeal. On 7 Sept. 1868, the 18th anniversary of the day he reached the "French shore" of Newfoundland, Alexis Bélanger died, exhausted by his difficult pastoral charge. In accordance with his wishes, he was buried at Saint-Roch-des-Aulnaies on 29 September.

Without repudiating the country of his birth, or neglecting the Gaelic speaking Catholics for whom he obtained religious assistance in their own language, Alexis Bélanger devoted nearly 30 years to the poor and despised French population on the islands and coasts of the Gulf of St Lawrence, and supported them in their will to survive.

RENÉ BÉLANGER

AAQ, 210 A, XVIII, XIX; 301 CN, I. ASQ, Fonds Plante, 198; Séminaire, 110, no.36. [J. J. Audubon], *Audubon's America; the narratives and experiences of John James Audubon*, ed. D. C. Peattie (Boston, 1940), 228–29. *Rapport sur les missions du diocèse de Québec* . . . , no.21 (mai 1874), 46–48. Allaire, *Dictionnaire.* Carrière, *Hist. des O.M.I.*, III, 229; IV, 22, 35–36, 38. René Baudry, "L'abbé Alexis Bélanger, missionnaire . . . ," SCHÉC *Rapport*, 25 (1957–58), 103–9.

BELCHER, CLEMENT HORTON, publisher and bookseller; b. 5 March 1801 at Cornwallis, N.S., only child of Benjamin Belcher Jr and Sarah Starr; m. 6 June 1826 at Halifax his first cousin, Mary Jane Starr, and they had six daughters and three sons; d. 23 May 1869 at Halifax.

Clement Horton Belcher's grandfather, Benjamin Belcher Sr, one of the earliest settlers of Cornwallis, was a prosperous landowner, trader, and member of the assembly. Belcher's father died in 1802 and his mother married Walter Carroll Manning of Halifax three years later. Thus Clement was probably brought to the city as a small child and received all his education there.

Belcher first served as apprentice to James Hamilton, the proprietor of one of the province's largest dry goods establishments. His stepsister's husband, George Eaton, operated Halifax's only bookstore and on Eaton's death in October 1822 Belcher, at the age of 21, took over the stock and established himself in the thriving business, which he ran for the next three decades. Late in 1823 he extended his interests to the publication of the *The farmer's almanack, for the year of our Lord 1824* . . . and continued to issue it annually. In 1832 the name was changed to *Belcher's farmer's almanack.*

Belcher began his almanac only a year after the appearance of *The letters of Agricola* . . . , in which John Young* urged the farmers of the pro-

vince to abandon their traditional methods for a more scientific approach to agriculture, and it is likely that Belcher was influenced by Young's commonsense theories. After extensive reading in agricultural literature he began to intersperse the pages of the *Almanack* each year with valuable suggestions and hints on the management and maintenance of a farm. Meticulous and methodical, Belcher made every effort to ensure that his information was reliable. Consequently it was only reluctantly that he permitted the inclusion of weather prognostications, always a popular feature. The *Almanack* eventually became an almost indispensable tool – a business directory, almanac, and book of reference combined – and Belcher's name a household word throughout the province. After his death the publication's goodwill passed to the firm of McAlpine and Barnes, but the *Almanack* continued under the originator's name until publication ceased in 1930.

Belcher also appears to have been the compiler of the short-lived *Nova Scotia temperance almanack*, issued annually from 1835 to 1837. His interest in publishing extended to a wide variety of titles, including the second edition of Thomas Chandler HALIBURTON's *A general description of Nova Scotia* . . . (Halifax, 1825) and the first two parts of Maria Frances Ann Morris*' *Wild flowers of Nova Scotia* (Halifax and London, 1839–40).

Belcher was a man of broad interests, both in business and in private life. When the Western Stage Coach Company was organized in 1828 he was one of the promoters, serving as agent until its disbandment with the coming of the railroad in the 1850s. An ardent flyfisherman, he delighted in casting the streams of the countryside for salmon and trout, deploring the use of live bait as a form of murder. He was a devout Anglican, worshipping at St George's Church, where he served as senior warden during the incumbency of the Reverend Robert Fitzgerald UNIACKE. In later years he devoted much of his time to the militia and at death held the rank of colonel of the 6th Halifax Regiment. An unabashed tory, "a politician of the old school," he openly opposed the views of Joseph Howe*, not always to his material advantage. In 1857, through Howe's influence, the £10 in pay due him as adjutant of the 3rd Halifax Regiment was deliberately withheld, though his brother officers were paid without question.

From all accounts Belcher was an amiable man noted for his integrity and concern for the community. At his death the *Morning Chronicle* wrote that "throughout life he preserved an equanimity of disposition that endeared him to all'' and in later years the *Halifax Herald* described him as ''in truth an exemplary gentleman, one of the old stock and style.''

SHIRLEY B. ELLIOTT

PANS, MG 4, no.18, record of marriages and deaths for Cornwallis Township, 1760–1825; MG 5, Camp Hill Cemetery (Halifax), August 1844–July 1869 (mfm. copy); RG 5, R, letter to J. J. Marshall, 21 March 1859. *Halifax Herald*, 14 Oct. 1892. *Morning Chronicle* (Halifax), 24 May 1869. *Novascotian*, 31 May 1869. *The army list of local forces of Nova Scotia* . . . (Halifax, 1866). *Belcher's farmer's almanack*, 1824–1930. *Directory of N.S. MLAs.* A. W. H. Eaton, *The history of Kings County, Nova Scotia* . . . (Salem, Mass., 1910).

BÉLESTRE-MacDONELL, JOHN. *See* MAC-DONELL, JEAN-FRANÇOIS-MARIE-JOSEPH

BELL, ANDREW, historian and journalist; fl. 1827–63.

Little is known of Andrew Bell's life before he came to Canada in 1858, and nothing at all of his birth and family. A Scottish background, a good education, and a superior intellect are revealed to us through his works. Bell tells his readers that he sojourned in Belgium, and that he ''lived long'' in France (where he had gone about 1827 for health reasons) gaining there an ''intimate knowledge of the character of the French people.'' He spent a year in the United States in 1835–36 and recorded his experiences in *Men and things in America* (1838).

Bell was evidently living in Glasgow about 1850 when a friend presented him with a package of manuscript letters by General James Wolfe*. Bell stated in print that these letters ''excited a desire'' in him to learn more about Wolfe's life. Related to this interest, no doubt, was an assignment from the publishers of his *Historical sketches of feudalism* (1852) to prepare a memoir of Wolfe for a proposed biographical collection, ''Lives of the illustrious.'' Bell was still in Glasgow in 1856, supporting himself as a ''literary lecturer and private teacher of French,'' and he was an early member of the Glasgow Archaeological Society which was founded in that year.

It may have been Bell's interest in Wolfe which attracted him to Canada, for he says that ''within a few hours of first setting my foot upon Canadian soil'' he paid his ''heart's devoirs'' at Wolfe's monument in Quebec City. This event took place no later than September 1858; by then he had become editor of the Montreal *Pilot*, a Reform daily newspaper owned and printed at that time by Rollo Campbell*. In 1859 he was referring to Canada as his adopted country and was campaigning for a national celebration to mark the centennial of the battle of the Plains of Abraham. Favourably taken up by members of the English Canadian press, the proposal was well received in Britain and the United States, and Bell was confident it would be also in France. But he was astonished by the opposition expressed in the French Canadian press ''in the most bitter, nay even insulting terms.'' On the anniversary day of the battle, 13 Sept. 1859, he lectured on Wolfe at the mechanics' institute in Montreal and the resulting pamphlet gives the impression that he was more naïve than malicious; notwithstanding his stated purpose, to honour Louis-Joseph de Montcalm* and Wolfe equally, he was clearly obsessed by his veneration of Wolfe (''my hero'' he called him) and by a patriotism more British than Canadian. In any case, the circumstances were inauspicious for one who, the day after the address, was announced as about to embark on a translation of François-Xavier GARNEAU's *Histoire du Canada*.

It was publisher John Lovell* who engaged Bell for the delicate task of translating ''the best Canadian History extant,'' to be entitled ''The New and Comprehensive History of Canada,'' hardly a rendering of the original title. According to the announcement which appeared in the Montreal *Pilot* on 14 September, Lovell had obtained Garneau's approbation to publish a translation of his new third edition of 1859 ''with such modifications as would make it acceptable to the entirety of our people, whether of British or French origin.'' Garneau, however, in a letter to *Le Journal de Québec* on 15 Oct. 1859, cautioned the public that he had ceded to Lovell only the right to make a faithful and correct translation; any observations provided by the translator should appear as footnotes. Bell executed his commission with dispatch: publication of the three volumes, containing over 1,200 pages of text, was announced on 26 Oct. 1860 in the *Pilot*, under the title *History of Canada*. The *Pilot* stated that Bell had ''performed his duty with fidelity,'' but French Canadian reviewers, as well as Garneau himself, were quick to point out that the translation was not at all faithful. Moreover, Bell was accused of making changes to please Anglophones and of including notes and insertions that were quite hostile to the original spirit of Garneau's work. Nonetheless, the responsibility clearly rested with Lovell, the contracting party with Garneau, and Lovell was evidently more concerned with the market for his publication than with scholarship. No doubt Bell's work was prepared for English readers, rather than for English and French as Lovell had announced, but one must take note of Bell's avowed intention to modify Garneau's text, and his prefatory notice did state that his work was a "*free*, rather than a slavishly *literal* translation." The controversy continues to the present day. A revised second edition in two volumes was published by Lovell in 1862; the third edition was published by Richard Worthington of Montreal in 1866, and Belford Brothers in Toronto put out another "third" edition in 1876. The revisions in the 1862 edition were minor, and most probably made by Bell before he left Canada; the later editions are unchanged.

Andrew Bell was listed in the Montreal directory for 1859 as editor of the *Pilot*, and in 1860–61 as a journalist and lecturer. By May 1862, he was living in a poor district of the port of Southampton, England, and was described as an insurance agent and "teacher of English and French languages." Bell had left Canada, perhaps because his "intimate knowledge" of the French character had served him so ill there. After July 1863 he disappears from sight, and new material in the 1863 edition of Bell's *Historical sketches of feudalism* was contributed by a different person.

WILLIAM F. E. MORLEY

[The commonness of the name Andrew Bell has vitiated many of the biographical sources in Canada and Britain. A reading of the relevant sections of Bell's own works (including title-pages and preliminaries), and of Montreal newspapers and directories contemporary with Bell's sojourn in that city, furnished primary clues, which were then pursued through correspondence with institutions in the British cities in which Bell had lived: the city and university libraries of Glasgow, Edinburgh, and Southampton, and the city archives of Glasgow and Southampton. Generous staff consulted graduate registers, city directories, rate books, transactions of societies, and other local sources, at my request, as well as appropriate biographical and bibliographical sources. I have been quite unable to identify further Bell's *New annals of old Scotland* and his memoir of Wolfe in "Lives of the illustrious." I must also acknowledge the assistance of Professor Pierre Savard, who is preparing a critical edition of Garneau's works.

Andrew Bell published *Men and things in America, being the experiences of a year's residence in the United States, in a series of letters to a friend* (London, 1838) under the pseudonym A. Thomason; Bell's own name appears, however, on the second edition of this work, published at Southampton, Eng., in 1862. His *Historical sketches of feudalism, British and continental; with numerous notices of the doings of the feudalry in all ages and centuries* (London, 1852), was republished in 1863 under the title *A history of feudalism, British and continental. . . .* After *British-Canadian centennium, 1759–1859; General James Wolfe, his life and death . . .* (Montreal, 1859), Bell published his

creative translation of François-Xavier Garneau, *Histoire du Canada . . .* (3ᵉ éd., Québec, 1859) under the title *History of Canada, from the time of its discovery till the union year (1840–1)* (3v., Montreal, 1860). Second and third editions of this work were published in two volumes at Montreal in 1862 and 1866; another third edition appeared at Toronto in 1876. W.F.E.M.]

Notes and Queries (London), 11 Oct. 1851 and following numbers. *Pilot* (Montreal), 14 Sept. 1859, 26 Oct. 1860. *Glasgow Post Office directory . . . ,* 1856. *Mackay's Montreal directory,* 1858–60.

BELL, JOHN, HBC chief trader and explorer; b. *c.* 1799 on the Island of Mull, Scotland; d. 24 June 1868 at Saugeen, Ont.

John Bell joined the North West Company in 1818 as an apprentice clerk. His early years with that company, and, following the coalition of 1821, with the Hudson's Bay Company, were spent in the Winnipeg River area. In 1824 Bell was transferred to the company's Mackenzie River District; while there he married Nancy, daughter of Peter Warren DEASE, an HBC chief factor. In the winter of 1825–26, Bell was appointed clerk at the company's most northerly post, Fort Good Hope.

The HBC board in London and Governor George Simpson* were eager to expand trade westwards from the Mackenzie. They thought that the Colvile (now Colville) River, recently discovered at the Arctic coast by Peter Warren Dease and Thomas Simpson*, flowed from the southeast and would provide a route for this expansion. They therefore gave instructions to Bell in 1838 for exploration west of the Mackenzie. In the summer of 1839 he explored the Peel River from its junction with the Mackenzie, and the following year he established a post, Fort McPherson, on its banks; he was to be in charge of the post until 1845. Appointed chief trader in 1841, Bell crossed the mountains to the west of the Peel in 1842 and descended what was called the Rat River (later the Bell River) to its junction with the Porcupine. On the latter river he was deserted by his Indian guide and had to return to Fort McPherson. It was not until 1845 that he successfully followed the Porcupine River to its confluence with the Yukon. In 1846 at the height of his achievements Bell left the area on account of ill health. His exploration had paved the way for the highly profitable expansion of the company's trade to the Yukon River *via* a practicable route. Robert Campbell*'s route, discovered in the 1840s, from Fort Simpson to the Yukon River *via* the Liard and Pelly rivers proved to be infinitely more arduous.

In the summer of 1847 Bell returned from furlough in Canada to conduct an advance party north from York Factory for the expedition of 1848–49 in search of Sir John Franklin* to be led by Sir John RICHARDSON and Dr John Rae*. His services to the expedition over the winter of 1848–49 were chiefly to organize living accommodation at Fort Confidence and ensure a supply of provisions. Against his wishes Bell was retained by the company in its Mackenzie River District after 1849, taking charge of the district in 1850–51.

At his own request, and in line with the views of Rae who did not consider Bell fitted to the command of the district because of his fear of responsibility and insufficient knowledge of business methods, Bell left Mackenzie River in 1851 first for Oxford House and then Cumberland House where he took charge of the district, 1852–53. From 1853 to 1857 Bell supervised the company's Athabasca District from Fort Chipewyan. Following a year's furlough (1857–58), spent at least partly in Montreal, Bell's final years with the HBC were spent in Canada East at Sept-Îles and at Weymontachingue in the Saint-Maurice District. He resigned because of ill health in March 1860.

Bell settled at Saugeen where he farmed. He died there in 1868, leaving two sons and five daughters. His son Peter Warren Bell was in the employ of the HBC from 1852 to 1895, attaining the rank of chief factor.

JOAN CRAIG

HBC Arch. A.1/62, p.75; A.11/28, ff.285d., 303d.–4; A.33/2, f.75; A.34/1, p.100; A.44/5, p.13; B.80/a/7, 4 June 1828; B.80/a/16, 25 June, 3 Aug. 1839; B.134/b/14, p.700; B.134/b/19, f.387; B.134/c/101, f.156; B.134/c/108, f.381; B.134/c/111, f.22; B.157/a/1; B.200/a/5, 14 Sept., 30 Oct., 10, 13 Dec. 1824; B.200/b/12, ff.2d.–3d.; B.200/b/15, ff.5–6; B.200/d/37, f.2; B.239/f/12, f.11; B.239/g/5,f.7;B.239/k/2,pp.31,62,86,125,154,176,197, 220, 249, 271, 318, 380, 401; B.239/k/3, pp.12, 47, 71, 99, 120, 139, 454, 476; D.4/23, f.160, p.211; D.4/67, f.30; D.4/69, pp.39–40; D.4/70, f.248; D.4/71, ff.121, 133; D.4/74, pp.112, 387–88; D.4/75, f.372d.; D.4/77, f.35d.; D.4/78, ff.307d.–9d.; D.4/79, ff.224, 229; D.5/7, f.250; D.5/15, ff. 464–64d.; D.5/28, ff.378 78d.; D.5/48, f.153; D.5/51, f.436; E.4/2, f.2d.; E.11/2, f.93; F.4/32, p.979. Somerset House (London), Probate Department, will of John Bell, 1 July 1869. *Documents relating to NWC* (Wallace). *Hargrave correspondence* (Glazebrook). HBRS, III (Fleming).

BELL, JOSHUA, shoe manufacturer and retailer; b. *c.* 1812 in Ireland; d. 24 Dec. 1863 at his home in Hochelaga (Montreal, Que.), without issue.

Joshua Bell and his brother Thomas immigrated to Canada probably between 1815 and 1825 with their father Alexander, a shoemaker by trade. Joshua was one of nine children. At an unknown date, he married the daughter of the Reverend John Hutchinson; she died before 1861.

Joshua Bell's career is difficult to trace. The name is known particularly through a brief account in Ægidius Fauteux*'s *Patriotes de 1837–1838.* Fauteux states that Bell, at the age of 44, took part in the rebellion, sought refuge in the United States, and returned to Montreal "before the proclamation of the general amnesty, for in 1845 he and his brother Thomas took over the management of the firm founded in 1824 by their father Alexander." There were, however, two Joshua Bells, both shoemakers, and the Joshua Bell who took part in the uprising had no connection with the footwear establishment of J. and T. Bell Boot and Shoe Manufacturers.

The Joshua Bell who died in 1863 at the age of 51 was a partner in this firm; in his will of 1861 the two brothers were called "Boot and Shoe Merchants." Moreover, in the 1861 census the household of Joshua Bell is listed as including himself, aged 48 and born in Ireland, his brothers Thomas, 46, and Samuel, 30, his widowed sister and her two sons, a niece, and a servant. Except for the latter, who was a Catholic, they all gave their religion as Wesleyan Methodist. The three brothers stated their trade was footwear. The 1842 census mentions a Joshua Bell, a shoemaker from Ireland, then between 21 and 30 years of age, who was married and a Methodist. So far everything fits.

The Joshua Bell who took part in the rebellion and is mentioned by Fauteux is probably the man listed in the 1825 and 1831 censuses. The latter gives him as a shoemaker and a Baptist. The ages shown in both censuses do not agree with the age Joshua Bell, manufacturer, would have been at this time, but do agree with Fauteux's mention of 44 years of age at the time of the rebellion. In addition a series of transactions between 1822 and 1834 relating to a house on Rue Saint-Paul show it as being rented originally to a Joshua Bell who identified himself at first as a shoemaker and later as a leather merchant. Fauteux also quotes a letter written by the Patriote Joshua Bell in 1838, in which he informed Ludger Duvernay* of his intention to leave for the western United States and of the possibility "that he might not return." This Joshua Bell may indeed never have returned. Our Joshua Bell was in business for himself in 1842 as a manufacturer of footwear. The first Montreal directory of 1842–43 contains the following entry: "Bell, Joshua, Boots and Shoes, 209 St. Paul Street." Two years later the directory notes that he also had a stock of imported

Benjamin

footwear, and a private fitting room for his female clientele.

In 1847–48 the firm of Joshua and Thomas Bell, manufacturers of boots and shoes, was on Rue Notre-Dame. The partnership of the two brothers is thought to date from 1845, but it is unlikely that at that date Joshua and Thomas took over from their father Alexander. According to some sources Alexander founded the establishment in 1824, or in 1819 according to one. Certainly Joshua owned the business before 1845, but no trace of a footwear factory owned by Alexander Bell has been found; all that is certain is that on 6 May 1825 an Alexander Bell, shoemaker, had a protest drawn up to enable him to enter into possession of a house on Rue Saint-Paul. To further complicate matters, there are death certificates for two Alexander Bells, both shoemakers (one is styled shoemaker and the other cordwainer), whose deaths occurred on 5 June 1838 and 28 Aug. 1839. It is probable that the latter was Joshua Bell's father, since his certificate bears the signatures of two witnesses, Joshua and Thomas Bell. In any case the dates 1819 or 1824 at which the Bell firm is presumed to have been founded both derive from late 19th century promotional notices (1893 and 1894), and are unreliable; it was a well-accepted practice for a business house to claim its establishment at the earliest date possible. These dates no doubt correspond approximately to the arrival of the Bell family in Montreal, and conceivably to the opening of a small cobbler's workshop, but certainly not to the starting of a mechanized boot and shoe factory.

At the time of Joshua Bell's death, however, J. and T. Bell was one of the larger footwear factories in Montreal. In the 1861 census it listed 70 employees (50 men and 20 women) and an annual production worth $60,000. William John Patterson*'s report for the year 1863 gives the annual production of the city of Montreal as nearly $2,000,000; thus the Bell firm would represent more than three per cent of the total city production, a proportion that seems correct. Indeed, in 1871 the enterprise ranked as a medium-sized factory. In addition to his share in the factory, Joshua Bell owned a 28-acre farm in the parish of Sainte-Marguerite-de-Blairfindie (L'Acadie).

Joshua Bell's career gives a glimpse of the beginnings of the mechanized footwear industry in Montreal; although we cannot affirm that he was the first to take an interest in it, he was certainly a pioneer.

JEAN-CLAUDE ROBERT

ANQ-M, État civil, Méthodistes, New Connection, 1839; St James, 1838–39, 1863; Greffe de Joseph Belle, 13 févr. 1861, 8 janv. 1864; Greffe de Peter Lukin, fils, 28 févr. 1822, 3 avril 1823, 6 mai 1825, 15 janv. 1828, 12 mars 1833, 15 févr. 1834; Testaments, Register of wills probated, no.679. ASQ, Fonds Viger-Verreau, 015-A. Bibliothèque de la ville de Montréal, Salle Gagnon, Fonds Ægidius Fauteux. PAC, MG 17, A7-2-3, sér.II, 13; RG 31, 1825 census, Montreal County; 1842 census, Montreal City; 1861 census, Montreal Centre Ward; 1871 census, Montreal.

"Papiers de Ludger Duvernay," *Canadian Antiquarian and Numismatic Journal* (Montreal), 3rd ser., VI (1909), 127–28. W. J. Patterson, *Report on the trade and commerce of the city of Montreal for 1863 . . .* (Montreal, 1864). *L'Ami du peuple, de l'ordre et des lois* (Montréal), 23 déc, 1837. *Montreal Gazette*, 26 Dec. 1863. *Montreal Herald*, 28 Dec. 1863. Ivanhoë Caron, "Papiers Duvernay conservés aux Archives de la province de Québec," ANQ *Rapport*, 1926–27, 145–258. Fauteux, *Patriotes*, 106–7. *Montreal directory*, 1842–63. *Montreal illustrated, its growth, resources, commerce, manufacturing interests, financial institutions, educational advantages and prospects . . .* (Montreal, 1894). *Montreal in 1856; a sketch prepared for the celebration of the opening of the Grand Trunk Railway of Canada* (Montreal, 1856), 45. F. W. Terrill, *A chronology of Montreal and of Canada from A.D. 1752 to A.D. 1893, including commercial statistics, historical sketches of commercial corporations and firms and advertisements . . .* (Montreal, 1893), 96. P.-A. Linteau, "Les Patriotes de 1837–1838 d'après les documents J.-J. Girouard," *RHAF*, XXI (1967–68), 281–311.

BENJAMIN, GEORGE, journalist, politician, and Orangeman; b. 15 April 1799 in Sussex, England; he was married and had 12 children; d. 7 Sept. 1864 at Belleville, Canada West.

Little is known about George Benjamin's family background and early life. He immigrated to North America as a young man, resided for a time in North Carolina, and came to Upper Canada about 1830. He at first lived in York (Toronto) where he became acquainted with James Hunter Samson, member of the assembly for Hastings and the leading barrister of Belleville. Induced by Samson, Benjamin purchased a printing press and, establishing himself as a printer in Belleville, began publication in 1834 of the *Intelligencer*, a newspaper that consistently upheld a conservative point of view.

Benjamin probably joined the Orange Order at this time, in company with Conservative leaders of the Newcastle District (including George Strange BOULTON, John Brown, MHA for Durham, and Colonel John Covert*) who were attempting to turn the Orange lodges into conventional Conservative clubs. Benjamin appears to have been acceptable to Belleville Conservatives and to governing circles in Toronto for he was soon appointed a captain in the Belleville militia. In spite of his status he served in the ranks of a volunteer company which repelled Canadian rebels and American infiltrators in the Gananoque area in 1838. This action undoubtedly enhanced his prestige in the politics of Hastings County. He promoted the building of a plank road between Belleville and Camden, and finally, with the support of an American entrepreneur, made the project a financial success. Benjamin also initiated the macadamizing of roads in his district.

His early appointments included that of notary public in 1836 and town clerk of Belleville from 1836 to 1847; he was appointed registrar of Hastings County, town clerk of Thurlow, and clerk of the Belleville board of police in 1847. When Hastings County was separated from the Midland District in 1849, Benjamin was one of the commissioners appointed to settle the financial aspects of the separation. For a time he served as councillor and reeve of Hungerford Township and from 1847 until 1862 was warden of Hastings.

Benjamin acquired these lucrative and relatively prestigious offices through his political influence and that of his friends, Ogle Robert Gowan*, Edmund Murney, and Samson. The appointments helped Benjamin consolidate his power in the county, but his connections with the Orange lodges brought him wider prominence. In 1846 he became grand master of the Orange Order in British North America, supplanting its founder, Gowan, who was preoccupied with his legislative career. At that time there were nearly 50,000 Orangemen in Upper Canada who, since 1836, had become an important element in the electoral strength of the Tory party. However, as Orange leader, Gowan on several occasions had denounced the Family Compact, and he had advocated responsible government in an 1839 pamphlet. Although an associate of John A. Macdonald* in the 1840s, Gowan was regarded as "unrespectable" and an outsider by ultra Tory and Compact leaders such as Sir Allan MACNAB. Conservative Orangemen thus felt the need for a less provocative and more conciliatory grand master and Benjamin appears to have met this need. In 1851 he helped secure the repeal of the legislation against Orange processions, only two years after Orange participation in the attacks on Lord Elgin [BRUCE] following the passage of the Rebellion Losses Bill.

Benjamin and Gowan had worked together in organizing the British American League in 1849 to combat annexationist and republican sentiments. But in 1852, when Gowan had moved from Brockville to Toronto, he decided to challenge Benjamin's leadership of the Orange movement. By this time Gowan was identified with John A. Macdonald's policy of maintaining an alliance between the Conservatives of Canada West and G.-É. Cartier*'s Bleu party in Canada East. It is not clear whether Gowan's or Benjamin's supporters were in the majority at the vital grand lodge meeting in Kingston in 1853, but Gowan, the more forceful and less scrupulous of the two, succeeded in reasserting his leadership. Gowan's attack on Benjamin's leadership was more than a personality clash: Benjamin's followers withdrew to form a schismatic grand lodge which rejected the Conservative alliance with the Bleus. Thus, although a moderate by temperament and in his previous associations, Benjamin found himself at the head of the anti-clerical wing of Orangeism which supported George Brown*'s voluntarist policies. The majority of Orangemen probably shared Benjamin's suspicions of the Bleu alliance. Benjamin, however, had not been active as grand master (an average of only eight new lodges a year had been founded by him) and did not have a strong personal following.

After the schism Gowan undertook a tour of the eastern counties of the province, founded 124 lodges in 1854, and reported in June 1855 that of 589 lodges, only 150 paid dues to the schismatic grand lodge. He noted with satisfaction that the pro-Benjamin Bytown *Orange Lily and Protestant Vindicator* and the Toronto *British Canadian* had both ceased publication. A hard working and imaginative politican in local affairs, Benjamin had little sympathy with Gowan's conception of higher political combinations, and because his personal influence hardly extended beyond his own district, he could not hope to compete effectively with Gowan who was well known in the province. Benjamin nevertheless kept the schismatic lodge in being and forced Gowan to accept an agreement whereby both grand masters resigned in 1856, permitting the reunion of the movement under the neutral George Lyttleton Allen. Once the schism was healed, it was John Hillyard Cameron*, rather than Benjamin, who led Orange opposition to the Bleu alliance.

Benjamin was elected by a substantial majority as member of the legislature for North Hastings in 1856, after the resignation of Edmund Murney. Benjamin had been defeated in the same riding in 1848, and his election in 1856 marked the beginning of a modest but useful parliamentary career that lasted until 1863. He favoured "rep. by pop.," but voted for separate schools and generally supported Macdonald's alliance with the

Benning

Bleus. Benjamin was, in fact, a moderate Conservative whose interest in Orangeism was political. He became leader of the "extreme Protestant" wing only after Gowan decided to drive him from office. Benjamin had to make concessions to the anti-clerical sentiments of the electorate, but the essential moderation of his policy is indicated by his vote for the incorporation of the Catholic Ladies of Loretto, for which he was rebuked by the *Globe*, and which undoubtedly lost votes for him in the closely contested election of 1857. But Benjamin was really more concerned with the administrative aspects of parliamentary life. He was credited with saving the government $500,000 as a member of the parliamentary printing committee, for which he received a grant of $2,000.

In 1862 he again sought election as councillor for Hungerford and warden for North Hastings, but his election was voided on technical grounds. He did not contest his seat in the provincial election of 1863, and died after a long illness the following year.

HEREWARD SENIOR

George Benjamin was the author of *Short lessons for members of parliament . . .* (Quebec, 1862), a guide to parliamentary rules and practice. PAC, MG 24, C34. *Elgin-Grey papers* (Doughty), I, 408. Loyal Orange Assoc. of British North America, Grand Lodge, *Annual report* (Toronto), 1853, 1856, 1865. Loyal Orange Assoc. of British North America, Grand Lodge, *Annual report* (Bytown [Ottawa]), 1854. *Brockville Recorder*, 9, 23 Oct. 1856. *Daily News* (Kingston, [Ont.]), 9 Sept. 1864. *Globe*, 9 Sept. 1864. *Intelligencer* (Belleville, [Ont.]), Jan.–March 1862. *Montreal Gazette*, 8 July 1854. *Orange Lily and Protestant Vindicator* (Bytown [Ottawa]), 4 Feb., 4 March 1854. *Toronto Patriot*, 14 Sept. 1864. *Weekly Post* (Montreal), 14 Aug. 1846. Armstrong, *Handbook of Upper Canadian chronology*, 130, 145, 198. *CPC*, 1862, 1863. Morgan, *Bibliotheca Canadensis*, 27. *Political appointments, 1841–65* (J.-O. Coté), 98, 101, 112. Wallace, *Macmillan dictionary*, 49. Careless, *Brown*, II, 22. Creighton, *Macdonald, young politician*, 195, 308, 328.

BENNING, CLEMENT PITT, merchant, building contractor, politician, and magistrate; b. 1785 probably in Great Britain; m. Susan Penny of St Jacques, Nfld, and they had at least two sons and three daughters; d. 30 May 1865 at Burin, Nfld.

Clement Pitt Benning's origins and early life are obscure. In 1804 he immigrated to Placentia Bay, Nfld, as agent for the firm of William Spurrier of Poole, England. Apparently originally an Anglican, Benning converted to Roman Catholicism probably at the time of his marriage. After the bankruptcy of the Spurrier firm in 1829, Benning went into the fishery business with his own boats at Burin. Later he became a building contractor and did construction and repair work on government buildings in several communities throughout the district. In the 1840s he was associated, in the joint venture of a Burin-Placentia ferry service, with the Falle family, the wealthiest Protestant, non-Anglican merchants in the area.

Benning was also involved in the public life of the colony. In 1831 he was appointed conservator of the peace for the Burin and Placentia districts. In the 1842 election for the Burin seat in the assembly Benning, a local merchant, was pitted against a St John's faction led by Henry David Winton*, editor of the *Public Ledger*, and leading critic of Roman Catholic clerical influence in island politics. Benning won the seat. Choosing not to run in 1848, Benning became the Liberal candidate in Burin four years later, again opposing Winton.

The Burin election of 1852 was important for the Liberal party. Its open alliance with the Roman Catholic Church, which supported its campaign for responsible government, had tended to confine the movement to a sectarian cause. The Conservative party, solidly entrenched in all the Anglican districts, resisted responsible government as a Catholic plot to gain ascendancy and attempted to organize Protestants against the reform campaign, which was depicted as a purely religious struggle. The Liberals recognized the urgency of acquiring Protestant support and this burden was pointedly imposed upon them late in 1851 when the British government rejected responsible government because no "preponderance of opinion" had been shown to favour such a change. This rejection was interpreted to mean that the Liberals needed to win non-Anglican Protestant support, and, therefore, in 1852 had to elect candidates in one or both of the only two constituencies which did not have either Roman Catholic or Anglican majorities. In the four-member Conception Bay riding there had been a long-standing agreement among the Catholics, Anglicans, and Wesleyan Methodists to divide the seats equitably among themselves, but in the single-member constituency of Burin where Wesleyans held the balance of power there was no such pact. This riding could then be truly regarded as the key to the responsible government movement.

Benning was admirably qualified as a candidate to draw together Roman Catholics and dissenting Protestants. He had joined the trend away from the Church of England noticeable on the island in the preceding decades, especially in the Burin district. He had had during his career contact with Protestant business people such as the Spurrier and Falle families. As well, the Burin district was relatively free from St John's conservative mercantile influence. Its Wesleyans and Anglicans had been feuding publicly over the former's demands for the right to baptize, marry, and bury their co-religionists and to have their own schools.

Benning won the election and in the assembly joined the Liberals and Wesleyans in championing education, electoral redistribution, and responsible government. In 1855 he was re-elected and became part of the Liberal majority which inaugurated the first responsible government in Newfoundland's history. He retired from politics before the 1859 election to serve as stipendiary magistrate in Lamaline. Six years later he died in Burin.

JOHN P. GREENE

Methodist Missionary Soc. Archives (London), Incoming correspondence, Newfoundland, 1843–44, 1851–52 (mfm. at PANL). PANL, GN 2/1, 1804–64; 2/2, 1825–59, 1863–64. Nfld., House of Assembly, *Journal*, 1843–48, 1853–59. *Morning Courier and General Advertiser* (St John's), 1853, 1855. *Newfoundlander*, 1842–48, 1852–53, 1855. *Newfoundland Indicator* (St John's), 1844. *Newfoundland Vindicator* (St John's), 1842. *Patriot* (St John's), 1852–53, 1855. *Public Ledger* (St John's), 1842–48, 1852–53, 1855. Greene, "Influence of religion in the politics of Nfld., 1850–61." E. A. Wells, "The struggle for responsible government in Newfoundland, 1846–1855" (unpublished MA thesis, Memorial University of Newfoundland, St John's, 1966).

BENOÎT, *dit* **Livernois, JULES-ISAÏE**, businessman and photographer; b. 22 Oct. 1830 at Longueuil, Lower Canada, son of Amable Benoît, *dit* Livernois, a farmer, and Desanges Beaudry; m. 9 May 1849 Élise L'Hérault, *dit* L'Heureux, and they had four daughters and two sons; d. 11 Oct. 1865 at Quebec, at the age of 34.

Jules-Isaïe Benoît, *dit* Livernois, was a person of feverish activity, energetic, persistent, and venturesome. He was destined for a rural existence, but quite early left his father's farm, a discouraging environment ill suited to his spirited temperament. He launched into a series of commercial activities. Taken on first as a clerk in a business house at Quebec, he then became in succession the owner of a store at Baie-du-Febvre (Baieville) in 1851, a bakery and a large store at Richmond, and two other commercial establishments beside the tracks of the Grand Trunk Railway. A victim of unfavourable circumstances, he was betrayed by some of his employees and went bankrupt. In 1853 he embarked for the United States, hoping to find the wherewithal to repay his creditors. After going round the Americas via Cape Horn, he reached San Francisco, where he succeeded in building "a large steam laundering plant." His business was prospering when his family suddenly recalled him to Quebec. In a hurry to sell his undertaking, he made it over to his chief employee, who disappeared without paying him after having resold the establishment to a third person. Penniless again, Livernois was obliged to serve as a sailor and to cross the Isthmus of Panama on foot to make his way home. In Panama he contracted a virus which would lead to his early death.

Around 1855, undaunted by his earlier experiences, Livernois (he was then 24) started a book-selling and sewing machine business at Quebec. It was apparently at this time that he began to take an interest in photography, a new art which had been firmly established in the town five or six years earlier. His first studio was announced in the Quebec directory for 1857–58 under the heading "photographers, daguerreotypers etc." It reads: "Livernois, Mr and Mrs, photographers, 32 St. John u.t. and 31 des Fosses Sr." Photographic technique was sufficiently developed for him to be able to offer photographs printed on paper, or tinted with oils, and ambrotypes (photographs on glass). He also gave instruction in the art.

During his eight years as a professional photographer, Livernois, characteristically, maintained two and sometimes three studios in Quebec Upper Town and the more popular *faubourg* Saint-Roch. In 1863 a study trip took him to England, Scotland, and Paris, but "anxiety about his family" soon brought him back home. As his health was steadily deteriorating, his doctors advised him to take treatment at Florence, in the United States. There he hoped to recover but received instead a diagnosis of impending death. He died at Quebec on 11 Oct. 1865. Among the friends present at his funeral was Louis-Prudent Vallée, a well-known Quebec businessman and photographer.

Jules-Isaïe Livernois's insatiable curiosity prompted him to undertake many diverse activities and led him away from the beaten track. Within his profession he was remarkable, as his contemporary, Henri-Raymond Casgrain*, makes clear: "Photography would have been no more than a trade for him, as for many others, if he had not had the intelligence to enhance its practice by unselfish research. He set out in zealous pursuit of pictures, portraits, views, engravings, and old paintings that might be of interest.

Besserer

In this way he accomplished something of real value by popularizing and preserving precious objects buried in dust and liable to perish. This fine collection, which a short while ago it would have been impossible to obtain, now has its place in the albums of all art lovers." Thanks to the care taken by the descendants of Livernois, many pages of these albums are extant, and they reveal important aspects of the cultural history of 19th century Quebec.

Jules-Isaïe's son Jules-Ernest Livernois*, and his grandson Jules, followed in his footsteps. The photographic firm he founded is one of the rare examples in Canada of a business enterprise that reached its centenary.

LOUISE HAMEL-MINH

[The only study of Jules-Isaïe Benoît, dit Livernois, *Jules Livernois* by Henri-Raymond Casgrain, was published in Quebec a year after the death of the photographer. The information it contains, some of it difficult to verify, was probably obtained in interviews with Benoît's widow. L.H.-M.]

ANQ-M, État civil, Catholiques, Saint-Antoine (Longueuil), 23 oct. 1830. ANQ-Q, État civil, Catholiques, Saint-Roch (Québec), 9 mai 1849, 14 oct. 1865. *McLaughlin's Quebec directory*, 1855–58. *Quebec directory*, 1858–66.

BESSERER, LOUIS-THÉODORE, notary, soldier, politician, and businessman; b. 4 Jan. 1785 at Château-Richer, near Quebec, son of Johann Theodor Besferer, known as Jean-Théodore Besserer, a German military surgeon and a Calvinist, who came to Canada in 1776, and Marie-Anne Giroux, a Canadian; d. 3 Feb. 1861 at Ottawa. By his first wife, Angèle Rhéaume of Quebec, whom he married on 25 Feb. 1830, and his second, Margaret Cameron of Bytown (Ottawa), he had 12 children.

Louis-Théodore Besserer was a pupil at the Petit Séminaire de Québec, then studied under Félix Têtu to become a notary; he was admitted to the profession on 28 Aug. 1810. Antoine Roy describes him as "a man of good counsel and an alert financier, sound and rarely at fault in his judgement, who quickly won the confidence of his fellow citizens and built up a fine clientele."

At the beginning of the War of 1812, Besserer was a lieutenant in the 2nd militia battalion of the Quebec City district. He was transferred to the 6th battalion on 20 March 1813 and on 25 September was promoted captain. He enjoyed the confidence of the governor, Sir George Prevost*, who entrusted him with a number of special civilian missions, among them the establishing of settlers along the Portage road between Rivière-du-Loup and the Quebec and New Brunswick border. Like many others, he received a land grant for his military services; Besserer chose his in the township of Horton in the Eastern Townships. After the war he returned to his notarial practice and business affairs at Quebec.

He represented the county of Quebec in the House of Assembly from 7 Oct. 1833 to 27 March 1838. Although he agreed with the Ninety-Two Resolutions, he was one of the Patriotes of the Quebec region who, more prudent and deliberate, preferred constitutional methods to rebellion, as advocated by the Montreal Patriotes. The difference of mentality between Montreal and Quebec was never more evident. Seeing the turn political agitation was taking at Montreal, Besserer refused to follow Louis-Joseph Papineau*. However, he escaped arrest in 1838 only by reason of his business relations with the British authorities; he was nevertheless forced to retire from politics. He remained on bad terms with Papineau's friends, who never forgave him his moderation.

Disappointed and embittered by political events, and distressed over the death of his first wife, Besserer retired in 1845 to an immense estate he had purchased in 1828 near Bytown (Ottawa). A shrewd businessman, he had it subdivided into building sites, and gave Bishop Patrick Phelan* a lot for a church and school in order to attract buyers; he also had several streets laid out, one of which still bears his name. This speculation brought him a fortune. With other fellow citizens he was concerned with the incorporation of Bytown as a town, which took place in 1847. He died on 3 Feb. 1861 at Ottawa.

A practical man and an opportunist, Besserer rapidly adopted English customs and attitudes. In fact, his family origin, his business connections, and his second wife's family all led him to identify more and more with English Canadians.

JEAN-YVES GRAVEL

PAC, MG 30, D62, 4, pp.597–604. P.-G. Roy, *Fils de Québec*, III, 22–24. Lucien Brault, *Ottawa old & new* (Ottawa, 1946). "Louis-Théodore Besserer," *BRH*, XXXII (1926), 479–81. Antoine Roy, "Les Patriotes de la région de Québec pendant la rébellion de 1837–1838," *Cahiers des Dix*, 24 (1959), 241–54. P.-G. Roy, "Les Besserer de la province de Québec," *BRH*, XXIII (1917), 30–31.

BETHUNE, DONALD, shipowner, lawyer, and politician; b. 11 July 1802 in Williamstown, Charlottenburg Township, Upper Canada, youngest of nine children of the Reverend John Bethune* and Véronique Waddin; d. 19 June 1869 at Toronto, Ont.

Donald Bethune's early education was obtained at the grammar school of his brother John* in Augusta Township and at John STRACHAN's school in Cornwall. Another of Donald's brothers, Alexander Neil Bethune*, was Strachan's protégé. At age 14 Donald began articling in law under the prominent Brockville lawyer and politician, Jonas Jones*, and in 1823 was called to the bar of Upper Canada. In 1826 he was appointed commissioner of customs for the Midland District and between 1826 and 1835 he was twice appointed judge of the Bathurst District Court and once of the Prince Edward District Court. In Kingston, where he had settled in 1824, competition between lawyers was rigorous. Of necessity Bethune began to diversify his interests. He became involved in local banking politics and ran as an independent conservative in the 1828 House of Assembly elections, defeating the influential incumbent Christopher Hagerman*. His two years in the assembly were undistinguished and he in turn was defeated by Hagerman in 1830.

While continuing his association with the Kingston branch of the Bank of Upper Canada, as both a local director and solicitor, Bethune began to dabble in the shipping and forwarding business. Business contacts for these activities were provided by his brothers, and by his father-in-law, Peter Smith, an early settler and notable businessman of Kingston, whose daughter Janet (Jennet) Bethune had married in 1826. Bethune launched his first steamboat in 1833. The pattern of his initial experience was to be repeated throughout his career as an owner of steamboats on Lake Ontario. He quickly ran out of cash as did his brothers, James Gray and Norman, with whom he had close financial dealings. Their conduct aroused the ire of the cautious William Allan*, president of the Bank of Upper Canada, who wrote to John Macaulay* in 1833: "I am perfectly sick of . . . hearing of the many traffics and speculations entered into as long as they can draw Dft. [drafts] or get Notes discounted at the *Bank*." It was beyond his comprehension that Donald Bethune could "ask for *time* and indulgence" and that he was involved "in business as much out of the way of what he ought to be . . . in [as this]. . . ." If Allan ever confronted Bethune with this advice, it was ignored.

Bethune's headquarters were at Cobourg between 1840 and 1843. Attempting to capitalize on his prestige as lieutenant-colonel of militia in the Cobourg area during the rebellion and border problems of 1837–40, Bethune ran as an independent conservative in Northumberland South in the election of 1841. Branded a "troublesome

person" by Sir George Arthur* because of his challenge to Hagerman and his business dealings, and because he was considered a follower of Sir Allan MacNab, Bethune did not receive the backing of influential Toronto Tories and was defeated by George Morss Boswell.

He then devoted himself to his shipping interests. Awarded the government contract for mail delivery in 1840, he quickly arranged route and rate agreements with potential competitors such as John Hamilton*, Hugh RICHARDSON, Thomas Dick*, and Andrew Heron, and between 1840 and 1842 purchased five steamers from the Niagara Harbour and Dock Company. Liberal credit was extended to Bethune by William Cayley*, then president of the dock company, by the Bank of Upper Canada of which Cayley was a director, and by the Commercial Bank of the Midland District. In 1842, Bethune had an interest in, if not sole ownership of, at least ten Lake Ontario steamboats.

Bethune moved his operations to Toronto after 1843. Aspiring to monopoly, he was faced with only one major competitor by 1846 – Hugh Richardson of Toronto, owner of three vessels. Price-cutting ensued and as a shrewd observer, John ELMSLEY, put it, "Bethune and Richardson I look upon as gone loons . . . they are now running against each other to their mutual destruction." When Richardson declared bankruptcy in the summer of 1846, Bethune probably anticipated no financial difficulties. But by 1845 he had already severely overextended his credit, and the purchase of one or more of Richardson's boats in 1847 sealed his fate. Desperate, he mortgaged boats in favour of his major creditor, the Bank of Upper Canada. His wife's uncle, John David Smith, endorsed for him a note for £16,000 which both he and Bethune ultimately failed to meet. Bethune raised rates for the transport of goods and passengers, and even ran unsuccessfully for the assembly in Toronto in 1847 on a platform decrying the lack of protection for the merchants of Canada's inland seas. All his measures failed. Beset by the recession of 1848, new competition, decaying equipment, and a debt to the Bank of Upper Canada exceeding £30,000, as well as innumerable debts to merchants along the shores of Lake Ontario, Bethune's business collapsed late in 1848. Sued for non-payment of debts, he was forced to hand over his boats to the sheriff of York for public auction. The bank, however, could not afford to let Bethune go under and therefore leased the mortgaged boats to him. By 1851, despite rate agreements with competitors, Bethune was again bankrupt. In 1853 he left for England with £4,000 of company

Billaudèle

funds, and by 1855 all of his boats had been sold.

Bethune returned to Canada in 1858 after what he probably hoped would be the last suit concerning his bankruptcy. To his chagrin he was forced by the master in chancery to assume liability for part of his debts. He settled in Port Hope and resumed the practice of law. Two pieces of evidence indicate that he had attained some degree of prosperity by 1864: he was being bothered by old creditors for repayment of debts and his prowess as a lawyer was recognized by his being named QC.

Donald Bethune's business activities had no permanent results for Upper Canada. Yet his career is important as a significant example of the reckless promotion characteristic of both water and rail transportation. Banking methods were loose and credit was easy; owners and operators were often prepared to seek profits at the expense of customers and creditors. Bethune's career accurately reflects the expansive tempo of the times.

PETER BASKERVILLE

MTCL, William Allan papers. PAO, Macaulay (John) papers; Robinson (John Beverley) papers. PAC, MG 24, A40, 13; D24; RG 1, E3, 52; RG 5, A1, 210; RG 68, 1, General index, 1651–1841. QUA, Thomas Kirkpatrick papers, letterbooks, 6, p.20; James Sutherland papers. UTL-TF, MS Coll. 56, MS Coll. 78. *Arthur papers* (Sanderson), III, 175. *British Colonist* (Toronto), 1845–52. *Cobourg Star* (Cobourg, [Ont.]), 1839–41. *Examiner* (Toronto), 1845–52. *Globe*, 1845–52. *Journal of Education for Ont.*, XXII (1869), 104. E. E. Horsey, *Kingston, a century ago; issued to commemorate the centennial of Kingston's incorporation* (Kingston, Ont., 1938). S. F. Wise, "Tory factionalism: Kingston elections and Upper Canadian politics, 1820–1836," *OH*, LVII (1965), 205–25. A. H. Young, "The Bethunes," *OH*, XXVII (1931), 553–74.

BILLAUDÈLE, PIERRE-LOUIS, priest, Sulpician, and superior of the Séminaire Saint-Sulpice in Montreal; b. 20 Nov. 1796 at Tourteron (dept of Ardennes, France), son of Pierre Billaudèle and Catherine François; d. 19 Oct. 1869 in Montreal.

Pierre-Louis Billaudèle began his secondary education under the direction of a priest, and in 1812 went into the Petit Séminaire de Charleville, dept of Ardennes, where he entered the priesthood. In 1813 he began his career as an educator by becoming tutor to a local nobleman's children. In 1816 he entered the Grand Séminaire de Charleville for his theological studies, and there he received holy orders.

On 30 Nov. 1819, a few months before his ordination to the priesthood, his bishop ap-pointed him director of the Petit Séminaire de Charleville, a position he combined with teaching and preaching. After five years of this absorbing ministry, he obtained permission to enter the Society of Saint-Sulpice. He spent two years in the novitiate at the Solitude d'Issy-les-Moulineaux near Paris (1824–26), and then was sent to the Grand Séminaire de Clermont-Ferrand. He remained there nearly 11 years, first as professor of philosophy, then as director of philosophy students and professor of dogma. Thus he was an experienced priest when he was asked to go to Montreal in 1837 to develop the educational work of Saint-Sulpice. He arrived in Montreal in November, accompanied by two other Sulpicians and the first four Brothers of the Christian Schools to come to Canada [see Louis ROBLOT].

Billaudèle was entrusted at first with a ministry at Notre-Dame de Montréal. As part of his work, he was responsible for giving a course of religious instruction, and because of his preaching ability he quickly attracted a large audience. He was soon obliged to add teaching ethics to the ecclesiastics of the Collège de Montréal to his duties. Billaudèle was thus moving towards the important position soon to be given to him, the direction of the first Grand Séminaire de Montréal.

This institution was founded in November 1840 and was immediately placed under the direction of the priests of Saint-Sulpice. On the recommendation of Joseph-Vincent Quiblier*, superior of the Séminaire Saint-Sulpice, Bishop Ignace Bourget* accepted Pierre-Louis Billaudèle as its first director. The latter's knowledge of theology and spirituality, his affable nature, and his experience of seminary life in France, all spoke in his favour. His position remained a delicate one, however; he had to introduce in Montreal the regulations governing the Sulpician seminaries in France, thereby imposing a new kind of life, with a spirit, customs, and traditions unknown to Canadians. Because of Billaudèle's skill and tact, the change was made smoothly. The small number of seminarists also facilitated his task: during the six years of his administration there were never more than 30.

On 21 April 1846 Billaudèle was elected superior of the Sulpicians in Canada, in succession to M. Quiblier. It was a radical change for him. Used to the calm, regular life of the seminary, he would have to direct an extensive and complicated operation at a time when everything in the parish of Notre-Dame and the teaching houses was being questioned. The parish first engaged his attention. Three weeks after his election, Billaudèle received a letter from Bishop

Bourget raising the matter of the deficiency of personnel and the subdivision of the parish. The council of the seminary entirely shared the bishop's concerns, but lack of resources and of priests prevented it from deferring to his wishes.

Several incidents delayed the solution of the problems raised by the bishop: the latter's trip to Europe in 1846–47, during which he discussed the subdivision and administration of the parish of Notre-Dame with the superior general of the Sulpicians; and the typhus epidemic, brought on by the arrival of nearly a thousand Irish in early June 1847, which occupied the bishop on his return. As parish priest of Notre-Dame, Billaudèle mobilized almost all the staff of the seminary, the Collège de Montréal, and the religious communities of the parish to meet the needs of the sick. During the epidemic, which lasted nearly three months, the seminary lost five of its members; several others, stricken by the disease, were forced to give up all their activities for several months, which made the problem of recruitment even more serious. In the end, it was necessary to await the arrival of the French visitor, Étienne-Michel FAILLON, in 1849, before attempting to solve the problems relating to the parish and to education.

At the first meeting with the visitor, the council of the seminary decided to build three subsidiary churches within the boundaries of the parish of Notre-Dame: one at Notre-Dame-de-Grâces, another in the *faubourg* Sainte-Anne, and a third in the *faubourg* Sainte-Marie. Bishop Bourget approved only the first two. Then in July 1852 fire destroyed the cathedral and the bishop's palace and in 1853 Bishop Bourget agreed to the seminary's offer to reconstruct the church of Saint-Jacques and make it a subsidiary of Notre-Dame.

In a letter to Billaudèle in April 1846, Bishop Bourget had suggested several other measures designed to strengthen the parish ministry. Long before the churches were built Billaudèle made a serious effort, both as superior and as parish priest, to follow his bishop's advice. He increased considerably the number of pastoral retreats, so as to be able to reach all classes of society. He reorganized the teaching of religion by entrusting the priests of the parish with the catechisms preparing children for first communion and confirmation, and he re-established the *catéchismes de persévérance* for young people leaving school at an early age. Pastoral visits in the town and the suburbs became more frequent and more regular. In addition, pious associations and charitable organizations experienced renewed growth. Existing associations and congregations were augmented by new ones including the Association de l'Amour de la Très-Sainte-Vierge, established in 1847 by Billaudèle, and the Saint-Vincent de Paul Society conferences, introduced in the parish in 1848.

The problem of the location of the grand seminary was of even greater interest to Billaudèle. At the time the institution was founded, it had been understood that its installation in a wing of the Collège de Montréal was only temporary. In 1850 the council of the seminary decided to erect its building near the church of Notre-Dame, on the site of the old seminary built by François Dollier* de Casson. Construction began immediately, and in 1853 the wing intended for the priests responsible for parish ministry was completed. There work stopped, for it had been decided in the mean time to look for a much larger lot. In 1854, during Faillon's second visit to Quebec, the decision was taken, at last, to construct the new building on the site of the Fort de la Montagne. The visitor's council approved the plans of the new grand seminary on 25 Aug. 1854, and in October the superior general, Joseph Carrière, ratified the decision. On 8 Sept. 1855 Billaudèle laid the foundation stone, one of the last official ceremonies over which he presided as superior. On 21 April 1856 he warned the council of the seminary that because of poor health he would not accept re-election for a third term.

During the last 12 years of his life, Billaudèle devoted himself almost entirely to preaching. Until the last he was able to make the most of his exceptional oratorical gifts: a voice of magnificent quality, elegant diction, an elevated mind, fertile imagination, prodigious memory, and great facility for expression and improvisation. He adapted readily to all audiences, and directed countless retreats, in the diocese of Montreal and neighbouring dioceses. This beneficent but exacting work finally exhausted him. During the last year of his life Billaudèle had to retire to the community's infirmary; he passed away in October 1869, after 50 years in the priesthood.

ANTONIO DANSEREAU

ASSM, 11; 21; 24, Dossier 2; 25, Dossier 1. Allaire, *Dictionnaire*. Henri Gauthier, *Sulpitiana* (2e éd., Montréal, 1926). Léon Pouliot, "Inventaire analytique de la correspondance de Mgr Ignace Bourget pour 1846," ANQ *Rapport*, 1965, 91. Léon Pouliot et François Beaudin, "Inventaire analytique de la correspondance de Mgr Ignace Bourget . . . [1847–50]," ANQ *Rapport*, 1966, 195; 1967; 1969, 3. Louis Bertrand, *Bibliothèque sulpicienne, ou histoire littéraire de la Compagnie de Saint-Sulpice* (3v., Paris, 1900), II,

311–12. [Pierre] Boisard, *La Compagnie de Saint-Sulpice; trois siècles d'histoire* (s.l., s.d.). [A.-C.-G. Desmazures], *M. Faillon, prêtre de St. Sulpice; sa vie et ses œuvres* (Montréal, 1879), 231–47. Frédéric Langevin, *Monseigneur Ignace Bourget: deuxième évêque de Montréal* (Montréal, 1931), 190–93. Pouliot, *Mgr Bourget*, I, II. Pierre Rousseau, *Vie de M. Pierre-Louis Billaudèle, grand-vicaire et dixième supérieur du séminaire de Montréal* (Montréal, 1885). Rumilly, *Hist. de Montréal*, II. Émile Boucher, "L'œuvre sulpicienne de la formation cléricale, les supérieurs du grand séminaire," *Le Séminaire* (Montréal), XXII (1957), 219–23. "Le grand séminaire de Montréal de 1840 à 1857," *Annuaire du grand séminaire* (Montréal), 3 (1930–31), 84–87. Olivier Maurault, "Grand séminaire de Montréal, I: son histoire," *Le Séminaire* (Montréal), V (1940), 9–64. Pierre Rousseau, "Notice biographique sur le révérend messire Pierre Billaudèle, s.s.," *L'Écho du cabinet de lecture pariossial de Montréal*, XII (1870), 274, 365, 408, 535, 620. "Vie de Monsieur Pierre-Louis Billaudèle, premier directeur du grand séminaire de Montréal," *Annuaire du grand séminaire* (Montréal), 3 (1930–31), 74–84.

BLACK, MARTIN GAY, merchant and banker; b. 19 Nov. 1786 in Halifax, the son of the Reverend William Black* and Mary Gay; m. 3 Jan. 1809 Frances Smith of Westmorland, N.B., and they had seven daughters and six sons; d. 26 Oct. 1861 in Halifax.

Martin Gay Black, eldest son of the founder of the Methodist movement in Nova Scotia, was raised in a home dedicated to establishing Methodism in a colony whose officialdom scorned John Wesley's evangelical religion. Educated at the latitudinarian Anglican academy in Windsor before 1802, Black followed his maternal grandfather in trade and by 1807 was established in business in Halifax with his brother-in-law James Hamilton. After dissolution of their firm in 1809, Martin Gay continued to supply British and East Indian goods and, like several Haligonian businessmen, rose to commercial prominence during the Napoleonic wars. By the late 1820s he had apparently retired from mercantile activities. In 1825 Black was an original partner in the Halifax Banking Company; he was its first secretary, and eventually served as president from September 1859 until his death. From 1832 to 1859 he owned, and rented out, the substantial wharf adjoining the Enos Collins*' property on which the bank stood. In addition, he invested prudently in local financial ventures and private loans.

In 1839, when Lieutenant Governor Sir Colin Campbell* sought to broaden the representation of his councils, Black was offered a seat on the Legislative Council. Declining the honour previously accorded five of his seven fellow bankers, he explained that his "habits and feelings [were] much more in accordance with the life of a private than a public character." Yet his life did not lack a public role. By 1814 he was a trustee of Zoar Chapel, and although this early appointment probably derived from his father's dominance of the Methodist organization, Black remained a steward of both chapel and circuit. When interdenominational and charitable institutions, as well as the Methodists, sought his efficient handling of their too meagre resources, he served for many years as treasurer of the Nova Scotia Methodist District, the local missionary society, and the Nova Scotia Bible Society. He was also more briefly an officer of such associations as the Poor Man's Friend Society, the Royal Acadian Society, the Halifax Visiting Dispensary, the Protestant Orphans' Home, and the YMCA. During half a century he subscribed, albeit nominally, to nearly every benevolent institution initiated in the city.

Black's life reflected the conservative, trade-oriented character of Methodism in Nova Scotia. His transition from merchant to banker and his active participation in interdenominational organizations, however, made him one of the church's most distinguished members. Contemporaries noted above all his "unostentatious usefulness."

S. BUGGEY

Brunswick Street United Church (Halifax), register of marriages, christenings, and burials, pp.29, 41, 74 (mfm. at PANS). Halifax County Court House (Halifax), Registry of deeds, index, 1749–1861, book 46, ff.184–85; book 55, ff.241–42; book 127, ff. 210–12. Halifax County Court of Probate (Halifax), no.1015, will of Martin Gay Black. Methodist Missionary Soc. Archives (London), Correspondence, box 11, nos.20, 102; box 12, no.34; box 13, no.65; box 15, no.177; box 21, nos.120, 125, 200 (mfm. at PAC). PANS, MG 20; RG 1, 244, no.91 (M. G. Black to R. D. George, Halifax, 23 March 1840); no.103 (address to Sir Colin Campbell). PRO, CO 217/171, f.208; 217/173, f.5; 217/174, ff.111–13.

Halifax Young Men's Christian Assoc., *Annual report* (Halifax), 1855–56, 1859, 1861–62. N.S. Bible Soc., *Report* (Halifax), 1819–55. Wesleyan Auxiliary Missionary Soc., N.S. District, *Annual report* (Halifax), 1827–52. *Acadian Reporter*, 6 Sept., 11 Oct. 1823; 13 April, 3 Aug. 1833; 12 Sept. 1835. *Halifax Journal*, 13 May 1816, 13 Oct. 1817, 4 Nov. 1833. *Novascotian*, 4 May 1825; 16 Jan. 1832; 10 Jan., 3 July 1833. *Nova Scotia Royal Gazette* (Halifax), 7 July 1807; 24 May 1808; 12 Jan., 21 Feb., 28 March 1809; 4 March, 6 May, 15 July 1812; 27 Oct. 1813. *Presbyterian Witness*, 2 Nov. 1861. *Provincial Wesleyan* (Halifax), 30 Oct. 1861. *Weekly Chronicle* (Halifax), 21 April, 5

May, 3 Nov. 1809; 4 May 1810; 17 June 1814; 5 June 1818. *Belcher's farmer's almanack*, 1837–61. Cyrus Black, *Historical record of the posterity of William Black* . . . (Amherst, N.S., 1885), 35. Ross and Trigge, *History of the Canadian Bank of Commerce*, I, 50, 52, 101, 106–7, 432. T. W. Smith, *History of the Methodist Church within the territories embraced in the late conference of Eastern British America* . . . (2v., Halifax, 1877–90), II, 315–16, 457. T. B. Akins, "History of Halifax City," N.S. Hist. Soc., *Coll.*, VIII (1895), 95, 146, 150, 152, 165, 182, 197, 271.

BLACK, WILLIAM, shipper, merchant, and office-holder; b. 1771 in Aberdeen, Scotland; m. Jane Billopp, and they had five children; d. 18 June 1866 in Fredericton, N.B.

William Black spent his early life in Aberdeen where he took an arts degree at Marischal College. In 1798 he immigrated to Saint John, N.B., to join his brother John*, who had already established a prosperous shipping and timber export business, John Black and Company. In 1808 John Black moved to Halifax, leaving the New Brunswick branch of the firm in William's hands. By 1812 it dominated Saint John's timber trade. Aside from developing their own fleet of ships, the Blacks established branches of the firm at Fredericton, St Andrews, Montreal, and on the Miramichi River. This commercial circuit was closed by their contacts in the West Indies and at Aberdeen and Greenock in Scotland, and by their position as the principal New Brunswick supplier of masts to the British Admiralty. By 1812 they possessed one of the largest business enterprises in British North America. The brothers Black further strengthened their position in the loyalist-dominated society of Saint John by their marriages to the daughters of Christopher Billopp*, a leading loyalist businessman and member of the Council of New Brunswick.

Doubtless this combination of circumstances led to William Black's appointment to the Council in 1817; Lieutenant Governor George Stracy Smyth* was adding new members to that body to reduce the influence of the executive and judicial officers of government in it. The decade following his appointment was an uneventful period for the Saint John businessman, highlighted only by the succession crisis of 1823 following Smyth's death when Black joined with another councillor in supporting Billopp's unsuccessful claims to the presidency of the Council and to the right to administer in the absence of a governor. His political fortunes rose sharply in the years following the arrival of Lieutenant Governor Sir Howard DOUGLAS, who appointed Black to the mayoralty of Saint John in 1828 over the opposition of several members of the city's Common Council. The

following year Douglas returned to England on leave of absence, and the Colonial Office proscription against the holding of executive posts by members of the judiciary cleared the way for Black's appointment to the presidency of the Council over the heads of two Supreme Court judges.

Black's two-year administration of New Brunswick during Douglas' absence was clouded by conflict. The assembly and the Colonial Office were involved in discussions concerning the control of crown lands and the disposition of the customs revenue in the province [*see* E. B. Chandler*]. At the same time, the Council itself was divided about giving support to the controversial commissioner of crown lands and surveyor general, Thomas BAILLIE. Black's reactions to these problems reveal a Briton whose metropolitan loyalties had been tempered by his experiences as a Saint John businessman. He consistently upheld the constitutional prerogatives of the imperial government, and displayed a profound mistrust of both the legal establishment represented in the Council and the movement towards local autonomy and popular sovereignty within the assembly. Thus he supported Baillie against his loyalist enemies in the Council, advocated the removal of the puisne judges of the Supreme Court from the Council, and condemned as "sweeping and extravagant" the demands of the assembly that it should control the casual revenues of the province. But if Black was prepared to acknowledge the constitutional sovereignty of the British government, he was equally prepared to argue that this authority should never be used to the economic detriment of the colony. In 1829, in the face of British disapproval, he strongly defended the colonial bounty on wheat grown in New Brunswick on the grounds that it was necessary to assist the development of a viable milling industry in Saint John, and the following year he led the provincial assault on the British government's proposed reduction of tariffs on imports of foreign wood products into Great Britain.

Black surrendered the administration of the province on the arrival of the new lieutenant governor, Sir Archibald Campbell*, on 8 Sept. 1831. He had little influence with Campbell and his successors. One of his last major functions as administrator had been to make recommendations to the Colonial Office regarding the creation of separate Legislative and Executive councils; in the subsequent reorganization in 1832 he was relegated to the Legislative Council. He served as president of that body from 1843 until his death in 1866, though he rarely presided in the last

Blackadar

decade of his life. During these years he was twice appointed mayor of Saint John, in 1832–33 and again from 1840 until 1843.

William Black was a Conservative, a Scottish Episcopalian, and a founder and leading member of the St Andrew's Society of Saint John. He had evidently withdrawn from direct management of his trading activities in the 1820s, though he had large holdings in the city for many years afterward, and may have continued to invest in many of the shipping and financial enterprises of the 1830s and 1840s. Neither of his sons followed him into business.

T. W. ACHESON

[Unfortunately there remains little documentation relating to Black's early business activities. The best sources for his political life are PRO, CO 188/39, 188/41; N.B., Council, *Journals*, 1817–29; and Legislative Council, *Journals*, 1832–66. There are also scattered references to the Black family in the Saint John newspapers of the early 19th century; Common Clerk's Office, Saint John, N.B., Common Council of Saint John, minutes, 1828–33, 1840–43; and City and County of Saint John, Court of Probate, Records, book D, pp.146–55; E, pp.84–85 (mfm. at PANB). The principal secondary sources include Hannay, *History of N.B.*; I. A. Jack, *History of St. Andrew's Society of St. John, N.B., Canada, 1798 to 1903* (Saint John, N.B., 1903); MacNutt, *New Brunswick*; and D. S. Macmillan, "The 'new men' in action: Scottish mercantile and shipping operations in the North American colonies, 1760–1825," *Canadian business history, selected studies, 1497–1971*, ed. D. S. Macmillan (Toronto, 1972), 44–103. T.W.A.]

BLACKADAR, HUGH WILLIAM (the name is sometimes written **Blackader**, but he signed **Blackadar**), newspaper printer and publisher; b. 13 Jan. 1808 at Halifax, N.S., the only son of Hugh and Amy Blackadar; m. *c.* 18 Feb. 1835, Mary Sharpless, who died childless in 1839, and secondly, on 4 Oct. 1840, Sophia Coleman, by whom he had 11 children; d. 13 June 1863 at Halifax.

Born into a family of shipwrights and artisans working at the Halifax dockyard, Hugh William Blackadar became a printer's apprentice in 1820 under John Munro, publisher of the *Halifax Journal*, a newspaper begun in 1781 by John Howe Sr. There is no record of Blackadar's early activities in Halifax. In March 1835, however, he was called upon by the prosecution during Joseph Howe*'s libel trial to establish that Howe had published an allegedly slanderous letter in the *Novascotian*. When Blackadar failed to reply, doubtless out of sympathy for a fellow-publisher and liberal, Howe admitted the letter had been printed in his paper.

In July 1835 Blackadar established himself as an independent publisher with the purchase of the fledgling *Weekly Mirror* from John Bowes. The newspaper had a limited audience, however, and Blackadar did little to alter its bland format; the final edition appeared on 13 Jan. 1837, with the notice that it was being discontinued because of a paucity of subscribers.

In 1836 in partnership with John English, Blackadar had purchased the *Acadian Recorder* from Philip J. Holland, brother of the paper's founder, Anthony Henry Holland*. The successful Blackadar-English association continued until the latter's death in July 1857, when ownership passed to Blackadar; after 1863 the *Recorder* was published by his three sons. Although various people occupied the *Recorder*'s editorial chair, policy was controlled ultimately by Blackadar and English. Under their direction the *Recorder* continued the stand for liberal reform developed by the Holland brothers, becoming second only to Howe's *Novascotian* in its independent editorial policy. Where the Hollands had maintained a platform of deliberate but discreet agitation, however, Blackadar and English became highly vocal in their support of Howe's struggle to gain greater colonial autonomy. The *Recorder* also championed social progress; when in 1842 the Baptist *Christian Messenger* refused to print Howe's controversial letters denouncing sectarian colleges, Blackadar, himself a Baptist, published them. Although such independent actions created many enemies, Blackadar and English consistently maintained a publication noted for the "fairness and impartiality" which they had advertised in their prospectus for the new *Acadian Recorder* on 14 Jan. 1837.

During the 1850s, however, the tone of the *Recorder* became somewhat conservative. The political patronage of the Liberal administration under responsible government alienated Blackadar, perhaps in part because he had been overlooked for the office of queen's printer. Howe's anti-Catholic campaign further estranged the *Recorder*, likely because English was Catholic. In any case, during Blackadar's final years, the *Recorder*, although maintaining a liberal platform, denounced the vicissitudes of party politics.

In private life, Blackadar had little desire for public notice. Publishing was his only interest and until his final days he could be found setting type in the *Recorder* office. He was remembered as "a perfect Encyclopedia" of information on Halifax, its inhabitants, and its naval activities. It was not for himself, however, that Blackadar was ultimately remembered, but rather for the liberal

54

tone and impartiality of his *Acadian Recorder*, qualities which lasted long after he had gone.

LOIS K. KERNAGHAN

PANS, MG 5, Camp Hill Cemetery (Halifax), records, 1844–78; RG 32, 151, 18 Feb. 1835; 153, 3 Oct. 1840. Duncan Campbell, *Nova Scotia in its historical, mercantile and industrial relations* (Montreal, 1873). Tratt, "Survey of N.S. newspapers." *Acadian Recorder*, 16 Jan. 1913. D. C. Harvey, "Newspapers of Nova Scotia, 1840–1867," *CHR*, XXVI (1945), 279–301. J. S. Martell, "The press of the Maritime provinces in the 1830's," *CHR*, XIX (1938), 24–49. [J. Murray Beck, Charles St C. Stayner, and Peter B. Waite gave information and advice for the preparation of this biography. L.K.K.]

BLACKBIRD. *See* ASSIGINACK, JEAN-BAPTISTE

BLAIR, ADAM JOHNSTON FERGUSSON. *See* FERGUSSON BLAIR

BLAKE, WILLIAM HUME, lawyer, politician, and judge; b. 10 March 1809 at Kiltegan, County Wicklow (Republic of Ireland), the son of Dominick Edward Blake, a Church of Ireland clergyman, and Anne Margaret Hume, the daughter of William Hume, a wealthy Irish parliamentarian; d. 15 Nov. 1870 at Toronto, Ont.

William Hume Blake belonged to an ancient and influential Irish family centred in Galway. His branch of the family had been converted from Roman Catholicism to Protestantism in the 18th century, and Hume, as he was usually called, grew up in his father's rectory. He was given a sound education, receiving a BA from Trinity College, Dublin, in 1828. From that year until 1831 he studied medicine in Dublin, but he apparently gave it up because he was repelled by the crudities of the dissecting room. In 1832 he married his first cousin Catherine Hume*, a pious, intelligent, and ambitious woman, who provided stability and leadership for the family of four children they were to have.

In 1832 Blake left Ireland on a chartered vessel as one of a group of prosperous and well-educated relatives and friends. Among them were the Reverend Benjamin Cronyn*, future Anglican bishop of Huron, the Reverend Dominick Edward Blake, Hume's eldest brother, George Skeffington CONNOR, a lawyer and Hume's brother-in-law, a number of evangelical Anglican clergymen, Hume's widowed mother and two single sisters, and other relatives by marriage. The group was dominated by the clergymen who, with the cooperation of the archbishop of Dublin and Archdeacon John STRACHAN of York (Toronto), were seeking placements in Upper Canada. They arrived in Quebec City in September 1832, and Hume and Dominick Blake proceeded to Middlesex County, Upper Canada, where Dominick became rector of Adelaide and Hume took land at Bear Creek, near Strathroy. Hume began to clear the land and built a primitive log house in which his son, Dominick Edward*, was born in October 1833. But the Blakes soon discovered that they were not suited to pioneer life and in the fall of 1834 moved to Toronto, where Hume studied law under Simon E. Washburn. A second son, Samuel Hume*, was born in 1835. In February 1838 Blake was called to the Upper Canadian bar. He also had a private income which enabled him to take his son Edward to Ireland in 1836 for a "change of air," and it was supplemented by the money Catherine earned giving music and language lessons. Blake and his wife, who demonstrated intense affection for their two sons and two daughters, were deeply involved in educating their children.

Blake became an outstandingly successful lawyer, active in most areas of legal practice. He participated in several spectacular criminal cases, built a large equity practice, and was quickly recognized as one of the leading chancery lawyers in Canada West. His preference was for practice in the Court of Nisi Prius, which he considered the stepping stone to prominence in business, the judiciary, and government. His early eminence was revealed in 1841 when Governor General Sydenham [Thomson*] attempted to appoint him a judge of the Surrogate Court of the Home District. Blake declined the honour, but in 1848 was named a QC.

Hume Blake was an aristocratic Anglican, without a liberal or radical background in Ireland, yet, like many successful Irish Anglicans, he favoured the reform rather than the conservative side in politics. A brilliant speaker, and a man whose loyalty was unquestioned in the rebellion of 1837–38, during which he served as paymaster of a government battalion, Blake was useful to the Reformers during the difficult years following the rebellion. In spite of his youth he emerged during the early 1840s as an important Reform leader. At that time he entered a legal partnership with two active Reformers, Joseph Curran Morrison* and George Skeffington Connor, and also formed associations with such key Reform leaders as Robert Baldwin* and Francis Hincks*. In 1843 Baldwin, then attorney general for Canada West, entrusted Blake with "the Crowns business on the Eastern Circuit." Blake had a significant role in the bitter and divisive election of 1844, following the resignation of the Baldwin – L.-H. LA FONTAINE government over

Blake

a disagreement with Sir Charles Metcalfe* about whether a responsible ministry or the governor controlled patronage. At an important Reform meeting in Toronto Blake moved a resolution identifying responsible government as an Englishman's right: "Ministerial Responsibility to the people of this country for every act of the Executive connected with our local affairs, is an essential ingredient of our Constitution." Blake contested the 2nd riding of York against the incumbent Tory, George Duggan*. He defended the British connection, and assured the electors "that your conservatism, like my own, consists of attaining for our fellow countrymen that control over the exercise of executive power in all its branches, which is enjoyed without question in England." Blake lost and was bitter about the "slander and falsehood more foul and base than ever yet disgraced an electoral contest." Later in 1844 Blake, his earlier defeat still rankling, agreed to run in a by-election in Simcoe, telling the electors that he did so regardless of the recent victory in the general election of moderate Conservatives led in Upper Canada by William Henry Draper*, who, he said, had won through shameful abuses. Though Blake strongly attacked Draper's "friend of the Governor" stance as "dangerous [and] subversive of all liberty," he declined to campaign actively and was soundly defeated early in 1845 by William Benjamin Robinson*. Robert Baldwin Sullivan*, however, attributed Blake's defeat to the influence of the Orange Order, "the source of power and influence in great things. . . ."

Blake continued to be politically active, and Hincks even suspected that he aspired to the Reform leadership. Blake ran in the 3rd riding of York in the election of 1848 and again placed heavy emphasis on the attainment of responsible government. In spite of his absence from Canada because of illness during the campaign, he secured an easy victory. The election resulted in a sweeping Reform victory, and La Fontaine and Baldwin were asked to form a ministry. Baldwin wanted Blake to become solicitor general for Canada West, a post to which he was suited because of his talents and interests. At this time there was no clear convention about solicitors general being members of the cabinet. Blake's counterpart for Canada East, Thomas Cushing Aylwin*, had occupied a seat in cabinet in 1842–43, and in 1848 resumed his place in the cabinet. Blake learned that he would not have a cabinet seat and resented this invidious distinction. At the same time strong retrenchment men like Hincks opposed any unnecessary cabinet appointments on grounds of cost. Hincks finally

suggested a compromise which removed the difficulty: Aylwin was appointed a judge, and Blake accepted office on 22 April 1848. Governor General Lord Elgin [BRUCE] reported to Colonial Secretary Lord Grey that the "Solicitors-General are not to be in the Council. . . ." Blake suffered some embarrassment over the incident: the anti-government *Montreal Gazette* meanly suggested that Blake had refused a cabinet place because he would not associate "with certain of the Ministry." In the necessary by-election Blake easily secured re-election in 3rd York.

His ministerial position was important, despite his lack of cabinet status. A modern historian has said that 19th century solicitors general were theoretically supposed to conduct the "non-political" legal work of the government, but that in practice they and the attorneys general ruled on points of law submitted by other departments. The law officers co-ordinated much of cabinet business, directed political strategy in parliament, and made rulings – not always on points of law – which were considered rulings of the whole cabinet. It is clear that Blake did in fact attend cabinet meetings, and at the close of his ministerial career was bitterly attacked by the Conservative Toronto *British Colonist* for "meddling in the affairs of Government. . . . [Blake], perhaps as much as [any] member of the executive, controlled the measures of Government, without appearing to have a seat at the Council Board." Nevertheless, Blake also had much detailed and non-political work connected with his office which involved appearances in court and a great deal of travel.

Blake was often a sick man during the 1840s. He experienced "severe attacks of gout" and suffered from a mysterious malady whose symptoms were irritability, anxiety, and instability. In 1847 a friend told Blake there was "no mean" in his "efforts and anxieties, it is all extreme. . . . It is one of the inseparable qualities of a too ardent nature." So serious was Blake's condition that in mid September 1847, during the election campaign, he, Catherine, and Edward took an extended European tour. In London Blake learned that he might be suffering from liver and heart ailments. After wintering in Paris, where Hume and Edward witnessed the sacking of the Tuileries in February 1848, the family returned to Toronto in the spring. But Hume's nervous illness continued, often precipitated by "severe mental exertion." With the pressures of the solicitor generalship he had assumed, he had so deteriorated by August 1848 that Catherine asked Baldwin "to persuade him as much as *possible to abstain from everything calculated to engage too deeply, or excite too* . . . fully his ardent enthusiastic mind. . . . I know the weakness of his mind is such, that he cannot enter *moderately* upon any occupation. . . .''

In 1849, at La Fontaine's insistence, the Reform government introduced a bill for the payment of losses incurred during the rebellion in Lower Canada in 1837–38. Blake disagreed with the policy, and his explanation in a letter to R. B. Sullivan reveals much about his general approach: ''This incurable disposition to waste our strength and means in toilsome and dangerous efforts to acquire mere baubles, and those, too, somewhat dangerous ones, whilst we neglect great and noble objects . . . will sooner or later be our ruin. Whether we are to exist as an appendage of Great Britain or annexed to the States, whatever is to be our condition, our very existence as a country depends upon the completion of our navigation. . . . Why should not our thoughts and energies be fixed upon our condition and the means of its improvement, instead of conjuring up the whole race of infernal spirits to plague and torment us. . . .'' Moreover, Blake resented the fact that the government's supporters from Canada West, most of whom opposed the measure, were not consulted until after the bill had been tabled in the legislature. He nevertheless felt obliged to support it. Indeed on 15 and 16 Feb. 1849 he delivered a major speech on the bill, analyzing the Upper Canadian political situation in pre-rebellion days, and taking as his theme the difference between self-serving loyalty to the person of a governor and his misguided policies and a higher loyalty to the maintenance of a free constitution. With controlled, relentless fury he turned the loyalty question back on the Tories: ''I have no sympathy with the would be loyalty of honorable gentlemen opposite, which, whilst it affects at all times peculiar zeal for the prerogative of the Crown, is ever ready to sacrifice the liberty of the subject. . . . True British loyalty owes allegiance alike to the Crown and the constitution.'' Unfortunately, Blake allowed his address to become a demagogic assault on the Tory members, whose disagreement with government policy was characterized as ''factious opposition'' and who were seen as racial murderers: ''I did feel disposed to advise them to . . . propose the erection of a gibbet before every French Canadian's door, and offer up an holocaust of 700,000 men to appease the *British* feelings of Canada.'' Sir Allan Napier MacNab received vicious treatment, being described as a rebel to the constitution and the country. Blake's speech was a sensation. *La Minerve* described it as ''replete with logic, with master-strokes of argument

and proof – severe, irrefragable, ironical, cutting,'' and said Blake proved himself ''decidedly a great orator.'' But he himself admitted that he had acted rashly: ''Had I come with more mature preparation, with a note or two for my guidance possibly my language might have been more measured.'' In defence of a policy with which he disagreed, Blake had intensified the bitterness of partisan warfare and accentuated the personal hatreds that disfigured political debate.

The response from Conservative members was immediate and nasty. Several duelling challenges were issued, one by John A. Macdonald* on Friday, 16 February. A duel was prevented by the quick action of the speaker. Macdonald made proper submission to the house but Blake was unavailable. On the Monday he appeared at the bar of the house to explain. It was assumed then, and has been since, that Blake could not be found late on 16 February because he wished to avoid facing Macdonald in an ''affair of honour.'' Blake had to admit privately that he had failed to display ''that cool measured step which ought to have distinguished the Solicitor-General.'' A proud and sensitive man, after submitting himself to the humiliation of appearing at the bar of the assembly, and doubtless knowing that he had been labelled a coward, he submitted his resignation because of the ''painful position in which some persons have thought it right to place me. . . .'' La Fontaine refused the resignation, and Blake's career was saved.

Other rash acts followed. When the parliament buildings in Montreal were burned in April after the Rebellion Losses Bill had passed, Blake had to be dissuaded from addressing the arsonist mob which might very well have lynched him. With the city given over to riot, Blake armed himself ''with a thick walnut ruler'' and to the horror of his wife ''paraded the town alone. . . .'' When La Fontaine released several Tory rioters Blake argued passionately with him that ''he had disgraced himself forever & rendered the govt contemptible.'' In May he wounded two rioters with a pistol when a mob attacked Têtu's Hotel during a ministerial banquet. The excess of ''feeling'' which he admitted to his brother was thus sustained for a lengthy period.

Had La Fontaine accepted Blake's resignation, Blake would have left office without completing the massive reorganization of Upper Canada's judicial system for which he is best remembered. In 1843 Blake had accepted appointment, along with Robert Easton Burns and James C. P. Esten, to a commission charged with examining the ''practice and proceedings'' of the Court of Chancery. Court reform had been a sensitive area, for the entire legal structure had been profoundly unpopular for many years. Many left-wing Reformers regarded the equity court as a device whereby lawyers exploited a vulnerable public, and advocated instead a simplified, less expensive system of legal administration. Many lawyers, however, wanted an enlarged court of chancery, additional common law court services, and an improved appeals system. There was a third motive force for legal reform at work behind the scene. Although Blake's private views remained secret, he regarded many of Upper Canada's powerful superior court judges as Tory hacks. He attributed his electoral defeat in 1845 to the intimidation by Conservative judges of many lawyers who might otherwise have aided the Reform party in elections. In 1845 he complained to Baldwin that "it is the thought of offending judges whose decrees are absolute, and who thus hold the fate of transgressors in their hand which has driven the bar into the ranks of our opponents." Blake wanted to reduce the authority of the judges, whom he accused of acting as a veritable "inquisition," and argued, "Give us the court of appeal, and you do more to liberalise the bench & bar than can well be conceived." He also shared with many professional colleagues the view that the single Court of Chancery judge, Vice-Chancellor Robert Sympson Jameson*, was incompetent. Indeed in 1845 Baldwin accused Blake of supporting judicial reform "for the sole purpose of getting rid of [Jameson]."

The commissioners investigating the Court of Chancery reported to Draper's Conservative régime in 1845 without making any recommendations for fundamental changes, but Blake's criticisms made during their investigations were clearly regarded as representative of the legal profession. In 1845 he publicly expressed his views in *A letter to the Hon. Robert Baldwin . . . upon the administration of justice in western Canada*, arguing that the existing system was defective because there was no effective appeals system, and because the Court of Chancery under a single judge had neither healthy respect for the law nor true freedom for the citizen. The solution was relatively simple: the Court of Queen's Bench should be divided into two common law courts; there should be three equity judges in a reformed court of chancery; and a court of appellate jurisdiction should be provided by "the assemblage of these several judges, in a court, to be termed the Court of Exchequer Chamber. . . ."

In spite of Baldwin's profound reservations, Blake took up his proposed reforms when he entered the ministry in April 1848. He was encouraged to proceed by the legal profession, and he consulted with the judges before his reforms were introduced as a series of bills in March 1849. They secured fairly easy passage through the assembly and received royal assent on 30 May 1849. Two superior common courts "of equal and concurrent jurisdiction and of equal dignity," Queen's Bench and Common Pleas, were established, each with three judges. The chief justice remained on the Queen's Bench. Chancery was enlarged by the addition of two vice-chancellors, and a Court of Error and Appeal, consisting of the judges of all three courts and presided over by the chief justice, was established. Restricted appeals to the queen in her privy council were still permitted. Blake's most constructive work as a minister was thus accomplished.

Yet Blake's rash behaviour during the riots and annexation crisis in the same spring of 1849 must have confirmed any doubts Baldwin retained about Blake's suitability for office. It probably accounts in part for the decision to remove Blake from the government. His appointment as chancellor of Upper Canada was logical in view of his high standing as an equity lawyer, though Conservatives and Clear Grits concluded that he had reformed the Court of Chancery in order to create a personal sinecure worth £1,250 per annum. He was offered the post on 10 Sept. 1849 and assumed his new office on 1 Jan. 1850. Baldwin, who had been far from enthusiastic about Blake's legal reforms, was to leave politics in 1851 when a majority of Upper Canadian Reform members indicated by vote their opposition to Blake's reformed Court of Chancery. When explaining his decision to leave public life Baldwin made it clear that the reforms had been inspired by Blake, though he acknowledged that as attorney general he himself was ultimately the "party responsible."

Blake's later years were busy, and probably unhappy. Nonetheless he functioned efficiently as leader of the court, at least for a time. He cleared away a mass of business that had accumulated during the indolent regime of Jameson. Contemporaries considered his work successful, and W. R. Riddell*, the historian of the courts of Upper Canada, found Blake's judgements "entitled to respect, but from changed circumstances and practice they are now little quoted."

Blake always had a profound interest in university affairs, and from 1843 to 1848 served as the first professor of law at King's College, Toronto, beginning with an annual salary of £100. As an Anglican and a lawyer he defended the college against the secularization movement, even to the point of working with John Strachan, who was a long-time enemy of the Blake family. Nevertheless Blake accepted as inevitable Baldwin's scheme to secularize the college in 1849. He intensified his involvement with higher education in 1853, when he accepted the chancellorship of the University of Toronto. His term was unpleasant. After 1854 he had to deal with Allan MacNab's government; his relationship with Governor General Sir Edmund Walker HEAD, who took an intimate interest in the university, was marred by bitter quarrels, especially over the appointment of a Tory, John Langton*, as vice-chancellor. Blake also involved himself in internal university feuds concerning the management of Upper Canada College and the building committee for University College. In 1856 he resigned the university chancellorship.

His health again broke down in 1856, and he discovered that he had diabetes. There being no cure, he could only seek rest and medical advice abroad. His problems were complicated by the financial panic of 1857, which badly damaged his investments and forced him to live frugally. Hume and Catherine returned to Canada in September 1857, but he was unable to attend to his duties for long periods of time and finally resigned as chancellor of Upper Canada on 18 March 1862. Blake had declined a knighthood in 1859 but accepted an appointment as a judge of the Court of Error and Appeal in 1864, a post for which he qualified as a retired chancellor.

In 1864 John A. Macdonald appointed Blake chairman of the Railway Postal Service Commission which was to examine the Grand Trunk Railway's request for a higher postal subsidy from the government. The request had been denied by the preceding Reform government, but Macdonald was resolved to assist the politically potent railway. He considered Blake "a man of large and liberal ideas in money matters," and Blake's committee duly recommended further assistance to the Grand Trunk and other lines.

The commission did its work in Quebec City from January to March 1865. Blake and his wife enjoyed their renewed participation in public life, but he was still seriously ill; and to his other afflictions he now added "impairment of vision." His financial problems continued, and his peace was disturbed by unhappy disputes, often over money, with his brother's children. He was forced to seek a calmer atmosphere abroad in 1867. Yet contacts with people became more and more "painful inflictions." He was able to take great pleasure in his elder son's political success during the early years of confederation, but never

recovered his health. Until his death in 1870 he was a pathetic figure, wracked by physical pain, nervous incapacity, and ruined hopes.

William Hume Blake was a tragic figure. He possessed enormous natural abilities, and an excellent education had increased an almost limitless capacity to assimilate new knowledge and ideas. Unfortunately, his physical and mental impairments, difficult to diagnose in the 20th century but nonetheless real, prevented him from fully realizing his powers. Thus he was an unstable man with enthusiasm but also an excess of passion. In law his abilities resulted in immediate and spectacular success, but he failed to sustain this drive and opted for a political career. In office he demonstrated fervent devotion to British freedoms and oratorical brilliance, but his instability resulted in frustration, rashness, and overzealous partisanship, which were an embarrassment to his colleagues. On the bench he was able to function successfully, though for only a few years. Yet as a lawyer and politician he made a major contribution to court structure and as a judge his efforts to adapt English authority to the needs of Canadian economic development were of particular significance.

DONALD SWAINSON

[The author is indebted to Professor R. C. B. Risk for valuable assistance in preparing the legal aspects of this biography. D.S.]

MTCL, Robert Baldwin papers. PAC, MG 24, B14; MG 26, A; MG 30, D111. PAO, Blake family papers, I, 1. W. H. Blake, *A letter to the Hon. Robert Baldwin ... upon the administration of justice in western Canada ...* (Toronto, 1845); *Separate report of Mr. Blake's speech on the rebellion losses* (Montreal, 1849). Can., Prov. of, Executive Council, *Copy of a report of a committee ... for the performance of the railway postal service* . . .([Quebec], 1865); Legislative Assembly, *Journals*, 1844–45, 2, app.J.J.; 1848–49. *Documentary history of education in U.C.* (Hodgins), IV–VIII, XI–XV. *Elgin-Grey papers* (Doughty). "The Hon. William Hume Blake," *Canada Law Journal* (Toronto), new ser., VI (1870), 281–83. [Catherine Hume (Blake)], "The riots of 1849 in Montreal," *CHR*, XV (1934), 283–88. [John Langton], *Early days in Upper Canada: letters of John Langton from the backwoods of Upper Canada and the audit office of the Province of Canada*, ed. W. A. Langton (Toronto, 1926); "The University of Toronto in 1856," *CHR*, V (1924), 132–45. Macdonald, *Letters* (Johnson and Stelmack). Reform Assoc. of Can., *Proceedings at the first general meeting* (Toronto, 1844). *British Colonist* (Toronto), 1844, 1849, 1851. *Globe*, 1844, 1848–49, 1870, 1895. *Cyclopaedia of Canadian biog.* (Rose, 1886). Dent, *Canadian portrait gallery*, III. *Political appointments, 1841–67* (J.-O. and N.-O. Coté). D. R. Beer, "Transitional toryism in the 1840's as seen in the political career of Sir Allan Mac-

Nab, 1839–1849'' (unpublished MA thesis, Queen's University, Kingston, Ont., 1963). C. R. W. Biggar, *Sir Oliver Mowat, a biographical sketch* (2v., Toronto, 1905). Creighton, *Macdonald, young politician.* A. W. Currie, *The Grand Trunk Railway of Canada* (Toronto, 1957). Dent, *Last forty years.* Hodgetts, *Pioneer public service.* J. D. Livermore, "Towards 'a union of hearts': the early career of Edward Blake, 1867–1880" (unpublished PH D thesis, Queen's University, Kingston, Ont., 1975). George Metcalf, "The political career of William Henry Draper" (unpublished MA thesis, University of Toronto, 1959). Joseph Pope, *Memoirs of the Right Honourable Sir John Alexander Macdonald, G.C.B., first prime minister of the dominion of Canada* (2v., Ottawa, [1894]). Read, *Lives of the judges.* W. R. Riddell, *The bar and the courts of the province of Upper Canada, or Ontario* (Toronto, 1928); *The legal profession in Upper Canada in its early periods* (Toronto, 1916); *Upper Canada sketches: incidents in the early times of the province* (Toronto, 1922). Joseph Schull, *Edward Blake: the man of the other way (1833–1881)* (Toronto, 1975). Sissons, *Ryerson.* W. S. Wallace, *A history of the University of Toronto, 1827–1927* (Toronto, 1927). G. E. Wilson, *The life of Robert Baldwin; a study in the struggle for responsible government* (Toronto, 1933). W. N. T. Wylie, "Toronto and the Montreal annexation crisis of 1849–1850; ideologies, loyalties and considerations of personal gain" (unpublished MA thesis, Queen's University, Kingston, Ont., 1971). *Toronto World*, 21 June 1892.

BLAKE, WILLIAM RUFUS, actor and theatre manager; baptized 5 Dec. 1802 at Halifax, N.S., first child of William Blake and Charlotte Herring; m. in August 1826 Caroline Waring, *née* Placide, an actress, and they had one son; d. 22 April 1863 at Boston, Mass.

Born of Irish parents, William Rufus Blake was known for his rich humour and *raconteur*'s skill. His widowed mother is said to have encouraged him to take up a medical career, but Blake determined upon a stage life. He first played on the Halifax stage from 1817 to 1819 with a troupe of visiting American actors which included Thomas Placide. The company's internal disputes and financial collapse as well as Blake's indifferent press notices can hardly have been encouraging. By 1824 he had nonetheless acquired sufficient stage skill to obtain a *début* at the newly opened Chatham Garden Theatre in New York City. During the next seven years the young actor appeared in several New York playhouses, travelled on tour for a short time, and was stage manager for the opening seasons of Boston's Tremont Theatre in 1827 and the renovated Walnut St Theatre in Philadelphia in 1829. In the summer of 1831 he and his wife starred with Vincent DeCamp's company in Montreal and Quebec before he returned to his native town to fit up a theatre and organize a company of actors.

In Halifax Blake leased the city's only theatre, a three-year old building known simply as "The Theatre." There, after renovation, he offered a broad selection of comedies, melodramas, and farces from the London and American stages. The members of his small but versatile company were all Americans, though officers of the British army garrison and transient actors joined them occasionally. Talent, enthusiasm, and high-priced tickets made the theatre both respectable and successful at first. Further remodelling of the building and an expanded company of which "the female department" was rated "equal to that of any company in the U. States" marked the opening of the second season. Blake himself was acknowledged by the *Boston Gazette* to be "favorably known to the public as a first rate genteel comedian."

Yet, despite high prospects, the theatre failed. Not enough townsmen were willing to support theatrical entertainments. Moreover, attendance dropped in the face of the threat of cholera spreading from the United States and the onset of a new economic depression in the winter of 1832–33. Blake's extravagant management of the theatre, as illustrated by his elaborate new productions, also contributed to its demise. After the theatre closed in June 1833, "a large quantity of *splendid scenery* . . . and an extensive wardrobe of *Elegant dresses*" were offered for sale; one stage set was said to have cost £85. Blake's extravagance appeared again in the interior embellishments of New York's Olympic Theatre, built for him and Henry E. Willard in 1837, and described as "a parlor of elegance." Blake managed this theatre from September 1837 until February 1838.

Except for British tours in 1839 and 1840, which included an unsuccessful appearance on the London stage, Blake confined the remaining years of his career to the United States. In Boston, New York, and Philadelphia he was both actor and stage manager, notably at the Walnut St Theatre again (1845–48) and at Burton's Old Broadway Theatre in New York (1848–52). Abandoning management in the last decade of his life, he played in the most famous American companies of the day – Wallack's and Laura Keene's – reputedly at some of the highest salaries on the New York stage. One of the foremost comedians of his age, Blake was acquainted with most important theatrical personalities in America during his 40 years of playing.

As a young man, slim and handsome, Blake played the gamut of leading male roles in genteel comedies. By the late 1830s, however, increasing corpulence led him to the study of old age. Several contemporaries considered his sentimental and comic old men – "Geoffrey Dale" in *The last man*, "Jesse Rural" in *Old heads and young hearts*, "Lord Duberly" in *The heir at law*, "Old Dornton" in *The road to ruin*, and "Sir Peter Teazle" in *The school for scandal* – as unsurpassed, and regarded Blake himself as "a positive epitome of fun and humor."

S. BUGGEY

[For Blake's years in Canada newspapers are virtually the only reliable sources. His early role is lightly covered in the 1817–19 issues of the following Halifax newspapers: *Acadian Recorder, Free Press, Halifax Journal, Nova Scotia Royal Gazette*, and *Weekly Chronicle*; his Halifax theatre is treated more fully in the 1831–33 issues of the town's *Acadian and General Advertiser, Acadian Recorder, Halifax Journal*, and *Novascotian*. The *Montreal Gazette* and *Quebec Mercury* record and comment upon his Canadian tour of July to September 1831. His experiences in London can be traced through the *Age* (London), April to July 1839. An obituary can be found in the *Acadian Recorder*, 2 May 1863. S.B.]

St Paul's Anglican Church (Halifax), register of baptisms, 1791–1816 (mfm. at PANS). *DAB*. T. A. Brown, *A history of the New York stage, from the first performance in 1732 to 1901* (3v., New York, 1903). W. W. Clapp, *A record of the Boston stage* (Boston and Cambridge, Mass., 1853; repr. New York and London, [1968]). J. N. Ireland, *Records of the New York stage from 1750 to 1860* (2v., New York, 1866; repr. 1966). S. B. Smith, "The Walnut Street Theatre, 1809–1834" (unpublished MA thesis, University of Delaware, Newark, 1960), 72–74. Lester Wallack, *Memories of fifty years* (New York, 1889). A. H. Wilson, *A history of the Philadelphia theatre, 1835 to 1855* (Philadelphia and London, 1935; repr. New York, 1968). [Joseph Jefferson], "The autobiography of Joseph Jefferson," *Century Illustrated Monthly Magazine* (New York), XXXIX (1889–90); XL (1890).

BOSTON, JOHN, lawyer, businessman, and sheriff; b. 1786 in Scotland; d. 6 March 1862 in Montreal, Canada East.

John Boston, leaving his parents in Scotland, arrived in Montreal in June 1802, and with the aid of his older brother, Thomas, quickly joined the Montreal mercantile élite dominated by Scots like himself. Apprenticed "under written indenture" in March 1805 to David Ross, a prominent member of the Montreal bar, Boston, after five years of continued clerkship and examination, received a commission as advocate at law in Lower Canada and opened a lucrative law practice in Montreal devoted largely to land transactions. A charter member and sometime president of the St Andrew's Society of Montreal, the Montreal Curling Club, and the Brothers in Law Club, a coterie of 15 Montreal lawyers, Boston undoubtedly profited from association with influential friends. His second marriage, on 16 Nov. 1826 to Margaret Walker, daughter of a wealthy merchant, William Walker, assured his economic and social standing and extended his economic interests. (Boston's first wife, Isabella Stewart, whom he had married on 17 Dec. 1814 had died on 7 Dec. 1821, leaving him with two daughters.)

Boston himself possessed intelligence, talent, industry, and charm and readily gained the respect of his professional colleagues and the larger civic community. In January 1827 a public meeting named Boston to a committee of nine to advise on the incorporation of Montreal. An officer of the Montreal militia, in 1821 he held the rank of lieutenant. From 1833 until 1835 he served as president of the Advocates Library and in 1838 received a QC. In 1839 he and Hughes E. Barron became joint sheriffs of the Montreal District; he served alone from March 1841 until William Foster Coffin*'s appointment in February 1842, and again from 1851, when Coffin resigned, until his death. As sheriff his annual salary in 1855 was £857 with an unlimited expense account which some years climbed as high as £4,231, not to mention fees from subsidiary services attached to the office. In election years, for example, he was *ex officio* district returning officer and he also acted as commissioner for receiving affidavits. Apart from his office duties, supervising a deputy and two clerks, the sheriff was administrator of the Montreal jail which boasted an annual intake of approximately 1,600 people, some simply disorderly or homeless overnight guests. In 1852, Wolfred NELSON, inspector of jails for Lower Canada, criticized the administration of the Montreal jail, particularly its finances. Prices were often double their market value and there was "a total absence of proper management." But he assigned the blame to the jailer, Thomas McGinn.

Boston, however, never neglected his railway, bank, and land interests. He owned shares and held directorships in, among others, the Bank of Montreal, the Montreal Provident and Savings Bank, the Montreal and Lachine Railroad Company, the St Lawrence and Atlantic Railroad, and the Grand Trunk Railway Company. He possessed extensive land in the city and the country, including the fiefs and seigneuries of Thwaite and St James. Although he purchased land primarily for its social and economic value, Boston advocated agricultural reform and experimented himself. In 1855 he sent samples of his pressed peat to the Paris exhibition.

Botsford

Described as a man of "urbanity," Boston possessed educational interests. He belonged to the Montreal Mechanics' Institute, the Montreal Library Association, and the Natural History Society. One of the principal promoters of the Montreal High School incorporated in 1845, he served as the corporation's first chairman.

When Boston died at age 75, still sheriff of Montreal, the Montreal section of the bar decreed a month's mourning for a man they described as marked by a sense of integrity, hospitality, and civic duty – qualities, however, which never inhibited his Midas touch.

CARMAN MILLER

ANQ-M, État civil, Anglicans, Christ Church, 17 Dec. 1814; Presbytériens, St Andrews (Montréal), 8 March 1862; Greffe de J. C. Griffin, 7 avril 1853; Greffe de J.-M. Mondelet, 22 sept. 1823. Atwater Library Archives (Montreal), Mechanics' Institute of Montreal, minute books. BUM, Coll. Baby, Corr. générale, letters of John Boston, 13 April 1835, 29 Aug. 1836, 13 Jan., 20 July, 10 Aug. 1838. McCord Museum, The Brothers in Law minute book, 1827–33. Can., Prov. of, Legislative Assembly, *Journals*, 1852–53, I, app.B; IV, app.H.H.; 1854–55, III, app.B; VI, app.D; IX, app.F.F. *Montreal Gazette*, 16 July, 10 Dec. 1825; 20 Nov. 1826; November 1861–May 1862. *Montreal Transcript*, 13 Oct. 1844–1 March 1845. *Pilot* (Montreal), 15 Aug. 1861–15 Nov. 1861. *Quebec Gazette*, 10 June 1802, 24 May 1821. *Quebec Mercury*, 8 March 1862. *Alphabetical list of merchants, traders, and housekeepers in Montreal* (Doige). *Canada directory*, 1851, 1857–58. *Montreal directory*, 1845–51. *Montreal pocket almanack . . .* , 1859, 49. *Quebec directory*, 1847–48. Atherton, *Montreal*, II, 381, 420–31. A. W. P. Buchanan, *The bench and bar of Lower Canada* (Montreal, 1925). Denison, *Canada's first bank*, II, 86. F.-J. Audet, "Shérifs de Montréal," *BRH*, VIII (1902), 200. L.-P. Desrosiers, "Mes tablettes," *Cahiers des Dix*, 12 (1947), 75–92. Victor Morin, "Clubs et sociétés notoires d'autrefois," *Cahiers des Dix*, 14 (1949), 187–222.

BOTSFORD, WILLIAM, politician, office-holder, and judge; b. 29 April 1773 at New Haven, Conn., son of Amos Botsford* and Sarah Chandler; m. in 1802 probably at Saint John, N.B., Sarah Lowell Murray, *née* Hazen, and they had eight sons and a daughter; d. 8 May 1864 at Westcock, Westmorland County, N.B.

William Botsford's family settled in Annapolis Royal, N.S., in 1782, and then moved to Westcock near Sackville, N.B., in 1784. Educated at Yale College, he took his degree in 1792 and received an MA in 1796. Botsford studied law at Saint John, in the office of Jonathan Bliss*, then attorney general and later chief justice, and was called to the bar in 1795.

On 12 May 1795 Botsford was made deputy clerk of the Supreme Court and deputy registrar of the Admiralty Court. In 1803 when Gabriel George Ludlow* became president of the Council, Botsford succeeded him as judge of the Court of Vice-Admiralty, a post he held for five years. The highlight of this phase of his career was the celebrated *Falmouth* case. For some years New Brunswickers and Nova Scotians had been chartering American ships to smuggle their cargoes of local goods into the United States. The exchange of goods took place on the islands of the Passamaquoddy Bay, part of the disputed border territory between Maine and New Brunswick. George Leonard*, the zealous superintendent of trade and fisheries, was determined to smash this trade and in 1805 seized the *Falmouth*, an American sloop engaged in the plaster trade, at Snug Cove on Moose Island. The agent for the American ship was Colin Campbell, the customs collector at St Andrews, N.B., and the cargo was owned by his son. At stake was whether or not Moose Island was American territory and whether these informal trading arrangements tolerated by the British customs officials for several years were legal. Botsford's judgement supported Leonard's action and criticized the customs officers for exceeding their authority. His ruling effectively asserted Britain's right to Moose Island and the waters adjacent to it. The legality of the judgement was not questioned, but the political and economic repercussions reached both London and Washington. The Colonial Office ordered Leonard to desist from seizing ships, and the Americans and local traders had their day until the boundary was finally settled in 1842.

Botsford resigned from the Court of Vice-Admiralty in 1808 and moved with his family to Westmorland to be near his father, whose health was failing, and to look after his own extensive lumbering and shipping interests in that region. On his father's death in 1812 William Botsford was elected to the assembly for Westmorland County. Four years later he was appointed solicitor general and thus became a member of the Council. The following year Botsford was chosen speaker of the house, a post that his father had held for 26 years.

In 1823 a vacancy occurred in the Supreme Court. Botsford had been recommended by Ludlow for a position in the court as early as 1807, but, to the surprise of the legal establishment, which favoured Botsford, Lieutenant Governor George Stracy Smyth* nominated Edward James Jarvis*. A friend of Botsford's father, James Morse, of Cumberland County, N.S., made use of influential friends in London, including the Duke of Wellington, to prevent the approval of Jarvis' appointment, and in April 1823 Botsford was elevated to the bench instead. That year he was also appointed an assessor in the Court of Chancery. In accordance with custom, he was made a member of the Council, a position he held until his resignation in 1834. In 1832 he became vice-president in the Court of Governor and Council, for hearing and determining causes relating to marriage and divorce.

Botsford's knowledge of the law and the humanity which he displayed caused him to be held in the highest regard by all classes. In 1827 he presided over the famous "Masonic Trial," a libel case about a document containing charges against a mason read by another mason in a lodge room. The defence held that no publication had occurred as the proceedings were conducted in secret. The case was without precedent but Botsford ruled in his charge to the jury that reading the charges before a number of people constituted publishing in the eyes of the law. The defendant was assessed damages of one penny.

In 1836 Botsford wished to retire, but the lack of a pension restrained him. By 1845 he found it impossible to continue owing to age and submitted his resignation. The assembly was asked by the lieutenant governor to consider granting Botsford a pension, but it decided against such an allowance by a vote of 14 to 13. Botsford was keenly disappointed but not even the colonial secretary's letters were able to convince the assembly, which feared creating a dangerous precedent.

Botsford spent the remainder of his long life at Westcock, where he was an active layman in the Church of England. Several of Botsford's sons achieved prominence in various fields; Bliss*, before his elevation to the bench, served as speaker of the assembly. Hazen and Chipman also served in the assembly, Amos Edwin* became a senator, LeBaron a well-known medical man, and Blair was a sheriff and warden of Dorchester Penitentiary.

C. ALEXANDER PINCOMBE

N.B. Museum, Botsford family papers, 1784–1839; Chipman family papers, 1764–1789; Hazen family papers, 1720–1889. PANB, RJU/S/ju. Ward Chipman, *The question relating to the right of the United States of America to the islands in Passamaquoddy Bay* (1805) (copy in PRO, CO 188/13). F. C. Bell, *A history of old Shediac, New Brunswick* (Moncton, N.B., 1937). J. W. Lawrence, *Footprints; or, incidents in the early history of New Brunswick* (Saint John, N.B., 1883); *Judges of N.B.* (Stockton), 77, 211, 280–99. MacNutt, *New Brunswick*, 139–40, 187–89, 228.

BOUCHER, CYRILLE, journalist and lawyer; b. 30 July 1834 at Saint-Rémi, Lower Canada, son of François-Xavier Boucher, a journeyman, and Félicité Roy; d. 9 Oct. 1865 at Montreal.

When Cyrille Boucher was born the parish of Saint-Rémi-de-La-Salle, created by canonical decree six years before, was developing rapidly under the impetus given by its priest, Abbé Pierre Bédard. Thanks to Bédard, Boucher began his classical studies at the age of 17 under the Sulpicians at the Collège de Montréal. In the prize-giving of July 1852 his name appeared only once on the honours list: he placed first in religious instruction, as he was to do unfailingly each year. He was remarkably successful as a student in his subsequent years. During his third, or poetry year, for unknown reasons, he left the college.

In September 1855 Boucher was admitted without fee to the Collège Sainte-Marie. Its rector and founder, Father Félix Martin*, exempted him from the belles-lettres class and advanced him to rhetoric under a remarkable educator, Father Jean-Baptiste-Adolphe Larcher*. Among his classmates were Joseph Royal* and Joseph-Édouard Lefebvre* de Bellefeuille. In 1856 poverty forced him to break off his studies. He turned to teaching at the Collège Masson, which the parish priest of Terrebonne, Abbé Adrien Théberge, had founded in 1847 with the help of the seigneur, Joseph Masson*. During the leisure which his apparently limited teaching duties left him, Boucher indulged in an orgy of reading, principally it seems of the works of Veuillot. Boucher's first known article, "Essai sur le guerrier," which appeared in *La Minerve* on 26 Nov. 1856, was a direct paraphrase of Veuillot's work *La Guerre et l'homme de guerre*, published the year before. Adolphe Ouimet*, under the pseudonym Sophog Velligul, in 1858 put together a pamphlet against Boucher in his series *Les contemporains canadiens*, in which he claimed that this essay was simply "outright plagiarism" of Veuillot.

While teaching, Boucher had thus begun to try journalism. He contributed to *La Patrie* and *La Minerve*. But it was primarily when he began to contribute to *Le Courrier du Canada* and received the advice of the experienced editor in chief Joseph-Charles Taché*, that he undertook a journalistic career in earnest. Articles in the paper from 1 to 4 July 1857 took issue with the thesis of Abbé Jean-Joseph Gaume, who had unleashed a widespread controversy in France over the use of pagan authors in Catholic colleges. Félix Dupanloup, bishop of Orléans, France, had disputed the validity of Gaume's thesis that the pagan classics contributed to the moral decadence of adolescents. In his articles Boucher recapitulated Dupanloup's arguments. Abbé Norbert Barret, of the College de L'Assomption, quickly replied in the Gaumist vein. The Boucher–Barret controversy was just a harmless prelude to Abbé Alexis Pelletier*'s furious campaign eight years later against the authorities and the teaching of the Séminaire de Québec. Hence Boucher is at the origin of the first vehement assertion of ultramontanism in Quebec; later, the arguments that Boucher defended as editor of *L'Ordre* foreshadowed the phase of ultramontanism which would be initiated by the publication of the "Catholic programme."

In September 1857, when he was ending his controversy with Abbé Barret, Boucher was about to return to study at the Collège Sainte-Marie, where a law school had been created in May 1851. Among other somewhat peculiar characteristics, this school had only one professor, François-Marie-Uncas-Maximilien Bibaud*. Leaving aside McGill University, which was attended by few young French Canadians, Bibaud monopolized the teaching of law at Montreal. The students at Saint-Marie (who numbered 14 when Boucher joined them) were compelled to take only the bar examinations. The programme of study was by no means exacting, and classes were held three times a week. An energetic man, Boucher was able to continue to contribute to newspapers while studying law. In December 1857, with the help of Ouimet, now his friend, he founded the weekly *La Guêpe*, and was for a while its principal editor.

Until he entered law school, Cyrille Boucher had acted as a *franc tireur* in Catholic journalism. On his return to Montreal, he began to take an active part in the bishop of Montreal's offensive against the Institut Canadien. In three pastoral letters published on 10 March, 30 April, and 31 May 1858, Bishop Ignace Bourget* condemned the liberalism professed by the leading figures of the institute. As a result some 135 members resigned and founded the Institut Canadien-Français, which was established on 16 December 1858. According to Boucher, this institute immediately took "a truly national direction." Bishop Bourget's act of authority was only a dramatic expression of a bitter resistance to the Institut Canadien's influence, which was thought to be harmful to young Montreal Catholics. This resistance was embodied principally in the Union Catholique of the Collège Sainte-Marie and the parish Cabinet de Lecture of the Sulpicians.

The Union Catholique had started in 1854 first in the form of a congregation, then of an academy. On 16 April 1858 Boucher was chosen its secretary. He was also an active member of the literary circle of the parish reading room, which was organized on 2 Feb. 1857 with a programme of "instruction, teaching, and dissemination for the religious and moral sciences and the arts, by the circulation of books and newspapers and public readings or lectures."

The Union Catholique contributed to the common struggle by founding the newspaper *L'Ordre*, the first number of which appeared on 23 Nov. 1858. The initiative for this venture came from Joseph Royal who brought in his friend Cyrille Boucher, and a little later Joseph-Édouard Lefebvre de Bellefeuille and Louis Beaubien*, all four former students of the Collège Sainte-Marie and members of the directorate of the Union Catholique. The idea of a Catholic paper was attributed to Canon Venant Pilon of the bishopric of Montreal; Denis-Benjamin VIGER guaranteed the necessary financial assistance for the publication. Boucher would have liked a daily paper, but they decided finally on two issues a week. On 5 March 1860 *L'Ordre* became a tri-weekly publication, and its format was enlarged. But on 15 November the paper passed into other hands, and the ultramontane *L'Ordre* was succeeded by the moderate liberal *L'Ordre*.

According to the founders' plan, *L'Ordre* was to be essentially a journal of opinion, devoted to the defence of truth in the religious, national, and political spheres. Although all the editors considered themselves as equals in a fraternal team, Boucher soon stood out as their leader, and the task of presenting the programme devolved on him. He frequently drafted the press review and alternated with Royal in attending the sittings of the assembly; into this review and the report of the parliamentary debates he occasionally slipped moral reflections, on men and events, whose sharp tone often sparked controversy. Already feared because of his irrepressible and uncompromising spirit, he soon became the target at *L'Ordre* for partisan attacks. He was a trouble-maker and his undeniable influence on the young people of his time, the voters of the future, threatened to upset many plans. From then on Boucher set about attacking not only the liberal democrats of the Institut Canadien and their organs *Le Pays* and *Le Courrier de Saint-Hyacinthe*, but also the supporters of George-Étienne Cartier* and *La Minerve*, the Conservatives' paper.

In the initial article outlining his programme, Boucher had asserted unequivocally that the paper would be independent of parties. "Our place in the press," he wrote on 26 Nov. 1858,

". . . is above the parties manœuvring in today's political arena; our duty is to state the truth to every man, frankly and without deference to public opinion, without fear and without shameful compromise, as soon as we perceive that anyone is departing from it." Being an inflexible idealist, Boucher could not tolerate the compromises to which the leaders of the Conservative party resorted to stay in power in this period of unstable governments: "A grovelling and gutless politics is not what my country needs; it is destined to be governed in a more noble fashion." The young paladins of *L'Ordre* proved so virulent in their criticism of Cartier's party that Joseph-Charles Taché, the editor in chief of *Le Courrier du Canada*, thought it advisable to bring his young *confrère* to a more realistic appreciation of Canadian politics: "People may certainly censure what they believe reprehensible," wrote Taché on 23 Feb. 1859, ". . . but to set oneself to destroy a party which, whatever its failings in other respects, after all represents order and sound ideas, and to do so for the benefit of the wrong party, is something we fail to understand, and it distresses us."

But Boucher and his friends turned a deaf ear to Taché's appeals, and continued to cut and thrust. Since *La Minerve* shifted in matters of principle and refused to attack the liberal theses of the democrats, *L'Ordre* unmasked the latter, thanks to Lefebvre de Bellefeuille, who published his "Essai sur le rougisme" in the issues of 13 to 27 May 1859: "Properly speaking a *Rouge* is one who seeks (1) the separation of church and state; (2) the abolition of the right of property; (3) the sovereignty of the people. Accordingly, a *Rouge* is one who supports and upholds three abominable principles, which promise anarchy and disastrous consequences and can never find acceptance in the conscience of an enlightened Christian." This analysis of the liberal theses drew its inspiration from the works of Veuillot. An influence upon French Canadian journalists had never before been as evident. It became even more obvious when Boucher and Royal had occasion to express opinions on the Italian war of 1859. Catholics saw the movement for Italian unity, carried out under the principle of nationalism, simply as an attempt on the part of hostile forces to reduce the church to impotence, since its outcome was the annihilation of the temporal power of the pope. Among ultramontanes, Veuillot probably sustained most forcefully and eloquently this thesis which totally disregarded the Italian people's aspirations for their country's independence. Cyrille Boucher and Joseph Royal adopted the ultramontane point of view from the outset, so that *L'Ordre* was nothing but the Canadian offshoot of *L'Univers* in Paris in its reporting of Italian affairs.

It was with a commentary on Castelfidardo, which on 18 Sept. 1860 marked the defeat of the small papal army, that Boucher ended his regular and acknowledged collaboration with *L'Ordre*. His three colleagues were to follow his lead. Indeed, circumstances forced the team to this course. The two promoters of the enterprise died within a short time of each other, Canon Pilon on 30 Nov. 1860 and Viger on 13 Feb. 1861. Deprived of the support of their counsellor and their financial backer, they resigned on 25 June 1861. The printer Jacques-Alexis Plinguet*, who had actually owned *L'Ordre* since 15 Nov. 1860, succeeded in getting the leader of the Lower Canadian Liberals, Antoine-Aimé Dorion*, to take over the paper.

Apart from an occasional contribution to *L'Écho du cabinet de lecture paroissial*, Cyrille Boucher no longer worked as a journalist. He was called to the bar in December 1861, and he no doubt was completely engrossed in his new profession, for he appeared in public only on two occasions: at the Union Catholique on Sunday 8 June 1862, when he spoke on "the part played by the papacy in society," and at an evening reunion of former students of the Collège Sainte-Marie on 26 Sept. 1865, when he figured in the programme along with Honoré Mercier*, Napoléon Legendre*, and Charles-Chamilly de Lorimier*.

He died suddenly on the morning of 9 Oct. 1865, and was buried in his native parish. "Some time later," according to Lefebvre de Bellefeuille, "a frightful rumour reached us: he was said to have been buried alive." Ten years afterwards journalist Oscar Dunn* was still repeating this story.

Joseph Royal, in his account of Boucher's life in *L'Ordre* on 11 Oct. 1865, gave this description of his colleague: "M. Cyrille Boucher was tall and well proportioned; he had a magnificent forehead and slightly aquiline nose; the cast of his features showed an extraordinary firmness, that was quickly belied by the expression in his eyes. His face, when animated, was truly handsome and masculine. His gentle, lively glance revealed all the goodness and spontaneity of his proud nature."

François-Edmé Rameau* de Saint-Père was of the opinion that in the great world of the Paris press a most brilliant success would have greeted Boucher, so unquestionable was his literary talent. "But," according to Laurent-Olivier David*, "like many young men he lacked patience and perseverance. To resign oneself to

Boucher de Niverville

poverty for several years when one has talent and ambition requires a very resolute character."

Did he leave a manuscript of a novel entitled "Émilie de Bruneville," as Henry James Morgan* and *La Minerve* of 17 Sept. 1864 asserted? No trace of it has been found.

PHILIPPE SYLVAIN

[This biography is a synthesis of a study entitled "Cyrille Boucher (1834–1865), disciple de Louis Veuillot," published in the *Cahiers des Dix*, 37 (1972), 295–317. The basic source for Boucher is an unpublished study by Father Paul Desjardins, "Cyrille Boucher," to which is attached an anthology of Boucher's articles. This study, preserved at the ASJCF in the Papiers Paul Desjardins, deserves publication. Another unpublished work of 48 pages, deposited in the same archives under the classification 3162, proved helpful in determining Boucher's share in the ultramontane Catholic reaction that affected Montreal from 1858 on: "Apologie de l'Union catholique," written around 1864 by Father Firmin Vignon*. P.S.]

Le Courrier du Canada, juill.-sept. 1857. *La Guêpe* (Montréal), 1857–58. *La Minerve*, 1856–58. *L'Ordre* (Montréal), 23 nov. 1858–25 juin 1861. Morgan, *Bibliotheca Canadensis*, 41. Sophog Velligul [Adolphe Ouimet], *Les contemporains canadiens* (Trois-Rivières, 1858), 23–33. L.O. David, *Mélanges historiques et littéraires* (Montréal, 1917), 256; *Souvenirs et biographies, 1870–1910* (Montréal, 1911), 8. Paul Desjardins, *Le collège Sainte-Marie de Montréal* (2v., Montréal, 1940–[44]), II, 60–75. C.-A. Gareau, *Aperçu historique de Terrebonne* (Terrebonne, Qué., 1927), 37–38. Olivier Maurault, *Le collège de Montréal, 1767–1967*, Antonio Dansereau, édit. (2e éd., Montréal, 1967), 198. Oscar Dunn, "Une pièce inédite de Cyrille Boucher," *Revue canadienne* (Montréal), XII (1875), 642. Henri Gauthier, "Le Cabinet de lecture paroissial," *Revue canadienne*, nouv. sér., VIII (1911), 387–400. J.-É. Lefebvre de Bellefeuille, "Cyrille Boucher," *Revue canadienne*, XLIX (1905), 67–69. É.-Z. Massicotte, "Adolphe Ouimet," *BRH*, XXXII (1926), 57. L.-A. Prud'homme, "L'honorable Joseph Royal; sa vie, ses œuvres," *Revue canadienne*, XLIX (1905), 36–66.

BOUCHER DE NIVERVILLE, LOUIS-CHARLES, lawyer, politician, and sheriff; b. 12 Aug. 1825 at Trois-Rivières, Lower Canada, son of Joseph-Michel Boucher de Niverville, a seigneur, and Josephte Laviolette; m. in 1852 Éliza Lafond, daughter of Antoine Lafond, a farmer of Nicolet; the couple had no children; d. 1 Aug. 1869 at Trois-Rivières.

A descendant of the illustrious Pierre Boucher* and member of a family that was still influential at Trois-Rivières, Charles Boucher de Niverville prepared early for a professional career. He studied at the Séminaire de Nicolet from 1837 to 1844, then received legal training at Trois-Rivières under lawyers Antoine Polette* and Louis-Eusèbe Désilets. He was called to the bar on 2 May 1849. He soon became one of the most popular local lawyers, both at Trois-Rivières where he had "almost all the commercial clientele," and in the rural districts, where his prodigious memory and prompt and reliable judgement were much admired. So successful was he that he sometimes earned between $10,000 and $20,000 a year. His colleagues acknowledged his merit by twice electing him *bâtonnier* of the bar of Trois-Rivières; on 28 June 1867 he became a QC.

Political life did not attract Boucher de Niverville until quite late in life. In 1856 Napoléon Bureau* had tried earnestly to persuade him: "It is time for people of your age to assume control of public life in your district." Boucher de Niverville hesitated to commit himself, for he was drawn more to society life, horse racing, and cock fighting. He took the step in 1863 and became mayor of the town of Trois-Rivières. Two years later, following Joseph-Édouard TURCOTTE's death, 252 electors begged him to stand in the provincial by-election in the riding of Trois-Rivières; he accepted, announcing his electoral programme would be to continue the policy of Turcotte and the businessmen who had fought at his side: support of plans for confederation and for the intercolonial railway, improvements to the Trois-Rivières–Arthabaska railroad and to the Collège de Trois-Rivières, and the transfer of the Collège de Nicolet in order that the Collège de Trois-Rivières would no longer have a competitor in the region. Boucher de Niverville was elected by acclamation in mid January 1865, took his seat on 24 January, and spoke in the assembly for the first time in early February. His friends enthusiastically congratulated him, and Odilon-Zéphirin Hamel wrote to him: "We have seen the noble C. B. Niverville show himself worthy of the name he bears, and sustain the cause of our great country with strength and courage."

During this same session Boucher de Niverville made the most important speech of his career: on Friday 10 March 1865 he gave his support to the Quebec Resolutions. Niverville had prepared himself by asking the advice of two "eminently qualified" members of the clergy. One was Abbé Louis-François Laflèche*, who on 2 March 1865 had written him a long letter in which he explained that confederation alone offered "in reality a last hope," and that, as worked out by "the men foremost in experience, talent, intelligence, knowledge of political affairs, and patriotism," it was "the best thing for us in the present circumstances.'' Inspired partly by the ideas of his former teacher, Boucher was not afraid to affirm that with confederation the rights of French Canadians would be well protected, that those of the French language would be more extensive, and emigration to the United States would cease. In the 1867 elections Boucher de Niverville was elected to two levels of government for Trois-Rivières. In parliament he concerned himself particularly with a railway that would connect Les Piles (Grandes-Piles) and Trois-Rivières, but he had little success. This railway, which had been requested since 1852, was not built until 1879.

Charles Boucher de Niverville gave up politics in 1868, and retired to Trois-Rivières to ''the coveted retreat known as the office of sheriff,'' as a contemporary put it. Did he feel that he already bore the inescapable mark of illness? In 1867 he had resolved to ''break for ever with Bacchus,'' but he had been unable to keep his word; similarly his passion for horses had not diminished, even if, as it was said, ''his ventures on the turf'' had made inroads into his fortune. In 1869 a disease of the lungs and liver struck him down. He made serious preparations for his death, and drew up a will by which he left his personal property to his wife and his real estate to the parish priest of Trois-Rivières for the benefit of the poor. He died on 1 Aug. 1869, leaving ''the memory of a most warm-hearted person, and of a man of talent who might have won a higher position than he did.''

NIVE VOISINE

ASTR, Archives de la famille Boucher, K 2, 46–100. Can., prov. du, *Débats parlementaires sur la Confédération*, 946–51. *Le Constitutionnel* (Trois-Rivières), 2 août 1868. *Le Journal de Québec*, janv.-févr. 1865. F.-J. Audet, *Les députés de la région des Trois-Rivières (1841–1867)* (Trois-Rivières, 1934). Raymond Douville, ''Charles Boucher de Niverville, son ascendance et sa carrière politique,'' *Cahiers des Dix*, 37 (1972), 87–122.

BOULANGER, CLÉMENT (baptized **Clément-Quentin**), Jesuit priest; b. 30 Oct. 1790 at Saint-Clément (Meurthe-et-Moselle, France), son of Pierre Boulanger, a farrier, and Marguerite Receveur; d. 12 June 1868 at Nancy, France.

Born during the French revolution, Clément Boulanger was 24 years old when the Society of Jesus was re-established in France. As a young priest and teacher of theology he decided in 1823 to enter the noviciate of Montrouge, near Paris. Eleven years later, after he had taught theology at Saint-Acheul, France, and at Madrid, he was allowed to profess the four vows.

In February 1842 Boulanger was appointed provincial of the Jesuits in France. He superintended the reconstitution of the Jesuits in Canada that year. The last Canadian Jesuit, Father Jean-Joseph Casot*, had died at Quebec in 1800. At the request of Bishop Ignace Bourget* of Montreal, and then of Father Jean Roothaan, the general of the society, Father Pierre Chazelle*, who had founded the Kentucky mission in 1830, was made responsible for recruiting, primarily in France, the nine Jesuits who arrived at Montreal on 31 May 1842 [*see* Rémi-Joseph TELLIER]. Thanks to a carefully maintained correspondence, the provincial was able to follow closely the establishment of the Jesuits sent to the country with Chazelle.

By July 1842 the Jesuits had assumed responsibility for the parish of Laprairie, where a year later they set up a noviciate. However, the college for which they had been summoned was slow in starting. Their services were already being sought in New York and Toronto. In 1844, responding to the request of Michael Power*, the first bishop of Toronto, Boulanger divided the territory of the Canadian mission: Chazelle, who continued as superior, gave his attention to Canada West, while Father Félix Martin* directed the mission of Canada East.

In 1844, to link more closely the administrative centres, then poorly served by the slow process of correspondence, Father Boulanger suggested that a visitor with full powers to negotiate with the French missions be sent to America. On 1 April 1845, after he had completed his duties as provincial, he was appointed visitor and went to Kentucky. Shortly after arriving he decided to suppress this mission and replace it by the one in New York, where the Jesuits took charge of St John's College at Fordham. Boulanger established his residence at New York, as superior general of the French missions, which he had united in 1846 and named the New York–Canada mission. He lived in New York until the end of his term in 1855, except for a period in 1849 when he stayed at the Collège Sainte-Marie at Montreal to settle problems of the Canadian mission. He returned to Montreal in 1855 before becoming superior of the new Jesuit residence at Nancy in October 1856. From 1861 to 1865 he was rector of the Collège de Laval in France. He finally retired to Nancy, three years before his death in 1868.

An affable and wise counsellor, Clément Boulanger was particularly suited to settle difficult situations with apparent ease.

GEORGES-ÉMILE GIGUÈRE

The correspondence of Clément Boulanger and various

documents related to the re-establishment of the Jesuits in Canada during the 19th century are in the ASJCF and various archives of the Society of Jesus in Rome, New York, Chantilly, and Lille, France.

Archives départementales de Meurthe-et-Moselle (Nancy), État civil, Saint-Clément, 30 oct. 1790. Joseph Burnichon, *La Compagnie de Jésus en France; histoire d'un siècle, 1814–1914* (4v., Paris, 1914–22), II, 141, 209, 227, 237, 270, 369, 394, 544; III, 93, 145, 248, 298, 569, 597. *Les établissements des jésuites en France depuis quatre siècles . . .* , Pierre Delattre, édit. (5v., Enghien et Wetteren, Belgique, 1949–57), I, 590; II, 609, 828, 833, 839, 1050; III, 760, 772, 1327, 1351; V, 2, 14. G.-É. Giguère, "La restauration de la Compagnie de Jésus au Canada, 1839–1857" (2 MS volumes in the author's possession; copies are available in various archives, libraries, and houses of the Society of Jesus). F. X. Curran, "Archbishop Hughes and the Jesuits," *Woodstock Letters* (Woodstock, Md.), 97 (1968), 5–56; "The founding of Fordham University and the New York mission, 1846–1850," *Archivum Historicum Societatis Iesu* (Rome), XXVI (1957), 285–94; "The Jesuits in Kentucky, 1831–1846," *Mid-America* (Chicago), new ser., XXIV (1953), 242–46. G. J. Garraghan, "Fordham's Jesuit beginnings," *Thought, Fordham University Quarterly* (New York), XVI (1941), 17–39.

BOULTON, GEORGE STRANGE, lawyer, militia officer, public servant, and politician; b. 11 Sept. 1797 at Greenbush, near Albany, N.Y., third son of D'Arcy Boulton* and Elizabeth Forster; m. in 1824 Elizabeth Boulton (d. 1836) by whom he had three children, and in 1840 Anna Maria Berk, *née* Walton, of Schenectady, N.Y.; d. 13 Feb. 1869 at Cobourg, Ont.

The Boulton family came to Upper Canada about 1800 and George Strange Boulton attended John STRACHAN's school at Cornwall. When the family settled in York (Toronto) about 1807, he was one of the first pupils enrolled at the Home District Grammar School of the Reverend George Okill STUART. He was admitted to the bar in 1818 and began practice in Port Hope. About 1824 Boulton moved to Cobourg upon his appointment as registrar of Durham County, a post he held until his death.

Boulton had served during the War of 1812, at the age of 15, and at the outbreak of the rebellion in 1837 he hastened to Toronto to offer his services as a militia officer to Sir Francis Bond Head*. For many years he was colonel of the 4th militia district of Upper Canada.

In politics George Boulton was described as "remarkable for his adherence to the conservative cause – which he never once failed to uphold to the day of his death." He was first elected to the House of Assembly for Durham in 1824, but his election was declared void in 1825 and he did not contest the subsequent by-election. Boulton was successful in his second attempt to enter the assembly, in 1830, and continued to represent Durham until 1841. During the election of that year one of the supporters of his successful opponent, John Tucker Williams, was killed. Boulton denied that he had "hired Bullies or Loafers," declaring that Williams' supporters had come to the polls armed and his own supporters had taken up sticks in self-defence. Yet Boulton, a kindly man who was noted for his benevolence, especially to the poor, arranged a subscription for the family of the man killed.

In the assembly, Boulton supported his brother, Attorney General Henry John BOULTON, in voting for the expulsions in the early 1830s of William Lyon MACKENZIE, and continued to vote against Mackenzie even after his brother was dismissed as attorney general over the issue. In 1834 Boulton opposed a clause in the bill to incorporate the town of York which proposed voting by secret ballot in municipal elections. Largely because of his speech the "vote by ballot," which he considered "a mean and despicable mode of voting . . . that tended to encourage deception . . . falsehood and misrepresentation," was rejected by the assembly.

In June 1847 Boulton was appointed to the Legislative Council. A member until confederation, he took his duties in the council seriously and spoke with effect on a subject when strongly moved. During debate on amendments to the Land Act in 1847, Boulton supported Robert Baldwin Sullivan*'s proposal to make available low-priced or free lands to encourage settlement by immigrants.

A devoted member of the Church of England and a member of the Church Society from its inception in 1843, Boulton was also a commissioner of the Cobourg Town Trust from 1858 until his death. Secure socially and financially, he took his private and public position as his due. Unlike his elder brother, Henry John, George Boulton excited neither envy nor fear. He could be a forceful and influential debater, but he seems to have attended to his parliamentary duties more in the sense of *noblesse oblige* than from any motive of personal ambition or gain.

HEREWARD SENIOR

Colonial Advocate, 1824–25. *Globe*, 20 Feb. 1869. *Toronto Patriot*, 1833–34, 1841, 1847, 3 March 1869. J. R. Robertson, *Old Toronto: a selection of excerpts from "Landmarks of Toronto,"* ed. E. C. Kyte (Toronto, 1954), 307. U.C., House of Assembly, *Journal*, 7 Jan. 1831. Armstrong, *Handbook of Upper Canadian chronology*, 81, 124. CPC, 1862. *Political appointments, 1841–65* (J.-O. Coté), 55. Wallace, *Macmillan dictionary*, 73.

BOULTON, HENRY JOHN, lawyer, office-holder, judge, and politician; b. 1790 in Kensington, England, second son of D'Arcy Boulton* and Elizabeth Forster; m. in 1818 Eliza, daughter of Ephraim Jones* of Brockville, Upper Canada; d. 18 June 1870 at Toronto, Ont.

Henry John Boulton was born at Holland House in a fashionable suburb of London, the son of a London barrister and grandson of Sir John Strange, master of the rolls. His family immigrated in the 1790s to Rensselaer County in New York and about 1800 to Canada, seeking, as Boulton later said, "a wider field for our energies." Boulton probably attended John STRACHAN's school at Cornwall, as did his three brothers, before beginning legal studies in 1807 in York (Toronto) where his father was solicitor general. Boulton went to England in 1811 to continue his law studies at Lincoln's Inn. He spent three years in a solicitor's office in London, then two years at Oxford beginning in 1814. He subsequently studied under a special pleader and was called to the English bar from the Middle Temple; he was admitted to the bar of Upper Canada on 5 Nov. 1816.

With a solid foundation in English law and considerable intellectual ability and ambition, Boulton returned to Canada where, despite the quick temper he could display in court, he succeeded John Beverley ROBINSON as solicitor general in 1818 at age 28; Robinson succeeded Boulton's father as attorney general. In 1829 Henry John Boulton became attorney general himself, again succeeding Robinson. Although the patronage of these legal offices was thus confined, Boulton, like his father and Robinson before him, filled the posts so ably and impartially that even Francis Collins*, an outspoken critic of the Family Compact who was editor of the *Canadian Freeman*, testified to his fairness.

Boulton was elected to represent Niagara in 1830, styling himself an independent rather than a ministerial candidate. In his election address, he assured the voters that "in the house he should fearlessly represent their interests as if he held no . . . office under the Crown." Thus, from the beginning of his parliamentary career, Boulton was identified with an independent position or even a "liberal cast," as the *Niagara Reporter* suggested in 1833. Yet the *Canadian Freeman* in 1830 called Niagara a "rotten borough" and referred to Boulton as a "ministerialist"; William Lyon MACKENZIE described him and his brother George Strange BOULTON "as bad as bad can be, perhaps the very worst members any country or nation can be afflicted with," and headed his "Black List" in the *Colonial Advocate* with Boulton's name.

As attorney general Boulton skirmished with the more radical Reformers who disliked his proposed bills in 1830 and 1832 for the incorporation of York. They also resented his legalistic arguments to Lieutenant Governor Sir John COLBORNE who in January 1833 refused the request of Reform sympathizer Father William John O'Grady* to have Colborne lift the suspension as pastor of York imposed on him by Bishop Alexander Macdonell*. Yet in the O'Grady case Boulton's action prompted no swift reaction from Irish Roman Catholics such as he was later to provoke in Newfoundland. In York Boulton had the support of Macdonell who had formed a working alliance with the administration in the interest of his co-religionists.

Boulton also provoked Reformers by supporting the repeated expulsions of Mackenzie from the assembly in 1831 and 1832. With Solicitor General Christopher Hagerman* Boulton complained of the cordial reception given Mackenzie by Lord Goderich, the colonial secretary, when he presented grievances to the authorities in 1832. As a result of Mackenzie's mission to London, Goderich sent a dispatch to Colborne in November 1832 advising the administration to drop its attacks on the reformer and to institute several financial and political reforms. The Legislative Council refused to accept the dispatch, and in violent debates in the assembly many Tories showed that they were as opposed as Reformers to imperial commands which clashed with their own interests. Boulton's language was characteristically extravagant, and he was described at a public meeting in Brockville in January 1833 as "the first man in the Province who ever attempted to agitate the question of separation from the Mother Country." Late in April 1833 Boulton and Hagerman were dismissed from their offices by the imperial government.

Boulton deeply resented his dismissal. He publicized the correspondence between himself and Colborne's civil secretary, Major William Rowan*, "so as to not leave room for unfounded or injurious rumours as to the cause of our dismissal," and he asked Rowan to state specifically the breach of public duty for which he was removed from office. Rowan replied that it was Boulton's promotion of the repeated expulsions of Mackenzie from the assembly; the Colonial Office had raised constitutional objections which it had conveyed to Colborne and through him to Boulton. Boulton maintained that he had never been informed by Colborne of the Colonial Office's objection. He journeyed to England to seek redress, and the imperial government acknowledged that his removal had been unwarranted. He was immediately offered the more lucrative post of chief justice of Newfoundland, and arrived in that colony in November 1833.

The Supreme Court had been established in the colony only seven years and Boulton's predecessor, Chief Justice Richard Alexander TUCKER, had been removed for what Governor Thomas John Cochrane* and others considered a recalcitrant attitude and "a mixing of political duties with his judicial ones." It was a charge difficult for any chief justice in Newfoundland to avoid since he was also expected to act as president of the Council, which exercised both executive and legislative functions.

Boulton seemed to answer the wish of the Newfoundland administration for a man well versed in English criminal law, able to frame new laws and to remodel the courts and judicial procedures. He set to work with a will. After consultation with the law officers and assistant judges of the Supreme Court, he first changed the method of empanelling juries. Under his new regulations the sheriff was to summon 48 jurors, rather than the previous 18, from which 12 would be drawn by lot; this was the system then used in Britain. For special juries 40 names would be drawn by lot from the 75 qualified grand jurors to form a list from which the opposing lawyers would alternately strike off names, to a total of 12 for each side; the remaining 16 would comprise the special jury.

Among the eligible grand jurors were the Reform leaders, Patrick Morris*, John Kent*, Patrick Doyle, and Laurence O'BRIEN, and five other Roman Catholics; the remainder were leading Protestant merchants of St John's. The Reformers attacked the new rules, which, they claimed, "allowed conservatives to strike off any person who was supposed to differ from him in interest or opinion" and they alleged "that the Attorney-General [James SIMMS] availed himself of [this practice] in all the political trials since the alteration was effected." Undoubtedly the law officers had felt some anxiety that the Reform leaders might not act with the strictest impartiality in cases involving their partisans. In August 1835 Daniel O'Connell presented a petition from the Reformers to the British House of Commons for the removal of Boulton as chief justice. Boulton journeyed to England and apparently satisfied the Colonial Office of the propriety of his actions, for Under-Secretary Sir George Grey defended him in the house.

Early in 1834 Boulton framed a law to incorporate a law society and to regulate the admission of barristers and attorneys to the bar. The Reform opposition claimed that the new rules disbarred aspiring lawyers who could not afford the fees charged by qualified attorneys with whom they had to apprentice themselves for five years.

The fact that in most of these disputes Boulton was the innovator and the Reformers defended tradition and ancient usages became apparent again in several cases in 1834 and 1835 involving the credit arrangements of the fisheries. For instance, seamen were accustomed to receiving their wages, not from the "planter" who had hired them for the voyage, but from the merchant who received the proceeds of the voyage. Boulton claimed that the seamen were deprived of all security for the payment of their wages under such arrangements, but the fishermen and Michael Anthony Fleming*, the Roman Catholic bishop, pointed out that the planter was simply a "steward" and usually without sufficient means to guarantee wages. The chief justice also annoyed fishermen by altering the writ of attachment so that a fisherman's boat and tackle could be seized for debt, a harsh measure which took from the fisherman his means of engaging in the fishery on his own. The third custom he overturned, in a case involving Patrick Morris, was the practice of "current supply"; Boulton said that past creditors, and not the supplying merchant – in this case, Morris – had a superior and prior claim to the proceeds of a voyage. In normal commerce such practices would be unquestioned, but these changes in the prosecution of the fishery in Newfoundland brought charges from the Reformers that Boulton shook "the confidence which induced merchants to afford to planters the means of carrying on their fishing voyages." In the tense political situation of the early 1830s political leaders could play on the fears of the fishermen and stigmatize Boulton as the author of injustice and bigotry.

At the opening of the Central Circuit Court in 1835 Robert John Parsons*, editor of the liberal *Newfoundland Patriot*, published a caricature of Boulton's address to the grand jury, entitled "Stick a pin here: the beneficial effects of hanging illustrated." Boulton then charged Parsons with contempt of court, fined him £50, and sentenced him to three months in jail, asserting that the article "strikes at the very independence of the seat of Justice. . . ." He would have been wiser perhaps to have ignored the article, for when O'Connell brought the case to the attention of the British government, British law authorities decided that although Boulton's decision was strictly legal, the "practice for many years . . . of this country was against him"; the sentence against Parsons was remitted. A second petition against Boulton prepared by the Reform leaders was printed in the *Patriot* on 2 Feb. 1836. These efforts to vilify Boulton did not go unanswered. Some 900 residents of St John's, including merchants, professional men, 17 captains, six carpenters, and 12 illiterates, sent a memorial to the colonial secretary on Boulton's behalf.

During an assembly inquiry in 1837 into judicial administration, at which John Valentine Nugent* was both chairman and a witness against Boulton, direct attacks were made on the chief justice. Morris, who had a genuine concern for the Irish fishermen of Newfoundland and whose suspicion of Protestant ascendancy was shared by Bishop Fleming, repeated his longstanding charges that the chief justice "has exhibited . . . great partiality on the bench; his adjudications have been unjust, arbitrary, and illegal, biassed by strong party prejudices. . . . [He] has totally subverted the ancient laws and customs of Newfoundland." When the house ordered that Morris' lengthy speech be printed, Boulton instituted a libel suit for £2,000 damages against Morris, Kent, and Nugent. Boulton proposed the unusual move of stepping down from the bench and acting as his own counsel while the two assistant judges presided, but the case was never heard.

Acting on the report of its committee, the assembly sent Morris, Nugent, and Dr William Carson* to London at the end of 1837 to seek Boulton's removal and to ask that in future the chief justice not be a member of the Council. Boulton also left for London to answer the charges. He was not without defenders. In his brief was a deposition from John Stark, registrar of the Northern Circuit Court of Newfoundland, who asserted that crime and litigation had decreased in late years, "a clear proof that the laws are now more certainly administered and better understood," and that Boulton was "just, impartial, upright and independent in his decisions and decrees." Expressions of support were also sent from Boulton's assistant justices, the members of the grand jury, 928 residents of St John's, the Chamber of Commerce, 39 merchants and lawyers, and the deputy sheriff of Harbour Grace, all attesting to his integrity, ability, and impartiality.

The assembly delegation to London was joined by Bishop Fleming, who wrote to one of Boulton's most outspoken critics, Father Edward Troy*, of the "truly flattering reception of the delegates at the Colonial Office" and stated that it appeared certain that "Mr. Boulton is disposed of." With O'Connell as one of their spokesmen, the Reform leaders were confident of success. A committee of the Privy Council, to which Boulton's case was referred, criticized the vehemence of the Reformers' memorial and found no evidence of "any corrupt motive or intentional deviation from his [Boulton's] duty as a Judge"; however, the committee noted much "indiscretion in the conduct of the Chief Justice" in participating in party controversies in Newfoundland, and recommended that he be removed from office. Lord Glenelg, the colonial secretary, had, in January 1838, already decided on Boulton's dismissal, and the latter's request for a new appointment was turned down by the Colonial Office.

Thus at age 50, with a family of eight children and bereft of office for a second time, Boulton returned to private practice in Toronto. His old constituency, Niagara, welcomed him back and returned him as an "independent" to the newly created assembly of the Province of Canada in 1841, and he was appointed a QC in 1842. In the new house it soon became apparent that Boulton did not support William Henry Draper*'s moderate Conservative ministry on many questions. Contemptuous as ever of public favour or disdain, Boulton made up his mind in favour of responsible government, and openly supported Robert Baldwin* by 1843. As chairman of a meeting called in Toronto on 6 Feb. 1844 to establish the Reform Association of Canada, Boulton stated that, "after considerable experience of Colonial Office Government . . . he was convinced, that to ensure the British connexion and Canadian prosperity, it was absolutely necessary that the people of Canada should have the entire management of their own local affairs." This association with the Reformers brought the wrath of the Conservative press down upon him. The *Montreal Gazette* spoke of Boulton as "that lord of Misrule . . . an office-seeker and demagogue." The editor of the newly established Montreal *Pilot*, Francis Hincks*, defended Boulton, pointing out that his stake in the country "is so large as to make him much more interested in promoting its prosperity, than he would be by securing for himself what, people who have never tasted them, imagine to be the sweets of office."

Boulton's support of the liberals resulted in his losing the Niagara seat in 1844, but in December 1846 he was appointed a member of the Executive Council. In 1847 he was given the safe Reform seat of Norfolk, and was described by the Conservative *Toronto Patriot* as being "brought forward on the ultra-radical ticket." One of his chief contributions as a supporter of the administration of Robert Baldwin and Louis-Hippolyte La Fontaine was to move successfully the amendment to the 1849 Rebellion Losses Bill that excluded those convicted in 1837–38 from the financial benefits of the bill, a device

71

which finally persuaded the reluctant rank and file Reformers from Canada West to accept the measure. Yet Boulton was never at home among the Reformers and by 1850 he was again an "independent" member, advocating, as did his nephew, William Henry Boulton*, the elective principle in the Legislative Council. He further asserted his individuality by proposing an amendment to the Reform government's speech from the throne which was essentially a demand for representation in parliament according to population. Boulton did not seek re-election in 1851, but continued to practise law in Toronto until 1860 or 1861 when he retired. In 1855 he had been manager of the Canadian section of the Paris exhibition.

Throughout his lifetime, Boulton remained an individualist and was consequently abused as an office-seeker, bigot, unbending tory, and ultra-radical. He was a man of energy and ability with connections that assured him a place in politics, but his inability or unwillingness to conciliate opposition did not permit him to fit into any party. This temperament was manifest in his frequent outbursts of defiance, which could and often did turn political defeat into personal disaster. Yet Boulton was a colourful personality in the assembly, and his parliamentary career cannot be considered a failure. Although forcefully expressed, his opinions were conventional, supporting Sir John Colborne in the 1830s, responsible government in the 1840s, and, later, elective institutions and "rep. by pop."

With regard to his years in Newfoundland, Boulton's severest critics were historians D. W. Prowse* and Bishop Michael Howley*, both of whom relied largely on the hostile assembly investigation and memorial seeking Boulton's removal. Prowse adds, without evidence, a charge of personal meanness. Yet Boulton's concern for individuals in several cases he heard indicates that he was not always the stern, inflexible judge. Charges of religious bigotry are also difficult to sustain. His wife was a Roman Catholic who once on leaving church spoke out indignantly against Father Troy's denunciation of her husband. Like his Protestant contemporaries, Boulton disliked Roman Catholic clerical involvement in politics, and he privately criticized Father Troy's withholding the services of the church from Roman Catholics for political reasons. A modern historian has concluded, as Prowse did, that Boulton was "the scapegoat, not only of the popular party, [which was] enraged by his bias in the Council and by his inflexibility on the Bench, but of the Colonial Office which had assigned him to these incompatible offices."

He was an enigma to his contemporaries. Newspapers confined themselves to the barest death notices. The Toronto *Leader* and *Patriot* simply reprinted the biography, probably written by Boulton himself, which appeared in Henry J. Morgan*'s *Sketches of celebrated Canadians*, but added that he "was respected by the whole community and was in every sense a good and worthy citizen," a direct contradiction of J. C. Dent*'s comment in his book, *The last forty years*, that Boulton was neither respected nor popular.

HEREWARD and ELINOR SENIOR

Henry John Boulton was the author of *A short sketch of the province of Upper Canada, for the information of the labouring poor throughout England, to which is prefixed thoughts on colonization* . . . (London, 1826). There are Henry John Boulton papers in the possession of Lawrence Lande (Montreal). PAO, Boulton (Henry John) papers. *Antidote* (Brockville, [Ont.]), 22 Jan., 12 Feb., 7 May 1833. *Canadian Freeman* (York [Toronto]), 21 Oct. 1830, 2 May 1833. *Colonial Advocate*, 7 Oct. 1830. *Correspondent and Advocate* (Toronto), 9 July 1835. *Leader*, 20, 22 June 1870. *Montreal Gazette*, 7 March 1844. *Niagara Reporter* (Niagara, [Ont.]), 16 May 1833. *Pilot and Evening Journal of Commerce*, 15 March, 9 April 1844. *Toronto Patriot*, 12 July 1847, 29 June 1870. Morgan, *Sketches of celebrated Canadians*, 263–64. Wallace, *Macmillan dictionary*, 73. Careless, *Brown*, I, 49–50, 112, 118. Creighton, *Macdonald, young politician*, 103, 123, 138. Dent, *Last forty years*, I, 104, 344, 350–51; 380; II, 151, 208–9, 233. Gunn, *Political history of Nfld.*, 18–64. M. F. Howley, *Ecclesiastical history of Newfoundland* (Boston, 1888), 329–30, 366, 380–83. Prowse, *History of Nfld.* (1896).

BOURCHIER, HUGH PLUNKETT, army officer; b. *c.* 1800, son of Major-General John Bourchier of Ardcloncy, County Clare (Republic of Ireland), and of his wife, *née* Macnamara; d. 24 Jan. 1862 on Point Frederick, near Kingston, Canada West, leaving his widow, one son, and four daughters.

Hugh Plunkett Bourchier, whose brother Thomas was later a naval hero in the 1st China War of 1839–42, entered the British army in 1814 and served in Portugal and at Gibraltar. He fought under the Duke of Wellington in France with the 19th Light Dragoons. In 1837 Bourchier came to Canada as a captain in the 93rd Regiment and after some time at Halifax and Toronto was posted adjutant of Fort Wellington near Prescott, Upper Canada, under Colonel Plomer YOUNG. In May 1839 he succeeded Thomas Fitzgerald as town major of Kingston.

In his new post Bourchier assumed responsibility for all the physical aspects of the military establishment at Kingston. The town major also led state processions, countersigned the police permits required for passage over the international boundary during emergencies, and assumed other functions when necessary during the absence of senior officers. Thus, Bourchier, who was town major at Kingston until his death, served at various times as commander of the forces in Canada West, commander of the Kingston garrison (1855–62), acting assistant deputy adjutant-general, and deputy assistant quartermaster-general of the forces. He was promoted brevet colonel in 1859.

Bourchier also participated in the volunteer militia movement at Kingston, made possible by the passage of the Militia Act of 1855. Holding the rank of colonel in the Canadian militia, he commanded for five years the three volunteer companies raised at Kingston: the predominantly Roman Catholic infantry unit which James O'Reilly* helped raise, another infantry unit raised by David Shaw and John Sutherland, and a cavalry unit raised by Maxwell William Strange, the last two dominated by members of the Orange Order. At the time of the outbreak of the Civil War in the United States he was one of the few senior military officers in Canada West who did not perceive Irish Roman Catholics as a major threat to the security of Canada and who was willing to admit them to important military roles. His influence might have enabled the militia in Kingston to avoid Orange domination at a time when moderation was most needed in view of Fenian threats against Canada, but he resigned on 13 Aug. 1861 because of ill health and was succeeded by Strange. Bourchier died less than a year later of heart disease, aggravated perhaps by overwork during the *Trent* crisis.

As town major Bourchier had played an important and visible role in the military life of Kingston. He was also an active and prominent participant in the social life of the community. An obituary commented that "his urbanity of manner and careful consideration for others gained him many friends."

GEORGE MAINER

PAC, RG 8, I (C series), 1284, pp.1–2, 179–81. PAO, Kingston Garrison order book, 1837–38 (mfm. copy). PRO, CO 42/614, p.71; 42/627, pp.141–47. *Globe*, 28 Jan. 1862. O'Byrne, *Naval biographical dictionary* (1849). J. W. Spurr, "The Kingston Garrison, 1815–1870," *Historic Kingston* (Kingston, Ont.), 20 (February 1972), 14–34.

BOUTILLIER (Bouthillier), THOMAS, doctor, Patriote, and politician; b. 9 Oct. 1797 at Quebec, son of Guillaume Boutillier, gentleman usher of the black rod, and Anne-Françoise Normand; d. 8 Dec. 1861 at Saint-Hyacinthe, Que.

After studies at the Séminaire de Saint-Hyacinthe and at the University of Philadelphia, Thomas Boutillier was authorized to practise medicine on 4 June 1817 and took up residence at Saint-Hyacinthe. In 1826 he married Eugénie Papineau, a cousin of Louis-Joseph Papineau*; she died four years later, leaving him a daughter.

An unsuccessful candidate in the 1832 elections, Boutillier was returned as member of the assembly for the county of Saint-Hyacinthe in 1834, at the time of the last electoral campaign before the insurrection. In 1836 he was the representative of a group of Saint-Hyacinthe citizens who presented a petition to Governor Gosford [Acheson*], in which they declared themselves supporters of order and public peace, but stated their intention of "springing to the help" of their Montreal compatriots if the latter were attacked.

In 1837 he took part in the battle of Saint-Charles at the head of some 100 men. Like many insurgents, he had to take refuge in the United States. He went via Burlington and Montpellier to Vermont. With Louis-Joseph Papineau, Robert Nelson*, Edmund Bailey O'Callaghan*, Édouard-Étienne Rodier*, and Cyrille-Hector-Octave Côté*, he belonged to the group of Patriotes who arranged to meet at Middlebury, Vt, on 2 Jan. 1838, to discuss the resumption of the rebellion. Although several refugees were embittered against Papineau, Boutillier disagreed, stating in June 1838 that Papineau "has made mistakes, but he is not a traitor to his country." By the summer of 1838 Boutillier had returned to Saint-Hyacinthe, where he endeavoured to collect money that was owing to Ludger Duvernay*, the former publisher of *La Minerve* who was still in the United States. Still a suspect himself, Dr Boutillier was placed under surveillance during the uprising in the autumn of 1838.

But Boutillier had given up his radical leanings. In a letter to Duvernay in 1839, he said he was happy to learn that the paper Duvernay was thinking of publishing in the United States would be a moderate one. In 1840 he was not sorry to see that petitions against the union were having a limited success. Like Louis-Hippolyte LA FONTAINE, he believed that the combining of the Upper and Lower Canadian Reformers would make it possible to end "racial prejudices" and obtain "the redress of grievances." In 1841, in the first elections held under the union, Boutillier was returned unopposed as member of the assembly for Saint-Hyacinthe. In 1844 he had some difficulty in defeating Louis-Antoine Dessaulles*, a young man of 24, who was Papineau's nephew and travelling companion to Paris, and the son of Jean Dessaulles*, seigneur of Saint-Hyacinthe and former member for Richelieu and Saint-Hyacinthe counties. Boutillier was, of course, a supporter of the out-going Reform ministers La Fontaine and Robert Baldwin*, whereas Louis-Antoine Dessaulles favoured the administration which included Denis-Benjamin VIGER. When a petition was presented to the assembly for the annulment of this election, the committee responsible for examining it maintained Boutillier in his seat.

When, however, Papineau returned to Canada after an eight-year exile, Dr Boutillier worked actively to encourage an understanding between him and La Fontaine. In a confidential letter to the latter, he even offered to give up his seat to the former speaker of the House of Assembly of Lower Canada. When Papineau was visiting Saint-Hyacinthe, where his brother André-Augustin and his sister Rosalie Dessaulles lived, Boutillier had a long interview in his own home with the former leader of the Patriote party. But, somewhat disappointed, he was obliged to write to La Fontaine: "I believe that M. Papineau does not wish to return immediately to public life."

In the 1847–48 elections it was the turn of lawyer Louis-Victor Sicotte* to try his strength against Boutillier. Sicotte, the defeated candidate, obtained 35 per cent of the votes in the county but only 20 per cent in Saint-Hyacinthe. On both the provincial and the municipal levels, Boutillier and Dessaulles opposed one another. Thus, in the autumn of 1849, when Dessaulles declared in a long letter published in *L'Avenir* that he favoured the annexation movement, Boutillier was one of those who, with George-Étienne Cartier* and Augustin-Norbert MORIN, signed the loyalist manifesto which appeared in *La Minerve* on 15 October under the title: "Protest against the separation of Canada from England and its annexation to the United States." In 1849 and 1850, Boutillier was involved in getting Saint-Hyacinthe incorporated as a town, and he worked on the committee responsible for drawing up the bill. Here again he was in open conflict with Dessaulles. The law of 12 Aug. 1850 partially reflected his views in that it placed the non-urbanized territory up-river from the church outside the town limits, but it exempted the forests and farms within the boundaries of Saint-Hyacinthe from municipal taxes, as Dessaulles wanted. In the subsequent municipal elections, Boutillier was defeated in his district, but Dessaulles won in his and was chosen mayor.

Thomas Boutillier decided not to stand in the provincial elections of 1851. It is said that he was among those who contributed to the founding of *Le Courrier de Saint-Hyacinthe* in 1853. In 1854 he became "inspector of land offices for Lower Canada"; he was responsible for writing the *Rapport des travaux de colonisation de l'année 1855* and the results of an inquiry into the causes of emigration to the United States. He died at Saint-Hyacinthe in December 1861.

In his political career Thomas Boutillier was typical of the group of Patriotes who, after 1840, moved away from Papineau and collaborated with La Fontaine within the French Canadian Reform party.

JEAN-PAUL BERNARD

Thomas Boutillier, *Rapport des travaux de colonisation de l'année 1855* (Toronto, 1856); also published in English as *Report of the progress of settlement in the townships of Lower Canada during the year 1855*. ANQ-Q, AP, Coll. Papineau, boîte 39, lettre de L.-A. Dessaulles à L.-J. Papineau, 24 juill. 1848. Bibliothèque nationale du Québec (Montréal), Soc. historique de Montréal, Coll. La Fontaine, lettres 343, 358, 404, 409, 659. PAC, MG 30, D62, 6, pp.33–52. Can., prov. du, Assemblée législative, *Rapport du comité spécial nommé pour s'enquérir des causes de l'émigration du Canada aux États-Unis d'Amérique ou ailleurs* (Québec, 1858). *Elgin-Grey papers* (Doughty), I, 389; IV, 1510, 1594, 1598–99, 1602. *L'Avenir*, 3 nov. 1849. *Le Courrier de Saint-Hyacinthe*, 13, 31 août 1867. *La Minerve*, 15 oct. 1849, 12 déc. 1851, 10 déc. 1861. Ivanhoë Caron, "Papiers Duvernay conservés aux Archives de la province de Québec," ANQ *Rapport*, 1926–27, 183, 185–87, 193, 209, 213, 224, 233. Fauteux, *Patriotes*, 136–38. J.-P. Bernard, "La pensée des journalistes libéraux de Saint-Hyacinthe, 1853–1864" (thèse de MA, université de Montréal, 1958), 3–6; *Les Rouges*, 67, 95–97. C.-P. Choquette, *Histoire de la ville de Saint-Hyacinthe* (Saint-Hyacinthe, Qué., 1930), 142, 144, 166–69, 200–1, 244–45, 265; *Histoire du séminaire de Saint-Hyacinthe depuis sa fondation jusqu'à nos jours* (2v., Montréal, 1911–12), I, 185–87, 206; II, 238. Hamelin et Roby, *Hist. économique*, 43, 86–87, 184. Monet, *Last cannon shot*.

BOWEN, EDWARD, lawyer, judge, and politician; b. 1 Dec. 1780 at Kinsale (Republic of Ireland); m. in 1807 Eliza, daughter of James Davidson, a doctor in the Royal Canadian Volunteers; they had eight girls and eight boys including Edward Henry who became a judge; d. 11 April 1866 at Quebec.

Edward Bowen came to Lower Canada in 1797, after finishing his secondary education at Drogheda Academy (Republic of Ireland). His great-aunt, the wife of receiver general Henry Caldwell*, brought him to Quebec City. Bowen studied law, probably in the offices of Jonathan

Sewell* and John Caldwell*, and in 1803 was authorized to practise. Through influential connections, he enjoyed government patronage (posts as clerk and assistant clerk of various courts, 1801–5, lieutenant of militia, 1804–12, and then captain, 1812–27). In 1808, at the request of Governor Sir James Henry Craig* and on condition that he leave private practice, he acceded to the post of attorney general of Lower Canada. But London had already chosen Norman Fitzgerald Uniacke* for this post. Although he had to withdraw, Bowen found solace in becoming the first king's counsel in 1809; in this capacity and that of attorney general *pro tempore* during Uniacke's absence (summer 1810 – January 1812), he drew attractive emoluments (more than £600 for 1811 alone). In 1812, thanks to Sir George Prevost*, he became, at the age of 39, judge of the Court of King's Bench at Quebec. At that time he declined the Colonial Office's offer of the post of attorney general of Upper Canada. He also held other well-paid offices: French translator for the Executive Council (1816–17), and French secretary of the province (1816–24/26?). He received a total stipend that usually exceeded £1,000 a year, especially after 1817 when the salary of judges rose to £900 a year (£2,500 in 1864). He sat as president of the Court of Appeal in certain cases (1839–43), and was promoted chief justice of the Superior Court in 1849. In earlier days he had advocated a reform of the judicial system (1815), and had shown his impatience at the delays in court when several judges sat together (1820). In 1818 he had heard a case involving the conflicts between the North West Company and the Hudson's Bay Company at Red River [see Thomas Douglas*, Lord Selkirk].

Politically, and again at Craig's request, Bowen represented the county of William Henry (Sorel) in the assembly from 1809 to 1812. He campaigned as a member of the British party. He looked after the interests of his county by trying to persuade the government to build a post office and roads there, to improve its school, and to change its seigneurial tenure into free and common socage tenure (a question still unresolved in 1829). In 1813 he signed a congratulatory address to Prevost. He took part in 1822–23 in drafting and presenting the Quebec petition against a projected union of the two Canadas which the signatories thought would only arouse fears and jealousies. Entering the Legislative Council in 1824, he was even its president *pro tempore* in 1834, and supervised the renovation of the council rooms in 1828. Bowen had in no way drawn closer to the Parti Canadien. He had sought Sewell's opinion, in 1814, about the advisability of imprisoning the staff of *Le Spectateur* for libel. In 1825, like other British judges, he took it upon himself to refuse a writ of summons drawn up in French. Augustin-Norbert MORIN, under the pseudonym of a "law student," replied in a letter which was soon made public reminding him of French language rights in Lower Canadian courts. In 1835–36 an uncompleted inquiry by the assembly challenged his conduct as a judge. And in 1839 he termed Sir John COLBORNE's recall to England a mistake.

From 1814 on, Bowen complained continually about his financial difficulties and the ruin threatening him. In fact, he was involved in disputes with some of his creditors, including a J. Davidson (probably his brother-in-law John) who sold 9,700 acres of his lands between 1818 and 1821, and the Bank of Montreal (1826). He none the less managed to get his numerous children educated, and he took advantage of generous land concessions from a government favourably disposed towards him. Some pieces of land were also acquired by purchase. Only part of his holdings are known: six lots in the township of Melbourne (1802–5), six in the township of Tewkesbury (1807), lots at Sorel (1812) and Laprairie (LaPrairie), 5,351 acres in the township of Jersey (1823–29), with the promise of a second concession he was seeking (1828–29), and 540 acres on the Kennebec highway (1837). In 1863 in an endeavour to hasten the passage of a bill to increase judges' pensions he got John Sandfield Macdonald* to intercede with Louis-Victor Sicotte*, attorney general of Canada East.

Bowen's financial embarrassment did not prevent his being active in various movements, such as the Incorporated Church Society in the diocese of Quebec, of which he was vice-president from at least 1849 to 1854, the Quebec Fire Society in 1805, 1815, and 1819, and Quebec Emigrant Society in 1821, and the Ladies Compassionate Society in 1821. He also contributed to subscriptions for the victims of Waterloo in 1815, an Anglican girls' school in 1816, poor relief in the district of Quebec in 1818, and the erection of a monument to Wolfe* and Montcalm* in 1828.

Family relationships, social connections, his numerous offices, and obvious ability all ensured Edward Bowen a place in the élite of important colonial officials who, together with the British commercial bourgeoisie, monopolized the executive power and state patronage (positions, land speculation, contracts), and controlled much of the legislative power. Unlike many of this group, Bowen had a good knowledge of French and of French laws.

JEAN-PIERRE WALLOT

Bowes

BUM, Coll. Baby, Corr. générale, Edward Bowen to Judge Pyke, 5 May 1820; lettre de Guérout et Lemesurier à Louis Gareau, 20 déc. 1820; lettre de l'abbé Joyer à Mlle de Lavaltrie, 19 déc. 1820. PAC, MG 23, GII, 10, pp.2343–44, 2382–91, 2394–97, 2426–29, 2449–60, 2469–77, 2482–85, 2511–14, 2537–48, 2991–93, 3156–59, 3195–98; GIII, 3, 1, pp.132, 146; 13, p. 143; MG 24, B1, 183, pp.700–1; B3, 1, pp.50–51, 53ff.; 3, pp.289ff.; B14, 8, pp.1778–83, 1789–91; B30, 2, pp.1016–17; K11, p.81; MG 27, II, D10, 12, pp.1930–36; MG 30, D62, 6, pp.61–112; RG 1, L3ᴸ, 4, pp.1213–16, 1299, 1531, 1568; 7, pp.2107, 2148; 8, pp.2387–99, 2449, 2494–95; 13, pp.5115–18; 14, pp.5224–27, 5250, 5344; 19, p.8706; 46, pp. 23629ff., 23647–49, 23656ff., 23664–69, 23674–81, 23683–86, 23697, 23712, 23749, 23753–54; 52, p.26790; 53, pp.26826–30; RG 4, A1, S (32 letters and documents concerning Edward Bowen from 1802 to 1840); B8, 18, pp.6453–57; B28, 135, no.1581; B46, 3, p.1342; RG 8, I (C series), 30, pp.69–72; 113, p.70; 115, pp.78, 88–89; 246, p.62; 278, pp.149, 158, 160; 279, pp.22, 38, 269; 386, pp.11–12; 509, p.141; 599, pp.100, 102; 601, p.55; 603, pp.116, 118, 120, 123, 126, 134, 176; 634, pp.28, 253, 307, 356; 688A, pp.13–14, 20, 22; 833, pp.19, 21–23; 1218, pp.31, 34, 44, 50, 106, 137; 1695, p.3; RG 68, 1, General index, 1651–1841; 1841–67. Private archives, J. E. Colborne (Mackrell, Eng.), Sir John Colborne papers (copies in PAC, MG 24, A40, 24, 2 Nov. 1839). PRO, CO 42/107, p.337; 42/109, p.128; 42/110, p.2; 42/112, pp.224, 311; 42/117, pt.1, p.25; 42/117, pt.2, p.246; 42/122, p.243; 42/130, pt.2, pp.321, 324 (transcripts at PAC).

Bas-Canada, chambre d'Assemblée, *Journaux*, 1800–37; Conseil spécial, *Journaux*, 1838–41. Can., prov. du, Assemblée législative, *Journaux*, 1841–61. *Quebec Gazette*, 1800–20, 1837–40. Le Jeune, *Dictionnaire*, I, 238. P.-G. Roy, *Les juges de la prov. de Québec*, 75. G. Turcotte, *Cons. législatif de Québec*, 97. Chapais, *Hist. du Canada*, III, 123, 192; IV, 74, 91, 114–15. Christie, *History of L.C.*, IV, 208–10.

BOWES, JOHN GEORGE, merchant, entrepreneur, and politician; b. *c.* 1812 near Clones, County Monaghan (Republic of Ireland); m. Ann Hall, and they had nine children; d. 20 May 1864 at Toronto, Canada West.

John George Bowes came to Upper Canada from Ireland in 1833 and was employed by his brother-in-law Samuel E. Taylor, a York (Toronto) merchant. When Taylor died in 1838 Bowes wound up the business, served as manager for the Messrs Benjamin who occupied Taylor's business premises, and then with another brother-in-law, John Hall, opened a successful wholesale dry goods business. By 1840 they were able to buy the Toronto business of Buchanan, Harris, and Company when the latter transferred its operations to Hamilton.

Bowes soon acquired a reputation as an astute businessman, and his genial personality made him popular among Torontonians. It was said that few had warmer personal friends. Of medium height and well built, he was a handsome man who enjoyed vigorous exercise. His contemporaries circulated many anecdotes concerning his physical prowess, and affectionately called him "an ugly customer in a row."

During his lifetime Bowes held numerous important and responsible offices: he was president of the Toronto and Guelph Railway Company, an incorporator in 1852 of the Grand Trunk Railway, president of the St Patrick's Society, and president of a savings society, in addition to serving on the boards of directors of numerous commercial and financial enterprises. He had a reputation for personal generosity to both charitable institutions and needy individuals. Though a Conservative in politics, his principles and views were generally liberal. With Adam Wilson* he was credited with successfully urging the establishment of scholarships to permit exceptional common school graduates to attend the Toronto Grammar School.

As his prosperity and popularity increased, Bowes sought public office. In 1847 he was appointed a common school trustee by city council and three years later was elected an alderman for St James' Ward. He was chosen mayor of Toronto by the city council in 1851, 1852, and 1853. Both as a Toronto merchant and as mayor, Bowes was anxious to promote the city's metropolitan aspirations. But his eye for profitable investment and his interest in the expansion of Toronto's commerce led to his involvement, with Francis Hincks*, in a celebrated conflict of interest scandal in 1853 – "the £10,000 job."

To encourage the building of the Ontario, Simcoe, and Huron Union (later called the Northern) Railway from Toronto to Collingwood, the city of Toronto invested £50,000 in the railway's stock, payable in city debentures bearing interest at 6 per cent. The railway, in turn, agreed to use the debentures as payment to the contractors building the road. Anxious to obtain working capital, the contractors endeavoured to sell them on the open market. But the bylaw under which they were issued had been defective, chiefly because it failed to establish a provincially required sinking fund to retire the debentures. The issue was further complicated because current interest rates had risen to 7 per cent, and the best offer the contractors received was for 75 per cent of the debentures' face value. At this point Bowes approached Hincks, who was both premier and inspector general of finance, and proposed that they purchase the bonds jointly at a discount of 20 per cent. This purchase was not known to the city council. Bowes was at this time arranging for the council to petition for a provincial act authorizing the city to refinance its debt and issue new debentures redeemable at par in ten years. Hincks and Bowes were then able to exchange their depreciated bonds for new ones which they soon sold in England, through Hincks' financial connections, at a discount of 2 per cent, giving a profit on the whole transaction of £8,237.

When these events became public a great uproar ensued. Hincks and Bowes were accused by their political opponents and the opposition press of corruptly manipulating the price of the debentures for their personal advantage. Committees of investigation were set up by the provincial legislature and the city council. Their reports absolved the two partners of having acted dishonestly; the city council, in particular, while deeply regretting Bowes' want of candour, held that his services to the city should exempt him from further censure. Cries of "whitewash" arose and five aldermen and three councilmen resigned in protest. In the next municipal elections all eight were successful, while only two of the 13 who had supported Bowes were re-elected. The city sued Bowes for his share of the profit on the transaction. The Court of Chancery did not find Bowes guilty of fraud, but held that since he was acting as the city's trustee he must pay over his profits to it. Bowes withdrew briefly from public life.

He soon regained his popularity, and in 1854 was elected one of Toronto's representatives in the assembly. Though he was a Wesleyan Methodist, Bowes opposed secularization of the clergy reserves, and he supported expansion of the separate school system in Canada West, arguing that schools established for Protestants in Canada East should be matched by facilities for Catholics in Canada West. He thereby earned the bitter enmity of George Brown* and the Toronto *Globe*. Bowes also promoted the interests of Toronto in the assembly by introducing or supporting bills for the settlement of the city's northern boundary, for the erection of waterworks, and for encouraging waterfront development. He served the mercantile community by advocating an improved bankruptcy law and by introducing bills to incorporate the British Bank of Canada and to amend the charter of the Colonial Bank of Canada.

In 1856 he re-entered municipal politics and was elected an alderman for St David's Ward, and in 1861 was again elected mayor – this time by the electorate at large. Bowes spent lavishly on his election campaigns, and established a political power base among the Irish population of Toronto which enabled him to win re-election as mayor in 1862 and 1863. While Bowes was mayor the city bought its first fire engine and opened a privately owned street railway, becoming one of the first cities in North America to acquire this "symbol of progress and pride." Licensed by council in March 1861, the railway had six miles of track and was carrying 2,000 passengers daily in December. Bowes at one time held a controlling interest in the railway. In January 1864, when the separate school controversy was at its height, he sought a seventh term as mayor. He was defeated by the provincial grand master of the Orange lodge, Francis Henry Medcalf*, who was vigorously supported by the *Globe*.

When he died in 1864 Bowes left a widow and nine children. His funeral was attended by all classes of the city. The *Globe* remarked that "as a business man he had few equals in the community," and that although "shrewd, observant and calculating," he was "to all a kind, generous man." His fellow councillor, Samuel Thompson*, believed him "far the ablest man who had ever filled the civic chair."

W. G. ORMSBY

PAC, MG 24, D16; MG 29, E29, 23. PAO, Mackenzie-Lindsey papers; Toronto City Council papers, 1850–54, 1856–64. *Journal of Education for U. C.*, XVII (1864), 77. Hincks, *Reminiscences*, 355–58. *Globe*, 1851–64. *Leader*, 1851–64. *Montreal Gazette*, 1853–54. Toronto, City Council, *Report of the debate in the city council . . . in reference to the £50,000 city debentures . . .* (Toronto, 1853); *The report of the debate in the city council on . . . the report of the special committee appointed to investigate in reference to the issuing of city debentures . . .* (Toronto, 1853); *Report of the select committee appointed to inquire into the issue and sale of city debentures* (Toronto, 1853). *The Canadian men and women of the time: a hand-book of Canadian biography of living characters*, ed. H. J. Morgan (2nd ed., Toronto, 1912). Careless, *Brown*. Creighton, *Macdonald, young politician*. Davin, *Irishman in Can.*, 279–82. P.G.Goheen, *Victorian Toronto, 1850 to 1900: pattern and process of growth* (Chicago, 1970). Middleton, *Municipality of Toronto*, I. "Mayors of Toronto," *Toronto Calling, the Monthly Magazine of Toronto Life*, I (January 1951), 5.

BOYER, LOUIS (he sometimes signed **Boyer**, *dit* **Quintal**), mason, merchant, and land owner; b. 30 Nov. 1795 at Montreal, son of François Boyer and Josette Boutonne; d. 21 Dec. 1870 in the same town.

Louis Boyer's career is an interesting illustration of upward social mobility. He was called a mason at the time of his first marriage, on 2 Oct. 1820, to Élisabeth Mathieu, *dit* Laramée, and his father-in-law, Joseph, of Montreal, was called a carter. The witnesses, described only as uncles of the couple, informed the parish priest that

Boyer

they, "like the husband and wife, could not sign their names." At his second marriage, on 14 July 1836, at Saint-Joseph-de-Chambly, Boyer described himself as the "Sieur Louis Boyer, merchant." His wife, Marie-Aurélie Mignault, was the daughter of the postmaster of Saint-Denis-sur-Richelieu and the niece of the parish priest of Chambly, Pierre-Marie MIGNAULT. The bridegroom's nephew Louis Boyer, a certain John Elliott, esquire, two priests, James Moore, and Charles La Rocque* attended the ceremony. Unlike the first marriage, all the participants signed the register. On 24 Dec. 1870, at Boyer's burial, there was an impressive number of witnesses, including the mayor of the town William Workman*, Judge Joseph-Amable Berthelot*, Senator Jacques-Olivier Bureau, and Romuald Trudeau*. Two Montreal papers, *La Minerve* and the *Gazette*, carried an obituary. It seems that the death of his first wife, on 24 March 1836, marked a decisive break in Boyer's life, rather as if it allowed him a fresh start. He had been absent from his wife's funeral, his will, drawn up on 23 Aug. 1832, had made no provision for her, and he remarried with speed. Was there a desire to forget the past, or to efface it?

The early part of Louis Boyer's career is somewhat obscure. According to John Douglas Borthwick*, he was one of the masons who built the Rideau canal and the Kingston prison. The first contracts for the Rideau canal were assigned in the spring of 1827, and never lasted more than three years. In any case, in 1829 Boyer was living at Montreal, and gave his profession as purveyor of bacon.

It was in foodstuffs that Louis Boyer was to build the fortune that would be systematically invested in landed property. Gradually, as successive notarial contracts were drawn up, the designation "purveyor of bacon" gave place to that of merchant, even businessman. In the Montreal directory of 1842–43, he was "Provision merchant," and in 1852–53 "Provision and fur merchant." Towards the end of his life, the directory styled him "Provision and produce merchant." He dealt in pork, beef, cut meats, butter, and cheese. This part of the provision trade would undergo a phenomenal expansion in the second half of the 19th century.

Louis Boyer worked on his own for a short time, then on 13 April 1832 went into partnership with Joseph Vallée, Fleury-Théodore Serre, *dit* Saint-Jean, and Philippe Turcot Sr, "all purveyors of bacon, furs, and other commodities." The company was capitalized at £6,500, of which Boyer contributed £2,000. It was called Vallée, Boyer et Compagnie at Montreal, and Vallée,

Saint-Jean et Compagnie at Quebec (the company had a branch at Quebec from its beginning). The firm lasted at least ten years; set up originally for three, it was extended for another three years on 18 July 1835 by an endorsement to the original contract, and Vallée et Boyer still appears in the directory of 1842–43, under the heading "Provision merchants." During the next decade Louis Boyer apparently carried on on his own. In 1856–57, however, another company, Boyer and Hawley Provision and Fur Merchants, appears at the same address. Towards the end of his life he went into partnership with his sons as Louis Boyer et fils. In 1868 he gave up all commercial activity, leaving his premises to his two eldest sons and investing $80,000 in their company (Boyer, Hudon et Compagnie). They traded in foodstuffs, spirits, and other commodities.

Louis Boyer's interest in landed property began early in his career. In 1819, when he was a mason, he had exchanged a site in the *faubourg* Saint-Laurent, which he had received from his sister. After 1829 especially his activity in this sphere expanded, paralleling his career as a merchant to such an extent that Boyer's biographer portrayed him first of all as a landed proprietor. A series of real estate transactions made him by the end of his life one of the biggest property owners in Montreal. Boyer's example confirms the theory that landed property constituted the preferred basis of economic activity for the French bourgeoisie. In addition to properties outside the town, around 1870 Louis Boyer possessed 21 urban lots which totalled more than 1,000,000 square feet. The name of *faubourg* Boyer was even given to one of his large landholdings.

Banking also interested Louis Boyer. He was listed as an honorary director of the Montreal City and District Savings Bank from its inception in 1846, and in 1870 he owned 104 shares in the Banque Jacques Cartier, of which he was a director. On 12 Dec. 1847 he was elected churchwarden of the parish of Notre-Dame in Montreal, and he was a member of the Montreal Board of Trade. At the time of his death his estate was valued at more than a million dollars. Five children, including the politician and merchant Louis-Alphonse, were born of his second marriage.

JEAN-CLAUDE ROBERT

AJM, Registre des sépultures, cimetière de Notre-Dame-des-Neiges, 21 déc. 1870. ANQ-M, État civil, Catholiques, Notre-Dame (Montréal), 30 déc. 1795, 2 oct. 1820; Saint-Joseph-de-Chambly, 28 mars 1836; Greffe de Joseph Belle, 11 juill. 1854; Greffe de J.-O. Bureau, 7 janv., 17 oct. 1871; Greffe de J.-M. Cadieux, 9 déc. 1819; Greffe de Peter Lukin, fils, 2 mars 1819, 13 avril, 23 août 1832. Can., *Doc. de la session*, 1870, III, no.6. W. J. Patterson, *Report of the trade and commerce of the city of Montreal, for 1863* . . . (Montreal, 1864). L.-W. Sicotte, *Extraits des livres de renvoi des subdivisions de la cité de Montréal* (Montréal, 1874). *Gazette* (Montreal), 23 Dec. 1870. *La Minerve*, 22 déc. 1870. Borthwick, *History and biographical gazetteer*, 442; *Montreal*, 47. H. W. Hopkins, *Atlas of the city and island of Montreal, including the counties of Jacques Cartier and Hochelaga* . . . (n.p., 1879). *Montreal directory*, 1842–68. J. P. Heisler, *The canals of Canada* (Canada Historic Sites: Occasional Papers in Archaeology and History, 8, Ottawa, 1973), 81–86. T. T. Smyth, *The first hundred years; history of the Montreal City and District Savings Bank, 1846–1946* (n.p., n.d.), 15, 165. H. P. Hill, "The construction of the Rideau Canal, 1826–1832," *OH*, XXII (1925), 117–24. P.-A. Linteau et J.-C. Robert, "Propriété foncière et société à Montréal: une hypothèse," *RHAF*, XXVIII (1974–75), 45–65.

BOYS, HENRY, surgeon, university administrator, and office-holder; b. 8 Nov. 1775 probably at Sandwich, Kent County, England, the son of William Boys, a prominent surgeon and topographer, and Jane Fuller; m. Maria da Purīfecacao Alves of Lisbon, Portugal, and they had ten children; d. 23 April 1868 at Barrie, Ont.

Henry Boys received the degree of MD from the University of Aberdeen in 1805, and later became a member of the Royal College of Surgeons of London. For 30 years he served in the medical departments of the British army and the Royal Navy, and in the department of the paymaster-general of the forces. He served throughout the Peninsular war as assistant to his brother, deputy paymaster-general to the Duke of Wellington's army.

The obligations of a large family forced Boys to commute his half pay in 1833, and emigrate to Whitby in Upper Canada. Here, besides being licensed to practise medicine, he became coroner, collector of customs, and judge of the Court of Requests. During the rebellion of 1837–38, he acted as medical officer to the loyalist forces.

On 11 July 1839 Colonel Joseph Wells*, a man of unquestioned honesty but little accounting ability, was dismissed as bursar and registrar of the University of King's College in Toronto after hopelessly mismanaging its financial affairs. Lieutenant Governor George Arthur*, who had been requested by Lord Fitzroy Somerset, military secretary of the Horse Guards, to find Boys a position, exercised his prerogative as chancellor of the university and named Henry Boys to fill the vacant position. The council of King's College accepted Boys as bursar and registrar, from 27 July 1839.

Boys did not treat his new position as a sinecure but worked assiduously to put the financial affairs of King's College in order. His office was required to handle receipts of more than £15,000 annually and to keep records of the more than 1,800 separate accounts of the university. Boys and his assistants also carried on an extensive correspondence, drew deeds, and recorded the minutes of the King's College council. His preoccupation with these and other routine tasks prevented Boys from carrying out a much needed overhaul of the defective accounting practices which had been instituted by Wells. It also prevented him from discovering the full implications of activities of certain clerks; in addition to their petty speculation in university lands, of which he had some knowledge, they had used their office surreptitiously to threaten in their own interest creditors of the college who happened to own valuable lots.

When evidence of irregularities in university land transactions came to light in 1845, William Charles Gwynne*, professor of anatomy and physiology and a member of the college council, instigated a full investigation into the state of the bursar's office. Far from finding Boys unconscientious or incompetent, the committee of inquiry remarked upon his honesty and the "unremitting attention which he pays to his duties . . . and to the ample Evidence afforded by the manner in which his Books are kept, to his accuracy and knowledge of Business." Boys was similarly cleared of any imputation of misconduct by the commissioners, including Robert Easton BURNS, appointed in 1848 to inquire into the affairs of the university and Upper Canada College.

Efforts by the Reform party to secularize the university had moved King's College into the political spotlight. Boys, in his 75th year in 1850, had already decided to resign. He was apprehensive of "the stability of this appointment, owing to the strong political feelings prevailing about the university." He also found the work too burdensome at his age and the remuneration insufficient for the support of his wife and seven dependent children. On 17 Oct. 1850, some nine months after the act creating the University of Toronto came into effect, he submitted his resignation as bursar. After an audit of his accounts, the resignation was accepted and, in December, the university senate voted Boys a generous retirement gratuity of £750.

Henry Boys spent the remaining years of his life in Barrie, where he and his family had gone to live with his eldest surviving son. Here Boys contributed his professional services to the relief of the poor and pursued studies in entomology.

Brennan

He was a fellow of the Linnean Society and donated his entomological collection to the University of Toronto. He died on 23 April 1868.

D. W. RUDKIN

PAC, MG 24, A13, 6; E1, 19; RG 1, L3, 55, bundle 18, no.73; RG 5, B9, 62, p.525; C1, 198, no.16217; RG 7, G1, 71; RG 68, 1, General index, 1841–67, pp.167, 170. PRO, CO 42/416. University of Toronto Archives, A-68-011 (Office of the Chief Accountant), 109, Final report of the commissioners of inquiry on the affairs of King's College University and Upper Canada College, pp.46–47, 249–70; A-70-005 (Senate), Minutes, book 1, 7 Dec. 1850, 11 Jan. 1851; A-70-024 (Board of Governors), King's College Council letterbook, 1839–44, 1, p.1; King's College Council minute book, 1837–42, 2, pp.99–102, 110–11, 120–21, 143; A-72-050 (Office of the Chief Accountant), 14, package 1d, Boys to P. B. De-Blaquière, 17 Oct. 1850; package 1e, draft minute, 16 Nov. 1850. *Arthur papers* (Sanderson). Can., Prov. of, Legislative Assembly, *Final report of the commissioners of inquiry into the affairs of King's College University, and Upper Canada College* (Quebec, 1852). *Globe*, 29 April 1868. [John Macara], *The origin, history, and management of the University of King's College, Toronto* (Toronto, 1844). [John Strachan], *A brief history of King's College in Upper Canada, from its first germ in 1797, to its suppression in 1850 . . .* (Toronto, 1850).

The Canadian men and women of the time: a handbook of Canadian biography of living characters, ed. H. J. Morgan (2nd ed., Toronto, 1912). *The city of Toronto and the Home District commercial directory and register with almanack and calendar for 1837 . . .*, comp. George Walton (Toronto, [1837]). *The Toronto almanac and royal calendar, of Upper Canada . . .* (Toronto), 1839. Canniff, *Medical profession in U.C.* W. S. Wallace, *A history of the University of Toronto, 1827–1927* (Toronto, 1927). W. F. A. Boys, "Early days of the university," *University of Toronto Monthly*, II (December 1901), 1–36. W. S. Wallace, "The first two bursars of the university," *University of Toronto Monthly*, XXV (1924–25), 211–13.

BRENNAN, JAMES, Wesleyan Methodist New Connexion minister; b. 1812 in Ireland; m. and had two daughters; d. 7 May 1866 at Hamilton, Canada West.

James Brennan came to Kitley Township, Upper Canada, as a child. The Brennan home was often visited by Henry Ryan* and James Jackson*, who seceded from the Methodist Episcopal Church in 1828 to found the Canadian Wesleyan Methodist Church, an independent Canadian sect which featured greater lay participation in its government. Through the influence of Jackson, James Brennan in 1830 decided to become a prayer leader, exhorter, and local preacher in this church, and in 1831 he was appointed an itinerant preacher on trial on the Lansdown circuit.

In 1833, Brennan was sent as superintendent minister to the Trafalgar circuit, where after two years he was received as a minister in full connection and transferred to the Goulbourn circuit. In 1836, in addition to his circuit duties he was responsible for serving the Lansdown District, comprising the Lansdown and Goulbourn circuits, as chairman. Brennan began in 1837 a series of four successive one-year stations. While at Waterford and St Thomas in 1839, he was chairman of the London District, and in 1840 he became chairman of the Welland Canal District.

The Canadian Wesleyan Church, under pressure from declining membership (which fell from 2,528 in 1835 to 1,879 in 1840), from a shortage of itinerant preachers, and from an unmanageable deficit, merged in 1841 with the English Methodist New Connexion Church to form the Canadian Wesleyan Methodist New Connexion Church. The Protestant Methodists joined the new church in 1843. The church in Canada was a mission of the church in Great Britain, and the Canadian superintendent was appointed by the British conference. Brennan was elected to preside at the annual conference in 1846, and in his presidential address declared that while his denomination had had "trials to pass through of a painful and disagreeable nature," many circuits had built fine new churches and parsonage houses, which he considered signs of progress.

After terms at various places in both western and eastern Upper Canada, Brennan returned to Ancaster in 1848, and the following year became chairman of the Hamilton District extending from Owen Sound to the Welland Canal. With some circuits stretching across 70 miles and including as many as eight townships, Brennan often travelled 500 miles and preached 30 times every four weeks. In 1850 he was compelled to retire because of ill health. He settled in Hamilton as a supernumerary minister and assisted some adjacent circuits. After two years he was able to return to ministerial work, but in 1853 he was forced to retire permanently. He continued to give occasional service, and after a series of protracted meetings extending over a period of a month, arranged by the Cavan circuit in 1865, he suffered severe lung hemorrhages; he died the following year. The minutes of the conference of 1866 record that Brennan was "affectionately remembered as a powerful and effective preacher, a faithful and devoted pastor, and a Christian gentleman."

The church with which he had been so closely identified since its founding in 1841 had suffered from the same lack of money and men as its predecessor and from the scattered nature of its circuits. Overshadowed by the larger Wesleyan Methodist and Methodist Episcopal churches, it made little headway in towns and cities and at its peak had only some 8,000 members. In 1874 it severed the connection with the British conference and merged with the Wesleyan Methodist Church in Canada.

ALBERT BURNSIDE

Canadian Wesleyan Methodist Church, *Minutes of the annual conference*, (Hamilton, [Ont.]), 1835–36, 1839–41. Canadian Wesleyan Methodist New Connexion Church, *Minutes of the annual conference* (Hamilton, Toronto, London, [Ont.]), 1846, 1848–49, 1866. *Christian Messenger* (Montreal; Toronto), 1845–47. Cornish, *Cyclopædia of Methodism*, I. Albert Burnside, "The Canadian Wesleyan Methodist New Connexion Church, 1841–1874" (unpublished DTH thesis, Toronto Graduate School of Theological Studies, 1967). *The centenary of the Methodist New Connexion, 1797–1897*, ed. George Packer (London, [1897]). J. E. Sanderson, *The first century of Methodism in Canada . . .* (2v., Toronto, 1908–10), II. William Williams, "Historical sketch of the Methodist New Connexion Church in Canada," *Centennial of Canadian Methodism* (Toronto, [1891]), 95–126.

BREW, CHARTRES, gold commissioner and judge; b. 31 Dec. 1815 at Corofin, County Clare (Republic of Ireland), eldest son of the Honourable Tomkins Brew, stipendiary magistrate of Tuam, County Galway; d. 31 May 1870 at Richfield, B.C.

At age 20 Chartres Brew joined the volunteer British Legion which left England under George de Lacy Evans in 1835 to fight in the Carlist wars. After recovering from severe wounds, he entered the Royal Irish Constabulary in 1840. On the outbreak of the Crimean War in 1854 he volunteered for the commissariat, and on 1 Feb. 1856 became assistant commissary-general. Awarded the Crimean Medal with three clasps, he returned to Ireland to serve in the constabulary and in 1857 held the position of inspector in the city of Cork.

In August 1858 Brew was recommended to the colonial secretary, Sir Edward Bulwer-Lytton, for the office of chief inspector of police for the new gold colony of British Columbia at a salary of £500. Bulwer-Lytton had chosen to rely on stipendiary magistrates and a constabulary to maintain law and order among the thousands of miners arriving at the Fraser River goldfields. As inspector of police, Brew was to assist Governor James Douglas* in forming a force similar to the Irish Constabulary. Military protection (and duties such as surveying and road building) were to be provided for the colony by the Corps of Royal Engineers under Colonel Richard Clement Moody*. Brew left Southampton on 4 September and after a journey full of vicissitudes, including shipwreck, arrived at Victoria on 8 November. He immediately visited Langley and the diggings at Yale and on his return to Victoria requested permission to commence his duties.

Brew's initial plan was to have a police force of 150 men, trained and equipped locally, organized along military lines, and centrally controlled. Douglas doubted the wisdom of recruiting police from a mining population which included so many Americans and requested that 60 members of the Irish constabulary be sent to form a nucleus. In January 1859 Douglas learned that a bitter dispute had broken out between the justice of the peace at Hills Bar and the gold commissioner at Yale and that the notorious Ned McGowan, a refugee from California vigilante justice, was organizing his followers at Yale against constituted authority. On 10 January Douglas appointed Brew chief gold commissioner and ordered him to sail for Yale the same day with three constables. Though the trouble subsidized, Brew recommended the establishment there of a force of 20 constables. The constables recruited from among the miners by the former gold commissioner, he reported, were "nearly all a worthless set of loungers." He had already succeeded in having two young Irishmen, Thomas Elwyn* and John Carmichael Haynes*, appointed constables and he added William George Cox* to their number. Brew now thought 150 Irish constabulary should be obtained for the colony and Douglas concurred, but when the cost was made clear and the British government refused to bear the expense, the plan was dropped.

Brew was far from happy about his unfulfilled expectations: his office had not materialized and his request for an allowance for expenses had been ignored. Douglas, in fact, had quietly absorbed him into the magistracy, though the appointment as chief gold commissioner was supposed to be temporary. During the 1859 mining season Brew found himself performing regular duties of a gold commissioner: collecting miners' licences, recording claims, and settling claims disputes. On 23 April 1859 Brew asked to be relieved of his duties. Instead Douglas kept him at Yale until May when he finally formally recognized his title as chief inspector of police. Although Brew kept up the struggle until October to have a police corps for the whole colony organized, no step was taken, and the magistrates in the gold districts continued to select their own constables, employing only those who were

Brew

"*absolutely* and *indispensably* necessary." This situation remained until the fear of general Indian insurrection in spring 1864 led Governor Frederick SEYMOUR to centralize the police force, put it under his own control, and fix the size of the constable establishment. It never became a paramilitary force, and although Brew kept the title and salary of inspector of police he had authority only over the constables in his own district.

Brew's abilities were such, however, that he came to be relied on for multifarious functions by Douglas and later by Seymour. In October 1859 he became chief magistrate at New Westminster. On 1 Sept. 1862 he was appointed acting treasurer of British Columbia to replace Captain William Driscoll Gosset and held the position for two years. For six months after Colonel Moody's departure from the colony, Brew served as acting chief commissioner of lands and works. Concurrently he was justice of the peace and judge of the small debts court. He was a natural choice for membership in the colony's first Legislative Council, and from 1864 until 1868 he served as an appointed member.

In addition, Brew's judicial and police experience continued to be appealed to. It was to Brew and the New Westminster Volunteer Rifle Corps that Seymour turned in 1864 when he feared the Indian uprising after the Bute Inlet attack [*see* KLATSASSIN; Alfred Penderell Waddington*]. Brew (accompanied by Seymour) led one expedition and W. G. Cox another to apprehend the murderers after they had scattered into the interior plains. Brew's party had to cross the Cascade Mountains and make a 250-mile march to Puntzi Lake to join Cox. In mid August, when the Indians' capture seemed imminent, Seymour departed, leaving Brew, "an experienced Magistrate, a man of admirable temper and discretion, full powers for holding a Court of Justice in the Chilcotin country."

In 1867 when a violent dispute over a claim on Grouse Creek led to the defiance of the gold commissioner's order by 500 miners, Seymour called upon Brew "to undertake another most disagreeable, dangerous and unhealthy duty." On 4 September Brew was ordered to replace Henry Maynard Ball as gold commissioner and take temporary charge of Cariboo. He accompanied Chief Justice Joseph Needham* to Richfield for the investigation of the dispute, and remained at hand after Needham had resolved the "Grouse Creek War" by finding in favour of the company whose claim had been jumped. In October Brew was appointed county court judge, and his remaining days were spent as magistrate

and gold commissioner at Richfield. There he developed a scientific interest in mining and secured the esteem and respect of the mining community by his impartiality. He supervised the rebuilding of Barkerville after its destruction by fire in 1868, seeing to improvements in its layout and safety requirements.

By June 1869 Brew was "suffering from acute rheumatism, a complaint which then prevailed in Cariboo." In March 1870 his accounts as gold commissioner were in arrears owing to his increasing debility: "For some weeks I have not had sufficient strength even to sign my name," he reported to Victoria. After several months' confinement with a painful illness, he died at Richfield on 31 May 1870. The inscription on the tablet over his grave bears the tribute of his friend Judge Matthew Baillie Begbie*: "A man imperturbable in courage and temper, endowed with a great and varied administrative capacity, a most ready wit, a most pure integrity and a most humane heart." In 1859, after "Ned McGowan's War," 80 miners at Yale had paid Brew an equally notable tribute when they praised his ability to give justice while keeping "the kind feelings and respect of all." Brew never created the police force he had planned, but Douglas and Seymour regarded him as without equal in the role of gold commissioner and stipendiary magistrate. He established a standard of conduct that enabled the Irishmen whom he attracted to serve the gold commissioner to maintain peace in the goldfields at the height of production with no more than 18 constables in regular employment.

MARGARET A. ORMSBY

Chartres Brew's correspondence for the period 1858–59 is printed in *The early history of the Fraser River mines*, ed. F. W. Howay (PABC Memoir, VI, Victoria, 1926).

PABC, B.C., Colonial Secretary, correspondence outward, January 1867 – December 1870 (letterbook); Gold Commissioner, Cariboo, correspondence outward, 11 Dec. 1866 – 15 Aug. 1870 (letterbook); Governor, despatches to London, 1858–63, 1863–67, 1864–67, 1868–69 (letterbooks); Lands and Works Dept., correspondence outward, August 1861– May 1865; Colonial correspondence, Chartres Brew correspondence; G.B., Colonial Office, despatches to B.C., no.11, 2 Sept. 1859, enclosure, Chartres Brew, testimonials; Miscellaneous papers relating to Chartres Brew; O'Reilly coll., Chartres Brew, Diary excerpt, 26 Aug. – 1 Sept. 1858; letter to Capt. Travaillot, 19 Jan. 1859. PRO, CO 60. B.C., Legislative Council, *Journals*, 1864–69. G.B., Parl., Command paper, 1859 (2nd session), XXII, [2578], pp.297–403, *British Columbia: papers relative to the affairs of British Columbia, part II. . . . British Colonist* (Victoria), 10 June 1865. *Cariboo*

Sentinel (Barkerville, B.C.), 4 June 1870, 21 Sept. 1872. F. J. Hatch, "The British Columbia police, 1858–1871" (unpublished MA thesis, University of British Columbia, Vancouver, 1955). E. S. Hewlett, "The Chilcotin uprising: a study of Indian-white relations in nineteenth century British Columbia" (unpublished MA thesis, University of British Columbia, 1972). M. A. Ormsby, "Some Irish figures in colonial days," *BCHQ*, XIV (1950), 61–82.

BRISTOW, WILLIAM, political journalist; b. 25 Dec. 1808 in Birmingham, England; last known to be living in 1868.

As a young English immigrant in Quebec City, Bristow plunged into the agitation for reform of parliament in Lower Canada and for union with Upper Canada. In 1836 he wrote articles for the *Union* in support of constitutional reformer Andrew Stuart* and in 1837 became secretary of the Quebec Constitutional Association, which included as members Stuart, Thomas Cushing Aylwin*, George Pemberton, and John Neilson*. In letters to Neilson's *Quebec Gazette* in 1841 Bristow described responsible government for United Canada and backed Robert Baldwin*'s resolutions introduced in the assembly of the Province of Canada.

Bristow next did editorial work for the Montreal *Times and Daily Commercial Advertiser*, a Reform newspaper founded in 1841; he contributed also to the *Pilot and Journal of Commerce*, founded by Francis Hincks* in Montreal in 1844 – the same year George Brown* founded the *Globe* in Toronto. He was a leading contributor to the *Canadian Economist* from the time of its founding by the Free Trade Association in 1846. Bristow gave a public lecture on "Free trade" in Montreal in 1846.

"The atrocious condition in Kingston Penitentiary" under the Tory warden Henry Smith provided Bristow with another editorial subject. The penitentiary, long an institution proudly displayed to such travellers as Charles Dickens, was now the subject of rumours of corruption, nepotism, and serious maltreatment of prisoners. In 1848, during the ministry of Baldwin and Louis-Hippolyte LA FONTAINE, Bristow was among the five commissioners, including George Brown and Adam FERGUSSON, appointed to investigate conditions in the penitentiary. Hearings were held in Kingston; then in November–December 1848, Bristow and Brown toured American penal institutions, returning to Montreal to draw up the commission's report. This report urged the dismissal of Warden Henry Smith and proposed wide reforms of the Canadian penal system.

The Montreal *Pilot*, in which Hincks was inactive after January 1848 when he joined the ministry, was now an object of Conservative attack, and its offices were wrecked during the riots over the Rebellion Losses Bill of April 1849 [see James BRUCE]. Rollo Campbell*, who had become the new owner, offered editorship of the paper to Bristow. In his hands, the *Pilot* rallied Reform opinion in Canada East. It also led the opposition to the Tory British American League, and to annexationism, which reached its peak of influence during the fall of 1849. Bristow spoke against annexation to the mechanics' institute in Montreal in January 1850 in a lecture entitled "The commercial prospects of Canada." Acknowledging the evils rising from fiscal impediments to Canadian trade, he nevertheless insisted on Canada's greater advantages in contrast to the United States because of the St Lawrence. The speech was extensively quoted in English periodicals, including the London *Times*, and brought Bristow a letter of congratulation from Earl Grey, via Lord Elgin [Bruce], the governor general. Lord Elgin, reporting that October to Lord Grey on a political banquet held in Montreal, included an account of another speech by Bristow, which urged interprovincial connections and the "spirit of Federation."

Meantime the report on the abuses at Kingston Penitentiary had been published, and had stirred the wrath of John A. Macdonald*, political ally of Warden Smith. Macdonald attacked the commission in Parliament in 1850 and again in 1851, asking for a committee of inquiry into its work. In a letter of 1851, Macdonald growled, "I hope Bristowe will meet the fate of his co-Commissioner Brown, who has been completely hoed out at Haldimand." Bristow had now been appointed member of the new board of Kingston Penitentiary, and, with Brown, the first paid government inspector of the institution.

Bristow continued to edit the *Pilot* until 1854, supporting the government of Hincks and Augustin-Norbert MORIN, and emphasizing its efforts to open new channels of trade. In the 1854 election Bristow ran in Montreal, but was defeated by John Young*. Returning to journalism, he established the *Argus* in 1854. Reform forces were regrouping, and Bristow's *Argus* entered into debate with *La Minerve*. He focused on the mutual economic advantages for the Canadas in these days of railway expansion. The *Argus* also attacked the ministry of the Liberal-Conservative coalition, alleging abuses in departmental organization.

In May 1856 Bristow was called as a witness by a parliamentary committee of inquiry into the charges hurled by Macdonald against Brown and the penitentiary commission. Bristow's testimony stressed the joint nature of the commission's work, and the meticulous methods it had followed in taking evidence. Ultimately Macdonald was rebuked by the committee for his accusations of the suborning of witnesses and false recording or suppressing of evidence. But the politically biased committee refused to take a clear stand on the extent to which there might have been errors in the original report.

Bristow continued to be a personal friend of Brown, and was listed among those attending a Grit convention in Toronto in November 1859. The *Argus* had ceased publication in November 1858, and Bristow had become editor of the *Montreal Transcript*, owned by John Lovell*. In 1862 he was appointed with Thomas Storrow Brown* and George Sheppard* to a financial and departmental commission to inquire into "the efficiency of the system of keeping the public accounts and the manner in which they were checked and audited," and later acted as editor of the report of this commission, 1863–64. Bristow then announced his editorial days were ended. In 1864, when the *Quebec Daily Mercury*, floundering after the defeat of John Sandfield Macdonald*, lost its editor, the rival *Quebec Gazette* called, "Ho, Mr. William Bristow ... able writer," suggesting that the veteran journalist might take over the editorship. But Bristow remained in Montreal through a period of depression in the newspaper world, when many papers, including the *Transcript* and the *Pilot*, were in financial difficulty.

Bristow was among the earlier members of the Canadian Press Association, founded in 1859; his name appears in the association's lists of 1868. We lose sight of him after that. Bristow's work as a political journalist had been consistently hard-hitting – a little heavy in tone for today's taste, but with an undeviating emphasis on the development of Canadian economic strength through the expansion of water and rail transport.

ELIZABETH WATERSTON

William Bristow, *The commercial prospects of Canada; a lecture delivered before the Montreal Mechanics' Institute, on Tuesday evening, January 29, 1850* (Montreal, 1850). Can., Prov. of, *First report of the financial and departmental commission, May, 1863* (Quebec, 1863); *Second report of the financial and departmental commission, February, 1864* (Quebec, 1864); Legislative Assembly, *Journals*, 1849, III, app.B.B.B.B.B. Hincks, *Reminiscences*. Macdonald, *Letters* (Johnson and Stelmack), I, 178, 501. *Argus* (Montreal), 1854–58. *Montreal Transcript*, 1858–60. *Pilot* (Montreal), 1849–54. *Canada, an encyclopædia*, V. *The Canadian newspaper directory . . .* (Montreal,

1892), 17–56. Morgan, *Bibliotheca Canadensis. A history of Canadian journalism . . .* (2v., Toronto, 1908–59), I. Careless, *Brown*, I. Christie, *History of L. C.* W. H. Kesterton, *A history of journalism in Canada* (Toronto, 1967).

BROKEN ARM. *See* Maskepetoon

BROOKING, THOMAS HOLDSWORTH, merchant and leader in the campaign for representative government in Newfoundland; b. at Stoke Fleming, Devon, England, and baptized in St Petrox Church, Dartmouth, 8 Aug. 1790, son of Thomas Brooking, tide-waiter at Dartmouth, and Hannah Channel; m. in 1816 at St John's, Nfld, Frances Mclea, the daughter of a Scottish merchant, and they had three sons and three daughters; d. 13 Jan. 1869 in London, England.

Thomas Holdsworth Brooking came to Newfoundland in 1806 or 1807 as a mercantile clerk, possibly to work for the Torquay firm of Hunt, Stabb, Preston, and Company, but more probably for Hart, Eppes, Gaden, and Robinson of St John's and London. In any case in 1818, when the Newfoundland partner of the latter firm, George Richard Robinson, retired to "head office" in London, Brooking became its resident junior partner, and the company traded as Hart, Robinson, and Company. In 1822 the senior partner retired and the firm became Robinson, Brooking, and Garland; the other member was Joseph Bingley Garland of Poole who had a large independent trade to Trinity and Bonavista bays.

It became Brooking's turn to retire to "head office" late in 1831, and the local establishment was left in the hands of a new junior partner, William Jaffray Hervey. Brooking never again returned to the island and the local business was run by a succession of agents and partners, including for a while two of his sons, George Thomas and Marmaduke Hart. Garland's death in 1840 and Robinson's retirement in 1850 left the firm completely in the hands of Brooking and his sons, although at the time of Brooking's death a St John's man, Frederick Joseph Wyatt, held a number of shares as the "Newfoundland partner." Expensive litigation between the two sons, however, resulted in the disappearance of the company in 1873.

Brooking was typical of the mercantile élite that dominated Newfoundland during the first half of the 19th century: he came out as young man with little wealth but good connections, apprenticed to a flourishing concern, and eventually owned it. Lucky in the choice of Hart, Robinson, and Company, which survived the prolonged post-1815 depression in the fish trade, Brooking moved quickly into a position of prominence and power. From the outset he was assured of a respectable place in the social structure of St John's, dominated as it was by a small group of fish merchants and the beginnings of a professional class of lawyers and doctors. Almost invariably the older members retired in middle age to Britain, and young, literate men were given unusual freedom and authority. Newfoundland itself was in a state of transition from a "migratory fishery," visited by thousands but inhabited by few, to a populous and dynamic community, which in 1815 numbered up to 60,000 souls. Before 1800 hardly any merchants settled in the island, and thus when Brooking arrived he found a young man's paradise. Institutions of government were few and the St John's middle class naturally assumed every function of responsibility and power it could. Inevitably it came into conflict with the governor and his small group of civil servants, and the period of Brooking's residence in Newfoundland was one in which this élite gradually wrested authority from the rulers, and brought about the establishment of representative government in 1832.

A glance at Brooking's ever widening involvement in the affairs of Newfoundland illustrates both the natural manner in which the mercantile leaders took their place at the head of society and the growth of agitation for local and political change which characterized the period. His first public service was in 1812 when he served on a committee which organized a lottery to raise money for road construction. The fact that the roads had to be constructed by private subscription illustrates the deficiencies of the government and its revenues at the time; it also shows the interest of the mercantile élite in "improvements," especially because they were living in the colony the year round. By 1816 Brooking was serving as foreman of the grand jury – an institution that was the only representative body on the island. From then until his departure from Newfoundland Brooking stayed in the forefront of social and political life. He was appointed chairman of a group which attempted to build a merchant's hall, churchwarden of the Anglican church in St John's, and the first fire warden for the east end of the town. He was a founding member of a committee to establish contact with the by now almost extinct race of Beothuks [see William Eppes CORMACK], treasurer of the St John's amateur theatre, president of the St John's Library Society, member of the vestry society for the establishment of evening lectures, for years president of the St John's Chamber of Commerce, chairman of the Amateurs of the Turf,

and a founder of the Newfoundland Fisherman's and Shoreman's Association. In 1825 his social prominence was recognized by his appointment as colonial aide-de-camp to the governor with the rank of lieutenant-colonel in the militia.

However, Brooking's concerns were more serious than this mundane if strenuous pursuit of worthy causes might suggest, and he gradually became identified with the cause of social and political change on the island. With a few other merchants, such as Patrick Morris* and William Thomas, he was ahead of his fellows in seeing the need for change and for mobilizing the middle class shopkeepers, tradesmen, and planters of St John's behind reform. They were also the only people in Newfoundland who could put up with the politically brilliant but personally abrasive character of Dr William Carson*, first and best propagandist for reform. Brooking's senior partner, George Richard Robinson, who was elected Tory member of parliament for Worcester in 1824, represented the reformers in the British corridors of power.

Brooking's first introduction to wider social problems came early in 1817 when the great fire in St John's, after two years of depression and bankruptcy in the fishery, created unimaginable misery for the poor of the town. The depression continued and in 1821 the grand jury presented an address, probably drafted by Brooking as foreman, advocating government action to relieve distress, and even urging emigration from Newfoundland either to Great Britain or to mainland North America. The immediate need was met by the British government but the deeper problems of poverty remained, and in 1822 Brooking was appointed to yet another committee to alleviate the condition of the poor. That year he also began his long and deep interest in education by forming a committee to establish a charity school.

As he became more deeply involved in the chaos and poverty of life in post-Napoleonic Newfoundland, he gradually realized that radical change was needed to cure the ills of her society. In 1819 he seems to have wanted only some kind of municipal body in St John's which could control "nuisances" and deal with the ever present menace of fire, but he soon found himself following Carson and Morris in agitation for wholesale reform of the laws as they related to Newfoundland. By the early 1820s they were becoming convinced that only the introduction of some form of representative government could alleviate the moral and material condition of the island. In 1824 the reformers' agitation resulted in three new pieces of imperial legislation that swept away the ancient system of government

Brown

and introduced reforms in the judicial and administrative structure of the island.

The new legislation was hardly revolutionary, but it was of symbolic importance in signalling the end of the British government's policy of dealing with Newfoundland as a fishery rather than a colony. It provided for a non-elective executive council to which Brooking was appointed, but neither he nor the other reformers were satisfied and agitation continued. However, the purpose of the battle had now changed from convincing the British government of the need for reform to overcoming divisions in Newfoundland society – particularly the apathy of most inhabitants, especially outside St John's, towards the whole question of government. For example, the new legislation provided for the establishment of a municipal corporation in St John's and Brooking was prominent in trying to persuade the inhabitants to support it. Despite his efforts the proposal was heavily defeated. Unable to solve a local problem, the reformers turned to the larger question of obtaining "local" government for the entire colony. Brooking and his partner Robinson played a continuous and a vital role in the campaign since their wealth and prominence gave it respectability in England. Robinson presented petitions in parliament while Brooking chaired the increasingly numerous reform meetings in St John's. In 1831, when Brooking retired to England, representative government was about to be introduced, and he sailed with the plaudits of all ranks and classes, Irish and English, Protestant and Catholic, in his ears. Everyone basked in the feeling of amity and cooperation which the campaign had created. Four years later Newfoundland society was bitterly divided and the Protestant merchants, now the Conservative party, who had so staunchly supported the advent of local government were strenuously demanding that the experiment be abandoned on the grounds that Newfoundland was not fit for freedom. Thomas Holdsworth Brooking was willing to admit that he shared their view.

Brooking's life was of course by no means over; he was only 41 when he left Newfoundland and his business continued and flourished for nearly 40 years more. However, his interests in England seem to have turned from social or political questions towards a concentration upon his business, as typified by the joint speculation in Prince Edward Island land with Samuel CUNARD and others, and the firm's great involvement with Lloyd's of London. The excitement of reform was replaced by the private affluence of Victorian commerce.

KEITH MATTHEWS

Cathedral of St John the Baptist (Anglican) (St John's), marriage register, 1816. H. M. Customs and Excise Library (London), Customs 65/3, Outport letters (Dartmouth), June 1788. PANL, GN 2/1, March 1819, October 1821, October 1822, 19 Oct. 1825; Nfld., Surrogate Court, St John's, Minutes, December 1816. PRO, BT 107/472, December 1818; CO 194/68, 344; 194/71. St Petrox Anglican Church (Dartmouth, Devonshire, Eng.), baptismal and marriage registers. G.B., *Statutes*, 5 Geo IV, c.51, c.67, c.68. *Newfoundlander*, September 1828, March 1829, 15 Jan. 1869. *Newfoundland Mercantile Journal* (St John's), 7 Aug. 1818–9 March 1820; May, November, 22 Dec. 1822. *Public Ledger*, December 1828, February 1829–March 1832. *Royal Gazette* (St John's), February 1812; March 1817; September 1830; 18 Dec. 1831; 8 Dec. 1840; 11 Nov. 1852; 13 Jan., 4 May 1869; 21 Jan. 1873; 24 June 1907. Gunn, *Political history of Nfld.*, 79–80. A. H. McClintock, *The establishment of constitutional government in Newfoundland, 1783–1832* ... (London, 1941). Keith Matthews, *The class of '32* (Maritime History Group pub., Memorial University of Nfld., St John's, 1974).

BROWN, JAMES, farmer, teacher, and politician; b. 6 Sept. 1790 at Glamis near Dundee, Scotland, son of James Brown and Janet Douglas; m. in 1817 Sarah Sharman, by whom he had four sons and three daughters, and in 1842 Catherine Gillespie, *née* Cameron, by whom he had four sons and three daughters; d. 18 April 1870 at Tower Hill near St Andrews, N.B.

James Brown was educated in Scotland and immigrated in 1810 to St Andrews, arriving "a friendless boy" on the brig *Hector*. He bought land at Tower Hill in Charlotte County where he farmed and taught school for a number of years.

Brown unsuccessfully contested a Charlotte County seat in the assembly in the 1827 general election, but was returned in 1830 and held the seat in the 1834, 1837, 1842, and 1846 elections. Like most other MHAs Brown did not have strong party affiliation, though he was closest to such Reformers as Lemuel Allan Wilmot* and Charles Fisher*. He supported measures which were considered progressive and which contributed to the material development of the province, and he opposed the maintenance of special privileges. His ability and his dedication to the improvement of New Brunswick were recognized by his appointment in 1838 as government supervisor of the great road from Fredericton to St Andrews. The construction of this road to link Charlotte County with the capital was important to Brown, since he had himself often travelled from Tower Hill to Fredericton on foot and on horseback. He devoted a great deal of effort to the project, and the experience he gained in road and bridge construction was to prove useful in later years.

86

Brown's experience as a teacher was called upon in 1844 when he was appointed, along with Dr Sylvester Zolieski Earle* and John GREGORY, to examine the condition of grammar schools in the province. Throughout the latter part of the year he made copious notes on the numerous schools he visited in the southern and western part of the province. The report of the commissioners, presented to the assembly in February 1845, resembles Brown's comments in his notes and diary entries in the incisive and sometimes harsh judgements of educational progress and the abilities of teachers. Brown considered the Wesleyan Academy in Sackville to be "perhaps, the very best Educational Establishment in the Province."

His continuing interest in education and in equality of opportunity was recognized again in 1854 when he was appointed, with John Hamilton Gray*, Egerton Ryerson*, John William Dawson*, and John Simcoe Saunders* to inquire into the state of King's College, Fredericton [see Edwin JACOB]. They examined the organization and administration of Brown University in Providence, Rhode Island, as a model. Their study and consequent recommendations resulted in the creation by an act of 1859 of the nondenominational University of New Brunswick to replace King's College. Brown's last major contribution to New Brunswick's educational system was an extensive new school act relating to the administration of parish schools which he drafted and which the legislature passed in 1858.

In 1849 Brown had been authorized, along with Dr James ROBB of King's College, to accompany Professor James Finlay Weir Johnston* on his 2,000-mile tour of the province to report on the condition of agriculture. The commission was an important part of the government's programme to encourage the development of agriculture, and Johnston's report is a landmark in agricultural investigation, much of it remaining valid more than 100 years later.

Brown was defeated in the general election for the assembly of 1850 but was appointed to the Legislative Council. He resigned his seat in 1854 and successfully contested the Charlotte County riding in the assembly election of that year. He then became an executive councillor and surveyor general in the Charles Fisher government. The following year he was appointed to the Board of Works, and during 1855 and 1856 carried out extensive examinations of the public works of New Brunswick. His diary for the period contains a thorough report of the state of roads and bridges at that time.

In 1856 Brown resigned with the Fisher government and he was not a candidate in the ensuing general election. According to his diary he was suffering the effects of a serious and prolonged illness, as well as experiencing financial difficulties. The following year he was re-elected as a member of the Fisher government and reappointed as surveyor general. During this administration there were accusations of mismanagement in the granting of crown lands, one of the surveyor general's major responsibilities. The legislature initiated a special inquiry and in response Brown submitted his resignation, although it was not accepted. The inquiry's report, submitted 26 March 1861, did reveal that there were abuses on the part of officials of the department in the sale of lands, but Brown's honesty was not seriously questioned.

In the 1861 general election Brown was defeated and resigned his office. Almost immediately he was appointed an emigrant agent and left on a year-long trip to Britain to promote immigration to New Brunswick. An account of his nostalgic return to his homeland was recorded in a report published in 1863. He also published some promotional literature on immigration to New Brunswick. In July 1864 Brown ran again for the Charlotte County seat, but was defeated probably for his opposition to confederation. He retired to his home at Tower Hill, where he died in 1870.

The constant preoccupation of Brown's public life had been the improvement of the lot of the common man. Throughout his career he always maintained the stance of a liberal, advocating the virtues of a sound public education system, the material development of the province along the lines of the progressive American states, and a free and open society, unhampered by the strictures of a privileged class. He was brought up a Presbyterian, but as an adult joined the Universalist Church in St Stephen, which was more to his liking. On occasion he would attend a Methodist service in Fredericton, but commented in his diary that he found the "trappings" offensive. Such an attitude, typical of his outlook on life, was also reflected in his opposition in the legislature to a resolution in 1860 to invite the Prince of Wales to visit New Brunswick. Since the province was in debt, Brown declared, public money should not be spent for such an occasion. As might be expected, he was a supporter of the temperance movement.

During his years in the legislature Brown did not play a significant role in determining such constitutional issues as control of the casual revenues, responsible government, and confederation. His importance lay instead in his contribu-

Brown

tions to the social and economic development of the province through his concern for education, agriculture and land policy, transportation, and immigration. Perhaps it was inevitable that the practical Scottish immigrant should give leadership as a builder rather than as a constitutional authority.

MICHAEL SWIFT

James Brown was the author of . . . *New Brunswick, as a home for emigrants: with the best means of promoting immigration, and developing the resources of the province* (Saint John, N.B., 1860), and *Report of Mr. Brown's mission to Great Britain and Ireland, for the promotion of emigration to New Brunswick* (Fredericton, 1863). Brown also wrote some poetry but the only example found was "Devil's reply to Robert Burns," *Acadiensis* (Saint John, N.B.), III (1903), 219–23, written in honour of the Burns' centennial in 1859.

N.B. Museum, James Brown, Journal (photocopy). PANB, J. C. and H. B. Graves, "New Brunswick political biography," VI, pp.3–4; RED/be/5; REX/mi/ex, draft minutes, 1845, 1849, 1854, 1859, 1861; RNA/c/3. UNBL, MG H9 (Lilian Mary Beckwith Maxwell papers). N.B., House of Assembly, *Journals*, 1845, 1849, 1854, 1858–59, 1861. *Royal Gazette* (Fredericton), 1844, 1849, 1854, 1861. MacNutt, *New Brunswick*. L. M. B. Maxwell, *How New Brunswick grew* (Sackville, N.B., 1943). D. F. Maxwell, "Hon. James Brown," *Acadiensis* (Saint John, N.B.), III (1903), 184–91. L. M. B. Maxwell, "James Brown," *Maritime Advocate and Busy East* (Sackville, N.B.), 41 (1950–51), no.4, 9–13.

BROWN, PETER. journalist and author; b. 29 June 1784 at Edinburgh, Scotland, the son of James Brown and Jean Lyon; m. in 1813 Marianne Mackenzie, and they had six children; d. 30 June 1863 at Toronto, Canada West.

Peter Brown, whose father was a successful builder, became a textile and general merchant. By the 1830s he owned a large wholesale warehouse and was a respected burgess of Edinburgh. As an earnest and well-read Whig-Liberal, moreover, he supported the swelling reform movement in Great Britain, and especially in Edinburgh itself. Accordingly, he was named collector of assessments in the reformed civic administration elected in 1835. But the next year his office became involved in the loss of some £2,800 of public funds that had been mixed up with his private accounts. There was no allegation of dishonesty, and friends who had guaranteed him made good the money. Yet Brown greatly felt the blow to his reputation and determined to make restitution. He found he could not, because of spreading world depression, and so decided to emigrate to America to recoup his fortunes. In April 1837 he and his elder son, George*, aged 18, set sail for New York.

There they started a small dry goods business, which flourished sufficiently to enable Peter's wife and four other children to join them in 1838. But Peter soon acquired an interest in political developments in the United States, and began writing for the New York *Albion*, a journal of the British emigrant community. Though a parliamentary liberal, he was not a universal suffrage democrat and found sizeable gaps between the Americans' claims of liberty and the corruption and demagogy of their mass politics. Also a fervent abolitionist, he detested the presence of slavery. Hence he was impelled to write a strong rejoinder to an American critique of things British, *The glory and shame of England*, written by C. E. Lester in 1841. Brown's own volume, *The fame and glory of England vindicated*, published the next year, was a trenchant comparison of British and American institutions and policies that gained considerable attention in Britain, the United States, and in the neighbouring British North American colonies. Perhaps as a result, Peter decided to give all his attention to writing on public affairs. In July 1842 he launched a little weekly of his own, the *British Chronicle*, intended for the Scottish community in the New York area and in nearby Canada.

The newspaper flourished and soon became engaged with the issue then dividing Scotland, the "Great Disruption" of the Presbyterian Church, when the Free Church separated from the main established body. A staunchly evangelical Presbyterian, Peter was eloquent in supporting the Free Kirk party in his paper. Consequently, an invitation came to him from leading Free Kirk adherents in Canada to take up the Presbyterian struggle on the colonial front. He accepted, terminated his first paper in July 1843, and began the *Banner* in Toronto the following month.

His son George worked closely with him on this weekly, as he had on its predecessor. Together, they soon took the *Banner* into the political conflict in Canada as well as into the Presbyterian religious dispute. The paper indeed became a stalwart supporter of the Reformers' campaign for responsible government. Their political involvement led to the founding of a wholly political Reform organ, the Toronto *Globe*, by George Brown in March 1844. Peter and his son Gordon* helped to write and edit it, while George still assisted with the *Banner*, both being published in the same office.

By 1848, however, the *Globe* was demanding increasing attention, the *Banner* had witnessed the successful establishment of a Canadian Free Church, and Peter was aging. In July 1848 his paper ceased publication, but he still gave himself loyally and busily to his son's *Globe*. Early in 1850 he retired from journalism, though he remained active for years more in the Toronto Anti-Slavery Society and other philanthropic or reform-inspired groups. Indomitably eager for a political or intellectual argument, yet the soul of kindliness and courtesy, he died in Toronto the day after his 79th birthday.

J. M. S. CARELESS

[The biographical material used comes from my study, *Brown of "The Globe"*, especially chap. 1 of vol. I. J.M.S.C.] Peter Brown, *The fame and glory of England vindicated* . . . (New York and London, 1842).

BRUCE, JAMES, 8th **Earl of Elgin** and 12th **Earl of Kincardine**, colonial administrator; b. 20 July 1811 in London, England, second son of Thomas Bruce, 7th Earl of Elgin and 11th Earl of Kincardine, the "saviour" of the "Elgin Marbles," and of Elizabeth Oswald; d. 20 Nov. 1863 at Dharmsala, India.

James Bruce, as a younger son until 1840, had to fit himself for work, and the career he actually followed owed much of its success to his education and to his early preparation for an occupation. He was educated at Eton and Christ Church, Oxford, and became one of a brilliant group of Eton and Christ Church graduates, many of whom were later associated in politics and the colonial service.

Bruce studied intensively, so much so that he injured his health and had to forego a double first for a mere first. Nevertheless he left Oxford not only widely read in classics but having "mastered" on his own, so his brother recorded, the philosophy of Samuel Taylor Coleridge. The latter, with its stress on the organic nature of society in which the members and interests are dependent on one another, was a suggestive and intriguing acquisition for a young man who was to lead, with the ready address and genial charm already apparent at Oxford, fragmented and unformed societies towards a new coherence in self-government.

On graduating in 1832, Elgin returned to Scotland to assist in the management of the family estates, and to read and think. But he had a political career in view. In 1834 he addressed a *Letter to the electors of Great Britain*, in which he showed himself a liberal-conservative of the model of Sir Robert Peel, and of the cast of thought derived from the philosophy of Coleridge. He failed to win election in the county of Fife in 1837 because of entering late, but in 1840 was returned for Southampton. He seconded the amendment to the address which brought down Lord Melbourne's government in 1841. But already in 1840 he had become on the death of his elder brother the heir to the earldom, and on his father's death in 1841 had to give up, as a Scottish peer, hopes of advancement as a member of the House of Commons.

In 1842, however, he accepted appointment as governor of Jamaica, and went there with his new wife, Elizabeth Mary Cumming-Bruce. Unhappily for the health of the latter, who was pregnant, the party suffered shipwreck on the way. In Jamaica Elgin found a society divided by racial differences and suffering the effects of an economic depression brought on by the abolition of slavery in 1833, circumstances not unlike those he was to find later in Canada. He also found a classic model of the old colonial constitution from which Canadian Reformers were seeking to escape. Jamaica was thus in many ways a preparation for Canada. It also gave Elgin an opportunity to use his personal charm and public diplomacy in turning men's thoughts to practical improvements and moderate politics.

In 1846, saddened by the loss of his wife and concerned for his own health and that of his daughter, Elgin returned on leave to England. The new colonial secretary in Lord John Russell's Whig administration, Lord Grey, was impressed with Elgin's performance in Jamaica and urged him, without success, to continue there. Grey then invited Elgin to assume the governorship of Canada. The acceptance of a Whig appointment by Elgin, and the appointment of a Tory by Grey, forecast the non-partisan role which Elgin was to play in his new post. By coincidence, this new political character was underlined by his marriage to Lady Mary Louisa Lambton, daughter of Lord Durham [Lambton*] and niece of Lord Grey. He was thus, publicly and privately, splendidly fitted to carry out the mission Grey had given him, to elaborate and confirm the practice of responsible government in the British North American provinces. Grey had made the idea explicit by his analysis of the conditions which stood in the way of responsible government in Nova Scotia in his important dispatches of 3 Nov. 1846 and 31 March 1847. Elgin's conduct in Canada defined through practice the form of responsible government and he was to expand it into a major anticipation of the Canadian nationhood which was yet in embryo. His private correspondence with Grey was in fact an agenda of what was to be done in British North America during the next generation.

Elgin reached Canada on 30 Jan. 1847, and at once met the incumbent Conservative govern-

Bruce

ment. It had been elected in 1844 following the resignation of the Robert Baldwin*–Louis-Hippolyte LA FONTAINE government and, although committed to support the governor and to resist the application of responsible government, it had itself under the leadership of William Henry Draper* become in effect a party government. There was some anticipation that Elgin as a Tory would assume direction of the government, but others thought that, as a governor sent by a Whig administration to recognize responsible government, he would dismiss the Draper ministry and call the Reformers to office. Elgin did neither. He had determined before his arrival not to be "a partisan governor," as his predecessor Sir Charles Metcalfe* had seemed to be. He would assume "a position of neutrality as regards mere Party contests." This was the first step in confirming in Canada what he felt certain it was his mission to ensure, what he termed "constitutional Government." By that he meant government by the full body of conventions controlling the formation and functioning of the cabinet and the role of governor general as the representative of the crown. In short, it was the parliamentary monarchical government then being confirmed by use in the United Kingdom.

Elgin accordingly made it clear that he would support Draper either in a new session of the legislature, or in his endeavours to strengthen his position in parliament by seeking support from the French followers of La Fontaine. Elgin himself wrote to Augustin-Norbert MORIN to suggest French support for the ministry, the more readily as he accepted Draper's opinion that the existing division of parties, with the Tories looked upon as the "English" party and the Reformers the "French" party, was no more than transitory. But Morin and his associates, whom Elgin considered essentially conservative, declined Elgin's proposal and the alliance did not occur at that time.

Having failed in its bid for French support, the government requested dissolution late in 1847, and the Reform party won a decisive victory in the ensuing election. The ministry, defeated in parliament, resigned as a body. The practice since 1841 had been simply to reshape ministries with some former members in the new, but when Elgin invited La Fontaine to form a ministry, he did so as leader of a party. Elgin, as a neutral governor, thus accepted the first administration deliberately based on party in Canadian history. In placing the crown which he represented above party politics, and in leaving the power to govern in the hands of a ministry of the leaders of a defined and organized party, Elgin revealed what

he meant by constitutional government. The party character of the ministry meant also that the cabinet was collectively responsible through the prime minister for policy and administration. The governor would no longer be head of the government responsible for its acts in all matters of local administration and legislation. Nor would he have a voice in matters of local patronage as Metcalfe had wished to have, but to prevent the establishment of a Jacksonian spoils system he had to ensure that major and permanent civil servants, being politically neutral, should have security of tenure.

Elgin had, of course, duties as an imperial officer, specific instructions from the colonial secretary, some voice in decisions concerning defence and foreign relations, as well as control of Indian affairs and other as yet untransferred imperial responsibilities; these precluded his playing an altogether neutral role. And both he and Grey had to act judiciously and tactfully in re-modelling the simple and archaic governmental procedures of Canada to deal with the complex administrative and conventional practices of British cabinet government. Elgin was thus, in confidential fashion, a far more active governor than his new definition of the office implied. Fortunately, La Fontaine, Baldwin, and Francis Hincks* desired the same ends as he did, and trusted him, so that the process of creating full parliamentary government went forward smoothly. Not that it was a mere matter of office organization; party control of patronage meant of course that hundreds of public offices went to French Canadians, others to English Reformers, both of which groups had had scant access to public employment before. Elgin put the finish to his new version of his office by traditional ceremony and entertainment, and also by less formal visits, official ceremonies, and public speeches. His personal charm aided greatly in all this, as did his personal simplicity.

The new Reform ministry, which was sworn in on 11 March 1848, marked the coming to power of French Canadians as members of a party, not as individuals, and represented as well the outcome of the long agitation for colonial self-government. It soon had to face, with Elgin's guidance and advice, the consequences of economic and external changes in the critical years from 1846 to 1850.

The first was the repeal in 1846 of the Corn Laws; it had precipitated the collapse of the old colonial system, and had impelled Russell and Grey to base their policy in British North America on the recognition of full responsible government in local matters. Another problem was the famine migration from Ireland to Canada and the United States in 1847. Not only did it bring to Canada some 70,000 Irish immigrants in that year, many of whom were to create burdens because of the ravages of cholera, but it also made real the possibility of Irish Americans striking at Great Britain through British North America. Elgin had to keep watch on Irish organizations and meetings in Montreal and on the Irish agitators of Boston and New York. Discontent in Ireland might too easily blend with discontent in Canada.

To these concerns was added in 1847 the financial and commercial depression which followed the collapse of the railway boom in the United Kingdom. Coming upon the repeal of the Corn Laws and the loss of guaranteed British markets for Canadian goods, commerce in Canada was completely disrupted. The falling off of trade, the increase of bankruptcies, and the collapse of investment values may well have been caused by the depression alone, but it was natural for Canadian businessmen to attribute them to the ending of the familiar protective system.

The Canadian constitutional revolution of 1848 may have forestalled an echo in Canada of the European liberal revolutions of that year begun in France. That there was apprehension is corroborated by the reaction to the return of Louis-Joseph Papineau* from exile in Paris. He came out eloquently and strongly as the critic of the "sham" of responsible government, and set out to become again the leader of French national feeling. The popularity he acquired almost immediately caused some fear among the French Canadian supporters of the Reform party. But the French ministers, aided by Elgin, set out to undermine his popularity and reduce him to an isolated figure mouthing the battle cries of an age of perpetual opposition. They remorselessly and cruelly succeeded in damping down the embers of revolution in Canada, although dissension continued in the activities of the republican and annexationist Rouges, the heirs of Papineau.

It was fortunate, in view of the next stage of the Canadian crisis, that Papineau had probably been reduced to impotence by the end of 1848. For, even if Papineau were powerless, there was a measure, required by both justice and policy, which was to demonstrate clearly to French Canadians that responsible government was not a sham but a reality. The indemnification of those who had suffered damage by acts of the troops and government in suppressing the rebellion of 1837 in Lower Canada (it had been done for Upper Canada) had been taken up by Draper's ministry, and a royal commission had recom-

mended payment for losses incurred by those not actually convicted of rebellious acts. The Draper ministry took no action, but clearly an administration headed by a French Canadian and supported by the French Canadian members of the assembly and under attack by Papineau, had, in policy as well as justice, to take it up. The Rebellion Losses Bill was passed by majorities of both Lower and Upper Canadian members despite the Tory opposition's cry that it was a bill to pay "rebels."

Fully to understand Elgin's dilemma in dealing with the bill, it is necessary to realize that the Tory opposition, as well as the government, were testing responsible government and learning the new rules, and that Elgin was their mentor little less than he was that of his ministers. For the most part they, and especially their leader Sir Allan Napier MacNab, were simply old-fashioned Tories, not sure that the new regime might not lead to a continuation of earlier conditions when ministries acquired permanency, only this time it would be a Reform ministry with French Canadian support. MacNab's remarks early in the debates on the bill are suggestive: "We must make a disturbance now or else we shall never get in." He knew also that the governor general, as an imperial officer, might properly decline to sanction the "paying of rebels," and that he could in any case dissolve the parliament or reserve the bill for the decision of the imperial government. MacNab was thus trying to force Elgin into using the powers left him under responsible government.

Elgin refused to be turned away from the role he had assumed. His ministry had an unshaken majority; there was no indication that an election would alter that fact and much that it would provoke racial strife in Lower Canada. The matter was also local, not imperial; it was therefore to be dealt with locally by the governor's assent; if his superiors disagreed, they could recall him. If he reserved the bill, it would simply embroil the imperial government in local Canadian affairs and perhaps provoke another Papineau rising with American and Irish aid. So he drove down to the parliament house on 25 April 1849, and gave his assent to the bill.

The immediate result was a violent attack by a mob of "respectable" demonstrators on the governor's carriage as he drove away. The next was the deliberate burning of the parliament buildings by the same mob, followed by rioting in the streets and attacks on the houses of La Fontaine and Hincks. Montreal was at the mercy of an organized and aggressive Tory and Orange mob, which conservative citizens either actively

Bruce

joined or refrained from resisting. When Elgin returned to meet parliament on 30 May to receive an address, his carriage was again assaulted with missiles and he carried off a two-pound stone thrown into it. The home of La Fontaine was again attacked, and one man killed by its defenders. Elgin remained outside the city for the rest of the summer in order not to provoke yet another outburst, with the possibility of racial violence. This course, although criticized by some as cowardice, showed great moral courage and was an important measure of his powers of restraint. His ministers could not be quite as quiescent. Government went on, but the troops were called in and the police were increased. Their policy, modelled on Elgin's conduct, was, however, not to answer defiance with defiance, but to have moderate conduct shame arrogant violence. In the end the policy succeeded, but only at the cost of suffering the climax of Tory Montreal's frantic despair. In October 1849, after frequent indications of what was to come, there appeared the Annexation Manifesto which advocated the political and economic union of Canada and the United States and was signed by scores of persons of political and commercial significance. It was an act of desperation, the act of men whose world had been turned upside down, the empire of protection and preference ended, the empire of the St Lawrence centred on Montreal disrupted, British "ascendancy" replaced by "French domination."

MacNab's role in the outcry and riots against the Rebellion Losses Act had failed to coerce Elgin or to force his recall; at bottom the Annexation Manifesto was a reply to Elgin's firmness. If the queen's representative was to welcome French Canadians to power in equality with the English and to convert the commercial system of the old empire into a new system of local government, free trade, and sentiment based on common institutions and common allegiance, the embittered loyalists and financially embarrassed businessmen of Montreal thought annexation an alternative so just it would be given for the asking. To men thinking in the old terms Elgin could seem only a traitor or a trifler. Elgin was neither. He foresaw a nation of diverse elements founded on the temperate exercise of tested institutions and conventions. So did Grey and the Russell government, which showed its approval by advancing Elgin to the British peerage with a seat in the House of Lords. So did his ministers. The men who had signed the manifesto while holding commissions from the crown, as many Tories did, were required to abjure the manifesto or forfeit their commissions. Montreal, which had

attempted to coerce the parliament and government of all Canada, was declared unfit to be the seat of government.

These measures stemmed the violence of the outraged Montrealers. Moreover, the general current of events turned the attention of businessmen everywhere to more congenial pursuits. By 1850 prosperity was returning to Montreal and Canada. In prosperity even responsible government and "French domination" could be tolerated. MacNab called on Elgin and was politely received. Responsible government and all it implied – French Canadians in office, British, not American, conventions of government, efficiency in public finance and the civil service, local decision-making and local control of patronage – had been tested in the fires of riot and the threat of annexation.

Much remained to be done, and Elgin's further four years in Canada called for the exercise of the same talents as did the turbulent year 1849. There were local reforms to be carried out, such as the abolition of the clergy reserves and of seigneurial tenure in Lower Canada. The latter was a clearly local issue and was dealt with by the Canadian parliament. But the clergy reserves, governed by an imperial act of 1840, could not be touched without an act of parliament of the United Kingdom enabling the Canadian legislature to deal with them. The question invited the same appeal to Britain as the Rebellion Losses Act had done, especially as nothing could more symbolize an empire and a nation across the seas than a common established church. Elgin recommended that the imperial parliament be asked to end the act of 1840 and leave the future of the reserves to the Canadian parliament. After repeated efforts were foiled by opposition of the bishops in the House of Lords, this action was taken and in 1854 the reserves were ended, but on terms respecting vested interests. In the same year seigneurial tenure was abolished.

That this legislation was the work of a Liberal-Conservative Anglo-French party in coalition pleased Elgin, as such a union was the outcome of the regime of local decisions by moderate and responsible men which he had made possible in Canada. But more exhilarating, no doubt, was the long delayed conclusion of the Reciprocity Treaty with the United States, the final act of Elgin's personal diplomacy. Foreseen as early as 1846 in Canada as a necessary outcome of the dismantling of the protective system, reciprocity had been repeatedly defeated in the United States for lack of evident advantage to American economic interests and because of its implications as a possible prelude to annexation, a step which would upset the balance of free and slave soil in the expanded republic of 1848. The inducements of free navigation on the Canadian section of the St Lawrence and of access to the fisheries of the Atlantic provinces removed American objections that it conferred no benefits on the United States. In 1854 the British government acknowledged the need to lobby Congress. Elgin went to Washington and in a diplomatic *tour de force* persuaded the Southern senators that reciprocity would prevent, not provoke, annexation. It was a brilliant climax to seven years of intense persuasion, in which he had established the conventions of constitutional, monarchical, and parliamentary government in Canada, and ensured that prosperity without which he believed, as had Durham, Canadians could not be expected to prefer self-government in the empire to annexation to the United States.

Elgin returned to Britain in December 1854. Despite approaches, he remained outside active politics there. In 1857 the dispute with the empire of China over the lorcha *Arrow* and British trading rights in Canton led to his commission by the Palmerston government as a special envoy to China. The mission was delayed by the need to assist in the suppression of the Indian Mutiny. In 1857, however, in consort with a French envoy, Elgin made his way by armed force into Canton, and in 1858 negotiated at Tientsin with representatives of the imperial government a treaty providing for a British minister to China, additional trading rights, protection of missionaries, and an indemnity. He then went to Japan where he concluded a commercial treaty. He returned to England in 1859 and accepted, as did other former Peelites, office in the new Palmerston government. He became postmaster general, not the best use of his talents which were diplomatic rather than administrative. However, in 1860, as a result of the Chinese government's refusal to implement the Treaty of Tientsin, Elgin was again sent with an Anglo-French military force and a French colleague to ensure the acceptance of the treaty. The army advanced to Peking and, after the murder of some English captives, the Summer Palace of the emperors was burned on Elgin's decision to avenge the insult and to enforce the signature of the treaty.

In 1861 he was appointed viceroy and governor general of India, but over-exertion on an official tour in 1862 brought a fatal heart attack the next year. There is no evident connection between Elgin's service in Jamaica and Canada and that in the Far East and India. The same decisiveness and diplomatic skill are apparent. But it is perhaps the unusual degree to which he sympathized with the Chinese he encountered and perceived the difficulties of a decadent empire that was most remarkable. He set out to understand India also, not by study of the conventions of the British regime, but in travelling among the people. It was the same desire and capacity to understand the society in which he was to govern that had enabled him to assist in creating in Canada a locally acceptable government of moderates between the extremes of race, partisanship, and tradition. What was extraordinary in Elgin's career in Canada was his immediate and imaginative mastery of his role, and the creative spirit in which he developed it.

W. L. MORTON

Elgin-Grey papers (Doughty). *Letters and journals of James, eighth Earl of Elgin*, ed. Theodore Walrond (London, 1872). R. S. Longley, *Sir Francis Hincks; a study of Canadian politics, railways, and finance in the nineteenth century* (Toronto, 1943). D. C. Masters, *The reciprocity treaty of 1854: its history, its relation to British colonial and foreign policy and to the development of Canadian fiscal autonomy* (London and Toronto, 1936). Monet, *Last cannon shot.* J. L. Morison, *British supremacy & Canadian self-government, 1839–1854* (Glasgow, 1919); *The eighth Earl of Elgin . . .* ([London], 1928). G. N. Tucker, *The Canadian commercial revolution, 1845–1851* (New Haven, Conn., 1936).

BRUCE, JOHN, primary school-teacher and inspector of schools; b. probably in 1801 in the county of Perth, Scotland; d. 19 Jan. 1866 at Lachute, Canada East.

Little is known of the first 50 years of John Bruce's life beyond the fact that he was living in Montreal before 1830 and taught there successfully for a number of years. On 2 March 1852 Bruce was appointed inspector of Protestant schools in Montreal, in Huntingdon County, and in part of Châteauguay and Argenteuil counties, under the 1851 school act which created the post of inspector and set their number at 23. The district under his jurisdiction contained 198 schools in 15 municipalities and his annual salary was $800.

From the beginning of his appointment, John Bruce took a remarkably keen interest in the advancement of teaching. In March 1853 he sent an important memorandum to the school-teachers of his district, with two parts: general directives to the trustees, teachers, and pupils themselves on the functioning of the schools, and instructions or pedagogical advice to the masters who wished to improve their teaching methods. In his statement Bruce deplored the incompetence of many teachers, attributing it to the poor salaries and scant social esteem they commanded, which in turn led to an unstable teaching body. In 1853, in his reply to the commission under Louis-Victor Sicotte*, which was investigating the state of education in Lower Canada, Bruce again stressed the incompetence of teachers: "as a body, they are, with few exceptions, much below what I would call good Common School teachers."

From 1853 to 1866 Bruce inspected the schools in his district many times. His official correspondence and inspector's reports are full of discerning remarks concerning the condition of the teachers, and of realistic assessments of the state of the schools in his district. Bruce supplemented his action on the pedagogical front by lectures on education, which included discussions of the importance of language, physical education, and a teachers' association; he also published an impressive series of articles in the *Journal of Education for Lower Canada*, founded in 1857 for educators. Several of these articles appeared in French in the *Journal de l'Instruction publique*.

John Bruce's conscientious efforts had their reward, according to his own report of the schools for which he was responsible. An extract in the *Journal of Education* begins: "Mr Bruce gives as favorable an account of the progress of the schools in this district of inspection during the year 1859 to 1860 as in his previous report, a progress which, he observes, was more than usually apparent in over one half the schools. The pupils of at least five eighths of the schools inspected showed much aptitude and were very intelligent; and an unmistakable sign of progress was the fact that many of the children appeared to understand the value of instruction, and the advantages to be derived therefrom, much better than formerly. It was also satisfactory to observe that in some municipalities the ratepayers entertained sounder views on this subject than formerly, and were not ignorant of the value of a good system of teaching. The Inspector also notices with evident pleasure the improvements introduced in the methods of instruction followed in the schools. More pains were now taken to cultivate the intellectual faculties of the children. . . ."

Bruce died while he was addressing the students of Lachute College in January 1866. He had devoted a good many years of his life to the task of teaching, and as a school inspector had rendered outstanding service to education; he had also contributed to the founding of such institutions as Lachute College (1855) and Huntingdon Academy.

LOUIS-PHILIPPE AUDET

[John Bruce's correspondence and the reports he wrote as inspector of schools to the superintendent of education, are held in ANQ-Q, QBC 27. He wrote several articles on education for the *Journal of Education for Lower Canada* (Montreal), 1859–66. L.-P.A.]

ANQ-Q, QBC 27, nos.195–209, 214–19, 234. Can., prov. du, Assemblée législative, *Journaux*, 1852–53, III, app.X; IV, app.J.J. Morgan, *Bibliotheca Canadensis*, 53. Lionel Allard et Gérard Filteau, "Un siècle au service de l'éducation, 1851–1951; l'inspection des écoles dans la province de Québec" (2v. polycopiés, [Québec, 1951]), I, II (copy at ANQ-Q). André Labarrère-Paulé, *Les instituteurs laïques au Canada français, 1836–1900* (Québec, 1965), 153, 171–74, 180.

BRUNEAU, FRANÇOIS-JACQUES, magistrate and councillor of Assiniboia; b. December 1809 at Lac Vert (Green Lake, Sask.), illegitimate son of Antoine Bruneau and a pure Cree or a Métis; d. 26 June 1865 at Saint-Boniface (Man.).

The father of François-Jacques Bruneau was probably a voyageur for the North West Company; he seems to have been related to Bruneaus prominent in Quebec society and also to Julie, wife of Louis-Joseph Papineau*. Since François-Jacques' grandparents came from Poitou, he was of recent European origin, which was not common among the Métis. Those who could referred to themselves as grandchildren of "Frenchmen from France" in an effort to achieve equal footing with their half-breed compatriots, who were mostly of recent Scottish or English ancestry.

In 1814 François-Jacques Bruneau went to Montreal with his father, where he was baptized on 28 October, and in 1822 came to the Red River Settlement. He registered in the Saint-Boniface school directed by Abbé Jean Harper; it became a classical college the following year. In 1827 he indicated a wish to enter the priesthood, news that could only please Bishop Joseph-Norbert Provencher* because of Bruneau's ability to speak the Cree language. But in 1829, when he was in first year, the first student of the college to reach that level, he decided to become a teacher. He married Marguerite Harrison, daughter of a Cree mother and a North West Company employee, probably in 1831, and abandoned teaching for farming. The censuses of Assiniboia between 1832 and 1849 indicate how his family, his property and livestock, and his carts for the transport trade, all increased. Eleven children were born to him; one of his sons, Athanase, served as a guide to Lord Milton [Wentworth-Fitzwilliam*] and Dr Walter Butler Cheadle* in 1862.

By 1849, in terms of Assiniboia, Bruneau was well off. He had also become involved in civic affairs. In July 1843 he had appeared before the Council of Assiniboia as a leading Métis in a delegation requesting a distillery (which would give the Métis an opportunity to sell their grain surplus) and regular changes in the police force (so that more of them might share in the running of the country). The return of Louis RIEL Sr from Lower Canada during the summer of 1843 took the attention away from Bruneau until 1849. Bruneau did act as honorary deacon in 1845 at the ordination into the priesthood of Alexandre-Antonin Taché*, later bishop and archbishop of Saint-Boniface, but he took such a minor part in events at this time that he even stood aloof from the attempt to obtain the dismissal of Adam Thom*, the francophobe recorder of Rupert's Land and councillor of Assiniboia. Bruneau was in a way typical of the Métis educated at Red River, who always remained diffident in the presence of the whites or half-breeds educated elsewhere. He was conciliatory, like the other Métis eventually named to the Council of Assiniboia, and easily influenced by established authority, civil or religious.

Bruneau rallied to the Métis in the spring of 1849 when, with the arrest of Pierre-Guillaume Sayer* for infringing the Hudson's Bay Company's commercial monopoly, their discontent reached its climax. Bruneau joined a vigilance committee. He alone among its members sat on the jury at Sayer's trial, although Riel was more in the public eye. Bruneau did not, however, sign the petition presented to the Council of Assiniboia in May 1849 after the trial requesting the removal of Thom and the appointment of a bilingual recorder and of French speaking Canadians and Métis to the council. Still he was one of two French Canadians and three Métis, "men of common sense able to judge soundly," recommended for appointment to the council by Bishop Provencher and approved by the Métis at a large gathering prior to their summer hunt. George Simpson*, the governor of Rupert's Land, did not share the bishop's opinions, however, and the company in London hesitated when he spoke of illiterates. Only Abbé Louis-François Laflèche* was made a councillor, in July 1850.

At this time, Bishop Provencher once again urged upon Simpson the importance of naming French Canadians and Métis to the council. Simpson, then at Red River, looked more carefully at Bruneau's candidacy, and finally recommended him to the London authorities as "a man of sound standing in the settlement & of fair education" whose appointment would promote peace among "the Canadian Half-breeds [who] form a very large proportion of the inhabitants,

and feel that they are not put on a footing of equality with the other classes in the community." In 1851, Simpson's suggestion received the support of Eden Colvile*, the governor of Rupert's Land, who also desired the appointment of Bruneau, among others, as a means of balancing the clerical element in the council.

Bruneau had been named magistrate in one of Assiniboia's judicial districts in the fall of 1850, and in 1851 was made its president or judge. On 29 March 1853 he finally took the oath as councillor of Assiniboia, the second French speaking layman after Cuthbert James Grant* to do so. He soon occupied a variety of posts paying annual salaries between £12 and £25, including that of judge in several districts. He attended council regularly but was not a vocal member.

According to contemporaries, Bruneau was approachable and courteous. A man of simple tastes, he liked to read books borrowed from the library of the HBC or of the bishop. On two occasions he defended his tutor, Bishop Provencher, in the *Nor'Wester* when it did not sufficiently recognize his contribution as an educator and civilizing influence in Red River. Bruneau always had great respect for Provencher and his successor, Taché, although he did not always share their attitudes in civil matters; he disapproved, for example, of Taché's stand in council for a duty on alcoholic beverages to curb their importation. Bruneau, who knew how to conciliate the more powerful, proposed and got accepted an amendment to exempt imports from Britain.

Bruneau died in 1865, a victim of a typhoid epidemic in the colony that also killed his wife. In 1870 only three of their daughters and one of their sons were living. He had served the authority of the HBC faithfully, without harming the interests of his Métis compatriots but also without contributing greatly to their political, social, or economic advancement.

LIONEL DORGE

ACAM, RLB, 2, p.54. Archives de l'archevêché de Saint-Boniface (Man.), Notes de Mgr Cloutier sur les commencements de l'histoire religieuse de ce pays. Cours donnés les jeudis par Mgr Taché à partir du 15 décembre 1881 à la fin de mai 1882; Registres des baptêmes, mariages et sépultures, paroisse Saint-Boniface, 1825–35, 28 juin 1865. Archives de la Société historique de Saint-Boniface (Man.), Dossier François Bruneau. Archives de l'évêché de Trois-Rivières, Correspondance Taché-Laflèche, 18 juill. 1865. HBC Arch. D.4/23, 5 Jan., 21 April 1838; D.4/70, 30 June 1849; D.4/71, 9 May, 2, 5 July 1850; D.5/25, 27 June 1849; D.5/34, 16 Aug. 1852; E.5/6, ff.3d.–4; E.5/7, ff.19d.–20; E.5/8, ff.3d.–4; E.5/9, ff.4d.–5; E.5/10, ff.4d.–5;

Brunet

E.5/11, ff.3d.–4 (mfm. at PAC). PAC, MG 9, E3, 1–3. *Les bourgeois de la Compagnie du Nord-Ouest: récits de voyages, lettres et rapports inédits relatifs au Nord-Ouest canadien*, L.-F.-R. Masson, édit. (2v., Québec, 1889–90; réimpr. New York, 1960), I, 59, 400. *Canadian North-West* (Oliver), I, 38–39, 63, 66–67, 80, 307, 352, 361, 368, 389–555. J. J. Hargrave, *Red River* (Montreal, 1871), 349. HBRS, XIX (Rich and Johnson), lxxxiii–lxxxv, xc, cxiv, 208. [J.-N. Provencher], "Lettres de Monseigneur Joseph-Norbert Provencher, premier évêque de Saint-Boniface, Manitoba," Soc. historique de Saint-Boniface, *Bull.*, III (1913), 94, 120, 122, 127. *Nor'Wester*, 14, 28 Feb., 14, 28 April 1860; 1 April, 14 Sept. 1861; 6 July, 3 Aug. 1865. Morice, *Dict. historique des Canadiens et Métis*, 53–54. Giraud, *Le Métis canadien*, 902–3, 905–63. Ross, *Red River Settlement* (1957), 239. A.-H. de Trémaudan, *Histoire de la nation métisse dans l'Ouest canadien* ([Montréal, 1935]), 135. F.-J. Audet, "François Bruneau," *BRH*, XXXVII (1931), 274–78, 600–1. J.-J. Lefebvre, "La vie sociale du grand Papineau," *RHAF*, XI (1957–58), 483–84. [Louis] Mailhot, "François Bruneau," *Les Cloches de Saint-Boniface* (Saint-Boniface, Man.), XLV (1946), 69–72.

BRUNET, ALEXANDRE-AUGUSTE (he signed Auguste), priest, Oblate of Mary Immaculate, missionary; b. 7 Oct. 1816 at Pont-en-Royans (dept of Isère, France), son of Jean-Baptiste Brunet, a merchant, and Marie Blain; d. 27 June 1866 at Montreal.

Alexandre-Auguste Brunet attended the Collège de Saint-Marcellin and the Petit Séminaire de Côte-Saint-André in Isère. In 1837 he joined the army but left it the following year and completed his studies at the Petit Séminaire. He was admitted to the noviciate of the Oblates of Notre-Dame de l'Osier on 14 Aug. 1841, took his perpetual vows there on 15 Aug. 1842, and began his theological studies. He was sent to Canada at the end of 1843, and Bishop Ignace Bourget* ordained him priest at Longueuil on 29 Aug. 1844.

Father Brunet and Father Eusèbe Durocher were the first Oblates to undertake the difficult work as missionaries to the lumber camps on the Gatineau and Ottawa rivers. He went there as early as January 1845, but in November returned to Longueuil to devote himself to parish missions. He was recalled to the lumber camp mission in 1849, and lived at Bytown (Ottawa) where he ministered to young lumbermen on their way through the town. He was also engaged in directing the seminarists and gave a few courses at the local college. At the same time he took charge of preaching and was chaplain at the mother house of the Grey Nuns. His favourite work, however, was in the lumber camps among the employees whom he visited regularly and called his "dear children." Brunet left a small manuscript entitled "Le guide des voyageurs," dedicated to Joseph-Bruno Guigues*, bishop of Bytown. The work, drafted after 1848, contains a series of canticles, a kind of treatise on the "temporal and spiritual duties of the voyageur" and "religious exercises for the voyageur." The canticles, set to familiar tunes such as "Quand Marianne s'en va au moulin" or "Un Canadien errant," showed the missionary's concern to adapt himself to the mentality of the faithful. In September 1855 Brunet had to give up his ministry because of poor health. He went to the Oblate residence of Saint-Pierre-Apôtre at Montreal, to devote himself once more to popular preaching in Canada and in several American dioceses.

At this time the preaching in Illinois of the former Oblate, Charles-Paschal-Télesphore Chiniquy*, was attracting people away from the Roman Catholic Church, and Bishop Anthony O'Regan of Chicago turned to Bishop Bourget for assistance. The latter passed on the request to Mgr Guigues who demurred somewhat, asserting that the mission was far away and they were short of men; finally, in October 1858, Fathers Lucien-Antoine Lagier* and Brunet were sent to fight the schism. They exercised their apostolate first at Bourbonnais; then Brunet went to Kankakee while Lagier took over the mission at St Anne, Ill. Following their preaching, "about 150 schismatics" returned to the practice of the Catholic religion. When the missionaries were preparing to return to Canada, Chiniquy had Father Brunet arrested, "on the false pretext," *Le Canadien* wrote, "that the reverend Father had accused him of having had the church at Bourbonnais burned down in 1853." Thanks to a bond of more than $2,000 put up by the Catholics of Kankakee, Brunet was able to return immediately to Canada. Chiniquy brought a libel action against Brunet, however, in the circuit court of Kankakee, which began on 13 April 1859. The missionary was ordered to pay Chiniquy damages amounting to $4,625. An appeal was launched and a new trial was held in January 1860. The jury sustained the verdict of guilty but reduced the fine to $2,500. The bishop of Chicago then decided to bring the case before the United States Supreme Court, but later abandoned the plan. Brunet declared himself insolvent and was forced to go to prison in May 1861. He thus obliged Chiniquy to pay his board in prison, instead of his paying Chiniquy the damages fixed by the judge. An enterprising Catholic managed to engineer Brunet's escape after three months of confinement, and the priest returned to Montreal in August. The affair seems to have had no sequel.

Even though his imprisonment played a large part in destroying his already impaired health, Brunet none the less continued to preach until he was stricken with paralysis in 1866. He died in June, leaving behind him the memory of a good-humoured and simple man who had distinguished himself by his zest for work.

GASTON CARRIÈRE

AHO, Auguste Brunet, "Le guide des voyageurs . . ."; Nérée Gingras, "Mémoire du procès du père Brunet, oblat, de sa condamnation, de son emprisonnement, de son évasion de la prison de Kankakee . . .". Archives départementales de l'Isère (Grenoble), État civil, Pont-en-Royans, 7 oct. 1816. Archives des Sœurs grises de la Croix d'Ottawa, Correspondance Bruyère, 21 janv. 1845. Archives provinciales O.M.I. (Montréal), *Codex historicus*, Montréal, I, 157–62 (copies at AHO). *Rapport sur les missions du diocèse de Québec . . .*, no. 10 (mars 1853), 88–95; no. 11 (mars 1855), 17–21. *Le Canadien*, 26 nov. 1858. *Notices nécrologiques des O.M.I.*, I, 273–99. Carrière, *Hist. des O.M.I.*, I, II, IV. [C.-P.-T. Chiniquy], *Mes combats, autobiographie de Charles Chiniquy, apôtre de la tempérance du Canada* (Montréal, s.d.). Marcel Trudel, *Chiniquy* (2e éd., [Trois-Rivières], 1955), 209. Gaston Carrière, "Une mission tragique aux Illinois; Chiniquy et les oblats," *RHAF*, VIII (1954–55), 518–55. Léo Deschâtelets, "Le guide des voyageurs," *La Bannière de Marie-Immaculée* (Ottawa), XLVIII (1940), 82–92.

BUCHANAN, ALEXANDER CARLISLE, public servant; b. 25 Dec. 1808 at Common Green, a large farm near Omagh in County Tyrone (Northern Ireland), son of James Buchanan and Elizabeth Clarke; m. 3 Nov. 1840 Charlotte Louise Caldwell, daughter of Edward BOWEN, chief justice of the Superior Court of Lower Canada, and they had four sons and two daughters; d. 2 Feb. 1868 at Quebec.

Alexander Carlisle Buchanan received part of his education in Ireland before his father, who ran a linen business there until 1816, was appointed British consul in New York and brought his family to the United States. In 1825 Alexander Carlisle came to Canada and he and his brother, Robert Stewart, were partners in business, apparently in Montreal.

Buchanan's uncle, also named Alexander Carlisle Buchanan, was the British agent for emigration at Quebec from 1828 until 1838. At least as early as 1833 the younger Buchanan (who sometimes added Jr to his signature) looked after the immigration office during the winter while his uncle took a leave of absence for his health. He did so regularly from 1835 to 1838, when the elder Buchanan resigned because of illness. In that year the British government appointed Buchanan chief agent "for the Superintendence of Emigra-

tion to [Lower and Upper] Canada." He had lived in Quebec perhaps from 1833 and continued to reside there until his death.

Buchanan was not an officer of the Canadian government, although he worked in Canada; he exercised a limited supervision over other emigration agents appointed by British authorities to such strategic locations as Montreal, Kingston, Toronto, and Hamilton. After 1848, however, he submitted his annual reports to the Executive Council of the Province of Canada before transmission to London. In the following years his title gradually changed to that of chief emigration agent and he was required to present his reports to the Legislative Assembly. In 1852 the Canadian government established a Bureau of Agriculture, one of whose responsibilities was immigration, and in 1855 Canada assumed the total cost of immigration services within the province. After the Department of Agriculture and Statistics was established in 1862 Buchanan's reports were included in those of the minister. Thus by the 1860s Buchanan had ceased to have the status of an imperial official and had become a Canadian civil servant, an evolution brought about by the achievement of responsible government in Canada.

Buchanan's exercise of his functions was affected by the inefficient and uncoordinated administration of immigration matters by the colonial government. The Bureau of Agriculture had been formed originally to take over some of the tasks of the Department of Crown Lands, which, however, retained a role in the promotion of immigration until 1862. The lack of clear purposes and prestige for the bureau is evident in the fact that it had no fewer than nine ministers between 1852 and 1862; moreover, it was the presidents of the Executive Council who were until March 1862 *ex officio* ministers of agriculture, and their many duties inevitably distracted them from the bureau's work, of which immigration was only one part. In 1862 the Department of Agriculture and Statistics became solely responsible for immigration and the situation improved, particularly with the appointment, in 1864, of Thomas D'Arcy MCGEE as minister and Joseph-Charles Taché* as first deputy minister.

The bureau's weaknesses had increased the burden on and enhanced the importance of its permanent officials among whom Buchanan was the one most concerned with the promotion of immigration. Quebec was the major port of entry, and when immigrants landed there Buchanan met them with information about transportation, employment, and land for purchase. For this purpose he collected information from subordinate agents in Canada and from employers, farmers, and landowners. He also sent this material to government emigration officers in Britain as well as to anyone interested in encouraging emigration, such as shipowners and landowners. Buchanan even undertook to have promotional literature distributed on the Continent. He took seriously one of the main purposes of his office, the protection of immigrants when they arrived. Often bewildered and uninformed about North America, they were easy prey for unscrupulous tricks. To safeguard their funds Buchanan sent them directly to locations where they could quickly find suitable work. Moreover, to guard immigrants from "runners" who sold tickets to destinations far inland, usually in the United States, he directed them to specific Canadian steamship companies and railway offices. Indeed occasionally between 1854 and 1862 Buchanan himself engaged in selling tickets and in remitting money to emigrants in Europe. He finally ended these business connections because of criticism, although a government investigation in 1861–62 showed he had not abused his position.

Buchanan's experience with immigration at the Canadian end and his knowledge of the conditions in Europe led him in 1852 to advocate sending Canadian emigration agents to Europe. Despite the support of the secretary of the Bureau of Agriculture, William HUTTON, and of two prominent politicians, Philip Michael Matthew Scott VANKOUGHNET and McGee, nothing was done until 1859. And it was actually the commissioner of crown lands, VanKoughnet, rather than the minister of agriculture, John Ross*, who first sent an emigration agent, Anthony Bewden HAWKE, to England in 1859.

Hawke returned in 1860, and Buchanan was sent to England in 1861 and 1863 on short term missions. He continued Hawke's work of advertising Canada but, as the department's most experienced senior official, he was given much wider duties. He was to consider the establishment of Canadian emigration agencies in the United Kingdom and the advertising of Canada on the Continent, including France, Switzerland, and Poland. The Canadian government most consistently sought to attract farmers with capital, farm labourers, and female domestic servants. Buchanan was the central distributing agent for Canadian publicity and supervised the other temporary agents promoting emigration to Canada. His report dated 30 Oct. 1861 accounted for work done and also made far-reaching recommendations, including a permanent Canadian agency for London which would perform consular functions as well as those of a central emigra-

tion agency. Much of what he proposed for an emigration agency was instituted in 1866 when William Dixon* was sent to Liverpool, and in 1869 Dixon was transferred to London where a central emigration agency with consular functions was put into effect.

Buchanan's chief contributions to Canada's development were his careful administration of the immigration agency at Quebec and his consistent support for a Canadian presence overseas particularly in the form of emigration agencies. From 1838 to 1868, about 866,000 immigrants came to Canada chiefly from the British Isles, and for many thousands who landed in Quebec, Buchanan provided the first official guidance to their new life in Canada. It is impossible to measure the benefits to Canada's growth of his sympathetic treatment of them. His knowledge and good sense gave weight to his opinions and enabled him to maintain harmonious relations with the Canadian emigration agents who were sent to Europe in the 1860s.

WESLEY B. TURNER

[Alexander Carlisle Buchanan sent great quantities of emigration literature to Europe, but aside from official reports and pamphlets he apparently published no writing of his own. A pamphlet, *Emigration practically considered; with detailed directions to emigrants proceeding to British North America, particularly to the Canadas; in a letter to the Right Hon. R. Wilmot Horton, M.P.* (London, 1828), often attributed to him, was almost certainly written by his uncle, although the younger Buchanan may have had a hand in the publication of the second edition in 1834. W.B.T.]

PAC, RG 4, A1, S-203, mai–nov. 1836; S-227, 1re partie, 10 janv. 1830; S-245, 17 août 1830; S-296, 1re partie, 31 déc. 1832; S-313, 5 nov. 1833; S-344, 26 sept. 1835; S-392, 1re partie, 23 déc. 1837; B28, 40, no.2378; C1, 234, no.2535; 338, no.1675; RG 17, AI, ser.1, 3, 8, 18–19; ser.2, 2–4; AIII, ser.1, 1–2. Can., *Sessional papers*, 1867–68, III, no.3. Can., Prov. of, *Sessional papers*, 1860, III, no.18; 1861, III, no.14; IV, no.23; 1862, V, no.32; 1863, III, no.4; 1864, III, no.32; 1865, II, no.6. *Montreal Gazette*, 1829–31, 4 Feb. 1867. *Quebec Gazette*, 6 Nov. 1840, 3 Feb. 1868. A. W. P. Buchanan, *The Buchanan book; the life of Alexander Buchanan, Q.C., of Montreal, followed by an account of the family of Buchanan* (Montreal, 1911), 197–230, 234–35. H. I. Cowan, *British emigration to British North America; the first hundred years* (Toronto, 1961). Hodgetts, *Pioneer public service*, 40, 226–43, 251, 255. W. B. Turner, "Colonial self-government and the colonial agency; changing concepts of permanent Canadian representation in London, 1848 to 1880" (unpublished PHD thesis, Duke University, Durham, N.C., 1970).

BUELL, WILLIAM, journalist and politician; b. 28 Feb. 1792 at Elizabethtown (Brockville),

Upper Canada, eldest son of Martha Naughton and William Buell*, the loyalist founder of Brockville; m. first, Mary-Ann Angelica Story, by whom he had three children, secondly, Deborah Dockstader, by whom he had four children, and thirdly, Catherine Dockstader; d. 29 April 1862 at Brockville.

William Buell was educated in a local school financed largely by his father and at Les Cèdres, Lower Canada. An Anglican in his early years, he spent most of his adult life as a Presbyterian. He was decorated for participating in 1813 in the battle at Crysler's Farm and in the attack on Ogdensburg, N.Y., led by "Red George" MACDONELL.

Buell inherited 125 acres of prime land in the Brockville area, operated a book store in the town from at least 1830 until 1852, and was editor of the *Brockville Recorder* from 1823 to 1849. Under his editorship and with the aid of his brother, Andrew Norton Buell*, the *Recorder* became a prominent newspaper which supported reform causes and expounded the views of much of eastern Upper Canada. During the 1820s and early 1830s it particularly represented the interests of Brockville expansionists such as James MORRIS who were attempting to develop a system of canals on the St Lawrence River so that Brockville could compete with other commercial centres such as Kingston and York (Toronto). When the flow of Upper Canadian trade shifted from the St Lawrence to Toronto and the Erie Canal in the late 1830s and 1840s, the *Recorder* increasingly articulated the views of comparatively static agrarian and business interests in Leeds County. Buell came to recognize that Brockville would be surpassed by other centres and that canal and railway developments were disastrously expensive. He opposed costly public works projects because he believed they overtaxed the poor and encouraged corruption.

Buell inherited from his father a long-standing local rivalry with the loyalist and Tory families of Solomon* and Ephraim Jones* and Levius Peters Sherwood*. The competition seems to have been motivated only occasionally by personal animus; usually it emanated from pronounced ideological differences, intense political ambitions, and competition for government patronage. Despite the intensity of the rivalries, the four old families between 1820 and 1860 frequently submerged differences and cooperated in economic and social ventures, especially during the early 1830s, when they campaigned for increased autonomy for Brockville (which became Upper Canada's first town under the authority of a police board in 1832), the construction of locally owned steamships, and the improvement of the St Lawrence transportation system. William Buell played a prominent role in these joint efforts.

This frequent cooperation, however, did not produce harmonious political relationships. From 1801 until the 1860s the four families struggled for political supremacy in the Brockville area, and the Joneses and Sherwoods often joined forces to thwart the Buells. William Buell was a stable and effective leader whose ability frequently enabled his family and the Reform cause in Leeds to equal the Tory forces.

The arrival in the 1820s and 1830s of thousands of Protestant Irish immigrants who settled in the interior townships complicated political competition in Leeds. Viewed suspiciously by older settlers and unfamiliar with the colony's economic, social, and political institutions, the Irish soon became a discordant local element. Organized in Orange lodges, they constituted a powerful Conservative voting bloc under the leadership of Ogle R. Gowan*. In the provincial election of 1830 Buell and his Reform running mate, Mathew H. Howard, defeated Gowan and Henry Sherwood* in Leeds, but Gowan received more votes than Sherwood and only 70 less than Buell. In the assembly Buell became a strong supporter of a decentralized education system, temperance legislation, cautious economic expansion, and liberal political reform.

Between elections Buell used the *Recorder* to fight Gowan, who employed a series of financially troubled newspapers he operated in Brockville. In the 1834 election Buell and Howard were opposed by Gowan and Robert Sympson Jameson*, the attorney general. The election was conducted at the village of Beverly, an Orange stronghold. Widespread drinking, violence, and intimidation, especially of Reform voters, marked the election. Buell and Howard withdrew and on their appeal the Reform-dominated assembly ordered a new election, but Lieutenant Governor Sir John COLBORNE again designated Beverly as the polling place. In the election held in March 1835 Buell and Howard again charged intimidation and appealed to the assembly, which passed a special election act designating four polling stations in Leeds County, thereby making it difficult for Gowan's supporters to disrupt the voting. Buell and Howard easily won the by-election of 28 March 1836. In the summer of 1836 Sir Francis Bond Head* called a new general election. Gowan and the old Tory families buried their differences and formed a strong anti-Reform coalition in Brockville and throughout Leeds to support Head. The county election, held at Beverly, saw Buell and the Reformers soundly defeated.

Following this reversal, Buell entered a period of relative political inactivity. He was a devoted monarchist and an adherent of the British liberalism of Robert* and William Warren Baldwin*. He favoured an extended franchise, responsible government, and educational reform, and advocated an increasing role for the press as educator. Like the Baldwins in Toronto, he withdrew from the Reform movement as William Lyon MACKENZIE and other radicals gained influence. When rebellion broke out in 1837, Buell was the first local militia officer to report for duty against the rebels. In 1838 he led his battalion to Prescott to resist the Patriot invasion.

After the rebellion Buell started a long campaign to restore the Reform cause in the county. The *Recorder* increasingly voiced the attitudes of eastern Upper Canadian farmers, and Buell expounded on the need for agrarian reform, reduced government expenditures, regional improvements, and local control. His campaign was in part rewarded in 1848, when, though he lost his own bid for a seat in Brockville, his nephew, William Buell Richards*, won easily in Leeds County. Richards and his brother, Albert Norton Richards*, were to become important Reform politicians in the 1850s and 1860s.

William Buell sold the *Recorder* in 1849 to David Wylie* and William Sutton and became a gentleman farmer, spending much of his time in Brockville. He was mayor of the town in 1856 and 1857; his term of office was featured by cautious expenditure and careful administration. Buell retired to his farm in 1858 and died there in 1862.

IAN MACPHERSON

PAC, MG 24, B75. PAO, Buell (Andrew Norton) papers. *Brockville Recorder* (Brockville, [Ont.]), 1830–49. *Gazette* (Brockville, [Ont.]), 1828–32. T. W. H. Leavitt, *History of Leeds and Grenville, Ontario, from 1749 to 1879, with illustrations and biographical sketches of some of its prominent men and pioneers* (Brockville, Ont., 1879). G. R. I. MacPherson, "The code of Brockville's Buells" (unpublished MA thesis, University of Western Ontario, London, Ont., 1966). Hereward Senior, *Orangeism, the Canadian phase* (Toronto, 1972). E. M. Richards, "The Joneses of Brockville and the Family Compact," *OH*, LX (1968), 169–84.

BULL COLLAR. *See* PEENAQUIM

BULLER, Sir ARTHUR WILLIAM, member of the Executive Council and the Special Council of Lower Canada and head of a commission of inquiry into education; b. 5 Sept. 1808 at Calcutta, India, son of Charles Buller, a civil servant in Bengal, and Barbara Isabella Kirkpatrick; m. Annie Templar in 1842; d. 30 April 1869 in London, England.

Arthur William Buller received his primary education at Edinburgh and entered Trinity College, Cambridge, where he obtained a BA (1830) and MA (1834), before being called to the bar. On 27 May 1838 Arthur William and his brother Charles* reached Quebec with Lord Durham [Lambton*], whom the British parliament had instructed to investigate the situation in Lower Canada following the rebellion. Noting the deplorable state of education in the province, Durham on 4 July made Buller a commissioner responsible for conducting an inquiry into it. Buller, who had become a member of the Executive Council of Lower Canada on 28 June, was to "proceed with the utmost despatch to inquire into and investigate the past and present modes of disposing of the produce of any Estate or Funds applicable to purposes of Education in Lower Canada. . . ." His commission further stipulated that it was "expedient and desirable that such a system of education should be established as may conduce to the diffusion of knowledge, religion and virtue," and Buller was to make suggestions with this end in view. To carry out his undertaking, Buller could question individuals, consult public documents, laws, and official papers, and if necessary co-opt assistant commissioners possessing the same authority.

Anxious to complete his inquiry successfully, Buller, with the assistance of his secretary Christopher Dunkin*, prepared a questionnaire for prominent persons and priests of each parish in order to collect as much information as possible about the organization of the school system. However, the majority of people able to provide him with useful data dissociated themselves from the inquiry, and some even attempted to prevent its completion. Buller then had recourse to an associate, who collected information and classified it, and had some of it sent to Buller in England after his departure in November. The inquiry was conducted with numerous consultations, and received newspaper publicity. Bishop Jean-Jacques Lartigue* of Montreal agreed in spite of his distrust to give the commissioner information about the Catholic schools in his diocese. *Le Populaire*, a Montreal newspaper directed by Hyacinthe-Poirier LEBLANC de Marconnay, published 21 articles on education from 23 July to 29 Oct. 1838. Dr Jean-Baptiste Meilleur* also replied to Buller's invitation, and outlined his views on education in a series of seven articles, published in *Le Populaire* in August 1838 and reprinted in *Le Canadien* of Quebec. All the suggestions, which were well received, did not however correspond with the purposes of the investigators, who wanted to anglicize the French Canadians. The inquiry, begun 1 August, was concluded in November 1838, such a brief period being clearly insufficient time for an accurate appreciation of a complex situation.

Buller's report, curiously, was dated 18 Nov. 1838 (three days before he left for England), but was presented to the British parliament in June 1839. It consisted of two parts: one on the past and present state of education in Lower Canada, the other on a future system of national education. In the first part, which contained the results of his inquiry, Buller studied the content and application of the various school acts since 1801. He repeatedly insisted that education grants had served political ends, and had helped only to further the interests of the Parti Canadien of Louis-Joseph Papineau*, rather than those of the schools. In addition he stressed the sterling qualities of the common people of Lower Canada and of Canadian women, criticized the unimaginative farming practices of the Canadiens, and praised the seminaries run by the Catholic clergy, particularly the seminary of Quebec and the work of Abbé John Holmes*.

After this brief historical outline, Arthur Buller sketched his new school system, based on the anglicization of French Canadians, the exclusion of politics from schools, religious instruction, and the imposition of an obligatory school tax. To attain the first objective, Buller proposed that the youth of both races should be brought together as often as possible in the same schools and through games and social activities. After some thoughts on how politics might be kept out of the schools, Buller tackled the delicate problem of religious instruction. As there were a certain number of points on which all Christians agreed, he advocated the creation of a committee responsible for selecting biblical passages acceptable to all, and preparing commentaries for each section of the catechism. If any one of the religious denominations found this teaching inadequate, it could add the religious instruction it deemed essential after school. This proposal aroused serious objections on the part of the Catholics, who thought the Catholic church alone should be responsible for education. For their part, the Protestants considered that Buller's plan undermined the very principle of free interpretation of the Bible.

To settle the problem of school financing, Buller suggested a direct tax be imposed. In his opinion the taxpayers (landed proprietors) and the public treasury should provide at least an equal amount, state aid from then on being only complementary to the voluntary efforts of each school district.

Further on in his report, the commissioner foresaw the establishment of primary, model, and normal schools, institutions of higher or academic learning, and a university at Quebec. He also insisted on the training of good teachers who would be expressly forbidden to engage in political activity, on pain of dismissal. To Buller's way of thinking the new school system must be based on the close control of teaching. He therefore devised a plan of inspection and supervision for the future national schools from which the Catholic clergy would be totally excluded.

Buller's report, which advocated a system of education inspired by those of the United States and Prussia, and sought primarily to unify the two races of Lower Canada by anglicizing French Canadians, was far from perfect. Prepared rapidly by an official who was completely ignorant of the problems peculiar to Lower Canada and had stayed in the country only briefly, the report contained erroneous statements and unrealizable plans. On the other hand, it offered some interesting suggestions, for instance concerning the exclusion of politics from schools, recruitment of future masters, teaching of agriculture in the normal schools, and improvement of teachers' salaries. Other proposals, such as the establishment of municipalities responsible for local problems, of the post of superintendent of education, and of a permanent education fund accruing from the Jesuit estates, the clergy reserves, and compulsory taxes, were to appear in the various school acts of the 1840s. In 1841 Buller's report, which was ill received by Canadian religious authorities, inspired Charles-Elzéar Mondelet* to write his *Letters on elementary and practical education*. The latter influenced the drafting of an education bill which was presented by Governor Sydenham [Thomson*] and passed on 18 Sept. 1841.

Arthur Buller was also a member of the Special Council from 22 Aug. to 2 Nov. 1838. He returned to England on 21 November. In 1840 he was appointed crown attorney in Ceylon, and held this post until 1848. He was made a judge of the Supreme Court of Calcutta and served in that capacity until 1858. Buller died in April 1869 in London, after being a member of the British House of Commons for ten years.

LOUIS-PHILIPPE AUDET

101

Bunch Sonego

[J. G. Lambton], *Lord Durham's report on the affairs of British North America*, ed. C. P. Lucas (3v., Oxford, 1912), III; *Le rapport de Durham*, M.-P. Hamel, trad. et édit. (Montréal, 1948). *Le Populaire* (Montréal), août–sept. 1838. Boase, *Modern English biog.*, I, 469. *Debrett's illustrated peerage and baronetage of the United Kingdom of Great Britain and Ireland* (London, 1868). Desjardins, *Guide parlementaire*. L.-A. Desrosiers, "Correspondance de Mgr Lartigue et de son coadjuteur, Mgr Bourget, de 1837 à 1840," ANQ *Rapport*, 1945–46. L.-P. Audet, *Hist. de l'enseignement*, I, 386–403; *Le système scolaire*, VI. L.[-A.] Groulx, *L'enseignement français au Canada* (2v., Montréal, 1931–33). André Labarrère-Paulé, *Les instituteurs laïques au Canada français, 1836–1900* (Québec, 1965).

BUNCH SONEGO, CATHERINE. *See* NAHNE-BAHWEQUAY

BUNN, JOHN, doctor, councillor of Assiniboia, and magistrate; b. probably in 1802 at an HBC post on Hudson Bay, son of Thomas Bunn and Sarah McNab who was of part-Indian blood; d. on 31 May 1861 at Red River; an Anglican, he was buried in St John's Cathedral cemetery.

Most of John Bunn's early childhood was spent with his family at York Factory (Man.) where his English-born father was employed as a writer by the Hudson's Bay Company. Whatever uncertainty the death of his mother in 1806 brought into his life, young John was well cared for by his father and by his Scottish grandfather, John McNab, a surgeon and the chief factor at York Factory. Thanks to their generous assistance, he attended a good school in Edinburgh and then began to study medicine at the University of Edinburgh. In 1819, when he had only two years' medical training, not enough to graduate, he was persuaded by McNab to accept a position as surgeon at Moose Factory. Upon reaching Moose Factory in September of that year, Bunn had grave misgivings about the wisdom of his grandfather's decision in sending a not yet fully qualified doctor into the wilderness of Rupert's Land. Uneasy as he was about his future, during the next five years Bunn gained considerable experience by serving the HBC as a surgeon at several posts as well as on the company's ship, the *Eddystone*.

With no real taste for a nomadic existence, Bunn in 1824 left the HBC service and moved to the Red River Settlement to begin a private medical practice. Here, in the vicinity of Middlechurch, he lived with his father who had retired two years earlier. Here too, on 23 July 1829, he married Catherine Thomas, the daughter of his father's close friend Thomas Thomas*, a former governor of the Northern Department.

Because of his family connections and his professional status, Bunn was able to move easily in the influential circles of Red River society. A witty, good-natured, and vigorous man, with a dark complexion and a handsome bearing, Bunn the doctor was as popular with the HBC establishment as he was with the half-caste population of the settlement.

Feeling the need to upgrade his qualifications, Bunn again attended the University of Edinburgh during the 1831–32 academic session, and returned to Red River in 1832 not with a degree but as a licentiate of the Royal College of Surgeons at Edinburgh. He was happy to come home to his wife Catherine who had cheered him with her affectionate letters while he was abroad. A little over a year after his return, on 3 Jan. 1834, came her death, and he never remarried. He and his three small boys, one of whom was Thomas*, continued to live comfortably in his father's household which was ably managed by his half-breed stepmother Phoebe Sinclair Bunn.

From 1835, when he became a member of the Council of Assiniboia, until his death, John Bunn was usually the only doctor in the settlement, and he mingled his private practice with public medical work. Beyond his private earnings, he received from the council during this period an annual salary of £100 as compensation for his free services to the poor of Red River. In the absence of a hospital and a pharmacy, and with shortages of essential medicines and vaccines, Bunn found himself struggling to control the scourges of whooping cough, scarlet fever, influenza, measles, and cholera that made their appearance in Red River from time to time. Dressing cuts and bruises and setting fractured limbs, providing remedies for common colds, and calling upon sufferers in their homes, all were among his routine activities and helped to make him a highly respected family physician.

In addition to his concern for the health of the Red River community, Bunn, as one of the most active councillors of Assiniboia, played a significant part in local government. His work on the council, which he approached with a pragmatic outlook and with an initimate knowledge of the affairs of Red River, was intended to encourage the development of an orderly society and the cultural and material growth of the settlement. Partly through his strong support of Eden Colvile*, governor of Rupert's Land, who regarded him as "the most sensible man in the Settlement," the government of Assiniboia, which had collapsed under the administration of Major William Bletterman Caldwell* in the late 1840s, was again made effective. Besides steering the council into voting financial aid for the Red River Agricultural Association and for the expansion of educational facilities, Bunn during his tenure as chairman of the Board of Public Works from 1856 to 1861 induced the council to spend a good deal of money on the construction of roads and the bridging of streams tributary to the Red and Assiniboine rivers.

The HBC's belief in John Bunn's ability, integrity, and sound judgement – a belief shared by an overwhelming majority of the inhabitants of Red River – led to his appointment to a variety of legal posts: magistrate of the Lower District, 1837–1849; coroner of Assiniboia, 1849–1861; sheriff and governor of the jail, 1856–1861; and, finally, recorder of Rupert's Land, 1858–1861, in which capacity he directed the proceedings of the General Quarterly Court of Assiniboia. In conducting the business of the recordership Bunn reached the height of his authority as a judicial administrator, and was faced with the most serious cases in Assiniboia. Individuals were brought before him in court for manslaughter, robbery, debt, and the illegal sale of liquor.

Diligent and conscientious in his many tasks, John Bunn drove himself at an exhausting pace. At the same time, he could relax and was fond of the merry Red River balls, and by reading professional journals and English newspapers he kept in touch with the medical field and the outside world. Proudly aware of his mixed English, Indian, and Scottish heritage, he was representative of important strands in the Red River civilization of the mid 19th century.

H. C. KLASSEN

PAM, MG 2, C21, John Bunn to Donald Ross, 12 March 1848. *Canadian North-West* (Oliver), I, 61–62, 268–69, 280, 314, 353, 358, 360, 368, 387, 395–96, 420, 423–25, 430–31, 433–34, 446–47, 478. *Hargrave correspondence* (Glazebrook), 158, 181, 342, 452. HBRS, XIX (Rich and Johnson), c-cv, 24–25, 213–16. Mactavish, *Letters of Letitia Hargrave* (MacLeod), liv, 105, 143–44, 169–70. *Nor'Wester*, 1859–62. "Private letters from the fur trade," ed. Clifford Wilson, HSSM *Papers*, 3rd ser., no.5 (1950), 28. *Pioneers of Man.* (Morley *et al.*), 34–35. Denis Bayley, *A Londoner in Rupert's Land: Thomas Bunn of the Hudson's Bay Company* (Chichester, Eng., 1969), 14–15, 31–32, 39–40, 57–60, 62–63, 65–67, 69–71, 73–75, 88, 92–97. W. J. Healy, *Women of Red River; being a book written down from the recollections of women surviving from the Red River era* (Winnipeg, 1923), 26, 49–50, 201, 216–19. R. B. Mitchell, *Medicine in Manitoba; the story of its beginnings* ([Winnipeg, 1955]), 37–46. R. St G. Stubbs, *Four recorders of Rupert's Land; a brief survey of the Hudson's Bay Company courts of Rupert's Land* (Winnipeg, 1967), 91–134. S. P. Matheson, "Floods at Red River," HSSM *Papers*, 3rd ser., no.3 (1947), 13. E. A. Mitchell, "A Red River gossip," *Beaver*, outfit 291 (spring 1961), 9, 11. Ross Mitchell, "Doctor John Bunn," *Beaver*, outfit 269 (December 1938), 50–53; "Early doctors of Red River and Manitoba," HSSM *Papers*, 3rd ser., no. 4 ([1949]), 39–41.

BUNNING, MARIA (the name is sometimes written von Bunning), named **Sister Mary Martha**; sister in the Congregation of the Sisters of St Joseph, foundress and first superior of the Sisters of St Joseph of the diocese of Hamilton; b. 1824 in the parish of Husen or Husum, Kingdom of Hanover (West Germany), daughter of Wileum and Ellen Bunning; d. 13 June 1868 at Toronto, Ont.

When Maria Bunning came to America she lived in the St Louis area on the Mississippi River. At age 21 she entered the Congregation of the Sisters of St Joseph of Carondelet at St Louis and received the religious habit. In August 1848 she professed the vows of perpetual poverty, chastity, and obedience, taking the name Sister Mary Martha. She began work in the order's convent, boarding school, and orphanage, and with Mother Delphine Fontbonne, a pioneer of the American community, taught in St Vincent's School, the first parochial school in St Louis.

The 45-member St Louis community lost three sisters during the cholera epidemic of 1849–51, when requests for their help, especially in caring for homeless children, increased. In 1850 Sister Martha was sent with Mother Delphine to Philadelphia to operate an orphanage, a school, and a hospital, and while there she became the superior of St Ann's Widows' Asylum.

Despite limited personnel and heavy commitments the Sisters of St Joseph answered an urgent appeal of Bishop Armand de Charbonnel* of Toronto to extend their charitable work to Canada. After a week's journey by boat and stage coach from Philadelphia, Mother Delphine, Sister Mary Martha, and two other sisters arrived on 7 Oct. 1851 in Toronto, where they were met by John ELMSLEY and other representatives of the Catholic community.

On 19 April 1852, at the request of Vicar General Edward John GORDON of Toronto, Sister Mary Martha and two novices moved to Hamilton. Sister Martha was appointed superior, and Gordon provided a house for a convent and orphanage. In 1853 the separate schools of the city were placed under the direction of the sisters, who also opened a private school at their convent. Seven sisters from Toronto helped in the work, and novices from Hamilton were sent to Toronto to be trained. In response to Mother Martha's appeal for contributions to support the orphanage, the citizens of Hamilton donated the proceeds of a public concert in 1853; this became an annual event, known as the Orphans' Festival, and it provided a major portion of the orphanage's financial assistance for over 100 years. In the early years the festival engaged professional talent and was responsible for bringing noted singers and entertainers to Hamilton. Gradually, the children began performing shows written by the sisters, for which they also composed music and designed costumes. Ever mindful of the orphans, Mother Martha and her sisters collected money, food, clothing, and wood in the city of Hamilton, throughout the diocese, and in outlying areas as far as Goderich. Farmers offered horses and wagons to transport the sisters and the supplies they collected. Despite the physical hardships of the expeditions, made even in winter, and the ridicule of some who criticized the sisters' collections as begging, they remained a means of support for the orphans for many years. A government grant of $600 was procured in 1856 through Sir Allan Napier MacNab, a benefactor of the sisters. The grant was given annually and was increased in later years. During the cholera epidemic of 1854, and in the typhus epidemic that followed, Mother Martha witnessed the self-sacrifice of her sisters who cared for the afflicted immigrants throughout the city. On some occasions their ministrations included the burial of the dead.

John Farrell*, who became bishop of Hamilton in 1856 when the diocese of Toronto was divided, encouraged the Sisters of St Joseph to expand their charitable and educational activities. At this time the Hamilton convent became the motherhouse and noviciate for the Hamilton diocese, and a new convent was opened in 1857. Between 1852 and 1862, 23 novices were received into the Hamilton congregation and by 1862 the community numbered approximately 28. Under Mother Martha's capable management branch houses were opened in quick succession in Paris, Brantford, and Oakville, and a hospital and a home for the poor and destitute were established in Guelph in 1861.

The arduous responsibilities of her office weakened the health of Mother Martha, who, saddened by misunderstandings involving her authority, resigned in August 1862. She returned to St Louis and resumed teaching; in 1865 she was appointed superior of a hospital and home in Erie, Pa. Realizing that her health was declining, Mother Martha obtained permission to visit Toronto, where she died a few days after her arrival.

In the short period of 10 years in Canada, Mother Martha Bunning had laid a solid and lasting foundation for the Sisters of St Joseph of Hamilton. She responded to the needs of her time by establishing orphanages, schools, hospitals, and homes for the aged which continued to flourish under the guidance of her community.

SISTER MARY ROSE PAUTLER

Archives of the Sisters of St Joseph of Philadelphia Community Archives (Philadelphia, Pa.), envelope 9 (Canada: Toronto, Hamilton, London, 1851–52). Sisters of St Joseph of Carondelet Community Archives (St Louis, Mo.), Maria Bunning, act of profession, August 1848. Sisters of St Joseph of Hamilton Archives (Hamilton, Ont.), Annals of the congregation, 1852–1927. Sisters of St Joseph of Northwestern Pennsylvania Community Archives (Erie, Pa.), letter to Mother Martha Bunning, 10 Sept. 1866. Sisters of St Joseph of Toronto Archives (Toronto), Annals, I (1851–1914); Catalogue of names of the sisters, 1851–68; Obituary book (1851–90). *Erie City Dispatch* (Erie, Pa.), 11 April 1868. *Constitutions of the Congregation of the Sisters of St. Joseph of Hamilton . . .* (Hamilton, Ont., 1937). D. M. Dougherty *et al.*, *Sisters of St. Joseph of Carondelet* (St. Louis, Mo., 1966), 71. Sister Mary Agnes, *The Congregation of the Sisters of St. Joseph: Le Puy, Lyons, St. Louis, Toronto* (Toronto, 1951), 80. *Hamilton Review* (Hamilton, Ont.), 2 May 1952.

BURNS, ROBERT, Presbyterian minister, educator, author, and secretary of the Glasgow Colonial Society; b. 13 Feb. 1789 at Barrowstowness (Bo'ness), West Lothian, Scotland, one of eight sons and at least one daughter of John Burns and Grizzell Ferrier; m. first Janet Orr (d. 1841), by whom he had three surviving children, and secondly in 1844 Elizabeth Bell Bonar; d. 19 Aug. 1869 in Toronto, Ont.

Robert Burns came from a middle class commercial background. The strong evangelical Presbyterian faith of his father, a merchant and later a customs officer and factor, profoundly influenced the children, four of whom became Church of Scotland ministers. Burns attended a parochial school at Barrowstowness from 1795 to 1801 when he entered the University of Edinburgh; he began his theological training in November 1805. He was licensed to preach by the presbytery of Edinburgh on 28 March 1810, and ordained on 19 July 1811. His first permanent appointment was to Laigh Kirk (St George's) of Paisley, where he remained until May 1843 when he led part of his congregation out of the Church of Scotland in the disruption. He ministered to St George's (Free Church) until March 1845.

An indefatigable and well-received pamphleteer and author, Burns figured prominently in many contemporary Scottish controversies, supporting reform politics and the radical wing of the Church of Scotland. Between 1838 and 1840 he was the last editor of the once-powerful *Edinburgh Christian Instructor and Colonial Religious Register* which he used to further both the evangelical cause and interest in colonial missions. Acutely concerned with urban poverty, and striving to extend the role of the church, like his contemporary Thomas Chalmers, he organized Sabbath schools and tract and Bible societies and laboured on behalf of charity schools and infirmaries. He was especially concerned with getting relief for the weavers of Paisley who were hard hit by the depression which followed the Napoleonic wars. Although from one point of view anti-intellectual, believing as he did that the uncontrolled pursuit of scientific knowledge without regard to the teachings of the church could only lead to error, Burns was a member of various philosophical and literary societies. The University of Glasgow had awarded him a DD in 1828 in recognition of his literary and philanthropic endeavours.

Throughout his life Burns was vehemently anti-Roman Catholic and considered it his duty to preach against those "systems of priestcraft which are based on allegiance to a foreign power, and are in their tendency inimical to the rights of local subjects and the interests of public morals and of public safety." It was this anti-Catholicism, coupled with his fascination with the colonies, that prompted him to champion the French Canadian Missionary Society founded in Montreal in 1839. Through speaking tours, committee work, and fund-raising, he supported its efforts to evangelize French Canadian Catholics.

Burns' interest in North America had been awakened at university, which had a large group of students from America, and strengthened by his brother George's pastorship in Saint John, New Brunswick. Horrified by the widespread unemployment and crushing poverty in Paisley, he encouraged his parishioners to emigrate to North America. In 1825 he took a leading role in the formation of what was to be commonly known as the Glasgow Colonial Society, which ministered to the religious needs of emigrant Scots. As the society's principal secretary until its merger with the Colonial Committee of the Church of Scotland in 1840, he selected and dispatched over 40 missionaries, made innumerable fund-raising tours, and lobbied the British government and the church's general assembly on behalf of the colonial church. The society linked emigrant Scots to their homeland and strengthened the Presbyterian Church in British North America in its initial period of development. Realizing that Scotland could not supply all the missionaries

required, Burns also encouraged the establishment and expansion of Presbyterian colleges such as Dalhousie in Halifax, Queen's in Kingston, and Knox in Toronto, to educate local men for the ministry.

Shortly after the disruption in 1843, the Free Church sent five of its members, including Burns, on a highly successful three-month tour of the eastern United States to solicit funds and vindicate its stand. In April 1844, in response to repeated calls from a group in Montreal headed by John REDPATH, Burns began a triumphal two-month tour from Niagara to Halifax in which he eloquently presented the Free Church position. He argued that the church's influence in society should be extended and that clerical control over church affairs should be increased. He expounded the traditional doctrine that while church and state were separate and equal, the state should admit the universal sovereignty of God by endowing the Church of Scotland and legislating in accordance with scriptural teachings as interpreted by its ministers. Many Canadian Presbyterians supported the principles upheld by the seceders, but problems of conscience, the acceptance of state aid, the nature of various church unions, and other local concerns complicated the decision to take action. Burns' tour did not cause the disruption in British North America, but it certainly helped consolidate the already vocal secessionist sentiment which led to the formation in 1844 of the Synod of the Presbyterian Church of Canada (Free Church) in Canada West and Free Church synods in the Maritime provinces.

Within a few months of his return to Scotland in 1844 Burns received calls from Redpath, James Court, and James Orr in Montreal and from Isaac Buchanan*, Peter BROWN, and George Brown* of Knox Church, Toronto. The latter offer included an interim appointment as professor of divinity at the newly established Knox College. Although Burns felt that he would be of greater service in Canada, it was the lure of a chair, long denied him in Scotland, that settled the issue. Even before the Colonial Committee of the Church of Scotland (Free) urged that he go, Burns had decided to accept the Toronto offer. He taught divinity until 1847.

He was inducted into Knox Church on 23 May 1845. He soon became enmeshed in controversy; at that evening's banquet he sided with the proponents of total abstinence and signed the pledge, an unpopular stand in Presbyterian circles. By this gesture Burns hoped to encourage the lower classes to avoid alcohol which he felt to be especially harmful in a new society. For the next 11

Burns

years Burns proved a faithful and dynamic pastor, striving to enlarge his congregation and to involve them in church affairs. He established Bible classes, young men's associations, and mutual improvement circles, and sought to persuade his elders to take a more active part in church government.

This same energy and enthusiasm catapulted him into the affairs of the church in general. He was unanimously elected moderator of the Canadian Free Church for the 1845–46 session, both out of gratitude for his previous labours on behalf of the colonies and as a visible symbol of the bond between Scotland and Canada. He was, however, too volatile and opinionated to preside successfully over the synod; in 1845 he drafted a note to the general assembly of the Presbyterian Church in the United States in which he spoke in inflammatory language of the evils of slavery. The Canadian synod had to take the unusual step of revising his note. Characteristically, Burns had taken an immovable stand based upon his own long-standing convictions; his disruptive and argumentative approach was often to alienate people who might otherwise have supported him. He continued to be an influential member of the synod, struggling to preserve the original evangelical fervour of the church. To this end he established and served on a variety of committees to fight the desecration of the Sabbath, establish an active programme for distribution of Bibles and tracts, and conduct pastoral visitations. He helped found in 1847 and was a member until 1856 of the Home Mission Committee which controlled both the internal and the external missionary work of the Free Church in Canada. In 1850–51 he was successful in persuading the Reverend John Black* to become its first missionary in Rupert's Land and in the same year obtained church funding for the Buxton Mission among blacks in western Upper Canada. In 1854 Burns encouraged the church towards greater independence and world responsibility by directing its preliminary attempts to enter the foreign mission field, especially India.

In the 1840s and 1850s Burns also undertook repeated missionary tours, for personal reasons or at the request of the synod, to "survey the religious state of the British provinces of North America." He met great numbers of laymen and clergy, preached the evangelical gospel, and helped consolidate the church's membership in settled areas and expand it into new ones. He visited the United States, New Brunswick, and Nova Scotia in 1847, raising money for the erection of churches and collecting books for the Dalhousie library. He visited the Maritimes in 1849 and again in 1858, when he also toured Newfoundland. In addition, almost every year he went on a summer or a winter tour of some area of the Province of Canada or the northern United States. He also made numerous trips to Great Britain on behalf of a variety of causes, including abolition of slavery. The zeal and geniality he displayed on these tours made him one of the most widely known and respected figures within the Free Church.

Burns was never interested in expansion of the church at the expense of its doctrine, however. To him its purity was vital to the success of its mission. He battled against the increasingly popular voluntarist stand taken by such people as the Reverend Andrew Ferrier of Brantford, who maintained that the church should not accept any state funds. Burns believed that the state had an obligation to support one or more established churches, and argued as well for a strong, centralized organization capable of maintaining discipline and unity of purpose. In the synod and in the pages of the Toronto *Banner* from 1846 to 1848 he vigorously opposed the proposals for union with the United Presbyterian Church in Canada. Burns always claimed he was not opposed to union provided that the United Presbyterians renounced their key doctrine of voluntaryism and accepted all the principles of the Free Church.

Curiously, Burns' anti-voluntaryism and his belief in the "Headship of Christ" over the state did not stop him from becoming a founding and prominent member, along with Adam Fergusson and George Brown, of the Anti-Clergy Reserves Association, established in 1850. He maintained that since the clergy reserves were used almost exclusively for the benefit of the established Church of Scotland and the Church of England they were a divisive factor detrimental to a new society where many denominations and sects coexisted. They should, as a consequence, be abolished and the proceeds used to support both common schools and academies where "the Word of God shall be distinctly recognized as the basis, and as the guardian of education." There is strong suspicion that Burns argued out of pique at seeing his church cut off from state funds, and out of hatred for the "Residuals," who had remained within the established Church of Scotland, and the Anglicans, whom he deemed little better than Roman Catholics.

In Burns' estimation, the clergy were duty-bound to take an active role in guiding the affairs of the community. Thus his concern for the poor and disadvantaged, aroused in Scotland, continued in Canada. He aided in 1846 the Irish and in 1847 the Highland famine relief committees, and he was also prominent in the anti-slavery and Negro missionary cause for many years. Once settled in Toronto Burns became an officer of the Anti-Slavery Society of Canada and helped formulate the Free Church's strong stand on the issue. He was a moving force behind the Elgin Association established in 1849 to aid communities of fugitive slaves in Canada, and worked to secure financial backing for it; in 1860, for example, he joined the Reverend William King* in a fund-raising tour of Great Britain.

On his arrival in Canada West in 1845, Burns had been appalled by the dearth of public schooling. Primarily to improve the quality of the students entering Knox College to study theology, he founded in 1845 the Toronto Academy to teach English, Latin, philosophy, and rhetoric; he also served as chairman of its board of directors. He advocated a non-sectarian, state-supported educational system extending from elementary school to university, but he did not fear that such a system would result in "non-Christian" education because the state which would run the schools would be controlled by a Christian society. In 1848 the *Banner* published a report he had written on the Toronto elementary schools which deplored the minor role of the churches in education, the quality of instruction, and the poor qualifications of teachers. From 1846 to 1849, in a series of newspaper articles, he argued for a single non-sectarian, state-run university, free of religious tests, which was achieved in 1849 with the establishment of the University of Toronto. Burns was not, however, averse to private schools. In 1853, for example, he urged the establishment of seminaries for girls to serve the wealthy Presbyterian families who were sending their daughters to Anglican and Roman Catholic schools.

Burns' relations with his congregation were not always easy, as his many activities might suggest. His frequent and prolonged missionary tours caused his congregation to feel neglected. As early as 1847 he had been brought before the presbytery on a charge of absenting himself from his pulpit without authorization. The case was dismissed but the acrimony remained. His application in 1852 for the chair of history at the University of Toronto did not ease matters. Burns' passionate temperament also increased his problems. Between 1851 and 1853 he repeatedly condemned as fraudulent the American Society for Meliorating the Condition of the Jews which, with the support of many Protestant clergy, was collecting funds in Toronto. Although he was

vindicated in the end, his impetuous handling of the unsavoury case alienated many former supporters in his congregation and, more important, some of his fellow ministers, including Michael Willis*, professor of divinity at Knox College. A bitter, protracted quarrel with G. A. Piper, superintendent of the Knox Church Sunday School, grew worse in 1855 when Piper and one of his supporters, J. M. Campbell, were elected elders. Burns felt that Piper had repeatedly defied his authority as pastor and declared the two elders unfit to serve. Although Burns had often argued for greater involvement of laymen in church government, his nature did not allow him to let any area of church polity escape from his direct control. The quarrel seriously split the Knox congregation.

Burns had also run into conflict at Knox College. When he had accepted the combination of pulpit and teaching post in 1845 he had put aside his evangelical criticism of dual offices: it was a necessity when few qualified persons were available. He had given himself wholeheartedly to the college, teaching first theology and then church history; he had also personally collected between 2,000 and 3,000 volumes for its library. By 1847, however, his thorny nature and evangelical zeal were causing discord among the staff and students. The synod, citing the problem of plurality of office, requested Burns' resignation from the college in 1847, and later that year appointed Michael Willis professor of divinity. Willis considered Burns a man "prone to rash statements and hasty decisions on character," and relations between them were never cordial. Nevertheless, between 1847 and 1856 Burns maintained his ties with the college, giving guest lectures, helping prepare new students, and working for the financial well-being of its members.

In 1856 a reconciliation was arranged between Burns and Willis, soon to become principal of Knox College, which enabled the synod to appoint Burns professor of church history and evidences at the college. Burns, whose position at Knox Church had become intolerable because of conflicts with some parishioners, resigned his pastorship and returned to his first love and chief concern throughout his years in Canada – the education of a native clergy. He taught until 1864 when advancing age forced him to retire. He was made emeritus professor and continued to play an active role in college affairs until his death.

Although he mellowed considerably in his later years, Burns in 1862 wisely refused the moderator's post in the united synod formed by the Free Church and the United Presbyterians in 1861. He became revered for his once-fiery strug-

Burns

gle for doctrinal purity, for his role in the disruption of 1843, and for his lifelong dedication to the expansion of the Presbyterian Church in North America and Asia. He represented the Canada Presbyterian Church at the Scottish General Assembly of 1868 and 1869, where he was able to fulfil his ambition of seeing the Canadian church recognized as the leading overseas affiliate of the Free Church of Scotland.

H. J. BRIDGMAN

[Robert Burns periodically burnt his correspondence, with the result that the Burns papers at UCA contain primarily sermon, lecture, and study notes, some of which are in shorthand. Other useful sources in Canada are Glasgow Colonial Soc., correspondence and *Reports*, 1825–35; Can. Presbyterian Church, *Minutes of the Synod* (Toronto), 1861–69; Presbyterian Church of Canada, *Minutes of the Synod* (Toronto), 1844–61; all found at UCA. Also used were PAC, MG 24, D16 and J14; and QUA, William Morris papers. Sources in Scotland include Scottish Record Office (Edinburgh), Church of Scotland records; and GD.45, sect.3, p.481 (mfm. at UCA); and at the National Library of Scotland (Edinburgh), MSS 3430–49 (Lee papers). Newspaper sources include *Edinburgh Christian Instructor and Colonial Religious Register*, 1810–40; *Banner* (Toronto), 1843–48; and *Globe*, 1844–69.

The most comprehensive listings of Burns' published works are to be found in *British Museum general catalogue* and *National union catalog*. The autobiographical sections in *The life and times of the Rev. Robert Burns . . . including an unfinished autobiography*, ed. R. F. Burns (Toronto, 1872) are accurate, but the rest is less reliable. Notman and Taylor, *Portraits of British Americans*, II, contains a short biographical sketch and a photograph of Burns in later life. William Gregg, *History of the Presbyterian Church in the dominion of Canada . . .* (Toronto, 1885), although dated, is still the most comprehensive account of the Presbyterian Church prior to 1875. I. S. Rennie, "The Free Church and the relations of church and state in Canada, 1844–54" (unpublished MA thesis, University of Toronto, 1954), and Moir, *Church and state in Canada West*, add much to an understanding of the general background for clerical affairs in Canada, while J. H. S. Burleigh, *A church history of Scotland* (London and Toronto, 1960), provides a good introduction to the Scottish heritage. H. J. B.]

BURNS, ROBERT EASTON, lawyer and judge; b. 26 Dec. 1805 in Niagara (Niagara-on-the-Lake), Upper Canada, eldest of the five children of the Reverend John Burns and his wife Jane; d. 12 Jan. 1863 at Toronto, Canada West.

Robert Easton Burns (named after the Reverend Robert Easton* of Montreal) was the son of a Presbyterian minister of the Associate Synod of Scotland who emigrated to Upper Canada from Pennsylvania in 1804 and settled first in Stamford, then in 1806 at Niagara. Burns was educated at home and later at the Niagara District Grammar School where his father served as master. In 1822, at age 16, he was admitted as a student-at-law with John Breakenridge in Niagara. Burns completed his legal training in 1827 and was admitted to the bar of Upper Canada in that year. He established an office in St Catharines, and for the next nine years practised successfully in the Niagara, St Catharines, and Hamilton areas.

His ability led to his appointment as judge of the Niagara District on 16 July 1836. Burns, however, was not happy with the routine duties of a district court, and he resigned his post in the spring of 1838. He moved to Toronto and entered into a partnership with Christopher Alexander Hagerman*, then attorney general of Upper Canada. Hagerman had an extensive practice and needed a partner to relieve him of some of its work. Burns practised extensively in the Court of Chancery, and followed that court when it moved with the seat of government to Kingston in 1841. In 1844 the court moved back to Toronto, and, upon his return, Burns entered into a partnership with Oliver Mowat* and Philip M. M. S. VAN-KOUGHNET, two recently admitted lawyers. The firm of Burns, Mowat, and VanKoughnet was one of the largest in Toronto at that time. On 19 Aug. 1844 Burns was appointed judge of the Home District; he gave up his partnership with Mowat and VanKoughnet the next year when an act was passed forbidding district court judges from engaging in private practice. He served the court for four years, during which time he wrote *A letter on the subject of division courts* (1847), his only published work. Addressed to the attorney general of Canada West, it suggested improvements in the system of division courts, especially in the area of jurisdiction over small claims, based on legislative changes in Great Britain in 1846.

Burns resigned from the bench in 1848 and entered again into private practice, this time with John Duggan of Toronto. However, in late 1849 he and Henry John BOULTON were nominated to fill the vacancy on the Court of Queen's Bench left by the death of Hagerman. Through the influence of Francis Hincks*, Burns received the appointment as puisne judge of this court on 21 Jan. 1850. He sat on the court until his death. During his career, Burns was an active bencher of the Law Society of Upper Canada, serving on several committees and as treasurer of the society in 1849–50. He was popular with the law students and was for many years elected president of the Osgoode Club, a student organization.

He was also active in the affairs of the University of Toronto. On 20 July 1848, he, and John Wetenhall* and Joseph Workman*, were appointed by the government of Louis-Hippolyte LA FONTAINE and Robert Baldwin* commissioners to investigate the financial affairs of the University of King's College and of Upper Canada College. Their report, presented in 1852, was severely critical of the financial management of both institutions [see BOYS]. On 11 Dec. 1857 Burns was appointed chancellor of the University of Toronto, succeeding William Hume BLAKE, and he retained this post until the end of 1861.

Burns was married first, on 10 Feb. 1835, to Anne Flora Taylor of St Catharines by whom he had four sons. She died in September 1850, and Burns married in 1856 Britannia Warton of Toronto; she died in 1858. Burns himself died at his Toronto home in 1863.

His legal career was not brilliant but he applied himself diligently to his work as lawyer and judge, and his decisions were well considered and well delivered. He was noted for his integrity and liberal views. "He was," writes David B. Read*, "eminently a self-made man, of plodding habits and honesty of purpose, which obtained favourable recognition from all who knew him."

BRIAN H. MORRISON

R. E. Burns, *A letter on the subject of division courts: with proposed alterations in the jurisdiction and details of the system* (Toronto, 1847). Can., Prov. of, Legislative Assembly, *Final report of the commissioners of inquiry into the affairs of King's College University, and Upper Canada College* (Quebec, 1852). *Globe*, 13 Jan. 1863. *Leader*, 13 Jan. 1863. *Upper Canada Law Journal* (Toronto), IX (1863), 29–31. Read, *Lives of the judges*. William Gregg, *History of the Presbyterian Church in the dominion of Canada . . .* (Toronto, 1885). *Historic sketches of the pioneer work and the missionary, educational and benevolent agencies of the Presbyterian Church in Canada* (Toronto, 1903).

BURR, ROWLAND, contractor and landowner; b. March 1798 in Pennsylvania, the son of Rheuben Burr and Elizabeth Cleever; m. in 1819 Hester Lamoreaux, and they had one son and five daughters; d. 6 Oct. 1865 at Toronto, Canada West.

Rowland Burr's father, a farmer and carpenter, settled near Aurora, Upper Canada, in 1805. Rowland took over his father's carpentry business at age 17, and three years later acquired farm land in Vaughan Township and built a grist mill and sawmill on it. In 1836 he sold a 100-acre farm on Yonge Street and the property in Vaughan Township. He moved to Toronto for a year and then bought a property on the Humber River. This land was subdivided, the village of Burrwick (Woodbridge) was established, and Burr had a sawmill, flour mill, and woollen factory built. Burr eventually sold these and other mills constructed later to John William Gamble*. Burr moved in 1846 to Weston, where he acquired more land. In 1851 he built a large house in Toronto, in which he lived for the rest of his life, and at this time also built other houses in Toronto which he rented or sold. He continued to acquire land in Lambton, York, and Simcoe counties, and by 1855 was expecting annual revenues of $3,700 from an estate he valued at $42,000. He gave up building in the mid 1850s, but mortgages, loans, rents, land trades, interest, and timber revenues kept him prosperous. William Lyon MACKENZIE described him as "well to do" in 1857, at a time when Burr considered his worth at nearly $70,000.

Burr was best known for his advocacy of a canal linking Toronto with Georgian Bay via the Humber and Holland rivers, Lake Simcoe, and the Severn or Nottawasaga rivers. It was thought that the trade of the rapidly developing American western states and the undeveloped lands of the Hudson's Bay Company would proceed by this route. Burr twice travelled the route on foot, committees composed of representatives from Canadian and American cities were formed in the mid 1850s to support the plan, and surveys of proposed routes were commissioned, but the project did not progress beyond a turning of the sod in 1859 because developmental capital was scarce owing to depression and the preference for investment in railways. Burr nevertheless maintained an interest in the canal. The *Elora Observer* described him in 1859 as "that inimitable Burr, who sticks, as a good Burr ought to do, to the Georgian Bay Canal, as a panacea for all evils. . . ."

A temperance advocate, Burr published in 1860 a pamphlet of extracts from an 1834 British parliamentary inquiry into intoxication, and in 1861 he petitioned the legislature for a "Prohibitory Liquor Law." He also played a minor role in the Reform movement in Canada West, and at the Reform convention of 1859 stressed that the success of municipal government since 1849 augured well for the success of federation, should it occur. He urged reform of the operations of the Court of Chancery after becoming involved in cases concerning mill and water rights on his property, and after 1859 supported George Brown*'s suggestions for constitutional changes.

It was a source of pride to Burr that he "never saw the Ritious forsaken or his seed Beging

Burrage

Bread,'' and he attributed his success to hard work, temperance, and the Proverbs of Solomon.

ELWOOD H. JONES

[Rowland Burr was the compiler of *Minutes of proceedings in the House of Commons of the imperial parliament, in the session of 1834, relative to an inquiry into the extent, causes and consequences of the prevailing vice of intoxication* (Toronto, 1860). His papers are among those of his son-in-law and executor, William Tyrrell*, in UTL-TF, MS Coll. 25. E.H.J.]
Elora Observer (Elora, [Ont.]), 16 Nov. 1859. *History of Toronto and county of York*, I. K. M. Lizars, *The valley of the Humber, 1615–1913* (Toronto, 1913), 76. E. L. Morrison and J. E. Middleton, *William Tyrrell of Weston* (Toronto, 1937). G. E. Reaman, *A history of Vaughan Township; two centuries of life in the township* ([Toronto], 1971). C. B. Todd, *A general history of the Burr family, with a genealogical record from 1193 to 1891* (2nd ed., New York, 1891).

BURRAGE, ROBERT RABY, Church of England clergyman and educator; b. 1794 in Norwich, England, son of Robert Burrage; d. 5 Dec. 1864 in Montreal.

Robert Raby Burrage was admitted to Corpus Christi College, Cambridge, in 1813 where he studied classics. He came to Lower Canada in 1816 to take charge of the Royal Grammar School of Quebec. Shortly after his arrival, on 23 Dec. 1817, he married Elizabeth Chapman. He was ordained deacon on 23 Aug. 1819, and priest on 9 Sept. 1820, by Jacob Mountain*, first Church of England bishop of Quebec. In addition to his teaching duties, Burrage was named missionary at Pointe-Lévi in 1819. Within a few years his ministry was extended to include the "Protestant settlers in parts adjacent" to Lévis. In 1833 he was acting chaplain to the garrison in Quebec, and in 1839 he became secretary to the Clergy Reserves Corporation which handled the administration of the lands granted by the crown for the support of Protestant clergy in Lower Canada.

Burrage's main contribution was in the field of education. He was master of the Royal Grammar School of Quebec from its establishment in 1816 to its dissolution in 1836. This school came under the controversial Royal Institution for the Advancement of Learning established in 1801 to administer Lower Canada's first public educational system. But this system was not particularly effective because of the lack of a central administrative body (a board and secretary were appointed only in 1818) and poor financial support, and because the French Canadian population feared schools controlled by an English establishment. Between 1801 and 1818, by local initiative and grants from the assembly, only 37 schools were set up and not all lasted. From 1814 to 1829 the assembly struggled in vain with governors and councils to pass legislation for a more appropriate system. Opposition to the Royal Institution came from the Roman Catholic hierarchy principally because it feared too much English Protestant influence, but also because the institution's grammar schools in Quebec and Montreal, as well as in Kingston [see George Okill STUART], were being funded through revenues of the Jesuit Estates. In Quebec City, for example, from 1816 to 1832, the school received annually £200 for the master and £90 for rent. From 1832 to its closure the Quebec school was supported by annual grants of the legislature.

Burrage's connection with the Royal Institution led him to disagreements with the Roman Catholic clergy. In 1822 he became a visitor of its school in Pointe-Lévi along with the parish priest of Saint-Joseph-de-Lévis (Lauzon), Michel Masse, but Masse resigned in 1823 because he had not been consulted in the appointment of a new teacher. This incident was unfortunate since Pointe-Lévi was one of the few parishes where the parish priest had cooperated in the administration of a Royal Institution school, something the institution's board was trying to encourage but with virtually no success. In 1823, invited to testify before a committee of the assembly, Burrage blamed the attitude of parents and the Roman Catholic Church for the poor state of education in Lower Canada. He recommended expansion of the work of the Royal Institution. In neither instance did Burrage's actions help the institution in establishing a working relationship with the Roman Catholic Church.

The driving force behind the growth of the Royal Institution in the 1820s was the Reverend Joseph Langley Mills*, its first secretary. He was in England from 1829 to 1832 and Burrage was acting secretary from February to December 1831. When Mills died shortly after his return, Burrage followed him as secretary from October 1832 until May 1856. In 1846, in poor health, he was placed on retirement allowance from the church though he continued to act as secretary of the Royal Institution; he remained in residence at Pointe-Lévi. Later he practised his ministry in the diocese of Montreal: in 1860 he was in Laprairie, and from 1862 to 1864 in Hochelaga when once again, shortly before his death, he retired.

By the 1830s the role of the Royal Institution in public education was declining rapidly as a result of the Syndics' Act of 1829, which gave to trustees elected in each parish authority for the administration and construction of schools, and of subsequent legislation. It now concentrated its attention on McGill University. As secretary during the 1840s and 1850s, Burrage witnessed a particularly controversial period in McGill's early history. The board of the Royal Institution held funds willed to McGill and acted also as official visitor of the college [*see* John Bethune*]. There were numerous disagreements between the board of the institution and the board of governors of McGill over budgets, academic appointments, and administration. Fortunately, this situation came to an end on 6 July 1852 when the two boards were combined.

During his career Burrage held relatively important posts as clergyman and educator, and was linked closely to the evolution of public education in Lower Canada and of McGill University. It is difficult to evaluate his personal impact upon the religious and educational events of this period, but any adequate study of them must make reference to him.

RÉAL G. BOULIANNE

ANQ-M, État civil, Anglicans, Christ Church, 1853–65. McGill University Archives (Montreal), Royal Institution for the Advancement of Learning, incoming correspondence, 1820–64; letterbooks, 1820–58, 1–6; minute books, 1837–56. QDA, 56 (B–10), pp. 65–83; 80 (C–9); 81 (C-10); 96 (D–15); 100 (D–20). Can., prov. du, Assemblée législative, *Journaux*, 1841–46. L. C., House of Assembly, *Journals*, 1816–37. Church of England, Diocese of Montreal, *Proc. of the Synod* (Montreal), 1860; 1862; 1863; 1864. *Journal of Education for Lower Canada* (Montreal), February–March 1865, 34. *Journal of Education for U.C.*, XVII (1864), 186.

L.-P. Audet, *Le système scolaire*, III, IV. R. G. Boulianne, "The French Canadians under the Royal Institution for the Advancement of Learning, 1818–1829" (unpublished MA thesis, University of Ottawa, 1964); "The Royal Institution for the Advancement of Learning: the correspondence, 1820–1829, a historical and analytical study" (unpublished PHD thesis, McGill University, Montreal, 1970). Cyrus MacMillan, *McGill and its story, 1821–1891* (London and Toronto, 1921). T. R. Millman, *Jacob Mountain, first lord bishop of Quebec, a study in church and state, 1793–1825* (Toronto, 1947); *Life of Charles James Stewart*. G. W. Parmelee, "English education," *Can. and its provinces* (Shortt and Doughty), XVI, 445–501.

BURTON, JACK. *See* ANDERSON, JOHN

C

CADRON, MARIE-ROSALIE, *dite* **de la Nativité** (**Jetté**), founder of the Institut des Sœurs de Miséricorde (Institute of the Sisters of Mercy); b. 27 Jan. 1794 at Lavaltrie, Lower Canada, daughter of Antoine Cadron, *dit* Saint-Pierre, farmer, and of Rosalie Roy, *dit* Desjardins; d. 5 April 1864 at Montreal.

For 50 years Rosalie Cadron led a life similar to that of most women of her time. On 7 Oct. 1811, at age 17, she married Jean-Marie Jetté, and 11 children were born of this marriage; she became a widow on 14 June 1832. But in 1845, after 13 years of widowhood, and freed of her family responsibilities, her life took a new direction that was to have lasting significance for the social and religious history of Montreal.

For five years, in the privacy of her home, the widow Jetté had been looking after a number of unwed mothers, with a broadmindedness rare for that period and a real sense of human values. At the same time, Bishop Ignace Bourget* was convinced that, with Montreal fast becoming a large city, it was essential to help unwed mothers, rejected by their families and held in contempt by society. The bishop also thought that the church should create new religious communities, free of traditions or previous hampering ties, to meet new needs of society. The widow Jetté therefore seemed to him to be destined to carry forward and lend stability to his charitable activity for unwed mothers by founding a community devoted "to works of temporal and spiritual mercy."

On 1 May 1845, despite the opposition of her children, who anticipated that Montreal society would disapprove, Rosalie Jetté went to live with a "penitent" in the *faubourg* Saint-Laurent, on Rue Saint-Simon, in a small house given for the new work by Antoine-Olivier Berthelet*, a rich citizen of Montreal and a regular benefactor of Bishop Bourget's charities. The nascent community reached the decisive stage of its foundation on 16 Jan. 1848, when its founder and her female collaborators made their religious profession. Once she had become Sister Marie of the Nativity the widow Jetté refused any position of authority in her community, since she deemed herself incapable of properly directing the organization during the period of development that lay ahead. However, working in the background,

Caldicott

she had a share in all the activities of the institute, including the reception of penitents, the care of new-born children at the "maternity room," attendance on the sick in their own homes until 1862, and visits to prisons.

In 1851, after living in the home on Rue Saint-Simon, and in the more spacious but still shabby houses on Rue Wolfe and Rue Sainte-Catherine, she had the satisfaction of seeing the community permanently settled in a mother house on Rue Campeau. In particular, in the succeeding years, she was glad to find the public shaking off its Pharisaical aversion to unwed mothers and increasingly recognizing the usefulness of her community. Finally, in 1859, she welcomed the founding of the secondary order of the Madeleines as the unhoped-for complement to her endeavours; the sisters of this order, recruited from among the penitents, were allowed to take religious vows and lived within the community, obeying particular rules of dedication to contemplation.

When after five years of illness and isolation Sister Marie of the Nativity passed away in 1864, the community whose spirit she had shaped had proved its worth. It was then composed of 33 professed religious, 11 novices and postulants, 25 Madeleines and other women attached to the institute. The community had given asylum to 2,300 unwed mothers, as well as relieving other misfortunes when the occasion arose.

The widow Jetté's charity had triumphed over the prejudices of her day. To a large extent she had succeeded in solving a delicate social problem, and the Hôpital de la Miséricorde, which played an essential role in the history of Montreal, stood as a witness to this until 1973.

ANDRÉE DÉSILETS

Archives de l'Institut des Sœurs de Miséricorde (Cartierville, Qué.), Mémoire sur l'origine et les progrès de l'établissement de Sainte-Pélagie à Montréal jusqu'en 1867. *Mélanges religieux*, 1848–52. É.-J. [-A.] Auclair, *Histoire des Sœurs de Miséricorde de Montréal; les premiers soixante-quinze ans de 1848 à 1923* (Montréal, 1928). P.-H. Barabé, "Mère de la Nativité, sa miséricorde," *Autour de Mgr Bourget: centenaires* (Ottawa et Hull, Qué., 1942), 73–89. P.-A. Fournet, *Marie de la Nativité et les origines des Sœurs de Miséricorde, 1848–1898* (Montréal, 1898). Pia Roseau [Rita Piuze-Balthazar], *Grand-mère Rosalie; vie de Mère de la Nativité, fondatrice des Sœurs de Miséricorde* (Montréal, 1964).

"La chapelle de l'Institut de la Miséricorde," *La Semaine religieuse de Montréal*, XIII (1889), 209–10. "Couvent de la Miséricorde; vêture et profession religieuse," *La Semaine religieuse de Montréal*, LXXXVIII (1929), 510–11. "La crèche; chez les Sœurs de Miséricorde," *La Semaine religieuse de Montréal*, XLVIII (1906), 357–60. "Nouvelle mission des Sœurs de Miséricorde à Green Bay, état du Wisconsin," *La Semaine religieuse de Montréal*, XXXVI (1900), 243–45. "L'œuvre de la crèche des Sœurs de Miséricorde," *La Semaine religieuse de Montréal*, XLII (1903), 335–36. "Profession religieuse chez les Sœurs de Miséricorde," *La Semaine religieuse de Montréal*, XLI (1903), 207–8. "Les Sœurs de la Miséricorde," *La Semaine religieuse de Montréal*, II (1883), 43–45. "Les Sœurs de Miséricorde à Montréal–Ottawa–New York–Winnipeg–Edmonton–Green Bay," *La Semaine religieuse de Montréal*, XXXVII (1901), 13–14. "Sœurs de Miséricorde; vêture et profession," *La Semaine religieuse de Montréal*, XCIII (1934), 76–77. "Sœurs de Miséricorde; vêture et profession religieuse," *La Semaine religieuse de Montréal*, LXVI (1915), 152.

CALDICOTT, THOMAS FORD, Baptist clergyman; b. probably on 21 March 1803 in Long Buckby, Northamptonshire, England, son of Joseph and Nancy Caldicott; d. 9 July 1869 in Toronto, Ont.

Thomas Ford Caldicott's father was a lay preacher and a deacon in the Baptist church at Long Buckby. After leaving school Thomas learned the trade of shoemaker, but his interest in preaching led him to further study. When no opening as a student at a Baptist college was available to him, he began a day-school in Leicester, while continuing his studies and serving as a lay preacher.

By 1827 Caldicott had immigrated to Canada, and become connected at Quebec with the 79th Foot, first as tutor to the family of the commanding officer, then as regimental schoolmaster. He accompanied the regiment successively to Montreal, Kingston, and York (Toronto). At York he was received on 22 May 1831 into the membership of the recently formed March Street Baptist Church, where the Reverend Alexander Stewart was minister. Caldicott was appointed a deacon on 3 July 1832, and licensed a lay preacher on 2 Oct. 1832, being known as the "soldier preacher."

In 1833, assisted by his brother Samuel, Caldicott opened the York Commercial and Classical Academy, a private school offering "a practical secondary education as opposed to the classicism of Upper Canada College." Caldicott also had a stationery and book store. He was prominent in the York Mechanics' Institute, founded in December 1830. He served as secretary of the Young Men's Society, formed in 1831, and delivered "a most able and impressive essay on the worth of the soul" at one of its first meetings. Caldicott participated in the organization meeting at York in January 1832 of the Upper Canada

Religious Tract and Book Society and served as a committee member in 1833–34; he was also a director of the York Auxiliary Bible Society from 1833–35. The preaching ministry was his goal, however, and in 1834 his ordination to the Baptist ministry took place in Chinguacousy Township, Upper Canada. At this time he was characterized as "a vigorous thinker, an effective speaker and a good singer."

Seeking wider opportunities for his ministry, in 1835 Caldicott moved to the United States, where for the next 25 years he served Baptist churches in Lockport, N.Y., in and near Boston (including the Baldwin Place Church) in Massachusetts, and at Williamsburg (New York City), N.Y. His broad interests led him into active participation in denominational affairs. He was honoured by election to many offices, and by a DD from Madison (Colgate) University, Hamilton, N.Y., in 1852, and he was in constant demand as a preacher. Stressing the importance of an educated ministry, he supported the work of the Northern Baptist Education Society, serving on its board of directors in many capacities, including that of full-time secretary from 1848 to 1850.

In November 1860 Caldicott returned to the Toronto church, now named Bond Street Baptist Church. His nine years in this church were described as "the solid rock foundation upon which is built the present prosperity of the Baptist church in Toronto." Here, as in his American pastorates, he promoted strongly the idea of "systematic beneficence"; the weekly offering system was adopted, clearing his church of debt, abolishing pew rents, and increasing its contributions to missions. For a short time in 1861–62 he assisted Robert Alexander Fyfe* in the editorial duties of the *Canadian Baptist*, but he had little liking for literary work. His heart was in his pulpit and pastoral duties.

Caldicott's friend and biographer, William Stewart*, characterized his discourses as "pre-eminently scriptural, methodical, and practical." Two sermons preached at Baptist conventions were particularly noteworthy: one on "Systematic Beneficence," at the Hamilton convention of 1863, and the other at the important Ingersoll convention of 1867 when his opening sermon was a factor in launching the Canadian Baptist foreign mission enterprise in India. Many organizations and committees profited by his leadership in the 1860s, among them the Upper Canada Bible Society of which he was a director, the Upper Canada Tract Society, and the Toronto branch of the Evangelical Alliance. But he does not seem to have been connected with any of the controversial issues of his day, secular or religious. He was

an excellent host, full of wit and interesting anecdote. Of portly build and commanding presence, "a man of sterling worth, of broad culture," he was regarded with esteem and deep affection by his contemporaries.

MARGET H. C. MEIKLEHAM

Canadian Baptist Archives, McMaster Divinity College (Hamilton, Ont.), Caldicott papers. T. F. Caldicott, *A concise history of the Baldwin Place Baptist Church . . .* (Boston, 1854); "The convention sermon: 'O Lord, revive thy work, Habakkuk 3:2'," *Canadian Baptist* (Toronto), 31 Oct. 1867; *Hannah Corcoran: an authentic narrative of her conversion from Romanism, her abduction from Charlestown, and the treatment she received during her absence* (Boston, 1853); *Systematic beneficence: a sermon preached before the annual meeting of the Baptist Missionary Convention of Canada West, in the city of Hamilton, October 21, 1863* (Toronto, 1863). *Canadian Baptist* (Toronto), 15, 22 July, 19 Aug. 1869. *The Baptist encyclopædia . . .*, ed. William Cathcart (2v., Philadelphia, 1881). *Directory of the Jarvis St. Baptist Church, Toronto, August, 1897* (Toronto, 1897), 49–64; app., pp.51, 53, 56–57, 61, 63. *Robertson's landmarks of Toronto*, I, 464; II, 756; IV, 424. William Stewart, "Thomas Ford Caldicott, D.D.," *McMaster University Monthly* (Toronto), IV (1894–95), 145–54.

CALF RISING IN SIGHT. *See* PEENAQUIM

CAMPBELL, ARCHIBALD, notary and seigneur; b. 29 June 1790 at Quebec, son of Archibald Campbell, a businessman, and Charlotte Saxton; d. 16 July 1862 at Bic, Lower Canada.

Archibald Campbell's father was a loyalist who came to Quebec soon after the American revolution and grew rich in the timber trade. Archibald Jr studied law under Jacques Voyer, and was authorized to practise on 6 June 1812. He volunteered for service in the War of 1812. On 18 May 1821 he was appointed king's notary at Quebec. This title, granted to only five notaries between 1821 and 1838, was largely honorific, but certain financial advantages were attached to it, since the holder had exclusive right to receive contracts in which the king had an interest. Lord Dalhousie [Ramsay*] is thought to have granted this privilege to Campbell for exceptional services rendered to the imperial authorities.

For 50 years Campbell practised in the city of Quebec. François-Xavier GARNEAU trained in law with him, and Campbell became his friend and protector. A patron of the arts, Campbell also helped the painter Antoine-Sébastien Falardeau* to spend some time in Italy, and encouraged the endeavours of the dramatist and poet Pierre Petitclair*, who transcribed documents in his office. He was a music lover and belonged to all the musical societies in the city of Quebec. Thanks to his efforts the Quebec Music Hall, the finest of the period in Canada, was constructed. With his brother-in-law William SHEPPARD, Campbell appeared among the founders of the Literary and Historical Society of Quebec on its royal charter (1831).

On 18 Oct. 1822 he purchased the seigneury of Bic in exchange for land he owned at Quebec. The Protestant seigneur was able to secure the goodwill of his Catholic *censitaires*. At Quebec, Campbell was active in commercial and philanthropic societies such as the Quebec Charitable Firewood Society (1844), the Society for the Erection of an Hotel in the City of Quebec (1852), the Quebec and Trois-Pistoles Navigation Company (1852), the corresponding committee at Montreal of the Colonial Church and School Society (1855), and the Stadacona Club of Quebec (1861). Contemporaries praised his generosity, which he displayed for example at the time of the fire in the Montcalm district of Quebec on 7 June 1862, when more than 100 houses were razed by the flames. He carried out his duties as a member of the commission responsible for assisting needy seamen to the satisfaction of all.

Archibald Campbell died on his seigneury at Bic on 16 July 1862. A large number of those prominent in the city of Quebec, including members of the professions, the magistrature, and the Board of Trade, attended the imposing funeral service. The newspapers praised the loyalty and generosity of the king's notary.

PIERRE SAVARD

DCB, Dossier André Garon. *Morning Chronicle* (Quebec), 18, 26 July 1862. *Quebec Gazette*, 18 July 1862. *Quebec Mercury*, 19 July 1862. P.-G. Roy, *Inv. concessions*, III, 153, 156. George Gale, *Historic tales of old Quebec* (Quebec, 1923), 256–57. J.-D. Michaud, *Le Bic, les étapes d'une paroisse* (2v., Québec; 1925–26). J.-E. Roy, *Hist. du notariat*, II, 412–14. P.-B. Casgrain, "La maison Montcalm sur les remparts, à Québec," *BRH*, VIII (1902), 256–67. P.-G. Roy, "Le notaire du roi, Archibald Campbell," *BRH*, XXXII (1926), 736–39.

CARY, GEORGE HUNTER, lawyer and politician; b. 16 Jan. 1832 in Woodford, Essex, England, the eldest of the ten children of William Henry Cary and Elizabeth Malins; m. Ellen Martin on 6 Nov. 1858; d. 16 July 1866 in London, England.

The son of a surgeon, George Hunter Cary was educated at St Paul's School and King's College, London. Following in the footsteps of his uncle, Sir Richard Malins, a distinguished barrister, judge, and Conservative MP, Cary was called to the bar of the Inner Temple on 13 June 1854 and moved to Lincoln's Inn where he "practised regularly & with some success in the Equity Courts." Early in 1859 Cary was recommended to Sir Edward Bulwer-Lytton, British colonial secretary, for the post of attorney general for British Columbia by a former instructor, Sir Hugh McCalmont Cairns, solicitor general of England, who had himself been a pupil of Malins. Bulwer-Lytton was responding to Governor James Douglas*' appeal for "gentlemen of the best education and ability" to assist him in administering the new gold colony on the mainland.

Cary arrived in Victoria, Vancouver Island, on 26 May 1859. Douglas was impressed with his background, intelligence, and energy and appointed him also acting attorney general of Vancouver Island in August 1859; one week later Cary announced his candidacy to represent Victoria Town in the second House of Assembly for Vancouver Island. In the ensuing contest, which was marked by charges of irregularity and foul play, Cary defeated Amor De Cosmos*, an anti-government "reformer." Cary went on to serve as Douglas' *de facto* minister of finance in the Vancouver Island assembly from 1860 to 1863. When in 1861 the Colonial Office required British Columbia officials to reside on the mainland, Cary refused to move from Victoria and gave up his appointment as attorney general of British Columbia, whereupon Douglas appointed Henry Pering Pellew Crease* to the post while Cary remained attorney general for Vancouver Island. Instead of seeking re-election to the assembly in 1863, Cary obtained a three-month leave of absence from the attorney generalship and set off for the Cariboo goldfields, officially to recover from a "general nervous debility" but in reality, according to Edward Graham Alston*, in an attempt "to return with enough of the ready to live for the rest of his days in serene leisure."

Controversy had attended Cary wherever he went. He had not been in Victoria long before he was arrested for "riding furiously" across the James Bay bridge; six weeks later, when charged with disturbing the peace, he went to jail rather than post the required bond. In 1861 he provoked a public outcry by covertly attempting to purchase the springs providing the town's main water supply, which were widely regarded as public property. His brawling in the town and intemperate conduct in court became a matter of public comment; he once assaulted a defendant on the street with a horsewhip only to emerge from the encounter with a "much damaged" face. In June 1863 Douglas was describing him as "excitable and overbearing in manner" and as a person whose actions "provoked hostility and made many personal enemies; defects which detract from his general usefulness as a member of the administration."

On Vancouver Island Cary had aspired to the life of a country gentleman. By 1861, in addition to one or two houses in England, he owned about 400 acres of land in and around Victoria and over 1,400 acres on Sallas (Sidney) Island. Two years later he began construction of "Cary Castle," a spacious residence commanding a magnificent view of the Strait of Juan de Fuca, in which he planned to spend the rest of his days. Unfortunately his ambition far exceeded his financial resources and he was forced to sell the mansion before it was completed.

Cary's sojourn in the Cariboo goldfields in 1863 resulted in both financial and professional setbacks and markedly affected the state of his health. To a long-standing eye affliction and recurrent attacks of rheumatism were added new signs of increasing mental instability. During the summer of 1864 Douglas' successor as governor of Vancouver Island, Arthur Edward Kennedy*, accused Cary of taking excessive legal fees from the government for out-of-court services and of other financial irregularities. Rather than defend himself against Kennedy's charges, Cary resigned.

By 1865 it was apparent to all that Cary was mentally unbalanced. Early in September his relative, Arthur Stanhope Farwell*, reported seeing him in his garden sowing "peas among potatoes at 12 at midnight with a candle." A week later Dr John Ash* certified him to be insane, and Farwell, Dr John Sebastian Helmcken*, and others persuaded him to return to England by contriving a telegram announcing that he was to be appointed lord chancellor at a salary of £15,000 per annum. Escorted by Robert Burnaby*, Cary and his wife left Victoria on 16 Sept. 1865. He died the following July in London at the home of an aunt, attended by his youngest brother.

Truculent, vain, and eccentric, Cary was nevertheless a person of some consequence in colonial Vancouver Island. Even his enemies respected his powers of articulation and considerable intellectual ability. The great tragedy of his career was the gradual derangement of his mind. He played a leading role in shepherding government legislation through the island's second House of Assembly, a contribution that looms larger when contrasted with the utter paralysis of the third and final house when there was no comparable spokesman. His most lasting legacy to the island and the province was Cary Castle; it was acquired by the government in 1865 and, until its destruction by fire in 1899, served as the official residence for the queen's representative.

JAMES E. HENDRICKSON

PABC, Henry Maynard Ball, Journal, 1865; B.C., Governor, Despatches to London, 12 Oct. 1858–25 Oct. 1859, 25 Oct. 1859–14 Sept. 1863, 14 Sept. 1863–31 Dec. 1867 (letterbook copies); Colonial correspondence, Colonial secretary correspondence (B.C.), 1858–63; Crease coll., Henry Pering Pellew Crease; Crease legal papers; Arthur Stanhope Farwell, Diary, 10 Jan. 1864–25 Jan. 1867; John Sebastian Helmcken, "Reminiscences" (5v., typescript, 1892); Vancouver Island, Governor, Despatches to London, 10 Dec. 1855–9 June 1859, 8 June 1859–28 Dec. 1861, 12 Jan. 1862–12 March 1864 (letterbook copies); Vancouver Island, House of Assembly, Minutes, 2 Aug. 1859–5 March 1860, 1 March 1860–6 Feb. 1861, 26 June 1861–27 Feb. 1863. PRO, CO 60/1–17 (mfm. at PABC); CO 305/1–20 (mfm. at PABC). [J. S. Helmcken], *The reminiscences of Doctor John Sebastian Helmcken*, ed. Dorothy Blakey Smith ([Vancouver], 1975). *Daily British Colonist and Victoria Chronicle*, 1859–66. *Law Times* (London), 17 June 1854, 28 July 1866. *New Westminster Times* (Victoria), 17 Sept. 1859. *Victoria Gazette*, 17 Sept. 1859.

CARY, THOMAS, printer and newspaper editor; b. 7 March 1797 at Quebec, son of Thomas Cary*; m. first, in 1817, Mary Ann Dorion, daughter of Peter Dorion, a merchant, and secondly, in 1835, Eliza Heath Ellen Noyes, widow of Josias Wurtele, a merchant; d. 16 Jan. 1869 at Quebec.

Thomas Cary Sr came to Canada in the 1780s. In 1797 he opened a lending library in Quebec where readers could obtain books on subscription and enjoy "the use of a periodical room from 10 o'clock in the morning to 3 o'clock in the afternoon." This library remained in the Cary family until 1835, and in 1830 its catalogue contained 5,314 titles, including 799 in French. In 1805 Cary Sr established the *Quebec Mercury,* to look after the interests of the English, Conservative, and Protestant minority of Lower Canada. During this first decade of the 19th century, so important for relations between the two ethnic groups, Cary made himself the spokesman for the quartet of Sir James Craig*, H. W. Ryland*, Jonathan Sewell*, and Jacob Mountain*, which according to historian Arthur Lower represented "the quintessence of eighteenth-century English toryism in all the depth of its intolerance, its lack of imagination, its devotion to a narrow fixed range of ideas and institutions, its total inability to see how the world looked to other people." Cary's vitriolic style and his violent attacks on French Canadians and *Le Canadien*, contributed greatly to the creation and maintenance of animosity.

In 1805 Thomas Cary Jr, who had more liking for an active life than for study, entered the *Mercury* as a typographer. Subsequently he held many positions at the printing-house – which was almost a government house – and at the newspaper. He became editor of the paper in 1823 on his father's retirement.

The *Mercury* began as a bi-weekly; in 1832 it became a tri-weekly, and in 1863 a daily. Its page make-up was seldom uniform. Thus, the front page might have commercial advertisements, parliamentary news, or an agricultural column. Foreign news drawn from American papers had fairly good coverage, but it was to local news, particularly advertisements, that the *Mercury* gave most space. As long as the Carys owned a library, the paper announced sales of their volumes, and the public auctions held by Joseph Cary, Thomas's brother, were similarly featured. Occasionally poems were published. But the real interest of the *Mercury* lies in its stand on the political issues of the day. Cary Jr, following his father's example, identified himself closely with the English establishment and Conservative policies. He never missed an opportunity to justify the attitude of the British government and of English authorities in Lower Canada. He claimed that in this way he was respecting public opinion, the portion which, as he made clear, deserved consideration. The ill-tempered Francophobia of the early *Mercury* was, however, moderated with the years. From 1828 to 1848 the *Mercury* was owned jointly by Thomas Cary and George-Paschal DESBARATS. In 1855 Cary, in his turn, handed over the editorship of the newspaper to his son George Thomas.

In his youth Thomas Cary had taken part in the War of 1812, and he continued, at least in the 1820s, to serve as adjutant in the 3rd battalion of Quebec militia. Later he advocated introducing the municipal system in his town and participated in the movement that led the House of Assembly of Lower Canada to incorporate the city of Quebec. In the first municipal elections in 1833, Cary was elected alderman of the Saint-Louis district. He was an active member of the Church of England, and in the 1850s was a member of the central committee of the Church Society of the diocese of Quebec; for a long time he was a churchwarden of the Quebec Cathedral.

When he died at the age of 81, the dean of the Quebec press, he received many tributes of respect. The Quebec *Morning Chronicle* summed them up the most aptly: "The deceased was a generous and obliging member of the Press, and an upright, kind-hearted citizen. His agreeable manners made him popular with all classes, and he was a worthy representative of the good old school."

MARC LA TERREUR

ANQ-Q, État civil, Anglicans, Cathedral of the Holy Trinity (Quebec), 27 Dec. 1817, 25 Nov. 1832, 19 Oct. 1842, 16 Jan. 1869. *Quebec Daily Mercury*, 1805–19, Jan. 1869. *Almanach de Québec . . .* , 1820, 1852–53. *Quebec directory*, 1843–69. Antonio Drolet, *Les bibliothèques canadiennes, 1604–1960* (Ottawa, 1965). Henri Têtu, *Historique des journaux de Québec* (2ᵉ éd., Québec, 1889).

CASAULT, LOUIS-JACQUES, priest, professor, superior of the Séminaire de Québec, rector of Université Laval; b. 17 July 1808 at Saint-Thomas-de-Montmagny (Montmagny, Que.), son of Louis Casault and Françoise Blais; d. 5 May 1862 at Québec.

Jean-Baptiste Casault, grandfather of Louis-Jacques, arrived in Canada in 1759 from the parish of Saint-Pierre-Langers, near Granville, Normandy. He never forgot his native land and provided his grandson with a living link with France until the boy was almost an adolescent, for he died at the venerable age of 87 and was buried on 11 June 1822 at Saint-Thomas-de-Montmagny.

At an early age Louis-Jacques was placed in a school in his parish, and was initiated into the rudiments of Latin. A gifted and unusually studious child, he made such rapid and auspicious progress that his parents thought they should make sacrifices in order to give him the advantages of a higher education. On 1 Oct. 1823 he entered the Petit Séminaire de Québec, where he was a brilliant student for five years. But when he came to Quebec nothing about him predicted future success; according to one of his classmates: "L.-J. Casault was already old for a pupil in the Thirty-sixth [the preparatory class], as it was called then. Brought up in the country, he had attended only small schools – Heaven knows what they were like at that time – and showed every sign of excessive reserve and great shyness. In short, his comrades' first impression of him was far from favourable; but opinion soon changed. In the first lessons he received, his remarkable talents were revealed; and while the little rascals who had made fun of the new boy continued to grope along at the bottom of the Thirty-sixth class, at one stride he took the lead and soon had to be transferred to another class, so that fresh material could be provided for his eager mind and more noble awards put within his grasp." According to that remarkable educator

Abbé Jérôme Demers*, then superior of the Séminaire de Québec and a professor of physics, young Casault was "the best pupil he had encountered throughout his long career."

At the conclusion of his classical studies, Louis-Jacques Casault decided on the priesthood. On 5 Oct. 1828 he received the tonsure from Bernard-Claude Panet*, bishop of Quebec. While studying theology, Abbé Casault was employed as classroom supervisor and as a teacher in the fourth, third, and second years. He was ordained priest on 27 Nov. 1831, and a few days later Bishop Panet appointed him curate to Abbé Félix Gatien, who since 1817 had been parish priest of Sainte-Famille-du-Cap-Santé. Three years later, in the autumn of 1834, Casault's inclination for study and teaching brought him back to the Séminaire de Québec, where he was to spend the rest of his life.

There he was assigned to teach physics, which finally was being separated from philosophy. He held this chair from 1834 to 1854, except when other responsibilities claimed him. In the opinion of one of his former pupils, "as a teacher he was remarkable for the clarity and brevity of his explanations, which were always affectionate and kindly in manner; and from his customarily diffident words, there invariably sprang light." Abbé Casault became a member of the community of the seminary on 14 Aug. 1840, and the next day joined the seminary council. He was director of students from 1843 to 1851 and in this office showed concern for maintaining strict discipline. No experience was more dreaded than having "to appear before M. Casault." He knew that one of the best ways to combat unruliness among pupils was to show a great deal of interest in them and seek by all possible means to improve their lot. He had the playgrounds enlarged at the Petit Séminaire; he beautified the estates of Maizerets (Quebec) and Petit-Cap (Cap-Tourmente) at Saint-Joachim; and he instituted an annual festival in honour of Bishop François de Laval*.

But Abbé Casault's principal accomplishment was the founding of Université Laval at Quebec, the plan for which he took from the abbés Jérôme Demers and John Holmes* who counted him their favourite disciple. Several years before Bishop Ignace Bourget* publicly advocated the establishment of a university at Quebec in 1851, Abbé Casault, "who understood" according to Abbé Jean-Baptiste-Antoine FERLAND, "that a university is not only, as some might think, a college with the power to confer degrees or give diplomas, but also an establishment distinct from and superior to colleges, in the nature and extent of its teaching," had carefully studied all the issues related to higher learning, and particularly the functioning and structure of European universities. Casault published historical notes in L'Abeille on Oxford University (17 and 24 Jan. 1850), and the academies of France (30 May, 5 and 20 June 1851), with the intention, apparently, of preparing opinion for the plan he foresaw must soon be put before the public. Almost every evening of the year 1849–50 he talked to his friend Abbé Charles Trudelle, a teacher of the second year, about his favourite subject, which had become almost an obsession.

In 1851 Abbé Casault succeeded Abbé Louis GINGRAS as superior of the Séminaire de Québec. He now possessed the authority and influence necessary for translating his plans into reality. But Bishop Bourget took the initiative; in a letter to the archbishop of Quebec, Pierre-Flavien TURGEON, on 31 March 1851, he suggested that Turgeon entrust to the Séminaire de Québec the task of founding a university, which he saw as a provincial university under the jurisdiction of the bishops of the ecclesiastical province of Quebec: the Séminaire de Québec would be at the head of the structure and its constituent members would be the various colleges, who would thus be "raised to the status of university colleges."

At Quebec, Abbé Casault and the directors of the seminary, who had been calculating their resources in money and men, had been thinking more and more seriously about setting up a university, but being realistic, and no doubt distrustful of the bishop of Montreal's grandiose plan, they had concluded that to secure its future prospects such an institution should begin modestly and be subject to a single authority. In their view, it should not be a provincial university under the jurisdiction of the bishops of the ecclesiastical province, but a diocesan university, attached directly to the Séminaire de Québec, with the archbishop as its supreme head. On 30 March 1852 Abbé Casault communicated their proposal to Bishop Turgeon, who on 12 April forwarded to Bishop Bourget this "plan for the establishment of a university at Quebec." After much hesitation the bishop of Montreal perforce accepted what Quebec had decided. In a letter of 4 May to Turgeon he refers to the fact that "all the steps [had been] taken at Quebec to ask the Pope for a bull for canonical establishment, and the government for a bill of incorporation, for the university establishment that it [had been] decided should be set up there." On 10 May the council of the seminary, with Abbé Casault presiding, adopted two texts: the petition to be addressed to Queen Victoria and the draft of a university charter to be presented to her.

Casault

Abbé Casault had already seen to securing the approval of Lord Elgin [BRUCE], governor general of Canada since 1 Oct. 1846. Elgin deplored the fact that there were already too many universities in the country. But they served only the Anglophone population: King's College, which became the University of Toronto, founded in 1827; McGill College at Montreal, 1829; Victoria College at Cobourg, Upper Canada, 1841; Queen's College at Kingston, Upper Canada, 1842; and Bishop's College at Lennoxville, Lower Canada, 1843. Casault stressed to Elgin that the Francophone group should be provided with at least one university. Ferland noted: "He surprised the noble lord by the lucidity of his exposition and the elevated nature of his views." When the archbishop of Quebec's letter of 10 May 1852 corroborated Casault's verbal assurance that the Séminaire de Québec possessed the necessary means to found a university, that a draft charter had been drawn up, and that the date on which the future university would open its door to students had been projected, Elgin hesitated no longer to support the project. On 13 May Étienne Parent*, who had held the post of assistant secretary of the Province of Canada since 1847, gave Bishop Turgeon the copy of an order in council, dated the previous day, which outlined the merits of the establishment of a Francophone university for the Catholic population of Lower Canada.

On the same day Bishop Turgeon forwarded to Elgin a copy of the draft university charter and requested him to facilitate the steps being taken by Abbé Casault, who was leaving in two days for Europe accompanied by a secretary, Abbé Thomas-Étienne Hamel*, at that time a seminarist. On 5 June the provincial secretary got in touch again with Bishop Turgeon to inform him of a new order in council, which announced that the governor general would give his approval of the seminary's petition to the queen. In London the royal charter was granted with dispatch. On 26 June the Colonial Office undersecretary notified Abbé Casault, who had recently arrived in the British capital, that he had received his petition and was now awaiting the governor general's report. On 7 July the same official informed Casault that he had received a letter from Lord Elgin recommending the granting of a royal university charter to the seminary of Quebec. On 16 July the colonial secretary, Sir John Pakington, informed Lord Elgin that he had received his communiqué; Pakington had advised the queen to grant the privilege requested, and the queen had proved to be in favour of the plan. On 9 August the archbishop of Quebec in turn was informed by the governor's aide-de-camp of the success of Abbé Casault's negotiations. The charter was accepted as the directors of the seminary had drafted it. At Casault's request it was dated 8 Dec. 1852. The official document reached Quebec on the following 14 January.

Rome did not proceed as expeditiously as London. Abbé Casault had gone there in July 1852, armed with a letter dated 12 May from Bishop Charles-François BAILLARGEON, the coadjutor of Quebec, which introduced him as being "sent to the Holy See to request the establishment of a Catholic university in this province." The secretary of the Propaganda had replied at that time that "the sovereign pontiff might grant the request of our lord bishops of Canada more readily when he no longer had cause to fear that the privileges he accorded would be rendered useless by the ill will of the civil authority." Abbé Casault reminded him of this in a letter of 21 Jan. 1853, forwarding an authentic copy of the charter just received at Quebec: "I hope that this document will be found satisfactory, and that it will persuade His Holiness to grant the favour requested on our behalf." The reticence of Rome is explained by the fact that Great Britain, currently a victim of "papal aggression," was refusing to recognize the dioceses that Pius IX had created by his brief of 29 Sept. 1850; nor did London want to grant legal existence to the Catholic university of Dublin. But on receiving the charter the pope signed a brief, dated 6 March 1853, authorizing the archbishop of Quebec to confer degrees in theology. Université Laval was not awarded a pontifical charter, however, until 15 May 1876 by the bull *Inter varias sollicitudines*.

Thus the university was born. Abbé Casault and the directors of the seminary, wishing to baptize it with a name which would be universally acceptable, "anxious also that the glory with which it might shine should be shared by the founder of the seminary, called it Université Laval." According to the charter, the two offices of superior of the seminary and rector of the university would henceforth be inseparable. Superior of the seminary since 1851, Abbé Casault, therefore became the first rector of the university. He was assisted by a council composed of the directors of the seminary and the three most senior titular professors of each faculty. The first session of the new council was held on 21 Feb. 1853. As no faculty yet existed, the only participants, besides the rector, were the directors, the abbés Joseph Aubry, Félix Buteau, Michel Forgues*, Léon Gingras, Louis Gingras, Edward John Horan*, and Elzéar-Alexandre

Taschereau*. Université Laval was to include four faculties: theology, law, medicine, and arts.

The faculty of theology could not be created immediately: there were too few ecclesiastical students, and the needs of the parochial ministry were so manifold and pressing that the seminarists could not yet be given time to devote themselves freely to the study of the sacred sciences. This faculty was thus not inaugurated until 1866.

By contrast, the faculty of medicine was organized and had begun to function as early as 1853. There had been a school of medicine at Quebec since 15 May 1848. The council of the university found in this school the members from which to form a group of professors able to undertake the teaching of medicine. Six of these professors left their chairs to accept an equivalent position at the university. They were Jean Blanchet*, professor of general pathology, who was elected dean, Charles-Jacques FRÉMONT, professor of external pathology and surgery, James Arthur Sewell, professor of internal pathology and special therapeutics, Jean-Zéphirin Nault, professor of materia medica and general therapeutics, Jean-Étienne Landry*, professor of descriptive and surgical anatomy, and Alfred Jackson, professor of tocology.

It was not so easy to create the faculty of law, and the first move to set it up was not made until 1854. After numerous negotiations two professors were obtained, Augustin-Norbert MORIN, judge of the superior court, who was appointed professor of natural law and the law of nations on 13 June 1854, then dean of the new faculty, and Jacques Crémazie*, who was appointed professor of civil law on 4 September. On 12 June 1855 the university council was able to add Judge William Badgley* as professor of criminal law, lawyer Jean-Thomas Taschereau* as professor of commercial law, and lawyer Joseph-Ulric Tessier* as professor of procedure. Unfortunately their pursuits outside the university prevented most of these professors from preparing and giving courses, so that for some years the teaching in the faculty was limited to civil and Roman law.

Civil law was looked after by Jacques Crémazie, and the teaching of Roman law was assigned to Auguste-Eugène Aubry, who began his course on 15 Jan. 1857. Aubry had been recruited in Paris by Abbé Thomas-Étienne Hamel, then a student at the École des Carmes. The Casault-Hamel correspondence throws interesting light on the qualities required of the candidate and his position at Quebec. On 22 Feb. 1855 Casault wrote to Hamel: "He must be young

(about 30), religious, have solid talent, be studious, express himself readily with a good delivery, and finally be a doctor of law." The rector then specified the professor's working conditions and salary: "The task he will have here is to teach Roman law. . . . The periods in the faculty last at least an hour, and he will have six a week except during the holidays. The salary he may expect will be 800 piastres for the first year. If we are satisfied with him, we will add 100 piastres to this sum for the second year and so on for the following years, with the proviso that once it has reached 1,200 piastres this salary will remain fixed." Abbé Casault added at the end of his letter that if the future professor were a "talented, hard-working man" he could "easily increase his income greatly through activities compatible with the duties of this post."

Certain professors more than liberally utilized this method of adding substantially to their salary, for on 20 Dec. 1856 the rector informed Hamel that the law faculty "was functioning badly," to the point that he feared it would give itself "a very unsavoury reputation" in the public eye. Jacques Crémazie was "in reality the only professor who is doing his job." As for Dean Augustin-Norbert Morin and William Badgley, both judges of the Superior Court of Lower Canada, they were no doubt too preoccupied with their duties to attend effectively to their teaching. "Our judges," added Casault, "are valuable for the honour they bring us, we need others for the work." On 28 Sept. 1857 Casault wrote to tell Hamel that Aubry had that month "asked to be given the courses in criminal and commercial law" "abandoned" by Judge William Badgley and lawyer Jean-Thomas Taschereau.

Aubry was to give supplementary courses in the faculty of arts. This faculty, the fourth to be organized, was the least privileged. According to Camille Roy*, the reason was that "One could not indeed establish university teaching in the arts and sciences at Quebec at a period when it would have been difficult to recruit enough students. Young people who had received their first literary or scientific training in our colleges and Petits Séminaires were not concerned with furthering their education in this direction. They were obliged to establish themselves immediately in society, to earn their living by entering one of the liberal professions; they began their studies in theology, law, or medicine immediately on completing their classical programme, and they had neither time nor money to devote to arts and sciences at the university level. Hence Université Laval, in its first years, did not deem it appro-

Casault

priate to set up university chairs in the faculty of arts."

Unable to organize regular courses in arts and sciences, the university instituted public classes or evening lectures. Aubry began in September 1857 with a course on universal history, which was a great success. He gave lectures three times a week during the university sessions 1857–58 and 1858–59, concluding the course on 14 April 1859. At that time his colleagues in the faculty of arts were Jules Tailhan, a French Jesuit who had been lecturing in philosophy since September 1858, and Abbé Jean-Baptiste-Antoine Ferland, who taught Canadian history.

Casault, as rector, in addition to looking after the organization of teaching in the faculties, had provisionally housed the staff of the new university in a building of the seminary, and he had to see to the construction of the university buildings. In 1853 he called in architects and contractors to discuss plans and estimates. In May 1854 a site was acquired adjoining the seminary, and a new street mapped out from the ramparts to Rue Sainte-Famille. This university street would link together the central block, whose corner stone was laid on 21 Sept. 1854, the medical faculty building, erected the same year, and the university residence, completed in September 1855. The architect who drew up the plans of the central building and the residence was Charles Baillairgé*, nephew of architect and sculptor Thomas Baillairgé* and protégé of Abbé Jérôme Demers.

But it was not enough to build in stone. It was above all necessary to build in men, in other words to train competent professors. On 26 Aug. 1853 abbés Louis Beaudet, Alphonse Marmet, and Cyrille-Étienne Légaré had left for Europe to study humanities at the École des Carmes in Paris. The following year Abbé Thomas-Étienne Hamel joined Beaudet and Légaré – Marmet having died – to take classes in mathematics. Beaudet, Légaré, and Hamel returned to Quebec, the first two as bachelors of arts, the third as a bachelor of mathematical sciences. When Abbé Casault terminated his rectorship he thus was able to say that, although he had provided for the housing of his teaching staff and student body with a certain munificence – denounced by some as extravagance – he had nevertheless not neglected the academic training of his professors, since their ranks already included three with degrees from the Sorbonne. For its part, Rome had conferred the degree of doctor of canon law on Abbé Elzéar-Alexandre Taschereau, after he had spent two years, 1854–56, on the banks of the Tiber.

Despite frail health, Abbé Casault had valiantly assumed an office beset by problems of all kinds, some directly related to the functioning of the university, others to the affiliation of the colleges. Université Laval had been founded to serve the Francophone population. The charter authorized the university council to grant the diploma of *bachelier ès arts* to the pupils of all Catholic colleges in Lower Canada. Regulations therefore had to be drawn up for the secondary schools that would be as uniform and equitable as possible. Submitting all candidates to the same examinations would create a healthy spirit of emulation. Casault indicated this aim in a letter of 18 Feb. 1853 to the archbishop of Quebec, who conveyed it to all the bishops of the province and through them to the seminaries and colleges of the dioceses. The rector had attached to his letter a draft statute in 13 articles governing the obtaining of a *baccalauréat ès arts* and admission to the university. This draft became the "Règlement provisoire pour les épreuves du baccalauréat ès arts et de l'inscription, dans L'Université Laval," and was published for the first time in the *Annuaire . . .* of 1856–57.

With the obvious exception of the Petit Séminaire de Québec, which had the first two *bacheliers*, Pierre Roussel and Benjamin Paquet*, the colleges deemed the Laval statute too exacting. "Extreme opposition" to the programme of university examinations drawn up at Quebec was expressed, especially in the Montreal region where in 1858 some college directors considered that the affiliation of their institutions to Laval should not necessitate such a close control by the university of the *baccalauréat* examinations and admission. But Casault remained adamant: "It is quality and not quantity that is needed at Université Laval," he constantly repeated. He was encouraged to maintain this policy of excellence by such colleagues as Abbé Michel-Édouard Méthot*, who in his biography of Casault was to praise the former rector for not deviating from the line of conduct that he had established for himself: "The *Baccalauréat ès Arts* is the diploma that opens the door to all the others. . . . Now how can one ensure that candidates from diverse institutions have acquired the sum of literary and scientific knowledge that is everywhere required of an educated young man? The idea of giving all the classical colleges the power to confer this degree on their own pupils was too dangerous for M. Casault to consider for one moment. He saw no other way than to oblige all candidates indiscriminately to take a serious examination on all the subjects of which secondary education is

120

normally comprised.'' When he was about to leave his post as rector, Abbé Casault sent Bishop Baillargeon, the administrator of the diocese, a long disquisition in three letters dated 1, 3, and 4 June 1859, in which he vigorously defended the standards he believed worthy both of Université Laval and of the institutions that would agree to be affiliated to it, with a view to furthering the progress of university and classical education in the province.

In 1860 Abbé Elzéar-Alexandre Taschereau succeeded Abbé Casault as superior of the Séminaire de Québec and rector of Université Laval; the latter accepted the directorship of the Grand Séminaire and resumed the teaching of theology. As a member of the university council, assistant superior, and vice-rector from 9 April 1862, when this post was created, he was in a position to give his colleagues the benefit of the experience he had so laboriously acquired. But already, at less than 54 years of age, he foresaw his end. On the eve of the first day of the year 1862 the staff of the university had presented him with his portrait, painted by Théophile HAMEL and, in Ferland's words, ''a perfect likeness.''

Abbé Casault had been in feeble health for many years. He suffered particularly from gout, and an acute attack of this disease brought about his death on 5 May 1862. He was given an impressive funeral in the cathedral of Quebec, and buried in the crypt of the seminary chapel. His coffin bore an inscription in lead; its text was reproduced on a marble epitaph unveiled in the former exterior chapel on 8 Jan. 1863 and transferred in 1909 to the present chapel. On the campus of the university at Sainte-Foy on the outskirts of Quebec, an unpretentious stele reminds recent generations of the one who, by virtue of the ''very great'' part he ''took in its establishment,'' is entitled to be ''proclaimed the founder'' of Université Laval.

PHILIPPE SYLVAIN

Archivio della Propaganda Fide (Rome), Scritture riferite nei Congressi: America Settentrionale, 6 (1849–57). ASQ, Université, 38–40, 100ff. *L'Abeille* (Québec), 8, 13 mai 1862. *Le séminaire de Québec* (Provost), 468–69. F.-É. Casault, *Notes historiques sur la paroisse de Saint-Thomas de Montmagny* (Québec, 1906), 243. C.-F. Cazeau, ''Allocution de M. le grand vicaire C.F. Cazeau,'' *Souvenir consacré à la mémoire vénérée de M. L.-J. Casault, premier recteur de l'université Laval* (Québec, 1863), 7–10. F.[-X.] Gatien et David Gosselin, *Histoire du Cap-Santé depuis la fondation de cette paroisse jusqu'à 1830 . . . continuée depuis 1830 jusqu'à 1887* (Québec, 1899), 165. F.-A.-H. Larue, ''Éloge funèbre prononcé par F. A. H. Larue, M.D.L.,'' *Souvenir consacré à la mémoire vénérée de M. L.-J. Casault, premier recteur de l'université Laval* (Québec, 1863), 35–58. M.-É. Méthot, ''Notice biographique sur Louis-Jacques Casault,'' *Souvenir consacré à la mémoire vénérée de M. L.-J. Casault, premier recteur de l'université Laval* (Québec, 1863), 11–33. Camille Roy, ''L'abbé Louis-Jacques Casault, fondateur et premier recteur de l'université Laval,'' *La Nouvelle-France* (Québec), II (1903), 209–22. Philippe Sylvain, ''Auguste-Eugène Aubry (1819–1899),'' *Cahiers des Dix*, 35 (1970), 191–226; ''Les difficiles débuts de l'université Laval,'' *Cahiers des Dix*, 36 (1971), 211–34. Philippe Sylvain et Antonine Gagnon, ''La vie quotidienne de l'étudiant universitaire québécois au XIXe siècle,'' SCHÉC *Rapport*, 39 (1972), 41–54.

CASSEGRAIN (Casgrain), OLIVIER-ARTHUR, lawyer and writer; baptized 6 Oct. 1835 at L'Islet, Lower Canada, son of Olivier-Eugène Casgrain, notary and seigneur of L'Islet, and Marie-Hortense Dionne; d. 9 Feb. 1868 at Quebec.

Olivier-Arthur Cassegrain was educated at the Collège de Sainte-Anne-de-la-Pocatière, where he ''distinguished himself by his good conduct, studiousness, and love of letters.'' He then enrolled in the faculty of law of the Université Laval at Quebec. ''More inclined to literature than law,'' he published regularly in *Le Courrier du Canada* during his legal training. His first article, ''Soirée d'universitaires,'' was published 28 Dec. 1857 and made such a marked impression on Joseph-Charles Taché*, the newspaper's editor, that the following year he had him report on the Canadian history lectures which Abbé Jean-Baptiste-Antoine FERLAND was giving to enthusiastic audiences. Cassegrain's reports were published up to 1862 and were reprinted from 1859 on in the *Journal de l'Instruction publique*.

Cassegrain was called to the bar in 1860 and for some time practised at Quebec, but he continued to write. That year he published in *Le Courrier du Canada* ''L'héros de Sainte-Foye,'' a poem that was highly commended by Édouard Sempé, a French poet staying briefly in Montreal. Cassegrain was part of a lively group that gathered at La Mansarde du Palais with Louis-Honoré Fréchette* and Alphonse Lusignan*. During this period he wrote *La grand-tronciade; ou itinéraire de Québec à la Rivière-du-Loup*, a long poem of nearly 100 pages that was published in 1866 after it had been read to his friends at La Mansarde. Fréchette recalled the event in his poem ''Reminiscor''; Léon-Pamphile Le May* judged the poem somewhat severely, and took the poet to task for having attempted too large a scale. In 1863 Cassegrain collaborated with Pascal-Amable Dionne, who was also a lawyer, in writing for the *Revue canadienne* a satirical poem, "La Tauride," inspired by a lawsuit concerning two bulls found on the public highway.

On 8 Aug. 1865, at Quebec, Cassegrain married Félixine Hamel, and in July 1867 took a position in the office of the clerk of the province of Quebec. He died on 9 Feb. 1868 at age 32, after a long illness.

JOHN HARE

[O.-]A. Cassegrain, *La grand-tronciade; ou itinéraire de Québec à la Rivière-du-Loup; poème badin* (Ottawa, 1866). [O.-]A. Cassegrain et P.-A. Dionne, "La tauride," *Revue canadienne* (Montréal), I (1864), 297–302. *Le Courrier du Canada*, 28 déc. 1857, 1858–1862, 10 févr. 1868. Edmond Lareau, *Hist. de la littérature canadienne*. L.-P. Le May, "Notice bibliographique sur *La grand-tronciade* de M. A. Cassegrain," *Revue canadienne* (Montréal), III (1866), 441–42.

CAZES, CHARLES DE, politician; b. in 1808 in Brittany; d. 4 Oct. 1867 at Montreal.

The notary Charles de Cazes landed at Quebec in 1854 with his wife, Constance Arnaud, and his children. He immediately settled in the Eastern Townships. By a contract drawn up on 11 Oct. 1854, de Cazes purchased a piece of land of about 100 acres, at a cost of £100, in the sixth concession of Shipton Township (near Danville). Charles de Cazes's coming to Canada cannot be placed within any general movement, although the 1850s showed a slight increase in French immigration to Lower Canada. But his settling in the Eastern Townships is explained by the nationalist policy of the civil and religious authorities of French Canada, which aimed at increasing the numbers of French and Catholic inhabitants in a region where the newcomers were almost entirely Anglo-Saxon.

De Cazes quickly established himself in Lower Canada and soon shared with the leaders of his adopted country the ideal of making the Eastern Townships a French community. In the elections of 9 July 1861, he was elected MLA for Richmond-Wolfe and thus became the first person of French origin and the first Francophone representative of the Eastern Townships to sit in the Legislative Assembly of United Canada. Although he began as a declared independent in parliament, he soon supported the Liberal-Conservatives of George-Étienne Cartier* and gave his attention particularly to immigration, settlement, and agriculture. In the majority of his speeches, as in the occasional article he published in newspapers, he showed concern for the future of French Canada. A lecture on "The organization of agriculture," delivered at the Institut Canadien of Quebec and printed in *Le Courrier du Canada* of 6 May 1863, is of great interest for historians of the period. In it de Cazes describes the disastrous state of agriculture in Lower Canada in the 1860s; he deplores the lack of an agricultural policy, which he considers the cause of the woefully inadequate immigration; finally, he sets forth his hope that an organizational framework for agriculture would naturally bring about the creation of that industry and then other industries according to need.

The parliamentary career of Charles de Cazes was short. In the 1863 election he lost the mandate of Richmond-Wolfe to William Hoste Webb*. Thus removed from politics, he was appointed inspector of schools for the constituencies of Saint-Hyacinthe, Bagot, and Rouville. While carrying out his duties he was stricken by a disease of the liver to which he succumbed on 4 Oct. 1867 at Montreal, where he was undergoing treatment. He was buried at Wotton, near his wife who had died a few years earlier. He was survived by two married daughters in France, and by two sons in Canada: Charles, who became a papal Zouave, and Paul-Marie*. The latter was called to the bar in 1869, practised law at Saint-Hyacinthe, and contributed to several newspapers. He entered the Department of Public Instruction in 1886, later becoming its secretary, and published several historical works.

ANDRÉE DÉSILETS

JIP, octobre 1867, 134. *Le Courrier de Saint-Hyacinthe*, 8, 10 oct. 1867. *Le Courrier du Canada*, 12 juill. 1861; 21, 31 mars, 2, 11, 28, 30 avril, 2, 7, 21, 26 mai, 16 juin 1862; 13 févr., 4, 6, 26 mars, 8 mai, 22, 26 juin 1863; 30 sept., 2 oct. 1865; 8, 9, 10 oct. 1867. *Le Pionnier de Sherbrooke* (Sherbrooke, Qué.), 11, 18 oct. 1867. *Richmond Guardian* (Richmond, Que.), Oct. 1867. *The Canadian men and women of the time: a hand-book of Canadian biography of living characters*, ed. H. J. Morgan (2nd ed., Toronto, 1912). *Cyclopædia of Canadian biog.* (Rose, 1888), 378. Desjardins, *Guide parlementaire*. *The encyclopedia of Canada*, ed. W. S. Wallace (6v., Toronto, 1935–37), II, 17. Le Jeune, *Dictionnaire*, I, 480. P.-G. Roy, *Les avocats de la région de Québec*, 84. L. S. Channell, *History of Compton County and sketches of the Eastern Townships, district of St. Francis, and Sherbrooke County* (Cookshire, Que., 1896). Maurice O'Bready, *Histoire de Wotton, comté de Wolfe, P.Q.* (Sherbrooke, Qué., 1949), 126–27. "Charles de Cazes," *BRH*, XLII (1936), 87. "Les disparus," *BRH*, XXXIII (1927), 95.

CHABOT, JULIEN, *canotier*, innkeeper, shipbuilder and owner; b. 20 Jan. 1801 at Saint-Laurent, Île d'Orléans, tenth of the 18 children of François Chabot, a farmer, and Marie-Françoise Pépin, *dit* Lachance; m. 2 Feb. 1830 Suzanne

Carrier, and they had eight children; d. 10 Aug. 1864 at Lévis.

A little before 1820, Julien Chabot settled in Lévis, and with his brother Laurent plied the trade of *canotier*. At that time communications between Quebec and Lévis generally were provided by these *canotiers*, usually natives of the Île d'Orléans, who carried people, light merchandise, and even cattle in boats 25 to 30 feet long. Chabot subsequently diversified his activities. At the end of the 1820s he apparently became one of those innkeepers called *passager* because they lodged travellers in transit.

Around 1828 the horse-boat appeared on the St Lawrence; this was a flat barge with paddle wheels turned by horses, which made crossing safer and increased the transport capacities between the two shores. Julien Chabot undertook at that time to build and operate one, in partnership first with Auguste Bégin, and, after 1838, with his widow. According to Pierre-Georges Roy*, Julien Chabot was the first to equip his horse-boat with a steam engine.

In 1843, when Jean-Baptiste Beaulieu put the steamboat *Charles-Édouard* in service between Quebec and Lévis, Julien Chabot set about building a bigger one, the *Dorchester*. Thus he competed with Beaulieu on the St Lawrence for several years. After building barges and small light boats on his property at Pointe-Lévi, Chabot tackled the building of steamboats, although he entrusted the machinery (motors and accessories) to another contractor, as is shown by a contract he made with Benjamin Franklin Tibbits, an engineer and brother of James Tibbits, a shipbuilder at Lévis.

In the 1850s, Julien Chabot used his steamboats mainly for towing in the port of Quebec and on the St Lawrence. At this time he also made his son Julien* a partner in his undertakings. When the St Lawrence Tow Boat Company, which included most of the tugboat owners of the port of Quebec, was organized in 1863, Julien Sr became one of its directors. After his death his son was to have important interests connected with the port of Quebec.

Julien Chabot and his brother Laurent joined businessmen and "ferrymen" of Pointe-Lévi in helping to found the Parish of Notre-Dame-de-la-Victoire at Lévis in 1850. When the church and presbytery were being built and the cemetery enlarged, they backed the parish priest Joseph-David Déziel*, by giving land, granting long-term loans, and participating in the collection of funds.

Julien Chabot died in this parish on 10 Aug. 1864, after an active career in the Quebec-Lévis "ferry trade" and in towing on the river and in the port of Quebec. In competitive times he was able to foresee and take advantage of changing maritime techniques, and he left the image of an ambitious and progressive entrepreneur.

MARC VALLIÈRES

ANQ-Q, État civil, Catholiques, Notre-Dame de Lévis, 13 août 1864; Greffe d'Archibald Campbell, 10 déc. 1851; Greffe de J.-B. Couillard, 12 août 1829, 8 juin 1833, 14 avril 1838; Greffe de F.-M. Guay, père, 27 avril 1859. Can., prov. du, *Statuts*, 1863, c. 59; Conseil législatif, *Journaux*, 1857, IV, app.9. *Le Journal de Québec*, 11 août 1864. *Canada directory*, 1857–58. *Cyclopædia of Canadian biog.* (Rose, 1888), 381–82. Frère Éloi-Gérard [Talbot], *Recueil de généalogies des comtés de Beauce-Dorchester-Frontenac, 1625–1946* (11v., Beauceville, Qué., [1949–55]), II. P.-G. Roy, *Dates lévisiennes* (12v., Lévis, Qué., 1932–40), I, II; *Profils lévisiens* (2 sér., Lévis, 1948), 1re sér., 18–29; *La traverse entre Québec et Lévis* (Lévis, 1942).

CHANDLER, JAMES WATSON, lawyer, politician, and judge; b. 18 July 1801 in Cumberland County or Colchester County, N.S., son of Samuel Chandler, loyalist, and Susan Watson, and cousin of Edward Barron Chandler*; m. 5 Jan. 1843 at St Andrews, N.B., Julia Hatheway, and they had at least one daughter and three sons; d. 3 Oct. 1870 at Moncton, N.B.

James Watson Chandler was educated in public schools in Nova Scotia and studied law. He moved to New Brunswick about 1829 and was admitted to the bar of that province as an attorney in the same year and as a barrister two years later. He established a law practice in St Andrews in 1829 and remained there until 1867.

Chandler took an active interest in the affairs of Charlotte County and held a number of important local offices. He served as judge of the Inferior Court of Common Pleas (1838–40, 1860–64), justice of the peace (1860–65), judge of the Court of Probate (1864–66), and commissioner for taking affidavits in the Supreme Court (1865–66). He also served from 1852 to 1854 with William Boyd KINNEAR and Charles Fisher* on a commission appointed by the provincial government to consolidate and codify provincial statutes and to examine the courts of law and equity and the law of evidence. The results of this study were published in three volumes in 1853–54.

After unsuccessfully contesting a Charlotte County seat for the assembly in the elections of 1846 and 1854, Chandler was elected for that county in 1857 and served until his defeat in the election of June 1861. In May 1858 Chandler requested Samuel Leonard Tilley*'s support in obtaining the position of speaker of the assembly but when the office became vacant in 1859 he was

Chandler

not nominated. In politics Chandler was a liberal; during the election campaigns of 1854 and 1857 he declared that he was in favour of the principle of responsible government, extension of the franchise, universal education, and free trade. In 1866 he supported confederation and was re-elected.

Chandler served in the legislature until 19 June 1867 when he gave up his seat to accept an appointment as county court judge for Westmorland, Kent, and Albert counties. He was one of five district court judges appointed for New Brunswick at confederation. Subsequent to his appointment, Chandler moved to Dorchester, N.B., and continued in his capacity as judge until his death in October 1870.

A man of considerable ability in his profession, he made a significant contribution in matters affecting the jurisprudence of the province. The *Morning News* noted on 4 Oct. 1870: "While in the Legislature he was considered a standard authority on intricate questions of law during the passage of bills through the House of Assembly affecting the jurisprudence of the country."

J. M. WHALEN

N.B. Museum, Ralph Hewson, "Chandler family" (typescript). PAC, MG 27, I, D15, Chandler to Tilley, 18, 21, 26 Nov., 2 Dec. 1857; 12 Jan., 17 May, 13 Aug., 26 Oct. 1858; 9 May, 4 July, 20 Sept. 1859; 25 April 1860; 18 Jan. 1861; 9 July 1866; 11 July 1867. PRO, CO 193/25–48, blue books, 1842–65. PANB, J.C. and H.B. Graves, "New Brunswick political biography" (copy at UNBL). *Daily Morning News* (Saint John, N.B.), October 1870. *St. John Daily Telegraph and Morning Journal* (Saint John, N.B.), October 1870. *Standard* (St Andrews, N.B.), January 1843; October 1846; May, June 1854; June 1861; March 1865; June 1866; May, June 1867; October 1870. *Hutchinson's New Brunswick directory, for 1865–66 . . .* , comp. Thomas Hutchinson (Saint John, N.B., [1865]). *The merchants' and farmers' almanack . . .* (Saint John, N.B.), 1840–41, 1843–46, 1852–53, 1855–63. *New-Brunswick almanac*, 1864–66. Lawrence, *Judges of N.B.* (Stockton). W. C. Milner, *History of Sackville, New Brunswick* (Sackville, 1934).

CHANDLER, SAMUEL, waggon maker, farmer, miller, and rebel; b. 8 Oct. 1791 at Enfield, Conn., son of Joseph Chandler and Lydia Hawkins; m. first Hannah Chapin (d. 1815), and they had two children; m. secondly in 1818 Ann McKelsey, and they had 11 children. d. 25 March 1866, at Colesburg, Iowa.

In 1818 Samuel Chandler was living in Albany, N.Y., but he moved to near Lundy's Lane, Upper Canada, before 1820. Within two years he had established a waggon making business at St Johns (St Johns West) in Welland County. A radical in politics, he was suspected by the local authorities of treasonable activities prior to the 1837 rebellion. On 10 Dec. 1837 the fleeing rebel chieftain, William Lyon MACKENZIE, came to him, and Chandler led him to safety in the United States. Chandler was later present at the rebel occupation of Navy Island, and despite the failure of this venture remained an enthusiastic Patriot. He helped form the Canadian Refugee Relief Association in March 1838.

On 20 June 1838 Chandler was a guide for a band of Patriots who raided the Short Hills area of the Niagara District. Led by James Morreau and joined by Linus W. Miller*, they entered St Johns, robbed a few inhabitants, then set fire to an inn in order to capture ten Lancers. Although Chandler may have opposed the attack initially and did secure the release of two of his neighbours from the raiders, during the raid itself he reportedly advised the robbery of an elderly resident and wanted the execution of the Lancers. The latter, however, were freed.

Chandler and most of those implicated were quickly arrested. Morreau was executed on 30 July, and Chandler himself was tried on 2 August. He was sentenced to death, but was instead banished to Van Diemen's Land (Tasmania) for life. In December 1841 he and a Short Hills comrade, Benjamin Wait, escaped and made their way to the United States. Settling first near Jackson, Mich., Chandler and his family moved to Iowa in 1843. Here he lived out his days as a farmer and miller.

COLIN READ

[L. W. Miller, *Notes of an exile to Van Dieman's Land: comprising incidents of the Canadian rebellion in 1838, trial of the author in Canada, and subsequent appearance before her majesty's Court of Queen's Bench, in London, imprisonment in England, and transportation to Van Dieman's Land . . .* (Fredonia, N.Y., 1846; repr. East Ardsley, Eng., 1968), 17–30, 94, contains a highly coloured account of the Short Hills raid and of the roles played in it by Miller and the other participants. A comprehensive account of the raid can be obtained from PAC, RG 5, A1, 179–221; *St. Catharines Journal* (St Catharines, [Ont.]), 7 Dec. 1837–1 Nov. 1838; E. C. Guillet, *The lives and times of the Patriots: an account of the rebellion in Upper Canada, 1837–1838, and the Patriot agitation in the United States, 1837–1842* (Toronto, 1938; repr. 1968), 32, 84, 104–13, 206, 209–10, 221–22; and E. A. Cruikshank, "A twice-told tale (the insurrection in the Short Hills in 1838)," *OH*, XXIII (1926), 180–222. PAC, MG 24, I26, 65, report by Robert Laidlaw, contains a transcript of the trials of the raiders, and Benjamin Wait, *Letters from Van Dieman's Land, written during four years imprisonment for political offences committed in Upper Canada* (Buffalo, N.Y., 1843), 60–61, 268, 354–55, is valuable for its description of the escape by Chandler and Wait from

Van Diemen's Land, as well as for the information it contains on the attempts made in England to prevent the transportation of Chandler, Wait, and others to the penal colony. Harvey Reid, *In the shadow of the gallows: a true story of an Iowa pioneer* (Maquoketa, Iowa, 1902), consisting of articles reprinted from the *Jackson Republican* (Maquoketa, Iowa), deals mainly with Chandler's fortunes after his capture and draws heavily on Wait's work. L. B. Duff, "Samuel Chandler of St. Johns," Welland County Hist. Soc., *Papers and Records*, V (1938), 115–49, is the best source on Chandler. c.r.]

PAO, Mackenzie-Lindsey papers, Mackenzie papers, box 1835 to March 1838, "Navy Island memoranda, 1837," [18 Dec. 1837]; box April to December 1838, Nelson Gorham to W. L. Mackenzie, 29 July [1838]; letter [M. A. Reynolds] to W. L. Mackenzie, 28 Aug. 1838; clippings, item 4682. Lindsey, *Life and times of Mackenzie*, II, 118–21.

CHAPPELL, EDWARD, naval officer and author; b. 10 Aug. 1792 at Hothfield, Kent, England; m. 5 Oct. 1819 Elizabeth Wood (d. 1842), and they had one daughter; d. 21 Jan. 1861 in London, England.

In 1804 at age 12 Edward Chappell signed on board the *Kingfisher* at the Sheerness naval base near the village where he was born. During the Napoleonic wars he saw action in several ships from the Mediterranean to the West Indies. He helped in 1805 to cut out a Spanish privateer from under the heavy batteries of the La Guaira fortress on the Venezuelan coast. In 1811 Chappell was made a lieutenant, after commanding a gunboat at the siege of Cadiz, Spain, in which almost all the crew was killed or wounded and he himself severely injured.

He served in warships off Tunis and Toulon, and then joined the sloop of war *Rosamond*, which sailed to Newfoundland in 1813 and Hudson Bay in 1814 to patrol the British North American fisheries. During these voyages he recorded his observations in two journals, which were later published as *Voyage of his majesty's ship Rosamond to Newfoundland and the southern coast of Labrador* and *Narrative of a voyage to Hudson's Bay*. In the first of these journals Chappell described the summer cruise of 1813 in Newfoundland and Labrador waters, at a time when almost everyone lived along the coastline and by means of the fishery. After reaching St John's at the end of May the *Rosamond* sailed around the south and west coasts of Newfoundland on her way to guard the fisheries on the Labrador coast, returning by the same route in autumn, and left St John's for England in December. During this voyage Chappell noted the isolated settlements of whites, Indians, and Inuit (Eskimos) on the west coast of Newfoundland

and the coast of Labrador; the crowded streets and lively social life of St John's at the end of the fishing season; and extraordinary natural features, such as the unusual castle-like rock formations of Chateau Bay in the Strait of Belle Isle. Like other visitors, however, Chappell condemned the system of economic exploitation whereby the fish merchants were able to "amass the most splendid fortunes with an inconceivable rapidity; whilst the middling and lower classes of fishermen may toil from year to year, with patient and unremitted industry, and yet find themselves, in their old age, many degrees worse off than when they first crossed the Atlantic."

In May 1814 the crew of the *Rosamond* learned that she had been ordered to Hudson Bay, and eight men, including the captain, left the ship in Suffolk, England. The ship convoyed two Hudson's Bay Company ships and a Moravian mission brig across the Atlantic, and then proceeded to York Factory on Hudson Bay, returning by the same route in the fall. The rugged natural grandeur of the Arctic, with its mountains and icebergs, awed the young naval lieutenant. Chappell first met Arctic Inuit on 31 July, when he went ashore at Cape Saddleback in Hudson Strait. Although he refuted some earlier farfetched descriptions of Inuit, a number of his own conclusions were naïve. Noting the natives' small hands and feet, for example, he reasoned that "the same intense cold which restricts vegetation to the forms of creeping shrubs has also its effect upon the growth of mankind, preventing the extremities from attaining their due proportion." He described more accurately the seal hunt and the importance of that animal to the natives' way of life. Chappell did sketches of Inuit huts and kayaks, later included in his *Narrative*, and traded for sealskin clothes and white feather gloves. He knew a few common Inuit words but could not communicate with the natives in any depth. Chappell later defended his work against a critic in the *Quarterly Review* (London) by maintaining that he had daily contact with the natives and, unlike any European in the previous 40 years, had been admitted to their homes. But most of his observations on Inuit society and beliefs were superficial.

At York Factory, Chappell dined on venison steaks and buffalo tongue, to the tunes of Highland bagpipers, and joined some Crees to hunt reindeer. He described briefly in his journal the trading operations of the HBC, referring the reader, for the western portions of the company's vast domains, to the journals of Alexander Mackenzie*. Chappell believed the Indians would become more industrious if the company's

Chartrand

monopoly were ended, and if they got a better deal for their furs.

On both his trips Chappell took part in every experience open to him with youthful buoyancy and resilience and talked to a wide range of people, from Moravian missionaries to Indian chiefs. In his books, which were essentially works of description and travel to be read by the British upper classes, he gives us glimpses of frontier societies which contained few educated people and about which little had been written. He displays, however, some understandable biases: Roman Catholic priests were jolly and rotund; Irishmen were turbulent drunkards; Indians and Inuit, although generally regarded as being good-natured and hospitable, were patronized in regard to their customs, religion, and drinking habits.

Chappell appears to have had no further connection with North America after the cruises of 1813 and 1814. Following the second voyage he presented some Inuit handicrafts to Cambridge University. After the Napoleonic wars, he served on warships patrolling the English Channel against smugglers. Promoted to commander in 1826, he supervised for the next 12 years the steam packet postal service around the British Isles. His superiors praised him as a hardworking officer whose conduct was pervaded by a "deep and moral sense of justice and truth." In 1838 Chappell was made a captain and two years later circumnavigated Britain in the steamer *Archimedes* in order to assess the newly developed screw propeller. He became an authority on steam navigation, giving evidence to committees of the British House of Commons, and advising the Board of Trade on legislation. In 1841 he went on half pay in order to manage the Royal Mail Steam Packet Company, which ran vessels to the West Indies. He retired from the navy in 1853 and was promoted rear-admiral in 1858, three years before his death.

WILLIAM H. WHITELEY

Edward Chappell was the author of *Narrative of a voyage to Hudson's Bay in his majesty's ship Rosamond containing some account of the north-eastern coast of America and of the tribes inhabiting that remote region* (London, 1817); *Voyage of his majesty's ship Rosamond to Newfoundland and the southern coast of Labrador* . . . (London, 1818), which also appeared as *Reise nach Neufoundland und der sudlichen Kuste von Labrador* . . . *nebst einer Beschreibung der Insel Cuba, und besonders der Stadt Havanna im Jahre 1817* . . . (Jena, 1819); and *Reports relative to Smith's patent screw propeller* . . . (London, 1840). PRO, Adm. 9/24, 36/17116, 37/919. Somerset House (London), Principal Probate Registry, Letters of administration, Edward Chappell, 6 Feb. 1861. G.B., Adm., *The commissioned sea officers of the Royal Navy, 1660–1815*, ed. D. B. Smith *et al.* (3v., n.p., [1954?]), I, 160; *Navy list*, 1811–61. O'Byrne, *Naval biographical dictionary* (1849), 186–87. *Quarterly Rev.* (London), XVIII (1817–18), 199–223.

CHARTRAND, VINCENT (sometimes called Vincennes), master-sculptor and painter; b. 18 July 1795 at Saint-Vincent-de-Paul (Laval, Que.), son of Vincent Chartrand and Marie-Charlotte Labelle; d. unmarried 26 March 1863 in his native parish.

As early as 1810 Vincent Chartrand was attending Louis-Amable Quévillon*'s school of sculpture at Saint-Vincent-de-Paul (commonly known as Les Écorres). Chartrand is mentioned in 1822 as a journeyman sculptor of René Saint-James*, *dit* Beauvais and he became a master-sculptor in 1824, when he went into partnership with Pierre-Salomon Benoît, *dit* Marquet, a Beloeil sculptor. The latter contract was suspended two years later, on 8 May 1826, revived in 1828, and terminated in 1834. During this period the names of Chartrand and Benoît were continually associated in important undertakings. In January 1826 the partners undertook to make a new vault and carve bas-reliefs in the parish church of Saint-Vincent-de-Paul. In that year they also worked on a new jube in the old church of Saint-Ours. The last assignment of the partnership appears to have been on the Île Dupas, where in 1831 substantial payments (£3,624) were made to the two sculptors for interior decoration of the church.

On 8 April 1833, seriously ill, Chartrand dictated a will to notary Jean-Baptiste Constantin of Saint-Vincent-de-Paul. This testament is important because it contains a list of parishes to which Chartrand bequeathed money through his partner. These were probably places where the sculptor had exercised his talents. Vincent Chartrand recovered quickly from his illness, however, and after the partnership contract expired in 1834 he abandoned interior architecture and worked exclusively as a sculptor. Benoît apparently had taken advantage of Chartrand's skill for developing the sculptural detail of buildings, while reserving the structure for himself. Concern with the craftsman's skill rather than with the over-all conception was characteristic of the Quévillon school. Thus the carvers concentrated on their tasks in the workshop during the winter months, and in summer went to the site to set the units in place; the ensemble (retable, vault, pulpit, and pew) would not necessarily have been conceived as a unit, as the Baillargé works in the Quebec region were.

The second part of Chartrand's career is distinguished by only a few pieces of sculpture. At Sault-au-Récollet, in 1836, the artist completed a pulpit "whose elegant form and finely carved details excite the admiration of all connoisseurs." The pulpit at Saint-Jean-Baptiste-de-Rouville, decorated with reliefs of the four evangelists with the apostles on the banisters, is also his work. His carved figures, such as the one of St Charles-Borromée done for the church at Lachenaie in 1843, and other reliefs and statues, are equally remarkable. From 1845 to 1853, Chartrand made the furnishings for the church of Caughnawaga, in particular three retables, a high altar, and the pulpit. The crowning achievement that, as it were, redeems the whole is undoubtedly the high altar, whose delicate and careful workmanship is in the purest Quévillon tradition.

The sculptures of Vincent Chartrand are gradually being distinguished from the productions of the Quévillon school as a whole. His paintings, however, remain relatively unknown. According to oral tradition, the artist had real talents as a painter. Noticing the daring *décolleté* of a portrait of Mme Charlotte Pépin, he, it is said, touched it up skilfully. In his second will, dictated in 1838, the artist bequeathed to the Sisters of Providence and to the hospice Saint-Pierre of Saint-Vincent-de-Paul an impressive set of pictures and a collection of prints; the latter represented precious material for a painter of religious themes in the 19th century. Chartrand presumably was the creator of these paintings for few artists of the period possessed collections of religious pictures they had not painted themselves. Finally, at the time of his death in March 1863 Vincent Chartrand bequeathed to his brother Toussaint, a doctor at Saint-Janvier, two paintings done by his own hand, one portraying his father and the other the archangel Gabriel.

Although as yet little known, Vincent Chartrand's work will occupy an increasingly important place in the history of Quebec art as the study of 19th century religious art in the Montreal region develops.

LUC NOPPEN

ANQ-M, État civil, Catholiques, Saint-Vincent-de-Paul (Laval), 18 juill. 1795, 26 mars 1863; Greffe de J.-B. Constantin, 14 sept. 1822, 23 févr. 1824, 2 juin 1828, 8 avril 1833, 21 nov. 1838, 17 mars 1863. IBC, Centre de documentation, Fonds Morisset, Dossier Vincent Chartrand; Dossiers Caughnawaga; île Dupas; Saint-Jean-Baptiste-de-Rouville; Saint-Ours; Saint-Vincent-de-Paul; Sault-au-Récollet. Gérard Morisset, *Coup d'œil sur les arts en Nouvelle-France* (Québec, 1941). Émile Vaillancourt, *Une maîtrise d'art en Canada (1800–1823)* (Montréal, 1920), 75–76.

CHAUSSEGROS DE LÉRY, CHARLES-JOSEPH, public servant, coseigneur of Rigaud-Vaudreuil, mayor, and county warden; b. 2 Sept. 1800 at Quebec, eldest son of Charles-Étienne Chaussegros* de Léry and Josephte Fraser; d. 4 Feb. 1864 at Saint-François-de-la-Beauce (Beauceville, Que).

Charles-Joseph was descended from the younger branch of the Chaussegros de Léry family, famous in Canadian military history. He studied at the Petit Séminaire de Québec from 1814 to 1818; thereafter for several years no record of him has been found. Like his father, he enjoyed the favour of the government, and he began his career in the public service on 12 April 1838 when Sir John COLBORNE appointed him deputy clerk of the Special Council of which his father at the same time became a member. When parliament reopened after the union of the Canadas, Chaussegros de Léry's appointment as deputy clerk of the Legislative Council was approved, on 23 July 1841. But as the clerk, James FITZGIBBON, was absent most of the time in England, the deputy clerk assumed entire responsibility for the post before he officially became the titular holder on 2 June 1847. Chaussegros de Léry decided, however, on 31 March 1850, to give up public service and devote himself exclusively to his Rigaud-Vaudreuil seigneury at Saint-François-de-la-Beauce. He subsequently was urged on more than one occasion to return to public life, as the representative of the county. Although he refused this honour, he reluctantly resigned himself to becoming mayor of Saint-François, then on 11 March 1860 warden of the county, a position he still held at the time of his death.

On the death of their father in 1842, Charles-Joseph and his brother Alexandre-René* had inherited conjointly the seigneuries of Rigaude-Vaudreuil and Sainte-Barbe-de-la-Famine, with their mother as usufructuary. However, Charles-Joseph, on the pretext that he was the elder, administered his father's estate until his own death as if he were sole owner. Before 1850 the Chaussegros de Léry family, who lived at Quebec, spent only the summer months on its lands in Beauce. When he left the public service, Chaussegros de Léry went to reside permanently at Saint-François-de-la-Beauce, and became a veritable father for his *censitaires*; he took an interest in their material and social welfare, and when necessary settled their differences. Eventually nobody called him anything but "M. Charles."

He began to amass his small fortune (with which he was not ungenerous) mainly from the time when the Beauce region appeared to be the Eldorado of Canada. The discovery of gold in the form of nuggets went back to 1834; it had been a purely chance discovery which at first had had few repercussions. But as it had occurred on his seigneury, Chaussegros de Léry wished to make the most of his chances. In return for a promise to hand over 10 per cent of the gross revenue to the public treasury, he obtained for his family, by letters patent dated 18 Sept. 1846, the exclusive and perpetual licence to mine precious metals on his lands and those of his *censitaires* on the Rigaud-Vaudreuil seigneury. After having the lands in question explored by John P. Cunningham, he undertook a mining operation himself, but found, as he put it, not an "atom of gold." Nor did his employees. In 1851 the Chaussegros de Léry family leased its mining rights to the Chaudière Mining Company, which was managed by Dr James Douglas* of Quebec. It made some success of the operation, and paid a royalty to the lessors.

As years passed, free right to search for gold was allowed to the farmers of the region, in return for a quarter of the gold found. But their primitive techniques and lack of loyalty reduced revenues, and they even began to speculate with the claims. Chaussegros de Léry's licence had already been challenged before the legislative authorities by his *censitaires*, who claimed to own the subsoil beneath their farms. Hence, before the expiry of the lease to James Douglas in 1863, Chaussegros de Léry prepared another for 15 years, made out to Messrs Parker, Hagens and Co. But he never learned the results of this action, for he died on 4 Feb. 1864 of a heart ailment. His brother Alexandre-René continued to mine the gold deposits.

Chaussegros de Léry, a man respected and mourned by all, was given a magnificent funeral at Saint-François-de-la-Beauce, and was buried in the church, a seigneur's privilege. On 30 Aug. 1851 he had married Mary O'Hara, an Irish woman from Quebec, who was an excellent helpmate; they had no children.

HONORIUS PROVOST

ANQ-Q, AP-G-40. PAC, MG 30, D62, 18, p.892. Bas-Canada, Conseil spécial, *Journaux*, 1838–39. Can., prov. du, *Doc. de la session*, 1863, VII, no.53; Assemblée législative, *Journaux*, 1865, I, app.7; Conseil législatif, *Journaux*, 1841. *Le Journal de Québec*, 22 févr. 1864. P.-G. Roy, *Fils de Québec*, III, 108–10. W. J. Anderson, *The valley of the Chaudiere, its scenery and gold fields* (Quebec, 1872). William Chapman, *Mines d'or de la Beauce; accompagné d'une carte topographique* (Lévis, Qué., 1881), 9–11. J. P. Cunningham, *Remarks on the mineralogical character of the seigneury of Rigaud, Vaudreuil, district of Quebec; dedicated to the proprietors, Charles and Alexander DeLery, esquires* (Montreal, 1847). Benjamin Demers, *Notes sur la paroisse de St-François de la Beauce* (Québec, 1891), 14–26. P.-G. Roy, *La famille Chaussegros de Léry* (Lévis, Qué., 1934). James Douglas, "The gold fields of Canada," Literary and Hist. Soc. of Quebec, *Trans.*, new ser., II (1864), 51–66. P.-G. Roy, "Les mines d'or de la Beauce," *BRH*, II (1896), 186.

CHEWETT, JAMES GRANT, surveyor, architect, contractor, and financier; b. 9 Nov. 1793 at New Johnstown (Cornwall), Upper Canada, second son of William Chewett* and Isabella Macdonell (McDonald); d. 7 Dec. 1862 at Toronto, Canada West.

Although James Grant Chewett's family moved from Cornwall to the new provincial capital of York (Toronto) in 1797, he was educated at his birthplace by John STRACHAN, thus coming into contact with many of those who later would form the Family Compact. About 1810 he entered the surveyor general's office where his father was deputy surveyor general (senior surveyor and draftsman). James' 30-year career in that office was interrupted by service during the War of 1812 as a lieutenant in the 3rd York militia regiment, commanded by his father; he fought at York and was paroled after the capture of the town in April 1813. Chewett was named a deputy surveyor in 1819, and became the deputy surveryor general on his father's retirement in 1832. When the capital was moved to Kingston in 1841 he retired with a pension of £135 per annum. He was responsible for the surveys of several townships located north and west of York, around Lake Simcoe, and near Kingston.

Chewett also displayed talents as an architect and contractor. In 1829 he designed part of the legislative buildings at York, and in 1832 he constructed as a private venture the town's first office building complex, the Chewett Block, on land he owned. He became a member of the building committee for St James' Church (Church of England) in York in 1832, and of the committees which superintended the construction of a new Home District jail (completed in 1840) and the Provincial Lunatic Asylum (1845). His plans for the St Lawrence Market (1831) were rejected.

In 1833 Chewett was appointed a justice of the peace for the Home District and, with Hugh RICHARDSON and William Chisholm*, to the commission superintending harbour improvements. When a permanent harbour commission was established in 1850 he was the appointee of the provincial government and was elected chairman by his fellow commissioners. During his chairmanship the first efforts were made to narrow and stabilize the Western Gap by land fill. He acted as curator for the Literary and Philosophical Society of Upper Canada in the early 1830s. He also served Toronto as an alderman for St George's ward in 1838–39.

Chewett displayed a lifelong interest in Toronto's financial development. He was one of the incorporators in 1833 of the town's first insurance company, the British America Fire and Life Assurance Company. In 1855 he became chairman of the provisional board and one of the original directors of the Canada Permanent Building and Savings Society (later the Canada Mortgage Corporation). Following his retirement from government service Chewett was elected to the board of directors of the Bank of Upper Canada; his financial conservatism enabled him to become vice-president in 1849 but he resigned in 1856 in disagreement with the policies which were to lead to the bank's collapse in 1866. He became the first president of the Bank of Toronto in 1856: his conservative and cautious nature provided the ideal leadership for a fledgling institution in a time of financial difficulties. He retained the presidency until his sudden death in 1862. To his children he left a substantial estate in the form of commercial property in Toronto and $76,000 in stocks in local financial institutions.

Chewett had married Martha Smith Robison of Kingston in 1825. They had two sons and one daughter; the eldest, William Cameron, though trained in medicine, became a prominent businessman in Toronto.

A trusted, talented, and industrious member of Upper Canada's early Toronto-based ruling group, Chewett's leadership and experience were often sought after for developments in that city. His many-sided career, especially his entrance into the financial world after 1841, demonstrate that members of the Family Compact did not necessarily become inactive with responsible government. Many, such as Chewett, were in fact able to turn their interests and ambition from government office to financial and commercial ventures and to enjoy much the same success.

ROBERT J. BURNS

PAO, RG 1 (catalogue entries for J. G. Chewett); RG 22, ser.7, 14–33. York County Surrogate Court (Toronto), will of James Grant Chewett. *Globe*, 9 Dec. 1862. *Town of York, 1793–1815* (Firth). *Town of York, 1815–34* (Firth). Armstrong, *Handbook of Upper Canadian chronology. Brown's Toronto city and Home District directory, 1846–7* (Toronto, 1846). *Brown's Toronto general directory, 1856 . . .* (Toronto, [1856]). Chadwick, *Ontarian families. The city of Toronto and the Home District commercial directory and register with almanack and calendar for 1837 . . .*, comp. George Walton (Toronto, [1837]). *York commercial directory, street guide, and register, 1833–4 . . .*, comp. George Walton (York [Toronto], [1833]). D. C. Masters, *The rise of Toronto, 1850–1890* (Toronto, 1947). Middleton, *Municipality of Toronto. Robertson's landmarks of Toronto*, I, 356, 362. W. A. Sims, "James Grant Chewett," Assoc. of Ont. Land Surveyors, *Annual report* (Toronto), no.36 (1921), 112–17.

CHIPMAN, WILLIAM HENRY, merchant, farmer, and politician; b. 3 Nov. 1807 in Cornwallis, Kings County, N.S., second son of the Reverend William Chipman and his first wife, Mary Dickey; m. 6 Jan. 1831 Sophia Araminta Cogswell, and they had nine children; d. 10 April 1870 in Ottawa, Ont.

About 1764 William Henry Chipman's grandfather, William Allen Chipman*, had moved with his family from Rhode Island to Cornwallis where he had eventually built a sizeable fortune as merchant, farmer, and landowner and had held several elective and appointive positions in the county. William Henry's father carried on the family businesses, established his own large farm, took a leading role in the Baptist Church, assisted in the founding of that church's Horton Academy (1828) and Acadia College (1838), and held numerous public offices in Kings County, including justice of the peace. There was, then, a well-established family tradition of public service and business enterprise.

William Henry Chipman probably received little formal education as public facilities were scarce in Nova Scotia during his youth and King's Collegiate School at Windsor, N.S., remained closed to "Dissenters." The education that he did receive was of a more practical kind: at an early age Chipman was sent to Saint John, N.B., to the firm of Leverett DeVeber, apparently a family friend, to learn business and merchandising practices.

After his return to the Cornwallis district, Chipman began his long and successful career in business and farming, which he pursued relatively independently of his father's enterprises. By the early 1850s he was a properous merchant dealing in general merchandise. His speculations in land and his dealings in mortages in Cornwallis Township seem to have been more lucrative. During the 1830s and 1840s, he had acquired an impressive array of properties and held mortgages on even larger tracts of land. He also held mortgages on sailing vessels and loaned money to business ventures in the Kings County region. At his death the *Novascotian* credited him with "the largest fortune in that section of the province."

Clare

In addition to his full business career, William Henry Chipman also followed family tradition in local politics. As early as 1832 he began serving as both clerk of the peace and clerk of licences for Kings County, filling the former position for 35 consecutive years. He also served after 1834 as deputy prothonotary, and after 1853 as prothonotary for the county, and between 1842 and 1855 as registrar of the Court of Probate. At various times he was appointed to investigate payment offered for land appropriated for public use, and served on county committees to examine such questions as the need for a poor-house in the area. The local school district also had Chipman's energetic attention, as he paid the largest sums for maintaining the school and gave the most in making up recurrent operating deficits.

The climax of Chipman's public career came in 1867 with his election as an anti-confederate member of parliament for Kings County to the first House of Commons of the new dominion. Again he was following family precedent, as the Chipmans appear to have been staunchly Reform or Liberal from the late 1830s. Elected with a large majority, Chipman joined fellow Nova Scotians in their battle for repeal of the union or better terms for their province. Although a follower of Joseph Howe*, Chipman was by no means subservient. At the stormy anti-confederate convention held in Halifax in August 1868, Chipman openly opposed Howe on the best means of obtaining repeal. He proposed that all anti-confederate members of the Nova Scotian assembly and the House of Commons "should forthwith tender their resignations" as "the best method of settling the difficulty between the Local and Dominion members and beyond all this, the most effectual way of obtaining repeal." This was not, however, the policy adopted, and so Chipman and the other "antis" continued to sit in the House of Commons. His parliamentary career was cut short by a sudden and fatal attack of smallpox in the spring of 1870 in Ottawa. The day after his death the house adjourned on the motion of Howe, seconded by Sir John A. Macdonald*, and heard eulogies in which even Charles Tupper* joined, referring to him as "a member of one of the oldest and most respected families in his Province."

That Chipman was not universally popular even in Kings County, however, was made quite clear soon after his death, when his son, Leverett DeVeber Chipman, announced his intention of seeking his father's House of Commons seat. An anonymous broadside of 31 July 1872, signed "An Elector," denounced the Chipman "compact" – "this old and corrupt ring." There is no clear indication that resentment against "a family who has always monopolized the principal offices of this county" was widespread, but the fact that it was voiced at all is a significant comment on the impact of the Chipman family.

William Henry Chipman, with his numerous political offices and wide business interests, in many respects represented the height of the Chipman family influence in Kings County. Some of his children followed distinguished careers in the medical and political professions, but the dominant role of the Chipman family in Kings County was largely at an end.

BARRY M. MOODY

Acadia University Archives (Wolfville, N.S.), MS Box 82 (school district 3, Cornwallis), Parade School, accounts, 1857–62; MS Box 91 (records of town meetings, Cornwallis, 1795–1862). Kings County Court House (Kentville, N.S.), Probate record books, nos.2, 3. PANS, MG 1, 181–218 (Chipman family papers). *To the electors of Kings County, by an elector* (Kentville, N.S., 1872). *Christian Messenger* (Halifax), 13 April 1870. *Novascotian*, 11, 18 April 1870. *A Chipman genealogy, circa 1583–1969, beginning with John Chipman (1620–1708), first of that surname to arrive in the Massachusetts Bay colony . . . ,* comp. J. H. Chipman III (Norwell, Mass., 1970). *Directory of N.S. MLAs.* A. W. H. Eaton, *The history of Kings County, Nova Scotia . . .* (Salem, Mass., 1910).

CLARE, JAMES ROBERT, HBC chief factor; b. 1 Nov. 1827, son of Stephen Clare; m. 23 May 1861 Margaret, daughter of Thomas Sinclair, Red River merchant, at Lower Fort Garry (Man.); d. 3 Jan. 1867 at London, England.

Following an education at the Royal Naval School in Camberwell (now in London), a year's counting-house experience, and brief training in shorthand and surveying, James Robert Clare was appointed apprentice clerk by the Hudson's Bay Company in 1845. He arrived on 8 September at Moose Factory where he spent the 1845–46 season. Except for a season at Edmonton House (1847–48) under Chief Factor John Edward HARRIOTT, and one as chief trader in charge of the company's Rainy Lake District (1856–57), Clare served at York Factory from 1846 to 1864. Initially an assistant in the counting-house, Clare, under Chief Factor James HARGRAVE, rose by the early 1850s to take charge of the accounts of the Northern Department of Rupert's Land and by 1858 of York Factory itself. Clare saw York at the height of its mid century importance as supply depot for the north and when it began to decline in the late 1850s as a result of the company's adoption of the overland

Coates

route via St Paul (Minn.) and Upper Fort Garry. In 1861, at the time of his marriage, Clare went with his bride to England on furlough.

Clare, chief factor from 1862, was transferred from York in 1864 to Upper Fort Garry where he took charge of the company's Red River District. He also acted in place of William MACTAVISH as chief officer of the Northern Department during Mactavish's absences from Red River between 1864 and 1866. In late 1866 Clare went to England on private business and died unexpectedly in London from dysentery in January 1867. He was survived by two sons and by his widow, who remarried and continued to live in Red River.

Clare's early death was a serious loss to the company, depriving it of a most able and vigorous officer. His training, experience, and outlook would likely have fitted him for an important position in the changed circumstances of the company after 1870.

JOAN CRAIG

HBC Arch. A.1/78, p.126; A.5/14, pp.353–54; A.6/39, p.308; A.6/41, pp.18, 25, 49, 52–53; A.10/17, ff.385–87d.; A.10/69, f.133; A.11/98; A.11/118, ff.404–6, 464; A.12/9, f.176; A.12/43, f.213–13d.; A.12/44, ff.34d., 194d.–96, 261–61d.; A.16/63, f.58; A.16/64, f.38; A.16/66, f.258; A.33/2, ff.321, 323; A.36/1b, pp.60–62; A.44/4, p.90; B.60/d/87, f.2d.; B.134/c/124, 27 Feb. 1873; B.135/a/150, 8 Sept. 1845; B.135/a/151, 1, 2 June 1846; B.154/a/49, 18 June 1848; B.154/b/10; B.239/c/13, f.59; B.239/k/3, pp.171, 192, 211, 218, 232, 254, 275, 297; B.239/u/1, ff.72d–73; C.1/676, f.3d.; C.1/677, f.21; C.1/855, ff.1d., 3, 7, 52; D.4/54, pp.328–30; D.4/68, p.374; D.4/75, pp.778–79; D.4/76a, ff.357–60, 862–65; D.5/15, ff.57, 59–62d.; D.5/21, f.54; D.5/25, f.506; D.5/26, f.640; D.5/28, ff.13d., 400d.–1d.; D.5/43, ff.524f. PABC, Thomas Lowe journal, 1843–50, 25 May 1848 (mfm. at HBC Arch.). PAM, MG 7, B4, register of marriages, 1860–83, 23 May 1861 (mfm. at HBC Arch.). J. J. Hargrave, *Red River* (Montreal, 1871), 411. Mac-Tavish, *Letters of Letitia Hargrave* (MacLeod). W. J. Healy, *Women of Red River; being a book written down from the recollections of women surviving from the Red River era* (Winnipeg, 1923), 46. A. C. Gluek, "The fading glory," *Beaver*, outfit 288 (winter 1957), 50–55.

COATES, RICHARD, musician, painter, sawmill owner, and organ builder; b. 30 Nov. 1778 at Thornton Dale, Yorkshire, England, the son of Richard Coates and Dorothy Reynolds; m. on 5 Nov. 1805 Isabella Smith, and they had at least three children; d. 29 Jan. 1868 in Aldborough Township, Ont.

Nothing is known about Richard Coates' education. He is reported to have played in a British army band during the Peninsular War and to have been a bandmaster at the battle of Waterloo. On 13 May 1817 he arrived at Quebec where he stayed for 15 months before settling at York (Toronto). Like Louis Dulongpré* of Montreal, Coates was active in both music and the fine arts. Henry Scadding* recalled Coates as "an estimable and ingenious man, whose name is associated in our memory with the early dawn of the fine arts in York. Mr. Coates, in a self-taught way, executed, not unsuccessfully, portraits in oil of some of our ancient worthies." When he petitioned for land as a settler in 1824, he described himself as a painter at York. In 1831 Coates moved to Trafalgar Township, east of present-day Oakville, where he acquired land and set up a water-powered sawmill and a threshing mill. His business prospered and he and his sons were esteemed for their honesty and pleasant banter. Shortly after 1860 the economic depression forced Coates to leave the Oakville area, and he spent his last years on a farm, part of which is now in the village of Rodney.

Although Coates does not appear ever to have been a resident of Hope (Sharon), Upper Canada, he was associated for several decades with the Children of Peace, a religious group led by David WILLSON who inhabited that village. It is not known whether he was a member of the group, but its musical and artistic needs provided an outlet for his talents. He painted the symbolic pictures for the temple at Sharon, titled "Peace" and "Plenty," in which a modern art critic has detected some of the "naïve quality of early Quebec ex-votos." At various times he acted as choirmaster or bandmaster for the Children of Peace and also gave individual lessons on various instruments. William Lyon MACKENZIE heard Coates play the "concert horn" in the small orchestra at Sharon in 1829. Undoubtedly much of the credit for the excellence of the band and the choir at Sharon belongs to Coates.

Although Coates was probably Toronto's first resident painter, he is best known as an organ builder, a craft to which he could bring his musical training and his interest in mechanical gadgets. He is reputed to have built seven organs. Of three that he made for the Children of Peace, the first, built about 1820 and preserved at Sharon, may be the oldest surviving, if not the first instrument of its kind built in Canada. It has no keyboard but two barrels with ten sacred tunes each, nearly all of which are British in origin. It is probably the organ Mackenzie described as "full-toned and soft-set." The second organ was similar in design but had three barrels of ten tunes each, including traditional ballads and hymns. It was placed in the study of the leader of the Chil-

Cochrane

dren of Peace, but later had other owners. The third organ was built in 1848 for the Second Meeting House at Sharon. It has a keyboard and approximately 200 pipes and is the largest of the known Coates organs. It has been displayed in the Sharon Temple since about 1913. At the age of 79 Coates was commissioned to build a keyboard organ for St Jude's Church at Oakville; it gave the congregation "great satisfaction" until it was discarded about 1899. Scadding remembered that even in his Toronto days Coates had one of his own organs in his home; it is still in family hands.

Coates is also reputed to have built a four-foot telescope for his own use, an "elegantly-finished little pleasure yacht, of about nine tons burden," as well as a "pulmoter," a gadget to revive drowning persons which was successfully used on the Toronto waterfront to save dogs, though not human beings.

HELMUT KALLMANN

W. L. Mackenzie, Sketches of Canada and the United States (London, 1833). Scadding, Toronto of old (1873). Landmarks of Can. J. R. Harper, Early painters and engravers; Painting in Canada, a history (Toronto, 1966); A people's art: primitive, naïve, provincial, and folk painting in Canada (Toronto, 1974). Helmut Kallmann, A history of music in Canada, 1534–1914 (Toronto and London, 1960). A. H. Lightbourn, Saint Jude's Church, Oakville, 1842–1957, an historical sketch ([Oakville, Ont., 1957]). Emily McArthur, A history of the Children of Peace (Newmarket, Ont., [n.d.]). C. E. McFaddin, "A study of the buildings of the Children of Peace, Sharon, Ontario" (unpublished MA thesis, 2v., University of Toronto, 1953). H. C. Mathews, Oakville and the Sixteen: the history of an Ontario port (Toronto, 1953). Tim Classey, "The old pipe organ," York Pioneer (Toronto), 1974, 67–69. E. W. Trewhella, "The story of Sharon," Newmarket Era (Newmarket, Ont.), 14 June 1951–27 March 1952.

COCHRANE, JOHN JAMES, engineer, land agent, auctioneer, and politician; b. c. 1827, probably in Scotland; d. 6 March 1867 at Victoria, B.C.

John James Cochrane apprenticed in Scotland as a millwright and engineer; his first employer, the manager of Shotts Iron Works, Edinburgh, described him as "a young gentleman of great intelligence, ability, energy and skill." Cochrane subsequently worked for several years for the Board of Northern Lighthouses in Scotland as a superintendent of construction of several difficult projects.

Cochrane arrived in New Westminster, British Columbia, at the end of 1858 with letters of high praise from his former employers. For a period of six months he worked in and around New Westminster as a civilian surveyor and engineer under Colonel Richard Moody*. This employment ended when Governor James Douglas*, because of budgetary difficulties, ordered in the summer of 1859 that all civilian surveyors be dismissed and their work be taken over by Royal Engineers.

Cochrane subsequently moved to Victoria, where he soon became an active and well-known resident. At first he was employed by the government, and he undertook such assignments as superintending the construction of the Race Rocks lighthouse and inspecting work being done at Pemberton Portage on the new Harrison Lake – Lillooet route to the Cariboo gold mines. Soon afterwards he entered the real estate and auction business. His excellent training and experience continued to be recognized and he was appointed an assessor of real estate for Victoria in 1860, a member of the Victoria Harbour Commission in 1861, and a member of the General Board of Education of Vancouver Island in 1865. He entered politics, and from 1864 to 1866 was the member for Saanich in the Legislative Assembly for Vancouver Island. He took a leading part in the successful effort to have the capital moved from New Westminster to Victoria in 1866.

Cochrane died suddenly, aged 40, leaving a wife and four children.

HELEN B. AKRIGG

PABC, John James Cochrane correspondence. Daily British Colonist and Victoria Chronicle, 8 March 1867.

COCKBURN, Sir FRANCIS, soldier: b. 10 Nov. 1780 in England, the fifth son of Sir James Cockburn, 6th Baronet of Langton, and his second wife, Augusta Anne Ayscough; m. in 1804 Alicia Sandys; d. 24 Aug. 1868 at East Cliff, Dover, England.

Francis Cockburn entered the 7th Dragoon Guards as a cornet at age 19 and through purchase of commissions and promotion rose to the rank of captain in 1804. He served in South America in 1807 and in the Iberian Peninsula in 1809 and 1810. On 27 June 1811 he arrived in Canada as a captain in the Canadian Fencibles and in September of that year was promoted major. During the War of 1812 Cockburn displayed himself as a competent and diligent officer. He led successful raids against enemy forces in 1813 at Red Mills, N.Y., south of Prescott, Upper Canada, and in 1814 at the Salmon River in Franklin County, N.Y. In November and December 1814 Cockburn commanded a company of Canadian Fencibles which, with a detachment of sappers and miners, traversed what would become the "Penetang Road" between Lake Simcoe and Penetanguishene on Georgian Bay. Cockburn's report to Sir Thomas Sydney Beckwith, quartermaster-general for Upper and Lower Canada, favoured the British scheme of establishing a naval base at Penetanguishene.

After 22 July 1814 Cockburn served at York (Toronto) and at Kingston in the Quartermaster-General's Department for Upper Canada. On 26 June 1815 his abilities were recognized by his elevation to the rank of lieutenant-colonel in the New Brunswick Fencibles and his appointment as assistant quartermaster-general for Upper Canada. In addition to his regular duties he was responsible for settling and provisioning the first groups of immigrants and disbanded soldiers to arrive in Upper Canada under Colonial Secretary Lord Bathurst's plan for assisted emigration. Some 1,500 people were established near Perth in the Bathurst District in mid 1816, and in September Cockburn made an important early report on settlement in this area.

Cockburn was transferred from Kingston to Quebec to become deputy quartermaster-general for Upper and Lower Canada on 10 Jan. 1818. As senior officer in the department he was responsible for the military settlements in Upper Canada at Perth (established in 1816), Richmond (1818), Lanark (1820), and the Bay of Quinte area and Glengarry County (1815), and in Lower Canada on the Rivière Saint-François (1816). With characteristic industry Cockburn enlarged his Quebec office (which, he complained in 1819, was "literally filled with settlers from Morning to Night"), dealt with settlers' petitions, and conducted numerous tours of the settlements. His reports provide valuable evidence of the early growth of these settlements. They also reveal in Cockburn, who himself held land in the Bay of Quinte area, a great personal interest in the development of the Rideau Lakes district: it was he who urged the plan of settlement adopted with the establishment of Richmond in 1818, and his belief in the potential prosperity of the district was demonstrated in his founding of Franktown in Beckwith Township, a village with his own name which he hoped would become a major trading centre. Cockburn's work in these settlements officially ended with the cessation of military control on Christmas eve 1822, but he continued to superintend them until June 1823.

While serving at Quebec, Cockburn gained a special knowledge of Canada. In 1821 he accompanied Lord Dalhousie [Ramsay*] on a tour of inspection of over 1,600 miles, which extended to the military posts on the western frontier of Upper Canada. Cockburn Island, a hamlet, and a township in the Manitoulin district bear his name in recognition of his part in this tour. The following year Cockburn surveyed the Gaspé Peninsula to determine its potential for settlement. His most notable journey, however, was as attendant to the Duke of Richmond [Lennox*] on his fateful tour of Perth and Richmond in August 1819; Cockburn's diary remains the main source for the events leading to the commander-in-chief's tragic death of hydrophobia.

Cockburn began an extended leave of absence from the Quartermaster-General's Office at Quebec in July 1823, when he returned to England. In 1825 he was one of the five commissioners, including John Davidson, asked to fix the price of lands to be purchased in Upper Canada by the Canada Company. The following year Cockburn was an important witness before a British parliamentary committee which asked him to prepare a report on past programmes of assisted emigration. Cockburn recommended strong government support of emigration, including an 18-month supply of provisions for settlers. He suggested settlement in the Gaspé and Ottawa regions and between lakes Simcoe and Huron, as well as along a line of communication between New Brunswick and Lower Canada. Cockburn opposed assisted settlement in the Eastern Townships because he felt the French Canadians and their seigneurial system offered a better barrier against the United States.

In 1827 the undersecretary of state for the colonies dispatched Cockburn on a tour of British North America to determine which remaining lands were suitable for settlement and to make tentative arrangements for possible future immigration. In his 1828 report Cockburn saw little room for further settlement but he recommended that six townships be laid out in New Brunswick in the tract between the Petitcodiac and Miramichi rivers. Again he stressed the importance of a strong communications link between New Brunswick and the Canadas.

Cockburn's tour in 1827 was his last involvement in the affairs of British North America. He had assiduously pursued his career in Canada, although his determination when frustrated could produce in him a saturnine disposition. Nevertheless, his commanding officers always expressed confidence in his abilities and frequently praised his performance of his duties.

On 30 July 1829 Cockburn joined the 2nd West India Foot, and in September of that year was ordered to British Honduras, where from 1830 to 1837 he was superintendent of the colony. From 1837 to 1844 he served as governor and commander-in-chief of the Bahamas; he had been knighted in 1841. In 1846 he was elevated to the rank of major-general, and on 26 Dec. 1853 was appointed colonel of the 95th Foot. He became lieutenant-general in 1854 and general in 1860, and died in 1868.

ED MCKENNA

PAC, MG 24, A14 (includes Cockburn's journal); F29; RG 8, I (C series), nominal index. PRO, CO 42/182, pp.11–16; CO 42/198, pp.3–14. PAC *Report*, 1897. G. B., Parl., House of Commons paper, 1825, XIX, 215, pp.461–74, *Canada Company: minutes of the intended arrangements between Earl Bathurst, his majesty's secretary of state, and the proposed Canada Company*; 1826, IV, 404, pp.1–381, *Report from the select committee on emigration from the United Kingdom*; 1826–27, V, 88, pp.1–2, *Report from the select committee on emigration, 1827*; 237, pp.3–224, *Second report from the select committee on emigration from the United Kingdom, 1827*; 550, pp.225–882, *Third report from the select committee on emigration from the United Kingdom, 1827*; 1828, XXI, 109, pp.359–78, *Emigration: return to an address of the Honourable the House of Commons . . .* ; 148, pp.379–482, *Emigration: further return to an address of the Honourable the House of Commons. . . .* Gates, *Land policies of U. C.* Andrew Haydon, *Pioneer sketches in the district of Bathurst* (Toronto, 1925). J. S. McGill, *A pioneer history of the county of Lanark* (Toronto, 1968). H. [J.W.] and Olive Walker, *Carleton saga* (Ottawa, 1968).

COCKRAN, WILLIAM (the name is sometimes written Cochrane, an error arising from a family arrangement whereby his son, the Reverend Thomas Cochrane, used this spelling), Church of England clergyman and missionary; b. 1796 or 1797 in Chillingham, Northumberland, England; d. 1 Oct. 1865 in Portage la Prairie (Man.).

Little is known of the Reverend William Cockran before his arrival in the Red River Settlement with his wife Ann and an infant son on 4 Oct. 1825. Cockran, a Scot, was apparently raised a Presbyterian, becoming a member of the Church of England as a young man. Both Cockran and his wife were of relatively humble origin: according to J. W. Brooks of the Church Missionary Society, "he would not suit a congregation in England – his origin is low – his wife, though a discreet and pious woman, was a servant maid – his manners unpolished and indicate his origin . . . his dialect broad and vulgar even as a scotchman." Cockran, Brooks reports, "was bred up to agriculture," employed as "under bailiff in Scotland," and later "set up a small school for children at Ordsall." His knowledge of husbandry and his intense desire to serve as a missionary made him a suitable candidate for the Church Missionary Society. A medical report on this physically "very big and vigorous man" that found him unsuitable for tropical climates was probably responsible for his selection as the third CMS missionary to be sent to Rupert's Land. Cockran was ordained deacon 19 Dec. 1824 and priest 29 May 1825, barely a week previous to his departure for the Red River Settlement.

Cockran arrived in the settlement at a critical juncture in the affairs of the Anglican mission and the development of Red River. The Reverend John West*, who had come in 1820 to establish the mission, and the Reverend David Thomas Jones*, who succeeded West in 1823, had determined the particular nature of the mission's relationship with the Hudson's Bay Company and with the Roman Catholic missionaries at Saint-Boniface (Man.). Much, however, remained to be accomplished. The principal challenge facing Jones and Cockran was the evangelization of the large numbers of mixed-bloods migrating from the trading posts of the interior to Red River especially after the amalgamation of the HBC and the North West Company in 1821. For business and philanthropic reasons the HBC encouraged supernumeraries in and about their posts to move to Red River where they would come under the influence of churches, schools, and civil government. Those mixed-bloods whose antecedents linked them to Lower Canada, the Métis, settled as buffalo hunters to the south and west of the junction of the Red and Assiniboine rivers and were ministered to by French Canadian Roman Catholic priests. Those mixed-bloods who derived from British progenitors, largely Orkneymen, and who were known as half-breeds or Country-born, settled to the north of the junction of the two rivers and came under the auspices of the Anglican mission. Their numbers were such that they soon overshadowed the few families of Presbyterian Kildonan Scots farmers, the original settlers brought by Selkirk [Douglas*]. As a majority of the Country-born families were not headed by a British-born parent they had little if any knowledge of the technical, economic, and social skills necessary for success as agriculturalists in a sedentary community. If the Anglican mission was to succeed, the cultural ways of the Country-born had to be adapted to circumstances in Red River. Quite quickly Cockran perceived that evangelization was not enough; "civilization" was equally important.

In 1827 Cockran therefore resolved to expand the farming operations of the mission at Upper Church (later St John's). The reduction of expenses for supplies was the principal reason he cited to win the support of his co-worker, Jones, and the directors of the CMS. It soon became evident that Cockran had had other reasons. Besides providing additional means of alleviating the poverty of his parishioners, the farm became a practical demonstration of the skills settlers needed for success in Red River. During visits among his parishioners Cockran instructed young and old alike in the most rudimentary techniques associated with the handling and care of farm animals and the planting, harvesting, and storing of vegetable and grain crops. But a knowledge of technical skills was not enough. Men who had spent their lives as servants of the HBC, which gave responsibility for the necessities of life and the planning of daily tasks to the officer in charge, were ill equipped to manage their riverlot farms. Cockran found himself acting also as an administrator and financial adviser. Still other problems arose. The Country-born, familiar with the social usages of the trading post, had difficulty adjusting to the society of the settlement. Cockran was called upon to mediate disputes within families and between neighbours. Frequently it was Cockran who aroused his parishioners to take cooperative action in the interests of the whole parish. From the pulpit, in the Sunday and day schools, and during visits, Cockran preached the message of evangelical Anglicanism, but inseparable from his religious message were the precepts of social behaviour which he felt were necessary if the Country-born were to survive as a Christian and civilized community in Red River.

In 1829, leaving Jones to carry on missionary work at Upper Church and Middle Church (later St Paul's), Cockran followed the flow of settlement northward down the Red River to establish Lower Church (later St Andrew's) at Grand Rapids. Here, amidst a population of bewildered and destitute Country-born settlers, he repeated the programme he had initiated at Upper Church. In 1832 when the Indian school, founded by West, was transferred to his care, he established a school of industry, which trained the boys in weaving, carpentry, and husbandry, and instructed the girls in spinning and other domestic duties.

Cockran's success at Lower Church led him to try a similar program with PEGUIS' band of Saulteaux, residing at the northern extremity of the settlement. With the assistance of a Country-born catechist, Joseph Cook, Cockran commenced his work with this band in 1831. It was difficult. The Saulteaux were far less responsive to the missionary's efforts than the Country-born settlers. But with patience and compassion Cockran instructed, pleaded, cajoled, and, on one occasion at least, threatened physical coer-

cion to win the support of a hesitant few. The increasingly enthusiastic support of Peguis was instrumental in crowning his efforts with some measure of success. In 1836 he began the construction of a church in the Indian Settlement (later St Peter's) to mark his labours among these people.

In the later 1830s Cockran's zeal waned. Believing that civilization was as important as evangelization, he was keenly disappointed that neither his Country-born nor his Indian parishioners adopted British practices to the extent he felt was necessary for their temporal success and their spiritual salvation. It was evident to him that they chose to maintain many of the cultural elements of the trading post and the trapline. Their homes collectively might look like a British country village, but their life was much different. Hunting, trapping, and tripping, occupations which Cockran frowned upon, continued to attract many of the Country-born and the Indians for at least part of the year. And in other areas of their social life older ways persisted, a noteworthy example being their child-rearing practices to which Cockran never completely reconciled himself. Self-doubt now began to mark his journal entries and letters. He also struck out at what he believed were the shortcomings of his co-workers, Jones, and the directors of the CMS. But the full sting of his pen and tongue was reserved for the officers of the HBC and, to an extent, Governor George Simpson*.

Cockran's work at Lower Church and the Indian Settlement was a success in that large numbers of Indians were attracted to Red River. Indeed the exodus from the interior reached such proportions that the company's officers became alarmed. No doubt their alarm would have increased had they been aware that Cockran saw in this migration the means of evangelizing a far larger number of Indians in Rupert's Land. Rather than having to journey into the interior and establish missions in areas unsuitable for settled agrarian communities, Cockran would encourage the Indians to move to the region of Red River and establish river-lot farms. The officers of the company and Simpson replied to Cockran's challenge to their livelihood by placing numerous barriers in the way of the migrants. Cockran, already suffering doubts concerning the value of his work, replied with vehemence. His relations with Simpson remained fairly cordial, but most of the company's officers do not emerge in a favourable light in Cockran's reports. Quite possibly as a result of this experience Simpson gave some encouragement to the Wesleyan Methodists for missionary work in the in-

135

Cockran

terior. They proposed to Christianize but not civilize the Indians. Their appearance early in the 1840s further disturbed the distraught Cockran.

In the same decade Cockran faced a new problem in the free trade movement among the mixed-bloods, directed against the company's monopoly [see Louis RIEL]. Cockran himself had reservations concerning some of the policies and actions of the company, but considered it the principal supporting power behind many of the settlement's institutions. These same institutions enshrined British practices that Cockran wished to inculcate in his parishioners. A victory for the free traders would create a less hospitable environment for the goals he sought. In his mind he saw the Country-born and Indian settlers forced to abandon their farms and return to the forests of the interior. In these circumstances Cockran began to take a less jaundiced view of the worth of his own work and the value of the company to his missionary labours. Perhaps in earlier years he had hoped for too much too soon. His support for the company grew when the increasing presence of the Métis in the free trade movement suggested the possibility of a French and Roman Catholic ascendancy in Red River.

The arrival of British troops in the settlement in 1846, which seemed to dispel the threat posed by the free traders, and the coming the previous year of the Reverend Robert James allowed Cockran to act on his plans to retire. Since 1840 he had been discussing this possibility with the directors of the CMS. Although he suffered from a hernia and nervous exhaustion Cockran would not abandon his work until an adequate replacement had been found. Sensing that he would not be happy in Britain, Cockran left Red River with his family in 1846 for Toronto. The next year, through the kind assistance of Simpson, they were back in Red River, Cockran apparently much improved in health. Accepting the chaplaincy of the company offered by Simpson, Cockran took up residence close to Upper Church where he worked with the Reverend John Macallum.

During the next few years Cockran saw a number of changes in Red River to which he adjusted with difficulty. In 1849 he welcomed the appointment of the Reverend David Anderson* as the first Church of England bishop of Rupert's Land. In recognition of Cockran's past services and the example he could offer to young missionaries, the bishop made him archdeacon in 1853. Cockran did not enjoy his clerical duties at St John's where his abilities as a missionary, which had made him the most respected and influential person at Grand Rapids and the Indian

Settlement, were not appreciated by the more sophisticated parishioners. His support for the unpopular recorder Adam Thom*, when pressure from the Métis persuaded Governor Simpson to request that Thom step down as recorder for the court of Assiniboia, and for the ineffective Governor William Bletterman Caldwell* isolated him from his congregation. Nor did all his parishioners sympathize with the uncompromising position he took in the scandal involving Captain Christopher Vaughan Foss and Chief Factor John Ballenden*'s wife. When a dispute with the Presbyterian Kildonan Scots emerged, concerning the disposition of their claims to privileges associated with the church and graveyard at St John's, Cockran did not facilitate an accommodation. Other similar incidents indicated that the aging missionary was not in harmony with new circumstances.

No doubt Cockran leapt at the chance to succeed the Reverend John SMITHURST at the Indian Settlement in 1851; there he was in his element. In the same year he went up the Assiniboine to choose a site for a CMS mission. He recommended a location known as Portage la Prairie. The next year a few of his former parishioners from St Andrew's established river-lot farms at this place, and in succeeding years more settlers from St Andrew's made the same journey. In 1855 they constructed St Mary's Church. In 1857 Cockran left the Indian Settlement to work among the Saulteaux and Country-born at Portage la Prairie. By 1860 lands to the east had been taken up. Under Cockran's guidance St Margaret's was constructed at High Bluff and St Anne's at Poplar Point. His son Thomas, ordained in the Church of England in 1852, assisted him in Portage la Prairie.

At St Mary's Cockran found ample reason to appreciate his experience as a councillor, since 1835, on the Council of Assiniboia, the local governing body in Red River. As Portage la Prairie was beyond the boundaries of Assiniboia the settlers had to administer their own affairs. Difficulties arose as disputes between individuals rapidly took on the dimensions of family feuds. The kinship connections that had regulated social life at Grand Rapids and that could be traced back to the trading posts of the interior in the previous century complicated the administration of local government. Only an individual such as Cockran, respected by all and familiar with the intricate workings of the system, could be a stabilizing influence. On more than one occasion his influence calmed a potentially disruptive situation.

In 1865, with his health failing, Cockran again

136

retired to Toronto. Medical treatment seemed to restore him to full vigour. Returning to the west the same year, he left St Mary's in the capable hands of his son-in-law, the Reverend Henry George, to work among the settlers at Westbourne (Man.). A sudden chill caused his return to his daughter's house in Portage la Prairie where he died. He was buried in the churchyard at St Andrew's, the scene of his early labours and noteworthy accomplishments.

Traditionally Cockran's career has been evaluated in terms of his contribution to Anglican missionary enterprise in Rupert's Land. Perhaps a more meaningful basis for examining his career is the experience of the Country-born community in the generation following his death. The presence of Canadians in Red River and Portage la Prairie heralded the coming of a new order. As this new order was established, the original inhabitants, Indian and mixed-blood, paid a heavy price in human suffering. The Métis in particular were virtually destroyed as a people. Apparently the Country-born did not experience the same disruption and suffering. Part of the explanation is to be found in their culture and especially those features of it which enabled them to adapt to change. More than any other person the Reverend William Cockran was responsible for encouraging much that allowed them to enter a new age with a minimum of pain.

J. E. FOSTER

[The most extensive source materials available on the Reverend William Cockran are the documents at the CMS Arch. (London), Northwest Missions, incoming and outgoing correspondence, containing his letters and journals; the PAC holds microfilm of this material. For information before 1825 see the CMS Arch., G/AC3. There are infrequent references to Cockran in HBC Arch. D.5/1–26.

Canadian North-West (Oliver), I, contains brief references to Cockran's legislative career. The section written by Donald Gunn*, covering the years to 1835, in Donald Gunn and C. R. Tuttle, *History of Manitoba . . .* (Ottawa, 1880), attempts to be fair in its examination of the work of the Anglican clergy but the author's Presbyterian bias is evident. HBRS, XIX (Rich and Johnson) covers the turbulent decade of the 1840s and the aftermath; Boon, *Anglican Church*, contains a short, factual account of Cockran's career. A. C. Garrioch, *First furrows; a history of the early settlement of the Red River country, including that of Portage La Prairie* (3rd ed., Winnipeg, 1923), 84–128, is particularly useful for Cockran's career at Portage La Prairie. R. B. Hill, *Manitoba; history of its early settlement, development and resources* (Toronto, 1890), has factual errors (note the incorrect spelling of Cockran's name), but complements Garrioch's work. Colin Inkster, "William Cockran," *Leaders of the Canadian church*, ed. W. B.

Heeney (2 ser., Toronto, 1918–20), 2nd ser., 41–61, is a sympathetic but anecdotal treatment by a descendant of one of Cockran's parishioners. As with Gunn and Tuttle, the Presbyterian interest in Red River is emphasized by Alexander Ross* in *Red River Settlement* (1856); although Ross did not know certain pertinent facts, his criticism of Anglican missionary labours reflects an intelligent contemporary analysis. Apparently based upon CMS documents, the contemporary account by Sarah Tucker, *The rainbow in the north: a short account of the first establishment of Christianity in Rupert's Land by the Church Missionary Society* (London, 1851; repr. New York, 1852; London, 1853, 1856), 19–146, emphasizes Cockran's work at the Indian village. J.E.F.]

A brief sketch of the life and labours of Archdeacon Cockran (London, n.d.). J. E. Foster, "The Anglican clergy in the Red River Settlement, 1820–1826" (unpublished MA thesis, University of Alberta, Edmonton, 1966); "The Country-born in the Red River Settlement, 1820–1850" (unpublished PH D thesis, University of Alberta, Edmonton, 1973). A. N. Thompson, "The wife of the missionary," Canadian Church Hist. Soc., *Journal* (Toronto), XV (1973), 35–44.

COLBORNE, JOHN, 1st **Baron Seaton**, soldier and colonial administrator; b. 16 Feb. 1778 at Lyndhurst, Hampshire, England, the only son of Samuel Colborne and Cordelia Anne Garstin; d. 17 April 1863 in Torquay, Devonshire, England.

An orphan at age 13, John Colborne was educated at Christ's Hospital, London, and Winchester College. He entered the army as an ensign in the 20th Regiment in 1794, winning his subsequent promotions to field marshal without purchase. Though not aggressive, he was concerned that his achievements should be recognized, and on occasion successfully drew attention to an earned but unawarded promotion.

Promoted captain-lieutenant in 1799, he saw active service at Helder (Netherlands), and as captain in Egypt, Malta, and Sicily. In 1806 he became military secretary to General Henry Edward Fox, commander in Sicily and the Mediterranean. He was promoted major in 1808 by Sir John Moore, who made him his military secretary. He accompanied Moore to Sweden and Portugal; at Coruña (Spain) Moore's dying request was that Colborne be gazetted lieutenant-colonel. Between 1809 and 1811 he exchanged units twice before joining his long-time regiment, the 52nd Regiment of Oxfordshire Light Infantry, one of the famous three forming the Light Brigade.

After service under the Duke of Wellington in the Iberian Peninsula at Ocaña, Busaco, and Albuera, he assumed command of the 52nd and in January 1812 was severely wounded in leading the attack at Ciudad Rodrigo. Though perma-

Colborne

nently disabled in one arm, he returned to active service in July 1813, assuming temporary brigade command for the battles of the Nivelle and the Nive in the Pyrenees. He again commanded the 52nd early in 1814 at Orthez and Toulouse (France). With the peace he was promoted colonel in 1814, becoming one of the first to receive a KCB in January 1815. He meantime assumed new duties as aide-de-camp to the Prince Regent, and military secretary to the Prince of Orange, commander of Britain's forces in the Netherlands.

One of the most significant events in Colborne's career took place in 1815, following Napoleon's escape from Elba. Ordered to Belgium, the 52nd formed part of Major-General Sir Frederick Adam's Light Brigade, charged with maintaining communications on the extreme right of the British line at Waterloo. This position confronted a substantial part of Napoleon's famed Imperial Guard, and was designed to prevent any move to bend the British line. When, on 19 June 1815, the Imperial Guard was observed to be preparing a northern charge in column through the allied lines, the Light Brigade was moved forward and assumed a flanking position facing east to direct its fire into the side of the advancing French column. When the moment came, however, and after the brigade had discharged its early volleys, Colborne, acting without authority but with boldness and brilliant initiative, swung the 52nd out of line and led it in a daring charge that immediately swept back the Imperial Guard in a rout. As the Guard fell back in confusion, the rest of the French army collapsed in complete disarray along the road to Charleroi. Colborne's bold stroke has been credited with assuring victory at Waterloo, although Wellington never acknowledged its decisiveness. Nonetheless, the "colonel of the 52nd" was widely acclaimed, and was awarded honours by England, Austria, and Portugal.

In the long peace that followed, Colborne remained strongly attached to the military, but he also undertook a succession of civil appointments. In these posts much of his success derived from his distinguished military reputation and great character, but much also was owing to the charm and graciousness of his wife, Elizabeth, daughter of James Yonge, rector of Newton Ferrers, Devonshire. From their marriage in 1813, Colborne acquired a large family, including two sons destined to become generals, and a household notable for its warmth, simplicity, and generosity. It was an important balancing asset for a civil governor whose military bearing and natural reserve were unrelieved by a quick, almost impetuous manner. But behind his abrupt-

ness, a dutiful, disciplined nature had been moulded by several acute bereavements, by rigorous training, and above all by a deep religious conviction. The Anglican faith surrounded Colborne in his step-father, Thomas Bargus, his father-in-law, and brother-in-law, all of them Anglican clergy; in his devout wife; and in his friends, such as Henry Phillpotts, bishop of Exeter, whose brother George* was Colborne's aide-de-camp in Upper Canada. As he advised his son James, attend "to the study of Christ and study of yourself, which is the wisest preparative for all that may happen to us." Beyond its implications for personal conduct, religion also served for him as a guarantor of order and hierarchy in society and government. His own simplicity and lack of display, however, rescued him from the charge of sanctimoniousness.

Colborne's promotion to major-general in 1825, and his tenure as lieutenant governor of Guernsey from 1821 to 1828, strengthened his reputation for effective administration and popular leadership. In many respects he served his apprenticeship in Guernsey for his role as Upper Canada's ablest governor. There Colborne built on the work of Sir John Doyle, who had achieved major fiscal, communications, and harbour improvements. Following the post-war depression and the bitter contest between Guernsey and Whitehall over proposals to revise the Corn Laws, Colborne sought to restore the islanders' loyalty. His appointment happily coincided with that of a new chief civic magistrate, Daniel De Lisle Brock, a distinguished Guernsey landowner and brother of Sir Isaac Brock*, whose military and civil duties Colborne would assume seven years later. A second Guernsey man, Major-General Sir Thomas Saumarez*, had served as commandant at Halifax and president of the Council and commander-in-chief of New Brunswick during the War of 1812. Thus Colborne could find in Guernsey's tiny society both inspiration and interest in the affairs of Britain's North American colonies.

The Colborne-Brock administration quickly re-established public confidence with impressive additions to the road system, indirect taxation for general improvements, increases in regular communication with England, the introduction of a first iron foundry, the construction of new quays and public markets, a reversal of the pattern of steady emigration, and a general increase in the value of agricultural lands and urban facilities. The pattern would be repeated by Colborne in Upper Canada. In three particular ventures, his experience had even closer parallels. First, Colborne counteracted a great rise in the strength of "sectaries," chiefly Wesleyan Methodists, by strengthening the establishment of the Church of England; second, with Brock's help, he laid the ground for removing the tithing system which encouraged strong anti-Anglican resentment; third, he re-established a boys' preparatory school, Elizabeth College, to strengthen education, the state religion, and a governing élite.

On 14 Aug. 1828 Colborne was gazetted lieutenant governor of Upper Canada, succeeding Sir Peregrine Maitland*, and arrived at York (Toronto) on 3 November. His was not to be an easy governorship: Maitland's imperious conduct and his wife's social pretentions had helped turn an early, natural, conservative leadership into an unnatural Tory establishment. This Family Compact had become increasingly resented by rural agrarian radicals, urban malcontents such as William Lyon MACKENZIE and Francis Collins*, religious nonconformists such as Egerton Ryerson*, American-born and Jacksonian sympathizers such as Marshall Spring Bidwell*, and moderates such as Robert* and William Warren Baldwin*, whose preference for conservative measures was qualified by disquiet over the ruling caste's arrogance. Colborne's arrival prompted unusual expectations of redress of grievances and of a liberal conduct that must strain his natural conservatism and soldierly concepts of constitutional limitation and duty. His military background had prepared him to take a hard line on constitutional responsibility and sovereign authority. He would not be a party to a direct colonial challenge to prevailing constitutional forms. His concern for Guernsey's interests, however, had prepared him for some of Upper Canada's challenges. Shrewd changes in the Legislative Council's composition, decentralization from York, independence from cliques of advisers, and executive enterprise and efficiency might serve as substitutes for root-and-branch constitutional reforms.

Colborne's new capital was only one-seventh the size of his last, and his style would be appropriate to the village status of little York with its 2,200 inhabitants. The simplicity of his manner and the lack of ostentation of his household soon set many minds at rest. Pressed to intervene in the *causes célèbres* of Judge John Walpole Willis* and the Francis Collins libel trial, which had been turned to good account by the radicals, he stood firm with the ordinary processes of the law and of appeal, and exerted a modest, successful pressure to have these issues resolved sympathetically by the imperial authorities.

But Colborne had arrived in York soon after the most exciting election in the colony's history, in which the Reformers had won a resounding victory. His capital, however, had upheld the Tory candidate and leader of the Compact, John Beverley ROBINSON. Plainly, Colborne was caught between fires. On the one hand were the over one-third of York householders with government connections, the prospering merchants, and purveyors to the Compact, and across the province the sub-branches of Compact support shored up by a disquieted but still moderate rural populace. But Colborne could recognize, too, a party of legitimate protest led by men like Bidwell, John ROLPH, and the Baldwins, and abetted by the extravagant exaggerations of others, of whom Mackenzie was among the more responsible. Moreover, his position was further compromised by the ambiguity of the situation in Britain. A select committee of the British House of Commons in the fall of 1828 had sharply criticized the Legislative Council's hold over the province, the claims of the Church of England for special consideration, and Archdeacon John STRACHAN's cherished plans for an Anglican university. But Colborne's old commander, the Duke of Wellington, was now prime minister, and it was doubtful whether the liberalism of the Commons' declaration would ever influence the Iron Duke. Colborne himself declared that the report had "done much harm in both Provinces, by furnishing the disaffected with arguments that suit their views. . . ."

Faced with an assembly-elect anxious to convene and to begin its Augean tasks, Colborne employed caution, conciliation, and affability to ease a difficult situation. Far from being made captive by the prejudices of the Family Compact, he brought his own convictions from his previous governorship. Purposely he avoided close association with the Compact's leaders, notably with Strachan, whose "Ecclesiastical Chart" and university plans had probably ensured the Reformers' 1828 electoral victory. Robinson's elevation to the chief justiceship in July 1829 also eased his task by reducing Robinson's room to manoeuvre openly as a principal Compact strategist and by furnishing the opportunity to call a York by-election, allowing the moderate Robert Baldwin to win an assembly seat. When the Reformers challenged that the speaker, not the governor, must issue an election writ, Colborne graciously acceded, and still another election in 1829 returned Baldwin.

Judgements of Colborne's early performance led to growing confidence in him. The 1829–30 assembly passed much sound legislation supporting road construction, commercial improve-

Colborne

ments, relief from War of 1812 losses, and the encouragement of agricultural societies – enterprises with which Colborne had been closely associated in Guernsey.

In other matters, however, things proceeded less harmoniously. In the 1829 session Mackenzie introduced his famous 31 grievances and resolutions, several of which challenged Colborne to declare himself on basic constitutional issues, such as judicial independence, church establishment, local control of the province's internal affairs, and the composition and role of the Executive and Legislative councils. Sir John would not champion constitutional positions that he felt must properly be determined in England; but he did transmit his opinion to the imperial authorities that the constitution was unsatisfactory and that Whitehall should investigate. Colborne treated the assembly as a debating group, and expressed concern over the Legislative Council's frequent intransigence in blocking strongly supported assembly measures, but he was not ready to strengthen the assembly itself. Partly, his reluctance arose from his interpretation of his constitutional position, but part may also be ascribed to the province's general prosperity. This economic health provided such indirect revenues that during his first years in Upper Canada Colborne did not have to ask the assembly to vote supplies, a circumstance strongly qualifying his view of its role and powers.

Another source of potential trouble rested in religion. Despite Colborne's early attempts to remain aloof from, indeed to criticize, Strachan's active political role, he was not one to dissemble about his own religious convictions. His ideas of religious organization were as orthodox as his canons of military conduct. "Sectaries" were guerillas; the denominations must be preserved and enlarged. In Guernsey he had witnessed a remarkable growth in the number of sects, and particularly in the number of Wesleyans, but a contemporary account held that their introduction had invigorated the Anglican clergy. In Upper Canada Colborne was alarmed at the Methodists' great increase in strength, at the fact that the strong Reform assembly of 1828 was often called the "saddlebag assembly," and that in 1829 the Methodists were gaining enormous support with their hard-hitting new journal, the *Christian Guardian*. Moreover, the editor, Egerton Ryerson, was clearly sympathetic with many of the causes of Mackenzie. Colborne would inevitably confront the Methodists, but his experience in Guernsey led him to seek better ways than Strachan's to support his church's establishment.

The early evidences of the new governor's in-

dependence, rectitude, and conservatism soon disarmed all but extremists on both sides. Moreover, he indicated his readiness to effect changes in the Legislative Council's composition by appointing new members from outside the York clique, even if he would not admit his own constitutional competence to change its functions. Such carefully considered accommodation had its effect in the election forced upon the province by George IV's death in 1830. Having achieved much at the assembly's committee level but little cohesion as party men, the Reformers lost heavily, holding only 17 of 51 seats. Colborne's reputation brought moderates and conservatives into a new and sympathetic assembly. For the remainder of his term, despite Mackenzie's increasing radicalism, Colborne displayed considerable initiative and leadership. Often ignoring the squabbling of Reformers and radicals, he single-mindedly pursued his own "good works." That he also failed to inform his superiors at the Colonial Office of many of these activities was partly a consequence of his dedication; partly, too, a result of having too many masters – six colonial secretaries in the nine years of his incumbency.

Colborne concentrated on making practical improvements in communications, roads, bridges, and market facilities which were beneficial to a sparsely settled colony. He was also determined to increase the size and improve the quality of the British community in Upper Canada through immigration and education. Government should provide assistance to needy immigrants, and expect services in clearing land and improving roads in return; the result would be early employment and sustained morale. When York's expansion was blocked by a military reserve, the governor relocated the reserve; to improve communications he personally paid £1,175 to repair the Don and Humber bridges, challenging the assembly to reimburse him.

Town improvement was important, but rural growth should also be encouraged. Reducing isolation would attract more people and more capital. Colborne's strategy was to concentrate upon a few townships, building well initially to encourage an early maturity and solvency. At Cobourg, Peterborough, and London he deployed new agencies for the settlement of immigrants, and encouraged the establishment of local immigrant societies. In 1829 he introduced the so-called Ops Township experiment, later extending it to Douro, Oro, and Dummer townships, up the Ottawa valley, and in the southwest between Colonel Thomas Talbot*'s lands and the Huron Tract. According to the experiment's plan, access roads were built to new settlements, temporary shelters in the new districts were provided, and a series of immigration agencies was established at Montreal, Prescott, and Cobourg. Supplies were sold cheaply by government agents until the newcomers were well settled. Indigents who had faithfully effected their own improvements but who lacked cash had their payments delayed or were given employment artificially stimulated to enable them to pay. Reformers in the assembly objected to the high costs of the programme of assisted settlement and resented the executive's unilateral use of public funds; Conservatives resented the encouragement given to indigent immigrants who, they were convinced, would soon swell the ranks of the "democrats." But both the assembly and the Colonial Office were expected to support Colborne's ambitious projects – often after they had been instituted without prior consultation.

Colborne's colonizing purpose was two-fold: to attract more of the masses of emigrants leaving England and thereby to reduce the proportion of American immigration and influence in Upper Canada. As late as 1833 he considered establishing a western subdivision of the province centred in London, in an effort to combat the forces of "republicanism" in the west. Measured by the increased number of immigrants and reduced re-emigration to the United States, he was highly successful. Moreover, partly because of his leadership in meeting the cholera epidemic of 1832, York became a resort for refugees from other localities seeking better preventive measures and treatment. Consequently, the high rate of immigration persisted from 1830 to 1833, the province's population growing by 50 per cent, and York's better than doubling.

With so many new English settlers and such a record of smooth adjustment, Colborne correctly predicted by 1834 that the province's political stability, by which he meant a conservative and industrious electorate, was assured. With his further programme of attracting to rural Upper Canada a class of gentlemen farmers from the ranks of British doctors, clergy, and half-pay officers, he may be excused to some degree if he did not draw to Whitehall's attention the intemperate criticisms of Mackenzie's minority. He believed that the best military and political policy was to ensure a large, secure population who would eschew grievance-mongering and rally to the defence of their interests. The fine line between Colborne's high-minded policy and the Compact's narrow pursuit of its own interests, however, was not always clear, and in his religious policies he invited disaster.

Colborne had been unwilling in 1828 to accept Strachan's proposal for a university in an unde-

veloped colony. Nor could he respect Strachan's tactics in strengthening the bond between his church and the interests of society. Consequently, he withheld support from King's College, turning instead to his Guernsey experience by creating first a classical English preparatory school, Upper Canada College, which was to produce an educated student body ready for university training. Colborne valued his own schooling, and throughout his life he pursued the classics, mathematics, rhetoric, history, and modern languages. Overwhelming his council and his Whitehall superiors with his organizational zeal, he brought the school into operation with a half-dozen highly qualified masters such as Joseph Hemington Harris* imported from the ranks of the English clergy. That the Methodists had been laying plans for an Upper Canada Academy was not lost on Sir John, but his pupils would be the sons of "gentlemen." Colborne's diversion of public school reserves funds and university money to his new school guaranteed opposition from all sides.

The second evidence of Colborne's fatal obstinacy in religious matters is his means of securing education and improved conditions for the Indians. Despairing of the Church of England's efforts, ironically he turned to the mission-minded Methodists. But in a series of secretive negotiations, Colborne encouraged the British Wesleyan leaders in preference to Ryerson's Canadian Episcopals, thus raising once again the old cry of Maitland's day that the Canadian Methodists were disloyal. Although ostensibly the British Wesleyans were encouraged to return for the sake of the Indian missions, their coming would also fulfil Colborne's goals of strengthening the anti-American and anti-republican spirit of Upper Canada and of challenging "natural" conservatives like Ryerson to loosen their radical ties and moderate their opposition to church establishment. The divisiveness of his tactics, however, undermined his conservative, unifying purpose.

The governor's most controversial act was his designation of rectory lands for the Church of England, an action in train since 1831 but taken only on the eve of his departure from Upper Canada in January 1836. Justification for designating 15,000 acres of the clergy reserves and another 6,600 acres of crown lands specifically to the endowment of 44 Anglican rectories across the province rested in the 1791 Constitutional Act and in the ambiguity of instructions from various colonial secretaries, but Colborne's timing was extraordinarily inappropriate. He successfully opposed his council's intent to add a spiritual jurisdiction to a comprehensive land endowment

Colborne

– and thus to affirm a formal establishment of the Church of England – but such distinctions were lost on radicals, Reformers, and many moderates. The rectories crisis undoubtedly precipitated the unrest of 1837, and was among the factors which had prompted the colonial secretary, Lord Glenelg, to recall Colborne early in 1836.

Arriving in New York in late May 1836, however, Colborne unexpectedly received a dispatch from Glenelg appointing him commander-in-chief of the forces in the Canadas. Colborne felt that Glenelg appointed him to the post to indicate his respect for him despite his having had to remove him from Upper Canada and because he was an experienced military leader whose presence in Lower Canada might encourage moderation and discourage civil disorder. Colborne's knowledge of Lower Canada was probably confined to the impressions he had gathered while staying with members of the English speaking community in Montreal from February to May 1836.

Dutifully, Colborne journeyed to Montreal, despite his private criticisms of Governor General Lord Gosford [Acheson*] for bringing a regiment to Lower Canada from Halifax, a move Colborne thought unnecessary and likely to cause alarm. During the summer of 1837 he did not anticipate a rebellion, believing instead that the public meetings addressed by Louis-Joseph Papineau*, though "of a very seditious character," would "produce little effect here." Nonetheless, by October he had fortified Quebec, ordered military supplies, and recruited troops to be in readiness for a possible uprising. Throughout the fall the political situation worsened; on 13 November Colborne's wife wrote that "the whole country has . . . apparently changed its nature in the short space of the last fortnight, and become interested in a revolution." With the outbreak of rebellion on 16 November, Colborne quickly marshalled the regular and militia forces, even drawing on Upper Canada's regulars, so confident was he of his earlier preparations in the upper province. Snow-shoes and 100 sleighs were prepared for the troops; £100 was spent to shut Quebec's long-unused and rusted gates; veterans of Colborne's 52nd turned out enthusiastically; and Colborne personally led 2,000 men, with artillery, against the rebels. By late December 1837 the insurrection had been put down.

Colborne, however, could not look forward to an early retirement, for meantime Governor General Gosford had abruptly resigned, and it would fall to Sir John as administrator to deal with the late rebels. Colborne preferred that the rebels, having been dealt with firmly in the field, should be treated generously in the courts. The decision, however, would not rest with him. In late February 1838, word arrived that Whitehall further proposed that martial law should end, the constitution be suspended, a special council established, and a special commission under Lord Durham [Lambton*] sent to Canada to govern and to prepare recommendations for the future government of the Canadas. On 29 May 1838 Durham landed at Quebec and assumed authority.

Colborne's early relations with the new governor general were good, and his preference for firm but humane treatment of the late rebels influenced Durham's decision to banish the leaders to Bermuda. But in other matters they differed. Sir John was sceptical of Durham's proposal for union of the two provinces because he felt it would encourage the importation of Lower Canada's serious troubles into the upper province. He also saw the union as simply a means of politically overwhelming the French Canadians and thereby adding the alarming prospect of assimilation to their existing unrest. Colborne was even less sympathetic with the measure of colonial self-government, however limited, that Durham proposed for the new union. Moreover, his confidence in Durham's judgement grew weaker on longer acquaintance. Despite his anxiety to resign – and his wish to gain the governorship of the Ionian Islands – Colborne yielded to Glenelg's request that he remain because he enjoyed the confidence "of all persons . . . to a degree to which it is clear no other could attain." Promoted lieutenant-general, his services were urgently needed by fall when, first, Lord Durham abruptly resigned his special commission and returned home, and, second, fresh unrest threatened in the lower province. During November 1838 Colborne was engaged in putting down even more effectively and swiftly a new insurrection. In mid December he was gazetted governor general amidst a series of courts-martial dealing severely with the second group of rebels. Colborne believed that an extended period of firm, semi-military, but enlightened rule would defuse the situation and provide Lower Canada with time to readjust to British colonial institutions. He did approve of Durham's resignation because it would allow him to extend this period of firm readjustment, and he agreed with Durham that it was necessary to teach the British authorities some of the realities of the Canadian situation.

Because of his handling of the rebellion and its aftermath, however, Colborne became known

Colborne

to Québecois as "le Vieux Brulôt," a symbol of brutality, of Anglo-Saxon fanaticism, and of anti-Catholicism. Historians from François-Xavier GARNEAU and Thomas Chapais* to Lionel Groulx* have condemned him for the seeming ruthlessness of his part in crushing the Lower Canadian rebellions. It was Colborne's conviction, however, that Gosford's equivocal and dilatory tactics had encouraged the growth of a rebellious population. Moreover, although on several occasions the rebels' numbers would melt away overnight before the actual engagements, Colborne's intelligence had reported substantial numbers of armed and concentrated dissidents. Having been recalled from New York as a military commander, he had made appropriate preparations, fatefully employing numbers of local English speaking volunteers in the expectation of meeting larger forces than proved in the event. The volunteers, and many of the British regulars, it was concluded by contemporaries such as Lieutenant E. Montagu Davenport and historians such as Robert Christie* and Chester New*, were enflamed by the guerilla tactics of the Patriotes, by the sadistic murder of a courier, Lieutenant George Weir, and by the fatigue and frustrations of operations conducted in bitter weather under exhausting conditions. The disruption of communication between Colborne's headquarters and his two field commanders, lieutenant-colonels Charles Stephen GORE and George Augustus WETHERALL, further complicated operations and left great discretion and responsibility with those officers for the conduct of their men. The rebels' resort to churches, convents, and strongly constructed stone houses as points of defence forced the use of artillery and of dangerous frontal attacks by the government's forces. All of these circumstances contributed to unauthorized, even forbidden, pillage in the aftermath of a bitter campaign.

How much Colborne was informed of the troops' excessive behaviour is problematical. Even at the height of his earlier military successes he had been known for his efficiency, not for ruthlessness, and since 1821 he had devoted himself to the arts of civil administration. Perhaps with better field communication he might have put firmer constraints upon his men and his commanders. Some evidence of his civil concern for French Canadians may rest in his resentment that Charles Poulett Thomson*, whom he considered too much the genial diplomat to contain unrest and enlighten the British authorities on the serious racial and political problems Canada faced, was to be given the mandate to serve as governor in the days following the rebellions. Colborne had

apparently not conceived such an animosity toward the French Canadians that he could not in good conscience contemplate serving as governor in a period of firm but humane recovery from the troubles of 1837–38.

On learning that Whitehall proposed sending yet another viceroy as governor general, but wished to retain his services as commander-in-chief, Colborne's patience broke. The idea of asking him to remain under Thomson, when the latter's policy of conciliation and moderation must make Colborne's actions appear even more Draconian, determined him to leave at the earliest opportunity. Colborne believed the new governor would have been greatly assisted had union come about under his own superintendence, and he would not "stand behind his amiable, conciliating, propitiating successor." At Quebec, on 19 Oct. 1839, Sir John yielded office to Thomson, and was invested with the GCB. Several days later, aboard the frigate *Pique* at Montreal, someone rallied a large crowd of well-wishers with the cry, "One cheer more for the colonel of the 52nd"; on 23 October Sir John left Quebec and Canada.

In England Colborne was widely recognized and rewarded for his distinguished military career and his 16 years of service in Guernsey and Canada, being named a privy councillor, receiving a pension of £2,000 annually, and being elevated to the peerage as Lord Seaton of Seaton, Devonshire, on 14 Dec. 1839. He continued to take an interest in Canadian affairs from the House of Lords. In 1840 he combined with Lord Gosford to oppose Thomson's proposed union; simultaneously, he allied with Lord Ripon (formerly Lord Goderich) and with Henry Phillpotts to try to stop Thomson's clergy reserves bill; in 1850 and 1853 he combined with the Duke of Argyll, the Church of Scotland's senior advocate in the Lords, to try to stop legislation enabling the Canadian parliament to dispose of the clergy reserves, which would lead to secularization. But these moves were mostly in vain, and his activities were already centred elsewhere.

From 1843, when he was made a GCMG, until 1849, he served as lord high commissioner of the Ionian Islands. In 1854 he was promoted general, and named colonel of the 2nd Life Guards. From 1855 to 1860 he served in Ireland as commander of the forces and as a privy councillor, as well as attending to his own considerable estates in County Kildare. In 1860, on his retirement, he was raised to England's highest military rank and honour, field marshal. After a short period of failing health, however, he died, aged 85, at Torquay.   ALAN WILSON

143

Colby

MTCL, Robert Baldwin papers. PAC, MG 24, A25; A40; B11; B18; RG 5, A1, 90–170; RG 7, G1, 69, 74–75. PAO, Macaulay (John) papers; Mackenzie-Lindsey papers; Robinson (John Beverley) papers; Strachan (John) papers. PRO, CO 42/388–427; 43/42–45. U.C., House of Assembly, *Journals*, 1828–36. Dent, *Canadian portrait gallery*, III. *DNB*. D. B. Read, *The lieutenant-governors of Upper Canada and Ontario, 1792–1899* (Toronto, 1900).

H. I. Cowan, *British emigration to British North America; the first hundred years* (Toronto, 1961). Craig, *Upper Canada*. Jonathan Duncan, *The history of Guernsey; with occasional notices of Jersey, Alderney, and Sark, and biographical sketches* (London, 1841). Aileen Dunham, *Political unrest in Upper Canada, 1815–1836* (London, 1927; repr. Toronto, 1963). J. W. Fortescue, *History of the British army* (13v., London and New York, 1899–1930). Gates, *Land policies of U.C.* William Leeke, *The history of Lord Seaton's regiment (the 52nd Light Infantry) at the battle of Waterloo . . .* (2v., London, 1866). J. D. Purdy, "John Strachan and education in Canada, 1800–1851" (unpublished PHD thesis, University of Toronto, 1962). G. C. M. Smith, *The life of John Colborne, Field-Marshal Lord Seaton, G.C.B., G.C.H., G.C.M.G., K.T.S., K.St.G., K.M.T. . . .* (London, 1903). Wilson, *Clergy reserves of U.C.* G. C. Patterson, "Land settlement in Upper Canada, 1783–1840," in Ont., Dept. of Archives, *Report* (Toronto), 1920. Helen Taft Manning, "The colonial policy of the Whig ministers, 1830–37," *CHR*, XXXIII (1952), 203–36, 341–68.

COLBY, MOSES FRENCH, physician and politician; b. 2 July 1795 in Thornton, N.H., younger son of Samuel Colby and Ruth French; m. 10 July 1826 Lemira Strong, and they had two sons and one daughter who lived to adulthood; d. 4 May 1863 in Stanstead Plain, Canada East.

Samuel Colby moved his family to Derby, Vt, in 1798, and they were among the pioneers in that settlement. At the age of 19, Moses French began the study of medicine with the local doctor in Derby. He left to attend medical lectures at Yale College in New Haven, Conn., in 1817 and graduated from Dartmouth College in Hanover, N.H., in 1821. He then began to practise in Derby. Although a boundary line separated Derby from Stanstead, Lower Canada, the people of both shared social interests, and he was named an officer in the newly formed chapter of the Stanstead Masonic Golden Rule Lodge. In 1828 Colby entered the School of Practical Anatomy at Harvard College. There he made the acquaintance of Dr Augustus Addison Gould, president of the Massachusetts Medical Society, with whom he long sustained an interesting correspondence, some of which was published. He returned to his practice in Derby with an MA.

In 1832, after passing a rigid examination before the Quebec Medical Board, Dr Colby moved to Stanstead, whose two physicians had died. His outstanding professional work and continued studies soon placed him at the head of his profession in the Eastern Townships and in northern New England. He published a pamphlet, *New views of the functions of the digestive tube* in 1860 and contributed valuable articles to the *Boston Medical and Surgical Journal* and other periodicals. He also offered his own remedies for sale: newspapers advertised "Dr. M.F. Colby's anti-costive tonic and pills, a Canadian Remedy," in the 1860s.

Colby was also public-spirited. In January 1837 the Conservative families of Stanstead had prevailed upon him to seek election to the assembly after the resignation of John Grannis, one of two members for Stanstead; the other was Marcus Child*, who supported the Patriote party. The *Missiskoui Standard*, a Conservative newspaper founded in 1835 by James Moir FERRES, endorsed Colby as a man of high principles. Colby agreed with the views expressed by Conservatives in Stanstead who, although they were opposed to some of the Legislative Council's policies, did not favour an elective council, which they felt would put too much power into the hands of French Canadians. Neither did he think that the way to improve the government was through revolution. Dr Colby served in the assembly from 13 Jan. 1837 to 27 March 1838, when it was replaced by the Special Council. In 1839 Colby was sued by Robert Nelson*, the former Patriote, allegedly because of an operation performed in 1833 in Vermont. Nelson appears, however, to have been retaliating for Colby's refusal to support him during the rebellion.

In the first election after the union of the two Canadas in 1841 Moses Colby and Reformer Marcus Child contested Stanstead County. Colby declared himself "an advocate for the free and unfettered exercise of the elective franchise, for a system of responsible government that would secure the country against fraud and malversations of office," and for taxation only with the consent of the people legitimately expressed through their representatives. He was, however, defeated by Child.

In 1847 Colby was appointed surgeon in the Stanstead Regiment of militia. Another indication of his wide interests appeared in the *Stanstead Journal*'s comment in September 1848 on his fine Ayrshire cattle shown at the Stanstead County fair at Barnston. For a number of years before his death in 1863 Colby was in feeble health, prematurely worn out by overwork in a day when good physicians were few. He had had a sincere concern for his patients and was regarded as an able, inquiring, and forceful man and doctor. His eldest son, Charles Carroll*, represented Stanstead in the House of Commons from confederation to 1891.

MARION L. PHELPS

M. F. Colby, *New views of the functions of the digestive tube by M. F. Colby, M.D., of Stanstead, C.E.* (Rock Island, Que., 1860). BCHS Arch., W. F. Beattie, "The times of Marcus Child." PAC, MG 30, D62, 8, pp.632–36. Private archives, C. C. Colby (Sabinel Island, Fla.), Colby family papers. *Missiskoui Standard* (Frelighsburg, Que.), January 1837. *Stanstead Journal* (Rock Island, Que.), 28 Dec. 1854; 12 April, 22 Nov. 1860; 8 Jan. 1863. *Vindicator and Canadian Advertiser* (Montreal), 7 Jan. 1837. *Cyclopædia of Canadian biog.* (Rose, 1886), 564. B. F. Hubbard, *Forests and clearings; the history of Stanstead County, province of Quebec, with sketches of more than five hundred families,* ed. John Lawrence (2nd ed., Montreal, 1963), 151–53. *Stanstead County Historical Society centennial journal* (2v., n.p., 1965–67), II.

COLEBROOKE, Sir WILLIAM MacBEAN GEORGE, soldier and colonial administrator; b. 9 Nov. 1787 in Charlton, Kent, England, son of Lieutenant-Colonel Paulet Welbore Colebrooke, Royal Artillery, and a Miss Grant; m. in 1820 or 1821 his cousin Emma Sophia Colebrooke, and they had three daughters; d. 6 Feb. 1870 at his home in Salthill, near Slough, Buckinghamshire, England.

Born to a family with a strong military tradition, William Colebrooke entered the Royal Military Academy at Woolwich and in 1803, at the age of 15, was commissioned a lieutenant in the Royal Artillery. His military career was distinguished but not outstanding. From 1805 to 1809 he served mainly in Ceylon and from 1809 to 1810 in India. The next year he went to Java, and in 1813 was a member of a mission to Sumatra. He served in Bengal in 1814 but then returned to Java until the island was restored to the Dutch in 1816. In 1817 he served with the Indian army in various campaigns and in 1818 and 1820 with the force sent to suppress piracy and the slave trade in the Persian Gulf.

In 1821 Colebrooke returned to England, and in January 1823 was appointed to the Commission of Eastern Enquiry. The work of this royal commission took Colebrooke to the Cape of Good Hope (Republic of South Africa) from 1823 to 1826 and to Mauritius in 1827 and 1828, but its most significant achievements were in Ceylon. After conducting extensive investigations there from 1829 to 1831, Colebrooke returned to Britain and produced in 1831 and 1832 a series of reports advocating far-reaching social, econom-

ic, and political reforms. His proposals, ranging from the abolition of the caste system and of all forms of legal discrimination to the destruction of any vestiges of mercantilism and the acceptance of a more liberal form of government, show clearly that Colebrooke was influenced by the liberal and humanitarian spirit of contemporary Britain. Colebrooke's reports brought about sweeping changes in the administration of Ceylon and made the island a model for other British crown colonies. Probably for his work on the commission Colebrooke was awarded a knighthood and in September 1834 became lieutenant governor of the Bahamas, where he served from 1835 until 1837, when he became governor general of the Leeward Islands. In both positions Colebrooke's main task was to deal with the problems created by the abolition of slavery, and through his concern for the welfare of the freed slaves he strengthened his reputation as an enlightened governor. In July 1840 he left Antigua and after an extended leave was appointed lieutenant governor of New Brunswick on 26 March 1841.

Colebrooke arrived in Fredericton in April 1841, but his reputation as a liberal governor had preceded him. "He came among us," the Saint John *Morning News* declared, "as a 'Responsible Government' man, to carry out in spirit the system introduced by [Sir John Harvey*]." Under Harvey, Colebrooke's predecessor, New Brunswick had been the most tranquil colony in British North America. By appointing to his Executive Council men who could command the confidence of the assembly, Harvey had introduced a rudimentary form of responsible government to New Brunswick, and by exchanging the revenues derived from the sale of crown lands for a permanent civil list, he had made himself extremely popular with the assembly. Yet New Brunswick was still a politically immature society, divided into a number of geographic interests with no overriding sense of community. Since under the Harvey system the provincial executive had no control over the vast revenues controlled by the assembly through its own appropriations committee, local and group interests took precedence over the general welfare and the colony's financial resources were frittered away on purely local projects. "Your excellency will not probably be long in making the discovery," the *Morning News* correctly predicted for Colebrooke, "that the boasted harmony existing between the different branches of the government, was the harmony of the leaders in each, banded together to advance their own power and interest, and in which the general interest had no

Colebrooke

concern.'' While the timber trade flourished and provincial revenues were abundant, few voices were raised in opposition to the *status quo*. Harvey's departure, however, coincided with the beginning of a two year depression. The widespread economic distress of the "hungry forties" brought a growing demand for fiscal reform and Colebrooke soon became the champion of the reformers.

Colebrooke's programme of reform was modelled upon the policy pursued by Lord John Russell and Lord Sydenham [Thomson*] in the Province of Canada. To revive New Brunswick's flagging economy through a series of large-scale public works, Colebrooke requested a loan from the British government, to be made conditional upon the assembly's acceptance of financial control by the executive. While sympathetic to Colebrooke's objectives, neither Russell nor his successor as colonial secretary, Lord Stanley, were prepared to follow the Canadian precedent and grant an imperial loan for internal improvements in the colony. Nonetheless, Colebrooke still held out hope for a loan if the assembly put its financial affairs in order and in his speech from the throne on 19 Jan. 1842 advocated the establishment of a system of municipal government, the creation of a provincial board of works, and the surrender to the executive of the authority to initiate money bills in the assembly. In spite of Colebrooke's inducements, this programme ran into overwhelming opposition. John Wesley Weldon resigned from the Executive Council, leaving only Charles Simonds* to defend Colebrooke's measures in the assembly. Although supported by Lemuel Allan Wilmot*, these measures had little appeal to the majority of its members, who were not prepared to abandon a system which placed patronage in their hands, and on 9 Feb. 1842 a motion of John PARTELOW, leader of the opposition to Colebrooke's proposals, that "it is not expedient to make any alteration" in the existing system of appropriations was carried 18 to 12. A bill to allow for municipal incorporation was passed by the assembly, but rejected by the Legislative Council where the speaker, Chief Justice Ward Chipman*, opposed Colebrooke's reforms. After adjourning the assembly, Colebrooke refused to authorize the expenditures it had passed and issued a circular outlining the financial difficulties faced by the province. Realizing the futility of another appeal to the existing assembly, he dissolved it, but the assembly elected in January 1842 was as intransigent as its predecessor. Its first act was to elect Weldon as speaker and on 14 Feb. 1843 it approved by 24 to seven a motion that "nothing

should induce the House to surrender its undoubted and inherent right to initiate all Grants of Money for the Public Service.''

Colebrooke could see the weakness of his position and in March and April 1843 broadened the base of his Executive Council by adding Hugh Johnston*, Edward Barron Chandler*, John MONTGOMERY, Robert Leonard Hazen*, and Wilmot. Although the reconstructed council was a coalition representing all factions in the legislature, the leading figures in the new government were Johnston, Hazen, and Chandler, who had opposed Colebrooke's reform programme and who formed the nucleus of the compact which was to dominate New Brunswick politics for the next decade. Colebrooke had capitulated to his opponents and although in his dispatches he frequently castigated the assembly's financial practices, he made no further effort to change them. Since 1843 also saw a revival of the timber trade and a return to prosperity, political harmony was restored to the province and the assembly showed its contentment in 1844 by passing a resolution supporting Sir Charles Metcalfe* in his struggle with the assembly of the Province of Canada.

Although Colebrooke was initially embarrassed by the assembly's interference in the affairs of Canada, he soon found their defence of the royal prerogative useful. For several years Colebrooke had been seeking an appropriate official position, first in the West Indies and then in New Brunswick, for his private secretary, Alfred Reade, but had been able to offer him only a few comparatively ill-paid posts. Colebrooke's concern for his protégé was undoubtedly strengthened by Reade's marriage in October 1844 to his eldest daughter, Frances Elizabeth. An opportunity finally presented itself on Christmas Day 1844 with the death of the provincial secretary, William Franklin Odell*, and Colebrooke promptly appointed Reade to the position. No decision could have been more surely calculated to outrage native New Brunswickers than the appointment of an Englishman to one of the most lucrative offices in the colony. In 1834 the appointment of Sir James Carter*, an Englishman, as a puisne judge had led to an outburst of protest and a promise by the Colonial Office that patronage would thereafter be distributed to natives of the province. Reade's appointment clearly contradicted this principle and led to the resignation of Johnston, Hazen, Chandler, and Wilmot from the Executive Council. The first three simply declared that Reade was unsuitable for the position of provincial secretary, but Wilmot took the broader constitutional position that the office of provincial secretary should become a political appointment made by the lieutenant governor on the advice of the Executive Council. The appointment was strongly condemned by the assembly which on 20 Feb. 1845 passed by 22 to nine a motion of non-confidence in the much weakened Executive Council.

Colebrooke justified his decision on the grounds that the provincial secretary, who had access to the lieutenant governor's correspondence, should be free "from all party influences" and portrayed himself as a man above party defending the royal prerogative against the assembly's encroachments. His argument did not convince the Colonial Office which realized that it was only Wilmot who had challenged the governor's theoretical right to make the appointment and that Wilmot and his supporters had failed to carry in the assembly resolutions to that effect. Moreover, the Colonial Office objected to the appointment; James Stephen, the permanent under-secretary, felt it to be "injudicious and indefensible," "a great job" that legitimately "provoked" the people of New Brunswick, "the model of loyalty and good order to all our North American possessions." Sharing these views, Lord Stanley refused to confirm the appointment.

Although disappointed, Colebrooke immediately attempted to reforge the coalition of the previous year by inviting Hazen, Chandler, and Johnston, but not Wilmot, who had taken a more extreme constitutional position than the others, to rejoin the Executive Council. They declined to serve unless the existing councillors, who had upheld Colebrooke's actions, resigned. For the rest of 1845 Colebrooke stuck by the councillors who had defended him, but, bowing to the inevitable, they resigned prior to the opening of the legislature in February 1846. Hazen, Chandler, Johnston, George Shore*, and Charles Jeffery Peters* formed a new council, which was, as the *Morning News* reported, "decidedly Compact." After the election of October 1846, and the return of a large number of new members, Colebrooke even offered to reappoint Wilmot, but the latter demanded the right to nominate half of the council. Colebrooke would not agree. Alexander Rankin*, Thomas BAILLIE, and George Stillman were added to the council, and Wilmot and his followers remained in opposition to form the nucleus of the Liberal party of the future. In fact, the beginnings of a party system in New Brunswick were laid during this period.

For the rest of his tenure of office Colebrooke was careful not to disturb the *status quo* again. Even the decision of the 3rd Earl Grey to concede responsible government to New Brunswick in 1847 made little immediate difference, since the Executive Council was already, as Colebrooke reported, "virtually responsible to the Assembly in so far that its tenure must be understood to depend on its possessing the confidence of the Assembly." Colebrooke hoped that before the principle of responsible government was fully implemented, the assembly would agree to create municipal councils and surrender to the executive the right to initiate money bills, but was dissuaded by his Executive Council from advocating measures that might "perhaps lead to embarrassment at the very close of His Excellency's administration of the Government." Colebrooke accepted this argument and left the details of the transition to a system of ministerial responsibility to be worked out by his successor, Sir Edmund Walker HEAD. In April 1848 Colebrooke left New Brunswick to become governor and commander-in-chief of British Guiana (Guyana), a post he held only briefly before transferring to a similar position in Barbados in August 1848. He served there with distinction until 1856 and then returned to service with the army, rising to the rank of general in 1865.

Colebrooke's reward for his services in New Brunswick was his appointment as a CB (Civil Division) in 1848, but ironically he is remembered in the history of the province chiefly for the *débâcle* of the Reade affair. Few governors were more conscientious or better intentioned. Colebrooke had a fertile imagination and a plethora of proposals to improve New Brunswick society through better communications with Canada, an improved system of education, an immigration policy which would discourage paupers, and an encouragement of agriculture to replace the timber trade as the basis of New Brunswick's economy. Few of Colebrooke's proposals had positive results and his propensity for advocating reforms was not universally admired either by the very conservative colonial legislature or by his almost equally conservative superiors in London. James Stephen complained that Sir William "is greatly addicted to throwing out immature suggestions and impracticable schemes. This results from the sleepless activity of his mind, and his eminent public spirit. But it is a considerable practical inconvenience." Nonetheless, many of the reforms Colebrooke advocated were sensible and were pursued more successfully by his successors. The more harmonious transition from imperial control to local self-government in New Brunswick than in either Canada or Nova Scotia was undoubtedly owing chiefly to the immaturity and fragmentation of New Brunswick society,

Comeau

the lack of organized political parties, and the colony's economic dependence upon the timber trade; but the personal respect in which Colebrooke was held was at least partially responsible and he was subjected to far less criticism than contemporary governors in Canada and Nova Scotia. George Edward Fenety*, not an uncritical admirer of the colony's governors, found Colebrooke "a thoroughly constitutional Governor and well-meaning man," who was "highly esteemed by the people of New Brunswick."

PHILLIP BUCKNER

[There is no collection of Sir William Colebrooke's papers but scattered letters are to be found in N.B. Museum, Edward Barron Chandler papers; Hazen coll.; Webster coll. The major primary source is PRO, CO 188/72–104. See also PRO, CO 54/121, Colebrooke to Goderich, 28 Jan. 1832; WO 76/361, "Statement of the services of W.M.G. Colebrooke"; and PANB, REX/mi/ex, draft minutes, 1841–48.

Among the contemporary printed sources are: Fenety, *Political notes and observations*; N.B., House of Assembly, *Journals*, 1841–48; *Morning News* (Saint John, N.B.), 1841–48; *New Brunswick Courier*, 1842–48. For biographical sketches of Colebrooke see: N.B. Museum, Ganong MS coll., box 37, G. B. Alleyne, "Sketch of the life of Colebrooke" (1923); Boase, *Modern English biog.*, I, 672; *The Colonial Office list for 1864 . . .*, ed. A. N. Birch and William Robinson (London, 1864); *DNB*, which is largely based on the *Times* (London), 10 Feb. 1870; Wallace, *Macmillan dictionary*.

The essential secondary source is W. S. MacNutt, "The coming of responsible government to New Brunswick," *CHR*, XXXIII (1952), 111–28. Also useful are the same author's "New Brunswick's age of harmony: the administration of Sir John Harvey," *CHR*, XXXII (1951), 105–25; "The politics of the timber trade in colonial New Brunswick, 1825–40," *CHR*, XXX (1949), 47–65; *New Brunswick*; and *Atlantic provinces*. Of some use are *The Colebrooke-Cameron papers, documents on British colonial policy in Ceylon, 1796–1833*, ed. G. C. Mendis (2v., [London], 1956); Hannay, *History of N.B.*; D. G. G. Kerr, *Sir Edmund Head, a scholarly governor* (Toronto, 1954); K. F. C. MacNaughton, *The development of the theory and practice of education in New Brunswick, 1784–1900: a study in historical background*, ed. and intro. A. G. Bailey (Fredericton, 1947); J. L. Miller, "A study of New Brunswick politics at the beginning of the era of free trade and reciprocity" (unpublished MA thesis, University of New Brunswick, Fredericton, 1950); W. P. Morrell, *British colonial policy in the age of Peel and Russell* (London, 1966); G. E. Rogers, "The career of Edward Barron Chandler – a study in New Brunswick politics, 1827–1854" (unpublished MA thesis, University of New Brunswick, Fredericton, 1953); V. K. Samaraweera, "The Commission of Eastern Enquiry in Ceylon, 1822–1837: a study of a royal commission of colonial inquiry" (unpublished DPHIL thesis, University of Oxford, 1969). P.B.]

COMEAU, ANSELM-FRANÇOIS, farmer, businessman, politician, and magistrate; b. 2 Dec. 1793 at Comeauville, N.S., second son of Major François Comeau and Marguerite Melanson; m. in 1824 Marie-Gertrude Amirault (d. 4 Sept. 1865), and they had four sons and five daughters; d. 27 Nov. 1867 at Comeauville.

Anselm-François Comeau was the grandson of François (Maza) Comeau and Félicité Le Blanc, the first family to settle at Comeauville. Although there were no regular schools in the area during his youth, he received instruction from an itinerant school-teacher, Louis Bunel, who taught in the vicinity of Comeauville from 1798 to 1825. A late 19th century local history suggests that Comeau worked at farming, lumbering, and fishing but also had some intellectual interests. The books he kept as clerk of Clare Township from 1831 to 1837 show a good handwriting and precise spelling in both French and English. He owned a small farm and a sawmill, and in 1835 was appointed postmaster of Clare. He also owned 1,000 acres of land in Digby County.

Clare Township was part of the Annapolis County constituency in the assembly until the 1840 general election. When it was given its own seat, Comeau declared himself a Reform candidate. According to the *Yarmouth Herald*, on 13 Nov. 1840, he was the sole contestant, but in a report two weeks later the same newspaper noted that Frederick Armand Robicheau, a Clare resident who had been a Reform party candidate in Digby Township, had shifted his candidacy to his home riding. The polls favoured Comeau, referred to in newspaper reports as "Samuel Commo."

He was re-elected in 1843, 1847, and 1851, but apparently took no active part in the assembly debates, usually supporting the Reformers. In 1848 he was appointed magistrate in Clare. He did not stand for re-election at the end of his fourth term in the assembly but was appointed to the Legislative Council in July 1855, the first Acadian in the Maritime provinces to be so honoured. He continued to serve in the council until his death in 1867. The Halifax *Novascotian* had kind words for him: "No politician can ever leave behind him a fairer record than Anselm Comeau. True always, despite all temptation, to what he believed the right, he has left behind him a memory free from all spot or stain." Since Comeau's time the Acadians of Digby County have almost always been Reform or Liberal party supporters.

J.-ALPHONSE DEVEAU

The record books of the township of Clare are in the possession of Mr Jean-A. Comeau, Little Brook, N.S.

Centre acadien, Collège Sainte-Anne (Church Point, N.S.), paroisse de Sainte-Marie, registres et lettres du père Sigogne, 1818–29, 1840–44. Centre d'études acadiennes, université de Moncton (Moncton, N.-B.), Placide Gaudet, "Notes généalogiques sur les familles acadiennes, c.1600–1900" (copy at PAC). N.S., Dept. of Lands and Forests, Land survey map no.6. *Novascotian*, 3 Dec. 1840, 16 Dec. 1867. *Yarmouth Herald* (Yarmouth, N.S.), 13 Nov., 5 Dec. 1840; 5 Dec. 1867. *Directory of N.S. MLAs*, 69. P.-M. Dagnaud, *Les Français du sud-ouest de la Nouvelle-Écosse: le R. P. Jean-Mandé Sigogne, apôtre de la baie Sainte-Marie et du cap de Sable, 1799–1844* (Besançon, France, 1905), 175. [J.-]A. Deveau, *La ville française* (Québec, 1968), 192–94. I. W. Wilson, *A geography and history of the county of Digby, Nova Scotia* (Halifax, 1900), 319.

CONGER, WILSON SEYMOUR, merchant, sheriff, and politician; b. 1804 at Hallowell, Upper Canada, first son of Peter Conger and Elizabeth Stapleton, *née* Seymour; he was married and had no children; d. 27 July 1864 of tuberculosis at Peterborough, Canada West.

Wilson Seymour Conger may have operated the furniture factory at York (Toronto) where Paul Kane* was employed. Kane between 1834 and 1836 painted portraits of Conger and his wife. In 1829 Conger was at Cobourg where he soon entered municipal public life. In 1831 he was secretary of the building committee of the Upper Canada Academy (later Victoria College). He ran as a Reformer in Northumberland riding in 1834, advocating a Trent valley canal, a tariff on American agricultural produce, adoption of the secret ballot, popular election of the Legislative Council, and the abolition of primogeniture. He lost to Alexander McDONELL and John Gilchrist*. He opposed the William Lyon MACKENZIE radicals and supported the government during the Rebellion of 1837.

Conger was involved in the formation of the Cobourg and Peterborough Railway Company in 1835, and sat on the Cobourg Board of Police from 1837 to 1841, serving as president of that body in 1839. He moved to Peterborough after being appointed sheriff of the Colborne District on 22 Dec. 1841, and was sheriff of Peterborough County from 1849 until 1856.

At Peterborough Conger's interest in municipal improvements did not abate. In 1848 Conger, Judge George Barker Hall, Frederick Ferguson, and Charles Perry drafted the resolutions which led to the bill incorporating Peterborough. Conger was a town councillor from 1850 to 1859 and mayor in 1856, reeve of North Monaghan Township in 1854 and deputy reeve in 1857, and Peterborough County warden in 1859. He was also Peterborough's first chief engineer. In 1851 the

county council rejected a proposal by Conger which would have wrested control of the rear townships from land speculators and absentee owners and opened them up for settlement. He suggested that municipalities purchase crown lands for nominal sums, and sell them to settlers. The proceeds would have been used to establish a permanent common school fund and to build good roads in the county.

Conger was elected MLA for Peterborough in an 1856 by-election after John Langton* resigned the seat to become auditor general. He ran as a supporter of the Conservative government, defeating his Reform opponent, Frederick Ferguson, who was supported by George Brown* in accusing Conger of holding on to his post as sheriff while seeking election. Conger endorsed separate schools if they were self-supporting, thereby winning the bulk of the Roman Catholic vote. In the assembly he dealt mainly with local issues such as roads, temperance legislation, revision of the Common School Act, and construction of the Trent canal. In the general election of 1857 he was defeated by Thomas Short.

In June 1858 George Brown charged in the committee on public accounts that Conger had been a party to the withholding of £2,000 worth of municipal debentures during their transfer from Wolford Township to the town of Peterborough. Conger was sued by the town and lost the suit in 1859, despite attempts by Conservative friends on the town council to protect him. Nevertheless, Conger was re-elected to the legislature by acclamation in 1863 as an independent. He died in office at a time when his committee work dealing with the Trent canal proposal was nearing completion.

KENNETH W. JOHNSON

City of Peterborough, Ont., Office of the Chief Clerk, Corporation of the Town of Peterborough, minutes, 1850–63. Municipal Council of the County of Peterborough, *Minutes of proc.* (Peterborough, [Ont.]), 1850–63. *Cobourg Star* (Cobourg, [Ont.]), 1834–35. *Peterborough Examiner* (Peterborough, [Ont.]), 1856–64. *Peterborough Review* (Peterborough, [Ont.]), 1853–64. G. W. Craw, *The Peterborough story: our mayors, 1850–1951* ([Peterborough, Ont., 1967]). E. C. Guillet, *Cobourg, 1798–1948* (Oshawa, Ont., 1948). T. W. Poole, *A sketch of the early settlement and subsequent progress of the town of Peterborough . . .* (Peterborough, [Ont.], 1867).

CONNOLLY, SUZANNE, a Cree Indian, designated in documents as Suzanne "Pas-de-Nom" or "la Sauvagesse," wife of William Connolly*, fur-trader; b. *c.* 1788, probably northwest of Lake Winnipeg; d. 14 Aug. 1862 in the Grey Nuns convent at Saint-Boniface (Man.).

Connolly

William Connolly, born at Lachine, Province of Quebec, in 1787, entered the service of the North West Company about 1801. Two years later, at Rat River House, a post within a short distance of Nelson House, he took as his wife by "the custom of the country" a 15-year-old Cree girl, Suzanne. This marriage arrangement, usual in the fur trade prior to the arrival of clergy in the west, was by the consent of the two parties, with a gift probably being given to the Indian father. William Connolly and Suzanne lived for 28 years in the various trading posts at which he was stationed, and they were to have six children. In 1831 chief factor Connolly left the fur trade and went to Saint-Eustache, Lower Canada, with his Indian wife and children. Four or five months later Suzanne and her children moved to Montreal where they boarded at one time with a sister of William. On 16 May 1832, William Connolly married in a Catholic church his second cousin, Julia Woolrich, daughter of a well-to-do merchant. He had first obtained a dispensation from the bishop on the grounds that his marriage with the Indian woman had no validity.

A trader returning to civilization had to choose whether to leave his Indian wife in the wilderness, either abandoned or under the protection of another trader, or to take her with him, which was not always the best solution for her. Among fur-traders, Alexander Mackenzie* made the first decision, Daniel Williams Harmon* the second. Testimony that Connolly had intended to be faithful to Suzanne when he first arrived in Lower Canada was given later by the priest who baptized their two younger children. Governor George Simpson* in a letter dated 2 Dec. 1832 wrote: "You would have heard of Connolly's marriage – he was one of those who considered it a most unnatural proceeding 'to desert the mother of his children' and marry another; this is all very fine, very sentimental and very kind hearted 3000 miles from the civilized world but is lost sight of even by Friend Connolly where a proper opportunity offers."

Connolly's second marriage may not have been happy. James Keith*, HBC chief factor in charge of the Montreal Department, writing in 1841 to Simpson, his brother-in-law, said of Connolly: "He is completely under petty coat government – & dare invite no one without special permission." The same year Connolly wrote to Simpson thanking him for providing passage back to Red River that spring for Suzanne and her younger children: "They will be much happier there than here, and their removal has taken a heavy weight off my mind." In a will made in 1848, Connolly left his considerable property to Julia and her two children. He died the following year.

Suzanne, who had taken up residence in the Grey Nuns convent at Red River in 1841, was supported by Connolly and later by Julia. She died 14 Aug. 1862. Two years later, on 13 May, John Connolly, Suzanne's eldest son, launched an action in the Superior Court against Julia Woolrich claiming one-sixth of one-half of his father's estate. At issue was whether Connolly's marriage to Suzanne "by the custom of the country" was legal, and whether a community of property existed between them. The court heard evidence from the few surviving traders on the marriage practices in the fur country in the early decades of the century, and decided in favour of the plaintiff. Julia, and later her heirs (she died on 27 July 1865), fought the case through the Court of Appeals and the Court of Revision. The last court rendered a decision on 7 Sept. 1869, which supported that of the lower courts, with one of the five judges dissenting. Julia's heirs appealed to the Privy Council in London, but before this body could deal with the case an out-of-court settlement was reached by the disputants.

The significance of the trials was the judgement that marriage with an Indian woman, entered into only with the consent of the two parties, was valid, at least if followed by long co-habitation, and that the children of such a union were entitled to share in the disposition of the father's property. The same decision 30 years earlier might have caused consternation among retired fur-traders living in civilization, but by 1869 nearly all were dead. Suzanne Connolly has the distinction of being the only Canadian woman the legality of whose marriage became a case for the Privy Council. Before her death she had the satisfaction of knowing that her daughter Amelia was Lady Douglas, wife of Sir James Douglas*, governor of Vancouver Island and the crown colony of British Columbia.

BRUCE PEEL

HBC Arch., B.135/c/2, 2 Dec. 1832; D.5/6, f.131d., 16 April 1841; D.5/7, f.274d., 10 Aug. 1841. "Cour d'appel; présents – Les Hons. Duval, Caron, Badgley, Loranger, MacKay; jugement rendu le 7 septembre 1869; Johnstone et al: – (reprenant l'instance de Julia Woolrich), appelants, et John Connolly, intimé," *La Revue légale* (Montréal), I (1869), 253–400. HBRS, II (Rich and Fleming), 209, "Superior Court, 1867: Montreal, 9th July, 1867; *Coram* Monk, J.; no.902, *Connolly* vs. *Woolrich* and *Johnson* et al., defendants *par reprise d'instance*; Indian marriage – question as to validity," *The Lower Canada Jurist/Collection de décisions du Bas-Canada* (Montreal), XI (1867), 197–265. Sylvia Van Kirk, "The role of women in the fur trade society of the Canadian west, 1700–1850'' (unpublished PHD thesis, University of London, 1975).

CONNOR, GEORGE SKEFFINGTON, farmer, lawyer, politician, and judge; b. 1810 in Dublin (Republic of Ireland), the son of a successful Dublin lawyer; m. in 1830 Eliza Hume, the sister of Catherine Hume*, and they had no children; d. 29 April 1863 at Toronto, Canada West.

George Skeffington Connor entered Trinity College, Dublin, at age 14 and received a law degree in 1830. He and his wife immigrated to Canada in July 1832 in the company of his brother-in-law, William Hume BLAKE, and also with the Reverend Benjamin Cronyn* and several other relatives and friends. After a long quarantine at Grosse Île because of a cholera epidemic the party separated, Connor settling near Orillia in Oro Township where he tried his hand at farming. In 1834, however, he returned to Ireland and travelled on the Continent.

He received an honorary call to the Irish bar in 1838, a law degree and position at the bar being considered an "honorable" and "liberal" profession for an Irish gentleman of private means who might not intend to practise. After his return to Canada Connor was called to the Upper Canadian bar in 1842; since he had a degree he did not have to article. With William Hume Blake and Joseph Curran Morrison* he then established a legal firm in Toronto. The firm was "very successful," but after several years Connor withdrew to form a partnership with George Boomer, who later became a Toronto police magistrate.

In September 1848 Connor replaced W. H. Blake as professor of law at King's College, Toronto, from which he received an annual salary of £250. A student later recalled that "he lectured with great care, and instructed the students in a manner as agreeable to them as it was elegant and useful." He taught at King's until it was closed in 1850 and at the University of Toronto until 1853, when all professional faculties were abolished. In 1849 Connor had received an honorary LLD from the University of Dublin, and in November of the same year had been elected university solicitor by the King's College Council, replacing James Edward SMALL. Connor was the University of Toronto's solicitor until August 1858 when he resigned to accept political office, but became its chancellor in January 1863 shortly before his death.

Connor had been appointed a QC in November 1850 and shortly after became a bencher of the Law Society of Upper Canada. In 1856 he was appointed one of the commissioners for consolidating the statutes of Upper and Lower Canada, and he took particular interest in revising the real property acts. As a defence lawyer he was involved in several cases that received public attention, including the Lawrence W. Mercer trial, which involved the purchase of the office of sheriff in Norfolk County, and the James Fleming murder trial.

From 1843 Connor had been politically associated with the Reformers. In 1844 he was a candidate in Simcoe riding but was defeated by William Benjamin Robinson*. When Robert Baldwin* suggested in 1846 that Connor run in the next election, he declined, maintaining that he lacked the necessary reputation and that it would be unfair to his legal partners. In 1857 Connor was elected by a majority of one vote in the riding of Oxford South, and was appointed solicitor general without an executive council seat in the "Short Administration" of George Brown* and Antoine-Aimé Dorion* in August 1858. In the assembly Connor advocated the incorporation of Ingersoll as a town, but his activities as a member were not noteworthy. He was re-elected in 1861 but resigned early in 1863 when he was appointed a puisne judge of the Court of Queen's Bench.

At his death from an epileptic seizure in April 1863 the Toronto *Globe* described him as "an excellent Irish gentleman in speech and manner." He had a reputation for being more fond of literature than of law and he was "a good French scholar."

R. LYNN OGDEN

MTCL, Robert Baldwin papers. PAC, RG 1, E1, 82, p.49; RG 5, C1, 604, no.245; 715, no.1389; RG 68, 1, General index, 1841–67. University of Toronto Archives, A-70-005 (Senate), Minutes, book 2, 14 Sept. 1858; March, May 1863; A-70-024 (Board of Governors), King's College Council minute book (17 Jan.–29 Dec. 1849), 4, p.57; A-72-050 (Office of the Chief Accountant), box 12, package 1c, T. E. Campbell to H. Boys, 13 Sept. 1848; Connor to H. Boys, 16 Sept. 1848. *Globe*, 30 April 1863. *Irish Canadian* (Toronto), 6 May 1863. Read, *Lives of judges. The University of Toronto and its colleges, 1827–1906*, ed. W. J. Alexander (Toronto, 1906). W. S. Wallace, *A history of the University of Toronto, 1827–1927* (Toronto, 1927).

COOK, WILLIAM FRANCIS, merchant, shipbuilder, and office-holder; b. 4 Feb. 1796 at or near Guysborough, N.S., third child of Benjamin Cook and Philomela Hull; m. first, on 5 May 1822, Eliza Cunningham (d. 1850), and they had eight children; m. secondly, in the mid 1850s, Caroline Brown, and they had one child; d. 8 April 1862 at Canso, N.S.

Apparently Francis Cook was apprenticed to

Cooke

Thomas Cutler*, a Guysborough merchant, in whose service he was brought up and in whose firm he eventually became a partner. In 1816, likely through Cutler's influence, he was made clerk of licence by the Court of Sessions; he also served as gauger, as hog reeve, and as an inspector and culler of dry and pickled fish. In 1822 Cook left R. M. Cutler and Company and established his own business in Guysborough. He dealt in general merchandise, and he likely purchased the fish he shipped to Halifax whence it was reshipped by larger firms to the West Indies. He may even have shipped directly to the West Indies himself. He also owned seines and engaged directly in the fishery. Between 1836 and 1849 his shipyards launched a number of brigs, schooners, and barques.

Francis Cook served as a vestryman in Christ Church (Church of England), Guysborough, from April 1822 to March 1823. However in 1823 he was listed as a teacher in the newly formed Methodist Sunday School, and in 1830 he and his wife were among the seven original founding families of the "Society of People called Methodists" in Guysborough. In 1837 Cook was appointed justice of the peace, in 1838 judge of common pleas, and in 1840 assistant judge of the Inferior Court and Sessions of the Peace. He served as a trustee of Guysborough Academy in 1848 and was an officer of the local temperance society, being president in the 1848–49 term.

For many years his business flourished and by 1842 Cook paid the fourth highest assessment in Guysborough County. In the late 1840s, however, Cook had serious financial difficulties, being unable to repay loans chiefly from Halifax merchants. With outstanding mortgages of about £1,000, his business was placed in the hands of assignees early in 1850 and in 1851 his Guysborough operation was sold by the sheriff for debts. In 1850, following his wife's death, Cook moved to Canso where he re-established as a merchant. In May the Court of Sessions appointed him the weigher of flour and meal for Canso and in 1853 he became a commissioner for giving relief to insolvent debtors and for taking affidavits to hold to bail. By the late 1850s he was again in the fishery, maintaining a boat and employing four men. He also had the small subsistence farm that most Nova Scotians, regardless of their station, found convenient, if not necessary.

A relatively minor figure in a community decreasing in importance, Francis Cook is nevertheless interesting as a typical middleman in the Nova Scotia fishery. The business of shipping fish was a risky one, and it made or destroyed the fortunes of hundreds of Nova Scotian entrepreneurs.

JOHN N. GRANT

Christ Church (Anglican) (Guysborough, N.S.), records (mfm. at PANS). Guysborough County Registry Office (Guysborough, N.S.), deeds. Guysborough United Church (Guysborough, N.S.), records (mfm. at PANS). PANS, MG 20, no.98; RG 1, 175, 449; RG 12, census of Nova Scotia, 1860–61; RG 34–311, P1–P4, 1785–1879. *Eastern Chronicle* (Pictou, N.S.), 1862. *Provincial Wesleyan* (Halifax), 1862. *Royal Gazette* (Halifax), 1851. *Belcher's farmer's almanack*, 1824–62. H. C. Hart, *History of the county of Guysborough* (2nd ed., [Windsor, N.S., 1895]). A. C. Jost, *Guysborough sketches and essays* (Guysborough, N.S., 1950).

COOKE, THOMAS, Catholic priest, missionary, bishop; b. 9 Feb. 1792 at Pointe-du-Lac, Lower Canada, eldest son of John Thomas Cooke and Isabelle Guay; d. 31 March 1870 at Trois-Rivières.

Thomas' father, a native of Ireland, ran away from home and stowed on a ship bound for Canada. The captain soon discovered him, and on reaching Montreal placed him under the care of the commandant of Île Sainte-Hélène, through whose initiative he was trained as a miller. Around 1790 John Thomas Cooke went to Pointe-du-Lac, where he worked at the mill of seigneur Nicolas Montour*, then became a miller at Cap-de-la-Madeleine; he was murdered in December 1808.

By then Thomas was already a boarder at the Grand Séminaire de Québec. The parish priest, Urbain Orfroy, had introduced him to French and Latin and then sent him in 1804 to the Collège de Nicolet, which had just opened. There he had shown himself "ingenious and virtuous," and his superiors had invited him to take his philosophy at the seminary of Quebec, starting in the autumn of 1808. A year later, Bishop Joseph-Octave Plessis* appointed him professor of Latin and bursar at the new Collège de Saint-Hyacinthe. He returned to the Grand Séminaire de Québec in 1811, and while studying theology acted as form-master and professor at the Petit Séminaire. Bishop Plessis ordained him priest on 11 Sept. 1814.

The new priest immediately found himself fully occupied. He was both curate at Rivière-Ouelle and secretary to the parish priest, Bishop Bernard-Claude Panet*, coadjutor to the bishop of Quebec. In four years he officiated at 508 baptisms, 125 marriages, and 221 burials, as well as dealing with the coadjutor's heavy correspondence. In the autumn of 1817 Bishop Plessis, pleased with his work, appointed him missionary at Baie des Chaleurs. Abbé Cooke immediately took Caraquet, N.B., as his centre for the missions entrusted to his care, from Belledune to the Baie du Vin. For six years he continually travelled throughout his vast territory to bring the comfort of religion to a thousand scattered settlers. He spread the gospel, did not mince his words with the varied population of Micmacs, Acadians, Irish, and Scots, and was not afraid to resort to extreme measures (expulsion from the church, a good caning) to correct drunkenness and loose living; he also became a builder and started or completed the construction of five churches and two presbyteries. The young missionary gave so much of himself that his health was affected, and in 1822 he had to ask to be recalled. He left Caraquet for good in November 1823.

After a few months' rest at Pointe-du-Lac, Abbé Cooke was appointed parish priest of Saint-Ambroise-de-la-Jeune-Lorette (Loretteville), with responsibility for the parish's Indian mission and the Irish settlement at Valcartier. Here he spent the most rewarding years of his life. His parishioners appreciated his piety and charity; he was unsparing in his devotion to his white parishioners, and even more to the Indians, for whom he had a particular affection; as a change from his labours, he taught school to young Canadians and Hurons, and accompanied soldiers on their fishing expeditions, where he proved to be a good companion, "gay, teasing, even a songster, as soon as he stepped into a fishing boat." He none the less continued to direct his parish "like a religious community."

Because of his reputation the bishop of Quebec appointed him parish priest of Trois-Rivières, a parish where piety and good order left something to be desired. Abbé Cooke arrived there in September 1835, with the titles of parish priest of Trois-Rivières and Cap-de-la-Madeleine, vicar general, and member of the corporation of the Séminaire de Nicolet. He immediately set to work. According to a contemporary, "he made ingenious use of everything [retreats, indulgences, confraternities] to achieve his ends: the improvement and sanctification of his flock." He brought in Abbé Charles-Paschal-Télesphore Chiniquy* and Bishop Charles-Auguste-Marie-Joseph de Forbin-Janson*, who by their eloquence profoundly stirred the people of Trois-Rivières and inaugurated there as elsewhere in Lower Canada an era of Catholic revival.

Thomas Cooke was appointed first bishop of the diocese of Trois-Rivières on 8 June 1852 and consecrated on 18 October. The diocese extended from Maskinongé to Sainte-Anne-de-la-Pérade, from Yamaska to Saint-Pierre-les-Becquets, and from the upper Saint-Maurice to the American border. The new office changed him little, for he remained above all a parish priest and pastor. Unfailingly courteous with laymen and gentle with children, Bishop Cooke became increasingly demanding of himself and others. An impetuous Irishman, he readily lost his temper, and blasted offenders without compromise or equivocation, but his anger almost always ended in a resounding laugh which disconcerted those who did not know him intimately; he was a witty and skilful talker, and his conversation was enlivened by clever and piquant rejoinders which sometimes went beyond acceptable limits. His charity was proverbial at Trois-Rivières, where he always showed himself a lover of order and justice. Bishop Cooke stayed out of ideological quarrels, for, according to a contemporary, "he understood little about the questions that so engrossed the minds of some." Thus in 1863, when he was obliged to take a stand concerning the creation of a Catholic university at Montreal, he wrote to the archbishop of Quebec: "I shall vote as Your Excellency does, if you are against it. You will please be good enough to inform me, indeed to send me a résumé of the reasons that I can use in my reply." In 1867 he left it to his coadjutor, Bishop Louis-François Laflèche*, to draw up a text which was strongly in favour of confederation, and he agreed to sign it although he considered it "too political."

Bishop Cooke's achievements during his episcopacy were not all spectacular, for he wanted first to organize the new diocese. He was alert to the needs of his flock and clergy; he gave particular attention to pastoral visits, and established ecclesiastical conferences and an annual retreat for his priests. Despite the manifest opposition of a section of the clergy, who favoured developing the Collège de Nicolet, and of the faithful, who were already sufficiently in debt, he allowed the college of Trois-Rivières to be established in 1860, and undertook to provide ecclesiastical staff for it. The cathedral of Trois-Rivières is the principal monument commemorating his episcopacy. He announced its construction in a pastoral letter of 16 March 1854, and requested the people of his diocese to contribute to the building of this mother church. Some of the faithful found the burden too heavy and protested. Moreover, through inept speculation and bad financial administration, the diocese was on the verge of bankruptcy. Indeed, anticipating the construction of a northern railway, the bursar had bought a large number of building sites at Trois-Rivières. But the railway did not appear, the land did not

Cooney

increase in value as anticipated, and the episcopal corporation was obliged to sell at a low price. Building of the cathedral was undertaken all the same and it was consecrated on 29 Sept. 1858. But Bishop Cooke was soon forced to disclose his financial difficulties. His clergy and people were warned, and Abbé Louis-François Laflèche was instructed to visit all the parishes in the diocese and meet all the creditors. Through generous gifts and private settlements bankruptcy was averted, and the debt of $96,000 wiped out in the years that followed. Bishop Cooke came into conflict with some of his clergy over another issue concerning money. In December 1856, by decree, he required the parish priests to pay him ten per cent of their revenues. The richest priests, particularly those on the south shore, challenged the bishop's right to impose a levy on them. The dispute assumed dangerous proportions before it was resolved by compromises in 1857 and 1862, when promissory notes given by the parish priests replaced the real ten per cent. But a certain animosity remained as a forewarning of the extensive manoeuvring from 1870 to 1880 to get a diocese created at Nicolet.

Endless toil, continual difficulties, and particularly the divisions among clergy and faithful, rapidly undermined the bishop's health. Increasingly crippled by rheumatism, and weakened by heart disease and leg pains, Bishop Cooke gradually handed over his powers to his successor. In September 1861 he took Abbé Louis-François Laflèche out of the Séminaire de Nicolet, appointed him bursar of the bishopric, and gave him full authority to clear up the financial situation; in 1867 he made him his coadjutor *cum futura successione*, and after 11 April 1869 entrusted him fully with the administration of the diocese. Bishop Cooke spent his remaining months in increasing seclusion, giving himself to meditation and devotions to the Virgin and St Joseph. He died on 31 March 1870, aged 78 years and one month.

NIVE VOISINE

AAQ, 311 CN, VI. Archives du séminaire de Nicolet (Nicolet, Qué.), Lettres des directeurs et autres à l'évêque de Québec, 1814–74, I–V. ASTR, Papiers Mgr Albert Tessier, Q1, C20. *L'Opinion publique*, 30 mai, 6 juin 1872; 6 févr. 1879. Marie-Stanislas-du-Sacré-Cœur, "Introduction à une biographie de Mgr Thomas Cooke" (thèse de DES, université Laval, Québec, 1965). *Les ursulines des Trois-Rivières depuis leur établissement jusqu'à nos jours* (4v., Trois-Rivières, 1888–1911). Edgar Godin, "Mgr Thomas Cooke, missionnaire de la baie des Chaleurs, 1817–1823," SCHÉC *Rapport*, 20 (1952–53), 43–48.

COONEY, ROBERT, Methodist clergyman, journalist, and author; b. 24 June 1800 in Dublin (Republic of Ireland); m. in 1837 Susan Catherine Shaw of Halifax; d. 17 March 1870 in Toronto, Ont.

Robert Cooney's father was a clerk in a Dublin mercantile firm and was described by Robert as "well to do, and very respectably connected." An Irish Gael and a Roman Catholic, he had married a girl who was Anglo-Irish and Church of England but who was converted to Catholicism and became a strong adherent. With her encouragement Robert Cooney began studies for the priesthood. The young Cooney was inspired not only by the priests who frequented his home, but also by Irish political leaders such as Daniel O'Connell, whom he frequently saw at mass.

In 1824, six years after the death of his father, Cooney abandoned his studies, immigrated to New Brunswick, and found employment in a Newcastle mercantile firm. He also found support for his ambitions for the priesthood in the person of the Reverend William Dollard*, later the first Roman Catholic bishop of Fredericton, under whom he renewed his theological studies. Cooney often accompanied Dollard on his pastoral rounds.

For a brief period Cooney worked for an unnamed barrister, who apparently had a great influence on him, but the real turning point in his life came in 1828. In the elections of that year, Cooney was asked, as an educated Irish Catholic, to help deliver the decisive Catholic vote to Joseph CUNARD, the timber and shipping baron of the Miramichi, even though it was well known that Bishop Angus MacEachern* supported Cunard's Catholic opponent, James DeWolf Fraser. Cooney agreed to support Cunard because he considered him more "liberal" than Fraser. Cunard received the critical Irish vote and was elected. Bishop MacEachern retaliated by having Cooney "read from the altar." To protest this "alliance of Scots" and "Jesuitism," Cooney left the Catholic Church.

Between 1829 and 1831, Cooney wrote for the *Gleaner* at Chatham, and gathered notes for his best known work, *A compendious history of the northern part of the province of New Brunswick and of the district of Gaspé, in Lower Canada*, which he dedicated to Cunard. In 1832 he took his manuscript to Halifax for publication by Joseph Howe*. During his visit to that town, Cooney was converted to Methodism, and soon began preaching. He was stationed in the next few years at Murray Harbour, P.E.I., and Liverpool, Halifax, and Guysborough, N.S., and was ordained in 1837. The next year he was transferred to Odelltown, Lower Canada, where he opposed the uprising which occurred in that town in 1838. After serving in Stanstead and Montreal in Canada East and Toronto in Canada West, he returned to New Brunswick in 1847, and preached at Carleton, Saint John, and St Stephen.

He was an extremely popular lecturer in the Saint John Mechanics' Institute, and during the early 1850s he prepared a rambling apologia, *The autobiography of a Wesleyan Methodist missionary*. Not as well known as his *History*, Cooney's autobiography is perhaps the more important work. It includes lengthy discussions of theological questions and defences of the Methodist Church, as well as observations on people and places encountered during Cooney's itinerant ministry, although, as a modern commentator has noted, it is "irritatingly skimpy when touching on important events of which he was a witness." Cooney discusses both the nature of his times and the difficulties faced by a cultivated and talented young man from Georgian Dublin in adjusting to the brutal realities of backwoods New Brunswick. The Catholicism which had inspired his youth was not the Catholicism he found struggling for survival in the Miramichi. If he resented the Highland hegemony of Bishop MacEachern, he had also discovered, perhaps for the first time, that all Irishmen were not the equal of O'Connell.

Cooney left New Brunswick in 1855, and after a brief stay at Saint-Jean in Canada East, moved on to preach in Canada West at Guelph (1856–57), London (1858–59), and St Catharines (1860–61). There he lived in retirement from 1862 to 1868 when he returned to Toronto. Although he continued to write and lecture, he became more interested in theological questions. Cooney was apparently a well-respected minister within his church; by 1858 two universities had honoured him with degrees. His death in 1870 went almost unnoticed in New Brunswick, but in 1896 his *History* was republished in Chatham, N.B., and Cooney's memory reaped the reward he deserved as an observer and recorder of history.

P. M. TONER

[Robert Cooney], *The autobiography of a Wesleyan Methodist missionary, (formerly a Roman Catholic), containing an account of his conversion from Romanism, and his reception into the Wesleyan ministry; also reminiscences of nearly twenty-five years' itinerancy in the North American provinces . . .* (Montreal, 1856); *A compendious history of the northern part of the province of New Brunswick and of the district of Gaspé, in Lower Canada* (Halifax, 1832; repr. Chatham, N.B., 1896). Wesleyan Methodist Church in Can., *Minutes* (Toronto), 1870. *Christian Guardian*, 23 March 1870. *Gleaner* (Chatham, N.B.), 1829–31. *Morning News* (Saint John, N.B.), 1853–57. *New Brunswick Courier*, 1 July 1837. *St. John Daily Telegraph and Morning Journal* (Saint John, N.B.), 29 March 1870. Cornish, *Cyclopaedia of Methodism*. Morgan, *Bibliotheca Canadensis*. Story, *Oxford companion*. T. W. Smith, *History of the Methodist Church within the territories embraced in the late conference of Eastern British America . . .* (2v., Halifax, 1877–90). W. O. Raymond, "Robert Cooney, first historian of northern and eastern New Brunswick," N.B. Hist. Soc., *Coll.* (Saint John), no. 10 (1919), 67–85.

COOPER, WILLIAM, sea captain, shipbuilder, farmer, miller, land agent, and politician; b. probably 4 Nov. 1786 in England; d. 10 June 1867 at Sailors Hope, P.E.I.

Virtually nothing is known about William Cooper's life before his arrival on Prince Edward Island about 1819. According to an account probably based on oral family tradition, he ran away to sea at age 11, was with the British navy at the battle of Trafalgar, and subsequently sailed the seven seas as a ship's captain.

The earliest known reference to Cooper on the Island is 6 Nov. 1819, when his wife, Sarah Glover, gave birth to their second son at Fortune Bay in eastern Kings County. Cooper had settled on a farm appropriately named "Sailor's Hope," where he built a home and took up stock raising. He also erected a grist mill, and in 1826 built a 72-ton ship called the *Hackmatack*.

Cooper was soon involved in the most controversial social and political problem in 19th century Island history – the land question. Since 1767 practically all the land in the colony had been in the hands of a small number of absentee proprietors, and with few exceptions settlers had no alternative but to become their tenants. In Lot 56, where Cooper lived, the general frustration found violent expression in the summer of 1819 when Edward Abell, the agent of the proprietor, Lord James Townshend, was murdered by an irate tenant from whom he had been attempting to extract rent. On 26 Feb. 1820 Lord Townshend appointed Cooper as Abell's successor.

Cooper was reputedly one of the more efficient of an apparently negligent and often corrupt class of land agents. Thomas Heath HAVILAND, who was to succeed him some nine years later in Lord Townshend's employment, claimed that Cooper had granted leases to almost 60 tenants; his figure was noteworthy since most settlers were reluctant to take out leases, thereby acknowledging the proprietor's claim to land and farms which, by dint of hard work and occupation, they thought should rightfully be their own. Moreover, Lord Townshend's terms were comparatively harsh: the usual lease in the colony ran for 999 years but Cooper was instructed to lease land lying "contiguous to the Sea Shore" for a period not exceeding 84 years, and land more than five miles inland for not more than 200 years. Furthermore, each tenant was to pay half the costs of executing his own lease.

In 1829 Cooper was dismissed by Lord Townshend for somewhat obscure reasons. In later years his political enemies frequently alleged that Cooper had misappropriated funds, a charge which Haviland supported in 1860 before the land commission and which Cooper never seemed quite able to refute convincingly. It was perhaps not entirely coincidental that by 1830 he had apparently undergone a change of heart amounting almost to a religious conversion, and had become the lifelong, implacable foe of the absentee proprietors.

Cooper was first elected to the assembly in a bitterly disputed by-election in Kings County in 1831. He ran on the platform of "Our country's freedom and farmers' rights." The voting was interrupted by a riot, and Cooper, fearing for his life, hid in a nearby barn. It was only after a lengthy investigations by a committee on privileges and elections – and then by a margin of a single vote – that he was allowed to take his seat.

Cooper's radical and uncompromising position on the land question, enunciated on 27 March 1832 in his first major speech as an MHA, set him apart from his fellow assemblymen: "The more I consider the Escheat question, the more plain it appears to me, that nothing less than a general Escheat will do justice to, or satisfy the inhabitants of this Island." By the 1830s the escheat issue had had a long tradition in Island politics. Advocates of escheat (i.e. confiscation) wanted a special court established to investigate land titles, and to decide whether the conditions attached to the original land grants of 1767 had been fulfilled. By the terms of these grants, proprietors were to pay annual quitrents to the crown, and settle each lot with at least 100 non-British Protestants within ten years. In no township had these conditions been fulfilled exactly as laid down. Thus Cooper and his political associates maintained that practically all the land in the Island should be escheated and regranted in small tracts to *bona fide* settlers. This heady doctrine, promising redistribution of virtually all landed property in the colony, proved attractive to a populace comprised largely of small tenant farmers, who, upon the satisfaction of a modest property requirement, shared with freeholders the right to vote.

During the 1830s Cooper became the founder and leader of an informal Escheat party, and proceeded with considerable energy and skill to polarize Island politics on the single issue of land tenure. Perhaps in an attempt to steal Cooper's fire, the more conservative members of the assembly were quick to express themselves in favour of a moderate escheat. But an 1832 assembly bill providing for a court of escheat, with vague jurisdiction, was vetoed by the British government, and Cooper was able to discredit his political opponents by claiming that, as a group comprised largely of land agents, lawyers, and others of the local élite, they were obviously opposed to reform. Cooper argued that they had conspired with the absentee proprietors to misrepresent the situation on the Island, and thus to frustrate the expressed wishes of the people. Cooper's message was clear: if the tenant voters wanted freehold tenure, they must elect honest, courageous men from among themselves, men in whose self-interest it was to present the true state of affairs to the crown. Then, in response to such obvious oppression and injustice, redress would be forthcoming.

Cooper's agitation contributed to a violent mood among the tenantry, many of whom refused to pay rents and on occasion banded together to threaten rent collectors and sheriffs physically. But Cooper himself was always careful to keep within the law, and appears not to have been the man to lead an actual armed uprising. He did maintain that "a degree of public excitement" was required to impress upon the British government the necessity of reform, and to this end he organized frequent public meetings at which he advised tenants to withhold the payment of rent, notably a large meeting at Hay River on 20 Dec. 1836, where several hundred tenants unanimously endorsed a 34-clause petition to the king requesting a court of escheat. As a result of his activity in the countryside, Cooper was committed to the custody of the assembly's sergeant-at-arms during the 1837 and 1838 sessions.

Cooper justified his actions by a sort of homegrown ideology – based largely on the writings of Sir William Blackstone and John Locke – which maintained that the labour invested by settlers in clearing their land gave them titles naturally superior to the allegedly forfeited claims of the absentee proprietors. These ideas, already well developed by 1832, changed little in the following years. In an 1855 assembly speech, for example, he supported his call for escheat by citing Blackstone's *Commentaries*, and by quoting Locke: ". . . the labour of a man's body and the work of his hands, we may say are properly his.

Whatsoever then he removes out of the state that nature hath provided and left it in, he hath mixed his labour with, and joined to it something of his own, and thereby making it his property.''

Cooper's credibility was diminished, however, by the fact that he continued to pay the rent on his own land to Lord Townshend, a fact which Thomas Irwin proclaimed in a full-page advertisement in the *Royal Gazette* in December 1834. Thus he remained secure in the possession of his farm at a time when his neighbours were risking eviction and keeping the countryside in turmoil by accepting his advice to withhold rents. This sort of inconsistency in Cooper's behaviour, as well as his tendency on occasion to stretch the truth close to the breaking point in his public pronouncements, gives some credence to Lieutenant Governor Sir Charles Augustus Fitz-Roy*'s description of him as ''an artful person although very illiterate, possessed of much low cunning and perfectly unscrupulous in making any assertion to serve his purpose.''

The apex of Cooper's political career came with the decisive victory of the Escheat party in the election of 1838, when it won 18 of the 24 seats. This essentially agrarian-populist uprising represented a major upheaval in Island politics: never before had the assembly been dominated by such a democratic element, and never had so many of its members been themselves tenant farmers. When the house met in January 1839 Cooper was elected speaker by a vote of 16 to six.

With a clear popular mandate to pursue land reform, Cooper immediately proceeded to carry out a scheme he had long advocated – an official delegation from the Island legislature to the colonial secretary in London. The assembly chose Cooper himself to present the colony's request for a court of escheat and several other land reform measures, and in the summer of 1839 he embarked for England. The trip was a disaster. Lord John Russell, the newly appointed colonial secretary, refused even to grant Cooper an audience, choosing instead to send directly to Fitz-Roy in Charlottetown his negative reply to the petitions and remonstrances of the Island assembly. Cooper remained a short time in London, consulting with the well-known radical parliamentarian Joseph Hume about presenting the Island's case to the British House of Commons. But parliament was not in session, and early in October Cooper wrote to a correspondence committee of the Island assembly that he was returning home ''by the first opportunity.'' It was an admission of defeat.

Cooper's prestige never fully recovered. In the legislative session of 1840 he was criticized by some of his own supporters; one of the more articulate of them, Alexander Rae*, remarked that while he was in England a ''lethargy'' seemed to have ''almost paralyzed his natural powers.'' However, in the face of strong attacks by such members of the opposition as Edward Palmer* and Joseph Pope*, the Escheators rallied behind Cooper and over the next several years endorsed a good deal of radical land reform legislation. One bill passed in 1840 was ''to authorize the Crown to purchase the Lands, and to regulate the settlement of the Inhabitants . . .''; another attempted to exempt tenants from having to pay quitrents and land assessments. However, those few bills which were acceptable to the Legislative Council faced veto by the colonial secretary in London. The years 1839–42 thus produced virtually no legislation which ameliorated the plight of the tenants. The Escheat party was defeated in the election of 1842, and rapidly disintegrated. Although Cooper was himself re-elected, he apparently began to lose interest in politics for he was absent from the house during the sessions of 1845 and 1846 and did not contest the 1846 election.

During these years his attention once again turned to the sea and shipbuilding, apparently in the Souris–Fortune Bay area: in 1844 he registered the *Flora Beaton*, in 1845 the *Sea Walker*, in 1846 the *Malvina*, in 1847 the *Plenty*, and in 1849 the 182-ton brigantine, *Packet*. In the *Packet* he and his family, which included at least three daughters and six grown sons, sailed from Fortune Bay on 5 Dec. 1849 bound for California, where gold had recently been discovered. With Cooper as captain, the *Packet* sailed around Cape Horn and arrived at San Francisco on 20 July 1850. There the ship and part of the cargo of lumber and agricultural implements were sold. After about six weeks Cooper decided to return to the Island; but the other members of his family, including his wife, chose to remain in California. In November 1851 Sarah Cooper and one son Oscar died of cholera in San Francisco. Three more sons were killed by Indians in 1852 and 1861 and another died from natural causes in 1853. Of the six Cooper sons who went to California only one, John W., outlived his father.

Upon his return to the Island Cooper once again took up residence at Sailor's Hope. By 1855 he was back in the assembly, still a fervent advocate of escheat. During his absence in California the Island had achieved responsible government, and in 1853 the legislature had enacted a bill to bring about land reform by enabling the Island government to purchase the estates of willing proprietors. This land could then be resold in small tracts to tenants. Although Cooper was nominally a Liberal supporter he embarrassed his political colleagues, including Premier George Coles*, by charging them with spending the people's money to purchase land to which he maintained the proprietors had no rightful claim or title. In these criticisms he was supported by the veteran Escheator John Macintosh*. Cooper sat in the assembly until 1862. He died on 10 June 1867 at Sailors Hope.

Until recently William Cooper has not received adequate treatment by Island historians, perhaps because he has always been looked upon as slightly disreputable – an alienated anti-establishment figure who by his advocacy of radical schemes threatened the social order. Paradoxically, it is for this same reason that more recently he has begun to be viewed as somewhat of a hero.

It is difficult to determine whether or not Cooper thought that the confiscation of the proprietors' land was literally possible. In retrospect, however, escheat must be regarded as a visionary doctrine which had almost no chance of realization. The proprietors had owned their estates for so long that the British government could hardly sanction such a major social and economic upheaval on the meagre grounds that some highly impracticable 60-year-old conditions had not been met. Possibly Cooper felt that the agitation around the issue of escheat would force the British government to take some effective action to redress the genuine grievances of the tenantry. In this too he failed, perhaps because he was unwilling to carry his agitation to the point of an armed uprising.

Nevertheless, Cooper's real achievements are considerable. In both organization and doctrine the political movement he founded was the undoubted forerunner of the reform-minded Liberal party, which led the struggle for responsible government in the 1840s. In addition, because Cooper brought the issue of land reform so forcefully into the political arena it could never again be ignored. Thus he deserves much of the credit for the gradual improvement in the condition of the tenants which more practical reformers such as Coles managed to bring about in the following decades.

Cooper remains an enigmatic figure – a visionary, an adventurer, and a pre-Marxist advocate of an ideology to support and justify the cause of an oppressed class, yet a man with evident weaknesses and inconsistencies. An obituary in the *Examiner* under the heading "An old veteran departed" seems to strike a fair and judicious balance in assessing Cooper's career: ". . . although he was deeply censured for the alleged extravagance of his views on the Escheat ques-

tion, he was long admired by the majority of his fellow Colonists for the boldness with which he urged those views; and we believe all parties and classes gave him credit for sincerity."

HARRY BAGLOLE

[William Cooper has been the subject of no substantial biography or biographical sketch, and no collection of his papers has come to light. Furthermore, attempts to obtain information from his descendants living in the United States have been unsuccessful. The main outline of Cooper's life, therefore, has been pieced together from diverse sources. Perhaps the most important of these is J. H. McDonald, "The story of the Cooper family," *Maple Leaf* (Oakland, Calif.), XXX (1936).

Additional information has been obtained from the following sources. PAPEI, T. H. Haviland rent books, Lot 56, ff.66–67; P.E.I., Shipping registers, 1815–50 (mfm.). PRO, CO 226/49–64; 227/8. P.E.I., Dept. of Health, Division of Vital Statistics, Records of St Paul's Church (Charlottetown), book 3, p.186; Supreme Court, Estates Division, liber 7, f.340 (will of William Cooper, probate proved 29 June 1867) (mfm. at PAPEI). *Abstract of the proceedings before the Land Commissioners' Court, held during the summer of 1860, to inquire into the differences relative to the rights of landowners and tenants in Prince Edward Island*, reporters J. D. Gordon and David Laird (Charlottetown, 1862), especially 5–8, 237–38. P.E.I., House of Assembly, *Debates and proc.*, 1855–62; *Journal*, 1830–46, 1855–62. *Colonial Herald* (Charlottetown), 1837–44. *Examiner* (Charlottetown), 1855–62, 17 June 1867. *Islander*, 1855–62. *Royal Gazette* (Charlottetown), 1830s, 1840s. F.W.P. Bolger, "The demise of quit rents and escheats," *Canada's smallest province* (Bolger), 99–114. Clark, *Three centuries and the Island*. MacKinnon, *Government of P.E.I.*, 105–19. Weale and Baglole, *The Island and confederation*. H.B.]

COPWAY, GEORGE. *See* KAHGEGAGAHBOWH

CORMACK, WILLIAM EPPES (Epps), explorer, entrepreneur, philanthropist, agriculturalist, and author; b. 5 May 1796 at St John's, Nfld, second of four children of Alexander Cormack; d. unmarried on 30 April 1868 at New Westminster, B.C.

William Eppes Cormack was the son of a Scottish merchant who arrived in St. John's about 1783 as a partner in the firm of Hart, Eppes, and Company trading mainly in lumber and miscellaneous supplies to Quebec and the West Indies; his mother was a daughter of William Eppes, assistant commissary and merchant in that town. After 1805 the family moved to Scotland. William studied at the universities of Glasgow and Edinburgh and graduated MA from the latter. A lasting influence was Professor Robert Jameson of Edinburgh, who inspired his interest in natural history, especially in botany, geology, and mineralogy, and was to act as adviser and mentor in Cormack's wide-ranging career of exploration and scientific collection.

Cormack left Scotland about 1818 to lead a group of Scottish immigrants to Prince Edward Island where they settled on the Hunter River near Charlottetown and where Cormack was land agent for David Rennie, a Glasgow merchant. But Cormack's restless energy seldom permitted him to restrict his activities to any one occupation or to reside long in any one place. Late in 1821 or early 1822 he returned to St John's where there were family business and property interests. John Peyton of Twillingate described him at this time as tall, lithe, and energetic and with great powers of endurance.

Within a few months Cormack had determined to undertake a task never before attempted by a European, to explore the interior of Newfoundland. Despite more than three centuries of English presence in Newfoundland, settlement was still in 1822 confined to the coast; the interior of the island was almost unknown. In undertaking his journey Cormack had three aims: to satisfy his geographical curiosity about the interior and its resources, to further colonization by opening up the hinterland, and to establish friendly contact with any surviving native Beothuks, or "Red Indians."

Governor Charles Hamilton*'s opposition to the expedition deprived Cormack of the participation of an enthusiastic volunteer, Charles Fox Bennett*, then the governor's aide-de-camp and a magistrate. Cormack's only companion was Joseph Sylvester, a young Micmac hunter from Bay d'Espoir. The month of July 1822 was spent in training for the crossing; Cormack and Sylvester walked the 150 miles from St John's to Placentia and back by way of Trinity and Conception bays. This trial reassured Cormack about the reliability of his companion (and presumably reassured Sylvester about Cormack), indicated to him the equipment required, and convinced him that the best season for the attempt would be early autumn when subsistence could be most easily procured from the land. The route was to be a direct crossing through the centre of Newfoundland, from Trinity Bay on the east coast to St George's Bay on the west.

On 30 August, lightly equipped, Cormack and Sylvester went off on their expedition. The travellers sailed from St John's to Bonaventure, a fishing settlement on the west side of Trinity Bay near present-day New Bonaventure, and from there on 3 September up the north arm of Random Sound. Early on the morning of 5 September Cormack and his guide struck inland through heavily wooded terrain towards the summit of the coastal range. Progress was slow and painful through the thick growth and the oppressive heat and flies. Within five days the character of the land had begun to change; marshes and open rocky spots became common. After crossing Clode Sound River they noticed that the land began to rise and soon found themselves on a great granite ridge, the highest point of which, The Look Out, afforded the travellers a last view of the sea coast; to the west Cormack noted that the "mysterious interior lay unfolded below us, a boundless scene, an emerald surface; a vast basin." Though the journey was to prove protracted and hazardous, at the beginning the travellers' buoyant spirits were supported by the richness of wild fruit and the signs of abundant game. Having consumed their provisions, and determined to adopt the self-dependent mode of Indian life, on 11 September they descended from the heights of the coastal ridge into the interior of east-central Newfoundland.

The area they were now traversing was for the most part composed of fine black compact peat mould covered with wiry grass, immense steppes, or "savannas," as Cormack called them, stretching northward and southward, with running water and lakes, often skirted with woods, lying between them. The month spent crossing this land was laborious, with repeated detours around bodies of water, though Cormack and Sylvester occasionally made crude rafts to cross the larger lakes. Day after day they walked 20 to 30 miles in order to advance five to seven miles westward. Yet Cormack's subsequently published *Narrative* everywhere bears witness to the care and acuteness of his observations, jotted down at the end of each day, and embracing the conditions of weather, soil, flora, and fauna. The only mountain in this whole territory, a granite peak of solitary splendour rising conspicuously from the plain, Cormack named Mount Sylvester in honour of his companion.

By early October they had reached the centre of the island and came across a hilly ridge, which Cormack named, after his Edinburgh teacher, Jameson's Mountains (now Jamieson Hills), and which marked a change of landscape. They soon found themselves at Pipestone Pond, which Cormack named Serpentine Lake, near the easterly pivot of the Micmac canoe route from the west to Bay d'Espoir. Sylvester proposed that they should abandon the expedition and proceed south to Bay d'Espoir. But despite his apprehension of being overtaken by winter before they could reach the west coast, Cormack was deter-

Cormack

mined to continue and a new agreement with his guide, which included promises of some foodstuff and a round-trip visit to Europe, was worked out before they once again stepped westward.

The land now became a series of mountains in irregular succession, and notes on the geological formations Cormack observed bulk large in the *Narrative*. While surveying one of the lakes between the mountains Cormack spotted the camp of a Montagnais named James John who had come from Labrador with his Micmac wife for his second hunting season in Newfoundland. They were entertained that night by their hosts, the woman at Cormack's request singing several songs in her own tongue, and Sylvester astonishing them with tales of what he had seen in St John's. From the Montagnais they learned that the Beothuk country lay nearby but that at this season these Indians were probably well to the north at Red Indian Lake. John also told them that St George's Bay was about two weeks' walk away, if they knew the best way to travel. After a day's rest Cormack and Sylvester continued their journey.

On 16 October they awoke to find the ground covered with three feet of snow. Dependent on game for provisions, and with winter fast approaching, Cormack was more than ever anxious to press on, even though the journey was taxing the strength of both men. A thaw two days later enabled them to continue and that day they came upon the camp of some Micmac hunters where once again they were hospitably received. These Micmacs were members of a band of some 150 Indians whose territory embraced the south-central and southwest parts of the interior; these natives told Cormack of the distribution of the interior between their own tribe, a smaller group of Labrador Montagnais, and the native Beothuks. They confirmed that Cormack would be unlikely to encounter the Beothuks so far south at that time of year.

Resuming their journey on 21 October the travellers now found progress slow in the mountainous country covered with low, dense foliage, frozen ponds, and deep snow. Moreover, the game birds had disappeared. Cormack felt his strength failing and knew "that it would not obey the will and drag along the frame beyond two weeks more." On 29 October they found another camp of eight Micmacs. Still a five-day walk from the coast, Cormack engaged two of these to accompany them on the final stage of the journey. On the evening of 1 November, from the summit of a snowy ridge, Cormack at last saw St George's Bay. In the last stages of exhaustion, he pressed down the precipitous Flat Bay Brook and

on 4 November reached the Jersey and English settlers on the coast. A few days later he took leave of Sylvester, who proposed to remain on the coast with his own people for the winter.

Since all European and other vessels had left the west coast a month before, Cormack rested for ten days at St George's, and then set out southward along the coast, hoping that by walking and travel by small boat between the scattered fishing villages he would reach Fortune Bay in time to take passage on one of the large mercantile firms' vessels before all had sailed to Europe for the season. On 16 December, after "a four month excursion of toil, pleasure, pain, and anxiety," Cormack took passage from Little Bay, Fortune, and reached Dartmouth, England, on 10 Feb. 1823.

Only one of Cormack's original three objects had been successfully achieved: his plan of geographical discovery. He explored and described the interior of the island with an accuracy no subsequent traveller has matched; his *Narrative* is the undisputed classic of Newfoundland travel. His botanical observations were the most important since those of Sir Joseph Banks* in 1766, and his account of the mineralogy and geology of the interior paved the way for Joseph Beete JUKES in 1840 and for the extension in 1864 to Newfoundland of William Edmond Logan*'s geological survey by Alexander Murray* and James Patrick Howley. Cormack failed in his other two aims, however. The opening of the interior through railway, roads, and settlement lay almost a century away. When J. G. Millais, the other great traveller of Newfoundland's interior, published his work in 1907, it could still be appropriately called *Newfoundland and its untrodden ways*, for with the exception of Grand Falls the island, after four centuries of European settlement, still had no town of any importance out of sight or smell of the sea. Cormack also failed to establish contact with the Beothuks, but in this enterprise he had yet to exhaust his persistent efforts.

He spent the winter and spring of 1823 in Scotland where Professor Jameson examined and helped identify the rocks brought back from Newfoundland. On 22 July Cormack wrote Lord Bathurst, the British colonial secretary, enclosing a sketch of the interior of the island and a short account of the route followed, drawing particular attention to the state of the Beothuks and expressing his intention to pursue further inquiries into their condition, as well as to examine further the natural resources of the colony. No response to this letter has been found. A few days later he sailed for St John's.

During the rest of the decade Cormack resided

principally in that town where in 1825, in partnership with John Thompson, a merchant from Greenock, Scotland, he engaged in the provisions and lumber trade with Canada. His leisure he devoted to the investigation of the flora of the colony, sending specimens of plants to the Linnean Society, preparing a monograph on the British and French fisheries in America, joining the agitation for representative government [*see* Laurence O'Brien; Brooking], and above all furthering attempts to open communications with the remaining Beothuks. On 2 Oct. 1827 he formed the Beothic Institution to establish contact with the Red Indians; it numbered among its members leading figures of the Newfoundland community as well as Professor Jameson, John Barrow, secretary to the Admiralty, and John Inglis*, Anglican bishop of Nova Scotia. Cormack himself was president and treasurer and was indefatigable in his efforts to promote the institution's aims. These culminated in his second journey to the interior of the island in 1827.

Accompanied by three Indians, a Canadian Abenakis, a Labrador Montagnais, and a young Micmac from the island, Cormack left St John's by sea in mid-September. Bad weather prevented the party from pursuing its intended northerly route inland from White Bay and they entered the country, on 31 October, at the mouth of the Exploits River in Notre Dame Bay. After 30 days, having traversed some 200 miles of the interior, the expedition returned, exhausted. In a moving passage Cormack described their discovery of Red Indian Lake, the central winter residence of the Beothuks, which was now deserted. Among the ruins of the camp, reposing on one of the wooden repositories for the dead, they found the skeleton of Mary March [Waunathoake*]. No living Beothuk was seen, though traces at Badger Bay Great Lake convinced Cormack that a party of the unfortunate tribe, soon to disappear without a trace, had been there with two canoes the year before.

All his efforts now went towards finding these survivors. Believing that the presence of Europeans on an expedition diminished the chances of establishing friendly contact with the tribe, Cormack organized under the sponsorship of the Beothic Institution two further expeditions to the unexplored area in the north of the island using trusted Montagnais and Micmacs. The capture of three Beothuk women by a party of furriers in 1827 spurred these efforts, but both expeditions failed to locate the Beothuks. Through it all Cormack remained an intent student of these Indians: he collected for the institution numerous objects of their material culture and, as the host

for several years in St John's of the last known survivor of the tribe, Shawnawdithit*, he collected valuable information about her people, their habits, beliefs, movements, and language. There is evidence that Cormack believed these tragic people to be of Scandinavian origin. But, depressed by what seemed to him the lack of vigorous interest by the local authorities, he gradually despaired of preventing the extirpation of the indigenous people of Newfoundland.

By the autumn of 1828 Cormack was writing to John Inglis about plans for "a change of profession." Early in the new year the business partnership with Thompson was dissolved. On 10 January he forwarded to Inglis his manuscript on the fisheries, undertaken, he explained, for the Natural History Society of Montreal. At the end of the month he sailed for Liverpool, England, to become for a while the guest of John McGregor*, the Scottish writer and statistician who had lived in Prince Edward Island. Various projects were in his mind including a volume entitled "Sketches of Newfoundland interior, aborigines or Red Indians, fisheries, &c.," evidently a consolidation of the several manuscripts on which he had been working for a number of years. He returned to St John's in May 1829, and further reduced his business by leasing his waterfront premises; he was also declared insolvent.

Cormack was in Prince Edward Island around 1830, settling British immigrants and exporting grain to Britain. In 1836 he left for Australia. An offer to Sir George Murray* of the Colonial Office "to cross and explore New Holland and New South Wales in any direction" had been made as early as 17 Sept. 1829, but of his career in Australia few details survive other than that he cultivated tobacco with much success for two or three years. He left for New Zealand in 1839 and purchased extensive lands from the natives for raising horses and cattle. He also exported spars to London for the Admiralty and continued his botanical collecting. He was forced to leave New Zealand when trouble arose with the British government which interfered with the enterprises of the first settlers. He appears to have gone to California around 1848–49, and there engaged in various mercantile and mining pursuits as well as in experimental horticulture.

Apart from occasional visits to Britain, and another brief visit to Newfoundland in 1862, Cormack's later years were spent in British Columbia. He was active in promoting representative government in the colony and served in the municipal government of New Westminster where he resided. He was instrumental in establishing an agricultural society in the colony and,

Counter

as its secretary, corresponded with the Royal Highlands and Agricultural Society of Scotland on the possible production of various feed grains and grasses. He was also, as usual, an untiring collector of the flora and fauna of the west coast, and he interested himself in Indian affairs. In 1862 he helped prepare the ichthyological section of a British Columbia exhibition. He was the correspondent, acquaintance, or friend of Sir William Hooker, Michael Faraday, Thomas Hodgkin of the Aborigines Protection Society, John McGregor, the British writer John Wilson, and his university friend the 2nd Marquis of Breadalbane.

To the end he was a lover of field sports; passionately fond of fishing and skating, in 1855 he revised and expanded a treatise on skating by Robert Jones. At the age of 70 he could still astonish his friends by his graceful evolutions on the ice. A friend of his later years speaks of his "buoyant and happy disposition, genial and kindly; his manners were suave and dignified." He died after a month's illness in April 1868.

In Newfoundland a granite cairn marks the spot at which Cormack and Sylvester crossed what is now the Bay d'Espoir Highway on their way westward, and an inland agricultural community on the banks of the Humber River, established in 1947, bears his name.

G. M. STORY

[W. E. Cormack's accounts of his travels appeared in the following forms: W. E. Cormack, "Account of a journey across the island of Newfoundland, in a letter addressed to the Right Hon. Earl Bathurst, secretary of state for the colonies, &c. &c., with a map of Mr Cormack's journey across the island of Newfoundland," *Edinburgh Philosophical Journal*, X (1823–24), 156–62; "Report of Mr W. E. Cormack's journey in search of the Red Indians in Newfoundland, read before the Boeothick Institution at St John's, Newfoundland," *Edinburgh New Philosophical Journal*, VI (1828–29), 318–29; *Patriot* (St John's), 27 Oct., 3, 10, 17, 24 Nov., 1, 8 Dec. 1856; *Narrative of a journey across the island of Newfoundland, the only one ever performed by a European* (St John's, 1856; repub. 1873); J. P. Howley, *The Beothucks or Red Indians; the aboriginal inhabitants of Newfoundland* (Cambridge, Eng., 1915), 130–68, 189–96; *Narrative of a journey across the island of Newfoundland in 1822*, ed. F. A. Bruton (London and Toronto, 1928). He also wrote "On the natural history and economical uses of the cod, capelin, cuttle-fish, and seal, as they occur on the banks of Newfoundland, and the coasts of that island and Labrador . . . ," *Edinburgh New Philosophical Journal*, I (1826), 32–41. He was the editor of Robert Jones, *The art of skating practically explained . . .* (London, 1855). G.M.S.]

Arts and Culture Centre (St John's), Provincial Reference Division, Census of the district of St John's,

1794–95; W. E. Cormack to John Peyton, 28 Oct. 1828. Memorial University of Newfoundland, Maritime History Group Archives (St John's), Cormack file. PABC, Colonial correspondence; John Copland correspondence; W. E. Cormack correspondence. PRO, CO 194/66. *British Columbian* (New Westminster, B.C.), 9 May 1868. *Newfoundlander*, 19 Sept. 1827; 22 May, 26 June, 9 Aug. 1828. *Patriot* (St John's), 20 Oct. 1856. *Public Ledger* (St John's), 14 Dec. 1827; 24 June, 2, 5 Sept. 1828. *Royal Gazette* (St John's), 18 Sept., 6, 13 Nov., 1827; 19 Feb. 1828; 1 July, 21 Oct. 1829. Keith Matthews, *A "who was who" of families engaged in the fishery and settlement of Newfoundland, 1660–1840* ([St John's], 1971), 90. J. P. Howley, *The Beothucks or Red Indians; the aboriginal inhabitants of Newfoundland* (Cambridge, Eng., 1915), 129–252. J. G. Millais, *Newfoundland and its untrodden ways* (London, 1907), 24–30, 197–99. J. G. Rogers, *Newfoundland* (Oxford, 1911), 159–69.

COUNTER, JOHN, baker, entrepreneur, and politician; b. 18 April 1799 in Devonshire, England, second son of Susannah and John Counter; m. in April 1822 Hannah Roode of Kingston, Upper Canada, and they had six children, two dying in infancy; d. 29 Oct. 1862 at Kingston.

John Counter came to Kingston with his parents about 1820. At first a baker and confectioner, he later expanded his commercial interests into transportation and real estate. In 1831 he bought waterfront land in Kingston and a year later built a handsome combined residence and commercial building (demolished in 1973) which he named Plymouth Square. He had added to this building three times by 1840 and had also extended his waterfront holdings.

Counter's first recorded investment in Kingston was in August 1826 when he bought a £25 share in the Cataraqui Bridge Company. In January 1836 he formed, and was first chairman of, the Kingston Stave Forwarding Company based on Garden Island opposite the town. A joint stock company, it became Calvin, Cook, and Counter in 1838. Counter left the firm in 1843, and Delano Dexter Calvin* and Hiram Cook expanded the business to include shipbuilding; the firm continued until 1914. Counter also formed the Marine Railway Company for ship repair and shipbuilding in April 1836. He started it with his own capital, then opened it to public subscription. It expanded into supporting industries and came to include a sawmill, an iron foundry, extensive shops, and wharfage rights.

At a public meeting on 30 Dec. 1835 Counter moved a resolution, seconded by John Mowat*, urging the incorporation of Kingston as a town. Counter continued to promote the measure, judging that it would bring increased business and improve property values, and signed the petition

162

which finally brought incorporation in 1838. He
sought a council seat in the town's first election
but was defeated. However, he served as mayor
in 1841, 1842, and 1843, and was the first mayor of
the city of Kingston in 1846. Elected again in
1850, 1852, 1853, and 1855, he resigned in June
1855 because his shares in the local gas company
were considered to constitute a conflict of interest. In 1851, Counter, whose politics were expressed as "Kingston," was nominated by the
Reformers to run against John A. Macdonald* in
the Kingston City riding but he refused to campaign. He did oppose Macdonald in 1854 but received only 265 votes to Macdonald's 437.

Counter had been instrumental in forming the
Board of Trade in Kingston in December 1839.
As its president (he was the first to hold that post)
he organized in 1841 a canvass of the town to find
accommodation for government officials when
Kingston became the home of the parliament of
the united Province of Canada, giving up his own
home to the vice-chancellor, R. S. Jameson*, and
renting the new offices of the Marine Railway to
the government. In 1842, as mayor, he went to
England to borrow money so the town could
erect a municipal building befitting the then capital of the province [see William COVERDALE].
With Macdonald he gave a clock for the tower of
the new building, completed in 1844, which became the city hall when Kingston was incorporated as a city in 1846. A strong supporter of the
Wesleyan Methodists, Counter donated generously to the building fund for the Victoria Street
chapel in 1847. He gave the land and laid the
cornerstone, on 17 April 1851, for the Sydenham
Street Church, and he served on its management
committee.

Before the Grand Trunk Railway came to
Kingston in 1856, Counter started a car ferry to
Cape Vincent (N.Y.), hoping to make Kingston
the distribution centre for American goods in
Canada. To speed up and improve this service he
promoted the Wolfe Island, Kingston, and Toronto Railroad and the Wolfe Island Railway and
Canal Company. The latter project, a canal
across Wolfe Island, which he had conceived in
1836, was incorporated in 1851 and finally put in
operation in 1857. By then, other railways provided alternatives to the Cape Vincent–Kingston
route and it was completed too late to be
profitable.

Counter borrowed heavily to support his
numerous interests and also to open the first subdivision in Kingston. In 1852 he had the highest
assessment in the city. In October 1855 he could
not meet a large mortgage payment and his
financial obligations forced him into bankruptcy.

At the time Counter's business enterprises began
to fail his personal life was beset with tragedy.
Within ten years he lost his brother, two grandchildren, his two sons, and his wife. The country
house he built in 1847, named South Roode to
honour his wife, was taken over by a bank in
1856, the same year that his extensive holdings
were disposed of by chancery sale.

John Counter died six years later at the home of
his son-in-law, in virtual obscurity. Only a brief
notice appeared in the local newspaper on the
death of a man who had devoted his life to the
welfare of his adopted home.

MARGARET S. ANGUS

Anglican Church of Canada, Diocese of Ontario, Synod
Archives (Kingston, Ont.), St George's parish register,
1822. Cataraqui Cemetery (Kingston, Ont.), gravestones. Kingston Registry Office (Kingston, Ont.), records for water lot 22; park lot 2 and subdivisions; and
farm lot 22, east ½. PAC, RG 31, 1861 census, Kingston City, ward 2. QUA, Kingston Town Council, proceedings, 1838–45; Kingston City Council, proceedings, 1846–55. *British Whig and General Advertiser for
Canada West* (Kingston, [Ont.]), 7 April 1838, 21 Nov.
1843, 29 Jan. 1844. *Chronicle & Gazette* (Kingston), 20
April 1835; 2, 16, 23 Jan., 2 March, 20 April 1836; 7 Dec.
1837; 17 Aug., 7 Dec. 1839; 7 March 1840; 24 Feb., 7
April 1841; 7 April, 16 May 1842. *Chronicle and News*
(Kingston), 7 Dec. 1848, 11 Aug. 1849, 14 Jan. 1853, 16
March 1855. *Daily News* (Kingston), 18 July 1854; 12
June, 10 Oct. 1855; 28 March 1856; 2 Nov. 1861; 29 Oct.
1862. *Kingston Chronicle*, 7 Aug., 15 Sept. 1826.
Creighton, *Macdonald, young politician*, 140, 171.
E. E. Horsey, *Kingston, a century ago; issued to com-
memorate the centennial of Kingston's incorporation*
(Kingston, Ont., 1938).

COVENTRY, GEORGE, journalist and antiquarian; b. 28 July 1793 at Wandsworth (now part
of London), England; his father was a ward of
Baron Dimsdale of Thetford and his mother was
Elizabeth Thornbarrow; d. unmarried on 11 Feb.
1870 at Toronto, Ont.

George Coventry's mother died when he was
three years old and he was educated at various
boarding schools in England until he began working in his father's merchant firm in London. He
demonstrated his interest in literary pursuits by
publishing a book on the letters of Junius in 1825
and in 1830 a work on the revenues of the Church
of England. Coventry immigrated to Upper
Canada in 1835 and settled in the Niagara District, where he probably worked as a clerk. He
witnessed the occupation of Navy Island by rebels led by William Lyon MACKENZIE in the
winter of 1837 and the burning of the American
ship *Caroline* by government forces under Andrew Drew*. Coventry wrote an account of these

Coverdale

events which was in many ways inaccurate and showed his Tory prejudices.

In 1838 he assisted in the inspection of the Grand River when the directors of the Grand River Navigation Company were promoting the sale to the provincial government of privately held company stock. In the same year he served as a clerk for William Hamilton MERRITT in his milling business at St Catharines, and in 1840 was employed as a clerk on the Welland Canal. In December 1846 Coventry became editor of the *Prince Edward Gazette* at Picton, which he co-owned with J. O. Dornan. The newspaper, "a bad concern" from which Coventry suffered financially, ceased publication in April 1847. He returned to the employ of Merritt and probably helped him write his report of 1850 as commissioner of public works and his study of the Welland Canal published in 1852. In 1857 Coventry was working as a customs broker at Cobourg, but seems always to have lived on the edge of poverty.

Coventry's major Canadian work resulted from his appointment in 1859 by the legislature of the Province of Canada to gather and transcribe documents relating to the early history of Upper Canada. The appointment, which was gained through Merritt's influence, ended in 1863. The papers gathered by Coventry are now housed in the Public Archives of Canada, but have largely been superseded by more complete and better copies. In 1861 Coventry had also taken a leading part, along with Merritt, Egerton Ryerson*, and John George Hodgins*, in the formation of an Upper Canadian historical society. The members hoped to collect and publish historical documents and the reminiscences of early settlers.

Coventry lived in Cobourg after 1849 and often contributed to the *Cobourg Sentinel* poems typical of the newspaper verse of the period. Flower and vegetable gardening was his hobby and he was active in the local horticultural society. He was dignified in appearance, polite, and urbane, and was able to read and write French.

J. J. TALMAN

PAC, MG 24, K2 contains about 2,600 pages of George Coventry's miscellaneous correspondence, notes, poems, drafts of letters, sermons, accounts, historical notes, and the prospectus and subscription lists of his newspaper. [George Coventry], "A contemporary account of the Navy Island episode, 1837," ed. W. R. Riddell, RSC *Trans.*, 3rd ser., XIII (1919), sect.II, 57–76; "A contemporary account of the rebellion in Upper Canada, 1837," ed. W. R. Riddell, *OH*, XVII (1919), 113–74. J. P. Merritt, *Biography of the Hon. W. H. Merritt . . .* (St Catharines, Ont., 1875). Morgan,

Bibliotheca Canadensis, 83. "George Coventry – a pioneer contributor to the history of Ontario, 1793–1870," *OH*, XIX (1922), 5. J. J. Talman, "Some precursors of the Ontario Historical Society," *OH*, XL (1948), 13–21.

COVERDALE, WILLIAM, carpenter and architect; b. in 1801 in England, son of Christopher Coverdale; m. Catherine Delmage and had five children; d. 28 Sept. 1865 at Kingston, Canada West.

Little is known about William Coverdale before he came to Kingston in 1832 or 1833. According to family tradition his father was born in the shadow of York Minster and the family came to Lower Canada about 1810. The first two children of Catherine and William Coverdale were born at Île aux Noix, Lower Canada. The earliest mention of Coverdale in Kingston appears in the St George's Church parish register, recording the birth of a son on 23 Sept. 1833.

Kingston in the 1830s was attracting many persons in the building trades. In 1832 the rebuilding of Fort Henry was started and contracts were being let for the General Hospital; work began on the Provincial Penitentiary the next year using day labour. A master carpenter like Coverdale would find ready work. He became the "master builder" at the penitentiary when John Mills, who had been brought from Auburn, N.Y., was dismissed in June 1834. Hired at one-fifth less pay, Coverdale held the post 14 years and in that time the main building and gatehouse were slowly constructed, mostly with convict labour. In 1848 a bill, introduced by Henry SMITH, son of Warden Henry Smith of the penitentiary, passed parliament; the bill cut the architect's salary and increased that of the warden. Coverdale resigned and, because of the constant difficulties he had experienced with the warden, refused reappointment when the salary was restored; Edward Horsey was appointed in his stead.

In 1859 Coverdale also became the architect – the term he had used to describe himself after 1842 – for the asylum in Kingston and continued on this project to his death. The building he planned was erected mainly by convict labour and took over eight years to finish; the centre and the east wing were formally opened in March 1865.

The penitentiary and asylum buildings, both still standing, mark the beginning and end of Coverdale's work in Kingston. Between his activities on these two grim and massive works, he designed and built every manner of structure. The residences he planned ranged from workmen's cottages to country mansions. Although his account book lists a few commissions in an area extending from Prescott to Port Hope and up to Perth, most of his work was in Kingston.

In 1844 Coverdale took over the superintendence of the building of Kingston's magnificent town hall from George Browne*. When the rear wing burned in 1865, he prepared plans for its rebuilding, carried out after his death by his son, William Miles Coverdale. The brewery, tannery, and bakery he designed are gone, but the Kingston churches still remain: St Paul's, St James, and St John's, all Anglican, and Sydenham Street Church, begun in 1851 for the Wesleyan Methodists, Coverdale's own church affiliation.

Only a few of Coverdale's plans have been found and some are very like those in the builders' manuals of the 1820s and 1830s which he had in his library. Although he built in a variety of styles, the Regency influence is strong in many of his buildings. Several of the best known houses in Kingston, such as Roselawn and the Mowat house, were planned by Coverdale, and other large Kingston residences built in the late 1830s, for which no architect has been identified, may also be his work.

MARGARET S. ANGUS

Anglican Church of Canada, Diocese of Ontario, Synod Archives (Kingston, Ont.), St George's parish register, September, October 1833. PAC, RG 11, ser.1, 38–41. QUA, Kingston Town Council, proceedings, 1844–45; Kingston City Council, proceedings, 1846–66; Portsmouth Village Council minutes, 1865; Queen's records, D6, 17 Nov. 1848. *Chronicle & Gazette* (Kingston), 22 March 1844. *Daily British Whig* (Kingston), 5 April 1869. *Daily News* (Kingston), 14 Jan. 1852, 8 Sept. 1862, 29 Sept. 1865. U.C., House of Assembly, *Journal*, 1835, app.20.

CRAIGIE, WILLIAM, physician and educationist; baptized 11 March 1799 at Belnaboth, parish of Towie, Aberdeenshire, Scotland, the son of William Craigie and May Ness; m. Mary Campbell, and they had nine children; d. 10 Aug. 1863 at Hamilton, Canada West.

William Craigie studied at Marischal and Aberdeen colleges in Aberdeen, the University of Edinburgh, and Trinity College, Dublin. In 1820 he became a licentiate of the Royal College of Surgeons of Edinburgh and established a medical practice at Midclova in the parish of Kildrummy, Aberdeenshire. He published in 1828 a paper on tracheotomy in the *Edinburgh Medical and Surgical Journal*.

Craigie immigrated to Upper Canada in 1834 and settled in Ancaster. After successfully appearing before the Medical Board of Upper Canada in April 1835, he was licensed to practise medicine. Soon after he arrived he also began working for the improvement of education and joined with others to found a school, the Ancaster Literary Institution, which opened in 1837. They hoped to provide a better quality of education than that available in the common schools. Craigie was secretary of the institution and corresponded with the council of King's College and later the Committee of Commissioners on Education seeking financial support for the school. In a submission to a committee appointed by Lieutenant Governor Sir George Arthur* to investigate education in the province, he advocated in 1839 a normal school for the training of teachers, provincial funding of education, and the establishment of village common and district grammar schools with varied curricula which would include reading, writing, arithmetic, classics, modern languages, and mathematics. He also proposed adequate salaries and superannuation for teachers, good Canadian textbooks, non-denominational religious instruction, and a central board of education for Canada West with subsidiary boards for each municipal district.

In 1845 he moved to Hamilton where he soon became a leader in educational, cultural, and scientific affairs. As school trustee he was largely responsible for the opening in 1853 of the Hamilton Central School despite strong opposition from William Munson Jarvis and the Reverend John Gamble Geddes* who favoured establishing common schools in each ward. Craigie organized in 1850 the Hamilton Horticultural Society, an offshoot of the mechanics' institute, of which he was a director. He was a member of the Board of Arts and Manufactures for Upper Canada and an elder of the Presbyterian Church. The meteorological records he had kept since coming to Canada were published in Canadian periodicals, and he contributed monthly meteorological reports to the *Hamilton Spectator* for a number of years. In 1854 he published a list of indigenous plants of the Hamilton area, a pioneer effort compiled for the Hamilton Scientific Association of which he was first recording secretary.

Dr Craigie was popular and respected both as a scholar and as a physician, and in 1861 he was appointed medical referee for the Canada Life Assurance Company. He was one of the attending physicians at the deathbed of Sir Allan Napier MACNAB just a year before his own death in 1863. He appears in a contemporary cartoon, "A Grave Scene," which depicts the struggle of the Anglican and Roman Catholic clergy over MacNab's body; Craigie is shown in the eccentric garb he wore in later years and with the "twa dogs" who were always at his heels.

KATHARINE GREENFIELD

Crawford

William Craigie was the author of "Case in which tracheotomy was successfully performed," *Edinburgh Medical and Surgical Journal*, 29 (1828), 83–85; "Mean results for each month of eleven years, (1835 to 1845 inclusive), of a register of the thermometer and barometer, kept at Ancaster, C.W.," *British American Journal of Medical and Physical Science* (Montreal), II (1846–47), 7–9; "Meteorological observations at Hamilton," *Canadian Journal*, II (1853–54), 187–88; and "List of indigenous plants found in the neighbourhood of Hamilton, with the dates of their being found in flower and examined," *Canadian Journal*, III (1854–55), 222–23. *Documentary history of education in U.C.* (Hodgins), III. "The late Dr. Craigie," *Canadian Illustrated News* (Hamilton, [Ont.]), II (1863), 174–75. Morgan, *Bibliotheca Canadensis*. Canniff, *Medical profession in U.C.* Hamilton Assoc. for the Advancement of Literature, Science and Art, *100th anniversary, 1857–1957* (Hamilton, Ont., [1957]). Hamilton Horticultural Soc., *Centennial year book and garden guide, 1850–1950* (Hamilton, Ont., 1950). J. G. Hodgins, *The establishment of schools and colleges in Ontario, 1792–1910* (3v., Toronto, 1910), I. J. H. Smith, *The Central School jubilee re-union, August, 1903, an historical sketch* (Hamilton, Ont., 1905). *Hamilton Spectator*, 19 June 1909.

CRAWFORD, GEORGE, businessman and politician; b. 1793 at Manor Hamilton, County Leitrim (Republic of Ireland), the son of Patrick Crawford, a farmer, and Jane Munse; m. first, in Ireland, Margaret Brown, by whom he had six children, and secondly, Caroline Sherwood, by whom he had 14 children; d. 4 July 1870 at Brockville, Ont.

George Crawford, who received little education, became a cloth merchant. He immigrated to Upper Canada with some capital in the early 1820s and farmed in the counties of Halton and then of York. After "a few seasons" he gave up agriculture and moved to York (Toronto), where he became a contractor. According to a later report he "rapidly accumulated a large fortune" through construction contracts on the Rideau, Cornwall, and Beauharnois canals. He was also a director of the Provincial Mutual and General Insurance Company, a director of the Grand Trunk Railway, and president of the Brockville and Ottawa Railway Company. A member of the militia in 1837, Crawford was later promoted lieutenant-colonel of the 3rd battalion of Leeds militia. He also served as a warden of St Peter's Anglican Church in Brockville.

Crawford moved from Toronto to Brockville in the mid 1840s. Although he curtailed his business activities at this time, he remained an important businessman and in Brockville was at the centre of a complex of family relationships which linked him to prominent businessmen and to both Tory

and Reform politicians. His second wife was the daughter of Adiel Sherwood*, a prominent Conservative; his brother John, also a contractor, was an alderman and mayor of Brockville; his son John Willoughby* married a daughter of Levius Peters Sherwood* and sister of the Tory leader Henry Sherwood*; and a daughter married John Ross*, a prominent Reformer and president of the Grand Trunk Railway.

In 1845 Crawford was appointed a commissioner for settling rebellion losses claims in Upper Canada, and from 1845 to 1847 was a member of the Brockville Board of Police. In 1849 he began a brief sojourn in agitational politics when he joined the first branch of the British American League to be established, at Brockville. The league was formed mainly by Tories to consider the effects on Canada of Britain's dismantling of the mercantile system. When the league endorsed British North American union in July 1849 it appointed a committee which included Crawford, John William Gamble*, George MOFFATT, and Ogle Robert Gowan* to confer with leaders from the Maritime provinces concerning the matter. At a "Great Demonstration" of Tories in Brockville in September of that year Crawford supported a Canadian protective tariff. At a meeting in Toronto in November, however, after the appearance of the Annexation Manifesto in Montreal, Crawford changed his position, and with Hugh Bowlby Willson* endorsed the annexation of Canada to the United States. In December 1849 he wrote to Edward Goff Penny*: "I have no doubt of a large increase in the number of those who will be in favour of a peaceable separation from the mother country before another year goes over our heads. . . ."

Crawford was one of few Upper Canadian Tories to support annexation; no evidence indicates he supported the cause for long. He quickly overcame the stigma of disloyalty and entered politics as a reliable Conservative, defeating George Sherwood in Brockville in elections for the assembly in 1851. He was re-elected in 1854 but did not stand in 1857. In 1858 he narrowly defeated William Henry Brouse* in St Lawrence division in elections for the Legislative Council; he served continuously until 1867, when he was appointed to the federal Senate.

A 19th century biographical work commented that as a legislator Crawford "did but very little talking, being known as a worker." This is a fair assessment. His rare interventions in debate were terse and often concerned minor business matters. At the same time he was in regular communication with Conservative leaders about problems related to patronage, elections, his town and region. Crawford was sympathetic towards the aspirations of French Canadians and an enthusiastic supporter of Montreal, arguing in 1859 that Ottawa be made the capital because that location would inevitably benefit Montreal.

Three of Crawford's sons became influential in their own right – John Willoughby as a financier, manufacturer, railway promoter, and Conservative politician; James as a contractor and Conservative MP for Brockville from 1867 to 1872; and Edward Patrick as rector of Trinity Church in Brockville.

DONALD SWAINSON

ANQ-Q, AP-G-203, lettre no.8. PAC, MG 24, B40; MG 26, A, 337, 507–8, 511–13, 516–18. *Elgin-Grey papers* (Doughty). "Parliamentary debates" (Canadian Library Assoc. mfm. project of the debates in the legislature of the Province of Canada and the parliament of Canada for 1846–74), 1846–65. *Brockville Recorder* (Brockville, Ont.), 1849, 1870. *Globe*, 1870. *Thompson's Mirror of Parl. . . .* (Quebec), 1860. *Canadian biographical dictionary*, I. *Canadian directory of parl.* (Johnson). *CPC*, 1867. *Political appointments, 1841–65* (J.-O. Coté). *Political appointments and judicial bench* (N.-O. Coté).

Cornell, *Alignment of political groups*. T. W. H. Leavitt, *History of Leeds and Grenville, Ontario, from 1749 to 1879, with illustrations and biographical sketches of some of its prominent men and pioneers* (Brockville, Ont., 1879). W. N. T. Wylie, "Toronto and the Montreal annexation crisis of 1849–1850; ideologies, loyalties and considerations of personal gain" (unpublished MA thesis, Queen's University, Kingston, Ont., 1971). C. D. Allin, "The British North American League, 1849," *OH*, XIII (1915), 74–115. "The annexation movement, 1849–50," ed. A.G. Penny, *CHR*, V (1924), 236–61. G. A. Hallowell, "The reaction of the Upper Canadian Tories to the adversity of 1849: annexation and the British American League," *OH*, LXII (1970), 41–56. D.[W.] Swainson, "Business and politics: the career of John Willoughby Crawford," *OH*, LXI (1969), 225–36.

CRESSWELL, SAMUEL GURNEY, naval officer and artist; b. 25 Sept. 1827 at King's Lynn, England, third son of Francis Cresswell, banker, and Rachel Elizabeth Fry (her mother, Elizabeth Fry, *née* Gurney, was a distinguished philanthropist); d. 14 Aug. 1867, unmarried, at King's Lynn.

From his childhood, Samuel Gurney Cresswell expressed a keen desire to go to sea rather than pursue a formal education at Harrow as his older brothers had done. His parents, having sought the advice of Sir William Edward Parry*, an intimate family friend "in whose judgement . . . [they] had perfect confidence," decided that Samuel, aged 14, would enter the Royal Navy.

He served as midshipman until September 1847 on board HMS *Agincourt* under Sir Thomas John Cochrane* in the China Seas. Stationed then at Portsmouth, England, on HMS *Excellent*, he was promoted mate 6 April 1848. In May 1848 he was appointed to HMS *Investigator* on Sir James Clark Ross' Arctic expedition in search of Sir John Franklin*. On 10 Sept. 1849 he was promoted 2nd lieutenant.

Within three weeks of his return to England in November 1849, Cresswell voluntarily rejoined *Investigator* as a member of Robert John Le Mesurier McClure*'s Arctic expedition in search of the northwest passage. Bound for the Bering Strait, the men set sail in January 1850 and encountered the first ice west of Barrow Point in August. On 26 October a travelling party from McClure's ship, held fast off Banks Land, discovered that Prince of Wales Strait connected to Viscount Melville Sound. Melville Island, first discovered 34 years earlier by Parry who had approached from the opposite direction, was clearly seen by the members of the party from their elevated position to lie across the entrance to Prince of Wales Strait. They had indisputable proof of the existence of a northwest passage.

Excessively heavy ice conditions during the summers of 1851 and 1852 prevented McClure's expedition from making progress eastward, and forced their wintering in 1851–52 and 1852–53 at the Bay of Mercy. The expedition was faced with the prospect of starvation but was located on 6 April 1853 by a sledge party sent by Captain Henry Kellett*, commander of HMS *Resolute* on the Franklin search expedition under Captain Sir Edward Belcher*. Cresswell with 24 invalids followed McClure on the 170-mile trek to Kellett's winter camp at Dealy Island located off Melville Island. Arriving in good health, Cresswell volunteered to continue overland about 300 miles to Beechey Island in the hope of meeting a ship. On 2 August, Captain Edward Augustus Inglefield arrived in HMS *Phoenix* on which Cresswell, triumphantly bearing McClure's dispatches to the Admiralty, set sail for England on the 23rd. He arrived in England with the first news, himself the living proof, of the discovery of the long-sought northwest passage. At a public dinner held in his honour by his native townsmen on 26 Oct. 1853, coincidentally the third anniversary of the discovery, he recounted the highlights of the voyage. Fitting tribute was paid by Rear-Admiral Parry, the person who had been influential in Cresswell's career and felt a personal responsibility for his safety.

Cresswell, while on the Ross and McClure expeditions, executed numerous water-colours

Crooked Arm

which today provide a valuable pictorial record of the crews' activities and Arctic terrain. Some of his sketches, suitably ironed flat from their rolled up state and placed in an album, were presented personally to Queen Victoria with a request for permission to dedicate a volume of lithographic views after the drawings to her majesty. The resulting folio volume, published in 1854 in London, was entitled *A series of eight sketches in colour . . . of the voyage of H.M.S. Investigator*. His drawings were also used to illustrate *The discovery of the north-west passage by H.M.S. "Investigator,"* edited by Sherard Osborn* and published in London in 1856.

Subsequently Cresswell served on HMS *Archer* in the Baltic during the Russian War until his promotion to commander on 21 Oct. 1854. While stationed in the China Seas in 1857 as commander of HMS *Surprise*, he was promoted captain on 17 Sept. 1858. During this posting Cresswell met with ill health from which he never fully recovered. He retired in February 1867 and died a few months later.

W. M. E. COOKE

S. G. Cresswell, *Dedicated . . . to her most gracious majesty the queen, a series of eight sketches in colour (together with a chart of the route) . . . of the voyage of H.M.S. Investigator . . . during the discovery of the north-west passage* (London, [1854]).

[The author was kindly granted access to primary sources held in a private collection in England. W.M.E.C.] National Maritime Museum (London, Eng.), MS 58/128 (mfm. at PAC). *The discovery of the north-west passage by H.M.S. "Investigator", Capt. R. M'Clure, 1850, 1851, 1852, 1853, 1854*, ed. Sherard Osborn (London, 1856). Can., *Sessional papers*, 1911, XIII, no.21a, 229–455. *Gentleman's Magazine*, CCXXIII (July–Dec. 1867), 407. *Illustrated London News*, 24 Aug. 1867. *Norfolk Chronicle* (Norwich, Eng.), 29 Oct. 1853. *Bibliotheca Americana; a dictionary of books relating to America from its discovery to the present time*, ed. Joseph Sabin et al. (29v., New York, 1868–1936), V, 76; XI, 17–18. Boase, *Modern English biog.*, VI, 758. G. B., Adm., *Navy list*, 1843–68. [Katharine Fry], *Katharine Fry's book*, ed. Jane Vansittart (London, 1966). C. R. Markham, *The Arctic navy list; or, a century of Arctic & Antarctic officers, 1773–1873; together with a list of officers of the 1875 expedition and of their services* (London, 1875). *The late Captain S. Gurney Cresswell, R.N.* ([King's Lynn, Eng., 1867]).

CROOKED ARM. *See* Maskepetoon

CROWDY, JAMES, office-holder; b. 1794 in England; d. 17 April 1867 at Newton Abbot, Devon, England.

James Crowdy served as clerk of the Council and colonial secretary of Cape Breton Island from 1814 until 1820 when Nova Scotia absorbed that previously independent colony. On 15 Sept. 1831 Crowdy with his wife, Elizabeth (Eliza) (d. 1836), and family arrived in St John's from Bristol, England, to take up new duties as Newfoundland's colonial secretary and clerk of the Council. In addition to these appointments he was collector of crown rents, which brought his total official yearly income to £800.

Crowdy's arrival coincided with the introduction of representative government in Newfoundland and the establishment of a local legislature. As colonial secretary, Crowdy was appointed to the new Council in July 1832. He appears to have acted as conciliator between Governor Thomas John Cochrane* and the more independent members of the Council. This role was tested during the first session of the assembly when the revenue bill for 1833 introduced new duties on spirits. The president of the Council, Chief Justice Richard Alexander TUCKER, with the support of Attorney General James SIMMS, opposed the bill. Tucker and Governor Cochrane, who objected to such attempts to deny the government revenue, were locked in a struggle until Tucker resigned his office and left the island. Throughout the dispute Crowdy supported the governor and the revenue bill, a position later vindicated by the British colonial secretary.

Crowdy was responsible for creating a crisis in 1836 when as Newfoundland's colonial secretary he did not make certain that the great seal was attached to the election writs issued through his office. Chief Justice Henry John BOULTON advised Governor Henry Prescott* that by this deficiency the election was invalid. Since it was found at the same time that the great seal might not have been attached to the election writs for 1832, all legislation passed by that assembly was in danger of being invalidated. Although Boulton's opinion was supported by Attorney General Simms, the British colonial secretary, Lord Glenelg, held that Crowdy's technical error could not be allowed to undermine the operation of the government. He ordered that a new election be held. However, Crowdy's carelessness caused a bitter controversy between the Reform group including Dr William Carson* and Patrick Morris* and the merchants and officials like Crowdy gathered around the governor. Indeed, some Reformers suggested that Crowdy's omission had been a deliberate attempt to discredit representative government in Newfoundland. In the midst of these difficulties Crowdy made a powerful alliance by marrying in September 1838

Caroline Augusta, daughter of Councillor John Dunscombe, a prominent St John's merchant.

The continuing conflict between the Council and the assembly led to the Council's refusal in 1841 to pass legislation sent up from the assembly, including the election and supply bills. As a result, the legislature was suspended and a parliamentary inquiry was held in London. Crowdy was one of a delegation to England to present the views of the Council, which sought the abolition of representative government. The chief result of this inquiry was the amalgamation of the assembly and the Legislative Council into one chamber with 15 elected members and ten appointed by the governor, a scheme first devised by Lord John Russell for the constitution of New South Wales. Crowdy was appointed to the new legislature and in 1843 was elected speaker at the insistence of Governor Sir John Harvey*, despite the objection of Lord Stanley, British colonial secretary, that Crowdy's two public offices were incompatible. Remaining in the speaker's chair until the dissolution of the amalgamated legislature in 1848, Crowdy was reasonably successful in gaining the passage of legislation and in quieting the conflict between the Reformers and the conservative colonial officials. His close connection with Governor Harvey and the governor's heavy personal indebtedness led to rumours that Harvey was under financial obligation to Crowdy. Indeed, a loan to Harvey from Crowdy's personal resources raised questions about Harvey's independence. Chief Justice John Gervase Hutchinson Bourne sent accusations of improper financial arrangements between the two men to the Colonial Office, and, although he dismissed the charges, Lord Stanley admonished Harvey for the "incautious and ill-considered" action of borrowing from persons on whom he could confer advantages.

The year 1848 brought the return of representative government in virtually the same form as in the 1832–41 period, and Crowdy was again appointed to the Legislative Council. The Reformers led by Philip Francis Little* waged a campaign for responsible government until the new system was introduced in 1855. One of the principal advantages to them of a responsible executive would be the chance to eliminate those office-holders who held place at the pleasure of the governor or of the British colonial secretary, rather than of the assembly. Office-holders such as Crowdy worked unsuccessfully to defeat the movement for responsible government but after the Reformers' victory in the election of 1855 were forced to resign.

Apart from his many official duties Crowdy

had taken little part in the social or economic life of St John's. He had been involved in few of the social and charitable activities which were the acknowledged duty of a person of his social station. After his resignation from the Legislative Council in 1855, he retired to England with a generous pension of £400 from the government of Newfoundland. He died 12 years later.

DAVID J. DAVIS

Church of St John the Baptist (Anglican) (St John's), Registers of marriages and baptisms, 1838–51. PANL, GN 1/1, 1843; GN 9/1, 6 Oct. 1831. PRO, CO 195/18. Nfld., *Blue book*, 1843, 1845, 1857. *Newfoundlander*, 1831, 1835, 1852. *Newfoundland Patriot* (St John's), 1840. *Royal Gazette* (St John's), 1853. *Times and General Commercial Gazette* (St John's), 1867. Garfield Fizzard, "The amalgamated assembly of Newfoundland, 1841–1847" (unpublished MA thesis, Memorial University of Newfoundland, St John's, 1963). Gunn, *Political history of Nfld*. Leslie Harris, "The first nine years of representative government in Newfoundland" (unpublished MA thesis, Memorial University of Newfoundland, St John's, 1959), 65–67. Prowse, *History of Nfld*. (1895), 450.

CUMMING, (Cummings), CUTHBERT, HBC chief trader; b. in 1787 in Banffshire, Scotland; d. 5 April 1870 at Colborne, Ont.

Cuthbert Cumming became a North West Company clerk at Fort Dauphin in 1804, and remained in the Swan River District until 1828 with the exception of one year on leave and one at Red River. In these years he took an Indian wife who bore him seven children, and his concern for them is a recurring theme in his papers; he made provision for them in his will. In this period also he formed lifelong friendships with other fur traders such as James HARGRAVE, John George McTavish*, and John Siveright*; the latter pictured him as "open, friendly & consistant." Reorganization of the fur trade in 1821 with the amalgamation of the North West and Hudson's Bay companies had no immediate impact upon Cumming's way of life. He remained a clerk with the HBC for several years, then was promoted chief trader in 1827; Governor George Simpson* described him as "a very fit man to come forward."

In 1828 Cumming was transferred to the Montreal Department, where he was a complete stranger. His financial position began to improve, but his frustration with the work he was asked to perform increased. First he had to cope with the Ottawa lumbermen at the Chats, who were opposed to the fur trade; on the other hand many lumbermen and contractors on the Ottawa River were also traders. He met equally fierce competi-

Cunard

tion in the Saint-Maurice region where he replaced Robert McVicar in 1830. In 1832 he went on leave to Britain, and received a hoped-for western appointment on his return. But a last-minute change of plan sent him in 1833 to Mingan, Lower Canada, on the north shore of the Gulf of St Lawrence, where for several successive winters he found himself completely cut off from the rest of the world with little work to do and little reading or society available.

Cumming eventually received an appointment to Fort Pic on the north shore of Lake Superior in the spring of 1841. There in 1842 he married Jane McMurray, daughter of Thomas McMurray* whom he had replaced at the post. It was perhaps the difference of 26 years in their ages that prompted a friend's remark: "Everyone knows their own circumstances and state of affairs best." They had three sons. In 1843 Cumming reluctantly left the Pic, which he described as "that snugg corner" though it was not a flourishing post, and returned to the Swan River District. The buildings at Fort Pelly had been destroyed by fire in 1843, and Cumming's first task was to rebuild them. Worse, he became convinced that the maintenance of an operation at Fort Pelly and the use of the Swan River transport route were errors in company policy. His journal expresses his dissatisfaction with limitations on the prairie fur trade and concern for the decreasing numbers of buffalo, which brought famine to the Indians. He was seeing the end of an era. Nostalgia overcame him when he wrote to Hargrave about his determination to leave the service: "I march the ensuing summer [1844] and through [throw?] my chains to the dogs. I must be a freeman. . . ."

A freeman he was for more than a quarter of a century. At Colborne, in Northumberland County, he was listed as "Cuthbert Cummings, gentleman." The sharpest picture of him in these years comes from one of his old friends, George Barnston*, writing in 1846 to Hargrave "[We] found Cummings the 'Noble Burgundy' seated in all his breadth and Majesty, on the Hall Bench, a perfect picture of ease and contentment. As soon as we entered, with great agility, he squared up to John George [McTavish], and set himself in Boxing attitude, seemingly jealous of the honor of rotundity being contested with him. You would have laughed to have witnessed the graceful movements of these sparring Birds of so like a feather." Cumming lived till the age of 83.

Elizabeth Arthur

HBC Arch. A.34/2, 1832; A.36/5, wills of Cuthbert Cumming, 30 July 1828, February 1844; B.159/a, 1817–19, 1824–26. Private archives, J. F. Klaus (Pelly, Sask.), Fort Pelly journal, 1843–44. *Canadian North-West* (Oliver), I, 657, 673, 690. *Documents relating to NWC.* (Wallace). *Hargrave correspondence* (Glazebrook). HBRS, III (Fleming). Mactavish, *Letters of Letitia Hargrave* (MacLeod). *The county of Northumberland directory, for 1870–71*, comp. J. C. Conner (Toronto, 1869), 61. J. F. Klaus, "Fort Pelly: an historical sketch," *Saskatchewan History* (Saskatoon), XIV (1961), 81–97.

CUNARD, JOSEPH, timber merchant, shipbuilder, and politician; b. 1799 at Halifax, N.S., son of Abraham Cunard, merchant, and Margaret Murphy; m. 12 April 1833 Mary Peters of Bushville, N.B., and they had four sons and one daughter; d. 16 Jan. 1865 at Liverpool, England.

After attending the Halifax Grammar School Joseph Cunard entered his father's firm in that town. About 1820 Joseph and his brother Henry went to Chatham, N.B., on the Miramichi River where they opened a branch of the family company, known as Joseph Cunard and Company; their older brother Samuel was also a partner in the branch. They immediately purchased a wharf and a store and were soon involved in lumbering, milling, and shipping on the south side of the river.

In 1832 Joseph Cunard was described as one of the wealthiest and most influential merchants in the province. At Chatham his firm owned several mills, including a large steam mill which began operations in 1836 and sawed 40,000 feet of lumber a day. In the same town the firm also had a brickworks, several stores, a counting house employing 30 people, and at least two shipyards. Mills were constructed farther down river and a store was opened in Shippegan. In 1830 stores were opened at Kouchibouguac and Richibucto in Kent County, and in 1841 William Raymond could report that Cunard had done £100,000 of business with him in Kouchibouguac and that he had paid approximately one third of this sum in ships. Cunard's operations in Kent County made Richibucto for a short time the third largest shipping port in New Brunswick. In 1831 the company purchased stores, houses, and other buildings at Bathurst and the next year began shipping timber. Exports of lumber from Bathurst rose from 1,300 tons in 1829 to 26,500 tons in 1833.

Cunard's shipbuilding activities were extensive. A number of vessels were built for him in the years 1827–38, but by 1839 he had two shipyards of his own in Chatham. There he had at least 43 vessels built, including the *Velocity*, the first steamboat constructed on the Miramichi, which was launched in 1846. Cunard began building ships at Bathurst in 1839 and from 1841 to 1847 was the only shipbuilder in the area. Between 1839 and 1847 he built at least 24 vessels at Bathurst. At his shipyards at Richibucto and Kouchibouguac, which began operations around 1840, he had at least nine vessels constructed in the years 1840–47.

By 1841 Joseph's brothers were no longer active in the Miramichi firm and he was given a free hand in it, although Samuel continued as a partner until 1846 and continued to advise his brother on his various entrepreneurial schemes.

Cunard made Chatham his headquarters and was active in local affairs and politics. He was a justice of the peace, member and chairman of the Board of Health for Northumberland and Gloucester counties, and commissioner of lighthouses. In 1828 he became an MHA for Northumberland County, retaining his seat until his appointment to the Legislative Council in 1833. From 1838 until his resignation in 1846 he was also a member of the Executive Council, though he was not an influential figure in that body and was rarely involved in any controversy. As chairman of the Board of Health, Cunard was involved in the establishment of a lazaret on Sheldrake Island in 1844 [see François-Xavier-Stanislas LAFRANCE]. Four years later he joined the other members of the Board of Health and the lepers living on that island in opposing the desire of the local magistrate to move the quarantine station for arriving immigrants from Middle Island, which Cunard owned, to Sheldrake Island. The buildings were, nonetheless, moved in 1848, but later that year the government decided to move the quarantine station to Chatham.

A massive man standing over six feet tall and weighing over 200 pounds, Cunard loved galloping through Chatham from his mills to his store or home and was often seen shouting orders to his men as he supervised their work on horseback. He drove to church in a coach with footmen in livery. His magnificent home was lavishly furnished, and peacocks wandered through its grounds. For the opening of his steam mill in 1836 some 300 people were invited to a large banquet. Often on his return from trips to England, he was greeted in Chatham by salutes of cannon and ringing of church bells. Occasionally he sent word from Richibucto that he was on his way home so that the people of Chatham would have time to organize a suitable welcome. "He was loved and hated, admired and feared, brusque, good-hearted when he wanted to be, grasping, domineering – all the contradictory qualities that made up that hard, crude, lavish Miramichi life of a century ago."

In 1839 Joseph Cunard accompanied his brother Samuel to England, where Samuel obtained a contract to carry the transatlantic mail by steamship. Although there is no evidence to show that Joseph played any part in these negotiations, he was given a triumphal reception on his return to Chatham. It was not yet realized that the development of steam power would mean the end of wooden ships and the end of the prosperity of the Miramichi area.

Cunard had many enemies as well as admirers. Upon his first arrival in Chatham, he had entered into bitter rivalry with the firm of Gilmour, Rankin, and Company, which was already firmly established in the Miramichi area. One of the earliest disputes between the two firms was over large timber reserves on the northwest Miramichi and the Nepisiguit rivers. As part of Thomas BAILLIE's plans for development of the timber industry, Cunard had been granted over 500 square miles of these excellent reserves in 1830–32 on condition that he improve the streams by erecting sluices and clearing obstacles. No other firm was interested in this area until Cunard proved that operations there could be profitable. When Cunard failed to carry out the promised improvements, Alexander Rankin* led an attack on his privileges. In 1833, on instructions from the Colonial Office, Cunard was forced to relinquish the reserves. This was the first battle he lost to the Rankin firm.

The quarrels continued over ownership of timber, trespass on mill reserves, and the election of candidates to the assembly. The rivalry was particularly bitter in the "fighting elections" of 1842–43 in Northumberland County, when Cunard supported John Thomas Williston and Rankin backed John Ambrose STREET. Crowds of 500–1,000 men fought during these election campaigns and troops were eventually sent to restore order. Street's election was another defeat for Cunard.

Cunard's recklessness and his overextension of his resources caused him continual trouble. In 1842 the Cunards faced bankruptcy. At the same time, the provincial government took action against Joseph Cunard to force him to settle his accounts with the government. The Executive Council appointed a committee to investigate his debts; it recommended that Cunard post bonds of £3,000 and that his timber, which had been seized earlier, be released. It also recommended an investigation into the conduct of the deputy surveyor in the area, Michael Carruthers, some of whose actions seemed designed to damage Cunard's business to the advantage of Gilmour, Rankin, and Company. Carruthers was later transferred out of the county. Cunard managed to

Cunard

survive the difficulties but by 1847 was unable to meet his obligations. Depressed economic conditions, strong competition from Gilmour, Rankin, and Company, and reckless expansion of his enterprises all played a part in his downfall. In November 1847 he declared bankruptcy. A panic ensued in Chatham where hundreds of men depended on him for work. An angry crowd confronted him in the streets with cries of "Shoot Cunard," but with two pistols in his boots Cunard stood his ground and is supposed to have demanded, "Now show me the man who will shoot Cunard." The crowd then dispersed. According to the newspapers, between 500 and 1,000 people were out of work as a result of Cunard's failure and many left the area in search of employment elsewhere. A number of small firms in the area also went bankrupt. The timber trade of the Miramichi area was depressed for many years partly as a result of Cunard's failure, but shipbuilding revived and boomed in the 1850s.

In 1849 Cunard left New Brunswick but returned shortly in an unsuccessful attempt to settle his affairs. His debts were not finally cleared up until 1871 and Samuel Cunard apparently assumed most of the burden of his brother's failure. Joseph finally left Chatham in 1850 and moved to Liverpool, England, where he entered the ship commission business as a partner in the firm of Cunard, Munn, and Company. In 1855 he formed a new company, Cunard, Brett, and Austin, which became Cunard, Wilson, and Company in 1857. These firms, working on a commission basis for colonial merchants and lumbermen, sold ships and lumber and purchased goods. The latter firm was still in operation at the time of Joseph's death in 1865.

Cunard was a colourful individual who played a major role in the commercial activities of Northumberland, Restigouche, Kent, and Gloucester counties. His failure in the late 1840s was to affect the economy of the area seriously for many years.

W. A. SPRAY

Mariners' Museum (Newport News, Va.), Indenture between Samuel, Joseph, and Edward Cunard, and Charles Walton, William George Driscoll, and Robert Carter, 11 April 1842 (photocopy in N.B. Museum). N.B. Museum, "One of the noted sons of Kent Co., N.B.: Honourable Joseph Cunard, industrialist and member of Legislative Council" (typescript); Webster coll., Sir Howard Douglas, letterbook (typescript), p.221. PANB, Cunard-Raymond letterbooks and diary, 1840–53 (mfm.); J. C. and H. B. Graves, "New Brunswick political biography," XI, pp. 24–25; Samuel Merchandising family papers, M. Samuel to Messrs Moses, Son, and Davis, 26 March 1842; REX/le/l–g, Head, letterbook, 1848–50, p.153; REX/pa/Register of appointments and commissions, 1785–1840, pp.31, 48, 99, 101, 140–41; REX/pa/Surveyor general's correspondence, 1843, I(a), 3; II(a), 2; REX/px, 20, pp.1886–91; 24, files 5–6; 65; 116, file 2; RLE/S55/pe/202; RLE/S63/pe/218; RNA/c/9/3/22; RPS, Letterbook, 1842–45, pp.15, 25; 1845–47, pp.214, 225, 341, 367; 1847–50, pp.135, 163, 201–2, 209–10, 227–28, 253. PRO, CO 188/42, 30 Nov. 1831; 188/43, 16 Jan. 1832; 188/46, 14 Oct. 1833; 188/99, 26 Feb. 1847; 188/106, 23 Oct. 1848; 188/108, 20 Feb. 1846, 29 March 1849.

Gleaner (Chatham, N.B.), 13 Aug. 1833; 8 Dec. 1835; 16 Feb., 12 July, 4 Oct. 1836; 30 April, 7 May 1839; 6 June 1846; 15 Feb. 1848; 29 June 1850; 27 Jan. 1851; 17 Nov. 1855; 21 Jan., 4, 11 Feb. 1865. *Miramichi Advance* (Chatham, N.B.), 10 June 1880. Esther Clark Wright, *The Miramichi: a study of the New Brunswick river and of the people who settled along it* (Sackville, N.B., 1944), 44–51. Hannay, *History of N.B.*, II, 19. MacNutt, *New Brunswick*, 216, 230, 240, 275–76, 288, 321. Louise Manny, *Shipbuilding in Bathurst* (Fredericton, 1965), 3–7; *Ships of Miramichi: a history of shipbuilding on the Miramichi River, New Brunswick, Canada, 1773–1919* (Saint John, N.B., 1961), 24–33; "Colossus of Miramichi," *Atlantic Advocate* (Fredericton), 55 (1964–65), no. 3, 37–41.

CUNARD, Sir SAMUEL, merchant, shipowner, and entrepreneur; b. 21 Nov. 1787 at Halifax, N.S., second child of Abraham Cunard and Margaret Murphy; m. 4 Feb. 1815 at Halifax Susan Duffus (1795–1828), and they had two sons and seven daughters; d. 28 April 1865 in London, England.

Samuel Cunard's father was a descendant of German Quakers who had immigrated to Pennsylvania in the 17th century. His mother's family had immigrated from Ireland to South Carolina in 1773 and to Nova Scotia with the loyalists a decade later. In 1783 Abraham Cunard came with the British forces to Halifax where he was employed as a foreman carpenter in the army. On 7 Oct. 1799 Edward Augustus*, Duke of Kent, commander-in-chief in British North America, appointed Abraham master carpenter to the Contingent Department of the Royal Engineers at the Halifax garrison; he continued to work for the army until his retirement on 22 Oct. 1822.

Abraham Cunard did not limit his career to his official duties. During the French revolution and the Napoleonic era the British army and navy greatly expanded their facilities at Halifax, creating a need for more houses, wharves, and commercial premises. Ignoring the stipulation of his appointment that he "give up every other occupation," from the 1780s to 1812 Abraham slowly acquired property in the north suburbs near the dockyard, some of which he rented. He was careful to obtain water rights for all lots fronting the harbour in order to build wharves.

The Cunards are remembered as a thrifty family, with Samuel knitting a sock as he drove the family cow to pasture, and the boys selling vegetables from their father's garden at the town market or to neighbours. Although he probably attended the Halifax Grammar School, Samuel was largely self-educated. He always emphasized the importance of a plain English education for a business career, but his own sons Edward and William received a classical education at King's Collegiate School and King's College, Windsor, N.S.

Samuel early proved to be a shrewd trader and at the wharves bought goods which he sold in town. Although he did not follow his father's trade, he had an extensive knowledge of timber. His father's acquaintance among the military enabled Samuel to train as a clerk for the Royal Engineers; from 1811 to about 1812 he was first clerk at the engineers' lumber-yard at a salary of 7s. 6d. daily and £20 lodging money annually.

About 1812 the firm of A. Cunard and Son was founded to enter the timber and West Indian trade. It had been granted considerable excellent timber land in Cumberland County, some of which was free and some purchased, and was selling timber abroad, chiefly in Britain, and to the Halifax Dockyard. The Cunards also profited from the War of 1812. They were licensed by Governor Sir John Coape Sherbrooke* to trade with the United States as early as 6 July 1812, and traded with New England. They imported goods from Britain valued at £6,272 in January 1814, and took part in the trade with Castine, Maine, after the British army captured that port.

The Cunard fortunes are reputedly based on the shrewd purchase at Halifax of an American prize (name unknown) with a valuable cargo. It is known, however, that the Cunards' schooner *Margaret*, on a voyage from Martinique to Halifax in 1814, was captured by an American privateer. Fortunately for her owners she was recaptured on 16 March and brought into Halifax, where Judge Alexander Croke* of the Court of Vice-Admiralty returned the schooner to the Cunards upon payment of one-eighth appraised value for the ship and cargo of sugar, molasses, and rum.

The Cunard firm continued to be active in the West Indian trade. Customs returns in 1813 and 1814 show them importing spirits, molasses, brown sugar, and coffee from Martinique, St Lucia, Dominica, Jamaica, Guadeloupe, Trinidad, Demerara, and Surinam. A. Cunard and Son also acted as agents for various ships owned by others; these included in 1813 the *White Oak*, owned in Bermuda, and in 1814 the Liverpool schooner *Harlequin*.

Samuel Cunard was under middle height, with a well-knit frame, a mouth showing strength of character and decision, and brow and eyes indicating intelligence. As he was to write to his daughter Jane, government positions did not offer enough opportunities for an ambitious young man and "frequently lead to old age with a small pittance but little removed from poverty." A merchant, however, with patient industry generally succeeded. Throughout his life Samuel was to carry out his belief that no one succeeded without application and close attention to business, and he was long remembered for his brisk step, quick and ready movements, and his air of "push." He had the skill to choose for his staff men of high calibre who were hard and faithful workers and to inspire them to work as quickly as he did.

As an able-bodied young man during the War of 1812 Samuel volunteered for service in the 2nd battalion of the Halifax Regiment of militia and eventually became a captain. He was selected by the Halifax Court of Quarter Sessions as one of the citizens to organize a night watch to patrol the town after the disturbances in 1817. Samuel had become a member of the exclusive Sun Fire Company on 11 Feb. 1809 and was president in 1821. In this period Halifax was protected by volunteer fire companies which were as renowned for social activities such as balls and sleigh rides as for fighting fires. From 1821 to 1835 he was to serve as one of the firewards appointed by the Halifax Quarter Sessions to direct those fighting the flames and to decide on demolitions to stop the spread of fire.

By the end of hostilities between Britain and the United States in 1815, Samuel had become accustomed to conducting business in a wartime economy. Immediately after the war the Cunard firm continued to expand. That summer the Cunards purchased at a public sale for £1,325 two lots in the north suburbs of Halifax which were no longer needed by the military, in order to construct wharves and warehouses. Surveyor General Charles Morris* supported their successful petition for water rights 500 ft out into the harbour in front of property they owned on Water Street because of "their well known character, for active exertion and enterprize in useful improvements and commercial pursuits."

With the withdrawal of most of the British naval and military forces, trade diminished and unemployment grew. This situation was aggravated by the arrival of large numbers of immi-

Cunard

grants. Lieutenant Governor Dalhousie [Ramsay*] selected Samuel Cunard and Michael Tobin to assist penniless immigrants arriving from Europe and Newfoundland at Halifax, and in the autumn of 1817 gave them £100, which they used largely to transport newcomers to districts in the province where they could find work or obtain board on farms for the winter in return for their labour. To help Haligonians on the verge of starvation Tobin and Cunard opened a soup kitchen which distributed 100 gallons of soup daily. In the winter of 1820 Cunard, Tobin, and John Starr administered a soup house at an expense of 50s. daily, where 320 people received one meal each day, and in 1821 the provincial legislature granted £33 to continue its operation.

Although probably hampered by lack of capital Samuel decided to diversify and expand the Cunard business. From his position with the Royal Engineers he had become acquainted with army and navy officials and the company was soon known for prompt assistance to the admirals and generals and for obtaining needed supplies; it was paid generously with money or favours. The Cunard firm contracted to carry the mail by sailing packet between Halifax and Boston and Halifax and St John's, Nfld; it also sometimes carried the Bermuda mail after the British naval dockyard was moved there in 1819. A. Cunard and Son had also tendered in 1815 to supply a 100-ton vessel for government service to protect the trade and fisheries and prevent smuggling, to sail to New York for mail in winter, to transport the lieutenant governor on official tours, and to move men or supplies to military outposts. The firm purchased a vessel for £1,500, and after inspection by naval officers it was taken into service as the sloop *Earl Bathurst*. In the summer of 1817, however, Lord Dalhousie decided that a larger vessel was required. The Cunards sold the sloop for £375 and bought the *Chebucto* in England for £2,960. This brig was hired for government service at £2,400 sterling per annum. Although Samuel estimated annual expenses of £2,325, including depreciation, complaints were made from Halifax and London to Colonial Secretary Lord Bathurst that Cunard had boasted about profits of £1,930 on the vessel and an additional profit because British bills of exchange had a premium of 15 per cent at a time when foreign currency was scarce. In consequence the lieutenant governor was instructed to advertise for tenders in 1822; the lowest bid was for £1,500 annually from Cunard, who explained to Sir James Kempt* that the firm had no other employment for the brig and was reluctant to dismantle her. An estimate made at the time for the

Colonial Office of the annual operating costs for the services requested of this type of vessel was £1,400. The Cunards ran this service for the government until 30 June 1833.

By the early 1820s Samuel had become virtual head of the Cunard firm. His parents moved to a farm at Pleasant Valley (Rawdon Gold Mines) in Hants County, and he became responsible for his younger brothers as well as his own wife and children; he also assisted his wife's family when the business of his father-in-law, William Duffus, failed. Abraham Cunard died at Rawdon on 10 Jan. 1824 and on 1 May S. Cunard and Company formally emerged. Abraham's will appointed his older sons Samuel, William, and JOSEPH as trustees of his property, and on 15 Dec. 1826 a settlement was made: for the sum of £1,550 Samuel and Joseph, the surviving trustees, transferred Halifax property to another brother, Edward, who had been taken into the business about 1825 to run the Halifax office after acting as master of various vessels owned by Samuel. Four days later Edward sold to Samuel one of the lots, which Samuel already occupied, and one-third of three water lots for £550, and to Joseph a one-third share for £500. The younger brothers John, Thomas, and Henry did not share in the assets of the firm.

Apparently each of the Cunard brothers acted individually rather than as a company in buying and selling wooden sailing ships. The large number of *Margaret*s (after their mother) and *Susan*s (after Samuel's wife) and the frequent re-registrations make determining the exact numbers difficult, but Samuel had at least 76 sailing ships registered at Halifax between 1817 and 1850, and Edward registered five more vessels built by Alexander Lyle of Dartmouth in 1840–41 which are usually attributed to Samuel's ownership. Of the 76 it is estimated that 28 were sold abroad, 21 sold in Halifax, two in Pictou, one in Newfoundland, three in the West Indies and one in Saint John, 14 unknown, and six wrecked. Of the 28 sold abroad, ten were disposed of in London, ten in Liverpool, and one each in Hull, Bristol, Aberdeen, Dundee, Banff, Belfast, Limerick, and Galway.

Except for his mail boats Samuel Cunard kept his vessels for only a few years, to be sold when he needed replacements or saw an opportunity for profit. At first he bought former prizes, but later purchased ships constructed in Nova Scotia and Prince Edward Island. Before 1827 Samuel sold some ships locally. Beginning in that year, however, he sold a few ships abroad from Halifax each year; three vessels registered in 1826 were sold in Britain in the summer of 1827.

Even during bad winter weather in the 1820s Cunard's vessels were sailing to and from the West Indies bringing in rum, molasses, sugar, and some coffee, and carrying out dry and pickled fish, hoops and staves, mackerel, alewives, codfish, lumber, tea, and oil. Mostly he used his own ships. Besides trade with the Miramichi area and with Newfoundland, Cunard imported cargoes from London and Liverpool of dry goods, anchors, cables, coal, and even a fire engine in 1827 ordered by the Halifax Fire Insurance Company; from Philadelphia flour, meal, and fruit; from Boston naval stores, flour, tobacco, and seeds; and from New York corn, wheat, apples, nuts, and books.

During the 1820s Cunard prospered. The adjustment to peace in Nova Scotia had been aggravated by crop failures, the readmission of the Americans to the fisheries (under the British-American Convention of 1818), the lowering of imperial duties on foreign timber, and the removal of the Royal Navy's dockyard facilities to Bermuda in 1819, but provincial trade expanded after 1824. The emergence of young entrepreneurs like Cunard and Enos Collins*, alert to every opportunity for increasing their capital, was assisted by the death or retirement of an older generation of merchants, such as James Fraser*, James Moody*, William Forsyth*, and John Black*, most of whom had been financed from abroad, and by the return of others to Britain with their profits as soon as the war ended. Earlier businesses were branches of British merchant houses, but now native Nova Scotians began to dominate the business scene.

Both Cunard and Collins joined in petitions in 1820 from Halifax merchants to the assembly to ask for bounties on flour to allow Nova Scotians to compete with the Americans in the West Indian trade and for a duty on flour imported from the United States. Cunard's increasing importance in business circles is shown by his election to the Chamber of Commerce of the reorganized Nova Scotia Commercial Society in 1822; he was its president in 1834.

The Cunards' brig *Prince of Waterloo* engaged in the whale fishery off Brazil from 1819 to 1821, and in 1827 Samuel Cunard, Joseph Allison*, and Lawrence Hartshorne were trustees for the Halifax Whaling Company, which employed the *Pacific*. In 1834 and 1836 the Cunards' ship *Susan and Sarah* went on whaling voyages, and their 421-ton *Rose* returned to Halifax in April 1839 after a two-year voyage with 2,400 barrels of black and sperm oil to learn that there were not enough funds left to pay her the full government bounty of £2 per ton.

Cunard subscribed £1,000 for stock in the Shubenacadie Canal Company and was chosen a vice-president in 1826. Along with Collins, Martin Gay BLACK, and five others, he was an original partner of the Halifax Banking Company formed on 1 Sept. 1825, subscribing £5,000 of its £50,000 capital. In 1831 the partners of this company held more than one-third of the provincial funded debt totalling £21,459, Cunard's holdings being £506 as compared to £2,559 for Henry Hezekiah Cogswell* and £450 for Collins. There were objections in other parts of the province to the concentration of so much wealth in the capital. Cunard withdrew from the company in 1836, becoming a resident director of the Bank of British North America. Possibly this move was influenced by the fact that the Bank of Nova Scotia, formed in 1832 as a rival of the Halifax Banking Company, was the bank used by the General Mining Association.

Samuel Cunard was one of the small shareholders in the Annapolis Iron Mining Company, incorporated by the legislature of Nova Scotia in 1825 to smelt and manufacture iron in Annapolis County; the largest shareholder was Cyrus Alger of Boston. After some success the enterprise was abandoned because the American shareholders wished to concentrate on the sale of pig iron in the United States, and the Nova Scotians on manufacturing finished products, but the company may also have been influenced by a yield lower than anticipated.

Cunard was always looking for opportunities to expand his business. On 9 Jan. 1826 he made a proposal to Lieutenant Governor Kempt to lease the Cape Breton coal mines for 30 years at £6,000 per annum and a royalty of 2s. per chaldron on coal shipments over 60,000. He stipulated that Sydney be made a free port and emphasized the value of the American market and the necessity of investing capital in the equipment at the mines and of building wharves and breakwaters. A month later Kempt observed to Robert John Wilmot-Horton at the Colonial Office that if Sydney were made a free port, the demand for coal would increase so much that the Cunards' proposed lease and royalties would not be large enough, but he admitted that "The Messrs. Cunards are Persons of Considerable Capital quite equal to carry on this Establishment & perfectly acquainted with the Country." Later that year, however, the rights to exploitation of the province's minerals were granted to the General Mining Association, and Cunard's bid failed [*see* Richard SMITH].

Cunard was more successful in obtaining the tea agency from the East India Company. When

Cunard

he learned in July 1824 of the proposal to ship cargoes of tea directly from Canton to Quebec in East India Company ships, he went to London to explain to the company the transportation problems of contrary winds and ice for ships sailing from Quebec to provide the Maritime provinces with their annual tea supply. On 11 Feb. 1825 Cunard and Zealmon Wheeler of Venner, Brown, and Wheeler, Saint John, N.B., applied jointly for the contract to import tea into Halifax and Saint John on the same terms as Forsyth, Richardson, and Company of Montreal [*see* James Bell FORSYTH], the agents for the Canadas. It was hoped that the lower prices offered by these firms would prevent smuggling of tea from the United States. Previously most of the tea exported from London to Nova Scotia and New Brunswick had been shipped by Bainbridge and Brown, London commission merchants and ships' brokers, who purchased it at East India Company auctions in London. Bainbridge and Brown offered to sign bonds as security for Cunard and Wheeler. However, Cunard alone received the agency for the Atlantic provinces. John Bainbridge, an active member of a committee of London merchants trading in British North America which was particularly interested in the timber trade, was appointed provincial agent for the Nova Scotia legislature on 23 Feb. 1826, and remained Cunard's friend until his death.

After the first 6,517 chests of tea shipped directly to Halifax from China by the East India Company arrived, a public sale was held at Cunard's warehouse on 19 June 1826. Quarterly auctions at the stone warehouse by Cunard's wharf, with Cunard as auctioneer, became customary. He retained the agency until 1860.

In the 1830s Cunard was re-exporting equal amounts of tea to New Brunswick and Newfoundland, some packages to Jamaica, Bermuda, Demerara, and Barbados, some to Forsyth, Richardson, and Company at Montreal late in the season before navigation of the St Lawrence River was closed, and a few packages and chests each autumn to Prince Edward Island, without paying duty. In 1831 Enos Collins attempted to oust Cunard from the tea agency. Possibly Cunard was exaggerating his profits to his colleagues in the Halifax Banking Company. Between October 1825 and April 1831 he remitted approximately $95,362 in Spanish dollars and £85,754 sterling to the East India Company.

Cunard sold about two-thirds as much tea as Forsyth, Richardson and Company. Although Cunard's commission on East India funds was only 2 per cent, it was useful to have large sums of money available, even for a short period, to help finance his own operations. He may have used some of the capital for financing his part of the steamship line in 1839 by withholding payments to the East India Company, for he was prompt with his remittances until 1840. In that year and the following the company had to request Cunard to remit the balance due; he did so soon afterward.

Although in later life Samuel Cunard declared that "he kept his politics to himself," he was a strong supporter of the Tory party. In April 1826 he was persuaded by "merchants and other respectable inhabitants" of Halifax County to offer himself as a candidate for election to the provincial assembly and issued an election card. He withdrew early from the contest, however, because he objected to the candidates and voters having to waste three weeks on an election campaign at such a busy season of the year for farmers and fishermen, and thus allowed the other candidates to be elected by acclamation.

Cunard owed his appointment to the Council of Twelve in 1830 to his position in the mercantile community; by that time his fortune was estimated at £200,000. He took his seat in the Council on 6 Nov. 1830 after the Brandy Election [*see* Collins], and Joseph Howe* expressed in the *Novascotian* the hope that "the same liberal and expansive views which have distinguished Mr. Cunard as a merchant, may be observable in his legislative character. He is wealthy and influential – he need fear no man, nor follow blindly any body of men; and we trust that he will not disappoint the hopes which many entertain of the benefit to be derived from his weight in the counsels of a branch, that, at the present moment, is really in no good odour throughout the Province." Alexander STEWART, a member of the assembly for Cumberland and a strong advocate for the Bank of Nova Scotia, objected to another appointment from the capital.

For the first three years Cunard faithfully attended both executive and legislative meetings of the Council, and was active on committees dealing with public accounts and revenue and the value of coinage. He was motivated by what he thought would be best for business. However, Cunard expected the same efficiency from public servants as from his own employees. In 1832 a committee of three councillors – Cunard, H. H. Cogswell, and Joseph Allison – investigated a complaint against William Cleveland, county treasurer, in his capacity as clerk of the licence, for allowing too many people to sell spirits without a licence, and reported that Cleveland "is an inattentive careless Officer, and has for a long time neglected to perform the duties of his office in a vigilant and effective manner. . . ." Cleveland was dismissed.

As the 1830s progressed the Council of Twelve came increasingly under attack by the Reformers, who objected particularly to the fact that five councillors, including Cunard, were directors of the Halifax Banking Company. Cunard also had increasing influence in British business and governmental circles. When Reformer William Young* met Colonial Under-Secretary Henry Labouchere in London on 16 June 1839 he declared that "we were perfectly aware of all the influence at work against us, that of the Bishop [John Inglis*], S. Cunard, Col. [John] Yorke &c."

During most of 1834 and 1835 Cunard was absent from Council meetings. He was present for most of 1836 and 1837, but not active on committees. He remained an executive councillor when the Council was divided into executive and legislative branches in 1838, but attended only a few meetings between 1838 and 1840, when he had become involved in the beginnings of his transatlantic steamship line. Thus he probably did not mind being asked to resign on 1 Oct. 1840 at the request of Lord Falkland [Cary*] to make room for Reformers in the coalition. He was allowed to retain the title of "Honourable."

The Tory press was indignant that Cunard, "the greatest benefactor Nova Scotia ever had . . . is deemed unfit to have a seat in the councils of his country. . . ." The Reformers, however, said Cunard should not be in the Executive Council because he "is no statesman . . . nor does he aim at the amelioration of the political condition of his countrymen." In 1844 the editor of the *Morning Chronicle* wrote bitterly against the address of the Halifax Tories to Sir Charles Metcalfe* which expressed concern about the "mischievous effects of party and intemperate Legislation." "This is a gross libel upon the people of Nova Scotia. Who utters it? Cunard, Collins & Co. The Old Bankers of the Old Council – who were dismissed by her Majesty from power, for their ultra-Toryism, and unfitness for office . . . who used the power with which they were clothed, for their own benefit and the benefit of their friends, *regardless of the wishes or interests of the people.* . . ."

After the breakdown of the coalition of Tories and Reformers in December 1843, the Tories formed a government under James William Johnston* with a bare majority over the Reformers. By-elections became crucial, including one in the spring of 1845 in Pictou, where Cunard exerted his influence for the Tories and apparently arranged with local Reformers for a Tory victory by acclamation in return for a few minor offices for the Reformers. Howe was angry because there was no hope of defeating the Tories before the next election: "Such a treaty is worthy of such a negotiator, and will long be held in remembrance as a proof of the gentleman's talents for diplomacy, and the gullibility of the men with whom he had to deal." But in the 1847 elections for responsible government Cunard assured Howe of his neutrality.

The success of the Cunard firm in its early years had been based in large part on the timber trade with Britain, which was encouraged by the tariffs placed on Baltic timber during the Napoleonic wars. In 1821, when the British government announced its intention of reducing the Baltic duties, Cunard had been chosen by the Halifax Chamber of Commerce to deliver to the colonial secretary a petition to keep them. The expansion of the Cunard firm into the Miramichi area of New Brunswick was a natural outgrowth of its timber interests. The Cunards may have been at Chatham as early as 1820, and Samuel Cunard received a deed to Egg Island on 13 July 1821. After the Miramichi fire of 1825, Joseph and Henry Cunard used the capital of the family firm for the aggressive building of a timber empire over the south bank of the Miramichi in rivalry with Alexander Rankin*. This rivalry became so important to Joseph that he ceased to worry about profits and when questioned about the prices Cunard brothers were selling at said: "We don't give a damn so long as we sell more deals than Gilmour, Rankin & Co." The business was conducted as Joseph Cunard and Company, the partners being Joseph, Samuel, Edward, and Henry (who withdrew in 1841 to farm at Woodburn). The Halifax-based firm of S. Cunard and Company provided most of the goods required by Joseph Cunard and Company, and shipped to Miramichi, Richibucto, and Bathurst most of the food products and manufactures needed by the lumbermen, the shipbuilders, and their families. It received in return shingles, staves, lumber, dry and pickled fish, salmon, and alewives, which they sold in the West Indies. S. Cunard and Company also sold tea and rum to Gilmour, Rankin, and Company and to Joseph Samuel at Miramichi.

The timber business necessitated large amounts of capital because two years elapsed between shipment of supplies to lumber camps and the receipt of cash from the sale of lumber. The situation was aggravated by the wildly fluctuating timber market in Britain. Bainbridge and Brown, writing from London to John Ward and Sons at Saint John on 20 Oct. 1826, reported

Cunard

poor prices for ships and timber in London and Liverpool and remarked: "We have two of Cunards Miramichi cargoes at the Clyde & two at Leith & cannot sell a stick. . . ." However, the demand for timber rallied in the 1830s and the Cunards expanded.

Samuel tried to control his headstrong younger brother Joseph. He wrote from Halifax on 28 Nov. 1838 to protest the additional capital sunk in a grist mill, pointing out the folly of discounting at 90 days and then having to pay four or five per cent for drawing funds in Saint John. Customarily merchants met their obligations by issuing notes or bills of exchange which were circulated like cheques; Joseph Cunard and Company in Miramichi issued large numbers for the convenience of the trade as there were no banks in the district. The notes were payable in Halifax at the office of S. Cunard and Company. In 1839 nearly every remittance received from the Miramichi by Halifax merchants consisted principally of Cunard's notes; "Publicola" (Richmond Robinson, a law student with William Young) speculated in the *Acadian Recorder* on 2 Nov. 1839 that these notes in circulation amounted to £80,000. In Samuel's absence his son Edward Cunard denied that more than £10,000 had ever been in circulation, and insisted that the amount outstanding was £4,000. "Publicola" observed that this postponement of settling debts would allow the firm to pocket quietly £1,000 through interest saved, and also warned the merchants of Halifax that in a financial panic Samuel Cunard could refuse to honour the notes because they had been issued by Joseph.

In the 1830s the West Indian trade diminished in importance for Nova Scotia merchants because of increased American competition and a decline in sugar production. S. Cunard and Company was bringing in only enough rum, molasses, and sugar to supply lumbering operations in Miramichi and Prince Edward Island. The clear-sighted and enterprising head of the firm turned its warehouses into bonded warehouses for other firms, and attempted to expand its trade with Britain in such goods as flour, dry goods, cordage, and glass, as Halifax was still the leading wholesale centre of the Atlantic provinces.

By the spring of 1834 the depression in Nova Scotia had deepened. In Halifax there were 600 houses for rent, shops were glutted with produce, and cash was locked up in the banks. Cunard was astute in avoiding failure. He had already competed to secure the contract to provide wharf space in Halifax for the General Mining Association. The long-established firm of Belcher, Binney, and Company had expected to be agents for the English mining company, but, when the company's engineer, George Blackwell, had returned to England strongly recommending Cunard's wharf and warehouses, Cunard's offer was accepted in 1827. At first Richard Smith, a mining engineer from England, acted as general agent in Nova Scotia as well as superintendent of operations, but since the GMA monopoly was resented by local capitalists, in 1834 the association shrewdly appointed Cunard as their local business agent and a director of the corporation.

When Cunard became GMA agent, the company owed the Bank of Nova Scotia over £16,000. By 9 April 1835 the overdraft had risen to £25,480 and at the request of William Lawson*, president of the bank, Cunard reduced it by £6,000. In the financial crisis of 1837 the board prevailed on Cunard to reduce it to £10,000. In 1839 Cunard's Halifax firm was awarded the contract to supply coal to the Halifax Dockyard, but his own ships seldom carried coal cargoes.

In December 1842 Cunard attempted to counter the popular supposition that the GMA was reaping large profits by stating that "no interest or return" had "yet been paid." Large capital expenditures had been made in expectation of almost unlimited demand for coal in the United States, but the company was meeting increasing competition from American anthracite coal. When the United States increased its tariff on foreign coal in 1842, Cunard asked the Nova Scotian government for a reduction in royalties and threatened that the GMA would lay off miners unless the government agreed; the royalties were reduced and the annual £3,000 rent was waived. Cunard's letters reveal his complete devotion to the interests of the corporation. As the GMA monopoly became steadily more unpopular over the years, Cunard became the buffer in conflicts between the British and Nova Scotian governments and in disputes between miners and owners. Yet it was acknowledged that under "his guidance and management the operations of the Company" were wisely and properly conducted. Cunard's connections with the GMA gave him a power base in Pictou County where he wielded political and business influence behind the scenes.

While in England in 1838, Cunard was approached about forming a Prince Edward Island land company by George Renny Young* of Halifax, who was in London as legal counsel for a number of landowners in Prince Edward Island to present to Colonial Secretary Lord Glenelg their case against any escheat of their lands [see William COOPER]. Cunard was easily persuaded to join Andrew Colvile (agent for the 6th Earl of Selkirk), Robert Bruce Stewart, and Thomas Holdsworth BROOKING, Young's father-in-law, in forming a joint stock company called the Prince Edward Island Land Company with a local board comprised of Young, Samuel Cunard, and Joseph Cunard. They purchased the 60,000-acre estate of John Hill for £10,000 and the mortgage on the 102,000-acre estate of John Cambridge for £12,000 sterling, £8,400 of which was paid immediately with the backing of London bankers Prescott, Grote, and Company and of the Liverpool Union Bank. Samuel and Joseph Cunard held six-tenths of the shares, Colvile two-tenths, and Brooking and Young one-tenth each.

In August 1838 Young and Cunard went to Prince Edward Island to visit their estates and to discuss the land tax with Lieutenant Governor Sir Charles Augustus FitzRoy*. They assured him that they wanted "a common line of policy between the Proprietors and their tenants calculated to restore peace and to promote the prosperity of the Island." At a meeting in Charlottetown on 20 Oct. 1838 a disagreement over the appointment of a solicitor for the land company split the board when Young insisted upon his younger brother Charles, and Samuel upon his son-in-law James Horsfield Peters*. This quarrel resulted in Samuel's buying out his partners on 26 March 1839, but it left ill feeling with the Youngs.

In the early years Cunard reserved the rights to all timber fit for shipping, shipbuilding, or exportation on leases which he granted; the timber taken off paid for the land. With his land purchases in Prince Edward Island, Samuel obtained the right to collect £2,535 in arrears of rent on the Cambridge estate. Many tenants paid but some cattle and land were seized for past rents by his agent, J. H. Peters, in 1842 and 1843, and new leases issued to new tenants. On Lot 45 in Kings County about 300 people assembled on 17 March to reinstate forcibly a man named Haney into possession of a house and farm from which he had been legally ejected; 50 soldiers had to be sent from Charlottetown to restore order on the Cunard estates.

As an alert shipowner Cunard was aware of the development in steam vessels and noticed increasing numbers of such vessels at Liverpool and on the Irish Sea. In 1825, in anticipation of the proposed steamship service by the American and Colonial Steam Navigation Company of Great Britain around the British Isles and once a fortnight to Halifax and New York, negotiations were begun for a steamboat between Quebec and Halifax to connect with the mail packets from Falmouth, England. With contrary winds sailing ships sometimes took 23 days to reach Quebec from Halifax. The Lower Canadian legislature offered £1,500 in three annual instalments and the Nova Scotian house offered £250, but no capitalists were attracted until subsidies were doubled in 1830. Samuel Cunard was only one of over 200 shareholders (including his brothers Henry and Joseph) from Quebec and the Maritimes in the Quebec and Halifax Steam Navigation Company formed in 1830 and incorporated the next year. Among prominent businessmen and merchants of Lower Canada were John Forsyth*, William PRICE, Sir John Caldwell*, Noah Freer, George Black*, and William Walker. Samuel was elected head of the Halifax committee of the shareholders.

The contract for building the steamship was given to John Saxton Campbell and Black. The ss *Royal William*, launched 27 April 1831 at Cape Cove, Quebec, sailed to Halifax on 24 August, calling at Miramichi (where Joseph Cunard was her agent) and Pictou. J. G. Denter, second engineer on board, later recalled that Samuel Cunard repeatedly visited the *Royal William* and inquired into every particular regarding her speed, sea qualities, and consumption of coal. Unfortunately for the owners the outbreak of a cholera epidemic at Quebec in 1832 forced the ship into quarantine at Miramichi and Halifax; it sat idle a large part of the season and suffered heavy financial losses. In the spring of 1833 the steamship which had cost £16,000 to build was sold at Quebec to the mortgagees for only £5,000. In a letter of 7 May 1833 to Sir Rupert George, Nova Scotia's provincial secretary, Cunard bitterly blamed the Quebec committee for allowing the frost to burst the pipes and injure the machinery and he stated, "I do not think . . . [the provincial bounty] should be paid in consequence of the Boats only making one trip during the whole Season. . . . They have already received £3,975 from this Province the whole of which is lost by the Management of the Quebec Committee and the object in view frustrated."

Although rapid communication was imperative for colonial merchants, the mails for America were still carried by the Falmouth packets taking 30 to 70 days to cross the Atlantic. On 7 Nov. 1838 the British Admiralty advertised for tenders to carry mails by steam from England to New York via Halifax. Two tenders were received from Britain but neither was satisfactory. The closing date had passed before Cunard heard the news in Halifax. Believing "that steamers properly built and manned might start and arrive at their destination with the punctuality of railway

Cunard

trains on land," he sailed to England to submit his own plan for an "ocean railway," with a letter from Nova Scotia's lieutenant governor, Sir Colin Campbell*, reminding the Colonial Office that Cunard was "one of the firmest supporters of the Government" with "a good deal of influence in this community. . . ."

Fortunately the comptroller of steam machinery and packet service and advisor to the Admiralty was Arctic explorer William Edward Parry*, who remembered with pleasure his service as a young naval officer at Halifax during the War of 1812. On 11 Feb. 1839 Cunard offered to provide steamboats of not less than 300 h.p. to carry the mails from England to Halifax and back twice monthly, and also to provide a branch service in boats of not less than 150 h.p. to Boston, and one from Pictou to Quebec while the navigation was unobstructed by ice. For this he asked £55,000 sterling yearly for ten years, and he promised to have the steamers ready by 1 May 1840. The Admiralty accepted Cunard's offer.

In order to obtain steamships Cunard consulted James Cosmo Melvill, secretary of the East India Company. He recommended Robert Napier, a foundry owner and engineer in Glasgow who had provided steamships for the company. On 25 Feb. 1839 Cunard wrote to William Kidston and Sons of Glasgow (who had had a branch in Halifax) asking them to obtain estimates from Napier. The latter offered to build a vessel of 800 tons and 300 h.p. for £32,000 but agreed to lower his price to £30,000 when Cunard ordered three vessels. Napier, a leader in establishing Glasgow as a great steamship-building centre, decided before the contract was signed with Cunard on 18 March 1839 that these steamships would have to be larger for safe Atlantic voyages and offered to provide the extra work on the engines at no additional cost if Cunard would pay for the structural changes. The Nova Scotian agreed, indicating he wanted "to shew the Americans what can be done in Glasgow and that neither Bristol or London Boats can beat them."

When Cunard could not sell stock in his steamship company in Britain or America, Napier approached a fellow shareholder in the City of Glasgow Steam-Packet Company, James Donaldson, a wealthy cotton broker. Donaldson consulted George Burns of Glasgow, who controlled the Belfast trade and was interested in shipping as well as the commission business. Burns "entertained the proposal cordially," inviting Cunard to meet David MacIver, an ambitious young Scot, who was the agent for small firms in the coastal trade. After various negotiations Burns persuaded some friends to form a co-partnership on 14 May 1839 to take over Cunard's mail contract. In a few days £270,000 was subscribed for "The Glasgow Proprietors in the British and North American Royal Mail Steam Packet Company." At first Cunard subscribed £55,000 for his 110 original shares but that amount was only gradually paid up; in the final arrangements of 23 May 1840 Cunard subscribed £67,500, George Burns £5,000, his brother James £5,000, and David and Charles MacIver £4,000.

The Glasgow investors were businessmen – cotton brokers, West Indian merchants, insurance brokers, iron merchants, warehousemen, textile manufacturers, produce merchants, shipping agents, and so on. Some of them were now seeking outlets for capital because of the decline of the West Indian trade, but most were interested in steamship companies. There was no Nova Scotian capital except for Cunard's investment, the financial losses of the *Royal William* making it difficult to raise money locally.

Haligonians were delighted with Cunard's contract and immediately subscribed £8,000 to build a new hotel for the expected passengers. On 9 April 1839 the Halifax *Times* rejoiced that a "new era will commence in Provincial prosperity from the moment the first steam packet reaches Halifax – and . . . the time is not far distant when it will become the centre of steam navigation for the whole American continent." That spring, however, a meeting of Boston merchants requested larger steamships to run directly through to Boston, instead of a branch service from Halifax, and offered to provide a suitable pier and dock and facilities for a quick transfer to railways. Cunard agreed, and finally the Maritimes realized that Boston had become the western terminus instead of Halifax.

The first scheduled steamer, *Britannia*, arrived at Halifax at 2 a.m. on 17 July 1840 with Cunard and his daughter Ann on board, discharged passengers and mail as quickly as possible, and sailed on to dock at East Boston at 10 p.m. two days later. There Cunard received a warm welcome and 1,800 invitations to dinner. The *Acadian Recorder* commented: "We are quite sanguine that our Boston neighbours *calculated* right when they so nobly encouraged Mr Cunard's splendid project. His steamships will enable Boston to become more important than New York in a little time. . . ." It was the Bostonians who called the line the Cunard Steam Ship Company or the Cunard Line of Packet Steam Ships long before the company was legally incorporated as the Cunard Steamship Company in 1878. The regular service of the Cunarders increased foreign trade to Boston by 100 per cent in one year. Yet the expectations of both Halifax and Boston to become the centre of navigation for the whole North American continent failed because geography gave Montreal and New York access to richer hinterlands.

Although historians of Nova Scotia, Scotland, or England assume that the partner in the enterprise from their own country deserves sole credit for the success of the steamship line, available evidence indicates that all important actions were undertaken after consultation among the major partners, although Burns superintended ship-building activities and financing, Cunard had special responsibility for negotiations with the British government over contracts, and the MacIvers managed the operations of the fleet at Liverpool. A letter from David MacIver in Liverpool in 1841 chided Cunard for his low spirits over difficulties about the application to the British government for a second contract and the low profits. MacIver argued that this had been an experimental year and we "are now arrived at that point where we must turn this experience to profit."

Difficulties with his own financial affairs added to Cunard's concern over the lower-than-expected profits of the steamship contract. Although he blamed his brother Joseph's loose business methods for their financial crises, he himself was overextended because of his Prince Edward Island land purchases and his borrowing to pay Robert Napier, and because the sailing ships built by Joseph and Samuel were selling slowly. These problems coincided with a cyclical downturn in the British economy. When Cunard, Ingram, and Company in London (formed to handle Cunard's interests in England) failed to accept drafts, it precipitated the crisis of 1842.

On 25 Sept. 1841 Cunard had borrowed £15,000 sterling from the British and North American Royal Mail Steam Packet Company for two years and mortgaged his 110 original shares and all rights in the company and in five steam vessels registered in Glasgow. Profits and dividends on shares of stock and commissions due to Cunard or his son Edward as the company's agent in North America were to be used to pay interest on the loan and to pay up the stock subscription. Samuel was allowed five per cent on the gross earnings of the ships (which amounted to about £8,000 to £10,000 annually). This sum was to be placed to his credit until the steamship shares were fully paid up; then his creditors would receive any profits made.

Cunard was considered to be one of the wealthiest men in Nova Scotia when he suddenly departed London for Halifax by one of his steam-

ships to escape a writ of attachment for £2,000 taken out against him by Leyland and Bullen, Liverpool bankers. Cunard's escape in March 1842 had been assisted by Duncan Gibb, a timber merchant and for many years Liverpool agent for Pollok, Gilmour, and Company, who had hidden him in a cottage and then provided a boat to row him out after the steamer had left her moorings. Cunard had arranged with most of his creditors for three years in which to discharge his obligations. His property was mortgaged for £47,000 and he owed about £130,000 sterling but claimed assets of £257,000.

Acting as his father's attorney in March 1842, Edward Cunard Jr was trying to collect as much money as possible, and even sold his father's farm in Rawdon. William Henry Pope* later claimed that three lots purchased in Prince Edward Island in 1839 for £9,600 were resold in 1842 for £25,000. On 9 and 11 March 1842 Samuel Cunard and his brother Edward mortgaged their warehouses, wharves, and premises on the east side of Water Street in Halifax for £9,000 at 6 per cent interest to Samuel's good friend, Stephen Wastie DeBlois, a merchant and auctioneer at Halifax. John Duffus, Cunard's brother-in-law and a dry goods merchant, used his influence with the directors of the Bank of Nova Scotia and the Bank of British North America, of which Cunard was a director, to provide assistance in preventing his bankruptcy. A special meeting was held by the directors of the Bank of Nova Scotia on 5 April 1842, and four days later a directors' by-law was suspended to allow a £45,000 loan secured by Duffus. The president of the bank, Mather Byles Almon*, along with Duffus, Alexander Murison, James Boyle Uniacke*, and Joseph Starr, became trustees for the property of Samuel, Edward, and Joseph Cunard. In June and July 1842 the Bank of Nova Scotia reluctantly paid £4,000 sterling to enable the Cunards to liquidate the debt due to Leyland and Bullen to prevent a fiat of bankruptcy being issued against Samuel.

The trustees of Cunard's English creditors were Charles Walton, William George Prescott, and Robert Carter, all leading London businessmen. Among creditors were the Bank of Liverpool, North and South Wales Bank, and Prescott's bank in London, as well as others who had probably advanced shipbuilding supplies or were commission merchants.

Cunard was 55 years old in 1842 and might have been looking forward to some relaxation, perhaps retiring to a small estate as did many English merchants. He must have enjoyed being entertained in London, at parties given by such hostesses as Mrs Caroline Sheridan Norton, and

Cunard

his difficulties must have hurt his pride. He had to give up his directorship in the Bank of British North America. The English creditors allowed the Cunards living expenses but they could not leave their places of business in Nova Scotia and New Brunswick without permission from the trustees, and Edward Jr and Robert Morrow had to go to England for the firm. Ironically, in the midst of Samuel's financial crisis the citizens of Boston forwarded a large silver vase as a testimonial to the frequent, rapid, and safe steamship service between Liverpool, Halifax, and Boston.

Resolutely Samuel devoted his attention to the widespread interests of the Cunards. Shipbuilding activities were increased both in New Brunswick and at Alexander Lyle's shipyard in Dartmouth. In the fall of 1845 Cunard was one of the sponsors of a meeting to discuss the controversial proposal of an English company to construct a railway from Halifax to Quebec [see W. S. MOORSOM], but the project collapsed amidst personal and political rivalries. Samuel and Edward Sr attempted to separate their business from Joseph's and the co-partnership was advertised to be dissolved on 31 Dec. 1845. But late in 1847 Joseph Cunard's enterprise on the Miramichi collapsed and during 1848 the timber trade in New Brunswick dropped to one-third of the 1847 value. As Joseph's ships and timber remained unsold in Liverpool, he admitted that the burden of his misfortunes in business had "in a great measure fallen" on his brother Samuel. Nevertheless, profits from the steamship company steadily paid off the loan borrowed from the Nova Scotia trustees and a formal deed was signed 1 April 1846 reconveying the steamship company stock to Samuel and his son. It is estimated that they received about £20,000 a year between 1841 and 1844 from commissions for the agency in Halifax and Boston and from dividends on the stock. The Bank of Nova Scotia loan was paid off on 11 Dec. 1850.

Cunard must have been delighted to resume his visits to Britain and to take a more active part in the steamship company. Even before his brother Edward died in 1851, Samuel evolved the pattern of travelling back and forth between England, Nova Scotia, Boston, and New York. With the help and experience of Henry Boggs, a longtime Halifax employee, he let his younger son William and his nephew James Bain Morrow run the Halifax firm, which was finding the GMA agency increasingly profitable. One or two of his daughters usually accompanied him on his visits to England.

In the negotiations of 1846 for the renewal of the mail contract of the steamship company, Cunard revealed great diplomacy and tenacity. Merchants and manufacturers in England objected to the renewal and the Great Western Steam-Ship Company of Bristol appealed for an open competition. The chancellor of the exchequer, Henry Goulburn, in defending the Cunard contract, differentiated the company from its competitors and stated that "this establishment owed its origin entirely to the activity of the colonists of Nova Scotia and its neighbourhood, and he for one would be sorry to do anything against the zeal and activity of the colonists." A ten-year contract with Cunard, George Burns, and Charles MacIver, with a yearly subsidy of £145,000, provided for weekly voyages from Liverpool alternating to Boston and New York after 1 Jan. 1848. By that date both the company and the British Post Office realized the necessity of New York sailings because of competition with the Oceanic Steam Navigation Company. Edward Cunard Jr was transferred to the New York office, and in 1849 married the daughter of a New York merchant. MacIver had become sole partner of D. and C. MacIver after his brother David's death in 1845, and in the next three decades became the leading figure among Liverpool shipowners. By 1867 the Burns, Cunard, and MacIver families owned all the shares in the company.

In the 1850s the English line had intense competition from the American Collins Line, which had faster, larger, and more luxurious ships and twice as large a subsidy from the American government, and from the Inman Line which by 1857 was carrying one third of the Atlantic passenger trade. The Cunard line met this increased competition with bigger ships, which recaptured the speed record from Collins and then lost it again. After two of Collins' steamers were shipwrecked, the Cunards stressed their reputation for safety. The competition ended when the Collins Line became bankrupt in 1858, but by the mid 1860s a score of companies were competing for passengers on the transatlantic route, and the Cunard firm had to turn to iron screwships which were more economical with coal consumption and which had more space, despite Cunard's preference for paddle-wheelers.

Cunard always seemed able to reach an understanding with the officials controlling post office contracts, for he wrote from London to his daughter Jane on 24 May 1850: "I have succeeded in making some very good arrangements about my contract have got it extended four years beyond the former period & some other advantages – they are always very good to me." The

Canadian government wished arrangements to be made on the termination of the existing Cunard contract for the St Lawrence mail service to be transferred to the Allan Line (owned by Hugh Allan* of Montreal), but while negotiations were still underway, the Cunard contract was renewed four years early. This 1858 contract required the Cunard line to provide at least eight vessels of 400 h.p., and weekly service from Liverpool to New York and a fortnightly service to Halifax and Boston for an annual subsidy of £173,340. The Cunard steamer stopped calling at Halifax after 1867.

The British government supported Cunard in part because of the strong recommendations from naval and military officers about the fitness of the Cunard vessels for war purposes and their more efficient convertibility into men-of-war as compared with any other vessels under contract for the packet service. With the outbreak of the Crimean War, Cunard immediately placed his ships at the service of the British government and advised the Admiralty about obtaining and adapting other steamships for war service. Eleven ships of the Cunard fleet were used to carry troops, horses, and supplies to the Crimea and two became hospital ships. On 9 March 1859 in recognition of the valuable services rendered by the steamship line, particularly during the Crimean War, Cunard was knighted.

Samuel had given his English residence as his permanent address for the first time on the 1858 contract, the year George Burns retired from active management in the company, but Cunard continued to maintain his home in Halifax also. Only his youngest daughter Elizabeth remained with her father; the others had married English army officers stationed at Halifax.

Cunard was still regarded by the Colonial Office as an expert on the Maritime provinces. By 1860 he had become the largest and most influential land proprietor in Prince Edward Island and was considered by the British government to be the landlords' spokesman. When the Island legislature requested a special land commission to settle disputes between landlords and tenants on the Island, the Duke of Newcastle consulted Cunard about appointments to the proposed commission. Not all the proprietors agreed to be bound by the commission's award but the most important did. The commission discovered that Cunard had 971 tenants in 16 townships on 999-year leases with terms of 1s. sterling per acre; the 64,889 acres leased (out of 134,293) should have paid £3,435 annually, but the average rent collected for the previous three years had been only £2,310. Some tenants had paid in cash and some in produce. By 1860 arrears of rent amounted to £17,073. In 1859 Cunard's agent, George W. Deblois, had remitted profits of about £2,000 in Island currency to Cunard in London.

The land commission proposed that the operation of the Land Purchase Act of 1853, brought in by George Coles*' Liberal government, should be extended to the whole Island, the British Treasury guaranteeing the sum of £100,000, and that a system of compulsory sale by arbitration should be organized. Immediately upon publication of the commissioners' report in the Island newpapers, Cunard was writing to Newcastle on 2 Oct. 1861 as "one of the largest proprietors in the Island" to object to the proposal that the tenants be allowed to have their farms valued by arbitrators. He argued that although the maximum purchase price was to be the value of the rent for 20 years, the arbitrators might decide that a fair price was two or three years' rent. He feared that arbitration would subject the proprietor to enormous costs – perhaps half the value of the farm. Newcastle vetoed the Island assembly's attempt to implement the commissioners' proposals. Many Islanders blamed the influence of the London proprietors for the British government's refusal to provide funds to buy out the landlords and for not forcing them to compulsory sale by arbitration. Because Cunard and other landlords knew the Islanders would be disappointed by the failure of the commission, they made another offer after consultation among themselves, to be open for a five-year period from 1 May 1862, which would let tenants buy land at a price equivalent to 15 years' annual rent. The Executive Council of Prince Edward Island refused it.

All the proprietors found it difficult to collect their rents during the ensuing agitation sparked by the Tenant League. Cunard wrote to the Colonial Office on 24 Feb. 1863: "There is no tenant on the Island who cannot pay his rent, if he is industrious and sober," but pointed out that "while the agitation is kept up by designing people, rent will not be paid nor money laid up to purchase farms; time is wasted and money spent in attending political meetings." That year the Island government had appointed Edward Palmer* and W. H. Pope to proceed to England to confer with the Colonial Office and the landlords. In October their request for implementation of the land commission's recommendations was forwarded by the Colonial Office to Cunard who objected to forgiving arrears of rent and to the proposed terms of sale to tenants. He pointed out that from 1841 to 1862 he had paid £8,641 for land taxes to the Island government on his own

Cunard

and his son's uncultivated lands, at a rate double that of cultivated land. Since the devaluation of Island currency reducing the pound sterling to 16s., Cunard claimed, the value of his rent and sales of land had been lowered by 25 per cent. He compared the 1863 rent paid by his tenants on the Island to that paid by a farm labourer in Britain "who cannot get shelter for his family for double that rate per week."

Pope declared that the Island was "Ireland on a small scale," vigorously disputed many of Cunard's contentions, and called upon the landlords to compromise. The Colonial office listened to Cunard's demand that neither the Island legislature nor the imperial government should interfere "with our property, in any manner different from that in which private estates in England could be dealt with." Despite these years of argument, the Cunard holdings of 212,885 acres were sold to the Island government in July 1866, a year after Cunard's death, for $257,933.30; the rents had become difficult to collect, and cash was needed to pay the legacies left to his daughters.

In his will Cunard left his real and personal estate to his sons Edward and William and £20,000 to each of his six daughters. In June 1865 Henry Boggs wrote from London to M. B. Almon: "I miss our old friend Sir Samuel C – I think he has left £600,000 – this is a good large sum for him to have accumulated since *the date* that you and I remember him to have had little or nothing – so much for Steam in 20 Years. . . ." Other sources estimated his fortune as £350,000.

Although early in life Cunard was imperious, he learned diplomacy and became a skilful and persuasive negotiator. His contemporaries admired him for the contribution to transatlantic communication by the line popularly called by his name. Without Cunard's prestige and diplomacy, the contract signed after his death in 1867 was far less favourable, paying only £80,000 annually for a weekly service from Liverpool to New York. Dividends which had been eight per cent under the old partners, dropped to two per cent or less.

In the early years of his career Cunard took a prominent part in community activities, St George's Anglican Church in Halifax, and various charitable organizations as well as mercantile affairs which extended throughout the Atlantic provinces. Although he supported the Halifax Mechanics' Institute with a handsome donation when it was organized in 1832, and was praised as "a gentleman whose purse is never closed when a good work needs encouragement," he did not take an active part in its meetings. He was one of the charter members of the Halifax Athenaeum

established in December 1834. Most of his local activities were tapering off in the 1850s; he ceased to be lieutenant-colonel of the 2nd battalion of the Halifax militia in 1857, and after 19 years as president of the Halifax Steam Boat Company, he resigned in 1855. One of his first official appointments, on 9 April 1816, had been as commissioner of lighthouses on the Nova Scotia coasts. He retained his interest in lighthouses for the rest of his career, and in 1852, when he was consulted on the subject by Provincial Secretary Joseph Howe, he stated: "Altho I am occasionally absent from home I leave behind me those who are competent to do the duty and when I am here I do not spare myself and my experience may be considered worth something."

Cunard was gratefully remembered for employing his capital in shipbuilding activities in the hard times of the 1830s because this enterprise had circulated money "where there would otherwise be poverty and stagnation." He could be ruthless to a rival or an enemy, but, although legally he could have refused to assume Joseph's debts, the Halifax firm gradually made payments to the creditors year after year.

In the opinion of William James Stairs*, Cunard was "the ablest man I have ever known as a merchant of Halifax" – "he made both men and things bend to his will." His competitiveness and his obsession not to waste time were important characteristics of his personality. Peter Lynch, a prominent Halifax barrister, recalled Cunard as cool, calculating, a man of keen perception whose whole mind was devoted to carrying out any project he had in hand. Nevertheless Cunard was admired at home and abroad as a successful colonial and for his contributions to the steamship trade. He was one of the first native Nova Scotians to build a business empire, but, like the successful British businessmen and officials who made their fortunes in the colonies, he retired to England where his descendants settled. True to his family motto "By perseverance" he had overcome obstacles to become an English merchant prince.

PHYLLIS R. BLAKELEY

[Although many libraries and repositories and museums have items about the Cunard Steamship Company, no large collection of the letters and papers of Samuel Cunard himself has been located. The account books, ledgers, and letter books of the Halifax branch of S. Cunard and Company were destroyed when the firm's north pier and the Cunard office building and warehouse were demolished in 1911 and 1917. The attic of the old warehouse had been full of chests of old manuscripts and business papers and Dr Archibald

MacMechan* was told that it took three months to burn them on the wharf.

In 1919 Mr J. Noble Foster, managing director of S. Cunard and Company of Halifax, found 44 documents in the attic of Cunard Coal Company which were presented to the PANS. These documents are stock, dividend, and agency accounts of the British and North American Royal Mail Steam Packet Company from 1840 to 1847, some correspondence with Samuel Cunard's partners, George Burns and David MacIver, and with the British Post Office, and the Pictou mail contract.

The Cunard Steamship Company archives were deposited at Liverpool University in 1973, and cover the period from about 1840 to 1945. However, most of the manuscript material dates from the incorporation of the company in 1878, and there is little from the period when it was a private partnership and when Samuel Cunard was active. Professor Francis E. Hyde has been commissioned to write a history of the Cunard Steamship Company and an inventory is being prepared. There is material collected by the publicity department of the company and copies of Cunard material from other repositories.

There are letters from Samuel Cunard in the official correspondence of the Maritime provinces and Quebec, and the Colonial Office, Secretary of State, Admiralty, War Office, Post Office and Treasury, and the East India Company. There are several letters to Robert Napier in the Glasgow Museums and Art Galleries, and some personal letters to his daughter Jane (Mrs G. W. Francklyn) which were handed down to his descendants are now at the Public Archives of Nova Scotia. P.R.B.]

Bank of Nova Scotia Archives (Toronto), Customer ledger, 1841–50 (A5:C3); President's letterbook, 1832–40 (A3:B2); President's private minute book, 1834–56 (A3:A1). Glasgow Museums and Art Galleries, Dept. of Technology, Napier papers, S. Cunard to R. Napier, 13 June 1840, and another dated Thursday morning. Halifax County Court House (Halifax), Registry of deeds, index, 1749–1861 (mfm. at PANS). Halifax County Court of Probate (Halifax), no.C189, will of Abraham Cunard; no.422, estate of Edward Cunard; no.1772, copy of will of Sir Samuel Cunard (mfm. at PANS). Hants County Court House (Windsor, N.S.), Registry of deeds, book 11:157, 159; 26:296 (mfm. at PANS). India Office Records (London), [East India House Archives], B/177 – B/178, Court minutes, 1824–26; E/1/156 – E/1/162, Miscellaneous letters received, 1825–28; Z/B/29 – Z/B/96, Index of court minutes, 1824–58. Mariners' Museum (Newport News, Va.), Indenture between Samuel, Joseph, and Edward Cunard, and Charles Walton, William George Driscoll, and Robert Carter, 11 April 1842 (photocopy in N.B. Museum). N.B. Museum, Ward family papers, Business correspondence, British agency correspondence; Bainbridge & Brown, 1822–33; Firm of John Ward & Sons records, Letterbooks, 1832–36, 1839–44. Postal Headquarters Archives (London), POST 51/12, 1839–54, Samuel Cunard, Boston – Halifax, etc., Contracts; POST 51/16, 1841–58, Samuel Cunard, George Burns, David MacIver, United Kingdom – Nova

Scotia, etc., Contracts; POST 51/41, 1867–68, Edward Cunard, John Burns, Charles MacIver, United Kingdom – New York and Boston, Contracts; POST 51/42, 1867, William Cunard, Henry Boggs, J. B. Foord, Halifax, Bermuda and St Thomas, Contracts; POST 51/91, 1853, American mail service, Formation by Samuel Cunard, Correspondence. PAC, MG 24, B29, 43 (mfm. at PANS); RG 8, IV, 130, 136, 138, 160–61; RG 42, I, 9–42. PANS, MG 1, 18–83 (M. B. Almon papers, 1827–68); 248 (Sir Samuel Cunard papers); MG 2, 724–25; MG 12, 2d, nos.3, 4; RG 1, 63–89, 112–19, 225–61, 291–95, 304–14, 458–61, 501 A; RG 5, P, 57–59, 119–25; RG 20, A; RG 31, Treasury papers, Impost and excise, 1812–39; Light duties, 1810–39; Customs permits, 1831–39; RG 39, J, 7–80. PAPEI, P.E.I., Records of land registration, General indexes to 1872; Rent books, Cunard estate. PRO, CO 217/146, ff.36, 41; 217/150, f.345; 217/152, ff.65–70; 226/94–96; T 28/20, p.40 (transcript at PAC). University of Liverpool Library, Cunard Steamship Company records. G. B., Parl., House of Commons paper, 1839, XLVI, 566, pp.271–78, *Mails conveyance contract* . . . ; 1846, XLV, 464, pp.195–232, *Halifax mails: Halifax and United States mail contract* . . . ; 1851, LI, 406, pp.37–38, *Mail steamers (Halifax and United States)* . . . ; 1864, XLI, 528, pp.649–802, *Prince Edward Island: return to an address* . . . . G. R. Young, *A statement of the "Escheat question," in the island of Prince Edward; together with the causes of the late agitation, and the remedies proposed* (London, 1838). *Liverpool Transcript*, 18 May 1865. *Novascotian*, 1824–50. *Weekly Chronicle* (Halifax), 1808–21. *Belcher's farmer's almanack*, 1825–65. *Burke's peerage* (1953). *East India register and army list* (London), 1845–60. *East-India register and directory* (London), 1825–44. *Gore's directory for Liverpool and its environs* . . . (Liverpool), 1839–64. *Memoirs and portraits of one hundred Glasgow men who have died during the last thirty years* . . . (2v., Glasgow, 1886). B. G. Orchard, *The second series of the Liverpool Exchange portrait gallery: being lively biographical sketches of some gentlemen known on the flags* . . . (Liverpool, 1884), 104–12. F. L. Babcock, *Spanning the Atlantic* (New York, 1931). P. R. Blakeley, *Glimpses of Halifax, 1867–1900* (Halifax, 1949). F. W. P. Bolger, *Prince Edward Island and confederation, 1863–1873* (Charlottetown, 1964). J. M. Brinnin, *The sway of the grand saloon: a social history of the north Atlantic* (New York, 1971). G. F. Butler, "Commercial relations of Nova Scotia with the United States, 1783–1830" (unpublished MA thesis, Dalhousie University, Halifax, 1934). J. M. Cameron, *The Pictonian colliers* (Halifax, 1974). *Canada's smallest province* (Bolger). Esther Clark Wright, *The Miramichi: a study of the New Brunswick river and of the people who settled along it* (Sackville, N.B., 1944). H. C. Conrad, *1683–1891, Thones Kunders and his children* . . . (Wilmington, Del., 1891). [H.] K. Grant, *Samuel Cunard, pioneer of the Atlantic steamship* (London and Toronto, 1967). Edwin Hodder, *Sir George Burns, bart., his times and friends* (London, 1892). F. E. Hyde, *Liverpool and the Mersey: an economic history of a port, 1700–1970* (Newton Abbot, Eng., 1971). A. A. Lomas, "The in-

185

Cunnabell

dustrial development of Nova Scotia, 1830–1854" (unpublished MA thesis, Dalhousie University, Halifax, 1950). A. R. M. Lower, *Great Britain's woodyard; British America and the timber trade, 1763–1867* (Montreal and London, 1973). Archibald MacMechan, *Samuel Cunard* (Toronto, 1928); also published as "The rise of Samuel Cunard," *Dal. Rev.*, IX (1929–30), 202–10. Louise Manny, *Ships of Miramichi: a history of shipbuilding on the Miramichi River, New Brunswick, Canada, 1773–1919* (Saint John, N.B., 1961). James Napier, *Life of Robert Napier of West Shandon* (Edinburgh and London, 1904). B. G. Orchard, *Liverpool's legion of honour* (Birkenhead, Eng., 1893). Ann Parry, *Parry of the Arctic: the life story of Admiral Sir Edward Parry, 1790–1855* (London, 1963). C. H. Philips, *The East India Company, 1784–1834* (2nd ed., Manchester, 1961). John Rankin, *A history of our firm, being some account of the firm of Pollok, Gilmour and Co. and its offshoots and connections, 1804–1920* (2nd ed., Liverpool, 1921). Ross and Trigge, *History of the Canadian Bank of Commerce*, I. Frank Staff, *The transatlantic mail* (Southampton, Eng., and New York, 1956). W. J. Stairs, *Family history, Stairs, Morrow; including letters, diaries, essays, poems, etc*. (Halifax, 1906). J. C. Arnell, "Samuel Cunard and the Nova Scotia government vessels *Earl Bathurst* and *Chebucto*," *Mariner's Mirror* (Cambridge, Eng.), 54 (1968), 337–47. R. G. Graves, "Letter about the parents of Sir Samuel Cunard," *Truro Weekly News* (Truro, N.S.), 21 Nov. 1957. D. C. Harvey, "Hopes raised by steam in 1840," CHA *Report*, 1940, 16–25. "The Honourable Samuel Cunard, and ocean steam navigation," *Provincial, or Halifax Monthly Magazine*, II (1853), 29–36. T. E. Hughes, "The Cunard story," *Sea Breezes* (Liverpool), new ser., 39 (1965), 503–19, 584–600, 663–81, 742–63. Peter Lynch, "Early reminiscences of Halifax – men who have passed from us," N.S. Hist. Soc., *Coll.*, XVI (1912), 194–96. J. S. Martell, "Early coal mining in Nova Scotia," *Dal. Rev.*, XXV (1945–46), 156–72. A. M. Payne, "The life of Sir Samuel Cunard, founder of the Cunard Steamship Line, 1787–1865," N.S. Hist. Soc., *Coll.*, XIX (1918), 75–91. Richard Rice, "The Wrights of Saint John: a study of shipbuilding and shipowning in the Maritimes, 1839–1855," *Canadian business history, selected studies, 1497–1971*, ed. D. S. Macmillan (Toronto, 1972), 317–37.

CUNNABELL (Cunnable), WILLIAM, printer and publisher; b. 24 May 1808 in Halifax, N.S., son of John Cunnabell and Nancy Leonard; m. 7 Aug. 1842 Margaret Athol, *née* Dechman, and they had six children; d. 31 Dec. 1868 of dropsy in Halifax.

William Cunnabell shared what seem to have been family characteristics of quiet integrity, willingness to innovate, friendliness, and a dislike of contention and discord. He served his printer's apprenticeship in Halifax with Philip J. Holland of the *Acadian Recorder*, and about 1836 took over the printing and publishing business of his brother, Jacob Sparling Cunnabell, which had originated in 1824 with the publication of the first monthly newspaper in Nova Scotia, the *Acadian Magazine; or, Literary Mirror*. During his 30-year business career, William Cunnabell was associated with the publication of a host of newspapers in Nova Scotia, though he seldom assumed much editorial control. One of these, the *Morning Herald and General Advertiser*, which appeared in the early 1840s, was the first penny paper in Nova Scotia. Prominent among his publications were Methodist periodicals, beginning with the *Methodist Quarterly*, the *Christian Gleaner*, and the *Wesleyan* in the 1830s, and including the *Provincial Wesleyan* in the 1840s. In fact, the volume of material he published for the Methodist Church indicates that during this period he was probably its unofficial printer and publisher. In addition, Cunnabell undertook to publish periodicals aimed at improving the cultural life of colonial society, such as the *Pearl*, a weekly "devoted to polite literature, science, and religion" which was sold to John Sparrow THOMPSON in 1837, and the *Psalmody Reformer*, a monthly journal with "a simple and comprehensive method of imparting instruction in vocal music" and including what may have been the first sheet music to be printed in the province. Like most colonial publications of the time, Cunnabell's papers were usually short-lived. Apparently not enough Nova Scotians were willing or able to take out the subscriptions necessary to guarantee financial stability.

In 1839, to improve his expanding and diversified enterprise, Cunnabell imported a new "Washington" press. Probably the most important publication to come off his press during these years was *The Nova-Scotia almanack*, first issued by his brother Jacob in 1834. William Cunnabell continued it after 1837, twice changing its name; it lasted until 1861, when fire on the premises ended this publication. The Cunnabell issues were undoubtedly the most artistic and innovative of all the early Nova Scotia almanacs, with especially beautiful woodcuts to grace the calendars. Although *Belcher's farmer's almanack* was longer lived, was probably more financially successful, and averaged about 80 pages to Cunnabell's 60, its format and contents changed little; Cunnabell's almanacs, on the other hand, were more varied, including from time to time featured articles on British royalty, ships' signals, and a calendar of local events for the past year. Cunnabell also published *Cunnabell's city almanac and general business directory* in 1842, one of the first compendiums of its kind in the province.

In addition, Cunnabell did a variety of general job printing for the Halifax community. His advertisements boasted of facilities to print "Commercial and Law Blanks, Exhibition, Business, and Visiting Cards, Small and Large Bills and Posters," as well as "Book and Rule Printing, Circulars, Music Printing, &c," with a special service of "Printing on Satin and Parchment." Numerous pamphlets were printed, including religious, scientific, and political tracts, poetry, and military guidebooks. The books printed or published by Cunnabell's firm represented a fair proportion of local printing of the time, and tended to deal with religious themes. Among these books were John William Dering GRAY's *A brief view of the scriptural authority and historical evidence of infant baptism . . .* (Halifax, 1837), Matthew Richey*'s *A memoir of the late Rev. William Black . . .* (Halifax, 1839), T. B. Akins*' *A sketch of the rise and progress of the Church of England in the British North American provinces* (Halifax, 1849), and J. G. Marshall*'s *Sermons on some of the principal doctrines and duties of Christianity* (Halifax, 1862). The Cunnabell establishment also published the Gospel of St John in the Micmac tongue.

William Cunnabell's publications reflect little of the political and sectarian quarrels of the period. Although the printer was a Methodist and was obviously given the patronage of the Methodist community, the religious controversies represented in his publications were mainly doctrinal in nature. It was his deliberate policy to present "news without views" and to publish items of literary and artistic merit. Seemingly rather conservative in outlook, Cunnabell was, at the same time, willing to experiment with a variety of publishing projects and to spend money and effort in improving his printing business.

GERTRUDE TRATT

[William Cunnabell was associated with the publication of the following Halifax newspapers: *Acadian Magazine; or, Literary Mirror*, 1826–28; *Acadian Telegraph*, 1837–38; *Advertiser and Business Directory*, 1849–?; *Christian Gem*, 1845; *Christian Gleaner*, 1833–38; *Methodist Quarterly*, 1832–38; *Monthly Magazine*, 1830–33; *Morning Herald and Commercial Advertiser*, 1840–42; *Morning Herald and General Advertiser*, 1843–48; *Morning News*, 1840s; *New Era*, 1851–?; *Nova Scotia and New Brunswick Wesleyan Methodist Magazine*, 1832; *Pearl*, 1837; *Provincial Wesleyan*, 1839–56; *Psalmody Reformer*, 1853–?: *Reporter*, 1860–64; *Weekly Miscellany*, 1863–64; *Wesleyan*, 1838–40; *Youth's Preceptor*, 1853–?. Cunnabell also published *The Nova-Scotia almanack* (Halifax), 1837–41, *Cunnabell's Nova-Scotia almanac* (Halifax), 1842–50; *Cunnabell's Nova*

Scotia almanac, and farmer's manual (Halifax), 1851–59, 1861; and *Cunnabell's city almanac and general business directory, for the year of our Lord 1842* (Halifax, 1842). G.T.]

Brunswick Street United Church (Halifax), records, 1829–1902 (mfm. at PANS). PANS, MG 5, Camp Hill Cemetery (Halifax), register of burials, August 1844 – December 1878 (mfm.); RG 1, 451; RG 5, P. 59, 123; RG 35, A, 1–3, Halifax assessments, 1817–41. St Matthew's Presbyterian Church (Halifax), session papers, 1819–1936 (mfm. at PANS). E. J. Connable and J. B. Newcomb, *Genealogical memoir of the Cunnabell, Conable, or Connable family, John Cunnabell of London, England, and Boston, Massachusetts, and his descendants* (2v., Jackson, Mich., 1886–1935), I, 145, 147, 151. *Halifax, N.S., business directory, for 1863 . . .*, comp. Luke Hutchinson (Halifax, 1863). H. W. Hopkins, *City atlas of Halifax, Nova Scotia, from actual surveys and records* ([Halifax], 1878). *Hutchinson's Nova Scotia directory, for 1864–65 . . .*, comp. Thomas Hutchinson (Halifax, [1864]). *McAlpine's Halifax city directory . . .* (Halifax), 1875–86. Tratt, "Survey of N.S. newspapers." F. E. Crowell, "New Englanders in Nova Scotia," *Yarmouth Herald* (Yarmouth, N.S.), 10 Nov. 1931 (copy in PANS, scrapbook 109, p.168). D. C. Harvey, "Newspapers of Nova Scotia, 1840–1867," *CHR*, XXVI (1945), 279–99.

CUTHBERT, ROSS, co-seigneur, lawyer, politician, and pamphleteer; b. 17 Feb. 1776, baptized 25 February in Montreal's Christ Church (Anglican), third son of James Cuthbert* Sr, from whom he inherited the seigneuries of Lanoraie and Dautray, and Catherine Cairns; m. Emily Rush, at Philadelphia, and they had at least three children; d. 28 Aug. 1861 at Berthier-en-Haut (Berthierville), Canada East.

Ross Cuthbert received his secondary education at the English Catholic college in Douai (dept of Nord), France. He was called to the bar of Lower Canada in 1803 and apparently practised law at Quebec (1803–4), Montreal (1805–6), Trois-Rivières (1807–10), and then again at Montreal. The swift expansion of international trade and growing urban problems prompted Governor Sir James Henry Craig*, in January 1810, to appoint him inspector of police and president of the Court of Quarter Sessions at Quebec with an annual salary of £500; he continued to hold these offices until 1815. In his work, for example during the special sessions of the court dealing with the streets of Quebec (1816, 1818, 1819), Cuthbert showed his concern for stricter control of urban life. At the beginning of the War of 1812 Sir George Prevost* appointed Cuthbert an honorary member of the Executive Council, a post he held until 1824. In this capacity he helped draft an address of thanks to Prevost in 1813, and an address of support for Jonathan Sewell* in 1814 following criticisms by the assembly. Cuthbert was a member of the assembly at various times and also held numerous offices: commissioner for the administration of the Quebec penitentiary (1811–29); justice of the peace, at various times between 1810 and 1824, in the districts of Quebec, Montreal, Trois-Rivières, Saint-François, and Gaspé; commissioner for oaths from 1812 on; and member of the Royal Institution for the Advancement of Learning (1818–22?). He also took part in various movements and contributed to numerous causes: the Quebec Fire Society (1812), the Loyal and Patriotic Society (1813), commissions for the education of all classes (1815) and for the instruction of the poor (1816), and the Quebec Emigrant Society (1820). In 1817 he went to London to obtain from the cabinet an appointment as judge, which Craig and Prevost had allegedly promised him. After 1829 he seems to have retired from public life.

As representative for Warwick County in the House of Assembly of Lower Canada (1800–10, 1812–16, 1820), Cuthbert led an active political life. In 1815 some even thought of him as a candidate for speaker of the assembly. He systematically opposed the Parti Canadien (in 1809 he went so far as to denounce secretly a contributor to Le Canadien), and advocated the enlightened assimilation of French Canadians. In L'aréopage, published at Quebec in 1803, he deplored the ignorance of the French Canadian population, its blind attachment to a system of antiquated, dusty French laws, and the unscrupulousness of its lawyers. In 1809 he published An apology for Great Britain . . . to answer Denis-Benjamin VIGER's Considérations . . . (published earlier that year) and the arguments of the Canadiens in defence of their survival as a separate "nation." According to him, their dream was fanciful: they failed to recognize the basic fact that Lower Canada, a barely emerging colony, would be gradually developed by primarily British immigrants. The French Canadians, a tiny minority in

the empire and ultimately in their own province, an unambitious and listless people, had every interest in cooperating in their inevitable assimilation, which would bring a more homogeneous society and access to positions and trade. In 1810 Cuthbert tackled a totally different subject with his New theory of the tides, in which he attempted to explain the tides as the result of the evaporation of great bodies of water. In 1817, in London, he worked on another political pamphlet, "The character of passing events," which does not seem to have been published.

Seigneur, lawyer, active citizen, militant Britisher, Cuthbert was, like many merchants, a typical member of the British party in the House of Assembly of Lower Canada in the early 19th century.

JEAN-PIERRE WALLOT

Ross Cuthbert, L'aréopage (Québec, 1803); An apology for Great Britain, in allusion to a pamphlet, intituled, "Considérations, &c. par un Canadien, M.P.P." (Quebec, 1809); New theory of the tides (Quebec, 1810).
BUM, Coll. Baby, Corr. générale, lettres de Ross Cuthbert, 17 oct. 1806; 13 avril 1807; 22 janv., 13 juin, 25 oct. 1808; 5 avril 1814 (copies at PAC). PAC, MG 8, G19, 22; MG 24, B1, 1, p.419; RG 4, A1, S; B8, 18, pp.6446–49; RG 8, I (C series), 284, p.104; 374, p.71; 387, pp.58–59; 688E, pp.376, 438, 440; 689, p.137; 694, pp.34–36; 1218, p.414; 1221, p.96. PRO, CO 42/141, pp.173–76; 42/157, pp.75ff.; 42/170, p.110; 42/172, p.90; 42/177, pp.97, 118 (mfm. at PAC). Bas-Canada, chambre d'Assemblée, Journaux, 1791–1837; Conseil spécial, Journaux, 1838–41. Can., prov. du, Assemblée législative, Journaux, 1841–61. Le Canadien, 1809. Quebec Gazette, 1800–20. John Hare et J.-P. Wallot, Les imprimés dans le Bas-Canada, 1801–1840, bibliographie analytique (Montréal, 1967), nos.55, 194, 228. Le Jeune, Dictionnaire, I, 457. Morgan, Bibliotheca Canadensis, 88. Wallace, Macmillan dictionary, 168. Christie, History of L.C., II, 166. Édouard Fabre-Surveyer, "James Cuthbert, père, et ses biographes," RHAF, IV (1950–51), 74–89. Régis Roy, "Cuthbert," BRH, XL (1934), 627–29.

D

DALTON, JOHN, Franciscan priest and Roman Catholic bishop of Harbour Grace, Nfld; b. c. 1821 in Thurles, Tipperary (Republic of Ireland); d. 5 May 1869 at Harbour Grace.

In 1839 John Dalton arrived in Newfoundland where his uncle, Charles Dalton, was a Francis-

can priest at Carbonear. In 1840 John also entered the Franciscan Order and enrolled at St Isidore's College in Rome where he was ordained in 1849. He returned to Newfoundland later that same year. Dalton was then appointed curate at Carbonear to assist his uncle. When Charles Dalton was later transferred to Harbour Grace, John became parish priest in Carbonear. In the spring of 1856 Newfoundland was divided into two Roman Catholic dioceses, and on 1 June John Dalton was consecrated bishop of the newly created diocese of Harbour Grace, which included Labrador. For the first few years the new bishop continued to live at Carbonear but following the death of his uncle he moved in 1860 to Harbour Grace, which remained the episcopal seat of the diocese until it was moved to the industrial town of Grand Falls in 1956.

By the 1850s Newfoundland's Roman Catholic bishops were accustomed to playing significant roles in the political life of the Island. Dalton was no exception, and during the 1859 and 1861 elections he took an active part in the campaigns in his diocese, especially in the Harbour Grace and Harbour Main districts [see HOGSETT]. For these interventions he was roundly criticized by the Protestant Conservative press in St John's. Nevertheless, he was not as politically prominent as his older, more experienced colleague, Bishop John Thomas MULLOCK of St John's, who was a close friend of Liberal leader Philip Francis Little*.

Dalton was a busy and effective religious leader and administrator. He directed missionary activities on the Labrador coast by sending a priest there each summer with the migratory fishing crews, many of whom came from the town of Harbour Grace. He also improved the educational facilities in his diocese and commenced construction of the Harbour Grace Cathedral of the Immaculate Conception. His pastoral letter of 1 June 1865, in which he granted permission for Roman Catholic fishermen to fish on 15 August, the date of the Feast of the Assumption, provided they gave the proceeds of their day's catch to the church, is the earliest known documentary evidence of the origins of a custom still existing in some communities. It was also during his episcopacy that the first native Newfoundlander was ordained priest at Carbonear in 1856.

SHANNON RYAN

John Dalton's "Pastoral letter," 1 June 1865, is in the possession of Mgr J. M. O'Brien, Harbour Grace, Nfld. *Newfoundlander*, 1856, 1869. *Royal Gazette* (St. John's), 1869. *Centenary of the diocese of Harbour Grace, 1856–1956*, [ed. R. J. Connolly] (St John's, 1956). Gunn, *Political history of Nfld*. Prowse, *History of Nfld*. (1896).

DALY, Sir DOMINICK, civil servant, politician, and colonial administrator; b. 11 Aug. 1798 at Ardfry, County Galway (Republic of Ireland), son of Dominick Daly and Joanna Harriet Burke, *née* Blake; d. 19 Feb. 1868 in South Australia.

The ancient Daly family of Galway into which Dominick was born had, through natural ability and judicious intermarriage, joined the governing class by the end of the 16th century, and attained nobility by the mid 19th. Dominick's father, himself a commoner, had noble connections and his wife was the sister of Joseph Henry Blake, 1st Baron Wallscourt. Young Dominick, third son of this auspicious alliance, studied at the Roman Catholic St Mary's College, Oscott, near Birmingham. After school, and an extended visit to an uncle who was a banker in Paris, he returned to Ireland, where his family arranged his appointment as private secretary to Sir Francis Nathaniel Burton*, lieutenant governor of Lower Canada. In 1823 Daly went with Burton to Canada, prompted by the Colonial Office's warning that the Canadians would tolerate no more absentee office-holders.

In Lower Canada Daly worked hard and unobtrusively, while his employer so ingratiated himself with the French Canadians that in 1823 the assembly raised his salary and granted him a house rental allowance. Then, from 1824 until the autumn of 1825, Burton acted for Governor Dalhousie [Ramsay*] who was in England enlightening the Colonial Office about the problems of government in Canada. In an attempt to displace Dalhousie as governor, Burton endeavoured to undermine Dalhousie's policies, and King George IV had personally to intervene on the governor's behalf. In 1826, Daly returned with Burton to England, where Burton continued his campaign to ruin Dalhousie. Burton failed to have the governor ousted, but he did foist upon him young Daly who returned to Quebec in 1827 with instructions to Dalhousie to appoint him provincial secretary for Lower Canada.

Daly was to remit his £500 salary as provincial secretary to the former incumbent, absentee Thomas Amyot, retaining for himself the considerable fees accruing from the post. Amyot was a favourite in official London circles, and even in the new climate of opinion about absenteeism no minister whether Whig or Tory was willing to take any action more drastic than to suggest that the income be considered a pension rather than a salary. Daly was content to accept the arrangement, and was sworn to secrecy, as Lord Stanley explained, to prevent the assembly's certain refusal to grant his salary should it become known that Amyot was to receive it. Dalhousie, who wanted to select his own provincial secretary, protested bitterly against Daly's appointment. He charged that Daly was too young, irresponsible, and inexperienced for such an important position, but a Colonial Office re-evaluation vindicated Daly's qualifications and he retained the post.

As provincial secretary Daly was in charge of preparing all official documents, including proclamations, as directed by the governor either alone or in conjunction with the Legislative Council, and in his care was the official government correspondence. Daly followed Burton's example and ingratiated himself with his co-religionists, the French Canadians, by sympathizing with many of their grievances. His conscientiousness and impartiality in his work won respect and confidence, which made his post-rebellion transition from provincial secretary *cum* civil servant to provincial secretary *cum* politician so easy. Daly was also active in civic life, serving, for example, in 1836 on the administrative board of the new normal school in Quebec along with such notables as René-Édouard Caron*, mayor of Quebec, John Neilson*, and Hector-Simon Huot. Thus leading Canadians were exposed to his genial personality and old-fashioned gallantry which enhanced his hard-earned reputation for diligence, "integrity and usefulness." Personally, Daly had followed his family's model by marrying, on 20 May 1826, Caroline Maria Gore, third daughter of the influential Colonel Ralph Gore of Barrowmount, County Kilkenny, who was then on military service in Quebec.

At the time of the rebellions of 1837–38 Daly does not appear to have made any direct statement of his views, and this silence seems to have induced both sides to believe that he sympathized with them. After the rebellions Daly was one of the few high-ranking officials Lord Durham [Lambton*] retained in office, for such antagonists as Sir John COLBORNE and political leader Louis-Hippolyte LA FONTAINE both recommended Daly in superlatives. In Durham's administrative group, Daly was associated with such British radical Whigs as Edward Gibbon WAKEFIELD, with whom he was to retain close and politically significant ties.

Durham designed a new colonial administrative system, and Lord Sydenham [Thomson*] was to implement it. Daly alone of the Lower Canadian office-holders survived the transition into the union of the provinces. Under the old system his office had been non-partisan, but under the new régime of 1841 it was regarded as one to be obtained by election. Sydenham therefore persuaded Daly to resign and find a seat in the assembly. Daly successfully contested the Eastern Townships constituency of Mégantic,

and on 10 Feb. 1841 Sydenham appointed him provincial secretary for Canada East, and three days later a member of the Executive Council.

From 1841 until 1843 Conservatives and Reformers both found Daly an acceptable associate. Then and later he applied himself most diligently to his duties as provincial secretary, to which were added on 21 Dec. 1841 those of a member of the Board of Works. He gave these duties priority over routine parliamentary proceedings. He attended the assembly when possible but seldom participated, for though a charming conversationalist in private, he was not a good public speaker. In the council Daly believed it his duty to give freely of his long experience and to be as agreeable as possible. Thus his experience made him a valued member of Sydenham's first administration. In the session of 1842 he was equally valued by his colleagues in the reconstructed Reform administration led by Robert Baldwin* and La Fontaine, who voluntarily retained him as provincial secretary. They considered him a colleague in good standing throughout the administration of Sir Charles Bagot*, and, for a while, that of Sir Charles Theophilus Metcalfe*. It took the ministerial crisis of 1843 to define clearly Daly's political views.

Daly's personal amiability, his sympathy for the French Catholics of Lower Canada, and his diligence had been taken by the Reformers as proof of political compatibility. In reality, Daly was a truly non-political man who believed that a combination of conscientious attendance to duty and loyalty to the sovereign was sufficient to determine his fitness to retain office. When his colleagues began quarrelling with Governor Metcalfe over such issues as ministerial accountability for all legislation and the right to patronage, Daly supported the governor simply because he was, as governor, her majesty's representative in Canada. Soon Baldwin began to speak of forcing Metcalfe's hand by resigning along with the other members of the council. Forty-two years of age, without an independent income, believing that his office was a permanent one contingent merely on the governor's favour, Daly alone of Baldwin's colleagues demurred. It had been a total misreading of his character to expect him to resign for political reasons; in supporting Metcalfe in 1843 he was consistent with his own principles if not with those of his colleagues.

A month before they resigned, Daly's colleagues attempted to destroy his reputation by appointing a select committee to decide whether he should be impeached for having advised Lord Sydenham to appropriate the proceeds from the sale of marriage licences. The arrangement regarding Amyot was also exposed. The select committee completely exonerated Daly, but not before he had been publicly defended by Edward Gibbon Wakefield, his new political adviser and the self-styled confidant of the beleaguered Metcalfe. Wakefield disclosed the rift between Daly and his colleagues, which Baldwin denied as false and "grossly presumptuous," though within a few weeks that rift was to become public knowledge.

On 27 Nov. 1843 La Fontaine and Baldwin announced their resignation. Then, accompanied by all their colleagues except one, they filed off the treasury benches; Daly alone remained. Two days later, after Baldwin had presented the case of those who had resigned to the assembly, Daly outlined the governor's side of the issue: the governor refused to relinquish what he held to be prerogatives of the crown. Baldwin and his colleagues, on the other hand, stressed that their own accountability for the governor's actions required him to accept either their advice or their resignations.

For about nine months the ministry consisted of Daly, William Henry Draper*, and Denis-Benjamin VIGER. The accession of Viger and Draper to office bettered Daly's unenviable position, but for the next several months the governor was unable to find anyone else to join his three councillors. Henceforth Daly had to face the hostility of Reformers, who believed he had betrayed them. On one occasion the irrepressible drunkard Thomas Cushing Aylwin* became so provoked in the assembly that he challenged the phlegmatic Daly to a duel. The duel on 26 March 1845, one of Canada's last, was concluded without injury to either party, though shots were fired. Whenever possible, however, Daly maintained silence in the assembly. He preferred to concentrate on his official duties, which on 1 Jan. 1844 were expanded when he became provincial secretary for both sections of United Canada. By 2 Sept. 1844 three more appointments to the ministry had been made: Viger's cousin Denis-Benjamin Papineau*, William Morris*, and James SMITH. With these men as proof that he could manage without La Fontaine or Baldwin, Metcalfe called general elections, and the ministry was vindicated by a victory.

Daly himself was again returned for Mégantic. He continued to survive political upheavals, as well as the negotiations, in 1845 and 1847, between the Draper-Viger administration and various French Canadian Reform politicians, designed to achieve a ministry more responsive to the French Canadian majority from Lower Canada [see Draper; Caron]. The Reformers tried to make his exclusion a *sine qua non* of their entrance into a reconstructed council, but both times Daly's colleagues refused to sacrifice him. Nonetheless, though Daly retained his seat in the general elections of 1847–48, the Reformers won a majority in the assembly, and on 10 March 1848 La Fontaine and Baldwin replaced him and his colleagues in the council. For the first time since 1822, the "perpetual Secretary" was out of work.

The new governor, Lord Elgin [BRUCE], recognized Daly's case as one of "great hardship": "he resigned a permanent office on the introduction of Responsible Government, at the request of the Governor for the time being – by supporting Lord Metcalfe at the period of his rupture with his first council he rendered himself especially obnoxious to the Party who are now about to come into power. Deprived of office he has no means of subsistence. . . . No one in this Colony has in my opinion similar claims upon Her Majesty's Govt." Daly completely agreed, and hastened to seek reassurances from Elgin that he would be provided for. When they were forthcoming, he resigned his seat in parliament and returned to England, having first rejected Elgin's offer of the administration of a Bahamian island. In England, however, Daly was persuaded by Wakefield to make excessive demands on Lord Henry George Grey at the Colonial Office, which led Grey to refuse him any government in the colonial service. Instead, Daly was named to a commission inquiring into the condition and claims of the New and Waltham forests. He held this position until the close of the commission in 1850–51. The following year, 1852, he was finally given a minor government, the lieutenant governorship of Tobago in the West Indies. There he accomplished nothing, for ill health forced him to leave after only six months.

In 1854 Daly was transferred to Prince Edward Island as lieutenant governor. He arrived on 12 June 1854 and received a warm welcome; for the next five years he proceeded to justify it by the firmness, moderation, and ability with which he administered the Island, self-governing for only three years. Almost immediately after Daly's arrival, elections were held. The results were unfavourable to the Conservative government headed by John Myrie HOLL which thereupon resigned, in compliance with the tenets of responsible government. The new Liberal government of George Coles* struggled on over the years with decreasing majorities, until the assembly had to be dissolved a few months after the elections of July 1858. Lieutenant Governor Daly respected the workings of responsible government, despite a tendency to advise and counsel more than was necessary, and he followed the example of his predecessor Sir Alexander BANNERMAN in opposing any attempts to exclude the executive from the legislative branches, such as were planned by the Tory government which came to power in 1859 just after Daly left the colony. The first Catholic governor of the Island, Daly was mistrusted by the Conservative party whose supporters came in large measure from the Protestant population; they often accused him of partiality towards the Liberals.

Legislation during the Daly administration included formalizing the provisions of the Reciprocity Treaty of 1854, the controversial acquisition of the large Worrell Estate by the government [see William Henry Pope*], the incorporation of Charlottetown and of the Bank of Prince Edward Island in 1855, and the establishment of a normal school, formally opened by Daly in 1856.

The most serious issue in the Island was the land question. In Durham's words, when the Island was in the "very cradle of its existence," it had been given up "to a handful of distant proprietors." During Coles' term of office the Liberals endeavoured to remove some of the abuses of the large landholdings. In 1855, after a number of unsuccessful attempts at ameliorative legislation, they passed a limited measure on behalf of certain tenants and squatters being ejected from their lands which would indemnify them for improvements they had made. Daly was undoubtedly torn between his liberal sympathies and his respect for the rights of property, and he was eventually pleased that he had only to inform the house that the Colonial Office had rejected the bill, thus preserving his popularity in the Island.

In 1858 Daly announced his resignation in the same speech in which he mentioned the rumours of a federal union of British North America. On 19 May 1859 he prorogued the assembly and delivered his farewell address, rejoicing at the harmony which had existed between the different branches of government throughout his tenure of office. There had been in fact harmony only between himself and the Liberals. In the same month Daly left the Island, hailed as one of its most popular administrators, and honoured by having been named a knight bachelor in 1856.

Back in England, Daly waited almost two years for another post. It came in October 1861, and it was to South Australia which had once figured so largely in Wakefield's colonization schemes. Daly was to replace Sir Richard Graves MacDonnell* as governor and commander-in-chief, at a time when Australia was rough and turbulent, racist, and unsettled politically. In addition, his religion was an even more serious handicap than it had been in Prince Edward Island, where almost half of the population was Catholic. In Protestant South Australia his religion put him at a disadvantage faced by no other governor. Preceded and protected by no special reputation, he was at first attacked bitterly. Finally, in this country which had achieved responsible government only in 1855, where political parties were a thing of the future, and 40 years saw 41 governments formed on single issues, Daly's personality and impartiality erased the suspicions felt on account of his Catholicism.

Daly died "in harness" on 19 Feb. 1868, from the debilitating anaemia which had for some months given him a noticeable pallor and taken away much of his energy. He left behind Lady Daly and five children, four of whom continued to live in South Australia. A fifth, Malachy Bowes Daly*, later became lieutenant governor of Nova Scotia. At funeral services in Protestant churches across South Australia, the governor's popularity, his "troops of friends," his fairness and affability were eulogized and mourned.

Sir Dominick Daly was a colonial administrator of no special genius apart from luck and skill in finding influential sponsors and an ability to project an image of himself as a man of "high honor and integrity, of polished manners and courteous address – a good specimen of an Irish gentleman. . . . He was possessed of judgment and prudence, tact and discretion – in short, a man to be trusted." His conscientiousness and impartiality earned him the praises of men of all political persuasions in Canada, until his indifference to politics, his lack of "political passion," were so forcibly demonstrated in 1843. Only then did former friends and colleagues become bitter political enemies. Daly was an adherent of the old colonial system who tried to perpetuate that system in the Canadas long after it had been replaced by a new régime. Later, however, in Prince Edward Island and Australia, he respected the principles of responsible government, though he always gave priority to the rights of the crown and vested interests, priorities typical of a man of his aristocratic background. In all his colonial appointments he undertook to fulfil his duties creditably, and he served with distinction, if not with brilliance.

ELIZABETH GIBBS

Debates of the Legislative Assembly of United Canada, I–IV. *Elgin-Grey papers*, I, 118–19, 148, 184, 298–99, 319. *Examiner* (Charlottetown), 18 Nov. 1861, 18 May 1868. Hincks, *Reminiscences. Select documents in Australian history, 1851–1900*, ed. C. M. H. Clark (Sydney, 1955). Dent, *Canadian portrait gallery*, III, 69, 71. *Political appointments, 1841–65* (J.-O. Coté), 27, 41.

[M.] E. [Abbott] Nish, "Double majority: concept, practice and negotiations, 1840–1848" (unpublished MA thesis, McGill University, Montreal, 1966), 87–97, 151–233, 234–82. L.-P. Audet, *Le système scolaire*, VI, 117, 251–52. Paul Bloomfield, *Edward Gibbon Wakefield, builder of the British Commonwealth* ([London, 1961]), 268–69. L. C. Callbeck, *The cradle of confederation; a brief history of Prince Edward Island from its discovery to the present time* (Fredericton, 1964), 168. Duncan Campbell, *History of Prince Edward Island* (Charlottetown, 1875), 112–15, 119, 121. Gertrude Carmichael, *The history of the West Indian islands of Trinidad and Tobago, 1498–1900* (London, 1961), 311, 435. Leonard Cooper, *Radical Jack; the life of John George Lambton, first Earl of Durham, etc.* (London, 1959). Creighton, *Macdonald, young politician*. Davin, *Irishman in Can.*, 168, 431. Dent, *Last forty years*, I, 86–87, 300, 323–24; II, 123–24. R. S. Longley, *Sir Francis Hincks; a study of Canadian politics, railways, and finance in the nineteenth century* (Toronto, 1943). MacKinnon, *Government of P.E.I.*, 86, 97, 105–12. J. P. MacPherson, *Life of the Right Hon. Sir John A. Macdonald* (2v., St John's, 1891), I. Douglas Pike, *Australia: the quiet continent* (Cambridge, Eng., 1962), 105–26. *Racism or responsible government: the French Canadian dilemma of the 1840's*, trans. and ed. [M.] E. [Abbott] Nish (Toronto, 1967). Ernest Scott, *A short history of Australia* (6th ed., London, 1936), 209–84. Helen Taft Manning, *The revolt of French Canada, 1800–1835: a chapter in the history of the British Commonwealth* (Toronto, 1962), 140, 267. G. E. Wilson, *The life of Robert Baldwin; a study in the struggle for responsible government* (Toronto, 1933), 99, 101, 107.

DAOUST (D'Aoust), CHARLES, lawyer, journalist, and politician; b. 23 Jan. 1825 at Beauharnois, Lower Canada, son of Charles Daoust, farmer, and Françoise Dandurand; m. 16 Dec. 1856 Angèle Doutre, and they had one son; d. 27 Feb. 1868 at Montreal.

The year 1825 was an auspicious one for the small town of Beauharnois, for in an interval of two months two children were born there who, through the spoken and written word, would become leaders of the democrat or Rouge party: Charles Daoust and Joseph Doutre* (b. 11 March).

Charles Daoust's childhood was marked by the events of 1837–38, during which his father was imprisoned in Montreal. Young Charles had probably attended one of the two schools established at Beauharnois on 2 May 1830 in conformity with the 1829 primary school act. He had then received a classical education at Chambly, on the Richelieu, at the Collège de Saint-Pierre, founded in 1825 by Abbé Pierre-Marie MIGNAULT; the reputation of this establishment was enhanced by Abbé Charles La Rocque*, its director during 1835–36. Daoust entered the college in 1836, and proved a diligent and talented student. He excelled in Latin, Greek, and English and had a fervent but enlightened devotion to French literature. His favourite author was Chateaubriand; in poetry, Lamartine seems to have been a determining influence on his taste, judging by the romantic alexandrines of his "Douleur amère," a poem dated 1845 and published in *Le répertoire national*.

In 1844, under the influence of his mother, Daoust began to prepare for the priesthood, but the following year he turned to the study of law at Montreal under Irish lawyer Lewis Thomas Drummond*. He was called to the bar of Lower Canada on 27 Oct. 1847. In the same year, he was one of 13 contributors to *L'Avenir*, a Montreal newspaper that George Batchelor and Jean-Baptiste-Éric DORION had just started. Although the paper's articles were anonymous it was not long before the liveliness of Daoust's pen was noticed; he was, according to Laurent-Olivier David*, "an unusual writer." Thus, to attribute to him the little comedy, "La Tuque bleue," which appeared in early August 1848 in *L'Avenir* and which depicted George-Étienne Cartier* running away at top speed from the battle at Saint-Charles, required only a step, or rather a stride, which took the angry Cartier to the office of *L'Avenir*, where he furiously berated Daoust. Dorion tried to intervene, but Cartier brushed him aside contemptuously. In the end it was against Joseph Doutre that Cartier agreed to fight with pistols on the slopes of Mount Royal, then, when the police arrived unexpectedly, near Chambly. No blood was shed, but honour was saved!

The lawyer succeeded the journalist. Daoust was at Beauharnois in 1851 and practised law there. That year he lost his mother; two years earlier his only brother, Dr Roger Daoust, had died at sea. In Montreal, however, the brisk, neatly turned articles of the collaborator of *L'Avenir* had not been forgotten. In 1852 *Le Pays*, the new Montreal organ of the liberal cause, began publication with Louis-Antoine Dessaulles*, Louis Labrèche-Viger*, and Joseph-Adolphe Hawley as editors successively in its first year. In March 1853 an appeal was made to the practised pen and known dedication of Daoust, who became editor. His youthful petulance had been replaced by a moderate tone that fitted in perfectly with the orders of the owner, printer Jacques-Alexis Plinguet*, and the shareholders of the journal, who, according to Edmond Lareau*, had planned to "rally those who had been set at variance by *L'Avenir*'s effrontery and exaggerations." Thus, when the

Daoust

fiery Italian orator Alessandro Gavazzi paid a short visit to Montreal at the beginning of June 1853, Daoust disapproved of his "violent declarations" against Catholicism. "These questions are too thorny, in Canada above all," he commented, "for it to be prudent to raise them."

His enthusiastic yet circumspect editorials certainly played a large part in the success of the democrat candidates during the elections of 1854. He was elected MLA for the county of Beauharnois and his election was hailed by *Le Moniteur canadien* on 3 Aug. 1854 as "one of the finest triumphs of democracy." Even relentless opponents of the liberals, such as Joseph-Charles Taché* and Pierre-Joseph-Olivier Chauveau*, who used the pseudonym Gaspard Le Mage in their diatribe entitled *La pléiade rouge*, had to soften the sting of their satire in regard to Daoust, a "tall, unpolished, vigorous and not very handsome fellow, who none the less wins the affection and esteem of those who know him." According to them, "M. Daoust, with pen in hand, despite great presumptuousness and lack of refinement, has usually shown more tact and good sense than democracy customarily admits of."

Victory has an intoxicating quality. "The future belongs to democracy," Daoust exclaimed exultantly in a carefully developed editorial of *Le Pays*, on 29 Aug. 1854. He discerned in "that inviolable law which presides over the formation and development of societies . . . the will of the Creator, of the supreme legislator. . . . In Canada," he concluded, ". . . barely three centuries have passed and absolute government no longer exists except in our memories, and the nobility has completely disappeared; only the democratic element remains, standing on these two ruins, and it grows in spite of or rather because of the obstacles to its growth." One of the obstacles to the progress of Canadian democracy was certainly, in the eyes of Daoust and his friends, the increasingly less discreet opposition of the clergy. In the election campaign in Beauharnois, Daoust had experienced the hostility of two parish priests. This clerical opposition increased during the 1856 session when the democratic MLA Joseph PAPIN made his plea for non-confessional schools. Daoust supported the Papin proposal. During the same session, George Brown* was attacking the separate schools of Upper Canada; it is not surprising then that in 1857, after the Papin motion, the clergy were much more predisposed against the Rouges than in 1854. Hence the 1857–58 elections were somewhat disappointing to the liberals, who lost a number of seats. Papin was defeated in L'Assomption, and Daoust in Beauharnois by Gédéon Ouimet*.

Daoust was to be called to account personally by the highest authority in Montreal diocese, Bishop Ignace Bourget*, in one of three pastoral letters published on 10 March, 30 April, and 31 May 1858 against the Institut Canadien and the liberal press. The letter of 31 May was an unqualified condemnation of liberalism, a condemnation that took its arguments from the encyclical of 15 Aug. 1832, *Mirari Vos*, which specifically rejected the liberal thesis of the separation of church and state. It happened that on 8 Feb. 1858, at a banquet offered by political friends, Daoust had exclaimed: "Since I have been engaged in public affairs, I have always been of the opinion that the church and the state should have a separate existence, each leading its own life, and should not become identified in a common action." After quoting this "impious language," but without indicating the author and the source, Bishop Bourget added: "you recognize, dearly beloved brethren, the supporters of unbridled liberty, of whom the common Father has just spoken. He, who writes under the divine inspiration of the Holy Spirit, proclaims agreement between empire and priesthood as propitious and salutary."

At that date Daoust was still editor of *Le Pays*, but he had secured the collaboration of a French emigrant Henri-Émile Chevalier*. Plinguet, the owner of the liberal paper, doubtless alarmed by the effect of the episcopal censures on its circulation, had made over his rights to the Société Dorion et Cie in June 1858. A year later, Daoust in turn retired from *Le Pays*; Chevalier remained sole editor until November 1859 when young Médéric Lanctot* took over. Daoust went into partnership with his brothers-in-law Joseph and Gonzalve Doutre* and was happy to abandon journalism for the more peaceful life of a lawyer. A member of the Institut Canadien, whose "real qualities of vitality" he had commended in a lecture of December 1853, he was elected its president in 1860. At that time he noted the situation of the group had been "more brilliant." But at least there remained "the strength and glory of the institute": "Here, there are freedom of thought, freedom of discussion, liberalism, tolerance; no exclusion, and no censure."

In January 1864 Daoust returned to journalism, when he succeeded Louis-Antoine Dessaulles, who had been editor of *Le Pays* from 1 March 1861 to the end of December 1863. He was warm in his praise of Dessaulles, specifying that he would not strike as hard as his predecessor, but his intention was to "strike as accurately." Like all his *confrères* in the Canadian press, Daoust commented repeatedly on the great question stirring public opinion, the confederation of the provinces of British America. He was not the least scathing of the liberal journalists in his denunciation of a system that would diminish the influence of the Lower Canadian representatives in the central parliament, leave that parliament the important financial matters, and make of the local assembly of Lower Canada "little more than a large municipal council." But the die had been cast. The plan of confederation was approved by the Legislative Assembly of the Province of Canada on the night of 10 March 1865, which, Daoust indignantly asserted, was "the most iniquitous, the most degrading act witnessed by the parliamentary régime since the betrayal of the Irish representatives who sold their country to England for positions, honours, and gold."

Charles Daoust remained editor of *Le Pays* until the autumn of 1865, when he was replaced by young Alphonse Lusignan*. His health undermined by tuberculosis, he passed away at his home in Montreal in February 1868, at age 43. He was survived by his wife and his only son, whose Christian names, Charles-Roger, would keep fresh his own memory and that of his beloved brother.

PHILIPPE SYLVAIN

PAC, MG 30, D62, 9, pp.838–40. *L'Avenir*, 1847–50. *Le Pays*, mars 1853–mai 1859, janv. 1864–oct. 1865, 29 févr. 1868. Fauteux, *Patriotes*, 195–96. Bernard, *Les Rouges*. L.-O. David, *L'Union des deux Canadas, 1841–1867* (Montréal, 1898), 135. Ægidius Fauteux, *Le duel au Canada* (Montréal, 1934), 273–78. Edmond Lareau, *Mélanges historiques et littéraires* (Montréal, 1877), 39. Augustin Leduc, *Beauharnois, paroisse Saint-Clément, 1819–1919; histoire religieuse, histoire civile, fêtes du centenaire* (Ottawa, 1920), 95–96, 158, 168. Gaspard Le Mage [P.-J.-O. Chauveau et J.-C. Taché], *La pléiade rouge* (Québec, 1854), 10. *Le répertoire national, ou recueil de littérature canadienne*, James Huston, édit. (2e éd., 4v., Montréal, 1893), III, 212–14. Robert [Philippe] Sylvain, *Clerc, garibaldien, prédicant des deux mondes: Alessandro Gavazzi (1809–1889)* (2v., Québec, 1962), II, 391; "Libéralisme et ultramontanisme," *Shield of Achilles* (Morton), 225–26.

DARLING, Sir CHARLES HENRY, soldier and colonial administrator; b. 19 Feb. 1809 in Annapolis Royal, N.S., eldest son of Major-General Henry Charles Darling and Isabella Cameron, daughter of a former governor of the Bahamas; d. 25 Jan. 1870 in Cheltenham, England.

When Charles Henry Darling was born, his father was a lieutenant-colonel attached to the militia in Nova Scotia. In December 1826, following an education at the Royal Military College at Sandhurst, England, he began a military career as ensign in the 57th Foot. He was stationed with his regiment in New South Wales between 1826 and 1831, and for part of this time was assistant private secretary, then military secretary, to his uncle, Governor Sir Ralph Darling. He became a lieutenant in 1830, and in 1831 obtained leave to re-enter Sandhurst as a student in the senior department. He remained there until 1833, when he was appointed military secretary to Lieutenant-General Sir Lionel Smith, under whom he served in Barbados and the Windward Islands, 1833–36, and then in Jamaica until 1839.

Darling retired from the army in 1841 as a captain following two years in command of an unattached company. He had married twice, first, in 1835, the daughter of Alexander Dalzell of Barbados, who died in 1837, and in 1841 the eldest daughter of Joshua Billings Nurse, member of the Barbados Legislative Council; she died in 1848. Between 1843 and 1847 Darling served as agent general for immigration in Jamaica under the governorship of Lord Elgin [BRUCE]; he became a member of the Legislative Council and adjutant-general of militia. After Elgin's departure he was to serve again as a governor's secretary.

Darling served as lieutenant governor of St Lucia from 1847 to 1851, and of Cape Colony (South Africa) during the absence of the governor in 1851. In that year he married Elizabeth Isabella Caroline Salter of Stoke Poges, Buckinghamshire. From May to December 1854 Darling again administered the Cape Colony. At this time he was appointed governor-in-chief of Antigua and the Leeward Islands, but the colonial secretary, Sir George Grey, asked him to go to Newfoundland instead.

Darling was sent to Newfoundland to smooth the way for responsible government, which the incumbent governor, Ker Baillie Hamilton*, had made difficult by his anti-Liberal partisanship. In March 1855 Hamilton was told of his transfer to Antigua, and Grey remarked that Darling would "have the advantage of meeting the new assembly, and commencing the responsible system without any former connexion with the Politics of the Island." Hailed as a man of experience in colonial affairs by the attorney general, Edward Mortimer Archibald*, Darling commenced his governorship by announcing the inauguration of responsible government. He came close to serious trouble, however, because he arrived without instructions to divide the old Council into its necessary executive and legislative parts, as was the established practice in colonies with responsible government. Happily for Darling the key members of that Council were anxious to go. Attorney General Archibald, Colonial Secretary James CROWDY, and Surveyor General Joseph Noad* arranged that their resignations would be accepted if the new assembly to be elected in May 1855 indicated a Liberal leadership. Subsequently the election returned a clear Liberal majority and on 22 May the new assembly passed resolutions designating Philip Francis Little*'s Liberal party the victors and the only possible source of the first Executive Council under responsible government. A stiff-necked governor could have insisted on his prerogative to decide that issue, but Darling let the slight pass with a mere rebuke to the assembly in the speech from the throne on correct constitutional practice.

The resolution in favour of Little's party had the effect of dissolving the old régime, and Darling's willingness to accept them surprised the Liberal members who had expected a fight. Fortunately, too, the Liberals were strong enough in the assembly to vote down resolutions proposed by Hugh William Hoyles*, leader of the Conservative and Protestant opposition, which charged Darling with unconstitutional conduct. Two productive sessions followed in 1855 and 1856. This era of relatively good feelings, though brief, was aided by the improved economic conditions resulting from the Reciprocity Treaty of 1854 with the United States in which Newfoundland had been included. However, the hoary French shore problem soon disrupted the harmonious political scene.

Since 1783 the French had claimed exclusive rights of fishery on Newfoundland's western coast from Cape St John to Cape Ray; Newfoundlanders steadily challenged this claim and asserted a concurrent right to the fishery. In 1856 Henry Labouchere, the British colonial secretary, reopened negotiations with France on the basis of modifications of the 1851 proposals made by Sir Anthony Perrier, the British negotiator. Governor Hamilton had condemned the Perrier proposals to the satisfaction of the colony, but Darling now endorsed many of Labouchere's suggested modifications, which would divide the French shore into two exclusive sections, one French and one British, and acknowledge the French right to take bait on the south shore; he argued that since the Americans could take bait there under the Reciprocity Treaty, it would be impossible to prevent the French from doing so. Though Darling did not accept all the terms of Labouchere's new proposals, it was believed that his dispatch of July 1856 to Labouchere strengthened the colonial secretary's resolve to complete the convention of 14 Jan. 1857. When it was presented a month later, the Newfoundland assembly and Legislative Council vehemently condemned it. Darling then declared himself "absolutely helpless" to implement the convention in the face of such unanimous opposition. Eventually Labouchere withdrew the convention, and sent off a dispatch promising "that the consent of the community of Newfoundland is regarded . . . as the essential preliminary to any modification of their territorial or maritime rights."

Seriously compromised by this triumph of the assembly's views, though he had heeded its protest, Darling left the colony in February 1857, amid bitter criticism, to become governor of Jamaica. Perhaps his new appointment was not a means of extracting him from Newfoundland, because it came in February before the protest had fully developed, but his alleged role in the negotiations may have hindered his usefulness to the colony.

In 1863 Darling received his last appointment, as governor of Victoria (Australia), among the best appointments of the colonial service. This one, however, ended abruptly in 1866 after a disagreement between Darling and the colony's Legislative Council. He returned to England to live in Cheltenham where he died in 1870. He had been knighted in 1865 for "his long and effective public services."

FREDERIC F. THOMPSON

PRO, CO 194/144–51. *Royal Gazette* (St John's), 15 May 1855–28 April 1857. *ADB. DNB*. G.B., WO, *Army list*, 1827–41. Gunn, *Political history of Nfld*., 139–49. Thompson, *French shore problem in Nfld*., 25–47.

DEASE, PETER WARREN, HBC officer and Arctic explorer; b. 1 Jan. 1788 at Mackinac (Mackinac Island, Mich.), son of Dr John B. Dease, captain and deputy superintendent of the Indian Department, and Jane French, possibly a Roman Catholic Caughnawaga Mohawk; d. 17 Jan. 1863 at *côte* Sainte-Catherine (Montreal), Canada East.

Peter Warren Dease was named after Admiral Sir Peter Warren*, the captor of Louisbourg, Île Royale (Cape Breton Island) in 1745 and a paternal relative. Raised in Montreal, Dease at age 13 was engaged to the XY Company on 11 April 1801 at a salary of £75 plus food, lodging, and clothing for a six-year term in the "Indian or North West Country." Following the amalgamation of the XY and North West companies in 1804, he was made a clerk in the North West Company and was posted to the Athabasca Department and then to the Mackenzie River District, being stationed at Fort Chipewyan and at posts on the Mackenzie River and north of Great Slave Lake. During the near warfare between the North West and Hudson's Bay companies, Dease was with the party that waylaid Colin Robertson* at Grand Rapids below Île-à-la-Crosse about 28 June 1820.

With union of the two companies in 1821, Peter Warren Dease and his brother John Warren were appointed chief traders in the HBC; Peter Warren attended the first meeting of the Council of the Northern Department at Norway House in August 1821, where he was appointed to the Athabasca District. Early in 1823, Governor George Simpson* instructed Dease to undertake during the summer an exploration of the Finlay and other rivers west of the Rocky Mountains and parallel to the Mackenzie River. Dease received the instructions too late to start from Fort Chipewyan before spring break-up, with the result that Samuel Black* took charge of western explorations for 1824, and Dease was seconded to John Franklin*'s "Land Arctic Expedition" for outfits 1824–25, 1825–26, and 1826–27.

At Fort Chipewyan in May 1820 Dease had "promptly and kindly" provided information about the natives and geography to Franklin for his first expedition to the Arctic, and for the second expedition Franklin requested his services in obtaining provisions, managing Indian and voyageur support, and constructing a base on Great Slave Lake. During the winter of 1824–25 Dease procured fish from Great Slave Lake and helped make peace between the Copper Indians (or Yellowknives) and the Dogribs, so that they would hunt for the expedition. In July 1825 he superintended the construction of Fort Franklin on Great Bear Lake. Dease Bay (Dease Arm) on that lake and Dease River (which flows into it) commemorate his services to the Franklin expedition.

Dease continued in the Mackenzie River District with headquarters at Fort Good Hope from 1827 until 1830. He was promoted chief factor 23 Jan. 1828, a reward for his aid to Franklin, and in July 1830 he was appointed to Fraser Lake in New Caledonia (British Columbia).

In the spring of 1831 Dease assumed sole charge of the New Caledonia District from William Connolly*, and he transferred his station to Fort St James on Stuart Lake. The district now showed large profits, said to be £8,000 in 1834. Dease was popular among his men as he was "most amiable, warm hearted, sociable." He brightened life at Fort St James with feasts of "roasted bear, beaver and marmot" and games of chess, backgammon, and whist; he played remarkably well on the violin and flute "for the fort's musical soirees." He was praised by his superiors for having established a new order of things at Fort St James, particularly in the introduction of cattle from Fort Vancouver (Vancouver, Wash.) and the encouragement of farm-

ing. In 1835, with a leave of absence, he was replaced by Peter Skene Ogden*.

In June 1836 the council assigned Dease to command the Arctic exploring expedition launched by the HBC to fill in the gaps left by the expeditions of naval officers Franklin, Frederick William Beechey*, and George Back* in the search for the northwest passage. George Simpson's young cousin, Thomas Simpson, who had joined the HBC in 1829 and had recently caused a disturbance among the Métis at Fort Garry (Winnipeg), was made second-in-command with responsibility for surveying and scientific investigations. The expedition, with 12 men, was to explore westward from the mouth of the Mackenzie River and eastward from Franklin's Point Turnagain on the Kent Peninsula.

Dease was joined at Fort Chipewyan on 1 Feb. 1837 by Simpson, who had made an astounding overland trip of 1,277 miles from Red River in a mere 62 days. They left the post on 1 June 1837, and at Fort Resolution on Great Slave Lake Dease vaccinated all the young natives. They reached the mouth of the Mackenzie River on 9 July. By 23 July they had progressed to Return Reef (Alaska), Franklin's farthest west point in 1826, which he had not attained until mid August. But on 31 July they had to abandon the sea because of ice. The following day Simpson set out overland from "Boat Extreme" on the remaining 60 miles to Barrow Point, which the Beechey expedition had reached from the west. Borrowing a native oomiak at Dease Inlet, Simpson reached Barrow Point on 4 August where he took possession of their discoveries for Britain. The reunited party reached the mouth of the Mackenzie on 17 August and Fort Norman on 4 September. There they received instructions to explore east of the Coppermine River in 1838. From Fort Norman Simpson wrote of being "sore" at not being given command, and that winter, from the winter quarters built for them at Fort Confidence on Great Bear Lake, wrote that "Dease is a worthy, indolent, illiterate soul, and moves just as I give the impulse," and that since he himself had "the *exclusive* honour of . . . uniting the Arctic to the Western Ocean" he felt entitled to promotion to chief trader.

The expedition of 1838 was disappointing because of the "extraordinary duration of the ice." In June they ascended the Dease River and crossed the Dismal Lakes which Simpson had discovered during a 95-mile exploration of seven days in March and April. Reaching the mouth of the Coppermine River on 1 July, they were imprisoned by ice until 7 July, Dease using the time to collect plants. After a "desperate" struggle

Dease

with the "same cold obdurate foe," they rounded Cape Barrow on 29 July. Their boats were finally stopped on 9 August at Cape Flinders, three miles south of Franklin's 1821 encampment at Point Turnagain. Government expeditions were expected to turn back on 20 August, a result of the disaster of Franklin's first journey, but Simpson proceeded on foot with five HBC servants and two Indians. When he returned to Dease on 29 August he had traced 100 miles of coast and had named Victoria Land (Island) and Cape Pelly. The party returned to the Coppermine River on 3 September, reaching their winter quarters across "the barren grounds" on 14 September. Simpson was soon blaming their failure on Dease's caution, adding that Dease, whose family had joined him in late August 1837, was "so much engrossed with family affairs, that he is disposed to risk nothing." To his brother, Simpson complained that he was "like Sinbad the sailor, hampered with an old man on my back." Dease, in truth, was concerned about their provisions and the possibility of being recalled from the expedition that autumn.

Dease and Simpson spent a second winter at Fort Confidence and in 1839 they again attempted to explore to the eastward. From the mouth of the Coppermine River Simpson explored the Richardson River which had been discovered in 1838, and on 3 July the sea ice opened. But their boats only attained Cape Barrow on 18 July. Ten days later they doubled Cape Alexander (near Simpson's farthest of 1838) and discovered Dease and Simpson Strait (now Simpson Strait) separating King William Island from the mainland. It led to the mouth of the Great Fish River (Back River). On 16 August they reached Montreal Island where they discovered a cache left by George Back. Thus, they had filled in the gaps left by the explorations of Franklin and the voyages of Beechey and Back. It remained to determine the relationship of the Boothia Peninsula, separating them from the Gulf of Boothia, to the continent. Although it was now time to turn back, they reached, and named, Cape Britannia on 17 August; Simpson also made a run of 40 miles to the northeast of Cape John Ross, where he named his farthest point the Castor and Pollux River, after the expedition's two boats. There he asserted (erroneously because of seriously restricted visibility) that five miles to the east the coastline turned south, thus denying the existence of the Isthmus of Boothia. En route back to the Coppermine, the expedition explored late in August the south coast of King William Island. They reached the Coppermine on 16 September after winter had set in in earnest. But they had completed the longest voyage performed in boats

on the polar sea, and they had more than fulfilled the mandate of the company's instructions.

After "boisterous and inclement" weather they reached Fort Simpson (District of Mackenzie) on 14 October. There Simpson completed his "Narrative of the Expedition" before departing for Upper Fort Garry (Winnipeg) on 2 December. He had requested permission to make a new expedition in the Gulf of Boothia himself ("Fame I will have but it must be *alone*," free from "the extravagant and profligate habits of half-breed families") but Governor Simpson was still unwilling to give his impetuous cousin independent command and Dease had taken leave. In June 1840 Simpson set out for England to ensure he received major credit for their discoveries and to appeal for the new expedition. En route to St Paul (Minn.), moody and overwrought, he killed two of his four Métis companions, and then, it is assumed, committed suicide.

In three summers Dease and Simpson had explored the Arctic coast through 60 degrees of latitude at a cost to the HBC of £1,000 and, except for the transit of the Boothia Peninsula, they had completed the long-sought survey of the northwest passage. That Simpson was the more daring is beyond doubt, but Dease's logistical abilities in organizing supplies, recruiting and maintaining discipline among his men, keeping peace among the natives, and managing the swift movement with a simplicity of equipment while living off the land in so far as possible assured the success of these arduous expeditions despite the disappointments of 1838. Governor George Simpson had been more than justified in refusing to give his erratic and self-seeking cousin independent command.

Dease, who was granted furlough for 1840–41 to seek medical attention in England for eye trouble, was at Norway House for the council in June 1840, and then at Red River, where, already a grandfather (he had had four sons and four daughters), he married his fur trade wife, Élizabeth Chouinard, a Métis, on 3 Aug. 1840. Dease and Simpson had each been granted a pension of £100 a year by Queen Victoria in June, "for their exertions towards completing the discovery of the North West Passage," and it was rumoured that Dease would be knighted, "which," said Letitia Hargrave [Mactavish*], "diverts the people here as they say Mrs Dease is a very black squaw & will be a curious lady." However, Dease, "with that modesty which was part of his nature," declined the knighthood. He was introduced to the HBC Committee in London in October. His furlough was extended until his retirement from active duty on 1 June 1843.

Dease settled on a farm at *côte* Sainte-

Catherine near Montreal in early 1841. He was joined by his family from Red River, and it was said by James Keith*, an HBC chief factor, that he was governed "by his Old Squaw & Sons. She holding the Purse strings & they spending the Contents *par la Porte* et *par les fenetres*." At *côte Sainte-Catherine*, Dease had 20 years of "comfortable and much respected" retirement. Three sons predeceased him and the fourth died in 1864.

George Simpson's perceptive remarks in his famous "Character Book" of 1832 remain the best commentary on Peter Warren Dease: "Very steady in business, an excellent Indian Trader, speaks several of the Languages well and is a man of very correct conduct and character. Strong vigorous and capable of going through a great deal of Severe Service but rather indolent, wanting in ambition to distinguish himself in any measure out of the usual course. . . . His judgement is sound, his manners are more pleasing and easy than those of many of his colleagues, and altho' not calculated to make a shining figure, may be considered a very respectable member of the concern."

WILLIAM R. SAMPSON

Peter Warren Dease and Thomas Simpson are the authors of three articles published in the *Journal* of the Royal Geographical Soc. of London: "An account of the recent Arctic discoveries . . . ," VIII (1838), 213–25; "An account of Arctic discovery on the northern shore of America in the summer of 1838," IX (1839), 325–30; "Narrative of the progress of Arctic discovery on the northern shore of America, in the summer of 1839," X (1840), 268–74. An extract of a letter by Dease was published in the *Edinburgh New Philosophical Journal*, XXX (1840–41), 123–24, under the title "On the cultivation of the cerealea in the high latitudes of North America."

HBC Arch. A. 34/2, f.7. PABC, Peter Warren Dease, Correspondence outward, 1837–38; Miscellaneous documents relating to Peter Warren Dease, 1801. *Canadian North-West* (Oliver), I, 624, 627–28, 709–10; II, 724, 726, 737, 799, 816, 836. *Documents relating to NWC* (Wallace). HBRS, III (Fleming). Thomas Simpson, *Narrative of the discoveries on the north coast of America; effected by the officers of the Hudson's Bay Company during the years 1836–39* (London, 1843). L. H. Neatby, *In quest of the north west passage* (Toronto, 1958), 122–24, 127. Alexander Simpson, *The life and travels of Thomas Simpson, the Arctic discoverer* (London, 1845), 255–57, 276, 300–1, 304, 334, 339.

DE HAVEN, EDWIN JESSE, naval officer and explorer; b. 7 May 1816 at Philadelphia, Pa., son of William De Haven and Maria McKeever; m. in 1844, Mary Norris Da Costa; d. 1 May 1865 in his native city.

Edwin Jesse De Haven, who was of Dutch descent, entered the United States Navy on 2 Oct. 1829 as a midshipman. After serving on various ships in the West Indies, he was appointed in 1839 to the *Vincennes*, commodore ship of the discovery squadron of Commander Charles Wilkes, and spent the following three years in exploration in Antarctica, the Pacific islands, and on the west coast of North America. He received the thanks of the Navy Department for saving several lives when one of the expedition's ships was wrecked at the mouth of the Columbia River, and he was commissioned lieutenant in September 1841. He was then attached to the Naval Observatory in Washington, D.C., under the celebrated oceanographer, Matthew Fontaine Maury, and served afloat during the Mexican War (1846–47).

Early in 1850 a wealthy New York merchant, Henry Grinnell, with the assistance of the United States government, equipped an expedition to share in the search for the lost ships of Sir John Franklin*; De Haven's polar experience and his scientific attainments procured him its command. The first Grinnell expedition, consisting of the brigs *Advance* and *Rescue*, manned by 33 officers and men, entered the Arctic by way of Baffin Bay and Lancaster Sound, and in August 1850 reached the entrance of Wellington Channel in company with a number of British rescue vessels, naval and private. There De Haven shared with Captain Erasmus Ommanney of the Royal Navy and the Scottish whaler William Penny* in the discovery of relics which indicated that Beechey Island was Franklin's winter quarters in 1845–46. Thirty miles west the expedition's progress was blocked by ice, and De Haven, who had been ordered not to winter over, parted from his British consorts to return home. His ships were soon frozen in, however, and driven by southerly gales 60 miles up the hitherto unexplored Wellington Channel; there was still enough daylight for identification of features on both sides of the strait. When the winds subsided a steady ice-drift carried the helpless ships back past Penny's winter quarters to the east and out into Baffin Bay; from late September 1850 to 5 June 1851 the crews endured sickness and privation locked in the ice out of sight of land. De Haven then brought his ships over to the Greenland shore and restored his scurvy-stricken crews with fresh meat and vegetables generously furnished by incoming British whalers. In a courageous attempt to renew the search he was again ice-bound in Baffin Bay in company with Captain William Kennedy* and French naval officer Joseph-René Bellot* aboard *Prince Albert* sent by Lady Franklin [Griffin*]. The Americans sailed for home on 19 Aug. 1851.

De Lisle

In the meantime Penny had spent early summer 1851 in a survey of Wellington Channel, and in ignorance of the American achievement had given to their discoveries names of his own choosing, which were duly transferred to Admiralty charts. This injustice to De Haven aroused fiery protest in the American press; American names were restored, but in a curious manner: it is certain that the present Grinnell Peninsula lies beyond De Haven's area of survey. Penny's findings, more extensive and the first to be published, naturally overshadowed the earlier American survey. Moreover, De Haven forfeited the renown justly his by leaving it to his surgeon, the colourful Dr Elisha Kent Kane, to write the history of the expedition.

After four years of arduous work making soundings on the American coast, De Haven ended his sea service in 1857 with health and eyesight impaired. He was retired with the rank of lieutenant in 1862 and died in 1865. His record gives the impression of a zealous, capable, and hard-working officer whose services were not sufficiently recognized.

L. H. NEATBY

Baker Library (Dartmouth College, Hanover, N.H.), Stefansson coll., Grinnell scrapbook. J.-R. Bellot, *Memoirs of Lieutenant J. R. Bellot . . . with his journal of a voyage in the polar seas in search of Sir John Franklin . . .* (2v., London, 1855), I, 197–261. E. K. Kane, *The U.S. Grinnell expedition in search of Sir J. Franklin; a personal narrative* (London and New York, 1854). Sherard Osborn, *Stray leaves from an Arctic journal; or, eighteen months in the polar regions, in search of Sir John Franklin's expedition, in the years 1850–51* (London, 1852). *DAB*. L. H. Neatby, *In quest of the north west passage* (Toronto, 1958), 138–40; *The search for Franklin* (New York, [1970]), 119, 127–34, 146–47. Albert Gleaves, ''The De Haven Arctic expedition: a forgotten page in American naval history,'' U.S. Naval Institute, *Proc*. (Annapolis, Md.), 54 (1928), 579–91.

DE LISLE (Delisle), AUGUSTIN (also known as Augustin-Stanislas), notary and botanist; b. at Montreal and baptized 4 Nov. 1802, last child of Jean De Lisle* de La Cailleterie and Suzanne Lacroix-Mézières; d. 8 Jan. 1865 at Varennes, Canada East.

Augustin De Lisle received his classical education at the Collège de Montréal from 1813 to 1822. His first wife was Henriette, daughter of Pascal Trudel and Marie Charbonneau, whom he married on 18 May 1825 at Sainte-Famille-de-Boucherville. His second was to be Charlotte-Henriette, daughter of Joseph Ainsse Jr, seigneur of the Île Sainte-Thérèse, and Charlotte Vigneau;

they were married on 15 May 1844 at Sainte-Anne-de-Varennes. He received his commission as a notary on 17 Dec. 1827, and practised his profession for nearly 17 years at Boucherville, then at Montreal (1845–47), Saint-Henri-de-Mascouche (1847–54), and again at Montreal until 1858. He was appointed curator of the Montreal Bar library in 1854, and held this position until his death.

As early as 1825, De Lisle, who inherited from his father a liking for the sciences, turned to the study of botany and started an herbarium. The majority of his manuscripts, however, date from after 1852, when he was living at Saint-Henri-de-Mascouche and visited Abbé Louis Gagné, a fellow enthusiast of the sciences staying at the local parish priest's house. Thus De Lisle dedicated to Abbé Gagné, for his birthday in 1852, his ''Hortus Eremi . . .'' in which were described the trees and plants of Gagné's garden, of the parish, and of the neighbourhood. In 1859 Jean-Baptiste Meilleur*, who had known De Lisle at the college and who corresponded with him, mentions a work on Canadian plants that De Lisle was trying to get published. This is probably ''Essai, arbres arbrisseaux et arbustes du Canada dont le bois de service, les gommes, ont été présentés à l'Exposition de Paris, 1855,'' a notebook of 142 pages with a few illustrations. Only one other notebook, more voluminous, seems to have been made ready for publication. Entitled ''Petite pharmacie végétale . . .'' and dated 1857, this manuscript comprises 271 pages and enumerates and describes the plants which have properties and medicinal qualities that may be domestically useful. The author mentions his authorities, such as Charlevoix* and Asa Gray, evidence of his considerable erudition. A reading of his manuscripts and notes reveals a sound knowledge acquired through regular consulation of the works of the great botanists of the period, botanizing excursions, and the practice of horticulture. This knowledge is manifest in the numerous notes at the bottom of the pages of a copy of *Flore canadienne . . .* which Abbé Léon Provancher* had presented to him, as well as in a manuscript prepared in 1856 and entitled ''Phytographie et taxonomie, catalogue de plantes du Canada, cueillies et classées par la comtesse Dalhousie, présentées en 1827 à la Société historique de Québec, avec remarques et notes par A.D. . . .'' A final manuscript, dated 1863 and unfinished, is called ''Entretiens de deux jeunes botanistes canadiens dans l'isle de Montréal et quelques paroisses environnantes.''

As well as being meticulous and methodical, De Lisle must have been modest. All his manuscripts bear only his initials, or a pseudonym, such as "un amateur de botanique montréalais" or "un amateur de botanique canadien." It was as the latter that he signed his only publication, a letter in *La Minerve* on 10 March 1859. It was an erudite and objective contribution to the controversy between Meilleur and Pierre-Joseph-Olivier Chauveau* over the name to be given to *Sarracenia purpurea*, a plant first described by Michel Sarrazin* which Chauveau wrongly called "Sarrazine."

Although his achievement in botany was not outstanding, since his manuscripts remained unpublished, De Lisle gave valuable assistance to Abbé Provancher when the latter was compiling his *Flore canadienne*. Provancher mentioned him particularly in *Le Naturaliste canadien*: "In the compiling of our *Flore*, we were able to avail ourselves of the kindness of this gentleman in order to obtain a great deal of information concerning the geographical distribution of our plants." Of the various amateurs who helped Provancher, such as Judge Louis-David Roy*, Bishop Edward John Horan*, and Jean-Baptiste-Antoine FERLAND, De Lisle was certainly the most scholarly and persevering.

LÉON LORTIE

Institut botanique de Montréal, Papiers Augustin De Lisle. "Correspondance," *Le Naturaliste canadien* (Québec), 2 (1869–70), 150–52. *La Minerve*, 10 mars 1859. Allaire, *Dictionnaire*. J.-E. Roy, *Hist. du notariat*, III, 95. Léon Lortie, "Deux notaires amateurs de science: Jean De Lisle et son fils Augustin-Stanislas De Lisle," RSC *Trans.*, 3rd ser., LV (1961), sect. I, 39–47; "Notes sur le 'Cours abrégé de leçons de chymie' de Jean-Baptiste Meilleur," Assoc. canadienne-française pour l'avancement des sciences, *Annales* (Montréal), 3 (1937), 261. É.-Z. Massicotte, "La famille de Jean De Lisle de La Cailleterie," *BRH*, XXV (1919), 175–86. *Le Naturaliste canadien* (Québec), 5 (1872–73), 230.

DERBISHIRE, STEWART, public official; b. perhaps in 1794 or 1795 in London, England, son of Dr Philip Derbishire of Bath, England, and Ann Masterton of Edinburgh, Scotland; d. 27 March 1863 in Quebec, Canada East.

Stewart Derbishire was of a type common enough in 19th century Canada, the middle class English adventurer. He drifted through a number of careers in England before coming to Canada. First an ensign in the 82nd Foot, he then studied law and was called to the bar in 1830. He gained some notoriety in 1832 as defence lawyer for the Dorchester labourers accused of machine smashing. His legal career gave way to journalism, for the Whig *Morning Chronicle*. He went to Spain as its correspondent in 1837 during the civil war. Typically he could not maintain journalistic neutrality. He joined the Carlist side and later fought with the British forces, under General George de Lacy Evans, which intervened in 1837. For his services Derbishire was decorated by the queen of Spain.

On his return to England the quiet life in George St, Adelphi, made him restless. He was ready to throw over his new journal, the *Atlas*, which he had begun to edit in the fall of 1837, when he heard of the mission of Lord Durham [Lambton*] to Canada. Writing to Durham in January 1838, Derbishire impressed the earl sufficiently to obtain employment. He arrived in New York in April and there began the first part of his mission, gathering information on rebel activities and on the causes of the Lower Canadian uprising.

Derbishire's reputation as an advanced Whig won him interviews with William Lyon MACKENZIE, John ROLPH, and Edmund Bailey O'Callaghan* in New York, Denis-Benjamin VIGER in Montreal, and more humble folk throughout Lower Canada. Derbishire reported to Durham in May 1838 that the *habitants* had "no practical grievances," that it was "the malaria of political agitation" which had produced the rebellion. The malaria, he felt, was still active; Derbishire found alarming signs of rebel activity throughout the border region of the province. His constant warnings during 1838 and 1839 to Durham, Lieutenant Governor George Arthur* of Upper Canada, and Sir John COLBORNE won him something of a reputation as an alarmist. Although Arthur was impressed by Derbishire and was inclined to continue his services after Durham's departure, Colborne warned that Derbishire was "*very* credulous" and that he should not be encouraged.

Derbishire served other functions, beyond excited reporting. He was Durham's press agent, cajoling and threatening editors into writing favourably about Durham's régime. And in November 1838, in an effort to summon reinforcements to Lower Canada, he carried dispatches from Canada to Fredericton and Halifax in a hazardous winter dash through the wilderness.

His official employment ended with Durham's departure in November 1838. Derbishire then spent some time in the United States gathering information on the Maine–New Brunswick border dispute for the British government. In 1840 he returned to Montreal to edit the *Morning Courier*. Re-establishing his close ties with government under Governor General Sydenham

Désaulniers

[Thomson*], Derbishire allowed the *Courier* to be used as a vehicle for official propaganda. He got his rewards in 1841. Under Sydenham's patronage, Derbishire was elected to the assembly for Bytown (Ottawa), although he had no connection with it. That September he was appointed queen's printer along with George-Paschal DESBARATS of the *Montreal Herald*. The latter position proved more durable than the former. Despite his constant boasts of close relations with the governors general, Derbishire was a poor member of parliament, unskilled even in managing local patronage. He was saved from the embarrassment of electoral defeat by new legislation which prohibited the queen's printer from sitting in parliament; as a result, he did not stand for re-election in 1844. He remained queen's printer until his death in 1863.

The income from the post eased Derbishire's chronic financial difficulties. His first wife was wealthy but they were estranged; she and their children remained in England while Derbishire adventured in Canada. So serious were his personal financial problems that he was declared outlaw in England in 1841 for absconding on debts. His appointment as queen's printer and the death of his wife in 1842 resolved some of his entanglements. But his finances were never easy, for as an obituary noted, "His hospitality was proverbial" and he was generous to a fault towards the needy. His second marriage, however, was happier than the first. He left at his death six children from the two marriages.

The queen's printer died at the capital, Quebec, on 27 March 1863. His grandiloquent career ended with a suitably ostentatious funeral attended by two cabinet ministers, three judges, and an impressive array of military officers.

MICHAEL S. CROSS

PAC, MG 24, A27, 37; A40, 23, pp. 6878–84; B14, 2, pp. 287–301, 321–26, 344–49; 5, pp. 932–34, 941–49; 12, pp. 2540–49; I9, 4, pp. 1009–40, 1044–45, 1056–59, 1066, 1075–90, 1104, 1108–10, 1116–30, 1136–42, 1147–60, 1190–1205, 1211–13, 1221–34, 1243–45, 1255–59, 1265–70, 1276–85, 1290–98; 5, pp.1301–7, 1318–22, 1327–36, 1350–52, 1356–59, 1367, 1372–82, 1483–86, 1491–1500, 1519–37, 1548–49, 1568–70, 1592–94, 1598–99, 1605–8, 1620–49, 1657; 6, pp.1680–81, 1709; 13, pp.3978–98; 19, pp.4817–18; 22, pp.5900, 5929; RG 1, E1, 77, pp.204–5. PRO, WO 44/30–32 (mfm. at PAC). *Arthur papers* (Sanderson), II, 179–84, 189–93; III, 69–70, 75–76, 167–68, 203, 305–6, 319–20, 354–55, 464–65, 471–72. [Stewart Derbishire], "Stewart Derbishire's report to Lord Durham on Lower Canada, 1838," ed. Norah Story, *CHR*, XVIII (1937), 48–62. [Charles Grey], *Crisis in the Canadas, 1838–1839: the Grey journals and letters*, ed. W. G. Ormsby (Toronto, 1964), 177. *Bytown Gazette* ([Ottawa]), 1840–44. *Montreal Transcript*, 31 March 1863. *Quebec Daily Mercury*, 28, 31 March 1863. *Cyclopædia of Canadian biog.* (Rose, 1888). Lucien Brault, *Ottawa old & new* (Ottawa, 1946), 140–49.

DÉSAULNIERS, ISAAC-STANISLAS. *See* LESIEUR-DÉSAULNIERS

DESBARATS, GEORGE-PASCHAL, printer, publisher, and businessman; b. 11 Aug. 1808 in Quebec City, third son of Pierre-Édouard Desbarats*, assistant clerk of the Legislative Assembly of Lower Canada and printer, and Marie-Josephte Voyer; d. 12 Nov. 1864 in Montreal.

Educated at the Reverend Daniel Wilkie*'s grammar school in Quebec City, George-Paschal Desbarats became apprenticed to James George, merchant, and then to a lumber merchant in Lower Town. In 1826 his father's illness forced him to concern himself with the family's interest in their printing office, which Thomas CARY had bought into. After the death of his father in 1828 he gradually took over this interest with the mutual consent of the other heirs. He was associated with Cary for a number of years; details of the contractual agreements between them are lacking but there is some evidence that the partnership was a strained one. Their joint imprint appears on various government documents from 1831 to 1842, mainly the *Journals* of the Legislative Council of Lower Canada. A statement in an obituary of Desbarats in the *Quebec Daily Mercury* that he was joint owner with Cary of that newspaper between 1828 and 1848 remains to be substantiated.

In 1841 for the first time Desbarats's name appeared with that of Stewart DERBISHIRE on government publications. In September of that year they were named to be jointly "Her Majesty's Printer and Law Printer in and for the Province of Canada." They continued this partnership until Derbishire's death in 1863, when Malcolm Cameron* became Desbarats's associate for the short time he still lived. During these years Desbarats lived in Kingston, Montreal, Toronto, and Quebec as the capital changed location.

In this period the queen's printer was responsible for printing and distributing laws and the official government newspaper, only a fraction of the total government output. Continuing earlier procedures, from 1841 to 1859 the Legislative Assembly and the Legislative Council each had its own printer as well; from 1860 to 1866 one printer served both houses. Desbarats and Cary were printers to the assembly in 1841; Desbarats and Derbishire were printers to the council in 1843.

Apart from his official printing Desbarats received the commission to reprint Samuel de Champlain*'s works, edited by Abbé Charles-Honoré Laverdière*. The completed works were finally published in 1870 under the imprint of his son, George-Édouard*. With his son, George-Paschal subsidized and published *Le Foyer canadien*; *recueil litteraire et historique* from 1863 until his death; the former carried on until 1865.

Desbarats was an astute and successful businessman. In 1847, with Derbishire, he bought the Ottawa Glass Works at Pointe-à-Cavagnal (Como-Est, Que.), the first glass factory in the province and then just in a formative stage [see François-Xavier DESJARDINS]. He invested in the St Lawrence and Atlantic Railroad and in 1849 wrote a pamphlet on its behalf, *The St. Lawrence and Atlantic Railroad: its position as a private undertaking, and advantages as a national work*. He is mentioned in documents as acting secretary of the Montreal Mining Company (1847) and president of the St Lawrence Mining Company (1854). At the time of his death he owned an extensive mining tract north of Lake Huron, the Desbarats Location, bought in 1847, land in the Chaudière valley where gold was being prospected, and much other property and land.

George-Paschal Desbarats held the commission of lieutenant-colonel in the militia and was a long time member of the Natural History Society of Montreal and the Horticultural Society. He was married three times: in 1836 to Henriette Dionne, daughter of Amable Dionne*, legislative councillor, by whom he had one son, George-Édouard; in 1841 to Charlotte Selby, daughter of Dr William D. Selby, by whom he had another son; in 1849 to Jessie-Louise Pothier, daughter of Jean-Baptiste-Toussaint Pothier*, legislative councillor, by whom he had two daughters.

AILEEN DESBARATS

G.-P. Desbarats, *The St. Lawrence and Atlantic Railroad: its postion as a private undertaking, and advantages as a national work* (Montreal, 1849).

Desbarats family papers are in the possession of the Desbarats family in Montreal. Can., Prov. of, Legislative Assembly, *Journals, 1841–64*. "*Canadian Illustrated News*" : *a commemorative portfolio*, ed. Peter Desbarats (Toronto, [1970]). St Lawrence Mining Company, *Report of the president and directors . . .* ([Quebec, 1854]). *Globe*, 12 Nov. 1864. *Le Journal de Québec*, 14 nov. 1864. *La Minerve*, 14 nov. 1864. *Montreal Gazette*, 14 Nov. 1864. *Morning Chronicle* (Quebec), 12 Nov. 1864. *Quebec Daily Mercury*, 12 Nov. 1864. *Union* (Ottawa), 17 Nov. 1864. Beaulieu et Hamelin, *La presse québécoise*, I, 19, 23. O. B. Bishop, *Publications of the government of the Province of Canada, 1841–1867* (Ottawa, 1963), 49–62. Le Jeune, *Dictionnaire*, I, 499. G. F. Stevens, *Canadian glass, 1825–1925* (Toronto, 1967). "Les disparus," *BRH*, XXXIV (1928), 241. Réjean Robidoux, "*Les Soirées canadiennes* et *le Foyer canadien* dans le mouvement littéraire québécois de 1860, étude d'histoire littéraire," *Revue de l'université d'Ottawa*, XXVIII (1958), 411.

DESJARDINS, FRANÇOIS-XAVIER, merchant and Patriote; b. c. 1802, probably at Saint-Benoît, Lower Canada, son of Joseph Desjardins and Marie-Josephte Prévost; d. 14 Nov. 1867 at Saint-Michel-de-Vaudreuil (Vaudreuil), Que.

François-Xavier Desjardins's activities remain little known until his participation in the disturbances of 1837–38. On 17 Dec. 1823 Desjardins, identified as "a merchant of upper Vaudreuil," married Mary Delesderniers, daughter of John Mark Crank Delesderniers of Vaudreuil, in St Andrew's Presbyterian Church (St Andrew and St Paul) in Montreal. Three girls and a boy were born of this union. Apparently Desjardins's commercial activities were flourishing at the time of his marriage, since he owned five pieces of land at Pointe-à-Cavagnal (called Como by about 1860, and today Como-Est).

When the 1837–38 insurrection broke out Desjardins joined the ranks of the Patriotes of Vaudreuil and Lac-des-Deux-Montagnes. His participation in the patriotic movement even led to two confinements in prison (from 16 Dec. 1837 to 28 Feb. 1838 and from 4 Nov. to 17 Dec. 1838), as a result of denunciations made by John Augustus MATHISON, leader of the local British loyalists, a justice of the peace, and a long-standing rival of Desjardins. According to these detailed denunciations, Desjardins and his brother Fabien were local Patriote leaders. He held meetings at his house and allegedly helped to recruit and arm about 150 habitants to defend the village of Saint-Benoît. The arms and ammunition may have been supplied to them by his cousin Alselme Desjardins, owner of a foundry at Rigaud who provided ammunition to Dr Jean-Olivier Chénier* of Saint-Eustache. In addition, Desjardins was accused of giving financial support to William Whitlock, an American sympathizer, who roused the local British to revolt by his numerous writings. Although he denied these accusations, Desjardins was probably one of the organizers of the insurrectional movement in its initial stages. He may have taken part in the

Destroismaisons

armed conflict in December 1837, but no charge was preferred against him.

After this political unrest Desjardins resumed his commercial activity in partnership with his brother Fabien. On 20 Aug. 1845, nine months after the death of his first wife, Desjardins, who then styled himself a businessman, married Virginie Laviolette at Saint-Jérôme. In the same year he participated in the industrial revival on the seigneuries of Vaudreuil and Rigaud by promoting a glass works at Pointe-à-Cavagnal.

On 24 Sept. 1845 Desjardins went into partnership, for a period of eight years, with Marc-Damase Masson*, Jules-Édouard Bardy, and François Coste, all of Montreal, to set up and run a glass works. The establishment, with its furnaces and outbuildings, was to be constructed on a piece of land that Desjardins leased to the company; the agreement was to be in effect as long as the buildings were used for the manufacture of glass. As well as supplying £150, each shareholder of Masson et Compagnie was assigned a specific task. Desjardins was responsible for selling the manufactured products in the Vaudreuil area. Before the construction of the plant was completed, however, the new company experienced its first disappointments. On 16 December Desjardins withdrew from the partnership with his share of the investment and profits, which amounted to £305. In February 1846 he refused to transfer to the shaky firm another strip of land needed for its expansion, alleging that its request could not be justified. During the succeeding years the company changed hands several times, becoming in 1847 the Ottawa Glass Works, under the ownership of Stewart DERBISHIRE and George-Paschal DESBARATS, queen's printers. From 1851 on the company, then known as the Canada Glass Works Company Limited, was to make headway; its progress slowed again around 1875. Desjardins received rent from the land at least until 1851.

After the more or less successful glass works venture, Desjardins's only known occupations are those of justice of the peace, coroner, and militia captain. He probably continued to take an interest in business and his ownership of Île Cadieux in the Lac-des-Deux-Montagnes perhaps indicates that he was fairly well off.

MARCEL BELLAVANCE and GÉRARD GOYER

ANQ-M, État civil, Presbytériens, St Andrew's (Montréal), 17 déc. 1823; Greffe de J.-O. Bastien, fils, 1er nov. 1844. ANQ-Q, QBC 25, Événements de 1837–1838, nos.116, 1064–65, 1067–69, 3888, 3890, 3894. Archives judiciaires, Terrebonne (Saint-Jérôme, Qué.), Registre d'état civil, Saint-Jérôme, 20 août 1845.

Archives paroissiales, Saint-Michel-de-Vaudreuil (Vaudreuil, Qué.), Registres des baptêmes, mariages et sépultures, 18 nov. 1867. Fauteux, *Patriotes*, 207. R.-L. Séguin, *Étude monographique relative à la paroisse de Saint-Thomas d'Aquin d'Hudson, comté de Vaudreuil* (Rigaud, Qué., 1947). G. F. Stevens, *Early Canadian glass* (Toronto, [1961]). R.-L. Séguin, "La famille Delesderniers," *BRH*, LVIII (1952), 131, 133; "La verrerie du haut de Vaudreuil," *BRH*, LXI (1955), 119–28.

DESTROISMAISONS, THOMAS-FERRUCE PICARD. *See* PICARD

DESTROYER. *See* PEGUIS

DEWAR, EDWARD HENRY, Church of England clergyman, theologian, and author; b. 31 Aug. 1812 at Amherstburg, Upper Canada, only son of Lieutenant John Dewar of the Canadian Fencibles regiment and his wife Maria; married twice, having one son by his first wife, Amy, and twin daughters by his second wife, Caroline Elliott, whom he married in 1859; d. 24 Oct. 1862 at Thornhill, Canada West.

Shortly after Edward Dewar's birth his father died. Edward received his early education at Hamburg (Republic of Germany), and matriculated at Exeter College, Oxford, on 27 Jan. 1831. He received a BA in 1834 and an MA in 1837, and was therefore in Oxford at the genesis of the Oxford Movement in the Church of England by which he was greatly influenced. After his ordination he is known to have taught and was chaplain at the Royal Sussex County Hospital, Brighton, for six months in 1840 before returning to Hamburg as chaplain to the British residents. There he completed in 1844 *German Protestantism, and the right of private judgment in the interpretation of Holy Scripture*.

This work was a scathing attack on German liberal Protestantism. Scripture, Dewar argued, could be interpreted by recourse either to the principle of church authority, "Catholicity," or to that of private judgement, "Rationalism." The latter principle had in Germany permitted the "wildest speculations of fancy" from Luther onwards. Dewar, competent in the German language, traced increasing error through Wolff, Kant, Schelling, Hegel, and the Neo-Hegelians. He contrasted the melancholy state of religion in Germany with that in England, "excelled by no nation upon the earth for piety," where catholicity was upheld. His book was important for its presentation of current German philosophy to English readers; Bishop John STRACHAN described it as "well known" in Canada.

Dewar returned to Canada in 1851. He assisted

the Reverend H. B. Jessopp in establishing the Cobourg church grammar school, and he and his wife looked after the boarders. In October 1852 he became rector of St John's church in Sandwich (Windsor), C.W., and despite ill health he played a notable part in the early development of Windsor. He built its first Anglican church, All Saints', which opened on 10 Sept. 1857, and served as its rector while retaining his previous charge. Hopeful of rescuing the young from "grovelling pastimes," he was a founder in 1855, and president in 1857, of the mechanics' institute with its public library. He examined the children of the Protestant common school, yet championed in synod the right of all Protestant denominations to have their own separate schools. He was also interested in agricultural education.

In October 1855 the first issue of a 16-page monthly, the *Churchman's Friend*, appeared at Paris (later moving to Windsor), edited by Dewar and the Reverend Adam Townley. Its aim was to explain and defend in simple language "true Church principles" in line with the high church theology of the Oxford Movement, and in 1857 it supported Alexander Neil Bethune* for bishop of the new "western diocese" which became the diocese of Huron. Dewar had earlier asked Strachan to nominate directly a candidate for clerical and lay approval in order to forestall the likely election of the evangelical Benjamin Cronyn*. After a controversial career the magazine died in 1857; Dewar attempted unsuccessfully to launch another in 1858.

Dewar was appointed rector at Thornhill, C.W., near Toronto, on 1 Oct. 1859. His wish to move to a place where he might be more influential in church affairs long antedated Cronyn's election as bishop and had been frustrated mainly by Strachan's desire to have "one of the most able and presentable of my clergy" on the borders of the diocese to "make some amends for our deficiencies on other parts of our border." Dewar proved in 1861 a strong defender of Trinity College, Toronto, against Cronyn's charges of Romish teaching by Provost George Whitaker*. In 1861 and 1862 Dewar was chosen a delegate to the provincial synod. His parishioners, however, complained of neglect.

Strachan regretted Dewar's early death, recognizing his many contributions to the church. "He was not only a good churchman, and well read, but one on whom I could at all times depend. His manners were not indeed very polished and I found him distant and reserved, yet always correct and ready to support the right course."

CHRISTOPHER HEADON

E. H. Dewar was the author of *The Church Society of the Diocese of Toronto: a letter addressed to the incorporated members* ([Windsor, Ont., 1858]); *German Protestantism, and the right of private judgment in the interpretation of Holy Scripture: a brief history of German theology* . . . (Oxford and London, 1844); *The history of the English language: a lecture delivered at Cobourg, C.W., March 15th, 1852* (Cobourg, [Ont.] 1852); *A letter to Dr. A. Neander . . . containing some remarks on his review of a work, entitled, "German Protestantism, and the right of private judgment in the interpretation of Holy Scripture"* (Oxford and London, 1845); *National calamities; a call to repentance: a sermon preached April 18th, 1855* . . . (Toronto, 1855); *Plain words for plain people: an appeal to the laymen of Canada, in behalf of common sense and common honesty, being a review of the "Strictures" on the two letters of Provost Whitaker* (Toronto, 1861); *Specimens of the early-German Christian poetry of the eighth and ninth centuries* . . . (London and Hamburg, 1845).

PAO, Strachan (John) papers, letterbook, 1854–62, letters to Edward Dewar; no date package 8, personalia, "Memorandum giving a short sketch of the Rev. E. H. Dewar." Trinity College Archives (Toronto), Strachan (John) papers, ser.1, 7 March 1851; 3, 10 May, 11 June 1855; 31 Oct. 1862. *Churchman's Friend* (Paris; Windsor, [Ont.]), 1855–57. Church of England, Diocese of Huron, *Minutes of the Synod* (London, Ont.), 1858; Diocese of Toronto, *Proc. of the Synod* (Toronto), 1861–63. *Windsor Herald* (Windsor, [Ont.]), 17, 24 Feb., 27 Oct., 22 Dec. 1855; 14 March, 28 Nov., 26 Dec. 1856. C. F. Headon, "The influence of the Oxford movement upon the Church of England in eastern and central Canada, 1840–1900" (unpublished PH D thesis, McGill University, Montreal, 1974).

DICKSON, SAMUEL, lumber manufacturer and industrialist; b. 1810 in County Cavan (Republic of Ireland); d. 26 April 1870 at Peterborough, Ont. He was married and had five daughters.

Samuel Dickson emigrated from Ireland to the Peterborough area in 1830 and found employment as a distiller with John Hall, also a native of County Cavan, a fellow Presbyterian, and prominent local businessman. Hall owned the Mill Reserve on the Otonabee River at Peterborough which included a grist- and sawmill, but financial difficulties forced him to relinquish ownership of the property in 1838. Dickson, recognizing the advantages of the river bank location for waterpower, rented the mill from its new owner and began to manufacture pine lumber in 1839.

The key to the expansion of Dickson's business was control of adequate water-power to allow larger milling operations. He had abandoned the Mill Reserve by 1851 and built a new mill across the river in Otonabee Township. Later Dickson also built a steam mill on the eastern side of Little Lake. The steam mill, however, was soon exchanged with the lumber firm of Ludgate and McDougall for mill rights on the old Mill Reserve. This last transaction was a calculated effort by Dickson to gain riparian rights on both sides of the Otonabee River at a centrally located site with abundant water-power; by 1870 he had amassed power rights which gave him virtual control of the river in Peterborough.

The rise in production of Dickson's mills reflected his skilful acquisition of sites and a rapidly growing market for Peterborough timber. In the early 1840s Dickson was producing square timber for the British market, as well as sawn lumber. The Reciprocity Treaty of 1854 encouraged lumbermen like Dickson to increase their production by opening a large American market to Canadians.

The impact of the American market was demonstrated by a dramatic rise in the production of lumber in Peterborough County. In 1851 it produced 11,589,000 board-feet, whereas in 1861 its production increased to 63,599,000 feet. Dickson's mill had an output of 1,000,000 board-feet in 1851, 800,000 feet being produced for the foreign market and the rest for the domestic market. By 1866, despite several short-term slumps in the lumber trade during the late 1850s and early 1860s, the Dickson Lumber Company had increased its production to 6,000,000 board-feet per year. To reach this market Dickson shipped his lumber to Port Hope on Lake Ontario and from there to Albany, N.Y., which served as the distribution centre for the major markets on the eastern seaboard of the United States.

Dickson's production at Peterborough was surpassed in the 1860s only by that of Campbell and Company at Nassau Mills, George Hilliard at Blythe Mills, and Ludgate and McDougall, Little Lake. His firm had not only improved its physical plant but had also acquired large new timber limits, moving its logging operations north from Buckhorn into the fine pine stands in the townships of Cavendish, Anstruther, Harvey, and Anson. As well, Dickson had established a large flour mill to help supply his camps and had set up a woollen factory just below his power dam in Peterborough.

In 1870 Samuel Dickson's invested capital in his sawmill operation alone was approximately $100,000 and the mills provided jobs for over 150 men. He was beginning to develop his large real estate and water-power interests for other industrial purposes besides the manufacture of sawn lumber. Having brought his son-in-law, T. G. Hazlitt, into the company in 1865 as assistant manager, Dickson apparently felt freer to plan new business ventures, to participate more fully in public affairs, and to take a more active role in the affairs of the Presbyterian Church. A lifelong Conservative, he was elected to the Peterborough town council in 1870. But Dickson's career was cut short after he fell into the spring torrent of the timber-choked Otonabee River on 25 April 1870; he died of his injuries the following day.

PETER GILLIS

PAC, MG 26, A; MG 55/24, 341; National Map Coll., "Romaine's map of the town of Peterborough and village of Ashburnham . . ." (1875); RG 1, L3 (index); RG 31, 1851 census, Otonabee Township; 1871 census, Ontario, district 56, schedule 6 (industrial census), town of Peterborough. Thomas White, *An exhibit of the progress, position and resources of the county of Peterboro . . .* (Peterborough, [Ont.], [1861]). *History of the county of Peterborough, Ontario . . .* (Toronto, 1884). A. R. M. Lower, *The North American assault on the Canadian forest: a history of the lumber trade between Canada and the United States . . .* (Toronto and New Haven, Conn., 1938; repr. New York, 1968). T. W. Poole, *A sketch of the early settlement and subsequent progress of the town of Peterborough . . .* (Peterborough, [Ont.], 1867). *Peterborough Examiner* (Peterborough, Ont.), 5 May 1906.

DOLLARD, PATRICK, Roman Catholic priest; b. 1 March 1804 at Glenmore, County Kilkenny (Republic of Ireland); d. 12 Feb. 1868 at Kingston, Ont.

Patrick Dollard was educated at the ecclesiastical seminary in Waterford, Ireland, and, in response to appeals from Canada for missionaries, immigrated to Montreal where he studied theology at the Grand Séminaire de Saint-Sulpice. Early in 1836 he was ordained by Bishop Jean-Jacques Lartigue* of Montreal and assigned to Kingston, Upper Canada. Dollard had been ordained early at the request of Bishop Alexander Macdonell* of Kingston who was in great need of help. In May 1836 Dollard took up his duties at St Joseph's Cathedral.

From all contemporary accounts he was a good and pious priest. During the rebellion of 1837 when loyalist militia crowded the town and during the epidemics of cholera and typhus, he counselled his parishioners and administered the sacraments. He was admired for his disregard of the danger of infection and for his unceasing work.

Dollard was appointed vicar general to Bishop Rémi Gaulin* who in 1842 entrusted him with directing the construction of St Mary's Cathedral. In this capacity Dollard raised the necessary funds by subscription in Kingston and Quebec, kept the accounts, and supervised the construction, much of the labour being volunteered by parishioners. The cost of the cathedral has been estimated at $90,000. The cornerstone of the church was laid early in 1843 by Bishop Patrick Phelan*, Gaulin's coadjutor, and the church was being used by its congregation as early as 1846, though construction was not completed until 1848. Dollard was appointed first rector of the cathedral; as vicar general to bishops Gaulin, Phelan, and Edward John Horan* he was administrator of the diocese in 1857 and 1862. He also served periodically as Roman Catholic chaplain to the military garrison at Kingston.

Dollard was deeply involved in the Roman Catholic struggle for educational rights from his arrival in Kingston until his death. The sisters of the Congregation of Notre Dame first established a Catholic school in Kingston in 1841, and in 1853 the Christian Brothers also started a school. After 1848 a common school board provided funding, but it was withdrawn in 1854 because of changes in the school act. The following year a Roman Catholic school board, on which Dollard served as a member and for several years as chairman, was established to supervise and fund separate schools.

Dollard was noted for his amiability of character and the purity of his life, and was widely consulted by townspeople on many matters from the spiritual to the political. He was in great demand as a confessor and spiritual director for religious as well as lay people; his sermons were models of erudition and practicality and displayed a gifted mind in theology and scripture.

B. J. PRICE

Archives of the Archdiocese of Kingston (Kingston, Ont.), unpublished letters and ecclesiastical documents. *Daily British Whig* (Kingston), 14, 15, 17 Feb. 1868. *Daily News* (Kingston), 13 Feb. 1868. *Weekly British Whig* (Kingston), 20 Feb. 1868.

DONEGANI, JOHN ANTHONY (baptized Jean-Antoine; not to be confused with Guiseppe Donegana, another Montreal hotel-keeper), tavern-keeper, businessman, municipal politician, and seigneur; b. 6 Aug. 1798 in Montreal, eldest son of Joseph and Thérèse Donegani; d. 6 July 1868 in Montreal.

Approximately 50 families of Italian origin lived in Montreal in the half-century before confederation. Most were from northern Italy and found employment in the grocery, tavern, or hotel trades. Among the innkeeping families were the Bonacinas, the Delvecchios, the Rascos, and the Doneganis. John Anthony's grandfather, Guiseppe, immigrated to Montreal in 1794 from Moltrazio in Lombardy with his wife, three sons, daughter, and nephew, Joseph Donegani.

Guiseppe Donegani established himself as an innkeeper, but returned to Italy in 1802. His offspring remained in Montreal and prospered.

In 1797 Guiseppe Donegani's daughter, Thérèse, had married her 40 year old cousin, Joseph. A year later, John Anthony was born; two other sons, Joseph and Guillaume-Benjamin, followed. The three boys attended the Collège de Montréal and Guillaume-Benjamin became Montreal's first Italian physician. After his father's death in 1816 John Anthony took over the family's tavern business in the *faubourg* Récollet, and began speculating in real estate. In partnership with his brother Joseph, he owned property on the island of Montreal, at Laprairie (La Prairie) on the south shore of the St Lawrence, and on Perrot Island. In 1829 he bought for £2,700 the seigneury of Foucault (Caldwell's Manor) on the Richelieu River near the American border. The seigneury, inhabited largely by loyalists, included five schools, a mill, and a fine manor house. In 1842 Donegani sold it to Joseph-Frédéric Allard of Chambly.

John Donegani was a scrappy individual who spent much time in the courts. In 1827 a bitter court battle began between the three Donegani brothers and their uncle Joseph, a successful merchant, manufacturer of mirrors, and proprietor of a well-known tavern, Les Trois Rois. The three brothers, who hoped to obtain real estate in Montreal left by their grandfather, contended that their uncle, an alien, could not inherit property in Canada, and that they, born in Canada, were the only legitimate heirs. The complex case involved French civil law in Lower Canada and the rights of aliens in France and England. The lower courts in Montreal in 1828, the appeal courts in 1832, and the Judicial Committee of the Privy Council in 1835 all upheld the claims of the brothers who were allowed to take possession of the property.

The 1830s and 1840s were boom years for ambitious Montreal businessmen like John Donegani. While other entrepreneurs profited from banking, commercial, and industrial expansion, Donegani made a fortune from rising property values. By 1847 he owned at least 65 properties in Montreal; in a good year in the mid 1840s he made up to 60 land transactions, many involving thousands of pounds. His properties were concentrated in the old commercial district, but he also participated in the west-end expansion along Rue Saint-Antoine, a prestige residential area. Construction of the Montreal and Lachine Railroad, started in 1846, further enhanced the value of his west-end properties.

In the years from 1833 to 1835 and from 1840 to

Donegani

1843 Donegani was a member of the Montreal City Council; in 1837 after the first municipal charter was allowed to lapse he was named a justice of the peace. As a member of the first council Donegani joined Jacques Viger*, John TORRANCE, Charles-Séraphin Rodier*, and other members of the commercial class in directing development in the growing city. They were concerned with three major problems: expansion of the commercial district along Saint-Paul and Commissaires streets (where Donegani had extensive properties), improvement of the city's roads, sewers, and waterfront, and protective measures against cholera epidemics. As chairman of the roads committee Donegani had to placate angry residents from the Sainte-Catherine and Saint-Urbain streets area who complained that the combination of sewage in the streets and the lack of sidewalks made the roads almost impassable.

Donegani made his political sympathies clear during the tumultuous events of 1837–38. He did not ingratiate himself with conservatives when, as JP, he led the 1st Royals against the Doric Club, a secret society dedicated to maintaining strong links with Britain. In November 1838 he was arrested without warrant by Robert Weir*, proprietor of the *Montreal Herald*. After testifying that he had committed no wrong Donegani was released. Later he became a patron of French Canadian literary and cultural activities. In January 1841 a public meeting to encourage the formation of an institute of literature, science, and the arts was held at his home [*see* Nicolas-Marie-Alexandre VATTEMARE]. Throughout the 1840s he continued to press for expanded cultural facilities. In 1845 he provided land on Dorchester Street to the Jesuits on which they built the Collège Sainte-Marie. The site was evaluated at more than £8,000 but Donegani sold it to the Jesuits for £2,250 with the stipulation that a daily mass would be said for him until the last of his children died. In 1849 he signed the Annexation Manifesto.

Donegani's social standing kept pace with his financial successes. His first business associate had been Joseph-Maximilien Bonacina, an Italian partner of his father. In 1819 he listed himself as a tavern-keeper, a decade later he was a seigneur, and in 1840 he was described simply as a "gentleman." His various places of business and residence are also an indication of his changing status, culminating in offices on Rue des Commissaires and a lavish home among the élite on Côte Saint-Antoine (Westmount). In May 1830 Donegani had married Rosalie-Louise-Geneviève Plamondon, the daughter of Louis Plamondon, a Quebec City lawyer. They had a son and a daughter. As a landowner, municipal politician, and magistrate Donegani seems to have been accepted into the inner circle of Montreal's French Canadian bourgeois class. After the death of his brother Joseph in 1837 Donegani participated in real estate deals with Antoine-Olivier Berthelet*. For legal advice Donegani turned to George-Étienne Cartier*; his notary was Théodore-Benjamin Doucet.

At the end of the 1840s, however, John Donegani fell on hard times. The circumstances are not clear but by the early 1850s he owed the Banque du Peuple, of which he had been one of the first directors, over £30,000. To forestall his creditors Donegani ceded his property to members of his family and in February 1850 declared himself bankrupt. The Banque du Peuple brought him to court and seized his possessions. After 1855 little was heard of the aging and bankrupt Donegani.

Montreal was changing and Donegani was a man of the pre-confederation era. Old Montreal was giving way to the new centre-town commercial district. The Italian taverns and hotels with their charm and cuisine were now gone, replaced by new centre-town hotels with large capital investment and oriented to the railway trade. In the face of industrialization and the growth of capital in the Montreal area, the roles of the tavern-keeper, small entrepreneur, and seigneur were diminishing in importance. It was fitting and ironic that Donegani should die on Rue Sainte-Catherine, symbol of the new Montreal.

BRIAN J. YOUNG

ANQ-M, Documents judiciaires, Contrats de shérif, Louis Gugy, 1827–29; Greffe de T.-B. Doucet, 17 déc. 1846. ANQ-Q, QBC 16, 3, f.292; QBC 25, Événements de 1837–1838, no.1029. AVM, Procès-verbaux du conseil municipal, 9 juin, 12 juill., 5 sept., 24 oct. 1834, 17 juin 1837; Rôles d'évaluation, 1847. *Canadian reports; appeal cases: appeals allowed or refused by the judicial committee of the Privy Council on appeal from the dominion of Canada*, ed. W. E. Lear (24v., Toronto, 1910–16), I: *1828–1850. The English reports . . .* (176v., Edinburgh and London, 1900–30), XII. *Lower-Canada reports* (17v., Montreal and Quebec, 1851–67), III. *Montreal Gazette*, 10 May 1853. *L'Ordre* (Montréal), 10 juill. 1868. *Vindicator and Canadian Advertiser* (Montreal), 3 Oct. 1837.

Alphabetical list of merchants, traders, and house-keepers in Montreal (Doige). *Montreal directory*, 1843–44, 1848, 1856–57, 1862–63, 1867–68. J. I. Cooper, *Montreal: a brief history* (Montreal, 1969). Oscar Handlin, *Boston's immigrants, 1790–1865; a study in acculturation* (Cambridge, Mass., 1941). Kathleen Jenkins, *Montreal, island city of the St Lawrence* (New

York, 1966), 296. Rumilly, *Hist. de Montréal*, II, 305. A. V. Spada, *The Italians in Canada* (Canada Ethnica, VI, Ottawa and Montreal, 1969), 54–56. F.-J. Audet, "1842," *Cahiers des Dix*, 7 (1942), 238–40; "Les Donegani de Montréal," *BRH*, XLVII (1941), 65–75. "Seigniory of Foucault," Missisquoi County Hist. Soc., *Report* (Saint-Jean, Que.), 1913, 34–43.

DOOLITTLE, LUCIUS, Church of England minister; b. 23 May 1800, possibly in Lyndon, Vermont, and baptized 30 June 1822 in the parish of Charleston, Hatley, Lower Canada, perhaps the son of Jesse Doolittle, resident of Lyndon in 1800; d. 18 May 1862 at his sister's home in Milwaukee, Wis., and buried on 30 May in Lennoxville, Canada East.

Lucius Doolittle spent his early years in Hatley where he was engaged in business under an uncle. He entered the University of Vermont in 1824. In 1825–26 he taught school at Hatley, presumably during the long vacations then permitted by the university for that purpose. He was involved in Phi Sigma Nu, a literary society.

In 1818 Doolittle became acquainted with the Reverend Charles James Stewart*, then missionary of the Society for the Propagation of the Gospel in Hatley. Doolittle decided to become a member of the Church of England and was encouraged by both Stewart and Bishop Jacob Mountain* to prepare for the Anglican ministry. In 1827, when he withdrew from the university without completing his course, he was nominated for an SPG scholarship and he read theology under the Reverend Thomas Johnson who had succeeded Stewart at Hatley. He was ordained deacon by Stewart, now bishop of Quebec, in October 1828 and was licensed to a mission on Chaleur Bay. In November 1829 he was ordained priest, and with his wife Clarissa Goss Lawrence, whom he had married the previous month, returned for four arduous years to his mission, stretching 100 miles along the coast.

In October 1833 Doolittle was put in charge of the Eastern Townships mission of Sherbrooke and Lennoxville. He served there until 1847, and in Lennoxville alone from 1847 to 1862. In 1838 he was awarded an honorary MA degree by the University of Vermont.

In 1847, a brick church, called St George's, was opened, replacing the original wooden church at Lennoxville. Doolittle was foremost in overseeing its construction from 1845 to 1847 and in providing it with suitable furnishings, including a bell and an organ. He obtained a font in Italy when on a visit to Europe in 1852. St Peter's Church, Sherbrooke, similar to the Lennoxville church, was also built during Doolittle's incumbency.

George Jehoshaphat MOUNTAIN, who was appointed suffragan to Bishop Stewart in 1836 and who became bishop of Quebec in 1837, had long planned to establish a theological seminary in the diocese of Quebec and had considered Trois-Rivières as a possible site. As principal of the nascent McGill University from 1823 to 1835, and president of the Royal Institution for the Advancement of Learning from 1838, Mountain also strove to advance higher education under Anglican auspices in Montreal. But when in 1840 Doolittle and a group of local laymen proposed to locate a seminary combined with a liberal arts college at Lennoxville and offered land and money, the bishop's agreement was quickly obtained. The growing uncertainty of the status of the church in McGill's direction undoubtedly influenced Mountain to adopt the Lennoxville plan in which the position of the Church of England would be unquestioned [*see* John Bethune*]. Doolittle also pointed out that a private school for boys which he had begun in 1836 had gained a measure of success and would provide a feeder for the college.

Bishop's College, which obtained its charter in 1843, began its long career in 1845 [*see* Jasper Hume Nicolls*]. Doolittle served as bursar of the college from 1845 to 1856, without remuneration, and he was also a trustee. He bequeathed a capital sum to endow divinity bursaries which are still being awarded. Both contemporaries and later historians give due credit to Doolittle's part in this large educational venture. Bishop Mountain, in an appreciative reference to Doolittle in his episcopal charge of 1862, asserted: "he may be called, in one sense, the founder of Bishop's College." Doolittle's own foundation was named the "Grammar School in connection with the College," and continues today as Bishop's College School.

Because Doolittle published nothing and little of his correspondence remains, his personality is elusive. It is certain from the preamble to his will that he was a man of deep religious faith, closely attached to the church of his adoption. He was untiring in his activities despite much ill health, shrewd in business dealings, sound in judgement, and full of faith in the realization of his dreams. The Reverend Ernest HAWKINS, SPG secretary, who visited Lennoxville in 1849, described Doolittle as "a kind, generous, simple hearted man." Such was the respect accorded to him that Bishop James William Williams*, who had once been in charge of the grammar school, recalled that an invitation to his house was "equivalent to a

Dorion

command which no one would dream of disobeying." Mrs Doolittle died in 1848. They had no children.

T. R. MILLMAN

Bishop's University Library (Lennoxville, Que.), Copy of the last will and testament of Lucius Doolittle, 28 Nov. 1861; Letters of Charles James Stewart to Lucius Doolittle, 1828–35; Letters of George Jehoshaphat Mountain to Lucius Doolittle, 1828–33, 1848. QDA, 53 (B-7), pp.38, 42–43; 68 (B-22), p.80; 91 (D-10); 92 (D-11); 94 (D-13). University of Vermont Archives (Burlington), Annual catalogue, March 1825; Treasurer's account, 9 Feb. 1825–3 May 1827. USPG, Journal of a visit to British North America and the United States in 1849 by the secretary of the society, Ernest Hawkins (copy at Anglican Church of Canada, General Synod Archives, Toronto).

A memoir of George Jehoshaphat Mountain, D.D., D.C.L., late bishop of Quebec . . . , comp. A. W. Mountain (Montreal, 1866). *Memoir of the Rev. Archibald Campbell Scarth, M.A., D.C.L., Rector of St George's Church, Lennoxville . . .* , [ed. Henry Roe] (Sherbrooke, Que., 1904). G. J. Mountain, *A charge delivered to the clergy of the diocese of Quebec at the triennial visitation . . . on 1st July 1862* (Quebec, 1862); *A journal of visitation in a portion of the diocese of Quebec by the lord bishop of Montreal, in 1846* (London, 1847); *A journal of visitation to a part of the diocese of Quebec by the lord bishop of Montreal, in the spring of 1843* (London, 1850). *Sherbrooke Gazette* (Sherbrooke, Que.), 14 June 1862. Soc. for the Propagation of the Gospel in Foreign Parts, *Report*, 1829, 1830, 1834, 1840. J. W. Williams, *A sermon preached by the right reverend the lord bishop of Quebec at the consecration of the chapel of Bishop's College, Lennoxville, June 14, 1878* (Montreal, 1878). *General catalogue of the University of Vermont and State Agricultural College, Burlington, Vermont, 1791–1900* (Burlington, Vt., 1900). D. C. Masters, *Bishop's University, the first hundred years* (Toronto, 1950). *Parish anecdotes, St James' Church, 1822–1845; St George's Church, 1845–1904*, ed. Lilian Watson (Lennoxville, Que., [1966]).

DORION, JEAN-BAPTISTE-ÉRIC, store clerk, journalist, pioneer settler, and politician; b. 17 Sept. 1826 at Sainte-Anne-de-la-Pérade (La Pérade), Lower Canada, son of Pierre-Antoine Dorion* and Geneviève Bureau; d. 1 Nov. 1866 at L'Avenir, Canada East.

Jean-Baptiste-Éric Dorion's father was a fifth-generation descendant of Pierre Dorion, who in 1684 had left Salies-de-Béarn (dept of Basses-Pyrénées, France) to emigrate to Canada. On 21 Feb. 1814 Pierre-Antoine signed a marriage contract with Geneviève, daughter of Pierre Bureau, merchant of Trois-Rivières. Pierre-Antoine was also a merchant and acquired a tidy fortune mainly in the timber trade. But a *débâcle* on the Rivière Sainte-Anne ruined him, and made it impossible for him to give all his children more than an elementary education though he had sent his first four sons, Nérée, Antoine-Aimé*, Hercule, and Louis-Eugène to the Collège de Nicolet.

Jean-Baptiste-Éric was baptized with his twin brother François-Edmond on 23 Sept. 1826, by parish priest Joseph Moll; his godfather was Dr Jean-Baptiste-Curtius Trestler and his godmother was the wife of Joseph Dorion, who had been unsuccessful as a candidate in Hampshire County in the 1824 election. Thus, in a sense, politics had marked his entry into the world; they were to hold him until his last breath.

They were also a part of his family. On both the local and the national level, Pierre-Antoine Dorion steadfastly championed the principles of Louis-Joseph Papineau*. He was elected a school inspector in August 1829, and vigorously opposed parish priest Marc Chauvin, who wanted to establish a school run by the parish council; Pierre-Antoine wished to build a school to be run by public trustees, in accordance with the provisions of the 1829 school act. He was MHA for Champlain county from 20 Oct. 1830 to 27 March 1838, and it was at his house that Papineau, in 1836, held meetings that brought together MHAs and Patriote supporters. He presided at the annual banquet of the Société Saint-Jean-Baptiste at Saint-Ours, during which a toast was drunk to the king of England, enlivened by a comment that was impertinent to say the least: "Let him not forget that there is no form of government whose prerogative is immovable, no political power, whether created yesterday or a thousand years ago, which cannot be abrogated in ten years or tomorrow."

Jean-Baptiste-Éric therefore grew up in an atmosphere of liberal fervour. He was a mischievous, noisy child, and the family bestowed on him the title of "enfant terrible." His political opponents, in particular Joseph-Édouard Cauchon*, were only too glad to revive this nickname later, and it has stuck like a tunic of Nessus to his career and his memory. Since his father's financial distress forced him to break off prematurely the schooling he had begun under the iron hand of the authoritarian Craig Morris, Jean-Baptiste-Éric went first to Quebec to study English, then in 1842 to Trois-Rivières, where he took a job as store clerk to support himself. The following year, this self-taught young man had recourse to two means of intellectual stimulus that would be beneficial to him in the future, a discussion group and a newspaper. He was an active member of the Société Littéraire de Trois-Rivières and as editor and printer published a small paper, *Gros Jean l'Escogriffe*. He even tried his hand at being an author, publishing *Un souvenir pour 1844*.

Following his elder brother Antoine-Aimé, since 1842 a lawyer practising in Montreal, he moved to Montreal himself in 1844, and on 17 December took part in the founding of the Institut Canadien. It was replacing two short-lived societies, the Société des Amis and the Lycée Canadien. Turning to account his early journalistic experience at Trois-Rivières, he launched at Montreal *Le Sauvage*, with the help of George Batchelor; only two numbers appeared, 24 June and 3 July 1847. It was followed by *L'Avenir*, whose first issue came out on Friday, 16 July. A bi-weekly at first, *L'Avenir* became a weekly on 23 October and appeared on Saturdays. When Batchelor left Montreal for the United States in November, Dorion remained sole managing director of the paper, which he owned with his brother Antoine-Aimé. The year 1847 consequently represented for Jean-Baptiste-Éric a period of intense activity. Although the inspiration behind *L'Avenir*, in September he had added to his time-consuming occupations the duties of secretary of the Société Mercantile d'Économie, which he and friends, who were also store clerks, had just founded. This organization had as its purpose to "encourage Canadian store clerks to save their salaries and make every effort to diffuse commercial knowledge among the class of young men concerned with trade."

Dorion was elected second vice-president of the Institut Canadien at the beginning of November 1847. He therefore had at his disposal a double tribune, a newspaper and a discussion club, where he could develop his views on a question that deeply concerned him: a more practical education directed towards trade and industry. In 1849 he would demand for Montreal the opening of a commercial school. Trade was, in his eyes, "the regulator of material progress, the vanguard of civilization." Second to trade and industry, Dorion attached great importance to the development of agriculture, especially in the Eastern Townships where intensive settlement was taking place. He already saw that this region could draw a large proportion of the young French agricultural population of Lower Canada, who were being attracted towards the United States. His brother Abbé Hercule, who had been a missionary and colonizer since 1843, was established at Wickham, near Drummondville, where two of his other brothers, Nérée and François-Edmond, were engaged in trade. It is not surprising, then, that Dorion should take the initiative in urging the Institut Canadien and the

Société Mercantile d'Économie to study the settlement problem, after Abbé Bernard O'Reilly, a young Irish priest serving in the Eastern Townships, had inserted in *Le Canadien* (Quebec) of 12 Oct. 1847 an article stressing the importance for the French Canadian community of settling its own sons on this territory, rather than letting them cross the American border. At Dorion's instigation, the "Association pour le peuplement des Cantons de l'Est" was founded. Enthusiasm was maintained for a certain time. Bishop Ignace Bourget* and Louis-Joseph Papineau stood surety for the movement. But the collaboration of these two men in an undertaking could not last long. From the beginning one might have expected that water and fire could not be joined with impunity! By the end of 1848, political and ideological differences had shattered the association. Dorion could only point to one settlement resulting from the association, Roxton, which in 1851 numbered 1,222 inhabitants.

For some months quarrels increased in the French Canadian group. Their origin was attributed to Papineau, who demanded the "repeal of the Union [of the Canadas]." *L'Avenir*, under the influence of Louis-Antoine Dessaulles*, Papineau's nephew, had finally come round to the great man's way of thinking, while the bishop of Montreal, worried by the turn of events in Europe, where Pius IX had just been driven from Rome, firmly supported in his pastoral letter of 18 Jan. 1849 the government of Louis-Hippolyte LA FONTAINE and Robert Baldwin* against the "revolutionaries" of Papineau and *L'Avenir*. Bishop Bourget rightly feared the influence of *L'Avenir*. Dorion, who about 15 April 1848 had given up his work as a clerk in a business firm to concentrate on the newspaper, watched its circulation grow from month to month. From 700 copies in April 1848, it reached 1,200 with 1,050 subscribers by the end of November. Faced with this unquestionable success, both clerical and political opponents banded together in fierce defence. The "enfant terrible" bore the brunt of the attack. In one incident his efforts were vain: George-Étienne Cartier*, during the episode of "La Tuque bleue" [see Charles DAOUST], refused to duel with him on the pretext that he did not want to fight a child. To Dorion's extreme humiliation, Joseph Doutre* was chosen instead! But on 16 May 1840 Dorion took his revenge; on Rue Saint-Vincent, he assaulted Hector-Louis Langevin*, editor of *Mélanges religieux*, and received a fine of 25 "shillings."

Cartier and Langevin represented *L'Avenir*'s main adversaries, the La Fontaine–Baldwin party and the clergy, *Mélanges religieux* being

Dorion

the unofficial organ of the diocese of Montreal. "It was just like the men who created the scheme of Union and of English responsible government," stated the editorial of 11 Sept. 1849, "to collaborate with those who cursed their compatriots in 1837 and delivered them without a qualm to their bloody enemies."

In addition, L'Avenir had been debating the question of tithes since 30 Sept. 1848, a campaign it pursued until it ceased publication in 1852. Dorion believed he had a "duty" to end "the greatest abuse of which the agricultural population of Lower Canada can complain"; they indeed bore the burden alone. For Dorion, the clergy were the enemy of all reform, because, paradoxically, they were too attached to their tithes. Did not priests teach contempt for the wealth of this earth? How then was one to explain their thinking only of acquiring riches? Tithes did not exist in France or in the United States. Why should not Canada free itself of this anachronistic custom and replace it by uniform payment for all ecclesiastics?

In defiance of the supporters of responsible government, L'Avenir preached annexation to the United States. Here again it met stubborn resistance on the part of the clergy, which was, as Pierre-Joseph-Olivier Chauveau* wrote, "the body most strongly opposed to annexation and the most sincerely loyal." This antagonism increased still further when Dorion's paper began its campaign for the abolition of seigneurial tenure. The clergy now saw itself violently taken to task by the democrats, because it owned seigneuries. The Séminaire de Québec was especially singled out. Dorion was inexhaustible in his sarcasms concerning "that leech," "seigneurial tenure," that "privileged caste" which "waxes fat on the sweat of the people," and "in the dark, nibbles at the cake which has been dangled above the masses, at their expense and unknown to them." He closely linked annexation and the abolition of seigneurial tenure. It was his hope that once the former was accomplished, "the people will be sovereign master," since they will no longer be under the protection of the "King-Masters and Seigneurs." These extremist arguments naturally aroused a storm of protest in conservative and clerical ranks. But even among the well-wishers in the group now called the Rouges, several shared the opinion of Papineau, who deplored "the exaggerated nature of L'Avenir's views on reform."

Soon Dorion and his friends would face a terrible ordeal. On 18 Feb. 1850, Louis-Joseph-Amédée Papineau* wrote in his diary: "Last night when we were going to bed a fire broke out, and its glow lit the whole town. We judged

that it was on Rue Saint-Paul, or the street beside the water, near Place Jacques-Cartier. Indeed we learn this morning that it was *number 106 Rue Saint-Paul*! The Institut Canadien and its volumes! L'Avenir and its printing shop and its press!" To this material disaster was added a much more painful blow for the managing director of L'Avenir: on 17 Dec. 1851 his brother in arms and closest collaborator in the editing of the newspaper, Gustave Papineau, Louis-Joseph Papineau's son, in whom his father had recognized "much talent," although "too fiery" a temperament, died in the flower of his youth after a six-month illness. In the same year Dorion experienced a serious political reverse. After the ministry of La Fontaine and Baldwin resigned and was replaced by that of Francis Hincks* and Augustin-Norbert MORIN, he was a candidate in Champlain county in the November 1851 election. He defended the democrats' programme which he had reformulated in plain language in L'Avenir on 4 January. The abolition of tithes and of seigneurial tenure, the repeal of the Union, and "finally and above all" the independence of Canada and its annexation to the United States were obviously the points closest to his heart. The electorate did not respond favourably to his efforts. He was obliged to withdraw, after the first day of voting, in favour of Thomas Marchildon.

To complete his misfortune, his paper was in difficulty. From one edition per week, L'Avenir went to one every ten days in October 1851 and to one every fortnight the month after. Already those who styled themselves "the true democrats in Canada" were busy laying the foundation for a new paper, Le Pays (Montreal), which would support a moderate liberalism. Louis-Joseph-Amédée Papineau noted receiving the prospectus on 2 Jan. 1852, and the first number appeared on 15 January. Six days later L'Avenir announced it would cease publication: it had then 927 subscribers. It reappeared sporadically from 17 June on, and finally ended on 24 Nov. 1852. A most important stage in Canadian liberalism came to a close with the disappearance of the paper Jean-Baptiste-Éric Dorion had sustained by dint of sacrifice: the "enfant terrible" of the peaceful parish of Sainte-Anne-de-la-Pérade had become, thanks to his newspaper, the "enfant terrible" of Canadian politics.

Before leaving Montreal he published a pamphlet, *Institut-canadien en 1852*; because of the destruction of the archives in the fire of February 1850 this pamphlet remains an irreplaceable source for the history of the institute from its beginnings until that fateful date. Dorion recalls some of his personal history when he expresses delight at seeing that "the Institut Canadien is now the rendez-vous of the intelligent and active youth of our city, which meets every Thursday evening to discuss publicly any questions that interest, instruct, and amuse at the same time. The library and newsroom become more important from day to day, and are an inexhaustible source from which young people can daily derive knowledge of history, the arts, sciences, and letters, as well as all subjects of practical utility" (they were stocked with 1,600 volumes and subscribed to 64 papers). The institute, which had 350 members in Montreal, extended its educational influence through branches in some ten urban centres in Canada. Dorion had identified himself so closely with the Institut Canadien that when he left Montreal for Durham, near Drummondville, some part of it went with him. In December 1856, scarcely three years after he had established himself as a pioneer settler, he founded the Mechanics' Institute of Drummond county.

Dorion came to Durham when his missionary brother Hercule was leaving it to take over the parish of Sainte-Anne-d'Yamachiche. Abbé Dorion had had an active part in transferring the centre of worship for the region from Wickham to Durham, where a temporary chapel had been erected on a piece of land he had purchased on 13 Jan. 1848 from settler Charles-Auguste Boucher. This initiative had caused sharp recriminations at Wickham, particularly when it was noticed that Jean-Baptiste-Éric Dorion was making his home near this chapel. There were suspicions of connivance between the two brothers, of an attempt by the priest to prepare a better future for his younger brother.

The latter displayed at once, in this tiny setting, the indomitable energy of which he had so often given proof on the wider stage of Montreal. He soon obtained a post office for the village, to which he gave the name of the newspaper that had just died: L'Avenirville (L'Avenir). A store and a small sawmill brought new life to the little centre. But above all this relentless anti-cleric, this voracious foe of priests, was seen busily engaged in bringing quickly to fruition his brother Hercule's plans for a brick church to replace the chapel. Called Saint-Pierre-de-Durham, it was completed in 1854. Later a presbytery was built through his efforts. These manifold activities had nevertheless left him time to marry. On 21 June 1853, at Saint-Joseph-de-Soulanges, he wed Marie Abby Victoria Hays, daughter of Eleazar and Josephte Trestler. Three boys and a girl were born of this union.

Dorion soon won the settlers' friendship by a politeness that was in no way obsequious, a tact-ful manner, and a willingness to give practical day-to-day help. He was therefore banking on a genuine popularity when he took part in the election of 1854, which saw the democrats take 16 of Canada East's 65 seats. Among them were 11 members of the Institut Canadien. Arthur Buies* was to call them in his *Réminiscences* "the brilliant group of 1854." Dorion was one of those elected, beating his opponent by 1,061 votes in the united counties of Drummond and Arthabaska.

In the assembly, he rejoined his elder brother Antoine-Aimé, who had been returned by the city of Montreal. With the reputation as a tough fighter he had acquired at *L'Avenir*, this incorrigible man took good care to be true to himself. Hence he quickly became the favourite target for the partisans of the reform party. Gaspard Le Mage (the pseudonym of Joseph-Charles Taché* and Pierre-Joseph-Olivier Chauveau), inserted articles in *Le Journal de Québec*, *Le Canadien*, and *La Minerve* (Montreal), and these were then put together in a brochure, *La Pléiade rouge*, which, *Le Pays* had to admit, displayed "wit and attic elegance." It painted a vitriolic portrait of Jean-Baptiste-Éric Dorion: "The skull of an old man on the face and body of a child, eyes starting from his head, an excessively wide mouth, thin, compressed lips through which emerges a strident, nasal and cracked voice." The country had for a moment vainly thought it could breathe more easily when *L'Avenir* foundered. Dorion had decided to go and beget "in the Bois-Francs, deep in our age-old forests," "a swarm of little men in his image," "practising among themselves the democratic and social virtues, and cursing in their small hearts the *sbirros* and the tyrants."

This sarcasm revealed the importance political opponents attributed to Jean-Baptiste-Éric Dorion, whose contributions during assembly debates made their mark every time. He was particularly concerned to have the uncultivated land that settlers were already occupying in the township of Durham made over to them by the squatters' bill; he proposed unsuccessfully that the united counties of Drummond and Arthabaska be divided to give each of them the right to elect a representative; he attacked the plan for the confederation of the provinces of British America, on which discussions had begun, and he did so with all his strength. He remained obsessed until his last days with this threat that hung over his compatriots, being convinced that a confederation would gradually submerge the Francophone element in an Anglophone ensemble.

But above all he spoke passionately on the bill to abolish seigneurial tenure. Like his democrat

Dorion

friends, he did not find the act favourable enough to the *censitaires*. Under the pseudonym "Frère de Jean-Baptiste," he wrote a pamphlet, *Tenure seigneuriale*, whose sub-title, *Paie, pauvre peuple, paie!*, clearly indicated its tone and content. The exploitation of the settlers, "betrayed, pillaged, sold" at the time of the redemption of seigneurial rights, foreshadowed, in his eyes, the exploitation that would be visited on French Canadians by the federal union which was being more and more discussed: "It's going fine, Baptiste! The great Union of all the British provinces is upon us. Now that we are attached to Upper Canada, I would wager that the mission of the new governor is to tie us by our feet to New Brunswick, Nova Scotia, Prince Edward Island, and Newfoundland! How enviable is this plan for us Lower Canadians! What influence we would have in parliament: one Canadian against seven Englishmen!"

During the 1857–58 elections, Dorion stood again in Drummond and Arthabaska, but was defeated by a Conservative, Christopher Dunkin*. He was no more successful in Maskinongé. Only nine representatives with Antoine-Aimé Dorion as leader formed the new group of French Canadian Liberals in the assembly. This modest success, which marked a distinct falling off since 1854, was attributed to a more widespread intervention of the clergy in the elections than had occurred in 1851 and 1854. In Jean-Baptiste-Éric Dorion's case, one of the arguments propounded by the Liberals, non-denominational education, had certainly contributed to his defeat, for, from the time of his founding of the Mechanics' Institute in Drummond county, he had not hesitated to debate there the question of the teaching of religion in school, and obviously, to suggest a liberal solution.

Returning to private life, he now gave more time to running his estate, which included land, a store, and a small sawmill. But his management always lacked clear purpose, so that although he had a good income he never became rich. The very spirit of intransigence in discussion, the uncompromising polemicist, he was signally weak in his dealings with his servants and those around him. His employees abused a situation in which supervision tended to be remote, for Dorion took refuge in his house as much as he could in order to read. "His life," wrote one of his biographers, "was spent in reading, reading ceaselessly, persistently, so great was his eagerness to learn. His wife, who had a liking for amusement, found this life too *literary*, and complained about the boring tranquillity of an existence in which books, papers, and journals formed the major part." But if anyone who met him was not put off by his icy seriousness – he was rarely seen to laugh – he was found to be obliging. The farmers of L'Avenir and the neighbourhood did not hesitate to consult him about their difficulties. He himself sometimes brought them together, for when he gave a supper party or organized an evening gathering, he invited the whole parish.

Dorion returned to public life in 1861, when he was re-elected for Drummond and Arthabaska. Although he did not know it, his days were numbered. He was not yet 40 years old, but a serious cardiac affliction threatened a premature end. No doubt he had a premonition of his own fate in the sudden death of his twin brother François-Edmond, on the morning of 8 June 1862. But he took no notice of it and gave of himself unsparingly, particularly during the election, when he travelled through one county after another in a small cart drawn at a spanking pace by two grey horses. "Here's the enfant terrible," people would exclaim when he arrived with a foaming team. Victory was assured for the Liberal supporters, as Dorion had no equal in confounding an adversary at meetings.

When he founded the first French language newspaper in the Saint-François valley, *Le Défricheur* (L'Avenir), published first in November 1862, he was proud to style himself a "farmer and representative of the people." He was a *Jean Rivard*, whose story Antoine Gérin-Lajoie* had just told in fictional form: "our story," confirmed Dorion in *Le Défricheur* of 11 December, "and that of all our neighbours, with little difference." He strove to carry through the motto he had given to his paper: "Work ennobles." His articles were rich in practical advice to farmers for improving their agricultural methods. He had often tested these opinions in the field. He also took an interest in forest and mining resources. But the farmer often gave place to the MLA, and then there were long reflections on the evils of confederation, which he energetically fought in the assembly: "I am opposed to confederation," he exclaimed, "because I perceive countless difficulties related to the joint powers granted to local and general government on several matters. These conflicts will always turn to the advantage of the general government and to the detriment of the sometimes very legitimate claims of the provinces." One of Dorion's last political acts was to sign the manifesto of the 20 MLAs opposed to confederation and addressed to the colonial secretary, Lord Carnarvon.

Dorion was an avowed anti-cleric even in his

everyday conversation, never missed an opportunity for a sarcastic remark about the clergy, and even brought an action, which he lost, against the Oblate father Joseph-Marie Royer, who had preached a parochial retreat at L'Avenir in January 1861. Yet Dorion went to services in his parish fairly regularly. It is true, however, that he kept his distance from the sacraments. Thus on 1 Nov. 1866, All Saints' Day, he attended mass "in a devout frame of mind and with a book in his hand," according to the unequivocal testimony of parish priest Abbé Pierre-Trefflé Gouin, in a letter written that day to the vicar general Louis-François Laflèche*. Abbé Gouin added that for the collection in the church on behalf of the victims of fire on 14 October at Saint-Sauveur and Saint-Roch in Quebec, Dorion had to borrow his offering: "In giving, this morning, he gave of his poverty."

At about two o'clock that afternoon, Dorion was travelling to Richmond when he was stricken with a heart attack. He was rushed home, and soon passed away. On 5 November he was given an impressive funeral, his brother, the parish priest of Yamachiche, officiating. His other brother, Antoine-Aimé, leader of the Lower Canadian Liberals, was in the first row, lost in grief. Jean-Baptiste-Éric lies in the little cemetery at L'Avenir, under an epitaph which preserves his familiar name, "L'Enfant Terrible."

The disappearance of such a controversial man produced a variety of commentary in the press. But his brothers in arms of the Institut Canadien, in whose founding he had participated and of which he had been one of the vice-presidents, then president from November 1850 to 1851, owed him a special tribute. It was rendered by the president, Louis-Antoine Dessaulles: "J. B. E. Dorion was one of the most clear-sighted minds that have graced our country. A tireless worker, his energy and perseverance literally knew no bounds. An elevated spirit, an upright and honest nature, an exceptional soul, he belonged to that phalanx of public figures, unfortunately too small in this province, whose motto at all times and places is: Everything for one's country, nothing for oneself."

Apart from the final remark, which shows the mark of the political partisan, one can agree with Dessaulles' judgement. Even Dorion's anticlericalism can be explained by the events in which he was involved and the combats he waged with his vizor raised. In the middle of the last century tolerance was generally the Christian virtue that was the most cheerfully mocked.

PHILIPPE SYLVAIN

J.-B.-É. Dorion was the editor of *Institut-canadien en 1852* (Montréal, 1852), and the author of *Un souvenir pour 1844 . . .* (Trois-Rivières, 1844), and *Tenure seigneuriale; paie, pauvre peuple, paie!* (Québec, 1855). The last work was published under the pseudonym "Frère de Jean-Baptiste." ANQ-Q, AP, Coll. Papineau, Louis-Joseph-Amédée Papineau, Journal d'un Fils de la liberté, 1835–38 (typescript). ASTR, Papiers J.-Napoléon Bureau, correspondance 1860–69. *L'Avenir*, 1847–52. *Le Défricheur* (L'Avenir, Qué.), 1862–66. Institut canadien, *Annuaire* (Montréal), 1866. Bernard, *Les Rouges*. Maurice Carrier, "Le libéralisme de Jean-Baptiste-Éric Dorion" (thèse de doctorat d'université, université Laval, Québec, 1967). J.-R. Rioux, "L'Institut canadien; les débuts de l'Institut canadien et du journal *l'Avenir* (1844–1849)" (thèse de DES, université Laval, 1967). J.-B. St-Amant, *Un coin des Cantons de l'Est, histoire de l'envahissement pacifique mais irrésistible d'une race* (Drummondville, Qué., 1932).

DORMER, HENRY EDWARD, soldier; b. 29 Nov. 1844 at Grove Park, near Warwick, England, the fourth son and youngest child of Joseph Thaddeus Dormer, 11th Baron Dormer, and Elizabeth Anne Tichborne; d. unmarried on 2 Oct. 1866 at London, Canada West.

The Dormers had largely remained Roman Catholic after the English Reformation, had provided distinguished servants for the Tudor and Stuart monarchs, and were among the more notable recusant British families; military service in British and later Austrian forces was a tradition. Henry Edward Dormer was sent to St Mary's College, Oscott, near Birmingham, in 1855. A year later he was compelled to withdraw because of poor health and spent the next four years with private tutors. Much of the deep piety that marked his later life could be seen developing in his interest in the family's private chapel and in his unusual thoughtfulness towards others. In 1860 he returned to St Mary's College to prepare for the examinations for an army commission. He was gazetted ensign in the 4th battalion of the 60th Regiment (King's Own Royal Rifles) in November 1863. An older brother was Lieutenant-General Sir James Dormer who served with the British army in Egypt in the 1880s and in India in the 1890s.

After basic training at Winchester, Henry Dormer joined his battalion at its base in Dublin. In 1865 the regiment, now absorbed into the Royal Green Jackets, was sent to London, Canada West, as part of the imperial troops guarding the Canadian frontier against Fenian attacks and possible American intervention. Dormer himself arrived in London on 24 Feb. 1866. Not yet 22 years of age and with every

Dorval

material advantage before him, he embarked on a life of deep Christianity and self-denial.

Dormer had been profoundly influenced spiritually by the history of his own family and by a deep attachment to the Order of Preachers or the Dominicans. A sister, to whom he was devoted, belonged to the Dominican Priory of Stone in Staffordshire, and in London he found the only Catholic church, St Peter's, staffed by Dominican friars brought from Kentucky in 1861 by the first bishop of London, Pierre-Adolphe Pinsoneault*. Dormer's spirituality was at once mystical and active. When off duty, and often through the night, he would worship to the point of ecstasy in either St Peter's Church or the chapel of the Sacred Heart Convent. He also attended constantly to the poor, the sick, and the inebriated. He bestowed money, his own clothes, food, and other necessities upon those in want, and gave generously of his time and effort to the poor and lonely sick. He gave religious instruction to children at St Peter's Church and to soldiers and brother officers if they requested it. At the end of September 1866, while nursing a woman ill from typhoid fever, he caught the disease and died from it on 2 October. He had just made up his mind to enter the Order of Preachers.

Ensign Dormer received the military funeral usually reserved for officers of higher rank. Contemporary accounts all state that at his death people said "The saint is dead!" In 1922, with devotion to Dormer's memory still flourishing, Bishop Michael Francis Fallon* established a *cultus* in the diocese of London as a prelude to eventual canonization. He renewed this directive in 1930, and Bishop Thomas Kidd* gave the same encouragement in 1950. Dormer's centennial was celebrated on 2 Oct. 1966 in London by representatives of church and state. His remains were reburied with full military honours in the military section of St Peter's Cemetery, and a public memorial service was held.

JOHN K. A. O'FARRELL

London Free Press, 3–4 Oct. 1866. *Burke's peerage* (1970), 822–24. [A. T. Drane], *Biographical memoir of the Hon. Henry Edward Dormer, late of the 60th Rifles* (London, 1867; repub. in *A thousand arrows; biographical memoir of the Hon. Henry Edward Dormer, late of the 60th Rifles* ([London, Ont., 1970]). J.K.A. Farrell [O'Farrell], "The history of the Roman Catholic Church in London, Ontario, 1826–1931" (unpublished MA thesis, University of Western Ontario, London, Ont., 1949); *The world of Henry Edward Dormer in 1866, a thousand arrows; biographical memoir of the Hon. Henry Edward Dormer, late of the 60th Rifles* ([London, Ont., 1970]). B. W. Kelly, *The Hon. Henry Edward Dormer (King's Royal Rifles), 1844–1866* . . . (London, 1930). J. K. A. O'Farrell, "The world of Henry Edward Dormer in 1866," and Mary Turner, "Biographical sketch of the Honorable Henry Edward Dormer, 1844–1866," *A thousand arrows; biographical memoir of the Hon. Henry Edward Dormer, late of the 60th Rifles* ([London, Ont., 1970]), 8–29 and 30–47 respectively.

DORVAL, MARIE-LOUISE, *dite* **Sainte-Élisabeth**, superior of the Congregation of Notre-Dame and educator; b. 7 June 1794 at Sainte-Famille, Île d'Orléans, daughter of François Dorval and Élisabeth Godbout; d. 1 Aug. 1866 at Montreal.

The Congregation of Notre-Dame had had a mission on the Île d'Orléans since 1685. Marie-Louise Dorval was therefore in very early contact with the sisters, and decided while still young to join them. On 26 June 1815, after her parents' death, she entered the noviciate, and two years later made her profession under the name of Sister Sainte-Élisabeth.

During the first 14 years of religious life, Sister Sainte-Élisabeth taught at the missions of Pointe-aux-Trembles (Neuville) and the lower town of Quebec, the boarding-school at Montreal, and the mission at Saint-François-de-la-Rivière-du-Sud (Saint-François-Montmagny). The tasks Sister Sainte-Élisabeth was subsequently given in her community are evidence of the quality of her work as a teacher. After being mistress of novices at Montreal from 1831 to 1837, she went as director to the boarding-school at Montreal, then to the one in the lower town of Quebec. Thus she supervised the transfer of the latter establishment to the *faubourg* Saint-Roch, where the parish priest Zéphirin Charest* requested the services of the sisters of the congregation. Sister Sainte-Élisabeth is therefore regarded as the founder of the convent of Saint-Roch, which was the extension of the first mission of the "Daughters of Mother Bourgeoys [Marguerite Bourgeoys*]" at Quebec. From 1844 to 1970 the convent of Saint-Roch was to have an influence on the history of Quebec by providing an education which took a variety of forms in response to the geographic and social changes in Quebec society.

From 1848 to 1855, Sister Sainte-Élisabeth carried out the most important duties in the community, first as assistant then from 1849 as superior. The life and work of the community, which in 1850 comprised 148 sisters and 27 missions, developed steadily. Five new missions were opened: Sainte-Croix de Lotbinière (1849), Saint-Eustache (1849), Sainte-Anne-d'Yamachiche (1852), Sainte-Anne-de-la-Pérade (1855), and Villa-Maria at Montreal (1854).

While she was watching over this expansion of the congregation, Sister Sainte-Élisabeth preserved the unity of the community whose mother house was at Montreal. In 1854 the question of establishing a noviciate at Quebec was again raised. In 1702 Sister Marguerite Le Moyne* de Sainte-Marie had refused the request made by Bishop Saint-Vallier [La Croix*] for a noviciate at Quebec, thus following the position taken by Mother Bourgeoys herself. Sister Sainte-Élisabeth wanted to remain faithful to the spirit of the founder, and rejected a plan that implied the division of the community into two institutes. In 1855 it was decided that the congregation would not set up a noviciate at Quebec, but that it would send there missionary sisters proportionate in number to the novices from the Quebec diocese.

In 1856, a year after the end of her term as superior of the community, Sister Sainte-Élisabeth was invited to take part in the missionary endeavours of the congregation. On 2 June 1856 Bishop Colin Francis MacKinnon* of the diocese of Arichat, Nova Scotia, went to Montreal to ask the congregation to establish a first mission at Arichat on Île Madame. Despite her advanced age, Sister Sainte-Élisabeth accompanied the four sisters responsible for the mission. On their arrival the sisters, who did not speak English, were surprised to find a solely Anglophone population at Arichat and to have no other interpreter but the bishop, "whereas they had been promised something else." Sister Sainte-Élisabeth stayed nearly three months at Arichat. When she left for Montreal, the work was well underway. The sisters had started classes on 26 June 1856 in a house given to them by the bishop, which became known as the Academy. By July the enrolment had risen to 100, and the missionaries had also agreed to take in boarders; they did this by rearranging the Academy and a second house which the bishop had made over to them for this purpose. The congregation worked at Arichat until 1900, when the council-general ruled that since the number of pupils was insufficient the mission should be closed.

On her return to Montreal Sister Sainte-Élisabeth had to retire to the infirmary, for her health no longer allowed her to take part in the community's activities. She lived there for ten years, until her death in 1866.

ANDRÉE DÉSILETS

Archives de la Congrégation de Notre-Dame (Montréal), Annales du couvent d'Arichat fondé en 1856 (2v.); Archives C.N.D.; Biographie des sœurs décédées depuis le 17 août 1855 jusqu'au 14 juin 1871, 99–107 (typescript); Correspondance de sœur Sainte-Élisabeth. Lemire-Marsolais et Lambert, *Hist. de la CND de Montréal*, VI–X.

DOUGLAS, GEORGE MELLIS, doctor; b. at Carlisle, Scotland, where he was baptized on 11 July 1809, son of George Douglas, a Methodist minister, and Mary Mellis; d. 2 June 1864 on the Île aux Ruaux, Lower Canada.

In 1822 George Mellis Douglas went to Utica, N.Y., at the urging of his brother James*, who was practising medicine there. He attended to the latter's affairs while learning medicine. James had to flee from Utica, however, because he feared prosecution for dissecting cadavers, an illegal act at the time, and he settled at Quebec on 13 March 1826; George Mellis joined him there a few days later. Since there were no medical boards in Quebec or Montreal, young Douglas was examined by a committee appointed by the governor and received authorization to practise medicine on 13 Nov. 1827. He apparently carried on his profession with his brother until 1831.

At that period cholera was claiming many victims. It had come from India, spread through England and especially Ireland, and was brought to Quebec every year by the many immigrants. In 1832, as a precautionary measure, Lord Aylmer [Whitworth-Aylmer*], then governor general, set up a provincial board of health and two quarantine stations controlled by the army, one 33 miles down river from Quebec at Grosse Île, and the other at Gaspé, where ships from Europe had to stop for inspection. George Mellis Douglas, who had been a justice of the peace for the Gaspé district since 1831, was appointed medical superintendent of the Gaspé quarantine station on 20 June 1832. While holding this post, he assisted Dr Charles Poole, the medical superintendent of Grosse Île. On 9 May 1836 he succeeded him, at the salary of 25s. a day. This was a heavy year for Douglas since in the Quebec region cholera accounted for 3,452 victims during the summer.

On 31 July 1839 Douglas married Charlotte Saxton Campbell, daughter of Archibald CAMPBELL, a royal notary at Quebec; seven children were born to them. In 1841 he bought a piece of marshy land at the east end of Grosse Île and had it drained and brought under cultivation. As the people of the island found it hard to obtain food, Douglas sold the produce of his farm, particularly milk; nevertheless, he was reproached for this trading. In 1847, to meet the typhus epidemic then raging, he improved conditions at the island hospital by adding some 50 beds to the existing 200. However, the epidemic exceeded all

Douglas

forecasts; by 20 May, 30 vessels from Ireland had carried 12,519 immigrants, of whom more than 1,200 had perished at sea or died on their arrival. The hospital took in up to 2,500 patients at a time, but was no longer adequate. Some of the volunteers who had come to Douglas' aid, including four of the 26 doctors, died; the others were stricken with the fever. Douglas himself did not escape. Yet thanks to the treatment used by him and his colleagues the murderous epidemic was stemmed towards the end of October, although more than 5,000 bodies lay in the cemetery of Grosse Île. In Canada there were 17,300 victims.

In July 1849 a new cholera epidemic struck the town of Quebec, causing more than 1,200 deaths. On Grosse Île, however, Douglas had only some 50 patients to treat. In 1853, a year after the last serious epidemic in the province, Dr Anthony von Iffland* was appointed assistant medical superintendent on Grosse Île. Four years later the quarantine station was placed under the Bureau of Agriculture and Statistics. Douglas found staying on the island less attractive, apparently because of conflicts of interest with Iffland and financial problems. Moreover, he was spending more of his time in England, where in 1858 he married Suzan Cleghorn of Nevis, Scotland, by whom he had a son; his first wife had died six years earlier.

In March 1861 the station on Grosse Île was closed, and on 19 April Douglas was appointed "deputy medical inspector" of ships anchoring in the roadstead of the Rivière Saint-Charles and alongside Cap Diamant. When Gross Île was reestablished as a quarantine station on 22 April 1863, Douglas resumed his post of medical superintendent. Sick and depressed (his second wife had died on 21 Nov. 1860), he learned in March 1864 that steps were being taken to appoint Iffland in his place. On 1 June he went to the Île aux Ruaux (northeast of Île d'Orléans), which he had acquired in 1848 and where he had built a sumptuous house that was still heavily mortgaged. That evening he stabbed himself, and died the next day. The coroner returned a verdict of suicide while temporarily deranged.

George Mellis Douglas was a highly respected doctor, who published a number of articles in medical journals about his professional activities on Grosse Île and the illnesses he had cared for there. For example, in 1847 he expounded his theory of the non-contagiousness of cholera, which contradicted that of Dr William Marsden. The discovery of the cholera vibrio in 1885, however, was to prove Marsden right. Douglas was a faithful member of the Literary and Historical Society of Quebec and was its secretary in

1842–43. Throughout his career, he distinguished himself by his devotion to duty as well as by his honesty and uprightness.

SYLVIO LEBLOND

George Mellis Douglas is the author of "On the natural history of the 'Ursus IV Americanus' or American black bear," Literary and Hist. Soc. of Quebec, *Trans.*, IV (1843), 56–64; he also published several articles in the *British American Journal of Medical and Physical Science* (Montreal) in 1847–48. Bureau d'enregistrement de l'île d'Orléans (Saint-Laurent, Qué.), Registre B, 3, no.149; 5, no.410. Bureau d'enregistrement de Québec (Québec), Registre B, 25, no.9773. PAC, RG 1, E1, 85, pp.66–75, 126; 87, pp.432–33, 437–39; 90, pp.327–28; E8, 24, ff.1–5; 74, ff.1–5; 80, ff.9–10; RG 4, A1, S-284, 18 juin 1832; B28, 39; 51, 11 août 1826, 12 nov. 1827. Private archives, Mrs F. N. Douglas (Lakefield, Ont.), correspondence.

Le Canadien, 2 déc. 1836, 9 juill. 1845, 10 janv. 1849, 24 mai 1852, 3 juin, 1ᵉʳ août 1864, 2 mai 1870. [James Douglas], *Journals and reminiscences of James Douglas, M.D.*, ed. James Douglas Jr (New York, 1910), 121, 128, 131. *Morning Chronicle* (Quebec), 3 June 1864. *Quebec Daily Mercury*, 3, 4 June 1864. Heagerty, *Four centuries of medical history in Can.*, I, 106–30, 179–211; II, 25–39. J. A. Jordan, *The Grosse-Isle tragedy and the monument to the Irish fever victims* (Quebec, 1909). M. D. Noble, *A long life* (Newcastle upon Tyne, Eng., 1925), 50–51. [Robert Whyte], *The ocean plague: or, a voyage to Quebec in an Irish emigrant vessel, embracing a quarantine at Grosse Isle in 1847 . . .* (Boston, 1848). Sylvio Leblond, "Le docteur George Douglas (1804–1864)," *Cahiers des Dix*, 34 (1969), 145–64; "James Douglas, M.D. (1800–1886)," Canadian Medical Assoc., *Journal* (Toronto), 66, (1952), 283–87; "La médecine dans la province de Québec avant 1847," *Cahiers des Dix*, 35 (1970), 69–95; "William Marsden (1807–1885); essai biographique," *Laval médical* (Québec), 41 (1970), 639–59. C. A. Mitchell, "Events leading up to and the establishment of the Grosse Ile quarantine station," *Medical Services Journal, Canada* (Ottawa), XXIII (1967), 1436–44.

DOUGLAS, Sir HOWARD, soldier, educator, author, inventor, and colonial administrator; b. 23 Jan. 1776 at Gosport, England, son of Sir Charles Douglas* whose naval force relieved Quebec in 1776, and his second wife, Sarah Wood; m. July 1799 Anne Dundas of Edinburgh, Scotland, and they had three daughters and six sons; d. 9 Nov. 1861 at Tunbridge Wells, England.

Howard Douglas grew up near Edinburgh under the care of an aunt, Mrs Helena Baillie. Educated at the Royal Military Academy, Woolwich, he passed out as a 2nd lieutenant of the Royal Artillery on 1 Jan. 1794. He commanded the artillery of the northern district of England during an invasion scare in the spring of 1795 and in August sailed for Quebec as senior officer of a detachment of troops on the *Phillis*. It was wrecked off Little Bay Head, Cape Ray, Nfld, and the few survivors rescued were taken to the fishing port of Great Jervais on Fortune Bay, Nfld, where they spent the winter. After three months in Halifax, Douglas proceeded to Quebec City. In the summer of 1796 he commanded a schooner sent down the St Lawrence by the governor of Lower Canada, Robert Prescott*, to investigate rumours of a French fleet heading for Quebec. In 1797 and 1798 he served in Kingston, Upper Canada. While in Canada, Douglas formed a liaison with a young lady of Quebec City, by whom he had a daughter. He returned to Britain in 1798 as mate on a trading brig. A letter written to the British secretary of state for war in December 1812, emphasizing the importance of strengthening British naval power on Lake Ontario, reveals Douglas' continuing interest in the defence of the Canadas and a sound appreciation of the strategic situation.

Following service with the Royal Artillery, the Royal Horse Artillery, and Congreve's Mortar-Brigade, Douglas had been appointed commandant of the senior department of the Royal Military College at High Wycombe, England, in 1804, and afterwards inspector-general of instructions. From this position, which he held until 1820, he influenced a generation of imperial and Indian army officers. He eventually became widely known as a military theorist and teacher. Proficient in mathematics, he wrote on military bridges (1816), fortifications (1819), and naval gunnery (1820), and later on naval tactics (1832), and, after his North American governorship, on naval warfare with steam power (1856). He was also an inventor, notably of an improved reflecting circle or semicircle for land and marine surveying patented in 1811. He became a Fellow of the Royal Society in 1812.

Douglas saw further military service as assistant quartermaster-general. He played an important role in the embarkation of the troops after the battle of La Coruña in Spain on 18 Jan. 1809, and took part in directing the artillery attack on Flushing in Holland (Netherlands) later in the same year. From August 1811 to September 1812, in the north of Spain, he helped to co-ordinate the efforts of the British forces with the Spanish regular and guerilla armies.

Promotion to major-general in 1821 made Douglas eligible for a colonial governorship. One of the first vacancies was that of lieutenant governor and commander-in-chief in New Brunswick, following the death of George Stracy Smyth* on 27 March 1823. He secured the post with the aid of highly placed political and military supporters, and on 28 Aug. 1824 arrived in New Brunswick to assume his duties. He proved by far the most popular of New Brunswick's colonial governors. He was charming, fond of talk, and always ready to listen to others, but the roots of his popularity lay deeper, in a contagious optimism which matched the mood of the turbulent, expansive society taking shape in New Brunswick. He had the restless energy and inventiveness of an ambitious man who enjoyed using his enormous powers in the service of a community of which he seems to have become fond and whose future he sought consciously to mould.

In 1825, while temporarily commander-in-chief of the Atlantic region of British North America, he visited the main places in his command and toured the outports along the east and north coasts of New Brunswick, which no lieutenant governor had previously visited. This region, at the time a single large county, Northumberland, was enjoying prosperity from the timber trade but suffering from the absence of law and order. Douglas reorganized the local government, naming two new counties, Kent and Gloucester, with shiretowns at Liverpool and Bathurst. In Northumberland, fearing the continuation of "those killer rival feelings" between Newcastle and the town he renamed Chatham, he tried to persuade the local magistrates to accept his policy of promoting the development of one urban centre for the county, in Chatham, a seaport and road junction where a road from Fredericton could join a projected road between Halifax and Quebec. The magistrates, however, insisted on Newcastle as shiretown. A road to the Canadas, he felt, would be needed along the Gulf shore in case of war, and he urged the governor of Canada, Lord Dalhousie [Ramsay*], to ask the assembly of Lower Canada to begin the section from the St Lawrence River to the New Brunswick border. As an inducement he sent the governor a sketch of the "uncommonly fine" site for the town he had named Dalhousie, near where the road would enter New Brunswick.

On 19 Sept. 1825 Government House in Fredericton was burned to the ground, and three weeks later, on 7 October, fires burned over 6,000 square miles of forest from the north shore of Miramichi Bay to the Oromocto River valley. Newcastle was destroyed in 15 minutes, and from the villages and farms people fled into the Miramichi to escape the flames; 160 people were killed. Douglas personally directed the fire fighting in Fredericton where 80 houses and stores were destroyed. It was probably then that he earned the awesome respect of the people of

Douglas

New Brunswick. The *New Brunswick Courier* on 10 Oct. 1825 described him as "our active and indefatigable Governor . . . through whom wonders absolutely were effected." He sent an agent to Quebec to purchase supplies, launched a public subscription, and toured the stricken Miramichi area while it was still burning.

Douglas had begun a reorganization of the provincial militia on his arrival. By 1831, he reported to the Colonial Office, it had 15,708 men, about 11,000 of them armed, all organized into regiments, completely officered, and drilled according to a simple code he had devised; there were two small troops of mounted militia and "three very good Companies of Field artillery." His successor, Sir Archibald Campbell*, an orthodox old soldier, thought this force of little value, but Douglas' experience in Spain had bred in him great faith in popular armies.

It was a dispute over the ownership of territory lying between Maine and New Brunswick that had led Douglas to try to strengthen the colony in this way. Efforts by British and American commissioners, appointed under the Treaty of Ghent in 1814 to settle the boundary line, had reached an impasse. In 1826 a party led by John Baker raised the American flag in the Madawaska settlements whose French-speaking residents were enrolled in the New Brunswick militia and voted in New Brunswick elections; Madawaska lay astride the route between Fredericton and Quebec City and Baker's group "opposed the postman in the prosecution of his duties." In 1827 Baker was apprehended and in May 1828 tried before the New Brunswick Supreme Court; his sentence was a fine and a jail term. There was an outcry in Maine, while in British North America Douglas was acclaimed for his firm action. Years later he stated that if he had received an order to halt proceedings, he would have disobeyed it and resigned his position. Authorities in Washington, including President Andrew Jackson, remarked on the correctness of Douglas' conduct throughout the affair. The boundary question was eventually referred to arbitration by the king of the Netherlands and in March 1829 Douglas was called to England to act as adviser to the British delegation. His presence at The Hague when the Belgians asserted their independence in 1830 led to his being employed on a secret mission of observation on the Dutch frontier.

All areas of New Brunswick life felt the influence of Douglas' restless activity. Deploring the New England Company's policy of taking Indian children from their families to be educated, he wanted families kept together, with adequate reserves for Indians who lived by hunting and gathering, and with freehold titles and government encouragement for Indians who farmed. He opposed the sending of Protestant missionaries to the Indians, and wanted the legislature to pay an allowance to enable a Roman Catholic missionary to live among them. He encouraged the establishment of rural schools. He persuaded the province to construct lighthouses on the coast and tried to get interprovincial cooperation for building rescue stations on isolated points. He tramped through the woods around Mount Douglas to lay out a new road between Saint John and Fredericton. Upon both imperial and colonial governments he urged the need for a canal across the Isthmus of Chignecto, a sluiceway around Grand Falls, and a suspension bridge across the mouth of the Saint John River. He supported planned immigration from Great Britain but objected to the British government's encouragement of pauper emigration which brought large numbers of destitute and unskilled persons to Saint John. He promoted agricultural societies and fairs. In Fredericton new stone public buildings, Government House, King's College (University of New Brunswick), and a barracks, were built during his term of office [*see* J.E. WOOLFORD]. The city's social life was stimulated by the lively Douglas family, some of whom were active water-colour painters.

Douglas had been appointed to New Brunswick at a time when Lord Liverpool's government, spurred on by parliamentary criticism and by permanent officials in the Treasury and the Board of Trade, was adopting a policy of retrenchment and reform, including reductions in parliamentary spending in the colonies and development of centralized Treasury control over colonial revenues and expenditures. Critical of the new economists who looked upon the empire as a burden, Douglas was also convinced that colonial interests were not being sufficiently considered and that the relationship between Britain and her colonies was being undermined. He saw the North American colonies as a source of strength to Britain and as capable of becoming a dynamic federation, escaping the instability he believed inherent in the emerging American democracy. The removal of restrictions on colonial trade in 1825, he felt, might "lead to an Union or Confederation of these Provinces hereafter, under the protection of Great Britain . . . [or] an Union with those States which have already emancipated themselves." In the same year he protested against a dispatch from the colonial secretary, Lord Bathurst, instructing him to ask the assembly to guarantee the expenses of the colony's civil government for a ten year period.

The small British parliamentary vote, of less than £5,000 a year for the civil government of New Brunswick, was money wisely spent in a colony which cleared 1,100 ships, employing 11,000 seamen, from its ports each year. So long as British officials were paid by parliament, he argued, New Brunswickers did not object to their presence. But dependence of the executive for salaries on assembly votes would greatly strengthen democratic forces and weaken the Council which "operated by keeping a high tone, and a tight hand, upon the Lower House, as well in executive affairs, as in Legislative measures." Fortunately for Douglas' relations with the assembly, this issue became theoretical when in December Lord Bathurst withdrew his instruction because of the province's losses in the Miramichi fire and its expense for a new Government House. In 1827 the Canning government withdrew the parliamentary grant but it was restored, though reduced, by the Wellington government in 1828 and continued until 1830.

The Treasury, however, was less aware of colonial susceptibilities than the Colonial Office. In December 1825 it ordered that imperial customs officers in the colonies be paid from colonial funds, rather than receiving fees on ships entering and leaving colonial ports. In 1826 more than £9,000 of revenue were diverted from the assembly to pay these officers at Saint John, St Andrews, and Miramichi. The assembly regarded the salaries as exorbitant and the Treasury action as illegal since the Declaratory Act of the British Parliament in 1778 had required that money raised under imperial trade legislation be turned over to colonial assemblies. Douglas agreed substantially with the assembly, as did Lord Bathurst and James Stephen, legal counsel to the Colonial Office, but they were able to gain only limited concessions from the Treasury. In 1828 Douglas reported correspondence among members of neighbouring assemblies in an attempt to co-ordinate opposition to the British government's policy – a form of interprovincial cooperation of which he disapproved.

In his handling of the volatile assembly Douglas showed a talent for political management. At first he found it to be arbitrary in decision, swayed by American ideas, given to a "quick transition of votes" even on important occasions, and much influenced by private feeling. The assembly of 1827 was more to his liking: "there is here, a loyal and truly British feeling," he reported to Huskisson, the colonial secretary in May 1828. The change in his attitude came about in part from the close relationship that developed between Douglas and Richard Si-

monds*, speaker in the new house. The leading members of the assembly in 1828 were, Douglas asserted, favourable to making a permanent settlement of the civil list and the customs house salary question and he asked the colonial secretary for permission to negotiate. But the Treasury was not prepared to settle and the issues were allowed to disturb the province for a further seven years.

A persistent source of difficulty for Douglas was the power of Thomas BAILLIE, who had been appointed commissioner of crown lands and surveyor general in 1824. Baillie held a Treasury commission which made him largely independent of the governor in the financial management of public lands, the main source of crown revenue. Baillie was very much in the public view, since his department dealt directly both with the timber merchants and with the settlers. He also made himself conspicuous by his style of living. When Douglas pointed out to the Colonial Office that Baillie's fees provided an excessive income, Baillie's office was divided. By 1827 Douglas was complaining of actions taken by Baillie "in defiance of my control," and warning of protests from the Council and assembly against acts which they pronounced to be illegal and which Douglas called "most indiscreet." Douglas disapproved of the new land regulations introduced by the Colonial Office in 1827, as placing too much emphasis on public land as a source of revenue to the exclusion of community interests. He favoured planned land settlement with government assistance to settlers, aimed at building a population with the attitudes of English yeomen. He was, however, willing to see large areas sold to companies which would bring capital as well as settlers into the province. He complained about the cost of running Baillie's department and in 1828 urged the Colonial Office to abolish the post of commissioner of crown lands and restore the control of public lands to the Council. He was also asking for authority to negotiate a surrender of the crown's control of the timber fund, quit-rents, and waste lands to the legislature to ensure a permanent provision for the civil list. In his dispute with Baillie and in his position on customs house salaries, Douglas clearly identified himself with colonial opinion and spoke firmly for colonial interests.

Douglas is chiefly honoured today as a founder of the University of New Brunswick, to which he gave a fund for an annual prize, still presented, the Douglas Gold Medal. Just before his appointment as lieutenant governor, the assembly had passed an act supporting the College of New Brunswick, with the understanding that a new charter would be obtained removing religious tests. Douglas accepted this objective, arguing that a college which was open to all would keep the youth of the province from seeking higher education in the United States and that a single adequately endowed institution was preferable to a number of denominational colleges. But the colonial secretary was pressed by a resurgent ecclesiastical establishment in England to oppose efforts to secularize colonial university education. Douglas proceeded with plans for the college and was active in choosing a site and arranging for a fine Georgian building. The royal charter he presented with a flourish of optimistic rhetoric on New Year's Day 1829 was, however, far less liberal than the one that had been sought: King's College, Fredericton, of which he was the first chancellor, was clearly an Anglican institution. Yet his mastery of New Brunswick politics is most clearly evident in his success in persuading the assembly, with its non-Anglican majority, to make grants for the operation of the new college and to pay more than half the cost of the new college building.

It is doubtful whether the Douglas magic could have continued to be successful in the tense political atmosphere of British North America in the early 1830s. He was fortunate to be in New Brunswick in the prosperous years 1824 and 1825 when crown revenues were flourishing, and to be serving a colonial secretary who permitted him a good deal of discretion in using those revenues to encourage social development.

On 19 Feb. 1831, three months after the Whigs came to power in England, Douglas resigned his New Brunswick position in order to carry on a public campaign in defence of the protection which British North American timber enjoyed in the British market. Douglas published three editions of a pamphlet entitled *Considerations on the value and importance of the British North American provinces*. When a government bill to reduce the duties on Baltic timber entering Britain was rejected by the House of Commons, Douglas was acclaimed for saving the North American timber trade; in New Brunswick a public subscription was raised to send him a service of silver plate. But in England he was out of favour. His hard line on the Maine-New Brunswick boundary question was unacceptable to the Whig ministers, and he was opposed both to the Reform bill and to the emancipation of slaves.

After being an unsuccessful Conservative candidate for parliament in 1832 and 1835, Douglas served as lord high commissioner of the Ionian Islands with command of the troops there from 1835 to 1841. In the islands he introduced a new code of laws based on the Greek model, known as the Douglas code. He served as MP for Liverpool from 1842 to 1847, speaking frequently on military questions and drawing on his North American experience in opposing free trade measures. He continued his scientific studies and speculation, being particularly fascinated by the technical questions of ship armour and the development of propellers for steamships. He received many decorations and honours, both Spanish and British, in the course of his career, including CB in 1814, KCB in 1821, GCMG in 1835, and GCB in 1841. Specifically related to the New Brunswick phase of his career was a DCL from Oxford University in 1829.

D. MURRAY YOUNG

The *DNB* article on Douglas contains a list of his published works, though one entry, *Observations on the proposed alterations of the timber duties* (London, 1831), is attributed to Douglas mistakenly. Specifically relevant to North America is *Considerations on the value and importance of the British North American provinces and the circumstances on which depend their further prosperity and colonial connection with Great Britain* (London, 1831). British Museum (London), Add. MS 40878. General Register Office (Edinburgh), Sir Howard Douglas, letters, 1825–28 (mfm. at PANB). PANB, REX/mi/ex, minute books, 1824–30; REX/px, draft minutes, 1824–30. PAC, MG 23, C6, ser.1, 7–8; MG 24, A3, 1–5; RG 7, G8, B, 6–11, 47–49. PRO, CO 188/29–42; 189/12–13. UNBL, BC-MS, Sir Howard Douglas letterbooks, I-IV. *Gentleman's Magazine*, CCXI (January-June 1862), 89–91. G.B., Parl., *Hansard*, 1842–47. N.B., Council, *Journals*, 1823–31; General Assembly, *Acts*, 1823–31; House of Assembly, *Journals*, 1823–31.

Agatha Armour, *Lady Rosamond's secret: a romance of Fredericton* (Saint John, N.B., 1878). S. W. Fullom, *The life of General Sir Howard Douglas, bart., G.C.B., G.C.M.G., F.R.S., D.C.L., from his notes, conversations, and correspondence* (London, 1863). Hannay, *History of N.B.*, I. R. S. Lambert, *Redcoat sailor; the adventures of Sir Howard Douglas* (Toronto, 1956). MacNutt, *New Brunswick. The University of New Brunswick memorial volume*, ed. A. G. Bailey (Fredericton, 1950). D. M. Young, *The Colonial Office in the early nineteenth century* ([London], 1961). W. C. Milner, "Sir Howard Douglas," *Educational Rev.* (Sackville and Moncton, N.B.), XXXV (1920–21), 216–17, 242–44.

DOUSE, WILLIAM, land agent and politician; b. 19 May 1800 in England; m. Esther Young, and they had 12 children; d. 5 Feb. 1864 in Charlottetown, P.E.I.

After immigrating to Prince Edward Island from Devizes, Wiltshire, in the early 1820s William Douse took up farming, shipbuilding, brewing, and auctioneering, and eventually pursued with some success the buying and selling of seed and produce. In 1833 he was named land agent by the 6th Earl of Selkirk and given power of attorney over the huge Island estate which had been assembled in 1803 in southern Queens County for the colonization scheme of the 5th Earl of Selkirk [Douglas*]. With more than 100,000 acres it was second in size only to that of Samuel CUNARD and his brother Edward. Douse remained land agent until the estate was purchased by the government in 1860. Late in 1833 Douse attempted to expand his control to other estates. A legal battle to be named land agent to John Stewart*, in which Douse and H. D. Morpeth, the former agent, both claimed to be Stewart's properly authorized agent, ended only when Stewart was declared insane in 1834 and the court decided in favour of Morpeth.

Douse had a long career in the assembly. He was first elected in 1834 in Queens County and with two exceptions won every election he contested until his retirement in 1862. He was an uninspired member of the house and spoke only on routine business affecting his district. As an agent he was strongly identified with the proprietors; yet probably because he obtained many local improvements, he managed to retain the support of tenants, which was necessary since his district covered much of the Selkirk estate. Edward WHELAN suggested in the *Examiner* in 1850 that Douse's tenants dared not refuse their votes because of rent-roll power he held over them, but this charge was not substantiated. Two incidents of vandalism in 1836 and 1841 directed against Douse's property in the district indicate, however, that he was not universally popular.

When Douse first entered the house the Escheat movement, headed by William COOPER, was gaining momentum. Selkirk's tenants had not been as active as those of other landowners, for the estate was known for long-term leases and reasonable arrangements to purchase, the two chief deficiencies complained of on other estates. However, in the fall of 1837, Lieutenant Governor Sir Charles Augustus FitzRoy* published a circular letter calling on all proprietors to grant to their tenantry better terms and conditions of settlement. By February 1838 Douse was complaining to Selkirk that tenants who had shown no previous sympathy for escheat (confiscation) were now refusing to pay their rents. Douse did not run in the 1838 election and was defeated in an 1840 by-election, but in 1842 when it had become obvious that the Escheat party had failed in its bid to make changes in the land system he was again returned.

Douse's important group of supporters from the Selkirk estate were largely Scots, and in 1846 strong national feelings added to political and religious differences between Protestants and Roman Catholics brought them into conflict with the Irish in the same district. Owing to several incidents of violence at the polls the assembly declared the election void. The by-election which followed in March 1847 was the bloodiest in Island history. At least three were killed in a riot in the Belfast district and the Irish, it was alleged, had dragged their dead away to be buried secretly. Douse and his running mate, Alexander Maclean, finally entered the assembly after being unopposed in a second by-election.

Douse became a landowner as well as agent in 1855 when he purchased 14,000 acres of the Selkirk estate, a move which may have been prompted by inquiries about possible purchase by the government of the whole estate.

On Douse's death Edward Whelan noted in the *Examiner* both Douse's extreme conservative views as a land agent and his popularity with the tenants for his fairness. It was significant that his funeral procession was one of the largest in the history of the colony.

H. T. HOLMAN

William Douse was the author of *A reply to the Hon. Charles Young's last will and testament bequeathed to his late constituents, the electors of the third electoral district of Queen's County* (Charlottetown, 1840). P.E.I., Supreme Court, Estates Division, liber 6, f.328 (will of William Douse) (mfm. at PAPEI). PAC, MG 19, E1, ser.1, 50, pp.19056–313. PRO, CO 226/71, pp.546–56. *Abstract of the proceedings before the Land Commissioners' Court, held during the summer of 1860, to inquire into the differences relative to the rights of landowners and tenants in Prince Edward Island*, reporters J. D. Gordon and David Laird (Charlottetown, 1862). P.E.I., House of Assembly, *Debates and proc.*, 1855, 1857, 1860–61; *Journal*, 1833–62. *Examiner* (Charlottetown), 15, 22 June, 11, 27 July 1850; 5 Oct. 1857; 8 Feb. 1864. *Islander*, 15 Feb. 1845; 1, 8, 15 May, 21, 28 Aug. 1846; 8 Jan., 9, 16, 23 March 1847; 2 June 1854. *People's Journal* (Charlottetown), 10, 24 Oct. 1857. *Prince Edward Island Register* (Charlottetown), 30 Oct. 1824, 23 Oct. 1826, 14 Aug. 1827, 11 May 1830. *Protestant and Evangelical Witness*, 6 Feb. 1864. *Ross's Weekly* (Charlottetown), 11 Feb. 1864. *Royal Gazette* (Charlottetown), 2 Nov. 1830 – 23 May 1841, 14 Feb. 1843.

DOW, WILLIAM, brewer and businessman; b. 27 March 1800 at Muthill, Perthshire, Scotland; d. 7 Dec. 1868 at Montreal.

The son of a brewmaster, William Dow emigrated to Canada in 1818 or 1819 with substantial experience in brewing. He was employed as foreman at Thomas Dunn's brewery, one of the few in Montreal at that time; by November 1829 Dow was a partner and was joined by his younger brother, Andrew, who had also trained as a brewer. Known as William Dow and Company after 1834, the year of Dunn's death, the firm prospered and became one of the principal competitors in Montreal to Molson's, the largest brewery in the city. Like some of his competitors William Dow was also engaged in distilling and in this business too he was a major local supplier. By 1863 his plant was producing some 700,000 gallons of beer in comparison to the Molson's 142,000 gallons. As his business grew, Dow took in other partners besides his brother (who died in 1853). During the early 1860s he was joined by a group of associates, headed by Gilbert Scott, to whom he eventually sold the business for £77,877 in 1864; it kept his name.

By that time Dow was already a wealthy man with a number of highly remunerative investments in other enterprises besides brewing and distilling. Through the 1840s he put considerable sums into Montreal real estate: in one transaction in 1844 he paid £5,580, mostly in cash, for four pieces of property. Investing also in railways and banks, Dow became important in this expanding sector of Montreal's economic life. He was a director of the Montreal and New York Railroad Company (which had a line between Montreal and Plattsburg, N.Y.) from 1847 to 1852 and invested nearly £10,000 in its shares, an unusually large sum for anyone to put into a single joint stock company in that era. Dow was one of the Montreal promoters who merged this railway with its major competitor, the Champlain and St Lawrence, in 1855, after a vicious rate war threatened to bankrupt both companies. He also had a small investment in the St Lawrence and Atlantic Railroad and served briefly on its board of directors (1852–53). A shareholder in the City Bank, he was also a director of the Bank of British North America and the Montreal Provident and Savings Bank. Although a determined rival of the Molsons in the beer and whisky business, he was their associate in 1854 in the formation of still another Montreal bank, Molsons Bank [see William Molson*], which was later incorporated into the Bank of Montreal. Compartmentalization of their lives, especially in business, was characteristic of most Montreal businessmen and, indeed, was probably essential for success in this era of constantly expanding frontiers of enterprise.

Dow was a director of the Montreal Insurance Company between 1839 and 1852 and a member of the group which formed the Sun Life Insurance Company in 1865. His many other local corporate ventures included the abortive company organized in 1849 by John Young* to build a canal between the St Lawrence River and Lake Champlain, the Montreal Steam Elevating and Warehousing Company founded in 1857, the City Passenger Railway Company in 1861, and the Montreal Stock Exchange in 1852. Though not himself a shipowner, he invested in shipping companies and was one of the pioneer investors in the Atlantic Telegraph Company. In 1854 he and Hugh* and Andrew Allan*, William Edmonstone, and Robert Anderson of Montreal formed the Montreal Ocean Steamship Company with a capital of £500,000 to provide regular steamer connections between Great Britain and Canada.

Although a bachelor, Dow lived in baronial style in an immense, richly decorated stone mansion named Strathearn House at the top of Beaver Hall Hill in Montreal and also nearby in the country on his estate at Côte Saint-Paul. At his death, on 7 Dec. 1868, the house and the bulk of his estate, estimated to be in excess of £300,000, were left to his brother's widow and her four daughters.

GERALD TULCHINSKY

ANQ-M, Greffe d'I. J. Gibb, 20 mai 1844; Greffe de James Smith, 13 nov. 1864. Château de Ramesay (Montréal), Antiquarian and Numismatic Soc. of Montreal, no.104. O'Keefe Brewing Company Ltd. Archives (Montreal), correspondence relating to the launching of the Atlantic Telegraph Co., 1857; last will and testament of William Dow, 22 Nov. 1868. PAC, RG 4, A1, S-299, 2e partie, p.159; C1, 173, no.3363; RG 30, 389, Lake St-Louis and Province Line Railway, stock ledger, 1851–54. Can., Prov. of, *Statutes*, 1849, c.180; 1854–55, c.44; 1857, c.178; Legislative Assembly, *Proceedings of the standing committee on railroads and telegraph lines . . .* (Quebec, 1851), 244–65. *Canada Gazette* (Montreal), 5 Jan. 1850. *Gazette* (Montreal), 9, 11, 12 Dec. 1868. *Montreal Herald*, 10 Dec. 1868. *Morning Courier* (Montreal), 24 Feb. 1849. *Alphabetical list of merchants, traders, and housekeepers in Montreal* (Doige). *The Montreal almanac . . .*, 1839. *Montreal directory*, 1847–52.

Merrill Denison, *The barley and the stream; the Molson story; a footnote to Canadian history* (Toronto, 1955). G. H. Harris, *The president's book; the story of the Sun Life Assurance Company of Canada* (Montreal, 1928), 23. *Historique de la brasserie Dow, 1790–1955* (s.l., s.d.). *Montreal old and new, entertaining, convincing, fascinating; a unique guide for the managing editor*, ed. Lorenzo Prince et al. (Montreal, n.d.), 92. *The National Breweries Limited; 25ème anniversaire, 1909–1934* (n.p., n.d.), 18. Émile Vaillancourt, *The history of the brewing industry in the province of Quebec* (Montreal, 1940), 39.

DOYLE, LAURENCE (Lawrence) O'CONNOR, lawyer, editor, and politician; b. 27 Feb. 1804 in

Halifax, N.S., eldest son of Laurence Doyle and Bridget O'Connor; m. in 1833, on Île Madame, N.S., Sarah Ann Driscoll (d. 25 Jan. 1841); d. 28 Oct. 1864 in New York City.

For Laurence O'Connor Doyle, the son of a Roman Catholic merchant in Halifax, educational opportunities were limited: the Halifax Grammar School was under Church of England supervision and King's College at Windsor, N.S., required its students to adhere to the 39 Articles. Doyle, therefore, spent seven years at Stonyhurst College, a Roman Catholic institution in Lancashire, England, before returning to Halifax in 1823 to study law with Richard John Uniacke*, the old attorney general. While still a student in Uniacke's office, he prepared the Roman Catholics' petition to the assembly for modification of the test oath. On 22 Jan. 1828 Doyle became an attorney and on 27 Jan. 1829, a barrister. Thereafter he practised law in Halifax.

Meanwhile, along with Joseph Howe*, Thomas Chandler HALIBURTON, and others, Doyle had become a member of "The Club," a literary society in imitation of the "Noctes" in *Blackwood's Magazine* in Britain. Its humorous, vigorous satires on the follies and affectations of the day appeared irregularly in the *Novascotian* between 8 May 1828 and 23 June 1831. As time passed Doyle became something of an incorrigible punster, and was regarded by Howe as the wittiest man he had ever encountered.

It was natural for a young man of Doyle's position, personality, and talents to become involved in the stirring political issues surrounding the struggle for responsible government. In 1832 when three new constituencies were added to the existing two in Cape Breton Island (one for Cape Breton County, one each for Arichat and Sydney townships), Doyle decided to run in a by-election for Cape Breton County. After visiting the island, however, he chose the Arichat seat on Île Madame, because, as he later said, "I would be equally honored by representing the only Catholic Township in the Province, as by representing the largest County." Doyle's political ally, William Young*, offered himself for one of the two Cape Breton County seats, and resentment against these two outsiders from Halifax was heard on the hustings. Furthermore, long-standing jealousies between Arichat and Sydney were revived, partly because the latter had been made a free port during a resurgence in coal mining in 1828. Doyle decided his chief opposition would come from the supporters of Richard SMITH, superintendent of the General Mining Association, an English company based at Sydney, and a candidate for one of the two Cape Breton County seats against Young and James Boyle Uniacke*. Doyle felt that Smith was the agent of an all too powerful body in the province, and that the rest of the island would be deprived of fair representation by Smith's connections with Sydney. Doyle campaigned in both ridings. He, Young, and Uniacke were returned, but Young's election was contested and Smith ultimately declared the winner.

Doyle quickly became recognized in the house as a convinced Reformer. He argued that Cape Breton Island deserved more than five members in a 44-seat assembly because its "area and population . . . were equal to 1–5th of the whole Province." In 1834 Solicitor General Charles Rufus Fairbanks* submitted a scheme for improving the great roads of the colony by borrowing £100,000 in England. Doyle seized the occasion to advocate changes in the road and bridge service. Traditionally MHAS had the right to allocate the sums of money for the great roads and divide the remainder among the counties for the maintenance of their crossroads, as well as to designate road commissioners in their constituencies. Doyle strongly favoured Fairbanks' proposal to take away this patronage which, in his opinion, had engendered corruption, but the house was unwilling to abandon the practice. Doyle also claimed that Cape Breton Island needed at least 200 miles of great roads, and that opening communications would thrust the island forward half a century.

Doyle was critical of the British government's announcement in 1834 that it intended to begin collecting quitrents if the assembly did not agree to a guaranteed annual grant of £2,000 for the salaries of the lieutenant governor, provincial secretary, and judges. He ridiculed "the horrible humbug of Quit Rents." Doyle was concerned about greater self-government for the province. Early in 1836 he moved in the assembly that an address be sent to the king expressing dissatisfaction at the sending of persons from England to fill positions in the colony, particularly in the Customs Department. This system was "insulting and injurious to the natives and residents of the Country, from whose pockets the Salaries were now taken. . . ."

His views regarding constitutional reform for Nova Scotia were enunciated in support of Alexander STEWART's 1834 resolution calling for changes in the composition, procedure, and functions of the council. Doyle's commitment to open council meetings was carried into the next election campaign, when at a nomination meeting in Halifax on 9 Nov. 1836 he moved a resolution, seconded by Howe, that the Halifax MHAS be requested to pledge themselves against doing any business with the council while its meetings were held in secret. In the next session Doyle moved a series of resolutions that the council be open to the public. Doyle also agreed with Stewart in 1834 that the council, which had only one member not a resident of Halifax, was defective in composition: "it is the feeling that they have no voice in that Council . . . that makes [the people of Cape Breton Island] dissatisfied . . . and seek for a severance of the connection." He thought, however, that Stewart's proposal to increase the membership of the council by selecting additional members from the province should be altered to include election of the whole council. He seconded an unsuccessful resolution for a council "in part composed of one member for each County and District, to be elected by Freeholders of a certain rank."

Doyle continued these reform initiatives after his re-election for Arichat Township late in 1836. He strongly supported Howe's 12 resolutions of 1837 which culminated in an address to the crown demanding an elective legislative council, and was dissatisfied with the 1838 decision of the colonial secretary, Lord Glenelg, to create separate Executive and Legislative councils but to make no substantial change in their composition. To strengthen the people's control over their representatives, he sponsored the Quadrennial Act for an assembly term of four rather than seven years; passed by the assembly in 1837, it did not become law until 1840.

In the 1840 elections Doyle again offered himself as a candidate in Arichat Township, but withdrew in favour of Henry Martell, thus honouring a four-year old agreement with his Acadian constituents to support Martell when he came forward. Doyle was not in the house again until 1843. Meanwhile the Nova Scotian Reformers were encouraged by Lord John Russell's dispatch of 16 Oct. 1839, according to which councillors were thenceforth to be appointed "during pleasure," or on a political basis, according to their usefulness to the lieutenant governor; by the recall of Lieutenant Governor Colin Campbell* in 1840; and by the fact that James Boyle Uniacke had come over to their side. Not all the Reformers, however, approved of the decision of Howe, Uniacke, and James McNab to join a coalition government with James William Johnston* and the Conservatives in that year. Doyle agreed with Herbert Huntington*'s refusal to accept office, because, as he later stated, not enough Reformers were included in the coalition.

During the early 1840s Doyle increased his interest in Irish affairs. He had been a member of the Charitable Irish Society of Halifax since 1828,

serving as vice-president in 1828–29, 1838–41, and 1846–47, and president in 1829–32, 1843–44, and 1847–48. He was also the first president of the St Mary's and St Patrick's Temperance Society of Halifax in 1843. Moreover, he was an ardent advocate of the repeal of the union of Great Britain and Ireland. Repeal agitation had been revived in Ireland in the early 1840s by Daniel O'Connell, who was imprisoned in 1843. During that year Doyle presided at meetings in Halifax of the Repeal Association, was a member of its correspondence committee, and was editor of the *Register*, a Halifax newspaper devoted to Ireland's affairs, at least from 10 Jan. to 30 May 1843. The following spring he took over the political department of the paper.

At the time of the 1843 election Doyle was concerned that the Roman Catholics and Irishmen of Halifax were being viewed with "distrust" by their Liberal allies: "Our nationality, too fervid and impassioned it was said, has given umbrage even to some portion of the Liberal Press. . . ." Doyle was to have been a candidate for Halifax County but the four sitting MHAs were eventually renominated for the Reform interest and the Catholic community was passed over. Doyle was convinced that his repeal activities were responsible and was reported as complaining that it was "illiberal and unjust, that the whole Catholic population of the Town should be disfranchised because he sympathized with his countrymen in Ireland." The Catholics did not participate in the election, and were thus partly responsible for the defeat of the Reformer William STAIRS by the Tory Andrew Mitchell Uniacke* in Halifax Township. But, with elections not yet simultaneous in all constituencies, a reconciliation brought Doyle onto the Reform ticket with Howe in Halifax County; they were elected without opposition. This brief Catholic defection may have helped the J. W. Johnston ministry to retain office from 1843 to 1847.

Late in 1843, disillusioned by the turn of events, the three Reformers left the coalition government, and the final stage in the struggle for responsible government began. The Reform party won the election of 1847 and Doyle was successful in Halifax Township. He became a member of the new Reform ministry on 2 Feb. 1848. On 2 Oct. 1850 he resigned from the Executive Council, though he continued to represent Halifax Township from 1851 to 1855. Doyle's interest in reform and in local concerns continued. He long favoured a general system of education available to all classes, urging it in the assembly as early as 1840. He supported Horton Academy at Wolfville, N.S., but opposed the creation of a college there because he believed the colony did not have the resources requisite for the support of a university. In 1845 he sponsored a motion in the assembly against the improvident practice of endowing sectarian colleges. Like many Liberals, Doyle spoke out against the pressure temperance societies were exerting on politicians. He used his powers of ridicule to label as claptrap the talk of members of the house who advocated temperance yet scrambled for the money from duties on rum.

In 1844, when the legality of the 1820 reannexation of Cape Breton Island to Nova Scotia was in question before the Judicial Committee of the Privy Council, Doyle spoke for his former constituents: "If rights had been wrested from the inhabitants of Cape Breton contrary to their wishes, and they now desired self-government, let them have it." Doyle also took a leading part in an effort to widen the franchise from its base on 40s. freehold and to end the practice of temporarily transferring freeholds in order to create votes. In January 1851 he sponsored an act for better regulation of elections, which extended the franchise to those males who had paid poor or county taxes in the year before an election. But while some evils were eradicated by this measure, it was itself subject to abuse, especially in the preparation of lists of ratepayers and receipts for taxes.

Over many years Doyle asserted the rights of the province to its mineral resources, then entirely controlled by the General Mining Association. In 1850 he was appointed to a committee on mines and minerals with responsibility for reviewing this company's activities in Nova Scotian coal mining. The committee recommended an appeal to the Judicial Committee of the Privy Council to clarify the company's legal rights and to the British government to end the monopoly. Eventually, in 1858, arrangements were made to terminate the monopoly and give the province control over the coal mines. Like many others Doyle was interested in railway development, and he saw it as assisting another of his concerns: a "closer and more intimate union" within a strong British empire.

In 1855 Doyle ended his career in the assembly and a few years later moved to New York to reside with his sister and practise law. There he died at the age of 60. Joseph Howe had written glowingly of him in 1855: "he was the only man [I] ever knew who had not an enemy . . . and who, if ubiquity and immortality could be conferred by universal suffrage, everybody would vote should enliven every scene of festivity down to the end of time."

CHARLES BRUCE FERGUSSON

PAC, MG 24, B29, 2, pp.404–6; 55, p.48 (mfm. at PANS). PANS, RG 1, 175, p.505; 176, p.31; 259, doc.94; RG 5, GP, 11, request for appointment, 25 April 1828; RG 7, 34, L. O. Doyle to L. M. Wilkins, 26 Aug. 1855; Vertical MSS file, J. B. Uniacke to Neil McDougall, 12 April 1832. St Peter's Roman Catholic Church (Halifax), records (mfm. at PANS). Albyn [Andrew Shiels], *The preface, a poem of the period* (Halifax, 1876). Howe, *Speeches and letters* (Chisholm). [Joseph Howe], *The speeches and public letters of the Hon. Joseph Howe*, ed. William Annand (2v., Boston, 1858). N.S., House of Assembly, *Debates and proc.*, 1855. *Acadian Recorder*, 10 Nov. 1832, 9 Nov. 1833, 25 March 1837. *British Colonist* (Halifax), 14 May 1855. *Christian Messenger* (Halifax), 10, 24 Nov., 1 Dec. 1843. *Colonial Standard* (Pictou, N.S.), 8 Nov. 1864. *Guardian* (Halifax), 4 Nov., 2 Dec. 1840; 27 Jan. 1841. *Halifax Journal*, 12 Nov. 1832. *Halifax Reporter*, 1 Nov. 1864. *Mechanic and Farmer* (Pictou, N.S.), 18 Nov. 1840. *Morning Chronicle* (Halifax), 22 March 1844. *Novascotian*, 1832–55, 7 Nov. 1864. *Nova Scotia Royal Gazette* (Halifax), 27 Jan. 1841. *Register* (Halifax), 1843–46. *Sun* (Halifax), 12 June 1848. *Times* (Halifax), 5 Feb. 1839. *Weekly Chronicle* (Halifax), 13 April 1821. *Belcher's farmer's almanack*, 1847, 1849, 1855.

Beck, *Government of N.S.* J. G. Bourinot, *Builders of Nova Scotia; a historical review, with an appendix containing copies of rare documents relating to the early days of the province* (Toronto, 1900). Anthony Traboulsee, *Lawrence Kavanagh, 1764–1830; his life and times, including brief sketches of the history of Nova Scotia (Acadie) and Cape Breton Island (Isle Royale) . . .* (Glace Bay, N.S., 1962). George Mullane, "A sketch of Lawrence O'Connor Doyle, a member of the House of Assembly in the thirties and forties," N.S. Hist. Soc., *Coll.*, XVII (1913), 151–95. D. J. Rankin, "Laurence Kavanagh," CCHA *Report*, 1940–41, 51–76.

DUFRESNE, NICOLAS, Sulpician priest and missionary; b. 10 Sept 1789 at Montreal, son of Louis Dufresne and Marie Arbour; d. 10 July 1863 at Montreal.

Nicolas Dufresne was a brilliant pupil at the Collège de Montréal from 1797 to 1806. At the end of his studies, he was still too young to go into theology and accepted the position of formmaster at the college. He held this charge for six years until his ordination to the priesthood on 18 Oct 1812.

Despite Dufresne's ardent desire to be admitted to the Sulpicians, Bishop Joseph-Octave Plessis* of Quebec kept him in his diocese, and appointed him curate at L'Islet for two years. He then became parish priest in charge of the mission of Caughnawaga with the care of Lachine and later of Châteauguay, and finally, in 1819, parish priest of the Iroquois mission at Saint-Régis, on Lac Saint-François.

In 1824 Nicolas Dufresne received permission

to join the Sulpicians. Shortly afterwards, at the suggestion of the bishop of Quebec, the sacred Congregation of the Propaganda decided to appoint him coadjutor to the bishop. Dufresne was determined to avoid episcopal honours and duties and immediately begged Antoine Duclaux, the superior general of Saint-Sulpice, to intercede with the papal nuncio in Paris. The appointment was not made.

For ten years Dufresne exercised his ministry at Notre-Dame in Montreal, among both the parishioners and the religious communities. At all times he distinguished himself by a gentle firmness, moderation, and prudence. These qualities were responsible for his appointment in 1834 to the difficult post of director of the mission of Lac-des-Deux-Montagnes (Oka). He had barely taken up his duties when his name was again put forward, this time as coadjutor to the bishop of Montreal. Bishop Jean-Jacques Lartigue* supported his candidature, but the opposition of Joseph-Vincent Quiblier*, the superior of Saint-Sulpice in Canada, thwarted the plan.

During his administration of the mission until 1857, Dufresne experienced trying moments. He had to face the Iroquois, who disputed the Sulpicians' right of ownership of the seigneury of Lac-des-Deux-Montagnes. Around 1789 the British courts had acknowledged that the Iroquois had no right to the seigneury, but as title-deeds for the Sulpician seminary had not been drawn up, the Iroquois for some years had continued to appeal to the courts. With the seigneurs' permission, they did have the right to cut timber for personal use, but not for trade. They gained the support of the Algonkin chieftains and succeeded in stirring them up against the seminary. All Dufresne's firmness and skill were needed to calm them and dissuade them from apostasy.

Despite these difficulties, the mission made some progress. A temperance society, established following the visit of Bishop Charles-Auguste-Marie-Joseph de Forbin-Janson*, almost completely eliminated drunkenness among the Algonkins and Iroquois. In 1849, at the time of Étienne-Michel FAILLON's visit, it was decided to entrust the boys' school to the Brothers of the Christian Schools. They were so successful that the school soon had to be enlarged and the number of teachers increased. Three years later, the seminary established a model farm to introduce the young Indians to agriculture. This measure was not successful, and the school had to close in 1860.

In 1857, because of his age and poor health, Dufresne was recalled to the Séminaire de Montréal. He later returned to the mission on several occasions to assist the missionaries, in particular at the time of a retreat in 1858 and, shortly afterwards, during the pastoral visit of Bishop Ignace Bourget*, for whom he acted as interpreter to the Iroquois. He died at the Séminaire de Montréal on 10 July 1863.

ANTONIO DANSEREAU

ASSM, 8, A; 36, André Cuoq, "Notes inédites pour servir à l'histoire de la mission du Lac-des-Deux-Montagnes" (typescript). Allaire, *Dictionnaire. Almanac de Québec . . . ,* 1807–12. Henri Gauthier, *Sulpitiana* (2e éd., Montréal, 1926). Lemire-Marsolais et Lambert, *Hist. de la CND de Montréal,* VI, VII, IX. Olivier Maurault, *Le collège de Montréal, 1767–1967,* Antonio Dansereau, édit. (2e éd., Montréal, 1967), 198. Rumilly, *Hist. de Montréal,* II, 212. J.A. Cuoq, "Anotc Kekon," RSC *Trans.,* 1st ser., XI (1893), sect.I, 178–79.

DUNCOMBE, CHARLES, physician, politician, and a leader of the rebellion of 1837 in Upper Canada; b. 28 July 1792 at Stratford, Conn., eldest of the five children of Thomas Duncombe and Rhoda Tyrrell; m. first in 1813, Nancy Haines, by whom he had three daughters and one son; she died in 1857, and he married, about 1858, Lucy Millard, by whom he had one son; d. 1 Oct. 1867 at Hicksville, Calif.

Although born in Connecticut, Charles Duncombe grew up in New York State, first in Stamford, Delaware County, and later in Middleburg, Schoharie County. After receiving his early education from his mother, he taught school and then studied medicine at the college of the One Hundred and One Members of the Medical Society of the City of New York. In 1819 he moved to the town of Delaware, Upper Canada, and on 5 October was licensed to practise by the Upper Canada Medical Board. He moved to St Thomas in 1822 and practised medicine there until 1828 when he settled in Burford Township in Brant County. There he built a large and lucrative medical practice. He had been appointed surgeon to the 2nd battalion of the Middlesex militia in 1825, and in January 1832 he became a member of the Medical Board. Always interested in medical education, he trained his two brothers, David and Elijah, before they studied for medical degrees at Fairfield Academy in Herkimer, N.Y. With Dr John ROLPH, Duncombe founded the Talbot Dispensatory at St Thomas in 1824, the first medical school in Upper Canada, an effort which failed in its first term. Duncombe invested the proceeds of his large practice in land (his homestead was the site of the village of Bishopsgate), and he owned large holdings in Burford, Brantford, and, in his wife's name, at Springfield in Elgin County.

Duncombe

A major interest for Duncombe was the masonic order. He was the first master of the Mount Moriah lodge at Westminster in 1820. In masonic affairs he showed both qualities of leadership and his rebellious instincts. When Simon McGillivray* was sent from Britain as provincial grand master, Duncombe led a delegation of western Upper Canadian masons to meet him at York (Toronto) in September 1822. Duncombe objected to the appointment of officials by British masons, insisting upon the right of Canadians to choose their own leaders. Temporarily reconciled by McGillivray, the doctor remained unhappy with Canadian freemasonry. Western lodges, discontented with the inactivity of the provincial organization after 1830, met at London, Upper Canada, in February 1836 to establish an independent grand lodge. Fittingly, the future rebel Duncombe was elected grand master. The grand lodge disappeared in the political and economic troubles of 1836–37, but Duncombe remained an ardent mason even after his exile; he was a founding member of the Washington lodge in Sacramento, Calif., in 1852.

The doctor turned politician in the election of 1830. He and Charles Ingersoll were returned for Oxford County to the 11th Upper Canadian parliament. In contrast to his later reputation as a radical, he was very much a moderate and an independent in his first term. Generally he voted with the Tories for public improvements such as banks and canals, and on issues involving government officers such as the granting of generous salaries to officials – not surprising positions for the representative of an area badly in need of public works to take. His own inclinations are indicated more accurately by his stand on political questions where the interests of his constituents were not at stake. He invariably voted with the advanced Reformers for such measures as vote by ballot, jury trials, secularization of the clergy reserves, independence of judges, and greater colonial autonomy. His major area of expertise was education and he advocated use of the crown lands to generate financial support for common schools.

His pragmatic and independent approach was best illustrated in the controversy over the expulsion from the House of Assembly of William Lyon MACKENZIE. When the issue arose in December 1831 Duncombe agreed with the Tories that Mackenzie had libelled the house in his newspaper, the *Colonial Advocate*. But he opposed expulsion of the radical, arguing a reprimand was sufficient. This sensible middle ground won Duncombe no friends on either side. Mackenzie attacked him as an enemy of free speech and as a "false reformer." Opposing the doctor's re-election in 1834, the *Colonial Advocate* denounced him as "that prince royal of performers" and, in his bombastic "Legislative black list" Mackenzie placed him among "the uncompromising enemies of the peace, happiness, and welfare of the people. . . ." The refrain was picked up by radicals in Oxford who repudiated Duncombe and nominated candidates to oppose him. Their efforts were unsuccessful as Duncombe easily won re-election.

In his second parliament Duncombe was much more of a Reform regular, perhaps because the issues had altered, with the political and humanitarian questions on which he held advanced liberal ideas at the forefront. He was one of the busiest and most productive members of the house. During the 1835 and 1836 sessions he chaired most of the committees on financial affairs and dominated debate on social questions. On 10 April 1835 the assembly established a select committee to plan a lunatic asylum and to investigate school systems and other social issues. Three doctors, Duncombe, Thomas David Morrison*, and William Bruce, were named commissioners. All the investigation, however, much of it carried out during a tour of the United States, and the writing would be done by Duncombe and the report would represent his most important contribution to Canadian public life.

His report on lunatic asylums, in February 1836, drew heavily on the experience of the Massachusetts Lunatic Hospital. The suggestion of constructing an expensive hospital, to operate on the theory that insanity was an illness, was radical in a province which locked lunatics in jails. Equally progressive was his report on prisons the same month. He called for the operation of the Kingston penitentiary along the lines of the Auburn Prison in New York, instituted in 1825. Its rigid ban on communication among prisoners was harsh but the Auburn system with its individual cells and meaningful work was a considerable advance over previous systems. Duncombe's own views were more liberal yet. He rejected revenge as a suitable social goal and opposed flogging of prisoners. He stressed the environmental causes of crime, especially in relation to juvenile offenders, who, he said, must receive sympathetic treatment and must be segregated from hardened criminals. Some of Duncombe's ideas would be implemented a decade later when the Kingston penitentiary was reformed; similarly the 1840s would see his basic suggestions for the insane introduced in the Toronto Lunatic Asylum.

The Reformer's greatest impact was made by

229

Duncombe

his report on education of February 1836. He was thoroughly convinced of the necessity of an educated population: education reduced the tendency to intemperance and crime, it taught people to live and work together, and it alone made the population capable of governing itself. The education of which he spoke was practical; the classics were of limited use in the real world for which education should prepare students. Crucial was adequate financial support for common schools and teacher education, and he recommended the appropriation of £15,000 annually, a sum to be supplemented by property taxes on freeholders.

A bill embodying Duncombe's views on education passed the assembly on 4 April 1836, only to be rejected by the Legislative Council. Many of its provisions, however, would be introduced under the administration of Egerton Ryerson* in Canada West and would form the basis for Ontario's education policy until the act of 1871: local assessment, elective school boards, regular inspection of schools, female education, creation of normal schools, female teachers, prescribed textbooks, and non-sectarian religious instruction.

Favouring such political reforms as an executive responsible to the elected house, Duncombe had returned to the good graces of the radicals by 1836. Now supported by Mackenzie for re-election, Duncombe was one of the few Reformers that year to withstand the Tory sweep of the province. And he was then chosen by the Constitutional Reform Society, a group of moderate Reformers, founded in 1836 with William Warren Baldwin* as its president, to carry to England its complaints against alleged corruption and interference in the election by Lieutenant Governor Francis Bond Head*. Arriving in London in September 1836, Duncombe had the Reform charges laid before the House of Commons by Joseph Hume. But the colonial secretary, Lord Glenelg, would not even see the Canadian delegate. It was a devastating experience for the moderate Duncombe. Along with many Reformers, he had held a naïve faith in British justice, and he had been convinced that the troubles of Canada stemmed from domestic misrule which Britain, if aware of the true situation, would rectify. In Duncombe's sharp disillusionment can be read a major cause of the rebellions. As he wrote to Robert Baldwin*, he now felt that the people of Canada, "if ever they have good government . . . must look among themselves for the means of producing it. . . ." His bitterness, and resultant radicalism, was heightened by personal tragedy: a fire devastated his property and, while he was on his way to England on his futile mission, his only son was thrown from a horse and killed, aged 14.

Duncombe virtually withdrew from public life on his return to Upper Canada in November 1836. That, in his melancholy, he was prepared for independence is clear. When he decided upon rebellion is more difficult to determine. The traditional interpretation is that he was involved in the rising agitation in the autumn of 1837, that he was informed by Mackenzie in November that an uprising was planned, and that he then raised an army in the London District to join the Yonge Street forces. The interpretation appears to rest upon two sources: John Charles Dent*'s 1885 history of the rebellion and a deposition given to London District magistrates on 17 Dec. 1837 by Peter Coon, a Burford blacksmith. Other depositions, and impressionistic evidence, cast doubt on this interpretation. Certainly meetings were being held in the London District from the beginning of December, but none of the participants placed Duncombe at any of them until 8 December, after the rising on Yonge Street led by Mackenzie. The doctor's friend Elisha Hall, of Oxford County, wrote to him on 6 December advising him to avoid involvement in the rebellion; it seems likely that Hall would have known if Duncombe had been committed to action by that date. Donald M'Leod*, the Patriot general in the border war of 1838 and another close associate of Duncombe, reported in a book published in 1841 that Duncombe had held back from agitation until 8 December, when he heard a warrant had been issued for his arrest. He then took arms in despairing self-defence. Adding force to this argument is the tension which existed between Mackenzie and Duncombe in 1838. Mackenzie felt his compatriot had never been fully committed to the cause, and correspondence in 1838 makes it clear that Mackenzie had not taken Duncombe into his confidence during the agitation in October 1837, though they had spent a week together at Niagara in that month. Although the evidence remains slight, General M'Leod's account now seems the most plausible.

With its reluctant leader, the virtually unplanned rising in the London District was fated to fail. Gathered at Scotland village, southwest of Brantford, the rebel force of 300 dispersed on Duncombe's orders when, on 13 December, they received news of Mackenzie's defeat at Toronto and of the approach of a loyalist army under Allan Napier MacNab. Hiding with relatives and supporters, Duncombe made his way out of the province over the next two weeks, crossing to Detroit disguised as a woman.

Duncombe's movements in the United States

are difficult to follow. Certainly he was at Detroit in February 1838 when he helped plan and supply weapons for the Patriot raid led by M'Leod on Fighting Island. In March he lectured on the Patriot cause at Cleveland and while there joined in planning a full-scale invasion of Upper Canada on 4 July, plans which were still-born. Later that year he helped shape tactics for the attacks on Sandwich (Windsor) and Prescott. Despite this activity, Duncombe wavered at times in his commitment to the cause. By June 1838 he was ready to join Marshall Spring Bidwell* in disillusioned retirement. In September, however, he had recovered his ardour and took a leading role in the Cleveland convention of the Hunters' Lodges. Although some, including Mackenzie, suspected him of being a secret agent for the United States government, his commitment at Cleveland seemed genuine enough. Applying the knowledge he had gained in the Upper Canadian assembly, he proposed to the convention the formation of a "Republican Bank" which would both finance the Patriot war effort and, by its radical example, democratize banking in the United States. It was an idea he would pursue for the next three years through memorials to the United States Congress and through his book, *Duncombe's free banking*, published in 1841.

As the Patriot cause collapsed Duncombe wandered the northern United States lecturing and practising medicine. Although he was pardoned on 20 April 1843 he showed no interest in returning to Canada. Rather, he went west, to gold-rush California in 1849, settling in Sacramento. Successful in his profession and serving on the town council, he remained in Sacramento until 1856 when he purchased a farm near Hicksville in Sacramento County. His passionate interest in emancipation of the slaves drew him into Republican politics. Elected to the state legislature in 1858, he was unseated because he was an alien – a nice touch of irony for a politician from Upper Canada, so long torn by its own alien question. By the time he was elected again, in 1863, Duncombe had taken American citizenship and he served a term in the California house. He was prosperous and happy, feeling the American Civil War had vindicated his life-long confidence in free institutions and the cause of human liberty.

In 1867 Charles Duncombe was partially paralysed by sunstroke. He never recovered. On 1 Oct. 1867 he died. He was interred in the masonic plot of the Sacramento City cemetery under a headstone which read, fittingly, "A Friend of Liberty." He was that. He was, as well, one of the most dedicated, intelligent, and progressive of Upper Canada's politicians. Remembered, if at all, as the leader of the fiasco at Scotland, he should more properly be recalled as the father of 19th century social legislation in Ontario and as a public figure of rare integrity.

MICHAEL S. CROSS

Charles Duncombe was the author of *An address to the different lodges upon the subject of a joint stock banking company bank* (n.p., n.d.); *Duncombe's free banking: an essay on banking, currency, finance, exchanges, and political economy* (Cleveland, Ohio, 1841); and *Memorial to Congress upon the subject of Republican free banking* (Cleveland, Ohio, 1841).

MTCL, Robert Baldwin papers, 42, no.69; 44, no.1; E. C. Guillet coll., Rebellion of 1837 papers; Scrapbook of clippings from American newspapers on the Canadian rebellion of 1837–38, 1835–43. PAC, MG 24, B38; RG 1, E1, 62, p.381; RG 5, B36. PAO, Mackenzie-Lindsey papers, clippings and notations, file no.1841; Mackenzie section, D. M'Leod to [Van Rensselaer], 1 March 1838; circular, Canadian Refugee Relief Association, 29 March 1838; A. K. Mackenzie to W. L. Mackenzie, 3, 7, 25 April, 10 June 1838; James Reid to [W. L. Mackenzie], 19 April 1838; James Mackenzie to W. L. Mackenzie, 12 July 1838; [A. C. Smith] to W. L. Mackenzie, 23 Sept. 1838; Peter Baxter to W. L. Mackenzie, 26 Oct. 1838. PAO, Snyder (J.M.) papers, deposition of John Beard, 10 Dec. 1837; Misc. MSS, C. Duncombe to E. E. Duncombe, 7 Feb., 25 Dec. 1835; 27 June 1865; RG 1, A-I-6, 16, C. Duncombe to R. B. Sullivan, 16 May 1837; 21, E. Tufford to S. B. Harrison, 6 Aug. 1842.

Documentary history of education in U.C. (Hodgins), II. "The Hunters' lodges of 1838," ed. E. P. Alexander, *New York History*, XIX (1938), 64–69. Donald M'Leod, *A brief review of the settlement of Upper Canada by the U.E. Loyalists and Scotch Highlanders in 1783; and of the grievances which compelled the Canadas to have recourse to arms . . .* (Cleveland, Ohio, 1841), 134–39, 192–94, 210–16. U.C., House of Assembly, *Journal*, 1831–38. *Colonial Advocate*, 1830–34. *Constitution* (Toronto), 1836–37. *Correspondent and Advocate* (Toronto), 1834–37. *Daily Bee* (Sacramento, Calif.), 2 Oct. 1867. *Palladium of British America and Upper Canada Mercantile Advertiser* (Toronto), 8 Jan. 1838. *Union* (Sacramento, Calif.), 7 Oct. 1867.

H. H. Bancroft, *Works* (39v., San Francisco, 1886–90), XXIII (*History of California*, VI), 721; XXIV (*History of California*, VII), 296. Dent, *Upper Canadian rebellion*, I, 217, 340, 375; II, 151–58, 238, 301–2. *The history of the county of Brant, Ontario* (Toronto, 1883), 377–83. O. A. Kinchen, *The rise and fall of the Patriot Hunters* (New York, 1956), 35–45, 125–26. Kathryn Morris Wilkinson, *Duncombes in America with some collateral lineages* (Milwaukee, Wis., 1965). R. C. Muir, *The early political and military history of Burford* (Quebec, 1913), 117–63. J. R. Robertson, *The history of freemasonry in Canada from its introduction in 1749 . . .* (2v., Toronto, 1899), I, 1041, 1106, 1159; II, 22–26, 51–53, 187–93. J. D. Wilson, "Foreign and local influences on popular education in Upper Canada, 1815–1844'' (unpublished PH D thesis, University of Western Ontario, London, Ont., 1970), 187–95. Fred

Landon, "The Duncombe uprising of 1837 and some of its consequences," RSC *Trans.*, 3rd ser., XXV (1931), sect. II, 83–98.

E

EASTMAN, DANIEL WARD, Presbyterian minister; b. 2 Sept. 1778 in Goshen Township (N.Y.), third child of Tilton Eastman and Polly Owen; m. first, on 21 Nov. 1800, Elizabeth Hopkins (d. 1844), by whom he had nine or ten children, secondly, Mrs Bridget Lowe (d. 1853), and thirdly, Margaret Hinton, *née* Merritt; d. 4 Aug. 1865 in Grimsby Township (West Lincoln Township), Canada West.

Daniel Ward Eastman had a profound religious experience at age 14 and became a communicant, presumably of the Presbyterian Church; he believed himself called by God to the ministry. He was educated at Goshen Grammar School and North Salem Seminary (Academy), and pursued further theological studies, probably in private. The Morris County Associated Presbytery, in New Jersey, which leaned to Congregationalism, licensed Eastman to preach, probably in March 1800. He came to Canada with a caravan of immigrants headed by his father-in-law, arriving at Beaver Dams near St Catharines in June 1801. There, in July, he first preached in Canada. Soon after he moved to Stamford (now in Niagara Falls) where he found a Scottish community with a "small but creditable" church building. Eastman resided in Stamford for a year and during that time purchased 50 acres of "wild land" near Beaver Dams on which he built a log house.

Thus began a long, rigorous, dedicated ministry which earned him the unofficial title of "Father of the Presbyterian Churches in the Niagara and Gore districts." There were in 1800 but four other Presbyterian ministers in Upper Canada: John Bethune*, Jabez Collver*, John Ludwig Broeffle, and Robert McDowall*. As there was no presbytery in Upper Canada, Eastman was ordained at Palmyra (East Palmyra), N.Y., on 9 June 1802 by the Ontario Association (which later merged with the Presbytery of Geneva). Ordination was required for a full ministry, including a licence to marry.

In his early years in Upper Canada Eastman preached regularly at Drummondville (Niagara Falls), Stamford, and Beaver Dams. He also visited other centres from Fort Erie to Ancaster, "carrying the Good News of salvation to solitary settlers, and preaching the Word to willing listeners, by the wayside and in the settlements." Later, between 1815 and 1819, he went as far west as Long Point and London. In 1804 Eastman was reinforced in the Niagara peninsula by John Burns, and in 1808 by Lewis Williams; a son who became a lay preacher later assisted him. He was always concerned with establishing permanent congregations; a group for which he was responsible in the Niagara peninsula became known as "Mr. Eastman's seven churches." During the War of 1812, when church buildings and schools were occupied as barracks and hospitals, Eastman spent much time ministering to the sick and wounded. From 1815 to 1819 he lived in Barton (Hamilton); he then moved to a farm he owned in Grimsby Township, where one of his seven churches was established. During his career Eastman performed some 3,000 marriages, thus greatly augmenting his annual stipend which for a long time seldom exceeded $50 plus some payment "in kind."

The first presbytery in Upper Canada was the Presbytery of the Canadas, organized in 1818 by men rejecting the strict voluntaryism which called for the complete separation of church and state. Eastman joined in 1820, the year it became the Synod of the Canadas. The synod dissolved in 1825 and in 1830 Eastman joined its successor, the United Presbytery of Upper Canada (the United Synod of Upper Canada after 1831). He withdrew in 1833 to found with A. K. Buell of St Catharines and Edward Marsh of Hamilton the Niagara Presbytery. It never affiliated with a higher court.

The rebellion of 1837 had a disastrous effect on the Niagara Presbytery, which by then had seven or eight ministers, mostly recent American immigrants, and 25 churches. Some ministers left Canada, having sympathized with the rebels; others were suspect. There was no stigma attached to Eastman, and he rejoined the United Synod in time to participate in its merger in 1840 with the Presbyterian Church of Canada in Connection with the Church of Scotland. In the disruption of 1844 he cast his lot with the Free Church group.

Failing eyesight forced Eastman to retire about 1851 but he continued to preach occasionally. He became totally blind about 1856 and died in 1865. In his physical and spiritual stamina, Eastman was a true pioneer. Gifted with a powerful voice, he was also an appealing singer who used hymns effectively in his services. Only one of his sermons, dated 1800, is extant; although lacking in maturity it is thoughtfully constructed and shows the influence of the modified Calvinism of the disciples of Jonathan Edwards who stressed "disinterested benevolence." It contains the promise of the forcible, yet warm, evangelical preaching for which Eastman became noted.

GEORGE L. DOUGLAS

Presbyterian Church in Can. Archives (Toronto), D. W. Eastman, "God is love" (sermon, 1800); Harriet Hagar collection of Eastman papers. UCA, H. S. McCollum, Presbyterian scrap book, pp.140–42, 145–46, 170–73, 175–80, 185–88; included are articles written by McCollum for the *Canada Presbyterian* (Toronto), the most important of which are "Canadian Presbyterian history," no.v, 19–20 and no.VII, 322–24, in new ser., II (1878–79). UCA, Presbyterian Church of Can., Presbytery of Hamilton, Minutes, 1844–57. Can. Presbyterian Church, *Home and Foreign Record* (Toronto), V (1865–66), 26–27. *Narrative of the origin of the churches and of the state of religion within the bounds of the "Niagara Presbytery" of Upper Canada* (St Catharines, [Ont.], 1834). Presbyterian Church of Can., *Minutes of the Synod* (Toronto), 1844–61. Presbyterian Church of Can. in Connection with the Church of Scot., *Minutes of the Synod*, 1831–45; *Acts and proc. of the Synod*, 1846–75. United Presbytery of Upper Canada, *Minutes*, 1830–31. United Synod of Upper Canada, *Extracts from the minutes*, 1832–33. *History and genealogy of the Eastman family of America . . .*, comp. G. S. Rix (2v., Concord, N.H., 1901), I, 192, 405–8.

F. H. Foster, *A genetic history of the New England theology* (Chicago, 1907), 52–61, 94–103, 107–86, 369–400. E. H. Gillett, *History of the Presbyterian Church in the United States of America* (rev. ed., 2v., Philadelphia, Pa., [1873?]), I, 156, 207–15, 380, 389–90, 401, 437–40; II, 114. J. H. Hotchkin, *A history of the purchase and settlement of western New York, and of the rise, progress, and present state of the Presbyterian Church in that section* (New York, 1848), 31–35, 40–41, 98–103, 376–77. "Loyalist and pioneer families of West Lincoln, 1783-1833," comp. R. J. Powell, *Annals of The Forty* (Grimsby Hist. Soc. pub., Grimsby, Ont.), 4 (1953), 54–56.

ECCLES, HENRY, lawyer; b. in 1817 in the parish of Weston, near Bath, England, eldest son of Hugh Eccles, a captain of the 61st Regiment, and his wife Elizabeth; d. 3 Nov. 1863 at Toronto, Canada West.

The Eccles family immigrated to Canada in 1835 and lived at Niagara (Niagara-on-the-Lake) until 1841. Young Henry received no formal education; instead, his father, a gold medallist of Trinity College, Dublin, educated him at home. Henry afterwards articled with James Boulton in Toronto. He was admitted to the Law Society of Upper Canada on 3 Aug. 1840 and was called to the bar in the spring of 1842. In 1842, also, he married Jane Lelièvre, the daughter of Captain Francis T. Lelièvre, at one time the assistant commissary general of Canada; one child, a son, was to be born to them. In 1853 Eccles was elected bencher of the Law Society, and in 1856 he was appointed queen's counsel. From 1854 until his death his law partner was Charles Ingersoll Carroll, and James H. Doyle was also a partner from 1856 to 1861.

Henry Eccles took little part in public affairs. Although his father and his younger brother William, a St Catharines lawyer, were active supporters of George Brown* and the Reformers, and he was himself sympathetic to the Reform cause, he was content to spend his time in the company of his family and a small circle of friends. In law, however, he was renowned for his logic, his deductive thinking, and his exceptional ability to simplify issues for a jury. At a time when accurate and concise pleadings were often crucial to a case, his peers considered him to be one of the best pleaders of his day. The addresses he made to juries at the end of his cases were looked upon as models. In addition, his appearance was imposing for he was tall and erect, and his voice was pleasing and described as musical.

JOHN HOVIUS

Globe, 3 Nov. 1863. *Leader*, 3 Nov. 1863. *Solicitors' Journal and Reporter* (London), VIII (1863–64), 71. *Brown's Toronto general directory, 1856 . . .* (Toronto, [1856]). *Brown's Toronto general directory, 1861 . . .*, comp. W. R. Brown (Toronto, [1861]). *Caverhill's Toronto city directory, for 1859–60 . . .*, comp. W. C. F. Caverhill (Toronto, n.d.). Morgan, *Sketches of celebrated Canadians*, 276–77. *The Upper Canada law directory, for 1857*, comp. J. L. Rordans (Toronto, 1856). *The Upper Canada law list, 1858*, comp. J. L. Rordans (Toronto, 1858). *The Upper Canada law list for 1860–61*, comp. J. L. Rordans (Toronto, 1860). *The Upper Canada law list* [1862], comp. J. L. Rordans et al. (Toronto, 1862). E. H. Jones, "The Great Reform Convention of 1859" (unpublished PHD thesis, Queen's University, Kingston, Ont., 1971).

ELGIN, and Earl of KINCARDINE, JAMES BRUCE, Earl of. *See* BRUCE

ELLICE, EDWARD, merchant-banker, landowner, and politician; b.23 or perhaps 27 Sept.

Ellice

1783 in London, England, second son of Alexander Ellice* and Ann (Anne) Russell; m. first on 30 Oct. 1809 Lady Hannah Althea Bettesworth, *née* Grey, daughter of Charles, 1st Earl Grey; m. secondly on 25 Oct. 1843 Lady Anne Amelia Leicester, *née* Keppel, daughter of the 4th Earl of Albemarle; d. 17 Sept. 1863 at Glen Quoich, near Glengarry, Scotland.

Edward Ellice (nicknamed "The Bear," probably for his financial acumen) derived his North American ties from the commercial interests and landholdings he inherited. His Scottish father and four uncles, having established themselves in the fur trade and other ventures in Schenectady (N.Y.), extended their operations in the 1770s to London and Montreal. Though amassing and retaining large investments in New York, increasingly the family business was conducted by Robert Ellice and Company in Canada and by Phyn, Ellice, and Company in England. These firms concentrated on the financing, provisioning, and marketing aspects of the fur trade, as agents for the North West Company, the XY Company, and the reorganized North West Company. Alexander Ellice established other important links with Canada when, in 1780, he married Ann Russell in Montreal, and when, on 30 July 1795, he purchased the seigneury of Villechauve, commonly called Beauharnois, a largely undeveloped estate of 324 square miles, west of Montreal on the south shore of the St Lawrence.

Little is known of Edward Ellice's early life within his family, which "commuted" between London and Montreal. He was enrolled in the public school at Winchester, and in 1797 he matriculated at Marischal College, Aberdeen, from which he graduated in 1800 with an MA. He entered his father's London establishment as a clerk and soon became its principal figure; after his father's death in 1805, he acquired control of the estate and the family's commercial empire. Ellice quickly became a prominent merchant-banker and shipowner in the City, trading in furs, fish, sugar, cotton, and general merchandise in North and South America, the East and West Indies, and Europe. With his special interests in North America, he emerged as a spokesman for the "Canada Trade" and helped found the Canada Club in 1810 to pressure the government on behalf of colonial commerce.

Ellice made extended visits to Canada and the United States between 1802 and 1807. Noting the ruinous rivalry among the Montreal trading houses, and their competition with the Americans and the Hudson's Bay Company, he unsuccessfully offered in 1804 to purchase the outstanding shares of the HBC for £103,000, hoping to amalgamate and rationalize the Canadian trade and thus to profit personally. The incident is evidence of Ellice's sharpness and rapid ascent in the business world. Similarly indicative is the facility with which he borrowed £150,000 in 1813 from the Bank of England to ease a war-induced cash shortage in his business dealings.

The "empire of the beaver" was a source of personal wealth, and, in Ellice's view, strategically important to Britain in her evolving rivalry with the United States. Between 1805 and 1820 Ellice augmented his role in the fur trade, extending large lines of credit to the NWC, and personally disposing of its furs on the London market with great shrewdness. Although there was occasional friction with the wintering and Montreal partners, the relationship with Forsyth, Richardson, and Company and with McGillivrays, Thain, and Company was generally good, that with Mackenzie and Company less satisfactory. In 1815 Ellice offered to become the sole London agent for the Montreal-based trade but its persistent divisions prevented such a rearrangement. With a view to hampering the ambitions of Lord Selkirk [Douglas*], Ellice also purchased a small interest in the HBC, enabling him to challenge, albeit unsuccessfully, the Red River grant in 1812. Ellice early questioned the validity of the HBC monopoly; when that proved unassailable, he promoted the merger of the NWC and HBC, waging a propaganda campaign and petitioning the British government to resolve the worsening situation in North America. Finally, in 1820, Ellice (and by virtue of his financial resources, probably Ellice alone) was able to bring to fruition the negotiations which saved both companies from bankruptcy. The arrangement agreed to by Ellice, Simon* and William McGillivray*, and Andrew Colvile resulted in the consolidation of the trade under a reorganized Hudson's Bay Company in 1821. Their precarious financial affairs made the solution acceptable to the Montreal merchants and the old HBC; by hastening the necessary legislation through parliament and securing the subsequent royal grant licensing the new concern, Ellice presented the wintering partners with a *fait accompli* which they were powerless to resist. After another reorganization in 1824, and the bankruptcy of McGillivrays, Thain, and Company, Ellice, now a director of the HBC, emerged as the sole representative of the former NWC active in the trade. He was ensured a substantial continuing income, especially after he aggressively assumed the liabilities of the collapsing Montreal partners in exchange for their HBC shares. The most important result of the merger, however, and perhaps the most satisfying for Ellice, was the retention under British control of the western territory, now much enlarged by the terms of the 1821 licence.

Ellice's intimate connections with the financial and political élite proved valuable to the new HBC. For example, in 1837, taking advantage of Ellice's influence with the Melbourne government, the company sought a renewal of its licence five years before the scheduled expiration. Similarly, when the initial influx of American settlers into Oregon threatened the company's operations there, Ellice consulted the ambassador of the United States about how to avoid a confrontation. It was suggested that the United States would relinquish its pretensions to the area north of the Columbia River if Britain agreed to concede part of her claim to the contested territory along the Maine–New Brunswick border. An accommodation of these two territorial disputes could not be reached before Melbourne's ministry fell in 1841, but Ellice, over the strenuous objections of Lord Palmerston, the former foreign secretary, persuaded the Whigs, now in opposition, to accept the Webster-Ashburton Treaty. Then, when the Oregon question appeared ripe for resolution in 1844–45, Foreign Secretary Aberdeen sought Ellice's advice, which was that the HBC had no absolute need for the territory between the Columbia River and the 49th parallel. The British government now had an excellent bargaining lever, for it could appear to compromise with the Americans, allowing President James Knox Polk to secure Senate approval for the Oregon Treaty. It might be questioned whether the conceded territory was unnecessarily abandoned, but the possibility of war and/or incessant riparian boundary disputes suggests that Ellice's advocacy of the artificial boundary had much to recommend it. His support of compromise in both disputes was based upon a realistic perception of the position and long-term interests of Britain. The maintenance by the HBC of its position, and hence a British presence, in what became British Columbia served the interests both of the company and of Canada.

In the 1850s substantial challenges to the HBC appeared; in Canada, dissatisfaction was aroused because the company's control over the Red River area was a barrier to settlement; in England, envy of its exclusive trading privileges and ideological objections to monopoly, which was regarded as anachronistic in the era of free trade, kindled antagonism. In and out of parliament Ellice successfully turned back repeated attempts to test the validity of the HBC charter.

Using his access to the cabinet, his parliamentary seat, his City connections, and his carefully cultivated liaison with the press, Ellice guarded the company's position. British administrations, by no means hostile to the company, found Ellice a useful intermediary. As unofficial spokesman for the HBC – he refused an invitation to become governor for personal reasons and for fear of adding fuel to the controversy – Ellice laid out the terms which, after much delay, settled the company's status. In response to a petition of the Canadian ministry, the Colonial Office succeeded in having the famous select committee of the House of Commons appointed in 1857. Ellice employed customary behind-the-scenes legerdemain. The committee's report upheld the charter and recommended renewal of the licence with the understanding that some territory would be ceded, if and when desired by Canada, providing Canada undertook to maintain order in the transferred area. No mention was made of compensation for the company – Ellice had earlier informed the government that £1,000,000 would be required – but in other respects the report endorsed Ellice's previous position. In June 1863, after political mismanagement and confusion, a settlement satisfactory to the HBC governing board was made whereby the chartered rights and territorial claims were sold for £1,500,000 cash to a group of investors headed by Edward William Watkin*. Ellice now disposed of his remaining interest in the company which, he was fond of saying with modest exaggeration, "I built ... as it now is." No longer as optimistic about the maintenance of order and authority in the west, he looked back on the not inconsiderable achievements of the HBC with pride. It was left to others to arrange the transfer of the territory to Canada, thus ensuring that it remained out of American hands.

Edward "Bear" Ellice, the fur baron, was also the *grand seigneur* of Beauharnois. For 60 years, he was concerned with the management of the inherited lands in Canada and New York, which at maximum exceeded 450,000 acres. Ellice, an absentee landlord, personally inspected his property only twice, in 1836 and 1858, yet he tried to give as much personal direction as he could, especially to the seigneury. From all appearances, the *censitaires* were satisfied with Ellice as seigneur. Actual management of all his holdings, and of the income derived from them, was necessarily entrusted to resident agents and to Ellice's commercial connections in Montreal and New York. It was difficult for Ellice to cope with legislative restrictions and judicial challenges, and with agents who occasionally ignored his

Ellice

instructions, but he could never bring himself to emigrate to end these frustrations.

Ellice gradually sold parts of his New York and Upper Canadian lands but the seigneury at Beauharnois and adjacent land in Godmanchester and Hinchinbrook townships were not as easily disposed of. Ellice's expenditures to develop his estates prior to the 1830s often exceeded his income; for example, on the seigneury alone he built numerous mills, schools, churches, post offices, taverns, a court house, stage depots, and steamboat wharves. He underwrote road construction and surveys in 1834 for a canal on the St Lawrence (the Beauharnois) and in 1836 for a railway south from Montreal via the seigneury toward Albany. The resident agent at Beauharnois ran a model farm, complete with imported breeding stock.

Such outlays for the seigneury could only be profitable with sufficient settlement. In the 1820s Ellice began to try to eliminate the system of feudal tenure which prevented him from disposing of individual parcels in fee simple. This was the aim of the Canada Tenures Act of 1825, an outgrowth of the Union Bill of 1822 which Ellice had unsuccessfully promoted. Under the act, Ellice chose to effect a re-grant of the seigneury in 1830. This permitted lands to be sold outright, although only 10,000 acres could be sold in the ensuing decade. The tenure issue remained a bone of contention until 1854, when Canadian legislation was passed establishing workable financial arrangements. In the interim, Ellice sold the entire seigneury in 1839 for £150,000. However, the purchaser, the North American Colonial Association of Ireland [see Edward Gibbon WAKEFIELD], suffered from inefficient management and insufficient capital, and Ellice had to repossess the seigneury to protect his investment.

Ellice had other business interests in North America. His largest and most profitable investments were in the United States, but at various times his portfolio included investments in Canadian harbour and railway bonds, government securities, the Welland Canal Company, the Canada Company, and the Bank of Upper Canada. He regularly took back mortgages on lands he sold. In the last 25 years of his life, all of his North American investments, including the fur trade and land, probably generated a gross annual income approaching £20,000, no mean fortune for the times. Various expenses reduced this figure by at least 25 per cent, and a significant portion of the remainder was reinvested in North America.

Ellice was often accused in the press of exploiting his political and financial position to benefit himself and his fellow investors at the expense of the Canadian population. Certainly he never neglected his own interests – he told his son: "Politics must never be allowed to interfere with business" – but the criticism was not entirely warranted. In some cases, such as the Welland Canal Company and Canada Company, Ellice's holdings were small, and taken up contrary to his business judgement. Indeed, in these two instances and others, he was highly critical of the management and deplored the consequences for Canada. Moreover, despite the low rate of return which his British North American investments yielded, Ellice for more than 60 years made significant efforts to improve economic conditions.

The most important contributions made by Ellice, moreover, did not appear in his account books; rather, they lay in the reformulation of British policy towards North America during this crucial period. Ellice possessed three assets which gave him an almost unique influence: his knowledge of the North American situation was unmatched among his contemporaries in Britain; he had a large and sustained personal incentive in seeing that nothing of importance affecting North America went unnoticed in London; and, by virtue of his ready access to the councils of decision over some 50 years, he enjoyed unusual political leverage by which he repeatedly pressured the British government to take action he judged necessary for the Anglo-American-Canadian situation.

Ellice's first marriage, to Lady Hannah Althea Grey, gave an *entrée* to the Whig aristocracy and the means to embark on a lifelong career in politics. Elected to the House of Commons in 1818, he became the principal Whig spokesman on finance, banking, and trade. A leading liberal or "Radical" in the party, Ellice became chief election manager, party publicist, and chief whip in the House of Commons when the Whigs took office in 1830 under his brother-in-law, Earl Grey [Charles Grey]. Ellice's success in these party endeavours was the result of strenuous exertion, discretion, numerous contacts with all shades of political opinion, and innovative party management. He insisted on the adoption of a general caucus of the Whigs, devised the party registration associations – two lasting features of British politics – and played an active role in the adoption of the Reform Act of 1832 and the Emancipation Act of 1833. As secretary of the Treasury (1830–32) and secretary-at-war (1833–34), and as a private member until his death, he furnished a liaison between the numerous factions, such as that of Lord Durham [Lambton*] and his "Radical" supporters, which made up the Whig and, subsequently, Liberal parties.

In the two decades after the collapse of Lord Melbourne's ministry in 1841, Ellice refused repeated requests to enter the cabinet or accept a colonial post, or to go to the House of Lords to augment party strength there. He became instead the "Nestor" of his party. Financially secure, the owner of an extensive estate in the Scottish Highlands and a luxurious town-house in London, he refused to retire from politics. He attended parliament regularly, and was actively concerned about all the major issues under debate. Leaders of both parties called upon him for assistance and advice.

The precarious balance of political power in Britain enabled Ellice to exert a measurable influence on the re-orientation of British imperial policy on behalf of freer trade, stimulation of colonial economic development, and gradual devolution of the empire. For instance, he was highly critical of the government's policy towards the Canada Company, pointing out on several occasions how a more realistic system of land sales might speed development. His most notable early effort to remedy the slow pace of Canadian development came in the abortive Union Bill of 1822 [see John Beverley ROBINSON and Louis-Joseph Papineau*]. Ellice persuaded the ministry to draft a bill largely along lines he suggested and to introduce it in the House of Commons. He had previously secured what he regarded as a commitment from other members to forego extensive debate, believing that only a *fait accompli* could succeed in preventing further French obstruction and in fostering English predominance in Lower Canada. When criticism was unexpectedly voiced in the house, the embattled ministry abandoned the scheme. Only the Canada Trade Act (1822) and, ultimately, the Canada Tenures Act (1825) were salvaged from the original proposal, measures which sought to meet some of the problems confronting the English minority. An important result of the episode – an ironic one in view of mounting criticism of Ellice as a malevolent "conspirateur" – was Ellice's growing realization of the difficulties of legislating for the colonies from London, and a reinforced determination to contemplate self-government for them. This advanced position is clear from his testimony to the Canada Committee of the House of Commons in 1828, and from his advice to the Colonial Office and to colonial governors such as Sir James Kempt* in the 1820s and 1830s. Unfortunately, successive ministries "cared nothing for Canada except as an occa-

sional makeweight in the political game." It required the rebellions of 1837–38, which threatened the Melbourne government, to create a situation that could no longer be ignored.

Ellice made an extended visit to North America in June–October 1836, and in the wake of the 1837 rebellions he saw an opportunity to pressure the government into decisive action. In early January 1838 he first presented to Sir Henry George Grey a concise proposal for a federal union of the two Canadas, and a limited measure of ministerial responsibility. He revived the suggestion that Lord Durham be sent as governor general, with "large powers both for the exercise of authority and conciliation." After consulting Ellice, Durham agreed to undertake the mission. Ellice gave Durham advice and introductions to colonial society, and safeguarded in parliament and the cabinet Durham's freedom of action. Ellice also persuaded his son Edward to accompany Durham as his private secretary. In the course of Durham's mission, Ellice continued his liaison between the Melbourne ministry and its mercurial representative, and tried to cushion the impact of some of Durham's actions (such as the appointments of Thomas Edward Michell Turton and Wakefield). When the ministry abandoned Durham over the banishment of the leading rebels, Ellice continued his efforts to ensure that Durham would produce recommendations and to prevent Melbourne's ministry from collapsing under political pressure. But while Durham was still in Canada, Ellice denounced in the press the reported proposals for a highly democratic, all-inclusive federation of the North America colonies as too difficult to achieve. When Durham returned to London in anger at the end of November 1838, Ellice succeeded in persuading him to abandon such a scheme, and to adopt several features from his own memorandum, "Suggestions for scheme for the future government of the Canadas" (21 Dec. 1838), recommending a federal union of the two provinces. Each of the principal recommendations of Durham's famous *Report*, semantic differences notwithstanding, had been advanced in Ellice's memorandum.

The leaking of the *Report* in early February 1839, in which Ellice may have had a hand, forced the ministry to move. It was a politically explosive issue for Melbourne's tenuous coalition. The cabinet first considered Ellice's "Suggestions," agreed upon them as a basis for legislation, and ordered printing of a bill based on them. However, this decision was reversed two days later. Finally, after two aggravating months, Lord John Russell, the new colonial secretary, proposed

Ellice

two measures, providing for temporary continuation of the emergency power in the hands of a new governor, and recommending Ellice's scheme of union; the first narrowly passed, and it was agreed that consideration of the second would await dispatch of Durham's successor.

Despite the severe strain these events imposed on his relations with the cabinet, Ellice continued his efforts. He provided Charles Edward Poulett Thomson* (Lord Sydenham), Durham's successor, with "advice and assistance" and he reiterated to Russell the need to give Thomson adequate authority to deal with the pressing financial and political crisis; he insisted that "the principle of union being determined upon, it is infinitely better to allow people to settle for themselves, the conditions and provisions, on which it may appear most expedient for the interests of both provinces to carry it into effect." Thomson's instructions and Russell's famous dispatch of 16 Oct. 1839 testify to the imprint of such thinking, when the government remained opposed in principle to "responsible government."

Thomson established a coalition ministry in February 1840; the British government reintroduced its bill in March, and Ellice gave the measure his "unqualified approbation" though he had some doubts about the legislative union now proposed. In June, Ellice (using the leverage of Tory pressure) induced the ministry to drop certain "municipal clauses" deemed a threat to property holders, and the act was finally passed. The measure, which paved the way for responsible government as it evolved in practice under Sydenham, Sir Charles Bagot*, Sir Charles Theophilus Metcalfe*, and Lord Elgin [BRUCE], represented the consummation of Ellice's efforts to force upon a most reluctant ministry some realistic proposals for colonial reform and confederation. It was Ellice's hope that with this step Canada would remain a British state, with sufficient economic self-reliance to resist the dynamic encroachment of the United States, and would advance politically to the point of managing its own destiny effectively. Such hopes might not be fulfilled until at least 1867, but the decisions taken in 1839–40 came at an important, possibly critical, juncture in the transformation of the British colonial system. In these decisions Ellice made his greatest impact on imperial policy.

After 1841 Ellice took a less dramatic but not insignificant part in the making of imperial policy. He proved sympathetic, for instance, to Bagot's efforts to bring Robert Baldwin* and Louis-Hippolyte LA FONTAINE into the government. When the implications of freer trade and responsible government were revealed in the increases in Canadian tariffs and the passage of the Rebellion Losses Act, Ellice accepted the colonial action in principle but questioned the perpetuation of British governance. Fear of possible civil strife and possible American intervention, however, persuaded him against Britain's precipitate withdrawal. Rather, Ellice urged that the British government consider again a federation of the North American colonies, and pursue reciprocal trade arrangements between them and the United States.

In the 1850s Ellice further suspected the efficacy of British colonial policy, in the face of ever increasing colonial self-confidence. He became convinced that "no British administration can be tempted again to dispute the sovereign will of the Canadian people, fairly represented in their legislature." Yet he hoped that Britain would still act to guard against "their passions and impulses" and preserve individual rights and liberties. But in the latter years of the decade, with the Canadians opting for what Ellice considered excessive democracy, leading to political deadlock and fiscal insolvency, he found less virtue in maintaining the imperial connection. He saw no reason to subject the British crown to unnecessary embarrassment and responsibility, though he insisted that the colonists themselves should cut the "silken thread." These views found resonance in both Conservative and Liberal administrations.

Ellice's last visit to the United States and Canada in 1858 reinforced his impression of the growing strength of the former and its impact on Anglo-American relations. His concern was evident in his approach to the HBC, and explicitly set forth in a lengthy and perceptive memorandum on the colonies submitted at the Duke of Newcastle's request in 1861. He urged again the adoption of a federal system comparable to his 1838 scheme which he alleged had been rejected as "too great a parody on the American Constitution." Some such step he saw as the only means of preventing the annexation of British North America to the American union, an eventuality made more likely, he argued, by the American Civil War.

Death brought Edward Ellice's long career to an end shortly before confederation, preventing him from seeing his goal achieved. In his final years Ellice's only son, Edward, and his daughter-in-law, Katherine Jane Balfour, were his frequent companions. Edward, who was an MP almost as long as his father, was also a businessman, with interests ranging from the HBC, of which he became deputy governor in

1858, to financially disastrous Scottish railways. Though he assisted for a time in the management of the Ellice North American investments and acted as interrogator for his father on the HBC select committee, Edward Jr had but slight contact with North American affairs in later life. The sale of the seigneury in 1867 to the Montreal Investment Association marked the passing of that Ellice connection with North America.

Edward "Bear" Ellice may never have forgotten his immediate self-interest when Canada was involved, but it would be hard to argue that the policies he recommended, and the information he supplied to British and Canadian ministries and to American cabinets, was inimical to their long-term mutual interests. Far from being simply an entrepreneur concerned with profits and power, he proved consistently broadminded, perceptive, and determined to pursue a policy solely on its merits. If he shared prevailing British and American assumptions about the place of the French populace in an English colony, he was at least able to temper the prejudices of his colleagues (Lord Durham included) and insist on a measure of equity for both founding peoples. Much of what he proposed was not taken up immediately; the results of the delay – rebellion, bloodshed, financial distress, and retarded political and economic maturity – were the very consequences Ellice worked so hard to avoid. Edward Ellice was a man with a passion for anonymity; yet the letters of condolences which poured in to Glen Quoich from people in all walks of life bear eloquent testimony to the wisdom, warmth, and generosity of a man whose important contributions to the expansion and survival of the British empire in North America ought not to be overlooked.

JAMES M. COLTHART

[There has been to date no complete biography of Edward Ellice. The material contained herein is drawn largely from my thesis, "Edward Ellice and North America" (unpublished PH D thesis, Princeton University, Princeton, N.J., 1971) and from research on Ellice's career after 1841 undertaken for that dissertation but not included therein because of limitations on length. The only other studies of Ellice are one now in progress by John Clarke, fellow of All Soul's College, Oxford, and one by D. E. T. Long, "Edward Ellice" (unpublished PH D thesis, University of Toronto, 1941).

Of necessity, the above account relies largely on primary materials. The major source of manuscript material on Ellice is the Ellice papers, National Library of Scotland (Edinburgh). Copies of a portion of this collection are found in PAC, MG 24, A2. Other important British manuscript sources are the Grey of Howick papers at University of Durham, Dept. of Palæography

and Diplomatic (2nd Earl Grey, box 13; 3rd Earl Grey, boxes 84–88, 142); the Lord John Russell papers at the PRO (PRO 30/22), and at the British Museum (Add. MSS 38080); the Holland House papers and 1st Viscount Halifax papers at the British Museum (Add. MSS 51587 and 49531–93); the 1st Lord Brougham papers and Joseph Parkes papers at University College Library, University of London; the 1st Viscount Halifax papers (A 4/103/1) in the archives of the Earl of Halifax, Garrowby (Yorkshire, Eng.), and the Lambton papers in the archives of the Earl of Durham, Lambton Castle (County Durham, Eng.). Other scattered (but occasionally important) sources in Great Britain, Canada, and the United States are listed in the bibliography of my thesis.

Ellice, by inclination a man with a passion for anonymity, has largely escaped the sustained attention of previous historians. Different aspects of his career are touched upon in: J. S. Galbraith, *The Hudson's Bay Company as an imperial factor, 1821–1869* (Toronto, 1957); Arthur Aspinall, *Politics and the press, c. 1780–1850* (London, 1949); Austin Mitchell, *The Whigs in opposition, 1815–1830* (London, 1967); D. H. Close, "The general elections of 1835 and 1837 in England and Wales" (unpublished D PHIL thesis, Oxford University, 1967); R. H. Fleming, "Phyn, Ellice and Company of Schenectady," *University of Toronto Studies, History and Economics, Contributions to Canadian Economics*, IV (1932), 7–41; W. S. Wallace, "Forsyth, Richardson and Company in the fur trade," RSC *Trans.*, 3rd ser., XXXIV (1940), sect.II, 187–94. Passing reference is made to the non-North American aspects of Ellice's multifaceted career in studies of British and Continental politics, economic development, imperialism, and in many contemporary diaries, journals and other accounts, cited in my bibliography. J.M.C.]

ELMSLEY, JOHN, naval officer, entrepreneur, office-holder, and philanthropist; b. 19 May 1801 at York (Toronto), Upper Canada, son of John Elmsley* and Mary Hallowell; m. Charlotte Sherwood and they had seven sons and three daughters; d. 8 May 1863 at Toronto.

When John Elmsley was born his father was chief justice of Upper Canada and the next year took on the same post in Lower Canada. John Elmsley Sr died in 1805 and Mary Elmsley returned to England with young John, his brother, and two sisters. Probably on the advice of a maternal uncle, Admiral Benjamin Hallowell, John entered the Royal Navy in 1815 as 1st class volunteer on *Tonnant*, and for the next nine years served on the Irish, North American (from 1818 to 1821), and Nore stations. In 1824 he was promoted lieutenant, but he had become disheartened with a profession which had "for its sole object the destruction of the Human Species" and retired on half pay.

Elmsley went to live with his mother at Wad-

Elmsley

don in Surrey, England, and intended supplementing the education he had received by teaching himself science and mathematics in order to qualify for a post on a naval surveying vessel. Instead, it was decided that John would return to Canada and manage the extensive land holdings acquired by his father. He arrived at York in 1825 and, with the assurance that came from a background which opened the doors of "all the Elite of the Upper Canadian Metropolis," became a gentleman farmer on his large property at York and a manager of an estate. An eligible, well placed, and reputedly wealthy bachelor, he participated fully in the social life of the capital despite a privately expressed complaint of the "emptiness and frivolity [of what] is termed High Life and fashionable Society." In September 1830 he became a member of the Executive Council and in January 1831 of the Legislative Council. He was first elected a director of the Bank of Upper Canada in 1828 (he was re-elected in 1829, 1830, 1832, and 1834) and in 1831 was one of the largest shareholders with some 330 shares. He was a founder of the Home District Agricultural Society in 1830 and was to hold the posts of president and secretary. He was one of the incorporators of the British American Assurance Company in 1833 and a major shareholder in the Welland Canal Company, and in 1836 was one of the promoters of the City of Toronto and Lake Huron Rail Road Company; he subscribed £100 to the railway and was elected a director in 1837.

On 12 Sept. 1831 Elmsley married Charlotte, daughter of Levius Peters Sherwood*, a judge on the Upper Canadian Court of King's Bench. Because she was a Roman Catholic, a marriage service was held first at St Paul's Catholic Church before the Reverend William Peter MacDonald* and another at the Anglican St James' Church before John STRACHAN. A long trip to Europe followed. On the Elmsleys' return to York in 1832 John's attendance at St James appeared less regular, then ceased altogether. In August 1833 he announced to the Roman Catholic bishop, Alexander Macdonell*, his intention, "with the most hearty joy and satisfaction," to join the Catholic Church. He wished to maintain secrecy, however, because his mother "would be most terribly shocked to learn that I had embraced a Religion against which she has ever entertained the most violent prejudices." Less than six months later Elmsley printed and distributed 5,000 copies of a translation of a work defending the doctrine of transubstantiation written by the Catholic bishop of Strasbourg, which he had first seen in Europe. "I feel quite unable to gainsay it," Elmsley reported to Strachan in forwarding a copy to him,

and "unless the subject of the Bishop's argument can be overthrown, I must, of necessity, no longer abstain from receiving Communion in that Church, where alone the real presence of our Blessed Lord . . . in the Sacrament of the Eucharist, is acknowledged." Strachan quickly replied, in an open letter to his congregation, to what he saw as an attempt by Elmsley, "even before his final conversion, to labour for the conversion of others." A vigorous debate and more pamphlets followed, including Strachan's *The poor man's preservative against popery* (1834) and a refutation of Strachan's arguments by W. P. MacDonald.

The fortunes of the Catholic Church were at a low ebb at York when Elmsley joined it. A long dispute between Bishop Macdonell and an earlier incumbent at York, William J. O'Grady*, was still simmering despite Macdonell's suspension of O'Grady in 1832. The conversion of so eminent a public figure as Elmsley at such a trying time appeared to Macdonell as providential and Elmsley was soon one of the bishop's principal advisers in the diocese. He also played a leading lay role in Toronto as a church warden at St Paul's, the city's only Catholic church. It was not long, however, before Elmsley found himself among detractors and in conflict with the incumbent, Patrick McDonagh. To overcome the apathy he found among members of the congregation towards their duties, Elmsley suggested to Macdonell in 1835 that the parish be deprived of priests for several months. A recommendation that 2*d.* be collected at the church door from all worshippers on Sundays was accepted, and led to a dispute with McDonagh who refused to cooperate in levying what he considered an unjust "impost." After the advice of Elmsley and other church wardens that McDonagh be removed was not taken, Elmsley resigned his post in 1836.

Elmsley's fortune was based on land and, as many others in Upper Canada did, he speculated heavily in UEL location rights after an 1830 order-in-council facilitated their transfer. His activities came to the notice of Sir John COLBORNE, who in 1833 recommended to the Executive Council a measure to curb the traffic. To Elmsley the proposed measure was in its "retrospective operation a Breach of good faith." He protested so strongly in council that Colborne demanded an apology. Elmsley soon resigned as executive councillor, explaining to the Toronto *Patriot* that he could not "fearlessly express my real sentiments and opinions if opposed to the government for the time being without incurring the risk of dismissal." Reformers were jubilant at this breach within the Family Compact and there was some speculation that Elmsley would join Reform ranks. In 1836 Sir Francis Bond Head* saw Elmsley as a man "inclined to liberality" when he reappointed him to the Executive Council. Later, in his *Narrative*, Head described Elmsley as "perhaps the most ultra-reformer in the Legislative Council." In 1835 Elmsley had established the private, joint-stock Farmers' Bank with George Truscott and served as its first president. The bank and the Home District Mutual Fire Company, of which he was to be a director in 1844, were both projects associated with Reformers.

Despite his earlier private misgivings about a military career Elmsley offered his services at the outbreak of the rebellion in 1837. He commanded one of the boats under the charge of Captain Andrew Drew* when the *Caroline* was cut loose on the Niagara River, and he later claimed to have fired the shot that killed Amos Durfee, the only known casualty in the episode. Elmsley also served on the St Lawrence River and in June and July 1838 was in command of the steamer *Thames* on the western Upper Canadian frontier. A provincial marine was established in summer 1838; he was put in charge at Toronto and given command of the *Chief Justice Robinson*. On board this vessel, on 28 Nov. 1828, Elmsley received an urgent request from Lieutenant Governor Sir George Arthur* to proceed with some 50 or 60 men to Lake Erie to assist Drew. Elmsley had agitated unsuccessfully about his rank in the provincial marine – he wanted the equivalent to his lieutenant-colonelcy in the militia and felt entitled to a rank above Drew's – and now, faced with serving under Drew in an inferior rank and concerned that the status of his men was also in jeopardy, Elmsley reopened the question with Arthur on 29 November. Again rebuffed, Elmsley resigned his commission and agreed to order his next in command to proceed to Lake Erie. The force still did not leave, and it was soon revealed that Elmsley in an address to his men had informed them they were no longer bound by their oaths of service as the grades promised when they enlisted were not in effect. To some his words were treasonable. Arthur deemed his actions "prejudicial to the interests of the province and to the good of the Queen's Service," and found it impossible to meet Elmsley in the Executive Council. Elmsley rejected an investigation by the council and demanded instead a general court martial, which was refused. He was suspended from the council on 28 Jan. 1839 and later dismissed. That Elmsley, who had earlier in 1838 been described as "a wrong headed man but brave as a lion and devotedly attached to all that is British," was loyal Arthur did not doubt, but his actions were ill advised.

Elmsley continued to sit in the Legislative Council until the union of Upper and Lower Canada in 1841. By then he was devoting himself largely to the management of his lands, steamship enterprises, and increasingly, church and philanthropic activities. In 1841 he became captain of the steamer *Cobourg* which plied the Kingston – Toronto route with stops at Cobourg and Port Hope. The next year he purchased with Donald BETHUNE the 475-ton *Niagara* from John Hamilton* and became its captain on the Toronto – Kingston route in the Royal Mail line. He changed the ship's name to *Sovereign* in 1843 and continued as captain and part-owner until summer 1844 when he sold his interest, having lost, he claimed later, £1,200. He also participated in boating events in Toronto and was joint president with Hugh RICHARDSON of the Toronto Regatta held in September 1842. He joined the Toronto Boat Club (later the Royal Canadian Yacht Club) in 1853.

Though land still occupied much of Elmsley's attention after 1841 he appears to have been disposing of property he had accumulated. He had sold some of his large estate in Toronto and after the rebellion moved to the northern edge of it at Clover Hill. He retained close contacts with the clergy in Toronto and from about 1852 acted as the bishop's secretary. When the construction of St Michael's Cathedral began in 1845 he organized work "bees," arranged much of the financing, and in 1848 when work was completed he and fellow convert S. G. Lynn guaranteed its mortgages so that it could be consecrated. In 1851 Elmsley took the 234-ton *James Coleman* on a run as far as Halifax, perhaps in order to raise funds for the cathedral.

Elmsley was liberal in the donations and in the time he volunteered to the Catholic Church and Catholic education, evidence of a deep commitment to his adopted faith. He helped build the first Catholic school in Toronto in 1841. He conducted catechism classes in city schools, donated prizes, and led children to Mass on Sundays. First elected a school trustee in 1841, he was a strong promoter of the establishment of separate schools in the city, founded an early commercial school in Toronto, and acted as agent in Toronto for separate schools throughout Canada West. He assisted the establishment in Toronto of the Sisters of St Joseph in 1851 (donating two acres of his Clover Hill estate for their convent) and of the Christian Brothers in 1851. He attempted to persuade Jesuits to open a college in Toronto in 1850 by holding out the promise of a site. When classes at St Michael's College outgrew the bishop's palace Elmsley donated four lots to the Basilian fathers for the college on condition that they build a parish church. He was a founder of the Widows and Orphans Asylum (which became the House of Providence) and an incorporator of the Toronto Athenaeum in 1848 and the House of Industry in 1851. After St Basil's Church was built near his home in 1856 he attended it daily and organized in 1857 its chapter of the St Vincent de Paul Society. He was the chapter's first president and retained the post until April 1863 when his health began to fail. He died in May, having made provision for his body to be buried in St Michael's Cathedral and his heart to be deposited in the west wall of St Basil's Church.

HENRI PILON

The most important pamphlets published on the occasion of John Elmsley's conversion were: [J.-F.-M. Le Pappe de] Trevern, *Extract from a celebrated work entitled an amicable discussion on the Church of England and on the Reformation in general . . .* , trans. William Richmond (York [Toronto], 1833); W. P. MacDonald, *Remarks on Doctor Strachan's pamphlet against the Catholic doctrine of the real presence of Christ's body and blood in the Eucharist . . .* (Kingston, [Ont.], 1834); John Strachan, *A letter, to the congregation of St. James' Church, York, U. Canada, occasioned by the Hon. John Elmsley's publication, of the bishop of Strasbourg's observations, on the 6th chapter of St. John's Gospel* (York [Toronto], n.d.), and *The poor man's preservative against popery, containing an introduction on character and genius of the Roman Catholic religion . . .* (Toronto, 1834).

Archives of the Archdiocese of Toronto, Macdonell papers, AB13–18; AB29–33; AC29–30; Add. ser.1, Macdonell, 1835; 1836; 1837. PAC, RG 1, E3, 18, pp.6–8; 23, pp.52–53; 24, pp.6–11, 110–11; RG 5, A1, 212, pp.116511–19, 116672–80; RG 7, G1, 72, p.405; 88, p.268; 94, pp.32–40. PAO, Elmsley-Macaulay papers; Macaulay (John) papers. PRO, Adm. 9/30, no.1223; CO 42/418, ff.49–70, 91–91v; 42/456–57. University of St Michael's College Library (Toronto), John Elmsley, notebook, 1823–41. UTL-TF, MS coll. 78. *Canadian Freeman*, 14 May 1863. *Colonial Advocate*, 1830–34. F. B. Head, *A narrative* (London, 1839). *Patriot* (Toronto), 1833–34. W. P. Bull, *From Macdonell to McGuigan, the history of the Roman Catholic Church in Upper Canada* (Toronto, 1939). Mary Hoskin, *History of St. Basil's parish, St. Joseph Street* (Toronto, 1912). *Jubilee volume, 1842–1892: the archdiocese of Toronto and Archbishop Walsh*, ed. J. R. Teefy (Toronto, 1892), ix, 92–93, 149–53, 210, 224, 244, 260, 297–98. *Robertson's landmarks of Toronto*, I, 124–26, 296–99; II, 864–902. *The story of St. Paul's parish*, ed. Edward Kelly ([Toronto], 1922). Brother Alfred [A. J. Dooner], "The Honourable John Elmsley, legislative and executive councillor of Upper Canada (1801–1863)," *CCHA Report*, 1936–37, 23–40; reprinted in Brother Alfred, *Catholic pioneers of Upper Canada* (Toronto, 1947), 195–224.

ERMATINGER, FREDERICK WILLIAM (usually known as **William**), soldier and officeholder; b. in 1811 probably in Sault Ste Marie, Upper Canada, son of fur-trader Charles Oakes Ermatinger* and Charlotte Kattawabide (Cattoonalute), daughter of an Ojibwa chief; d. 22 Jan. 1869 at Montreal.

Frederick William Ermatinger, a descendant through his father of a Swiss merchant who settled in Canada shortly after the Conquest, had family connections with the British military, Montreal's official class, and French Canadian society. His uncle, Frederick William Ermatinger*, was postmaster and sheriff of Montreal from 1810 to 1827, and his brother, Charles Oakes Ermatinger, was captain of the Royal Montreal Cavalry during the 1840s; his wife, Caroline-Élisa, whom he married on 14 July 1845 at Saint-Ours, was of the prominent Juchereau Duchesnay family.

Ermatinger studied law in the office of Samuel GALE from 1829 to 1834. He was admitted to the bar on 23 Sept. 1844 but never practised. His military career began in the Royal Montreal Cavalry in which he was a lieutenant by 1833. He served in Spain during the Carlist wars from about 1835, first with the British Legion and then in the Spanish service, reaching the rank of lieutenant-colonel. In 1839 he returned to Montreal where he was appointed police commissioner of the city on 16 Feb. 1842. In 1843 the offices of inspector and superintendent of police were combined and Ermatinger was given the new post.

As police superintendent, Ermatinger was charged with assisting in curbing civil disturbances when they went beyond the control of the local magistrates. In 1843 two strikes, the first in March by workmen on the Lachine Canal and the second three months later by canal workers at Beauharnois, resulted in rioting. Ermatinger was sent with troops to quell the riot at Lachine and was placed in charge of the inquiry following the Beauharnois riot. The workers involved in the Beauharnois strike were demanding higher wages (3s. instead of 2s. 3d.), to be paid semiannually in place of annually, and shorter hours (they wanted a 12-hour day). They also did not want to have to pay for the shanties they lived in while employed on the canals, and there were complaints that they were compelled to purchase their food from company stores when it could be procured at less cost from local farmers. Ermatinger was later assigned the task of organizing canal police at both Lachine and Beauharnois.

During the disturbances in Montreal in April and May 1849 and again in August following the passage of the Rebellion Losses Act [*see* James Bruce], Ermatinger was instrumental in organizing joint action by police and troops. In 1850 he led the police in establishing order during a riot over the question of the annexation of Canada to the United States. Both Ermatinger, as superintendent of police, and his elder brother, Charles Oakes, as chief of police in Montreal, were wounded in June 1853 when a mob attacked Zion Church where the ex-Barnabite Alessandro Gavazzi was lecturing [*see* Charles Wilson*]; the brothers had attempted to keep rioters from entering the church. Early in the 1850s Ermatinger organized, at the request of the provincial government, the Water Police, a corps of about 30 men recruited largely from former soldiers and men of the Royal Irish Constabulary, its purpose being to protect wharves and canal shipping in the vicinity of Montreal and generally to deal with disturbances of the peace in Canada East.

Ermatinger remained police superintendent until 1855. In 1856 he became field inspector of the active volunteer militia of Canada East. It was to him that George-Étienne Cartier*, attorney general of Canada East, turned in 1864 to undertake new duties as a police magistrate on the American border when tension was increasing because of the threat of raids by Fenians. Ermatinger was able to maintain good relations with American border authorities and, when Fenians began making border raids, he kept his own government informed of Fenian movements. The exposure and strain of this work, however, undermined his health, and in 1866 he was appointed to the lighter post of joint clerk of the crown and peace in Montreal with Louis-Antoine Dessaulles*. But he was again pressed into service as a police magistrate; in the same year he was sent to Sweetsburg (Cowansville) in the Eastern Townships to command the government police while Fenian prisoners were being tried.

At his death in 1869, Ermatinger's wife was left with a family of four sons and one daughter to care for but she appealed in vain for a widow's pension, even though her husband had been one of the most important men in the Montreal civil service for almost 30 years.

Colonel Ermatinger was an able, courageous, and reliable public servant, tall and commanding in appearance, whose experience in civil disturbances made him eminently valuable to the authorities. In an era when political tensions pervaded both private and public relationships, he remained aloof from political entanglements and carried out his duties as police superintendent under several different administrations over a period of 15 years. His success in handling riotous mobs of all kinds came from a combination of firmness, courtesy, and forbearance towards the rioters. In 1853, for example, he refused to identify those who had injured him during the Gavazzi riot.

Elinor Senior

McCord Museum, McCord papers, M. Aylmer to D. R. McCord, 17 July 1901; Edward Ermatinger to D. R. McCord, 31 May 1913; C. O. Ermatinger to D. R. McCord, 29 April 1912, 9 April 1917; Military papers, misc. no.2, M5728.

PAC, MG 19, A2, ser.4; MG 26, A, 240, p.106391; 241, p.107046; 472, pp.235157–59; RG 8, I (C series), 319, pp.82–85; 616, pp.238, 249, 255, 289. Can., Prov. of, Legislative Assembly, *Journals*, 1843, II, app. T; 1851, I, app.B. [Edward Ermatinger], "Edward Ermatinger's York Factory express journal, being a record of journeys made between Fort Vancouver and Hudson Bay in the years 1827–1828," ed. C. O. Ermatinger and James White, RSC *Trans.*, 3rd ser., VI (1912), sect.II, 67. *Gazette* (Montreal), 12 July 1850; 6 March, 10 June 1853; 23 Jan. 1869. *Montreal Transcript*, 4 March 1843. P.-G. Roy, *La famille Juchereau Duchesnay* (Lévis, Qué., 1903), 353–57.

ESSON, JOHN, merchant and politician; baptized 6 Nov. 1804 in Aberdeen, Scotland, first child of Charles Esson, millwright, and Elizabeth Whyte; m. 10 Jan. 1836 Harriet Ann Leonard, and they had 11 children; d. 4 March 1863 in Halifax, N.S.

Emigrating from Scotland, John Esson joined his stepbrother Charles and his uncle Adam in Halifax about 1823. From his uncle he learned the grocery trade, and by the mid 1830s had set up his own store. In 1847 his assistant, Robert Boak Jr, became his partner in John Esson and Company, a domestic wholesale grocery firm, and in 1854 the two men, with John Taylor, formed a second company, Esson, Boak, and Company, to carry on trade in the West Indies. In the latter year, James Parker became an associate in John Esson and Company, but five years later Esson sold his share in this firm to his son William and to Alexander Stephen. In 1863 the senior partner's continuing interest in Esson, Boak, and Company was valued at $200,000. By the mid 1850s Esson's financial acumen had been recognized by his appointment to directorships in such organizations as the Bank of Nova Scotia, the Indisputable Life Policy Company, the Union Marine Insurance Company of Nova Scotia, and the Halifax Fire Insurance Company. He was president of the latter from 1858 to 1863. Although his financial interests encompassed a diversity of firms, his principal investments were in property, county mortgages, banks, and development enterprises.

During this period Esson also established himself as a concerned townsman. Active in the North British Society after 1832, he became its president in 1847. He served on the committee of management of the Halifax Mechanics' Institute in 1840 and acted as a fire warden from 1841 to 1849. An original subscriber to the British North American Association, he sat on its committees for the advancement of Nova Scotian interests in manufacturing and the fisheries. Later he was president of the Halifax Agricultural Society. His various civic appointments in the 1850s, such as governor of the Poor's Asylum and commissioner of the cemetery, were routine and responsible rather than controversial.

Only after his election as an MHA, however, did Esson become fully a public figure. Quietly active in the Reform party by 1840, Esson was elected in 1851 to the Halifax County seat left vacant by Joseph Howe*'s transfer of his candidacy to Cumberland. Frequently Esson headed the Halifax poll in subsequent elections. After the reorganization of districts in 1859, Esson sat until his death for the eastern division of the county. He was a regular though not unswerving adherent of the Liberal government, steadfastly supporting such party priorities as Howe's railway policy but rarely debating in the assembly upon principal issues. He did speak, however, on behalf of municipal autonomy and was a staunch defender of the authority of the corporation of Halifax. Moreover, he sought to promote the particular needs and interests not only of his business colleagues but also of his poorer constituents by regularly bringing before the assembly such issues as railway damages and road allowances. His view of the temperance movement might best be described as pragmatic; although his business included the sale of rum, he willingly presented his constituents' petitions favouring prohibition. His most important position within the house was his long-standing membership, including the chairmanship from 1856 to 1863, of the public accounts committee. In the latter year, he declined an appointment to the Executive Council. A contemporary observer of the assembly found Esson "very quiet, but not inscrutable," and Howe observed that "not many men had ever passed from the halls of legislation, leaving behind them so few enemies, and so many personal friends."

S. BUGGEY

General Register Office (Edinburgh), Register of births and baptisms for the parishes in Aberdeen, 1 Aug. 1795, 22 Nov. 1799, 6 Nov. 1804. Halifax County Court House (Halifax), registry of deeds, index, 1749–1865. Halifax County Court of Probate (Halifax), no.1127, estate of John Esson. PAC, MG 24, B29, 3, pp.684–87; 8, pp.491–92. PANS, MG 3, 154; RG 35, A, 1–3, Halifax assessments, 1817–41, and road tax records. St Matthew's Presbyterian Church (Halifax), no.47a, burials, p.66, no.48, marriages, p.347; baptisms, various pages (mfm. at PANS). *Constitution and bye laws of the British North American Association, organized at Halifax, Nova Scotia, 18th Feb., A.D., 1851* (Halifax, 1851). *Acadian Recorder*, 31 July 1841; 7 June, 26 July 1856; 7 March 1863. *Morning Herald and Commercial Advertiser* (Halifax), 23, 30 Oct. 1840. *Novascotian*, 8 Jan. 1855, 4 April 1859, 9 March 1863. *Sun* (Halifax), 1 Jan. 1847, 6 March 1863. *Belcher's farmer's almanack*, 1837–63. *Directory of N.S. MLAs. Halifax and its business: containing historical sketch, and description of the city and its institutions . . .* (Halifax, 1876). J. S. Macdonald, *Annals, North British Society, Halifax, Nova Scotia, with portraits and biographical notes, 1768–1903* (Halifax, 1905).

ESTEN, JAMES CHRISTIE PALMER, lawyer and judge; b. 7 Nov. 1805 at St George, Bermuda, the son of James Christie Esten, chief justice of Bermuda, and Ester Palmer; m. in 1832 at Exeter, England, Ann Frederica Hutchison, and they had several children; d. 24 Oct. 1864 at Toronto, Canada West.

James Christie Palmer Esten's childhood was spent in Bermuda and Virginia. He was sent to England to be educated at the Charterhouse School, London, and then entered Lincoln's Inn. He was called to the bar, and practised in London and at Exeter, becoming an expert in conveyancing and other aspects of land law.

In 1836 Esten immigrated to Upper Canada to pursue a career in retail merchandising. But when, in March of the following year, the Court of Chancery was established for the province, Esten had the opportunity of renewing his career as an equity lawyer, and with a reasonable expectation of success, since few lawyers in Upper Canada were expert in equity law. He was admitted as a barrister in 1838, and until 1849 enjoyed a growing practice.

In 1843 the Robert Baldwin*–Louis-Hippolyte LA FONTAINE ministry established a commission to investigate the Court of Chancery in the hope of simplifying its practice and reducing costs to suitors. Among those appointed to the commission were three prominent equity lawyers – Robert Easton BURNS, William Hume BLAKE, and Esten. The report of the commissioners was presented to the government in 1845; many of its recommendations were implemented in 1849. The major revision, however, the enlargement of the court from one to three judges, was not among the 1845 recommendations. William Blake, Baldwin's solicitor general, became the chancellor, and Esten a vice-chancellor; Robert Sympson Jameson* remained a vice-chancellor. Esten sat as a judge in equity from the fall of 1849 until his death in 1864. Along with Blake, he was instrumental in further simplifying the operations of the court, and in promulgating new orders in May 1850. When Jameson retired late in 1850, the master in chancery, John Godfrey Spragge*, was appointed a vice-chancellor. Over the next decade he, Blake, and Esten largely settled the practice of the court.

Esten wrote the decisions in many of the cases before the Chancery Court, particularly those which dealt with the rights of parties to mortgages. He died at Toronto in 1864, a respected member of the legal profession and of the Chancery bench.

ROBERT HETT

Can., Prov. of, Legislative Assembly, *Journals*, 1844–45, 2, app.J.J.; 1850, app.O. *Globe*, 26 Oct. 1864. *Journal of Education for U.C.*, XVII (1864), 171. *Reports of cases adjudged in the Court of Chancery of Upper Canada . . .*, comp. Alexander Grant (29v., Toronto, 1850–83), I–II. *Upper Canada Law Journal* (Toronto), X (1864), 281. Read, *Lives of judges*. W. R. Riddell, *The bar and the courts of the province of Upper Canada, or Ontario* (Toronto, 1928). H. C. Wilkinson, *Bermuda from sail to steam; the history of the island from 1784 to 1901* (2v., London, 1973).

EVANS, THOMAS, soldier; b. 9 March 1777, near Wolverhampton, Staffordshire, England, the son of Richard Evans; d. 11 Feb. 1863 at Quebec.

Thomas Evans volunteered for the British army in 1793 and later claimed that his "juvenile exertions" at that time resulted in the enlistment of "more than 150 men for the Service." An unusually active and ambitious officer, he purchased an ensign's commission in the 113th Foot, then served in the 93rd Foot, and became a lieutenant in the prestigious 8th, or King's Regiment, on 11 Oct. 1796. He saw active service in the West Indies with the 93rd, participating in the taking of Demerara and Berbice (both now part of Guyana). En route to England in 1797, however, his ship was captured by the French, and he was kept in close confinement for several months at Saintes, France.

Evans rejoined the 8th Regiment early in 1798 and won special recognition for his services as lieutenant and adjutant during the Egyptian campaign of 1801. On 19 Nov. 1803, while serving at Gibraltar, he purchased his captaincy – an advancement influenced by the patronage of the Duke of Kent [Edward Augustus*] and Evans' commanding officer, Colonel Gordon Drummond*. Shortly after Drummond's promotion to major-general on 1 Jan. 1805, Evans was seconded to his staff as aide-de-camp. He served the first half of 1808 with the 8th, but by August he was in Quebec, again seconded to Drummond, now second in command in British North America. Evans was later military secretary to Drummond until the general's recall in the summer of 1811. At that time Captain Evans was posted to Upper Canada as brigade-major to Major-General Isaac Brock*.

Promoted on merit to a majority on 16 Feb. 1812, Evans assumed onerous additional duties as deputy adjutant-general in Brock's command on the outbreak of war with the United States in June. In his dual staff role he was primarily responsible for preparing the expedition which compelled the surrender of General William Hull's army at Detroit on 16 August. His brilliant handling of reinforcements at Queenston on 13 October, following the death of Brock, proved a vital contribution to Major-General Roger Hale Sheaffe*'s victory in that crucial battle.

Although honoured with a lieutenant-colonel's brevet retroactive to 13 Oct. 1812, Evans returned to the 8th as a major at the end of January 1813. He commanded five companies of his regiment in Sir George Prevost*'s combined operation against the American base at Sackets Harbor, suffering three wounds in that ill-starred venture. He recovered, however, in time to play important roles in the expulsion of the Americans from Forty Mile Creek on the Niagara peninsula in June and in the remaining actions of the campaign of 1813.

Late in the winter of 1813–14 Evans commanded six service companies of the 2nd battalion of the 8th, as well as 230 seamen posted to the fleet at Kingston, on a forced snowshoe march through the wilderness from New Brunswick to Quebec. Successfully completing this assignment in March, he then proceeded to Upper Canada and the command of the 8th's 1st battalion, winning commendation for effective leadership at the battle of Chippawa on 5 July, and at Lundy's Lane on the 25th. He was wounded for the fourth time in the abortive assault on Fort Erie on 15 August, but continued on active service until the end of the war, by which time he had won ten honourable mentions in dispatches and general orders.

Evans assumed command of the 2nd battalion of the 8th in Montreal in February 1815 and returned to the United Kingdom with the battalion in August. On 14 March 1816 he exchanged for a majority in the 70th (Glasgow Lowland) Regiment and two days later was created a CB. He returned to Canada in 1816 and joined the 70th in Kingston in July. During the next 11 years he served with that distinguished regiment – frequently as its commanding officer – in Kingston, York (Toronto), Quebec, and Montreal. Moreover, he commanded the garrison in Lower Canada from June 1824 to September 1825 during the absence of Governor General Dalhousie [Ramsay*].

Posted from Canada to Ireland in August 1827, the 70th subsequently garrisoned Gibraltar during 1834–36 and Malta during 1836–38. Evans had purchased its immediate command on 24 Sept. 1829, and had been granted its colonelcy on 22 July 1830. He retired from active service on promotion to major-general in 1838. Promoted lieutenant-general in 1851, he was subsequently honoured with the colonelcy of the 81st, and promoted general on 18 May 1855.

Evans' connections with Canada had been given further personal continuity by his marriage in Montreal on 12 March 1810 to Harriet Lawrence, daughter of an eminent loyalist, Judge Isaac Ogden*. Evans lived in Montreal from 1848 until shortly before his death, and six of his eight children were born in Canada. One of his four sons, Richard John, became a prominent businessman in Toronto and Montreal after serving 18 years in the British army, principally in India; his daughter Catherine Maria married in 1847 Isaac Hellmuth*, an evangelical Anglican clergyman who was then vice-principal of Bishop's College in Lennoxville and completed his career in Canada as bishop of Huron; Emily Anne married in 1856 Adam Crooks*, later attorney general and minister of education for Ontario. In retirement Evans actively supported Hellmuth's promotion of evangelical Anglicanism in Canada, and it was he who offered to assist the financing of a church in Montreal of which Hellmuth would be rector, a project that incurred the wrath of Francis FULFORD, high church bishop of Montreal.

It was said of General Evans that he participated in some 42 general actions and minor affairs and that testimony was borne to his distinguished conduct on almost 70 different occasions. It is also recorded that in his last seven years with the 70th, "he was never forced to order corporal punishment or to see his court-martials reversed." Such tributes are exceptional in the annals of the British army.

JOHN W. SPURR

PRO, WO 17, Monthly returns, Nova Scotia and dependencies, 1808; Canada, 1808–27; WO 25/798, no.4479. *Select British documents of the Canadian War of 1812* (Wood). *Montreal Transcript*, 17 Feb. 1863. G.B., WO, *Army list*, 1794–1839. *Hart's army list*, 1840–63, especially 1863, p.364. *Montreal directory* (Mackay), 1848–62. William Kingsford, *The history of Canada* (10v., Toronto, 1887–98), VIII, 239.

F

FAILLON, ÉTIENNE-MICHEL, priest, Sulpician, professor, and historian; b. 29 Dec. 1799 at Tarascon, dept of Bouches-du-Rhône, France, son of Jacques-Michel Faillon, surveyor, and Claire Raoûx; d. 25 Oct. 1870 in Paris.

Étienne-Michel Faillon attended the *lycée* of Avignon and the Séminaire d'Aix-en-Provence, then continued his theological studies with the Sulpicians in Paris. Ordained priest on 18 Sept. 1824, he became a member of this community, and stayed a year in the novitiate at the Solitude d'Issy-les-Moulineaux, near Paris, where the priests who were to work in the grand seminaries were prepared. There he met the future superiors of the seminary of Saint-Sulpice at Montreal: Joseph-Vincent Quiblier*, Pierre-Louis BILLAUDÈLE, and Joseph-Alexandre Baile*.

From 1826 to 1829 Faillon taught dogmatic theology at the Grand Séminaire de Lyon. In his first years of teaching Faillon prepared two hagiographical accounts for his pupils, and more especially for clergy engaged in pastoral work in working-class environments: *Vie de M. Démia, instituteur des Sœurs de S. Charles . . .* (Lyon, 1829), and *Vie de M. de Lantages, premier supérieur du séminaire de Notre-Dame du Puy* (Paris, 1830). In 1829 he was appointed a professor in the Paris seminary. In addition to giving instruction in patristics, he took an interest in the history of the training of clerics and in the subject of catechisms. His responsibility for catechism led him to write a *Directoire des associées du catéchisme de persévérance de Saint-Sulpice* (Paris, 1830), and *Histoire des catéchismes de Saint-Sulpice* (Paris, 1831), and also a *Méthode de Saint-Sulpice dans la direction des catéchismes* (Paris, 1832).

In 1837 Faillon left Paris to become director of the Solitude. His new duties were less immediately connected with teaching, but they did not divert him from intellectual work. A first edition in two volumes of the *Vie de M. Olier, fondateur du séminaire de S. Sulpice accompagnée de notices sur un grand nombre de personnages contemporains* (Paris), which he had begun early in 1830, appeared in 1841. The French historian René-François Rohrbacher drew inspiration from this work for his monumental 29-volume *Histoire universelle de l'Église catholique* (Paris, 1842–49). Faillon's life of Jean-Jacques Olier was particularly appreciated by ultramontanes: "an extraordinary book . . . the most admirable biography I have read," exclaimed Louis Veuillot. The Paris journal *L'Université catholique* considered it a book "written in the German manner," one characterized by concern for erudition. The book's great merit is that it recreates the social and religious context of Olier's work. This important study had three editions in Faillon's lifetime and a fourth edition appeared three years after his death; two English editions were published in 1861 and 1885. In the fourth edition the first volume recounts the origin of Olier's apostolate among the clergy; the second, the portion of his life devoted to ministering in the parish of Saint-Sulpice. The third discusses the work of the seminaries. Some critics, for instance in the *Semaine religieuse* of Paris, see in it a "model of its kind." Faillon was to publish other significant works in Europe, conforming to a type of apologetic history that 19th century Catholics found particularly palatable.

The Sulpician historian made three trips to Canada, staying about seven years in all, from October 1849 to June 1850, from May 1854 to September 1855, and from November 1857 to June 1862. As assistant general of the society, he was responsible for visiting the Sulpician houses in America, and he made contact with the women's communities at Montreal established under the French régime. His experience in the field of hagiography led him to agree to write the biographies of their founders, Marguerite Bourgeoys*, Marie-Marguerite d'Youville [Dufrost* de Lajemmerais], and Jeanne Mance*. In this way Faillon shared in the religious revival of the 1840s in the diocese of Montreal.

His prolonged visits in Canada enabled Faillon to accomplish here a great deal of work important beyond the literary sphere. His biographies, it is true, were for him a form of evangelization, aimed at encouraging the Montreal communities to return to the spirit of their founders. Faillon, however, also turned his attention to the codifying of the regulations of these congregations; he even drew up a travel regulation for the nuns of the Congregation of Notre-Dame. When he be-

came involved in the question of the division of the Montreal parish of Notre-Dame [*see* Ignace Bourget*], he also naturally took an interest in the smooth running of Sulpician affairs.

With a more specific pastoral intention, Faillon gave the nuns of Mother Bourgeoys at Montreal a statue of Our Lady of Mercy, which came originally from Avignon and was reputed to be miraculous. Abbé Adam-Charles-Gustave Desmazures* related: "Several illnesses considered incurable for many years were cured almost instantaneously by the oil in the statue's lamp; several people in peril of death and given up by doctors recovered their health; several of the crippled, paralytic, or disabled who had long suffered were made whole. Devotion to the statue spread so widely that imitations were made in various sizes. They were soon to be found in all the principal churches of the region and in different communities."

During his third stay at Montreal, Faillon played an important role in the propagation of the cult of the Virgin. In July 1860 he preached at the inauguration of the church built in honour of Our Lady of Mercy. The miracles continued, and Faillon recorded prodigies attributable to the Madonna's intervention. He visited those miraculously healed, going even to the *pays d'en haut*; he collected the testimony of doctors and confessors, and noted the amazing events; at Saint-André d'Acton (Acton Vale) parish priest Narcisse-Édouard Ricard pointed out five families that had received favours. Thus, in 1861 he declared some 30 miracles authentic and these were reported with enthusiasm in the religious press. In addition to spreading the faith in this way, Faillon was involved in developing the cult of St Joseph, both in Canada and in Europe. In 1843 he had published a tract entitled *Sentiments de M. Olier sur la dévotion à saint Joseph* (Saint-Denis, France), which was reprinted in 1854. Four years later 40,000 copies had been sold in Canada. In 1859 Faillon published at Montreal a voluminous *Vie de saint Joseph, composée d'après les vues communiquées à M. Olier.* . . . Faillon also played an important role for the church at Montreal in developing catechisms for first communion and *catéchismes de persévérance*.

Nevertheless, Faillon's major achievement is his *Histoire de la colonie française en Canada*, which he undertook seriously during his second voyage. He consulted the archives of the Montreal and Quebec communities and the notaries' registers in the two towns. He was assisted by several copyists, who transcribed documents under his direction. In France, he completed his

Faillon

documentation at the Archives de la Marine and the Ministère des Affaires Étrangères. He also visited the great Paris libraries, and looked through the collections of Saint-Sulpice, the prefecture at Versailles, the archdiocese and prefecture at Rouen, and the British Museum in London. He thus assembled in 30 volumes in quarto documentation for a history of New France in some ten volumes. His achievement was more modest than his ambition: before his death he had published only the first three volumes of his *Histoire de la colonie française*. This monumental work along with his earlier biographies and his life of the recluse Jeanne Le Ber*, which appeared in 1860, represent some 4,000 pages published on Canadian history by Faillon.

His *Histoire* appeared during the years (1864–69) he spent at Rome as procurator general of the society. He returned to Paris in 1869, and died during the disturbances of 1870. Educated within the church that had accepted the Concordat, and under masters who had experienced the revolution of 1789, Faillon allied himself with the aggressive and apologetic spirit of his time. He was profoundly attached to the cult of the Virgin Mary, and often dedicated his works to the mother of Jesus; he also wrote a *Vie intérieure de la Très-Sainte Vierge . . .* (2v., Rome, 1866). His faith in providence was exceptional; in his correspondence, as in his historical works, one has the impression that, compared with its omnipresence, "second causes" are of no importance. A witness of the French revolutions of 1830 and 1848, he came to consider these "misfortunes" as calamities willed by God for the sanctification of the church. The political upheavals of 1870 accompanying his last days brought out a *leitmotif* that in a sense was the synthesis of a life consecrated to God: "they will not take Jesus Christ away from us," he liked to repeat to those at his bedside. Moreover, all his historical writings, as he recognized himself, were intended to be a literature of edification.

His writings are, indeed, thoroughly impregnated with his profound religious convictions. Faillon's characters act only at the dictation of God or the devil. In the last analysis, they are no more than instruments programmed according to the two cities of St Augustine: hence the miracles, apparitions, visions, and ecstasies succeeding one another in a rhythm that our secular mentality rejects. Providence intervenes everywhere, even at the most unexpected moment. For example, we know that the founders of Montreal encountered stiff opposition to their plans. Faillon explains it as providential, for it obliged the founders to write *Les véritables motifs de messieurs et dames de la Société de Nostre Dame de Monreal; pour la conversion des Sauvages de la Nouvelle-France* ([Paris], 1643). Without this document the providential origin of the founding of Montreal would not be known. Fire destroyed the first establishment of Marguerite Bourgeoys: Faillon sees here the hand of providence, for this misfortune allowed the congregation to set itself up in the heart of the town, a more suitable place than the port area in view of the later development of the city. Many examples of this type could be given. They would only illustrate more clearly the supernatural atmosphere that surrounds Faillon's narratives.

Faillon's historical thinking cannot, however, be reduced simply to a belief in providence and exaltation of Christian virtues. His *Histoire de la colonie française* recognizes worldly reality. The only contemporary historian in the country with recourse to legal archives, he unhesitatingly presents aspects of criminality in Montreal. A number of pages on population and economic life contain little moralizing or reference to supernatural causality. Thus, to explain the small number of immigrants to New France, Faillon mentions the harsh climate, the absence of precious metals, and the poverty of the settlers, which was attributable to the monopoly held by those trading in beaver. If Canadian historians have often been indignant that the trading companies did not fulfil their obligation to promote settlement, Faillon notes without animosity that the merchants found a colony of trading posts to their advantage.

Faillon makes interesting observations on ways of life in general. The history of labour, on the other hand, brings him back to moral reflections. In New France those in charge, like the ordinary settlers, got down to the job. The author sees this as an indication of social equilibrium since the privileged were not exempt from manual work. In the colony resourcefulness was born of necessity. Here Faillon detects the origin of the French Canadian handyman he observed in the 19th century. He ventures some discerning remarks about the quality of the labour force; he notes that Montreal had a better supply of specialized workers than Quebec. In short, economic and social history is not completely ignored by the Sulpician historian. It is unfortunate that the three volumes published stop in the 1680s, although the author had intended to continue his account to 1836. Other tasks absorbed him, and thus Canada was deprived of possibly one of its most complete historical syntheses.

Faillon was read a great deal and has been often quoted. Despite a regional focus centred on

Faribault

Montreal that was the despair of the clergy of the city of Quebec, his work contains an exceptional wealth of information. His well-documented synthesis was a model for several Canadian historians from a methodological point of view. All things considered, Faillon's historical thought and the strengthening of clerical structures kept pace with each other; the former justified the latter, and gave it a quality of legitimacy. The ultramontanes, such as Bishop Ignace Bourget, could see in his thought the justification of their struggle against the "liberal" bishops of Quebec. Hence the 19th century rivalry between Quebec and Montreal acted as a distorting mirror for the historians of New France.

SERGE GAGNON

[Étienne-Michel Faillon left an extensive correspondence, as well as some important manuscripts. An inventory of the Faillon papers in the Archives de la Compagnie de Saint-Sulpice (Paris) appeared in ANQ Rapport, 1969. Several of Faillon's letters were printed in *Lettres à Pierre Margry de 1844 à 1886 (Papineau, Lafontaine, Faillon, Leprohon et autres)*, L.-P. Cormier, édit. (Québec, 1968). In 1948 the Grey Nuns of Montreal printed a work entitled *Lettres adressées aux sœurs grises de Montréal*, which reproduces the correspondence addressed to the community by Faillon. The Archives de la Congrégation de Notre-Dame (Montréal) also possesses some letters, as well as a travel regulation for the use of the community, from Faillon's pen. Other letters are found at the Archives générales des Religieuses hospitalières de Saint-Joseph (Montréal), the Archives paroissiales de Notre-Dame de Montréal, and the ASSM. In fact only rarely does an old collection of private archives in Quebec not contain some of the historian's letters; letters can be found, for example, at the ACAM, the ASQ, and the Bibliothèque de la ville de Montréal.

Faillon, whose name never appears on the title pages of his volumes, is the author of a number of historical works on Canada. They include: *Vie de Mme d'Youville, fondatrice des Sœurs de la Charité de Villemarie dans l'île de Montréal, en Canada* (Villemarie [Montréal], 1852; réimpr. Saint-Jovite, Qué., 1971); *Vie de la sœur Bourgeoys, fondatrice de la Congrégation de Notre-Dame de Villemarie en Canada, suivie de l'histoire de cet institut jusqu'à ce jour* (2v., Villemarie, 1853); *Mémoire pouvant servir à l'histoire religieuse de la Nouvelle-France* (2v., Paris, 1853); *Mémoires particuliers pour servir à l'histoire de l'Église de l'Amérique du Nord* (4v., Paris, 1853–54); *Vie de Mlle Mance et histoire de l'Hôtel-Dieu de Villemarie dans l'île de Montréal, en Canada* (2v., Villemarie, 1854); *L'héroïne chrétienne du Canada ou vie de Mlle Le Ber* (Villemarie, 1860) (this volume was translated into English under the title *The Christian heroine of Canada; or, life of Miss Le Ber* (Montreal, 1861); and *Histoire de la colonie française en Canada* (3v., Villemarie, 1865–66).

There are two important but highly flattering biog-raphies of Faillon: [A.-C.-G. Desmazures], *M. Faillon, prêtre de St. Sulpice; sa vie et ses œuvres* (Montréal, 1879); and [F.-R. Gamon], *Vie de M. Faillon, prêtre de Saint-Sulpice* (Paris, 1877). For a more complete account of Faillon's writings, as well as of the articles written on him in various journals *see*: L.-G. Deland, "Bio-bibliographie de M. Étienne-Michel Faillon, p.s.s." (thèse de bio-bibliographie, université de Montréal, 1946). S.G.]

Archives départementales des Bouches-du-Rhône (Marseille), État civil, Tarascon, 30 déc. 1799.

FARIBAULT, GEORGES-BARTHÉLEMI, lawyer, public servant, and bibliographer; b. 3 Dec. 1789 at Quebec, son of Barthélemi Faribault, merchant and later notary, and Marie-Reine Anderson, whose father was one of Fraser's Highlanders; d. 21 Dec. 1866 at Quebec.

Georges-Barthélemi Faribault probably spent some years at John Fraser's school at Quebec, and then received a secondary education interrupted from time to time. He trained in law in the office of Jean-Antoine Panet* and was licensed to practise law on 15 Dec. 1810.

An official of the House of Assembly of Lower Canada from the summer of 1812 on, Faribault became a lieutenant in the 6th battalion of light infantry on 20 March 1813, and in 1815 was appointed clerk of committees and papers (parliamentary archives). On 19 June 1821 he married Marie-Julie, daughter of Joseph-Bernard Planté*, a notary and MHA for the county of Hampshire (Portneuf) from 1796 to 1808. They were to have three children: the first two died in infancy; the youngest, Georgina-Mathilde, married the painter Théophile HAMEL in 1857. Faribault was already the third most senior officer in the house when he was appointed translator into French on 3 Dec. 1828. Then on 16 Nov. 1835 he became assistant clerk of the house, a post he held until his resignation on 9 May 1855.

In 1830 Faribault, who was familiar with legislative documents, accustomed to indexes, registries, and reference works, and interested in the activities of the Literary and Historical Society of Quebec, which had been founded in 1824, devised plans for collecting and cataloguing works on North America and particularly Canada. From 1832 on, he corresponded regularly with the Montreal antiquarian Jacques Viger*. On 14 Sept. 1835 he commemorated the landing of the native of Saint-Malo, Jacques Cartier*, by unveiling a monument, an initiative which put him in contact with Europe as did the purchase of Canadian books in Paris and London. Honorary librarian of the Literary and Historical Society of Quebec and adviser to Étienne Parent*, the librarian of the assembly, Faribault examined

249

Faribault

historical works, biographies, bibliographies, historical dictionaries, and booksellers' catalogues. Throughout 1836 he was corresponding with Viger, when the latter was minutely annotating and completing the manuscript of Faribault's *Catalogue d'ouvrages sur l'histoire de l'Amérique, et en particulier sur celle du Canada....* This first Canadian bibliography appeared in 1837. It was designed "to be of use to those who might feel disposed to write a fuller history of Canada than any of those currently available": William Smith*'s history printed in 1815 and published in 1825, the five abridged volumes (1832–36) of protonotary and pedagogue Joseph-François Perrault*, and the first part of Michel Bibaud*'s *Histoire du Canada* . . . (Montréal, 1837), all of which went beyond the period covered by Pierre-François-Xavier de Charlevoix*'s history (1744).

This *Catalogue* of printed works, which published the results of the continued collection of material for the library of the house, does not, however, account for the interest increasingly being taken in official archives and historical manuscripts. Already Denis-Benjamin VIGER in England, and Abbé John Holmes* in France (1836–38), had become copyists, before changes in the location of parliament after the union made the need for inventories and measures to protect the parliamentary archives more evident, and led the House of Assembly to create special committees (1845–47) on the state of the archives, a subject on which Faribault reported in September 1847. The Literary and Historical Society of Quebec, which was subsidized by the government and presided over by Faribault in 1844 and from 1849 to 1859, began to publish manuscripts. In 1842 it had received offers of copies of documents from the French archivist Pierre Margry, and it sent Andrew William Cochran*, a judge of the Court of Queen's Bench, to make copies at Albany, N.Y. He was followed there, thanks to steps taken by Faribault, by Félix Glackmeyer, who was commissioned by the government to transcribe (November 1845 – March 1846, summer 1846) the collection of documents relating to the French colonial period that had been gathered by John Romeyn Brodhead.

Faribault, a diligent and tireless researcher, was in these years sought out frequently for advice and opinion. Jacques Viger continued to suggest subjects of research to him; the American historian George Bancroft, on the recommendation of Louis-Joseph Papineau*, visited him in 1837. Faribault corresponded with John Neilson*; on 21 Nov. 1848 he briefed Louis-Hippolyte LA FONTAINE and drew his attention to the risk that "50 cases containing the files or documents of the different sessions of this legislature from 1791 to 1837" might be destroyed. He wrote to the mayor of Saint-Malo, France, in 1843 when the Literary and Historical Society was publishing Cartier's *Voyages* . . . , corresponded with the philanthropist Nicolas-Marie-Alexandre VATTEMARE (1841–47), and ensured the exchange of legislative documents between France, the United States, and Canada; he carried on all these initiatives in collaboration with Adolphe de Puibusque, the French literary critic, writing and visiting him in Canada and France.

During the riot in Montreal on 25 April 1849, which Faribault termed "outrage and infamy," the parliament buildings were burned, and the libraries and archives of the two legislative houses were destroyed. To attempt to repair "the irreparable," the government sent Faribault on a European mission as an agent and special delegate to form a new parliamentary and national library. From 3 Oct. 1851 to 3 July 1852, in London and Paris, with a credit of £4,400, Faribault bought English and French volumes, visited ministries, and solicited gifts while distributing a few Canadian publications, and through Margry ensured that a plan for transcribing documents relating to New France was carried out (1852–55).

On 1 Feb. 1854, two years after this work of reconstructing the collection, the parliamentary library was again destroyed by fire. Jacques Viger confided at that time to Faribault: "Your misfortune [is that] people are more conscious of you in this than of the country." On 9 May 1855, after 43 years of service and the grant of an annual pension of £400 until his death, Faribault resigned. It was at the very time of the celebrated voyage from France of *La Capricieuse*, commanded by Paul-Henry de Belvèze*, to be followed by the establishment of a French consulate at Quebec in 1859. While in retirement, Faribault presided again over the Literary and Historical Society of Quebec (1858–59), and for two years prepared the setting up of a monument in commemoration of Montcalm*; this was unveiled at Quebec on 13 Sept. 1859, 100 years after the defeat on the Plains of Abraham. Faribault, who had been a widower since 1852, died in December 1866, a few months after the historians François-Xavier GARNEAU and Abbé Jean-Baptiste-Antoine FERLAND. By this time the government was undertaking more and more systematically the reprinting of historical documents, and François-Marie-Uncas-Maximilien Bibaud*, Abbé Louis-Édouard Bois*, Abbé Charles-Honoré Laverdière*, and Father Félix Martin* were continuing the historiographical tradition.

The patient labour of this "archaeologist," a public servant of refined and aristocratic courtesy, who spoke in 1835 of the "reign of law and order" and in 1848 of "Europe in flames," warrants an attention not thus far paid to his initiative in collecting documents which were essential for the beginnings of historiography in Quebec, and also suggests an evaluation of the ideological implications deriving from the fact that a generation of polygraphers and historians were linked socially with the political and religious powers. A bibliographer "to whom historical science is indebted for such eminent services," Faribault, through books, booksellers, and archivists, had found the way to a free cultural exchange.

YVAN LAMONDE

Georges-Barthélemi Faribault left his personal collections to the Séminaire de Québec and to Université Laval; Father Charles-Honoré Laverdière was his executor. These papers can be consulted at present at ASQ, in the Fonds Viger-Verreau, Saberdache bleue, and carton 60, liasses 12–29; in Polygraphie, VI, 81A. Other Faribault papers are located at ANQ-Q.

The PAC also has copies of documents from Albany and Paris relative to New France, which were collected through Faribault's efforts (MG 8, A1). Letters from Faribault are also found in the Neilson collection (MG 24, B1), in the Denis-Benjamin Viger papers (MG 24, B6), and in the La Fontaine papers (MG 24, B14). Further interesting information on Faribault can be found in the P.-G. Roy papers (MG 30, D58), and the F.-J. Audet manuscripts (MG 30, D62, 12, pp.662–63). Another important source is the Vattemare collection in the New York Public Library. Official documents relating to Faribault's appointments and to his trip to Europe in 1852 are in the *Journals* of the House of Assembly of Lower Canada (1812–37) and of the Legislative Assembly of the province of Canada (1841–66).

Faribault was the author of *Excursion à la Côte Nord, au-dessous de Québec; nouvel établissement aux Escoumains, anciens vestiges sur l'île aux Basques* (Québec, 1849), and he compiled *Catalogue d'ouvrages sur l'histoire de l'Amérique, et en particulier sur celle du Canada, de la Louisiane, de l'Acadie, et autres lieux; avec des notes bibliographiques, critiques et littéraires* (Québec, 1837).

ANQ-Q, État civil, Catholiques, Notre-Dame de Québec, 3 déc. 1789, 19 juin 1821. Archives du séminaire de Nicolet (Nicolet, Qué.), Succession Bois, IV, 3:44 (23 mars 1861). Bibliothèque de la ville de Montréal, Salle Gagnon, MSS, Pierre Margry, 31 mars 1855. BUM, Coll. Baby, Doc. divers, M1394–96. New York Public Library, Alexandre Vattemare, Copypress letterbooks, 9v., no.3. PAC, RG 9, 1, A3, 12, pp.18–19; RG 68, 99, p.234. *Lettres à Pierre Margry de 1844 à 1886 (Papineau, Lafontaine, Faillon, Leprohon et autres)*, L.-P. Cormier, édit. (Québec, 1968). *Le Canadien*, avril–mai 1849. *La Minerve*, 17 juin 1844, 3 mai 1847, févr. 1854. *Montreal Transcript*, 10 April 1852. *Quebec Gazette*, September 1835.

Catalogue de la bibliothèque du parlement (2v., Québec, 1857–58), II, 1448. *Catalogue of books in the library of the Legislative Assembly of Canada* (Montreal, 1846). P.-G. Roy, *Fils de Québec*, III, 45–47. H.-R. Casgrain, *Faribault et la famille de Sales Laterrière* (Montréal, 1912). *The centenary volume of the Literary and Historical Society of Quebec, 1824–1924*, ed. Henry Levers (Quebec, 1924). Guy Frégault, "La recherche historique au temps de Garneau (la correspondence Viger-Faribault)," *Centenaire de "l'Histoire du Canada" de François-Xavier Garneau; deuxième semaine d'histoire à l'université de Montréal, 23–27 avril 1945* (Montréal, 1945), 371–90. *Notice sur la destruction des archives et bibliothèques des deux chambres législatives du Canada, lors de l'émeute qui a eu lieu à Montréal le 25 avril 1849* (Québec, [1849]). P.-G. Roy, *La famille Faribault* (Lévis, Qué., 1913). N.-E. Dionne, "Historique de la bibliothèque du parlement à Québec, 1792–1892," RSC *Trans.*, 2nd ser., VIII (1902), sect.I, 3–14. J. F. Kenney, "The public records of the province of Quebec, 1763–1791," RSC *Trans.*, 3rd ser., XXXIV (1940), sect.II, 87–133. W. K. Lamb, "Seventy-five years of Canadian bibliography," RSC *Trans.*, 3rd ser., LI (1957), sect.II, 1–11. Fernand Ouellet, "L'histoire des archives du gouvernement en Nouvelle-France," *La Revue de l'université Laval* (Québec), XII (1958), 397–415. Élisabeth Revai, "Le voyage d'Alexandre Vattemare au Canada: 1840–1841; un aperçu des relations culturelles franco-canadiennes: 1840–1857," *RHAF*, XXII (1968–69), 257–99. J.-E. Roy, "Les archives du Canada à venir à 1872," RSC *Trans.*, 3rd ser., IV (1910), sect.I, 57–123.

FELLER, HENRIETTE. *See* ODIN

FERGUSSON, ADAM, agriculturalist and politician; b. 4 March 1783 at Woodhill, Perthshire, Scotland, the son of Neil Fergusson, sheriff of Fifeshire, and Agnes Colquhoun; m. first Jemima Blair, *née* Johnston, by whom he had eight children, and secondly, in 1833, Jessie Tower; d. 25 Sept. 1862 at Waterdown, Canada West.

Adam Fergusson, a lawyer by training and country gentleman by inclination, was a wealthy magistrate and deputy lieutenant of Perthshire. He was also a director of the Highland Society of Scotland, an agricultural association which published a journal, supported exhibitions, and encouraged improved farming methods. In 1831 the society sent him to Canada and the United States to investigate the state of agriculture and the potential for emigration. His report to the directors was published in 1832 and reprinted in 1833 as an appendix to his own work, *Practical notes made during a tour in Canada, and a portion of the United States*. In 1834 he issued a new edition of the *Practical notes* which incorporated observations made during another visit to North America in 1833. H. J. Morgan* quotes the *Montreal Gazette*'s observations on the 1834 edition: "unambitious in style, it is level in every capacity;

Fergusson Blair

strong in its collection of useful information, and correct in its general reflections. . . .'' Fergusson was impressed with the opportunities for immigrants, and brought his family to Canada in the summer of 1833. He settled near Waterdown in East Flamborough Township where he built his home, Woodhill. In 1834 he and James Webster bought 7,367 acres in Nichol Township on part of which they established the village of Fergus. Webster built a grist mill and sawmill; Fergusson ''offered to build a church as soon as a Church of Scotland clergyman could be obtained.''

Fergusson commmanded a militia unit during the Rebellion of 1837, and in its aftermath proposed unsuccessfully that British regiments be recruited for a short term of active service and encouraged to settle permanently in groups after being disbanded. Politically reliable communities in Upper Canada and a basis for a trained militia would thereby be established. He again demonstrated his loyalty to the British connection when he opposed annexation to the United States in 1850, maintaining that many potential immigrants would wish to remain under the British flag.

A farmer by avocation, Fergusson sought to improve the conditions and quality of Upper Canadian agriculture by encouraging selective livestock breeding, the development of new feeds, crop rotation, soil analysis, and improved drainage techniques. He was one of the first to import pure-bred, short-horned cattle from Britain and donated the Fergus Cup to be awarded in annual competition for the best-grade Durham heifer. He often contributed articles to agricultural journals in Britain and the United States and in 1839 tried to obtain a government loan to aid the publication of an Upper Canadian agricultural journal based in St Catharines. As early as 1843 he advocated a central agricultural society for Canada West and he was the first president of the Agricultural Association of Upper Canada organized in 1846. From its inception in 1850 until his death he was a leading member of the Board of Agriculture of Upper Canada, which co-ordinated the activities of various agricultural associations to make them more effective in developing and promoting good agricultural practices. The board also supported and distributed books and periodicals to educate farmers, and organized an annual agricultural exhibition in the province. A senator of the University of Toronto from 1856 until his death, Fergusson encouraged the establishment of a chair of agriculture at the university and was credited with bringing Dr Andrew Smith* from Scotland to found the veterinary school at Guelph which opened in 1863.

Fergusson, whom Sir George Arthur* described as ''a gentleman from Scotland, highly respectable and intelligent,'' was an appointed member of the Legislative Council of Upper Canada and then of the united province from 1839 until 1862. In 1838 he had described himself as a Liberal who supported the British Reform Bill of 1832; he favoured constitutional reform in Canada and opposed special privileges for any church. He wanted ''to safeguard the best interests of the people, to watch for money recklessly spent and to uphold the bond between Great Britain and Canada.'' His unquestioned loyalty and prestige lent respectability to the Reform cause. In May 1848 he was appointed chairman of the commission of inquiry to investigate the management of the provincial penitentiary near Kingston. The commission recommended the dismissal of the warden, Henry Smith, collected considerable evidence of the maltreatment of prisoners and of inefficient administration, and prepared the way for reforms such as the appointment of permanent salaried inspectors, begun in 1851.

Fergusson was actively involved in Reform party organization after 1844, and was chairman of the Reform conventions of 1857 and 1859. With George Brown*, William McDougall*, and others, Fergusson prepared the resolutions for the 1859 convention which condemned the union as a failure and advocated constitutional changes leading to confederation. But he was not well and was to suffer a paralytic stroke in 1860. He died two years later. Of his seven sons, Adam Johnston FERGUSSON BLAIR became a prominent Reform politician, and Robert Colquhoun Fergusson became governor of the Union Bank in London, England.

ELWOOD H. JONES

Adam Fergusson was the author of *On the agricultural state of Canada, and part of the United States of America* (Cupar, Scot., 1832) and *Practical notes made during a tour in Canada, and a portion of the United States, in MDCCCXXXI* (Edinburgh and London, 1833; 2nd ed., 1834). PAC, MG 24, B40; D16; RG 68, 1, General index, 1651–1841; 1841–67. *Arthur papers* (Sanderson). *Globe*, 1858–68. *Leader*, 26 Sept. 1862. *London Free Press*, 12 Nov. 1859. *CPC*, 1863. Morgan, *Bibliotheca Canadensis*. Notman and Taylor, *Portraits of British Americans*. A. E. Byerly, *Fergus; or the Fergusson-Webster settlement, with an extensive history of north-east Nichol* (Elora, Ont., [1934?]). Careless, *Brown*. G. C. Patterson, ''Land settlement in Upper Canada, 1783–1840,'' Ont., Dept. of Archives, *Report* (Toronto), 1920.

FERGUSSON BLAIR, ADAM JOHNSTON (he added Blair to his surname in 1862 when he inherited the Blair estate in Scotland on the death without issue of his elder brother), lawyer and politician; b. 4 Nov. 1815 in Perthshire, Scotland, the son of Adam FERGUSSON and Jemima Johnston; d. unmarried on 30 Dec. 1867 at Ottawa, Ontario.

Adam Johnston Fergusson was educated in Edinburgh and immigrated to Upper Canada with his parents in 1833. The family settled in Nichol Township in the Wellington District, where his father helped found the town of Fergus. In 1839 Fergusson was called to the Upper Canadian bar and began to practise law in Guelph. In 1842 he was named the first judge of the Wellington District Court and a colonel in the local militia. Universally regarded as a man of high personal integrity, he was persuaded to become the Reform candidate for Waterloo in the general election of late 1847, and resigned from the bench in order to be eligible. James Webster, his father's old partner in local land settlement ventures, was declared elected but he was unseated on petition, and on 8 Feb. 1849 Fergusson took his seat. He was re-elected in 1851. He represented Wellington South from 1854 until 1857 when he resigned in order to seek election to the Legislative Council. In 1860 he was elected by acclamation to an eight-year term as legislative councillor for the Brock division. After 1862 he lived on his father's estate near Waterdown, where he pursued his interest in agricultural improvements.

Following the retirement of James MORRIS, Fergusson Blair in March 1863 was appointed receiver general in the ministry of John Sandfield Macdonald* and Louis-Victor Sicotte*. The moderate Reform administration was committed to the double majority principle and at the time was opposed by George Brown*, publisher of the *Globe* and leader of the Reform Grits, because of its lack of commitment to representation by population. Brown had hoped that Fergusson Blair, who was considered an influential western Upper Canadian Reformer, would remain outside the cabinet as a staunch Grit critic of Sandfield Macdonald; his appointment was considered a victory for the premier, whereas the *Globe* described it as a "shame." In May 1863 the government was reconstructed with Antoine-Aimé Dorion* replacing Sicotte as Lower Canadian leader; Fergusson Blair became provincial secretary. He acted as Sandfield Macdonald's chief political agent in the Waterloo-Wellington area, especially during the general election in the summer of 1863 and in the Waterloo North by-election of April 1864. In the latter contest he helped defeat Michael Hamilton FOLEY, who had been dropped from the cabinet and who with Sicotte now opposed the Reform ministry.

Sandfield Macdonald resigned on 21 March 1864 and he advised Governor General Monck* to ask Fergusson Blair to attempt the formation of a coalition ministry. Fergusson Blair suggested to Sir Étienne-Paschal TACHÉ, the old Quebec City Conservative, a coalition cabinet of four Reformers and two Conservatives from Upper Canada, with four Bleus and two Rouges representing Lower Canada. His attempt failed, however, because Taché was reluctant to serve with the Rouge leader Dorion whose radical proposals, he charged, would tend to "mutilate" some Canadian institutions.

Instead, the Great Coalition of John A. Macdonald* and George Brown was formed in June 1864 to solve the political stalemate and implement confederation. Fergusson Blair supported the coalition, and in the Legislative Council, while unsuccessfully arguing that the character of the proposed new provincial constitutions should be discussed first, he voted for the Quebec resolutions. In December 1865 Brown left the coalition cabinet and early the following year Fergusson Blair took his place as president of the council. Relations between Fergusson Blair and Brown improved in 1866, but in 1867, as confederation approached and it became evident that Macdonald intended to maintain some form of coalition, Fergusson Blair and Brown fell out. With his Reform colleagues in the ministry, William Pearce Howland* and William McDougall*, Fergusson Blair supported continued coalition, although Brown was suspicious of Macdonald's motives and urged the re-establishment of clear-cut party distinctions. In June 1867 the three Reform "traitors" called a pro-coalition caucus in Toronto in an unsuccessful attempt to sway the Reform convention away from Brown. Later John A. Macdonald appointed Fergusson Blair to the Senate and made him president of the privy council in the first dominion cabinet. But his career was cut short by his premature death.

On his passing the *Globe* forgave him his "political mistakes," claiming that he had remained "in spirit" with his Reform friends; he had been a "sound lawyer" and "an able politician whose retiring habits prevented him from rising to the position to which his talents entitled him." It was a measure of his local reputation that the village of Carlisle in Waterloo County was renamed Blair in his honour.

BRUCE W. HODGINS

PAC, MG 24, B30; B40. PAO, Clarke (Charles) papers. Can., Prov. of, *Confederation debates. Globe,*

Ferland

1862–67. *Guelph Herald* (Guelph, Ont.), December 1867–January 1868. *London Free Press*, 1862–67. *CPC*, 1863. A. E. Byerly, *The beginning of things in Wellington and Waterloo counties . . .* (Guelph, Ont., 1935); *Fergus; or the Fergusson-Webster settlement, with an extensive history of north-east Nichol* (Elora, Ont., [1934?]). Careless, *Brown*, II. W. L. Morton, *Critical years*.

FERLAND, JEAN-BAPTISTE-ANTOINE, priest, professor, and historian; b. 25 Dec. 1805 at Montreal, Lower Canada, son of Antoine Ferland, a merchant, and Élizabeth Lebrun de Duplessis; d. 11 Jan. 1865 at Quebec.

Little is known about Jean-Baptiste-Antoine Ferland's paternal ancestry. His father, who was born at Saint-Pierre, Île d'Orléans, died before Jean-Baptiste-Antoine's birth. Thus, when he became a priest, Jean-Baptiste-Antoine was for a long time the financial support of his mother. She was the daughter of Jean-Baptiste Lebrun* de Duplessis, who had arrived in Canada in 1755 as a volunteer in the French armed forces. At the beginning of the English régime, Jean-Baptiste-Antoine's grandfather, and godfather, had formed a friendship with Francis Maseres*, who was attorney general of the Province of Quebec from 1766 to 1769 and whose political views he shared. In 1778 Maseres wrote to him: "I do not know if you have learned English, but a man of your intelligence and talent ought to have done so." It does seem that, by his maternal ancestry at least, Ferland belonged to a family that had been converted to "bilingualism" from the beginning of the English régime. He learned English as a boy and when he was only eight years old his mother moved to Kingston, Upper Canada. There he met his cousin Julia Catherine BECKWITH, whose novel *St. Ursula's convent, or the nun of Canada, containing scenes from real life*, would be published in 1824; he was to correspond with her during his studies at the Collège de Nicolet.

In 1816, through the influence of Abbé Rémi Gaulin*, a missionary in Upper Canada and later bishop of Kingston, Ferland entered the Collège de Nicolet, where, as the protégé of Bishop Joseph-Octave Plessis* (whose biography he later published), he achieved a brilliant record in classical studies: in 1821 he was first in the philosophy class. In 1822 he chose the ministry, and the following year, still only a candidate for the priesthood, he became Bishop Plessis's temporary secretary. In 1828 Ferland was ordained priest at the age of 22, not an unusual age at this period when the shortage of priests encouraged early ordinations.

On 14 September, the day of his ordination,

Abbé Ferland was appointed curate of the Quebec parish of Notre-Dame (1828–29). He then served as curate at Fraserville (Rivière-du-Loup) and at Saint-Roch in Quebec, and in 1834 became first chaplain of the Marine and Emigrant Hospital at Quebec. From 1834 to 1841 he was successively parish priest of Saint-Isidore (near Lévis), Sainte-Foy, and finally Sainte-Anne-de-Beaupré. In 1836 he accompanied Bishop Pierre-Flavien TURGEON, then coadjutor to the archbishop of Quebec, on his visit to the Gaspé; 25 years later Ferland published an account of this trip. Because of his knowledge of English, Ferland was often called upon during his years as a parish priest to minister to Anglo-Catholic minorities. The devoted attention he gave to Irish immigrants on Grosse Île, stricken with typhus in 1847 [*see* George Mellis DOUGLAS], earned him great respect among the Irish community of Quebec.

In 1841 Abbé Ferland returned to the Collège de Nicolet, where he remained nine years. He was professor of literature, history, and philosophy, and rose through the administrative hierarchy of the institution, becoming dean of studies (1841–50), director (1842–48), and superior (1848–50). The intellectual curiosity of a future historian developed in these years, during which he also took up botany. He was interested in social and political questions, and read the *Mélanges religieux* and the *Quebec Gazette* to some of his students; they took notes in English to familiarize themselves with the second language. Encouraged by the episcopacy, Abbé Ferland devoted himself particularly to historical studies, and in 1842 supported and sponsored the founding at the college of a literary society, where subjects drawn from national history were discussed.

At the end of the 1840s the college faced financial difficulties, due in large part to scarcity of students. The deficits were such that there was talk of selling the building to the state for conversion into a penitentiary. Abbé Ferland, who was then superior, quietly informed his bishop that if the difficulties appeared to have been caused by his own bad administration, he would gladly leave the college. To increase the number of boarders, he asserted, they should perhaps think of imitating the Collège de L'Assomption and the Collège de Saint-Hyacinthe, which allowed their students to take meals outside the institution. Meanwhile the deficit persisted, and at the beginning of term in September 1849 there were only 70 boarders. Ferland attributed this drop to the scarcity of money in circulation. In December of that year the superior voiced to Bishop Turgeon his anxiety over the college's financial situation, since the amounts receivable from boarders' fees for the previous two years totalled only £600. Claiming that he was ill-suited to administration, he hoped that he might be appointed a parish priest. To his more intimate friend Abbé Louis-Jacques CASAULT, Ferland gave a somewhat different version. He had already confided to Casault in 1847 that he had joined the staff of the college against his wishes. He called himself a victim of "vexations . . . aimed at the office [of superior] and not at the person." The refusal to take financial aid from the government, which other similar institutions accepted at the time, was in his eyes the determining cause of the inglorious state of Nicolet.

Ferland resigned his post as superior during the summer of 1850, and then divided his time between research, teaching, and a number of administrative and pastoral tasks. He lived at Quebec as he was counsellor to the archdiocese. He was appointed treasurer of the Society for the Propagation of the Faith and drew up its annual report. In 1852 he visited Anticosti Island (where he heard the legend of the sorcerer Gamache). In 1855 he was appointed military chaplain in the episcopal city. Then in 1858, at the request of Bishop Charles-François BAILLARGEON, the archdiocesan administrator, he visited the Catholic population settled on the Labrador coast, and assisted the Oblate François Coopman at Mécatina.

It was during the 1850s that Abbé Ferland's career as an historian took shape. In 1854 he had been appointed a professor at Université Laval in the faculty of arts (of which he became dean in 1864), and was assigned a course of public lectures on the history of Canada. This task made it necessary for him to visit archival collections in Europe in 1856–57, one of his concerns being the transcription of documents. Indeed, the Séminaire de Québec had undertaken to pay half the expenses of his trip to France, on condition that he obtain copies of "all that he deems of interest concerning America and Canada in particular." For several years after his return his public lectures attracted an audience whose actual size and composition are difficult to specify. However, it seems that this stocky, stout little man, intelligent and lively if not particularly eloquent, drew fair-sized crowds. According to Antoine Gérin-Lajoie*, a pupil of Ferland's at Nicolet, his lecture on the years of the Conquest was delivered before a gathering of 300 to 400 persons. The lecture series, which Ferland would have liked to extend to the constitutional régime, was published in two volumes in 1861 and 1865.

However, his premature death prevented him from supervising the printing of the second, which stopped at the Conquest. At his death Jean-Baptiste-Antoine Ferland left a library of modest proportions, as well as a small sum saved for his old age; these he bequeathed to the Asile du Bon-Pasteur at Quebec, where he was chaplain from 1853 to 1856.

The beginning of Ferland's literary vocation is usually traced to the publication in 1852 of *Histoire du Canada, de son Église et de ses missions depuis la découverte de l'Amérique jusqu'à nos jours . . .* (Paris), by Charles-Étienne Brasseur* de Bourbourg. Ferland's *Observations sur un ouvrage intitulé "Histoire du Canada,"* which was published in 1853 but first appeared in the form of articles in *Le Journal de Québec* in January and February of that year, is indeed the first monograph Ferland wrote for which he could familiarize himself with national history. But this work is not itself enough to explain why Abbé Ferland was adopted by the clergy during the 1860s as a spokesman for its interpretation of the past. The voluminous history of Canada by the historian priest has rather to be fitted into the social struggle of the 19th century, in the course of which the clergy emerged victorious over the increasingly marginal élite nurtured on European doctrinal liberalism. During the first half of the 19th century the Catholic clergy in Canada, weak in relation to the bourgeoisie, had been somewhat roughly handled by historians. In the 1840s, 30 years after the anti-clerical and anti-French-Canadian history of William Smith*, François-Xavier GARNEAU became the defender of liberal values in his interpretation of Canada's past. A nationalist, his version of the facts could be considered preferable to that of Michel Bibaud*. Garneau's *Histoire du Canada* was seen by the French Canadian professional class as a compensation for the defeat of 1837–38. A clerical version of Canada's history began as early as 1845 with a refutation of Garneau's interpretation of François de Laval*; two pamphlets devoted to the prelate were published that year, one by Abbé Louis-Édouard Bois*, the other by Abbé Brasseur de Bourbourg. But during the 1850s neither Brasseur de Bourbourg's synthesis nor Abbé Étienne-Michel FAILLON's works succeeded in creating unanimity within the Catholic clergy. Although Brasseur de Bourbourg's interpretation was ultramontane, it tended to serve the liberals by freely condemning the action of the episcopate as too timid about "encroachments" by the state. For his part, Faillon had attacked the ecclesiastical dignitaries of

Ferland

Quebec for being unjust towards Montreal. In the 1860s the time seemed to have come to reach unanimity on the historical role of clerics, in order to encourage some sort of consensus about the growing ascendancy of the clergy over the destinies of French Canada. To this task Ferland dedicated his efforts.

His *Cours d'histoire du Canada* is indeed a reply to the liberals, as well as to the historian priests who wrote too much about the conflicts that had divided the clergy throughout the country's history. An attentive reader of Ferland's synthesis is aware of his concern to create an image of an ideological unanimity for churchmen. Any references to the conflicts between church and state that divided the leaders of New France are timid. The Quebec historian assigns a role to the church at Montreal with no hint of the rivalries that had been uncovered by Faillon and that Abbé Henri-Raymond Casgrain*, in his biography of Marie de l'Incarnation [Guyart*] in 1864, also wanted to attenuate. In Ferland's synthesis, everything unfolds as if the clergy had scarcely ever had to contend with acute problems that brought it into conflict with civil authority. According to him, the people followed the illustrious examples of virtue offered by both lay and religious leaders, trod the path they traced, and conformed to the models of behaviour they proposed. Similarly, the Amerindians obeyed the missionaries, the example of white Christians and the word of the Gospel having sufficed to convince them of the truth of Christianity.

Apart from this central preoccupation to demonstrate the beneficent influence of clergy and Catholicism on colonial society, Ferland succeeded more markedly than any other French Canadian writer in the 19th century in describing the Amerindian civilization without the discriminatory attitude towards the aboriginal races so characteristic of the time. He realized that the Amerindians felt alienated in the presence of Europeans. Hence, he explained, their relentless opposition to the white man. True, Ferland's Amerindians are cruel and bloody, but, as he said, this was "Indian politics." To him, their actions were perhaps as valid as those of the settlers, whom he condemns on occasion for misusing force or for lacking frankness and justice in their dealings with the native peoples. We owe to Ferland the condemnation of the kidnappings perpetrated by Jacques Cartier*, the military alliance of Samuel de Champlain* with the Hurons, and the behaviour of Jacques-René de Brisay* de Denonville towards the "enemy" of the whites. The Amerindians' social organization prompted Ferland to write pages totally missing in traditional French Canadian historical works. When it was fashionable to stress the superstitious nature of indigenous beliefs, Ferland took a close interest in what he called their "theology" and studied the "Indian philosophers." Amerindian society seems to have favoured strongly a respect for individual liberties, an observation which made it possible for the author to explain why treaties of peace or military alliance, which do not bind individuals, were as a rule little honoured. On the other hand, an ultramontane could not remain neutral when noting the existence of liberalism even among the Amerindian tribes. "Many comparisons could be made," wrote Ferland, "between the Iroquois confederacy and the federation of the United States. Both founded on the principle of the liberty of man, they have to a great extent adopted its consequences: assemblies of the nation, the state, the commune, frequent councils, numerous stump-orators; independence of men, women, and children; and, in the midst of all these liberties, slavery." It is not surprising that such a parallel was drawn by an author who had read widely in the history of the United States and who corresponded regularly with the historian John Gilmary Shea.

When it was published Ferland's *Cours d'histoire du Canada* was praised by the critics. The work corresponded to the nationalist clerical ideology that was beginning to dominate French Canadian thinking. It was during the 1880s that the conception of history elaborated by the clergy was censured by liberals. In his *Histoire des Canadiens-français, 1608–1880 . . .*, published in eight volumes at Montreal from 1882 to 1884, Benjamin Sulte* disputed certain interpretations of Abbé Ferland. Since the latter's work was in some ways a story of missionary endeavour, one can readily understand that Sulte's condemnation of missionary activity must of necessity imply censure of the authors who had extolled it. But the isolated attacks of a few liberal *francs-tireurs* were not enough to imperil Ferland's credibility. In the conservative context of the second half of the 19th century, he was preferred to his adversary. Did not the French liberal Eugène Réveillaud, in his *Histoire du Canada et des Canadiens français, de la découverte jusqu'à nos jours*, published in Paris in 1884, style Ferland an ultramontane historian? In the last decades of the 19th century, this was sufficient to make him a herald of the whole truth.

Serge Gagnon

[The works of J.-B.-A. Ferland are relatively numerous and have each received at least two editions. *Observations sur un ouvrage intitulé "Histoire du*

Canada," etc. par M. l'abbé Brasseur de Bourbourg (Québec), which had first appeared in *Le Journal de Québec* on 22, 25, 29 Jan. and 1 Feb. 1853, appeared in pamphlet form that year and was republished in Paris in 1854. After *Notes sur les registres de Notre-Dame de Québec* (Québec, 1854; 2ᵉ éd., 1863), Ferland published his most important historical work, *Cours d'histoire du Canada* (2v., Québec, 1861–65). A second edition appeared in 1882, and a third, under the title *La France dans l'Amérique du Nord*, was published at Tours, France, and Montreal in 1929. Finally, in 1969 an American company reprinted the first edition. In 1863 *Le Foyer canadien; recueil littéraire et historique* (Québec), I, 70–312, published a long article by Ferland entitled "Notice biographique sur Monseigneur Joseph Octave Plessis, évêque de Québec." In 1864 T.B. French brought out an English translation of it in book form: *Biographical notice of Joseph Octave Plessis, bishop of Quebec* (Quebec); in 1878 the work entitled *Mgr. Joseph-Octave Plessis, évêque de Québec* was published at Quebec.

In the 1860s Ferland published a number of articles that were to have several editions: first a "Journal d'un voyage sur les côtes de la Gaspésie," which appeared in *Les Soirées canadiennes; recueil de littérature nationale* (Québec), 1 (1861), 301–476. In 1877 and 1879 reprints of this article were published in book form at Quebec under the title *La Gaspésie*. Finally, Ferland signed two articles in *La Littérature canadienne de 1850 à 1860* (2v., Québec, 1863–64), I: "Louis Olivier Gamache" (pp.259–74), and "Le Labrador" (pp.289–365). These articles were published in 1877 as *Louis Gamache, le Labrador, opuscules* (Québec). This volume, commonly called *Opuscules*, was subsequently published in several editions.

Manuscript sources concerning Jean-Baptiste-Antoine Ferland's life and work are not substantial and often of little interest. Research at the ASQ, the Archives de l'université Laval, and the Séminaire de Nicolet furnished little information; nor did the Ferland papers preserved at the AAQ in the T series. Significant printed sources are also rare, probably because of the dearth of manuscript material. However, literary critics have given a good deal of importance to the literary and historical work of Ferland. For more detail about the studies that proved useful in the writing of Ferland's biography, the reader is referred to *J.-B.-A. Ferland; textes*, T.-M. Charland, édit. (Montréal et Paris, 1958). The reader may also find it advantageous to consult the following: *Le Monde illustré* (Montréal), 30 août 1890; J.-A.-I. Douville, *Histoire du collège-séminaire de Nicolet, 1803–1903, avec les listes complètes des directeurs, professeurs et élèves de l'institution* (2v., Montréal, 1903), I; and Frère Fernando [Gérard Bédard], "L'abbé Jean-Baptiste-Antoine Ferland; son œuvre historique et littéraire" (thèse de MA, université de Montréal, 1953). s.g.]

FERRES, JAMES MOIR, journalist, politician, and public servant; b. in 1813 in Scotland; m. in 1834 at Montreal Sarah Robertson, a native of Aberdeen; d. 21 April 1870 in Kingston, Ont.

The young James Moir Ferres arrived at Montreal in 1833. His academic success as a student at the Grammar School, and later at Marischal College, in Aberdeen, led to a brief teaching career in Montreal at Edward Black*'s school and soon after to his assuming charge of the academy at Frelighsburg in the Eastern Townships. There, in 1835, he founded with Joseph D. Gilman a weekly newspaper, the *Missiskoui Standard*, the first of a series of platforms from which Ferres expressed his powerful opinions. Unfortunately, as even a friendly source observed, "He seemed only to think of how he could best damage or destroy." Until his departure from the editorship of the *Standard* in December 1836, Ferres maintained a strongly anti-Patriote policy, urging the townships' resistance to the "pseudo" reform and mounting "despotism of a few" in the lower province.

Ferres' strident Toryism attracted the attention and approval of Adam Thom*, editor of the *Montreal Herald*, on whose urging he moved to Montreal, apparently late in 1836, to take up a position. He became editor of the *Herald* in 1839. His firm support for Governor General Charles Edward Poulett Thomson* led to his appointment in June 1840 as secretary of the Montreal Turnpike Trust. He remained an active Tory partisan, however, and, expecting to be dismissed, prudently resigned his office when the Reformers took over the government in 1842. He became editor of the *Montreal Herald* again until 1843 when, on the death of the proprietor, Robert Weir, he left the paper over "a difference of opinion" with the trustees of the estate. On the return of the Conservatives to power in 1844, Ferres was appointed revenue inspector for the second division of the District of Montreal; the Reformers considered this "a vile political job," created especially for him "for having been useful to Mr. Smith [James SMITH]," the new Tory member of the Executive Council from Missisquoi. This lucrative position ended abruptly with the formation of the Louis-Hippolyte LA FONTAINE and Robert Baldwin* ministry in 1848. It immediately removed Ferres for participating in the late elections in Shefford County, civil servants being forbidden to engage in such activity. The incident provoked a lively provincial debate which Ferres fuelled by sarcastic letters to the *Montreal Gazette*, widely reprinted, ridiculing Lord Elgin [BRUCE], the Reform party, and the partisan nature of responsible government.

In December 1848 Ferres became editor and chief proprietor of the *Montreal Gazette*, immediately taking a lead in the local business

Ferrie

community against the British "madness of Free Trade." He soon turned violently anti-French Canadian over the rebellion losses legislation of the Reformers. The sparks from the verbal "fiery cross" he promised to forward through the Anglo-Saxon community contributed immeasurably to the general Tory agitation in the city and the consequent burning of the parliament buildings in April 1849. Throughout the winter Ferres had railed against the bill as "a nefarious attempt at robbery" of the Anglo-Saxon population by "an insignificant French nationality in a corner of Canada." In the aftermath of the destruction of the parliament buildings, Ferres, a victim of his overheated syntax, was among the small group arrested for arson. He was, nevertheless, soon released on bail and the case evidently never came to trial.

Although he believed annexation to be a probability, Ferres nevertheless considered the Montreal Annexation Manifesto of October 1849 as a hasty approach, preferring instead a cautious movement towards independence. By early 1850 he had become critical of any union because of his objections to slavery in the United States.

Ferres remained editor of the *Montreal Gazette* until 1854 when the journal was sold to John Lowe and Brown Chamberlin*. That year he entered parliament as a Tory from Missisquoi-East, defeating another Tory, Bartholomew Conrad Augustus Gugy*; he was returned for Brome, a subdivision of his previous riding, in 1858. His political career was undistinguished and, declining to contest the seat in 1861, he accepted a position on the newly created Board of Inspectors of Asylums and Prisons.

With his fellow inspectors Ferres urged a programme of general prison reform. In 1868 he became chairman of the board, and in May 1869, at the request of Sir John A. Macdonald*, warden of Kingston Penitentiary. During the following months, plagued by failing health, he instituted reform measures balanced by a degree of economic retrenchment. He died in April 1870. Ferres had created numerous enemies throughout his public life, but his successor at Kingston claimed that he had ". . . greatly advanced the cause of humanity and civilization among the . . . inmates . . . ; that he is generally regretted by them, forms not the meanest tribute to his memory."

LORNE STE. CROIX

PAC, MG 30, D62, 12, pp.723–27. Can., *Sessional papers*, 1867–68, VIII, no.40; 1870, II, no.5; 1871, III, no.6. Macdonald, *Letters* (Johnson and Stelmack), I, 233–34. *Gazette* (Montreal) 13, 20 Dec. 1848, 16 Feb., 11, 23 Oct. 1849, 30 Jan. 1850, 18 Nov. 1853, 26 April 1870. *Missiskoui Standard* (Frelighsburg, [Que.]), 8 April 1835–6 Dec. 1836. *Pilot and Journal of Commerce* (Montreal), 6, 11, 13 April 1848. Beaulieu et Hamelin, *Journaux du Québec*. *Canada directory*, 1857–58. Atherton, *Montreal*, II, 301. L. [-A.] Groulx, *Notre maître le passé* (3 sér., Montréal, 1924–46), 3ᵉ sér. L.-P. Turcotte, *Canada sous l'Union*, II, 112. "Les disparus," *BRH*, XXXII (1926), 436.

FERRIE, ADAM, industrialist, merchant, shipowner, and politician; b. 15 April 1777 at Irvine, Ayrshire, Scotland, 16th child of James Faerrie and Jean Robertson; d. 24 Dec. 1863 at Hamilton, Canada West.

Unlike most of Montreal's Scottish-born businessmen during the 19th century, Ferrie immigrated when middle-aged, after a highly successful commercial career in Glasgow. In his autobiography he describes the help given him by his father and elder brothers who had been trading successfully for many years to both the East and the West Indies and had interests in London and Liverpool sugar refineries. In 1792, at age 15, Ferrie opened a profitable cotton printing shop at Irvine; by 1799, when he moved to Glasgow, he had three factories in Scotland, and in 1811 he opened another in Manchester, England. His principal outlets were provided by ship captains, including several of his brothers, who accepted his goods on consignment for sale in their ports of call; many cargoes came to Quebec and Montreal. Ferrie himself occasionally visited foreign markets in Europe. By 1815 he had an estate of £70,000 and an annual trade of £100,000. He lost most of his fortune during the next few years, mainly through the failure of business associates whose notes he had endorsed, and he was forced to rebuild by augmenting his consignments to Canada, the Mediterranean, and Brazil. He spent some years in Jamaica attempting to re-establish himself.

In the hope of improving his sales to Canada and establishing his sons, Ferrie in 1824 set up his own firm in Montreal. He formed a partnership with William Cormack who had been associated for many years with Hector Russell and Company, a Montreal dry goods house. In 1825, with £35,000 capital supplied by Ferrie, the new firm, Ferrie, Cormack and Company, to which his son, Colin Campbell, was sent, began business in dry goods, hardware, groceries, and stationery on St Paul Street, Montreal's commercial centre in the early 19th century. Ferrie even built a vessel for the firm's trade, the 300-ton *General Wolfe*. Heavy initial losses forced him to take charge of the business himself; after a brief visit to Canada in 1826 he moved to Montreal with his family in May 1829.

Ferrie readily saw that western Upper Canada provided a rapidly increasing market for imported manufactured goods and, like a number of his competitors, he decided to establish a branch in that region. His sons Colin Campbell and Adam Jr, who had been in business with their father, chose Hamilton as the base for their Upper Canadian operations, which were now substantial, especially from York (Toronto) to Niagara. Ferrie conducted the Montreal end of the business, and his sons built up a profitable trade in the Hamilton area, establishing branch stores in nearby Preston (Cambridge), Brantford, Nelson, and Dundas during the early 1830s.

At Montreal, Ferrie, in addition to imports, was also involved heavily in exporting. He suffered enormous losses on flour, pork, beef, and butter shipments to Great Britain in 1842, but apparently recovered later to a level of considerable comfort. Suffering again through the bankruptcy of friends, Ferrie took an interest in revisions of bankruptcy legislation during the early 1840s. A supporter of the Montreal Committee of Trade, Ferrie took an active part in organizing it as the Board of Trade in 1842.

An outspoken radical reformer in Scotland, Ferrie eschewed any affiliation with Lower Canadian radicals during the troubled 1830s. In the organizations to which he belonged, such as the Constitutional Association, he counselled firm but balanced loyalism, to keep "the furiously loyal within moderate bounds as to their hatred of the French Canadians." Most loyalists in Montreal, he later recalled, "were so prejudiced as to assert that [French Canadians] were all traitors in their hearts whatever they might pretend." Ferrie earned little thanks for urging his friends to be less virulent and for the open contempt shown to the activities of the "set of silly puppies calling themselves the Doric Club."

Ferrie maintained the same independence and determined loyalism combined with a strong distrust of most politicians during his career in public life. In 1840 he was appointed by Lord Sydenham [Thomson*] to the municipal council governing Montreal and served on a number of committees until his resignation in 1843. Appointed also to the Legislative Council in 1841, he remained a member until his death. He seems to have regarded these honours more as duties, that of councillor, with its high costs of living away from home, being an expensive one. Despite his strong reform sympathies, Ferrie quickly developed a pronounced distaste for most Canadian Reformers. Reflecting later on the politics of the late 1840s and early 1850s, he remembered only "bickerings and low personalities between the place men and the place hunters, between the 'ins' and 'outs.'" Francis Hincks* and Louis-Hippolyte LA FONTAINE were "pretended Liberals" and "base creatures" who "seemed so wholly corrupt as to be insensible to shame."

Aside from his support of the St Andrew's Society, which he helped to organize in 1834, Ferrie directed his philanthropic efforts into unusual projects. He assisted personally in helping cholera-stricken immigrants in 1832 and 1834; during the 1830s he took a leading part in attempting to relieve the city's poor of high bread and fuel costs inflicted by combines of bakers and fuel dealers. From 1837 to 1840 he headed the committee managing the Montreal Public Bakery, a cooperative established to produce bread for sale "at the cheapest possible rate." The bakers countered by selling at less than cost and forced the cooperative out of business. A woodyard he established on a similar basis also collapsed with Ferrie personally bearing a substantial loss.

Ferrie invested little in the Montreal railway schemes of that era, but had strong interests in banking. He was active in the formation of the City Bank of Montreal, was a large shareholder in Hamilton's Gore Bank, and supported the City and District Savings Bank of Montreal. His other joint-stock ventures included the Ottawa and Rideau Forwarding Company, the Montreal Fire Assurance Company, and the Montreal Gas Company.

His wife, Rachel Campbell, had 12 children of whom six survived infancy. As most of them settled in Hamilton, Ferrie decided to retire there and in 1853, at age 76, he left Montreal, one suspects without much regret. He died in Hamilton on Christmas eve, 1863.

GERALD TULCHINSKY

[Adam Ferrie], *Autobiography, late Hon. Adam Ferrie* (n.p.,n.d.); *Letter to the Rt. Hon. Earl Grey, one of her majesty's most honorable Privy Council and secretary of state for colonial affairs; embracing a statement of facts in relation to emigration to Canada during the summer of 1847* (Montreal, 1847). General Register Office (Edinburgh), Register of births and baptisms for the parish of Irvine. HPL, Ferrie papers, inventory. McGill University Libraries, Dept. of Rare Books and Special Coll., MS coll., Ottawa and Rideau Forwarding Company, minutes of meeting, 29 March 1837. PAC, MG 24, B1, 11. *Hamilton Spectator*, 29 Dec. 1863. *Montreal Gazette*, 29 Dec. 1863. *Montreal Transcript*, 21 Jan. 1840. *Morning Courier* (Montreal), 20 June 1849. *Montreal directory*, 1841–53. *Political appointments, 1841–65* (J.-O. Coté), 55. G. Turcotte, *Cons. législatif de Québec*, 132–33.

Finlayson

Campbell, *History of Scotch Presbyterian Church*, 487. *Hist. de la corporation de la cité de Montréal (Lamothe et al.)*, 204. Adrien Leblond de Brumath, *Histoire populaire de Montréal depuis son origine jusqu'à nos jours* (Montréal, 1890), 370. T.T. Smyth, *The first hundred years; history of the Montreal City and District Savings Bank, 1846–1946* (n.p., n.d.), 14–15. F.-J. Audet, "1842," *Cahiers des Dix*, 7 (1942), 241. "Origins of the Montreal Board of Trade," *Journal of Commerce* (Gardenvale, Que.), 2nd ser., LV (April 1927), 28–29. Adam Shortt, "Founders of Canadian banking: the Hon. Adam Ferrie, reformer, merchant and financier," *Canadian Bankers' Assoc., Journal* (Toronto), XXXII (1924–25), 50–63.

FINLAYSON, DUNCAN, HBC officer and governor of Assiniboia; b. *c.* 1796, possibly in Dingwall, Scotland; d. 25 July 1862 in London, England.

Duncan Finlayson and his elder brother, Nicol*, sailed from Orkney in 1815 for three years' service as writers (the apprentice rank below clerk) in the employ of the Hudson's Bay Company. After working under James Curtis Bird* at Red River, "the seminary for men of talent" according to Governor George Simpson*, Duncan Finlayson succeeded Colin Robertson* in 1820–21 as supervisor of the Peace River District. During the next four years, he won the attention of the governor and received consistent reports as a "highly respectable well educated good clerk & Trader, [who] looks to promotion through merit." However, an accidental gunshot wound forced him to go to England for medical treatment in 1825 and perhaps influenced his appointment as clerk at Red River from 1826 to 1831. Under the wise direction of Chief Factor Donald McKenzie*, Finlayson was promoted chief trader (1828), attended the councils of the Northern Department (1828 and 1830), and assisted with trade at Fort Garry (Winnipeg). Rapid promotion (he became chief factor in 1831) was proof of his high reputation with his colleagues and Simpson's private assessment in 1832 was even greater tribute: "A highly upright honorable correct man of good Education and superior abilities to most of his colleagues. Has great influence with and is much liked by his Equals, inferiors and the Natives. . . . Firm cool and decisive, one of our best Legislators and most effective practical men . . . he may be ranked high among the most respectable and efficient men of his class."

After his promotion in 1831 Finlayson travelled west to the valuable Columbia River Department which he was to supervise upon the departure of Dr John McLoughlin*. Unexpectedly, McLoughlin chose to remain on the Columbia.

Finlayson went on leave in 1834–35 and left the district in the spring of 1837. His chief contribution there was in the coastal trade. He purchased the brig *Lama* from William Henry McNeill* in 1832, sailed three times to the Sandwich Islands (Hawaii), supervised the *Beaver*'s first trip in 1836, and recommenced negotiations with the Russians to supply provisions at Sitka (Alaska) and thereby undercut American competition for furs. He also surveyed the agricultural potential of the Puget Sound area (Wash.) and founded Fort McLoughlin on Dowager Island (B.C.) in 1833.

Evidence concerning Finlayson's relationship with McLoughlin, who kept command of the Columbia Department until 1846, is scanty but one can surmise that the two chief factors maintained at least formal politeness. They did, however, differ on several occasions. Finlayson's criticism in 1833 of the Stikine post project and, more important, his support for the *Beaver* in 1836 conflicted with McLoughlin's plans to establish posts rather than conduct trade from ships. Both McLoughlin and Finlayson were to be in London, however, in 1838–39 during company negotiations with the Russians concerning provisions and trade on the Pacific coast.

Finlayson had travelled to Scotland in 1837. He dined at the Simpson family home in London almost daily from February to May and the entry in his journal for 25 May, "Heard first intimation from a certain quarter," might have been anticipated. Isobel Graham Simpson*, George Simpson's sister-in-law, married Duncan Finlayson in Bromley-by-Bow, Middlesex, on 10 Nov. 1838, in the presence of Simpson and McLoughlin. The marriage settlement provided income and dividends from a portfolio of investments, and perhaps a dowry from the Simpson family.

Finlayson became the governor of Assiniboia in the spring of 1839. Joined by his wife a year later, he supervised the Red River community, oversaw HBC interests, and contributed to the stability and grace of local society throughout his five years at Upper Fort Garry. During his tenure the judicial system of the colony was reorganized by the newly appointed recorder, Adam Thom*. At the same time agriculturalists were encouraged to develop methods and products appropriate to the environment. Finlayson recruited settlers for the proposed HBC colony in Puget Sound and, in 1841, he sent 23 families to the Pacific under James Sinclair* in a vain attempt to stave off American penetration of the disputed territory. He faced continual problems related to "freedom of trade" but carefully avoided open confrontation. Challenges from merchants James

Sinclair and Andrew McDermot*, and from Pembina trader Norman Wolfred Kittson*, had only begun when Finlayson left Red River [*see* Alexander Christie*]. His term was considered a success; Alexander Ross* concluded that he had "laid a solid basis, not only for the prosperity of the white man, but also for the Christian civilization of its aboriginal inhabitants."

In 1844 Finlayson and his wife moved to Lachine, Canada East, where he was to supervise the Montreal Department and assist George Simpson. They soon found that they were to live with, and help, the Simpson family. A small, ill-contrived house, Finlayson's continuing ill health, and, no doubt, the governor's temper, encouraged them to spend at least three winters in England during the next decade. In addition to the daily administration of the department, Finlayson travelled to Washington in 1848 with Simpson and Henry Hulse Berens for negotiations on company land claims, and assisted when in England with the publication of two books on Red River and the fur trade by Alexander Ross. He retired from service on 1 June 1855 but, at his own request and with the strong support of Simpson, he was reappointed to the Lachine post six months later. When he retired in 1859 and took up permanent residence in London, he was elected to the committee of the company.

A dominant feature of Finlayson's personality was his firm adherence to a high standard of personal conduct. Combined with moral uprightness was a sincere concern for the native peoples within the fur trade empire. In his record of the 1831 trip to the Columbia, Finlayson had condemned the treatment of the natives by his "licentious" Canadian crew. In Columbia and Red River he supported the missionary enterprises as best he could. His principal heir, after the death of his wife, was the Church Missionary Society of England, which, according to Finlayson's wishes, was to establish additional missionary stations in HBC lands for the conversion of natives to Christianity.

Finlayson rose from apprentice clerk to director of his company and acquired many luxuries. His postings in later years were doubtless affected by the influence he acquired by marriage but were also due to his own abilities. His influence upon the administration of the company was undoubtedly dependent upon the will of the governor but no one was closer to Simpson after 1840. In Finlayson, ability was linked with fortune.

GERALD FRIESEN

HBC Arch. A.1/70, p.83; A.10/38; A.34/1, p.27; A.34/2, no.25; A.36/6; D.6/3; E.12/1; E.12/2, add. M/2; E.12/3–4. PABC, Donald Ross papers, letters of Duncan Finlayson to Donald Ross, 1845–52. PAM, MG 2, B5, Andrew McDermot to Alexander Christie, 30 Nov. 1846; C14, letters of Duncan Finlayson to Alexander Ross, 59, 124–25. PAC, RG 31, 1851 census, Lachine. *Canadian North-West* (Oliver), I, 35–78, 262. *Documents relating to NWC* (Wallace). *Hargrave correspondence* (Glazebrook). HBRS, I (Rich); III (Fleming); IV (Rich); VI (Rich); XXIV (Davies and Johnson). Mactavish, *Letters of Letitia Hargrave* (MacLeod). I. [G. Simpson] Finlayson, "York Boat journal," ed. A. M. Johnson, *Beaver*, outfit 282 (September 1951), 32–35; (December 1951), 32–37. *Times* (London), 1 Aug. 1862. Rich, *History of HBC*, II. Ross, *Red River Settlement* (1972), 121, 341–42.

FISET, LOUIS, lawyer, judge, protonotary; b. 20 Aug. 1797 at Quebec, son of Pierre Fiset and Ursule Maufet; m. 8 May 1821 at Quebec Mary Powers; d. 4 Jan. 1867 in the same town.

Louis Fiset studied under the protonotaries Joseph-François Perrault* and John Ross, and was called to the bar on 4 Jan. 1822. He then practised law at Quebec until 1844. Fiset was never a member of the assembly, but he soon became the friend and counsellor of many politicians of the day: Elzéar Bédard*, Augustin-Norbert MORIN, René-Édouard Caron*, Jean-François-Joseph Duval, Étienne Parent*, and John Neilson*. He was therefore involved in all the political developments from 1822 to 1838. He took part in the elections of the time and supported the Parti Canadien, which became the Patriote party in 1826. In the 1834 elections, for example, he organized the campaign of Amable Berthelot* and René-Édouard Caron, candidates in Quebec's Upper Town. According to *Le Canadien*, he was the *éminence grise* behind the Patriotes of the Quebec region during this period.

On 25 April 1834, following the presentation in the house of the Ninety-Two Resolutions, *La Gazette de Québec* published a short play entitled "La première comédie du Statu Quo," written by Louis-David Roy*, a lawyer, and Georges-Barthélemi FARIBAULT, clerk of the House of Assembly. The principal characters in this comedy were the moderate Patriotes of the Quebec region, Étienne Parent, Elzéar Bédard, Hector-Simon Huot, Louis Fiset, and François-Xavier GARNEAU. They were satirized as brawling republicans who delighted in quarrelling among themselves.

When the disturbances of 1837–38 occurred, Louis Fiset, although struggling against the tory party, feared the consequences of the rebellion, and joined the majority of his Quebec friends in rejecting it in favour of continuing their opposition by constitutional means. Thus he was one of

Fisher

the principal organizers of the great assembly that took place on the Quebec Esplanade on 31 July 1837. At this assembly of more than 8,000 people, according to *La Gazette de Québec*, Louis Fiset, together with Duval and Neilson, castigated those who were sabotaging the parliamentary régime, advocating smuggling, and fomenting revolution. Proclaiming his loyalty to democratic institutions, Fiset proposed sending a petition to the queen, to assure her of the loyalty of her Canadian subjects and ask her to end the abuses and dissensions from which Canadians were suffering. Nevertheless, in the autumn of 1838, when a warrant was issued for Augustin-Norbert Morin's arrest, Fiset, although he did not share all Morin's ideas, hastened to assist him to escape and to hide papers that might have compromised him. Furthermore, after the arrest on 26 Dec. 1838 of Étienne Parent and Jean-Baptiste Fréchette, respectively the editor and printer of *Le Canadien*, Louis Fiset was one of those who supported the paper during this difficult period.

Louis Fiset was appointed judge of the district of Gaspé on 23 April 1844, but could not adapt to the climate of the region and to the arduous journeys necessitated by the administration of justice in this remote area. His health was deteriorating daily, and he resigned his position after two years. On 27 June 1846 he accepted from the government of William Henry Draper* and Denis-Benjamin VIGER the office of protonotary of the district of Quebec, left vacant by Hector-Simon Huot's death. Fiset gave up this office on 10 Oct. 1861 in favour of his son, Louis-Joseph-Cyprien*, a lawyer and poet. He died at his home in Rue Mont-Carmel at Quebec, on 4 Jan. 1867, at the age of 69.

CLAUDE VACHON

ANQ-Q, AP-G-79; AP-P-184; QBC 25, Événements de 1837–1838, no.3249. PAC, MG 30, D62, 12, pp.801–5. *Le Canadien*, 28 juill., 2, 4 août 1837, 7 janv. 1867. *La Minerve*, 8 janv. 1867. *Le Pays*, 10 janv. 1867. Beaulieu et Hamelin, *Journaux du Québec*, 179–80. P.-V. Charland, "Notre-Dame de Québec: le nécrologe de la crypte ou les inhumations dans cette église depuis 1652," *BRH*, XX (1914), 310, 338. P.-G. Roy, *Les avocats de la région de Québec*, 163; *Fils de Québec*, III, 84–86; *Les juges de la prov. de Québec*, 205. N.-E. Dionne, *Les trois comédies du "Statu Quo" 1834* (Québec, 1909). "Protonotaires du district de Québec," *BRH*, X (1904), 117. Antoine Roy, "Les Patriotes de la région de Québec pendant la rébellion de 1837–1838," *Cahiers des Dix*, 24 (1959), 250.

FISHER, WILFORD, merchant, shipowner, and office-holder; b. 1786 at St Andrews, N.B., son of Turner Fisher and Esther Foster; m. Sarah Elizabeth Ingalls, and they had two children; d. 6 May 1868 at Grand Manan, N.B.

As a youth of 18 Wilford Fisher moved with his family to Grand Manan Island where they applied for and received a land grant. Though this was at a time of immigration from New England and competition for land, his father's record as a Boston-born loyalist who had joined the Royal Navy and become a sailing master presumably aided the claim. Wilford Fisher probably received no more than elementary education, but his intelligence and natural ability, combined with a gift for leadership and planning, soon launched an amazing career. He acquired land at Priest Cove and ownership of High Duck Island, near Woodwards Cove, where he built a plant for salting and processing herring and ground fish. On this cove he also operated as a general merchant, outfitted fishermen, and received exclusive rights to the catches. He thus became "laird of the port" and a leading figure in the larger island community.

Commissioned a captain in the 3rd battalion of the Charlotte County militia in 1832, Fisher was responsible for the weekly drill and general training of a company. With no immediate threats of enemy action, many looked upon the militia as an objectionable and unnecessary burden that interfered with their calling as fishermen. As early as 1836, Fisher was appointed one of the magistrates for the island and was expected to attend sessions at St Andrews, the shiretown, where by-laws were made and local officials appointed. Because of his position he had virtual control of the constables, hog reeves, and other officials, as well as administering and interpreting the law between sessions.

His name appears as one of the prime subscribers on many petitions to the provincial government, and he evidently wrote a majority of these submissions. Consequently he was one of the few leading citizens consulted by visiting officials. He served as chairman at meetings of the local inhabitants, such as that of 8 Sept. 1838, called to inform the master of a British fisheries patrol vessel about the intrusion of American fishermen. One of his petitions to government requested that "the islands in the Passamaquoddy, And Grand Manan be erected into a separate and distinct County," though this was never acted upon. By 1838 Fisher was a director of the Bank of Charlotte County, an indication of his progressing fortunes. In the same period, as a commissioner for roads, he had authority to auction off contracts for sections of highway improvements, receiving a commission on the government funds expended.

In the decade following 1820 the Church of England had established St Paul's Church on a reserved lot at Grand Harbour. Fisher was the largest subscriber toward the cost of the "parsonage house" and a regular contributor to the Church Society of the archdeaconry. As a mission church, St Paul's had depended upon the ministry of students and short term rectors. In 1832, after spending two summers there as a student rector, the Reverend John Dunn was posted to this island parish. At first he and Fisher appear to have got on well. Soon, however, trouble developed over management of the glebe lots where there was some of the finest virgin timber available, for which the church received a stumpage fee. Fisher was interested in shipbuilding as well as the potential lumber trade; Dunn was under pressure from his parishioners who wanted access to the timber and resented a monopoly by one individual. Dunn accused Fisher of attempting to control elections to the vestry of persons likely to support his proposals. The breach widened, and soon there were two camps, one supporting the rector, the other supporting the magistrate.

On the night of 9 Oct. 1839 Dunn and others living nearby were roused from their sleep to see St Paul's Church in flames. Rushing to the scene, but too late to save it, they found, casting a gruesome shadow, a figure hung in effigy dressed so as to leave no doubt that it represented the rector. The deliberate destruction of the church had repercussions far beyond the confines of the parish, symbolizing as it did open conflict between church and state.

William Boyd KINNEAR was sent to Grand Manan to conduct an investigation, and on circumstantial evidence such as the clothing of the effigy a charge of arson was laid against "Wilford Fisher and others." The case was tried in the Supreme Court at St Andrews in April 1840, where the jury acquitted the accused without even leaving its box. In 1844 Dunn was willingly transferred to Douglas, N.B., where he served until his death in 1849.

Exoneration by the court did not, however, still the clamour against Fisher. Prior to the fire there had been complaints; now petitions and letters were rushed to Fredericton charging misdemeanours and worse in his capacity as road commissioner, magistrate, and holder of other public positions. On 3 Sept. 1840 militiamen were ordered to march from Grand Harbour to the parade grounds at Woodwards Cove, "but all refused except very few." Ordered out again on 4 and 5 September, they still refused to obey and were in fact in mutiny against authority. The militiamen asked for the government's help, "before we are condemned to that state of slavery which has too long been suffered to deprive us of our rights as British subjects. . . ." Saint John businessman Lauchlan Donaldson, sent to investigate the new disorders, said of Fisher: "he has been much more the Dictator of this location, than [Sir John Harvey*] has been or is Governor of the Province, and to such an extent, that for years I have called him 'Emperor of Grand Manan, King of the Duck Islands.'" Despite such a harsh appraisal, no action was taken, though militia training was allowed to lapse for a time.

In a petition to the assembly on 6 Feb. 1841, Fisher recounted how he had been "unjustly charged with setting fire to the Episcopal Church," causing him heavy pecuniary expense and other serious loss, and asked for "such relief as may be deemed just and reasonable." A select committee reported a week later that they could not in principle recommend a grant of money be made, although praising "the high character and respectability of Mr. Fisher."

For a time it appeared Fisher would be forced to leave his island domain. In a letter to Donaldson he wrote: "now I am perfectly willing to leave the Island . . . but I will never be drove off." However, he soon had picked up the threads of his affairs and even ventured into new enterprises. He joined with Harris Hatch and Thomas Wyer, both of St Andrews, as a commissioner for running a packet, carrying mail and passengers between the shiretown and the county islands. On 26 Dec. 1845 he was appointed first postmaster for Grand Manan, serving until 1854. Though still in favour with mainland officials, he fared less well locally, and when he died in 1868 his total estate was valued at only $9,500. His will stipulated that he should be buried at North Head alongside his mother, but "*never at Grand Harbour.*"

The complete story about the burning of St Paul's may never be revealed, but a distinguished and perhaps impartial observer, William Fitzwilliam Owen*, proprietor of Campobello Island and a New Brunswick MHA, noted on 24 March 1842: "Mr. Fisher has within my knowledge been made the butt of a most wicked and atrocious conspiracy against his life, his peace and his character."

L. K. INGERSOLL

PAC, MG 9, A1, 96–109, enclosures, "Complaints against local officials." John Dunn *et al.*, *Church burnt: statement of the proceedings arising from the burning of the Episcopal Church at Grand Manan* [together

FitzGibbon

with a sermon] (Grand Manan, N.B., 1839) (incomplete copy at Grand Manan Museum). References to Fisher can also be found in articles written or edited by L. K. Ingersoll for the *Grand Manan Historian* (Grand Manan Island, N.B.), "The great debate of 1877," XII (1968), 47–51, 68–69; "Grand Manan as part of the new dominion," XI (1967), 10; [M.H. Perley], "The Perley report on the fisheries of Grand Manan (1850) . . . ," X (1966), 12–15; [John Robb], "Report by Captain John Robb, R.N., on the state of the fisheries, the condition of the lighthouses, the contraband trade, and various other matters in the Bay of Fundy . . . (1840) . . . ," IX (1965), 8–11; "Report of the commissioners appointed . . . to procure information respecting the state of the herring fishery at Grand Manan . . . (1836)," VII (1964), 42–44.

FitzGIBBON, JAMES, soldier and public servant; b. 16 Nov. 1780 at Glin (County Limerick, Republic of Ireland); son of Garrett (Gerald) FitzGibbon and Mary Widenham; m. in 1814 Mary Haley, and they had four sons and a daughter who lived beyond infancy; d. 12 Dec. 1863 at Windsor Castle, England.

James FitzGibbon's father, a farmer and weaver, had a small holding on the Knight of Glin's estate in Ireland. James left school at age 11 and at 15 enlisted in the Knight of Glin's Yeomanry Corps where he was soon promoted sergeant. In 1798 he joined the Tarbert Infantry Fencibles, an Irish home service regiment, from which he was recruited into the 49th Regiment of the British army. His battle initiation was at Egmond aan Zee, Holland, in 1799. He served as a marine in the battle of Copenhagen (1801), for which he received the Naval General Service Medal. In 1802, FitzGibbon landed in Quebec with the 49th Regiment; he remained in Canada for 45 years.

FitzGibbon's commanding officer, Lieutenant-Colonel Isaac Brock*, encouraged him to improve his education by private study and obtained promotions for him without the usual purchase of commissions. He became sergeant-major in 1802, ensign and adjutant in 1806, and lieutenant in 1809. He resigned as adjutant in 1812, in order to have time to study for promotion, but the War of 1812 intervened.

During the war FitzGibbon demonstrated personal initiative. In August 1812 he escorted a brigade of boats with military stores from Montreal to Kingston, navigating the St Lawrence River rapids in view of the American shore. The following January he took 45 sleighs with stores from Kingston to Niagara. In June 1813, after the battle of Stoney Creek, in which he participated as a company commander, FitzGibbon obtained permission to select "50 chosen

men to be employed in advance of the Army, and with authority to act against the Enemy as he pleased and on his own responsibility solely." Operating from John De Cou's stone house near Beaver Dams, FitzGibbon's men harassed enemy troops and observed their movements. The Americans, based at Fort George (near the town of Niagara), resolved to send an expedition to dislodge FitzGibbon's force. Some 500 American troops, led by Lieutenant-Colonel Charles Boerstler, marched from Fort George to Queenston, encamped there for the night, and proceeded next morning, 24 June, towards Beaver Dams. On entering a beech wood they were ambushed by 400 Indians commanded by Captain William J. Kerr* and Captain Dominique Ducharme*. The battle had been raging for three hours when FitzGibbon rode up to the Americans, hoisting a white handkerchief. He bluffed them into believing that they were greatly outnumbered and that more Indians were expected, and Boerstler surrendered.

FitzGibbon was widely praised for achieving the surrender of 462 American officers and men to his "46 rank and file." General Edward Baynes commended him for his "most judicious & spirited exploit," and the *Montreal Gazette* spoke of "the cool determination and the hardy presence of mind evinced by this highly meritorious officer." FitzGibbon's fellow officers presented him with a gold medal. The coveted promotion came in October 1813, when FitzGibbon was appointed captain in the Glengarry Light Infantry Fencibles.

But the Indians felt cheated of the military credit due them. In 1818 Captain Kerr obtained a letter from FitzGibbon in which he acknowledged that at Beaver Dams the Indians "beat the American detachment into a state of terror, and the only share I claim is the taking advantage of a favorable moment to offer them protection from the Tomahawk and the Scalping Knife." It also became known later that FitzGibbon had received advance warning of the American attack from Laura Secord [INGERSOLL], who had walked from Queenston by a circuitous route of 20 miles to bring him the warning. FitzGibbon certified this fact for Mrs Secord in 1820, 1827, and 1837. In the 1827 certificate he stated that because of the information she had brought to him he had "placed the Indians . . . together with my own Detachment in a Situation to intercept the American Detachment."

After his coup at Beaver Dams, FitzGibbon served mainly in reconnaissance, observing the movements of American troops. The Glengarry Light Infantry Fencibles were disbanded in 1816 and FitzGibbon went on half-pay until 1825 when he sold his commission. He became a militia colonel in 1826.

FitzGibbon began his public service career in 1816, as clerk in the office of the adjutant-general of militia for Upper Canada. His salary was small and his family kept increasing, so he left his post early in 1819 to establish a land agency in York (Toronto) in partnership with Benjamin Geale. His income almost doubled in two years, but in 1821 he returned to his clerical position with an increase in salary. Two years later he became assistant adjutant-general of militia, and in 1827, clerk of the Upper Canadian House of Assembly. Until 1841, FitzGibbon also served in other capacities in the Home District for varying lengths of time: commissioner to administer oaths to members of the assembly and to administer the oaths of office and allegiance, justice of the peace, chairman of the Court of Quarter Sessions of the Peace; register of the Court of Probate and commissioner of customs. He was also appointed one of two commissioners to report on the La Guayra settlers at Guelph, a member of the building committee for Upper Canada College, one of three commissioners to complete the Parliament House, and member of the Board of Health for York and vicinity in the aftermath of the 1832 cholera epidemic. FitzGibbon was indebted mainly to lieutenant governors Sir Peregrine Maitland* and Sir John COLBORNE for his appointments which, however, carried little power or prestige. It is not surprising that William Lyon MACKENZIE selected FitzGibbon as a prime example of government patronage. FitzGibbon's political sympathies were Tory, and after Mackenzie's printing press was destroyed in 1826, he had collected donations to help pay the fines of the young men involved. Reformers charged that his appointment as clerk of the House of Assembly came as a reward for this action.

FitzGibbon was a prominent mason, and from 1822 to 1826 he held the highest office in Upper Canada as deputy provincial grand master (the provincial grand mastership was retained in England). He was secretary of the Society for the Relief of Strangers in Distress, and was a founding member, in 1831, of the York Mechanics' Institute.

With his Irish background, FitzGibbon was an effective peacemaker among Irish immigrants. He was sent to Perth by Lieutenant Governor Maitland in 1824 when violence erupted in Ramsay Township between the Irish Catholic immigrants and the Scottish and Protestant older settlers. By "reasoning with both parties, and soothing the irritated feelings of all," FitzGibbon restored peace. Again, in 1836, when Irish canal workers were accused by settlers at Cornwall of rioting and murder, FitzGibbon was sent to investigate. Lieutenant Governor Sir Francis Bond Head* supplied him with arms for distribution to the local militia if required, but they were not needed. FitzGibbon rode up and down the canal on horseback and "by remonstrance and amicable advice" succeeded in preserving order.

FitzGibbon also urged Orange and Catholic Irish in Canada to end their animosity for one another. He discouraged Orange parades and stopped a violent riot in York in 1833 by jailing the participants. FitzGibbon himself was a Protestant whose father had renounced the Roman Catholic faith probably to avoid discrimination under the anti-Catholic laws in Ireland during the 1780s.

When a dangerous riot among Tories and Reformers occurred in York in 1832, FitzGibbon showed that his talent as riot-breaker was not limited to clashes among his own countrymen. He single-handedly broke up the fighting in front of Mackenzie's printing plant. When Mackenzie challenged him to call out the troops FitzGibbon threatened to take him to jail as the chief cause of the riot. Instead, FitzGibbon took Mackenzie home and thrust him inside his own door.

FitzGibbon's chief assets in handling rioters were his military bearing and exceptional strength, his courage and wit. But he was also impulsive and sometimes indiscreet, and these characteristics led him into a customs scandal in 1830 involving his assistance to William Bergin, a York merchant, in obtaining the release of a shipment of allegedly smuggled pork. FitzGibbon defended his involvement in the affair by claiming that Bergin had not smuggled the pork and had previously helped him to "pacify the Roman Catholics."

The rebellion of 1837 brought FitzGibbon to the peak of his career. He anticipated the outbreak of insurrection and urged Lieutenant Governor Head to take appropriate measures for defence. Head obstinately refused, and even sent all the regular troops to Lower Canada to help put down the revolt there. FitzGibbon took some precautionary measures on his own, thereby irritating Head and his Executive Council who accused him of being over-zealous and an alarmist. On 4 December, however, Head appointed FitzGibbon acting adjutant-general of militia. That night the first two casualties occurred, and the following evening FitzGibbon, defying Head's orders, posted a militia picket on Yonge St under the command of Sheriff William Botsford JARVIS. The picket intercepted a rebel force marching to

FitzGibbon

Toronto where they expected to be joined by hundreds of sympathizers. Both sides fired a round of shots and fled in panic.

It was decided to attack the rebels on Thursday, 7 December. FitzGibbon then learned that Head had asked Allan MacNab, a militia colonel and speaker of the assembly, to lead the attack. Humiliated, for he was the senior and most experienced militia colonel in the province, Fitz-Gibbon protested vigorously, and at the last moment Head gave him the command. But just when resolution was essential, FitzGibbon suffered a mental crisis. Besides being agitated over his conflict with Head, he faced "an organization of the most difficult nature [he] had ever known." Over 1,000 volunteers had to be formed into companies and equipped with arms that very morning. FitzGibbon had had no experience in organizing troops for battle. He retired to his office, fell on his knees in prayer, then, his composure restored, accomplished his task. At noon, he led the troops up Yonge St to the music of bands and the cheers of citizens. The rebels were soon put to rout, after which, on orders from Head who had accompanied the troops, John Montgomery*'s tavern and the house of rebel David Gibson were burned. Next day, FitzGibbon, deeply wounded by Head's treatment, resigned as acting adjutant-general of militia. He served as judge advocate, however, in the 1838 court martial that followed the rebellion.

The remaining years of FitzGibbon's life were marred by bitterness and his persistent struggle to achieve financial stability and the reward that eluded him. FitzGibbon had been in financial trouble throughout his life. His debts had started to accumulate in 1806 when he had to equip himself as ensign and adjutant, and every army promotion led to additional expenses. He had his sons educated at Upper Canada College and in law and generally lived beyond his means. The Bank of Upper Canada threatened to sue him in 1843 for money he had borrowed to pay some of his creditors, but the threat was never carried out.

In May 1838 the citizens of Toronto held a public meeting and expressed gratitude to Fitz-Gibbon for "rescuing them from the horrors of a civil war," but the financial gift they proposed to raise by subscription never materialized. The imperial authorities objected to the 5,000 acre land grant requested of the queen by the two houses of the Upper Canadian legislature in 1838, and instead suggested that FitzGibbon be given a pecuniary reward for his civil and military services. A bill designed to overcome the objections was passed in 1839 but was disallowed, and a similar bill in 1840 was ignored by the British government. Appeals on FitzGibbon's behalf from Sir Augustus D'Este, a grandson of George III, to the colonial secretary, Lord Stanley, and from governors general Sir Charles Bagot* and Sir Charles Metcalfe* to the legislature of the united Canadas were also ignored. Members of the legislature from Canada East had no personal interest in FitzGibbon but agreed to support any pledge made by the former Upper Canadian assembly. Only in 1845, however, did the legislature reward him with the sum of £1,000, which was half the total of FitzGibbon's debts and less than half the estimated value of the land grant originally proposed. FitzGibbon tried in vain to persuade the British government to supplement his reward, arguing that he had saved Upper Canada for the empire. In 1847 he assembled all his documentation in a pamphlet entitled *An appeal to the people of the late province of Upper Canada*, but this achieved nothing.

In 1841 FitzGibbon had become clerk of the Legislative Council of the Province of Canada, but increasingly he absented himself from the office while continuing to draw his salary. His physician, Dr William Winder, said of FitzGibbon in 1845 that he had a "temperament highly sanguine and nervous," which, along with "disappointments and distresses of no ordinary character," had produced "a state of mental irritation, prostration, and despondency, and loss of memory. . . ." He had become querulous and bitter, and was his own worst enemy. The council lost patience in 1846, declaring that FitzGibbon had "virtually transformed the Office into a sinecure," and retired him on pension.

FitzGibbon had been a conscientious, capable, and zealous public servant until he became overburdened with debt and obsessed by the injustice of the long delay in granting him his well-earned reward. He was intensely loyal and had a keen mind but he lacked the education, social background, and wealth that would have enabled him to penetrate the higher ranks of office in the army or government.

He went to England in 1847 and did not return. Through the influence of Lord Seaton [Colborne], FitzGibbon was accepted in 1850 as a military knight at Windsor Castle. There he lived on a small allowance in comfortable quarters provided by the crown, using his Canadian pension to pay off his debts. FitzGibbon died at 83 and was buried in the crypt of St George's Chapel.

RUTH McKENZIE

MTCL, James FitzGibbon, "Narrative of occurrences in Toronto, Upper Canada in December 1837." PAC,

MG 24, A13, 3, pp.409–11; MG 29, D61, 7, pp. 2980–3019; RG 5, A1, 46, p.22487; 78, pp.41932–34; 84, pp.45661–63; 87, pp.47608–9, 47619–20; 97, pp.54439–46, 54452–55; 116–17, pp.65533–36; 128, p.70543; 166, pp.90524–31; 167, pp.91357–743; 194, pp.108276–80; 205, pp.113624–26; C1, 82, no.2887; RG 7, G16, C, 36, pp.162–69; RG 8, I(C series), 679, pp.130–42; 684, pp.198–99; 686, pp.121–29; 924, p.24; 1170, pp.58, 281–82; RG 68, 4A, 77–79, 83, 112, 114, 151. PAO, Robinson (John Beverley) papers, "Notes on the rebellion of 1837, December 7, 1837"; Tupper (F.B.) papers, correspondence, FitzGibbon to Tupper, 1845–50. PRO, CO 42/373, pp.134–69; 42/439, pp.436/38A; WO 12/6035–44.

"Battle of the Beaver Dams," *Niles' Weekly Register* (Baltimore, Md.), X (March–September 1816), 119–21. Can., Prov. of, Legislative Assembly, *Journals*, 1844–45, 102, 396, 400; Legislative Council, *Journals*, 1846, 134, 183, 186–87, 199, 205–6, 211. *Canadian Freeman* (York [Toronto]), 15, 22, 29 July 1830. *The documentary history of the campaign upon the Niagara frontier in the year 1813*, ed. E. A. Cruikshank (Welland, Ont., 1902). *Documents, selected from several others, showing the services rendered by Colonel FitzGibbon, while serving in Upper Canada, between the years 1812 and 1837*, [comp. A. F. D'Este] (Windsor, Eng., 1859). [James FitzGibbon], *An appeal to the people of the late province of Upper Canada* (Montreal, 1847); [   ], "The history of a life," *London Rev. and Weekly Journal of Politics, Literature, Art and Society*, I (1860), 62–63 (repr. in Morgan, *Sketches of celebrated Canadians*, 192–96). *Patriot* (Toronto), 3 Aug. 1838. U.C., House of Assembly, *Journal*, 1838–40.

E. A. Cruikshank, *The fight in the beechwoods, a study in Canadian history* (2nd ed., Welland, Ont., 1895). Dent, *Upper Canadian rebellion*. M. A. FitzGibbon, *A veteran of 1812; the life of James FitzGibbon* (Toronto, 1894; repr. 1972). Ruth McKenzie, *Laura Secord, the legend and the lady* (Toronto and Montreal, 1971). [A. B. Murphy] Jameson, *Winter studies and summer rambles in Canada* (3v., London, 1838), I, 126–33. J. R. Robertson, *The history of freemasonry in Canada from its introduction in 1749 . . .* (2v., Toronto, 1899). F. H. Armstrong, "The York riots of March 23, 1832," *OH*, LV (1963), 61–72. J. K. Johnson, "Colonel James FitzGibbon and the suppression of Irish riots in Upper Canada," *OH*, LVIII (1966), 139–55.

FOLEY, MICHAEL HAMILTON, journalist, lawyer, and politician; b. 1820 at Sligo (Republic of Ireland); he and his wife Katherine had eight children; d. 8 April 1870 at Simcoe, Ont.

Michael Hamilton Foley immigrated with his parents in 1822 to Port Colborne, Upper Canada, where he was educated. He later taught school briefly in Louth Township. Unhappy with a teaching career, between 1845 and 1853 he edited successively the *Long Point Advocate and Norfolk County General Advertiser* (Simcoe), the *Norfolk Messenger* (Simcoe), and the *Brant Herald* (Brantford) while studying law. In 1851 he was admitted to the Upper Canadian bar, and in 1854 he won election to the legislature for Waterloo North as a Reformer. Rising quickly in Reform ranks and backing George Brown*'s call for representation by population, Foley held the office of postmaster general in the short-lived ministry of Brown and Antoine-Aimé Dorion* in August 1858. At the Reform convention held in Toronto in November 1859 he spoke eloquently against dissolution of the Canadian union and won the admiration of the eastern Upper Canadian delegates who opposed constitutional change. He had reservations about William McDougall*'s compromise motion calling for separate governments for Upper and Lower Canada and "some joint authority" for common matters – reservations that aroused Brown's displeasure. Foley argued that justice to Upper Canada in the way of representation and schools could not long be denied or even he would have to become a dissolutionist. But he maintained that union was beneficial to all, that Upper and Lower Canada were "in partnership," and that change under a united Reform ministry would soon come.

Foley had tried for several years without success to reconcile the two opposed groups within the Reform party: the western Grits under George Brown's leadership, and the followers of Robert Baldwin* such as Sandfield Macdonald*. In 1859 rumours circulated that Foley would either head a reunited Reform ministry or join in a coalition with George-Étienne Cartier*'s Bleus and John A. Macdonald*'s Conservatives. In the spring of 1860, Foley, Sandfield Macdonald, and Josiah Blackburn* of the *London Free Press* attempted to bypass Brown's leadership and block all moves, including Brown's federalist proposals, which tended toward disruption of the union. Foley and Sandfield Macdonald hoped to forge an alliance with Louis-Victor Sicotte*, the leader of moderate Reform in Canada East. But Brown fought back, and a vehemently personal clash between Brown and Foley rang through the columns of the *Globe* and the *Free Press*. Foley urged liberals not to be seduced by "the tortured misrepresentations of ill-natured and sour-minded seekers after sectional supremacy, nor by the ungenerous and malicious coloured emanations of the biddable scribblers who follow in their wake." Yet, in the west, support for Brown was strong, and Foley was denounced for disrupting the unity achieved through McDougall's compromise at the Reform convention. Under extreme political pressure from his constituents and Brown, Foley deserted Sandfield Macdonald

Forbes

and voted in the assembly for Brown's resolutions in favour of remodelling Canada along federal lines. In 1861 Foley supported a resolution for representation by population, yet he also seconded Sandfield Macdonald's resolution urging adoption of the principle of "double majority."

In the election of 1861 Brown was defeated, and the Upper Canadian Reform caucus, boycotted by Sandfield Macdonald, early in 1862 elected Foley house leader over Oliver Mowat*, a disciple of Brown. The fortunes of moderate Reform and of Foley seemed to be on the rise. Yet, when the Conservative forces fell in May 1862, Governor General Monck* did not choose Foley or Sicotte but Sandfield Macdonald as premier. Foley, it was alleged, drank too much, lacked sufficient stature, and might have appeared, especially to Lower Canadians, too sectional. Instead of the coveted attorney generalship, Foley had to be satisfied with the office of postmaster general. In that post he initiated steamer mail service to the head of Lake Superior.

Sandfield Macdonald, who people claimed had a strong propensity to distrust Irishmen, was always suspicious of Foley's loyalty. When in May 1863 the ministry was reconstructed, Brown was able to persuade him to drop Foley in favour of Mowat. Foley was enraged; in the election that followed, he was successful in Waterloo North as an independent Reformer opposed to the ministry but, he stressed, dedicated to Reform principles.

When the house met in August 1863, Foley seconded Sicotte's motion condemning the reconstructed Reform ministry led by Sandfield Macdonald and A.-A. Dorion. This attack on his former colleagues permanently destroyed Foley's credibility with Reformers. In his own constituency the *Berlin Telegraph* correctly called his behaviour the "shipwreck of his political fortunes" and a "serious breach of good faith." From then until the fall of the Reform government in March 1864, his political behaviour was erratic.

As part of a vain and transparent attempt to make the succeeding Conservative ministry of Sir Étienne-Paschal Taché and John A. Macdonald appear a coalition, Foley was again appointed postmaster general. But the *Berlin Telegraph* asserted that Waterloo North would not return an "opponent of liberal measures," and Foley was defeated in the ensuing by-election. Before the election, Luther Holton*, the outgoing finance minister from Montreal, wrote Brown that if men like Foley could be re-elected in western Upper Canada to support such a government,

"there would really seem to be little use in troubling ourselves about politics at all."

Foley went back to his law practice, and resided primarily in Simcoe. Between his defeat in 1864 and the election of 1867, he tried at times to refurbish his Reform credentials. The sole effect of his attempts was to alienate him from the Conservatives. He did editorial work for the *Simcoe Reformer*, but his drinking became much more serious. In 1867 he ran unsuccessfully both in Wellington North for the House of Commons and in Norfolk North for the provincial legislature, having received no help from either Macdonald, prime minister or premier.

Despite his frustrations and bitterness, Foley was usually affable and witty, adept at making life "hot for his opponents, even if he had once in a while to take a little liberty with the facts." Although he was an Anglican he played on the popularity of his Irishness to solicit Irish Catholic votes. The *London Free Press* noted at his death that he had had "habits which seriously interfered with his official duties . . . ," that he was better on the "stump" than in the legislature, and that his premature death was regrettably caused by alcohol.

BRUCE W. HODGINS

PAC, MG 24, B30, B40; MG 26, A. PAO, Clarke (Charles) papers; Mackenzie-Lindsey papers. Can., Prov. of, Legislative Assembly, *Journals*, 1857. *Globe*, 1858–64. *London Free Press*, 1858–64. *Quebec Daily Mercury*, 1862–64. Careless, *Brown*, II. Davin, *Irishman in Can*. B. W. Hodgins, "The political career of John Sandfield Macdonald to the fall of his administration in March 1864: a study in Canadian politics" (unpublished PHD thesis, Duke University, Durham, N.C., 1964). E. H. Jones, "The Great Reform Convention of 1859" (unpublished PHD thesis, Queen's University, Kingston, Ont., 1971). W. L. Morton, *Critical years*. James Young, *Public men and public life in Canada* . . . (2v., Toronto, 1912).

FORBES, CHARLES JOHN, military official and politician; b. 10 Feb. 1786 in Gosport, Hampshire, England, ninth child of Robert Forbes and Elizabeth Cobb; m. Sophia Browne on 20 June 1815, and they had seven children; d. at Carillon, Canada East, 22 Sept. 1862.

Educated at the College of Altona in Denmark, (today in the Federal Republic of Germany), Charles John Forbes joined the Commissariat Department of the British army at age 19 in 1805. Daring, personable, and capable, he rose from a lowly clerkship to the rank of deputy commissary general in a few years. He spent most of his early military career in the Mediterranean area, serving in the Ionian Islands, in Egypt in 1807 (where he was imprisoned for some months), and in Sicily. He was also employed in 1813–14 in the Peninsular campaign and was present at the battle of New Orleans in January 1815. On 9 July 1817 he retired from the army on half pay.

After seven years of retirement spent with his wife and children at Corfu, in Italy, and in France, Forbes returned to the commissariat in 1824 and was ordered to Nova Scotia. One year later he was transferred to Montreal where, as deputy commissary general in charge of acquiring and transporting all supplies required by the army in his district, he remained for eight busy years. In 1833 he was sent to Jamaica and served there until sickness forced him to go to England two years later. On 13 Jan. 1836 he retired from the commissariat for the second time and was placed again on half pay.

While stationed in Montreal, Forbes had been responsible for providing the supplies needed to build the canals on the Ottawa River. He had purchased a large estate in 1827 near the eastern end of these works, at the village of Carillon. According to a relative, Forbes was a terrible speculator. He strenuously recommended that the entrance of the Carillon Canal be located on his property when plans for its construction were being made, but was unsuccessful. Forbes left his family at Carillon when he was transferred to the Caribbean in 1833, and to that quiet spot this worldly and well-travelled Englishman – who had spent more than 30 of his 50 years away from England – returned to settle permanently after his retirement in 1836.

The calm of Carillon was shattered in the fall of 1837 by the increasing political agitation in nearby Lac-des-Deux-Montagnes. Forbes' role in the events of that year illustrates how useful the British authorities found military officers who had retired to the countryside. From early October onward, Sir John COLBORNE relied on Forbes for confidential information about the activities of the Patriotes at Saint-Benoît. On 22 October, after Colborne had decided to check the increasing unrest north of Montreal by moving a detachment of regulars from Bytown (Ottawa) to Carillon, Forbes leased a large stone building to the army to serve as a barracks for the troops. In mid November Forbes reported "Sedition . . . now reigns paramount." On 28 November, after the battles at Saint-Denis and Saint-Charles in the Richelieu Valley [see Charles Stephen GORE; George Augustus WETHERALL], Colborne urgently requested Forbes to raise "a thousand men" to counter the increasing strength of the

Patriotes in the county of Deux-Montagnes. Forbes recruited over 800 in less than two weeks. Although command of these volunteers was given to Major Henry Dives Townshend, the officer commanding the garrison at Carillon, "General" Forbes – as he was styled locally – accompanied the men to Saint-Benoît where on 15 Dec. 1837 they met Colborne's army advancing from Saint-Eustache [see Maximilien GLOBENSKY]. The following day, according to one of the volunteers, Alfred W. Stikeman, Forbes was with Colborne and his staff when the village was put to the torch. Together they watched "the whole of the troops galloping through the flames . . . everybody plundering, bringing hoard, stealing horses, furniture, sleighs, etc." Later, Forbes' volunteers were accused of outrageous acts of pillage as they returned home. The volunteers did not deny the charge; however, they did maintain that they were following the example set by the regulars. Sir John Colborne, of course, denied that the regulars had engaged in pillaging.

Following the troubles of 1837, Forbes enjoyed life at Carillon to the full. Like a true Tory squire, he entered into public affairs with zest. From 1837 until his death he served as a magistrate, and, following a by-election in 1842, represented the county of Deux-Montagnes in the Legislative Assembly for two years. On his estate Forbes was energy incarnate, pursuing experiments in agriculture, plunging into speculative (and unprofitable) enterprises from brewing to running a ferry, and revelling in the role of congenial host to countless visitors – governors, bishops, old soldiers, and seemingly dozens of relatives. Energetic and hospitable to the end, Charles John Forbes died at Carillon on 22 Sept. 1862 at age 76.

JOHN BESWARICK THOMPSON

BNQ, Soc. historique de Montréal, Coll. La Fontaine, lettres, 300 (mfm. at PAC). Dept. of Indian Affairs and Northern Development (Ottawa), Parks Canada, National Historic Parks and Sites Branch, Hyacinth Lambart, "The Carillon barracks" (typescript, [1964]). MTCL, Forbes family papers. PAC, MG 24, A40, 10, pp.2703–4; 11, p.2946; 12, pp.3417–21; Γ87, 1, pp.52–53, 90; I69; RG 8, I (C series), 51, p.94; 55, pp.21–23; 75, pp.74–140; 136, pp.93–121; 170, pp.143–49; 368, pp.145–51. PRO, WO 42/17/160; 44/21, p.231; 55/1917; 61/2. Canada, Prov. of, Legislative Assembly, *Journals*, 1842, 1843. G.B., Parl., House of Commons paper, 1837–38, XXXIX, 357, pp.517–18, *Lower Canada and Upper Canada: further copies or extracts of correspondence relative to the affairs of Lower Canada and Upper Canada. . . . Montreal Gazette*, 18 Jan. 1830, 7 Nov. 1837, 21 April 1842.

Forrester

Montreal Transcript, 11 Nov. 1837. *Novascotian*, 20 Jan. 1830. *The British North American almanac . . . 1864 . . .* , ed. James Kirby (Montreal, 1864). Cyrus Thomas, *History of the counties of Argenteuil, Que., and Prescott, Ont., from the earliest settlement to the present* (Montreal, 1896).

FORRESTER, ALEXANDER, Presbyterian clergyman and educationist; b. 1805 in Scotland; m. in 1841 Margaret Tweddale Davidson, who died in 1861; d. 20 April 1869 during a visit to New York City and was buried at Truro, N.S., survived by three daughters and one son.

Alexander Forrester was educated at the University of Edinburgh between 1821 and 1825. He subsequently had several posts as a tutor while he undertook theological studies in the Church of Scotland during the halcyon years of the eminent theologian and social leader, Thomas Chalmers. Forrester was licensed to preach in 1831 and in 1835 was ordained by the presbytery of Wigtown as assistant minister of the parish of Sorbie in Galloway. For eight years he ministered to Sorbie and nearby Garlieston as assistant to the Reverend Elliott Davidson, whose daughter he married.

In 1843 Forrester and many of the Sorbie congregation joined the secession led by Chalmers from the established church. Shortly thereafter Forrester was inducted as first minister of Free Middle Church of Paisley. The industrial area provided greater scope for his evangelical and educational interests which led him to establish numerous schools and preaching stations. He was particularly cognizant of the needs of the labouring population, an enthusiasm not shared by wealthier members of his congregation.

In 1848 his fellow minister, John Macnaughton, of Paisley Free High Church, returned from Nova Scotia with details of the promising prospects for a theological training college there. With only four days' notice, Forrester volunteered to visit Halifax. He arrived on 30 Jan. 1848, a Sunday, and climbed directly from the harbour to conduct morning service at St John's Church. In his capacity as deputy from the Colonial Committee of the Free Church, Forrester stayed in Nova Scotia for six months serving at St John's and supervising the Free Church college in Halifax. With tireless energy and zeal he conducted three Sunday services, gave lectures on three evenings, and each day taught four hours of logic, "mental science," Latin, and Greek to the students of the Free Church college and their juniors in the church's Halifax Academy. On 4 May, the day after the college recessed, he set out on a tour of Nova Scotia and New Brunswick to raise funds for the college endowment fund.

On 24 June he left for Scotland, but his missionary ardour had been fired and he accepted the call from St John's Church to return as its pastor. He arrived back in Halifax on 18 October, was inducted on 16 November, and on 1 Jan. 1849 laid the foundation stone of Chalmers' Church, a Gothic edifice into which the St John's congregation moved on 14 Oct. 1849. Until 1855 Forrester also served the Free Church by travelling widely in Nova Scotia, Prince Edward Island, New Brunswick, Newfoundland, and Bermuda to raise funds for its college and home mission scheme and to supply vacant charges.

During the same period he frequently contributed articles, mostly unsigned, to the *Presbyterian Witness* relating to the church at home and abroad, education, science, and agriculture. He reached other audiences by means of his lectures on botany, geology, natural philosophy, and biblical prophecy to the Halifax Mechanics' Institute (of which he was president in 1852–54), to the young men of his own congregation and those of the YMCA (established in 1854), and to a wider public from the lecterns of the city's public halls. His leanings towards non-sectarian Protestantism found expression through participation in the Nova Scotia Bible Society, Micmac Missionary Society, Sabbath Alliance, and prayer meetings, while his public-spiritedness was reflected in executive duties for industrial and agricultural exhibitions, as well as exhibits sponsored by the city's horticultural society of which he was corresponding secretary.

Forrester's interest in the Nova Scotian educational system, eventually his major preoccupation, was fostered not only by his incessant peregrinations and conscientious supervision of his church's schools in Halifax, but more decisively by his role as one of the nine city school commissioners between 1850 and 1855. He and fellow commissioner John Sparrow THOMPSON were two-man committees for most of the board's functions. The resulting acquaintance with the city's public schools led Forrester to campaign for better school books, compulsory city assessment, and teacher training. In 1854 he was asked to become superintendent of education in succession to John William Dawson*. Forrester accepted the post the following winter after resigning the charge of Chalmers' Church, and he also became principal of the projected provincial normal school. He began by inspecting the educational systems of New England, New York, and Canada in the spring of 1855, and by holding close to 50 public meetings throughout the province in the summer of that year to stimulate interest in teacher training.

After decades of debate over the need for teacher training, the new co-educational normal school opened at Truro on 14 Nov. 1855 with about 60 students. Since the introduction of the monitorial system in Nova Scotia in the 1810s, various proposals had been made by the managers of schools for a non-sectarian normal school. In Halifax the Royal Acadian School, the National School, and the school conducted by the Colonial Church and School Society pioneered teacher training. Such work had also been sustained in the institution at Boularderie in Cape Breton established by graduates of the Glasgow Normal School. It was Dawson, however, who campaigned most effectively for the establishment of a provincial normal school and the government finally undertook the venture after Dawson's lack of success led him to resign in disgust. Consequently, it fell to Forrester to preside over the inauguration of the institution demanded by his predecessor. Shortly afterward he was awarded an honorary doctoral degree by Presbyterian Princeton College in New Jersey.

From 1855 until 1863 Forrester observed a rigorous routine of instruction in natural science and the theory and practice of education for two terms at the normal school, and inspection of the province's schools during the recesses in April and October, when he lectured on education and held teachers' institutes. In 1857 the model or practice schools for about 200 pupils, divided into primary, intermediate, and high departments, opened under his supervision at Truro. From 1858 to 1860 he edited, financed, and largely wrote the *Journal of Education and Agriculture, for the province of Nova Scotia*, an immensely informative and handsomely produced monthly periodical. His enthusiasm for agriculture in the curriculum of the normal school resulted in his appointment as provincial agricultural commissioner between 1859 and 1863 and thereafter he served as an *ex officio* member of the re-established Central Board of Agriculture. He revisited Europe only in 1863, on a working holiday which included visits to teachers' colleges in Scotland, England, France, and Belgium.

Forrester's annual reports as superintendent of education, like those of Dawson, advocated assessment, centralization, and inspection of Nova Scotian schools. His insistence on quality as well as quantity underlay his demands for better schoolhouses, a graded system of primary, intermediate, and high schools, and the recognition of teachers' qualifications through licensing and improved remuneration. His pronounced streak of independence is illustrated by his well-publicized petition to the government in 1862 containing almost 6,000 names and demanding compulsory assessment as the only way of improving the school system of a province whose inhabitants were still markedly illiterate.

In 1864–65 many of Forrester's incessant demands for improvement were met in Charles Tupper*'s legislation for free schools supported by compulsory assessment and greater centralization and supervision through a council of public instruction and a system of school inspectors. But in the reorganization Forrester found himself unexpectedly relieved of the pre-eminent position as superintendent. Until his death he remained principal of the normal school, working in harmony with the new superintendent, and he now had time for his natural history specimens and the organization of his normal school lectures into a manual for teachers, *The teacher's text book* (1867).

As an educationist, Forrester was more a popularizer than an innovator. In common with liberals of his day he believed in the contribution of education to national improvement, prosperity, security, and morality. His conception of schooling and teacher training was closely patterned on David Stow's ideas as embodied in the Glasgow Normal School, ideas that were current in Nova Scotia before Forrester's arrival. Stow's system (derived from Johann Heinrich Pestalozzi), which Forrester styled "the natural system," emphasized the training of the child's moral, intellectual, and physical attributes, which Forrester considered as much interdependent as the animal, vegetable, and mineral kingdoms of science. His enthusiasm for science, especially for horticulture and agriculture, explains his determination to establish a model experimental farm at the Truro institution; it foreshadowed a provincial agricultural college but such an institution was during Forrester's tenure largely frustrated by the parsimony of the local government. His intention to secure grants from the same officials, in addition to free tuition for student teachers, was also unsuccessful. Many of the expenses of the early years were borne by Forrester himself.

Although his contemporaries acknowledged Forrester's praiseworthy exertions on behalf of education and utter selflessness in discharging his duties, they also considered him over-ambitious in his plans for the normal school and something of an autocrat as superintendent. As long as he

Forrester

retained both positions he was criticized as being a power unto himself. The separation of the offices in 1864 represented a resort to checks and balances under the watchful eye of the government-appointed Council of Public Instruction as much as it did an administrative reform.

In an age of continuous sectarian antagonism and renewed Protestant-Catholic strife, Forrester inevitably had difficulty in walking the knife edge of neutrality deemed desirable in a public servant. As an ordained minister of the highly energetic and numerically predominant Presbyterian Church in Nova Scotia, he was bound to be accused of Protestant bigotry and Presbyterian partiality; moreover, as a "foreigner" he could be reproached with ignorance of the province. Catholics distrusted him because of his opposition to legislative enactment for separate schools and insistence on the use of the Bible for moral education. Forrester apparently went to some lengths to appease them by refraining from association with such ultra-Protestant organizations as the Protestant Alliance, established in response to "papal aggression" and local Irish intransigence. Yet there was no doubting his anti-Catholicism; like many contemporaries he referred repeatedly to the Catholic Church as the "Man of Sin" and maintained an interest in Protestant union and the distribution of the Bible which was partly inspired by the utility of these measures as antidotes to Romanism. At the same time Protestants of other denominations were critical of Forrester. They identified the normal school as a Presbyterian institution, especially since the overwhelming majority of normal students were Presbyterians. At the same time, they interpreted Forrester's support of Dalhousie College, which he saw as a means of providing a high quality liberal education by concentrating resources in one large-scale, amply endowed institution, as an attack on the government support of denominational colleges. Possibly as a sop to other Protestants, he withdrew from the courts of his own church.

To add to the complexities, Forrester was a forthright supporter of the Liberal party. During the controversy over separate schools and the transfer of Catholic allegiance from the Liberals to the Baptist-dominated Conservatives in the mid 1850s, Forrester's sympathies for the Liberal cause became something of a religious crusade. At the mundane political level, his behind-the-scene machinations for the defeat of Charles Tupper in the Cumberland County election of 1857 were fruitless and aptly rewarded by his own demotion at the hands of the Conservative leader seven years later. It was also no coincidence that in 1864 Forrester was succeeded by a subordinate, Theodore Harding Rand, a Baptist and a layman.

Ironically, the free school legislation which Forrester did so much to promote not only meant his eclipse as educational leader but also the virtual failure of the Truro college as the province's teacher training school. Because of the increased demand for teachers under the new legislation, Rand had to approve a permissive licence which in effect undermined the Truro institution by making graduates of every secondary school in the province eligible to teach. Forrester's disappointments together with his lingering evangelical predilections led him to espouse the foreign missionary cause successfully blossoming in the Presbyterian church after the union of the Free Church Synod and the Synod of Nova Scotia (Secession) in 1860. But old age discouraged him from volunteering for the South Seas, and his continued devotion to the circumscribed and degraded arena of the normal school was apparently enough to hasten the demise of the once robust Scotsman.

JUDITH FINGARD

Maritime Conference Archives of the United Church of Canada, Pine Hill Divinity Hall (Halifax), Chalmers' Presbyterian Church, session book, 1843–1904; Free Church of Scotland, Colonial Committee, notices and minutes, 1843–70 (mfm.). PANS, MG 2, 736–42; RG 14, 65, records of the board of commissioners of schools for the City of Halifax; 70; 81. Alexander Forrester, *Address to the people of Nova Scotia, on the support of common schools* (n.p., n.d.); *Duty of the legislature of Nova-Scotia with respect to collegiate education* (Halifax, 1852); *The object, benefits and history of normal schools, with act of legislature of Nova Scotia anent normal schools, &c* (Halifax, 1855); *The present war: a discourse preached in Chalmers' Free Church, on Wednesday, the 17th May, 1854 . . .* (Halifax, 1854); *Provincial normal and model schools: brief review of the history of provincial normal and model schools, with prospective arrangements, viewed more especially in relation to the community of Truro* (n.p., [1865]); *Register and circular with brief history and condition of the Normal School of Nova Scotia, 1862* ([Halifax, 1862]); *The sustentation of the Gospel: a sermon preached at the opening of the Synod of the Free Church of Nova-Scotia, at Halifax, June 25th, 1851* (Halifax, 1851); *The teacher's text book* (Halifax, 1867). *Journal of Education and Agriculture, for the province of Nova Scotia* (Halifax), 1858–60. *Journal of Education for Nova Scotia* (Halifax), 1866–70. N.S., House of Assembly, *Journals and proc.*, 1856–70. *Acadian Recorder*, 23 Jan. 1858, 17 May 1862. *British Colonist* (Halifax), 24 April 1869. *Christian Messenger* (Halifax), 25 May 1864. *Evening Express* (Halifax), 4 Jan. 1861, 16 May 1862. *Presbyterian Witness*, 1848–72. J. B. Calkin, *Old time customs, memories and traditions and other essays* (Halifax, 1918), 175–88. J. Willoughby, *Progress of education in Nova Scotia during fifty years, and lights and shadows in the life of an old teacher* (Halifax, 1884). D. C. Harvey, "The establishment of free schools in Nova Scotia," *Journal of Education* (Halifax), 4th ser., X (1939), 1074–80; "The origin of our normal school," *Journal of Education*, 4th ser., VIII (1937), 566–73. Robert Harvey, "From pulpit to platform: Alexander Forrester," *N.S. Hist. Quarterly*, 2 (1972), 349–65. N. K. VanBuskirk, "Dr. Alexander Forrester," *Journal of Education*, 4th ser., XIV (1943), 181–86.

FORSYTH, JAMES BELL, merchant; b. 25 Dec. 1802 in Kingston, Upper Canada, son of Joseph Forsyth and Alicia Robins; d. 1 April 1869 in Quebec.

James Bell Forsyth belonged to one of Canada's leading commercial families. Through his grandparents he was connected to the important London trading house Phyn, Ellice, and Company. A subsidiary of this company was Forsyth, Richardson, and Company of Montreal in which two of his uncles, Thomas and John Forsyth*, were partners; this firm prospered in the fur trade and expanded into other activities such as the agent and forwarding business. Another uncle, James Forsyth, was associated with Lloyd's of London. The web of Forsyth family and commercial relationships extended to England, Scotland, and throughout the colony.

James Bell Forsyth was the eldest of a family of six. His father came to Canada in 1784 and was named agent for Forsyth, Richardson, and Company in Kingston. As a member of Canada's élite, young James received his education in Kingston and in England. In 1821 in partnership with William Walker he went to Quebec City as agent for Forsyth, Richardson, and Company. He cemented his entry into Quebec society in 1828 by marrying Frances Bell, second daughter of Matthew Bell*, a wealthy Trois-Rivières businessman and the lessee of the historic Saint-Maurice ironworks. Forsyth was also fortunate in his choice of Walker as his business partner. Walker had emigrated from Scotland in 1815 and, unlike Forsyth, was an enthusiastic participant in politics. After their partnership ended in 1838, he was to be a member of the Special Council which governed Lower Canada from 1838 to 1841, deputy for Rouville (1842–43), a legislative councillor from 1842 until his death in 1863. Throughout his political career he acted as a spokesman for the commercial class and particularly for the Quebec City timber interests. Walker had lumber coves at Sillery and Pointe-à-Pizeau, and speculated in real estate. He served as director of the Quebec branch of the Bank of Montreal (1844), chairman of the board of the Quebec Gas Company, president of the Quebec City Board of Trade (1840–49), chairman of the Quebec branch of the Colonial Life Assurance Company (1847), and president of the Quebec Fire Insurance Company (1852). He was the first chancellor of Bishop's University.

With a well-established Quebec partner, a timely marriage into a prominent family, and the power of a leading Montreal trading house behind him, Forsyth's success was almost guaranteed. He established himself in Quebec City at an opportune moment. Between 1790 and 1845 the city tripled in size to 46,000 and its English speaking population grew steadily in numbers and importance. In 1819 Quebec counted 3,246 Protestants among its 15,237 inhabitants; in 1861 one-fifth of the city's 51,109 people were of Anglo-Scottish origin. As well as dominating the timber trade and shipbuilding, they played a central role in the city's military and political life. Like their Montreal partners, Forsyth, Walker, and Company carried on a varied business. In the 1820s the basis of their strength may have been their monopoly as East India Company agent. From their warehouse on the India wharf in Quebec City, Forsyth, Walker, and Company held annual tea sales. The partnership also became active in the passenger business. In 1826 they announced passenger space on a tea ship from Canton which was continuing to London. Insurance was another natural extension of the forwarding business and Forsyth, Walker, and Company became Quebec agent for the Alliance British and Foreign Life Assurance Company (1830). When the Forsyth, Walker partnership broke up in 1838, Forsyth joined with Alexander D. Bell to form the Forsyth, Bell Company; it became agent for the Royal Insurance Company. In 1863 Forsyth was a director of the Accident Assurance Company.

Forsyth's career was characterized by participation in a variety of enterprises. Speculation in land was a family tradition. In 1834 Forsyth, Walker, and Company was granted 18,777 square feet of crown land in Quebec City and in 1839 Forsyth received an additional 22,760 square feet. Lord Durham [Lambton*] named the Forsyths as one of 105 families who had received a total of 1,404,500 acres of crown land outside the seigneuries; James Bell Forsyth's share was 10,000 acres. Forsyth's father-in-law helped in land deals along the Quebec City waterfront. In one important transaction Matthew Bell sold his son-in-law the valuable point of land between the Saint-Charles River and the St Lawrence. Forsyth also owned property along the waterfront at Lévis and elsewhere in the Canadas. Forsyth

Forsyth

realized large profits from his land holdings. In 1840 he was awarded £1,400 after arbitration in a Quebec City land dispute. Two years later he predicted profits of £20,000 from his Gaspé lands and £10,000 to £20,000 from his Montreal properties; he owned considerable acreage and a mill in the Kingston area and anticipated a profit of £2,000 if the capital of the new province were to be established in Kingston.

Forsyth's most ambitious land scheme was a colonization project for Megantic County. In partnership with Robert Hunter Gairdner and William PRICE he organized the Quebec and Megantic Land Company in 1838. Imitating the British American Land Company, they offered to buy 225,000 acres of "waste" crown lands in Megantic County and proposed to settle as many as 20,000 British immigrants within 70 miles of Quebec City. Despite pressure, the scheme was rejected by the Colonial Office.

Although Forsyth continued to carry on a varied business – shipping pianos, selling insurance, investing in ships, speculating in real estate – by the 1840s he was primarily interested in the timber trade. Capitalizing on his Upper Canadian and British contacts, he specialized in timber from the Lake Ontario region [see John COUNTER]. Forsyth was instrumental in helping the Calvin, Cook, and Counter Company of Garden Island get established; he made representations on behalf of Delano Dexter Calvin* to his old friend, John Solomon Cartwright* of the Bank of Upper Canada, urging him to give Calvin "fair play." Forsyth's backing of Calvin paid off. In 1839 Calvin's consignment with Forsyth's company amounted to £58,000; Forsyth's profit on the Calvin account was £1,800. By 1842 business was so good that the company ordered six barges to handle the Upper Canadian trade. Forsyth travelled regularly to England to sell timber and by the 1840s his price book and annual review of the timber trade, published as the *Forsyth, Bell timber circular*, had become the standard index of timber prices.

The construction of railways upset the balance of St Lawrence lowlands. In 1850 Quebec City was near the peak of its strength. Twenty years later it was declining in commercial importance, isolated by the St Lawrence from railways to the United States, and increasingly under the influence of Montreal. Forsyth sensed the significance of railways, and like many of his contemporaries assumed that the iron horse was synonymous with progress and civilization. In 1858 he supported a railway to the Pacific. With an imperial subsidy of £8,000 a mile the "bonds of iron" would unify the Anglo-Saxon world.

In the last two decades of his life Forsyth supported virtually every railway that might serve Quebec City from the south shore of the St Lawrence. He was a director of the Quebec and St Andrews Railway (1850), the Quebec and Richmond Railway (1850), and the Grand Trunk Railway (1852). In 1856 he sold property in Lévis to the Grand Trunk. He also served on the boards of two smaller railways: the Quebec and Melbourne (1849) and the Chaudière Valley (1864). Forsyth's enthusiasm for railways was, however, restricted to those that served his interests on the south shore of the St Lawrence. As a promoter of the Grand Trunk he was opposed to the plan of Hector-Louis Langevin* and Joseph-Édouard Cauchon* to build a railway along the north shore between Quebec City and Montreal. Feelings were strong and in 1860 he felt obliged to reassure Langevin that he would not speak against the North Shore Railway to his friends on the London money market.

Forsyth had proved himself a flexible entrepreneur, able to make the transition from furs and tea to timber, and from sail to steam and railways. His wealth, contacts, and family connections brought him a variety of directorships. As well as being honorary secretary of the Quebec and Montreal Telegraph Company (1847), he was a director of the Cap Rouge Pier, Wharf, and Dock Company (1853), the Quebec Warehouse Company (1858), the Canadian Loan Company (1853), the St Lawrence Navigation Company (1861), the City of Quebec Hotel Society (1853), and the Tadoussac Hotel Sea Bathing Company (1865). His associates on these boards of directors represented a "Who's Who" of mid 19th century Lower Canadian commercial power. In Montreal his associates included John Joseph Caldwell Abbott*, Charles John Brydges*, Luther Hamilton Holton*, George-Étienne Cartier*, John Young*, and Peter McGill [McCutcheon*]. Among his Quebec City associates were George Pemberton, William Price, William Rhodes, George Irvine, Joseph-Édouard Cauchon, and Weston Hunt.

Forsyth and Walker both played leading roles on the Quebec City Board of Trade which until 1850 acted primarily as spokesman for the English speaking commercial community. In 1842 Charles Langevin and Pierre Langlois were among the few members with French Canadian names. During the 1830s Forsyth prepared the board's annual reports, and served as secretary and as a member of the boards of arbitration. In the 1840s the board largely represented the lumber and shipbuilding interests. When Walker replaced Forsyth as the board's leading figure in

1840 its major concern was the maintenance of the Navigation Acts which gave a preference to Canadian timber in British markets. In 1841 Walker presented a petition to the Legislative Assembly asserting that the Quebec City timber dealers felt "alarm" at the prospect of changes in the system of protection. By 1849 the battle was lost: the Navigation Acts were repealed and the Board of Trade fell under the control of free traders.

Quebec City's merchant class lived a comfortable life. With the danger of fires and epidemics in the lower town, many merchants had moved to the upper town by 1830. After his marriage Forsyth lived in a fine house on Rue Sainte-Anne facing the Esplanade. Although he continued to refer to himself as an Upper Canadian, Forsyth was fond of Quebec City. In 1840 he moved out of town to Cataraqui on the fashionable Chemin Saint-Louis; this estate was rented by the government as a residence for the Prince of Wales during his visit to Quebec in 1860. Here on the cliffs above the St Lawrence and the Sillery lumber coves, surrounded by convents and the estates of timber barons and shipbuilders, he raised his family of two boys and two girls. In 1850 his wife's health failed and she died of "decline."

A photograph of Forsyth taken four years before his death gives the impression of a stern and self-possessed individual. His full beard offset his portliness and baldness. Forsyth was a man of expensive tastes, who ordered his boots and furniture from London and whose wine cellar in 1839 included four hogsheads of madeira. He was a great traveller whose business took him regularly to England for meetings with bankers, brokers, exporters, and insurance men. He knew Europe well. In 1860 he took a lengthy pleasure trip to the East and published an account of his travels, *A few months in the East; or, a glimpse of the Red, the Dead, and the Black seas.*

English speaking society in Quebec was close-knit in its social as well as its commercial life. Forsyth was a founder of the prestigious Literary and Historical Society and of the less intellectual Stadacona Club. He met his business associates at the Quebec Exchange and served on its managing committee (1828). While enjoying their wealth and status, Forsyth and his fellow merchants took seriously their responsibilities as leaders of Quebec's English speaking community. Forsyth was an active mason and was vice-president of the St Andrew's Society (1838). A prominent Church of England layman, he was a member of the select vestry of the parish of Quebec (1847) and served for years as vice-president of the Church Society; in 1861 he dedicated his book on his travels to Bishop George Jehoshaphat MOUNTAIN. Providing a suitable cemetery for Quebec's Protestants was another task which Forsyth shouldered as a trustee of the Protestant Burial Ground committee (1857).

While Quebec's English speaking community left the care of needy French Canadians to Roman Catholic institutions, they showed a persistent concern for the welfare of immigrants. Forsyth's motives were mixed: a sense of Christian charity and duty, a fear of cholera epidemics, a wish to see Canada populated by British peoples, and the fact that he had lands for colonization and timber ships that provided cheap steerage passage for immigrants.

As a Lower Canadian Tory, Forsyth was distressed by political developments in the 1830s and 1840s. "Everything seems so out of joint," he wrote shortly after the rebellions of 1837. Opposed to Lord Durham's plan for union government he dismissed responsible government as a "delusion." Forsyth had great faith in the strength of Anglo-Saxons. Although threatened throughout the world, they were destined "to be the great civilizers of the countless masses in India and China." However, eastern peoples did have their use. He proposed that Chinese labour be imported to build Canadian railways and that 250,000 Indian troops be dispatched to England "to stand shoulder to shoulder on English ground" to fend off threatening Europeans.

A confident man with an empire view, Forsyth seems to have had little contact with the French Canadian community. With his business connections, his church, his social club, his library and country home, he had a secure and separate existence.

On 1 April 1869 Forsyth died of a heart attack. He was buried in Mount Hermon Cemetery only a short distance from where he lived, surrounded by the tombstones of his English speaking friends and associates.

BRIAN J. YOUNG

[J. B. Forsyth], *A few months in the East; or, a glimpse of the Red, the Dead, and the Black seas, by a Canadian* (Quebec, 1861). ANQ-Q, Greffe d'E. B. Lindsay, 22 June 1833; AP-G-134/12, lettre de J. B. Forsyth à H.-L. Langevin; AP-G-219/1, 26 Oct. 1832, 20 April 1841. ASQ, Seigneuries, 12, no.38. McCord Museum, Notman Photographic Archives, no.15396. QUA, John Solomon Cartwright papers, J. B. Forsyth to John Cartwright, 24 Nov. 1837, 13 Nov. 1839, 1 May 1840, 10 June 1841, 8 Sept. 1842, 23 Feb. 1844; Matthew Bell to John Cartwright, 16 Oct. 1841. *Montreal Gazette*, 4 Dec. 1831, 10 Nov. 1838. *Morning Chronicle* (Quebec), 23, 28 June 1847, 30 Jan. 1856, 28 Dec. 1858. *Quebec*

Foster

Mercury, 10 Oct. 1826. Langelier, *List of lands granted.*

D. D. Calvin, *A saga of the St Lawrence: timber & shipping through three generations* (Toronto, 1945). Drolet, *Ville de Québec*, III. George Gale, *Historic tales of old Quebec* (Quebec, 1923); *Quebec twixt old . . . and . . . new* (Quebec, 1915). Hamelin et Roby, *Hist. économique.* P.-A. Lamontagne et Robert Rumilly, *L'histoire de Sillery, 1630–1950* ([Sillery], Qué., 1952). A. R. M. Lower, *Great Britain's woodyard: British America and the timber trade, 1763–1867* (Montreal and London, Ont., 1973). Fernand Ouellet, *Histoire de la Chambre de commerce de Québec* (Québec, [1959]); *Hist. économique.* W. F. Butcher, ''The 'English' of Quebec City,'' *Hermès* (Québec), 3 (1953–54), no.2, 24–29. W. S. Wallace, ''Forsyth, Richardson and Company in the fur trade,'' RSC *Trans.*, 3rd ser., XXXIV (1940), sect.II, 187–94.

FOSTER, SEWELL (Stephen Sewell), physician, medical officer, and politician; b. 22 Nov. 1792 at Oakham, Mass., son of Samuel Foster and Patty Wilkings; d. 29 Dec. 1868 in Knowlton, Que.

On 7 Feb. 1813 young Sewell Foster married Sally Belknap of Dummerston, Vt. Two years later he was licensed by the Vermont Medical Society, and then practised in Newfane, Windham County, Vt., until 1822. In that year the Fosters and their four children joined a group of young pioneers who needed a doctor to accompany them as they followed such Newfane emigrants as the Knowltons [*see* Paul Holland KNOWLTON] and Robinsons into the Lower Canadian wilderness of the future Shefford and Brome counties. Foster settled for a year at the pioneer settlement of Frost Village in Shefford County, moved to Waterloo, in the same county, then returned to Frost Village to live on his farm.

After attending medical lectures in Quebec City and obtaining his provincial licence on 15 Feb. 1830, Foster began an extensive practice; he was one of the few doctors in the huge area from Yamaska Mountain to Missisquoi Bay, Stanstead, Sherbrooke, and Melbourne. He was appointed by Governor Dalhousie [Ramsay*] as surgeon to Colonel John Jones' Battalion, and from 18 May 1859 until his death he served, with Dr John Brown Chamberlin, as joint coroner for the Bedford District. Dr Foster also attended lectures at McGill College's new medical faculty and by his diligent studying and practical experience won professional acclaim and honorary degrees from universities in England and Scotland. After the profession was organized provincially under the College of Physicians and Surgeons of Lower Canada in 1847, Foster sat as a governor until ill health forced his resignation in 1866. His widespread professional contacts notwithstanding, Foster devoted himself above all to his private practice. His kindness to his patients, his unflagging courage and energy in reaching them, whether by canoe or through uncleared forest on foot or horseback, working night after night, made him a folk hero to the people of the townships.

Foster was more than his community's physician. He was a justice of the peace and commissioner for small causes in Shefford County, and a founder, officer, and active supporter of the Frost Village Academy. A Congregationalist in Vermont, Foster became an enthusiastic supporter of the Church of England, whose bishops, Charles James Stewart* and George Jehoshaphat MOUNTAIN, were his personal friends.

His position as a community leader and his support of the local Conservative party leader, Paul Holland Knowlton, led Foster temporarily into politics. He was defeated in the general elections of 1834 in Shefford County. When in 1841 Knowlton was appointed to the Legislative Council, Foster easily took over as member for Shefford in the Legislative Assembly, campaigning as a Unionist candidate against Alphonso Wells; in 1844 he defeated Reformer John Easton Mills. In the assembly he seldom participated in debates, and when in 1847–48 Reformer Lewis Thomas Drummond* defeated him, Foster gladly returned to medicine.

In the autumn of 1857 Foster moved from Frost Village to Knowlton. There ''the old Doctor'' continued his practice and his support of education, temperance, and other social reforms, until he died on 29 Dec. 1868. He left his widow, five daughters (one adopted), and seven sons including Shefford registrar Hiram Sewell, Senator Asa Belknap*, Dr William Hershall (Herschel), and Judge Samuel Willard. Among the hardy pioneers of the Eastern Townships, Sewell Foster stood out as a lion. He threw himself into his community's social, judicial, religious, and political life, and his considerable achievements, his charismatic personality and selflessness, made him one of its outstanding pioneers.

ELIZABETH GIBBS

BCHS Arch., Stephen Sewell Foster papers. *Debates of the Legislative Assembly of United Canada*, I–VI (the author has also consulted the MS debates for 1848). *Waterloo Advertiser* (Waterloo, Que.), 7 Jan. 1869. *Canadian biographical dictionary*, II, 266–67. F. C. Pierce, *Foster genealogy; being the record of posterity of Reginald Foster, an early inhabitant of Ipswich, in New England . . .* (Chicago, 1899). Cornell, *Alignment of political groups*, 5, 16, 24. C. M. Day, *History of the Eastern Townships, province of Quebec, dominion of Canada, civil and descriptive, etc.* (Montreal, 1869); *Pioneers of the Eastern Townships: a work containing official and reliable information respecting the formation of settlements; with incidents in their early history; and details of adventures, perils and deliverances* (Montreal, 1863). J. P. Noyes, *Sketches of some early Shefford pioneers* ([Montreal], 1905), 101–3. E. M. Taylor, *History of Brome County, Quebec, from the date of grants of land therein to the present time; with records of some early families* (2v., Montreal, 1908–37), I, 192–95.

FOULIS, ROBERT, engineer, artist, entrepreneur, and inventor; b. 5 May 1796 in Glasgow, Scotland, son of Andrew Foulis, a Glasgow publisher, and his wife whose maiden name was Dewar; m. first, in Belfast, Elizabeth Leatham, and they had one daughter; he also had two surviving children by a second marriage; d. 28 Jan. 1866 in Saint John, N.B.

Robert Foulis was a contemporary of Michael Faraday, the famous English scientist, and those who knew them both as young men considered Foulis the greater genius. Foulis studied surgery at the University of Glasgow but abandoned the medical field because of ill health and apprenticed to an engineer. As a journeyman he went to Belfast where he worked as a painter and where he met his first wife; she died shortly after their daughter's birth in 1817. Foulis decided to begin a new life in America and intended to settle in Ohio. Rough weather forced his ship ashore on the coast of Nova Scotia and he made his way to Halifax in 1818 where some Scottish friends persuaded him to remain. He earned a living at Halifax as a portrait painter and as teacher of painting at "Mrs. Burns' English and Commercial Academy." In 1822 he moved to Saint John where he worked as a civil engineer.

A man of many talents, in 1825 he started New Brunswick's first iron foundry at Saint John (which he sold in 1835), and in 1826 he was commissioned by the provincial government to survey the Saint John River from Fredericton to Grand Falls. He was also responsible for fitting up the *John Ward*, the second steamboat to ply the river. Active in the cultural activities of his adopted city, he was a frequent lecturer in chemistry and other subjects at the Saint John Mechanics' Institute, which he helped to organize. In 1838 he established a "School of Arts" to bring educational opportunities to the residents of Saint John and to supplement his income. The school's programme included "instruction of Youth in the rudiments of Mechanical and Experimental Philosophy and the Fine Arts; [and] for instructing by popular Lectures and Experimental Illustration, an Evening Class for Artizans, where the practical application of the Sciences to the useful Arts will be demonstrated."

Foulis is credited with inventing an apparatus for decomposing coal to make illuminating gas. He is also said to have invented an electric dynamo, but to have made no use of the invention. In 1853 he conceived the idea for what was undoubtedly his greatest invention, a steam foghorn, and a year later a committee of the New Brunswick legislature reported favourably on this invention. From time to time between 1854 and 1859 he agitated for the installation of his fog-horn on Partridge Island in Saint John harbour, but no action was taken by the assembly. In 1859 T. T. Vernon-Smith obtained Foulis' plans and was granted permission to erect a steam foghorn, the first to be installed anywhere in the world, on the island. Foulis petitioned the assembly and in 1864 the house passed a resolution recognizing Foulis' claim as inventor of the foghorn and of the coded system of telegraphing associated with its use. However, this was the extent of the recognition granted to him and he has not been credited with the invention, which is ranked by later historians as one of the most outstanding in the development of navigation aids.

The coded steam fog-horn was evidently later patented by an American who realized its financial potential. Business naïveté or preoccupation with other projects may explain why Foulis failed to patent such an obviously important invention. He died in poverty in Saint John in 1866. He had been truly a man of great genius, but unfortunately the Saint John environment did not nurture scientific and technological endeavour. Exchange of ideas with peers and financial support – the necessary stimulants for the development of scientific excellence – were lacking.

CHARLES MACKINNON

N.B. Museum, Ganong MS coll., Scrapbooks, 3, "In the time of Gesner" (undated newspaper article). PAC, MG 27, I, D15, Robert Foulis to S. L. Tilley, 5, 17, 23 Feb. 1859. N.B., House of Assembly, *Journals*, 1838, 1854, 1864. *Morning News* (Saint John, N.B.), 29 Jan. 1866. *Hutchinson's New Brunswick directory, for 1865–66 . . .* , comp. Thomas Hutchinson (Montreal, [1865]). J. J. Brown, *Ideas in exile: a history of Canadian invention* (Toronto and Montreal, 1967). P. G. Hall, "A misplaced genius," *New Brunswick Magazine* (Saint John), I (1898), 247–56.

FOWELL, WILLIAM NEWTON, naval officer; b. 5 June 1803 probably at Torbryan, Devon, England, third son of the Reverend John Digby Fowell, rector of Torbryan, and Sarah Knowling.

an heiress; m. 29 May 1841 Theana Holland, daughter of John Holland, of Clapham, Surrey, by whom he had three daughters during his residence in Canada; d. at Leycroft, Taunton, Somerset, on 17 June 1868.

William Newton Fowell joined the Royal Navy on 26 March 1819 and won commendation as a midshipman on the schooner *Lion* for services against pirates in the West Indies in 1822–23. He served with distinction as mate on the small schooner *Pickle* in the capture on 6 June 1829 of the powerful and notorious West Indian slaver, the *Boladora*, and was wounded while serving as mate of the *Gambia* during the so-called "Barra War" of 1831–32, a minor West African campaign mounted to extend British interests inland along the Gambia River. He won his lieutenant's commission on 12 Aug. 1834, and during the next three years served successively on Sir George Cockburn's flagship *President* in North American and West Indian waters, on *Comus* in the same area, and on *Inconstant* from 15 July 1836. From the *Inconstant* he was posted on 17 Aug. 1838 to be 1st lieutenant at Kingston on the *Niagara*, the headquarters of Captain Williams Sandom*, commander on the lakes of Canada.

Sandom commanded an improvised flotilla of civilian steamers which had been hastily acquired and lightly armed by the government to protect the border against possible incursions by Canadian rebels who had fled to the United States in 1837 and their American sympathizers organized into militant Hunters' Lodges. On 12 Nov. 1838 Lieutenant Fowell, in command of the 150-ton war steamer *Experiment*, prevented a landing of such an invading force at Prescott, forcing the large "pirate" steamer *United States* and its satellites, the *Paul Pry* and two schooners, to abandon their enterprise. Nonetheless, one of the invading flotilla succeeded in landing a force of Americans and a few Canadians commanded by Nils von Schoultz* a few miles below the town, where they occupied a six-storey stone windmill and a number of adjacent stone buildings. After a bloody, three-day battle, Schoultz was forced on 16 November to surrender to a strong force of British regulars and Canadian militia commanded by Major Plomer Young and Lieutenant-Colonel the Honourable Henry Dundas. Meanwhile, Fowell had used the *Experiment* effectively to prevent reinforcements from reaching the windmill. For his zeal and gallantry in this battle Fowell was commended by the magistrates and citizens of Prescott, his commanding officer, and the lieutenant governor of Upper Canada, Sir George Arthur*. A more tangible recognition of his services was his promotion to the rank of commander on 4 July 1839.

Fowell succeeded Sandom in mid-summer 1843, and commanded the *Montreal* on Lake Erie from 3 April 1843 until 26 July 1844 when he assumed command, successively, of the ironclad *Mohawk* (150 tons) and the *Cherokee* (750 tons) on Lake Ontario with headquarters at Kingston. He was then posted to the United Kingdom at his own request, and left Kingston on 26 July 1848.

Fowell retired in 1853 having been promoted captain with seniority from 6 Aug. 1852. His final promotion, to rear-admiral, took place in 1867.

JOHN W. SPURR

Chronicle & Gazette (Kingston, [Ont.]), 1838–47. *Gentleman's Magazine*, CCXXIV (January–May 1868), 397. G.B., Adm., *Navy list*, 1819–68. O'Byrne, *Naval biographical dictionary* (1849), 374. W. L. Clowes *et al.*, *The Royal Navy, a history from the earliest times to the present* (7v., London, 1897–1903), VI, 268. G. F. G. Stanley, "Invasion: 1838," *OH*, LIV (1962), 237–52.

FOX, JOHN C., piano manufacturer; b. in 1832 in New York City; he apparently married; d. 14 Jan. 1868 at Kingston, Ont.

John C. Fox trained both as a musician and as a manufacturer of pianos in the United States and in Europe. He set up a firm in New York City to make pianos, J. C. Fox and Company, and he arrived in Kingston, Canada West, in February 1861 to sell pianos made by this firm. By June he had a branch store in Kingston and within a year had started a piano factory. He was a resident of Kingston by 1862, when he appears to have discontinued the New York City firm. In September 1862, he competed in the provincial exhibition in Toronto and won first prize for the best piano. He supplied pianos for visiting musicians and, a skilled musician himself, performed at local concerts and directed charity musicals.

Fox expanded his business in January 1864, buying a large distinctive stone building while retaining the earlier factory as a branch of the new one. He also improved the quality of the instruments he produced: on 23 Sept. 1865 he received a patent for a modified sounding board. He "bound the free border of the piano sounding board with a cast iron band and thus made it free of any tendency to spring upwards or downwards." He later advertised "Double Iron Clad Pianos for Defiance," explaining that they defied competition in both price and beauty of tone.

Fox had by then the largest piano factory in Canada. He employed over 60 men, many of them skilled artisans, and completed six pianos a week. He had sales agents in Picton, Cobourg, Toronto, Hamilton, and London. However, over-expansion, along with a fire at his branch factory in May 1867 and the collapse of the Commercial Bank in October, brought financial failure. On 16 Dec. 1867 Fox was declared insolvent. Early that month he had received head injuries in a sleighing accident, and he died in January 1868. Among his effects were a fine organ and a Cremona violin. He was buried in New York City.

Fox's patent for the sounding board was sold to F. C. Cline who carried on the business for a time. All the materials and tools later went to Charles Rappe, later Rappe, Weber, and Company, who manufactured pianos for many years in J. C. Fox's building.

MARGARET S. ANGUS

Frontenac County Registry Office (Kingston, Ont.), abstract of town lot 4. *Daily News* (Kingston), 19 Feb. 1861 – 7 Feb. 1868. *Mitchell & Co.'s Canada classified directory for 1865–66* (Toronto, n.d.), 76. *Mitchell & Co.'s general directory for the city of Kingston, and gazetteer of the counties of Frontenac, Lennox and Addington, for 1865* (Toronto, 1865), 58, 60.

FRANCHÈRE, GABRIEL, fur-trader, merchant, and author; b. 3 Nov. 1786 in Montreal, son of Gabriel Franchère, merchant, and Félicité Morin (Miron, Marin); d. 12 April 1863 in St Paul, Minn.

Gabriel Franchère's ancestor, a ship's surgeon, came to Quebec from France in the middle of the 18th century. His father achieved modest success in commerce, eventually became master of the port of Montreal, and was called the "dean of merchants and *marguilliers*" when he died in that city in May 1832. Gabriel probably had some formal education, but nothing is known of his life prior to the spring of 1810. Then, hoping to advance himself in the proposed enterprise of John Jacob Astor* on the Columbia River, he signed on as clerk, one of a number of clerks and voyageurs recruited in Montreal, and set sail from New York on an adventure that determined the course of his life.

The founding of the Pacific Fur Company and the establishment of a post at the mouth of the Columbia River were part of Astor's plan to dominate the American and perhaps the continental fur trade. The Astor empire was built upon sales and purchases of fur, tea, sandalwood, post provisions, and Indian trade goods, as well as general merchandise and shipping, and extended from the United States to both Europe and the Orient. The activities in the Pacific as well as the expanding fur trade in western North America required a fortified headquarters, which Fort Astoria would provide. The fort was established in 1811 but the prospect of hostilities after war with Britain broke out in 1812 and the aggressive com-

petition of the North West Company forced the sale of the assets of the Pacific Fur Company to the Nor'Westers in October 1813.

Franchère, a mere clerk in Astor's vast plan, was a member of Duncan McDougall*'s party which in 1810 made the difficult voyage around Cape Horn to the Columbia under the disturbing guidance of Captain Jonathan Thorn of the *Tonquin*. Franchère demonstrated his ability and common sense in the daily struggles at the outpost, observed the competition between the two companies, and finally returned to Canada with some of the survivors of the Astor enterprise in a party of Nor'Westers in 1814. But his work for the expedition was less significant than his valuable narrative of its progress, the only chronicle by one whose entire service was passed at the fort.

Franchère had kept a diary with the innocent intention of describing precisely, for family and friends, "what I had seen and learned," and he prepared a manuscript for publication just five years after the events. This manuscript was edited by Michel Bibaud*, a respected Montreal journalist and author, who made extensive revisions and additions for its publication in 1820. The book soon became a rare and valued item in Lower Canada, and also established Franchère's reputation as a traveller and writer. The best single account of the Astor enterprise, it became a central source for Washington Irving's *Astoria*, a minor factor in the debates in the Congress of the United States over the Oregon boundary in 1846 (Franchère was invited to Washington at that time by Senator Thomas Hart Benton), and a frequently cited record of the fur trade's relations with Indians in the era. The Oregon dispute, and the appearance of narratives of Astoria not only by Irving but also by Ross Cox* and Alexander Ross*, prompted an English translation of Franchère's account, published in 1854. Based on Bibaud's text, it was prepared by Jedediah Vincent Huntington, a prominent American writer, who worked with the author to clarify the perspective and increase the drama of the tale. No less than four versions of Franchère's story have been published since, each with extensive notes and introduction.

Upon his return from the Pacific Franchère had apparently settled into the Montreal fur-trade community. On 24 April 1815 he married Sophie Routhier, the "true girl" who "was still waiting for him," and family records suggest that he remained in the city, or near by, for the following 19 years. It is certain that he was the chief agent of the American Fur Company in Montreal from 1828 to 1834. The company enjoyed great success in these years, earning close to $200,000 in profits annually, and the Montreal office played a modest part by supplying some of the 400 to 500 *engagés* who laboured on Astor's behalf for $80 to $200 per year. Franchère advertised for the trip men, travelled to several towns to enlist them, paid notaries to draw up engagements, arranged the purchase of flour and pork and spirits for the voyage to the Mackinac (Mich.) headquarters, and handled the inevitable problems of search and arrest associated with the many "deserters and delinquents" who accepted cash advances and headed for the woods.

When Astor left the fur trade in 1834, another Astorian, Ramsay Crooks*, assumed control of the American Fur Company. Franchère agreed to direct the company's agency at Sault Ste Marie, Mich., and was thus, once again, a frontier trader and merchant. In 1842 he became the New York agent of Pierre Chouteau, Jr, and Company. He founded his own fur commission house in Brooklyn in 1857 and was probably engaged in this business at the time of his death.

His years in New York had their difficult moments, particularly after the failure of the American Fur Company in 1842 when, according to a friend, he acted "in an extremely honorable manner, [and] sacrificed his own personal fortune to assist in meeting its liabilities." But in this era too Franchère established closer contacts with the French Canadian community on both sides of the border. He was recognized as the founder of the first American branch of the Société Saint-Jean-Baptiste, about 1850, encouraged local literary evenings, and wrote several articles for Montreal newspapers. In 1853 he was given a public welcome on a visit to Montreal and an address signed by 100 leading citizens for his work as president of the New York society.

Franchère and his wife had had eight children in their years in Montreal and Sault Ste Marie, six of whom survived childhood. When Sophie died in 1837, Franchère had been concerned about his two young daughters but a chance introduction to a widow, Charlotte Prince, in Detroit, provided a happy solution to his difficulties in 1839. Franchère was a respected member of the communities in which he lived. An appropriate comment was provided by an acquaintance, Benjamin Parke Avery of Minnesota, who described him as being "of very simple and correct habits, which insured him good health and cheerful spirits. He possessed a blithe disposition, veined with a kindly humour; was very active and intelligent, exceedingly kind-hearted, true to his adopted country, and had a firm faith in the Christian religion."

GERALD FRIESEN

[At least five editions of Gabriel Franchère's journal have been published: *Relation d'un voyage à la côte du Nord-Ouest de l'Amérique septentrionale, dans les années 1810, 11, 12, 13 et 14*, Michel Bibaud, édit. (Montréal, 1820); *Narrative of a voyage to the northwest coast of America in the years 1811, 1812, 1813, and 1814; or, the first American settlement on the Pacific*, ed. and trans. J. V. Huntington (New York, 1854) (repr. in *Early western travels, 1748–1846; a series of annotated reprints of some of the best and rarest contemporary volumes of travel . . .*, ed. R. G. Thwaites (32v., Cleveland, Ohio, 1904–7)), VI; *A voyage to the northwest coast of America*, ed. M. M. Quaife (Chicago, 1954); *Journal of a voyage* (Lamb); *Adventure at Astoria, 1810–1814*, ed. and trans. H. C. Franchère (Norman, Okla., 1967).

A number of American archives hold material on Franchère: Bayliss Public Library (Sault Ste Marie, Mich.), documents on the American Fur Company and letters of Franchère from 1834 to 1840; Clarke Historical Library (Central Michigan University, Mount Pleasant), Franchère papers, 1834–40, J. R. Livingston papers, 1832–48, in the Sault Ste Marie coll.; Detroit Public Library, Burton Hist. Coll.; Minn. Hist. Soc. (St Paul), Franchère papers and H. H. Sibley papers; Mo. Hist. Soc. (St Louis), American Fur Company papers, 1802–58; N.Y. Hist. Soc., American Fur Company papers. G.F.]

PAC, MG 19, B2, 1–6. [Washington Irving], *Astoria; or, anecdotes of an enterprise beyond the Rocky Mountains*, ed. E. W. Todd (Norman, Okla., 1964). "Une lettre au chirurgien Jacques Franchère," É.-Z. Massicotte, édit., *BRH*, XXXVII (1931), 348–51. *La Minerve*, 5 mai 1863. *New York Times*, 15 April 1863. [F.-M.-U.-]M. Bibaud, *Le panthéon canadien; choix de biographies, dans lequel on a introduit les hommes les plus célèbres des autres colonies britanniques* (2e éd., Montréal, 1891), 100. Tassé, *Les Canadiens de l'Ouest*, I, II. Alexandre Belisle, *Histoire de la presse franco-américaine; comprenant l'historique de l'émigration des Canadiens-français aux États-Unis, leur développement, et leurs progrès* (Worcester, Mass., 1911), 12, 45, 432. K. W. Porter, *John Jacob Astor, business man* (2v., Cambridge, Mass., 1931; repr., New York, 1966), II, 819, 830–32. F.-J. Audet, "En marge d'un centenaire: André Jobin, Benjamin Holmes, Gabriel Franchère, régisseurs," *La Presse* (Montréal), 23 déc. 1933. B. P. Avery, "Death of a remarkable man," Minn. Hist. Soc., *Coll.* (St Paul), VI (1894), 417–20.

FRASER, JAMES DANIEL BAIN, druggist, scientist, and entrepreneur; b. 11 Feb. 1807 in Pictou, N.S., the son of Daniel Fraser, a merchant, and Catherine McKay; m. 20 Dec. 1831 Christiana MacKay, and they had at least seven children; d. 4 May 1869 in Pictou from a "chronic liver disease."

James Daniel Bain Fraser's mother was a daughter of Roderick McKay, a blacksmith and one of the last survivors of the Scottish immigrants who arrived at Pictou on the *Hector* in

1773. Part of Fraser's early education may have been at Pictou Academy under the tutelage of Thomas McCulloch*. The family apparently moved to Halifax prior to 1812, left again for Pictou in 1818, went to Saint John, N.B., around 1820, and returned to Pictou in 1824. There in June of that year Fraser opened a drug store. Two of his brothers, Robert Grant and Thomas Roderick, were in the same business; a third brother, John, was a professional diver in Europe.

Fraser soon developed diverse business interests. He was the local agent for the Eastern Stage Coach Company, which on 18 June 1828 began a service between Halifax and Pictou that lasted for 13 years. Despite government contracts and subsidies, the company was only a marginal success. In 1840 he opened a stone quarry at West River, N.S., and shipped grindstones to Boston. He also found time to hire a diving apparatus to recover the guns of HMS *Malabar* which had foundered off Prince Edward Island in 1838. He afterward complained bitterly about the settlement he received from the naval authorities. His was a pioneer effort in underwater salvage on the Maritime coast. Throughout this period he continued to expand his drug business, serving eastern Nova Scotia and points as distant as Halifax and Charlottetown, P.E.I. By 1841 he had three shops in Pictou.

Fraser kept thoroughly abreast of happenings in his field and had seen the notes concerning Sir James Young Simpson's use of chloroform at a childbirth in England. At the poor-house in Halifax on 9 Feb. 1848 Dr William Johnston Almon* amputated the thumb of a patient who had been given chloroform. A large number of doctors, including Daniel McNeill Parker*, were present. In mid March Almon used chloroform during the amputation of a leg above the knee. According to the *Royal Gazette*, "The Chloroform made use of on this occasion (on the purity of which the producing its characteristic effect depends) was manufactured by J. D. B. Fraser Esq., Chemist, of Pictou."

Probably encouraged by the two successful uses of chloroform, Fraser administered the drug to his wife at the birth of their seventh child, Robert Peden Fraser, on 22 March 1848, thus becoming the first druggist to manufacture and use chloroform at a childbirth in what was to become Canada. Immediately rumblings were heard from fellow Presbyterians who did not, as yet, accept the use of any pain-killing drugs during childbirth. It has been suggested that Fraser was censured by the Court of Session of Prince Street Church (Pictou) for his act, but no evidence is available. It is probable, however, that he left that church, for neither the birth of his seventh child nor his own death is entered in the church records.

Fraser filled several positions in municipal government, including commissioner of streets, 1837–41, member of the Board of Health, 1845–48, and fire warden, 1852–62. On 31 Dec. 1841 he was made a justice of the peace for Pictou County. He was persuaded in 1845 to offer himself as the Liberal standard bearer in a by-election against the Tory Martin I. Wilkins*, later attorney general of Nova Scotia. The election was a wild contest. Even a 10-foot high fence erected down the main street of Pictou to separate the contending parties failed in its purpose and a riot ensued. The election was nullified, but Fraser did not enter the subsequent by-election. In the provincial election of 1863 he carried the Liberal banner in Pictou West, but was unsuccessful. With the advent of the confederation struggle he sided with his old friend Joseph Howe*.

Fraser had a variety of other interests. He was in 1834 one of the first members of the Pictou Literary and Scientific Society, where he introduced many of the newest scientific discoveries, and a member of the Agricultural Society founded in 1837. He also became a charter member of the Oriental Division, Sons of Temperance, in 1841 and rose to become grand worthy patriarch of this powerful organization in 1861.

During the 1850s he turned his attention to the coal fields of Pictou County. He discovered in 1859 the Stellar coal seam. This contained a high-grade coal shale from which top quality coal oil was extracted, but by 1864 the venture had been abandoned following the drilling of the first oil well in the United States. With Sir Hugh Allan* and a New York business syndicate, Fraser formed the Acadia Coal Company in that year to work the MacGregor seam (named for James Drummond MacGregor*). Besides these mining ventures he was a director (1857–61) and president (1862–69) of the Pictou Gas Light Company and a director (1865–68) of the Pictou Home Marine Association.

In his final years Fraser appears to have slowed the hectic pace of his younger days. Within the community he was viewed as "a hardy Scot" of "honest purpose, manly integrity and active public spirit." He died after a lingering illness, leaving an estate worth $14,000. The Pictou *Colonial Standard* eulogized: "His kindness and charity to the poor and afflicted were proverbial and his labours in the cause of Temperance placed him in

Fraser

the front rank as an advocate of that social reformation.''

ALLAN C. DUNLOP

Dalhousie University Library (Halifax), Pictou Literary and Scientific Society, minutes, 1834–55. PANS, MG 1, 319–27 (Fraser family papers); Vertical MSS file, Pictou, pharmacy. *Colonial Standard* (Pictou, N.S.), 11 May 1869. *Royal Gazette* (Halifax), 15 March 1848. *Belcher's farmer's almanack*, 1835–70. *Fiftieth anniversary of the Nova Scotia Pharmaceutical Society, 1875–1925; historical notes, lists of officers and members* (Halifax, 1925). George Patterson, *A history of the county of Pictou, Nova Scotia* (Montreal, 1877).

FRASER, SIMON, fur-trader and explorer; b. at Mapletown (near Bennington, Vt) in 1776; d. on his farm near St Andrews, Stormont County, Canada West, 18 Aug. 1862. He was the eighth and youngest child of Simon Fraser, who was descended from the Frasers of Culbokie and Guisachan, a cadet branch of the Frasers of Lovat, and Isabella Grant, daughter of the laird of Daldregan.

Simon Fraser's parents joined the noted migration of Highlanders, mostly Roman Catholics like themselves, who came to New York in the *Pearl* in 1773. After spending about a year in Albany the Frasers moved to Mapletown, where they settled on the farm on which the explorer was born. They soon encountered anxious times in Mapletown. The area was in dispute between New York and New Hampshire, and conflicting land titles cost them 60 of their 160 acres. Much more serious was the outbreak of the American Revolution; the Frasers were loyal to the British crown, whereas the community was strongly in sympathy with the rebel cause. In spite of abuse and persecution, Simon Fraser Sr was active in the loyalist interest. He came of a military family (two of his brothers had been officers of the celebrated 78th Regiment, Fraser's Highlanders, and had fought with James Wolfe* at Quebec), and he determined to join the British forces at the first opportunity. This came in 1777, when General John Burgoyne* led his ill-fated expedition into the region. Simon Fraser and William, his eldest son, enlisted in July and took part in the battle of Bennington on 17 August, when the British were decisively defeated. Then or soon after Fraser was apprehended by the Americans and taken to Albany, where he was imprisoned under such rigorous conditions that he died in little more than a year.

When the war ended, Isabella Fraser determined to move to Canada. Captain John Fraser*, one of the brothers who had served in Fraser's Highlanders, had settled in Montreal and had been appointed a judge of the Court of Common Pleas. In 1784, with his help, Isabella and her younger children were able to join her son William, who had taken up land at Coteau-du-Lac, west of Montreal.

In 1790, when young Simon was 14, he was sent to Montreal, where Judge Fraser took charge of him. He received some schooling, but his education was brief for in 1792 he was apprenticed to the North West Company. The choice of a career in the fur trade was not surprising. It was a major part of the commercial life of Montreal at the time, two of Isabella Fraser's brothers were engaged in it, and the Frasers were related to Simon McTavish*, the dominant personality in the North West Company.

Virtually nothing is known about Fraser's activities during the next dozen years. Records and letters occasionally refer to a Simon Fraser but there were at least four men of the name in the service of the North West Company in the 1790s and it is seldom possible to say with certainty which individual is meant. It is known that he was serving as a clerk in the Athabasca Department in 1799, and it is probable that he spent most of his time there. He was obviously well regarded and a successful trader, for the minutes of the meeting of the partners of the company held at Grand Portage (Minn.) on 30 June 1801 record that ''It was unanimously Resolved'' that Fraser and five others ''should be admitted Partners of the North West Company for one Forty sixth share each, their Interest in the same to Commence with the Outfit of the Year 1802.'' To have gained a partnership at the age of 25 was no mean achievement.

For a decade or more the Nor'Westers had been interested in exploring the far west, with two purposes in view. One was an increase in trade; the country west of the Rockies might well prove to be a rich new source of furs. The other was the discovery of a practicable travel route to the Pacific coast over which supplies could be brought into the area and furs taken out, because the old supply route from Montreal would be so long that transportation costs would swallow up profits. There was the further possibility that direct trade might be established between the Pacific coast and the fur markets of China.

Alexander Mackenzie* had tried to find a route to the coast in 1789, but the Mackenzie River had led him to the Arctic Ocean instead of the Pacific. In 1793 he reached the Pacific, but by a route so difficult that it was considered useless for purposes of trade. Western exploration then ceased for a time, largely because of a personality and policy clash between Mackenzie and McTavish. By the time Fraser became a partner, Mackenzie had joined others in the rival XY or New North West Company that was offering the Nor'Westers such vigorous, costly, and violent competition that no men or resources could be spared for expansion. This state of affairs ended in 1804, when McTavish's death was followed within a few months by the union of the North West and New North West companies.

To avoid friction, Mackenzie was excluded from the management of the combined concern, but the Nor'Westers were less indifferent to his discoveries than they had appeared to be. The coalition cleared the way for the resumption of western expansion, and in 1805 Fraser was given responsibility for extending operations to the country west of the Rockies. Mackenzie's expeditions had been primarily reconnaissance trips; Fraser's assignment, by contrast, reflected a definite decision to build trading posts and take possession of the country as well as to explore travel routes. He deserves therefore to rank as the pioneer of permanent settlement in what is now the mainland of British Columbia.

In the autumn of 1805 he ascended the Peace River and built Rocky Mountain Portage House at the eastern end of the Peace River Canyon. This post was intended to be both a trading post and a base for the push across the mountains. It is clear that Fraser had been instructed to re-examine Mackenzie's route up the Peace and Parsnip rivers, over the divide that separated the watersheds of the Peace and the Fraser, and thence down the Fraser, which was still believed to be the Columbia. Indian reports of impassable rapids and canyons had caused Mackenzie to turn back in the vicinity of Alexandria; Fraser was to press on down the river and put the Indian tales to the test.

He was accompanied by John Stuart*, who was to be his companion and invaluable lieutenant on most of his travels, and James McDougall*, a younger clerk. Soon after Rocky Mountain Portage was established, Fraser and McDougall set off to build an advance post farther west. They went up the Peace, turned up the Parsnip, and found the Pack River, which led them to Trout Lake (McLeod Lake). The Sekani Indians there were friendly and a small fort, Trout Lake Post (Fort McLeod), was built – the first permanent white settlement west of the Rockies in what is now Canada. During the winter the *engagé* left in charge when Fraser and McDougall returned to Rocky Mountain Portage deserted his post, and McDougall was sent back to look after the company's property. This move

had an important result, for McDougall, having heard Indian reports of a much larger lake to the west, went to investigate and discovered the "Carriers' Lake" (Stuart Lake). It was in the heart of the country inhabited by the Carriers and obviously provided an excellent site for a trading post. Fraser decided to combine the building of this post with the exploration he planned to undertake in 1806. McDougall had learned that a river of some kind drained Stuart Lake into the Fraser River, and Fraser's plan, which he duly carried out, was to go down the Fraser until he came to this river (it turned out to be a combination of the Nechako River and its tributary the Stuart River) and ascend it to Stuart Lake.

Just before leaving Rocky Mountain Portage, Fraser sent the winter's harvest of furs to Dunvegan (Alta). It included 14 packs from Trout Lake – the first furs traded west of the mountains. Fraser was delighted with their quality. "The furs are really fine," he noted in his journal. "They were chiefly killed in the proper season and many of them are superior to any I have seen in Athabasca. . . ."

Break-up was late in 1806; it was 20 May before the Peace was clear of ice and Fraser and Stuart could start up the river. The travellers encountered many difficulties. Most of the rivers and creeks they followed were in freshet and swift currents impeded their progress. Good bark for canoe-building was lacking at the Portage, and the old and makeshift craft with which they set out had to be replaced at Trout Lake. Their ten crewmen were an unskilled and unsatisfactory lot; most of them suffered from illness or injuries along the way. Fraser evidently had a copy of Mackenzie's journal, and in his own indulged occasionally in derogatory remarks about "the Knight's" explorations. Mackenzie had failed to notice either the Pack River or the Nechako, and Fraser remarked on 5 June that he "could prove that he seldom or ever paid the attention he pretends to have done. . . ." But when he himself struggled over the height of land and encountered the rapids, rocks, fallen trees, and other hazards on the Bad River (as Mackenzie had named James Creek), he was compelled to admit on 10 July that Mackenzie had described it "with great exactness. It is certainly well named and a most dangerous place. . . ."

Fraser faced further difficulties at Stuart Lake, which he finally reached on 26 July. A post (the future Fort St James) was built there, but few goods were available with which to barter for furs. The salmon run was late and the Indians were near starvation; Fraser and his men were soon in a like state. He had intended to return to

Fraser

the Fraser River and trace at least part of its course before winter, but lack of goods and provisions forced him to postpone this major part of his mission. Instead, he sent Stuart to visit Fraser Lake, which the Indians had described, and later he and Stuart built there the post subsequently called Fort Fraser. The whole area Fraser named New Caledonia, because, it is believed, the country reminded him of his mother's descriptions of the Scottish Highlands.

To his distress, no supplies or additional men reached Fraser until the autumn of 1807, and the exploration of the river had to be postponed until 1808. All he could do in the interval was establish Fort George (Prince George), on the river near the mouth of the Nechako, which was both a good site for a trading post and a convenient starting point for the trip downstream.

The party of 24 that left Fort George in four canoes on 28 May 1808 included Fraser, Stuart, Jules-Maurice Quesnel*, a young clerk, 19 other company employees, and two Indians. From the start they were greeted by Indian reports that the river below "was but a succession of falls and cascades" which they would find impossible to pass. Even the portages were extremely difficult, so much so that they tempted Fraser's crews to run rapids almost regardless of danger in order to avoid the immense labour of carrying canoes and cargoes around obstructions. In many places steep, high banks made it impossible to leave the river, once launched upon it, and the canoes would have been helpless if they had come without warning to rapids or falls. The river was in freshet; at one point it rose eight feet in 24 hours. By 10 June, Fraser was convinced at last that the Indians were right in contending that it was madness to descend the river itself. Some distance above the site of Lillooet the canoes were stored on a scaffold in a shady spot, goods that could not be carried were cached, and the party pressed forward on foot.

Travel on land proved to be almost as great an ordeal as travel by water. "I have been for a long period among the Rocky Mountains," Fraser wrote, "but have never seen any thing equal to this country, for I cannot find words to describe our situation at times. We had to pass where no human being should venture." Occasionally it was practicable to take to the river again, but they were then involved in the difficulties of borrowing, or, on at least one occasion, virtually commandeering canoes from the Indians.

Fraser showed great skill in dealing with the Indians. Friendly relations had to be established with those encountered along the way, and there was also the delicate matter of passing from the territory of one tribe to that of another. By means of the two Indians he had with him, he saw to it whenever possible that the tribe next to be visited had been warned of his coming and assured that his intentions were friendly. Nevertheless he was ever on the alert for trouble. "However kind savages may appear," he wrote on 20 June, "I know that it is not in their nature to be sincere in their professions to strangers. . . . It is certain the less familiar we are with one another the better for us." The natives were numerous; crowds numbering hundreds were met several times and on one occasion Fraser estimated that 1,200 had assembled.

All went reasonably well until he reached the mouth of the river, where the Cowichans were first suspicious and then openly hostile. Fraser was unable to go as far into the Strait of Georgia as he wished to do, and when he hurried back up the river the Indians pursued and harassed his party as far as the vicinity of Hope. Scores of canoes closed in repeatedly with the intention of upsetting Fraser's canoe, but each time they were fended off successfully and without casualties on either side. The Indians finally abandoned the chase, but Fraser's men were left completely exhausted and discouraged.

The supreme test of Fraser's leadership came when many of his men determined to leave the river and try to find their way back to Fort George independently. He "remonstrated and threatened by turns" and insisted that the only hope of safety lay in keeping together. His journal for 6 July records the sequel: "After much debate . . . we all shook hands, resolving never to separate during the voyage; which resolution was immediately confirmed by the following oath . . .: 'I solemnly swear before Almighty God that I shall sooner perish than forsake in distress any of our crew during the present voyage.' After this ceremony was over all hands dressed in their best apparel, and each took charge of his own bundle." Fort George was reached safely on 6 August. The journey down the river had taken 36 days and the return trip 37 days.

There has been considerable debate as to whether Fraser actually reached the mouth of the river, largely because he expressed in his journal his "great disappointment in not seeing the *main ocean*, having gone so near it as to be almost within view." But the Musqueam Indian village, which he visited, was at the mouth of the Fraser River and he paddled some distance beyond it in the direction of Point Grey. Fraser's remark was made under the impression that the ocean was near at hand, whereas in fact it was still about 140 miles away, beyond Vancouver Island.

The journey that had been carried through with such effort and heroism ended for Fraser in disappointment and a sense of failure. The river would be of no use as a travel route, and at its mouth he discovered that the latitude was about 49°. "This River, therefore, is not the Columbia," Fraser wrote sadly. "If I had been convinced of this fact where I left my canoes, I would certainly have returned from thence." Like Mackenzie's journey to the Arctic, the expedition had been a useless enterprise from the point of view of the North West Company.

Fraser left New Caledonia in 1809, attended the annual rendezvous at Fort William (Thunder Bay, Ont.), and then went on leave. When he returned to duty in 1810 he was assigned again to the Athabasca Department, where he remained until 1814. For much of this time he was in charge of the Mackenzie River District. After a second leave in 1814–15 he went to Fort William with the spring brigade from Montreal and travelled on to Red River, where he immediately became involved in the strife between the North West Company and the colony established by Lord Selkirk [Douglas*] which the Nor'Westers regarded as a threat to the fur trade. He was one of the partners who escorted Miles Macdonell*, governor of the colony, to Fort William as a prisoner in the summer of 1815. The violence of the clash between the North West Company and the Hudson's Bay Company was not to Fraser's liking; he made a determined effort to retire, but was persuaded finally to return to Athabasca for one more year. Like many of the Nor'Westers he was doubtless aware that mischief was planned in Red River in 1816; he was one of those who arrived "judiciously late" for the rendezvous that year, and so kept clear of the Seven Oaks massacre on 19 June when Robert Semple*, the governor at the Red River Settlement, and 19 of his men were killed in a clash between half-breeds and colonists. Nevertheless he was one of the partners arrested by Lord Selkirk at Fort William; he was taken in September to Montreal where he was promptly released on bail. He was back at Fort William in 1817, when the North West Company regained possession of the post, but this was evidently his last appearance in the fur trade.

Fraser, with five other partners, was tried at York (Toronto) in 1818 for "treason and conspiracy" and "accessory to murder," but all were acquitted. By that time he had settled on farm lands on the Raisin River, near St Andrews; the 1861 census records that his holdings then consisted of 240 acres valued at $4,000. He had engaged in a number of enterprises, including a sawmill and a grist mill, but they did not prosper.

He was greatly handicapped by a severe knee injury suffered when serving as captain of the 1st Regiment of the Stormont militia during the rebellion of 1837–38. The small pension he received was little compensation for an injury which, as he informed Governor General Charles Bagot*, had been "the cause of reducing him from a state of comparative affluence to penuery, owing to his not being capable to attend to his ordinary business." The rest of his long life was passed in straitened circumstances.

On 7 June 1820 Fraser married Catherine, daughter of Captain Allan Macdonell, a prominent resident of nearby Matilda Township. Five sons and three daughters grew to maturity. Fraser was one of the last surviving partners of the North West Company when he died on 18 Aug. 1862. His wife died the next day, and they were buried in a single grave in the Roman Catholic cemetery at St Andrews.

Fraser's fame rests upon his remarkable journeys in the years 1805–8. These are recorded in considerable detail in his three journals and 11 contemporary letters. Writing to John Stuart, he described his 1806 journal as being "exceeding ill wrote worse worded & not well spelt," but his narratives are direct and frequently dramatic. The versions now available are "fair copies," a term for somewhat revised versions of the originals. The most important of them is the account of the 1808 expedition down the Fraser River.

Possessed of great physical courage and endurance, Fraser remained calm and determined in the face of dangers and difficulties. Few feats of exploration surpass his journey to the sea and back in 1808. Nevertheless, recognition of his achievement was slow in coming. A son and daughter received small pensions from the government of Canada in 1890, but little popular interest was aroused until the government of British Columbia organized a centennial celebration of the journey in 1908. An exhibition was held and a memorial column was unveiled on the bank of the Fraser at New Westminster; a bust by Louis Hébert* was added to the column in 1911. The HBC placed a marker and inscription on his grave in 1921. The journey down the Fraser was re-enacted in 1958, the 150th anniversary, when British Columbia was celebrating its own centenary.

W. KAYE LAMB

[Simon Fraser's "Journal of a voyage from the Rocky Mountains to the Pacific Ocean, performed in the year 1808" is preserved at MTCL. Transcripts of a fragment of Fraser's second journal, 1808, and of his journal for 1806 are at the Bancroft Library, University of California, Berkeley; the original copies of the two journals have been lost. The Bancroft Library also possesses transcripts of 11 letters written by Fraser in 1806 and 1807, four of which can also be found as original letterbook copies at the PABC. In addition, there are Fraser family papers in the possession of Mr Donald C. Fraser, Fargo, N.D. Copies of all these and of various other documents have been collected in PAC, MG 19, A9. The 1806 journal is printed in PAC *Report*, 1929, 109–59, and the 1808 journal in *Les bourgeois de la Compagnie du Nord-Ouest: récits de voyages, lettres et rapports inédits relatifs au Nord-Ouest canadien*, L.-F.-R. Masson, édit. (2v., Québec, 1889–90; réimpr. New York, 1960), I, but the versions printed are imperfect and, in the case of the 1806 journal, garbled. Both journals, the fragment of the second journal for 1808, the letters of 1806–7, and other primary documents have been collected and edited by W. K. Lamb in *The letters and journals of Simon Fraser, 1806–1808* (Toronto, 1960), which also includes a biographical introduction. w.k.l.]

Documents relating to NWC (Wallace). Alexander Mackenzie, *History of the Frasers of Lovat, with genealogies of the principal families of the name . . .* (Inverness, Scot., 1896). Morice, *History of northern interior of B.C.* (1905). John Spargo, *Two Bennington-born explorers and makers of modern. Canada* ([Bradford, Vt.], 1950). E. O. S. Scholefield, "Simon Fraser," *Westward Ho!* (Vancouver), III (1908), 217–31, 440–45; IV (1909), 61–76, 138–44.

FRÉMONT, CHARLES-JACQUES, doctor, surgeon, and professor; b. 17 Oct. 1806 at Quebec, son of Charles-Pierre Frémont, a businessman, and Charlotte Voyer; m. 8 Jan. 1845, at Quebec, Cécile Panet, daughter of Judge Philippe Panet*, and they had eight children; d. 20 Dec. 1862 at sea.

Charles-Jacques Frémont began his education at the Séminaire de Québec, but had to interrupt it when his parents decided to move to Montreal. He completed his studies at an English school there, then started medical training under Dr John Stephenson, a founder of the Montreal Medical Institution in 1822. On 16 Nov. 1829 Frémont was licensed to practise medicine and surgery. He intended to carry on his profession at Saint-Thomas-de-Montmagny (Montmagny), but in the end settled at Pointe-Lévi (Lauzon, Lévis).

Some years later Dr Frémont left Pointe-Lévi for Quebec, where his practice grew steadily. Living in the capital made it possible for him to take a more active role in the medical life of Quebec. He was able to participate in the activities of the Société Médicale de Québec, giving lectures and taking part in discussions. In 1835 he stayed for a short time at the quarantine station on Grosse Île [*see* George Mellis DOUGLAS]. In 1837 the governor general, Lord Gosford [Acheson*], a great admirer of Frémont, appointed him assistant to Dr James Douglas* at the Marine Hospital, then called the Marine and Emigrant Hospital. But Douglas, who considered Frémont much too young, refused to take him, claiming that he wished to work with a doctor as competent as himself. Dr Joseph Painchaud* was immediately appointed. Douglas, honouring professional ethics, insisted on informing Frémont of the reasons for his refusal; as a result of this encounter, the two became close friends. Douglas was indebted to Frémont over a number of years informally for his "success in surgical operations" but Frémont was his regular assistant only for a few months in 1847. Douglas described him in his diary as "an honest, an upright, and a high-minded gentleman, and with a thorough knowledge of his profession." He added: "Had I been aware that on the appointment of the six visiting physicians [to help Douglas] I would have been deprived of the assistance of Dr. F., I would at once have placed my commission at His Excellency's disposal."

In 1845 Frémont helped set up the École de Médecine de Québec and from 1849 to 1852 he gave courses there in the theory and practice of surgery. In 1845 also he and doctors Joseph MORRIN and James Douglas founded the Asile de Beauport; he and Douglas even underwrote the financial deficits of this undertaking. Frémont became director in 1849 and devoted himself unsparingly to it until his death.

In 1852 the authorities of the Université Laval invited Dr Frémont to become a professor in the new faculty of medicine, which opened in 1853. On 9 Sept. 1856 he agreed to replace the first dean of the faculty, Dr Jean Blanchet*, who had just died. For seven years he made the development of the faculty his first concern; in particular he organized its internal management, and established regulations concerning the anatomy and dissection room, the anatomical theatre, and the clinic – still in its early stages – at the Hôtel-Dieu. Indeed his first act was to improve working conditions both at the Hôtel-Dieu clinic and at that of the Marine and Emigrant Hospital which opened in 1857. In June 1858 he instituted a schedule of honoraria for the courses being offered at the faculty.

Under Frémont's deanship the programme of studies was revised, improved, and completed. In December 1858 he instituted a course in clinical manipulation to be given by Dr François-Alexandre-Hubert La Rue*. Thanks to the dean, the latter also had the opportunity to learn how to handle a microscope, so that in 1862 the faculty offered its students a course in microscopic anatomy. In July 1860 Frémont obtained a grant for Dr Alfred Simard which allowed him to take a clinical course in Belgium. In addition, he provided for the development of the faculty library, had an ice room installed and the pathology museum finished, and increased the number of professors.

Charles-Jacques Frémont, widely known as a dedicated man, was for many years the doctor of the Quebec prison and visiting doctor to the Hôtel-Dieu, where "his kindness and attention were fully appreciated." In 1860, in addition to his medical activities, he paid a visit to the pope as the delegate of Canadian Catholics. On that occasion Pius IX conferred upon him the title of Knight Commander of the Order of St Gregory the Great.

In October 1862 Frémont set off on a rest trip to Egypt accompanied by his wife. As his health was deteriorating, he decided to return, but died on 20 December on board the liner *Bohemian* en route to Portland, Maine. He was buried on 31 December at Quebec.

CHARLES-MARIE BOISSONNAULT

ANQ-Q, AP-G-85/3; État civil, Catholiques, Notre-Dame de Québec, 17 oct. 1806, 8 janv. 1845, 20 déc. 1862. [James Douglas], *Journals and reminiscences of James Douglas, M.D.*, ed. James Douglas Jr (New York, 1910). Université Laval, *Annuaire* (Québec), 1852–53. M.-J. et George Ahern, *Notes pour servir à l'histoire de la médecine dans le Bas-Canada, depuis la fondation de Québec jusqu'au commencement du XIXe siècle* (Québec, 1923), 235–39. Père Alexis [de Barbezieux], *Histoire de Limoilou* (Québec, 1921), 108, 111. C.-M. Boissonnault, *Histoire de la faculté de médecine de Laval* (Québec, 1953), 180–83. P.-B. Casgrain, *Mémorial des familles Casgrain, Baby et Perrault du Canada* (Québec, 1898). P.-G. Roy, *La famille Frémont* (Lévis, Qué., 1902), 29–34. C.-M. Boissonnault, "Création de deux écoles de médecine au Québec," *Laval médical* (Québec), 39 (1968), 547–49.

FRIEL, HENRY JAMES, journalist, politician, and public servant; b. 1823 at Montreal, son of Charles Friel; d. 16 May 1869 at Ottawa, Ont.

Henry James Friel was born of Irish Catholic parents. In 1827 the family moved to Bytown (Ottawa), Upper Canada, where Charles Friel operated a general store. Orphaned in the 1830s, Henry Friel apprenticed to Alexander James Christie*, proprietor of the *Bytown Gazette*. Friel proved to have all of the qualities necessary for a 19th century journalist: he was intensely political, he had an instinct for controversy, and he wrote well. His literary career began in 1845–46, when he contributed four articles on the Ottawa valley to the Montreal magazine, the *Literary Garland*. They confirm the judgement of the contemporary critic, Henry James Morgan*, that Friel was "a terse and vigorous writer of undoubted ability."

In October 1846 Friel and John George Bell purchased the Bytown *Packet*. It was a noisy, controversial paper which, under Friel's direction, made surprising impact for the Reform party in a traditionally Tory community. Friel strengthened his voice in 1848 by marrying into one of Bytown's leading families. His wife was Mary Anne, daughter of prominent merchant Daniel O'Connor. The Friels would have a number of children, but only three lived beyond infancy. Friel also began a busy career of social service: he was a founding member of the Bytown Mechanics' Institute (serving several times as its president) and was active in the affairs of St Joseph's Roman Catholic parish and in the Catholic charity, the St Vincent de Paul Society. During the 1860s he was a member of the council of the Ottawa Board of Trade and a director of the Ottawa Gas Company.

Friel was at the centre of most political disputes in Bytown. In September 1849, when rioting broke out over a proposed visit by Governor General Elgin [BRUCE], Friel was among those arrested for abetting the looting of the government arsenal at Hull to supply arms to the Reform rioters. He had already entered active politics more legitimately when he was elected to Bytown's first town council in September 1847. Although defeated for re-election in 1848, he became a school trustee the following year.

The struggle to maintain a Reform newspaper was a financial drain. After the election in 1848 of the liberal government of Louis-Hippolyte LA FONTAINE and Robert Baldwin*, Friel became an avid seeker of patronage. When government printing contracts could not make the *Packet* profitable, he sold it in October 1849 to Robert Bell*. A civil service position then became Friel's goal. He was successful in 1850, being appointed clerk of the Carleton County Court and deputy clerk of the crown, posts he held until 1857.

Friel was elected alderman for Bytown's East Ward in 1850, 1853, and 1854, and in the latter year was chosen mayor by his fellow aldermen. He attempted to move into provincial politics in 1854, but was defeated for the Bytown seat. It was the first of three unsuccessful tries: in 1863 he ran in Prescott, and in 1867 he was bested by Richard William Scott* for the Ottawa seat in the Ontario Legislature. His municipal career remained successful, however, and when Bytown became the city of Ottawa in 1855, Friel continued as a dominant force. He was alderman

Frothingham

from 1855 to 1858, and in 1864, 1865, and 1867. He was three times mayor, in 1863, 1868, and 1869, dying in office.

Friel had returned to journalism in 1858 when he established the Ottawa *Union* as a popular Reform paper modelled on the American "penny press." His first partner was his brother-in-law, Roderick O'Connor, who also operated the Catholic newspaper, the *Tribune*. In 1860 Friel took a new partner, civil engineer George Hugo Perry*. The paper expanded from a weekly to a tri-weekly in 1861, and to the *Daily Union* in 1865. It was chiefly concerned with protecting Ottawa's position as capital and as a linchpin in the union of the Canadas. As a result, the *Union* became a staunch opponent of the confederation scheme, which might endanger these Ottawa interests, and of those Reformers, such as George Brown*, who supported confederation.

In 1866 Friel sold the *Union* to its rival daily, the *Ottawa Times*. He busied himself with local politics and with his agency for the Royal Insurance Company. On 10 May 1869 Mrs Friel gave birth to a son. Henry Friel caught a severe cold the same night and it rapidly developed into lung congestion. On 16 May Mayor Friel died, aged 45. The city he had served so long gave him a grand state funeral, and he was laid to rest in the Ottawa Catholic Cemetery at Sandy Hill, on 19 May 1869.

MICHAEL S. CROSS

H. J. Friel was the author of "The Calumette: a passage from Tom Clifden's *Ottawa sketches*," "Lake Colonge, from Tom Clifden's *Ottawa sketches*," "Lake des Alumettes, from Tom Clifden's *Ottawa sketches*," and "The misanthrope" in the *Literary Garland* (Montreal), new ser., III (1845), 520–22; IV (1846), 84–86, 235–37, and 343–57, respectively.

MTCL, Robert Baldwin papers, 37, no.70; 46, nos.30–36; 60, no.32; 70, no.31. PAC, MG 24, B55; I9, 12, p.3744; 20, pp.4967–70; 32; I107; RG 8, I (C series), 617, pp.57–59. *Daily Union* (Ottawa), 1865–66. *Ottawa Citizen*, 1851–69. *Ottawa Times*, 1865–69. *Packet* (Bytown [Ottawa]), 1846–51. *Union* (Ottawa), 1858–65. *Illustrated historical atlas of the county of Carleton (including city of Ottawa), Ont.* (Toronto, 1879; repr. Port Elgin, Ont., 1971), xix, xxviii–xxix. Morgan, *Bibliotheca Canadensis*, 131. *The province of Ontario gazetteer and directory . . .* , comp. Henry McEvoy (Toronto, 1869), 352–58. Alexis de Barbezieux, *Histoire de la province ecclésiastique d'Ottawa et de la colonisation dans la vallée de l'Ottawa* (2v., Ottawa, 1897), I, 146–47. Lucien Brault, *Ottawa old & new* (Ottawa, 1946), 76–77, 86–89, 115–16, 200, 253. M. S. Cross, "Stony Monday, 1849: the rebellion losses riots in Bytown," *OH*, LXIII (1971), 177–90. R. U. Mahaffy, "Ottawa journalism, 1860 to 1870," *OH*, XLII (1950), 205–11.

FROTHINGHAM, JOHN, merchant; b. June 1788 in Portland, Maine, son of Judge John Frothingham of the Massachusetts Superior Court and his wife Martha; d. 22 May 1870 in Montreal.

John Frothingham was thrown on his own resources at an early age. He entered the hardware firm of Samuel May in Boston and in 1809 was sent to Montreal to open a branch outlet. On his arrival he joined a small but growing group of Americans, mainly from New England and New York, who were involved in Montreal's expanding commerce. Although the American community of Montreal experienced some social and business discrimination after the War of 1812 it continued to grow and prosper. Frothingham himself suffered early business setbacks but re-established himself in the hardware business in partnership with his younger brother, Joseph May Frothingham; the latter died at age 32 in 1832. In 1836 Frothingham formed a partnership with William Workman*, and their firm became the largest hardware and iron wholesale firm in British North America. In 1853 the partners moved to larger premises and about the same time began to manufacture some of their own merchandise.

Frothingham was a promoter and shareholder in a number of companies and associations that were formed during the expansion of the 1840s, among them the Montreal Board of Trade, the St Lawrence and Atlantic Railroad, the Montreal Stock Exchange, and the Canada Inland Steam Navigation Company. He was also associated with the British and Canadian School of Montreal and the Montreal Horticultural Society. His principal outside business interest, however, was the City Bank of Montreal. Formed in 1831, it was the first to be successful in breaking the monopoly of the Bank of Montreal in the city. The Montrealers who formed the new bank may have been unable to secure credit from the Bank of Montreal, but the early shareholders' lists suggest that the American investors, mainly from New York, who supplied most of the initial capital were motivated by a desire for profit. Frothingham was associated with the bank from its origins, along with John Molson*, William Ritchie*, François-Antoine LAROCQUE, Thomas A. Begley, Joseph Vallée, John Easton Mills, Stanley Bagg*, and William Lyman* – a group consisting mainly of Americans and French Canadians. Frothingham held a substantial quantity of the bank's stock; he served on its board for at least 16 years and was president from 1834 to 1849 when he resigned. The bank had sustained heavy losses in 1849 and he may have felt that he had to assume personal responsibility. He was succeeded as president by Workman.

As his business affairs prospered, Frothingham, like many of his more successful colleagues, adopted a grand style of living. During the 1840s, when it was becoming fashionable among the local merchants to move from their dwellings above the Rue Saint-Paul shops to large homes on the slopes of Mount Royal, Frothingham built the baronial mansion Piedmont, which was used as the governor general's residence when parliament met in Montreal.

Frothingham was not involved in politics at either the provincial or the municipal level, and was content, it seems, with a business role. His diary, which he kept for many years, reflects only passing interest in current political affairs. His son John joined the business and in 1859 Frothingham retired to live quietly on his estate. A Presbyterian, he was a generous contributor to the Protestant schools of Montreal, to Queen's College at Kingston, and to McGill University. Two sons, and a daughter, Louisa Goddard, wife of John Henry Robinson Molson, survived him.

GERALD TULCHINSKY

McCord Museum, Antiquarian autographs. PAC, MG 27, I, E10A. Private archives, J. I. Cooper (Tillsonburg, Ont.), John Frothingham diary. Can., Prov. of, *Statutes*, 1841, c.90, c.97; 1844–45, c.25; 1852–53, c.146; 1857, c.169; 1859, c.122; Legislative Assembly, *Journals*, 1843, II, app.S. L.C., *Statutes*, 1833, c.32; House of Assembly, *Journals*, 1835, app.J. *Gazette* (Montreal), 10 Feb., 8, 15, 19, 29 March 1831; 12 March 1849; 23 May 1870. *La Minerve*, 25 mai 1870. *Montreal Herald*, 23 May 1870. *Montreal Transcript*, 15 Feb. 1840. *Pilot* (Montreal), 2, 5 April 1844; 11 May 1853. *Lower Canada almanack . . .*, 1840. *Montreal almanac . . .*, 1839. *Montreal directory*, 1841–50. G. J. J. Tulchinsky, "The Montreal business community, 1837–1853," *Canadian business history, selected studies, 1497–1971*, ed. D. S. Macmillan (Toronto, 1972), 131.

FULFORD, FRANCIS, Church of England minister and bishop; b. 3 June 1803, at Sidmouth, Devon, England, second son of Baldwin Fulford and Anne Maria Adams; m. in October 1830 Mary Drummond of Fawley, Hampshire, England; 9 Sept. 1868 in Montreal, Que.

Francis Fulford came of old west country stock. He was educated at Blundells School and at Exeter College, Oxford (BA 1827, MA 1838, and DD 1850). After ordination in 1828 he had extensive parochial experience in western England and at Croydon, Cambridgeshire, before becoming minister of Curzon Chapel, Mayfair, London, in 1845. He was also chaplain to the Duchess of Gloucester, an office which may have provided an entrée to court. In 1834 he had begun to figure in meetings of the Society for the Propagation of the Gospel and formed a close friendship with its secretary, the Reverend Ernest HAWKINS. In 1848, Fulford became editor of the *Colonial Church Chronicle and Missionary Journal*, an independent periodical favouring the SPG's programme. At this point, he appears as a capable, energetic man ready to assume responsibility. He wrote with clarity and simplicity.

Fulford moved on the fringes of the church reform commonly known as the Oxford movement. With its principal tenet, complete freedom of the church from any state interference, he was in full accord. He protested when in 1843 Edward Bouverie Pusey, the real leader of the movement, was forbidden to use the university pulpit at Oxford; later, on visits to England, Fulford would stay with Pusey. With John Henry Newman he had friendly correspondence. Long afterwards, when Newman had become a Roman Catholic, Fulford delivered a sympathetic review of his *Apologia pro vita sua* in Montreal. Yet Fulford professed admiration for the English and generally for the Continental reformers of the 16th and 17th centuries. His pamphlet, *The progress of the reformation in England* (1841), is an index of his independent position: "[Our] Anglo Catholic Church was a reformed church." He drew encouragement from its spread overseas, in the English colonies and in non-English countries.

The choice of Fulford for the projected diocese of Montreal probably came through his association with the SPG. The division of the diocese of Quebec was a project of long standing. George Jehoshaphat MOUNTAIN used the title bishop of Montreal as suffragan to Charles James Stewart*, and even when he succeeded him as bishop of Quebec, allegedly to keep the claims of Montreal before the authorities in Britain. By 1849 the necessary funds for an episcopal endowment were available. Hawkins inspected the proposed diocese of Montreal and conferred with Lord Elgin [BRUCE] and Bishop Mountain. The Montreal clergy and laity were understandably disturbed, and their leader, the Reverend John Bethune*, tried to marshal opinion in favour of a conference that would recommend a candidate for consecration. Bethune professed to fear that the Executive Council, consisting of "members of the Church of Rome, Protestant Dissenters and only two or three Episcopalians," would make the recommendation. In the event, the Colonial Office seems to have turned to the SPG and the Reverend Francis Fulford was its choice.

Letters patent were issued by the queen in 1850 setting up the diocese of Montreal and naming

Fulford

Francis Fulford lord bishop, a title enjoyed by only one other Canadian prelate, the bishop of Quebec. The diocese was coterminous with the judicial district of Montreal, an elongated triangle with its base on the United States border, its western boundary on the Ottawa River, and its eastern at the districts of Trois-Rivières and Saint-François. Christ Church, the old Protestant parish church of Montreal, was designated as the cathedral. Since the legality of letters patent in colonies exercising self-government was in question, Fulford later supplemented his through legislation by his diocesan synod. He was consecrated on 25 July 1850 in Westminster Abbey by the archbishop of Canterbury, John Bird Sumner, four English bishops, and one Canadian bishop, John STRACHAN of Toronto.

On 15 Sept. 1850, Fulford was enthroned in Christ Church as the spiritual head of some 25,000 adherents of what contemporaries called "the United Church of England and Ireland." In the main they were Anglophones, but there were French speaking families and congregations in the Richelieu valley and elsewhere, such as Sainte-Thérèse, Rawdon, and Saint-Hyacinthe, missions among the Germans in the Ottawa settlements, and one for Abenaki Indians at Saint-François-de-Sales (Odanak). The complexities of his charge Fulford explored in a quick survey in the late autumn. In town and country-side he found depression, spiritually and materially. "The people are disunited & . . . few . . . [are] in reality Church people." Their horizons were narrow; that they were parts of a *societas perfecta et universalis* they had no comprehension. Fulford did not despair. He liked his clergy, who numbered 48. As he came to know his people Fulford began to draw out his own lines.

In diocesan administration he had a clear field, since before 1850 there had been no special provision for the Montreal area. He began with what was closest, a cathedral chapter with dean and canons, which would exercise authority during the bishop's absence or in the event of his death. Actually, the chapter's powers were limited to the management of the cathedral church and membership was honorific. Nevertheless, John Bethune could boast that he was the first dean of any Anglican jurisdiction in North America. In 1855 Bishop Fulford named an archdeacon for the whole diocese; he became the executive assistant, a hard-worked, much-travelled dignitary. To encourage local initiative, Fulford in 1859 marshalled the missions and parishes into four rural deaneries, St Andrews (northern), Hochelaga and Iberville (central), and Bedford (southern). Ruridecanal meetings of laity and clergy made possible projects beyond the resources of a single charge, did something to break down isolation, and smoothed decision-making at higher levels. The efficiency and *esprit de corps* the diocese rapidly achieved may be ascribed largely to Fulford's local organization.

Fulford inherited a Church Society. Ten years old in 1850, the society was divided between the dioceses of Quebec and Montreal. This association of fee-paying members, charged with the administration of finances, was reorganized by Fulford into committees (education, church extension, etcetera) and he encouraged branches in the missions. Much of the society's effectiveness was owing to its principal officers – Thomas Brown Anderson*, the treasurer, and Strachan Bethune*, the legal adviser – and to its élite of lay members who included George MOFFATT and William Badgley*.

In synodical organization Fulford showed great persistence. As early as July 1851, the Montreal Church Society debated the possibility of setting up a synod. To his primary visitation (January 1852), Fulford directed each of his clergy to bring two laymen, although traditionally the visitation was exclusively clerical. Observation of a diocesan convention of the American Protestant Episcopal Church reinforced his preference for strong "lay influence." Two meetings of Montreal clergy and laity in 1853 were held to consider William Ewart Gladstone's bill before the British parliament to "amend the laws relating to the Church in the Colonies." Fulford, ready to set up a synod, was surprised when clerical and even lay opposition showed itself. The laymen were chiefly lawyers, such as Thomas Cushing Aylwin*, who affected to believe that the overseas church, cut off from the state, could not govern itself. Fulford adroitly took advantage of the opposition by obtaining Canadian legislation giving legal recognition to the synod in 1857 and 1858.

A constitution proposed for synod observed three "orders": bishop, clergy, and laity. The lay members would be communicants elected by the various charges; the Church Society, in contrast, was composed of fee-paying members. Another difference was the power the synod would have to enact regulations (canons) binding on its members. (When in 1867 the Church Society was merged with the synod and thus disappeared, all authority was brought under representative and responsible control.) To be legal, canons of the synod would require the concurrence of the three orders. Many of the original opponents of the synod now opposed what they called "the Bishop's veto," since the bishop formed one order. Fulford out-manœuvred this group, and the constitution he wished was adopted in 1859.

Financing of the diocese was a continuing preoccupation. Apart from the episcopal endowment (capital £10,000), there was no regular income. Following 1854, as part of the clergy reserves settlement, the diocese received about £10,500 when the clergy commuted their life interest in the reserves in favour of the church. The Church Society (and after 1867 the synod) began diocese-wide collections to maintain the clergy. Grants were made by the SPG but, in Fulford's view, they would have to be eliminated as soon as possible. To make the charges of the diocese self-supporting, he instead encouraged systematic giving by their people, and favoured local endowments in money or in land. Between 1859 and 1864 the SPG also assisted in the acquisition of glebes, contributing over £1,100.

Within the diocese after 1854 lay some 190,000 acres of undisposed clergy reserve land, roughly estimated at £30,000. Fulford doubted the validity of the Church of England's claims, and also the wisdom of pushing them. Nevertheless, he signed with his fellow bishops a petition to the British government for their retention. In 1855 he commented with detachment on the progress of secularization, deploring Strachan's vigorous protests, although admitting that they were "[all] too true as to facts." Possibly, like his predecessor, Bishop Stewart, Fulford appreciated contemporary Canadian attitudes towards the public endowment of denominational bodies, and was unwilling to expose his church to obloquy.

Early in his episcopate Bishop Fulford considered extensive church building but hope of it was dispelled as he came to grips with diocesan finance. Only after destruction by fire in December 1856 of the old cathedral on Notre-Dame St could anything on a large scale be done. A new site was secured on Sainte-Catherine St and Frank Wills designed a church generally resembling Fredericton Cathedral (itself apparently inspired by Snettisham Church in Norfolk). The new cathedral, opened on Advent Sunday 1859, completely satisfied Fulford's hopes: "There is no building to compare with it on this Continent." A less subjective judgement would describe it as a fine example of Gothic architecture, although of minute proportions.

Francis Fulford was deeply concerned with schooling in all its phases. From his first arrival he took an active part in Bishop's University, from which he secured a number of his clergy. He was vice-president and enjoyed with the bishop of Quebec (the president) visitorial powers. With McGill University his relations were cooler, pos-

sibly because of John Bethune's embroilment in that institution.

Parochial schools and the perennial problem of supplying staff drew him into the earliest and possibly the most serious controversy of his episcopate. In 1851 he was informed that the Colonial Church and School Society proposed to enter his diocese. This organization, formed by the amalgamation of other religious or educational societies, was controlled by a committee in England which posted missionaries (pastors and schoolmasters) and set up schools independently of the diocesan bishops. Fulford's position was the more difficult since one of his principal Montreal clergymen, William Bennett Bond* of St George's Church, became the local agent of the society. At the same time Fulford had to recognize the benefits of trained teachers. A compromise was made. He became the president of the Montreal Committee of the Church and School Society, and hence effectively director of local operations; thus his episcopal authority was recognized. The society maintained schools throughout the diocese, and in Montreal replaced the declining National School [see John Bethune]. In 1853 the society introduced William Henry Hicks*, an experienced teacher, as headmaster of a central, or teacher-training, school in Montreal, which supplied masters and mistresses for the diocesan schools; in 1856 Fulford permitted it to act as the Normal School of McGill University, and it became the chief supplier of Protestant teachers for Quebec.

The society was a factor in Fulford's work among Francophones. It maintained the churches and schools at Iberville and Sabrevois begun by William Plenderleath* Christie. At Saint-Jean a training college was organized to prepare the French speaking teachers and ministers required, chiefly in the missions round Lac Maskinongé and on Île Jésus, for congregations of converted French Canadians and also for groups of Anglo-Canadians, who, through living among French Canadians, had become French speaking. In 1859 a more concerted effort was made with the incorporation of the Church of England Mission to the French-speaking population of British North America, with Fulford as chief patron. He had little in common with the French Canadian Missionary Society, which contained few Anglicans. Not a proselytizer, he was, however, determined his church should minister to both English and French.

In 1860 Bishop Fulford became the first metropolitan of the ecclesiastical province of Canada. Petitions in favour of creation of a province had begun much earlier. In 1861 letters

Fulford

patent declared Montreal to be the metropolitan see with Fulford and his successors enjoying the dignity. To him legal vexations fell early. The bishop of Huron, Benjamin Cronyn*, was disposed in 1861 to question Fulford's authority under the letters patent. Fulford's reply was decisive: "I told him that I was in the Chair & meant to keep it – that I should never stultify myself or insult the Queen [by permitting a question on the validity of the letters patent]." However, more powerful dissolvents were at work. Decisions of the imperial Privy Council on several disputes in 1863–65 involving the metropolitan of South Africa destroyed the authority of letters patent. In Canada legislative action by the provincial synod provided a new, contractual basis of authority, and Fulford's powers as metropolitan were never effectively challenged.

Nonetheless, in 1864 the bishop of Huron again tried, with the counsel of Edward Blake*, his son-in-law, and Adam Crooks*; their legal opinion came close to invalidating the system of provincial synodical administration. Fulford was fortified by a contrary opinion from his chancellor, Strachan Bethune. John Hillyard Cameron*, however, the distinguished Canada West lawyer, insisted that the provincial synod rested on consensus, buttressed by a Canadian statute, as well as on the letters patent, and since Blake and Crooks had admitted the synod might be based on "voluntary association," even Bishop Cronyn was silenced.

In 1863 Fulford consecrated James William Williams* bishop of Quebec on the authority of a royal licence; in 1867, when Alexander Neil Bethune* was made suffragan to Strachan, election by the synod of the diocese of Toronto was deemed sufficient before the consecration. Thus it fell to Bishop Fulford as metropolitan to signal the autonomy of the Canadian church.

Fulford was engaged throughout 1862 in a lengthy and complicated debate with Archdeacon Isaac Hellmuth* of Huron. Eleven years earlier Hellmuth had been one of Fulford's subjects in the Montreal diocese, and the two had differed over a real estate deal involving Hellmuth's father-in-law, Thomas EVANS, who had promised an interest-free loan and land for a church on Sherbrooke St, with Hellmuth to be the first incumbent. In Fulford's view, Hellmuth had irretrievably compromised himself. Late in 1861 Hellmuth was sent on a collecting tour in England for the theological institution Bishop Cronyn proposed in London, Canada West. This plan reflected the quarrel between Bishop Cronyn and Trinity College, Toronto, of which, as metropolitan, Fulford was forced to take cognizance. Deeply deploring it, he was indignant to

learn that in England Hellmuth claimed evangelical clergy to be at a "discount" in the Canadian church and positive Protestant teaching to be lacking in Canadian colleges. Between April and July, Fulford launched three hard-hitting pastoral letters condemning Hellmuth's extravagances. The dispute over the Montreal church was raked out and Hellmuth was bracketed with Father Charles-Paschal-Télesphore Chiniquy* as "a very astute and successful collector of funds" – a cutting comparison considering some of Chiniquy's transactions. Fulford may have won in the polemics, but his victory scarcely contributed to harmony within the ecclesiastical province.

Fulford preached before the triennial convention of the American Protestant Episcopal Church at Philadelphia in October 1865. It was a momentous meeting, being the first of any national representative body after the ending of the Civil War. Fulford's closest contacts had been with the bishops of New England and New York, but he had received clergymen from the Confederacy into his diocese. Fulford wrote: "Mine was a very plain ordinary sermon except that it just did hit the right note . . . & the breach, I trust, is effectively healed." The continuing fellowship with the church in the United States was shown on 6 June 1867 when four American bishops (Maine, Vermont, Illinois, and Virginia) took part in the consecration of the Montreal cathedral.

In 1867, Fulford took an active part in the first world meeting of Anglican prelates at Lambeth, England. As early as 1852, in a letter to Hawkins deploring the defection of friends "to Rome," he wrote, "Nothing will tend more to stop that evil than some real united action of all the Reformed Episcopal Churches, our own, home, colonies, Scotch & American." The appearance in 1860 of *Essays and reviews*, disturbing to conservative theologians, and, beginning in 1863, the protracted scandal in South Africa, favoured his pleas. He returned to the theme in the first provincial synod of 1861 and at the second, in 1865, his views were put in a formal resolution to the archbishop of Canterbury. With Bishop Samuel Wilberforce of Oxford, perhaps the chief English advocate of the conference, Fulford was on intimate terms. At the conference itself, Fulford pressed for a strong declaration of independence of the church, and possibly as recognition was asked to preach on 28 Sept. 1867 before the final meeting in Lambeth Church. (For some unexplained reason Fulford was absent when the historic group photograph of this first Lambeth Conference was taken.)

On this same visit to London Fulford had a

leading part in another event: "Saturday 16 Feb[r]. I attended at St. George's Hanover Square and officiated at the marriage of the Honble [John Alexander Macdonald*] Attorney Gen'l for Upper Canada and president of the Delegates." This is one of his few references to the meeting in London of the Canadian political leaders negotiating the final terms of the British North America Act.

For some years Fulford's health had been failing, but in spite of this his last months of life were especially laborious in activities of the diocese. On 9 Sept. 1868 he died. He had intended to make the findings of the Lambeth Conference the subject of the forthcoming synod's deliberations, determined as he was to head off a discussion of ritualism, already a divisive issue elsewhere in Canada. With ritual as such he had no quarrel, but he disliked ecclesiastical finery. He preached in a plain black gown, often extemporaneously.

Anthony Trollope would not have found Bishop Fulford a sympathetic subject. He had few interests beyond the care of his scattered and struggling flock, but this care included more than spiritual comfort and guidance. He had a keen aesthetic sense and was one of the founders of the Montreal Art Association. He was interested also in adult education, conceived along self-help lines, and thus supported the Montreal Mechanics' Institute and the Church of England Young Men's associations. Within his own communion Fulford stressed the virtues of self-support and self-government, from the level of the individual mission to the ecclesiastical province itself. The characterization of him as "master-builder" was not unwarranted.

JOHN IRWIN COOPER

Francis Fulford, *A letter to the bishops, clergy, and laity of the United Church of England and Ireland in the province of Canada* (Montreal, 1864); *A pastoral letter addressed to the clergy of his diocese* (Montreal, 1851); *A pastoral letter to the clergy of his diocese* (Montreal, 1851).

Anglican Church of Canada, Diocese of Montreal, Synod Archives (Montreal), Correspondence with the secretaries of the SPG, 1850–60 (photocopies); Francis Fulford, miscellaneous notes, memoranda. Anglican Church of Canada, General Synod Archives (Toronto), C. H. Fulford, "Life of Bishop Fulford" (typescript). *The Lambeth conferences of 1867, 1878, and 1888, with the official reports and resolutions, together with the sermons preached at the conferences*, ed. R. T. Davidson (London, 1889). *A memoir of George Jehoshaphat Mountain, D.D., D.C.L., late bishop of Quebec . . . ,* comp. A. W. Mountain (Montreal, 1866). C. R. Bell, *General index of the proceedings of the first eleven synods of the diocese of Montreal . . .* (Montreal, 1872). Notman and Taylor, *Portraits of British Americans*, I, 15–23. *The controversy between the lord bishop of Montreal and the Ven. Archdeacon Hellmuth, with opinions from the press and letters from correspondents . . . ,* ed. A. E. Taylor (London, [Ont.], 1863). J. I. Cooper, "The beginning of teacher training at McGill University," *A century of teacher education, 1857–1957, addresses delivered during the celebration of the centenary of the McGill Normal School (Montreal, 1957); The blessed communion; the origins and history of the diocese of Montreal, 1760–1960* ([Montreal], 1960). T. R. Millman, *Life of Charles James Stewart.* C. F. Pascoe, *Two hundred years of the S.P.G.: an historical account of the Society for the Propagation of the Gospel in Foreign Parts, 1701–1900 . . .* (2v., London, 1901). *The progress of the reformation in England, to which are added two sermons, by Bishop Sanderson . . .* (London, 1841). [J.] F. Taylor, *The last three bishops, appointed by the crown for the Anglican Church of Canada* (Montreal, 1869).

FULLER, THOMAS HORACE, lawyer and politician; b. *c.* 1816 probably in Arichat, Cape Breton Island, son of John Fuller, sheriff of Richmond County, N.S., and Mary Oakley, and brother of Hyacinth Huden Fuller*, Nova Scotia MLC; m. 1 Feb. 1849 at Arichat to Margaret Lanigan, and they were apparently without issue; d. 24 Aug. 1861 at Arichat.

Thomas Horace Fuller studied law probably at Arichat; he became an attorney on 29 Nov. 1847 and barrister on 4 Dec. 1848. On 18 Feb. 1850 he was appointed registrar of probate for Richmond County, an office he held until 1859. He apparently continued to practise law.

Fuller was elected a Liberal member of the Nova Scotia assembly for Richmond County at a by-election on 16 May 1855. The latter election was disputed by Charles Fortnum Harrington, the Conservative candidate, who alleged that a number of his supporters had been intimidated and prevented from voting by partisans of Fuller armed with cudgels, pistols, and revolvers; a select committee of the house, however, declared that Fuller had been duly elected.

Meanwhile Fuller became involved in the arrangements being made for the proposed St Peters Canal to connect the Bras d'Or Lakes in Cape Breton Island with the Atlantic Ocean. In 1853 the provincial legislature passed an act for the construction of the canal, and in 1854 the government set up a commission of three to supervise the work, appointing James W. McLeod as chairman and Isaac LeVesconte* as another member; the premier, William Young*, solicited Fuller's aid in securing, with the assent of the MHA for Arichat Township, Henry Martell, a suitably qualified third commissioner. Fuller himself was considered acceptable by the government, and although Martell desired it, he got the appointment, with the premier later regretting a third party had not been chosen.

Fulton

In July 1854, to counteract rumours that funds for the canal might not be available because of the province's railway building, Fuller and LeVesconte arranged with a Royal Engineer, P. J. S. Barry, to commence work on 1 September. The work was not begun on that date, however, and Barry could not devote all his attention to the task. Fuller continued as a commissioner until 1856 when work, under C. W. Folsom as engineer in 1855 and 1856, was suspended. Costs of the canal, estimated at about £17,750 by Barry in 1853, eventually reached about £75,000 or $300,000 by the time it was finally completed in 1869.

The religious controversies of the 1850s, sparked by such developments as Joseph Howe*'s recruitment efforts for the British forces in the Crimea and the Gourley Shanty Riot, led to a split in the Liberal ranks. On 8 Feb. 1857 the Young government was defeated on a vote of non-confidence when Fuller, a Roman Catholic, and nine other Catholic members and Protestants representing Roman Catholic constituencies crossed the floor of the assembly to vote against the government.

In the election on 12 May 1859, Fuller, an opposition candidate, was defeated. He then petitioned against the election of C. F. Harrington on the ground that the latter, as a judge of probate, was ineligible, but he did not enter into a recognizance in regard to the petition and the matter was dropped. Fuller subsequently returned to his law practice in Arichat where he resided until his death.

CHARLES BRUCE FERGUSSON

Notre-Dame de l'Assomption Church (Arichat, N.S.), records. PANS, MG 2, 733, nos.456, 457, 468, 485; 734, nos.977, 1000; RG 1, 176, p.4; 200, 19 June 1854, 6 May 1856, 20 June 1859; 263, doc.47; 264, docs.60, 100; RG 5, R, 77, 1856; James Laurie's report on the St Peters Canal, 16 July 1858. St Peter's Roman Catholic Church (Halifax), records (mfm. at PANS). N.S., House of Assembly, *Debates and proc.*, 1855–59; *Journal and proc.*, 1854–55, app. 20; 1856–60. *Acadian Recorder*, 7 May 1859, 31 Aug. 1861. *British Colonist* (Halifax), 31 May 1855. *News* (Sydney, N.S.), 20 May 1854. *Novascotian*, 2 Sept. 1861. *Belcher's farmer's almanack*, 1852, 82; 1856, 83; 1858, 96; 1859, 101; 1860, 35, 99.

FULTON, STEPHEN, merchant, shipowner, shipbuilder, and politician; b. in 1810 in Wallace, Cumberland County, N.S., son of William Fulton; m. first Julia Ann Heustis, who died childless in 1844; m. secondly Sarah Elizabeth Black, and they had two sons and five daughters; d. 23 Oct. 1870 of typhus at Wallace.

Stephen Fulton's great-grandfather, Thomas Fulton, emigrated from Ireland and settled in Cumberland in 1769. Nothing is known of Stephen's early life, but his father was apparently a farmer. At age 20 Stephen was converted to Methodism and took an active role in his church for the rest of his life, serving as circuit steward, leader, and trustee. By the 1850s Fulton had become a merchant and shipowner in Wallace at a time of rapid economic development on the north shore. He was not deeply involved in shipping, but in the mid 1850s he built or commissioned four vessels, of which two were soon sold in Newfoundland and one in Liverpool, England. Apart from extensive land holdings, probably inherited from his father, his main business activity was as a merchant and ship-chandler. Eventually he constructed a warehouse, a wharf, and a sawmill. At his death he left his business to his son Allison, whom he had admitted as a partner some years previously, and the bulk of his land to his other son, William.

During the 1840 provincial election Fulton was recruited as a last-minute Tory candidate in Cumberland County when the incumbent, Andrew McKim, died during the campaign. Only 30 when he entered the assembly, Fulton had neither the experience nor the temperament to make a marked impression. It was 1845 before he first was appointed to a standing committee, and not until 1854 did he chair a standing committee, the committee on printing, which controlled lucrative forms of patronage. Although a consistent Tory supporter in the 1840s, he was not a violent partisan. The legislation he introduced as a private member tended to deal with county roads, lighthouses, and pilotage. He was a member of the Sons of Temperance and on one occasion his refusal to drink wine at Government House caused ill will with Lieutenant Governor John Gaspard Le Marchant*.

In 1850 Joseph Howe* proposed that the government build a railway from Halifax through Cumberland to connect with a proposed railway in New Brunswick. Fulton, like other Tories, not only feared the centralization of political power inherent in this government project, but was also unenthusiastic about a rail link to Canada. He recognized, however, that such a railway would tie into a proposed link to Portland, Maine. North shore merchants were usually interested in improved communications with the United States, and there would be an opportunity to compete with New Brunswick for a share of the trade between the United States and Prince Edward Island. Thus, Fulton supported the railway enough to be compelled in 1851 to vote against

Conservative leader James William Johnston*. In the 1851 general election tension developed between Fulton and other Tory candidates when he refused to support their vituperative campaign against the railway and Howe, who was also contesting a Cumberland seat. Two candidates withdrew, however, and Fulton and Howe were elected by acclamation. Fulton's political conversion was a victory for Howe, but in 1852 the assembly set aside the election because of improper election procedures. In the ensuing by-election Fulton reasserted his support for Howe and using a sectarian appeal to his fellow Methodists emerged at the head of the poll.

Despite this success Fulton continued to face opposition in his county, particularly evident in 1853 in a petition signed by several hundred shipyard workers in Wallace protesting against his support of the railway. With Howe's help he managed to obtain funds for several county projects, and in April 1854 he was appointed minister without portfolio in the Liberal administration of James Boyle Uniacke*. This appointment was part of an important shift in alignment in which a second Tory, Lewis Morris Wilkins*, became provincial secretary and a third, Stewart Campbell*, became speaker [see KILLAM]. Fulton's position was not helped when the assembly decided to build the long-awaited railway not through Cumberland but to Hants. In the Joggins area he also faced opposition from the General Mining Association, which objected to the government's attack on its mining monopoly. In 1855 Fulton was defeated by Charles Tupper* and Alexander MacFarlane*, but in 1857 the Liberal government, before being forced to resign, appointed him *custos rotulorum* of Cumberland. He also lost the 1859 election, in part owing to a recent adjustment of the border with New Brunswick, changes in the election law which deprived him of several hundred votes, and an unusual action of the sheriff in disqualifying voters in the election.

This campaign marked the effective close of Fulton's political career. He had served as a justice of the peace since 1842 and was not removed as *custos rotulorum* when the Tories came to power in 1863. Fulton had served as a trustee of the local academy from 1842 to 1858, and from 1862 until his death as a school commissioner in his county. He was a supporter of Tupper's free school legislation of 1864–65. He may also have been the Stephen Fulton who was appointed to conduct the provincial census in 1861.

Fulton later abandoned his preference for trade ties with the United States and spoke in favour of confederation. He declined to run in the 1867 election but seconded the nomination of his old rival, Tupper.

Apart from his involvement in the railway controversy, Fulton had not played a large role in provincial politics and his death in 1870 attracted little notice. He had been a useful member of the assembly, however, and his career illustrates the strong influence of county politics on the tone and conduct of provincial affairs. Furthermore, his independent approach shows why political innovations and clear party divisions were so difficult to introduce in Nova Scotia.

K. G. PRYKE

Cumberland County Court of Probate (Amherst, N.S.), book E (1842–72), ff.359–62, will of Stephen Fulton (mfm. at PANS). PANS, RG 5, R, 62, 1851–52; 88, Cumberland election, 1859. *Morning Chronicle* (Halifax), 1870. *Novascotian*, 1840–60. *Wesleyan* (Halifax), 1840–60. *Some North Cumberlandians at home and abroad, past and present* (North Cumberland Hist. Soc. pub., 2, [Pugwash, N.S.], 1965). Cyrus Black, *Historical record of the posterity of William Black . . .* (Amherst, N.S., 1885). *Ships of the North Shore: Pictou, Colchester and Cumberland counties*, comp. P. R. Blakeley and J. R. Stevens (Maritime Museum of Can., Occasional paper, 11, Halifax, 1963).

G

GAGGIN, JOHN BOLES, public servant; b. probably in 1830 or 1831 in County Cork (Republic of Ireland); d. 27 May 1867 at Wild Horse Creek, Kootenay district, B.C.

A former lieutenant in the Royal Cork Artillery militia and a member of a "most respectable" Anglo-Irish Protestant family, J. Boles Gaggin arrived in Victoria, Vancouver Island, on 10 April 1859. In June he was appointed chief constable at Yale, B.C., and on 4 Oct. 1859 magistrate and assistant gold commissioner at Port Douglas, the southern terminus of the Harrison-Lillooet trail to the gold mines. Here he also served as justice of the peace, county court judge, deputy collector of customs, and sub-commissioner of lands and works. Governor James Douglas* praised him for his "commendable promptness" in seeing that the trail was kept open, and the people of his district declared themselves "perfectly satisfied" with his decisions as a magistrate.

"A favourite with all classes on the mainland," according to his obituary, Gaggin was apparently too open-hearted and generous for his own good. H. P. P. Crease* once admonished him: "Try and keep out of good companie, you old 'father of the fatherless.'" Dr W. B. Cheadle*'s diary records the kindness shown to travellers by this "regular jolly Irishman from Cork," but adds that "'The Judge' turned out a 'whale for drink.'" Douglas also considered him "zealous and well disposed, but deficient in judgment," and other officials found him far from reliable.

On 23 Nov. 1863 Douglas suspended Gaggin on a charge of tampering with his accounts, and sent a fellow magistrate, Philip H. Nind, to investigate him. On 12 December Nind exonerated Gaggin completely. Nevertheless the governor did not lift the suspension until 3 March 1864, and even then he declared it "in the interest of the public service" to remove Gaggin from Port Douglas to temporary duty at Lillooet. Touched to the quick by this reflection on "an honorable name transmitted to me untarnished through generations" Gaggin appealed on 14 March 1864 to the Colonial Office, but the officials there left the problem to Douglas' successor as governor, Frederick SEYMOUR. Despite Gaggin's "faults as a public officer," Seymour felt he had been "treated without sufficient consideration for his character," and offered to restore him to his former appointment. But Gaggin now asked for reasons of health to be left at Quesnelle Mouth (Quesnel) where Seymour had placed him on 14 June. Soon the accounts there were "in great confusion," and Gaggin was ordered back to Port Douglas where, because the new road through the Fraser canyon had by this time almost superseded the old Harrison-Lillooet trail, his duties were much lighter than before.

In January 1866 the magistracy at Port Douglas was abolished. After some misgiving on the part of the acting colonial secretary, Gaggin was appointed magistrate for Kootenay but placed under the direct supervision of Peter O'Reilly, who had charge of the entire Columbia and Kootenay district. On 8 June 1866 Gaggin arrived at Wild Horse Creek, where he found "first rate fishing and shooting" and few official duties. O'Reilly reported privately that he "found Gaggin remarkably well & as kind as ever" and that Gaggin had "knocked off the drink *in toto*, excepting Larger beer."

In November 1866 the colonies of British Columbia and Vancouver Island were united, and in the necessary reduction of the civil list Gaggin was dismissed. He had been ill for some time before he died at Wild Horse Creek on 27 May 1867, it was thought from the shock of hearing that the Kootenay district constable had been murdered that same day. The two lie buried side by side in the cemetery at Wild Horse Creek.

DOROTHY BLAKEY SMITH

PABC, Henry Maynard Ball, Journal, 1865; B.C., Colonial Secretary, Correspondence outward, 1859–67 (letterbook copies); A. T. Bushby, Diary, 1874; Colonial correspondence, W. G. Cox correspondence; J. B. Gaggin correspondence; P. H. Nind correspondence; Peter O'Reilly correspondence; Crease coll., Henry Pering Pellew Crease, Correspondence inward, 1862–63; Private miscellaneous letters, 1864–65; O'Reilly coll., Peter O'Reilly diaries, 1859–67. J. B. Gaggin's commission as ensign in the City of Cork Regiment of Militia of Artillery, 20 Jan. 1855, and as lieutenant in the Royal City of Cork Regiment of Militia of Artillery, 1 Aug. 1855; and testimonials signed by the bishop of Killaloe and Ireland, 1 Jan. 1859, Lord Bandon, 15 Nov. 1858, and Lieutenant-Colonel A. J. Wood, 2 Dec. 1858, are also at PABC. PRO, CO 60/17, James Douglas, "Confidential report upon the character and qualifications of the principal officers of this government," enclosure in Douglas to Duke of Newcastle, 18 Feb. 1863; CO 60/17–18, dispatch no.18, James Douglas to Duke of Newcastle, 8 April 1864; CO 60/19, dispatch no.33, Frederick Seymour to Edward Cardwell, 5 Sept. 1864 (mfm. at PABC).

B.C., *Blue book*, 1859–67. W. B. Cheadle, *Cheadle's journal of trip across Canada, 1862–1863*, ed. A. G. Doughty and Gustave Lanctot (Ottawa, 1931; repr. Edmonton, 1971). *Daily British Colonist and Victoria Chronicle*, 12 April 1859; 3, 15 Aug. 1860; 15 April, 4 July 1867. *Hart's army list*, 1856. *Cranbrook Courier* (Cranbrook, B.C.), 4 Dec. 1952. M. A. Ormsby, "Some Irish figures in colonial days," *BCHQ*, XIV (1950), 63.

GALE, SAMUEL, lawyer and judge; b. 1783 at St Augustine (Florida), son of Samuel Gale, assistant paymaster of English forces in North America, and a Miss Wells, originally from Brattleboro, Vt; d. 15 April 1865 at Montreal, Canada East.

Samuel Gale came to Canada with his parents, ardent loyalists who left the United States after the American revolution. He received his early education at Quebec, where his father was secretary to Governor Robert Prescott*. He studied law in Montreal and was called to the bar on 8 March 1807.

An opponent of Governor Sir George Prevost*, he was critical of the latter's actions during the War of 1812, and made veiled attacks on him in letters published in the *Montreal Herald* and later put together in a pamphlet entitled *Nerva, or* a collection of papers published in the "Montreal Herald" (1814). At the point when James Stuart* and the members representing the French Canadian majority were attacking the English judges, and particularly Judge Jonathan Sewell*, whose dismissal they sought, Nerva reminded its readers of recent events in Ireland in such a way that they could transpose them to Lower Canada. Blaming Prevost mistakenly for yielding to "factious" elements, Gale asked the authorities to take a firmer stance.

He served as lawyer for Lord Selkirk [Douglas*], founder of the Red River colony, when the latter had difficulties with the North West Company, and in 1815 he went west to defend his client's interests. In 1817 he published Notices on the claims of the Hudson's Bay Company and the conduct of its adversaries (Montreal).

In the spring of 1828 Gale went to London and in May and June gave testimony on three occasions before the committee of the House of Commons inquiring into the government of Canada. He represented in particular the inhabitants of the Eastern Townships, who claimed their interests were harmed because French Canadians were in a majority in the House of Assembly. On their behalf he called for better highways and asked that the courts apply English law in the region, particularly in land tenure. He also requested that the Eastern Townships be better represented in the assembly and that English immigration to them be encouraged. Finally, he declared himself in favour of the union of Upper and Lower Canada.

On 23 Aug. 1834 Samuel Gale was appointed by Lord Aylmer [Whitworth-Aylmer*] a judge of the Court of King's Bench at Montreal, to replace Norman Fitzgerald Uniacke*, who had resigned. In 1835 he sat temporarily at Trois-Rivières. The members of the Patriote party in the assembly protested against the appointment of the man who had testified for the bureaucrat party before the House of Commons committee in 1828, and the colonial secretary, Spring-Rice, could not refrain from writing to the governor: "At all times, but more particularly at a moment like the present, I feel it of the highest importance that no persons who can be considered as strong political partizans should be placed on the Bench of Lower Canada. . . . When I advert to the line adopted by Mr Gale before the Committee of 1828, and his connection with the measures of those times, I very much fear that he will be looked upon with distrust by a very considerable portion of the community in Canada. . . . Under those circumstances . . . I am not disposed, as at

present advised, to recommend the confirmation of his appointment." Lord Aylmer persisted, and Gale remained a judge despite fresh protests by the members of the assembly. In 1837, in a detailed judgement, Gale maintained the right of the crown to establish martial law and suspend habeas corpus.

As a lawyer and judge, Gale enjoyed the respect and admiration of his colleagues even if he had adversaries. He retired on 25 April 1848 because of poor health, and died at Montreal on 15 April 1865.

J.-C. BONENFANT

[Samuel Gale], Nerva, or a collection of papers published in the "Montreal Herald" (Montreal, 1814); Notices on the claims of the Hudson's Bay Company and the conduct of its adversaries . . . (Montreal, 1817); a second edition was published under the title: Notices on the claims of the Hudson's Bay Company: to which is added a copy of their royal charter (London, 1819). Bas-Canada, chambre d'Assemblée, Journaux, 1835–36, app.E. Montreal Gazette, 17 April 1865. P.-G. Roy, Les juges de la prov. de Québec, 233.

GARNEAU, FRANÇOIS-XAVIER, notary, poet, and historian; b. 15 June 1809 at Quebec, son of François-Xavier Garneau and Gertrude Amiot-Villeneuve; m. on 25 Aug. 1835, at Quebec, Marie-Esther Bilodeau, and they had ten children; d. during the night of 2–3 Feb. 1866 in his native town.

François-Xavier Garneau's ancestor, Louis Garnault, came originally from Poitou, landed at Quebec around 1659, and settled at L'Ange-Gardien, on the Beaupré shore. His descendants made their home at Saint-Augustin, west of Quebec, but the historian's father went to live in the faubourg Saint-Jean at Quebec (now the parish of Saint-Jean-Baptiste). At the beginning of the 19th century Quebec had 8,000 inhabitants, the majority of whom were French speaking. It was the seat of the government of Lower Canada and of both Catholic and Anglican dioceses. The English speaking group (English, Scottish, Irish), who held positions in the government, the garrison, and the world of trade and industry, constituted an important segment of the population of this town, where architecture, habits, and customs all served as reminders that Quebec had been the capital of New France.

François-Xavier's father, with neither wealth nor a profession, met the needs of his growing family by being in turn a saddler, a carter, the captain of a merchant schooner, and finally an innkeeper. There were three children born after François-Xavier: David, who became a busi-

Garneau

nessman at Quebec, Honoré, who enlisted in the American army at the time of the war against Mexico, and Marie-Émélie, who married Charles Routier of Quebec.

Young Garneau, whose lively mind apparently attracted attention quite early, was put in the local school, which was run by an aged teacher known as "le bonhomme Parent." Tradition has it that he was a serious and brilliant pupil. One of the earliest memories Garneau recounted concerns his fondness for history. In his *Voyage en Angleterre et en France* . . . , published in 1855, he recalled that his grandfather Jacques Garneau of Saint-Augustin liked telling him the story of the naval battle he had witnessed in 1760 between the *Atalante*, commanded by Jean Vauquelin*, and two English frigates.

In 1821, when Garneau was 12 years old, he had absorbed all the knowledge that "le bonhomme Parent" could offer. That year he entered a school which had been opened in the basement of the chapel of the Congrégation des Hommes de la Haute Ville through the efforts of Joseph-François Perrault*. Garneau spent two years here in what was called a "mutual" school, in which teaching was conducted according to the method of English educator Joseph Lancaster, the most advanced pupils being used as instructors. Garneau became an instructor, and his diligence brought him to Perrault's attention. When he left the school, Garneau wanted to enter the Séminaire de Québec, the only college in the district where boys could get a normal classical education. His parents lacked the means to provide for their child's education and the seminary was reluctant to assist the young pupil who felt no attraction to holy orders. Garneau had therefore to abandon the hope of studying humanities. Perrault, who was clerk of the Court of King's Bench and his patron, offered him a job in his office. For two years the young man benefited from the experience and culture of the clerk, in whose house he sometimes spent his evenings. Perrault, an old man who had read and travelled widely and who belonged to a family active in the army and administration of New France, gave Garneau and his clerks English, Latin, and history lessons, and placed his library at their disposal.

In 1825 Garneau chose the profession of notary. He was introduced to Archibald CAMPBELL, a notary in charge of the most respected office in the town of Quebec. Young Québecois, such as Pierre Petitclair*, a poet and dramatist, and Antoine-Sébastien Falardeau*, the future painter, also served their apprenticeship there. On 22 June Campbell and Garneau signed the indentures covering the latter's legal training: the

notary undertook to teach the practices of his profession and to pay the young clerk £13 a year for the next five years. Garneau devoted himself to his work and took advantage of his leisure to delve into his master's library, which contained a good collection of English, Latin, and French classical works. In this way he continued to teach himself Latin, which he had begun to study under Perrault, and he eventually was able to read Horace at sight. He also learned Italian on his own, and improved his English by reading Byron, Milton, and Shakespeare.

At the end of August 1828 Garneau set off on a journey with an Englishman who had asked Campbell to recommend a companion whose expenses he would pay. The travellers went to Saint John, New Brunswick, proceeded to Boston by boat, then went to New York. Garneau spent some 20 days visiting the great American city. From New York they went via Albany and Rochester to Buffalo, then travelled overland to Niagara Falls. They finally returned to Quebec by way of Queenston, York (Toronto), and Kingston. Later, in his *Voyage*, Garneau recalled this long trip, which allowed him to see the United States and Upper Canada for himself.

After five years of legal training, Garneau took his examination on 23 June 1830 and received his commission as a notary; however, he took a year of further training. During this period Garneau began to try his hand at poetry: on 31 Aug. 1831, displaying a certain indulgence, *Le Canadien* of Quebec published a topical poem entitled "Dithyrambe: Sur la mission de Mr Viger, envoyé des Canadiens en Angleterre."

By his own testimony, Garneau had long been dreaming of visiting the old world, the "cradle of genius and civilization." On 20 June 1831, with his modest savings in his pocket, he sailed for London. He reached his destination a month later, and devoted most of his time to visiting and studying the English capital. On 26 July he set out for France, anxious to know the country of his ancestors. Two days later he arrived in Paris, in the midst of the celebrations marking the anniversary of the July revolution: the young man was delighted to see France resolutely committed to liberalism. He immediately set out to explore the *Ville lumière*; he spent several evenings at the theatre, and during the day visited museums and libraries. He also went to see Isidore-Frédéric-Thomas Lebrun, the scholar.

On 9 Aug. 1831 Garneau returned to London. Montreal MHA Denis-Benjamin VIGER, who had been sent by the House of Assembly to make numerous representations to the Colonial Office, including a request that Attorney General James

Stuart* be dismissed, suggested that Garneau become his secretary. Garneau had expected to return home in the autumn but changed his plans and accepted the offer. Thus for a year he copied reports for Viger. At the same time he learned something about Canadian and British policy. His correspondence shows he was highly critical of the colonial régime and the institutions introduced into Lower Canada by Great Britain. While Viger lodged at the luxurious London Coffee House, Garneau lived in a boarding house on Cecil Street, near Charing Cross, where another gifted young MHA, Joseph-Isidore Bédard*, son of Pierre-Stanislas Bédard*, also lived. The delegate from the Lower Canadian assembly entertained a great deal, which gave the young secretary an opportunity to meet and hear some of the great figures of Canadian and British politics, such as William Lyon MACKENZIE, the Upper Canadian Reformer, John Arthur Roebuck*, a member of the British parliament and an ally of French Canadians, and John MacGregor*, a publicist and statistician who was to gain public attention by his writings about Canada. Garneau also met the Irish patriot Daniel O'Connell and was impressed by his gifts as a speaker. During his free time the young secretary attended concerts, went to the theatre, and was an interested observer of popular meetings and parliamentary debates during the period of electoral reform in 1832.

Since 1830 many refugees had flocked to London. Garneau had occasion to meet the Poles who had chosen exile after the tragic dénouement of the Warsaw insurrection in 1831. He struck up a friendship with Dr Krystyn Lach-Szyrma, at whose house he met several Polish refugees. Many liberal-minded members of the House of Commons were well disposed towards the Polish cause, and supported the principles of the new Literary Society of the Friends of Poland, of which the poet Thomas Campbell was president. Elected to the society on 15 Aug. 1832, Garneau presented a specially composed poem, "La liberté prophétisant sur l'avenir de la Pologne," in which he recounted the history of a country divided and sorely tried by the bloody events of the years 1830 and 1831.

At the end of the summer of 1832 Garneau had the opportunity to undertake a second trip to Paris, this time with Viger and MacGregor. The trip, which deepened his knowledge of France, lasted from 15 September to 3 October. In Paris Garneau again saw Lebrun, who was working on a book on Canada: thus began an exchange of views which went on for some years. He also met Amable Berthelot*, a lawyer and scholar from Quebec who later became his benefactor. The winter of 1832–33 was for Garneau as studious as the preceding one. Compatriots visiting London brought news of the bloody riot at Montreal during the elections of May 1832. At the end of the winter Garneau decided to return home. His father had died on 7 Aug. 1831, and his mother was in poor health.

After his return to Quebec on 30 June 1833, Garneau seems to have been hesitant about his future. Although this period of his life is less well known, it is clear Garneau was writing poetry. From 19 July to 18 October Le Canadien published at least six of his poems, including "Souvenir d'un Polonais," which seems to be a poem of recollections addressed to his friend Lach-Szyrma, "Le Canadien en France," an elegy composed in Europe, and "La Coupe." Only the last piece, composed in July 1830, is dated. Garneau thought of becoming a journalist, a difficult means of earning a livelihood at the time. On 7 Dec. 1833 the first number of the paper L'Abeille canadienne, founded and edited by Garneau, and printed by Jean-Baptiste Fréchette, was published at Quebec. The paper proposed to encourage "the spread of knowledge and a liking for reading." It was an unpretentious weekly, and ceased publication two months later, on 8 Feb. 1834, without attaining the longevity of papers such as the Penny Magazine of London, or the Magasin pittoresque of Paris, which Garneau had wanted to imitate in order to further popular education.

In February 1834 Garneau, with no marked enthusiasm, began to work as a notary in the office of Louis-Théodore BESSERER, with whom he had gone into partnership in the summer of 1833. In the whole of 1834 he wrote only two poems, "Le Premier Jour de l'an, 1834," and "Chanson Québec," which Le Canadien, as always, loyally published. Politics already seemed to be preoccupying his leisure. He followed closely the conflict, then reaching its peak, between the House of Assembly, dominated by French Canadians, and the Legislative Council and the executive. Elzéar Bédard*, Augustin-Norbert MORIN, and Louis-Joseph Papineau* had taken the lead by presenting the 92 Resolutions in the assembly. Garneau assisted Étienne Parent*, the guiding spirit of the revived Le Canadien, which vehemently defended French Canadian nationality. In March 1834 Garneau became secretary of the constitutional committee, and thus laid himself open to attack by the Quebec Gazette, a resolute supporter of the status quo.

In May 1836, less than a year after his marriage, Garneau parted company with Besserer, and opened his own office on the Côte de la Montagne; but he does not seem to have been happy in the performance of his duties. In 1837 he became cashier in the Bank of British North America, and two years later an employee of the Quebec Bank. He continued to practise as a notary on occasion, and drafted a dozen acts a year between 1837 and 1842.

Garneau's political activity in the years 1837 to 1840 is little known. Although his contemporaries did not comment on it and his correspondence for this period has not been discovered, his poems and his interpretation of events in *Histoire du Canada depuis sa découverte jusqu'à nos jours* (published in 1845) enable us to affirm that on the whole he favoured Papineau's ideas.

It is during 1837 that the first clear signs of Garneau's vocation as an historian can be detected. In *Le Canadien* of 15 February he published an historical piece on the combats and battles "waged in Canada and elsewhere in which Canadiens have taken part." His first writing of this kind, it emerged from the same patriotic inspiration as his poems. True, in 1832 in London, he had copied a French officer's diary of the siege of Quebec at his employer's request, and Viger had published this document in 1836, but we cannot argue from this fact that Garneau had decided to write the history of his country during his stay in England. In 1837 history was of interest to an increasingly wide public which, like Garneau himself, wanted to understand the present and find reasons for hope in a past which they believed to be glorious, but which had been recounted by Anglo-Saxons such as Robert Christie*, William Smith*, and John MacGregor with their compatriots in mind. Moreover, the works published in French could not satisfy the new generation of Patriotes. In 1833 Lebrun had published in France a *Tableau statistique et politique des deux Canadas*, which despite its abundant detail was lacking in subtlety of perception. Since 1819 Michel Bibaud* had been writing well-documented historical articles, but these supported the *status quo*, and therefore alienated some readers. Jacques Viger*, Amable Berthelot, and Jacques Labrie* were reasonably competent antiquaries with limited historical vision. Most recently, between 1831 and 1836 Joseph-François Perrault had published an *Abrégé de l'histoire du Canada* in five volumes which was a worthwhile attempt at popularization but dull and confused.

Although Garneau took a serious interest in history from 1837 on, it was the union of the Canadas, a measure endangering the survival of the French Canadian nation, that unquestionably confirmed his vocation as an historian and prompted his determination to write a history of Canada. By so doing, Garneau sought to revive the courage of fellow citizens who experienced misgivings and doubts; he proposed to arouse their will to live, and he wanted to combat the British contempt for the "Canadiens." On 24 Jan. 1840 he signed and circulated a resolution against the Act of Union, which was adopted at a protest meeting attended by Étienne Parent, John Neilson*, and Louis-Édouard Glackmeyer*. Nevertheless the Act of Union was passed, and its application roused indignation. On 22 Feb. 1841, in a long article in *Le Canadien*, Garneau again attacked the imperial enactment, and demanded the maintenance of the French language, which was no longer constitutionally guaranteed.

Garneau, however, continued to try to develop his compatriots' liking for literature. With Louis-David Roy*, he launched a semi-literary, semi-scientific weekly, *L'Institut, ou Journal des étudians*, first published on 7 March 1841. In the autumn of 1840 a resourceful Frenchman, Nicolas-Marie-Alexandre VATTEMARE, had come to Canada as the "guest" of Denis-Benjamin Viger, bringing with him a book exchange plan that had the warm support of the civil and religious authorities and of prominent citizens. At Quebec, *Le Canadien*, Napoléon Aubin*'s *Le Fantasque*, and *L'Institut, ou Journal des étudians* welcomed his proposal enthusiastically. On 13 March 1841 Garneau's paper reported the formation of a general committee, chaired by John Neilson, whose object was to found an institute as inspired by Vattemare, a sort of federation of the cultural societies in the town of Quebec, to foster wider diffusion of knowledge and bring "classes" and "races" closer together. But Vattemare's plan was short-lived. It clashed with the interests of the societies – the Literary and Historical Society of Quebec for example – who were jealous of their autonomy. Furthermore, the project came at a bad political juncture (the union of the Canadas had been proclaimed on 10 Feb. 1841), and it remained only a plan. Yet the foundation in 1847 of the Institut Canadien of Quebec, of which Garneau became a mainstay, can be partly explained by the enthusiasm aroused by Vattemare's projects. After the latter left Canada the two men kept up a correspondence for a long time.

In September 1842, through the good offices of his friend Parent, Garneau obtained the post of French translator to the Legislative Assembly. This position left him free time for reading, and gave him easy access to the valuable library assembled by Georges-Barthélemi FARIBAULT. As a member of the Literary and Historical Society of Quebec, he could also draw upon the rich collection of this association, which had been founded in 1824. In June 1843 Garneau sent *Le Canadien* an article on the voyages of Jacques Cartier*, a prelude to his full-scale historical work. Although he was absorbed by his *Histoire du Canada*, which had become the great passion of his life, Garneau nevertheless kept in close contact with political and national life. In 1842 he helped found the Société Saint-Jean-Baptiste at Quebec [*see* Pierre-Martial BARDY]. He was opposed to the autocratic policy of Governor General Lord Sydenham [Thomson*], but was later well disposed towards Sir Charles Bagot*, who looked favourably upon the French population; it was Garneau who drafted the appropriate address on Bagot's departure in March 1843. In January 1844 Garneau and others petitioned for the return of the political exiles who had left the country in 1837. That year, with the help of Louis-Édouard Glackmeyer, he obtained the post of clerk of the city of Quebec, which meant an increased salary but less leisure time, and riveted him to a task which he scarcely found appealing. From 1835 to 1845 Garneau published 14 poems, including "Au Canada," "À lord Durham," "L'Hiver," "Le Dernier Huron," "Les Exilés," and "Le Vieux Chêne." His best pieces, "Le Dernier Huron" and "Le Vieux Chêne," are imbued with patriotic feeling, and point to his *Histoire du Canada*.

In August 1845 the first volume of Garneau's *Histoire* was published at Quebec. The work is preceded by a "Discours préliminaire," in which the author recalls the development of historical criticism in the west since the Renaissance and outlines his ideas concerning the philosophy of history; it is divided into five books and 16 chapters; it begins with two introductory chapters on the discoveries and explorations of the late 16th century. The volume describes events in New France from its beginnings until 1701, when peace was concluded with the Indian tribes. The best pages are those dealing with the work of Samuel de Champlain*, Bishop François de Laval*, the wars between Hurons and Iroquois, the new machinery of government in 1663, and the state of the English colonies in 1690; in analysing these colonies he offers an interesting parallel with New France, one that has become famous.

The book seems to have been well received at first. But soon after its publication, the papers published letters and reviews which judged the *Histoire du Canada* severely. Anonymous authors, frequently clergymen, reproached Garneau for his defence of freedom of conscience, his regrets that French authorities had excluded the Huguenots from Canada, and especially his criticisms of Bishop Laval's authoritarianism. Doubts were frequently cast on the religious convictions and the nationalism of the writer, who was called a "philosopher," a "Protestant," and an "ungodly" man. Garneau seems to have been deeply mortified by this display of hostility.

At the time the first volume of the *Histoire du Canada* was published, Garneau went to Albany, where the archives of New York State were located, to consult their collections of copies of official documents held in the French national archives. Here he again met his friend Edmund Bailey O'Callaghan*, a Patriote who had taken refuge in the United States in 1837 and become the state archivist. This new source of documentation provided fuller material for the second volume of the *Histoire du Canada*, which was published in April 1846. The narrative covers the period from 1683 to 1775. Garneau first recalls the fate of Louisiana and that of Acadia, then discusses trade from 1608 to 1744, before reconstructing in detail the war of the Conquest. The brilliant French victories are recounted with spirit, France's neglect of her colony is denounced, François Bigot* and his clique are held up to shame. The last book of the second volume discusses the early years of the British régime, beginning with the military era which Garneau regarded as odious, and ending with the Quebec Act, or more precisely with the first difficulties with the rebellious American colonies. This second volume, which seldom deals with ecclesiastical questions, does not seem to have caused the impassioned controversies that followed publication of the first. And from Paris Garneau received unexpected support. In 1847 Lebrun published in the *Nouvelle Revue encyclopédique* a laudatory review of the *Histoire du Canada*, which several Quebec papers, including *Le Canadien*, hastened to reprint.

In 1846 Garneau went to Montreal to examine the four volumes of documents and reports on New France that Louis-Joseph Papineau had had copied in Paris at the request of the government of United Canada. However, the heavy work he undertook affected his health. At the beginning of 1847 he had an epileptic seizure (he had suffered from epilepsy since 1843), complicated by attacks of typhoid and erysipelas, which prevented him from continuing his work at the rate he had anticipated.

In 1848, 19 poems Garneau had written between 1832 and 1841 were published in James

Garneau

Huston*'s *Le répertoire national, ou recueil de littérature canadienne*. His growing reputation as an historian heightened his renown as a poet. The year 1848 was printed as the publication date of the third volume of the *Histoire du Canada*, relating events from 1775 to 1792, but the work did not in fact come out until March 1849. Local critics, according to Garneau, seemed to have nothing to say. Garneau's reputation as an historian now appeared solidly established. His proclamation in the third volume that religion and nationality were united had disarmed the clerical critics, as Garneau stressed in May 1850 in a letter to O'Callaghan. As a token of goodwill the archbishop of Quebec, Joseph Signay*, opened the episcopal archives to him. In May 1849 the legislature granted Garneau $1,000 for a new edition of the *Histoire du Canada*. The author already had in mind considerable improvements in both content and style. Severe and exacting, Garneau sought perfection, correcting, shaping, and completing his text.

Distinguished travellers passing through Quebec paid calls upon the historian. Two Frenchmen, Xavier Marmier who came in 1849 and Jean-Jacques Ampère in 1851, described their pleasant memories of time spent in the company of a "cicerone" as learned as he was patriotic. François-Edmé Rameau* de Saint-Père, who also met Garneau, continued an interesting correspondence with him. The most spectacular visit was that of Paul-Henry de Belvèze*, the commander of *La Capricieuse*, which called at Quebec in 1855; the French officer, to whom Garneau had presented a copy of the *Histoire du Canada*, asked that the author be introduced to him, and saluted him as "the national historian of Canada."

The narrative of the first edition of the *Histoire du Canada* (totalling more than 1,600 pages) had scarcely gone beyond the year 1792. Resuming his work, Garneau proceeded with an account of historical events up to 1840, and also obtained more sources for the purpose of the second edition. He was able to draw on several useful sources: to the documents in the archdiocesan archives at Quebec, and those at Albany, was now added the official correspondence of the English governors of Canada up to the period of Lord Dalhousie [Ramsay*], which was placed at his disposal by the governor Lord Elgin [Bruce] as a sign of his esteem. In the autumn of 1852 the second edition of the *Histoire du Canada* was published in three volumes. Garneau had made countless stylistic emendations and expanded the documentation of this work. He had also provided an account of events from 1792 to 1840,

stressing the constitutional struggles. This addition was published in instalments intended as a supplement for the subscribers to the first edition. After the description of the reign "of terror" of Sir James Henry Craig* and of the War of 1812, Garneau gave particular attention to the struggle between the Patriote leaders and the English oligarchy surrounding the governors. England's policy, after raising a few hopes, proved hostile to the Canadian Patriotes. The disturbances of 1837 and 1838 broke out and were harshly put down. The union of the two Canadas proved to be a catastrophe for French Canada, according to Garneau. In his general conclusion he urged French Canadians to remain true to themselves by refraining from political and social ventures.

The *Histoire du Canada* continued to meet with success and attracted wider critical attention. Théodore Pavie, a literary critic from Anjou who had travelled in North America in his youth, gave a favourable account in the 15 July 1853 number of the celebrated *Revue des deux mondes* of Paris. In *Le Correspondant* (Paris) of 25 Dec. 1853 another Frenchman, Louis-Ignace Moreau, analysed the work at length and censured it in terms reminiscent of the ecclesiastical criticisms stimulated by the publication of the first volume of the first edition. In Boston, Orestes Augustus Brownson, who was then a liberal Catholic, praised the *Histoire du Canada* eloquently in the October 1853 issue of *Brownson's Quarterly Review*.

Yielding, as he said, to the persuasion of friends, Garneau published his recollections of travel in England and France in *Le Journal de Québec*, from 18 Nov. 1854 to 29 May 1855. The text started as travel notes, then took the form of a diary, which was expanded through his later readings. In the spring of 1855 he brought his material together in a volume entitled *Voyage en Angleterre et en France dans les années 1831, 1832 et 1833*, which was published by Augustin Côté*. Once the volume was in print, Garneau distributed ten copies to his friends, and immediately received crushing comments; he was criticized for lapses in style and his republican ideas were deplored; certain passages directed against former Patriote leaders, who supported the government under the union, such as Augustin-Norbert Morin (who however was not named), provoked reservations and displeasure. Hesitant and embittered, Garneau asked his publisher to destroy the copies not yet distributed, and only a few volumes were saved. The *Voyage* remains a document of prime importance for understanding Garneau's formative years.

In 1855, at the time his *Voyage* was printed,

Garneau was severely taken to task by the son of historian Michel Bibaud, François-Marie-Uncas-Maximilien Bibaud*. In a bitter pamphlet entitled *Revue critique de l' "Histoire du Canada" de M. Garneau*, Bibaud took pleasure in pointing out the incorrect phrasing as well as the errors of date and the contradictions scattered throughout the work of this self-taught man. Bibaud, who spoke of "charlatanism in history," was displeased with the book's general ideology, which was the direct opposite of the one animating the *Histoire du Canada, et des Canadiens, sous la domination anglaise* (Montréal, 1844) by his father, which was hostile to the Patriotes. Bibaud's exaggerated statements came too late, however, to undermine seriously Garneau's high reputation.

On the occasion of a competition launched by the editor and printer Côté in 1856, Garneau wrote an *Abrégé de l'histoire du Canada depuis sa découverte jusqu'à 1840, à l'usage des maisons d'éducation*. It was a dull little book, in the form of questions and answers, from which the historian took care to eliminate anything that might offend the clergy. Fortified by the *imprimatur* of the archbishop of Quebec, the manual enjoyed considerable success. In his biography of Garneau, Pierre-Joseph-Olivier Chauveau* recalls that by 1882 the book had sold 30,000 copies. Garneau wrote it without enthusiasm, as if it were a lengthy punishment inflicted on a schoolboy, and without paying much attention to Chauveau's suggestions that he should make it more attractive and better suited to young readers.

Meanwhile Garneau was preparing a third edition of *Histoire du Canada* with the help of his son Alfred*. Since the publication of the second edition the historian had gained access to yet more primary sources. Georges-Barthélemi Faribault, who had succeeded in interesting the Canadian government in keeping archives, had had numerous documents copied, and these were available to researchers from the autumn of 1853. In addition, Abbé Jean-Baptiste-Antoine FERLAND had brought back from France a large number of documents to which Garneau had partial access. He also used the fifth and sixth volumes of the *History of the late province of Lower Canada . . .* by Robert Christie, which had been written in a very different spirit from his own. Garneau the perfectionist re-examined his entire *Histoire du Canada* for the new edition: not a page escaped correction, a substantial number of additions and changes were made, the narrative was filled out by new documents, and the style was carefully revised and polished. In 1859 the third edition, the last in Garneau's lifetime, was published. It ensured him the title of "national historian." Tirelessly he set to work on a fourth edition, which his son Alfred was to bring to completion in 1882 and 1883. But his health was daily becoming more delicate. Garneau had been a member of the Council of Public Instruction since its formation in 1859, but found himself obliged to give up his office in May 1862. In 1864 illness forced him to resign as clerk of Quebec.

The *Histoire du Canada* had continued to be well received. French historian Henri Martin quoted Garneau approvingly. The Institut Canadien of Quebec made him its honorary president. A Briton who had settled in Canada, Andrew BELL, translated the *Histoire*, at the same time adapting it somewhat freely for the Anglo-Saxon public. The historian protested vigorously against the undertaking, which in his opinion distorted his work. Despite these reservations, Bell's translation, published in 1860, was a definite success, and was re-issued in 1862. In our day the English speaking public still knows Garneau's work through Bell's translation.

There are no documents to provide the means for sketching a portrait of Garneau. He was reserved in nature and lived a quiet life. Those close to him have left us little to go on. His correspondence was voluminous, according to Abbé Henri-Raymond Casgrain* and Chauveau, but only some hundred letters remain. What is known about Garneau comes principally from three of his contemporaries, notary Louis-Michel Darveau*, Chauveau, and Casgrain, whose descriptions written after his death show contradictions and also some idealization. Below medium height, and with a high forehead, Garneau had a meditative appearance. Timid, seemingly even gentle and conciliatory, he was yet firm and "almost obdurate" in certain matters. He showed a nervous hesitation, an embarrassment probably linked to the progress of the disease he had suffered from since 1843. He was most at ease in small, intimate gatherings. His diligence in work was legendary. A self-taught man in a world where the influential almost all received a classical education, Garneau seemed sensitive to the point of touchiness. This characteristic helps explain his concern to revise his work constantly, and his intractability in the defence of his ideas.

Those ideas are known primarily through his *Voyage* and his *Histoire du Canada*, though his poems and his correspondence are valuable. In Europe he admired the France of 1830 and even more England, which was evolving towards increasing political liberty. Did he occasionally feel drawn to republican institutions? Certain pages

Garneau

on the United States and France seem to suggest that he did. In the religious sphere he supported the distinction between the spiritual and political in a period when ultramontanism was spreading: hence the accusations of Gallicanism and liberalism levelled against him even well into the 20th century. Casgrain and Chauveau conjure up for us a fundamentally religious Garneau, but his son Alfred recounts the "conversion" of his "Voltairian" father on his death bed. In his work Garneau showed little interest in religion itself, but rather dealt with the relations of the two powers, church and state. Above all, Garneau was concerned about his nationality. His life and work were marked by constant preoccupation with defending the right to survival of his compatriots, "the Canadiens," who were threatened by "the Anglo-Saxon race." With time, Garneau's thinking moved towards the consensus that circumstances imposed on his era. The famous, oft-repeated conclusion he published in 1848, advising his compatriots to shun ventures fraught with danger for a small nationality, reveals the distance his thought had travelled over a ten-year period.

Garneau was intellectually a self-made man. From his parents, who had had no education, he could receive no more than encouragement. His literary culture, vision of the world, ideas on man and on his country, even his principles and methods as an historian, Garneau owed to a thirst for knowledge and great industry. It seems likely Garneau acquired much of his knowledge from extensive and varied reading. In literature, he had read the classicists, the encyclopaedists, and the romantics; in history, he felt at home in contemporary historiography, particularly in the company of Augustin Thierry; he also did a great deal of general reading and examined Canadian and foreign newspapers. Garneau's accomplishments were achieved with difficulty because of his straitened circumstances. It should be noted that to be able to continue his historical work, he had sought the help of his father-in-law and of city hall in Quebec, and the favours granted by parliament and by several friends. He brought up his family in an atmosphere saddened by frequent bereavements, for in the 20 years between 1835 and 1855 he fathered ten children of whom seven died in childhood.

As a writer Garneau was a poet, an historian, and a memorialist, a journalist on occasion, and a letter-writer when need arose. His manner of writing closely reflects his character and situation. His style is on the whole correct, and it is both terse and tentative. He strives for realism and clarity of expression, and his language demonstrates in its own way the weaknesses of a society still not well equipped with schools. Yet, despite unquestionable faults of vocabulary, grammar, and style, and the fact that he was entirely self-taught, Garneau redeems undeniable blunders in his writing by the vigour of the phrasing, by the narrative drive, and by the original vision of reality his words, clauses, and paragraphs convey. He was the first in Quebec to infuse poetry with romantic rhythm and colour; he was the first also to conceive the idea of a coherent and well-documented panorama of national history. As a writer Garneau was not given to elaborate detail, nor did he possess the brilliance of certain great authors; his skill lay in the inspiration that quickened his poems and in his dynamic style of narration. Garneau was aware that his work was not without flaws. That is why he continually reworked his material and still was never satisfied; he learned his art by writing, and was always conscious of his limitations.

A portrait of Garneau as a writer completes and in some ways confirms the portrait of the man. His poetry reveals his sensitivity and his vision of the world; the *Histoire du Canada* displays his learning as an historian and his ideas on the life of a nation; the *Voyage* gives his observations on London and Paris against the background of the two great ancient cultures. Garneau wrote laboriously, impelled by a vocation that slowly took shape, and above all by a sense of duty. As an artist he did not seek to dazzle; the writer was content to convince. As a creator he can be situated somewhere between the thinker who loved the age of enlightenment and the scholar who had reflected deeply on the art of the historian Thierry. He also had many romantic inclinations and a natural bent for meditation.

An attack of epilepsy, complicated by pleurisy, brought about Garneau's death during the night of 2–3 Feb. 1866. The historian died in a house on Rue Saint-Flavien, in which, notwithstanding a persistent and widely held legend, he had lived only during the last years of his life. From 1854 to 1864 he had resided, first as a tenant then as owner, in a dwelling on Avenue Sainte-Geneviève.

The news of Garneau's death was sent by the newspapers throughout French Canada, and his passing was felt as a bereavement by the whole nation. A committee was established to erect a monument and to assist his family. On 15 Sept. 1867, about a year and a half after his death, a memorial was unveiled in the Belmont cemetery, on the Sainte-Foy heights. On this occasion, Chauveau, in a moving homage to his late friend, made one of the finest speeches of his career. It is true that Garneau's star had waned a little after the publication in the 1860s of Abbé Ferland's *Cours d'histoire du Canada*, since its emphasis upon the religious dimension of the history of New France ensured its lasting success in Catholic and conservative French Canada. None the less, nobody disputes Garneau's title as "national historian." Another edition of his *Histoire du Canada* was the occasion for fresh praise and wider distribution. Early in the 20th century (1913–20), his grandson, Hector Garneau, published in Paris an updated version of the *Histoire du Canada*, based on the first edition. The reactions and comments it aroused once more testified to the importance of the *Histoire* in the French Canadian consciousness. Between 1944 and 1946 it was re-issued again – in the eighth edition – treated not so much as a classic text as a synthesis, brought up to date and unrivalled in its field. The centenary of the first edition was honoured in 1945 in impressive ceremonies at Montreal, Quebec, and Ottawa, and led to demonstrations in which patriotism vied with concern for historical knowledge.

Textbooks of literature and anthologies give a special place to Garneau, who is generally considered the greatest French Canadian author of the 19th century. Although since the 1950s historians have moved away from his primitive method of reconstructing the past, Garneau's ideas still engender a good deal of interest today, and, reaching across generations, link up with the permanent aspirations of French speaking Canadians. The name of Garneau was given during his lifetime to a street in Quebec. Today, a college offering general and professional courses in the city of Quebec bears his name. Throughout French Canada, a considerable number of streets, parks, schools, lakes, and rivers, and a township, recall the memory of the man who wanted to give his compatriots reasons not to despair, and grounds for living to the full their destiny as Frenchmen in North America.

PIERRE SAVARD and PAUL WYCZYNSKI

[From 1831 to 1841 Garneau published a number of poems in various newspapers, primarily *Le Canadien*. Nineteen of his poems were printed in *Le répertoire national, ou recueil de littérature canadienne* (Montréal, 1848), edited by James Huston. Garneau's principal work, however, is *Histoire du Canada depuis sa découverte jusqu'à nos jours* (3v., Québec, 1845–48, et suppl., 1852). Two other editions (1852, and 3v., 1859) were published during his lifetime, and from 1859 until his death in 1866, Garneau was preparing, with the help of his son Alfred, a fourth edition (published in Montreal in 1882 and 1883). Three new editions were published in Paris, each in 2v., under the direction of Hector Garneau, the historian's grandson (1913–20, 1920, 1928). Finally, an eighth edition, in 9 volumes, was prepared by Hector Garneau for the centenary of the *Histoire*'s first publication and was published in Montreal from 1944 to 1946. In 1860, Andrew Bell published a translation of Garneau's work entitled *History of Canada, from the time of its discovery till the union year (1840–1)* (Montreal) which was republished in 1862, 1866, and 1876. Garneau is also the author of *Voyage en Angleterre et en France dans les années 1831, 1832 et 1833* published in Quebec in 1855. This work was first printed in instalments in *Le Journal de Québec* from 18 Nov. 1854 to 29 May 1855. About two years before Garneau's death an abridged version of his *Voyage* was published in *La littérature canadienne de 1850 à 1860* (2v., Québec, 1863–64) and was reprinted in 1881. In 1968, Paul Wyczynski published an annotated critical edition of the original text of the *Voyage*. Finally in 1856 Garneau published *Abrégé de l'histoire du Canada depuis sa découverte jusqu'à 1840, à l'usage des maisons d'éducation* (Québec); new editions appeared in 1858, 1876, and 1881. Alfred Garneau and Pierre-Joseph-Olivier Chauveau prepared a section covering the period from 1840 to 1881 for the 1881 edition.

Sources of information for Garneau's life are few, and virtually nothing is known of certain periods. The registers of births, marriages, and deaths and his notarial register, preserved at ANQ-Q, provide the essential facts. Only some hundred letters remain of what was a large correspondence, according to Henri-Raymond Casgrain in 1866; these letters are, however, full of information on the man and his work. Contemporary newspapers provide some of his writings (especially the poems) and some traces of his activity. The thousands of legal notices scattered through Quebec City newspapers between 1854 and 1864 are of little interest to the historian's biographer. We have, of course, Garneau's poetic and historical work and especially his account in his *Voyage*, which is rich in information about the man himself and the nature of his ideas.

Garneau's first biographers could give personal accounts of his life. Abbé Casgrain published *Un contemporain: F. X. Garneau* (Québec) just after Garneau's death. He knew the historian during his declining years; his portrait of him tries to conceal the disputes caused by *Histoire du Canada* in the years after 1845. Pierre-Joseph-Olivier Chauveau knew Garneau well, and traced the older man's life for the fourth volume of the 1882–83 edition of *Histoire du Canada*. Despite several gaps attributable to his faulty memory, this biography is still the most complete. Chauveau's own temperament and his concern to unite French Canadians led him to present a picture of Garneau that conforms to the nationalist ideal of the early 1880s which saw an optimistic future for French Canada under the protective wing of her leading citizens and the church. In his long analysis of *Histoire du Canada*, Chauveau concentrates on the most conciliatory statements of Garneau, and he praised French Canada's recovery since 1850. The striking portrait that Chauveau drew of Garneau's physical and mental qualities has often been repeated in anthologies. In *Nos hommes de lettres*, published in

Montreal in 1873, notary Louis-Michel Darveau depicted Garneau as a victim of the clergy and of narrow-minded readers, and such first-hand testimony must be considered. Alfred Garneau did not publish anything about his father, but his correspondence provides much private information, unavailable elsewhere. In his introduction to the fifth edition (1913–20), Hector Garneau, Alfred's son, describes the life of "the national historian," adding several new facts, no doubt learned from family sources. His François-Xavier Garneau favours secularization and is less conciliatory than the man depicted by Casgrain and Chauveau, and his portrait rekindled debate on the meaning of Garneau's work, especially his treatment of religious questions.

In 1926, Gustave Lanctot* published *François-Xavier Garneau* (Toronto) which was reprinted with minor changes in 1946 as *Garneau, historien national* (Montréal). It is a well-informed study, and its judgements are carefully considered. Since that time various works, the most important of which are listed in the bibliography of the critical edition of the *Voyage* prepared by Paul Wyczynski, have added to our knowledge of Garneau. Additional material can be found in the archives of the Projet Garneau at the Centre de Recherche en Civilisation Canadienne-Française at the University of Ottawa, which is described in the centre's *Bulletin* of April 1973. A critical edition in 12 volumes of François-Xavier Garneau's complete works is being prepared for publication by the authors of this biography. It will include a descriptive and critical bibliography of his life and works.   P.S. and P.W.]

GAUTIER, JEAN-BAPTISTE SAINT-GERMAIN, *dit. See* SAINT-GERMAIN

GEORGE, JAMES, Presbyterian minister and educator; b. 8 Nov. 1800 at Muckhart (Perthshire, Scotland), son of James and Elizabeth George; d. 26 Aug. 1870 at Stratford, Ont.

James George, the son of a crofter, spent his childhood near Kinross and, after elementary schooling, became a weaver at Auchterarder. The local Presbyterian minister, recognizing his ability, persuaded him to study for the ministry and gave him private tuition. George entered Dollar Academy in 1822, then matriculated in St Andrews University. In 1825 he graduated in arts from the University of Glasgow and entered Divinity Hall to study theology. He also taught in a Glasgow charity school. In 1855 the University of Glasgow conferred upon George the honorary degree of DD.

Imbued with radical social ideas and strongly opposed to the Tory policies of Lord Melville in Scotland and of the ministry of Lord Liverpool, George immigrated in 1829 to the United States, joining his brothers who had settled in Delaware County, N.Y. He may have married before leaving Scotland; his first wife, Margaret, was buried there in 1834. After entering the ministry of the Associate Reformed Church, he preached in New York State in Philadelphia and Fort Covington. He later said that his stay in the United States cured him of his radical republicanism.

In July 1833 he moved to York (Toronto), Upper Canada, where he was received into the secession United Synod of Upper Canada, and was given the charge of Scarborough. Within a year he built up an active congregation which he took with him into the Presbyterian Church of Canada in Connection with the Church of Scotland. He was elected moderator of the synod in 1841.

At the time of the uprising led by William Lyon MACKENZIE in December 1837, George marched into Toronto at the head of the "Men of Scarboro" to support the government. In a sermon preached at the time, one can see how thoroughly George had repudiated his earlier radicalism. Civil government, he said, should be obeyed as an institution of "divine appointment," and rebellion could be justified only in extreme cases when a government "nullified its own claim to obedience." George stayed with his Scarborough congregation for 17 years with only one interval, from October 1847 to May 1848, when he was stationed in Belleville. Up to 1853 he is said to have preached 1,700 sermons, each one written out in full. From these and later sermons a selection was made by his son-in-law, the Reverend Donald Ross, and published as a posthumous volume.

In 1846 George received a part-time appointment as interim professor of systematic theology at Queen's College, Kingston. He lectured annually for six weeks while the Toronto presbytery supplied his pulpit in Scarborough. In 1852 he was appointed by the synod as a clerical member of Queen's board of trustees, and the following year was made professor of mental and moral philosophy. With the resignation soon after of Principal John MACHAR, George became the acting head of the college with an increment of £100 in salary and the rank of vice-principal. During his term of office Queen's acquired its first permanent home; a medical and a law faculty (the latter was short-lived) were added to those of arts and theology.

In 1854 George was partly instrumental in bringing the Reverend George Weir from Scotland to Queen's as professor of classical literature. His early relations with the young professor were as cordial as they were with Weir's sister who, for the first year, acted as her brother's housekeeper. Trouble began in 1856 with the circulation of an anonymous letter attacking George and the board of trustees for their mismanagement of the college preparatory school. It was traced to the school's headmaster, H. J. Borthwick, who was summarily dismissed. When Borthwick then applied to enter Queen's as a divinity student, George refused to admit him to his classes and attempted to have his conduct investigated by the college senate, a move blocked by Weir who voted against it. George then made a formal complaint about Weir and Borthwick; when the board later pressed George to admit Borthwick to classes, he resigned as trustee, vice-principal, and professor of theology, retaining only the chair in mental and moral philosophy.

In 1859, when William LEITCH became principal, George and Weir were summoned before the board and admonished to end their continuing altercation for the good of the college. The feud remained in abeyance until the autumn of 1861. On his return from a visit to Scotland, Weir charged that his "sister bore a child in March 1855 – a son – at this moment a living likeness of yourself [George], and known from the hour of its birth only by your name – of which child she has uniformly and solemnly affirmed that you are the father." George categorically denied the charge, and at first demanded a full investigation by the trustees; he then changed his mind and decided to resign for reasons of health. The board promptly accepted his resignation, to take effect at the end of the spring term in 1862, and declined to take any further action on Weir's charges.

Frustrated by what he considered to be the board's pusillanimous attitude, Weir retaliated by lampooning the "immoral professor" of moral philosophy in an anonymously printed mock-heroic poem of 16 cantos. According to Leitch, who considered Weir to be mentally unbalanced, he also read to students and anyone who would listen, "the most indelicate and licentious details" from letters dealing with the alleged affair between his sister and George. When George left Queen's in 1862 to become minister of St Andrew's Church in Stratford, Weir transferred his antagonism to Leitch and so disrupted the college that the board of trustees dismissed him in 1864.

In Stratford, George had a successful ministry. He healed rifts in the small congregation and so increased its membership that a much larger church was needed. He was active also in community affairs, serving on the school board and acting as chaplain of the St Andrew's Society. His second wife, Barbara Ross, whom he had married 20 Dec. 1845, had died a few years later, and some time before leaving Queen's he married

Janet Kerr. Both minister and wife were popular with the Stratford congregation and worked together to make a new church possible. When it was opened on 13 Jan. 1869, a debt of only $1,400 remained to be paid. George died in 1870, survived by his wife and three daughters by his first wife, two sons by the second, and two girls and a boy by the third.

No hint of scandal marked George's ministry in either Scarborough or Stratford. Robert Ure, who preached the funeral sermon, made oblique reference to the troubles at Queen's in affirming his belief that George's record "impartially considered will be found to contain nothing that seriously affects the lustre of a noble character or the general consistency of a life devoted to the service of God." A long encomium also gave him unstinted praise as pastor, teacher, pulpit orator, writer, and conversationalist; it even commented upon his "rich vein of genuine humour," a quality singularly lacking in his published works.

It is difficult to assess the Weir–George dispute which once rocked Queen's. George appears to have been self-important and resentful of criticism; Weir, envious, ambitious, paranoiac. However indiscreet George may have been, it seems highly improbable that he was Miss Weir's seducer. The evidence, at best, is circumstantial and one can only resort to the old Scottish verdict, "not proven."

H. P. GUNDY

[James George], *Thoughts on high themes: being a collection of sermons from the mss. of the late Rev. James George, D.D. . . .* (Toronto, 1874). Other writings by James George are listed in *Bibliography of Canadiana* (Staton and Tremaine); *Bibliography of Canadiana: first supp.* (Boyle and Colbeck); *Canadiana, 1698–1900, in the possession of the Douglas Library, Queen's University, Kingston, Ontario* (Kingston, 1932), 47–48; and *Catalogue of pamphlets in PAC* (Casey), I.
Perth County Surrogate Court (Stratford, Ont.), will of James George, dated 19 May 1868; codicil, 15 Aug. 1870; affidavit, 29 Aug. 1870 (copy at PAO). QUA, Queen's records, B, 1846–62; D1, 1846–64. *Argus; a Commercial, Agricultural, Political and Literary Journal* (Kingston, [Ont.]), 1862. *Chronicle and News* (Kingston), 1847–62. *Daily British Whig* (Kingston), 1849–62. *Daily News* (Kingston), 1851–62. *A historical and statistical report of the Presbyterian Church of Canada, in Connection with the Church of Scotland, for the year 1866* (2nd ed., Montreal, 1868). *Memorials of the life and ministry of the Rev. John Machar, D.D., 1796–1863, late minister of St. Andrew's Church, Kingston* (Toronto, 1873). "On appeal from the Court of Chancery: Weir v. Mathieson," *Reports of cases adjudged in the Court of Error and Appeal*, comp. Alexander Grant (2nd ed., 3v., Toronto and Edinburgh,

Gesner

1885), III, 1123–63. *Presbyterian* (Montreal), XXIII (1870), 239–46. Presbyterian Church of Can. in Connection with the Church of Scot., *Minutes of the Synod*, 1834–36; *Abstract of the minutes of the Synod*, 1837–45; *Acts and proc. of the Synod*, 1846–71. *Stratford Beacon* (Stratford, Ont.), 2, 9, 14 Sept. 1870. *Stratford Herald* (Stratford, Ont.), 31 Aug. 1870. William Gregg, *History of the Presbyterian Church in the dominion of Canada* ... (Toronto, 1885).

GESNER, ABRAHAM, physician and surgeon, geologist, and inventor; b. 2 May 1797 in Cornwallis Township, N.S., third son of Colonel Henry Gesner and Sarah Pineo; d. 29 April 1864 at Halifax, N.S.

The Gesner family was of German origin. About the middle of the 18th century Abraham's grandfather, Nicholas Gesner, came from the Netherlands and settled in the Hudson valley near Tappantown (Tappan, N.Y.). When the American revolution broke out he had a large and prosperous farm, but being of loyal sentiments he was dispossessed by the insurgents. His twin sons, Abraham and Henry, 16 years of age, joined the loyalist forces, fought throughout the war, and then came to Nova Scotia. Their land grant in New Brunswick proved unsuitable for farming, and they remained in Nova Scotia, purchasing, in 1785, a small farm in Cornwallis Township, Kings County. There Henry married Sarah Pineo, daughter of an Acadian family. In 1807 and again in 1812 Abraham Sr and Henry petitioned for a grant of land in the Annapolis valley, and the former was awarded 500 acres in Wilmot Township. Meanwhile the brothers had purchased a large farm near Chipman Corner, about three miles northeast of Kentville. We must assume that when Abraham Sr moved to Wilmot he turned over the Chipman Corner farm to Henry, for the latter lived there the remainder of his life.

Abraham Jr, along with his brothers, received the elementary schooling of rural children in the early 19th century: reading, spelling, and "ciphering." When he was 21 he set out to make his own way. He tried shipping horses from Nova Scotia to the West Indies, but was twice shipwrecked, once off Bermuda and once off Nova Scotia. Deciding not to risk a third venture, he returned to his father's farm, and, in 1824, married Harriet, daughter of Dr Isaac Webster of Kentville and sister of William Bennett WEBSTER. Tradition has it that Dr Webster's consent was obtained on the condition that Abraham accept his financial help to enrol as a medical student in London. The following year he began to study medicine at St Bartholomew's Hospital under Sir Astley Paston Cooper, and surgery at Guy's Hospital under Dr John Abernethy. He appears to have taken lectures also in mineralogy and geology, for on completion of his medical course he brought back to Nova Scotia not only a medical diploma but also a keen interest in the earth sciences.

Gesner settled in Parrsboro, on the north side of Minas Basin, and began to practise medicine. He deliberately chose Parrsboro because it lies in an area rich in mineral occurrences and curious geological features. As he made his visits to patients, either on foot or on horseback, he recorded observations and gathered specimens. Soon he had a representative collection and a fund of knowledge, not only of the local area, but also of Cape Blomidon across the basin and of the Chignecto shore north to Joggins. He acquired such geological books as were available, and was especially impressed with a paper on the geology and mineralogy of Nova Scotia written by Charles Thomas Jackson and Francis Alger of Boston. Using this as his model, Gesner, in 1836, wrote his first book, *Remarks on the geology and mineralogy of Nova Scotia* (Halifax). It had a more popular manner than its predecessor and it improved somewhat on the subdivisions of the geological regions of the province. As a result of this work Gesner was asked in 1837 to examine certain areas in New Brunswick for coal, and the following year was engaged by the government of that province to make a geological survey. His is said to be the first appointment of a government geologist in a British colony.

Gesner moved with his family to Saint John in 1838, and for the next five years spent his summers on geological field work and his winters classifying his specimens and writing his reports. For the first three years he concentrated on the more accessible southern parts of the province, but in the last two he extended his explorations to the north and northwest, pushing his way up turbulent streams and over rugged mountains seldom seen by white men. His assistants and guides were mostly Indians, who were not always prepared to travel as hard and as far as their leader. The observations made and the conclusions reached as a result of these five field seasons were recorded in successive annual reports as provincial geologist from 1839 to 1843. He described all the mineral occurrences and geological features he saw, and classified the different rock formations of the province into five "districts." He recorded the occurrence of fossil plants and deduced that there was an association between these and the presence of coal seams. His generalizations were embodied in a geological map of southern and central New Brunswick, published 54 years later. In addition to recording the geology and natural resources, Gesner included in his reports graphic descriptions of picturesque scenery and accounts of curious incidents of history and travel. He was enthusiastic about the potentialities of his adopted province, and did not hesitate to predict the future development of its riches.

Gesner's geology, by modern standards, is crude, and is marred by errors in identification and correlation of various formations. But by the standards of the 1840s it was of high quality, quite in the same rank with most of what was being done in the United States and Europe. In England he was highly respected as a geologist, and was elected a fellow of the Geological Society of London. Yet in one respect Gesner was behind the geology of his own time. He had little knowledge of fossils and almost none of their use in stratigraphic correlation, a technique that had been known for over 50 years. Had he been able to employ this method he would have avoided some of the errors for which he was later criticized. Nevertheless, he laid the foundations of geological knowledge in New Brunswick, on which later workers such as Sir John William Dawson*, Robert Wheelock Ells*, and George Frederick Matthew* were to build.

A different kind of error had more serious and immediate consequences for Dr Gesner. With no experience in practical mining, he was not able to make a realistic appraisal of the economic potential of the mineral occurrences he discovered. Thus his enthusiasm saw in every galena vein or coal seam a lead mine or a coal field. But some people who accepted his appraisals and attempted to develop such occurrences were disappointed in the quality, extent, or accessibility of the product. The value of Gesner's survey was strongly questioned by such disappointed investors, with the result that in 1842 the Legislative Assembly of New Brunswick refused to provide funds for that year's field work. Gesner went ahead anyway, with the authorization of Sir William COLEBROOKE, the lieutenant governor, completing his summer's explorations and writing his final report. Only a few copies were ever published, and his map was relegated to the archives.

Gesner had borrowed from friends to finance the work of 1842. Biographers disagree as to whether or not he was ever paid by the New Brunswick government, but in 1842 he was seriously in debt, with no funds immediately available. Therefore he felt justified in retaining the large collection of minerals, wildlife specimens,

and ethnological artifacts that he had accumulated during his travels, and using them as the basis for a public museum. His former Micmac Indian guides were employed as assistants; they thought highly of the doctor and called him by a name meaning Wise Man. But the Gesner Museum, open by April 1842, was a financial failure, and its proprietor was now worse off than before, with no buyer for the collections. Gesner's creditors, who were also his friends, took over the collections in lieu of repayment, although it was obvious that they did this out of charity, for they promptly donated the objects to the Saint John Mechanics' Institute. There the Gesner collections were displayed for a time, but eventually went into storage. In 1890 they were acquired by the Natural History Society of New Brunswick. This acquisition has led to the tradition that the New Brunswick Museum was founded by Abraham Gesner, whereas in fact that museum had been established independently by the society in 1870. Gesner's museum was one of the first two established in Canada, the other being the museum of the Geological Survey of Canada, begun by William Edmond Logan* at Montreal.

While still a resident of Saint John in 1841, Gesner had purchased the Chipman Corner farm from his father, giving a mortgage in part payment. One reason for this action was perhaps his father's advancing years. The doctor probably also realized that his position as provincial geologist was soon to terminate. In fact, he wound up his affairs in Saint John in 1843 and returned to Cornwallis Township to settle down as a farmer and general practitioner.

Had Gesner been willing to confine his restless intellect to farming and "doctoring" he might have prospered, but the world would have been poorer. Instead, he spent much of his time and no doubt some of his small income on scientific experiments. He became interested in "galvanism," that is, current electricity, and expanded the experiments of Faraday and others to construct electric generators and motors. In order to provide insulation for the large amounts of copper wire used in such devices he designed a machine for winding yarn around the wire.

In 1846 or earlier Gesner turned to the investigation of hydrocarbons. During the voyages to the West Indies he had probably seen the great pitch lake of Trinidad, and he stated in later years that it was with material from there that he began his experiments. By means of a specially designed retort he was able to distil this bitumen and obtain among other products a light oil, which could be used much more effectively than sperm

Gesner

oil in argand lamps, the last word in domestic illumination at that time.

In 1846 the government of Prince Edward Island invited Gesner to make a geological survey of that province. He accepted, and in addition to his field work undertook a series of public lectures in Charlottetown. According to Gesner's own account, it was at one of these lectures, in August 1846, that he gave the first public demonstration of the preparation and use of the new lamp fuel. However, a Charlottetown newspaper of the time reports his lectures as having been given in June and September, and in August printed a letter from the doctor in the field. The lectures, which were very popular, were mostly on geology or electricity, but on 19 June his subject was "caloric" (heat), and for his experiments he needed the extra space of the court house instead of the mechanics' institute. This must have been the occasion of his demonstration of the new hydrocarbon lamp fuel. His audience was enthusiastic, but little knew that they were witnessing the birth of the petroleum refining industry. Gesner returned to Nova Scotia in late September and resumed his many activities at the Chipman Corner farm.

One of these activities was the writing of reports and books. In 1846 he published a geological map of Nova Scotia and also the report of his survey of Prince Edward Island. The following year one of his two major works, *New Brunswick, with notes for emigrants*, appeared. Not only were the natural resources of that province described, but also the topography, natural history, ethnology, and commerce. A similar, shorter account on Prince Edward Island appeared the same year. At this time also he was appointed commissioner to the Indians of Nova Scotia, and in this capacity submitted a report in 1847.

The success of his lecturing and writing, and the difficulties of operating a large farm while carrying on a medical practice, led Gesner, early in 1848, to sell the Chipman Corner property back to his father, or, more correctly, to exchange it for the original mortgage of 1841. He then moved to Sackville, a village north of Halifax. His son George says this move was in 1850, but it must have been in 1848, for the Chipman Corner home had been sold that year. From Sackville he went to Halifax, his son says in 1852. But we have records of his activities in Halifax in 1851, so again the move must have been earlier, probably 1850. In Halifax he made the acquaintance of Thomas Cochrane*, 10th Earl of Dundonald, who after an incredible career as a naval warrior was now, in his 75th year, commander-in-chief of the North American and West Indian station of the Royal Navy. Dundonald had long been interested in the improvement of illumination, and had acquired control of the Trinidad bitumen deposits in the hope of exploiting them for fuel. Although 22 years younger, Gesner had at last found a kindred spirit in this legendary hero and firm believer in the virtues of technology. The all-too-short period of their association must have been the happiest of Gesner's life. With Dundonald's encouragement and probable participation he resumed his experiments with the hydrocarbon lamp fuel.

The major problem was finding raw material for the distillation process. The Trinidad pitch lake was a long sea voyage away. But in 1849 renewed interest was taken in a deposit of a natural bitumen now known as albertite (named for Albert County) occurring in eastern New Brunswick. Gesner tried to acquire the mining rights for this deposit, and began his operation. However, he was partly anticipated by William Cairns, who purchased the coal-mining lease for the area. Cairns had Gesner's men forcibly expelled from their workings, and Gesner brought suit against Cairns for trespass. The case appeared to hinge on whether or not the deposit was coal; if so, it would be covered by Cairns' lease. At a preliminary trial in Halifax in 1852 the decision was that it was asphaltum, not coal. Later the same year, however, a more elaborate trial was held in Albert County, New Brunswick. Expert witnesses were called by both Gesner and Cairns to testify as to whether the Albert material was asphaltum or coal; curiously enough, each gave his opinion in favour of the side that employed him. At the end, however, Judge Lemuel Allan Wilmot* instructed the jury that Cairns' lease included "and other minerals," and the material was certainly a mineral. With this bias the jury found in favour of Cairns, adding their opinion that the material was coal.

Gesner was more bitter about this injustice than over any of his previous disappointments, and he referred sarcastically in after years to the jury of farmers who transformed asphaltum into coal, although the judge had left the jury with little choice. Meanwhile, back in Halifax Gesner had been trying to organize a company to manufacture and sell the new lamp fuel. One of his first actions was to coin a name for it. As one residue of the distillation was a kind of wax, Gesner decided to call his lamp fuel wax-oil. So he combined the Greek words κηρός, and 'ἔλαιον, and came up with "keroselain" and "keroselene", but finally decided on "kerosene" as neater and more analogous with such established names as benzene and camphene. This christening must have been in 1850, for we find the name being used in his publicity ventures in 1851. These included illuminating the citadel courtyard with a lamp hung from the east signal yard arm.

Lack of interest in Halifax, and the shattering blow of the Albert County trial, must have finally convinced Gesner that the future of kerosene was elsewhere. In 1853 he moved to New York City. Probably he had already made arrangements with businessmen there, for Horatio Eagles, Erastus W. Smith, Philo T. Ruggles, and others formed the Asphalt Mining and Kerosene Gas Company, with Gesner as chemist. On 27 June 1854 Gesner obtained U.S. patents nos. 11,203, 11,204, and 11,205 for "Improvement in kerosene burning-fluids." The three patents are essentially the same in text, but cover respectively what Gesner called "A", "C", and "B" kerosene. "A" kerosene was the lightest fraction, what was later called volatile hydrocarbon and subsequently gasoline. The patent states that it could be used with a jet of air to produce a luminous flame, a forecast of the gasoline vapour lamp. "B" kerosene was somewhat less volatile, and was intended mainly for mixing with the other grades. "C" kerosene was the lamp fuel, which soon came to be known as "coal-oil" or "carbon-oil."

Although the manufacture of kerosene in the 1850s was mainly from New Brunswick albertite or Scottish "boghead" coal, Gesner states in his patents that he obtained it from "petroleum, maltha, or soft mineral pitch, asphaltum, or bitumen." It is worthy of note that coal is not mentioned. The essential point of Gesner's patents was in the temperatures of distillation, all less than 427°C (800°F). Also crucial was the purification process, in which the original distillate was decanted, the liquid fraction redistilled, then treated with sulphuric acid to separate impurities and with "calcined lime" to absorb water and neutralize the acid. Finally the liquid was distilled a third time, to obtain the three grades of kerosene.

Under Gesner's guidance the Asphalt Mining and Kerosene Gas Company set up a factory at Newtown Creek on Long Island. Modern engineers have admired the efficient design shown in the published plans. The name of the company was changed to the North American Kerosene Gas Light Company. The brothers John H. and George W. Austen were engaged as sales agents. By 1857 kerosene was being advertised as an illuminant and lubricant throughout the United States and the British American provinces. John H. Austen found a simple, inexpensive lamp burner in Austria, and brought it to America to sell as the Vienna burner. The Kerosene Company prospered, and Gesner lived comfortably in Brooklyn, N.Y., a prominent figure in the local church and community. But ill fortune was about to strike again.

The first cloud was the appearance in 1857 of a rival manufacturer, Samuel Downer of South Boston, Mass. His product was inferior in quality to Gesner's kerosene, and he was soon glad to pay a royalty for the use of Gesner's name and process. A more serious threat came from abroad. In 1848 a Scottish chemist, James Young, working in Manchester, had distilled boghead coal to produce a light lubricant. He subsequently found that with purification it served as an excellent lamp fuel. Unaware of Gesner's earlier discovery, he obtained a British patent in 1850 and an American patent in 1852 for what he called "paraffine-oil." When Young's product began to meet competition in the late 1850s from Gesner's kerosene, he brought suit for patent infringement and won. The value of Gesner's patents was thus seriously impaired. Thereafter the Kerosene Company had to pay royalties to Young to continue the manufacture of the lamp fuel. The final blow came in 1859, when the commercial production of petroleum began on a frenzied scale in northwestern Pennsylvania and southwestern Canada West. By converting to petroleum as the raw material, a change made easy by Gesner's flexible design, the kerosene factories began producing the illuminant at about one-quarter its former cost. The age of the kerosene lamp and the petroleum industry was launched but Gesner benefited little. He had made his contribution to refining technology and he was replaced as the chemist of the Kerosene Company.

For a time he stayed in Brooklyn, practising medicine and writing a book that would have been a claim to fame in itself. This was entitled *A practical treatise on coal, petroleum, and other distilled oils* (1861). In this modest volume Gesner outlined the history of natural hydrocarbons, described the various source materials for distillates, and gave highly practical accounts of how to build and operate a hydrocarbon refining factory. This work, and its second edition completed in 1865 by George Weltden Gesner, became the textbook for petroleum refining and was translated into several other languages. But Abraham Gesner derived little profit from it.

At last, in 1863, disappointed and tired but still full of plans for the future, Gesner returned to Halifax and began preparing the edition of his *Practical treatise* which would be published in 1865. At this time he took out Nova Scotia patent

Gibson

no. 108, for the manufacture of kerosene. Unfortunately it was 17 years late. He was now famous, and was appointed professor of natural history at Dalhousie University. With his broad interests in geology, natural history, and ethnology, his experience as a practical chemist, and his proven ability as a public lecturer, he would have been a great success as a professor and his courses would have been immensely popular. But again the reward for originality and hard work was denied him and he died in Halifax on 29 April 1864.

Dr and Mrs Gesner had seven sons and three daughters for whom they provided a Christian home and a good education. Two sons carried on their father's work as chemists and metallurgists, one became a United States Army surgeon who served in the American Civil War, and another was a distinguished Episcopal clergyman. With such an admirable family it is hard to understand why their father's grave in Camp Hill Cemetery, Halifax, was left unmarked for 69 years. It remained for Imperial Oil Limited, mindful that their great refinery across the harbour was the direct descendant of Gesner's retort, to erect a handsome shaft over his grave in 1933 and inscribe on it a tribute to the pioneer geologist and the founder of the hydrocarbon refining industry. In 1969 the Historic Sites and Monuments Board of Canada set up an impressive monument to Gesner in front of his former home at Chipman Corner.

According to his son George Weltden, Abraham Gesner was of medium height but with broad shoulders. His eyes were black and piercing, and his hair remained black all his life. The published portrait shows him as partly bald, with heavy side-whiskers, perhaps in emulation of his friend Lord Dundonald. He played the flute and the violin, and was fond of the old Scottish airs. He loved to tell stories, and joined in the laughter as fully as his audience. He was abstemious, his only indulgence being an occasional good cigar. His religion was important to him and he was an active member of the Church of England in Nova Scotia and the Episcopal Church in Brooklyn.

Abraham Gesner was a man who believed that science was good, and that through technology it could make a better world in which to live. This philosophy, together with his religion, enabled him to meet his many disappointments without self-pity, and to pick up the pieces and go on to the next project with undiminished enthusiasm. If he could come back today and see the great aircraft now propelled over continents and oceans by his kerosene, he would be delighted but not surprised.

LORIS S. RUSSELL

[The above account includes statements that are at variance with previously published biographies of Abraham Gesner, or which do not appear in those biographies. The author's sources for these are as follows. The Gesner ("Gisner") petitions for land grants are preserved in PANS, RG 20, A, 28, 43, 48. Copies of deeds covering purchases and sales of land by the Gesners in Cornwallis Township are in the Registry of Deeds for Kings County, Kentville, N.S. From these, and with the help of Mr Durrell Sutton of Port Williams, Mr Ernest Eaton of Upper Canard, and Miss Muriel Murray of Chipman Corner, the author located in 1966 the former Gesner home and the site of the original kerosene distillation. Gesner's lectures and other activities in Prince Edward Island are reported in the Charlottetown *Islander* of 1846. Accounts of Gesner's activities in Halifax in the early 1850s appear in the Halifax *Morning Chronicle*. Sale of the Gesner collections to the Natural History Society of New Brunswick is recorded in that society's *Bull.* (Saint John), no.IX (1890), 33–35. The gravestones of Gesner's father and mother and his brother Henry are still legible in St John's Anglican churchyard at Port Williams. Copies of the Gesner and Young patents were obtained from the United States and Canadian patent offices. L.S.R.]

See also: Abraham Gesner, *The industrial resources of Nova Scotia: comprehending the physical geography, topography, geology, agriculture, fisheries, mines, forests, wild lands, lumbering, manufactories, navigation, commerce, emigration, improvements, industry, contemplated railways, natural history and resources, of the province* (Halifax, 1849); *New Brunswick, with notes for emigrants: comprehending the early history, an account of the Indians, settlement, topography, statistics, commerce, timber, manufactures, agriculture, fisheries, geology, natural history, social and political state, immigrants, and contemplated railways of that province* (London, 1847); *A practical treatise on coal, petroleum, and other distilled oils* (New York, 1861; 2nd ed., rev. G. W. Gesner 1865). G. W. Gesner, "Dr. Abraham Gesner – a biographical sketch," N.B. Natural History Soc., *Bull.*, no.XIV (1896), 2–11. G. F. Matthew, "Abraham Gesner: a review of his scientific work," N.B. Natural History Soc., *Bull.*, no.XV (1897), 3–48. Kendall Beaton, "Dr. Gesner's kerosene: the start of American oil refining," *Business History Rev.* (Boston), XXIX (1955), 28–53. L. M. Cumming, "Abraham Gesner (1797–1864) – author, inventor, and pioneer Canadian geologist," Geological Assoc. of Can., *Proc.* (Toronto), 23 (1971), 5–10. L. K. Ingersoll, "A man and a museum," N.B. Museum, *Museum Memo* (Saint John), 4, no.1 (March 1972), 2–5. K. A. MacKenzie, "Abraham Gesner, M.D., surgeon geologist, 1797–1864," Canadian Medical Assoc., *Journal* ([Toronto]), 59 (1948), 384–87. Ian Sclanders, "He gave the world a brighter light," *Imperial Oil Rev.* (Toronto), 39 (February 1955), 22–25. W. A. Squires, "Abraham Gesner: a short biography of New Brunswick's first provincial geologist," *Atlantic Advocate* (Fredericton), 53 (1962–63), no.5, 92–95.

GIBSON, DAVID, surveyor, politician, and public servant; b. 9 March 1804 in the parish of

Glammis, Forfarshire (Angus), Scotland, the son of James Gibson and Margaret Watson; d. 25 Jan. 1864 at Quebec City.

David Gibson, whose father was a tenant farmer, was apprenticed at 15 to a land surveyor in Forfarshire. Once his term was completed in 1824, he decided to practise in North America. Inquiries brought a negative response from a friend in Virginia but Gibson's uncle, Alexander Milne, in Markham Township, Upper Canada, replied that it appeared quite easy to qualify as a surveyor in the province. Gibson took this answer as a sign that work was available.

After obtaining letters of introduction he set out for Quebec in 1825. He procured work surveying the Lower Canadian–United States border, but even with the help of Lord Dalhousie [Ramsay*], with whom family friends had influence, he was unable to obtain permanent employment. Armed with letters of introduction from Dalhousie, Gibson moved to his uncle's farm in Upper Canada, turning down an offer of a highly paid position in a grocery firm in Montreal.

Despite his uncle's optimism, Gibson did not immediately receive work. However, Lieutenant Governor Sir Peregrine Maitland*, primed by Dalhousie's letter, advised Gibson to apply as soon as work became available. This he did and, upon passing the provincial examination, was appointed in December 1825 a deputy surveyor of roads and in September 1828 surveyor of highways for the southern part of the Home District. These posts, together with surveying for farmers in the neighbourhood, gave him more than enough employment.

In 1828 Gibson married his cousin Eliza Milne. The following year Gibson bought a lot on Yonge Street at Willowdale in York Township, and began to take an increasing interest in public affairs. In 1831 he was elected president of the York Temperance Society. At about the same time he became an avid Reformer, organizing and speaking at Reform meetings, presenting petitions, and assisting William Lyon MACKENZIE. In 1834 and 1836 Gibson was elected to the assembly for the 1st Riding of York, and he gained a reputation as a reasonable but forceful proponent of radical reform. Perhaps as a reward for his assistance to the Reform cause, the Toronto City Council gave him jobs surveying streets and sidewalks, and he made a report on the feasibility of bringing water into Toronto from various sources. Gibson served as secretary of the York Township meeting in 1836, and as chairman in 1837. He was also a prosperous farmer, winning prizes from the Home District Agricultural Society and selling stock at ever increasing prices.

Gibson was acknowledged by members of all parties as a moderate and sensible Reformer, not one who would be expected to take part in an uprising. In fact, he learned that the rebellion of December 1837 was likely only two days before it began, when Mackenzie, who misrepresented the nature and strength of the movement, told Gibson to choose his side. Once he learned the true nature of affairs, Gibson stuck by his decision to join, in the belief that wrong as the rebellion was, it could still bring denied reforms. During the rising at Toronto he protected the loyalist prisoners held at Montgomery's Tavern from mistreatment and led them to safety when government forces under James FITZGIBBON and Allan MACNAB shelled the tavern. For this he was much praised by the prisoners after their release, but his farm was nevertheless ordered burned by Sir Francis Bond Head*.

After the skirmish at Montgomery's Tavern, Gibson hid near Oshawa for a month. He then escaped across Lake Ontario and commenced a surveying business in Lockport, N.Y., where he carefully avoided involvement in the border troubles of 1837 and 1838. He also avoided Mackenzie, who called him a coward in print, because Gibson had left the battle at Montgomery's. After a short period of hardship, Gibson found employment as an engineer on the Erie Canal and brought his family to Lockport. He prospered, bought a farm, and, despite obtaining in 1843 a pardon for the charge of treason, remained in the United States and even applied for citizenship in 1846.

In 1848 he was dismissed from his job on the Erie Canal, probably because of a change of party in the local government. At that time he decided to return to his farm in Upper Canada, which had been managed for him by relatives during his absence. Gibson was soon doing well again. He was immediately given employment as a provincial land surveyor. From June 1848 to August 1849 he surveyed the Durham Road and the town plot of Durham in Grey County. His sons James and William acted as chain-bearers, and later became prominent surveyors. In 1851 he was appointed a member of the board of Canada West to examine candidates for the position of surveyor. He also attempted to regain his old seat in the legislature in that year in order to defend his views on the strict separation of church and state. His defeat by John William Gamble* ended his political career, but his economic fortunes continued to rise. In August 1853 John ROLPH, then commissioner of crown lands, with whom Gibson had remained friends, appointed him inspector of crown lands agencies and superintendent of colonization roads for Canada West, a position he occupied until his death. In 1861–62 he was also

313

Gildersleeve

responsible for supervising the surveying of roads in the Algoma region.

Gibson was raised in the Church of Scotland but, upon coming to Canada, his interest in religion waned. After the rebellion he decided that he had neglected the spiritual life of his four sons and three daughters. He began attending the Methodist Episcopal church of his wife, but he also attended a Baptist church.

Between 1828 and 1856 Gibson surveyed much of Simcoe, Grey, Huron, and Bruce counties, as well as townships in Wellington, Wentworth, Ontario, and Dufferin counties. Between 1854 and 1863 he also surveyed, inspected, and superintended the construction of the important Elora, Saugeen, Goderich, Southampton, Garrafraxa, Peterson, Muskoka, and Victoria colonization roads which opened up vast areas of Ontario for settlement. He travelled throughout Canada West in the course of his work, yet still was able to visit and manage his farms in Lockport and Willowdale. He and his sons also owned an "extensive" sawmill in Parry Sound which was sold shortly before his death. By 1860 Gibson was spending less time in the field and more in Quebec to attend to general office work and meetings of the board of examiners. At his death in 1864 he was well off, with developed and undeveloped properties throughout Canada West, as well as his two farms.

RONALD J. STAGG

PAC, MG 24, B15; RG 5, A1, 180. PAO, Gibson (David) papers; RG 1, A-I-4, 34–35; A-II-6, 3; CB-1. *Christian Guardian*, 19 March 1831. *Globe*, 27 Jan. 1864. *Muskoka and Haliburton* (Murray). *Illustrated historical atlas of the county of York* . . . (Toronto, 1878; repr. 1969). M. A. FitzGibbon, *A veteran of 1812; the life of James FitzGibbon* (Toronto, 1894; repr. 1972). P. W. Hart, *Pioneering in North York; a history of the borough* (Toronto, 1968). Assoc. of Ont. Land Surveyors, *Annual report* (Toronto), 31 (1916), 51–54.

GILDERSLEEVE, OVERTON SMITH, lawyer, businessman, and politician; b. 13 Jan. 1825 at Kingston, Upper Canada, eldest of the eight children of Sarah Finkle and Henry Gildersleeve; d. 9 March 1864 at Kingston. He married Louisa Anne, daughter of William Henry Draper*, 16 Aug. 1850; there were no children.

Henry Gildersleeve arrived in Kingston from Gildersleeve (part of Portland, Conn.) in 1816, and developed a flourishing shipping and shipbuilding business. He helped construct the *Frontenac*, the first steamboat on Lake Ontario, in 1816, and is sometimes called "the father of steam navigation on the Lakes." Overton Smith Gildersleeve was educated in Kingston. He took up the study of law in 1843, was called to the bar in 1849, and began practising in Kingston in 1850. Henry Gildersleeve died 1 Oct. 1851, four months after the death of Overton's young wife, and at age 26 Overton became the head of the family shipping business, holding a majority of the stock in each ship, and the head of a household consisting of his mother, two sisters, and two brothers. He also succeeded his father as a director of the Kingston Marine Railway Company; it built all types of vessels for lake, river, and ocean traffic, and had an iron foundry, a sawmill, a hotel, and extensive wharfage rights.

With the launching of the *Bay of Quinte* in April 1852, Gildersleeve had three steamboats operating between Bay of Quinte ports and Cape Vincent (N.Y.). He had also taken his father's place, with John COUNTER and others, in the promotion of the Wolfe Island Railway and Canal Company which was expected to provide a shorter and more protected route between Kingston and Cape Vincent. The canal was completed in 1857; it continued to be used until 1890, but it carried little traffic and was not a profitable venture.

Competition from railways began, by the latter part of the 1850s, to affect the shipping business which had earlier undergone a period of great expansion. Rivalry between railways and steamboats led to competition between boatlines for passengers. In June 1854, for example, Gildersleeve engaged in racing and rate-cutting to force Belleville competitors to withdraw their boat within a month. Usually he offered passage between Kingston and Belleville, including stateroom and berth, for 5s., but during one season he provided the same service for 15d. By 1860 Gildersleeve was offering a round trip three-day excursion to Quebec City, with a quadrille band on board, for a special fare of $15.50. Similar excursions were conducted to other river and lake ports.

With the decline in lake traffic Gildersleeve joined John Hamilton* in re-forming Hamilton's Royal Mail Line and they became the principal stockholders in the new Canadian Inland Navigation Company. Gildersleeve and Hamilton bought up other steamers for service on their run between Hamilton, Toronto, Kingston, and Montreal. Gildersleeve was also a promoter of branch railways in this period – the Cataraqui and Peterborough incorporated in 1852 and the Kingston and Newburgh Railway in 1856.

Elected alderman in Kingston in 1854, Gildersleeve replaced Counter as mayor in June 1855 when Counter was forced to resign. Gildersleeve was elected mayor in 1861. In politics he was a Liberal, actively supporting Oliver Mowat* in the elections for the Legislative Assembly in 1861 and running unsuccessfully against John A. Macdonald* for the Kingston seat in 1863. On his death in 1864 his brother, and law partner since 1859, Charles Fuller Gildersleeve, took over the family business.

MARGARET S. ANGUS

Anglican Church of Canada, Diocese of Ontario, Synod Archives (Kingston, Ont.), St George's parish register, 1825. QUA, E. E. Horsey, "The Gildersleeves of Kingston, their activities 1816–1930" (typescript, 1942); Kingston City Council, proceedings, 1854–62. *Chronicle and News* (Kingston), 30 May 1854; 16 March, 22, 27 Nov. 1855. *Daily British Whig* (Kingston), 21 April 1836, 17 Nov. 1855. *Daily News* (Kingston), 17 Aug. 1850; 24 Oct. 1851; 28 April, 6 May 1852; 12 April 1861; 10 March 1864. A. G. Young, *Great Lakes saga; the influence of one family on the development of Canadian shipping on the Great Lakes, 1816–1931* (Toronto, 1965), 43–52.

GILL, IGNACE, businessman and politician; b. 15 March 1808 at Saint-François-du-Lac, Lower Canada, son of Thomas Gill, a farmer, and Catherine Bazin, and greatgrandson of Samuel Gill who as a child was kidnapped by the Abenakis of Saint-François at Salisbury (Mass.) in 1697; d. 1 Sept. 1865 at Saint-Thomas-de-Pierreville (Pierreville, Que.).

Ignace Gill worked as a clerk in the store of Michel Lemaître, then in that of the Mackenzies at Baie-du-Febvre (Baieville, Que.), where he learned English. He opened his own store around 1830 in a former presbytery of the Abenaki mission of Saint-François-de-Sales (Odanak). The Gill family had always been considered part of the tribe; however in 1833 the Abenakis, "tired of the authority of the Gills over the tribe," requested the government to strike the family off the list of tribe members drawn up by the Indian Department. When Gill ceased to run his store in 1850, he engaged in various activities: the timber trade, the building of barges, and the administration, as agent, of the Pierreville seigneury owned by François-Xavier Biron.

Ignace Gill was active in the public life of his village. He was appointed justice of the peace in 1835. On 18 June 1837, at a meeting protesting Lord John Russell's resolutions, he was named a member of a committee responsible for obtaining signatures to a petition to the American Congress requesting free trade with the United States; many people desired this *rapprochement* after London refused to accept the Ninety-Two Res-

olutions. After the suppression of the rebellion, however, he was recommended to Sir John COLBORNE as the person most suited to hold the office of stipendiary magistrate in his region. Later, in 1850, he fought against the *éteignoirs* of the county of Yamaska, whose members, like those of Saint-Grégoire-le-Grand in the county of Nicolet (Larochelle), set fire to the schools in protest against the 1846 law that had re-established the school tax [*see* Jean-Baptiste Meilleur*]. For years he was president of the Yamaska County Agricultural Society, and he was mayor of the parish of Saint-Thomas-de-Pierreville in 1862 and 1863.

Gill, a Conservative, was a successful candidate for the county of Yamaska in the 1854 election. His re-election in 1857, however, was difficult: the *enfant terrible* Jean-Baptiste-Éric DORION came to assist the Liberal candidate, Dr Roch-Moïse-Samuel Mignault. The malcontents claimed that the Abenaki women had been dressed in greatcoats and made to vote for "cousin" Gill. Gill was defeated in the 1861 elections. He died on 1 Sept. 1865, remembered as a profoundly religious and eminently charitable man.

On 30 Jan. 1832, at Baie-du-Febvre, Ignace Gill had married Elizabeth, daughter of Allen McDougald and Marie McPherson; then in September 1850, at Drummondville, he took as his second wife Jane Henrietta, daughter of William Robins and Margaret Anderson. By his first wife he had a son, Charles-Ignace, later a judge of the Superior Court and father of Charles-Ignace-Adélard*, painter and poet. The financier Louis-Adélard Sénécal* bought Gill's estate and in 1866 founded the Pierreville Steam Mills Company for the exploitation of timber. Family souvenirs are still preserved in the brick house built by Gill at Odanak in 1854.

THOMAS-M. CHARLAND

Le Journal des Trois-Rivières, 12 sept. 1865. T.-M. Charland, *Histoire de Saint-François-du-Lac* (Ottawa, 1942); *Histoire des Abénakis d'Odanak (1675–1937)* (Montréal, 1964). C.[-I.] Gill, *Notes historiques sur l'origine de la famille Gill et histoire de ma propre famille* (Montréal, 1887).

GILLESPIE, ROBERT, merchant and businessman; b. 1785 at Douglas, Lanarkshire, Scotland; d. 3 Sept. 1863 in London, England.

Robert Gillespie came to Montreal in 1800 to join his older brother, George Gillespie*, a partner in the firm of Parker, Gerrard, and Ogilvy which was one of the major components of the XY and, later, the North West companies. There

Gillespie

is no evidence that Robert ever served the firm in the northwest as a wintering partner; he seems to have worked only in the company's Montreal offices where he and his brother rose quickly to become its principal partners. In 1816 the firm changed its name to Gillespie, Moffatt, and Company. George MOFFATT was the principal associate and others involved were Samuel Gerrard*, Jasper Tough, John Jamieson, James Blackwood Greenshields, and Robert Patterson. By the early 1820s Gillespie's function in the company was the management of its London offices. Whether for his work or for personal reasons he moved to Britain in 1822 and he remained there until his death. By 1842 partners of Gillespie, Moffatt, and Company in Quebec, Toronto, and London provided important links with the major commercial centres of Canada and Britain. During these years copartnership arrangements were commonly made and within this framework there were regular changes of personnel as contracts usually lapsed at three or five-year intervals. Robert Gillespie and George Moffatt, however, were always the principal partners as the business grew and diversified during the 1840s.

Gillespie, Moffatt, and Company was the largest importing house in Montreal, and sold a wide variety of British manufactured goods. The firm was also extensively engaged in trade with the West Indies; by 1837 it was trading regularly between Quebec and Jamaica with its own and rented ships. Besides at least one vessel of its own, the firm also held interests in a number of Quebec-based ships. Its huge Montreal warehouse, owned by Gillespie, had room for 10,000 barrels of flour, 20,000 bushels of wheat, and 7 to 8,000 barrels of beef and pork as well as special facilities for inspecting, packing, and coopering pork. In addition, the firm was the Canadian agent of the London-based Phoenix Assurance Company, one of the first companies to sell fire insurance in Canada.

Robert Gillespie was involved in most of the controversies respecting Canadian trade, taking the side of the Montrealers who argued for liberalization of British regulations. During the political turmoil in Lower Canada of the late 1820s [see Denis-Benjamin VIGER], he appeared as a witness before the select committee of the British House of Commons on the civil government of Canada. Reflecting the general assumptions and aspirations of most English speaking merchants in Lower Canada, Gillespie recommended the establishment of registry offices and the political union of the Canadas as measures which would greatly improve business conditions. He pointed out that, because of the unavailability of registry offices, information about mortgages and other encumbrances could not be easily obtained thus retarding both settlement and investment in the province. Many Canadian merchants invested their money in Britain, he asserted, rather than in the inhospitable environment of Lower Canada.

Like many other merchants Gillespie supported efforts to improve Canadian transportation facilities in order to make Montreal a more competitive entrepôt; he was a director of the Company of Proprietors of the Lachine Canal, a group formed in 1819 to build a canal around the rapids a few miles upstream from Montreal. The company failed to raise sufficient capital and the project was taken over in 1821 by the Lower Canadian House of Assembly as a public work and completed in 1825. In addition to his interests in Gillespie, Moffatt, and Company, Gillespie became involved in a number of other Canadian business ventures. One was the British American Land Company formed in 1834 with London backers who included, besides Gillespie, Edward ELLICE, another former Montreal merchant then living in Britain; also involved were George Moffatt, and Peter McGill [McCutcheon*]. This company's vast holdings of land in Lower Canada's Eastern Townships became a political issue during the later 1830s, but the company nonetheless continued and eventually prospered. An early supporter of the Bank of Montreal, Gillespie served during the 1820s as its London agent. By 1836, however, again in company with London financiers, he helped to found the Bank of British North America which became a powerful competitor of the Bank of Montreal.

Gillespie appears to have prospered in Britain. Besides a London residence, he maintained a Scottish country seat, Springhill, in his native county of Lanark, not far from his brother George's estate of Biggar Park. Robert Gillespie died in London in 1863 leaving a modest estate valued at less than £50,000. Of his two daughters and three sons only Robert Jr seems to have developed any financial interest in Canada. Robert lived for some years in York (Toronto) where, in 1832, he opened a branch Gillespie, Jamieson, and Company. Later he moved to Britain, and in 1853 joined a group of London and Liverpool investors who formed the Canadian Steam Navigation Company which for two years operated a line of steamships between Liverpool and Montreal.

GERALD TULCHINSKY

ANQ-M, Greffe de Henry Griffin, 16 sept. 1842. BUM, Coll. Baby, Doc. divers, G2, 1820–30. Château de

Ramezay (Montréal), Antiquarian and Numismatic Society of Montreal, no.707. General Register Office (Edinburgh), will and codicils of Robert Gillespie, 4 Jan. 1864. McGill University Libraries, Dept. of Rare Books and Special Coll., ms coll., Frederick Griffin papers. PAC, RG 1, L3^L, 126, pp.62161–232; RG 42, I, 175, p.14. Can., Prov. of, *Statutes*, 1847, c.101; 1852–53, c.131. G.B., Parl., House of Commons paper, 1828, VII, 569, pp.375–733, *Report from the select committee on the civil government of Canada* (repr. Quebec, 1829). *Montreal Gazette*, 15 Feb. 1845.

Campbell, *History of Scotch Presbyterian Church*, 265. D. [G.] Creighton, *The empire of the St. Lawrence* (Toronto, 1956). Denison, *Canada's first bank*, I, 220. R. C. McIvor, *Canadian monetary, banking and fiscal development* (Toronto, 1961), 38. *Montreal business sketches with a description of the city of Montreal, its public buildings and places of interest, and the Grand Trunk works at Point St. Charles, Victoria bridge, &c., &c.* (Montreal, 1864), 183–87. Phoenix Assurance Company Ltd., *First in the field* ([Toronto, 1954]), 13. *Semi-centennial report of the Montreal Board of Trade, sketches of the growth of the city of Montreal from its foundation . . .* (Montreal, 1893), 46. Gerald Tulchinsky, "Construction of the first Lachine Canal, 1815–1826" (unpublished ma thesis, McGill University, Montreal, 1960), 39; "Studies in the development of transportation and industry in Montreal, 1837 1853" (unpublished phd thesis, University of Toronto, 1971), 480.

GINGRAS, LOUIS, secular priest and superior of the Séminaire de Québec; b. 5 Sept. 1796 at Saint-Olivier (Saint-Mathias, Quebec), son of Charles Gingras and Marie-Charlotte Blanchard, *dit* Raynaud; d. 6 March 1866 at Quebec.

Louis Gingras had as a benefactor Abbé Joseph Signay*, then parish priest of Sainte-Marie-de-Monnoir (Marieville), who sent him in 1810 to complete his studies at the Collège de Montréal. There the young man began his clerical training in 1817 and taught successfully for three years. He was ordained priest, however, at Quebec on 5 Nov. 1820. His protector had by then become the parish priest of the cathedral, and Gingras remained with him as curate until 28 Sept. 1821, when Bishop Joseph-Octave Plessis* appointed him missionary at Memramcook, New Brunswick. His health having deteriorated, he was recalled to the Quebec region. He became parish priest in turn of Sainte-Foy in 1825, of Saint-Pierre, Île d'Orléans, on 1 July 1826, serving also Saint-Laurent from 1827, and finally of Cap-Saint-Ignace from 10 Oct. 1832.

On 8 Aug. 1833 Gingras sought and obtained admission to the Séminaire de Québec. After a year's probation he was not only made a member of the community, but became its bursar, which gave him access to the directors' council. During his administration he appears to have concerned himself particularly with the seigneury of Île-Jésus. He was elected superior of the seminary in July 1848, and presided over part of the deliberations that led to the creation of the Université Laval. After three years in office he stepped down in favour of Abbé Louis-Jacques CASAULT, in order to devote himself to the teaching of theology. It was probably as a theologian that Abbé Gingras was summoned by Archbishop Pierre-Flavien TURGEON, in August 1851, to sit on the first provincial council of Quebec. He continued as a member of the seminary council, and as such was one of the nine priests to sign the petition of 1852 asking Queen Victoria to grant the charter of the Université Laval. Although his name disappears from the list of teachers at the seminary after 1854, Gingras had further opportunities to show his perspicacity and decisiveness when its superior, Casault, died unexpectedly in 1862, and when its building burned in 1865. Gingras, almost blind during the last 12 years of his life, resigned from the council in 1865, and died in March 1866.

A tradition has been handed down in Gingras' family to the effect that he once refused a mitre, and indeed it is conceivable that Abbé Signay, who became bishop of Quebec in 1833, may have thought of taking his former protégé as a coadjutor.

Honorius Provost

AAQ, 210 A, XII, 493, 501, 530; XIII, 217; XIV, 100; XV, 159, 282; 101 CM, 30. ASQ, mss, 676, pp.36–37, 146–54; Polygraphie, XXVI, 48; Séminaire, 75, no.9. *L'Abeille* (Québec), 13 mars 1879. Université Laval, *Annuaire* (Québec), 1867–68, 26–30.

GIROUX, ANDRÉ-RAPHAËL, sculptor and architect; b. 21 April 1815 at Charlesbourg, near Quebec, son of Michel Giroux, carpenter, and Marie-Anne Pageot; d. 25 Dec. 1869 at Saint-Casimir, Quebec.

The name Giroux was connected with religious architecture long before the beginning of André-Raphaël's career. Indeed, at the beginning of the 19th century an outstanding group of this family, which had originally settled at Beauport, was active in various building trades at Quebec, particularly in the *faubourg* Saint-Roch. In his will Thomas Baillairgé* bequeathed to Giroux his sketch books, his architectural manuals, and some tools; presumably Giroux served his apprenticeship with the master and received his training as sculptor and architect on Baillairgé's numerous building sites. The name of André-Raphaël Giroux, sculptor, first appears in the record in 1838, when he married Sélina Bédard at Quebec. She died soon afterwards and he married again on 22 Oct. 1844, his second wife being Adélaïde Michaud.

From 1847 to 1850 André-Raphaël Giroux worked on the chapel of the Hôtel-Dieu of Quebec, where he carved the side altars according to Thomas Baillairgé's plans. In 1853 Giroux's design for the new high altar of the church of Saint-Roch was chosen over those of Thomas Fournier* and Louis-Thomas Berlinguet. He executed this work the following year, and left Ancienne-Lorette, where he seems to have lived from 1850 to 1853, to settle in the *faubourg* Saint-Roch of Quebec. From 1853 on, he was also involved in the interior decoration of the church of Notre-Dame-de-la-Victoire, Lévis. In 1854 he agreed to undertake the interior decoration of the chapel of the Sisters of Charity at Quebec, following the plans of Charles Baillairgé*, Thomas' nephew; this work was praised in the Quebec papers at the dedication of the chapel. When the wing for the Université Laval at the Séminaire de Québec was built in 1857, Giroux again collaborated with Charles Baillairgé.

Paralleling Giroux's career as a sculptor was his work as an architect after 1858. He planned and built the Saint-Joseph and Saint-Thomas wings of the Ursuline convent, Quebec, and in 1859 drew up the plans and specifications for a church at the Percé mission. He also had a share in drafting the plans for the Saint-Laurent church, on Île d'Orléans.

A second phase in André-Raphaël Giroux's career began at Cap-Santé in 1859, where his work truly became original. In partnership with a master-plasterer, and using his own plans, Giroux began work on the whole of the church's interior architecture (completed in 1863). In 1861 he opened a second large building yard at Saint-Pierre-les-Becquets (Les Becquets, Que.), where he saw to the completion of the church interior and the construction of a sacristy (finished in 1866). Working without respite, André-Raphaël Giroux accepted a contract in 1862, proposed by the parish council of Saint-Casimir, for the completion of the interior of that church (finished in 1868). While directing these three large work sites on opposite shores of the St Lawrence, Giroux, whose reputation as an architect now seemed established, was also called upon to intervene as an expert when conflicts occurred between churchwardens and contractors, notably at Deschaillons in 1862.

This increasing volume of work did not, however, bring prosperity. In 1867, to cover his mortgages, Giroux was forced to cancel his agreement as a contractor with the parish council of Saint-Casimir, and to complete this undertaking while being paid as a day labourer. Although completely ruined, he undertook the interior architectural work for the church of Gentilly in 1869, the year of his death. Two of his sons, Alfred and Eugène, took over from him there; they were joined around 1880 by their younger brother, Joseph, who was sometimes an architect, sometimes a contractor; the latter's sons, during the first half of the 20th century, were to be the pillars of the Giroux dynasty of Saint-Casimir, contractors of high repute in the field of ecclesiastical architecture.

In what is customarily called the Thomas Baillairgé school, the place occupied by André-Raphaël Giroux is important. He shared in most tasks undertaken by the master-architect towards the end of his career, and the plans he devised at that time continued those of Baillairgé. More interesting, however, is Giroux's work as sculptor and architect after Thomas Baillairgé's death. From the beginning, at Cap-Santé, André-Raphaël Giroux displayed a creativity vastly superior to that of Thomas Baillairgé's other followers. Generally he kept alive the architectural detail typical of the Louis XVI style, but imbued it with a lightness and a decorative grace unknown before. His interiors are, moreover, well designed, for his sculptural skill ensured that architectural elements would be prominent rather than buried under superfluous ornament. An innovation was the projection of retables into the sanctuary, in which he freely employed curved form to give artistic unity to the design. Elongated lines characterized his style. Thus, more than the Baillairgés, Giroux heralds the monumentality of architecture in the second half of the 19th century. Coming just before the generation of architects who were to introduce into Quebec the eclectic architecture of the European 19th century, André-Raphaël Giroux is an important link in the chain that unites them to Thomas Baillairgé.

LUC NOPPEN

AJQ, Greffe de C.-A. Lemay, 30 avril 1862. ANQ-Q, Greffe de Joseph Bernard, 23 nov. 1859, 27 mars 1863; Greffe d'Henri Bolduc, 2 mars 1852; Greffe de Charles Cinq-Mars, 6 mars 1854; Greffe de C.-M. Defoy, 13 mai 1841; Greffe de F.-L. Gauvreau, 17 mai 1848, 13 sept. 1853; Greffe de James Haney, 23 déc. 1869; Greffe de A.-Archange Parent, 4 mars 1818. Archives des ursulines de Québec, Journal, 18, 30 oct. 1858, 21 sept., 6 nov., 1859; 19, 17 juin 1860, 6 mars 1861. Archives du monastère de l'Hôtel-Dieu de Québec, Livre des dépenses de la communauté, 9, pp.301–3, 321–22, 406; 10, pp.3–4; Livre des recettes et des dépenses de la communauté, 1825–57, pp.364–79, 406, 425. Archives judiciaires de Richelieu (Sorel, Qué.), Greffe de Paul Payan, 2 nov. 1864, 9 sept. 1865. Archives paroissiales, Saint-Casimir (Saint-Casimir, Qué.), Livres de comptes et de délibérations, 1868; Saint-Jean-Baptiste (Deschaillons, Qué.), Livres de comptes, III (1861–1915), dépenses 1867; Saint-Laurent (île d'Orléans, Qué.), Livres de comptes, V (1863–1900), 7 avril 1860; Saint-Pierre (Les Becquets, Qué.), Livres de comptes et de délibérations, 1861, 1866; Devis de la voûte par André Paquet; Saint-Roch (Québec), Livres de comptes et de délibérations, 21 févr., 2 avril 1848, comptes de 1853. ASQ, C 4, p.472; Polygraphie, XIX, 59. IBC, Centre de documentation, Fonds Morisset, Dossiers Giroux; Charles Baillairgé; Dossiers Cap-Santé; Deschaillons; Gentilly; Lévis; Notre-Dame-de-la-Victoire; Québec; Saint-Roch; Saint-Pierre-les-Becquets; Yamaska. *Le Courrier du Canada*, 3 janv. 1870. *Le Journal de Québec*, 4 mai 1854, 13 sept. 1856, 4 août 1859. *La Minerve*, 21 août 1873. Gérard Morisset, *Le Cap-Santé, ses églises et son trésor* (Québec, 1944); "L'influence des Baillairgé," *Technique* (Montréal), XXVI (1951), 307–14.

GLADMAN, GEORGE, fur-trader and explorer; b. 23 June 1800 at New Brunswick House, an HBC post on Brunswick Lake (Ont.), son of the fur-trader George Gladman and of an Indian woman; d. 24 Sept. 1863 at Port Hope, Canada West.

George Gladman entered the service of the Hudson's Bay Company in 1814 under his father at Eastmain House. He served as clerk at Moose Factory from 1819 to 1834, and, after a year's furlough in England, at Cumberland House in 1835–36. Promoted chief trader in 1836, Gladman was at York Factory and Norway House (1836–41), Upper Fort Garry (1841), and Oxford House (1842–45). While in the northwest he married, probably in 1837, Harriet, daughter of Thomas Vincent* of the HBC, who was the abandoned wife of R.D. Stewart of the same company; they were to have six children. After 31 years in the HBC service Gladman retired in 1845 to settle at Port Hope. Here he opened a store, which did not prosper, and his health also gave him trouble. In 1849 he re-entered the company's service at the King's Posts on the lower St Lawrence at Tadoussac, but resigned again in 1853 to return to Port Hope.

Gladman's retirement was, however, interrupted by his being chosen leader of the Canadian exploring expedition to Red River in 1857. The parliamentary inquiry by a select committee of the British House of Commons in February and March of 1857 into the petition of the HBC for renewal of its licence had added to the interest already awakened in Canada in the future of British northwest America. Indeed merchants of Toronto and Hamilton wished to share, or take over, the trade of St Paul (Minn.) with Red River, and farmers in Canada West saw it as a region which might afford new farm lands.

On 11 May 1857 the Legislative Assembly of the Province of Canada also appointed a select committee, to inquire into the agricultural possibilities of the northwest. This committee heard witnesses, and as was natural in view of his experience and accessibility, Gladman was one. The committee's recommendation that an expedition be sent to explore the route to Red River and the area's agricultural prospects was acted on by the government on 18 July. Gladman was appointed head of the expedition, on which he was accompanied by his son Henry and by Simon James Dawson*, engineer, and Henry Youle Hind*, geologist and naturalist; Dawson and Hind had special instructions. The expedition left Toronto on 23 July 1857, and its organization was therefore hurried. Its instructions proved to be unclear: Gladman was to lead the expedition to Red River, but Dawson and Hind were expected to make observations along the way. There was thus some difference of purpose, and probably in consequence Gladman went on ahead of the other parties to Fort Frances, on Rainy Lake, to secure canoemen and then on to Red River to make preparations for the arrival of the others. All might have been well had he indeed made adequate provision in the settlement for the oncoming party, most of whom were to work and winter there. By his own report he did, but Hind and other members were dissatisfied, and relations between Gladman on the one hand and Hind and Dawson on the other grew strained.

Dawson was to remain at Red River during the winter of 1857–58, but Hind and Gladman both returned to Toronto, the latter arriving in September. Hind set about writing his report of the 1857 expedition and making plans for a similar expedition in 1858 to go as far as the Saskatchewan River. It was at first assumed that Gladman would lead it. But to the complaints already sent to the provincial secretary from Red River by Hind and Dawson, Hind now added a formal list of eight objections against Gladman ranging from his alleged refusal to give Hind a light canoe for explorations on the way to Red River to failure to make adequate arrangements for the arrival of the Hind and Dawson parties there. Gladman, in his replies to the criticism made of his work, responded amiably to the chief commissioner of crown lands, Philip Michael Matthew Scott VanKoughnet, and to the provincial secretary,

Globensky

Thomas-Jean-Jacques Loranger*, and made no countercharges. His defence was that he could not be held wholly responsible for the conduct of the expedition as the instructions had not put him fully in charge and it had in fact been given three leaders.

He accepted quietly the government's decision not to use his services again and cheerfully resumed his retirement. He returned to Port Hope where he died in 1863.

W. L. MORTON

PAC, RG 5, C1, 523, 543. Can., Prov. of, Crown Lands Dept., *Report on the exploration of the country between Lake Superior and the Red River Settlement* (Toronto, 1858), 185. G.B., Parl., House of Commons paper, 1857, *Report from the select committee on the HBC*. Mactavish, *Letters of Letitia Hargrave* (MacLeod). W. L. Morton, *Henry Youle Hind: explorer, geologist, promoter* (Toronto, 1976). L. H. Thomas, "The Hind and Dawson expeditions, 1857–58," *Beaver*, outfit 289 (winter 1958), 39–45.

GLOBENSKY, MAXIMILIEN, soldier, b. 15 April 1793 at Verchères, Lower Canada, son of Dr Auguste-France Globensky, of Polish extraction, and Marie-Françoise Brousseau, *dit* Lafleur de Verchères; m. first Élisabeth Lemaire Saint-Germain, by whom he had four daughters and one son, and secondly Marie-Anne Panet on 3 March 1851 at Sainte-Mélanie; d. 16 June 1866 at Saint-Eustache, Canada East.

Maximilien Globensky is remembered because of his participation in the War of 1812 and the disturbances of 1837 at Saint-Eustache. He enlisted in the Canadian Voltigeurs during the war with the United States, and took part in the battles of Châteauguay, Lacolle, and Ormstown. On Lieutenant-Colonel Charles-Michel d'Irumberry* de Salaberry's recommendation, he was given the rank of 2nd lieutenant on 24 March 1813 for recruiting 12 men. When peace was restored, he was promoted 1st lieutenant on 8 Feb. 1815. He was also granted half pay, which he continued to receive until his death, and 500 acres of land in Buckingham County. This grant he was able to exchange for other land in the Plantagenet Township, Upper Canada. On 11 Dec. 1826 he became a captain in the 1st militia battalion of York County, Lower Canada. Ten years later, on 12 April 1836, he acquired 933 acres in Drummond County.

On 27 Nov. 1837, only a few days after the battles of Saint-Denis and Saint-Charles, the military authorities asked Globensky to raise 60 volunteers, and entrusted him with command of the group. According to his son Charles-Auguste-Maximilien, Globensky recruited his men from "the most highly regarded, the most respectable and the most comfortably off" citizens of Saint-Eustache. On 14 Dec. 1837, when the British soldiers opened fire on the Patriotes at Saint-Eustache, these volunteers were stationed on an island opposite the village, blocking the escape of fugitives across the frozen surface of the Rivière des Mille-Îles. The next day Globensky was instructed by Sir John COLBORNE to maintain order at Saint-Eustache after the defeat of the Patriotes and the departure of the regular troops for nearby Saint-Benoît.

If his son is to be believed, Globensky cannot be held responsible for the abuses committed at Saint-Eustache. On the contrary, reports his son, despite his family's hostility towards the Patriotes and the differences of his sister Hortense* with some of them, his attitude towards them was kindly and he also sought to protect them from needless cruelty, for example by preventing soldiers and volunteers from outside the area from totally destroying the village. But there are no documents bearing specifically on his attitude during these dark hours except the favourable testimony collected by his son. There is no doubt, however, that volunteers of Maximilien Globensky's company did take part in the depredations. According to Colborne, the officials of Saint-Eustache and Rivière du Chêne were the perpetrators of the destruction. It is true that the commander-in-chief thus relieved his regulars of all responsibility. Although Colborne's argument concerning the desire for revenge on the part of the local pro-government faction is not without logic, one must remember that Globensky's son himself admitted that some volunteers under his father's orders might have carried out reprisals.

In any case, Globensky's assistance was appreciated by the government, since on 4 Nov. 1838 he was asked to raise a group of volunteers to counter the insurrection of the Hunters' Lodges. Meanwhile he had acquired 200 acres in Arthabaska County. On 12 Sept. 1845 Maximilien Globensky ended his career in the Lower Canadian militia with the title of lieutenant-colonel. He was still prepared for military duty towards the end of his life, since he offered his services to the government in the 1860s when the *Trent* affair and the threat of a Fenian invasion aroused fears of an armed conflict with the American republic.

Globensky always thought of himself as a soldier, but evidence from one document suggests that he may have engaged in business of some kind during the quiet years he spent at Saint-Eustache. His motto, "God and my King," reveals the convictions of a soldier who always discharged his duties with dignity. Some years after his death in 1866, he was attacked for having taken up arms against the Patriotes by political opponents of his son, who was elected as a Conservative in the 1875 by-election in the county of Deux-Montagnes. Charles-Auguste-Maximilien then undertook to defend his father's memory in *La rébellion de 1837 à Saint-Eustache*, which he finished in 1877 but did not publish until 1883. His interpretation of 1837 roused the wrath of Laurent-Olivier David* and a sharp and interminable controversy ensued in *La Minerve* and *La Patrie* about the meaning of the 1837 rebellion and of the events at Saint-Eustache.

JEAN-PIERRE GAGNON

ANQ-M, État civil, Catholiques, Saint-François-Xavier-de-Verchères, 15 avril 1793. PAC, MG 8, G29, 15, p.5487; RG 1, L3, 93, pp.46243–45; RG 8, I (C series), 1, p.28; 187, p.117; 797, p.83; 798, p. 23; 1039, pp. 15, 123, 125, 165; 1170, p.154; 1172, p.111; 1202, pp.19, 31, 39; RG 9, I, A5, 5; 14, p.273. PRO, CO 42/280, p.260. Charles Beauclerk, *Lithographic views of military operations in Canada under His Excellency Sir John Colborne during the late insurrection* (London, 1840). *La Minerve*, 23 juin 1866. *Quebec Gazette*, 18 Dec. 1837.

Langelier, *List of lands granted. Liste de la milice du Bas-Canada, pour 1829* (Québec, [1829]). *Mariages du comté de Joliette (du début des paroisses à 1960 inclusivement)*, Lucien Rivest, compil. (4v., Montréal, 1969), II. Émile Dubois, *Le feu de la Rivière-du-Chêne; étude historique sur le mouvement insurrectionnel de 1837 au nord de Montréal* (Saint-Jérome, Qué., 1937). [C.-A.-M. Globensky], *La rébellion de 1837 à Saint-Eustache précédé d'un exposé de la situation politique du Bas-Canada depuis la cession* (Québec, 1883). Ludwik Kos-Rabcewicz-Zubkowski, *Les Polonais au Canada* (Ottawa et Montréal, 1968), 12, 14–17, 48, 50, 53, 162. *The Polish past in Canada; contributions to the history of the Poles in Canada and of the Polish-Canadian relations*, ed. Wiktor Turek (Toronto, 1960), 101–22. "Feu M. C. A. M. Globensky," *Le Courrier de Saint-Hyacinthe*, 14 févr. 1906. Jacques Prévost, "Les Globensky au Canada français," SGCF *Mémoires*, XVII (1966), 156–61.

GODEFROY DE TONNANCOUR, LÉONARD, politician; b. 7 Nov. 1793 at Saint-Michel-d'Yamaska, Lower Canada, fifth child of Marie-Joseph Godefroy de Tonnancour and Catherine Pélissier, *dit* La Feuillade; d. 29 Jan. 1867 at Saint-Michel-d'Yamaska.

Léonard Godefroy de Tonnancour belonged to the sixth generation of one of the oldest seigneurial families in Lower Canada. His father gained fame through his part in the resistance to the American invasions of 1775–76 and 1812. He was a representative in the first House of Assembly of Lower Canada, and he instilled in his children a respect for the old seigneurial traditions, in a setting where the interests of the military aristocracy and the requirements of an active public life were combined.

In 1806, at 13, Léonard entered the Séminaire de Nicolet. When he finished his studies in 1812, he decided to work as administrator and farmer on the family estates. In early 1832 his father was feeling the burden of age and decided to make his will. The Labadie seigneury went to the eldest son, Marie-Joseph. The other children were to receive equal shares in the Yamaska seigneury and a part of the Saint-François seigneury, with entail of the estate to their children. Joseph Godefroy de Tonnancour further bequeathed to each of his children 100 acres of land in the township of Acton, given to him by the government for services rendered.

In the same year, Léonard Godefroy de Tonnancour was elected to represent the county of Yamaska in the assembly. The atmosphere was tense in Lower Canada at that time. The quarrel over government finances, the 1822 plan of union, bad harvests, and scarcity of land hardened the attitudes of a number of leading French Canadians, and the Patriote party set up local organizations to rally the country people. But Godefroy de Tonnancour, whose interests were tied to those of his social group, was more inclined to support the government. In 1837 he refused to follow the Patriotes of his parish. At Saint-Denis-sur-Richelieu, where he had gone to visit his mother-in-law, they treated him to a "charivari." A popular celebration in the 18th century, the charivari acquired a distinctly political significance during the disturbances. Indeed, opponents of the Papineau party were not infrequently threatened by Patriote gatherings.

After the disturbances the Patriotes of the Saint-Michel-d'Yamaska region became more moderate and did not oppose Godefroy de Tonnancour so strongly. In 1838 he abandoned public life, and was content to lead a peaceful existence with his family, enjoying the income from his estates. He was well regarded by his parish priest and the people of his district; he died quietly at Saint-Michel-d'Yamaska in the year of confederation. On 14 Sept 1835 he had married Marguerite Cherrier, and they had nine children.

RICHARD CHABOT

ANQ-Q, QBC 25, Événements de 1837–1838, nos.2816, 2833. *Le Populaire* (Montréal), 2 oct. 1837. F.-J. Audet, *Les députés des Trois-Rivières, 1808–1838* (Trois-Rivières, 1934), 14–21. F.-J. Audet et Edouard

Goldsmith

Fabre Surveyer, *Les députés de Saint-Maurice et de Buckinghamshire, 1792–1808* (Trois-Rivières, 1934), 41–46; *Les députés au premier parlement du Bas-Canada, [1792–1796]* . . . (Montréal, 1946), 67. J.-A.-I. Douville, *Histoire du collège-séminaire de Nicolet, 1803–1903, avec les listes complètes des directeurs, professeurs et élèves de l'institution* (2v., Montréal, 1903), II, 129. Alexandre Dugré, *La Pointe-du-Lac* (Trois-Rivières, 1934), 14–21. P.-G. Roy, *La famille Godefroy de Tonnancour* (Lévis, Qué., 1904).

GOLDSMITH, OLIVER, author and civil servant; b. 6 July 1794 in St Andrews, N.B., son of Henry Goldsmith and Mary Mason, and grandnephew of Oliver Goldsmith, the Anglo-Irish poet; d. unmarried 23 June 1861 in Liverpool, England.

As a youngster Oliver Goldsmith tried his hand at a number of professions and trades. He worked at the Halifax Naval Hospital but was nauseated by current medical practices; he was apprenticed to an ironmonger who discharged him for idleness; he then worked for a bookseller, and subsequently in a lawyer's office. Finally, through the influence of his father, who was first assistant commissary general in Halifax and who took charge of the commissariat in New Brunswick in 1810, Oliver began work as a civilian volunteer in the British army's commissariat at Halifax in 1810; his appointment was confirmed in December 1814.

Goldsmith was to hold various positions during a long career in the commissariat. It was interrupted in its early stage by visits to Liverpool, London, and Plymouth for much of 1817, and a circuitous return to Nova Scotia via New York, Boston, and Maine, where he was shipwrecked on Hat Island early in 1818. After his return he was posted first to Halifax, then transferred to New Brunswick in 1833, and, rising steadily in rank and responsibility, found himself ordered to Hong Kong in 1844. He served there until March 1848 and in October of that year was appointed to Newfoundland where he led, by his account, a socially full and an intellectually satisfying life, helping to organize a masonic lodge and a mechanics' institute. He attained the rank of deputy commissary general in 1853. Retiring in June of that year on half pay, he sailed for England where he spent his time in leisurely travel including an extended visit to Ireland. In 1854 Goldsmith was pressed into service once again, and was posted to Corfu until ill health forced his return to England in 1855 and his retirement on half pay. He lived in Liverpool with his sister until his death.

Goldsmith's career as a writer seems to have followed a whimsical and sporadic course. He later noted that in 1822 he had dabbled in amateur theatre in Halifax, and that he had written some verse. *The rising village*, a narrative poem of 528 lines in pentameter couplet, was first published in 1825 in London. Goldsmith later wrote: "In my humble poem, I . . . endeavoured to describe the sufferings they [the loyalists] experienced in a new and uncultivated Country, the Difficulties they surmounted, the Rise and progress of a Village, and the prospects which promised Happiness to its future possessors." It has become recognized as an important example of early Canadian verse as well as a valuable commentary on contemporary life and conditions in the Maritimes and an expression of the aspirations of a pioneer society.

Comparisons have always been made between this poem and the famed work of Goldsmith's great-uncle, *The deserted village*. Goldsmith himself felt such comparisons were unfair, although he seems to have been making a response, certainly in spirit, to the earlier poem. Contemporary commentators were on the whole generous, including a reviewer in the *Canadian Review and Magazine* in February 1826, who found the author "indeed worthy of the relationship he bears to that great genius." Goldsmith claimed, however, that adverse criticism squelched his creativity, and that he "abandoned the Muses"; but a reworked text of his poem together with a number of shorter poems published in Saint John, N.B., in 1834 is evidence to the contrary. The other verse included in this edition was of an occasional and social nature, intended as entertainment and diversion rather than as a serious literary statement.

Goldsmith's *Autobiography* remained undiscovered until Reverend W. E. Myatt found it in the family papers and published it with valuable annotations in 1943. Only 24 pages in type, it seems to be a telescoped, and, in places, incorrectly remembered version of some events in Goldsmith's busy and long life. It nevertheless provides interesting information on the life of a man who is widely regarded as Canada's first native-born poet to write in English.

MICHAEL GNAROWSKI

Oliver Goldsmith's *The rising village, a poem* (London, 1825) was republished with additional poetry as *"The rising village," with other poems* (Saint John, N.B., 1834); it was also republished as *"The rising village" of Oliver Goldsmith* . . . , ed. Michael Gnarowski (Montreal, 1968). *See also*: [Oliver Goldsmith], *The autobiography of Oliver Goldsmith, published for the first time from the original manuscript of the author of "The rising village,"* ed. W. E. Myatt (Toronto, 1943), and *The manuscript book of Oliver Goldsmith, author* of "The rising village," ed. E. C. Kyte (Toronto, 1950). Desmond Pacey, "The Goldsmiths and their villages," *University of Toronto Quarterly*, XXI (1951–52), 27–38.

GOODHUE, GEORGE JERVIS, merchant, landowner, and politician; b. 1 Aug. 1799 at Putney, Vt, son of Josiah Goodhue, a prominent physician in both Vermont and Massachusetts, and Rachel Burr; d. 11 Jan. 1870 at London, Ont.

George Jervis Goodhue was one of three brothers who immigrated to Canada. Charles Frederick Henry went to Sherbrooke, Lower Canada, and Josiah Cosmore settled in the St Thomas, Upper Canada, area before moving on to Chicago, where he sat on the first city council in 1835.

George Jervis received some education at Amherst, Mass., before coming to the London District in 1820 at the age of 21. He soon became a general merchant, distiller, and pearl-ash maker in Westminster Township. By 1827 he had a branch at Ancaster from which he brought most of his supplies. In 1825 he had returned to New England to marry Maria Fullerton of Chester, Vt; she died in 1828 leaving an infant daughter. In 1831 he married Louisa Matthews, the daughter of Captain John Matthews*, former member of the House of Assembly for Middlesex; they had two sons and four daughters. One daughter was to marry a son of Bishop Benjamin Cronyn* and another married Francis Wolferstan Thomas*, general manager of Molsons Bank.

The establishment of London as the district capital in 1826 presented Goodhue with the opportunity of becoming a really wealthy man. By 1830 he was located on the Court House square where he "sold everything the settlers wanted and bought everything they had to sell." Two years later he formed a profitable partnership with Laurence Laurason* as "Laurason and Co.," general merchants, and, for a short period before 1836, agents for the Bank of Upper Canada (Goodhue and Laurason were later both directors of the bank, the former holding that office from 1848 to 1854). The partnership was dissolved amicably in 1840, Goodhue reportedly receiving $40,000 for his share of the store. During the 1830s he was also involved in railway speculation, being one of the incorporators in 1834 of the London and Gore Railroad Company (later revived as the Great Western Railway), along with Allan MacNab, Dennis O'Brien, and Laurason, and in 1836 of the Niagara and Detroit Rivers Rail Road Company. Neither venture was successful and his losses may have been the reason for his lack of interest in developmental projects at a later date.

Goodhue had held some minor offices in Westminster and London townships; he was made postmaster of London in 1830, although not naturalized until 1834, and kept the appointment until 1852. When London was incorporated as a village in 1840, he was elected to the council for St George's ward and became the first village president by vote of the councillors. He did not run for re-election, but was appointed one of the district magistrates after the union of 1841. Then, in 1842, when Louis-Hippolyte La Fontaine and Robert Baldwin* needed a member from western Upper Canada for the Legislative Council, Goodhue's pro-reform attitudes, or rather those of his brother Josiah Cosmore and of his father-in-law, stood him in good stead. Further, in spite of his Congregational background, he had become a member of the Church of England. The stumbling block to his appointment to the upper house was the need for the approval of the local Methodists. Goodhue accordingly attended a Methodist missionary meeting and poured the contents of his purse, reported as $50, on the table; the appointment duly followed. In the upper house he played a merely nominal role until ill health prevented his attendance in the mid 1860s. He was not appointed to the Senate in 1867.

After 1840 he concentrated on land speculation and mortgages, and, to quote the family biographer, "the care of his estate became the occupation of his life." Goodhue's interest in land speculation had begun as early as 1830 when he purchased 30 acres north of the settlement and opened this land as London's first subdivision. In the years following, his operations rapidly expanded. Profiting from the rebellion of 1837 he acquired in 1841 some of the lands confiscated from the rebel Anthony Van Egmond*. He also purchased crown lands, particularly in Huron County, and acquired other property by purchase and foreclosure of his mortgages, on which he charged interest rates which varied from 6 per cent in prosperous times to 24 per cent in the depression years after 1857. When he died he had interests in London itself and in the counties of Elgin, Grey, Huron, Kent, Lambton, Middlesex, Oxford, Perth, and Simcoe. The value of his estate was about $650,000.

Just before he died, Goodhue dictated his will to one of London's best-known lawyers, Henry Corry Rowley Becher*. It provided that the bulk of his estate would not be distributed until after his wife's death. The family unanimously opposed this clause and at their request the MPP for London, John Carling*, had a private bill passed in the Ontario legislature breaking the will.

Gordon

Another member, Edward Blake*, realizing that this bill set a precedent for legislative interference with estates, immediately introduced another bill which provided that in future any such measure would be referred to the appropriate legal authorities for advice before legislative action was taken. Both bills became law in 1871. Becher still refused to distribute the estate and on appeal the case was heard before a committee of nine judges, including William Henry Draper*, John Godfrey Spragge*, Oliver Mowat*, and John Hawkins Hagarty*. Their 1873 judgement supported Becher. The heirs then attempted to have a second statute passed to circumvent the judicial objections. Because of the Blake act this second bill was referred to a group of the same judges, who reported against it. The estate was only distributed after Louisa's death in 1880.

Clarence T. Campbell correctly stated that Goodhue was "a man of business, who thought of little else than business." In his activities he was neither better nor worse than any of the other Upper Canadian pioneer merchants who rose to wealth as their region opened up. London was one of the last areas of the province to be settled, however, and in his case the memory of his great wealth and the tales of the harshness of his business activities have not yet died. Indeed the legend of Goodhue as a sort of tight-fisted Midas has become deeply rooted in western Ontario folklore.

FREDERICK H. ARMSTRONG

Middlesex County Surrogate Court (London, Ont.), no.668 (will of G. J. Goodhue); no.1980 (will of Louisa Goodhue). PAO, RG8, I-7-F-2, box 20, nos. 9, 68; box 25, nos. 157, 158. UWO, 128 (George J. Goodhue papers). E. J. Carty, "The diary of H. C. R. Becher," *London Advertiser*, 6 Nov.–24 Dec. 1926. *Daily Advertiser* (London), 12, 15 Jan. 1870. *London Free Press*, 17 Jan. 1870, 2 Aug. 1880. "Re Goodhue [in appeal]: Tovey v. Goodhue; Goodhue v. Tovey," *Reports of cases adjudged in the Court of Chancery of Ontario*, reporter Alexander Grant (29v., Toronto, 1861–83), XIX, 366–455. C. T. Campbell, *Pioneer days in London; some account of men and things in London before it became a city* (London, Ont., 1921), 29–33, 68, 84–85, 88, 91, 119. J. E. Goodhue, *History and genealogy of the Goodhue family in England and America to the year 1890* (Rochester, N.Y., 1891), 40–41, 71–73, 144–45. *History of the county of Middlesex* (Brock), 71, 74, 112, 140, 195, 216, 221, 225, 231, 258–59, 264, 340, 568, 573. F. H. Armstrong, "Depression of 1857," *London Free Press*, 5 May 1971; "George Jervis Goodhue: pioneer merchant of London, Upper Canada," *OH*, LXIII (1971), 217–32.

GORDON, EDWARD JOHN, Roman Catholic priest; b. 1 Nov. 1791 in Dublin (Republic of Ireland), son of Francis Gordon and Margaret McKernan; d. 15 Oct. 1870 at Hamilton, Ont.

Edward John Gordon's parents died when he was a child and he was brought up by an uncle living in County Wicklow. In 1811 Gordon, who had been baptized into the Church of Ireland, was converted to the Roman Catholic faith through the influence of a brother. He then lived with a parish priest of County Wicklow, with whom he studied humanities until 1814, when he went to live with his brother in Woolwich, England. In 1817 he came to Canada. He was one of the first students to enter the newly opened seminary at St Raphael, Upper Canada, and after three years of theological studies he was ordained by Bishop Alexander Macdonell* on 29 Jan. 1829.

Gordon's first year of ministry was spent at St Raphael as bursar and as a teacher at the seminary and in helping in the neighbouring missions. Early in 1830 he was appointed to York (Toronto) to assist Father William John O'Grady* in the parish of St Paul's. O'Grady felt that although Gordon's "talents or acquirements may possibly not be of the first order . . . he is blessed with solid judgment and piety, together with a sufficient portion of prudence and good sense to regulate his conduct in the duties assigned to him." Gordon also served as an itinerant missionary in the York area. His first missionary journey, made during the winter season and without the aid of a horse, to the townships north of Toronto, including that of West Gwillimbury which had never before been visited by a Catholic clergyman, was described in a letter he wrote on 11 March 1830 to Macdonell and is indicative of his lifelong zeal: "The difficulties, hardships and expenses of my mission were forgotten, when I witnessed the fervour of our poor people in complying with their spiritual duties, their willingness to contribute to the support of a clergyman and the fervent prayers they offered to Heaven for your Eternal welfare, in thus giving them the means of complying with their duty." In 1833, when O'Grady and Macdonell were in conflict, the bishop ordered Gordon to leave O'Grady's house as his "presence there has been and is a virtual approval of his [O'Grady's] disobedient, contumacious and schismatic conduct. . . ." Gordon denied disloyalty to his bishop.

Soon after, Gordon was sent to Kingston to look after the back missions and remained there six months. Gordon was appointed the first resident clergyman in the Niagara peninsula on 23 April 1834 and completed, at Niagara in 1835, its first Catholic church. He was responsible for the missions in the area around Niagara and near the falls, and in 1842 also assumed the charge of the district of St Catharines for a short time. On 31 Oct. 1846 he went to Hamilton and Waterdown, with privileges as rural dean in the Gore, Talbot, and Niagara districts, but two weeks later he replaced Father William Peter MacDonald* at St Mary's Church in Hamilton. In 1851 he also became vicar general to Bishop Armand de Charbonnel* of Toronto, who assigned Father Auguste Carayon as his assistant.

The establishment of the new diocese of Hamilton in 1856 saw John Farrell* named first bishop and Gordon first vicar general, a post Gordon continued to hold for the rest of his life. Gordon also remained rector of St Mary's, which had become the cathedral church, though he was in semi-retirement because of ill health after 1862. The church was destroyed by fire in August 1859 at a loss of $20,000 and Gordon was instrumental in replacing it; the corner-stone of the new cathedral was laid within 40 days of the fire, and the church was dedicated on 21 May 1860.

Gordon had also been instrumental in bringing the Sisters of St Joseph to Hamilton in 1852 and persuaded Sister Mary Martha [BUNNING] and two novices to found a convent and orphanage in a house he provided. He was active in the establishment of separate schools in Hamilton, which were placed under the charge of the sisters in 1853, and donated a lot to be used for a school. During the cholera epidemic of 1854 Gordon and Carayon attended to the spiritual needs of the victims.

Edward Gordon visited Ireland twice, in 1839, and in 1864, en route to Rome to visit Pope Pius IX. He died in Hamilton six years later at the age of 78 and was buried beneath the cathedral.

J. S. McGIVERN

Archives of the Archdiocese of Toronto, Macdonell papers, AB24–AB25; BBO4; CA14–CA18; Bishops Power and de Charbonnel letterbook. W. P. Bull, *From Macdonell to McGuigan, the history of the Roman Catholic Church in Upper Canada* (Toronto, 1939). [W. R.] Harris, *The Catholic Church in the Niagara peninsula, 1826–1895* (Toronto, 1895). Theobald Spetz, *The Catholic Church in Waterloo County . . .* ([Toronto], 1916). *The story of St. Paul's parish*, ed. Edward Kelly ([Toronto], 1922).

GORDON, GEORGE NICOL, Presbyterian clergyman and missionary; b. 21 April 1822 at Cascumpeque (Alberton), P.E.I., son of John Gordon and Mary Ramsey; d. 20 May 1861, at Eromanga, New Hebrides.

In 1786 George Nicol Gordon's father had come to Prince Edward Island with his parents from Scotland via Shelburne, N.S. In 1813 John Gordon and his family became tenants on the estate of Samuel CUNARD, whose alleged unfair practices as landlord they fought for many years; in 1850 they were forcibly evicted. George Gordon was able to get only limited schooling in the area and then worked on his father's farm and as a tanner.

In 1848 Gordon underwent a deeply moving religious experience, and in 1850, at age 28, he enrolled in the academy attached to the Presbyterian Free Church College in Halifax, N.S. The following year he studied briefly at the Presbyterian Church's Theological Hall at West River, Pictou County, N.S., and then returned to Halifax where he began regular studies at the Free Church College. While studying he was instrumental in securing in 1852 the establishment of the Halifax City Mission and became its first missionary. The next year he offered himself as a foreign missionary to the Board of Foreign Missions of the Free Church Synod of Nova Scotia and was accepted for service in the New Hebrides in the South Pacific. By the spring of 1854 he had completed his formal studies. In 1855 he undertook a missionary preaching tour of Prince Edward Island, was ordained that September in Pictou, and soon thereafter left for London, England, to study medicine. It was in London that he met Ellen Catherine Powell, who was prepared to become a missionary's wife despite rather frail health. They were married in June 1856.

The Gordons set out from London for the New Hebrides on the London Missionary Society's vessel, *John Williams*, at the end of July 1856. In June 1857 they reached Aneityum, where John Geddie* of Nova Scotia had maintained a virtually solitary but highly successful Presbyterian mission since 1848. Finally, on about 15 June 1857, the Gordons landed at Dillon's Bay on the island of Eromanga. There the pioneer missionary of the society, John Williams, had been killed in 1839, and the society had subsequently sent Samoan and Rarotongan teachers to prepare the way for a European missionary. During the 1840s and 1850s Eromanga had often been visited by sandalwood traders, chiefly from Sydney, New South Wales; by 1857 there were several permanent trading stations, including at least one at Dillon's Bay, not far from the site chosen for the mission settlement.

During their four years in Eromanga the Gordons endured many hardships, especially Mrs Gordon's frequent attacks of malaria which eventually necessitated the removal of the mission house to a healthier location on a nearby hill. Gordon was a powerful, energetic man, and as a skilled tradesman was particularly well qualified

Gordon

for the physical labour of early missionary work. With only a few native helpers he built a house, a church, and other buildings. Ten weeks after his arrival he had translated the Ten Commandments into the Eromangan dialect of Melanesian, and later translated and personally printed many other religious and educational works, including scriptural passages. He held regular services, ran a school at Dillon's Bay, and often visited other parts of the island. Gordon wrote occasionally for the *Presbyterian Witness* of Halifax, edited by his friend the Reverend Robert Murray*, and for the London *Missionary Register*. By 1861 he had won a small number of adherents on the island, who had renounced the traditional practices which the Gordons found objectionable, wore clothes, attended classes and services, and observed the Sabbath. Gordon was at first unconvinced of the value of native teachers in pioneer missionary work, and for a long time refused to train a body of local helpers. This refusal limited the range of his influence and effectiveness, and probably contributed to the misunderstandings which were to result in the Gordons' deaths.

In January 1861 a trading vessel brought people infected with measles to Dillon's Bay. The Eromangans ignored Gordon's warning to avoid contact with the ship, and the disease, complicated by dysentery, spread rapidly throughout the island. Many deaths and great misery followed. At about the same time a series of cyclones devastated crops and threatened famine for the survivors of the epidemic. By dispensing medicine and caring for the sick, Gordon tried to mitigate the effects of the disaster. Traditionally, Eromangans believed that disease, death, and natural disaster always resulted from sorcerers' magic, and suspicion of sorcery immediately fell upon Gordon, who had predicted the ravages of the epidemic and who seemed immune to its effects.

In mid May Gordon's local assistants warned him to move his household back to the coast and the protection of friendly islanders. He refused. On 20 May 1861 he was ambushed at work and murdered by a group of nine Eromangans. One of the assassins then killed Mrs Gordon with his hatchet at the door of the mission house. She and her husband were both to be described as "martyrs" by Gordon's younger brother, James Douglas*, later also killed on Eromanga. His *The last martyrs of Eromanga . . .* , attributed their deaths to the malicious influence of sandalwood traders. Several traders who were hostile to the missionaries seem indeed to have fanned the anger of some Eromangans against Gordon and his God. Gordon's own actions, however, appear to have been at least as important. He wrote in his diary: "[The disease] was preceded by nearly a universal opposition to the gospel, and much murder and idolatry. I felt sure that God would visit them in judgment and warned them most solemnly but a few days before they were attacked. The chiefs . . . can hardly persuade their people that this is not the finger of Jehovah." In a long letter published in the *Evangelical Christendom* of London on 6 April 1861, he emphasized the severity of the epidemic of measles, the growing tension, and the recent great "wickedness of this people." Gordon's tragedy was that the islanders regarded him as the means by which divine retribution was called down upon them. Geddie, an experienced missionary, questioned the "propriety and prudence of denouncing temporal judgment," and considered that Gordon's words had certainly contributed to the suspicions against him.

Gordon was a dedicated and devoted missionary, but his limited success on Eromanga resulted at least in part from a lack of judgement which coincided with his more admirable qualities. Thus courage and independence led him to eschew native help in proselytism and to ignore warnings about the dangers he faced; his fervent commitment to his religion led him publicly to denounce traditional attitudes and behavior, with fatal results.

BRONWEN DOUGLAS and BRUCE W. HODGINS

J. D. Gordon, *The last martyrs of Eromanga: being a memoir of the Rev. George N. Gordon and Ellen Catherine Powell, his wife* (Halifax, 1863); [ ], *The sandalwood trade and traders of Polynesia* (Halifax, 1862). *Evangelical Christendom* (London), 6 April 1861. Presbyterian Church of the Lower Provinces of British North America, *Home and Foreign Record* (Halifax), I (1861). *Presbyterian Witness*, 5, 21 Oct., 7 Dec. 1861. *Reformed Presbyterian Magazine* (Edinburgh), October 1861. *Samoan Reporter* (Leulumoega, Samoa), May 1862. George Patterson, *Missionary life among the cannibals: being the life of the Rev. John Geddie, D.D., first missionary to the New Hebrides; with a history of the Nova Scotia Presbyterian mission on that group* (Toronto, 1882). H. A. Robertson, *Erromanga, the martyr isle*, ed. John Fraser (London, 1902). Robert Steel, *The New Hebrides and Christian missions, with a sketch of the labour traffic, and notes of a cruise through the group in the mission vessel* (London, 1880).

GORDON, JOHN, naval officer; b. 1792, the seventh child of George, Lord Haddo, and Charlotte Baird; d. 11 Nov. 1869 in London, England.

Shortly before John Gordon's birth his father died. John entered the Royal Navy on 15 April

1805, attained commander's rank on 15 June 1814, and served for ten months on the Newfoundland station. He was promoted post captain on 31 Dec. 1818. He then went on the inactive list for 26 years. Personal influence, however, may have brought Gordon the command of the 50-gun frigate *America* on the Pacific station on 22 Feb. 1844. At that time his brother, the 4th Earl of Aberdeen, was foreign secretary, and another brother, William, was a lord of the Admiralty and an associate of Sir George Francis Seymour, commander-in-chief of the Pacific station at Valparaiso, Chile. Gordon, whose duties would include transporting specie to England, could expect his appointment to prove lucrative since about one half of one per cent of all specie conveyed by British ships from Latin America to England was the captain's legal share.

In February 1845 the British government sent Gordon in the *America* from England to Oregon to give naval support to the Hudson's Bay Company during the Oregon boundary dispute. After a laborious voyage Gordon arrived off Cape Flattery on 28 Aug. 1845 and, missing the entrance to Fort Victoria, Vancouver Island, sailed on to Port Discovery. There he ordered Lieutenant William Peel, son of the British prime minister, and Captain Henry W. Parke to proceed to Fort Vancouver (Vancouver, Wash.) to ascertain "the actual state of the Country on the Banks of the River Columbia, and the district called Oregon." Gordon's instructions to Peel of 2 Sept. 1845 also told him to give the Americans no "cause of jealousy or offence," except in self-defence, and to cooperate with Chief Factor John McLoughlin*. At Fort Vancouver Peel conferred with Henry James Warre* and Mervin VAVASOUR about their secret military reconnaissance in Oregon.

In September 1845 while the *America* lay at Port Discovery, Gordon spoke about Oregon with HBC Chief Factor James Douglas*, who reported that Gordon "does not think the country worth five straws and is surprised that Government should take any trouble about it. . . . He did not appear at all friendly to the Hudsons Bay Company, and told me plainly that we could not expect to hold the entire country." Roderick Finlayson* at Fort Victoria reported Gordon as saying about Vancouver Island that he would not give "one acre of the barren hills of Scotland for all that he saw around him" and that Gordon, "a great deer stalker," considered the hunting and fishing on Vancouver Island to be much inferior to that of Scotland. "What a country where the salmon will not take the fly." He agreed with Peel, however, when the latter returned from his mission, that if the 49th parallel were to be the boundary, Vancouver Island, possessing good harbours, commanding the Juan de Fuca and Georgia straits, and soon to be the company headquarters in the region, must be retained. He also advocated freedom of navigation in the straits. Gordon dispatched Peel with the information that had been gathered to London, which Peel reached by 10 Feb. 1846. It augmented British knowledge about Oregon at a critical time in the negotiations Lord Aberdeen was conducting with the United States on the future of Oregon. Gordon's recommended boundary, as conveyed by Peel, was the one proposed by the British and accepted by the Americans.

Gordon left Port Discovery in the *America* on 26 Sept. 1845 bound for Honolulu. Rear-Admiral Seymour instructed him to remain in the northeastern Pacific and watch the movements of the United States Navy because he feared American designs on upper California. Although Gordon appreciated this threat, he came under great pressure to return to England from merchants at Mazatlán, Mexico, who wanted a safe repository for their wealth in case of war. Laden with Mexican specie worth nearly $2,000,000 according to Gordon's estimate, the *America* reached England on 19 Aug. 1846. Gordon was court-martialled on 26 August at Portsmouth for leaving his station without orders. The charge was "fully proved" and he was "severely reprimanded," but the suspicion that he had sought personal gain was removed. Although not relieved of his command, Gordon accepted retirement on generous terms on 1 October. He rose on the retired list *pari passu*, was promoted admiral in 1863, and died in 1869.

BARRY M. GOUGH

HBC Arch. B. 226/b/1, ff. 35–36d. Maritime Museum of B.C. (Victoria), "H.M.S. *America*, 1810–1867," [comp. P. W. Brock] (typescript). National Maritime Museum (London), JOD/42 (Journal of Lieutenant Thomas Davies, H.M.S. *America*, 1844–47, in the Pacific, and in H.M.S. *Cygnet*, 1850–52, off West Africa). PRO, Adm. 1/5561–62, 1/5564, 1/5568; 13/103–4; 53/1946. Warwick County Record Office (Warwick, Eng.), CR 114A/414/1 (Seymour of Ragley papers), Seymour order book. HBRS, VII (Rich), liv. O'Byrne, *Naval biographical dictionary* (1849), 411. Walbran, *B.C. coast names*. B. M. Gough, *The Royal Navy and the northwest coast of North America, 1810–1914: a study of British maritime ascendancy* (Vancouver, 1971), 50–83; "H.M.S. America on the north Pacific coast," *Oreg. Hist. Quarterly* (Portland), LXX (1969), 293–311.

GORE, Sir CHARLES STEPHEN, soldier; b. 26 Dec. 1793, son of Arthur Saunders Gore, 2nd

Gore

Earl of Arran, and Elizabeth Underwood; m. 13 May 1824 Sarah Rachel, daughter of James Fraser*, legislative councillor of Nova Scotia, and they had six children; d. at London, England, 4 Sept. 1869.

The Honourable Charles Stephen Gore entered the army in 1808, and on 4 Jan. 1810 was promoted to a lieutenancy in the 43rd Regiment. Joining the 43rd in Spain in July 1811, he participated in the investment and storming of the great fortresses of Ciudad Rodrigo and Badajoz, and in all the actions of the Light Division from 1812 until 1814.

Appointed in 1812 aide-de-camp to Major-General James Kempt*, in August 1814 he accompanied him to Canada, where Kempt was appointed to command the Montreal District. He returned to England on the general's recall, and served him with gallantry during the Waterloo campaign. On 15 June 1815 he had been gazetted a captain in the 85th Regiment in which he was promoted to a majority on 21 Jan. 1819. After five years of regimental duty, which included the capture and occupation of Paris, Major Gore was seconded as ADC to Kempt on the latter's appointment to the command of Nova Scotia and its Dependencies. They reached Halifax on 2 June 1820. Promoted lieutenant-colonel on 18 Sept. 1822, Gore then served in Jamaica as deputy quartermaster-general until 1826 when, on exchange, he became deputy quartermaster-general for British North America. Promoted major-general on 9 Nov. 1846, Gore became, as of 1 April 1847, the general officer commanding Canada's Eastern District at Montreal.

During the insurrection of 1837, Gore, after nearly 20 years on staff, played a conspicuous if controversial role. Appointed by the commander of the forces, Sir John COLBORNE, to lead an expedition against Saint-Denis and Saint-Charles, dissident villages some 20 miles east of Montreal on the Richelieu River, he arrived at Sorel by steamer on 22 November, accompanied by a deputy sheriff representing the civil power. Gore had at his disposition an infantry column composed of four companies of the 24th and 32nd regiments, a small detachment of artillery with a howitzer, and a token troop of the Royal Montreal Cavalry (also known as the Montreal Volunteer Cavalry). He was to proceed against Saint-Denis, headquarters of Dr Wolfred NELSON, one of the ablest of the insurgent chiefs, while Lieutenant-Colonel George Augustus WETHERALL advanced north from Fort Chambly against Saint-Charles.

Despite freezing rain and next to impassable roads, Gore determined on a night march in order to surprise his objective, and at 10 p.m. his slender column, now reinforced by two companies of the 66th Regiment, was en route. He thus missed a courier, Lieutenant George Weir of the 32nd, who had been dispatched by Colborne with urgent orders for his field commander to await reinforcements or, if engaged, to retire in the face of superior force. To avoid insurgents he thought to be at Saint-Ours, Gore took a minor inland road and the nearly exhausted British force did not reach Saint-Denis until nearly 10 a.m. on the 23rd, just when Lieutenant Weir, who had been arrested during the night, was sadistically murdered near the south end of the village. Gore found Nelson's men – probably some 700, but only some 120 with firearms of any description – fully alert and blocking his advance from two strong stone buildings and a stout street barricade. Although his own strength did not exceed 300, Gore attacked. By 3 p.m., however, his infantry had been outgunned, his howitzer had proved useless, ammunition was in perilously short supply, rations were non-existent, and he had suffered some 22 casualties. Moreover, George-Étienne Cartier* had just crossed the Richelieu with 100 well-armed reinforcements, and Nelson had promptly ordered a counter-attack.

The defeated British limped into Sorel on 25 November, the day of Wetherall's victory at Saint-Charles. Gore left for Montreal later that day, but by the evening of the 30th, his original command reinforced by five additional companies (three of the 32nd, one of the 24th and the 83rd), two guns, and 12 Montreal cavalry, he was back in Sorel for a second attack on Saint-Denis. On Saturday, 2 December, he re-entered Saint-Denis unopposed. There followed two days of unrewarding searches, looting, and burning, and by Sunday night some 50 buildings had apparently been gutted or destroyed. According to a reputable observer, Lieutenant E. Montagu Davenport, the regulars were set to work to destroy the property of known insurgents, but Gore had issued strict orders against pillage, and a picket patrolled the streets to prevent it. Nonetheless the troops got out of hand, and many houses were wantonly destroyed or at least set alight. While Dr Nelson's distillery was being demolished, Davenport noted, houses along the road to Saint-Ours were burnt, an act of indiscriminate arson he attributed to the vengeance of the volunteers.

Early on the 4th Gore set out for Saint-Hyacinthe in pursuit of Louis-Joseph Papineau* and other insurgent leaders. Later that same day, at Saint-Denis, the hideously mutilated body of

Lieutenant Weir was discovered. Two days later Gore proceeded to Sorel, leaving three companies to garrison Saint-Denis, and returned to Montreal on the 7th with the 32nd who were bearing Weir's body.

Colonel Gore suffered considerable censure, primarily in Patriote circles, because of the burnings in Saint-Denis. In fact, in February 1849, he was viciously attacked on the subject by Henry John BOULTON during the legislative debates on the Rebellion Losses Bill. Sir Allan Napier MacNab rose to his defence, but the charge was not given quietus until, in a subsequent session, Boulton not only retracted but asserted he had Gore's authority to state that he had used every exertion to prevent the burnings and had given orders for recalcitrants to be hailed before drumhead courts martial and flogged. Curiously the responsibility for orders to destroy insurgent property never became a public issue, but as similar burnings took place at Saint-Charles and Saint-Eustache, it must be assumed that such orders emanated from headquarters itself [see John Colborne]. Writing in the early 1850s, the historian Robert Christie* attempted a rational explanation of the Saint-Denis and similar incidents: "There are occasions when the passions of men become uncontrollable by human authority and, unhappily, this was one of them." The truth of this observation is obvious, yet the fact remains that a military commander is indisputably responsible for the conduct of his men if, in fact, he is physically and mentally able to exercise that responsibility.

On 4 July 1849, Gore was posted to Kingston as commander, Canada West. However, during the last years of his tenure in Montreal he had not enjoyed the full confidence of Lord Elgin [BRUCE] who wrote of Gore, at a time when passage of the Rebellion Losses Bill was causing concern for order, that it was "generally believed that his judgement could not be relied on in difficulties." But Kingston was an eminently "safe" posting, and after three uneventful and popular years there Gore was ordered to Halifax on 20 Sept. 1852 with the command of Nova Scotia and its Dependencies. In June 1855 he finally embarked for the United Kingdom, on recall. His final promotion was to general in February 1863, and his last appointment, dated December 1868, was to the lieutenant governorship of Chelsea Hospital in London. His honours included the Peninsular medal (nine clasps), the Waterloo medal, CB (1838), and GCB (1867).

It was said of Colonel Gore in 1837 that he was a better QMG than he was a field commander. But his personal bravery was never questioned, his long career on staff was successful, if not brilliant, and he proved himself an effective, considerate, and much respected district commander in British North America.

JOHN W. SPURR

PAC, RG 8, I (C series), 1275. PRO, WO 17/1518, 17/1536–58, 17/1830–35, 17/2367–69, 17/2399–402 (mfm. at PAC). E. M. Davenport, *The life and recollections of E. M. Davenport . . . written by himself; "notes of what I have seen and done," from 1835 to 1850* (London, 1869), 49–65, 69–72. *Elgin-Grey papers* (Doughty), I, 166. Daniel Lysons, *Early reminiscences, with illustrations from the author's sketches* (London, 1896), 69–76. *Montreal Gazette*, November-December 1837, February-March 1849. Boase, *Modern English biog.*, I, 1184. *Burke's peerage* (1967), 105. *DNB*. G. B., WO, *Army list*, 1809–39. Hart's *army list*, 1840–69. *Historical records of the 91st Argyllshire Highlanders, now the 1st battalion Princess Louise's Argyll and Sutherland Highlanders . . .*, comp. G. L. J. Goff (London, 1891), 336. L.-N. Carrier, *Les événements de 1837–1838* (Québec, 1877), 75–78, 82–85. Christie, *History of L. C.*, IV, 451–70. William Kingsford, *The history of Canada* (10v., Toronto and London, 1887–98), X, 53–61, 68. Joseph Schull, *Rebellion: the rising in French Canada, 1837* (Toronto, 1971), 73–77, 79, 84–88.

GOULET, ELZÉAR, mail carrier, member of the court martial which condemned Thomas SCOTT; b. 1836 at Saint-Boniface, Red River Settlement, son of Alexis Goulet and Josephte Siveright; drowned 13 Sept. 1870 in the Red River at Winnipeg, Man.

Elzéar Goulet was descended from Canadian *voyageurs* who had come west with Pierre Gaultier* de Varennes et de La Vérendrye and his sons. His mother was the daughter of John Siveright*, a factor of the Hudson's Bay Company at Fort Pelly, Rupert's Land. Two older brothers become prominent in the early political affairs of Manitoba.

Goulet received some schooling at Saint-Boniface. In 1859 he married at Pembina, Dakota Territory, Hélène Jérôme, *dit* Saint-Matte, an orphan, brought up as the ward of her uncle Joseph Rolette*, pioneer merchant, freighter, and politician of Pembina. Elzéar and Hélène Goulet had six children. From 1860 to 1869 Goulet carried the mails from Pembina to Upper Fort Garry (Winnipeg). During this period Goulet became an American citizen.

In 1869 Goulet joined the forces of Louis Riel* at Upper Fort Garry and became second in command of the Métis irregular armed force commanded by Ambroise-Dydime Lépine*. On 3 March 1870, together with Lépine, Janvier

Gourlay

Ritchot, André Nault*, Joseph Delorme, Elzéar Lagimodière, and Jean-Baptiste Lépine*, he served as a member of the court martial for Thomas Scott, accused of treason against the provisional government. Goulet supported imposition of the penalty of death by the court. On 4 March he, together with André Nault, acted as escort for Scott when he was taken from Upper Fort Garry and shot by a Métis firing squad.

On 13 Sept. 1870 Goulet was recognized in the hamlet of Winnipeg by a member of the Canadian faction who had been a prisoner of Riel during the period of the provisional government. This man, whose identity cannot be determined, and two uniformed members of the expedition of Garnet Joseph Wolseley*, pursued Goulet, apparently to apprehend him for complicity in the death of Scott. Goulet fled on foot to the Red River and tried to swim to safety on the Saint-Boniface side. His disappointed pursuers threw rocks, one of which struck him on the head, stunning him, and he drowned. When the body was recovered the following day, it bore the mark of a blow on the head.

Goulet's drowning took place within a month of the arrival of the Wolseley expedition at Red River and just 11 days after the arrival of Manitoba's first lieutenant governor, Sir Adams George Archibald*. The coroner, Curtis James Bird*, who had held the office under the Council of Assiniboia, was absent. Archibald appointed two HBC magistrates, Salomon Hamelin* and Robert MacBeth*, to conduct an inquest with the assistance of Henri-Jean McConville, a lawyer newly arrived from Montreal. Subpoenas were issued and 20 witnesses heard. One of John Christian Schultz*'s followers and one of Wolseley's soldiers were identified as having been among Goulet's pursuers and warrants for their arrest were prepared. No arrests, however, were ever made.

The circumstances at Red River at the time of Goulet's death were unsettled. During the same period another Métis and an Irish-American were killed and two others, one of whom was André Nault, badly beaten, by unidentified assailants. All were acts of revenge for the death of Scott and no official action to punish the culprits was ever taken, apparently for fear of bringing on a general uprising. Members of the Canadian faction who favoured annexation to Canada were angry at what they considered the treason of Riel and his supporters during the preceding year, while the Métis and other Red River natives felt justified in their resistance to Canadian aggression and were deeply resentful of the proscription of Louis Riel and the others who had forced Canada to bargain for possession of Rupert's Land. The government at Ottawa was informed of the details of the death of Goulet but apparently left all initiative about it to the reluctant local authorities.

J. A. JACKSON

PAM, MG 3, D1; MG 5, B2. Can., *Sessional papers*, 1871, III, no.5; V, no.20. *Globe*, 3 Oct. 1870. Morice, *Dict. historique des Canadiens et Métis*, 127–28. Dom [J.-P.-A.] Benoit, *Vie de Mgr Taché, archevêque de Saint-Boniface* (2v., Montréal, 1904), II, 85–126. R. B. Hill, *Manitoba; history of its early settlement, development and resources* (Toronto, 1890). Stanley, *Louis Riel*. L.-A. Prud'homme, "La famille Goulet," RSC *Trans.*, 3rd ser., XXIX (1935), sect.I, 23–41. *Manitoba Free Press* (Winnipeg), 3 Aug. 1911. *Winnipeg Telegram*, 18 July 1911.

GOURLAY, ROBERT FLEMING, scientific farmer, reformer, and author; b. 24 March 1778 at Craigrothie, Fifeshire, Scotland, third of four children of Oliver Gourlay, a substantial landowner, and Janet Fleming; m. first in 1807 Jean Henderson, and they had four children, and secondly in 1858 Mary Reenan; d. 1 Aug. 1863 in Edinburgh, Scotland. In memory of his mother, who died in 1827, he took Fleming as his middle name.

Robert Fleming Gourlay's tumultuous moment at the centre of the Upper Canadian stage was foreshadowed in his earlier life. He received a gentleman's education, graduating MA from St Andrews in 1797, and studying agriculture for two more years at the University of Edinburgh. In 1799 he carried out for Arthur Young, secretary of the Board of Agriculture, a study of the condition of farm labourers in two English shires which was later published and cited by Thomas Malthus. From 1800 to 1809 he managed one of his father's farms and from 1809 to 1817 was tenant to the Duke of Somerset at Deptford Farm, Wiltshire. In both places he earned a reputation as an improving farmer and kindly landlord.

Gourlay was an agrarian radical with strong similarities to William Cobbett; both detested the Poor Laws, sympathized with the rural poor, and hoped to restore them to the world that enclosing landlords had stolen from them. They also shared a taste for personal invective. Unlike Cobbett, Gourlay was a dreamer and a visionary; out of his brain, teeming with two generations of radical polemics, he spun "new political edifices" for the transformation of a corrupted world. Some of his radicalism he inherited from his father, who had welcomed the French revolution. Gourlay himself was a democrat of a kind, but his political thought was deeply contradictory. Believing at once in human perfectibility and in the evil of all government because of the inherent vices of mankind, he proposed elaborate systems of reform, whether for land redistribution or universal education, plainly requiring complex bureaucracies to administer. These reforms he hoped to achieve by peaceful petitioning, a form of political action that depended upon corrupt governors reforming themselves, or stepping aside, when confronted by the united voice of the people.

A specific plan for organising the people, and for obtaining reform independent of parliament . . . to the people of Fife . . . of Britain!, an overgrown pamphlet published in London in 1809, is typical of his early writings. In it, Gourlay saw governments as conspiracies of the powerful to shackle mankind by "mysterious ceremonies" and "subtle machinery," as great engines defended by the forms and quibbles of lawyers and by those "whitewashers of iniquity," the kept clergy. Governments promoted war, abhorred by Gourlay together with all other forms of violence, solely for the selfish ends of the powerful classes. Revolution would sweep away the rotten structure, nor need revolution under proper supervision be bloody and violent; "it depends all on the management." Change would come not from the "tainted pool" of aristocracy but from "the dwellings of the poor"; through universal suffrage a simple form of government and the rule of "pure unhampered virtue" would be created.

Gourlay's specific plan (or "darling system") divided Britain into voting units of 300 on a literacy suffrage. Every May Day, at six in the morning, voters would march, in dead silence, into their polling places, and there confront a voting machine of "curious workmanship." In turn, each voter would deposit 30 voting balls in his choice of 300 chambers. At noon, the 30 men so elected were to converge with their fellows from neighbouring parishes upon a district centre, there to repeat the process. By seven in the evening, county representatives to a national assembly would have been chosen; their first task would be the preparation of a petition to the king; and they would have "nothing to do with the present Parliament." In a revealing passage Gourlay envisioned man regenerated by his system, and himself as architect of the new world of virtue: "Lord of artless truth, of simple nature, if e'er, in time regenerating, thou giv'st me office, let it be this, to burn the lumber of antiquity! . . . O rescued man! O noble savage! now again thyself, when this is done, I'll meet thee on the smooth green lawn, and sketch the outline of our future garden."

"Through life," Gourlay disarmingly said of himself, "I have been enthusiastic in my pursuits." At Deptford Farm, both enthusiasm and bad judgement brought him into collision with his neighbours and with the Duke of Somerset. His efforts to found a national organization of tenant farmers against great landlords, "the last cohort of feudal power," caused his expulsion from the Bath and Wiltshire agricultural societies. With the duke he waged a long and costly lawsuit over the terms of his lease; the price of victory was loss of tenancy and impoverishment.

During these years, through practical philanthropy and incessant pamphleteering, Gourlay made his chief concern the state of the rural poor. Why, he inquired in his address *To the labouring poor of Wily parish* (1816), should millions be expended on bloody wars when "not one in ten of you has been taught to read or write"? From a reading of Malthus he drew an optimistic answer: it was not man – "a ductile animal, and a good one, when not crossed with tyranny" – but the system that was at fault. Vicious institutions like the Poor Laws had pauperized and brutalized the peasantry, and deprived them of motive and opportunity to better their condition. He petitioned parliament to abolish them and to educate the poor as part of a vast scheme of national regeneration. In another petition, to the House of Commons in 1817, he argued for a vast transfer of land to the poor. Property ownership would transform them. His simple plan (and bureaucratic nightmare) provided for governmental acquisition of 100 acres in every parish in England, to be parcelled out in half-acre allotments to paupers. Prompt payment of rent and proper tillage would win promotion from pauper to "parish holder." £100 in a government savings bank would bring a government-built cottage of that value, and the rank of "cottage holder"; a further £60 meant the rank of "freeman" and eligibility for parish office. Thus the poor would achieve both respectability and independence.

"I am quite a radical, but I am one of my own sort," Gourlay said of himself with much truth. "I am known both in England and in Scotland because of my peculiar opinions, and these opinions are by many misunderstood." It was with this reputation that he departed in 1817 for Upper Canada, in hopes of retrieving his fortunes. His wife, a niece of Robert Hamilton*, had inherited 866 acres in Dereham Township, and her cousins, Thomas Clark* and William Dickson*, had both visited Deptford Farm and suggested emigration. Gourlay landed at Quebec on 31 May, intending to return to England in the autumn.

Gourlay

In Upper Canada he was to be accorded an importance he had never attained in Britain. The province was simmering with discontent. The end of the war with the United States had ended wartime prosperity as well. Immigration had slowed to a trickle, partly because of an imperial decision, strongly endorsed by the local administration, to forbid the granting of land to Americans. Those who had suffered losses at American hands during the war had not been compensated; militiamen who had served actively had not been awarded their promised lands. Discontent was particularly acute in the Niagara District, not only because it had been the chief cockpit of the war, but also because its local oligarchy, headed by Dickson and Clark and including Samuel Street*, Robert Nichol*, and the heirs of Robert Hamilton, held huge amounts of wild land that only immigration would render profitable. In April 1817, Nichol had boldly moved in the assembly at York (Toronto) for the lifting of the ban upon Americans and for the sale of the crown reserves. Only Lieutenant Governor Francis Gore*'s hurried prorogation prevented the adoption of all Nichol's resolutions. Gore was also forced to dismiss Dickson, a legislative councillor, from the commission of the peace because of his refusal to deny the oath of allegiance to prospective American settlers. Here, among the province's ruling class, were ready-made collaborators and a set of grievances for Gourlay to exploit, should he so choose.

For six weeks Gourlay stayed with Thomas Clark, nursing his mosquito bites and absorbing the Niagara viewpoint of provincial affairs. He was downcast to find that Clark could lend him no money because his capital was tied up in land, and that his wife's property was unsaleable "because of an illegal and arbitrary order of the Lieutenant Governor," that is, the ban upon American immigration. After a walking tour of the Genesee country of New York, however, he decided to prolong his stay. He had resolved to become a land agent, he told his wife, "to cross the Atlantic annually, and at once make my own fortune, establish a grand system of emigration, and render Upper Canada prosperous and happy." As well, in keeping with the long-established tradition of Scottish agricultural and statistical scholarship, he intended to compile a statistical account of the province.

To these several ends, he prepared an address to the resident landowners of Upper Canada, and appended to it a list of 31 questions based upon those used by Sir John Sinclair in his *Statistical account of Scotland*. It was this source, and no secret design, that inspired the well-known 31st question: "What, in your opinion, retards the improvement of your township in particular, or the province in general; and what would most contribute to the same?" Through introductions provided by his Niagara friends, Gourlay met most of the leading men of York (with the notable exception of John STRACHAN), secured the permission of Samuel Smith*, administrator of the province, for insertion of his address in the *Upper Canada Gazette*, and mailed an additional 700 copies to township officials. While in York he also applied for a land grant. It appears he asked for special consideration, probably because he required a large acreage to float his emigration scheme.

The address was a skilful and effective appeal, though some found it patronizing. Disavowing any interest in political matters, Gourlay contrasted the province's actual state with its rich prospects. Since Upper Canada had been peopled chiefly by the poor, inevitably it had a society "crude, unambitious and weak." What was needed was not the resumption of American immigration but a plan to attract British capitalists to invest in the province and to bring out immigrants. Should that happen, then a superior society "with all the strength and order and refinement" of Britain would spring up. Gourlay proposed his statistical account as a first step in the awakening of British interest, and invited Upper Canadians to hold township meetings in order to reply to his questionnaire.

In February 1818, while township meetings were still being held in many parts of the province, Gourlay abruptly altered his tone and tactics. In a second address, he announced that he had changed his mind about American immigration; Governor Gore, he thought, should have been impeached for forbidding it. Were Upper Canada part of the United States, its lands would double in value. Gourlay was not advocating annexation, though many so construed him. He was, however, throwing down the gauntlet to the provincial government, accusing it of "a system of paltry patronage and ruinous favouritism" and calling for a legislative inquiry into the state of the province followed by a commission to proceed to England with the results.

Gourlay's decision to challenge the colonial government and one of its central policies, and to come forth not as scientific investigator but in his more accustomed guise as anti-authoritarian, was a fateful one. He offered a number of reasons for it. On a walking tour through western Upper Canada, a region settled mainly by Americans, he had found them to be "active, intelligent, friendly, and adept in the arts of settlement."

Moreover, he "could not help sympathizing" with the plight of his friends Dickson and Clark because of the ban on American immigration. As well, his application for land had been refused "by the dirty ways of Little York" and "the loathsome things of the Land Granting Department" (on the quite proper ground that he was not proposing to become an actual settler). In this, he detected the hand of that "monstrous little fool of a parson," Strachan. Though that supposition was incorrect, he was probably right in laying at Strachan's door the fact that not a single township report had come in from the populous Home District, and only scattered reports from districts east of York. Strachan had tried to persuade Chief Justice William Dummer Powell* and Samuel Smith that Gourlay was a "dangerous incendiary" when he had seen the first address in type at the government printer's, and he continued to work against him behind the scenes.

All these setbacks, in combination with a number of depressing letters from his wife about Deptford Farm, threw him into "an absolute fever of care, perplexity and feeling." Through the columns of the *Niagara Spectator* he poured out an extraordinary torrent of abuse against "the vile, loathsome and lazy vermin of Little York" and others hostile to him. During his provincial tours, he had picked up scandal as well as statistics, and the facility and vehemence with which he now drew upon it shook the genteel little polity of Upper Canada to its foundations. When Thomas Clark ventured to caution him, Gourlay heedlessly rushed a reply into print. Why, he asked Clark, should someone who had "contended with the second Peer of England" moderate his language when dealing with a contemptible little man who "has got on horseback." Strachan should stop dabbling in politics and get himself to a penitentiary, as should his tool, the Reverend John Bethune* Jr, "a fool, a busybody and a slanderer."

Even more important in polarizing opinion was Gourlay's third address, published on 2 April 1818. He had written it "at a downsitting" on hearing that Smith had prorogued the legislature because of a collision between the two houses over money bills, thus killing an assembly motion for a legislative inquiry into the state of the province. "*The Constitution of the province is in danger*," he announced; "*all the blessings of social compact are running to waste.*" In sweeping language, open to the most damaging interpretation, he declared that "it is the *system* that blasts every hope of good; and till the system is overturned, it is vain to expect anything of

value from change of Representatives or Governors." The constitution of the province being useless, he called for a direct approach to the Prince Regent through a series of meetings at the township and district levels, culminating in a provincial convention at York to draft a petition. Debate was to be avoided; "the one thing needful" for his followers to keep in mind was "a radical change of system in the government of Upper Canada."

Though Gourlay lost his most powerful allies at this point – Clark, for example, warned the people of Niagara against "visionary enthusiasts" and the possible illegality of conventions – by early May a Niagara District meeting had been held and a draft petition adopted. One thousand copies of this petition and the Niagara proceedings were printed, and in May and June Gourlay set about distributing the pamphlet through eastern Upper Canada, arousing great controversy. In a blow-by-blow account of his eastern tour in the *Spectator*, he told his readers that the "grovelling wretches" he encountered in the east had "never soared into the regions of benevolence because they cannot see through the midst of their own iniquity." In Kingston he clashed with Daniel Hagerman, John Macaulay*, and Stephen MILES, and in Prescott with Jonas Jones*. Philip VanKoughnet* followed him about ripping down his placards. At Cornwall he was assaulted by Richard Duncan Fraser*, a magistrate; in Kingston he was horsewhipped by Christopher Hagerman* for refusing to withdraw from the press a story that Hagerman's brother "was many years confined in the States' prison for forgery, now reported to be hanged."

In both Kingston and Cornwall Gourlay was charged with seditious libel. In April, at Strachan's urging, the administrator had directed Attorney General John Beverley ROBINSON to seize the first opportunity for prosecution in order to check "the very threatening career now entered upon." In Robinson's opinion, both the third address and the Niagara pamphlet contained grossly libellous passages subversive of government. Though he feared that if acquitted Gourlay would be "immediately elevated into a Champion for liberty against imaginary oppression," the Kingston charge was laid at his instance; that of Cornwall was R. D. Fraser's own idea.

Members of the administration were particularly apprehensive about the coming convention. Robinson, for instance, thought conventions extremely dangerous "as they pointed out the mode by which popular movements, on pretences less specious than the present, can be effected." On 4

Gourlay

July he compared "Mr. Gourlay's wild measures" to those proceedings "which in another era and in other Colonies of the British Empire, terminated in Rebellion." But neither he nor the judges could find any clearly constitutional means to suppress the convention and to punish its most active members.

The convention met in York from 6 to 10 July 1818. It was an anticlimax. Only 14 of the 25 elected district representatives came; Gourlay had hoped for 25 to match the assembly's numbers. Although Strachan alleged that Gourlay "directed them like children," the members showed themselves nervous about the stir they had created. They decided to call themselves "The Upper Canadian Convention of Friends to Enquiry" to distinguish their meeting from "conventions formed to control and command public affairs." Instead of a petition to the Prince Regent, they voted to present one to the new lieutenant governor, Sir Peregrine Maitland*, and to ask him to call provincial elections. Gourlay himself seems to have been disconcerted by the poor attendance and by the criticism he received from two delegates. His own speech was singularly flat; and had it not been for his trials, he later claimed, he would have abandoned the convention on its second day "to get out of the mud of Little York by its own shifts."

Gourlay was tried in Kingston on 15 August and in Brockville on 31 August. In both cases he defended himself; in both the jury found him innocent. Immediately after his second acquittal, he went to New York, hoping for recent letters from his wife. During his sojourn in Upper Canada, she had been braving his creditors, scraping up rent for the farm, and warding off the duke's agents. From her husband she had heard that "I have all eyes on me here," and that "our affairs are banished from my mind by my present avocations." In response to the plea to "come home my dearest Gourlay" that awaited him in New York, Gourlay sent his wife a power of attorney to do what she could, for "the very effort of thought" about Deptford Farm was "painful." "I am tossed on the capricious wave," he wrote, "and my destiny is beyond my direction." By October he was back in Kingston organizing township meetings to call for a provincial election. At about the same time his wife gave up the farm and took the children to Edinburgh.

Gourlay's control over events in Upper Canada melted even more rapidly than his prospects at home. Maitland, persuaded that Gourlay was "half Cobbett and half Hunt," obtained from the legislature, with only one dissentient in the assembly, an act banning seditious meetings. He then refused to accept from the Friends to Enquiry the petition on which so much effort had been expended, because the convention was "an unconstitutional proceeding." Gourlay's counterblast, a letter headed "Gagged, gagged, by Jingo!" caused the arrest of the editor of the *Spectator*, Bartimus Ferguson*, on a charge of seditious libel. The warrant was issued by William Dickson and William Claus*, on information from Isaac Swayze*, a Niagara assemblyman and a confidant of Dickson's. Swayze informed Maitland's secretary that Gourlay himself would shortly be "in Safe Keeping" or else "sent across the River."

On 18 Dec. 1818 Swayze swore before the same two legislative councillors that Gourlay was a person of "no particular or fixed place of residence," that he was "an evil minded and seditious person," that he had not been an inhabitant of the province for the previous six months (having been out of the country), and that he had not taken the oath of allegiance (that is, in Upper Canada). These allegations were carefully framed to fit the provisions of the sedition act of 1804, originally passed to meet an apprehended danger from French revolutionaries and Irish radicals, and never before used against a British subject. Gourlay was to contend for the rest of his life that as a British subject the act could not apply to him, yet it is clear from the express intentions of the framers, from the sweeping language of the act itself, and from the construction given it by the judges in an opinion of 10 Nov. 1818 that he fell within its scope.

A particularly vicious provision of the act placed the burden of proof upon the accused. When Gourlay, in an appearance before Dickson and Claus, "did not give full and complete satisfaction," he was ordered to leave the province as the act provided. On his refusal to obey, he was committed on 4 Jan. 1819 to Niagara jail to await trial. Except for a court appearance in York on 8 February to seek bail, a relief denied him by the chief justice as expressly forbidden by the act, he remained in jail until 20 August.

It was not the government which had taken the initiative in applying this "unchristian, unconstitutional, wicked, deceitful, atrocious" act. Maitland and his advisers believed with some reason that Gourlay's influence was in decline. Strachan's view was that his arrest was inexpedient, that sooner or later the ordinary laws of libel would have tripped him up, and that Gourlay himself was "an object of pity" who "from his youth has been restless and turbulent." Maitland told the Colonial Office that he was "perplexed" by the arrest, but had decided to let the law take its course. Gourlay had been trapped, not by government, but by the inconvenient revival of what Strachan called "long dormant" Niagara loyalty. To Dickson and some of his friends, Gourlay had outlived his usefulness, and, with a new and tough-minded governor, become a positive danger to themselves. Seeking to re-establish their positions at York, they threw Gourlay to the wolves. Gourlay himself blamed Dickson alone; "your cousin," he wrote his wife, "has proved himself little better than a madman."

From jail Gourlay continued to write vigorously in the *Niagara Spectator*, including a fourth address to the resident landowners on 20 May. Further publications in June were voted libels by the assembly, and he was more closely confined. Want of vent for his pen and the excessive heat of his cell broke his spirit and his health. At his trial on 20 Aug. 1819, according to Gourlay and to John Charles Dent*, whose graphic account in *The story of the Upper Canadian rebellion* seems to be based in part on eyewitness testimony, he was mentally incapable of defending himself. Robinson, his prosecutor, termed Gourlay's description of the trial "a tissue of falsehoods," but there is little reason to doubt its substantial accuracy. In any event the jury's verdict was a foregone conclusion, since in essence the trial was to determine whether or not the accused had disobeyed a legal order to leave the province. On 21 August Gourlay was on the New York side of the Niagara, a free man and a banished Briton.

The chief monument to Gourlay's stay in Upper Canada was his *Statistical account*, which he published in two volumes (a third was projected but not published) in London (1822). Its shrillness, irrelevancies, and disorder reflected his bitter sense of grievance and the mental depression which followed the death of his wife in 1820. With all its deficiencies, however, it is easily the best compendium of information about Upper Canada for his period. Though Gourlay made no attempt to analyse them, the 57 township reports he printed present an unrivalled picture of provincial social and economic life.

It is less easy to discern Gourlay's relevance to the provincial reform movement, though some have contended for it. Beyond providing the useful myth of his martyrdom at the hands of a reactionary oligarchy, and perhaps some useful organizational techniques, he seems temporarily to have short-circuited reform. His egotism obscured its aims, his style brought it disrepute, and his petitioning technique was a tactical blind alley. In a real sense Gourlay was not a Upper

Canadian but a British and imperial reformer. "I have little care about Canada," he later said, "my chief efforts were made . . . for the poor of England." He disclosed no real programme until the publication of his letter "To the parliamentary representatives of the people of Upper Canada" (otherwise "my clodhopping brothers – most august legislators"), written from Niagara jail on 7 June 1819. Here he argued (and the township reports bore him out) that the chief impediment to Upper Canadian growth was the existence of huge amounts of idle land in public and speculative hands. The more rapidly that land was converted to productive use the better, and therefore he proposed direct imperial control of land granting, the taxation of cultivated and wild lands, both public and private, and the use of the revenue and the provincial credit so established to finance both British emigration and large-scale developmental projects. In advocating the taxing of wild land and the sale of crown reserves he was only a few years in advance of his time, and in suggesting by these means the alleviation of English poverty through financed emigration he directly influenced Edward Gibbon WAKEFIELD. Yet had he disclosed these ideas at an earlier point in his Upper Canadian career, it is most doubtful whether he would have won any following whatever.

The rest of Gourlay's long life was warped by his Upper Canadian experience and his quest for vindication. His flair for self-advertisement and for martyrdom never deserted him. In 1822 he won notoriety in the press as the "amateur pauper" by cracking flints on the roads of Wily parish. In 1824 he was committed to Cold Bath Fields as a dangerous person of unsound mind, having tapped Henry Brougham with a riding crop in the House of Commons lobby for failing sufficiently to advocate his cause. He chose continued incarceration rather than give weight to the charge of insanity by seeking bail. His chronicle of this episode, *An appeal to the common sense, mind and manhood of the British nation* (1826), declared that "the world is still against me, the same world which poisoned Socrates, crucified Christ, and imprisoned Galileo." Released in 1828, he stood unsuccessfully for the chair of agriculture at Edinburgh in 1831 and for parliament in 1832. In 1833 he went to stay with friends in Ohio, but failed to interest Ohioans in a statistical account of their state or in a project to sink pits to sea level to furnish data about the earth's crust. The same fate befell the plans he submitted to a number of cities for their improvement. Bostonians, for example, were cold to his suggestion for a 40-foot addition to Faneuil

Hall because it had "no length sufficient for its width." From 1846 to 1856 Gourlay lived in Scotland, running for parliament in 1846 on a platform of "a bed, an umbrella and a bannock." In 1856 he returned to Upper Canada to settle on his land at Dereham. At age 80 he contested the riding of Oxford and married Mary Reenan, his 28-year-old housekeeper. Neither venture proving successful, he left Upper Canada for Edinburgh, living there until his death.

Through all these years Gourlay sought justice from British and colonial authorities. This quest was chronicled, in part, in *The banished Briton and Neptunian*, his personal newspaper, bound together in 39 numbers and published in Boston in 1843. Despite everything, he remained "A Briton, and to Britain ever shall be true." Thus, at the time of the Upper Canadian rebellion, he publicly damned William Lyon MACKENZIE, whom he thought lacked stability, for his treasonable conduct, and provided Sir Francis Bond Head* with information about Patriot activities in the United States. From time to time his cause was taken up by sympathetic Canadian politicians, but he frustrated them all by his rejections of pensions and pardons as insulting. He wanted nothing less than a reversal of history. To the end, he remained convinced of the rightness of his cause and the wickedness of those who had crushed him. John Neilson*, who tried to help in 1841, told him in a kindly letter that "you must not suppose, that in the difficulties in which you engaged in Canada, you also were entirely exempt from error." But, Gourlay replied, that was precisely the point: "I *was* exempt from error, and I do most earnestly beg you to review all my writings in Canada, and detect error if you can."

S. F. WISE

[Some of Robert Gourlay's publications, notably *The banished Briton and Neptunian: being a record of the life, writings, principles and projects of Robert Gourlay* . . . (Boston, 1843) and *Chronicles of Canada: being a record, of Robert Gourlay* . . . (St Catharines, [Ont.], 1842), contain primary material no longer extant elsewhere, such as material from missing files of the *Niagara Spectator* (Niagara, [Ont.]). Gourlay's other printed works include *A specific plan for organising the people, and for obtaining reform independent of parliament . . . to the people of Fife . . . of Britain!* (London, 1809); . . . *To the labouring poor of Wily parish* ([Bath, Eng.], 1816]); *General introduction to statistical account of Upper Canada, compiled with a view to a grand system of emigration, in connexion with a reform of the Poor Laws* (London, 1822; repr. [East Ardsley, Eng.], 1966, and London, 1966); *Statistical account of Upper Canada, compiled with a view to a grand system of emigration* (2v., London, 1822; repr. [East Ardsley,

Eng.], 1966, and [New York, 1966]); and *An appeal to the common sense, mind and manhood of the British nation* (London, 1826).

The only full length biography of Gourlay, Lois Darroch Milani, *Robert Gourlay, gadfly: the biography of Robert (Fleming) Gourlay, 1778–1863, forerunner of the rebellion in Upper Canada, 1837* ([Thornhill, Ont., 1971?]), contains much material, especially from Scotland, which is unavailable elsewhere. The introduction to R. F. Gourlay, *Statistical account of Upper Canada*, ed. S. R. Mealing (Toronto, 1974), is a most perceptive and balanced account, and is especially good on the Scottish background to Gourlay's statistical work. s.f.w.]

PAC, MG 24, B33; RG 5, A1. PAO, Gourlay family papers; Macaulay (John) papers; Robinson (John Beverley) papers; Strachan (John) papers. PRO, CO 42/359–62. *Niagara Spectator* (Niagara, [Ont.]), 1818–19. Sir John Sinclair, *The statistical account of Scotland: drawn up from the communications of the ministers of the different parishes* (21v., Edinburgh, 1791–99). [John Strachan], *The John Strachan letter book, 1812–1834*, ed. G. W. Spragge (Toronto, 1946). S. D. Clark, *Movements of political protest in Canada, 1640–1840* (Toronto, 1959). Craig, *Upper Canada*. Dent, *Upper Canadian rebellion*. E. A. Cruikshank, "Post-war discontent at Niagara in 1818," *OH*, XXIX (1933), 14–46. W. R. Riddell, "Robert (Fleming) Gourlay," *OH*, XIV (1916), 5–133.

GRANT, WALTER COLQUHOUN, soldier and settler; b. 27 May 1822 in Edinburgh, Scotland, the only child of Colquhoun Grant and Margaret Brodie; d. 27 Aug. 1861 in Saugor, India.

Walter Colquhoun Grant was born to a military family, his father having been chief of the intelligence department of the army commanded by the Duke of Wellington at Waterloo. Both of Grant's parents were dead by 1829, and he was raised by a cousin, William Brodie, in Forres, Morayshire, Scotland. Grant followed family tradition and at age 24 became the youngest captain in the British army, in the 2nd Royal North British Dragoons, known as the Scots Greys. In 1848 he was at the Royal Military Academy, Sandhurst. The loss of a reported £75,000 inheritance through the failure of his bank, however, forced Grant, now beset by rising debts and pressing creditors, to leave the army.

In the summer of 1848, before he left Sandhurst, Grant learned that the Hudson's Bay Company was to be given proprietary rights to Vancouver Island, which he considered "a grand field for fresh & vigorous enterprise." In communication with the HBC, Grant agreed to purchase 200 acres of land, and, in accordance with the company's provisions, establish settlers on it. The HBC, which officially took possession of the island on 13 Jan. 1849, was in urgent need of maps of Vancouver Island to facilitate land sales, and appointed Grant its surveyor at a yearly salary of £100. After initial difficulties in attracting settlers, Grant did succeed in recruiting eight Scots, including a farm manager, labourers, and house builders, who sailed for the island at the beginning of 1849, their passages paid by Grant. He also arranged that the Church of Scotland would supply a clergyman to be schoolmaster on Vancouver Island, but the minister died on the voyage out. Grant dispatched carriage harnesses, sawmill machinery, sporting rifles, tools, seeds, cricket equipment, and surveying devices, but the expenses involved in his immigration plans plunged him into further financial difficulties before he left England. With the assistance of his uncle, Sir Lewis Grant, he purchased 100 of the 200 acres he wanted, and he obtained from the HBC an advance on his first year's salary as surveyor.

In the spring of 1849 Grant sailed from Scotland via Panama (where he ran out of money and drew on the HBC for £100), and California, to Fort Victoria, which he reached on 11 Aug. 1849. Approaching the fort from his landing near Clover Point, he mistook a milk cow for a buffalo and shot it, much to the consternation of the company. He found his eight settlers disgruntled from their two months' wait for him. He set about claiming the quantity of land he had bought, expecting to find 200 acres of "prairie land" near Fort Victoria, but this land was still in the company's possession. James Douglas*, the chief factor, suggested that he settle at Metchosin; instead he chose a site on Sooke Basin, 25 miles northwest of Fort Victoria, suitable for building a sawmill. Grant and his men began building a house, named Achaineach (Gaelic for Ravensfield), which was constructed of squared logs and cedar shakes and defended by two cannon. Soon he and his men had some 35 acres under cultivation. In 1850 he installed a small water-powered mill at the mouth of a stream at the northeast end of Sooke Basin to cut the abundant timber found nearby.

The increasing involvement with his estate made Grant's surveying duties take second place. Pressed by the company to send back sketches on tracing paper to London as soon as possible, Grant in his role as company surveyor of Victoria district completed the base lines for the proposed municipal area and established the perimeter for the acreage of John Tod* (the only other colonist to have come to the island by September 1850), but did not complete his assignment of dividing the area into sections. Hampered by lack of assistance and time, Grant tendered his resignation in March 1850 and finally gave up the survey in September, leaving the colony without a surveyor's services.

Grant, however, was now short of capital and was betraying a lack of ability in managing men. He ran up large accounts with family, friends, banks, and the company; Sir George Simpson* observed that Grant had "a peculiar talent for getting into the pockets of his friends." Grant claimed in March 1850 that he had been forced to dismiss half of his men for misconduct and had lost others through desertion, although most of them later settled on land of their own. He had some difficulty with the Sooke Indians over theft and vandalism and urged that two regiments be stationed on Vancouver Island, but he received no protection from the authorities in Fort Victoria or London. Later, Grant claimed that he had established "a friendly intercourse with the native tribe of savages." By late 1850 the depressed condition of the economy, caused in part by the California gold rush, which affected prices and drained off settlers and labour, hit Grant hard. His spirits, also, were much affected by the solitariness of his existence as a colonist and in October 1850 he visited the Hawaiian Islands, returning to Sooke in February 1851. During the summer he rented his farm to one of his former servants and left for the Klamath gold mines in Oregon. After spending almost two years there, he arrived in San Francisco in August 1853. He returned to Vancouver Island for the last time in September 1853 and sold his property to John Muir*, another non-company settler, who went on to develop a profitable lumber business at Sooke. Grant quit Vancouver Island in mid November 1853.

Associates of Grant on Vancouver Island, such as Governor Richard Blanshard*, the Reverend Robert John Staines*, and James Yates, were in agreement with his complaints about the company's lack of interest in colonization. Grant's objections to company rule, expressed even before he left England, concerning the high cost of land, heavy royalties on the export of lumber, and the exclusive rights of trade of the company, were confirmed by his experiences as a colonist. Yet Grant made numerous contributions to the development of British colonization on the island. He was the first white person independent of the HBC to settle on the island, and its first inland surveyor. He was the founder of Sooke, and a promoter of Scottish immigration. He introduced cricket, and left his equipment to Staines' boarding school. He imported seeds of broom in order that the hills around him might benefit from it and also take on the hue of his native Scotland. He was a pioneer in the lumber

Gray

industry at Sooke, though in this as in many of his projects he was unsuccessful. A swordsman, hunter, conversationalist, and spendthrift, he was a unique addition to the colonial society dominated by the company. James Douglas wrote that Grant was "an unfortunate man who has been an absolute plague to me since he came to the Island." Eden Colvile*, another company servant, thought Grant's "flightiness almost amounts to lunacy." John Sebastian Helmcken*, however, remembered him as "a splendid fellow and every inch an officer and a gentleman."

Upon his return to Britain Grant re-enlisted in the British army, and served during the Crimean War as lieutenant-colonel of the cavalry of the Turkish contingent. At the time of his death at age 39, he was brigade-major of Lucknow in central India. He had retained, however, his interest in Vancouver Island, and wrote from India in December 1857 to the secretary of the Royal Geographical Society that once the mutiny was settled and if Vancouver Island were "not in the meantime provided with a better governor," he would certainly accept the post "provided government felt disposed to take the [colony's] affairs seriously in hand." In 1857 and 1859 he prepared papers concerning the island for the Royal Geographical Society in London which were published. They are distinct contributions to the early literature concerning the potential for colonization on an island that he had been unable, because of circumstances and certain personal traits, to influence as he had wished.

BARRY M. GOUGH

[W. C. Grant was the author of "Description of Vancouver Island, by its first colonist," Royal Geographical Soc., *Journal* (London), 27 (1857), 268–320, and "Remarks on Vancouver Island, principally concerning townsites and native population," Royal Geographical Soc., *Journal* (London), 31 (1861), 208–13. Important letters are in "Two letters from Walter Colquhoun Grant," ed. J. E. Hendrickson, *BC Studies*, 26 (summer 1975), 3–15. B.M.G.]

Royal Geographical Soc. Archives (London), Correspondence files, W. C. Grant to secretary, 16 Dec. 1857, 23 Nov. 1858, 15 March 1859. Scottish Record Office (Edinburgh), Brodie of Brodie papers, box 11, bundle 5, W. C. Grant to William Brodie, 29 Aug. 1848, 8 Aug. 1851. *Gentleman's Magazine*, CCXI (July–December 1861), 572. Royal Geographical Soc., *Journal*, 32 (1862), cviii; *Proc.* (London), I (1857), 487–90. [C. J. D.] Haswell, *The first respectable spy: the life and times of Colquhoun Grant, Wellington's head of intelligence* (London, 1969). D. A. Fraser, "British Columbia's first settler," *Public School Magazine* (Victoria), III (1920), 44, 46, 48. W. E. Ireland, "Captain Walter Colquhoun Grant: Vancouver Island's first independent settler," *BCHQ*, XVII

(1953), 87–125; "Pioneer surveyors of Vancouver Island," Corporation of B.C. Land Surveyors, *Report of proc. of the annual general meeting* (Victoria), 1951, 47–51. *Daily Colonist* (Victoria), 12 July 1931, 8 July 1956. *Vancouver Daily Province*, 10 March 1950 (magazine section). *Victoria Daily Times*, 2 April 1949.

GRAY, JOHN WILLIAM DERING (often known as **I. W. D. Gray**), Church of England clergyman and editor; b. 23 July 1797 in Preston, N.S., son of the Reverend Benjamin Gerrish Gray*; m. Avis Phillips Easson of Jamaica; d. 1 Feb. 1868 in Halifax, N.S.

John William Dering Gray's father had been sent to Preston as a Church of England missionary to a group of Maroons, transferred there after the British conquest of Jamaica. In 1818 Gray earned a BA from King's College in Windsor, N.S. (he received an MA in 1826 and a BD and DD in 1846 from the same institution). He then spent a year in England where he was ordained in 1820.

Upon his return to Nova Scotia a few years later, Gray may have been given the parish of Amherst. In 1826 he was appointed curate in Trinity Church, Saint John, N.B., where his father had become rector. Gray himself became rector in 1840 and served until November 1867 when he retired owing to ill health. He then went to Halifax to live with his son, Benjamin Gerrish Gray, and died there a few months later. He had fulfilled his duties as a minister conscientiously. He was, as his contemporaries testified, an active and inspiring rector.

Gray's convictions and character also impelled him to participate in the religious controversies of his time and to assume the leadership of the evangelical or low church party in the Church of England in the Maritimes. His theological writings were aimed first at stopping Anglican defection to the Baptist Church [*see* James Walton NUTTING] and later at preserving the Anglican communion from Tractarian or Romanizing tendencies. The consecration of John Medley* as bishop of Fredericton in 1845 and of Bishop Hibbert Binney* of Nova Scotia in 1851, both decidedly high church, precipitated a conflict within the Anglican community over matters of theology and church management. However, the roots of this conflict, the passions it evoked, and the issues at stake reflect as much the social, economic, and political life of Saint John as its religious persuasion. In a number of Anglican parishes of the Maritimes, and especially in Saint John, feelings of autonomy had been nurtured by frontier conditions and not countered by absentee or overworked bishops. Furthermore, although Saint John was growing in population and prosperity, the city's élite was seeing political power shift to Fredericton. Concerns for faith and social position had also been increased by the influx of Irish immigrants in the 1830s and 1840s and the selection of Saint John in 1845 as the see of the first Roman Catholic bishop of New Brunswick, William Dollard*. Gray was the rector of the wealthiest parish in Saint John and his statements of religious principle in pamphlets and letters to local newspapers, notably the *New Brunswick Courier*, reflected the struggle of Saint John to further its autonomy and influence. The quarrels reached a peak during the late 1840s and early 1850s, when the advent of free trade and the implementation of responsible government were also severely disrupting the economic and political *status quo* of the town.

A first flurry had occurred in 1836 when Gray's parish refused to join the Church Society of the archdeaconry of New Brunswick, ostensibly because it objected to the society's constitution, although Gray's opponents contended that it was more likely that the Saint John parish was unwilling to share its wealth with poorer parishes and missions. Some of Gray's parishioners and other clergymen of the town donated individually to the society and formed a dissenting nucleus within Saint John which became active and venomous in subsequent years. Dr LeBaron Botsford, Judge Robert PARKER, and Dr Robert BAYARD supported Gray against such men as William Wright, advocate general and a church warden, the Reverend Richard Berrian Wiggins, and the Reverend Frederick Coster.

In the early 1840s Gray was apparently one of several Maritime clergymen who entertained hopes of becoming bishop (his rivals included Archdeacon George Coster* of Fredericton, Archdeacon Robert WILLIS of Nova Scotia, and the Reverend Edwin JACOB of King's College, Fredericton). When Medley was installed in 1845, Gray and his supporters unsuccessfully opposed the new bishop's decision to place his see in Fredericton rather than Saint John. After the Saint John parish joined the Church Society in 1846 and thereby doubled the society's previous income with its contribution of £1,400, internal rivalries within the society increased and threats of secession were heard. Gray opposed Medley over the questions of church ritual, prayer books, the building of the cathedral and St Anne's Chapel in Fredericton, the request for funds for these projects, and the bishop's "abuses of power" in nominating clergy, which undermined the established New Brunswick practice of allowing congregations to choose their own clergy, and

in attempting to introduce synods, which would "augment the powers vested in the Colonial Bishops." The opposition led by Gray, however, appears as more than a theological dispute; it reflects the concerns of a frontier town caught in a centralizing network and losing control over its destiny.

In 1850 Gray decided to publish and edit a newspaper, the *Church Witness*. He bore the responsibility for six years, when the paper fell into other hands and toward 1860 eventually failed. Gray resuscitated it in 1865 and assisted it with his pen until shortly before his death. An editorial in the first issue indicates how strongly he identified with the ideals of the Reformation period: "We . . . propose to conduct our paper upon what we conscientiously regard as the *true* principles of the Church . . . as settled by her Reformers of the sixteenth century. . . . New and strange opinions as they may arise from time to time . . . to disturb the faith, we shall watchfully and steadfastly resist. We desire thus simply to speak the truth in love, thus earnestly to contend for the faith once delivered to the saints." The weekly's pages were given over to the fight against the danger of "perversion" to Catholicism inherent in the high church movement, and opposition to the "tyranny" of the bishop. In later years, Gray became concerned about the dangers of rationalism presented by the broad church movement.

The paper's uncompromising low church stand earned Gray adherents in the whole Maritime region as well as fierce enmity from the established Anglican circles in Fredericton and Halifax. Nova Scotia's Bishop Binney was as much the butt of Gray's attacks as Medley. For instance, through active involvement in the affairs of King's College, Windsor, Gray tried to prevent Binney's gaining absolute control over the teaching of theology at that institution; Gray served for many years on the board of governors, founded the New Brunswick branch of the Alumni Society, and spent time in England in 1838–39, in 1846, and in 1860 soliciting funds for its support.

Gray had the loyalty and respect of many and after his death the *Church Witness* (quoting the Halifax *Morning Chronicle*), praised him as "the ripest scholar and most thoroughly finished Theologian of the Church in these Colonies. . . ." Even Medley once described him as "a zealous clever useful man." But because his views ran counter to the initiatives of Medley and his collaborators and pupils, he has tended to be regarded by some local historians as a troublemaker or, at best, a sincere but misguided leader. His own admiration for the plainness and inde-

Gregory

pendence of the 16th century divines is perhaps a more useful indication of the tradition he represents.

GENEVIÈVE LALOUX JAIN

J. W. D. Gray's publications include: *A brief view of the scriptural authority and historical evidence of infant baptism; and a reply to objections urged in the treatise of E. A. Crawley, A.M.* (Halifax, 1837); *A letter to members of the Church of England, in reply to a letter from Edmund Maturin, M.A., late curate St. Paul's, Halifax, N.S.* (Saint John, N.B., 1859); *A reply to the Rev. F. Coster's defence of the "Companion to the Prayer Book"* (Saint John, N.B., 1849); *A reply to the statement of the Rev. Mr. Wiggins, A.M., showing the causes which have led to his retirement from the curacy of Saint John* (Saint John, N.B., 1851); *A sermon, preached at Trinity Church, in the parish of St. John, N.B., on the 8th December, 1857, and designed to recommend the principles of the loyalists of 1783* (Saint John, N.B., 1857); *A sermon, preached at Trinity Church, Saint John, N.B., on Sunday, 24th November, 1839, upon resuming his duties in the parish, after an absence of twelve months in England* (Saint John, 1839); *A sermon, preached at Trinity Church, Saint John, New-Brunswick, on Sunday, January 22, 1837* (Saint John, 1837); "Sermon, preached in Christ's Church, Fredericton, on Sunday, 8th February, 1846, being the day before the anniversary meeting of the society," Diocesan Church Soc. of N.B., *Report of proc.* (Saint John), 1846; *A sermon preached in Trinity Church, Saint John, March 4, 1849, on the providential rescue of that church from fire, on the night of the 26th February, 1849* (Saint John, N.B.,1849); *A sermon, upon the death of . . . William IV . . .* (Saint John, N.B., 1837); *Sermons upon the second Advent of our Lord, preached at Trinity Church, St. John, in December, 1864* (Saint John, N.B., 1865); *Trinity Church and its founders: a sermon preached on New Year's Day, 1854 . . .* (Saint John, N.B., 1854).

N.B. Museum, Jarvis family papers, William Jarvis, "The Church of England in New Brunswick in its relations with the state" (11 March 1863); Trinity Anglican Church (Saint John, N.B.), baptismal records, 1835–67. Robert Bayard, *A statement of facts, as they occurred at the late annual meeting of the Diocesan Church Society; with a reply to some misstatements and expositions in the Rev'd F. Coster's defence of the "Companion to the Prayer Book"* (Saint John, N.B., 1849; 1875). *Church Witness* (Saint John, N.B.), February 1850 – March 1868. Fenety, *Political notes and observations. Morning News* (Saint John, N.B.), November 1867, February 1868. R. B. Wiggins, *A review of the Rev. Dr. Gray's "Reply" to the "Statement of some of the causes which have led to the late dissention in the Episcopal Church" in this city* (Saint John, N.B., 1851); *Statement of some of the causes which have led to the late dissention in the Episcopal Church, in the city of Saint John* (Saint John, N.B., 1851). William Wright, *Observations on Dr. Bayard's mis-called "Statement of facts, as they occurred at the late annual meeting of the Diocesan Church Society"* (Saint John, N.B., 1849).

F. G. H. Brigstocke, *History of Trinity Church, Saint John, New Brunswick, 1791–1891* (Saint John, N.B., 1892). Philip Carrington, *The Anglican Church in Canada, a history* (Toronto, 1963). S. D. Clark, *The developing Canadian community* (2nd ed., Toronto, 1968); *The social development of Canada, an introductory study with select documents* (Toronto, 1942). V. G. Kent, "The Right Reverend Hibbert Binney, colonial Tractarian bishop of Nova Scotia, 1851–1887" (unpublished MA thesis, University of New Brunswick, Fredericton, 1969). W. Q. Ketchum, *The life and work of the Most Reverend John Medley, D.D., first bishop of Fredericton and metropolitan of Canada* (Saint John, N.B., 1893). *Leaders of the Canadian church*, ed. W. B. Heeney (3 ser., Toronto, 1918–43), 1st ser. MacNutt, *New Brunswick*. L. N. Harding, "John, by divine permission: John Medley and the church in New Brunswick," Canadian Church Hist. Soc., *Journal*, VIII (1966), 76–87.

GREGORY, JOHN, civil servant; b. 13 Oct. 1806 in Edinburgh, Scotland; m. in 1833 Mary Grosvenor of Fredericton, N.B., and they had eight sons and four daughters; d. 29 Oct. 1861 in Fredericton.

Little is known of John Gregory's early life except for his later indication that he had been a mechanic's son. He came to New Brunswick about 1820 and probably served with the 74th Regiment stationed in Fredericton at that time. In 1825 he became a clerk in the office of the provincial secretary and subsequently was clerk to the Legislative Council until his death.

Concern for the education of his family brought Gregory into local prominence and notoriety. In 1844, Gregory and assemblymen James BROWN and Sylvester Zolieski Earle* comprised a special committee appointed by Lieutenant Governor Sir William COLEBROOKE to investigate provincial grammar and parochial schools. Their report, later published in pamphlet form, provided overwhelming evidence of the incompetence of teachers and the inadequacies of education generally but especially in the parish schools. It strongly recommended the establishment in Fredericton of a teacher-training school, a model school, and a provincial board of education, measures aimed at creating an educational system of higher quality for the whole population. A subsequent inquiry in 1846 into the grammar schools supported the findings and recommendations of the 1844 committee. In 1846, however, the assembly passed an act to reform not the more numerous parish schools but only the grammar schools, which generally served the affluent sector of New Brunswick society in or near the principal urban centres. More extensive educational innovations came, after prodding from Lieutenant Governor Colebrooke, in a parish schools act of 1847 which provided for a training and model school under the newly constituted Board of Education. Gregory became the board's secretary at a salary of £100 per year.

Joseph Marshall* d'Avray, the master of the training school appointed under the same act, who arrived from Mauritius in 1848, indicated in his speech at the opening of the school that his views on education and teacher training were similar to those contained in the 1845 report of Gregory and his fellow inspectors. However, as one educational historian has observed, Gregory seemed to detect a note of condescension toward parish schools in some of d'Avray's remarks, suggesting these institutions were "schools for colonials of a static lower order." If Gregory did gain this impression, he was probably reflecting the suspicion and hostility of some New Brunswickers against the appointment of outsiders. Gregory may also have sensed the impending decline of his own influence in educational circles with the arrival of the urbane and well-qualified d'Avray. Whatever the reasons, hostility soon developed. In April 1848 d'Avray complained to Colebrooke that the Board of Education was disinclined to accept or sanction any improvement "not emanating from themselves. . . . Many of them are entirely guided by the opinion and views of their Secretary, who is nothing more than a Theorist like themselves." For his part, Gregory criticized d'Avray's first report, complaining to Colebrooke that d'Avray did not understand the province's representative form of government.

On 21 April 1849 the King's College Council received a memorial from Gregory complaining about certain aspects of the new county scholarships which meant that his eldest son would be ineligible. Despite Gregory's repeated requests and angry letters to the local press, the council refused to modify the regulations. Gregory wrote to the Fredericton *Head Quarters* on 22 June 1849 insisting that another son had been "wronged" by the manner in which "certain parts of the Collegiate School examination" had been conducted. On 30 June 1849 he publicly appealed to Bishop John Medley* to ask the Collegiate School Committee to reinstate a third son, ten-year-old George, who had been expelled. A heated exchange in the *Head Quarters* between Gregory and George Goodridge Roberts, the school's principal and a close friend of d'Avray, failed to resolve the issue, although the King's College Council, which became involved, admitted that the expulsion had resulted from the father's intemperate remarks.

A petition from Gregory to Lieutenant Governor Sir Edmund Walker HEAD was read in the assembly on 7 March 1850; it asked for copies of the headmaster's letters outlining the expulsion, and an accounting of all public money paid in 1849 toward the upkeep of the school and stipends to the collegiate staff. Gregory received the information but continued efforts until 1854 did not get redress of his grievances.

In 1853, in his role as secretary of the Board of Education, Gregory became involved in a bitter debate with d'Avray, now superintendent of education, professor of modern languages at King's College, and part-time instructor at the Collegiate School. Once again, the initial point involved another of Gregory's sons, but in several caustic letters to the press, which criticized d'Avray's views on education, Gregory raised the question from a personality clash to a conflict between opposing educational philosophies. D'Avray was accused of being an "élitist" favouring classical training for the minority attending the grammar schools while restricting the parish schools to elementary instruction.

In 1854 d'Avray's office of superintendent took over the duties of secretary of the Board of Education and Gregory lost his position. Several times during the 1850s he tried unsuccessfully to win a seat in the assembly. His sons went on to successful careers, several in the professions. Gregory's angry and well-publicized confrontations with educational authorities could be dismissed as the extreme and at times irrational behaviour of an over-zealous parent, but his complaints were raised as part of a widespread discontent with an education system which served the wealthy at the expense of the bulk of the population.

RICHARD WILBUR

PANB, REX/pa/Education papers, University of New Brunswick, 1850–59. PAC, MG 9, A10, 5, p.277 (mfm. at UNBL). UNBL, King's College, College Council, minutes, 1849–51. *Documents before the Council of King's College, in the case of the expulsion of George Gregory from the Collegiate Grammar School, and minutes of the council . . .*, comp. John Gregory (Fredericton, 1850). *Head Quarters*, 22 June 1849, 1861. N.B., House of Assembly, *Journals*, 1851, app., "Report of secretary of Provincial Board of Education." *Royal Gazette* (Fredericton), 1833; 30 Oct. 1861. *Hutchinson's New Brunswick directory, for 1865–66 . . .*, comp. Thomas Hutchinson (Montreal, [1865]). *Lovell's Canadian dominion directory for 1871 . . .* (Montreal, [1871]). *The old grave-yard, Fredericton, New Brunswick: epitaphs copied by the York-Sunbury Historical Society Inc.*, comp. L. M. B. Maxwell ([Fredericton], 1938). K. F. C. MacNaughton, *The development of the theory and practice of education in New Brunswick, 1784–1900: a study in historical background*, ed. and intro. A. G. Bailey (Fredericton, 1947), 122–43.

Grollier

GROLLIER, PIERRE-HENRI, priest, Oblate of Mary Immaculate, and missionary; b. 30 March 1826 at Montpellier (dept of Hérault), France, son of Jean-Jacques Grollier, baker, and Thérèse-Catherine-Rose Giniès; d. 4 June 1864 at Fort Good Hope (Northwest Territories).

In October 1847, Pierre Grollier, a student at the Grand Séminaire of Montpellier, decided, as a result of a lecture given by Father Jean-Claude-Léonard BAVEUX, to enter the noviciate of the Oblates at Notre-Dame de l'Osier (dept of Isère). He made his profession on 15 Oct. 1848. After completing his studies at Marseilles, he was ordained priest on 29 June 1851 by Charles-Joseph-Eugène de Mazenod, bishop of Marseilles and founder of the Oblates.

Grollier worked at the sanctuary of Notre-Dame-de-la-Garde at Marseilles (1851–52) before embarking for America in the spring of 1852. Bound for the missions of the northwest, he reached Saint-Boniface on 27 June. He left there on 8 July to go to the Lake Athabasca mission at Fort Chipewyan, where he lived from 1852 to 1856 and from 1857 to 1858. In 1853 he founded a mission at the Fond-du-Lac trading-post, which had been re-established recently by the Hudson's Bay Company on Lake Athabasca among the Caribou Eaters. He stayed for fairly long periods among these Indians during the years 1853 to 1856 and in 1858. He was called to the Île-à-la-Crosse mission (Saskatchewan) in 1856 and remained a year there, ministering to the Montagnais. From 1858 to 1859 he stayed at Fort Resolution.

His zeal increased by the arrival of an Anglican missionary in the north in 1858, Grollier, already a seasoned traveller, set forth on lengthy apostolic expeditions to beyond the Arctic circle. He founded and visited missions at Fort Simpson (1858–60), Fort Providence (1858–59), Fort Rae (1859), and Fort Norman (1859–60). In 1859 he was given the task of setting up and directing the mission at Fort Good Hope, where he spent the last years of his life, although continuing to visit the numerous missions he had founded. In 1860 he went to Fort McPherson on the Peel River, where he met Loucheux Indians for the first time. He also visited the Inuit (Eskimos) there, and on 14 September assembled the two groups and made them promise to live in peace.

A victim of severe asthma in 1861, Grollier found his journeying arduous. His superiors therefore gave him some associates and offered to send him to a less demanding post, but he refused to leave his neophytes. He stated that he would not become a burden on the mission, since "missionaries do not have long illnesses." The poverty and lack of comfort of these missions imposed great privations. At Fort Good Hope Father Grollier lived in a house measuring 22 by 18 ft, which served as church, parlour, dining room, kitchen, and sleeping quarters.

In the Mackenzie River region the HBC agents did not look favourably on Catholics, but they were usually courteous and hospitable. However, Grollier, a man of great energy, severe on himself, and little inclined to moderation, was given a cold reception by certain company agents at Peel River in September 1860: they refused to give him lodging and food. In Grollier's eyes, it was the Anglican missionaries who were the enemy, from whom the Indians, pagan or Catholic, should be protected. Yet, in a way typical of religious attitudes in the 19th century, the Anglicans were scarcely better disposed towards him.

As the first Catholic missionary to meet the Inuit of the northwest, Grollier was delighted to learn, in 1862, that his demands had resulted in the creation of the apostolic vicariate of Athabasca, of which Bishop Henri Faraud* became the incumbent. Two years later Grollier died and in accordance with his wishes was buried between two Indians in the cemetery of the Fort Good Hope mission.

GASTON CARRIÈRE

Archives de l'archevêché de Saint-Boniface (Man.), Correspondance de l'archevêché (mfm. at AHO); Alexandre Taché, Notes sur l'établissement de la mission d'Athabaska (mfm. at AHO). Archives départementales de l'Hérault (Montpellier), État civil, Montpellier, 30 mars 1826. Archives générales O.M.I. (Rome), Dossier Pierre-Henri Grollier (mfm. at AHO); histoire de la mission de Notre-Dame-des-Sept-Douleurs établie au fond du lac Athabasca (mfm. at AHO). Archives provinciales O.M.I. (Edmonton), Dossier Grollier (mfm. at AHO). *Notices nécrologiques des O.M.I.*, I, 169–76. P.-J.-B. Duchaussois, *Aux glaces polaires; Indiens et Esquimaux* (Lyon, France, [1921]), 384–95. Herman Klingler, *Conquérants sans terre, l'aventure des missionnaires*, Pierre Chambard, trad. (Tours, France, 1956), 189–203. Morice, *Hist. de l'Église catholique*, II, 29, 50, 55, 66, 98, 103, 116, 118, 156, 172, 179, 184; III, 258. Gaston Carrière, "Fondation et développement des missions catholiques dans la Terre de Rupert et les Territoires du Nord-Ouest (1845–1861)," *Revue de l'université d'Ottawa*, XLI (1971), 397–427; "Glorieux centenaire d'un grand missionnaire, le père Henri Grollier, o.m.i.," *La Bannière de Marie-Immaculée* (Ottawa), LXXII (1964), 40–44.

GUIBORD, JOSEPH, typographer, member of the Institut Canadien; b. 31 March 1809 at Sainte-Anne-de-Varennes (Varennes, Que.), son of Paul Guibord, *dit* Archambault, and Marie-Anne Célerier, *dit* Roch; on 2 June 1828, at Montreal, he married Henriette Brown, and they had at least ten children; d. 18 Nov. 1869 in Montreal.

It is known that in 1838 Joseph Guibord and John Lovell* were printing *Le Populaire* (Montreal). Later Guibord went to work in Louis PERRAULT's printing house. Acknowledged to be skilful and even to be one of the best typographers in Canada, Joseph Guibord was entrusted by Abbé André-Marie Garin, a missionary in the northwest, with the task of printing a catechism in an Indian language, which was published in 1854. Guibord is thought to have introduced stereotype printing in Canada, and to have had a part in printing the first book to be stereotyped in the country. At the time of his death he was foreman in Perrault's firm.

Nothing predestined Guibord to the dubious fame he enjoys today. Around his mortal remains, however, was waged the last and fiercest battle between the liberals of the Institut Canadien and the ultramontanes. Following a decree of the Inquisition (July 1869) condemning the doctrines "contained in a certain yearbook," the *Annuaire de l'Institut Canadien pour 1868*, and placing it on the Index [*see* Gonzalve Doutre*], the parish priests of the diocese of Montreal on 29 August proclaimed an ordinance issued by Bishop Ignace Bourget*: "He who persists in the desire to remain in the said Institut or to read or merely possess the above-mentioned yearbook without being so authorized by the Church deprives himself of the sacraments at the hour of his death." Three months later Joseph Guibord was near death; he was then a member of the Institut Canadien. In one of the certified documents later sent to Cardinal Alessandro Barnabo in Rome, Louis-Antoine Dessaulles* stated that Joseph Guibord received absolution and communion at his bedside. However, he wrote, "the confessor, learning that Guibord was a member of the Institut, hastily returned to tell him that he ought never to have given him absolution, and demanded his resignation as a member." Guibord's refusal made him, in the eyes of the religious authorities, a rebel and a public sinner, and thus barred him from the church's rites and from burial in consecrated ground. This excommunication aroused the anger of the members of the Institut Canadien, who then prompted Henriette Brown Guibord to take the priest and the churchwardens of the parish of Notre-Dame to court. It was a famous and unfortunate case which went up through many courts and was not decided until 1874. At that time the Privy Council

in London ordered that Guibord be buried in the cemetery of Côte-des-Neiges [*see* Charles-Elzéar Mondelet*; Alexis-Frédéric Truteau*; Joseph Doutre*]. Bishop Bourget, using his power to bind and to loose, to bless and to curse, then declared the place of burial forever "under an interdict and separate from the rest of the cemetery." And the bishop further pronounced. "There rests a rebel who has been buried by force of arms."

According to his contemporaries, Joseph Guibord was a worthy man, the last to deserve this misadventure.

JEAN-ROCH RIOUX

ANQ-M, État civil, Catholiques, Notre-Dame de Montréal, 2 juin 1828, 18 nov. 1869. Fraser-Hickson Library (Montreal), Archives de l'Institut canadien de Montréal. *The Guibord affair*, ed. L. C. Clark (Toronto and Montreal, 1971). Le Jeune, *Dictionnaire. Notices généalogiques sur la famille Guibord* (Ottawa, 1914). *La Presse* (Montréal), 1er avril 1967. Théophile Hudon, *L'Institut canadien de Montréal et l'affaire Guibord; une page d'histoire* (Montréal, 1938). Adrien Thério, "Les grandes batailles de Mgr Bourget: l'Institut canadien, l'affaire Guibord et l'université de Montréal," *Perspectives/Le Nouvelliste* (Trois-Rivières), 9 (1967), no.20, 29–37; "Mgr Ignace Bourget: novateur audacieux et lutteur intrépide," *Perspectives/Le Nouvelliste*, 9 (1967), no.19, 15–23.

GUILLET, LOUIS, notary and politician; b. 28 Jan. 1788 at Sainte-Geneviève-de-Batiscan (Que.), son of Jean-Baptiste Guillet, merchant, and Marguerite Langlois; d. 28 Oct. 1868 in the village of his birth.

On 6 Feb. 1809 Louis Guillet was admitted to the profession of notary; he practised at Sainte-Geneviève-de-Batiscan until 1863. The high reputation he soon acquired in his particular circle enabled him to render important services in several fields: thus on 22 May 1830 he was appointed a commissioner for the opening of a road in the parish of Saint-Stanislas-de-la-Rivière-des-Envies; on 5 August of the same year he became a justice of the peace. A few years later, on 10 June 1836, he was appointed a commissioner to oversee the building of a bridge over the Sainte-Anne River. Following the disturbances in Lower Canada in 1837, Guillet was authorized on 21 Dec. 1837 to receive the oath of allegiance of the settlers on the Batiscan seigneury; finally on 2 April 1838 he was appointed commissioner for small causes in the same seigneury.

In 1836 the question of setting up registry offices in Lower Canada for the preservation of deeds or contracts concerning real estate (sales, wills, mortgages, conveyances, transfers, guardianships, and trusteeships), was revived. In reply to a questionnaire sent by a special committee of the Legislative Council, Guillet wrote on 29 Jan. 1836: "I would submit . . . that registry offices are not at all necessary and that they will be more annoying than useful to those living in country districts." He suggested instead that "deeds signed before a notary and creating mortgages should be considered public deeds, and the notary should be obliged to give discovery of [these documents] to anyone who asked." Guillet wanted to prevent registry offices from proliferating. In 1830 offices had already been set up in the counties of Drummond, Sherbrooke, Stanstead, Missisquoi, and Shefford, where the majority of inhabitants were English speaking and real property was held in free and common socage. In 1831 similar offices had been opened in the counties of Ottawa, Beauharnois, and Mégantic, and in 1834 in the counties of Deux-Montagnes and L'Acadie. Then, in 1841, against Guillet's advice, the Special Council of Lower Canada extended the registration requirement to all landed and real property in Lower Canada, whether held in free and common socage or in fee. It also established registry offices in each judicial district, where the district court sat. These measures were designed to avoid "the serious losses and evils resulting from secret and fraudulent conveyancing of landed property, from the mortgages on the latter, and from the uncertainty and insecurity attaching to land titles in this province." On 30 Aug. 1842, in pursuance of his notarial activities, Louis Guillet applied, unsuccessfully, for nomination as the agent for certain fiefs in the district of Trois-Rivières. On 25 Oct. 1851 and on 4 Dec. 1860, he was appointed census commissioner.

Guillet was a candidate in the 1844 election, in which the Reformers faced the supporters of Governor Charles Metcalfe*, and was elected on the Reform ticket in the county of Champlain. His mandate was renewed in the 1847–48 election, when he defeated the Conservative Joseph-Édouard TURCOTTE. He therefore sat in the opposition until 1848, and subsequently became a loyal supporter of the government of Louis-Hippolyte LA FONTAINE and Robert Baldwin*. In the 1851 elections, however, the Conservative Thomas Marchildon won in Champlain over Jean-Baptiste-Éric DORION, a representative of the radical Liberals, and Guillet, spokesman of the moderate Liberals.

Louis Guillet had married Louise Leclerc at Sainte-Geneviève-de-Batiscan. They had one son and two daughters.

LOUIS-PHILIPPE AUDET

PAC, MG 30, D62, 14, pp.790–91. Bas-Canada, *Statuts*, 1830, c.8; 1831, c.3; 1834, c.5; Conseil spécial, *Ordonnances*, 1840–41, c.30. Can., prov. du, *Statuts*, 1843, c.22; 1854–55, c.99. *Elgin-Grey papers*, IV, 1510, 1595–96, 1598–99, 1602. *Guide des sources d'archives sur le Canada français, au Canada* (Ottawa, 1975), 19–20. F.-J. Audet, *Les députés de la région des Trois-Rivières (1841–1867)* (Trois-Rivières, 1934), 68–70. Cornell, *Alignment of political groups*, 24, 30. J.-E. Roy, *Hist. du notariat*, II, 557–94.

GUITTÉ (Guité), P.-J., newspaper printer and publisher, native of France; fl. 1846–67.

In 1846 P.-J. Guitté first appears in Canadian history as printer of *L'Écho des campagnes*, a paper of "popular news for farmers" of Berthier-en-Haut (Berthierville). Four years later *L'Avenir*, the official organ of the Rouges, mentions his name in its list of representatives for this region. On 24 Feb. 1853, Guitté and A. de Grandpré founded *Le Courrier de Saint-Hyacinthe* and recruited Louis Delorme*, a Saint-Hyacinthe lawyer, to look after the political orientation of the new paper. Liberal and moderate, *Le Courrier de Saint-Hyacinthe* supported the ministry of Francis Hincks* and Augustin-Norbert MORIN. However, it withdrew rapidly from this position, for a year later the paper asserted that Morin's Liberal party ought to be ashamed of its leaders. From 21 Aug. 1854 to 14 Sept. 1860 Guitté was the sole "owner-publisher" of *Le Courrier*. During this period he acquired in succession three assistant editors just beginning their careers as journalists: a young Frenchman, Claude Petit, Médéric Lanctot*, and Raphaël-Ernest Fontaine*. At this time the newspaper plainly supported the Rouges and *Le Pays* of Montreal, particularly concerning education and the influence of the clergy in politics, and thereby incurred the censure of the seminary and bishopric of Saint-Hyacinthe.

After seven years at *Le Courrier*, Guitté sold the paper in September 1860. The Prince of Wales' visit to Saint-Hyacinthe perhaps provoked this decision. The paper's report of the occasion had read: "The Prince is not a handsome fellow in the ordinary sense of the word, far from it. An overlong, slightly hooked nose, eyes of a pale, lack-lustre blue, a thoroughly juvenile appearance, make him a decidedly insignificant figure. . . . All in all, we expected *something better*." The article had caused some astonishment among the local populace, and several people had considered such remarks out of place. *Le Courrier* agreed to publish a retraction of the "hastily written article," but maintained that despite the personal charm of His Highness the visit had been "the least instructive and the most frivolous event imaginable."

After Guitté's departure *Le Courrier*, under Delorme's direction, rapidly began to oppose the Rouges. In September 1861, stressing that "for more than six months the Liberal population of the district of Saint-Hyacinthe has had no organ among the country's newspapers," Guitté founded *Le Journal de Saint-Hyacinthe*. With Guitté and Fontaine the journal in fact took up the tradition of *Le Courrier* in the years 1854–60. *La Minerve* considered it merely "*Le Pays*' tail." After he had owned *Le Journal* for two years, Guitté made it over to Ed. Lecours et Compagnie.

In November 1866 Guitté and Wilfrid Laurier* went into partnership and acquired *Le Défricheur*, a paper published since 1862 at L'Avenir by Jean-Baptiste-Éric DORION. When the latter died on 1 Nov. 1866, one of his creditors, businessman Louis-Adélard Sénécal*, and the Rouges were uneasy about who would take over the paper. At this point Guitté and Laurier assumed responsibility, the first as printer, the second as editor. For a time they continued to publish at L'Avenir, but on 20 Dec. 1866 a notice to the readers stated that "on 1 January next the offices and printing plant of *Le Défricheur* will be transferred to the village of Victoriaville, Arthabaska station." *Le Défricheur* of Laurier and Guitté announced that it intended to continue Dorion's work by defending the Rouges and the opponents of confederation who gravitated towards *L'Union nationale* at Montreal. The paper crossed swords with Conservative papers such as *Le Journal des Trois-Rivières*, *L'Union des Cantons de l'Est*, and *Le Pionnier de Sherbrooke*. It was in its pages that Laurier, two weeks before having to give up his editorship because of illness, and a few months before confederation, wrote an article pointing out that union had imperilled French Canada, and that it must "ask for and secure free and separate government." Contrary to what has generally been said, *Le Défricheur* appeared until the end of March 1867, when the management warned the subscribers that publication would have to be suspended because of Laurier's health.

With *Le Défricheur*'s disappearance we lose track of Guitté. Little is known as yet of his personal life, but of his career it can be noted that he was connected with the Rouge party, printed and published newspapers in two of the regions where *rougisme* was particularly strong, and was in contact with many important Liberals from 1854 to 1867.

JEAN-PAUL BERNARD

ASSH, A, F, Chroniques de l'abbé Tétreau, févr. et juill. 1853. *L'Avenir*, 18 déc. 1850. *Le Courrier de Saint-Hyacinthe*, 21 août 1854, 31 août, 4, 7, 18 sept. 1860. *Le Défricheur* (L'Avenir et Victoriaville, Qué.), 20, 28 nov., 13, 20 déc. 1866, 7, 21 mars 1867. *Le Journal de Saint-Hyacinthe* (Saint-Hyacinthe, [Qué.]), 7 oct. 1861, 7 sept. 1863. *La Minerve*, 1er mars, 5 oct. 1861. *Le Pays*, 1er déc. 1866. Beaulieu et Hamelin, *Journaux du Québec*, 5, 241–43; *La presse québécoise*, I, 181–83. J.-P. Bernard, "La pensée des journalistes libéraux de Saint-Hyacinthe, 1853–1864" (thèse de MA, université de Montréal, 1958), 11–21; *Les Rouges*, 284–87. C.-P. Choquette, *Histoire de la ville de Saint-Hyacinthe* (Saint-Hyacinthe, Qué., 1930), 528. Rumilly, *Hist. de la prov. de Québec*, I, 54. O. D. Skelton, *Life and letters of Sir Wilfrid Laurier* (2v., Toronto, 1921), I, 39–40. J. R., "Le 'Courrier de Saint-Hyacinthe'," *BRH*, X (1904), 30–31.

GURNETT, GEORGE, journalist, politician, and magistrate; b. Horsham or Lewes, Sussex, England, *c*. 1792, the son of George and Anne Gurnett; d. 17 Nov. 1861 at Toronto, Canada West.

George Gurnett's early life is obscure, but it is known that in the mid 1820s he emigrated from England to Virginia, where he was superintendent of a tan-yard and something of a radical in politics. He then came to Ancaster, Upper Canada, where some of his family may have already settled. After obtaining press and type from Albany, N.Y., Gurnett began to publish the *Gore Gazette* on 3 March 1827, with the motto "All Extremes are Error." At first he corresponded with William Lyon MACKENZIE, but they soon disagreed. In late 1827 Gurnett supported the Tory Allan MACNAB when he was charged with contempt by the assembly during its investigation of the "Hamilton Outrage," in which Sir John COLBORNE was hanged in effigy. In 1829 Gurnett moved to York (Toronto), renaming his paper the *Courier of Upper Canada*; the first issue appeared in February 1830, and it soon became one of the town's chief Tory organs.

When Toronto was incorporated in 1834 Gurnett was elected a councilman for St George's ward, and the next year became one of its two aldermen. Gurnett held this office continuously until 1850. From the first he played a leading role on the committees of council, and was one of the judges in the minor cases heard in the city court. He was almost always chairman of the finance and assessment committee and of the board of works. Gurnett formed one of a group of staunch Tories, which included George Taylor Denison*, Thomas Carfrae*, and John Craig, who vigorously opposed the Reformers when they had a majority in 1834 and 1836. Gurnett helped Orange leader Ogle Robert Gowan* defeat Mackenzie in

Gurnett

York County in the provincial election of 1836, fought on the question of loyalty.

In January 1837 the Tory-dominated city council elected Gurnett fourth mayor of Toronto by a majority of 18 to one. The Tory *Royal Standard* jubilantly asserted that the "triumph of Conservatism is now complete." Gurnett's mayoralty, although marked by much quarrelling among the Tory councillors, saw the first amendment to the city's Act of Incorporation, which improved the basis of assessment and established a two-year term for the council. But the city had to cope with the depression of 1837 and was forced to issue its own paper money because it could not borrow sufficient funds. Despite these problems some sewer-building and macadamizing of roads were accomplished; a second market, St Patrick's, was built with the aid of public-minded citizens such as D'Arcy Boulton* Jr, who donated the land. Improvements were also begun on the harbour by a commission which included Gurnett and Hugh RICHARDSON. In September 1837 Gurnett was appointed a magistrate of the Home District and shortly afterwards district clerk of the peace, an office he held until 1861. He sold the *Courier* in 1837 to Charles Fothergill*.

Like Lieutenant Governor Sir Francis Bond Head*, Gurnett and the city council were ill prepared for the outbreak of rebellion in December 1837. At the end of October they had accepted custody of some 6,000 guns which, with their ammunition, were stored at city hall, unprotected. Although he did cooperate with James FitzGibbon in preparing for the defence of the city, Gurnett was not instrumental in the loyalist victory. John Powell, who had played a dramatic role in the rebellion, defeated him in the elections for mayor from 1838 to 1840.

The city election of 1841 was unusually vicious. The Reformers and moderates in provincial politics, including Robert Baldwin*, James Edward SMALL, and Francis Hincks*, did their utmost to get rid of Gurnett and the old corporation, whom they regarded as a left-over collection of inept Compact Tories. Robert STANTON, who beside Gurnett appeared as a moderate, ran against him in St George, but lost. As the Reform *Mirror* said, "We are left another year in the power of the odious, detestable corporation." It was generally assumed that Gurnett would again be chosen mayor; however, Alderman William Henry Boulton* charged that he was renting a house to a brothel keeper and was therefore morally unacceptable. George Monro* was elected mayor by the council, defeating both Gurnett and Powell.

Throughout the 1840s Gurnett was active on committees, including those connected with the harbour and wharves, gas and waterworks, and education. As chairman of the board of health in 1847 he displayed his usual energy in combatting the typhus epidemic. During this period he began to moderate his politics with the changing times. Breaking with his former Orange connections, he was physically attacked when he tried to stop the Orange parade in 1844. When the council again elected him mayor in 1848 his main opposition was an Orange leader, George Duggan*, who opposed him again unsuccessfully in 1849 and 1850. Gurnett also gained Reform support by refusing to sign a petition protesting the 1849 Rebellion Losses Bill.

During his second mayoralty Gurnett continued to show his meticulous attention to the work of the city and its committees. He became a city representative on the permanent harbour commission established in 1850. After the devastating fire of 7 April 1849 he was chairman of the committee to rebuild the St Lawrence Market which chose William Thomas* as the architect.

Gurnett sat regularly as a judge in the city court, and when the provincial government decided in 1850 to establish both a police magistrate's court and a recorder's court for Toronto, he was an obvious candidate for the first post. George Duggan's candidacy for both jobs was endorsed by city council, but Robert Baldwin appointed Gurnett the first police magistrate. Approval of his appointment in the radical and liberal press showed how the times and Gurnett's image had changed. He assumed office in January 1851, and for the next decade gave general satisfaction as police magistrate. He was also a member of the police commission established in 1858.

Gurnett was not very active outside the council. While at Ancaster he had joined the Gore militia, and served as a major during the rebellion. He was a lieutenant-colonel of the sedentary militia when he died. A supporter of St James' Cathedral, he was also one of the incorporators of the unsuccessful City of Toronto Gas Light Company in 1836.

Gurnett's first wife died in 1835 and in 1841 he married Catherine Darby of Trafalgar. At least six children died in infancy, but two daughters and his second wife were still living when he died suddenly of a stroke. Although John Ross Robertson* regarded Gurnett as a "Tory among the Tories, a Church and King man first, last and every time," his course in politics was somewhat circular, from an early commitment to reform, which had moderated by the late 1820s, to a high Tory stance in the 1830s, and finally to an acceptance of responsible government in the 1840s. These changes were perhaps expedient, perhaps a reflection of a gradual conversion to a more democratic outlook. As a conscientious and able administrator he helped give Toronto efficient civic government.

FREDERICK H. ARMSTRONG

City of Toronto Archives, Toronto City Council, Minutes, 1834–50. PAC, RG 68, 1, General index, 1651–1841, p.304; 1841–67, pp.287, 311, 315. PAO, Mackenzie-Lindsey papers, M. Crooks to W. L. Mackenzie, 30 Jan. 1827; William Wallace to Mackenzie, 6 May 1839; Toronto City Council papers, 1834–50. *Arthur papers* (Sanderson). *Globe*, 18–20 Nov. 1861. *Mirror* (Toronto), 15 Jan. 1841. F. H. Armstrong, "Toronto in transition: the emergence of a city, 1828–1838" (unpublished PHD thesis, University of Toronto, 1965). B. D. Dyster, "Toronto, 1840–1860: making it in a British Protestant town" (unpublished PHD thesis, University of Toronto, 1970). M. A. FitzGibbon, *A veteran of 1812; the life of James FitzGibbon* (Toronto 1894; repr. 1972), 197–209. Johnston, *Head of the lake* (1967), 77–78, 95, 154. Middleton, *Municipality of Toronto*, I, 169, 195–204, 211, 227, 247, 417–18, 444; II, 742, 791–96. *Robertson's landmarks of Toronto*, VI, 190.

H

HALE, JEFFERY, philanthropist; b. 19 April 1803 at Quebec, son of the Honourable John Hale* and Elizabeth Frances Amherst; d. a bachelor 13 Nov. 1864 at Tunbridge Wells, Kent, England.

Jeffery Hale was educated in England, enlisted in the Royal Navy at age 14, and served in it for ten years. At one time during this period he was in India, where together with his brother Edward* he was under the orders of his uncle, William Pitt Amherst, Earl of Amherst, the governor general. He left the navy in 1827, some time after obtaining the rank of lieutenant, in order to help, then to replace his ailing father as receiver general of Lower Canada. His hopes of succeeding him on his death in 1838 unfortunately came to nothing. Jeffery Hale does not seem to have held any other lucrative post subsequently.

At Quebec, Hale soon became interested in benevolent societies and Anglican religious organizations: the British and Foreign Bible Society, the London Religious Tract Society, the Quebec Mission Society, and the Protestant Ladies' Asylum of Quebec all received his attention. His greatest efforts, however, were devoted to education. He set up on 16 June 1833 the first English Sunday school at Quebec, the Free Chapel Sunday School, and in its session of 1835–36 he also submitted to the assembly a request for financial assistance for the British and Canadian School Society of the District of Quebec. The aim of this society, founded in 1823 in the Saint-Roch district by Joseph-François Perrault*, was to ensure the advantages of elementary education to young Anglophones of the poorer classes. In 1837, when the legislature's help was no longer sufficient, Hale, as one of the directors of the society, announced in *Le Canadien* of 6 November that a fund had been launched to assist this institution. It is not surprising that his name appeared at the head of the list in the act incorporating the society on 9 June 1846. Furthermore, according to the *Journal of Education*, Hale founded and maintained several other schools. Letters from family correspondence make clear the affection he had for these schools and their students. His will, moreover, contained provisions intended to ensure the continued existence of his Sunday school.

Jeffery Hale also sought to encourage thrift: he was one of the founders of the Quebec Provident and Savings Bank (Banque de Prévoyance et d'Épagnes de Québec) in 1847. He interested himself in the health and welfare of his fellow-countrymen: in his will he left £9,000 (about $36,000) for the founding of a hospital to care for Protestants of all denominations; Jeffery Hale's Hospital is one of Quebec's principal hospitals today. He also took part in the founding of Victoria Hospital in 1855.

Jeffery Hale had the reputation of achieving perfection in the tasks he undertook. His settlement of his father's estate, his struggle to expand education, his commitment to charitable works are examples. Journalists and historians describe him as an eminently respectable citizen, a true Christian, and one who did not propose to abdicate his responsibilities; writing to his brother Edward on 29 Nov. 1843, he clearly expressed opposition to the absolute power of the Anglican bishop in the Church Society.

Although not a person of the first rank, Jeffery Hale played an active role in the Anglican community of Quebec; the importance of his participation in the financing and vigorous maintenance of charitable works are well illustrated by a com-

Haliburton

ment in the *Morning Chronicle* shortly after his death: "the several schools he mainly supported from his own private means will, it is to be feared, be placed in pecuniary embarrassment."

ROBERT GARON

ANQ-Q, AP-P-931. AVQ, Rôles d'évaluation et d'imposition, 1864–66. McCord Museum, Hale family papers. PAC, MG 23, G II, 18. *Journal of Education for Lower Canada* (Montreal), February–March 1865, 34. *Le Courier du Canada*, oct. 1864–févr. 1865. *Morning Chronicle* (Quebec), 8 Dec. 1864. *Quebec Gazette*, 19 Dec. 1864. A. R. Kelley, "The Quebec Diocesan Archives, a description of the collection of historical records of the Church of England in the diocese of Quebec," ANQ *Rapport*, 1946–47, 206, 222. *McLaughlin's Quebec directory* (McLaughlin), 1855–67. P.-G. Roy, *Fils de Québec*, III, 118–19. L.-P. Audet, *Hist. de l'enseignement*, I, 356–76; II, 3–52; *Le système scolaire*, VI, 205–9. Denison, *Première banque au Canada*, II, 85. Hamelin et Roby, *Hist. économique*, 429–30. André Labarrère-Paulé, *Les instituteurs laïques au Canada français, 1836–1900* (Québec, 1965), 92. *Storied Quebec* (Wood *et al.*), III, 80–82. "La famille Hale," *BRH*, XXXVIII (1932), 750.

HALIBURTON, THOMAS CHANDLER, politician, judge, and author; b. 17 Dec. 1796 at Windsor, N.S., the son of William Hersey Otis Haliburton and Lucy Chandler Grant; d. 27 Aug. 1865 at Isleworth, Middlesex, England.

The ancestry and upbringing of Thomas Chandler Haliburton were the deepest and most enduring influences upon his political views and career. The first North American Haliburton had been an obscure wig-maker, but Thomas Chandler's grandfather, William Haliburton, who had migrated to Nova Scotia in 1761, and his father were both successful lawyers who in later life became judges. Their achievement within an essentially tory system reinforced the political faith of three generations of Haliburtons. This faith was further strengthened by a consciousness of lineage. Haliburton's grandfather believed that he was descended from the Haliburtons of Newmains and Mertoun on the Scottish border – maternal ancestors of Sir Walter Scott – and although he could not prove it legally, the Nova Scotian Haliburtons nevertheless considered themselves to be gentry because they were of that stock. Haliburton's inherent toryism was given a strong anti-republican bias through the sufferings of his mother's people, the Grants, during the American War of Independence, and by their tragic death at sea while en route to Saint John, N.B., to settle loyalist claims.

Haliburton was educated at King's Collegiate School in Windsor, N.S., and later at King's College, Windsor, from which he graduated in 1815.

There an indoctrination into the correct principles upon which the tory Anglican establishment was based was confirmed by his association with the sons of leading professional men in the Atlantic colonies who were being prepared to take their fathers' places. To this ethos was added the study of Greek and Roman literature; while imparting useful lessons in the form and beauty of language that were later to stand Haliburton in good stead, it provided examples of a society which believed that history was essentially the sum of wars and politics directed by great men drawn mainly from aristocratic families.

The period in which Haliburton grew up was also an important influence. Great Britain's struggle with France and with the republican United States gave the added stimulus of patriotism to tory attitudes and the stigma of traitor to democratic ones. The advent of peace in 1815, however, left Nova Scotia with an inflated economy and brought an end to the protective colonial policy of the British government which had occasioned upwards of two decades of prosperity. The security – and the spoils – of office then became something precious to be fought for, and it took at least 15 years from the end of the Napoleonic wars before this struggle for control of government offices became crystallized into anything like an ideological combat between "privilege" and "democracy" and nearly a decade longer before it became apparent that toryism in its Burkean sense was not only seriously threatened but doomed.

Haliburton's political life fits into these circumstances with a remarkable inevitability. In 1820 he was admitted to the bar and began a lucrative law practice at Annapolis Royal. Six years later he became the MHA for Annapolis Royal in the Nova Scotian assembly. From 1826 to 1829 he conducted himself in that house as befitted a tory who had as much regard for the responsibilities as for the rights of privilege, and who was sufficiently free from dependence upon patronage to exercise his personal independence. Thus he took sides with the governor and the Council in supporting the right of Britain to regulate such matters as commerce and crown lands. At the same time he backed measures for the internal development of Nova Scotia, notably the subsidization by the assembly of a public school system and support for the permanent endowment of Pictou Academy. He also urged the removal of the declaration against popery from the assembly oath, which was passed unanimously by the assembly in 1827. Since few members of the legislature could afford such a consistent position, Haliburton soon found his enemies on one question to be his friends on another and was accused of inconsistency. His considerable powers of oratory and ridicule, often marred by prolixity, were the delight and exasperation of the house; on one occasion, when the Council disallowed a common schools bill which he had supported, Haliburton denounced the councillors as "twelve dignified, deep read, pensioned old ladies, but filled with prejudices and whims like all other antiquated spinsters," and subsequently received a motion of censure from the assembly. His presence in the assembly became a nuisance to both the governing Tories and the reform elements. When in 1829 Haliburton applied for the position in the Inferior Court of Common Pleas which his father's death had left vacant, he was quickly elevated to the bench.

Haliburton's subsequent political career in Nova Scotia was confined almost entirely to his large body of writing. From 1827 to 1837, although a tory, he maintained with decreasing conviction in his celebrated humorous *Clockmaker* series the point of view that political ideologies are superficial and that they were no cure for the ills of Nova Scotia. All they accomplished was to mask a naked struggle of individuals for power and money. While maintaining this position, Haliburton remained, despite his toryism, on terms of deep personal friendship with Joseph Howe*, the leading Nova Scotian Reformer. With the arrival in Canada in 1838 of Lord Durham [Lambton*], a renowned British liberal, Haliburton realized a vital threat to everything he felt he stood for, and from this point onward the political aspects of his writings reveal a committed tory partisan who felt that combatting radicalism justified any means that could be used for the purpose. As the cause of toryism became more hopeless, Haliburton became more extreme in its advocacy, and in his old age opposed many measures which as a young man he had supported in the Nova Scotian legislature.

Haliburton remained a judge in the Inferior Court of Common Pleas from 1829, holding twice-yearly sessions at four county towns at an annual salary of £405 plus travelling expenses, until the office was abolished in 1841. Then, through the direct personal influence of Lord Falkland [Cary*], the lieutenant governor, Haliburton was appointed to the Supreme Court of Nova Scotia at an annual salary of £560 plus travelling fees. In 1854 he offered to retire from this office, provided the pension of £300 per annum that had been granted to judges of the Inferior Court of Common Pleas at the time their office had been abolished were given to him. This offer was not accepted by the legislature, and in 1856 Haliburton retired from the bench on grounds of ill health. He immediately took up residence in England, a country he had been visiting frequently since 1816. After lengthy and deplorable litigation and political manœuvring, which culminated in an appeal to the Judicial Committee of the Privy Council, Haliburton succeeded in 1862 in obtaining his pension quite against the will of the Nova Scotian legislature and the wishes of the Nova Scotian people.

As a judge, Haliburton was conscientious, upright, intelligent, adhering to the spirit rather than to the letter of the law; he was, however, in no sense a great judge, and his propensity for punning and his strong sense of the ludicrous, although often enlivening an otherwise dull courtroom session, did not add to his reputation or that of the judiciary in Nova Scotia.

Despite judicial duties, the demands of his writing, and a busy social and family life, Haliburton found time for some business activity in Nova Scotia. He was president of the agricultural society in Windsor, the owner of six stores and a considerable length of wharfage in that town, the proprietor of a gypsum quarry, and president of a joint stock company which owned the bridge across the Avon at Windsor. After he moved to Britain his business ventures continued to be largely colonial, maintained as much for the advancement of the colony as for his personal profit. He was the first chairman of the Canadian Land and Emigration Company, which in 1861 purchased an extensive area of unoccupied country in Haliburton and Victoria counties in Canada West for purposes of settlement (a village there now bears his name). Moreover, in a startling reversal of his earlier opposition to the recommendations of Lord Durham on federalism, Haliburton became in 1862 a member of the first board of the British North American Association of London to promote provincial union and spread information about the colonies.

In England he settled at Isleworth, near Richmond, and in 1859 became the Tory member for Launceston in a British House of Commons dominated by the "Little Englander" majority of Lord Palmerston and William Gladstone. Haliburton soon found himself handicapped by a party in opposition which had, he believed, made too many compromises to suit his convictions, and by ideas which most Englishmen felt belonged to the last century. He was also impaired by gout and a throat complaint that made him difficult to hear and understand, and by a reputation for wit which had been established on paper only. Haliburton, therefore, found his career as an MP not only ineffectual and frustrating to him-

Haliburton

self but boring to other members less interested in colonial affairs than he was. He did not offer himself for re-election at the conclusion of his term in 1865.

Haliburton's public career as summarized above is a tribute to a twofold persistence – a sufficient sense of the value of public office to wish to serve his fellow human beings in a political and judicial capacity, and a sufficient sense of the value of public life in terms of privilege and money to wish to extract the greatest possible fee for his services. It shows also Haliburton's ability to carry out his duties with diligence and competence. Of the higher political and juridical gifts – the ability to work with others and to evolve new principles to meet changing situations – his career shows hardly a glimmer. Haliburton could make a good living out of public employment and provide routine service in exchange. His contemporary, Joseph Howe, could do much more. Haliburton's reputation today comes from the literary strings on his bow.

In 1816 Haliburton had married Louisa Neville, and the couple had 11 children, three of whom died in infancy. One son, Robert Grant*, became a distinguished anthropologist and antiquarian, and another, Arthur Lawrence*, enjoyed an outstanding career in the British army and civil service. In 1856 Haliburton married Sarah Harriet Owen, widow of Edward Hosier Williams, of Eaton Mascott, Shrewsbury.

As a man, Haliburton's most distinguishing characteristic was a thoroughgoing, if somewhat coarse-fibred, appetite for life. He was the uxorious husband of two wives, a connoisseur of good food, good drink, good horses, and good conversation. He availed himself of all the privileges and emoluments of his rank and sought to augment these privileges on every possible occasion. Although he could be a convivial companion to anyone in a bar or tavern while on circuit, he was nevertheless extremely conscious of formal social proprieties, and at his own home, whether in Annapolis Royal, Windsor, or in England, he condescended to associate only with his equals or betters, even though he knew that such a course of conduct in Nova Scotia could not make him popular.

Although a practising Anglican and, in his youth, a friend of the celebrated Abbé Jean-Mandé Sigogne*, Haliburton was most at home drinking and exchanging stories with robust men whose interests were earthy rather than spiritual. In Halifax he was associated with a group of amateur *literati* known as "The Club," who contributed articles to Joseph Howe's newspaper, the *Novascotian*, between 1828 and 1831, and

among whose members were Howe and Laurence O'Connor DOYLE. Haliburton's principal literary companions were Howe in Nova Scotia and Richard Harris Barham and Theodore Hook in England. Like the 18th-century squires whom he resembled, he saw only absurdity in a religion that went beyond the social and moral functions of the church to any excess of feeling; and he was singularly blind to the emotional glories and sectarian disputes which characterized the religious life of contemporary Nova Scotia.

But although as conscious as a man could be of the rights and privileges owing to *noblesse*, Haliburton was equally conscious of the responsibilities. His name is high on the list of charitable donations in his parish, and his writing, his agricultural activities at Windsor, and his parliamentary and judicial offices are strong testimonials to his desire by instruction, precept, and example to point the way to Nova Scotians in particular and English speaking people everywhere to what he considered more desirable ways of social and moral thought and action. He may have indulged his appetites to the detriment of his constitution, but there is an equal case that the breakdown in his health came about quite as much as a result of his labours in the general service of humanity. The fact that he was an intelligent man who cared greatly for causes and objects outside himself by identifying them with himself is the principal source of both his success and his failure.

Haliburton's literary work was varied and abundant. Considering the demands of his more important creative works, and his other public responsibilities, Haliburton managed to put an amazing amount of time into the compilation and composition of histories, pamphlets, and anthologies, which alone would have given him a considerable reputation among 19th-century colonial writers. Although like so many of his contemporaries, amateur and professional, he tended to see history as the struggles of individuals against a background of politics and war, and his sources of information were often meagre and secondary, he could be, when he wished, more effective than most in his arrangement of material and his strong, muscular prose was superior to most.

Haliburton's *A general description of Nova Scotia*, long thought to have been the work of Walter Bromley*, published in 1823 and reprinted in a pirated form in 1825, is a remarkable production for a young lawyer. But it did not suit its composer and was superseded in 1829 by *An historical and statistical account of Nova-Scotia*. This work won its author a vote of thanks from the legislature of his province. The first volume contained a history of the province. Dealing mainly with Nova Scotia before the British occupation, part of its narrative described in graphic terms the expulsion of the Acadians; through Nathaniel Hawthorne, it gave Henry Wadsworth Longfellow the germ of his popular poem *Evangeline* and furnished the Acadian people with a version of the "expulsion" which has tended to transform myth into history proper. The second volume was packed with information on the geography of the province.

These initial attempts to write history combined practical and academic motives. Much of the material in both works is information designed for the use of prospective settlers from Britain and the United States. In the second of them Haliburton set out to provide Nova Scotia with a past, and this he compiled out of sources ranging from Tobias George Smollett's well-known history of England to obscure and inaccessible documents and reference books. Probably the difficulty in getting many of the sources of these histories and the relatively limited time at his disposal led Haliburton to paraphrase consciously or unconsciously much of the material. As an historian his curiosity and stylistic vigour were aroused more by the "human interest drama" of history than by the more prosaic analysis of causes and processes. Although at this early stage in his intellectual development as an historian he tended to accept the past uncritically as he read it in the works of other men, he did independently argue a position on the expulsion of the Acadians that transcends national prejudice.

Haliburton made another attempt at the writing of formal history, *The English in America*, which appeared in two volumes in London in 1851 and in New York as *Rule and misrule of the English in America* in the same year. It is a thesis history attempting to prove that the earliest settlers of New England possessed an independent democracy, which they exercised by default of the British colonial authority, and that therefore the American republic had come about not by revolution but by enlargement and improvement on the part of colonists who had a unique training in self-direction. The corollary, of course, was that the French colonies and the rest of British North America, having come into being under truly colonial circumstances, ought therefore to remain colonies. The work is well written and the thesis well argued, but the book's reputation has been largely destroyed by its plagiarism from Richard Hildreth's *History of the United States of America* . . . (6v., New York, 1848–52). The

plagiarism was so blatant as to be beyond excuse, and in fact Haliburton never offered one. Why he should have borrowed from Hildreth is incomprehensible unless he was pressed for time and had to meet a publisher's deadline. A paucity of original sources might have forced him to rely upon Hildreth for information, but he had at his disposal a superior style in which to recast Hildreth's material.

The least considerable of Haliburton's longer writings are two political tracts published in 1839, *The bubbles of Canada* and *A reply to the report of the Earl of Durham*, which reflect Haliburton's concern with Lord Durham's appointment as governor general and commissioner to the colonies of British North America. Seeing this appointment, quite rightly, as threatening the tory position as never before, he realized, too, that if the threat were to be countered, action would have to be taken to influence public opinion without delay. Accordingly, Haliburton determined to use his reputation as a humorist to obtain a hearing, and he worked quickly and under pressure rather than taking time to shape his work carefully. But in the case of *The bubbles of Canada*, the British reading public resented the fact that a book advertised as being by a celebrated humorist and bearing a title strikingly similar to that of a current bestseller by Sir Francis Bond Head* turned out to be a pedestrian exercise in partisan political invective. And in both pamphlets, Haliburton's haste overpowered his sense of form and accuracy, while the intensity of his partisan feelings led him to unmeasured statements that undermined the credibility of his position. He seems to have written each paragraph in the heat of the moment, seizing on any pretext afforded by Lord Durham's actions and statements, and never to have examined his completed work to see whether his points contradicted one another. Only an exercise of sustained irony could have redeemed these pamphlets and made them effective, and it is conspicuously absent.

Haliburton accused Lord Durham of misrepresenting the efforts of past colonial administrators to govern Britain's North American colonies. He disagreed particularly with Durham about the past and future treatment of the French. As a conquered people they had been given too many concessions, and their rebellion was, in his opinion, an indication of the danger of giving freedom to the colonies. He opposed Durham's suggestion of a federal union on the ground that it would only give a greater field for demagogues and would expedite the move of the British North American colonies toward fur-

Haliburton

ther independence from Britain. He opposed Durham's advocacy of the union of Upper and Lower Canada and his recommendations for responsible government.

Haliburton's international and enduring reputation as a writer, however, is based on *The clockmaker; or, the sayings and doings of Samuel Slick, of Slickville*, of which 22 instalments had appeared in the *Novascotian* newspaper before a book of that title was issued by Joseph Howe at Halifax in 1836. *The clockmaker*, second series, was published in London by Richard Bentley in 1838, and the third series in 1840. These series were frequently reprinted in Britain and the United States. For a time at least in the mid 19th century Haliburton and his work had a vogue on both sides of the Atlantic which rivalled that enjoyed by Charles Dickens.

The clockmaker can be regarded as a series of moral essays pointed by satire or as a picaresque novel whose plot is more episodic than that of most. The Squire, narrator and *persona* of the author, and Sam Slick, a Yankee clockmaker, travel through contemporary Nova Scotia. On their wanderings somehow or other every incident they encounter becomes an apt illustration of a political or social trait which can often be summed up by a maxim. Interest throughout the book, therefore, is not dependent on suspense but rather on the inherent liveliness of each incident, the appropriateness of the meaning which it illustrates, and the author's brilliant use of characterization, language, anecdote, and point of view.

Sam Slick is the only character in *The clockmaker* who really matters – the Squire and Mr Hopewell serve merely as foils or exponents of tory views. In chapter after chapter attention is sustained by the vanity, the ingenuity, and the linguistic skill of that Yankee of Yankees, Sam Slick. It has been argued that the character of Slick lacks consistency not only throughout the books in which he appears but even within the pages of a single book, that his speech reflects the dialect of many different areas of America rather than that of a single one, and that he is a theatrical person rather than a flesh-and-blood human being. It is true that the Sam Slick of *The clockmaker* is most unlike that of *The attaché; or, Sam Slick in England*, published in two series in 1843 and 1844 and slanted toward a different audience. In the latter book, the peaceful Yankee pedlar has become a swaggering bully. Those who criticize this change perhaps do not notice that the American at home is not the same animal as the American abroad in unfamiliar surroundings. Against these strictures it may be pointed

out too that *The clockmaker* and *The attaché* are organized on the principle of the chapter unit and that therefore Sam Slick is only required to dominate each chapter. It may be further argued that Slick himself is something of a folk-hero combining the diverse and sometimes conflicting ingredients that make up a national character.

Like the Greeks, the Yankees were great gatherers during their wanderings of tales and linguistic peculiarities; a knowledge of these could by "soft-sawder" and "human natur" be converted into dollars and cents, and Slick's eclectic argot was in his own day merely an exaggeration of the norms of speech of a group of men whose like have now largely disappeared. Be that as it may, if Slick is today merely a stage character, he is one at least in the same sense as the personages of Dickens and Molière.

By his use in *The clockmaker* of Sam Slick, Haliburton was able to deliver a balanced judgement with respect to the Americans, the British, and the Nova Scotians. His judgements were two-edged. He admired the English for their traditions and institutions, of which he felt himself to be a part. He criticized them because they refused to alter their traditions when faced with new conditions, and because they patronized the colonies. He disliked the Americans for their braggadocio, their opportunism, and for having defeated Great Britain in war. At the same time, he admired their industry, efficiency, and adaptability. Haliburton saw the Nova Scotians as a people who possessed fundamental British virtues, but who were ruining themselves by maintaining an unrealistic standard of living in the face of depressed circumstances more than 15 years after the close of the Napoleonic wars. Instead of following the Yankees' example and improving their lot by practical means, they were squandering fast-vanishing opportunities in futile religious and political battles. Sam Slick, in Haliburton's hands, becomes in his industry and practicality an example for Nova Scotians to follow and in his uncouth manners and vanity the epitome of those qualities his creator despised. Out of his deeds and observations emerges Haliburton's vision of a possible Nova Scotian life combining the conservative principles of Edmund Burke with the practice of frontier practicality and industry.

Much research has gone into the sources of *The clockmaker*. It is valid, but to a great degree irrelevant. Certainly Haliburton was familiar with Thomas McCulloch*'s "Letters of Mephibosheth Stepsure" which had appeared in the Halifax *Acadian Recorder* in 1821–22. In all likelihood he was also familiar with Seba Smith's *Life and writings of Major Jack Downing, of*

Downingville, away down east in the state of Maine (Boston, 1833), and with the rip-roaring frontier type of American humour displayed by the anonymous author of the *Sketches and eccentricities of Col. David Crockett of west Tennessee* (London, 1833). Haliburton no doubt adapted material from these and from other similar sources to suit his purpose, but the fact that he did so in no way explains why his work rose to prominence (more than 70 editions of *The clockmaker* have been published since 1836) while the other works cited above remain to this day in obscurity.

What was needed for a North American work to become popular in Great Britain, and by that popularity to shine with reflected glory in the still colonial literary circles of the United States, was for it to be deeply rooted in tradition but at the same time to present that tradition in a sufficiently striking way as to seem more original than in fact it was. In *The clockmaker* Haliburton united two traditions, both popular in England for over a century. The first was the moral essay illustrated by the pointed anecdote so much a feature of the *Spectator* and the *Tatler* of London; the second was the popular tradition on the English stage of exploiting the dialect and character eccentricities of foreigners. By combining both, Haliburton assured himself of the minor success which such popular entertaining writers as Charles James Lever and Theodore Hook were enjoying, but by adding a moral earnestness intelligently rooted in an environment that was genuine and believable but sufficiently remote from British readers to have a romantic charm, he was able to achieve a much greater success of a more lasting nature.

Haliburton unites two very different stylistic elements in *The clockmaker*. The narrative parts are written in the typical literary prose of the 18th century. The conversational parts – notably Sam Slick's – are stage pieces in which Haliburton becomes a prose poet, bold in metaphor, piling adjectival climax upon climax without fear of barbarism. In fact, he did for the dialect of his time what Robert Burns did for Lowland Scots. The purist would say that both wrote a bastard language, but to most others their writing is a successful *tour de force*.

Of the three series of *The clockmaker*, the first was undoubtedly the best. Not only does a writer tell his best stories first but he usually tells them best if he tells them in his own good time. In the first series Haliburton worked at his own pace as the book ripened naturally out of the milieu in which he found himself. His principal biographer, V. L. O. Chittick, is probably correct when he suggests that the main purpose of each of the three series was slightly different: the first was to stimulate the Nova Scotians to self-help in order to solve their immediate financial difficulties; the second was to put down the Reform movement, which Haliburton dismissed as a sham whereby self-seeking politicians sought by creating a new ideology of "democracy" to supplant administrators who were in all respects their superiors; and the third was directed more to an English audience than to Nova Scotians, to persuade the Colonial Office not to grant responsible government to Nova Scotia. These were tasks of increasing difficulty which Haliburton failed to surmount completely in the second and third series of *The clockmaker*. A crisis in his personal relations with Joseph Howe in the 1840s is a further confirmation that Haliburton was rapidly losing the balance with respect to the political and economic realities in Nova Scotia that was one of the strengths of *The clockmaker*, first series.

In *The attaché* Haliburton presents his hero as a member of the American legation "to the Court of Saint Jimses." This is undoubtedly Haliburton's most ambitious work. In it he tried to improve on his reputation as a satirist by turning his examination of human foibles from their peripheral manifestations in Nova Scotia to their centre in Britain. He was unsuccessful for several reasons. In the first place, he knew Nova Scotia and Nova Scotians well, whereas his relatively facile impressions of Britain blurred the ambiguities that result when actual experience encounters idealized preconception. Secondly, when writing *The clockmaker*, Haliburton had a more secure position in Nova Scotia, and in the current political struggle the chances of the Tories obtaining the upper hand seemed considerable; in consequence, he was able to express himself without fear or favour and with relative objectivity and freedom from bitterness. When he wrote *The attaché*, however, circumstances had altered considerably. In England he was a small frog in a large puddle, and, in consequence, often undercut his own harshest criticisms of British society in order not to offend powerful acquaintances. Thirdly, the plot of *The attaché* vitiated against the book having as great a success as *The clockmaker*. In the latter work Sam Slick, as a travelling entrepreneur, could display positive as well as negative qualities and remain both the centre of interest and the moral centre of the book. In *The attaché* Slick as an American diplomat out of his depth is mainly relegated to a negative role as the butt of satire while the book's more serious views are aired by such dull charac-

Haliburton

ters as the Reverend Mr Hopewell and Squire Poker. Fourthly, English toryism, which from the perspective of Nova Scotia in the earlier book had appeared to be a consistent application of the principles of Burke, now to Haliburton at first hand seemed to be the compromised conservatism of such politicians as Sir Robert Peel. Haliburton's hatred for radicals and liberals, therefore, deepened and the tone of his political writing became more extreme, masking by its violence and bitterness his innate despair. Last, but scarcely least, Haliburton's British audience found itself less willing to laugh at its own errors and shortcomings than it had been to laugh at those of the Nova Scotians in his earlier books.

Given these factors, it is surprising that *The attaché* became as respectable a popular and literary success as it did. Even the most condemnatory critics in Britain found much to praise in the books, and the sales, though smaller than those of *The clockmaker*, were quite substantial. Haliburton still remained the seemingly inexhaustible *raconteur* and master of racy frontier diction and the excellence of this quality was by itself sufficient to obscure the fact that much more often in this work than in *The clockmaker* the gap in probability between the anecdote and the meaning which the author applied to it had become too great for ready acceptance.

By comparison, *Sam Slick's wise saws and modern instances; or, what he said, did, and invented*, published in 1853, and *Nature and human nature*, published in 1855, are light-weight works. In these books, Haliburton presents Sam Slick almost entirely for the purpose of entertaining his audience, and to an intelligent reader few things are quite so dreary as a set of funny stories told merely for the sake of being funny. If any reader doubts the role of moral earnestness in elevating Haliburton's humour to universal interest, let him first read *The clockmaker* and then read either of these books. Conversation, however dull, with a purpose is never quite devoid of interest; conversation, however witty, maintained solely for the sake of conversation inevitably becomes garrulity. What is missing in both *Wise saws and modern instances* and *Nature and human nature* is the author's heart.

Aside from Sam Slick, the book which gained Haliburton the greatest notoriety was *The letter-bag of the Great Western; or, life in a steamer*, published in 1840. Much of this book was composed for the diversion of the other passengers on Haliburton's steamship voyage from Bristol to New York in 1839. The form and tone derive from Haliburton's memory of *The expedition of Humphry Clinker* by T. G. Smollett, a writer who in his fondness for indecorous humour and exaggeration of the eccentricities of character was a kindred spirit. The book's ostensible function was the advertisement of the advantages of travel by steamship, but few, after reading the passengers' accounts of their voyage, would, if they took them seriously, ever venture off shore. The book's principal sources of amusement – infirmities of the human body (seasickness), the peculiarities of spelling and grammar that arise from faulty or defective education, the cultural mores of other races and lower classes, and the outrageous punning – all these are the very subjects which the 18th century critics condemned as sources of satire. *The letter-bag of the Great Western* played to the gallery with cheap humour and deserved the opprobrium with which commentators almost universally greeted it. Even a modern assumption that Haliburton the punster was an unconscious metaphysician reducing the world to a universal harmony of absurdity does not help. Such a game just is not worth the candle.

Traits of American humour, by native authors and *The Americans at home; or, byeways, backwoods, and prairies* are compilations by Haliburton from well-known works of American humour and from obscure American periodicals and newspapers of the first half of the 19th century. Despite undue reliance upon other authorities in compiling his preface, and despite almost negligible editing, these two works remain in the words of Haliburton's biographer, Chittick, "Two unrivalled collections of a distinctively literary type now no longer written, and two rich storehouses of the dialect curiosities, odd customs, and hard living conditions which once prevailed in an America that has all but vanished."

The old judge; or, life in a colony, published in 1849, is Haliburton's farewell to the Nova Scotia that he never succeeded in refashioning to his heart's desire; it is filled with love and nostalgic regret. Sombre, realistic, and more varied in its nature than Haliburton's other works, it is the most satisfying of all his books, although it never attains the surface brilliance of *The clockmaker*. It is constructed upon the same plan as *The clockmaker*. Nova Scotia is seen through the eyes of an English tourist who is visiting his friend, the old judge, and who is accompanied on his tour of the province by another friend, Lawyer Barclay. To the observations and adventures of the tourist are added the memories and observations of his friends and the other personages whom they encounter during their wanderings. Most notable among these is Stephen Richardson, the Nova Scotian eccentric, a kind of colonial Sam Slick and one of Haliburton's few other character creations who could compete with Sam in interest and credibility. Through his sketches of men and women, through his recounting of melodramatic events on an isolated frontier, through his description of social life in the past, Haliburton reveals in *The old judge* a vein of romantic sentiment little indulged in in his other work and narrative talents which had he cultivated them might have made him the first considerable novelist to have emerged in what is now Canada. Not excepting *Roughing it in the bush; or, life in Canada* by Susanna [Strickland*] Moodie, it remains the most graphic picture of colonial society in British North America that we have.

The season ticket, published in 1860, is made up of a series of articles previously contributed during 1859 and 1860 to the Dublin *University Magazine*. Its plan is like that of *The letter-bag of the Great Western* except that a train takes the place of a steamboat and conversations take the place of letters. It is also reminiscent of the *Clockmaker* series. Squire Shegog acts as recorder and interlocutor and Mr Ephraim Peabody and the Honourable Lyman Boodle, senator from Michigan, replace Sam Slick and the Reverend Mr Hopewell. There is the usual mixture of partisan politics combined with acute observation, garrulity tempered with original and apt statement, but the general effect is dull. Chittick, however, maintains that its quality of interest lies in its major purpose: the programme of a thorough going British imperialist who advocates "a three-fold policy for developing intercommunication between the motherland and the colonies." In this work, Haliburton proposed that Great Britain subsidize transatlantic steamers between its ports and the colonies, complete the Intercolonial Railway and continue it to Lake Superior, and provide a "safe, easy, and expeditious route to Fraser's River on the Pacific." Like Joseph Howe, Haliburton was arguing for the development of a colonial empire with an improved communication system, but he felt that such remote colonies as Australia and New Zealand could not be sufficiently linked by communication to prevent them from going their own ways. They ought, therefore, to be given their independence as soon as feasible and allowed to fend for themselves. Haliburton further argues for the substitution of a permanent colonial council of appointees from the colonies in place of the Colonial Office, and he raises the possibility of colonial representation in the British parliament. He would, a generation later, surely have recognized a kindred spirit in Joseph Chamberlain.

In addition to the works cited above, Haliburton privately printed and distributed two pamphlets, *An address on the present condition, resources and prospects of British North America*, and *Speech of the Hon. Mr. Justice Haliburton, M.P., in the House of Commons . . . the 21st of April 1860, on the repeal of the differential duties on foreign and colonial wood*. Haliburton was, at the time of the publication of the latter pamphlet, either too ill to see it through the press properly or so lacking in concern with respect to it that he must never have seriously proof-read it.

Much has been made by Chittick and others of Haliburton's inability to alter his views in relation to changing circumstances as Joseph Howe and other notable contemporaries had been able, albeit slowly and painfully, to do. In Haliburton's defence, it may be stated that these others did not have the same weight of ingrained doctrination to overcome. Moreover, Edmund Burke's political theories are still as intellectually defensible as any others, and it must have seemed to the class-conscious Haliburton that the men who upheld them were with respect to education and ability infinitely preferable to those who opposed them. Chittick was right, however, in his main assumption. In so far as there was a crippling factor in Haliburton's life and writing, it was the fact that, say, do, or write what he would, Haliburton knew himself to be a colonial and that on this account all his achievement would be patronized in the very places that he considered to be his own true spiritual home. Yet the will to dominate against odds persisted and, in his writing at least, he by turns flattered, wheedled, bullied, and threatened the British in an almost successful attempt to enter the shrine of their hearts that Dickens and Tennyson enjoyed; it is to his credit that he came close to succeeding.

Although happy in his social activities, Haliburton in his later work developed an inclination toward melancholy which cannot be entirely explained by his failing health. It flowed from his frustrated idealism. Believing passionately in the toryism of Edmund Burke, he had the misfortune to live during the period of that ideology's decline on both sides of the Atlantic – a decline as evident among the Tories themselves as among the uncommitted. Haliburton had no confidence in the British Conservative leader, Peel. He felt that the word "Conservative" was only another way of writing the word "Liberal," and cumulative events only served to deepen this conviction.

There are many reasons why Haliburton's greatest success was achieved as a writer. He early discovered that words were more amenable to government than events and that writing could give him the quick success that his imperious and hasty nature demanded. One factor in his abandoning an active political career for a judicial one was that it gave him more leisure in which to write. To the sense of proportion which he had acquired through his classical studies and his reading of 18th-century prose was added an ear sensitive to the rhythms and nuances of colloquial speech at the very time on the North American frontier when the laxity of education was enabling that speech to run riot in a picturesque and racy manner not known in the English language since Elizabethan times.

Haliburton's use of language added American to Lowland Scots on the list of English variants which a writer could use with a fair chance of winning appreciation and acclaim. In this regard, he paved the way for that great democratic prose epic of America, *The adventures of Huckleberry Finn*. Furthermore, his gregarious and sociable nature enabled him to study at first hand the many individual and unusual types which were fostered by the isolation and social freedom of a frontier. At the same time, his knowledge, derived from both reading and experience, of traditional propriety and genteel British behaviour gave him a frame of reference within which to place these excesses.

It is ironic that Haliburton, the arch-tory, should have become the "father of American humour" in the most democratic sense. The success and popularity of Sam Slick established at the same time the vogue of the folk hero, the man whose ability and humanity do not depend upon education, position, and ancestry but upon his own intrinsic ability to cope with circumstance. Sam Slick, in his vices and virtues, is the epitome of Jacksonian democracy.

Recent thesis histories of Canadian literature – particularly those that see fear and awe of nature as the mark of an archetypal Canadian writer – have had little to say about Haliburton. With him human nature is everywhere and physical nature is nowhere. In his work, Europeans who "gush" about such physical wonders as Niagara Falls are satirized whereas native Americans are seen as either speculating as to their possible commercial use or are too busy with their own concerns to notice the backdrops against which those concerns take place.

There are essentially two types of humour: one which is fixed and eternal; another whose appeal is transitory. This last must be rewritten with every passing generation. Eternal humour, of which Swift is the great example, in its purest form seizes upon some dichotomy in a fundamental area of human concern between the ideal and the actual and presents it stripped of accidental or temporary circumstances. Transitory humour applies accidental or temporary circumstances of either language or place to certain stock human situations, and by an exploitation of novelty – which soon exhausts itself through over-popularity – brings these situations to momentary life. A classic example of this genre is vaudeville humour. Although the proportions are mixed, there is more vaudeville humour than true humour in the work of Haliburton, and as a result many readers today find the once admired dialect dated and the anecdotes not only told in a pace and form that are strange to them but dependent upon circumstances with which they are no longer concerned. There is reason, therefore, to suppose that in time more and more of Haliburton's work will pass out of the domain of "popular" reading into the domain of literary history. It is not inconceivable that *The old judge*, which is interesting for other factors besides its humour, will ultimately become the most widely read of all Haliburton's writings.

The modern reader will not lose a sense of Haliburton's imaginative energy – the almost unrivalled power of sustained comic invention which he displays in both use of language and choice of incident through thousands of pages of the Sam Slick series, with a minimum of repetition and a remarkable evenness of quality. It is true that he risks – and ultimately achieves – over-exposure, but a fraction of the invention and ingenuity displayed in these books would have made the reputation of many another writer.

During his own lifetime, Haliburton was not valued in Nova Scotia. His books received there the most unfavourable reviews and were not apparently popular or appreciated. This does not mean that Nova Scotians were more sensitive to satire than were Americans and British. They knew him for his social exclusiveness and overbearing ways and for his desire for the privileges of office. Satire, however well intentioned and executed, is not appreciated from objectionable sources. With the appearance, however, of a new generation of Nova Scotians and with the development after confederation of a growing cultural nationalism, something approaching a Haliburton cult began to appear in Nova Scotia. A Haliburton Club was established in Windsor in 1884 to promote the knowledge of Canadian literature in general and of the works of Haliburton in particular.

Like all colonists the Nova Scotians were slower than the inhabitants of the metropolis to honour one of their own. In 1858 Oxford University awarded Haliburton the honorary degree of DCL for services to literature. He was the first colonial to receive that degree. In fact, he was more than that. He was the only colonial in the 19th century to achieve an international reputation in literature, and it is doubtful whether any writings from British North America, with the possible exception of the works of Stephen Leacock*, have since been able to make the impact upon the English speaking world which Haliburton's works have. These factors help us to understand Haliburton's success, but, as in all work that captures the human imagination on a large scale, much credit must be given to that indefinable yet magnetic individuality which for want of a better term we call genius.

FRED COGSWELL

[Most of T. C. Haliburton's works were republished many times. The following list indicates their first date of publication: *A general description of Nova Scotia, illustrated by a new and correct map* (Halifax, 1823); *An historical and statistical account of Nova-Scotia* (2v., Halifax, 1829); *The clockmaker; or, the sayings and doings of Samuel Slick, of Slickville* (1st ser., Halifax, 1836; 2nd ser., London, 1838; 3rd ser., London, 1840); *The bubbles of Canada* (London, 1839); *A reply to the report of the Earl of Durham* (London, 1839); *The letter-bag of the Great Western; or, life in a steamer* (Halifax, 1840); *The attaché; or, Sam Slick in England* (1st ser., 2v., London, 1843; 2nd ser., 2v., London, 1844); *The old judge; or, life in a colony* (2v., London, 1849); *The English in America* (2v., London, 1851), republished as *Rule and misrule of the English in America . . .* (2v., New York, 1851); *Traits of American humour, by native authors*, ed. [T. C. Haliburton] (3v., London, 1852); *Sam Slick's wise saws and modern instances; or, what he said, did, and invented* (2v., London, 1853); *The Americans at home; or, byeways, backwoods, and prairies*, ed. [T. C. Haliburton] (3v., London, 1854); *Nature and human nature* (2v., London, 1855); *An address on the present condition, resources and prospects of British North America . . .* (London and Montreal, 1857); *The season ticket* (London, 1860); *Speech of the Hon. Mr. Justice Haliburton, M.P., in the House of Commons . . . the 21st of April 1860, on the repeal of the differential duties on foreign and colonial wood* (London, 1860).

Watters and Bell, *On Canadian literature*, 101–4, contains a partial listing of secondary literature on Haliburton, but there is a great need for a complete, up-to-date bibliography. Many editions and articles have appeared since the last full bibliography, A. H. O'Brien, *Haliburton ("Sam Slick"): a sketch and bibliography* (Ottawa, 1910). In fact, the best single bibliography is that appended to V. L. O. Chittick, *Thomas Chandler Haliburton: a study in provincial toryism* (New York, 1924).

The periodical literature on Haliburton tends to cover the same ground again and again. Some of the best critical work appears in the introductions to various modern editions. Among the more notable of these are [T. C. Haliburton], *Sam Slick*, ed. R. P. Baker (New York, 1923); *The clockmaker . . . (first series)*, ed. R. L. McDougall (Toronto, 1958); *The old judge . . .*, ed. R. E. Watters (Toronto and Vancouver, [1968]); and *The Sam Slick anthology*, ed. R. E. Watters (Toronto, [1969]). F.C.]

HALL, ARCHIBALD, physician, educator, and editor; b. 8 Nov. 1812 in Montreal, son of Jacob Hall, hatter, and Rebecca Ferguson; m. Agnes Burgess on 17 May 1838 in Montreal, and they had two children; d. 14 Feb. 1868 in Montreal.

Archibald Hall obtained his first education at the Royal Grammar School of Montreal under Alexander Skakel* and in his early years developed a strong love for the study of natural history. In 1828 he commenced medical training by apprenticeship to Dr William Robertson* of the Montreal General Hospital. The following year Hall registered as a medical student at the McGill College Medical Faculty and attended for three academic sessions. In November 1832 he transferred to the University of Edinburgh where he received the doctorate of medicine in 1834.

Shortly after graduation, Hall returned to Canada and in 1835 began practising medicine in Montreal. He was also appointed to the McGill Medical Faculty in 1835 and served as a member of that faculty until his death, holding the posts of lecturer on materia medica (1835–42, 1849–54), lecturer on chemistry (1842–49), and professor of midwifery and the diseases of women and children (1854–68). Hall was also on the staff of the two hospitals affiliated with McGill University at that time, the Montreal General and the University Lying-In, and as professor of midwifery was physician *accoucheur* to the latter institution.

Hall's interest in natural history continued after he had chosen medicine as a career. The subject of his doctoral thesis was the respiratory function of plants. Two years after graduation he forwarded to Edinburgh a collection of Canadian plants. In 1839 he prepared for the Natural History Society of Montreal a lengthy memoir on the mammals and birds of the district of Montreal; he was awarded the society's silver medal and a part of the memoir was published in the *Canadian Naturalist and Geologist*.

Throughout his professional life, Archibald Hall was actively concerned with medical education and licensing. He played a prominent role not only in his medical school and teaching hospitals but also in the College of Physicians and Surgeons of Lower Canada, a provincial licensing body of which he became vice-president in 1856 and president in 1859. A vigorous supporter of the McGill Medical Faculty with its British roots, his forthrightness frequently brought him

Hamel

into conflict with those of differing views. His avowed intent, as he himself wrote, was to "state the truth, irrespective of persons, and fearless of consequences."

Hall's chief claim to remembrance is his work as a medical journalist. When he launched in 1845 with the assistance of Robert Lea MacDonnell* the *British American Journal of Medical and Physical Science* (which became the *British American Medical and Physical Journal* in 1850 and continued until 1852), there had only been two earlier Canadian medical journals and both had lasted less than two years, the *Journal de médecine de Québec/Quebec Medical Journal* founded in 1826 by Dr François-Xavier Tessier*, and the *Montreal Medical Gazette* founded by Drs Francis BADGLEY and William Sutherland in 1844. From 1860 to 1862 Hall was editor of another medical journal, the *British American Journal.*

Hall was a good writer and he probably welcomed the opportunity the journals provided to air his views, always strongly held, on virtually any subject he chose. Nevertheless, the task of editor was not easy. Relatively few Canadian medical men had the time, inclination, or even ability to furnish original articles on medicine, and such articles should be the mainstay of professional journals which primarily must disseminate information useful in practice. As a result, considerable space was allotted to abstracts or reprints from British and American journals. There were many medical news items, particularly from the McGill Medical Faculty and the Montreal General Hospital, as well as reports of meetings, including those of the Montreal Medico-Chirurgical Society which Hall himself had helped found in 1843. All this meant a heavy work load for an editor with many other duties, including a busy medical practice. But Hall's chief worry was financial support. The number of potential subscribers was small and advertising had not yet become an important source of revenue. There was always the danger that the editor might have to assume personal responsibility for debts incurred. Editorship thus required courage and a willingness to make substantial sacrifices, qualities which Hall possessed in abundance.

E. H. BENSLEY

Archibald Hall, *An apology for British and colonial medical degrees or strictures on the report of the special committee of the Legislative Assembly on the laws relative to the practice of physic, surgery and midwifery in Lower Canada* (Montreal, 1853); *Letters on medical education . . . addressed to the members of the provincial legislature of Canada* (Montreal and Kingston, [Ont.], 1842); "On the mammals and birds of the district of Montreal," *Canadian Naturalist and Geologist* (Montreal), VI (1861), 284–309; VII (1862), 44–78, 171–93, 289–316, 344–76, 401–30; "On the past, present, and future of the faculty of medicine of McGill University; an introductory lecture delivered at the opening of the session 1866–67," *Canada Medical Journal and Monthly Record of Medical and Surgical Science* (Montreal), III (1866), 289–302.

ANQ-M, État civil, Anglicans, Christ Church, 8 Nov. 1812, 17 May 1838. McGill University Archives (Montreal), McGill University student register. PAC, RG 4, B28, 53, pp.1748–49. "The late Archibald Hall, M.D., L.R.C.S.E.," *Canada Medical Journal and Monthly Record of Medical and Surgical Science* (Montreal), IV (1868), 429–32. *Gazette* (Montreal), 17 Feb. 1868. *Montreal Herald*, 17 Feb. 1868. McGill University, Faculty of Medicine, *Annual calendars* (Montreal). Morgan, *Bibliotheca Canadensis*. Abbott, *History of medicine*, 68–69, 72, 87–88. H. E. MacDermot, *History of the Canadian Medical Association, 1867–1921* (Toronto, 1935), 4, 120, 128, 131, 133–34, 155; *A history of the Montreal General Hospital* (Montreal, 1950), 15, 26, 31, 61. M. E. Abbott, "The faculty of medicine of McGill University," *Surgery, Gynecology and Obstetrics* (Chicago), 60 (1935), 242–53. D. C. MacCallum, "Reminiscences of the Medical School of McGill University," *McGill University Magazine* (Montreal), 2 (1903), 124–48. H. E. MacDermot, "Early medical journalism in Canada," Canadian Medical Assoc., *Journal* (Toronto), 72 (1955), 536–39.

HAMEL, THÉOPHILE (baptized **François-Xavier**), painter; b. 8 Nov. 1817 at Sainte-Foy, near Quebec, one of nine children of François-Xavier Hamel, a farmer, and Marie-Françoise Routhier; d. 23 Dec. 1870 in Quebec.

On 16 May 1834, at age 16, Théophile Hamel became an apprentice to the most prominent artist at Quebec, Antoine Plamondon*, by a contract between Théophile's father and the artist. Plamondon undertook, for a period of six years, to "show and teach him . . . the art of painting and everything involved therein, not concealing anything from him." Until he was 22, Théophile worked under Antoine Plamondon, experiencing no other influence. It seems that the master's touchy nature made it impossible for him to meet others in the profession. Hamel's contract further stipulated that the young man must "not frequent taverns, gambling dens, or other houses of doubtful repute."

Théophile Hamel began his career with encouragement from three leading social groups interested in art: the clergy, politicians, and businessmen. In October 1840 a correspondent of the *Quebec Mercury* reported that in Hamel's studio he had seen a magnificent sketch of an ecclesiastic. The following year, Hamel painted a portrait of Abbé David-Henri Têtu (still hanging in the church of Saint-Roch at Quebec) and one of Amable Dionne*, a politician. In 1842, Mme Marie Bilodeau and her daughter Léocadie were portrayed with great delicacy of touch. Finally, during the same year, he did a large canvas, painted with bold strokes, on a religious theme inspired by a picture in the Desjardins collection [see Louis-Joseph Desjardins*], *Jésus au milieu des docteurs*. This canvas is still preserved in the church at Saint-Ours. Hamel's principal themes were established; from then on he would not change.

As his master had done, Théophile Hamel decided to make a trip to Europe. On 10 June 1843 he sailed on the *Glenlyon*, a merchant ship bound for London. Tradition has it that he stayed mainly in Italy and Belgium, and spent some time in Paris. In fact the letters we possess concerning his journey prove that Théophile stayed in Rome from summer 1843 to summer 1845. In October 1844 a Canadian priest records meeting him in Rome, when, after a year and a half in Italy, he seems to have been experiencing financial difficulties. The priest launched a dramatic appeal to the Canadian government through *Le Journal de Québec*: "But must it be said? This young man is here in Rome at his own expense; . . . should not our government follow the example of the French government and the other governments who maintain so many resident students in Rome, and come to the aid of this brilliant young artist?" To support his request, the cleric even stated that the Accademia di San Luca would have awarded Hamel first prize if he had not been debarred because he had not participated in the work of the academy long enough.

This assertion raises the whole question of young Hamel's artistic activity in Italy. In a letter of 26 Aug. 1843, the artist states that on his arrival in Rome he had been admitted to the various academies of painting, and had chosen the Académie Royale de France. But it is unlikely that Hamel was actually admitted to this academy: under the directorship of Victor Schnetz (1841–46), the academy had to face continuous financial difficulties; moreover, the Villa Medici, where the academy was housed, contained only five painting studios, and had so little space that Alexandre Cabanel's arrival in 1845 as the sixth boarder created serious problems of accommodation. The Canadian priest's letter of 19 Oct. 1844 speaks of the Accademia di San Luca. This academy, which had been founded in Rome around 1588, and had an unusual history,

had declined and thus numerous private schools had been formed which called themselves academies. They were schools organized by artists in their own houses; it was easy to get oneself admitted to them. Several towns, including Florence, had the same system. Hamel may well have enrolled in these academies and followed their teaching.

From Rome, Théophile Hamel went directly to Venice, and there at the end of August 1845 he was busily copying Titians. Nothing is known of his movements in France and Belgium, but there are some fine works executed in Europe. The Madeleine Hamel collection at Quebec contains magnificent drawings and some water-colours. The spontaneity of certain sketches is in happy contrast with the stiffness of the majority of his pictures. What became of other works executed during his travels? No mention was made of them when he returned in August 1846. His arrival in Quebec was, however, widely commented on in the newspapers. All observed that the artist had travelled extensively, and stressed his long stay in Italy. *Le Canadien*'s note that he had brought back Italian and Belgian paintings was the only mention of his movements outside Italy. After 1870, simply on the basis of a notice published in *Le Courrier du Canada* (Quebec) the day after his death, all his biographers speak of his stay in Belgium. This stage in Hamel's artistic training remains obscure, and the vigour of the great Flemish masters does not seem to have made much change in his style of painting. On the other hand, most of his portraits show the influence of Titian.

Barely a month after his return to Quebec, Théophile Hamel opened a studio at 13 Rue Saint-Louis. Every week-day, from nine in the morning to four in the afternoon, the public was invited to visit it. Fourteen months later, in the autumn of 1847, the painter went to live in Montreal and remained there for two and a half years.

The Quebec phase of Hamel's career really began in October 1851, when he took up permanent residence in the city itself. Antoine Plamondon had already retired to Neuville and Cornelius Krieghoff* had not yet come to Quebec. On 9 Sept. 1857, at age 39, the already well-known artist married Georgina-Mathilde Faribault, daughter of Georges-Barthélemi FARIBAULT, and they were to have at least five children; only two, Julie-Hermine and Théophile-Gustave, reached adulthood.

As a result of his work as an artist, Théophile Hamel was able to live comfortably; he bought a house, and a notarial register indicates a large number of financial transactions. For example, in 1858 he lent his brothers, who were trading partners, the tidy sum of £2,000. He received appeals from distant parish councils in Quebec – that of Rimouski, for instance, to which he loaned £200 – and also from neighbouring farmers. Between 1863 and 1869 he granted several loans, amounting to £1,600. For several years after his death on 23 Dec. 1870 his widow continued to carry out such transactions.

In addition to prosperity, Théophile Hamel had won the respect of the élite. His work merits careful scrutiny for the close relation between its themes and the social groups from which his commissions came. He was appointed official portrait painter by the government in June 1853, and entrusted with the task of painting the portraits of the speakers of the assemblies and legislative councils since 1791. This honour was equivalent to recognizing him as the best painter of his day. The first series of portraits consisted of 14 canvases representing the speakers of the assembly. To fulfil these orders, he found it necessary to travel outside Quebec. In October 1853 he went to New York to do the portrait of Marshall Spring Bidwell*, who had been speaker of the assembly of Upper Canada. That year he painted Sir Allan Napier MACNAB of Canada West, and had the portrait lithographed. As the government travelled between Quebec and Toronto, the artist was obliged to follow it to execute his commissions. Since several speakers had died or were living abroad, Hamel had to be content with copying family paintings of Alexander McDonell*, Levius Peters Sherwood*, Jean-Antoine Panet*, Joseph-Rémi Vallières* de Saint-Réal, Michel-Eustache-Gaspard-Alain Chartier* de Lotbinière, and Augustin Cuvillier*. The complete assignment was dispatched to Toronto at the end of November 1856. From then on he was able to concentrate on the portraits of the speakers of the Legislative Council. In December 1856 nine portraits were finished. On 30 Jan. 1858 a second series of 14 portraits was completed, eight copied from family portraits and six from life. Five speakers could not be portrayed because there was no documentary material. These two series of portraits were to form "the nucleus of a national and historical gallery," to which some wanted to add the canvases of Paul Kane*. When the government settled in Ottawa in 1866, the portraits were taken there. After surviving the fire which destroyed the parliament buildings in 1916, the majority were hung in the corridors surrounding the Senate and the House of Commons, where they can still be seen. Others are in the National Gallery of Canada.

Hamel also painted for the government a series of historical portraits: Champlain*, Charlevoix*, Montcalm*, Wolfe*, Lévis*, Murray*, Sir George Prevost*, John Neilson*, Andrew Stuart*, and Louis Bourdages*; in March 1866 these were added to numerous others already hanging in the parliament buildings. His portrait of Jacques Cartier* is a special case. On his return to Canada in 1846, Hamel had made a copy based on a copy of an original attributed to François Riss and preserved at Saint-Malo; Hamel's painting had been sent to the Literary and Historical Society of Quebec. This copy was reproduced on dollar bills and stamps, and in text-books. Hamel seems also to have made several replicas in oils, since in 1860 the Legislative Assembly and in 1870 the Institut Canadien at Quebec each received one.

The aristocracy and bourgeoisie provided further scope for Hamel's activity as a portrait painter. In 1841 he had done portraits of Charles-Hilaire TÊTU and of his wife. During his stay at Montreal, in response to the Mailhot family's request, he painted Dr Alfred Mailhot, who died in 1847 during the typhus epidemic. In 1849 he put on canvas the features of the future mayor of Montreal, Charles Wilson*. The chief justice, Jean-Roch ROLLAND, had his portrait done in 1848. In 1853 a subscription was started at Quebec to pay for the portrait of mayor Narcisse-Fortunat Belleau*. A similar subscription was undertaken in 1862 for Mayor Thomas Pope. Dr Marc-Pascal de Sales Laterrière* and his wife Eulalie-Antoinette Dénéchaud each ordered their portrait during the year 1853. Joseph MORRIN, a doctor and seventh mayor of Quebec from 1855 to 1858, was also painted by Hamel. Several members of the Hamel family and intimate friends such as Cyrice Têtu and his wife were preserved for us by his brush. His parents, painted in 1843, are perhaps, along with Mme Louise Racine, the sole representatives of the habitants. We know of only one picture of his wife, and one of his father-in-law, the bibliographer Georges-Barthélemi Faribault. On several occasions Hamel painted his own children, those of his brother Abraham, and those of his nephew Ernest Hamel. Of all these portraits from his own family group, three self-portraits painted in 1837, 1846, and 1857 have given rise to the most discussion.

Hamel's talents as a portrait painter also tempted the clergy: abbés, bishops, deans, and vicars general proved eager to display the trappings of their dignity. Several founders were also portrayed, at the request of grateful church people: Louis-Jacques CASAULT, the first rector of the Université Laval; Abbé Joseph-David Déziel* of Lévis, with the plans of the college he had just established; the Reverend Patrick McMahon*, with his hand resting on the plans of St Patrick's Church. The newspapers of the period all mention the picture of Abbé Charles-Paschal-Télesphore Chiniquy*, which was lithographed in 1848. *Le Journal de Québec* expressed the wish "that the portrait of M. Chiniquy will grace all the dwellings of the numerous families who should be grateful to this tireless missionary; and there are many of them." Bernard-Claude Panet*, archbishop of Quebec from 1825 to 1833, Abbé Louis Proulx*, priest of the parish of Notre-Dame de Québec in 1850 and 1851, and Vicar General Antoine Langevin were also painted by Théophile Hamel. This impressive array of ecclesiastics dressed in surplices, capes, and richly embroidered stoles should not make us forget humble churchwardens such as François-Xavier Paradis of the council of Quebec's Saint-Roch parish; the subtle portrayal of Paradis constitutes a high point in Théophile Hamel's art. Few other works can match the animation of this face, with its intelligent look, or the gracefulness of the pose. The hands, one of which holds an address of thanks drafted by the parish councillors, contrast with so many inert and expressionless hands given to other persons by Hamel. Nuns seldom appear in his work. The picture of Sister Marie-Rose [Eulalie Durocher*] was painted a few hours before the death of the co-founder of the community of the Sisters of the Holy Names of Jesus and Mary. "When they returned from the cemetery and saw the picture placed at the feet of the Virgin whom the mortal remains of the founder had just left, sisters and pupils cried out together: 'It is she! It is our Mother! She is going to speak!'" This is one of the most beautiful 19th century pictures of a nun.

The outline of his work clearly shows that Théophile Hamel painted all the most respectable elements in mid 19th century Canadian society. The most prominent politicians and doctors, mayors of Quebec and wives of important persons, had their portraits done by the artist.

A whole section of Théophile Hamel's work still remains obscure. Almost nothing is known of his religious compositions. Some ten canvases deal with the New Testament: *Sainte Geneviève* (Notre-Dame-des-Victoires at Quebec), a *Pèlerin* (1846), a *Christ mort* (Sisters of Charity of Quebec, 1860), *Saint Raphaël* (Verchères),

Vierge et enfant (1867), *Jésus au milieu des docteurs* (Saint-Ours), *Saint Laurent présentant les pauvres au gouverneur de Rome* (Musée du Québec), and *La Présentation de Jésus au temple* (chapel of the Jesuit fathers at Quebec, 1862; copy of a picture by Louis de Boullongne). The Old Testament was of little interest to him, providing only two subjects: *Les Filles de Jethro* has disappeared, as has *Samson poursuivant les Philistins*, a picture for which Charles-René-Léonidas d'Irumberry* de Salaberry is said to have posed. A single religious composition is concerned with contemporary events: *Le Typhus* (church of Notre-Dame-du-Bon-Secours at Montreal, 1847), which shows the Sisters of Charity looking after the sick. The limitations of the artist show up clearly in these large-scale works.

The arrival of the Desjardins collection in Quebec at the beginning of the 19th century was not an unmixed blessing. Many of the compositions of these European painters were so superior to local products that artists came to prefer copying to creating. Painters such as Joseph Légaré* and Antoine Plamondon adopted the reassuring path of the copyist. Hamel followed suit. It is not surprising that a painter who was associated almost exclusively with one particular type of portrait – a solitary individual, seen full face or three quarters, generally seated – and who refused to paint husbands and wives on the same canvas, should feel at a loss with a subject in which a crowd of individuals had to be arranged. Hamel made several copies. The most famous is *Le Repos de la Sainte-Famille pendant la fuite en Égypte*, after a picture attributed to one of the Vanloos, which is preserved in the cathedral at Quebec. Hamel's picture was damaged by fire on 5 May 1866 and replaced by another copy, for which Hamel received 70 louis. From this copy Hamel probably made several replicas, including those in the churches of Saint-Jean-Baptiste at Quebec and Notre-Dame-de-Liesse at Rivière-Ouelle. He is thought to have made several copies of a *Descente de croix* attributed to Peter Paul Rubens. One must remember that for most people at that period a good copy was worth almost as much as an original.

Théophile Hamel's range of subjects is narrow. Indeed, his work is essentially portraiture. His few religious compositions, still little known, are largely copies. To this list can be added some drawings, a landscape, and a still life. There are no historical and mythological themes. Should one see here a lack of imagination? Must one conclude that he could not organize large-scale

Hamel

compositions? Answers to these questions will lead to an evaluation of the importance of Théophile Hamel's artistic production.

A close examination of the portraits of adults painted by Hamel suggests several comments. First, he never ventured to portray two adults on the same canvas. His master Plamondon had taught him how to make a face stand out, with a simple technical handling. Hamel adhered to it all his life. He chose positions presenting the fewest problems. He seated his model, placed himself at the same height, then painted the subject full face or slightly in profile. Although he sometimes avoided the hands of his subjects, he painted them more often than did Plamondon. Before 1843 these hands are unhappily stiff: witness the portraits of M. and Mme Dionne (about 1841), Michel Bilodeau (1842), and his father and mother (1843). After Hamel's return from Europe, the hands remain heavy although the fingers are flexed to some extent and there is some mobility of the wrist. The portraits of René-Édouard Caron* (1856), Mme Marc-Pascal de Sales Laterrière (1853), and Cécile Bernier (1858) make us forget the primitive character of the hands of the 1840s. The men have an elbow placed on the back of their chair or hold a book, the women have their hands crossed demurely. The unusual pose of Mme Laterrière is in itself surprising. The flowing lines, set off by the grace of the long hands, give this picture a charm and freshness that are rare in Hamel.

Generally, Théophile Hamel's portraits lack richness of detail. The rather stiff dignity of the personages takes its place. Usually the model stands out against a completely unrelieved background, although sometimes a heavy curtain serves as back-drop. In either case, light is concentrated at the level of the face and this creates a majestic effect which customarily is found in pictures of saints. More infrequently, a window suggests a landscape beyond. The artist even tried to indicate that Mme Charles-Hilaire Têtu and her son were set in a landscape, and were, indeed, outside. But the heavy tasselled hangings, like those in the *Jeune fille en rose* of Plamondon, and the dull landscape, make the back-drop insipid; we are brought back inside again, rather clumsily. The enormous squat columns that are the chief element of the décor for the portraits of Abbé Louis-Jacques Casault, René-Édouard Caron, and Mme Cyrice Têtu appear scarcely more felicitous. The introduction of a child allowed some modification in the composition. The arrangement is then similar to that of the portrait of a man with his elbow on a chair. Thus the pose of Mme Têtu and her son Eugène resembles that of Charles Wilson. The lack of boldness of these portraits appears evident as soon as they are compared with *La Comtesse d'Haussonville* of Jean-Auguste-Dominique Ingres (1845), the portrait of *Lavoisier et sa femme* (1788) by Louis David, or the *Frédéric Villot* (1832) of Eugène Delacroix.

Does Hamel show more imagination in the minor details? He avoids difficulties by simplifying to the utmost his handling of delicate lace work (Mme Rolland), women's hair (Mme Belleau), and even jewellery. We may compare in this respect the portrait of *Mme Marcotte de Sainte-Marie* by Ingres (1826) with that of *Mme Charles-Hilaire Têtu et son fils Eugène*. Whereas the long pendant worn by the first woman harmonizes with her eccentric hair style and the neck of her dress to create a lively, almost fanciful work, the simple presentation of the piece of jewellery Mme Têtu leaves forgotten on her lap accentuates the stillness of the composition. The shawl Mme Rolland put on her chair is a pale reflection of the one enveloping the shoulders of Mme Philibert Rivière in Ingres' painting (1805). A further detail enables us to evaluate this desire for simplification. The lion's head, a common ornament on the chairs of the period, appears in the pictures portraying Abbé Casault and Sir Allan MacNab. It looks like a rough sketch beside the one painted by Ingres in the portrait of Philibert Rivière. These circumstances help us to understand more readily why Hamel only needed a morning to produce an entire portrait.

The range of feelings expressed in this imposing gallery of personages is restricted. Hamel's greatest successes are his portraits of men, in which he excels in conveying the importance the models attach to the prestige of their position. Charles Wilson lifts his chin with superb dignity. The powerful torso of Melchior-Alphonse de SALABERRY supports an imposing head at once both grave and affable. In the churchmen, a certain gentleness usually tempers the coldness (Abbé Antoine Langevin) or the complacency (Abbé Édouard Faucher) reflected in the eyes. The female faces express a gentle resignation more evocative of nuns than of women anxious to please. Yet the candour of Cécile Bernier, the subtle smile of Mme Dessane, and the slightly worried expectancy of Mme Marc-Pascal de Sales Laterrière show a sensitive grasp of the delicate interplay of feelings in young women who were admired, despite the restraints of their deportment and dress. With very rare exceptions (Mme Georges-Barthélemi Faribault and Mme

362

René-Édouard Caron) all the women Hamel painted wear heavy dresses as discreet as their faces.

The absence of any sensuous element in the majority of Hamel's feminine models is matched by the rarity of a smile in the children. *Gustave et Hermine Hamel* (Musée du Québec) pose with a too docile gravity. The babies, such as the infant Jesus the Redeemer, look concerned. The little *Léocadie Bilodeau*, *Ernest Morisset*, and *Olympe et Flore Chauveau* are among his best achievements.

The considerations discussed here make it possible to take a comprehensive view of Théophile Hamel's production. The severe restraint of the technique gives to most of the artist's works a solidity further accentuated by a general dark tonality contrasted with some warm tones. His brush scarcely touches his backgrounds. Garments sometimes shimmer, but rarely. It is astonishing, therefore, that Hamel should have been described as "a fanatic for detail." The backgrounds of some canvases barely have a layer of paint, and he seldom puts paint on thickly. From this point of view, the portrait of Salaberry constitutes a happy exception. On the bullions of the epaulets, on the buttons and the collar, vigorous brush strokes produce a pearly grey sparkle that contrasts effectively with the red of the uniform. More subdued strokes bring out the angle of the epaulets. Rich blacks, browns, and greys, freely used, create surprising effects in juxtaposition with a brilliant garnet-red or crimson.

Théophile Hamel's real originality is in the faces of his subjects. The variety and delicacy of several of these testify to the artist's psychological acumen. He concentrated his solid sketching abilities there, with the abundance of commissions certainly one of the reasons. Within the severe framework he imposed on all his models, Hamel succeeded in varying expressions and in bringing out the revealing features.

Hamel did not get this strict economy of means either from the Flemish painters or from the neo-Classics or the French Romantics. Titian was his master as much as if not more than Antoine Plamondon; his letters say so and his works prove it fully for most of his composition exists in Titian. *L'Homme au gant* in the Louvre may have provided him with his arrangement of a man seated, with an elbow on a piece of furniture and a hand at rest. This arrangement is repeated exactly in the portraits of Charles Wilson, Archibald CAMPBELL, James Stuart*, and Jean-Roch Rolland. The minor details such as windows, landscapes, columns, and curtains are also found in Titian.

Hamel hardly ranks as a painter of religious compositions. Yet he attached enough importance to these pictures to send two of them to the 1867 Paris exposition. Apparently *Sainte Geneviève* and the *Vierge à l'enfant* were shown with a self-portrait and the portrait of Salaberry. The heavy treatment of the saint, seated in a bergère before an ill-defined landscape, and the lack of originality with which the Madonna and child are represented, are surprising in an artist who had reached the summit of his career. His other religious compositions must be studied in comparison with the canvases in the Desjardins collection and those of Plamondon. Several are copies, such as *Jésus au milieu des docteurs*, after Samuel Massé's picture at Saint-Antoine-de-Tilly, itself a copy of an unknown master.

Several of Théophile Hamel's works were not executed in the presence of the model. Others were done both with the model and with a daguerrotype. Finally there are the copies. The large-scale religious subjects required much of the artist's time, and a skill in composition he did not possess. Parish councils were readily satisfied with copies, which had the advantage of being cheaper.

This leads to the question of the sources of Théophile Hamel's art. Can we find an evolution by starting from his sources? He was helped by several factors. First was the talent of his master Antoine Plamondon, through whom he made contact with the pictures of the Desjardins collection. In addition, certain bold flights of fancy of Plamondon captivated him. We certainly owe to Plamondon's influence the magnificently successful self-portrait of 1837. The freshness of its landscape, the vigour in each undulation of the foliage, and the ease of the pose were to give place to a more sober approach.

Théophile Hamel's studio and a great part of his equipment were destroyed by fire in 1862. We possess, however, a series of 24 prints which had belonged to him: studies of mouths and noses, faces, warriors, an *Agrippine*, and a *Saint Bernard*. The latter may have inspired his *Saint Hugues*, painted in 1849. A small girl's face resembles that of the eldest daughter of Mme Jean-Baptiste Renaud (1853). A study of a male nude perhaps became the insipid central figure of *Saint Laurent présentant les pauvres au gouverneur de Rome*. All this work is of little value.

His studies in Italy marked him profoundly. Although he admired Rubens, Titian became his real master, and the Italian classical tradition moulded his work more than any other artistic movement.

Three elements constantly recur in his painting. First, dignity: within the limited range of feelings in his many portraits there is always present the considerable nobility that primarily characterizes his art. Second, verisimilitude: contemporary critics never ceased to praise the likeness between his portraits and the models, his most enduring merit. Finally, the very restraint of the technique, which gives most of his works a solidity accentuated by the contrast of dark and warm tones; though the brush seldom lingers to catch reflections and sharp contrasts, his technique, acquired during a long apprenticeship of six years and perfected by copying the great masters, never falters.

Théophile Hamel succeeded in finding a style which suited his temperament and the aspirations of Canadian society in the 1850s. A quiet, steady person, he never felt attracted to venture into complex composition and chromatic brilliance. His training and his desire to live in the upper social strata predisposed him towards an art characterized by nobility. His influence marked the generation that followed. Napoléon Bourassa*, Ludger Ruelland*, his nephew Joseph-Arthur-Eugène Hamel*, who all worked in his studio, and Sister Marie de l'Eucharistie, who died in 1946, perpetuated his manner into the 20th century. The study of Théophile Hamel's work throws light on the art of a whole century.

RAYMOND VÉZINA

[The main outlines of Théophile Hamel's biography were established in Le Courrier du Canada shortly after his death and have come down to us unchanged. The extensive documentary material available in archives now makes it possible to describe the man more closely and to re-evaluate his artistic work. R.V.]

AJQ, Greffe de Philippe Huot, 8 janv. 1867. ANQ-Q, AP, Coll. Bourassa, Boîte 1, lettres de Napoléon Bourassa à Théophile Hamel, 10 mai, 29 juin 1852, 14 déc. 1855, 28 juin 1857, 11 sept. 1861, 13 avril 1864, 7 juin 1868, 12 juin 1869, 24 juill. 1870; État civil, Catholiques, Hôpital Général de Québec, 8 nov. 1817; Notre-Dame-de-Foy (Sainte-Foy, Qué.), 23 nov. 1852, 28 nov. 1855, 5 mai 1859; Notre-Dame de Québec, 2 août 1822, 29 août 1827, 30 mars 1830, 22 sept. 1840, 26 oct. 1842, 31 janv. 1844, 30 août 1860, 24 nov. 1862, 26 sept. 1864, 29 nov. 1865, 23 déc. 1870; Greffe de Joseph Petitclerc, 5 juill. 1834, 27 déc. 1841, 10 juin 1843, 10 juill. 1851, 11 févr. 1854, 11 mars 1856, 8, 23 sept., 8 oct. 1857, 31 août 1858, 20 avril 1861, 24 janv. 1863. Archives de la résidence des Jésuites (Québec), Diariums du supérieur, cahier 1915–16, 130; Procès-verbaux du conseil de la congrégation Notre-Dame de Québec (congrégation des hommes), I, 192–93, 218; II, 208. Archives paroissiales, Immaculée-Conception (Saint-

Ours, Qué.), Livres de comptes, 31 juill. 1831, 4 nov. 1842; Notre-Dame-de-Foy (Sainte-Foy, Qué.), Livres de comptes, 1843; Notre Dame de Québec, Livres de comptes et délibérations, 7 mai 1867; Saint-Charles (Saint-Charles-de-Bellechasse, Qué.), Registres de la fabrique, 1856; Saint-Charles-des-Grondines (Grondines, Qué.), Livres de la fabrique, 18 janv. 1846, 23 févr. 1847. Archives paroissiales de Saint-Roch (Québec), Livres de comptes et délibérations, 31 oct. 1862. Archives privées, Anne Bourassa (Montréal), correspondance de Théophile Hamel avec sa famille de 1843 à 1867. Archives privées, Madeleine Hamel (Québec), lettre de Théophile Hamel à Cyrice Têtu, 11 juin 1844; Alphonse Leclerc à Théophile Hamel, 27 avril 1870; livre de comptes de Théophile Hamel. ASQ, C 51, 19 mai 1858; Fonds Casgrain, Lettres, IV; Fonds Viger-Verreau, 38, no. 287, 19 févr. 1847; Journal du séminaire, 24 févr. 1853, 31 déc. 1861, 22 avril 1862, 10 juin 1867, 12 avril 1868, 22, 27 déc. 1876; Plumitif, 21 oct. 1852.

Can., prov. du, Assemblée législative, Journaux, 1844, 1853; Conseil législatif, Journaux, 1861. L'Ami de la religion et de la patrie (Québec), 21 avril, 6 oct., 3 nov. 1848. L'Aurore des Canadas, 25 avril 1843; 14 août 1846; 15 juin, 2 nov. 1847; 18 nov. 1848. Le Courrier du Canada, 26 déc. 1870. Daily Colonist (Toronto), 24 Nov. 1856. Le Journal de Québec, 18 avril, 5 oct., 10 juin 1843; 15 sept. 1846; 11 nov. 1848; 16 oct. 1851; 29 janv., 25 juin, 19 nov. 1853; 27 nov. 1856; 30 janv. 1858; 4 déc. 1862; 16 févr., 21 mai 1867; 9 avril 1870; 3 juill. 1889. La Minerve, 16 sept. 1847; 30 mars 1848; 25 juill. 1850; 15 oct. 1853; 31 mars 1860; 22, 24 mars 1865. Morning Chronicle (Quebec), 20 June 1853, 28 July 1858. Quebec Mercury, 27 Oct. 1840.

R. H. Hubbard, Antoine Plamondon/1802–1895, Théophile Hamel/1817–1870; two painters of Quebec (Ottawa, 1970), 34, 40, 43. Georges Bellerive, Artistes-peintres canadiens-français; les anciens (Québec, 1925), 43–51. William Colgate, Canadian art, its origin & development (Toronto, 1943), 26–38. P.[-J.-B.] Duchaussois, Rose du Canada, mère Marie-Rose, fondatrice de la Congrégation des Sœurs des saints noms de Jésus et de Marie (Montréal, 1932), 287–89. J. R. Harper, La peinture au Canada des origines à nos jours (Québec, 1966), 79, 90–93, 130, 136, 145, 235, 423. Gérard Morisset, Coup d'œil sur les arts en Nouvelle-France (Québec, 1941). P.-V. Chartrand, "Les ruines de Notre-Dame," Le Terroir (Québec), V (1924–25), 100–3, 126–30, 153–57, 162, 438–39. Hormidas Magnan, "Peintres et sculpteurs du terroir," Le Terroir (Québec), III (1922–23), 342–54, 410–22.

HARGRAVE, JAMES, HBC chief factor; b. 19 Nov. 1798 in Hawick, Scotland, son of Joseph Hargrave and Jane Melrose; d. 16 May 1865 at Brockville, Canada West.

The son of a humble, devout Lowland Scot, James Hargrave received a good education and a strict upbringing. After graduating from Fysshe's Academy in Galashiels at 18, he began teaching school in a nearby village. In 1819 he persuaded his father, an estate manager, to follow the example of relatives and emigrate to Canada where he believed the family was assured of a brighter future. Hargrave himself arrived in 1820 and entered the service of the North West Company; he helped his parents to settle comfortably on a farm near Beauharnois, Lower Canada.

During his first winter in the fur trade, Hargrave served as an apprentice clerk at Sault Ste Marie (Ont.). In the spring of 1821 he travelled to Fort William (Thunder Bay, Ont.) where he attracted the notice of the influential Nor'Wester John George McTavish*. After the union of the North West and Hudson's Bay companies in 1821, Hargrave was retained as a clerk by the HBC and spent the next season at York Factory under McTavish, now a chief factor. In 1823, Hargrave was appointed to the Lower Red River District. Here he spent the next four winters but travelled with the brigades to York every summer. In 1827, having distinguished himself as a "Clerk, Warehouse & Shopkeeper," he was stationed permanently at York Factory, the company's entrepôt on the shores of Hudson Bay. During the hectic summer months which saw the arrival of the fur brigades from the vast Northern Department and the annual ships from England, Hargrave had to cope with piles of invoices and accounts or heaps of trade goods to be sorted for the various districts. The departure of the fur-laden ships in early fall signalled a welcome period of relaxation. Hargrave derived particular pleasure from the newly arrived books and newspapers, "those precious fruits of civilization," which helped to beguile many a long winter evening. Hunting also broke the monotony of the counting-house. He wrote jauntily of sallying forth on snowshoes "wrapt up in treble folds of Duffle & DeerSkin" to brave "the terrors of an Arctic sky."

Governor George Simpson* was impressed by Hargrave, whom he described as a man of "highly correct conduct and character," with a "clear headed" grasp of general business. Simpson favoured his early promotion, but Hargrave lacked experience in trading with the Indians, could speak none of the native languages, and had a reputation for being sour-tempered. Although he secured a chief tradership in January 1833, when he assumed the management of York, he was not officially given charge of the York Factory District until 1835.

Hargrave, who suffered from ill health, took a year's furlough in 1837. While touring in Scotland, he was warmly received by the family of his friends WILLIAM and Dugald Mactavish*, both of whom were in the HBC's service. Hargrave soon felt he had found the ideal wife in their older

sister Letitia*. Unlike many of his contemporaries, Hargrave had resolved not to marry a native woman because he was determined to leave the Indian country as soon as he had accumulated enough money to live in comfort. He was unexpectedly called back to York Factory early in 1838, but returned to Scotland in the fall of 1839, and married Letitia on 8 Jan. 1840. Hargrave brought his bride to York Factory by the annual ship and was extremely gratified that she adapted so readily to life on Hudson Bay. He was to find much happiness in their four children, all born at the Factory.

Family considerations urged James Hargrave to press for a long-promised chief factorship. For nearly a decade he had managed an important and burdensome post, but with the decline of the fur trade in the 1840s, he began to despair of achieving financial security. Moreover, he felt frustrated by the governor's refusals to allow him to attend the annual meeting of the Council of the Northern Department at Norway House (Man.) because his services were too essential to permit even a short absence from York. Promotion to chief factorship eventually came in January 1844. By this time Hargrave longed to move his family to a post nearer "the civilized world." York's severe climate often left him crippled with rheumatism, and he had grown excessively corpulent under the sedentary routine. In 1846, when he returned from his only trip to the council, he went on furlough with his ailing wife. A firm believer in "a good moral & religious education," Hargrave placed his son Joseph James* at school in Scotland. The family returned to York Factory in the summer of 1847, and remained there, to Hargrave's chagrin, for another four years. He was increasingly aggravated by the lack of trained men, the heavy demands of private orders from the Red River colony, and the loss of the supply ship *Graham* in 1849 which threatened his carefully regulated system. In the summer of 1851, Hargrave gratefully relinquished York to William Mactavish and journeyed overland to take charge of Sault Ste Marie, the supply depot for the districts of Lake Huron and Lake Superior. His wife joined him the next summer.

Sault Ste Marie brought only disappointment and sorrow to James Hargrave. A kind, genial man in private, he observed strict propriety in business, and so irritated his easy-going American customers. His private expenses were also much greater than anticipated. Hargrave's grief at the sudden death of his wife in September 1854 was compounded by the loss of his youngest child a few months later. He left the Sault in the sum-

Harriott

mer of 1855 for Scotland, where the affairs of his wife's family devolved heavily upon him. Refused further leave because the governor deemed him the only man qualified to replace the ailing William Mactavish at York, Hargrave returned to his old post in 1856. He finally retired officially from the company's service 1 June 1859 after a year's leave of absence in Scotland.

Throughout his career Hargrave was a prodigious letter writer, corresponding with officers all over the HBC's vast domains. His draft letter books, which give much detail about the logistics of the trade, reveal his assiduous attempts to satisfy the needs of every district with fairness and economy. His private letters, where he appears as esteemed friend and confidant, constitute the richest surviving record of life in western Canada during the first half of the 19th century. Besides providing valuable commentary on fur trade society with its blend of Indian, British, and French customs, these letters also contain much specific information about the personal lives of many of Hargrave's contemporaries.

Paradoxically, Hargrave himself remained aloof from the main stream of fur trade life – he was never the trader who spent the winter bartering pelts and the summer travelling hundreds of miles by canoe and York boat. Rather he served as the administrative king-pin whose efficient management at York was crucial to the success of the far-flung trade of the HBC.

In June 1859, shortly before returning to Canada from Scotland, Hargrave was married again, to Margaret Alcock. After a year in Toronto, he settled on a substantial property, Burnside House, at Brockville. Hargrave did not have long to enjoy the fruits of his labours: he died five years later at the age of 66 and was buried beside his first wife in St James' cemetery, Toronto.

SYLVIA VAN KIRK

[The correspondence of James Hargrave, which amounts to 26 volumes, is preserved at PAC (MG 19, A21, ser.1). Of the letters written to Hargrave (vols. 1–20), only a small number have been published in *Hargrave correspondence* (Glazebrook). Hargrave's own letter books (vols. 21–26) are unpublished. s.v.k.]

HBC Arch. A.33/3, ff.210–24; A.34/1, f.104; A.34/2, f.34; A.36/7 (will and papers concerning the Hargrave estate). McGill University Libraries, Dept of Rare Books and Special Coll., MS coll., James Hargrave diary (mfm. at HBC Arch.). PABC, Donald Ross papers, James Hargrave letters, 1839–51. PAC, MG 19, A2, ser.2, 1, pp.111–65. Mactavish, *Letters of Letitia Hargrave* (MacLeod).

HARRIOTT, JOHN EDWARD, HBC chief factor; b. 1797 in London, England, a son of John

Peter PRUDEN's sister; d. 7 Feb. 1866 in Montreal, Canada East.

In 1809 John Edward Harriott entered the service of the Hudson's Bay Company as an apprentice. He went out in the company's ship *King George*, apparently spent the winter at York Factory, and in 1811 went to the Saskatchewan District. At the age of 17 Harriott was described as five ft seven in. in height, "fair, long hair, slender . . . sober, modest and obedient, rather idle and illiterate." He remained in the Saskatchewan district until 1822; was with the Bow River expedition of 1822–23, led by Donald McKenzie*; then at Carlton House, 1823–26, and Fort Assiniboine, 1826–28; and in the Columbia District, 1828–32. In 1832–34 he had charge of Piegan Post in the Saskatchewan District among the Slave Indians of the Bow River country. When Piegan Post was abandoned because of scarcity of trade, Harriott re-established Rocky Mountain House, a difficult post where his skill in Indian relations clearly stood him in good stead. From 1834 to 1854 he alternated between this post and Edmonton House, except for service at Pembina in 1848–49; he was in charge of the Saskatchewan District from Edmonton House in 1841–42 and 1847–48 in the absence of John Rowand*.

Apparently an exemplary employee, Harriott had been promoted clerk during the season of 1816–17, chief trader in 1829, and chief factor in 1846. His uncle, John Peter Pruden, who had left him in charge of Carlton House in 1818, recommended him as "a very promising and interested young man well acquainted in the way of Trade" and "much beloved by the Natives, of a good Temper and very obedient to his Superiors." Even Governor George Simpson* gave him an excellent character. In 1832 he described him as "A finished trader. Speaks Cree like a native and is a great favourite with Indians; has much influence likewise with the people and is generally esteemed by his colleagues. Strong, active and fit for severe duty. Mild tempered, well disposed, and bears an excellent private character. Came to the country when quite a boy so that he is deficient in regard to education, but in every other respect he is a very effective man." Father Pierre-Jean De Smet* described him as a "most amiable gentleman" and Paul Kane* in 1847 found him a kind, considerate, and even lavish host at Edmonton House.

Harriott married three times within the network of family relationships that came into being in the service in the first half of the 19th century. His first marriage to his cousin Elizabeth, daughter of Pruden, ended with her death under tragic circumstances, though their precise nature is shrouded in legend. In 1838 Harriott married Anne (Nancy), daughter of John Rowand, to whom he had been contracted in 1835–36. By 1846 they appear to have had four daughters and two sons. Nancy Harriott died in 1850. In 1853, with what his father-in-law considered unseemly haste, Harriott married Frances, sister of Dr John BUNN of Red River.

Harriott retired to the Red River in 1855; his will, made in 1858, indicates also some period of residence in Montreal. He had prospered in the service and in his will was able to dispose of an estate of over $10,000, not including "a house, property, cattle, horses, carriage, carriols." A strong family man, he had made a generous allowance to his mother until 1844 and in his will he remembered his brother and three sisters and provided handsomely for his widow and his younger children. To his daughter by his first marriage, Margaret, who had married John Rowand Jr, he left £50 "to purchase a gold watch or anything she may fancy to keep in remembrance of her affectionate father."

LEWIS G. THOMAS

[Apart from the account in HBRS, II (Rich and Fleming), Harriott's career can be followed in the surviving journals in HBC Arch. of the posts in which he served. There are also some references to his affairs in PABC, Donald Ross papers. L.G.T.]

HBC Arch. A.16/60–63; A.31/2–4; A.34/e, f.17; A.36/7; A.44/6, f.180.

HARRIS, FREDERICK WARREN, manufacturer; b. 1823 in Lancaster, Mass., son of Emery Harris, manufacturer, and Sally Wilder; d. 13 July 1863 at Montreal.

Frederick Warren Harris attended Harvard University and graduated in 1845. While still an undergraduate he became interested in mechanical inventions, and spent considerable time and money developing a number of his own. After graduation he moved to Middlebury, Vt, where he opened a cotton factory. He soon began taking an interest in the Canadian market, as a considerable portion of his production was being sold in Montreal, the traditional metropolis of northern Vermont. He realized that the expanding market in Canada could be more readily exploited by producing goods there in order to avoid the new 12½ per cent general duty on imports. Harris was also excited by the possibilities offered by the hydraulic power resources of the Lachine Canal which by the early 1850s had attracted large-scale industrial development.

Harris probably arrived in Montreal in 1852 or 1853. An unknown manufacturer with limited means, he nevertheless impressed a number of Montrealers as a shrewd businessman. Ira Gould and John Young*, the two owners of the St Gabriel Hydraulic Company, which controlled water rights at the St Gabriel lock on the Lachine Canal, thought Harris to be a good enough risk that in 1853 they extended a cash loan of £1,000 and at the additional cost of £1,500 also erected a three-storey mill, called the St Gabriel Cotton Mills, to start him in business. Despite some difficulties – a major one being the lack of trained operatives – Harris invested £6,500 within the first two years in up-to-date machinery: willows, pickers, carding and drawing machines, 1,500 spindles, and 46 looms. He was engaged principally in manufacturing denim cloth at the rate of 300 yds daily and employed 70 people, mainly women and children. In 1855 he added at a cost of £3,000 a batting and wadding mill with carding and other machines capable of producing 6,000 yds of wadding and 1,200 lbs of batting each day.

In 1857 a fire in the factory seriously impaired production and a secret investigator for R. G. Dun Company reported that Harris had "little or no means." Within three years, however, he was back in business and thriving. A short time later he set up a large woollen factory beside the cotton mill. When he died at the early age of 40 Harris' factories were doing well. Not only had he become one of the city's major industrialists, but he was also one of the pioneers of Montreal's textile manufacturing industry which was to be such an important component of its economic life by the end of the 19th century.

GERALD TULCHINSKY

Baker Library, Harvard University (Cambridge, Mass.), R. G. Dun Co. credit ledger, Canada, 5, pp.4, 40, 53. *Montreal Gazette*, 16 July 1863. *Montreal Herald*, 14 July 1863. *Quinquennial catalogue of the officers and graduates of Harvard University, 1636–1930* (Cambridge, Mass., 1930), 244. *Montreal in 1856; a sketch prepared for the celebration of the opening of the Grand Trunk Railway of Canada* (Montreal, 1856), 40.

HARRIS, MICHAEL SPURR, lumberman, shipbuilder, and businessman; b. 22 Sept. 1804 in Annapolis Royal, N.S., son of Christopher Prince Harris and Elizabeth Spurr; m. 11 May 1826 Sarah Ann Troop, and they had five sons and three daughters; d. 26 Jan. 1866 at Moncton, N.B.

Michael Spurr Harris' grandfather, Samuel Harris, came to Annapolis County with the first of the New England planters in 1761. Michael is thought to have been involved in the family lumber business in Annapolis, but in 1821 moved to Saint John, N.B., where, after a period of apprenticeship, he became a carriage maker. A few years later he moved to Norton in Kings County to carry on his trade. On 27 July 1836, at the small community on the Petitcodiac River known as The Bend (Moncton), Harris purchased about 11 acres of land including a section of marsh along Hall's Creek. There he began farming, opened a store, built a wharf on the Petitcodiac about a quarter of a mile from his property, and began to export timber to Great Britain. In 1845 Harris built a fine new residence, which became Moncton's first hospital more than 30 years after his death.

The profits from his lumber exports as well as his frequent visits to British ports made him a well-known New Brunswick figure. He was appointed deputy sheriff for Westmorland County on 30 Dec. 1845. Six years later Harris built his first ship in the yards on Hall's Creek, the 782-ton *Flora*, first of five ships built for Joseph Salter*, another prominent Moncton businessman. In 1859 he laid the keel of the brig *Isabella*, the last ship known to be launched from his yards. The collapse of Salter's firm and setbacks in the Liverpool market brought to an end Moncton's "golden age" of shipbuilding in the late 1850s.

Harris was a shareholder of the Westmorland Bank organized in 1854 and an active promoter of the Petitcodiac Wet Dock Company in 1855. The latter proposed to harness the great tides of the Bay of Fundy by a series of brick retaining walls built around a diverted channel of Hall's Creek to enable a vessel to dock, load or unload cargo, and sail all on the same tide. Owing to lack of capital the plan was never implemented. Harris was a strong supporter of civic incorporation and his name appears among the citizens who signed a petition to the assembly 30 Jan. 1855, which resulted in the "Bend of the Petitcodiac" becoming the town of Moncton on 12 April 1855.

In 1861 Harris was elected the mayor of the town, and later served as a magistrate. He was a strong supporter of responsible government, an intercolonial railway, the union of the Maritime provinces, and eventually confederation of all the British North American provinces. He saw the economic potential of Moncton as an industrial centre with rail and shipping connections, which later came about partly as a result of the entrepreneurial capacity of two of his sons, John Leonard and Christopher Prince, and his son-in-law John Albert Humphrey. Although Harris spent only 30 years in Moncton, he became one of its leading citizens and his death in 1866, following a lingering illness, was widely mourned.

C. ALEXANDER PINCOMBE

N.B. Museum, Edward Barron Chandler papers, 1821–70. PAC, RG 31, 1851 census, Moncton parish (mfm. at PANB). Westmorland County Registry Office (Dorchester, N.B.), libro O, ff.578–79 (deed 7149, 23 Aug. 1836). N.B., House of Assembly, *Journals*, 1854, 626–39; 1855, 100, 103–4, 256. *Moncton Times* (Moncton, N.B.), 11 Dec. 1889, June 1927. *Cyclopaedia of Canadian biog.* (Rose, 1888). W. A. Calnek, *History of the county of Annapolis, including old Port Royal and Acadia, with memoirs of its representatives in the provincial parliament, and biographical and genealogical sketches of its early English settlers and their families*, ed. and completed by A. W. Savary (Toronto, 1897; repr. Belleville, Ont., 1972), 523–24. E. W. Larracey, *The first hundred: a story of the first 100 years of Moncton's existence after the arrival in 1766 of the pioneer settlers from Philadelphia, Pa.* (Moncton, N.B., 1970). C. A. Pincombe, "The history of Monckton Township (ca.1700–1875)" (unpublished MA thesis, University of New Brunswick, Fredericton, 1969), 133–34, 158, 178, 181, 304–6. S. T. Spicer, *Masters of sail: the era of square-rigged vessels in the Maritime provinces* (Toronto, 1968), 83–84, 95–96.

HARRIS, ROBERT WILLIAM, merchant and entrepreneur; b. *c.* 1805 at Bogmount Grange, Crosskeys, County Antrim (Northern Ireland); d. 22 March 1861 in London, Canada West.

Robert William Harris was the son of a small farmer whose family traced its Ulster roots back to the late 17th century. At 14 he began working in a Dublin dry goods business. Subsequently he moved to Liverpool, then came to Canada in 1830 where he worked for William Guild Jr and Company, dry goods merchants in Montreal and, from 1832, York (Toronto). When Peter* and Isaac Buchanan* took over the firm in 1834, Harris, as an expert in the dry goods trade, proved indispensable and earned a partnership in their firm, Isaac Buchanan and Company, within a year. Harris' responsibilities grew rapidly; in 1840 when the firm opened its Hamilton branch with John Young* also a partner, it was called Buchanan, Harris, and Company. Harris himself moved to Hamilton in 1844. In the early 1850s he became a partner with the two Buchanans in their principal firm, Peter Buchanan and Company of Glasgow, and spent much time in Liverpool managing Buchanan, Harris, and Company's new office there. It had been his lifelong ambition to achieve such a place in the British business world, yet he was happier in Hamilton and settled there again in 1854. He had no capital in 1835, but by 1856 his capital in the business exceeded $360,000.

Harris' integrity and growing business eminence, and Peter Buchanan's support, led to his election as president of the Great Western Railway of Canada in 1849 and of various subsidiaries in later years. Harris saw his office as a form of public service, for which he declined payment. However, he did hope to assist Hamilton and his own business and to keep Sir Allan MacNab from making excessive raids on the company's treasury. As the line moved from promotion through construction to operation, he was active in most policy deliberations, though C. J. Brydges*, whom Harris had helped to select as managing director, became the more important figure. By 1856, Harris considered that he could safely retire. Instead, when Isaac Buchanan sought to force the Great Western to build a branch along the strategic "southern route" from the Niagara River to Amherstburg and invoked Harris' name in support of the idea, the Great Western's board, which felt that no new branches should be authorized, demanded that Harris resign. It was a sad end to seven years of devoted service.

A shy man, Harris made few friends and never married. After the deaths of his brother and father, he took growing responsibility for his relatives in Ireland. He employed several nephews in the business and arranged a partnership for William Muir, husband of his favourite niece, Eliza Harris, in the London, Canada West, branch of the business. In so assisting relations he rejected the Buchanans' argument that he was often misguided in his family loyalty. In 1837–38 Harris had commanded a Toronto volunteer company, but he consistently opposed what he termed "the compact" in Toronto and in Hamilton. Increasingly he was disillusioned by the corruption he saw on all sides in Canadian politics.

A riding accident in 1850 left Harris permanently lame. After 1856 his mental and physical health deteriorated, and the tendency was hastened by his railway reverses and losses suffered by the Buchanans' business in the 1857 depression. In 1860, Peter Buchanan wrote Harris out of the business; he feared death was near for Harris and that the large payments he knew Harris had provided for in his will were beyond the business' ability to pay. Harris, who now lived quietly in London with his niece, protested Buchanan's action but to no avail. Nevertheless, his heirs ultimately realized $70,000 from the business before it went bankrupt in 1867, much less than the $300,000 Harris had provided for. Harris

died dependent on others and largely neglected by former business acquaintances. He was buried in Paris, Canada West.

Douglas McCalla

PAC, MG 24, D16; RG 30, 1–2, 5, 10–11, 19. *Hamilton Spectator*, 25, 27 March 1861. M. F. Campbell, *A mountain and a city, the story of Hamilton* (Toronto, 1966). Johnston, *Head of the lake* (1958). G. R. Stevens, *Canadian National Railways* (2v., Toronto and Vancouver, 1960–62), I. P. D. W. McCalla, "The Buchanan businesses, 1834–1872: a study in the organization and development of Canadian trade" (unpublished DPHIL thesis, University of Oxford, 1972); "Peter Buchanan, London agent for the Great Western Railway of Canada," *Canadian business history, selected studies, 1497–1971*, ed. D. S. Macmillan (Toronto, 1972), 197–216.

HARRISON, SAMUEL BEALEY, lawyer, miller, politician, and judge; b. 4 March 1802 in Manchester, England, son of John and Mary Harrison; d. 23 July 1867 at Toronto, Ont.

Samuel Bealey Harrison grew up at Foxley Grove in Berkshire and early turned towards a legal career. At 17 he was admitted to the Middle Temple as a special pleader; he gave up this practice when he was called to the bar in 1832. He then carried on a private law practice in London and compiled *Harrison's digests*, an analytical digest in four volumes of all the important cases determined in the House of Lords, the courts of common law in banc and nisi prius, and the Court of Bankruptcy from 1756 to 1834. Also important was his revision of the standard edition of William Woodfall's *The law of landlord and tenant* . . . (probably published in 1837).

Harrison's promising legal career in England was cut short by ill health, and in 1837 he dramatically altered his life. Immigrating to Upper Canada, he bought a section of the former Mississauga Indian reserve near Bronte (Oakville), where he built a grist and saw mill and prepared for the life of a gentleman farmer and miller.

Nevertheless, his legal writing was well known, and men of his ability were desperately lacking in the colony. In June 1839, "most unexpectedly to himself," he was requested to act as civil secretary to Sir George Arthur*, lieutenant governor of Upper Canada. For the next four years Harrison was also involved in politics and renewed his legal activities. He was called to the Upper Canadian bar in September 1839 and was appointed a justice of the peace for the province in 1840.

It was his brief political interlude that proved to be the most remarkable phase of Harrison's public life. Yet it was a role that has proved singularly difficult to evaluate. From 1841 to 1844 he acted as government leader in the assembly of the Province of Canada, rivalled Robert Baldwin* for control of the Upper Canadian Reformers, and played a critical part in the struggle for responsible government. But all this was accomplished in a "behind-the-scenes" fashion that mystified his contemporaries and left a record so sparse that historians long ignored him. He made no appeals to the public, deliberately refrained from committing himself in writing, was reluctant to do so in conversation, and was ambiguous when he did talk. The historian John William Kaye described him as "unassuming and unaffected[;] making no display of his talents, he still got through his business in such a manner as to justify a belief in their existence."

As civil secretary Harrison conducted careful investigations and prepared several reports for the lieutenant governor and the Executive and Legislative councils on the economic and social problems facing the colony in the chaotic aftermath of 1837–38. Perhaps it was his genius for clear and unemotional analysis which commended him to the new governor general, Charles Poulett Thomson*, who in August 1840 became Lord Sydenham. After leaving Arthur's service Harrison became a key man in Sydenham's plans.

Once he had achieved the union of Upper and Lower Canada in February 1841, Sydenham set out to make the union work. This was not easy since the French Canadians hated its assimilationist aims, and the Upper Canadian Tories disliked it almost as strongly for wedding them to the French Canadians. The Reformers who followed Baldwin, on the other hand, hoped to use the union as a vehicle for achieving responsible government, a principle the governor was under instructions from the Colonial Office not to concede. Yet Sydenham was optimistic: "I can make a middle Reforming party I am sure which can put down both [the Tories and Baldwin Reformers]." Harrison, whom Sydenham described as "the best man I have," was to lead this projected party.

On 13 Feb. 1841 Harrison was appointed to the Executive Council as provincial secretary for Canada West. Sydenham's skilfully assembled council was comprised of men of every political group in Canada except French Canadians. Yet soon the Upper Canadian Tories and Reformers were in opposition. Through gerrymander, patronage, and the use of troops the governor secured in the election that spring an over-all majority of moderate Reformers and Conservatives committed to support him, but Harrison was defeated in Hamilton by the Tory leader Sir Allan Napier MacNab. An attempt in Kent led to a further defeat, but he was finally returned for Kingston on 1 July 1841.

Once in the assembly, Harrison took control of the largest single block of members, the "Moderate Reformers," acting as co-government leader with William Henry Draper* who commanded the small group of "Moderate Conservatives." In practice Harrison was soon handling virtually all government initiatives in the assembly, since Sydenham disliked Draper and tended to use him only when oratorical eloquence was needed. In 1842 came the governor's reorganization of the colony which, backed by a £1,500,000 loan from the imperial government, introduced a brief period of remarkable prosperity. To Harrison, whose administrative ability Sydenham greatly admired, and to Dominick Daly, the provincial secretary for Canada East, was entrusted, in Sydenham's own words, "the whole internal management of the Province" for this reorganization. Most of the imperial loan was to be spent on the construction and improvement of canals, and Harrison was deeply involved in the planning. He was one of the five members of the newly created Board of Works under the chairmanship of H. H. Killaly*.

In the legislature Harrison and his colleagues introduced the Common Schools Bill which established a general system of publicly supported primary schools in the united province. In August 1841 they also introduced the District Councils Bill which first established elective municipal government in Canada West. Harrison appears to have done most of the drafting of these two bills. The rough passage of the second measure must have strengthened Harrison's identity as a moderate, attacked as it was by the Tories for its "unprecedented liberalism" which would "pave the way for the introduction of Republican institutions" and by some Reformers as "a complete system of despotism" which, because it provided for the appointment of district wardens, centralized power to an extent "for which there is no example in the whole civilized world."

The main political crisis of the session came on 3 Sept. 1841 when Robert Baldwin moved five resolutions calling explicitly for responsible government. Since many moderate supporters of the government were pledged to this principle, the government was endangered, but both Harrison and Sydenham were prepared. Each of Baldwin's resolutions was parried with a counter-resolution by Harrison which sounded much the same and was accepted by the members, including Baldwin, who were committed to responsible government. Though greeted at the time as "the Magna Carta of responsible government," the Harrison resolutions ignored the principle of a governor *having* to act on the advice of the Executive Council, stating only that he should listen to such advice and that the council "ought" to be comprised of persons having the confidence of the assembly – concessions well within the colonial secretary's instructions to Sydenham.

Yet it was important that many Canadians now thought responsible government an established fact. Harrison himself, though he had helped Sydenham's manœuvre, was willing to make more of the principles behind the resolutions when dealing with Sydenham's successor, Sir Charles Bagot*. In a kind of double-bluff Harrison had helped to defeat Baldwin's resolutions, yet he had actually made a move towards real responsible government at the same time. Nor did his performance damage Harrison's reputation as a "good liberal." Baldwin, with five to seven supporters, could not afford to offend the 19 to 21 moderates from Upper Canada who consistently supported Harrison, and had to reaffirm his political confidence in Harrison, though not in the whole ministry. In private, the "ultra" Reformers were confused and annoyed by Harrison's performance. Francis Hincks* described him as "a spy and a traitor," and shortly afterwards as "at heart a liberal."

Harrison's political importance initially declined under the administration of Bagot, because Draper, whom Bagot found more congenial, became government leader. Many moderate Reformers who had supported Harrison and Sydenham were beginning to drift to Baldwin's party once Sydenham's magical brilliance had been removed. Characteristically, Harrison did not appear resentful or perturbed. Perhaps he considered his practical administrative duties more important than the degree of political support he could muster in the assembly. In February 1842 he was named one of three directors of the Welland Canal which had been taken over by the government and in March one of the three commissioners superintending work on the Lachine Canal. Nevertheless, the defection of Harrison's former supporters precipitated the crisis of Bagot's administration.

Bagot was aware of what was happening, and attempted to counterbalance the sagging support in the centre of his ministry by strengthening the left and the right. Hincks, impressed by the practical achievements of the Sydenham régime, had broken with Baldwin and entered the council in June 1842; and in July so did Henry Sherwood*,

the arch-Tory mayor of Toronto. But this apparent master stroke to broaden the government's support did not achieve its purpose. In a letter to Bagot on 11 July 1842 Harrison had in his usual manner dispassionately analysed the stand of each member of the assembly and proved conclusively that the government would fall when the assembly met in September if it remained constituted as at present, and that neither Sherwood nor Hincks would strengthen it. Harrison added that he would feel bound to resign from the Executive Council in accordance with his resolutions of the previous September; other councillors would undoubtedly do likewise. Bagot could then govern personally, dissolve the assembly, or call on Baldwin and Louis-Hippolyte LA FONTAINE to form a new ministry. Harrison felt that the only sensible course was the third one, and that if Bagot took it quickly and on his own initiative he would avoid the humiliation of having it forced upon him later.

Draper took a similar position. Like Harrison, he was convinced that the key was to abandon the original assimilationist aims of the union and invite La Fontaine's Reform group into the government. Draper was willing to resign to facilitate matters. The joint advice from what one historian has aptly termed "the right and left bowers" of his ministry convinced the governor. On 28 July 1842 he wrote to Colonial Secretary Lord Stanley asking for permission to admit the French members. Much of Bagot's crucial dispatch was a paraphrase of Harrison's letter; indeed, a good deal of it was direct, though unacknowledged, quotation.

The imperial government rejected Bagot's request. However, parliament met on 8 September, before Stanley's dispatch had reached Canada, and it became clear that the government would soon fall. Bagot invited La Fontaine to join the ministry, but La Fontaine's demand for four seats in the council and for the inclusion of Baldwin caused Bagot to hesitate. Harrison and Draper on 12 September called an extraordinary meeting of the Executive Council in the absence of the governor and its members threatened to resign *en masse* if La Fontaine's demands were not met. Bagot acceded; the Tory councillors left, and the council was reconstructed with moderate Reformers and the Baldwin–La Fontaine group. Harrison, still provincial secretary, was named government leader in the assembly.

Although Harrison was recognized as head of the new ministry by Bagot, the council rallied behind Baldwin and La Fontaine in creating an all-Reform administration. Only the "nonpolitical" Dominick Daly and Harrison remained

Harrison

independent of Baldwin's direction. When in 1843 the capital was moved from Kingston to Montreal, Harrison, as member for Kingston, resigned in protest from the Executive Council on 30 September. Characteristically he did so after publicly stating he was in no way bound to take such a course. Equally characteristically, when Baldwin and Hincks hoped to dissuade him, they could think of no one on close enough personal terms with Harrison to approach him. During Bagot's administration Harrison had played his most constructive role in politics, but also demonstrated his inability or unwillingness to be either a true party leader or a good follower.

Governor Sir Charles Metcalfe*, who had succeeded Bagot in March 1843, was under orders from the Colonial Office to make no more concessions to the Reformers and to keep patronage firmly in his own hands. When Baldwin and La Fontaine challenged him on the latter point Metcalfe stood by his instructions, and the whole of the Executive Council except Daly resigned late in November 1843. On 1 December the former ministers read out in the assembly the Harrison resolutions of September 1841, claiming that Metcalfe had contravened them; resolutions supporting Baldwin and La Fontaine were passed by the assembly. Metcalfe denied abrogating the Harrison resolutions and prorogued the assembly.

Harrison's position as author of the resolutions and as the most prominent independent Reformer was pivotal, but he again acted with studious ambiguity. In the debate of 1 December he "appeared partly to approve, partly to condemn the late ministry," supporting the ex-ministers on some divisions while abstaining on others. When Metcalfe invited him to join a caretaker government with Daly, Draper, and Denis-Benjamin Viger* he first accepted and then declined, pleading confusion in his personal finances. In January 1844 Hincks made two determined efforts to get Harrison to pledge he would not actively oppose the ex-ministers, but Harrison's response was non-committal. Then, towards the end of the month, Harrison sounded out back-bench Reformers to see how many would support him if he formed a government himself – a course Egerton Ryerson* had long been urging on him. When this attempt came to nothing, Harrison professed a desire to retire from politics and asked Metcalfe to appoint him to the next vacancy in the judiciary. Metcalfe, though nearly as annoyed at Harrison as Hincks and Baldwin were, grudgingly acquiesced.

Harrison's actions in the Metcalfe crisis were thus obscure and confusing, but they were significant. The fact that he contemplated joining a ministry under Metcalfe made it clear that he disagreed with Baldwin. The disagreement helped to crystallize some moderate thinking, and there were soon those who claimed that after Harrison's resignation the Reform ministry had gone too far too quickly and no longer represented the majority of Upper Canadians, a notion often stressed in the elections in the fall of 1844 in which Baldwin's followers were soundly defeated in Canada West. Harrison's ambiguous position may have contributed to that defeat. Harrison himself was returned for Kent, but in January 1845 he received his appointment to the bench. At the announcement of his resignation from the assembly "there was a perfect storm of 'Hear, hears' from all sides" of the house, reflecting Harrison's enigmatic conduct.

Harrison was appointed a QC and judge of the Surrogate Court of the Home District, then of York County, where he remained until his death 22 years later. In addition he was made judge of the District Court for the Home District in 1848. Some thought he would eventually become a justice of the Court of Queen's Bench, but he was owed no political favours, and his scruples about the death penalty were a bar to promotion. Contemporaries, however, felt that his long tenure in York County did much to raise the prestige of the county courts.

Of the many fields of public welfare which had come under his purview as provincial secretary, education was the one interest he continued most actively. Appointed to the Board of Education for Canada West when it was first established in 1846, Harrison was unanimously chosen chairman in 1848 after the death of Bishop Michael Power*. In July 1851 he replaced Henry Sherwood on the senate of the University of Toronto.

Harrison's first wife, Mary Harman, whom he had married in England in 1831, died in Canada, and in 1852 he married Ellen Humphreys, the widow of Colonel Colley Lyons Lucas Foster*. They settled in Toronto with a home on Dundas St which Harrison nostalgically called Foxley Grove after his father's house in England. His hobby was horticulture and his garden and conservatory included a number of specimens unique in North America. He died on 23 July 1867. His wife survived him by 38 years; they had no children.

Despite his long judicial tenure, Harrison's brief political career is more significant. Although he kept his position through changing ministries under Sydenham, Bagot, and Metcalfe, his abrupt and voluntary departures first from the Executive Council and then from politics make it clear he was no placeman. The key to his policy would seem to be that though he believed progress towards responsible government both good and inevitable, he understood it could be severely set back by a premature clash with the Colonial Office. If gradual constitutional advance was his aim, he contributed significantly to its achievement. His part in introducing the resolutions of 1841 and in sponsoring the entry into government of Baldwin and La Fontaine in 1842 certainly forwarded responsible government; his role in partially outmanœuvring Baldwin on both these occasions and in contributing to the latter's defeat in the election of 1844 did much to avert a confrontation with the imperial government until, by 1847, the Colonial Office itself was willing to accept the concept of internal self-government for the Canadas.

GEORGE METCALF

Bibliothèque nationale du Québec (Montréal), Société historique de Montréal, Coll. La Fontaine. MTCL, Robert Baldwin papers. PAC, MG 24, A13; E1; RG 4, C2, 2, 24; RG 5, B30, 1–6; C1, 882–85; C4, 2–5. PAO, Harrison (Samuel Bealey) papers. PRO, CO 42/437–517; 537/140–43. *Arthur papers* (Sanderson). Can., Prov. of, Legislative Assembly, *Journals*, 1841–44. *Documentary history of education in U.C.* (Hodgins), IV. Hincks, *Reminiscences*. Scadding, *Toronto of old* (1873). [C. E. P. Thomson], *Letters from Lord Sydenham, governor-general of Canada, 1839–1841, to Lord John Russell*, ed. Paul Knaplund (London, 1931). *British Colonist* (Toronto), 1838–44. *Christian Guardian*, 1838–44. *Examiner* (Toronto), 1838–44.

Careless, *Union of the Canadas*. Dent, *Last forty years*. C. [B.] Martin, *Empire & commonwealth: studies in governance and self-government in Canada* (Oxford, 1929). H. C. Mathews, *Oakville and the Sixteen: the history of an Ontario port* (Toronto, 1953). Sissons, *Ryerson*. R. S. Woods, *Harrison Hall and its associations, or a history of the municipal, judicial, and educational interests of the western peninsula* (Chatham, Ont., 1896). George Metcalf, "Samuel Bealy Harrison: forgotten Reformer," *OH*, L (1958), 117–31.

HART, JULIA CATHERINE. *See* BECKWITH

HARWOOD, ROBERT UNWIN, merchant and politician; b. 22 Jan. 1798 at Sheffield, England; his mother was Elizabeth Unwin; d. 12 April 1863 at Vaudreuil, Canada East.

Robert Unwin Harwood came to Canada in 1821 to work for the family-owned wholesale hardware house of John Harwood and Company of Montreal, then managed by his brother John. Young and handsome, Robert won the hand of Marie-Louise-Josephte, the eldest daughter of

the late Michel-Eustache-Gaspard-Alain Chartier* de Lotbinière, seigneur of Vaudreuil, Rigaud, and Lotbinière; they were married on 15 Dec. 1823. Before his fortunate marriage Harwood had been an obscure petitioner seeking from the crown a grant of 200 acres of unlocated land in some remote township north of Montreal. After his wedding, he moved in a more select society, serving, for example, on the grand jury for criminal cases several times between 1824 and 1828 with John Molson* Jr, Peter McGill [McCutcheon*], George MOFFATT, and other prominent Montreal merchants.

Following his wife's inheritance of the seigneury of Vaudreuil in 1829, Harwood exchanged trade and Montreal society for the countryside. His first years in Vaudreuil were spent attending to long-neglected seigneurial matters, renewing the *censitaires'* contracts, and building a new manor house for his growing family which eventually numbered ten children. "My occupations are at present so great," Harwood wrote in 1830, declining an appointment as justice of the peace, "that I could not do my duty as a magistrate."

During the 1830s provincial politics somewhat diverted Harwood from parochial problems, but after 1840 he again turned his full attention to the seigneury. He made generous donations to the churches, schools, and needy individuals of Vaudreuil. He pursued reforms in agriculture and transportation; this interest he called "a hobby," but it was based on a sound grasp of problems and genuine concern for improvement. Harwood, who was usually referred to as seigneur, was one of the few to commute seigneurial property into freehold tenure, doing so between 1846 and 1853. Rather than relying solely on rents for his income, he used the right of *banalité* to begin a large-scale milling operation in 1841. Towards the tenants he was less businesslike. He preferred leniency to litigation in the collection of seigneurial dues. His liberal attitude led his disapproving brother in England to say in 1852 that "the management of property to advantage is a talent not possessed by many and certainly not by our family"; however, it also prompted *La Minerve* to remark, around the same time, that "Mr. Harwood's conduct as a seigneur has been and remains irreproachable." All in all, Harwood was a rare example of an English speaking seigneur who gained the respect and affection of his people. After his death *La Minerve* noted that "few seigneurs were as well liked by their *censitaires* as he was."

Harwood's political career, although curious, was of less significance. In 1832 he was appointed

Hatheway

to the Legislative Council of Lower Canada, but as a moderate and youthful member he had little influence on its decisions during the constitutional tension in the 1830s. Following the troubles of 1837–38, in which he played no part, Harwood was one of the moderates added to the Special Council in September 1839. His term was short, as the Special Council last met in June 1840.

Not appointed to the Legislative Council after the union, Harwood eschewed active participation in politics until 1847 when he stood for election in Vaudreuil as a Reform candidate. He was defeated then and again in 1851 and 1854. He was finally elected to the assembly from Vaudreuil in January 1858. In 1860 he resigned his seat and won election to the Legislative Council for Rigaud. Thus his political career came full circle – from a young appointed member of the upper house to an old elected member of it.

Harwood died at the manor house in Vaudreuil in April 1863. "The Hon. Robt. Harwood was much respected," it was noted, "indulgent to his tenantry, of unspotted reputation, courteous and considerate to all with whom he had relations."

JOHN BESWARICK THOMPSON

Bureau d'enregistrement de Vaudreuil (Qué.). Terrier des mutations de la seigneurie de Vaudreuil, 1829–63. McGill University Libraries, Dept. of Rare Books and Special Coll., MS coll., Robert Unwin Harwood papers. PAC, MG 24, I119, Seigneurie de Lotbinière, 1821–65, pp.74–114; RG 1, L3ᴸ, 136; RG 4, A1, S-244, p.152; B12, 1; B30, 115; B72, 39, 43, 49. Private archives, Henri de Lotbinière Harwood (Vaudreuil, Qué.), Harwood family papers. Can., Prov. of, Legislative Assembly, *Journals*, 1842, I, app.Z; 1851, III, app.U.U.; 1852–53, VII, app.P.P.P. L. C., Special Council, *Journals*, 1839; House of Assembly, *Journals*, 1829, app.Ee (A). *La Minerve*, 16 déc. 1847; 13 janv. 1848; 16, 19 déc. 1851; 16 avril 1863. *Montreal Gazette*, 30 April 1846, 5 Feb. 1851, 16 Oct. 1860. *Montreal Herald*, 9 June 1821, 1 May 1822, 3 Feb. 1849. *Vindicator and Canadian Advertiser* (Montreal), 1 Sept. 1835. *The British North American almanac and annual record for the year 1864: a hand-book of statistical and general information*, ed. James Kirby (Montreal, 1864), 308. E. C. Royle, *An historical study of the Anglican parish of Vaudreuil* (Hudson Heights, Que., 1952), 49.

HATHEWAY, CALVIN LUTHER, author and surveyor; b. 17 Sept. 1786 in Burton, Sunbury County, N.B., son of Ebenezer Hatheway, loyalist; m. 8 Nov. 1809 Sarah Harrison, and they had at least three children; d. 23 Aug. 1866 at Saint John, N.B.

Calvin Luther Hatheway spent his early life in Sunbury County where he became a land surveyor in 1809 and took an interest in "an im-

proved system of agriculture." He moved to Saint John in the early 1820s, and there earned the rank of adjutant and later major in the 2nd battalion of the Saint John County militia, in which he continued to serve until 1842. He also served as justice of the peace for the city and county of Saint John from 1838 to 1844.

Hatheway resided in Saint John until the mid 1840s when he moved to Maugerville and later Sheffield in Sunbury County. His work as a surveyor, however, took him to many parts of the province. On 1 June 1822 he was appointed deputy surveyor of lands for Charlotte County. In the period 1836–38, during the New Brunswick–Maine boundary dispute, Hatheway as a surveyor presented valuable evidence to the British government in support of the British claim. In 1845 he made a survey of the Grand River, Madawaska County, for the Crown Lands Office, and in 1848 served as deputy land surveyor for Sunbury County. During the period 1849–54 he was appointed a deputy for the surveyor general's office.

It was no doubt his knowledge of the geography of the province that induced him to write *The history of New Brunswick* in 1846. It was to serve as a manual and guide for the traveller, student, businessman, and emigrant. The work contains a brief sketch of the founding and early settlement of the province by the loyalists, as well as a description of its various counties, natural resources, and boundaries. The book reveals that Hatheway considered the blacks settled near Loch Lomond as "a tax upon the charity of the public" and thought that the Malecites on the upper Saint John River should abandon their "roving habits" and apprentice their children to "English occupations." He also supported those who were opposed to municipal corporations as recommended by Lord Durham [Lambton*].

Five years after Hatheway's death, in 1866, his son George Luther* became premier of New Brunswick.

J. M. WHALEN

N.B. Museum, C. L. Hatheway, correspondence, 1836–48; papers, 1 June 1822; Ganong MS coll., W. F. Ganong, "The province of New Brunswick"; Wilmot United Church, records, 1794–1892. PAC, MG 27, I, D15, Hatheway to Tilley, 28 Sept. 1862, 25 Aug. 1863. PANB, REX/px, 43, pp.589–606. G.B., Parl., House of Commons paper, 1849, XXXVIII, 593, pt.II, pp.377–474, *Emigration (North American and Australian colonies).* . . . C. L. Hatheway, *The history of New Brunswick from its first settlement, containing a geographical description of the province* . . . (Fredericton, 1846). *Morning Telegraph* (Saint John,

N.B.), 25 Aug. 1866. *Royal Gazette and New Brunswick Advertiser* (Saint John, N.B.), 20 Nov. 1809. *St. John Daily Telegraph and Morning Journal* (Saint John, N.B.), 6 July 1872. W. G. MacFarlane, *New Brunswick bibliography: the books and writers of the province* (Saint John, N.B., 1895). *The merchants' and farmers' almanack* . . . (Saint John, N.B.), 1840–41, 1843–46, 1852–53, 1855–63. *New-Brunswick almanac*, 1825–36, 1838–39, 1842, 1849–51. Lorenzo Sabine, *Biographical sketches of loyalists of the American revolution, with an historical essay* (2v., Boston, 1864; repr. Port Washington, N.Y., 1966). Wallace, *Macmillan dictionary*.

HAVILAND, THOMAS HEATH, office-holder, land agent and proprietor, banker, and politician; b. 30 April 1795 or 1796 in Cirencester, Gloucestershire, England; d. 18 June 1867 in Charlottetown, P.E.I.

After holding a minor position in the Naval Victualling Office in Chatham, England, Thomas Heath Haviland immigrated in 1816 to Prince Edward Island. There he became provost marshal, a post he later described as "a sinecure." In August 1817 he was appointed naval officer, another sinecure and a position which was abolished eight years later, leaving him with an imperial pension of £159 sterling. This was the starting point for an impressive accumulation of offices: in July 1823 he was named to the Council; in the following year, despite his lack of legal training, he became assistant judge of the Supreme Court, a largely honorary position with no fixed salary; in 1830 he was appointed colonial treasurer, and during his tenure he successfully collected the Island's first land tax (on the average around £1,425 per annum, a sum which increased about 50 per cent the year after he left office); and in November 1839 he vacated the latter position to become colonial secretary, registrar, and clerk of the Executive and Legislative councils. As clerk of the Legislative Council he had to resign from that body; he had been its first president following its separation from the Executive Council in March 1839.

While in these strategic official positions Haviland had become local overseer of entrepreneur Thomas Burnard Chanter*'s various interests, and land agent to Sir George Seymour, Lord James Townshend, and the trustees of the Selkirk estate. Eventually he became a large landed proprietor in his own right; in 1852 he described himself as owner of Lot 56 and parts of Lots 8, 40, and 43. Thus most of his holdings were concentrated in rural Kings County, where one of his paying tenants was the Escheat politician William COOPER, whom he had succeeded in 1829 as agent for Lot 56, then owned by Townshend. At the time of his death he also owned a substantial amount of real estate in Charlottetown and Georgetown.

Because of his many public offices (executive, legislative, and judicial) and his vested interests in the leasehold system, Haviland became known as the perfect embodiment of the old régime before the arrival of responsible government in 1851 with the formation of George Coles*' Reform administration. Edward WHELAN in that year described his accumulation of offices as "an instance of monopoly that no other colony can parallel." The interlocking nature of the local élite was illustrated in 1841 when the report of an assembly investigation revealed, among other things, that Haviland had family connections with seven of his eight fellow executive councillors. His influence and prestige appear to have grown over the years, to the point that Whelan believed him to have been "the master-mind of the cabinet" of Sir Donald Campbell*, the reactionary lieutenant governor in the late 1840s. When responsible government came, Haviland was forced to relinquish his offices (except for his assistant judgeship, which he retained until 1854). At the insistence of the Colonial Office he was granted a pension of £200, a sum which he complained was "so slender" as to be "Inadequate . . . to the pecuniary sacrifice which I am subjected to." A few weeks earlier he had reported his income from salaries and emoluments for 1850 (excluding his pension as retired naval officer) as amounting to some £668.

Haviland was generally credited with the characteristic virtues usually ascribed to his social type: courtly manners and sound judgement in the discharge of his official duties. Whelan described him as "decidedly the ablest and best informed man of the party to which he belongs." But, like many beneficiaries of the old régime, he did not make a rigid distinction between serving his own interests and those of the colony. An investigation in 1849 revealed that he was involved in questionable financial proceedings as accountant general in the Court of Chancery, a minor position he had held since 1831. Two years later the new Reform government conducted a well-publicized inquiry into his exaction and retention for his private purposes of fees for his services between 1840 and 1850 as "private secretary," an office which had no official existence. After a report by the investigating committee demanding that Haviland be required to refund some £796 to the treasury, Lieutenant Governor Sir Alexander BANNERMAN referred the controversy to London. Although there had been significant substantive and procedural errors on

Haviland

Haviland's part, which had resulted in his personal gain and a minimum of public scrutiny, Lord Grey [Henry George Grey], the colonial secretary, was more impressed by the fact that political motives appeared to lie behind the allegations. He declined to intervene against Haviland, and requested that the Reformers let the matter drop. After seeking legal advice, they decided to comply with Grey's wishes. This unsavoury affair may have been a factor in Haviland's decision in late 1852 to return to England for an extended period. Prior to his departure he appointed his son, Thomas Heath* Jr, his agent.

Yet Haviland's extensive interests and connections on the Island brought him back after seven months, and he resumed a highly influential role in local politics. He entered the electoral arena in March 1854, and won a by-election for Princetown, the closest thing to a rotten borough in the colony, by a vote of 59 to 51. He was promptly appointed to the Tory Executive Council which had taken office in the previous month under John Myrie HOLL. Despite a sweeping Liberal victory in June of that year, he was re-elected. He remained a member of the assembly through 1858, albeit attending irregularly and missing the session of 1856 because of a visit to England. In the later 1850s he and Thomas Heath Jr, also an assemblyman, both prominent Anglican laymen, played an important and forceful role in bringing forward the question of the use of the Bible in the schools, over which the Liberals would eventually be toppled from office [see Coles].

Haviland had been elected mayor of Charlottetown, traditionally a Tory stronghold, in 1857, and he was annually re-elected without serious opposition until his death owing to a disease of the kidneys and bladder. He was among the minority of Islanders who favoured confederation in the mid 1860s. At the time of his death Whelan wrote that "He was *the* representative man of the old conservative party. Without brilliant talents, his judgment was of the highest order; he filled every situation in the colony to which a colonist could aspire, short of the gubernatorial chair." Thomas Heath Jr became lieutenant governor at the end of the 1870s. Haviland had married twice: on 8 Jan. 1822 to Jane Rebecca Brecken, who died on 28 March 1839; and on 4 Jan. 1848 to a widow, Amelia Janetta Emslie, *née* Boyd. In addition to Thomas Heath Jr, he had at least five daughters; each of these children received a substantial legacy.

As elder statesman of the old Family Compact, Haviland had wielded tremendous power and influence in the political and economic life of Prince Edward Island for most of his long career. He had been a central figure in every administration between 1823 and 1851, and for much of that time he was the most influential councillor. As well as being an extensive landowner, he was president of the Bank of Prince Edward Island from the second annual meeting of shareholders in 1858 until his death. William Henry Pope* stated in an obituary: "With two generations of the inhabitants of this Island, the name of the deceased gentleman has been a household word. He was more generally known to them than any other individual in the community."

IAN ROSS ROBERTSON

[Detailed information on T. H. Haviland's business connections will be found in PAPEI, P.E.I., Land Registry Office, Land conveyance registers; for his agencies to Seymour, the Selkirk trustees, Townshend, and Chanter, his purchase of Lot 56, his marriage settlement of 1848, and his assignment of agency to T. H. Haviland Jr, *see*, respectively, liber 31, f.259; liber 34, f. 637; liber 35, f.396; liber 43, f.297; liber 56, f.1; liber 63, f.467; and liber 65, f.428. For Haviland as land agent and landlord, see *Abstract of the proceedings before the Land Commissioners' Court, held during the summer of 1860, to inquire into the differences relative to the rights of landowners and tenants in Prince Edward Island*, reporters J. D. Gordon and David Laird (Charlottetown, 1862), 7–8, 237–40; and PAPEI, T. H. Haviland Rent books, Lot 56 from 1845 (2v. and index). His will, dated 21 June 1865, will be found in P.E.I., Supreme Court, Estates Division, liber 7, f.330 (mfm. at PAPEI).

A wealth of information on Haviland's administrative and political career can be found in PAPEI, P.E.I., Executive Council, Minutes, 24 July 1823, 20 March 1854; P.E.I., House of Assembly, *Journal*, 1834, 28; 1840, 70; 1841, 151, app.N; 1846, app.K; 1847, 128, 136; 1848, 61, 78; 1849, 18, 85, 105, 125–27, 131, 134–36, 142–45, apps.H, V, X; 1850 (1st session), 18, 22–23, 44–45; 1850 (2nd session), 14–15, app.G; 1851, 8, 19–21, 25–27, 30–31, 35–37, 49, 51–53, 119, 131, 136–42, apps.D, H; 1852, 31, 160–63, app.A; 1853, app.E; 1854, 24; 1856, 87, app.E; 1857, 35–36; P.E.I., House of Assembly, *Debates and proc.*, 1857, 7, 42, 54, 91–92, 119; 1858, 7, 61; PAPEI, P.E.I., Lieutenant Governors' record group, Commission book I, pp.120, 181, 192, 222, 228; Commission book II, pp.8–9, 62, 121–22; P.E.I., Legislative Council, *Journal*, 1839 (2nd session), 10; 1840, 6; P.E.I., *Acts*, 1851, c.3, s.4; PRO, CO 226/65, 5; 226/67, 44; 226/69, 326, 340, 427; 226/71, 251, 259–61, 288, 293–300; 226/79, 48, 84–86, 235–300; 226/80, 238; 226/82, 118, 225–31; 226/83, 87, 123, 182. Also *see* PAPEI, Bank of Prince Edward Island, minute book, 1856–82; Central Academy, minute book, 50–51; Henry Jones Cundall, letterbook, 27 March 1867 – 26 May 1871, p.20.

For newspaper sources on Haviland, see *Examiner* (Charlottetown), 14, 28 Aug. 1847; 8 Jan. 1848; 19 Jan.,

13 April, 4 May, 26 June 1850; 19 May, 9, 23 June, 7 July 1851; 21 Jan., 4 Aug. 1856; 22, 29 June, 6 July, 10 Aug. 1857; 22 Feb., 1 March, 12 April, 9 Aug. 1858; 22 Aug. 1859; 7 Aug. 1860; 27 July 1863; 18 June, 2 July 1866; 24 June 1867 (obit); 12 Sept. 1895; *Islander*, 27 Aug. 1847; 7 June 1850; 3 Dec. 1852; 15 July 1853; 10, 17 Feb., 3, 10, 17, 24 March, 16, 23, 30 June, 21 July 1854; 3 April, 14 Aug. 1857; 21 June 1867 (obit.); *Monitor* (Charlottetown), 6 July 1858; *Prince Edward Island Gazette* (Charlottetown), 26 Jan. 1822; *Prince Edward Island Register* (Charlottetown), 19 Jan. 1830; *Protestant and Evangelical Witness*, 25 June 1864; *Royal Gazette* (Charlottetown), 2 April, 3 Dec. 1839; 8 May 1849; 14 July 1851; 26 Jan., 6 Dec. 1852; 21 Feb., 24 Oct. "Extra," 14 Nov., 5 Dec. 1853.

Obituaries to Haviland are also found in *Gazette* (Montreal), 5 July 1867; *Herald* (Charlottetown), 19 June 1867; *Summerside Journal* (Summerside, P.E.I.), 20 June 1867; *Summerside Progress* (Summerside, P.E.I.), 24 June 1867.

Useful secondary sources are Duncan Campbell, *History of Prince Edward Island* (Charlottetown, 1875), 194–96; Greenhill and Giffard, *Westcountrymen in P.E.I.*, 70–71, 94, 98–99, 101, 107–9, 116–17, 137, 155, 189, 216; W. S. MacNutt, "Political advance and social reform, 1842–1861," *Canada's smallest province* (Bolger), 116–19; *Report of the city of Charlottetown for the year ending 31st December, 1877 . . . and a synopsis of city affairs from the date of its organization to 31st December, 1876* (Charlottetown, 1878), 97; and Robertson, "Religion, politics, and education in P.E.I.," 17, 19–23, 34–35, 47–49, 60. i.r.r.]

HAWKE, ANTHONY BEWDEN, immigration agent; b. in England, probably in the late 18th century; d. 11 Aug. 1867 in Whitby, Ont. He and his wife Eliza had two sons and three daughters.

Anthony Bewden Hawke came to Upper Canada after the War of 1812 and settled near Bath, Lennox (Lennox and Addington) County. A Tory in politics, he became a justice of the peace in the Midland District in 1825 and in the Home District in 1837. In 1832 Lieutenant Governor Sir John COLBORNE employed him as an agent at Lachine, Lower Canada, to assist immigrants proceeding to Upper Canada. The next year he was in York (Toronto) in charge of an emigrant office. His duties were to provide information to immigrants about transportation routes and the availability of employment, and occasionally to direct settlers to newly opened regions and give them financial assistance. In 1841 he was transferred to Kingston where his duties were similar but also included providing temporary work in the town for immigrants who were penniless. He had returned to Toronto by 1850. Hawke, as chief emigrant agent for Upper Canada from about 1835, exercised authority over other agents in Canada West, and, in turn,

was subordinate to A. C. BUCHANAN, the chief emigrant agent at Quebec.

In June 1859 Hawke was sent to Britain as Canadian emigration agent, the first since Thomas Rolph* had acted as agent there from 1839 to 1842. Hawke went with instructions to consider the possibility of having Canadian agents in Europe to promote emigration, to investigate the government's emigration advertising, to publicize Canada's land regulations, and to examine the Canadian exhibit at the Crystal Palace in London. In January 1860, Hawke was ordered to open an emigration office in Liverpool – the first such Canadian agency overseas. His chief duty was to promote emigration by hand-bills, pamphlets, and advertisements in newspapers, but he was also to publicize Canada's resources to encourage British interest in investment and trade. The government was supporting other emigration agents in Britain and on the Continent as well as conducting an extensive advertising campaign in 1860, but its policy was a tentative one and all the agents were temporary. The only hint of permanency was Hawke's Liverpool agency.

Hawke conscientiously travelled about England, meeting with government officials and businessmen and distributing publicity materials. Although his efforts did not appreciably influence British emigration to or trade with Canada, his services were useful: for the first time the Canadian government had its own agent in Europe who gave full time to emigration tasks and who was well acquainted with problems of immigrants in Canada. As a result, the government received recommendations appropriate to Canadian conditions. Hawke favoured the establishment of a permanent Canadian agency in Britain, and his opinion added weight to similar views expressed in Canada by other immigration officials such as Buchanan and William HUTTON, and by some politicians, including Thomas D'Arcy McGEE and P. M. M. S. VanKOUGHNET.

After his return from England in 1860, Hawke continued his agency work in Toronto until 1864 when he retired because of age and ill health. Hawke's major importance lies in his work to aid immigrants arriving in Upper Canada and in his mission to England during 1859 and 1860. It laid the groundwork for the later permanent Canadian agency, opened by William Dixon* in Liverpool in 1866 and transferred to London in 1869.

WESLEY B. TURNER

PAC, RG 1, E1, 56; L3; RG 7, G20, 2; RG 17, AI, ser.2, 1492–93; AIII, ser.1, 2392; ser.3, 2398. Can., Prov. of, Legislative Assembly, *Journals*, 1852–60. *Whitby*

Hawkins

Chronicle (Whitby, Ont.), 5 Oct. 1865, 15 Aug. 1867. *Commemorative biographical record, county York*, 115–16. W. B. Turner, "Colonial self-government and the colonial agency: changing concepts of permanent Canadian representation in London, 1848 to 1880" (unpublished PHD thesis, Duke University, Durham, N.C., 1970).

HAWKINS, ERNEST, Church of England clergyman and secretary of the Society for the Propagation of the Gospel in Foreign Parts; b. 25 Jan. 1802 at Hitchin, Hertfordshire, England, the son of Henry Hawkins and Anne Gurney; m. in 1852 Sophia Anna Lefroy; d. 5 Oct. 1868 in London, England.

Ernest Hawkins attended Balliol College, Oxford, and received from the university his BA in 1824, his MA in 1827, and his BD in 1839. After ordination he became a fellow of Exeter College, Oxford, and also served as under-librarian of the Bodleian Library. In 1844 he was made a prebendary of St Paul's Cathedral, London, and in 1850 he succeeded Francis FULFORD, bishop designate of Montreal, as minister of Curzon Chapel in London. In 1838 he had been appointed assistant secretary, and in 1843 secretary, of the Society for the Propagation of the Gospel, the Church of England missionary organization. After a successful career in this post, he resigned in 1864 on his nomination as canon of Westminster.

During his 26-year service with the SPG, Hawkins bore heavy responsibility for the welfare of hundreds of Anglican clergymen and their families in British North America and throughout the world. In 1838, for example, the SPG supplied £12,254 to 99 missionaries in the dioceses of Quebec and Nova Scotia. Thirty-eight missionaries in Upper Canada were being paid from clergy reserves income and 28 in Nova Scotia received salaries from the British parliament. In 1864, with the addition of the North West Territories and British Columbia, there were 234 Anglican missionaries in British North America. Through his personal acquaintance with the missionaries of the society, many of them sent from England, and from his knowledge of their work through regular correspondence, he gained an extensive understanding of the church's life. Moreover, from its formation in 1841 until 1864 he was honorary secretary of the Colonial Bishoprics Council, an organization for the extension of the colonial episcopate. In this capacity he was involved in setting up new dioceses and appointing bishops to them: John Medley* to Fredericton in 1845 and Francis Fulford to Montreal in 1850. He was also concerned with the formation of the dioceses of Huron in 1857 and Ontario in 1861, to which respectively Benjamin Cronyn* and J. T. Lewis* were elected by the Canadian laity and clergy. Relations between the SPG and the bishops in British North America were generally cordial, though some, like Cronyn, objected to what they saw as the society's high churchmanship.

In 1849 Hawkins paid a private visit to the eastern United States and British North America. In the course of the tour he kept a journal, an incisively written document which, supplemented by letters to English correspondents, gives an absorbing account of places visited, persons met, and travelling conditions. Apart from a desire to see SPG missions at first hand, Hawkins was also concerned with establishment of a new policy of the society towards them. Many parishes themselves provided a house and church and a small stipend to the missionary, but the SPG salary of £100 and £125 was still highly valued by many clergy because of its regularity. Hawkins felt nevertheless that certain missions could become self-supporting. Thus from the 1830s to the 1860s the number of SPG-supported missionaries increased, while the aid required by them decreased. Missions in Upper Canada, for example, after 1832 were receiving income from the sale of clergy reserve lands, and, in certain cases after 1836, from endowments granted by Lieutenant Governor Sir John COLBORNE. Consequently, support for the diocese of Toronto ended in 1858, and the dioceses of Montreal, Huron, and Ontario finally became self-supporting in the early 1880s. The dioceses of Fredericton and Nova Scotia, however, continued to receive support into the first decade of the 20th century, the diocese of Quebec until 1900, and Newfoundland until 1922.

During his visit in 1849 Hawkins was careful to consult the bishops on matters of missionary policy, beginning with George Jehoshaphat MOUNTAIN at Quebec. The two men discussed with Governor General Lord Elgin [BRUCE] the establishment of the new diocese of Montreal. Elgin asked Hawkins to be the first bishop of the projected diocese, but he refused the offer. From Montreal Hawkins proceeded to Kingston, where on 19 August he took part in a large service in which 136 persons were confirmed and 12 deacons and five priests ordained by Bishop John STRACHAN. In Toronto he was hospitably entertained by Strachan, whom he much respected. Hawkins in London frequently sought support among British politicians for measures concerning education and the clergy reserves which Strachan and the Anglican church in Canada desired. Writing about his visit, Hawkins observed:

"We went over again the perennial question of the Clergy Reserves – his Lordship lays down his arms and surrenders." Two years later Hawkins assisted Strachan in founding Trinity College by donating £2,000 in SPG funds and seven and one half acres of valuable land. He also encouraged Strachan to call a synod with lay representation in order to strengthen the Canadian church which, with the achievement of responsible government in Canada, could no longer rely on friends in London to protect its interests.

Hawkins went next to Niagara Falls, which greatly impressed him, journeyed to Detroit and Sarnia, then turned east again to Toronto, Kingston, and Montreal, visiting several SPG missions on the way. He went to Bytown (Ottawa) and afterwards took a tour through the Eastern Townships, spending a short time at Bishop's College, Lennoxville. From Quebec he proceeded to Rivière-du-Loup; he thought the SPG's yearly donation of £100 there could be better used elsewhere, since "next to nothing is doing at this place." At Fredericton he stayed for a week with Bishop John Medley, who that same year stated there would be only "12 missions out of 40 which would support a Clergyman in common decency" if the society abandoned its aid to his diocese. A call at Saint John was followed by a short visit to Bishop John Inglis* near Windsor, Nova Scotia. Hawkins then returned to England. He visited Toronto again in 1853.

During his years with the SPG Hawkins edited a number of small publications with the general title *The church in the colonies*. Several of these tell in great detail about the journeys of Bishop Edward Feild* of Newfoundland with whom Hawkins was on intimate terms. Others relate the travels of bishops Inglis, Medley, Mountain, and Strachan. All are of great historical interest. Hawkins also edited the series *Missions to the heathen*; two of its numbers dealt with F. A. O'Meara*'s Indian missions on Lake Huron. He directed the publication in 1844 of the *Colonial church atlas* which included maps of Canadian dioceses. He also wrote histories of the dioceses of Quebec, Toronto, and Fredericton. A number of other historical, biblical, and devotional works came from his pen.

The quarter century during which Hawkins served the SPG was a period of unprecedented expansion. Voluntary subscriptions rose from £16,557 in 1838 to £91,703 in 1864, and the number of overseas dioceses increased from 8 to 47. In both 1838 and 1863 the SPG spent approximately one-third of its income on British North American missions. After Hawkins' death a writer in the London *Guardian* eulogized him for his

tact, judgement, breadth of mind, and absence of party feeling, and concluded: "He was one of those men who do unseen much of the real work of life." A recent historian of the SPG writes of him as perhaps the greatest secretary that the society has ever had; certainly no English churchman made a greater impact on Anglican development in eastern Canada from 1838 to 1864.

T. R. MILLMAN and J. L. H. HENDERSON

Ernest Hawkins was the author of *Annals of the diocese of Fredericton* (London, 1847), *Annals of the diocese of Toronto* (London, 1848), *Annals of the diocese of Quebec* (London, 1849), *Historical notices of the Church of England in the North American colonies previous to the independence of the United States . . .* (London, 1845), and editor of *Documents relative to the erection and endowment of additional bishoprics in the colonies; with a short historical preface* (London, 1844). USPG, Hawkins papers. *Church*, 1, 15 Sept. 1853. *Guardian* (London), 7, 14 Oct. 1868. Soc. for the Propagation of the Gospel in Foreign Parts, *Report* (London), 1869. *DNB*. W. F. France, *The oversea episcopate; centenary history of the Colonial Bishoprics Fund, 1841–1941* (Westminster, Eng., [1941?]). H. P. Thompson, *Into all lands; the history of the Society for the Propagation of the Gospel in Foreign Parts, 1701–1950* (London, 1951), 111, 154.

HAYES (Hays), MOSES JUDAH, businessman and office-holder; b. 1799 in Montreal, only son of Andrew Hayes and Abigail David; d. 12 Nov. 1861 in Montreal.

Moses Judah Hayes' father, a New York City merchant freeman of Dutch origin, moved to Montreal around the year 1763. He rapidly established himself as a successful merchant and a prominent member of the nascent Jewish community centred around the 'Shearith Israel Synagogue. Moses, though following faithfully his family's mercantile vocation and religious obligations, possessed a keener interest in public office and civic affairs.

In his early years Hayes held a clerkship in the Royal Engineers' Office which he shortly resigned to devote more time to his family's business interests. Although he possessed considerable valuable city real estate partly inherited from his David relatives, and served as a director of several corporations, notably Joseph Masson*'s gas company and the Montreal Provident and Savings Bank, fortune seemed to escape his grasp. In 1832, for example, he launched a company, in which he and his brother-in-law Isaac Valentine of Trois-Rivières were the major shareholders, to purchase the Montreal waterworks and city baths from Thomas Porteous for

Hayes

the sum of £60,000. Hayes, despite major improvements in the system, replacing the four-inch piping with ten-inch piping and installing a more powerful steam pumping engine, failed to improve this company's troubled business record. In 1845, after several years of public agitation, Hayes readily sold the waterworks to the City of Montreal for £50,000. The failure in 1848 of the Montreal Provident and Savings Bank from mismanagement, and a depreciation of stocks, securities, and real estate, complicated his business affairs since he, as managing director from February 1845 to April 1846, had borrowed from it extensively. From 1848 to 1852, a period of depressed conditions generally, the Bank of Montreal issued to Hayes repeated protests for the non-payment of loans he had endorsed. Hayes, however, was far from destitute. Soon after the sale of the waterworks, he had opened an elegant hotel and theatre on his valuable property in Dalhousie Square, to replace the Molson Theatre demolished in 1845. Hayes House, a four-storey stone structure with a theatre in the back, was administered by George F. Pope, the former manager of Donegana's Hotel. Winter entertainment featured a German orchestra and Viennese dances. But in 1849, following the burning of the Parliament Building, Hayes did not hesitate to rent the building to the parliament of the United Canadas on a six-month lease at £125 per month. Three years later during the great fire of 1852 Hayes House itself burned to the ground, and Hayes (his wife, Abigail Levy, having died in 1840 leaving him with five children) lived the rest of his life in a boarding house.

Hayes, a strong man "of restless vigour and energy," reaped greater rewards from his community service and civic endeavours. Throughout his life he gave time and resources for the betterment of the Jewish community. In 1826 Hayes and Benjamin Hart* initiated the drive which gave the Shearith Israel congregation a new synagogue in 1838. He served as councillor and president of his congregation and in 1847 helped establish the Hebrew Philanthropic Society.

Hayes' public activities, however, ranged well beyond his religious community. A member of the masonic Provincial Grand Lodge with the office of sword bearer, he also belonged to the Montreal Mechanics' Institute, serving it for several years as recording secretary, and the County of Montreal Agricultural Society, being president from 1846 to 1851.

Hayes' active participation in the civic life of the city helped establish the right of Jewish Canadians to public office. In August 1837 Hayes and Benjamin Hart, both quiet but firm friends of the government and the Montreal Tory merchants, accepted appointment as justices of the peace, the first Jewish Canadians to hold the post; Hayes retained it until his death. In 1849 the city named him to the Central Board of Health. Hayes' reputation for justice and fair play led to his appointment in 1854 as city police chief with the rank of captain and control over some 100 constables, a far from comfortable post in this era of religious and ethnic strife. Nevertheless he performed his difficult duties with apparent success.

Moses Judah Hayes died, from a heart attack, on 12 Nov. 1861. He had earned, despite his unfortunate business record, the respect and confidence of his community, and had helped establish the right of men of his religious faith to public office.

CARMAN MILLER

ANQ-M, État civil, Spanish and Portuguese Synagogue (Montreal), 1840–62; Greffe de J. C. Griffin, 4 août 1846, 17 nov. 1847, 30 mai, 27 sept. 1848, 10 avril, 8, 22, 29 juin, 17 nov. 1849, 5 févr., 17 juill. 1850, 17 nov. 1851. Atwater Library Archives (Montreal), minute books of the Mechanics' Institute of Montreal, 7 July 1829. AVM, Procès-verbaux de conseil municipal, 19 janv. 1844. Can., Prov. of, Legislative Assembly, *Journals*, 1850, I, app.A; 1851, I, app.Q. "Extracts from the register kept by the prothonotary of His Majesty's Court of the King's Bench, for the district of Montreal," *Canadian Jewish Archives* (Montreal), I (1955), no.1, 3. *Montreal Daily Star*, 30 Dec. 1896. *Montreal Gazette*, 23 Nov. 1825, 3 Dec. 1831, 13 Nov. 1861. *Montreal Transcript*, 1 March 1845. *Pilot* (Montreal), 15 Nov. 1861. *Quebec Gazette*, 3 Jan. 1833. *Alphabetical list of merchants, traders, and housekeepers in Montreal* (Doige). Canada directory, 1851, 1857–58. *Montreal directory, 1849*, 357. *Montreal pocket almanac . . .* (Montreal), 1849–50.

Camille Bertrand, *Histoire de Montréal* (2v., Paris et Montréal, 1935–42), II, 74. Kathleen Jenkins, *Montreal, island city of the St Lawrence* (New York, 1966). [John] Richardson, *Eight years in Canada; embracing a review of the administrations of lords Durham and Sydenham, Sir Chas. Bagot and Lord Metcalfe, and including numerous interesting letters from Lord Durham, Mr. Chas. Buller, and other well-known public characters* (Montreal, 1847). Rumilly, *Hist. de Montréal*, II, 317. B. G. Sack, *History of the Jews in Canada*, trans. Ralph Novek [and ed. Maynard Gertler] ([2nd ed.], Montreal, 1964), 132. F. C. Smith, *The Montreal water works* (Montreal, 1913). F. W. Terrill, *A chronology of Montreal and of Canada from A.D. 1752 to A.D. 1893, including commercial statistics, historical sketches of commercial corporations and firms and advertisements . . .* (Montreal, 1893), 83, 115. F.-J. Audet, "1842," *Cahiers des Dix*, 7 (1942), 244. Gérard Malchelosse, "Les Juifs dans l'histoire canadienne," *Cahiers des Dix*, 4 (1939), 184. Léon Trépanier, "C'est un Israëlite qui a occupé le plus longtemps le poste de chef de police de la ville de Montréal," *La Patrie* (Montréal), 2 avril 1950.

HEAD, Sir EDMUND WALKER, colonial administrator; b. 16 Feb. 1805 at Wiarton Place, near Maidstone, England, son of Sir John Head and Jane Walker; m. 27 Nov. 1838 Anna Maria Yorke and they had three children; d. 28 Jan. 1868 at London, England.

Edmund Walker Head's grandfather had immigrated to South Carolina but after losing his holdings as a loyalist sympathizer during the American revolution he returned to England. Edmund's father held an Essex living for many years. Edmund himself received his schooling at Winchester, and in 1823 entered Oriel College, Oxford, as a fellow-commoner. He took his BA in 1827. For two years he travelled on the Continent, then became in 1830 a fellow of Merton College, Oxford, where he was lecturer in classics and held various offices. During the next few years he continued his travels, in Italy, Spain, and Germany, an experience which gave him a foundation for his later writing on European art and literature; he was also to become one of the most accomplished linguists and philologists of his generation. In 1836, while retaining his fellowship and presumably because of financial reverses in his father's family, he began his civil career. He was named an assistant Poor Law commissioner, his area being the west of England and a part of Wales. After his marriage in 1838 he resigned his college fellowship according to the rules of the university. Earlier that year Head had succeeded his father as 8th, and last, baronet.

In 1840 Head was promoted assistant Poor Law commissioner for the metropolitan area of London and late in 1841 was appointed one of three chief commissioners under the Poor Law Act of 1834. Resident in London, he continued his literary pursuits, especially a work on schools of European painting which was published in three volumes from 1846 to 1854. When the Poor Law Act lapsed in 1847, Head lost his emolument of £2,000 and in compensation he was offered an appointment as lieutenant governor of New Brunswick at £3,000, succeeding Sir William MacBean COLEBROOKE. He assumed this post on 11 April 1848, in Fredericton, having brought with him his family and a private secretary, Richard Theodore PENNEFATHER.

It had been apparent at the time of Head's appointment that the Colonial Office was concerned to implement in New Brunswick a considerable advance towards "Responsible Government," in particular some measure of ministerial accountability. Its policy of requiring the maintenance of confidence in the Executive Council by a majority of the elected members of the legislature was known and in part implemented in Canada and Nova Scotia, but in the confused political state and frontier society of New Brunswick there had been no real opportunity for principles to become incorporated into practice. Thus a new governor in New Brunswick still had to be prepared to direct as well as to invite advice, to instil vigour in administration as well as to counsel prudence in the management of resources, and to encourage self-reliance as an antidote to the tendency of blaming all economic evils on the home government. In a province of 200,000 inhabitants, widely separated by geography and by patterns of settlement and commercial development, the new governor had his work cut out for him.

On 20 May 1848 Head formed what has been described as the first "responsible" government in New Brunswick. He retained in the Executive Council two previous members, Edward Barron Chandler* and Robert Leonard Hazen*, and continued William Boyd KINNEAR as solicitor general; he added Lemuel Allan Wilmot* as attorney general, John Richard PARTELOW as provincial secretary, and Charles Fisher*, among others. In a situation without recognized "parties" Hazen had been the ostensible leader in the assembly, as Chandler had been in the Legislative Council. Wilmot and Fisher were regarded as "reformers"; Partelow had been mayor of Saint John, and was noted for his skills in political "management." Characteristically, Head now referred to the council a host of petty grievances of a kind previously left to the governor and encouraged members to draw up considered proposals for recommendation to him. He summed up his position on 21 July 1849 thus: "A Governor's power is mainly that nothing can be done without him."

One of the main problems of the colony in 1848–49 was the economic necessity of regaining some balance between its speculative lumber trade and the until then booming shipbuilding enterprises, on the one side, and its neglected agriculture and its fisheries on the other. Head welcomed the evidences of interprovincial cooperation which both led to and flowed from a conference on fisheries at Halifax in 1849. The most attractive solutions to pressing economic problems, however, appeared to be threefold: railways, reciprocity with, or annexation to the United States. If a railway could be constructed between Halifax and Quebec, employment would

Head

rise and immigration, especially from Britain, would be encouraged. Following the report of a survey, various proposals were made involving the home government as guarantor for the interest on loans needed for its construction; the home government was unwilling, however, to enter into any such arrangement, and so between 1849 and 1851 the negotiations virtually came to a standstill. Various promoters in British North America, Joseph Howe* a prime enthusiast among them, overstated their case by making it appear that Britain owed something to the North American provinces in compensation for the removal of their preferred entry into British markets in 1849. To the threats of annexation which were heard in 1849 Head provided a measured answer in an important dispatch to Lord Grey on 15 September: "The words 'annexation' or 'independence' are heard as subjects for discussion in the mouths of persons whose loyalty was their peculiar pride. . . . 'Annexation' for the most part represents nothing but the desire of access to the markets of the United States & 'independence' expresses a feeling that . . . the connection is not valued by the Mother Country." The opening of markets came eventually by reciprocity in trade with the United States established by the treaty of 1854 embracing Canada and the neighbouring provinces. As early as 1849 it became apparent that participation by the United States was predicated on opening the North Atlantic fishing grounds to American fishermen, but the advantages of reciprocity were generally held to outweigh any temporary disadvantages. Specific New Brunswick interests were, however, advanced meanwhile by free trade with Nova Scotia in 1848 and by Head's advocacy of a uniform British North American currency in silver.

One of the consequences of economic stresses and of agitation over railways, fisheries, and reciprocity was a stirring of interest in some closer union of the British North American provinces. Writing to Colonial Secretary Lord Grey in March 1849, Head had tried to moderate the impact of some of the language used in the legislature expressing disappointment at the failure of the railway proposals: "[The] depression of our material interests and the want of importance implied in a diminished consciousness of identity with the Mother Country have naturally directed the eyes of stirring and intelligent men to some source of colonial importance which may compensate for these losses, and thus it is that the notion of an union of the British North American Colonies has embodied itself. . . ." This line of thought was further developed in a lengthy memorandum written some time during the winter of 1850–51. Head was to write, more than once, that separation from Britain was not an inevitable consequence of progress in democratic government. His incisive summary of the basic requirements of federalism for Canada was linked with the vision of a new nation which should extend from sea to sea, in which the forms and the substance of the British constitution should come to maturity, and in which the inhabitants should "stand in conscious strength and in the full equipment of self-government as a free people bound by the ties of gratitude and affection." It seems clear that Head's interest in a federal structure, no doubt whetted and strengthened by discussions with Lord Elgin [BRUCE] in 1850, remained a steady and intriguing concern although he was to vary his opinion of its practicality from time to time.

In 1850 Head had to face the problem of appointing a successor to Chief Justice Ward Chipman* and the event underlined how little cohesiveness there was among members of the Executive Council, as well as the extent to which the lieutenant governor had still to rely on his own responsibility. When no unanimous expression of opinion came from the council, Head took the matter into his own hands. Having apparently ascertained that Chandler, leader in the Legislative Council, was less set on receiving the office than he had earlier suggested, Head recommended that James Carter*, the senior puisne judge, be named chief justice and that Lemuel Allan Wilmot be appointed to the bench. It is known that Head did not further consult the Executive Council about these appointments, nor inform it until after Lord Grey had approved, and Carter and Wilmot had accepted, the appointments. Some local animosity resulted, and in 1851 an attempt was made by the six members from Saint John to bring down the government by combining criticism of the governor's conduct with an expression of lack of confidence in the council. But the tactic did not succeed; only one member of the council resigned, Charles Fisher, who had in any case failed of re-election to the legislature in 1850, and at the end of his calculated gamble Head was able to bring into the council two of the "dissidents," Robert Duncan Wilmot* and John Hamilton Gray*. His assessment of the degree to which public feeling was agitated, and of the necessary extent of his responsibility as governor in a matter he insisted must be dealt with on judicial and not on partisan political grounds, turned out to be remarkably accurate.

It was characteristic that, the immediate political storm having abated, Head seized the opportunity to outline a legislative programme for deliberate consideration during 1851. It embraced proper procedure for the initiation of money votes, proper registration of voters, county authority for certain county requirements, approaches to an elective legislative council, commutation of judges' fees as a charge on the civil list, better regulation of the common schools, and the appointment of a statutory commission to consider changes in legal procedure for readier access to the courts. Some enabling legislation resulted.

Head also began in New Brunswick the encouragement of public education and the arts for which he was distinguished all his life. He brought an old friend, the geologist Sir Charles Lyell, and Professor James Finlay Weir Johnston* of Durham, an agricultural scientist, to the province to give public lectures. He secured the appointment of a commission of inquiry for King's College, Fredericton, where in 1850 there were more professors than students, and a meagre course of studies largely in the classics. Two of the commissioners were Egerton Ryerson*, superintendent of education for Canada West, and John William Dawson*, then superintendent of education in Nova Scotia and later principal of McGill University [see Edwin Jacob]. The governor gave evidence before the commission based on his experience in the University of Oxford and his conviction that means to study the sciences, medicine, and law were needed for the colony.

Lord Grey had stated in 1851 that Head's appointment "was the best hit he had made since he had been in office." No doubt such an assessment lay behind the Duke of Newcastle's decision to appoint him governor general in succession to Lord Elgin. The latter may indeed have proposed Head as his successor. Head had declined an offer of Guiana, as he was in 1864 to decline Ceylon, ostensibly on grounds of Lady Head's health, but he accepted Canada with alacrity, and travelled from Fredericton to Quebec without returning to England. He was sworn in on 19 Dec. 1854.

In the larger colonial arena of Canada the governor's initiative was less obvious – indeed Head encouraged the practice by which he did not as a matter of course attend meetings of his Executive Council – but the practical problems were no less constant. From 1854 onward the permanency of the union of the Canadas stood in some doubt. Economically, the advantages of the Reciprocity Treaty in part offset the effects of the loss of protected entry into British markets, but there was continuing unrest as a sequel to many unwise speculations, both public and private, for

example in the timber trade, flour milling, railway shares, and some bank stocks, all of which, together with general business activity, had declined between 1847 and 1849 and were slow in recovering. Politically, there was uneasiness about the possibility of a legislative majority in one province of the union imposing some measure on the other province. The convention of requiring a double majority was in fact threatening to imperil the union itself. Sir Allan Napier MacNab's days as leader were numbered but he had declined to retire voluntarily and the governor did not want publicly to disavow him. In his own words, Head "sat still," and in May 1856 when three members of the council, including John A. Macdonald*, resigned, ostensibly because there was a majority of Upper Canadian members against them, the governor used the occasion to reconstitute the government. The new administration of Macdonald and Étienne-Paschal Taché had to repudiate the "obnoxious dictum" of double majority although the concern about it did not die. It may be said that the real emergence of party government dates from the disappearance of MacNab, as in 1856 moderate Conservative John A. Macdonald took over from him and began to make common cause with George-Étienne Cartier* in Canada East; George Brown* headed a Reform persuasion which discovered affinities with some of the Rouges, chiefly led by Antoine-Aimé Dorion*. But party organization of itself could not avail against the crippling effects of the "double majority," nor did ministerial coalitions have any stability until 1864, after Head's time.

It was federation, however, of which Head was to be the most eloquent single advocate, which would in the end provide the basis for effective political cooperation. The Colonial Office might say, drily, in 1858, that no difficulties had arisen for which federation was an obvious solution; they thought of it as a "device chiefly favoured by politicians." Head attempted to demonstrate that so far from being an "abstract" question it was an intensely practical matter, and a means of giving a proper sense of importance to the queen's subjects in British North America. He regarded federation as a question on which the duty and interest of Britain seemed to coincide; and what the Colonial Office implacably regarded as "a barren symmetry" in 1858, Head continued to champion as the condition of "something like a national existence" (a phrase used by Lord Durham [Lambton*]).

Head's strongest advocacy came after he had analysed the practicability and possible consequences of a lesser union of the three Maritime provinces. In writing to the colonial secretary, Henry Labouchere, in September 1856 he had said that knowledge and experience had changed his belief in the practicability of a legislative union of Canada with the three "lower colonies." In such a union, he added, the "process" would be a long one, and he could have "no personal interest" in the matter. In London the following year (July 1857) he wrote again to Labouchere that a legislative union of the three lower provinces would be "more practicable" than a federal union with Canada, but that the lesser union "would not in any way prejudice the future consideration of a more extensive union." He remained flexible and appears never to have given up wholly the idea of a federal union of all the British North American provinces. When it came forward again it was in character that Head should also outline the parliamentary mechanism for achieving it: the queen's sanction of the principle, then a conference of provincial delegates whose working conclusions should be incorporated into a statute of the parliament at Westminster. But the content was intended to be Canadian, originating in British North America, and it was not contemplated that there should be interference or dictation from London.

Head's advocacy of federation was hastened and crystallized by two developments: speculation about the future of the Hudson's Bay Company territories west of the Great Lakes and the choice of a capital for the Province of Canada. By diligent study from 1856 on he learned a good deal about the extent and resources of that vast area at a time when the Colonial Office was imperfectly informed and even the London officers of the HBC were hazy about administrative details. He was also a correspondent of Edward ELLICE, a leading figure in the company. In the early part of 1857, probably following discussions in Toronto with Robert Lowe, vice-president of the Board of Trade, Head prepared an extensive memorandum on the future of the company's territories and the steps by which some of the more accessible parts of them might be politically linked with Canada and opened up for settlement. Head was in London in 1857 when the select committee on the HBC was deliberating, and there was a considerable resemblance between his known views and the final conclusions of the committee. Its report identified the Red River and Saskatchewan areas as suitable areas for early settlement, foreshadowed arrangements for local government, and urged the cession of designated areas to Canada "on equitable principles."

The political crisis sparked by the question of the capital of the Province of Canada, which had had a migratory seat of government for several years, began in March 1857 when both houses of the Canadian legislature addressed the queen asking her to exercise her royal prerogative and choose "some certain place" for the capital. The governor invited the five principal cities (Kingston, Montreal, Ottawa, Quebec, and Toronto) to send in statements of their claims. Publicly Head said it would be inappropriate for him to appear to offer any advice on behalf of the Executive Council on a matter specifically referred to the queen's discretion. Privately, he wrote a confidential memorandum coming down strongly on the side of Ottawa, albeit as the least of several evils, and there seems little doubt that it was on the strength of this representation that the queen made her choice of Ottawa in late 1857 (Head was in England at the time). Legislative turmoil followed in 1858: there were 14 separate divisions before Ottawa was confirmed. Also in the meantime the celebrated "double shuffle" occurred.

This sudden change of ministries arose directly out of a vote on the capital question. The government led by Cartier and Macdonald chose it as an occasion to resign. Head sent for George Brown, but warned him, as a governor was constitutionally entitled to do, that because there had been a general election only the year before and there was doubt whether Brown and his colleagues did indeed command the support of a majority in the legislature, he could not give any pledge that he would grant a dissolution if it should be asked for. Brown, Dorion, and their associates were sworn into office but, under the prevailing usage, they thereby forfeited their seats in the house until returned at by-elections. The opposition then carried a vote of no confidence; Brown asked for dissolution, which Head, against the background of his previous warning, refused. Brown's administration thereupon resigned, on the crest of a spate of journalistic venom in the *Globe* which never relaxed during Head's remaining residence in Canada. Cartier was asked by Head to form the government, and he, Macdonald, and their colleagues, by shifting portfolios and adroitly relying on an ingenious interpretation of the relevant act (20 Vict., c.17), avoided the necessity of seeking re-election. The manoeuvre was legal under the existing law, but it looked like sharp practice, and was widely condemned. One of the sequels was a ministry pledge in August 1858 to seek a federal solution of difficulties which were by then widely recognized as inescapable otherwise. Though his own conduct in the events surrounding the double shuffle was hotly questioned on the one side, and publicly and officially vindicated on the other, Head was thereafter less happy in his working relationships, partly because his last months in Canada were also overlaid by painful domestic affliction (the death by drowning of his only son) and recurring ill health.

The governor accompanied the Prince of Wales and the Duke of Newcastle on the royal tour in Canada and the United States in 1860. He travelled to England on leave, and after his return to Quebec in February 1861 expected to be only a caretaker until his successor should arrive. Even so, the strains and tensions within Canada meant continuing attention to some everyday "practical" questions. Reciprocity with the United States had opened the way to many new channels of trade, though the impact upon transportation and communication was not immediately recognized. Yet no authority was prepared to build other than local lines without financial guarantees from Britain, and when the several provinces failed to agree on shared contributions for an intercolonial line, the matter was dropped until the years after Head's departure. He had to live through the economic and political consequences of this uneasy situation.

Head continued to seek improvement in everyday relations with the government of the United States. He had called on President Franklin Pierce in Washington in 1854 during the Crimean War, and was constantly anxious for the effect upon Canada of civil war between the North and the South which he long foresaw. His dispatches of 1860 and interviews during his brief return to London in the autumn of that year pressed upon the home government the urgency of safeguarding Canadian (and British) interests. When civil war did break out in 1861, Head's last year of office, the vexed questions of effective defence for Canada and the public requirement of maintaining a steady neutrality towards the United States were his major preoccupations. He steadfastly refused to sanction public attempts to enlist men in Canada for the Northern armies, or to allow export of arms to any American source.

The changed nature of his office, when Head left it in October 1861, is underlined by the considerable difficulty of the Colonial Office in naming his successor. After a number of refusals, the post was accepted by Viscount Monck*. In September the colonial secretary had written to Head to thank him "for the manner in which you have always co-operated with me for the good of the Colony and the spirit in which you have conducted the business in circumstances which whilst they render the Governor but little dependent on the Secretary of State enable him to keep that Functionary in a state of constant effervescence if he is either too much afraid of responsibility or too little inclined to consult the home authorities." After his return to England Head made one brief essay into politics by contesting, unsuccessfully, an election in the Yorkshire riding of Pontefract. In April 1862 he was appointed one of the three unpaid civil service commissioners and served until his death six years later.

On 2 July 1863, however, on the reorganization of the proprietorship of the HBC, Head was elected its governor. The reorganization reflected in part the imagination and driving energy, on both sides of the Atlantic, of Edward William Watkin*, who had visited Canada in 1861 in the interest of bondholders of the Grand Trunk Railway Company, and who now combined this interest with a proposal to build a telegraph line from Halifax to British Columbia and a wagon-road westward from the head of Lake Superior. Watkin saw in the reorganized company an encouragement to his large designs. On the other hand the governor and committee were convinced before the end of 1863 that their interests required some satisfactory definition of the company's rights and responsibilities in its territories under the terms of its charter, even if this involved the creation of new political authorities to deal with increasing settlement and the mounting problems of law and order. Sir Edmund as governor of the HBC was unwilling to proceed as rapidly as Watkin wished. For two months he discussed with the colonial secretary, the Duke of Newcastle, the possible transfer of authority and compensation for the company's territorial and mineral claims. But Newcastle (who may indeed first have suggested Head's governorship to the old HBC proprietors) would not recommend for Head's proposed crown colony on the prairies a basis either of money payments to the HBC or a sharing of land with it. Newcastle left office in mid 1864 and there was no real progress on transfer or compensation until shortly before Head's death in 1868.

Sir Edmund was evidently much at home in the literary world of London of these years. He had been made KCB and a privy councillor in 1857; his colonial service over, Oxford and Cambridge conferred honorary degrees upon him, and he was elected a fellow of the Royal Society. He served as both secretary and treasurer of the Athenæum, the famous literary club. He died suddenly in 1868, of a heart attack, although he had long feared that the mild epilepsy he suffered from might become a threat to his health. He had left many memorials other than his official achievements, among them the architecture of University College, Toronto, in whose design he had taken great interest, and works on art, poetry, the Norse sagas, and philology which he published from 1833 to 1864.

Any assessment of the importance of Head in the office of governor general makes it clear that Head confirmed some enduring characteristics. The queen's representative was not a figurehead; he had (then as later) the right to warn, to guide, to intervene in an emergency such as in 1858. Head had shown discernment about the situation of the Canadas. There are few more eloquent passages in our political literature than his memorandum, written at some time before July 1858: "Gratitude for past indulgence or forbearance is no bond in politics . . . the federal principle – the assumption that two communities holding a sort of quasi independence were going to live together – was implied by the previous giving of equal representation to each. The poison of disunion had been left in the political system, ready at any moment to influence to the utmost the rivalry of race, language and worship which would at any time be kept down only by the greatest tact on the part of the Govt. & the utmost forebearance on the p[ar]t of all. . . ." Yet Head was convinced of the real necessities of Canadian unity. After seven years in the rough and tumble of Canadian politics in the 1850s he could write: "It should never be forgotten that the interests of Upper and Lower Canada are essentially the same. The St. Lawrence as the outlet to the ocean of the vast system of inland lakes is a link which must bind them inseparably together if they are to retain their place as the chief colony of England in America, and to achieve future greatness as the home of a united people."

In these same turbulent years, any alert governor would have had to take account, as Head did, of two slow decisive movements. The first was the continuing education of British political leaders in the meaning of responsible government. The second was the linking together of the lessons of political experience with an innate feeling of self-importance in the minds of British subjects overseas, and the corollary that political leaders would in the long run have to profess disinterested motives and high standards of conduct, and respond with clear administrative vigour.

His own concept of his office developed against a background in which, on many matters, he got no real assistance or guidance from the Colonial Office itself. He, more than any of his predecessors, had to make his own decisions. The Colonial Office once argued that if the home government entirely disapproved of Head's proposals for federation, the governor "would be left with no alternative but to resign his office,

with the effect of increasing greatly the difficulties and embarrassment of Government at home." But that, after all, had been one of the plain implications of responsible government in Canada, and Head knew it as well as anyone in Downing St. This understanding was a positive achievement in the progress of parliamentary government in Canada. The vigour of Head's ideas, the invariable clarity and grace with which he expressed them, his understanding of the physical necessities of government and of those human qualities which make its course run smoothly and swiftly, all added to the stature of his office and to his own claims for affectionate remembrance.

JAMES A. GIBSON

[This biography is based largely on D. G. G. Kerr's study, *Sir Edmund Head, a scholarly governor* (Toronto, 1954), on which the author collaborated, and on the author's dissertation "The life of Sir Edmund Walker Head, baronet" (unpublished PHD thesis, Oxford University, 1938). These works include detailed bibliographies concerning Sir Edmund Walker Head. To them should be added J. A. Gibson, "The Colonial Office view of Canadian federation, 1856–1868," *CHR*, XXXV (1954), 279–313; "The Duke of Newcastle and British North American affairs, 1859–1864," *CHR*, XLIV (1963), 142–56. J.A.G.]

HEAVISIDE, MARY (Lady Love), artist and lithographer; baptized 25 June 1806 in Halifax, N.S., youngest daughter of Thomas Heaviside, a dry goods dealer and later a prosperous lumber merchant, and his wife Elizabeth; fl. 1806–66.

Mary Heaviside was educated in England where she also studied art. On 16 July 1825 she married Lieutenant-Colonel James Frederick Love, who had entered the 52nd Light Infantry in 1804, had fought in the Napoleonic wars at La Coruña and at Waterloo under Sir John COLBORNE, and had come out to New Brunswick as an inspecting field officer of militia. He was stationed in the years 1825–30 at Saint John and St Andrews.

In this period Mary Love apparently developed both her interest and her skill in drawing. In 1830 she executed at least two sketches which were signed "Drawn on stone by M. Love" and lithographed by John B. Pendleton of Boston, Mass., whose firm, established in 1826, had first produced lithographs commercially in the United States. Entitled "A view near St. Andrews, New Brunswick (Chamcook)" and "A view on the St. Croix River, New Brunswick," Mary Love's two lithographs have been described by a modern art historian in the 1960 New Brunswick Museum

Art Bulletin as probably the first lithographs drawn on stone in Canada by a Canadian-born artist. The sketches, charming and sensitively delineated scenes, compare favourably with the work of other artists of the early 19th century.

The *Bulletin* suggests that Pendleton would likely have published a set of at least four sketches, and that the two illustrations used by Joseph Bouchette* in *The British dominions in North America . . .* (2v., London, 1832), which were signed "By a Lady," were Mary Love's work. These, "New Government House, Fredericton, N.B." and "Barracks and Market Square, Fredericton, N.B.," seem to be drawn in the same style as Mrs Love's known sketches. Another unsigned plate in Bouchette's book, "On the Kennebeckasis near St. John," seems attributable to her as well.

The illustrations "by a Lady" in a book of poetry entitled *A peep at the Esquimaux. . . ,* published in London in 1825, have sometimes been attributed to Mrs Love. The drawings were largely based on illustrations by Captain G. F. Lyon in the journal of an Arctic voyage by W. E. Parry* published the year before. Conjectures about the identity of the "Lady" who was their author are unsupported by convincing evidence.

After postings in Great Britain and the Mediterranean Lieutenant-Colonel Love was back in British North America in 1838, when he commanded a column during the rebellion in Lower Canada. He was subsequently commander on the Sarnia frontier from 1838 to 1840. Mary Love, it seems, continued her work as an artist, since H. J. Morgan* quotes a newspaper of the period which stated that she had made finely executed water-colour sketches of the Eastern Townships and other parts of Lower Canada, and expressed the wish that "the fair artist may consent to their being published, when Mrs. Love's taste and genius will be made as manifest to the world as her kindly and graceful manners have been appreciated, wherever she has resided in Canada."

Mary Love's husband was in England once more early in the 1840s. He held various military posts including that of governor of Jersey (1852–56) and was knighted in 1856. Lady Love was in London with him at the time of his death on 13 Jan. 1866. She had no children. Efforts to trace her later life and determine the date of her death through descendants of her sisters Ann Maria, the wife of Archdeacon Robert WILLIS of Halifax, and Jane, the wife of Alexander Wedderburn* of Saint John, have yielded no further information.

PHYLLIS CREIGHTON

The author would like to thank Donald C. Mackay for providing valuable information. St Paul's Anglican Church (Halifax), register of baptisms, 1791–1816 (mfm. at PANS). *Arthur papers* (Sanderson), I, 441–42; II, 219–21, 318, 401; III, 54–55, 64–65, 104. *Gentleman's Magazine*, CCXX, (January–June 1866), 442. Boase, *Modern English biog.* (1965), II, 562. *DNB*. Harper, *Early painters and engravers. Types of Canadian women and of women who have been connected with Canada*, ed. H. J. Morgan (Toronto, 1903). N.B. Museum, *Art Bull.*, ([Saint John]), V, no.1 (September 1960), [10–12]. Judith St John, "A peep at the Esquimaux through early children's books," *Beaver*, outfit 296 (winter 1965), 38–44. *Ottawa Citizen*, 11 Feb. 1963.

HELLIWELL, THOMAS, merchant and forwarder; b. in 1795 or 1796 at Todmorden, Yorkshire, England, eldest son of Thomas Helliwell and Sally Lord; m. first Mary Wilson (d. 1833), by whom he had six children, and secondly Ann Ashworth, by whom he had seven children; d. 9 March 1862 at Toronto, Canada West.

Thomas Helliwell Sr, a small cotton manufacturer, immigrated to Niagara, Upper Canada, in 1818, with his family. His son Thomas remained behind to wind up his father's affairs in Yorkshire. In 1819 Thomas Jr arrived in Drummondville (Niagara Falls) and there operated a store with three of his brothers. In 1821 Thomas Sr with Thomas' help erected a brewery, malt house, and distillery on his 10 acres along the Don River north of York (Toronto). They named the site Todmorden and the area, which also had milling establishments of the Skinner and Eastwood families, became known as the Don Mills. Thomas Jr established himself in York the same year as an agent for the business, which came to include grist and paper mills, as well as the brewery and distillery. From his location at Market Square in York, Thomas purchased grain for the mills, sold its beer and other produce, and expanded the Helliwell property holdings along the waterfront. In 1828 his name was listed among those given town water lots, valuable for wharves and dock storehouses; William Lyon MACKENZIE thought these grants were an attempt to win support for John Beverley ROBINSON, the Tory candidate for York in the election that year. Thomas' brothers, John, Joseph, and William, shared at various times in the operation of the business at Todmorden after the death of their father in 1825; from 1835 until its destruction by fire in 1847 the business was called "Thomas Helliwell and Bro."

Helliwell was involved in civic activities in York. In 1825 he served on a committee which purchased a six-acre public burial place (known

Henderson

as Potter's Field) north of York. He was also the principal signatory of an 1840 petition to Toronto City Council requesting alterations in the plans for market buildings so that the petitioners themselves could build along the Market Square. He was as well a justice of the peace for Toronto.

His occupation is given in 1856 as "forwarder" and his place of business as Helliwell's Wharf. He was probably then an agent for his brothers' businesses: Joseph rebuilt the flour mills at Todmorden, and William established saw and grist mills at Highland Creek, Canada West. At his death in 1862 Thomas Helliwell had been a resident and businessman in Toronto for 40 years and he had contributed to the early commercial development of both the Don Valley and the Toronto waterfront.

DIANNE NEWELL

MTCL, William Helliwell, diary, 15 Feb.–15 July 1833; reminiscences, 1889. PAO, Street (Samuel) papers, 24 Aug. 1853; Toronto City Council papers, petition of Thomas Helliwell *et al.*, 16 March 1840. Todmorden Mills Museum (Toronto), Sarah Helliwell diary, 1 Jan.–14 March 1847. *Town of York, 1815–34* (Firth). *Illustrated historical atlas of the county of York . . .* (Toronto, 1878; repr. 1969). *Toronto directory*, 1833–63. *History of Toronto and county of York. Robertson's landmarks of Toronto*, II, 617, 1035.

HENDERSON, ANDREW, schoolmaster; b. *c.* 1797 in County Fermanagh (Northern Ireland); m. in 1815 Susannah Slack, and they had seven children who survived him; d. 25 April 1869 at Annapolis Royal, N.S.

On Saint Patrick's Day, 1818, the 21-year-old Andrew Henderson, son of an itinerant Methodist preacher, sailed from Ireland for Saint John, N.B., with his 19-year-old wife and their two children. Shortly after their arrival they lost their infant son and were cheated of their savings by relatives. Henderson, with little formal education but a lively mind, tried manual labour on the Saint John wharves, then moved his family to Fredericton. Later he wrote: "I was sometimes engaged with a little school; sometimes mending old shoes and making new ones; sometimes tilling the ground and earning by the sweat of my brow my daily pittance; lastly I was lumbering." In the lumber camps his health collapsed, and in 1820 the family crossed the Bay of Fundy to Annapolis County where Henderson remained for the rest of his life.

Henderson continued studying while teaching, first for three and a half years in Wilmot Township. At that time he also started the first Sunday school in the county. In 1824 he opened the first school in Bridgetown, where he was also secretary-treasurer of the library, an active temperance worker, Sunday school teacher, and lay preacher. He was instrumental in founding the first Methodist church in Bridgetown.

When he moved to Annapolis Royal in 1832, Henderson established a boarding and day school with the help of a generous legislative grant. About 1837, on a 150-acre farm outside the town, he set up Albion Vale Academy, constructing a building, supplying a library of 200–300 volumes and other equipment, and using the large 15-room farm-house as his home and residence for the boarders. These came from a considerable distance – Halifax, Saint John, Bermuda. At one time there were 21 boarders and about 30 day pupils in the school, girls being accepted as day pupils. His older children also taught in the school: George at 14 was licensed to teach English grammar and even at age 11 Eliza taught a class of 11 girls.

In advertising the school in 1838, Henderson emphasized the "pleasant and agreeable" environment for the students, as well as the quality of the education provided: "All branches necessary to form a good English, Mathematical and Commercial Education are here taught, nor are the moral and religious duties neglected." His students were prepared for a variety of occupations, including school-teaching, business, or seafaring. They got their exercise by sawing wood for the many woodboxes.

All was not easy, however. Despite his many letters and petitions to the legislature, the grants were not renewed after a number of years, perhaps because Henderson was a Methodist, or perhaps because another school was opened in Annapolis Royal. In 1847 he sold the farm and school and moved back to Annapolis Royal, where he became postmaster, a storekeeper, and "an able magistrate." He may have returned to schoolmastering at a later date.

His life of unremitting struggle and little material reward brought praise from men like Joseph Howe*, and he was particularly recognized for his judgement about the guidance of his students.

MINERVA TRACY

PANS, MG 5, Annapolis Royal Cemetery inscriptions; RG 14, 45, Albion Vale and Annapolis Academy; Vertical MSS file, Andrew Henderson, Annapolis Academy. *Novascotian*, 25 Sept. 1828, 10 May 1869. W. A. Calnek, *History of the county of Annapolis, including old Port Royal and Acadia, with memoirs of its representatives in the provincial parliament, and biographical and genealogical sketches of its early English settlers and their families*, ed. and completed by A. W. Savary

(Toronto, 1897; repr. Belleville, Ont., 1972). E. R. Coward, *Bridgetown, Nova Scotia; its history to 1900* ([Bridgetown, N.S., 1955]), 75–80. J. F. D. Fry, "350 years of education in Canada's oldest settlement, Annapolis Royal, N.S." (unpublished MED thesis, Acadia University, Wolfville, N.S., 1965), 52. C. I. Perkins, *The romance of old Annapolis Royal, Nova Scotia, Port Royal, 1604* (n.p., 1934; rev. ed., n.p., 1952). T. W. Smith, *History of the Methodist Church within the territories embraced in the late conference of Eastern British America* . . . (2v., Halifax, 1877–90), II. Grace Tomkinson, "An old schoolmaster speaks," *Dal. Rev.*, XIV (1934–35), 33–41.

HEPBURN, JOHN, seaman and Arctic traveller; b. in 1794 at Whitekirk, East Lothian, Scotland; d. on 5 April 1864 at Port Elizabeth (South Africa).

After a little education at the local parish school, John Hepburn spent his early years as a cowherd by the Firth of Forth. In about 1810 he became an apprentice seaman, and he spent the next three years sailing between Newcastle and London. At the end of his apprenticeship, he sailed to North America on a trading vessel, and on the return voyage he was shipwrecked, taken prisoner by an American privateer, and later handed over to the Royal Navy. In 1818 he served as able seaman in the navy under Lieutenant John Franklin*'s command on the brig *Trent* during Captain David Buchan*'s expedition to Spitsbergen. In 1819 he was selected to accompany Franklin, Dr John RICHARDSON, George Back*, and Robert Hood* on an overland expedition to explore the coast eastwards from Coppermine River (Northwest Territories). Although 20 Canadian voyageurs accompanied them, the officers found Hepburn indispensable and by far the most reliable, honest, courageous, and hard working of their subordinates. In 1821, when the party was struggling half-starved from the Arctic coast back to Fort Enterprise, Hepburn, though scarcely any stronger than the rest, tirelessly gathered fuel and the *tripe-de-roche* that served as food when the others felt too weak to do so. At Fort Enterprise only Hepburn and Richardson found strength to keep searching for food and fuel until help arrived, even though Hepburn's limbs were then badly swollen.

On their return to England in 1822, Franklin used his good offices at the Admiralty on Hepburn's behalf. In one recommendation he wrote that Hepburn's conduct "during a period of extreme difficulty and distress was so humane and excellent as to merit the highest promotion that his situation in life entitles him to. . . ." As a result of Franklin's efforts, Hepburn was promoted second master in the navy and received a comfortable situation at Leith, Scotland, in charge of a small ship that supplied naval vessels with stores. Later he was made a warder at Haslar Hospital. He remained in contact with Franklin: mutual respect and the common experience of hardship had given rise to a warm friendship between the humble seaman and his chief. When, in August 1836, Franklin became lieutenant governor of Van Diemen's Land (Tasmania), Hepburn sailed with him. He had, by this time, married, but no details of his marriage are known.

In Van Diemen's Land he first served as superintendent of government house, then as superintendent of the Point Puer convict establishment for boys. Franklin returned to England in 1844, but Hepburn seems to have remained until about 1850. The search for Franklin's missing northwest passage expedition was at its height on his return. Lady Franklin [Jane Griffin*] insisted he take part in her second *Prince Albert* searching expedition: "You must not attempt to say (for I know you always think humbly of your merits) that you are not competent, for we all believe & know that you are." But Hepburn needed no persuading and answered that "there is no employment on earth I should prefer to the forwarding of your amiable views, and I will most readily strain every nerve in my search of my worthy Chief."

Prince Albert, commanded by William Kennedy* and with Hepburn as supercargo, sailed north from Aberdeen on 22 May 1851, and wintered at Batty Bay, Somerset Island. Hepburn had hoped to lead one of the sledging parties in spring 1852 but his health was not equal to the task. His services were therefore rather limited, but he nonetheless won the trust and admiration both of Kennedy and of Joseph-René Bellot*, the second in command. Kennedy gave Hepburn charge of the ship when the sledging parties were out, and Bellot loved to listen to Hepburn's yarns about his earlier days with Franklin.

After the expedition's return home in autumn 1852, Hepburn remained for some years in Britain. Anxious about his health, which had been poor since the expedition of 1819–22 and was further shaken by the second Arctic voyage, he went to the Cape of Good Hope early in 1856 to take up a government appointment. He was ill for many months before his death in 1864.

Of all the hundreds of ordinary seamen who served in the Canadian Arctic during the 19th century, Hepburn was undoubtedly the best known. He was a simple man with little education, yet he won the love and respect of many who were far above his station in life. Franklin's devotion to him is amply illustrated; Lady Franklin, Richardson, Kennedy, Bellot, and others wrote of him with admiration and affection. It was not only courage and endurance in the field that won him such respect. He was humble and almost excessively modest: in Van Diemen's Land, he was rather embarrassed by his elevated status and by Franklin's ambitions for him, and Richardson wrote in 1851: "he always spoke of himself with much diffidence." But, above all, Hepburn's unfailing loyalty and devotion to Franklin commanded admiration. His return to the Canadian Arctic in his old age, "as the best tribute he can render, of his affection for his old commander," was indeed a touching sequel to their long friendship.

CLIVE A. HOLLAND

Scott Polar Research Institute (Cambridge, Eng.), MS 248/106 (letters and notes of Lady Franklin and Sophia Cracroft, January–March 1851), pp.246, 251–53, 269; MS 248/107 (letters and notes of Lady Franklin and Sophia Cracroft, March–May 1851), pp.10, 13, 36, 39, 92, 101; MS 248/463/1 (Sir John Richardson to Sophia Cracroft, 7 April 1851); MS 395 (Sir John Franklin to George Back, 14 Feb. 1835). J.-R. Bellot, *Journal d'un voyage aux mers polaires exécuté à la recherche de sir John Franklin, en 1851 et 1852* (Paris, 1854). John Franklin, *Narrative of a journey to the shores of the polar sea in the years 1819, 20, 21 and 22 . . .* (London, 1823). William Kennedy, *A short narrative of the second voyage of the Prince Albert, in search of Sir John Franklin . . .* (London, 1853), 30–31, 114–15. *Voyages of discovery and research within the Arctic regions, from the year 1818 to the present time . . .* , ed. John Barrow, (New York, 1846), 230, 278. C. R. Markham, *The Arctic navy list; or , a century of Arctic & Antarctic officers, 1773–1873; together with a list of officers of the 1875 expedition and of their services* (London, 1875). K. [E. Pitt] Fitzpatrick, *Sir John Franklin in Tasmania, 1837–1843* (Melbourne, Aust., 1949), 25, 45. H. D. Traill, *The life of Sir John Franklin . . . with maps, portraits, and facsimiles* (London, 1896). F. J. Woodward, *Portrait of Jane: a life of Lady Franklin* (London, 1951), 198, 277–79. "An East Lothian polar explorer," *Haddingtonshire Courier* (Haddington, Scot.), 22 Aug. 1913.

HIANVEU, *dit* **LAFRANCE, FRANÇOIS-XAVIER-STANISLAS.** *See* LAFRANCE

HILTON, JOHN, furniture manufacturer; b. late 1791 or early 1792 in England; m. Elvira Healy (Healey) on 31 Dec. 1816 in Montreal, and they had a large family; d. 19 June 1866 in Montreal. Sons with him in his business were William, John Fisher, and James Henry.

John Hilton seems to have been related to Henry Hilton, a cabinetmaker from England, who was working in Montreal by 1808. (John named two of his sons Henry, both of whom died in infancy, and another James Henry.) By 1820 John Hilton had his own business. Three years later he took James Baird as partner. Hilton and Baird set up in Place d'Armes; Edmond Baird replaced James in 1833. In 1845, when the partnership was dissolved, the business style of Hilton's firm became J. and W. Hilton (John and his son William).

For the next quarter of a century Hilton's was one of the most prestigious furniture establishments in the country. The showrooms alone occupied six floors in the building that Hilton eventually acquired on Rue Saint-Jacques. In 1856 the firm had more than 80 employees – the weekly payroll was then £116 – and a yearly output that was valued at £20,000 to £30,000. What newspapers referred to as the "well known reputation" of the firm was due to the fact that John Hilton, by his own definition, was a man who "would rather do than talk." This craftsman, born in the 18th century, who successfully adapted to the mechanical developments of the Victorian age, summed up his business philosophy at a banquet given him by his workmen in 1864: "I . . . never hesitated to invest all the means in my power in those appliances to labor, so necessary to keeping pace with the requirements of the age." His factory was distinguished by its "numerous engines."

Yet there was still a place for hand work; and here Hilton made an incidental contribution to the history of Canadian literature: he employed the woodcarver-poet Charles Heavysege*, who composed at his workbench and wrote his work down at home. He is even said to have brought Heavysege to Canada from England in 1853. John Reade*, the poet and journalist, saw it as the mistake of Heavysege's life that he left Hilton's employment.

Rich carving in accordance with Victorian taste, fine woods (rosewood, mahogany, black walnut), and fine polishing characterized Hilton's best furniture. It was to be seen in the most fashionable houses: Peter McGill [McCutcheon*], president of the Bank of Montreal, had Hilton furniture; Hugh Allan* furnished the library of his mansion, Ravenscrag, from Hilton's. When the Ottawa Hotel opened on Rue Saint-Jacques, Hilton supplied the furniture. Harriet Beecher Stowe stayed at the hotel and was so struck by its "finely furnished" appearance that she noted it in her published impressions of Montreal.

Hilton was one of those whose furniture represented Canada at the Great Exhibition in London, in 1851. Sir William Logan* records that when Queen Victoria was shown the chairs of another Montreal manufacturer, Reed and Meakins, she had difficulty suppressing a smile of amusement. The quick-witted attendant on duty in the Canadian section hastily explained that Canadian furniture was not intended to compete with English manufactures. Hilton's furniture, however, received favourable notice in overseas journals for ''bold carving'' and a felicitous harmony of design and wood. Moreover, while other Montreal furniture manufacturers of the period were often in reality more importers than manufacturers, Hilton emphasized his own production, attempting to match Canadian furniture against an increasing flood of imports from the United States.

In community as well as business affairs Hilton was a prominent figure. He was one of the original incorporators of the Montreal Mechanics' Institute in 1845. He was also a trustee of St James Street Methodist Church, a generous contributor to its building fund in 1846, and a staunch supporter of other Methodist causes.

After his death in 1866 his sons continued the furniture business, but, with John Hilton gone, it dwindled, and ten years later was out of existence. Several of Hilton's workmen branched out on their own, including James Morice, his one-time foreman, and Frank Smith, another foreman, to whom his association with John Hilton was an advertising asset long after the great warehouse on Saint-Jacques was closed.

John Hilton was to Montreal what the firm of John Jacques* and Robert Hay* was to Toronto. In the transition of a craft to an industry he was an innovator with mechanization and mass production, and the only one of the earlier cabinetmakers of the city to survive the growing demands of industrialization. Indeed he played a major role in establishing furniture-making as an industry of considerable importance for Montreal in Victorian times. In the words of a testimonial presented to him two years before his death, he ''led, rather than followed in the wake of improvement, and . . . acted upon the principle, that the appliances to labor are progressive.''

ELIZABETH COLLARD

ANQ-M, État civil, Anglicans, Christ Church, 20 Dec. 1808; Presbytériens, St Gabriel Street Church, 31 Dec. 1816, 18 Oct. 1817. Archives of the Mount Royal Cemetery Company (Outremont, Que.), register of burials, 10 April 1825, 15 Feb. 1837, 21 June 1866. St James United Church (Montreal), Register of births, marriages, and burials, 19 Aug. 1830, 10 Nov. 1832, 19 June 1866. *Canadian Courant and Montreal Advertiser*, 14 Aug. 1809. *Gazette* (Montreal), 27 Aug. 1833, 21 May 1845, 8 April 1846, 12 April 1861, 30 March 1864, 10 Dec. 1869. *Montreal Herald*, 21 June 1866. *Times and Daily Commercial Advertiser* (Montreal), 23 April 1845. *Great exhibition . . . official descriptive and illustrated catalogue . . .*, ed. Robert Ellis (4v., London, 1851), II, 965–66. *The illustrated exhibitor . . . comprising sketches, by pen and pencil of the principal objects in the Great Exhibition of the industry of all nations, 1851* (London, 1852), 278. *Montreal directory*, 1842–76. [T. M. Gordon], *The Mechanics' Institute of Montreal founded 1840; one hundredth anniversary, 1840–1940* ([Montreal], n.d.), 11. B. J. Harrington, *Life of Sir William E. Logan, Kt., first director of the Geological Survey of Canada* (Montreal, 1883), 271–72. G. E. Jaques, *Chronicles of the St. James St. Methodist Church, Montreal, from the first rise of Methodism in Montreal to the laying of the corner-stone of the new church on St. Catherine Street* (Toronto, 1888), 8, 84, 90. *Montreal business sketches with a description of the city of Montreal, its public buildings and places of interest, and the Grand Trunk works at Point St. Charles, Victoria Bridge, &c., &c.* (Montreal, 1864), 77–81. *A sketch prepared for the celebration of the opening of the Grand Trunk Railway of Canada* (Montreal, 1856). C. M. Whyte-Edgar, *A wreath of Canadian song, containing biographical sketches and numerous selections from deceased Canadian poets* (Toronto, 1910), 35–36. L. J. Burpee, ''Charles Heavysege,'' RSC *Trans.*, 2nd ser., VII (1901), sect.II, 21. Elizabeth Collard, ''Montreal cabinetmakers and chairmakers: 1800–1850,'' *Antiques* (New York), CV (1974), 1132–46.

HOGG, JAMES, poet and journalist; b. 14 Sept. 1800 in Leitrim (Republic of Ireland); d. 12 June 1866 at Fredericton, N.B.

James Hogg arrived in Saint John, N.B., in 1819 after receiving some education in Ireland. By mid 1820s he was employed by Henry Chubb* on the *New Brunswick Courier*, a newspaper that served as an incubator for a number of prominent New Brunswick journalists. There Hogg learned his trade and in the pages of the *Courier* had his first poems printed. In 1825 Chubb issued Hogg's *Poems: religious, moral and sentimental*, a 228-page book containing 67 poems, which was probably, as has been claimed, the first volume of poetry published in New Brunswick.

Some time later Hogg moved to Fredericton and may have tried farming and business for a while. By 1844 he had launched his own newspaper, the *New Brunswick Reporter and Fredericton Advertiser*, to which he devoted the rest of his life. In its pages he emerged as a prominent New Brunswick journalist as well as a respected poet.

Hogg's poetry has mainly curiosity value today, though it was considered to be well above the ordinary in the 19th century. He was invariably linked to James Hogg, the ''Ettrick

Hogg

Shepherd," a distant relative and contemporary, and some of their works have possibly been confused by observers. Hogg's poetry was mostly lyrical, though he did write some narrative verse. "The Hermit of Woodford" in his *Poems*, a typical long tale about the "Lord of Leitrim," is a medieval romance in the style of Sir Walter Scott. His lyrical poems about dreams and women are again imitative, yet they are often attractive in imagery and sentiment. Hogg also wrote odes and elegies, but as W. G. MacFarlane said in 1895: "Every verse of Gray's elegy is a polished gem. Hogg's are gems, but in the rough." Even in his later poems, in the *Reporter* or as pamphlets, Hogg never quite wrote memorable verse, nor did he experiment with themes or forms. Journalism and publishing had become more important to him.

Unlike other newspapers started in the 1840s and 1850s, the *Reporter* survived and became the most successful weekly in the province. Hogg's commitment to responsible government, it was later claimed, was one of his reasons for starting the paper. Throughout the 1840s he backed Charles Fisher* and Lemuel Allan Wilmot* in their fight with the "compact," and when Fisher formed the first Reform government in 1854, Hogg saw the advent of "liberty, progress and true reform." He concurred with the new government's various reforms, especially the financial changes of Samuel Leonard Tilley*, the provincial secretary, which included giving the power to initiate money grants to the executive. Though certainly not a democrat, Hogg approved the limited franchise offered by the Reform Bill of 1855. He championed the move towards a public, non-sectarian school system, but he also showed the anti-Catholicism typical of the day. In 1859, for example, he initiated a prolonged controversy by printing a rumour about the flogging by a Roman Catholic priest of a Northumberland County boy who had read a Protestant Bible. Hogg, recognized as a strong Protestant, had published the *British North American Wesleyan Magazine* from June 1846 to May 1847, and John Medley*, Anglican bishop of Fredericton, had turned to him from 1850 to 1852 to print the *New Brunswick Churchman*. It was probably Hogg's Protestantism that led him to the prohibition movement, for he was a stout defender of Tilley's Prohibition Act of 1855.

Hogg's press served a multiplicity of uses, and that was part of his success. In 1846, for example, he published the *Young Aspirant*, a journal designed exclusively for children, and during the 1850s he printed the *Journal* of the New Brunswick Society for the Encouragement of Agriculture, Home Manufactures, and Commerce.

Newspaper reporting and politics had a rough and ready character about them at the time, and it was the customary partisanship that created the war between Hogg and the *Reporter* on one side and Thomas Hill* and the Fredericton *Head Quarters* on the other. Hill could be both brilliant and vitriolic and he turned both qualities on the Fisher government and Hogg. Hogg was outclassed in the verbal warfare which surrounded the publication of a letter in the *Reporter* on 11 July 1856 questioning Hill's loyalty, but he won in the end: a suit for libel initiated by Hill was decided in Hogg's favour by Judge L. A. Wilmot. On 3 March 1858 Hill resigned from the *Head Quarters*, which declined rapidly, while the influence of Hogg and the *Reporter* grew.

Confederation was to be Hogg's last battle. He had pressed for a British North American union intermittently since the 1840s. Throughout 1864 and 1865, when the union scheme was badly mauled in New Brunswick, the *Reporter* stood firmly with Tilley, its advocate. Not the least of the reasons for the newspaper's support was the Intercolonial Railway, a line Hogg expected to pass through Fredericton. The defeat of confederation in the 1865 election was compared to the coming of spring which "may be delayed for a time by contending elements, but [whose] advent is nevertheless sure and certain." On 12 June 1866, in the midst of the second and ultimately successful confederation election, Hogg unexpectedly died. For some months he had been unwell, and his son Thomas had gradually taken over the management of the *Reporter*. Thomas Hogg continued his father's work until he was tragically killed in a hunting accident on 25 Oct. 1875.

Producing a weekly newspaper had provided Hogg with the luxury of time to clarify his thoughts and freshen his prose. The *New Brunswick Reporter* consequently gave the province moderately responsible journalism during a period of extremes. In a small way he also contributed to the "flowering tradition" in poetry that grew in Fredericton. At his death a fellow newspaperman called Hogg "one of the most able and intelligent editors in the province."

C. M. WALLACE

N.B. Museum, Robert Wilson scrapbook. *Hill v Hogg* (1858), 9 New Brunswick Reports 108. James Hogg, *Poems: religious, moral and sentimental* (Saint John, N.B., 1825). *Morning News* (Saint John, N.B.), 15 June 1866. *Morning Telegraph* (Saint John, N.B.), 16 June

1866. *New Brunswick Courier*, 1820–30. *New Brunswick Reporter and Fredericton Advertiser* (Fredericton), 1844–75, especially 22 June 1866, 3 Nov. 1875. Harper, *Hist. directory.* C. C. James, *A bibliography of Canadian poetry (English)* (Toronto, 1899). W. G. MacFarlane, *New Brunswick bibliography: the books and writers of the province* (Saint John, N.B., 1895). Morgan, *Bibliotheca Canadensis.* Wallace, *Macmillan dictionary.* A. G. Bailey, *Culture and nationality . . .* (Toronto and Montreal, 1972), 44–57. D. R. Jack, "Acadian magazines," RSC *Trans.*, 2nd ser., IX (1903), sect.II, 173–203. W. G. MacFarlane, "New Brunswick authorship, introduction," *Dominion Illustrated* (Montreal), VII (1891), 401–2.

HOGSETT, GEORGE JAMES, lawyer and politician; b. 1820, probably at St John's, Nfld, second son of Aaron Hogsett, high sheriff of Newfoundland; d. 15 June 1869 at St John's.

George James Hogsett was born into a family of some prominence and was educated in Church of England schools. He studied law under William Bickford Row and was called to the bar on 21 Dec. 1846. At his death he was described as the oldest practising barrister in Newfoundland, never having been raised to the silk.

Hogsett was elected to the assembly for Placentia and St Mary's in 1852, and was re-elected in 1855 and 1859. He held the posts of chairman of the Board of Works and, briefly, solicitor general under the Liberal administration of Philip Francis Little*. Upon the retirement of Little from politics in 1858, Hogsett became attorney general under John Kent* and held this appointment until the defeat of the Liberal party in the spring of 1861. He was himself defeated in Harbour Main in 1861, but won in 1865 and held the seat until his death four years later.

Like his father Hogsett was active in the Benevolent Irish Society, becoming secretary in 1855. He must have converted to Roman Catholicism by this time as he was in charge of the society's celebrations for the consecration of the new cathedral in St John's in 1855.

Hogsett gained notoriety in 1861 during the stormy election contest at Harbour Main. The contestants were all Roman Catholics [*see* John Thomas MULLOCK]. The local Catholic clergy, fathers Kyran WALSH and J. O'Connor, actively campaigned for Hogsett and his running mate, Charles Furey, who were also supported by Bishop John DALTON of Harbour Grace. The opposing candidates, Patrick Nowlan and Thomas Byrne, had taken a position independent of the Liberal party in the months before the election and on polling day the supporters of each faction came to blows. Because the 36 men of

Salmon Cove, largely partisans of Hogsett and Furey, were required to vote at Cat's Cove, a centre of opposition strength, Father Walsh led some 250–300 Harbour Main residents to protect them. Violence resulted when the people of Cat's Cove fired upon the crowd with sealing guns, leaving one dead and ten wounded. The Salmon Cove men then retreated to Harbour Main to record their votes. Under pressure from an angry crowd supporting Hogsett and Furey, the returning officer, Patrick Strapp, gave them a certificate of return. The Hugh William Hoyles* government, however, invalidated the Harbour Main returns, and left the assembly to decide the winners.

When Hogsett attempted to take one of the Harbour Main seats in the assembly a few weeks later, he was forcibly removed by the police and thrown into the arms of the huge and sympathetic crowd outside. As news of his ejection from the house spread, the crowd began to attack the property of Hogsett's opponents and to stone the troops who had been called out. Eventually two rioters were killed and one fatally wounded. Hogsett's claim to the Harbour Main seat was ultimately set aside by the assembly. Soon afterward he helped to organize a petition to the queen calling for the removal of Governor Sir Alexander BANNERMAN for his anti-Liberal partisanship and for his dissolution of the assembly. Hogsett failed to win a by-election in St John's in 1861. During the summer of that year he took over the editorship of the St John's *Record.*

When Hogsett ran again in 1865 the important issue was confederation with the other British North American colonies, a move he consistently opposed. He denounced his Liberal colleagues, John Kent and Ambrose Shea*, when they joined the coalition government of Frederic Bowker Terrington Carter*, and he himself became leader of the Liberal rump around which the anti-confederates rallied. He may have weakened his leadership in 1868 when, moved by the economic distress of the colony, he admitted that he would "wish to see any terms brought down by Government and to investigate them . . . [and] that he would like something that would lift the people out of their present degraded state." By the spring of 1869, realizing the continued strength of anti-confederate feeling, he again took a vigorous anti-confederate stand, but the leadership of the party had passed to Thomas Glen*.

Hogsett was one of the ablest debaters and most active members of the assembly. He could with justice boast that he had never given a silent vote. As a convert to Roman Catholicism, he had to contend with the hostility of his former co-religionists, especially such a politician as Hugh Hoyles. But he could take the offensive himself and in the late 1860s did not hesitate to label his former Liberal chiefs as "a set of state paupers and legalized robbers." He never evaded an unpopular stand. When many politicians were courting local votes by their distribution of poor relief, Hogsett urged that relief to the able-bodied poor be reduced and that they be stimulated to self-reliance by supplementing fishing with farming. As economic distress grew in the 1860s, he objected to any increase in the pauper grant of seed potatoes, presumably because they were being eaten rather than planted.

Hogsett seems to have been financially well off, as he claimed he paid the election expenses of Ambrose Shea on several occasions. He was married and at the time of his death left three small children.

ELINOR SENIOR

Nfld., House of Assembly, *Journal*, 1861, app., "Harbor Main election; evidence taken before the select committee appointed to inquire into the contested election for the district of Harbor Main," 59–92; 1866, 69; 1868, 20. *Courier* (St John's), 16 June 1869. *Morning Chronicle* (St John's), 28 Nov. 1865; 2, 9, 16 Feb., 6 March, 16 June 1869. *Patriot* (St John's), 17 March 1866, 13 April 1867, 12 June 1869. *Public Ledger* (St John's), 2 June 1865. *Notable events in the history of Newfoundland: six thousand dates of historical and social happenings* (St John's, 1900), 234. *Centenary volume, Benevolent Irish Society of St. John's, Newfoundland, 1806–1906* (Cork, Ire., [1906?]), 48, 101. Gunn, *Political history of Nfld.* Prowse, *History of Nfld.* (1896), 466, 488. Elinor Senior, "The origin and political activities of the Orange Order in Newfoundland, 1863–1890" (unpublished MA thesis, Memorial University of Newfoundland, St John's, 1959), 27, 38. Frederick Jones, "Bishops in politics: Roman Catholic v Protestant in Newfoundland, 1860–2," *CHR*, LV (1974), 408–21. E.C. Moulton, "Constitutional crisis and civil strife in Newfoundland, February to November 1861," *CHR*, XLVIII (1967), 251–72.

HOLL, JOHN MYRIE, farmer and politician; b. 16 Aug. 1802 in Lambeth, London, England, eldest son of John M. Holl and Ann Lewis; d. 6 April 1869 in London.

John Myrie Holl spent his early life in England where he was educated at Cheam School in Surrey. In 1825 he married Ann, daughter of William Smart, a London silk manufacturer, and they had six sons and one daughter; for about ten years they lived near Bideford, Devon. At age 34, Holl immigrated to Prince Edward Island with his wife and family.

Shortly after his arrival in 1836 Holl purchased over 600 acres of land in Lot 32 near Charlottetown which he called Kenwith after his Bideford home. He had a practical interest in farming and soon became an active member and, by 1855, president of the Royal Agricultural Society. His holdings outside his own farm were marginal; however, between 1850 and 1854 he was involved in extensive land transactions when he acted as one of the trustees of the large estate of Charles Worrell, eventually purchased by the Island government in 1854 [*see* William Henry Pope*].

Lieutenant Governor Sir John Harvey* remarked in 1836 that "Persons of Mr. Holl's class are exactly the description of Emigrant most wanted in this Colony," and after the creation of separate Legislative and Executive councils in 1839, Harvey's successor, Charles Augustus FitzRoy*, appointed Holl to the Legislative Council, describing him as "an independent Gentleman resident in Queen's County entirely unconnected with the Government, or with the Proprietors or Tenantry." Although for several years Holl eluded any party designation, during the 1840s his class background was reflected in his stand on land tenure and responsible government. By 1841 a quasi-feudal system of tenure was clearly evident on the Island with over two-thirds of the land occupied by leaseholders. A radical Escheat party, led by William COOPER, had gained ascendancy in the assembly by advocating forfeiture of unsettled lands and their resale on a freehold basis. Under the influence of the absentee proprietors the Colonial Office rejected as impractical both escheat and the later proposal, a land purchase act authorizing the crown to buy out absentee owners. Holl endorsed the principle of voluntary sale as a settlement of the land question but agreed with a majority of the Legislative Council that the crown and the proprietors should approve any measure passed. A profound respect for property caused Holl in the early 1840s to oppose any legislation tending to interfere with land titles.

The struggle for responsible government was intimately tied to the land tenure question for it was generally understood that free land would be the first objective of a popularly controlled executive. As a landowner Holl might have feared such a change in the constitution; yet in the late 1840s the interpretation of the responsible system on the Island was fluid enough to encompass supporters who might have evaded its literal implementation. Holl voted for the 1847 resolutions favouring responsible government and his appointment to the Executive Council the same year was hailed by Reformers as an endorsement of their cause. As the issue of principle sharpened, however, Holl subscribed to the British view that "time and the natural progress of events" were necessary before the small Island society would have the requisite property, education, and leisure for self-government. But the impatient Liberal majority in the assembly, led by George Coles*, used their newly acquired control of supply to force the issue. In 1851 Holl and the other executive councillors had to resign to make way for a new executive possessing the confidence of the elected majority.

Debate concerning the application of the responsible principle soon brought Holl to the forefront of the conservative forces of Island politics. The first responsible cabinet under Coles' leadership was based on the system whereby departmental heads held their seats in the legislature until they lost the confidence of the house. Slow colonial adjustment to cabinet discipline soon resulted in a Liberal split over a salaries bill which would put public officers above suspicion by replacing fees with fixed salaries. Since the concession of self-government Edward Palmer*, Conservative leader in the assembly, and Holl in the Legislative Council had argued that the independence of the legislature would be better preserved and more responsibility obtained if salaried departmental officers did not hold seats in the legislature. A summer election gave the Conservatives an opportunity to promote non-departmentalism, a policy of administrative and legislative separation with strong American overtones. Coles, already in trouble over high education taxes, lost his appeal to the people and in February 1854 was defeated by a Conservative majority in the assembly. In April 1854, as senior member and leading Conservative in the Legislative Council, Holl became the first Conservative premier under responsible government.

The Holl administration lasted but four months. A large Liberal majority in the appointed Legislative Council fought the Conservatives' major legislation – the Maine liquor law prohibiting sale of alcoholic beverages, an appropriation bill, and a salaried officers' bill excluding government members from departmental office. Siding with the Liberals, Lieutenant Governor Sir Alexander BANNERMAN opposed the Conservative view of the practice of responsible government as un-British and boldly dissolved the assembly on a technicality, against the wishes of his Executive Council. While Palmer fought an election in June, Holl with Thomas Heath HAVILAND represented the Island at a conference in Quebec

on the Reciprocity Treaty under negotiation between Britain and the United States. Coles' return by the enlarged electorate led the Conservatives to resign in July.

Holl's opposition to the extension of democracy and his agency for the Worrell estate increased his identification with the landed interest. His worst fears of popular government seemed to be realized in the new assembly. He saw the 1855 acts compensating tenants for improvements and imposing a tax on the nominal rent of proprietors as a type of class legislation compelling owners of land to sell to the local government under the Land Purchase Act of 1853, a situation he described as "a species of Legislative Robbery." The conviction that "Louis Blanc's Communist Doctrines in so far as P.E. Island is concerned are no longer theory" undoubtedly influenced Holl's decision to return to England in 1855.

In June of that year 300 prominent citizens of the Charlottetown area presented Holl with a farewell address emphasizing his public and private contribution to the community. During 19 years' residency he had supported and led the Auxiliary Bible Society and the Colonial Church Society; he had been a justice of the peace, a commissioner for prison discipline, a member of the Board of Health, and a commissioner for superintending the construction of the Colonial Building (Province House). All shades of the political spectrum acknowledged his judgement and prudence. His conservatism, a personal concern for measured economic and social progress, might have been seen as a positive force in another developing colony. In 19th century Prince Edward Island, however, the overwhelming desire for freehold tenure would not tolerate moderation. Two of Holl's sons remained to farm the Kenwith estate and continued their father's interest in the agricultural improvement of the Island.

MARY K. CULLEN

Useful information was supplied by Mr F.M. Holl in a letter to the DCB, 23 June 1962. PANB, REX/le/1g, Harvey, Letterbook, 28 Oct. 1836 – 18 July 1837, p. 10. PAPEI, P.E.I., Executive Council, Minutes, 1837–55 (mfm. at PAC); Records of land registration, general indexes to 1872. PRO, CO 226/54, 222–27; 226/60, 254–55; 226/71, 566; 226/73, 9–11, 384–85; 226/83, 87–88, 92, 123, 126–29, 141–45, 148, 234–39; 226/84, 217; 226/85, 221, 225–31. P.E.I., Legislative Council, *Journal*, 1840–55. *Examiner* (Charlottetown), 13 Nov. 1847. *Haszard's Gazette* (Charlottetown), 1 Feb., 20 July, 30 April, 4, 11, 18, 21 May, 8 June, 3 Aug., 5 Oct. 1853; 15, 18, 25 Feb., 15, 19, 29 April, 3, 6, 17, 20, 31 May, 7 June, 1, 5, 12 July, 2, 5 Aug., 6 Sept. 1854; 13

Holmes

June 1855. *Islander*, 24 May, 7 June 1844; 5 April 1845; 28 March 1846; 30 April, 12, 19 Nov. 1847; 13 Oct. 1848; 5 July 1850; 28 May 1852; 8 April, 27 May 1853; 17, 24 Feb., 17 March, 21 July 1854; 16 Feb., 15 June 1855. *Royal Gazette* (Charlottetown), 4 Aug. 1840; 30 March, 1 May 1841; 26 March 1844; 25 March 1845; 13, 27 April 1847; 9, 16 May 1848; March 1849; 21 July 1851; 29 March, 3, 5 April 1852; 4 April 1853. *Times* (London), 26 April 1866. *Prince Edward Island almanack . . .* (Charlottetown), 1853. *The Prince Edward Island calendar . . .* (Charlottetown), 1836–37, 1840–41, 1843–45, 1847, 1850–51, 1855. *Canada's smallest province* (Bolger). W. R. Livingston, *Responsible government in Prince Edward Island: a triumph of self-government under the crown* (University of Iowa studies in the social sciences, IX, no.4, Iowa City, 1931). MacKinnon, *Government of P.E.I.*, 61–85. D. C. Harvey, "Dishing the Reformers," RSC *Trans.*, 3rd ser., XXV (1931), sect.II, 37–44.

HOLMES, BENJAMIN, businessman, politician, and public servant; b. 23 April 1794 in Dublin (Republic of Ireland), son of Thomas Holmes and Susanna Scott; m. 5 June 1819 in Montreal Élisabeth, daughter of Dr Daniel Arnoldi* and Élisabeth Franchère, and they had several children; d. 23 May 1865 at Montreal.

In 1797, Thomas Holmes, his wife, and his son Benjamin sailed for Canada. Their ship was subsequently captured by a French frigate and taken as a prize to Cadiz, Spain. The Holmes family, including young Andrew Fernando* born during the detention in Spain, eventually reached Canada in 1801. Little is known of their early life in Montreal, but it is evident that the family enjoyed moderate financial security, if not wealth. At age 18 Benjamin Holmes joined the firm of Henderson, Armour and Company as a clerk, and soon entered the employ of Horatio Gates and Company in the same capacity. However, the War of 1812 interrupted his commercial apprenticeship with Horatio Gates*. Probably influenced by his father's earlier military career, Benjamin joined the Canadian Light Dragoons, receiving a lieutenant's commission on 30 Jan. 1813.

Young Holmes saw action during the Niagara campaign of that year. His adventures terminated abruptly on 3 Oct. 1813 when he was taken prisoner by the advancing American army. Holmes remained confined at Frankfort, Ky, evidently until July 1814 when a general exchange of prisoners of war was effected. He subsequently received, on 8 Aug. 1814, a new commission as ensign with the Canadian Fencibles.

With the return of peace in 1815, Holmes briefly formed a commercial partnership with Benjamin Delisle at Perth, Upper Canada. However, in November 1817 he became a discount clerk with the fledgling Bank of Montreal, thereby commencing "one of the most interesting and most important careers in the early history of Canadian Banking." By 1827 Holmes had risen to the position of cashier (general manager). As the bank's day to day director for virtually the next 20 years, he contributed perhaps more than any other individual to the institution's early development. Often arbitrary and inflexible in his procedures, Holmes' adroit defence of his approach invariably overcame opposition. At the same time, his non-political, uncontroversial public stance was a decided asset during the late 1820s and 1830s when much of the local business community associated with the bank was openly hostile to the rising Patriote party. Nevertheless, with the outbreak of violence in 1837–38, Holmes, as lieutenant-colonel of the battalion of Montreal Light Infantry, actively participated in suppressing the rebellions, and thereby greatly increased his popularity among the Montreal English speaking community.

In the aftermath of the rebellions Holmes accepted public office, being returned on 8 April 1841 from the City of Montreal, together with fellow Tory George MOFFATT, to the first parliament of the united Canadas. During the first session he concerned himself primarily with securing favourable financial legislation, in particular the renewal of the charter of the Bank of Montreal, from which he was on leave of absence. Despite Holmes' reputation as an independent man of unorthodox manner, his unqualified public support, on 19 Sept. 1842, for the newly restructured and largely Reform ministry of Louis-Hippolyte LA FONTAINE and Robert Baldwin* was thoroughly unexpected. "No dealer in prosy speeches," Holmes bluntly explained his conversion: "He . . . had taken his seat in Parliament with prejudice for his guide – the veil had since fallen from his eyes, and he was ready to act cordially with gentlemen of French origin."

The Montreal Tory press might coldly disapprove of Holmes' "ratting," but the Reformers praised his liberalism. During Montreal's municipal elections of 1 Dec. 1842, the first since the city's reincorporation in 1840, Holmes was returned as councillor from the West Ward, and later, in council, elected an alderman, in both instances with the enthusiastic support of the local Reform organization. His term as alderman expired in March 1846.

The value of Holmes' political involvement diminished with the resignation of the La Fontaine–Baldwin government in November

1843, and, the Bank of Montreal having suffered in his absence, he resigned from the assembly on 1 Feb. 1844. As a politician, Holmes had largely ignored the occasional editorial barb in the Tory journals, and, once back in Montreal, he attempted to function routinely as the bank's major administrative figure. In the autumn of 1845, however, his suspension of payments on the estimates of the apparently nearly bankrupt Board of Works was interpreted as a political act by the Conservative administration. Faced with government censure of the bank and personal abuse by the Tory press, Holmes resigned as cashier on 21 Feb. 1846.

Seemingly undaunted, Holmes, on 31 Aug. 1846, formed a partnership with John Young* for produce merchandising and railway promotion. In this politically less sensitive position he was more readily accepted by the local business community, and consequently exerted considerable influence within Reform circles. During the elections of January 1848, Holmes was returned to the assembly, together with the party leader, Louis-Hippolyte La Fontaine, from the City of Montreal. Though disappointed at his omission from the Reform ministry, he actively supported the new government through the agitation over the Rebellion Losses Bill, and then broke with the party in 1849 over the annexation issue. Like fellow liberal Montreal businessmen Luther Hamilton Holton* and Jacob De Witt*, Holmes was more inclined to be Rouge than Reform. He signed the Montreal Annexation Manifesto and, on 12 Dec. 1849, helped to form the local Annexation Association, of which he was elected first vice-president. During the violent municipal election of March 1850, Holmes narrowly captured the West Ward for the annexationists but failed, in council, to win election as mayor.

With the exception of the Montreal mayoral contest of 1860 (he lost by 24 votes to the incumbent Charles-Séraphin Rodier*), Holmes had largely withdrawn from active politics by the mid 1850s. His commercial partnership had expired in December 1849, a victim of his annexationist activities, although his position within the business community had strengthened. An early promoter and vice-president of the St Lawrence and Atlantic Railroad, Holmes became on its amalgamation with the Grand Trunk Railway in July 1853 vice-president of the latter, from which he resigned in 1858. By an unlikely coincidence, he was elected, in November 1853, a director of the Bank of Montreal as well, a position he maintained until his death in 1865. On 23 Dec. 1863, the ministry of John Sandfield Macdonald* and Antoine-Aimé Dorion* be-

lately recognized Holmes' previous political service by appointing him receiver of customs at Montreal. At the time of his death the bitterness that had once marred his public life had long since disappeared.

LORNE STE. CROIX

PAC, MG 30, D62, 16, pp.1–45. *Debates of the Legislative Assembly of United Canada*, II, 101. Hincks, *Reminiscences. La Minerve*, 27 mai 1865. *Montreal Gazette*, 21 July 1814; 24 Sept. 1842; 3 Feb. 1844; 4 March, 14 Sept. 1846; 13 March 1850; 19 July 1853; 24 May 1865. *Montreal Herald*, 24 May 1865. *Montreal Transcript*, 11 Nov. 1841; 24, 27 Sept., 3 Dec. 1842; 23 Feb., 1 April 1843. F.-J. Audet, *Les députés de Montréal*, 245–46. Chapais, *Hist. du Canada.*, V. Denison, *Canada's first bank*, I, 103, 266, 294, 393; II, 3, 22–31, 420. Dent, *Last forty years. Hist. de la corporation de la cité de Montréal*, (Lamothe *et al.*). Monet, *Last cannon shot.* William Weir, *Sixty years in Canada* (Montreal, 1903), 44.

HONORAT, JEAN-BAPTISTE (baptized **Jean-Baptiste-André-Pascal**), priest, Oblate of Mary Immaculate, missionary; b. 18 May 1799 at Aix-en-Provence, France, son of Jacques-Christophe Honorat, candlemaker, and Marie-Thérèse Bremond; d. 23 Dec. 1862 at Notre-Dame de l'Osier (dept of Isère), France.

Jean-Baptiste Honorat belonged to a Catholic family which remained faithful to religion in spite of the Revolution of 1789. His father desired to take him into the family business, but at age 18 he entered the Oblates and was ordained priest in 1821. During his first 20 years as a priest, he lived in close association with the founder of the community, Bishop Charles-Joseph-Eugène de Mazenod, and proved an obedient, almost excessively zealous missionary. As a result, although he had little inclination for administration, he was called upon to occupy important offices. He was fourth assistant general and was superior first (1825–27) of the house of Notre-Dame-du-Laus (dept of Hautes-Alpes), of Nîmes (1827–30), of Marseille (1830–37), and then (1837–41) of Notre-Dame-des-Lumières (dept of Vaucluse) which he founded. On 13 Aug. 1841, in response to the invitation of Bishop Ignace Bourget*, Mazenod entrusted him with the founding of the first Oblate establishment in Canada.

On 2 December Father Honorat arrived at Montreal, with fathers Pierre-Antoine-Adrien Telmon, Jean-Fleury Baudrand, and Lucien-Antoine Lagier*, and the lay brothers Basile Fastray and Pierre-Jean-Louis-François Roux. Two days later Bishop Bourget appointed Hon-

Honorat

orat parish priest of Saint-Hilaire (Mont-Saint-Hilaire), the first base of the Oblates in Canada. The following summer (August 1842), the community moved to Longueuil to be closer to the bishopric of Montreal. As first superior of the Oblates in Canada, Honorat took an active part in setting up Oblate missions in the Montreal region, the Eastern Townships, and the areas of the Ottawa, Saint-Maurice, Saguenay, and Red rivers. Nevertheless, in 1844 Mazenod wanted to entrust the direction of the young, expanding community to a more skilful administrator and a more adaptable leader. Father Honorat bowed willingly to this decision. He handed over his office to his *confrère* and friend Father Joseph-Bruno Guigues*, and became superior of the new Saguenay mission of Saint-Alexis-de-la-Grande-Baie.

On 15 Oct. 1844 Honorat arrived in the Saguenay region, accompanied by fathers Augustin-Médard Bourassa, Pierre Fiset, and Flavien Durocher*. The Oblates' responsibility was to lay the foundations of an organized church in this forest region, which had been opened to settlement only six years earlier. While his missionaries carried on their ministry among the native peoples of this vast area, Honorat endeavoured to organize the religious life of the new settlers by creating parishes and building churches and schools.

The society that was developing in the Saguenay area with a mixture of agriculture and timber as its base had a strong effect on Honorat. Because of its monopoly of lumbering the Price Company was ensured control of the region. The population, poor and still sparse, was under the domination of Peter McLeod*, partner of William PRICE and chief of operations in the region. McLeod, an unbending advocate of Protestantism, represented in Honorat's eyes a grave threat to the Catholics there. Moreover, to him McLeod symbolized economic dictatorship, for not only did the company pay employees with vouchers redeemable in goods in its stores, but it also resorted to intimidation to enslave the population. The ministry of the Oblate superior in the Saguenay rapidly became a social commitment, a struggle against exploitation and poverty. His opposition to McLeod was so violent that the two men barely avoided coming to blows. Honorat, a man of action, resolved to pursue the struggle along another line. In 1846, believing that settlement based on agriculture was the way to protect the population from the monopoly in the lumber trade and to do away with poverty, he founded an agricultural parish, Le Grand-Brûlé (Laterrière). He invested the meagre resources at his disposal

in this "liberating" venture, as he liked to call it.

Laterrière was a veritable financial abyss for the little community and a cause of great irritation among the Quebec diocesan clergy. Several priests who thought the Oblates already occupied too big a place in the Saguenay did not forgive Honorat, a Frenchman, for pushing his action so far, and for compromising the relations of the church with the masters of the region through open conflict. The archbishopric of Quebec, thinking his management overbold, sought his recall. Father Guigues finally yielded to repeated pressure from Quebec. In August 1849 Father Honorat left the Saguenay, leaving behind him an Oblate house in serious difficulty. Lacking financial means, and increasingly isolated, it had to close its doors some time later, to the great relief of champions of clerical-capitalist collusion in the Saguenay.

On his return to Montreal, Father Honorat gave his attention to preaching and spiritual exercises. On 26 July 1850, at Montreal, he founded the Community of the Sisters of St Ann. During the next eight years, Father Honorat was a member of the provincial council, a bursar, and, after a short period as director of the house at Plattsburgh, N.Y., in late 1856 and early 1857 he went to Ottawa as superior of the bishop's palace, the residence of Bishop Guigues. On 27 Oct. 1858 he was recalled to France. He died there four years later, at age 63, following an apoplectic seizure.

Jean-Baptiste Honorat, one of the men responsible for increasing the role played by the Oblates in Canada, is still remembered as a distinctive figure of the Saguenay region in the 19th century. Throughout his life he was an authentic missionary who was more concerned with men than with things.

NORMAND SÉGUIN

AAQ, 71 CD, Oblats de Marie-Immaculée, I. Archives de l'évêché de Chicoutimi (Chicoutimi, Qué.), Paroisse 9, Cote 5, 3, RR. PP. Oblats. Archives générales O.M.I. (Rome), Correspondance Jean-Baptiste Honorat, 1841–1852 (photocopy at AHO). Archives provinciales O.M.I. (Montréal), Ancienne maison, Saguenay, région de Grande-Baie et de la Côte-Nord, 1844–52; Correspondance des autorités ecclésiastiques, Diocèse de Québec, 1844–1904; Correspondance des autorités oblates, Autorités générales, 1848–69; Correspondance des autorités oblates, Procure générale, 1848–92. *Notices nécrologiques des O.M.I.*, I, 69–76. Gaston Carrière, *Hist. des O.M.I.*, I–V; *Planteur d'églises; J.-B. Honorat, oblat de Marie-Immaculée* (Montréal, 1962). J.-P. Simard, "Une fondation pas comme les autres: le Grand-Brûlé," *Protée* (Chicoutimi, Qué.), 1 (décembre 1970), 31–36.

HOOPER, JOHN, printer, teacher, stationer, journalist, and author; b. 1791 in Cornwall, England; d. May 1869 at Saint John, N.B.

Hooper came to Saint John about 1817 as a printer and schoolmaster, eventually becoming proprietor of a bookbinding and stationery business on Market Square. In 1827, in partnership with James Stevenson, he commenced publication of the *British Colonist*. First a literary journal carrying extracts from such British periodicals as *Blackwood's Magazine*, it later acquired the character of a newspaper.

In the spring of 1830 Hooper published an article signed "Hampden" which, according to Attorney General Charles Jeffery Peters*, was "a gross libel on the judges and the whole administration of justice within the province." Written by Thomas Gardner of Fredericton it represented, without offering names, judges, lawyers, sheriffs, and clerks of the courts as being "unjust, cruel and rapacious." Because it appeared at a time of great public hostility to the administration of the crown lands and the customs establishment, Peters despaired of getting a jury that would convict Hooper for libel against authorities. When the case came to trial in January 1831, the judge, Ward Chipman*, directed the jury to find Hooper guilty. Its verdict was guilty of publication without malice and the case was stayed, though the writer of the article was later fined £30. Hooper had conducted his own defence on the principle of freedom of the press, and public opinion supported him.

That Hooper was a firebrand is shown by his letter of a few weeks after the verdict to Henry Chubb*, publisher of the *New Brunswick Courier*, offering a duel for alleged defamation of character in a private quarrel. Yet in 1836 Hooper joined the staff of the *Weekly Chronicle*, an ultra-conservative paper founded that year to defend the unpopular policies of Thomas BAILLIE at the Crown Lands Office; he worked there until it ceased publication in 1860.

W. S. MacNutt

John Hooper wrote *The advantages of emigrating to the British colonies of New Brunswick, Nova Scotia, etc.* . . . (London, 1832); *Emigration to the North American colonies: recommended to the attention of capitalists, agriculturalists, mechanics, and others* . . . (London, 1832); and *Practical information for emigrants including details . . . of the province of New Brunswick* (n.p., 1832). *New Brunswick Courier*, 22 Jan., 9 April 1831. Harper, *Hist. directory*, 49. W. H. Kesterton, *A history of journalism in Canada* (Toronto, 1967). MacNutt, *New Brunswick*, 223, 237–38. J. S. Martell, "The press of the Maritime provinces in the 1830's," *CHR*, XIX (1938), 29.

HOWARD, JAMES SCOTT, public servant; b. 2 Sept. 1798 in Bandon, County Cork (Republic of Ireland), son of John Howard and Mary Scott; m. 8 June 1822 in Fredericton, New Brunswick, Salome, daughter of New Brunswick MLA Archibald McLean*, and they had three children; d. 1 March 1866 in Toronto, Canada West.

James Scott Howard left Ireland in 1819. He settled briefly in Fredericton but moved on to York (Toronto) in 1820. Shortly after his arrival he was appointed to the staff of the York post office. He was later to describe his position as that of "chief and only assistant to . . . [William Allan*] in his respective offices of Postmaster, Collector of Customs, Inspector of Licences, and Treasurer of the [Home] District." When Howard succeeded Allan as postmaster on 2 July 1828, Allan wrote officially that the department was fortunate to have a person so well acquainted with the duties and so faithful in all respects. Thomas STAYNER, who was his chief, consulted him on many postal problems such as franking and the transport of mail through the United States, and also praised his service.

Consequently it was with surprise that Howard found himself removed from his post by Lieutenant Governor Francis Bond Head* on 13 Dec. 1837 during the Upper Canada rebellion. Howard, aware of suspicion against him, had written on 9 December to Charles Berczy*, surveyor of the post office, asking for an investigation. Assured that there was nothing against him except that he had associated too much with "those people," Howard learned late in January 1838 from Stayner that Head suspected him of compliance with the aims and plans of the rebels because he had contact with John and Joseph Lesslie and of having appointed mostly sympathizers with the revolutionary party to the Toronto post office. Head's doubts were reinforced by the fact that Howard did not take arms against the rebels.

In answering these accusations Howard stressed his political neutrality, stating that as postmaster he had never attended a political meeting or voted, and that he had proof of Stayner's commendation of such a course. Nor had he been asked to leave his post and take up arms. Undoubtedly Howard's defence was accurate enough, but Head could neither understand nor tolerate Howard's neutrality; he wanted a zealously loyal man in charge of the post office. In February 1838 the case was brought before Lord Glenelg, the colonial secretary, who consulted both Head and Head's successor in Upper Canada, George Arthur*. Head stood firm; Arthur, though agreeing, obtained a report from the

Huntley

Executive Council in May, signed by Robert Baldwin Sullivan*, Allan, and Augustus BALDWIN, which granted Howard's political neutrality, but upheld Head's action. In the unsettled atmosphere of Upper Canada Glenelg let the matter rest.

There can be little doubt of Howard's neutrality or his loyalty in the years of the rebellion. He may have had some friends with radical leanings, but they only demonstrated his impartiality. He certainly was not in league with William Lyon MACKENZIE, a long-time critic of post office administration, who during the rebellion entered Howard's house, harassed his wife, and commandeered provisions for the rebel troops. Howard was plainly a victim of Head's precipitate action during the turbulence of the rising.

In the years that followed Howard continued his efforts to have himself returned to the post office or to have some recompense made. Nor was his case forgotten by others; in 1840 Francis Hincks* suggested in the *Examiner* that at least the government could have appointed the wronged Howard to the commission established that year to investigate the post office in the Canadas. However, a position was found for Howard in 1842 as treasurer of the Home District. He subsequently became treasurer of the united counties of York and Peel and held this office until his death. He was named to the General Board of Education at its formation by the Common School Act of 1846. When it became the Council of Public Instruction in 1850, Howard continued as a member and served until his death; he was cited for his valuable service, "especially in financial matters during and since the erection of the Toronto Normal School." In 1828 Howard had been appointed to a committee established to superintend the publication of the Wesleyan Methodist *Christian Guardian*. He was treasurer of the Irish Relief Fund in 1847, secretary of the Upper Canada Bible Society from 1846 to 1860, and treasurer of the Upper Canada Tract Society.

MARION BEYEA

MTCL, William Allan papers, 6. PAO, Howard (MacLean) papers; RG 2, B-3. PRO, CO 42/448, 42/454. *Examiner* (Toronto), 4 Nov. 1840. J. S. Howard, *A statement of facts relative to the dismissal of James S. Howard, esq., late postmaster of the city of Toronto, U.C.* (Toronto, 1839). *Town of York, 1815–34* (Firth). Chadwick, *Ontarian families*, II, 188. *Commemorative biographical record, county York*. Dent, *Upper Canadian rebellion*.

HUNTLEY, Sir HENRY VERE (baptized **Henry Veel**), naval officer and colonial administrator; b. 1795 and baptized 29 Nov. 1796, third son of the Reverend Richard Huntley and Ann Webster of Boxwell Court, Gloucestershire, England; d. 7 May 1864 in Santos, Brazil.

Little is known of Henry Vere Huntley's early life except that he entered the British navy at age 14. His formal education was probably limited, although in later years he did indulge a literary bent. Following the Napoleonic wars he remained in the navy and served in many exotic parts of the world, rising to the rank of commander in 1838. After 30 years of distinguished naval experience he became lieutenant governor of the British settlements on the River Gambia in western Africa in 1839.

Huntley's health appears to have suffered from the African climate, and in 1841 he returned to England to accept the lieutenant governorship of Newfoundland. However, the Colonial Office withdrew the offer in favour of Sir John Harvey*, and sent Huntley to Prince Edward Island instead. On 9 October, prior to his departure from England, he was knighted. Five weeks later he arrived in the island colony, which was then absorbed in struggle over the land question. Huntley was sympathetic to the rights of property, and was pleased by the electoral defeat in mid 1842 of the radical Escheators led by William COOPER, who had controlled the assembly for four years. In early 1843 a public meeting at New London declared the government to be conducted "for the benefit of a couple of dozen of land Speculators, their connexions, dependents, and parasites," and gave the resolution to their assemblyman, Duncan MacLean, for publication. Huntley directed that MacLean, whom he had privately described as "most violently revolutionary," be prosecuted for libel against the government. The prosecution was successful, but at Huntley's request sentence was not passed; the case was simply to serve as a warning. However, the Escheators, blocked by the parliamentary process, concentrated their efforts, with some success, on direct action in the countryside, such as preventing evictions and resisting collection of rents. The burning of the home of a Cunard agent in March 1843 caused Huntley to send soldiers to eastern Kings County. These actions, and his friendship with such unpopular landlords and agents as Father John McDonald* and James Horsfield Peters*, firmly identified the governor in the popular mind as a servant of the local Family Compact.

Yet the alliance between Huntley and the Charlottetown oligarchy did not endure. His official correspondence first betrayed reluctant disillusion because of the failure of the Tory-dominated assembly to make adequate provision for the repair of his official residence or to augment his salary. His annual allowance of £1,000 met only about two-thirds of his expenses, and by early 1844 he apparently found it necessary to withdraw his patronage from several, though not all, public organizations. But there was another, larger point of difference, one in which Huntley had the full backing of the Colonial Office: under the leadership of the speaker, Joseph Pope*, the assembly consistently overspent its revenues. Huntley believed this fiscal unorthodoxy to be a demagogic device to cultivate the approval of rural Islanders, whom he considered incapable of appreciating more enlightened policies. On both issues, the maintenance of official dignity and the state of the treasury, the governor believed Pope's majority to be lacking the moral courage to do more than reflect rural prejudices.

An impetuous man, prone to direct and dramatic actions, Huntley decided to make public his views on the necessity of balancing revenues and expenditures. Against Pope's wishes, he included pointed observations on the public debt in his addresses to the assembly in 1845 and 1846 (unaccountably, historians W. Ross Livingston, W. S. MacNutt*, and Wayne E. MacKinnon have interpreted these remarks as references to supposed private debts of Pope). Tension continued to increase over financial questions, and in March 1846 Pope charged in the assembly that Huntley's "underhanded proceedings" were a "degradation" of him as an executive councillor and legislator. Huntley then suspended Pope from the Executive Council for these and related remarks. Pope, with the support of an aroused assembly, appealed to the Colonial Office for reinstatement. Lord Grey, the British Colonial secretary, sustained the appeal and directed that any further proceedings be dropped, not least because they had arisen from words uttered in the assembly. Vindicated, Pope then resigned from the council.

The controversy with the speaker, which generated a staggering volume of correspondence between Charlottetown and London, had also made unbridgeable the gulf between Huntley and the local élite, which supported Pope. The governor sought a new alliance and in April 1847 appointed a leading Reform assemblyman, George Coles*, to Pope's seat on the council. Accepting constitutionally erroneous advice from the majority in the assembly, Huntley required Coles to submit to the unusual procedure of a new election, which he won. But the divisive nature of the appointment was revealed when an influential executive councillor, Colonial Secretary Thomas Heath

HAVILAND, publicly voted against Coles. Pleased to have the new, if limited, leverage of a seat on the council, the Reformers raised petitions for the continuance of Huntley's term beyond six years. Alarmed, the Tories circulated a contrary petition and sent it to London with a three-man delegation, which included Pope and Edward Palmer*, an executive councillor who had resigned explicitly for the purpose. The opposing petitions simply reinforced Grey's conviction that Huntley should be relieved at once. He left for England on 30 Nov. 1847, much to the chagrin of the Reformers.

Huntley appears to have led a rather chequered existence after his departure from the Island. Less than a year later, after being held briefly in jail, he declared insolvency in England. Although he seems to have been in debt prior to his arrival on P.E.I., in court he attributed his financial plight to the insufficiency of his salary as governor. By 1850 he had led a company of miners to California. In the late 1840s and the 1850s he published several pedestrian books on a variety of subjects, including a description of California. At the time of his death in 1864 in Santos, Brazil, he was back in the British overseas service as a consul. He had been married twice: first, on 20 Sept. 1832 to Anne Skinner (d. 1855) and then in 1859 to Miss Drury of Harrow, Middlesex, England. He was survived by at least two sons and a daughter.

Sir Henry Vere Huntley had gone to Prince Edward Island as a career naval officer with nothing in his background to suggest liberal propensities. His early dispatches reveal him as entirely disposed to adopt the views of the local élite. Yet by the conclusion of his tenure he was allied with one of the most militant and progressive reform movements in British North America. He was even advocating what he called responsible government, although his understanding of it seems to have centred on the responsibility of executive councillors to resign when not in harmony with the governor. His conversion to the cause of reform does not appear to have been the product of a slow maturation of convictions. It owed more to his wilful personality, which together with a rigid sense of duty had led to his estrangement from the Island's Family Compact. Once the disaffection became complete, the oligarchy with great vindictiveness waged, in Edward WHELAN's words, "an exterminating war." The strategy of Huntley's new defenders, such as Whelan (who had once called him "the Gambian Crocodile" because of his desire for an increase in salary), was to exploit the split to their own advantage.

Huntley had been placed in an almost impos-

Huot

sible position: between a truculent popular movement and a deeply entrenched oligarchy possessing a greater sense of permanence than any governor. It is difficult to imagine what he could have done to lessen the social tensions which, combined with quarrelsome personalities, made Island politics notoriously bitter and turbulent. Yet, faced with this situation, Huntley did not display remarkable talent or diplomacy. Indeed, because of his excessive sensitivity to slight, his impulsiveness, and, to a considerable extent, his blunders, he became one of the most beleaguered men to occupy government house in Prince Edward Island.

IAN ROSS ROBERTSON

H. V. Huntley's publications include: *California: its gold and its inhabitants* (2v. in 1, London, 1856), also published as *Adventures in California* (London, n.d.); *Observations upon the free trade policy of England, in connexion with the Sugar Act of 1846 . . .* (London, 1849); *Peregrine Scramble; or, thirty years' adventures of a blue jacket* (2v., London, 1849); *Seven years' service on the slave coast of western Africa* (2v., London, 1850).

PAPEI, Central Academy, Minute book, 83–84, 93, 95, 104; H. V. Huntley to Webster Huntley, 10 May 1842 (copy). PRO, CO 226/62–65, 226/67–72, 226/76, especially 226/62, 113–16, 184; 226/63, 337; 226/64, 3–15, 30–31; 226/65, 86–93, 131–36, 139–50, 155, 190–235, 250–56, 260–61; 226/67, 36–43, 192–207, 273–75, 298–305; 226/68, 25–29, 140–47, 161–62, 296, 496–98; 226/69, 90, 100–2, 129–33, 152–94, 287–90, 317–35, 453–54, 479–89, 501–5; 226/70, 104–313; 226/71, 44–45, 61–64, 67–73, 105–6, 148–59, 246–67, 287–376, 420–31, 472–93; 226/72, 56–59, 111–48; 226/76, 234–36. *Elgin-Grey papers* (Doughty), I, 68–69, 72–73; IV, 1375–78. P.E.I., House of Assembly, *Journal*, 1845, 6, 95; 1846, 6, 96–99, 114–17, 123; 1847, 7–8, 145. *Colonial Herald* (Charlottetown), 4 Sept., 13 Nov. 1841. *Constitutionalist* (Charlottetown), 2, 9, 16 May 1846. *Examiner* (Charlottetown), 7, 14, 21 Aug., 2, 16 Oct., 27 Nov., 4, 11 Dec. 1847; 11 Sept. 1848; 12 Feb. 1850; 4 July 1864. *Islander*, 30 June, 7 July 1843; 12 Jan., 29 March, 5 April 1844; 8 Sept. 1848; 1 July 1864. *Palladium* (Charlottetown), 7, 11 Sept., 16 Nov., 14, 28 Dec. 1843; 4, 18 Jan., 7 March, 11, 18 April, 9 May, 28 Dec. 1844. *Ross's Weekly* (Charlottetown), 14 July 1864. *Royal Gazette* (Charlottetown), 16 Nov., 7 Dec. 1841; 14, 28 March 1843; 19 March 1844; 23, 30 Nov., 14 Dec. 1847; 8 Oct. 1850. *DNB*.

W. R. Livingston, *Responsible government in Prince Edward Island: a triumph of self-government under the crown* (University of Iowa studies in the social sciences, IX, no. 4, Iowa City, 1931), 20–36. Peter McCourt, *Biographical sketch of the Honorable Edward Whelan, together with a compilation of his principal speeches; also interesting and instructive addresses to the electors of the second district of King's County, and a brilliant lecture entitled "Eloquence as an art"* (Charlottetown, 1888), 5–8. MacKinnon, *Government of P.E.I.*, 30–31, 40, 49, 73, 78–81, 170. W. E. MacKinnon, *The life of the party: a history of the Liberal party in Prince Edward Island* (Summerside, P.E.I., 1973), 14, 19. J. C. MacMillan, *The history of the Catholic Church in Prince Edward Island from 1835 till 1891* (Quebec, 1913), 45–46. MacNutt, *Atlantic provinces*, 231–34. Robertson, "Religion, politics, and education in P.E.I.," 33–37. W. S. MacNutt, "Political advance and social reform, 1842–1861," *Canada's smallest province* (Bolger), 114–21.

HUOT, MARIE-CATHERINE, *dite* **Sainte-Madeleine,** superior of the Congregation of Notre-Dame; b. 30 April 1791 at L'Ange-Gardien, below Quebec, daughter of Jacques Huot, a farmer, and Catherine Plante; d. 7 Jan. 1869 at Montreal.

Catherine Huot was educated by her mother, who had studied under the sisters of the Congregation of Notre-Dame at Sainte-Famille, Île d'Orléans. As a young girl she learned about the sisters through her mother and formed the desire to join them. After making her profession on 28 Sept. 1809, Catherine Huot, now Sister Sainte-Madeleine, worked in the community at Montreal, then taught from 1812 to 1820 at the missions of Saint-Denis-sur-Richelieu, Quebec, and Rivière-Ouelle. She then returned to Montreal, where she soon was given the institution's most important positions; she carried these responsibilities for 46 years, until her death.

Mother Sainte-Madeleine was superior from 1828 to 1840, 1843 to 1849, and 1855 to 1861; thus she presided over the destinies of the Congregation of Notre-Dame during a period of remarkable development which matched the rhythm of growth of the church at Montreal. The statistics of the community are testimony: in 1828 the congregation numbered only 80 sisters, this limit having been imposed by an episcopal decree of 1698; as a result of the cancelling of this restriction by Bishop Ignace Bourget* in 1843, it counted 459 in 1869. At Montreal, the congregation had only the boarding school of the mother house and the day school of Notre-Dame-des-Victoires in 1828; in 1869 it controlled two boarding schools (Villa-Maria and Mont Sainte-Marie) and four academies (Saint-Denis, Saint-Vincent, Sainte-Anne, and Saint-Patrice), as well as nine schools, which had been founded mainly by the Sulpicians for the children of workmen or Irish immigrants. These schools were originally free, and the sisters went to them "in the morning after mass, by carriage," and returned "in the evening at five o'clock." But the congregation's expansion took it beyond Montreal as far as Rimouski and Baie-Saint-Paul on the shores of the St Lawrence,

Sherbrooke in the Eastern Townships, and Huntingdon; 21 missions were thus founded.

Under Mother Sainte-Madeleine's administration, the congregation prepared the ground for a great missionary advance, thus particularly meeting the needs of Irish Catholics. In 1828, in addition to the mother house, it had only 17 missions, all Francophone, whereas in 1869 there were 68, including five new ones in Ontario, eight in the Maritimes, and five in the United States. Anxious for integration into the communities which accepted them, the sisters agreed at that time to give instruction that was exclusively in English and this decision established the bilingual and bicultural character of the Congregation of Notre-Dame.

The extensive recruitment and rapid expansion of the congregation under Mother Sainte-Madeleine's superiorship were accompanied by the adoption of a new direction in education. The history of the community seems to indicate that since the Conquest the congregation had been intellectually behind the times. The sisters had confined themselves "to watchfulness against the inroads of Protestantism, without seeking, for the glory of religion, to make the Catholic schools more distinctive." They had early begun to teach English, but it was not until 1830 that they extended the programme of secondary studies to almost all branches of knowledge, from grammar, geography, arithmetic, history, chemistry, mineralogy, etcetera, to embroidery, drawing, and vocal and instrumental music, even to the guitar. And the quality of their teaching was noted, not only in the papers of the day, but also in the report of the superintendent of education for Lower Canada, which deplored the lack of preparation of teachers except for the sisters of the congregation.

During this era of educational progress and missionary expansion, the Congregation of Notre-Dame itself experienced the events that were to give a definitive form to its government and consolidate its existence in the church: the institution of the office of general in 1864, the approval of the congregation by Rome in 1876, and the sanction of its rules in 1889.

The evolution of the congregation on such a large scale in the 19th century did not depend solely on an environment that favoured initiative and generosity. It was due to the intelligence and idealism of religious women to whom society entrusted a great number of responsibilities. Seen in this perspective, Mother Sainte-Madeleine is a prototype, representative of a pivotal period in the social history of Montreal and the province.

ANDRÉE DÉSILETS

Archives de la Congrégation de Notre-Dame (Montréal), Biographie des sœurs décédées depuis le 17 août 1855 jusqu'au 14 juin 1871 (typescript); Correspondance de Mère Sainte-Madeleine; Notices historiques, écoles de la Commission scolaire de Montréal. Can., prov. du, Assemblée législative, *Journaux*, 1856, II, app.16. *Mélanges religieux*, 10 sept. 1841, 5 avril 1842, 21 avril 1843. L.-P. Audet, *Le système scolaire*, IV, V. L.[-A.] Groulx, *L'enseignement français au Canada* (2v., Montréal, 1931–[33]). Lemire-Marsolais et Lambert, *Hist. de la CND de Montréal*, VII, 145, 158. C. E. Phillips, *The development of education in Canada* (Toronto, 1957). *Vie de la mère Sainte-Madeleine, supérieure de la Congrégation de Notre-Dame de Montréal, par un ancien supérieur de communauté* (Montréal, 1876).

HUTCHINSON, ROBERT, merchant, officeholder, and politician; b. 19 Jan. 1802 in Charlottetown, P.E.I., son of Samuel Hutchinson and Elizabeth Wilder; m. 24 May 1829 Susanna Harvie, and they had two surviving daughters; d. 30 April 1866 at his home in Charlottetown.

After the death of his father in 1803, Robert Hutchinson was brought up by his mother who kept a tavern in Charlottetown. At an early age Robert opened a dry goods and groceries store in that town. In 1829 he was appointed jailer of Queens County jail. During the 15 years he occupied this post he continued his business across the street but resided in the prison with his wife who acted as matron. In 1844, when his father-in-law, Nicholas Harvie, was appointed jailer, Hutchinson advertised the opening of a new store.

A Conservative by family tradition, Hutchinson appreciated the relationship between politics and office in Prince Edward Island. In 1847 he joined a number of influential merchants, magistrates, and members of the legislature from Charlottetown in petitioning against the reappointment of Governor Sir Henry Vere HUNTLEY, whom they accused of identifying with George Coles* Reformers and of naming to office "persons unqualified by education or position in society." Under the new governor, Sir Donald Campbell*, Hutchinson was appointed a justice of the peace for Queens County and a commissioner for prison discipline and for adding hard labour to prison sentences.

As magistrate he gained a reputation for "painstaking and judicious" application of the law. He resigned his magistracy in February 1852 on grounds of unconstitutional interference by Governor Sir Alexander BANNERMAN in commuting without reason or notice the prison sentence of a woman tried before him. Reappointed, he joined 11 other magistrates who in November 1853 re-

Hutton

signed in protest against the conduct of Edward WHELAN at a public meeting and his "unfit" appointment as a JP. Although the governor chose to keep Whelan on the roll of magistrates, Hutchinson returned to his office, probably during 1854, and held the position for life.

Hutchinson's involvement in municipal administration began in 1837 with his election as a town assessor at the annual meeting of Charlottetown residents, which took place under the authority of the Pump and Well Assessment Act passed in 1833 and revised in 1843. He was elected the town's assessment treasurer from 1837 to 1845, 1st lieutenant of Fire Engine Company no. 2 from 1844 to 1846, and captain from 1846 to 1853. In addition he served as commissioner to superintend the erection of a wharf (1843), member of the board of health (1847), and commissioner for furnishing cornmeal for the relief of destitutes (1848).

In the early 1850s, when local newspapers were advocating the incorporation of Charlottetown, Hutchinson, with the majority of citizens, opposed what he saw as the burden and expense of municipal institutions. By 1855, however, the population of the town had reached 6,500 and rural assembly members felt overburdened with city affairs. An act for the incorporation of Charlottetown passed the legislature in March 1855 and the first council elections were held in August. Robert Hutchinson's extensive civic experience made him the unopposed choice as first mayor.

In his initial year in office Hutchinson set up the officers and machinery of civic government and directed the formulation of the first by-laws; some 32 had passed by August 1856, The independent manner with which Hutchinson proceeded irked some of his Conservative friends who accused him of selling out to the Liberals. At the 1856 council elections Hutchinson found himself running on the Liberal ticket for mayor. He won but the bitter residue of a partisan contest surfaced in public accusations by William Henry Pope* that Hutchinson's victory resulted from an anti-Irish, anti-Catholic appeal, charges that cannot now be substantiated or disproved. During Hutchinson's mayoralty the small budget allotted by the assembly to Charlottetown prevented substantial public improvements. The streets were partially lighted by gas and sidewalks laid out and gravelled, but Charlottetown lacked sewage and water systems for many years.

In 1857 Hutchinson did not intend to stand for office, but was hastily nominated on the eve of election day. He lost to Thomas Heath HAVILAND. Hutchinson's two-year régime was marked by competence, if fussiness. The *Examiner* suggested the principal complaint against him was that "he made too much a hobby of his office (all that was human of him was absorbed in his ministerial functions)," but praised his "patience, perseverance and industry."

In January 1859 Hutchinson was appointed to the Island Legislative Council. As councillor he promoted the abolition of imprisonment for debt and provision to Charlottetown of a site for a public market house. After the council was made elective in 1862 Hutchinson retired, devoting himself exclusively to his mercantile affairs.

MARY K. CULLEN

Charlottetown City Hall, Charlottetown City Council, Minutes, 1855–56. PAPEI, P.E.I., Executive Council, Minutes, 1770–1867 (mfm. at PAC). P.E.I., Supreme Court, Estates Division, liber 7, f.2.9 (mfm.). PRO, CO 231/26, 77. St Paul's Church (Charlottetown), Baptismal records, 1777–1826, book 3; 1827–53, book 2; Charlotte parish, Marriage register, 1827–53, book 1. P.E.I., House of Assembly, *Journal*, 1845; Legislative Council, *Debates and proc.*, 1859–63; *Journal*, 1859–63. *Examiner* (Charlottetown), 1855–66. *Haszard's Gazette* (Charlottetown), 1853–56. *Islander*, 1847–66. *Morning News and Semi-Weekly Advertiser* (Charlottetown), 1844–45. *Royal Gazette* (Charlottetown), 1837–53. *The Prince Edward Island calendar*... (Charlottetown), 1844–45, 1847, 1855–63. *Canada's smallest province* (Bolger). MacKinnon, *Government of P.E.I.*, 275–79.

HUTTON, WILLIAM, farmer, teacher, and public servant; b. 22 Dec. 1801 at Summer Hill, near Dublin (Republic of Ireland), seventh child of the Reverend Joseph Hutton and Mary Swanwick; m. Frances McCrea of Strabane, County Tyrone (Northern Ireland), and they had five daughters and one son; d. 19 July 1861 at Quebec City.

Educated in Ireland, William Hutton apprenticed to a farmer before farming himself. He immigrated in 1834 to New York but decided to settle instead near Belleville, Upper Canada, where he purchased a farm. Unable to support his family by this means he also taught school, and was superintendent of common schools in the Victoria District from 1844 to 1850. He was a justice of the peace for the district from 1840 until his appointment in 1842 as warden; he held the latter office until it became elective in 1846. The district council appointed Hutton their clerk in the following year and, subsequently, the district auditor, but he held these posts only a short time. In 1848 he became a part-time provincial arbitrator for the Board of Public Works and in 1852 a clerk in the customs branch of the department of the inspector-general, Francis Hincks*, a cousin who often helped Hutton's career.

Hutton had already shown an interest in the improvement of Canadian agriculture by organizing in 1841 a district agricultural society. In 1851 his essay, "Agriculture and its advantages as a pursuit," won a gold medal from the Johnstown District Agricultural Society, and in 1852 he received an award from the Board of Agriculture of Upper Canada for his "Report on the state of agriculture in the county of Hastings." Spurred by ambition and interest, he sought the position of secretary to the Bureau of Agriculture created in 1852 but, instead, became secretary of the Board of Registration and Statistics in 1853. When the bureau absorbed the board in 1855 he became its secretary. His position in the bureau, his enthusiasm for Canada's prospects, and his connection with prominent Reformers, notably Hincks, probably account for his dispatch on a mission to promote emigration from England and Ireland during the winter of 1853–54. He lectured widely and also arranged for the publication by Edward Stanford of London of an emigrant guide entitled *Canada: its present condition, prospects, and resources*. It was the first of two pamphlets he produced for promoting immigration, and he also contributed to a refutation of observations of Canada by an English visitor, James Caird. His style was direct and informative. His writings were probably helpful to emigrants because they were based on his experiences and observations as an immigrant, a farmer, and a civil servant, familiar with different parts of the province.

As secretary of the Bureau of Agriculture, with a small staff under him, Hutton prepared the annual statistical reports, granted patents and copyrights, arranged for Canadian displays at exhibitions in Europe and the United States, assisted local agricultural societies, advised the government on the opening of colonization roads, and corresponded with the emigration agents who were sent to Europe beginning in 1859 with A. B. HAWKE. He was conscientious and a capable public servant; he prepared the 1852 census with classifications and analyses of the statistics so that the general public could easily understand them and in 1855 his plan for a reorganization of the Bureau of Agriculture was accepted. He was in many ways the ideal *laissez-faire* mid-Victorian: a believer in self-help, a constant pursuer of personal and community improvement, and a supporter of public education as a means of personal and social betterment.

WESLEY B. TURNER

William Hutton was the author of "Prize essay on agriculture and its advantages as a pursuit" and of "Report on the state of agriculture in the county of Hastings," *Canadian Agriculturalist and Trans. of the Board of Agriculture of Upper Canada* (Toronto), IV (1852), 1–7 and 194–98 respectively; of *Canada: its present condition, prospects, and resources, fully described for the information of intending emigrants* (London, [1857]); and of *Canada: a brief outline of her geographical position, productions, climate, capabilities, educational and municipal institutions . . .* (Toronto, 1857; 2nd ed., Quebec, 1860; 3rd ed., 1861). The latter was published in French as *Le Canada: courte esquisse de sa position géographique, ses productions, son climat, ses ressources, ses institutions scolaires et municipales, ses pêcheries, chemins de fer . . .* (2e éd., Québec, 1860). In addition, Hutton was a contributor to *Caird's slanders on Canada answered & refuted! . . .* (Toronto, 1859). PAC, RG 17, A1, ser.2, 1491–93; AIII, ser. 1, 2393. Can., Prov. of, Legislative Assembly, *Journals*, 1852–60; *Sessional papers*, 1863, III, no.4. *Morning Chronicle* (Quebec), 20 July 1861. [G. E. Boyce, *Hutton of Hastings: the life and letters of William Hutton, 1801–61* (Belleville, Ont., 1972), is an interesting and most informative work. W.B.T.]

I

INGERSOLL, LAURA (Secord), heroine; b. 13 Sept. 1775 in Great Barrington, Mass., eldest daughter of Thomas Ingersoll and Elizabeth Dewey; d. 17 Oct. 1868, at Chippawa (Niagara Falls, Ont.).

When Laura Ingersoll was eight, her mother died, leaving four little girls. Her father remarried twice and had a large family by his third wife. In the American War of Independence, Ingersoll fought on the rebel side, but in 1795 he immigrated to Upper Canada where he had obtained a township grant for settlement. His farm became the site of the modern town of Ingersoll. He ran a tavern at Queenston until his township (Oxford-upon-the-Thames) was surveyed. Within two years, about 1797, Laura married James Secord, a young merchant of Queenston. He was the youngest son of a loyalist officer of Butler's Rangers, who had brought his family to Niagara in 1778. James and Laura Secord were to have six daughters and one son.

They lived first at St Davids but soon settled in

Ingersoll

Queenston. Early in the War of 1812, James, a sergeant in the 1st Lincoln militia, was wounded in the battle of Queenston Heights and was rescued from the battlefield by his wife. The following summer, when neither side had a firm hold of the Niagara peninsula, Laura heard on 21 June 1813, probably by listening to the conversation of some American officers dining at her house, that the Americans intended to surprise the British outpost at Beaver Dams and capture the officer in charge, Lieutenant James FITZGIBBON. It was urgent that someone warn FitzGibbon and, since James was disabled, Laura resolved to take the message herself early the next morning.

The distance to the outpost by direct road was 12 miles but Laura feared she would encounter American guards that way and chose a roundabout route. She went first to St Davids where she was joined by her niece, Elizabeth Secord, and then to Shipman's Corners (St Catharines). Elizabeth became exhausted and Laura continued alone, uncertain of the way but following the general direction of Twelve Mile Creek through fields and woods. That evening, after crossing the creek on a fallen tree, Laura came unexpectedly on an Indian encampment. She was frightened, but after she explained her mission to the chief he took her to FitzGibbon. Two days later, on 24 June 1813, an American force under Colonel Charles Boerstler was ambushed near Beaver Dams by some 400 Indians led by Dominique Ducharme* and William Johnson Kerr*. FitzGibbon then persuaded Boerstler to surrender with 462 men to his own 50 men. In the official reports of the victory no mention was made of Laura Secord.

The Secords lived in poverty in the postwar years until 1828 when James, who had received a small pension because of his war wound, was appointed registrar, then judge (in 1833), of the Niagara Surrogate Court. In 1835 he became collector of customs at Chippawa. He died in 1841 leaving Laura without financial resources. She ran a school for children in her Chippawa cottage for a brief period. Petitions to the government for a pension and other favours were unsuccessful.

Laura Secord was 85 before she achieved wide public recognition for her heroic deed. While visiting Canada in 1860, the Prince of Wales (the future Edward VII) learned of Laura's 20-mile walk. She had prepared a memorial for the prince describing her war-time service, and she also had placed her signature among those War of 1812 veterans who presented an address to him. After Albert Edward returned to England, he sent Mrs Secord a reward of £100. She died in 1868, at the age of 93, and was buried beside her husband in Drummond Hill Cemetery, Niagara Falls.

Laura Secord became celebrated as a heroine in history, poetry, and drama, after 1860. Legends grew; the favourite was that she had taken a cow with her on her walk, for camouflage, and that she had milked it in the presence of American sentries before leaving it behind in the woods. In fact, Mrs Secord never mentioned a cow and it is unlikely that she encountered an American sentry. William F. Coffin* apparently invented the episode for his book *1812, the war and its moral* (1864). According to another story, Laura had walked through the woods at night, on her bare feet. But she herself said, "I left early in the morning," and though she may have lost a slipper in the woods or fields, she was far too sensible to have started out barefoot. Her popular fame was such that two monuments were erected in her honour, one at Lundy's Lane in 1901, the other on Queenston Heights in 1910. Her portrait was hung in the parliament buildings at Toronto, and a memorial hall was established in the Laura Secord School at Queenston.

Some 20th century historians, however, have questioned her place in history. For example, W. Stewart Wallace* in *The story of Laura Secord: a study in historical evidence* (1932) concluded from the available documents that Mrs Secord had undoubtedly taken a message to FitzGibbon, probably on 23 June, but that she had arrived too late for her information to be of value. Lieutenant FitzGibbon had said in his report on the battle of Beaver Dams: "At [John] De Cou's this morning, about seven o'clock, I received information that ...the Enemy...was advancing towards me...." It was argued that this information, brought by Indian scouts, was Fitzgibbon's first warning. Wallace also cited a certificate written by FitzGibbon in 1837 testifying that Mrs Secord had brought warning of an American attack; unfortunately FitzGibbon gave no specific date, and he wrote, he said, "in a moment of much hurry and from memory."

The puzzle of the chronology and of Laura's role in the events was solved when two earlier testimonials came to light, both written by FitzGibbon, in 1820 and 1827, to support petitions the Secords had made to the government. In the 1827 certificate, FitzGibbon said that Mrs Secord had come "on the 22d day of June 1813," and that "in consequence of this information" he had placed the Indians in a position to intercept the Americans. Thus he made it clear that Laura's warning had indeed made the victory possible at Beaver Dams. It was a significant victory, and for her part in it Laura Secord became justly known as the heroine of the War of 1812.

Laura Secord typified pioneer women in her courage, endurance, and resolution in the face of adversity. FitzGibbon remembered her as a person of "slender frame and delicate appearance," but underneath was a strong and persistent will.

RUTH MCKENZIE

[The main documentary evidence of Laura Secord's heroic deed is found in the petitions she and her husband made to the government and in three certificates by James FitzGibbon, all now at the PAC. The petitions are in MG 24, 175 (n.d.); RG 5, A1, 46, pp.22844–45; 108, pp.61567–68; C1, 52, no.3157; 59, no.222; and the FitzGibbon certificates are in RG 5, A1, 46, p.22487 (1820); 84, pp.45661–63 (1827); C1, 82, no.2880 (which encloses the 1837 certificate). Laura Secord's memorial to the Prince of Wales in 1860 is in RG 7, G23, 1, file 2. Official reports of the battle of Beaver Dams are in RG 8, I (C series), 679, pp.132–41. In PAO, Misc. 1933, is "The story of Laura Ingersoll Secord, wife of Captain James Secord, as related by Laura Secord Clark, grand-daughter of Laura Secord to Mrs. George S. Henry."

Laura Ingersoll's birth and marriage records are missing but the approximate date of her marriage is known from circumstantial evidence. Two birth dates appear in biographies and family histories – 13 Sept. and 19 Dec. 1775. The former was confirmed as correct by Mrs Secord's granddaughter, Laura Louise Smith, in E. J. Thompson, "Laura Ingersoll Secord," Niagara Hist. Soc., [Pubs.], no.25 (Niagara-on-the-Lake, Ont., 1913), 10.

Among the published material are two letters Laura Secord wrote about her walk to Beaver Dams, the first for Gilbert Auchinleck, in "A history of the war between Great Britain and the United States of America, during the years 1812, 1813, & 1814," Anglo-American Magazine (Toronto), III (1853), 467n (the series of articles appeared as a book under the same title (Toronto, 1862; repr. London, 1972); and the second for B. J. Lossing, now in PAC, MG 24, K2, 13, pp.396–98, an edited version of which is in B. J. Lossing, The pictorial field-book of the War of 1812 . . . (New York, 1869), 621n. Charles B. Secord related his mother's deed in a letter to the Church, 18 April 1845. W. F. Coffin, 1812, the war and its moral; a Canadian chronicle (Montreal, 1864), 146–53, first introduced Laura Secord as a heroine. The Niagara Mail (Niagara, Ont.) reported on the prince's gift to Mrs Secord, 27 March, 3 April 1861, and on her death, 17 Oct. 1868. The best of the early biographies is E. A. [Harvey] Currie, The story of Laura Secord, and Canadian reminiscences (Toronto, 1900; St Catharines, Ont., 1913). W. S. Wallace, The story of Laura Secord: a study in historical evidence (Toronto, 1932), raises questions about Mrs Secord's contribution. Ruth McKenzie, Laura Secord, the legend and the lady (Toronto and Montreal, 1971), reassesses the evidence and Laura Secord's place in history. R.M.]

IRONSIDE, GEORGE, public servant; b. probably c. 1800 in the area of Amherstburg, Upper Canada, son of George Ironside* and a woman who was possibly of Ojibwa descent; d. 14 July 1863 at Manitowaning, Manitoulin Island, Canada West.

George Ironside Sr joined the Indian Department in the 1790s as clerk and storekeeper to agent Matthew Elliott* at Amherstburg, eventually rising to the post of Indian superintendent. Beginning as a clerk under his father at Amherstburg about 1826, George Ironside Jr followed him as superintendent there for a 15-year period. He took part in the events that followed the rebellion in Upper Canada in 1837; on 4 Nov. 1838 he led some 40 or 50 Indians to help repulse the Patriot force that had landed at Windsor. In 1845 he succeeded Captain Thomas Gummersall Anderson* as northern superintendent at Manitowaning. Ironside was involved in the negotiations conducted by William Benjamin Robinson* which resulted in the signing in September 1850 of the Robinson treaties for the surrender of lands along Georgian Bay and north of lakes Huron and Superior; this event marked what was probably the high point of his tenure of office.

As the decade of the 1850s passed, it became obvious that the original hopes for Manitoulin Island would not be met. Sir Francis Bond Head*'s notion of using the island as a reserve for all the bands in Upper Canada had been quickly abandoned, as few even from central and north central Upper Canada went to the island. Moreover, the lesser aim of using the government supported Indian community of Manitowaning, where the Church of England was active in educational and pastoral work, as a model for others to emulate had to be given up when the Indians gradually abandoned it to return to their traditional ways of hunting and fishing. With the failure of the Manitoulin Island experiment, Indian fears of white encroachment increased rapidly in the late 1850s and resulted in growing discontent. The signing in 1862 of the Manitoulin Treaty for the surrender of the island, which Ironside helped William McDougall* and William Spragge to negotiate by persuading the Indians around Manitowaning to support the government's intentions, brought the situation to a head [see Jean-Baptiste ASSIGINACK].

Anti-government feeling was particularly potent among the people in the eastern end of the island around Wikwemikong. The Indians of this flourishing, predominantly Roman Catholic settlement had felt betrayed by the 1862 treaty, which they saw as part of a design on the part of

407

Irumberry

the government "to deprive them of their Island." The chiefs at Wikwemikong had, with only two exceptions (who, it was claimed by some, were not representative or had been appointed illegally by Ironside), refused to sign the treaty. In December 1862, a few months after it was signed, a number of white families were expelled from Wikwemikong, along with some Indian families who disagreed with the majority there over the treaty; Chief Francis Tehkummeh, a signatory of the treaty, was forced to seek refuge with Ironside at Manitowaning. In July 1863 William Gibbard, fisheries commissioner for the Great Lakes, came to the island to arrest the chiefs responsible for the incidents. Encouraged by two Roman Catholic missionaries at Wikwemikong, Auguste Kohler and Jean-Pierre Choné, the Indians mounted a physical force and resisted; Gibbard withdrew with his force and a captive Indian who was charged for his involvement in the expulsion of a white family from an island off Manitoulin. The confrontation demonstrated the intensity of Indian feeling after the 1862 treaty. The deteriorating situation affected Ironside's health, and in the midst of the excitement surrounding the incident he died suddenly on 14 July 1863, probably of a heart attack.

Conscientious, humane, and knowledgeable, Ironside in many ways represented the best type of Indian Department employee, who often carried out the daily tasks of Indian administration without any recognition being given his efforts. The Indian Department was robbed of one of its most experienced officers at a time when such men were most needed. The tradition of service in the Indian Department was to persist in the family for at least three generations, George Jr's son, McGregor Ironside, succeeding him briefly as northern superintendent.

Douglas Leighton

PAC, RG 10, 498–527, 568, 572–73, 586, 722. Enemikeese [Conrad Vandusen], *The Indian chief: an account of the labours, losses, sufferings, and oppression of Ke-zig-ko-e-ne-ne (David Sawyer), a chief of the Ojibbeway Indians in Canada West* (London, 1867). *Evening Times* (Hamilton, [Ont.]), August 1863. *Globe*, 27, 30 July, 3, 5–8, 12, 21, 22, 24 Aug. 1863. *Irish Canadian* (Toronto), 5, 12, 26 Aug., 2, 16 Sept., 21 Oct. 1863. *Morning Chronicle* (Quebec), 1, 4, 7, 10, 12 Aug. 1863. *Quebec Daily News, Commercial and Shipping List*, 3–5 Aug. 1863. *Quebec Gazette*, 31 July, 7 Aug. 1863. *Sarnia Observer* (Sarnia, [Ont.]), 31 July, 7, 14 Aug. 1863. R. A. Douglas, "'The battle of Windsor,'" *OH*, LXI (1969), 137–52.

IRUMBERRY DE SALABERRY, MELCHIOR-ALPHONSE D'. *See* Salaberry

J

JACOB, EDWIN, educationist and Church of England clergyman; baptized 9 Dec. 1793 in Painswick, Gloucester, England, son of John and Namaria Jacob; d. 31 May 1868 at Cardigan, York County, N.B.

Little is known of Edwin Jacob's family background but his extensive education suggests a certain level of affluence and social position. In 1811 he entered Corpus Christi College, Oxford, a college founded in 1516 to provide a classical education, which in Jacob's day had chairs only in Greek, Latin, and theology. He was granted his BA in 1815, an MA in 1818, and from 1820 to 1827 he was a fellow of his college. Ordained a Church of England clergyman in 1827, he served for two years as rector of St Pancras, Chichester, and in 1829 was awarded a DD from Oxford.

Married to Mary Jane Patterson, daughter of an official of the East India service, Jacob's influential friends included Sir Howard Douglas, lieutenant governor of New Brunswick (1823–31), who recommended him as vice-president and principal of King's College, Fredericton, when it received a royal charter in 1829. He was also appointed to the chair of divinity. Jacob arrived in the colony with his young family on 11 Oct. 1829, and took up residence near the Nashwaak River. In addition to his college duties he served as missionary to the parish of St Marys and the surrounding country. He also built up a thriving farm at Cardigan to augment his small college income, insufficient for a family of two daughters and six sons. In 1840 Jacob hoped he would become bishop of the new see of New Brunswick, which was in prospect; Bishop John Inglis* of Nova Scotia apparently supported him, but three years later when the archbishop of Canterbury created this see, he named the Reverend John Medley* of Exeter Cathedral the first bishop.

During the 1840s the entire New Brunswick educational system, including King's College, came under attack by reforming critics and liberal educationists, who had long regarded the college

408

as the bastion of Tory privilege and Anglicanism; its learned principal shared in its unpopularity, especially after responsible government was introduced, a change "most distasteful" to the "worthy Doctor who had no sympathy with Colonial political progress," as the Fredericton *Head Quarters* later noted. Partially succumbing to these pressures, the predominantly Anglican assembly passed a bill in 1845 taking the college presidency from the archdeacon of the Church of England in New Brunswick and barring Jacob and the other professors from membership on the college council, which was now open to non-Anglicans. In 1849 Jacob argued that a proposed suspension of the chair of divinity was contrary to the college's charter and that, if it was carried out, he would be unable to meet his financial obligations, including maintenance of his farm, which he felt was contributing "to the agricultural importance of my adopted country." An appeal to Sir Howard Douglas, no longer lieutenant governor but still, after 14 years, a visitor of the college, saved the divinity chair, but Jacob's stipend was reduced by two-thirds.

Calls for change continued. In 1851, when the assembly debated a motion to convert the college to an agricultural school, Jacob denounced the move in his encaenial address: "We must not listen to the cry which calls us from the pursuit of truth and virtue to the lower paths and grosser occupations of the multitude." The motion was defeated, but the new lieutenant governor, Sir Edmund Walker HEAD, saw the need for change. He had already helped to establish an engineering course and in 1852 he suggested a study of the college to rescue it from "a position of comparative inaction and consequent danger." Jacob was named to a three-man study committee but it accomplished little. Two years later, Albert James Smith*, a strong supporter of the Methodist college at Sackville, argued that an institution with only 15 students did not warrant public support and introduced a bill to discontinue the £2,200 grant to King's College. A bitter debate lasting 15 days ended when the house accepted Head's suggestion for a commission of inquiry. The five members were John Hamilton Gray*, James BROWN, and John Simcoe Saunders* of New Brunswick, John William Dawson*, superintendent of education for Nova Scotia, and Egerton Ryerson* of Canada West. Their report, released in 1855, brought a new public attack on the college, but because of the general instability of the provincial governments, its recommendations were not debated until 1858.

By an act of 1859 which incorporated the report's major recommendations, King's College became the University of New Brunswick, a non-denominational provincial university. The chair of theology which Jacob had held for 30 years was abolished, and he was demoted to a professorship of classical and moral philosophy. Jacob appealed to the Duke of Newcastle, arguing that an act of a provincial legislature could not supplant a royal charter, but Lieutenant Governor John Henry Thomas Manners-Sutton* had assured the concurrence of the Colonial Office in the assembly's decision. Refusing to recognize the new order, Jacob was finally pensioned off in 1861. Even then, he had to be evicted from the university premises; when confronted in his classroom, he had but one student, his daughter. In the ancient Oxonian tradition, to the end he was endeavouring, as he said, "to communicate knowledge intrinsically valuable, with the disposition to use it for the common benefit." He died in seclusion on his farm in 1868.

According to historian W. S. MacNutt*, Jacob "was probably the only public functionary in the province upon whom the political changes of the passing years had made utterly no impression." An official memorial volume of the university was somewhat kinder: noting that "much of the opposition which greeted his efforts was ignorant, short-sighted and misguided," it concluded that "social and cultural conditions in the young colony were simply not ripe for work of the kind and standard he was prepared to offer."

RICHARD WILBUR

PANB, REX/pa/Education papers, University of New Brunswick, 1815–90. UNBL, Edwin Jacob file; King's College, College Council, minutes, 1829–61. *Head Quarters*, 22 Aug. 1866, 3 June 1868. Edwin Jacob, *Sermons intended for the propagation of the Gospel* (Fredericton, 1835). *A catalogue of all graduates in divinity, law, medicine, arts and music, who have regularly proceeded or been created in the University of Oxford, between October 10, 1659, and December 31, 1850 . . .* (Oxford, 1851), 358. Hannay, *History of N.B.*, II, 145–66. G. H. Lee, *An historical sketch of the first fifty years of the Church of England in the province of New Brunswick (1783–1833)* (Saint John, N.B., 1880). MacNutt, *New Brunswick*. Desmond Pacey, "The humanist tradition," *The University of New Brunswick memorial volume*, ed. A. G. Bailey (Fredericton, 1950), 61–62.

JARDINE, ROBERT, businessman, railway promoter, and office-holder; b. 12 Jan. 1812 at Girvan, Ayrshire, Scotland, son of Alexander Jardine, mason, and Helen Davidson; m. 30 Oct. 1834 at Saint John, N.B., Euphemia Reid, for-

Jardine

merly of Kildonan, Scotland, and they had four daughters; d. 16 June 1866 at Saint John.

Jardine apparently had some schooling in Scotland and dabbled in both law and business before immigrating to Saint John in the early 1830s. Shortly after arriving, he entered the employ of Barnabas Tilton, a grocer. In 1838 or 1839 he and his brother Alexander, who had joined him in 1835, took over the business and changed the name to Jardine and Company.

Throughout the 1840s and 1850s the Jardines expanded their operation into a significant enterprise, importing staples and exotics from around the world: Java coffee, Puerto Rican molasses, British seed, American tobacco, Peruvian fertilizer, Canadian flour, African cocoa, and Nova Scotian fish, as well as agricultural implements ranging from rakes and scythes to the most recent innovations in machinery. Robert Jardine also acquired a large farm named Woodside about a mile east of Saint John where he raised Ayrshire cattle and attempted new farming techniques. These interests led him to the Saint John Agricultural and Horticultural Society, of which he was several times president, and the New Brunswick Society for the Encouragement of Agriculture, Home Manufactures, and Commerce, of which he was vice-president in 1851.

Agriculture was never more than a hobby to Jardine. By 1851 he was president of the Saint John Gas Light Company and of the New Brunswick Electric Telegraph Company, and a director of the Saint John Water Company, the Saint John Hotel Company, and the Fredericton and Saint John Electric Telegraph Company. He was, in addition, vice-president of the Saint John Chamber of Commerce, president of the St Andrew's Society of Saint John, and a school trustee for the parish of Simonds. A leading citizen in Saint John civic affairs, he gained special commendation in 1854 during the cholera epidemic when, as president of the Saint John Water Company, he pressed forward in establishing a pure water system that was to last for decades.

Railways, however, became Jardine's great interest. He emerged as the leader of the businessmen of Saint John who envisioned their city as the prosperous east coast railway centre. Jardine attended the railway convention in Portland, Maine, on 31 July 1850 [see John Alfred Poor*] and returned to Saint John to help organize the European and North American Railway Company in order to build a line linking Saint John with the United States on the west and the Gulf of St Lawrence on the east. The company began with construction of a line from Saint John to Shediac. Jardine was president by the time the first sod was turned on 14 Sept. 1853.

During 1853 and 1854 work on the railway progressed satisfactorily, but by 1855 everything had stopped and the assembly called upon Jardine to explain. In the face of difficulties with the English contractors, Peto, Brassey, Betts, Jackson, and Company, Jardine fought valiantly to save what was being called "The Great Bubble Railway." In the end the provincial government bought out the contractors and arranged to complete the line as a public project. Jardine was the logical candidate to complete the work, for he was a faithful supporter of the Liberal government, especially of Samuel Leonard Tilley*, the provincial secretary and a director of the European and North American. Construction was held up, however, when Lieutenant Governor John Henry Thomas Manners-Sutton* put the government out of office over Tilley's Prohibition Act of 1855 and called on John Hamilton Gray* and Robert Duncan Wilmot* to form a government. In the 1856 election Jardine ran as a candidate against Gray and Wilmot in Saint John but was badly defeated.

Within a year, however, Tilley and the Liberals were back in power, and by August 1857 Jardine was the chief commissioner of railways for New Brunswick. Between 1857 and 1860 he and the European and North American were the subject of three commissions of inquiry by the assembly, and Jardine was vilified by the opposition press. The first commission, reporting in 1858, found some small irregularities. The second inquiry in 1859, before which Jardine spent long hours, concluded that the railway "will be a first class road, of superior description, well and solidly built." Still, Jardine had been criticized and there were some cabinet members who did not like him. He was incensed by the insults he felt he had experienced and complained to Tilley of the committee's use of "anonymous slanders & calumny, by calling for, listening to & publishing as evidence the assertions – not on oath – of discharged servants and confessedly malicious and disapointed men of no character or standing." He publicly resigned as commissioner of railways. When Tilley refused to let him go, another attack opened up on "Mr. Tilley and Mr. Jardine and the Smasher junta" and a third commission of inquiry was appointed. Two reports were submitted, a laudatory majority and a condemnatory minority. Gray, the Conservative leader, supported the majority opinion that the railway was a "thoroughly constructed road" and that Jardine was an admirable man. The 108-mile railway from Saint John to Shediac was completed on 8 Aug. 1860.

Jardine then urged Tilley to move on with the "*line* from Saint John to the State of Maine . . .

410

immediately." Though sympathetic, Tilley had other priorities and Jardine was left to manage the European and North American. Edward Watkin* declared that Jardine was "one of the best informed on Railways he had ever met, and the Railway over which he presided was the best in construction and management on this continent."

Jardine was responsible for New Brunswick railways until 22 March 1865 when he resigned as commissioner upon the defeat of Tilley's government in the confederation election. For two years he had been considerably crippled by an attack of paralysis. On 16 June 1866, when out for a drive, he fell ill, and almost immediately died, apparently of a heart seizure. After Robert's death Alexander Jardine continued to operate Jardine and Company until his retirement in 1875. He died in February 1878.

Robert Jardine was a practical, industrious, and highly successful Scot who made several contributions to his adopted city and province. His great work was the European and North American and for that he was given a unique honour. In 1868 a locomotive built in Saint John was named the *Robert Jardine*. On a steel front panel was painted the "engine portrait" of Jardine, now in the New Brunswick Museum.

C. M. WALLACE

N.B. Museum, Edward Barron Chandler papers, Jardine to Chandler, 26 Feb. 1857; Jardine family papers; Marriage register B (1828–39); Tilley family papers. PAC, MG 27, I, D15. N.B., House of Assembly, *Journals*, 1855–61. *Morning Freeman* (Saint John, N.B.), 1859–60. *Morning News* (Saint John, N.B.), 1840–60, 18 June 1866. *Morning Telegraph* (Saint John, N.B.), 19 June 1866. *New Brunswick Courier*, 22 June 1839, 1840–60. *New-Brunswick almanac*, 1851, 1854, 1856, 1860, 1864. I. A. Jack, *History of St. Andrew's Society of St. John, N.B., Canada, 1798 to 1903* (Saint John, N.B., 1903). N.B. Museum, *History Bull.* (Saint John), I (August 1952).

JARVIS, WILLIAM BOTSFORD, sheriff, politician, land speculator, and entrepreneur; b. 4 May 1799 at Fredericton, New Brunswick, third and youngest son of Stephen Jarvis* and Amelia Glover; d. 26 July 1864 at Toronto, Canada West.

In 1809 Stephen Jarvis moved to York (Toronto) where his cousin William* was a prominent local official. William Botsford Jarvis attended the district school at York, under George Okill STUART and later John STRACHAN. He became in 1818 clerk of the provincial secretary's office where a cousin, Samuel Peters Jarvis*, was acting head. Here he remained until 1827 when he was appointed sheriff of the Home District; he retired from that position only in 1856, in favour of his nephew, Deputy Sheriff Frederick William Jarvis.

Jarvis contested three provincial elections for the town of York. In 1830 he was narrowly defeated by moderate Robert Baldwin* in a by-election, but was successful later that year against the same opponent when a new election was called upon the death of King George IV. Jarvis pressed for York's incorporation as a city, while objecting to the change of name to Toronto, and though he was a Tory (he was president of the British Constitutional Society, the political arm of the Tories, during the 1836–38 period), he advocated voting by ballot in municipal elections because he felt his constituents wanted it. In 1834 he was defeated by a moderate, James Edward SMALL. Jarvis and William Lyon MACKENZIE engaged in a bitter personal feud and when the rebellion came he ordered, as leader of the loyalists' picket, the single volley which disrupted the rebels' march on Toronto on 5 Dec. 1837. In 1841 Jarvis returned to politics as a Toronto alderman but resigned in early 1842 when the council failed to choose him as mayor.

Like other members of the official class, Jarvis engaged in land speculation in and around Toronto. Along with Joseph Bloor he subdivided land to create the village of Yorkville north of what is now Bloor Street. He also initiated a short-lived tramway service on Yonge Street to render this land more accessible and valuable. Although he was to clash with his cousin S. P. Jarvis over the allocation of family debts and a trust fund in later years, he was for a time associated with him in various financial dealings and land speculation.

In 1834 Jarvis was chairman of a committee to plan a railway from Toronto to Lake Simcoe and was one of the first directors when the project was revived in 1844. He was also one of the petitioners for the establishment of the first local insurance company, the British America Assurance Company, in 1832, and was an incorporator of the Toronto Dry-Dock Company (1847), the Toronto, Hamilton, Niagara, and St Catharines Electro-Magnetic Telegraph Company (1847), the Toronto Island Bridge Company (1857), and the Accident Assurance Company (1863).

Though a member of the social élite of the town, Jarvis, as sheriff, witnessed much of the brutal and degrading side of 19th century life and tried to improve the living conditions of Toronto's citizens. He was a vice-president of the Toronto Mechanics' Institute for many years, a member of the Board of Health during York's cholera epidemic of 1832, and a commissioner to superintend the construction of the Provincial Lunatic Asylum (1845). When the Board of Arts

411

Jebb

and Manufactures for Upper Canada was established in 1857, to award prizes to local scholars and artists, Jarvis was its first president.

Jarvis' social affiliations reveal a gregarious and outgoing personality. A mason, he joined the St Andrew's Lodge in 1841 and was a charter member of the Ionic Lodge in 1847. He was vice-president of the St George's Society and of the Toronto Turf Club, and member of the Toronto Club and the Toronto Boat Club (later the Royal Canadian Yacht Club). He was also associated with the Provincial Agricultural Association in the mid 1830s (as president), the district and local agricultural societies, the Toronto Horticultural Society, and the Toronto Athenaeum. In 1824 he had purchased from Small the home he called Rosedale, from which that region of Toronto obtained its name. In 1827 Jarvis married Mary Boyles Powell, granddaughter of Chief Justice William Dummer Powell*; they had two sons and three daughters.

Jarvis is usually thought of as the sheriff of the Family Compact, the man who resisted Mackenzie's forces and who presided at the executions of Samuel Lount* and Peter Mathews* in 1838. He was indeed a high Tory, "an ardent politician of the old and nearly extinct school," an obituary described him, but he was also the man who freed the debtors in York's jail to save them during the cholera epidemic of 1834. In a career only partially characterized by his official and political activities he showed a keen interest in the development of Toronto and in the welfare of its residents, and ended his life a respected patriarch of his adopted city.

ROBERT J. BURNS

MTCL, William Dummer Powell papers. PAC, MG 24, I47. PAO, Jarvis-Powell papers. York County Surrogate Court (Toronto), will of William Botsford Jarvis. *Globe*, 27 July 1864. *Town of York, 1815–34* (Firth). Armstrong, *Handbook of Upper Canadian chronology*. *Brown's Toronto city and Home District directory, 1846–7* (Toronto, 1846). Chadwick, *Ontarian families*. *The city of Toronto and the Home District commercial directory and register with almanack and calendar for 1837 . . .*, comp. George Walton (Toronto, [1837]). *The Toronto almanac and royal calendar, of Upper Canada . . .* (Toronto, 1839). A. G. Meredith, *Mary's Rosedale and gossip of "Little York"* (Ottawa, 1928). Middleton, *Municipality of Toronto*.

JEBB, Sir JOSHUA, military engineer; b. 8 May 1793 at Chesterfield, Derby, England, eldest son of Joshua Jebb and Dorothy Gladwin; m. first Mary Legh Thomas, by whom he had four children, and secondly, Lady Amelia Rose Pelham; d. 26 June 1863 at Chesterfield.

Joshua Jebb graduated from the Royal Military Academy at Woolwich and was commissioned 2nd lieutenant in the Royal Engineers in 1812. The following year he rose to 1st lieutenant and was posted to Canada. He was recommended for his participation in the battle of Plattsburgh on 11 Sept. 1814. Jebb remained in Canada after the war and performed minor duties for the military in Brockville and Quebec, including service as a commissioner to evaluate damaged buildings and estimate costs of repairs and construction.

His most significant work in Canada, however, was his survey of a canal route between Kingston and the Ottawa River. The War of 1812 had demonstrated to Sir George Prevost*, Sir Gordon Drummond*, and other officers that American forces could easily cut the strategic St Lawrence supply and communications link between Upper and Lower Canada. They felt that a route remote from the boundary was needed. In April 1816 Jebb was instructed to survey the Rideau chain of lakes and rivers with a view to developing it by means of canals into a secure, interior communication route. Surveys of the Rideau route had been made in 1783 and 1812 and Jebb's task was to provide specific plans for a canal's construction. He was also instructed to assess the suitability of the adjacent terrain, especially along the St Lawrence river front, for settlement by retired British soldiers.

By June 1816 Jebb had completed the survey. His report recommended a route from where the Rideau emptied into the Ottawa River westward to Irish Creek, approximately five miles south of Smiths Falls. The route then followed this creek to Irish Lake, at which point Jebb, concerned to keep the costs low but eager nevertheless to use novel concepts wherever possible, proposed to build a five-mile long marine railway instead of a canal to a navigable point on the shallow Gananoque stream. An abandoned iron forge nearby could be used to make the rails and the road would be of great economic value to settlers in the area. By means of canals and locks the Gananoque would lead to Whitefish and Cranberry lakes and then by way of the Cataraqui River to Kingston on Lake Ontario.

Shortly after Jebb's report was presented military settlements were established at March, Richmond, and Perth. His route, however, was not followed by Colonel John By* when construction of the Rideau Canal began in 1826. By felt that the low water level in Irish Creek and the lack of continuous flow to the Cataraqui River made Jebb's scheme impracticable.

Still in the army, in 1820 Jebb returned to England where he used his engineering skills to design several prisons, most notably that at Pentonville, regarded for long as a model. He also exerted a strong influence on the management of penal institutions. Jebb opposed transportation of convicts in favour of employing them on public works in England. Appointed surveyor general of prisons in 1837, he served in 1844 as a commissioner to investigate punishment for military crimes and the same year became inspector general of military prisons.

Jebb retired from the army as a lieutenant-colonel in 1850 and was appointed chairman of the managing board of all convict prisons. He received the ranks of colonel in 1854 and major-general in 1860; he was created a KCB in 1859. Jebb died in 1863 after serving for two years as a commissioner to consider the construction of a portion of the Thames embankment.

KENNETH E. KIDD

Water-colours painted by Sir Joshua Jebb while he was in Canada are preserved in the Bushnell Collection, Peabody Museum, Harvard University, Cambridge, Mass. A list of Jebb's publications can be found in the *DNB*. PAC, RG 8, I (C series), nominal index; RG 11, ser.1, 38. PRO, WO 55/857–87. *Encyclopedia Canadiana*, V, 345–46. G.B., WO, *Army list*, 1804–39. *Hart's army list*, 1840–64. R. [F.] Legget, *Rideau waterway* (Toronto, 1955). Ont., Dept. of Energy and Resources Management, *History of the Rideau waterway* (Toronto, 1970).

JETTÉ, MARIE-ROSALIE. *See* CADRON

JOHNSON, JOHN MERCER, lawyer, politician, and office-holder; b. October 1818 in Liverpool, England, son of John Mercer and Ellen Johnson; m. 9 Oct. 1845 Henrietta, daughter of Adam Dixon Shirreff, high sheriff of Northumberland County, N.B., and they had 12 children of whom six lived beyond infancy; d. 8 Nov. 1868 at Chatham, N.B.

John Mercer Johnson Sr was a Liverpool merchant who immigrated to Chatham in 1818 and became a commission merchant and auctioneer. Largely involved in community affairs, holding at different times the offices of magistrate, coroner, and high sheriff of Northumberland County, he headed several organizations at the time of his death in 1859. John Mercer Johnson Jr arrived in Chatham in 1821. Upon completion of his early education in the Northumberland County Grammar School, he studied law at the office of John Ambrose STREET in Newcastle. He was admitted to the New Brunswick bar as attorney on 13 Oct. 1838 and as barrister in October 1840. The same year he entered a law partnership with

C. A. Harding of Newcastle; each of them had an office in their respective home towns a few miles apart. In October 1847 he entered into a similar partnership with Peter Mitchell* of Newcastle, which lasted for five years. Later in life his law partner was William Wilkinson.

In 1837 Johnson served as secretary of the Young Men's Debating Society in Chatham. He was secretary in 1846 of its mechanics' institute, giving several lectures on phrenology. Perhaps out of a sense of public responsibility rather than inclination he gave land in 1851 for a temperance hall in Chatham. By 1866 he was also an officer in the Union Lodge of Good Templars. At various times he held the minor local posts of hog-reeve, tax collector, assessor, and firewarden in the parish of Chatham.

In the non-party political system of the time, Johnson was originally considered a conservative, but he was elected to the New Brunswick assembly in July 1850 as a liberal in favour of "Responsible Government to the full extent." He also supported municipal corporations, retrenchment in expenditures, and reciprocity with the United States. In the assembly he quickly established himself as "an excellent speaker" with colourful debating style. When William Johnstone Ritchie*, the leader of the opposition, resigned over Lieutenant Governor Sir Edmund Walker HEAD's appointment of executive councillors in 1851, Johnson emerged as one of the leaders in the weakened opposition.

The success of the reformers in the 1854 election led to the creation of the Charles Fisher* government. Johnson represented New Brunswick's north shore in the council, being appointed solicitor general, a position he held until Lieutenant Governor John Henry Thomas Manners-Sutton* dismissed the government in May 1856 over the Prohibition Act of 1855. Johnson was returned in the election of June 1856 and in a subsequent election in May 1857, following the disintegration of the government of John Hamilton Gray* and Robert Duncan Wilmot*. Again he was appointed to the council, this time to the portfolio of postmaster general, a position he held from June 1857 until November 1858, when he was forced to resign. Johnson was little interested in administrative detail and left clerks to do the work of the department. The result was chaos and a public scandal. His enemies branded him "a political charlatan, a cheat, an imposter, an empty vapourer, a spiritless swaggerer, who pocketed a salary he never earned."

Johnson remained on the council without portfolio until he was elected speaker on 11 Feb. 1859. He was quite at home amid the passionate and rough debates of the period. Even Lieutenant Governor Arthur Hamilton Gordon*, a young upper class Englishman, considered Johnson "one of the ablest men in the house, a good speaker and a ready debator, but very deficient in that judicial calmness & dignity which should characterize the occupant of the Speaker's chair." It was his failure to look after detail, however, that remained his main problem. "That incorrigible man Mr. Johnson is again the stumbling block" was the complaint of a secretary who needed his signature.

Samuel Leonard Tilley*, the new premier, had a much higher opinion of Johnson and, following the resignation of Attorney General Albert James Smith* in 1862, had Johnson appointed attorney general, a position he retained until 1865.

A consistent advocate of confederation, Johnson was a New Brunswick delegate to the Charlottetown and Quebec conferences in the fall of 1864 with Tilley, Edward Barron Chandler*, William Henry Steeves*, and J. H. Gray. He favoured a legislative as opposed to a federal union, but considered it impracticable. Consequently, he argued at Quebec for a strong central government. "Enumerate for Local Governments their powers," he declared, "and give all the rest to the General Government, but do not enumerate both." He was, at the same time, somewhat inconsistent, arguing against federal powers of reservation and disallowance. The judicial system had a special interest for him and he believed that the federal government should control all courts.

Johnson was defeated narrowly in the first confederation election in 1865 when the Smith anticonfederate government came to power. But he led the poll in the May 1866 vote that paved the way for the London conference, which he attended in December, and for confederation the following year. He resigned from the provincial assembly in June 1867 to run for the Canadian House of Commons, and on 4 Sept. 1867 he became the first federal representative for Northumberland County.

A contemporary described Johnson as being "of slender form, airy gait, and proud appearance; his complexion is dark, with a very sharp and piercing eye." A keen sense of humour and a ready wit served him well in the legislature, especially as speaker.

Unwell for more than a year, Johnson was seriously ill for two months prior to his death in 1868. He died of "Dropsy of the Stomach" due in part to "social excesses." He was, according to Gordon, "a habitual drunkard and gambler," which may explain some of his difficulties. Despite his shortcomings, Johnson was popular with his constituents and his colleagues. Tilley wrote of him: "A more intimate acquaintance with him will not diminish your respect for his talents and Gentlemanly bearings."

JAMES A. FRASER AND C. M. WALLACE

Old Manse Library (Newcastle, N.B.), John Brown papers, J. M. Johnson, correspondence and legal papers. PAC, MG 27, I, D15; RG 31, 1851 and 1861 censuses, Chatham parish, Northumberland County, N.B. PANB, J. C. and H. B. Graves, "New Brunswick political biography," I: Northumberland County marriage records, 2. PRO, CO 188/143, Gordon to Cardwell, 8 May 1865. St Paul's Anglican Church (Bushville, N.B.), baptismal records (mfm. at PANB). UNBL, MG H12a, Gordon to Newcastle, 31 Dec. 1862; 1864. *Documents on the confederation of British North America ...*, ed. G. P. Browne (Toronto and Montreal, 1969). *The union of the British provinces: a brief account of the several conferences held in the Maritime provinces and in Canada, in September and October, 1864, on the proposed confederation of the provinces ...*, comp. Edward Whelan (Charlottetown, 1865; repr. Summerside, P.E.I., 1949). *Daily Sun* (Saint John, N.B.), 21 Aug. 1902. *Gleaner* (Chatham, N.B.), 1845–68. *Head Quarters*, 28 July 1858. *Morning Freeman* (Saint John, N.B.), 4 Nov. 1858. *Morning News* (Saint John, N.B.), 5 Aug. 1850, 1 Dec. 1854. *New Brunswick Courier*, 6 Nov. 1858. *Union Advocate* (Newcastle, N.B.), 12 Nov. 1868. *Canadian directory of parl.* (Johnson).

JOHNSTON, WILLIAM, agitator and pirate; b. at Trois-Rivières, Province of Quebec, 1 Feb. 1782, the son of loyalist James Johnston, a sergeant in Edward Jessup*'s corps of loyalist rangers; d. 17 Feb. 1870 at Clayton, N.Y.

Although his formal education was limited, "Bill" Johnston learned blacksmithing and boat building as a youth in Ernestown Township, Upper Canada, and in the years 1804–13 operated first a lake freighting business and then a store in Kingston. In 1810 he married an American citizen of Washington County, N.Y., Anna Randolph, a step which he later described as being the root of his troubles. He served in 1812 as a private in the 1st Regiment of Frontenac militia but in 1813 was imprisoned at Kingston on suspicion of being an American agent in communication with Commodore Isaac Chauncey*'s fleet; Johnston always denied the charge. He escaped from prison and defected to the American forces, leaving behind, by his own account, property to the value of $20,000. His role during the remainder of the war is obscure, but it certainly included spying and making small raids on British shipments of supplies and mail. He afterwards claimed to have personally known and to have earned the gratitude of both Chauncey and General Jacob Brown.

During the 1820s and 1830s Johnston acquired a reputation as a smuggler operating between French Creek (Clayton), N.Y., and the Kingston area. In this period several of his relatives in Upper Canada were subjected to harassment because of alleged contacts with "the notorious traitor and pirate William Johnston."

When William Lyon MACKENZIE fled to Buffalo, N.Y., in mid December 1837, Johnston offered his services to the Patriot cause. He was briefly on Navy Island, Mackenzie's headquarters, and there received a Patriot "naval commission." On 22 Feb. 1838 he was one of the leaders along with Rensselaer Van Rensselaer* of the abortive Hickory Island raid, near Gananoque. After this failure he began a series of independent border raids with a small number of followers from a secret base in the Thousand Islands, his most notorious exploit being the capture of the Canadian passenger steamship *Sir Robert Peel* at Wells Island (Wellesley Island) on the night of 29–30 May 1838. He planned to use the captured ship as a pirate vessel with which to seize other British lake steamers, but a lack of manpower (he had only 13 men) made this plan impossible and the *Sir Robert Peel* was burned in American waters after being looted. Rewards for his capture, £1000 by Lord Durham [Lambton*] and $500 by the governor of New York, were then offered.

On 10 June 1838 Johnston issued a proclamation as "Commander-in-Chief of the naval forces and flotilla" declaring that he led a movement for "the independence of the Canadas." During the summer of 1838 he continued to make periodic raids on shipping and property although continually pursued by both British and American forces. He attended the convention of the secret Hunters' Lodges in Cleveland in September 1838 where he was given the title "Commodore of the Lower division on Lake Ontario"; as such he took an inglorious part in the American raid led by Nils von Schoultz* on Prescott (the battle of the Windmill) in November 1838 during which he ran his ship aground and never reached the Canadian shore. He then surrendered to American authorities – "the weather growing cold." Released on bail early in 1839 he resumed, on a reduced scale, his hit-and-run incursions from the Thousand Islands. After he was finally captured in the winter of 1839, he was sentenced in February 1840 to jail in Albany for one year but escaped in May. He was never recaptured and ultimately received a federal pardon, but in any case by the time of his escape the Patriot movement as a whole had virtually ceased to exist. He spent the rest of his life in the area of Clayton, where his six children and his brother John also settled. He was appointed lighthouse keeper on Rock Island, then was tavern keeper at Clayton.

Bill Johnston's contemporaries on both sides of the border agreed that he possessed extraordinary courage, strength, and resourcefulness; but he was also uncouth, a braggart, and of dubious honesty. Because of his unsavoury reputation it has generally been supposed by Canadian historians that he was simply a criminal whose piratical activities were undertaken for his own enrichment, yet his numerous letters to Mackenzie from 1837 to 1840 strongly suggest a higher motive. He was a convinced republican who believed sincerely in a government and a society more democratic than those he had left in Upper Canada. He was not, however, in any sense a revolutionary. He had no faith in a spontaneous Canadian uprising. In American terms his political views were conservative. In the 1830s and 1840s he consistently supported the Whig party of Henry Clay and William Harrison against the Democrats of Martin Van Buren. His motives for joining the Patriot movement were straightforward: in his own words he wished to "drive the two countries at it" in the hope of an American victory, or, failing this, to create as great a financial drain on the British Treasury as possible. Though he too finally became disillusioned with the struggle to liberate the Canadas, he was true to the cause longer than most of the other border agitators. "You can depend upon me to stick to the Patriot cause as long as I have breath" he told Mackenzie in March 1840; "I don't go to sleep as many of our pretended friends do."

J. K. JOHNSON

PAC, MG 24, C10; RG 5, A1, 195, 203, 208, 223; B41, 4; RG 7, G6, 4; G9A, 3–5, 7–9; RG 8, I (C series), 608–14, 1274, 1717; RG 9, I, B1, 16–18, 20, 23–24, 31, 34–36, 39. PAO, Mackenzie-Lindsey papers. PRO, CO 42/280, 42/282, 42/285–86, 42/290, 42/297, 42/300, 42/445, 42/451, 42/459, 42/461, 42/463.

JONES, THOMAS MERCER, Canada Company official and banker; b. in England in 1795; d. 2 Oct. 1868 in Toronto, Ont.

In 1815 Thomas Mercer Jones commenced an apprenticeship with the London mercantile firm of Ellice, Kinnear, and Company. With the help of his mentor in the firm, Edward ELLICE, Jones rose to a position of responsibility and gained the reputation of being "steady to a proverb." Ellice was also deputy governor of the Canada Company, the huge land and colonization venture chartered in 1826. It was intended that the Canada Company be granted the crown reserves and a large portion of the clergy reserves in Upper Canada in return for an annual payment to the government of Upper Canada which in effect would release the provincial executive from financial dependence on the elected assembly. The clergy reserves were excluded from the plan because of the objections of John STRACHAN, Church of England archdeacon and later bishop of Toronto, and the Upper Canada Clergy Corporation, but in their place the company was granted the Huron Tract, a 1,000,000-acre triangle bordering on Lake Huron. The company, whose court of directors was based in London, commenced its operations in Canada under the superintendence of the Scottish novelist John Galt* in 1827, but his poverty of business experience caused confusion in the company's affairs. When the directors determined to replace Galt by two commissioners in 1829, Jones was offered, through Ellice's influence, a co-commissionership along with William Allan*, the financial pillar of the Family Compact in Upper Canada.

Jones arrived in Upper Canada in early 1829. Originally his contract was for one year, but the directors were so impressed with the regularity in the accounts and the increased sales he and Allan soon established that they persuaded him to stay on. Allan managed the sale of the scattered crown reserves, while Jones administered the settlement of the Huron Tract. He carried out his duties from Toronto, where in 1832 he married Elizabeth Mary, daughter of John Strachan.

Jones soon became convinced that the company's future depended mainly on the Huron Tract, and with the grudging approval of the directors undertook in the mid 1830s a number of projects to promote and improve the area. He operated a company-owned steamship, but the vessel was frequently locked up by Goderich's silty harbour bar. Costly efforts to improve the harbour failed, as did extensive ventures in lumbering in the tract. Moreover, the times were not ripe for ambitious improvements since the number of immigrants who settled in the Huron Tract was adversely affected by recurrent cholera epidemics, slightly improved economic conditions in Britain, and uneasiness in Upper Canadian politics.

By the late 1830s Jones was effectively lord and master of the Huron Tract. He moved from Toronto and lived in a lavish mansion in Goderich overlooking Lake Huron. His conservative social and economic standing had brought him in 1833 into William Lyon MACKENZIE's celebrated list of Family Compact members. Opposition to his rule and to the considerable swagger of the Canada Company was forming, however, both in the province and in London. The company and its commissioners were vehemently opposed by Reformers in the assembly who objected to its monopolistic rights and practices and its close alliance with the Family Compact. Damaging criticism also came from a local group, the "Colborne Clique," made up of educated and wealthy landowners who had bought large portions of company land in Colborne Township north of Goderich and resented the power over local affairs exercised by the Canada Company. The Colbornites demanded a bridge across the Maitland River to give proper access to their property but Jones, for the company, was reluctant to make the expenditure in an area which had been almost entirely sold off. A newspaper feud and mounting public pressures forced the establishment in 1840 of a provincial commission to investigate the company's affairs. The commission prepared only a preliminary report which, although identifying certain misdemeanors, largely cleared the company of any charges that it had grossly violated its charter. This verdict was due in part to the untiring efforts of Frederick WIDDER, a new Canada Company commissioner sent out from England in 1839 as an eventual replacement for the aging William Allan. An enterprising and responsible officer, Widder by 1841 had taken sole command of the Toronto office.

Jones' stock was still high with the London court of directors but in the 1840s he began to dabble openly in local politics, a policy the directors had always expressly forbidden. In the 1841 provincial election the Reform candidate in Huron County was a former Canada Company employee turned staunch supporter of the Colborne Clique, the eccentric William "Tiger" Dunlop*. In opposition to him Jones first nominated John Longworth, the company's unpopular chief engineer, and then James McGill STRACHAN, his brother-in-law and legal counsel to the Canada Company. A violent campaign followed and Strachan was elected with a plurality of ten votes. Dunlop's supporters petitioned for an inquiry, however, which proved Strachan's support was based on unpropertied voters, and Dunlop was declared elected. The London directors cautioned Jones against further political manoeuvrings.

Jones also came into conflict with the Colbornites in the early 1840s over local control of the government. Governor Sydenham [Thomson*]'s municipal reforms of 1841 created a system of district governments in which elected local officials had the power to impose taxes and administer local public institutions. The Colborne Clique, dominating the Huron District Council, attempted in 1842 to tax the Canada Company's wild lands. Jones and the company fought this move in the courts and a compromise was not achieved until 1846.

In these years competition between the two commissioners was developing. Widder was actively soliciting the support of the directors; Jones, forced to deal with day-to-day complaints of settlers in the field, could not match his rival's grandiose schemes, though in 1844 Jones' father-in-law, Bishop Strachan, wrote to the directors lavishing praise on Jones' efforts. Then, when Widder made an offer for the company to take over the administration of the clergy reserves, Strachan, under the pseudonym Aliquis, published in 1845 a series of open letters condemning Widder and his system of leasing company lands. Jones was mortified and denied, it would seem quite honestly, any prior knowledge of the letters. By 1850 Jones was clearly the junior of the two commissioners and Goderich a mere branch of the Toronto office.

Jones' interests gradually became solely the interests of the Huron area and Goderich. He had served as an officer of the Huron County militia in the late 1830s and was warden of the district in the mid 1840s. Indeed, his activities became perfectly complementary to the views of the Colbornites. Together they perceived that unless a railway could return Goderich to prominence, it would be overshadowed by growing towns such as Stratford and Guelph to the east. The Colborne Clique in 1852 supported construction of the Buffalo, Brantford, and Goderich Railway from Buffalo to a terminus at Goderich which would become a major port funnelling the trade of lakes Huron and Michigan to upstate New York. Widder and the court of directors supported the rival Toronto and Guelph Railway, to run through Guelph and Stratford and eventually to Sarnia, which they considered the best port on Lake Huron; Goderich would then simply terminate a branch line from Stratford. To the directors' amazement, Jones announced company support for the Buffalo–Goderich route. In late 1852 he was dismissed. The company, mindful of his earlier services, granted him a sizable pension of £400 per annum.

Jones had gained much sympathy in Huron County. Remaining in Goderich, he was agent for the Bank of Montreal from 1852 until his wife's death in 1857, when he moved to Toronto. There he lived in retirement until his death in 1868. Two sons, Charles Mercer Jones and Strachan Graham Jones, survived him.

ROGER D. HALL

[The primary source for materials relating to Thomas Mercer Jones is the Canada Company's records at PAO. Since Jones' responsibility in the company's operations was so great, he figures prominently in almost all the Canadian records from the time of his appointment in 1829 until his dismissal in 1852. Of particular value in this study were: Proceedings of the general courts, 1 (1826–54); Minutes of the Court of Directors, 2–6 (1826–54); Minutes of the committees, 2–7 (1826–69); Commissioners' letters and reports, 1–2 (1826–34); Correspondence from the commissioners (originals), 1830–37; Letters to Court of Directors from Frederick Widder, 1–3 (1839–45, 1852, 1853–59); Correspondence to the commissioners, 2–5 (1834–77); "Miscellaneous Correspondence, Canadian Office"; and *Annual report* (London), 1824–70. R.D.H.]

National Library of Scotland (Edinburgh), Edward Ellice papers. PAO, Misc., 1840, Daniel Lizars, "Report, upon the affairs and influence of the Canada Company . . ." (Toronto, 14 Jan. 1840); Misc., 1840, J. T. W. Jones to Sir George Arthur, "Preliminary and confidential report of an enquiry into the affairs of the Canada Company" (2 Nov. 1840); Strachan (John) papers. Aliquis [John Strachan], *Observations on the history and recent proceedings of the Canada Company; addressed in four letters to Frederick Widder, esq., one of the commissioners* (Hamilton, [Ont.], 1845).

H. I. Cowan, *British emigration to British North America; the first hundred years* (Toronto, 1961). Gates, *Land policies of U.C.* R. D. Hall, "The Canada Company, 1826–1843" (unpublished PHD thesis, Cambridge University, 1973). H. J. M. Johnston, "Transportation and the development of the eastern section of the Huron Tract, 1828–1858" (unpublished MA thesis, University of Western Ontario, London, 1965). C. G. Karr, *The Canada Land Company: the early years, an experiment in colonization, 1823–1843* (Ottawa, 1974). R. C. Lee, "The Canada Company, 1826–1853; a study in direction" (unpublished MA thesis, University of Guelph, Guelph, Ont., 1967). Norman Macdonald, *Canada: immigration and colonization, 1841–1903* (Toronto, 1966). Wilson, *Clergy reserves of U.C.* H. J. M. Johnston, "Stratford and Goderich in the days of the Canada Company," *OH*, LXIII (1971), 71–85. G. C. Patterson, "Land settlement in Upper Canada, 1783–1840," Ont., Dept. of Archives, *Report* (Toronto), 1920.

JUKES, JOSEPH BEETE, geologist and author; b. 10 Oct. 1811 at Summerhill, near Birmingham, England, eldest child and only son of John Jukes and Sophia Beete; m. in September 1849 Georgina Augusta Meredith, and the marriage was childless; d. 29 July 1869 in Dublin (Republic of Ireland).

When Joseph Beete Jukes was only eight years old, his father, a manufacturer, died, leaving a

Jukes

strong-willed widow who was resolved that the lad should be educated for the clergy. Consequently, on completion in 1830 of his grammar school studies at Wolverhampton and at King Edward's School, Birmingham, young Jukes was sent to St John's College, Cambridge. Although he pursued classical and mathematical studies, an interest in geology led him to attend the lectures and spirited geological "excursions" of the Reverend Professor Adam Sedgwick. Even before graduating BA in 1836 (he obtained an MA from Cambridge in 1841), Jukes had given up any plans of being ordained. Undecided about his future, he geologized in the midland and northern counties for almost two years, supporting himself by giving public lectures and courses on geology. By 1842 he had become a member of the Geological Society of London.

In 1838 the Newfoundland assembly proposed a geological survey of the colony to search for any valuable mineral resources. Jukes was offered the post of geological surveyor by Lieutenant Governor Henry Prescott* on the recommendation of William Whewell, president of the Geological Society of London. Jukes arrived at St John's, Nfld, on 8 May 1839, and spent that month familiarizing himself with the local geology and investigating supposed coal occurrences (one on the outskirts of St John's proved to be slaty rock and the other near Harbour Grace was bog iron). During a visit to Bell Island late in May, he failed to identify its valuable iron ore deposits and instead mapped them as "reddish stone."

Prior to 1839 Newfoundland's coastline had been carefully charted by Royal Navy hydrographers but the interior was virtually unknown except for the single track of William Eppes CORMACK's crossing from Trinity Bay to St George's Bay in 1822. The lack of maps combined with the difficulty of rugged inland travel satisfied Jukes that he would have to restrict his efforts to coastal regions. The legislature increased the original survey grant to permit the chartering of the *Beaufort*, a 37-ton ketch, which on 16 June sailed out of St John's harbour. The shoreline and islands of Conception and Trinity bays were mapped and prospected during a five-week cruise, but the search for ore proved fruitless. On learning this disappointing news, Governor Prescott advised Jukes to proceed to Newfoundland's west coast where coal was known to occur. It was politically expedient that the survey produce results as soon as possible in order to justify its cost. On 30 July the *Beaufort* headed for the west coast. In early September Jukes, guided by a Micmac named Sulleon, located coal on a small creek near upper Grand Pond (Grand Lake). Nine days later a west coast

settler led Jukes to a second coal location near Barachois Brook. Jukes returned to St John's in mid November and before the year was out submitted to the governor a slim folio entitled *Report on the geology of Newfoundland*.

On 3 March 1840 Jukes and a Norwegian naturalist, Dr Stüwitz, left St John's and sailed to "the ice" on the sealer *Topaz* to find out if ice floes contained the same kind of boulders as those found in diluvium (they are now known to originate from glaciers). While Jukes was still at sea a supply bill including road and survey appropriations was rejected by the Council in the political conflict between that body and the assembly, but eventually Governor Prescott persuaded the house to vote £450 to provide for the continuance of Jukes' salary and survey expenses. The 1840 mapping programme began with a survey of southern Avalon Peninsula and Placentia Bay, followed by geological exploration of the northeastern coastline from Brigus on Conception Bay to the Bay of Exploits. Jukes ascended Exploits River as far as Great Falls (Grand Falls) in company with John Peyton of Toulinguet (Twillingate). In mid October Jukes was back in St John's, and then returned to England.

In his full geological report, which first appeared in London in 1842 as part of his *Excursions in and about Newfoundland*, Jukes acknowledged that "the practical results of this survey are but few, and . . . rather of a negative . . . character," though he thought they might be useful "in restraining rash speculation." The Newfoundland assembly's attempt to publish his geological report separately was vetoed by the Council, but it appeared in 1843 under the financial sponsorship of Lieutenant Governor Sir John Harvey*, who had succeeded Prescott.

Jukes' accomplishments as geological surveyor of Newfoundland had established his professional reputation. In 1842 he was attached as naturalist to a surveying expedition in Australasian waters. Shortly after his return to England in 1846, he was appointed to the Geological Survey of Great Britain, and in 1850 he accepted the local directorship of the Irish branch of the Geological Survey. Though he came to dislike administration, for 19 years he directed the preparation of more than 40 memoirs on the geology of Ireland. In a landmark paper published in 1862 Jukes demonstrated the importance of stream (fluvial) erosion compared with the lesser role of marine (wavecut) erosion in the genesis of recent landscapes. This contribution along with later studies by American geologists in the western United States laid the foundations of geomorphology. In 1853 Jukes had become a fellow of the Royal Society. In 1866 he was appointed to the British royal commission on coal. A head injury suffered in a fall in 1864 triggered a decline in Jukes' health, and on 29 July 1869 he died in Dublin. His friend Thomas Huxley memorialized him as "an upright, generous man, of considerable scientific powers."

Jukes' geological report on Newfoundland had no apparent effect on island history or on future geological work in the colony; Sir William Logan* rarely referred to his work, and in 1864 James Richardson* spoke of Newfoundland as geologically a "new field." Jukes' work was purely a preliminary reconnaissance, and surveyors, legislators, civil servants, and entrepreneurs in the colony appear to have found it of little value. Jukes' principal legacy to Canada is a valuable record of Newfoundland society in 1839–40. He came into contact with Micmacs, mummers, cod fishermen, and seal hunters, and reported on the hospitality of the colony's inhabitants from the humblest outport to the governor's mansion. He was struck by the coarse, primitive manners and customs and the plain, rugged lives of the people, but unlike some other observers he concluded that "the mass of the people are not habitual drunkards." Despite some disappointment with the "want of manly independence and self-reliance" of the lower classes, whom he felt were too easily led, he found Newfoundlanders "simple, honest, industrious, goodnatured and hospitable" with "the virtues of all hardy races exposed to the toils and dangers of the adventurous life."

RICHARD DAVID HUGHES

J. B. Jukes was a prolific writer. A bibliography of his published works can be found in *Letters and extracts from the addresses and occasional writings of J. Beete Jukes,* ed. [C. A. Jukes (Browne)] (London, 1871). His writings relating to Newfoundland include: *Excursions in and about Newfoundland, during the years 1839 and 1840* (2v., London, 1842); *General report of the Geological Survey of Newfoundland, executed under the direction of the government and legislature of the colony during the years 1839 and 1840* (London, 1843); *Report of the progress of the Geological Survey, during 1840* (St John's, 1840); *Report on the geology of Newfoundland, December, 1839* (St John's, 1839); and "Report on the geology of Newfoundland," *Edinburgh New Philosophical Journal,* XXIX (1840), 103–11.

DNB. *Mapoteca geologica Americana; a catalogue of geological maps of America (North and South), 1752–1881, in geographic and chronologic order,* comp. Jules and J. B. Marcou, (Washington, 1884), 36. E.[B.] Bailey, *Geological Survey of Great Britain* (London, 1952), 35–36, 41–42, 50, 68–70, 73–76. J. W. Clark and T. M. Hughes, *The life and letters of the Reverend Adam Sedgwick . . .* (2v., Cambridge, Eng., 1890), I, 521; II, 490. G. L. Davies, *The earth in decay; a history of British geomorphology, 1578–1878* (London, 1969), 317–33. J. S. Flett, *The first hundred years of the Geological Survey of Great Britain* (London, 1937), 55, 59, 76, 92, 116–17. Archibald Geikie, *Life of Sir Roderick I. Murchison, bart.; K.C.B., F.R.S.; sometime director-general of the Geological Survey of the United Kingdom, based on his journals and letters . . .* (2v., London, 1875), II, 326–29; *Memoir of Sir Andrew Crombie Ramsay* (London, 1895), 105, 176, 215–18, 294–96. D. W. Thomson, *Men and meridians; the history of surveying and mapping in Canada* (3v., Ottawa, 1966–69), I, 155. H. B. Woodward, *The history of the Geological Society of London* (London, 1907), 228–32. [T. H.] Huxley, "Joseph Beete Jukes," Geological Soc. of London, *Quarterly Journal,* 26 (1870), pt.II, xxxii–xxxiv.

K

KAHGEGAGAHBOWH (Kahkakakahbowh, Kakikekapo) (known as **George Copway**), Methodist missionary, author, lecturer, and herbal doctor; b. 1818 in Upper Canada near the mouth of the Trent River, the son of John Copway, a Mississauga chief and medicine man; d. January 1869 at Lac-des-Deux-Montagnes (Oka), Que.

George Copway as a boy shared the traditional migratory existence of his parents, who lived by fishing, hunting, and trapping in the Rice Lake area. In 1827 his parents were converted to Christianity, and early in the 1830s he began to attend occasionally the Methodist mission school at Rice Lake. One of his first white teachers was the Reverend James Evans*, later to be known as the inventor of Cree syllabics.

In July 1834 Copway was invited by Evans' successor, the Reverend Daniel McMullen, to help with the mission work of the American Methodist Episcopal Church among the Ojibwa on Lake Superior. With his uncle John Taunchey, his cousin Enmegahbowh (John Johnson), and John Cahbeach he departed for the west. Working as an interpreter and school teacher, Copway spent the winter of 1834 at Kewawenon

Kahgegagahbowh

Mission on the south shore of the lake, and the winters of 1835 and 1836 at La Pointe (Wisconsin), farther west. During the course of the last winter at La Pointe he helped the Reverend Sherman Hall translate the Acts of the Apostles and the Gospel of St Luke into Ojibwa.

Copway's missionary superiors recognized his intellectual talents and in 1838 sent him to a church school in Illinois, where he studied until the fall of 1839 and then returned to Canada. At the Credit River mission in the summer of 1840 he married a white woman, Elizabeth Howell, a friend of the wife of Kahkewaquonaby* (Peter Jones). Called back to Wisconsin and Minnesota for a missionary tour, the Copways left for the west immediately after their marriage. They were back in Canada in the fall of 1842. After he was accepted as a preacher by the Wesleyan Methodist Canadian conference, Copway left on a three month missionary tour of Upper Canada with the Reverend William Ryerson*. Posted the following year to the Saugeen Mission (near Southampton), he transferred in 1844 to Rice Lake, returning to the Saugeen in 1845. That summer the Ojibwa General Council elected him vice-president of their assembly. His election was clearly the highpoint of his missionary career, for later that year first the Saugeen band, then that of Rice Lake, accused him of embezzlement. During the summer of 1846 he was imprisoned for several weeks by the Indian Department, and expelled from the Canadian conference of the Wesleyan Methodist Church.

In disgrace, Copway left for the United States where he had an extraordinary career. Early in 1847 appeared his autobiography entitled *The life, history, and travels of Kah-ge-ga-gah-bowh*, and at once he enjoyed great popularity. His book, the first written by a Canadian Indian, became a bestseller, running through six editions by the end of the year. In it he vividly described his youth among his people and his subsequent career as a Methodist missionary. He made no reference to his expulsion from the church and incorrectly claimed in the title that he was an "Indian Chief," but some of the information can be verified as accurate. In 1851 an epic poem, *The Ojibway conquest*, was published under Copway's name. It was not his own work. In 1898 Julius Taylor Clark, then living in Topeka, Kans., claimed that he had written it over 50 years earlier and allowed Copway to publish it under his own name in order to "raise funds to aid him in his work among his people."

Evidently Copway's training as a Methodist preacher had admirably equipped him for the extensive lecturing he undertook in the late 1840s.

In addresses "from South Carolina to Massachusetts" he advocated the establishment of a 150-square-mile Indian territory on the northeastern side of the Missouri River. There the 100,000 Indians of the "North West" could be exposed to "the cause of Education and Christianity." Under a white governor the "well educated" Indians would administer the territory, replacing "the elder Indians" whose "prejudicial views," Copway claimed, "have ever unfitted them to become a fit medium of instruction to their people."

Before his next book, *The traditional history and characteristic sketches of the Ojibway nation*, appeared in 1850, Copway secured a great following, even among the intellectual community. The young historian Francis Parkman*, for example, met him in March 1849 and noted in a letter to a friend, "I liked him much and wanted to see more of him. . . ." A month before in Boston the poet Henry Longfellow had befriended Copway, whom he described as the "Ojibway preacher and poet." When Copway left in 1850 on a European tour, described in his *Running sketches of men and places, in England, France, Germany, Belgium, and Scotland*, Longfellow gave him a letter of introduction to the German poet Ferdinand Freiligrath. With the appearance of the first issue of the short-lived weekly, *Copway's American Indian*, on 10 July 1851, Copway obtained letters of support from the eminent ethnologists Lewis Henry Morgan and Henry Rowe Schoolcraft, from Parkman, and from the novelists James Fenimore Cooper and Washington Irving.

As early as November 1849, however, Parkman had remarked that Copway's "scheme of settling the Indians is a flash in the pan, or rather he has no settled scheme at all, and never had any." Apparently Copway had repeatedly asked him for money; in a letter of November 1850 Parkman commented on his annoying "applications" "for pecuniary aid." Slowly others must have come to share Parkman's negative opinion of the man; support for his weekly evaporated and it ceased in the fall of 1851.

By the late 1840s Copway was a confused individual. His dilemma — one which might have tormented a number of the Mississaugas educated in Methodist schools — stemmed from his divided loyalty. On the one hand, he sought favourable recognition from the white man, and on the other he retained a deep love of his own people. In early 1849, for example, he wrote an article for Boston's *Flag of Our Union* in which he termed the United States "the eagle of freedom," and included a passionate statement of his admiration for white Americans: "What else could I do but love and esteem the American people? I love their Bible and their institutions." Elsewhere he wrote in a different vein. As he stated in the second and all the subsequent editions of his *Life*: "The white men have been like the greedy lion, pouncing upon and devouring its prey. They have driven us from our nation, our homes, and possessions. . . ."

Little documentary evidence of Copway's activities from 1851 to 1867 survives. Apparently he remained in the United States. Longfellow wrote Freiligrath in December 1858: "Kagegahgabow is still extant. But I fear he is developing the Pau-Puk-Keewis element rather strongly." Longfellow's comparison of Copway with the mischief maker in his epic poem, "Hiawatha," showed his own loss of faith in his Indian friend.

It was once thought, on the basis of information supplied by Enmegahbowh, Copway's cousin, that he died at Pontiac, Mich., about 1863. But in 1867 he appeared in Detroit advertising his services as a practitioner of the "healing art," and inviting "all who are sick" to "come and be cured."

In the summer of 1868, after apparently abandoning his wife and daughter, Copway arrived alone at Lac-des-Deux-Montagnes, a large Algonkin-Iroquois mission northwest of Montreal. Because of his remarkable cures with herbs, leaves, flowers, bark, and roots, Copway was quite popular at first with both tribes. To the resident Sulpician missionary, Abbé Jean-André Cuoq*, the former Methodist preacher described himself as a pagan. After he announced that he had come to study and embrace Roman Catholicism, however, the Iroquois avoided him. At that time the Iroquois at the station were on the verge of converting to Methodism to protest the Catholics' claim of ownership of the reserve. Copway now became the Sulpicians' native champion. When the Iroquois' Methodist allies brought the French Canadian apostate, Charles-Paschal-Télesphore Chiniquy*, to the mission, Copway convinced most of the Algonkins not to attend his services. On 17 Jan. 1869 Copway was baptized by the Sulpicians as "Joseph-Antoine." But several days later, the ex-Methodist preacher, who had momentarily returned to the traditional religious beliefs of his native people, suddenly died, on the night before his first communion as a member of the Catholic Church.

DONALD B. SMITH

Kahgegagahbowh was the author of *The life, history, and travels of Kah-ge-ga-gah-bowh, (George Copway) a young Indian chief of the Ojebwa nation . . .*

(Philadelphia, 1847), republished as *Recollections of a forest life; or, the life and travels of Kah-ge-ga-gah-bowh . . .* (London, [1850]); *The life, letters and speeches of Kah-ge-ga-gah-bowh or G. Copway . . .* (New York, 1850); *The traditional history and characteristic sketches of the Ojibway nation* (London, 1850; repr. Toronto, 1972); and *Running sketches of men and places, in England, France, Germany, Belgium, and Scotland* (New York, 1851).

ASSM, 8, A; 36, André Cuoq, "Notes inédites pour servir à l'histoire de la mission du Lac-des-Deux-Montagnes" (typescript). PAC, RG 10, vols. 409–10, 511, 532, 2221. UCA, Mission register for the Credit River Mission. Victoria University Library (Toronto), Peter Jones coll., Peter Jones papers, box 3, letterbook. [J. T. Clark], *The Ojibway conquest; a tale of the northwest . . .* (New York, 1850). [J. F. Cooper], *The letters and journals of James Fenimore Cooper*, ed. J. F. Beard (6v., Cambridge, Mass., 1960–68), I. "La Pointe letters," ed. F. T. Sproat, *Wisconsin Magazine of History* (Madison), XVI (1932–33), 203–9. [H. W. Longfellow], *The letters of Henry Wadsworth Longfellow*, ed. Andrew Hilen (4v., Cambridge, Mass., 1966–72), III–IV. [Francis Parkman], *Letters of Francis Parkman*, ed. W. R. Jacobs (2v., Norman, Okla., 1960), I. *Christian Guardian*, 20 Sept. 1837. *Copway's American Indian* (New York), 10 July 1851. *Detroit Free Press*, 6, 11 Sept., 1 Oct. 1867. J. C. Pilling, *Bibliography of the Algonquian languages* (Washington, 1891). *Life of Henry Wadsworth Longfellow, with extracts from his journals and correspondence*, ed. Samuel Longfellow (2nd ed., 2v., Boston, 1886).

KAY, THOMAS, merchant; b. 1810 in England; d. 17 Nov. 1863 at Montreal.

Like almost all of Thomas Kay's early life, the time of his move from his native England to Montreal is unknown. By 1842, at age 32, he had established himself and his English-born wife Mary Lucy with their two small children in their own home in Montreal, and had become moderately visible in the city's mercantile scene.

Among the great merchants of the booming Montreal of the early 1840s Thomas Kay was considered a lesser businessman, though one with considerable promise. He was already the principal owner of a prosperous general merchandising firm. His influence in the venture grew steadily as he found more and more capital for expansion, and from 1844 on he ran it under the name of Thomas Kay and Company. Acting as an importer from Glasgow, Liverpool, and London, he regularly supplied Montrealers with such goods as shoes, cottons, hardware, and wines. He tied up much of his money in the farm produce trade, buying large quantities of flour, pork, and beef from Canada West for sale to local consumers and for export to the industrial centres of the United Kingdom.

For his sizable profits in the overseas trade in

Ketchum

bread-stuffs Kay had come to rely in part upon the preference provided by the British Corn Laws. He consequently viewed uneasily the new order triggered by the repeal of these laws in 1846. Yet he tried to adjust to it, and in March 1846 joined other Montreal businessmen such as John Young* and Luther Hamilton Holton* in founding the Free Trade Association of Montreal. A member of the association's council, Kay felt that he had a great deal to gain by urging the relaxation of restraints upon the Canadian economy and the opening of the St Lawrence waterway to American vessels. Within a year or so, however, the beginning of hard times turned his attention away from the principles of free trade and competition. The world-wide depression of 1847–49 badly affected his business activities. It did not ruin him, but the threat seemed real enough to justify his decision to seek, together with hundreds of other disheartened commercial men in the city, a way out through the annexation of Canada to the United States. He indicated his support of annexationism in October 1849 by signing the manifesto of the Montreal Annexation Association. With its swift collapse a few months later, he pushed annexationist thoughts out of his mind and found new hope for his business operations in the good times that returned to Montreal as the 1850s began.

Continuing to meet with success in his commercial affairs, Kay also had an ongoing interest in financial, economic, and social endeavour. In 1841 he had helped to organize the Montreal Provident and Savings Bank. Throughout the 1840s and early 1850s he was a director of the Montreal Fire, Life and Inland Navigation Assurance Company. A founder of the Montreal Board of Trade in 1842, he was a member of its council in 1846 and 1855–57, and as its president in 1859 he worked with characteristic diligence to encourage the city's economic growth. In September 1863 he contributed $2,000 to the building of the Montreal Protestant House of Industry and Refuge.

During the closing years of his life Kay lived in a large two-storey, stone house on Dorchester St. A Wesleyan Methodist, he was buried in Mount Royal Cemetery. The leading pall-bearers at his funeral were John Young and James Ferrier*, two prominent Montreal citizens who were undoubtedly impressed with his solid, if unspectacular, accomplishment in business and his active interest in the development of the city.

H. C. KLASSEN

Montreal Board of Trade Archives, Minutes of the general meeting, 1842–63, pp.21–22, 188, 204, 216, 265–83. PAC, RG 31, 1842 census, Montreal, Queen's Ward; 1861 census, Montreal, St Antoine Ward. *Elgin–Grey papers* (Doughty), IV, 1487–94. *Montreal Gazette*, 1835–63. *Montreal Herald*, November 1863. *Canada directory*, 1851. *Montreal directory*, 1844–46. *The centenary of the Montreal Board of Trade* (n.p., n.d.).

KETCHUM, JESSE, tanner, politician, and philanthropist; b. 31 March 1782 at Spencertown, Columbia County, N.Y., fifth son of Jesse Ketchum and Mollie Robbins; m. first Ann Love (d. 1829), by whom he had three sons and three daughters, and secondly Mary Ann Rubergall, by whom he had three children; d. 7 Sept. 1867 at Buffalo, N.Y.

Following the death of his mother when he was six years old, Jesse Ketchum was taken into the home of a tanner in Spencertown where he probably learned the tanning trade. Unhappy in his foster home because his efforts to attend school were frustrated, Ketchum ran away at the age of 17 to join his brother, Seneca, who had come to Upper Canada in 1796 and was farming on Yonge St north of York (Toronto).

On the outbreak of the War of 1812 some recent arrivals from the United States left Upper Canada rather than serve in the militia or swear allegiance to the crown. One such individual, John Van Zandt, an American tanner at York, was obliged to dispose of his property at once, and no doubt at a sacrifice. Ketchum was the purchaser. Like other merchants, he profited greatly from the wartime demand for supplies for the troops. A shrewd businessman, Ketchum invested his profits in town property in York, and also bought and sold farms in the county of York.

At the beginning of the war Ketchum joined the 3rd Regiment of York militia, and was among those paroled after the capitulation of York to the Americans in 1813. Nevertheless, his loyalty came under suspicion during the brief American occupation, and he was one of those whom Attorney General John Beverley ROBINSON was subsequently directed to have arrested and tried if, upon inquiry, that action seemed justified. No arrest occurred, but the episode no doubt had a lasting effect upon Ketchum.

Ketchum was a public spirited and generous man. He subscribed to the rebuilding of the Don bridges after the war; he became a member of the Society for the Relief of Strangers in Distress (renamed the Society for the Relief of the Sick and Destitute in 1828); and he was on the board of health. After the passage in 1816 of the Common Schools Act, which provided legislative support for administrative costs but not for the erection of school buildings, Ketchum subscribed to the building fund of the first common school in York. It was completed in 1818, and he was elected by the townspeople to its board of trustees. In 1832 he provided at his own expense for an infant school for children under seven.

Ketchum first became opposed to the Family Compact and sympathetic to the radical party in 1820 as a result of John STRACHAN's involvement with the common school of York; Strachan persuaded Lieutenant Governor Sir Peregrine Maitland* to withhold funds for the school, and, when the elected trustees resigned, was successful in replacing their choice of teacher, Thomas Appleton, with his own Anglican nominee, Joseph Spragge*. A second factor was the clergy reserves question. Although a Methodist himself, Ketchum was no narrow sectarian. He attended St James' Anglican Church when it was the only church in York, and, with gifts of land and money, he helped to establish a Methodist chapel in 1818, as well as a secessionist Presbyterian church (later Knox Presbyterian Church) in 1820. He taught Sunday school in the Methodist church and took a keen interest in Sunday schools of all denominations. In 1823 he founded the York Sunday School Union to establish libraries for children attending these institutions. This broad-minded man was chosen chairman of a public meeting called in December 1827 to protest against Strachan's famous "Ecclesiastical Chart" and his efforts to secure the clergy reserves wholly for the Church of England. Ketchum's name headed the list of those from the Home District who, in 1828, petitioned for a liberalization of the charter of King's College. In 1831 another petition was drawn up by Ketchum and Egerton Ryerson* and signed by "Friends of Religious Liberty," asking the imperial parliament to place all denominations in the province on a footing of equality and to appropriate the clergy reserves to general education and public works.

By 1828 Ketchum had become well known as an opponent of the Family Compact. In that year the county of York elected him and William Lyon MACKENZIE to the assembly. Ketchum held his seat until 1834, when he declined to run again, disliking the hurly-burly of politics. During these years he had so much influence with Reformers, supported them so fully, and worked so closely with Mackenzie for constitutional and other reforms that his opponents called him "King Jesse" and Mackenzie "King Jesse's jackal." Ketchum opposed the expulsions of Mackenzie from the assembly, did his best to have him reinstated, and in the process suffered in the York riots of 1832.

Ketchum's withdrawal from political life in 1834 did not mean withdrawal from public affairs. He helped to organize the Canadian Alliance Society, founded in December 1834 to further the demand for reform, and he was an active member of the society's vigilance committee which collected much of the material Mackenzie included in *The seventh report . . . on grievances* (1835). When in 1836 Sir Francis Bond Head* dismissed the Executive Council and replied rudely to delegates presenting a petition of public protest, Ketchum helped to draw up the indignant and sarcastic response of the Reformers, and he and James Lesslie* were delegated to deliver it to the lieutenant governor. Ketchum continued to hope to secure reforms by peaceful means, though talk of rebellion began in 1837. He did not attend the meeting of Reformers at John Doel*'s brewery on 31 July 1837, because he knew that Mackenzie would propose a *coup d'état*. He refused to sign the resulting declaration of Toronto Reformers, broke with his former political associates, and took no part in the rebellion.

Soon after the rebellion Ketchum, though he remained in Toronto, moved his tannery to the outskirts of Buffalo, a location which gave his business wider prospects and which provided security for his son, William, who had fled Upper Canada in the aftermath of the rebellion. Moreover, the Toronto site had now grown too valuable for use as a tannery. Ketchum invested his profits from the Buffalo tannery in nearby farm lands which, as the city expanded, became very valuable. He had many interests to keep him in Toronto, including large real estate activities. In 1845, however, he decided to turn over his property in Toronto to the children of his first marriage and, with his second family, move to Buffalo where his extensive real estate developments now required his presence.

In Ketchum Toronto lost a generous citizen who had given building lots to his employees and who, before leaving for Buffalo, secured employment for them. He was vice-president of the York Temperance Society, founded in 1830, and built two halls for the society's meetings. He was a founder of the Upper Canada Bible Society in 1828, and of the Upper Canada Tract Society established in 1832. He also endowed these societies with funds to enable them to present prize books annually to school children and to the Sunday schools. He was a founder, in 1830, of the Home District Savings Bank which served the town's working class, and two years later helped to organize the York Mechanics' Institute. In Buffalo Ketchum continued his benevolences to churches, schools, and temperance societies and

Kierzkowski

he made annual gifts of books to the school children. He died in 1867. On the day of his funeral the schools of the city were closed in his honour.

LILLIAN F. GATES

Scadding, *Toronto of old* (1873). *Town of York, 1793–1815* (Firth). *Town of York, 1815–34* (Firth). E. J. Hathaway, *Jesse Ketchum and his times: being a chronicle of the social life and public affairs of the capital of the province of Upper Canada during its first half century* (Toronto, 1929). Lindsey, *Life and times of Mackenzie. Municipality of Buffalo, New York; a history, 1720–1923*, ed. H. W. Hill (4v., New York and Chicago, 1923). Sissons, *Ryerson.*

KIERZKOWSKI, ALEXANDRE-ÉDOUARD (baptized **Alexander Edward**), civil engineer, seigneur, and politician; b. 21 Nov. 1816 in the Grand Duchy of Poznań and baptized 20 Oct. 1817 at Odolanów (Poland), son of Filip Jakub Kierzkowski, an officer in the Polish army, and Maryanna Ludwika Liebermann; d. 4 Aug. 1870 at Saint-Ours, on the Richelieu River, Que.

In 1830–31, despite his youth, Alexandre-Édouard Kierzkowski followed his father's example and took part as an officer of the Polish national army in the campaign against the Russians. It concluded with the defeat of the Polish army and, like numerous other Polish patriots, Kierzkowski found refuge in France, according to a certificate dated 25 Aug. 1832 and signed in Paris by a member of the Polish committee. Kierzkowski completed his studies in Paris at the École Centrale des Arts et Manufactures in 1838, and received a diploma as a civil engineer. He arrived in the United States in 1841 and the following year settled in Canada. From 1842 to 1844 he was a civil engineer with the Board of Works.

On 15 May 1845 Kierzkowski married Louise-Amélie Debartzch; the same day, his compatriot and colleague at the École Centrale in Paris, Édouard-Sylvestre Rottermund*, married her sister, Caroline Debartzch. The girls were daughters of the Honourable Pierre-Dominique Debartzch*, who was also of Polish extraction. Kierzkowski had two sons, who died bachelors. By his marriage he acquired part of the seigneuries of Saint-François-le-Neuf, Cournoyer, Debartzch, and L'Assomption. He made his home at that time at Saint-Marc, on the Richelieu.

In 1852, having noted that land banks had furthered the development of agriculture in his native country, Kierzkowski published at Montreal a pamphlet entitled *The question of the seigniorial tenure of Lower Canada reduced to a question of landed credit*, which also appeared in French. In it he advocated the setting up of a land bank system for the redemption of seigneurial rights. Investment security, regular interest payments, and reimbursement of capital at the expiry of the term were guarantees which in his opinion would make it possible to obtain the necessary capital at an advantageous rate for the borrowers. He also suggested reforms to the mortgage system. It does not seem, however, that Kierzkowski's proposals were seriously considered by the government when it initiated the reform of the seigneurial system in 1854; the civil code of 1866 did secure the abolition of concealed mortgages which he had requested.

Kierzkowski was one of the directors of the Agricultural Society of Lower Canada in 1852, and was vice-president of the mechanics' institute. In addition he held the office of justice of the peace. On 16 Aug. 1855 he was appointed major of the Richelieu district militia, then on 13 Nov. 1862 lieutenant-colonel. He also commanded the 2nd militia battalion of Saint-Hyacinthe, and was assistant quartermaster-general of the 5th military district of Canada East. Kierzkowski was interested in the building of railways. He acquired four shares in the St Lawrence and Atlantic Railway, which was built under the direction of his countryman Casimir Stanislaus Gzowski*.

On 2 Nov. 1858 Kierzkowski was elected to the Legislative Council for the Montarville division, and on 13 July 1861 was chosen as the representative for the county of Verchères in the Legislative Assembly. On both occasions, however, Kierzkowski was debarred from his seat following decisions by the committees responsible for judging disputed elections. On 10 Sept. 1867 he was elected to the House of Commons as Liberal member for the county of Saint-Hyacinthe; he remained an MP until his death on 4 Aug. 1870.

His wife had died in 1850, and on 21 Oct. 1868 Kierzkowski married Caroline-Virginie, daughter of the Honourable François-Roch de Saint-Ours and cousin of his first wife; the church granted them dispensation from the second degree of affinity. By his second marriage he had one daughter. In his *Histoire de la seigneurie de Saint-Ours*, Azarie Couillard-Després* describes Kierzkowski as a handsome man, with "fine blue eyes and fair hair. He had a sharp wit which he knew how to use effectively but was a man of tact and sensitivity and always in great demand at family gatherings." Kierzkowski is thought to have brought back from a trip to Poland a few handfuls of earth, and to have asked that they be placed with his coffin, so that he might rest in Polish soil.

L. KOS-RABCEWICZ-ZUBKOWSKI

424

A.[-É.] Kierzkowski, *La question de la tenure seigneuriale du Bas-Canada ramenée à une question de crédit foncier* (Montréal, 1852), which also appeared in English as *The question of the seigniorial tenure of Lower Canada reduced to a question of landed credit*. PAC, MG 27, I, E32, 1, 2. Can., Prov. of, *Report of the commission appointed to inquire into the affairs of the Grand Trunk Railway* (Quebec, 1861); Legislative Assembly, *Journals*, 1863. [F.-M.-U.-]M. Bibaud, *Le panthéon canadien; choix de biographies, dans lequel on a introduit les hommes les plus célèbres des autres colonies britanniques* (2e éd., Montréal, 1891), 124–25. *Canada directory*, 1857–58. *CPC*, 1867. G. Turcotte, *Cons. législatif de Québec*, 248–49. Wiktor Turck, *Polonica Canadiana; a bibliographical list of the Canadian Polish imprints, 1848–1957* (Toronto, 1958), 58. C.-P. Choquette, *Histoire de la ville de Saint-Hyacinthe* (Saint-Hyacinthe, Qué., 1930), 132, 287. [Azarie Couillard-Després], *Histoire de la seigneurie de Saint-Ours* (2v., Montréal, 1915–17), II, 99–100; *La première famille française au Canada, ses alliés et ses descendants* (Montréal, 1906), 240. Ludwik Kos-Rabcewicz-Zubkowski, *The Poles in Canada* (Canada Ethnica, VII, Ottawa and Montreal, 1968), 21–26, 47–50; "Alexandre-Édouard Kierzkowski, patriote polonais, réfugié au Canada (1816–1870)," *BRH*, LX (1954), 175–80. "L'honorable Alexandre-Édouard Kierzkowski," *BRH*, X (1904), 86.

KILLAM, THOMAS, merchant, shipowner, and politician; b. 8 Feb. 1802 in Yarmouth, N.S., the son of John Killam (d. 1842) and Sarah Allen; m. first in 1823 Sophia Corning (d. 1839), by whom he had a son, and secondly in 1841 Elizabeth Gale Dudman, by whom he had five sons and three daughters; d. 15 Dec. 1868 at Digby, N.S.

Thomas Killam's father was a Yarmouth shipowner and merchant who helped establish the Marine Insurance Company, built a sawmill on Cape Fourchu, and took an active part in developing local public services. Thomas was probably educated in the private school which operated in part of his father's house. He gained early experience in the family business and probably served at sea in the 1820s. As his father began to reduce his business activities, Killam became prominent in his own right.

In 1839 he built his first vessel, *Sophia*, a 92-ton schooner, and until 1865 he constructed, commissioned, or purchased from one to six vessels almost every year. During the 1840s almost all of Killam's ships were schooners or brigantines, of less than 400 tons, often built for the fisheries; one, a barque, was 628 tons. By 1852 he was experimenting with barques of over 800 tons and in 1861 he commissioned from John Richards, a noted local builder, the 1,459-ton *Research*, for $15,000. Between 1839 and 1865 he owned some 60 vessels, 25 of which were lost at sea, although

he himself probably had a substantial interest in no more than 16 at any given time; others in Yarmouth owned far more. Some shares in these ships might be held by suppliers, ships' captains, and other merchants. Occasionally Killam was joint owner with various relatives by marriage and with his own sons, especially George, but not with his several uncles, prominent shipowners in their own right. Thus the family name, attached to many Yarmouth ships, did not designate a coherent organization despite some cooperation among the Killams. These relatively small, flexible businesses could adapt more quickly to fluctuations in trade.

Killam steadily developed a general trade between North America and Great Britain, which had many hazards. Yarmouth merchants insisted that provincial regulations covering pilotage fees, lighthouse duties, and reporting to customs clerks discriminated against the outports and coastal shipping, and reflected Halifax mercantile interests. These merchants also had to cope with fluctuations in Atlantic trade. On 1 Jan. 1862 the firm of Killam, Son, and Dudman, established in 1849, failed with a total cost to Killam of $85,000. Nevertheless he continued in the carrying trade, speculating in such commodities as iron rails, lumber, and grain. In Yarmouth he also expanded his business as a ship-chandler and as a dealer in fishing supplies, iron, cordage, coal, meat, and flour. His success as a merchant was partly explained by his ability to keep a large amount of assets in accounts receivable, rather than in fixed assets, so that he had a continuous turnover of capital. At his death, his estate had a gross value of $290,810 with $96,255 in shipping and $129,231 in accounts receivable, though it also included $44,538 in bad debts. He operated a tightly controlled, well-organized business.

Following his father's example Killam became in 1837 a director of the newly established Yarmouth Marine Insurance Association. He remained associated with this company and also purchased shares in the Acadian Insurance Company (established 1858) and the Atlantic Insurance Company (1865). Yarmouth's financial growth, attested to by the presence of these new insurance companies, and the failure of the Halifax banks to service Yarmouth's needs, resulted in the formation of the Bank of Yarmouth in 1863, of which Killam served as a director until his death.

Killam looked on material possessions as a fruit of social mobility and not as an inherited right. He supported a broadened franchise, but was unconcerned with schemes to improve the position of the workingman or the poor, beyond

Killam

helping to obtain a better jail for Yarmouth. Killam was willing, when he turned to politics, to use the political support of the shipwrights and joiners in the Yarmouth shipping industry, many of whom were Acadians from Argyle, N.S., and who succeeded in forming an association in 1834, which by 1851 had 150 members. He was noted for individual acts of kindness to his associates, but he had no interest in the fraternal and benevolent societies of his day. He did, however, serve as director of the Wesley Chapel from 1839 and helped finance the construction of the Methodist church built in Milton in 1865. He was also involved in the establishment in 1858 of a private school for the sons of local merchants, and became a director of the Yarmouth Academy, donating $1,000 to the building fund in 1864.

Throughout his business career Killam had dealings with the provincial legislature, whether to obtain a lighthouse or to incorporate a company. In 1847 he was elected to the assembly as a supporter of the popular Herbert Huntington* and as a Reformer opposed to Tory élitism. A successful businessman, Killam was an important addition to the Reformers. Although never an eloquent speaker Killam soon appeared on several select committees, often with Joseph Howe* and George Renny Young*, dealing with such issues as insurance, acts of incorporation, and conditions of business partnerships. He became a member of the influential public accounts committee in 1849, and then chairman from 1853 to 1856 and again in 1859, where he furthered the interests of the mercantile community. He was opposed to the development of manufacturing in the province. He also preached the liberal slogans of free trade, though he was prepared in 1850 to agree that the power of the state should be used in the fisheries to force the Americans to grant trade concessions to Nova Scotia. With other Nova Scotian merchants Killam felt that the Reciprocity Treaty of 1854 provided an opportunity to supplant the American merchants who had previously controlled much of the trade in fish.

Killam's belief that government should not be involved in economic affairs caused him to be concerned in 1849 when Howe proposed a government telegraph company. Construction of a line was begun by the Nova Scotia Electric Telegraph Company, but a group of businessmen, including Killam, secured control of the company in the mid 1850s. In 1850, when Howe first advanced his scheme for a publicly financed railway from Halifax to Windsor, N.S., Killam began to denounce the ministry, and in 1851 he voted against the government almost as often as did

James William Johnston*, the leader of the Conservative party.

Returned as the member for Yarmouth County in the 1851 election, Killam continued to distinguish himself as a leading opponent of the Reform ministry. With the support of another Reformer, Edward Lothrop Brown of Horton Township, Killam played an important role in helping the Tories defeat Howe's railway plans in 1853. Yet unlike many Tories, Killam looked on railways with distaste and foreboding, although he was not opposed to technological innovation. He saw railways not as the symbol and agent of modern progress, but as an expensive undertaking fostered by a clique of Halifax businessmen trying to make the entire province pay for a project which would lead only to their own aggrandizement. Killam's criticism contained a bitter irony: at a time when Killam and his fellow merchants were expanding the shipping trade and needed public support, the legislature was debating whether it would devote the bulk of provincial revenues to the railways. Despite the government's defeat in 1853, railway fever, which in Killam's view resulted in a frantic attempt to grasp a puff of smoke, finally proved to be too strong, and a board of commissioners was established in 1854 to construct a railway from Halifax to Windsor.

Killam's often virulent attacks on Howe and other Reform leaders precluded his appointment to the Reform ministry, which in 1848 had seemed assured. Yet he continued to be known as a Reformer and to serve on committees dealing with business matters. Gradually, however, he became convinced that the Reform ministry was spitefully discriminating against his county by refusing to finance local projects. Killam's estrangement, which meant the ministry was losing the support of its more radical supporters in the assembly, was part of the same process which resulted, in 1854, in the introduction of two former Tories, Lewis Morris Wilkins* and Stephen FULTON, into the Reform ministry, and the election of another, Stewart Campbell*, as speaker.

As Killam moved away from the Reformers he increased his interest in protecting the rights of the assembly member and in limiting the ministry's power. He became an enthusiastic supporter of an elective upper house, a broadened franchise, and municipal institutions to replace the existing Quarter Sessions. Although J. W. Johnston supported these measures as a means of carrying out the old Tory principle of a division of power, Killam was more interested in protecting the power of the people against an overly strong executive. Some members, how-

426

ever, feared a reduction of their political influence in their counties if routine local issues were handled by municipal bodies. A general incorporation bill was rejected but several members, including Killam, demanded and received in 1855 an act allowing for the local option to incorporate. Yarmouth did so in 1856, but a petition from Yarmouth, prompted by the higher taxes resulting from incorporation, led the legislature to repeal the town's incorporation in 1858, much to Killam's disgust. This set-back, and the failure to establish an elective upper house, meant that the attack on the cabinet system was not successful and Killam was becoming more isolated in the house.

Killam had been re-elected in 1855, for the first time as a Conservative. He played no direct role in the defeat of the Reform ministry in early 1857. After the triumph of J. W. Johnston and the Conservatives, he did not receive a cabinet position, perhaps because of his long antagonism to sectarian privileges. He was an uncomfortable supporter of the new ministry as it continued with the railway construction begun by the Reformers. He followed the Conservatives into opposition, however, when the Liberals returned to office under William Young* in 1860. Although by temperament he seemed more content in opposition, he appeared on few committees after 1859 and introduced little legislation. Despite his service to the Conservatives he was again passed over for the ministry in 1864. He was appointed to the railway committee but soon resigned in protest against Charles Tupper*'s flamboyant scheme to expand the provincial railway system.

Tupper got approval for his railway schemes in 1864, over the objections of six members, mainly from the western counties, and ultimately ensured the necessary financing through the scheme of colonial union, which included federal absorption of the provincial debt. This connection between confederation and railways might have been sufficient to provoke Killam into opposing colonial union, but he also saw as inevitable higher tariff duties, a commitment to industrial growth, and acceptance of intercolonial, rather than continental, trade. With his life-long support for a maritime mercantile economy, Killam found the creation of a political and economic unit out of the British North American colonies ridiculous. To the assembly in 1866, with map and pointer, he "proceeded to show that the natural home of B.N.A. was with and among the old Colonies. . . ." He was not so much advocating joining the United States as defending the *status quo*. When the legislature committed the province to colonial union in 1866, Killam still

objected and with his long-time opponent, Joseph Howe, helped establish a province-wide anti-confederate corresponding committee.

Passage of the British North America Act in 1867 changed the anti-confederate agitation in Nova Scotia. Killam had intended to retire from politics, but now ran successfully in Yarmouth for the new federal parliament. At its fall session in 1867 he refrained from debate until a new tariff bill was introduced. In a restrained fashion he reaffirmed his belief in free trade and mildly objected to tariff increases on imported flour which blatantly discriminated against Nova Scotian interests. His opposition stiffened when he returned to Yarmouth and found that a public meeting had denounced the tariff and supported the growing provincial campaign for a delegation to England to repeal Nova Scotia's participation in confederation. Of the federal members from Nova Scotia only James William Carmichael of Pictou and Killam publicly agreed with the provincial ministry that resuming their places in parliament would constitute a recognition of confederation and they refused to return to Ottawa.

Yarmouth remained a vociferous centre of opposition to union. At a public meeting in July 1868 broad hints were dropped that unless repeal was granted Nova Scotia should seek entry into the United States; Killam, who had long professed support for republican institutions, probably sympathized with the agitation. But in Yarmouth, and in the province generally, there was dissension among the anti-confederates, especially between the provincial ministry and the federal wing, led by Howe. Killam looked on the anti-confederate cause as a people's movement and on any division among the leaders as a betrayal of the true source of political power. Moreover, as a life-long liberal, Killam would not follow Howe into a compromise with the Conservative John A. Macdonald* or a coalition with Tupper. In his own county Killam was able to keep the anti-confederates together but he had little influence elsewhere in the province.

Killam's death, amid the feud between Howe and the provincial ministry, passed almost unnoticed. Of the major Halifax papers, only the Roman Catholic *Evening Express* published an obituary, in which the editor referred to Killam's defective education, inadequate command of words and grammar, and strong prejudices, and added: "To be obliged to yield, even when in the wrong, he considered not only a misfortune, but a disgrace." Yet the paper also concluded that almost every important issue in Nova Scotia for the past 25 years bore his mark and that he had been the leader of the anti-railway policy in Nova

Kincardine

Scotia. The extent to which Killam apparently had quickly become an anomaly in Nova Scotia is perhaps best illustrated by the fact that his son Frank, at 24, pulled the Liberal party together in Yarmouth, won his father's federal seat at a by-election in 1869, and became president of the Western Counties Railway Company in 1870.

K. G. Pryke

N.B. Museum, Tilley family papers. PAC, MG 24, B29; MG 26, F. PANS, RG 5, P, 124. Yarmouth County Court of Probate (Yarmouth, N.S.), will of Thomas Killam. Can., House of Commons, *Debates*, 1867–68. N.S., General Assembly, *Statutes*, 1848–67; House of Assembly, *Debates and proc.*, 1848–67. *Evening Express* (Halifax), 1863–68. *Morning Chronicle* (Halifax), 1863–68. *Novascotian*, 1847–63. *Yarmouth Herald* (Yarmouth, N.S.), 1863–68. *Yarmouth Tribune* (Yarmouth, N.S.), 1855–68.

G. S. Brown, *Yarmouth, Nova Scotia: a sequel to Campbell's "History"* (Boston, 1888). J. R. Campbell, *An answer to some strictures in Brown's sequel to Campbell's "History of Yarmouth . . ."* (n.p., 1889). J. C. Farish, *Yarmouth, 1821; a reprint of articles published in the "Yarmouth Herald," 1892* ([Yarmouth, N.S.], 1971). *Our dominion; historical and other sketches of the mercantile and manufacturing interests of Fredericton, Marysville, Woodstock, Moncton, New Brunswick, Yarmouth, N.S., etc.* (2v. in 1, Toronto, 1889). D. F. Warner, *The idea of continental union; agitation for the annexation of Canada to the United States, 1849–1893* ([Lexington, Ky.], 1960).

KINCARDINE, JAMES BRUCE, Earl of ELGIN and Earl of. *See* BRUCE

KING, EDWARD HAMMOND, soldier, printer, and publisher; b. 12 July 1832 at Stoke Damerel, Devonshire, England, son of Major John William King of the 21st Fusiliers and Anne Robinson; m. 14 Sept. 1854 Harriett Nice Holmes, and they had one son and two daughters; d. 7 March 1861 on an island, later named Edward King Island, in Barkley Sound off Vancouver Island, and buried at Alberni, B.C.

Edward Hammond King entered the British army as an ensign in the 94th Regiment in May 1851 and was promoted lieutenant on 3 March 1854. He transferred to the 27th Regiment in February 1855 and on 10 August became paymaster of the 59th Regiment. He served in India and China, was invalided home, and retired from the army on 16 Oct. 1857. He then became a superintendent in the Welsh Constabulary, but resigned after a few months probably because he was not promoted chief constable.

Restless and dissatisfied, King set out in 1859 with his family for Vancouver Island intending to enter government service either as a police officer or as an accountant. Failing in this plan, he turned to printing and publishing. His first venture, with Leonard McClure, was the *Government Gazette for the Colonies of Vancouver Island and British Columbia*, which carried official notices and proclamations for the two colonies. It was first issued on 10 Sept. 1859; on 13 March 1860 the two men sold it to George Elmes Nias. In the meantime King had launched two more papers. With the assistance of Coote M. Chambers he published the *New Westminster Times* in Victoria, whence it was shipped by steamboat to the mainland city; it ran from 17 Sept. 1859 to 3 March 1860 when McClure became proprietor. For the *Victoria Gazette*, whose first issue appeared on 5 Dec. 1859, King and McClure appropriated the name of the city's first newspaper which had ceased publication on 26 November. The life of the second *Victoria Gazette* was short: King sold it to Nias on 16 April and it ceased to appear in July.

In 1860 King became involved in a libel suit in Victoria. Edward Edwards Langford*, a leader of the radical faction in the colony and a candidate for a seat in the assembly, published an election address in which he attacked Governor James Douglas* and his administration. A parody was issued anonymously and circulated throughout the town. Discredited, Langford withdrew from the election on 5 Jan. 1860. He believed King to be the printer of the pamphlet and instituted a libel suit. The case was heard before Chief Justice David Cameron* in April. Because Langford refused to answer questions in cross-examination a non-suit was entered. Langford, who had been ordered to pay the costs of the action, later charged King's counsel, George Hunter Cary, with fabricating the bill. The charge against Cary was dismissed for want of evidence. On leaving the court King, a principal witness, encountered Edward Graham Alston*, a barrister who had been watching the proceedings with great amusement. A heated exchange ensued and King assaulted Alston. King was arrested immediately and on 6 November sentenced to a month's imprisonment for contempt of court. On 17 November, in response to a petition signed by prominent citizens of Victoria, Governor Douglas pardoned King.

In March 1861 King, acting as a special constable for the government, investigated the wreck of the *Florencia* on 31 Dec. 1860. On his way back to Victoria he was obliged to take shelter in Dodger Cove in Barkley Sound. An avid hunter and fisherman, he died there on 7 March as a result of gunshot wounds in a hunting accident.

SYDNEY G. PETTIT

PABC, Colonial correspondence, E. H. King correspondence; Colonial correspondence, Police Dept, Victoria correspondence, 1860; Vancouver Island, Governor, despatches to London, 8 June 1859–28 Dec. 1861 (letterbook); 12 Jan. 1862–12 March 1864 (letterbook), James Douglas to Newcastle, 14 Feb. 1863. PRO, WO 25/158–59; 25/802, ff.255–56; 76/167; 76/171–72. *Daily British Colonist* (Victoria), 5 Jan., 17, 19, 21, 26 April, 3, 6–10, 13–15, 17, 20 Nov. 1860; 22 Jan., 27, 28 March 1861. G.B., WO, *Army list*, 1817–58. Walbran, *B.C. coast names*, 285–86. S. G. Pettit, "The trials and tribulations of Edward Edwards Langford," *BCHQ*, XVII (1953), 5–40. Madge Wolfenden, "The early government gazettes," *BCHQ*, VII (1943), 171–90.

KING, GEORGE, stevedore, shipbuilder, and shipowner; b. about 1798, possibly of loyalist descent, in Lower Cove, Saint John, N.B.; d. 21 Nov. 1867 at Halifax, N.S.

George King is first mentioned on a Saint John ship register in 1850 as the owner of the new ship *American* and was described there as a "stevedore." According to an obituary, he was able to leave this occupation "by dint of industry, sobriety and assiduous attention to business." From 1850 until his death King registered 23 vessels, of which 22 were newly built and 20 fully rigged ships; he was the sole builder of 13 of the 23 vessels and the joint builder of another six. The first four were built by John Storm, with whom King was in partnership from 1853 to 1857. Most of King's ships were soon sold to Liverpool owners, and the sales were frequently financed by Fernie Brothers, who were probably King's correspondents in Liverpool, as they were for many British North American shipowners. A glimpse of the financial scale of King's business is given in the "certificates of sale" which he registered in the years 1861 to 1864 for his eight new ships of a combined tonnage of 9,487 and minimum sale price of £95,900.

As King's health deteriorated, he sought a change of climate by sailing to Liverpool on 2 Sept. 1867 with his son Frederick on the maiden voyage of the last ship he built, *Trial Wave*. At Liverpool his health continued to fail; he set out to return to Saint John, but died en route at Halifax. The next day the Saint John *Morning News* commented: "He has been so long and so extensively connected with the shipbuilding interests of this city, that for years past his name has been familiar as a household word."

George King had married Mary Ann Fowler, of Kings County, N.B.; they had at least five sons and one daughter. His second son, George Edwin*, became an MHA, premier of New Brunswick, and judge of the Supreme Court of Canada.

RICHARD RICE

PRO, BT 107/95–109/253; "Vessels built in Saint John and transferred to Liverpool," comp. E. C. Wright. *Morning News* (Saint John, N.B.), 22 Nov. 1867. F. W. Wallace, *Wooden ships and iron men: the story of the square-rigged merchant marine of British North America, the ships, their builders and owners, and the men who sailed them* (Boston, 1937; repr. Belleville, Ont., 1973). Clarence Ward, "Old times in Saint John, 1850," *Saint John Globe* (Saint John, N.B.), 17 Aug. 1912.

KING, WILLIAM. *See* PEGUIS

KINNEAR, DAVID, journalist; b. in 1805 or 1807 in Edinburgh, Scotland; d. 20 Nov. 1862 at Montreal.

Son of a celebrated Scottish banker and educated for the law, David Kinnear came to Lower Canada after a youthful involvement in the literary circle of Sir Walter Scott, John Gibson Lockhart, James Hogg, and John Wilson, a brief experience in London business, and a quick tour of the United States and Upper Canada. He settled in 1835 near Sherbrooke, bore arms against the rebels in 1837, and took part in the restoration of order as justice of the peace and stipendiary magistrate, 1839–40. In later years he lived in Montreal, but maintained a residence also at Napierville.

Montreal in the 1830s had two conservative, pro-British, "anti-patriot" papers, the *Montreal Herald*, owned by Robert Weir* and edited after 1838 by Robert Weir Jr, and the *Montreal Gazette*, owned by two more Scots, Hew Ramsay and Robert Armour Jr. Kinnear, a friend of Ramsay, joined the *Montreal Gazette* as a reporter in 1838 and became editor-in-chief in 1839. He moved to the *Montreal Herald* in 1843 when Robert Weir Jr died, and became its editor-in-chief in 1844. The *Herald* and the *Gazette* both battled against the *Pilot and Journal of Commerce* and the Toronto *Globe*, the Reform position, and the "rebel-paying measures" of the Rebellion Losses Bill.

In 1846 Robert Weir Sr retired and D. Kinnear and Company bought the *Montreal Herald*, the co-owners being Kinnear, Andrew Wilson, James Potts, printer, John Stewart, and Edward

Kinnear

Goff Penny*, reporter on the *Herald* since 1842. The *Gazette* had a new editor and proprietor in James Moir FERRES, and the two papers were growing politically distant. By 1848, Kinnear, now senior partner and editor of the *Herald*, had become the mouthpiece of the Montreal mercantile interests. In particular, he voiced their dismay at British free trade measures and changes in the British navigation laws that seemed to put Canadian merchants at a disadvantage in competition with American shippers. Sir Robert Peel's free trade bill of 1846, for instance, was interpreted as destroying Canadian revenue from a protected trade.

The 1849 movement for annexation grew in part out of this dismay, and Kinnear became a leader of the movement. In June 1849 the *Herald* discussed cautiously in editorials the possibility of joining the United States, in light of the belief that Britain was "prepared to bid adieu to the colonies." In October, Kinnear was one of the first to sign the Annexation Manifesto, and the *Herald* printed full news of annexation meetings in rural ridings. Kinnear was elected a councillor of the Montreal Annexation Association, on an executive which included John REDPATH, John TORRANCE, Jacob De Witt*, and Antoine-Aimé Dorion*. When some annexationists were demoted from judicial and administrative positions, the *Herald* in January 1850 objected bitterly. Indignantly, Kinnear also protested that the *Herald* had not been financed from the United States: "Not one farthing!" he thundered. In March, Kinnear accepted nomination for a municipal office on an annexationist platform, but withdrew before election day, recognizing that the annexation issue did not fit into municipal politics.

The *Herald* gradually shifted from supporting annexation to urging protection by tariffs. Kinnear's editorials reflect the turning of his attention to more perennial, though still urgent matters: the new temperance laws, capital punishment, pot-holes in local roads.

In the 1850s sharper competition with the *Gazette* led Kinnear to put in the first steam press in Canada East and make a new drive for business patronage. The *Herald* outstripped its rivals in advertisement: between 1845 and 1863 it attracted 97,141 new advertisers, much the highest aggregate of any Montreal paper. As editor of an increasingly commercial paper, Kinnear turned his interest to the Welland Canal and railways. By 1860 he had five steam presses, capable of printing 12,000 copies per hour.

David Kinnear died of dysentery in Montreal on 20 Nov. 1862, leaving behind his wife Mary and a large family. After his death ownership of the paper went to Penny, Andrew Wilson, and Mary Kinnear, operating as Penny, Wilson, and Company.

From the Scotland of *Blackwood's Magazine* and the *Edinburgh Review*, David Kinnear had brought a tradition of firmness and eloquence to the conservative cause. His swing to annexationism and away again, traceable in the daily editorials of the *Herald*, illuminates one unexpected shift in conservative views during the mid-Victorian period.

ELIZABETH WATERSTON

"The annexation movement, 1849–50," ed. A. G. Penny, *CHR*, V (1924), 236–61. *Montreal Gazette*, 1838–62. *Montreal Herald*, 1838–62. Beaulieu et Hamelin, *Journaux du Québec*, 100. *Canada, an encyclopædia*, V, 165, 186, 226. *The Canadian newspaper directory* ... (Montreal, 1892). Morgan, *Bibliotheca Canadensis*, 212. C. D. Allin and G. M. Jones, *Annexation, preferential trade and reciprocity; an outline of the Canadian annexation movement of 1849–50, with special reference to the question of preferential trade and reciprocity* (Toronto and London, [1912]), 74, 82, 118–20, 269, 274, 282, 289, 293. *A history of Canadian journalism* ... (2v., Toronto, 1908–59), I. W. H. Kesterton, *A history of journalism in Canada* (Toronto, 1967). S. M. E. Read, "An account of English journalism in Canada from the middle of the eighteenth century to the beginning of the twentieth, with special emphasis being given to the periods prior to confederation" (unpublished MA thesis, McGill University, Montreal, 1925), 144. Rumilly, *Hist. de la prov. de Québec*, I. Thomas White, *Newspapers, their development in the province of Quebec* (Montreal, 1883).

KINNEAR, WILLIAM BOYD, lawyer, judge, politician, and office-holder; b. 2 Oct. 1796 in Dorchester, N.B., son of Andrew Kinnear, a loyalist and a member for Westmorland County in the first assembly in New Brunswick, and Letitia Boyd, both natives of County Derry (Northern Ireland); m. in 1830 Janet Muir of Edinburgh, Scotland; d. 22 Feb. 1868 in Saint John, N.B.

William Boyd Kinnear's Anglo-Irish, Anglican, loyalist background guaranteed him a role in the public affairs of New Brunswick. His first position, at age 17, was in the military pay office in Saint John. Three years later he began to read law in the Saint John office of Charles Jeffery Peters*, and was admitted to the bar in 1819. In 1827, during a visit to Halifax, he left the Church of England in favour of the Baptist faith [see James Walton NUTTING]. He was later cited by the Baptists as both a valuable prize and an irreplaceable asset.

His success as a barrister gained for him respect and influence. In 1828 he was appointed recorder of the city of Saint John and in 1830 was elected to the assembly for the city of Saint John, taking his seat two years later. As a member of the assembly Kinnear was a consistent supporter of the governor, even though he was increasingly involved with the success of the Baptist movement. He became active in the founding of the Baptist Seminary in Fredericton, and Acadia College in Wolfville, N.S. In 1833 Kinnear became a judge of the Court of Vice-Admiralty and he was named to the Legislative Council in 1839. He resigned from the assembly at that time.

Seven years later he was appointed solicitor general of the province, whereupon he relinquished the offices of recorder and judge and moved to Fredericton. Kinnear served as solicitor general with a distinction admitted by all shades of political opinion. He was displeased with the chaotic state of New Brunswick law, which made the administration of government difficult and often worked to the disadvantage of the ordinary citizens of the province. In the summer of 1851 Kinnear was appointed chairman of a special law commission with Charles Fisher* and James Watson CHANDLER as members. It was charged with the revision of the statutes of New Brunswick, and the simplification of judicial procedure in the courts of the province. After two years' work the commission concluded that "the practice of the law must . . . be founded more on the principle of common sense than on ancient precedent," and recommended sweeping reforms in the civil law and in its practice and regulation; although all of the proposals were not adopted, the report of the commission served as a basis for legal reform. Soon afterward Kinnear revised the statutes themselves into three comprehensive volumes.

The work of Kinnear as solicitor general, and his contribution as chairman of the law commission, fully justified his elevation to a vacant seat on the Supreme Court. He expected such an appointment, but politics overtook him. When the "smashers" gained power in 1854 [see Charles Fisher], they were determined to pursue their own ideas of responsible government. Kinnear lost his position as solicitor general, despite his pledge to work within the principle of responsibility. He also lost any chance he might have had for an appointment to the Supreme Court.

His public career at an end, Kinnear returned to Saint John, where he served as clerk of the peace and judge of probate. He devoted his later years to education, and his numerous and wide-ranging lectures to the mechanics' institute were well attended and well received. Although he was

a member of the Senate of the University of New Brunswick, his primary interest remained the Baptist Education Society.

As a public figure Kinnear had brought common sense to government and its function. As a religious leader, he brought to the Baptist movement respectability and energy.

P. M. TONER

N.B. Museum, Kinnear family papers. N.B., *Report of the commissioners for revising and consolidating the laws of the province of New Brunswick* (3v., Fredericton, 1853–54); *The revised statutes of New Brunswick . . .* (3v., Fredericton, 1854–55). I. E. Bill, *Fifty years with the Baptist ministers and churches of the Maritime provinces of Canada* (Saint John, N.B., 1880). Lawrence, *Judges of N.B.* (Stockton).

KIRKPATRICK, THOMAS, lawyer and politician; b. 25 Dec. 1805 at Coolmine House, Clonsilla, near Dublin (Republic of Ireland), fourth son of Alexander Kirkpatrick and Marianne Sutton; m. in 1829, Helen, daughter of Alexander Fisher*, a judge of the Midland District of Upper Canada, and they had five sons and three daughters; d. 26 March 1870 at Kingston, Ont.

Thomas Kirkpatrick came to Canada in 1823 and settled at Kingston where he read law in the office of Christopher Hagerman*. He was called to the bar in 1828 and established a flourishing practice in Kingston. From 1828 until 1845 he was collector of customs at Kingston, a lucrative position he probably owed to the influence of Hagerman whom he succeeded in the post. He became a QC in 1846.

Although he was not considered a brilliant lawyer, Kirkpatrick was a successful one and had a reputation for integrity and soundness of judgement especially in business matters. He was president of the Kingston Permanent Building Society and was the local solicitor of the Bank of Upper Canada from about 1837 until its collapse in 1866 and local solicitor to its trustees until his death. He was also a director of the bank on six occasions between 1846 and 1853 and a trustee of the property of James MORTON, one of the bank's largest debtors.

Kirkpatrick was a staunch Conservative who was influential in Kingston and Frontenac County politics; he took an active interest in local affairs. He was elected first mayor of the town of Kingston in 1838 but had to be disqualified as a non-resident. In 1847 he was elected as the city's second mayor. After being defeated by Alexander Campbell* in a bid for the Legislative Council in 1858, he became MP for Frontenac in the first dominion parliament in 1867.

Klatsassin

Kirkpatrick was an example of the sober upper middle class which ruled the cities and towns of Ontario until the end of World War I. Kirkpatrick's descendants retained their influence in Kingston after his death; his son, George Airey*, succeeded his father as MP and in 1892 was appointed lieutenant governor of Ontario.

M. L. MAGILL

QUA, Thomas Kirkpatrick papers; Kirkpatrick-Nickle legal records. *Daily British Whig* (Kingston), 28 March 1870. Armstrong, *Handbook of Upper Canadian chronology*. *Canadian directory of parl.* (Johnson). Chadwick, *Ontario families*.

KLATSASSIN (Klatsassan, Klattasine), Chilcotin chief; executed 26 Oct. 1864 at Quesnellemouth (Quesnel), B.C., and was apparently survived by two wives and several children.

The Chilcotins were a semi-nomadic hunting and fishing tribe of British Columbia inhabiting most of the Chilcotin River drainage basin and some adjoining territory. They had long and hostile relationships with some adjacent tribes – the Carriers and Lillooets, and some of the Shuswaps – but were in the main friendly with the Bella Coolas and the Canyon Shuswaps. Their social structure was loose, and their sense of unity as a tribe weak. The nature of leadership among the Chilcotins is not clear, but it is apparent that although it could be informal the hereditary principle also played a part, at least in the period following contact with whites.

The Chilcotins' relationships with white fur-traders before the years of the gold rush had been strained, and most had experienced only superficial contacts with missionaries. In 1862 a smallpox epidemic wiped out probably one-half to two-thirds of the tribe. In that year also Alfred Waddington* began work on a trail inland from Bute Inlet to run through Chilcotin territory. Many Chilcotins were attracted to the coast to work as packers for the construction crews.

In the spring of 1864 some goods left at Bute Inlet were discovered to have been stolen. A white man questioned a group of Chilcotins regarding the theft. Receiving no satisfaction, he took down their names, then told them that they would all die. The Chilcotins, who believed that it was possible to bring harm to others through spirits, doubtless thought that the white man had acquired a power of life and death over them through what seemed powerful magic, the writing down of their names. Their earlier experience of smallpox added to the effect of the threat as not long before smallpox had reached them in 1862 a white man was said to have threatened to bring it on them. His statement may have been merely a prediction rather than a threat, but it and the epidemic that followed had their effect on the Chilcotins when a threat really was made against them in the spring of 1864.

To the Chilcotins who had come to the Bute Inlet region, wiping out the whites seemed not only a revenge for the threat made there but also the only way to prevent the whites from bringing smallpox. This threat of smallpox was the chief immediate cause of the "Chilcotin Uprising" of 1864. Less direct causes were the Chilcotins' previous experience with other tribes and with whites, and a desire for plunder.

One of the Chilcotin chiefs was Klatsassin, described as athletic and bold-looking, with a great under-jaw. Although perhaps not a hereditary chief, he was nevertheless influential because of his physical vigour, intelligence, and commanding personality. On 29 April 1864 he and a number of other Chilcotins arrived at the ferry site about 30 miles up the Homathko River which led off Bute Inlet. Klatsassin shot the lone ferry-keeper, Tim Smith, and the Chilcotins plundered the stores, obtaining gunpowder and 30 pounds of balls.

About one mile above the ferry Klatsassin and his party met a Homathko Indian and the Chilcotin chief Telloot (Taloot, Tellot), who had come down to the Bute Inlet area in 1863 looking for work. Apparently Telloot had been employed by whites before and a written reference to his character said he was a "faithful and trustworthy guide." The artist Frederick Whymper*, who had employed him as a guide in the Bute Inlet area in 1864, described Telloot as "an Indian of some intelligence." He was a much older man than Klatsassin and an influential chief of a section of the tribe. Church of England clergyman R. C. Lundin Brown* later mentioned him as "a man of great authority with his tribe."

Klatsassin told Telloot how he had killed the ferryman and after some argument Telloot joined Klatsassin. The Homathko who had accompanied Telloot hurried down-river, while Klatsassin, Telloot, and their party went up-river to the main road camp and there joined other members of their tribe. At dawn next morning (30 April) the Chilcotins attacked the 12 unsuspecting road-workers at the main camp. Only three escaped. Next the four workmen at the advance camp about two miles up-river were attacked; all perished. Proceeding into the interior to escape possible pursuit, Klatsassin and his followers (some 16 men and an undetermined number of women) reached Nancoontloon (Anahim) Lake where they were joined by more Chilcotins. They ambushed a pack-train; three whites were killed, but five escaped and reached Bentinck Arm. A settler at Puntzi Lake was also shot and his house looted, then destroyed.

Governor Frederick SEYMOUR of British Columbia reacted swiftly. He sent an expedition under Police Magistrate Chartres BREW to the Homathko on 15 May, and another from Alexandria under Gold Commissioner William George Cox* which penetrated to Puntzi Lake. Brew returned to New Westminster and Seymour himself accompanied a second expedition under Brew which met Cox at Puntzi Lake on 6 July; both expeditions searched the country to the southwest. Cox later received several messages from Klatsassin and Telloot, and on 15 August they and six others came to Cox's camp-site. Apparently they interpreted a message from Cox in reply as guaranteeing their freedom and their lives. Cox, however, regarded their coming as an outright surrender and was not ready to admit any such guarantee had been made.

The eight Indians were taken to Quesnellemouth. Two, having no specific charges against them, were freed; Chedékki, sent to New Westminster for trial, escaped on the way. Chief Justice Matthew Baillie Begbie* sentenced Klatsassin, Telloot, Tahpit, Chessus, and Piel (or Pierre, Klatsassin's 18-year-old son) to be hanged. Lundin Brown acted as their spiritual counsellor. By means of an interpreter he instructed the prisoners in Christian teachings over many days. The Chilcotins had already been in either direct or indirect contact with Roman Catholic missionaries and at first, seeing that Brown had no crucifix about his neck, were somewhat dubious of his credentials as a true priest. But before the time of their execution they had accepted him and satisfied him as to their repentance and true faith.

A crowd of about 200 gathered to watch the execution on 26 October. Brief prayers were said in Chilcotin, Brown having now gained some knowledge of it, and, as each prisoner was blindfolded, he gave a blessing in their language. Tahpit suddenly called out to his fellow-prisoners to "have courage." Then, addressing the Carrier Indians who had gathered, he said, "Tell the Chilcoatens to cease anger against the whites," and added: "We are going to see the Great Father."

Klatsassin's role in almost every part of the Chilcotin uprising was a prominent one, and he was evidently the instigator and main planner. Without his forceful leadership it could not have been carried on for as long as it was. Yet the fact that he embarked on such a hopeless course shows how little he understood the position of his own people and the overwhelming strength of the white man.

EDWARD SLEIGH HEWLETT

PABC, Colonial correspondence, M. B. Begbie correspondence; Miscellaneous material relating to Fort Chilcotin, "Fort Chilcotin" (typescript). PAC, RG 7, G8, C, 26 April–20 Dec. 1865 (copies at University of British Columbia Library, Special Coll. Division). University of British Columbia Library, Special Coll. Division (Vancouver), Robie L. Reid papers, material on Alfred Waddington. Ross Cox, *The Columbia River; or scenes and adventures during a residence of six years on the western side of the Rocky Mountains . . .*, ed. E. I. and J. R. Stewart (Norman, Okla., 1957). Frederick Whymper, *Travel and adventure in the territory of Alaska, formerly Russian America – now ceded to the United States – and in various other parts of the north Pacific* (London, 1868).

British Columbian (New Westminster, B.C.), 28 May, 2 Nov. 1864. *Daily British Colonist* (Victoria), 15 Nov. 1862, 6 July 1863, 12 May 1864. *Daily Press* (Victoria), 4 Sept. 1862. *Victoria Daily Chronicle*, 12, 29 May 1864. R. C. L. Brown, *Klatsassan, and other reminiscences of missionary life in British Columbia* (London, 1873). R. B. Lane, "Cultural relations of the Chilcotin Indians of west central British Columbia" (unpublished PHD thesis, University of Washington, Seattle, 1953). A.-G. Morice, *The great Déné race* (Vienna, n.d.); *History of northern interior of B.C.* (1904); *History of the Catholic Church*, II. E. S. Hewlett, "The Chilcotin uprising of 1864," *BC Studies*, 19 (autumn 1973), 50–72. F. J. Saunders, "'Homatcho'; or, the story of the Bute Inlet expedition, and the massacre by the Chilcoaten Indians," *Resources of British Columbia* (Victoria), III (March 1885), 5–8; III (April 1885), 5–6.

KNOWLTON, PAUL HOLLAND, pioneer industrialist, soldier, and politician; b. 17 Sept. 1787 in Newfane, Vt, son of Silas Knowlton and Sally Holbrook, grandson of the Honourable Luke Knowlton, judge of the Supreme Court of Vermont in 1786 and a loyalist sympathizer; d. 28 Aug. 1863 in Knowlton, Canada East.

Silas Knowlton took up in 1796 the British government's offer of wild land in Canada made earlier to his father, who had been too old to accept it. Paul Holland was only 11 when he came to the future Stukely Township in Lower Canada, but he remembered the struggles of pioneer life. The family of three boys and one girl was left motherless in 1800 and Paul Holland was sent back to his grandparents in Newfane to be educated. He returned to Stukely in 1807 and on 22 Sept. 1808 married Laura Moss, a schoolteacher of Bridport, Vt. Not having any children of their own, they adopted a boy and a girl of his brother Luke's large family.

Knowlton

In 1815, after farming in Stukely, Paul Holland Knowlton moved to Brome Lake in Brome Township where he cleared a farm, built a home on the lake, and operated a store and distillery. In 1827 he was appointed agent to dispose of the unsold land in Brome Township for its absentee owners; a few years later he had purchased much of the land himself. The early proprietors had mortgaged most of the land in the township so that settlers were discouraged from purchasing; under Knowlton's management and ownership the mortgages were discharged and the land disposed of. On 26 Oct. 1830 he became representative for the newly formed Shefford County in the House of Assembly of Lower Canada, and held the seat until 9 Oct. 1834.

In that year Knowlton became one of the first corresponding members from the Eastern Townships of the Literary and Historical Society of Quebec; the early local interest in history he encouraged survives today in the Brome County Historical Society. Knowlton was also president from 1834 to 1836 of the Shefford County Agricultural Society formed at a meeting over which he presided in Waterloo on 15 June 1834; one of the first county agricultural societies in Lower Canada, its formation was assisted by a bill "to make more ample provision for the encouragement of Agriculture" promoted by Knowlton himself in the legislature.

Knowlton moved in 1834 from his farm on Brome Lake to a site beside a large stream flowing into the lake. Here he took up water rights, first erecting a sawmill to produce building materials. He built a large house with offices attached, a smithy and its shop, a pearlashery, and later a store and a grist mill which became the nucleus of the village of Knowlton, called Coldbrook until its post office was set up in 1851. These facilities enhanced the value of the wild land in the neighbourhood, much of which either belonged to him or passed through his hands.

During the rebellion of 1837 in Lower Canada Knowlton helped arm and equip 400 men in Shefford Township and was promoted lieutenant-colonel of the Shefford battalion of militia on 1 Dec. 1837. A detachment under his command captured one of the Patriote leaders, Dr Wolfred NELSON, in the Shefford area on 12 Dec. 1837. His Shefford Volunteers were also "on guard at Granby . . . to protect the families and property from American sympathizers and Canadian refugees." Colonel Knowlton assisted in furnishing the Missisquoi militia with arms and ammunition for the battle at Moore's Corner (Saint-Armand-Station) on 6 Dec. 1837. He received the special thanks of Sir John COLBORNE who called him in

1838 to sit on the Special Council which governed Lower Canada while it was under martial law.

Mention of these activities in an English newspaper had a curious sequel. Miss Sarah Knowlton of Darley Dale, Derbyshire, England, wrote to Knowlton claiming that she was a relative. Knowlton visited her and they kept up a correspondence. In April 1845 he learned that she had died leaving him heir to her fortune.

Knowlton was named to the Legislative Council of the Province of Canada on 9 June 1841. He was active throughout the 1840s in voicing the needs of the Eastern Townships. In 1846 he introduced a bill to facilitate the partition of lands in the Townships, and in 1847 served on a commission which made recommendations to prevent immigrants to Canada from being induced by American speculators to settle in the United States. In 1847 also, he and Philip Henry Moore* of Missisquoi objected in local newspapers that the recently adopted free trade would mean too heavy competition for Canadian goods in the home market and called for protective legislative action. Knowlton had also objected in 1846 to the inequality of representation in the Legislative Council: Canada West had 18 members but Canada East only 15. Nor did he and Moore feel one member from the Townships was enough, but, according to Knowlton, in speaking to the governor, Charles Murray Cathcart*, on this subject they might as well have "addressed a horse block."

Knowlton signed the Annexation Manifesto of 1849, thus placing himself among those who felt that, with the economy of the country at its lowest ebb, union in a great North American confederacy of states would be a particular benefit to Canada East. When it came to a decision between loyalty to the British crown and the progress of his country Knowlton firmly supported the latter. As a result he lost his military commission, at the special request of the member from Shefford, Lewis Thomas Drummond*, who according to a local newspaper wanted a friend appointed to the position.

Knowlton's interest in his own area remained constant. In 1849 he obtained, through his influence as a legislative councillor, a grant for a road through Brome Township that brought traffic to Knowlton. He gave land and funds for the building of a high school in 1854 in Knowlton, just as he had earlier contributed to the erection of the Anglican church and rectory. To Knowlton also goes the credit for securing Brome County in 1855 out of parts of Stanstead, Shefford, and Missisquoi counties. He was elected first warden of the county, and became first president of the

Brome County Agricultural Society on 12 July 1856. He worked to have the counties organized into districts for judicial purposes, and in 1857 Brome County became a part of the judicial district of Bedford.

The *Advertiser and Eastern Townships Sentinel* was started in Knowlton in 1856 by Lucius Seth Huntington*, who acted as editor, and Knowlton, who provided influence and financial support. Articles in the early issues reflect some of Knowlton's political views, especially that the interests of rural districts were not fairly represented in parliament. In 1860 Knowlton and Moore took up a lively issue in the paper by appealing for a meeting before a forthcoming election of a new legislative councillor which would determine that henceforth the voters would be represented in parliament by residents of the Townships. When Knowlton felt that the editor had become too radical, the partnership was dissolved.

Paul Holland Knowlton died on 28 Aug. 1863 at his home in Knowlton. Many memorials of his liberality remain in the village of Knowlton, including the Paul Holland Knowlton Memorial Museum in the original high school he assisted. All through his career he had kept the progress of the province as his first goal and he became inseparably connected with the history of his own area.

MARION L. PHELPS

BCHS Arch., VII, Paul Holland Knowlton papers. Franklin County Registry Office (St Albans, Vt.), marriage records, 22 Sept. 1808. L.C., House of Assembly, *Journals*, 1830. *Advertiser and Eastern Townships Sentinel* (Knowlton and Waterloo, [Que.]), 8, 29 Feb. 1856, 10 May 1860, 3 Sept. 1863. *Montreal Herald*, 26 May 1847. *Philipsburg Gleaner* (Philipsburg, [Que.]), 23 Feb. 1847. *Stanstead Journal* (Rock Island, [Que.]), 9 April 1846. G. Turcotte, *Cons. législatif de Québec*, 9, 132–33. C. M. Day, *History of the Eastern Townships, province of Quebec, dominion of Canada, civil and descriptive, etc.* (Montreal, 1869), 256. J. P. Noyes, *Sketches of some early Shefford pioneers* ([Montreal], 1905), 15. *Stanstead County Historical Society centennial journal* (2v., n.p., 1965–67), II, 85. C. H. W. Stocking, *The history and genealogy of the Knowltons of England and America* (New York, 1897), 118. E. M. Taylor, *History of Brome County, Quebec, from the date of grants of land therein to the present time; with records of some early families* (2v., Montreal, 1908–37), I, 164–65, 169, 281. Cyrus Thomas, *Contributions to the history of the Eastern Townships: a work containing an account of the early settlement of St. Armand, Dunham, Sutton, Brome, Potton, and Bolton; with a history of the principal events that have transpired in each of these townships up to the present time* (Montreal, 1866), 235–37, 267–71. "The Moore's Corner battle in 1837," Missisquoi County Hist. Soc., *Annual report* (Saint-Jean, Que.), 1908–9, 70–71. "Parliamentary representation of Missisquoi from the beginning of parliaments in Canada," Missisquoi County Hist. Soc., *Annual report* (Saint-Jean, Que.), 1907, 29–30.

KOUGH, PATRICK, builder, architect, politician, and office-holder; b. *c*. 1786 in County Wexford (Republic of Ireland); d. 9 Nov. 1863 at St John's, Nfld.

Patrick Kough came to St John's about 1804 as a boy with little education; he became a carpenter, and later a successful building contractor. He built the stone court house and jail at Harbour Grace in 1830–31. Shortly after finishing it he replaced the roof of the newly constructed Government House in St John's after a wind storm had blown it off; his completion of the court house on time and for the stipulated price had earned him the job.

In 1826 Kough had become captain of the fire company founded in St John's that year. He was also a member and officer of the Benevolent Irish Society and at various times served as chairman, treasurer, and secretary of the society's Orphan Asylum school after it opened on 17 Feb. 1826. By 1833 he was president of the St John's Mechanics' Society.

Appointed superintendent of Newfoundland's public buildings in 1834 at £50 a year, Kough continued in this position until his death. From 1847 to 1849 he was superintending inspector for the construction of the Colonial Building, opened on 28 Jan. 1850, where the assembly met until 1959; he had been influential in having the site of this building changed from that of the present court house, a wise decision since the steepness of the latter location was not suitable for the Grecian design. Kough's government appointment evidently allowed him to work on other contracts in St John's. In 1835 he built St Thomas' Church [*see* WIX]; he supervised the building of an addition to the Orphan Asylum in 1841 and the rebuilding of its school in 1857, as well as the construction of the convent of the Sisters of the Presentation of the Blessed Virgin Mary in 1850 [*see* MOLONY].

In the first assembly election under representative government in 1832, Kough, a Roman Catholic, ran for one of the St John's seats, against Reformers William Carson* and John Kent*, who were actively supported by the Roman Catholic bishop, Michael Anthony Fleming*; Kough, Kent, and William Thomas were elected. After his defeat Carson petitioned unsuccessfully for Kough's disqualification from

Labatt

the assembly because he had worked on government construction jobs before his election, but the house dismissed the petition. No rules had been enacted about disqualifications; Carson himself was drawing a salary as district surgeon when he was elected in a by-election of 1833 and the colonial treasurer, Patrick Morris*, was sitting in the assembly. During the next three years Kough was a prominent and active member, serving on committees dealing with the fisheries and with finance.

In the next general election in 1836, Kough and two colleagues of the mercantile party, Nicholas Gill and John Thomas Grieve, were bitterly opposed by the leading Catholic clergy and by most of the Roman Catholic population of the town. Kough and his Catholic supporters were dubbed "Orange Catholics" and in some instances were denied the right of attending church and the use of the sacraments. On the day of the election Kough and his colleagues resigned from the contest, alleging intimidation, and joined in a petition to declare the election void. When a new election was held in 1837 Kough, like some others of the mercantile group, did not run. In November 1836 he had sued Robert John Parsons*, the pro-liberal editor of the *Newfoundland Patriot*, for libellous statements made in that paper and was ultimately awarded £100 in damages. Kough was not again

active in the political life of the colony until 1860–63, when he sat in the Legislative Council.

Kough was interested in farming; he developed a large farm, Ken Mount, on the western outskirts of St John's, and for a time in the 1850s was president of the Agricultural Society. He also served on the Roman Catholic Board of Education. His widow Mary, two sons, and six daughters survived him.

Governor Thomas John Cochrane* wrote that Kough was one of the most respectable men in St John's, an efficient member of the assembly, and the most trustworthy builder in the town. At the time of his death the *Newfoundlander* lauded his "probity and consistency of conduct."

FABIAN O'DEA

PANL, Nfld., Dept. of Surveyor General, W. R. Noel, "Plan of St. John's" (1849). PRO, CO 194/95–99. *Newfoundlander*, 23 Aug. 1832; 28 Feb., 14 March 1833; 12 Nov. 1863. *Public Ledger*, 11 Nov., 27 Dec. 1836; 16 May 1837; 20 Jan., 3 March 1857. *Royal Gazette* (St John's), 18 Feb. 1828, 1 Feb. 1859, 17 Jan. 1860. Gunn, *Political history of Nfld*. H. W. LeMessurier, *The Church of Saint Thomas and its rectors, 1836–1928* (St John's, [1928]). *The story of the Colonial Building, seat of parliament from 1850 to 1960, now the home of the Newfoundland and Labrador provincial archives* ([St John's], 1972).

L

LABATT, JOHN KINDER, farmer and brewer; b. 1803 at Mountmellick (County Laoighis, Republic of Ireland), eldest of the seven children of Valentine Knightley Chetwode Labat (Labatt), whose Huguenot ancestors came from the Bordeaux region of France, and his wife Jane; d. 26 Oct. 1866 at London, Canada West.

Little is known of the early life of John Kinder Labatt. In August 1833 he married Eliza Kell, a relative of the great Norwich banker, Daniel Gurney, at Twickenham, Middlesex County, England. They were to have five sons and nine daughters. John and his wife immigrated to Upper Canada and in January 1834 purchased a 200-acre tract from the Canada Company in Westminster Township, just south of the town of London. In 1843 he acquired 200 acres adjacent to his lot from Colonel Thomas Talbot* for £50. He prospered in farming, sent his sons to the Caradoc Academy, the best boarding school in the region, and in 1844 played a leading role in the

construction of Christ Church (Church of England) at Glanworth.

In 1846–47, possibly because of temporary difficulties with his English investments which were being handled by his father-in-law, Labatt visited Great Britain and considered remaining there, but the high cost of living sent him back to Canada. He sold his farm and invested £2,000 in the brewery operated by his friend Samuel Eccles, located, as it still is, on the south branch of the Thames at the foot of Talbot St. This was the oldest brewery in London, having been established by John Balkwill in 1827–28, then acquired by William Balkwill and Thomas W. Shepherd before it was sold to Eccles in 1847. Labatt and Eccles, as the firm was called, was soon producing three brands, XXX, XX, and X; Labatt prospered sufficiently to be able to buy Eccles' interest when the latter retired in 1854. Labatt then changed the name to the London Brewery, and advertised himself as a brewer, maltster, and

436

dealer in barley, malt, and hops. He was assisted by his eldest sons Ephraim and Robert; they later purchased their own brewery at Prescott, Ont., from a younger son, John, who joined his father in 1864.

Labatt was also active in the affairs of London. He was a member of the town council for St David's Ward in 1850–51 and of the council of the Board of Trade in 1863. Interested in transportation ventures, he was one of the principals of the Proof Line Road Joint Stock Company, which extended communications north of London after 1849, and an incorporator of the London and Port Stanley Railway in 1853. He also helped establish the London Permanent Building and Savings Society and the Western Permanent Building Society, which were absorbed by the Huron and Erie Savings and Loan Society in 1865 and 1866 respectively. He was a parishioner of St Paul's Cathedral (Church of England) and was prominent in aiding the needy of London in the great depression of the late 1850s.

When John K. Labatt died in 1866 his estate was valued at $16,000. The firm was purchased by his son John under the terms of the will and the presidency of the company remained with John, then with John's sons John S. and Hugh F., until 1956. The corporation became a public company in 1945 and was controlled by the family trust until 1964, by which time it was one of Canada's largest breweries.

FREDERICK H. ARMSTRONG

Labatt family records are in the possession of Mrs Hugh F. Labatt of London, Ont., and of John Labatt Limited (London, Ont.). London Public Library and Art Museum (London, Ont.), Edwin Seaborn coll., Medical history, p. 369; Medical doctors, pp. 178, 446, 584. Middlesex County Surrogate Court (London, Ont.), will and inventory of J. K. Labatt, 25 April 1864, probated 13 Nov. 1866. Gore Gazette (Ancaster, [Ont.]), 24 Nov. 1827. Inquirer (London, [Ont.]), 15 Nov. 1844. London Free Press, 29 Oct. 1866. London Times (London, [Ont.]), 1 Oct. 1847. "John Labatt, London, Ont.," The newspaper reference book of Canada ... (Toronto, 1903), 411. History of the county of Middlesex (Brock), 196, 233, 285, 362, 372, 473, 575. London and its men of affairs (London, Ont., n.d.), 68, 70, 133.

LABELLE, LUDGER, lawyer, journalist, and politician; baptized 7 April 1839 in the parish of Notre-Dame in Montreal, son of Jean-Baptiste-Napoléon Labelle and Éloïse Leclaire; d. 29 Dec. 1867 at Montreal.

Ludger Labelle's childhood was saddened by the death of his mother, who for many years had been "in a decline." His father, an artisan who had been at the Collège de Montréal with Louis-Hippolyte LA FONTAINE and had thought of becoming a priest, saw that he received a sound education. After attending primary school, Ludger studied at the Collège de Montréal from 1850 to 1857; he then chose the legal profession. He was called to the bar on 3 July 1860, and went into partnership with Joseph-Alfred Mousseau*, the future leader of the Quebec Conservative party.

Labelle, according to his brother-in-law André-Napoléon Montpetit*, had "a brilliant mind, an extremely likable nature," and he rapidly emerged as one of the most promising young professional men. By 1861 he was a captain and staff officer in the Chasseurs Canadiens, a militia corps which the superintendent of police, Charles-Joseph Coursol*, recruited during the Trent affair. For Labelle, law was primarily a means of livelihood. He had a bent for journalism, and he was intellectually drawn towards politics. Described by Laurent-Olivier David*, who knew him well, as "the most unorganized person imaginable," Labelle drafted at night the articles he published. While a student, he had been for a time editor of the paper La Guêpe, which had been started by Cyrille BOUCHER in 1857. Later, at Montreal, Labelle founded Le Colonisateur, which first appeared on 2 Jan. 1862. This bi-weekly numbered among its contributors prominent young Conservatives such as Mousseau, David, and Joseph-Adolphe Chapleau*, and advocated colonization as "the surest means of preserving intact the precious trust of our faith and traditions." Le Colonisateur reflected the interests of its editors in the arts, science, and literature; it proclaimed a genuine political independence but never hesitated to defend the Bleus and fight the Rouges. Well written, but not a paying proposition, the paper came to an unceremonious end when on 27 June 1863 the printer Pierre Cérat refused to continue to print it.

For Labelle Le Colonisateur had been merely a stepping-stone to politics. He had rallied to the Liberal-Conservative banner, and his first political success came in 1863 when he was elected a councillor for the Sainte-Marie district in Montreal, an office he held until his death. He and his friends dreamed of still greater successes and were dumbfounded by the announcement in June 1864 of a coalition of parties to set up a Canadian confederation. They split into two camps. Chapleau and Mousseau remained loyal to their party, but in the summer of 1864 Labelle joined Médéric Lanctot* and the young Turks who opposed confederation and were in revolt against George-Étienne Cartier*.

Labillois

While conducting a vigorous campaign with Lanctot to bring politics to the mass of the people and to mobilize them, Labelle started the Saint-Jean-Baptiste Club, where the opinions expressed privately corresponded to those *L'Union nationale*, Lanctot's paper, was voicing aloud. The club was started either in the autumn of 1864 or during the winter of 1865, and had a meeting-place, initiation rites, and a password. It included members of the assembly, lawyers, business-men, and, the final ironic touch, the Montreal chief of police, Guillaume Lamothe, and a number of police officers. With this organization the club was more noisy than dangerous, but it managed to worry the establishment. Judge Charles-Joseph Coursol, infuriated as much by the club's relentless opposition to Cartier as by the fact that it had given shelter for a month to one of the Confederates who had made a raid in October 1864 against St Albans, Vt, ordered its dissolution.

The club had some success in politics. It ensured the defeat by a merchant-grocer of young Chapleau in the elections for the municipal council, and it got Labelle re-elected. The son of a workman, Labelle had remained close to his roots. Short and puny, he had retained the awkward bearing and impulsive movements that were the mark of his working-class origins. Affable and courteous, he knew "the names of most of the workers in the East division of Montreal, as well as those of their wives and children," according to L.-O. David. Labelle maintained with his Sainte-Marie electors a political relationship typical of rural circles.

The unconditional support of his electors helped Labelle to establish himself as the leader of young dissident Conservatives and Lanctot's right hand man. Their role became clear in the 1867 elections. Both men tried their strength, unsuccessfully, against Cartier in Montreal East: Lanctot sought election to the House of Commons and Labelle to the provincial legislature. It is the duel between Lanctot and Cartier that is remembered, and the role of Labelle is underestimated. Throughout the whole summer he went from door to door and harangued the electors in the streets and at popular meetings. André-Napoléon Montpetit, his comrade in arms, later recalled the hard campaign of 1867: "We have had few men as skilful in organization, as shrewd in method, as wily in expedients, as persevering, not to say unrelenting."

Labelle emerged from this electoral campaign emotionally broken and financially ruined, and seems to have abandoned the struggle at that time. He was living with his father and aunt.

Disillusioned, he returned briefly to the practice of law, which ill suited his bohemian inclinations. Like his brother Elzéar, he had a poet's soul, with a particularly lively gift for rhyming songs. Labelle died in December 1867, remembered as a man endowed with a noble and charitable nature, a just spirit, and a shrewd mind.

HUGUETTE FILTEAU and JEAN HAMELIN

[Ludger Labelle did not leave any private papers. Contemporary newspapers note his political activities but reveal nothing of his professional and private life. Laurent-Olivier David, who knew him well, drew a faithful portrait of him in *Mes contemporains* (Montréal, 1894), but no further attempt has been made to investigate this intriguing person. He has received only passing mention in historical works. É.-Z. Massicotte* in *Faits curieux de l'histoire de Montréal* (Montréal, 1922) and Victor Morin* in his article "Clubs et sociétés notoires d'autrefois," *Cahiers des Dix*, 16 (1951), 233–70, describe the Club Saint-Jean-Baptiste and sketch Labelle's role in it. Labelle figures briefly in Léon Trépanier*'s articles on Montreal, "Figures de maires," and "Guillaume Lamothe (1824–1911)," in *Cahiers des Dix*, 22 (1957), 163–92, and 29 (1964), 143–58, respectively, as well as in Robert Rumilly, *Hist. de Montréal*. J.H. and H.F.]

ANQ-M, État civil, Catholiques, Notre-Dame de Montréal, 7 avril 1839. PAC, MG 30, D62, 17, pp.27–32. Elzéar Labelle, *Mes rimes*, A.-N. Montpetit, édit. (Québec, 1876), 15–16, 21. *Le Colonisateur* (Montréal), 2 janv. 1862–27 juin 1863. *Le Pays*, 31 déc. 1867.

LABILLOIS (La Billois), CHARLES-MARIE, surgeon; b. 8 July 1793 at Ploërmel (dept of Morbihan, France), son of Jean-Pierre Labillois, a district secretary, and Périnne-Louise Gaillard; d. 16 Sept. 1868 at Restigouche, Que.

Charles-Marie Labillois was a surgeon in the French Marine before arriving in 1816 at Miguasha, Lower Canada. That year he married Émilie Meagher, sister of John Meagher, who was later MHA for the county of Bonaventure; they were to have ten children. He practised medicine for more than 30 years, then in 1849 was invited to look after the sick in the leper hospital at Tracadie, N.B.

Leprosy had probably appeared in Gloucester and Northumberland counties at the beginning of the century but the provincial authorities did not take an interest in the fate of the unfortunate people stricken with it until the 1840s. In April 1844 they created the first county board of health; its members included Joseph CUNARD, an influential shipbuilder, and François-Xavier-Stanislas LAFRANCE, parish priest of Tracadie. In that year a lazaret was established on Sheldrake Island in Miramichi Bay; five years later, in

July 1849, a leper hospital was opened at Tracadie.

Although their living conditions had improved, the lepers, with the support of their families and the inhabitants of neighbouring parishes, demanded the appointment of a doctor for the establishment. The new board of health set up in April 1849, agreed that Dr Labillois, who was well known for having cured several lepers in the Baie des Chaleurs region, should visit the hospital and treat the sick. However, as no provision had been made to remunerate a resident doctor for his services, the board refused to guarantee Labillois a salary. He none the less cared for the 31 patients in the hospital from September 1849 to January 1850. According to the secretary of the board, James Davidson, Labillois cured a fair number of lepers and improved hygienic conditions in the establishment. With no further guarantees, Dr Labillois worked there for six more months in 1850.

On 19 Dec. 1850, soon after his departure, Labillois wrote to the board of health to say that "almost all the sores of both old and new patients have been cured." Nevertheless, following an inquiry conducted by Dr Robert Gordon – who, as it happened, was to replace Labillois in 1851 – the board concluded that Labillois had hospitalized some non lepers, to "make people believe that there had been cures," and rejected Labillois' assertions. Labillois in turn contradicted the conclusions of the report of a medical commission which had been set up in 1844 by the lieutenant governor of the province, Sir William MacBean George COLEBROOKE, and included Dr Gordon; Labillois maintained that the sick at Tracadie were suffering from syphilis and not leprosy. However, when certain patients whom he had declared cured returned to the hospital he was further discredited. Judged incompetent, but to some extent the victim of a coterie, Labillois is thought to have left Tracadie without ever having been remunerated. His activities until his death in 1868 are unknown.

In any event, Labillois' stay at Tracadie benefitted the sick. His presence, devotion, and treatments effected many improvements, which were confirmed both by James Davidson and by the chaplains of the leper hospital, Abbés Lafrance and Ferdinand-Edmond Gauvreau*, and by the lepers themselves. The medical aid he gave was certainly appreciated, for in 1860 Abbé Gauvreau and 212 other signatories were still demanding his return.

GÉRARD GOYER

Archives départementales, Morbihan (Vannes), État civil, Ploërmel, 8 juill. 1793. Archives judiciaires, Bonaventure (New Carlisle, Qué.), Registre d'état civil, paroisse Saint-Joseph-de-Carleton, 18 sept. 1868. N.B., House of Assembly, *Journals*, 1850–53. *Les Courriers des Provinces maritimes* (Bathurst, N.-B.), 12 juill. 1894. *Le Moniteur acadien* (Shédiac, N.-B.), 16 oct. 1868. Patrice Gallant, *Les registres de la Gaspésie (1752–1860)* (6v., s.l., s.d.), III, 300. Heagerty, *Four centuries of medical history in Can.*, I, 161–67. F.-M. Lajat, *Le lazaret de Tracadie et la communauté des Religieuses hospitalières de Saint-Joseph* (Montréal, 1938), 19–155. [J.-]É. Lefebvre de Bellefeuille, "Les lépreux de Tracadie," *Revue canadienne* (Montréal), VII (1870), 545–74.

LACOMBE (Truillier, *dit* Lacombe), PATRICE, notary and writer; b. 20 Feb. 1807 at the Lac-des-Deux-Montagnes mission (Oka, Que.), son of François-Xavier Truillier, *dit* Lacombe, merchant, and Geneviève Adhémar; d. 6 July 1863 at Montreal.

Patrice Lacombe studied at the Collège de Montréal from 1816 to 1825. He displayed there an aptitude for a happy turn of phrase, to judge by the prize lists, where he is recorded as receiving first prizes for translation from Latin and for Latin dissertation. He was admitted to the profession of notary on 31 Dec. 1830, and two years later entered the service of the Society of Saint-Sulpice, as their business agent. The management of the immense possessions of the Sulpicians did not take all his time, as the quantity of acts he signed shows.

Lacombe's life as a notary seems not to have been marked by any unexpected occurrences. On 7 Jan. 1835, at Saint-Joseph-de-Maskinongé (Maskinongé, Que.), he married Léocadie Boucher, widow of John Dies Nelson; Lacombe left no heirs. All his obituary notices attributed to him the qualities of a well-ordered life: integrity, affability, respectability. Without giving any precise information, they said that he encouraged literature.

Patrice Lacombe would certainly have sunk into oblivion if he had not written a short novel, which first appeared in the *Album littéraire et musical de la "Revue canadienne"* in 1846 and was then published by James Huston* in *Le répertoire national.* . . . "La terre paternelle" tells the story of a peasant family, the Chauvins, beset by misfortune because of the younger son's departure for the *pays d'en haut*. To prevent the elder son from following his example the father gives him his land, but under onerous conditions. He is soon forced to take it back, and decides to rent it out in order to buy a business. This does not prosper, and he has to declare bankruptcy. Having lost his land, he goes off, an exile, to the city, where he and his son become water carriers.

La Fontaine

The family then knows hardship and hunger. After ten years of this miserable existence the elder son dies, and Chauvin, for lack of money, has to surrender him to the charnel-house and to every kind of profanation. Luckily the younger son returns from the northwest with his pockets well lined, and the family is then able to recover their land and their lost happiness.

This little novel is not remarkable as a piece of writing but is notable for having inaugurated regionalist literature in Quebec. While other writers, such as Joseph Doutre*, Eugène L'Écuyer*, or Pierre-Georges Boucher* de Boucherville, were striving to follow the French serialists, Lacombe endeavoured to describe the "pure and simple customs" of a countryside whose people bear "the greatest adversities with resignation and patience." But although it is the prototype of the "roman de la terre paternelle," which was to have more than 60 examples, Lacombe's story is not a stereotype for this kind of writing. It was more than half a century later that Damase Potvin* wrote of elderly fathers who want to bequeath their land to their only son. The son, lured by the city, leaves his home, only to meet degradation and disillusionment. In some of the stories he dies, or he may return home recognizing his error. Such a concept of rural life was still in a primitive form when Lacombe wrote, and could not suggest to him all the possible effects he might produce. But, though his writing was not of the liveliest, he wrote correctly, and often managed scenes that had colour, for instance the sketch of the voyageurs' inn, the auction at the door of the church, the realistic description of the squalid house in the *faubourg* Saint-Laurent, and finally the return of the voyageurs from the *pays d'en haut*. For a modest effort, this novel accomplished much.

MAURICE LEMIRE

Patrice Lacombe's *La terre paternelle* was first published in February 1846 in *Album littéraire et musical de la "Revue canadienne"* (Montréal). It has been reprinted at least 11 times, the last in 1972. A complete description of the reprints can be found in D. M. Hayne and Marcel Tirol, *Bibliographie critique du roman canadien-français, 1837–1900* ([Québec et Toronto], 1968), 95–97.

ANQ-M, Greffe de Patrice Lacombe, 1831–63. Archives judiciaires, Terrebonne (Saint-Jérôme, Qué.), Registre d'état civil, Lac-des-Deux-Montagnes, 21 févr. 1807. *JIP*, juill.-août 1863, 121–22. *Le Journal de Québec*, 9 juill. 1863. *La Minerve*, 7 juill. 1863. *Le Monde illustré* (Montréal), 10 sept. 1892. Albert Dandurand, *Le roman canadien-français* (Montréal, 1937), 29–37. D. M. Hayne, "Les origines du roman canadien-français," *Le roman canadien-français, évolution-témoignages-bibliographie* (Montréal et Paris, [1964]), 55–57. *Histoire de la littérature française du Québec*, Pierre de Grandpré, édit. (4v., Montréal, 1967–69), I, 178–84. Léopold Lamontagne, "Les courants idéologiques dans la littérature canadienne-française du XIXᵉ siècle," *Littérature et société canadiennes-françaises*, Fernand Dumont et J.-C. Falardeau, édit. (Québec, 1964), 101–19. J.-E. Roy, *Hist. du notariat*, II, 85–87. Richard Lessard, "Patrice Lacombe, auteur de *La terre paternelle*," *BRH*, XLVI (1940), 180. Réjean Robidoux, "Fortunes et infortunes de l'abbé Casgrain," *Revue de l'université d'Ottawa*, XXXI (1961), 209–29.

LA FONTAINE (Ménard, *dit* La Fontaine), Sir LOUIS-HIPPOLYTE (he signed LaFontaine; the spelling Hypolite is used on certain documents including his certificate of baptism), politician and judge; b. 4 Oct. 1807 at Boucherville, Lower Canada, third son of Antoine Ménard, *dit* La Fontaine, a carpenter, and Marie-Josephte Fontaine, *dit* Bienvenue; d. 26 Feb. 1864 at Montreal.

Louis-Hippolyte La Fontaine attracted attention at an early age. At the Collège de Montréal, where he began classical studies in 1820, he rapidly distinguished himself by a love of work and an astonishing memory. His fellow students called him "the big brain." He was considered the most gifted, although he always came second in his class. (According to an oft-told story Louis-Joseph Plessis, who always was first in the class, later became a drunkard and for several years sponged off La Fontaine.) At recess, La Fontaine was acknowledged as the most energetic and most skilful, particularly at tennis in which he had no rival. Because of his strong personality and competitive spirit, however, he could not put up with the college régime for long. At the end of his *belles-lettres* year he left to become a clerk in the office of the lawyer François Roy.

Called to the bar in 1828, La Fontaine rapidly built up a substantial practice and soon was known as a gifted advocate. He made an advantageous marriage at this time. On 9 July 1831, at Quebec, he married Adèle, the daughter of Amable Berthelot*, a wealthy lawyer, bibliophile, collector, and politician. La Fontaine thus laid the foundations of a fortune and legal career both of which would be noteworthy. Even when he was a law student he had become interested in politics. At the request of his friends Ludger Duvernay* and Augustin-Norbert MORIN, he published his critical views on law and politics in *La Minerve*. Hence it is not surprising that he took part in electoral campaigns at the end of the 1820s. In 1830 he entered active politics, and was easily elected to the House of Assembly of Lower Canada for Terrebonne. He was re-elected just as easily in 1834.

In the assembly the young member rapidly demonstrated his solid support of the most impassioned leaders, Louis Bourdages* and Louis-Joseph Papineau*. On 21 May 1832, he accompanied Papineau into the thick of the riot at Place d'Armes, Montreal, which marked the election of Daniel Tracey*; and in 1834, after MHA Dominique MONDELET accepted a post on the Executive Council and his brother Charles-Elzéar Mondelet* opposed the 92 Resolutions, La Fontaine replied for the Patriote party in a violent pamphlet entitled *Les deux girouettes, ou l'hypocrisie démasquée*. Until the beginning of the insurrection in 1837, he loyally went with Papineau to the stormiest meetings, and appeared in Quebec dressed in the Patriote style in a jacket of cloth woven locally. And he was becoming known as one of the most anticlerical MHAS; his pamphlet, *Notes sur l'inamovibilité des curés dans le Bas-Canada* (1837), recalled to Bishop Joseph Signay* of Quebec the acid writings of the precursors of the French Revolution. But it seems that the approach of hostilities caused a totally unexpected reversal of his feelings, which he never explained. Some saw political opportunism in the change, but it is more likely that La Fontaine, a practical politician, lost confidence at that moment in both the party's strategy and some of its objectives. He had been aggressive and fiery; from November 1837 on, he showed a surprising skill for political manoeuvre and compromise. He would later prove to have a profound understanding of the principles of the British constitution and of their importance for the survival of French Canadians.

Four days before armed violence broke out at Saint-Denis, on 23 Nov. 1837, La Fontaine wrote to the governor, Lord Gosford [Acheson*], urging him to convene parliament immediately. He then went to Quebec with his colleague James Leslie* for a personal interview with the governor on 5 December bringing to him a new request, signed this time by 13 other MHAS, including his father-in-law Amable Berthelot and his friend Augustin-Norbert Morin. When Gosford refused to call parliament, La Fontaine left for London, arriving at the end of December. He met frequently with the parliamentary representatives of the English reform party, Edward ELLICE and Joseph Hume, before going to Paris in March 1838. Returning to America on 11 June, he stopped at Saratoga, N.Y., to greet Papineau and arrived at Montreal on 23 June. There he rejoined his wife; for six months she had devoted herself to visiting her husband's former colleagues imprisoned since his departure, and had been endeavouring, with considerable sacrifice, to meet the needs of their families. When hostilities resumed in November, La Fontaine himself was imprisoned, as were his friend and partner Joseph-Amable Berthelot* and other politicians, including Denis-Benjamin VIGER, Jean-Joseph Girouard*, and Charles-Elzéar Mondelet. He was released on 13 December after questioning and no charges were laid against him.

During the events of this year, La Fontaine was unquestionably the man of compromise, and the skilful spokesman both of the imprisoned Patriotes and of the former moderates who had put their trust in the flexibility of British institutions and who considered La Fontaine's visit to London a final attempt at a constitutional solution to Lower Canada's problems. He had won the confidence of Canadian politicians and the respect of the government. It was he who was chosen as legal adviser to the prisoners granted amnesty by Lord Durham [Lambton*] in June 1838, and who served as intermediary between the government and those deported to Bermuda. He also placed himself at the disposal of the governor's secretaries, Charles Buller* and Edward Gibbon WAKEFIELD, for discussions on the general political situation. Ultimately it was he who drafted the documents that led the authorities to free him and his friends late in 1838. Most important, in his exchanges with Lord Gosford, Edward Ellice, Joseph Hume, Charles Buller, and Edward Gibbon Wakefield, he put forward the most lucid analysis of French Canada's situation and most clearly outlined the remedies for its troubles. Thus, he mapped out his own programme in the decade to come.

For the immediate future, La Fontaine insisted on two points: a general amnesty for those guilty of rebellion, and an indemnity for its victims. Since in his opinion no impartial jury could be found to judge the rebels, the British government would gain through clemency. And if in addition the imperial government would consent to compensate the innocent, it might even persuade French Canadians to forget the repression. The questions of amnesty and indemnity were to be the young Canadien leader's priorities, and their settlement would be one of his principal achievements. Since several of his letters to Ellice on these matters are in Lord Durham's papers, it is reasonable to suppose that his opinion may have influenced the partial amnesty proclaimed by the governor in 1838; again in 1842 it was he who took the first steps towards the final

441

La Fontaine

pardon of the exiles in 1845. He would obtain the *nolle prosequi* in favour of Papineau in July 1843; and finally he would propose in 1849 the famous Rebellion Losses Bill which marked his accession, amid drama and violence, to the summit of political power.

During the years 1837–38, La Fontaine's political thinking was shaped. For him, "Canadiens have become British subjects by treaty. They must be treated as such." As British subjects, French Canadians had a right to an assembly. The young politician therefore insisted that the legislature, suppressed in March 1838, should be restored. "Without it," he wrote to Berthelot, "we will certainly become just like the Acadians," legally incapable of reforming their institutions and influencing their destiny. As British subjects, French Canadians had the right in the assembly to exercise their preponderant and majority influence on the government. According to La Fontaine, if the Parti Canadien had been admitted to the governor's council the disturbances would have been averted, and political and social harmony maintained. "It is a great mistake," he wrote to Ellice, "to suppose that there is no means of rapprochement between the two parties. I do not hesitate to repeat what I have so often said, in Canada and in England, that it is easy to re-establish harmony among the majority in the two political parties, for their interests are the same. It is even a long felt need. Let local government in all its administrative and social dealings cease to make or to allow distinctions of race, let it advance openly towards a liberal but firm policy, let it abstain from favouritism towards the privileged classes. You will see harmony restored more quickly than one might think." Indeed La Fontaine was convinced that it was through the union of the French and English of Lower Canada in a single party that the liberal transformation of institutions would be accomplished, to the best interests of the Canadiens and of Great Britain. The "political disturbances" were due to the government's discriminatory practices and would therefore end with the complete application of the principles of the British constitution, according to which political distinctions were based on "opinions" rather than "origins." The "bastard, unnatural government" before 1837 had encouraged Canadien leaders to look towards the republican institutions of the United States; in future "the soundest policy is to leave us no reason to envy them." In stressing that "opinions" rather than ethnic "origins" were the basis of parties, La Fontaine, although unaware of it, shared the views of the Upper Canadian Reformer Francis Hincks*.

But in spring 1839, the Durham Report captured the attention of La Fontaine and of the Canadiens. The report defined the kind of government that La Fontaine had described in his letters to Ellice, a system in which the governor must undertake to follow the advice given by his Executive Council, which in turn would always be "responsible" to the elected house. Ministerial responsibility, applied to Lower Canada alone, would have meant that French Canadians would have predominated in the colony's government. Hence La Fontaine could not do other than accept it. But, in conjunction with responsible government, Durham recommended the union of Upper and Lower Canada. This measure, much less acceptable to the "nationalists" of the two colonies, was anathema in Lower Canada. Almost all the political leaders, and especially Papineau, had fought it since 1822, and Lord Durham was clearly proposing it in 1839 with assimilation as its purpose. With his keen sense of realities, La Fontaine was able to see that union could help his people. It would lead to promising solutions to the colony's economic and social problems, and in particular, through ministerial responsibility, provide the political instruments necessary for the reform of Lower Canadian institutions, which still reflected the absolutist and arbitrary structures of the old régime. He was therefore ready to agree to it. Twelve years later he recalled his decision: "after having carefully examined the rod by which it was intended to destroy my countrymen, I beseeched some of the most influential among them to permit me to use it, to save those whom it was unjustly designed to punish – to place my countrymen in a better position than they had occupied before. I saw that this measure enclosed in itself the means by which the people could obtain that control upon the Government to which they have a just claim."

He needed courage, for in the months following the publication of the Durham Report Lower Canadians were hostile to the recommendations. Everything conspired to turn French Canadians against union: the provocative actions of Governor Charles Edward Poulett Thomson*, the offensive attitude of Upper Canadian members during the debate on union in the House of Assembly at Toronto, and, even more significant, the vital fact that the provisions of the bill adopted by the imperial parliament during the summer of 1840 did not recognize responsible government. La Fontaine summed up the principal objections to the act: "It is an act of injustice and despotism, in that it is imposed on us without our consent; in that it deprives Lower Canada of its legitimate number of representatives; in that it deprives us of the use of our language in the proceedings of our legislature, against the assurance of the treaties and the *word* of the governor general; in that it forces us to pay, without our consent, a debt we have not contracted; in that it permits the executive, under the guise of the civil list, and without the votes of the people's representatives, to take illegally an enormous part of the country's revenues.''

The principal leaders of opinion, journalists and politicians, and especially John Neilson* at Quebec and Denis-Benjamin Viger at Montreal, rejected union outright and fought for its repeal. "Finding ourselves alone," La Fontaine recounted later, "we could not hide from ourselves the fact that it was impossible to arouse either the town or the countryside, so discouraged were they by events."

On 25 Aug. 1840, less than ten days after it was learned that union had received royal sanction, La Fontaine published his "Adresse aux électeurs de Terrebonne," in which he showed himself a realistic and adroit politician by making the following distinctions concerning the plan of union. Although some people reject it, he wrote, "does it follow that the representatives of Lower Canada . . . should commit themselves in advance and unconditionally to seek the repeal of Union? No, they ought not to do it. They should wait before deciding on a course whose immediate result would be perhaps to subject us again, for an indefinite time, to the liberticide legislation of a Special Council, and to leave us with no representation at all." According to La Fontaine, union would allow a party to be set up on Reform principles rather than on nationality: "Reformers in the two provinces form an immense majority . . . . [Those of Upper Canada] must protest against provisions that subjugate their political interests and ours to the whims of the executive. If they failed to do so, they would place the Reformers of Lower Canada in a false position in relation to themselves, and would thus run the risk of delaying reform for many years. They, like us, would have to endure the inevitable discord with those who oppose them. Yet we share a common cause. It is in the interest of the Reformers of the two provinces to meet on the legislative level, in a spirit of peace, union, friendship, and fraternity. United action is more necessary than ever." It was union also that would make possible the responsible government promised to Upper Canada but denied to Lower Canada. "For myself," added La Fontaine, "I do not hesitate to say that I am in favour of the English principle of responsible government. I

see in its operation the only possible guarantee of a good, constitutional, and effective government. The inhabitants of a colony must have control of their own affairs. They must direct all their efforts towards this end; and, to achieve it, the colonial administration must be formed and controlled *by* and *with* the majority of the people's representatives." The conclusion was clear. Union was the price that must be paid for responsible government, "the driving force of the English constitution," and the means whereby French Canadians would regain all that the less acceptable recommendations of the report sought to take from them. It was also the indispensable condition for a transformation of institutions in an orderly manner, in peace and liberty, and with due regard for the parliamentary institutions to which French Canadians had become accustomed.

La Fontaine had discussed these ideas in his correspondence with Francis Hincks. Between 12 April 1839 and 30 Jan. 1840 the two Reformers had exchanged some ten letters in which they both expressed the view that a political party should be based on common principles rather than on interests of class or origin, and the conviction that together they could create such a party. The Toronto journalist knew he did not have sufficient support to get his plans for reform in Upper Canada accepted without the aid of the French Canadian representatives; La Fontaine knew that he needed the Upper Canadian influence to overcome both the conservative forces that were still strong in Lower Canada and the prejudices of London against his countrymen. On 17 June 1840 Hincks summed up his idea in a letter to La Fontaine: "Your countrymen would never obtain their rights in a Lower Canadian Legislature. You want our help as much as we do yours . . . . Our liberties cannot be secured but by the Union." For La Fontaine there remained the task of convincing his compatriots.

He was ready. He was in great demand as a lawyer and had an extensive and influential clientele. He was considered to be a rich man. In 1840 he was sufficiently so to authorize Parisian friends to extend credit to Louis-Joseph Papineau. By then he and his partner Lewis Thomas Drummond* already owned a large block of houses and stores at the corner of Saint-Jacques and Saint-Lambert streets in Montreal, and two years later he purchased land on Rue Lagauchetière for £5,200. Furthermore, his activities during the rebellion had earned him the reputation of being pragmatic and resolute. And indeed he had the practical bent of those who solve difficulties easily. His correspondence re-

La Fontaine

veals that he was able to distinguish the important from the secondary. He liked fine points of law, the precise data of a problem; he distrusted theory and valued neither philosophy, which he had never studied, nor fiction, nor poetry. He was not a thinker. In private life he was dour and uncommunicative, had few friends, seldom went out, and shunned social gatherings. In public life, he spoke dispassionately, without excess of emotion. In fact, it was his physical appearance that helped him command attention. Slightly above average height, he walked with a slow, measured tread. His black eyes, his calm, set expression gave him an air of self-assurance. Some thought him pretentious. He bore a striking resemblance to Napoleon, did his hair after the manner of the emperor, and adopted the habit of inserting the fingers of his right hand between the buttons of his jacket. It was said that he was ambitious. But he commanded the respect of all by his ability. The combination of ambition and doggedness made him capable of displaying extraordinary steadfastness and restraint; his difficult, cold nature invested him with an air of mystery which his supporters saw as disinterestedness.

La Fontaine devoted the next ten years of his life to attaining his goals. First, he had to get union accepted. A proven leader at 32, he had to manoeuvre adroitly among the old political hands. He knew the importance of not dividing politicians in a time of crisis, and therefore supported his elders in everything that was not contrary to his tactic of accepting union as a means of obtaining responsible government. He took part in meetings at Quebec and organized others at Montreal to protest the terms of union proposed by London. In April 1840 he clearly intimated his disapproval by refusing the post of solicitor general offered him by Governor Thomson. At the same time, he worked hard to get the ideas of his "Adresse . . ." accepted. After the first elections of the new régime had been announced, he worked to find candidates who would support him. In July 1840 he went to Toronto to meet his Upper Canadian allies, and in September received Hincks at his home in Montreal. He also went to Quebec several times to coordinate the efforts of Étienne Parent* and Morin in favour of union. His stand did not always make him friends. When the polling stations were opened at Terrebonne in March 1841 he withdrew from the struggle, making way for Dr Michael McCulloch; the latter had the support not only of Governor Thomson's followers but also of those Patriotes who sided with Neilson and Viger. Despite this personal setback, due as much to his desire to avoid compromising his leadership by an elec-

toral defeat as to the fear that the presence of numerous braggarts in each camp would lead to violence, the election results throughout the province brought him a certain satisfaction. He had succeeded in convincing French Canadians to take part in the voting, and he could count on the backing of a good half-dozen members of the assembly. And his defeat at Terrebonne allowed him to test the spirit of solidarity of his allies.

Robert Baldwin*, leader of the party in Upper Canada, had been elected in two counties. On learning of La Fontaine's defeat, he resigned his York seat and offered it to the Lower Canadian leader. La Fontaine was elected easily on 23 Sept. 1841, after spending three weeks among the Torontonians, accompanied by Étienne Parent. Ties of deep friendship linked him from then on with Baldwin. He was to consult him on all matters bearing on politics and the constitution and to tell him all the events of his personal life. The relationship lasted until Baldwin's death in 1858. Apart from Joseph-Amable Berthelot, La Fontaine's papers reveal no one else with whom he had such intimate personal relations.

Elected MLA, La Fontaine continued his campaign in support of union in a more assured manner. At each by-election, he took steps to secure candidates favourable to his ideas. He won the confidence of several MLAS who had been elected under Neilson's banner. He also worked at making his message more widely known. In 1841 he offered advantageous terms to Ludger Duvernay to get him to return from exile and establish *La Minerve* again. This newspaper was to move quickly again to the forefront in the Montreal area, and was entirely devoted to La Fontaine's interests. He also encouraged the founding of *Le Journal de Québec*, whose editor Joseph-Édouard Cauchon* always remained loyal to him.

In the summer of 1842, the political situation had become such that the new governor, Sir Charles Bagot*, realized he could no longer work with parliament without turning to La Fontaine. After two weeks of difficult negotiations, the young leader took the oath as attorney general for Canada East and head of the provincial administration. The date was 19 Sept. 1842. On his recommendation Augustin-Norbert Morin, Robert Baldwin, and Quebec lawyer Thomas Cushing Aylwin* also entered the government. A vote of 55 to five expressed the confidence of the assembly. Of the Lower Canadians, only John Neilson had voted in the negative.

La Fontaine was now in a position to prove that union could serve French Canadian interests. He set to work with a will. In less than a year he

444

secured the repeal or amendment of the measures of the Sydenham régime that had most displeased French Canadians. He had the electoral law modified in order to establish a polling station in each parish, and thus diminish violence during elections. To increase French Canadian influence, he secured the adoption of a new electoral map of Canada East redrawn particularly in the areas of the Montreal and Quebec suburbs. He had the capital transferred from Kingston to Montreal, took the first of numerous steps to obtain amnesty for those condemned in 1837–38, and to restore the use of French as an official language in the records of the legislature and of the courts. La Fontaine paid particular attention to patronage. He knew that through it he could probably best demonstrate to his fellow countrymen that union could serve their interests. He gave important posts in the government to men like Étienne Parent and René-Édouard Caron*, clerk and president of the Executive and Legislative councils respectively. And he opened up careers and posts at all levels for all classes; the well-to-do he summoned to the Legislative Council, the modest habitant he had appointed land agent or census commissioner. "Patronage is power," the Upper Canadian MLA James Hervey Price* wrote to Baldwin on 6 Feb. 1843, and La Fontaine fully intended to show that French Canadians had arrived.

It was precisely on the question of patronage that he encountered the opposition of Governor Sir Charles Theophilus Metcalfe*, who had replaced Sir Charles Bagot in March 1843. Metcalfe did not understand responsible government in the way that La Fontaine did. He refused to agree to follow the advice of the council and its leader, and when La Fontaine persisted, there developed in November 1843 what journalists of the day called "the Metcalfe crisis." La Fontaine and his ministers, with the exception of the provincial secretary Dominick DALY, resigned *en bloc*. The house supported them, and the governor had to go in search of other councillors.

The years 1843 to 1847, when he was leader of the opposition, were La Fontaine's most difficult. His health deteriorated and on several occasions he was forced to take to his bed for a week or two. At the end of November 1846 he had to undergo an operation to relieve his rheumatism, which left him weak for three months. In the summer of 1847 he went to Newport, R. I., to recuperate. In January 1848 he was again under medical treatment. During these same years Adèle La Fontaine too was quite ill. They also experienced the grief of losing their niece and adopted daughter, Corine Wilbrenner, who died

on 4 Nov. 1844 at the age of 13. "You have children," La Fontaine wrote at that time to Baldwin, "we have not. Corine was our adopted daughter. Her death will, I am afraid, exercise a great influence on my plans and calculations."

In the political sphere, La Fontaine had to secure the loyalty of his own people without the use of patronage, and, after the defeat of the Reformers in the general election of 1844, without the hope of soon regaining it. In fact, the election results seemed to justify the views of those who had opposed the union of the Canadas and the union of the Reformers. Canada West returned a majority for Governor Metcalfe and the new government of William Henry Draper*. But Canada East elected 29 supporters of La Fontaine out of 42 members. Thus the partisans of the two groups were almost evenly divided, and two French Canadians, Denis-Benjamin Viger and Denis-Benjamin Papineau*, had joined the Executive Council in order to rally their countrymen to the governor's side. They envisaged a loose collaboration with Canada West and resorted to the principle of double majority. This principle, which subsequently was more fully elaborated, favoured a temporary coalition of the majority in Canada East with the majority, no matter which party, in Canada West, to last as long as both were satisfied with the arrangement. La Fontaine opposed the principle in theory and in practice. For him ministerial solidarity was an essential condition of responsibility. And he was convinced that even if responsibility could theoretically be exercised without solidarity, Lord Metcalfe would never agree to commit himself to follow the directives of his council. Whatever theoreticians might argue about the principle, La Fontaine was right about Metcalfe. Moreover, neither the British prime minister, Sir Robert Peel, nor the colonial secretary, Lord Stanley, accepted the principle of responsible government for Canada. La Fontaine knew the concession would have to be wrung from them. "I know you think we shall never get Responsible Govt." Hincks had written to him on 17 June 1840, "that the Ministry are deceiving us – granted – *But we will make them give it whether they like it nor not.*"

La Fontaine's tactics were to keep the electors aware of his belief in responsible government. The challenge – in the event it was not met so successfully – was to avoid demagogy, violence, and compromise. By the end of 1843, La Fontaine began to identify responsible government with survival. It was not difficult for him to do so. Control of the executive by the spokesmen of the majority was in fact the best guarantee that

La Fontaine

French Canadian national institutions, threatened by the conclusions of the Durham Report, would be protected, as La Fontaine's brief period in power in 1842 and 1843 had demonstrated. And to regain power, unity must absolutely be preserved. "What our countrymen must fear most in the present circumstances and at all times," he announced as the heading for his programme for 1844, "is division. One cannot be too strongly persuaded of the great truth that union is strength. Let this word be, particularly at this moment, our rallying cry." All must accept their mutual responsibility, and the "traitors" and "*vendus*" were those intent on dividing French Canadians. La Fontaine was clever. By taking the theme of unity, he was helping his party to benefit from the French Canadian habit of voting *en bloc*. In addition, he was using irony. The champion of British parliamentarianism and union, he was busy seeing that the label of *vendu* was pinned on the brother and the cousin of the principal nationalist of his generation. This theme, that *la survivance* could be achieved only by the united effort of all French Canadians voting together, has, or course, remained almost a cardinal tenet of Quebec nationalist ideology ever since.

La Fontaine's political skill is also illustrated in his use of the language question. The proscription of French as an official language by the Act of Union had been one of the main points in the imperial policy of assimilation, and it was perhaps the one most resented by French Canadians. Realizing their concern, La Fontaine manoeuvred to identify his party's cause with the question of language and thus gain for himself the full emotional allegiance of his followers. It is true that although the Act of Union gave no support to official use of French, French Canadians had come to realize that in their daily lives the law had little meaning. They continued to speak French, their schools taught it, their newspapers maintained it. Moreover if French had no official status at the seat of government, bilingual civil servants such as Étienne Parent imitated La Fontaine himself and wrote their reports in French, while such notables as the bishops of Quebec and Montreal corresponded with successive governors general and their secretaries in their own language. Several French Canadian politicians delivered their first speeches in parliament in French. And in 1844, at the opening of the second parliament of the union, Sir Charles Metcalfe reverted to the old Lower Canadian custom of having the clerk of the Legislative Council read a formal French translation of the speech from the throne. In 1844, however, La Fontaine, as leader of the opposition, began to raise the issue, making it, as his enemies averred, "a claptrap for popularity."

His newspapers and his partisans accordingly began to refer to their leader's first speech to the union parliament, in Kingston on 13 Sept. 1842. La Fontaine had begun in French and had been interrupted after a few sentences by a member who asked that he speak in English. After some reflection La Fontaine had grandly retorted: "Has he [the honourable member] already forgotten that I belong to that nationality which has been so horribly illtreated by the Act of Union? . . . He asks me to deliver in a language other than my maternal tongue the first speech I have to deliver in this house! I distrust my ability to speak the English language. But . . . even if I knew English as well as French, I would still make my first speech in the language of my French Canadian countrymen, if only to protest solemnly the cruel injustice of that part of the Act of Union which aims to proscribe the mother tongue of half the population of Canada. I owe it to my countrymen, I owe it to myself." At the time the incident attracted little notice. But two years later La Fontaine's propagandists saw to it that no Canadian elector would ever forget it. The leader of the opposition was to emphasize the language problem at every opportunity. Until the end of the decade he managed to manoeuvre almost every debate in the house onto grounds that turned a vote for his opponents into a vote against the French language. By mid 1848, La Fontaine had succeeded in identifying his party with the language issue – indeed, the new governor general, Lord Elgin [BRUCE], complained that he spoke of nothing else. When he finally came to power he wished to inaugurate his government by proclaiming a new language policy. He did this by having Lord Elgin read the speech from the throne in French at the opening of parliament on 18 Jan. 1849.

No doubt La Fontaine was sincere. His public letters and his private official communications were always written in French. His reports as attorney general were bilingual, as were his letters of resignation as head of the government in 1843 and 1851 and his letter of thanks to Lord Elgin when he received his baronetcy. He gradually progressed towards nationalism, moved at first by party spirit (especially when he was again in opposition), and some years later by personal ambition. In his correspondence during 1837 and 1838, his "Adresse aux électeurs de Terrebonne," and his exchanges with Hincks, he showed his concern to obtain reforms which would satisfy and serve the two Canadas. His

446

analysis of the problems of French Canadians was in strictly political terms. But in 1854 he reached the point where he confused political and social with national concerns . . . and with his personal interests. When he accepted the title of baronet, he wrote Lord Elgin a letter in which such distinctions were indeed subdued: "I shall be the first French Canadian on whom this dignity has been conferred. I am equally the first, and in addition the only French Canadian to have been made attorney general and chief justice of my native country. . . . Rest assured, My Lord, that I can appreciate the motives which have prompted you to act on this occasion as on many others, the desire to prove to my countrymen of French origin that political and social inferiority is no longer their lot, and that all doors will be open to [them] as to their fellow citizens of other origins." He seems however to have had some reservations about adopting nationalist stances. A few weeks after his resignation in 1851, when *Le Journal de Québec* was discussing an administrative question in a distinctly nationalist tone, he reminded Joseph-Édouard Cauchon of certain past rebukes. The latter replied: "I recall what you said to me with regard to the national question; but I replied to you that it was the only chord that could be struck successfully." And La Fontaine, with his keen sense of reality, accepted the inevitable . . . and his hereditary title of baronet.

The same realism probably inspired him in the construction of his party's electoral machine. He knew how elections were won. When in opposition, he set up a network of agents who could keep him informed at all times about the opinions, prejudices, needs, and desires in each county. At election times, these agents were readily transformed into speakers and candidates. Early in 1844, he asked Hincks to come to Montreal to coordinate operations. With the help of organizers such as Joseph-Édouard Cauchon for the Quebec region and George-Étienne Cartier* in Montreal, the Upper Canadian Reformer set up a team that was always ready, during brawls and riots, to cheer "good" candidates, besiege polling stations, and batter opponents. The team demonstrated its strength in a by-election in Montreal in April 1844, and, later, during the general elections of 1844 and 1847–48. It included French Canadians and Irishmen and created the atmosphere of a battlefield in the electoral struggles, especially in Montreal, where the Tories had previously won their greatest victories.

The team of French Canadians and Irish was also Catholic. Quietly, and perhaps inadvertently, La Fontaine found himself towards the end of his opposition years again at the head of a party that was increasingly seeking support from clerical circles. After 1843, his supporters had begun to improve their relationships with the clergy, who had gradually come to look upon politicians more favourably. Just as the latter needed clerical backing among the electors, the clergy for its part knew it must give up its old behaviour. Union had marked the end of the urbane, aristocratic approach through which the bishops of Quebec and the British governors had so carefully merged the interests of altar and throne. Now that real political power was slipping from the hands of the governor into those of the electors, the clergy had to begin to deal directly with electors and politicans, if it wanted the church to continue to exercise the influence that it genuinely believed to be its right. Politicians were therefore welcomed with increasing cordiality at the seminary and the bishop's palace, and La Fontaine himself won the regard of the episcopate, particularly the new bishop of Montreal, Ignace Bourget*.

Despite early distrust, Bishop Bourget and La Fontaine were born to understand each other. Both were authoritarian and stern leaders, with the same stubborn character, the same profound sense of duty, and the same political skill. In 1845 and 1846 the debate about the bills on education and on the Jesuit estates led La Fontaine's supporters and the clergy to form a lasting alliance. La Fontaine's opposition ensured that the education act was satisfactory to the ultramontanes. The discussion on the Jesuit estates helped to enlarge the gap between the supporters of Denis-Benjamin Viger and the Papineau clan on the one hand, and those of the clerics and La Fontaine on the other. Following liberal doctrine Viger claimed the state had the right to dispose of the Jesuit estates as it thought fit; La Fontaine and his followers argued that these revenues belonged by right to the church. After 1846 the clergy was to prove one of the great social forces working for the principle of responsible government.

To what extent was this cooperation a moral compromise for La Fontaine? It is hard to say. When he was young he was reputed to be anticlerical. But at the same time he seems to have been faithful in his religious observances. At official dinners he made a large sign of the cross before sitting down; and he had been known to prostrate himself in the street before the Holy Sacrament, when it was being carried publicly for the communion of the sick. In 1855 he accepted the title of knight commander in the pontifical order of St Sylvester, which Bishop Bourget had recom-

La Fontaine

mended for him to Pius IX. But La Fontaine received this decoration with a touch of humour, which might suggest that his public demonstrations of religion were not wholly sincere. "For myself," he confided to his friend, French historian Pierre Margry, "I cannot tell you to what I am to attribute my parchment and my two crosses, unless it is to my well-known piety, of which I can imagine you would never have had any idea." At the time of his death in 1864, another friend, the devout Abbé Étienne-Michel FAILLON, wrote to Margry: "That is how he died, after postponing from day to day his return to God. . . . He sacrificed himself for others, left few possessions; and despite all that, he did nothing for God and has appeared before Him empty-handed."

Whatever his personal beliefs, as leader of the opposition La Fontaine was subjected to pressures from both opponents and supporters. He found himself gradually involved in an alliance with the church. He had wanted to break with the particularist and republican nationalism of the Patriotes, and in 1840 had denounced the dangers of an inward looking nationality. In 1848 he was once more at the head of a party to which he had given unity and a firm structure, but it too was moving towards a particularism quite as rigid as that of the republicans in the 1830s.

In the 1847–48 elections La Fontaine and his supporters won a resounding victory. He was elected in Montreal by a majority of 1,400 votes, and in Canada East as a whole his followers succeeded in 32 out of 40 counties. In Canada West, 23 Baldwinite Reformers were elected. The new governor, Lord Elgin, acknowledged that responsible government must finally be instituted. He agreed to entrust the government to the leader of the majority party in the house, and to undertake to follow his advice. Early in March 1848 La Fontaine was therefore sworn in as attorney general. He was the first Canadian to become prime minister, and the first French Canadian elected by his own people to direct their national aspirations.

In power again, La Fontaine took up the work that had been interrupted when he resigned in 1843. The Lower Canadian exiles were now back in the country; several of them had even come to thank him personally for his efforts on their behalf. There remained the indemnities to be paid to the victims of the soldiery of Sir John COLBORNE.

For La Fontaine, the Rebellion Losses Bill was no more than justice. It was designed as a broad, unstinting gesture that would finally put to rest the bitterness of 1837. But for many in Montreal's commercial class, already suffering the trials of deep financial depression, and for many of the Tory politicians who had just lost political control of Lower Canada for the first time since 1791, the issue became a symbol. They reacted with the primitive, panic-stricken fury typical of the recently dispossessed. When Lord Elgin gave royal assent to the bill, a mob broke into the parliament building and set it afire. On the next day, 26 April 1849, the mob rushed to La Fontaine's house, broke in, smashed woodwork and his costly period furniture, pulled off window sills and shutters, ripped up floors, and shattered china and glass. They set fire to the stables, burned several coaches, and pulled up a dozen saplings from the orchard. Later, in August, when some opponents of La Fontaine were arrested, the mob returned to the attorney general's home. This time he was ready: the house was dark but a group of his friends including Étienne-Paschal TACHÉ and Charles-Joseph Coursol* waited behind the shutters with guns. As the rabble moved towards the front door, shots rang out on both sides; before the rioters had fled, six were wounded, and one, William Mason, was dead. Rumours that La Fontaine would be assassinated filled the city. Twice he was assaulted on the street, and when he testified at the inquest into Mason's death at the Hôtel Cyrus, it was set ablaze.

The riots of 1849 appeared to La Fontaine as a revealing counterpart of the rebellion ten years earlier. If not in lives lost, at least in national bitterness and property damage, the reaction of the Montreal Anglophones had several parallels with the "violence" of 1837–38. There was even a "rebellion losses" aftermath: La Fontaine's supporters claimed damage for the destruction of their property: Morin £34, Francis Hincks £34, the Grey Nuns £65, and La Fontaine himself £716. They did not claim it from the provincial government, however, but from the municipal administration of Montreal, headed by Édouard-Raymond Fabre*, a political adversary of La Fontaine. But these outrages against his person and property only served to enhance the prestige of the prime minister.

During his tenure of office, from March 1848 to October 1851, La Fontaine entrusted Hincks with economic and commercial questions, and Baldwin with legal reform and with land utilization in Canada West. He retained responsibility for the courts and the distribution of patronage in Canada East. Hence, in the first session of the new parliament, he presented bills to institute the Court of Queen's Bench, a court of appeal with four judges. In addition, he created the Superior Court as a court of original jurisdiction and a circuit court for small causes. Thus the broad outlines of judicial organization in Canada East were drawn in 1849–50.

In his administration of patronage, the prime minister utilized his network of agents and relied on the advice of his organizers, Caron, Cauchon, Cartier, and Drummond. He wanted to make certain that by a judicious allotment of favours all French Canadians would become permanently involved in self-rule. For two generations the Canadien professional class had been struggling to secure an outlet for its ambitions: now, with a kind of bacterial thoroughness, its members began to invade every vital organ of government, and assume hundreds of positions as judges, queen's counsellors, justices of the peace, medical examiners, school inspectors, militia captains, postal clerks, mail conductors. And as the privileges and salaries of office percolated down to other classes of society, French Canadians came to realize that responsible government was no longer just an ideal. It was also a profitable fact. Henceforth, thanks to La Fontaine, all French Canadians would be guaranteed the possibility of room at the political top.

The prime minister did not escape setbacks. Three times, in 1849, 1850, and 1851, he put a bill before the house to increase the number of members for each section of the province from 42 to 75. He insisted that the representation of Canada East and West should remain equal, and he wanted the regions within each section to be equally represented. His bill never received the two-thirds majority required. In 1850 and 1851 La Fontaine was again in the minority over the clergy reserves and seigneurial tenure. On these questions he was absolutely determined to respect vested interests. He knew his ultramontane supporters feared that the secularizing movement prevalent in Canada West, especially with regard to the clergy reserves, would spread to Canada East. "As appetite grows the more it feeds on," Drummond wrote to him about those who supported secularization in Canada West, "these hungry sectarians, after dividing up the clergy reserves, will perhaps not hesitate to lift a sacrilegious hand against the private properties of our religious communities." Resolution of the question was, however, postponed.

As for seigneurial tenure, La Fontaine certainly favoured its reform, even its abolition. He had already proposed this in his "Adresse aux électeurs de Terrebonne" in 1840. But since then his alliances had led him in a conservative direction. He therefore insisted that the seigneurs should receive compensation. On 14 June 1850 he proposed in the house that a committee should be set up chaired by Drummond, with instructions to prepare a bill. The following year, when the committee proposed to redeem the rights of the seigneurs by forcing them to accept an amount fixed by the legislature, La Fontaine contended that such action would be confiscation. Finally he succeeded in getting this question postponed also; but meanwhile, on a point of order, he found himself in the minority among French Canadians for the first time since union. Only eight representatives voted with him, whereas his strongest allies, including Drummond, Cauchon, and Cartier, supported the majority.

His authoritarian temperament made it difficult for him to accept even this small setback. Hence he resolved to hand in his resignation. In any case, for some months he had been tired and sick. The dampness of winters in Toronto, which he had had to endure since the capital had been transferred to Canada West in 1850, had aggravated his rheumatism. He was overburdened with work and plagued by insomnia and headaches. On 6 March 1850, he had written to Joseph-Amable Berthelot to say that if paradise was in store for those who had experienced only tribulation in this life, he would most surely obtain his passport. In November 1850 he confided to Lord Elgin that he was weary of public life. Then, during the winter of 1851, his wife also began to complain of rheumatism. The resignations of Baldwin on 27 June 1851, and of Hincks on 15 September, profoundly distressed him. On 26 Sept. 1851, after one last meeting of the Executive Council, held at Niagara Falls, he handed his own resignation to Lord Elgin.

He had attained all the objectives he had set himself in the years 1837–40. Union had been accepted; the rebels had been pardoned and the victims compensated; responsible government had been secured. He had established the structures which would enable Jean-Baptiste Meilleur* to undertake the reform of education, Morin to bring about the transformation of the seigneurial régime and make the Legislative Council an elective body, and the clergy to further their efforts of colonization. He had succeeded in stimulating and coordinating the activity of his colleagues. And his greatest success had been to give expression through the institutions of the country to the social aspirations of the liberal bourgeoisie.

In Montreal, La Fontaine returned to the practice of law with his former partner Joseph-Amable Berthelot. His reputation as a logical, firm, and precise speaker preceded him in the courts, where law students and young lawyers often went to hear him argue. His coolness and

La Fontaine

self-control were much admired: he persuaded by force of ideas rather than by sonorous periods or brilliant words. His influence also extended to business circles. At the time of the great fire in Montreal in 1852, it was he who was chosen by the city council to negotiate a loan. Then, on 13 Aug. 1853, after the death of Sir James Stuart*, he was appointed chief justice of the Court of Queen's Bench, the tribunal which he had reorganized in 1849. He sat there for the first time on 1 July 1854.

Throughout the final decade of his life La Fontaine was burdened by illness. "At 40, one is still young," he wrote to Pierre Margry on 4 Nov. 1859; "at 52, with health daily undermined by too sedentary a life that has already ruined the strongest constitution a poor mortal was ever privileged to possess, one perceives that the years are numbered." His hair had gone white, and he was becoming fat. In the early 1860s his corpulence had become distressing for him.

He travelled to recover his health. For nearly a year, from the summer of 1853 to the spring of 1854, he made the "grand tour," stopping in London, where he stayed with Lord Elgin, in Florence, and in Rome, where he was received in audience by Pius IX. He spent several months in Paris and visited museums and art galleries. It was during this stay that his resemblance to Napoleon I sent a stir of excitement through the old soldiers at the Invalides. It was also on this voyage that he had become a friend of the historian Pierre Margry, a regular and interesting correspondent. In 1862–63 he spent a further ten months in Paris for medical treatment; he was accompanied by his brother-in-law, Charles-François-Calixte Morrison, parish priest of Napierville. Meanwhile, in 1855, 1856, 1857, and 1859 he had been obliged to take to his bed following attacks of rheumatism, "an unpleasant companion who persists in visiting me." But Lady La Fontaine had died before him. On 27 May 1859, at the age of 46, she passed away after a long illness.

On 30 Jan. 1861, he remarried at Montreal; his second wife was Julie-Élisabeth-Geneviève (Jane) Morrison, 39 years old, widow of Thomas Kinton, an officer in the Royal Engineers, and mother of three girls aged ten, eight, and six. She came originally from Maskinongé and was descended from the first Bouchers. La Fontaine, who had taken an interest in genealogy since his retirement from public life, wrote to Margry: "Thus, she and I have a common ancestor." The new Lady La Fontaine nursed her husband during his last years: he spoke of her as his "sister of charity." She also gave him the joy of father-hood. A son, Louis-Hippolyte, was born on 11 July 1862.

Called upon to preside over the special tribunal of 13 judges set up in 1855 to rule on the claims resulting from the 1854 act on seigneurial tenure, La Fontaine became engrossed in the history of the feudal system and of civil law in Canada. He cherished the hope of publishing a scholarly study of the customs of New France and Lower Canada. His correspondence reveals his numerous contacts with genealogists and archivists in France, England, and Canada. "Again and again I go through the registers of the parishes at Quebec, Montreal, and 3 Rivières," he wrote to Margry on 4 Nov. 1859. He was thoroughly tired of politics. In 1853 he was already showing signs of this disenchantment. When visiting Florence he had met the painter Napoléon Bourassa*. "Your leaving politics," the young man is said to have remarked, "must have provoked a deep commotion in our country?" "As for reaction, my young friend," La Fontaine had replied, "I saw only that of the people who rushed forward to take my place." He began to associate with such historians and men of letters as Abbé Faillon, Jacques Viger*, Georges-Barthélemi FARIBAULT, and François-Xavier GARNEAU. In 1859 he published an essay on slavery in Canada, and, between 1860 and 1864, several unsigned articles on genealogy. He contributed regularly to *La Minerve* and to the *Annales* of the Société Historique de Montréal. However, his history of law was never completed.

On 25 Feb. 1864 La Fontaine had an apoplectic fit in the judges' chambers. He was taken home, where he gathered his son in his arms, made the sign of the cross, and lost consciousness. He received extreme unction from the vicar general, Alexis-Frédéric Truteau*, and died during the night. At his funeral, presided over by Bishop Bourget, 12,000 persons gathered. Lady La Fontaine gave birth to a second son on 15 July, but he died in 1865; his elder brother, Louis-Hippolyte, followed him to the grave in 1867. Lady La Fontaine lived until 1905.

For French Canadians, La Fontaine's accomplishments put an end to the period of the sterile nationalist claims of the Papineau type. His work opened up new directions in the areas of administration, law, education, settlement, and politics. It was proof of the power of national unity and of cooperation among those whom history and geography had brought together. Despite the Act of Union, which was clearly directed against French Canadians, La Fontaine was able to demonstrate that cultural survival depended not on constitutional documents but first and foremost on the collective will to live and on enthusiasm engendered by reform. Convinced of the interdependence of the two Canadas, and refusing to follow those who in his opinion failed to understand true grandeur, he transmitted to future generations through his accomplishments his confidence that their cultural fulfilment was linked to the vitality and flexibility of the parliamentary system of Great Britain. Thanks to him, a great and new hope was born.

By his decision to use British principles to strengthen his own nationality, La Fontaine did more than ensure the cultural survival of French Canadians. He also became one of the founders of the future Commonwealth of Nations. For within a century after the French Canadians solved their national problem by political evolution rather than armed revolt, other peoples on continents the Canadians of the 1830s and 1840s had barely heard of made use of the same pattern to achieve their own cultural destinies, and, like the French Canadians, managed not only to gain their collective freedom according to their masters' own principles but also to accede in peace to ruling their rulers. Thus the practice of La Fontaine's own life – radical nationalism, imprisonment for rebellion, shift to moderation, and the first prime ministership of a newly self-governing nation – became, a century later, the classic pattern of colonial leaders in most parts of the commonwealth.

For the tradition of Canada as a whole his lasting contribution is obvious as well: he is the father of parliamentary democracy on this continent; or, as he himself expressed it in the play on his name which he officially chose as a motto when he was created a baronet: *Fons et origo*.

A strange man he was: stubborn, introverted, pragmatic, ambitious; a man of few friends, who loved his country, not with wild passion, but with a devotion hard and steady. He was difficult to love, but he made it much more difficult not to admire him.

JACQUES MONET

[The most important primary material on Louis-Hippolyte La Fontaine is found in the La Fontaine collection at the Bibliothèque nationale du Québec (Montréal), in the Robert Baldwin papers at the MTCL, and in the Henry Vignaud papers at the William L. Clements Library (University of Michigan, Ann Arbor); the latter includes his letters to Pierre Margry.

Other archival collections include significant items for La Fontaine's life and work: at the PAC, the governors' correspondence (MG 24, A), especially the Elgin-Grey papers (MG 24, A10, 21–37); at ANQ-Q, the Collection Papineau and the Langevin papers (AP–G–134); at the AAQ and the ACAM, the correspondence of bishops Signay, Lartigue, and Bourget. In addition, contemporary newspapers contain a great deal of information on La Fontaine's activities.

La Fontaine was the author of *Les deux girouettes, ou l'hypocrisie démasquée* (Montréal, 1834); *Notes sur l'inamovibilité des curés dans le Bas-Canada* (Montréal, 1837); *Analyse de l'ordonnance du Conseil spécial sur les bureaux d'hypothèques* . . . (Montréal, [1842?]); and with Jacques Viger, *De l'esclavage en Canada* (Montréal, 1859).

Biographies of La Fontaine by L.-O. David, *Sir Ls. H. Lafontaine* (Montréal, 1872), by A.-D. De Celles, *Lafontaine et son temps* (Montréal, 1907), and by S. B. Leacock, *Baldwin, Lafontaine, Hincks; responsible government* (Toronto, 1907), have been superseded by the more recent works by W. G. Ormsby, *The emergence of the federal concept in Canada, 1839–1845* (Toronto, 1969), by [M.] E. [Abbott] Nish, "Double majority: concept, practice and negotiations, 1840–1848" (unpublished MA thesis, McGill University, Montreal, 1966), and by Jacques Monet, *Last cannon shot*. The *Last cannon shot* includes a more detailed bibliography for Louis-Hippolyte La Fontaine. J.M.]

Correspondence between the Hon. W. H. Draper and the Hon. R. E. Caron; and, between the Hon. R. E. Caron, and the Honbles. L. H. Lafontaine and A. N. Morin . . . (Montreal, 1846). *Hommages à La Fontaine; recueil des discours prononcés au dévoilement du monument de sir Louis Hippolyte La Fontaine en septembre 1930* . . ., Clarence Hogue, édit. (Montréal, 1931). *Lettres à Pierre Margry de 1844 à 1886 (Papineau, Lafontaine, Faillon, Leprohon et autres)*, L.-P. Cormier, édit. (Québec, 1968), 13–55). *Catalogue de la bibliothèque de feu sir L. H. Lafontaine baronnet, juge en chef, etc.* . . . (Montréal, [1864?]). Réjane Soucy, "Bio-bibliographie de sir Louis-Hippolite Lafontaine, bart." (thèse de bibliothéconomie, université de Montréal, 1947). Olivier Maurault, "Louis-Hippolyte La Fontaine à travers ses lettres à Amable Berthelot," *Cahiers des Dix*, 19 (1954), 129–60.

LAFRANCE (Hianveu, *dit* Lafrance), FRANÇOIS-XAVIER-STANISLAS, Roman Catholic priest and educator; b. 26 Feb. 1814 in Quebec, son of Louis-Charles Hianveu (Hyanveux), *dit* Lafrance, a bookbinder, and Marie-Angélique-Émilie McDonell (McDonald); d. 27 Nov. 1867 at Barachois, N.B.

François-Xavier-Stanislas Lafrance's first ambition had been to become a doctor but the typhoid outbreak of 1837 changed his mind, and in September of that year he entered the Petit Séminaire de Québec. The following year he heard a sermon by a family friend, Bishop Bernard Donald MacDonald*, of Charlottetown, P.E.I., on the need for priests to work in the Acadian parishes. Lafrance went to Prince Edward Island with the bishop in 1838 and after studying at St Andrew's College was ordained

Lagorce

in Rustico on 2 April 1841. For the next 26 years Lafrance worked among the Acadians.

He was a curate during the summer of 1841 in Rustico itself and then moved to Saint John, N.B. From 1842 to 1852 he served as vicar at Tracadie, N.B., where he was also responsible for the neighbouring parishes of Pokemouche-en-Haut, Pokemouche-en-Bas, Neguac, and the Indian mission of Burnt Church. His first task was to organize the parishes, for until his arrival the cure had been attached to Caraquet. He had some basis on which to build, for between them the settlements at Pokemouche had a chapel and a schoolhouse. The teacher, however, usually taught in several places and spent only six or seven weeks at one time in any village. Neguac had a wooden chapel but Burnt Church had only the ruins which gave the settlement its name. Tracadie's fine church had been completed in 1823 but the community had no school. For ten years Lafrance expanded and rebuilt churches and carried out all the normal duties of a parish priest. He also established a school at Tracadie despite the difficulty of obtaining permanent staff.

His most remarkable achievement during these ten years, however, was his work in the establishment of the lazaret at Tracadie. The existence of leprosy in New Brunswick had not been remarked at the beginning of the 19th century, but by 1844, after Lafrance led a delegation of prominent citizens to Fredericton to urge government action, Lieutenant Governor Sir William COLEBROOKE established a commission, which included among others Lafrance, Joseph CUNARD, and Alexander Rankin*, to cope with this scourge. That year Lafrance assisted in the movement of lepers to Sheldrake Island. In 1849 he supervised the establishment of a permanent refuge for lepers at Tracadie [see Charles-Marie LABILLOIS], which was maintained and developed until the repeal of the Leprosy Act in 1971.

In 1852 Lafrance was transferred to Memramcook, the centre of an Acadian population of some 4,000, with responsibility for the neighbouring parishes of Petitcodiac, Irishtown, Scoudouc, and Moncton. Here in 1854 he set about the founding of Collège Saint-Thomas. In his appeals to parishioners for funds he stressed that as far as education was concerned the Acadians had never been justly treated. His vision was to provide the Acadians with their own élite of priests, merchants, doctors, lawyers, and even judges. During his tenure of office at Memramcook, however, his efforts had no real success. Lack of episcopal support meant the closing of the college

in 1862. His last action as vicar of Memramcook, in June 1864, was to welcome as his successor Father Camille Lefebvre*, who was able to succeed where Lafrance had failed. The college he established that same year as the Collège Saint-Joseph exists today as the Université de Moncton.

François-Xavier Lafrance spent the last three years of his life as the vicar of Barachois. His death in 1867 came before the results of his initiative bore much fruit, but his actions played a major role in the organization of Acadian life during the 19th century.

NAOMI GRIFFITHS

Centre d'études acadiennes, université de Moncton (Moncton, N.-B). *L'album souvenir des noces d'argent de la Société Saint-Jean-Baptiste du collège Saint-Joseph, Memramcook, N.B.* ([Moncton, N.-B., 1894]). P.-F. Bourgeois, *Vie de l'abbé François-Xavier Lafrance . . .* (Montréal, 1913). U.-J. Bourgeois, *L'abbé F.-X. Lafrance, premier curé de Tracadie* ([Moncton, N.-B.], 1962), where his name is given as François-Xavier-Stanislas de Kostka Hienveu Lafrance.

LAGORCE, CHARLES-IRÉNÉE, priest, Cleric of St Viator; b. 6 June 1813 at Saint-Hyacinthe, Lower Canada, son of Charles Lagorce, notary, and Marie-Angèle Morin; d. 23 Feb. 1864 at Sainte-Claire, on the Etchemin River, and buried at Saint-Hyacinthe.

Charles-Irénée Lagorce was educated at the Séminaire de Saint-Hyacinthe. He was ordained priest on 30 July 1837 and appointed to the parochial ministry, serving as curate at Saint-Denis on the Richelieu (1837–38) and at Sorel (1838–41), then as parish priest at Sainte-Anne-des-Plaines (1841–44) and at Saint-Charles on the Richelieu (1844–48). At Saint-Charles Abbé Lagorce attempted to give instruction to a deaf mute, Antoine Caron. From his initiative sprang the Institution des Sourds-Muets in Montreal.

With the support of Bishop Ignace Bourget*, Lagorce actually started a class for deaf mute boys on 27 Nov. 1848 in the hospice of Saint-Jérôme-Émilien, in the Québec *faubourg* of Montreal, assisted by a man named Reeves, himself a deaf mute. On Sundays Lagorce gave lessons to deaf mutes of both sexes, usually in a room in the Asile de la Providence [see Albine Gadbois*]. After several changes to ensure the progress and stability of the undertaking, it was established canonically by a pastoral letter of Bishop Bourget, dated 30 Aug. 1850. Lagorce immediately began a regular teaching programme for deaf mute boys in a three-storey building at Côte Saint-Louis (Montreal).

But devotion was not enough to make up for shortage of well-trained staff. On the advice of the founder, Bishop Bourget decided to entrust the work to a religious community. Lagorce therefore went to France in May 1851 in order to learn the teaching methods used by those religious who might agree to come to Canada. Unsuccessful among the religious of the Congregation of the Holy Cross at Le Mans (dept of Sarthe), he turned to the Clerics of St Viator at Lyons. In mid January 1852, no doubt with better service to deaf mutes as his aim, Lagorce entered the noviciate at Vourles. He took his first vows there in July, returned to Montreal with Brother Joseph Fayard on 4 September, and went to L'Industrie (Joliette), where the Clerics of St Viator had been established since 1847 [see Antoine MANSEAU].

Lagorce resumed his teaching first at L'Industrie, where he took in seven or eight deaf mutes, then at Côte Saint-Louis in August 1853. He was director of the Institution des Sourds-Muets and priest in charge of the developing parish. But soon the task became too heavy for him. A sick man, he gave up teaching in June 1855, and handed over to his community (which in fact he left in August 1856) the responsibility of continuing his work, content that the institute was in excellent hands and knowing that his was the honour of founding it. After numerous ups and downs Brother Jean-Marie-Joseph Young (Yung), in the years 1856 to 1863, gave the institute its greatest development. Lagorce again tried life in a religious order, this time among the Fathers of the Holy Cross, and he ended his days at the Trappist monastery of Sainte-Justine-de-Langevin, which he had entered in 1862.

Lagorce's life in itself is not of particular interest. In 1848, when an institution for deaf mutes was started, Bishop Bourget was already looking for a founding priest. The work would have borne fruit at the same time without Lagorce's zeal. But the founding of the Institution des Sourds-Muets illustrates two points in the religious history of Canada. If the church was the guiding spirit behind so many social undertakings in a country already involved in urbanization and social development, it was because its ideal of charity compelled it, as a duty, to fill the gaps left by the state and society. In February 1832 the parliament of Lower Canada had actually authorized the creation of a school for deaf mutes at Quebec, and had undertaken to support it financially. A layman, Ronald MacDonald*, had been put in charge, after he had studied, at Hartford, Conn., methods calculated to ensure its success. But in 1836 the legislature had withdrawn its encour-agement of the newly begun project so that in 1849 there were in Canada 1,100 deaf mutes dependent on the charity of the Roman Catholic Church. In addition, Lagorce's undertaking proved that the religious communities usually were best able, through the coordination and continuity of their efforts, to ensure the permanence and stability of any charitable organization in the essentially Francophone Lower Canada of the 19th century. It was therefore in response to the needs of society that European religious communities were brought in or that new Canadian religious communities were established. Thus Bishop Bourget's zeal proved to be far sighted and adapted to the requirements of his day.

ANDRÉE DÉSILETS

Archives des Clercs de Saint-Viateur, Province de Montréal (Montréal), II, N, États de service du père Irénée Lagorce; P, Institut des sourds-muets. *Le Courrier de Saint-Hyacinthe*, 26 févr. 1864. *Mélanges religieux*, 12 févr. 1850. Allaire, *Dictionnaire*. Le Jeune, *Dictionnaire*, I, 391. [J.-P. Archambault], *Une œuvre sociale: l'Institution des sourds-muets* [. . .] (Montréal, 1949). Antoine Bernard, *Les Clercs de Saint-Viateur au Canada* (2v., Montréal, 1947–51), I, 650. *Notices historiques sur l'Institution catholique des sourds-muets pour la province de Québec dirigée par les Clercs de Saint-Viateur, Mile-End, Montréal* (Mile-End, 1893). Hector Tessier, *Saint-Viateur d'Outremont* (Outremont, Qué., 1954).

"Centenaire de l'Institut des sourds-muets, 1848–1948," *L'Ami des sourds-muets* (Montréal), octobre 1912, 70–84; avril-mai 1948, 25–40. "Les écoles des sourds-muets à l'exposition de Chicago," *La Semaine religieuse de Montréal*, XXII (1893), 117–22. "L'Institution catholique des sourds-muets de Montréal," *L'Ami des sourds-muets*, juillet-août 1939, 138–49. "Institution des sourds-muets," et "L'Institution des sourds-muets au Mile-End, Montréal," *La Semaine religieuse de Montréal*, XIX (1892), 299–302 et 237–239, 313–16. "Numéro-souvenir du 75e anniversaire de l'Institution des sourds-muets, 1848–1923, célébré le 16 mars 1924," *L'Ami des sourds-muets*, mars-avril 1924, 118–32. Corine Rocheleau-Rouleau, "Parler est chose facile, vous croyez," *RHAF*, IV (1950–51), 345–74. P.-G. Roy, "Les commencements de l'Institution des sourds-muets à Montréal," *BRH*, XXX (1924), 70–79.

LAMBLY, JOHN ROBERT, sail-maker and registrar; b. 25 Jan. 1799 in Rochester, England, eldest child of Captain John Lambly, harbourmaster of Quebec, and Frances Richardson; d. 31 Jan. 1863 in Leeds, Canada East.

The parents of John Robert Lambly had been married at Quebec on 31 Aug. 1797, and lived in Rochester before coming back to Quebec on 18 May 1802. At age 14 John Robert, although hop-

Land

ing to become a sail-maker, began to study for the notarial profession. The boy's wishes finally prevailed and in 1816 he was sent to London, England, to serve his apprenticeship as a sail-maker. Letters from his father in Quebec contained good advice for his son to "write French often and keep constant attention to that language," to attend church, and especially to read the bible and prayer book. John Robert evidently completed his apprenticeship in the fall of 1819, and sailed for Quebec in the spring of 1820. An item in the *Quebec Gazette* of 1 Aug. 1820 announcing the opening of a sail loft on 12 June 1820 by John Robert Lambly confirms that he set up a business immediately upon his return from England.

Lambly did not continue long at the sail-making trade. He became one of the first settlers in Halifax Township, in the Eastern Townships, moving there, it is believed, in 1827. He may not have relished the sail-making business as much as he had anticipated. Moreover, the building of Craig's Road to connect Quebec with Richmond may have been an incentive to leave Quebec, especially since two of his future brothers-in-law were moving into the area on the northeast shore of Lake William. They established their families in forest clearings, as did Lambly, who married Ann Mackie of Quebec City on 23 April 1828. Seven children were born of this marriage. The Lambly family had thus settled in the region prior to the coming of the Scots from Arran in 1829.

On 30 May 1843 Ann Lambly died; on 15 Jan. 1845 John Robert married Elizabeth Pierce Bailey of the township of Ireland, and they had ten children. On 3 April 1844, he had been appointed registrar of Mégantic County by the government and had moved with his family to Leeds where the registry office was located. Thus at 45 John Robert returned to a type of notarial work for which he apparently had had some early training.

He remained registrar until 1862 when the county seat was moved to Inverness and his son William Harvard succeeded him. John Robert was also president of the Mégantic County Agricultural Society for many years, and first mayor of the municipality of Mégantic in 1854 and of Leeds Township in 1855.

Wesleyan Methodism in Mégantic County seems to have had its oldest organized existence in the Leeds circuit with preaching at various stations before 1864. John Robert Lambly was one of the local preachers who filled appointments in Ireland, Saint-Ferdinand-d'Halifax (Halifax), Inverness, and Saint-Sylvestre (Beaurivage), and he canvassed the county in the interest of temperance reform. In 1855 he became deputy grand worthy patriarch of the Society of Temperance. His religious influence was reflected in the careers of his children. Two sons, Osborn Richardson and James Bankier, became ministers, and William Harvard became internationally known for his work in prohibition.

John Robert Lambly died in Leeds on 31 Jan. 1863, having made a worthwhile contribution to the development of Mégantic County and the Eastern Townships.

MARION L. PHELPS

ANQ-Q, État civil, Anglicans, Cathedral of the Holy Trinity (Québec), 23 April 1828. Private archives, Harry Lambly (San Francisco), "The Lamblys, lore and legend." *Christian Guardian*, 11 March 1863. *Men of today in the Eastern Townships*, ed. V. E. Morrill and comp. E. G. Pierce (Sherbrooke, Que., 1917), 22. D. M. McKillop, *Annals of Megantic County, Quebec* (Lynn, Mass., 1902), 65.

LAND, ROBERT, pioneer, farmer, militia officer, and public servant; b. 10 April 1772 in Pennsylvania, sixth of the seven children of Robert Land and Phebe Scott; m. Hannah Horning of Barton Township, Upper Canada, and they had nine children; d. 21 Nov. 1867 at Hamilton, Ontario.

Robert Land, who is sometimes also designated Jr or II to avoid confusion with his father and second son, fled with his mother, a sister, and a younger brother from what is now Wayne County, Pennsylvania, to New York in May 1779 for protection from rebel harassment after his father, a magistrate under the colonial government of Pennsylvania, joined the British forces as a dispatch carrier. In 1783, while his father was based at Niagara (Niagara-on-the-Lake), Robert and the others embarked with the first fleet of loyalists for the Saint John River (New Brunswick) where his mother was granted 200 acres of land at Parr Town (Saint John). In 1791 they made their way to Upper Canada and joined Robert Land Sr who, in the meantime, had become one of the first settlers at the Head-of-the-Lake (later Hamilton).

As "the son of a zealous and active Loyalist," Robert Jr petitioned for land in 1795 and was granted 200 acres in Middlesex County. Following military service in 1812–14, he received an additional 500 acres in Caledon Township (Peel County). He lived in Barton Township on land originally granted to his father, farming several hundred acres in the area.

In 1804 Land had begun a military career that was to span a period of 43 years by joining the West Lincoln militia as lieutenant. When the War

454

of 1812–14 began, he entered the 5th Lincoln militia as lieutenant in Samuel Hatt*'s company of flankers and was granted a medal and clasp for action at the surrender of Detroit. On the morning of the battle at Queenston Heights, 13 Oct. 1812, his company was the only force present at Queenston. He next took part in the skirmish at Frenchman's Creek. At Stoney Creek, acting under orders of Colonel John Harvey*, he is credited with helping to prevent a junction between American troops landed at Burlington Beach and the main force at Stoney Creek. After the battle of Lundy's Lane, Land, his nephew Joseph Birney, and Major Hatt, were recommended for the medal of the Loyal and Patriotic Society by their commanding officer, Colonel Andrew Bradt, having behaved "with every mark of intrepidity during the action saving the Major who was severely wounded." After the war Land maintained his active connection with the militia; he was gazetted lieutenant-colonel of the 3rd Gore militia in 1830, and commanded the post at Hamilton during the rebellion of 1837–38. In 1847, at age 75, he retired from command of the 2nd Wentworth militia.

Land was appointed commissioner of customs for the Gore District in 1834; he was reappointed in 1840 and resigned in 1847. He also served as postmaster for the district for a period around 1847. He was appointed general commissioner of the peace on four occasions between 1827 and 1838, and an associate justice of the Court of Oyer and Terminer and General Gaol Delivery for the counties of Wentworth, Halton, and Brant on 12 March 1852. Land was a member of the Church of England and the Masonic Order; he had been initiated in the Barton Lodge on 7 Nov. 1796 and at his death was believed to be the oldest mason in Canada.

He died at his home and was given a funeral on 24 Nov. 1867 attended by "the Volunteers of the City, together with the mayor and civic authorities, and a large representation of the Masonic fraternity." "A very large number of private citizens joined in the procession and thus lent testimony to the great respect in which the deceased gentleman was held by all classes of the community with which he has been so long identified."

R. BRIAN LAND

HPL, Land papers; Land family papers. PAC, RG 1, L3, L, bundle 1, no.55. PAO, Strachan (John) papers, Andrew Bradt to C. Foster, 25 Jan. 1815. *Daily Spectator* (Hamilton), 22, 25 Nov. 1867. I. L. Alton, *Descendants of Robert Land, 1736–1818, & Phebe Scott, 1733–1826* ([Burlington, Ont., 1970?]). George Laidler, "The story of the Land family," *Wentworth Bygones* (Hamilton, Ont.), 1 (1958), 14–26.

LAROCQUE, FRANÇOIS-ANTOINE (he signed **LaRocque**), businessman; b. 19 Aug. 1784 at L'Assomption, Que., son of François-Antoine Larocque, first representative for the county of Leinster (L'Assomption), and Angélique Leroux, daughter of Germain Leroux, merchant of L'Assomption; d. 1 May 1869 at Saint-Hyacinthe, Que.

Shortly after his father's death on 31 Oct. 1792, young Larocque, who had studied at the Collège de Montréal, was sent to the United States to learn English. He was to prefer expressing himself in that language for the rest of his life. In 1801, through his uncle Laurent Leroux*, who had established Fort Resolution (N.W.T.) in 1784, he joined the XY Company as a clerk, working in the region of the Assiniboine River from 1802 to 1804. When this company was absorbed by the North West Company in 1804, he continued to work as a clerk in the Upper Red River department. In the autumn of 1804 he left Fort Assiniboine, with Charles Mackenzie, Jean-Baptiste Lafrance, and four other voyageurs, to go to the Mandan villages on the banks of the Missouri. There, on 25 November, he met the American captains Meriwether Lewis and William Clark, who were under orders to explore the upper Missouri and the northwest as far as the Pacific Ocean. Larocque suggested accompanying them, but when they refused he continued alone on his own expedition. The *Journal of Larocque from the Assiniboine to the Yellowstone, 1805* contains the description of the first visit of whites to the country of the Crows since the expedition of Louis-Joseph Gaultier* de La Vérendrye in 1742, and throws a new light on distinctive features of the Mandans and the Minnetarees (Gros-Ventres-Hidatsa).

In 1806 Larocque left the northwest for Montreal, where he founded an unsuccessful business firm. During the War of 1812 he was an ensign in the 3rd militia division of Lower Canada, then a captain in the 5th battalion of Chasseurs Canadiens. He was taken prisoner in October 1813, held at Cincinnati, and set free six months later when prisoners were exchanged. On his return to Montreal after the war, he was decorated with the Châteauguay medal. At Montreal, on 26 Jan. 1818, he married Marie-Catherine-Émilie Cotté, daughter of the merchant Gabriel Cotté*.

In 1819 Larocque was one of the founders of the Bank of Montreal, and remained a member of its board of directors until 1826. When the bank

Larocque

was founded, he was one of the principal French Canadian shareholders, along with his uncle Laurent Leroux and Augustin Cuvillier*. Larocque was also actively engaged in trade. He was a partner of Joseph Masson*, then organized his own business in 1832 under the name of Larocque, Bernard, et Compagnie. During the insurrection of 1837, Larocque was affiliated with the Fils de la Liberté, but did not take up arms. Nevertheless he was imprisoned in Montreal in April 1838 "for having an article on Canada printed and sold at Montreal."

In September 1841, after the marriage of his only son François-Alfred-Chartier to Amélia Berthelet, daughter of Antoine-Olivier Berthelet*, he retired from business, and led a quiet life until June 1853. At that time he undertook a long trip to the principal cities in the United States, including Cincinnati where he had been a war prisoner. Larocque was by then concerned only with his eternal salvation, and this journey of nearly a year was in effect a long pilgrimage. In 1855 he entered the Hôtel-Dieu of Saint-Hyacinthe run by the Grey Nuns, and here he spent the last years of his life in retreat and study.

Like many of his contemporaries, Larocque had achieved success on the basis of the fur trade. Moreover to him fell "the honour of having opened up the upper Missouri basin to penetration by Canada." Founding member and one of the rare French Canadians to be a director of the Bank of Montreal, partner in the firm of Masson, Larocque, Strong, and Company, and founder of Larocque, Bernard, et Compagnie, he was a highly respected businessman, in both English and French circles, in the first half of the 19th century.

ANDRÉ L. J. LAMALICE

[F.-A. Larocque], *Journal of Larocque from the Assiniboine to the Yellowstone, 1805*, ed. L. J. Burpee (Ottawa, 1910); a French edition was published in 1911. PAC, MG 19, A18; C1, 3; MG 30, D62, 17, pp.620–715. *Les bourgeois de la Compagnie du Nord-Ouest: récits de voyages, lettres et rapports inédits relatifs au Nord-Ouest canadien*, L.-F.-R. Masson, édit. (2v., Québec, 1889–90; réimpr. New York, 1960), I, 299, 402. *Le Canadien*, 16 mai 1838. [Meriwether Lewis], *History of the expedition under the command of Lewis and Clark*, ed. Elliot Coues (3v., New York, 1965), I, 228. Denison, *Première banque au Canada*, I, 104, 173, 211.

LAROCQUE, JOSEPH (perhaps **Joseph-Félix**), HBC chief trader; b. *c.* 1787; d. 1 Dec. 1866 at Ottawa, Canada West.

Joseph Larocque, whose brother FRANÇOIS-ANTOINE was also active in the fur trade, was the son of François-Antoine Larocque, member for the county of Leinster (L'Assomption) in the first parliament of Lower Canada, and Angélique Leroux, and may have been the child, baptized François, born 20 Sept. 1786 at L'Assomption, Province of Quebec. If this identification is accepted, Joseph would have been 15 years old when he was a clerk in the XY Company in 1801. At this time, the XY Company was challenging the dominance of the North West Company. When they settled their differences Joseph Larocque transferred to the NWC and was sent to serve on the upper Churchill (or English) River. He is known to have been at Lake La Ronge in 1804 and at Fort des Prairies in 1806. He was transferred to the Columbia River Department of the North West Company, but no details of his career are known until he appears in 1812 in the neighbourhood of Fort Kamloops (Kamloops, B.C.), among the Shuswap Indians. In 1813 he joined John George McTavish* in his descent of the Columbia River and take-over of Fort Astoria (Astoria, Oreg.) from the Pacific Fur Company. Larocque spent the next three years in the Columbia River Department, travelling much, often with dispatches, and managing posts among the Flatheads and at Okanagan, Fort Kamloops, or Spokane House, until in 1816 he returned over the mountains from Fort George (Astoria, Oreg.) to Fort William (Thunder Bay, Ont.), carrying dispatches.

In the spring of 1817 Larocque was again sent west to the Columbia, taking strong reinforcements for the Nor'Westers as their struggle with the Hudson's Bay Company gathered momentum. Athabasca and Île-à-la-Crosse were, however, the main areas of trading opposition, and Larocque was brought back over the mountains to Fort Chipewyan; he was arrested at Fort Wedderburn in May 1820 for complicity in the outrages perpetrated at Île-à-la-Crosse by Peter Skene Ogden* and Samuel Black*, on warrants sent into the Indian country by Lord Selkirk [Douglas*]. Colin Robertson* of the HBC, who, in effect, made the arrest, described Larocque as "one of the Principle bullies" of the NWC. Robertson provided canoe transport to take him down to Montreal to stand trial, but in June 1820 a strong party of Nor'Westers captured the brigade of canoes at the Grand Rapids of the Saskatchewan and Larocque was freed. He was sent back to Athabasca, where the "grand push" was to be made by the North West Company. In September George Simpson* found him one of the two men in command at Île-à-la-Crosse, and though he appears to have gone "into the mountains" to escape possible arrest, along with Black and

456

other "outlaws and felons" (as Simpson called them), he was reported to be most uneasy at the way in which the Nor'Westers were behaving and to be a man of great spirit.

On the coalition of the Hudson's Bay and the North West companies in 1821 Larocque was accepted into the joint concern as a chief trader and served in the English River district and at Edmonton House and Lesser Slave Lake. In 1825 he was sent to the lower St Lawrence, where he was responsible for the Mingan seigneury, whose fur trade and fishing the HBC rented until 1831. Neither activity was profitable and the seigneury was kept going largely as a challenge to the lessees of the King's Posts until the posts were bought out in 1831. Larocque had retired in 1830, with a fortune of 15,000 louis (approximately $60-75,000) to which he added when he married Archange Guillon-Duplessis in March 1833.

In 1837, when rebellion broke out in the Canadas, Larocque went to France, where he lived until 1851. He retained his interest in Canada. In 1843 he donated £225 for the construction at Willamette (Oreg.) of a college, Saint-Joseph, for French Canadians. On his return to Montreal he continued his philanthropic activities. He and his wife retired to the convent of the Grey Nuns at Ottawa in the fall of 1857 and he helped establish the Hôpital Général there. He died in 1866 leaving his fortune to the Grey Nuns.

E. E. RICH

Ross Cox, *The Columbia River; or scenes and adventures during a residence of six years on the western side of the Rocky Mountains . . .*, ed. E. L. and J. R. Stewart (Norman, Okla., 1957), 121–22, 138, 194–95, 229, 323. *Documents relating to NWC* (Wallace), 219, 460. Franchère, *Journal of a voyage* (Lamb), 118. *Hargrave correspondence* (Glazebrook), 59, 65. HBRS, I (Rich), 31, 41, 222, 445; II (Rich and Fleming); III (Fleming). *New light on the early history of the greater northwest: the manuscript journals of Alexander Henry, fur trader of the North West Company, and David Thompson . . .*, ed. Elliot Coues (3v., New York, 1897), II, 752, 916. Tassé, *Les Canadiens de l'Ouest*, II, 321–38.

LASCELLES, HORACE DOUGLAS, naval officer; b. 20 Sept. 1835 in Yorkshire, England, seventh son of Henry Lascelles, 3rd Earl of Harewood, and Lady Louisa Thynne; d. a bachelor, 15 June 1869, at Esquimalt, B.C.

Horace Douglas Lascelles entered the Royal Navy in 1848 and saw service in India, China, and on the west coast of Africa. He came to the Esquimalt Station in HMS *Topaze* in March 1860 as 1st lieutenant, having received his promotion in 1855. After the death of its commander, he succeeded to the command of the gunboat *Forward* in November 1861. In this capacity he participated in several excursions against coast Indians who menaced settlers on Vancouver Island and its adjacent islands in the 1860s.

On such an expedition in April 1863, Lascelles in the *Forward* bombarded and devastated the village of the Lamalchi band of Cowichans on Kuper Island during a concerted search for the murderers of a settler, Frederick Marks, and his married daughter, Caroline Harvey. In Victoria, Charles William Allen, editor of the *Evening News*, made a harsh criticism of the exertions of the *Forward* in his newspaper, taunting Lascelles for "running away" without apprehending the malefactors. Lascelles was enraged. He had brought Marks' widow and five children back to Victoria and had then returned to the scene of action. Allen was lured on board the *Forward* on 20 May 1863, confined, and taken out to sea. Escaping by diving overboard, he was recaptured, and eventually put ashore. Allen filed suit for $25,000 against Lascelles for assault and battery, and the case came before Judge David Cameron* of the Supreme Court of Vancouver Island. The jury found for the plaintiff and Allen was awarded $1,000 for damages and costs.

Lascelles, a man of means, figured prominently in the social life of Victoria, especially in riding and horse racing circles, and when not on active service was always to be seen at race meets and queen's birthday celebrations at Beacon Hill. Lascelles reportedly sought the hand of Catherine Anne Wigham who in December 1862 married instead Gilbert Malcolm Sproat*, a businessman and government official. Lascelles invested in real estate on Vancouver Island and founded the Harewood coal mine near Nanaimo, of which Robert Dunsmuir* was resident manager. He was closely associated in Victoria with James Johnson Southgate, a retired ship-master engaged in commission business, and with him financed the building of a commercial block shortly before his death.

Returning to England in 1865, Lascelles retired the following year with the rank of commander but, in company with Southgate, took up residence at Esquimalt in 1868. He died on 15 June 1869, and was interred with full naval ceremony at the Naval Cemetery on the same day as Governor Frederick SEYMOUR. The Victoria *Colonist* in lengthy accounts described him as being "generous to a fault" and deeply interested in the advancement of Vancouver Island. A stained-glass window in St Paul's Anglican Church, Esquimalt, given by the Harewood family, and a

Leblanc

number of place names commemorate his life on the west coast.

MADGE WOLFENDEN

Daily British Colonist and Victoria Chronicle, 1860–63, 16 June 1865; 1 June 1866; 24 Aug. 1868; 16, 17, 22 June 1869; 23 April 1879. Daily Evening Express (Victoria), May, November 1863. Evening News (Victoria), 1863. Burke's peerage (1885). Walbran, B.C. coast names. James Audain, From coalmine to castle; the story of the Dunsmuirs of Vancouver Island (New York, 1955). Edgar Fawcett, Some reminiscences of old Victoria (Toronto, 1912). B. M. Gough, The Royal Navy and the northwest coast of America, 1810–1914: a study of British maritime ascendancy (Vancouver, 1971). D. W. Higgins, The passing of a race and more tales of western life (Toronto, 1905). L. B. Robinson, Esquimalt, "place of shoaling waters" (Victoria, 1948). Daily Province (Vancouver), 19 Jan. 1922, 7 Feb. 1940. Victoria Daily Times, 30 Dec. 1938. Madge Wolfenden, "The early government gazettes," BCHQ, VII (1943), 171–90.

LEBLANC DE MARCONNAY, HYACINTHE-POIRIER, writer and journalist; b. 20 Jan. 1794 in Paris, France; d. 17 Feb. 1868 in the same city.

Leblanc de Marconnay's family, which was elevated to the nobility in the early 16th century, was of Poitou extraction. Hyacinthe-Poirier seems to have been the son of a former page of the Orléans family. He was accepted as an apprentice in the masonic lodge of Clémente Amitié in Paris in 1820 and became a master mason nine months later. In 1828 he reached the 32nd degree. Brother Leblanc changed his masonic allegiance, moving from the Grand Orient (1820–27) to the Scottish rite (1827–34), and returning to the Grand Orient (1834–68). Nine of his publications reveal his activity in the lodges.

Leblanc de Marconnay probably arrived in Canada in 1834, and he began his career in this country by publishing an account of the election that autumn in the county of Deux-Montagnes, which had been marred by irregularities. Jean-Joseph Girouard* and William Henry Scott*, representatives of the Patriote party, had been elected, but Frédéric-Eugène Globensky and his brother-in-law, James Brown, had withdrawn because they had little chance of winning. The latter two had prevented the partisans of Girouard and Scott from voting at Saint-André-d'Argenteuil, but at Saint-Eustache they and the men they had brought along had had to retreat. Leblanc de Marconnay praised the courage and tenacity of the Canadians who supported the Patriote party. This account was published in part on 17 Nov. 1834 in La Minerve, of which he had been an editor since 5 September; it later appeared under the title of Relation historique des événements de l'élection du comté du lac des Deux Montagnes en 1834. . . . He wrote for Le Populaire during the difficult years of 1837–38, and for L'Ami du peuple, de l'ordre et des lois from August 1839. In February 1840, even before publication of L'Ami du peuple ceased, Leblanc de Marconnay was an editor of L'Aurore des Canadas. He left the country during that year.

Leblanc de Marconnay at first supported the Patriotes and Louis-Joseph Papineau*, siding with the "Franco-canadiens" in the interests of their having fair representation in the House of Assembly; he continued his support until the day when, as he wrote to Sir Charles Bagot* on his return to Paris, fools incited them to rebellion. But though he asserted that his aim was to show that French Canadians had the right to keep their autonomous institutions, one cannot help but see in Leblanc de Marconnay a turncoat and a social climber. Not only had he gone from La Minerve to Le Populaire with Léon Gosselin and shamelessly castigated the Patriotes, but as early as 1836 he had published a violent diatribe against Louis-Hippolyte LA FONTAINE, Edmund Bailey O'Callaghan*, and Louis PERRAULT in La petite clique dévoilée . . . , labelling them hypocrites, rabid democrats, a clique of carping critics, and even accusing them of wanting to overthrow Papineau. In February 1840 he told John Neilson* in confidence that at Montreal the petitions against the union of Upper and Lower Canada were contrived by La Fontaine, Côme-Séraphin Cherrier*, Charles-Elzéar Mondelet*, and the group of hot-headed Patriotes who were seeking to take up the work of Papineau. He stated that he was not invited to participate in these petitions, although the paper he edited, L'Aurore des Canadas, had declared itself against union. According to him, it had no doubt been presumed that he would oppose the operations in which this group wanted to engage. What seems to have been his last publication at Montreal was a refutation of the Histoire de l'insurrection du Canada written by the Patriote leader in exile; this refutation appeared in 1839, and was generally attributed to Clément-Charles SABREVOIS de Bleury. It is not surprising that once back in Paris Leblanc de Marconnay should write to Bagot, on 23 Oct. 1841, that he had been in the confidence of all parties, and would willingly return to Canada if he were offered a suitable position. He announced at the same time that he was preparing a work, "Véritable situation des Canadas," which, however, does not seem to have been published.

Leblanc de Marconnay appears to have taken

part in masonic activities during his stay in Canada. Long after his return from America, he wrote a letter to the Albion Lodge at Quebec, in his capacity as secretary of the Clémente Amitié Lodge in Paris, in which he stated that he had attended a number of meetings at Montreal lodges. Leblanc de Marconnay also took an interest in the theatre. He wrote a comic opera which he had performed in Paris in 1831, as well as an interlude in two parts, performed in 1835 and 1836 at the Théâtre Royal in Montreal, and a comedy in one act, *Valentine, ou la Nina canadienne*.

CLAUDE GALARNEAU

[H.-P. Leblanc de Marconnay], *La petite clique dévoilée, ou quelques explications sur les manœuvres dirigées contre la minorité patriote qui prit part au vote sur les subsides, dans la session de 1835 à 1836, et plus particulièrement contre C. C. Sabrevois de Bleury, écuyer, avocat du Barreau de Montréal, membre de la chambre d'Assemblée du Bas-Canada* (Rome, N.Y., 1836); *Relation historique des événements de l'élection du comté du lac des Deux Montagnes en 1834; épisode propre à faire connaître l'esprit public dans le Bas-Canada* (Montréal, 1835); *Le soldat, intermède en 2 parties, mêlé de chants, exécuté sur le théâtre Royal de Montréal (Bas-Canada) en 1835 et 1836, arrangé par M. Leblanc de Marconnay* (Montréal, 1836); *Valentine, ou la Nina canadienne, comédie en un acte* (Montréal, 1836). Bibliothèque nationale de France (Paris), Fonds français, no. 29971, Nouvelles acquisitions françaises, no. 1074. PAC, MG 24, A13, 5, pp.30–32; B1, 10, pp.17–18, 66–69. *L'Ami du peuple, de l'ordre et des lois* (Montréal), 1839. *L'Aurore des Canadas*, 1840. *La Minerve*, 17 nov. 1834. *Le Populaire* (Montréal), 1837–38. [C.-C.] Sabrevois de Bleury, *Réfutation de l'écrit de Louis Joseph Papineau, ex-orateur de la chambre d'Assemblée du Bas-Canada, intitulé "Histoire de l'insurrection du Canada . . ."* (Montréal, 1839). Monet, *Last cannon shot*. P.-G. Roy, *Toutes petites choses du régime anglais* (2 sér., Québec, 1946), 2e sér., 5–6. Caubet, "Le F. Leblanc de Marconnay," *Le Monde maçonnique; revue de la franc-maçonnerie française et étrangère* (Paris), 10 (1867–68), 700. J.-N. Fauteux, "Débuts du journalisme au Canada français," *Le Journaliste canadien-français* (Montréal), I (1955), 27. E.-Z. Massicotte, "Leblanc de Marconnay," *BRH*, XXVI (1920), 177–79. Benjamin Sulte, "Leblanc de Marconnay," *BRH*, XVIII (1912), 353–54.

LECLÈRE (Leclerc), PIERRE-ÉDOUARD, notary, police superintendent, and businessman; b. 10 Feb. 1798 at Montreal, son of Pierre Leclère, *dit* Lafrenaye, a merchant, and Marie-Anne Bourg; d. 5 May 1866 at Montreal, Canada East.

In 1813 Pierre-Édouard Leclère began his training as a clerk under Louis Chaboillez*, but after the latter died in July of that year he entered the office of notary Jean-Marie Mondelet*, and, in 1819, that of notary André Jobin*. Having worked with "these three masters," he managed, with some difficulty, to obtain a commission as a notary in 1825. On 10 Jan. 1820 he had married Josephte, daughter of Jean-Baptiste Castonguay, a fur-trader; they were to have 17 children.

In the decades preceding the union of Upper and Lower Canada, the Patriote party and the administration of Lower Canada opposed one another in a struggle to secure the loyalty of the population. The story of the Patriotes' activities is known, but there is less information about government officials and sympathizers. Pierre-Édouard Leclère's career must be put into this context. Leclère became superintendent of the Montreal police in 1830 and, charged with reorganizing it, made himself the champion of law and order. His mandate was renewed at the time of Montreal's incorporation in 1832, and he supervised the organization of a police corps for the town. His jurisdiction extended to the entire district of Montreal. In the troubled years that followed, Leclère openly declared his opposition "to the immoral and disruptive effects of the measures recommended by speakers at popular meetings," and in particular to the pernicious encouragement given by the Patriotes to clandestine importing of goods.

Leclère planned and took part in attempts by the governor's associates to infiltrate the Patriote party, large public gatherings, and the Fils de la Liberté. In 1838, with the authority of a justice of the peace and of a commissioner of small causes, he supported the Special Council that governed Lower Canada, issued summonses, signed search warrants, and authorized police searches at the office of *La Quotidienne* and the arrest of its editor François Lemaître. His jurisdiction went beyond the boundaries of Montreal, according to the evidence of documents such as warrants of arrest for citizens of Saint-Hyacinthe and Saint-Jean signed by Leclère. In particular he had the border villages kept under surveillance.

Thanks to a vast network of informers, which constituted a veritable secret police, and to a reward system, Leclère had individuals spied on and forwarded his information to the governor's secretary, Dominick DALY, and the attorney general, Charles Richard OGDEN. He was also able to follow movements between Canada and the United States, since he controlled the issue of permits for entry to the United States. The informers in his employ were even audacious enough to infiltrate Canadian refugee circles in the United States. Félix Poutré*, a journeyman of Saint-Jean, was entrusted with one of these intelligence missions in 1838.

In partnership with John Jones, Leclère had become the owner of the *Canadian Spectator* in 1826 and of *L'Ami du peuple, de l'ordre et des lois* from 1832 to 1836. In 1835 he had started *Le Journal du Commerce*, which lasted less than a year. At *L'Ami du peuple* Leclère was aided by Joseph-Vincent Quiblier*, superior of the Sulpicians and "unofficial" director of the paper. Leclère's vast knowledge of the events of 1837–38 were to make him some years later a competent member of the commission to consider compensation for rebellion losses. In 1840 he had moved to Saint-Hyacinthe, where he practised as a notary until 1859 and held the office of stipendiary magistrate until 1843.

Convinced that a shipping line was the indispensable complement to the building of railways, Leclère became a shareholder in the Société de Navigation de la Rivière Richelieu in 1845 (later the Richelieu Company) and its president in 1850 [*see* Jacques-Félix Sincennes*]. He was active in his region's agricultural society, and became president of the Agricultural Society of Lower Canada.

JEAN-LOUIS ROY

ASSH, A, F, Fonds Pierre-Édouard Leclère. PAC, MG 30, D62, 28, pp.158–292. Ivanhoë Caron, "Inventaire des documents relatifs aux événements de 1837 et 1838, conservés aux Archives de la province de Québec," ANQ *Rapport*, 1925–26, 216–17; "Papiers Duvernay conservés aux Archives de la province de Québec," ANQ *Rapport*, 1926–27, 152–53. Fauteux, *Patriotes*, 115–16. C.-P. Choquette, *Histoire de la ville de Saint-Hyacinthe* (Saint-Hyacinthe, Qué, 1930). *Hist. de la corporation de la cité de Montréal* (Lamothe *et al.*), 110–11. F.-J. Audet, "Pierre-Édouard Leclère (1798–1866)," *Cahiers des Dix*, 8 (1943), 109–40.

LE GALLAIS, WELLMEIN WILLIAM, Church of England clergyman and missionary; baptized 21 July 1833 at St Helier, Jersey, son of Richard Le Gallais and Susan Mason; m. 21 June 1859 Fanny Harriet Loftus, *née* Langrishe, of St John's, Nfld, and they had four daughters and one son (one daughter married Edward Patrick Morris*); d. 27 Oct. 1869 near Isle aux Morts, Nfld.

Wellmein William Le Gallais went to Newfoundland sometime in the 1840s as a clerk in the firm of Nicolle and Company, Jersey merchants at La Poile. There, under the influence of the Reverend Jacob George Mountain, an able Tractarian recruit to the diocese of Bishop Edward Feild*, Le Gallais offered himself for the ministry.

In 1854 he was admitted to Queen's College, St John's, where he completed his theological and pastoral training by 1857, and was made deacon the same year. He was put in charge of the mission at Channel, on the south coast of Newfoundland, and ordained priest two years later. He set a pattern of Tractarian missionary endeavour by saying morning and evening prayer daily and celebrating communion every Sunday. Like other efficient Church of England clergymen in this period, he also founded a Church Provident Society in the early 1860s as an insurance against distress through bereavement, sickness, or unemployment. Members, who had to be regular communicants of the church, made quarterly payments into a fund. Bad behaviour was punished by expulsion. Le Gallais also organized courses of lectures during the winter months when fishing was impossible, and set up a lending library to provide the reading matter always scarce in an isolated community.

Le Gallais' 12 years of missionary work ended abruptly when, returning in a small boat from a sick call to Isle aux Morts, he was caught in a gale and drowned. Bishop Feild mourned the loss of "perhaps the most active and useful of our Missionaries in Newfoundland." A successful missionary with concern for the spiritual and material needs of his parishioners, Le Gallais had been a fine product of Feild's policy of training and using former clerks, schoolmasters, and scripture readers when candidates educated at universities were not available. Like many other missionaries in Newfoundland he lost his life in the church's service.

FREDERICK JONES

USPG, D39, Feild to secretary, 31 Oct. 1869. Soc. for the Propagation of the Gospel in Foreign Parts, *Report* (London), 1864, 36. *Mission Field* (London), 1 March 1870. *Newfoundlander*, 23 June 1859. *Times and General Commercial Gazette* (St John's), 6, 10 Nov. 1869. [C. F. Pascoe], *Classified digest of the records of the Society for the Propagation of the Gospel in Foreign Parts, 1701–1892 . . .* (5th ed., London, 1895), 858.

LEITCH, WILLIAM, Presbyterian clergyman and educator; b. 20 May 1814 at Rothesay on the Isle of Bute, Scotland, son of John Leitch, a customs officer, and Margaret Sharp; m. Euphemia Paterson in 1846, and they had four sons; d. 9 May 1864 at Kingston, Canada West, and was buried at Monimail, Fifeshire, Scotland.

At age 14 William Leitch suffered a serious accident which confined him to his room for many months and was the occasion of his taking up the study of mathematics and science. He attended the grammar school at Greenock and the University of Glasgow where he received a BA in 1837 with the highest honours in mathematics and science. He obtained an MA from Glasgow in 1838, and the university conferred a DD on him in 1860. As a student at Glasgow he lectured on astronomy and was observatory assistant to Professor John Pringle Nichol. He retained his interest in science all his life and was later said to be "a distinguished astronomer, naturalist and mathematician."

In 1839, after two years at the University of Glasgow Divinity Hall, Leitch was licensed to preach as a minister of the Church of Scotland. He did not break with the church during the "great disruption" of 1843. In that year he was ordained and presented by the Earl of Leven to the parish of Monimail in the presbytery of Cupar. For the next 16 years he gave himself up to his parish duties, to his studies, and to the work of the General Assembly. There, as convenor of the committee on Sabbath schools, he interested himself particularly in popular education. He was a man of genial personality who made many warm friends.

In 1859 two trustees of Queen's College at Kingston, the Reverend John Barclay and Alexander Morris*, were sent to Scotland to find a successor to the retiring principal, the Reverend John Cook*. The General Assembly recommended Leitch to them, although expressing the belief that he might have a more distinguished and useful career in Scotland. He was already well known for the writings on science and religion he had published in the *Scottish Review* and other periodicals. It may have been a special interest in educational matters that induced Leitch to leave these agreeable occupations in order to build up the little college at Kingston.

Leitch was appointed principal of Queen's at a salary of £600 a year from 1 June 1860. He arrived at Kingston in October and expressed much pleasure at the quality of the students there, pronouncing them "quite equal to the students at home." He was optimistic about the future of the college. During his principalship he did much to develop the theological faculty, and he added to the existing faculties of theology, arts, and medicine the new but short-lived faculty of law in 1861. He accepted for Queen's the management of the local observatory, of which N. F. Dupuis* was appointed "observer," and the accompanying responsibility of arranging for public lectures on astronomy and other scientific subjects. In 1862 he published his best known work, *God's glory in the heavens*. He was also associated with Dr George Lawson*, the professor of chemistry,

in establishing a botanical garden and in the founding at Kingston in 1860 of the Botanical Society of Canada, of which he became president in 1861, and of the society's *Annals*, to which he contributed.

For the first year or two of his principalship Leitch was deeply involved in the question of university education in Canada West. Along with S. S. Nelles*, the principal of Victoria University at Cobourg, he claimed for Queen's, as a constituent college in the provincial university at Toronto which had been envisaged by the University Act of 1853, a share in the endowment and the government of the university. He believed that university education should be carried on in colleges, and he advocated following the Scottish pattern of a number of small colleges at various places throughout the province conducting their own teaching in their own way and requiring their students to write university examinations for a university degree. In 1861 a commission which included Leitch's friend and colleague on the Queen's board of trustees, John Paton, proposed a plan by which the colleges might be associated with the University of Toronto in the manner suggested by Leitch. Under this plan too, the colleges would have secured the needed support from the university endowment. Hoping that the plan might be adopted, Leitch for a time served on the senate of the University of Toronto and as a university examiner. The senate, however, was strongly opposed to the views of the commissioners, and its influence brought about the rejection of the proposals. The University of Toronto retained complete control of the entire endowment. Fortunately, the provincial government had in 1860 increased its grants to Victoria and Queen's from $3,000 to $5,000 yearly.

Leitch, as a distinguished clergyman and scholar and as principal of Queen's College, was welcomed by the Synod of the Presbyterian Church in Canada in Connection with the Church of Scotland. His name was entered on the roll of the synod in the month of his nomination as principal, November 1859. Absences in Scotland prevented his attendance at the synod meeting held in 1861; he was elected moderator for the year 1862–63.

At Queen's, however, Leitch was facing disappointment and failure. The college was deeply divided by personal quarrels and by conflicts of principle which had arisen between the senate and the board of trustees. The professors at Queen's, most of them graduates of Scottish universities, claimed life-long tenure of their "chairs" and maintained that the senate, although created by the board of trustees, could,

LeMesurier

once created, exercise its powers of academic discipline independently of the board. The question of the distribution of powers within the college was a difficult one. Leitch, having no previous knowledge or experience of the complexity and bitterness of academic quarrels or of the special problems of Queen's, underestimated the seriousness of the situation. He accepted too readily the views of the trustees and gradually found himself alienated from almost all his academic colleagues. Out of a staff of some 12 professors, three, James GEORGE, Lawson, and John Dickson*, resigned and two, John Stewart and George Weir, were dismissed during his administration of three and a half years: a result not so much of Leitch's policy as of deep-seated disagreements and resentments which had built up over the previous decade under a series of overworked acting principals. Leitch's health, never robust, broke under the strain, and he died after considerable suffering in May 1864.

HILDA NEATBY

William Leitch's writings include *God's glory in the heavens* (London and Edinburgh, 1862; 1863); *Introductory address at the opening of Queen's College, Nov. 8, 1860* (Montreal, 1860); and *Vindication of the General Assembly's resolution to accept grants in aid, as offered in the despatch of the hon. the court of directors of the East India Co., of July, 1854* (Edinburgh, 1857); as well as articles in Botanical Soc. of Can., *Annals* (Kingston, Ont.); British Assoc. for the Advancement of Science, *Report* (London); *Good Words* (London); and *Scottish Rev.: a Quarterly Journal of Social Progress* (Glasgow).

QUA, Queen's records, B, 1859–64; D1, 1859–64. *Documentary history of education in U.C.* (Hodgins), XVI–XVIII. *Presbyterian* (Montreal), XV (1862)–XVII (1864). Presbyterian Church of Can. in Connection with the Church of Scot., *Acts and proc. of the Synod*, 1860–64. Notman and Taylor, *Portraits of British Americans*, I, 258–66. D. D. Calvin, *Queen's University at Kingston: the first century of a Scottish-Canadian foundation, 1841–1941* (Kingston, Ont., 1941).

LeMESURIER, HENRY (sometimes spelled **Lemesurier**, but he signed LeMesurier), soldier and businessman; b. 17 Nov. 1791 on the island of Guernsey, son of Haviland LeMesurier, commissary general in the British army; d. 25 May 1861 at Quebec.

Following his father's example, young Henry chose a military career; he served under Wellington in 1811 in Spain, where he lost his right arm. This wound ended his active service and caused him to enter the Commissariat Department in London. His new duties brought him to Canada at the time of the War of 1812. He left the army on half pay after the war, and on 3 Oct. 1815, at Saint-Denis-sur-Richelieu, he married Julie, daughter of Pierre-Guillaume Guérout, a merchant and representative for Richelieu in the first parliament of Lower Canada. The chaplain of the armed forces officiated.

Between 1818 and 1823 Henry LeMesurier lived at Quebec, and rapidly assumed an important role, principally as an agent for clients in the export of squared timber to the British Isles. He then set up the firm of LeMesurier and Company with William Henry Tilstone, a Quebec lawyer; in 1830, when he took Havilland LeMesurier Routh into partnership, the firm became LeMesurier, Tilstone, and Company. The same partners subsequently set up LeMesurier, Routh, and Company of Montreal, and, in association with John Egan*, John Egan and Company of Aylmer. To ensure the shipment of timber, LeMesurier chartered ships or used those he already owned. He had at least four ships built in the Quebec shipyards between 1825 and 1847. As deputy master of Trinity House at Quebec, then as master from 1846 to 1861, he also took an interest in the training and movements of the St Lawrence pilots and in the upkeep of lighthouses. In this latter post he received a salary of £250 a year until 1855, and from then on £300.

LeMesurier took an active part as well in the Quebec Committee of Trade, which in 1842 became the Quebec Board of Trade. He was one of its members from at least 1832, its president from 14 Nov. 1833 to 2 July 1838, and its vice-president in 1848–49, as well as being a member of the Board of Arbitration on several occasions between 1843 and 1856.

He was also involved in setting up and incorporating several companies: the Quebec Fire Assurance Company (1829), the Quebec Exchange (1830), the Quebec and Halifax Steam Navigation Company (1831), the Quebec and Lake Superior Mining Association (1847), the Quebec and Richmond Rail-way Company (1850), of which he was the director, the Quebec and St Andrews Rail-road Company (1850), and the Grand Trunk Railway Company (1852), of which he was one of the first directors.

After 1855 Henry LeMesurier gradually withdrew from business, and his son Henry entered the timber trade. He established himself at Sillery cove, and on 1 Jan. 1859 went into partnership with his brother Edward, as LeMesurier and Brothers.

After returning from England where he had stayed during the winter of 1860–61, Henry LeMesurier died suddenly at Quebec on 25 May

1861, at age 69. The *Quebec Gazette* described him as "affable in manner and possessed of all the characteristics of a gentleman of the Old School."

MARC VALLIÈRES

ANQ-M, État civil, Anglicans, Garrison, 3 Oct. 1815. ANQ-Q, AP-G-219/1–4; État civil, Anglicans, Cathedral of the Holy Trinity (Québec), 28 May 1861; Greffe de John Childs, déc. 1836; Greffe de E. B. Lindsay, 22 mai 1826, 21 juin 1830; Greffe de L. T. McPherson, 29 mars 1830. Bas-Canada, *Statuts*, 1829, c.58; 1830, c.15; 1831, c.33. Can., Prov. du, *Doc. de la session*, 1845–61 (Maison de la Trinité de Québec, Rapport annuel); *Statuts*, 1841, c.92; 1847, c.69; 1850, c.116, c.117; 1861, c.99. *Canada Gazette* (Quebec and Toronto), 19 May 1855, 31 Dec. 1858. *Le Journal de Québec*, 28 mai 1861. *Quebec Gazette*, 27 May 1861. F.-J. Audet et Édouard Fabre Surveyer, *Les députés au premier parlement du Bas-Canada [1792–1796]* . . . (Montréal, 1946), 266–67. *Canada directory*, 1857–58. *Montreal directory*, 1843–73. Morgan, *Sketches of celebrated Canadians*, 234–35. *Quebec directory*, 1847–62. Hamelin et Roby, *Hist. économique*, 107. P.-A. Lamontagne et Robert Rumilly, *L'histoire de Sillery, 1630–1950* ([Sillery, Qué., 1952]). Fernand Ouellet, *Histoire de la Chambre de commerce de Québec* (Québec, [1959]), 105. Narcisse Rosa, *La construction des navires à Québec et ses environs; grèves et naufrages* (Québec, 1897), 52. G. R. Stevens, *Canadian National Railways* (2v., Toronto and Vancouver, 1960–62), I, 87.

LEMIEUX, FRANÇOIS-XAVIER, lawyer and politician; b. 9 Feb. 1811 at Lévis, Lower Canada, son of Gabriel Lemieux and Judith Bonneville; d. 16 May 1864 in the town of his birth.

In 1647 Gabriel Lemieux, of Rouen, Normandy, immigrated to Quebec with his half-brother Pierre. In 1655 he received from the grand seneschal, Jean de Lauson*, title-deeds to a piece of land with a river frontage of three *arpents* and a depth of 40 *arpents*. François-Xavier Lemieux was descended from this old Pointe-Lévi family.

After attending the Séminaire de Québec, Lemieux studied law in the office of the future judge Jean-Baptiste-Édouard Bacquet. He was called to the bar on 1 April 1839, and from then on practised at Quebec, dividing his time between law and politics. His political career began on 12 July 1847, when he became MLA for Dorchester County in the assembly of united Canada. His opponent, Elzéar-Henri Juchereau* Duchesnay of Sainte-Marie-de-la-Beauce, was a Reformer like himself; his victory was not therefore one of political opinions but of the lower county (Lauzon) over the upper (Beauce), and probably one of an economy moving from the agricultural

tradition to industrialization. Until the dissolution of the government of Henry Sherwood* and Denis-Benjamin Papineau* on the following 7 December, Lemieux sat with the strongest opposition since union. He supported the manifesto of the "Comité constitutionnel de la réforme et du progrès" [*see* René-Édouard Caron*], launched on 8 Nov. 1847, whose fundamental principles Louis-Hippolyte LA FONTAINE adopted in his political programme of 1848.

During the ministry of La Fontaine and Robert Baldwin*, Lemieux made himself "the chief organizer, both in parliament and in the country regions," of the movement for the abolition of seigneurial tenure. A member of the commission formed for this purpose in 1851, he was the author, with Lewis Thomas Drummond*, of a bill that was rejected in the assembly in 1852 but formed the basis for the law of 1854. He was also closely involved in the incorporation of the Grand Trunk and the construction of its sections connecting Lévis to Richmond and Rivière-du-Loup.

In 1854, when the new county of Lévis was detached from the counties of Dorchester and Beauce, Lemieux was elected there by acclamation. On 27 Jan. 1855, since he was "the stuff of which ministers are made," and had distinguished himself in parliament in recent sessions, he became commissioner of public works in the cabinet of Allan Napier MACNAB and Étienne-Paschal TACHÉ. He continued to hold this office in the Taché–John A. Macdonald* ministry, from 24 May 1856 to 25 Nov. 1857. Taché's retirement brought about the dissolution of the Taché–Macdonald government, and Lemieux stayed out of the new ministry of Macdonald and George-Étienne Cartier*. Like Joseph-Édouard Cauchon* and Drummond, he apparently was not ousted but retired voluntarily, although on this occasion Cartier did sacrifice some of his party in order to attempt a reconciliation of all political groups, even the most radical. Indeed, in the December 1857 elections Lemieux was elected on the Liberal-Conservative ticket, and voted accordingly in the following session. Lemieux, however, did not feel bound to the Liberal-Conservative party, and on 2 Aug. 1858 he entered the "48-hour government" of George Brown* and Antoine-Aimé Dorion* as receiver general. From then on his support was given unreservedly to the moderate Liberal wing led by Louis-Victor Sicotte*, and he was defeated in the 1861 elections by his former Liberal opponent Joseph-Goderic Blanchet*, who had just joined the Liberal-Conservative party. The moderate Liberals recorded gains in the Quebec region, but

Lenoir

this defeat clearly showed that Lévis remained loyal to one party, to the point of rejecting its representative of 15 years' standing, and that, seven years after the official union of the Conservatives and the moderate Reformers of the two Canadas, party lines were finally taking firm shape in the famous coalition of Francis Hincks* and Augustin-Norbert MORIN.

On 15 Sept. 1862 Lemieux was elected by acclamation to the Legislative Council for La Durantaye; on the following 1 May he was appointed *bâtonnier* of the Quebec bar. But his physical strength was failing, and on 16 May 1864 he died at Lévis. In the political history of the union, when political parties had a precarious existence, Lemieux was one of the men who forced the opposition party to repudiate its radicalism, and who marked the transition between the Rouge party of Louis-Joseph Papineau* and the Liberal party of Wilfrid Laurier*.

ANDRÉE DÉSILETS

Can., prov. du, Assemblée législative, *Troisième rapport et délibérations du comité spécial de l'Assemblée législative . . . au sujet de la tenure seigneuriale* (Québec, 1851). *Le Courrier de Saint-Hyacinthe*, 3 août 1858. *Le Courrier du Canada*, 1847–64. *Le Journal de Québec*, 1847–64. *La Minerve*, 1847–64. *Montreal Gazette*, 13 July 1861. *Quebec Mercury*, 3 Aug. 1858. *CPC*, 1864. Desjardins, *Guide parlementaire*. Le Jeune, *Dictionnaire*. Bernard, *Les Rouges*, 149, 191. Chapais, *Hist. du Canada.*, VII, VIII. Cornell, *Alignment of political groups*, 108. P.-G. Roy, *L'église paroissiale de Notre-Dame de la Victoire de Lévis; notes et souvenirs* (Lévis, Qué., 1912). *Glanures lévisiennes* (4v., Lévis, 1920–22), IV; *Profils lévisiens* (2 sér., Lévis, 1948), 1re sér., 65. L.-P. Turcotte, *Canada sous l'Union*, II, 322. Andrée Désilets, "Une figure politique du XIXe siècle, François-Xavier Lemieux," *RHAF*, XX (1966–67), 572–99; XXI (1967–68), 243–67; XXII (1968–69), 223–55. Lucien Serre, "La plus ancienne souche des Lemieux," *BRH* XXXIV (1928), 112–16.

LENOIR, *dit* **Rolland, JOSEPH**, lawyer and poet; b. 15 Sept. 1822 at Montreal, son of Nicolas Lenoir, *dit* Rolland, a saddler, and Marie-Angélique Cazelet; d. 3 April 1861 at Montreal.

Joseph Lenoir, *dit* Rolland, was a brilliant student at the Collège de Montréal from 1835 to 1843. He was drawn to poetry at an early age, and during the literary exercises at the prize-giving in July 1843 he read *Le Génie des forêts, ode*, a poem that was published in *La Minerve* on 4 Jan. 1844. In 1840, influenced by the patriotic poetry of François-Xavier GARNEAU, he had composed his *Chant de mort d'un Huron*.

Lenoir studied law and was licensed to practise on 28 Sept. 1847. In 1848 he opened an office in Montreal, then went into partnership with Joseph Doutre*. He was not really drawn to the profession, however, and practised it little. Lenoir, who had married Félicité Latour on 22 June 1847 at Lachine, managed to provide for the needs of his family – he had six children – through translating and journalism.

He was one of 13 contributors who in 1847 founded the newspaper *L'Avenir*. This paper was considered very liberal and had links with the Institut Canadien in Montreal, of which Lenoir was an active member. On 6 Feb. 1852 he presented an important study at the institute on the civilization of peoples, which was published in *Le Pays* three days later; in this study he maintained that literary development and the arts were stimulated more under republican institutions than any other form of government, and that the country in which education and letters "have a place of honour is eminently civilized." Extensive reading in the institute's library led him to give at least three lectures on civilization, the humanities, and history. From 1853 to 1855 Lenoir contributed to *La Ruche littéraire*, founded in February 1853 by Henri-Émile Chevalier*. In 1857 he became assistant editor of the *Journal de l'Instruction publique*; at the same time he held the two posts of "clerk of French correspondence [and] librarian" in the Department of Public Instruction.

The years 1848 to 1853 constituted Lenoir's most intense period of poetic production; more than half of his known poems date from these years. In 1848, for example, he published several poems and short stories in the *Album littéraire et musical de la "Revue canadienne."* At the end of 1852 Lenoir was planning to publish his poetry in a collection entitled "Les voix occidentales, ou chants nationaux." However, a lack of subscribers caused him to cancel the project. It was not until 1916 that Casimir Hébert* published *Poèmes épars de Joseph Lenoir-Rolland, 1822–1861*, a collection of some 20 poems of that period. Lenoir is thought to have edited a collection of songs *Lyre (nouvelle) canadienne ou chansonnier de tous les âges*, published in Montreal in 1858. On 27 March 1860 *La Guêpe* reproduced a short story by Lenoir, "Légina, légende chippeouaise"; unfortunately, another story, announced in the same issue, was never published. On the occasion of the Prince of Wales' visit to Montreal in August 1860, he published a guide to the town, *Montréal et ses principaux monuments*.

Probably one of the best French Canadian

poets before Émile Nelligan*, Lenoir enjoyed wide popularity in the 1850s. Louis-Honoré Fréchette* thought he "was almost the only [poet of that period] who was able to free himself from the mythological paraphernalia with which the 18th century was infatuated and all the conventional circumlocutions that Abbé Delisle [Jacques Delille] had made fashionable." Lenoir was well acquainted with contemporary literature and several influences are discernible in his poetry. He drew from the early Romantic writers, especially Lamartine, an extreme sensibility and a liking for exotic themes. On the other hand, his study of English poets added a vigour to his thought which was expressed in his poetry in marked hostility against institutions and authorities. Yet his boldness was accompanied by apprehension, since his most virulent lines were signed with pseudonyms such as Un Canadien, Peuple, or Jean Meunier.

Some 40 of Lenoir's poems have never been published in collected form. Their tone varies, ranging from the sentimental to the violent and even towards the macabre. Although Lenoir was a talented poet, he was unable to break away from his models. Yet in his own way he demonstrated the desire for literary and political freedom that characterized the generation of 1845. The hard realities of life in a "society of philistines," to quote Octave Crémazie*, were, however, too much for his sensitive soul. More than a century after the death of Lenoir, *dit* Rolland in April 1861, his work still remains scattered in newspapers and journals.

JOHN HARE

[Joseph Lenoir, *dit* Rolland], *Montréal et ses principaux monuments* (Montréal, 1860); *Poèmes épars de Joseph Lenoir-Rolland, 1822–1861*, Casimir Hébert, édit. (Montréal, 1916). The poem "Les Deux Voix" is not by Lenoir. J.H.]

PAC, MG 30, D62, 18, pp.843–47. *Album littéraire et musical de la "Revue canadienne"* (Montréal), 1848. *La Guêpe* (Montréal), 27 mars 1860. *La Minerve*, 4 janv. 1844. *Le Pays*, 9 févr. 1852. Monique Biron, "Essai bio-bibliographique sur Joseph Lenoir-Rolland, poète canadien" (thèse de bibliothéconomie, université de Montréal, 1948). Gabriel Leclerc, "L'introduction du romantisme dans la poésie canadienne-française" (thèse de MA, université de Montréal, 1950), 62–74. J. d'A. Lortie, "Les origines de la poésie au Canada français," *Archives des lettres canadiennes* (Montréal), IV (1969), 44–46.

LEOLO. *See* LOLO

LÉONARD, JEAN-CLAUDE. *See* BAVEUX, JEAN-CLAUDE-LÉONARD

LÉRY, CHARLES-JOSEPH CHAUSSEGROS DE. *See* CHAUSSEGROS

LESIEUR-DÉSAULNIERS, ISAAC-STANISLAS (he signed **Isaac Désaulniers**), priest, professor, and superior of the Séminaire de Saint-Hyacinthe; b. 27 Nov. 1811 at Sainte-Anne-d'Yamachiche, Lower Canada, son of François Lesieur-Désaulniers, farmer and member of the assembly, and Charlotte Rivard-Dufresne; d. 22 April 1868 at Saint-Hyacinthe.

During his classical studies at the Séminaire de Nicolet, Isaac-Stanislas Lesieur-Désaulniers came in contact with Lamennais's philosophy of certitude grounded in the general reason of mankind, or common consent, communicated by revelation and tradition. Désaulniers became a priest in 1829. He was immediately appointed professor of sciences (1829–33), then of philosophy (1831–33), at the Séminaire de Saint-Hyacinthe, where Lamennais's ideas fired his colleagues Jean-Charles Prince*, Joseph-Sabin Raymond*, and Joseph La Rocque* with enthusiasm; they in turn were supported by Bishop Jean-Jacques Lartigue*, administrator at Montreal of the diocese of Quebec.

Conscious of the importance of intellectual exchange and concerned with the excellence of "his" seminary, Bishop Lartigue sent Désaulniers to the Jesuit university at Georgetown (Washington, D.C.), to study science and English, "without neglecting theology." Désaulniers and his brother François, who was well regarded as a professor of science and philosophy at the Séminaire de Nicolet, were the first French Canadian clerics to undertake advanced study abroad. Désaulniers stayed at Georgetown from June 1833 to July 1834, studying science and familiarizing himself further with Lamennais's philosophy of common consent, which was probably taught according to Jean-Marie Doney's *Nouveaux éléments de philosophie*. . . . He returned to Saint-Hyacinthe with a "tinge of democratic liberalism," just when the controversy (October 1833–September 1834) between Abbé Jacques Odelin*, a Cartesian, and the professors of the seminary, fervent supporters of Lamennais, had been ended by the encyclical *Singulari nos* of Gregory XVI, which condemned Lamennais's *Paroles d'un croyant*. Profoundly discouraged, Désaulniers taught physics (1834–39, 1844–47), as well as returning to philosophy (1837–49), which he taught with the aid of the eclectic manual by Abbé Jérôme Demers* of the Séminaire de Québec. Demers was resolutely opposed to Lamennais,

Lesieur-Désaulniers

did not take common consent as a criterion of certainty, and showed himself more distinctly Cartesian in his treatment of the problem of ideas.

Désaulniers had been ordained on 30 July 1837, and because of his "determined, independent character" was requested to "be on his guard" during the disturbances of 1837–38; moreover, with his colleagues, he signed a statement justifying the teaching at the seminary, and guaranteeing that "moral philosophy" was taught in orthodox fashion according to the "fundamental principles of society" and "the duties of the citizen with regard to the government."

Like a fair number of clerics of the time, Désaulniers contributed to the "popular press"; he argued polemically about scientific questions in *La Minerve* in 1837 (on the identification of a celestial body), and in the new *Mélanges religieux* in 1841 (on the safety of lightning conductors). Increasingly absorbed in the life of the seminary, he introduced the teaching of agricultural chemistry, and also of political economy (1845), and taught theology (1847–52). In 1847 he became "a beggar going from presbytery to presbytery" to collect the funds needed to build a new seminary.

Désaulniers was able to undertake a voyage in Europe and the Near East (16 Aug. 1852–28 March 1854) through the generosity of the family of Louis-François-Roderick (Rodrigue) Masson*, a seminary pupil for whom he was to act as guide. This voyage shaped his subsequent thinking and conduct. Already acquainted with the eastern United States, Désaulniers now discovered France, Italy, Austria, Germany, Switzerland, Belgium, Spain, Greece, Turkey, Palestine, Malta, and England. He visited the physical laboratories and libraries of many colleges and universities. In France, he went "first to the office of *L'Univers*," then met the philosopher Pierre-Célestin Roux-Lavergne, Father Auguste Gratry, Abbé Théodore Combalot, as well as a son of Louis-Gabriel-Ambroise de Bonald and a grandson of Joseph de Maistre. His Italian tour led to Rome, the "centre of the world," where he met Father Giovanni Perone and visited the universities. St Thomas Aquinas was virtually omnipresent: Désaulniers saw his manuscripts, his room, and his crucifix at Rome and Naples. Before returning from this pilgrimage to the fountainhead, he was appointed superior of the seminary (1853); he was to hold this office with no teaching duties until 1860. He was absent again only when, at the request of Bishop Ignace Bourget*, he was in Illinois (November 1856–June 1857), and attempted in vain to bring around his former friend,

the "schismatic" Charles-Paschal-Télesphore Chiniquy*.

Désaulniers once again taught philosophy from 1860 to 1868. After "wandering" from Cartesianism to eclectic philosophy by way of Lamennais's philosophy of common consent, he had become a fervent adherent of the philosophy of St Thomas Aquinas, which he had discovered during his voyage in Europe and probably studied deeply during his term as superior. He read, translated, and taught the doctrines of the *Doctor angelicus*; in lectures given in the Cabinet de Lecture of the parish of Montreal and before the Union Catholique of Saint-Hyacinthe, he spread the "truth" of St Thomas' word as it related to the history of philosophy, to the origin of knowledge, to authority, capital punishment, and the theory of power.

Released from his duties as superior, Désaulniers collaborated with his *confrère* Joseph-Sabin Raymond in the anti-liberal offensive of the day. He promoted the venture of the papal zouaves of the "militant" and soon "triumphant" church. He preached in honour of the defenders of the Holy See who had fallen at Mentana and Castelfidardo, and gave lectures on Rome and the Holy Land. He outlined a bishop's duties on the occasion of the consecration of Bishop Charles La Rocque*, and expressed approval of the writings of Bishop Louis-François Laflèche* at the time of his consecration. Désaulniers became vicar general in 1866, and supported Raymond in a controversy with liberal Louis-Antoine Dessaulles* by criticizing in April 1867 a lecture given by the latter in 1863 on "progress." Désaulniers died on 22 April 1868 and was buried at Saint-Hyacinthe, where numerous "persons of note" gathered for the occasion.

The philosophical development of this learned priest of Saint-Hyacinthe is to a certain extent representative of the pattern of Lamennais's influence in Quebec; through his travels Désaulniers discovered Thomism as a truth, some 25 years after the condemnation of Lamennais and the standardization of eclectic philosophy by means of the "manual" of Abbé Demers had together left a philosophical void. Around 1860, when clerical authority was growing in Canada and elsewhere, this independent and determined scholar, who initially had commented in public only on purely scientific matters, turned increasingly towards an anti-liberal conservative proselytism. A cleric and professor of philosophy, his knowledge was his power.

YVAN LAMONDE

ACAM, RLB, 1, pp.50, 216; 2, p.160; RLL, 7, pp.48, 107–8, 301–2, 467, 492; 8, pp.176, 321; 9, pp.69, 227; 901.009, 837–3. ASQ, MSS, 626, p.26. ASSH, A, F, Grands cahiers, I, 97–99, 125f.; III, 2f., 8; IV, 19f., 48f., 58, 74–79, 97f., 108, 123–27; A, G, Correspondance des supérieurs, 1860–70, chemises 177, 187; Fonds Isaac Désaulniers; A, M, Lettres d'affaires, B, 127f. BUM, Coll. Baby, Corr. générale, lettre de J. Désaulniers, 24 avril 1859. PAC, MG 24, B59, Cahier de notes, p.14. JIP, juill.–août 1868, 96–97. L'Avenir, 28 juill. 1847, juin–juill, 1857. Le Courrier de Saint-Hyacinthe, 4 sept. 1864; 21, 24, 28 nov. 1865; 27 mars 1866; 6, 9, 13 avril 1867; 25 janv., 23 avril 1868. L'Écho du cabinet de lecture paroissial, janv.-févr., 15 mars, 15 oct., 1er nov. 1864; 1er févr., 1er juill., 1er août 1865, 15 août 1866. Le Journal des Trois-Rivières, 1er mars 1867. Mélanges religieux, 16 juill., 6, 13, 20 août 1841. La Minerve, avril-mai 1837, 14 avril 1857, Le Pays, 7 mai 1867. La Revue canadienne (Montréal), 9 août 1855.

Lucien Beauregard, "La part de M. Isaac-Stanislas Désaulniers à l'introduction du thomisme au Canada français vers l'époque de la renaissance religieuse de 1840 à 1845," Historiographie de la philosophie au Québec (1853–1970), Yvan Lamonde, édit. (Montréal, 1972), 113–30. Napoléon Caron, Histoire de la paroisse d'Yamachiche (précis historique) (Trois-Rivières, 1892). C.-P. Choquette, Histoire du séminaire de Saint-Hyacinthe depuis sa fondation jusqu'à nos jours (2v., Montréal, 1911–12), I. L.-O. David, Monsieur Isaac S. Désaulniers; prêtre, professeur de philosophie au séminaire de Saint-Hyacinthe (2e éd., Montréal, 1883). J.-A.-I. Douville, Histoire du collège-séminaire de Nicolet, 1803–1903, avec les listes complètes des directeurs, professeurs et élèves de l'institution (2v., Montréal, 1900), II, 143. [J.-S. Raymond], Éloge de messire I. S. Lesieur-Desaulniers prononcé à la distribution des prix du séminaire de St.-Hyacinthe, le 7 juillet 1868 (Saint-Hyacinthe, Qué., 1868). Émile Chartier, "Figure d'éducateur, messire Isaac-Stanislas Désaulniers (1811–1868)," RSC Trans., 3rd ser., XLII (1948), sect.I, 29–41.

LILLIE, ADAM, Congregational minister and educator; b. 18 June 1803 at Glasgow, Scotland; d. 19 Oct. 1869 at Montreal, Que.

Adam Lillie as a child fell under the religious influence of Ralph Wardlaw, a Congregational minister in Glasgow then at the height of his pulpit eloquence. Lillie joined the church at age 18, and, hoping to become a minister, studied intermittently for several years at the University of Glasgow, where he won a prize in classics. While he was at Glasgow, however, he offered his services to the London Missionary Society, an interdenominational organization largely supported by Congregationalists. In preparation for his future work Lillie was sent to the Theological Academy at Gosport, Hampshire, directed by David Bogue, a founder of the LMS. Graduating in 1826, he was ordained at Stockwell Independent Church, London, on 28 March and a month later he and his wife Elizabeth sailed for India. He was stationed in Belgaum, but found the climate so injurious to his health that he returned to Glasgow a year later.

Weakened by his ordeal, Lillie hesitated to undertake the full responsibility of a church and supported himself as a private tutor preparing students for the university and at the same time assisting the Reverend John Watson in his church in Edinburgh. One of the students whom he prepared for matriculation in 1829 was a young Canadian, Henry Wilkes*. At Wilkes' urging, and with the aid of £20 from the London Missionary Society, Lillie came to Canada in 1831 to start a Congregational church wherever it might be needed. Wilkes' family lived in Brantford, Upper Canada, and had already shown their Independent sympathies by starting a union Sunday school. They invited Lillie to join them in founding a church. A church roll was started in 1834 and enlarged so rapidly that they were able to erect a frame building in 1836.

In the period following the Napoleonic wars considerable numbers of Scottish and English Congregationalists immigrated to British North America, usually to urban areas where they engaged in commerce. Most were educated in the rudiments of trade, and they were usually modestly independent financially. Liberal in their political and social ideas, they emphasized the importance of popular education beyond the classroom (through such groups as the mechanics' institutes) and civic involvement in social movements against intemperance, slavery, and church establishment. Mildly Calvinistic in their theology, the Congregationalists were also closely aligned with the Baptists because of their insistence on congregational autonomy and religious equality.

In 1839 the Congregational church in Guelph sent Ludwig Kribs to Lillie to be trained for the ministry; in order to have more space for students he moved that year to Dundas, and began serving the Congregational churches in both Dundas and Hamilton. The following year his class in theology had increased to five students, and the Congregational Union of Upper Canada agreed to establish the Congregational Academy of British North America in Toronto. Later that year the academy opened, and there Lillie, with the help of a tutor, taught 64 students between 1840 and 1864. Meanwhile, in 1836, Henry Wilkes had returned to Canada as minister of Zion Church in Montreal and agent of the LMS in Canada. Wilkes and his associate, J. J. Carruthers, in 1842 formed in that city a small training institute for ministers, the Congregational Theological Insti-

Lind

tute, but the number of students was not encouraging and in 1845 they decided to unite with the Toronto college and send their students to Lillie. The combined college in Toronto was renamed the Congregational Theological Institute in 1846.

In spite of his heavy duties in the college, Lillie was secretary of the Congregational Union of Upper Canada from 1842 to 1844, and published a lecture on educating the ministry which he had delivered at the opening of the academy in Toronto in 1840. Two lectures, delivered before the Toronto Mechanics' Institute in March 1852, were also published in the *Quebec Gazette* and the *Journal of Education of Upper Canada*, where they attracted considerable complimentary attention. They were later published in a volume which included a statistical appendix concerning the future of the united counties of Leeds and Grenville. His third publication, *Canada: physical, economic, and social*, directed at prospective immigrants, contained detailed maps of Canada, geographical and agricultural information, a description of the economy and of transportation facilities, and a discussion of governmental and cultural institutions. Lillie was also a frequent contributor to the Congregational magazines, the *Harbinger*, and its successor, the *Canadian Independent*. The University of Vermont, in a state with a strong Congregational tradition, honoured him with a DD in 1854. In 1850 Lillie had been a founding member of the Anti-Clergy Reserves Association and in the 1860s served as a member of the University of Toronto senate.

In the census of 1851 Congregationalists in Canada had numbered 11,674 compared to 914,561 Roman Catholics, 280,619 Methodists, and 268,592 Anglicans. The Congregational Church's growth in the following decade required more ministers. In 1864, because of the increasing number of students, it was decided to move the college from Toronto to Montreal, where Wilkes and Dr George Cornish, who were experienced in training ministerial students, could also be used as professors. Lillie, who taught theology and church history, remained principal, while Cornish taught Greek testament and exegesis and Wilkes homiletics and pastoral theology. Lillie travelled between Montreal and Toronto, where his wife and eight children remained, as his work dictated. At his death in 1869 the *Canadian Independent* said that "no man had a higher estimate than Dr. Lillie of the requirements of the Christian ministry, in respect to intellectual endowment and culture . . ." and that

he had always given to his students the "choicest fruits of his own reflection and research. . . ."

EARL B. EDDY

Adam Lillie was the author of *Canada: its growth and prospects; two lectures delivered before the Mechanics' Institute, Toronto . . .* (Brockville, [Ont.], 1852); *Canada: physical, economic, and social* (Toronto, 1855); and with W. P. Wastell, *Ministerial education; two discourses delivered in the Congregational chapel, Toronto . . .* (Toronto, 1840). *Canadian Independent* (Toronto), November 1869. *Harbinger* (Montreal), 15 July 1842. E. B. Eddy, "The beginnings of Congregationalism in the early Canadas" (unpublished THD thesis, Emmanuel College, Toronto, 1957). John Robertson, *History of the Brantford Congregational Church, 1820–1920* ([Brantford, Ont.], n.d.). John Waddington, *Congregational history* [1200–1880] (5v., London, 1869–80), IV. John Wood, *Memoir of Henry Wilkes, D.D., LL.D., his life and times* (Montreal and London, 1887).

LIND, HENRY, Church of England clergyman, missionary, and teacher; b. in 1805 in England; m. with two children; d. 19 May 1870 at St George's, Nfld.

Nothing is known about Henry Lind until he first appeared in Newfoundland in 1829, a lay missionary of the Newfoundland School Society employed as a schoolmaster at Port de Grave on Conception Bay. He and his wife taught there with such success that within a year there were 150 pupils in the day school, 60 in the Sunday school, and 36 in the adult classes.

In 1840 Aubrey George Spencer*, the first Anglican bishop of Newfoundland, decided to expand the number of clergy by ordaining the society's schoolmasters even though they lacked degrees or formal theological training. Lind was made deacon and moved to Catalina on Trinity Bay. Ordained priest in 1841, he was transferred to Heart's Content on Trinity Bay. He took over a large mission of nine settlements and five churches, and for most of his time there he pursued a quiet missionary existence. It was a poor mission, however, which in 1855–57 was unable to send any contributions to the Newfoundland Church Society's missionary fund.

Early in 1856, just before Lind was to depart for England on a leave of absence, Bishop Edward Feild* received a message from a married woman who accused Lind of having had "criminal connection with her." At Feild's request Lind signed a statement denying the charge, and then left for England. After Lind's return a few months later Mr Ollerhead, magistrate of Heart's Content, "spread and magnified" the report of

Lind's supposed adultery, even though the woman had signed an affidavit declaring Lind was innocent. Lind may have tactlessly antagonized the magistrate, for Bishop Feild later claimed: "The trouble was got up by a wicked man to get rid of a disagreeable cleric."

When some of the parishioners of Heart's Content denied Lind entry to the church, Feild consented to legal action being taken against Ollerhead for slander. The case was to be heard in May 1856, but after witnesses first for the defence and then for the prosecution failed to appear, it was adjourned. Persuaded by Ollerhead that Lind was afraid to prosecute, the people of Heart's Content ostracized Lind and asked for his dismissal. But Feild refused to act without a legal decision. The case finally opened in November 1856, but it had to be abandoned when a juror was taken ill. It was not continued as Bryan Robinson* and Hugh William Hoyles*, the prosecution lawyers, felt that the evidence against Lind had already been shown to be too weak to credit.

Feild announced his belief in Lind's innocence and moved him in 1857 from Heart's Content to St George's Bay area on the other side of Newfoundland. Legal expenses were paid by the Newfoundland Church Society and the Society for the Propagation of the Gospel. Privately Feild said: "I have never had any matter which gave me so much distress, and I may say misery, since I have been in the Diocese." At his new station Lind functioned as a competent missionary, and from 1857 to 1864 kept a diary which gives detailed and interesting accounts of local customs. There he died in 1870.

Lind was an undistinguished missionary whose grasp of church principle Feild found wanting. He is an example, however, of a clergyman who had the misfortune, as did two contemporaries, the Reverend William Kepple White of Harbour Buffet and the Reverend John Cyrus A. Gathercole of Burin, to offend a local magistrate and acquire notoriety as the subject of the intolerance possible in a small, claustrophobic community.

FREDERICK JONES

PANL, P6/A/9 (Henry Lind, diary, 1857–64 (photocopy)). USPG, D9B, 753–56, 783–88, 873–76, 891–97, 899–904, 925–28. Prowse, *History of Nfld.* (1896).

LINTON, JOHN JAMES EDMONSTOUNE, journalist, teacher, and abolitionist; b. 1804 at Rothesay (Isle of Bute, Scotland); m. in November 1829 Margaret Dallas; d. 23 Jan. 1869 at Stratford, Ont.

Apparently a teacher with the United Secession Church and a lawyer before coming to Upper Canada from Perthshire in 1833, John James Edmonstoune Linton was one of the original settlers of Stratford. He had been directed there by an agent of the Canada Company, for which in the 1840s he wrote three emigration handbooks. He began by farming and opened his first school in Stratford, while his wife started a school in nearby North Easthope Township; they jointly conducted night classes in 1834–35. Linton then entered business as a public notary and conveyancer, interested himself in the growing temperance movement, and promoted an agricultural society (of which he became secretary in 1841).

Linton joined those agitating for separation of the Stratford area from the Huron District. His views brought him into conflict with J. C. W. Daly*, local representative of the Canada Company, and Linton saw himself as a "public watchdog." A common desire to see Stratford made a district capital brought the opposing groups together by 1846, however, and in 1847 Linton persuaded John PRINCE to present a bill to the assembly for the creation of a district of Peel, only to see the bill withdrawn. When the ministry of Robert Baldwin* and Louis-Hippolyte LA FONTAINE was formed early in 1848, he helped Malcolm Cameron* draft a bill by which the eastern section of Huron became Perth County – a name apparently chosen solely by Linton. As a result he was hailed in Stratford for his "indefatigable exertions and untiring perseverance." In 1850 he was appointed clerk of the Court of Requests and clerk of the peace, a post he held until his death. He also promoted the construction of railways to Stratford in the 1850s.

That Linton had left Scotland in 1833, immediately following the explosive 1832 assembly of the Church of Scotland which led directly to the disruption of 1843, may have been coincidental, but he was involved in religious disputes throughout his life. In 1845 he began attacking the American Tract Society, which supplied religious literature to Canadian churches through the Upper Canada Tract Society, for its pro-slavery stance. Because the American group refused to distribute anything on slavery, Linton concluded that the society, as well as the American Board of Commissioners for Foreign Missions and the American Sunday School Union, supported "the peculiar institution." He wrote letters to and took out advertisements in local and New York newspapers, and distributed tracts at his own expense. He charged his own church with "false fellowshipping" through the Presbyterian Board

Litchfield

of Publications of Philadelphia. In addition, from 1853 to 1856 he often wrote for Canada West's most substantial newspaper for fugitive slaves, the *Provincial Freeman*, and he launched his own paper, the *Voice of the Bondsman*, in Stratford in 1856. He distributed 5,000 free copies of the first issue in November and 7,000 copies of a second issue in December, but finding few subscribers he abandoned his effort early in 1857. He had also initiated in April 1854 an irregularly published pamphlet series entitled *Challenge*, which continued through 24 issues until 1860 and was devoted to the temperance and sabbatarian movements; he did not neglect to remind his readers of the links between slavery and drink. He also wrote an abolitionist pamphlet and with Thomas Henning, secretary of the Anti-Slavery Society of Canada, prepared *Slavery in the churches, religious societies, &c., a review* (Toronto, 1856), which indicted Baptists, Congregationalists, and Wesleyan Methodists.

In the final analysis, however, Linton was ineffective as an abolitionist, for he was so outspoken, indeed vicious, and so much a perfectionist that even the patient philanthropist of abolitionism in New York, Lewis Tappan, asked to be relieved of further correspondence with him. The only results of Linton's efforts were the decisions taken by the Upper Canada Tract Society in 1856 to obtain American tracts through its own rather than through American agents, and by the Canadian Presbyterians to turn away from the Presbyterian Board of Publications and to obtain their publications from Scotland. Unhappily, Linton was a typical Canadian abolitionist, unable to seek out constant allies in American anti-slavery movements because he could not separate his hatred of slavery from an intense dislike for the United States. Instead, his principal sustenance came from the Bristol and Clifton Ladies' Anti-Slavery Society and the Edinburgh Ladies' Emancipation Society. At the annual meeting of the Canadian Anti-Slavery Society in 1857 Linton was thanked for his efforts on behalf of abolitionism. Thereafter, perhaps because of illness, he became increasingly silent and interested himself in relief for the poor of Stratford. He was observed in 1859 carrying a bottle of wine to a dying man (notwithstanding his temperance sentiments) and he opened a soup kitchen. He died at age 64, having seen the Stratford he helped found elevated to the status of a town and the slavery he hated abolished in the republic to the south.

ROBIN W. WINKS

[*Letters from settlers in Huron District, C.W.*, comp. J. J. E. Linton (London, 1842?)]. [J. J. E. Linton], *The life of a backwoodsman; or, particulars of the emigrant's situation in settling on the wild land of Canada* (London, 1843; repr. 1850). J. J. E. Linton, *A prohibitory liquor law for Upper Canada, being a bill for an act to prohibit the sale by retail, &c., with remarks, and other documents* (Toronto, 1860). J. J. E. Linton and Thomas Henning, *Slavery in the churches, religious societies, &c., a review* (Toronto, 1856). [*Statements from settlers on the Canada Company land in the Huron District*, comp. J. J. E. Linton (London, 1842?)].

Dr Williams's Library (London), Estlin papers. Library of Congress (Washington), Manuscript Division, Lewis Tappan papers. PAC, RG 7, G20, 59. *Globe*, 1856–57. *Provincial Freeman* (Windsor; Toronto; Chatham), 1853–56. *Voice of the Bondsman* (Stratford, [Ont.]), 1856–57 (the only surviving copy is at the UWO). *Windsor Herald* (Windsor, [Ont.]), 6 June 1856. W. S. and H. J. M. Johnston, *History of Perth County to 1967* (Stratford, Ont., 1967). William Johnston, *History of the county of Perth from 1825 to 1902* (Stratford, Ont., 1903). A. L. Kearsley, *Paths of history in Perth and Huron* (Stratford, Ont., 1963). Robina and K. M. Lizars, *In the days of the Canada Company: the story of the settlement of the Huron tract and a view of the social life of the period, 1825–1850* (Toronto and Montreal, 1896). A. L. Murray, ''Canada and the Anglo-American anti-slavery movement: a study in international philanthropy'' (unpublished PHD thesis, University of Pennsylvania, Philadelphia, 1960). Winks, *Blacks in Can.*.

LITCHFIELD, JOHN PALMER, journalist, physician, and educator; b. 1808 in London, England, probably the son of John Charles Litchfield, a surgeon in the Haymarket; m. Louisa Maddock; d. 18 Dec. 1868 at Kingston, Ont.

There is considerable doubt whether John Palmer Litchfield earned a medical degree. At various times he maintained that he had received one from the University of Heidelberg (West Germany), that he was a lecturer recognized by the Royal College of Surgeons, and that he was a fellow of the Linneaen Society – none of which was true. By his own description he was connected in the mid 1830s as a ''physician'' with the London Infirmary for Diseases of the Skin and the Westminster General Dispensary. He became a medical journalist and contributed a series of lectures on diseases of the skin to *Lancet* and the *Medical Gazette* in 1835. From 1836 to 1838 he apparently contributed articles on a variety of subjects to such British monthly periodicals as *Bentley's Miscellany*. He emigrated to Australia in 1838 and in June of that year was appointed without salary as inspector of hospitals for South Australia. In 1840 he was briefly a member of the managing board of Adelaide's first hospital, a clay hut. He continued as an active journalist with the *Adelaide Independent and Cabinet of Amusement* and cam-

470

Little Chip

paigned vigorously for the development of public health services. When a new general hospital was opened in Adelaide in 1840, however, Litchfield was not reappointed to the hospital board and his post as inspector was abolished. He diverted his attention to the pauper insane, but failed to acquire funds for an asylum and convalescent home from the governor of the colony, George Gawler. At the same time his credentials were questioned and he had so overextended his credit that he was imprisoned for debt in 1841. He was released upon promise of repayment and in 1843 returned to England. From 1843 to 1845 he was employed as a European correspondent for various London newspapers. He claimed to have been medical superintendent for a minor lunatic asylum at Walton, near Liverpool, from 1845 to 1852. In 1853 he emigrated to Boston where he wrote editorials for the *International Journal* of New York, Boston, and Portland, Maine, and was listed in local directories as a physician with the Invalid Food Office.

Litchfield came to Canada in 1853, and acted for a time as editor of the Montreal *Pilot and Journal of Commerce*, a Reform newspaper which supported Francis Hincks*. In March 1855 he was appointed by a Montreal civic committee to head a delegation to promote the city's manufactures at the Paris exposition. At the same time the ministry of Augustin-Norbert Morin and Allan Napier MacNab appointed him superintendent of the criminal lunatic asylum near Kingston. Litchfield and some male patients resided in J. S. Cartwright*'s house, known as Rockwood, while others were housed in Kingston Penitentiary. After Cartwright's estate was purchased by the provincial government in 1856 the stables were renovated to house 24 female patients previously confined in the penitentiary. The building of a permanent institution began in 1859, but the gradual transfer of patients from the penitentiary was not effected until construction was completed in 1868. At Rockwood, Litchfield espoused what were considered advanced moral treatment views, and opposed mechanical restraint and segregation for all but the most violent patients.

During his tenure as medical superintendent of the asylum, Litchfield maintained close connections with the fledgling Queen's College at Kingston. From 1855 until 1860 he held successively the chairs of forensic and state medicine, obstetrics, and, after 1860, institutes of medicine. His lack of credentials became known in Kingston, but his lectures were popular. They ranged widely over such subjects as medical jurisprudence and insanity, the causes of violent insanity, and contemporary improvements in understanding the causes and in the treatment of lunatics.

Litchfield was also active in civic affairs, and in 1860 was elected president of the Kingston Electoral Division Society for Promoting Agriculture, Horticulture, Manufacture, and Works of Art. After 1861 he withdrew from this association to become a member of the Botanical Society of Kingston. By 1865 he was ailing and no longer able to continue his numerous interests. Litchfield remained as titular head of Rockwood Asylum for the next three years, and died of heart disease in his own hospital at age 60.

Litchfield had demonstrated an uncommon adaptability in his chosen professions of journalism and medicine. There are sufficient grounds to suspect his credentials, although not his abilities, as a practitioner of both. The literary achievements which he himself professed cannot readily be verified in the anonymous underworld of Victorian popular culture. His medical qualifications were twice proven false, first in South Australia and later in Canada. Yet he seems to have been able to master the nuances of practical treatment through careful observations of skilled clinicians, and was alive to new techniques and theories of treatment promulgated in popular medical journals. By the 1850s he had acquired enough experience both as a newspaperman and an urbane exponent of moral treatment to erase his earlier embarrassment in Adelaide. Times had also changed, and the second discovery at Rockwood that Litchfield lacked a medical degree went virtually unnoticed in the prosperous colony of Canada West in the 1850s. As an esteemed professor of Kingston's expanding college, Litchfield was beyond formal rebuke and even moral reproach.

A. W. Rasporich and I. H. Clarke

[The authors would like to thank Dr George K. Raudzens and Janet K. Cooper of Macquarie University, Sydney, Australia, for their research assistance. A.W.R. and I.H.C.]

John Palmer Litchfield was the author of "The acarus scabiei," which appeared in *Lancet* (London), I (1835–36), 251–52. Other writings he claimed are listed in Morgan, *Bibliotheca Canadensis*, 226–27. QUA, Thomas Gibson, "The astonishing career of John Palmer Litchfield, first professor of forensic medicine at Queen's University, Kingston" (typescript, c. 1939). *Daily British Whig* (Kingston), 1855–68. *The institutional care of the insane in the United States and Canada*, ed. H. M. Hurd (4v., Baltimore, Md., 1916–17), IV.

LITTLE CHIP. *See* Peguis

471

Livernois

LIVERNOIS, JULES-ISAÏE BENOÎT *dit. See*
Benoît

LOGAN, ROBERT, fur-trader, merchant, and
councillor of Assiniboia; b. 1773, in either Scotland or the West Indies; d. 26 May 1866 at Red
River (Man.).

There is little record of the early life of Robert
Logan. His father was a planter in the West Indies, but after a slave rebellion destroyed their
holdings in the Caribbean the family moved to
Montreal. Robert completed his education there
and became fluently bilingual.

In 1801 Logan entered the service of the North
West Company, and from 1806 to 1814 represented it at the post of Sault Ste Marie. He
became disgruntled at his lack of progress and
returned to Montreal in 1814, "a dissatisfied win-
terer." He was persuaded by Colin Robertson*
to transfer to the Hudson's Bay Company. After
assisting Robertson in the preparation of his
outfit for a thrust into the Athabasca country,
Logan accompanied the brigade to the *pays d'en
haut*.

Logan wintered at Île-à-la-Crosse and in 1815
he was placed in charge at Rock Depot (Gordon
House) on Hayes River. In 1818 he assumed
supervision of the company's business at Rainy
Lake (Lac La Pluie). Despite his apparent success Logan was unhappy as an employee and
preferred to strike out on his own. The opportunity came quickly. He was requested by Lord Selkirk [Douglas*] to oversee his affairs at Red
River in the absence of Alexander Macdonell*,
governor of the Red River Settlement. Although
the sources are inconclusive, it appears Logan
may also have served briefly as sheriff of Red
River. In any case, he left the HBC probably late
in 1819, established himself at Red River, and
began a long and varied career in the newly opening west.

As early as 1822, Sir George Simpson* wrote
to Andrew Colvile that "Logan is the best settler
about the place without exception; is sober, industrious and active, has a little spirit of enterprise and improvement about him, with the
command of a little money." His capital was
turned to advantage. In 1825 he purchased the
remains of Fort Douglas and a windmill for £400.
The windmill powered the first grist mill in Red
River and the enterprise prospered. Logan received ten per cent of all the grain he handled.
Over the years he engaged in the wholesale trade,
was an outfitter to the fur brigades, and became
one of the busiest importers in the district. Logan
was also a partner in the Buffalo Wool Company.

His prominence in business affairs led him,
almost inevitably, into the public life of the small
community. In 1823 the General Quarterly Court
of Assiniboia recommended his appointment as a
councillor. In 1835 he was appointed a justice of
the peace for the Third District, and in the administrative reorganization of 1837 became a
magistrate for the Middle District. He resigned
from this office, as well as from the council, in
1839 because of ill health. Five years later, however, he accepted the position of chairman of the
Board of Public Works, a post for which his wide
business interests suited him admirably. Logan
once again undertook the duties of magistrate in
1850. Throughout these active years he was frequently consulted by the HBC on Indian affairs.

Robert Logan was twice married. On 13 Jan.
1821 he married Mary, a Saulteaux Indian, just
prior to the baptism of their daughter Ann on the
same day. Up until that time they had lived together according to the "custom of the country,"
but after settling permanently in Red River Logan
felt constrained to regularize his domestic affairs.
Mary Logan died in 1839 and the following year
Robert married a widow, Mrs Sarah Ingham.
Twelve children were born to Robert Logan during his first marriage and four during the second.

All the family ceremonies in Red River took
place in Upper Church (St John's Cathedral) despite the fact that Logan was a Presbyterian. The
lack of a Presbyterian church was especially
curious since most of the original European immigrants to the colony were Scottish crofters
brought out by Selkirk. After many promises and
many disappointments about a minister, Logan
was pleased to be a member of the committee
which secured the services of the first Presbyterian minister in Red River, the Reverend
John Black*, in 1851.

The concluding years of Robert Logan's life
were spent attending to his many business enterprises and those of his children in whose careers
he took a direct and continuing interest. He remained apart from the growing factionalism of
Red River which would erupt three years after his
death in 1866 in the insurgency of the Métis.
Despite his public activities, he was a businessman and thought of the future of the Canadian
west in that context.

J. E. Rea

PAC, MG 19, E1, ser. 1 (mfm. at PAM); E3. PAM, MG
2, A5, C3, C23; MG 7, B7, register of baptisms,
1813–79; register of marriages, 1820–82; register of burials, 1821–75; MG 14, C23. *Canadian North-West*
(Oliver). [Nicholas Garry], "Diary of Nicholas Garry,
deputy-governor of the Hudson's Bay Company from
1822–1835 . . .," ed. F. N. A. Garry, RSC *Trans.*, 2nd

ser., VI (1900), sect.II, 73–204. HBRS, II (Rich and Fleming); XIX (Rich and Johnson). Ross, *Red River Settlement* (1957), 144–45, 176–78, 346–48. Ross Mitchell, "Robert Logan of Red River, 1775–1866," *Manitoba Pageant* (Winnipeg), 13 (1967–68), no.2, 19–23.

LOLO (Leolo), JEAN-BAPTISTE (known as **St Paul**), HBC employee, trader, and Indian spokesman; b. 1798, probably of French and Iroquois parents; d. 15 May 1868 at Thompson's River Post (Kamloops), B.C.

Jean-Baptiste Lolo entered the fur trade as an interpreter, perhaps with the North West Company. By 1822, when he is first mentioned in Hudson's Bay Company records, he was stationed at Fort St James, and was later at other New Caledonia posts. In 1825 he visited York Factory, probably as an HBC employee on a transport brigade from the western posts. From 1828 intermittently until his death he worked for the HBC at Thompson's River Post, on the east bank of the North Thompson River, and became influential throughout the district. In 1832 Samuel Black*, the trader in charge, admitted that the fort would be "lame without him." He served as interpreter, tripman, and postmaster, but his real importance was as an unofficial liaison officer between the company and the Indians of all the interior Salish tribes. Respected by both, Lolo helped maintain the balance of power between them with remarkable dexterity. In 1841 the company accorded Lolo the courtesy title of chief, apparently as a measure of appeasement after he had been flogged by William Thew, the violent-tempered trader in charge of the post at Fraser Lake, and Indian retaliation seemed imminent.

When the company moved its post across the river in 1843 Chief Trader John Tod* left Lolo on the old site, even building him a house. Here he traded independently with the Indians and bred horses on a tract of pasture extending northeast. By the 1850s HBC traders were acknowledging his enterprise by adding to his missionary nickname St Paul, "Mr." and "Capt.," titles he relished. He achieved transient prosperity as a miner and trader during the brief Tranquille gold rush of 1859–60 but quickly fell into debt with the company.

Travellers through the area have left personal impressions of Lolo. Dr Walter Butler Cheadle* reports in 1863 that Lolo spoke "a curious mixture of French, English & Indian," and called himself "un Canadien." Weary from his arduous trip across western Canada with trying companions [*see* O'BEIRNE], Cheadle also found Lolo grasping and self-important. Lieutenant Richard Charles Mayne*, however, on a visit to Kamloops in 1859 had been more favourably impressed. He admired Lolo's courage in crossing a turbulent river with a crippled knee, "swearing in a French jargon peculiar to himself," and rejoiced in this vivid character.

St Paul's domain was on part of land designated an Indian reserve in 1862 by William George Cox*, despite protests from the HBC. He lived on it in reduced circumstances doing a little trading in loose association with the company until his death. "Mr. Capt. St. Paul" left a large family of at least seven sons and four daughters (including Sophia, Tod's wife), but they did not stay in the area, and his land became part of the general property of the Kamloops Indian band. His restored house still survives as part of the Kamloops Museum.

MARY BALF

HBC Arch. B.188/e/1; B.239/g/2, 4, 8, 12, 22–25; B.239/1/2, 3, 5, 13–16; B.239/x/4a, p.321. PABC, Colonial correspondence, chief commissioner of lands and works correspondence (B.C.), 1860, Donald McLean to H. M. Ball, 12 March 1860, encl. in chief commissioner of lands and works to Governor Douglas, 10 April 1860. [W. B. Cheadle], *Cheadle's journal: being the account of the first journey across Canada undertaken for pleasure only, by Dr. Cheadle and Lord Milton, 1862/1863*, ed. John Gellner (Toronto, n.d.), 190. *Daily British Colonist* (Victoria), 28 May 1861, 8 Dec. 1865. R. C. Mayne, *Four years in British Columbia and Vancouver Island: an account of their forests, rivers, coasts, gold fields, and resources for colonisation* (London, 1862), 76, 119–21, 126–27. Morice, *History of northern interior of B.C.* (1904), 151–53, 200. G. D. Brown, "A further note on Captain St. Paul," *BCHQ*, III (1939), 223–24. G. D. Brown and W. K. Lamb, "Captain St. Paul of Kamloops," *BCHQ*, III (1939), 115–27. "John Tod: 'Career of a Scotch boy,'" ed. Madge Wolfenden, *BCHQ*, XVIII (1954), 215–16, 225, 235.

LOVE, MARY, Lady Love. *See* HEAVISIDE

M

MABEY, PAUL, merchant and politician; b. *c.* 1786 at Bedeque, P.E.I., son of George and Mary Mabey; d. unmarried 21 March 1863 at Pownal Point, P.E.I.

McAskill

Paul Mabey's parents arrived at Charlotte-town, P.E.I., from Shelburne, N.S., in July 1784. Qualifying for a land grant, they settled at Bedeque with other loyalists. About 1800 the family moved to Charlottetown, where Paul became a clerk, along with young Robert Hodgson*, for Benjamin Evans, a prominent merchant. By 1811 he was president of the local New Harmonic Society, and trustee for a piece of land held by the local Wesleyan Methodist Society. Soon after he became a partner of Evans and by 1819 had his own business. In 1823 he was referred to as a merchant of considerable property who had rapidly acquired a fortune.

In 1817 he had been elected as one of the two members of the assembly for Charlottetown and Royalty; he held that seat until 1830. When in 1822 acting Receiver General John Edward Carmichael, son-in-law and close associate of Lieutenant Governor Charles Douglas Smith*, revived a demand for the payment of quitrents, Mabey joined a group led by John Stewart* which sought the dismissal of the governor. Smith's relations with the assembly had been stormy since 1818 and he had governed without an assembly since August 1820. The group petitioned High Sheriff John MacGregor* to call meetings in each county to discuss grievances. At the Queens County meeting on 6 March 1823, over 800 householders and freeholders adopted resolutions critical of Smith's administration. A committee composed of Mabey, Stewart, Mac-Gregor, and four others was chosen to embody the resolutions in a petition to the king, which was subsequently circulated around the Island for signatures. After the publication of these proceedings, Stewart escaped to England with the petition, but Mabey and the others were charged with contempt of the Court of Chancery because they had accused Ambrose Lane*, master in chancery and also Smith's son-in-law, of levying extraordinary charges in cases brought before him. They appeared before a crowded and noisy court on 27 October with Smith presiding. Uneasy about the disturbed state of the colony, Smith suspended proceedings and placed the accused in the custody of the sergeant-at-arms. Mabey told Smith that the committee considered his actions illegal and that they would not remain in custody. On 30 October they were released and the case was dropped. Mabey continued the attack on Lane with several letters to the *Register*, to which Lane made little attempt to reply.

After Smith's dismissal in 1824, Paul Mabey spent his remaining six years in the house actively attending to its business and involved in most of the important committees. He was de-feated in the 1830 elections and never again ran for office. He remained active in the militia and was a well-known Charlottetown figure. About 1856 his mental condition deteriorated and in 1861 he was adjudged to be of unsound mind.

E. G. CARROLL

PRO, CO 226/39, pp.202–10. *Islander*, 13 Dec. 1861. *Prince Edward Island Register* (Charlottetown), 13 Sept. 1823–24 Jan. 1824. *Vindicator* (Charlottetown), 27 March 1863. J. P. Tanton, "Memories of the past – continued," *Prince Edward Island Magazine* (Charlottetown), I (1899–1900), 348.

McASKILL, ANGUS, farmer, businessman, and "Cape Breton Giant"; b. in 1825 on Harris in the Hebrides, Scotland, one of 13 children of Norman McAskill and Christina Campbell; d. a bachelor on 8 Aug. 1863 at Englishtown, N.S.

About 1831 Angus McAskill immigrated with his family to Cape Breton where his father was seeking better economic opportunities. Norman McAskill settled on a 100-acre farm on the south side of St Ann's Harbour in a district called "Englishtown" because its inhabitants "had not the Gaelic."

For a few terms Angus McAskill attended the one-room school run by Alexander Munro, a graduate of King's College, Aberdeen. McAskill was no larger than other children as a boy, but he kept growing. At 14 he became known as St Ann's big boy or *Gille Mor*, and he continued to grow in his 20s until he became so tall that his father lifted the roof of the family home and raised the ceilings of the kitchen and living room. Angus worked with his father and brothers on the family farm. He was also a fisherman. In a pioneer community which admired strength and had many strong men he was called "the big giant" and was remembered because he could carry a 60-foot beam on his shoulder, set a 40-foot mast into a schooner, throw a man weighing 300 pounds over a woodpile 10 ft high and 12 ft wide, pull the bow off a fishing dory when a crowd of fishermen hauled back on the stern as a joke, and lift grindstones as easily as sugar lumps. Fortunately he had a "mild and gentle manner," and was always helpful.

Crop failures in 1847 and 1848 caused economic depression in Nova Scotia, and induced Angus to accept the offer of a visitor to St Ann's to go on a tour as a curiosity. In July 1849 he toured Lower Canada and in 1850 the United States. When he reached his full growth his agents reported his height as 7 ft 9 in., his weight 425 pounds, his shoulders 44 in. wide, and the palm of his hand 8 in. wide and 12 in. long. In 1863 he was wearing boots 17½ in. long. He had deep-set blue eyes and a musical, if somewhat hollow voice. Despite his huge size he was perfectly proportioned.

In 1852 and 1853 he was exhibited in the United States and may have appeared at P. T. Barnum's museum in Philadelphia or New York; in 1853 the giant toured the West Indies and Cuba. Descriptions of his presentation to Queen Victoria, however, are apocryphal. McAskill was often involved in wagers over his weight-lifting ability. The story of one of these wagers is often told. Some bystanders on a pier in New Orleans or New York bet that he would be unable to lift an anchor weighing about 2,700 pounds. He lifted it and walked with it on his shoulder. However, in replacing it on the pier, his grip slipped and the anchor dropped pinning him beneath it.

The giant returned to St Ann's about 1854 with a "snug fortune" and bought farms and a grist mill from some of those who had emigrated to New Zealand with the Reverend Norman McLeod. He is said to have established salmon fishing on a commercial basis at St Ann's. He also operated a general shop at Englishtown in a building he had erected to suit his size, and where he did much of his business by barter. McAskill died after a lingering illness which local doctors described as "brain fever."

The Giant McAskill and Highland Pioneers' Centennial Museum at the Gaelic College of Celtic Folk Arts at St Ann's perpetuates his memory and contains some clothing and furniture used by the giant.

PHYLLIS R. BLAKELEY

PANS, RG 1, 449/52C, census of 1838; RG 20, C, nos.55, 56. Victoria County Court of Probate (Baddeck, N.S.), 1863, A24 (letters of administration and inventory of the estate of Angus McAskill). *Acadian Recorder*, 15 Aug. 1863. *Novascotian*, 7 Oct. 1850, 11 April 1853, 17 Aug. 1863. *Yarmouth Herald* (Yarmouth, N.S.), 14 Nov. 1850. P. R. Blakeley, *Nova Scotia's two remarkable giants* (Windsor, N.S., 1970). W. A. Deacon, *The four Jameses* (Ottawa, 1927), 123–49. J. D. Gillis, *The Cape Breton giant; a truthful memoir* (Halifax, 1926). Albert Almon, "The Cape Breton giant . . . ," *Cape Breton Mirror* (Glace Bay, N.S.), January 1952, 12–14; February 1952, 12–13; March 1952, 12–13.

MACBETH, GEORGE, landowner, entrepreneur, and politician; b. 4 Nov. 1825 at the Red River Settlement (Man.), eldest of the eight children of George Macbeth and Catherine Sutherland; d. 3 June 1870 at London, Ont.

George Macbeth's parents, from Leirobol in Kildonan, Sutherland County, Scotland, were evicted in the Highland clearances and arrived at the Red River Settlement in 1815. In 1838 the family travelled to Upper Canada by canoe, to farm first at Port Talbot, Dunwich Township, and later in Euphemia Township.

About 1839 young George began to work for their neighbour, Colonel Thomas Talbot*, and gradually became what Edward Ermatinger* described as "at once a personal attendant and business and farm manager." In 1848 Talbot's nephew, Richard Airey*, took over the Port Talbot estate, and Macbeth and Talbot then visited Great Britain and the Continent, returning in 1849. The following year, Talbot and his nephew quarrelled. Talbot then made a settlement with Airey, transferring one-half of his estate to him, and in a will named Macbeth the beneficiary for almost all the remainder, valued at about £50,000. The bequest was not surprising considering Talbot's split with his family, his high opinion of Macbeth's character and faithfulness, and Macbeth's genuine affection for him; nevertheless, the Airey family, which knew of the provisions of the will, was furious and felt that a mere servant had absconded with property rightfully theirs. Since Talbot lived another three years, had constant access to his solicitor, H. C. R. Becher*, and made a second similar will in 1852, the settlement was of his own choosing.

In 1852, after having again accompanied Talbot to England, Macbeth married Anne Gilbert Sanders (d. 1911), daughter of John Sanders who had rented Talbot's old residence at Port Talbot. The Macbeths shortly moved to London, Canada West, taking Talbot with them. He died at their home in February 1853. Macbeth was now a wealthy landowner with interests in Bayham, Dunwich, London, Malahide, and Southwold townships. About this time he built a large London residence, Bleak House, and became one of the gentry of the region.

When the new riding of Elgin West was established in 1854 in an area which included much of his estate, Macbeth ran successfully as the Conservative candidate against Archibald McIntyre. In 1857 he was re-elected, defeating W. A. McKinnon, editor of the Hamilton *Daily Banner*. In 1861 he was less lucky; he defeated John SCOBLE, but was unseated for election corruption on 23 Feb. 1863. He then turned to municipal politics; when Frank Smith* retired as alderman of the sixth ward of London in March 1867, Macbeth was elected to succeed him. He was re-elected in 1869.

With his large land holdings Macbeth was naturally interested in steamboat and railway development. In 1855 he was one of the incor-

McCann

porators of the Amherstburg and St Thomas Railway (and was involved in its consolidation into the Niagara and Detroit Rivers Railway Company in 1859) and of the St Clair, Chatham, and Rondeau Railway, and he was a director of the London and Port Stanley Railway from 1857 until the mid 1860s. In the 1860s he was also connected with numerous other incorporations: the Petroleum Springs Road Company in 1861, the City of London Oil Company, the Bank of London, and the North Shore Transportation Company in 1866, the Canada Chemical Manufacturing Company in 1867, and the Merchants' Express Company of the Dominion of Canada in 1868. Few can have been profitable.

Macbeth was active in the militia and established in 1866 the 25th Elgin volunteers, of which he held the lieutenant-colonelcy until his death. He joined St George's masonic lodge in London in 1854 and was on the original board of trustees of St James' Presbyterian Church in 1860, although he appears to have sometimes supported the Church of England. Macbeth had suffered from liver trouble and had intemperate habits but his death came unexpectedly in 1870. He was buried beside Talbot. His estate was valued at $120,000, and he left six children the eldest of whom, Thomas Talbot Macbeth, was county judge of Middlesex from 1904 to 1930.

George Macbeth remains a controversial person because of the Talbot inheritance. Yet he was of a kind and genial nature, was generally popular in the London and Elgin region, and socially was accepted by the local squirarchy.

FREDERICK H. ARMSTRONG

London Public Library and Art Museum (London, Ont.), Edwin Seaborn coll., Diaries, diary of William Elliot, III, pp.5226, 5468–69. Middlesex County Surrogate Court (London, Ont.), will of George Macbeth, 28 Nov. 1866; codicil, 2 June 1869; probated 15 June 1870. PAC, RG 9, I, C6, 20, p.63; RG 68, 1, General index, 1841–67, pp.124, 126–27. UWO, 1 (Sir Richard Airey papers); 10 (H. C. R. Becher papers). Can., Prov. of, Legislative Assembly, *Journals*, 1862, 79–80, 301; 1863, 36; *Statutes*, 1854–55, c.182; 1861, c.88; 1866, c.90. Can., *Statutes*, 1868, c.91. Edward Ermatinger, *Life of Colonel Talbot, and the Talbot settlement, its rise and progress . . .* (St Thomas, [Ont.], 1859), 217–20, 225. "The Richard Airey – Henry C. R. Becher correspondence," ed. M. A. Garland, *Western Ontario History Nuggets* (London, Ont.), 36 (1969). *Daily Advertiser* (London), 3, 6 June 1870. *London Free Press*, 4, 6 June 1870. George Bryce, *The romantic settlement of Lord Selkirk's colonists, [the pioneers of Manitoba]* (Toronto, 1909), 325–27. F. C. Hamil, *Lake Erie baron: the story of Colonel Thomas Talbot* (Toronto, 1955), 255, 266–68, 273–91. *History of the county of Middlesex* (Brock), 120, 251–52, 317, 332, 893–94. J. J. Watts, "Political personalities and politics in western Ontario from 1854 to 1867" (unpublished MA thesis, University of Western Ontario, London, 1958), 19, 21–22, 24–25.

McCANN, ROSANNA (named **Mary Basilia**), Sister of Charity and educator; b. 1811 in Ireland; d. 27 Oct. 1870 in New York City.

Little is known about the childhood of Rosanna McCann. She came to Maryland as a child and received her education with the Sisters of Charity of Emmitsburg, Maryland. At age 18 she entered that congregation, receiving the name Sister Mary Basilia. Her religious community, begun by Elizabeth Ann Bayley Seton in 1812 and the first religious institute for women to have its native foundation in the United States, was one response to the tremendous influx of Catholic immigrants in the early 19th century which made necessary the development of a variety of organizations within the church. The Sisters of Charity were to give temporal and spiritual service to those in need, particularly in the fields of health and education. With the growth of the congregation and the success of its various apostolates, requests for sisters came from many parts of the United States. Sister Mary Basilia served in Baltimore and Frederick, Md, and in Martinsburg, W. Va, as teacher and superior. In 1842 she was sent to New York City, where there were now eight missions and 62 sisters.

In 1845 the New York houses were separated from the Emmitsburg administration, and a second motherhouse was established there in order to give a concentration of authority and supervision. Each sister on mission in New York was allowed to choose whether she would remain or return to Emmitsburg. Sister Mary Basilia, recognizing the needs in the New York area, decided to stay in that diocese. In the spring of 1847 the new motherhouse, Mount Saint Vincent, was dedicated. In the same year the Sisters of Charity of New York received a request from Bishop William Walsh* of Halifax for sisters who would work in his diocese. One hundred years after its founding the city was conscious of the need for organized forms of Catholic education. An affirmative answer to the request was deferred, but when it was repeated two years later four sisters were chosen for this northern mission. With her experience as a successful and tactful administrator, Sister Mary Basilia was named superior.

The sisters arrived in Halifax on 11 May 1849. Bishop Walsh had prepared a convent for them, a four-storey wooden structure, close to St Mary's Cathedral. Originally built as a parochial school, it was now to be utilized as a convent, an elementary girls' school, and an orphanage. Sister Mary Basilia and her three companions began their work immediately: 200 girls were registered, and the formal opening of St Mary's Girls' School took place on 27 May. Since 1821 there had been some financial help from the Nova Scotia government for private schools. Those who could pay met a small tuition charge, but the majority of the pupils were "free scholars." In 1850 the first report of the new Board of School Commissioners for Halifax spoke in glowing terms of the "large Day School . . . conducted by the Sisters of Charity," gave the registration as 400 pupils, and noted a grant of $50 "from the Treasury." Succeeding reports continued to be complimentary, and the financial help increased. Sister Mary Basilia's work as an educator was not confined to the classroom of an elementary school. Night classes for illiterate adults and for those who had not completed their elementary school education were also organized. Furthermore, at the end of their first year in Halifax, the sisters were caring for 20 orphans, children of immigrants whose parents had died of ship fever as they journeyed across the Atlantic during the years of the great famine in Ireland; in 1854 St Mary's Orphan Asylum was said to be housing 16 orphans.

In the same year Bishop Walsh wrote to New York that there was work enough for six more sisters, but to no avail. Instead, in 1856, the establishment of a Canadian motherhouse was approved by Rome and Sister Mary Basilia became the first mother superior of the Sisters of Charity of Halifax, at that time the only independent English-speaking congregation of religious in Canada. The noviciate was established at St Mary's and postulants admitted. A convent was opened for which property was purchased in the north end of the city. Here the sisters took a particular interest in the blacks, and special classes were provided for them in the convent.

Mother Mary Basilia has been described at this time as "in appearance tall and erect; she had a dark complexion and very penetrating black eyes, which would kindle with disapproval, or beam with sympathy and kindness, as the occasion called . . . a person of vast experience, a clever business woman, and a genuine Sister of Charity."

In December 1858 there were 14 professed sisters in the young congregation. Mother Mary Basilia felt that she could return to New York. Two years later she was sent to Jersey City, N.J., to supervise a new mission, where she worked for the last decade of her life. In 1870, a few months before her death, she returned to Halifax for a visit. There were now over 50 sisters and five convents; there were also plans for a new motherhouse in Rockingham, N.S., under whose roof Mount Saint Vincent Academy would be founded three years later.

Today, more than a century after Mother Mary Basilia's death, the Sisters of Charity of Halifax have become an international congregation, numbering over 1,400 sisters, with convents in British Columbia, Alberta, Quebec, New Brunswick, and Nova Scotia; in Massachusetts, New York, New Jersey, and Washington; and with missions in Peru and the Dominican Republic. As well as education from pre-school classes through university, the work of the sisters in Canada embraces hospital and paramedical services for the sick, supervision of child care institutions, and the care of the aging.

SISTER FRANCIS D'ASSISI

PANS, RG 14, 29, "Minutes of the board of school commissioners for the city of Halifax," 1850–64, 1 Nov. 1864 – 7 Nov. 1865. *Acadian Recorder*, 11 May 1849, 14 Aug. 1852, 14 Aug. 1870. C. I. White, *Life of Mrs. Eliza A. Seton, foundress and first superior of the Sisters or Daughters of Charity in the United States of America; with copious extracts from her writings, and an historical sketch of the sisterhood from its foundation to the present time* (New York, 1853). Sister Francis d'Assisi, *Mother Mary Basilia McCann, first mother superior of the Halifax daughters of blessed Elizabeth Seton, 1811–1870* (Halifax, 1968). M. R. Hoare, *Virgin soil; Mother Seton from a different point of view* (Boston, [1942]). Annabelle [McConnell] Melville, *John Carroll of Baltimore, founder of the American Catholic hierarchy* (New York, [1955]). Sister Maura [Mary Power], *Sisters of Charity, Halifax* (Toronto, [1956]). T. H. Raddall, *Halifax, warden of the north* (Garden City, N.Y., 1965). M. de L. Walsh, *The Sisters of Charity of New York, 1809–1959* (3v., New York, n.d.).

McCLEARN, MATTHEW (the name is sometimes written **McLarn**, or **McLearn**, but he signed **McClearn**), captain, merchant, ship owner, and politician; b. 8 April 1802 in Port Mouton (then often spelled Port Matoon), N.S., youngest of ten children of Robert McClearn, a farmer, and Sarah West; d. 18 Jan. 1865 at Tobago, W.I.

There is no record of Matthew McClearn's early life or education. In 1828, at age 26, he was sailing vessels for his uncle, Joseph Freeman*, of Liverpool, N.S., in the West Indies trade. On 9 Dec. 1830 in Liverpool he married Sophia Darrow, the sister of a prominent captain and ship owner, John L. Darrow; their only child, born in 1839, was named after him. McClearn acquired a well-located piece of waterfront property in

McClure

Liverpool from his father and mother in 1831. After his father's death later that year, he inherited a generous portion of the estate and assumed responsibility for his mother and an unmarried sister.

For 12 more years he sailed in the West Indies trade. During this time he developed a reputation for "intrepidity and coolness in scenes of danger." McClearn added a substantial piece to his waterfront holdings, and built up enough capital to acquire, in 1843, a 57-ton schooner, the *Dolphin*. As its master he began the first regular packet service between Liverpool and Halifax. In 1848 the *Dolphin* was replaced by the 78-ton schooner *Liverpool*. In 1854 McClearn formed a partnership with John Day who took over as master. It appears that McClearn left the packet business when his partnership was dissolved in 1856.

Once his business allowed him more time in Liverpool, McClearn entered into the public and social life of the community: he became a member of the Liverpool bowling alley; he served on committees to rebuild the court house and to organize Liverpool's exhibits in the Halifax Industrial Exhibition of 1854; he carried out several responsible commissions for Liverpool organizations in Halifax; he was an active member of the Wesleyan Congregation; he joined the temperance movement.

In 1855 McClearn was elected by acclamation to the House of Assembly as a Conservative, "thus showing," according to the editors of the *Liverpool Transcript*, "the esteem in which he was held by men of all parties and creeds, during a period when party feeling ran high, and political contests were carried on with much bitterness." He was also on the popular side of the temperance question although he did not pursue the cause in the legislature. He attended regularly and looked after constituency business, but did not enter into debate on more general issues. The session was one of turbulence and infighting which he appears not to have relished, for he decided not to seek re-election in 1859.

During his years in the packet business, McClearn was also shipping fish and lumber to the West Indies and importing flour, meal, molasses, salt, and other foodstuffs for his wholesale and retail business in Liverpool. By 1857 he had joined with his brother-in-law to form Darrow and McClearn, General Commission Merchants and Ship Agents. As the West Indies trade expanded in the 1850s and early 1860s, he also engaged in shipbuilding. He and others built, in 1856, the 154-ton *Oxford*; in 1859, the 163-ton *Vulcan*; in 1863, the 260-ton *Undine*, for interests in Bermuda; and in 1864, the 267-ton *Annie*. Both the *Church Times* of Halifax and the *Liverpool Transcript* commented on the "Fine lines – beautiful mould and superior workmanship" evident in vessels built under his supervision.

McClearn decided to sail south with the *Annie* on her maiden voyage in 1864. On the trip he caught yellow fever and died at Tobago in January 1865. His portrait hangs in the house he built in Liverpool, with a painting of the *Annie*.

CATHERINE PROSS

Various materials in private collections have been useful in the preparation of this biography: R. J. Long, "The annals of Liverpool and Queen's County, 1760–1867" (1926) in the possession of Seth Bartling, Liverpool, N.S. (typescript at Dalhousie University Library, Halifax; mfm. at PANS); Liverpool Gauger's Book, 1821–40, in the possession of Hector MacLeod, Liverpool, N.S.; McClearn family bible, in the possession of John D. McClearn, Liverpool, N.S. PANS, MG 1, 827, 848; MG 4, no.80, Grand Jury Records, Queens County, N.S., 12; RG 14, 56 (Queens County), 1849. Queens County Registry of Deeds (Liverpool, N.S.), Matthew McClearn from Robert and Sarah McClearn, 1831; Matthew McClearn from Robert McClearn, 1831; Matthew McClearn from John L. Darrow, 1841. *Liverpool Transcript* (Liverpool, N.S.), 1854–65. N.S., House of Assembly, *Debates and proc.*, 1856–69.

McCLURE, LEONARD, printer, journalist, and politician; b. 25 Dec. 1835 at Lisburn, near Belfast (Northern Ireland), son of Adam McClure and his second wife Margaret Wilson; d. 14 June 1867 at San Francisco, Calif., survived by a wife to whom he had been married "but a short time."

Leonard McClure was brought up to the printing trade, serving his apprenticeship on the *Northern Whig* of Belfast. At an early age he left Ireland and is said to have been a parliamentary reporter in London before emigrating to Australia, where he "engaged in his profession," probably in the gold colony of Victoria between 1855 and 1858. In November 1858 he began to publish the *Morning Star* in Sacramento, Calif.

By September 1859 McClure was in Victoria, Vancouver Island, printing the *Government Gazette for the Colonies of Vancouver Island and British Columbia* and the *New Westminster Times* (printed in Victoria despite its name) in association with Edward Hammond KING. After the first *Victoria Gazette* ceased publication in November 1859, the name was appropriated by King and McClure for a new paper. In March 1860 McClure separated from King, taking over the *New Westminster Times* and moving its printing to the mainland capital.

In New Westminster McClure soon became prominent in a group that was demanding an end to the rule from Victoria of Governor James Douglas* over the mainland of British Columbia and the establishment of representative institutions for the mainland colony. The municipal council of New Westminster, elected after the incorporation of the town in July 1860, became their base and in August McClure was chosen the council's first president. In December 1860 he initiated a petition for a "British Columbia Convention," but the election for delegates saw a split over tactics. McClure's "government" slate, which saw the convention as an unofficial legislature to advise the governor, was defeated by a "reform" slate which wanted a separate governor and representative institutions. It was probably backers of the reform slate who bought out McClure's printing plant and installed John Robson* as editor of a new paper, the *British Columbian*.

By February 1861 McClure had bought the plant of the defunct *Victoria Gazette*, in which he had earlier been associated with King. He resigned from the municipal council and moved the *New Westminster Times* back to Victoria. In March it became the Victoria *Press*, which he published tri-weekly and then daily until October 1862 when he sold the plant to David William Higgins* and James Eliphalet McMillan. That same month the New Westminster reformers were preparing to send a visiting Canadian politician, Malcolm Cameron*, to England as their delegate to press again for a separate governor and representative institutions. McClure, who it appears was already going to England to promote a mining speculation, succeeded in getting an endorsement from a Victoria public meeting as a co-"delegate" from Vancouver Island, but he failed to get recognition from the Victoria municipal council, let alone from the assembly or the colonial government. Cameron seems to have had little influence on the termination in 1864 of Douglas' governorship of British Columbia and the inauguration there of a legislative council. The Colonial Office also declined to recommend McClure's proposed changes in the Legislative Council and the House of Assembly of Vancouver Island or his suggested wholesale removal of officials.

Returning to Victoria in February 1864, McClure in March became editor of the reform paper, the *British Colonist*, whose operation had passed in 1863 from founder-editor Amor De Cosmos* to a group of his employees. Under McClure's "exclusive control," the *Colonist* in 1864 reflected changes in reform opinion about the new governor of Vancouver Island, Arthur Edward Kennedy*, whose position on the civil list and control of land revenues soon dampened hopes that he would be more liberal than his predecessor.

By late 1864, as Vancouver Island revenues dropped with the petering out of the gold-rushes on the mainland, the question of future relations with British Columbia dominated politics. McClure's advocacy of a legislative union and a tariff for revenue won him a seat in the assembly in February 1865. Although the assembly had already passed a resolution in January agreeing to "such constitution as Her Majesty's government may be pleased to grant," the Colonial Office delayed action, knowing that many British Columbians opposed union. As finances worsened, the assembly led by De Cosmos and McClure fought the governor over rival plans for retrenchment. An attempt in 1866 by the assembly to cut the number of officials and increase spending on public works was turned back by the Legislative Council, and the resulting deadlock ended only with the expiry on 2 Sept. 1866 of the legislature's term. In the 1866 session McClure delivered what has remained the longest speech in the annals of the legislature in Victoria. To prevent extension of the time for redemption of tax-sale lands by people he considered speculators, McClure spoke continuously for 16 hours from 2 p.m. 23 April 1866 to 6 a.m. the next morning.

In August 1866 it became clear that the impending union would continue the nominated legislative council system of British Columbia, and McClure headed an unsuccessful last-ditch attempt to save representative institutions. The refusal of colonial self-government led McClure increasingly to favour annexation to the United States. By October he was posing the alternatives of "good and cheap government, under British rule, if possible, under the American Republic if it cannot be otherwise obtained." Annexation had, however, only minority support even in Victoria. McClure had lost his editorship of the *Colonist* and much of his political influence when the *Colonist* amalgamated with the rival *Chronicle* in June 1866. In July McClure and a partner, W. Mitchell, started the *Evening Telegraph*, but the failure of McClure's campaign in favour of annexation is reflected in the failure in December of the Telegraph. At the end of December 1866 McClure left the colony for San Francisco, where he was editor of the *Times* until his final illness.

Contemporaries agreed that Leonard McClure was a writer and speaker of talent, but charged him with a lack of political principle. Where his own views can be distinguished, McClure ap-

McDonald

pears as a somewhat radical democrat. Inconsistencies in his position can best be attributed to a very competitive newspaper field in which he, unlike his fellow journalists De Cosmos and Higgins, was not able to establish a secure base. For a short time, however, he was a public figure equal in importance to either of them. His espousal of annexation and his early death have unfairly affected his stature.

H. Keith Ralston

PABC, Colonial correspondence, Attorney general's correspondence (B.C.), August–December 1862, Leonard McClure to H. P. P. Crease, 29 Oct. 1862, encl. in Crease to colonial secretary, 29 Oct. 1862. PRO, CO 305/21, pp.336–40; 305/25, pp.205–6 (mfm. at PABC). G. B., Parl., Command paper, 1866, XLIX, [3667], pp.119–64, *Papers relative to the proposed union of British Columbia and Vancouver Island*; 1867, XLVIII, [3852], pp.282–332, *Further papers relative to the union of British Columbia and Vancouver Island....* *Alta* (San Francisco), 15 June 1867. *British Columbian* (New Westminster, B.C.), 13 Feb. 1862, 13 May 1863, 21 May 1864. *Daily British Colonist* (Victoria), 15, 16, 27 Jan., 7, 27 Feb. 1861; 20–30 Oct., 5 Nov. 1862; 4 March, 6 Oct. 1863; 1864, especially 22 Feb., 21 March, 9 July, 10, 20, 23, 29 Aug., 5, 27 Oct.; 1865–66, especially January–February 1865, 25 April 1866. *Daily British Colonist and Victoria Chronicle*, 25 June, 3 July, 29 Aug., 2, 3 Oct., 19, 24, 27 Dec. 1866; 25, 26 July 1867. *Daily Chronicle* (Victoria), 6 Nov. 1862, 18 March 1864, 25 April 1866. *Evening Post* (Victoria), 24 April 1866. *Evening Telegraph* (Victoria), July–December 1866, especially 5 July, 20, 21, 29 Aug., 12, 25, 29, 30 Sept., 1–5 Oct. *New Westminster Times* (New Westminster, B.C.), 24 Sept.–24 Dec. 1859; 3 March 1860; 2, 13 Feb. 1861. *Press* (Victoria), 1861–62, especially 9 March, 6 April, 27 Aug., 15 Oct. 1861. *Times* (San Francisco), 15 June 1867.

E. C. Kemble, *A history of California newspapers, 1846–1858*, ed. H. H. Bretnor (Los Gatos, Calif., 1962), 165. Barry Mather and M. [L.] McDonald, *New Westminster: the royal city* ([Don Mills, Ont.], 1958), 35–36. P. F. Palmer, "A fiscal history of British Columbia in the colonial period" (unpublished PHD thesis, Stanford University, Calif., 1932). R. L. Smith, "Governor Kennedy of Vancouver Island and the politics of union, 1864–1866" (unpublished MA thesis, University of Victoria, 1973). L. A. Wrinch, "Land policy of the colony of Vancouver Island, 1849–1866" (unpublished MA thesis, University of British Columbia, Vancouver, 1932), 123–68.

McDONALD, DONALD, Presbyterian clergyman, author, and hymnist; b. 1 Jan. 1783 in Drumcastle near Rannoch in Perthshire, Scotland, son of Donald McDonald and Christan Stewart; d. 21 Feb. 1867 in Southport, P.E.I.

Little is known of Donald McDonald's early years in Perthshire. His father had been a McKay and had fought in the Highland army under Prince Charlie, but after the battle of Culloden in 1746 he changed his name to McDonald and settled on a farm on the border of Rannoch. The family was amongst those caught up in the wave of revivalism which swept over many regions of Scotland in the late 18th and early 19th centuries. In 1808 Donald McDonald entered the University of St Andrews to prepare for the ministry; after working for a time as a tutor to a chieftain's family and as a farm labourer, he completed his studies in 1816 and was ordained a clergyman of the Church of Scotland. He did not settle into a routine parish ministry but elected to serve as a missionary in the Highlands of Glengarry for the next eight years.

There is no reliable record of McDonald's activities at this time, but in later years a persistent rumour existed to the effect that while in the Highlands he developed a drinking problem which at least partially accounted for his emigration to Cape Breton Island in 1824. Although he arrived in British North America in possession of a letter stating that he was a properly ordained minister in good standing, McDonald never eliminated completely the suspicion that he had incurred the disfavour of the Church of Scotland.

After two years in the Bras d'Or Lake area of Cape Breton the restive McDonald, then 44, moved to Prince Edward Island which was in a period of rapid growth and change owing to a heavy influx of immigrants, mostly from Scotland. On the Island, in 1827, he underwent a deep spiritual awakening. This experience, which McDonald regarded as the unmistakable touch of God, marked the beginning of an outstanding 40-year ministry among the people of Prince Edward Island. By the time of his death in 1867 he had single-handedly established a parish of some 5,000 members and adherents, which covered the full length of the Island, and which included at least 12 congregations and several preaching stations.

Known to his people simply as "The Minister," McDonald was constantly on the move, sometimes preaching every night in both Gaelic and English. He never married, and, from 1827 to 1867, with no home of his own, he lived, literally, with his people. Although he was in some respects an austere, imperious individual and exercised an almost autocratic control over his congregations, his people – mostly fellow Scots – appear to have regarded him with great warmth and affection. In doctrine he was often stern and dogmatic, the essence of unbending Calvinism; but an acquaintance once described him as a "hearty" individual with a "keen appreciation of the humorous,'' and his frequent, and often impulsive, acts of kindness to the needy, whether they were his followers or not, were widely acknowledged during his lifetime and became part of his legend after his death.

McDonald's ministry on the Island was characterized by some exceptional features. During two revivals, in 1830 and 1860, religious excitement among his followers rose to a fevered pitch and many hundreds were "awakened" and "set free" under the influence of his impassioned preaching. His ministry frequently gave rise to physical manifestations or "works" of spiritual excitation. The response during the first revival was so extraordinary that McDonald became unalterably convinced he was God's specially ordained instrument, and his labours on the Island were part of the divine plan for gathering the chosen people into the church before the imminent arrival of the millennium. This theme, which included the notion that his followers were members of the "ten lost tribes" of Israel, was extensively elaborated by McDonald in *The subjects of the millennium*, published in 1849. He also published in 1845 *A treatise on the holy ordinance of baptism*, a rigorously partisan attempt to establish the true scriptural mode and meaning of Christian baptism and to discredit those – in this case the Baptists – who thought differently. In 1874 a number of McDonald's followers arranged for the publication of a manuscript entitled *The plan of salvation*, a brief, incomplete study of types and antitypes, which was found among his papers after his death.

Besides doctrinal dissertations McDonald also composed hymns and spiritual songs. Most are extremely long and somewhat didactic, but they occasionally achieve a fine lyric quality and, when set to well-known tunes of the period, proved to be popular. Only the Psalms were permitted during the worship period in the church, but his hymns were frequently sung during the less formal introduction to it. A first collection, *Spiritual hymns*, was published in 1835; several years later, expanded editions included also compositions of some of McDonald's elders. This songbook was still in use in some congregations more than a century later.

In addition to being a forceful, evocative personality, McDonald was also an adept and tactful organizer. Thus, in spite of the intensely spiritual nature of his ministry, he was always able to exert sufficient personal authority and control to prevent serious discord or fragmentation. During his 40 years of leadership he imposed stability and order upon what was a potentially turbulent situation. "The Minister," however, left no apparent heir, and after his death the question of leadership soon created factionalism.

Although he maintained a nominal connection with the mother church and always regarded himself as a Church of Scotland cleric, McDonald manifested a persistent independence of thought and action. He was not radically innovative or unorthodox, but did freely adapt his ministry to the frontier situation in which he found himself, and both his teachings and techniques were clearly conditioned by the Island and its people. Consequently, the church he founded was in large degree a unique and autonomous Island body. Many of his followers, indeed, referred to it as "Mr. McDonald's Unattached Church."

McDonald remained active and alert until his death in his 85th year. His funeral was one of the largest ever held on the Island. A lengthy obituary in the *Islander* acknowledged that he had been "one of the most remarkable men of his time" and that "tradition will long preserve the memory of MINISTER MCDONALD."

DAVID WEALE

[Privately held material used in the preparation of this biography includes: minutes of meetings, financial records, a copy of McDonald's last will and testament, and a number of unpublished hymns, which were in the possession of the late Mr Nathan Bears, Brooklyn, P.E.I.; baptismal records of Orwell parish at the eastern end of McDonald's charge, in the possession of the Reverend William Underhay, Charlottetown; and baptismal records of the De Sable parish at the western end of his charge, in the possession of the Reverend David Compton, Hampton, P.E.I.

McDonald's published works include: *The plan of salvation* (Charlottetown, 1874); *Spiritual hymns* (Charlottetown, 1835; 1840); *The subjects of the millennium, traced in their downward progress from their ancestry through the three pre-millennial dispensations; together with a scriptural view of the new Jerusalem; coming of Messiah; sacred numbers, and signs of the times; the end of the world, and the last judgment; and scriptural views of the millennial church* (Charlottetown, 1849); and *A treatise on the holy ordinance of baptism . . .* (Charlottetown, 1845; 1898).

For obituaries of McDonald see: *Herald* (Charlottetown), 6 March 1867; *Islander*, 1 March 1867; and *Summerside Progress* (Summerside, P.E.I.), 4 March 1867. The most comprehensive source of biographic material is Murdoch Lamont, *Rev. Donald McDonald: glimpses of his life and times* (Charlottetown, 1902). *See also* J. M. MacLeod, *History of Presbyterianism on Prince Edward Island* (Chicago, 1904).   D.W.]

McDONALD, GEORGE RICHARD JOHN. *See* MACDONELL

McDONALD, JOHN (known as John McDonald of Garth), NWC partner and farmer; b. *c.* 1771 at

McDonald

Garth, a family estate near Callendar, Perthshire, Scotland, son of John McDonald, army captain; d. 25 Jan. 1866 at Gray's Creek near Cornwall, Canada West. He apparently had five children by his first wife, an Indian, and six by his second, a niece of Hugh McGillis of Williamstown.

John McDonald's withered right arm (which led to his being called "Le Bras Croche") prevented him from following the family tradition of a career in the British army. He left for Canada in April 1791 bound to the North West Company as a clerk. Although in his "Autobiographical Notes" written in 1859 McDonald may have overemphasized his importance in the NWC, he was to participate in many of the major events of the western fur trade during the crucial years 1795 to 1814. Pugnacious and daring, he proved a valuable trader and a tenacious opponent in the struggle between the North West and Hudson's Bay companies. Under the tutelage of Angus Shaw*, McDonald served as clerk at Moose Lake (Man.), Fort George (Alta), and Fort des Prairies. He was in charge of the building of Fort Augustus (later Fort Edmonton) in 1795 and of Rocky Mountain House (Alta) in 1799. By 1802, two years after becoming a wintering partner in the NWC, he replaced Shaw at Fort des Prairies, the largest department in the north.

After completing a furlough in 1804, McDonald wintered at Île-à-la-Crosse (Sask.), but the next season he returned to Fort des Prairies Department, where he established New Chesterfield House. Falling ill, he passed the winter of 1808 in Montreal with his sister Magdalen, wife of William McGillivray* of the NWC; elected to the Beaver Club, he amassed a huge entertainment bill. In the spring McDonald returned inland to share the charge of the Red River Department with John Wills* and probably to help establish Fort Gibraltar (Winnipeg). In 1811 he carried supplies to the explorer David Thompson* in the Kootenay Range of the Rocky Mountains.

McDonald then went to England to participate in his company's assault by sea on Fort Astoria (Astoria, Oreg.) and in February 1813 he sailed from London with Donald McTavish* on the *Isaac Todd*. At Portsmouth he offered a lucrative contract to a young woman, Jane Barnes, to sail with him to the Columbia, thereby bringing the first white woman to the North Pacific coast. McDonald transferred to the *Raccoon* in mid-voyage and soon after was badly burned in an explosion. He nevertheless took charge of Fort Astoria upon his arrival 30 Nov. 1813, two weeks after an overland party of Nor'Westers had purchased the post from the American Fur Company [see Gabriel FRANCHÈRE]. The *Isaac Todd*,

with McTavish, did not arrive until 22 April 1814, 18 days after MacDonald had embarked with a brigade of about 80 Nor'Westers in ten canoes for Fort William (Thunder Bay, Ont.).

When the brigade arrived at Red River, the "Pemmican War" between the NWC and the HBC was in progress [see Miles Macdonell*]. The attempt on the part of the HBC to prevent the Nor'Westers from living off country provisions (mainly pemmican brought in by Indians and Métis), thus forcing them to import supplies from Montreal, had induced the NWC to respond by preparing to destroy the colony established by Selkirk [Douglas*]. McDonald mediated a peace between the Nor'Westers at Red River and the Selkirk colonists, but he was criticized by the NWC partners at the annual meeting in Fort William and his agreement was disavowed.

McDonald retired in November 1814 and sold his two shares in the company. He then devoted over a year to socializing in Montreal. He left Montreal early in 1816 and purchased a farm at Gray's Creek near Cornwall. Over the years he added to his original holdings. He was active in the local Presbyterian church, and served as judge of the surrogate court of Glengarry from 1832 to 1844. Like many of his companions he adapted with remarkable ease to the sedentary life of a successful farmer. But McDonald always retained a lively interest in the west as letters he wrote to Edward ELLICE and William Henry Draper* about its future development demonstrate. His autobiography, written at the suggestion of his son De Bellefeuille, recalls the highlights of the career of a spirited young man who shared the lives of great explorers and empire builders and who played a significant if not central role in the huge dramatic adventure of the Canadian fur trade. Accurate in essence if not in detail, McDonald's self-portrait reveals the myth and perhaps much of the truth of the North West Company.

C. M. LIVERMORE and N. ANICK

The original of John McDonald's "Autobiographical Notes, 1791–1816" is at McGill University Libraries, Dept. of Rare Books and Special Coll. The PAC has had a copy since 1920 (MG 19, A17). McDonald's notes are published in *Les bourgeois de la Compagnie du Nord-Ouest: récits de voyages, lettres et rapports inédits relatifs au Nord-Ouest canadien*, L.-F.-R. Masson, édit. (2v., Québec, 1889–90; réimpr., New York, 1960), II, 1–59.

McCord Museum, McDonald, A. de Lery, family papers, James McDonald to A. de Lery McDonald, 11 Oct. 1887; North West Company papers, Beaver Club minute book, 16 April 1809, 1814–16; North West Company papers, 5 July 1796–1 Aug. 1859. McGill University Libraries, Dept. of Rare Books and Special Coll., MS coll., John McDonald of Garth papers. PAC, MG 19, B1. Ross Cox, *The Columbia River; or scenes and adventures during a residence of six years on the western side of the Rocky Mountains ...*, ed. E. I. and J. R. Stewart (Norman, Okla., 1957). *Documents relating to NWC* (Wallace). HBRS, XXVI (Johnson). [Duncan McGillivray], *The journal of Duncan M'Gillivray of the North West Company at Fort George on the Saskatchewan, 1794–5 ...*, ed. A. S. Morton (Toronto, 1929). *The Oregon country under the Union Jack; postscript edition; a reference book of historical documents for scholars and historians* (2nd ed., Montreal, 1962), 166–68, 635–36. J. G. Harkness, *Stormont, Dundas, and Glengarry: a history, 1784–1945* (Oshawa, Ont., 1946), 392, 419.

McDONELL, ALEXANDER, immigration and land agent and politician; b. 1786 in Scotland; d. 29 Nov. 1861 at Peterborough, Canada West. He married but the name of his wife is not known, and he apparently had no close relatives when he died.

Alexander McDonell probably came to Canada in 1804 with his uncle Alexander Macdonell*, later Roman Catholic bishop at Kingston. He served as an ensign or cadet in the War of 1812 and saw action at least once in the attack on Sacket's Harbor on 29 May 1813. He was established in Peterborough in 1825 when it was still only the depot for Peter Robinson*'s settlement of 2,000 assisted immigrants from the south of Ireland. His public career began in August that year when Robinson hired him first as a guide and then, from 1 Sept. 1825 to 31 Jan. 1829, as a clerk at 10s. a day. Robinson's first favourable impression of McDonell as "an intelligent and respectable young Man, well acquainted with the Country" was confirmed by experience, and McDonell played an increasingly important part in locating the settlers until, in the spring of 1827, Robinson left him in charge of the settlement. McDonell's duties with Robinson's settlers merged into a wider role as agent for the Crown Lands Department in the Newcastle District after Robinson became commissioner of the department in 1827.

In the early years of McDonell's agency his friendship with Robinson, his supervision of poor immigrants assisted by the Upper Canadian government, and the large numbers of independent immigrants flocking to his district all combined to give him considerable importance in the land office. He gradually lost his special place as these conditions, and his own interests, changed, but he did not finally retire as agent for Northumberland and Durham counties until 1843. He had, in the meantime, turned to politics and he was

elected to the House of Assembly for Northumberland in 1834.

Because he was well known as their land agent, McDonell was very much the candidate of the back townships. He offered pro-British sentiments and "the good old sterling qualities," while relying for support on his past reputation and his prominence in urging the development of the region, notably as one of the commissioners for the improvement of navigation on the Trent waterway system. He was re-elected easily as a constitutionalist in 1836, and in 1837 he was locally prominent as colonel of the 2nd battalion of Northumberland militia. By 1841 his platform, which he had not modified, was less popular, and he was defeated in the first election in the united province by his radical opponent, John Gilchrist*.

In his later years, McDonell withdrew from his life as "an active and useful public man" to involve himself in business ventures. His duties as land agent had included responsibility for the timber on crown lands. In the 1840s and 1850s he himself acquired timber limits on the Bonnechère and Petawawa rivers and engaged in lumbering. Although he had been an active Roman Catholic, he must also have broken with the church in these years, for his body was refused a Roman Catholic burial "because of his not living to their requirements."

WENDY CAMERON

PAO, RG, A-I-4, 2–4, A-I-6, 8–12, 17, 20–23, 25, 28, 30, 32. PRO, AO 2/34, pp.48–55. *Cobourg Star* (Cobourg, [Ont.]), 10 Sept.–29 Oct. 1834, 15 June–13 July 1836, 24 Feb.–31 March 1841. *Peterborough Examiner* (Peterborough, [Ont.]), 5 Dec. 1861. *Valley of the Trent* (Guillet). T. W. Poole, *A sketch of the early settlement and subsequent progress of the town of Peterborough ...* (Peterborough, [Ont.], 1867).

MACDONELL, DONALD, soldier, politician, and public servant; b. 17 Jan. 1778 at Greenfield (Inverness-shire, Scotland), son of Janet Macdonell (Aberchalder) and Alexander Macdonell* (Greenfield); d. 13 June 1861 at Quebec, Canada East.

Donald Macdonell, who came to Charlottenburgh Township, Upper Canada, in 1792 with a group of Highlanders led by his father, was a member of a Scottish Catholic family long prominent in the military and political affairs of the Eastern District. The family included his father, Colonel Alexander Macdonell, JP, his uncle John Macdonell* (Aberchalder), first speaker of the Upper Canadian House of Assembly, and his brothers Colonel Duncan Macdonell, who in 1857

Macdonell

was to succeed his father in the command of the 2nd Regiment of Glengarry militia, Colonel John Macdonell*, member of the assembly and aide-de-camp to General Isaac Brock*, and Alexander Greenfield Macdonell*, member of the assembly and sheriff of the Ottawa District.

Donald Macdonell (and his brother Duncan) attended John STRACHAN's school at Cornwall. He served during the War of 1812 as captain, rising to lieutenant-colonel of the 2nd Regiment of Glengarry militia and assistant quartermaster-general of militia for the Midland District. He was present in October 1812 during the attack on Ogdensburg, and in February 1813 was part of the force under the leadership of Colonel George MACDONELL which captured it. His own war service and that of his brother John, who died heroically with Brock at Queenston Heights, gained him an appointment as registrar of Glengarry County immediately after the war. He resigned in 1819, however, to become sheriff of the Eastern District, an office which he obtained through the influence of Chief Justice William Dummer Powell* and which he retained until 1838. He was elected to represent Glengarry in the assembly in 1834 and sat until 1841 when he did not stand for re-election. His political views were solidly conservative.

During the rebellion years Macdonell raised and led a force of Glengarry Highlanders which was on active duty on the Lower Canadian frontier in 1837–38 and which in November 1838 took part in the relief of Beauharnois, where Patriote forces had taken over the seigneury of Edward ELLICE. He expected to receive the command of one of the incorporated militia corps which continued in service after 1838. Despite frequent applications he was unable to relieve his growing financial hardship by further government employment until 1845, when he served briefly as superintendent of police for the Williamsburg canals on the St Lawrence River. The following year, having secured the recommendation of 57 members of the Legislative Assembly, he was appointed deputy adjutant-general of militia for Canada West. He filled this post until his death.

This government service meant following the provincial capital in its several moves. Previously Macdonell had lived almost all of his life at Cornwall, Canada West. There he married Elizabeth Macdonell, daughter of Ranald Macdonell (Leek), a Scottish loyalist. They had five sons and two daughters.

J. K. JOHNSON

PAC, RG 1, E3, 70; RG 5, C1, 78, 86, 148–49, 151; RG 8, I (C series), 26, 60, 169, 195, 221; RG 9, I, B5, 1–7. A. N. Bethune, *Memoir of the Right Reverend John Strachan, D.D., LL.D., first bishop of Toronto* (Toronto and London, 1870), 148. U.C., House of Assembly, *Journal*, 1834–40. Chadwick, *Ontarian families*, I, 9. W. L. Scott, "Glengarry's representatives in the Legislative Assembly of Upper Canada," CCHA *Report*, 1939–40, 41–42.

MACDONELL (McDonald), GEORGE RICHARD JOHN (known as Red George), soldier; baptized 15 Aug. 1780 at St John's, Nfld, son of John McDonald (Leek), who in 1780 was commander of Fort Townshend, Nfld; d. 16 May 1870 at Wardour Castle, Wiltshire, England.

George Richard John Macdonell was commissioned an ensign in the 55th Foot in the British army on 15 Sept. 1796. He rose to lieutenant on 4 May 1798 and then transferred to a vacant captaincy in the 8th Foot on 4 Sept. 1805. He may have been on active service in Europe prior to the commencement of his North American career in 1808, when the 8th Regiment was posted to Nova Scotia and subsequently to the Canadas.

In December 1811 the settlers in Glengarry County who had come to Canada as a disbanded military unit in 1804 with Bishop Alexander Macdonell* became alarmed by the growing hostility between Britain and the United States. They proposed that they be re-embodied as a fighting force. Sir George Prevost* agreed, and chose their clansman, Red George Macdonell, as recruiting agent for the new force, the Glengarry Light Infantry Fencibles. He was given the brevet rank of major in the new militia force in February 1812, but enlistment was so slow that the ambitious Macdonell was not given his next brevet commission until 8 Feb. 1813.

As a new lieutenant-colonel Macdonell succeeded to the command of Fort Wellington at Prescott, and on 22 Feb. 1813, exceeding his orders to make a demonstration of strength, he attacked Ogdensburg, N.Y. His successful assault across the ice with a mixed force of regulars and militia ended the occupation of Ogdensburg by American forces for the remainder of the war. His action helped secure the St Lawrence link between Upper and Lower Canada but did not stop American harassment along the St Lawrence River, as Macdonell later claimed.

After recovering from wounds received at Ogdensburg, Macdonell took command of the 1st Light Infantry Battalion at Kingston. When Wade Hampton's American forces began advancing upon Montreal, Prevost ordered Macdonell and his militia force to march into Lower Canada. At the battle of Châteauguay on 26 Oct. 1813 Macdonell ably commanded the reserves under Lieutenant-Colonel Charles d'Irumberry* de Salaberry. Although losses on both sides were light, Hampton retreated and refused to participate in subsequent plans to attack Montreal. Hence this British victory stopped the only concerted American effort which could have cut the St Lawrence River supply lines between Montreal and Upper Canada and forced the latter to capitulate.

Macdonell recognized the vulnerability of the St Lawrence as the single supply line and in November 1814, at the end of the war, he explored an alternative route along the Rideau River and lakes. His plan for a canal of temporary dams and rough wooden structures was very different from the precise engineering work done under Colonel John By* a decade later.

The Rideau survey was undertaken as part of Macdonell's duties as inspecting field officer of militia. Immediately after assuming this new position in June 1814, Macdonell also took command of the Cornwall district. Until the fall of 1815 he was responsible for training and commanding the Stormont and Glengarry militia and for the protection of transportation on the St Lawrence River in that neighbourhood. From Cornwall he went to Fort George (Niagara), York (Toronto), and Kingston inspecting and training militia units until he was granted leave of absence on 3 Oct. 1816.

Macdonell returned to England in 1816 and married the Honourable Laura Arundel in 1820. When the 8th Foot was called to active duty in 1821 Macdonell transferred to a vacant half-pay position in the 79th Foot. He was apparently unable to find a position acceptable to his own sense of prestige and his wife's social position. Although he was created a CB in 1817 and awarded a medal for Châteauguay, Macdonell was never satisfied with this recognition of his services. During the half century after the war Macdonell revealed a sense of personal grievance; he appealed to the public for recognition and to the secretary for war for recompense. In a scarcely veiled anonymous article in *Colburn's United Service Magazine* in 1848, Macdonell claimed that England's "transatlantic empire" was saved by his "personal exertions" in 1813. To Earl Grey he wrote in 1850 that Ogdensburg was "of one hundred times more political Importance" than Nelson's victory at Trafalgar. Furthermore he accused the Duke of York and Allan McLean*, speaker of the Upper Canadian assembly from 1812 to 1820, of denying him a medal for Ogdensburg because he was a Roman Catholic.

Macdonell claimed in 1817 that the idea of a

Rideau Canal defence work "had occurred, exclusively to me, in the beginning of 1813" and that Sir George Prevost had promised him a reward of 2,000 guineas if he could prove the practicality of his plan. He did not receive the reward because the Colonial Office maintained in 1818 that earlier plans for a military canal had existed. The Colonial Office also refused to recognize Macdonell's weakly supported contention that he had inspired Sir Isaac Brock*'s successful campaign tactics at the beginning of the war. Tragically, this energetic officer who had displayed such perspicacity on the battlefield had completely lost his sense of judgement.

CAROL M. WHITFIELD

PAC, RG 8, I (C series), Index entries to G. R. J. Macdonell. PRO, CO 42/177, 42/180; WO 1/563, Macdonell to Grey, 8 April – 4 June 1850; WO 17/1514–15, 17/1519–20. Philalethes [G. R. J. Macdonell], "The last war in Canada," *Colburn's United Service Magazine and Naval and Military Journal* (London), 1848, pt.1, 425–41. G.B., WO, *Army list*, 1795–1871. J. M. Hitsman, *Safeguarding Canada, 1763–1871* (Toronto, 1968). George Raudzens, " 'Red George' Macdonell, military saviour of Upper Canada?" *OH*, LXII (1970), 199–212.

MacDONELL (McDonell), JEAN-FRANÇOIS-MARIE-JOSEPH (usually called **John MacDonell-Bélestre** or **John Bélestre-MacDonell**), lawyer; b. 21 Oct. 1799 at Montreal, son of Angus (Ignace) MacDonell, a Scottish artillery lieutenant, and Marie-Anne Picoté de Bélestre; d. 1866 at Saint-Anicet, Canada East.

In 1812, the year his father died, Jean-François-Marie-Joseph MacDonell left the Collège de Montréal, where he was a student. A few years later, he was studying law under James Stuart* of Montreal. He was called to the bar there on 3 Aug. 1821.

MacDonell was a friend of Ludger Duvernay*, and in 1834 he made his garden on Rue Saint-Antoine available to the journalist and his friends for the first Société Saint-Jean-Baptiste celebration. The 60 or so guests, Irishmen, Americans, and Canadians, included Thomas Storrow Brown*, Clément-Charles SABREVOIS de Bleury, Louis-Hippolyte LA FONTAINE, Edmund Bailey O'Callaghan*, and George-Étienne Cartier*. The mayor of Montreal, Jacques Viger*, presided at the banquet, and speeches alternated with songs composed for the occasion. Toasts were drunk to the people, to Louis-Joseph Papineau*, Louis Bourdages*, and Elzéar Bédard*, to the Irish Reformer Daniel O'Connell, the Reformers of Upper Canada, the government of the United

McDougall

States, and the "liberal" clergy. The participants decided the festival should be celebrated annually. In 1836, however, the Reformers were divided. The "radicals," loyal to Papineau, celebrated the day at the Hôtel Rasco, on Rue Saint-Paul, while the "moderates," who favoured Bédard and Sabrevois de Bleury, met in MacDonell's garden. On this occasion, MacDonell claimed to be the originator of the festival. Needless to say, Duvernay's *La Minerve* did not give much publicity to this public demonstration of dissidence. In 1837 the scenario was the same: while 100 Patriotes dined at the Hôtel Nelson, the moderates, including Sabrevois de Bleury, MacDonell, and Frédéric-Auguste QUESNEL, had a final celebration at MacDonell's house.

Despite this split MacDonell was arrested in November 1838 because of his leanings towards the Patriotes. He stood trial in 1839 and was released after a few months' detention. He then returned to his profession, and practised law in Montreal until 1850. At that time he moved to Saint-Anicet, where he died in 1866.

In 1835 MacDonell had married Elizabeth Pickell, sister of lawyer John Pickell, MHA for the town of William Henry (Sorel).

MICHÈLE GUAY

PAC, MG 30, D62, 19, p.678; 20, pp.648–61. *La Minerve*, 30 juin 1836. Fauteux, *Patriotes*. Rumilly, *Hist. de Montréal*, I, 141. Benjamin Sulte, "La Saint-Jean-Baptiste," *Mélanges historiques*, Gérard Malchelosse, édit. (21v., Montréal, 1918–34), XV, 40, 111–17. [F.-A.-]H. Larue *et al.,* "Les fêtes patronales des Canadiens-français," *Revue canadienne* (Montréal), VII (1870), 485–96.

McDOUGALL, JOHN, businessman; b. 25 July 1805 at Coldstream, Scotland, son of John McDougal and Janet Wilson; d. 21 Feb. 1870 in the parish of Vieilles-Forges (Saint-Michel-des-Forges), near Trois-Rivières, Que.

Because precise information is not available, the McDougall families of Quebec are often confused. This confusion is all the more natural because three McDougall families came from Berwickshire, Scotland, to Canada in the 19th century. The John McDougall family of Trois-Rivières, which won fame at the Saint-Maurice and L'Islet ironworks under the name of John McDougall and Sons, was not the John McDougall family that owned the Montreal company "Caledonia Foundry" and bought the Saint-Pie-de-Guire ironworks in 1874; George McDougall, who from 1876 to 1879 operated the Saint-Maurice ironworks in partnership with Alexander Mills McDougall under the name of G.

and A. McDougall, was a member of yet a third branch. Apparently there was no relationship between the first McDougall family and the second, but the first and third were linked by marriage. What the three families had in common – which helps to jumble the whole issue – is the fact that all were to a varying extent involved in the metallurgical industry in Quebec, and that the theatre of their operations was bounded by the triangle Trois-Rivières – Saint-Pie-de-Guire – Drummondville.

John McDougall, founder of the Trois-Rivières branch of McDougalls, had married Margaret Purvis before he crossed the Atlantic in the 1830s; he is believed to have arrived at Trois-Rivières in 1833. Almost nothing is known of his activities during the next 20 years, except that he may have worked at a distillery and brewery. At the time he became mayor of Trois-Rivières (from 1855 to 1857), John McDougall had for several years owned a general store and a number of plots of land; he was also president of the Three Rivers Gas Company, and he was described as a "steamboat agent" in a protest lodged against him by lumberman William PRICE. Price complained that the proceedings McDougall had instituted against him on 6 Aug. 1855 in the Circuit Court of Trois-Rivières to recover the sum of £36 4s. 9¹/₂d. were injurious to his reputation. This grievance of William Price, if it were known to be justified, might shed light on McDougall's character.

In the provincial elections of 4 and 5 Jan. 1858 John McDougall ran against William McDonell Dawson in the county of Trois-Rivières. In his electoral address Dawson associated himself with the "Liberal party of reform and progress" of the former team of Robert Baldwin* and Louis-Hippolyte LA FONTAINE whose principles were now adopted by the "moderate party of the day," while McDougall, without propaganda and fanfare, blandly proposed to give "[his] support, in parliament, to the 'Moderate party.'" Despite the subtlety of these distinctions, Dawson emerged victorious from an election in which there were violent confrontations between the supporters of the two camps. McDougall protested Dawson's election. He thus added fuel to a newspaper quarrel between the readers of *L'Ère nouvelle* (pro-Dawson) and *L'Écho du St-Maurice* (pro-McDougall), each of whom denounced the reprehensible attitude of the opponent. During the ensuing lawsuit the defendant produced testimony by François Brousseau that John McDougall had attacked and beaten him with a walking-stick in the Saint-Louis district polling-booth. Although McDougall did not win the case, it is difficult to assess his temperament on the basis of this election brawl. Similarly the action brought by Marie Hamel on 28 Jan. 1858, a few weeks after the election, accusing McDougall of having raped her on 29 Dec. 1857, is hardly more illuminating. The plaintiff and her husband, Louis Bertrand, were former employees who had been dismissed by the accused. At the time of the inquiry, the judges concluded that Marie Hamel's complaint did not even warrant proceedings at law. Was McDougall a victim of partisan manoeuvres to destroy his reputation? The electioneering customs of the time lead to this conclusion.

If McDougall's short incursion into politics was a failure, his career as a businessman presents quite a different picture. In addition to the business activities already mentioned, McDougall was a member by 1858 of the board of directors of the North Shore Railway Company; a promotional notice of this company introduced him as a director authorized "to receive the payments required on the shares of the said company that were owned by shareholders living in the district of Trois-Rivières, and to give receipts therefor." In the absence of exact data in the documentation available, it is impossible to determine McDougall's role in this railroad company, the part he played in the Three Rivers Gas Company or as steamboat agent, or indeed the length of time he held these positions. We do not even know exactly the nature of his business activity although he is listed in notarial documents as merchant, independant grocer, "general merchant," and later iron merchant.

During the 1850s McDougall acquired some land at Trois-Rivières; he owned a mortgage on four lots in the township of Arthabaska; and he had an "immense estate" called Moulin Rouge, at Sainte-Anne-d'-Yamachiche (Yamachiche) by 1857, when he received four lots and acquired the property of the Johnston heirs. It would be logical to suppose he obtained this land so that he could either supply his store with foodstuffs or carry on trading in timber, unless he was simply engaged in land speculation. What is certain is that when he offered to purchase the Saint-Maurice and L'Islet ironworks he had capital at his disposal.

The whole story of the Saint-Maurice ironworks, from its beginning in the 1730s until its demise in 1883, was marked by periods of depression and growth, stops and starts. In 1861, two years after the partners Andrew Stuart* and John R. Porter went bankrupt, the government, as mortgage holder, seized the establishment. In the following year Onésime Héroux bought it for $7,000. The metallurgical industry in the Saint-Maurice region was probably threatened when the Radnor ironworks were built in the future village of Fermont (adjoining the parish of Saint-Maurice) by Auguste Larue, George Benson Hall*, and Joseph-Édouard TURCOTTE in 1854 and the L'Islet ironworks were established beside the stream at L'Islet (Ilet) on the west bank of the Rivière Saint-Maurice by Dupuis, Robichon et Compagnie in 1856. John McDougall was to turn this situation to his advantage by purchasing the Saint-Maurice and L'Islet ironworks.

The process by which he acquired these undertakings illustrates his business sense. On 15 Dec. 1862 he both initialled a contract of sale with the former owners of the Saint-Maurice ironworks (Porter and Stuart) and concluded a deal with the owner of the L'Islet ironworks. Through notary Louis-Zéphirin Duval, John Porter and Company sold McDougall the equipment it still possessed at the Saint-Maurice ironworks and in the neighbourhood. Of the $1,000 cost of this transaction, McDougall immediately paid $300 representing the value of the iron mine and of the moulds for heavy casting. John McDougall then signed with Louis Dupuis, the sole owner of the L'Islet ironworks since March 1862, an agreement by which the latter undertook not only to deliver to McDougall before 15 Nov. 1863 various types of cast-iron stoves, cauldrons, axle-boxes, moulds for pipes, and "250 barrels of pig-iron," but also not to supply these kinds of articles to other merchants.

A year later, on 16 April 1863, McDougall acquired the L'Islet ironworks from Dupuis, who apparently preferred to sell rather than to declare bankruptcy. The land sold consisted of a piece three *arpents* wide by 25 deep, in the north-east range of the Saint-Félix concession in the parish of Notre-Dame-de-Mont-Carmel, on which the L'Islet ironworks had been set up; these encompassed "several edifices, a furnace, sheds, a casting-shop, houses, stables, cowsheds, and other outbuildings." McDougall also bought four other pieces of land in the Saint-Félix concession, as well as "all the items and articles necessary for the operation of the ironworks." The figure for this transaction was £2,000 at current rates or $8,000, according to the contract; however, it was stipulated that McDougall would pay this sum by undertaking to discharge the numerous mortgages encumbering the property of Louis Dupuis. The mortgages in question and the interest accruing thereon were apportioned as follows: $805.30 to Louis-Charles BOUCHER de Niverville, $808.31 to Moses E. Hart, $541.87 to John Houliston, $127.75 to Luc Précourt, and

McDougall

$5,694.08 to Amable Prévost: a total of $7,977.31. In the end Dupuis received only $22.69. Furthermore, as a guaranty of the act of sale, which in fact was a statement of bankruptcy, the "caster" Louis Dupuis, who could not write, had to mortgage his property at Trois-Rivières for $1,200 in favour of McDougall.

McDougall had had the equipment of John Porter and Company in his possession since December 1862 and on 27 April 1863 assumed control of the Saint-Maurice ironworks, which Onésime Héroux sold to him for $4,300. A cash payment of $1,075 was made to Héroux immediately, and McDougall undertook to pay the balance of $3,225 to the government, in equal annual instalments until November 1865, to discharge its mortgage on the ironworks. McDougall did indeed pay off this mortgage, interest included, on 8 Feb. 1866, according to the acceptance of satisfaction of mortgage signed by Marie Héroux, the former wife of Onésime Héroux, on 26 April 1867. McDougall's new domain included "houses, barns, sheds, cowsheds, stables, coal storage space, a flour mill, a large furnace, a foundry, a casting-shop, forges, and other outbuildings." However, the seller, a merchant of Saint-Barnabé, did not surrender his property completely; he kept a portion of the land adjoining the stream on which were "a large brick shed and a sawmill."

Research has thus far provided scant data on which to base an estimate of production at the Saint-Maurice ironworks. It seems that in 1865 they produced about 90 tons per week, and that the annual average was some millions of pounds. Apparently in 1870, with about a hundred men employed, half of them at the foundry, an output of about four tons a day was obtained. We know nothing of the conditions under which these employees worked, or of their salaries, except that according to Dollard Dubé they were paid either "with vouchers exchangeable at the store" or in money.

The growth and expansion of McDougall's economic activities, and his determination to involve his sons, led to the formation of a partnership on 26 April 1867. The firm of John McDougall and Sons took the form of a partnership in two sections. The first, relating only to the general store at Trois-Rivières, established the parity of each partner (John McDougall Sr, John McDougall Jr, and James McDougall) in profit-sharing; at the management level, the two sons were to give all their time to the store, while the father would free himself from it completely in order to devote his energies more effectively to administration of the ironworks. The second sec-

tion, relating to the Saint-Maurice and L'Islet ironworks, included the eight sons; each owned an eighteenth of the shares, except for William who held one-ninth; the father retained half of all the shares. This proportion applied to both profits and losses.

The place of residence of each of the partners in 1867 was indicative of both the level of their participation and the importance of the Saint-Maurice ironworks: John Sr, Robert, George, and David lived at the Saint-Maurice ironworks, Alexander Mills lived at the L'Islet ironworks, and John Jr, James (who for a time was to be a banker), William, a lawyer, and Thomas resided at Trois-Rivières. In 1869 they were still living in the same places except for the youngest, Thomas, who was now in Montreal; in 1873 he married the oldest daughter of George Baptist*.

Although the distribution of shares and activities within John McDougall and Sons was necessary for accounting purposes it had in reality an artificial quality, for the firm's metallurgical sector and its commercial sector (the general store) overlapped. In fact, one transformed raw material and the other sold the finished product. The most demanding activity was undoubtedly the ironworks. Not only was it necessary to oversee the various operations, but the blast furnaces had to be supplied with charcoal. This fuel, needed for the reduction of the ore, came from numerous surface deposits of "hydrated iron oxide," and was provided by the surrounding forest. However, one had to possess the wooded areas, or take steps to purchase the timber cuts of the small local landowners. Thus, when John McDougall and Sons was founded, it owned 38 pieces of land in the parish of Mont-Carmel, specifically, in the concessions of Saint-Félix, Saint-Louis, Saint-Michel, Saint-Mathieu, and Saint-Flavien; to these were added 14 sections in the fief of Saint-Étienne, one in the fourth concession of Shawinigan Township, and the former estate of Thomas Burn at Mont-Carmel. The policy of purchasing land reached a culmination on 22 Nov. 1867, when the commissioner of crown lands sold McDougall 62 lots in the Cap-de-la-Madeleine seigneury, at a unit price of $24.00. These lots, each 60 acres in size, were located in the concessions of Saint-Louis, Saint-Michel, Saint-Mathieu, and Saint-Flavien.

The above inventory, although not exhaustive, seems to reveal the dynamic drive of John McDougall and Sons. In the absence of precise data on the production of the ironworks, the store sales, and the balance-sheets, the analysis cannot be taken any further. It is possible, of course, that, in addition to the motives listed earlier, the

1867 deed of partnership was dictated by a need to enlarge the credit margin. At the time the company's debts stood at $11,500, and they were still increasing in 1869. The interesting point is that its creditors were closely or distantly related to the McDougall family. Mrs Janet Purvis, John Campbell's widow, to whom the firm owed $2,500, was probably a relative of Margaret Purvis, the wife of John McDougall; Anne Paterson, widow of Quebec merchant John Paterson, to whom they owed $9,000, was the eldest daughter of John McDougall.

The Saint-Maurice McDougall family included, in addition to the father and mother, eight boys and three girls. The latter were: Anne, who married John Paterson in 1847; Janet Wilson, who married Montreal accountant Robert Nilson in 1871; and Margaret, who became the wife of Montreal merchant Robert Linton in 1867. The boys distinguished themselves in business, politics, or one of the professions. All the children survived their father, who died on 21 Feb. 1870, and whose burial was the occasion for a procession of more than "fifty vehicles [. . . that followed] the hearse from the Vieilles Forges du Saint-Maurice" to Trois-Rivières.

After the death of its founder, the firm of John McDougall and Sons entered an extremely trying phase during which the sons experienced serious difficulties in keeping their metallurgical operations profitable. Numerous factors, including the gradual exhaustion of iron ore and the effects of the international banking crisis of 1873–79, explain the decline. Nevertheless, John McDougall and Sons did not appear to suffer from the restricted credit characterizing banking relations in Quebec during this crisis: from 30 June to 27 Oct. 1875 the Trois-Rivières branch of the Quebec Bank gave them a credit of $80,500. When they were unable to meet payments, either as a result of the poor productivity of their ironworks or because they were selling at a loss, they were obliged to mortgage the Saint-Maurice and L'Islet ironworks on 8 Nov. 1875; thus covered, the bank extended the date of reimbursement of the $80,500 debt by four years.

Subsequently, on 8 Dec. 1876, John McDougall Jr and his brother Robert relinquished their shares in the Saint-Maurice ironworks to a member of the third McDougall family, George McDougall. The latter, in partnership with Alexander Mills McDougall under the name of G. and A. McDougall, presided over the destinies of the Saint-Maurice ironworks until 1879, at which time Alexander Mills, who had closed the L'Islet ironworks the preceding year, sold his investments and left the Saint-Maurice

region. Under the sole direction of George McDougall, the Saint-Maurice ironworks continued to function at a slow pace from 1879 to 1883, when a new international monetary crisis closed it down for good.

GEORGES MASSEY

AJTR, Greffe de la paix, dénonciation et plainte de Marie Hamel, 28 janv. 1865; déposition de François Brousseau, 1er févr. 1858; Registre d'état civil, St Andrew's Presbyterian Church, 1876–89. ANQ-TR, État civil, Presbytériens, St Andrew's Church, 1846–75; Greffe de R.-Honoré Dufresne, 22 nov. 1867; Greffe de Petrus Hubert, 17 mars 1857, 8 janv., 26 févr. 1858, 5 nov. 1859, 15 déc. 1862, 16 avril 1863, 26 avril 1867, 6 janv. 1868, 3 mai 1869, 8 nov. 1875; Greffe de F.-L. Lottinville, 14 mars, 14 mai 1850, 23 mars 1854, 2 mars, 22 sept. 1855. Le Constitutionnel (Trois-Rivières), 28 févr., 23 mai 1870. L'Ère nouvelle (Trois-Rivières), 10, 14 déc. 1857; 14 janv., 15, 22, 25 févr., 5 avril 1858. Cyclopaedia of Canadian biog. (Rose, 1886). Brouillette, Le développement industriel. Ernestine Charland-Rajotte, Drummondville, 150 ans de vie quotidienne au cœur du Québec (Drummondville, Qué., 1972). Une page d'histoire de Trois-Rivières et la région, magnifique essor industriel (Trois-Rivières, 1954). Albert Tessier, Les forges Saint-Maurice, 1729–1883 (Trois-Rivières, 1952); Les Trois-Rivières: quatre siècles d'histoire, 1535–1935 (2e éd., s.l., 1935). "La famille McDougall," BRH, XXXIII (1927), 401–3. Daniel McDougall, "The final half-century of charcoal iron production in Quebec, 1861–1911," Canadian Mining Journal (Gardenvale, Que.), 92 (1971), no.8, 30–34.

McGEE, THOMAS D'ARCY (he signed both McGee and M'Gee), journalist, poet, and politician; b. 13 April 1825 in Carlingford, County Louth (Republic of Ireland), fifth child of James McGee and Dorcas Catherine Morgan; assassinated 7 April 1868 in Ottawa.

Thomas D'Arcy McGee's formative years were spent in Ireland. His mother's family was reputed to have been involved in the 1798 Irish rebellion. His father worked for the Coast Guard Service, and in 1833 was transferred to Wexford, the town where the memories of the bloody 1798 rebellion were the most vivid. D'Arcy's mother died shortly after the family's arrival in Wexford; he obtained an informal elementary education in a Catholic "hedge school." He was influenced at an early age by Father Theobald Mathew's temperance movement, by Daniel O'Connell's campaign to repeal the union between Ireland and Great Britain, and by the work of Celtic scholars published in the Dublin Penny Journal.

D'Arcy McGee left for North America in 1842, one of almost 93,000 Irishmen who crossed the Atlantic that year, the greatest number in any one

McGee

year before the famine. McGee's father had married again, and the stepmother was not popular with the children. He travelled the classic route to North America, sailing on a timber ship from Wexford to Quebec, and continuing to New England, where he was welcomed to the home of his mother's sister in Providence, R.I. He then moved to Boston to look for work. Soon after his arrival he was asked to address the Boston Friends of Ireland celebrating the Fourth of July. It was his first recorded public address in America, and it revealed a hostile attitude towards British rule in Ireland: "The sufferings which the people of that unhappy country have endured at the hands of a heartless, bigoted, despotic government, are well known to you. . . . Her people are born slaves, and bred in slavery from the cradle; they know not what freedom is." The speech made a favourable impression, and the 17-year-old immigrant was asked to join the staff of the *Boston Pilot*, New England's principal Catholic newspaper.

McGee was taken on as the *Pilot*'s travelling agent, and for the next two years travelled through New England collecting overdue accounts and new subscribers. He also lectured to the scattered Irish population of New England, describing the movements begun in Ireland by Daniel O'Connell and Father Mathew. During the same period he contributed 40 articles to the *Pilot* on the history of literature in Ireland. The response to his articles was enthusiastic, and McGee was asked to become editor of the newspaper; his first editorial appeared on 13 April 1844, on his 19th birthday.

McGee edited the *Pilot* for a year. In his editorials he urged the Irish in America to support Ireland's struggle for nationality, arguing that the Irish in America would never be recognized as equals until Ireland was recognized as a nation. The young editor also defended Irish Catholic immigrants against hostile Protestant and nativist opinion and led a successful campaign for the establishment of evening schools for adult immigrants. He published two books in Boston during his first stay in the United States: *Eva MacDonald, a tale of the United Irishmen* (1844) and *Historical sketches of O'Connell and his friends* (1845).

While in Boston, McGee had the opportunity to comment on Canada, and his perspective was distinctly Irish. At first, he urged the Irish in Canada to support Robert Baldwin* and Louis-Hippolyte LA FONTAINE, and wrote that " 'Repeal of the Union' is the Irish for 'Responsible Government.' " When a correspondent informed him that in Canada the Tories were more tolerant towards the Catholic Church, McGee answered: "The Tories! Well may the Catholics of Canada exclaim, 'Oh, save us from our friends!' " Later, the annexation of Texas and the Oregon boundary dispute led McGee to reconsider his views on Canada and to see it in a new light. He now confessed that he could find no reason for Canada's remaining separate from the United States: "The United States of North America must necessarily in course of time absorb the Northern British Provinces. . . . One vast Federal Union will stretch from Labrador to Panama. A river like the St. Lawrence cannot safely be left in European hands. . . . Either by purchase, conquest, or stipulation, Canada must be yielded by Great Britain to this Republic."

McGee was offered in 1845 a position with the *Freeman's Journal* in Dublin and in June returned to Ireland. He reported on the proceedings in Dublin of the Repeal Association organized by Daniel O'Connell and then moved to London where he covered the parliamentary session of 1846 which repealed the Corn Laws. While working for the *Freeman*, however, McGee became closely associated with Young Ireland, an enthusiastic group of Irish nationalists who believed that self-government was a fundamental principle of nationality, and who were trying to develop a sense of Irish identity by their contributions to journalism, history, and literature. McGee contributed two volumes to their "Library of Ireland," *Gallery of Irish writers* in 1846 and *A memoir of the life and conquests of Art MacMurrogh* in 1847. He also began to contribute to the *Nation*, Young Ireland's journal. Finally he was asked to resign from the *Freeman*. McGee transferred to the *Nation* just after his 21st birthday.

In July 1846, Daniel O'Connell announced his support for the new Whig government which promised Irish reform; McGee supported the leaders of Young Ireland when they resigned from the Repeal Association and established the Irish Confederation to promote what they believed were the original aims of the association, repeal of the union between Ireland and Great Britain. He was a principal speaker at all of the new association's public meetings and was elected secretary in June 1847. On 13 July 1847 he married Mary Theresa Caffrey. The couple were to have five daughters and one son, but only two daughters survived their father.

The Irish Confederation was frustrated in the general elections of 1847, and a radical faction developed which called for armed action. When the radicals were purged from the Confederation at the beginning of 1848 McGee supported the conservative leadership. But the French revolution of February persuaded the conservatives to adopt a revolutionary course of action, and McGee now participated in the plans for an Irish rebellion. He was actually arrested for sedition on the eve of his first wedding anniversary, but the charges were dismissed the next day. The government suspended habeas corpus in Ireland towards the end of July, and the Irish Confederation appealed to the country for armed support. McGee was dispatched to Scotland where he was to collect an expedition of armed sympathizers, but the main resistance did not last two weeks and McGee's expedition did not embark. He returned to Ireland; when he could not obtain a following in the northeast he left again for the United States.

McGee arrived in Philadelphia in October 1848, and issued a public letter describing recent events in Ireland. He blamed the Irish clergy for the rebellion's failure and signed the letter defiantly, "Thomas D'Arcy McGee, A Traitor to the British Government." He then moved to New York City and started his own newspaper, the *Nation*, in which he tried to arouse American sympathy for the liberal and nationalist revolutions in Europe and supported the annexation movement in Canada as a part of the same cause. His newspaper became a forum for Irish Canadian opinion on the subject. However, McGee antagonized the bishop of New York by supporting the Roman republic against Pope Pius IX, and by the end of 1849 he had alienated Irish republicans in New York when, following yet another shift in position, he began to support a new Irish reform movement which planned to work within the existing Irish constitution. The dispute became personal, and two Irish republicans, who were to become Fenian leaders, challenged McGee to a duel. The combination of clerical and republican opposition forced him to leave New York in the spring of 1850.

McGee returned to Boston where he started another newspaper, the *American Celt and Adopted Citizen*. He now emphasized Irish interests in America and supported a naturalization campaign among the Irish of New England. He also published *A history of the Irish settlers in North America* (1851) to demonstrate that the Irish had made a significant contribution to the history of North America. When the pope appointed an English episcopacy in 1851, anti-Catholic opinion was aroused in Britain and America, and McGee, unable to endure the charge made by Catholics that he was contributing to the nativist campaign by attacking the clergy, made his peace with the Catholic Church.

He moved the *American Celt* to Buffalo in the summer of 1852, but it did not prosper. McGee and his newspaper returned to New York City in the summer of 1853.

For the next four years, McGee worked on behalf of the Catholic interests in the United States, condemning revolutionary liberalism as a threat to Christianity and civilization. He completed three books during this period: *A history of the attempts to establish the Protestant reformation in Ireland* (1853), *The Catholic history of North America* (1855), and *A life of the Rt. Rev. Edward Maginn* (1857). Gradually McGee became more critical of the United States, arguing that American society required the tempering influence of Catholicism to balance the disorderly tendencies of the New World. By 1855 he was urging the American Irish Catholics to leave the eastern cities and to found a colony in the newly opening west where they could recover their Celtic and Catholic character. He was the principal organizer of the Buffalo Emigrant Aid Convention of 1856, but the project failed when it aroused the opposition of the Catholic hierarchy in the east who insisted that the Irish had neither the skills nor the capital necessary for colonization. McGee believed, however, that the eastern hierarchy was afraid an exodus of Catholics would jeopardize the financial situation of their dioceses.

In the spring of 1857 McGee moved to Montreal. He came at the invitation of leaders of that city's Irish community who expected him to promote their interests. His attitude toward Canada had changed from the days when he supported annexation: after his reconciliation with the Catholic Church, McGee defended Canada as a place where Catholic rights were recognized. He had visited Canada in the fall of 1852 and in the winter of 1856. After the Irish rebels of 1848 were granted amnesty, McGee lectured in Ireland in 1855 and urged emigrants to choose Canada over the United States.

In Montreal McGee's first effort was another newspaper, the *New Era*, which he published for one year. The newspaper was designed to launch his career in Canadian politics, and it concentrated on attacking the influence of the Orange Order and defending the Irish right to representation in the assembly. McGee also devoted considerable space in the *New Era* to the future of Canada, and outlined a programme for the development of what he called "a new nationality." This included proposals for extensive economic development by means of railway construction, the fostering of immigration, and the application of a protective tariff. McGee also urged economic

McGee

cooperation between Canada and the Maritime colonies and suggested that this would lead to "a federal compact" among the provinces. A federal system, McGee argued, would solve Canada's constitutional problems and provide for the survival of French Canada. McGee urged Canadian colonization of the Hudson's Bay Company territory, but, at the same time, called for a policy which would allow for the integration of the native people of the western territory into the new order; his plan included the establishment of a separate province for the native people and extensive Canadian economic assistance.

McGee's concept of the "new nationality" was based on the desirability of developing an alternate experience in North America to that of the United States. An essential characteristic of Canada's experience was its relationship with Great Britain, and McGee's solution to the problem of retaining the connection between them yet providing for Canadian sovereignty was a proposal that one of Queen Victoria's younger sons establish a Canadian dynasty in a "kingdom of the St. Lawrence." Equally important in McGee's mind was the development of a distinctive Canadian literature. After asking, "Who reads a Canadian book?" he went on to suggest ways in which Canadian literature might be encouraged, including tariff protection for Canadian publishers. Much of McGee's Canadian programme was derived from the nationalist theories of Young Ireland, and he applied them to the particular circumstances of Montreal and British North America during the economic depression of 1857. Later he described his programme as his "national policy," and its tenets influenced the course of his public life in Canada.

In December 1857 D'Arcy McGee was one of three members elected to represent Montreal in the Legislative Assembly. He had been nominated by the St Patrick's Society of Montreal and his property qualification was obtained by public subscription among the Irish community. When the Conservative government nominated Henry Starnes* to oppose him, McGee joined himself with Luther Hamilton Holton* and Antoine-Aimé Dorion* against John Rose*, George-Étienne Cartier*, and Starnes. Holton, Dorion, and McGee were all returned, and it was believed that the Irish vote had decided the contest.

In parliament McGee supported the short-lived Reform government of George Brown* and Dorion during the 1858 session, and when they left office he sat in opposition to the coalition of Cartier and John A. Macdonald*. Outside the assembly, McGee developed a political organiza-

tion among the Irish Catholics of Canada West and urged them to support George Brown's Reformers. He also tried to change the Reform party so that it would be acceptable to both sections of the province. At the very time the 1859 convention of western Reformers adopted a federal policy, McGee and three other members of the opposition from Canada East issued a manifesto endorsing a federal union of the two Canadas. It was rumoured that McGee had persuaded the western Reformers to consider the Irish national school system as a model for solving the school problems of Canada West.

McGee's hopes of winning Irish Catholic support for a reconstructed Reform party under George Brown did not survive long after the 1861 general election when McGee's school policy was attacked in a public letter signed by the Roman Catholic hierarchy of Canada. McGee was himself re-elected in 1861, but Brown went down to defeat and believed that his failure was due to John Joseph Lynch*, the Catholic bishop of Toronto. McGee's alliance with Brown ended when Richard William Scott* introduced his separate school bill which the *Globe* categorically opposed and McGee supported. Nevertheless, McGee continued to oppose the Conservatives after the 1861 election. When the Cartier-Macdonald government was defeated on its militia bill in 1862, McGee was asked to become president of the council in the moderate Reform administration of John Sandfield Macdonald*. McGee immediately went to work on a programme to reform the civil service and tried to have all matters of immigration transferred to his office. Despite his government's retrenchment policy, McGee urged economic expansion and chaired the Intercolonial Railway conference which met in September 1862 at Quebec. When Sandfield Macdonald's government supported the railway, Dorion resigned; when the railway scheme fell through, Dorion returned and McGee was dropped from the cabinet. In the general election that followed, McGee announced he would run as an independent and declared: "I intend to adhere to the national policy I have always advocated and acted upon. . . ." The Sandfield Macdonald–Dorion government decided to nominate a candidate to oppose McGee, and McGee then supported Cartier and Rose against Holton and Dorion. On this occasion, McGee, Cartier, and Rose were returned.

As McGee moved from the Reformers to the Conservatives, he renewed his public efforts on behalf of the programme he had outlined in the *New Era*. During the summer of 1863 he wrote several public letters and contributed two articles

492

to the *British American Magazine* in which he defined a destiny for British America. British America and the United States, McGee argued, both enjoyed a freedom native to their continent and unknown in Europe. Americans had developed their freedom into a republican system of government, and, although it was a magnificent experiment, it had many shortcomings. British Americans, on the other hand, had not separated from Britain and had developed their institutions along different lines. By retaining a system of constitutional monarchy, they had achieved a better balance between their natural freedom and the need for authority. Their society was more orderly and more free. "To the American citizen who boasts of greater liberty in the States, I say that a man can state his private, social, political and religious opinions with more freedom here than in New York or New England. There is, besides, far more liberty and toleration enjoyed by minorities in Canada than in the United States." McGee was fond of citing the example of minority rights and he brought this to the attention of the Irish press, contrasting the position of the Irish in "British and Republican North America." In the summer of 1863 McGee took his appeal for British American nationality to New Brunswick and Nova Scotia. He addressed audiences in Saint John and Halifax, and used the same arguments he had put forward in Canada. "I invoke the fortunate genius of a united British America, to solemnize law with the moral sanction of religion, and to crown our fair pillar of freedom with its only appropriate capital, lawful authority, so that, hand in hand, we and our descendants may advance steadily to the accomplishment of a common destiny."

McGee became the minister of agriculture, immigration, and statistics in the Conservative government which was formed after the defeat of Sandfield Macdonald's second administration in 1863. He retained that office in the "Great Coalition," and was a Canadian delegate to the Charlottetown and Quebec conferences of 1864. At Quebec, McGee introduced the resolution which called for a guarantee of the educational rights of religious minorities in the two Canadas.

The years which inaugurated confederation coincided with a crisis in Ireland, and the crisis touched McGee. The Irish Republican Brotherhood, popularly known as the Fenians, had obtained wide support among the Irish in Great Britain and the United States, and appealed to the Irish in Canada. McGee openly opposed the movement, and based his opposition on two grounds: first, he objected to the republican programme for Ireland and urged the Irish to adopt the Canadian model of self-government within the British Empire; second, McGee attacked the Fenian plan to invade British America and called on the Irish in Canada to "give the highest practical proof possible that an Irishman well governed becomes one of the best subjects of the law and the Sovereign." When he visited Ireland in 1865 as the Canadian delegate to the Dublin International Exposition McGee addressed an audience in Wexford, the town where he had spent his boyhood, and spoke on the Irish immigrant in Canada and the United States. He also described his career as an Irish rebel as "the follies of one and twenty." This "Wexford Speech" attracted great attention in Ireland, Britain, the United States, and Canada, and McGee was accused of being a turncoat and a traitor to Ireland.

By 1866, McGee was in political trouble with his Irish constituents in Montreal. He had antagonized the Irish vote and had become a liability in Canadian politics. He was not invited to the London conference in 1866, nor was he included in the first dominion government. As the federal general election of 1867 approached, McGee was expelled from the St Patrick's Society, and the society's president, Bernard Devlin*, was nominated to oppose him. Although McGee was returned for Montreal West, he had lost the Irish vote and was defeated as a candidate for Prescott in the Ontario provincial election. He now expressed a desire to leave politics. John A. Macdonald promised him a civil service post for the summer of 1868, and McGee intended to turn his full attention to literature and Canadian history. He was dead before the appointment was made.

McGee was assassinated in Ottawa during the early morning hours of 7 April 1868. He was buried a week later on his 43rd birthday. It was generally believed at the time that his murder was part of a Fenian conspiracy. Patrick James WHELAN, an Irish immigrant, was charged with the crime, found guilty, and hanged publicly in Ottawa on 11 Feb. 1869. The crown, however, never accused Whelan of being a Fenian, and the charges against other alleged members of the conspiracy were dismissed.

Aside from his public speeches and newspaper editorials, Thomas D'Arcy McGee left behind a significant body of literature. His first piece, *Eva MacDonald*, was historical fiction. The only other fiction he wrote was a drama intended for Catholic schools, *Sebastian, or the Roman martyr* (1861). All of his other prose work was historical, most of it propagandist and designed to justify a present position through historical argument. His best historical work was his last, *A popular history of Ireland* (1863). Its title was

McGillivray

significant: although McGee did some primary research, he depended on the work of other scholars and popularized their discoveries. The work was well received, and he was elected to the Royal Irish Academy.

McGee also published a large number of poems throughout his career under the pseudonym "Amergin," and 309 of them were collected and published after his death by his close friend, Mary Anne Sadlier [Madden*]. McGee's poetic style was lyrical when he expressed personal emotion; he used the ballad for historical subjects, and once expressed the ambition to write a ballad history of Ireland. As a poet, he was a part of the Young Ireland school which published in the *Nation*, and which included Thomas Osborne Davis, James Clarence Mangan, Sir Samuel Ferguson, and "Speranza," the future Lady Wilde and mother of Oscar Wilde. McGee's verse, his love of the Celtic past, his interest in history, and his political ideas were all consistent with the romantic milieu in which he lived.

D'Arcy McGee's personality and private life are difficult to evaluate, as very few of his private papers are available. He was well known for his speaking ability, being generally acknowledged as the finest public speaker in Canadian politics at the time. This ability was apparent from his earlier career, when he obtained a substantial part of his income from lectures and speaking tours. He never enjoyed an independent income, and always depended on writing, journalism, lectures, public subscriptions, and government appointments for income. He was generally in debt, and this condition contributed to the charge that he changed ideological and political positions for personal gain. The truth of this charge is difficult to determine accurately. His early flirtations with revolutionary liberalism and anti-clericalism, followed in later years by a passionate faith in Catholicism and conservatism, was a common pattern among many 19th century romantics. So too was the tendency towards personal escapism. Many prominent romantic personalities were acknowledged to be users of drugs, and McGee was known for his heavy drinking. This pattern of behaviour was most noticeable during times of stress, such as the crisis preceding his reconciliation with the church, the conflict with Sandfield Macdonald, and his confrontation with the Fenians. At the time of his death he had renewed his pledge of total abstinence, a pledge he had first taken from Father Mathew in Ireland.

ROBIN B. BURNS

T. D'A. McGee, *The Catholic history of North America; five discourses, to which are added two dis-* *courses on the relations of Ireland and America* (Boston, 1855); *Eva MacDonald, a tale of the United Irishmen* (Boston, 1844); *Gallery of Irish writers; the Irish writers of the seventeenth century* (Dublin, 1846); *Historical sketches of O'Connell and his friends . . .* (2nd ed., Boston, 1845; 4th ed., 1854); *A history of the attempts to establish the Protestant reformation in Ireland, and the successful resistance of that people; (time: 1540–1830)* (Boston, 1853); *A history of the Irish settlers in North America, from the earliest period to the census of 1850* (Boston, 1851; 5th ed., 1852); *A life of the Rt. Rev. Edward Maginn, coadjutor bishop of Derry, with selections from his correspondence* (New York, 1857; 2nd ed., 1860); *A memoir of the life and conquests of Art MacMurrogh, king of Leinster, from A.D. 1377 to A.D. 1417, with some notices of the Leinster wars of the 14th century* (Dublin, 1847; 2nd ed., [1886]); "A plea for British American nationality" and "A further plea for British American nationality," *British American Magazine; Devoted to Literature, Science, and Art* (Toronto), I (1863), 337–45, and 561–67; *The poems of Thomas D'Arcy McGee; with copious notes; also an introduction and biographical sketch,* ed. Mrs. James Sadlier [M. A. Madden] (New York, 1869); ed. Brady (2nd ed., Boston, 1869), *A popular history of Ireland . . .* (2v., New York, 1863).

Georges P. Vanier Library (Concordia University, Montreal), G. E. Clerk diary, 18 Sept. 1856–21 Dec. 1857; T. D'A. McGee coll. PAC, MG 24, B30; C16; MG 26, A, 46, p.18010; MG 27, I, E9; E12; III, B8; MG 29, D15; RG 1, E7. Royal Irish Academy (Dublin), Minute book of the Irish Confederation, 26 June 1847. *American Celt* (Boston, Buffalo, N.Y., and New York), 31 Aug. 1850; 31 May, 8 Nov. 1851; 18 May, 11 June 1853. *Boston Pilot,* 9 July 1842, 13 April 1844–17 May 1845, June 1845–May 1846, 7 Aug. 1847, 21 Oct. 1848. *Gazette* (Montreal), 3, 12 June 1863; 9 Dec. 1865; 15 April 1868. *Globe,* 13 Aug. 1858, 23 Aug. 1859. *Montreal Herald,* 26 Nov. 1856. *Nation* (Dublin), 19 Sept. 1846; 5 Feb., 15 July 1848; 22 June 1850; 8 March 1851; 4 Sept., 11 Dec. 1852; 2, 9 June 1855; 8 March 1856; 13, 20 May 1865. *Nation* (New York), 20 Jan., 31 March, 14 April, 1 Dec. 1849; 27 Jan. 1850. *New Era* (Montreal), 25 May 1857–1 May 1858. W. F. Adams, *Ireland and Irish emigration to the New World from 1815 to the famine* (New Haven, Conn., 1932). E. R. Cameron, *Memoirs of Ralph Vansittart* (Toronto, [1924]), 101–2. H. J. O'C. Clarke, *A short sketch of the life of the Hon. Thomas D'Arcy McGee, M.P., for Montreal (West) . . .* (Montreal, 1868). C. G. Duffy, *My life in two hemispheres* (London, 1898); *Young Ireland; a fragment of Irish history* (2v., London, 1880–83), II. M. G. Kelly, *Catholic immigrant colonization projects in the United States, 1815–1860* (New York, 1939). Isabel [Murphy] Skelton, *The life of Thomas D'Arcy McGee* (Gardenvale, N.Y., 1925), 373. T. P. Slattery, "*They got to find mee guilty yet*" (Toronto and Garden City, N.Y., 1972). [J.] F. Taylor, *Thos. D'Arcy McGee: sketch of his life and death* (Montreal, 1868).

McGILLIVRAY, ALEXANDER, Presbyterian minister; b. 1801 at Croy, Inverness-shire, Scotland; m. in 1837 Elizabeth McCormick Skinner, and they had 13 children; d. 16 Feb. 1862 at McLellan Brook, Pictou County, N.S.

Alexander McGillivray was educated at the parish school and at King's College, Aberdeen, and was ordained to the ministry of the Church of Scotland at Stornoway, Isle of Lewis, on 25 April 1832. That same year he heeded the call to preach to his fellow Scots in Nova Scotia and immigrated to the colony. After a short stay in Lochaber as the first resident pastor, he was inducted in 1833 as minister at Barney's River and Merigomish. Five years later he became pastor at McLellan Mountain, and ministered there until his death.

McGillivray was a mild, benevolent man, and little inclined to religious controversy. Partly for this reason, he stayed in Nova Scotia after the disruption of the Church of Scotland in 1843, when nearly all other Kirk ministers went home to Scotland to replace those who had joined the new Free Church of Scotland. Resisting entreaties from his family and departing colleagues to join the exodus, McGillivray preached and administered the sacraments to pastorless Church of Scotland people. For almost ten years this lone "shepherd of the Kirk" journeyed through the rugged terrain of eastern Nova Scotia and Prince Edward Island where thousands of Highlanders came to hear him preach in English and Gaelic. It is believed that he was the only Kirk minister on the eastern mainland of Nova Scotia for eight years. His work was easier after 1853, when three new Kirk ministers, G. W. Sprott, Alexander McLean, and Allan Pollok*, came out from Scotland in answer to his pleas for support. Realizing the need for a native clergy, McGillivray raised money to send George Monro Grant* and three other young men to study for the ministry at the University of Glasgow in 1853.

McGillivray's self-sacrificing and resolute character won him the love of his people. Queen's College at Kingston, Canada West, rewarded his efforts with an honorary degree in 1858. His own farm, as well as the support of his large following in the province, also brought a considerable measure of worldly prosperity, and several of his children received a professional education. Above all, by avoiding religious wrangles and maintaining cordial relations with clergy and laity of the Free Church, he aided in the development of a conciliatory spirit among Presbyterians, which helped to make possible the reunion of Presbyterians in British North America in 1875.

A. A. MacKenzie

McLellan Mountain Presbyterian Church (McLellan Brook, N.S.), records. James Robertson, *History of the mission of the Secession Church to Nova Scotia and Prince Edward Island from its commencement in 1765* (Edinburgh, 1847). *Eastern Chronicle* (Pictou, N.S.), 20 Feb. 1862. *Novascotian*, 24 Feb. 1862. John Doull, *Reverend Alexander McGillivray, D.D.* (Halifax, 1938). W. L. Grant and Frederick Hamilton, *Principal Grant* (Toronto, 1904). J. P. MacPhie, *Pictonians at home and abroad* (Boston, 1914).

MACHAR (Machir), JOHN, Presbyterian clergyman and educator; baptized on 18 Dec. 1796 at Tannadice, Forfarshire (Angus), Scotland, youngest of the nine children of David Machir, a small farmer, and Jean Walker; d. 7 Feb. 1863 at Kingston, Canada West.

John Machar's mother had been educated by her father, a classical scholar driven into obscurity through his attachment to the Young Pretender, Charles Edward. Her unusually strong traditions of piety and culture deeply influenced her son. He attended a local school at Tannadice and the grammar school at Brechin, then entered King's College, Aberdeen, where he obtained the degree of MA in 1814. Before being licensed to preach by the Church of Scotland in October 1819 he taught in a school at Inverurie, Aberdeenshire, acted as tutor in private families, and attended two sessions at the University of Edinburgh. While waiting for a permanent appointment he assisted in a number of parishes, including those of Brechin and Logie, and again tutored.

In 1826 the elders of St Andrew's Church at Kingston requested the Edinburgh Presbytery to nominate a minister to succeed the Reverend John Barclay. Machar was chosen and reached Kingston by way of New York early in September 1827. From then until his death he was honoured for his untiring pastoral work which was not confined to Kingston but extended to many surrounding districts then without regular church services. Despite poor health, partly the result of a severe attack of rheumatic fever in 1831, he also worked among the immigrants who passed through Kingston travelling west, many of whom became victims of the prevailing cholera epidemics.

In 1831 Machar was one of 14 ministers of the Church of Scotland who, along with five representative elders met at Kingston to establish the first Synod of the Presbyterian Church in Upper Canada. John Mackenzie* was elected first moderator in 1831; Machar became moderator in 1833. Machar was also secretary of the Religious Tract Society and of the Kingston Bible Society, a promoter of Sabbath schools, and a Presbyterian chaplain to the army in Kingston. In a period of rather bitter religious controversy he

Mackenzie

was notable for his friendly co-operation with clergymen of other denominations, particularly with his neighbour, the Reverend R. D. Cartwright of the Church of England. Together they worked to endow day schools in the Midland District for the benefit of those who could not afford the usual fees.

Machar was by taste a pastor and a scholar finding his recreation in his own unusually fine library. He is chiefly remembered, however, for the part he played in founding and fostering Queen's College at Kingston. He was among the 12 clergymen and 15 laymen named in the charter as the first board of trustees. One of the few who lived in Kingston and who could attend meetings regularly he was for over 20 years closely concerned with the management of the college and of its auxiliary school. For a number of years he conducted the classes in Hebrew. In 1846, as a result of the division of the church in Canada in 1844 following the "great disruption" of 1843 in Scotland, and of the failure to secure for Queen's a share in the King's College endowment, some thought that the college should be closed. It was then, at the request of the trustees, that Machar, while remaining pastor of St Andrew's, accepted the temporary position of principal of Queen's, in succession to Thomas Liddell*. The University of Glasgow accorded him the customary honour of the DD in the following year. He carried on until 1852 with a temporary, part-time, and constantly changing staff. He asked for no regular salary, and returned, in the form of bursaries, substantial portions of the honoraria voted by the board; the rest he devoted to paying off the debt on St Andrew's Church. The only tangible profit of these years to him was the magnificent folio edition of Walton's "Polyglot Bible" which now forms a part of the distinguished collection of bibles in Queen's University library.

Machar resigned as principal in 1852 but continued to serve until 1853 when he was at last allowed to retire in favour of the Reverend James GEORGE. He left Queen's in what may be termed a typical situation of precarious security. He continued to act as trustee until his death in 1863, and in 1855–57 he again took charge of the Hebrew classes. He had married in 1832, but the name of his wife is not known. His daughter, Agnes Maule Machar*, who was known as a writer of verse and short stories, published a brief biography of Machar in 1873. His son, John, a graduate of Queen's, practised as a lawyer in Kingston and was a member of the faculty of the abortive college of law at Queen's in 1880.

HILDA NEATBY

QUA, Queen's records, B; D1, 1840–63. [A. M. Machar], *Memorials of the life and ministry of the Reverend John Machar, D.D., late minister of St. Andrew's Church, Kingston,* (Toronto, 1873). *Presbyterian* (Montreal), XXVI (1873), 283.

MACKENZIE, WILLIAM LYON (he also used **McKenzie** and **MacKenzie**), merchant, journalist, politician, and rebel; b. 12 March 1795 at Springfield, Dundee, Forfarshire (Angus), Scotland, the only child of Daniel Mackenzie, a weaver, and Elizabeth Chalmers, *née* Mackenzie; d. 28 Aug. 1861 at Toronto, Canada West.

William Lyon Mackenzie's career can only be understood if the man and the legend are separated. Virtually all examinations of his life have concentrated on his political activities from 1824 to 1838, and such concentration has helped to develop the legend. Because he was most active in periods of stress when the post-Napoleonic despotism was breaking down, new waves of technology were shaking society, and the North American continent was being transformed from wilderness to farmland, his advocacy of radical changes brought him quickly into prominence. Moreover, his colleagues and opponents were less colourful. Fortune let him initiate a rebellion which to later generations seemed crucial in forging Canadian institutions and in establishing a national spirit of democracy, justice, and freedom from oppression. As a legend, Mackenzie has a role and importance that Mackenzie the man could never achieve. Thus he is one of the most documented and discussed and yet one of the most frequently misunderstood figures in Canadian history. He himself laid the basis for the confusion which has surrounded his career. He regularly recorded his own past and his objectives in great detail but his commentaries were often based on a faulty memory, or spurred by the exigencies of the moment.

Both branches of Mackenzie's family came from Glenshee, in the parish of Kirkmichael, north of Dundee. His parents married at Dundee on 8 May 1794; his mother, the elder by 17 years, was a widow. On 9 April 1795, three weeks after Mackenzie's birth, the father supposedly died, but no record of his burial exists. Although Charles Lindsey*, Mackenzie's son-in-law and first biographer, stressed that Mackenzie and his mother suffered hardship, relatives looked after their welfare. Mackenzie certainly retained some fond memories of his youth at Dundee: "here also I was partly educated, and here I passed some of my happiest days . . . unencumbered with care." His mother's influence cannot be over-estimated. Like her son, Elizabeth Mackenzie was extremely proud, but unlike him she was deeply religious, a convert to the Secession or anti state-support branch of Presbyterianism which often produced reformers. Mackenzie early rebelled against her religious observances but retained a strict, puritanical outlook throughout his career.

Willie, as he was called, although the family also used Lyon, entered the Dundee parish school at age five, with the help of a bursary. He was subsequently taught at a Mr Adie's school, but proved difficult to discipline. With the meticulousness which later made his filing system such a weapon against opponents, he listed by year and type the 958 books he read from 1806 to 1820. At 15 he was the youngest member of the commercial news room of a local newspaper. He also belonged to a scientific society where he met Edward Lesslie. Lesslie and his son James* were to be Mackenzie's patrons throughout his life.

Mackenzie was apprenticed to several tradesmen in Dundee, but by 1814, with Lesslie's backing, he and his mother were operating a general store and circulating library at Alyth, 20 miles north of Dundee; the business was bankrupted during the post-Napoleonic depression. Mackenzie's last years in Britain are obscure. He returned briefly to Dundee, worked for a canal company in Wiltshire in 1818, visited France, and went to London, where he probably began newspaper writing. He later said that he led a dissipated life from 17 to 21, when he gave up gambling and drinking. On 17 July 1814 his illegitimate son James had been born at Alyth. Nothing is known of the mother, Isabel Reid, but Elizabeth Mackenzie assumed responsibility for the child.

In 1820 Mackenzie sailed to Canada with John Lesslie, another son of Edward. He worked briefly on the Lachine Canal, and wrote for A. J. Christie*'s Montreal Herald, but soon moved to York (Toronto) where he worked for Lesslie in a book and drug company. Mackenzie was immediately impressed with Upper Canada, which was to become his spiritual home. Before the end of 1820 he was writing for the York Observer under the name "Mercator." In the summer of 1822 the rest of Edward Lesslie's family came to Canada with Mackenzie's mother and the girl she had chosen as William's wife, Isabel Baxter (1805–73) of Dundee. Married in Montreal on 1 July, they were to have 13 children. Isabel was to make an ideal wife for Mackenzie, strong of body, yet submissive and uncomplaining through the many exigencies of his career.

Later that year Edward and John Lesslie established a branch store in Dundas. They provided the capital and Mackenzie was resident partner, dealing in drugs, hardware, and general merchandise, as well as operating a circulating library. Mackenzie also received a crown land grant, but his partnership with the Lesslies did not thrive and quickly degenerated into quarrelling so bitter that Peter Paterson* Sr had to act as intermediary in its dissolution in January 1823. Mackenzie unsuccessfully attempted to carry on but by October 1823 he had moved to Queenston. There he again attempted a business and became acquainted with Robert Randall*, a member of the assembly. Randall died in 1834, and Mackenzie, as executor and partial heir to the estate, was to wage a 20-year battle over Randall's land claims. When business at Queenston proved unsatisfactory Mackenzie started his most famous newspaper, the Colonial Advocate. The first number appeared on 18 May 1824 with the avowed purpose of influencing voters in their choice of representatives in the approaching election. Initially, Mackenzie supported the British connection, primogeniture, and the principle of clergy reserves, but he also praised American institutions. The Advocate quickly ran into financial difficulties, and into problems with the post office and with its agents. Mackenzie was partly at fault for sending copies to many influential non-subscribers, a parallel to his habit of writing to anyone of consequence.

In November 1824 he transferred his operations to York, where he became increasingly critical of the Tory establishment as his debts increased. Although, according to Charles Lindsey's estimate, circulation at the beginning of 1825 was 825 copies, Mackenzie was soon faced with a rival Reform paper, Francis Collins*' Canadian Freeman, and from July to December 1825 the Colonial Advocate suspended publication. Yet in October Mackenzie purchased a new printing press and type from the United States. Early in 1826 he began to consider changing to an agricultural journal or selling to Charles Fothergill* and returning to Dundas as a merchant. An editorial change was taking place that spring. His attacks on leading Tories such as William Allan*, the Boulton family, and George GURNETT became more scurrilous, but yellow journalism, admittedly common to other editors, failed to improve circulation. In May 1826 he fled to Lewiston, N.Y., to avoid arrest for debt.

At this juncture Mackenzie was saved by an act of Tory stupidity. On 8 June 1826 a group of 15 young, well-connected Tories, perhaps organized by Samuel Peters Jarvis*, thinly disguised themselves as Indians, raided his York office in broad daylight, smashed the press, and threw

Mackenzie

type into the bay. The Tory magistrates did nothing to protect Mackenzie's property. As Jesse KETCHUM, a far-sighted Reformer, remarked: "the ministerial Party could not have done anything more against themselves." Mackenzie, back in York, took the eight major participants to court, refusing a £200 settlement. The case was heard in October with James Edward SMALL, Marshall Spring Bidwell*, and Alexander Stewart of Niagara acting for Mackenzie. The jury awarded compensation of £625, a sum far beyond the damage done. The settlement enabled Mackenzie to pay off his most pressing creditors and re-establish himself on a sound footing. He never ceased to refer to the trial, joining himself to such martyrs for Upper Canadian liberty as Robert Thorpe* and Robert GOURLAY. Yet his trial demonstrated that the Upper Canadian courts could be fair. Disgruntled Tories now began a campaign of minor harassment against the little Scot.

Mackenzie was becoming increasingly involved in the question of the political rights of American settlers [see John ROLPH]. As secretary of a committee to gather petitions for redress Mackenzie played a central part in the selection of Robert Randall to bear them to England in 1827. With the aid of English Reformers such as Joseph Hume, Randall persuaded Colonial Secretary Lord Goderich that an injustice was being done, and the Upper Canadian legislature was instructed to introduce measures giving American-born settlers full rights. To Mackenzie this incident proved the efficacy of petitioning London directly.

Another petitioner in London in 1827 was John STRACHAN, rector of York, who was seeking a charter for his proposed King's College, and pressing the claims of the Church of England to the proceeds from the sale of clergy reserve lands. Mackenzie and the Reverend Egerton Ryerson*, a Methodist leader, immediately protested Strachan's claims. Mackenzie declared his candidacy for the spring elections, and corresponded with English radicals such as Hume and Lower Canadian Reformers such as John Neilson*.

The riding Mackenzie chose to contest was the two-member county of York, which included present-day Toronto north of Queen St, and the counties of York, Peel, and Ontario. The population, to a large extent of American extraction, promised to be Reform oriented. Three other leading Reform candidates declared themselves: J. E. Small and Robert Baldwin*, both moderates, and the more radical Ketchum. When Mackenzie received less support than the others at meetings, he turned to stating his case in the

newspapers. As part of his newspaper campaign he published a "Black List" which dissected the opposition, but was himself taken to task by Collins and the Tory editors, the former dubbing him "William Liar Mackenzie." Mackenzie's tactics worked; he and Ketchum were victorious in a Reform landslide.

When the assembly met in early January 1829, it was Bidwell rather than Mackenzie who was elected speaker, the only position the Reform majority could then award its leader. Mackenzie, nevertheless, could now press for reforms. He immediately began organizing committees on agriculture, commerce, and the post office. As chairman of the last he clearly demonstrated that that British-controlled post office was run at a profit, and recommended transfer to local control. He also castigated the Bank of Upper Canada as a monopoly and as a limited liability company, an indication of his traditional agrarian conservatism, dislike of limited liability companies, and belief in hard money. He also opposed any further expenditures until the public debt was paid off, even though the debt had been largely created by public works essential to the colony. Later in this parliament he particularly criticized the Welland Canal Company for its close connections with the provincial executive and William Hamilton MERRITT's methods of financing the work. He involved himself as well in an altercation over whether or not the chaplain of the house should be an Anglican, a fine example of his inability to distinguish between the significant and the frivolous.

In March 1829 Mackenzie went to the United States to buy books for resale and to study the actions of the newly inaugurated president, Andrew Jackson. He saw the simplicity and low cost of the American government, as compared to that in Upper Canada, admired the spoils system – which could be a means of removing Family Compact officials - and approved of Jackson's hard money, anti-bank ideas. Mackenzie, like Jackson, whom he met, was an entrepreneurial radical who strongly supported the independent proprietor and farmer but was hardly an agent for the common man. He returned to York filled with admiration of the United States and its institutions, an attitude soon supplemented by a growing dislike of Great Britain.

The death of King George IV necessitated the dissolution of the legislature in May 1830 and a new election. But the atmosphere of the province was very different from what it had been in 1828. Sir John COLBORNE, a more competent and popular governor than Sir Peregrine Maitland*, was undermining the power of Strachan and his cohorts and strengthening the British character of the province through assisted immigration. Conversely the Reform-dominated assembly had had little success, partially through inexperience and disorganization, but also because legislation was blocked by the Legislative Council. In York riding Mackenzie obtained 570 votes to Ketchum's 616, and his nearest Tory opponent received 425. Over-all the Reform group won fewer than 20 of the 51 seats.

After the Reform defeat Mackenzie became frustrated with the democratic process in Upper Canada. Aside from his political conflicts he engendered further Tory hatred by violent personal attacks on all he disagreed with and by his attempts to politicize and reform any organization to which he belonged. For instance, when in the summer of 1830 the Tories organized an agricultural society, Mackenzie refused to subscribe yet insisted on speaking at its meetings. Around the same time he joined St Andrew's Church, established by leading Presbyterian Tories who supported the state-church connection. Mackenzie had attended Anglican St James Church, as was appropriate for members of the legislature, as well as the independent Presbyterian church. Once a member of St Andrew's, he began to agitate for its separation from any state connection, and the battle lasted four years, ending with the departure of both Mackenzie and the minister.

When the assembly met in January 1831 Mackenzie totally immersed himself in its proceedings, demanding inquiries into abuses, and, probably inspired by the reform movement in England, particularly insisting on a review of representation in the province. He chaired a special committee which recommended increased representation, especially for the growing towns, and such sound ideas as a single day's poll and vote by ballot. His riding of York, despite its radical voting record, became four single member ridings in 1833. On other points he was less constructive, and the new Tory assembly had little patience with his activities. Men with no love for Mackenzie were in control: Archibald McLEAN was the new speaker and the house leaders were Attorney General Henry John BOULTON and Solicitor General Christopher Hagerman*. Moreover, the Tory ministerial group were simultaneously angered by assaults from Sir John Colborne, who was reforming the Legislative Council and ignoring Strachan and the Executive Council. The British government elected in 1830 was also suggesting the transfer of certain revenues to the control of the colonial legislature in return for an established civil list.

The Reformers had long demanded control of these revenues, but Mackenzie nevertheless dubbed the enabling legislation the "Everlasting Salary Bill." Caught in a vice between Reformers and the Colonial Office, some exasperated Tory members unsuccessfully moved to oust Mackenzie from the assembly; he considered the motion a "sign of the times."

Mackenzie decided to appeal for redress to Britain, after the manner of the 1827 Randall mission. Throughout a great deal of 1831 he traversed the province, propagandizing and gaining signatures for petitions listing grievances; he also consulted with Lower Canadian Reformers. He gained many supporters, particularly among the new Irish immigrants and those of American descent. The Tories reacted by preparing counter petitions. When the legislature opened in November, Mackenzie was again demanding investigations of the Bank of Upper Canada, the Welland Canal, King's College, the revenues, and the chaplain's salary. The *Colonial Advocate* simultaneously became more strident. When he called the assembly a "sycophantic office," the Tory majority expelled him on 12 December by a vote of 24 to 15. The Tories' short-sighted action helped recreate his image as a martyr and raised him to a key position at the very time the system they represented was being changed by local moderates and a new attitude in England.

On the day of Mackenzie's expulsion a mob of several hundred entered the assembly and demanded that Colborne dissolve parliament. He refused, but the Tories were quickly to find that if expelling Mackenzie was one thing, keeping him out was another. At the by-election on 2 Jan. 1832 he was re-elected by 119 votes to one. He was presented with a gold medal worth $250, and to the accompaniment of bagpipes a victorious procession of 134 sleighs made its way down Yonge St, headed by one bearing Mackenzie and a small press casting off leaflets. It was his greatest moment.

The Tories could have had no better demonstration of his political strength, but some of his opponents, particularly H. J. Boulton and Allan Napier MacNab, lacked political acumen. On 7 Jan. 1832, in response to new attacks, he was again expelled, and again re-elected. The province was by now in a turmoil, with Mackenzie organizing petitions to London, and the Tories founding the contrary British Constitutional Society. Inevitably there were incidents. Mackenzie disrupted a meeting at York called by Bishop Alexander Macdonell* to express Catholic support for the government. In Hamilton, William Johnson Kerr*, a Tory magistrate,

Mackenzie

lured Mackenzie out of his hotel and had him beaten by thugs. In York, Irish apprentices, incensed at the attacks on the bishop, pelted Mackenzie and Ketchum with garbage on 23 March. Later the same day riots broke out again and Mackenzie was only rescued from injury by the intervention of magistrate James FITZGIBBON. He went into hiding until his departure for England in April 1832, after public meetings approved payment of his expenses.

In London Mackenzie met with such reformers as Joseph Hume and John Arthur Roebuck*, and wrote for the *Morning Chronicle* to get public support. The Whig colonial secretary, Lord Goderich, a moderate man of considerable perspicacity, wanted to gain information and to redress any reasonable grievances. On 2 July he received Mackenzie as a private citizen, along with Denis-Benjamin VIGER, from the Lower Canadian assembly, and the Reverend George Ryerson* of the Methodists. In this and subsequent interviews, Mackenzie felt he received a fair hearing. Goderich suggested Mackenzie report on Upper Canada, and was soon swamped with dispatches. Mackenzie found time to enjoy the sights of London, heard the debate in parliament on the Reform Bill, and presented his grievances to the British people in his *Sketches of Canada and the United States*.

As a result of Mackenzie's presentations, Goderich sent a dispatch to Colborne on 8 Nov. 1832 which advised financial and political improvements and a halt to the assembly's vendetta against Mackenzie. But the Tories had expelled him, *in absentia*, a third time early that month, only to see him re-elected by acclamation. Goderich's dispatch arrived in Upper Canada in January 1833, and set off a furor among the Tories, who were no more ready than the most radical Reformers to accept dictates from England that went against their interests. The Legislative Council refused to accept the dispatch; after a violent debate in the assembly the dispatch was only narrowly approved for printing. The house deprived Mackenzie of his vote in February 1833 and refused to call a new election. When news of this action reached Goderich he dismissed Boulton and Hagerman, the attorney general and solicitor general. Colborne protested to the Colonial Office and Hagerman and Boulton left for England to object. Meanwhile, a triumphant Mackenzie and his wife left London for a tour of England, Scotland, and part of France.

In April, however, Lord Goderich was replaced at the Colonial Office by the more conservative Lord Stanley, who reappointed Hagerman and made Boulton chief justice of Newfoundland. Within three months, it seemed, all Mackenzie had accomplished was undone, and for him the setback was decisive. His belief in appeals to England was destroyed and his orientation towards the United States was accelerated. His mercurial disposition swung to despair, although the trip to England had not been without success in effecting governmental changes and in showing the Tories to be self-seeking. Mackenzie's new attitude was symbolized by the disappearance of "Colonial" from the title of his newspaper on 5 Dec. 1833. He had returned to Canada in August and on 17 December was again declared expelled from the assembly. Later in December he was re-elected unopposed and twice unsuccessfully attempted to take his seat. It took Colborne's orders to get him sworn in, thus ending a thoroughly discreditable series of expulsions.

At this time Mackenzie split with Egerton Ryerson and the Methodists. When Ryerson had begun the *Christian Guardian* in 1829 Mackenzie had welcomed it, although Ryerson and the Methodists were to prove anything but radical on issues unrelated to the breakdown of Anglican religious privileges. Ryerson was also in England in 1832, negotiating a union of Canadian and British Methodists, and thereby preparing to accept state aid. On his return Ryerson repudiated radicalism and attacked Joseph Hume in the *Christian Guardian*. Mackenzie countered, and an exchange of acrimonies followed which helped alienate the colony's largest denomination, with the most widely circulated newspaper.

A new theatre of operations for Mackenzie appeared with the incorporation of York as Toronto on 6 March 1834. Both Tories and Reformers presented slates of candidates in its first election on 27 March. Mackenzie was elected alderman, and the Reformers obtained a majority on the council. Mackenzie was chosen Toronto's first mayor by his fellow councillors, defeating John Rolph. As mayor, Mackenzie was both head of council and chief magistrate for the city. Deeply in debt, the city had an inadequate assessment law and needed many public works. The council was quarrelsome and difficult to manage. Yet, such as his opportunities were, Mackenzie failed to grasp them. In attack the "firebrand" could be magnificent, but he could not apply himself to the city's problems. Instead, he spent time on his favourite causes or in preparing for the next provincial election. A typical politician of the era, he got rid of Tory officials, gave patronage to his supporters, and was readier to hear contested elections against Tories than Reformers. His demands that his dignity be recognized when presiding over either council or court were manifestations of his fierce personal pride. With little precedent and unsatisfactory associates, he had a difficult task, complicated by a cholera epidemic, but his mayoralty, the highest office he was to hold, demonstrates that he was not the man to institute the reforms he demanded. That much could be done in Toronto, with the same financial problems and many of the same council members, was to be shown by succeeding mayors, both Reform and Tory. By mid-summer 1834 the council was ineffectual. The Reformers were roundly trounced in the elections for the 1835 council, and Mackenzie received the smallest vote given any of the candidates for alderman in his own ward.

In the provincial election of October 1834, some months before his term as mayor was completed, Mackenzie won the 2nd Riding of York, and the Reformers a majority in the assembly. Their chances had not been hurt by the storm of criticism from both Reform and Tory sources, including Egerton Ryerson, which greeted Mackenzie's publication in May 1834 of Joseph Hume's "baneful domination" letter, with its seeming call for independence for the colonies, even by the use of violence. In November 1834, sure that his assembly seat gave him a platform from which to seek reform, and depressed over the Colonial Office's inconsistency in the matter of Hagerman and Boulton, Mackenzie ceased publication of the *Advocate*. It passed to fellow Reformer William John O'Grady*. When the new Reform-dominated house met it quickly removed, at Mackenzie's initiative, all record of his previous expulsions. It then appointed him chairman of a special committee which three months later produced the *Seventh report on grievances*, an idiosyncratic, ill-organized, but overwhelming compendium of major and minor grievances together with every possible remedy. Appointed one of the government directors of the Welland Canal Company by the assembly, Mackenzie made a penetrating examination of its financial affairs which resulted in a committee of the house condemning it for excessively bad management, although their report shied away from accusing the directors of the outright dishonesty which some of the evidence suggested.

Despite Mackenzie's efforts, there was little chance reforms would be instituted because the new lieutenant governor, Sir Francis Bond Head*, had been instructed by the imperial authorities not to make concessions and Colonial Secretary Lord Glenelg had condemned the report on grievances. Head, originally seen as a reforming governor, soon disagreed with the moderate Reformers, including Robert Baldwin and Rolph, whom he had appointed to the Executive Council; he quarrelled with the Reform majority in the assembly, dissolved the legislature, and personally campaigned against the Reformers in the ensuing election. Mackenzie wept when he learned of his personal defeat by Edward William Thomson in July 1836. He could not believe that the people had deserted their champion. Corruption was the answer! He did not consider the possibility that Head's loyalty cry, combined with damage to the Reform cause by his own quarrel with the Methodist press over Hume's letter, might have influenced the outcome.

Within days of his defeat Mackenzie rushed into print a new paper, the *Constitution*, although he had forsworn journalism "forever" in 1834. It was supposed to appear, symbolically, on 4 July. Mackenzie's flirtation with American constitutional practices was moving towards its zenith. But despite continued evidence of corrupt or unjust practices, such as the rejection on a technicality of his petition to the house for an investigation of his defeat, Mackenzie wrote only of constitutional change.

In the spring of 1837, however, the tone began to change. The arrival of Lord John Russell's "Ten Resolutions" which removed all assembly control over the executive in Lower Canada seems to have finally satisfied Mackenzie that nothing could be hoped for from the imperial government. Increasingly the *Constitution* had references to possible armed resistance to oppression, although it also stressed the need to carry out reform constitutionally. By the summer of 1837 Mackenzie was organizing committees of vigilance and political unions and during August and September carried the message of Toronto Reformers to a series of meetings in the Home District. Resolutions were passed expressing extreme concern over the present state of the colony and calling for a convention of delegates from the various townships and from Lower Canada to discuss remedies. Probably Mackenzie himself had much to do with the wording of many resolutions, a few of which vaguely suggested a resort to force, but there is evidence that he was ambivalent on the subject or even completely opposed to an armed rising. The purpose of the political unions, Mackenzie wrote, was only to convince the government of the solidarity of the people in desiring reform. As well, it seems that no preparations were made for a rising. Between late July and the end of October only one military training session was held north of Toronto, and as late as September none of the men who would later lead the rebellion appears to have known of plans for one.

Gradually, experiencing the abuse and physical attacks of Orange gangs on one hand and the support of large crowds on the other, Mackenzie came to the decision that the only way to sweep away the rule of Head and the Compact and their Orange supporters was to lead these enthusiastic crowds into Toronto to overthrow the government. But this action he knew would not be easy. The people might indicate their enthusiasm for reform by attending meetings and even, some of them, by attending shooting practice, but they were basically conservative; they would need a push to persuade them to action.

At first Mackenzie attempted to present them with a *fait accompli.* Around the middle of October he called a meeting of ten radical Reformers at the house of John Doel*, a common Reform meeting place. He offered a plan to use "Dutcher's foundry-men and Armstrong's axe-makers," employees of radical Reformers who were also important industrialists in the city, to seize the government that evening, after which a general call would be issued for support. Head was particularly vulnerable to such action for earlier that month, in response to a request from Colborne, he had sent to Lower Canada every regular soldier in the province. When objections to Mackenzie's proposed *coup d'état* were raised at the meeting, he proposed instead that the farmers be organized to resist the government.

To circumvent the essential conservatism of even the reform-minded segment of the population and obtain respectability for his movement, Mackenzie resorted to an elaborate deception. He approached Rolph and Dr Thomas David Morrison* with the information that there were people outside Toronto preparing for a descent on the city. With the aid of one of his principal supporters in the country, Jesse Lloyd*, Mackenzie produced a letter from Thomas Storrow Brown* of Montreal which he claimed (untruthfully) conveyed a secret message that the Reformers of Lower Canada were prepared to rise, but desired a diversionary action by Upper Canadian Reformers to draw off the British troops. Rolph and Morrison, not entirely convinced, asked Mackenzie to do a further survey of popular feeling north of Toronto. Instead, in the third week of November he called a meeting of Reform leaders from strongly pro-Reform areas outside the city. Assisted by Lloyd and perhaps Silas Fletcher*, Mackenzie convinced this group that they could, with the support of Rolph, Morrison, and some members of the Family Compact who were said to be in favour of the scheme, remove the government in Toronto.

Having set 7 December as the date for action, Mackenzie returned to Toronto and presented his completed plan to Rolph and Morrison. Although they protested at the high-handed manner in which Mackenzie had treated them, his arguments that supporters were ready overcame their resistance and they agreed to join once the force had entered Toronto. When Rolph suggested the need for a military leader, Mackenzie asked Colonel Anthony Van Egmond*, an ardent foe of the Compact and a man of extensive military background who lived in the Huron Tract, to take command of the rebel forces. On 15 November Mackenzie had published in his newspaper a draft constitution based mainly on the American model, but incorporating English radical Reform ideas and elements of utilitarianism. He now arranged for more blatant warnings of his intent to be published, and planned a notice for 29 November that a provincial convention would meet on 31 December. It has never been clear what Mackenzie expected to do if the rising succeeded. He probably intended to have a provisional government headed by Rolph hold office until the convention met, when the members could discuss the draft constitution and settle on a form of government for Upper Canada. His plan may not have been this fully developed, but certainly the elements mentioned had some part in his thinking.

Returning to the country north of Toronto on 24 November, Mackenzie set about haphazardly organizing his supporters, urging friends to recruit their neighbours. No attempt appears to have been made to coordinate activities with the rising in Lower Canada, where revolt had begun in the third week of November. At a large meeting on 2 December in Stoufferville (Stouffville), some 25 miles northeast of Toronto, Mackenzie presented an expanded version of the plan he had used two weeks before. The Lower Canadians had risen and were carrying all before them, thus barring troops from reaching Upper Canada from the sea. A general rising had been arranged across Upper Canada. His listeners were to march to Toronto and take over the government, not a difficult task as over half the city was prepared to join them, including Reformers such as Rolph and Morrison, and important men such as Peter Robinson*, George Herchmer MARKLAND, and John Henry Dunn*, who would not normally be considered Reformers but who had shown their sympathy by resigning from Head's Executive Council. What he required of his listeners was not fighting but simply an armed demonstration to overawe any small groups of die-hard Tories. Once the lieutenant governor had been seized, Rolph's provisional government would distribute all the reserve lands to the people, notably 300 acres to each participant in the march on Toronto. Those who did not participate might, like the Tories of the American Revolution, have their land confiscated. Mackenzie was satisfied that enough men would rally on the appointed date at John Montgomery*'s tavern on Yonge St, several miles north of the city.

On Friday morning, 1 December, Mackenzie wrote a "Declaration of Independence" which would be printed over the week-end and distributed before Thursday's march. It carefully did not specify what exactly was to be done or when, but it would prepare people for action when word of the "demonstration" at Toronto reached them. On Sunday, 3 December Mackenzie rode back towards Toronto. He learned that Rolph, upon hearing false rumours of preparations for defence by the government, had sent a message to Samuel Lount*, a Reform leader north of the city, requesting him to act with a few hundred men on Monday. Mackenzie tried to stop this action, but Lount and his men had already started to march south to Montgomery's.

On Monday night, after the first few score had arrived at the rallying point, a dispute arose as to whether the men, tired from a long day's march over muddy roads should go into Toronto immediately or wait till morning. Mackenzie's position is unclear, but he did decide that a scouting expedition, including himself, should check Toronto's preparedness. It met several persons investigating rumours, including Alderman John Powell, who, after killing Anthony Anderson, the only one of Mackenzie's men with military experience, escaped and warned the city.

By Tuesday Mackenzie had become so overwrought that his actions were extremely erratic. He spent much of the day attempting to inflict punishment on the families or property of individual Tories instead of marching his men into Toronto. The secondary commanders, such as Lount and David GIBSON, were astonished and tried to stop him and apologize to the victims. John Rolph, who had been sent by the lieutenant governor to dissuade the rebels from their plans, urged Mackenzie to enter the city in mid-afternoon. Finally, on Tuesday night Mackenzie and his force approached the city, but shots from a small party of loyalist guards led by Sheriff William Botsford JARVIS easily dispersed the confused marchers. Only now did Mackenzie

show some sense of the necessities of command, but his efforts to reorganize his forces, who had been led to believe they would meet little or no opposition, failed. Many men who had come for an armed demonstration and found instead a violent rebellion went home that night and the next day.

On Wednesday Mackenzie seized the mail coach which ran west of Toronto, while the majority of his forces, with new arrivals replacing men who went home on Tuesday, sat at Montgomery's Tavern. On the original day set for the rebellion, 7 December, the defenders of Toronto, armed by the government and reinforced by large numbers arriving from loyal areas outside the city, marched to Montgomery's and easily defeated the much smaller and poorly armed force of hard-core rebels and recent arrivals who had not yet learned the true situation. Van Egmond, reaching Montgomery's Tavern only a few hours before because of the change of date, had warned that the position was hopeless, but Mackenzie, highly agitated, had "put a pistol to his head" and ordered him to carry out what was a hopeless defence.

The ease with which most leaders of the rebellion and many of the rank and file escaped to the United States gives some support to Mackenzie's contention that the vast majority of people, both Tory and Reformer, did not actively oppose the rebellion and were favourable to reform, if not to rebellion. Still, Mackenzie suffered a great deal in trying to avoid his loyalist pursuers and reach the American shore near Niagara.

A growing interest in Canadian affairs among residents of the American frontier had been fed by a letter asking for assistance in the rising which Mackenzie had dispatched to a Buffalo newspaper from Montgomery's on 6 December. The arrival of Rolph at Lewiston had also caused a great commotion. Mackenzie reached the American side on 11 December and spoke to a sympathetic audience the next day concerning the desire of Upper Canadians to be free. He then interested himself in a scheme to invade Upper Canada, with the help of American volunteers commanded by Rensselaer Van Rensselaer*, from Navy Island in the Niagara River. Despite the arrival in the next several weeks of food, shot, cannon, and several hundred volunteers, the attempt failed because Van Rensselaer and Mackenzie disagreed on tactics and because British troops and Canadian militia led by Allan MacNab bombarded the island and destroyed the Patriot supply ship, *Caroline*. Many of the volunteers had already left when the American government

Mackenzie

warned the expedition to abandon the island or be prosecuted as criminals. At this time Mackenzie took his ailing wife, who had joined him, to Buffalo, and was arrested for having violated American neutrality laws. Released on bail, he returned to Navy Island, but on 14 Jan. 1838 Van Rensselaer insisted that the Patriot force withdraw to the American shore. Mackenzie settled in New York City that month.

He remained convinced for a time that a majority of Upper Canadians were ready to rise if given some sign of substantial aid, such as an invasion by sympathetic Americans. By the end of 1838, however, opposition from the American government, poor organization, and apathy prevented attacks against Canada. Mackenzie himself had taken little or no part in organizing raids after February 1838, and came to recognize that ill-organized expeditions, by increasing the pressure on the Upper Canadian government, intensified the persecution of Reformers without offering them any chance of freedom. In January 1839 he moved to Rochester, where in March he and John Montgomery founded an association to organize Canadian exiles and prevent further rash expeditions. Not all its resolutions were made public, but deduction suggests it would act against Canada only in case of war between the United States and Britain. Canadian exiles gave the association little support and funds were scarce. By late 1839 Mackenzie, beset by personal problems and discouraged by American attitudes and the failure of the association, turned his mind from thoughts of invading Canada.

In April 1838 the remainder of Mackenzie's family had crossed to New York, though he had little income to provide for them and large debts incurred before the rebellion. Generous supporters had lent enough money to start a newspaper, *Mackenzie's Gazette*, in New York in May 1838. At first, American interest in affairs on the border, curiosity about Mackenzie and his journalism, and a desire to help the Canadian cause, brought in many subscriptions. In August 1839, however, by attacking Whig banking policy, Mackenzie took sides in American politics for the first time. In December he attacked the Democratic government of Martin Van Buren as a tool of British tyranny because it had issued a neutrality proclamation. Gradually such political comments, and lagging interest in Canadian affairs, cut the number of readers and left Mackenzie in even more serious financial difficulties. Moreover, to his chagrin, many Canadian exiles, Rolph and Bidwell among them, would have nothing to do with him.

His trial for breaking the neutrality laws had finally been held in June 1839. Mackenzie, who fancied himself a legal expert, conducted his own elaborate and contorted defence, but was sentenced to a $10 fine and 18 months in jail. Already badly in debt, he found the added expense of carrying on his newspaper from prison the last straw. Cash donations and new subscriptions came in reply to his pleas for aid, but lack of money was a constant harassment. The *Gazette* appeared erratically.

Other factors made conditions worse. The unhealthy jail, set in a bog containing factory effluent, soon made Mackenzie very ill. In November one of his children was near death, and his wife became sick. The following month his mother, his greatest supporter through the many crises of his life, died. He learned that President Van Buren was loath to show him any mercy for fear of antagonizing Britain. By February 1840 Mackenzie was so depressed that he wrote a friend of being "entombed alive." He memorialized the grand jury of Monroe County, the governor of New York, the attorney general, and the secretary of state, even the president himself. Numerous petitions were also presented on his behalf. Mackenzie's memorials were at first carefully reasoned requests, later pleas, and finally harsh criticisms, a familiar pattern in his correspondence.

In May 1840 he was pardoned, after serving less than one year. With a keen sense of injustice he began to plot further violations of American neutrality, asking for "shrewd and daring fellows" to burn English-owned ships, barracks, and warehouses in Canada. The *Gazette* criticized American life for not being what it claimed, and Van Buren for his shabby treatment of Mackenzie. He was, however, too late for vengeance on either the United States or Britain. The frontier was settling down. In September 1838 Mackenzie had taken the first step towards becoming an American citizen. His future was now in the United States, a country with which he was already becoming disillusioned. Thus a recurring theme in Mackenzie's correspondence during these unhappy years was the question of amnesty. As others, including Louis-Joseph Papineau*, were granted relief, he became increasingly frustrated. Too proud to petition directly himself, although he admitted the rebellion was an error, he asked such influential Reformers as Isaac Buchanan* to intercede on his behalf. Meanwhile, he watched impatiently while the changing political picture to the north passed him by.

Money problems, inability to find work he wanted or would accept, increasing family illness and death, continued to make his life a misery. He was constantly a focus of controversy. Nevertheless, he retained his ability to attract such friends and patrons as Horace Greeley*. *Mackenzie's Gazette* died in December 1840 for want of donations and circulation, and the political patronage denied with the election of the Whig party. In April 1841 he successfully launched the *Rochester Volunteer*, which struggled through 17 irregular issues. In it Mackenzie examined Canadian affairs and attempted to whip up war between Great Britain and the United States over the trial of Alexander McLeod*, a Canadian arrested in New York State in November 1840 and charged with murder and arson for his part in the *Caroline* incident. Despite Mackenzie's efforts, American public opinion was not aroused and McLeod was acquitted. The affair provides a good example of Mackenzie's single-mindedness; in his determination to "free" Upper Canada by involving Americans he failed to grasp the possible consequences of his actions, including the ravaging of the province by war.

The *Volunteer* last appeared in September 1841, and Mackenzie, lacking both money and influence, voiced his disillusionment: " . . . the more I see of this country the more bitterly I regret the attempt at revolution at Toronto." In June 1842 he and his family left Rochester for New York City, where he worked at various publishing ventures but refused to accept an editor's post with a newspaper. In August, however, he became actuary and librarian of the mechanics' institute. The small salary of about $400 was supplemented by a dwelling. Though his duties were "rather wearysome," he was able to make ends meet. In April 1843 he took out American citizenship.

By that fall he was preparing a collective biography of 500 Irish Patriots, planning a new paper, and negotiating for a patronage appointment as an inspector in the New York Customs House. He ended his connection with the mechanics' institute and began publishing the *Examiner*, which failed after five issues. The customs post did not materialize, but the first part of *The sons of the emerald isle* appeared in early 1844, and came close to paying expenses. In July of that year he was appointed a customs clerk at a yearly salary of $700 but resigned in June 1845 when a conservative was appointed collector of customs.

While at the customs house Mackenzie copied, or appropriated, for publication the papers of Jesse Hoyt, a former customs official closely connected with President Van Buren and the Al-

bany Regency which long ran New York State. The Hoyt book sold 50,000 copies, but Mackenzie, who made nothing on the work, was criticized for publishing private papers simply to air scandals involving his enemy, Van Buren. Undaunted, Mackenzie proceeded with the second part of his Irish biographies and in April 1846 published a highly critical life of Van Buren.

In May 1846 Mackenzie went to Albany to cover the state constitutional convention for Horace Greeley's *New York Daily Tribune*. It proved to be a radical convention, establishing elected offices and abolishing institutions such as the Court of Chancery; its decisions greatly influenced Mackenzie's political opinions in Canada during the 1850s. He stayed in Albany until the spring of 1847, editing the *Albany Patriot*. Returning to New York, in the winter of 1847–48 he worked at the *Tribune* and edited almanacs for Greeley.

In February 1849 the Canadian administration of Robert Baldwin and Louis-Hippolyte LA FONTAINE brought in sweeping reforms, including an amnesty act. Mackenzie had written abjectly to James Leslie*, the provincial secretary, and was included in the amnesty. He immediately began a tour of Canada from Montreal to Niagara, though he claimed that he was not so much anxious to return permanently as he was to obtain the right to come back if he chose. Repatriation involved problems of employment. Mackenzie's independent ideas prevented him from working for Lesslie's Toronto *Examiner* – he deplored its annexationist sympathies – and he wanted his own paper. He was also worried about legal action on his debts. Although he visited Toronto and Niagara again late in 1849, he did not remain. In January 1850 Greeley, who had proven to be as patient a patron in the United States as the Lesslies had been in Scotland and Canada, gave him a job as Washington correspondent for the *New York Daily Tribune*, but in April 1850 he left that paper and by early May was again a Torontonian, though fearful as to his reception and unsure as to how he could support his family.

He continued to write for the *Tribune*, contributed to the *Niagara Mail*, and wrote regularly for the *Examiner*. Lesslie offered him a permanent position with the paper in order to further the cause of uncompromising radical reform, but Mackenzie would not commit himself to full-time work for any employer. Instead he pinned his hopes on the collection of money he believed was still owed him from the 1830s. York County paid him $1,200, and he received from the provincial government £250 for his services as a Welland Canal commissioner. He ignored his creditors for the present and concentrated on being re-elected to parliament. In the spring of 1851 he won the seat in Haldimand County, defeating among others George Brown*, editor of the *Globe*, who was at a disadvantage because of Mackenzie's current notoriety, and especially because of his own known anti-Catholic bias, in a riding with a large Catholic vote.

Once elected, Mackenzie supported measures of "true reform" no matter which party or faction in the assembly presented them. He became involved in many issues left unsettled from the 1830s, such as the clergy reserves, state aid to religious colleges, and the Court of Chancery. Always worried about government overspending and monopoly control, Mackenzie now became a foe of government aid to railways, and of railways which took state aid but had neither competitors nor public control to encourage economy and honesty while building. His long-standing suspicions of lawyers and the complications of law prompted him to introduce a measure to simplify and codify the law and to make it easy for citizens to plead their own cases. This latter measure, which he reintroduced in later sessions, was one of those policies which, together with his sometimes impish, sometimes waspish behaviour, caused him to be regarded as eccentric. On this and other measures he stood virtually alone, thus gradually earning the reputation of being harmless as well.

In 1851, however, he did not seem harmless. He carried out one of those damning investigations of government affairs for which he was always noted, and through his attacks on the Court of Chancery was considered instrumental in forcing the resignation of Robert Baldwin as premier. [*see* William Hume BLAKE]. It was also believed that Mackenzie, by campaigning against what he and Lesslie called "sham" Reformers, helped defeat several colleagues, including Baldwin, in the fall elections. As a result, Mackenzie could not be ignored in 1852 when Francis Hincks* was consulting with the new Clear Grit movement about a merger of Reform groups. Mackenzie was asked to attend the negotiations, but refused in order to maintain his "freedom of action." Once Rolph and Malcolm Cameron* had entered the ministry of Hincks and Augustin-Norbert MORIN, Rolph consulted Mackenzie on appointments in Haldimand and even offered him a well-paid job. This offer was refused when Mackenzie discovered the position would be specially created and would further burden taxpayers.

From this high point Mackenzie's importance gradually decreased. His attacks on government mismanagement and hypocrisy towards reform soon alienated Hincks and Rolph. His indignation against false Reformers reached new heights with the revelation in May 1853 of the "£10,000 Job" in which Hincks and Toronto mayor John George BOWES had made profits at public expense by dealing in railway debentures. Mackenzie also strongly attacked the government, including Rolph and Cameron, for selling out principle to secure office. He did one final bit of damage to his relationship with Rolph in March and April 1854 with a detailed assault on him in *Mackenzie's Weekly Message* (notably after Rolph had failed to consult Mackenzie over appointments in Haldimand) for what he asserted were Rolph's treasonable actions during the flag of truce missions at the time of the 1837 rising.

In other areas affairs also went badly for Mackenzie. In late 1852 he had managed to offend his greatest Canadian supporter and perhaps truest friend, James Lesslie, by refusing to allow him to edit an intemperate letter on crown lands policy. Lesslie closed the columns of the *Examiner* to him and, although they were reconciled, Mackenzie at that time founded his own paper, the *Message* (later the *Toronto Weekly Message*). Friends put up $2,000 and subscriptions poured in at first, but within a year the paper was in financial trouble. At the same time old creditors increasingly bothered him. His well-documented attacks on the government reached only a limited readership in the *Message*, and the orgy of official patronage and reckless spending by an obviously corrupt government sickened Mackenzie of the whole process of responsible government. These abuses made him anxious for "democratic" reforms so that the government would be controlled by the people rather than politicians. Almost all of the legislation he proposed in the early 1850s did not pass, however. Mackenzie also managed to alienate the most important critic of the government, George Brown, by constant public reference to the hypocrisy of Brown's Reform stance and to his impolitic attacks on Catholics. These actions served no purpose since Mackenzie regularly supported Brown in every election as the best of a bad lot.

Cut off from all the influential Reformers, disgusted with the politics of the day, in grave financial difficulties, by the summer of 1853 Mackenzie had started to question the value of the union as well. By mid 1854 he was convinced that the French Canadians received far more than they contributed, and all at the expense of Upper Canada. The answer, he increasingly believed, was to dissolve the union.

Mackenzie was given one more chance, in the

years 1854 to 1857, to help create over-all policy for the Reform movement. By 1854 his advice was being sought in correspondence from most of the founders of the Clear Grit movement, as well as other prominent Grits, including James Lesslie, David Christie*, Charles Lindsey, William McDougall*, and Alexander Mackenzie*; all felt Mackenzie was a true Reformer, if a somewhat muddled thinker. They were disillusioned with the Hincks-Morin brand of reform but supported Hincks as long as he was in office because the Tory alternative was unacceptable. When the government resigned in September 1854, a defeat which Hincks rightly or wrongly partially attributed to Mackenzie's well-argued attacks, they began to seek a more conscientious Reform party. Naturally enough they wanted to include Mackenzie.

In November 1854 Lesslie proposed uniting the *Examiner* and McDougall's *North American* with the *Message* and giving Mackenzie complete managerial and editorial control of this powerful "independent" journal. Mackenzie refused because others would hold stock in the journal, thus threatening his independence of action. His Grit correspondents next tried to get him to support Brown, whom they came to accept over the next year or two as the only viable leader, even if his reform principles were less satisfactory than they would have wished. But Mackenzie persisted in attacking Brown, though in 1857 he did briefly cooperate in establishing a Reform executive committee centred around the *Globe* editor. By that year only David Christie still attempted to include Mackenzie in any Reform grouping.

In the assembly Mackenzie doggedly advocated his own proposals. From 1854 to 1857 he successfully introduced measures to convert decimal currency, to simplify the handling of controverted elections, and to have mayors elected directly rather than by city councils, and he supported as well such popular measures as the abolition of the clergy reserves, the election of legislative councillors, privately financed railways, and reciprocity. As chairman of the finance committee in 1854–55 he dug out evidence of financial mismanagement and misuse of patronage so extensive as to embarrass the Conservative government of Sir Allan MacNab and John A. Macdonald*. His legislative accomplishments were impressive for a private member and his criticisms were pointed and effective, but his critics dismissed him because more was expected of him than of others. Mackenzie became convinced that the age was so corrupt and the union so intolerable a burden that little reform could be

accomplished. His financial problems worsened, making him even more misanthropic. In February 1855 he was forced to stop the *Message*, but he refused full-time jobs with the *Examiner* and the *Weekly Globe*. When the *Examiner* ceased, Mackenzie resumed the *Message* in December 1855, although he could not afford it. Finally, in March 1856, Lesslie, Archibald Alexander Riddell, and others started a campaign to raise funds to reward Mackenzie for his untiring efforts. About $7,500 was ultimately collected and though Mackenzie wanted a trip to England, a house was bought and a loan made to keep the *Message* alive.

In August 1858, his strength failing and having lost all hopes for the future of Upper Canada, he resigned his seat. He published the *Message* only sporadically and refused requests that he run for the Legislative Council or for mayor of Toronto. He abandoned ideas for a new Upper Canadian constitution, and increasingly through 1858 and 1859 discussed annexation to the United States if the people became thoroughly disillusioned with responsible government. When he resumed regular publication of the *Message* in June 1859, he called for independence from Britain and suggested that annexation would inevitably follow.

His spirits improved a little as donations to the "Homestead" fund were received. He approved of the list of necessary reforms produced by the Reform convention of 1859, although he refused to sit on one of the committees because he represented no riding. His removal from day to day politics also improved his spirits. Although he helped friends in the election of 1861, the *Message* all but ceased noticing political events and its final comments on the fate of Upper Canada showed a certain mellowness. Mackenzie now saw not annexation but some union of Britain, the United States, Canada, and Ireland as the answer to problems. He even enjoyed friendly relations with George Brown in 1861. In fact, in late June 1861, only two months before he died, Mackenzie was improved enough in spirit to toy with the idea of again running for the legislature.

He could not be called a happy man, nevertheless. His creditors plagued him, he felt himself growing old, and no help seemed in sight for his beloved province. In his last months, periods of mental confusion must have discouraged him, for he refused all medicine. On 28 Aug. 1861 Mackenzie suffered an "apoplectic seizure" which proved fatal.

During the 1850s Mackenzie's image of himself as a lone individual battling against overwhelming odds in an heroic struggle was reinforced by

Mackenzie

many letters praising his efforts, even if these were seldom successful. This praise probably as much as his own will sustained him in his struggle. Although he had the satisfaction of seeing George Brown adopt some of his ideas, his concern for popular democracy went largely unrewarded. He was not the leader in the 1850s that he had been in the 1830s: he was not an effective back-room political organizer; he did not hold the public meetings which had been his most effective means of reaching the people; and, as he quite rightly said, the age was too affluent. People were willing to accept corruption and mismanagement while their pockets were full. But although Mackenzie died without ever putting himself at the head of other men with similar views, the radical tradition he represented pervaded Ontario politics until well after confederation.

Historical evaluation of Mackenzie has continued to reflect the verdict of Charles Lindsey who in 1862 gave Mackenzie almost sole credit, or discredit, for the Upper Canadian rebellion. At the same time Lindsey elevated the rebellion to a place of respectability, incorrectly claiming that it was necessary to Canada's attainment of responsible government. But this essentially heroic conception of Mackenzie ignores certain aspects of his character and perpetuates certain historical misconceptions; to place him in balance it is necessary to consider the whole man. He was very much the typical merchant, proprietor, and entrepreneurial radical of his era who, despite his talk of improving the status of workers and farmers, resisted strikes in his own shop and could be as ruthless as any of the great merchants in collecting debts. He displayed little love for minorities, especially Jews and blacks, and though he wrote enthusiastic articles about elevating the poor, his accomplishments in this area do not equal those of Jesse Ketchum, the Baldwins, or John Strachan. A puritan with a mission and an indefatigable journalist compelled to thrust himself into the public eye, Mackenzie did much to popularize other people's ideas and expressed with complete sincerity the grievances felt by many Upper Canadians prior to the rebellion. The times were ripe for a man of his talents. However, his image as a solitary and fearless victim of Tory persecution ignores the fact that other Reformers also suffered and that the harassment was usually on a personal rather than an official basis and in numerous cases was occasioned by his own pugnacity. Despite his demand that others be consistent, he could not distinguish major grievances from trivia and was himself changeable. His economic thinking displays a dichotomy; he eulogized 18th century rural values, yet he admired the advance of commerce and technology. He resisted government intervention in the economy, but the development of Upper Canada was only made possible by long-term financing and public investment. Finally, the credit often given Mackenzie for creating a new political era in Canada through rebellion ignores the significance of new social and economic conditions, external influences, and the efforts of those moderate Reformers and Tories who actually negotiated new terms of government.

Though Mackenzie was consistent in his fear of monopolies, and in his demand for free government and an end to favouritism and prodigality, the events of his later years, which historians have badly neglected, show that he could not evolve beyond a certain set of ideas and that he never found an acceptable form of government in Upper Canada, the United States, or the union of the Canadas. His overwhelming urge to reform everything, his suspicion of all in power, and his fierce pride in his own independence suggest that Mackenzie's only decided policy was *je suis contre*. Yet the very determination with which he attacked those he saw as enemies of Upper Canada was always fuelled by his desire to somehow make his adopted home a better place. His deep love for Upper Canada and his fervent devotion to its exclusive interests would suggest that Mackenzie was, in essence, an early Ontario nationalist.

FREDERICK H. ARMSTRONG
and RONALD J. STAGG

[The two major collections of Mackenzie papers are those in the PAO (Mackenzie-Lindsey papers) collected by Mackenzie himself and those in the PAC (MG 24, B18) collected by William Lyon Mackenzie King*. The PAO collection has been augmented with facsimiles of Mackenzie correspondence from American collections such as the William Henry Seward papers at the University of Rochester Library (Rochester, N.Y.). Almost all of the pre-1837 Mackenzie papers were destroyed by his family during the rebellion, but a few letters from Mackenzie survive in the John Neilson coll. (PAC, MG 24, B1) and the Lesslie papers at the Dundas Hist. Soc. Museum (Dundas, Ont.). The latter collection, as well as the George Brown papers (PAC, MG 24, B40), contain material on Mackenzie's later career. Three collections at the PAC contain statements by various participants regarding his conduct during the rebellion: RG 1, E3; RG 5, A1; and PRO, CO 42 (mfm.). The Rebellion of 1837 papers at the PAO also contain useful material. A critical view of Mackenzie at the time of the rebellion, as well as some material on his later career, can be found in the John Rolph papers

(PAC, MG 24, B24). The David Gibson papers at the PAO contain occasional references to Mackenzie prior to and following the rising of 1837, as well as significant material concerning the rebellion itself and Mackenzie's involvement in it.

Available only in typescript form is a biography of Mackenzie written by W. D. Le Sueur* which deals principally with his political career (copies may be seen at the University of Toronto Archives, the PAC, and the PAO). The biography was challenged in the courts by the Lindsey family on the grounds that it misinterpreted material in the Mackenzie-Lindsey papers, and was never published.

Printed primary sources relating to Mackenzie's career are also numerous. The various publications of the government when he was a member should be noted, especially Upper Canada, House of Assembly, *The seventh report from the select committee on grievances . . .* (Toronto, 1835). A very useful account by a contemporary is F. B. Head, *A narrative* (London, 1839), which was published in 1969 edited by S. F. Wise. Mackenzie himself was a prolific writer of books and pamphlets. Most important of these are *A new almanack for the Canadian true blues . . .* (2nd ed., York [Toronto], [1833?]), written under the pseudonym Patrick Swift; *Sketches of Canada and the United States* (London, 1833); *Mackenzie's own narrative of the late rebellion, with illustrations and notes, critical and explanatory . . .* (Toronto, 1838); *The sons of the emerald isle, or, lives of one thousand remarkable Irishmen . . .* (New York, 1844); *The lives and opinions of Benj'n Franklin Butler . . . and Jesse Hoyt . . .* (Boston, 1845); and *The life and times of Martin Van Buren . . .* (Boston, 1846).

Mackenzie's own newspapers are invaluable sources, the main ones being the *Colonial Advocate*, 1824–34; the *Constitution* (Toronto), 1836–37; the *Correspondent and Advocate* (Toronto), 1834–37; *Mackenzie's Gazette* (New York), 1838–40; the *Rochester Volunteer* (Rochester, N.Y.), 1841–42; and *Mackenzie's Weekly Message* (Toronto), 1852–60. Selections have been made by Margaret Fairley, *The selected writings of William Lyon Mackenzie, 1824–1837* (Toronto, 1960), and A. W. Rasporich, *William Lyon Mackenzie* (Toronto, 1972). Another newspaper to be consulted is the *Canadian Correspondent* ([Toronto]), 1832–34; it was edited by William John O'Grady and took a radical view. Egerton Ryerson's *Christian Guardian*, begun in 1829, shows the Methodist view of Mackenzie's activities. Papers in opposition to Mackenzie were the *Canadian Freeman* (York [Toronto]) edited by Francis Collins, a Reformer, and the *Courier of Upper Canada* (Toronto) edited by George Gurnett, a Tory; only incomplete runs of these papers survive. The *Patriot and Farmers' Monitor* (Toronto), begun in Kingston in 1828, was edited by Thomas Dalton*, who moved from the Reform to the Tory camp. Mackenzie also wrote for a great number of newspapers which he did not edit, including Horace Greeley's *New York Daily Tribune* and James Lesslie's *Examiner* (Toronto).

An account of Mackenzie's Toronto appears in Scadding, *Toronto of old* (Armstrong) and a description and valuable documents in *Town of York, 1815–34* (Firth). The first major interpretation of Mackenzie's political career was by John Charles Dent* in *Last forty years* and *Upper Canadian rebellion*. The latter provoked a response by John King*, Mackenzie's son-in-law, *The other side of the "Story," being some reviews of Mr. J. C. Dent's first volume of "The story of the Upper Canadian rebellion," and the letters in the Mackenzie-Rolph controversy . . .* (Toronto, 1886). At the end of the 19th century two more accounts appeared: Robina and K. M. Lizars, *Humours of '37, grave, gay, grim: rebellion times in the Canadas* (Toronto, 1897), and D. B. Read, *The Canadian rebellion of 1837* (Toronto, 1896). A decade later the original Mackenzie biography by Charles Lindsey, *Life and times of Mackenzie*, was revised by G. G. S. Lindsey, Mackenzie's grandson, and published as *William Lyon Mackenzie* (Toronto, 1909).

Modern studies of the Mackenzie era began with Aileen Dunham, *Political unrest in Upper Canada, 1815–1836* (London, 1927; repr. Toronto, 1963). This work was followed many years later by Craig, *Upper Canada*. There are two modern biographies: William Kilbourn, *The firebrand: William Lyon Mackenzie and the rebellion in Upper Canada* (Toronto, 1956), and David Flint, *William Lyon Mackenzie: rebel against authority* (Toronto, 1971). S. D. Clark, *Movements of political protest in Canada, 1640–1840* (Toronto, 1959), provides a sociological analysis of the rebellion.

There is also a large periodical literature, including two comprehensive and analytical articles: Eric Jackson, "The organization of Upper Canadian Reformers, 1818–1867," *OH*, LIII (1961), 95–115, and F. C. Hamil, "The reform movement in Upper Canada," *Profiles of a province: studies in the history of Ontario . . .* (Toronto, 1967), 9–19. Articles more specifically on Mackenzie's career written by L. F. Gates, who is also preparing a biography of Mackenzie's later years, include "The decided policy of William Lyon Mackenzie," *CHR*, XL (1959), 185–208; "*Mackenzie's Gazette*: an aspect of W. L. Mackenzie's American years," *CHR*, XLVI (1965), 323–45; and "W. L. Mackenzie's *Volunteer* and the first parliament of united Canada," *OH*, LIX (1967), 163–83. R. A. MacKay provides an interesting discussion in "The political ideas of William Lyon Mackenzie," *Canadian Journal of Economics and Political Science* (Toronto), III (1937), 1–22. John Moir discusses his American journalism in "Mr. Mackenzie's secret reporter," *OH*, LV (1963), 205–13, and John Ireland [M.L. Magill] discusses the *Caroline* incident in "Andrew Drew: the man who burned the *Caroline*," *OH*, LIX (1967), 137–56. F. H. Armstrong has written "The York riots of March 23, 1832," *OH*, LV (1963), 61–72; "Reformer as capitalist: William Lyon Mackenzie and the printers' strike of 1836," *OH*, LIX (1967), 187–96; "William Lyon Mackenzie, first mayor of Toronto: a study of a critic in power," *CHR*, XLVIII (1967), 309–31; and "William Lyon Mackenzie: the persistent hero," *Journal of Canadian Studies* (Peterborough, Ont.), VI, no.3 (August 1971), 21–36. J. E. Rea has prepared a bibliog-

MacKinlay

raphy in "Rebellion in Upper Canada, 1837," HSSM, *Trans*. (Winnipeg), 3rd ser., no.22 (1965–66), 87–94, as well as "William Lyon Mackenzie – Jacksonian?" *Mid-America: an Hist. Quarterly* (Chicago), L (1968), 223–35. F.H.A. and R.J.S.]

MacKINLAY (Mackinlay, McKinlay, Mckinley), ANDREW, businessman and philanthropist; b. 1800 in Stirlingshire, Scotland, the son of John MacKinlay; m. first on 26 Jan. 1829 Barbara Goodfellow (d. 1833), by whom he had four children and secondly, on 8 Aug. 1836, Margaret Alardyce, by whom he had seven children; d. 29 Sept. 1867 at Halifax, N.S.

It is not known when Andrew MacKinlay immigrated to Nova Scotia, but by 1826 he had opened a book and stationery store in Halifax. In 1827 he was joined by his brother William, thus forming the firm of A. and W. MacKinlay. Initially, the MacKinlays concentrated on building a solid reputation as sellers of books, paper products, and writing implements. However, with increasing interest in education in the province during the 1850s, the firm expanded and began reprinting school texts. They were also the original publishers of some locally written books, including Dr Hugo Reid*'s *Elements of geography* . . . , printed in 1856 with B. Dawson of Montreal.

The subsequent success of the firm as publishers depended largely on a willingness to venture into areas neglected by their competitors. When the Irish National Series was authorized for provincial schools in the late 1850s, the MacKinlays stereotyped most of the volumes and reprinted them in Halifax, while their rivals impatiently awaited the arrival of their expensive American editions. Such an astute business manoeuvre paid off; in 1864 the firm was awarded the government contract for the Nova Scotia Series of Readers. Maps were another educational venture; the firm's 1862 chart of Nova Scotia received a bronze medal at the 1867 Paris exposition.

Over the years Andrew MacKinlay became associated with other local business concerns, the most notable being the Halifax Gas, Light, and Water Company, organized in 1840. In 1842 he was appointed a director and served as president from 1855 until his death. His business success enabled him to leave an estate valued at more than $38,000.

MacKinlay had first become involved with education in 1835, when he joined the mechanics' institute, an organization devoted to adult education in the natural sciences. According to the newspaper accounts of MacKinlay's early lectures, electricity and magnetism were his chief interests. He advanced rapidly in the institute, serving two long terms as president (1838–49, 1855–67); he was apparently a driving force behind the organization, since it was dissolved shortly after his death. His interest in education was evident in other fields as well. He was instrumental in the founding of the Presbyterian Free Church College in Halifax in 1848, and served as its chairman (1852–61) and as a board member (1864–67). From 1849 to 1867 he was a member of the board for Dalhousie College, and from 1852 to 1865 a school commissioner in Halifax.

MacKinlay's concern for community development was a second significant aspect of his career. During his lifetime he was associated with nearly 20 of the influential political, educational, and social organizations in Halifax. His involvement with civic affairs began in 1841 when he was chosen an alderman for the city of Halifax. He later served twice as mayor (1845–46, 1851–52). In 1846 he was appointed a justice of the peace with special jurisdiction over insolvent debtors, an office he retained until his death. In 1855 his long civic career was rewarded with the office of *custos rotulorum* for Halifax County, and he filled this position until 1867. The next year he was appointed chairman of the committee for erecting a new courthouse. At the time of his death he was chairman of the local committee for the Paris exposition, an office he had earlier held for the 1851 London exhibition.

His third great interest was the welfare of the young and handicapped. Although he was influential as a board member of the Protestant Orphans' Home (1860–67), his most lasting contribution in this field was his work with the Institution for the Deaf and Dumb, founded in 1856. In his capacity as board chairman (1857–67), MacKinlay did much to lay the foundations for the school's continued success and sound reputation.

Andrew MacKinlay was respected in Halifax as "a sagacious Scotchman of more than ordinary literary and scientific attainments, and of good business habits."

LOIS K. KERNAGHAN

PANS, RG 32, 35, no.64; Vertical MSS file, Andrew MacKinlay. St Andrew's Presbyterian Church (Halifax), records, 1818–1916 (mfm. at PANS). *Acadian Recorder*, 4 Oct. 1867. *Presbyterian Witness* (Halifax), 5 Oct. 1867. *Belcher's farmer's almanack*, 1833–67. W. P. Bell, *A genealogical study* (2v., Sackville, N.B., 1962). *The city of Halifax, the capital of Nova Scotia, Canada: its advantages and facilities* (Halifax, 1909).

Halifax and its business: containing historical sketch, and description of the city and its institutions . . . (Halifax, 1876).

McKINNON (M'Kinnon, MacKinnon), WILLIAM CHARLES, editor, author, and Methodist clergyman; b. 19 April 1828 at Sydney, N.S., the son of John McKinnon and named for his grandfather, William McKinnon*, loyalist and provincial secretary of Cape Breton; m. a Miss Crane, and they had two children; d. 26 March 1862 at Shelburne, N.S.

By 1844, at age 16, William Charles McKinnon had written several poems. That year he published a long work, entitled *The battle of the Nile; a poem, in four cantos*, which a modern writer has described as "an exercise in youthful colonial patriotism." He was also intensely interested in all branches of science, studying astronomy, navigation, and, particularly, geology, which became a lifelong interest. He began a work on ornithology, but it was unfinished at his death.

In 1846 he commenced publishing at Sydney what was then Cape Breton's only newspaper, the *Cape Breton Spectator* (later renamed the *Times and Cape Breton Spectator*). When this paper ceased publication in 1850 McKinnon issued the *Commercial Herald* for a few months. His political interests were liberal and he was attracted to republican views to such an extent that friends were alienated and financial support was withdrawn from his newspaper enterprise. He went to Boston in 1851, where he wrote briefly for magazines. Ill health caused his return to Canada in 1852.

His writing continued throughout this period. In 1850 he had published *St. Castine; a legend of Cape-Breton*, and in 1851, *Frances, or Pirate Cove*. His book *St. George: or, the Canadian League*, a tale published in 1852, was inspired by the "recent late rebellion" and was dedicated to Sir Edward Bulwer-Lytton "by his humble and ardent admirer."

Shortly after the publication of *St. George* he was strongly attracted to the Methodist ministry, and undertook studies directed by Robert E. Cranc on the Sydney circuit. He first preached at Bedeque, P.E.I., in 1853, then at Guysborough and Canso, N.S., in 1855, Bedeque again in 1856, and Middle Musquodoboit, N.S., in 1857. In 1857 he was ordained at Sackville, N.B., and became a minister at Shelburne, N.S., in 1861. There he died the following year at age 34.

McKinnon held strong views on many subjects. In addition to his early republicanism, which he later regretted, he waged fanatic pulpit and newspaper battles against Roman Catholics, Calvinists, and Baptists alike. In his more positive defence of the Methodist faith, he wrote clearly and effectively, and was a popular lecturer and newspaper correspondent.

MINERVA TRACY

W. C. McKinnon, *The battle of the Nile; a poem, in four cantos* (Sydney, N.S., 1844); *The divine sovereignty; a sermon . . .* (Halifax, 1861); *Frances, or Pirate Cove; a legend of Cape Breton* ([Halifax], 1851); *The papacy: the sacrifice of the Mass . . .* (Halifax, 1859); *St. Castine; a legend of Cape-Breton* ([Sydney, N.S.], 1850); *St. George: or, the Canadian League* (2v., Halifax, 1852). Wesleyan Methodist Church, Eastern British America Conference, *Minutes* (Halifax), 1862. *Provincial Wesleyan* (Halifax), 3 Feb., 10 March 1859; 21 March, 5 Sept. 1860; 2, 16 April, 18 June 1862. Cornish, *Cyclopaedia of Methodism*, I, 392. Wallace, *Macmillan dictionary*, 471. T. W. Smith, *History of the Methodist Church within the territories embraced in the late conference of Eastern British America . . .* (2v., Halifax, 1877–90), II, 198. D. C. Harvey, "Newspapers of Nova Scotia, 1840–1867," *CHR*, XXVI (1945), 292.

McLAREN, WILLIAM PATERSON, businessman and philanthropist; b. 6 May 1810 at Stirling, Scotland; d. 7 March 1866 at Hamilton, Canada West.

Little is known of William Paterson McLaren's parents and childhood. He was born in a region of Scotland from which emerged what a modern commentator has described as a "self-conscious new capitalist order of confident entrepreneurs." McLaren arrived in Upper Canada around 1829 and by 1838 had established himself in Hamilton. He was one of the first of the major wholesale merchants to profit from Hamilton's strategic location as *entrepôt* for the peninsular area. A major competitor, Buchanan, Harris, and Company, for example, did not open in Hamilton until the early 1840s by which time McLaren had developed strong community roots: his business was well positioned on Main Street and he had married a native Upper Canadian, Jane Evatt; they had at least four children.

As Hamilton expanded, so did McLaren's business. In 1852 he reorganized his wholesale firm to include Adam Brown*, a fellow Scot and his brother-in-law, as a junior partner. Brown represented the company in public and political affairs while McLaren forged extensive business links. After 1845 McLaren was involved in most of Hamilton's important entrepreneurial activities. A co-founder of the Board of Trade in 1845, he became its vice-president in 1852 and remained a member throughout the 1850s. Much time was devoted to the promotion and operation of such financial concerns as the Canada Life Assurance Company, the Western Permanent Building Society, and the Deposit and Savings Bank. Although a director of other endeavours such as the Hamilton Gas Light Company, McLaren's major interest outside his own firm was in transportation. He invested in Lake Ontario steamboats and was co-founder and director of the Burlington Bay Dock and Ship Building Company, but was particularly concerned with railways. Associated with the Hamilton and Toronto Rail-way soon after its formation in 1852, he was also one of the first merchants to become a director of the Great Western; for a brief period in the 1850s he was that road's chairman. In 1857 he refused the presidency of the Preston and Berlin Railway but remained a director. At that time he was also on the board of the Hamilton and Port Dover Railway and had just resigned as a director of the Galt and Guelph Railway.

The business web spun by McLaren was strengthened by family ties. In addition to one brother-in-law in his wholesale firm, another, Richard Juson, a wealthy wholesale hardware merchant and nail manufacturer, was co-director with McLaren in seven of his business concerns. F. W. Gates, father-in-law of McLaren's son, was on the Board of Trade and active with McLaren in two other business pursuits. Along with the merchant John Young* and financier Hugh Cossart Baker, McLaren and his associates formed one segment of Hamilton's business élite. Another faction was grouped around Isaac Buchanan* and Robert William HARRIS. In addition to being mercantile rivals, these men often clashed over railway affairs. Indeed it was due to Buchanan and Harris that McLaren was eased from the boards of directors of the Hamilton and Toronto and Great Western railway companies.

Other than through his business endeavours McLaren was not much involved with the community in which he lived, and he had no interest in politics. He contributed to an educational scholarship, was a trustee of the short-lived Hamilton Ladies College, and he and his wife established the McLaren Mission, a Free Church Presbyterian bible school. In the tradition of successful families he constructed a mansion known as Oakbank, a "combination Gothic revival and modified Loyalist stone residence," which housed the Prince of Wales during his visit to Hamilton in 1861.

Ill health forced McLaren to retire in 1860. Whether he was, as one obituary reported, "one of the wealthiest men in Upper Canada" is impossible to determine. His career does, however, offer insights into the nature of Upper Canada's business élite: the interlocking through family relationships and the merchant orientation are clear; the co-existence of humble McLaren Mission and sumptuous Oakbank likely reflect its sense of priorities.

PETER BASKERVILLE

HPL, Ferrie papers; Hamilton biography, William Paterson McLaren; Index to census and assessment rolls. PAC, MG 24, B4; D16, 14; D24, J. H. Greer to Donald Bethune, 1 Oct. 1851; RG 31, 1851 census, Hamilton, St Lawrence Ward. *Evening Times* (Hamilton, [Ont.]), 8 March 1866. *Examiner* (Toronto), 1845–55. *Hamilton Gazette*, (Hamilton, [Ont.]), 1852–55. *Hamilton Spectator*, 1847–61; 8 March 1866. *Canada directory*, 1857–58. *Hamilton directory* (Hamilton, [Ont.]), 1853, 1858. W. H. Smith, *Canada: past, present and future, being a historical, geographical, geological and statistical account of Canada West* (2v., Toronto, [1851–52]). M. F. Campbell, *A mountain and a city, the story of Hamilton* (Toronto, 1966). Johnston, *Head of the lake* (1958). R. L. Kelley, *The transatlantic persuasion: the liberal democratic mind in the age of Gladstone* (New York, 1969).

McLARN. *See* McCLEARN

McLEAN, ARCHIBALD, lawyer, politician, and judge; b. 5 April 1791 at St Andrews, Luneburg District, Province of Quebec, second son of Neil McLean and Isabella Macdonell; m. Joan McPherson, and they had seven children; d. 24 Oct. 1865 at Toronto, Canada West.

Archibald McLean's father was prominent in the Eastern District, serving at various times as sheriff, militia colonel, and judge. Archibald attended John STRACHAN's school in Cornwall and developed a lifelong friendship with its master. In 1809 McLean articled in law at York (Toronto) under William Firth*, then attorney general. The War of 1812 interrupted his legal studies and he became a subaltern in the 3rd Regiment of York militia. At the battle of Queenston Heights on 13 Oct. 1812, McLean was seriously wounded, but he crawled from the battlefield to a nearby village where his wounds were hurriedly dressed. His recuperation, prolonged because of an infection resulting from the late removal of a bullet, was not yet complete when the Americans attacked York on 27 April 1813. Still unfit for combat because of his illness, McLean buried the York militia's colours in the woods and escaped to Kingston. He was back in action on 25 July 1814 at Lundy's Lane, where he was captured by the Americans and held prisoner for the duration of the war.

In 1815, after declining a commission in the British regulars, McLean was called to the Upper

Canadian bar and entered the firm of William Warren Baldwin*. The following year McLean established his own lucrative practice in Cornwall. The McLean family were members of the Church of Scotland, leaders in the Cornwall area, and related through marriage to prominent local Scottish Catholics. It was to be expected, therefore, that as a rising member of the Family Compact, McLean should be elected to the assembly for the county of Stormont in 1820. In the assembly he gradually became a leading Tory member and an advocate of recognizing the rights of the Presbyterian Church as equal to those of the Church of England. McLean held the Stormont seat until 1834 when Cornwall was incorporated as a town and received its own seat. That year he won election as member for Cornwall and became speaker of the assembly in 1836. He again represented Stormont in the 13th parliament which opened 8 Nov. 1836.

Promoted colonel in the militia during the Rebellion of 1837, McLean was involved in routing the rebels in Toronto, commanding the left flank of the loyalist forces under Colonel James FitzGibbon in the attack on Montgomery's Tavern. McLean initially opposed the union of 1841 out of fear that Upper Canadians would be dominated by French Canadians. He saw responsible government as a danger to the British connection and to the ordered freedom and the recognition of class and property of the British tradition, but he quickly adjusted to the new reality.

Archibald McLean began his long judicial career with an appointment to the Court of King's Bench for the western circuit in March 1837; he was replaced as member for Stormont by his brother Alexander in December of that year. In 1850 he was transferred to the newly created Court of Common Pleas where he served with James Buchanan Macaulay* and Robert Baldwin Sullivan*. In 1856, when he was passed over as this court's chief justice in favour of William Henry Draper*, he returned to the Queen's Bench as a senior judge. In December 1860 McLean dissented in the case of John ANDERSON, a fugitive slave, and argued that he should be discharged: "in administering the laws of a British province, I can never feel bound to recognize as law any enactment which can convert into chattels a very large number of the human race." On 15 March 1862 he was appointed chief justice of the Court of Queen's Bench for Upper Canada. McLean was a Conservative from a prominent old Tory family. Nevertheless, in July 1863 Reform Premier John Sandfield Macdonald*, who had articled with

McLean and served under him on the western circuit, had him appointed to the less onerous post of presiding judge of the Court of Error and Appeal when Sir John Beverley ROBINSON died. McLean, now 72, was replaced as chief justice by Draper.

For many years McLean was president of the St Andrew's Society of Toronto. When he died in 1865 he was honoured by an impressive public funeral. The *Upper Canada Law Journal* commented that McLean "upon the bench was dignified and courteous; unsuspicious and utterly devoid of anything mean or petty in his own character, his conduct to others was always what he expected from them."

BRUCE W. HODGINS

PAO, McLean (Archibald) papers, Misc. coll., 1807–57. *Upper Canada Law Journal* (Toronto), XI (1865), 281–84. Read, *Lives of judges*. L. J. Blom-Cooper, *The language of the law* (New York, 1965). Craig, *Upper Canada*. J. G. Harkness, *Stormont, Dundas and Glengarry: a history, 1784–1945* (Oshawa, Ont., 1946). B. W. Hodgins, *John Sandfield Macdonald, 1812–1872* (Toronto, 1971). A. M. Macdonell, *Incidents in the life of the late Chief Justice Archibald McLean: seven years president of the St. Andrew's Society, Toronto* (n.p., n.d.).

McLEAN, DONALD, HBC chief trader and cattle rancher; b. 1805 in Tobermory, Isle of Mull, Scotland; d. 17 July 1864 in Chilcotin, B.C.

Donald McLean, a tall and powerful red-head, joined the Hudson's Bay Company in 1833 as apprentice clerk, serving in the Western Department for two years. He then joined expeditions in the Snake River country (Oreg.) under Thomas McKay and John McLeod*. In 1839 he was moved to Fort Colvile (near present-day Kettle Falls, Wash.) under Archibald McDonald*, and next year was promoted clerk at Flathead Post (Mont.); here he lived with a Spanish-Indian girl, from whom he separated in 1853 or 1854.

He was transferred to New Caledonia District in 1842, taking charge at times of the Chilcotin, Babine, and McLeod posts, and working at Fort Alexandria on the Fraser River under Donald Manson*. This district was the "Siberia of the fur-trade"; troublesome servants were moved here to cool off in the harsh climate on rations of three dried salmon daily. The men were rough and tough, as was the discipline meted out to them. Governor George Simpson* was thoroughly justified in condemning the "club law" enforced by Manson, McLean, and Paul Fraser, but perhaps reasonable methods had failed.

Sometimes, quite inexcusably, violence was

extended towards Indians by fur traders. In 1849 the Indian Tlelh killed Alexis Bélanger, a Métis in the HBC service, after considerable provocation. McLean, who was at that time at Alexandria, headed an unsuccessful manhunt, venting his spleen on Tlelh's relations by killing two men and a baby. He wrote to Manson of those sheltering Tlelh: "The black, ungrateful, blood-thirsty, treacherous, and cowardly scoundrels should have prompt justice for it; hang first, and then call a jury to find them guilty or not guilty." His superiors apparently accepted this attitude. The Indians remembered it as their dislike for the white invaders, and particularly McLean, increased.

In 1853 McLean was appointed chief trader, and two years later took charge of Thompson's River Post (Kamloops) when Fraser died. Here he improved horsebreeding and developed larger cattle herds; he also, with his growing sons, amassed livestock of his own. He soon was aware of gold in the area but the HBC suppressed news of it until 1857, when the fur trade autocrats gradually yielded to mining and colonial interests.

A naval officer, Lieutenant Richard Charles Mayne*, visiting Kamloops in 1859 praised McLean: "A finer or more handsome man I think I never saw." But HBC officials were not so impressed by his growing high-handedness, and he was ordered to headquarters at Victoria in 1860. He resigned the next year. The McLean clan moved their livestock to grasslands on the Bonaparte River; here they ranched, prospected, and ran "McLean's Restaurant" for travellers in the Cariboo country. Donald McLean had married Sophia Grant, a Colville Indian, at Fort Colvile in 1854, and now had a second family. He was apparently devoted and indulgent to all his children. The deaths of two moved him to verse of gentle resignation, contrasting strongly with his harsh public character.

During 1864 Chilcotin Indians, seemingly provoked by unprincipled private traders, the ravages of diseases introduced by the white men, and the probability of reserves being established, killed some 19 members of work parties building a road inland from Bute Inlet for Alfred Penderell Waddington*. Panic arose in Victoria, where a large-scale uprising was feared. A mass meeting there urged that "Captain McLean" lead a "Chilcoaten" expedition of vengeance, and he duly left the Bonaparte River, ostensibly under William George Cox*'s command. But, a self-confident individualist to the end, McLean scouted almost alone and was killed in an ambush. The murderers of the workmen were in-

duced to surrender, but McLean's slayer was sheltered by the Indians, who regarded his act as a just retribution for his victim's life of cruel violence.

McLean's older children became worthy settlers, but the three youngest, Allan*, Charley, and Archie, wild half-breeds disclaimed by both Indians and the immigrant white society, eventually ran berserk, and were hanged for murdering a constable in 1879. Ironically, the son of one was decorated in 1917 for bravery in killing 19 Germans single-handed.

MARY BALF

Kamloops Museum (Kamloops, B.C.), HBC journals, 1859–60; HBC letters, 1879. PABC, Donald McLean, miscellaneous papers. R. C. Mayne, *Four years in British Columbia and Vancouver Island: an account of their forests, rivers, coasts, gold fields, and resources for colonisation* (London, 1862), 115–21. *Daily British Colonist and Victoria Chronicle*, 4 Nov. 1863; 3, 4, 6, 30 June, 7, 11 July, 1, 8, 25 Aug. 1864; 11, 13, 14, 16, 18, 28 Dec. 1879; 1, 20 Jan., 16, 19, 20 March, 19 Nov. 1880. Morice, *History of northern interior of B.C.* (1904), 233, 239, 264–69, 272, 311. Mel Rothenburger, *"We've killed Johnny Ussher!": the story of the wild McLean boys and Alex Hare* (Vancouver, 1973), 3–21. "German killer returns home; Kamloops crowd meets hero of Vimy Ridge who was awarded DCM," *Kamloops Telegram* (Kamloops, B.C.), 11 Oct. 1917.

MacLEAN, PETER, merchant and Presbyterian clergyman; b. 1800 at Nigg on the island of Lewis in Scotland; m. in 1843 Flora Campbell Stalwart; d. 28 March 1868 at Stornoway, Scotland.

Peter MacLean spent the early years of his manhood as a successful merchant in Stornoway. At age 27 he experienced a deep religious conversion as a result of which he gave up his business to begin studies for the Presbyterian ministry. In winding up his affairs "he blotted out of his books all sums due to him by ministers."

Following the successful completion of his studies in arts and theology at King's College, Aberdeen, MacLean was licensed by the Presbytery of Lewis in 1836 and a year later he accepted a call to Cape Breton Island. The money required for his outfit and passage was furnished by the Edinburgh Ladies Association, which since 1828 had provided similar assistance to several Presbyterian missionaries bound for Cape Breton. He established himself at Whycocomagh, a small pioneer settlement, and began to preach throughout the countryside, eventually becoming a widely known evangelist. Powerfully built, with a voice to match, his sermons attracted large audiences, and "his preaching was accompanied by very extraordinary effects upon his hearers, not only mentally and spiritually, but also physically . . .''; some even followed him on his ministrations around the island. By preaching and travelling in all kinds of weather he fostered greater interest in religion among the people of the district. He also distributed bibles and encouraged the establishment of schools. The physical toll exacted by constant preaching and travelling forced him to return to Scotland in 1842 to rest. Recovering rapidly, he participated in the disruption of the Church of Scotland in 1843 and accepted a call to the Free Church congregation of Tobermory, Scotland. There, as in Cape Breton, his preaching was popular.

He revisited Whycocomagh in 1853 and presided at a communion which drew 5,000 people, with 200 boats in the bay and 500 horses tethered in the groves, reputedly the largest pentecostal service ever held in Cape Breton. After returning to Scotland he was called to Stornoway in 1855, but ill health in 1862 forced him to seek rest. In an effort to heal strife among Presbyterians in Cape Breton he returned there in 1866, though still in poor health. Upon his return to Scotland he suffered bronchial troubles and died soon afterward. A small church in the Wycocomagh district was named after him.

R. MacLean

Presbyterian Witness, 30 April 1898. John Murray, *The history of the Presbyterian Church in Cape Breton* (Truro, N.S., 1921). L. M. Toward, ''The influence of Scottish clergy on early education in Cape Breton,'' N.S. Hist. Soc., *Coll.*, XXIX (1951), 153–77.

McLEARN. *See* McCLEARN

McLEOD, EZEKIEL, Baptist clergyman and journalist; b. 16 Sept. 1812 in Penobsquis, N.B.; d. 17 March 1867 at Fredericton, N.B.

Whatever early education McLeod received was at Penobsquis, for he moved to Saint John as a young man and tried his hand at merchandising and milling. Soon, however, he was active in the Free Christian Baptist Church, entering the ministry in 1848. He then became an itinerant preacher in Westmorland County where, in association with the Reverend Samuel Hartt, he helped found a number of churches.

Though poorly educated, McLeod appears to have had considerable natural ability and practical insight. He became convinced that the evangelicalism of the Free Christian Baptist Church was being ridiculed because it was not properly understood and that public education was the answer. He returned, therefore, to Saint John in 1853 to establish the *Religious Intelligencer and Bible Society, Missionary and Sabbath School Advocate* under the sponsorship of the New Brunswick Baptist Conference. Though opposed by some in his church, the semi-monthly newspaper thrived and became a weekly in 1854. For the next seven years McLeod directed both the *Religious Intelligencer* and the Free Baptist Church of Saint John. In 1861 he moved to Fredericton where he presided over the largest Free Baptist chapel in the province and helped to establish others in the York County region. At the time of his death he stood out as the leader of his denomination in New Brunswick. The *Religious Intelligencer*, the most outspoken Protestant newspaper in the province, also made McLeod one of the best known Protestants.

From its inception the *Religious Intelligencer* united Protestant fundamentalism with an evangelical fervour for moral reform and public stewardship. Thus the paper supported Sunday schools, Bible societies, and foreign missions. Its moralistic tone and zealous anti-Catholicism were combined with a deep strain of humanitarianism. Slavery was condemned and the North supported in the American Civil War; cruelty to Indians was denounced; ignorance was fought with support for a public non-sectarian school system.

McLeod maintained firm control over the paper, leaving no doubt about his opinions. There were few more aggressive supporters of prohibition in New Brunswick. ''The question of Prohibition and Anti-Prohibition in St. John,'' he wrote in 1856 at the height of the struggle over Samuel Leonard Tilley*'s Prohibition Act of 1855, ''is fast assuming its true aspect, which is *Protestantism* and anti-Protestantism; and the sooner it becomes fully developed the better.''

Perhaps because of Tilley's leading role in the prohibition movement or his evangelical inclinations, McLeod became a forceful ally of Tilley's party and the confederation scheme. Throughout 1865 and 1866 the *Religious Intelligencer* was filled with articles on the dangers to Protestantism and the responsibilities of British subjects. ''The 'Protestant faith' and the 'open Bible' are in danger,'' he declared in an editorial on the sensitive York County by-election of November 1865, ''and the climax is, that . . . the people of York had better vote against the anti-Confederate candidate and for Mr. [Charles Fisher*].'' The anti-confederates were labelled as the ''Catholic Party'' in sympathy with Fenianism. Tilley encouraged McLeod and supplied him with suggestions and information. When the confederation party was returned to

McLeod

power in June 1866 the *Religious Intelligencer* announced proudly: "The people of this Province have not only fought the battle of Confederation, and won, but they have struck a blow against Fenianism and disloyalty. . . ."

Although McLeod received letters from Tilley and Fisher written in London in January 1867, informing him that all hurdles had been cleared, he did not live to see confederation. In March of that year he died of bilious fever. He was survived by his wife and nine children. One clergyman son, Joseph, continued to edit the *Religious Intelligencer*.

C. M. WALLACE

N.B. Museum, McLeod family papers. UNBL, MG HIO. *Morning News* (Saint John, N.B.), 20 March 1867. *Morning Telegraph* (Saint John, N.B.), 21 March 1867. *New Brunswick Reporter and Fredericton Advertiser*, 22 March 1867. *Religious Intelligencer and Bible Society, Missionary and Sabbath School Advocate* (Saint John, N.B.), 1853–67. Harper, *Hist. directory*. G. E. Levy, *The Baptists of the Maritime provinces, 1753–1946* (Saint John, N.B., 1946). Joseph McLeod, "A sketch of the history of the Free Baptists of New Brunswick," E. M. Saunders, *History of the Baptists of the Maritime provinces* (Halifax, 1902), 410–21.

McLEOD (MacLeod), NORMAN, Presbyterian clergyman; b. 17 Sept. 1780 at Point of Stoer, in the parish of Assynt, Sutherlandshire, Scotland; m. in 1812 Mary MacLeod, and they had ten children; d. 14 March 1866 at Waipu, New Zealand.

Norman McLeod received his early education at the local parish school of the Church of Scotland and for some years thereafter worked at fishing and farming. During this period he often experienced doubts about the true religious denomination for his salvation, and finally made a decision to follow the doctrine of Calvin. At age 27 he began studies for the ministry and entered King's College at the University of Aberdeen. He graduated in 1812 with the gold medal in moral philosophy. To complete his studies he registered at the University of Edinburgh but left before the end of his second term, having made a sharp break with the established Church of Scotland, caused partly by his deep opposition to its policy of patronage and to the lack of discipline in its clergy.

From 1814 to 1817 McLeod taught school at Ullapool, and, during the frequent absences of the local minister, read Scriptures and commented on them. Strongly outspoken in his criticism of the minister, and attracting large crowds to his own services, McLeod, who was not licensed by the Church of Scotland, soon came into conflict with the minister, and after two years found himself out of his teaching position at the church-controlled school. By this time McLeod had attracted a number of sympathizers who shared his criticisms of the established church. In order to support his family he returned to fishing and began to consider emigration. By July 1817 he had paid his debts and he then sailed from Loch Broom for Pictou, N.S. His wife and family soon followed.

Settling near Loch Broom in Pictou County, he was initially absorbed in the problems of pioneer life. However, he continued his preaching with messianic zeal and soon attracted a large number of followers, many of whom had come from the same region in Scotland. Unable to secure sufficient land so that he and his "Normanites" could live together and repelled by the rough frontier environment, McLeod decided to accept a call from a Scottish settlement in Ohio. A boat was built, dubbed the "Ark" by his critics, and a small group left to investigate the new location. En route, they stopped in St Ann's Harbour, Cape Breton, which they liked so well they decided to settle there. Returning to Pictou in the fall of 1819, they made preparations to bring their families; by April 1820 seven small boats had been built at Middle River. Despite storms the first group arrived safely on 20 May and eventually some 700 people set about clearing the forest and building their homes. So began the most theocratic community in the history of the province.

At St Ann's, McLeod's tremendous powers came into full flowering. Not only did he establish the first Calvinistic church in the district but he also secured a position as magistrate in 1823 and as a licensed teacher in 1827, though he had already started a school as early as 1822. In 1827 he was also ordained a minister of the Presbyterian Church by the Presbytery of Geneva in New York State. Now fully licensed, and independent of any Presbyterian body in Canada, McLeod, who could tolerate no restraint from other clergy, was in complete command at St Ann's. In addition to his schoolmaster's fees McLeod received the labour of every adult in his charge in clearing his land, planting and harvesting his crops, and building houses, barns, and ships.

The community grew and gradually prospered: "his congregation in St Ann's was the most temperate moral and orderly that ever existed in Cape Breton. . . ." Ruling in an autocratic fashion, McLeod led and exhorted his followers towards moral perfection. As the minister he could scold a person from the pulpit on Sunday for drunkenness; as a magistrate he could fine him on Monday. He even criticized his wife's bonnet during a Sunday sermon and quickly castigated anyone he suspected of moral laxity. On one occasion in his judicial capacity he ordered the tip of a boy's ear removed in punishment for a suspected crime. Some of his congregation eventually withdrew because of his autocratic manner. Not even the Presbyterian clergy in other parts of Cape Breton were spared from his censure and criticism. His preaching was described as "torrents of abuse against all religious bodies and individuals"; in 1843 he published a strongly worded tract entitled *The present Church of Scotland, and a tint of Normanism, contending in a dialogue.*

Partly because of the failure of the potato crop and the threat of famine during the late 1840s, he began to consider another move for the sake of his children, this time to Australia where his eldest son was already living. Such was his hold on his people that he convinced more than 800 to follow him, the first of six ships leaving in October 1851, the last in December 1859. After a brief period in Australia, the great majority eventually settled at Waipu, New Zealand, where once again McLeod was the dominant religious personality.

Sincere, courageous, and totally committed to his cause, McLeod could not be described as open-minded in religious matters. He died as he had lived, lamenting the world's madness.

R. MacLean

Norman McLeod's correspondence of 1835–51, available in PANS, MG 1, 570C, is published as [Norman McLeod], *Letters of Rev. Norman McLeod, 1835–51*, ed. D. C. Harvey (PANS *Bull.*, II, no.1, Halifax, 1939). Maritime Conference Archives of the United Church of Can., Pine Hill Divinity Hall (Halifax), L. D. Currie, "An epic of Cape Breton, or the story of Reverend Norman McLeod" (typescript). PANS, MG 1, 745 (Judge George G. Patterson papers), no. 58; G. G. Patterson, "History of Victoria County" (typescript, 1885); RG 1, 237, no.117; RG 5, P, 84, poor relief, 10 March 1848; RG 14, 5–6 (Cape Breton Island, 1803–95). T. C. Haliburton, *An historical and statistical account of Nova-Scotia* (2v., Halifax, 1829; repr. Belleville, Ont., 1973). [Norman McLeod], *The present Church of Scotland, and a tint of Normanism, contending in a dialogue* ([Halifax, 1843]). *Presbyterian Witness*, 11, 25 Aug. 1866.

C. W. Dunn, *Highland settler; a portrait of the Scottish Gael in Nova Scotia* ([Toronto], 1953). Gordon Macdonald, *The highlanders of Waipu, or echoes of 1745; a Scottish odyssey* (Dunedin, N.Z., 1928). N. R. McKenzie, *The Gael fares forth: the romantic story of Waipu and her sister settlements* (London, 1935). F. [McG.] McPherson, *Watchman against the world; the story of Norman McLeod and his people* (London, 1962). John Murray, *The history of the Presbyterian Church in Cape Breton* (Truro, N.S., 1921). G. G. Patterson, *More studies in Nova Scotian history* (Halifax, 1941). George Patterson, *A history of the county of Pictou, Nova Scotia* (Montreal, 1877); *Memoir of the Reverend James McGregor* (Edinburgh and Philadelphia, 1859). N. C. Robinson, *Lion of Scotland, being an account of Norman McLeod's forty years' search for a land where he and his followers could live as they wished* . . . (London, [1952]). Mrs Charles Archibald, "Early Scottish settlers in Cape Breton," N.S.Hist. Soc., *Coll.*, XVIII (1914), 69–100. A. J. Clark, "The Scottish Canadian pilgrims of the fifties," *OH*, XXVI (1930), 5–15. D. C. Harvey, "Educational experiments, 1825–32," *Journal of Education* (Halifax), 4th ser., VI (1935), 22–29. M. D. Morrison, "Migrations of Scotch settlers from St. Ann's, Nova Scotia, to New Zealand, 1851–1860," N.S. Hist. Soc., *Coll.*, XXII (1933), 73–95. L. M. Toward, "The influence of Scottish clergy on early education in Cape Breton," N.S. Hist. Soc., *Coll.*, XXIX (1951), 153–77.

McMICKING, THOMAS, gold-seeker, municipal official, and author; b. 16 April 1829 in Stamford Township (city of Niagara Falls), Upper Canada, eldest son of William McMicking and Mary McClellan; m. 12 July 1853 Laura Chubbock, and they had two girls and two boys; d. 25 Aug. 1866 near New Westminster, B.C.

Thomas McMicking's grandfather had come from Scotland and had settled at Stamford about 1780. Thomas attended the local public school and Knox College, Toronto. He was a teacher at Stamford and Queenston, and then in business at Queenston. In June 1861 he stood for election as the Clear Grit candidate at Niagara but was defeated by the Conservative John Simpson*.

In autumn 1861, when news of the rich gold finds in the Cariboo reached Canada West, Thomas was the leading spirit in organizing a party of 24 or 28 to travel overland to the Cariboo from the Queenston and St Catharines area. The party, including Thomas' youngest brother, Robert Burns McMicking*, left Queenston in April 1862. It travelled through the United States by rail and steamer to St Paul on the Mississippi, by coach to the Red River, and then by steamer to Fort Garry.

Other parties (perhaps as many as 20 from Canada West, two from Canada East, and one from New York State), were organized independently and travelled in much the same manner on their own to Fort Garry. At St Paul and Georgetown in Minnesota, or at Fort Garry, these parties bought animals, supplies, and Red River carts for the trek west. Thomas McMicking met the new governor of Rupert's Land, Alex-

McMicking

ander Grant Dallas*, at Georgetown on 12 May 1862. Dallas and his wife joined the Overlanders for the journey on the steamship *International* to Fort Garry.

On 5 July, at Long Lake just west of Fort Garry, 138 men from at least 15 of the original groups organized themselves into a single party; Thomas McMicking was elected captain with an advisory committee of 13, approximately one member for each original party. McMicking's group adopted rules governing its order of march, behaviour in camp and en route, and defence against possible Indian attack. McMicking wrote later in the year that "We found the red men of the prairies to be our best friends."

As McMicking's party proceeded westward, additional members, notably the family of Augustus Schubert who travelled with horse and buggy across the prairies, joined the group. Catherine Schubert was the only woman among the Overlanders, who had a policy of excluding women, thinking their presence inappropriate in large groups of men. Yet even this one family proved an asset for the morale and work of the expedition.

Two smaller parties followed the main contingent. One had left Toronto with 45 men (the largest number of any group) under the authoritarian leadership of former policeman Stephen Redgrave, but it was now split by dissension; some members transferred to other groups, including McMicking's. Redgrave himself was one of nine of the original Torontonians to join a group led by the adventurer Timolean Love in a futile attempt to find gold on the upper North Saskatchewan. After wintering there, and encountering Eugene Francis O'BEIRNE who delivered sermons and sponged upon them, most of Love's party crossed into the Cariboo in 1862. The other party was that of Dr Symington, and it followed the two others. Its movements and membership are little known; when Archibald McNaughton of McMicking's party fell back with an injured comrade he travelled with this group for a time.

The main party under McMicking reached Fort Edmonton, the last depot for supplies, on 21 July 1862. When it left eight days later, some of its members stayed behind to prospect before crossing the mountains the next year. McMicking crossed with pack animals, proceeding up the Athabasca and then the Miette River, and over the height of land by Yellowhead Pass to reach the upper Fraser and Tête Jaune Cache. Here, near starvation, McMicking's party was provisioned by a band of Shuswaps. Owing to disputes about the best route to follow, a meeting of those still with the party was held on 1 September dissolving the agreement of 5 July.

About 20 of the members, including Catherine and Augustus Schubert and their three children, chose to cross to the North Thompson. On it two drowned, and the remainder reached Thompson's River Post (Kamloops) destitute and near their end on 13 October; the next day Mrs Schubert, with the help of an Indian woman, gave birth to a fourth child, Rose, the first white girl born in the interior of British Columbia. The main party, including McMicking, had chosen instead to descend the Fraser River. Some went on rafts, at no loss of life, but of a group that used dugout canoes three drowned and one died of pneumonia after surviving an upset. Thomas McMicking, travelling by raft, reached Quesnelle Mouth (Quesnel) on 11 September. Here he drew up a summary of expenditures by the Queenston parties until that time. They worked out to $97.95 per person. He commented drily on their purchases: "Our mining tools were the only articles ... that we found to be unnecessary." He tried, although the season was late, to reach the diggings at Williams Creek, but turned back because of the weather and discouraging reports of miners departing for the coast.

Many of the Overlanders left the country without ever mining. As a gold seeking expedition the trek of the Overlanders of '62 was almost fruitless. A few returned to the Cariboo in 1863 but they found the gold deposits becoming exhausted. Late in 1862 Thomas McMicking went down from the Cariboo to New Westminster, where he was befriended, as many Overlanders were, by John Robson*, editor of the *British Columbian*. McMicking worked for a short time in a shingle mill. He also quickly prepared an interesting, well-written narrative of the journey which was published in the *British Columbian* between 29 Nov. 1862 and 23 Jan. 1863 in 14 instalments. This is the basic published primary document on the Overlanders.

Thomas McMicking's education and talents soon won him civic responsibility. In 1864 he was appointed town clerk for New Westminster and in April 1866 deputy sheriff. He was active in the affairs of St Andrew's Presbyterian Church and was a member of the volunteer Hyack Fire Company. On 26 June 1866 he was secretary of a meeting called to organize a local home guard, when news arrived from Canada of the Fenian raids. The corps subsequently elected him 1st lieutenant. A short time afterwards, however, on 25 August during a family visit to a friend ten miles below New Westminster, McMicking's second son William Francis, six years old, fell into the Fraser River. The father went to the rescue, but with his son was swept under a boom and drowned.

McMicking was one of the few who came to the British Columbia gold-rush overland from Canada as against the tens of thousands who came by sea. Apart from a handful in 1859, nearly all the Canadians who did arrive by land were in the three 1862 groups; their exact number is hard to determine, but Thomas McMicking's figure of 200 seems the most reliable. Their purpose in making the journey was not fulfilled but it had other positive results. The passage of the Overlanders through the Rocky Mountains helped to show that the geographical barriers to union between Canada and British Columbia could be overcome.

Many of the Overlanders who remained in British Columbia became outstanding contributors to the development of the province, a result undoubtedly of the self-sufficiency and of the organizational capacity developed by the journey. One of these was Robert Burns McMicking, a resident of the province till his death in 1915 and a central figure in the introduction of the telegraph, the telephone, and electric power into British Columbia.

VICTOR G. HOPWOOD

Thomas McMicking was author of an "Account of a journey overland from Canada to British Columbia during the summer of 1862 …," *British Columbian* (New Westminster), 29 Nov., 3, 10, 13, 17, 20, 24, 27, 31 Dec. 1862; 10, 14, 17, 24, 28 Jan. 1863 (typescript at PABC).

PABC, R. H. Alexander, Diary, 29 April–31 Dec. 1862; R. B. McMicking, Diary, 23 April 1862–29 April 1863; Miscellaneous material relating to Thomas McMicking, R. B. McMicking, memo, 3 Dec. 1912; Stephen Redgrave, Journals and sundry papers, 1852–75 (typescript); J. A. Schubert, Notes of conversation, 18 July 1930 (typescript). University of British Columbia Library, Special Coll. Division (Vancouver); A. L. Fortune, coll. of addresses and narratives (typescript); John Hunniford, Journal and observations (typescript). R. B. McMicking, "Second overland journey," *Year book of British Columbia …*, comp. R. E. Gosnell (Victoria, 1897), 100–2. J. B. Kerr, *Biographical dictionary of well-known British Columbians, with a historical sketch* (Vancouver, 1890), 253–61. Margaret McNaughton, *Overland to Cariboo; an eventful journey of Canadian pioneers to the gold-fields of British Columbia in 1862* (Toronto, 1896; repr., intro. V. G. Hopwood, Vancouver, 1973). M. S. Wade, *The Overlanders of '62*, ed. John Hosie (Victoria, 1931).

MacNAB, Sir ALLAN NAPIER, politician, businessman, land speculator, lawyer, and soldier; b. 19 Feb. 1798 at Newark (Niagara-on-the-Lake), Upper Canada, third of seven children of Allan MacNab and Anne Napier; d. 8 Aug. 1862 at Hamilton, Canada West.

Allan Napier MacNab's father had been a lieutenant in John Graves Simcoe*'s 2nd corps of Queen's Rangers which saw action in the American revolution. Put on half pay, he settled in York (Toronto) where he was denied further military preferment and a high civil placement. A sometime bankrupt, Allan MacNab struggled on the fringe of Upper Canada's Tory society. Into this rather unstable atmosphere Allan Napier Mac-Nab was born. Despite the family's financial problems, he briefly attended the Reverend George Okill STUART's Home District Grammar School at York. Contacts established by his father with the York civil and military establishment would be of use to him in his future career. Even more important, he absorbed his father's love of the military, intense social and economic ambitions, and perseverance under adverse circumstances.

In the War of 1812 MacNab, 14 years of age at its outbreak, gave full rein to his martial instincts. He saw action at Sackets Harbor, Plattsburgh, and Black Rock, N.Y., and at Fort Niagara. In March 1814 he was promoted ensign in the 49th Foot. His military career curtailed by regimental cutbacks at war's end, MacNab searched restlessly for alternative employment. In 1816 he entered the law office of Judge D'Arcy Boulton* Sr. That MacNab took nearly twice the average time to qualify at the bar was a result of his inadequate education and his preference for active work. Thus in his early years he dabbled in acting, carpentry, and land speculation, and in 1820 renewed his military connections as captain in the York militia. Even his marriage in 1821 to Elizabeth Brooke, daughter of a British soldier, failed to have a settling influence. Not until his wife's sudden death while giving birth to their second child in January 1825 did MacNab begin to exercise some discipline over his life. He was called to the bar in 1826.

He decided against staying at York, where the avenues to advancement seemed blocked by the Allan, Robinson, Boulton, and Strachan families. MacNab was always reluctant "to accept a minor part," and instead set up office as the first resident lawyer in the small but growing community of Hamilton, where he hoped advancement would be easier. Capitalizing on his father's relations with the Jarvis family, he quickly befriended William Munson Jarvis, sheriff of the Gore District, whose family provided crucial business and political support. Law contacts also drew him close to the important Chisholm family

519

MacNab

of Oakville and the Hatts of Ancaster. Moreover, John Beverley ROBINSON, also a veteran of 1812, secured for him the position of notary. In August 1827 he successfully defended several prominent Hamilton Tories charged with tarring and feathering George Rolph, a Reformer who had been accused of adultery and whose lawyer was William Warren Baldwin*. MacNab's legal practice benefited and within a year he had at least one student articling under him. He was now able to buy and develop land in the Hamilton area. Partly through the Chisholms, MacNab was appointed in May 1830 lieutenant-colonel of the 4th Regiment of Gore militia. Dependent on him at this time were four unmarried sisters, his recently widowed mother, and his two children. In September 1831 he married Mary Stuart, daughter of John Stuart, formerly sheriff of the Johnstown District, and niece of George Okill Stuart and Henry John BOULTON. The marriage provided further links to influential persons and was, as it turned out, a very compatible union.

MacNab understood well the mechanics of preferment, but it was chance that propelled him into the public eye. In 1829 he had refused to testify before a committee of the House of Assembly chaired by the Reformer W. W. Baldwin, which was investigating the hanging in effigy of Lieutenant Governor Sir John COLBORNE at Hamilton by a Tory mob. Prodded by William Lyon MACKENZIE, the house sentenced MacNab to ten days in jail for contempt. It is doubtful whether MacNab anticipated such an outcome. But he became a Tory martyr, an image he exploited effectively in the 1830 election when he and John Willson* defeated the Reformers in Wentworth County.

MacNab's first term in the assembly was inauspicious. He was convinced that it would be unwise to identify with any single group in a political atmosphere characterized by fluid factionalism. As a first step in increasing his political influence in the province MacNab sought to strengthen his ties in the Wentworth region. Political power was only as strong as one's regional roots and MacNab's required much cultivation. He thus sought, with William Hamilton MERRITT of St Catharines, the Chisholms of Oakville, and the Bethunes and Cartwrights of the Cobourg-Kingston area, to decentralize and redistribute the commercial and political power of the York clique. MacNab had to step lightly. Not only was he faced with stiff political opposition in Wentworth led by James Durand of Dundas, but also he was indebted both to York's financial institution, the Bank of Upper Canada, and to many York contacts for his current advancement.

W. L. Mackenzie, an ally of the Durands, had first priority. Bested by Mackenzie both in the assembly and at a political meeting in Hamilton, MacNab countered by seconding a motion in December 1831 to expel his rival from the assembly on grounds of libel. It was the first of five expulsions; in all MacNab was active. The significance of these expulsions soon transcended personal vengeance and even party strife. By spearheading the attack against the irascible editor, MacNab was able to gain power in the assembly and maintain a link with Tory York. This bridge was sorely needed as, in its shadow, intra-party manoeuvring and contending over the control of Upper Canada's commercial and economic power was occurring. The intra-party struggle was most evident concerning banks and land speculation.

Initially MacNab avoided direct conflict with York. While supporting John Solomon Cartwright*'s Commercial Bank at Kingston, in the hopes of managing its prospective Hamilton "agency," MacNab continued to give legislative assistance to the Bank of Upper Canada. In return he received liberal credit from the latter and, in March 1833, was appointed its solicitor for the Gore District. Using this credit and his own limited cash reserves, he increased his speculation in land. By May 1832 he owned some 2,000 acres of wild land in London, Gore, and Newcastle districts. Of more importance, by 1835 he had cornered much of the best land in the centre of expanding Hamilton. His holdings fluctuated dramatically and their total value at any one time is unknown, but he probably did become, as Sir Charles Bagot* stated in 1842, "a huge proprietor, perhaps the largest in the country."

Although evidence suggests that MacNab was not scrupulous in liquidating mortgages before resale, the initial payments on his land purchases represented a severe drain on his cash resources, especially in the early 1830s. The Burlington Heights property, on which the symbol of MacNab's social aspirations, the resplendent 72-room Dundurn Castle, would soon sit, had been purchased in November 1832 from J. S. Cartwright for £2,500, £500 more than MacNab had intended. Tragically, on the day the sale was completed, fire destroyed his Hamilton building projects causing between £5,000 and £10,000 damage. Moreover, he was ousted as president of the Desjardins Canal Company in 1834, after having mortgaged a large block of his own land as security for a government loan to the company in 1832. Contacts with the Tory hierarchy were also wearing thin. Some three years behind in payments to one important creditor, Samuel Peters

Jarvis*, the wily debtor claimed that Jarvis owed him for past services. In Jarvis' eyes the brash Hamilton lawyer was simply a "villain."

As credit tightened, MacNab faced the prospect of a confrontation with his creditors in York. But the clash was delayed by the death of Wentworth's land registrar. Whoever controlled this office could quietly acquire choice, undeveloped land in the Wentworth area without the necessity of a public auction. After a bitter struggle with James Durand, MacNab in April 1833 secured this appointment for his brother David Archibald. He had gained a seemingly impregnable hold over Wentworth's land development and, as a result, a firm grip on the county's commercial and political future.

It was a fleeting victory. Peter Robinson*, commissioner of crown lands, wishing to curb rampant speculation in land and thereby retain York's hold over Upper Canada's development, issued an order in council on 8 Nov. 1833 which tightened and centralized control over land speculation. This move undermined MacNab's coup and pushed him into open conflict with the capital. Interpreting the order in council as an attempt by York Tories to bypass local "dealers in Land" and monopolize profits, MacNab was irate. Within a month he sponsored a bill to incorporate the rival Gore Bank at Hamilton, criticized the excessive power of the Upper Canada and Commercial banks, and even temporized on supporting the bill to incorporate York as the city of Toronto.

Repercussions were immediate. The Legislative Council not only rejected his bank bill but also began to obstruct his real estate affairs by denying him privileged status at the central registry office and by ignoring his constant demands and complaints. With construction costs for Dundurn escalating, MacNab persevered and did realize some return on his land dealings in 1834. However, ultimate control over land continued to rest with Toronto.

By contrast, success was his in the field of banking. In this sphere he gained the support of prominent Hamilton businessmen as well as assistance from assemblymen who desired local banks for their own developing metropolitan areas. The Gore Bank was chartered late in 1835 with MacNab controlling a majority of its shares. At this point he opposed the chartering of further regional banks.

Freed of the financial restraints imposed by Toronto, MacNab continued both to expand his commercial domain and to consolidate his local political control. By 1837 he was the operator of a steamship line running between Rochester, Os-

wego, and Hamilton, the owner of an important dock on Burlington Bay, the chief promoter and president of the Hamilton and Port Dover Railway, an active director of the Great Western Railway, an insatiable land speculator, a builder, renter, and seller of houses and stores, and the owner of a tavern in Hamilton. His railway promotions increased the value of his land and in 1835 and 1837 he sold large blocks at solid profits. But MacNab's emphasis on his commercial career helped to split the Wentworth electorate into rural and urban divisions. With the exception of sponsoring town fairs, MacNab paid little attention to the rural vote and in the elections of 1834 he briefly retreated from the county to represent the new seat of Hamilton, the centre of his commercial affairs.

Although he was identified as a leading Tory, pragmatism rather than ideology shaped MacNab's commercial dealings. Tories in Toronto were his most prominent commercial opponents. Ignoring traditional trade channels with Britain, he was quite prepared to envisage the projected Great Western and Hamilton and Port Dover railways (the latter in connection with his steamship line) as mere links between the eastern and western United States. Nor was he loath to approach New York capitalists for financing. In fact, in the year of the Upper Canadian rebellion he made an impassioned plea for greater immigration of Americans, arguing, unlike most Tories, that "they were a useful and enterprising people and if admitted would be of great advantage to the country." He acknowledged that he would benefit from the sale of land to immigrants. He also criticized British interference in Upper Canadian banking affairs and even argued that British lawyers should be subject to probation before practising law in Upper Canada, as were Canadian lawyers in England. In cultivating his local roots, MacNab was prepared to contravene not only Toronto Tories but also the British Colonial Office.

His pragmatic actions show that MacNab is only partly encompassed by the term Tory. A supporter of the clergy reserves, he nonetheless believed that all denominations, including Roman Catholics, should have an equal share in the proceeds from them. Although an Anglican, he often attended a Presbyterian church, married a Catholic for his second wife, and opposed the rising Tory Orangeman Ogle Robert Gowan*, partly because of Gowan's strong Protestant stance. In 1836, indeed, he proclaimed his independence from all parties and partly in this guise was elected speaker of the house in 1837.

Certain Tory tenets did, however, strongly ap-

MacNab

peal to MacNab in the 1830s. He wanted class lines extended, not lowered or abolished. Even at the height of his conflict with Toronto officials, he favoured an appointed Legislative Council, suggesting only that its membership be made more representative. To be heard in ruling circles and to advance the economic and military policies he sought, MacNab attempted with some success to bypass the council, controlled as it was by Toronto Tories, and deal directly with Lieutenant Governor Sir Francis Bond Head*. In 1836 MacNab opposed responsible government because it would sever ties "with the Mother Country." Love of the military, while not exclusively a Tory phenomenon, was largely a preoccupation of the ruling group. Also, by building Dundurn Castle MacNab doubtless hoped to gain admission to the centre of the colony's social élite. But by 1837 it remained to be seen which element in MacNab's flexible alliance of Tory, commercial, and somewhat liberal characteristics would dominate.

The tensions in his personality and world view were brought into sharp focus by Mackenzie's ill-conceived rebellion in December 1837 and January 1838. With some 65 "hastily collected" men, MacNab sped by steamboat to Toronto where, encouraged by Head, he aspired to command the loyalist forces. Virtually all the British regulars in Toronto had been sent to Lower Canada to help suppress the rebellion there, but in Toronto Colonel James FITZGIBBON, a retired British regular and the adjutant-general of militia, refused to play a subordinate role to MacNab. A compromise was effected. Under FitzGibbon's nominal command, with MacNab leading the "Principal body," over 1,000 men marched north on 7 December to Montgomery's Tavern where they routed the rebels.

MacNab paid no heed to the complaints and schemes of the regular officers at Toronto who felt they had been ill treated by Head and himself. Following the victory at Montgomery's Tavern, Head placed MacNab in sole command of troops sent to the London District to suppress rebels led by Charles DUNCOMBE. The quality of MacNab's leadership was mixed. He faced extreme problems of communication, supply procurement, and control of raw, if eager, volunteers, but he also ignored certain basic operational procedures. He must share responsibility with the Commissariat Department for the hardships and decline in morale occasioned by delays in payment to militia and suppliers. The mobilization of over 1,500 men had been unnecessarily chaotic. As early as 14 December MacNab admitted that he had "at least six times as many men as I

require." However, he defended the value of his force as a threat and as evidence of local enthusiasm, maintaining that "the volunteers joining me in this District [London] would not be pleased to be dismissed and all left to the men of Gore." In the resultant confusion Duncombe, like Mackenzie before him, escaped to the United States.

In his treatment of rebel prisoners, MacNab acted to belie the image of himself as a close-minded Tory. He was able to appreciate degrees of involvement and, on his own initiative, he jailed only rebel leaders and allowed their "deceived" followers to remain free on their own recognizances. He even promised clemency to some. His concern for the common soldier also endeared him to the men under his command. MacNab believed that officers earned their subordinates' respect not only through courage in war but also by tempering strict justice with kindness and approachability off the battlefield. His relations with the militia were on the whole excellent, and he adroitly deflected criticism of mismanagement to the central command at Toronto and Montreal.

Mackenzie left his American sanctuary, re-entered Canadian territory, and occupied Navy Island on 13 Dec. 1837. Head continued to ignore his regular officers on staff and on 25 December dispatched the "popular" MacNab, complete with regular officers and naval support, to command forces on the Niagara frontier. With the active involvement of American sympathizers, the lieutenant governor admitted that the revolt had "assumed a new and different character," yet both he and MacNab reacted as they had earlier. Upper Canadian volunteers poured toward the frontier – some 2,000 by 29 December and over 3,500 by 10 January – yet supplies and billeting were inadequate and, more important, orders were vague. Head, while refusing to sanction an attack on the island, failed to spell out any alternatives such as a blockade of the island and its American suppliers. Neither MacNab nor Head seemed able to interpret contradictory reports about the strength or morale of their opponents; Colonel C. L. L. Foster*, a competent British regular, remained in Toronto; and Commander-in-Chief Colborne in Montreal was out of touch with the situation. MacNab alternated between drilling and dining. The weakness of the line of command became apparent when a dawn sortie on 29 December led by bibulous officers nearly ended in disaster. MacNab and his militia clearly lacked the discipline necessary for a passive containment of the rebels. Under MacNab's orders, on the night of 29 December,

MacNab

Andrew Drew*, a retired Royal Navy officer, led a contingent against the *Caroline*, an American boat supplying the rebels, and destroyed it in American waters.

Reaction was swift. An American citizen had been killed, and MacNab was indicted for murder in Erie County, N.Y. American newspapers became increasingly belligerent. Colborne immediately ordered Colonel Foster to take command of all regular and militia troops in the province, and Colonel Hughes, a British regular, to replace MacNab as commander at Niagara. Protesting that Hughes would receive "all the credit," although he and the militia had done "all the drudgery," MacNab finally had to yield to Colborne's perseverance. MacNab quit the frontier on 14 January, ironically the same night that Mackenzie and his rebels slipped unseen off Navy Island. While Colonel Hughes was occupying the nearly deserted island, the displaced MacNab was lobbying in Toronto for his lost command.

The intense emotional experience of the rebellion altered MacNab's flexible posture of the 1830s. A sense of having proven himself, strengthened by receiving a knighthood in March 1838, underlay his belief that the trappings of power and prestige were now rightfully his. He ignored the criticisms of Chief Justice John Beverley Robinson, William Henry Draper*, and Governor General Colborne concerning his role in the rebellion. He was also unaware that fundamental upheavals were about to occur in Upper Canada's political and social structure.

The decade of the 1840s was a time of complex political and economic change. Union of Upper and Lower Canada in 1841, abolition of the Corn Laws in 1846, and severe financial retrenchment presaged the establishment of responsible government in 1848. MacNab was not alone in his inability or reluctance to adjust to a new set of social, economic, and political priorities. Until the mid 1840s J. S. Cartwright, Henry Sherwood*, and a few other Tories supported MacNab's criticisms of imperial and domestic policy. Because MacNab was, after the retirement of Christopher Hagerman* early in 1840, the leader of this small group, many may have seen him as a caricature of a fossilized Tory. In fact he was not so much the advocate of an abstract political and social structure as he was the defender of his privileged place within the established structure. The vehemence of his resistance to the changes in the 1840s varied directly with his failure to procure a suitable placement.

In 1839 the British government and its chief representative in Canada, Charles Poulett Thomson*, soon to be Lord Sydenham, believed that the union of Upper and Lower Canada on the basis of equal representation and moderate, efficient leadership would lead to the assimilation of French Canadians and a more economical administration of the country. MacNab supported the economic aims of Thomson's union bill, but opposed it on cultural grounds because he felt that French speaking members would dominate the legislature and that Canada's traditional ties with Britain would be diminished. In March 1839 he, Sherwood, and several other Tories supported Cartwright's motions designed to secure dominance of the united legislature by loyal Upper Canadians. With important conservatives like W. H. Draper voting against them, Cartwright's motions were rejected.

After this defeat MacNab was prepared to work within the new union. He was even willing to accept Lord John Russell's definition in 1839 of responsible government: the Executive Council, although representative of the assembly, was responsible solely to the governor general, who was to have the right of executive selection and displacement as well as control of patronage. In this way traditional ties to and ultimate control by the crown would remain inviolate. In this way, too, MacNab assumed, the presence of the loyal could not be ignored.

In its relations with Canada during the late 1830s and 1840s the Colonial Office stressed the need for administrative expertise and economy, qualities which MacNab lacked. Financial stringency also directly affected him. His large fees as queen's counsel (an appointment he received in 1838) were closely scrutinized and only reluctantly granted in 1839 and 1840. Despite MacNab's protests, general command of the Gore militia was given to a more experienced officer during the Patriot disturbances of June 1838. Not only were MacNab's recommendations ignored in the militia reorganization of 1839–40, but also, because of cutbacks, he could no longer continue as an active officer. This loss of position meant a lower public profile, fewer patronage outlets, and a smaller cash income.

By mid 1841 he had focused his increasing discontent on the governor general. Sydenham encouraged his provincial secretary, Samuel Bealey HARRISON, whom he considered a talented political moderate, to seek election in Hamilton because MacNab had indicated he would run in Wentworth. When MacNab stood in Hamilton and defeated Harrison the awkward relations between Sydenham and himself became evident. Unable to agree on the right price for peace, both sides felt "ill-used" and betrayed.

523

MacNab

By ignoring the loyal, MacNab concluded, Sydenham was subverting the crown's true policy and must, therefore, be resisted. Unfortunately for MacNab's credibility, his statement of proper policy came suspiciously close to special pleading – who, after all, was more loyal than the gallant knight?

Although Sydenham could not pacify, he could and did isolate MacNab. Under Sydenham's tutelage, potential allies of MacNab such as Draper began to mould instead a party characterized by moderate views and able administrative talents. Short on support – he could count on six or seven votes in the legislature after the 1841 election – MacNab sought an agreement with the French Canadian party whereby the union would be ended and a dual administration bound by a common economic policy created instead. In common with Upper Canadian Reformers such as Robert Baldwin* and Francis Hincks*, MacNab realized that the French Canadians were the pivotal group within the union and that they could not or would not be assimilated, as Lord Durham [Lambton*] and Sydenham expected. Cut off from government preferment by Sydenham, MacNab reacted in a manner that had been successful in the past; he appealed directly to a higher authority. Inexplicably, or so it seemed to MacNab, a trip to England early in 1842 proved fruitless. The colonial secretary, Lord Stanley, denied him a baronetcy, and when a compromise appointment as adjutant-general of Canada West was botched by Sydenham's successor, Sir Charles Bagot, MacNab's bitterness knew no bounds. Increasingly isolated in the assembly – even Sherwood entered Bagot's government as solicitor general in July 1842 – MacNab behaved, as Bagot put it, "very factiously – and very ill."

In September 1842 MacNab was given his best opportunity to organize an effective party. The formation of the first Reform government of Baldwin and Louis-Hippolyte LA FONTAINE was opposed by Tories such as Sherwood and many moderate Conservatives. Draper withdrew from active politics and MacNab became leader of the disaffected Tory and moderate Conservative elements. But when the Reform government resigned in December 1843 over the question of patronage control, Sir Charles Metcalfe* called on Draper, the semi-retired moderate, to form a new administration. As Metcalfe later explained, MacNab was "so obnoxious to the Parties at present constituting the Majority in the House of Assembly . . . I could hardly place him in the Council."

Late in 1844 MacNab began to take stock. Old allies like Cartwright were leaving politics. Personal relations between MacNab and Draper had been strained at least since the *Caroline* affair. After his disappointments with colonial authorities, differences with Reformers no longer seemed so irreconcilable. Even on the crucial issue of loyalty he publicly admitted that Baldwin passed all tests. In fact he now distrusted Conservatives like Sherwood, who had deserted him on crucial questions in the past, more than many Reformers. The supple pragmatism evident prior to 1837 was beginning to reappear. As he confided to a friend, "perseverance and industry will soon carry me through all my misfortunes." From 1845 to 1847 his quiescent political behaviour can be attributed to a lucrative involvement in railways.

It was Sir Allan who, in July 1851, after consuming "one or two bottles of good port," fathered the famous phrase "all my politics are railroads." He was at various times after 1845 president of three companies, chairman of one, and a director of at least two others, involving service on the Great Western, 1845–54; Grand Trunk, 1854–56; Galt and Guelph, 1853–60; Hamilton and Toronto, 1853–56; Hamilton and Port Dover, 1854–60; North-West Transportation, Navigation, and Railway Company, 1858–60. He chaired the assembly's railway committee seven times between 1848 and 1857. George Brown* accused him of having "managed to make or mar every railroad scheme as he thought proper." MacNab in his public speeches and private letters encouraged this judgement. As was the case with many of MacNab's activities, however, the reality was more mundane.

In the pre-1850 exploratory period of railway development MacNab's indomitable energy and questionable scruples stood him in good stead. As the Great Western's president between 1845 and 1849 he was active at home and abroad. He tirelessly disarmed his two major competitors, the Niagara and Detroit Rivers Railway led by John PRINCE and the Toronto and Goderich Railway led by the venerable Toronto businessman William Allan* and championed in the assembly by MacNab's rival for the Tory leadership, Henry Sherwood. By branding the former road an arm of American capitalists and the latter an extension of the Canada Company, he gained support for the Great Western. He also made a clandestine arrangement with Prince who, in return for a rumoured emolument, withdrew his road from direct competition for three years.

Despite his criticisms of Prince's financing, MacNab, too, sought money south of the border and for a brief period even employed as an agent William Hamilton Merritt, the financial and political representative of the Niagara and Detroit railway. His contacts with British capitalists reveal a more sordid side of MacNab's railway career. He unloaded 55,000 Great Western shares to a syndicate headed by the notorious British railway king, George Hudson, who in turn attempted to sell these shares at inflated prices before the first call for capital was due. MacNab and Peter Buchanan* joined the syndicate in selling the as yet worthless stock. It mattered not to the speculator whether the buyer could supply capital beyond the initial premium, though the road could not be constructed if future calls for capital could not be met. Oblivious to this distinction, MacNab made a profit of £2,500. Because of a slumping economy, however, the syndicate could not unload all its shares, nor could it pay the first call. For £5,000 MacNab allowed them to return all but 10,000 shares. The railway's interests were secondary to those of MacNab's pocketbook. His profiteering, failure to locate secure sources of capital for the railway, ineptness as a manager, and declining parliamentary influence led to his being deposed as president of the Great Western (although he remained a director) in 1849.

For MacNab this was one of a series of setbacks. In 1846 his wife had died. In 1847 he was again unable to secure the adjutant-generalship. When Draper resigned in May 1847 Sherwood, from whom MacNab could hope for little sufferance, took over as government leader. Nor was he able to effect an alliance with Baldwin because, as one historian has noted, the Reformers were "strong enough . . . to neglect the knight's approaches." Although MacNab had been speaker since 1844 and expected re-election in 1848, the new Baldwin–La Fontaine government supported Augustin-Norbert MORIN instead. Having over-speculated in land (late in 1845 he and William Cayley* had purchased from George Rolph 145 acres in the town of Dundas for £7,200) his finances were chaotic, and creditors were eager "to put on the screws." Gout was a constant companion.

His frustration and anger were focused by the passage in 1849 of the Rebellion Losses Bill which MacNab believed rewarded past rebel activity. He reverted to the factious and bitter stance characteristic of him in 1843. Sustained by economic discontent in Montreal and scattered Upper Canadian urban centres, he both harangued and vilified Lord Elgin [BRUCE], the French, and the "disloyal" Reformers. Unlike some Montreal Tories, however, he did not condone the firing of the parliament buildings and the signing of the Annexation Manifesto. Rather he went to London and again made a personal appeal to higher authorities. Informed by the Colonial Office that British intervention in Canadian affairs by disallowing the act would be a contravention of responsible government, he returned home, defeated and somewhat subdued.

The obstreperous, arch-Tory element in MacNab was finally extinguished late in 1849. The moderate element, visible in the pre-rebellion era, came gradually to the fore and allowed him to bridge the gap between the extreme Tory and moderate Conservative factions. His moderate behaviour during the rebellion losses crisis, compared to that of many Tories, stood him in good stead. Gradually he became the Tories' leading spokesman on major issues. Having eased the leadership from Sherwood in 1849–50, MacNab, in the early 1850s, did his best to keep the high church, old Tory section in check. Aware in 1852, as he was in the early 1840s, that parliamentary strength ultimately depended on an alliance with French speaking members, he attempted to undercut the Upper Canadian Reform section of the Hincks–Morin government formed late in 1851 by approaching Joseph-Édouard Cauchon*, an able follower of Morin. Preliminary agreement on an alliance between them which would aim to guarantee "each section of the Province . . . the entire control of their respective legislation and administration" was reached, but the alliance was not put into practice at that date. A supporter of sectarian schools, MacNab also allowed the Conservatives he led to leave the secularization of the clergy reserves, an issue on which he had been moderate since the 1830s, an open question in the election of 1854.

MacNab's moderation in part facilitated the formation in September 1854 of a governing alliance between Upper Canadian Conservatives and the Hincks-Morin Reformers. It was opposed by a few arch-Tories and a larger group of Clear Grits led by George Brown. With MacNab as premier the coalition passed important pieces of legislation – restructuring of the militia, secularization of the clergy reserves, abolition of seigneurial tenure, and a measure to make the Legislative Council elective – which placed MacNab in the vanguard of political reform. The coalition of 1854 was possible because for moderate Conservatives and moderate Reformers, both French and English, economic ties transcended sectarian differences. A shared desire for economic rationalization was coupled with the

MacNab

French Canadian moderate Reformers' fear of the growing power of the Clear Grits. Like John A. Macdonald*, MacNab would seem to have been direct heir of Draper's moderate conservatism of the 1840s.

MacNab's political conduct in the 1850s, however, cannot be understood apart from his personal railway affairs. By 1850 specialized talents in railway management were required which MacNab did not have. As he came to realize that he could not wield real power, he increasingly began to covet its trappings. The 1850s were for him a quest for security, an endeavour, as he put it, "to wind up my distracted affairs – and make my children comfortable." The means he used were often unprincipled. For instance, he had been the Great Western's president when in 1847 Charles Stuart, the chief engineer, ran his survey through the laird's domain. As a director in 1851 MacNab sold part of his Burlington Heights property to the railway at an exorbitant price. By 1860 his profits from railways totalled in modern values around $400,000.

MacNab, privy to the shady manoeuvres of the promoters of a Great Western subsidiary, also attempted extortion. Peter Buchanan warned another promoter that "unless [MacNab] has confirmed in a formal way your acts in the Hamilton and Toronto, he could find little difficulty in driving a Coach and four through them." But MacNab could press only so far; there was also written proof that he himself had an interest in a construction contract for a road of which he was a director. Although his worried co-directors were quite willing to deceive shareholders, the government, and the general public, they drew the line at betraying their own colleagues. Not so MacNab. His skills obsolete, his reputation suspect, he was, in the words of an associate, "an excrescence which cannot be got rid of."

The Great Western tried to drop MacNab as a director in June 1854, and tentatively promised him a £5,000 retirement gift. MacNab accepted the promise and then turned to the Great Western's arch-rival, the Grand Trunk Railway, to whose policies concerning rate agreements and general competitive practices he had been inching closer as his relations with the Great Western deteriorated. Thus, the coalition government of 1854, sanctioned by Francis Hincks, a Reformer and long-time Grand Trunk promoter, and by John Ross*, president of that company, was politically palatable to MacNab primarily because as premier he could extort money from the Great Western while extending his influence into Grand Trunk circles. In 1854 one Great Western director pushed for "some immediate

arrangement . . . with MacNab for £5000 . . . [to] secure his continuance and support as Head of the Government." MacNab received the £5,000 in April 1855, but he was not as fortunate with the Grand Trunk. His precarious political control began to slip in 1855 and 1856. MacNab had rarely been in the assembly because he was crippled by gout, and some of his colleagues felt he had delayed the bill to make the Legislative Council elective. Objecting to the laird's narrow use of patronage, his increasingly weak leadership, and, no doubt, his attempts to gain power within the Grand Trunk, John Ross resigned from the coalition government in April 1856. Pleading lack of a sectional majority, the rest of the government members from Canada West resigned in May. Carried into the assembly, MacNab denied having opposed any liberal measures proposed by government. He got no support and resigned, whereupon John A. Macdonald constructed a new ministry including, with the exception of MacNab, most of the old. In November he was ousted as a director of the Grand Trunk. MacNab had played out his options: it seemed to many people that in politics as well as railways he was now totally expendable.

One further Great Western payment of £6,000 was given MacNab by its vice-president John Radcliffe, who in turn sought MacNab's help in purchasing a complex of lines collectively known as the Southern route. MacNab, doubtless amazed at Radcliffe's obtuseness, accepted with alacrity. Buttressed by a baronetcy (secured in July 1856 on the recommendation of the sympathetic governor general, Sir Edmund Walker HEAD) and the Great Western's £6,000 donation, he set sail for England.

Having achieved nothing for the Great Western, he returned briefly to Canada in 1857 to resign his seat in the legislature, and then went back to England. In 1859 he unsuccessfully contested the seat of Brighton in the British House of Commons. Weighted by financial problems and unsaleable land, he returned again to Hamilton to settle his affairs. Despite his gout he ran for the Legislative Council for the Western division in 1860, was elected, and became speaker in 1862. MacNab's move to the Legislative Council was eased by the prospect of a substantial land sale to the Conservative-controlled government. He received $20,000, but it was not enough to satisfy his many creditors. In August 1862 the laird of Dundurn died, a penniless debtor.

Even his death was controversial. While creditors argued over his effects, possession of his soul was fought for by the Anglican and Roman Catholic churches. The latter quarrel was won by his strong-willed Roman Catholic sister-in-law, Sophia Stuart. Although in 1855 MacNab's second daughter Sophia had married an English baron, the Viscount Bury, Sir Allan was left without a male heir. His only son Robert had died in 1834 and thus his many social distinctions could not be passed on.

Inept at planning and organization but a promoter and enthusiast in many commercial, military, and political schemes, MacNab cultivated an image at the expense of substance and his triumphs had about them a hollow ring. But because he was not completely of the feudal world or a member of its ruling class, or completely of the world of steam and entrepreneurial activities, he was able to serve as an unsteady link between both. In doing so he reflected many of the contradictions evident in Upper Canada during a period of intense economic, political, and social change.

PETER BASKERVILLE

[Allan Napier MacNab was a public and business figure for such an extended time that his letters, or references to him, can be found in almost all extant collections. For this reason only the most important sources consulted are listed. P.B.]

HPL, Ferrie papers; Hamilton biography, Sir Allan Napier MacNab. MTCL, William Allan papers; Robert Baldwin papers; Samuel Peters Jarvis papers. PAC, MG 23, L4; MG 24, A13; A15; A40; B4; B14; B17; D16; D18; E1, 2–40; G20; I25; MG 26, A, 539; RG 1, E3, 21, 49, 54; RG 5, A1, 115, 127, 138, 140–41, 184, 195, 217, 242; RG 7, G16, A, 3; RG 8, I (C series), 610, 924, 1227, 1272, 1274; RG 9, I, B3, 2, 5, 6; RG 30, 1–17. PAO, Cartwright (John Solomon) papers; Gilkinson (William and Jasper T.) papers; Jarvis-Powell papers; Macaulay (John) papers; Robinson (John Beverley) papers; Street (Samuel) papers. PRO, CO 42/439, 42/444. QUA, John Solomon Cartwright papers; Kirkpatrick-Nickle legal records; John Macaulay papers. UTL-TF, MS coll. 56. UWO, 144(Harris family papers).

Arthur papers (Sanderson). Can., House of Commons, *Journals*, 1870, app.1. Can., Prov. of, Legislative Assembly, *Journals*, 1841–62. *Debates of the Legislative Assembly of United Canada. Elgin-Grey papers* (Doughty). Macdonald, *Letters* (Johnson and Stelmack), I. *Opinions of the Canadian press of the Hon. Sir Allan Napier MacNab, bart., late speaker of the House of Commons in Canada* (London, 1859). U.C., House of Assembly, *Journal*, 1830–41. *British Colonist* (Toronto), 1838–54. *Colonial Advocate*, 1834. *Correspondent and Advocate* (Toronto), 1834–36. *Examiner* (Toronto), 1838–55. *Globe*, 1845–62. *Gore Gazette* (Ancaster, [Ont.]), 1827–29. *Hamilton Gazette* (Hamilton, [Ont.]), 1852–55. *Hamilton Spectator*, 1847–62. *Leader*, 1853–58. *Times* (Hamilton, [Ont.]), 1858–62. *Toronto Patriot*, 1832–44. Dent, *Canadian portrait gallery*, IV. Morgan, *Sketches of celebrated Canadians*. Notman and Taylor, *Portraits of British Americans*, II.

P. A. Baskerville, "The boardroom and beyond; aspects of the Upper Canadian railroad community" (unpublished PHD thesis, Queen's University, Kingston, Ont., 1973). D. R. Beer, "Transitional toryism in the 1840's as seen in the political career of Sir Allan MacNab, 1839–1849" (unpublished MA thesis, Queen's University, 1963). M. F. Campbell, *A mountain and a city, the story of Hamilton* (Toronto, 1966). Careless, *Union of the Canadas*. Craig, *Upper Canada*. [Charles Durand], *Reminiscences of Charles Durand of Toronto, barrister* (Toronto, 1897). Johnston, *Head of the lake* (1958). Marion MacRae, *MacNab of Dundurn* (Toronto and Vancouver, 1971). J. P. Martyn, "Upper Canada and border incidents 1837–38: a study of the troubles on the American frontier following the rebellion of 1837" (unpublished MA thesis, University of Toronto, 1962). C. F. Smith, "The political career of Allan Napier MacNab, 1825–1836; a study in determination" (unpublished MA thesis, University of Guelph, Guelph, Ont., 1971). W. S. Wallace, *The knight of Dundurn* (Toronto, 1960).

McPHELIM, FRANCIS, merchant and politician; b. 1811 in Donegal (Republic of Ireland), son of Peter and Catherine McPhelim; m. in 1839 Rosanna McGuirk of Saint John, N.B.; d. 14 Oct. 1866 in Buctouche, N.B.

Francis McPhelim immigrated with his family to Buctouche in 1821. Like his father he entered the mercantile and shipping business of that community. As a prosperous Irish Catholic, he soon assumed a position of leadership for his people in New Brunswick. In 1850 he was elected to represent Kent County in the assembly, and although he was pledged to the principle of responsible government, like most of his north shore colleagues he supported the "compact" party. During the first administration of Charles Fisher* and the "smashers" (1854–56), McPhelim became a leading Conservative, apparently because of his opposition to temperance. His role is uncertain in the political crisis which developed in May 1856 when Lieutenant Governor John Henry Thomas Manners-Sutton* forced the resignation of the "smashers" for their failure to repeal the Prohibition Act of 1855, but McPhelim was appointed postmaster general in the "compact" government which was formed at that time to support the governor's position. He thus became the first Roman Catholic appointed to the Executive Council, a recognition both of McPhelim's abilities and of the rising political power of the Irish in New Brunswick. Although the summer elections of 1856 were primarily concerned with temperance and the governor's prerogative, in parts of New Brunswick the contest was seen as one against "Rum and Romanism"; this emphasis helped to propel the Irish vote to the "compact" party and increased McPhelim's

McQueen

importance in the government. By July 1857 he and his "compact" colleagues were back in the opposition [see John Hamilton Gray*], where he spent the remainder of his political career.

McPhelim established a reputation as a moderate in religious matters, and, refusing to use Irish political power as a club, he sought instead to win concessions with a minimum of bitterness. He defended King's College, an Anglican institution, against the assaults of the Baptists and Methodists, and in turn won Church of England support in the matter of lower education. In 1858, when, during discussion of the Public Schools Act, a debate developed concerning the reading of the Scriptures in the parish schools, Protestant opinion was divided between fear and appeasement of the Catholics. The options seemed to be either Protestant schools or schools without religious instruction. But McPhelim proposed an amicable solution to the impasse, whereby the Scriptures would be read in the schools, but Catholic children would use the Douay Bible. When combined with the responsibility of teachers to inculcate Christian principles, the McPhelim amendment in effect gave legal status to Catholic denominational schools in New Brunswick; it was a small but significant victory for Catholic schools.

McPhelim's later career was marked by the same moderation. He supported the Intercolonial Railway continuously during the 1850s and 1860s, but preferred construction of the western extension of the European and North American Railway to the United States. When confederation was proposed, he refused to support the plan, but was too restrained in his condemnation to retain favour with his strongly anti-confederate constituents. He lost his seat in 1865, and later that year was appointed high sheriff of Kent County; he died the next year.

In a period not remembered for ethnic and religious tolerance, McPhelim's moderate leadership of the Irish was at least in part responsible for the relative social stability of New Brunswick.

P. M. TONER

N.B. Museum, Observer [E. S. Carter], "Linking the past with the present" (clippings). *Gleaner* (Chatham, N.B.), 1864–66. *Morning Freeman* (Saint John, N.B.), 1851–66. *Morning News* (Saint John, N.B.), 1853–66. *Morning Telegraph* (Saint John, N.B.), 1863–66. G. E. Fenety, "Political notes," *Progress* (Saint John, N.B.), 1894 (collected in a scrapbook in N.B. Museum and PAC). Hannay, *History of N.B.* Lawrence, *Judges of N.B.* (Stockton). MacNutt, *New Brunswick.*

McQUEEN, THOMAS, stonemason, journalist, politician, and poet; b. 9 Oct. 1803 in the parish of Kilbirnie, Ayrshire, Scotland; he married and had several children; d. 26 June 1861 at Goderich, Canada West.

Thomas McQueen's father was a labourer in a rural parish 20 miles southwest of Glasgow, and McQueen received little schooling because he was required to work. At the age of nine an accident left him convalescent for a long period and lame for the rest of his life. He developed an interest in books, although his reading never led him away from his origins. He went to work as a stonemason at 14 or 15, during years of intense labour unrest when working class journalism became established. Stimulated by the agitation for parliamentary reform in the 1820s and early 1830s, he wrote for the periodical press and lectured on the rights of the working man. He also published three volumes of poetry – much of a political nature – and issued a weekly series of essays and lectures on political economy, education, and morals.

In 1842 McQueen immigrated to Canada West and settled near Pakenham in the Bathurst District, immediately north of an established settlement of Glasgow weavers and other Scots. Although the rocky land of much of the district was ill suited to agriculture, he was impressed by the rent-free, cheap, and fertile land available elsewhere in Upper Canada and contrasted the settler's opportunities to prosper with "the revolting condition of the five-farthing per-yard weaver" in Britain whom the industrial system had "driven within the precincts of a lingering starvation." From 1842 to 1846 he worked as a mason throughout the Pakenham area. His journalistic instincts were not long in surfacing, and he began to contribute regularly to the *Bathurst Courier*, vigorously advocating secular education and deriding the claims of the Church of England.

In 1847 Malcolm Cameron*, a Sarnia merchant and radical Grit member of the assembly for Lanark, offered McQueen £100 a year to edit a paper in the newly settled Huron Tract. McQueen did not accept this offer, but in 1848 he moved to Goderich and on 4 February the first issue of the *Huron Signal* appeared with McQueen as editor and Charles Dolsen as publisher.

McQueen saw his principal task as the revival of the Reform party in Huron County, represented in the assembly by William Cayley*, a Tory lawyer from Toronto and a nephew of Bishop John STRACHAN. Huron was divided between conservative Ulstermen and reform-minded dissenting Scots, but the Reformers were fragmented and disorganized and in the *Signal* McQueen set out to give them a point of focus. He urged the farmers of Huron to elect "one of your own class," and denounced toryism as "the curse of the civilized world – the liberal meaning of it is to exalt and pamper a few individuals in luxuriant indolence, at the expense of the sweat and toil and degradation of the great mass of industrious mankind." McQueen's triumph came in 1851 when Malcolm Cameron defeated Cayley in Huron. By this time, as McQueen put it, he was "tired of living in the extreme verge of civilization in Goderich." In 1852 he took the editorship of a new Reform journal, the Hamilton *Canadian*, at £200 a year. During the next two years the *Canadian* developed from a weekly to a tri-weekly and McQueen acquired a province-wide reputation as an advocate of reform and temperance. Early in 1854 Francis Hincks* asked him to edit the Montreal *Pilot and Journal of Commerce* at £250 a year and he had offers from newspapers in Halton County, Belleville, and elsewhere. But he chose to return that year to Goderich and the *Huron Signal*.

In the election of the same year McQueen ran against Cayley on a radical Grit platform, promising to seek the abolition of the clergy reserves, separate schools, and seigneurial tenure in Lower Canada, and to work for reciprocity with the United States and a union of the British North American provinces. He was defeated by a strong Conservative turnout in the town of Goderich.

After 1854 McQueen took a special interest in evaluating agricultural methods and educating farmers in proper drainage, rotation of crops, drill husbandry, fencing, and the use of fertilizers and machinery. He bought an 800-acre property in Huron County and continued as editor of the *Signal* until his death in 1861.

H. J. M. JOHNSTON

Thomas McQueen was the author of *My gloaming amusements, a variety of poems* (Beith, Scot., 1831); *The exile; a poem, in seven books* (Glasgow, 1836); *The moorland minstrel* (Glasgow, 1840); and "Report on the county of Huron," Upper Canada, Board of Agriculture, *Journal and Trans.* (Toronto), II (1856–57), 172–203. *Bathurst Courier* (Perth, [Ont.]), 1842–48. *Huron Signal* (Goderich, [Ont.]), 3 July 1861. Morgan, *Bibliotheca Canadensis*, 273–75. Wallace, *Macmillan dictionary*, 487. Andrew Haydon, *Pioneer sketches in the district of Bathurst* (Toronto, 1925), 237–85. James Scott, *The settlement of Huron County* (Toronto, 1966), 247–49.

MACTAVISH, WILLIAM, HBC governor and governor of Assiniboia; b. 29 March 1815 in Edinburgh, Scotland, eldest son of Dugald Mactavish, a lawyer, and Letitia Lockhart; d. 23 July 1870 in Liverpool, England.

In 1792 Simon McTavish* of the North West Company introduced himself to the Mactavish clan chief, Lachlan Mactavish, and established a friendship which brought Lachlan's second son, John George McTavish*, into the Canadian fur trade in 1798. When he had become chief factor, John George McTavish in turn placed his nephews, William and Dugald*, into apprenticeships with the Hudson's Bay Company on 2 Jan. 1833.

William Mactavish sailed to Rupert's Land that summer, and was appointed to Norway House (Man.) under Donald Ross*. Writing to James HARGRAVE in December 1833, John George McTavish indicated the degree of personal influence involved in the introduction of apprentices: William "has been well educated but it depends greatly on the first master he has in this Country whether that education be of future use to him [.] Gov. [George Simpson*] promised me voluntarily that the boy should be placed under your eye his first winter, why this was departed from gives me uneasiness." In 1834, however, William was transferred to York Factory to work under Hargrave at his uncle's insistence.

From the outset William Mactavish's industrious habits won him the approval of company officers. Ross characterized him as "promising," and Hargrave thought that "his merits are indeed of the first order." As an apprentice clerk at York Factory he was trained in accounting and employed in the inventorying and preparation of shipments at this major supply depot. His older sister, Letitia*, reunited with William upon her marriage to Hargrave in January 1840, said that he "pad[ded] about as if he had the whole charge of the Factory, & is in the store from 1/2 past 4 A.M. till 8 at night." Apparently overwork frequently jeopardized the young accountant's health; he spent at least one winter recuperating at the Red River Settlement, in 1836. His ambition was rewarded, however, with a promotion in 1841 to the post of general accountant for the Northern Department and second in command of the factory.

With both his uncle and his brother-in-law to further his career, Mactavish's energetic efforts brought him up quickly through the ranks of the HBC. Hargrave was particularly interested in preparing Mactavish to succeed him at York. For

Mactavish

this reason both John George McTavish and Hargrave saw to it that Mactavish was continually brought to Simpson's attention, even arranging that in 1845 Mactavish should travel back from a furlough in England with Simpson. The following year Mactavish received his commission as chief trader and took temporary charge of York Factory in Hargrave's absence. Clearly Simpson had by this time begun to appreciate Mactavish's talents. In 1847, when it looked as though a new person would be needed to supervise the trade at Upper Fort Garry (Winnipeg) upon Alexander Christie*'s departure, Simpson made plans to move Mactavish to Red River, though, for some unexplained reason, they were not carried out. Instead Mactavish was placed in charge of Sault Ste Marie (Ont.) the following year. He returned to York Factory in 1850, and from 1851 to the autumn of 1856 had charge of it; he received his commission as chief factor in 1852. Replaced by Hargrave, who returned to York in 1856, Mactavish spent another furlough in England before assuming the new post of officer in charge of Upper Fort Garry, the most "troublesome and complicated charge" in Rupert's Land.

The man who came to Red River in 1857 was not only a thoroughly trained and efficient business administrator. The qualities of "mental calibre," "energy," and "determination" as well as "executive ability" were also observed in this "well-bred … Englishman." Tall, sandy-haired, and sporting "the Palmerston style of whiskers and a heavy moustache," he had a well-modulated voice and manner. A more intimate portrait of Mactavish is offered by his sister Letitia who described his love of fishing and hunting and his sense of humour. Essentially, she saw him as a "dreamer," with interests in such current theories as phrenology. "William," she wrote to her father, "has made himself acquainted with the notions of everyone who has got into difficulties with Church or State for being too far in advance of the world." He also applied his intellectual curiosity to the study of natural history in Rupert's Land, exchanging specimens and information with his friend Dr William Fraser Tolmie* of York Factory and with other HBC men in the territories. In 1862 he was a secretary of the short-lived Institute of Rupert's Land.

Shortly after coming to Red River, Mactavish ended a life of determined bachelorhood by marrying Mary Sarah McDermot, the mixed-blood Catholic daughter of businessman Andrew McDermot*. Although Mactavish's will provided for three "illegitimate daughters" in

Stromness, Scotland, the four "country-born" children that are known are by his wife Mary Sarah.

Mactavish's career underwent a dramatic change of direction when in 1858 he was appointed to replace Francis Godschall Johnson as governor of Assiniboia. He accepted the appointment under protest, and stated 11 years later that he would rather have been "a stoker in hell." He firmly believed that the administration of the fur trade and of the settlement should not fall to a single person. At the same time he felt himself unsuited to the political arena, particularly because the ever difficult office of company-appointed governor was becoming more so after 1858 with the increased number of Canadian settlers agitating for representative government and the annexation of Red River to Canada. If ever the HBC was an unpopular government, it was during Mactavish's period in office. Realizing this problem, he tried to secure a permanent military force from Britain, unsuccessfully; he also failed to mobilize what popular support may have existed for his government. Mactavish did not take an active and creative role in the fashioning of a new political structure. When, however, pressure for the reorganization of Red River came from both the Canadian party and the Métis he attempted to respond in what he considered the best interests of the settlement. As a result he drew criticism from all quarters, including his own superiors in the HBC.

Mactavish's position was further complicated by a multiplication of his responsibilities in the 1860s. For a brief time in 1861–62 he served as president of the courts of Red River and Rupert's Land when the HBC was unable to find a suitable recorder to succeed Dr John Bunn. Also, when Sir George Simpson died in 1860, Mactavish, in response to Simpson's wishes, was appointed acting governor of Rupert's Land. Although supervising a territory considerably smaller than Simpson's empire (the Western and Montreal departments were now "independent" and under separate authority), Mactavish still acquired a substantial administrative responsibility. Being a good fur trade administrator, however, he assumed the post without the reluctance he had shown for the political appointment. He was relieved as acting governor of Rupert's Land in 1862 when the company appointed Alexander Grant Dallas* as governor, but with Dallas' resignation in 1864 Mactavish became governor in his own right.

Thus it was as governor of Rupert's Land and governor of Assiniboia that Mactavish served throughout the Red River Rebellion of 1869–70. With powers which were in theory absolute, he alone could perhaps have short-circuited Louis Riel*'s Métis uprising, overruled Dr John Christian Schultz*'s vocal agitation, and overseen a less tempestuous transfer of Rupert's Land from the HBC to Canada in 1870. His lack of effective action might be seen as a reflection of his distaste for political office and his rapidly deteriorating health. It was also, however, a result of his own assessment of the situation at Red River. He believed that the majority of Red River inhabitants, both English and French speaking, supported at least passively the existing Council of Assiniboia. The opposition which flared up sporadically he considered to be the work of a few "designing demagogue[s]." His sympathies lay apparently with the older inhabitants of Red River, the Métis, the HBC people, and the descendants of the colonists brought by Selkirk [Douglas*], all of whom, he argued, should have had a voice in the transfer of Rupert's Land.

Although never condoning or authorizing Riel's provisional government, and gravely fearing the threatened seizure of HBC property by the Métis, Mactavish felt that the Métis had the right to demand a specific settlement with Canada. While attempting to obtain the aid of the Catholic clergy in persuading the Métis to wait for a legal settlement, he reported to the HBC in London in 1868 and 1869 his objections to the Canadian land claims and to the surveys which were preceding the legal transfer. Mactavish placed the blame for the unrest mainly on the Canadian party and to a lesser extent on the Canadian government. In his correspondence in the 1860s he had expressed continued concern for the way in which the *Nor'Wester* and men such as Schultz agitated against both company and Métis. At the same time he criticized the Canadian government for its refusal to consult the inhabitants of Rupert's Land about the transfer and its apparent attempt to assert authority before the transfer had taken place. He suspected that William McDougall*, the federally appointed lieutenant governor of Rupert's Land, with the Canadian government's sanction, was encouraging political disturbance so as to precipitate the fall of the HBC government and weaken the company's position in its attempt to obtain a £300,000 land settlement. Although the Canadian prime minister, Sir John A. Macdonald*, claimed that Mactavish had "never intimated that he had even a suspicion of discontent existing," Mactavish had certainly informed his superiors in London of it, and when he stopped at Ottawa on

his return from London in April 1869, he had an opportunity to warn the Canadian government of the difficulties as well, if Macdonald had been prepared to heed him.

With Riel's seizure of Upper Fort Garry on 1 Nov. 1869, Mactavish's government virtually came to an end. One of his last reluctant acts before being imprisoned by Riel was to issue on 16 November at McDougall's insistence a proclamation of the transfer of Rupert's Land to Canada. After this proclamation the legal status of Mactavish's government is uncertain, but for practical purposes Riel was in control.

Nevertheless, Mactavish continued to act as HBC governor of Rupert's Land to the best of his ability until his departure in May 1870. While Riel's prisoner, and under pressure from him, Mactavish authorized loans to the Métis in money and kind from the trading stores, which closed because furs and supplies were rerouted to avoid Upper Fort Garry. The company lost ground to its competitors both within and outside the settlement, and with the threat of financial losses the chief factors and chief traders expressed dissatisfaction with Mactavish's handling of the situation. It was as a fur trader rather than as a politician that Mactavish pointed out to Joseph Howe* on 14 May 1870 that any government which sought to remove as suddenly as the Canadian government had done the economic base of a hinterland would cause "widely spread misery and starvation [among the native inhabitants]: and the consequent disorders and embarrassment to the Government which spring from such scenes." The difficulties of Mactavish's dual responsibility at this time were compounded by his realization that he was dying. He had, in fact, been bedridden since the summer of 1869, and had conducted both government and fur trade affairs under the severe debilitation of advanced tuberculosis. Still, not until 15 Jan. 1870 did he draft his resignation from the company, declaring himself "so feeble as to be unfit for business of any kind." He was released from prison by Riel in February and on 17 May he and his family finally left for Scotland. Travelling via St Paul (Minn.) and New York, he reached Liverpool on 21 July where he died two days later.

Those who knew Mactavish in his capacity as governor of Rupert's Land or as governor of Assiniboia agreed with Mactavish's own evaluation of himself. Trained in the fur trade, he felt quite capable of administering Rupert's Land, and was respected in that capacity. By his own admission, however, he found many of the duties of the

McVicar

governor of Assiniboia "disgusting." A more forceful and decisive course by the governor might have averted the Métis rebellion, but Mactavish, whether through an underestimation of the hostility between the different groups at Red River, a lack of military power, or helplessness born of illness, chose not to act. Thus as governor of Rupert's Land he became not a master but a victim of his situation.

N. JAYE GOOSSEN

HBC Arch. A.11/96, 11 Dec. 1858; A.12/42, f.94; A.12/44–45; A.33/4, 5 July 1852; B.154/a/24, f.32; B.239/a/13, 2 Aug. 1850; B.239/a/148, 13 Aug. 1834; B.239/a/154, f.58; B.239/a/168, 16 Aug. 1848; B.239/a/176, 12 July 1851; D.9/1; D.10/1. PAM, MG 1, D2; D8, Ewen Macdonald to Robert Campbell, 16 March 1870; D14, 1792; MG 3, D1, Pierre Poitras to Louis Riel, 13 Feb. 1872; MG 7, B4, register of marriages, 1835–60, 17 Oct. 1836; MG 9, A76, file 93, Donald Ross to George Simpson, 19 Feb. 1834; George Simpson to James Hargrave, 30 June 1847. Somerset House (London), PPR/334, will of William Mactavish (copy at HBC Arch.). Begg, *Red River journal* (Morton). *Hargrave correspondence* (Glazebrook). Mactavish, *Letters of Letitia Hargrave* (MacLeod). *Nor'Wester*, 1861. F. E. Bartlett, "William Mactavish, the last governor of Assiniboia" (unpublished MA thesis, University of Manitoba, Winnipeg, 1964).

McVICAR (MacVicar, McVicker), ROBERT, HBC chief trader and author; b. before 1799, probably at Bowmore, Isle of Islay, Scotland; d. April 1864 at "The Station" (Thunder Bay), Canada West.

First employed as a Hudson's Bay Company clerk at York Factory, 1812–14, Robert McVicar spent the next 14 years in the Saskatchewan and Athabasca country, participating in the stirring events of the Hudson's Bay Company's rivalry with the North West Company, which often involved physical conflicts, and rising in the HBC's service. By the time he reached Île-à-la-Crosse in 1815, he had already acquired a reputation as a fighter; he was to clash at least twice with Simon McGillivray, the Métis son of William McGillivray*, and was held prisoner briefly by the Nor'Westers at Fort Chipewyan. His first winter command was at Fort Resolution, on Great Slave Lake, from 1819 to 1823. With the amalgamation of the fur-trading companies in 1821, McVicar became a chief trader. He gave assistance to the Arctic land expeditions of John Franklin* in 1819–22 and 1825–27 by purchasing and collecting supplies. It was Franklin, as justice of the peace, who married McVicar and Christina McBeath, the daughter of pioneers

brought out by Lord Selkirk [Douglas*], at Fort Chipewyan, probably in May 1827.

The pattern of McVicar's life altered with his transfer to the Montreal Department in 1827. He was sent to the Saint-Maurice District where competition from rival fur-traders was extremely keen. He was at first over-optimistic about overcoming this opposition, as he was about his own financial prospects when he retired from the HBC service in 1830 and settled in the Lac-des-Deux-Montagnes region. There he lived for a decade, building his home, Silver Heights, increasing his skill as a "practical farmer," working with the local agricultural society, developing his interest in immigration policy and politics, and helping to raise a volunteer force to suppress rebellion in the province in 1837. By the 1840s, McVicar's resources had dwindled and he was seeking employment, at a time when he did not have friends in office. Twice he considered a move to the United States. His hopes for a share in the development of Saugeen Township in the Huron Tract, and his ideas for the assistance of Scottish immigrants, sent in a series of letters in 1843 and 1844 to officials in the Department of Crown Lands, came to nothing, as did his request for an appointment as a crown land agent.

At Norval, Canada West, with his family in 1844, he finally received word of an appointment as inspector of clergy reserves for the Western District. The work was uncongenial and arduous, but it did pay 15s. per day for part of the next two years. He continued to reside in villages on the fringes of the Huron Tract. A number of his letters during this period were printed in 1853 as *Letters on emigration from the British Isles, and the settlement of the waste lands in the Province of Canada*. These letters to newspapers and to prominent officials urged the more rapid opening up of lands in Canada West, especially to Scottish settlement.

Eventually McVicar did receive an appointment as land agent and postmaster, apparently in 1860, but it was in the Lake Superior country, which he considered unsuitable for immediate settlement. In 1859 he had cleared a small piece of land several miles north of the HBC's establishment at Fort William (Thunder Bay), built a shanty, and applied for permission to purchase one or two hundred acres. No action was taken on this request; the commissioner of crown lands decided in 1863 that McVicar was too old to be an effective land agent.

McVicar was survived by two sons and two daughters who found the financial success he had been denied, in spite of his petitions and impressive references. The transition from the fur trade to a leading role in Canadian settlement ventures proved difficult for one without capital or influential friends, but McVicar's name continues to designate a bay on Great Bear Lake and the creek beside which he built the first house in what later became Port Arthur (Thunder Bay).

ELIZABETH ARTHUR

Robert McVicar, *Letters on emigration from the British Isles, and the settlement of the waste lands in the Province of Canada* (Hamilton, [Ont.], 1853), 1–116. HBC Arch. B.39/a, 1816–17; B.39/z, 11 Dec. 1817, 26 May 1818; B.89/a, 1815–16; B.181/a, 1819–21, 1824–25. *Hargrave correspondence* (Glazebrook). HBRS, I (Rich); II (Rich and Fleming).

MANSEAU, ANTOINE, priest, missionary, and vicar general; b. 12 July 1787 at Baie-du-Febvre (Baieville, Que.), son of a farmer, Antoine Manseau, and Marie Côté; d. 7 April 1866 at Montreal.

Antoine Manseau learned to read by the age of six, but in 1796 the death of his parish priest, Pierre-Victor Archambault, from whom he was taking lessons, interrupted his studies. In 1804 he left the family farm to serve as a clerk in the office of notary Étienne Ranvoyzé at Trois-Rivières, where he also learned English. He cancelled the contract that bound him to his master, in 1806, in order to undertake classical studies at Nicolet; these he completed at age 23. He entered the Grand Séminaire de Québec in October 1811, and immediately succeeded Abbé Pierre-Flavien TURGEON as secretary to Bishop Joseph-Octave Plessis*. A few months after his ordination in January 1814, he was sent to the Maritimes with "extraordinary powers" and ministered to the Chéticamp and Tracadie missions. This assignment to a vast territory enabled him to demonstrate that he was both a good walker and an excellent informant for the religious authorities there. When an apostolic vicariate was created for Nova Scotia in 1817, Manseau was recalled by Bishop Plessis and appointed parish priest of Les Cèdres, southwest of Montreal. Named in 1823 vicar general to the bishop of Quebec, Manseau was given responsibility for the missions of Upper Canada for two years during the absence of Alexander Macdonell*, the auxiliary bishop of that district. However, he had no faith in the effectiveness of these long trips, which took him away from his parish to a region he disliked. His transfer from Les Cèdres to Contrecoeur in 1827 coincided with a reply in the newspapers, signed by seven parish priests including Manseau, to the accusations of John Simpson*, MHA for York County. Simpson claimed, among other things,

that Catholic priests were exercising their influence in temporal affairs unconnected with religion.

In 1835, after a seemingly quiet period, Manseau was invited to become the auxiliary of the future bishop of Montreal, Jean-Jacques Lartigue*. He refused this offer, apparently because of the divergence of his views from those of Lartigue. Nevertheless, he was appointed vicar general to Lartigue in 1837, and three years later accepted the invitation of Bishop Ignace Bourget* to live in the bishop's palace and administer the diocese during the bishop's voyage to Europe. Interesting himself in the *Mélanges religieux*, he tried in vain to obtain the participation in it of the diocese of Quebec. He was prompted by two principal ideas: in order to ensure greater pastoral effectiveness, and in some measure for the sake of nationalism, the clergy should not meddle in politics, but should display unity of spirit and action. Life at the palace soon bothered him so much that he was obliged to take a long rest (1842–43).

On 23 Oct. 1843 Antoine Manseau was appointed parish priest of the village of L'Industrie (Joliette), and experienced a rejuvenation. On account of the poverty of the people, of whom "two thirds are day labourers," Barthélemy Joliette*, seigneur of Lavaltrie and owner of the church, presbytery, and cemetery, was almost the only one who provided for the needs of the clergy. Anxious about his autonomy and that of the church, Manseau strove to persuade the seigneur to give his wealth to the church during his lifetime rather than through his will. He alone stood up to the seigneur, whose generosities were above all investments that served his interests. In spite of tensions, and within the limits of their respective concerns, they managed to collaborate in various difficult projects: the incorporation of the parish of Saint-Charles-Borromée, which was contested by the neighbouring parishes, and the opening in 1846 of the Collège de Joliette near that of L'Assomption. By the time Joliette died in 1850, Manseau acknowledged his business competence to the point that in 1851 he ceded a plot of ground belonging to the parish council for the building of a market, which would raise the value of the church's lands. However, he could not take the place of the seigneur, and he recognized that only the introduction of manufacturing could check emigration to the United States.

It was in the interests of the church, although somewhat uneasily too, that Manseau gave his attention to the development of the Collège de Joliette and the coming of the Clerics of St Viator

Marconnay

[see Étienne Champagneur*]. Even before the arrival of Champagneur in 1847, he showed the bishops of Quebec and Montreal his distrust with regard to the coming of these Frenchmen and the introduction of independent bodies into the church. He hoped then that the Canadian branch of the congregation would separate from the mother house in France. He suggested in addition that the ownership of the college should not be given directly to this community, in order to allow future control by the bishop. Furthermore, he endeavoured to send recruits to the college and placed complete confidence in Canadians. In short, he was a not inconsiderable factor in the Canadianization of the congregation. But he was soon to divert his attention from this religious body to building a convent (1853) and establishing the Sisters of Providence in his parish (1855). In 1864 he retired to Montreal, where he died two years later.

The image left by Manseau is of an engaging but somewhat inscrutable man. Although preoccupied with the future of the diocese of Montreal, he always remained in contact with the authorities of the diocese of Quebec. Perhaps he was a man of action not content with the role of administrator, or a silent representative of the opposition to the bishop of Montreal.

BENOÎT LÉVESQUE

AAQ, 1 CB, V, 146–50, 155, 159, 163, 165; 303 CD, II, 18; 312 CN, II, 138–49; 320 CN, III, 109–38; 26 CP, II, 17; VI, 27; H, 228f., 280. ACAM, RLB, 1–3; RLL, 2, 5–7, 9; 420.080; 465.105. Archives de la Société historique de Joliette (Joliette, Qué.), Cartable Antoine Manseau, curé. Archives de l'évêché de Joliette (Joliette, Qué.), Cartable Saint-Charles-Borromée-de-L'Industrie, I. Archives des Clercs de Saint-Viateur (Outremont, Qué.), Dossier: Amérique (6v. polycopiés, Côteau-du-Lac, Qué., 1955–59), II–VI. Archives paroissiales, Saint-Antoine-de-la-Baie-du-Febvre (Baieville, Qué.), Registres des baptêmes, mariages et sépultures, 12 juill. 1787. Bulletin paroissial (Joliette, Qué.), oct.–nov. 1943. La Gazette de Joliette (Joliette, Qué.), 13, 20 avril 1866. Montreal Gazette, 20, 23, 24 Aug. 1827. Allaire, Dictionnaire. Ivanhoë Caron, "Inventaire de la correspondance de Mgr Bernard-Claude Panet, archevêque de Québec," ANQ Rapport, 1933–34, 235–421; 1934–35, 321–420; 1935–36, 157–272; "Inventaire de la correspondance de Mgr Joseph-Octave Plessis, archevêque de Québec," ANQ Rapport, 1927–28, 215–316; 1928–29, 89–208; 1932–33, 3–244; "Inventaire de la correspondance de Mgr Joseph Signay, archevêque de Québec," ANQ Rapport, 1936–37, 125–330; 1937–38, 23–146. É.-J.[-A.] Auclair, Histoire de la paroisse de Saint-Joseph-de-Soulanges ou les Cèdres (1702–1927) (Montréal, 1927), 113–36. J.-E. Bellemare, Histoire de la Baie-Saint-Antoine, dite Baie-du-Febvre, 1683–1911 (Montréal, 1911), 457–61. Antoine Bernard, Les Clercs de Saint-Viateur au Canada (2v., Montréal, 1947–51), I, 42–253. [Joseph Bonin], Biographies de l'honorable Bartelemi Joliette et de M. le grand vicaire A. Manseau (Montréal, 1874), 174–216. Carrière, Hist. des O.M.I., I, 77–78. Benoît Lévesque, "Naissance et implantation des Clercs de Saint-Viateur au Canada, 1847–1870" (thèse de MA, université de Sherbrooke, Sherbrooke, Qué., 1971), 165–287. J.-C. Robert, "L'activité économique de Barthélemy Joliette et la fondation du village d'Industrie (Joliette), 1822–1850" (thèse de MA, université de Montréal, 1971), 127–64. Wilfrid Caillé, "Messire Antoine Manseau et la paroisse Saint-Charles-Borromée de Joliette," SCHÉC Rapport, XVII (1949–50), 69–80. J.-C. Robert, "Un seigneur entrepreneur, Barthélemy Joliette, et la fondation du village d'Industrie (Joliette), 1822–1850," RHAF, XXVI (1972–73), 375–95.

MARCONNAY, HYACINTHE-POIRIER LEBLANC DE. See LEBLANC

MARKLAND, GEORGE HERCHMER (Herkimer), public servant; b. about 1790 at Kingston, Upper Canada, the only child of Thomas Markland* and Catherine Herchmer (Herkimer); his wife Anna died in 1847; d. 17 May 1862 at Kingston.

George Herchmer Markland, son of a prominent Kingston merchant, was educated by John STRACHAN at Cornwall. In 1810 the Reverend John Stuart* wrote of him as "a good, indeed an excellent young man" who wished to enter the Anglican ministry. In the same year John Beverley ROBINSON described Markland, then 20 years old, as "a good fellow, and very friendly," but added: "I prefer seeing a person at his age rather more manly and not quite so *feminine* either in speech or action." Markland did not enter the ministry. During the War of 1812 he served as an ensign in a company of Frontenac militia commanded by his uncle, Lawrence Herchmer (Herkimer).

In 1820 Markland unsuccessfully contested the riding of Kingston against fellow Tory, Christopher Alexander Hagerman*. Within a few weeks of his defeat he was appointed to the Legislative Council, probably through the influence of Strachan. Two years later, at age 32, he was made an honorary member of the Executive Council and, in 1827, a regular member. He was also appointed to the Provincial Board of Education in 1822. Though Markland spent several years in England in the mid 1820s, his absence from Upper Canada did not slow his advancement in the government. In 1828 he was appointed secretary receiver of the Upper Canada Clergy Corporation which administered the leasing of the clergy reserves. In the same year he became registrar of King's College, chartered in 1827, and was later involved with Sir John COLBORNE in the creation of Upper Canada College. From 1831 to 1838 he was also secretary and treasurer of the board responsible for the collection of money from the sale of school lands, and from 1828 to 1836 he served as an Upper Canadian arbitrator in the division of customs revenue between Upper and Lower Canada. In his positions of trust and in his roles as legislative and executive councillor Markland completely supported Strachan's religious and educational goals. In 1836, for example, he, Peter Robinson*, and Joseph Wells* formed the Executive Council which assented to Colborne's endowment of 43 Anglican rectories. In May 1833 he reached the apex of his career when he was made inspector general of public accounts. As in his previous positions of fiscal responsibility, he worked diligently and efficiently; he was, to all appearances, a model bureaucrat deserving the emulation of his fellow officials.

In June 1838 reports began to circulate in Toronto that Markland's habits were "derogatory to his character as a public officer." Lieutenant Governor Sir George Arthur* determined upon an investigation by executive councillors Robert Baldwin Sullivan*, William Allan*, Augustus Warren Baldwin, John Elmsley, and William Henry Draper*. Markland agreed that an inquiry was necessary to clear his name and unsuccessfully attempted to have Strachan made the sole investigator. Largely through circumstantial evidence, Markland was accused of having had sexual liaisons with a number of young men. Two witnesses stated during the inquiry that he had purchased the discharges of several young soldiers and had supported a law student allegedly in return for anticipated sexual favours, although those who had accepted his financial aid denied having been parties to illicit relationships. The law student, Frederick Creighton Muttlebury, stated that he had ended his financial dependence upon the inspector general because of Markland's increasingly bold and possessive attitude but he too denied any "criminality" on Markland's part. Margaret Powell, housekeeper of the government buildings, claimed that Markland had often met young men in the evenings at his office, and that on one occasion, while listening at his door, she had heard "such movements as convinced me that there was a female in the room, with whom some person was in connection," but only Markland and a young drummer emerged from the office. Another witness claimed that during a walk on the outskirts of town in 1835 "Markland had . . . put his hand in an indecent manner on my brother's person." Markland maintained his innocence to Arthur, and defended his private acts of benevolence, but did not testify on his own behalf. The week-long inquiry was quietly dropped in return for Markland's resignation as inspector general. His career in ruins, Markland returned to Kingston to live in virtual isolation. In the following month, after being pressed by his fellow officers, he resigned his commission as colonel in the Frontenac militia. He had resigned from the Executive Council in 1836 and was not re-appointed a legislative councillor in 1841. He never again held any public office.

Markland's problems did not end with his virtual banishment. In 1841 a legislative committee, chaired by John Simcoe Macaulay*, discovered that Markland as treasurer of the school lands fund was in default almost £5,000 for the period 1831–38. He did not deny responsibility for the deficit; the government was reimbursed through occasional payments and provisions in his will. In the mid 1840s Markland barely escaped civil suit by the council of King's College for his role in using college funds for the erection of Upper Canada College. Strachan intervened on his behalf and convinced the council that Markland had merely been acting on the orders of Sir John Colborne.

In 1838 Markland was a leading member of the Family Compact, probably ranking second only to J. B. Robinson among Strachan's protégés. His political and social eclipse was abrupt. No hint of the sexual scandal appeared in the contemporary press, and the account of it rests on official reports. Today only a few of Markland's letters remain, scattered in the correspondence of his friends and associates. Whether the charges made against him in 1838 were accurate or the result of gossip and innuendo will probably never be known with certainty. The witnesses, including two labourers, a gardener, a soldier, a servant, and a housekeeper, as well as a merchant, a law student, and a government clerk, seemed as shocked by the familiarity with which Markland, a gentleman, treated members of the lower class, as they were by the nature of the conduct of which he stood accused. Even the exact circumstances surrounding his defalcations from the school lands account remain unknown. He may have been guilty of no more than careless accounting, a common fault among 19th century Canadian officials. His sudden departure from office could have prevented him from balancing his accounts and led ultimately to charges being laid against him. The passing of his peers in the Family Compact elicited glowing eulogies from Reform and Conservative newspapers alike, but Markland's death in 1862 was noted in the Kingston *Daily British Whig* and in the *Globe* by identical two-line obituaries. Almost a century later W. S. Wallace* noted "the almost Egyp-

Marshall

tian darkness'' which has obscured Markland's career.

ROBERT J. BURNS

PAC, RG 1, E1, 56, pp.22–23, 25–26, 299; 57, p.78; E3, 50, pp.210–311; RG 5, A1, 201, pp.110995–1001, 111051–53; 203, pp.112399–403; 204, pp.113075–77; C1, 61, p.485; 62, p.515; 63, p.664; 66, p.1097; 140, p.8980; 143, p.9239; 540, p.182; RG 9, I, B7, 10, pp.51, 56, 58; 11, pp.285–92a. PAO, Irving (Æmilius) papers, box 59, pkg.62, item I, Markland mortgage; Macaulay (John) papers, J. B. Robinson to Macaulay, 24 July 1810; G. H. Markland to Macaulay, 2 May 1824, 23 Sept. 1825, 10 April 1843; Macaulay to Ann Macaulay, 5, 31 Aug. 1838; John Kirby to Macaulay, 25 Nov. 1838; Macaulay to J. Kirby, 27 Jan. 1839; Strachan (John) papers, letterbook, 1844–49, Strachan to G. H. Markland, 29 Dec. 1845; Strachan to Henry Boys, 28 Feb. 1848; RG 22, ser. 6–2, Frontenac County Surrogate Court, will of George Herchmer Markland, 30 July 1858. St George's Anglican Church (Kingston, Ont.), parish register of burials, 5 Jan. 1857–5 Nov. 1924, no. 271, 19 May 1862; vestry book, 1835–49, 23 March 1841.

A. N. Bethune, *Memoir of the Right Reverend John Strachan, D.D., LL.D., first bishop of Toronto* (Toronto and London, 1870), 16–17. Can., Prov. of, Legislative Assembly, *Journals*, 1841, I, app.K.K.; 1854–55, XI, app.S.S. *The parish register of Kingston, Upper Canada, 1785–1811*, ed. A. H. Young (Kingston, Ont., 1921). *Church*, 11 June 1847. *Daily British Whig* (Kingston, [Ont.]), 19 May 1862. *Globe*, 22 May 1862. *Upper Canada Gazette* (Toronto), 4 Oct. 1838. *Directory of the city of Kingston, for 1857–1858 . . . .*, comp. Thomas Flynn (Kingston, [Ont.], 1857). Wallace, *Macmillan dictionary*. Wilson, *Clergy reserves of U.C.*, 99–101, 123. Alison Ewart and Julia Jarvis, "The personnel of the Family Compact, 1791–1841," *CHR*, VII (1926), 209–21. W. D. Reid, "Johan Jost Herkimer, U.E., and his family," *OH*, XXXI (1936), 215–27. W. S. Wallace, "Two early officers of the university," *University of Toronto Monthly*, XXVII (1926–27), 207–8. S. F. Wise, "Tory factionalism: Kingston elections and Upper Canadian politics, 1820–1836," *OH*, LVII (1965), 205–23.

MARSHALL, JOHN JOSEPH, merchant and politician; b. 1807 in Guysborough, N. S., son of Joseph H. and Ann Marshall; m. Esther Maria Ballaine; d. 25 Oct. 1870 at Manchester, N.S.

Educated at the Sackville Grammar School, John Joseph Marshall was raised in a prosperous family in Guysborough County. Unlike most of the shore-dwelling families of Chedabucto Bay, the Marshalls were "all clerk and farmer, who didn't know a gunnel from a tholepin." They attained some political prominence: Marshall's grandfather, Joseph Marshall (a Georgia-born loyalist), and his uncle, John George Marshall*, were both Nova Scotia assemblymen. His father-in-law, John Ballaine, a Jersey Island merchant, also had sat in the assembly. Along with the Cutlers and Torys, they formed a powerful "compact" in Guysborough County.

As a merchant, Marshall ran a general store dealing in groceries, rum, fishing supplies, and smallware. Like many outport merchants, he left behind a reputation for tight-fisted shrewdness, partly because he is said to have seized properties for unpaid debts. He lived rather ostentatiously, and apparently did not leave much wealth.

Marshall served as justice of the peace in his community and in 1837 worked on a fisheries commission. In 1840 he was elected to the assembly to represent Guysborough County, a seat he held until 1859. Not surprisingly in view of his background, Marshall became associated with James William Johnston*'s Conservative group in the legislature. Outspoken to the point of brashness, he earned the active dislike of those he termed the "agitators" of the Reform party, whom he criticized for their "obsession" with party patronage. During the political turmoil of the 1840s, Reform papers assailed the "conceited, abusive, treacherous Marshall . . . packhorse for the Halifax Tories . . . the greatest nuisance who ever disgraced the floors of the House of Assembly," and derided him as the author of the "celebrated Goose Bill" of 1846, intended to prevent the straying of domestic waterfowl. Nevertheless Marshall's role in distributing government relief supplies during the hard times of the 1840s, and again in the late 1860s, did win him the gratitude of some people if the hatred of others.

In 1856 Charles Rohan offered the following portrait of Marshall's political personality in the *Acadian Recorder*: "He acquiesces in being called a Conservative, yet makes occasional headlong plunges into Radicalism . . . he is not at all given to generalizing or theorizing . . . altogether of a destructive turn . . . seems made for opposition . . . quick in decision and reply, quick to wound an opponent in debate . . . the very picture of saucy self-possession . . . yet he is genial and friendly with his opponents outside the House." Marshall spoke of himself, with arrogant independence, as a follower of no party. Obviously he chafed under the party discipline which responsible government made necessary.

He bitterly resented the British betrayal of Nova Scotian fisheries and shipping interests in the Reciprocity Treaty of 1854. While in opposition he particularly criticized railway expenditure and prohibitory liquor laws: "They want not only to stop our grog, but to rob us of our Road money." His abilities and his frequent support of the Conservatives, for whom he had sponsored some unpopular bills, won him the post of financial secretary in the Johnston administration from 1857 to 1860.

Marshall's opposition to union with Canada

brought him under attack from many of his associates who supported confederation. Along with John Angus Kirk, he was elected in 1867 to the Nova Scotia assembly for Guysborough County on an anti-confederate ticket. He served as speaker from 30 Jan. 1868 until his death in 1870, when William Annand*'s *Morning Chronicle*, although acknowledging his defence of Nova Scotian interests over the years, maintained the old enmities by dismissing his career as "not of a distinguished character."

A. A. MacKenzie

The Marshall family papers are in the possession of Gladys Marshall, Boylston, N.S. PANS, RG 7, 143. Howe, *Speeches and letters* (Chisholm). N.S., House of Assembly, *Debates and proc.*, 1855–59; *Journals and proc.*, 1855–56. *British Colonist* (Halifax), 1844. *Eastern Chronicle* (Pictou, N.S.), 1847. *Morning Chronicle* (Halifax), 1865–70. *Times* (Halifax), 1842. *Belcher's farmer's almanack*, 1860. *CPC*, 1869. *Directory of N.S. MLAs*. Charles Bruce, *The channel shore* (Toronto, 1957). A. C. Jost, *Guysborough sketches and essays* (Guysborough, N.S., 1950).

MARY BASILIA, Sister. *See* McCann, Rosanna

MARY MARTHA, Sister. *See* Bunning, Maria

MARY XAVIER, Sister. *See* Molony, Belinda

MASKEPETOON (Broken Arm, Crooked Arm, baptized **Abraham**), Cree Indian chief; b. probably in 1807 in the Saskatchewan River area; d. 1869 at a Blackfoot camp in central Alberta.

Maskepetoon was the leader of a small Plains Cree band which normally hunted south of Fort Edmonton, but at times ranged into what is now southern Saskatchewan and northern Montana. Early in life he gained a reputation as a warrior and was given the name Mon-e-guh-ba-now or Mani-kap-ina, Young Man Chief, by the enemy Blackfoot. According to a Methodist missionary, Egerton Ryerson Young*, Maskepetoon "was a magnificent looking man physically, and was keen and intelligent," although John Palliser*, in the journal of his 1857 expedition, considers him neither imposing nor fine-looking. Maskepetoon had a violent temper and as a young man was said to have scalped his wife Susewisk alive. He almost killed a Métis during a drinking bout near Fort Edmonton.

Late in 1831, while on a trading expedition to Fort Union on the Missouri River, Maskepetoon was invited to accompany three other chiefs, from the Assiniboin, Saulteaux, and Sioux tribes, to Washington, D.C., to meet President Andrew Jackson who wanted to establish peaceful relations with the western tribes and also to impress them with the might of his government. While in St Louis en route east, Maskepetoon was painted by the celebrated artist George Catlin. Upon his return to the west, Maskepetoon encountered at Fort Union in 1833 Swiss Prince Maximilian of Wied-Neuwied, who noted that "The chief of the Crees . . . Maschkepiton (the broken arm) . . . had a medal with the effigy of the President hung round his neck." In January 1848, the artist Paul Kane* met Maskepetoon near Fort Edmonton and recorded the chief's views on the failure of Christian missionaries to agree with each other and on the superiority of native beliefs.

During the 1840s, Maskepetoon had come under the influence of a Wesleyan Methodist missionary, the Reverend Robert Terrill Rundle*, and later was taught to read and write Cree syllabics by the Reverend Thomas Woolsey. As a result of these associations, Maskepetoon became a strong proponent of peace. Whenever the opportunity arose, he made peace with enemy tribes and attempted to keep his young men from going to war. In these years Maskepetoon's father was killed by a Blackfoot; when the Cree chief later met the killer on one of his missions, he invited the man into his lodge, forgave him, and presented him with a chief's costume. In April 1865 Woolsey baptized Maskepetoon under the name Abraham, with his wife receiving the name Sarah.

In 1841 Maskepetoon had been engaged by James Sinclair* of the Hudson's Bay Company to guide a party of emigrants from Fort Edmonton to the Oregon country. He took them along a previously unexplored route over what was later named Sinclair Pass and on to Fort Vancouver (Vancouver, Wash.). There he travelled on the HBC ship *Beaver* (1841), and claimed he would not be able to tell his people as they would not believe that a large ship could move on the ocean under its own power. Maskepetoon made further trips across the mountains in 1850 and 1854, on these occasions guiding Sinclair only as far as the west slope of the Rockies. In 1857 he was engaged by John Palliser's expedition to act as guide from the Qu'Appelle lakes (near Fort Qu'Appelle) to the elbow of the South Saskatchewan River (near Elbow); from the expedition's members he acquired the name Nichiwa, the Cree term for "friend."

In 1869, when hostilities broke out between the Crees and the Blood, Blackfoot, and Peigan tribes, Maskepetoon entered a Blackfoot camp alone and unarmed to negotiate peace. He was met and killed by a war chief, Big Swan. The dead chief became known to the Methodists as a "mar-

Mason

tyr of peace'' and was held up as an example of a man dying for his Christian faith. Some Crees, however, believed his actions were not those of a peacemaker, but of a warrior who demonstrated his bravery and scorn by entering an enemy camp unarmed.

Maskepetoon has been a hero in a variety of writings. In 1957 Maskepetoon Park, a wildlife sanctuary near Red Deer, Alta, was dedicated to the memory of the Indian peacemaker.

HUGH A. DEMPSEY

Glenbow-Alberta Institute Archives (Calgary), Reverend John McDougall papers, file A/M 137B/f.58; Reverend Robert Terrill Rundle papers, file A/R941. *Early western travels, 1748–1846; a series of annotated reprints of some of the best and rarest contemporary volumes of travel . . .* , ed. R. G. Thwaites, (32v., Cleveland, Ohio, 1904–7), XXIII, 13. [Charles Larpenteur], *Forty years a fur trader on the Upper Missouri; the personal narrative of Charles Larpenteur, 1833–1872*, ed. Elliot Coues (Chicago, 1933), 160. *Papers of Palliser expedition* (Spry), 138–40, 143–44, 602. *Paul Kane's frontier; including "Wanderings of an artist among the Indians of North America" by Paul Kane*, ed. J. R. Harper (Toronto, 1971), 142. George Simpson, *Narrative of a journey round the world, during the years 1841 and 1842* (2v., London, 1847), I, 241–42. J. P. Berry, *Maskepetoon, Alberta's first martyr to peace* (Toronto, [1945]). D. G. Lent, *West of the mountains: James Sinclair and the Hudson's Bay Company* (Seattle, Wash., 1963), 132–53, 246–61. J. [C.] McDougall, *Saddle, sled and snowshoe; pioneering on the Saskatchewan in the sixties* (Toronto, 1896), 197. John Maclean, *Vanguards of Canada* (Toronto, 1918). E. R. Young, *The apostle of the north, Rev. James Evans* (New York and Toronto, 1899), 139. J. E. Ewers, "When the light shone in Washington," *Montana; the Magazine of Western History* (Helena), 6 (1956), 2–11. Allen Ronaghan, "The problem of Maskipiton," *Alberta History* (Calgary), 24 (spring 1976), 14–19.

MASON, SOPHIA. *See* THOMAS

MASSUE, LOUIS-JOSEPH (known as Louis), businessman, politician, and public servant; b. 4 April 1786 at Varennes, Quebec, son of Gaspard Massue, co-seigneur of Varennes, and Josephte Huet Dulude; d. 4 July 1869 at Quebec.

Little is known about Massue's career, as is the case with so many Canadian businessmen. We do know, however, that while young he amassed a fortune in the import trade and the sale of dry goods and by 1818 had become one of the "richest" merchants in Quebec. In that year he was elected to the first board of governors of the Quebec Bank, and he held various positions of this kind over the years. He was a founder of the

Quebec Fire Insurance Company, and successively treasurer and president of the Canadian Fire Insurance Company. He also served as vice-president of the Quebec Provident and Savings Bank.

After becoming rich in his business, Massue gave up the undertaking that had made his fortune. In 1840 he was said to have "retired from business." His wealth in real estate at that time was impressive; in 1838 Massue held 40,000 acres, which made him the sixth largest owner of non-seigneurial land in Lower Canada. He also bought more than 3,600 acres in 1842 and 1843. Among these lands were properties in the townships of Blandford, Clarendon, Litchfield, and Bulstrode. Although changing the direction of his affairs, Massue maintained contact with the financial world. Thus in 1849 he was one of the trustees of the Quebec Provident and Savings Bank, and during the next two years was associated with the groups involved in railway projects.

In addition, Massue concerned himself with politics. Although he opposed the rebellion of 1837, he was against the union of the Canadas. In 1840, yielding to the urgent requests of several Quebec citizens, he agreed to be a candidate in the elections of the following year to choose the first parliament of united Canada. He suffered honourable defeat in the city of Quebec, owing to the limited number of Francophone electors and the massive support given by the army and public servants to his opponents Henry Black* and James Gibb, who backed the new constitutional régime. He was, however, elected alderman in 1841 and served until 1845. He was appointed legislative councillor in 1843, but had to relinquish this office in May 1851, in order to obtain the post of inspector of customs for the port of Quebec. At that time, any official holding a position which involved the handling of public funds was required to pay a deposit to guarantee the proper discharge of his duty. Massue had to put down £500 for this purpose, and his son-in-law Alexandre Lemoine and René-Édouard Caron* stood surety for £250 each.

For some years now, Louis-Joseph Massue had been in a disastrous financial position. The year 1849, with its serious difficulties, had brought him to bankruptcy, as it had many other businessmen. According to Ovide-Michel-Hengard Lapalice, the final blow for Massue had been the failure of merchant Pierre Boisseau. "The latter at that time owed considerable sums to the Quebec Bank, and Louis Massue, as one of the directors, shared liability." Massue, ruined, had to stand a powerless onlooker before the seizure and sale by auction of his properties. "It is my son-in-law," he wrote on 21 Sept. 1849, "who is supporting me at this moment, and until such time as I can obtain or procure some means of livelihood." Unlike many merchants, Massue did not believe that the solution to the economic problems of the day was to be found in the annexation of Canada to the United States, a proposal he publicly opposed.

On 13 Jan. 1824, Louis-Joseph Massue had married at Quebec Elizabeth Anne Marett, daughter of businessman James Lamprière Marett and Henriette Boone; two daughters were born of this marriage. He was the brother-in-law of Elzéar Bédard*. When Massue died, his contemporaries were unanimous in praising his integrity and his devotion to his fellow citizens. He certainly deserved their gratitude, for he had contributed to the progress of a number of movements and institutions.

JEAN-PIERRE GAGNON

[There is no biography of Louis-Joseph Massue that is even minimally satisfactory; only O.-M.-H. Lapalice has provided new information on his life. This article is based mainly on documents in the PAC and on certain newspapers, especially *Le Canadien*. J.-P.G.]

PAC, MG 30, D62, 20, pp.455–59; RG 4, B28, 135, no.1404; RG 9, I, A1, 9; A5, 5, 11. *Le Canadien*, 1er oct. 1840–12 avril 1841, 29 déc. 1848–12 mai 1851, 7 juill. 1869. Langelier, *List of lands granted. Liste de la milice du Bas-Canada, pour 1829* (Québec, [1829]). *Liste de la milice du Bas-Canada, pour 1832* (Québec, [1832]). O.-M.-H. Lapalice, *Histoire de la seigneurie Massue et de la paroisse de Saint-Aimé* (s.l., 1930).

MATHIESON, ALEXANDER, Presbyterian minister; b. 1 Oct. 1795 at Renton, Dunbartonshire, Scotland, son of George Mathieson, a soldier, and Janet Ewing; d. 14 Feb. 1870 at Montreal.

Alexander Mathieson was educated at local schools in Dumbarton and Stirling and graduated in 1814 from Glasgow University. He continued as a part-time student in theology, tutoring to support himself. In 1823 he was licensed to preach by the Church of Scotland and in 1826 the Reverend John Burns, minister of St Andrew's Presbyterian Church in Montreal, chose Mathieson as his successor.

The Presbyterians of St Andrew's (now St Andrew and St Paul), were among those who stood for a continued connection with the Scottish Kirk, also a cardinal conviction of Mathieson's. This wealthy congregation included many of the Montreal Scots merchant community, and his initial stipend was £250 yearly. By 1832 the church had a yearly revenue of £450 and a con-

gregation of 1,500. In 1835, led by such merchants as William Ritchie*, it adopted a constitution. That year Mathieson was active in founding the Montreal St Andrew's Society of which he became the first chaplain, an office he had held 25 times by 1869. In 1837, while on leave of absence in Great Britain and on the Continent, he resigned from St Andrew's, evidently hoping to find a parish in Scotland. He was unsuccessful but Glasgow University gave him a DD in 1837 and in the fall of 1838 he resumed his Montreal charge.

During these early years he strengthened Presbyterianism by helping found the Synod of the Presbyterian Church of Canada in Connection with the Church of Scotland (1831). He was elected its second moderator in 1832. The association about which he felt so strongly was thus maintained. With the Upper Canadian politician William Morris* he contended that the Presbyterian Church, as an established church of the empire, had a "right" to part of the clergy reserve revenues; in 1840 they triumphed and the Kirk obtained a share equal to half that of the Church of England. In the same year union with the Presbyterians of the United Synod of Upper Canada was effected. Mathieson first opposed this union, but accepted it when reference to connection with the Church of Scotland was retained in the title of the new body. At this time, too, he helped establish Queen's College at Kingston which would train Presbyterian clergy and educate students according to the ways of the Church of Scotland. Named a founder in the royal charter of 1841, he was a trustee from 1842 to 1868.

Mathieson was active in the 1840s in founding a committee to establish a mission to the French Canadians and in missionary work with the Highland Scots of the Eastern Townships. He was instrumental also in establishing in 1847 the Ministers' Widows and Orphans Fund and was on its board of managers until his death. In 1856 he was a founder of St Andrew's Home, established by the St Andrew's Society of Montreal for immigrants and homeless Scots.

The disruption in the Church of Scotland in 1843–44 quickly aroused controversy in the Canadas [see Robert BURNS]. Mathieson, naturally, stood uncompromisingly with those who remained faithful to the Church of Scotland. Although he lost some of his congregation to the Free Presbyterians, he gained many prominent members from rival St Gabriel's. St Andrew's thus became even richer and more influential. In 1847 the congregation purchased land on Beaver Hall Hill and in 1851 built a magnificent $64,000 church, copied after Salisbury Cathedral, which became known as the "Scotch Cathedral."

Mathison

Meanwhile, as was appropriate to a businessmen's church, St Andrew's had been incorporated in 1849. When it revised its constitution in 1850–51, one of the new trustees was Mathieson's friend William Edmonstone, with whom he toured the Maritime provinces in 1855 as a delegate for the synod, to strengthen contacts with fellow Presbyterians. As senior minister of the Church of Scotland in Canada, he was elected moderator for the second time in 1860. He opposed the move to unify the various Presbyterian synods which began about that time and resulted in the 1875 union.

In the last decade of Mathieson's life St Andrew's continued to prosper; he had a regular assistant and could spend his summers at his farm in the Eastern Townships. In 1869, his annual stipend was $3,600. Prosperous parishioners continued to join the congregation, including Andrew Wilson, co-proprietor of the *Montreal Herald*, and Sir Joseph Hickson*, general manager of the Grand Trunk Railway. When St Andrew's burned on 23 Oct. 1869 it was "amply insured," and additional funds were promptly raised to rebuild it.

Mathieson married in 1840 Catherine Elizabeth (1822–56), daughter of John Mackenzie, a prominent merchant of Montreal, which connected him with the leading commercial families of Esdaile, Fisher, and Torrance. They had two sons and four daughters. A portly man of venerable aspect, Mathieson died only three weeks after preaching his last sermon. He might have been more influential had he been less outspoken, especially on matters of church organization, and more willing to conciliate his opponents. He was almost always militant, frequently triumphant, and all too often intransigent, as were many of the clergy in 19th century Canada; yet, like John STRACHAN and Egerton Ryerson*, he accomplished much for his denomination, particularly in practical matters.

FREDERICK H. ARMSTRONG

Alexander Mathieson, *The moral and religious influences of autumn, a sermon in three parts, preached in Saint Andrew's Church, Montreal . . .* (Montreal, 1850); *A sermon, occasioned by the death of the late Mr. Robert Watson, preached in St. Andrew's Church, Montreal, April 8th, 1827* (Montreal, 1827); *A sermon preached in St. Andrew's Church, Quebec, on the 29th May, 1861, at the opening of the Synod of the Presbyterian Church of Canada in Connection with the Church of Scotland* (Montreal, 1861). Can., Prov. of, *Statutes*, 1849, c.154. Morgan, *Bibliotheca Canadensis*, 252. Notman and Taylor, *Portraits of British Americans*, I, 89–91. D. D. Calvin, *Queen's University at Kingston: the first century of a Scottish-Canadian foundation, 1841–1941* (Kingston, Ont., 1941). Campbell, *History of Scotch Presbyterian Church*, 746ff. James Croil, *Life of the Rev. Alex. Mathieson, D.D., minister of St. Andrew's Church, Montreal, with a funeral sermon, by the Rev. John Jenkins . . .* (Montreal, 1870). W. J. Rattray, *The Scot in British North America* (4v., Toronto, 1880–84), III, 851–54.

MATHISON, JOHN AUGUSTUS, soldier; b. 25 Dec. 1781 in London, England; m. in Saint-André-Est, Lower Canada, Harriet Vandenburgh; d. 5 Nov. 1868 at Hudson, Que.

A veteran of the Peninsular campaign, John Augustus Mathison retired on half pay as lieutenant of the 77th Foot in 1817. Three years later he came to Canada and purchased a farm in the seigneury of Vaudreuil, at Pointe-à-Cavagnal (Hudson), where impoverished farmers from northern England had begun to buy farms. Compared to the folk of his community, Mathison was both well educated and, with a modest but steady income from his army pension, quite wealthy. In 1826 he was appointed commissioner of small causes and justice of the peace, and he began to assume the role of squire of the district, being "constantly applied to in matters of difficulty and doubt."

Virtually every activity in this pioneer community was stimulated by Mathison's organizational ability. In 1829 he built a schoolhouse and appointed a teacher at his own expense to serve "the children of very poor parents." In 1832 he organized a campaign to collect money to construct an Anglican church. In 1846 he was the founder and first president of the Vaudreuil Agricultural Society. Mathison also held the ranks of major (1831) and lieutenant-colonel (1846) in the Vaudreuil militia and was the president of the British American League in the county in 1849.

Mathison's local leadership was most clearly shown in 1837–38. Vaudreuil had many Patriote sympathizers and was represented in the assembly by Charles-Ovide Perrault*, killed in the battle of Saint-Denis in November 1837. Late in that same month when Patriote agitation seemed to threaten the security of the English speaking minority in Vaudreuil, Mathison formed "a refuge in the woods of Canada" for the women and children of the area and organized the men to meet an expected Patriote assault. Although the attack did not occur, in early December Sir John COLBORNE authorized Mathison to transform his *ad hoc* guard into an active unit of volunteer militia. Following the battle of Saint-Eustache, the Vaudreuil Loyal Volunteers under Mathison's command disarmed the French inhabitants of the seigneury of Vaudreuil and patrolled it [*see*

François-Xavier DESJARDINS]; "they . . . were fortunate," noted bishop George Jehoshaphat MOUNTAIN, "to have such an officer to head them as Major Mathison."

Others had a less flattering view of Mathison's leadership. One critic, William Whitlock, in 1838 called him "a petty tyrant"; another, Robert Unwin HARWOOD, seigneur of Vaudreuil, in the same year claimed he was "unjust, partial and arbitrary." Autocratic Tory though he was, Mathison seems to have served his community well and was adept at obtaining governmental assistance for local needs such as in education and agriculture. No believer in democracy, Mathison was nevertheless popularly elected to several positions he held. Thus when his political adversaries caused him to lose his position as justice of the peace in 1847 because of a dispute about a new school law, the people of his community (about 100 English speaking families) responded by petitioning for his reappointment, and during the election of that year chose him as "a worthy and capable person to represent the county." As in the election of 1831, when he was defeated, and in the election of 1841, when he was suggested as a candidate to Lord Sydenham [Thomson*] but was finally passed over, Mathison was luckless in 1847 and withdrew before the vote was held.

With the advent of responsible government and of the dominance of commercial men over the gentleman farmers, the power of Mathison – and other Tories like him – waned and eventually vanished. Changing times brought younger leaders with more sophisticated techniques of control.

JOHN BESWARICK THOMPSON

ANQ-Q, QBC 25, Événements de 1837–1838, nos.1064, 3895. PAC, RG 4, A1, S-215, p.152; B30, 80; RG 8, I (C series), 1039, pp.106, 175; 1044, pp.3, 55, 175; RG 9, I, C2, 3; RG 19, E5, 3797, pp.1067–1271. Private archives, Miss Ethel Kyte (Darien, Conn.), Mathison papers. PRO, WO 31/322. Can., Prov. of, Legislative Assembly, *Journals*, 1843, II, app.J.J.; 1850, I, app.J. *Journal d'agriculture et transactions de la Société d'agriculture du Bas-Canada* (Montréal), janvier 1848, mai 1849. *La Minerve*, 9 août, 27, 30 déc. 1847; 3 janv. 1848. *Montreal Gazette*, 10 Dec. 1831. *Montreal Transcript*, 28 Dec. 1837, 3 Jan. 1848. E. C. Royle, *An historical study of the Anglican parish of Vaudreuil* (Hudson Heights, Que., 1952). J. B. Thompson, *Cavagnal, 1820–1867* (2nd ed., [Hudson, Que.], 1970).

MAURAULT, JOSEPH-PIERRE-ANSELME, priest, missionary, and historian; b. 27 Dec. 1819 at Saint-Louis-de-Kamouraska (Kamouraska, Que.), son of Cyriac Maurault, militia captain and merchant, and Émilie Sirois, *dit* Duplessis; d. 4 July 1870 at Saint-Thomas-de-Pierreville (Pierreville, Que.).

Joseph-Pierre-Anselme Maurault was descended from a Poitou family which had arrived at Quebec in 1656. He studied at the Collège de Sainte-Anne-de-la-Pocatière (1831–36) and the Petit Séminaire de Québec (1836–37). After teaching natural sciences at Sainte-Anne-de-la-Pocatière for two years, he served from 1839 to 1841 as the secretary of Bishop Pierre-Flavien TURGEON, coadjutor to the archbishop of Quebec. Ordained by Bishop Joseph Signay* on 10 Feb. 1842, Maurault served as curate at Saint-François-du-Lac, and visited the Têtes-de-Boules, Indians of the upper Saint-Maurice, in 1844, 1845, and 1846.

In 1848 Maurault was appointed parish priest of Saint-François-du-Lac. The following year he opened a new church there which was more central than the old one on the Île du Fort, downriver on the Saint-François. The inhabitants of Île du Fort had so strongly opposed the construction of the new church, decided upon in 1832, that the affair had gone to the courts. To satisfy the islanders, Maurault undertook to divide his parish. In 1852 he bought a piece of land on the east bank of the Saint-François; there, at his own expense, he built a church, which he proposed to make the centre for a new parish. Thomas COOKE, the bishop of Trois-Rivières, was at first displeased with this irregular procedure, without precedent in the history of French Canada. Eventually, however, he came round to Maurault's view, and entrusted to him the new parish, which was named Saint-Thomas-de-Pierreville. Thanks to the initiative of the priest and of his two brothers, Thomas and Jean-Élie, whom he had brought from Kamouraska, a village grew up around the new church. Favourably located for shipping, this village rapidly attained great prosperity.

From 1841, Maurault had been responsible for the Abenaki mission of Saint-François-de-Sales (Odanak) near Saint-Thomas-de-Pierreville. He quickly mastered the Abenaki language, and tried, without complete success, to counteract the efforts of Osunkhirhine* (also known as Pierre-Paul Masta) to bring Protestantism to the Indians. Maurault also wrote two reports, in 1856 and 1865, that are an important source of information on the Abenakis' way of life and character. In 1856 he presented a report to the special commissioners appointed to inquire into Indian affairs [*see* Richard Theodore PENNEFATHER]. In it he proposed that the Abenakis be set free from government tutelage, that they be accorded

Mayawassino

full citizens' rights, and that each receive a grant of good land in freehold for cultivation. But this report went unheeded.

The prosperity of Saint-Thomas-de-Pierreville roused the envy of the Abenakis. The Indians began to doubt the legality of all their land sales to the new arrivals. On 2 Feb. 1865 Maurault submitted a long report to the government, together with a petition from the owners concerned. He sought to have the tenure of the Abenakis' lands changed, so that the rights of the two parties would be protected.

At the suggestion of Abbé Henri-Raymond Casgrain*, Maurault decided to write *Histoire des Abénakis, depuis 1605 jusqu'à nos jours*, which appeared in 1866. With few records available and no access to government documents, he was forced to rely, for much of his history, on American and Canadian works about the colonial wars in which the Abenakis had fought beside the French. Hence the preponderance given to these wars in his book. The critics of the time were charitable towards this ambitious work, devoted to a tribe in danger of extinction.

Joseph-Pierre-Anselme Maurault died of pneumonia on 4 July 1870. The large number of priests who attended his funeral is evidence of the esteem in which he was held by the clergy of his time.

THOMAS-M. CHARLAND

J.-P.-A. Maurault, "Du lac St-Jean au Saint-Maurice," *Le Foyer canadien; receuil littéraire et historique* (Québec), IV (1866), 344–52; *Histoire des Abénakis, depuis 1605 jusqu'à nos jours* ([Sorel, Qué.], 1866). Archives de l'évêché de Nicolet (Nicolet, Qué.), Cartable Odanak; Cartable Saint-François-du-Lac; Cartable Saint-Thomas-de-Pierreville. PAC, RG 4, C1, 572; RG 10, vols. 592–95. Can., prov. du, Assemblée législative, *Journaux*, 1858, VI, app.21. *JIP*, juillet–août 1870, 105. *Rapport sur les missions du diocèse de Québec . . .*, 6 (juillet 1845), 131–45. *Le Journal des Trois-Rivières*, 7 juill. 1870. *La Minerve*, 15 juill. 1867. Arthur Bergeron, *Pierreville, 1853–1953; un siècle de vie paroissiale et l'aurore du suivant* ([Trois-Rivières], 1960), 11–18. T.-M. Charland, *Histoire des Abénakis d'Odanak (1675–1937)* (Montréal, 1964); *Histoire de Saint-François-du-Lac* (Ottawa, 1942). N.-H.-É. Faucher de Saint-Maurice, *Choses et autres; études et conférences* (Montréal, 1874), 60–65. Lareau, *Hist. de la littérature canadienne*, 207–9.

MAYAWASSINO. *See* MUSQUAKIE

MEIN, SUSAN (Sibbald), memoirist; b. 29 Nov. 1783 at Fowey, Cornwall, England, fifth daughter of Thomas Mein, physician in the Royal Navy, and Margaret Ellis; d. 9 July 1866 at Toronto, Canada West.

Susan Mein spent her childhood in Cornwall, first at Fowey, and then at Devonport where Thomas Mein was appointed inspector of hospital ships in 1795. From 1797 to 1800 she attended Belvedere House, a fashionable boarding-school in Bath, and, following her *début*, spent winters in London and summers in Scotland at Eildon Hall, her father's estate near Melrose. In 1807 she married William Sibbald, colonel in the 15th Regiment of Foot; they were to have two daughters and nine sons.

Susan Sibbald and her son Archibald came to Upper Canada in October 1835 to visit two other sons, William (founder in 1833 of a short-lived monthly literary magazine in York (Toronto), the *Canadian Magazine*) and Charles, who had both immigrated several years before. Mrs Sibbald purchased, probably for William and Charles, 500 acres and a log house on the south shore of Lake Simcoe, near the present site of Jackson's Point, and named it Eildon Hall. In March 1836 she returned to Scotland to find that her husband had died in her absence; the following October she arrived back in Canada with her three youngest sons to settle at Eildon Hall, carving out of the Canadian wilderness a thoroughly British oasis of culture and comfort. The estate soon boasted traditional gardens, imported trees, and a heated greenhouse; it became the setting for a social life which Susan made as similar as possible to that which the family had enjoyed in Britain. She was also instrumental in 1838 in building St George's Anglican Church on her property.

In September 1843 Mrs Sibbald returned to Britain, remaining there until 1856, when she came back to Canada with her second son, Captain Thomas Sibbald, author of *A few days in the United States and Canada, with some hints to settlers* (London, [1846]). Mrs Sibbald spent the remaining ten years of her life in Toronto, keeping up friendships she had made previously with Bishop John STRACHAN, Admiral Augustus Warren BALDWIN, Sir John Beverley ROBINSON, William Henry Boulton*, and other members of the Family Compact with whose attitudes she sympathized. She believed firmly in maintaining the class distinctions of the old world and saw the city's rising merchants and financiers as parvenus who were usurping social leadership. In her last years she often lamented the decline of old values and the disappearance of the first generation of Toronto's Tory families. She tried to pass on to her grandchildren her sense of loyalty to British customs and institutions and took pride that, in addition to her father and husband, eight of her nine sons held commissions in either the Royal Navy, the Indian army, or the Canadian militia.

While living in Toronto Mrs Sibbald wrote an autobiography of the first 29 years of her life, which was later edited by her great-grandson, Francis Paget Hett, and published in 1926. Her *Memoirs* show her to be an accomplished writer with a good sense of dialogue, discrimination in detail, and skill in characterization. Family friends who appear in the *Memoirs* include the satiric poet John Wolcot ("Peter Pindar"), novelists Sir Walter Scott and G. P. R. James, and painters William Owen and Henry Bone. The most delightful character in the *Memoirs*, however, is Susan Sibbald herself, with her sprightly outlook on life, sense of humour, and spirit of adventure. Her personality made it easy for her to adapt to life in Canada, and her letters reveal that she kept her zest for living undiminished in her old age. She died in Toronto in 1866 and is buried at Jackson's Point.

MARIAN E. FOWLER

PAO, Thomson (John), diaries, 1821–26, 1833–38. Sibbald Memorial Museum (Sibbald Point Provincial Park, Ont.), Sibbald papers, diary of Hugh Sibbald, 1842–44; diary of John Sibbald, 1840–42; Susan Sibbald, journals, 1849–66, and letters, 1858–66. [Susan Mein], *The memoirs of Susan Sibbald, 1783–1812*, ed. F. P. Hett (London, 1926). *Canadian Magazine* (York [Toronto]), January–March 1833. Craig, *Upper Canada*. F. P. Hett, *Georgina: a type study of early settlement and church building in Upper Canada* (Toronto, 1939), 85–86. Susanna [Strickland] Moodie, *Life in the clearings versus the bush* (London, 1853). M. E. Fowler, "Portrait of Susan Sibbald: writer and pioneer," *OH*, LXVI (1974), 51–64.

MERCER, ALEXANDER CAVALIÉ, soldier and artist; b. 28 March 1783 at Hull, Yorkshire, England, son of General Alexander Mercer, Royal Engineer, and Miss Dickson; m. 10 Oct. 1813 Frasquita (Fanny) Rice, and they had one son; d. 9 Nov. 1868 at Exeter, England.

Alexander Cavalié Mercer's early education took place in a variety of undistinguished private schools; these did not prepare him adequately to pass initially the entrance examinations for the Royal Military Academy at Woolwich, England, though he was eventually admitted. Upon graduating he took a commission as 2nd lieutenant in the Royal Artillery in 1799 because he "hardly looked upon Engineers as soldiers; and . . . [he] wanted to be a soldier." Promoted 1st lieutenant in 1801, Mercer served in the Cork district of Ireland between 1801 and 1805, to help keep order after the union of Ireland with Britain. During this time he suffered from ophthalmia. After spending the next two years at Woolwich, Northfleet, and Christchurch in England, he was ordered to South America where he participated in Lieutenant-General John Whitelocke's unsuccessful expedition to seize Buenos Aires for the British. By now a captain, Mercer was back in England by the end of 1808 where he remained until ordered to the Continent in 1815 as part of the Duke of Wellington's army; he fought at Quatre Bras and Waterloo. In the absence of Sir Alexander Dickson, the youthful officer was given command of G troop of the Royal Horse Artillery. During the battle of Waterloo he disobeyed Wellington's orders, and although the results were fortunate Mercer was disciplined. Reduced to half pay on 31 July 1816 he was forced to wait until 1821 to be reinstated to full pay; he nonetheless received the Waterloo medal, presented to all British officers who participated in Napoleon's defeat.

A careful observer, Mercer was considered by his son to be "a very good amateur artist" and it was this ability that he drew upon when writing about his experience in the Waterloo campaign; his journal, published posthumously in 1870 by his son, is an excellent description of the Lowlands and the Netherlands as the English found them in 1815, but it records only that portion of the battle which immediately affected Mercer.

Upon reinstatement Mercer was sent to Lower Canada in command of the 6th company of the 5th battalion of the Royal Artillery at Quebec; he arrived in Canada on board the *William Harris* on 7 July 1823. During this posting Mercer spent time at Quebec and Île Sainte-Hélène, and, using Kingston, Upper Canada, as a base, was a member of a board to survey the ordnance supplies in Upper Canada in 1824. Away from Canada during a long leave of absence from 1825 to 1827, Mercer again left the colony for England in 1829 and took up postings at Woolwich and then Devonport. On 22 Oct. 1837 Mercer, now a lieutenant-colonel, returned to British North America to command the artillery in Nova Scotia and remained at Halifax until 16 Aug. 1842. He made extensive tours of inspection throughout the Maritimes, and left an important water-colour record of many of the places he visited, especially Halifax and the surrounding region and Fredericton and the Saint John River valley. Although his paintings are now faded, he appears to have been one of the most original artists of the group of military topographers who documented the colonial landscape. The largest collection of his

Merritt

water-colours is preserved in the Public Archives of Canada.

In 1842 Mercer returned to England and a posting at Dover. He was promoted colonel in 1846, major-general in 1854, lieutenant-general in 1857, colonel-commandant in 1859, and general in 1865. He then left active service. He remained colonel-commandant of the 9th brigade of the Royal Artillery until his death.

M. BELL

PAC, RG 8, I (C series), 747, pp.151–52, 154. PANS, MG 12, HQ 31, p.119. PRO, WO 17/1527–33, 17/2384–89 (mfm. at PAC); WO 76/360. Royal Artillery Institution (Woolwich, Eng.), General A. C. Mercer papers, diary, 1786–1815. [A. C. Mercer], *Journal of the Waterloo campaign kept throughout the campaign of 1815*, ed. C. A. Mercer (2v., Edinburgh and London, 1870). *Battery records of the Royal Artillery, 1716–1859*, comp. M. E. S. Laws (Woolwich, Eng., 1952). *Hart's army list*, 1868. Francis Duncan, *History of the Royal Regiment of Artillery* (2v., London, 1872–73).

MERRITT, WILLIAM HAMILTON, soldier, merchant, promoter, and politician; b. 3 July 1793 at Bedford, Westchester County, N.Y., the son of Thomas Merritt and Mary Hamilton; d. 5 July 1862 at Cornwall, Canada West.

William Hamilton Merritt's father had served under John Graves Simcoe* in the Queen's Rangers during the American revolution, and after living in Saint John, N.B., from 1783 to 1785, and in South Carolina, he had settled in New York State. In 1796 Thomas Merritt petitioned Simcoe for land in Upper Canada and in the same year settled at Twelve Mile Creek (St Catharines), where in 1803 he was appointed sheriff of Lincoln County. In 1806 his son William Hamilton attended a school run by Richard Cockrel* at Ancaster and later at Niagara. Cockrel, a leading educator in Upper Canada and a land surveyor, taught Merritt mathematics and surveying. He also received some classical education from the Reverend John Burns, a Presbyterian minister at Niagara. Merritt rounded out his education in 1808 by a voyage to Bermuda with his uncle Nehemiah Merritt and by a visit to relatives in Saint John, where for a short time he attended a school run by Alexander McLeod. In December 1809 he returned to Upper Canada where he began to farm his father's land grant and an adjoining 200 acres in Grantham Township. Merritt also opened a general store which sold imported goods and took in exchange farm produce, lumber, ashes, and hides for shipment to Montreal.

Commissioned a lieutenant in the Lincoln militia shortly before the outbreak of the War of 1812, Merritt was called out on 28 June 1812 with the 1st troop of the Niagara Light Dragoons. He arrived at Sandwich (Windsor) one day after the fall of Detroit, but took part in the battle of Queenston Heights. After the troop was disbanded on 25 Feb. 1813, Merritt briefly and profitably engaged in the timber trade. On 11 March, however, he was appointed captain with orders from Brigadier-General John Vincent* to raise a troop of 50 Provincial Dragoons. Although Merritt complained at the time that the troop acted as "post boys and orderlies," it was placed on patrol duty and saw action in many major battles and minor skirmishes of the war. Illness kept Merritt from the fall of Niagara and the burning of Buffalo, but he fought at Lundy's Lane in July 1814 and was captured. He remained a prisoner in Cheshire, Mass., until the end of the war. While travelling back to Upper Canada Merritt stopped at Mayville, Chautauqua County, N.Y., where he married in 1815 Catharine Prendergast, whose family had lived near St Catharines before the war. They were to have four sons and two daughters.

Merritt now entered into a great variety of activities, beginning as a merchant in St Catharines with outlets in Niagara, Queenston, and the naval station on the Grand River. He sold dry goods, groceries, hardware, crockery, and books, for which he accepted cash and country produce. He also opened a land agency, although he does not seem to have been a major land speculator. In March 1816 Merritt purchased a mill site and small sawmill on Twelve Mile Creek and shortly after built a grist mill there. That same year he developed a salt spring on his property, built a potashery, and erected a small distillery. With the closing of the Grand River naval station and a general depression following the war, Merritt concentrated his mercantile activities in St Catharines, forming a partnership with his brother-in-law Charles Ingersoll. The depression, over-extension of the business, and bad debts caused them to fail in 1819, but eventually they paid off their debts to Montreal wholesalers. Merritt was left with his mills and other works in which he retained an interest until 1839.

Merritt is best known for his part in the promotion of the Welland Canal, linking lakes Ontario and Erie. The idea likely grew out of the need for water to run his mills on Twelve Mile Creek; by constructing a feeder canal he hoped to obtain water from the Welland River and its source, Chippawa Creek, the summit of which was two miles from his mill site. His plan to build a canal to connect the Welland River with Twelve Mile Creek soon grew into a plan to link the two Great Lakes. The canal would improve the St Lawrence transportation system by providing a cheap and convenient means for the products of western Upper Canadian farms to bypass the Niagara Falls portage and to proceed to Montreal and Great Britain. In September 1818 Merritt and a small party carried out a survey which later proved to have seriously underestimated the height difference between Twelve Mile Creek and the Welland River. Soon after, Merritt and 74 others petitioned the Upper Canadian legislature to order a survey by "some scientific men." The petition also revealed an awareness of the threat posed by the American plan to link Lake Erie with New York City by means of the Erie Canal and the Mohawk and Hudson rivers: "The grand object of the American people appears to be opening a navigation with Lake Erie, which design our canal, if effected soon, would counteract, and take down the whole of the produce from the Western country." Merritt's plan had sound economic grounds: only a canal linking lakes Erie and Ontario and the development of canals on the upper St Lawrence could restore Montreal to its dominant position in the western trade.

Merritt's project quickly encountered opposition. Those with interests in Niagara and Queenston faced ruin from the loss of the Niagara Falls portage. The project also encountered financial and political difficulties. Delays were caused by general depression, Merritt's own difficulties in 1818–19, and the political stalemate caused by the inability of Upper and Lower Canada to agree on the distribution of customs revenues between them. The Upper Canadian assembly was not idle, and a select committee in February 1823 recommended the construction of a canal from Burlington Bay to the Grand River. Strategic rather than industrial or trading considerations dictated this choice of route. Although Merritt had envisaged a canal built by the government, he now saw that for purposes of trade rather than defence a private company was essential. In 1823 he organized local meetings in support of his plan and sought incorporation; despite opposition from Niagara interests the Welland Canal Company was finally chartered by the Upper Canadian assembly on 19 Jan. 1824.

Merritt now faced the problem of organizing a company, raising funds, and finding personnel. He began his search for funds in York (Toronto), realizing that he needed the support of the colonial executive. John Henry Dunn*, the receiver general, subscribed and agreed to become president of the company (an agreement soon withdrawn). Attorney General John Beverley ROBINSON promised his support, and John STRACHAN played a leading part in the group. With encouragement assured in York, Merritt travelled to Montreal, stopping wherever he might enlist support, including Kingston, Gananoque, Prescott, and Cornwall. Although he received many promises, he got no subscriptions until he reached Quebec City. Funds raised in Upper and Lower Canada fell far short of the authorized capital of £40,000. Forced to look elsewhere, Merritt turned to the Upper Canadian government and to the United States. In August 1824 the directors of the company petitioned the assembly for a grant of waste lands in Wainfleet Township. Lieutenant Governor Sir Peregrine Maitland*, in referring the application to London, advised against approval, with defence in mind. Private investors in the United States remained, and in December 1824 Merritt set out for New York where he met John Barentse Yates, who advanced a large and crucial portion of the necessary funds. Merritt and Yates remained close associates in building the canal until the death of the latter in 1836. The American stockholders quickly proposed larger dimensions for the canal to accommodate sloops as well as boats.

With funds available, but with the dimensions unresolved, construction of the canal began on 30 Nov. 1824. Physical difficulties in construction, however, soon necessitated more capital. In 1825 a new charter allowing an increase of capitalization to £200,000 and permitting the enlargement of the canal to accommodate schooners was passed; it specified the branch of the Twelve Mile Creek that flowed through Merritt's property as the northern section. The 1825 act envisaged a single canal from Lake Ontario up the Twelve Mile Creek, and from that point two branches, one through a deep cut to the Welland River and a second through a cut to the Grand River. Construction went well until 9 Nov. 1828 when the excavation at the Deep Cut to the Welland collapsed. The contractor had encountered sand which would not support the weight of the high banks, and the funds spent on the cut were wasted. The level of water in the Deep Cut had now to be raised by a feeder supplied by a reservoir made by damming the Grand River. Despite these difficulties two schooners passed through from Lake Ontario on their way to Buffalo on 30 Nov. 1829. The canal, symbolically at least, had been opened. The Grand River section opened late in the following year. Between 1830 and March 1833 a channel was cut directly south from the Grand River feeder to Lake Erie at Gravelly

Merritt

Bay (Port Colborne). Merritt's canal had become a fact.

Physical and engineering problems had increased the Welland Canal Company's financial needs. When in 1825 the House of Assembly permitted an increase of capitalization it also had resolved to lend the company £25,000 and thus became a major participant in the project. Then, when failure to sell the additional shares in England or the United States threatened the company in 1827, the assembly had voted to purchase stock to the amount of £50,000; Lower Canada also voted £25,000. Early in 1828 Merritt realized that another £50,000 would be required for the remainder of the season. One proposal was to send an agent to England to secure the one-ninth of the estimated cost of production, subject to conditions, promised by the imperial government in 1826. After fruitless efforts to raise funds in New York and Philadelphia, Merritt sailed to England from New York on 16 March 1828. The House of Commons appropriated £50,000 sterling for the canal, and Merritt sold the remaining stock to English investors. The collapse of the Deep Cut, however, late that same year, again precipitated a financial crisis. Various expedients such as the issue of company scrip and the raising of loans enabled the work to continue. But when the canal was opened in its earliest form, the company was deeply in debt. Again Upper Canada voted assistance. With the increasing sums advanced by the province, the question of public ownership began to be raised. Merritt realized its inevitability but Yates still believed private capital could pay off all government grants and loans. In 1835 William Lyon MACKENZIE attacked the company's management for their identification of the canal with the Tories, thus undermining the efforts of Yates to raise private capital. The depression and rebellions of 1837 delayed public ownership, but in 1843 an act, containing long-term safeguards for the shareholders, ended the canal as a private concern.

To Merritt must go credit for the idea, the enlisting of government support, the raising of funds, and the general supervision of the canal project. His vision, however, quickly outgrew the Welland Canal, for as early as 1824 he had begun to dream of a St Lawrence system, with the rapids between Prescott and Lachine as the next place for improvement. In 1832 he, as "A Projector," published a pamphlet which advocated standardizing the dimensions of the canals and placing them under the sole direction of the legislature of Upper Canada. With the St Lawrence system opened, tributary streams which disgorged themselves into it, could, he said, be made navigable by private companies such as the Grand River Navigation Company with which he was involved as a director and adviser from 1834 to 1857. That company, using funds from the Six Nations band, improved transportation on the Grand River and gave the inhabitants of the area an inexpensive outlet to markets. Where natural water courses were not available, he suggested "rail roads" might be built. In 1836 he himself was identified with the Niagara and Detroit Rivers Railway Company which hoped to build a line between Buffalo and Detroit. Thus, despite his preoccupation with canals, Merritt saw early that railways should be an important part in Canadian transportation systems. For instance, because it was more economical to carry grain on the upper lakes in vessels too large for the Welland Canal, Merritt enthusiastically promoted the Welland Railway, completed in June 1859, between Port Dalhousie and Port Colborne. Using the facilities of the two ports, it did not compete with but supplemented the canal. His promotion of the first international suspension bridge over the Niagara gorge, opened for carriage travel in 1849 and rail in 1855, and his support in 1850 for a rail link between Detroit and Halifax also evidenced his broad views on transportation. He did not forget canals, however, and in 1852 spoke in St Catharines of vessels of 2,000 tons (at a time when ships of 1,000 tons were the exception) sailing from Lake Superior to the Atlantic.

An essential ingredient in Merritt's successful promotion of transportation schemes was his involvement in politics, although his political affiliation is hard to define. He sympathized with Robert Fleming GOURLAY following the War of 1812, but identified himself with the Tory party; he held the position of magistrate for the Niagara District from 1817 on and was reappointed after the union of 1841. But in politics Merritt simply advanced his own business and commercial interests. When the Family Compact was in power he supported it, and he changed his allegiance from Tory to moderate Reform to match the predominant mood of the union period. Merritt had first entered the Upper Canadian assembly for Haldimand in 1832 and was re-elected in 1834 and 1836; after the union he sat for Lincoln (North Riding, 1841–47, and Lincoln, 1848–60). In 1860 he resigned from the assembly and was elected to the Legislative Council for the Niagara division. In 1844 he had declined invitations from William Henry Draper* to join his ministry because he considered himself a long-standing supporter of

Robert Baldwin*. Merritt served as president of the Executive Council from 15 Sept. 1848 to 7 April 1850 in the government of Baldwin and Louis-Hippolyte LA FONTAINE, concentrating on public works and trade policy. After Lord Elgin [BRUCE] arrived in Canada in 1847, Merritt quickly urged on him the need to establish reciprocity of trade with the United States to increase markets for Canadian products after the abolition of the Corn Laws in 1846 and to make full use of the canal system. Elgin's early letters to Colonial Secretary Lord Grey clearly reveal the influence of Merritt, who with the encouragement of Elgin visited Washington in May 1848 and June 1849 to promote a reciprocity treaty. By the latter date, Elgin was convinced that because of commercial depression the choice was reciprocity or annexation. Early in September 1849 Merritt and La Fontaine discussed the same subject at Halifax with leaders of Nova Scotia and New Brunswick, but in Merritt's view the conference achieved little. On 7 April 1850 Merritt accepted the cabinet post of chief commissioner of public works, a position well suited to him; he diligently applied himself in pressing for the completion of the canal system to link inland waters with the ocean. His report for 1850 was a masterly analysis of the water transport system.

Although Elgin and many of his contemporaries considered Merritt a visionary, Elgin more than once affirmed his belief in Merritt's "large views." However, Elgin did say that Merritt though "honest" was "illogical" and "utterly unscrupulous in his mode of grouping together facts and figures when he has a case to make." For instance, Merritt's commitment to retrenchment in government spending clashed with his urging that the Cornwall and St Lawrence canal works be completed. Elgin considered fallacious Merritt's suggestion that a considerable portion of judicial expenses paid out of the general revenue be shifted to the municipalities, since the plan would transfer rather than abolish the costs. Merritt's other suggestions for financial retrenchment included abolishing all ports of entry and trusting to public opinion to discountenance smuggling, reforming the system of land sales, slashing the civil list and some pensions, and budgeting a fixed allowance to each department.

On 11 Feb. 1851 Merritt resigned from the Executive Council, later explaining that over the years he had been thwarted in his attempts to reduce public expenditure and to develop and sell crown lands to provide funds for canal and railway building. Another reason was that "public attention has been directed to Railroads and other new undertakings, on which the public credit is freely extended, while this great and important communication [the St Lawrence canal system], on which the future prospects of Canada in a great measure depend, has been virtually abandoned." As for political affiliations he said he had no connection with any parties. Henceforth, he would support measures that, in his judgement, would bring about those changes he deemed necessary for the prosperity of the country. In 1854 he supported the abolition of seigneurial tenure in Canada East and of the clergy reserves in Canada West. Though no longer in the Executive Council, Merritt continued to promote reciprocity, preparing in 1852 an address to the imperial government on the subject. Reciprocity was instituted by treaty in 1854. He was also endeavouring in 1852 to secure the returns of receipts and expenditures from each separate government in British North America with a view towards evaluating the financial possibilities of a union of the colonies.

The financial difficulties Merritt experienced in the 1840s and 1850s show that he was not always a successful businessman. He was a director of the Niagara Suspension Bridge Company incorporated in 1846, and of several small railways in the Niagara peninsula, as well as the St Lawrence Navigation Company. His close association with the Welland Railway Company from 1852 caused him severe financial loss in 1859, but the Niagara District Bank, which he promoted and incorporated in 1841, did prosper.

Merritt's public interests ranged far beyond transportation and trade. In 1843 he visited the United States to gather information for the government respecting the establishment of a provincial lunatic asylum. He worked on behalf of the survivors of the War of 1812 by obtaining medals for those who had fought at Detroit, Crysler's Farm, and Châteauguay, and played a leading part in the building of the second Brock monument at Queenston. He was active in the affairs of the Church of England, aided the establishment of Grantham Academy at St Catharines in 1829, and as a member of the Refugee Slaves Friends Society helped escaped slaves from the United States in the 1840s and 1850s. In his later years he encouraged the gathering of Canadian historical records from England and elsewhere, particularly relating to the United Empire Loyalists. In 1860 the library committee of parliament, through Merritt's influence, employed his son J. P. Merritt and George COVENTRY to gather documents. This early attempt at a na-

Mignault

tional archives ended in 1863, shortly after Merritt's death. Out of the project, however, had grown the Upper Canada Historical Society, formed in October 1861, to which Merritt subscribed.

Merritt was a compulsive worker who put in long days, often carrying on when incapacitated. Although happily married, he spent long periods away from his family, and his wife in turn spent much time with her parents in Mayville, N.Y. Their letters and diaries reveal in both a serious turn of mind with little sense of humour. Although not a teetotaler, Merritt was temperate. His contemporaries considered him a "strong and vigorous" speaker, but it was also thought that his "policy is too liberal – his conceptions too vast – his views too comprehensive to be comprehensible by all." Fittingly, he died aboard a ship in the Cornwall canal.

Today Merritt can be seen as one of the great figures in the history of Canadian transportation. But his large scheme for a system of canals linking the Great Lakes with the St Lawrence and the ocean, which finally came to fruition in 1849, was soon challenged by the new technology of railways. In 1853 the New York state legislature consolidated railways to connect New York with Buffalo and by early 1854 the Great Western Railway ran from the Niagara River Suspension Bridge to Windsor. Just as the Welland Canal had suffered from the earlier completion of the Erie Canal, the Great Lakes–St Lawrence canal system suffered from the competition of railways. Merritt's vision of an eastern Canadian transportation system involving waterways and railways was logical, practical, and consistently pursued. Even if his canal system did not achieve the economic benefits to Canada expected by Merritt, his vision foreshadowed the opening of the St Lawrence Seaway in 1958.

J. J. TALMAN

William Hamilton Merritt was the author of the following works, some of which were unsigned: *A concise view of the inland navigation of the Canadian provinces* . . . (St Catharines, [Ont.], 1832); *A brief review of the revenue, resources, and expenditures of Canada, compared with those of the neighboring state of New-York* . . . (St Catharines, 1845); *Letters, addressed to the inhabitants of the Niagara District, on free trade, &c*. (Niagara, 1847); *Brief review of the origin, progress, present state, and future prospects of the Welland Canal* (St Catharines, 1852); *A lecture delivered before the Mechanics' Institute of St Catharines, on the 21st day of January, 1857* (St Catharines, 1857); *Journal of events principally on the Detroit and Niagara frontiers, during the War of 1812* (St Catharines, 1863). The latter pamphlet was reprinted in *Select British documents of the Canadian War of 1812* (Wood), III, pt.II, 543–648.

PAC, MG 24, E1. PAO, Merritt (William Hamilton) papers (mfm. at PAC). "Campaigns of 1812–14: contemporary narratives by Captain W. H. Merritt, Colonel William Claus, Lieut.-Colonel Matthew Elliott and Captain John Norton," ed. E. [A.] Cruikshank, Niagara Hist. Soc., [*Pubs.*], no.9 ([Niagara-on-the-Lake, Ont.], 1902), 3–20. Can., Prov. of, Legislative Assembly, *Journals*, 1851, 1, app. T. *Elgin-Grey papers* (Doughty). *Farmers' Journal and Welland Canal Intelligencer* (St Catharines, [Ont.]), 1826–35. *St. Catharines Journal* (St Catharines, [Ont.], 1835–62. Chadwick, *Ontarian families*, I, 191–97. H. G. J. Aitken, *The Welland Canal Company: a study in Canadian enterprise* (Cambridge, Mass., 1954). J. P. Merritt, *Biography of the Hon. W. H. Merritt* . . . (St Catharines, Ont., 1875). A. R. M. Lower, "A half-forgotten builder of Canada (William Hamilton Merritt)," *Queen's Quarterly* (Kingston, Ont.), XLVI (1939), 191–97. D. C. Masters, "W. H. Merritt and the expansion of Canadian railways," *CHR*, XII (1931), 168–73.

MIGNAULT, PIERRE-MARIE, Catholic priest and vicar general; b. 8 Sept. 1784 at Saint-Denis on the Richelieu River, Province of Quebec, son of Basile Mignault, farmer, and Marie-Josephte Ledoux, both of Acadian ancestry; d. 5 Nov. 1868 at Montreal.

Following classical studies at the Collège de Montréal (1798–1806), Pierre-Marie Mignault spent a year with his parish priest, Abbé François Cherrier*, preparing for the priesthood. For the next academic year he went to the Séminaire de Nicolet, where he continued his theological studies and also served as bursar. Ordained priest on 18 Oct. 1812, he was appointed curate by Bishop Joseph-Octave Plessis*, first at the city of Quebec, then two years later at Halifax, which still formed part of the diocese of Quebec. After the parish priest at Halifax, Edmund Burke*, left for Europe, Mignault had to minister alone to about a thousand Irish Catholics. His correspondence with Bishop Plessis includes reference to occasional contact with Sir John Coape Sherbrooke*, the lieutenant governor of Nova Scotia, and this contact enabled him to write later: "I am quite familiar with the nature of British government, through having studied it here at Halifax." When Burke returned from Rome in 1817, as head of the new apostolic vicariate of Nova Scotia, Mignault went back to Lower Canada.

He was immediately appointed parish priest of Chambly, which had 3,000 parishioners in addition to the garrison. Religious life in the parish seemed to him superficial, and licentiousness too common. Working first by himself, then with the help of a curate, he was able to induce almost all the Catholics to take Easter communion. Neighbouring parish priests were envious of his success; Mignault retorted that he "had not asked for the position," which was in fact an important one for so young a priest. Spurred on by the example of the Protestants, who were building a combined church and school, Mignault opened two schools in October 1818, one Francophone and the other Anglophone. He also wanted to get signatures to a petition for the promotion of the teaching of the French language and the Catholic religion, but Bishop Plessis dissuaded him.

In 1821, however, Mignault joined the association to improve educational opportunities in the Chambly River area [see Charles La Rocque*]. Moreover, in 1825 Mignault founded the classical college at Saint-Pierre de Chambly, remaining its superior until 1844. There were many obstacles; he would have given up if he had not had strong religious and patriotic convictions, and had not also wished to "dispel the old and continually revived calumny that the clergy seeks to keep the people in ignorance." Despite his devotion, the institution, incorporated in 1836, was frequently in a precarious state. Debts, a small teaching body hastily assembled, pupils chosen somewhat at random, authority divided between the superior and various directors, and the introduction of a commercial course in 1839, brought an end to the classical programme at Chambly in 1844. Mignault unsuccessfully attempted on several occasions to revive classical studies in this establishment, which finally closed its doors in 1862.

Pierre-Marie Mignault also took an interest in the Canadians who had emigrated to the United States and settled on the shores of Lake Champlain. From 1818 to 1850 he set aside some 14 days each year for these people, who could not be ministered to for want of American priests. At his own expense Mignault went to the region, where he preached and administered the sacraments. In 1849, when Bishop Ignace Bourget* held an inquiry into the emigration of Canadians to the United States, Mignault was asked to give information on the conditions of life and the habits and customs of the emigrants.

By 1830 Mignault had become in succession vicar general of the dioceses of Boston, New York, and Albany; he earned the gratitude of the first bishop of Burlington, Louis de Goesbriand, among others: "Only with respect and gratitude can I utter the name of the Reverend Mignault, who had a true father's heart for the immigrant Canadians." In 1852 he received the title of apostolic chaplain from Pope Pius IX.

Although he had always upheld the bishops' authority, Mignault felt able to give them advice or submit plans to them. In 1854, with 15 other priests, he suggested to Bishop Bourget that a new diocese be set up, covering the south shore of the St Lawrence as far as the Richelieu. The reasons advanced were serious: the assurance of wealth and material resources to support a bishop and the need to guard and strengthen the faith in view of the large number of Protestants. However, the second provincial council of Quebec in June 1854 did not approve the proposal.

The last years of Mignault's life as parish priest of Chambly were hampered by illness and old age. He none the less founded a convent in 1855 and a hospital in 1858. In 1866 he resigned, and retired to the hospice of Saint-Joseph at Montreal, where he died two years later.

LUCIEN LEMIEUX

AAQ, 210 A, V, 124, 225; IX, 113; 515 CD, I, 139–50. Archives du diocèse de Saint-Jean-de-Québec (Longueuil, Qué.), Saint-Joseph-de-Chambly, 1A/44f., 47f., 50–52, 54, 66, 84, 89, 128, 134, 137, 159, 162. Archives paroissiales, Saint Denis sur Richelieu (Saint Denis-sur-Richelieu, Qué.), Registres de baptêmes, mariages et sépultures, 9 Sept. 1784. L'Ami du peuple, de l'ordre et des lois (Montréal), 10 juin 1835, 13 sept. 1839. L'Aurore des Canadas, 17 sept. 1839. Mélanges religieux, 16 juill. 1841. Allaire, Dictionnaire. J.-A.-I. Douville, Histoire du collège-séminaire de Nicolet, 1803–1903, avec les listes complètes des directeurs, professeurs et élèves de l'institution (2v., Montréal, 1903), II, 3, 5–7. A. A. Johnston, A history of the Catholic Church in eastern Nova Scotia (2v., Antigonish, N.S., 1960–71), I, 348, Lemieux, L'établissement de la première prov. eccl., 87–92. Yvon Charron, "Le collège classique de Saint-Pierre à Chambly," SCHÉC Rapport, 13 (1945–46), 19–38. Adrien Verrette, "La paroisse franco-américaine," SCHÉC Rapport, 15 (1947–48), 132. Mason Wade, "The French parish and survivance in nineteenth-century New England," Catholic Hist. Rev. (Washington), XXXVI (1950–51), 163–89.

MILES, EDWARD MADAN, surveyor; b. 14 March 1835 near Thornhill in Markham Township, Upper Canada, eldest son of Lawford Edward and Anna Miles; d. 9 Nov. 1866 at Weston (now in Metropolitan Toronto), Canada West.

Edward Madan Miles' parents moved to the island of Heligoland, then a British possession, soon after his birth. He attended school in Altona in the duchy of Holstein, and, following that, spent three or four years at sea. In 1851 he returned to Markham Township to farm on land purchased by his father in 1834. However, he was attracted by land surveying and became articled to John Stoughton Dennis* of Weston. Miles passed his final examination on 13 July 1857. A year later he accepted as a pupil his younger brother, Charles Falconer Miles.

Miles

In 1858 Edward Miles entered into a partnership with surveyor John Lindsay; he assisted in surveying military pensioners' lots and ordnance lands in Penetanguishene from November 1858 to January 1859, and the boundaries of the town plot of Keswick in May 1859. Soon after he formed a partnership with Charles Unwin, who in 1860–61 conducted surveys on the north shore of Lake Huron for the Crown Lands Department, which had decided to subdivide some townships and find new lines of communication. From May to October 1860 Miles was in charge of the survey of Macdonald Township in the Algoma District.

Miles is best known for the position he held as surveyor with the Canadian Land and Emigration Company, founded in London in 1861 with Thomas Chandler HALIBURTON as chairman. After lengthy negotiations the company had agreed to purchase from the Canadian government ten townships, *en bloc*, nine in the present county of Haliburton, and one, Longford, in Victoria County, which it proposed to divide into lots for sale to settlers. The cost to the company and the settlement duties required by the government were to be based on the number of acres considered fit for settlement as determined by a surveyor acceptable to both the company and the government. Miles was originally selected by the company but was not approved by the Crown Lands Department. The position was given to Brookes Wright Gossage, who by 1862 had more than 60 men working in the area. In 1863, after disputes had arisen between the department, the company, and Gossage concerning the location and quality of the land and the amount to be paid to Gossage, the company employed Miles independently as "inspecting surveyor." He re-examined Dysart, Dudley, Harcourt, Harburn, and Guildford townships and made a preliminary survey of the townsite of Haliburton. His estimate of the acres fit for settlement was far below that of Gossage, but, unfortunately for the Company, Gossage's figures were accepted in the final agreement between it and the Crown Lands Department. It was left to the settlers, struggling with rock and swamp, to prove the accuracy of Miles' report.

While Miles was employed by the company he was active in establishing the new settlement at Haliburton. He read the services in St. George's Church (Church of England) before the arrival of the first clergyman, the Reverend Frederick Burt, in the summer of 1865. He left the company shortly after this date. Returning to Weston, where he had maintained his home for some years, he entered into partnership with J.W. Farrand to operate a woollen mill on the Humber River. In the fall of 1866 Miles' hand was crushed in a burring machine and he died from lockjaw on 9 November.

In December 1859 he had married Louisa, eldest daughter of the Reverend William Arthur Johnson*, rector of St Philip's Church, Weston, and founder of the school that later became Trinity College School at Port Hope.

FLORENCE B. MURRAY

Ont., Dept. of Lands and Forests, Surveys Office, Instructions to land surveyors, Canada Land and Emigration Company surveys, 26 Feb. 1861–13 Jan. 1869 (mfm. copies at PAO). PAO, RG 1, B-IV, 82. *Daily Telegraph* (Toronto), 13 Nov. 1866. *Globe*, 13 Nov. 1866. *Leader*, 20 Nov. 1866. *Muskoka and Haliburton* (Murray). *Mitchell & Co.'s general directory for the city of Toronto, and gazetteer of the counties of York and Peel for 1866* (Toronto, 1866). H.R. Cummings, *Early days in Haliburton* (Toronto, 1963). Nila Reynolds, *In quest of yesterday* . . . ([Minden, Ont., 1968]). C. F. Miles, "Edward Madan Miles," Assoc. of Ont. Land Surveyors, *Annual report* (Toronto), 33 (1918), 186–87. "Charles Falconer Miles," Assoc. of Ont. Land Surveyors, *Annual report* (Toronto), 38 (1923), 142–48.

MILES, STEPHEN, printer, newspaper publisher, and Methodist minister; b. 19 Oct. 1789 at Royalton, Vt, son of Ephraim Miles; m. first 22 June 1812, Laura Spafford of Kingston, Upper Canada, and then 21 Aug. 1822 Lucinda Daniels of Windsor, Vt; d. 13 Dec. 1870 at Clark's Mills (Camden East), Ont.

At age 15 Stephen Miles was apprenticed to Nahum Mower*, a printer, in Windsor (Vt), and in 1807 immigrated with him to Montreal where they established the weekly *Canadian Courant and Montreal Advertiser*. In June 1810 Mower and Charles Kendall, a printer in his employ, issued a prospectus for a weekly newspaper to be published in Kingston. By the time the first issue of the *Kingston Gazette* appeared on 25 September, Mower had relinquished control to Kendall and Miles, though Mower was mentioned as co-publisher with Kendall since Miles was still technically an apprentice and under age.

In the early 19th century printers were often newspaper proprietors or publishers as well as editors; so it was with Kendall and Miles, though their editorials were brief and non-controversial. Of greater interest were articles submitted in response to the editors' general invitation to "gentlemen of science and leisure, the divine, the moralist, the poet, and the politician." John STRACHAN as "Reckoner" contributed 70 essays, and Richard Cartwright* as "Falkland," John Young* of Nova Scotia, and Barnabas

Bidwell* also wrote occasionally for the *Gazette*.

The partnership lasted until March 1811 when Miles withdrew to seek employment as a journeyman printer (having now completed the term of his apprenticeship), first in Plattsburgh, N.Y., and then in Montreal. In September 1811 Kendall sold the newspaper to Cartwright and a group of Kingston business and professional men. They recalled Miles and sold back the paper to him on easy terms. The issue for 17 Nov. 1811 was the first to be "printed and published by Stephen Miles." It was the only newspaper in Upper Canada to continue publication throughout the War of 1812–14, although its appearance was interrupted at times by Miles' militia duty and by his inability to procure paper. War news was prominent and first hand accounts appeared on the naval engagement of 10 Nov. 1812 in Kingston harbour and on the battle of Crysler's Farm.

In 1815, under government contract, Miles published the statutes of the 2nd and 3rd sessions of the 6th parliament of Upper Canada. Miles also reprinted Robert GOURLAY's first "Address to the resident landowners" from the *Upper Canada Gazette* (York) and his later letters and addresses from the *Niagara Gleaner*. At first a supporter of Gourlay, Miles turned against him as he indulged more and more in personalities. A break in their relations came when Gourlay castigated the Hagerman brothers, Daniel and Christopher*, along with John Macaulay*. Miles then published an unsigned editorial protest written, Gourlay discovered, by John Alexander Pringle, a Kingston civil servant. In an angry letter to the *Gazette*, Gourlay accused Miles of double dealing, of forswearing his Methodist principles, and of betraying him to the authorities, for it was on Miles' oath that Gourlay was first arrested for having published a libellous pamphlet. After Gourlay's acquittal, Miles published a pamphlet by John Simpson* highly critical of Gourlay. Gourlay's continued resentment was vented in letters to the press, a form of persecution which led Miles to sell the *Kingston Gazette* at the end of 1818 to Macaulay and Pringle; they changed the name to the *Kingston Chronicle* and retained Miles as printer but not editor. In 1821, however, Miles transferred his services as printer to the rival Kingston paper, the *Upper Canada Herald*, owned and edited by his brother-in-law, Hugh C. Thomson*.

A member of the Methodist group in Kingston, Miles was a class leader and occasional local preacher. In 1828 he left the *Herald* to establish the first religious weekly in Upper Canada, the *Kingston Gazette and Religious Advocate*, which ran from 20 June 1828 to 26 March 1830. It was outclassed after December 1829 by the official Methodist organ, Egerton Ryerson*'s *Christian Guardian*, but Ryerson in September 1830 paid tribute to its "many entertaining and profitable articles." Miles was by then engaged as printer of a Presbyterian journal, the *Canadian Watchman*, published by Ezra S. Ely. When it folded in 1831, he moved to Prescott and bought from J. Ketchum Averill the *Prescott Telegraph* which, re-named the *Grenville Gazette*, he published from January 1832 to April 1833.

At the end of April 1833, Miles sold the *Gazette* to Donald M'Leod* and returned to Kingston to become foreman in the pressroom of the *Chronicle*. Then, in 1835, Miles, aged 46, decided to give up the printing trade and was received on trial in the Wesleyan Methodist Church. He was ordained in 1840. By the time he was superannuated in 1851, he had served on 13 different circuits in what is now eastern Ontario, the more important of which were Gananoque, Bath, Marmora, Madoc, Newburgh, and Loughborough Township. As a preacher he was earnest and diligent, though considered ineffectual in the pulpit. As a pastor, however, he was popular and a general favourite with children. "Few ministers," it was said at the time of his death, "have been more beloved." Becoming blind late in life, he made his home with a married daughter at Clark's Mills, enfeebled in body and mind. He was survived by his daughter and by a son, Elijah, printer and proprietor of the *Hastings Chronicle* in Belleville.

H. P. GUNDY

[Stephen Miles wrote at the request of a friend an account of his early days as a printer in Kingston for the *Chronicle & Gazette*, 6 Jan. 1847; he also left a holograph account of the founding of the *Kingston Gazette* on the flyleaf of a bound copy of the first volume now in the Douglas Library, Queen's University (Kingston). Obituaries appeared in the Kingston *Daily News*, 16 Dec. 1870, the Toronto *Globe*, 19 Dec. 1870, the *Christian Guardian*, 14 Dec. 1870, and the Wesleyan Methodist Church in Canada, *Minutes* (Toronto), 1871. H.P.G.] G. H. Cornish, *Hand-book of Canadian Methodism* . . . (Toronto, 1867). William Canniff, *History of the settlement of Upper Canada (Ontario), with special reference to the Bay Quinté* (Toronto, 1869; repr. as *The settlement of Upper Canada*, intro. D. W. Swainson, Belleville, Ont., 1971). H. P. Gundy, *Early printers and printing in the Canadas* (Toronto, 1957; 2nd ed., 1964).

MILETTE (Millette), ALEXIS, carpenter, wood sculptor, and architect; b. 15 Feb. 1793 at Sainte-Anne-d'Yamachiche (Yamachiche, Que.), son of Joseph Milette and Judith Leblanc; m. 15 Feb.

Milette

1819 Marie, daughter of Jean-Baptiste Hébert, and they had 13 children, one of whom, Joseph-Octave-Norbert, became an architect and sculptor; d. 11 Oct. 1869 in his native parish.

There is no documented information about Alexis Milette's childhood and training. We know that his father was himself a sculptor and had at least one apprentice, Édouard Besse. Did Joseph Milette train his son? It is impossible to state that he did with certainty. Émile Vaillancourt* asserts, in *Une maîtrise d'art en Canada*, that Milette attended the workshop of Louis-Amable Quévillon* at the same time as Amable Gauthier*. Moreover, in 1821 Milette was associated with the latter in the decoration of the church of Sainte-Geneviève-de-Berthier; they may well have become acquainted at Quévillon's workshop at Saint-Vincent-de-Paul (Laval), a place commonly called Les Écorres. At this school the pupils learned the currently accepted styles of fine carpentry, wood carving, and gilding by working with the master and the advanced pupils.

In 1815 Alexis Milette obtained a contract to make and install "the wood panelling of the sanctuary and the interior ornamentation" of the church of Sainte-Anne-d'Yamachiche; he had probably just finished his training under Quévillon. The principle of team-work, apprenticeship, and the trade guild, which was used at Les Écorres, seems to have served as a model for Milette. Like several of Quévillon's pupils, he set up a workshop. The first associate to appear in connection with Milette's work is the sculptor's father Joseph, who is thought to have backed him financially and given him his shop; others were his brothers Michel, Bénoni, and Pierre; his son, Joseph-Octave Norbert; Joseph-Hengard Lapalice, who built numerous churches including Sainte-Trinité-de-Contrecœur, Saint-Paul-d'Abbotsford, Saint-Simon, and Sainte-Cécile (at Valleyfield); Moïse Berthiaume; and the brothers Joseph and Georges Héroux.

Throughout his career, Alexis Milette handled several contracts at the same time; moreover, his clients generally called upon his services more than once. His principal clients were the councils of the following parishes: Sainte-Anne-d'Yamachiche (1815–58), La Nativité-de-Notre-Dame-de-Bécancour (1817–22), Saint-Antoine-de-la-Baie-du-Febvre (1818–45), Sainte-Geneviève-de-Berthier (1822-29), Saint-Joseph-de-Maskinongé (1835), Sainte-Geneviève-de-Batiscan (1837), Saint-Aimé (1843), Saint-Michel-d'Yamaska (1843–52), Saint-Jean on the Richelieu River (1845–55), Saint-François-du-Lac (1849–56),

Saint-Joseph-de-Lanoriae (1864), and Saint-Barnabé (1864).

Like most French Canadian artists of the period, Alexis Milette had to turn his hand to all the varied forms of his art. Primarily a sculptor in wood, he was hired in this capacity, with the builder Jean-Baptiste Hébert, for the church of Saint-Michel-d'Yamaska; on other occasions he himself was builder, as for the church of Saint-Antoine-de-la-Baie-du-Febvre. In addition, he often had to supply plans for repairs, architectural modifications, or the decoration of church interiors and exteriors.

"The most fashionable sculptor of the day in the whole Trois-Rivières region" apparently enjoyed an excellent reputation among his contemporaries; the solidity and elegance of his buildings, in Louis XV style, were highly commended, and his ability to erect churches in keeping with the financial means of the parishes was generally acknowledged. Whether as sculptor or builder, Milette was strongly influenced in the decoration of church interiors by the plans of the architects who conceived the building. Thus at Baie-du-Febvre and Saint-François-du-Lac he worked according to the principles of Thomas Baillairgé*; at Lanoraie and Maskinongé we can see the architecture of Victor Bourgeau*. In this sense Milette's work is broadly comparable to that of Augustin Leblanc*, who also was torn between two spheres of influence: Quebec and Montreal.

MICHEL CAUCHON

ANQ-TR, Greffe de Petrus Hubert, 8 mars 1855. Archives judiciaires, Saint-Hyacinthe (Saint-Hyacinthe, Qué.), Greffe de P.-P. Dutalmé, 26 juill. 1814. Archives paroissiales, La Nativité-de-Notre-Dame-de-Bécancour (Bécancour, Qué.), Livres de comptes, II; Saint-Antoine-de-la-Baie-du-Febvre (Baieville, Qué.), Livres de comptes, I (1734–1819); Sainte-Anne-d'Yamachiche (Yamachiche, Qué.), Livres de comptes, 1789–1843; Saïnte-Geneviève-de-Berthier (Berthierville, Qué.), Livres de comptes, I, II; Saint-François-du-Lac (Saint-François-du-Lac, Qué.), Livres de comptes, III (1849–82); Saint-Michel-d'Yamaska (Yamaska, Qué.), Livres de comptes, I (1763–1843), II (1844–1907). IBC, Centre de documentation, Fonds Morisset, Dossier Alexis Millette. PAC, MG 30, D62, 21, pp.678–81. *Le Courrier du Canada*, 26 oct. 1864. *La Minerve*, 17 janv. 1860. Louis Carrier, *Catalogue du Musée du château de Ramezay de Montréal*, J.-J. Lefebvre, trad. et édit. (Montréal, 1962), 115. Napoléon Caron, *Histoire de la paroisse d'Yamachiche (précis historique)* (Trois-Rivières, 1892). O.-M.-H. Lapalice, *Histoire de la seigneurie Massue et de la paroisse de Saint-Aimé* (s.l., 1930). Émile Vaillancourt, *Une maîtrise d'art en Canada (1800–1823)* (Montréal, 1920), 91–92.

MOFFATT, GEORGE, businessman and politician; b. 13 Aug. 1787 at Sidehead, Weredale, Durham, England; m. first in 1809 an Indian whose name is not known (they had one son, Lewis), and secondly Sophia MacRae, by whom he had three sons; d. 25 Feb. 1865 in Montreal, Canada East.

After some schooling in London, George Moffatt came to Canada in 1801 at the age of 14 under the sponsorship of Montreal merchant John Ogilvy*. Further schooling with William Nelson at Sorel preceded his entry into his patron's firm, Parker, Gerrard, and Ogilvy, a major component of the XY Company. He later left them to join the firm of McTavish, McGillivray, and Company, the principal partner in the rival North West Company, and took part in a number of trips to Fort William (Thunder Bay, Ont.). In 1811 Moffatt set up his own firm in partnership with Alexander Dowie, a nephew of Sir Alexander Mackenzie*, which soon merged with Parker, Gerrard, and Ogilvy. After several changes the firm became known as Gillespie, Moffatt, and Company with Moffatt the principal Montreal partner and Robert GILLESPIE his associate in London. Although the firm became a major Montreal supply house for the fur trade, Moffatt was by no means totally committed to the North West Company; in 1809, while still working for McTavish, McGillivray, and Company, he was ready to join with Colin Robertson* in establishing an agency of the Hudson's Bay Company in Montreal.

After serving briefly during the War of 1812 with the Montreal volunteers at Laprairie under Charles-Michel d'Irumberry* de Salaberry, Moffatt aided Robertson, still an officer of the HBC, in his expeditions of 1815 and 1816 to the Athabaska country. He was one of Robertson's close friends and in 1819 put John McLoughlin*, a discontented wintering partner of the NWC, in contact with the HBC, thus paving the way for the coalition of the two great fur-trading companies in 1821 [see Edward ELLICE]. In facilitating the merger Moffatt was betraying an already failing cause: the NWC was losing money and had sacrificed much prestige during its protracted squabbles with Lord Selkirk [Douglas*]. As a major Montreal merchant Moffatt no doubt wanted a number of things which, to his mind, the merger would accomplish, among them the settlement of the NWC's debts, including some to Gillespie, Moffatt, and Company, and the elimination of competition and of generally chaotic conditions in the fur trade.

By 1821 Gillespie, Moffatt, and Company had become one of the major import-export houses of Montreal. It dealt in a wide range of imported manufactured goods, including groceries and dry goods and hardware, as well as the increasing volume of up-country staple commodities being shipped down the St Lawrence for foreign markets. The firm occupied large premises facing the Lachine Canal wharves, where it received its incoming shipments. Its affairs expanded substantially during the next decade and by the mid 1840s Gillespie, Moffatt, and Company received more seaborne goods than any other firm in Montreal, handling in 1845 alone the cargo of 15 foreign ships. By this time the company itself owned one large ship and was hiring several others each year to haul cargo overseas, much of it on consignment to Moffatt's British-based partners, Alexander and Robert Gillespie. A branch of the firm, Moffatt, Murray, and Company, was later opened in Toronto by Moffatt's eldest son, Lewis.

Like most of his business contemporaries, Moffatt had many other interests besides his own firm. He was an investor in the Lower Canada Land Company (formed in 1825) and a Canadian representative of the British American Land Company which had vast holdings in the Eastern Townships. Moffatt had his own substantial land holdings in Lower Canada including an island in the St Lawrence opposite Montreal. One of Moffatt, Gillespie, and Company's most important sidelines was insurance. The firm managed the Canadian branch of the Phoenix Fire Assurance Company which had had policies in the Canadas since 1804; by 1845, under Moffatt's management, the company had policies for £285,000 in Montreal. In that year a special inspector was sent from London and reported favourably on Moffatt's judgement in accepting risks in Montreal.

As a dominant figure in the city's commercial life, Moffatt was keenly interested in increasing its metropolitan mercantilist strength. He was active in a large number of enterprises which promoted Montreal's hegemony, including the Bank of Montreal of which he was a director from 1822 to 1835. He was also an early promoter of the pioneer Champlain and St Lawrence Railroad and a fervent promoter, major shareholder, and director of the St Lawrence and Atlantic Railroad; the latter, running 245 miles from Saint-Lambert opposite Montreal to Portland, Maine, was begun in 1845 and completed in 1853. His name was associated with many other ventures typical of the new economic activities emerging in the Canadas during the mid 19th century. He

Moffatt

was a director of the Montreal Mining Company, established in 1847 to exploit the copper deposits on the north shore of Lake Huron, and a promoter of the Marine Mutual Insurance Company of Montreal in 1851, Molsons Bank in 1854, the Canada Marine Insurance Company in 1856, and the Montreal Steam Elevating and Warehousing Company in 1857. Businessmen's clubs, where deals were often scouted or concluded, were a necessary adjunct to the commercial activity of a city, and Moffatt led in the formation of the exclusive St James Club in 1857. Other institutions reflecting Montreal's Anglo-Saxon commercial class which received Moffatt's support included the St George's Society, the Mountain Boulevard Company, the Montreal Cemetery Company, St George's Church, and McGill University.

The continuance of Montreal's key position in the import-export trade of Canada depended heavily on the ability of its harbour to handle an increasing volume of commodities and ocean-going ships. However, Montreal's commerce was severely hampered by high shipping costs since large ocean-going vessels could proceed up river only as far as Quebec, and there was a lack of adequate wharves. Along with fellow Montreal merchants, Moffatt sought to improve the harbour of Montreal and in 1830 had been designated chairman of the newly appointed harbour commissioners of Montreal. With his fellow members Jules-Maurice Quesnel* and Captain Robert S. Piper, he oversaw the erection of wharves at Montreal and initiated surveys of Lac Saint-Pierre to determine where the shipping channel should be dredged. Later, in the legislature, first as a member and in 1841 as chairman of a special committee, he was associated with efforts to deepen the channel. Moffatt had also been an original member of the Committee of Trade formed in 1822, and after it was reconstituted as the Montreal Board of Trade in 1842 was its president from 1844 to 1846; the question of harbour improvements occupied much of its time.

George Moffatt's legislative career began in 1831 when he took a seat in the Legislative Council of Lower Canada and assumed the mantle of his predecessor John Richardson* as spokesman for Montreal businessmen. During the increasingly tense 1830s the actions of the Legislative Council in rejecting or severely amending bills sent up from the assembly exacerbated tensions. Moffatt was in large measure responsible for increasing this animosity by instituting in 1832 criminal charges against two Montreal newspaper editors, Ludger Duvernay* of *La Minerve* and Daniel Tracey* of the *Irish Vindicator* and

Canada Advertiser, who had ridiculed the council. Their vindictive arrests and imprisonments set the stage for the violent election campaign in Montreal West in May 1832; Tracey, recently released from prison and now a popular hero, trounced the merchants' candidate Stanley Bagg*. Moffatt also had a hand in the tragic denouement to the election which took place on 21 May: as one of the magistrates of Montreal, he approached the garrison for assistance in keeping order at the polls and instructed the army to advance on a rioting mob; three persons were killed.

As the moral leader of the Lower Canadian English speaking community, Moffatt was one of the most active of the Montreal merchants who organized the "constitutionalists" of Montreal between 1832 and 1837. Although not as closely identified with the Constitutional Association of Montreal as John Molson* Jr or Peter McGill [McCutcheon*], Moffatt appears to have been a major behind-the-scenes-figure directing some of the most venomous attacks on French Canadians. He was probably one of the leading associates of Adam Thom* whose "Anti-Gallic letters" were published in the *Montreal Herald* during the autumn of 1835.

Moffatt and William Badgley*, a Montreal solicitor, went to London in the fall of 1837 to explain the position of the "British party" to the imperial government. In the aftermath of the Lower Canadian rebellion of 1837 Moffatt advocated to Colonial Secretary Lord Glenelg a moderate course in handling captured rebels, suggesting that only a few of the most serious offenders be banished. When Lord Durham [Lambton*] was appointed high commissioner of British North America in January 1838, Moffatt and Badgley provided him with a detailed memorandum outlining the major reforms they felt were necessary, including some which had been pursued unsuccessfully for decades by Lower Canadian merchants to create a more favourable business climate; a letter advising against the election of members of the Legislative Council was also provided. Moffatt accompanied Lord Durham to Canada and continued to offer advice on such matters as the disposition of prisoners. He also pressed for a legislative union with Upper Canada, which he considered was the best constitutional solution to the problems of Lower Canada. On 2 Nov. 1838 Sir John COLBORNE appointed Moffatt to the Special Council of Lower Canada following the suspension of the constitution. As a member of the executive of the Special Council he was one of Colborne's principal advisers.

The arrival of Colborne's replacement, Charles Poulett Thomson*, in October 1839 drastically altered Moffatt's status on the council. In a letter to Colonial Secretary Lord John Russell in December 1840, Thomson, now Lord Sydenham, described Moffatt as "the most pig headed, obstinate, ill tempered brute in the Canadas . . . whom I shall certainly not put in the new Legislative Council" of united Upper and Lower Canada. If Moffatt was to have a significant voice in union politics he had no choice but to sit in the Legislative Assembly. He was elected, with Sydenham's blessing, as one of the two members for the Montreal City riding in 1841. Moffatt had long supported union and it must have been with special pride that he sat in its first legislature. He resigned his seat on 30 Oct. 1843 to protest against the decision to move the capital from Kingston to Montreal, on the grounds that it was unfair to Canada West, but regained the seat in 1844, defeating Dr Pierre Beaubien* who had succeeded him the previous year.

Although Moffatt was never much at home in the assembly he was an assiduous member who was mindful of the interests of the Montreal English speaking business community. He introduced bills which originated in that community, including many from the Montreal Board of Trade, and which favoured its institutions, such as the Royal Institution for the Advancement of Learning and the High School of Montreal (but he also brought in bills on behalf of the Grey Nuns). He participated frequently in debates, especially in discussions on legislation affecting railways, usury laws, and McGill University. He served on several special committees during his six years in the house, including one in 1842 to consider the disposition of the Jesuit Estates.

Moffatt remained a conservative, but he now spoke with new-found moderation. He was far from being an anti-French reactionary; in the 1844–45 session he seconded Denis-Benjamin Papineau*'s motion favouring the reinstatement of French as an official language of debate and record in the Province of Canada and recanted earlier remarks in the assembly against the use of French. He also declared that he was prepared to support the payment of rebellion losses claims in Lower Canada. Civil disorder in Montreal and at Beauharnois during the early 1840s [see Frederick William ERMATINGER] was of special concern to Moffatt, and he sought to have the police forces augmented and placed under the control of the executive in order to increase their effectiveness.

Moffatt was not a candidate in the 1847 elections. He might have felt that he had already made whatever contributions he could towards the establishment of a favourable climate for business in Canada through the legislative process. But changes in British imperial policy at the end of the 1840s provoked violent reaction among Montreal Tories, many of whom signed the Annexation Manifesto of October 1849. Moffatt, although he had flirted briefly with Montreal free traders in 1847, remained aloof from annexationism. Instead, he became president of the Montreal branch of the British American League, an association of Conservatives and Tories formed to debate the problems created by the sudden disappearance of a protected imperial market for Canadian staples. The league included Harrison Stephens*, Thomas Wilson, John Esdaile, John Gordon MacKenzie, James Mathewson, and William Spier, all established Montreal merchants. In a manifesto published in the *Montreal Gazette* on 20 April 1849 Moffatt's group described themselves as "children of a monarchy, too magnanimous to prescribe, too great to be unjust." Their concern was for the "prosperity of Canada and with it the nation of which it forms a part." By using his extensive business and political influence throughout Canada, Moffatt hoped to undermine the annexationist menace by reconstructing a strong province-wide conservative organization. He visited Toronto and guided the sessions of the league's convention in July 1849 in Kingston where resolutions were passed calling for a study of the possibility of uniting the British American provinces, for retrenchment in public expenditure, and for protection for home industry. In Moffatt's opinion the resolutions demonstrated "that annexation had by no means captured the main forces of the tory-conservative party." A second convention in early November received a report from a committee which had discussed the proposal for union with representatives of the other colonies. Debate also ranged over a number of current economic issues, including reciprocity, annexation, free trade, and the renewal of protection.

The league underlined the fundamentally loyal character of Canadian political conservatism, but it made no lasting contribution to the political life of Canada and soon disappeared. Moffatt also retired from active politics at this time to concentrate on business. His association with banking and railway ventures in the 1850s indicates that he was alive to the entrepreneurial opportunities in finance and transportation in this era of rapid economic growth and change. He devoted considerable attention to the affairs of the Church of England in Montreal, where funds were being

Molony

collected for the erection of Christ Church Cathedral on Rue Sainte-Catherine.

A fervent empire loyalist to the end, Moffatt always publicly upheld the "British connection." When he died in Montreal on 25 Feb. 1865, he was probably the last of the small group of Montreal businessmen whose careers stretched from the era of the fur trade to the age of steam railway and heavy industry. They were entrepreneurs in a period of transition, who possessed the remarkable flexibility and diversity that enabled them to move easily from fur to wheat, hardware, dry goods, banking, insurance, mining, railways, and land speculation within one generation. Of them all, George Moffatt was in many ways the most representative.

GERALD TULCHINSKY

BUM, Coll. Baby, Doc. divers, G2, 1820–30. Conseil des ports nationaux (Cité du Havre, Montréal), Minute books, 22 Aug. 1846. McGill University Libraries, Dept. of Rare Books and Special Coll., MS coll., Corse family papers. PAC, MG 24, D11; RG 1, L3ᴸ, 126, 160–63; RG 42, I, 175, p.14. British American League, *Minutes of the proceedings of the second convention of the delegates . . .* (Toronto, 1849). Can., Prov. of, *Statutes*, 1847, c.67; 1849, c.164; 1851, c.202; 1856, c.124; 1857, c.178. *Debates of the Legislative Assembly of United Canada. Documents relating to NWC* (Wallace). *Elgin-Grey papers* (Doughty), I, 347, 411, 443. HBRS, II (Rich and Fleming). Macdonald, *Letters* (Johnson and Stelmack). *Select documents in Canadian economic history*, ed. H. A. Innis and A. R. M. Lower (2v., Toronto, 1929–33). [C. E. P. Thomson], *Letters from Lord Sydenham, governor-general of Canada, 1839–1841, to Lord John Russell*, ed. Paul Knaplund (London, 1931), 107. *Montreal Gazette*, 23 Jan. 1845, 27 Feb. 1865. *Montreal Transcript*, 21 April, 24 May, 14 July 1838. *Morning Courier* (Montreal), 16 May 1849. F.-J. Audet, *Les députés de Montréal*. Notman and Taylor, *Portraits of British Americans*, I, 113. *Political appointments, 1841–65* (J.-O. Coté). G. Turcotte, *Cons. législatif de Québec*.
C. D. Allin and G. M. Jones, *Annexation, preferential trade and reciprocity; an outline of the Canadian annexation movement of 1849–50, with special reference to the questions of preferential trade and reciprocity* (Toronto and London, [1912]). K. M. Bindon, "Journalist and judge: Adam Thom's British North American career, 1833–1854" (unpublished MA thesis, Queen's University, Kingston, Ont., 1972), 60ff. Careless, *Union of the Canadas*. Christie, *History of L.C.* E. A. Collard, *Oldest McGill* (Montreal, 1946); *The Saint James's Club; the story of the beginnings of the Saint James's Club* (Montreal, 1957). D. [G.] Creighton, *The empire of the St. Lawrence* (Toronto, 1956). R. C. Dalton, *The Jesuits' estates question, 1760–1888: a study of the background for the agitation of 1889* (Toronto, 1968). P. G. MacLeod, "Montreal and free trade, 1846–1849" (unpublished MA thesis, University of Rochester, N.Y., 1967), 114, 138–39, 166. Monet, *Last cannon shot. Montreal business sketches with a description of the city of Montreal, its public buildings and places of interest, and the Grand Trunk works at Point St. Charles, Victoria Bridge, &c, &c.* (Montreal, 1864), 103–7. Gustavus Myers, *History of Canadian wealth* (Chicago, 1914). C. W. New, *Lord Durham; a biography of John George Lambton, first Earl of Durham* (Oxford, 1929). Phoenix Assurance Company Ltd., *First in the field* ([Toronto, 1954]). Rich, *History of HBC*, II. *Semi-centennial report of the Montreal Board of Trade, sketches of the growth of the city of Montreal from its foundation . . .* (Montreal, 1893). Helen Taft Manning, *The revolt of French Canada, 1800–1835: a chapter in the history of the British Commonwealth* (Toronto, 1962). G. J. J. Tulchinsky, "Studies of businessmen in the development of transportation and industry in Montreal, 1837–1853" (unpublished PHD thesis, University of Toronto, 1971), 466. Adam Shortt, "Founders of Canadian banking: the Hon. George Moffatt, merchant, statesman and banker," Canadian Bankers' Assoc., *Journal* (Toronto), XXXII (1924–25), 177–90.

MOLONY, BELINDA (named **Mary Xavier**), sister of the Presentation of the Blessed Virgin Mary; b. 1781 in Tulla, County Clare (Republic of Ireland), the daughter of Francis and Catherine Maloney; d. 8 Oct. 1865 in St John's, Nfld.

Belinda Molony entered the convent of the Presentation nuns at Galway (Republic of Ireland) in 1822, and in 1825 pronounced her vows, taking the name Sister Mary Xavier. On 11 Aug. 1833 she, Mother Mary Bernard Kerwin, and two other sisters of the Presentation order left Galway for Newfoundland at the urging of Bishop Michael Anthony Fleming*. Previously the Benevolent Irish Society had established an Orphan Asylum school for the education of the poor children of both sexes in St John's. Bishop Fleming felt the girls should be withdrawn from the bad influence of the tutelage of men and association with boys for they might "lose much of that delicacy of feeling and refinement of sentiment which form the ornament and the grace of their sex."

Although the sisters reached St John's harbour on 21 Sept. 1833 – the first nuns to serve in Newfoundland – no account of their arrival was received in Galway until four months later. The community gave them up for lost, celebrated Solemn Requiem Mass for them, and burned copies of their vows.

Within a few weeks of their arrival the sisters had gathered and divided into classes girls of poor families in the settlement. They began teaching in a room at the rear of an old tavern, the "Rising Sun." The curriculum included grammar, literature, arithmetic, French, music, needle work, and Christian doctrine. Attendance at the convent school rose from 450 in 1833 to 1,200 by 1844. Later boys and adults were also taught in the school. There were several moves before a new convent was built in December 1844, but the St John's fire of 9 June 1846 reduced it to ashes. The sisters, who numbered eight in 1846, moved to Bishop Fleming's farm on the outskirts of the city until Bishop John Thomas MULLOCK arranged for the construction of a new convent on Cathedral Square in 1850.

In 1853 Sister Mary Xavier was made the first superior of a new convent in Harbour Main, the third branch house to be established. When the convent school opened in that town on 9 July 1853, 180 children attended. After three years Mother Mary Xavier became ill and returned to the mother house in St John's where she occupied herself by painting pious pictures on satin and making altar ornaments until her death at age 84.

BARBARA J. EDDY

Archives of the Presentation Sisters in Newfoundland (St John's), Annals of the Presentation Convent, Harbour Main; Correspondence, Sister Mary Xaverius Lynch to Mother Mary John Power, Sept. 1833; Sister Mary Xaverius Lynch to Sister Ann, 6 Jan. 1834; Sister Mary Magdalen O'Shaughnessy to Mother Mary John Power, 22 Sept. 1833; Sister Mary Magdalen O'Shaughnessy to Sister Mary Augustine, 21 Nov. 1833: Records of professions, deaths, and interments. *Morning Courier and General Advertiser* (St John's), 10, 12 June 1846. J. T. Mullock, *Two lectures on Newfoundland, delivered at St. Bonaventure's College, January 25, and February 1, 1860* (New York, 1860), 60. *Newfoundlander*, 18 June 1846. [Edward Wix], *Six months of a Newfoundland missionary's journal, from February to August, 1835* (London, 1836).

M. F. Howley, *Ecclesiastical history of Newfoundland* (Boston, 1888), 275–300. F. W. Rowe, *The development of education in Newfoundland* (Toronto, 1964). T. J. Walsh, *Nano Nagle and the Presentation Sisters* (Dublin, 1959), 255. "History of Presentation convents in Newfoundland," *Daily News* (St John's), 8 Dec. 1958, 24. "Presentation nuns in Newfoundland in 1833," *Evening Telegram* (St John's), 30 Jan. 1958, 30. "Presentation Sisters here since 1833," *Evening Telegram* (St John's), 6 Oct. 1961, 38.

MOLSON, THOMAS, brewer, distiller, miller, and merchant; b. 1 Sept. 1791 at Montreal, second son of John Molson* Sr and Sarah Insley Vaughan; d. 22 Feb. 1863 at Montreal.

No primary sources describe Thomas' childhood and adolescence. The earliest reference to him is in a letter written in 1811 by his elder brother John* to his father, John Sr, who was in England to purchase an engine for the Molsons' second steamship the *Swiftsure*, launched in 1812. The letter tells us that the two brothers were running the brewery at Montreal.

In 1816 Thomas went to England, where he married Martha Molson, his first cousin, without making a marriage settlement. On his return to Montreal, he entered into partnership with his father and two brothers, John and William*, under the name of John Molson and Sons. Thomas was made responsible for the brewery, and he expressed satisfaction at his early success. In December 1816 he recorded in his notebook: "The beer we have for sale now and the past month is far superior to any made in Montreal, viz. [Miles] Williams, [Francis and John] Chapman, [James] Stevenson, by the customers' account of it and their getting of us, viz. J. Molson and Sons, brewed by Thos. Molson." The partnership, which lasted seven years, managed all the family assets (most of which belonged to the father), including the brewery, ships, wharves and storehouses at Montreal and Quebec, and a hotel. An 1816 inventory of the business also listed a still. Thomas' notebooks indicate that he was experimenting with distilling by 1822, and that he attempted to export whisky to England through his brother William, who was then living at Quebec. In 1822 also, the St Lawrence Steamboat Company was founded and through it the Molsons would control all steamship navigation on the St Lawrence. Collectively they held 26 of the company's 44 shares; individually each held six and a half shares.

When the firm of John Molson and Sons came to an end in 1823, Thomas decided to leave Lower Canada, where the marriage laws imposed community of property on couples who had married without a marriage settlement. He thought of settling in England, but finally decided on Kingston, Upper Canada. He made two trips to England in 1823 and bought brewing equipment there. In July 1824 he purchased the Kingston brewery and land of Henry Murney. He settled at Kingston with his family and was a neighbour of Thomas Markland*, a founder of the "pretended" Bank of Upper Canada, who, after this bank was closed, had become an agent of the Bank of Montreal. Markland remained its agent until 1824, when an Upper Canadian law prohibited on its territory any branch of a bank established by a law promulgated by another government. During the ten years he spent at Kingston, Thomas lived a relatively quiet life. The town's newspapers only mention him in connection with his brewing and distilling business. In 1831 he bought a second business, Thomas Dalton*'s Kingston Brewery and Distillery. In the English style, he became the owner of the taverns connected with this business. He invested in land outside Kingston, buying a 100-acre parcel at Ameliasburg in 1828, and in 1829 300 acres at Portland, near Rideau Lake. In 1832 he helped found the Commercial Bank of the Midland District. Six of the 11 children of Thomas and Martha were born at Kingston. Five of them, Martha Ann (1824), John Henry Robinson (1826), Mary Ann Elizabeth (1828), Harriet Bousfield (1830), and William Markland (1833), survived their parents, as did John Thomas who was born at Montreal in 1837.

Thomas returned to Montreal in 1834 to go into partnership with his father and his brother William. William had just begun distilling at their businesses in Montreal, and Thomas was probably invited to come because of his experience as a distiller. Moreover, John Molson Sr, who was to die in 1836, had found a way of getting round the consequences of the community of property of Thomas and Martha: he would entail the breweries in Montreal on their eldest son, John Henry Robinson, on condition that Thomas and William manage them until his grandson reached the age of majority. The biography of William Molson [see *DCB*, X] describes the two brothers' partnerships from 1834 to 1852 as brewers and distillers (John Molson and Company in 1834, Thomas and William Molson in 1837, Thomas and William Molson and Company in 1838, and Thomas and William Molson and Company in 1848), and their joint personal and financial undertakings.

Throughout this long period Thomas diversified his interests and increased the holdings he shared with his brother William in the Montreal distillery. In the 1840s he bought several pieces of land and houses in the district near the distillery: in 1850 his statement for land taxes owing to the city of Montreal concerns 68 plots of land and houses. He bought a large farm at Sherrington, in Huntingdon County. In 1847 the New City Gas Company of Montreal was set up, in competition with the Montreal Gas Light Company, founded in 1836. From the beginning Thomas sat on the board of directors of the new company, which in 1848 acquired all the assets of the first; he became president in 1857, and in 1859 in recognition of long, valuable, and disinterested contribution to the company he received a silver service valued at £250 ($1,000). By 1846 he had become involved in a new investment in Upper Canada (until the end of his life he retained all his Kingston premises, which he had rented since 1834). This time he bought a distillery at Port Hope, Crawford's Distillery; then, in 1851, he acquired the large establishment known as

Brownston Mills, which included a flour mill, sawmill, and distillery. He leased the two distilleries, but until his death he ran the sawmill and flour mill through a manager, Robert Orr; he himself sold the flour on the Montreal Corn Exchange through his brokers, John and Robert Esdaile; this flour was intended for export to England. Molsons Bank was set up in 1853, in accordance with the 1850 law controlling private banks, and in 1855 it became a chartered bank; Thomas assisted its development by circulating its notes in the Port Hope region, and even in the American midwest when he bought grain at Chicago.

During the 1840s Thomas and his brother William built St Thomas' Church in the Sainte-Marie district of Montreal. The church was destroyed, as were 49 of Thomas' houses, in the great fire of 1852. Thomas built a new church in 1855, but fell out with the Church of England bishop of Montreal, Francis FULFORD, because he himself wanted the right to appoint the parish priest of his church. He then brought in a new Methodist sect of an aristocratic character, the Countess of Huntingdon's Connexion, founded in England in the mid 18th century. In 1857 parliament conferred upon the ministers of this church the right to keep registers of baptisms, marriages, and burials, and to celebrate marriages. In the same year, Molson had a college built for training clergy of the new sect; some 20 students were enrolled in 1858. However, in 1860 the church's minister, Alfred Stone, resigned; when British troops arrived in Montreal during the American Civil War, Thomas rented the college and several houses as army billets. The rental contract was renewed in February 1863, but this time it included the church itself. In his will Thomas bequeathed the temple and 11 houses to the Church of England, which had modified its rules to allow groups to own churches and appoint their own priests.

Thomas' eldest son John Henry Robinson had gone into partnership with him and his uncle William in the firm incorporated in 1848 as Thomas and William Molson and Company; at the same time, by two other contracts, the young man was given possession of the brewery bequeathed to him by his grandfather, and was released from the obligations of an apprenticeship deed by which he had been bound to Thomas and William since 1844. A new company bearing the same name and bringing together father and eldest son was formed in 1853, when William resigned. In 1859, by a new contract, Thomas' second son, William Markland, became a partner in the firm, which continued under the same name. However, another partnership, John H. R. Molson and Brothers, was formed in 1861; when John

Thomas joined his two elder brothers, Thomas ceased to be a partner; he leased his distillery, and granted a loan to the new company.

On 25 Aug. 1859 Thomas married Sophia Stevenson of Port Hope. During a trip with her to England, he planned to request the queen to elevate him to the peerage. Presumably this request was not presented, for no record of it exists in the Public Record Office, the Home Office, or the Privy Council. Thomas Molson died on 22 Feb. 1863 and was buried in the Protestant cemetery at Mount Royal, in the family vault that he and his brothers had constructed in 1860, at a cost of $15,000, to receive their own and their parents' remains.

Thomas Molson can be seen, in the context of 19th century entrepreneurship and the evolution of capitalism in the colonies, to be reacting against the structures of the dominant economic system, the large-scale export-import trade. Similarly he was unable to adapt to the joint-stock company then developing, as did his brother William. True, he did undertake large-scale export of flour, but only by selling to exporters at Montreal; he was also a shareholder of companies such as the New City Gas Company of Montreal, the Canadian Grand Trunk Railway Company, and Molsons Bank. But he was always and above all an industrialist who, with some exceptions, financed his undertakings himself, managed them directly, and personally looked after all phases of production and marketing. Thomas Molson gave little responsibility to his manager in the running of the sawmills and flour mill at Port Hope. Although he left a relatively large fortune (which can be assessed at a minimum of $1,000,000), he was not always capable of overcoming the fundamental contradiction of the firm that combines the functional relations of business and the emotional relations of family: witness the difficulties that constantly set him on the one hand against his elder brother, and on the other against his sons. Nevertheless by determination he built a successful career against all odds.

ALFRED DUBUC

[Sources of information on Thomas Molson are scattered in various archives. Among the most important are the following: the proceedings of the meetings of the board of directors and of the shareholders in the Molsons Bank Archives (preserved at the head office of the Bank of Montreal) and in the Bank of Montreal Archives; proceedings of the meetings of the board of directors in the Montreal Board of Trade Archives; proceedings of city council in the AVM; the registers of notaries Thomas Barron, I. J. Gibb, Henry Griffin, J. C. Griffin, J. S. Hunter, William Ross, and James Smith at ANQ-M; Molson papers at the Château de Ramezay (Montreal) and in the McCord Museum; the William Molson coll. in McGill University Libraries; and manuscript material at QUA and documents in the registry office in Kingston.

The most important repository is the Molson Company Archives (Molson's Brewery Ltd., Montreal), and its contents are described in an inventory prepared in 1955 (copy in PAC, MG 24, D1). The following volumes were consulted for this article: 144, 321–23, 327–28, 350–52, 355–57, 360–70, 372–74, 383–91. The Adam Shortt papers at the PAC (MG 30, D45) also contain interesting information on Molson. A.D.]

Merrill Denison, *Au pied du courant; l'histoire Molson*, Alain Grandbois, trad. ([Montréal], 1955); *Première banque au Canada*. Alfred Dubuc, "Thomas Molson, entrepreneur canadien: 1791–1863" (thèse de doctorat, université de Paris, 1969; en cours de publication). *Father's rest* (Montreal, n.d.). Georges Ripert, *Aspects juridiques du capitalisme moderne* (Paris, 1946). B. K. Sandwell, *The Molson family* (Montreal, 1933). B. E. Walker, *A history of banking in Canada; reprinted from "A history of banking in all nations"* ... (Toronto, 1909). F. W. Wegenast, *The law of Canadian companies* (Toronto, 1931). G. H. Wilson, "The application of steam to St. Lawrence valley navigation, 1809–1840" (unpublished MA thesis, McGill University, Montreal, 1961). Alfred Dubuc, "The advent of banking credit on the guarantee of warehouse receipts in Canada," *Canadian Banker* (Toronto), 70 (1963), no.4, 51–54; "La crise économique au Canada au printemps de 1848; quelques considérations tirées de la correspondance d'un marchand," *Recherches sociographiques* (Québec), III (1962), 317–22; "Montréal et les débuts de la navigation à vapeur sur le Saint-Laurent," *Revue d'histoire économique et sociale* (Paris), XLV (1967), 105–18.

MONDELET, DOMINIQUE, lawyer, politician, judge, and seigneur; b. 23 Jan. 1799 in the parish of Saint-Marc on the Richelieu River, Lower Canada, son of Charlotte Boucher de Grosbois and Jean-Marie Mondelet*, notary, member of the assembly (1804–9), and coroner of Montreal; d. 19 Feb. 1863 at Trois-Rivières, Canada East.

Dominique Mondelet studied at the Collège de Montréal and then articled with the distinguished lawyer Michael O'Sullivan*. He was admitted to the bar of Lower Canada on 18 Aug. 1820, and won immediate professional recognition. He served on committees of the Advocates Library and Law Institute of Montreal and was elected its president in 1834; in November 1832 he was named KC. He also found time to translate Thomas Moore's "Canadian Boat Song" into French. On 18 Feb. 1822 he had married in Montreal Harriet Munro, and they were to have eight children.

On 20 Nov. 1820 Mondelet was named major in the Pointe-Claire division of the militia, but seven

Mondelet

years later lost his commission for opposing the militia policies of Governor Dalhousie [Ramsay*]. In 1828 he began active service on the Montreal Committee of Correspondence set up by prominent politicians to gather evidence for the imperial authorities substantiating Canadian complaints against Dalhousie's administration. He co-authored the resolutions of 17 April chronicling Dalhousie's persecution of magistrates and militia officers, which John Neilson*, Denis-Benjamin VIGER, and Augustin Cuvillier* later presented to the British House of Commons in the form of a petition.

In 1831, aided by his radical younger brother Charles-Elzéar*, who had entered his law office, and endorsed by the Patriote party, Dominique successfully contested the assembly seat for Montreal County as a moderate Reformer; during the election campaign he expressed faith in Britain's new policy of conciliation. Mondelet insisted upon Lower Canada's right to internal self-government, at the same time stressing that demands upon Britain should be made "energetically, but still with respect and moderation." He also advocated educational and agricultural reforms, amendment of the road laws, appointment of an agent for Lower Canada in England, supervision of the notarial profession, and a better, cheaper, and faster administration of justice. Once elected, he immediately set to work, serving on 27 select committees, and assisting Frédéric-Auguste QUESNEL to design a reformed judicial system.

The first split between Mondelet and the Patriote party's radical wing occurred in 1832 when Dominique and Charles-Elzéar opposed the radical Dr Daniel Tracey* in the notorious "Massacre of Montreal" by-election, in which three of Tracey's supporters were killed. Then in November 1832, when Dominique accepted a post as an honorary executive councillor without portfolio, the radicals reacted violently, arguing that like Philippe Panet*, another deputy appointed to the Executive Council, he would serve as the administration's spokesman and spy in the assembly. Moderate Reformer John Neilson defended Mondelet's entrance into the council as introducing an element of ministerial responsibility into Lower Canada, a view similar to one George-Étienne Cartier* would later, in the 1840s, hold as Louis-Hippolyte LA FONTAINE's lieutenant. The radicals were adamant, however, and got Mondelet expelled from the assembly in a 32 to 27 vote. They referred to the expulsion of Robert Christie* as a precedent for their action, but the governor was unconvinced and sought an opinion on the legality of the assembly's action. Mondelet remained in the Executive Council,

his constituency unrepresented in the assembly, until 1834 when his expulsion was declared illegal. His feud with the radicals deepened when Charles-Elzéar Mondelet publicly opposed the 92 Resolutions, and reached its culmination in La Fontaine's bitter public attack on the Mondelets in Les deux girouettes, ou l'hypocrisie démasquée. This pamphlet appeared just before the general elections of 1834, and contributed to Dominique's failure to muster enough support to present himself as a candidate.

In 1835, as "Un Avocat," Mondelet defended himself and Charles-Elzéar with his Traité sur la politique coloniale du Bas-Canada . . . , aimed at Louis-Joseph Papineau* rather than his immature and excitable disciple La Fontaine. Mondelet warned against the organization of Patriote groups and the incendiary and anti-clerical articles in the popular press. He defended appointed legislative councils as institutions necessary to balance the rashness of popular assemblies, adding that, if these councils were made elective, they would merely represent the same interests as the assembly. As a radical youth he had supported elective councils, though advocating that their electoral basis be entirely different from that of assemblies.

Between printed sallies, Mondelet and Neilson cooperated in formulating policy. They were named commissioners to study American penitentiary systems with a view to establishing prisons in Lower Canada. In January 1835, in a comprehensive report in English, they listed relevant publications and documents concerning penitentiaries, building plans, estimates of construction and maintenance costs, and summaries of data from six northern states. There is no evidence to show how this report may have influenced penitentiary reform after the rebellion.

Politically, Mondelet remained unreconciled with the Patriotes. On 21 Dec. 1837 he was named among those to administer the general oath of allegiance, an unpopular function. In 1838 he was appointed to the hated Special Council, though he never attended a meeting or participated in its activities. From 10 May 1839, as deputy judge advocate, he prosecuted rebel prisoners, dealing severely with foreigners whose meddling in Lower Canadian affairs he deplored. He also came into direct professional conflict with his brother when he prosecuted prisoners whom Charles-Elzéar and his colleagues had defended in an earlier trial. This time the prisoners were sentenced to hang. Nonetheless, the two brothers continued to practise together, apparently unaffected by their clash in the courts.

On 15 June 1839 Mondelet temporarily replaced suspended Patriote sympathizer, Judge Joseph-Rémi Vallières* de Saint-Réal, on the Court of Queen's Bench in Trois-Rivières. In 1842, after Vallières de Saint-Réal was vindicated and promoted, Mondelet replaced him permanently on the bench. Prior to leaving Montreal for Trois-Rivières, he had supervised the distribution of £2,000 voted by the assembly to provide temporary accommodations for the insane.

Mondelet's first wife had died in childbirth during the traumatic year of 1837. A year later he was married again, to Mary Woolrich. By 1842 only six of his 11 children were still alive. For a time, however, death spared his family. In 1850 he was appointed to the Superior Court, still stationed in Trois-Rivières. That same year his eldest son was admitted to the bar, but another son in his teens died two years later. After years of "precarious health," Mondelet died of a stroke on 19 Feb. 1863, and was buried in the cathedral. Conscientious and dedicated, he had attended court to the last, though on the 18th "his mind was not possessed of its customary clearness and precision." Mondelet left vast and lucrative seigneurial holdings which he had inherited from his father in Saint-Michel-d'Yamaska (Yamaska) and Boucherville, together valued at over $55,000.

Dominique Mondelet's personality was characterized by independence of spirit, a cautious reformist approach to government, and an orthodox religious conviction. Friends and opponents alike acknowledged his professional brilliance, for his skill in law, his erudition, and his remarkable fluency were outstanding even in the competitive legal circles of Montreal. His capacity for hard work and his temperate politics attracted the support of other moderates such as Quesnel and Neilson when his radical political opponents were charging him with office-seeking and misrepresenting his dislike of violence as treachery to the nation. Mondelet's exclusion from the assembly was a great loss to the French Canadian people, and no less to be regretted because in the areas to which he subsequently turned he served with utmost integrity and conscientiousness despite the personal tragedies and disappointments he endured throughout his lifetime.

ELIZABETH GIBBS

[The best sources for a study of Dominique Mondelet are at the PAC, MG 30, in the Audet papers, 21, pp.740–808, and in Audet's *Les députés de Montréal*, pp.370–410. The selection of the Audet papers cited contains all Audet's work notes for his biography in *Les députés de Montréal*: correspondence with archives, libraries, and private persons such as Mondelet's grandson Charles-Dominique Gaudet; excerpts from parish registers, judicial archives, books, and articles, as well as the rough draft for his final study. An organized and extremely thorough historian, Audet has covered virtually all the available sources on Dominique Mondelet. His essay in *Les députés*, the final product, is as thorough and sympathetic a treatment of the subject as might be expected from the work notes. Audet's own biases and views on the events of the 1830s are expounded as well in letters to Charles-Dominique Gaudet.

Another excellent source is La Fountaine's *Les deux girouettes, ou l'hypocrisie démasquée* . . . (Montréal, 1834), since it is entirely devoted to attacking the Mondelet brothers and commenting on their political behaviour up until 1834. Dominique Mondelet's own pamphlet, written under the pseudonym of Un avocat, *Traité sur la politique coloniale du Bas-Canada, divisé en deux parties: opposition dans le gouvernement, licence de la presse, Conseil législatif par voie d'élection; réflexions sur l'état actuel du pays* (Montréal, 1835), is also informative. Its 67 pages are devoted to attacking policies of Papineau and the Patriotes, and to expounding Mondelet's own views on the political situation immediately prior to the rebellions. E.G.]

Archives paroissiales, Notre-Dame (Montréal), Registres des baptêmes, mariages et sépultures, 18 févr. 1822, 12 févr. 1838; Saint-Marc (Saint-Marc, Qué.), Registres des baptêmes, mariages et sépultures, 23 janv. 1799. *Documents relating to constitutional history, 1819–28* (Doughty and Story), 506–19. *Report of the state trials before a general court martial held at Montreal in 1838–9: exhibiting a complete history of the late rebellion in Lower Canada* (2v., Montreal, 1839). *Le Franco-Canadien* (Saint-Jean, Qué.), 3 mars 1863. *La Minerve*, 21 févr. 1863. *Quebec Daily Mercury*, 23 Feb. 1863. F.-J. Audet, "Commissions d'avocats de la province de Québec, 1765 à 1849," *BRH*, XXXIX (1933), 582. P.-G. Roy, *Les juges de la prov. de Québec*, 377. Story, *Oxford companion*, 531. G. Turcotte, *Cons. législatif de Québec*, 9.

Chapais, *Hist. du Canada*, III, 251; IV, 8–9. Christie, *History of L.C.*, III, IV, V. Alfred Duclos de Celles, *Lafontaine et son temps* (Montréal, 1907), 12–13. Maurice Grenier, "La chambre d'Assemblée du Bas-Canada, 1815–1837" (thèse de MA, université de Montréal, 1966). Helen Taft Manning, *The revolt of French Canada, 1800–1835: a chapter in the history of the British Commonwealth* (Toronto, 1962), 346–47, 356–57. Mason Wade, *The French Canadians, 1760–1967* (2nd ed., 2v., Toronto, 1968), I. F.-J. Audet, "Les Mondelet," *Cahiers des Dix*, 3 (1938), 191–216. Gérard Malchelosse, "Généalogie de la famille Mondelet," *BRH*, LI (1945), 54–55.

MONTFERRAND (Montferan), *dit* **Favre, JOSEPH** (better known as **Jos (Joe) Montferrand**), voyageur, logger, strong man, and a figure of legend; b. 25 Oct. 1802 at Montreal, son of François-Joseph Favre, *dit* Montferrand, voyageur, and Marie-Louise Couvret; d. 4 Oct. 1864 in his native town.

Montferrand

Joseph Montferrand, *dit* Favre (the Favre comes from his grandfather François Favre, *dit* Montferrand), belonged to the third generation of Montferrands in Canada. His grandfather, a soldier in the troops of the Chevalier de Lévis*, had settled at Montreal after the conquest of New France and opened a fencing salon. Powerfully built and renowned for strength, the Montferrands acquired a certain fame in the working class districts of Montreal, whose people made a fetish of physical skill and strength. According to Benjamin Sulte*, the *faubourg* Saint-Laurent where they lived had "some ten boxing halls and many taverns" in which foreign sailors and voyageurs engaged in combat, under the amused gaze of idle bystanders, sometimes including soldiers and citizens, who shared the popular love of the "noble art."

It was in this cosmopolitan, picturesque *faubourg* that Joseph Montferrand grew up. He was supposed to have learned the shorter catechism from his sister Hélène (he also had two brothers) and the art of foot fighting and boxing from his father, but his sister was born on 9 Nov. 1804 and his father died prematurely on 16 Sept. 1808. Joseph's natural gifts quite early won him respect as a *boulé* (from the English "bully"). At 16, Montferrand had almost reached his full height. Six feet four inches tall, he had a clear complexion, blue eyes, and fair hair, and did not look at all like a ruffian. His contemporaries seem to have been struck by the regularity of his features and his distinguished bearing. It was not so much his physical strength as his agility and litheness that were impressive. By trade he was a carter. Around 1818 he established himself as the cock of the *faubourg* Saint-Laurent by thrashing three hooligans who were terrorizing the neighbourhood. At the same period, before a crowd of boxing enthusiasts on the Champ de Mars, he took on an English boxer who had declared himself champion and had challenged him. With one punch he knocked him out. In 1820 or 1821, on his way through Kingston, Upper Canada, where his work as a carter had taken him, he beat a mulatto boxing instructor who was greatly admired by the garrison. These two exploits brought him fame. People began to say that Jos Montferrand "struck like the kick of a horse," and that he "used his leg like a whip."

Montferrand, along with many young people around him, was drawn to the west by the tales of the voyageurs who came to spend their money in the inns of his neighbourhood. In 1823, at the age of 21, he signed on with the Hudson's Bay Company, but nothing is known of his activities during his four years with it. In 1827 he became an employee of Joseph Moore, who was exploiting the pine forests of the Rivière du Nord, in Lower Canada. Subsequently he worked for Baxter Bowman, a lumberman with camps on the upper Ottawa River. In turn foreman, crib guide, and trusted agent of his employers, Montferrand lived a logger's adventurous life for 30 years. In the autumn he would leave Montreal with his men to proceed to the upper Ottawa, stopping at all the many taverns along the route. For months on end the men were busy felling trees, getting up at dawn and slaving away until nightfall. In spring the woodcutters became "raftsmen." Then the logs were driven down towards the lower Ottawa, where they were collected into cribs to be steered with the currents as far as the port of Quebec. The men lingered at Montreal and Quebec, where they were always ready to show off their strength and skill, and when the occasion arose to hire out their talents to the organizers of elections.

Montferrand enjoyed this roving life, which led him to spend part of his time in the "tough spots" of Lower Canada: the lumber camps, ports, and taverns, where the law of the strongest prevailed and where the fighters of each ethnic group valiantly defended the honour of their race. Because he was the strongest and quickest, Montferrand was king. But king though he was, he constantly had to defend his crown. On more than one occasion he had to take up a challenge or extricate himself from an ambush. His adventurous life was studded with exploits in which skill, speed, and strength were of prime importance. In 1828, on the Quai de La Reine at Quebec, Montferrand is said to have beaten a champion of the Royal Navy in the presence of a large crowd. The following year, on the oak bridge leading from Hull to Bytown (Ottawa), he managed, according to legend, to rout a band of "Shiners" [*see* Peter AYLEN] 150 strong. During the violent by-election of May 1832 at Montreal, he put to flight a band of braggarts who were threatening his friend Antoine Voyer; the latter, with one blow of his fist, had instantly killed an adversary whom Montferrand had once thrashed. In 1847, again at Montreal, he defeated a man by the name of Moore who was an American boxing champion. But later there were fewer such exploits.

No doubt Montferrand was feeling the weight of his years: from 1840 on he no longer went to the upper Ottawa region; he was content in spring and summer to direct the raftsmen who brought the cribs down to Quebec. Around 1857 he retired to Montreal to a house on Rue Sanguinet. He was only 55 but had declined physically; his back was bowed from constant rheumatic pain. But he was still king of the Ottawa River, and in his *faubourg* was worshipped as a hero. On 28 March 1864, Montferrand, whose first wife Marie-Anne Trépanier had died, married Esther Bertrand; after his death she bore him a son, Joseph-Louis, who grew to be as tall as his father. Montferrand died at his home on 4 Oct. 1864.

Well before his death, Montferrand was enshrined in a legend that was to embellish his life and magnify his exploits. The hero of this legend had two destinies, one given him by the oral tradition of folklore, the other by writers. Even in his lifetime, perhaps before the 1840s, Montferrand was a hero whose deeds were exaggerated in taverns, logging camps, and at home. André-Napoléon Montpetit* was to write: "Before I was eight years old Joe Montferrand had captured my imagination, his French Canadian personality blotting out the fanciful figures of the stories by [Charles] Perrault." Wilfrid Laurier* had written in 1868 that "no name, after that of the great Papineau [Louis-Joseph*], has become more popular, wherever the French language is spoken in the land of America." The most notable feats oral tradition seems to have attributed to him are routing the best known English, Irish, Scottish, and black bullies, scattering 150 "Shiners" on the bridge from Hull to Bytown, impressing his heel-mark on tavern ceilings by a fantastic somersault, and lifting his plough at arm's length with one hand. It is impossible to be precise about all these exploits, since no one knows to what extent Sulte's work, which was widely read, influenced the oral tradition. Montpetit wrote that "the popular panegryists have taken advantage of it [the tradition] to credit him with a host of stories and similar valorous deeds completely unconnected with him, while wantonly misrepresenting and distorting his real exploits." The Montferrand of tradition owes a lot to our innate need for the fanciful and the marvellous, but it is virtually certain that many of this hero's feats were designed to increase the self-esteem of the community and to exorcize popular fears. Heroes are for small groups what self-images can be for individuals.

As there is no collection of legends, it is impossible to follow the development of the oral tradition. Laurier, in 1868, was the first prose writer to attempt to popularize the hero. His work marked the beginning of Montferrand's third life, in which he was neither a real person nor a creation of folklore, but a popular figure whose image was transmitted first by the printed word (Montpetit, Sulte, etc.), then by the theatre (Louis Guyon*), then by song (La Bolduc [Mary Travers*], Gilles Vigneault). As a popular figure Montferrand came to embody the ideals, ethics, and aspirations of the French Canadian community. These writers retained and emphasized elements of the oral tradition which corresponded most closely to their vision of French Canadian society. The Montferrand of Montpetit and Sulte is the prolongation of the élite's clerical, rural, and nationalist ideology. He is not quite an altar boy but certainly resembles one. He has a gentle nature, he displays piety in his childhood, and when he makes his first communion a Sulpician points him out as an example. He has great trust in God and profound reverence for the Virgin Mary, and knows instinctively that he must only use his strength to redress wrongs and punish the wicked. He protects the children of his neighbourhood, and later the widows. He collects alms for the destitute and for those in prison. He does not like brawls, "but subordinates his temper to the dictates of the law and justice." The miscreants he chastises are always enemies of religion or the country or the people. If he accepts a challenge for honour's sake, he hands the takings of the fight to his defeated opponent. To those who suggest that he should take revenge, he replies: "I much prefer to forgive than to avenge." The real Montferrand had a weakness for the fair sex, but Montpetit keeps silent about his nocturnal gallantries "in order to display our hero against a background of poetry and light." For his part, Sulte proceeds to make this voyageur the prophet of colonization: on Bowman's farm at the Lac des Sables, near the Rivière du Lièvre, Montferrand is said to have urged that new territories be conquered, "otherwise the English will crush us." Thus 19th century writers sanctified and nationalized Jos Montferrand, just as the church sanctified popular festivals, place names, church and charitable groups, and the French Canadian society as a whole.

Both the stories of lumberjacks and the written material distributed by certain lumbering companies spread the legend and the popular tales through the forests of North America from Newfoundland to British Columbia. Sometimes Montferrand squares the Laurentian forests, sometimes he takes a roller to the plains of Saskatchewan, sometimes he notches a maple 600 feet high. George Monteiro has analysed the Montferrand legend in the United States. It is thought to have been imported by French Canadian immigrants to New England around the 1870s. Only at the turn of the century, apparently, did it spread to the tree-felling centres in Michigan, Wisconsin, and Minnesota. The hero was called Mouffreau, Mufferon, Maufree, Murphy, etc. Monteiro accepts Max Gartenberg's

Montferrand

theory that W. B. Laughead of the Red River Lumber Company first associated Montferrand with the celebrated Paul Bunyan, the legendary American hero, in material written for the company. It widely distributed Laughead's writings, in which Montferrand is reduced to the role of Bunyan's cook. This assimilated Montferrand bore little resemblance to the hero of the Canadian legend: "Joe Le Mufraw was enormously squat, shaggy, and wide. His feet and legs bulged like two mammoth black stumps sawed close to the ground . . . [He] was a man without a neck. His head merged with his shoulders like a black camel's hump."

The Montferrand legend creates two problems for historians. The first is to understand why French Canadian society valued strong men and physical strength so highly. Our hypothesis would be that the more a society feels weak and threatened the more it clings to giants. Legends are not simply a means of repression in society, but also serve to heighten a sense of importance, even to exalt. Between the situation of the French in North America and their cult of the strong man there is more than mere coincidence.

The second problem is to ascertain why, among the ten or so strong men credited with what were often legendary exploits, Montferrand so attracted the popular imagination and the attention of writers that he became an exemplary figure and in certain respects acquired the quality of myth. Laurier proposed an answer in 1868: "The secret of this popularity is that Joe Montferrand combined all the features of the national character, each as completely developed as humanly possible. In him undaunted bravery, muscular strength, thirst for danger, resistance to fatigue – the distinctive qualities of the race 50 years ago – were heightened to an almost miraculous degree. In a word, Joe Montferrand was the most truly Canadien of all Canadiens ever known." We can see three reasons: the personality of the hero, the place of his exploits, and the period in which he lived. Montferrand, an athlete endowed with a fine physical presence, who had never been on exhibition in a circus, was an engaging figure in his lifetime. The fact that a fair number of his deeds of valour were performed against the "Shiners" or the Orangemen in the Ottawa valley, which for 50 years was a no man's land where Irish and Canadiens, Catholics and Protestants, English merchants and French settlers were pitted against one another, made it possible for him to become a symbol at a time when a national ideology based on faith and language was about to be formulated. Because his exploits belonged to the period which saw the disappearance of the coureur de bois and the voyageur, and the suppression of the Patriotes by British soldiers, he was a proper hero for a nostalgic and anxious people in search of a symbol onto which it could project its fears, frustrations, and dreams. Unable to realize their visions, French Canadians, between 1840 and 1880, built a symbolic country in their ideology, their legends, their literature, and their art. In the struggle they continued to wage against the English and against nature, French Canadians found hope and greater self-respect in the Montferrand legend.

The legend has not died out. It still lives in town and countryside, and reappears with more vigour than ever in difficult periods. During the crisis of the 1930s, it was perhaps Montferrand that La Bolduc revived under the name Johnny Monfarleau. Early in the quiet revolution, the poet Gilles Vigneault made Montferrand a philosopher sitting on Cap Diamant. This new Montferrand, very different from the hero of preceding generations because he reflects the new values of Quebec culture, continues none the less to be a part of the symbolic country.

GÉRARD GOYER and JEAN HAMELIN

[Jos Montferrand still awaits his historian or folklorist. In the present state of research, it is impossible to distinguish clearly history from legend and to give their true proportions to both the voyageur and the figure of folklore.

This description of the real individual and of the legendary hero is based on Benjamin Sulte, *Histoire de Jos. Montferrand, l'athlète canadien*, published in Montreal in 1899. Sulte's text went through several editions prior to 1899: a first edition probably in 1883, a second in 1884, a third in the *Almanach du peuple* (Montréal) in 1896. Since 1899 Beauchemin of Montreal has evidently published several popular editions of Sulte's text. The reader should, however, consult Sulte's article entitled "Jos. Montferrand," which Gérard Malchelosse* annotated and published in volume XII (1924) of *Mélanges historiques* (21v., Montréal, 1918–34). In it Malchelosse provides the dates of the hero's genealogy and life. Further material was found in the anecdotal work of André-Napoléon Montpetit, *Nos hommes forts . . .* (Québec, 1884), of which certain passages were published in *L'Opinion publique* of 9, 16, 23, 30 Nov., 7, 21 Dec. 1871, and 25 Feb. 1875, as well as in *Le moniteur acadien* (Shédiac, N.-B.) of 3 and 10 Nov. 1881. Sulte borrowed from Montpetit, who had known Montferrand around 1863, probably through Montferrand's second wife, Esther Bertrand, who had been brought up by Montpetit's uncle.

Around 1866 young Wilfrid Laurier amused himself while resting at L'Avenir, Lower Canada, by writing a biography of Montferrand. To his friend Médéric Lanctot* he noted: "These stories were about Joe

Montferrand, and one day I perceived that unwittingly I had recounted almost the whole life of the famous voyageur.'' He gave his friend the task of publishing them in instalments in the weekly *L'indépendance canadienne* (Montréal), which, after two issues – 22 and 25 April 1868 – apparently ceased publication. We only have the introduction to the biography which contains a picturesque description of the town of Montreal. In the review *Asticou* (Hull, Qué.), no.8 (déc. 1971), 27–34, Gilles Lemieux published with an introduction ''La vie de l'illustre Joe Montferrand par sir Wilfrid Laurier.'' It is regrettable that we do not have the other parts of Laurier's article, which seems to be the first biography of Montferrand based on the oral tradition. Judging by the text of Laurier quoted above, it would appear that his biography follows that tradition more closely than those of Montpetit and Sulte, and that it was not influenced by the post-1850 clerico-nationalist ideology. Ludger Gravel's *Recueil de légendes illustrées* (Montréal, [1896]) and the articles on Montferrand in magazines and in the weekend press seem to be watered down versions of Sulte's work. We note also that Louis Guyon composed a play about Montferrand in 1903.

Jean Du Berger of Université Laval, who has kindly read this article, presents some of the oral traditions relating to Montferrand in his ''Introduction à la littérature orale'' (roneoed copy, Québec, 1971). In ''Histoire de Montferrand: l'athlète canadien and Joe Mufraw,'' *Journal of American Folklore* (Philadelphia), 73 (1960), 24–34, George Monteiro makes an interesting analysis of the Montferrand legend in the United States. Finally, the dates of birth, marriage, and death of Montferrand and his family have been checked in the ANQ-M, État civil, Catholiques, Notre-Dame de Montréal.   G.G. and J.H.]

MONTGOMERY, JOHN, shipbuilder, merchant, and politician; b. 12 May 1800 at Fox Point, P.E.I., son of Donald Montgomery and Nancy Penman; m. 6 Feb. 1834 Elizabeth Hamilton, and they had seven daughters and one son; d. 9 Jan. 1867 at Dalhousie, N.B.

John Montgomery's father was a magistrate in Prince County, P.E.I., and for many years a member of the assembly for the county. John was educated in public schools in Prince Edward Island and moved to New Brunswick, where he was among the first settlers of Dalhousie, a community laid out in 1826. There he established a shipyard in partnership with his brother Hugh, and they became leading shipbuilders and exporters of timber and fish. The great expansion in lumbering and shipbuilding along the Restigouche River, which had begun after the Miramichi Fire of 1825, brought about a rapid growth of the settlement and led to the creation of Restigouche County in 1837.

Montgomery took an active interest in the public affairs of Restigouche County and held a number of important county and parish offices. He was a justice of the peace, a justice of the Inferior Court of Common Pleas, an officer in the militia, a commissioner for solemnizing marriages, a commissioner of buoys and beacons for the port of Dalhousie, a commissioner for sick and disabled seamen, and a trustee of the Restigouche Grammar School. In 1848, 40 residents of Restigouche County complained to Lieutenant Governor Sir Edmund Walker HEAD that Montgomery was monopolizing local offices for himself and his friends. At that time the assembly had complete control over county and parish affairs, and as a MHA Montgomery's power to control local patronage was considerable.

Montgomery had a long career in New Brunswick politics. In April 1843 he had been appointed to the Executive Council and continued as a member of the council, without office, until February 1846. In the same year, he was elected to the assembly for Restigouche County and was re-elected in 1850. He was again appointed to the Executive Council in February 1853 and served until the new ''smasher'' administration took office in October 1854 [*see* Charles Fisher*]; he had, however, been re-elected in the 1854 elections. In July 1856 he was appointed surveyor general with a seat on the Executive Council in the administration of John Hamilton Gray* and held this post until June 1857. He was re-elected to the assembly in 1857 and again in 1861. He was in favour of confederation and was defeated in the anti-confederate election of March 1865. Subsequently he retired from politics.

A conservative, Montgomery was strongly opposed to universal suffrage and believed that the franchise should be based on property qualifications. He was an advocate of the north shore route of the Intercolonial Railway because he thought it would attract settlers and expand trade in the northeastern section of New Brunswick.

Montgomery was survived by his son William who was an MHA for Restigouche County from 1867 to 1874. His grandson, William Scott Montgomery, was the first mayor of the town of Dalhousie when it was incorporated in 1905.

Montgomery's initiative in the development of the lumbering and shipbuilding industry along the Restigouche and his prominence in public affairs at both the provincial and the local levels made him a man of considerable importance in 19th century New Brunswick.

J. M. WHALEN

PAC, MG 27, I, D15, Montgomery to Tilley, 9 July 1858, 8 Nov. 1859, 13 Nov. 1861, 10 Nov. 1863. PANB, J. C. and H. B. Graves, ''New Brunswick political biography'' (copy at UNBL); REX/px, 107,

Montigny

pp.5446–51 (mfm. at PAC). PRO, CO 193/25-48, blue books, 1842–65. *Gleaner* (Chatham, N.B.), 29 April 1834, 18 March 1865, 12 Jan. 1867. *Morning Telegraph* (Saint John, N.B.), March 1865, 24 Jan. 1867. N.B., House of Assembly, *Debates*, 1852, 1854–55, 1857, 1860. Thomas Pye, *Canadian scenery: district of Gaspé* (Montreal, 1866). *CPC*, 1869, 1871–74. *Commemorative biographical record, county York*, 113. *The merchants' and farmers' almanack . . .* (Saint John, N.B.), 1840–41, 1843–46, 1852–53, 1855–63. *New-Brunswick almanac*, 1825–36, 1842, 1849–51, 1864–66. *Prominent people of New Brunswick in the religious, educational, political, professional, commercial and social activities of the province; also a brief historical and biographical reference to New Brunswickers of the past and to others of the province who have attained prominence elsewhere*, comp. C. H. McLean ([Saint John, N.B.], 1937). G. B. MacBeath, *The story of the Restigouche: covering the Indian, French, and English periods of the Restigouche area* (Saint John, N.B., 1954). *Past and present of Prince Edward Island . . .*, ed. D. A. MacKinnon and A. B. Warburton (Charlottetown, [1906]). *Campbellton Graphic* (Campbellton, N.B.), 4 March 1915. *Daily Telegraph* (Saint John, N.B.), 10 May 1907. *Dalhousie News* (Dalhousie, N.B.), 25 Aug. 1955. *Telegraph-Journal* (Saint John, N.B.), 7 Nov. 1940.

MONTIGNY, CASIMIR-AMABLE TESTARD DE. *See* TESTARD

MOODIE, JOHN WEDDERBURN DUNBAR, army officer, farmer, public servant, and writer; b. 7 Oct. 1797 at Melsetter in the Orkney Islands, fourth son of Major James Moodie; d. 22 Oct. 1869 at Belleville, Ont.

J. W. Dunbar Moodie was born into a family with a tradition of military service. Two of his brothers served with the navy during the Napoleonic wars and Dunbar himself joined the army as a second lieutenant in the 21st Royal North British Fusiliers in 1813. He took part in the disastrous night attack on Bergen op Zoom in the Netherlands on 8 March 1814 and was shot in the left wrist while attempting to rescue comrades from a canal. He received a military pension for two years in compensation and was placed on half pay in March 1816.

In 1819 Moodie joined his elder brothers, Benjamin and Donald, in South Africa where he was able to indulge his love of field sports. He served for a time as magistrate at Umkomas, Natal, but returned to England in 1829 and began a writing career with an article about the attack on Bergen op Zoom in the *United Service Journal* (London) in 1831. In 1835 his *Ten years in South Africa* was published on terms of half-profits; the book was sufficiently popular to yield the author £64 13*s*. by April 1841.

Moodie had met Susanna Strickland* in 1830 at the home of a mutual friend, Thomas Pringle, then secretary to the Anti-Slavery Society. They were married on 4 April 1831, moved to Southwold, Suffolk, and then decided to immigrate to Canada in 1832 with the expectation of establishing a comfortable and secure future for themselves and their children (they were to have two girls and four boys).

Almost from the beginning that expectation was frustrated. Because their ship was becalmed off Newfoundland for three weeks, the voyage to Canada took two months. They first purchased a farm near Cobourg, Upper Canada, in October 1832, and moved to uncleared land in Douro Township in the spring of 1834, but their lives as settlers were marked by difficulties of adjustment and errors in judgement which led to their abandonment of the pioneer role for residence in Belleville in 1839. The story of their settling and the tribulations they experienced are vividly and dramatically recounted in Mrs Moodie's *Roughing it in the bush* (1852).

Following the outbreak of rebellion in Upper Canada Moodie served in the provincial militia, and in November 1839, as a result of a petition written by his wife to Lieutenant Governor Sir George Arthur*, he was appointed sheriff of Victoria District. Moodie remained sheriff of the district, then of Hastings County, until January 1863 when he resigned on the advice of the solicitor general, Adam Wilson*, while awaiting judgement on a charge that he had contracted an illegal arrangement in the appointment of a deputy. Although the judgement, issued in March 1863 by a grand jury presided over by John Hawkins Hagarty*, went against him, he was found to have transgressed unintentionally. During his later years Moodie experienced both ill health and financial distress. He suffered a partial paralysis of his left side in 1861, and he was unable to secure any remunerative position following his resignation as sheriff.

Most of Moodie's work as a writer was subsidiary to his wife's career and fame. Three of the sketches in the first edition of *Roughing it* were written by him, and together with Susanna he edited and contributed to the *Victoria Magazine*, published at Belleville from 1847 to 1848. His contributions include light verse, short stories, essays, and lectures. Although the essays are marred by a lack of logic in the development of his arguments, he is, through all of his prose, persistent in his advocacy of tolerance, liberty, and education. Indeed, an educational function was supposed to be the principal feature of the *Victoria Magazine*. Moodie's most interesting and graphic work is on South Africa, perhaps because his emigration there was an adventure which contrasted with his disappointed hopes in Canada. Even near the end of his life he considered immigration to Canada to have been a mistake.

CARL P. BALLSTADT

J. W. D. Moodie was author of *Scenes and adventures, as a soldier and settler, during half a century* (Montreal, 1866); *Ten years in South Africa, including a particular description of the wild sports of that country* (2v., London, 1835); and of the second volume of *Memoirs of the late war: comprising the personal narrative of Captain Cooke . . . the history of the campaign of 1809 in Portugal, by the Earl of Munster; and a narrative of the campaign of 1814 in Holland, by Lieut. W.D. Moodie* (2v., London, 1831). He also contributed to Susanna [Strickland] Moodie, *Roughing it in the bush, or life in Canada* (2v., London, 1852), and was a contributor to and an editor of the *Victoria Magazine* (Belleville, [Ont.]), 1847–48.

British Museum (London), Add. MSS 46640, 46654, 46676A, 46676B. *DNB.* Morgan, *Bibliotheca Canadensis.* A. J. G. Armytage, *Maids of honour: twelve descriptive sketches of single women who have distinguished themselves in philanthropy, nursing, poetry, travel, science, prose* (Edinburgh and London, 1906). C. P. A. Ballstadt, "The literary history of the Strickland family . . ." (unpublished PHD thesis, University of London, 1965). A. Y. Morris, *Gentle pioneers: five nineteenth-century Canadians* (Toronto and London, 1968). U. C. Pope-Hennessy, *Agnes Strickland, biographer of the queens of England, 1796–1874* (London, 1940).

MOORSOM, WILLIAM SCARTH,

soldier, civil engineer, and author; b. 4 July 1804 in Stakesby, Yorkshire, England, second son of Admiral Sir Robert Moorsom and his wife Eleanor; m. in 1831 in Halifax, N.S., Isabella Wilkins, daughter of Judge Lewis Morris Wilkins*; d. 3 June 1863 in London, England.

After his education at the Royal Military College, Sandhurst, William Scarth Moorsom was commissioned an ensign in the British army on 22 March 1821, and joined the 69th Regiment on 7 Nov. 1822. He went on half pay in the Cameron Highlanders before being raised on 8 April 1826 to captain in the 52nd Regiment, which he joined in Nova Scotia the following August. Before Moorsom returned to England with his regiment in 1831, he had explored most of mainland Nova Scotia, mapped Halifax harbour, commanded the small army detachment in Prince Edward Island, and served as acting deputy quartermaster general for the Nova Scotia command from November 1830 to September 1831.

As a result of his explorations, Moorsom published in 1830 *Letters from Nova Scotia, comprising sketches of a young country.* Written sententiously in the form of letters to friends in England, this volume of observations on the people, climate, geography, and economic prospects of the colony is the most complete picture available of Nova Scotia during the 1820s. A few cursory judgements and his derogatory comments on their society drew an angry reaction from some Nova Scotians, but Joseph Howe* pleaded in the *Novascotian* that the author be forgiven since he had helped to publicize the colony in England.

On 2 March 1832 Moorsom sold his army commission to care for his father, hoping to return to Nova Scotia shortly and settle on the land he had purchased in Hants County. Instead he sold the land in 1835 and was drawn into the English railway boom, developing a wide reputation as an excellent surveyor and engineer for several railways laid out over difficult terrain.

Although Moorsom never returned to Nova Scotia, he maintained a keen interest in the colony. In a letter to the *Novascotian* in 1835 he advocated a railway for Nova Scotia but did not press the matter again until 1844 when he drew up concrete proposals for a line between Halifax and Windsor. His ideas were picked up by Sir Richard Broun and William* and George Renny Young* who began to promote the construction of such a line in 1845. In two prospectuses placed before the public in the fall of that year Moorsom was named engineer-in-chief for the Halifax and Windsor Railway and one of the engineers for the Halifax and Quebec Railway. During the ensuing political fights over the merits of these two lines, Moorsom, unlike his associates on the provisional committees, never received criticism. Because of the nature of his assessment of the colony's prospects in *Letters from Nova Scotia* and his previous engineering experience, no one questioned his affiliation or judgement. The political squabbling among the promoters of these lines and between Liberals and Tories destroyed public confidence and neither railway was incorporated.

This was Moorsom's last flurry of involvement with Nova Scotia. Henceforth he directed his energy to engineering contracts and prolific writing for the *Proceedings* of the Institute of Civil Engineers. Shortly before his death in 1863 he published a *Historical record of the Fifty-Second Regiment,* a typical regimental history.

CAROL M. WHITFIELD

PANS, MG 12, HQ, 27–29; RG 1, 455, 456. W. S. Moorsom, *Historical record of the Fifty-Second Regiment (Oxfordshire Light Infantry) from the year 1755 to*

Morin

the year 1858 (London, 1860); *Letters from Nova Scotia, comprising sketches of a young country* (London, 1830). *Acadian Recorder*, 7 Jan. 1826–22 Oct. 1831, 3 Aug. 1863. *Halifax Morning Post*, 8 Nov.–23 Dec. 1845. *Novascotian*, 4 Jan. 1826–26 April 1832, 13 Jan. 1836, 3 Aug. 1863. *DNB*.

MORIN, AUGUSTIN-NORBERT, lawyer, politician, and judge; b. 13 Oct. 1803 at Saint-Michel (Saint-Michel-de-Bellechasse), Lower Canada, eldest son of Augustin Morin, a farmer, and Marianne Cottin, *dit* Dugal; m. 28 Feb. 1843 Adèle, daughter of merchant Joseph Raymond, and sister of Joseph-Sabin Raymond*, the superior of the Séminaire de Saint-Hyacinthe; they had no children; d. 27 July 1865 at Sainte-Adèle, Canada East.

Augustin-Norbert Morin was the eldest of 11 children who were the seventh generation of Morins in Canada. Despite his impressive height, Morin's health was delicate and at an early age he was subject to violent attacks of rheumatism which forced him to restrict his activities. The Morin family was not well off, and Augustin-Norbert owed his classical education to the intervention of the parish priest of Saint-Michel, Abbé Thomas Maguire*. The latter discovered that the boy, to whom he was teaching the catechism, had remarkable talent and intelligence. The parish priest sent his protégé to the Séminaire de Québec in 1815. Morin was consistently successful in his studies, according to his teachers.

When he left the seminary in 1822 Morin hesitated between law and the priesthood but finally chose law. In debt and without financial means, he had to earn money in order to study. He began to work for *Le Canadien*, with a dedication disproportionate to the pittance he received. When the paper ceased publication in 1823, Morin went to Montreal to study law under Denis-Benjamin VIGER. His financial worries were by no means over, however, for Viger was not exactly a generous man. The young clerk gave Latin and mathematics lessons in order to survive.

In 1825 he lashed out vociferously at Judge Edward BOWEN on French language rights in the law courts of the province. The experience with *Le Canadien*, far from dissuading Morin from journalism, apparently prompted him to return to this profession. As his duties in Denis-Benjamin Viger's office left him some leisure time, he decided to start a paper, which he named *La Minerve*. The first number was published on 9 Nov. 1826, but he had to suspend publication from the 29th of that month since the 240 subscriptions were not sufficient to cover expenses. Three months later Ludger Duvernay* bought the paper, and Morin undertook to continue as editor for six months. The founding of *La Minerve* was not received with joy by all Morin's friends. Étienne Parent* questioned whether it was useful for the Parti Canadien to have two papers, *Le Spectateur* and *La Minerve*, and also turned down Morin's offer that he become his parliamentary columnist: "the running of a paper may not be free of gall, but the debates are like the dregs." For more than ten years, even after he was called to the bar and entered parliament, Morin contributed to *La Minerve*, supplying Duvernay with well-written perceptive articles on topics as varied as politics, judicial decisions, theatre, literature, and agriculture.

Morin was authorized to practise law in 1828, after taking final examinations under three judges from the district of Montreal: James Reid, chief justice of the Court of King's Bench, and Louis-Charles Foucher* and Norman Fitzgerald, of the same court. Dividing his time between legal practice and journalism, the young lawyer began to become familiar with the workings of the law, took an increasing interest in the public administration of the country with a view to better informing readers of *La Minerve*, and thus admirably prepared himself for entering politics.

On 26 Oct. 1830 the electors of Bellechasse chose Morin, one of their own, to represent them in the House of Assembly. His entry into politics might appear a paradox in the light of descriptions of him by contemporary politicians. One asserted that "He looked more like a bishop on a pastoral visit than a politician out for votes." Morin remained true to his temperament, that of an assiduous worker: by 1831 he was able to inform Duvernay that he was a member of seven committees of the house, which required much work and prevented him from devoting time to his articles for *La Minerve*. In the house few topics failed to engage his interest. In 1831 he took steps on behalf of the widow of Dr Jacques Labrie*, former representative of the county of Deux-Montagnes, to obtain a special gift of £500 to allow her to publish a history of Quebec written by her husband. The next year Morin presented a petition on behalf of his friend Duvernay, who had been imprisoned for publishing statements attacking the composition of the Legislative Council. The sale of lands by Morin in the seigneury of Rivière-du-Sud exposed him to unsubstantiated accusations of embezzlement. Consequently, giving poor health as a pretext, the representative for Bellechasse resigned on 18 Dec. 1833. He was re-elected in a by-election on 25 Jan. 1834 by a majority of 41 votes. Re-election had ended the affair.

The year 1834 gave Morin the opportunity to distinguish himself. On 1 March the House of Assembly passed a resolution instructing the representative for Bellechasse to join Denis-Benjamin Viger in London to present the assembly's petitions on the state of the province. The work he accomplished in London received the most laudatory comments, both from Louis-Joseph Papineau* and from the whole house. A rumour even circulated that he might be appointed a judge. But with the political climate already overheated, Morin could not avoid taking a stand: it was he who in 1834 drafted the 92 Resolutions.

In February 1836 Morin was still numbered among the moderates. But he rapidly adopted the position of Papineau's group in their struggle against the Executive Council and over the question of supply bills. The representative for Bellechasse was swept up in the whirlwind of events, and after settling at Quebec towards the end of 1836 took an active part in the rebellion of 1837. Morin's radical stand conformed neither to his temperament nor to his usual conduct. His leadership in the revolt at Quebec was an undeniable failure. Although, according to Antoine Roy, he was "certainly one of the most level headed of those who took up the cause of the rebellion in 1837–1838, . . . he did not have the qualities of a leader. He lacked the energy and decisiveness essential to those who wish a cause that requires the support of the people to succeed." When a warrant for his arrest was issued, Morin took refuge in the woods of the parish of Saint-François-de-la-Rivière-du-Sud (Saint-François-Montmagny). Arrested on 28 Oct. 1839 he did not remain long in prison, for the accusation of high treason "was so ill founded that it was not considered necessary to undertake to prove it, even before the most accommodating court of the time."

The hazards of rebellion left Morin penniless, and more and more afflicted with rheumatism. He returned to the practice of law at Quebec, living alone in humble circumstances in a small house on Rue Desjardins. He had developed rather an aversion for politics, but the plan of union quickly revived his interest in public affairs. Under the personal influence of Louis-Hippolyte LA FONTAINE, who visited Quebec in December 1839, Morin was at first inclined to support the union of Upper and Lower Canada since it would foster an alliance with the Upper Canadian Reformers. But he was opposed to the bill as passed in England, since it did not provide for proportional representation in the assembly and granted neither ministerial responsibility nor control of

supply. Morin was elected member of the assembly for Nicolet on 8 April 1841, and although he aspired to the office of speaker he yielded to the suggestion of Francis Hincks* that it was better to consolidate the Reform party by supporting Augustin Cuvillier* as candidate.

Morin resigned on 1 Jan. 1842, and on 11 January became a judge for the districts of Kamouraska, Rimouski, and Saint-Thomas. His first term as judge was brief. Sir Charles Bagot* wanted Morin to take the position of clerk of the Executive Council, but he showed little interest in a post which would be "both too near to and too far from the political scene." He chose instead to become commissioner of crown lands, although this post necessitated procuring a seat in the legislature and giving up the office of judge. Morin was elected representative for Saguenay on 28 Nov. 1842 and resumed his political career.

The commissioner took his new responsibilities seriously. He insisted that his work should be based on personal knowledge. He acquired property and initiated many varied experiments, for example in growing potatoes, stock breeding, crop rotation, maple syrup production, and the experimental cultivation of plants such as grape vines. He made his experiments known to agriculturalists through articles in *La Minerve* and in specialized American agricultural journals. He also took an interest in the everyday problems of farmers, such as the building and maintenance of roads, the erection of mills, the use of casual farm help, and even the feeding of farmers' families. To ensure that his experiments would not be ignored, Morin carefully worked out programmes to be used in agricultural schools for farmers' sons detailing everything from the qualifications of the teaching staff to the syllabus itself. He was not a pure theorist. He assisted in founding new parishes to the north of Montreal: Val-Morin, Sainte-Adèle (from the name of his wife), and Morin-Heights began as a result of his action. His appointment as commissioner of lands had indeed strengthened his interest in agriculture, an interest which continued to grow.

In the general election of 1844 Morin was successful in the counties of Saguenay and Bellechasse. He chose to be member for Bellechasse as much for sentimental reasons as for political security. Although he was no longer one of the executive, Morin was mentioned as the future speaker of the new legislature, but no formal approach was apparently made to him. He devoted his energy to defending the cause of the Catholic clergy in the quarrel over the Jesuit estates, and drafted the School Act of 1845 which established the parish rather than the muni cipality as the basis of the school system. He also acted as an arbitrator in parochial disputes. His sound judgement and natural level-headedness ensured that in these special legal matters he did not take a radical stand.

In July 1846 the most controversial period of Morin's political career began. On 31 July he received a letter from William Henry Draper*, which contained an explicit invitation to join the Executive Council. Morin refused the offer on 10 August, affirming his solidarity with the Reform party. The matter seemed closed, but Lord Elgin [BRUCE] had not said his last word.

In a final effort to bring Morin and a number of Francophones, including René-Édouard Caron*, into the Executive Council, the governor general sent him a confidential note on 23 Feb. 1847. He expressed again his desire to see Morin join the council. To Morin's objection concerning his party he replied that he wished "to express his confident hope that objections, founded on personal or party differences (if such exist) will yield to the dictates of Patriotism and public duty." Morin's reply was not long in coming. He rejected the new offer but explained his motives more fully. His three years in opposition allowed no room for doubts about his patriotism, but, he clearly stated, he was opposed to the present government. It would be unreasonable in his view not to have a certain measure of unity in the council and his acceptance of a post would not create it. He further declared plainly that his party was ready for a coalition, but not at any price. He concluded by brushing aside the objection that the council lacked Francophone representation confessing he was "convinced that an addition based solely on considerations of origin, and in the circumstances offering all parties concerned only an equivocal position, could not be advantageous to the group for which this arrangement would be made."

This political document, said to be confidential, did not remain so for long: numerous leaks made it common knowledge. The Reformers were the first to get upset, as the old rivalry between Quebec and Montreal stirred up a lot of malicious gossip. The situation became even more difficult when Le Canadien began on 27 March to publish part of the famous document and garbled quotations from Morin. He was urged to reply to the Quebec paper and its virulent attacks, heavy with implication. Morin refused, for he "had considered that the word confidential imposed on him the obligation to keep private the action he took from the beginning of the negotiations and for several days after." And his leader Louis-Hippolyte La Fon-

taine declared that he had been perfectly aware of the situation from the outset: "I had to leave Morin free to use his judgement as he thought fit in the interest of the public weal, having always had the greatest confidence in his patriotism, sincerity, and disinterestedness." The crisis seemed to be resolved by the members' acceptance of Morin's interpretation and conduct.

The Reform party was returned to office in the 1847–48 elections, and Morin was elected speaker of the Legislative Assembly over Allan Napier MacNab by an overwhelming majority, obtaining 54 votes against 19 for his opponent, who had held the position since 1844. The newly elected member commanded respect even among his fiercest opponents.

In 1849, during the debate on the Rebellion Losses Bill, Morin displayed remarkable firmness. He had the galleries emptied when uproar persisted, and during the proceedings maintained discipline to an extent he had not shown before [see Bruce]. His imperturbable calm was tested when the parliament buildings in Montreal were set on fire by rioters. The story goes that he even asked for a formal motion of adjournment while the flames were licking the curtains in the hall where the members were sitting! And when the disturbances started again, Morin did not hesitate to have the building in which parliament was meeting guarded by a detachment of soldiers.

In the general election of October 1851 Morin changed counties, abandoning his native constituency of Bellechasse for Terrebonne, where he won easily. Since Louis-Hippolyte La Fontaine had given up his position as head of the government, Morin became the colleague of Francis Hincks. But he agreed to be the head of the Lower Canadian section of the government without enthusiasm. He held this post until January 1855, but his profound humility prevented him from being a leader of the stature of La Fontaine.

The legislative activity of the Hincks–Morin government was varied and substantial. Hincks was interested primarily in railways; Morin, as provincial secretary and commissioner of crown lands, was particularly concerned with the abolition of the seigneurial régime, the separate schools of Canada West, and especially the transformation of the Legislative Council into an elective body, a reform he had supported since the 1830s. He was so convinced that an appointed Legislative Council was incompatible with responsible government that in the 1851 election he had announced his intention of resigning if he did not obtain satisfaction on this point. By 24 Sept. 1852 he presented a series of resolutions to make the Legislative Council elective. However, it was not until 1856 that the MLAS passed such a bill, and it was accompanied by amendments that limited the effect of Morin's proposals. By making an elected Legislative Council and abolition of the seigneurial régime part of the Reform programme Morin had removed the most popular weapons from the arsenal of Louis-Joseph Papineau's Rouges; this action helped to secure the loyalty of the electorate to the Reformers. During these hectic years Morin devoted his leisure to preparing articles for agricultural journals, reading the latest books from France, and checking the standards of the agricultural experiments carried out on his property.

The general elections of 1854 were the first real set-back in Morin's political career. He was defeated in Terrebonne by a political unknown, Gédéon-Mélasippe Prévost, a "sign of the times," according to Le Journal de Québec. Bellechasse lost no time in seeking Morin's candidature, 319 electors from Saint-Michel, Beaumont, and Saint-Vallier signing a petition to that effect. The commissioner of crown lands was ultimately elected unopposed in the united counties of Chicoutimi and Tadoussac. And, from 11 September, Morin and all his colleagues from Canada East agreed to form a team with Allan Napier MacNab.

Ten days after the formation of the new government, Morin was present at the inauguration ceremony of Université Laval; he had had a part in its founding and he was dean of the faculty of law. During the ceremonies he received a doctorate in law, evidence of his fame and his eminence as a jurist.

Some months later, in January 1855, Morin resigned from the government because of failing health. He was appointed a judge of the Superior Court, from which he had to take long periods of rest. However, the indefatigable and energetic intellectual managed to found a legal journal, the Law Reporter, with Thomas Kennedy Ramsay*, a Montreal lawyer.

His withdrawal from public activity paved the way for the final work of his life. Because of his competence as a jurist and the quality of his personal judgement, the government asked him to become a member of the commission charged with codifying the civil law of Canada East. Morin consented on 2 Feb. 1858, but he was not officially appointed until 4 Feb. 1859. His colleagues were Charles Dewey Day* and René-Édouard Caron, the latter acting as chairman. Morin attacked this colossal task with uncommon energy. The work books deposited in the Archives du Séminaire de Saint-Hyacinthe

show Morin's concern for perfection. As the person responsible for civil law, he noted down every possible reference on all pertinent subjects, set out the law as established by judicial decisions based on a library of more than 400 legal works, and drew up a new text. The last report of the commission was submitted in November 1864 to the Legislative Assembly, which studied its seven reports in 1865. Morin was not destined to see the end of his task, for he passed away quietly on 27 July 1865, at Sainte-Adèle de Terrebonne. The new civil code of Canada East, a masterpiece of its kind, came into force on 1 Aug. 1866 [see George-Étienne Cartier*].

Morin was undoubtedly one of the great figures of 19th century Canada. Of indifferent health although unusual stature, he possessed few of the charms that rendered other politicians more attractive to their supporters. Nature had bestowed oratorical talent upon him in miserly fashion, and "art had in no way succeeded in correcting the work of nature." He was a fervent Patriote, and he had an integrity that was proverbial and undisputed by any adversary. He was a model of the zealous parliamentarian, regular in his attendance in the house, studying all subjects in depth, and assessing the short and long term consequences of every legislative measure. He was alert to developments in his time, neglecting nothing that might improve the economic life of his own people.

Yet "he was too modest and not aggressive enough to become a party leader." Perhaps also he was too idealistic, too much of a theorist, and too disinterested to feel himself at ease in the game of politics. Although his intelligence and his education set him above the renowned Papineau and La Fontaine, he was not able to command attention, even when he was the head of the Lower Canadian section of the government. His distinction and personal qualities were a drawback politically, and deprived him of a role to which he might have aspired. But no Canadian politician has ever had greater talents for so many diverse disciplines: truly, nothing human was alien to him.

JEAN-MARC PARADIS

[Documents relating to Augustin-Norbert Morin's political career are found primarily in PAC, MG 24, which includes the private papers of pre-confederation politicians. Especially useful were the La Fontaine papers (MG 24, B14), the Hincks papers (B68), and the Chauveau papers (B54). The Papineau and Bourassa collections at the ANQ-Q were also consulted. The Duvernay papers at the Château de Ramezay in

Morrin

Montreal (transcript in PAC, MG 24, C3) were helpful for Morin's activity in journalism. Miscellaneous material on Morin's studies and his notes in the areas of agriculture and law were consulted at the AAQ, ASQ, and ASSH. J.-M.P.]

L'Avenir, 1848–54. *Le Canadien*, 1840–55. *Le Journal de Québec*, 1843–44, 1850–55. *La Minerve*, 1831–37, 1842–50. *Quebec Gazette*, 1832–42. Le Jeune, *Dictionnaire*, II. Morgan, *Sketches of celebrated Canadians*. Wallace, *Macmillan dictionary*. Auguste Béchard, *L'honorable A.-N. Morin* (Québec, 1858). C.-P. Choquette, *Histoire du séminaire de Saint-Hyacinthe depuis sa fondation jusqu'à nos jours* (2v., Montréal, 1911–12), I. André Garon, "La question du Conseil législatif électif sous l'Union des Canadas, 1840–1856" (thèse de DES, université Laval, Québec, 1969). Antoine Roy, "Les Patriotes de la région de Québec pendant la rébellion de 1837–1838," *Cahiers des Dix*, 24 (1959), 241–54.

MORRIN, JOSEPH, doctor; b. 19 Oct. 1794 in Dumfriesshire, Scotland; m. 18 Jan. 1817, at Quebec, Catherine Evans, and they had six children; d. 24 Aug. 1861 at Quebec.

Joseph Morrin was four years old when he arrived at Quebec with his parents. He received primary and secondary education at the school run by the Reverend Daniel Wilkie*. His parents intended him to take up engineering, and consequently considered it pointless for him to continue his studies. Hence, apparently in 1809, the youth was entrusted to the care of a tradesman who was to give him some basic training. However, Morrin almost immediately became an apprentice of surgeon James Cockburn, who had been established at Quebec for some years, and was one of its few pharmacists. Morrin soon learned how to prepare medicaments, mastered the art of applying poultices, and assisted Cockburn with his operations. At the same time, he resumed studies at Wilkie's night school.

At this period, the city of Quebec had neither a medical school nor teaching hospitals. Anatomical dissection could be practised only on the corpses of common law criminals. Cockburn, with numerous patients at Quebec and in neighbouring villages, had established a hospital in lower town for sailors and victims of shipboard accidents. Consequently a pupil like Joseph Morrin found a great many advantages in working under Cockburn which students elsewhere did not enjoy since the latter had their courses read to them by their employers, and learned anatomical dissection by means of printed plates and drawings.

Because military doctors were scarce at Quebec, Morrin, despite his youth, was considered sufficiently competent by the military authorities to accompany soldiers disabled in the War of 1812 to Portsmouth, England. He went to London and without delay became a student at London Hospital, then under the direction of one of the ablest surgeons in England, Sir William Blizard. Morrin also studied for a short while in Edinburgh, but he failed the examinations of the Royal College of Surgeons. In fact he had not been able to complete the programme of study and the period of internship required for a diploma.

Morrin returned to Canada in 1814 and shortly after was appointed temporary assistant naval surgeon on the Great Lakes. He gave up this post a few months later and became assistant to his former employer James Cockburn, at Quebec. Licensed to practise medicine on 15 July 1815, Dr Morrin, in 1818 or 1819, set up his office in lower town and founded a sailors' hospital. As his practice grew he went into partnership with John Musson, then the senior chemist and pharmacist in Lower Canada, and settled in upper town.

Thanks to his talent and his interest in the community's welfare, Dr Morrin soon became an eminent member of the medical profession in the Quebec region. For many years after 1826, he was on the medical staff of the Hôtel-Dieu of Quebec. In 1826 he also took an active part in founding the Société Médicale de Québec of which he became the first president. He was a regular contributor to the *Journal de Médecine de Québec*, which had been started in 1826 by François-Xavier Tessier*. In 1830 he helped found the Marine Hospital, which was set up to combat epidemics but was not opened until 1834; he worked there with doctors James Douglas*, Joseph Painchaud*, and Anthony von Iffland*.

During the cholera epidemics of 1832 and 1834 Dr Morrin gave generously of his energy as a commissioner of the Quebec Board of Health. In 1847, when he was president of the commissioners of the Marine and Emigrant Hospital, he was just as unsparing and zealous in his efforts.

Morrin took part in the movement launched by a number of progressive doctors to establish a college of physicians and surgeons. This movement, supported by Painchaud, Daniel Arnoldi*, Wolfred NELSON, and others, led to the incorporation in 1847 of the College of Physicians and Surgeons of Lower Canada. The name of Morrin also was on the list of founders of the École de Médecine de Québec, which opened its doors in 1848 and became part of the medical faculty of Université Laval in 1852. Morrin was its first president. In 1849 he was a director of the asylum at Beauport, which he, James Douglas, and Charles-Jacques FRÉMONT had founded in 1845. He was also the doctor for the Quebec prison.

Anxious to render service and devote himself to the economic and social progress of his fellow citizens, he naturally became active in municipal politics. From 1836 on, Morrin participated in Quebec political life as justice of the peace responsible for the administration of the city [*see* Hippolyte Dubord*]. From 1840 to 1842, and from 1850 to 1854, he was alderman of Palais district, and in February 1855 was elected mayor, for a one-year term, by the members of the council. He held this post again from 1857 to 1858, becoming at that time the first mayor elected by the "qualified electors . . . duly competent to elect the members of the council," in conformity with the law of 19 June 1856.

During his first term as mayor, Morrin led the demonstrations marking the visit to Quebec of *La Capricieuse* in 1855 [*see* Paul-Henry de Belvèze*]. He endeavoured to obtain regular ship connections between Quebec and Great Britain, and to persuade the imperial government, to no avail, to recognize Quebec's claim to be permanent capital of Canada. Indeed the minutes of the council of 14 Sept. 1855 indicate that George-Étienne Cartier* even wrote to him that no "branch of the secretariat of the Department of Crown Lands [could] be left at Quebec at the time of the transfer of the seat of government" from Quebec to Toronto. Under Morrin, the city of Quebec reorganized its police services, and improved its street lighting and most of its administrative services. Mayor Morrin's most effective associate at that time was the clerk of court, historian François-Xavier GARNEAU.

During his second term, Morrin once more insisted on "Quebec's claims to become the capital of Canada." But the efforts of the mayor and his council yielded no better results. Still defending his city's rights, Morrin complained when the governor of Canada, returning from Great Britain to Toronto, failed to stop at Quebec. Sir Edmund Walker HEAD apologized, giving as a pretext his wife's poor health. Elections in Quebec at this time being scarcely untroubled events, the town council passed a regulation ensuring "the maintenance of peace during an electoral period." The Rue Saint-Jean was widened, and the mayor endeavoured to protect Quebec's interests during the negotiations regarding railway building on the north shore.

As president of the St Andrew's Society of Quebec, Morrin was one of its most loyal supporters for some 30 years. His medical knowledge, extensive for his day, his competence, and his untiring devotion to duty earned him such authority and respect that he had few professional rivals.

Joseph Morrin's name is still well known in Quebec. It designates a building, Morrin College, which since June 1868 has housed the oldest historical and literary society in the British empire (Great Britain excepted), the Literary and Historical Society of Quebec, founded on 6 Jan. 1824. Opened in 1862 thanks to a substantial financial contribution made by the doctor, Morrin College existed as a Protestant institution until 1902. Morrin also gave his name to a prize awarded each year by Université Laval, and conferred for the first time on 24 May 1859. It consisted of a sum of £500 bequeathed to the faculty of medicine to allocate according to its own terms and conditions.

CHARLES-MARIE BOISSONNAULT

ANQ-Q, État civil, Presbytériens, St Andrews (Quebec), 18 Jan. 1817, 24 Aug. 1861. ASQ, Université, 101-BG; 103-BA. AVQ, Procès-verbaux du conseil, 1854–58. Can., prov. du, *Statuts*, 1847, c.26; 1856, c.69. *Morning Chronicle* (Quebec), 2 Sept. 1861. *Quebec Gazette*, 26 Oct. 1864. Université Laval, *Annuaire*, 1868–69, 16. Abbott, *History of medicine*. M.-J. et George Ahern, *Notes pour servir à l'histoire de la médecine dans le Bas-Canada, depuis la fondation de Québec jusqu'au commencement du XIX*e *siècle* (Québec, 1923), 420–23. C.-M. Boissonnault, *Histoire de la faculté de médecine de Laval* (Québec, 1953), 139–41. Heagerty, *Four centuries of medical history in Can.*, I, 86. W. P. Percival, *The lure of Quebec* (Toronto, 1941), 112, 141. C.-M. Boissonnault, "Création de deux écoles de médecine au Québec," *Laval médical* (Québec), 39 (1968), 547–49. C.-A. Gauthier, "Histoire de la Société médicale de Québec," *Laval médical*, 8 (1943), 62–121. Sylvio Leblond, "L'hôpital de la Marine de Québec," *L'Union médicale du Canada* (Montréal), LXXX (1951), 616–26.

MORRIS, FREDERICK WILLIAM, physician; baptized 29 May 1802 at Halifax, N.S., eighth son of Charles Morris*(1759–1831), surveyor general of Nova Scotia, and Charlotte Pernette; m. 12 Nov. 1863 at Lunenburg, N.S., Janet Maria (Jessie) Solomon; they had no children; d. 4 Sept. 1867 at Halifax.

Frederick William Morris entered King's College, Windsor, N.S., in 1816, but did not graduate, perhaps because his right hand had to be amputated following a shooting accident in 1820. After his recovery he was apprenticed to Dr William Bruce Almon*, a leading Halifax surgeon. Morris continued his studies at the University of Edinburgh where he received his MD on 1 Aug. 1825. He visited hospitals in London and Paris at this time.

The early years of Morris' medical career are difficult to trace. By 1826 he was practising in

Morris

Lunenburg, and on 8 Oct. 1828 he was appointed a justice of the peace for Lunenburg County and attended the Court of Quarter Sessions for a year. In a letter written in 1859 he stated that he had practised in Annapolis, Lunenburg, Halifax, Dartmouth, and Rawdon. He published a pamphlet, *Remarks on spasmodic cholera*, in Halifax in 1832. In 1839 he advertised a 20-week course on chemistry at the Halifax Mechanics' Institute; one would therefore assume that he was practising in Halifax by that date.

On 10 Jan. 1840 Morris was one of the Halifax practitioners petitioning the Legislative Council to establish a public hospital. His name next appears in existing documents as founding member of the Halifax Medical Society on 7 May 1853. A member of its first council, in March 1858 he was elected its second vice-president. This society became the Medical Society of Nova Scotia on 21 March 1861, and Morris was chosen a member of its first council.

At a citizens' meeting in Halifax on 20 Feb. 1855 Morris became one of eight doctors on the board of governors of the newly founded Halifax Visiting Dispensary. The board also included eight businessmen, with William MURDOCH as president. On 23 April 1855 Morris was appointed the dispensary's resident physician with an annual salary of £100; he was to attend the clinic daily, dispense free medicine, visit the patients at home, and keep the records. Although the dispensary received small grants from the provincial government and the city, as well as voluntary contributions, it was always short of funds. Between 1855 and 1867 over 38,000 cases were treated there. Another important function was the training of medical students.

In the spring of 1861 Dr Morris administered a drug, "Indian Remedy," as a cure for smallpox. He also published in the local press several letters urging its use. At a meeting of the Nova Scotia Medical Society on 6 May 1861 Morris was asked to give notes of patients treated with this remedy. He did so, but the meeting decided by a vote of ten to one that he had "not had any reliable data" upon which to base his recommendation. Finally the society passed a resolution that "Dr. Morris by lending his name and authority to the sale and use of . . . [a] remedy . . . of the utility of which he appears . . . to possess no conclusive evidence, has violated the rules of this society . . . and his name should be erased from the list of members." Action taken at the Halifax Visiting Dispensary was less drastic; although five of the medical governors resigned in protest at the decision, its board only censured Morris and demanded his written assurance that he would no longer prescribe the "Indian Remedy" or any other medicine not recognized by the medical profession. Morris accepted their reprimand.

In September 1861 the Reverend James C. Cochran* tried to have Morris reinstated in the medical society and to convince the doctors who had left the dispensary to return. He failed on both counts as did Charles Tupper* when he attempted to have Morris reinstated in the society. Finally at its annual meeting on 7 Jan. 1862 the society amended its by-laws to enable a person who had been expelled to be readmitted on obtaining a favourable vote from two-thirds of the members present at a meeting. Shortly thereafter the secretary of the society wrote to Cochran stating that Morris should write expressing "his regret for the circumstances which led to the erasion of his name" and also expressing his "determination to avoid such unprofessional conduct in the future." Such a letter would probably have gained his readmission but there is no evidence that it was ever written.

Frederick William Morris continued his work at the dispensary until his death. The inventory of his will shows that he died almost in poverty, leaving his widow an estate of only $1,235. In 1867 the dispensary was reorganized; some of its functions were taken over by the Dalhousie Public Health Clinic in 1924, but it still provides medicine for outpatients at the Izaac Walton Killam Children's Hospital in Halifax.

PHYLLIS R. BLAKELEY

Halifax County Court of Probate (Halifax), no.1485, will of F. W. Morris, 1867. PANS, MG 1, 544 (T. H. Lodge, "Genealogy of the Morris family of Halifax" (typescript)); MG 20, no.179/1; no.181/1. St John's Anglican Church (Lunenburg, N.S.), register of marriages, 1817–65 (mfm. at PANS). St Paul's Anglican Church (Halifax), register of baptisms, 1791–1816 (mfm. at PANS). F. W. Morris, *Remarks on spasmodic cholera* (Halifax, 1832). Halifax Dispensary, *Report*, 1855, 1857, 1858, 1860–1959, 1962. *Acadian Recorder*, 22 Oct. 1825; 21 Nov. 1863; 14 Jan., 16 Feb., 6 Sept., 13 Nov. 1867; 10 April 1897. *Novascotian*, 20 Nov., 4 Dec. 1839; 23 Nov. 1863. M. W. Fleming, "The Halifax Visiting Dispensary – 100 years ago," *Nova Scotia Medical Bull.* (Halifax), XXXVI (1957), 106–9.

MORRIS, JAMES, politician, merchant, and banker; b. 1 Nov. 1798 at Paisley, Renfrewshire, Scotland, third son of Alexander Morris and Janet Lang; m. Emily Rosamond Murney, daughter of Henry Murney of Kingston, and they had nine children; d. 23 Sept. 1865 at Brockville, Canada West.

James Morris' family immigrated to Upper Canada in 1801 and settled briefly in Elizabethtown (Brockville). They returned to Scotland in November 1802, but later re-established themselves at Brockville, James arriving in 1808. He was educated partly at the academy of William Nelson, father of Wolfred NELSON, at William Henry (Sorel), Lower Canada. There is evidence that as early as 1820 James Morris was cooperating in business with his older brothers, Alexander* and William*. By 1836 James was cashier of the Commercial Bank of the Midland District at Brockville and his various enterprises prospered. He was a surety in the amount of a £5,000 bond when his brother William was appointed receiver general in the William Henry Draper* administration in September 1844. By 1860 he held 358 shares in the Commercial Bank, 80 in the Bank of Montreal, 18 in the Bank of Upper Canada, and 44 in the Niagara District Bank. He was engaged in mercantile and banking activity based at Brockville throughout his life and was one of the spokesmen for bankers in the assembly. Morris was associated at various times with W. H. MERRITT, and had a close understanding with Isaac Buchanan*, both liberals and businessmen of stature. Morris' daughter Janet married W. H. Merritt Jr.

Morris had entered public life in 1825 when he was first appointed a justice of the peace in the Johnstown District. In 1835 he was commissioned a coroner for the Bathurst District and he served on the Brockville Board of Police after 1832. He was involved in public meetings held at Brockville in that year which urged the government to press on with the building of canals to improve navigation on the St Lawrence River. On 20 Sept. 1838 he was appointed a commissioner to administer funds raised by debenture for building canals on the river, and he continued in this appointment throughout the period of canal building. The name given to Morrisburg honoured his work for the canals.

Morris was present on 11 Dec. 1839 at a public meeting in Toronto which proposed the establishment of a Presbyterian college at Kingston. Between 1840 and 1844 he was one of four trustees of Queen's College who dealt with finances and selected a site. In these same years he acted as a spokesman in the legislature for Presbyterian congregations in Montreal, Smiths Falls, and Brockville, aiding his brother William, who was leading the Presbyterian challenge to the clergy reserve legislation of Governor General Sydenham [Thomson*]. By the end of the decade, however, James Morris had joined the Church of England.

First elected to the legislature for Leeds at a by-election in July 1837, Morris retained the seat

until his appointment to the Legislative Council in November 1844. He had presented himself in 1837 as an independent, a "conservative," who supported the British connection but who was opposed to "establishing any church as dominant." He voted in favour of the union of the two Canadas, explaining that it was not a time for "faction." He was, however, a reformer, a liberal by temperament and insight. Adam FERGUSSON considered him in 1840 one of three true liberals of the older Reform tradition which antedated the Clear Grits. John Ross* feared in 1842 that he was more radical than A. N. Buell* and the allies of Robert Baldwin* in the eastern part of Canada West. Buell in November 1842 recommended Morris to Baldwin for appointment to the Legislative Council, describing him as a friend of liberals, who had used his status and position as a justice of the peace to protect them in the time of bigotry following the 1837 rebellion. In the tensions arising from the Rebellion Losses Bill and the Annexation Manifesto of 1849 Morris despondently wondered whether "as colonists we shall ever have peace." He considered the government's use of armed police to control the disturbances in 1849 and the unrest among railway workers in 1856 "wholly unnecessary and dangerous to the peace and liberties of the people."

It is clear that throughout the Baldwin era Morris was not of the inner circle, but a respected associate and supporter. On 22 Feb. 1851 he was appointed the first Canadian postmaster general in the Baldwin–LA FONTAINE ministry, when the responsibility for that service passed from the British to the Canadian government [see Thomas Allen STAYNER]. As public administrator he showed energy and considerable ability. Two days after his appointment he arranged that Sandford Fleming* design and engrave the first Canadian postage stamps, including the 3d. "Beaver," 6d. "Prince Albert," and 12d. "Queen Victoria." Also within days of his appointment he was in Washington negotiating the terms for a new postal treaty with the United States. It was Morris who reduced and standardized the postal rate for letters at 5¢, and who launched a policy of establishing post offices as widely as possible.

A member of the Board of Railway Commissioners from 1851 to 1853, Morris was also a government director of the Grand Trunk Railway from 1852 until 1854. On 16 Aug. 1853 he was appointed speaker of the Legislative Council, holding that office till the fall of the Francis Hincks* and A.-N. MORIN ministry in September 1854. His association with Hincks appears to have been intimate until about 1854, but after Hincks' defeat there were public recriminations, Hincks accusing Morris of communicating with his "malignant enemy," William McDougall*, the editor of the Clear Grit *North American*. However, Morris wrote in 1855 that the A. N. MacNab-Morin coalition which succeeded Hincks was a "political monstrosity" unequalled in any country. He was again speaker in the George Brown*-A.-A. Dorion* "Short Administration" in August 1858. Morris concluded his public career as receiver general in the ministry led by John Sandfield Macdonald* and L.-V. Sicotte*, serving from May 1862 till he was incapacitated by a stroke in November 1863.

Throughout his career Morris held a series of commissions in the militia, being appointed lieutenant in the 2nd battalion of Carleton militia in the Johnstown District on 20 Aug. 1821, lieutenant-colonel of the 3rd Leeds Light Infantry in June 1828, and lieutenant-colonel of the 1st battalion of Leeds militia on 5 Nov. 1846.

When Morris died the Toronto *Globe* spoke of the loss of one who had been a steady member of the Reform party through trials and triumphs, a man of great shrewdness, tact, and knowledge of affairs. J. C. Dent* was more restrained in referring to him as thoroughly upright and well intentioned but without any remarkable vigour or understanding.

P. G. CORNELL

MTCL, Robert Baldwin papers; James Morris papers. PAC, MG 24, D16, 48, pp. 39052–131; RG 8, I(C series), 275, pp. 28–39; RG 68, 1, General index, 1651–1841. PAO, Morris (Alexander) papers. QUA, William Morris papers; Queen's records, A3; B, 1840–44; D1, 1840–44. *Brockville Recorder* (Brockville, [Ont.]), 13 Dec. 1824–12 Oct. 1843. *Globe*, 30 Sept. 1865. Cornell, *Alignment of political groups*. Dent, *Last forty years*.

MORRISON, DANIEL, journalist; b. 29 July 1826 at Inverness, Scotland; m. in 1858 Charlotte*, daughter of John NICKINSON, and they had two sons and two daughters; d. 11 April 1870 in Toronto, Ont.

Daniel Morrison, son of a Church of Scotland minister, was raised and educated, apparently for a professional career, in Scotland. He immigrated to Upper Canada in 1847 and became a teacher and farmer in West Flamborough Township. Beginning probably in 1849 he wrote occasional vigorous and sarcastic items for the *Dundas Warder and Halton County General Advertiser*, the Reform newspaper founded by Robert SPENCE, and was its parliamentary correspondent in 1851. He replaced Charles

Lindsey* in 1852 as editor of the Toronto *Examiner*, owned by James Lesslie*, and in 1854 joined Lindsey at the *Leader*, which was owned by James Beaty* and supported the Hincksite Liberals. When the coalition government of Sir Allan Napier MacNab and Augustin-Norbert MORIN was formed in 1854, the *Leader* supported it and thereafter followed a moderate Conservative line. Morrison remained at the *Leader* until November 1857. Early in 1858 he and George Sheppard* bought the money-losing *Daily Colonist* from Samuel Thompson* with the intention of merging it with the *Leader*, thereby making it solvent and reducing the number of dailies in the overcrowded Toronto market. The merger was prevented by the joint action of the Grand Trunk Railway, which advanced money to the *Colonist*, and of John A. Macdonald*. The railway needed the government's support as well as the newspaper's, and the government wanted a dependable government paper in Toronto.

Morrison and Sheppard attempted to publish the *Colonist* with a degree of editorial independence unusual for a government organ. Yet the advantages of receiving contracts for government advertising and stationery were offset by the restraints exerted by political leaders to have the paper serve their own ends exclusively. Macdonald's anger with articles condemning the government's political practices and the refusal of Sheppard and Morrison to retract an article that defended George Brown* from a scurrilous personal attack by William Frederick Powell led to a break with the government. On 30 June 1858 Sheppard and Morrison wrote a celebrated editorial "Whither are we drifting?" that strongly condemned the Macdonald government. Arguing that it abused its executive power by placing party ahead of country, they were asserting that even a paper which supported the governing party must have independent opinion. Sheppard wrote Charles Clarke* that "Macdonald is now hunting us with the malignity of a fiend." On 9 July the *Atlas*, published by Samuel Thompson, was founded to support the government. The loss of government advertising and stationery contracts created further financial difficulty for the *Colonist*; Sheppard joined the *Globe* by the end of July, and Morrison resold the *Colonist* to Thompson on 12 Nov. 1858.

After unsuccessful speculation in railways with William Kingsford* and Isaac Buchanan*, Morrison in 1859 secured a civil service appointment, evidently as an arbitrator in the Public Works Department. On 19 March 1860 he became editor of the Quebec *Morning Chronicle*, and in the spring of 1861, of the *London*

Prototype, both owned by S. B. Foote. Exciting opportunities as a correspondent during the American Civil War may have drawn him to New York, where he worked for the *Tribune* and the *Times* and contributed articles to the *Scottish American* and the *Albion*. He returned to Canada for a while in 1864 to work on the Cayuga *Haldimand Tribune*, then went back to New York. In August 1868 Morrison joined John Ross Robertson*'s Toronto *Daily Telegraph*, which claimed to be an "advocate of liberal conservatism" whose "independence was not open to question," but was secretly supported by the Conservative party and the Grand Trunk Railway. It was agreed by this time, as Morrison and Sheppard had unsuccessfully attempted to demonstrate in 1858, that the most useful paper to a government was one which seemed strong and independent. Nevertheless, in return for support it was expected to give editorial backing on crucial issues.

Morrison, who was highly regarded by his peers as a newspaper writer, remained as managing editor of the *Daily Telegraph* until his death. An obituary stated: "There were vigour, and fire, and life, and force in those splendid articles of his."

ELWOOD H. JONES

PAC, MG 24, D16; MG 26, A. PAO, Clarke (Charles) papers; Mackenzie-Lindsey papers. UWO, MSS, VF 305 (W. Buckingham papers). Macdonald, *Letters* (Johnson and Stelmack), II, 154, 165. *Daily Colonist* (Toronto), 1858. *Daily Telegraph* (Toronto), 12 April 1870. *Leader*, 14 Dec. 1861. *Lundmarks of Can.*, I. Morgan, *Bibliotheca Canadensis*; *Sketches of celebrated Canadians*. Careless, *Brown*. Ron Poulton, *The paper tyrant, John Ross Robertson of the "Toronto Telegram"* (Toronto and Vancouver, 1971), 31–55. M. H. Lewis, "A reappraisal of George Sheppard's contribution to the press of North America," *OH*, LXII (1970), 179–98. J. J. Talman, "George Sheppard, journalist, 1819–1912," *RSC Trans.*, 3rd ser., XLIV (1950), sect.II, 119–34; "The newspaper press of Canada West, 1850–60," *RSC Trans.*, 3rd ser., XXXIII (1939), sect.II, 149–74.

MORTON, JAMES, brewer, manufacturer, contractor, and politician; b. 29 Aug. 1808, probably at Killylea, County Armagh (Northern Ireland); he was married and seven children survived him; d. 7 July 1864 at Kingston, Canada West.

James Morton came to Kingston in 1824, possibly as an apprentice or articled clerk to Thomas MOLSON who established a brewery and distillery there in that year. In 1831 Morton became a partner with Robert Drummond in a new brewery; when Drummond died in 1834, Morton bought his interest from his executors and continued to operate the business as the Kingston Brewery and Distillery.

Morton had been thoroughly trained as a shrewd businessman by Molson. His products, especially Morton's Proof whisky, enjoyed a reputation for quality, he was personally popular in Kingston, and his business prospered. After 1845 he began to invest in real estate and became a large owner of rental property in and around Kingston and as far west as Hamilton. He erected a large sawmill on land purchased at Trenton and produced more than 700,000 board feet of lumber per year, most of it for export to the United States. He also established a lumber yard and dock at Kingston. Apparently to free his brewery and lumber interests from dependence on local shipping lines, he became involved in lake shipping and by 1855 owned and operated seven or eight cargo ships.

An interest in railway contracting began in 1853 or 1854 when he became a silent partner in the small Kingston construction firm of Valentine and Hall which, in competition with Samuel Zimmerman*, was trying to obtain the contract to build a railway from Woodstock to Port Dover and Port Burwell on Lake Erie. Through Valentine and Hall, Morton met an engineer named Hand and with him built the Kingston section of the Grand Trunk Railway, completed in October 1856. In about 1854 Hand and Morton had purchased the works of Tutton and Duncan of Kingston which manufactured steamboat engines. They enlarged the factory, renamed it the Kingston Locomotive Works, and began to build railway engines. Hand soon left the partnership and Morton carried on alone.

By 1858 Morton had reached the peak of his prosperity. He purchased a house, St Helen's, from Thomas KIRKPATRICK and transformed it into Mortonwood, one of the most splendid homes in Kingston. But by 1860 Morton was bankrupt. His troubles were caused by a new railway venture and the collapse of the Upper Canadian financial system in the depression of 1857.

Isaac Buchanan* of Hamilton had gained control of charters to build a railway from Hamilton to Windsor, to be called the Great South Western Railway, but he had suffered heavy losses in his dealings. Morton apparently agreed in the late 1850s, against the advice of his friend and former solicitor John A. Macdonald*, to buy Buchanan's charters and thereby also receive the construction contracts involved. After numerous disputes and delays over terms of the transaction, Buchanan in 1859 sued Morton and was awarded

Mountain

damages of £50,000. Morton was unable to pay and the action ruined his already shaky credit. The economy of the province operated on a long-term credit system of bank drafts and promissory notes which were not backed by collateral in negotiable securities. The depression which began in 1857 at the end of the Crimean War, and the curtailment of foreign investment in Canadian railways, caused the collapse of this credit system. The drafts of Morton's debtors, which he had deposited with the Bank of Upper Canada to cover his own overdrafts, became worthless. A successful suit against his debtors by Morton would only ruin the buyers of his beer, whisky, lumber, and locomotives, and he would also find himself the owner of his debtors' only assets – heavily mortgaged real estate for which there was no market. Moreover, he had endorsed loans for numerous bankrupted friends which he was now obliged to repay. In 1859 his dept to the Bank of Upper Canada alone was $250,000.

Because of his troubles the bank limited Morton's line of credit and made it impossible for him to pay his creditors, many of whom successfully sued him. But the bank was reluctant to proceed against debtors in hard times. In order to obtain some security from Morton, the bank's new cashier, Robert Cassels*, obliged him to mortgage all his property but to continue operating his business. He was also forced in 1861 to lease his distillery, the only enterprise which was producing cash, for $20,000 a year to three trustees of the bank. From this amount Morton was paid $3,000 a year and the balance was applied to his bank debt. Morton's other creditors sold at auction several locomotives and the furniture in Mortonwood. The bank bought his furniture, however, and thus made it possible for him to continue living in his magnificent house.

Morton continued to be popular in Kingston. Through the influence of Macdonald he was elected to the assembly for Frontenac in 1861, defeating Sir Henry SMITH. His health was beginning to fail, however, and he rarely took his place in the house. He did not stand for re-election in 1864 and died later that year.

James Morton is representative of the early Canadian industrial entrepreneurs who became prominent after 1845 and had failed by 1867. They attempted to operate in a credit and financial system suited to an agricultural and commercial economy in which the leading businessmen were merchants who exported staple products such as lumber and wheat and imported manufactured goods. Large financial institutions which, by accumulating capital would make possible the operations of an industrial entrepreneur like Morton, had not yet been developed.

M. L. MAGILL

PAC, MG 24, D16; MG 26, A, p.94994. QUA, Kirkpatrick-Nickle legal records. *Daily British American* (Kingston, [Ont.]), 8, 11 July 1864. *J. of Education for U.C.*, XVII (1864), 105–6. Merrill Denison, *The barley and the stream; the Molson story; a footnote to Canadian history* (Toronto, 1955). Anne MacDermaid, "The visit of the Prince of Wales to Kingston in 1860"; and M. L. Magill, "James Morton of Kingston – brewer," *Historic Kingston* (Kingston, Ont.), 21 (March 1973), 50–61 and 28–36.

MOUNTAIN, GEORGE JEHOSHAPHAT, Church of England clergyman and bishop; b. 27 July 1789 in Norwich, England, son of Jacob Mountain* and Elizabeth Mildred Wale Kentish; d. 6 Jan. 1863 at Quebec.

The arrival of the Mountain family in Quebec City on 1 Nov. 1793 marked an important step in the establishment and development of the Church of England in Canada. George Mountain's father, Jacob, had come as the first bishop of the diocese of Quebec; his uncle, Jehosaphat Mountain*, and his cousin, Salter Jehoshaphat Mountain*, both became priests of the diocese; and George himself would become the third bishop. He was the first bishop of Quebec to grow up in Canada and the impressions of his youth created in him a deep and abiding love for the new country to which he was destined to devote himself.

George Mountain's early education was provided by a private tutor, the Reverend Matthew Fielde, under whose guidance he displayed an aptitude for literature and exhibited an enthusiasm for poetry which was maintained throughout his life. He himself published a volume of verse in 1846 entitled *Songs of the wilderness*, a collection interesting for what it reveals of the character and personality of its author, but far from memorable from a literary standpoint.

In 1805 George Mountain and his older brother Jacob returned to England to complete their education. The Reverend T. Monro of Little Easton, Essex, had charge of the boys until they went to Trinity College, Cambridge, from which George obtained his bachelor's degree without honours in 1810. His failure to win a fellowship at Downing College, Cambridge, led in 1811 to his return to Quebec. Always of a religious turn of mind, he had been confirmed by his father on 18 Sept. 1803, and on his return home, his decision to enter the priesthood firmly made, he placed himself as a student under the bishop's tutelage. Acting as his father's secretary he greatly relieved the heavy pressures upon him, and following his ordination as deacon on 2 Aug. 1812 in the Cathedral of the Holy Trinity he was appointed to assist Salter Jehoshaphat Mountain, the priest in charge of the cathedral. His diaconate coincided with the War of 1812 and in addition to his normal responsibilities the young clergyman volunteered for sentry duty on the walls of Quebec City.

In 1813 Mountain accompanied his father on his triennial visitation of the diocese and when they returned to Quebec the bishop considered his son sufficiently prepared for ordination. On 16 Jan. 1814 he was admitted to priest's orders, and until August of that year he served as "Evening Lecturer" at the cathedral in Quebec. On 2 August, George Mountain married Mary Hume Thomson of Quebec City and the couple departed to take up residence in the parish of Fredericton, New Brunswick.

During their three years in Fredericton the Mountains won the undying affection of the parishioners. Probably the most lasting of their contributions was the establishment of a local branch of the Society for Promoting Christian Knowledge, through which the foundations of an educational system were laid. In addition to his parish work Mountain also successfully undertook the posts of chaplain to the legislature and to the military forces.

George Mountain's return to Quebec in 1817 as officiating clergyman at the cathedral initiated a new phase of his career. His designation as "Official" of Lower Canada in 1818 was followed in 1819 by his receiving the degree of doctor of divinity from the archbishop of Canterbury and his appointment as a member of the Royal Institution for the Advancement of Learning. In January 1821 two archdeaconries were established in Upper and Lower Canada: George Mountain was created first archdeacon of Quebec and George Okill STUART, archdeacon of York (Toronto). Later in the same year the parish of Quebec was erected by letters patent and Mountain was made the first rector.

Over a short span of time Mountain had attained a position of seniority among the clergy of Upper and Lower Canada, and in the last years of his father's episcopate and for the entire period of Bishop Charles James Stewart*'s tenure (1826–36) he served the diocese as if he were already a consecrated assistant. It was not surprising then that on 14 Feb. 1836 he was consecrated at Lambeth Palace, London, as suffragan bishop in the diocese of Quebec under the title of bishop of Montreal, and that upon Bishop Stewart's departure for England the same year he assumed full diocesan responsibility. In 1837 he formally succeeded Stewart as bishop of Quebec, but he continued to use the title bishop of Montreal until 1850, when a diocese of Montreal was created. When Mountain became bishop, Quebec Diocese extended from the New Brunswick border to the westernmost reaches of Upper Canada. Beyond Upper Canada the territory was legally under the authority of the bishop of London, but for practical purposes the diocese of Quebec extended virtually to the west coast. According to an estimate prepared by Mountain for Lord Durham [Lambton*]'s *Report* in 1838, his clergy numbered 117, with 73 in Upper Canada and 44 in Lower Canada.

As bishop, Mountain was faced with the task of creating a sense of diocesan unity in a country where communication was a major problem. In view of the hardships involved, it is one of his most remarkable achievements that throughout his career he methodically and indefatigably toured his diocese injecting new spiritual life into his people. He had begun this journeying as an archdeacon, his most notable excursions being to the Gaspé coast in 1824 and 1826. Transportation was always largely a matter of chance and on the 1824 expedition Mountain walked 25 miles across the peninsula through unbroken forest in the company of Indian guides. On all his tours the living conditions of the people and the state of religion and education in every settlement at which he stopped were his prime concerns, but undoubtedly the most memorable of his journeys was his 1844 expedition to the Red River, the first such visit by an Anglican bishop [see John SMITHURST]. A handful of missionaries had been working there since 1820 and Mountain, after travelling nearly 2,000 miles largely by canoe or on foot, met with a warm reception from the mainly Indian and Métis population. His 18-day stay was an inspiration to the settlement but, more important, it was his plea that these people required greater assistance which stimulated the creation of the diocese of Rupert's Land in 1849 with David Anderson* as first bishop.

Gradually the original see of Quebec was subdivided: in 1839 the diocese of Toronto had been established with John STRACHAN as bishop, and in 1850 Francis FULFORD became the first bishop of the see of Montreal. In the later years of his episcopate no ventures show Mountain in a more courageous light than do his voyages to the Îles-de-la-Madeleine in 1850 and the Labrador coast in 1861. On the islands he discovered settlements which no non-Roman Catholic clergyman had ever before visited, and on the Labrador

Mountain

coast he met with a level of poverty for which all his years of experience had failed to prepare him. Just two years after his Labrador visitation, as he lay dying, Mountain's thoughts dwelt on the problems of that struggling mission and his final word before blessing his children was "Labrador."

One of George Mountain's life-long interests was the promotion of education in the Canadas. Upon his return to Quebec in 1817 he had formed a Quebec diocesan committee of the SPCK, and with its support he turned to the establishment of a system of "National Schools" for the purpose of educating at no cost to the parents those children who could not meet the academic or financial requirements of the already functioning Royal Grammar Schools, sponsored by the British government. The original National School in Quebec City opened in 1819, and here the Bell system of instruction was employed whereby older children acted as monitors to teach the younger students. In April 1823 the SPCK committee established the Quebec Sunday School for those children unable to attend regular weekday classes.

Mountain's influence is also to be traced in the histories of both McGill and Bishop's universities. Letters patent incorporating McGill College were issued on 31 March 1821 and an honorary teaching staff was appointed in 1824, Mountain being named principal of the college and professor of divinity, both of which positions he held until July 1835. Under Mountain's guidance McGill became an established, degree-granting corporation; nor did his resignation from the faculty terminate his relationship with the university. On Bishop Stewart's death in 1837 he succeeded to the presidency of the Royal Institution for the Advancement of Learning which had received in 1813 the estate of James McGill* in trust for the endowment of a college or a university. In that capacity he became locked in a bitter controversy with John Bethune*, the acting principal of McGill, whose policy of developing the university as an Anglican stronghold was alienating many of its supporters. Bishop Mountain would not accept a seat on the Board of Governors of McGill unless Bethune were removed from his post, and in 1846 the principal was ousted by the British government.

George Mountain's involvement with Bishop's University was of a more personal nature for it was his desire to obtain new clergy for his expanding diocese which mainly stimulated the erection of the Anglican sponsored college in the Eastern Townships village of Lennoxville. Its foundation and growth became something of a favoured project for Mountain and was by his own admission amongst the most personally satisfying of his accomplishments. The parish of Lennoxville offered generous financial assistance to see a university established in the neighbourhood [see Lucius DOOLITTLE] and royal assent was granted on 9 Dec. 1843. For its first ten years Bishop's functioned without the essential power of being able to grant degrees, and both Mountain and the first principal of Bishop's College, Jasper Hume Nicolls*, Mountain's nephew and son-in-law, worked ceaselessly to obtain a royal charter. Finally, under continued pressure, the Canadian government relaxed its opposition and a charter was granted on 28 Jan. 1853 creating Bishop's a university with the right to grant degrees in divinity, law, and medicine. Bishop Mountain's dream was realized, and at the same time of his jubilee celebration in 1862 a scholarship in his honour was established at the university.

It was during Mountain's episcopate that church government became an increasingly important issue and he was instrumental in laying the foundations for the system which is still functioning. The perplexing problem of financing his diocese made this development necessary. In the face of decreasing government support he organized in 1842 the Church Society of the Diocese of Quebec. It was designed, through a system of voluntary self-support, to assume the responsibilities for the salaries of missionaries and the building of new churches, but it also served as a stepping-stone to the creation of a diocesan synod. As the desire among the laity for responsible church government grew, Mountain initiated a correspondence with the other British North American bishops and under his auspices a conference was held at Quebec from 24 Sept. to 1 Oct. 1851 following which a plan for the erection of both diocesan and provincial synods was submitted to the archbishop of Canterbury.

In 1853 Mountain chaired a convention of colonial bishops in London, England, whose purpose was to legalize synodical government in all the colonies. The Colonial Church Bill failed to pass the British Parliament but eventually on 28 May 1857 an enabling act was passed by the legislature of the Province of Canada. Opposition from the evangelical part of the Anglican population, which sought to limit the power of the bishop for the advantage of the laity, forced delays and legal negotiations but Mountain was finally able to conduct his first synod session from 6 to 8 July 1859.

When the question of erecting a metropolitan see in Canada arose in 1860 Bishop Mountain was again a prime organizational force. It was felt by many that the honour of being metropolitan should go to Mountain, the senior bishop of the province. Mountain, however, realizing that his strength was failing, had requested the appointment of Bishop Francis Fulford of Montreal. In addition, even in the face of almost total opposition to a fixed metropolitical see, Mountain maintained that the responsibilities of metropolitan should be permanently attached to the diocese of Montreal.

One of the most contentious issues in Canada during the years of George Mountain's ministry was the disposal of the proceeds from the clergy reserves, and the Church of England's position that the revenue from the reserves should be put entirely at its disposal, despite the claims of other Protestant groups, was unwaveringly supported by Mountain. As archdeacon in 1825 he negotiated unsuccessfully with the British government concerning the sale of church lands to the Canada Land Company, an experience which served to increase his innate distaste for political dealings, but throughout the years of both his father's and Bishop Stewart's episcopates he staunchly supported their partisan views. Following his own consecration, Mountain maintained a voluminous correspondence in his efforts to stave off the eventual collapse of the Anglican defence of the reserves. Only once did an outside issue influence his thinking: in 1849 his anti-Americanism predominated when he thoroughly denounced the Annexationist movement although it had offered guarantees of Anglican endowment in return for political support in Lower Canada. This venture into political commentary was a highly uncharacteristic move.

George Mountain's entire ministry was given to the alleviation of human suffering and degradation and his social service efforts won for him great admiration. His work with immigrants and his devoted labour during the cholera and ship fever epidemics in 1832 and 1847 have become legendary. He numbered amongst his perennial concerns the conditions in the hospitals and jails in Quebec City and he served on the Jail Association for many years. Such foundations as the Quebec Asylum and the Church of England Orphan Asylum for Girls, which was organized by Mrs Mountain, received his constant attention, and he established a parochial lending library, a district visiting society, and a Church of England clothing society for the poor. The Church Home for Widows and the Finlay Home for Boys and Men were also the result of the work of Bishop Mountain and his wife.

In 1853 on his final visit to England the bishop was granted an honorary DCL by Oxford University. In his own diocese, for the 50th anniversary of his ministry on 2 Aug. 1862, he was honoured at a jubilee celebration in Quebec. Bishop Mountain's last public appearance was made on Christmas Day 1862 when he celebrated Holy Communion in the Cathedral of the Holy Trinity. The following day he developed a severe cold which turned into pneumonia and he died on 6 Jan. 1863. The grief expressed by the public and the funeral which was held at the cathedral in Quebec were in every sense fitting tributes to the life and work of one who had given himself completely to the people of his diocese.

MONICA MARSTON

G. J. Mountain, *Songs of the wilderness, being a collection of poems written on the route to the territory of the Hudson's Bay Co. in 1844 with notes* (London, 1846); *Visit to the Gaspé coast* (Quebec, 1943).

QDA, 24 (A-2), 9 Jan. 1821; 25 (A-2), 8 Sept. 1821; 33-b (A-4), 18 July 1850; 40-a (A-5–6), 12 June 1838; 40-c (A-5–6), 11 Feb. 1836; 118 (G-12); 119 (G-13); 120 (G-14); 121 (G-15). *A memoir of George Jehoshaphat Mountain, D.D., D.C.L., late bishop of Quebec . . .*, comp. A. W. Mountain (Montreal, 1866), 9–10, 14–15, 18, 22, 27–30, 33, 41, 44, 64–65, 84–85, 96, 122, 184, 186, 281, 318, 388, 407–15, 419–20, 423. J. I. Cooper, *The blessed communion; the origins and history of the diocese of Montreal, 1760–1960* ([Montreal], 1960). Ernest Hawkins, *Annals of the diocese of Quebec* (London, 1849). *Leaders of the Canadian church*, ed. W. B. Heeney, (3 ser., Toronto, 1918–43), 2nd ser. Cyrus MacMillan, *McGill and its story, 1821–1921* (London and Toronto, 1921). D. C. Masters, *Bishop's University, the first hundred years* (Toronto, 1950), 15. T. R. Millman, *Jacob Mountain, first lord bishop of Quebec, a study in church and state, 1793–1825* (Toronto, 1947), 181; *Life of Charles James Stewart*. [J.] F. Taylor, *The last three bishops, appointed by the crown for the Anglican Church of Canada* (Montreal, 1869). D. C. Masters, "The first provincial synod in Canada," Canadian Church Hist. Soc., *Journal*, IV (1962), 1–18; "G. J. Mountain," CHA *Report*, 1963, 89–101; "The Mountain family circle: a study in Canadian urban culture," RSC *Trans.*, 3rd ser., LII (1958), sect.ii, 21–31. F. C. Würtele, "The English cathedral of Quebec . . .," Literary and Hist. Soc. of Quebec, *Trans.*, new ser., XX (1891), 63–132.

MULLOCK, JOHN THOMAS, Franciscan priest, Roman Catholic bishop, writer, and educationist; b. 27 Sept. 1807 in Limerick (Republic of Ireland), the son of Thomas J. Mullock and Mary Teresa Hare; d. 29 March 1869 at St John's.

Eldest of 13 children of a wood-carver and manufacturer of church furniture, John Thomas Mullock was sent by the Franciscan Order at age 16 to study at St Bonaventure's Convent, Seville,

Mullock

Spain. He joined the order in 1825 and completed his education at St Isidore's College, the Irish Franciscan seminary in Rome. By special dispensation he was ordained priest at age 22 and returned to Ireland in 1829 to serve for 14 years as pastor, in Ennis, County Clare, in Dublin, and in Cork, and as recruiting agent for the colonial bishops. In 1843 he became father guardian of the Franciscan convent in Dublin, where he served until he was offered the position of coadjutor with right of succession to Bishop Michael Anthony Fleming*, the ailing vicar apostolic of Newfoundland, who had personally requested Mullock as his successor. Consecrated in Rome on 27 Dec. 1847, Mullock arrived in Newfoundland on 6 May 1848.

Before Mullock's arrival the see of Newfoundland had been erected and Bishop Fleming had become a suffragan of the archdiocese of Quebec. In 1850, on the advice of Mullock, Fleming successfully pressed for independence. That same year Fleming died and Mullock succeeded him. In May 1856 Mullock secured the creation of two dioceses, St John's with Mullock as its bishop, and Harbour Grace, with John DALTON as bishop. The St John's accounts published in 1856 showed a large and steady diocesan income. In 1851 Mullock had founded St Michael's Orphanage, and in 1857 he opened St Bonaventure's College in St John's, a Roman Catholic institution to provide a classical education "on the Irish model" for middle class Newfoundland boys and to serve as a seminary for an indigenous priesthood. In 1855, after 14 years of construction, the Cathedral of St John the Baptist was consecrated by Archbishop John Hughes of New York who laid the foundation stone of St Patrick's Church in St John's. Mullock built a new palace, an episcopal library, 11 new convents, and numerous churches, five of them in stone.

Mullock had inherited the powerful position enjoyed by the Roman Catholic Church in Newfoundland under Bishop Fleming. It had a privileged position in education, as it had schools under its own control but financed by the state, whereas the Church of England had to share schools with the Methodists. Fleming's church had garnered considerable popular support and increasing political power. Inspired by the spirit of Daniel O'Connell, whom he greatly admired, Fleming had openly interfered in politics, using boycotts, excommunications, and clerical sponsorship of candidates to advance the cause of the Liberal party and wrench control of government from the mercantile and Anglican establishment. Increasingly the Liberals were dominated by the Roman Catholic Church which alone had the capacity to secure a mass vote.

Yet the church felt aggrieved because the less numerous Anglicans had far more official patronage. The Church of England was growing in strength under its recently appointed bishop, Edward Feild*. It had launched theological attacks on Roman Catholicism. Moreover it had paid for its new cathedral out of a fund collected in Anglican churches after the fire of 1846 but which Roman Catholics asserted had been subscribed for all victims; they claimed they had not been compensated for the loss of a convent [see MOLONY].

Mullock himself was indignant at being refused the official salary which had been paid to Fleming as to other clergymen out of imperial funds, but which the British government in the 1840s had decided to cease granting on the death of incumbents. He felt insulted when the Colonial Office suggested that he put "Roman Catholic" in front of his title to satisfy Feild, who objected to another bearing the designation already held by an Anglican bishop, and it does not appear that he complied. In 1851, angry that the Anglican-dominated Legislative Council had removed him from his *ex officio* position on the Roman Catholic Central Board of Education, he threatened to organize a boycott of educational boards if he were not restored to office; he was reinstated.

Personally a kindly, hospitable man, he was described by Lieutenant-Colonel Robert Barlow McCrea, commanding officer of the Royal Engineers at St John's in the 1860s and a Protestant Conservative admirer of Mullock, as living in a "palace, fitted only for the residence of a plain, simple gentleman" with an "absence of worldly ostentation which commands unfeigned respect." Mullock, however, would not endure any public insult to his church or official position and would not tolerate grievances suffered by his community. Unlike Fleming he did not regard himself as an Irish missionary to Newfoundland but strove to become a Newfoundlander: he brought his relatives to live in St John's and he advocated better roads, steamship and telegraph communication with continental North America, and a native priesthood. Unlike Fleming also he was eager to receive native nuns and ordain native priests. He identified himself with his people and, with greater skill than Fleming, sought desired reforms by using his religious position for political ends.

When in early 1852 the Colonial Office refused to grant responsible government to Newfoundland, Mullock put all his moral authority behind the Liberal party. Although in private conceiving of the Liberals as the "Catholic Party," in public he was careful not to endanger their non-sectarian appeal. Yet a letter to the Liberal leader, Philip Francis Little*, soon became public in which Mullock denounced the existing political system as "irresponsible drivelling despotism, wearing the mask of representative institutions, and depending for support alone on bigotry and bribery," and demanded responsible government. The governor, John Gaspard Le Marchant*, described the letter as a "highly inflammatory document," and, in correspondence with the governor, Colonial Secretary Sir John Pakington criticized Mullock's decision "to take the part of a Political Leader, rather than to instil into the minds of the members of his persuasion the duties of forebearance and Christian charity." A modern historian of the Atlantic provinces has described Mullock's tone as "probably surpassing anything that had been produced in the whole story of reform in British North America."

Roman Catholics quickly consolidated behind their bishop and the Liberal party. At a mass meeting in St John's his letter was read to a cheering crowd, and responsible government at last became an issue which aroused excitement. With the bishop's blessing Roman Catholic priests acted as election managers for the Liberal party. Mullock argued that because they paid taxes they had the same rights as any other British citizens to vote and canvass; nothing in civil or canon law prevented them from exercising political influence. The *Pilot*, a Roman Catholic newspaper, went further and suggested, probably with Mullock's approval, that it was sinful to vote other than at the direction of the clergy.

This spiritual suasion, exercised, however, without the public boycotts and excommunications characteristic of Fleming, helped to secure a solid Roman Catholic vote for the Liberals without alienating the Methodist Liberals who had the balance of power in some crucial electoral districts [see BENNING]. In 1855 responsible government was won, and, following an election victory, Little became prime minister of an administration in which Roman Catholics had a dominant voice and the lion's share of patronage.

Mullock, nevertheless, was not entirely satisfied. An idealistic man, he was shocked to find corruption among Liberal politicians, who were expending road funds and poor relief not according to need but at the request of supporters. Early in 1856, in a private letter to the Board of Works, he complained that because of the poor state of roads in the colony the journey from St John's to Placentia took as long as one from the Baltic to the Mediterranean and urged that relief and road fund money should be distributed only for work done. Although not intended for publication, the letter appeared in newspapers and speculation about a possible breach between Little and his most powerful supporter flourished.

But Mullock continued to uphold the government, and was used by them to maintain mass support. When Little required help in securing rejection of the fisheries convention proposed in 1857 by the British government he turned to Mullock. A long and eloquent letter from the bishop, described by Governor Sir Alexander BANNERMAN as "the alarm bell which detonated the monster meeting of 16 February" called to protest against the British terms, stirred the people and helped in the rejection of the convention. Ambrose Shea*, speaker of the assembly, struck a typical note at a by-election in November 1857: "My friends, they say the Bishop is your Governor; well, what if he is! Is he not a good one, and who has a better right to govern you?"

Mullock's political strength was sufficient to secure the dismissal in 1858 of a legislative councillor, James Tobin*, who criticized him. He assisted the Liberals by naming candidates worthy of support, and under the leadership of John Kent* they won the 1859 election. But Mullock was becoming further disillusioned. He had thrown his influence behind the campaign for responsible government, helped the Liberals win elections, and spent time and energy keeping the party together, not for personal gain but for reform which he believed possible only through political action. Yet the politicians were using him to keep themselves in office while still neglecting the causes for which he had helped them, such as clean, efficient government, improvement of communications, and the curbing of excessive and politically motivated poor relief.

Mullock complained in 1860 that a committee set up to administer poor relief was favouring supporters of the government. Members of the assembly had gained the right to give poor relief to their constituents and some were using it as a bribe, thus competing with the priests for influence over the people. He was even more angry when Kent, in order to meet the demands of his supporters for a larger road fund, abandoned a bill to provide for local steamship communication, a project which Mullock had long desired. Indeed he had even gone to New York with Little to arrange for a steamship service for Newfoundland without the government's knowledge or support. Mullock publicly denounced the government for "legalised robbery" and attacked politicians who "take care of themselves, but do nothing for the people."

The government, thoroughly alarmed, quickly made arrangements for local steam communication and early in 1861 introduced new poor relief

Mullock

regulations. Mullock expressed his support for these measures in a letter which Kent read out to the assembly. But Ambrose Shea and many other Liberals of native origin, who were less under the sway of the clergy than Irish immigrants, opposed the second reform because it would have taken away from them the right to distribute relief. They were helped by a crowd which entered the chamber and caused the suspension of the sitting. Kent bowed to popular clamour and withdrew his reform soon after the incident in the assembly, thus losing the remainder of Mullock's confidence.

The bishop then issued a pastoral letter urging his clergy to watch the politicians, and wrote to Governor Bannerman describing the members of the assembly as "only the representative beggars of a set of paupers." Noting the split between Mullock and the Liberal politicians, whom he neither liked nor trusted, the governor felt that Mullock might approve of the dismissal of the Liberal government in February 1861 and its replacement by a ministry under Hugh William Hoyles*, a Protestant and a Conservative. The bishop hesitated before taking a position. He did not trust Kent, and the new government contained Laurence O'Brien, a wealthy Roman Catholic merchant. His mind was perhaps finally swayed by the fact that Bishop Feild of the Church of England published a letter in support of Hoyles. Worried about Protestant ascendancy, Mullock in a public letter described the election scheduled for May 1861 as a calamity. The last government had improved roads, postal communications, and education. Roman Catholic electors were exhorted not to give Protestants undivided power but rather to defend the gains of the past 40 years. Mullock urged all Catholics to listen to the clergy, who alone were benefactors of the people, promoters of improvement, and independent agents – "the founders and fathers of civilisation in Newfoundland."

This outburst frightened Protestant Liberals and alienated Roman Catholics who wished to be independent of clerical control in politics. Mullock appeared to equate Liberalism with Roman Catholicism and Roman Catholicism with the clergy. Methodists who had previously voted for the Liberals turned to the Conservatives, and many Roman Catholics refused to accept Mullock's leadership.

Tension was high on polling day. In Harbour Grace so great was the tumult that the magistrates refused to open the poll. In the district of Harbour Main the intervention of Father Kyran WALSH led to a clash in which the men of Cat's Cove killed one man and wounded ten others [see HOGSETT]. With no return for Harbour Grace and a contested return for Harbour Main, the election gave the Conservatives 14 seats and the Liberals 12. Neither side was sure of victory.

Mullock increased the excitement by allowing the publication, just before the opening of the legislative session, of correspondence between himself and the governor. He had claimed in a letter that a man from Spaniard's Bay had come to him for help because of "a body of armed men who wished to destroy the Roman Catholic Church and devastate all before them – as it appears a war of extermination is commenced against Her Majesty's Roman Catholic subjects in this Colony." When Bannerman rejected this story (it was subsequently revealed as a lie by the Spaniard's Bay man) Mullock replied by blaming Protestants for disrupting the peace of Newfoundland. He then preached a political sermon in his cathedral, comparing George Furey, the man killed at Cat's Cove, with Jesus Christ. Such allegations and statements were regarded by Henry WINTON's *Public Ledger*, the leading Protestant Conservative newspaper, as inflammatory.

At the opening of the assembly on 13 May 1861 the combined efforts of the military and some of the Roman Catholic clergy could not quell the riot which broke out. The tumult raged for four hours and was only ended by the soldiers opening fire and Mullock summoning the crowd to his cathedral by ringing the bells. Dressed in full pontificals, he exacted from the crowd a promise of good behaviour, and exposed for their veneration the Blessed Sacrament. Never was his power more clearly shown, but he had exercised it only when the rioting had been revealed as politically and practically disastrous, not four hours earlier when he might have curbed the disorders.

For several days violence continued. Bishop Feild was stoned, his theological college was partly burned, and Hoyles' summer cottage was destroyed. The returning officer at Harbour Main was punished by a mob for not having given the verdict to the clerically supported candidates, and threats of looting and violence were made at Harbour Grace. But Mullock made no attempt to restrain his people; indeed later in 1861 he encouraged popular discontent by initiating a petition to the British government for the removal of Bannerman, though Kent, Shea, and most of the Roman Catholic clergy refused to sign. The *Record*, popularly regarded as the voice of Mullock, threatened civil war if Bannerman sent troops to Harbour Grace for the by-election in November 1861. Bannerman, however, ensured a peaceful election by doing so. In a pastoral letter Mullock declared himself in favour of peace and order and repudiated the *Record*. The Conservatives were returned with a large majority.

Mullock was defeated, but his desire to direct politicians did not end. When the men of Cat's Cove, who had been imprisoned after conviction for manslaughter, were released by Bannerman early in 1862 in response to a petition signed by Kent, Shea, and many other prominent Liberals, Mullock angrily put Cat's Cove, where Furey had been "murdered," under his episcopal ban. No Mass was to be said and no sacraments administered for a year.

Mullock had gone too far, and his political influence suffered a sharp decline. Henceforth widespread clerical intervention was rare in the politics of Newfoundland. Sectarianism underwent a temporary decline and wealthy Roman Catholics gravitated towards the Conservatives. Mullock continued to rumble like a dormant volcano, but could safely be ignored; although critical of their actions, he never tried to upset governments. He began to live down the reputation he had gained among Canadian Roman Catholic bishops as "a firebrand and disturber of the peace." Instead, describing local politics as a "disreputable struggle for place, not principle," he advocated almsgiving, sobriety, and hard work as remedies for the depressed state of society. When the people of Burin and Placentia attacked users of cod seines he denounced violence and reminded them that "the powers that be are ordained of God." When confederation with the other British North American colonies became a political issue, he gave no guidance to his people, beyond a few ambiguous observations. His death after a long illness came in 1869, well before the crucial election of that year which decided that Newfoundland should not join Canada.

His funeral was an impressive occasion. The governor, Sir Anthony Musgrave*, attended the Requiem Mass, all shops closed in St John's, and all flags were at half-mast. The *St John's Daily News*, not a pro-Roman Catholic newspaper, commented that "He was universally loved and esteemed by the whole community for his amiable and kindly disposition." This eulogy, though truthful in part, seems to overlook the fact that in the island's politics he had been rash and not too scrupulous. Nevertheless he was widely respected for his real achievements and in private was often regarded with affection. He did much to enhance the self-respect and independence of the Roman Catholic community of Newfoundland. He made several episcopal visitations to remote parts of Newfoundland. When he became

bishop there were 46,785 Roman Catholics in Newfoundland, and when he died there were 60,567. He found 24 priests and left 35.

His political activities sprang from generous motives: "It is the duty of a Bishop to aid and advise his people in all their struggles for justice." This maxim led him to spur on his co-religionists to demand responsible government, to denounce Liberal politicians when they betrayed him, and finally, in indignant outbursts, to condone extremes of violence against a Protestant-led government. Yet realizing the error of such a strategy, in later life he threw his influence on the side of law and order.

Mullock was also a scholar. His publications demonstrate his pride in his native land, his devotion to the country of his adoption, his loyalty to his religious order, and his fidelity to the more ultramontane aspects of the 19th century Roman Catholic Church. An able linguist, fluent in Spanish, French, and Italian, he translated *The history of heresies* by Alfonso Maria de'Liguori, and a history of the Irish Franciscan province, attributed to Francis Ward, which he published in *Duffy's Irish Catholic Magazine* (Dublin) in 1847. Besides some sermons he also published *The life of St. Alphonsus M. Liguori* and *Two lectures on Newfoundland* given in St John's in 1860. The latter revealed his faith in his adopted land: "The present generation in Newfoundland . . . leaves a mighty inheritance to their children, and we are forming the character of a future nation."

FREDERICK JONES

J. T. Mullock was the author of *The Cathedral of St. John's, Newfoundland, with an account of its consecration* . . . (Dublin, 1856); *Circular letter . . . to the clergy and laity of the diocese of St. John's, on his return from the Eternal City, where he had been on the occasion of the canonization of the Japanese martyrs* (St John's, 1862); *The life of St. Alphonsus M. Liguori* . . . (Dublin, 1846); *Rome, past and present; a lecture, delivered in St. Dunstan's Cathedral, Charlottetown, Prince Edward Island, on Thursday, August 16, 1860* (Charlottetown, 1860); *A sermon preached . . . in the Cathedral of St. John's, on Friday, May 10th, 1861* (St John's, [1861?]); *Two lectures on Newfoundland, delivered at St. Bonaventure's College, January 25, and February 1, 1860* (New York, 1860), the first of which was published in *Lectures on Newfoundland* ([St John's, 1860]). He also translated A. M. de'Liguori, *The history of heresies, and their refutation; or, the triumph of the church* (2v., Dublin, 1847; 2nd ed., 1857).

Archives of the Archdiocese of St John's, E. Morris, diaries, 1851–70; J. T. Mullock, journals and diaries, 1850–69. PAC, MG 24, B51. PRO, CO 194/116–92. University of Nottingham Library (Nottingham, Eng.),

Murdoch

Newcastle MSS, letterbooks, 1859–64; colonial correspondence, 1849–64 (mfm. at PAC). R. B. McCrea, *Lost amid the fogs: sketches of life in Newfoundland, England's ancient colony* (London, 1869). *Newfoundlander*, 1848–69. *Public Ledger*, 1848–69. Greene, "Influence of religion in the politics of Nfld., 1850–61." Frederick Jones, "Bishop Feild, a study in politics and religion in nineteenth century Newfoundland" (unpublished PHD thesis, Cambridge University, 1971). MacNutt, *Atlantic provinces*. E. C. Moulton, "The political history of Newfoundland, 1861–1869" (unpublished MA thesis, Memorial University of Newfoundland, St John's, 1960). Prowse, *History of Nfld.* (1896). E. A. Wells, "The struggle for responsible government in Newfoundland, 1846–1855" (unpublished MA thesis, Memorial University of Newfoundland, St John's, 1966). E. B. Foran, "Right Reverend Doctor Mullock, bishop militant . . ."; E. P. Roche, "The Right Reverend John Thomas Mullock, D.D., 1807–1869 . . . ," *The centenary of the Basilica-Cathedral of St. John the Baptist, St. John's, Newfoundland, 1855–1955*, ed. P. J. Kennedy ([St John's, 1955]), 233–46 and 222–32. Frederick Jones, "Bishops in politics: Roman Catholic v Protestant in Newfoundland, 1860–2," *CHR*, LV (1974), 408–21.

MURDOCH, WILLIAM, merchant, banker, and philanthropist; b. 1800 in Perth, Scotland, the son of William Murdoch; d. unmarried 21 June 1866 in London, England.

Educated in Edinburgh, William Murdoch in 1820 joined the Glasgow dry goods business operated by his brother James. The following year William took a small consignment of dry goods to Halifax. Disappointed by his initial venture in trading, he resolved to return to Scotland, but was persuaded by a local merchant to remain. He opened a dry goods business near the ordnance; his brother joined him and became a partner in December 1831. Another brother, Charles, also joined the firm and after James' death was admitted as a partner in February 1845.

William Murdoch imported dry goods from Greenock, Scotland (where his father operated a business until his death in 1839), and supplies from Glasgow, Liverpool, and London. He also purchased goods at dock-side and on occasion from other Halifax merchants. During the 1830s he advertised cloth, twine, gunpowder, rails, linseed oil, pepper, butter, Congo tea, and various kinds of spirits. Murdoch soon became aware of the need for banking facilities in Halifax, and he supported the formation of the Halifax Banking Company in 1825. Dissatisfied with this company, or perhaps wishing to be more personally involved, he helped promote the establishment of the Bank of Nova Scotia in 1832 and remained a director until 1849. For over 25 years Murdoch devoted his considerable energy and talent to his business. He became an important wholesaler in the province, and perhaps because of this trade his firm in 1845 commissioned the construction of the brigantine *Perserverance*, which traded along the Cape Breton coast.

Gradually Murdoch also became involved in a variety of civic and social organizations. He was admitted to the North British Society in 1829, serving as president in 1847, and at various times he acted as director of the Highland Society. He was on the committee of the Halifax Reading Room in 1837 and 1838 and was a fire warden from 1837 to 1841. Frequently combining his business and civic functions, Murdoch served in 1839 as president of the Sun Fire Insurance Company. He was involved in the Halifax Hotel Company from 1841 to 1845 and was a member of a committee, organized in 1845, to promote a railway from Halifax to Quebec [*see* MOORSOM]. Beginning in 1847 he served successively as city auditor, ward auditor, magistrate, alderman, commissioner of public property, commissioner of the public cemetery, and, from 1853 to 1856, as a member of the provincial Board of Works.

Murdoch was involved in the 1850s in many activities that had a bearing on the development of an urban community. Associating urban growth with improved communications, transportation, and industrialization, in 1850 he joined the board of the Halifax-Dartmouth Steamboat Company and helped promote the Inland Navigation Company. In 1851 he served as commissioner in the Nova Scotia Electric Telegraph Company and in 1854 he organized a provincial exhibition of manufactures.

Murdoch was also interested in improving the social and intellectual climate of Halifax. He helped to establish the botanical gardens and sponsored a curling club and the Halifax Club. He was concerned with several religious and charitable institutions, such as the Protestant Orphanage and the Young Men's Christian Association.

Murdoch also had an involvement with the problems of public hygiene and community health services which sets him apart from moral reformers who preferred such private charities as the House of Refuge for Fallen Women. In addition to serving as director of the Halifax Water Company from 1849 to 1860, he began in 1849 to solicit funds for a general hospital. But in 1855, when he failed to raise sufficient funds, he became president of the newly founded Halifax Visiting Dispensary, which provided medical assistance to the poor under the supervision of Dr Frederick William MORRIS. The request of the dispensary's board for a legislative grant of £100 was initially rejected, but in 1857, unable to ignore the dispensary's success, the assembly finally agreed to vote a small subsidy. Not until 1867 was the Provincial and City Hospital officially opened.

Murdoch's time-consuming commitment to civic affairs (he does not seem to have taken any part in politics) required some readjustment in his firm and in January 1853 William M. Campbell became a partner. In addition Charles Murdoch dissolved his partnership with John Doull, a former clerk with the Murdochs, and devoted more time to the family firm. With a revitalized leadership W. and C. Murdoch and Company expanded its wholesale trade in the province. In 1856, however, William Murdoch retired from the firm to establish himself as a private financier. He invested heavily in banks in British North America, the United States, and Britain, and in American railway stocks, and had a reputation for backing young men wishing to go into business.

Apparently because of the economic and social limitations of Halifax, he moved in 1860 to London, England, where he purchased a fashionable home. He soon established a new business partnership, Murdoch, Nephews, and Slater, and once again became a private investor. In 1862 he helped establish the Imperial Bank, a modest affair at first, which specialized in financing commercial ventures connected with the colonies. The success of these numerous business activities is shown by the fact that in June 1866 his estate was valued at £480,000.

Although no precise calculation is possible, a large portion of this amount undoubtedly came from Nova Scotia and its transfer to England had represented a loss in available capital to the Halifax business community. His contemporaries did not consider this departure unusual and assumed that a man of Murdoch's wealth would move to England. Instead it was his bequests that drew attention. Not only did various relatives receive grants, but also the North British Society, St Matthew's Presbyterian Church, and the city hospital. In addition he left grants of £5,000 each to the Halifax Institution for the Deaf and Dumb and to the Asylum for the Blind. The nature of these grants, as much as their size, fully justifies his reputation as a "father of philanthropy" in Halifax.

K. G. PRYKE

Halifax County Court of Probate (Halifax), no.1396, will of William Murdoch (mfm. at PANS). *Acadian Recorder*, 1867–73. *Halifax Herald*, 4 July 1896. *Novascotian*, 1825–66. *Annals, North British Society,* Halifax, Nova Scotia, with portraits and biographical notes, 1768–1903*, comp. J. S. Macdonald (3rd ed., Halifax, 1905). *Belcher's farmer's almanack*, 1824–60. W. J. Stairs, *Family history, Stairs, Morrow; including letters, diaries, essays, poems, etc.* (Halifax, 1906).

MURPHY, MICHAEL, cooper, tavern-keeper, and Fenian leader; b. in 1826 at Cork (Republic of Ireland); d. 11 April 1868 at Buffalo, N.Y.

Michael Murphy came to York (Toronto), Upper Canada, from Ireland with his parents as a young boy. He received little formal education and was apprenticed to a cooper. Murphy eventually operated his own business for several years before purchasing a tavern in Toronto.

The late 1850s were years when feelings between Irish Catholics and Protestant Orangemen often ran quite high in Toronto and celebrations on St Patrick's Day (17 March) and on the anniversary of the Battle of the Boyne (12 July) were frequently accompanied by outbreaks of violence. The bloodiest of these "incidents," the St Patrick's Day riot of 1858 when one person was killed, prompted Michael Murphy and other prominent Irish Catholics in Toronto to create in that year the Hibernian Benevolent Society of Canada. Murphy became its first president. The society grew rapidly and branches were soon established in both Canada East and Canada West. It stressed its benevolent aims, "assisting . . . their distressed members, attending them in their sickness, and, in case of death, defraying their funeral expenses," but when its constitution was made public in 1865 it indicated that the society had evolved along secret and paramilitary lines to meet the needs of self-defence. In January 1863 the society acquired its own organ in Toronto, the *Irish Canadian*, which proclaimed that its "*printers, publishers, editors and stockholders* are HIBERNIANS"; Murphy was a provisional director when the paper was established.

By late 1864 the society was identified by many with the fast-growing Fenian Brotherhood in the United States, and Murphy himself was publicly accused by his most ardent critic, George Brown*'s Toronto *Globe*, of having attended a recent Fenian convention in the United States. In defence of himself and his organization, Murphy wrote in a letter to the *Globe* that the Hibernian Society was founded on "the principles of benevolence and self-defence." Its existence was justified on the grounds that "Orange excesses" and the apparent reluctance of the local authorities to protect Irish Catholics compelled the latter "to depend mainly upon themselves for the protection of their families and property." He insisted that there was "no connection what-

Murphy

soever between Fenianism and his organization," but he did admit that the Hibernians would always express "a heartfelt sympathy with any organization . . . having for its object the freedom and prosperity of the Irish people on Irish soil." Murphy had indeed attended the first national convention of the Fenians in the United States in November 1863.

Murphy was probably the most important of the small group of Canadian Fenians. His sympathy for the John O'Mahony wing of the Fenian Brotherhood in the United States, which supported revolution in Ireland, was known, and the authorities were aware that he was selling Fenian bonds and making financial contributions to O'Mahony. However, Murphy vigorously denounced the W. R. Roberts* faction of the brotherhood which openly advocated an invasion of British North America as a step towards the liberation of Ireland.

In March 1866, when rumours abounded of an imminent Fenian raid from the United States, and 10,000 volunteers were called out for duty, the Toronto Hibernians were determined to march on St Patrick's Day despite a decision by the St Patrick's Society not to hold a parade. Toronto authorities, led by Mayor F. H. Medcalf*, eventually permitted the march but only after Gilbert McMicken*, the chief of a government detective force, had arrived on the scene and had received Murphy's promise that his followers would "keep the peace." About 600 Hibernians paraded without incident, while 2,000 soldiers stood ready to intercede. Some of these men had been billeted in Murphy's tavern several days before.

In the days that followed, although no Fenian raiders appeared, the government of Canada, particularly Attorney General John A. Macdonald*, was now determined to prove that Murphy worked actively for the Fenians. However, before McMicken's "detectives" could accumulate sufficient evidence against him, Murphy was arrested at the Cornwall railway station on 9 April 1866. The Hibernian president and six companions had been on their way to Portland, Maine, to join the Fenian raid on Campobello Island. Instead, they were led to the local jail. Mayor William Cox Allen of Cornwall confiscated a considerable supply of weapons, ammunition, and money. Other Toronto Fenians were also arrested and sent to Cornwall.

The sudden arrests had not been ordered by Macdonald, but rather by his cabinet colleagues George-Étienne Cartier* and Alexander Tilloch Galt* who felt that the group should not be allowed to leave the country and thus escape Canadian surveillance. Macdonald was greatly annoyed, for he had given strict orders that the group should only be shadowed in order to gather more reliable evidence for use in a courtroom. Although no incriminating evidence could be found, not even by a spy "planted" in prison with Murphy, the prisoners were charged with treason for, as British subjects, having planned to participate in a raid on British territory.

The trials, set for the autumn assizes, were never held: on the night of 1 September Murphy and five followers escaped and fled across the border. The *Globe* fulminated over the escape, but other newspapers and even government officials expressed relief that the troublesome Murphy had slipped away. After all, the government prosecutor would have found it quite difficult to prove Murphy's complicity in a court of law. A sentence of outlawry was passed against Murphy at the October assizes in Cornwall, but three other prisoners were never tried.

Murphy was soon reported denouncing the Roberts Fenians for their recent raids on Canadian soil, especially that at Fort Erie [*see* Alfred Booker*], and on 11 September he appeared at Lewiston, N.Y., where he met a group of Toronto Hibernians. Shortly thereafter he moved to Buffalo and became the proprietor of the Irish Arms Hotel. His health was now failing rapidly, however, and business was poor because local Fenians suspected him of spying for the British and avoided his establishment. On 11 April 1868, at the age of 42, Murphy died of pulmonary tuberculosis. He left a wife and several children. His body was brought home to Toronto for burial and funeral services were held in St Michael's Cathedral.

Michael Murphy provided the strongest connection between Fenians and the Irish Catholic community in British North America. Most contemporaries considered Murphy and the inner circle of the Toronto-based Hibernian Society to be "the Canadian branch of the Fenian Brotherhood," but the number of Fenians was small; not even among the Hibernians were Fenians in a majority. In fact, Fenian supporters in British North America probably never numbered more than a thousand. Murphy was a man whose character was ill suited for revolutionary activities, for he was both vain and highly excitable and he lacked skill and discretion. He was an impulsive but sincere person, and he was convinced that by supporting the Fenian movement he was doing his patriotic duty for Ireland. At heart he was still an Irishman who "longed for the hour when Ireland should be free to manage her own affairs and enact her own laws within the shores of the island.''

W. S. NEIDHARDT

PAC, MG 26, A, 58, 236–37. *Globe*, 1864–66; 13 April 1868. *Irish Canadian* (Toronto), 1863–66, 15 April 1868. *Leader*, 1864–66. C. P. Stacey, "A Fenian interlude: the story of Michael Murphy," *CHR*, XV (1934), 133–54.

MUSQUAKIE (Mayawassino, Waisowindebay, also known as **William Yellowhead**), Ojibwa chief; d. 11 Jan. 1864 at the Rama Reserve, Canada West.

Musquakie has often been confused with his father, also called Yellowhead, who had preceded him as an Ojibwa chief. "The Yellow Head, Chief of Lake Simcoe," who visited the British fort at York (Toronto) in 1796 was probably the father, as was the Yellowhead who visited York and Niagara in 1797. It is also likely that the father was the Yellowhead responsible for keeping the Ojibwas of southern Upper Canada loyal to the British during the War of 1812. The elder Yellowhead was severely wounded in the defence of York in 1813, and as a result his son, who was also present, was then created a chief of the tribe. Four years later, "at the desire of his father," he assumed the position of head chief of the Ojibwas around lakes Simcoe and Huron.

In 1818 Musquakie took part, with several other Ojibwa chiefs, in a surrender of 1,592,000 acres of their territory to the British government in exchange for a "perpetual" annuity of £1,200; the area today forms part of Grey, Wellington, Dufferin, and Simcoe counties. Musquakie's father in 1815 had surrendered 250,000 acres in Simcoe County for which the tribe received £4,000. Musquakie and several hundred followers, however, continued to use their hunting grounds around Lake Simcoe after the treaties until in 1830 Sir John COLBORNE, disturbed by their migratory life, set aside lands for them at The Narrows (Orillia) and persuaded them to settle there. The government constructed dwellings, a meeting-house, and other buildings for them, and engaged a white settler to teach them farming. The Methodist missionary, Samuel Rose, was optimistic in 1831 about the Indians' condition and success in their new location. Musquakie had evidently been converted to Christianity some years previously, and his example was followed by his band.

By 1835 Musquakie's band at The Narrows and another Ojibwa band under Snake*, which had been settled in 1830 at Coldwater, had improved their lot considerably. Thomas Gummersall Anderson*, an Indian agent, submitted an enthusiastic report in that year which stressed that the tribes had made a successful transition from hunting to farming and that religion and education were increasingly important in their lives. Moreover, the Ojibwas had begun to construct furniture for themselves and to sell fish to neighbouring white settlers; they had also largely overcome problems of debt and drunkenness.

The next year, however, Lieutenant Governor Sir Francis Bond Head*, anxious to remove the Indians from areas which were now being claimed by white settlers, persuaded the Ojibwas at The Narrows and at Coldwater to surrender their lands and move to a reserve in the Rama-Longford Mills region. The treaty of surrender was drawn up, and Musquakie and his band bought with their annuity money some 1,600 acres in Rama Township. Before they were able to move, the government, alarmed by the disturbances in 1837–38 led by William Lyon MACKENZIE, called out the Ojibwas of lakes Huron and Simcoe as a local defence force. In the winter of 1838 members of several bands, including Musquakie, were camped at Holland Landing, where they experienced considerable hardship. The tribe was unable to do its winter hunting, and pay and provisions were stopped after a short period. Musquakie and other chiefs petitioned the government for supplies, claiming that starvation was imminent.

White settlers at Orillia and Coldwater also petitioned the government, demanding that the Indians be moved as soon as possible. In the summer of 1839 Musquakie and his band settled on the reserve in Rama Township, the other bands also establishing themselves in the same region. Houses and barns were again built for them, and farm implements and supplies provided. For the first few years the reserve flourished, exporting surplus produce to the surrounding white settlers. In 1842, however, Musquakie and several other chiefs claimed that they were being denied the proceeds from the land they had surrendered to the government in 1836. By the mid 1850s conditions on the reserve at Rama had deteriorated considerably; a government report of 1858 attributed the decline to a reduction in the number of supervising officers. Farm production had dropped off noticeably, and the Ojibwas had largely returned to hunting and basket-making. The Methodist missionary apparently neglected the Indians' education, and the buildings were all in decay.

Musquakie himself was less active in the affairs of his band and of the Ojibwas in general during the latter years of his life. In 1840, however, he had renewed the Ojibwa friendship treaty with the Six Nations, and in 1845 he had complained to Methodist officials of the tendency of missionaries to attempt to persuade the Indians to ignore the powers of their chiefs. Methodist ministers nevertheless continued to live and work in the Rama Reserve after 1845.

On his return from a mid-winter hunting trip in 1863–64, Musquakie was taken ill, and died shortly after. At that time his age "was supposed to be upwards of one hundred years," although the burial register of St James' Church, Orillia, lists his age as 95. A large gathering of whites and Indians attended his funeral out of respect for this influential chief who had often stressed his loyalty to the British crown. In his will Musquakie assigned his reserve lands and his hunting grounds to his nephew Isaac, and charged him to care for his wife Elizabeth and his daughter Jane; Isaac was designated head chief by Musquakie, but Joseph Benson Naingishkung became chief instead. Soon after Musquakie's death his wife petitioned the government for an increase in her pension, but it is not known if her appeal was successful.

Although the claims of several other persons have been advanced, it is generally believed that Musquakie is the origin of the name of the town and district of Muskoka.

In Collaboration

PAO, Misc. 1831, Rose papers, 1831–59. *Canada: Indian treaties and surrenders . . .* (3v., Ottawa, 1891–1912; repr. Toronto, 1971), I. *The correspondence of Lieut. Governor John Graves Simcoe, with allied documents relating to his administration of the government of Upper Canada*, ed. E. A. Cruikshank (5v., Toronto, 1923–31), IV. *Muskoka and Haliburton* (Murray). *Gazetteer and directory of the village of Orillia for 1866–7* (Toronto, 1866; repr. Orillia, Ont., 1967). *Guide book & atlas of Muskoka and Parry Sound districts, 1879* (Toronto, 1879; repr. Port Elgin, Ont., 1971). W. P. Bull, *From Strachan to Owen: how the Church of England was planted and tended in British North America* (Toronto, 1937). Pat Reid, *A history of Orillia* (n.p., n.d.). C. H. Hale, "Chief William Yellowhead: sketch of the life of William Yellowhead, head chief of the Chippewas, whose Indian name was Musquakie, 1769–1864," *Orillia portraits* (2nd ed., Orillia, Ont., 1966), 23–26.

N

NAHNEBAHWEQUAY (**Nahneebahweequa**, meaning upright woman; known as **Catherine Sutton**, *née* **Catherine Bunch Sonego**), Ojibwa spokeswoman; b. 1824 on the Credit River flats (Port Credit, Ont.); m. William Sutton, and they had seven children; d. 26 Sept. 1865 in Sarawak Township, Canada West.

Nahnebahwequay was the daughter of Tyatiquob (Bunch Sonego), of the Eagle totem, and Myarwikishigoqua (Mary Crane), of the Otter. Shortly after her birth her family visited the Grand River, where her uncle, Kahkewaquonaby* (Peter Jones), had recently converted many of his relatives to the Methodist Episcopal Church. The Sonegos accepted Christianity, and moved in the spring of 1826 with other Ojibwa converts to the Credit River to begin a Methodist settlement. The government erected 20 houses for them, paid for out of funds given the tribe for ceding their lands on the north shore of Lake Ontario. The Ojibwas (called "Mississaugas" by the Europeans) built a chapel, which also served as the school, and began to clear land.

Catherine attended the mission school until 1837, at which time she accompanied her aunt Elizabeth, the English wife of Peter Jones, on a year long trip to Great Britain. In January 1839 Catherine married an Englishman, William Sutton, who had immigrated to Canada in 1830. At the Credit mission, in addition to raising a family, she acted as a Methodist class leader.

In the summer of 1846 the Credit band considered moving to Owen Sound, but the poor quality of the land for farming convinced many of them that they should stay at the Credit. Three families, including the Suttons, did move. The Newash band at Owen Sound allowed the Suttons 200 acres on which they erected "a commodious house, barn and stable," and brought "40 to 50 acres into a good state of Cultivation."

From 1852 to 1854 they lived at the Garden River Reserve near Sault Ste Marie, where they superintended "the working of a Model farm [presumably under Methodist auspices] for the Benefit of the Indians." The Suttons went to a reserve in Michigan in 1854, where William was engaged in improving the Methodist mission. In 1857 they returned to Owen Sound and found that their property had been surveyed, laid out in town lots, and offered for sale by the government. In their absence, the Indian Department had secured the surrender of the Bruce Peninsula by treaty and refused to recognize the validity of the Suttons' land title. The local Methodist minister, Conrad Vandusen*, claimed that the crown had conducted its negotiations with an unofficial and unrepresentative group of Newash band members, but the superintendent of Indian affairs, Richard Theodore PENNEFATHER, maintained that: "The chiefs having no power to dispose to private parties of land belonging to the tribe, could not give a title, and [the Suttons'] written grant was therefore valueless." He also turned down Mrs Sutton's request for her share of the Newash band's annuities, "on the ground of her having married a white man, and having been absent from the country during the time for which she claimed payment."

In September 1857 Mrs Sutton was not allowed to buy back her land at public sale because, she was told, Indians could not purchase their ceded land. Kezhegowinninne* (David Sawyer) and Abner Elliott, a Newash Indian, were also denied the right to purchase the farms they had established. The three Indians in April 1858 unsuccessfully petitioned the Canadian legislature for title to their land or a fair remuneration for their loss. No redress was made by the government and in 1859 Catherine Sutton decided to journey to England to present their case to the colonial secretary and the queen.

Mrs Sutton travelled by way of New York, where a group of Quakers paid her passage to Britain and supplied her with a letter of introduction to Mr and Mrs Robert Alsop in England. Through the influence of the Alsops and their friend, the English reformer John Bright, Mrs Sutton met the colonial secretary, the Duke of Newcastle, in London. On 19 June 1860 she was presented to Queen Victoria, who noted in her private journal: "She speaks English quite well, and is come on behalf of her Tribe to petition against some grievance as regards their land." As a result of the direct intervention of the British government, the Suttons were allowed to buy back their land, but nothing was done for the other Indians.

Upon her return to Canada, Mrs Sutton, one of the few Indian women of her time to understand the "white man's ways," continued to argue for the native people's rights against the Europeans, who acted "as though their ideas of justice are that 'might is right.'" She severely criticized as "wholesale robbery and treachery" the government's attempt in 1861 to purchase Mani-

toulin Island – promised forever to the Indians in 1836 – for land-hungry white settlers.

During the last two and a half years of her life she suffered from poor health and died in 1865. Her husband survived her and continued to serve as a Methodist lay preacher until his death several years later. Through her mission school training, her first visit to Britain, and her marriage to an Englishman, Catherine Sutton had gained enough knowledge of the white man and sufficient confidence in his world to fight for her family's rights and for those of her people.

DONALD B. SMITH

Grey County and Owen Sound Museum (Owen Sound, Ont.), Journal of William Sutton. PAC, RG 10, vol. 2877, file 177181; RG 31, 1861 census, Sarawak Township; Keppel Township. PRO, CO 42/624, pp.355, 409, 428–29. UCA, Mission register for the Credit River Mission. *Christian Guardian*, 12 Jan. 1848; 2 April, 28 May 1862; 8 Nov. 1865. Enemikeese [Conrad Vandusen], *The Indian chief: an account of the labours, losses, sufferings, and oppression of Ke-zig-ko-e-ne-ne (David Sawyer), a chief of the Ojibbeway Indians in Canada West* (London, 1867), 119–37. Peter Jones (Kahkewaquonaby), *History of the Ojebway Indians; with especial reference to their conversion to Christianity* . . . (London, 1861); *Life and journals of Kah-ke-wa-quo-na-by (Rev. Peter Jones), Wesleyan missionary* (Toronto, 1860). Wesleyan Methodist Church in Can., Missionary Soc., *Annual report* (Toronto), 1845–46. *Illustrated atlas of the county of Grey* (Toronto, 1880; repr. Port Elgin, Ont., 1971), 17. *Daily Sun Times* (Owen Sound, Ont.), 30 Aug. 1960.

NAPIER, DUNCAN CAMPBELL, British army officer and office-holder; b. *c.* 1788 probably on the Island of Jersey; d. in June 1865 at St Helier, Island of Jersey.

Duncan Campbell Napier joined the Commissariat Department of the British army at an early age. He spent almost the whole of his active career in Canada, stationed in either Montreal or Quebec City where he was attached to the office of the governor general's military secretary. Although his career was hardly spectacular, it does provide some useful insight into the workings of the Indian Department in the half century before confederation.

Napier seems to have been attached to the military secretary's office from the time of the War of 1812. He had a variety of responsibilities; by 1825 he was in charge of army transport for the Montreal district, the resident Indian agent for the area, and secretary at Montreal of the Indian Department, responsible for all correspondence regarding the Indian population of Lower Can-

Nativité

ada. From 1830 to 1840 he was secretary at Quebec City and from 1840 until his retirement in 1857 secretary again at Montreal. Napier was the chief official in the Indian Department in the lower province for at least 32 years.

The Indians of Lower Canada were in a very different position from those of Upper Canada during the years Napier was concerned with Indian affairs. In North America, the traditional British policy was to negotiate the surrender of Indian lands through treaties, and then to sell these lands to incoming white settlers. This model was used in Upper Canada after 1791 and in the new dominion after confederation. French authorities in New France before 1763 had had quite another practice. They had entrusted the work of cultural assimilation to religious orders, setting aside land grants for that purpose. The ownership of these grants or reserves had been vested in the religious organizations rather than the Indians. Consequently, no Indian land surrenders had been signed and Roman Catholic missionaries had often acted in a double capacity as priests and as government Indian agents. After 1763, British authorities in the Province of Quebec thus found themselves administering a system of Indian-white relations whose roots lay in the province's French past.

Under the British system of Indian treaties, bands who gave up territory received compensation in the form of yearly presents, annual payments, and interest on the capital which accrued from the sale of surrendered land. From at least the time of the American revolution the army commissariat had been involved in the annual distribution of Indian presents. Because the Indians were also regarded as military allies, it seemed logical to put one of its officers in charge of the Indians of Lower Canada. After 1800 they came under the jurisdiction of the governor general, who made the military secretary responsible. By the time of the War of 1812 it had become necessary to appoint a permanent official in Lower Canada to oversee the duties of the military secretary's office with regard to the Indians and Colonel Napier was the first officer to be appointed. Napier was therefore subordinate to the military secretary. This administrative pattern persisted in Lower Canada until the Canadian government became responsible for Indian affairs in 1860 [see Richard Theodore PENNEFATHER], even though the Indians of Upper Canada were effectively under civil control after 1830.

Napier was responsible for a vast, ill-defined area whose Indians for the most part clung to the semi-nomadic hunting and fishing life of their an-cestors. He could do little to encourage the formation of fixed agricultural settlements which was the object of official policy. His correspondence was mostly with resident priests or other religious and dealt chiefly with the mundane matters of everyday administration: population statistics, requests for funds, and salary supplements. Many Indian bands went officially unvisited for years or simply dropped out of view altogether. This situation contrasted with the one in Upper Canada, where problems were fewer and administration more innovative [see Thomas Gummersall Anderson*].

Duncan Campbell Napier was a conscientious administrator who could do little more than maintain the Indian Department's *status quo* in Lower Canada. Advancing age lessened his effectiveness during his last years in office. His retirement in 1857 coincided with Britain's decision to retreat from Indian affairs in Canada. That retreat marked the real end of an administrative system which had become an anachronism. It is not known when Napier left Canada or how he spent the last years of his life.

Douglas Leighton

PAC, MG 30, D62, 22, pp.787–802; RG 10, vols. 22–25, 78–102, 141, 590–603, 655–655a. *Gentleman's Magazine* CCXVIII (January–June 1865), 801.

NATIVITÉ. *See* Cadron

NAWAHJEGEZHEGWABE (**Newechekeshequeby, Nawachjekezhegwabe**; signifying "the sloping sky"; known in English as **Joseph Sawyer**), member of the Eagle totem, soldier, and Ojibwa chief; b. 1786 in the Genesee country (western New York State); d. 8 Nov. 1863 at the New Credit Reserve, Tuscarora Township, Canada West.

Nawahjegezhegwabe, the son of Wahbanosay (Wabenose, Wobenosay), "a chief of the Mississauga Tribe of the Ojibway Nation," and Pakakis, his wife, was born in the territory of the Senecas, allies of the Ojibwas. The family apparently resided in the vicinity of the head of Lake Ontario (Hamilton, Ont.), and there Nawahjegezhegwabe learned to fish and hunt. In 1801 or 1802 the Reverend Joseph Sawyer*, a Methodist preacher, baptized Nawahjegezhegwabe as "Joseph Sawyer." At that time the Indian lived with surveyor Augustus Jones* and his family on their large farm at Stoney Creek. Shortly after his baptism, however, Nawahjegezhegwabe returned to his people and the faith of his forefathers. Once among his tribe, called Mississauga by the white settlers, he married Wetosy

(Jane Sawyer), a member of the Otter clan. A loyal supporter of the crown, he fought in the War of 1812 at Detroit, Queenston Heights, and Lundy's Lane.

Joseph Sawyer was tormented by spiritual conflict for 20 years following his conversion. As "his convictions of the truth of Christianity remained," he suffered from "terrible depressions" which led him to drink heavily. Being a "wiry and muscular" man, Sawyer proved "a terror to the whole band" when drunk; in such a state only several Indians could control him. The band considered him at that time to be completely under the control of the *Mahje-munedoo*, or evil spirit. "This was the only way," the white Methodist missionary Conrad Vandusen* wrote, that "they could account for his vile and vicious conduct." His "second" conversion to Christianity in 1824 would resolve his spiritual dilemma.

The native missionary Kahkewaquonaby* (Peter Jones), the son of Sawyer's sister Tuhbenahneequay and Augustus Jones, brought his uncle back to the Methodist Episcopal Church. Early in the spring of 1826 Sawyer moved with his family from the head of the lake to the Methodist Indian settlement then being formed at the Credit River, where he farmed and served as a class leader. Following the death of Chief James Ajetance (Ajetans) in 1829, the warriors in council elected Sawyer their head chief.

In conjunction with his fellow chief and nephew, Kahkewaquonaby, Sawyer sent many petitions to the lieutenant governor and the assembly at York (Toronto) seeking adequate protection for the Credit band's fishery and a firm title to their reserve. Probably Chief Sawyer's most eloquent appeal came when Sir Francis Bond Head* proposed that the band move from the Credit River to Manitoulin Island. After a dozen years of hard work the Mississauga hunters had become successful farmers. Consequently, Sawyer bluntly informed Head, they did not favour removal to a barren island: "Now we raise our own corn, potatoes, wheat; we have cattle, and many comforts, and conveniences. But if we go to Maneetoolin, we could not live; soon we should be extinct as a people; we could raise no potatoes, corn, pork, or beef; nothing would grow by putting the seed on the smooth rock."

Only when the government's intention not to give them secure title to their reserve was made clear did Sawyer and his council consider leaving the Credit River. Having made the decision to depart, they eventually accepted the invitation of the Six Nations tribe to settle in 1847 on a fertile tract on their reserve in Tuscarora Township, Brant County. Sawyer remained head chief at the New Credit until his death in 1863. On at least two occasions he was also elected president of the Ojibwa Grand Council of Upper Canada. His son Kezhegowinninne* succeeded him as head chief.

DONALD B. SMITH

UCA, Mission register for the Credit River Mission. *Canada: Indian treaties and surrenders . . .* (3v., Ottawa, 1891–1912; repr. Toronto, 1971). I, 34–40. [J. S. Carroll], *Past and present, or a description of persons and events connected with Canadian Methodism for the last forty years* (Toronto, 1860), 57–58. *Christian Guardian*, 12 Jan. 1848, 16 Dec. 1863. Enemikeese [Conrad Vandusen], *The Indian chief: an account of the labours, losses, sufferings, and oppression of Kezig-ko-e-ne-ne (David Sawyer), a chief of the Ojibbeway Indians in Canada West* (London, 1867), 18–21. Peter Jones (Kahkewaquonaby), *History of the Ojebway Indians; with especial reference to their conversion to Christianity . . .* (London, 1861); *Life and journals of Kah-ke-wa-quo-na-by (Rev. Peter Jones), Wesleyan missionary* (Toronto, 1860). Kahgegagahbowh (George Copway), *Recollections of a forest life; or, the life and travels of Kah-ge-ga-gah-bowh . . .* (London, [1850]). *Minutes of the General Council of Indian chiefs and principal men . . .*, comp. Henry Baldwin (Montreal, 1846). Benjamin Slight, *Indian researches; or, facts concerning the North American Indians . . .* (Montreal, 1844).

NELSON, WOLFRED, doctor, politician, and Patriote; b. 10 July 1791 in Montreal, third son of William Nelson and Jane Dies; m. in 1819 Charlotte-Josephte Noyelle de Fleurimont, and they had seven children; d. 17 June 1863 in Montreal.

There is little in Wolfred Nelson's family background or early life to suggest that he would become an opponent of British misrule in Canada and a champion of the civil rights of French Canadians. His mother was the daughter of a wealthy New York landowner who had lost his possessions by remaining loyal to the crown during the American revolution. Wolfred's father, a London-trained schoolmaster, had come to the Province of Quebec in 1781 and earned so high a reputation as a teacher that the British colonial authorities granted him a comfortable annual salary as an inducement for him to stay in the colony. When Wolfred was three the family moved to Sorel (officially named William-Henry although commonly called Sorel) where his father opened a school. There, in the stockaded British outpost at the mouth of the Richelieu River, he grew up. The family lived not far from the summer residence of British governors and Wolfred attended his father's school along with the sons of British officers.

At age 14 Wolfred Nelson was apprenticed to Dr C. Carter of the British army and in February 1811 he received his surgeon's licence. He remained in Sorel, suffering, in the words of a biographer, "the drudgery of a small military hospital" while hoping for advancement in the service. In January 1812 he learned that he was to be recommended as a hospital mate by the staff surgeon at Sorel, and a few weeks later his prospects for a military medical career were further brightened when Britain and the United States declared war. Nelson immediately petitioned Governor Sir George Prevost* for a commission and received an appointment as surgeon of the 5th battalion of embodied militia. This was a turning point in his life, although not in the expected direction. Until the War of 1812 Nelson's world had been that of Sorel's British élite – however humble that élite may have been – and its prejudices were his prejudices. "I was in my earliest days," Nelson recounted many years later, "a hot Tory and inclined to detest all that was Catholic and French Canadian, but a more intimate knowledge of these people changed my views." This intimacy began with his militia appointment. The headquarters of the battalion was at Saint-Denis, a prosperous French Canadian town of about 500 people several miles south of Sorel on the Richelieu River. In September 1813 when the battalion was called out to guard against an expected American attack, Nelson was its only English speaking officer. Following the war he established a practice at Saint-Denis.

Nelson's political conversion from Tory to Reformer had also begun, and in 1827 he entered politics. It was a dramatic entry, for he chose to run for the assembly in the "royal borough" of William-Henry which included his home town of Sorel and which traditionally had been the fief of the governor. In the campaign he revealed himself to be an implacable enemy of the established order. His opponent, James Stuart*, the attorney general of Lower Canada, was publicly supported by Governor Lord Dalhousie [Ramsay*]. At one meeting Nelson interrupted Dalhousie, who was speaking on Stuart's behalf, informed him that his conduct was unconstitutional, and forced him to cease his activities in the campaign. Nelson won the election by two votes, "to the astonishment and indignation of the respectable part of the inhabitants," according to the *Montreal Gazette*. An outraged Stuart then began a series of harassing legal actions to annul the election. Instead, the corrupt election practices which were exposed led to Stuart's dismis-

sal from the office of attorney general in 1831. "The Laws," wrote Nelson, "must be observed as much by those who govern as by those who are governed."

For reasons not now entirely clear – perhaps simply the difficulty of attending to his duties as a doctor while serving in the assembly – Nelson did not stand for re-election in 1830. The seven years that followed were perhaps his most successful. He visited Great Britain and the Continent to study medical institutions, established a large distillery at Saint-Denis, and was appointed a justice of the peace. His political views, however, did not soften with his material success. If anything, he became increasingly radical as the abuses of the governing oligarchy became more apparent. The assassination of his friend and political ally, Louis Marcoux, during the election of 1834 at Sorel, and the subsequent acquittal of the accused murderer by a packed jury in Montreal, particularly incensed him. In an interview in January 1836 with Governor Lord Gosford [Acheson*], in which Nelson protested against the abuses by the Executive Council, Nelson warned that "if the Habitans were left to themselves and if their leaders were insulted or abused in Montreal, that would be the signal of a war of extermination."

Indeed the conflict between the Patriote and constitutional parties, which saw French Canadians mostly on one side and English speaking – with a number of exceptions such as Nelson – on the other, was soon intensified from a war of words – editorials, speeches, and resolutions – to one of guns. In both contests Nelson fought in the front rank. In May 1837 he organized the first of many "anti-coercion meetings" held in the province that summer and proposed its first resolution which condemned the undemocratic measures recently advanced by Lord John Russell to resolve the troublesome political situation in Lower Canada. For his part in the meeting Nelson was relieved of his commission as magistrate. In October he was made chairman of the Assemblée des Six Comtés, where he again proposed the first angry resolution: "whenever any form of government becomes destructive . . . it is the right of the people to alter or abolish it." On 16 Nov. 1837 the government moved against the Patriotes by issuing illegal warrants against Nelson and 25 others on charges of high treason. Soon afterwards, Louis-Joseph Papineau* and Edmund Bailey O'Callaghan* joined Nelson at Saint-Denis where they decided to resist arrest, procure arms and ammunition for the people, and declare the independence of Lower Canada on 4 Dec. 1837.

The British authorities, however, decided to act long before that date. When they learned that the Patriotes were occupying Saint-Charles and that Papineau was with Nelson at Saint-Denis, they launched on the night of 22 November a two-pronged attack on the two Patriote strongholds. A brigade under Colonel George Augustus WETHERALL set out from Chambly to move against Saint-Charles at the same time that another brigade under Colonel Charles Stephen GORE left Sorel on a secret march to take Saint-Denis, which, according to an officer on the march, "was not supposed to be strongly held." The British tactics were not successful. Forewarned before dawn on the 23rd of the British approach by the capture of a British officer, Nelson went to reconnoitre the strength of their forces. Accounts differ as to exactly what followed, but it appears that Nelson returned to Saint-Denis determined to engage the British. He ordered the alarm bell rung, sent parties out to destroy bridges, and made preparations to resist from two stone houses at the north end of the town. He had informed Papineau of his reconnaissance trip, but he does not appear to have conferred with him regarding his intentions after his return. To the Patriotes with him he said: "A bit of courage, and victory will be ours."

The opposing forces at Saint-Denis may have appeared grossly mismatched, a country doctor and his collection of farmers and tradesmen against a veteran of Waterloo and his selected companies of seasoned regulars. But Nelson had grown up among British soldiers and he was not intimidated by the sight of their military uniforms. Also, among Nelson's angry, determined men were several first rate sharpshooters. On the other hand, although Gore was an earnest and hardworking deputy quartermaster-general he was not a brilliant tactician, and some of his men, who were part of an army which, in Wellington's words, collected "the scum of the earth," were waiting for a chance to slip away to the United States. Furthermore, the elements were in Nelson's favour. He and his snipers remained dry behind thick stone walls while Gore and his soldiers, after having marched all night in freezing November rain, had to manoeuvre in mud. From about nine a.m. until mid afternoon, Gore attempted in vain to push his men past the Patriote position. He was forced instead to order a retreat.

The victory at Saint-Denis electrified Lower Canada and made Nelson a hero among the Patriotes. Even the British grudgingly admitted that he was "far more determined, courageous and active than any of his brother traitors." But Patriote defeats followed the great victory and,

worse still, Papineau disappeared, "leaving us," Nelson later declared, "all in the lurch." In just over a week, the defenders of Saint-Denis had diminished to six. In the face of Gore's impending return, they fled to the woods on 1 December. For Nelson the aftermath was a nightmare. At Granby he became separated from his companions of Saint-Denis, and he wandered without food for ten days until he was captured by some volunteers near Stukeley in the Eastern Townships. He was then taken to Montreal to face trial on the charge of high treason. "Just before he started," wrote a friend to Mrs Nelson, "he desired me to write a few lines saying that he willed all the property he possessed to his dear wife and children." Nelson did not know at the time that Colonel Gore's soldiers had burned most of his property on their return to Saint-Denis. But he did know that martial law had been declared and that the penalty for high treason was death.

Nelson, however, did not even come to trial. After spending seven months in prison, he and seven others were banished to Bermuda after pleading guilty in a private letter to Lord Durham [Lambton*] of "rebelling against colonial misgovernment." In October 1838 another odd twist of fate, the disavowing of Durham's ordinance, allowed the exiles to leave Bermuda. By early 1839 Nelson had found his way to Plattsburgh, N.Y., near the Lower Canadian border, where he established a medical practice and was joined by his family. When asked what should be done to liberate Lower Canada, he replied simply: "At this moment we must let time and circumstances do their work, however slowly."

Time and circumstances did their work remarkably quickly. In 1842 Louis-Hippolyte LA FONTAINE, a friend who had offered to adopt one of Nelson's children just before the exiles left for Bermuda, took office as attorney general for Canada East and entered a *nolle prosequi* in Nelson's case. Nelson left Plattsburgh in August, to the regret of the people of that town, and moved his family to Montreal where once again he began a new medical practice.

Although he had vowed to stay out of Canadian politics when he returned, he kept his resolution for only two years. In 1844 La Fontaine requested him to stand for election to the assembly, and, fired by his indignation over Downing Street's refusal to adhere to the principle of responsible government, he was unable to refuse. For the next seven years he was the member for Richelieu. To the disgust of Tories, he restaked his old political position as the English speaking exponent of French Canadian rights and was a firm advocate of responsible government.

Nelson

During his parliamentary career there twice emerged the same angry man who had defied Dalhousie and defeated Gore. On the first occasion, in 1848, his opponent was Louis-Joseph Papineau. Back from exile and a member in the assembly, Papineau had begun manoeuvring to regain his leadership from La Fontaine by appealing to national prejudices. Nelson resented Papineau's thinly veiled efforts to split the Reform alliance that had finally gained power. When Papineau insinuated that the violence of 1837 was attributable to Nelson, the latter turned on the great man himself and finally revealed that Papineau had been quite prepared to use force and had indeed signed a declaration of independence in his house. He also exposed Papineau's hurried flight from Saint-Denis, only half an hour after the battle had started, and stated his belief that Papineau's escape had resulted in the ultimate defeat of the Patriote movement and all the misery that had followed. "It is perhaps a favour for which we should thank GOD, that your projects failed," he sneered, "persuaded as I am at present that you would have governed with a rod of iron." Possibly only a man of Nelson's reputation could have attacked so exalted a figure with such telling effect. Papineau's power and popularity were mutilated. But Nelson's own heroic stature was diminished by the vehemence of his attack; there is no doubt that in later years he regretted having made it.

A second outburst occurred during the fiery debate on the Rebellion Losses Bill [see James BRUCE] which Nelson had helped frame. Taunted by Tories with accusations of being a rebel and a traitor, Nelson replied that to "Those who call me and my friends rebels I tell them that they *lie* in their throats. . . . I tell those gentlemen to their teeth, that it is they and such as they, who cause revolutions, who pull down thrones, trample crowns into the dust and annihilate dynasties." He also offered to withdraw his own valid claim for losses, "wantonly inflicted as they were," but demanded that those who had suffered innocently be paid. When royal assent was given to the bill in April 1849, Nelson had the satisfaction of knowing that the measure would benefit materially his constituents in the Richelieu valley, exonerate his own actions of 12 years earlier, and by its very passage, establish the principle of responsible government for which Nelson had fought since the beginning of his political career 22 years before. A little over a year later he announced his retirement from politics.

Nelson was 60, but he was not to retire yet. As a reward for his services to the La Fontaine-Robert Baldwin* ministry he was offered the position of inspector of provincial penitentiaries and jails, an office for which he was ironically well qualified. As he himself explained, "My sojourn for seven months in the Montreal Jail gave me such a practical knowledge of prison affairs, the accursed abuses that prevailed there . . . and the uncalled for miseries that were inflicted on the prisoners [as] induced me to accept." With his characteristic energy he made a possible sinecure an important office. His reports on prisons, which have been described as "well written," contain much valuable information.

Nor did he retire from politics. In 1854 he defeated Édouard-Raymond Fabre*, a Papineau supporter, to become the first popularly elected mayor of Montreal. No study has been made of Nelson's career in municipal politics, but he appears by his speeches to have been a progressive administrator. In 1855 he urged the greater regulation of public services through the appointment of municipal inspectors. He favoured welfare for the poor when there was no work and he recommended that the municipal council seriously consider Sir James Edward Alexander's idea of creating a park atop Mont-Royal. He retired from municipal politics in 1856.

Nelson seems never to have retired from his first profession. He was always a doctor – for the wounded British soldiers after Saint-Denis, among his fellow prisoners, among the blacks in Bermuda, and on the Montreal waterfront during the 1847 epidemic of ship-fever. He is credited with having performed with his son, Dr Horace Henry Nelson, the first operation using anaesthetics in Canada. As mayor of Montreal he published at his own expense a useful pamphlet in both English and French on the prevention of cholera. In the assembly he drew up legislation for the teaching of medicine and the regulation of the profession. It comes as no surprise to find him putting medicine ahead of politics. In 1851 he wrote to his friend William Lyon MACKENZIE regretting having missed the opening of the session because of three or four serious cases. "I have endeavoured to put [them] into quite as good hands but my patients will not hear of it." Although Nelson's historical reputation rests upon his political activities, possibly his greater contribution lies in his long and honourable medical career. His services to thousands of people during his 50 years as a doctor, however, can never be known.

Wolfred Nelson revealed throughout his life a strong humanitarian concern, and actions in small events which reveal this quality are part of the accurate measure of the man. While being transported to Bermuda he feared that certain comments he had made regarding opportunities for escape that he had refused might implicate his jailer; he wrote the jailer to set the record straight and to commend him on his "humanity and due regard to the feelings of the prisoners." In 1854 he took the trouble to write a letter that helped the unpopular Tory colonel, Bartholomew Conrad Augustus Gugy*, disprove allegations of cruelty in 1837. Nelson gratefully recalled the kindness shown by his old opponent Gugy to Mrs Nelson following Gore's return to Saint-Denis. In the union Legislative Assembly he made his first speech in 1845 in French, a language proscribed at the time, and in 1849 he seconded an amendment to the Rebellion Losses Bill that prohibited him from making any claim for his own losses. On a cold January night in 1849 he acted as chairman of a meeting called to promote the abolition of capital punishment, which he termed "judicial murder." Wolfred Nelson died in Montreal on 17 June 1863 at the age of 71. The small white marker over his grave reads: "Here lieth God's noblest work, an honest man."

JOHN BESWARICK THOMPSON

Wolfred Nelson, *Practical views on cholera, and on the sanitary, preventive and curative measures to be adopted in the event of a visitation of the epidemic* (Montreal, 1854; a French edition was published in Montreal in the same year).
    PAC, MG 24, A27, ser.2, 26, pp.631–37, 652–53; A40, 9, pp.2273, 2344, 2432–34, 2457, 2475–77, 2574, 2589; 27, pp.8156, 8170; B14; B31, 1, p.40; B34; B37, 1, p.118; B82; RG 4, A1, S-112; S-203a; S-272, pp.73–74; S-507, pp. 73–75; S-586, pp. 42–42a; RG 8, I (C series), 281, p.222; 1717, p.59; RG 9, I, A7, 21. PRO, CO 42/274, 10–11 (mfm. at PAC). "Les Patriotes aux Bermudes en 1838, lettres d'exil," Yvon Thériault, édit., *RHAF*, XVI (1962–63), 267–72. *La Minerve*, mai-oct. 1848, juin 1863. *Pilot and Journal of Commerce* (Montreal), Nov.-Dec. 1844, Jan. 1849. *Vindicator and Canadian Advertiser* (Montreal), April-Dec. 1837. Borthwick, *History and biographical gazetteer.* Morgan, *Sketches of celebrated Canadians.* Abbott, *History of medicine.* Christie, *History of L.C.,* IV, V. Azarie Couillard-Després, *Histoire de Sorel de ses origines à nos jours* (Montréal, 1926). Monet, *Last cannon shot.* Wolfred Nelson, *Wolfred Nelson et son temps* (Montréal, 1946). B. B. Kruse, "The Bermuda exiles," *Canadian Geographical Journal* (Ottawa), XIV (1937), 353.

NICKINSON, JOHN, soldier, actor, and theatre manager; b. 2 Jan. 1808 in London, England, son of a Chelsea pensioner; d. 9 Feb. 1864 in Cincinnati, Ohio. He married first Ann Talbot, and was survived by a second wife, four daughters (Charlotte*, who married journalist Daniel MORRISON; Eliza, who married comedian Charles Peters; Virginia, who married actor Owen Marlowe; and Isabella, who married actor Charles M. Walcot Jr), and one son.

John Nickinson enlisted at the age of 15 as a drummer boy in the 24th Regiment of Infantry and became a sergeant in 1825. He was probably with the regiment when it arrived in Montreal in October 1829. He joined the 24th's theatre group, the Garrison Amateurs, formed in 1830 when the regiment was stationed in Quebec City, and in April 1833 interpreted "Karl" in *The miller and his men* and "Caleb Quotem" in *The review.* Such theatre groups were common in the British army; if there was little entertainment in the country in which they were stationed they promptly supplied it. The regiment returned to Montreal in 1833 and on 9 April 1835 Nickinson was again one of the principals in a production of *The miller and his men*; he also played in *The Irishman in London*. Both plays were put on in the Theatre Royal, provided for the occasion by John Molson*, for the benefit of the "theatrical fund." On 21 April Nickinson was producer-director of a benefit at the theatre.

The stage now started to dominate Nickinson's life. In 1836 he left the army to devote his full time to acting. He became a member of the company of Thomas Ward, the lessee of the Theatre Royal in Montreal, but on 7 Sept. 1836 was given a farewell benefit. Soon after he made his début in Albany, N.Y., and he became a member of the South Pearl Street Theatre. He returned to Montreal in 1841 to become part of the company playing at the Theatre Royal, and returned again for the 1843 season when he was lessee and manager of the theatre. However, he once more left for the United States, probably because of financial difficulties, and may have gone first to the Utica, N.Y., Museum. In 1848 he was the original "Dombey" in John Brougham's dramatization of *Dombey and son* at Burton's Theatre in New York. He became the stage manager of the Albany Museum in 1849. He subsequently played at the Franklin and Park theatres in New York City and was part of William Mitchell's Olympic Theatre. When the latter company closed in 1850 Nickinson began touring the United States, often performing his well-known interpretation of "Haversack" in *Napoleon's old guard.*

In 1852 Nickinson formed his own company which included W. J. Florence (who later became one of the leading comedians in the United States), C. M. Walcot Jr, and Charles Peters. The company was invited to tour Montreal, Quebec, and Toronto by T. P. Besnard. Nickinson became Besnard's partner in 1852 in the management of their theatres at Toronto and Quebec, and in 1853 became sole lessee of the Royal Lyceum in Toronto. His opening play was probably *The rough diamond*, first presented on 28 March 1853. During Nickinson's management, which lasted until 1858, many popular actors of the day were persuaded to come to the Lyceum, including James William Wallack, Jr and Sr. Nickinson's daughters Charlotte (who had earlier appeared briefly with her father in New York City) and Isabella began their stage careers there. Nickinson was seen by Toronto audiences in such character roles as "Midas" in the play of that name, "Aminadab Sleek" in *Serious family*, and "Haversack." By 1857 Nickinson was also the proprietor and manager of the Theatre Royal in Brantford. His company appeared regularly at Montreal, Quebec, Kingston, and Hamilton. He raised a militia company of rifles during his stay in Toronto.

In 1858 Nickinson left for the United States, although he remained owner of the Toronto Lyceum, and Owen Marlowe became its manager. However, he was again manager in 1860 when it changed its name to the Prince of Wales Theatre. He returned to the United States soon after, and was manager of Pike's Opera House in Cincinnati when he died in 1864.

MURRAY D. EDWARDS

Molson Archives (Montreal), "Early theatre in Montreal." *Cincinnati Commercial* (Cincinnati, Ohio), 11 Feb. 1864. Boase, *Modern English biog.*, I, 1445–46. T. A. Brown, *History of the American stage . . .* (New York, 1870), 265–66. *Types of Canadian women and of women who have been connected with Canada*, ed. H. J. Morgan (Toronto, 1903). J. E. Middleton, "Music and the theatre in Canada," *Can. and its provinces* (Shortt and Doughty), XII, 651–61. M. D. Edwards, *A stage in our past, English-language theatre in eastern Canada from the 1790s to 1914* ([Toronto], 1968). Franklin Graham, *Histrionic Montreal; annals of the Montreal stage with biographical and critical notices of the plays and players of a century* (2nd ed., New York and London, 1902; repr. New York, 1969), 83. H. P. Phelps, *Players of a century: a record of the Albany stage, including notices of prominent actors who have appeared in America* (2nd ed., Albany, N.Y., 1880; repr. New York, 1972). *Robertson's landmarks of Toronto*, I, 486–91. F. N. Walker, *Four whistles to wood-up: stories of the Northern Railway of Canada* (Toronto, 1953).

NIVERVILLE, LOUIS-CHARLES BOUCHER DE. *See* BOUCHER

NOAD, HENRY JOHN, businessman; b. 1812 in England, eldest son of John Batson Noad and

Rachel Street, of Woolwich, Kent; d. 18 Aug. 1870 at Montreal.

In 1819 or 1820 Henry John Noad's father settled with his family at Quebec, where he opened a grocery and liquor store. In 1824 he formed a company with Richard Rogerson of Upper Canada for the production and sale of potash. The family environment therefore encouraged an aptitude for business.

Henry John's beginnings in business are somewhat obscure. As early as 1831 he owned a store in Lower Town, and in 1833 he was a clerk in the employ of Charles-Félix Aylwin, a Quebec merchant. At the end of the 1830s he went to live on Rue Saint-Paul, where he traded in flour, corn, coal, oil, and wood, both on his own account and as a commercial agent. In 1854, with other Quebec businessmen, he financed the operations of James Tibbits, a shipbuilder, and acquired several ships assigned to the St Lawrence River trade. In addition, he purchased, rented, and sold various properties and pieces of land in Quebec. From at least 1845 on, Noad carried on his business under the firm name of H.J. Noad and Company, in partnership with his brother-in-law, William Henry Jeffery.

As well as managing his own undertakings, Noad was a member of several groups of entrepreneurs whose names became known when the following companies were incorporated: the British North American Electric Telegraph Association (1847), of which he was a director; the Quebec and Trois-Pistoles Navigation Company (1853); the Quebec and Saguenay Railway Company (1854); the St Lawrence Navigation Company (1861); the Quebec Marine Insurance Company (1862); the Quebec Elevator Company (1863); and the English and Canadian Mining Company (Limited) (1865). He was also a director of the Quebec Forwarding Company, the Quebec Exchange, and several savings banks. Most of the enterprises in which he invested time and money showed he had an entrepreneur's readiness to take risks as much as concern for diversifying his investments.

Henry John Noad also played an active role in the Quebec Board of Trade: he was a member of the board's council from 1841 to 1862, treasurer from 1844 to 1853, and president from 3 April 1854 to 7 April 1856. This continuous participation in the activities of the Board of Trade well illustrates his prestige in the business community of Quebec.

On his father's death in 1843, Noad assumed responsibility for his family, the youngest child, James Street, being 11. Subsequently his three brothers successively left Quebec to settle at

Montreal, where they embarked on various commercial ventures.

For reasons difficult to understand, linked perhaps with some nervous instability, Henry John Noad retired from business in the autumn of 1861. H. J. Noad and Company consequently was dissolved on 2 Dec. 1861 and placed in liquidation. William Henry Jeffery, Noad's former partner, then set up with James Street Noad the firm of Jeffery, Noad and Company, which took over the affairs of H. J. Noad and Company. On 28 Oct. 1864, Jeffery, Noad and Company was dissolved in its turn, and Jeffery withdrew, paying Henry John the sum of $140,000, the sole indication we possess of the scope of Henry John Noad's operations. On 2 May 1865 James Street and Henry John formed J. S. Noad and Company, which lasted only a year.

On 26 Nov. 1862 Noad had bought for $3,000 a 125-acre farm on the Rivière Saint-François, at Melbourne in the Eastern Townships. There he spent the last eight years of his life. On 18 Aug. 1870, while visiting his brother James, in Montreal, Noad took his own life with a revolver, by a bullet through the heart. At the coroner's inquest, the jury returned a verdict of death by suicide in a moment of mental derangement. His remains were shipped to Quebec by steamboat on 19 August, and the funeral was held on the 20th.

Henry John Noad, a bachelor, left a sizable fortune of about $70,000, numerous properties at Quebec, his farm at Melbourne, and a property at Swindon, Wiltshire, England. These assets were divided among his family. His youngest brother James inherited the business.

Henry John Noad's career is interesting in so far as it allows us to know more about the methods by which businessmen of British origin acquired their wealth. A close study of the notarial contracts made between the principal Quebec merchants would doubtless add a great deal to our knowledge of them, both as individuals and as a social group.

MARC VALLIÈRES

ANQ-Q, AP-G-219/1–4; État civil, Anglicans, Cathedral of the Holy Trinity (Québec), 1 Sept. 1820, 20 Aug. 1870; Greffe de William Bignell, 6 août 1840, 4 janv., 6 nov., 2 déc. 1843, 28 oct., 26 nov. 1864, 2 mai 1865; Greffe de N. H. Bowen, 1852–65; Greffe de W. D. Campbell, 20 oct. 1854, 2 mars 1859, 15 nov. 1860; Greffe de William De Léry, 9 juill. 1833, 29 nov. 1838; Greffe de S.-I. Glackmeyer, 1852–65; Greffe de L. T. McPherson, 1833–56; Greffe de Louis Panet, 21 sept. 1824, 8 août 1831. Archives judiciaires, Saint-François (Sherbrooke, Qué.), Greffe de G. H. Napier, 26 nov. 1862. Can., prov. du, *Statuts*, 1847, c.82; 1852–53, c.247; 1854–55, c.35; 1861, c.99; 1862, c.71; 1863, c.23; 1866, c.90. *Canada Gazette* (Quebec; Toronto), 10 Jan. 1852, 1 April 1854, 4 Jan. 1862. *Le Canadien*, 22 août 1870. *Gazette* (Montreal), 19 Aug. 1870. *Montreal Daily Witness*, 19 Aug. 1870. *Morning Chronicle* (Quebec), 20 Aug. 1870. *Canada directory*, 1857–58. Langelier, *List of lands granted. Montreal directory*, 1843–47. *Quebec directory*, 1847–62.

NORDBECK, PETER, silversmith and jeweller; b. 1789 in Germany, probably in Hanover; d. 7 Feb. 1861 in Halifax, N.S.

After serving the customary seven-year apprenticeship, Peter Nordbeck worked as a journeyman with silversmiths in Germany. By 1814 he had emigrated and settled in the British West Indies. Five years later he moved to Halifax and commenced business as a goldsmith and silversmith, entering into partnership with another capable silversmith, Henry Mignowitz, in 1824. This partnership was soon dissolved, but in August 1827 he formed Nordbeck and Company with Mignowitz and Robert Clarke as partners. Although Clarke soon left, Nordbeck and Mignowitz worked together until 1829.

Nordbeck's wife Caroline died in 1832, and in 1833 he married Grace, widow of John Langford, a London goldsmith who had worked in Halifax from 1809 until 1815. Nordbeck took her young son, James I. Langford, as an apprentice until in 1838 Langford set up on his own. Nordbeck also trained several other notable silversmiths, including Michael Septimus Brown*, William Veith, and George Witham.

During the 1820s Nordbeck made some jewellery and a quantity of table silver, varying this work with such excellent pieces as a snuff box, now in the Victoria and Albert Museum in London, England. After 1830 Nordbeck produced many notable examples of church communion silver, chalices, ciboriums, and patens, as well as large presentation goblets, tankards, mugs, and domestic silver. In 1832 he advertised that he had imported from England a patent "fly-press" enabling him "to make 'King's Pattern' plate of every description, also to strike up medals and ornaments of every sort." A wood-engraving shows the device with a large fly-wheel on a threaded shaft which drove the iron moulds down with great force. He may also have used it in producing brooches, lockets, and other pieces of gold and silver jewellery, many still treasured today. Several dated pieces, a magnificent gold and silver chalice with a gold paten for St Peter's Church, Pubnico, N.S., in 1835, and silver goblets presented as trophies for yacht races in 1836 and 1837, give some indication of the progress of his craftsmanship. Nordbeck also made regular

599

crossings to England to select fine goods for import, and his advertisements in the press show the variety of his stock.

On 9 Sept. 1859 fire destroyed his premises along with most of the business district of Halifax. Soon afterwards Nordbeck with other leading merchants commenced rebuilding Granville St, "at a cost and in a style far beyond the requirements of this city," according to Thomas Beamish Akins*. The rows of stone buildings with ingeniously varied fenestration of their Italianate façades comprise one of the few homogeneous blocks of early business buildings remaining in Canada.

Peter Nordbeck only occupied his fine new premises for a short time before his death at age 72. The interior of his store with its ornate gesso ceilings, carved pinewood decorations, and soaring Corinthian columns, remains almost intact over a century after he opened it.

DONALD C. MACKAY

[Examples of Peter Nordbeck's work in silver may be seen in the Provincial Museum of Nova Scotia (Halifax), the Canadiana Gallery of the Royal Ontario Museum (Toronto), the Victoria and Albert Museum (London), and the Henry Birks Collection (Montreal). D.C.M.]

N.S., Provincial Museum and Science Library, *Report* (Halifax), 1934–38. J. E. Langdon, *Canadian silversmiths, 1700–1900* (Toronto, 1966). D. C. Mackay, *Silversmiths and related craftsmen of the Atlantic provinces* (Halifax, 1973). Harry Piers and D. C. Mackay, *Master goldsmiths of Nova Scotia and their marks* (Halifax, 1948). T. B. Akins, "History of Halifax City," N.S. Hist. Soc., *Coll.*, VIII (1895). D. C. Mackay, "Goldsmiths and silversmiths," *Canadian Antiques Collector* (Toronto), 7 (February 1972), 22–26.

NORDHEIMER, ABRAHAM, musician, music dealer, and publisher; b. 24 Feb. 1816 at Memmelsdorf, near Bamberg (Federal Republic of Germany), sixth son of Meier Nordheimer, a cattle dealer, and Esther Nathan; m. Fanny Rosenthal, and they had at least three sons and two daughters; d. 18 Jan. 1862 in Bamberg.

Abraham Nordheimer's family had held property at Memmelsdorf in Bavaria for over a century, but, perhaps because of restrictive laws against Jews, a number of sons immigrated to the United States in the 1830s. Abraham and his brother Samuel* apparently went to New York in 1839 where an older brother Isaac, an Oriental scholar and author of a Hebrew grammar, had settled a few years earlier. It has been related that a Canadian officer met Abraham in New York and induced him to become music teacher to the

family of Sir Charles Bagot*. All that can be ascertained is that Abraham began advertising in the Kingston *Chronicle and Gazette* on 13 July 1842, six months after Bagot's arrival in Kingston, identifying himself clearly as a newcomer and a professor of music from Germany. He "begs to intimate to the inhabitants of this City, that he intends giving lessons on the Piano Forte, Violin and in Singing. Piano Fortes tuned." In November Nordheimer announced that he had opened a store which sold imported printed music and instruments. He is said to have formed and directed a musical society in Kingston; the *Chronicle and Gazette* in March 1844 notes that members of the Kingston Harmonic Society could obtain admission cards to its private concert at his store.

In June 1844 Abraham and Samuel Nordheimer opened a music store in Toronto where they promised to have always "on hand a large and well selected stock of English, French, Italian and German Songs . . . the newest and most popular Operas, Waltzes, Quadrilles . . . an assortment of the celebrated PIANO FORTES," as well as a "select Stock of PATTERNS for Needlework, and Berlin wool to match." The earliest Nordheimer publications were reprints of European music, but almost from the beginning they published Canadian compositions as well. The first plate number was assigned to Joseph Philip Knight's "Beautiful Venice"; a later item featured Canadian composer St George B. Crozier and dates from 1846. By about 1852 100 pieces had been published. Many of the original Canadian pieces were by Toronto musicians, including George William Strathy, Martin Lazare, Jules Hecht, and J. P. Clarke*. The longest work published in Abraham's lifetime was Clarke's *Lays of the maple leaf, or songs of Canada* (1853). The firm undoubtedly produced the largest number of Canadian sheet music publications before confederation and was probably the first to specialize entirely in music. The engraving and the paper of their publications are of a high quality.

The Nordheimer company filled a definite need in a rapidly expanding society. Although the firm did not build its own pianos until late in the century, as early as 1845 it had become the agent for such manufacturers as Stodart and others in New York and Boston. About 1848 a piano and music store was opened in Montreal and before Abraham's death branches were established in Hamilton and London. The Nordheimers also invited famous performers to visit Canada and established Nordheimer's Hall in Montreal.

The roles played by Abraham and Samuel are difficult to distinguish. As the elder brother and the only one whose name is associated with the Kingston years, Abraham must have been the guiding spirit. Abraham is also the only one whose name is recorded as a performer. As well as being a pianist and vocalist, in the 1840s he played the second violin in the Toronto Philharmonic Society, was its instrumental manager, and belonged to its committee. Abraham was an early member of the Toronto Hebrew Congregation (Holy Blossom) and, with Judah G. Joseph*, bought land in 1849 for the Jewish cemetery in Toronto. He was also an original director of the Canada Permanent Building and Savings Society established in 1855. He died on a visit to Germany, survived by his wife and a number of children. Abraham Nordheimer established a trade name that is still perpetuated as a brand name of Heintzman pianos and is the oldest such name in Canadian music.

HELMUT KALLMANN

Central Archives for the History of the Jewish People (Jerusalem), register of births, marriages, and deaths of Memmelsdorf, Bavaria, 1811–75. *Chronicle & Gazette* (Kingston), 13 July 1842, 2 March 1844. *Globe*, 10 Feb. 1862. *Toronto Patriot*, 7 June 1844. *Cyclopaedia of Canadian biog.* (Rose, 1886), 663–65. *1840–1903 . . . the house of Nordheimer . . .* ([Toronto, 1903]). *The Jew in Canada; a complete record of Canadian Jewry from the days of the French régime to the present time*, ed. A. D. Hart (Toronto and Montreal, 1926). B. G. Sack, *History of the Jews in Canada from the earliest beginnings to the present day*, trans. Ralph Novek (Montreal, 1945). D. J. Sale, "Toronto's pre-confederation music societies, 1845–1867" (unpublished MA thesis, University of Toronto, 1968). F. E. Dixon, "Music in Toronto, as it was in the days that are gone by forever," *Mail and Empire* (Toronto), 7 Nov. 1896.

NUTTING, JAMES WALTON, lawyer, editor, and office-holder; b. probably in 1787 at Kempt, Hants County, N.S., the son of John Nutting, a Boston loyalist, and Mary Walton; m. 9 July 1813 Mary Elizabeth MacLean, and they had three sons and two daughters; d. 7 July 1870 at Halifax, N.S.

James Walton Nutting probably obtained his early schooling at King's Collegiate School, Windsor, N.S. From 1804 to 1810 he attended King's College, distinguishing himself academically and graduating BA. In October 1810 he was admitted to the bar, and began work as a notary and tablion public in the office of William Thompson, prothonotary of the Supreme Court and clerk of the crown. In 1811 he replaced Thompson but was not officially appointed to the position until 30 May 1834. He was to hold this office to his death in 1870.

In the 1820s Nutting attended St Paul's Church at Halifax and was one of the socially prominent and well-educated people, including James William Johnston*, who were influenced by two early evangelicals in Halifax, Hibbert Binney Sr and Isaac Temple. This group became dissatisfied with the cold, formal services of the Church of England. When Bishop John Inglis* blocked the group's attempt in 1827 to secure the appointment of one of their number, John Thomas Twining*, to the vacant rectorship at St Paul's, they withdrew from the church. Subsequent endeavours to form an independent Episcopal church failed, and they organized the Granville Street Church (later the First Baptist) on 30 Sept. 1827. Nutting was among the first to be baptized; according to a contemporary he was "one of the first converts in Halifax to earnest religion. . . ."

Thereafter Nutting was prominent in the affairs of the Granville Street Church, whose congregation gave impetus to the Baptist education movement in Nova Scotia. He was one of the representatives of his congregation who attended an important meeting of the Nova Scotia Baptist Association at Upper Horton (Wolfville) on 23 June 1828, where recognition of the necessity for a school for potential Baptist leaders resulted in the organization of the Baptist Education Society. Nutting was appointed to the committee of management, which raised funds, chose Horton as the site of the new academy, secured the services of a teacher, and generally maintained the school for a few years after it opened on 1 May 1829. Similarly, in the 1830s Nutting wrote letters, published editorials, and travelled widely to acquire funds for a seminary of high literary distinction separate from the academy. Finally, after a long struggle, Queen's (Acadia) College opened on 21 Jan. 1839.

Much of Nutting's importance to the Baptist movement lay in his abilities as a newspaper editor. With John Ferguson he edited from 1834 to 1836 the *Baptist Missionary Magazine*, which was expanded in 1837 into a weekly newspaper, the *Christian Messenger*. Nutting and Ferguson made the *Messenger* the chief religious and political mouthpiece for Nova Scotia Baptists. Ferguson died in 1855 and the next year Nutting gave up his editorship and sold the paper, though he contributed articles occasionally after this date. The first years of the *Messenger* had been marked by a financial dispute with Joseph Howe* over a sum of money which Howe alleged was owed to him for printing the paper from 1837 to 1840, and which Nutting and Ferguson declined to pay because the money was owed by the Bap-

O'Beirne

tist Association. A bitter newspaper controversy ensued, and a number of Howe's Baptist supporters consequently bolted Reform ranks and sided with J. W. Johnston's Tory party in the 1843 election. In 1844 Howe denounced the paper as "the mere political engine of two or three intriguing lawyers and professors . . . only read by a section of the religious body to which it ostensibly belongs, and beyond that circle is regarded with well merited contempt."

During his lifetime Nutting was respected for his integrity. Described by a contemporary as "a scholarly, polished, old school gentleman and devout, God-fearing man," Nutting's break with the Church of England apparently did not diminish the esteem in which he was held. The governors of King's College conferred upon him an honorary DCL in 1868. Active in a number of organizations, he was secretary of the governors of King's College for a short period after 1818, governor of Acadia College, and honorary secretary of the Nova Scotia Barristers' Society, and was a subscriber to the Micmac Missionary Society. His main interest, however, was in the Baptist movement and its efforts in education.

WENDY L. THORPE

Acadia University Archives (Wolfville, N.S.), Baptist Education Soc., minutes and letters, 1838–41; reports, 1828–47; Edward Manning correspondence, 1778–1859. Granville Street Baptist Church (Halifax), minutes, 1827–41 (mfm. at PANS). St Paul's Anglican Church (Halifax), register of baptisms, 1749–1875; miscellaneous documents, 1824–63 (mfm. at PANS). *Acadian Recorder*, 9 July 1870. *Christian Messenger* (Halifax), 1837–56, 13 July 1870. W. B. Hamilton, "Education, politics and reform in Nova Scotia, 1800–1848" (unpublished PHD thesis, University of Western Ontario, London, Ont., 1970), 294. R. V. Harris, *The Church of Saint Paul in Halifax, Nova Scotia, 1749–1949* (Toronto, 1949), 164–83. R. S. Longley, *Acadia University, 1838–1938* (Wolfville, N.S., 1939), 13–37. E. M. Saunders, *History of the Baptists of the Maritime provinces* (Halifax, 1902), 180–203, 494–95; *A sketch of the origin and history of the Granville Street Baptist Church* (Halifax, 1877), 4–16. A. E. Coldwell, "History of our denominational press," *Messenger and Visitor* (Saint John, N.B.), 9 Oct. 1895.

O

O'BEIRNE, EUGENE FRANCIS (known as **Mr O'B**), adventurer and schoolmaster; b. *c.* 1809–11 at Newtown Forbes, County Longford (Republic of Ireland), sixth son of John O'Beirne, a farmer, and his wife Claire; d. sometime after 1864.

Eugene Francis O'Beirne was educated at St Patrick's College, Maynooth, County Kildare, about 1826–30, but was expelled before graduation and ordination to the priesthood. In 1834 he enrolled in Trinity College, Dublin, but he gave much time to two pamphlets attacking St Patrick's. Then from 1836 to 1839 he toured England giving anti-Catholic lectures and again attacking his old college. In 1842 he was admitted to St John's College, Cambridge, and the next year transferred to Clare College. He did not take a degree. After these years his career until he arrived in Canada is obscure, and the details he gave later to Viscount Milton [Wentworth-Fitzwilliam*] and Walter Butler Cheadle* have not been confirmed or refuted. It is certain that he arrived in Louisiana in the late 1850s, moved north after the outbreak of the Civil War, and unsuccessfully sought ordination in Minnesota in 1861 in the Episcopal Church, or a teaching position. In September of that year he arrived in the Red River Settlement with vague plans for starting a private school. Joseph James Hargrave* provides a lengthy account of him here.

In 1862 O'Beirne joined one of the parties of the "Overlanders" on their way to the Cariboo gold-fields [*see* Thomas MCMICKING]. His querulous disposition, insobriety, and abuse of hospitality by then were well known, and were experienced anew by the "Overlanders," who refused to take him beyond Fort Carleton. The Hudson's Bay Company gave him transport farther west, and he spent the winter of 1862–63 with the pioneer Methodist missionaries Thomas Woolsey and John Chantler McDougall* in the North Saskatchewan valley east of Edmonton. McDougall brought O'Beirne to Fort Edmonton in March 1863.

When Viscount Milton and Dr Cheadle, two venturesome young English travellers on their way overland to the Pacific, arrived at Edmonton in May 1863, O'Beirne was living in a miner's shack on the riverbank. He importuned them to take him across the mountains, which, against their better judgement, they agreed to do. The party, with horses and native guides, left Fort Edmonton in early June 1863, traversing heavily forested and swampy country, and crossing countless hazardous streams in the mountains. They arrived at Kamloops three months later, ragged and half-starved. O'Beirne had proved to be a helpless, quarrelsome, and uncooperative companion, although possibly his behaviour can be partially explained by the defects of his character and physique, and the fact that he was twice the age of his two hosts.

At Kamloops, Milton and Cheadle gave him supplies and arranged for him to proceed alone to Victoria. They subsequently reported in a later edition of their book, *The north-west passage by land* (first published in 1865), that O'Beirne had reached Victoria, and that he had gone on to San Francisco, where he boarded a ship to Melbourne, Australia, arriving there in January 1864. He embarked on a career as a tutor, according to Australians who later reported his peripatetic activities to Milton and Cheadle. At this point he disappears from history, and no record of his death exists in official records in Australia. The Canadian government immortalized him in 1918 by giving his name to a peak in the Yellowhead Pass.

So curious a character led some readers of *The north-west passage by land* to believe that "Mr. O'B" had been invented by the authors to add comic relief to their narrative. But he was in truth a real person, whom the tolerant young authors described somewhat more charitably than did Joseph James Hargrave and John Chantler McDougall.

Lewis H. Thomas

[For details on Eugene Francis O'Beirne's parentage, education, and career to 1861 *see* PAC, Tweed papers (MG 30, D159), which include a copy of Thomas Tweed, "Eugene Francis O'Beirne," an unpublished paper read at the annual meeting of the Canadian Hist. Assoc. in 1968. l.h.t]

E. F. O'Beirne, *An impartial view of the internal economy and discipline at Maynooth College* . . . (1st and 2nd ed., Dublin, 1835). W. B. Cheadle, *Cheadle's journal of trip across Canada, 1862 1863*, ed. Λ. G. Doughty and Gustave Lanctot (Ottawa, 1931; repr. Edmonton, 1971). J. J. Hargrave, *Red River* (Montreal, 1871), 199–201, 216–19, 221–29. [William Wentworth-Fitzwilliam] Viscount Milton and W. B. Cheadle, *The north-west passage by land; being the narrative of an expedition from the Atlantic to the Pacific . . . by one of the northern passes in the Rocky Mountains* (8th ed., London, 1875). J. [C.] McDougall, *Forest, lake and prairie; twenty years of frontier life in western Canada, 1842–62* (Toronto, 1895), 250–51; *Saddle, sled and snowshoe; pioneering on the Saskatchewan in the sixties* (Toronto, 1896), 17–18, 43–50. M. S. Wade, *The overlanders of '62*, ed. John Hosie (Victoria, 1931), 49–50.

O'BRIEN, DENNIS, pedlar and merchant; b. 1792 at Fermoy, County Cork (Republic of Ireland); d. 16 May 1865 in Westminster Township near London, Canada West.

Dennis O'Brien emigrated to the United States in 1811 and lived for a time in Maine. He moved to Upper Canada in 1820 and as a foot pedlar sold hardware and tinware for a few years in the western peninsula. With the establishment of London as a district administrative centre in 1826, O'Brien settled there and became London's first general merchant, obtaining his goods from Niagara. He was to be remembered as the first merchant in the area to reduce the prices of his goods to a level deemed a reasonable exchange for farmers' produce, in opposition to other merchants, most notably George Jervis Goodhue.

Typical of pioneer merchants, O'Brien soon branched out into related enterprises. He purchased a grist mill from Robert and Thomas Parke in December 1835, and he later operated a distillery in Westminster Township and engaged in land speculation. Pedlars in the western peninsula came to his store for their goods, and O'Brien was said to have controlled at one time a chain of general stores in such towns as Exeter, Goderich, Chatham, and Sarnia. In addition, he was one of the incorporators in 1834 of the London and Gore Railroad. He married Jane Shotwell of Delaware Township on 22 July 1834; they were to have at least three sons and two daughters.

In 1836–37 O'Brien erected the first brick business block, and the third brick structure, in London facing the court house square. As well as housing his own and other businesses, it served as the temporary barracks of the British garrison stationed in the town after the rebellions of 1837–38. O'Brien had the structure remodelled into London's largest hotel, the Western Hotel, after the great fire of 1845 which consumed his frame residence and former business establishment. He then left London to live on the Westminster side of the Thames. There is no evidence that he continued operating a general store after 1845.

O'Brien appears to have retired from business several times over the years, and often faced legal suits brought against him by creditors while losing thousands of pounds through not pursuing debtors – "his goodness of heart . . . [not allowing] him to oppress anyone in order to secure an honest debt. . . ." Despite his earlier adversities and the depression of 1857, O'Brien was said to have "lived through and surmounted his financial difficulties, and . . . was able to leave a very fair competency to his family. . . ."

O'Brien was active in the community as a prominent member of the Irish Benevolent Soci-

O'Brien

ety and was noted for his works of charity. When London was constituted a police village in 1840 he became the first councillor from St Patrick's ward. In politics he was described as "a Conservative or a Moderate Reformer."

Throughout his life he was noted for his uncompromising support of the Roman Catholic Church. At a time when a priest visited the London area only a few times a year, his house and store were "always open for the clergy and for all church purposes free of charge." He was one of the men instrumental in persuading Bishop Alexander Macdonell* to send a resident priest, Laurence Dempsey, to the St Thomas–London area, and by 1831 was London's agent for W. P. MacDonald*'s *Catholic*, Upper Canada's first Catholic newspaper, published at Kingston. At least one of his children was sent to be educated at the Academy of the Sacred Heart at Detroit, Mich. O'Brien's funeral marked one of the rare occasions in which a eulogy was preached in the Catholic church.

DANIEL J. BROCK

City of London Registry Office (London, Ont.), Abstract index, books 1, 2; instruments 2769 (1835), 2771 (1835). PAC, RG 31, 1851 census, Westminster Township, district 1. PAO, Macdonell (Alexander) papers, box 4, vol.6. St Peter's Cemetery (London, Ont.), records. UWO, 229 (Dennis O'Brien papers). *Canadian Free Press* (London, [Ont.]), 19 May 1865. *London Evening Advertiser*, 17 May 1865. *London Free Press*, 3 June 1865. *Upper Canada Times and London District Gazette* (London, [Ont.]), 5 March 1836. [Archie Bremner], *City of London, Ontario, Canada; the pioneer period and the London of to-day* (2nd ed., London, 1900), 46–47, 69, 94, 96. *History of the county of Middlesex* (Brock), 215–17, 220–21, 231, 311, 368–69, 838–39. C. T. Campbell, "The settlement of London," London and Middlesex Hist. Soc., *Trans.* (London, Ont.), III (1911), 10.

O'BRIEN, LAURENCE, merchant, banker, politician, and office-holder; b. 1792 in Clashmore, County Waterford (Republic of Ireland); m. in 1853 Margaret Manning of St John's, Nfld; d. 28 April 1870 near St John's.

Laurence O'Brien probably left Ireland for Newfoundland some time between 1808 and 1810. During these years the war-time prosperity of the Newfoundland fishery was attracting young men and women from southern Ireland and southwestern England. O'Brien may have come to Newfoundland as a mechanic, possibly as an apprentice, although the *Newfoundland Mercantile Journal* of 1819 lists a Laurence O'Brien as a publican. At the time of O'Brien's death an associate commented that he had risen from the lowest levels of society.

By the mid 1820s Laurence O'Brien and Company was engaged in the wholesale and retail trade in St John's, locally known as "dealing." As a dealer in this period, O'Brien would import various goods to sell in the St John's area for cash or credit. It was customary for dealers to advance goods to fishermen during the fishing season for a return from their catch of cod in the fall, and also to contract for dried cod to be sent abroad in their own ships or sold to larger suppliers. Moreover, an enterprising dealer might purchase and sell vessels for the export trade and the seal fishery. By the 1840s O'Brien owned between four and eight ships himself.

Eventually, O'Brien, through his extensive wholesale-retail trade, was importing coal from Sydney, N.S., vegetables from Prince Edward Island, lumber from the Miramichi in New Brunswick, molasses from Barbados, fishery salt from Cadiz, Spain, and manufactured goods from England. His establishment on Water Street grew to consist of a wharf, warehouses, and a retail store, with flakes for drying codfish on some of the roofs. In 1833 and again in 1846 O'Brien's premises were destroyed by fire, but he soon rebuilt. In the codfish trade O'Brien's involvement was small in comparison with such large merchants as Charles Fox Bennett*. O'Brien shipped cod abroad in his own ships or in foreign vessels to Brazil, Naples (Italy), Havana (Cuba), Leghorn (Italy), and Veracruz (Mexico); he also shipped pickled cod to the United States.

By 1850 O'Brien's commercial success was based especially on sealing, in which he had been engaged at least since 1837. The smaller investment necessary for sealing as compared with the inshore, Labrador, or Grand Bank fisheries allowed the two medium-sized mercantile firms of O'Brien and James Tobin* to contribute 15 to 20 per cent of the annual sealing fleet in the 1840s, the golden age of Newfoundland sealing. However, O'Brien's prominence did not survive the disastrous seal fishery of 1848 which reduced his fleet the next year to half its usual size. Smaller firms like O'Brien's did not have the financial resources to rebound from their losses as well as large establishments like Bowring Brothers or Job Brothers and Company.

Among O'Brien's other commercial activities was the formation of the Bank of Newfoundland in 1844. The leading merchants of St John's were displeased with the restrictive lending policy of Newfoundland's only bank, a branch of the Bank of British North America. The shares in the new bank were subscribed, its charter passed by the assembly, and the bank ready to commence business when the older bank's directors appear to have taken action to mollify the merchants; the Bank of Newfoundland was, therefore, wound up before it began. O'Brien was also a leading figure in the promotion of the Union Bank, a locally controlled commercial bank which opened in 1854. Similarly O'Brien was a member of the boards of directors of the Equitable Fire Insurance Company of London, the Standard Life Assurance Company, the Newfoundland Marine Insurance Company, and the Newfoundland Steam Tug Boat Company.

One of O'Brien's enduring interests was agriculture which he pursued on his estate, Rostellan, on the outskirts of St John's. He seems to have been particularly interested in grains, some of which he displayed in an exhibition in London in 1862. He served as president and member of the board of management of the Agricultural Society in St John's for many years.

Despite his humble origins in the Roman Catholic community, O'Brien's growing affluence in the 1830s and 1840s had thrust him into contact with the mainly Protestant mercantile community, and his name appeared with increasing frequency as a member of committees formed to undertake such public projects as cholera prevention. Yet O'Brien's position within the Irish Roman Catholic community was also important. Between 1838 and 1857 he was 11 times president of the Benevolent Irish Society, a quasi-charitable, quasi-political organization, and after 1859 was vice-patron of the society.

O'Brien's prominence in the St John's community brought him into the colony's politics. Like other Irish Roman Catholics O'Brien had supported the movement for representative government in Newfoundland. He had been one of 67 prominent supporters of the creation of a local legislature who had signed a public notice calling a meeting in September 1831 to discuss the slow progress of the local legislature bill through committee in the British House of Commons. O'Brien played a leading role in the meeting which drew up resolutions to be forwarded to the House of Commons [see BROOKING; ROCHFORT].

In 1840, when Patrick Morris*, one of the Reform leaders of the representative government movement, accepted a seat on the Council, a St John's assembly seat became vacant. O'Brien had at first joined in supporting James Douglas as the Reform candidate; but, whether motivated by personal ambition or by pressure from Bishop Michael Anthony Fleming*, O'Brien changed his mind and ran himself. With only the two Liberal candidates in the field, most of the merchants supported the Protestant Douglas, while John

Kent* and the Roman Catholic clergy of St John's backed O'Brien. O'Brien won by only eight votes out of 3,000 cast in a heated and violent election.

The legislature which O'Brien entered in 1841 was a battleground between the elected assembly and the appointed Council. Important legislation was in suspension since the Council had been using its power to amend or veto bills sent up from the assembly in order to frustrate the operation of the representative government the councillors disliked. Indeed in 1841 they refused to pass 19 bills, especially the electoral and supply bills. That year O'Brien was one of four delegates sent by the assembly to London to put its case against the Council to the British colonial secretary, Lord John Russell. As a result of a British parliamentary inquiry, the two bodies were amalgamated in 1842 into a single chamber with 15 elected and ten appointed members. The structure of the new legislature gave governor Sir John Harvey* control of its proceedings by use of a combination of appointed office-holders, particularly the speaker, James CROWDY, and elected Conservative merchants. This control was bitterly denounced by O'Brien and other Reform members, and in 1843 Governor Harvey appointed O'Brien to the Executive Council as a conciliatory gesture to the Reformers.

Although he attended the sessions of the legislature regularly, O'Brien did not take a major role in its proceedings, leaving the Reform leadership to Morris, Kent, and William Carson*. True to his mercantile background he supported increased duties to protect Newfoundland manufacturers. But unlike his Protestant colleagues he insisted on the rights of Roman Catholics to fairer representation and to more government jobs.

With the expiration of the trial period for the amalgamated legislature in 1848, Newfoundland returned to the old system of an assembly and an appointed Legislative Council. O'Brien was re-elected for St John's in that year. However, in 1850 he resigned from the assembly to accept an appointment to the Legislative Council to fill the vacancy left by the death of Patrick Morris the previous year.

O'Brien's new position in the council and his stature in the commercial world of St John's allowed him to play a unique role among his associates in the period leading to the introduction of responsible government in 1855. In a special meeting of the Commercial Society of St John's on 16 Feb. 1852, O'Brien was the only prominent merchant who refused to support a resolution proposed by C. F. Bennett and Thomas Row condemning responsible government as likely to lead to control of the executive by the Roman Catholic bishop, John Thomas MULLOCK, not by the assembly. In March of the same year O'Brien was the only dissenting voice from a council resolution opposing responsible government. He criticized the existing arrangement of representative government as defective, defended Newfoundlanders' right to responsible government, which had been granted in the neighbouring colonies, and demanded that Roman Catholics and Wesleyan Methodists be given their fair share of government patronage. With the institution of responsible government in 1855 O'Brien received his reward and was appointed president of both the Legislative and the Executive councils created under the new system. He was consequently administrator of the colony in 1863 before the arrival of Governor Sir Anthony Musgrave*.

The first two administrations of the new era were created from the Liberal party and were headed by Philip Francis Little* and John Kent. O'Brien was a member without portfolio while retaining his position as president of the Legislative Council. He apparently had little involvement in the formation of Liberal policy, but continued to defend his party in the mercantile community. With the dismissal of the Kent government by Lieutenant Governor Sir Alexander BANNERMAN in 1861, the Conservative leader, Hugh William Hoyles*, attempted to draw Liberal Roman Catholics into his new government. Only O'Brien accepted his proposal, and remained in the Hoyles administration through the contested elections and riots of 1861 [see Mullock] and all the bitterness of the succeeding decade. In 1866 Frederic Bowker Terrington Carter* formed a coalition administration made up of three members from the Hoyles government including O'Brien, and four Liberals, including Kent and Ambrose Shea*. O'Brien was still a member when he died in 1870.

In his progress from poor immigrant to affluent merchant, Laurence O'Brien adopted the hardfisted methods of other merchants, whether English or Irish, Protestant or Roman Catholic. Robert John Parsons*, writing in the *Patriot* at the time of the by-election of 1840, referred to O'Brien as a "hard-dealer" whose only qualification for election was to be "found in his iron chest wrung from the fishermen and mechanics of Newfoundland." O'Brien did not forget this aspersion cast on his motives; in 1849 he brought forth a petition from some of Parsons' constituents in St John's insinuating, wrongly it appears, that Parsons had misused funds he had received after the great fire of 1846. As his com-

mercial interests prospered, O'Brien came to have less in common with his Reform colleagues and moved closer to his Protestant mercantile associates in the Chamber of Commerce and the Legislative Council. Yet his interests in agriculture could have been part of an attempt to establish himself as a gentleman-farmer, rather than retiring to the British Isles as a large number of his Protestant colleagues would do. O'Brien was one of the earliest of Newfoundland mercantile and political figures to consider himself a Newfoundlander, not an Englishman or Irishman temporarily transplanted to Newfoundland.

DAVID J. DAVIS

Church of St John the Baptist (Roman Catholic) (St John's), marriage register, 1853. MTCL, R. H. Shepherd, "Three months in Newfoundland" (handwritten on blank pages at end of [Henry Winton], *A chapter in the history of Newfoundland for the year 1861* (St John's, 1861)). PANL, GN 1/1, 10 June 1840, 16 March 1843. R. B. McCrea, *Lost amid the fogs: sketches of life in Newfoundland, England's ancient colony* (London, 1869). Nfld., *Blue book*, 1845–57; House of Assembly, *Journal*, 1851, app., "Evidence taken before the select committee on the St. John's Hospital", 194–95. *Newfoundlander*, 1827–52, 1870. *Newfoundland Mercantile Journal* (St John's), 1819, 1826. *Patriot* (St John's), 1840, 1849–50. *Public Ledger*, 1827, 1870. *Royal Gazette* (St John's), 1840–53. *Times and General Commercial Gazette* (St John's), 1850, 1867. *Centenary volume, Benevolent Irish Society of St. John's, Newfoundland, 1806–1906* (Cork, Ire., [1906?]), 1–100. Garfield Fizzard, "The amalgamated assembly of Newfoundland, 1841–1847" (unpublished MA thesis, Memorial University of Newfoundland, St John's, 1963), 21–109. Greene, "Influence of religion in the politics of Nfld., 1850–61." Gunn, *Political history of Nfld.*, 66–159. Prowse, *History of Nfld.* (1895), 458–60.

O'BRIEN, LUCIUS JAMES, physician, editor, and civil servant; b. 26 July 1797 at Woolwich, England, eldest son of Captain Lucius O'Brien of the Royal Artillery and Mary Callender-Campbell; d. 14 Aug. 1870 at Ottawa, Ont.

Raised at Cork, Ireland, where his father was employed as a paymaster of the Ordnance Department, Lucius James O'Brien began the study of medicine at the University of Edinburgh in 1812. He received his MD in 1819; his thesis, entitled "De amaurosi," dealt with the loss of sight without visible cause. He had meanwhile joined the Royal College of Surgeons of London in 1817 and the Royal Medical Society of Edinburgh in 1818. O'Brien interned at the Royal Infirmary, Edinburgh, where he made a life-long friend, Sir Robert Christison, later professor of materia medica at Edinburgh. Christison once helped O'Brien disentangle himself from two duels after a student drinking party.

After graduation O'Brien established a practice at Cork. He married Rosalie Roche in 1822, and soon afterwards, for financial reasons, went to Jamaica as the assistant surgeon, later surgeon, of the Kingston Regiment. He also established a private practice in Kingston. William Canniff* has written of O'Brien's heroism during Sharpe's slave rebellion in 1831–32 but the story cannot be substantiated. O'Brien's wife died in 1825, and in 1830 he married Elizabeth Lindo (1801–94) of Constant Spring; there were several children by his two marriages.

In 1832 he decided to join his brother Edward George* in Upper Canada and settled at York (Toronto). He was licensed to practise in September. In 1833 he moved to Thornhill where he "soon had a large, if not very remunerative practice." While at Thornhill he helped, ironically, to establish a temperance society and he was appointed a magistrate of the Home District in 1837. He also became a member of the Upper Canada Medical Board; when it was replaced by the short-lived College of Physicians and Surgeons from 1839 to 1841, he acted as secretary and registrar.

Meanwhile, the rebellion of 1837 had brought O'Brien back to Toronto as a military surgeon. He again attempted to establish a practice in that city, was unsuccessful, and moved west to Beachville in Oxford County. By this time he was in serious financial difficulties brought on by drinking, but in July 1845 he wrote Edward stating: "I have in truth forsworn the baneful cause and for eighteen months been strictly a teetotaller, knowing that no half measures will avail. . . ." Lucius had also been trying for a chair at the university in Toronto since 1839 and in September 1845, the year after the medical faculty was formed, he was rescued from his difficulties by his appointment as professor of medical jurisprudence, a post he held until the faculty was abolished in 1853. He was a member of the board of trustees of the Toronto General Hospital (1847), a vice-president of the Upper Canada Bible Society (1840–53), a member of the editorial board of the *Upper Canada Journal of Medical, Surgical, and Physical Science* (1851–54), and was active in the Toronto Medico-Chirurgical Society.

O'Brien also became editor of the *Toronto Patriot*, which Edward purchased in 1848, until he disagreed with his brother over content and retired. Samuel Thompson*, who was the manager, described him as a "highly educated and talented, but not popular, writer." There

seems to be no basis for Canniff's statement that Lucius edited other papers.

By the mid 1850s, with both editorship and professorship gone, his practice unremunerative and his money, as Nicholas Flood Davin* asserts, lost through injudicious speculations, O'Brien was again in trouble. He was saved by the patronage of Inspector General William Cayley*, who obtained a secretaryship for him in his office in 1856. From that post he transferred to the Customs Branch in 1857, moved to Ottawa with the government in 1865, and at confederation was placed in charge of the books of the Excise Division, a post he held until his death.

Christison summed up his career: "O'Brien had his good parts, was a diligent prominent student, and in the hospital an acute observer and sound practitioner. Strange! sadly Strange! that the life of such a man should prove a failure." Though he was an affable person, a lively conversationalist, and a man of considerable ability, O'Brien's intemperance would appear to have frustrated his varied attempts to establish a successful career.

FREDERICK H. ARMSTRONG

L. J. O'Brien was the author of "On syncope, asphyxia and asthenia" and "On the non-contagious nature of scarlatina" in *Upper Canada Journal of Medical, Surgical, and Physical Science* (Toronto), I (1851–52), 7–10, and II (1852–53), 121–25, respectively.

MTCL, William Allan papers, City of Toronto and Lake Huron Railroad Company papers, 29 July 1846. PAC, RG 16, A4, 15, p.1. PAO, Toronto City Council papers, 21 Aug. 1847. [Robert Christison], *The life of Sir Robert Christison, bart.* (2v., Edinburgh, 1885–86), I, 113, 122–24; II, 289–94. *Documentary history of education in U.C.* (Hodgins), X, 208–20. [M. S. Gapper (O'Brien)], *The journals of Mary O'Brien, 1828–1838*, ed. A. S. Miller (Toronto, 1968), xvi, 172, 190, 205. Samuel Thompson, *Reminiscences of a Canadian pioneer for the last fifty years; an autobiography* (Toronto, 1884), 189. U.C., House of Assembly, *Journal*, 1839–40, I, app., "Minutes of the council of King's College for the year 1839," 379–81, 385. *Ottawa Citizen*, 12 May 1891. *Ottawa Times*, 15 Aug. 1870. Chadwick, *Ontarian families. The roll of pupils of Upper Canada College, Toronto, January, 1830, to June, 1916*, ed. A. H. Young (Kingston, Ont., 1917). Wallace, *Macmillan dictionary*, 556. Canniff, *Medical profession in U.C.* Davin, *Irishman in Can.* Heagerty, *Four centuries of medical history in Can.* Donough O'Brien, *History of the O'Briens from Brian Boroimhe, AD. 1000 to AD. 1945* (London, 1949), 217–18.

ODIN, HENRIETTE (Feller), founder of the French Canadian Protestant mission at Grande-Ligne, Lower Canada; b. 22 April 1800 at Montagny, canton of Vaud, Switzerland; d. 29 March 1868 at Grande-Ligne, Que.

Odin

In 1803 Henriette Odin moved with her parents to Lausanne, where her father had been appointed director of the canton's hospital and was later to be administrator of a penitentiary. In this environment she acquired some medical knowledge that would be helpful in her apostolate in Canada.

The visit of a Scot, Robert Haldane, to Geneva in 1816–17 brought about a "religious revival" there that led his adherents to break from the official Protestant church, which they accused of a rationalist interpretation of the Scriptures and erroneous teachings on grace, predestination, and christology. The dissidents were persecuted under a law passed in 1824 that made them liable to a punishment as severe as exile. Two years earlier, in 1822, Henriette Odin had married Louis Feller, a 41-year-old widower and father of three children of whom the eldest was 14. Feller, the director of the Lausanne police, was responsible for applying the law; although his wife did not subscribe at that time to the dissidents' credo, she could not tolerate their being hunted down, and in connivance with her husband did everything she could to protect them.

Little by little, her sympathy for them was transformed into an ardent faith, characterized by mystical impulses which her associates attributed to a morbid imagination, and indeed even to a neurosis resulting from the successive deaths, between 1822 and 1827, of her daughter (born the year of her marriage), husband, sister, and mother. She herself, stricken with typhoid fever, had to take a rest cure in the Jura. There she became convinced from reading the Bible that baptism could be administered only to believers, and on her return to Lausanne she was rebaptized by sprinkling, which was contrary to custom.

In 1828, about a year after Mme Feller had left the official church, the legal restrictions against dissidents were temporarily lifted. This gave the revival movement in Switzerland free rein for its initiatives. Theological discussions were revived; abundant and varied literature was disseminated; renewed efforts to proselytize were made through the founding of several biblical and missionary societies; controversy with Catholics was resumed; and new methods of spreading the gospel were introduced including colportage, preaching by itinerant pastors, and prayer meetings improvised in the most diverse places. These were not the only activities of the revival movement but through them it prospered and spread through Switzerland and France. Moreover several missionaries were sent to French Canada.

Mme Feller engaged herself in the Société des Missions Évangéliques de Lausanne which was founded in 1828. On the advice of the London Bible Society, this society sent to the Indians of Lower Canada Isaac Cloux, the missionary institute's first student, who finished his training somewhat hastily. Cloux found the work too difficult and returned to Switzerland in 1832, after little more than a year's absence. The evangelization of pagans was the sole objective of this society. It had categorically rejected the earnest request of some English residents of Montreal that it should devote itself to evangelizing French Canadians. For this reason when Henri Olivier, pastor of the dissident church at Lausanne, left for Canada in 1834, he had to sever his connections with the society since he had decided to work at Montreal rather than in the Indian territories. Mme Feller corresponded regularly with Mme Olivier, with whom she had been friendly at Lausanne. This exchange no doubt strengthened her intention to devote herself to the Canadian missions: in August 1835 she in turn left for Canada, accompanied by Louis Roussy*, who earlier had been a student at the missionary institute.

The experience of these missionaries among a people whom they at first described as "ignorant and superstitious" proved extremely painful. Olivier and his wife left the country after 15 months of work. Mme Feller and Roussy persisted, but at the cost of great frustrations. During the first year they had to abandon three schools which the Catholic clergy denounced. Colportage became increasingly difficult: the doors of houses were closed against them and they were sometimes ill treated. Unable to settle in towns and villages where the clergy exercised strict surveillance, they decided to withdraw to newly settled areas, where the clergy went infrequently and where the absence of public services inevitably encouraged good relations between neighbours.

This was the situation at Grande-Ligne, some ten miles south of Saint-Jean, when Mme Feller took up residence there in September 1836. The absence of a school and a doctor gave the missionaries their first means of spreading the gospel. They won the confidence of a number of families, so that at the time of the 1837 rebellion the little Protestant community numbered 16 converts and about ten sympathizers. However, with the revolutionary disturbances they were subjected increasingly to persecution. The Patriotes accused them of being supported by their English foes, and of not taking part in the movement. Then finally, in November, after a series of "charivaris" in front of Protestant homes, Mme

Feller and the converts, fearing the worst, fled to the United States.

The 1837 rebellion, nevertheless, marked a stage in the advance of Protestantism. The English and Swiss evangelists of Lower Canada saw it as an opportunity to overcome the influence of the clergy, the greatest obstacle to the conversion of French Canadians. At the time of the exodus Mme Feller already noted: "One of the fortunate repercussions of this war is that it has broken the priests' yoke; they have exerted no influence on the rebels, whom they tried to hold back by threats of excommunication; but nobody has taken any notice of them." Louis Roussy made the same kind of statement in Swiss, English, and American papers: "And it is not only at Grande-Ligne, it is in the region generally that the influence of the priest is diminishing." Mme Feller sounded the watchword: "The time is come, Canada is open."

The pathetic newspaper description of their exodus set in motion a wave of generosity in the United States and Switzerland. Thus when she returned to Grande-Ligne, Mme Feller was able to distribute supplies, seed for planting, and medicines to some 50 persons. She also suspended legal action against those who had pillaged the converts' dwellings, and went to Napierville to intercede on behalf of neighbouring inhabitants with Richard MacGinnis, who had been deputed by the government to receive statements and examine the accused. She could then write: "In general, the feeling of the people towards us has changed so much that I believe there is no house at Grande-Ligne which I cannot now enter." The task of spreading the faith was accomplished at Grande-Ligne through the free school, colportage, and preaching; like the Catholic clergy of the time, Mme Feller also became involved in charitable works.

The success of the Swiss missionaries in spreading the Protestant gospel, the hopes aroused by the anticlericalism of the insurrectionary period, and the desire for a measure of political security, prompted the English pastors and laymen of various religious denominations in Montreal to found a new society, the French Canadian Missionary Society. According to the constitution formulated after the founding meeting, in February 1839, its objectives were exactly those pursued at Grande-Ligne: to convert French Canadians to Protestantism without linking them to a precise denomination. How then is one to account for Mme Feller's refusal of the invitation to join the Montreal society? There is no easy explanation; at first sight a divergence of views about the age required for receiving bap-

tism seems to have motivated this refusal. But it is more probable that she was first and foremost jealous of her own independence and anxious to preserve her almost absolute authority at Grande-Ligne. Despite a clear affinity of belief with the Baptists of Montreal, she preferred affiliation with the distant Foreign Evangelical Society of New York, and then, after 1845, with a number of Baptist societies in Canada and the United States. Indeed from the beginning she declared an intention to remain free to refuse any affiliation.

Henriette Feller personally made eight fund-raising trips to the United States. As she spoke English badly, she took an interpreter who introduced her to the different religious associations, particularly the women's associations which she had helped to establish. While travelling, she continued to take an interest in administrative matters at the Grande-Ligne school and mission, and insisted that Roussy or his substitute report to her every two or three days. However, her graciousness, devotion, accessibility, and abounding affection for students in particular caused this authoritarianism to be forgotten. In her correspondence with them she asked the students to call her "mother," and signed herself "your affectionate mother, Henriette Feller."

Her health was a constant source of anxiety for her close associates. Illness frequently kept her bed-ridden. In 1855 an attack of pneumonia, from which she never fully recovered, forced her to rest for seven months in the southern United States. A trip to Switzerland in 1860–61 brought no improvement. She was stricken with paralysis in 1865, and until her death on 29 March 1868 was compelled to direct the mission from her room, which she could leave only with difficulty.

That year, the society begun at Grande-Ligne numbered in the Province of Quebec about 400 members, and possessed nine churches; at least seven pastors worked in these churches, not including the evangelists and colporteurs. The school at Grande-Ligne taught 34 students, and a larger number of students received primary instruction in various other localities. In short, Mme Feller's 32 years of missionary work in Canada yielded significant results; they were, however, diminished by steady emigration to the United States, which proved more attractive to a group of converts who had been banished from French Canadian society and recruited primarily from the working class.

To judge the results of her work by these figures alone would not do justice to Henriette Feller. She succeeded in setting up the first Francophone Protestant community in the province of

Ogden

Quebec, and inspired the work of several other reformed religious denominations which, around 1860, shared in trying to serve a small number of persons whom it was difficult to evangelize. Finally it should be noted that she managed to secure the collaboration of educated, influential French Canadians, among them the Patriote Dr Cyrille-Hector-Octave Côté*, and the defrocked priests Louis Normandeau* and Hubert-Joseph Tétreau*; she also obtained an education in Switzerland for a number of talented students who later played an important role in the mission, including Narcisse Cyr*, publisher and editor of the *Semeur canadien*, and the Reverend Théodore Lafleur*, a prominent member of the Institut Canadien of Montreal, director of the Protestant school at Longueuil, and an influential minister at the Grande-Ligne mission.

The memory of the founder is alive even today among the adherents of the ten or so Protestant churches that owe their existence to Henriette Feller.

RENÉ HARDY

Evangelical Soc. of La Grande Ligne, *Register* (Grande Ligne, Que.), March 1866. French Canadian Missionary Soc., *Report* (Montreal), 1842–60. *A memoir of Madame Feller; with an account of the origin and progress of the Grande Ligne Mission*, trans. and ed. J. M. Cramp (London, [1876]). Soc. des missions évangéliques de Lausanne, *Rapport* (Lausanne, Suisse), 1830–50. R.-P. Duclos, *Histoire du protestantisme français au Canada et aux États-Unis* (2v., Montréal, [1913]). Henri Fines, *Album du protestantisme français en Amérique du Nord* (Montréal, 1972). Théodore Lafleur, *A semi-centennial, historical sketch of the Grande Ligne Mission, read at the Jubilee gathering, Grande Ligne, Oct. 18th, 1885* (Montreal, [1886]). Léon Maury, *Le réveil religieux dans l'Église réformée à Genève et en France (1810–1850), étude historique et dogmatique* (2v., Paris, 1892). Daniel Robert, *Les églises réformées en France, 1800–1830* (Paris, 1961). E.-A. Therrien et al., *Baptist work in French Canada* (Montreal, 1954). Paul Villard, *Up to the light; the story of French Protestantism in Canada* (Toronto, 1928). W. N. Wyeth, *Henrietta Feller and the Grande Ligne Mission, a memorial* (Philadelphia, 1898). *Feuille religieuse du canton de Vaud* (Lausanne, Suisse), 1830–1860.

OGDEN, CHARLES RICHARD, lawyer, politician, and public servant; b. 6 Feb. 1791 in Quebec City, one of 11 sons of Isaac Ogden*, loyalist and puisne judge of the Court of King's Bench at Montreal, and Sarah Hanson; m. first, at Walcot, Somerset, England, in July 1824, Mary Aston, daughter of General John Coffin*, and they had two children, both of whom died at an early age; m. secondly, at Montreal in August 1829, Susan,

daughter of Isaac Winslow Clarke, deputy commissary general at Montreal, and they had four sons and a daughter; d. 19 Feb. 1866 at Edge-hill, near Liverpool, England.

Charles Ogden received his earliest education at the school of the Reverend John Doty* in Trois-Rivières, thereby establishing, apparently, his initial contact with that town. He completed his education in Montreal under the noted schoolmaster Alexander Skakel*. Upon being called to the bar on 21 Feb 1812, Ogden established his practice at Trois-Rivières but in a few years returned to Montreal where he formed a widely respected and lucrative law partnership with Alexander Buchanan*. During the War of 1812 he served an undistinguished term as lieutenant with the 1st battalion, then with the 8th, of the militia division at Trois-Rivières.

In May 1814 Ogden commenced a political career with his election to the House of Assembly for Trois-Rivières. Although a Tory, he represented this largely French Canadian constituency almost uninterruptedly for the next 19 years, by means of the tight control over local politics wielded by his supporters among the merchants, combined with the force of his own personality. His only electoral defeat occurred in 1824 while he was absent in England; he easily regained the seat in the contest of 1826.

A man from a prominent family, a successful lawyer and politician, Ogden early attracted official favour: an appointment as KC in 1816, as attorney general for the district of Trois-Rivières in 1818, and six years later, at the urging of Governor Dalhousie [Ramsay*], as solicitor general of Lower Canada. During the 1820s, when government candidates were virtually swept from the assembly, Ogden remained, representing, as one historian has claimed, "the advance guard of the Montreal party," a group which was anathema to the Patriotes.

In 1833 he was appointed attorney general for Lower Canada, and consequently resigned from the legislature in response to the Colonial Office's request that public officers maintain "a cautious abstinence" from politics. Yet, in the aftermath of the rebellions of 1837–38, Ogden's participation in events, as an intimate adviser to the hated Governor Sir John COLBORNE, as chief prosecutor of the arrested "rebels," as a member, after 1840, of the Special Council, and as provider of an official countersignature, in February 1841, to the proclamation of the union of Upper and Lower Canada, deepened the hostility with which he was regarded by French Canadians at large.

Ogden continued as attorney general for

Lower Canada into the union period, complying with the Colonial Office's new directives by re-entering the political sphere, and successfully contesting the borough of Trois-Rivières in the election of April 1841. He nevertheless bitterly resented the drastic reduction in his salary, from £4,000 to £1,500, and the curtailing, by the government's removal to Kingston, of his substantial Montreal law practice.

Following the close of the session of 1841, Ogden departed for Europe on a year's leave. In his absence, the government of William Henry Draper*, of which he was a member, resigned; he returned in 1842 to discover that Louis-Hippolyte LA FONTAINE had replaced him as attorney general for Canada East. Furthermore, the new Reform administration refused a suggestion that Ogden be offered a government pension. He returned almost immediately to England to seek official redress, probably with the aid of Lord Lyndhurst to whom he was related through his second wife, but without success.

In the spring of 1844, Ogden briefly revisited Canada to settle his affairs; he had been admitted earlier that year to the English bar at Lincoln's Inn and appointed attorney general of the Isle of Man. In 1857 he accepted the further appointment of registrar of the Liverpool Probate Court. He retained these positions until his death on 19 Feb. 1866.

LORNE STE. CROIX

ANQ-Q, AP-G-196. PAC, MG 30, D62, 23, p.191. Gentleman's Magazine, CXXXVI (July–December 1824), 176; CCXX (January–June 1866), 753. La Minerve, 23 juill. 1827. Montreal Gazette, 27 March, 7 Dec. 1824; 14 Sept. 1826. Montreal Transcript, 9 April 1844. F.-J. Audet, Les députés des Trois-Rivières (1808–1838) (Trois-Rivières, 1934), 12–17. Ivanhoë Caron, "Inventaire des documents relatifs aux événements de 1837 et 1838, conservés aux Archives de la province de Québec," ANQ Rapport, 1925–26, 153ff. Desjardins, Guide parlementaire. Notman and Taylor, Portraits of British Americans, III. P.-G. Roy, Les juges de la prov. de Québec, 395. Atherton, Montreal, II, 127. Archie Binns, Peter Skene Ogden: fur trader (Portland, Oreg., 1967). Christie, History of L.C., V. Dent, Last forty years, I, 244. A. E. E. Legge, The Anglican Church in Three Rivers, Quebec, 1768–1956 (Russell, Ont., 1956), 43. Lorenzo Sabine, The American loyalists (Boston, 1847), 219. Helen Taft Manning, The revolt of French Canada, 1800–1835: a chapter in the history of the British Commonwealth (Toronto, 1962), 83, 130. W. O. Wheeler, The Ogden family in America, Elizabethtown branch, and their English ancestry; John Ogden, the Pilgrim, and his descendants, 1640–1906, their history, biography & genealogy, ed. Lawrence Van Alstyne and C. B. Ogden (Philadelphia, 1907).

O'REILLY, GERALD, physician and surgeon; b. 11 Aug. 1806 at Ballinlough, County Meath (Republic of Ireland), seventh son of Gerald O'Reilly; d. 26 Feb. 1861 in Hamilton, Canada West.

Gerald O'Reilly was sent to Dublin to study medicine in 1823 and was apprenticed to James William Cusack of Doctor Steevens' Hospital. He remained with Cusack for more than five years, and obtained the diploma of the Royal College of Surgeons of Ireland and the diploma in midwifery in November 1829. O'Reilly then continued his studies in London and became a licentiate of the Society of Apothecaries, London, in July 1833. Shortly after this he immigrated to Hamilton, Upper Canada, and obtained the provincial licence to practise physic, surgery, and midwifery in January 1835.

O'Reilly was popular from the first, and counted among his early patients Allan MACNAB and Samuel Mills*. His practice extended from St Catharines to Brantford and over to Oakville; when he discontinued his country practice several years before his death, he remained in a leading position as a consultant. O'Reilly was examiner in principles and practice of medicine at the University of Toronto in 1856. He also held a commission as surgeon to the 3rd Gore militia, the "Men of Gore," and at the time of his death was surgeon to the jail at Hamilton, having occupied the office for nearly 20 years, and surgeon to the counties of Wentworth and Halton. As a practitioner, he had a large professional library and a good idea of mechanics – he usually made his own splints and other appliances to suit individual cases – and he was quick and expert in operations. He was also one of the first to administer chloroform for surgical operations in Canada.

O'Reilly was one of the founders and original shareholders of the Canada Life Assurance Company, and was one of the first assured by the company. He was also the first medical officer for the company in 1847, a position he held until a few years before his death. He was a member of the Loyal Hamilton Lodge Independent Order of Oddfellows, having joined the order in 1844, and was elected surgeon to the lodge the following year.

O'Reilly died suddenly, at the age of 54, as the result of pyaemia, after the removal of a small tumour of the leg. He was married to Henrietta, youngest daughter of Henry Harcourt Waters, of Hailsham, Sussex, England, and left four sons, three of whom became physicians, and two daughters.

CHARLES G. ROLAND

Ossaye

HPL, Land family papers, p.1843 (sick report of the 3rd Gore militia, 8 June 1838). Canada Life Assurance Company, *Prospectus and first and second annual reports*, (Hamilton, [Ont.], 1849), 4. Canniff, *Medical profession in U.C.*, 541–51. C. R. McCullough, "The O'Reillys of old," *Hamilton Spectator*, 26 May, 4 June 1932.

OSSAYE (Ossaie, Ossage), FRÉDÉRIC-M.-F., agronomist and agricultural journalist; fl. 1851–63.

Frédéric Ossaye had had a successful career in France where he had run a model farm for five years before he came to Canada in 1851. That August the Agricultural Society of Lower Canada, which had been set up in 1847 to coordinate and direct agricultural development in the province above the level of the district societies, gave him control of the first experimental farm in Canada East as teacher and supervisory director. The establishment of this model farm was one of the three major achievements of the society, which included the launching in 1848 of an official agricultural journal directed by William Evans* and an extensive inquiry in 1850 into the state of agriculture in Canada East. The rented farm was located at La Tortue (Saint-Mathieu), in the county of Laprairie, on the 500-acre estate of the society's president, Alfred Pinsonnault. It was short-lived. Upkeep and payment of insurance and taxes rapidly swallowed up the $800 that the budget plan called for, and the special grant expected from the assembly never materialized. Hence the society returned the farm to its owner in the spring of 1852, in a transfer completed with some difficulty. Ossaye and several others opposed the conditions of the transfer because improvements had been made to the farm and because Pinsonnault refused to pay the society a sum equal to the recorded profits, and retained what remained of the sum paid when the contract was signed.

In 1852 Ossaye published *Les veillées canadiennes; traité élémentaire d'agriculture, à l'usage des habitants franco-canadiens* at Quebec. The eight "veillées" were conversations between a Scottish farmer who had settled in Canada around 1835 and one of his neighbours who had taken agricultural lessons from the immigrant and had decided to follow his example. This method of engaging two or three questioners in discussion to enliven the teaching of a rather dry subject was not new. However, Ossaye's introduction of the Scottish farmer was an application of the current theory of agricultural journalists that agricultural knowledge should be obtained through practical example rather than books.

In 1853 Ossaye contributed to *La Ruche littéraire illustrée*, directed by Henri-Émile Chevalier*. In his articles on the agricultural education of women, Ossaye listed the duties of a farmer's wife: working in the garden, beautifying the farm, and cultivating flowers and small fruit. That year he published at Montreal a book entitled *Nouveau système de comptabilité agricole, ou méthode sûre et facile pour bien gérer les opérations d'une ferme*. Like several of his *confrères*, Ossaye tried to combat the negligence of the many inefficient farmers.

In 1857 Ossaye became one of the principal contributors to Joseph-Xavier Perrault*'s *Journal de l'agriculteur et travaux de la chambre d'Agriculture du Bas-Canada*. After December 1857 he even replaced the editor for a few months and he wrote for the journal until at least November 1858. Among Ossaye's demands in his articles was government intervention in agricultural affairs. In Canada as in England private societies and individuals were assuming responsibility for agricultural affairs; he thought this demonstrated a Protestant mentality.

After 1858 it is increasingly difficult to determine Ossaye's activities. It is known that he continued to work for some years in the agricultural sphere. He was a member – at least from 1859 to 1862 – of the Board of Agriculture of Lower Canada, which had been formed in 1852 and placed under the direction of the Bureau of Agriculture of the province of Canada. *Le Courrier de Saint-Hyacinthe* on 13 Sept. 1859 carried a notice that Ossaye, a friend of Félix Vogeli, had entered an agricultural machine he had made, a stump-remover, in a competition run by the Board of Agriculture. He received the gold medal for his invention. The competition is thought to have been held on a farm worked by Ossaye. Ossaye volunteered his services to Pierre-Joseph-Olivier Chauveau*, the superintendent of public instruction, for free agricultural lessons at the École Normale Jacques-Cartier at Montreal, and taught there in 1860. Finally, in 1863, he became involved, principally with Henri-Gustave Joly* de Lotbinière, in popularizing the cultivation of textile plants in the province. In a long article, published in the *Gazette des campagnes* on 15 July, he discussed the need to cultivate flax and hemp. These crops would supply clothes for local people, and open export markets "which would bring a considerable amount of capital" into the country. After this date all trace of him is lost.

Ossaye's career is characteristic of those of numerous Europeans who came to Lower Canada in the mid 19th century and worked in specialized and relatively new areas such as agronomy, veterinary medicine, and agricultural journalism.

MARC-A. PERRON

F.-M.-F. Ossaye, *Les veillées canadiennes; traité élémentaire d'agriculture, à l'usage des habitants franco-canadiens* (Québec, 1852); *Nouveau système de comptabilité agricole, ou méthode sûre et facile pour bien gérer les opérations d'une ferme* (Montréal, 1853). *Le Courrier de Saint-Hyacinthe*, 26 juill., 13 sept. 1859. *Gazette des campagnes* (Sainte-Anne-de-la-Pocatière, [Qué.]), 15 juill. 1863. *Journal d'agriculture et transactions de la Société d'agriculture du Bas-Canada* (Montréal), juin–août 1852. *Journal de l'agriculteur et travaux de la chambre d'Agriculture du Bas-Canada* (Montréal), mai 1857–novembre 1858. *La Ruche littéraire illustrée* (Montréal), 1853. [L.-] A. Desrosiers, *Les écoles normales primaires de la province de Québec et leurs œuvres complémentaires, 1857–1907* (Montréal, 1909), 107. M.-A. Perron, *Un grand éducateur agricole: Édouard-A. Barnard, 1835–1898; essai historique sur l'agriculture de 1760 à 1900* ([Montréal], 1955).

P

PANET, PIERRE-LOUIS, lawyer and chief road inspector (*grand voyer*); b. 21 Feb. 1800 at Montreal, son of Pierre-Louis Panet*, judge of the Court of King's Bench, and Marie-Anne Cerré; d. 31 March 1870 in Montreal.

The ninth child of a family of 12, Pierre-Louis Panet studied at the Collège de Montréal from 1809 to 1817. On 13 Feb. 1823, after some years of training, he was called to the bar. Three years later Panet gave up his profession, following his appointment by Governor Dalhousie [Ramsay*] on 29 Nov. 1826 to the post of chief road inspector for the district of Trois-Rivières.

This office, a legacy of the French regime, remained long after the conquest. In 1796 the statute on public highways divided the province of Lower Canada into three districts: Montreal, Quebec, and Trois-Rivières. However, the cities of Montreal and Quebec, which possessed their own highway systems, were not in the jurisdiction of the chief road inspector. According to this law, the chief inspector of a district was assisted in each parish, seigneury, or township by an inspector appointed by him for two years. The parishes were subdivided into a maximum of nine sections and administered by an assistant inspector, elected for two years by the property owners. Any person refusing to accept this office incurred a fine of £5. The law also required those who wanted a road, or who had the use of one, to construct or maintain it in summer and winter, in proportion to the extent of their land contiguous to the road.

The duties of chief road inspector demanded a "man of talent and judgement," since this person was responsible for laying out public highways and presided over the meetings that brought together all parties interested in opening up and financing a new road. It was he who, in the last resort, nominated those who would build and maintain the roads. His decisions were recorded in a report which was ratified by the court of sessions of the peace in each district. The chief inspector, once a year, also had to visit each division of his district and inspect the roads and bridges. While the inspectors supervised the assistant inspectors and conducted periodical inspections, the assistant inspectors ensured that the orders of the chief inspector were carried out, and punished those who through negligence or for some other reason contravened them.

On 28 Aug. 1827, at Montreal, less than a month after his appointment, Panet married Louise-Clorinthe Bouthillier, daughter of Lieutenant-Colonel Jean Bouthillier, commanding officer of the 3rd militia battalion of Montreal. Two children were born of this union; Mme Panet died in July 1832. In the following December Panet moved to Montreal, to succeed the Honourable Louis-René Chaussegros* de Léry as chief road inspector of that district, a post he held for eight years.

On 30 Dec. 1840 the Special Council passed an ordinance which abolished the existing structure, including the position of chief road inspector. The management of roads was transferred to the jurisdiction of municipal councils. From that date, Panet was a pensioner of the state. Suffering from acute rheumatism, he went to the United States for a while in search of a milder climate. The death in March 1870 of this man, who had maintained an image worthy of the reputation of the family from which he had sprung, ended the Montreal line of the Panets.

ROGER BARRETTE

PAC, MG 30, D62, 23, p.688. Bas-Canada, *Statuts*, 1796, c.9; Conseil spécial, *Ordonnances*, 1840–41, c.7. *La Minerve*, 1er avril 1870. *L'Opinion publique*, 6 juin 1872. P.-G. Roy, *Inventaire des procès-verbaux des*

Papin

grands voyers conservés aux Archives de la province de Québec (6v., Beauceville, Qué., 1923–32), III, 103–47, 208–22; V, 179–312; *La famille Panet* (Lévis, Qué., 1906), 197–200. "Le premier grand voyer," *BRH*, LXIX (1967), 19–20.

PAPIN, JOSEPH, lawyer and politician; b. 14 Dec. 1825 at L'Assomption, Lower Canada, fifth of the 11 children of Basile Papin, a well-to-do farmer, and Marie-Rose Pelletier; d. 23 Feb. 1862 in the town of his birth.

Joseph Papin was a brilliant pupil at the Collège de L'Assomption from 1835 to 1842; he then studied law in the office of Joseph-Ferréol Pelletier in Montreal and was called to the bar on 21 Dec. 1846. Joseph Papin rapidly made a name for himself. As a law student he had been one of the group that founded the Institut Canadien at Montreal in December 1844. He was elected its first vice-president in August 1845 and served as president from November 1846 until November 1847. In the May 1848 elections at the Institut Canadien, there was a confrontation between the party that backed *La Minerve* in support of Louis-Hippolyte LA FONTAINE, and the party that backed *L'Avenir*, which had declared itself for Louis-Joseph Papineau* and against the union. Antoine Gérin-Lajoie*, the editor of *La Minerve*, was narrowly defeated for president by Toussaint-Antoine-Rodolphe Laflamme*, a contributor to *L'Avenir*. Louis Labrèche-Viger*, Jean-Baptiste-Éric DORION, and Joseph Doutre* were elected to the executive committee, as was Joseph Papin, in the office of recording secretary; they were among the 13 who made up the committee of contributors of *L'Avenir*. Papin, and the young men of *L'Avenir* and Papineau's friends, belonged to the Association pour le Peuplement des Cantons de l'Est [*see* Louis Labrèche-Viger], and he was one of the signatories to the Annexation Manifesto of 1849.

In the 1851 provincial elections, Papin, Jean-Baptiste-Éric Dorion, Antoine-Aimé Dorion*, Joseph Doutre, and Joseph-Guillaume Barthe* all campaigned for Louis-Joseph Papineau, a candidate in the city of Montreal riding. When Papineau was defeated, Édouard-Raymond Fabre*, his friend and adviser, asked Joseph Papin and Louis Labrèche-Viger to test public opinion in the county of Deux-Montagnes, where by-elections had become necessary following the death of the elected candidate William Henry Scott*. In a large meeting held at Saint-André-Avellin, Papin was responsible for introducing Papineau, and on this occasion the latter's supporters were triumphant, presaging the Patriote leader's victory in July 1852 in the

Deux-Montagnes riding. A short time earlier, in the mayoral election for Montreal, Joseph Papin had campaigned for Fabre against Wolfred NELSON. In 1853 Papin was himself elected municipal councillor for the Sainte-Marie district, but his election was rendered void by a decision of the Superior Court in October 1854, because he was unable to furnish proof that he had been a landed proprietor in Montreal for at least a year prior to the election. During these years Joseph Papin was particularly active in the movement for the abolition of seigneurial tenure.

General elections were held in 1854, and Canada East returned a dozen Rouges to the assembly. *Le Pays*, quoting the *British Colonist* of Toronto, wrote that they were "beyond question among the most talented men sent to parliament by French Canadians since the Union." Joseph Papin, who had unsuccessfully offered himself to the group as leader in 1853, was elected in L'Assomption, where he defeated a young Conservative layer, Louis-Siméon Morin*.

As an MLA, Papin won renown through the issue of sectarian schools. In 1856 George Brown*, the leader of the Grits, raised the sensitive question of separate schools in Canada West and asked for suppression of Roman Catholic educational privileges. William Locker Pickmore Felton*, however, advocated the extension to Catholic schools in Canada West of the rights accorded Protestant schools in Canada East. At this point Joseph Papin proposed, on the basis of the principle of the separation of church and state and the equality of all religious persuasions, "the establishment throughout the province of a general and uniform system of free elementary education, supported entirely by the State, through a special fund which would be created for that purpose; . . . all schools should be open without discrimination to all children old enough to attend them, and no child should be exposed, by the nature of the teaching given, to seeing his religious beliefs or opinions attacked or offended in any manner." The Conservatives, for propaganda purposes, held that Joseph Papin and the Rouges had dared to advocate a school system from which religion would be banished. Long after 1856 Papin's proposal was quoted, as was the programme of *L'Avenir* in favour of annexation to the United States, as one of the iniquities of the Rouges. During the elections in late 1857 and early 1858, *La Minerve* of course recalled Papin's opposition to denominational schools; Papin was defeated in L'Assomption by the Conservative Louis Archambeault*, by a narrow margin of 16 votes.

After this reverse Papin was able to devote

more time to the practice of law. At the time of Bishop Ignace Bourget*'s first large-scale attacks on the Institut Canadien, Papin defended Médéric Lanctot*, a young law student in the office of Joseph Doutre and Charles DAOUST, who was accused of shattering the windows of the Œuvre des Bons Livres. Papin remained an active Liberal. Thus in the autumn of 1859 he took part in the discussions that led to the manifesto of the parliamentary opposition of Canada East, which advocated "the confederation of the two Canadas" as the solution to the political instability of the Canadian union [see Luther Hamilton Holton*]. In May 1858, after Joseph-Ferréol Pelletier's death, Joseph Papin became counsel for the town of Montreal, with an annual salary of $2,000. He held this office until his death.

In November 1857 Papin had married Sophie Homier; five years later, when he was only 36, he died of cancer. In a letter to Bishop Bourget of Montreal, Pierre-Férréol Dorval, parish priest of L'Assomption, wrote that he had taken an interest in Papin during his illness, and that Papin had renounced the Institut Canadien and received the sacraments before he died. Marie-Louise, his only child, was to be the mother of Joseph-Papin Archambault*, a Jesuit who was active in the 20th century.

A satirical pamphlet, *La pléiade rouge*, described Joseph Papin as "the Danton of the Mountain." It gave him credit only for a "fine physique" and a "powerful voice." But Joseph Papin was obviously more than a resounding speaker. A few days after his death the Rouge Henri-Émile Chevalier* wrote: "Canadian democracy has just suffered a considerable loss in the person of its most direct leader, M. Joseph Papin . . . and his premature death leaves in Canada a void difficult to fill." Laurent-Olivier David*, a moderate Liberal, wrote in *L'Opinion publique* in 1871 that "age, study, and reflection would have made him one of the most important statesmen and the most popular speaker in Lower Canada." In *Le panthéon canadien . . .*, François-Marie-Uncas-Maximilien Bibaud*, an author who cannot be suspected of a radical bias, presented Joseph Papin as "one of the most brilliant men to appear on the political scene at the time of the formation of the Liberal party."

JEAN-PAUL BERNARD

ACAM, 355.114, 862-2. ANQ-Q, AP, Coll. Papineau, no.541. AVM, Biographies autres que celles des maires et conseillers, Joseph Papin. PAC, MG 24, B40, 3, pp.460–62. Can., prov. du, Assemblée législative, *Journaux*, 1856, 246–47, 310–14, 615–18. *L'Avenir*, 31 déc. 1847, 24 mai 1848, 13 oct. 1849. *La Minerve*, 16, 25, 31 oct. 1851; 16 déc. 1857. *L'Opinion publique*, 24 août 1871. *Le Pays*, 5, 19, 29 août, 16 sept. 1854; 13, 17 mai 1856. [F.-M.-U.-]M. Bibaud, *Le panthéon canadien; choix de biographies, dans lequel on a introduit les hommes les plus célèbres des autres colonies britanniques* (2e éd., Montréal, 1891), 212–14. Borthwick, *Montreal*, 107. Le Jeune, *Dictionnaire*, II, 407. Morgan, *Bibliotheca Canadensis*, 299.

J.-P. Archambault, *La famille Papin (1653–1953)* (Montréal, 1953). Bernard, *Les Rouges*, 42, 45, 64–65, 71, 117, 120–21, 126–29, 147, 172–73, 249. L.-O. David, *Biographies et portraits* (Montréal, 1876), 81–205. *Hist. de la corporation de la cité de Montréal* (Lamothe et al.), 210–11. [L.-H. Huot], *Le rougisme en Canada; ses idées religieuses, ses principes sociaux et ses tendances anti-canadiennes* (Québec, 1864). *Institut-canadien en 1852*, J.-B.-É. Dorion, édit. (Montréal, 1852), 21–27. Gaspard Le Mage [P.-J.-O. Chauveau et J.-C. Taché], *La pléiade rouge* (Québec, 1854), 3–4. Monet, *Last cannon shot*, 286, 370, 383. Guillaume Saint-Pierre, "Les avocats de la Cité," *La Revue du Barreau de la province de Québec* (Montréal), 4 (1944), 345–60.

PAQUET, JOSEPH-MARIE, priest; b. 21 Nov. 1804 at Quebec, son of Joseph Paquet and Marie-Josephte Gagnon; d. 28 July 1869 at Montreal, and buried 13 August at Caraquet, N.B.

Joseph-Marie Paquet was still young when his father, described by Bishop Joseph-Octave Plessis* as a "brutal, drunken and jealous" man, deserted the family; his sickly mother had to bring up the family on her own. Young Paquet was entrusted to his maternal uncle Abbé Antoine Gagnon*, a parish priest and vicar general in New Brunswick, who sent him to the Séminaire de Québec. Here he completed classical studies (1816–25) and theology (1825–28). He was ordained priest on 28 Sept. 1828.

The following year he was appointed parish priest of Shemogue, N.B., a mission for which his uncle was responsible. Abbé Paquet's stay there was scarcely a happy one. The Acadians of New Brunswick disliked these "Canadian priests" who came to proselytize among them as though they were pagans. Indeed Abbé Gagnon, in a letter to the archbishop of Quebec, spoke of his parishioners as "Acadian fools" who "live in disorder . . . being a racial mixture of Indian, Negro, French, Spanish and even Italian, with all the natural and moral and intellectual defects of their origin."

After a year at Shemogue, Abbé Paquet became parish priest of Richibucto-Village where he remained until 1840. Like other missionaries on the east coast of New Brunswick he complained of the authoritarianism of his uncle and

Paré

protector, Abbé Gagnon. The first confrontation between the two men occurred in 1831, when a plan for building a seminary at Grande-Digue was proposed by the provincial legislature and by the bishop of Charlottetown, Bernard Angus MacEachern*, whose jurisdiction included the Catholics of New Brunswick. Gagnon, the local parish priest, wanted the title-deeds of the land and the future building in his own name. Abbé Paquet, the other missionaries, and the Acadians of Kent and Westmorland counties were offended by this. Gagnon, however, was unable to tolerate the idea of having to take orders from laymen and of being obliged to "bow and scrape to win their good will," and decided in 1832 to move to Barachois and to build a school there, on one of his many properties. Meanwhile Paquet openly supported the representative of the Acadians, Pascal Poirier. At a stormy meeting in September 1833 which was attended by the bishop of Charlottetown, and by those affected by the plan, including the spokesmen for the Acadians of Grande-Digue, Cocagne, Barachois, Buctouche, and Richibucto, Paquet angered his uncle "by opposing [him] in the presence of the bishop and numerous people." Gagnon then asked the archbishop of Quebec to recall or move Paquet, "in order to be freed of this harpy." In the end both plans for a seminary fell through.

From 1840 to 1848 Paquet was parish priest of Saint-Louis. In 1842 he again had to tackle his uncle, when a bishop was to be appointed for New Brunswick. Two candidates had been proposed, the vicars general Gagnon and William Dollard*, and at the request of Rome a meeting was called at Chatham to choose between them. When each obtained six votes in the ballot Paquet, as chairman, had to decide the issue, and declared in favour of Dollard. It is possible that the Irish clergy promised to support Paquet's own candidature as bishop in the event of Dollard's death, although Paquet never did obtain the mitre: Thomas Connolly* was appointed bishop of Saint John in 1852, after Dollard's death, and in 1860, when the diocese of Chatham was formed, James Rogers* was selected over Paquet who was then parish priest of Caraquet and later became Bishop Rogers' vicar general.

At Saint-Louis Paquet antagonized many of the parishioners when he decided to build a new church on the site of the old one. These parishioners wanted the church erected in a more central place and were fiercely opposed to Paquet's plan. When the church was dedicated, one of the malcontents got up in the middle of the sermon, and, leaving his place, "marched out, singing the hymn 'Au sang qu'un Dieu va répandre.' " The incident compromised Paquet and made his position at Saint-Louis untenable.

In his last months at Saint-Louis in 1848, Paquet had witnessed the general hostility among the tenant-farmers of Kent and Westmorland counties towards Vicar General Gagnon which led to the affair of the "rebels of Grand-Digue" [see Antoine Gagnon]. Because Abbé Hector-Antoine Drolet, the parish priest of Caraquet, had taken sides against Abbé Gagnon and Bishop Dollard, he was deprived of his office. When Paquet left Saint-Louis and went to Caraquet in September 1848 to take over the parish, he brought the bishop's order to withdraw from Drolet "all powers if he persisted in wishing to remain at Caraquet." The latter agreed to leave, and Paquet took over the charge, holding it without incident until his death in 1869.

RÉGIS BRUN

AAQ, 311 CN, I, 77, 80, 82, 87, 89, 144; III, 59; V, 80, 85, 87, 139–40. Archives of the Diocese of Saint John, N.B., Bishop MacEachern to Antoine Gagnon, 22 July 1832; lettre de Monseigneur Plessis à Antoine Gagnon, 28 nov. 1815. Centre d'études acadiennes, Université de Moncton (Moncton, N.-B.), 1.65-15 (Fonds Placide Gaudet, Placide Gaudet à Mgr C.-O. Gagnon, août 1895). Allaire, *Dictionnaire*, IV, 341. P.-F. Bourgeois, *Vie de l'abbé François-Xavier Lafrance . . .* (Montréal, 1913), 35. L.-C. Daigle, *Histoire de Saint-Louis-de-Kent: cent cinquante ans de vie paroissiale française en Acadie nouvelle* (Moncton, N.-B., 1948), 94. J.-U. Demers, *Histoire de Sainte-Rose, 1740–1947* ([Montréal], 1947).

PARÉ, HUBERT, businessman; b. 5 April 1803 at Saint-Denis, on the Richelieu River, Lower Canada, son of Léon Paré and Marie-Angélique Grenier; d. 24 Jan. 1869 at Montreal.

Nothing is recorded of Paré's boyhood; possibly he received his early education at the *école de latin* opened in 1805 at Saint-Denis. About 1819 he was in Montreal as a clerk in the employ of Félix Vinet-Souligny, grain merchant and shipowner. Paré rose to a partnership, married on 22 June 1835 Justine Vinet, daughter of Hippolyte Vinet and Marie-Anne Beaudry, and in the 1840s continued the grain business. In the 1850s he became a dealer in iron, and at the time of his death was a retail and wholesale hardware merchant. The shifts in his economic interests doubtless reflected the decline in cereal growing in Canada East and the rise of Montreal in the consumption and distribution of manufactured goods.

The organization of capital and the improvement of transportation also concerned Paré. Along with other representative French Canadians he was among the petitioners for setting up the Banque des marchands (1846) and the Banque Jacques Cartier (1861); his name also appears in the chartering of the Montreal City and District Savings Bank (1862). Paré had been one of the founders of the latter, when it was established, without incorporation, in 1846. The major commercial banks, the Bank of Montreal excepted, did not have savings departments; hence the desirability of an institution specializing in savings. Incorporation in 1862 regularized the bank's position and extended its services. Paré was active in encouraging the *fabriques* to insure their properties against fire under the provisions of the statutes of 1853 and 1854, incorporating the Mutual Assurance Association of the *fabriques*. He had a substantial stake in railways, £500 in St Lawrence and Atlantic stock and a directorship in the Montreal and Bytown, both lines being essential to Montreal's metropolitan outreach.

Hubert Paré's wealth enabled him to assist financially in the training of his brother, the future Canon Joseph-Octave Paré*, and three nephews who became priests. Perhaps through the influence of his brother, who was Bishop Ignace Bourget*'s secretary, he was brought into the main stream of Catholic action. He became one of the founders of the Société Saint-Vincent-de-Paul, established in Montreal on 19 March 1848, and an early member of the Société de Tempérance and the Société Saint-Jean-Baptiste; in all these he was frequently an office holder. The three societies were largely lay in membership and were designed to meet contemporary needs, charitable, moral, and cultural. Paré was also a member of the more traditional Congrégation des hommes de Ville-Marie, a men's moral improvement society that dated from the time of Maisonneuve [Chomedey*]. He was on the parochial committee that secured chimes for Notre-Dame Church. He and Mme Paré donated one of the tenor bells, stood as its godparents, and named it "Hubert et Justine."

He was active in business and in good works until his death on 24 Jan. 1869. Four days later he was accorded an impressive funeral, and burial in the crypt of Notre-Dame-de-Grâce.

Hubert Paré lived in the golden age of the tradesman. He was more than just a successful shopkeeper, who adroitly changed his wares to take advantage of new conditions. He illustrates the strong sense of personal responsibility so characteristic of the mid 19th century social conscience. His activity in numerous philanthropic and cultural organizations suggests the extent to which the example of the France of the Restoration penetrated French Canada.

JOHN IRWIN COOPER

ANQ-M, État civil, Catholiques, Notre-Dame-de-Grâce (Montréal), 28 janv. 1869. *L'Ordre* (Montréal), 26 janv. 1869. Borthwick, *Montreal*, 64–65. J.-B.-A. Allaire, *Histoire de la paroisse de Saint-Denis-sur-Richelieu (Canada)* (Saint-Hyacinthe, Qué., 1905), 246–47, 257, 260, 339–48. *Le diocèse de Montréal à la fin du dix-neuvième siècle, avec portraits du clergé; héliogravures et notices historiques de toutes les églises et presbytères, institutions d'éducation et de charité; sociétés de bienfaisance, œuvres de fabrique et commissions scolaires . . .* (Montréal, 1900), 48–51, 122–27. Olivier Maurault, *La paroisse; histoire de l'église Notre-Dame de Montréal* (Montréal et New York, 1929), 192–93, 198–99. Pouliot, *Mgr Bourget*, II, 159–60. J. I. Cooper, "The origins and early history of the Montreal City and District Savings Bank, 1846–1871," CCHA *Report*, XIII (1945–46), 15–25; "Some early Canadian savings banks," *Canadian Banker* (Toronto), 57 (1950), 135–43.

PARISIEN, NORBERT, Métis labourer involved in the 1869–70 rebellion; b. probably in the Red River Settlement; d. there 4 March 1870.

Norbert Parisien, whom Alexandre-Antonin Taché* identified as a "young French Métis," appears briefly in the history of the northwest in 1870. At this time he was employed at Upper Fort Garry (Winnipeg) chopping wood; his contemporaries describe him as simple-minded.

By early February 1870 the Red River Settlement appeared to be released from the months of tension following the Métis resistance to the transfer of the northwest to Canada. A provisional government had been organized by Louis Riel*, a bill of rights had been approved, and delegates to negotiate the transfer with Canada had been appointed. "Everyone appeared relieved that peace seemed once more certain," wrote Alexander Begg* in his diary. However, rumours began to circulate that a party of armed Canadians was preparing to force the release of prisoners taken by Riel on 7 Dec. 1869 and overthrow his government. The prospect of an armed conflict revived tensions "and, at one sweep," wrote Begg, "the Settlement was thrown back in a worse position."

On 15 February the Canadian party seized Parisien believing him to be a spy of Riel. Riel, however, claimed he was a partisan of the Canadian party. According to the account by Charles Arkoll Boulton*, who, along with Charles Mair* and John Christian Schultz*, was a leader of the Canadian party, Parisien escaped his guard, seized a gun, and while fleeing shot Hugh John

Parke

Sutherland, son of John (later Senator) Sutherland*, who died soon after. Parisien was recaptured and in Boulton's words was handled "severely." The following day, while he was being taken to Lower Fort Garry, he attempted to escape again, was shot by his guard, and later died of his wounds.

The incident, the first bloodshed in the rebellion of 1869–70, had a restraining effect on the Canadian party. The plan to release the prisoners and overthrow Riel was abandoned. However, a gulf had opened between the two sides, and on 17 February as members of the Canadian party were returning home nearly 50 were taken prisoner by Riel's men. Boulton was threatened with execution but was spared, it is said, partly by the pleas of Sutherland's parents. Another prisoner taken at this time was Thomas SCOTT, who was executed on 4 March.

HARTWELL BOWSFIELD

Alexander Begg, *The creation of Manitoba; or, a history of the Red River troubles* (Toronto, 1871), 276–90; *Red River journal* (Morton), 104–9, 307–16. Can., chambre des Communes, *Rapport du comité spécial sur les causes des troubles du Territoire du Nord-Ouest en 1869–70* (Ottawa, 1874), 21–23. "Letter of Louis Riel and Ambroise Lépine to Lieutenant-Governor Morris, January 3, 1873," trans. and ed. A. H. Trémaudan, *CHR*, VII (1926), 137–60. Morice, *Dict. historique des Canadiens et Métis*, 221–22. C. A. Boulton, *Reminiscences of the North-West rebellions, with a record of the raising of her majesty's 100th Regiment in Canada, and a chapter on Canadian social and political life* (Toronto, 1886), 100–23. Morice, *Critical history of the Red River insurrection*, 251–71.

PARKE, THOMAS, builder, architect, politician, journalist, and public servant; b. 1793 in County Wicklow (Republic of Ireland); d. 29 Jan. 1864 at St Catharines, Canada West.

An emigrant from Ireland, Thomas Parke came to York (Toronto), Upper Canada, in 1820. There he worked as a master carpenter in association with John Ewart* on the construction of the new parliament buildings at York (completed in 1829). In 1832 he moved to London where he had worked with Ewart in the late 1820s as foreman of all the carpentry work in the erection of the London District court house and gaol. Like many early London residents, such as George Jervis GOODHUE, Parke invested in land: with Robert Parke, possibly a brother, he purchased a block north of the London town plot in 1832. Although much of this land was sold as town lots, Thomas Parke completed a grist mill in 1833 on a portion fronting the north branch of the Thames River,

and in 1835 the mill and the surrounding land were sold to Dennis O'BRIEN. Thomas Parke was also interested in promoting a railway from London to the head of Lake Ontario; his name appears after that of Edward Allen Talbot* among the incorporators of the London and Gore Railroad in 1834. During the mid 1830s he played a leading role in the attempt to improve the navigability of the Thames River downstream from London.

In 1834 Parke, a Wesleyan Methodist, and the Quaker Elias Moore from Yarmouth Township won the two seats in Middlesex riding for the Reformers. After a stormy election in 1836, both retained their seats in Upper Canada's last parliament. Following the rebellion Parke joined Reformers Peter Perry*, James Lesslie*, and Francis Hincks* in 1838 in organizing the short-lived Mississippi Emigration Society for the settlement in the territory of Iowa of Canadians dissatisfied with political conditions in Upper Canada. That summer he accompanied Perry and Lesslie on a trip to Iowa to choose a site.

In order to further reform, particularly constitutional reform, Parke frequently contributed to various journals, and in 1839 founded the *Canada* (later *London*) *Inquirer* with George Heyworth Hackstaff. Special attention was given in it to "the introduction of responsible government, municipal institutions, public schools, free grants of land to actual settlers and the secularization of the clergy reserves." By January 1842 Hackstaff was sole publisher of the newspaper. An earnest supporter of Governor General Charles Poulett Thomson*'s efforts to unite the Canadas, Parke was said to have been "largely instrumental in securing the consent of the Upper Canada Legislature to the [union bill]." In June 1841, shortly after being elected representative from Middlesex to the first parliament of the Province of Canada, he was commissioned surveyor general. He did not contest Middlesex in 1844 but continued as surveyor general until the abolition of that office in March 1845. His political career was perhaps best summed up by Clarence T. Campbell who asserted that Parke was "not a very brilliant man, and not an extremist; a Reformer, and yet not very objectionable to the ruling clique."

After 1845 "unobtrusiveness" would be as much a part of him as "integrity, and upright character." He had been first commissioned a magistrate in July 1840, and in July 1845 he assumed the offices of collector of customs and collector of canal tolls at Port Colborne. In July 1860 Parke became collector of customs at Port Dalhousie (now in St Catharines) and collector of

618

canal tolls at the port of St Catharines; these positions he held until his death.

He married twice. His first wife, Sarah, by whom he had at least three sons and possibly a daughter, died on 29 March 1841. He appears to have had at least a son and two daughters by his second wife, Harriet Rose Wilkes. All four of Parke's sons became lawyers.

DANIEL J. BROCK

City of London Registry Office (London, Ont.), Abstract index, book 2; instruments 2769 (1835), 2771 (1835). Niagara North Land Registration Office (St Catharines, Ont.), instrument 5643 (1893). PAC, RG 31, 1861 census, St Catharines, district 7; RG 68, 1, General index, 1651–1841; 1841–67. Can., Prov. of, Legislative Assembly, *Journals*, 1846, I, app.C; *Sessional papers*, 1861, II, no.3. U.C., *Statutes*, 1834, c.29; 1837, c.113. *Canadian Emigrant* (Sandwich [Windsor, Ont.]), 9 Aug. 1834. *Colonial Advocate*, 10 May 1832. *Daily Advertiser* (London), 1 Oct. 1874. *Evening Journal* (St Catherines, [Ont.]), 30 Jan. 1864. *London Free Press*, 4 Feb. 1864. *London Inquirer* (London, [Ont.]), 8 Dec. 1840, 16 June 1841, 21 Jan. 1842. *Montreal Gazette*, 14 Nov. 1833. *St. Catharines Constitutional* (St Catharines, [Ont.]), 4 Feb. 1864. *St. Catharines Journal* (St Catharines, [Ont.]), 22 Aug. 1839. *St. Thomas Standard* (St Thomas, [Ont.]), 23 May 1844. *Upper Canada Times and London District Gazette* (London, [Ont.]), 5 March 1836. C. T. Campbell, *Pioneer days in London; some account of men and things in London before it became a city* (London, Ont., 1921), 64. *History of the county of Middlesex* (Brock), 220–21, 957–58. *London and its men of affairs* (London, Ont., n.d.), 132, 137, 183. R. S. Longley, "Emigration and the crisis of 1837 in Upper Canada," *CHR*, XVII (1936), 29–40. H. O. Miller, "The history of the newspaper press in London, 1830–1875," *OH*, XXXII (1937), 127–28.

PARKER, NEVILLE, lawyer and judge; b. 8 June 1798 in Saint John, N.B., second son of Robert Parker, a Boston loyalist who became ordnance storekeeper and comptroller of customs at Saint John, and Jane Hatch, daughter of another Massachusetts loyalist; m. 22 April 1821 in St Andrews, N.B., Elizabeth Margaret Sheddon Wyer, and they had ten children; d. 6 Aug. 1869 at St Andrews.

Neville Parker followed the customary path of the children of New Brunswick's small loyalist upper class in the early 19th century. He attended the Saint John Grammar School, King's Collegiate School at Windsor, N.S., in 1811, and then King's College, Windsor, from 1812 to 1816. After graduation he entered the legal profession, studying in the office of Ward Chipman* Jr. He was admitted to the bar in 1819 and began to practise in St Andrews.

By 1826 Parker was practising law in Saint John. Until 1834 he was in partnership with his brother, ROBERT, and then until 1838 with William Jack. In 1833, when Robert Parker resigned as judge of the Court of Vice-Admiralty, Neville Parker was given the position. In 1837 he was offered a place on the Executive Council by Sir John Harvey*, who recommended him to the Colonial Office as a "gentleman of the highest character and professional attainments." But before the appointment was confirmed in London, Parker was given in March 1838 the newly created post of master of the rolls. Because he had been a master in chancery since 1823 and by 1838 was the senior master, he was the logical choice for the position and appears to have held it with distinction until the office was abolished in a reorganization of the judiciary in 1854, which Parker and his fellow judges opposed. Parker then became a puisne judge of the Supreme Court. In 1860 he also became judge of the Court of Divorce and Matrimonial Causes, and served until illness forced his retirement in October 1868. After his appointment as master of the rolls, Parker resided in Fredericton, but at the time of his death he was visiting St Andrews.

Neville Parker was a prominent member of New Brunswick's establishment, but as a judge he was probably not above the average. Although James Hannay* remembered him as a "very dignified old gentleman," in his younger days he was known for his fiery temper. When still a youth he challenged General John Coffin* to a duel, but the latter, who was 67, declined the invitation. In 1834 Parker was one of the leaders in the protest of the provincial bar against the appointment of an Englishman, James Carter*, to the New Brunswick bench; his brother Robert had hoped to obtain the post. In 1846, when he was asked to serve with the lieutenant governor and Executive Council on a court to deal with cases of marriage and divorce, he refused on the grounds that extra funds were not provided for an usher and a suitable meeting-place for the court. The result was a prolonged and bitter conflict with Sir William COLEBROOKE and the Executive Council, to whom his actions seemed "a clear case of misbehavior." During the 1850s Parker repeatedly took the lead in defending high judicial salaries against the demands of the assembly for reductions. It was these actions rather than his judicial decisions which occasionally gave Neville Parker a prominence he otherwise neither sought nor merited.

PHILLIP BUCKNER

N.B. Museum, D. R. Jack, "Pre-loyalist biographical

Parker

data, and other notes'' (typescript of original notes in Saint John Regional Library), pp.33–35. PANB, REX/mi/ex, draft minutes, 10 Dec. 1846, 30 March 1847. PRO, CO 188/56, Harvey to Glenelg, 28 July 1837; 188/59, Harvey to Glenelg, 16 March 1838; 188/99, Colebrooke to Grey, 30 March 1847. Fenety, *Political notes and observations. Daily Morning News* (Saint John, N.B.), 7 Aug. 1869. *Morning Freeman* (Saint John, N.B.), 7 Aug. 1869. *St. Croix Courier* (St Stephen, N.B.), 12 Aug. 1869. *St. John Daily Telegraph and Morning Journal* (Saint John, N.B.), 7 Aug. 1869. *Political appointments and judicial bench* (N.-O. Coté). Hannay, *History of N.B.* Lawrence, *Judges of N.B.* (Stockton). James Hannay, "The Supreme Court," *Daily Telegraph* (Saint John, N.B.), 23 Dec. 1892.

PARKER, ROBERT, lawyer, politician, and judge; b. 26 June 1796 in Saint John, N.B., eldest son of Robert Parker and Jane Hatch and brother of NEVILLE; d. 24 Nov. 1865 in Saint John.

Robert Parker received his early education under the Reverend Roger Viets* after the opening of the Saint John Grammar School in 1807. He then attended King's Collegiate School at Windsor, N.S., in 1810–11 and King's College from 1811 to 1814, where he received his BA and MA. His classmates included Thomas Chandler HALIBURTON, afterwards a life-long friend. Parker became the first law student in the office of Ward Chipman* Jr, was admitted as an attorney in 1817, and was called to the bar in 1820. Born into the loyalist and Anglican establishment of New Brunswick, Parker's rise to prominence was assured, but he was undoubtedly assisted by his marriage in January 1820 to Susan Robinson, niece of John Robinson*, mayor of Saint John and a member of the Council. In 1820 Parker became a director and the solicitor of the Bank of New Brunswick, of which Robinson was president. In 1824 he received the lucrative post of recorder of the city of Saint John. In 1826 he was elected by acclamation to the assembly to fill a vacancy in Saint John created by Ward Chipman's appointment to the bench, and he was returned again in the general election of 1827.

A moderate conservative, Parker played an active role in the assembly, but politics was for him, as for many colonial lawyers, simply the quickest route to official advancement. He impressed the lieutenant governor, Sir Howard DOUGLAS, "as a gentleman of the first respectability and character at the Bar, of great talent, legal knowledge, and of principles thoroughly to be depended upon." Consequently, when the attorney general, Thomas Wetmore*, died in March 1828, Parker was appointed to the position during the absence of Charles Jeffery Peters*, the

solicitor general, and when the latter returned to accept the attorney generalship, Parker became solicitor general. Later in 1828 he also received the position of judge commissary of the Court of Vice-Admiralty, which he held until 1833 when the pressure of his work as solicitor general compelled him to resign. Since his political ambitions had never been great, he had not run for re-election to the assembly in 1830, and except for the occasional jibe at "discontented theorists," abstained from politics, devoting his time to legal business. Among other duties he served on an important commission in 1832–33 to investigate the judicial institutions of the colony. He practised law in partnership with his brother Neville from 1826 to 1834.

Robert Parker's diligence was rewarded in 1834. When the chief justice, John Saunders*, died, Sir Archibald Campbell* recommended that Parker should replace whichever puisne judge became chief justice. Parker's hopes were frustrated, however, for the vacancy on the bench created by the promotion of Ward Chipman was filled by an Englishman, James Carter*, much to the disgruntlement of the New Brunswick bar. Not until the death of another judge, John Murray Bliss*, later in 1834, did Parker become a puisne judge. Carter was to stand in Parker's way yet again, for when Chipman died in 1851, Carter, whose appointment had preceded Parker's by only a few months, became chief justice. Finally in 1865 Parker received the highest judicial position in the colony, largely by accident. Carter resigned in 1865 to allow Arthur Hamilton Gordon* to offer the post to the leader of the anti-confederate government of New Brunswick, Albert James Smith*. Smith declined the appointment and recommended Parker, who is said to have received Smith's support for having declared that "he would rather vote for a hedgehog than for a supporter of Confederation." Ironically, the promotion cost Parker £200 a year, since the salary of the chief justice had been reduced prospectively below that of the puisne judges. His appointment was short-lived for he died a few months later.

Arthur Hamilton Gordon described Parker as "the ideal judge and accomplished Gentleman." There can be little dispute over the latter claim. A devout Anglican, Parker was president for many years of the New Brunswick branch of the Auxiliary Bible Society and an avid supporter of the temperance movement in the province. He assisted many charities, served as a director of the Saint John Grammar School and on the board of governors of King's College, and actively participated in the Natural History Society. His performance as a judge is more difficult to measure. He was respected by the bar and admired as "the most efficient judge who has ever occupied the Bench of New Brunswick." But in judicial matters, as in political, Parker was a conservative; he believed the law should be administered impartially and severely. On one occasion when he realized that he had inadvertently purchased partridges out of season, he voluntarily paid the fine. James Hannay*, not an admirer of Parker, found him "one who lived very much out of the range of human sympathy" and criticized his harshness as a judge. Parker appears to have been an able and respected but not an outstanding or particularly beloved judge.

PHILLIP BUCKNER

N.B. Museum, D. R. Jack, "Pre-loyalist biographical data, and other notes" (typescript of original notes in Saint John Regional Library), pp.33–35. PRO, CO 188/37, Douglas to Huskisson, 31 March 1828; 188/45, Campbell to Goderich, 4 April 1833; 188/50, Campbell to Rice, 27, 31 Aug. 1834; 188/144, Cole to Cardwell, 27 Sept. 1865; Gordon to Cardwell, 28 Nov. 1865. Fenety, *Political notes and observations*. N.B., House of Assembly, *Journals*, 1826–29. *Daily Evening Globe* (Saint John, N.B.), 26 Sept., 27, 28 Nov. 1865. *Morning Freeman* (Saint John, N.B.), 30 Nov. 1865. *Morning Journal* (Saint John, N.B.), 27, 29 Nov. 1865. *Morning News* (Saint John, N.B.), 31 July, 3, 5, 10, 14 Aug. 1846; 27, 29 Nov. 1865. *Morning Telegraph* (Saint John, N.B.), 25 Nov. 1865. *New Brunswick Courier*, 23 June 1827, 28 Oct. 1834. Lawrence, *Judges of N.B.* (Stockton). James Hannay, "The Supreme Court," *Daily Telegraph* (Saint John, N.B.), 23 Dec. 1892.

PARKS, WILLIAM, merchant; b. 11 Feb. 1800 at Buckley, County Monaghan (Republic of Ireland); m. Ann Hegan in Ireland, and they had five sons and two daughters; sailed late in 1870 from Halifax for Liverpool aboard the ss *City of Boston*, which disappeared.

Although the surviving record does not admit of a personal portrait of William Parks, it is sufficient to indicate that during the middle decades of the 19th century he was a leader in the commercial and religious affairs of Saint John, N.B., when that port was a centre of commerce in British North America. Parks, somewhat typically for a prominent merchant of his day, had wide business interests. They extended from the operation of an import and retail establishment through shipowning and banking to the manufacturing of cotton.

William Parks had immigrated to New Brunswick in 1822 and settled in Saint John. He apparently began in the grocery and dry goods business. In the early 1840s he went into shipowning.

The 737-ton *Lady Sale*, built by Francis and Joseph Ruddock, was the first of nine vessels owned by Parks in the years 1843 to 1867, five of which were retained for long periods. Until 1846 he usually owned his vessels with John Hegan, with whom he may have been in general partnership and to whom he was probably related by marriage. In 1847 Parks went into partnership with his eldest son, Samuel. In the firm, styled as William Parks and Son, the father was the dominant partner at least until 1860. Samuel died in 1863 and another son, John Hegan Parks, a civil engineer, apparently took his place.

Shipowning was probably only of secondary interest to William Parks, who took a more or less important role in many of the commercial institutions of Saint John. He was an active member of the city's board of trade. By 1849 he was a director of the Commercial Bank of New Brunswick, which was long Saint John's largest bank, and he was president for the last seven years of his life. Parks was a substantial investor in the Saint John Gas Light Company, the Saint John Water Company, and, it would appear, the New Brunswick Marine Insurance Company. Moreover, he was a prime mover, and the president from 1865, of the locally much championed Western Extension Railway. This enterprise, which envisaged the western extension of the European and North American Railway from Saint John to the New England states, was seen by the anti-confederate forces in New Brunswick as the economic basis for an alternative to confederation with Canada, and as such drew heavy fire from those favouring confederation. The *Halifax Citizen* stated that "The New Brunswickers in laying down the rails to the boundaries, would be forging link after link of a chain which would inevitably bind them to the chariot wheels of the North" of the United States. Perhaps Parks' most commercially conspicuous venture was his founding in 1861 on Courtenay Bay of the New Brunswick Cotton Mill. His son John was also active in founding and running the mill and in due course inherited it. It is a tribute to William Parks' commercial acumen that the setting up of the cotton mill was well timed to take advantage of the general disruption in cotton manufacturing caused by the American Civil War.

Parks was prominent in the religious life of Saint John in the mid 1840s. In 1843–44 he led the Irish members out of the Scots-dominated St Andrew's Church to form Saint John Presbyterian, and he played the main part in obtaining Irish clergymen for the new congregation – Robert Irvine in 1844 and, after his resignation in 1852, William Elder. Parks was an evangelical

Partelow

of note, and served on the executives of the Bible Society and the Evangelical Union, an interdenominational organization of evangelical Christians founded in 1846 "to secure perfect equality in civil privileges among all denominations. . . ." He was drawn into the latter's political wing, the Election Society, which opposed the privileged position of the Church of England in New Brunswick. Parks stood for a time as a candidate for the society in the provincial election of 1846, but withdrew before the polling.

William Parks emerges as an energetic, respectable, and prominent entrepreneur of his time. Equally he appears as a man of his place, of Saint John. His business interests bore a peculiarly Saint John stamp; indeed his railway enterprise epitomized the strong current of anti-confederate opinion which was then running through the mercantile class of the port.

RICHARD RICE and T. W. ACHESON

N.B. Museum, Parks family papers. PAC, MG 9, A10, 5, p.7 (mfm. at N.B. Museum). PRO, BT 107–8. *Loyalist* (Fredericton), 22 Sept. 1846. *New Brunswick Courier*, 28 March 1846. *Canadian biographical dictionary*, II, 634–35. *The merchants' and farmers' almanack* . . . (Saint John, N.B.), 1849. Davin, *Irishman in Can.* MacNutt, *New Brunswick*.

PARTELOW, JOHN RICHARD, merchant and politician; b. 1796 at Saint John, N.B., son of a shoemaker, Jehiel Partelow; m. in 1819 Jane Hamlin Matthews, and they had eight daughters; d. 13 Jan. 1865 at Fredericton, N.B.

Of loyalist extraction, John Richard Partelow was educated in the public schools of Saint John and by private tuition. After working as a clerk in a Saint John store, he was by 1827 engaged in business as a general merchant. Partelow became prominent in 1823 as a partisan of Ward Chipman* Sr when the presidency of the Council was contested by Christopher Billopp* and Chipman following the death of Lieutenant Governor George Stracy Smyth*. At the time of his entry into the assembly in 1827 as a member for Saint John County, he enjoyed a public confidence probably unequalled by any other politician. He remained in the assembly until 1855.

Partelow's peculiar ascendancy in the assembly rested on his capacity to make its members agree on distribution of revenue among the constituencies. In an age when there was no minister of finance to produce an annual estimate of income and expenditure, the assembly's committee on appropriations allocated the roughly estimated available funds to the counties. Members for each county would then meet to divide the patronage. This system, later designated by Lord Sydenham [Thomson*] as "abominable," and often described as log-rolling, made every member of the assembly a distributor of the public funds. Partelow was chairman of both the appropriations and audit committees. Amid the annual bargaining he was the master, always able to achieve compromise. George Edward Fenety*, a contemporary journalist, saw him as one "who knew better than any other person in the legislature how to manipulate honourable members and mould them to his purposes." Jovial and hearty in his demeanour, he was sometimes jocularly called "the Chancellor of the Exchequer."

Partelow was not renowned for eloquence, but the leadership he acquired as chairman of the appropriations committee brought him to the fore in the contest to gain greater colonial autonomy in the 1830s. Early in the decade he was prominent, along with Charles Simonds* and Edward Barron Chandler*, in the assembly's agitation for control of the casual and territorial revenues, several times demanding from the executive information on the size of these revenues and on expenditures from these funds. Success came in 1837 when the British government agreed to turn over control of the casual and territorial revenues to the assembly in return for a guaranteed civil list. Partelow's influence was now immensely enlarged because of the vast increase in revenue at the disposal of the assembly. In an era of free spending he presided over the flow of public money for construction of roads and bridges, subsidies to schools, pensions and gratuities to those who deserved favour. His enhanced popularity did not wither with adverse times in 1841. In the election of 1842, when the province was rapidly sinking deeply into debt, he emerged, as usual, at the top of the poll for Saint John county.

In addition to his commanding position in provincial finances he held the provincial appointment of chamberlain of the city of Saint John from 1827 to 1843. During the 1840s the finances of the city were in a precarious state owing to the heavy expense of cutting streets through the rocks on which Saint John was built. His few enemies blamed him for the impending bankruptcy of the city but he remained at the height of public favour and served as mayor in 1847–48.

Though Partelow remained behind the scenes, all governments of the 1840s were dependent on his support. This became most apparent at the time of the crisis surrounding the appointment of Alfred Reade as provincial secretary in 1845, when Sir William COLEBROOKE was mortified by resignations in his Executive Council and was compelled to invite the dissidents to return on the conditions they made. Colebrooke was certain that the "sinister" machinations of Partelow behind the scenes were principally responsible for his humiliation. Yet at this stage Partelow could not be considered a reformer. He was eminently satisfied with the existing system of administration and disapproved of the idea of responsible government which appeared on the horizon in 1846–47. Fenety's unvarnished opinion was that he was "opposed to any change in the Constitution" and that he was "the most influential opponent of Responsible Government and Reform." Without holding any important provincial office, he was the master of the administration by reason of his grip on a financial apparatus that must be described as disorderly as well as popularly based.

Partelow's dominant position was recognized in 1848 when Lieutenant Governor Sir Edmund Walker HEAD introduced responsible government and reluctantly offered the provincial secretaryship to Partelow. The assembly had not surrendered the right to initiate money grants and only Partelow could manage it. "His opinion," said Head, "has the greatest weight in the assembly in all matters relating to money." In 1849 Partelow joined Lemuel Allan Wilmot* as a delegation to a Halifax conference to discuss reciprocity with the United States. He held the office of provincial secretary until Head's predominantly conservative coalition government led by E. B. Chandler and Robert Leonard Hazen* left office in 1854.

Partelow finished his career in a manner just as unusual as that by which he established his early ascendancy. In 1855 his former opponents, the so-called "smashers," led by Charles Fisher* and William Johnstone Ritchie*, on assuming office, bought the auditor generalship from Frederick Phillips Robinson for £350 and presented the position to Partelow, later increasing his salary. Lieutenant Governor John Henry Thomas Manners-Sutton* was at a loss to explain this transaction, so reminiscent of more unenlightened times before the arrival of responsible government. Partelow held the position until his death in 1865.

W. S. MacNutt

PANB, J. C. and H. B. Graves, "New Brunswick political biography." Fenety, *Political notes and observations. The old grave-yard, Fredericton, New Brunswick: epitaphs copied by the York-Sunbury Historical Society Inc.*, comp. L. M. B. Maxwell ([Fredericton], 1938). Hannay, *History of N.B.*, II, 78–82. MacNutt, *New Brunswick*.

PEENAQUIM (Pe-na-koam, Penukwiim, translated as seen from afar, far seer, far off in sight, and far off dawn; also known as **Onis tay say nah que im, Calf Rising in Sight**, and **Bull Collar)**, chief of the Blood tribe of the Blackfoot nation; b. *c.* 1810, probably in what is now southern Alberta, son of Two Suns; d. 1869 near the present city of Lethbridge, Alta.

From about 1840 until his death this Indian warrior was considered to be the leading chief of the Blood tribe, which hunted over much of what is now southern Alberta. Tribal tradition has still much to say about his deeds but it is difficult to assign dates or locations to such records. Peenaquim was a close friend of fellow chieftain Sotai-na*, and both had the reputation of being fearless in battle. On one occasion Peenaquim led a war party to raid the Crees. At the North Saskatchewan River they unexpectedly met a brigade of Hudson's Bay Company boats. Peenaquim was recognized as a chief, exchanged gifts and clothing with the chief factor, possibly John Rowand*, and left the brigade in peace. When the Bloods shortly after discovered a Cree camp, Peenaquim walked boldly into it and shot their chief, Handsome Man. Not long after, near the Sweetgrass Hills, Peenaquim and fellow chief Calf Shirt [Onistah-sokaksin*] led a three-day pursuit of nine Cree raiders and surrounded and killed them. In another battle, against the Assiniboins, he cut off the hand of one of their warriors. His most famous battle was against some Crow Indians. While he and Sotai-na were spying on their camp, Peenaquim deliberately flashed a mirror to let them know they were being watched. When the Crows attacked, Peenaquim, then known as Bull Collar, killed a chief bearing the same name and Sotai-na did the same.

Peenaquim had a large tribal following, estimated at the time of his death as being 2,500 people. Of these, some 260 were from his own band; called the Fish Eaters (Mamyowis), they had received that distinctive name when starvation had forced them to eat fish, a food they normally abhorred.

In about 1840, Peenaquim's sister, Medicine Snake Woman, married Alexander Culbertson, chief trader at Fort Union on the Missouri River. This alliance gave the Americans great influence among the Bloods and, at the same time, made Peenaquim the most powerful chief in the Blackfoot nation. He received many gifts from the traders, and also carried on a limited trade himself. An entry for 26 March 1855 in the Fort Benton journal indicates the chief's importance: "A party of Blood Indians arrived for trade, headed by Mr. Culbertsons Bro in Law, Gave

Peers

them a salute and hoisted our flag.'' When the American government negotiated a treaty with the Blackfoot tribes in 1855, Culbertson was prominent in the proceedings. The first to sign the treaty for the Bloods was Peenaquim, using his name Onis tay say nah que im [*see* Onistah Sokaksin].

Because of his close relationships with the Americans, Peenaquim usually hunted in southeastern Alberta and northern Montana, taking his tribe's robes and dried meat to Fort Benton on the Missouri River. By 1866 the influx of gold seekers into Montana had resulted in several conflicts, and in that year the chief took his followers north to southern Alberta between the Belly and Red Deer rivers. They were in danger of attack by Crees, but Peenaquim successfully kept his warriors at peace during this trying period.

In 1869, Peenaquim was among the first of his band to die in a devastating smallpox epidemic. During the winter of 1869–70 no less than 630 Bloods were victims. Shortly before his death, Peenaquim spoke to his people: ''The last hour of Pe-na-koam has come, but to his people he says, Be brave; separate into small parties, so that this disease will have less power to kill you; be strong to fight our enemies the Crees, and be able to destroy them.'' Peenaquim was buried in the valley of the Oldman River, just north of Lethbridge. He was described by one Montanan as ''the greatest chief Major Culbertson ever saw amongst the Blackfeet – having 10 wives and 100 horses,'' and William Francis Butler*, a visitor to Rocky Mountain House, said he was ''one of their greatest men.'' Peenaquim's chieftainship was taken for a few months by his older brother, Kyiyo-siksinum (Black Bear), and when the latter died in 1870 his nephew Mekaisto* (Red Crow) became chief of the Bloods and famous in his own right.

HUGH A. DEMPSEY

Private archives, H. A. Dempsey (Calgary), Interviews with John Cotton, 1953; Percy Creighton, 1954; Charlie Pantherbone, 1954; and Frank Red Crow, 1954 (unpublished field notes). W. F. Butler, *The great lone land: a narrative of travel and adventure in the north-west of America* (2nd ed., London, 1872). ''The Fort Benton journal, 1854–1856,'' ed. Anne McDonnell, Mont. Hist. Soc., *Contributions* (Helena), X (1940), 13, 26. H. A. Dempsey, *Crowfoot, chief of the Blackfeet* (Edmonton, 1972), 38–39. S. H. Middleton, *Kainai chieftainship; history, evolution, and culture of the Blood Indians; origin of the sun-dance* (Lethbridge, Alta., [1953]), 116, 133, 136, 157–58. J. W. Schultz and J. L. Donaldson, *The sun god's children* (Boston and New York, 1930), 170. J. H. Bradley, ''Characteristics, habits, and customs of the Blackfeet Indians,'' Mont. Hist. Soc., *Contributions*, IX, (1923), 256.

PEERS, HENRY NEWSHAM, HBC officer and British Columbia pioneer; b. 17 March 1821 at Lymington, Hampshire, England, son of Captain H. Peers; d. 27 March 1864 at Saanich, near Victoria, Vancouver Island.

Henry Newsham Peers attended the Royal Military Academy at Woolwich from which he was dismissed after 18 months. On 5 Jan. 1841 he was appointed to the Montreal Department of the Hudson's Bay Company as an apprentice clerk at a progressive salary of £20, £25, £30, £40, and £50 per annum. Peers sailed from England in March 1841 for Montreal. During 1841–42 and 1842–43 he served at Lachine, Canada East, where he ''gave great satisfaction'' but was ''dying to get away . . . to the North.''

Peers was transferred to the Columbia District as an apprentice clerk in 1843 and was attached to Fort Vancouver (Vancouver, Wash.) as a clerk under Richard Lane* and Thomas Lowe* until March 1848. In the fall of 1844, when a forest fire nearly engulfed Fort Vancouver, Peers was temporarily in charge of the fort's sawmill. His map of the fort showing the conflagration remains a prime source of information about structures and land use there. In June 1846 the Oregon Treaty established the 49th parallel as the boundary between the United States and British territories from the Rocky Mountains to the Pacific. The HBC was anxious to hold its Columbia trade, but because of the treaty it decided to abandon Fort George (now Astoria, Oreg.) at the mouth of that river. On 1 Aug. 1846, Peers left for Fort George to succeed Alexander Lattie and to superintend the erection of a house and store at Baker's Bay on the north side of the river. There he acted as port agent of the HBC.

That autumn Peers was elected to represent Vancouver County in the second regular session of the assembly established by the provisional government of Oregon. Peers' chief contribution was to prepare the Oregon petition of 19 Dec. 1846, which urged the United States Congress to confirm land titles, adopt measures for education, and establish navigational facilities on the Columbia River. The petition was tabled in the Senate a year later. Peers was re-elected in 1847, but did not attend the legislature. In its attempt to secure its claims to Fort Vancouver and surrounding lands after the Oregon treaty, the HBC assigned 640-acre holdings to individual employees who could be considered *bona fide* settlers by the Oregon government. Peers had claimed the square mile on which the flour mill west of the fort was located.

The 1846 treaty also caused the HBC to seek a route for its New Caledonia (now British Columbia) brigades which would use the Fraser River rather than the Columbia. In 1846 and 1847, Alexander Caulfield Anderson* explored routes from Kamloops to the lower Fraser, but elevation, deep snow lasting well into summer, risky river crossings, and excessive travelling time caused James Douglas* and Peter Skene Ogden* to reject his findings. During the summer of 1848, accordingly, Peers was detached from the New Caledonia brigade, to which he had been assigned for outfit 1848–49, and ordered to re-locate Anderson's 1846 route to the Fraser. Peers found a more practical route from Kamloops to the mouth of the Coquihalla River on which elevation and lingering snow were not so formidable. A new route was increasingly urgent because of American customs duties on goods landed at Fort Vancouver and the disruption of the Columbia River route by the massacre at the Whitman mission (near Walla Walla, Wash.) and the resulting Cayuse War. In October 1848, James Douglas instructed Peers to establish Fort Hope (Hope) on the Fraser River at the mouth of the Coquihalla. Peers was then to open a new road up the Coquihalla, thence up the valleys of Peers Creek and the Sowaqua River into the Similkameen valley. From there with the help of a son (or son-in-law) of Anderson's Indian guide in 1846, he would establish the route to Kamloops, via the Tulameen River and Otter Lake where they would rejoin Anderson's track of 1846. Peers' new route had just five encampments between Fort Hope and Otter Lake, and was faster than Anderson's 1847 route. He worked on the new road, which provided a viable all-British route from the interior, during the winter of 1848–49, and for outfit 1849–50 he was in charge of Fort Kamloops owing to the illness of John Tod*. Peers' route was ready for use by both outbound and inbound brigades in the summer of 1850 when more work was done, and by 1851–52 the route was finally settled and made passable for loaded horses.

In June 1850, Governor Sir George Simpson* informed Peers' father-in-law, James Murray Yale*, that Peers was to be stationed at the coal mines "where he will have a fair field for rendering conspicuous and valuable services to the Company," but Peers spent outfit 1850–51 as a clerk at Fort Langley where his "fur trade marriage" to Eliza Yale was solemnized on 13 July 1851. (Four daughters and a son survived their parents.) The Peers left Fort Langley in September 1851 for Cowlitz Farm, in what was to become Washington Territory in 1853, where Peers was in charge until 1857, when he went on furlough. At Cowlitz, he "turned all the rascals off" who had given the previous manager so much trouble and achieved a better balance sheet. Peers was commissioned a chief trader on 30 March 1853, and during the Indian wars of 1855–56, at the request of Governor Isaac I. Stevens of Washington Territory, assisted in raising a company of 39 mounted men to serve for three months as the 1st Regiment of the Cowlitz Rangers, of which he was captain. He never received compensation from the United States government for these services.

In September 1858, after his furlough, Peers and James H. Ray (whom Governor James Douglas described as "an American citizen . . . [of] very bad character") attempted to claim two square miles along the Fraser River at Fort Langley, which, it appeared, would become the capital of the mainland colony of British Columbia, then being created. They proposed to colonize the land with British subjects, but Douglas considered their claim an "attempt at squatting" which must "be put down by the strong hand, being a flagrant violation of the rights of the Crown." Later that month Douglas issued a proclamation that no lands had been sold and that, as title still rested with the crown, all squatters would be ejected and those attempting to sell land would be prosecuted. Peers, who had tried to sell his Vancouver Island farm during the summer of 1858, thereupon departed for England.

He retired from the HBC on 1 June 1859, and by November he was back at his Colquitz Farm just north of Victoria. He had purchased the 205 acres from the HBC in January 1852. During the winter of 1859–60, Peers had a saw and grist mill constructed, evidently with funds provided by Yale who bought adjacent property at that time. He spent the remaining four years of his life farming at Colquitz (to which he introduced California quail with the intention of stocking the island with game birds) and managing his various rural and city properties.

WILLIAM R. SAMPSON

Bancroft Library, University of California (Berkeley), A. C. Anderson, "History of the northwest coast" (1878) (typescript at PABC). PABC, B.C. law courts (Victoria), Probate records, papers no.539, H. N. Peers; Fort Vancouver, Correspondence outward to 1849; Thomas Lowe journal, 1843–50; Henry Newsham Peers journal, 1848; Yale family papers, Correspondence, James Murray Yale. *Daily British Colonist and Victoria Chronicle*, 3, 22, 27 Dec. 1859; 3 Jan., 21 Feb. 1860; 29 March 1864; 8, 9 June 1886. Dorothy

Peguis

Blakey Smith, "The first capital of British Columbia: Langley or New Westminster?" *BCHQ*, XXI (1957–58), 15–50. E. P. Creech, "Similkameen trails, 1846–61," *BCHQ*, V (1941), 255–67.

PEGUIS, (**Be-gou-ais, Be-gwa-is, Pegeois, Pe-gouisse, Pegowis, Pegqas, Pigewis, Pigwys**; also known as the **Destroyer** and **Little Chip**, and baptized **William King**), Saulteaux Indian chief; b. *c.* 1774 near Sault Ste Marie (Ont.); d. 28 Sept. 1864 at Red River.

Born in the Great Lakes area, Peguis was among the Saulteaux, or Ojibwa, who migrated west with the fur trade in the late 1790s, settling on Netley Creek, a branch of the Red River south of Lake Winnipeg. He welcomed the first settlers brought to the Red River area by Lord Selkirk [Douglas*] in 1812 and is given credit for aiding and defending them during their difficult years. When the main group of settlers arrived in 1814 to find none of the promised gardens planted or houses built, Peguis guided them to Fort Daer (Pembina, N.D.) to hunt buffalo. The children, weak from the journey, were carried on ponies provided by the Indians. The Saulteaux showed the settlers how to hunt and brought them along on their annual trek to buffalo country.

Peguis sided with the Hudson's Bay Company during its dispute with the North West Company, and after the Selkirk settlers had been attacked at Seven Oaks on 19 June 1816 [*see* Robert Semple*] he offered assistance to the survivors. The future grandmother of Louis Riel*, the first white woman resident in the West, Marie-Anne Gaboury*, whose husband was away when the Nor'Westers occupied Fort Douglas, was rescued by Peguis, and she and her children were kept safely in his camp for several weeks. Before the other settlers fled north to Norway House, they were befriended and fed by Peguis.

On 18 July 1817 Peguis was one of five Saulteaux and Cree chiefs who signed a treaty with Lord Selkirk to provide an area for settlement purposes. This included a strip of land two miles wide on each side of the Red and Assiniboine rivers, beginning at their confluence within the present city of Winnipeg and extending up the Red to what is now Grand Forks (N.D.) and up the Assiniboine to Rat Creek. Plots of land reaching six miles in each direction from Fort Douglas, Fort Daer, and Grand Forks were also included. In exchange, each tribe was to receive annual payments of 100 lbs of tobacco. This land treaty was the first to be signed in western Canada.

Colin Inkster*, a Manitoba politician, writing in 1909 remembered Peguis as "short in stature, with a strong, well-knit frame, and the voice of an orator." He was "clad in a cotton shirt, breech clout, red cloth leggings and over all a blanket wrapped loosely about him, his hair hung in two long plaits studded with brass ornaments, his breast decorated with medals." One of the latter was a medal presented to him by Lord Selkirk as a confirmation of the agreement of 1817. Peguis' appearance, however, was disfigured as part of his nose had been bitten off during a tribal quarrel in about 1802. As a result, he was known to some settlers as "The Cut-Nosed Chief."

Peguis and his followers, who in 1816 numbered 65 men, lived by raising corn, potatoes, barley, and other grain at their village on Netley Creek, as well as by hunting. Peguis was met at this village by Anglican missionary John West* in 1820 and later he supported missionary work among his followers [*see* William COCKRAN]. In 1836 St Peter's mission was built nearby to serve the Christian Indians, and on 7 Oct. 1840 Peguis gave up three of his four wives so that he could be baptized by the Reverend John SMITHURST. He and his remaining wife took the names William and Victoria King, and their children later adopted the surname of Prince.

Peguis was recognized and honoured by the HBC throughout his life, and in 1835 Governor George Simpson* gave him an annuity of £5 a year in recognition of his contributions. Peguis also carried with him a testimonial from Lord Selkirk which stated that he was "one of the principal chiefs of the Chipeways, or Saulteaux of Red River, has been a steady friend of the settlement ever since its first establishment, and has never deserted its cause in its greatest reverses."

Peguis was a welcome visitor to the Red River Settlement and, even after the threat of native hostilities had passed, his earlier support was remembered. However, in 1860 Peguis became dissatisfied with the white settlers when they began using lands not surrendered by his tribe, and he made a formal protest to the Aborigines' Protection Society. He also stated that the tobacco payment instituted in 1817 had been simply a goodwill token and that arrangements for the formal surrender of the land had never taken place. In addition, he questioned the right of the governor and Council of Assiniboia to make any laws which affected the unsurrendered area until after a further treaty was made. No action was taken by the authorities to rectify the situation until after the area was transferred to the Dominion of Canada in 1870; then Treaty No.1 was negotiated by Peguis' son, Mis-koo-kee-new, known as Red Eagle or Henry Prince, in August 1871.

Peguis did not live to see the treaty; he died in September 1864, and was buried in the graveyard of St Peter's Church. In 1924 a monument honouring the chief was erected in Kildonan Park, Winnipeg.

HUGH A. DEMPSEY

Morris, *Treaties of Can. with Indians*, 13–15, 298–300, 313–16. [John Tanner], *A narrative of the captivity and adventures of John Tanner (U.S. interpreter at the Sault de Ste-Marie) during thirty years of residence among the Indians in the interior of North America* (Minneapolis, Minn., 1956), 154. John West, *The substance of a journal during a residence at the Red River colony, British North America; and frequent excursions among the North-West American Indians, in the years 1820, 1821, 1822, 1823* (London, 1824; repr. [East Ardsley, Eng., and New York], 1966), 102–4. A. S. Morton, *History of the Canadian west*. W. L. Morton, *Man.: a history* (1957). A. E. Thompson, *Chief Peguis and his descendants* (Winnipeg, 1973). Colin Inkster, "Noble chief Peguis," *Manitoba Free Press* (Winnipeg), 17 April 1909. Betty Woods, "Peguis," *Western Producer* (Saskatoon, Sask.), 18 Aug. 1966.

PENNEFATHER, RICHARD THEODORE, office-holder; b. *c*. 1830, son of Edward Pennefather, a judge, and Suzan Darby; d. late in 1865 in Ceylon.

Richard Theodore Pennefather was the offspring of an Anglo-Irish family of soldiers and clerics. From 1848 to 1854 he was the private secretary of Sir Edmund Walker HEAD, lieutenant governor of New Brunswick, then came with him, still as private secretary, to the Province of Canada, when Head was made its governor general in 1854. A rather introverted, genteel young man, Pennefather was trusted by Head but never liked or understood by him. "He is young – about 21 – well-informed and a gentleman," wrote Head shortly after his arrival in Canada, "but I cannot say that he is particularly agreeable to me as he is so shy and reserved." Pennefather did not enhance his reputation with Head by marrying a young lady who, though respectable enough, was not considered at all pretty by the governor general. In September 1860, during the visit of the Prince of Wales to North America, Pennefather attracted a great deal of attention by falling into the river at Detroit as the royal vessel left the dock. The picture that results from all this is that of a fairly serious, aloof young man with a penchant for making *faux pas*.

In February 1856, Pennefather became the governor general's civil secretary and superintendent-general of Indian affairs in the Province of Canada. During his tenure the Indian Department was still in a state of change and the administrative confusions of the early 1840s had not yet disappeared. Indian affairs in Lower and Upper Canada had been administered separately after 1830, but in 1841 the Indians in the Province of Canada were placed under the authority of the governor general. In 1842, with the appointment of a royal commission to investigate the Indian Department, there had begun a wholesale change in the organization of the department. Indian affairs in the Province of Canada were then placed under the civil secretary who was *ex officio* superintendent-general; in Canada West superintendents and agents became directly responsible to the governor general through the civil secretary, but in Canada East responsibility for Indian affairs, although nominally in the charge of the civil secretary remained the concern of the military secretary (it was to him that Duncan Campbell NAPIER, the chief Indian affairs official in Canada East in the 1840s and 1850s, reported). Questions of jurisdiction were further complicated by the fact that British officials had been making it clear from as early as the 1820s that they hoped Canadian authorities would eventually assume the running of the Indian Department. The "little England" sentiment of the 1840s and 1850s strengthened this feeling; by the end of the 1850s, Britain informed Canada that the transfer must occur.

Pennefather, as superintendent-general, was the official head of the Indian Department, but its day-to-day affairs were largely in the hands of superintendents and agents, especially in Upper Canada. At the beginning of his service Pennefather was fortunately served by experienced officials, notably Napier in Canada East and Thomas Gummersall Anderson* in Canada West. They were, however, to resign in 1857 and 1858 respectively.

Pennefather's greatest contribution to Canada was his chairmanship of a three-man commission which conducted an inquiry from 1856 to 1858 into the Indian Department's operations. The report of 1858 provided a complete picture of the department and of the Indian bands of the province through use of a massive number of statistics. It was noted with surprise that efforts to "civilize" the Indians were still piece-meal despite almost 30 years of such a policy. Because the Indians did not respond to attempts at "civilization," and because of the lack of organization and funding in the department, conditions among the Indians were not good in the late 1850s [*see* George IRONSIDE]. The commission urged compassionate and effective treatment for the Indians' social ills. Feeling that administrative confusion was still responsible for many of their

Perley

problems, it urged the establishment of a centralized Indian Department with its own permanent head. This step was finally taken by the Canadian government in 1862, two years after the relinquishing of imperial control.

The transfer to Canadian authority in 1860 meant that Pennefather reverted to his position as Head's private secretary. He left Canada in 1861 when Head's term of office expired. He went to Ceylon where he was executive councillor and auditor-general from 1862 until his death in 1865.

DOUGLAS LEIGHTON

PAC, RG 10, vols. 116–18, 270–72, 714, 752–60. Can., Prov. of, Legislative Assembly, *Journals*, 1858, VI, app.21. Macdonald, *Letters* (Johnson and Stelmack), I. John Ferguson, *Ceylon in 1883: the leading crown colony of the British empire; with an account of the progress made since 1803 under successive British governors* (London, 1883), 243. Hodgetts, *Pioneer public service*, 205–25. D. G. G. Kerr, *Sir Edmund Head, a scholarly governor* (Toronto, 1954), 57. E. W. Watkin, *Canada and the States; recollections, 1851 to 1886* (London and New York, [1887]), 502.

PERLEY, MOSES HENRY, lawyer, entrepreneur, naturalist, author, and office-holder; b. 31 Dec. 1804 at Maugerville, Sunbury County, N.B., of pre-loyalist New Brunswick ancestry, son of Moses Perley and his cousin Mary Perley; m. 6 Sept. 1829 Jane Ketchum, and they had eight children; d. 17 Aug. 1862 on board the HMS *Desperate* off the Labrador coast.

Shortly before Moses Henry Perley's birth his father was accidentally killed. His mother moved to Saint John, N.B., when he was very young and he was educated there in the public schools. As a boy he spent his summers hunting, fishing, and trading with the Indians on the Saint John River and its tributaries. Perley's interest in the welfare of the Indians increased after an unfortunate incident in 1822 when he accidentally killed an Indian while target shooting. During these early years Perley became an avid sportsman and developed his intense lifelong interest in natural history.

Perley studied law and was called to the bar in 1830. As a young lawyer, he still found time to continue exploring the inland waterways of the province, to make frequent visits to Indian settlements, and to begin collecting information on the natural resources of the province which would later assist him in his business life and in his position as emigrant agent.

Between 1835 and 1838 Perley was involved in several business ventures, many of which were unsuccessful. He was secretary of the Lancaster Mill Company, bought mills on the Musquash River, and attempted to develop coal mines on the Salmon River in Queens County. Sometimes he was in partnership with New England interests and in the late 1830s was accused by Tory newspapers of being the leading promoter of American commercial interests in New Brunswick. An attempt to purchase 80,000 acres of land in Charlotte County failed when the Executive Council in 1836 refused to allow Perley to pay in instalments or to refund him money paid in advance for parts of the land which were found unsuitable when surveyed. Throughout his career Perley criticized the Crown Lands Office for restricting instead of encouraging development of the province's timber resources and the settlement of immigrants. Such opinions may have hurt his chances in 1836–37 when he tried to obtain assistance from the government, which harboured some opposition to land sales to Americans and to Perley's well-known connections with New England. Moreover his schemes were hampered by a scarcity of American capital for investment abroad created by economic problems in the United States in the late 1830s. Perley continued, nevertheless, to be involved with American businessmen in his own interest and to encourage foreign investment as a necessary means of developing the resources of the province. His American connections later proved useful when he figured in the reciprocity negotiations of 1854.

Perley's extensive knowledge of Indian settlements and his concern for the Indians' welfare resulted in his appointment as the province's commissioner of Indian affairs, an office without salary. Perley claimed to have received this appointment in 1839, but there are no records of his activity before 1841. With Lieutenant Governor Sir William COLEBROOKE's permission, he visited all the Indian settlements in the province, and in 1842 began preparing his first report, in which he protested against the encroachments of squatters on Indian lands. He recommended the crown continue to hold in trust the reserves granted to the Indians and that they be encouraged to form village settlements where schools could be established and regular visits could be made by doctors. He felt that this programme should be carried out without interfering with the Indians' way of life. Encouraged by the lieutenant governor to continue his investigative work, Perley again visited Indian settlements in 1842 and also the Micmac settlements on Prince Edward Island in 1842 and 1843. In the latter years he was offered the post of chief superintendent of Indian affairs for the province of Canada, but a new governor, Sir Charles Metcalfe*, was ap-

628

pointed before negotiations were completed. Perley's second detailed report on the reserves, submitted to the government in 1843, repeated his recommendations made the year before.

The Indians appreciated Perley's work and he was made a chief of the Malecites in 1839 and of the Micmacs in 1840. In 1842 he was elected "Wunjeet Sagamore" or "chief over all." He was often in their settlements – in February 1843 he complained that at times he had "not slept in a bed for two months together" – and he frequently addressed tribal gatherings dressed in Indian clothing.

Perley played a major role in the drafting of New Brunswick's Indian Act of 1844, which was designed in part to put into effect some of the recommendations of his reports, but at the same time would allow the government to sell some of the reserve lands and to put the money into a fund to be used for the benefit of the Indians. In his capacity as an honorary Indian chief, Perley sharply criticized the act as it was passed. He believed squatters would not be removed from the Indians' territory, and that the government sale of large sections of the reserves would provide little benefit for the Indians. When he attempted to send objections to the colonial secretary, Governor Colebrooke and his Executive Council refused to forward the letter. A committee of the council was appointed to study his criticisms; it reported that he had "an erroneous idea that its [the act's] provisions require the Government to make sale of the Indian Reserves and that thus the different Tribes would be deprived of their Hunting grounds and other settlements but partially formed by them." The committee claimed no government would use its powers in such a way, but the act did, in fact, enable the government to sell any part of the reserves which could be considered a hindrance to settlement if left with the Indians.

Under the provisions of the act Perley was appointed commissioner for Indian affairs for Saint John County. However, as the man most knowledgeable about Indian affairs throughout the province, he was sent in 1845 to Northumberland County to make inquiries into the claims of squatters on Indian lands, and in September of that year he was also appointed commissioner to act with local commissioners to put various provisions of the act into effect. He was also to visit all the reserves in the province, look into settlement of the Indians on them, and investigate squatters' claims. He soon found that adverse public opinion and government reluctance, particularly to remove squatters, hampered enforcement of the act. Squatters on the Tobique

Reserve informed him they would burn their buildings rather than pay for clear titles to the lands. In 1848 Perley pointed out that land was being sold on credit and not a penny had gone into the Indian fund. There was, therefore, no money to pay the local commissioners or to be used for the Indians. Perley recommended that sufficient land be reserved for the use of the Indians and that the government provide a fixed annuity for them. The provincial government was not favourable, and in July 1848, when Perley intervened in a dispute in Northumberland County, he was warned against such action where he lacked government authority. He took his protest to the lieutenant governor, Sir Edmund Walker HEAD. There is no record of a meeting, but soon after this time Head informed the colonial secretary that Perley would no longer be employed in Indian affairs, having exceeded his office by publicly criticizing the government's Indian policy.

Perley had often encountered difficulty obtaining reimbursement for his expenses in visiting the settlements but was told he would be repaid from the Indian fund "when funds are available." Although he was not paid a regular salary, he often received legal work from the government. He also continued to practise law and to carry on various business activities. After helping to establish the mechanics' institute in Saint John in 1838, he frequently lectured there on the history and resources of the province. He was also active in the formation of the Provincial Association in Saint John in 1844, the principal aim of which was the protection of manufacturing and agricultural interests by tariffs.

During the 1840s Perley undoubtedly became the best informed man in the province on rivers, natural resources, and fisheries. He believed the government had not done enough to develop these resources. In 1843 he began on his own a study of the fisheries of the Gulf of St Lawrence. The same year he also undertook the settlement of immigrants on lands near Saint John, collecting petitions from settlers wishing to purchase lots in Mechanic Settlement and Cork and signatures from those willing to sign bonds guaranteeing their purchases. He helped in laying out the two settlements and collected data on their progress for the government in 1843 and 1844.

Recognized as an able and energetic man, interested in the development of the province, Perley was appointed by the provincial government acting emigrant agent in June 1843 when illness struck Alexander Wedderburn*; a few months later his position was made permanent. He was now responsible for supervising the arrival of immigrants and the enforcement of quarantine

Perley

regulations; he also hoped to use his position as "an excellent field for promoting the settlement of the country and forwarding its best interests." Perley was resolute in his prosecution of captains and firms for violation of British government regulations in the transporting of immigrants to New Brunswick. He had to deal with shiploads of poor immigrants many of whom were suffering from smallpox, cholera, and other diseases, and frequently recommended assistance for them on their arrival. Perley and his staff could make cash advances to those in distress but they were not always reimbursed by the assembly; in 1846 he threatened to resign over these accounts. The matter was settled in 1847 when the British government stepped in to make Perley its emigrant agent in New Brunswick. By this double appointment his annual salary had increased from £100 to £300.

In 1847 one of his tasks was to find homes for 120 orphans, two of whom he took himself. With the support of many medical men in Saint John, he argued, unsuccessfully, against the New Brunswick government's choice of Partridge Island as a quarantine station. In 1851 he recommended that it encourage the emigration of young people from Britain, particularly girls between 14 and 16, who would easily find employment as domestic servants, and who would be helped to find proper homes by means of committees set up in the port towns. Perley prepared a handbook for emigrants, which the government agreed to publish in January 1855. He recommended in March 1855 that 1,000,000 acres of land be set aside for deserving British veterans, but nothing came of the proposal.

The New Brunswick government, in recognition of Perley's abilities, had frequently called on him for special work. In October 1846, when a route was being surveyed for a railway between Nova Scotia and Quebec, he was asked to report on the nature of the country, the mineral resources, the fertility of the soil, and the possibilities for settlement where stations might be located. He was also to study possible branch lines to various New Brunswick cities and towns, and the encouragement such railways would give to the Gulf of St Lawrence and Labrador fisheries. His report, submitted in December 1846, and reflecting the railway enthusiasm of the period, was well received by the government and the colonial secretary. At this time Perley was also preparing his report on the trees of New Brunswick, published in 1847, which was designed to promote the development of forest resources.

Perley was actively interested in other rail-ways, and was involved in the St Andrews and Quebec Railway Company for which in 1847 he spent three months in England. In 1848 he was asked to examine the route being surveyed by John Wilkinson* for the Saint John–Shediac Railway but the work was cancelled because the legislative grant would barely pay the expenses of the surveyor. He attended railway conventions, including the important one in Portland, Maine, in 1850 [see John Alfred Poor*]. In 1848 he persuaded the government to invite Professor J. F. W. Johnston* to New Brunswick to study its agricultural resources. He also spent some time in Fredericton in 1848 and 1849 helping to draft amendments to the Emigrant and Indian acts.

The fisheries provided Perley with another large interest. In 1849 he submitted a report on the New Brunswick fisheries of the Gulf of St Lawrence, which was supplemented later by further studies. In 1848 or 1849 he wrote a preliminary report on the fisheries of the Bay of Fundy and prepared a catalogue of its fishes (published in 1851 and 1852 respectively). In July 1850, after favourable response in New Brunswick and Britain to his reports, he was instructed to make further inquiries into the fisheries in the Bay of Fundy, whenever his duties as emigrant agent would allow. In his tireless study of the inland and sea fisheries in 1849–50 Perley covered some 900 miles, over 500 by canoe. In 1851 he drew up special instructions for the fishery wardens of Charlotte County and recommended the formation of fishery societies along the same lines as the agricultural societies, as well as the establishment of fishing colonies on the coast. Two years later he made further inquiries on the coast between Miramichi Bay and Baie Verte. In 1849 and 1852 he helped draft legislation to regulate sea and river fisheries. Between 1852 and 1854 he was deeply involved in compiling statistics on the fisheries for the negotiations between the United States and the British North American colonies which culminated in the Reciprocity Treaty. He spent considerable time in the United States at the request of the British ambassador, visiting Washington, New York, and Quebec during the negotiating process.

On his return from New York in November 1854 Perley was concerned about his own future. Except for his salary as emigrant agent he had received only his expenses for all his duties and he was "tired of working for the public without fee or reward." In 1855 he got this reward when he was appointed a fishery commissioner to enforce the Reciprocity Treaty, with an annual salary of £300, while continuing as emigrant agent. He was given permission in 1857 to visit London on business connected with his duties as commissioner, and in his capacity as emigrant agent was instructed to promote New Brunswick as a desirable place for British emigrants by publishing material he had collected concerning the resources of the province, and by arranging to sell it in London and other cities and ports. Perley suggested ways to promote emigration, most of which were, however, discarded by the New Brunswick government; for instance, one scheme involving assistance to immigrants was rejected as possibly only encouraging many to use New Brunswick as a stepping stone to Canada and the United States, while another to guarantee work for immigrants on such projects as railway construction was turned down because it was not in the government's power "to guarantee to Immigrants here employment either continuous or temporary or any specified rate of wages."

After Perley's appointment as fishery commissioner, several persons sought his position as emigrant agent. In 1858 many of his political allies, such as Edward Barron Chandler*, were no longer in power. The eagerness of Charles Fisher*'s new administration for reform included jobs for friends, and in May 1858 it was decided that Perley's duties as a fishery commissioner interfered with his duties as emigrant agent. Despite the hesitation of Lieutenant Governor John Henry Thomas Manners-Sutton* because Perley was serving the British as well as the provincial government, he was replaced as provincial agent by Robert Shives. Perley wanted to continue as agent for the British government but it decided that emigration having fallen off so much in recent years, his services, however competent, were no longer needed. He asked to be allowed to continue even without salary, but the governor rejected his offer because it might interfere with Shives' work.

In 1861 Perley was one of the owners of a new newspaper in Saint John, the *Colonial Empire*, which aimed to promote the union of the colonies, intercolonial free trade, railway extension, and the development of mineral resources and fisheries. It was critical of the Fisher administration and in that year Perley and his associates were responsible for bringing to light a scandal involving the Crown Lands Office which resulted in Fisher's resignation.

Continuing as fishery commissioner, Perley visited Prince Edward Island, Newfoundland, and other areas. In the summer of 1862 he became ill on board the *Desperate* while inspecting the fisheries off the Labrador coast. The captain wanted to bring him to Shediac for medical atten-

tion, but he insisted that "politically he would be ruined if he did not this season complete his surveys and visits to the different Bays and fishing stations." He died on board ship on 17 August and was buried at Forteau, Labrador.

Perley was a versatile, energetic man, and a prodigious writer of letters to government and friends on provincial affairs. Throughout his life he showed concern for the welfare of the Indians and the development of the resources of the province. Until the coming to power of the Reformers, he seems to have used his considerable influence with the government primarily to further what he considered the province's best interests. Successive lieutenant governors acknowledged his abilities and energy and availed themselves of his services. He was the most zealous emigrant agent the province ever had. Active as a lecturer and writer, he read widely on all subjects, and published a variety of books, including government reports, natural history, and fiction based on Indian legends. Though a self-trained naturalist, he was recognized as the leading ichthyologist in the Maritime provinces, and as one of the most authoritative in North America. There are few errors of importance in his work on the fish of New Brunswick. He laid the foundation of natural science in the province and was the founder of the Natural History Society of New Brunswick.

W. A. SPRAY

M. H. Perley was a prolific writer on many subjects. His several reports on Indians include *Report on Indian settlements, &c.* (Fredericton, 1842). His publications on the fisheries include *Report on the fisheries of the Gulf of Saint Lawrence* (Fredericton, 1849); *Report on the sea and river fisheries of New Brunswick, within the Gulf of Saint Lawrence and Bay of Chaleur* (Fredericton, 1850); *Report upon the fisheries of the Bay of Fundy* (Fredericton, 1851); and a one-volume collection of these reports entitled *Reports on the sea and river fisheries of New Brunswick* (Fredericton, 1852). He also wrote: *Descriptive catalogue (in part) of the fishes of New Brunswick and Nova Scotia* (Fredericton, 1852); *Handbook of information for emigrants to New-Brunswick* (Saint John, N.B., 1854; London, 1857); "Report on the forest trees of New Brunswick," *Simmonds Colonial Magazine and Foreign Miscellany* (London), XI (May–August 1847), 129–55, 314–24, 412–29; and "The progress of New Brunswick, with a brief view of its resources, natural and industrial," H. Y. Hind et al., *Eighty years' progress of British North America . . .* (Toronto, 1863), 542–653. He also contributed several articles to the *Sporting Rev.* (London).

N.B. Museum, Edward Barron Chandler papers, Colebrooke to Chandler (undated); Marriage register B (1828–39), p.31; N.B. Hist. Soc. papers, William Crane correspondence, M.H. Perley to William Crane, 19

Perrault

March 1837; Indian affairs, M. H. Perley to J. S. Saunders, 17 Aug., 27 Oct. 1846; M. H. Perley papers, personal correspondence, 1813–54 (typescript); Scrapbook 41, p.51; Tilley family papers, temperance; Webster coll. PANB, REX/le/l–g, Colebrooke, letterbooks, 1841–47, pp.29–31, 35–36, 51, 81, 84, 119–20, 200–2, 232–33, 245–47, 257, 269–70, 272–76, 283, 292–93, 300–1, 331; 1841–48, pp.19, 86, 92, 118–19, 131; Head, letterbook, 1850–54, pp.83–84, 373; Manners-Sutton, letterbooks, 1854–58, pp.57, 65, 68, 134, 137, 165, 171, 181, 200–1; 1858–61, pp.23, 46, 61; REX/mi/ex, duplicate minutes, 4, pp.39–42, 94, 158; 5, pp.89–90, 104, 111, 160, 192, 228–29, 266, 363, 389, 401, 414, 439, 449; 6, pp.51, 133, 230, 258, 361, 372, 447–48, 481, 549; 7, pp.194–96, 319–20, 452; REX/pa/Register of appointments and commissions, 1785–1840, pp.95, 141; 1840–57, pp.4, 34, 38–39, 44, 134–36; REX/pa/Surveyor general's correspondence, 1842, II(a); 1843, I(a), 2–3; 1844, II(d); REX/px, 22, pp.2842–45; 31, pp.398–99, 401, 515–19; 32, pp.13–14, 988–89; 33, pp.151–53, 156–61, 189–91, 202–5; 100, pp.2079, 2125–30, 2132–34; Indians, pp.269–73, 308–15; RLE/S55/zz, letter of M. H. Perley, 28 March 1842; RPS, letterbook, 1842–45, pp.216–17, 476–78, 494, 499; 1845–47, pp.66–67, 245, 255–56, 319, 498; 1847–50, pp.25, 71, 146, 161, 184–85, 208, 241, 295, 305, 310–11, 346, 359, 385–89, 430, 443, 458, 469, 567, 668; 1850–54, pp.60, 403, 465, 524, 544, 552; 1854–57, pp.116, 229, 448, 454, 460, 490–92, 510–11, 590; 1857–60, pp.32, 178. PRO, CO 188/106, 180–201, Head to Grey, 7 Aug. 1848; 205–23, "Memorandum on history of Indians"; 188/127, pp.544–45, 547–48, 585–86; 188/131, 8 Nov. 1854, pp.114–15, 464–70; 188/133, 9 Sept. 1862; 188/137, A. J. Thrupp to Sir A. Milne, 22 Aug. 1862.

Colonial Empire (Saint John, N.B.), 1861. *Elgin-Grey papers* (Doughty), I, 26–27; III, 1132–33; IV, 1328. Fenety, *Political notes and observations*, 45, 70, 93, 312, 337, 478, 483, 494–95. N.B., House of Assembly, *Journals*, 1847, app., "Railway and electro-magnetic telegraph," cxxxi–clxxxiv; 1848, app., "Quarantine buildings," xciii–xcv; 1849, app., "Emigrants," xcvi–cv; 1853, app., "Emigration," clxxiii–clxxxi; 1854, 340, 359–61; app., "Emigration," cclix–cclxiii; 1857–58, 88–95, 154. *DNB*. Harper, *Hist. directory*. *History and genealogy of the Perley family*, comp. M. V. B. Perley (Salem, Mass., 1906), 410–15. Morgan, *Bibliotheca Canadensis*, 305–6. MacNutt, *New Brunswick*. Philip Cox, "Life of Moses Henry Perley, writer and scientist," Miramichi Natural History Assoc., *Proc.* (Chatham, N.B.), IV (1905), 33–40. L. F. S. Upton, "Indian affairs in colonial New Brunswick," *Acadiensis*, III (1973–74), no.2, 3–26.

PERRAULT, JOSEPH-JULIEN, Roman Catholic priest and church musician; b. 8 May 1826 in Montreal, son of a merchant, Julien Perrault, and Marie-Sophie Gauvin; d. 22 Aug. 1866 in Varennes, Canada East.

Joseph-Julien Perrault received his basic education at the Collège de Montréal from 1836 to 1844, then began to study theology at the Grand Séminaire of Montreal. He completed his formal education at the Sulpician seminary in Paris, 1847–49. At the church of Saint-Sulpice he also directed post-communion instruction; on 22 Dec. 1849 he was ordained a priest. When he returned to Montreal he was admitted into the Society of Saint-Sulpice and from 1850 to 1853 taught at the Collège de Montréal. In 1853 he was appointed to the parish of Notre-Dame and from 1854 to 1862 was also director of the Congrégation des hommes de Ville-Marie. He helped to obtain new organs for the churches of these groups and to initiate a renovation of Notre-Dame Church. In 1862 Perrault was appointed chaplain of the Christian Brothers. On 9 March 1866 he suffered a stroke, and died a few months later. Well liked as a priest, and fluently bilingual, Perrault won a reputation as a fine orator.

It is as a musician that Perrault is best remembered. Although he learned to play the flute as a boy he never had the opportunity to study a keyboard instrument. Self-taught in music, he became a good score-reader and an inspiring chorusmaster. He conducted the parish choir of Notre-Dame from September 1859 until February 1861 in the absence of the regular choirmaster, Abbé Arsène-Louis Barbarin, and again from October 1863 until his final illness. His conducting included a Haydn mass for the Saint-Jean-Baptiste festival in 1860, and in the following year two performances of Félicien David's symphonic ode for choir and orchestra, *Le Désert*, and excerpts from Mozart's *Requiem*.

Although he did not aspire to professional status as a composer, Perrault was skilled enough to employ in his writing such technical devices as imitation and fugato; he had an instinctive feeling for effect and tone colour. His earliest known work is a four-part choral, *Salve Regina* (1849). Haydn was his favourite composer and model, but his best-known work, the *Messe de Noël, Deo infanti*, is patterned after the *Petite messe pour la nativité de Notre-Seigneur* . . . by the French composer Stéphane-Louis Nicou-Choron, which was made up of Christmas songs. Perrault's work integrates some 15 traditional noëls into an artistic whole, punctuated by contrapuntal passages and recitatives. He wrote the *Kyrie, Gloria, Sanctus*, and *Agnus Dei* in 1859–60 and added the *Credo* and *Magnificat* in 1865 for a Christmas day performance at Notre-Dame church. Perrault's other compositions, about 12 in all, were also intended for specific occasions, for example a *Tantum Ergo* for choir and orchestra for the Pentecost service in 1864. His *Messe des morts* was published, as was his edition of Henry de Thier, *dit* Du Mont's *Messe du second ton*, but Perrault also circulated litho-

Picard

graphed copies of his compositions. The *Messe
de Noël*, published posthumously in 1870, enjoyed popularity for a long time; a rearrangement
was issued in the 20th century by Eugène
Lapierre.

HELMUT KALLMANN

The best known of J.-J. Perrault's works is *Messe de
Noël, Deo Infanti*, A.-L. Barbarin et M.-A. Gosselin,
édit. (Montréal, 1870).
ASSM, 25, Dossier 3, 18 sept. 1866. *Le Canadien*, 24
août 1866. *L'Écho du cabinet de lecture paroissial*, 1er
sept. 1866. Allaire, *Dictionnaire*, I, 427. *Catalogue of
Canadian composers*, ed. Helmut Kallmann (rev. ed.,
Toronto, 1952). Ernest Myrand, *Noëls anciens de la
Nouvelle-France* (2e éd., Québec, 1907), 95–101. "Feu
messire Joseph-Julien Perreault," *Le Canada musical*
(Montréal), I (octobre 1866), 17–20. O.[-M.-H] La-
palice, "Les organistes et maîtres de musique à Notre-
Dame de Montréal," *BRH*, XXV (1919), 243–49.

PERRAULT, LOUIS, bookseller, publisher, and
printer; b. 8 Oct. 1807 at Montreal, Lower
Canada, son of Julien Perrault, a baker, and Eu-
phradine Lamontagne; m. 11 June 1833 Marguerite Roy, daughter of Charles-Fleury Roy, a merchant; d. 6 Jan. 1866 at Montreal.

Louis Perrault belonged "to one of the oldest
and most respected families in this country" according to Laurent-Olivier David*. His father
was typical of those Canadians who, without attaining great wealth, managed in the first quarter
of the 19th century to improve their social and
economic position considerably. A master baker,
then an agent for the coach service connecting
Montreal and Quebec, Julien Perrault identified
himself with the Patriotes, and opened his home
to the party's leaders and their passionate discussions. It was in this atmosphere that Louis
Perrault grew up. At the end of his studies at the
Collège de Montréal in 1826, he was undecided
whether to seek a career in law or in business.

In 1828 he and his brother-in-law Édouard-
Raymond Fabre* became partners in a firm importing books and variety wares, known as the
Librairie française. That year he spent some time
in France "to choose new merchandise" for their
firm, and greatly increased business connections
between the Montreal bookshop and numerous
European suppliers. After seven years the
difficult partnership was dissolved in 1835. Perrault found it hard to adapt himself to the budgetary constraints and accounting procedures that
explained his brother-in-law's success. He preferred to spend money for personal reasons
rather than reinvest profits in the joint venture.
Fabre undertook to continue running the bookshop alone. For his part Perrault then devoted his

time to printing and publishing newspapers, in
particular the *Vindicator and Canadian
Advertiser* (Montreal).

In 1837 his establishment was sacked by the
members of the Doric Club, and his work rooms
destroyed. His political commitment to the Patriote party forced him to take refuge in the United
States in 1837, and he remained there for 18
months. Perrault's correspondence reveals he
was active among political refugees in the United
States. He distributed information from *Le Pays*
(Montreal) to them, and was commissioned by
Ludger Duvernay* to collect money to assist
them. Perrault had been much disturbed by the
death of his brother Charles-Ovide*, killed at the
battle of Saint-Denis, by the dispersion of the rest
of his family, and by the destruction of his printing shop. He returned to Montreal in 1839 and
resumed his activities as a printer and bookseller,
but without much success. The last 20 years of
his life were difficult, marked by a long paralysis,
social and physical inactivity, and financial instability.

JEAN-LOUIS ROY

ANQ-Q, AP-G-69. *Le Canadien*, 5 janv. 1866. Ivanhoë
Caron, "Papiers Duvernay conservés aux Archives de
la province de Québec," ANQ *Rapport*, 1926–27,
176–77. Fauteux, *Patriotes*. David, *Patriotes*, 170.
É.-Z. Massicotte, "Louis Perrault," *BRH*, XLIX
(1943), 106–7.

**PICARD DESTROISMAISONS, THOMAS-FER-
RUCE** (he signed Thomas Destroismaisons),
priest and missionary; b. 12 Jan. 1796 at Saint-
Pierre-de-la-Rivière-du-Sud (Saint-Pierre-Montmagny, Que.), son of Philippe Picard Destroismaisons and Rosalie Fournier; d. 5 April 1866 at
Saint-François, Île d'Orléans, Canada East.

After completing his secondary education
at the Séminaire de Québec, Thomas-Ferruce
Picard Destroismaisons was sent to the Collège
de Nicolet to teach and to study theology
(1816–19). He was ordained priest on 17 Oct. 1819
in the cathedral of Quebec, and went immediately
to Saint-Hyacinthe to become curate of the
parish of Notre-Dame.

Since 1818 Abbé Joseph-Norbert Provencher*, the first missionary of Red River, had
been looking for "a priest and an ecclesiastic"
to assist him. Although he did not have all the
qualifications required by Provencher – an acquaintance with astronomy, a knowledge of
English and of the "Indian tongue," some
skill in construction, and an ability to lead people
– Abbé Destroismaisons was chosen by Bishop
Joseph-Octave Plessis* to become a missionary

633

Pigewis

in the west. He arrived in Red River on 12 Aug. 1820, four days before Provencher departed for Quebec. Even before his return in August 1822, Provencher was thinking of sending the young missionary back to Lower Canada "when he could be dispensed with," for he "is not too well liked." However, Destroismaisons remained and worked with the Indians at the Qu'Appelle River in 1823, at Pembina (North Dakota) in 1824, and at Red River during the summers. Despite great effort, he did not succeed in learning the language of the Indians he visited and had to use an interpreter. During his last years in the west, he was attached principally to the mission of White Horse Plain, of which he was the first officiating priest.

Finally, in 1827, Abbé Destroismaisons was discharged. Despite the partial failure of his missionary career, he was remembered with kindness by Bishop Provencher, who wrote to Bernard-Claude Panet*, bishop of Quebec: "M. Destroismaisons is a good priest full of good will. He will not give any trouble to his bishop." The civil authorities held him in high esteem; George Simpson*, governor of the Northern Department of the Hudson's Bay Company, even suggested him as a missionary for the King's Posts in the east.

In 1827, having returned to Lower Canada, Thomas Destroismaisons became the first parish priest of Saint-Urbain (Saint-Urbain-de-Charlevoix), where he devoted his attention particularly to the building of the church. From 1833 to 1850 he was the parish priest of Saint-Germain (Rimouski), with responsibility for several neighbouring missions. He was occupied with the building of a public hall at Saint-Germain and a church in the mission of Sainte-Luce, demonstrating again his aptitude for construction. These activities, and the great expanse of territory to be ministered to, tired him rapidly, and he wrote: "I did not feel myself endowed with the talents necessary for directing and administering one large parish, or rather several parishes." From 1848 he exercised his ministry less and less. Notwithstanding his fatigue, he asked to remain at Rimouski, where he felt himself well liked. Abbé Célestin-Zéphirin Rousseau, his curate, willingly conceded the truth of this claim, but considered it a result of the priest's innocent good nature: "Father Destroismaisons is the best man alive, and towards his parishioners he shows a kindness that is devoid of good sense. To all requests he replies with an interminable succession of *yeses*, but when it is a question of acting the *yeses* become ineffective." Only one group of persons missed this excessive kindness: the Irish

orphans. On various occasions two curates reproached the parish priest for ignoring these unfortunate children. The fact seems to be well authenticated, but an explanation is not apparent.

Despite his lack of enthusiasm, Abbé Destroismaisons was finally transferred in 1850 to the small parish of Saint-François, on the Île d'Orléans, where he died in April 1866.

NIVE VOISINE

AAQ, 330 CN, I. Archives de l'archevêché de Rimouski (Qué.), 355.106. [J.-N. Provencher], "Lettres de Monseigneur Joseph-Norbert Provencher, premier évêque de Saint-Boniface, Manitoba," Soc. historique de Saint-Boniface, *Bull.*, III (1913), 5–124. Morice, *Hist. de l'Église catholique*, I.

PIGEWIS (Pigwys). *See* PEGUIS

PLAYTER, GEORGE FREDERICK, Methodist minister, author, and journalist; b. *c.* 1809 in London, England; d. 24 Oct. 1866 in Frankford, Canada West.

Little is known about George Playter's early years. His literary interests and writing skill suggest that he went to good schools or was encouraged to educate himself. He was evidently raised in a Wesleyan Methodist home and was converted in his youth. Playter immigrated in 1832 to Montreal, where he was employed as a printer. Two years later he entered the Methodist itinerancy in eastern Upper Canada, and in 1838 he was ordained and stationed on the Ottawa circuit.

Although there is no reason to doubt the strength of Playter's religious commitment, he was seemingly not consumed by that zeal for souls which characterized so many of his brethren. This reticence, combined with his modesty, produced "a clear, terse and satisfactory preacher, very correct, who dealt very much with the conscience. Had he possessed as much passion as point, he would have been very powerful." His lack of success in the ministry doubtless strengthened his strong literary bent, though it was an avocation he hesitated to pursue because to his colleagues nothing was more important than their evangelical task. Playter was never wholly resigned to his ministerial lot.

The real significance of Playter's career lies in his work as editor, historian, and polemicist, roles in which he throws light on the development of Upper Canadian Methodism and particularly on the tensions in that community during the 1840s and 1850s. Canadian Methodist leaders were becoming concerned with the development of their church as a social institution. At the same time they did not wholly accept the British Wesleyan argument that the church should be politically conservative or remain aloof from politics. Moreover, though Canadian Methodist ministers were aware that their membership were becoming more liberal, they were unwilling to share their authority with the laity in the conference.

Although he was an immigrant and a convinced Wesleyan, Playter came out strongly against his English brethren in the conflict between the English Wesleyan representatives in Canada and their Canadian colleagues, which in 1840 resulted in the dissolution of the union between the two conferences. In two lengthy letters to the *Christian Guardian*, entitled "Voice from Canada" and "Second voice from Canada," Playter assailed the English conference for driving the two conferences apart. British Wesleyan leaders such as Joseph STINSON and Matthew Richey*, unable to enforce obedience on the part of the Canadian conference, established a rival Wesleyan church in Canada West following the dissolution. The actions of the British conference and its missionaries were based, Playter insisted, on a misunderstanding of the true character of Canadian Methodism which, despite its opposition to church establishment and its sympathy for responsible government, was as British in its attitudes and as loyal to the crown and British connection as the English body. There was thus no need to establish a genuinely English form of Methodism in the province; the attempt not only was a waste of resources but ran counter to the fundamental Methodist conviction that Methodists are one in every part of the world. "Persevere not in this work," he concluded, "Be yourselves again; and we shall be your friends."

Playter's firm stance in defence of the Canadian position helped to secure his election as editor of the *Christian Guardian* in 1844, when political as well as religious controversy was acute. In November 1843 the Reform ministry of Robert Baldwin* and Louis-Hippolyte LA FONTAINE had resigned over Governor General Sir Charles Metcalfe*'s refusal to follow the ministry's advice on questions of patronage. Playter contrived to maintain the newspaper's professed political neutrality and to avoid condoning the conservative position in support of Metcalfe taken by Egerton Ryerson*. In fact, Playter's sympathies, and those of many Methodist laymen and ministers, were more with the Reform ministers than with the governor. Playter also continued to criticize the British Wesleyan Methodists' demand that Canadian Wesleyans submit to their authority. His prophetic advocacy of foreign missions and of general Methodist union in British North

America as the solution to the continuing strife with the British conference earned him the dislike of those in the Canadian conference such as Anson Green* who were working quietly for an accommodation with the British. In 1845 a decrease in Canadian Methodist adherents led to new efforts for reunion with the English conference. Playter, as a leading anti-Wesleyan, was removed as editor of the *Guardian* in 1846 to facilitate the reunion which occurred in 1847. Not surprisingly, and again in anticipation of the tension that would develop later in the conference over the role of the laity in the governance of the church, Playter was one of the signatories in 1847 of a pamphlet which criticized the reunion negotiations for strengthening ministerial authority.

Playter resumed his work as a printer in Picton in 1847, but in 1849 he returned to the itinerancy and held several circuits until his early retirement in 1858. During his later years, Playter maintained his dissenting role, a position that reflected his awareness of the necessity to adapt the practices and the policy of Canadian Methodism in the face of a society less content with simplistic preaching and discipline and unwilling to perpetuate clerical oligarchy. But his principal endeavour in this period and his enduring contribution was the preparation of a two-volume history of Methodism in Upper Canada from its inception to 1847. The first volume was published in 1862; evidently the second was completed but the manuscript disappeared in the wake of Playter's untimely death.

The history of Methodism in Canada was the first account of the subject written by a Canadian minister and published in the province. It is a factual narrative covering the years from 1784 to 1828 based upon "the memories of the aged," periodicals, and printed documents. "This history," he wrote, "may be called the 'Acts of the Methodist preachers in the province of Canada,' with the motives, difficulties, and consequences." His account is reasonably dispassionate and concise, and shows a sensitive awareness of the limits imposed by the evidence. It is thus an invaluable record of "how the foundations of the Methodist Church were laid," and of the Methodist mission to the Indians. John Carroll*, Playter's friend and defender, would make effective use of his work in his massive *Case and his cotemporaries*.

Throughout his career, as Carroll noted, Playter was not a principal figure in the Methodist leadership. His death was barely noticed in the *Christian Guardian* and but for his *History* his memory would soon have faded entirely.

Point

Nevertheless, "he uttered nothing at random, nor anything not worth the uttering." His study of Methodism, editorials, and pamphlets, formed the outer dimensions of his personal world and are a thoughtful witness to the outlook and the concerns of Canadian Methodism in his generation.

G. S. FRENCH

G. F. Playter was the author of *The history of Methodism in Canada: with an account of the rise and progress of the work of God among the Canadian Indian tribes, and occasional notices of the civil affairs of the province* (Toronto, 1862); *Thirty-five reasons why I am not a member of the Episcopalian Church, commonly called the Church of England* (n.p., n.d.); and with David Wright *et al.*, *Considerations on the proposed reunion of the Canadian and English Wesleyan conferences* (Picton, [Ont.], 1847). *Christian Guardian*, 9 Dec. 1840, 10 Feb. 1841, July-October 1844, 1845–46. Wesleyan Methodist Church in Can., *Minutes* (Toronto), 1867. Cornish, *Cyclopaedia of Methodism*. Carroll, *Case and his cotemporaries*. French, *Parsons & politics*.

POINT, NICOLAS, Jesuit priest and missionary; b. 10 April 1799 in Rocroi, Ardennes, France, son of François Point, carpenter, and Marie-Nicole Boursois; d. 3 July 1868 at Quebec.

Born during an unsettled period in the history of France, the education of Nicolas Point was sketchy. His father's early death required him to take employment as a lawyer's drudge at 13 to help his widowed mother support a large family, of which he was, apparently, the eldest. Even as a young child he could sketch well and his mother encouraged his talent. Reading a life of St Francis Xavier engendered in him an interest in the missions and probably led him to apply for entrance into the Society of Jesus. He entered that order at Saint-Acheul, Somme, on 28 June 1819, and he was ordained a priest at Sion, Switzerland, on 20 March 1831.

At the request of Benoît-Joseph Flaget, first bishop of Louisville, Ky, he and several other Jesuits were sent in 1835 to open a college at Lebanon, Ky. That venture failed, and Point was sent to Louisiana where, under the direction of Antoine Blanc, bishop of New Orleans, he began Saint Charles College at Grand Coteau. The school opened in 1837, but did not prosper under Point's direction. In the spring of 1840 Point was called by his superiors to St Louis and sent to Westport (today in Kansas City, Mo.) to prepare for an expedition of six Jesuits, led by Pierre-Jean De Smet*, who were to open a mission among the Flatheads in the northwestern United States. Point worked there tirelessly for the following six

years. He established at least one mission, that of the Sacred Heart among the Skitswish (Coeur d'Alenes) at a site near the present Cataldo, Idaho. Throughout this period he kept a journal and made in it hundreds of sketches of Indians in every phase of their existence. Point also made many sketches which were to appear in De Smet's books.

At his own request, Point was recalled in 1847, and he went to Windsor, Canada West, to join his brother Pierre* who was in charge of a parish serving mainly Indians. In 1848 he was transferred to Wikwemikong, on Manitoulin Island, where the Indian mission of Sainte-Croix was conducted by the Jesuits. During his years there, he built a stone church, started schools for Indian girls and boys, established pious societies (chiefly in an effort to combat the effects of drunkenness), and encouraged large-scale agriculture among the Indians. In 1855 his health gave out and he was sent to the Jesuit house at Sault-au-Récollet (Montreal) to recover. It was there that he reorganized his journal, with its interleaves of drawings in colour. This precious work, composed of six ledger-sized manuscript volumes, he called "Souvenirs des Montagnes Rocheuses."

For most of the rest of his life Point was an invalid. In 1865 his superiors sent him to Quebec where he became a highly sought after adviser to the local clergy. He died at Quebec on 3 July 1868. He was so much admired by the clergy, particularly the canons, that they insisted on his burial in the crypt under the cathedral.

Point's work as an artist is said by some to be primitive, but it is also original in its technique. His paintings are especially valuable because they portray the daily life of several Indian tribes, the Flatheads, Blackfeet, and Skitswish for the most part, just before they were radically changed by the incursion of the white man.

JOSEPH P. DONNELLY

[Nicolas Point left a large body of manuscript material which is scattered through several archives. The Archivum Romanum Societatis Iesu (Rome), Epistolae praepositorum generalium ad patres et fratres Societatis Iesu, has a collection of his letters to the Jesuit general and of the baptismal records he kept while on the missions in the Oregon country. The Biblioteca Nazionale Centrale (Rome), Fondo Gesuitico, has the original journal and sketches Point made on a voyage by barge from the northwestern United States back to St Louis on his way to Canada. The Missouri Province Archives of the Society of Jesus (St Louis University, Mo.) has a small collection of letters and some pen and ink sketches of scenes he drew at the behest of Father Pierre-Jean De Smet. The ASJCF has

636

the manuscripts of Point's "Souvenirs des Montagnes Rocheuses" and Pierre Point's "Vie du P. Point."

There is no single work dealing with the life and work of Father Nicolas Point. The most available sources are: *Wilderness kingdom; Indian life in the Rocky Mountains: 1840–1847; the journals & paintings of Nicolas Point, S.J.*, trans. and ed. J.P. Donnelly (New York, 1967); a chapter entitled "Nicolas Point, Jesuit missionary in Montana of the forties," in G.J. Garraghan, *Chapters in frontier history; research studies in the making of the west* (Milwaukee, Wis., 1934); Léon Pouliot, "Le père Nicolas Point (1799–1868); collaborateur du P. De Smet dans les montagnes Rocheuses et missionnaire en Ontario," SCHÉC *Rapport*, IV (1936–37), 20–30. J.P.D.]

PORTER, CHARLES, Church of England clergyman and educator; b. 1779 or 1780 in Manchester, England, elder son of Thomas Porter, fustian calender; m. in 1808 Eleanor Wallace, daughter of Michael Wallace*, treasurer of Nova Scotia, and they had four sons and four daughters; d. 25 Nov. 1864 in Exeter, England.

Charles Porter received a classical education at Manchester Grammar School and proceeded in 1799 to Brasenose College, Oxford, taking his BA in 1803, MA in 1805, a BD in June 1815, and receiving a DD in June 1816. He became a private tutor in the university, and in November 1805 was appointed vice-principal of St Alban Hall, an old residential hall in Oxford. He was ordained deacon at Lincoln in June 1806.

In 1789 the legislature of Nova Scotia had enacted a statute providing for the foundation of a college at Windsor, N.S., to be named King's College, with a requirement that the president be a clergyman of the established Church of England. Prospects from England failing, the board of governors in 1790 chose as president William Cochran*, a graduate of Trinity College, Dublin, and the recently appointed head of the Halifax Grammar School. In 1802 a royal charter established a board of governors with authority to frame statutes for the college, conferred power to grant degrees, and appointed the archbishop of Canterbury as patron and the bishop of Nova Scotia as visitor. When, in 1803, the statutes were adopted, they prescribed that the president be a regular graduate of Oxford, Cambridge, or King's College itself. Cochran was thus displaced from the presidency. The first president under the charter, proposed by Archbishop John Moore as patron, was the Reverend Thomas Cox, DD, of Worcester College, Oxford. Cox arrived in Nova Scotia in October 1804, but died in October 1805.

In September 1806 the new archbishop, Charles Manners-Sutton, nominated Porter as Cox's successor on the recommendation of the

principal of Brasenose College. Against the advice of friends, Porter accepted the position, was ordained priest by the archbishop in March 1807, and arrived in Nova Scotia in July. Cochran, who had been almost continuously president since 1790, now found himself subordinated to an inexperienced man half his age. Porter became professor of divinity, Hebrew, and mathematics, while Cochran continued as professor of grammar, rhetoric, and logic. Instruction of the tiny student body in Greek and Latin was presumably divided between the two. Writing to the archbishop in January 1808, the bishop of Nova Scotia, Charles Inglis*, who had earlier favoured Cochran for the presidency, said of Porter that "he appears to be a modest, sensible, and worthy young man."

In November 1814 Porter went to England on six months' leave with a commendatory testimonial from the board. In July 1815, before returning, he wrote to the colonial secretary, Lord Bathurst, telling of the sacrifice he had made in going to Nova Scotia and the privation he had suffered, and suggesting "remuneration" for persons undertaking offices of importance and responsibility abroad.

Relations between Porter and Cochran, which may previously have been difficult, became embittered after Porter returned disappointed. In September 1817 the lieutenant governor, Lord Dalhousie [Ramsay*], attended the annual meeting of the governors at Windsor and recorded in his diary that because the two were "at open violent war with each other . . . the proceedings are in general a discussion of complaints and recrimination, extremely indecorous and unpleasant." Porter he described as "a strict disciplinarian, and rather an ill-tempered man," and Cochran as mild and amiable, with great appeal to the students. Dalhousie may have failed to note that Porter necessarily resided in the dilapidated college building and would thus be more immediately concerned with student discipline, while Cochran enjoyed a house in town.

In 1818 Porter also became rector of Newport, a missionary parish of the Society for the Propagation of the Gospel 14 miles from Windsor, a position he held, to the detriment of his health, until 1836. In November 1825 Porter went to England for his health, again with a commendatory testimonial. He requested from the under-secretary for the colonies, Robert John Wilmot-Horton, first, a pension, on the ground of ill health caused by arduous duties during 18 years, and then preferment in England. Both requests were denied, and he was again compelled to return to Nova Scotia.

Price

After his return, student indiscipline, which finally brought stern intervention by the visitor, Bishop John Inglis*, was a great trial for both Porter and Cochran. Then in July 1831 financial problems became especially serious. As part of its effort to reduce the financial burden which the colonies placed on the British treasury, the British government announced its intention to reduce by half the £1,000 annual grant to the college, and in March 1832 decided to terminate the grant altogether after 1833–34. Moreover, as a further economy, the same government was pressing for the union of the college with the non-denominational Dalhousie College, to be located in Halifax, but not as yet in actual existence. Porter was authorized by the governors to go to England to urge the case of the college in person. In England he found that any appeal on behalf of the college would fail. This left him with "no resources but to prefer his own personal claims." In June 1834 he returned to Nova Scotia, where he was subsequently informed of the grant of a pension by the British government, to begin on 1 April 1835. At the end of March 1836 he resigned the presidency, effective 1 October; as his successor the governors elected the Reverend George McCawley*, a former student under Porter.

In June 1837 Porter dispatched to England a medical certificate that he was suffering from a recurrent disabling affection of the larynx and trachea, and a recommendation from Bishop Inglis that he receive a pension for his service in the Newport parish. This additional pension was approved by the Treasury in September 1837.

Early that month, he and some of his family sailed from Halifax to Liverpool, and to seemingly inactive retirement in England. He first settled, perhaps for reasons of health, in the village of Alphington, on the outskirts of Exeter, and later moved to Exeter, where he died.

C. P. Wright

PANS, MG 1, 479–80 (transcript of letterbooks and journals of Bishop Charles Inglis). PRO, CO 217/97; 217/145, pp.547–48; 217/146, pp.857–59; 217/155, pp.915, 953, 957, 961–65; 217/164, pp.249–54. University of King's College (Halifax), Board of Governors, minute books. *The admission register of the Manchester School with some notices of the more distinguished scholars*, ed. J. F. Smith (4v., Manchester, Eng., 1866–74), II. *Brasenose College register, 1509–1909* (Oxford, 1909). T. B. Akins, *A brief account of the origin, endowment, and progress of the University of King's College, Windsor, Nova Scotia* (Halifax, 1865). H. Y. Hind, *The University of King's College, Windsor, Nova Scotia, 1790–1890* (New York, 1890). F. W. Vroom, *King's College: a chronicle, 1789–1939, collections and recollections* (Halifax, 1941).

PRICE, WILLIAM, lumber merchant and manufacturer of planks (deals); b. 17 Sept. 1789 at Hornsey, near London, England, third son of Richard Price and Mary Evans; d. 14 March 1867 at Quebec.

William Price's parents, originally from Wales, moved to Middlesex at the end of the 18th century. The family probably belonged to the upper middle class, and although its financial situation was precarious after Richard Price's death around 1804, William's mother, with eight children to provide for, was able to count on friends important in business and government. After a few years at Hammersmith College in London, William began to study law under a cousin, a lawyer of the Inner Temple, but had to give up this career. At age 14 he became an employee of Christoper Idle, a prominent London businessman. Six years later, on 10 May 1810, he landed at Quebec as a clerk in a branch of the Idle firm, at a wage of £135 a year. Much of the correspondence between Price and his family and friends during these early years has been preserved. These letters show that he was well educated in spite of his interrupted studies, and that family feelings remained strong despite distance. William's eldest brother David, who traded with Portugal and Latin America, assumed the role of father, and followed his younger brother's career closely, lavishing advice on him and arousing his ambition: "If you get nothing but your salary by going to Quebec," he wrote, "you are doing little better than stand still." And, in another letter: "I trust it may please Heaven to strengthen us; that we may finally succeed and stand in due season on an independent footing." This solidarity did not weaken with time: in 1817 William lent his savings to his brother Samuel who was on the verge of bankruptcy, and in 1843, when William himself was in difficulty, David went to Canada to give him moral and financial support.

Information on Idle's business in North America is imprecise. It may be this firm that, at the beginning of the Napoleonic wars, obtained a monopoly on orders of Canadian lumber for the Admiralty. Price devoted most of his time to filling such orders, travelling through the forests of Vermont, the Ottawa valley, and Upper Canada to select timber for masts. Planks cut in Lower Canada's sawmills completed the cargoes of square timber. The firm also imported wines and other goods, but the Quebec store does not seem to have had an important place in this trade.

Price's first biographers note his services during the War of 1812. A major in the militia, he is thought to have raised a cavalry corps, organized an artillery battery at Quebec, and acted as a courier for Governor George Prevost*. In any case, he was in Halifax by March 1813, where he negotiated for his employer the purchase of five ships intended for the Royal Navy.

In 1815 Price took over management of the Quebec office from William Oviatt, who returned to England. In the years of recession that followed, he concerned himself with supplying food to the Maritime provinces and undertook some business on his own account in the West Indian market, but without conspicuous success. The Idle firm, badly managed in England, was close to ruin, and Price was looking for financial backers and a form of partnership to enable him to take advantage of the experience he had acquired during his first ten years in Canada. He finally decided on the proposal made by Parker and Yeoman, timber brokers in London. The agreement concluded on 1 May 1820 created three distinct business firms, one in London, the William Price Company in Quebec, and the partnership of Peter McCutcheon*, known as Peter McGill, and Kenneth Dowie in Montreal. Following a new arrangement in 1823, Parker and Yeoman was succeeded by a company formed by James Dowie and Nathaniel Gould, in London, which from then on financed the entire undertaking, chartered ships, and disposed of colonial produce. After Kenneth Dowie left for Liverpool, Peter McGill continued to trade corn on his own in Upper Canada. At Quebec, the William Price Company specialized in the export of timber. Each of the four partners, Price, McGill, J. Dowie, and Gould, received a quarter of the shares and profits in each of the three firms, although the capital invested was not equal. Price, whose sole contribution was a sawmill of little value not far from Quebec, was chosen because of his reputation as an experienced businessman and his technical knowledge. As he was to do the major part of the work at the port of loading, he levied a commission of 5 per cent on his operations, which was added to his share of the profits.

Until 1843 Price always acted in the name of the company. He drew bills of exchange on Gould and Dowie for advances to local contractors, the preparation of cargoes, and the purchase of operation of sawmills. Canadian banks accepted only short term bills, which the London partners had to honour as they became due, even if about 18 months had to be allowed between the first outlay and the payment for delivery of lumber in England. At the least contraction of the market, the accounts of the Canadian partners were liable to be overdrawn.

At the time Price concluded these arrangements, the commercial climate was still unsettled. In the British House of Commons, the Liberals were violently attacking the exorbitant preferences granted Canadian timber during the war as being no longer justified. But in 1821 a commission of inquiry recommended only a minor readjustment, and, reinforced by these tariff advantages on the British market, the colonial timber trade soon entered a new period of expansion. The company's business followed the rhythm of general growth. After a quiet beginning, its volume of exports soared. It was exporting about 50 cargoes of lumber a year around 1827, then the average rose rapidly to 75, and from 1833 on nearly 100 ships left each year for England from Quebec and the ports of the lower St Lawrence. This represented a turnover of £70,000, and more.

Price was both an exporter of square timber and manufacturer of planks or deals. Bit by bit manufacturing outstripped strictly commercial operations, but the latter, as his first source of capital, was the foundation of his remarkable success. Like other Quebec lumbermen in this period, he bought from various contractors the pine and oak cribs that came down each spring from the Ottawa valley, Upper Canada, and the seigneuries upstream from Quebec. He often granted advances to his customers to help them set up a lumbercamp and dispatch lumber to Quebec, keeping their production for himself at a price fixed at the beginning of the winter. The loads were completed by staves and barrel hoops, as well as planks bought from local sawmills. The company had offices and a warehouse on Rue Saint-Pierre at Quebec, two roadsteads on the south shore, with wharves, breakwaters, and workshops, and a sawmill at Hadlow Cove. In the New Liverpool roadstead, at Lévis, the principal port of loading, there were some 60 employees during the shipping season.

A large part of the exports made by Price, perhaps the most important part, was intended for the shipyards of the Admiralty. Six or seven tenderers, representing large firms which had invested in the Canadian trade, wrangled over orders for masts and construction timber which would go as high as £150,000 or £200,000. Between 1830 and 1850 the firm of Brockelbank and Holt usually won out, and entrusted Price with the completion of the deal. These contracts, which extended over several years, were important for stability, because they reduced the impact of the commercial crises that jeopardized so many other colonial enterprises.

Most of the ships transporting timber to England were hired by Gould and Dowie, but the company also possessed a few barks and brigs,

Price

two three-masters, and several schooners for coastal trade. Between 1820 and 1850 some 40 vessels, built at Quebec and Montreal and in the shipyards of the upper St Lawrence, were registered in the name of Price and his partners. After 1850 Price apparently no longer equipped ships for transatlantic voyages, but he kept a fleet of schooners to serve his establishments, as well as steamships to tow sailing vessels in the Saguenay, and later on to link this region with Quebec.

Price deserves a special place in Canadian economic history primarily as a contractor. The profits realized in trade were gradually reinvested in sawmills and lumbering. Before 1830 the company bought almost all its planks from various small firms in Lower Canada. Price encouraged the owners to increase their production, financed them, and subsequently acquired the mortgaged sawmills. Thus, before 1838, the sawmills of Batiscan, Saint-Vallier, Bic, Rimouski, Métis (Métis-sur-Mer), La Malbaie, those of Anse-à-l'Eau and Moulin-Baude near Tadoussac, and those of Bytown (Ottawa) and Crosby in Upper Canada, were entered on the company's books. Often co-ownership was involved and usually Price was the owner in fact long before he held legal title.

He was already an important contractor downstream from Quebec when he established himself in the Saguenay region, a vast untapped expanse which the crown leased to the Hudson's Bay Company. Through one of his men, Alexis Tremblay*, dit Picoté, Price encouraged and financially supported a group of people from La Malbaie, who went to settle as squatters along the Saguenay. Between 1838 and 1842 this community, called the "Vingt-et-un," built nine sawmills at the mouths of the principal tributaries of the Saguenay. By 1840 Price was having planks for England loaded there, and two years later repurchased all the sawmills outright. Large numbers of settlers soon arrived and, as Price had foreseen, the government had to yield to the pressure for colonization. In 1843 the lands were put up for auction.

With astonishing rapidity, Price bought all the sawmill sites in the valley and fjord, and along the north St Lawrence shore on both sides of Tadoussac. To take on timber, ships came as far as Grande-Baie, the most important manufacturing centre before 1850. As early as 1842 Price was associated with the enterprises of Peter McLeod*, which were located at the mouths of the Chicoutimi, Moulin à Baude, and Shipshaw rivers. A Montagnais on his mother's side, Peter McLeod could claim his natural rights and install

sawmills in the upper Saguenay, a territory the HBC was attempting to retain. Similarly, by concluding agreements with other contractors such as William Charles Pentland, Félix Têtu and Frédéric Boucher, and Édouard Slevin and James Gibb*, Price managed to extend his monopoly from Tadoussac to Bersimis. He also controlled the north shore from La Malbaie to Rivière-Noir. At the same time, he consolidated his positions on the south shore of the St Lawrence by going into partnership with Pierre-Thomas Casgrain and Nazaire Têtu at Trois-Pistoles and John Caldwell at L'Isle Verte, and thus established himself in some ten villages between Montmagny and Cap-Chat. His partners were generally not in a position to export planks to England. So long as there were no other important outlets, Price's connections in England enabled him to monopolize the whole market without difficulty, and to wait for the right moment to redeem the other shares, a process he had completed by about 1860.

To supply the mills, Price acquired substantial reserves of timber. On the south shore, he bought the township of Armagh and part of the Rimouski and Métis seigneuries, some 240 square miles, but still only a tiny fraction of the area being exploited. According to the policy in force from 1826 on, contractors exploited the forests of the province as agents of the public domain in return for the annual payment of felling dues. Price, a skilful and discreet man, was able to get round the officers of the crown, oust competitors, foresee the needs of his enterprise long before they arose, and thus put his hands on about 7,700 square miles of forest, in addition to timber limits in the Ottawa valley of an extent hard to determine. These immense reserves were concentrated on each side of the Saguenay and to the northeast of Lac Saint-Jean.

The turning point in Price's affairs came in 1843, just after he had worked his way into the Saguenay region. Until then his partners had supported all his ventures, but suddenly relations became strained. The preference granted to Canadian timber was reduced and finally abolished, at a time when the English market was shrinking dangerously. The situation was aggravated by the near bankruptcy of McGill. Gould and Dowie ordered the liquidation of the company, limited the working capital until the final winding up, and insisted on full remittances at the end of each fiscal year. They criticized Price for his 5 per cent commission, blamed him for having tied up some £130,000 in sawmills, and ordered him to get rid of them forthwith. But in the middle of a slump, there obviously were no takers. The

1846 fire at Grande-Baie was a culminating stroke. So long as the William Price company had been borne along on the economic boom, the man had remained hidden behind a laconic business correspondence and uncontroversial balance-sheets. But when disaster struck, he made himself heard, and it was then possible to perceive what was behind his success. "If you fail or retreat or show your star to be on the wane, powerful enemies start up against you," he scribbled on a memo pad. An obstinate man, he rejected all advice. He would not close his sawmills, he would not go to England to wait out the crisis quietly. Instead he appealed to his brother David, who advanced him £6,000 and came to Canada to help him clear up his accounts. For four years he fought unceasingly to get from banks and former partners the means to preserve his credit and the forest empire he was building for his sons.

He already had three sons working with him. Rather than abandon the fight, he declared in a letter to McGill that he was ready to sell Wolfesfield, send his family to the country, and go to live with his sons in the company's offices. Wolfesfield, which he kept despite everything, was a magnificent property on the Plains of Abraham, acquired by Price at the time of his marriage in 1825 to Jane Stewart, one of the daughters of Charles Grey Stewart, a customs inspector at Quebec. The couple was to have 14 children. The father initiated the elder sons at an early age into his business, beginning with the technical side. When still young, they worked in the sawmills in the Saguenay and the lower reaches of the river. Price sent them to England as apprentices, and made them travel on the Continent and in Scandinavia to complete their training.

The old company continued to function while settling its accounts and narrowly escaped bankruptcy; at the same time Price used his credit with the government and the public to acquire new properties and timber limits in his own or his sons' names. Business recovered, and in 1849 annual production of planks in all the mills downstream from Quebec reached £90,000; about half of this came from Price's own sawmills. He quickly redeemed his partners' shares, and in 1853 the old company's timber represented no more than 10 per cent of exports. The founding of the company of William Price and Sons in 1855 was the realization of an ambition that had sustained him throughout his career.

He had no other ambition. He had been invited to be a member of the Legislative Council several times, but had refused. Politics were of no concern unless they served his interests directly, and for this end unofficial approaches were often most effective. As a young man he had many a good laugh over the debates that split the assembly of Lower Canada, and only a crisis as grave as the one that began in 1834 penetrated his indifference. He was a member of the subcommittee of the Constitutional Association formed at Quebec that year, but this brief entry into public life had no sequel. His contemporaries often said that in 57 years in Canada he scarcely ever took the trouble to vote. The fate of his business was linked more closely to imperial policy. Price and his partners followed attentively the "subversive" campaigns of the "Manchester school" that threatened their privileges, and they witnessed with dismay the collapse of the preferential system, but he was not among those who went so far as to advocate annexation. Moreover, his enterprises survived competition, and because of their geographical location long continued to be turned towards the British market.

At the end of his life, Price represented the Tory of the old school, for whom the motto was still "Ships, colonies, and commerce." He had been one of the founding members of the Quebec Board of Trade, and was a member of the Baron Club, and of the Literary and Historical Society of Quebec, but his work scarcely permitted him to mingle with the British officers and businessmen in exile at Quebec. He readily derided those who conducted their affairs from the seclusion of their offices. Price was a man of the lumbercamps and log-runs. "I have," he wrote to Dowie, "to find intelligent explorers and judge their reports, have roads planned and made, rivers cleared, lakes dammed, engage superintendents, contractors, engage men for them, buy their homes, cattle, hay, oats; engage schooners, . . . buy provisions . . . . I have to negotiate with the Commissioners of crown lands. It takes local influence, tact, vigilance. . . ."

As long as his strength permitted, Price spent most of his time at his businesses, making the trip to the Saguenay two or three times in winter by roads unsuitable for vehicles and sleeping in makeshift shelters. In 1861 the region already had about 12,000 settlers. It was a closed world which, except for the new agricultural enclaves to the south of Lac Saint-Jean, was entirely dependent on Price. Work in the sawmills and roadsteads in summer alternated with tree felling in the forest in winter. An improved sweating system totally cut these people off from the outside world, and bound them hand and foot to their master's pleasure. One had to push farther and farther inland to find pine and spruce of a good size. The settlers sowed seeds in the tree-stripped and burnt-out areas of the Baie des Hahas (Baie des Ha! Ha!), and Chicoutimi became the new centre of activities. Price ruled the region; charitable when his men were docile, he was ruthless towards those who disputed his dominion. "Everywhere the nobility and generosity of the Master are proclaimed," wrote Bishop Charles-François BAILLARGEON in a letter to him, on his return from a tour of the parishes and missions. Prominent citizens went further. According to Denis-Benjamin Papineau*, in Le Canadien: "This gentleman is without question the foster-father of this young settlement; his stores full of supplies and clothing of all kinds are open to everybody. It is eminently right that his humanity, his fairness and that of his agents, should win the confidence and hard work with which these poor people, in their zeal and gratitude, repay him." There were, it is true, a few discordant voices in this chorus of praise [see Jean-Baptiste HONORAT]. Rumour had it that Price had schemed underhandedly to get possession of McLeod's holdings, and in 1849 a few daring settlers even signed a petition to the governor, denouncing Price's monopoly of the land, saw and grist mills, and waterways blocked by booms. In the memorandum that he sent to Lord Elgin [BRUCE] refuting these accusations, Price quoted testimonies of gratitude such as the following: "Grandfather Price, I came here with my wife, my eight children, and barely enough to eat. Now I am all right, thanks to you."

Towards the end of his life, Price developed a fascination for agronomy. On every official visit to the Saguenay, there was an obligatory stop at one of his model farms. In other areas he could rely on well-chosen and well-trained managers, and on his sons, who were a credit to him. After he had been the representative in the assembly for the new county of Saguenay for a long time, David Edward was elected a legislative councillor in 1864. William Evan* lived more modestly in the Saguenay, and became well liked. Edward took care of the company's interests in England. Henry, the only one to marry, left to carry on trade in Chile, while young Evan John* continued his studies.

At the end of his career the government had presented Price with a timber slide a mile long, which brought the logs from Lac Saint-Jean over the Petite Décharge into the sawmills. Thanks to this shoot, the firm still loaded 500,000 planks each year for England, while a variety of products – boards, railway ties, fence posts, battens, and shingles – was taken by schooner to Canadian and American markets. Did the old man know that the forests were being depleted, and

that his sons lacked innovative ability? When he died at Wolfesfield in 1867, his long-established industry was no longer growing, but it had not begun to decline. The people of the Saguenay erected a statue to him on the heights of Chicoutimi. The country was changing rapidly, and was escaping the Prices. One by one the sawmills ceased to turn, but the family kept its forests and lands. Thirty years later a grandson, the second William Price*, came to the Saguenay to create the paper industry, reviving the fortune of the Prices and the economy of the region.

LOUISE DECHÊNE

[The Archives of the Price Company Limited (Quebec) hold account books, correspondence, memoranda, contracts, some of William Price's personal notes, and copies of various documents, maps, etc. The material is classified chronologically. A partial transcription of these documents by Mgr Arthur Maheux* is at ASQ. L.D.]

Bas-Canada, chambre d'Assemblée, Journaux, 1823–24, app.Z; 1828–29, app.V; 1834, app.A. Can., prov. du, Assemblée législative, Journaux, 1844–45, II, app.O.O.; 1846, I, app.A; 1847, III, app.E.E.E.; 1849, III, app.P.P.P.P. Quebec Gazette, 1806–21. Joseph Bouchette, The British dominions in North America; or a topographical and statistical description of the provinces of Lower and Upper Canada . . . (2v., London, 1832); A topographical dictionary of the province of Lower Canada (London, 1832). Langelier, List of lands granted. Notman and Taylor, Portraits of British Americans, III, 31–34.

Raoul Blanchard, L'Est du Canada français, province de Québec (2v., Montréal et Paris, 1935), II. Arthur Buies, Le Saguenay et le bassin du lac Saint-Jean: ouvrage historique et descriptif (3e éd., Québec, 1896). Christie, History of L.C., IV, 21–23. A. D. Gayer et al., The growth and fluctuation of the British economy, 1790–1850: an historical, statistical, and theoretical study of Britain's economic development (2v., Oxford, 1953). H. Y. Hind et al., Eighty years' progress of British North America . . . (Toronto, 1863). A. R. M. Lower, Settlement and the forest frontier in eastern Canada (Toronto, 1936); The trade in square timber (Toronto, 1933), 40–61. Ouellet, Hist. économique. [François Pilote], Le Saguenay en 1851; histoire du passé, du présent et de l'avenir probable du Haut-Saguenay au point de vue de la colonisation (Québec, 1852). Narcisse Rosa, La construction des navires à Québec et ses environs; grèves et naufrages (Québec, 1897). Louise [Saint-Jacques] Dechêne, "William Price, 1810–1850" (thèse de licence, université Laval, Québec, 1964). R. L. Schuyler, The fall of the old colonial system; a study in British free trade, 1770–1870 (London and Toronto, 1945). Horace Têtu, Résumé historique de l'industrie et du commerce de Québec de 1775–1900 (Québec, 1899). Tremblay, Hist. du Saguenay (1968). Arthur Maheux, "Un marchand de Québec: William Price," La Revue de l'université Laval (Québec), IX (1955), 717–22. Victor

Tremblay, "La fondation de Chicoutimi," *Sague-nayensia* (Chicoutimi, Qué.), 13 (1971), 59–61; "Le Saguenay il y a cent ans," *Saguenayensia*, 13 (1971), 91–97.

PRINCE, JOHN, lawyer, farmer, soldier, politician, and judge; b. 12 March 1796 probably at Hereford, England, eldest son of Richard Prince, a miller at Lugg Bridge, near Hereford, and his wife Mary; m. 17 June 1823 Mary Ann Millington and they had seven sons and one daughter; d. 30 Nov. 1870 at Sault Ste Marie, Ont.

John Prince was educated first by his uncle, a Church of England clergyman, and then at the Collegiate Grammar School, Hereford. In 1813 he was commissioned a lieutenant in the 1st Regiment of Herefordshire militia but left the regiment in 1815 to begin the study of law. He was admitted to the bar in 1821 and embarked upon what rapidly became a successful career, practising at Westerham, Kent, from 1821 to 1823, and at Cheltenham, Gloucestershire, from 1823 to 1833. In 1831 he joined Gray's Inn, London. He showed an interest in politics by campaigning in 1832 on behalf of the Whig candidate for Cheltenham for the House of Commons.

Prince was a respected lawyer. He could probably look forward to the rewards that would accompany advancement in his profession and the satisfaction of his political ambitions. But, in the summer of 1833, he suddenly abandoned his law practice, uprooted his family, and set off for the interior of North America. Family reasons explain Prince's unexpected move. His father appears to have been a ne'er-do-well. In 1826 Richard Prince was fined more than £1,100 for making malt illegally, and by 1832 the reputation he had acquired as a wastrel seems to have been profoundly embarrassing for his son. John relocated at Sandwich (now part of Windsor), Upper Canada, and at that remote outpost of the British world made an apparent attempt to hide, to escape the humiliations which he felt humankind wanted visited upon him.

At Sandwich Prince supported himself at first by the proceeds of his law practice at Cheltenham (indeed, this source appears to have accounted for much of his income for the rest of his life), and in a few years acquired park lots just beyond the town. These became the basis for his Park Farm on which he built a Regency cottage in 1835. It was turned away from the nearest road, another apparent manifestation of a desire to escape. From his diaries can be gleaned a frequently expressed wish to escape life altogether, although he was too devout to destroy himself. His struggle to flee also dominated his view of his adopted country, and for the rest of his life he entertained a hatred for "this wretched Country where man's Capital & killing Exertions go for nothing"; yet he felt driven to participate in public life, an urge all the more easily rationalized as it was a way of avoiding burgeoning domestic unhappiness. He was self-reliant, and conceived himself predestined to lead; consequently the led, those who depended on others and particularly on him, were to be despised. It is not surprising and it is consistent with his personality that his lifelong political watchword was independence.

In Upper Canada people of education were few and needed, and soon after his arrival Prince was named, in July 1835, a magistrate for the Western District. It was after the death of an infant son early in 1836 that Prince offered himself as a candidate for the two-member Essex riding in the House of Assembly. He ran as an independent and his popularity was already such that he headed the poll. In the house he proved a capable and energetic member, and he was particularly active in issues that affected his constituency. The year 1837, when he introduced and carried five bills, was perhaps the most successful in his parliamentary career. In that year he pushed through a bill to establish the Western District Bank, and with William Hamilton MERRITT he promoted a bill on land titles which he felt would induce British immigrants to remain in Canada rather than move on to the United States. He also attempted to regularize the land titles of non-naturalized "aliens" who had acquired land in Upper Canada. One of the bills he got passed was particularly dear to him; it prevented the killing of game out of season. In July 1836 he had been appointed chairman of the Court of Quarter Sessions in the Western District, and that autumn he accepted the presidency of the Niagara and Detroit Rivers Rail Road Company.

When the rebellion led by William Lyon MACKENZIE broke out in Upper Canada late in 1837 Prince volunteered to serve in the militia. In 1838 the main concern at Sandwich was the defence of the western frontier of Upper Canada against Patriot attacks from Detroit. He participated in the capture of the Patriot schooner *Anne*, which carried Edward Alexander Theller*, near Amherstburg on 9 Jan. 1838. He fought on 25 February in the battle of Fighting Island and on 3 March at the battle of Pelee Island when Patriots attempted landings in Upper Canada. A few days later he and a few companions captured the Patriot general, Thomas Jefferson Sutherland*, whom they found by accident wandering near Amherstburg. Prince was soon gazetted colonel of the 3rd Essex militia.

Prince

Prince's military career had been brief but noteworthy, and Lieutenant Governor Sir George Arthur* of Upper Canada considered it merited the "approbation of the Crown." Prince, however, had other concerns that summer: another son was born but his birth was complicated by the near death of Mary Ann Prince, and on 15 August Prince was called to the bar of Upper Canada. The danger of invasion of Upper Canada was not over, however, and British military authorities feared further attempts by Patriots from Detroit. On 25 November Prince was given command of the militia post at Sandwich and was asked to call out all militia regiments in anticipation of an attack. On 4 December more than 150 Patriots crossed to Windsor and took the town. Led by Prince the militia dispersed the invaders, 27 of whom were killed. During the battle Prince "resolved upon shooting at once and without a moment's hesitation every bandit who happened to be captured and brought in." By Prince's orders, five men were shot.

Arthur was at first shocked at the news of the summary executions. He felt that Prince had badly mismanaged the affair by failing to pursue the Patriots after their defeat and that "To make amends for what was wanting in the field, Colonel Prince determined upon severity after the affair was over." "That they well deserved such punishment is true enough, but it was a most unwise proceeding & is likely to occasion no small trouble." Arthur was dismayed too that Prince had published a report on the affair before notifying him, and, perhaps most of all, that his action was being widely applauded in Upper Canada, despite the possible consequences; Arthur feared that the result might well be war between Great Britain and the United States. But in the light of much public approval Prince was sustained in his command at Sandwich, and in March 1839 a military court of inquiry conducted by Colonel Richard Airey* exonerated him. Even Arthur admitted that "although never was anything equal to the mismanagement of Colonel Prince," "[m]ost *providentially* the affair at Sandwich terminated upon the whole well as a deterring example."

Prince's unorthodox course of action did not go unopposed in the Western District. "A cabal of *disappointed* persons . . . are formed against me," Prince reported, and his diary records the horsewhippings he inflicted on persons who he felt had insulted him. The Sandwich *Western Herald*, in turn, listed subscriptions it lost in coming out in support of Prince. But the more general feeling that the Patriots had received no more than they deserved sustained Prince's position among his constituents, the House of Assembly, and the militia. In 1839 he strengthened his support by introducing a bill to grant £40,000 to victims of the rebellion (passed in 1840). With the approach of elections in 1841 freeholders in both Essex and Kent solicited him as a candidate. He chose Essex and won easily.

Although Prince had not voted on the union of Upper and Lower Canada when it came before the Upper Canadian assembly he agreed with the proposal, with some misgivings. In 1839 he had supported a motion by Ogle R. Gowan* that the question be taken to the country, and in 1841 he concurred with Lower Canadian members that parts of the bill were objectionable and required modification. When he ran in 1841 he did so as a "constitutionalist" and a supporter of Governor Charles Poulett Thomson*. Mindful of his constituents, "a majority of whom were French Canadians," he supported Augustin Cuvillier*, whom he considered a moderate Reformer like himself, as speaker.

A son, his last, was born to Prince just after the 1841 election. In July a commission was ordered appointing him a queen's counsellor (it was not, however, actually issued for another three years). In the assembly he participated energetically in debate, but he avoided identification with any group or person and voted "as a Member entirely independent of the Executive." In 1843 when Robert Baldwin* and Louis-Hippolyte LA FONTAINE resigned from the ministry he stated that although he was an independent he had always supported the ministry and that as a partisan of responsible government he upheld the ministers' action. He was still not (and never would be) reconciled to Canada. In a questionnaire which he completed in January 1841 for Frederick WIDDER he said he would advise prospective British emigrants: "*exist* on bread and cheese and small beer at home rather than *live* if you can in North America." The climate was "most unhealthy" and "in the Country[,] society is of the worst description." "It is fit only for *laborers*, who by themselves and *their families* can till the earth. . . . [T]hey may do about as well as *good* laborers do in England." In the assembly he urged that the country be populated by "foreigners from all nations" who should enjoy full rights for acquiring and conveying lands provided that they were *bona fide* settlers, but he insisted that paupers, particularly British paupers, not be encouraged to come. It was substantial farmers that were needed in Canada.

Prince was appointed commissioner of bankruptcy for the Western District in 1844 and finally received his QC. He was nominated in the autumn to run again in Essex, then withdrew, reversed his withdrawal, and finally won the election handily. He had resigned the commissionership of bankruptcy before polling began. His first act in the assembly was to nominate Augustin-Norbert MORIN as speaker in opposition to Allan Napier MACNAB because the latter could not speak French. Prince generally supported Baldwin, now in opposition, but maintained his independent stance. His main concerns were petitions for constituents relating to local affairs and a bill for the protection of wild fowl. Early in 1845 Prince arranged for the judgeship of the Western District Court to go to a friend, Alexander Chewett of Sandwich. The closer relations with the Chewetts brought more domestic unhappiness, for Mary Ann Prince soon convinced herself that there was something amiss in her husband's solicitude toward Mrs Chewett during Judge Chewett's periodic bouts with what was described as illness. By the autumn of 1846 a separation seemed in prospect for the Princes, but to the colonel appearances were important.

Prince retreated even farther into political affairs and became a frequent platform speaker. In 1846 he was chosen to move the reply to the speech from the throne, and became a member with Étienne-Paschal TACHÉ and William Hamilton Merritt of the committee on railway bills. When the correspondence of William Henry Draper* and René-Édouard Caron* on the introduction of French Canadian members into the ministry was read in the house, Prince decried the actions of the French Canadian leaders. The longer he sat in the house, he said, "the more he became convinced that it was impossible to conciliate them on true British principles." He now felt that Baldwin "had not a morsel of British principle in his composition." He remained an independent, but now his support went to the Conservatives.

Mining and railway promotions also became an important outlet for Prince. He was president of the Niagara and Detroit Rivers Rail Road Company in 1846 when it tried to revive the charter granted ten years earlier for a railway to cross southwestern Upper Canada. The project, which would have competed with the proposed Great Western, was abandoned in 1847 when compensation in the form of Great Western stock was made to the directors of the company. Prince was also a promoter and major shareholder as well as incorporator in 1847 of the Montreal Mining Company and the British North American Mining Company. He became president of the latter in 1848. In addition he reported that he was a stockholder in the Lake Huron Silver and Copper

Mining Company and that he had expended his own money in its explorations. In 1849 he was an incorporator of the Huron Copper Bay Company. He was a member in 1848 and 1849 of the assembly's standing committee on railways and telegraph lines; railways, he said, were the "most important public improvement for industry and unity" which could be undertaken in the province.

Prince had run unopposed in Essex in the election of 1847. He continued his support of the Tories, and when MacNab and Morin were again proposed for the post of speaker in 1848 he supported MacNab, considering now that it was desirable but not indispensable that the speaker have a knowledge of French. He also reported that he had found Reformers "less liberal than the true liberal Conservatives in fostering and carrying out legitimate reforms." By 1849 he was ridiculing the use of French in the speech from the throne, and he strongly criticized the Baldwin–La Fontaine government. Despite his earlier support of compensation for rebellion losses in both sections of the province (he was rebellion losses commissioner for the Western District in 1846), he strongly opposed the Rebellion Losses Bill in 1849. It was the height of injustice, he declared, for Canada West and the Western District in particular to be saddled with the costs arising from compensation for losses in Canada East. There had not been rebellion in the Western District; instead, people there had been victims of invasions instigated by the rebellion in Lower Canada. Moreover, losses in Upper Canada had been defrayed from its own resources. He participated in public protests against the bill, and firmly supported MacNab in the house.

From experience within his own family Prince was convinced of the desirability of personal independence and self-reliance. It was but a short step, at a time of political upheaval, for Prince to depart from a life-time adherence to the colonial link and to want to apply the same principle to public affairs. He thus became an advocate of the independence of Canada, so that its only ties with Britain would be those of friendship. In April 1850 the government revoked Prince's QC (it was restored in 1852) after he had published these views, but Prince asked only for the independence of Canada and did not approve of the movement for annexation to the United States. Later that year Prince decided that he would leave Canada were he given the opportunity.

He did not leave and although he felt that the people were ungrateful for his efforts on their behalf and unworthy of his leadership, he offered

Prince

himself once more for election to the assembly in 1851. He won, but his desire to retreat from the world probably now included public life, and the importunities of mankind weighed more desperately on his mind. His great love remained hunting. He had obtained in 1848 permission to lease land for a hunting and fishing retreat at Rondeau on Lake Erie, but in January 1853 Mary Ann frustrated his efforts to retain it. In October he tried unsuccessfully to obtain the judgeship of the new county of Lambton. Also futile were efforts in May 1854 to be named chief superintendent of the Indian Department.

Prince did not contest the election held in July 1854. His son Albert ran in his place in Essex but lost to Arthur Rankin. Prince was bitter towards Rankin, and in this frame of mind intensified his efforts to escape Sandwich. In August he explored the possibility of obtaining the judgeship at Sault Ste Marie, which he had first visited the previous September and disliked. He was not successful and in early 1855 was refused the judgeship of Huron County. When war broke out in the Crimea in 1854 he made an offer to the government (which was not accepted) to raise troops.

Prince had believed for some years that Mary Ann was actively working for his ruin. In 1855 he was scandalized by his son Albert's marriage to a divorced woman, and it was easy for him to conclude that his children had turned against him as well. With a deep sense of having been wronged by his family Prince reversed his earlier decision to leave politics and in 1857 sought election to the Legislative Council in the Western division. He was successful, and for the next three years immersed himself in political activity. He was energetic in the council in representing his constituents (in 1857, for example, he obtained passage of a bill for the incorporation of Sandwich), in introducing bills for the incorporation of companies (including in 1857 the St Clair, Chatham, and Rondeau Ship Canal Company, and in 1858 the River St Clair and Two-Creeks Ship Canal Company, and in 1860 the Windsor Improvement Company), and in promoting favourite causes, including in 1857 a bill for the prevention of cruelty to animals. His last legislative contributions, early in 1860, were in the same pattern; they included another game preservation bill and a bill for the division of Sandwich Township into Sandwich East and West.

It was on 24 Feb. 1860 that Prince departed for the last time "the ungrateful Soil of ungrateful Essex." On 26 May at Quebec he received a letter from the attorney general for Canada West, John A. Macdonald*, which appointed him judge of the provisional district of Algoma. He also became chairman of the Court of Quarter Sessions and judge of the Surrogate Court when Sault Ste Marie was named the district town in October 1860. By July he had moved to Sault Ste Marie. His family was still at Park Farm and Mary Ann maintained that he had deserted them; in April 1861, however, she refused to join him. That summer he built Belle Vue Lodge east of Sault Ste Marie.

Prince soon felt himself beset by all sorts of annoyances. Early in 1863 he offered Belle Vue Lodge for sale and that autumn he attempted to resign his judgeship. In 1865 he embarked on a short autobiography, published in 1867 by John Fennings Taylor*. It is an engagingly written document in which he gave the world a very selective view of himself. He offered little of his English origins and career, no explanation for his removal to Canada other than love of adventure, nothing about his family, little about his political and judicial careers, and nothing about his railway and mining interests; there was, however, a great deal about his military career and his life as a sportsman.

Physically, John Prince was incredibly tough. In his 70th year he suffered an accident with a horse that required him to amputate his own left thumb with a penknife. In 1866 when there were threats of a Fenian invasion, the old soldier was offering to take military charge at Sault Ste Marie and vowing to execute Fenian prisoners summarily, just as he had the Patriot prisoners at Windsor. He still professed a belief in the need for Canadian independence; an independent Canada would not have been a target for the Fenians, and it would in addition eliminate American contempt for Canada.

In the latter part of 1866 Prince had mellowed sufficiently toward Arthur Rankin for whom he had nursed a hatred ever since the election of 1854 to approve of his parliamentary performance on behalf of Essex. That autumn he welcomed Rankin as a visitor at Belle Vue Lodge. On 12 Aug. 1867 Prince learned of his son Septimus' death of alcoholism. Before the month was out he was seeking to return to southern Upper Canada and applied for the judgeship of Toronto. Another Fenian alarm in spring 1868 sent Prince's mind back again to 1838. The supreme irony of his long life, however, was that by this time his love of independence had evolved into republicanism; he now questioned the wisdom of ever having defended Canada and the monarchy.

John Prince's tragic life ended on 30 Nov. 1870.

At his wish he was buried in a solitary grave on an island in the St Mary's River opposite Belle Vue Lodge.

R. ALAN DOUGLAS

Hiram Walker Historical Museum (Windsor, Ont.), John Prince diaries. PAC, RG 68, 1, General index, 1651–1841; 1841–67. *Arthur papers* (Sanderson). Can., Prov. of, Legislative Assembly, *Journals*, 1841–54; Legislative Council, *Journals*, 1856–60. *Debates of the Legislative Assembly of United Canada*, I–VII. *Elgin-Grey papers* (Doughty). U.C., House of Assembly, *Journal*, 1836–40. Notman and Taylor, *Portraits of British Americans*, II, 159–80. Cornell, *Alignment of political groups*. Dent, *Last forty years*. R. A. Douglas, "'The battle of Windsor,'" *OH*, LXI (1969), 137–52.

PROUDFOOT, WILLIAM, merchant, banker, and investor; b. probably in Scotland; last known to be living in 1866.

The age William Proudfoot sometimes gave himself would indicate that he was born in 1802, but this is a late date for a man who signed the address of farewell from the inhabitants of York (Toronto) to Lieutenant Governor Francis Gore* in 1817, who sat on the original board of the Bank of Upper Canada in 1822, and who was a magistrate by 1827. Coming to York, Upper Canada, about 1816 with no traceable antecedents, he almost immediately became a partner in the store of lawyer D'Arcy Boulton* Jr and continued the business alone after 1825, selling wholesale and retail groceries, wines, and dry goods. He retired in the late 1830s. He also collected land avidly, advancing loans on such security, and claimed "upwards of 70,000 acres" by 1858.

On the full organization of the British America Assurance Company in 1834 he became its governor (chairman), but gave way to William Allan* in 1836. Allan in 1835 had resigned as first president of the Bank of Upper Canada, tired of the political attacks the bank had had to sustain and of the supine or apathetic attitudes of his fellow directors. Two potential candidates with stronger claims than Proudfoot for the presidency of the bank, John Spread Baldwin* and John Henry Dunn*, were ruled out by the supposedly factious quality of their support; Proudfoot, on the other hand, seemed personally innocuous. Allan wrote privately that "Mr Proudfoot was not elected from the idea of his being by any means either equal to it or the best they could get. He was the only [one] who was a candidate for it. . . . Proudfoot has not stamina or nous." It was his inoffensiveness, almost to the point of nonentity, which partly explains his survival in office through 25 more annual meetings of the bank. Threats to his position, such as those sparked by Samuel Peters Jarvis* in the financially stringent years of 1843 and 1848, were defeated because many shareholders felt the challengers to be far more reckless, ambitious, and opinionated than Proudfoot. What ultimately secured him, however, was the weight of proxy votes which absentees were persuaded by his long tenure to entrust to him and his associates.

Despite Proudfoot's continuous presidency, the bank's cashier from its inception, Thomas Gibbs RIDOUT, with his strong family and political ties in Toronto, had far more real and acknowledged influence. When Proudfoot wished as late as 1858 to borrow money from Glynn Mills and Company, the bank's English agents, he still felt the need to introduce himself and to use Ridout's name to establish his credentials. This letter and the few others of his which survive show Proudfoot deficient in cogency, orderliness, and information, which made the cashier's influence both explicable and essential.

But neither Ridout nor Proudfoot was equal to the complexities of financing and politicking which the development of the Province of Canada forced on them. The Bank of Upper Canada had always been prone to over-extension of credit to the large landowners who were its directors and to their peers, and never more so than in the boom of the 1850s. The bank, moreover, received the government's business after 1850, and this drew it into the ruinous role of agent for the Grand Trunk Railway and into other dubious or tangled government concerns, of which the frauds of the tycoon Samuel Zimmerman* were the most crippling. The bank became an abject dependent of its clients and creditors. Proudfoot and Ridout, bewildered by proceedings too vast and murky for them to fathom, stepped down in April 1861, Ridout dying soon after of exhaustion and Proudfoot trying desperately to appease his own insistent creditors.

Proudfoot had married Caroline Brooks Stow in York on 25 May 1833. By 1846 they had moved into the newly built Kearsney House on Yonge Street, possibly the most spacious residence in the Toronto of that day, and in it Mrs Proudfoot acted as hostess to parties of hundreds at bazaars, balls, and musical and theatrical entertainments. In the early 1860s, however, Proudfoot had to bind the house over to the bank.

Proudfoot's last years are almost completely unrecorded. The final notice of him so far discovered, dating from 1866, suggests that he was once more speculating in lands north of Toronto. In the later 1860s his wife, her address usually given as London, Eng., was listed as a shareholder in various Canadian banks – moderate holdings which grew quickly. In 1872 she was referred to as "widow." Yet, despite Proudfoot's long span in the chair of the Bank of Upper Canada (and the civic, benevolent, and Church of England ventures he was invited to patronize), he left so little impress on the minds and memories of his contemporaries that his death apparently passed as unnoticed as his birth. He died, as he had lived, in conspicuous obscurity.

BARRIE DYSTER

City of Toronto Archives, Toronto assessment rolls, St David's Ward, Yonge St, 1845, 1846; St James' Ward, Yonge St, 1860, 1861, 1865, 1866; St Andrew's Ward, Adelaide St, 1864. MTCL, Samuel Peters Jarvis papers, Bank of Upper Canada papers, 1843, 1848; Larratt William Smith papers, transcripts of letters, 1848; diaries, 1856, 1858. PAC, MG 24, D16, pp.41715–893; D36; RG 1, L3, index. PAO, Macaulay (John) papers, 1835; Street (Samuel) papers, 1864. UWO, 128 (George J. Goodhue papers), J. R. Gowan to G. J. Goodhue, 4 April 1866. Can., *Sessional papers*, 1867–68, VI, no.12; 1869, III, no. 6; 1870, III, no.6; 1872, VI, no.13 (returns of shareholders in Canadian banks). Scadding, *Toronto of old* (1873), 401. *Town of York, 1815–34* (Firth). U.C., House of Assembly, *Journal*, 1832–33, app. "Report of select committee on the inland water communication of the province," 90–101. *Upper Canada Gazette* (York [Toronto]), 5 June 1817. *Toronto directory*, 1833–66. *Robertson's landmarks of Toronto*, I, 25; III, 296–97. Ross and Trigge, *History of the Canadian Bank of Commerce*. "Historical sketch of the British America Assurance Company," *Canadian annual review of public affairs, 1911*, ed. J. C. Hopkins (Toronto, 1912).

PRUDEN, JOHN PETER, HBC chief factor and councillor of Assiniboia; baptized 31 May 1778 in Edmonton, Middlesex, England, son of Peter Pruden and Margaret Smith; m. first, sometime after 1800, Nancy, a half-breed woman, by whom he had six sons and five daughters, and secondly, 4 Dec. 1839, Ann Armstrong; d. 28 May 1868 at Winnipeg (Man.).

John Peter Pruden entered the Hudson's Bay Company's service as an apprentice in 1791 and arrived at York Factory on Hudson Bay in September. He was probably brought into the company through the influence of Sir James Winterlake, its deputy governor from 1792 to 1799, who owned land at Edmonton, Middlesex. In 1795 Pruden accompanied James Curtis Bird* to Carlton House, Saskatchewan District, and in May 1796 moved to Edmonton House; both posts had been built in the autumn of 1795. In 1798 he became a writer, moving in 1799 to Buckingham House and returning in 1800 to Edmonton House where Bird was now in charge. Bird then sent him with two others to build a house half-way between the Edmonton and Acton (Rocky Mountain) houses; it was probably the house noted on 7 May 1800 by David Thompson* of the rival North West Company on his way out from Rocky Mountain House.

Pruden seems to have spent the next few years in the Saskatchewan District. He was in charge of Acton House for the winter of 1805–6 and remained there until 1807 when he took over for one year a new settlement near the mouth of the north branch of the Saskatchewan. Between 1809 and 1824 Pruden apparently spent most of his time in charge of Carlton House, located after 1810 at the Crossing Place on the south branch of the Saskatchewan. In the autumn of 1819 Pruden entertained John Franklin* while his expedition was preparing for its journey to explore the north coast of America. On the amalgamation of the North West Company and the HBC in 1821 Pruden was appointed a chief trader. He went on leave because of ill health in 1824 and took three of his sons to England.

Pruden returned the following year to take charge of Norway House. In 1826 he again took over Carlton, where he remained, becoming chief factor in 1836, until he retired in 1837 to the Red River Settlement. There he married Ann Armstrong, the governess of Red River Academy. Letitia Hargrave [Mactavish*] wrote in 1846 that she had heard Pruden was "the best man in the Settlement"; but she had also heard scandalous tales about Ann's conduct on her voyage out from England in 1835 and of Ann's intention of returning to England because "her husband being so vulgar, she can't live at peace with him." Thomas Simpson* of the HBC, on the other hand, described Ann in 1835 as "a pious, unaffected well read lady."

Pruden was appointed a councillor of Assiniboia in 1839 and became a member of the Board of Public Works in 1844 and its chairman in 1847. In August 1845 he had accompanied Métis hunters from Red River on an expedition into American territory, perhaps in his capacity as councillor of Assiniboia to keep an eye on freelance half-breed traders. Stopped by American cavalry, the Métis were told they could no longer hunt on these lands unless they became American subjects. Already angry with the HBC over its opposition to their rights as free traders and conscious of the possibility of war between Britain and the United States as a result of the Oregon question and other irritants, the Métis were receptive to the American offer of protection if they settled on the United States side of the border at Pembina. On his return Pruden reported to governor Sir John Henry Pelly of the HBC: "If a war ensues there is no doubt what side the half-breeds will take. The Soldiers boasted they were now strong enough to thrash daddy England." The arrival of 500 British troops in the Red River Settlement in 1846 did much to restrain this unrest.

Pruden lived in retirement until the age of 90. An imposing man, he was apparently of humble origin or at least limited education. His writing skill improved markedly with the passing of time and he seems to have made his way through the company ranks by competent and faithful ser-

vice. In 1798, when he had been with the company only seven years, he was described as "A steady young man promises fair to make a Valuable Servant . . . ."

W. H. Brooks

HBC Arch. B.20/a/1; B.60/a/1–5. PAM, MG 7, B7, register of baptisms, 1813–28, no.518; register of burials, 1821–75, no.635 (595). Somerset House (London), Probate Department, will of John Peter Pruden, 27 Feb. 1826 (copy at HBC Arch.). Private archives, A. G. Pruden (Winnipeg), Notes on John Peter Pruden. HBRS, I (Rich). Mactavish, *Letters of Letitia Hargrave* (MacLeod), 218. Thompson, *Narrative* (Tyrrell). A. S. Morton, *History of the Canadian west.* E. A. Mitchell, "A Red River gossip," *Beaver*, outfit 291 (spring 1961), 9, 11.

Q

QUESNEL, FRÉDÉRIC-AUGUSTE, politician, lawyer, and businessman; b. 4 Feb. 1785 at Montreal, son of Joseph Quesnel*, musician and poet, and Marie-Josephte Deslandes; d. 28 July 1866 at Montreal.

Frédéric-Auguste Quesnel's family was prominent in the social and political life of Quebec for nearly a century. His father became a leading figure of Boucherville, then a centre of French society. Of Joseph's 13 children, Frédéric-Auguste, or Auguste as he called himself, and Jules-Maurice* achieved success in politics and commerce; Joseph-Timoléon was involved in the 1837 Rebellion; a sister Mélanie married successively Joseph-Michel Coursol, a fur-trader, and Côme-Séraphin Cherrier*, a leading Montreal advocate and cousin of Louis-Joseph Papineau*.

Frédéric-Auguste Quesnel was raised at Montreal by his mother's step-father, a fur-trader named Maurice-Régis Blondeau*. Like his brothers he was educated by the Sulpicians at the Collège de Montréal from 1796 to 1803. Frédéric-Auguste was noted for the purity of the French he learned there, but, unlike his fellow pupil, Louis-Joseph Papineau, he probably imbibed also the conservative principles that were apparent in other graduates.

He studied law in the office of Stephen Sewell*, a future solicitor general. By the time he was admitted to the bar in 1807, Quesnel could speak English with the same facility as French. He practised as an attorney at Montreal and by 1819 had offices on Rue Notre-Dame. In this period he laid the basis of his fortune, in the fur

trade, with which his brother Jules-Maurice was deeply involved, and in various speculations that included land sales. When war broke out in 1812 he was already a captain in the 5th battalion of Montreal militia, which became the *Chasseurs canadiens* in 1814; in 1830 he was promoted major in the 4th battalion of Montreal.

Meanwhile Quesnel had entered the Legislative Assembly, representing Kent County (renamed Chambly in 1829) from 1820 to 1834. It was a two-member riding, and his co-members were first Denis-Benjamin Viger and then Louis-Michel Viger*. Quesnel, who was an elegant speaker, in the early years supported the Papineau and Denis-Benjamin Viger group. In 1822 he signed the petition against the bill which would have reunited Upper and Lower Canada and in 1823 spoke at the farewell dinner before Papineau left for England with John Neilson* to fight successfully against the bill.

In the 1820s Quesnel held many minor government positions: he was commissioner in 1821 for the commune of Boucherville, in 1829 to assist the judges of the King's Bench at Montreal, and in 1830 to erect a jail. He also appeared in 1830 on the board appointed to erect churches and parsonages at Montreal. During the 1829–30 session of the legislature he headed a committee to review the judicial system, which recommended a court of appeal and circuit courts. The measure passed the assembly, but was defeated in the Legislative Council. In 1831 he became a KC.

A moderate in politics, Quesnel found himself in increasing difficulties as Papineau became

Quesnel

more radical. In 1832 he took the constitutionally correct position that Dominique MONDELET's seat in the house should not be declared vacant on his appointment to the Executive Council, an issue on which his side was defeated 32 to 27. The next year he, John Neilson, Augustin Cuvillier*, and other moderates refused to back a resolution in favour of an elected upper house. In January 1834 Quesnel was one of the minority who clashed with the radicals over the speech from the throne. The final break came over the 92 Resolutions. As he stated: "to say in a few words what I think of them, I approve a great many, I reject several, but taken as a whole and as a single unit, I cannot approve them." Other moderates, such as Cuvillier and Neilson, took the same stand, and Neilson attempted, without success, to introduce more moderate resolutions, which Quesnel backed. Both men were condemned at a public meeting at Saint-Athanase-d'Iberville (Iberville, Que.). In the ensuing elections Louis Lacoste*, with Papineau's backing, ousted Quesnel at Chambly. Neilson, Cuvillier, and other moderates also disappeared from the legislature.

Quesnel's political activity was not over, for in 1836 he was elected to the board regulating the affairs of the newly created Montreal Normal School, with both Catholics and Protestants voting. Since Papineau and Dr Edmund Bailey O'Callaghan* were also elected, the contest had political overtones. At the same time Quesnel was helping to secure various contested seigneurial rights of the Séminaire de Saint-Sulpice. Petitions to successive governors, which he played a leading role in formulating, led to confirmation of most of the Sulpicians' claims in 1840. Meanwhile, as the political situation worsened in 1837, Quesnel, George MOFFATT, and Clément-Charles SABREVOIS de Bleury arranged a public meeting in support of the government on 6 July. In September Governor Lord Gosford [Acheson*] appointed Quesnel to the Executive Council.

When the rebellion broke out, Quesnel's brother, Joseph-Timoléon, was forced to flee to Montreal from his medical practice at L'Acadie and had to give up his magistrate's commission. By this time Frédéric-Auguste was condemned as a *vendu* by the Patriotes. He had not lost his authority however: in March 1840, at the head of a delegation of 300, he presented Governor Charles Edward Poulett Thomson* with a petition of 6,370 signatories opposing the union of Upper and Lower Canada.

In 1841 Quesnel was elected MLA for Montmorency County, without a contest, on an anti-union platform. Thomson (now Lord Sydenham) listed him as one of the members who consistently opposed his policy. In the legislature Quesnel supported Neilson and Robert Baldwin* in protesting the union, and later Louis-Hippolyte LA FONTAINE and Baldwin when they resigned in 1843. Yet in the following months some feared he might support the succeeding Tory government under pressure from Denis-Benjamin Viger. In the election of 1844 he was defeated in Montmorency County by another moderate, Joseph-Édouard Cauchon*.

Again, defeat did not end his political activities, for in 1845 Quesnel was appointed to the Royal Institution for the Advancement of Learning. In 1845–46 he was one of the commissioners investigating the Board of Works [*see* Hamilton Hartley Killaly*]; their report led to a reorganization of the department. His middle-of-the-road position is demonstrated by the fact that Tory leader William Henry Draper* recommended him for appointment to the Legislative Council in 1847, but La Fontaine and Baldwin actually appointed him in September 1848. He remained in the upper house until his death. There Quesnel strongly supported the Rebellion Losses Bill of 1849 and condemned the Annexation Manifesto which followed it. He always believed annexation to the United States would not be an improvement over British rule. In the battle for abolition of seigneurial tenure in 1854 Quesnel, closely connected with the Sulpicians and with the Hôtel-Dieu as tenant and then proprietor of the fief of Saint-Joseph, naturally fought for proper compensation of the seigneurs. Many of his suggestions were incorporated in the final legislation. For some years after 1857 he was a trustee on the commission settling the boundary between Canada East and Canada West.

Quesnel also had a highly successful business career. He became a director of the Banque du Peuple about 1848 and while he was its president, 1859–65, it knew steady growth and tranquillity. By 1864 he was apparently winding up his holdings, selling a property to William Workman* and Alexandre-Maurice Delisle* for $100,000; the town of Sainte-Cunégonde (later annexed to Montreal) grew up on this land. He had been active in the Saint-Jean-Baptiste society of Montreal, which elected him president in 1860.

With powerful features, flowing hair, and mutton-chop whiskers, Quesnel radiates authority from his portrait. He long maintained an extensive establishment on fashionable Rue Saint-Antoine, but his personal life was tragic. In 1813 he had married Marguerite Denaut at Boucherville. She died in 1820 and their two sons and three daughters also predeceased him. Quesnel's substantial estate largely passed to his nephew Charles-Joseph Coursol*.

Frédéric-Auguste Quesnel's political career exemplifies the problems faced by a moderate amid the tensions of the 1830s and 1840s. His later influence points up the often neglected fact that supporters of reform who nevertheless opposed Papineau frequently had successful political careers after the rebellion. Quesnel's achievements in commerce and finance demonstrate that a French Canadian could make his fortune in business. The respect which Quesnel achieved, and the possibility of old political feuds being forgiven in new circumstances, are evident in the list of mourners at his funeral, which included such diverse personalities as Charles Wilson*, Mayor Henry Starnes*, Jean-Baptiste Prat*, and Quesnel's sometime ally, sometime opponent, Louis-Joseph Papineau.

FREDERICK H. ARMSTRONG

Côme-Séraphin Cherrier, Quesnel's brother-in-law, prepared a "Biographie de l'honorable F.-A. Quesnel," which was printed in *La Minerve* (Montréal), 5 Sept. 1866, and reprinted in *L'Écho du cabinet de lecture paroissial*, 15 Sept. 1866, in *L'Opinion publique*, 10 Oct. 1872, and as a pamphlet under the title *L'honorable F.-A. Quesnel* (Montréal, 1878).

PAC, MG 24, B126; RG 68, 1, General index, 1651–1841, pp.9, 225–26, 272, 393; 1841–67, pp.22, 89, 131, 338. F.-J. Audet, *Les députés de Montréal*, 381–82, 415. *Political appointments, 1841–65* (J.-O. Coté), 56, 78, 85. Atherton, *Montreal*, II, 135, 149, 161. G.-É. Baillargeon, *La survivance du régime seigneurial à Montréal; un régime qui ne veut pas mourir* ([Montréal], 1968), 38, 45, 84. Chapais, *Hist. du Canada*, III, 123; IV, 11, 14, 32, 36, 38–39, 188; VI, 104. Cornell, *Alignment of political groups*, 5, 7, 16. R. S. Greenfield, "La Banque du Peuple, 1835–71, and its failure, 1895" (unpublished MA thesis, McGill University, Montreal, 1968), 1, 8, 33, 67. I.[-A.] Groulx, *Histoire du Canada français depuis la découverte* (4e éd., 2v., Montréal et Paris, 1960), II, 158. Olivier Maurault, *Le collège de Montréal, 1767–1967*, Antonio Dansereau, édit. (2e éd., Montréal, 1967), 196, 550. Monet, *Last cannon shot*, 43, 55, 64, 83–84, 146–47. Rumilly, *Hist. de Montréal*, II, 199, 203, 226, 257, 368–69. Helen Taft Manning, *The revolt of French Canada, 1800–1835: a chapter in the history of the British Commonwealth* (Toronto, 1962), 318, 356, 362. F.-J. Audet, "L'honorable Frédéric-Auguste Quesnel," *BRH*, XXXIII (1927), 399–400. É.-Z. Massicotte, "La famille du poète Quesnel," *BRH*, XXIII (1917), 339–42.

QUINAN, JOHN JOSEPH, Roman Catholic priest; b. 1834 at Halifax, N.S., son of Joseph W. Quinan; d. 7 April 1870 at Church Point, Digby County, N.S.

John Joseph Quinan was one of at least three brothers who entered the priesthood. A promising student at Saint Mary's College in Halifax, he was sent to Rome in 1850 by Bishop William Walsh* to study at the College of Propaganda. He returned to Nova Scotia in 1855 and spent nearly 18 months at Tracadie where he received further training for the priesthood under his uncle, Father John Quinan. It was here that he learned to speak French, a skill which contributed to his posting in 1857 to southwestern Nova Scotia. Quinan was ordained to the priesthood on 21 June of that year by Thomas L. Connolly*, bishop of Saint John, N.B., and soon after was sent to Yarmouth County.

He served there in the predominantly Acadian parishes of Saint-Michel at Tusket, Sainte-Anne at Eel Brook (Sainte-Anne du Ruisseau), and in the town of Yarmouth. It was at Eel Brook that he supervised the construction of a new church and a school. In 1867 he was transferred to the parish of Church Point, Digby County, and here, in April 1870, he died following a severe and lengthy throat ailment. He was buried in Halifax.

A popular personality among his parishioners, Quinan was one of the few priests of Irish background to serve successfully in a predominantly Acadian parish. The Catholic hierarchy in Nova Scotia, oriented more to the urban Irish community, had in the past neglected the faithful in southwestern Nova Scotia if they were unable to find French-speaking priests from within the archdiocese or from Quebec. In an obituary of Quinan, *Le Moniteur acadien* wrote: ". . . he was a model of the pious virtues which distinguish every good Christian, and displayed all possible zeal for religion and education." A further tribute was paid him on 15 May 1885 when a public meeting of the inhabitants of Tusket Forks, Yarmouth County, voted unanimously to change the name of their community to Quinan, in honour of one "who had greatly endeared himself to them and [who] was highly esteemed by all classes of the people of this County."

DAVID B. FLEMMING

PANS, MG 5, Holy Cross Cemetery (Halifax), 10 April 1870 (mfm.). *Casket* (Antigonish, N.S.), 2 July 1857. *Evening Express* (Halifax), 8 April 1870. *Le Moniteur acadien* (Shédiac, N.-B.), 22 avril 1870. *Yarmouth Herald* (Yarmouth, N.S.), 20 May 1885. T. J. Brown, *Place-names of the province of Nova Scotia* ([Halifax], 1922). *Place-names of N.S.* William Foley, *The centenary of St. Mary's Cathedral, Halifax, N.S., 1820–1920: a souvenir memorial* (Halifax, 1920). A. A. Johnston, *A history of the Catholic Church in eastern Nova Scotia* (2v., Antigonish, N.S., 1960–71), II.

QUINTAL, LOUIS BOYER, *dit. See* BOYER

R

RANKIN, ROBERT, timber merchant and ship-owner; b. 31 May 1801 at Mearns, Renfrewshire, Scotland, son of James Rankin and Helen Ferguson; d. 3 June 1870 at Bromborough Hall in Cheshire, England.

Robert Rankin's family were prosperous farmers in the Mearns parish. Between 1807 and 1813 Rankin received a good general education and a grounding in book-keeping at the Mearns school under James Jackson, an able dominie in the best Scottish tradition, many of whose pupils were to become business leaders.

In May 1815, after a few months in the counting-house of John Wilson, a Glasgow merchant, Rankin joined the office staff of the timber-importing firm, Pollok, Gilmour, and Company, at the thriving new port of Grangemouth on the Forth estuary, terminal of the Forth and Clyde Canal. The firm had been founded in Glasgow in 1804 by Allan Gilmour Sr and the brothers John and Arthur Pollok, also natives of Mearns. Rankin's elder brother, Alexander*, had served it since 1806, and in 1812 had gone to Miramichi in New Brunswick to found the branch-firm of Gilmour, Rankin, and Company. It was through his brother's influence that Robert Rankin had secured entry to the firm in the difficult post-war years of recession, and his rise was rapid. On 15 Dec. 1816 he was transferred to the head office in Glasgow, where he soon gained the approval of Arthur Pollok through his competence as book-keeper and accountant, and was appointed cashier of the firm at age 16.

By this time Pollok, Gilmour, and Company, through its Miramichi operations, had become the leading British firm in the North American timber trade. These operations had originally been planned by Allan Gilmour as a means of beating Napoleon's Continental System, which prohibited lumber exports from the Baltic to Britain. Now the firm owned more than 50 vessels engaged in the shipment of lumber and employed 700 men in the forests and sawmills of New Brunswick. The scale of these operations increased steadily as the trade boomed, and in 1818 Robert Rankin was selected by Gilmour to go out to the Miramichi branch to gain experience in the colonies.

Young Rankin was clearly regarded as a "coming man" in the firm, and a possible future partner. Assiduous in his labours in the Miramichi office, he soon gained a reputation as a skilful administrator and a shrewd bargainer with timber contractors. In 1820–21 he made a "prospecting trip" to the Saint John River to assess the timber of the area and recommended to the head office that another branch-firm be founded at Saint John.

During his years in Glasgow and on the Miramichi, Rankin's life was one of "Spartan self-discipline," according to his nephew John Rankin, the historian of Pollok, Gilmour, and Company, who examined his personal expenditure book. In Glasgow he had lived carefully in cheap lodgings, but gave regular church donations and gifts to charity. He had also sacrificed on clothing and food to take French lessons, realizing he would be working in the British North American colonies. In his first years in New Brunswick he lived frugally and saved hard. Although he received only £45 from his deceased father's estate in November 1817 after providing for his mother, by the end of 1822 he had accumulated nearly £400 in savings to his credit in the firm's books, a sum which represented practically all of his annual salary for four years' service on the Miramichi.

Rankin's career as an independent entrepreneur began early in 1822 when Pollok, Gilmour, and Company decided to set up the branch-firm in Saint John that Rankin had recommended. He had made an arduous overland journey from the Miramichi to Saint John in the spring of 1821 to transfer his capital in bullion form, but on arrival decided that the time was not quite ripe for commencing operations. A year later, however, he judged correctly that there would be a new timber boom and set up the firm of Robert Rankin and Company in Saint John. Within ten years, by his shrewdness in purchasing timber and dealing in imports of foodstuffs and lumbering stores, he made this branch-firm the most prosperous and successful of the Pollok, Gilmour, and Company enterprises, which also flourished in Bathurst and Chatham, N.B., Montreal, Quebec, Restigouche County, and on the Miramichi. Unlike other branch-firm managers, Rankin had a completely free hand to conduct the Saint John operation as he saw fit. He became, in fact, the guiding intelligence in the colonies of Pollok, Gilmour, and Company, a vast concern which by 1838 operated 130 vessels in the timber trade – making it the largest British shipowning firm – and employed no fewer than 15,000 men in its sawmills, on its wharves, and in the forests; it owned as well 2,000 horses and oxen for draught purposes. In the early 1830s the firm shipped out annually over 300 cargoes of timber. At Saint John Rankin had added to his lumbering concerns the building of ships and the importing of textiles, foodstuffs, and building supplies on a large scale – reputedly for more than half of the numerous merchants in the town. His success in Saint John was so great that by the early 1830s he was even influencing affairs in the head office in Glasgow.

John Rankin, who knew his uncle well, ascribed his success to "his perfect mastery of figures and of book-keeping, his love of order, quickness of decision, close eye on the leading markets and articles of produce and the fact that he was not only a good buyer, but, what few men are, a wise and competent seller, who would not regret if the buyer had a profit." It also appears that Rankin had a gift for clarity of thought and expression. His business letters were noted for their terseness and precision.

By 1830 Robert Rankin was wealthy and regarded as the leading shipowner and timber merchant of Saint John, but he continued to live frugally and unostentatiously. On 17 March 1829 he married Ann, daughter of John Strang, a prominent Scottish merchant of St Andrews, N.B., where, as in Saint John, commercial life was largely dominated by Scots. By 1837 he had prospered to such an extent that he was contemplating retiring, returning to Scotland, and purchasing a landed estate where he could take up livestock breeding, a pursuit which had interested him since his youth as a farmer's son. This possibility was easily within his reach financially, since he had now considerable investments outside the firm, in British railways, mining, insurance companies, and shipping.

His plans were altered by a crisis in the affairs of the firm in Glasgow in 1837, following a bitter quarrel among the founders. Since all parties considered that only Rankin could settle the dispute and take the leadership of the over-all concern, he left Saint John in the summer of 1838 with his wife and family. In Scotland he speedily arranged to buy out Gilmour for £150,000 and to reconstruct Pollok, Gilmour, and Company. Rankin, his brother Alexander, and Allan Gilmour* Jr of the Quebec branch now became the controlling partners. At Rankin's instigation, the head office was moved from Glasgow to Liverpool, to take advantage of the greater commercial opportunities there, particularly in the lumber trade, and a new subsidiary firm was established under the name of Rankin, Gilmour, and Company. In order to employ its large fleet fully in the winter months, branch houses were opened in New Orleans, La, and Mobile, Ala, where the company entered the rapidly expanding cotton trade.

As in New Brunswick, Rankin's business acumen ensured the firm's success in this new *milieu*. The diversification into cotton brought great profits, and by 1851 he was a member of the Dock Committee of Liverpool, the "inner ring" of influential merchants and shipowners. In addition to owning a fine residence in Liverpool, he had purchased the large estate of Bromborough Hall in Cheshire, where he engaged in cattle breeding and other rural pursuits. In 1857 he toured Canada and the United States with his family and was accorded what has been described as "an almost Royal reception" in many places, particularly in New Brunswick. Until his death in 1870, he remained in active control of the Pollok-Gilmour-Rankin "empire." His prestige in Liverpool can be judged by his election in January 1862 as chairman of the Mersey Docks and Harbour Board, described as "the highest honour Liverpool has to bestow." In 1865 he set up his son James as a country gentleman, buying for him two large estates in Herefordshire.

In his later years Rankin's public benefactions were numerous. He funded mechanics' institutes, temperance societies, and orphans' homes, and he contributed several large sums for the laying of the first Atlantic cable in the 1850s and 1860s. Early in 1869 his health began to fail, and despite a long Mediterranean trip the decline continued. The death of his daughter, drowned in Menai Strait, Wales, in August 1869, was a crushing blow to Rankin, who had already lost four of his seven children through childhood illnesses. He died the following June.

Rankin was a characteristic Scottish entrepreneur of his period, utterly devoted to his business with few cultural or public interests. His only outside interests were livestock breeding and the pursuits of a country gentleman in the last phase of his life. It is difficult to avoid the conclusion that except in matters pertaining to trade prospects, he was narrow in outlook. According to John Rankin, he was taciturn and far from sociable. Yet his industry, commercial percipience, financial ability, and organizational capacity, shown in the colonies and later in Liverpool, mark him as one of the outstandingly successful businessmen of his time. The Canadian timber trade and the New Brunswick shipbuilding industry owed much of the amazing progress they made between 1820 and 1850 to his sagacity and tenacity.

DAVID S. MACMILLAN

Redpath

General Register Office (Edinburgh), Mearns parish register, 1760–1801. Liverpool Record Office, City Council, minute books, 1851–55. University of Glasgow, Business History coll., Pollok, Gilmour, and Company, records. John Rankin, *A history of our firm, being some account of the firm of Pollok, Gilmour and Co. and its offshoots and connections, 1804–1920* (2nd ed., Liverpool, 1921). C. F. Fay, "Mearns and the Miramichi: an episode in Canadian economic history," *CHR*, IV (1923), 316–20. D. S. Macmillan, "The 'new men' in action: Scottish mercantile and shipping operations in the North American colonies, 1760–1825," *Canadian business history, selected studies, 1497–1971*, ed. D. S. Macmillan (Toronto, 1972), 69–103.

REDPATH, JOHN, contractor and industrialist; b. 1796 at Earlston, Berwickshire, Scotland; d. 5 March 1869 at Montreal, Que.

Of John Redpath's life in Scotland before he left at the age of 20, we know only that he trained as a stone mason. In the early 1820s he emerged as a major building contractor in Montreal, supplying the stone for the new Notre-Dame Church and the Lachine Canal in partnership with Thomas McKay*. The canal was one of the most important public works of the early 19th century in Lower Canada and in building its locks Redpath gained a sound reputation. In 1827 and 1828 McKay and Redpath were engaged in building the locks at Jones Falls on the Rideau Canal, "the most extensive engineering undertaking at any one location along the Canal." Redpath then seems to have returned to Montreal, although until 1831 he apparently retained an interest in a partnership with major contractors on the canal including McKay, Thomas Phillips, and Andrew White.

It is not clear what business Redpath pursued after he returned to Montreal. He was already well-to-do and moved rapidly to the highest level of the Montreal business community. In 1833 he was elected to the board of directors of the Bank of Montreal, the city's leading financial institution; until his death he was a director, after 1860 a vice-president, and a large shareholder. But like most of his wealthy colleagues Redpath put money into several enterprises of Montreal's burgeoning economy of the 1840s, 50s and 60s. An investor in the Montreal Fire Assurance Company and the Montreal Telegraph Company, and a director of both, he also invested substantial sums in Canadian mining ventures – some in the Eastern Townships – including the Belvedere Mining and Smelting, Bear Creek Coal, Rockland Slate, Melbourne Slate, and Capel Copper companies. In addition, he owned shares in a copper smelter, a large share of the Montreal Investment Association, and much of the most desirable mountainside property in Montreal, and he had investments in shipping, the Montreal Towboat Company and the Richelieu Company [*see* Jacques-Félix Sincennes*]. He was also a promoter of the Canada Marine Insurance Company, the Metropolitan Fire Insurance Company, and the Canada Peat Fuel Company.

Despite these many financial interests and substantial wealth, Redpath would not have stood out among many equals in Montreal had it not been for his decision in 1854 to begin construction of the first sugar refinery in the Province of Canada. His was one of the largest establishments among more than 20 new plants in the recently opened industrial belt along the Lachine Canal. Redpath had started several years earlier to purchase land along the canal from the Sulpicians, the provincial government having not long before authorized the use of the canal's water for industrial purposes. His seven-storey factory, whose towering smokestack became one of the city's landmarks, represented an immense investment for Redpath, the sole owner. He put £40,000 into land, buildings, and machinery, and disposed of a like amount in working capital. Within a year, he had more than 100 employees and was producing 3,000 barrels of refined sugar per month for the Canadian market. His plant depended entirely on supplies of cane sugar imported from the West Indies, much of it in his own ships, the *Helen Drummond* and *Grace Redpath*, named after his daughters. By 1862 he was importing about 7,000 tons of raw sugar annually. Under the protection of favourable tariffs conveniently established by the Canadian government in 1855 – the year Redpath's factory opened –the business prospered. By the mid 1860s another sugar refinery had been established in Montreal to compete with Redpath's. In 1859 Redpath had brought his eldest son, Peter*, and his son-in-law, George Alexander Drummond*, a young Scottish engineer, into the firm and made plans to retire gradually as more of his sons came of age, perhaps to enjoy his new country house, Terrace Bank, built on one of his Mount Royal properties overlooking the city where his substantial fortune had been founded.

Redpath had served a brief and undistinguished term as a member of Montreal's city council from 1840 to 1843, but he had provided the province with other useful services. During the late 1830s he was a member of the Lachine Canal commission. In 1839 he was appointed to the newly created provincial Board of Works, resigning on 24 April 1840, and in 1845 he served on the commission of inquiry into the management of the Board of Works along with William

Cayley*, Frédéric-Auguste Quesnel, George Sherwood, and Moses Judah Hayes [see Hamilton Hartley Killaly*].

Redpath was president in 1849 of the Montreal Annexation Association, which enjoyed broad, yet brief support from many of the city's prominent businessmen. Requests for assistance from other annexationists, including Hugh Bowlby Willson*, editor of Toronto's *Independent*, were forwarded to Redpath. There is a strong possibility that as an aspiring industrialist, who would have been concerned about markets for manufactured goods, Redpath was in part responsible for the emphasis in the association's manifesto on the supposed advantages for Canadian manufacturers in union with the United States. His concern was perhaps reflected in his announcement to the annexationists in October 1849 that thousands of skilled Canadian artisans were moving to the United States. With the rapid decline of annexationism in Montreal in 1850, Redpath turned his interest in public welfare onto surer paths.

He had always been a charitable man in the best Christian tradition. He supported established institutions such as the Montreal General Hospital, the Montreal Presbyterian College, and the mechanics' institute, all of which he served as a director, but he also, at the head of a small group, sought government assistance to fight Montreal's white slavery traffic and, working through the local Magdalene Asylum, to redeem "unfortunate females, many of whom are poor immigrants who have been decoyed into the abodes of infamy and shame which abound in this city." He also secured support for an insane asylum from the government, and helped establish the Protestant House of Industry and Refuge. A devout Free Church Presbyterian, Redpath was a founder of the Presbyterian Foreign Missions, the Labrador Mission, the Sabbath Observance Society, and the French Canadian Missionary Society; to the latter he left a substantial legacy.

Redpath had ten children by his first wife, Janet McPhee, whom he married in 1818. Following her death in 1834 he married Jane Drummond, and they had seven children. Only two of his sons, Peter and John James, appear to have joined the refinery. One of Redpath's daughters married John Dougall*, editor of the *Montreal Witness*, another Henry Taylor Bovey*, a well-known McGill University professor, and another George Alexander Drummond, who became the principal figure in the refinery and a prominent Montreal businessman.

Gerald Tulchinsky

Canada and Dominion Sugar Company Ltd. Archives (Montreal), Ledger, John Redpath and Son, p.44; Deeds files, 31 Dec. 1866. PAC, RG 4, C1, 121, no.259; 268, no.3063; RG 7, G20, 83–84, no.9558; RG 8, I (C series), 43, pp.181, 196–200; 45, pp.24–25; 221, pp.221–22; RG 11, ser. 1, 24; RG 42, I, 175, pp.43–44, 47, 62. Private archives, Mr Quinton Bovey (Montreal), will of John Redpath (photocopy). "The annexation movement, 1849–50," ed. A. G. Penny, *CHR*, V (1924), 236–62. Can., Prov. of, *Statutes*, 1841, c.98; 1859, c.115; 1864, c.98. *Elgin-Grey papers* (Doughty), IV, 1491. D. H. MacVicar, *In memoriam; a sermon, preached in the Canada Presbyterian Church, Côté Street, Montreal, on Sabbath, March 14th, 1869, on the occasion of the death of John Redpath, esq., Terrace Bank* (Montreal, 1869). *Pilot and Evening Journal of Commerce* (Montreal), 19 March 1844. *Select documents in Canadian economic history*, ed. H. A. Innis and A. R. M. Lower (2v., Toronto, 1929–33), II, 613–14. Borthwick, *History and biographical gazetteer*, 130. L. J. Burpee, *The Oxford encyclopaedia of Canadian history* (Toronto and London, 1926), 532. C. E. Goad, *Atlas of the city of Montreal . . .* (2nd ed., 2v., Montreal, 1890), I, xix, xxi. *Montreal directory*, 1841–53.

C. D. Allin and G. M. Jones, *Annexation, preferential trade and reciprocity; an outline of the Canadian annexation movement of 1849–50, with special reference to the questions of preferential trade and reciprocity* (Toronto and London, [1912]), 136. Campbell, *History of Scotch Presbyterian Church*, 388. Denison, *Canada's first bank*, II, 421. *Hist. de la corporation de la cité de Montréal* (Lamothe *et al.*), 204. R. [F.] Legget, *Rideau waterway* (Toronto, 1955), 106, 114, 116–18, 166–67, 220. O. J. McDiarmid, *Commercial policy in the Canadian economy* (Cambridge, Mass., 1946), 73. *Montreal in 1856; a sketch prepared for the celebration of the opening of the Grand Trunk Railway of Canada* (Montreal, 1856), 39–45. *Redpath centennial, one hundred years of progress, 1854–1954* (Montreal, 1954). Franklin Toker, *The church of Notre-Dame in Montreal; an architectural history* (Montreal and London, Ont., 1970), 43–44. G. J. J. Tulchinsky, "Studies of businessmen in the development of transportation and industry in Montreal, 1837–1853" (unpublished PHD thesis, University of Toronto, 1971), 425–29.

REID, JAMES MURRAY, HBC employee and merchant; b. 15 Oct. 1802 in the Orkney Islands; d. 24 April 1868 at Victoria, B.C.

James Murray Reid entered the Hudson's Bay Company's marine service about 1822 and became first officer of *Prince Albert* and later *Prince Rupert*, both of which voyaged out of London to Hudson Bay. In 1849 Vancouver Island became a British crown colony open to colonization and trade, and soon after the HBC gave Reid command of *Vancouver*, a new brigantine of 184 tons designed for the west coast service. The ship, the third of that name built by the HBC, set sail from London on 30 June 1852 and Reid arrived in Victoria in mid December with his wife Mary Petrie and their three daughters.

In 1853, after a busy trading season which included a voyage to the Sandwich Islands (Hawaii), *Vancouver* left Victoria for Fort Simpson with "outfits" for the northern posts. Within 50 miles of Fort Simpson she ran aground on treacherous Rose Spit off the northeastern tip of the Queen Charlotte Islands, and was set on fire to prevent the cargo, which included spirits, from falling into the hands of Indians. The loss of the ship was serious for both the company and the colony since all trade on the coast was disrupted.

Reid himself had lost his income and decided to enter business as an independent mercantile importer. He purchased waterfront lots for warehouse and wharf facilities in Victoria, and established connections with London wholesale houses. In 1858 he was joined by his son-in-law, William John Macdonald*. They profited greatly by the rapid growth of trade resulting from the Fraser River gold rush of that year. Their properties in Victoria included elegant 19th century brick buildings in Bastion Square. Reid was appointed port warden for Esquimalt and Victoria in 1859 and elected town councillor in Victoria in 1862. In that year he sold his business to devote himself to public service and remained prominent in civic and community affairs until his death.

FLORA HAMILTON BURNS

PABC, John Sebastian Helmcken, "Reminiscences" (5v., typescript, 1892). *Daily British Colonist and Victoria Chronicle*, 20 April, 1 Dec. 1859; 20 May, 18 Aug. 1862; 25 June 1863; 25 April 1868. Walbran, *B.C. coast names*. W. J. Macdonald, *A pioneer, 1851* ([Victoria?, 1851]).

RICHARDSON, EDWARD MALLCOTT, sculptor and landscape painter; b. 21 May 1839 at London, England, son of Edward Richardson and Eliza Austen; last known to be living in 1865.

The father of Edward Mallcott Richardson was a London sculptor and restorer of monumental effigies, and presumably he instructed his son in his own skills. In addition, the younger Richardson claimed in 1864 to have articled in England to a surveyor on the Great Northern Railway (opened in 1852) "for three years previously to taking to painting. . . ." "While I was with him," Richardson added, "he was engaged in the Grand Surrey Canal Docks and one or two minor railways &c."

In June 1859 Richardson was accepted as a probationer in the Royal Academy Schools, and he entered the School of Painting in London as "a life student" on 21 Dec. 1859. He was, he said, "for three years a pupil of Sir George Hayter, principal historical painter" to the queen. At that period the Royal Academy studentship was for seven years, but on 6 June 1862 Richardson left London for Vancouver Island aboard the steamer *Tynemouth*. On 19 Sept. 1862 he arrived in Victoria, and soon afterwards designed and executed an 18-foot-high stone monument erected in the local cemetery to the memory of John D. Carroll. The truncated and moss-grown remains of this once "handsome monument . . . in the Gothic style . . . most carefully finished in every part" may still be identified in Pioneer Square, adjoining Christ Church Cathedral.

During the mining season of 1863 Richardson sketched along the Harrison-Lillooet trail to the Cariboo goldfields, and in 1864 he was painting in Victoria. But the prosperity stimulated by the spectacular gold strikes of 1860–62 was fast receding, and the future for an artist was far from bright. On 18 May 1864 Richardson applied to the committee then organizing the Vancouver Island exploration party under Dr Robert Brown* "for the appointment of Artist . . . but should [the] committee decide on not sending an Artist as well as an Assistant Surveyor I would offer to undertake both duties." His application was unsuccessful. He is last heard of in the spring of 1865 when the newspapers reported that on 6 May he would hold a raffle of his paintings, which were said to be "valuable, and executed with a rare fidelity to nature and finished off with much care and artistic taste."

In all probability Richardson was one of the many adventurous young men who in 1862 threw up their prospects at home to join the flood of immigrants to British Columbia, victims of the highly optimistic, and highly unscrupulous, reports on the gold colony from the anonymous and persuasive pen of Donald Fraser*, the Victoria correspondent of the London *Times*.

DOROTHY BLAKEY SMITH

Three of E. M. Richardson's water-colours are at PAC, Picture Division, and four are at PABC. Greater London Record Office, All Souls, Langham Place, London, Register of baptisms, entry for E. M. Richardson. PABC, Robert Brown coll., E. M. Richardson to the committee of the [Vancouver Island] exploration party, 18 May 1864. Royal Academy of Arts (London), Students' register. Somerset House (London), General Registry Office, birth certificate of E. M. Richardson. Frederick Whymper, *Travel and adventure in the territory of Alaska, formerly Russian America – now ceded to the United States – and in various other parts of the north Pacific* (London, 1868). *Daily British Colonist* (Victoria), 19 Sept. 1862, 28 March 1863, 6 May

1865. *Vancouver Times* (Victoria), 5 May 1865. *Victoria Daily Chronicle*, 28 March 1863. J. R. Harper, *Early painters and engravers*; *Painting in Canada, a history* (Toronto, 1966).

RICHARDSON, HUGH, shipowner and captain, and office-holder; b. 12 June 1784 in London, England, second son of Thomas Richardson, a West Indies merchant; d. 2 Aug. 1870 at Toronto, Ont.

Hugh Richardson left school and went to sea in 1798, serving with distinction until he was taken captive by the French in 1810. Imprisoned at Verdun, Arras, and Paris, he was not released until 1818. He married that year and in the spring of 1821 he and his wife Frances came to Canada; they were to have a large family.

In 1823 he became a captain in the 2nd Regiment of militia at York (Toronto), under the command of John Beverley ROBINSON, was promoted major in 1830, and transferred to the reserve in 1831. Richardson was appointed a district coroner for Niagara in 1824, Newcastle in 1828, and Home in 1830. In 1825 he organized the construction of the steamer *Canada*, designed for the York-Hamilton-Niagara run. Its maiden voyage was on 7 Aug. 1826. Richardson went to England in 1827 to raise money to make himself managing-owner, but the purchase put him in financial difficulties. In 1832, although he had paid off £1,040 in interest and £300 in principal on his debts and had a net profit of £1,946, he was not prospering. "Sink I often think I shall – founder in the midst of a mine of gold, with a millstone about my neck," he wrote J. B. Robinson. Nevertheless, in 1835 he purchased the steamer *Constitution*, renamed *Transit*, operated that year on a semi-weekly circuit with stops at Toronto, Port Hope, Cobourg, Rochester, Hamilton, and Oakville. The next year the *Transit* took over the *Canada*'s Toronto–Niagara–Lewiston itinerary and the latter ship was sold for £1,400.

Deeply interested in the improvement of Toronto harbour, Richardson in 1833 had published a pamphlet, *York harbour*, which advocated several improvements. At his own expense he had lighted the harbour entrance until 1833 and provided buoys and beacons until 1837. In 1833 Richardson, J. G. CHEWETT, and William Chisholm* had been appointed commissioners to improve the harbour with a £2,000 grant, and in 1837–38 he and George GURNETT sat on another commission which for £2,375 extended the government wharf and built a new lighthouse.

Richardson supported the Church of England and had his sons educated at Upper Canada College. He was appointed a magistrate of the Home District in 1837. When the rebellion broke out that December, Lady Head, the Robinson family, and the wives and children of officials took refuge on Richardson's *Transit* in Toronto harbour at Archdeacon John STRACHAN's suggestion. On 7 December the *Transit* sailed to Niagara to warn that town of the rebellion, and in 1838 it was sometimes used to transport troops. Lieutenant Governor Sir Francis Bond Head* appointed Richardson to a special magistracy in 1838.

Apparently hoping to improve his finances by expansion, Richardson purchased the *Queen Victoria* from James Lockhart for £7,000 in 1839; in 1842 he had the *Chief Justice Robinson* constructed. Both ships joined the *Transit* on the Toronto–Niagara route, but rival American lines pushed Richardson into a disastrous rate-cutting war with a Canadian competitor, Donald BETHUNE. In 1846 Richardson declared bankruptcy, and in 1847 his fleet and other assets were sold at what he considered a poor price. Richardson moved to Montreal and captained the *John Munn*, plying between Montreal and Quebec. In 1849 he was captain of his former *Transit*, which was running as a ferry in the Montreal area.

Richardson was appointed first harbourmaster of Toronto in 1850. The post gave him an important social position in the city; by the 1860s it paid a salary of $1,600 and $300 for rent. The first board of harbour commissioners included his old colleagues, Gurnett and Chewett, as well as Thomas Clarkson* and Peter Paterson* representing the Board of Trade. With their cooperation Richardson began work on the harbour, which he felt was in an advanced state of decay. The Queen's Wharf was improved and extended, Kivas Tully* superintending much of the work. In addition the Western Gap was widened and repaired and the Eastern Gap (created by storms in 1858) came into use.

Though paralysed for about the last three years of his life, Richardson retained his office until his death. He was described by Henry Scadding* as "a man of chivalrous temperament. His outward physique, moreover, corresponded with his character. His form was lithe, graceful and officer-like." A popular figure in 19th-century Toronto, he probably did more than anyone else to develop its facilities as a lake port.

FREDERICK H. ARMSTRONG

Hugh Richardson, *York harbour* (York [Toronto], 1833). MTCL, Vaughan Maurice Roberts papers, 3, pp.1–112; 6, pp.43, 90; 15, pp.7–8. PAC, RG 1, E3, 89, pp.212, 214–17. PAO, Robinson (John Beverley) papers, 13 Jan. 1833, 22 March 1847, 29 March 1848, 1

Richardson

Dec. 1849; Street (Samuel) papers, 3 May 1839. *Daily Telegraph* (Toronto), 3 Aug. 1870. *Globe*, 3 Aug. 1870. Scadding, *Toronto of old* (1873), 548, 550–55, 558–63, 565, 572, 575–76. Erik Heyl, *Early American steamers* (6v., Buffalo, N.Y., 1953–67), II, 23, 37, 215; VI, 53, 70–71, 264–65. *Landmarks of Can.*, I, nos.517, 589, 2544. Middleton, *Municipality of Toronto*, I, 169, 440, 444–45, 460. *Robertson's landmarks of Toronto*, II, 850, 852–53, 856–57, 860–61, 864, 871–72, 878, 880–81, 888, 938.

RICHARDSON, Sir JOHN, surgeon, explorer, natural historian, and ichthyologist; b. 5 Nov. 1787 in Dumfries, Scotland, eldest of 12 children of Gabriel Richardson and Anne Mundell; m. first in 1818 Mary Stiven (Stivens) of Leith, Scotland, and secondly in 1833 Mary Booth of Stickney, England, by whom he had seven children, and thirdly in 1847 Mary Fletcher of Edinburgh; d. 5 June 1865 at Grasmere, Westmorland, England.

John Richardson's father was a prosperous brewer, provost of Dumfries for one term, and a magistrate for many years. Robert Burns was a close friend of the family and influenced John towards literary tastes that lasted all his life. Burns' oldest son and John Richardson attended the Dumfries Grammar School together. John always liked vigorous activity and outdoor life, encouraged by holidays near the Solway Firth and in the Galloway Mountains.

At age 14 he was apprenticed to his uncle James Mundell, a surgeon in Dumfries, and later to Dr Samuel Shortridge. He attended the medical school of the University of Edinburgh from 1801 to 1804, studying botany, geology, and Greek in addition to the usual subjects: anatomy, chemistry, materia medica, and therapeutics. From 1804 to 1806 he was a house surgeon at the Dumfries and Galloway Royal Infirmary, and in 1806–7 completed his qualification at Edinburgh. His teachers at Edinburgh included some famous figures in a period when its medicine was the model for the world.

Upon obtaining his licence at Edinburgh, Richardson volunteered for the Royal Navy, went to London, became a fellow of the Royal College of Surgeons, and was gazetted to his first ship, at Deptford (London). During sea duty in the Napoleonic wars, 1806–14, he was on six ships in succession and saw action in the Baltic, off Portugal, in the Mediterranean, and off Africa. In 1814 Richardson was appointed surgeon to the Royal Marines in North America. He joined them at Halifax, and was with Sir George Cockburn off the coast of Georgia when Cumberland Island and St Mary's were captured.

After the War of 1812–14 Richardson went on half pay and returned to Edinburgh to complete his doctorate. Besides medical subjects, he took botany and mineralogy with Robert Jameson, the geologist. He graduated MD in 1816, offering a thesis on yellow fever, with which he had had experience in Africa and North America. He set up a practice in Leith, which was not successful because of the post-war surplus of physicians. Here he married, and started a lasting friendship with Dr Francis Boott, the physician and botanist.

Richardson's Arctic service began in 1819 when he was assigned to John Franklin*'s first expedition as surgeon and naturalist. He then met Sir Joseph Banks* and Dr John Edward Gray (of the British Museum), who became his collaborator and friend for life. The Franklin party, which also included two midshipmen, George Back* and Robert Hood*, and John HEPBURN, seaman, went to Montreal, then to Cumberland House on the Saskatchewan River, where they wintered in 1819–20. Travelling 1,350 miles in 1820, they wintered at Fort Enterprise on Great Bear Lake. The summer of 1821 took them by canoe down the Coppermine River to its mouth at the Arctic Ocean and from there east $6^{1}/_{2}°$ by way of Bathurst Inlet and Melville Sound. On their return to Fort Enterprise they suffered from famine and cold, and would have perished except for the efforts of Richardson and Hepburn. Richardson felt compelled in defence of the weakened party to execute one of the voyageurs who had murdered Hood. Thanks to a difficult winter trip by Back in search of Indians, they were rescued by the Indian Akaitcho and brought to Fort Providence. In June 1822 they proceeded to Great Slave Lake and York Factory and then returned to England, having travelled some 5,550 miles in North America, much of it through unexplored country.

Richardson was granted leave to write three sections of Franklin's narrative of the expedition, the main one on zoology, and lesser ones on the geognostical material and the aurora. In Edinburgh he also worked up the section on mammals and birds for the journal of William Edward Parry*'s second Arctic voyage (1824).

In 1824 Richardson went on detached service as surgeon, naturalist, and second in command on Franklin's second Arctic expedition; the group travelled overland from New York to Albany, Niagara, Fort William (Thunder Bay, Ont.), Fort Chipewyan, Great Slave Lake, the Mackenzie River, and Fort Franklin on Great Bear Lake, where they wintered. In 1826 Thomas Drummond, who was assistant naturalist, explored the natural history of the Rocky Mountains, while Franklin and Richardson went to the mouth of the Mackenzie River. Franklin then explored the coast westward; Richardson, working in two boats with 11 men, mapped the coast eastward to the Coppermine River, some 900 miles. Regaining Fort Franklin, he made a canoe survey of the shores of Great Slave Lake and wintered at Carlton House. After the party's return to England by way of New York, with important collections, Richardson was granted leave to work on the account of his part in Franklin's expedition.

Richardson became chief medical officer at the Melville Hospital, Chatham, in 1828 and remained there for ten years. There, after his first wife's death, he married Mary Booth, a niece of Sir John Franklin. His greatest scientific book, the *Fauna Boreali-Americana* . . . , was published in four volumes, 1829–37, with William Swainson as collaborator on birds and the Reverend William Kirby on insects. Richardson was solely responsible for quadrupeds and fish. The work established him as one of the foremost biologists of his time.

In 1838 Richardson was assigned as senior physician to the Royal Naval Hospital at Haslar, near Portsmouth, and lived there for the remaining 17 years of his naval career. Here his second wife died and his marriage to Mary Fletcher occurred. At the time of his appointment Haslar Hospital was the largest naval hospital in the world and the biggest brick building in Europe. It had a reputation for good care of patients and outstanding clinical research. Haslar was headed in these years by a captain superintendent who was a naval line officer, not a medical man, with his own staff, and the senior medical officer was an inspector of hospitals and fleets, with his own professional staff. For several years Richardson had as captain superintendent the Arctic explorer Sir William Edward Parry, his close personal friend, and Haslar Hospital went well. Before and after Parry, the incumbents were not nearly so congenial.

Almost from the beginning of his stay at Haslar, Richardson had the responsibility for building up a library and museum. The museum became well known in and outside navy circles as an important centre for research in natural history and comparative anatomy. During the mid 19th century the Royal Navy sent many ships on geographical exploration. Their surgeons, often trained in natural history at Haslar Hospital under Richardson, sent back specimens of plants and animals, and the museum had an unparalleled collection of type specimens first described by Richardson. Alone, or in collaboration with others, he wrote papers and books based on the voyages and the specimens sent back by expeditions including those of Frederick William Beechey*, James Clark Ross, and Edward Belcher*.

Richardson made a last trip to the Canadian Arctic in 1848 when he had reached the zenith of his naval career and was 60 years old. In 1845 Franklin had sailed on his last Arctic expedition in command of *Erebus* and *Terror*. Richardson did not accompany him, partly because of important duties at Haslar Hospital. When, however, in 1848 fears for Franklin's safety forced the Admiralty to investigate, Richardson volunteered to look for his old colleague, and was named to command a search party with Dr John Rae*, a chief factor of the Hudson's Bay Company, and also skilled in Arctic travel. Their expedition started from Liverpool in March 1848 and proceeded to the estuary of the Mackenzie River in August by way of New York, Montreal, Fort William, Norway House on Lake Winnipeg, and Cumberland House. They next travelled by boat to Wollaston Land and Cape Kendall, and abandoned their boats at Icy Cove. They went overland to Fort Confidence on Great Bear Lake to winter. Extensive measurements were made of meteorological phenomena, including temperature, wind, and magnetic variations. In the spring of 1849 Richardson returned to England leaving Rae in command. As a search for Franklin this expedition was unsuccessful; no traces of the ships were found. Not until Rae's next trip in 1853 were the first definite relics obtained and the mystery of Franklin's fate solved. But Richardson's last expedition, as described in *An Arctic searching expedition* . . . (1851), was a model. Excellent arrangements for all phases of travel, especially food, shelter, and means of travel, prevented any privation, illness, or injury. The book dealt at considerable length with the ethnography of various Indian tribes and with the physical geography, geology, fauna, and flora of northern America.

After 48 years as a naval surgeon, Richardson retired from active duty in 1855, his age preventing his appointment as director general of the Medical Department of the Royal Navy. He and his family moved to Westmorland, and he lived his last ten years in Grasmere, at Lancrigg, originally a farmhouse, which his wife inherited. In retirement he remained busy. On Arctic matters the Admiralty often turned to its experienced Arctic officers, including Richardson, Francis Beaufort, Beechey, Back, Parry, Edward Joseph Bird, and James Clark Ross. Although never formally organized as such, the group came to be known as the "Arctic Committee" or the "Arctic

Richardson

Council" because of their consultative value. Richardson was also used by parliamentary committees, for example when the future of the HBC was under scrutiny in 1857. He acted as an expert witness on the geography of the Arctic, its past governance, and its future in agriculture and industry.

He continued to write in the field of ichthyology and polar subjects, publishing a number of books and articles. Being away from libraries and collections, he eventually gave up natural history and became a reader for the Philological Society's new dictionary, which became the *Oxford English dictionary*.

Sir John Richardson has to be judged in three careers: naval surgery, Arctic exploration, and biology. His chief contributions to naval surgery were three. First, he improved the standards of the nursing staff, Florence Nightingale being his friend and adviser in this effort. Second, he improved the care of the mentally ill, by converting it from restraint to regular ward-care along humane lines. Third, he was a pioneer in the use of general anaesthesia in naval surgery shortly after ether and chloroform were first used.

Richardson displayed both physical and mental qualities that place him high in the ranks of explorers of Canada. He was a man of great stamina, even into his 70s, and he had an unswerving resolution, a quality which saved Franklin's first overland Arctic expedition. Meticulous planning characterized his field work. Richardson's surveys along the Arctic coast were substantial contributions to the discovery of the northwest passage. He was an all-round natural historian and contributed important observations in geology, meteorology, mineralogy, and glaciology as well as in botany and zoology.

The two monumental works, *Fauna Boreali-Americana* . . . , edited by Richardson, and its companion *Flora Boreali-Americana* . . . , edited by Sir William Jackson Hooker, were based largely on specimens collected by Richardson in Franklin's first expedition and by Richardson and Drummond in the second. These books, primary sources for North American biology, opened up a whole new field of geographical natural history, that of the Arctic region, and were strong influences toward an ecological approach to natural history. Antarctic biology also received Richardson's attention in *The zoology of the voyage of H.M.S. Erebus and Terror, under Sir James Clark Ross . . . during the years 1838 to 1843 . . .* (2v., London, 1844–75), in collaboration with John Edward Gray and others.

The unique nature of the Haslar Hospital and the specimens brought back to it from discovery ships made Richardson the foremost ichthyologist of his time. From seas as far away as Australia, China, and Japan virtually every shipment contained fish not yet examined by taxonomists. The numbers of species described by Richardson, and the numbers of type specimens in the museum, were enormous. Although Richardson never held an academic post, his general influence on younger scientists was powerful, and his work in biology and geology has been considered important for Canadian science. Some of the young naval surgeons who were assigned to ships of discovery with duties as naturalists and who had got their training at Haslar Hospital from Richardson became, like Thomas Henry Huxley, professional biologists.

Richardson was a friend and colleague to many of the famous investigators of the day, including Richard Owen, Huxley, William Jackson Hooker and his son Joseph Dalton, Charles Lyell, Georges Cuvier, Louis Agassiz, John James Audubon, and Charles Darwin. While writing *The zoology of the voyage of H.M.S. Beagle . . .* in 1836, Darwin turned to Richardson for advice on matters of Arctic ecology and the taxonomy of Arctic animals. Richardson's contribution was mainly in providing information in areas where Darwin himself was not strong. He was a descriptive, not an experimental or theoretical biologist. His papers are characterized by wide learning, a concise, clear style, attention to accuracy in all details, elegance of illustration, and not much theorizing. He was the right man in the right place to contribute notably to systematics and taxonomy, and thus to the early development of Darwin's ideas.

In his Victorian time he held a respected place. His early work won him election in 1825 to the Royal Society of London. He was knighted in 1846 and made a CB in 1850. His hospital assignment enabled him to continue a highly productive scientific career, for which he received the royal medal of the Royal Society in 1856. Numerous animal species, several plant species, and a Canadian river, lake, bay, and mountain are named in his honour.

R. E. JOHNSON

[Sir John Richardson's writings are numerous. A complete bibliography of his printed books was published by M. F. Curvey and R. E. Johnson and of his articles in learned journals by M. A. Huntley *et al*. in the Soc. for the Bibliography of Natural History, *Journal* (London), 5 (October 1969), 202–17; 6 (April 1972), 98–117. The Burgh Museum (Dumfries, Scotland), Crombie bequest, has many letters of the Richardson family in Scotland; many letters from Richardson's friends, family, and professional colleagues may be found in the private Richardson-Voss collection owned by John Voss (1972), Chesham Bois, Amersham, Eng. The PRO, Adm. 8/196, contains Richardson's navy service record from April 1807 to June 1855. The only full-length biography of Richardson was written by the Reverend John MacIlraith, a nephew by marriage. The *Life of Sir J. Richardson* . . . (London, 1868) is weak on scientific matters but the author had access to a wealth of family letters and papers.   R.E.J]

DNB. C. S. Houston and M. G. Street, *The birds of the Saskatchewan River, Carlton to Cumberland* (Regina, 1959). J. J. Keevil *et al., Medicine and the navy, 1200–1900* . . . (4v., Edinburgh and London, 1957–63), IV, 70. Rich, *History of HBC*, II. J. B. Richardson, "A visit to Haslar, 1916," Royal Naval Medical Service, *Journal* (London), 2 (1916), 329–39. Humphrey Rolleston, "Sir John Richardson, C.B., M.D., L.L.D., F.R.S., the naturalist of the Naval Medical Service," Royal Naval Medical Service, *Journal*, 10 (1924), 160–72. D. A. Stewart, "Sir John Richardson, surgeon, physician, sailor, explorer, naturalist, scholar," Canadian Medical Assoc., *Journal* (Toronto), 24 (1931), 1–15.

RIDOUT, THOMAS GIBBS, banker; b. 10 Oct. 1792 near Sorel, Lower Canada, third son of Surveyor General Thomas Ridout* and Mary Campbell; m. first on 5 April 1825 Anna Maria Louisa Sullivan (d. 1832) and had two sons and one daughter, and secondly on 6 Sept. 1834 Matilda Ann Bramley and had six sons and five daughters; d. 29 July 1861 at Toronto, Canada West.

Thomas Gibbs Ridout moved with his parents to Newark (Niagara-on-the-Lake) in 1792 and to York (Toronto) in 1797. He was educated by John STRACHAN at Cornwall and, when 17 years old, was appointed deputy to his father, then registrar of deeds for York County. He also worked as a temporary clerk in several government departments. In 1811, armed with letters of introduction from Lieutenant Governor Francis Gore*, Ridout travelled to England in the hope of beginning a business career in one of the great London trading houses. British commerce, however, was suffering because of the Napoleonic blockade of European ports; Ridout returned to Upper Canada at the outbreak of war with the United States, and entered the 3rd Regiment of York militia as a lieutenant. He was appointed a temporary clerk in the Commissariat Department, possibly through the influence of his father who had previously worked in the department, and in September 1813 served on the Niagara frontier. In January 1814 Ridout was promoted deputy assistant commissary general at a salary of £500 and stationed at Cornwall. Following the examples of nepotism set by his own father and other members of the small govern-

ment clique at York, Ridout, within a month of his own appointment, procured as confidential clerk his 14-year-old brother John. During the remaining year of the war Ridout purchased supplies for the British forces on the upper St Lawrence, often from farmers and merchants in New York State. He remained with the Commissariat Department until 1820 when he retired on half pay. Probably while stationed at Quebec after the war, Ridout became enmeshed in the quarrel between his family and the Jarvis clan that led in 1817 to the duel in which Samuel Peters Jarvis* killed John Ridout.

T. G. Ridout was presented with an opportunity for civilian employment in 1821 when the Bank of Canada was incorporated by a group of government officers and York merchants. In January 1822 the bank's shareholders unanimously elected him its first cashier, or general manager, at a salary of £200. Ridout, who had handled and disbursed large sums of money during the war, was an obvious choice for the post. He was accepted by the capital's growing Tory clique because he was a member of one of York's first families, and by the emerging political moderates because of his own liberal views and those of his family. Ridout was soon on his way to Philadelphia and London to learn what he could of current banking practices, and to purchase plates and paper. In the bank's early years Ridout was an advocate of hard money policies and was backed by merchants such as John Spread Baldwin* against government supporters such as the Boultons, the Robinsons, and John Strachan who wanted an easier credit system and a greater flow of paper currency. However, one suspects that Ridout played a largely passive role in implementing bank policy since no effort was made to oust him when proponents of easier credit gained control of the board of directors in 1825. Once established in his post as cashier Ridout began to assume his rightful place as a second generation member of York's gentry. In 1824 he purchased from Andrew Mercer* for £500 his Sherborne estate on the northern edge of town, and in 1825 by his first marriage gained as brothers-in-law both Robert Baldwin* and Robert Baldwin Sullivan*.

The Bank of Upper Canada was considered by many in the 1820s and 1830s to be a virtual tool of the Family Compact. Ridout, testifying in 1835 before a select committee of the assembly, defended the bank's record and claimed that "every farmer or person in trade or in respectable circumstances, who can give unexceptional personal security, has a right to secure from the public banks reasonable accommodation in proportion to his means, without being considered to ask for favours." Its officers and directors of course interpreted the terms "respectable circumstances" and "reasonable accommodation," and the bank became a frequent target of radical reform criticism. William Lyon MACKENZIE's hatred of the Tory institution was so intense that in December 1837 he interrupted his march down Yonge St to Toronto to burn the house of Dr Robert Charles Horne*, chief teller of the bank and brother-in-law of its first president, William Allan*. Ridout for his part served from the beginning of the rebellion until the end of April 1838 as a captain in the Bank of Upper Canada Guard, a militia unit created solely to protect the bank and its coffers from rebel attack. Late in 1838 the tension generated by the Patriot attack near Prescott once more turned the bank into a fortress which temporarily held Ridout's family and that of R. B. Sullivan. But the bank survived the troubles of 1837–38 without incident and within a few months Ridout was giving more thought to the winter's assemblies and balls than to its physical defence.

The 1840s were for T. G. Ridout, now entering middle age, a period of increasing civic involvement. In 1841 he chaired the electoral committee supporting Reformer Isaac Buchanan*'s successful bid to represent Toronto in the assembly. Initiated as the first recruit of the St Andrew's Masonic Lodge in 1823, Ridout was provincial grand master by 1846. He was also involved in Toronto's St Andrew's Society, rising from second vice-president in 1843 to president in 1848–49 and 1849–50. He was the first president of the Toronto Mechanics' Institute upon its incorporation in 1847. In the same year Ridout, along with such Toronto notables as William Botsford JARVIS and Joseph Clarke Gamble*, founded the Toronto, Hamilton, Niagara, and St Catharines Electro-Magnetic Telegraph Company. He was as well treasurer of Trinity College for a short time before his death.

In 1850 the Bank of Upper Canada became the official government bank; soon both Ridout and the institution he represented were deeply enmeshed in the politics of railways and Ridout as well began to speculate in land. In 1852 he was an incorporator of the Grand Trunk Railway and, along with Peter* and Isaac Buchanan, of the Hamilton and Toronto Railway Company, an eastern extension of the major Buchanan enterprise, the Great Western Railway. At the same time Ridout tried unsuccessfully to persuade Peter Buchanan, then residing in Glasgow, to become the bank's London agent. In the following year the bank accepted the account of the Great Western, and Ridout's eldest son Thomas became, probably not coincidentally, an assistant engineer on that railway. Within a month T. G. Ridout received from Isaac Buchanan 40 shares of Great Western stock, enough to qualify him to become a director. The accommodation was not without its awkward moments, however; in 1854 Ridout was concerned because news of the bank's large loans to the Great Western seemed likely to lead to an effort in the legislature to force the government to remove its account. When this step was taken for other reasons two and a half years after Ridout's death, it was a major factor precipitating the bank's collapse.

Although the bank was becoming increasingly the subject of criticism and legislative inquiry, Ridout's personal fortune continued to improve. In 1853 his salary as cashier was raised from £750 to £1,000. Swept up in the speculative boom which preceded the depression of 1857, he estimated his Sherborne property to be worth £16,000, or £20,000 if subdivided, and was considering selling it although he was "in no hurry about it." When he did sell this land, a month before his death, he received $9,500 for it. He was also in 1853 developing several hundred acres near Port Hope. He had two streets laid out and planned to sell the 76 building lots for £30 to £35 each. He estimated that another 100 acres north of the town could be developed into one-acre properties worth £100 each. He also owned 100 acres "on the lake shore and harbour . . . where the Grand Trunk rail way is to be" and he estimated its worth at four to five times that of the land north of the town. He even confided to his wife that, after selling all this property, "I fancy I shall not bother myself any more about the Bank [of Upper Canada]." His grandiose plans were disrupted by the end of the speculative boom in 1857, and in his will he left the modest sum of $4,160.

The depression of the late 1850s adversely affected the fortunes of the Bank of Upper Canada as well as those of its cashier. Like many of his contemporaries Thomas Gibbs Ridout was unable to cope with the new economic situation; in addition, his health began to fail in the late 1850s. In April 1861 he retired in favour of the younger financier, Robert Cassels*, who admitted in his first report that the bank had suffered losses of $1,500,000, or half its capital, as a result of imprudent railway and land speculations. Ridout's health continued to deteriorate and he died at Toronto on 29 July 1861.

ROBERT J. BURNS

PAC, MG 24, D16, 52; RG 8, I (C series), 1171, p.20;

1203, p.215. PAO, Ridout papers. York County Surrogate Court (Toronto), will of Thomas Gibbs Ridout, 3 Nov. 1860; inventory of estate, 21 Sept. 1861. Can., Prov. of, *Statutes*, 1847, c.81; 1852, c.44. *Ten years in Upper Canada in peace and war, 1805–1815; being the Ridout letters . . .* , ed. Matilda [Ridout] Edgar (Toronto, 1890). *Town of York, 1793–1815* (Firth). *Town of York, 1815–34* (Firth). U.C., House of Assembly, *Journal*, 1835, app.III. *Globe*, 30 July 1861. *Toronto directory*, 1837–56. *One hundred years of history, 1836–1936: St. Andrew's Society, Toronto*, ed. John McLaverty (Toronto, 1936). R. M. Breckenridge, "The Canadian banking system, 1817–1890," Canadian Bankers' Assoc., *Journal* (Toronto), II (1894–95), 105–96, 267–366, 431–502, 571–660. E. C. Guillet, "Pioneer banking in Ontario: the Bank of Upper Canada, 1822–1866," *Canadian Banker* (Toronto), 55 (1948), 115–32.

RIEL, LOUIS, farmer, miller, and Métis leader; b. July 1817 at Île-à-la-Crosse (Sask.), eldest son of Jean-Baptiste Riel, *dit* L'Irlande, a voyageur, and Marguerite Boucher, a Franco-Chipewyan Métisse; d. 21 Jan. 1864 at Saint-Boniface (Man.).

In 1822 the Riel family returned to Lower Canada from the west, and Louis was baptized at Berthier-en-Haut (Berthierville, Que.) on 23 September. He attended a local school and learned the trade of carding wool. When he was 21, in 1838, he returned to the northwest in the service of the Hudson's Bay Company. That date, and the appearance of a flag called the "Papineau standard" among the Métis as mentioned by Alexander Ross* in *The Red River settlement*, cause one to wonder whether the elder Riel had had any part in the rebellion of 1837. Like his famous son, he was to become the champion of French and Métis rights in the northwest. For several years Louis was stationed at Rainy River. In 1842 he returned to Lower Canada and entered the noviciate of the Oblates of Mary Immaculate at Saint-Hilaire (Mont-Saint-Hilaire), but after a short while withdrew for lack of a sense of vocation. In the summer of 1843 he returned to the northwest and settled in the Red River colony.

Louis Riel's river lot in Saint-Boniface was near that of voyageur Jean-Baptiste Lagemodière and his wife, Marie-Anne Gaboury*. On 21 Jan. 1844 Riel married their daughter Julie, after a painful hesitation on her part between the attraction of a religious vocation and her duty to her parents, who favoured the match. Julie Riel's intense religious spirit was to have a great influence on her eldest son, Louis*, born in October 1844, one of 11 children.

That son was to be influenced also by his father's career. Louis Riel Sr early became a man of note in the French Canadian and Métis society of Red River, and showed sympathy with the free traders in furs who were challenging the monopoly of the HBC. This monopoly was tested in May 1849 in the trial of Pierre-Guillaume Sayer*, charged by the HBC with illicit trading; Riel emerged with the Reverend George-Antoine Bellecourt* as the adviser and leader of the Métis in support of Sayer. The jury returned a verdict of guilty but recommended mercy, and Sayer was freed. Riel promptly asserted that the outcome of the verdict was tantamount to a surrender of the monopoly, and his assertion was at once taken up by the Métis. The trade was indeed to be free thereafter. Riel also took up strongly the cause of representation of the Métis on the Council of Assiniboia and the use of French as well as English in the courts of Assiniboia. Success in these endeavours made him the leader of the French community in the 1850s.

Riel had also become a man of business. He worked for the establishment of a fulling mill in Saint-Boniface, and in 1847 opened a small mill on his farm with the support of chief factor John Ballenden*. But Riel had little success with his fulling mill. It is said he later attempted, with some success, to open and operate a carding and grist mill, hence his title of "miller of the Seine." In 1857 he ambitiously went to Montreal to buy machinery for a textile mill, but after his return with the equipment the venture failed.

In 1864 Riel died, mourned by his people as well as his family and not least by his son Louis, then at college in Montreal. If the elder Riel had failed as a businessman, he had created for his son a tradition of leadership which would alter the history of the northwest.

W. L. MORTON

Archives paroissiales, Sainte-Geneviève-de-Berthier (Berthierville, Qué.), Registres des baptêmes, mariages et sépultures, 23 sept. 1822. HBRS, XIX (Rich and Johnson). Tassé, *Les Canadiens de l'Ouest*, II, 353–79. A. S. Morton, *History of the Canadian west*, 805, 810, 816, 858, 880. Ross, *Red River Settlement* (1957), 239–40. Stanley, *Louis Riel*.

ROACHFORD. *See* ROCHFORT

ROAF, JOHN, Congregational minister; b. 5 July 1801 at Margate, Kent, England, son of a naval officer; d. 2 Sept. 1862 at Toronto, Canada West.

John Roaf was educated at a boarding school and was subsequently apprenticed to a printing firm in London. Evangelical preachers there aroused him to religion, and in 1819 he entered Hoxton Academy to study for the Congregational

Roaf

ministry. He became pastor of a chapel in Wolverhampton in 1823, and as "a minister of power and salvation" held that post with noteworthy success till 1837. He was active as well in such community concerns as the local board of health. He then accepted an invitation to become the agent of the Congregationalist Colonial Missionary Society in Upper Canada, where he would supervise the funds it provided to organize churches among the Congregational element that had grown increasingly through British immigration.

He arrived in Toronto in October 1837, and early the next year was asked to take the pastorate of a small Congregational body which had been organized there in 1834 and met in rented quarters. He began an energetic drive for a permanent building and for increased membership. Zion Church, opened on 1 Jan. 1840 and enlarged in 1843, became a leading centre of Congregationalism from which other sister churches in the city and province developed, given impetus by Roaf's vigorous example. The denomination had little general organization, however, because of its inherent belief in independent congregations; the Congregational Union of Canada (for both Canada West and Canada East) was not formed until 1853.

Roaf repeatedly entered into popular issues of the day, for he had an assertive personality and was as eloquent and as much at home on the public platform as in the pulpit. Moreover, his political and religious tenets impelled him to take part. He opposed any ecclesiastical ascendancy or connection between church and state, a view derived from his Congregationalist forbears, the Independent Puritans of the 17th century. On the one hand, the state should not interfere in religious affairs; on the other, there should be no privileged or state-recognized religious bodies. Through strict separation true civil and religious liberty would be attained. Roaf had participated in the anti state church movement in England in the 1820s to remove the political disabilities of the Nonconformists and end the official supremacy of the Church of England. In Canada he urged abolition of the clergy reserves, the public lands endowed to the Church of England. In 1838 he testified against the reserves before the commission of inquiry under Lord Durham [Lambton*], notably agreeing in his opinion with the Canadian Methodist luminary, Egerton Ryerson*.

During the 1840s Roaf similarly took part in the agitation against Anglican control of the provincial university, King's College. Its secularization was achieved in 1849 when the University of Toronto was established. In the early 1850s he was a significant figure in the Anti-State Church Association, which finally witnessed the abolition of the clergy reserves in 1854. He also was involved in school questions. He was one of a committee which included prominent Protestant clergymen named by the Toronto City Council in 1843 to devise a non-denominational pattern of tuition and control for Toronto schools in the new provincial system of public education. He believed in schools free of religious ties, but not in an educational system wholly state-supported. In 1852 he publicly opposed free education, arguing that it destroyed the responsibility of the individual citizen and represented "communism." On this issue, which made allies of right-wing opponents of public schooling and doctrinaire individualist liberals like himself, he unsuccessfully opposed Ryerson, then superintendent of education for Canada West.

Roaf found time as well to lecture at the Toronto Mechanics' Institute, to found the Toronto Temperance Reformation Society in 1839 (and later become its president), and to produce a number of works on religious topics, including many published sermons. He was a commissioner of the Toronto Lunatic Asylum, and so became embroiled in a controversy in 1853 concerning his son-in-law, Dr John Scott.

By 1854 his health was failing. He suffered from asthma and from overwork, and he had overtaxed a strong constitution. While he had a taste for business ventures – such as financing a larger Zion Church whose cornerstone he laid in 1855 – his judgement was not always sound. At this time he involved himself and his church in financial problems and consequent discord. Furthermore, the missionary effort he had directed to enlarge Congregationalism across the province also ultimately broke down, partly because of lack of harmony among its ministers, and partly because Roaf had been busy with so many other concerns. In 1851 the Colonial Missionary Society dropped the scheme under which he had served as its agent. Although the society continued to administer its funds in Canada under a committee, the expansionist phase of congregation-building had passed. Financially embarrassed, ill, disheartened, and disgruntled, Roaf retired from his pastorate in 1856. He spent his remaining years in relative obscurity, and died in Toronto "from asthma."

J. M. S. Careless

John Roaf was the author of *A catechism on the constitution and government of Christian churches* (Toronto, 1839); *Lectures on the millennium* (Toronto, 1844); and *Two sermons on baptism, delivered to his church* (Toronto, 1850). Other sermons he published can be found at UCA. UCA, Biography, Roaf, John (Rev.). [W. F. Clarke], *"In memoriam," the late Rev. John Roaf . . .* (Toronto, [1863?]). *Canadian Independent* (Toronto), October 1862. *Christian Guardian*, 10 Sept. 1862. *Globe,* 27 April, 9 May 1850; 31 Jan., 5 Feb. 1852. Middleton, *Municipality of Toronto*, I. J. E. Middleton and Fred Landon, *The province of Ontario: a history, 1615–1927* (5v., Toronto, [1927–28]), II, 869–71. Moir, *Church and state in Canada West.* Sissons, *Ryerson*, I.

ROBB, JAMES, educator and scientist; b. 2 Feb. 1815 in Laurencekirk, Scotland, son of Dr Charles Robb and Elizabeth Paterson; d. 2 April 1861 in Fredericton, N.B.

Little is known of James Robb's early life. After his father died, the family moved to Stirling, and from there he entered the University of St Andrews. In 1831 he enrolled in medicine at the University of Edinburgh, but never seems to have engaged in regular practice after graduation. In 1835 he attended lectures in natural history at the University of Paris and he visited several famous seats of learning in France, Germany, Switzerland, and Italy, making himself known to eminent scientists in these places. He also began a collection of minerals, fossils, plants, and shells at this time. In 1836, on the recommendation of Thomas Thomson, Regius professor of chemistry in the University of Glasgow, he was appointed lecturer at King's College, Fredericton, and in September 1837 arrived at that institution as its first professor of chemistry and natural history, teaching botany, zoology, physiology, anatomy, geology, and mineralogy, as well as chemistry.

In order to acquaint himself with New Brunswick's natural history, Robb set out, soon after arrival, on a long journey by foot and canoe through the wilderness of the province. Geological, mineralogical, and other data were collected on this and later excursions, and before long he was able to describe and interpret their own natural environment to his students at the college.

Robb was the first person in the province to attempt a systematic botanical collection, which, although classified on Linnean principles, was valuable for its extent and accuracy. Soon after his arrival in New Brunswick he combined his own geological, mineralogical, and botanical specimens with a collection donated by Abraham GESNER to create a museum at King's College, which grew to be the finest in the Atlantic provinces. His willingness to undergo hardship in securing data and his painstaking methods of work brought him an enviable reputation as a scientific investigator. Before long he was considered a possible successor to Sir William Jackson Hooker in the chair of botany at Glasgow, but he felt that his engagements in New Brunswick prevented him from accepting.

In contrast with the intellectual ferment Robb left behind in Scotland, he found in Fredericton little interest in scholarly pursuits. Some decline in its intellectual tone had occurred as the older generation of loyalists passed away and the materialism of the timber trade came to predominate. In the college the students preferred cricket to chemistry, but gradually the "pestilent spirits" were weeded out, and the remaining students were brought up to the level of the best in Scotland.

Robb became a founder and first president of a learned society, the Fredericton Athenaeum, to which he contributed papers on literary, historical, and scientific subjects. He served as president of the Fredericton St Andrew's Society from 1848 to 1852, 1854 to 1856, and 1858 to 1861. Although a deeply religious Presbyterian, he was far from being a sectary. In 1840, after his close friend Archdeacon George Coster*, president of the college, had persuaded him of the rightness of episcopacy, Robb joined the Church of England, an event which enabled him to sit as a member of the college council. On 17 Dec. 1840 he married the archdeacon's daughter, Ellen, and they had eight children. Although Robb and the family into which he married moved in the highest circles in the colony and he occasionally took part in musical evenings at Government House, his duties and interests left him little leisure for recreation. He gave several encaenial addresses at King's College, as well as popular lectures to the vice-regal set, the judiciary, members of the legislature, and other officials. A course in mineralogy was requested by the citizens of Saint John for the Christmas recess of 1841. The college library had to be organized. The new lieutenant governor, Sir William COLEBROOKE, asked for a report on the recently invented electro-magnetic telegraph. The report, which Robb co-authored, resulted in telegraphic communication between the capital and Saint John. Finding the populace ill-informed, he published in 1849 the *New-Brunswick almanac*, with much useful information not otherwise obtainable. He kept records of temperatures and precipitation in Fredericton and other New Brunswick towns, and gave a course of lectures on agricultural chemistry under the patronage of Lieutenant Governor Sir Edmund Walker HEAD. When Fredericton became a city in 1848, he was appointed to the first city council, declining, however, to be reappointed in 1850.

Robb

Robb, like many others, was concerned about the crisis resulting from the repeal of the imperial timber duties and, in 1849, of the Navigation Acts, and recognized that too great a dependence on this single extractive industry had been responsible for a marked neglect of agriculture and domestic manufactures. The province was consequently vulnerable to sudden and devastating fluctuations in the imperial market. To investigate how these circumstances might be offset, the government engaged a British agricultural scientist, J. F. W. Johnston*, whom Robb accompanied as guide and adviser on a 2,000-mile journey over the province; to Johnston's 1850 report he contributed an important geological map which represented an advance over the work of his contemporary, Abraham Gesner, New Brunswick's provincial geologist. Despite some errors, Robb established the true stratigraphic position of the red saliferous and gypsiferous rocks covering large areas of New Brunswick, and confirmed Sir Charles Lyell's contention that such formations were older than the coal measures. Although he rarely entered into public controversy, Robb was able, through his expert knowledge, to support Gesner in a famous unsuccessful lawsuit in 1852 concerning the identity of the mineral albertite, contending correctly that it was not coal.

Believing that Johnston's report did not give a fair estimate of agricultural possibilities, Robb took a leading part in forming the New Brunswick Society for the Encouragement of Agriculture, Home Manufactures, and Commerce; he became the first president in 1850, and then for some years its corresponding secretary. He encouraged farmers all over the province, disseminating accurate scientific information through the society's publications and himself contributing several important papers, including one on manures indicative of a thorough acquaintance with the advanced scientific practices of other countries. He believed farming to be the true foundation of civil society, but he also urged the diversification of industry to render New Brunswick more nearly self-sufficient.

While thus occupied Robb carried on his work at the college, corresponded with other scientists in America and Europe, and attended the great railway convention in Portland, Maine, in 1850 [see John Alfred Poor*] and, whenever possible, the meetings of the American Association for the Advancement of Science.

Partly as a result of his work with agricultural societies, he concluded that the people of the province must acquire both a knowledge of the conditions of their existence and a pride in local initiative if prosperity and progress were to be ensured. Accordingly he secured authorization in 1854 from Joseph Marshall* d'Avray, the chief superintendent of education, to prepare a history of New Brunswick for use in the schools. He gathered information on the languages and traditions of the Indians, as well as copies of many documents relating to the French régime, but he died before completing the work. In 1856 he published *Agricultural progress: an outline of the course of improvement in agriculture . . . with special reference to New Brunswick*, and saw a provincial Board of Agriculture established, a measure for which he had long contended. Robb was appointed secretary of the board and issued in 1861 a report which embodied practical proposals as well as something of his social philosophy.

By the mid 1850s King's College was threatened with extinction by a faction in the assembly that wished to divert its funds to sectarian colleges [see Edwin JACOB]. In his encaenial address of 1856 Robb made an able plea for the maintenance of the college. But the college was reconstituted as the University of New Brunswick in 1859 and there is good reason to believe that, had he lived, he would eventually have been offered the presidency of the university. He had now become so closely identified with the practical affairs of the province that his chances of suitable employment elsewhere had lessened, and his concern for his family beclouded his last years.

The multiplicity of tasks Robb undertook exceeded his strength and despite his substantial achievements and the esteem in which he was held, hardships persisted throughout his life. It was barely possible to marry on his meagre salary, and he never altogether lost the feeling of isolation from other scholars working in the fields in which he was most deeply interested. Sir John William Dawson* paid tribute to Robb's competence as a geologist. At his death, from pneumonia, he was widely mourned, and William Brydone Jack*, a colleague and the man who knew him best, referred to his death as a public calamity.

ALFRED G. BAILEY

[The principal primary source is UNBL, RG 62 (James and Ellen Robb, letters); there are also useful references in the College Council of King's College, minute book, II. Robb's own publications include *Agricultural progress: an outline of the course of improvement in agriculture considered as a business, an art, and a science, with special reference to New Brunswick* (Fredericton, 1856); papers and reports in the N.B. Soc. for the Encouragement of Agriculture, Home Manufactures, and Commerce, *Journal* (Fredericton), 1850–52; *Oration delivered at the encænia in King's College, Fredericton* . . . (Fredericton), 1839, 1849, 1852, 1856; and he helped compile N.B., Board of Agriculture, *Annual report* (Fredericton), 1861; and *New-Brunswick almanac*, 1849. The only published biographical sketch, by his successor as professor of chemistry and natural history, L. W. Bailey*, is "Dr. James Robb, first professor of chemistry and natural history in King's College, Fredericton, a sketch of his life and labours," N.B. Natural History Soc., *Bull*. (Saint John), no.XIV (1898–1904), 1–15. *See also* L. W. Bailey, *The study of natural history and the use of natural history museums: an address delivered at the encænia of the University of New Brunswick, June 27th, 1872* . . . (Saint John, N.B., 1872); and *New Brunswick Courier*, 6 July 1861. An interesting reference to Abraham Gesner and the controversy over albertite is to be found in J. W. Bailey, *Loring Woart Bailey; the story of a man of science* (Saint John, N.B., 1925), 81–82. There is much valuable material in Frances Firth (Gammon), "The history of higher education in New Brunswick" (unpublished MA thesis, University of New Brunswick, Fredericton, 1945). The nature and occurrence of the mineral albertite are dealt with in L. W. Bailey, "On some modes of occurrence of the mineral albertite," RSC *Trans*., 2nd ser., VII (1901), sect.IV, 77–83. For the context of Robb's work *see* R. A. Jarrell, "Science education at the University of New Brunswick in the nineteenth century," *Acadiensis*, II (1972–73), no.2, 55–79. A.G.B.]

ROBERTSON, THOMAS JAFFRAY, educator; b. March 1805 in Dublin (Republic of Ireland), youngest son of Charles Robertson, a Dublin portrait painter, and Christiana Jaffray; d. 26 Sept. 1866 at Toronto, Canada West.

As a youth Thomas Jaffray Robertson attended the Frinaiglian Institute in Dublin where he won many academic prizes before his graduation in 1820. He then entered Trinity College, Dublin; although unable to take his degree "through illness," he obtained honours in both science and classics. In 1827 he returned to Frinaiglian Institute as a teacher of classics, and the following year joined the Irish Office of Education. He reached high office in it when he was named chief inspector of the national schools of Ireland in July 1845. Two years later he accepted appointment as headmaster of the newly created Normal School in Toronto, a position that was to have gone to the headmaster of the national model schools in Dublin, John Rintoul, until his wife's illness forced him to withdraw.

Arriving in Toronto in September 1847, Robertson, a "tall, erect, well filled out" man of "strong, rugged character" and "direct ways," had to prepare at once for the first session of the Normal School which began on 1 November. Although he himself taught a variety of subjects for a total of five hours per day, his main interests were grammar, physical geography, and ancient and modern history. Three textbooks he wrote for publisher John Lovell*'s series of Canadian school books reflect his concern with the subject of grammar: *The general principles of language*; *An easy mode of teaching the rudiments of Latin grammar to beginners*; and *The rudiments of English grammar for beginners*.

As a teacher, Robertson "had little to do with the fine distinctions of psychology and child-study"; rather, he was known as a strict disciplinarian, and he instilled in his students "sturdy, energetic, thorough-going ways and methods." In an 1856 report on the grammar schools in the eastern section of Canada West, he lamented the insufficient attention being paid to the "inculcation of the habits of neatness, regularity, and order, so especially necessary in the training of youth." He also criticized the too great "dependence being placed on the Text-books and the recitation of lessons committed to memory." Similarly, his textbook prefaces reveal his opposition to rote learning and his belief in what he called the "conversational-method." "Mechanical" teaching he condemned, because it failed to seek out the general principles underlying a subject and because it tended to be reinforced by the "pandying" and "cowhiding" of children. One account asserts that *The general principles of language* "did much . . . to lift grammar from being a mere mechanical repetition of rules and exceptions to becoming the 'logic of the classroom.'" Despite his reputation as a strict disciplinarian, his students found him an earnest instructor and a kind friend. As a reward for work well done, he made a practice of taking his favoured students on yachting trips.

Yachting was Robertson's main leisure-time activity; in it "his genial nature was fully shown." He was one of the persons responsible for founding in 1852 the club that two years later became the Royal Canadian Yacht Club. From the outset Robertson held various leading offices in the club, including the top rank of captain (a title later changed to commodore) and that of vice-commodore. He remained on the club's executive until his death, and also won the first racing trophy at the RCYC, the Queen's Cup.

Robertson was granted a leave of absence for the school year of 1865–66 because of failing health, and he died while still in office. His successor as headmaster was a former student, J. H. Sangster*. Robertson was survived by his widow, Amelia Nelson of Dublin, and six children.

J. DONALD WILSON

Robinson

T. J. Robertson was the author of *Chronological chart of contemporary dates in the history of Judea, Israel, Nineveh, Babylon, Egypt, Syria, Persia, Greece, Phœnicia, Carthage, Troy and Rome* (Toronto, 1866); *An easy mode of teaching the rudiments of Latin grammar to beginners* (Montreal, [c. 1860]); *The general principles of language; or, the philosophy of grammar* (Montreal, 1860; 2nd ed., 1861; 3rd ed., 1864); *Grammar school tables for parsing Latin and English* (Toronto, 1866); and *The rudiments of English grammar for beginners* (Montreal, 1866).

Daily Telegraph (Toronto), 27 Sept. 1866. *Journal of Education for U.C.*, XIX (1866), 140–41. *Leader*, 2 Oct. 1866. *Documentary history of education in U.C.* (Hodgins), VII, VIII, XII. *Past principals of Ontario normal schools, January, 1905* ([Toronto, 1905]). David Fotheringham, "Thomas Jaffray Robertson, M.A.," *Toronto Normal School, jubilee celebration, 1847–1897: (October 31st, November 1st and 2nd); biographical sketches and names of successful students, 1847 to 1875* (Toronto, 1898), 10–12.

ROBINSON, Sir JOHN BEVERLEY, lawyer, politician, and judge; b. 26 July 1791 at Berthier, Lower Canada, second son of Christopher Robinson* and Esther Sayre; d. 31 Jan. 1863 in Toronto, Canada West.

John Beverley Robinson's father, a Virginia-born loyalist, had served in the Queen's Rangers in the closing stages of the Revolutionary War. The regiment was evacuated to New Brunswick and then disbanded in 1783. Christopher Robinson the following year married Esther Sayre, the daughter of a well-known loyalist clergyman, and in 1788 the family moved to Quebec, where John Beverley was born three years later. In 1792 they went to Kingston, Upper Canada, where Christopher was appointed surveyor general of the woods and reserves of Upper Canada; in 1794 he was called to the bar. Then, suddenly, on 2 Nov. 1798 he died. The Robinsons and their children, the eldest of whom was Peter*, age 13, had moved from Kingston to York (Toronto) only a short time before.

The seven-year-old John Beverley was sent to Kingston to live with and be educated by his father's friend, the Reverend John Stuart*, with whom he remained for four years. In 1799 the boy was enrolled in the school opened by the recently arrived John STRACHAN. Four years later Strachan was ordained a priest of the Church of England and given the charge at Cornwall, where he also re-established his school. Until 1807 Robinson lived in the Strachan household at Cornwall, his fees paid by Stuart and the executor of his father's estate, although Strachan had offered to take him free of charge. In the relationship of pupil and teacher was formed Robinson's life-long admiration for and friendship with Strachan.

At age 16 he left Strachan's tutelage to article in law with D'Arcy Boulton* Sr, the solicitor general of Upper Canada. He mixed easily with the young people of York's society, worked hard, read avidly, and when the assembly was in session, watched many of its debates. As a former pupil of Strachan and a bright, personable young man, he was drawn into Chief Justice William Dummer Powell*'s circle, a connection which helped him in his early career. In 1811, after Boulton had been captured by a French privateer on his way to England, Robinson had to move into the office of John Macdonell*, the newly appointed attorney general, to finish the last year of his articling.

During the spring of 1812, as war clouds blew north from the United States, Robinson volunteered to serve in one of the flank companies – special militia companies designed for regular service. When war was formally declared on 18 June 1812, these companies were called to train for active service. As one of those best qualified by education and family, Robinson was given an officer's commission. His role in the fighting was brief and glorious. He went with Isaac Brock* to the southwestern area of the province in August to repel General William Hull's invasion, and commanded the volunteers who accompanied the regulars to take formal possession of Detroit. The volunteers then took parties of prisoners back to York. In September the York flank companies were sent to reinforce the Niagara frontier. Robinson was temporarily in command of one of these companies when the invaders crossed at Queenston. Arriving there just moments after Brock's death, Robinson's company was ordered on another charge like that in which Brock had been killed. John Macdonell, commanding the militia flank companies, was mortally wounded, and the companies fell back. They were then sent on the long flanking march which led to victory in late afternoon.

When he returned to York with prisoners, Robinson was congratulated on his new appointment. Only after asking was he told that he had been made acting attorney general of the province. Powell's recommendation had secured him the post, although he was just 21 years old and not yet even a member of the bar. It was subsequently rumoured that Robinson's friendship with Powell's daughter, Anne, had won him the appointment, but in his later life, when he was displaced from power, Powell would still insist that Robinson had been chosen for his abilities. From 1812 to 1814 the young Robinson performed the functions of attorney general, giving legal opinions to the provincial government and handling crown prosecutions of criminals.

His most serious problem in the context of the war was the potential disloyalty of many recent immigrants to the province; most of these were Americans who, in moving westward to obtain land, had crossed into Upper Canada, and their loyalty, whether to the United States or to Upper Canada, was not strong. In retrospect, it is clear that relatively few settlers actually deserted to the Americans during the war, but there was evidently sufficient disaffected talk to upset the government and its leaders. The American invasion intensified the disaffection, and some prominent critics of the government prior to the war, such as Joseph Willcocks*, did desert. When a party of settlers from Norfolk County obtained arms from the Americans and returned to that area to terrorize their neighbours, a group of militia officers and volunteers acted to stop them and 18 of the renegades were taken in arms. The arrests gave government authorities the chance to make a deterrent example; the 18 were charged with treason and Robinson was made responsible for their prosecution. General Francis Rottenburg*, the provincial administrator, urged haste in holding the trial, suggesting that some of the accused, as militiamen, might be court-martialed. Robinson resisted Rottenburg's pressure and proceeded methodically to assemble evidence to hold civil trials for treason. Three of the 18 prisoners from Norfolk agreed to turn crown's evidence. Nineteen persons were finally tried: 15 from Norfolk, two indicted at York, and two who had surrendered voluntarily. The grand jury also indicted another 50 persons who had fled to the United States. The trials began at Ancaster on 7 June 1813 and lasted two weeks. Fourteen were found guilty, one pleaded guilty, and four were acquitted. Robinson subsequently recommended to Sir Gordon Drummond*, commander of the forces, that seven of the convicted should be executed, but Chief Justice Thomas Scott* added another, and on 20 July eight men were hanged. It is doubtful whether the name "Bloody Assize," used subsequently to describe the trials, was really deserved. Those executed had committed treason in wartime.

Robinson had also to prosecute normal criminal offences and to appear at the assizes in each district of the province. He was expected to provide names of people suitable to act as justices of the peace, and many administrative procedures required the attorney general to act on behalf of the governor. In addition, he had his own private practice. When D'Arcy Boulton returned to

Canada in the autumn of 1814 he was appointed attorney general because of his seniority in years of service. Robinson was given the post of solicitor general on 13 Feb. 1815.

The war's end and relief from its responsibilities gave Robinson, encouraged by Strachan, the opportunity to go to England for further legal studies and be called to the bar there. With Powell's aid, he was granted a leave of absence by the new provincial administrator, Sir George Murray*, and on 1 Sept. 1815 left York. By late October he was settled in London, where he was received graciously by Lord Bathurst, the secretary of state for war and the colonies. Among his sponsors at Lincoln's Inn was the solicitor general of the United Kingdom. Between terms of study he travelled to the Continent and to Scotland and northern England. His leave of absence was twice extended at full pay and a third time on half salary.

One of Robinson's letters of introduction had been to William Merry, the under-secretary for war. On his first call at the Merrys he met "an exceedingly fine, pretty little girl – a Miss Walker – there; very pleasant and engaging in her manner and appearance." On 5 June 1817 he and Emma Walker were married, and in early July they left England for Upper Canada. Robinson continued as solicitor general for a few months, but the promotion of Boulton to the bench led to his appointment as attorney general on 11 Feb. 1818.

As attorney general, Robinson received a salary which seems to have been regarded as a retainer, as well as fees for his work for the crown. He still pursued his private practice, and on his return from England in 1817 he had been retained by the North West Company to represent them in litigation against Lord Selkirk [Douglas*], an affair which would give him much notoriety. Following the destruction of his colony on the Red River by the Nor'Westers, Selkirk had hired a band of Swiss mercenaries, come to Canada, armed himself with a magistracy from Lower Canada, and headed west. He had seized Fort William (Thunder Bay) and its contents, expelling the NWC's people. The company, which had first contemplated civil action for damages, decided to press criminal charges of theft and assault against Selkirk in the Western District of Upper Canada. Robinson as attorney general was expected to prosecute. He returned his retainer to the company, but naturally was open to suspicion of a conflict of interest. His attempt to have an indictment preferred against Selkirk at Sandwich (Windsor) in September 1818 failed, as did a second bill, for conspiracy, which went to a jury. Shortly after, Robinson brought charges against the Nor-Westers for felonies against Selkirk and his people, but all the accused were acquitted.

The bitterness evident in the Selkirk affair was symptomatic of Upper Canada following the war. The collapse of the NWC's business in the American west simply exacerbated the already difficult economic situation in Upper Canada. The end of the war had brought a drop in farm prices. The war had also ended immigration from the United States so that land development had slowed and land prices had fallen. Damage to property, particularly in the Niagara peninsula, had been extensive and compensation was not yet being paid. The discontented soon found spokesmen.

Shortly after Robinson's return to Upper Canada in 1818, a Scot named Robert GOURLAY had appeared to scout a piece of land his wife owned in the western part of the province. Unduly influenced by his wife's relatives, Thomas Clark* and William Dickson*, who were large-scale land developers and speculators in the Niagara area, Gourlay blamed the government for its restrictive development policies and its discouragement of immigration by Americans. In order to get information for a proposed book Gourlay composed a questionnaire, to be printed in the *Upper Canada Gazette*, which invited information, complaints, and suggestions for improvements from landowners. Both Powell and Samuel Smith*, who was administering the government, approved the questionnaire and its intent, but Strachan, more suspicious, saw that it provided a vehicle for many Upper Canadians to express grievances.

Robinson, deeply involved in the Selkirk litigation, seems to have paid little attention to Gourlay until Smith, who had become alarmed by the spring of 1818, ordered him "to watch the progress of" Gourlay for an "occasion to check [him] by a criminal prosecution." In June Robinson rendered an opinion that Gourlay's third printed address was "grossly libellous" and "entirely subversive," but told Smith that prosecution should be considered carefully before any court action which might give importance to what would otherwise be an insignificant affair. Gourlay's meetings across the province Robinson considered "dangerous," however, because they pointed out "the mode by which popular movements on pretences less specious than the present can be effected."

Smith decided to act, giving the prosecution to Henry John BOULTON, the solicitor general. Gourlay was acquitted of a charge of seditious libel. However, the new lieutenant governor, Sir Peregrine Maitland*, at Strachan's urging, decided to silence the agitation, and the assembly, so recently critical of government, passed with only one dissenter an act "to prohibit certain meetings within this province." Under a statute of 1804 Gourlay was ordered to leave the province. He did not, and was arrested and jailed in mid January 1819. Robinson represented the crown at Gourlay's trial in Niagara the following August. Convicted of ignoring the order to leave the province, Gourlay was banished from Upper Canada.

The government, alarmed by the discontent voiced by Gourlay, decided that a spokesman was needed in the assembly for the lieutenant governor and his advisers in the Executive and Legislative councils. At the general election held in midsummer 1820 Robinson was returned for the town of York, and the labour of preparing, presenting, and defending government measures in the assembly thereafter fell mostly on his shoulders. Although he told his friend John Macaulay* that he was not fond of politics, Robinson continued in his leading role until 1828. The goals which Maitland and his chief advisers, Robinson and Strachan, set out to achieve in the 1820s were to promote economic development through the encouragement especially of British immigration and the construction of public works; the creation of a centrally controlled banking system like that advocated earlier by Hamiltonian federalists in the United States; the maintenance of the constitutional connection with Britain and of British political institutions; support for the Church of England, tolerance of some religious sects, and friendliness to Presbyterians and conservative Methodists; public support for elementary education; and avoidance of some aspects of the American experience, such as a wide electoral franchise and the separation of church and state.

When the assembly met in November 1821, Barnabas Bidwell*, the member for Lennox and Addington, took his seat. Bidwell, a former member of the United States Congress and state official in Massachusetts, had come to Canada in 1810 fleeing a charge of malversation of government funds in that state. Robinson thought him a "rascal" and was only too happy to promote any measure to get him out of the assembly. Like many other Upper Canadian Tories, Robinson saw Bidwell as the product of an American political system which, based on republicanism and reform, encouraged corruption and disloyalty in its adherents. The attorney general presented a petition to the house from some electors in Lennox and Addington who wanted Bidwell's election declared "null and void," thereby preserving the "pure and unsullied . . . dignity" of the assembly. After long debate in which Robinson played a prominent role, and a close decision, Bidwell was expelled and a bill was passed barring persons who had held office in the United States from standing for election. Yet Marshall Spring Bidwell*, after two disputed by-elections, was returned in his father's place in the general election of 1824. The episode was the beginning of the alien question which was to divide the province after 1824.

Robinson was also personally concerned with the government's desperate need for revenue. The legislatures of Upper and Lower Canada had failed to agree since 1819 on the division of customs duties between them. Both houses of the Upper Canadian legislature decided that the attorney general should go to England to persuade the imperial government to intervene in the deadlock. Robinson, his wife, and brother Peter, set off for London via New York in February 1822. Two days after their departure Anne Powell followed, against her family's wishes. She joined the Robinsons at Albany, but Robinson refused to allow her to sail from New York with them. She crossed in another packet which broke up in heavy weather on the rocky coast of southern Ireland. Anne's body was cast ashore. Her father, whose influence had waned with the coming of Maitland and who was in England seeking preferment, was crushed. Much against his wishes his daughter had pressed her attentions on Robinson for five years; the infatuation had now ended in tragedy.

Robinson's principal task in England was persuading the imperial government to enable Upper Canada to obtain some of the arrears in customs revenue due since 1819 and guarantee the province a share of future revenue. When he arrived he found, however, that the Colonial Office was considering a political union of the Canadas. A group of officials from Lower Canada, including Solicitor General Charles Marshall and Receiver General John Caldwell*, were pressing for such a union to create a predominantly Anglophone province whose legislature would be dominated by English speaking members. The colonial secretary and his senior officials, anxious to solve the political impasse in Lower Canada, seemed receptive to the plan. Robinson joined in the talks, but soon realized the discussions were unlikely to assist Upper Canada and pressed to have provision dealing with the financial problem inserted in the union bill. He won his point, but when the bill was introduced in the British parliament, it met unexpected opposition. The government withdrew it and Robinson was asked to

redraft the financial and trade provisions into a new bill, which became law as the Canada Trade Act in August 1822. The act established a comprehensive scale of import duties on goods from the United States entering Upper Canadian ports of entry on the Great Lakes. Shipping tolls on the St Lawrence were eliminated, and Upper Canada was paid one-fifth of the duties collected from 1 Jan. 1819 to 1 July 1824, with its share to be revised every three years thereafter.

Robinson was now ready to return home, but Lord Bathurst held him back as an adviser. Meanwhile he was completing his terms at Lincoln's Inn. He also began negotiations with the under-secretary for the colonies, Robert Wilmot-Horton, with whom he had dealt on the proposed union and trade bills, for a proper post office in York. He pressed Wilmot-Horton and the crown law officers for an opinion on whether persons who had been resident in Upper Canada for seven years but had not taken the oath of allegiance and become naturalized British subjects were legally able to hold land. Both Robinson and Maitland felt that immigrants should be legally secure in their lands but they were also fearful of the potential disloyalty of unnaturalized Americans and sought legislation to exclude aliens from the assembly. The imperial government was not, however, ready to make a hard ruling at this time.

Robinson also raised the question of war damages. Two boards of inquiry had assessed the value of the damages at £230,000 and £182,130 respectively, but no money had been paid. An unofficial committee in England, consisting of Edward ELLICE, Alexander Gillespie, and John Galt*, had been pressing for payment to some Canadian claimants since the summer of 1821. In the fall of 1823 the British government authorized Maitland to make an initial payment from imperial funds of one quarter of the second award, if the provincial government would pay another quarter. The rest of the claim was also to be shared equally. The result was disappointing to Robinson because the province was already in severe financial difficulties. Galt recommended that payment of the imperial funds should be handled through Gillespie's company, a Montreal and London mercantile and forwarding house; the money would thus be channelled through a company which was a creditor of many Upper Canadian businessmen. Henceforth Robinson had little use for Galt.

During the summer and autumn of 1822, Robinson and Wilmot-Horton saw each other constantly, becoming close friends. In discussing colonial policy they developed a project to en-

Robinson

courage British immigration to Upper Canada, believing it to be the way to offset the influence of predominantly American immigration, increase the Anglophone population in Canada, and maintain the British connection with the colonies. To Wilmot-Horton the plan, which received government approval in January 1823, would make "the redundant labour and the curse of the mother country, the active labour and blessing of the colonies." As they considered potential immigrants, their attention turned to Ireland as a source and they received encouragement and help from the Irish administration. Robinson's brother, Peter, was asked by the colonial secretary to supervise the migration to Upper Canada.

Discussion of the union of the two provinces had continued through the summer and into the autumn. Although he personally disliked the idea, Robinson had not spoken against it until signs of adverse public opinion in the Canadas began to arrive. He disliked the enlarged and strengthened elective assembly, and felt that English speaking Montreal merchants were merely trying to drag in Upper Canada to help with their own political and economic problems. When a new union bill was introduced to the British house early in 1823, it died in the face of vigorous opposition by the reformers who pointed out that French Canadians rejected the measure. Robinson in the meantime had been thinking of an alternative. His pamphlet on the plan, published in London in 1824, contained two papers by himself, one by Strachan, and one by James Stuart* of Quebec. Robinson proposed a union of all the British provinces in North America as a more effective deterrent to United States encroachment, and he argued that government officials would be more secure, for a civil salary list would be easier to pass in a single legislature. The union would be federal in nature with provincial governments, constituted as they now were, looking after local matters. The union parliament would consist of an upper house with members summoned from the provincial legislative councils by the governor general, and a lower house elected by the provincial assemblies or by electors meeting a fairly high property-requirement franchise. This parliament would "enact laws for the general welfare and good government of the United British Provinces." It could deal with religious matters, subject to the restrictions in the Canada Act of 1791, with commerce, and with defence. It could levy tariffs, whereas the provincial governments would depend on excise and land taxes. Such a proposal would strengthen the British hold in North America, for the Anglophone majority it would establish in the united legislature would be able to prevail over the French Canadians, whom Robinson considered conservative, agrarian, and opposed to commercial development. This concept of union, though rejected by the imperial government at the time, remained in Robinson's mind throughout his life.

In February 1823 he completed his terms at Lincoln's Inn and was called to the English bar. Strachan had urged him to attempt public life in England and was willing to provide a forgiveable loan of £1,500 for the purpose. More tempting was Lord Bathurst's offer of the chief justiceship of Mauritius at £3,500 per year, a salary greater than Robinson would ever earn on the bench, plus a housing allowance. But he preferred to stay in Canada: "One day or other we shall become a great people – that's certain – our boys may live to see it," he wrote Macaulay. He returned to York in early July 1823.

Robinson came back to York as one of the two most influential men in the province. The friendship which he and Strachan shared with Lieutenant Governor Maitland and the supporters they had in the Legislative Council and House of Assembly gave them much influence. As chief officer of the government during the 1820s Robinson was not the leader of a cohesive political party based on a constituency of support for policies across the province, but he was at the centre of a group of administrative officers and government supporters in the legislature who were bound together by friendships and common interests. This group, called the Family Compact by its Reform opponents, had fought together in the War of 1812 and was distinguished by support of the British connection, opposition to the United States, a desire to assimilate French Canadians into a "British" culture, and support of commercial development and the construction of public works. Strachan was the Compact spokesman on religious and educational matters, while Robinson led the group in the assembly. The Reformers nevertheless attributed more unity of purpose to the Compact than in fact existed; on banking, land, education, and religious policy the group was not always in agreement.

Robinson was once more returned for York in the 1824 elections, after a bitter campaign. William Lyon MACKENZIE, in the newly founded *Colonial Advocate*, remarked: "His abilities are greatly overrated; his flippancy has been mistaken by some for wit; but not by us. . . . We account him to be a vain, ignorant man." Robinson commented to the governor's secretary: "Another reptile of the Gourlay species has sprung up in a Mr. Mackenzie. . . . What vermin!" The narrowness of Robinson's victory signalled a change in the political temper of the assembly: in the coming sessions the house would be evenly divided between government supporters and opponents. The opposition was even more diffuse in character than the Compact group. Opposition members coalesced around a series of issues, primarily the alien question, but they were as often motivated by personal axes as by high ideals and ideology. There was a coterie of friends and supporters centred around Marshall Spring Bidwell, a few radicals influenced by the British Reform movement, a group who opposed the Church of England and its claims to church establishment, individuals some of whom disliked the government's land and development policies, or, like Robert Randall*, had personal grievances against the government.

The first session of the 9th parliament opened in January 1825 with much talk and little legislation. But behind the scenes the great issue of the 1820s was developing. The British courts had ruled that persons who had remained in the United States after 1783 and their descendants could not continue to be considered British subjects. Lord Bathurst in passing on the decision to Maitland late in 1824 advised him that neither Bidwell could sit in the assembly. But because so many people in Upper Canada would be adversely affected, in both their right to hold land and their civil rights, the dispatch was not acted on. Instead, Robinson and the colonial secretary discussed the matter when the former went to England in the summer of 1825. Since the imperial parliament would not act at that time, it was agreed that a bill of limited scope should be passed by the Upper Canadian legislature to confer the civil rights and privileges of British subjects upon those who had resided in Upper Canada for seven years and who would renounce their American citizenship.

There had been spirited public discussion of the issue for months prior to the meeting of the assembly in November 1825. Robinson's draft bills passed through the council but when he presented them to the house, explaining how the legislation would solve the problem, a storm of protest erupted. Robinson felt that the opposition deliberately misrepresented the government's position in arguing that the bills were a gratuitous insult to people born or long resident in Upper Canada. The opposition also questioned the right of a colonial government to act in this matter and the house passed an address asking the imperial parliament to intervene.

This parliament then gave the Upper Canadian legislature the power to naturalize persons resident in Upper Canada who met the qualifications of British naturalization laws, but instructions for modified legislation had not been received when the Upper Canadian legislature reconvened in December 1826. Robinson, knowing what the instructions from England would be, found himself fighting a politically popular bill introduced by John ROLPH, which provided that all resident settlers were to become British subjects unless they registered their dissent. When the imperial government's instructions finally arrived, Rolph's bill was amended by the attorney general to conform with them. Once more the opposition took exception to the Colonial Office's requirement that persons register their naturalization and again take an oath of allegiance. Robinson felt that they were arguing against the judgement of the courts and against a measure which would relieve people of disabilities arising from that judgement. After angry debate and the defection of members from the opposition, the amended bill was passed.

The enraged opposition sent Robert Randall to England to protest. Randall consulted both the colonial secretary and the radical parliamentary opposition; fear of raising the issue in parliament forced the new colonial secretary, Lord Goderich, to agree to instructions for a new bill which passed the Upper Canadian legislature in May 1827. All who had received land grants, held office, taken the oath of allegiance, or been resident in the province before 1820 were to be admitted to the rights of British subjects. No provision for renunciation of allegiance to foreign countries was made. This new bill was acutely embarrassing to Robinson and the government party in Upper Canada. After they had patiently accepted Colonial Office dictation and defended the unpopular decisions made, a new colonial secretary had bowed to pressure by the Upper Canadian opposition and undermined the colonial administration.

While the alien question was still at full heat in 1827, D'Arcy Boulton's replacement on the bench arrived in York. He was John Walpole Willis*, an equity lawyer, who was expected to serve only briefly on the Court of King's Bench until the provincial legislature created a court of equity in Upper Canada. He developed a dislike of Robinson, perhaps because by now so many in the province deferred to his legal abilities. The conflict came into the open when Willis presided over the trial of Francis Collins*, the fiery newspaper editor, whom Robinson was prosecuting on three charges of libel. Previously, and in the course of his trial, Collins charged that Robinson had been remiss in not laying criminal charges against some of those involved in the Samuel Peters Jarvis*–John Ridout duel ten years before, and in not prosecuting those who had destroyed William Lyon Mackenzie's press in 1826. From the bench, Willis agreed with Collins. Over Robinson's objections Willis ordered prosecution in both cases. The seconds in the duel, Solicitor General H. J. Boulton and James Edward SMALL, were acquitted of murder charges, and Mackenzie's tormenters were fined five shillings. Although Robinson deeply resented the criticisms of him implicit in these prosecutions, he then agreed at Willis' urging to drop the libel charges against Collins, who had precipitated the furor. Shortly after, Willis argued that the Court of King's Bench could not act without all its three members present, as it had done in the past. He withdrew from the bench, and thereby not only stopped the functioning of the provincial courts but brought into question the validity of all the court's previous decisions. Maitland, after seeking the advice of Robinson and Boulton, removed Willis from the bench.

The alien question, Willis' removal, and criticism of the clergy reserves were province-wide issues in the election of 1828. Robinson again won his seat narrowly, but his work was made more difficult by the fact that the new house was overwhelmingly anti-government and anti-Anglican. When Chief Justice William Campbell* retired in the spring of 1829, Robinson was appointed to replace him and resigned his seat in the assembly. He had refused the appointment in 1824 because he could not afford to give up his law practice for the salary of the chief justice. Robinson's elevation to the bench removed him in large part from political struggles, although his appointment carried with it the speakership of the Legislative Council and the presidency of the Executive Council.

As government leader in the assembly throughout the 1820s Robinson had demonstrated a legalistic and constitutional approach to the solution of problems which the opposition had handled in a more openly "political" fashion. He had shown a consistent concern for sponsoring a controlled, commercially based development of the province through the encouragement of immigration, the construction of public works, and the discouragement of land speculation. Although much interested in the welfare of the Church of England, he at times disagreed with John Strachan's passionate advocacy of its rights. Robinson seemed to have taken for granted the Anglican dominance of education and had been instrumental in preventing the sale of the clergy reserves to the Canada Company in

1826. Nevertheless, his critics in the assembly saw him grow in tact and caution, and he had been successful in pushing much basic housekeeping legislation through a sharply divided assembly.

Robinson lost his real influence with the appointment of the new governor, Sir John COLBORNE, in August 1828. Colborne did not lean on the advice of a few Compact councillors as had his predecessor. He was a conservative, but many of the leading men in the Compact party distrusted him. However, when the Reform-dominated assembly demanded that Robinson be removed from his political posts in the councils in accordance with the 1828 Canada Committee report which had recommended political independence for the judiciary, Colborne was quick to defend Robinson's worth. Although Robinson might not have objected to losing the posts "to save him from the drudgery of colonial politics," Colborne felt that he should continue at least in the speakership because his legal experience would be helpful in drafting legislation. The colonial secretary accepted the substance of the assembly's demand and ruled that no judges were to serve in the executive or legislative councils in future. Robinson remained a legislative councillor but was advised to confine his contributions to giving legal advice. He and Colborne became friends and Colborne consulted him on occasion over provincial affairs. Robinson remained the senior Tory in the province, a kind of figurehead. No one emerged in the assembly with his knowledge or effectiveness in debate. Only once, in 1832, did he break his cautious abstention from politics: to pen the reply of the Legislative Council to a dispatch from Lord Goderich which seemed to pay too much attention to Mackenzie and his grievances.

Robinson's relations with Colborne's successor, Sir Francis Bond Head*, were closer, and more cordial, though in personality they differed. Certainly many radicals saw them as working too closely together. Both agreed that an outward show of calm was necessary as rumours of rebellion began circulating in Toronto in the summer and fall of 1837. The chief justice willingly stood in the ranks of militia called out to resist Mackenzie. On 7 December, when the militia marched north to Montgomery's Tavern to defeat the rebels, Robinson sat in his study writing a history of the rebellion. Because of his advice and support during the crisis, Head recommended that Robinson be knighted, but Robinson declined the honour.

As chief justice, Robinson presided over the trials of those charged with insurrection or treason in connection with the rebellion and the Patriot invasions from the United States in 1838. Over 900 had been arrested, but most were released without trial and bound to keep the peace. Robinson presided daily over the actual hearings and passed sentence on those convicted. Thirty-seven men were sentenced to transportation or had death penalties commuted to that punishment, but on Robinson's recommendation only 25 were actually transported. Others were given prison sentences of a few years. However, it was Robinson's view that "some examples should be made in the way of capital punishment," and Samuel Lount* and Peter Matthews*, both leaders in the rebel movement who had pleaded guilty to high treason, were hanged.

Through discussions of the treatment of insurgents, Robinson came into contact with Sir George Arthur*, who had relieved Head in early 1838. Although the two were carefully formal to begin with, Arthur too succumbed to the knowledge and experience of his chief justice and relied upon his "friendly advice." When Governor General Lord Durham [Lambton*] visited Upper Canada for a few days in July 1838 he too took the opportunity to seek Robinson's views on a proposal to federate the British North American provinces in an elaborate political system of local and general governments with ill-defined areas of jurisdictional competence. Robinson made a number of comments on the scheme, objecting most strongly to suggestions that the legislative councils be abolished and that the elected assemblies control the entire provincial revenues. He had few illusions that his discreet advice would be heeded because "nothing but a notorious, factious opposition to government in the adviser is acknowledged as giving any value to Colonial opinions."

Ill health forced Robinson to ask for a leave of absence in the summer of 1838 so that he could seek medical advice in England. He and his family stayed with his wife's friends at Cheltenham. In December Colonial Secretary Lord Glenelg asked him to come to London to discuss Canadian affairs. It was the first of many interviews with influential British politicians, including Sir Robert Peel, the Conservative leader, who, in a period of unstable Whig governments, were reluctant to move decisively in formulating Canadian policy. At this time Robinson visited Durham, and found him still undecided about what to recommend in his report, trying to please both "the ballot and short parliament people" (radicals in England) and the British in the Canadas.

Durham's report was tabled in the House of Commons in February 1839. To his wife Robinson described it as "horrid," and he saw the sections on Upper Canada, which criticized the Family Compact, as "disgraceful and mischievous." He gave his opinion to Peel and the Duke of Wellington without delay. Once more, as in 1823, Robinson pointed out to colonial office officials that the union of the Canadas Durham recommended would only drag Upper Canada into the difficulties in Lower Canada. He foresaw that the assembly proposed would be closely divided between French and English and would give "no assurance of anything but bitter and hateful conflict." To attempt to submerge the French Canadians in the legislature would be to force them into a "close phalanx against the British portion of the Legislature," without any guarantee that the Anglophones would remain "faithful to British supremacy." To give the governor power temporarily to suspend elections was unfair to all the colonies. Reinvestment of control of colonial lands in the British government to encourage immigration was unwise since the colonial governments would be unwilling to give it up. The abolition of the clergy reserves he rejected, for the Protestants of the province would be left "destitute of any public provision to support the public worship of God, and to ensure the maintenance of religious instruction." The proposal that the governor carry out his responsibilities through heads of departments in whom the legislature placed its confidence was absurd. "The Assemblies of the Provinces . . . displayed a degree of selfishness (if not corruption), a prodigality, a negligence, a recklessness beyond what one can think credible . . . it is happy indeed that they have not had higher and greater interests at their mercy." Such a form of government would lead to "a servile and corrupting dependence upon Party"; it would be without parallel in the British empire and "in comparison with it the Republican Government of the United States would be strongly conservative."

In the following weeks Robinson made a number of his own confidential recommendations to deal with Canada's problems. What was needed were guarantees against American aggression, the restoration of order so that investment might once more flow into the Canadas, governmental forms to prevent the recurrence of disturbances, and financial assistance to Upper Canada to offset the effects of suspended immigration and a decline in commerce and revenue. Robinson's alternatives to Durham's plans for union included the annexation of Montreal to Upper Canada and the maintenance of separate provincial governments, with Lower Canada to be governed for up to 15 years by an appointed executive and a partly elected, partly appointed legislative council. To better control the rebellious Lower Canadian population he suggested various measures to assimilate French Canadians into the English language culture, including the use of English in government and the courts and the substitution of English for French civil law in Lower Canada.

In April Robinson came up to London. He saw Peel regularly and conferred with many leading Whigs and Tories in an effort to discredit Durham's report. The weakness of Lord Melbourne's ministry gave him some hope and the abandonment of a union bill offered in parliament in June 1839 seemed to augur well. Throughout the summer while he consulted physicians and tried to rest Robinson continued writing to Tory leaders and to supporters of the Anglican establishment and the clergy reserves.

During the summer the government placed the Canadian issue at the top of its list of priorities: Lord John Russell was appointed colonial secretary in August and shortly afterwards Charles Poulett Thomson* was appointed governor general of British North America. Robinson, who had had his leave extended to 1 March 1840, now anticipated for himself even more effort to fight the union. In the autumn of 1839 he began a short book criticizing the proposal. After a long introductory chapter on the geography and economy of the British North American provinces, it gave a detailed argument against the union bill as presented in June 1839. With the publication of *Canada, and the Canada Bill* in February 1840, Robinson had shot his bolt against the union project.

His efforts in the winter and spring of 1840 were turned to the clergy reserves. He met with leaders of the high church party in parliament such as Sir Robert Inglis and Henry Phillpotts, bishop of Exeter, to present his views. Early in 1839 the Tory majority in the Upper Canadian legislature had passed a bill providing that the income from the clergy reserves be applied to "religious purposes" in a manner to be determined by the British parliament, rather than by the Upper Canadian legislature. This reinvestment of the reserves in the crown was rejected by the British government on the grounds that the drafting of the bill had constitutional defects. Robinson was not unhappy at the rejection because he felt that this reinvestment merely opened use of the reserves' income to future political pressures. An act passed in August 1840 by the imperial parliament was something of an improvement, built on the principle of dividing the reserves among denominations, but giving a bigger share to the Church of England. Robinson's cultivation of pro-Anglican British politicians had proved effective. Most Anglicans in Upper Canada were aware that the imperial act was better than they could have obtained in Upper Canada, though few in 1840 could have been happy that this legislation provided support for other denominations as well.

The winds of change over the winter of 1839–40 were blowing hard. The Upper Canadian assembly voted to support the proposed union, and, in consequence, the English Tories, who had been neutral although sympathetic to Robinson and his arguments, decided to support the union measure. But Robinson's consorting with the Tories in England and his absence from the bench began to excite comment. In mid March Russell told Robinson that his presence in England was no longer required or welcome. After a few weeks of visiting and farewells, the Robinsons embarked from London.

The new union bill was introduced in the spring of 1840 just as they left. The Canadas were to be reunited for legislative and executive purposes. Equal representation in the assembly was accorded to each of the former provinces in order to ensure Anglophone domination. Other recommendations made by Durham were ignored or dealt with in different ways. The new governor general of the Canadas engineered an Upper Canadian solution to the clergy reserves by which one-half of the revenues were to be divided between the Anglicans and the Presbyterians, the other half, when funds permitted, among all denominations. He also introduced many of the administrative reforms advocated by Durham. But many of the points Robinson had argued had been accepted and incorporated in the bill. Legislative councillors were to hold office for life, executive responsibility to the legislature was not specified, and the courts were clearly established; indeed, his only objection would probably have been to the union itself and the basis of representation with its potential for political deadlock between French and English.

When Robinson and his family returned to Toronto the political climate of Upper Canada had completely changed. As a judge, he was effectively divorced from political life, and as an old Compact Tory he was excluded from political power. He made some effort to maintain the unity of the high Tories in Upper Canada, but their exclusion from office made this a difficult task. He no longer had personal contact with the governors, although Sir Charles Metcalfe*, after reading *Canada, and the Canada Bill*, corresponded with him.

Much of his time outside his legal duties in the next 20 years was devoted to the Church of England. He served on the executive of the Church Society, the body charged with managing the temporal affairs of the Toronto diocese as well as carrying out good works. He became a vice-president of the Society for the Propagation of the Gospel and was active in the Society for Promoting Christian Knowledge. He believed firmly in the union of church and state and the need for an established church because he felt the only secure basis for civil authority was religion. Hence he defended the clergy reserves, although his views about how to do so were more liberal than Strachan's. He was friendly with the leaders of the high church party in England and associated with them in Canada, but was never attracted by the Oxford Movement or the Tractarians or their followers in Canada. Whether or not he ever accepted a separation of church and state as did Strachan is uncertain. He was always hesitant to make religion a subject of political contention.

Robinson was not narrow in his religious views. He gave land and support to the Methodists because he felt their preachers had brought the Christian message to the frontier when no one else had. He appeared publicly several times in the 1840s and 1850s at meetings of the British and Foreign Bible Society, an organization to which normally only evangelical Anglicans belonged. He had played an active role in establishing King's College, an Anglican university in Toronto, and strongly defended its denominational character. "A college or university which professes to take the range of the sciences – and to send forth a youth in the world qualified to act his part in it – and yet carefully abstains from including any religious doctrine must be an abortion," he told Strachan in 1844. Following Robert Baldwin*'s act to secularize King's College in 1849, he advised Strachan that he should not be satisfied with merely a theological seminary, but that the Anglicans, like the other major denominations, should have their own college. Strachan and his supporters obtained a charter for the University of Trinity College in 1852; Robinson became its first chancellor, serving until his death.

In 1849 Governor General Lord Elgin [BRUCE] recommended Robinson for a knighthood as one means of placating the ultra Tories. Robinson told Elgin's secretary rather cynically that he would accept but that he hoped responsible government would not lead to a too generous creation of knighthoods. He was made instead a Companion of the Bath in 1850, but in 1854 was created a baronet of the United Kingdom.

His work as chief justice of the Court of Queen's Bench naturally occupied most of his time. He worked hard; there was seldom an arrears of business in the court. In fact, Robinson had specifically asked for legislation to allow the court to convene and render judgements after the regular terms as a means of speeding up procedure. The *Upper Canada Law Journal* noted in its obituary: "Few opinions will ever command more respect or carry more weight than those delivered by Sir John Robinson. They are remarkable for their lucid argument, deep learning, strict impartiality and pure justice." D. B. Read* observes that he tended towards severity in criminal matters. As a judge he was courteous and careful, if anything rather conservative. No man has served longer as chief justice than did Robinson, and his judgements are among those which merit a full examination by a legal historian of Canada.

His judgements seldom excited controversy. Two did, however: one in 1859 in which he gave a light sentence to an Orangeman charged with attempted murder following a public brawl, and the John ANDERSON extradition case which aroused intense public interest in both Canada and Britain. Anderson, a slave from Missouri, had, it was alleged, murdered a man in making good his escape to Canada. In 1860 the Court of Queen's Bench presided over by Robinson granted Anderson's extradition to the United States, but the Court of Common Pleas overturned the ruling on a technicality.

Robinson's years on the bench were financially comfortable, but his income was less than it might have been if he had remained at the bar. Indeed, with the help of his prosperous private practice in the 1820s he had built one of Toronto's best homes in Beverley House. He also accumulated a good deal of land, some of which he inherited from his brother Peter in 1838. In 1852 he owned 300 acres in Simcoe County, over 1,000 acres in York, some land in Ontario and Peel counties, and some 29 parcels elsewhere. Nevertheless he was by no means wealthy. He and his wife had four sons and three daughters. Three sons became lawyers; the youngest entered the British army and attained the rank of major-general. His second son, John Beverley*, entered politics, serving briefly in the cabinet before confederation and as lieutenant governor of Ontario in the 1880s.

Robinson

Robinson had never really liked the notoriety of political life; his career on the bench was probably most satisfying because it removed him from politics. He never seems to have thought of power as such; rather he accepted responsibility to govern and to be a public servant. He saw himself as part of the governing class, the "regularly bred," who must take up his duty. He thought that he acted in a liberal or benevolent way on principles which would preserve and strengthen an essentially good Upper Canadian society. His loyalist background, his education by Strachan, and his experience during the War of 1812 shaped his attitudes fundamentally. Looking back from the 1840s, he argued that the war had given Upper Canadians a sense of identity, a sense of anti-Americanism and of pro-British sentiment. He would long remember that many Upper Canadians had been lukewarm in defence against the United States, and remained suspicious of American-born settlers and those whose politics were "republican." Indeed, maintenance of the British connection was his major goal, a goal which could be attained only by encouraging immigration from Britain and by establishing British political institutions in Canada. That British political institutions changed during his lifetime made it difficult for him to adjust his thinking.

He saw what he described as "ancient and venerable institutions," "respect for rank and family," "the power of wealth," and "the control of numerous landlords over a grateful tenantry" as part of the essential fabric of a stable society. That these did not exist in Canada meant that government depended on "the presumed good sense, and good feeling of an uneducated multitude" which periodically could be led astray. Even late in life, when he had begun to feel that he had often been mistaken in his understanding of public wants, he still distrusted democracy. He believed always in a balanced constitution – an elected assembly, an independent upper house to act as a check on the assembly, and an independent executive which could be checked by both houses of the legislature and check them in turn. A society governed in this way could prosper through the work of its people.

Robinson was always a supporter of British immigration and of development. He subscribed to the stock of the Welland Canal Company and the Desjardins Canal Company because of the assistance they would give to the Upper Canadian economy. Nevertheless, as his comments on the United States in the 1830s indicate, he did not favour extravagant development and widespread credit to encourage it.

He was also an early advocate of British North American union. From 1823 onwards he saw such a union as preferable to the union of the two Canadas. The control of Canada by its Anglophone majority could only be ensured by bringing the Atlantic provinces into the union. By the 1840s many Upper Canadian Tories shared his views. His loyalism, his Anglicanism, and his distrust of democracy did not make him into a colonial, however. He would visit England often, be friendly with that country's leading men, and be offered attractive opportunities outside Canada, either in England or in other colonies, but his sense of duty and his love of Upper Canada kept him a Canadian. Indeed, in the last years of his life, he reconciled himself to the concept of responsible government as he saw it working and realized that it was the means by which the British connection could be maintained.

In the spring of 1861 Robinson suffered such a severe attack of gout that his work on the bench had to be curtailed. He was able to resign from the Queen's Bench on 15 March 1862, at which time he was appointed presiding judge of the Court of Error and Appeal. That fall he was again seized cruelly by gout but continued to serve until pain forced him to retire to his home in January 1863. On 28 January the aged Bishop Strachan gave him communion, and three days later he died.

ROBERT E. SAUNDERS

John Beverley Robinson was the author of *Canada, and the Canada Bill: being an examination of the proposed measure for the future government of Canada . . .* (London, 1840; repr. East Ardsley, Eng., and New York, 1967); *Remarks on the proposed union of the provinces* (n.p., 1839); and with Jonathan Sewell*, *Plan for a general legislative union of the British provinces in North America* (London, [1824?]), repub. in *General union of all the British provinces of North America* (London, 1824).

Sir John Beverley Robinson papers are in the possession of Christopher Robinson (Ottawa) (mfm. in PAC, MG 24, B9). MTCL, William Dummer Powell papers. PAC, MG 23, H I, ser.4, 1; MG 24, A40; RG 1, E1, 50–57; E3; RG 5, A1, 16–267; RG 7, G1, 55–95. PAO, Cartwright (John Solomon) papers; Jarvis-Powell papers; Macaulay (John) papers; Robinson (John Beverley) papers; Strachan (John) papers; RG 4, ser.A-1. PRO, CO 42/351–453 (mfm. at PAC).

Arthur papers (Sanderson). A. N. Bethune, *Memoir of the Right Reverend John Strachan, D.D., LL.D., first bishop of Toronto* (Toronto and London, 1870). *Correspondence between the Right Honourable Sir Robert Wilmot Horton, bart., and J. B. Robinson, esq., chief justice of Upper Canada, upon the subject of a pamphlet lately published entitled "Ireland and*

Canada'' (London, 1839). G.B., Parl., House of Commons, 1828, VII, 569, pp.375–733, *Report from the select committee on the civil government of Canada* (repr. Quebec, 1829). [J. G. Lambton], *Lord Durham's report on the affairs of British North America*, ed. C. P. Lucas (3v., Oxford, 1912). *Papers relating to the removal of the Honourable John Walpole Willis from the office of one of His Majesty's judges of the Court of King's Bench of Upper Canada* ([London?], 1829). *Statistical account of Upper Canada, compiled with a view to a grand system of emigration*, comp. R. [F.] Gourlay (2v., London, 1822). [John Strachan], *The John Strachan letter book, 1812–1834*, ed. G. W. Spragge (Toronto, 1946). [C. E. P. Thomson], *Letters from Lord Sydenham, governor-general of Canada, 1839–1841, to Lord John Russell*, ed. Paul Knaplund (London, 1931). *Town of York, 1815–34* (Firth). Upper Canada, House of Assembly, *Journal*, 1820–29; *The seventh report from the select committee on grievances . . .* (Toronto, 1835); Legislative Council, *Journal*, 1829–38. ''The late Sir John B. Robinson, baronet,'' *Upper Canada Law Journal* (Toronto), IX (1863), 57–66. *Canadian Freeman* (Toronto). *Colonial Advocate*. *Constitution* (Toronto).

II. I. Cowan, *British emigration to British North America, 1783–1837* ([Toronto], 1928). Craig, *Upper Canada*. Lois Darroch Milani, *Robert Gourlay, gadfly: the biography of Robert (Fleming) Gourlay, 1778–1863, forerunner of the rebellion in Upper Canada, 1837* ([Thornhill, Ont., 1971?]). Dent, *Upper Canadian rebellion*. Aileen Dunham, *Political unrest in Upper Canada, 1815–1836* (London, 1927; repr. Toronto, 1963). S. W. Jackman, *Galloping Head; the life of the Right Honourable Sir Francis Bond Head, bart., P.C., 1793–1875, late lieutenant governor of Upper Canada* (London, [1958]). Julia Jarvis, *Three centuries of Robinsons: the story of a family* ([Toronto, 1953]). Lindsey, *Life and times of Mackenzie*. Ged Martin, *The Durham report and British policy: a critical essay* (Cambridge, Eng., 1972). Moir, *Church and state in Canada West*. C. W. New, *Lord Durham; a biography of John George Lambton, first Earl of Durham* (Oxford, 1929). W. [G.] Ormsby, *The emergence of the federal concept in Canada, 1839–1845* ([Toronto], 1969). G. H. Patterson, ''Studies in elections and public opinion in Upper Canada'' (unpublished PHD thesis, University of Toronto, 1969). W. R. Riddell, *The bar and the courts of the province of Upper Canada, or Ontario* (Toronto, 1928); *The legal profession in Upper Canada in its early periods* (Toronto, 1916); *The life of William Dummer Powell, first judge at Detroit and fifth chief justice of Upper Canada* (Lansing, Mich., 1924). C. W. Robinson, *Life of Sir John Beverley Robinson, bart., C.B., D.C.L., chief-justice of Upper Canada* (Edinburgh and London, 1904). R. E. Saunders, ''John Beverley Robinson: his political career, 1812–1840'' (unpublished MA thesis, University of Toronto, 1960). W. S. Wallace, *The Family Compact: a chronicle of the rebellion in Upper Canada* (Toronto, 1915).

H. G. J. Aitken, ''The Family Compact and the Welland Canal Company,'' *Canadian Journal of Economics and Political Science* (Toronto), XVIII (1952), 63–76. D. R. Beer, ''W. H. Draper and the formation of the Conservative party,'' *CHR*, LIV (1973), 228–32. G. W. Brown, ''The Durham report and the Upper Canadian scene,'' *CHR*, XX (1939), 136–60. Terry Cook, ''John Beverley Robinson and the conservative blueprint for the Upper Canadian community,'' *OH*, LXIV (1972), 79–94. E. A. Cruikshank, ''John Beverley Robinson and the trials for treason in 1814,'' *OH*, XXV (1929), 191–219; ''A study of disaffection in Upper Canada in 1812–5,'' *RSC Trans.*, 3rd ser., VI (1912), sect.II, 11–65. Alison Ewart and Julia Jarvis, ''The personnel of the Family Compact, 1791–1841,'' *CHR*, VII (1926), 209–21. G. M. Gressley, ''Lord Selkirk and the Canadian courts, '' *North Dakota History* (Bismarck), XXIV (1957), 89–105. Robert Hett, ''Judge Willis and the Court of King's Bench in Upper Canada,'' *OH*, LXV (1973), 19–30. K. L. P. Martin, ''The Union Bill of 1822,'' *CHR*, V (1924), 42–54. W. G. Ormsby, ''The civil list question in the Province of Canada,'' *CHR*, XXXV (1954), 93–118; ''The problem of Canadian union, 1822–1828,'' *CHR*, XXXIX (1958), 277–95. W. R. Riddell, ''The Ancaster 'bloody assize' of 1814,'' *OH*, XX (1923), 107–25; ''The Bidwell elections: a political episode in Upper Canada a century ago,'' *OH*, XXI (1924), 236–44; ''Robert (Fleming) Gourlay,'' *OH*, XIV (1916), 5–133. R. E. Saunders, ''What was the Family Compact?'' *OH*, XLIX (1957), 165–78. William Smith, ''The reception of the Durham report in Canada,'' *CHA Report*, 1928, 41–54; ''Side-lights on the attempted union of 1822,'' *CHR*, II (1921), 38–45. W. M. Weekes, ''The War of 1812: civil authority and martial law in Upper Canada,'' *OH*, XLVIII (1956), 147–61. S. F. Wise, ''Conservatism and political development: the Canadian case,'' *South Atlantic Quarterly* (Durham, N.C.), LXIX (1970), 226–43; ''God's peculiar peoples,'' *Shield of Achilles* (W. L. Morton), 36–61; ''The rise of Christopher Hagerman,'' *Historic Kingston* (Kingston, Ont.), 14 (January 1966), 12–23; ''Sermon literature and Canadian intellectual history,'' United Church of Can., Committee on Archives, *Bull.* (Toronto), 18 (1965), 3–18; ''Upper Canada and the conservative tradition,'' *Profiles of a province: studies in the history of Ontario . . .* (Toronto, 1967), 20–33.

ROBLIN, DAVID, lumber merchant and politician; b. 19 April 1812 in Adolphustown Township, Upper Canada, fifth of the nine children of John Roblin and Mary Moore; m. in 1832 Pamelia Hawley, and they had ten children; d. 1 March 1863 at Napanee, Canada West.

John Roblin, an Adolphustown farmer and Methodist lay preacher, died when David was still a child. Largely ''self-educated,'' David opened a small general store in Richmond Township in 1832, moved his business to Napanee in 1841, and during the next decade expanded into the timber trade and speculation in United Empire Loyalist scrip with considerable success.

Like most Upper Canadian politicians of the period, Roblin entered politics through municipal channels. He was Richmond Township's first reeve (1841–57), and served as first warden

Roblot

(1849–57) of the United Counties of Frontenac and Lennox and Addington. He used his considerable municipal influence to promote the passage of the Grand Trunk Railway legislation, the construction of the Addington Colonization Road, and the rebuilding of the county courthouse and jail in Kingston. His political influence also gained him such dividends in the 1850s as a large timber limit in Frontenac from the Francis Hincks* administration, a Grand Trunk Railway sub-contract to build a bridge over the Napanee River, and an appointment as company arbitrator for the GTR in April 1854.

Roblin was not simply a political "railwayman," however, for Reform zeal ran through the family. Both his father and his cousin, John Philip Roblin*, sat in the assembly. David contested Lennox and Addington unsuccessfully in the 1844 and 1851 elections against the Tory incumbent Benjamin Seymour. Throughout his political career Roblin labelled himself a Reformer, and he was an admirer of Marshall Spring Bidwell*, Peter Perry*, and particularly Robert Baldwin*, whom he described in 1861 as "that good and great man, the lamented and ever-to-be revered champion of our liberties."

Victorious in the elections of 1854, Roblin, along with such colleagues as John Ross*, Angus Morrison*, and Sidney Smith*, was persuaded by Hincks to join the new Liberal-Conservative coalition. Though he continued to identify himself as a Baldwin Reformer, he supported John A. Macdonald* loyally on every major issue, including Macdonald's unpopular stand against representation by population.

Roblin survived the 1857 election, but the eclipse of his personal and political fortunes was already under way. Two unsuccessful legislative attempts, which he supported, to separate Lennox and Addington from Frontenac (in 1858 and 1860) alienated both his Addington supporters and the Kingston political triumvirate of Macdonald, Alexander Campbell*, and Sidney Smith. His lumber business, which had suffered severe losses in the 1857–58 depression following the collapse of the London, England, timber market, continued to decline, leading to the loss of his Frontenac timber limits and all his property except for the family home. In the election of 1861 he was defeated by the official Conservative candidate, Augustus F. G. Hooper*, a Newburgh merchant. Ill and bankrupt, Roblin retired from politics and died in 1863.

In 1857 Macdonald wrote of Roblin: "When I was in straits, he stood by me like a man & I can never forget him." Yet for all Roblin's faithful support of the Liberal-Conservative coalition, he continued to have a Reform identity, which was undoubtedly the root of his eventual defeat for it satisfied neither Clear Grits nor Conservatives in a period when the polarization of parties made the separate existence of the Baldwin Reform group both meaningless and irritating. The Toronto *Globe*, for example, castigated Roblin as a "Reform renegade," at the same time that the Conservative *Chronicle and News* of Kingston labelled him one of Macdonald's "most pliant instruments." Indeed it was the support of such coalition Reformers as Roblin that provided the precarious edge the Conservatives enjoyed in the assembly throughout most of the decade after 1854.

JAMES A. EADIE

Lennox and Addington Hist. Soc. (Napanee, Ont.), IV (Roblin family papers), A (David Roblin papers); V (John Stevenson papers) (copies at PAC). *Napanee Standard* (Napanee, [Ont.]), 1854–63. W. S. Herrington, *History of the county of Lennox and Addington* (Toronto, 1913), 151, 157, 206, 223, 275, 317, 341, 401–3. J. A. Eadie, "Politics in Lennox and Addington County in the pre-confederation period, 1854–1867" (unpublished MA thesis, Queen's University, Kingston, Ont., 1967); "The political career of David Roblin," Lennox and Addington Hist. Soc., *Papers and Records*, (Napanee, Ont.), XIV (1972), 48–63.

ROBLOT (Roblet), LOUIS, known as **Brother Aidant**, member of the Institute of the Brothers of the Christian Schools, director and visitor of the district of Canada and the United States; b. 5 Feb. 1796 at Talmay (dept of Côte d'Or), France, son of Claude Roblot and Madeleine Dadavant; d. 19 Sept. 1866 in Paris.

On 1 July 1817 Louis Roblot entered the noviciate of the Brothers of the Christian Schools at Langres, and soon was entrusted with positions of responsibility. From 1822 to 1831 he was director of the Christian Brothers' school at Bourbonne-les-Bains, then of the Saint-Médard and Saint-Enfant-Jésus schools in Paris. In 1831 Brother Aidant was authorized by his superior general to assume the important function of visitor to the French district of Nantes. Six years later he was sent to establish the Christian Brothers securely in Canada.

On two occasions, in 1718 and 1737, the Brothers Hospitallers of the Cross and St Joseph had come close to welcoming Brothers of the Christian Schools to New France. The two plans had failed, despite the visit of Brothers Denis and Pacifique to Montreal during the summer of 1737 [*see* Gervais Hodiesne*]. A century later the story was to be different. Yielding to pressure from Joseph-Vincent Quiblier*, superior of

Saint-Sulpice in Canada, Brother Anaclet, superior general of the Christian Brothers in Paris, authorized four brothers to leave for Lower Canada in 1837. On 10 October Brothers Aidant, Rombaud, Euverte, and Adelbertus left Le Havre on the steamship *Louis-Philippe*, and on 3 November they reached New York. Travelling by water and by the new railway from Saint-Jean on the Richelieu to Laprairie, they reached Montreal on 7 November, in time to observe barricades in certain streets because of the troubles of 1837. The disciples of Jean-Baptiste de La Salle were welcomed by Bishop Jean-Jacques Lartigue* and the Sulpicians, and the latter immediately took charge of them. Brother Aidant got to work so quickly that classes were opened two days before Christmas in a building opposite the seminary; he took in 240 pupils divided among three classes. On 22 Jan. 1838 Bishop Ignace Bourget* opened the school year with the mass of the Holy Spirit at Notre-Dame.

The Sulpicians, who were linked to the brothers by a long tradition of friendship, contributed greatly to the prosperity of the new community, going to "considerable expense" on its behalf. By 6 June 1838 the brothers were able to take up residence in their own house, and on 16 Nov. 1840 the Saint-Laurent School on Rue Vitré was opened. The school housed 860 pupils divided into eight classes, four in English. It was "a great step forward in the history of education in Montreal." The discipline and good behaviour of the students often aroused the admiration of distinguished visitors, among them Bishop Lartigue, Bishop Forbin-Janson*, and the governor general, Lord Sydenham [Thomson*].

In 1843, faced with an almost total lack of pedagogical material at the elementary level, Brother Aidant drafted three school texts, the first in Canada to be based on the methods of La Salle in France: an arithmetic textbook, a short history of Canada, and a concise geography.

The opening of a noviciate at Montreal in December 1838 and the successive arrival of new brothers from France allowed Brother Aidant, the visitor, to deal with the increasing number of requests for schools. Thus the brothers were able to open a school at Quebec in 1843, at Trois-Rivières in 1844, and at Baltimore, U.S.A. in 1845. On 11 Sept. 1847 Brother Aidant left for Paris, at the summons of his superior general. During the meeting that followed the decision was taken to establish a house at New York. By 18 November Brother Aidant was back at Montreal to resume his duties, which he fulfilled until his recall to France on 9 Dec. 1848.

After 11 years of Brother Aidant's administration, the Canadian and American district comprised five houses, including two in the United States. The brothers' schools had a total of 40 classes attended by 3,200 pupils; 56 brothers, including 16 novices, made up the staff. Only a few months after the pioneer's departure, the first French Canadian brother, Toussaint Dufresne, *dit* Brother Jean-Baptiste, became director and founded a school at Montmagny.

From 1849 to 1852 Brother Aidant was in charge of another equally difficult, new district, the Orient, which had a residence on the Bosphorus. He was then recalled to Paris, and in 1852 became one of the advisers of the superior of the institute assisting the latter's work as spiritual leader and administrator. While serving in this capacity Brother Aidant died in 1866, at age 70.

His work, with that of Brother Facile, his resolute successor as visitor in Canada, was to prove so significant that Georges Rigault, the official historian of the Brothers of the Christian Schools, was prompted to write: "Of all the districts founded in the 19th century, those of the Canadian regions and of Anglo-Saxon America will be numbered among the most flourishing."

FRANÇOIS DE LAGRAVE

Archives des Frères des écoles chrétiennes, District de Montréal (Laval), Historique du district: 1837–1967 (copies manuscrite et dactylographiée); Registres de prise d'habit du noviciat de Montréal: 1837–1965. Archivio della Propaganda Fide (Rome), Scritture riferite nei Congressi: America Settentrionale, 4 (1837–41), f.180. Archivio Fratelli delle Scuole Cristiane, Casa Generalizia (Rome), NO 400, 4; NO 432A, 10–12. Brother Angelus Gabriel, *The Christian Brothers in the United States, 1848–1948; a century of Catholic education* (New York, 1948), 78–79. J.-C. Caisse, *L'Institut des Frères des écoles chrétiennes, son origine, son but et ses œuvres* (Montréal, 1883), 49. Jacques Guibert, *Histoire de S. Jean-Baptiste de La Salle, ancien chanoine de l'Église métropolitaine de Reims, fondateur de l'Institut des Frères des écoles chrétiennes* (Paris, 1900), 587. *L'œuvre d'un siècle ; les Frères des écoles chrétiennes au Canada* (Montréal, 1937), 62–66, 73, 80, 85. Georges Rigault, *Histoire générale de l'Institut des Frères des écoles chrétiennes* (9v., Paris, 1937–53), V, 205; VI, 248, 358. Frère Symphorien-Louis [Stanislas Roberge], *Les Frères des écoles chrétiennes au Canada, 1837–1900* (Montréal, 1912). Yves Poutet, "Une institution franco-canadienne au XVIIIe siècle: les écoles populaires de garçons à Montréal," *Revue d'histoire ecclésiastique* (Louvain, Belgique), LIX (1964), 52–88.

ROCHFORT (Rochford, Roachford), JOHN, doctor and office-holder; b. in Ireland; m. on 6

Rolland

Feb. 1823 at Harbour Grace, Nfld, Elizabeth Cane (Cain), and they had five children; d. 2 Jan. 1865 at St John's, Nfld.

After receiving a medical education in Ireland or England John Rochfort arrived in St John's in 1820 and began to practise there. He was soon involved in local politics. That year a surrogate court sentence of 36 lashes to Philip Butler and James Landergan for contempt of court aroused widespread public discontent with the arbitrary and brutal sentences handed down by these courts. At a public meeting on 14 November called to appeal the sentence to the king, Rochfort played a prominent role and signed the resolutions along with Dr William Carson*, Patrick Morris*, and 13 other professional men and small merchants of St John's. Partly as a result of this protest the surrogate courts were abolished in 1824.

In 1822 John Rochfort moved to the thriving town of Harbour Grace, some 70 miles from St John's, where he became closely connected with the leading mercantile families of the area: the Dansons, the Packs, and the Thornes. He was also deeply involved with the Roman Catholic parish of Harbour Grace, especially in the establishment of a school there. In 1826 he was elected president of the newly formed St Patrick's School Society.

An 1828 newspaper advertisement announced Rochfort's return to practise in St John's, although his whole family does not appear to have moved to that town until June 1829. In St John's Rochfort joined the campaign for a local legislature for Newfoundland [see O'BRIEN; BROOKING]. A meeting was called in September 1831 to prepare petitions to the House of Commons in London asking for quicker passage of the bill to establish the legislature. Rochfort was one of 67 signatories to a petition, and a member of the committee selected to convey to the king and the House of Commons the meeting's resolutions calling for an elected legislature.

Rochfort's successful medical career during the 1830s led to his appointment in 1838 as one of four district surgeons for St John's. In February of the next year he was involved in a dispute at the government-run St John's Hospital; the commissioners of the poor had removed the patients at this institution from the care of the district surgeons, and after an unsuccessful protest to the governor, Rochfort refused to visit the hospital again. By 1850 Rochfort, as one of the most prominent Roman Catholics in St John's, was appointed to the Roman Catholic board of directors of the St John's Academy, in company with Bishop John Thomas MULLOCK, John

Kent*, Laurence O'Brien, and Philip Francis Little*.

With the election of the Little administration after the introduction of responsible government in 1855, Rochfort was appointed to the Legislative Council, a position of social prestige if little power. The following year he was also appointed by that government surgeon-in-charge of St John's Hospital. He continued in these positions until his death in 1865.

DAVID J. DAVIS

Church of the Immaculate Conception (Roman Catholic) (Harbour Grace, Nfld.), baptismal and marriage registers, 1820–27 (mfm. at PANL). Church of St John the Baptist (Roman Catholic) (St John's), baptismal and marriage registers, 1831–36 (mfm. at PANL). Nfld., *Blue book*, 1857. *Harbour Grace and Carbonear Weekly Journal and General Advertiser for Conception Bay* (Harbour Grace, Nfld.), 11 June 1829. *Newfoundlander*, 1828–34, 5 Jan. 1865. *Newfoundland Mercantile Journal* (St John's), 1820–26. *Royal Gazette* (St John's), 10 Jan. 1865. *Times and General Commercial Gazette* (St John's), 26 May 1855. Gunn, *Political history of Nfld.*

ROLLAND, JEAN-ROCH, lawyer, judge, member of the Executive Council, and seigneur; b. 11 May 1785 at Montreal, son of François-Roch Rolland and Angélique Boisseau; d. 5 Aug. 1862 at Sainte-Marie-de-Monnoir (Marieville, Que.).

Jean-Roch Rolland was called to the bar on 22 May 1806. After a brilliant and lucrative career of 24 years at Montreal, he was appointed judge of the Court of King's Bench at Montreal on 7 Jan. 1830. On 13 Feb. 1836 he was named acting resident judge for the district of Trois-Rivières, replacing the ailing Judge Joseph-Rémi Vallières* de Saint-Réal.

During the 1837–38 disturbances Judge Rolland played a somewhat special role in Lower Canada. Writs of *habeas corpus* served on Colonel George Augustus WETHERALL on 21 April 1838 ordered him to bring before judges Jean-Roch Rolland or James Reid the political prisoners Louis-Michel Viger* and Toussaint Pelletier. However, on 23 April Sir John COLBORNE had the law of *habeas corpus* suspended by an ordinance of the Special Council. This law, adopted in England in 1679, had been introduced in the Province of Quebec in 1784. Judges Philippe Panet*, Elzéar Bédard*, and Vallières de Saint-Réal refused to comply with the Special Council's ordinance and maintained that it was illegal. Judge Jean-Roch Rolland disagreed, arguing that the law of 1679 had never come into force in Canada. The sentences delivered by judges Panet, Bédard, and Vallières de Saint-Réal were quashed on appeal, their writs annulled by the Special Council, and all three were relieved of their offices by Colborne.

On 28 Dec. 1838 Jean-Roch Rolland was again appointed acting resident judge at Trois-Rivières to replace Judge Vallières de Saint-Réal. Meanwhile, on 28 June 1838, Rolland had been appointed to the Executive Council by Lord Durham [Lambton*], at the same time as Vallières de Saint-Réal. This puppet council, set up as a matter of form by Durham, disappeared on 2 Nov. 1838, the day before he left Lower Canada. On 17 April 1839 a commission called upon Rolland to preside over the provincial Court of Appeal in certain cases.

Eight years later, on 23 April 1847, Rolland was appointed chief justice of the Court of Queen's Bench, replacing Justice Vallières de Saint-Réal. In 1849 the Superior Court replaced the Court of Queen's Bench, and the provincial Court of Appeal was renamed the Court of Queen's Bench. Rolland was promoted to the latter court on 1 Jan. 1850, and retired from the bench on 26 Jan. 1855.

The Honourable Judge Rolland then went to live in his manor-house at Sainte-Marie-de-Monnoir, a seigneury he had acquired from Sir John Johnson* in 1826. He died there on 5 Aug. 1862, at age 77. On 1 March 1821, at Quebec, he had married Marguerite, the younger daughter of Jean-Baptiste-Philippe-Charles d'Estimauville*. Rolland and his wife had eight children; one of them, Charles-Octave, became a lieutenant-colonel in the militia and another, Henri-Auguste, a medical doctor.

CLAUDE VACHON

PAC, MG 30, D62, 26, pp.553–57. Le Jeune, *Dictionnaire*, II, 539. P.-G. Roy, *Les juges de la prov. de Québec*, 475. Garneau, *Hist. du Canada* (1882–83), III, 359–67. P.-G. Roy, *La famille d'Estimauville de Beaumouchel* (Lévis, Qué., 1909). F.-J. Audet, "Les juges de Trois-Rivières," *BRH*, VI (1900), 246. "L'honorable Jean-Roch Rolland," *BRH*, X (1904), 58. Antonio Perrault, "Le Conseil spécial, 1838–1841; son œuvre législative," *La Revue du Barreau de la province de Québec* (Montréal), 3 (1943), 213–15.

ROLLAND, JOSEPH LENOIR, *dit*. *See* LENOIR

ROLPH, JOHN, physician, lawyer, and politician; b. 4 March 1793 at Thornbury, Gloucestershire, England, son of Dr Thomas Rolph and Frances Petty; d. 19 Oct. 1870 at Mitchell, Ont.

John Rolph was the second of 18 children. His father, a surgeon, emigrated about 1808, staying briefly at Les Cèdres, Lower Canada, and then settling near Vittoria in Norfolk County, Upper Canada, where he died in 1814. The family was soon respected in the area, and noted for its hospitality. Two of the sons became Church of England clergymen: Romaine studied divinity under John STRACHAN and served in several parishes in Upper Canada; Thomas lived in England. Another son, George, became a well-known lawyer. A daughter married George Ryerson*.

John Rolph did not accompany his family to Canada, but continued his education in England. In 1809 he was admitted as a student of law at the Inner Temple (London). Immigrating to Upper Canada in 1812, he served during the war as paymaster of the London District militia. He also took up land near Port Talbot and in these years he and members of his family were on excellent terms with the arch-tory, Colonel Thomas Talbot*. In 1817 Rolph took the initiative in inaugurating the "Talbot Anniversary," honouring the founding of the settlement by the colonel in 1803. Soon afterward Rolph returned to England to resume his education. From 1818 to 1821 he studied both law and medicine at St John's College, Cambridge, and medicine at Guy's and St Thomas' hospitals in London. He also undertook studies leading to a divinity degree. He was called to the bar of the Inner Temple in 1821, and in the same year, soon after his return, to the bar of Upper Canada. In 1826, on a subsequent visit to England, he was admitted by examination to membership in the Royal College of Surgeons. He practised medicine in the province during the 1820s, although he did not apply for and receive his licence until 1829. In 1824 he wrote to Colonel Talbot, asking him to be the patron of the Talbot Dispensatory, which he and Dr Charles DUNCOMBE proposed to establish for the dual purpose of offering free medical advice and instructing students. The dispensatory soon disappeared from sight; it may have been projected mainly to establish good relations with Talbot.

Rolph's active pursuit of two professions made him widely known in the London District. On 2 Sept. 1824 William Lyon MACKENZIE in the *Colonial Advocate* stated that "there are thousands in the district, whom he has been the means of restoring to health and strength." He was soon drawn into politics and was elected in Middlesex County for the House of Assembly in 1824. Rolph now sacrificed whatever friendly ties he had with Talbot and quickly assumed the leadership of those members (soon to be called Reformers) who were opposing the official party (soon to be called the Family Compact); indeed, the assembly sessions from 1825 through 1828 were to a considerable extent dominated by a

Rolph

continuing political duel between Rolph and the attorney general, John Beverley ROBINSON. In an assembly not noted for learning, a man with Rolph's thorough and varied education, his good social background, and his powerful (if somewhat florid) eloquence, was best equipped to stand up to the highly competent and masterful attorney general.

Of all the issues before the legislature elected in 1824, the most controversial was the "Alien Question" – whether American-born settlers who had come into Upper Canada since 1783 were aliens and, if so, how they were to be naturalized. The question affected the political status, and possibly the property titles, of over half the province's population. Despite his English birth, Rolph embraced the cause of the American-born settlers, who were numerous in his own constituency; he saw it as a "popular" cause being attacked by the executive branch and the Legislative Council. More specifically, he denounced the habitual attacks of conservative loyalist members, many of them from the eastern part of the province, on everything American. He called upon Upper Canadians "to give over indulging in worthless slander of our neighbours and friends." Upper Canada had nothing to fear from American settlers; they had not fled from "a bad government and a barren soil" but had come willingly and were quickly developing a "deep personal interest" in the province and its institutions. After the assembly had passed resolutions demanding that resident American-born settlers be recognized as having all the rights of British subjects, Rolph went to England in the spring of 1826 as a spokesman of the Reform majority in the assembly to try to influence the Colonial Office to respond to the resolutions. In London he was courteously received and consulted and appeared to be satisfied with an act of parliament empowering the provincial legislature to pass a naturalization bill of limited scope; it would have to contain provisions such as a renunciation of allegiance to the United States and a public registry of naturalized Americans which many found repugnant. However, after Rolph returned to Upper Canada he introduced in December 1826 a bill which differed from imperial instructions and made the naturalization process much easier and more palatable to American-born settlers. (There is a certain air of mystery in the whole transaction – as in so many episodes in Rolph's career.)

The alien controversy reached new heights of bitterness in 1827. After some complicated legislative manœuvring, in which Rolph and Robinson both took leading parts, the assembly reluctantly and somewhat surprisingly passed a bill conforming to the Colonial Office's instructions, presumably on the assumption that no better measure was obtainable. Reformers opposed to the measure were determined on a further appeal to England and once again hoped that Rolph would represent them. He apparently decided that his professional obligations made another lengthy trip impossible and, instead, Robert Randall* was sent. The latter's mission was completely successful: the act, largely shaped by Robinson, was disallowed, and the assembly was invited to pass a measure to its own liking; it did so in 1828. Because of the leading part he had taken in the assembly Rolph could claim a large share of the credit for this outcome.

From 1825 to 1828 Rolph was also prominent in questions and controversies that were defining and sharpening political alignments in Upper Canada. He harked back to the wrongs done to "the martyred" Robert Fleming GOURLAY. He deplored the harsh treatment meted out to his colleague from Middlesex, Captain John Matthews*, whose army pension was suspended for remarks considered sympathetic to the United States. He defended Francis Collins*, editor of the *Canadian Freeman*, in his quarrels with the administration and, especially, with Robinson. Along with other Reform lawyers he criticized the "persecution" of Judge John Walpole Willis*. In the assembly he spoke against the "exclusive" claims of the Church of England (even though he was a member), attacked all connection between church and state, and defended the Methodists from John Strachan's criticisms. He sponsored a number of reform measures, most notably in an eloquent speech on a bill to abolish imprisonment for debt. In many of these activities he was closely associated with Marshall Spring Bidwell* and with Dr William Warren Baldwin* and his son Robert*. After the convincing Reform victory in the elections of 1828, and his own easy return in Middlesex, Rolph might have been chosen speaker; in any case in the short, Reform-dominated assembly of 1829–30 an unfriendly Tory observer noted that he led "the house like a flock of sheep."

Following this intense political activity, however, Rolph was not a candidate in the 1830 elections. One can only guess at his motives: perhaps he had concluded that political action in the assembly was futile as long as it had no control or influence over the lieutenant governor, the Family Compact, and the Legislative Council. Perhaps he had lost touch with his constituency, since he had moved eastward to Dundas some years earlier and had spent much time in York (Toronto), the provincial capital, as well as in

England in 1826. Perhaps he had found it impossible to do justice to his two professions and at the same time perform the time-consuming and often thankless duties of a political leader. In fact he was having to choose between law and medicine. Early in 1831 he wrote to Robert Baldwin: "Every day I become less and less efficient in these Law matters" and a few months later to W. W. Baldwin: "My time is wholly occupied in medical practice – I think of no other pursuit, I engage in no other: but it is laborious. Country practice must be so. . . ." He was accepting no new suits at law, and about 1832 he transferred the remainder of his practice to his brother George. (He might have been amused if he had known that, shortly afterward, the colonial secretary wrote confidentially to Lieutenant Governor Sir John COLBORNE that Rolph would be a suitable person for the vacant post of solicitor general.) By early 1832 he had moved to York, where he not only built up his practice but accepted students in what was apparently the only "medical school" in the province at that time. He was also active in establishing the mechanics' institute in York, where he gave popular lectures on a variety of subjects. Like other doctors in the town, he sought to relieve the sufferings of cholera victims in the epidemics of 1832 and 1834. In the latter year he was married to Grace Haines, of Kingston, a woman of strong character who shared fully in his career, particularly in the administration of his various medical schools. They were to have four children.

Early in 1834 York was incorporated as the city of Toronto, and in the elections for aldermen and councilmen Rolph's name headed the poll in St Patrick's Ward. There was general expectation that the Reform majority on council would elect him the city's first mayor. But the councillors apparently felt the honour should go to Mackenzie in recognition of the "persecutions" he had recently been suffering. When he learned of this plan, Rolph promptly resigned his seat and took no further part in municipal politics, leaving everyone to guess at his motives. Nor was he a candidate in the elections for the assembly in 1834, which resulted in a resounding Reform victory. Rolph's life now appeared to be devoted almost entirely to the practice and teaching of medicine, although he also served as a director and first president of the People's Bank, founded in 1835, with many leading Reformers, including Francis Hincks*, active in it.

Nevertheless, it was soon clear that Rolph was still a political force, all the more, perhaps, because he had recently been somewhat out of the public eye. At the end of January 1836 Sir Francis Bond Head* arrived in Toronto to replace Colborne as lieutenant governor. He found that the Executive Council had only three members, and that there was an immediate need to enlarge it. Although he felt instinctively antagonistic to Mackenzie and to the American-born Bidwell, Head was prepared to see the Executive Council broadened by the appointment of suitable men from outside the Tory ranks. Robert Baldwin and Rolph were obvious possibilities. Despite misgivings on Baldwin's part, he and Rolph, along with John Henry Dunn*, the receiver general, were sworn as members of the Executive Council on 20 Feb. 1836. Rolph and Baldwin were determined to be more than mere ciphers: they wished to be consulted regularly by the lieutenant governor, to have an influential voice in the dispensing of patronage, and to see "the Affairs of the Province . . . distributed into Departments, to the Heads of which shall be referred such matters as obviously appertain to them respectively." They succeeded in convincing the entire council to prepare a memorandum supporting this stand, which Head later stated had been taken at Rolph's initiative. The lieutenant governor at once rejected the memorandum, stating that in Upper Canada he alone could be the "responsible Minister," and inviting the council to resign if they felt that their "Principles" were being compromised. This they did on 12 March, thereby precipitating a political crisis which poisoned the political air of Upper Canada for many months.

Rolph, however, did not take any prominent part in the debate between Head and the "Constitutionalists" on the one side and the Reform and radical leaders of the assembly on the other. He was clearly identified with the Reform side, but with the moderate, "responsible" brand associated with the Baldwins, and not at all with Mackenzie or even with the actions and statements of the assembly majority. Thus he was not especially vulnerable when provincial opinion veered sufficiently to defeat the Reformers in the elections of 1836. It is curious – but unexplained – that Rolph chose this somewhat inauspicious time to return to politics. Although now a resident of Toronto, he stood as a candidate in Norfolk County, where he had long associations and where he was easily elected.

Reformers were outnumbered in the new assembly by more than three to one; with Mackenzie, Bidwell, and Peter Perry* all defeated and with Robert Baldwin still withdrawn from politics, Rolph once again found himself the leader of the party. He appears to have shared to the full the Reformers' indignation at the methods that, they felt, had been used to defeat them. "Orange

Rolph

violence, bribery and corruption, manufactured deeds, false evidence . . . and malicious official misrepresentation, and ultra tory returning officers, and the like abuses together with the aid of a state paid priesthood, turned the elections against us . . . there is not a baser or more unprincipled government in the world than the one we are now enduring here,'' Rolph wrote Baldwin in July 1836. The tone of this letter points to Rolph's role in the assembly in 1836 and 1837 and it may even help to explain why he was willing to flirt, in his own way, to be sure, with involvement in the rebellion.

In the assembly Rolph could of course achieve no legislative goals against the overwhelming Tory majority, but he could hearten Reformers by his oratory and by his persistent attacks on the Tories and their allies. The hostile Toronto *Patriot* on 20 Dec. 1836 paid him grudging tribute as ''the great leader of the minority, and the only one worth listening to,'' while denouncing his ''wily sophistry.'' His main interventions were two speeches on the clergy reserves in December 1836 and in the following month during the ''inquiry into the charges of high misdemeanors at the late elections preferred against Sir Francis Bond Head.'' In the first, which was widely reprinted and was in part a debate with Christopher Hagerman*, he asserted that a connection between church and state was always harmful to religion, as was the state endowment of any denomination, and he denied that the Church of England was established in Upper Canada; he ended by moving that the clergy reserves be sold and ''the proceeds [be applied] to the purposes of General Education.'' It is probable that much of Rolph's popularity as a Reform leader throughout his long career derived from his eloquent and consistent support for the voluntary principle in religion. The second speech contained a slashing attack upon Head, accusing him of having used ''the language of an agitator,'' of having treated ''the friends of reform . . . as enemies,'' and, in appealing ''from the throne to the passions of the people as 'Englishmen, Irishmen, Scotchmen and U.E. Loyalists,' [of having] forgot, yes sir, forgot the CANADIANS! . . .'' Rolph wondered whether Upper Canada would ''ever again have a free Election.'' It is impossible to know whether this remark was merely a rhetorical flourish or whether it indicated real despair over the prospects for peaceful change.

But, whatever despair Rolph may have felt, he took no visible part in the mobilizing of radical opinion and in the preparations for the armed uprising of December 1837. He and Mackenzie had never been intimates, or even working as-

sociates, and like his neighbour in Toronto, M. S. Bidwell, and his friends the Baldwins, he did not associate himself with the little editor's increasingly frenetic course in the latter months of 1837. How much he knew about Mackenzie's plans by November and how much he was consulted by Mackenzie are other, and perhaps unanswerable, questions. In the event of success Mackenzie would obviously need men of respectability and standing to assume leading roles and no one was better fitted for such a task than Rolph. Mackenzie later claimed, and went on claiming all his life, that shortly before the outbreak of the rebellion Rolph had agreed to become ''the Executive'' who would direct operations in secret until the time came to reveal his identity. Rolph denied this claim, and there is no evidence to support Mackenzie's assertion. But it is clear that Rolph was consulted by Mackenzie and it appears Rolph agreed that Mackenzie should continue to investigate the state of opinion north of the city at the end of October and in November. Later in November he also learned that Mackenzie had fixed on Thursday, 7 December, for the insurgents to assemble north of Toronto and advance on the capital. Rolph apparently had no part in this decision, but he did not report the information to the authorities. His complicity apparently went considerably further: as far as can be gathered, he agreed that in the event of success he would, in John Charles Dent*'s words, ''assume the direction of the Civil Government.''

From his vantage point within Toronto and his access to information and rumour, Rolph learned late on 2 December that the government intended to arrest Mackenzie and to take other precautionary measures. Rolph could see the uprising being nipped in the bud and he sent word to Samuel Lount* advising him to move on the city at once with 300 men in order to maintain the advantage of surprise. Lount received the message the next day and the men did begin to assemble at Montgomery's Tavern on Monday, 4 December. Mackenzie was furious at this turn of events, for there was still much to do before an effective operation could be mounted. On this same day, he conferred with Rolph outside the city, when the latter apparently advised abandoning the uprising. But it was now too late, and the men were moving down Yonge St.

On Tuesday, 5 December, occurred the single most controversial episode in Rolph's long career. In the morning Head decided to send a message to the rebels, under a flag of truce, advising them to return peacefully to their homes. After one or two other names had been canvassed, Robert Baldwin and Rolph were selected and agreed to undertake the mission. They met with the rebel leaders, who insisted on having the lieutenant governor's message in writing. Baldwin and Rolph returned to the city, only to find that Head had determined not to parley further with the rebels. They delivered this message to the rebels, again under a flag of truce, and the mission was at an end. The controversy surrounding this affair started a little more than a month later when Lount was captured and made a statement, prior to his execution, that on the first trip, Rolph "gave me a wink to walk on one side, when he requested me not to hear the message but to go on with our proceedings." If this account was correct, Rolph had obviously played a double, indeed a traitorous, role, posing as the trusted envoy of the lieutenant governor while counselling the rebels to attack the city. Rolph's version was that he had given this advice to Lount on the second trip, after he had delivered Head's message and when the truce mission was at an end.

Upon his return to the city in the middle of Tuesday afternoon Rolph apparently busied himself in urging radicals to arm themselves to join with Mackenzie's men, who were expected imminently. But hours passed and in the evening it was learned that the rebels, after an exchange of fire with an outpost guard, had precipitately retreated. As midnight approached and the loyal forces were clearly gaining strength and confidence, Rolph realized the insurgents' cause was hopeless and he sent out a messenger advising them to disperse. So far, his implication in the movement had not come to the attention of the authorities, but when on the morning of 6 December Dr Thomas David Morrison* was arrested and officials began to search Mackenzie's house and office, Rolph perceived that evidence of his complicity would probably come to light. With his accustomed self-control he casually walked westward from the centre of town to a spot where one of his medical students had a saddled horse waiting. He was stopped once by loyalist volunteers but allowed to pass after a doctor (a former student of his) vouched for him, and after riding all night he reached the Niagara River and exile in the United States. On 11 December the lieutenant governor issued a proclamation stating that facts had come to his knowledge indicating that Rolph "had been concerned in the traitorous attempt . . . to subvert the Government of this Province" and offering a reward of £500 for his apprehension. Head later stated to Lord Glenelg that "Dr Rolph has been proved to have been the . . . most crafty, the most bloodythirsty, the most treacherous, the most

cowardly, and . . . the most infamous of the traitors who lately assailed us." He further noted that on 20 Jan. 1838 Rolph, accused of having "combined, conspired and confederated, with the rebels," had been expelled from the assembly.

Rolph lived for more than five years in the United States, mainly in Rochester. At first he showed some interest in the Patriot activities along the border, and he occasionally corresponded with exiles from both Upper and Lower Canada. But he soon dissociated himself from such activities and began to re-establish himself as a doctor and medical teacher. Some Canadian students came to study under him. He managed to get a good deal of his property out of Toronto and he was presently joined by his wife. No doubt exile was bitter, but his was a good deal more comfortable than that of many who had been implicated in the rebellion, including Mackenzie, who later insisted that Rolph had failed to befriend him when he had been jailed in Rochester. Such aloofness on Rolph's part was not only characteristic but also not surprising in view of the accusations Mackenzie had been publishing. Mackenzie asserted that he had been the mere agent of the "Executive," John Rolph, that Rolph had ruined any chances of success by changing the date of the rebellion, and that his appearance with the flag of truce had discouraged the rank and file of the insurgents. Rolph prepared but did not publish a "Review of Mackenzie's publications . . . ," in which he accused Mackenzie of endangering the lives and liberty of Reformers by leaving evidence of the rebels' plans in Toronto and by publicizing the names of those associated with the movement. He laid the failure of the rebellion to Mackenzie's own mismanagement, especially the tardiness in moving on the city after the end of the flag of truce mission. The review, found later among his papers, was in the third person and, as usual, volunteered no information about Rolph's own actions or motives.

A grant of amnesty in 1843 permitted Rolph to return to Toronto that August. The event was greeted on a strictly party basis: the *Examiner* welcomed the return "of a man whose profound talents are calculated to ornament any department of life"; in the legislature Dr William Dunlop* remarked that Rolph and others "kept back and pushed better men than themselves forward to bear the brunt of the contest. If the sleek and wily traitor, Rolph, was to be pardoned . . . why not Mackenzie?" Rolph resumed his old residence and soon re-established his medical school and practice. At this time King's College

Rolph

was just getting under way, and Rolph's school was aimed at "medical students who do not intend to enter the University. . . . They would be conducted through the usual course of medical studies . . . and prepared for their diploma from the Medical Board." He assembled a competent staff, and for a time the school – incorporated in 1851 as the Toronto School of Medicine – flourished.

Meanwhile, Rolph had reappeared as a controversial figure in the public prints. In April 1848 the government of Robert Baldwin and Louis-Hippolyte LA FONTAINE dismissed Dr Walter Telfer, the medical superintendent of the Provincial Lunatic Asylum in Toronto, and replaced him with Dr George Hamilton Park, a brother-in-law of Rolph. There were adequate reasons for the dismissal and Park appears to have been suitably qualified for the post, but in a small community intensely interested in patronage and riddled with personal animosities, the incident became the centre of bitter partisan recriminations in the newspapers. Matters were intensified when Rolph, serving as acting superintendent in Park's absence, clashed with the asylum's board of commissioners. Personal relations between Baldwin and Rolph had never been fully restored after the flag of truce incident, and supporters of Baldwin saw Rolph's actions in a sinister light. James Hervey Price* called him "a black hearted rascal," determined "either to destroy the Baldwin ministry or to compel that ministry to alter the Bill for the Lunatic Asylum giving all power to Park that Rolph and his medical School might rule it for the School's benefit." The rift was widened when the Baldwin government dismissed Park in January 1849.

This incident coincided with a deepening split in the Reform party, as its radical or "democratic" wing (coming to be called the Clear Grits) became increasingly impatient with the Baldwin government's moderate and cautious policies. By-elections from 1849 to 1851 marked the growing strength of this group and in the fall of the latter year the tired and discouraged Baldwin resigned. It fell to Francis Hincks to reconstruct the Upper Canadian portion of the government and he decided that party harmony dictated the inclusion of two Clear Grits in the cabinet. The man above all others whom the Grits wanted included was Rolph.

Why they wanted him is less clear. As so often it is uncertain what part Rolph had played in the rise of the Clear Grits, although he was accused of writing anonymous anti-Baldwin articles in the *Examiner*. Perhaps the Clear Grits simply wanted a spokesman in the cabinet who was a powerful orator and who had been identified with Reform principles for more than a quarter-century. The *Examiner* asserted, "There is not a man in the entire ranks of our party whom the tories dread half as much as Dr. Rolph." In fact, however, as the *Globe* noted in November, Hincks had made a master stroke. Once two of their number (Malcolm Cameron* was the other) had accepted the responsibilities of office, the Clear Grits were bottled up and rendered ineffective.

Rolph was appointed commissioner of crown lands when the government of Hincks and Augustin-Norbert MORIN took office on 28 Oct. 1851. Governor General Lord Elgin [BRUCE], perhaps worried that the colonial secretary might query the inclusion in the government of one "whose conduct in 1837 was not above reproach," noted that "He is an Englishman, educated at one of the Universities and has a brother a Rector." Besides, the cry of "rebel" had lost much of its force since the Tory violence of 1849. In the general elections some weeks later, Rolph was a candidate in Norfolk County and was easily elected. In fact, his popularity with Clear Grits was so great that his name was mentioned as a possible candidate in several other constituencies.

The Hincks-Morin government, which held power until September 1854, was not especially distinguished, and Rolph did little to make it more so. He carried on a personal quarrel with his Clear Grit colleague Malcolm Cameron, and he further weakened the morale of the Grits by failing to press within the government for measures to which Grits were committed, including the secularization of the clergy reserves. Rolph developed a considerable talent for disappearing when critical votes were to be taken. He was apparently rather ineffective in the Crown Lands Department and was shifted to the presidency of the council and the Bureau of Agriculture in 1853. One observer felt that as a minister Rolph "showed how little talent he really possessed." By 1853 many Reformers were turning against him because of his continued association with Hincks despite the fact that the latter's railway deals were coming to light. The *Globe* denounced Rolph as "a sleek visaged man . . . deep, dark, designing, cruel, malignant, traitorous . . . [whose] manners are civil and insinuating. . . . It is thought that he is an agile man – he is certainly a slippery one." Hincks, who himself had often enough been the target of the *Globe's* attacks, came to share this harsh assessment when Rolph, dissatisfied with Hincks' policies and wishing to re-establish his standing with independent Reformers, deserted the government in September 1854. The ministry collapsed, and the two men parted amid mutual recriminations.

Three incidents in Rolph's life during the years of the Hincks-Morin government are worth noting. The first was the revival of the flag of truce controversy by a Conservative member from Toronto, William Henry Boulton*. Rolph had apparently been expecting an attack for he had taken the trouble, two months earlier, of securing an affidavit from Hugh Carmichael, who had been the bearer of the flag and was now in Rolph's employ, which completely corroborated Rolph's version: it stated that during the actual mission Rolph did not communicate separately with Lount or say "anything irrelevant to the Flag of Truce or against its good faith." Boulton accepted Rolph's explanations, but another member of the assembly, none other than Mackenzie, felt called upon to defend Lount's memory, and to go back over the whole story, in speeches, editorials, and, finally, a pamphlet. On Rolph's behalf, David GIBSON prepared a reply to Mackenzie, but Rolph did not use it; he wrote to Gibson that "the time has not yet arrived" to "repel" Mackenzie's charges.

The second incident involved that old source of controversy, the lunatic asylum. In 1853 the government, at Rolph's behest, secured the passage of a bill reorganizing the asylum; subsequently Dr Joseph Workman*, an associate of Rolph's, was appointed medical superintendent and another member of Rolph's school was made consulting physician. The reorganization improved the administration of the asylum, but to his critics the whole episode was but another example of Rolph's labyrinthine ways.

The third incident also raised the suspicion that Rolph used his influence in government to serve the interests of his medical school. In these years the legislature was sitting in Quebec, and Rolph was perforce removed from his school. Letters from his staff indicated that it was in a state of decline, unable to meet the competition of the medical faculty of the University of Toronto, and also probably suffering the competition of the recently formed Upper Canada School of Medicine, affiliated with Trinity College. In 1852–53 a bill passed through the legislature reorganizing the university by making it an examining and not a teaching body and thus abolishing instruction in the faculties of medicine and law. Rolph's school was no longer faced with competition from the university.

In the 1854 election following the break-up of the Hincks-Morin ministry, Rolph was re-elected in Norfolk, but he was now in opposition. He remained in the legislature until 1857 but attended infrequently, now more than ever a relic from a former age.

In his last 15 years Rolph resumed his career as a medical administrator, but with limited success. In 1854 the Toronto School of Medicine became affiliated with Victoria College, thus enabling its graduates to secure degrees from that institution, even though the latter was still located in Cobourg. Two years later, however, Rolph's entire staff resigned on the same day to remove themselves from his ineffective and autocratic leadership. They established a rival institution under the old name, and by legal action prevented Rolph from further using that name. Nevertheless, Rolph's students remained loyal to him; he secured new staff and continued as dean of the medical faculty of Victoria College, which conferred an honorary LLD on him in 1859. For the next decade Rolph was still highly regarded as a teacher, and still practised his profession, despite failing powers following a stroke in 1861. He no longer had the capacity to function effectively as dean, but refused to relinquish control. Finally, early in 1870, he was, in effect, forced to retire, and he went to live with his daughter and son-in-law in Perth County, where he died a few months later.

At the time of his death the controversies associated with Rolph's political career had receded into the distant past; there was a general willingness to pay tribute to him as a Reform leader, a medical teacher, and an orator, and to gloss over his weaknesses. But 15 years later dispute again erupted with the publication of the first volume of Dent's *The story of the Upper Canadian rebellion*, which disparaged Mackenzie and praised Rolph. Old Reformers sprang to the defence of Mackenzie, revived all the earlier charges against Rolph as devious, cunning, and self-seeking, and probably helped establish the picture of him that has widely prevailed. Rolph's own habitual secretiveness and the absence of adequate personal papers make it difficult now to draw a full and sympathetic portrait. But his contributions to the emerging reform movement in the 1820s and to medical education over a longer period will continue to be remembered, and the intricacies of his personality will continue to fascinate.

G. M. CRAIG

There are David Gibson papers in the possession of S. E. Gibson, Willowdale, Ont. (mfm. at PAO). Academy of Medicine, Toronto, William Thomas Aikins papers. MTCL, Robert Baldwin papers; William Warren Baldwin papers; J. H. Richardson, Reminiscences of the medical profession in Toronto, 1829–1905 (typescript). PAC, MG 24, B24; B40, J. H. Price to George Brown, 28 Dec. 1848. PAO, Clarke (Charles) papers; Macaulay (John) papers, R. Stanton to J. Macaulay, 21 Jan. 1830; Mackenzie-Lindsey papers. PRO, CO 42/380. Victoria University Library (Toronto), Victoria University records, papers relating to the Medical Department. "Dr. John Rolph's own account of the flag of truce incident in the rebellion of 1837," ed. C. B. Sissons, *CHR*, XIX (1938), 56–59. *Elgin-Grey papers* (Doughty), III, 917. F. B. Head, *A narrative* (London, 1839). [John Rolph], *The speech of the Hon. John Rolph, M.P.P., delivered on the occasion of the late inquiry into charges of high misdemeanors at the late elections, preferred against His Excellency Sir Francis Bond Head . . .* (Toronto, 1837). *Speeches of Dr. John Rolph and Christop'r A. Hagerman ... on the bill for appropriating the proceeds of the clergy reserves to the purposes of general education . . .* (Toronto, 1837). U.C., House of Assembly, *Journal*, 1825–38. *Canadian Freeman* (York [Toronto]), 1825–27. *Colonial Advocate*, 1826–34. *Examiner* (Toronto), 1843–44, 1848. *Globe*, 1848–54. *Long Point Reformer* (Simcoe, [Ont.]), 1853–54. *Mackenzie's Gazette* (New York), 1838. *Mackenzie's Weekly Message* (Toronto), 1852–54, including "extra" issued as *Head's flag of truce, or a defence of the memory of the late Colonel Samuel Lount . . .* ([Toronto, 1854]). *North American* (Toronto), 1850–51. *Simcoe Standard and Agricultural, Commercial, and Literary Gazette* (Simcoe, [Ont.]), 1852.

Canniff, *Medical profession in U.C.* Dent, *Upper Canadian rebellion.* C. O. Ermatinger, *The Talbot regime; or the first half century of the Talbot settlement* (St Thomas, Ont., 1904). [John King], *The other side of the "story," being some reviews of Mr. J. C. Dent's first volume of "The story of the Upper Canadian rebellion," and the letters in the Mackenzie-Rolph controversy . . .* (Toronto, 1886). Lindsey, *Life and times of Mackenzie.* G. M. Craig, "Two contrasting Upper Canadian figures: John Rolph and John Strachan," RSC, *Trans.*, 4th ser., XII (1974), sect.II, 237–48. N. B. Gwyn, "A chapter from the life of John Rolph," Academy of Medicine, Toronto, *Bull.*, IX (1935–36), 137–44. John Muggeridge, "John Rolph – a reluctant rebel," *OH*, LI (1959), 217–29. M. A. Patterson, "The life and times of the Hon. John Rolph, M.D. (1793–1870)," *Medical History* (London), V (1961), 15–33.

ROSS, DUNBAR, lawyer and politician; b. *c.* 1800 in the British Isles; d. 16 May 1865 at Quebec City.

Dunbar Ross immigrated to Canada while still a youth. He was called to the bar of Lower Canada on 2 Feb. 1834 and practised law in Quebec; in 1853 he was appointed a queen's counsel. In November 1843, when there was discontent over the selection of Montreal as capital of the united province, Ross wrote an essay entitled *The seat of government* which pressed Quebec's claims. The essay was considered at

that time a model of its genre in literature. In 1844, under the pseudonym Zeno, Ross published another widely read pamphlet, *The "crise" Metcalfe and the LaFontaine-Baldwin cabinet defended*, in which he whole-heartedly supported the decision of the ministry of Louis-Hippolyte LA FONTAINE and Robert Baldwin* to resign in December 1843 in protest against the policies of Governor Sir Charles Theophilus Metcalfe*. He accused Metcalfe of not consulting with the Executive Council in several official appointments and of usurping the council's power of patronage. The two issues, according to Ross, justified the resignation of the ministry. In the conclusion of his pamphlet, he asked the members of the house to study the constitutionality of Metcalfe's actions and to take action that would prevent the recurrence of similar acts by governors. His literary activity had the effect of bringing him quickly to the attention of both the Canadian public and the government.

Ross, a Reformer, made his direct entry into politics on 1 May 1850 by successfully contesting the riding of Mégantic recently vacated by the resignation of Dominick DALY. Ross continued to represent Mégantic in the Legislative Assembly until 6 Nov. 1851 when he was defeated by Conservative John Greaves Clapham. He contested the result but Clapham's election was upheld. In 1851 Peter Boyle De Blaquière*, a legislative councillor and chancellor of the University of Toronto, remarked in a letter to Lord Elgin [BRUCE] that he would have liked to see Ross chosen as solicitor general for Canada West. The Reform government of Francis Hincks* and Augustin-Norbert MORIN recognized Ross' talents by appointing him solicitor general for Canada East on 31 Aug. 1853 though he was not at that time in the assembly. In 1854 Ross was again returned to the assembly, this time for Beauce County, defeating F.-S.-A. Bélanger. He continued to hold the post of solicitor general in the ministries formed by Allan Napier MACNAB and Morin (1854–55), MacNab and Étienne-Paschal TACHÉ (1855–56), and then Taché and John Alexander Macdonald* (1856–57). The separate schools, seat of government, and double majority questions were all brought up during this period, and Ross republished his essay as *The seat of government of Canada* in 1856, adding to it material on "the Composition and Functions of the Legislative Council, and the 'Double Majority' Question." During his tenure as solicitor general Ross personally administered the crown's business, carrying out his duties with meticulous concern for the gathering of all necessary data. Although his manner was overbearing and somewhat brusque, he had a reputation for leniency and mercy in matters relating to criminal justice.

In 1857 Ross refused an appointment as judge of the district of Gaspé, and in 1858 he was re-elected for Beauce County. Increasingly bad health after 1860, however, made him unable to participate fully in either his political or his professional duties. He consequently retained his seat in the house only until 10 June 1861. Ross was residing in Quebec when he died on 16 May 1865 after suffering for five years from paralysis.

Ross, of whose personal background little is known, had been successful in establishing himself securely in professional and political circles. He was a member of Conservative-led governments, but he never veered from his early Reform principles. Dunbar Ross was remembered for his literary talent, political sense, and public spirit, and for his straightforwardness and sense of justice.

IRENE BILAS

Dunbar Ross, *The seat of government* (Quebec, 1843; 2nd ed., 1856; a French translation, *Le siège du gouvernement provincial* was published at Quebec in 1858); Zeno [Dunbar Ross], *The "crise" Metcalfe and the Lafontaine–Baldwin cabinet defended; letter of Zeno to the Legislative Assembly of Canada* (Quebec, 1844).

Debates of the Legislative Assembly of United Canada, III. *Le Journal de Québec*, 17 mai 1865. *Morning Chronicle* (Quebec), 17 May 1865. *Pilot* (Montreal), 7 Aug. 1850. *Quebec Daily Mercury*, 17 May 1865. Morgan, *Bibliotheca Canadensis. Political appointments, 1841–65* (J.-O. Coté). P.-G. Roy, *Les avocats de la région de Québec*, 383. Chapais, *Hist. du Canada*, V. Cornell, *Alignment of political groups*. Dent, *Last forty years*, II, 278–79. "Les disparus," *BRH*, XXXV (1929), 178. "L'honorable Dunbar Ross," *BRH*, XLII (1936), 89.

ROSS, Sir JAMES CLARK, explorer; b. 15 April 1800, possibly in Scotland, third son of George Ross and Christian Clark; d. 3 April 1862 in Aylesbury, England.

James Clark Ross' father, a London businessman, came from an eminent Wigtownshire family and was an older brother of Sir John Ross*, the distinguished Arctic explorer. James' early life came under his uncle's influence. Ten days before his 12th birthday he followed Commander John Ross, then a dashing young officer serving in the Napoleonic wars, into the Royal Navy and thus found his life-long career. He began as a first-class volunteer on *Briseis*, but obviously John, who was well connected in the navy, looked after his nephew's welfare, for he re-ceived quick promotions to midshipman and master's mate on the same vessel. Ross served continuously for six years with his uncle, and moved with him when the latter took command of *Actaeon* for service in the Baltic, the White Sea, and the English Channel, and then of *Driver* for service on the west coast of Scotland. It was while he was on *Driver* that John Ross was invited on 11 Dec. 1817 by his friend Sir George Hope, first lord of the Admiralty, to take command of an Arctic expedition to search for a northwest passage from Baffin Bay to Bering Strait. This invitation changed the lives of both Rosses; they were no longer typical career officers but polar explorers.

James Clark Ross, at 18, thus gained his first Arctic experience as a midshipman serving with his uncle in the 1818 search. The expedition's two ships *Isabella* and *Alexander* sailed from the Thames in April, with John Ross' second-in-command being Lieutenant William Edward Parry*, captain of the latter vessel. The well-equipped expedition was to enter Davis Strait, make observations on the currents, and sail north and west as far as the ice would allow. After taking his ships up the west Greenland coast, John Ross penetrated to the head of Baffin Bay. He observed the entrance of Smith Sound and, turning down the western shore of the bay, also saw the entrance of Jones Sound. Neither had been seen since William Baffin* named them; both were ice filled and Ross considered them dead ends. When the ships arrived off Lancaster Sound, however, the passage was clear and he sailed west until he seemed to see a range of mountains (he named them Croker's Mountains) blocking his way. He turned back and by mid November the *Isabella* and *Alexander* were once more in the Thames. James C. Ross had taken an active part in the many scientific observations made on this voyage, working especially closely with Captain Edward Sabine*, a supernumerary.

John Ross' quick return was severely criticized and the controversy set off by his expedition lasted for years. Ross never commanded another government expedition. The Admiralty had nevertheless immediately fitted out two stout bomb vessels, the *Hecla* and *Griper*, for another expedition, to be commanded by Parry. James C. Ross received an appointment as midshipman in *Hecla*.

The ships sailed in May 1819. After getting as far north as Sanderson's Hope on the Greenland coast, Parry turned west and forced a passage to the mouth of Lancaster Sound. There was clear sailing westward and Croker's Mountains proved to be a mirage. Coming to Prince Regent Inlet, which he named, Parry took time to push 120 miles down that waterway before continuing westward through Barrow Strait. Again James C. Ross was active making observations and Parry named one of the promontories of Melville Island Cape James Ross. The remarkable westward progress was halted at 112° 51′ and Parry turned back to an anchorage at Melville Island.

The long cold winter of 1819–20 was enlivened by the publication of a shipboard paper called the *North Georgia Gazette and Winter Chronicle* and by a series of theatrical productions. In these Ross and the other young midshipmen usually played the female parts. In the spring Ross got his first taste of sledging when Melville Island was crossed and surveyed. As soon as the ships were free from the ice on 1 August the expedition set sail and by early November Parry was back in London. His was the most successful of all the early 19th century Arctic expeditions for he had sailed halfway through the northwest passage. James C. Ross had spent his first winter in the Arctic, and it was only a beginning.

In May 1821 Ross accompanied Parry's next expedition, in *Hecla* and *Fury*, westward through Hudson Bay, still as a midshipman. He took an especially active part in the land surveys on this expedition, which spent two winters, the first at Winter Island and the second at Igloolik Island near the eastern end of Fury and Hecla Strait. He also served as naturalist, collecting birds, mammals, marine life, and plants. During the second winter he collected the first recorded specimen of the beautiful Ross's Gull. Fury and Hecla Strait was surveyed by land and Parry saw the opening at its western end into what is now called the Gulf of Boothia. The expedition returned home in the fall of 1823 and Ross learned that he had been promoted lieutenant on 26 Dec. 1822. His efforts as a naturalist were rewarded by his election as a fellow of the Linnean Society.

Parry's third expedition, in 1824–25, with the same two ships, was a disaster. Ross sailed this time as 2nd lieutenant in the *Fury* commanded by Henry Parkyns Hoppner. Davis Strait was reached in mid July, but it took all summer to cross Baffin Bay to Lancaster Sound and enter Prince Regent Inlet; Parry wintered on its eastern shore. Parry was not well and he relied heavily on the hard-working Ross for much of the scientific work. Ross continued his taxidermy, tested the thickness of saltwater ice, recorded temperatures, made magnetic and lunar observations, checked longitudes, and went on land excursions.

Summer freed the ships and Parry crossed over to the western side of the inlet. There, at the foot of an enormous precipice on Somerset Island, *Fury* was forced aground on 1 August at a place ever since called Fury Beach. Parry decided not to risk another winter in the Arctic with his crippled expedition; he was back in England on 12 Oct. 1825. James Ross had now spent every summer since 1818 in the Arctic and had wintered there four times.

After enjoying a summer out of the Arctic, Ross was made second in command of Parry's expedition to reach the North Pole. It was to reach the Pole by going north from Spitzbergen dragging boats on sledges over the ice in preparation for navigating the mythical "Open Polar Sea." *Hecla* again was commissioned and sailed on 4 March 1827. On 21 June the boats left the ship and after a 100-mile sail the long journey over the ice began. It proved impossible. Not only were the trudging men plagued by wretched travelling conditions – fog, rain, and sun softened the snow so that pulling sledges loaded with 200 pounds per man was nearly impossible – but the ice was moving south under them. For every ten miles they laboriously dragged the sledges only four miles were gained. They never reached 83°. Parry became snowblind and Ross was severely injured when squeezed between a boat and an icy hummock. On 26 July, after finding they had gained only one mile in five days, Parry turned back. Their farthest north was a little beyond 82° 45′, a record that lasted until 1875 but still 500 miles from the North Pole. Parry left the ship when it reached the Orkneys and Ross brought her into the Thames on 6 October.

James Clark Ross was now the most active experienced officer in Arctic matters in the Royal Navy, Parry having retired to become the Admiralty's hydrographer. Ross was a fine seaman, an authority on magnetism, and a good naturalist and taxidermist. He was rewarded with a commission as commander on 8 Nov. 1827, but without an appointment and on half pay. In 1829 he was still on half pay when his uncle Captain John Ross was preparing his privately financed expedition to attempt the northwest passage in the sidewheeler *Victory*. With a tender named the *Krusenstern* in tow, *Victory* sailed from Scotland on 13 June 1829. After an extended stop on the west coast of Greenland, Captain Ross crossed Baffin Bay and in August entered Lancaster Sound, then Prince Regent Inlet. The wreck of the *Fury* provided ample supplies of all kinds.

By the end of September it was impossible to go any farther south and the *Victory* was laid up in an anchorage named Felix Harbour. During the winter James C. Ross made a series of sledge journeys exploring the shore, which proved that Boothia was a peninsula as the Inuit (Eskimos) had told them and not an island as John Ross had hoped. James crossed what is now called James Ross Strait, and discovered and named Matty Island and Cape Felix. His farthest westward was Victory Point where the coastline turned. This part of the coast he named King William Land assuming it was part of the mainland – actually he was on King William Island.

Ice prevented the return of the *Victory* in the summer of 1830 and it was possible to move her only a few miles north of Felix Harbour, to an anchorage the party called Sheriff Harbour. Again she was roofed over and an observatory erected. The second winter's routine was like the first, but John Ross discovered he could keep his men free from scurvy if they ate an Inuit diet: plenty of fat. As spring approached James C. Ross began his sledging journeys again. His objective was to locate the North Magnetic Pole, which he did at eight in the morning of 1 June 1831. He set up the British flag, took possession of the North Magnetic Pole and adjoining territory in the name of King William IV, and erected a cairn. The location was established as latitude 70° 5′ 17″ north and longitude 96° 46′ 45″ west (the pole has since moved farther north and west). Ross returned to the *Victory* on 13 June after an absence of 28 days.

Again that summer the ship remained locked in the ice and could only be moved to another anchorage, named Victory Harbour (Victoria Harbour). During the interminable months of this third winter John Ross decided to abandon the ship as soon as the weather moderated, load boats and provisions on sledges, and go back to Fury Beach. James C. Ross was a tower of strength in this endeavour. The expedition was, however, forced to spend a fourth winter on Prince Regent Inlet. A lane of water finally opened up on 14 Aug. 1833, and on the 26th the expedition was picked up by a whaler in Baffin Bay. The Rosses, who had spent an unprecedented four and a half years in the Arctic, were received by William IV upon their return. James C. Ross was assigned to *Victory* at Portsmouth and on 28 Oct. 1834 received his well-deserved promotion to post-captain. He was voted the thanks of the Common Council of London and presented with a piece of silver plate from the subscribers of the Arctic Land Expedition (one of the groups organizing to rescue the Rosses if they had not returned).

In 1835 James C. Ross was ordered, as one of Britain's leading authorities on terrestrial magnetism, to conduct the first systematic magnetic survey of the British Isles. This survey lasted until 1838 but was interrupted in December 1835 when Ross was detached to take command of *Cove* to go to the relief of 11 whaling ships frozen in Davis Strait. He sailed in January 1836, but most of the whalers got back on their own before he returned to the survey in August. He had now spent eight winters and 15 navigation seasons in the Arctic regions, an unequalled record. He was offered a knighthood for his distinguished service, but for some reason refused it.

His experience in ice-filled seas and his knowledge of terrestrial magnetism made him the logical choice for commander of an Antarctic expedition to study this magnetism in extreme southern latitudes; the voyage was strongly supported by the British Association for the Advancement of Science and the Royal Society of London. In two strong bomb vessels, *Erebus* and *Terror*, Ross sailed for the southern hemisphere in September 1839. He spent the next three years there making geographical and magnetic observations and returning to Van Diemen's Land (Tasmania) and Australia during the winter. He discovered Victoria Land, McMurdo Sound, the Ross Sea, and the great Ross Ice Barrier, and added many lesser features to the map. The successful expedition returned home in September 1843. Ross now accepted a knighthood and married Ann Coulman on 18 Oct. 1843 in Wadworth. During five years of private family life in Aylesbury Ross, although not a fluent writer, wrote *A voyage of discovery and research in the southern and Antarctic regions during the years 1839–43*, one of the most important books ever written on the Antarctic.

When Ross married he had pledged himself not to take any further polar voyages. His wife released him, however, in 1848, when he was asked to command the first expedition to search for Sir John Franklin*. He sailed on this errand of mercy on 12 May 1848, in command of *Enterprise* and *Investigator*. Among his officers were two men who would become leaders in the next generation of Arctic explorers: Robert John LeMesurier McClure*, who later proved the existence of the northwest passage, and Francis Leopold M'Clintock*, who eventually found the remains of the Franklin expedition. Ross searched north into Wellington Channel and wintered his ships (his ninth and last winter in the Arctic) in Leopold Harbour at the northeast corner of Somerset Island. From here he surveyed the shores of Peel Sound, but found no trace of Franklin. During the summer his ships were carried out into Baffin Bay and in September were released from the ice. They were paid off at Woolwich on 26 November 1849. Although he had surveyed another 150 miles of unknown coast, the expedition failed in its main purpose.

Ross now lived quietly, enjoying the company of his wife and four children in Aylesbury. In 1856 he was made a rear-admiral. The next year Lady Ross died and Sir James never recovered from the shock.

ERNEST S. DODGE

[There are letters of James Clark Ross in the PRO, the Royal Geographical Soc., and the Scott Polar Research Institute (Cambridge, Eng.). Ross' great-granddaughter, Miss Esther Ross of London, also has some letters, but apparently most of his papers and diaries were burned. E.S.D.]

J. C. Ross, "On the position of the North Magnetic Pole," Royal Soc. of London, *Philosophical Trans.*, CXXIV (1834), 47–52; *A voyage of discovery and research in the southern and Antarctic regions during the years 1839–43* (2v., London, 1847). John Ross, *Narrative of a second voyage in search of a north-west passage, and of a residence in the Arctic regions during the years 1829, 1830, 1831, 1832, 1833 . . . including the reports of Commander . . . J. C. Ross, and the discovery of the Northern Magnetic Pole* (1st ed., London, [1834]; 2nd ed., 1835); *A voyage of discovery, made under the orders of the Admiralty, in his majesty's ships Isabella and Alexander, for the purpose of exploring Baffin's Bay, and inquiring into the probability of a north-west passage* (London, 1819). *DNB*. E. S. Dodge, *The polar Rosses: John and James Clark Ross and their explorations* (London, 1973).

ROW, WILLIAM BICKFORD, merchant, lawyer, politician, and office-holder; b. 3 Oct. 1786 at Torquay, Devon, England, son of John and Betty Row; d. 29 July 1865 in Taunton, Somerset, England.

John Row was a Torquay merchant engaged in trade between England and Newfoundland until 1811. The date of William Bickford Row's arrival in Newfoundland is unknown, but by 1804 he was agent at St John's for the English merchant, William Bickford. In 1809 Row joined his brother John in representing the firm of John Hill and Company of London and St John's, which carried on a wholesale-retail trade, supplying provisions for the fisheries. It was declared insolvent in 1811. The two brothers then became joint agents for administering the firm's debts, a function which W. B. Row continued until 1816. In May of that year he went into the supplying trade on his own account with a store in St John's. In this period of depression following the Napoleonic wars Row's enterprise does not appear to have prospered. On 15 May 1818 he entered a five-year partnership with William Vallance of Newton Abbot, Devon, with Row acting as the Newfoundland representative of the company.

In December 1823 Row began a long relationship with the newly organized St John's Commercial Society and its executive body, the Chamber of Commerce, when he was elected secretary-treasurer. The Commercial Society repeatedly elected him to the Chamber of Commerce. One of the half-dozen most prominent officers of the society, he became its legal representative in later years.

Row's legal career began in 1826 when he was one of the first lawyers to sign the barristers' roll of the reconstituted Supreme Court of Newfoundland. In 1834 he was elected first treasurer of the Law Society of Newfoundland. He maintained a successful practice until the early 1850s.

With his growing public prominence Row was soon involved in island politics. In 1832 he contested the first election for the assembly under representative government as one of three candidates for the three-seat district of St John's. Despite support from the St John's commercial community, the unfavourable results of the first day's voting persuaded Row to retire from the contest. Two years later he was returned to the house in a by-election for Trinity Bay in the place of John Bingley Garland, who had been appointed to the Council. He was again returned in 1836 and 1837 for Fortune Bay. Row was a Conservative, voting with such members as Robert Carter* and Newman W. Hoyles* and opposing Reformers such as William Carson* and John Kent*.

In February 1841 Row was appointed to the Council by Lieutenant Governor Henry Prescott*. When the existing form of government was suspended several months later and all legislative authority placed in an amalgamated legislature, Row became one of the ten appointed members of the new house. He also remained in the Executive Council. In the amalgamated house Row voted with his fellow appointed legislative councillors and the elected Protestant Conservative members, under the leadership of Attorney General James SIMMS. In 1844 Row introduced a bill to incorporate a second bank in St John's, the Bank of Newfoundland, in which he was one of the principal shareholders [see Laurence O'BRIEN].

In 1848 the Legislative Council and the assembly were again separated. Retaining his seat on the council, Row continued to support a conservative policy in such matters as redistribution of seats in the assembly, on which would depend control of the house in the approaching era of responsible government. In the debates on education in 1852 Row was particularly prominent, presenting petitions and defending the position of the Church of England leaders, Bishop Edward Feild* and Archdeacon Thomas Finch Hobday Bridge*, on the division of Protestant education funds with the Methodists. Row also fought to prevent the erosion of Anglican pre-eminence in the most lucrative public offices. In these debates he had the support of the Anglican majority in the council. In 1854 Row joined Edward Mortimer Archibald* and Hugh William Hoyles* in presenting the council's case to Colonial Secretary Sir George Grey against a hasty grant of responsible government.

Row's public career ended in 1855 when he had to resign along with the other appointed officeholders to make way for the new age of an executive responsible to the assembly. During his last years, Row retired to Devon. He died in 1865.

DAVID J. DAVIS

Memorial University of Newfoundland, Maritime History Group Archives (St John's), Row file. Nfld, House of Assembly, *Journal*, 1834–36, 1844; Legislative Council, *Journals*, 1853–54. *Newfoundlander*, 20 Sept. 1832. *Newfoundland Mercantile Journal* (St John's), 1816–27. *Public Ledger*, 14 Feb. 1851. *Royal Gazette* (St John's), 11 Oct. 1811, 4 Jan. 1816, 29 Aug. 1865. Greene, "Influence of religion in the politics of Nfld, 1850–61." Prowse, *History of Nfld* (1895), 421–80. R. W. Bartlett, "The legal profession in Newfoundland," *The book of Newfoundland*, ed. J. R. Smallwood (4v., St John's, 1937–67), III, 519–27.

RYAN, JOHN B., shipowner and Patriote; b. 1792 in St John's, Nfld; d. 13 Feb. 1863 in Quebec City.

About 1822 or 1823 John B. Ryan came to Quebec City where he engaged mainly in the steamship business on the St Lawrence. He made an important contribution to the improvement of travel on the river with the creation of a "People's Line" which, running in successful competition to the first established steamboats on the St Lawrence, particularly those of the Molsons, brought about a reduction in the cost of passenger travel. Quebec being at that time Canada's principal seaport, where many of the thousands of immigrants who landed every summer sought passage to Montreal, there was scope for business competition. Ryan also became one of the vibrant group of Irish in the trades and in commerce who were building for themselves a place in the political life of the city. A respected businessman, he was frequently called upon by friends and acquaintances to act for them as attorney or agent in money matters.

In politics Ryan was a reformer. As early as 1832, he wanted the recall of the governor general, Lord Aylmer [Whitworth-Aylmer*], and the institution of a civil governor for Canada. Ryan's circle of friends included members of the Patriote party such as Dr Edmund Bailey O'Callaghan*, Michael Connolly, and John Teed; he corresponded with Ludger Duvernay* before, during, and after the rebellion, acting as his agent in Quebec City. As a result of his activities, Ryan was forced to flee to the United States in 1837, along with his son John. He took up residence first in Vermont, living at one time or another in Chelsea or in Montpelier, and corresponded with rebel leaders in the United States; in January 1838 he offered to purchase guns, powder, and shot in Chelsea "to further the Sacred Cause . . . of opposing British misrule and British oppression in our native Country." He and his son John also tried to obtain printing supplies for Ludger Duvernay, then in Swanton, Vt. His first attempt to return to Canada in the spring of 1838 was blocked. In 1839 he was apparently living in New York City, for a son was born there that year. By 1844, however, he was back in Quebec City, and he was listed in a directory as agent for the steamship *Charlevoix* which he also owned.

The census of 1851 shows John Ryan and his Newfoundland-born wife, Deborah, as having a son and a daughter born in Quebec, as well as the son born in New York City; no mention is made of John Jr. It also stated "No religion" for Mr Ryan and Protestant for Mrs Ryan.

When John Ryan died in Quebec City, at the age of 71, obituary notices in rival papers either praised his noblemindedness (according to the *Quebec Daily Mercury* he had been "indifferent to money and devoted to projects of a public character") or condemned his political and religious ideas, but could agree that "Mr. Ryan lived long enough to witness the elevation of almost every one of his companions in trouble without sharing in their prosperity."

MARIANNA O'GALLAGHER

ANQ-Q, AP-G-68, nos.149, 159, 375, 544; Greffe de Louis Panet, 4 févr. 1837, 13 août 1842, 24 juin 1848. PAC, RG 31, 1851 census, Quebec (mfm. at ANQ-Q). "Papiers de Ludger Duvernay," *Canadian Antiquarian and Numismatic Journal* (Montreal), 3rd ser., V (1908), 167–68; VI (1909), 7–9, 108. *Morning Chronicle* (Quebec), 13 Feb. 1863. *Quebec Daily Mercury*, 14 Feb. 1863. Fauteux, *Patriotes*, 58. *Quebec directory*, 1844–45. *Quebec pocket almanac . . .*, 1849.

S

SABATIER, CHARLES. *See* WUGK, CHARLES-DÉSIRÉ-JOSEPH

SABREVOIS DE BLEURY, CLÉMENT-CHARLES, lawyer and politician; b. 28 Oct. 1798 at William Henry (Sorel, Que.), youngest son of Clément Sabrevois de Bleury, a soldier, and Amelia Bowers, daughter of a Halifax half-pay officer; d. 15 Sept. 1862 in his manor-house at Saint-Vincent-de-Paul (Laval), near Montreal.

Descended from a military family linked by marriage to Pierre Boucher*, Sieur de Grosbois, Clément-Charles was the last Sabrevois to bear the name Bleury. He spent his childhood at William Henry, where in 1800 and 1801 his father was commandant. He was brought up in a conservative Anglican milieu, where the dominant values were service to the king, parliamentary freedoms, and the interests of empire. From 1809 to 1815 he studied at the Collège de Montréal, then took legal training under his brother-in-law, Basile-Benjamin Trottier Desrivières-Beaubien, and was called to the bar in November 1819. Sabrevois de Bleury soon acquired a reputation as a sound legal practitioner, and won over Montreal's high society by his charm, elegant manners, and refined style of living. His family background and his skill in arms gained him a commission, on 29 Jan. 1825, as lieutenant in the 3rd Battalion of Montreal militia, and enabled him to rise quickly in the militia. On 24 Nov. 1830 he was promoted captain in the Chasseurs Canadiens; on 22 April 1838 he became a major and on 7 July 1848 he was appointed lieutenant-colonel commanding the Montreal Rifles.

Possibly at the Collège de Montréal, or through regular contact with members of the professions, Sabrevois de Bleury gradually discovered a "Canadian identity" which led him to embrace the Patriotes' cause. In July 1832, yielding to the party's pressing requests, he stood as a candidate for the assembly in Richelieu, following the resignation of François-Roch de Saint-Ours. He was then 33, and possessed all he required to win a resounding victory: a distinguished name, a reputation as a brilliant lawyer, the Patriote party's support. On 8 August he was returned by acclamation. In the house, Sabrevois followed Louis-Joseph Papineau*'s lead. He voted in favour of the expulsion of Dominique MONDELET in 1832 and for the 92 Resolutions in 1834, branding John Neilson* a turncoat because he opposed each of the resolutions. Like many other MHAs, Sabrevois de Bleury believed that political strategy by itself could overcome England's hesitation. But, also like many others, he had to change his view. From 1835 the prospect of armed resistance, the normal outcome of a strategy of "all or nothing," was taking shape and weakening the bonds of solidarity linking the heterogeneous elements of the Patriote party. The crisis occurred at the opening of the 1835 session, after the reply to the speech from the throne reiterated the party's firm positions: Sabrevois de Bleury followed the representatives from the Quebec region who rallied to the more moderate Elzéar Bédard*. Disturbed by England's concessions, and annoyed by the insulting campaign conducted against him in *La Minerve* and in his constituency by the Montreal radicals, Sabrevois de Bleury in a further step went firmly over to the government side. Twice in 1836 he fought a duel in defence of his honour, which had been scurrilously attacked first by Ludger Duvernay*, the owner of *La Minerve*, and then by Charles-Ovide Perrault*, the Patriote representative for Vaudreuil. The rupture was total and conspicuous. On 6 July 1837 Sabrevois de Bleury agreed to be vice-chairman of a gathering of the governor's supporters at which George MOFFATT presided.

Sabrevois de Bleury was not the stuff of which rebels are made. He was then nearly 40. He had a farm of 416 acres on the banks of the Rivière des Prairies and he liked to retire to the spacious manor-house crowned by his family's coat of arms which he had built there. He had also inherited part of the seigneury of Boucherville. At Montreal he had an apartment and a law office, and he lived lavishly, riding and fencing, keeping his own carriage, and associating with the last of the French nobility as well as with the important English businessmen who were well on their way up the social ladder. He readily accepted the invitation of the governor, Lord Gosford [Acheson*], to sit on the Legislative Council, serving as a member from 22 Aug. 1837 until its dissolution in 1838.

Sabrevois de Bleury had not been able to identify himself for long with either the habitants or the professional élite. He appeared more at home with Montreal's British Tories. In April 1837, he, Léon Gosselin, and others had founded *Le Populaire*, a newspaper promoting moderation and prudence. In that year he commanded the escort that took the political prisoners to the new prison in Montreal. In June 1839 he composed a reply to Papineau, who had attempted to justify his actions in "Histoire de l'insurrection du Canada," published in the Paris weekly *Revue du progrès politique, social et littéraire*. Signed Sabrevois de Bleury, the *Réfutation de l'écrit de Louis-Joseph Papineau*, an indictment of 136 pages, was probably dictated by Sabrevois and drafted by Hyacinthe-Poirier LEBLANC de Marconnay, the editor of *Le Populaire*. In this pamphlet Sabrevois de Bleury developed the argument that Papineau had "prepared, wanted, and even foreseen armed resistance," and must now accept responsibility for the country's misfortunes. A well-written piece enlivened with pungent judgements on men and events, this now forgotten pamphlet created a great stir in its day. Scandalmongers asserted that the signatory owed to it his appointment on 20 June 1839 as a member of the new Board of Works, and the following year his nomination by Governor General Sydenham [Thomson*] as alderman for the town council of Montreal, a post he held until 1845, and again in 1847. But the council, which was controlled by the Reform party, refused to choose him as mayor in 1842.

As a supporter of the Montreal Tory party, Sabrevois de Bleury made an ostentatious return to the political scene at the time of the political crisis created by Governor Charles Theophilus Metcalfe*'s personal government. He sided with Denis-Benjamin VIGER, and in the elections of November 1844 was returned for the county of Montreal with his friend George Moffatt. But he was not an unconditional government supporter. In 1845 he voted for Allan Napier MACNAB as speaker and for Denis-Benjamin Viger's motion to repeal the clause in the Act of Union forbidding the use of French in the legislature; in 1846, however, he opposed the use of the income from the Jesuit estates for the creation of a system of primary schools, preferring to back the bishops who wanted to use the income to found a university.

Sabrevois de Bleury soon realized that the support he had given the triumvirate of William Henry Draper*, Viger, and Denis-Benjamin Papineau* had discredited him forever in French circles. In 1847 he settled in his manor-house at Saint-Vincent-de-Paul, launching a programme to enlarge and improve the property. He was not a candidate in the 1847–48 elections. In 1849 he let himself be persuaded by his friend Moffatt to sign the Annexation Manifesto; then in 1854, for an unknown reason, he ran for election in the constituency of Laval, not supporting any party. He suffered the most bitter defeat in Canadian political history – he did not receive a single vote.

This staggering blow was the signal for his final retirement from public life.

On 16 Jan. 1823, at Saint-Roch-de-l'Achigan, Sabrevois de Bleury had married Marie-Élisabeth-Alix, daughter of Barthélémy Rocher, a merchant and lieutenant-colonel; they had no children. At his death, sheriff Louis-Tancrède Bouthillier, a nephew by marriage, bought the heavily mortaged manor-house.

IN COLLABORATION

[C.-C.] Sabrevois de Bleury, *Réfutation de l'écrit de Louis Joseph Papineau, ex-orateur de la chambre d'Assemblée du Bas-Canada, intitulé "Histoire de l'insurrection du Canada," publiée dans le recueil hebdomadaire "La Revue du progrès," imprimée à Paris* (Montréal, 1839).

Archives judiciaires, Richelieu (Sorel, Qué.), Registre d'état civil, Saint-Pierre (Sorel), 28 oct. 1798. Archives paroissiales, Saint-Roch-de-l'Achigan (Qué.), Registres des baptêmes, mariages et sépultures, 16 janv. 1823. PAC, MG 30, D62, 6, pp.71–186. *Le Populaire* (Montréal), 10 avril 1837–3 nov. 1838. F.-J. Audet, *Les députés de Montréal*, 249–75. Monet, *Last cannon shot*. É.-Z. Massicotte, "Les Sabrevois, Sabrevois de Sermonville et Sabrevois de Bleury," *BRH*, XXXI (1925), 133–37, 185–87.

SAINTE-ÉLISABETH, MARIE-LOUISE DORVAL, *dite*. *See* DORVAL

SAINTE-MADELEINE, MARIE-CATHERINE HUOT, *dite*. *See* HUOT

SAINT-GERMAIN, JEAN-BAPTISTE (sometimes written **Saint-Germain**, *dit* **Gautier**, but he signed Saint-Germain), secular priest; b. 1 April 1788 at Sainte-Famille-de-Boucherville (Boucherville, Que.), son of Jean-Baptiste Saint-Germain and Amable Sénécalle; d. 3 Dec. 1863 at Saint-Laurent, Montreal Island, Canada East.

Jean-Baptiste Saint-Germain attended the Collège de Montréal from 1798 to 1806. After completing his theological studies, he was ordained priest on 15 Sept. 1811. He was curate of the parish of Notre-Dame at Montreal for five years, then in 1816 took over the parish of Sainte-Anne-des-Plaines. In 1818 he became parish priest of Saint-Louis-de-Terrebonne.

From 1821 Saint-Germain became involved with the religious dispute centring on the role of the Séminaire de Saint-Sulpice in the town and district of Montreal. The French members of the seminary were fiercely resisting the establishment of an episcopate in Montreal which would put an end to the Sulpicians' traditional place and threaten their property. Saint Germain subscribed to the views of this group. As early as 1822, the assistant of Bishop Joseph-Octave Plessis* of Quebec in Montreal, Bishop Jean-Jacques Lartigue*, suspected Saint-Germain, along with Augustin Chaboillez*, the parish priest of Longueuil, and François-Xavier Pigeon, the parish priest of Saint-Jean-François-Régis (Saint-Philippe-de-Laprairie), of being members of a coterie that had circulated a petition by the priests of the diocese of Montreal against this establishment. In December 1828 Saint-Germain was one of the few priests of the district who refused to sign the petition against the transfer of the seigneurial rights and duties of Saint-Sulpice to the government, which the seminary desired. To protect its interests, the seminary attempted to have Saint-Germain appointed to the episcopate. On 25 Feb. 1833 he was appointed coadjutor to the bishop of Quebec by the Congregation of the Propaganda, but Gregory XVI never ratified the appointment. In March 1836, through the influence of Jean-Baptiste Thavenet*, the Sulpicians' agent in Rome, he ran unsuccessfully for the coadjutorship of the new diocese of Montreal. In 1842 Ignace Bourget*, who had become bishop of Montreal, still counted him among the episcopate's opponents. But the battle had lost its significance, and Saint-Germain took no further part in the disputes between the seminary and the bishop. He devoted his energies instead to reviving religious practice in the parish of Saint-Laurent; he had been its priest since 1829.

The crisis that had set Bishop Lartigue against the seminary had convinced the latter that it must protect its property by displaying unswerving loyalty. Since he shared the interests of the seminary, Saint-Germain found himself siding politically with the government's allies, who were strongly biased against the French Canadian lower bourgeoisie and its aspirations to national leadership. From 1834 on, he denounced the manœuvres of the "so-called Patriotes" and hoped for an episcopal pronouncement against their liberalism, which, through the 92 Resolutions, was spreading among the inhabitants. In November 1837 he refused to sign the clergy's petition to the government since, on the basis of his royalist theology, he approved its rigorous intervention. Yet the prevailing panic of the time appears in the notion, held by the entourage of Bishop Lartigue in November 1838, that the parish priest of Saint-Laurent would shortly be imprisoned for having supported the Patriotes. He was in fact appointed army chaplain in December 1839 as a reward for his steadfast opposition to the advocates of insubordination and revolution, with whom some of the clergy (includ-

ing Lartigue himself, Saint-Germain at one time claimed) were in sympathy.

At the height of the crisis, Saint-Germain, although leaning towards the ultra-loyalism of the Gallican party (the seminary), nevertheless showed keen interest in the new Italian liturgy and the most recent pastoral trends in France. In 1837 he had requested that a Way of the Cross be set up in his parish church, as well as an altar to Ste Philomène, the object of a rapidly developing popular cult. In the pastoral field, his ideas were similar to those of Bishop Bourget. He took part in the great preaching tour of Bishop Forbin-Janson*, and even prepared for the establishment of French missionaries in his parish, a plan that Bishop Bourget did not succeed in implementing during his trip to Europe in 1841. In addition, from 1845 on, Saint-Germain took steps to bring teaching brothers to Saint-Laurent. These negotiations bore fruit in May 1847 with the arrival of eight brothers, four sisters, and two priests of the Congregation of the Holy Cross, whom Saint-Germain supported financially, particularly in the founding of the Académie Industrielle (1849), which became the Collège de Saint-Laurent in 1861.

L. ROUSSEAU

AAQ, 12A, F, 165, 184; G, 196, 226v; 210A, XII, 434, 501, 511; XIII, 426, 502; XIV, 10, 13, 20, 86, 98, 310; XV, 266, 291, 420; XVI, 80, 394. ACAM, RLB, 1–12; RLL, 1–9; 355.105; 420.013. Archives de l'évêché de Saint-Jérôme (Saint-Jérôme, Qué.), 332.182 (1810–29), dossier Saint-Germain. ASSM, 11, tiroir 47; 27, tiroirs 95–97. Lemieux, L'établissement de la première prov. eccl. Pouliot, Mgr Bourget, I, 94, 127–28, 190. Rumilly, Hist. de Montréal, II. Sainte-Croix au Canada, 1847–1947 (Montréal, 1947), 39–40, 50–51, 53, 55–56, 58, 61–62, 64, 74, 125, 158, 201, 524–25, 533, 591.

ST PAUL. *See* LOLO, JEAN-BAPTISTE

SALABERRY (Irumberry de Salaberry), MELCHIOR-ALPHONSE DE, soldier, lawyer, and politician; b. 19 May 1813 at Saint-Jean-François-Régis (Saint-Philippe-de-Laprairie), Lower Canada, son of Lieutenant-Colonel Charles-Michel d'Irumberry* de Salaberry, the "victor of Châteauguay," and Marie-Anne-Julie, daughter of Jean-Baptiste-Melchior Hertel* de Rouville, legislative councillor; d. 27 March 1867 at Quebec.

Melchior-Alphonse de Salaberry was offered responsible and prestigious posts when he was very young because of his father's renown and the good name enjoyed in government circles by the families from which he was descended. Indeed he was barely 16 when his mother declined on his behalf the invitation of Lord Aylmer [Whitworth-Aylmer*] that he assume a rank in the army. Five years later, on 14 Aug. 1834, he was made aide-de-camp extraordinary. On 6 June 1836 he was appointed commissioner for small causes for the parish of Saint-Joseph-de-Chambly, and on 22 March 1837 was reconfirmed in his post. A few weeks earlier, on 24 February, he had been called to be a member of the grand jury summoned at the opening of the criminal court of the district of Montreal. On 22 August he became a member of the Legislative Council, but since the constitution was suspended on 27 March 1838 he did not take his seat.

Appointed lieutenant-colonel on 23 March 1837, Salaberry had commanded the 2nd battalion of Chambly militia during the autumn disturbances, and prevented the Patriotes from seizing Fort Chambly. During the ensuing months, however, five militiamen cast doubt upon his zeal in fighting the Patriotes. Four of them, John Pool, Thomas Cary, Louis Chaloux, and Jean-Baptiste Poudrette, in a joint statement dated 9 Jan. 1838, attributed his lack of eagerness to "downright pusillanimity and astonishing cowardice," and deplored that they still had to serve under such an officer. Nevertheless, it was apparent from Chaloux's retraction on 4 Feb. 1837 that one of Salaberry's officers, Lieutenant John McCutcheon, was responsible for this manœuvre. As early as November 1837 the latter had refused to comply with orders of his superior. On 15 January McCutcheon took up the charge of faint-heartedness, giving as particular ground for complaint that around 10 November Salaberry had refused to sign a declaration of loyalty to the government. However, McCutcheon's accusations proved to be without foundation and he was relieved of his post on 10 February.

Salaberry had the opportunity, three years later, to prove his loyalty. In 1841, in the first elections after the union, he stood as a candidate in the county of Rouville, and just managed to win over Timothée Franchère in a violent campaign that resulted in one death. In the Legislative Assembly, Salaberry and Alexandre-Maurice Delisle* were the only French-Canadians to support Lord Sydenham [Thomson*] and the government. In June 1841, for example, they voted against an amendment by John Neilson* seeking the repeal of the union by the British government. Salaberry remained in the assembly for only a short time. In June 1842 he had to resign to face the electorate again, because he had accepted from the government the lucrative office of clerk of the court for the district of Richelieu. He was defeated by William Walker, who was to

support the same parliamentary group. Salaberry was called to the Montreal bar on 4 Feb. 1845, and for some time practised with Robert-Shore-Milnes Bouchette*, before he was appointed on 23 April 1847 to work with Joseph Jones as coroner of Montreal. He gave up this post to accept, on 26 June 1848, that of assistant adjutant-general of the militia for Lower Canada. He held this high executive and administrative position until his death.

On 22 Sept. 1846 Melchior-Alphonse de Salaberry had married at Montreal Marie-Émilie Guy, daughter of Louis Guy, a legislative councillor. Eight children were born of this union. The son of a seigneur, Salaberry enjoyed a privileged existence; his very birth destined him to live in an exclusive social environment and to accede at an early age to positions that few people of more modest origins could hope to occupy. Like his father, he remained aloof from the Canadian nationalist movement of the day. At the time of the confrontation between Patriotes and British troops, Salaberry was already moving in the influential circles which would assure his personal future.

JEAN-PIERRE GAGNON

ANQ-Q, QBC 25, Événements de 1837–38, nos.3023, 3754–55, 3757, 3767, 3769–71, 3776, 3779–81, 3783, 3785. PAC, MG 24, G45, 5, p.1462; 6, p.1480; MG 30, D62, 27, p.309; RG 9, I, A5, 15; I, C6, 6. G. Turcotte, *Cons. législatif de Québec*, 19, 123–24. Thérèse d'Irumberry de Salaberry, *Regards sur la famille d'Irumberry de Salaberry; ses origines lointaines, sa branche canadienne* (Paris, 1953). Monet, *Last cannon shot*. P.-G. Roy, *La famille d'Irumberry de Salaberry* (Lévis, Qué., 1905), 119–22.

SAMPSON, JAMES, physician, educator, and public servant; b. 1789 at Banbridge, County Down (Northern Ireland), one of six children of Alicia Brush and the Reverend William Sampson; m. 10 May 1817 Eliza Chipman Winslow, daughter of Chief Justice Edward Winslow* of New Brunswick, and they had six children; d. 9 Nov. 1861 at Kingston, Canada West.

James Sampson was educated in Dublin and was trained at Middlesex Hospital and at York Hospital in Chelsea. He was appointed assistant surgeon to the 85th Foot in June 1811 and was dispatched to Canada. In March 1812 he was transferred to the Royal Newfoundland Fencible Infantry and served with this unit during the War of 1812. His surgical skill was of special value at Sackets Harbor in May 1813. In August 1814 Sampson was part of a small force commanded by Lieutenant Miller Worsley which eluded the

Sampson

American ships at the mouth of the Nottawasaga and reached Fort Mackinac at the head of Lake Huron; Sampson lost his surgical kit with the destruction of the schooner *Nancy* at Nottawasaga on 14 August. At Mackinac Worsley organized an attack force in four canoes which captured the United States schooner *Tigress* on 3 September and, still flying American colours, seized the *Scorpion* on 6 September. In August 1815 Sampson was transferred to the 104th Foot which did garrison duty at Quebec and Montreal in 1815 and 1816. His unit was disbanded in May 1817, at which time he married and went on half pay.

Fellow officers persuaded Sampson to take up private practice in Niagara in 1817. He later lived for a short time in Queenston and moved to Kingston in September 1820 to join the town's 14 civilian and military doctors. Sampson's ability, education, and personality soon made him a highly regarded surgeon and member of the community. His tall and magnificent appearance gave him a special kind of prominence among his fellow practitioners. His acquaintance with politically important men such as Samuel Peters Jarvis*, Christopher Hagerman*, John Macaulay*, and Charles Grant, Baron de Longueuil, gained him positions of importance, including an appointment as magistrate of the Midland District in August 1821. It is said that when Sampson was recalled to active duty in 1825 his friends and patients persuaded him to stay in Kingston by guaranteeing him a regular income through a yearly fee from each family as compensation for his half pay. He was consulting surgeon to governors general Sydenham [Thomson*], Charles Bagot*, and Charles Metcalfe* in Kingston from 1841 to 1844, and was a personal friend of Sydenham. In 1847 he received an honorary MD from McGill University.

Sampson was one of the three commissioners appointed by the assembly in January 1832 to superintend the building of a charity hospital for the sick poor in Kingston. The hospital was built by 1835 but no money was left for equipment, maintenance, or staff, and it remained empty until it served as the parliament building of the Province of Canada from 1841 to 1844, when Kingston was the capital. From 1845, when it opened as a charity hospital, Sampson was the chief surgeon, and he was soon faced by an influx of indigent immigrant patients during the typhus epidemic of 1847. He became the first elected chairman of the board of governors of the Kingston General Hospital in 1857 after a period of mismanagement, which meant reorganizing, with the assistance of some young doctors, the medical and financial operations of the hospital. He was also consulting surgeon to Hotel Dieu Hospital.

As a practising physician and member of the Medical Board of Upper Canada from 1822 until his death, Sampson trained and examined medical students and was acutely aware of the need for better training facilities. In 1854 he was chairman of the committee which organized the medical faculty at Queen's College, and was president of the faculty from 1854 to 1860 and professor of clinical and medical surgery.

Sampson was the first surgeon to the provincial penitentiary near Kingston from 1835 to 1861, and a leader in penitentiary reform. He objected to public viewing of prisoners and punishment of the mentally ill, and fought for the separation of the latter from criminals. In 1839 Sampson was on a commission of three appointed to erect a provincial lunatic asylum, but resigned when Toronto was chosen as the site. In 1848 conditions at the prison impelled him to ask the government to investigate the administration. The parliamentary commission, whose secretary was George Brown*, revealed inhumane treatment of prisoners and its recommendations led to the dismissal of Warden Henry Smith and his son Frank [see Henry SMITH]. Sampson encouraged local groups to send visitors to the prison and he assisted released prisoners.

Sampson held various government appointments: magistrate of the Court of Quarter Sessions, associate judge of the Court of Oyer and Terminer, and in 1838 commissioner for the improvement of navigation on the St Lawrence River. Because his poor patients paid nothing and the wealthy ones at their leisure, he supplemented his income as inspector of licences from 1829 to 1849. Other responsibilities included service on the Midland District Grammar School Board and the Kingston Board of Health. In September 1839 he was elected mayor of Kingston after Henry Cassidy's sudden death, and was re-elected in March 1840. He refused a third term in 1841. During the 18 months of his mayoralty, Kingston became the capital and suffered a great fire and a serious housing shortage. Sampson's next term as mayor in 1844 witnessed the departure of parliament, bitter recriminations from citizens who had empty new buildings and bankrupt businesses, widespread unemployment, and a huge civic debt for the new and unoccupied town hall. The city council had confrontations with butchers who refused to rent stalls in the new market wing, with building contractors who had not been paid, and with officials such as Robert Baldwin*, R. B. Sullivan*, and Francis

Hincks* who left Kingston without paying their taxes. The duties of mayor became too onerous for a busy doctor like Sampson; he resigned after he was bitterly attacked for including a few Catholics among the 25 constables appointed to police the Orangemen's 12th of July parade.

As an avocation James Sampson had an experimental farm from 1832, offering his prize wheat as free seed and his prize sheep for breeding. In the 1830s and 1840s he held high offices in the Midland District Agricultural Society and in such social organizations as the Turf Club and the St Patrick's Society.

During the rebellion of 1837 Sampson had been commander of the town guard until the militia was called up, and as major of the 3rd Regiment of Frontenac militia he was a member of the court martial at Fort Henry which condemned Nils von Schoultz* to be hanged. He resigned as major in October 1839.

Sampson had little interest in politics but an absorbing interest in the welfare of the poor and oppressed and in the improvement of medical training. He had unlimited patience with the sick and mentally ill, and no patience with humbug or dishonesty.

MARGARET S. ANGUS

Fenwick, Hale, and Sampson family papers are in the possession of Stephanie Hensley, London, Ont. Kingston General Hospital Archives (Kingston, Ont.), Papers and records, 1832–61. MTCL, Samuel Peters Jarvis papers, James Sampson to S.P. Jarvis, 24 Feb. 1820–23 Nov. 1823. PAC, RG 16, A1, 16, 7 and 15 July 1828; 17, 5 March 1829. QUA, Gibson coll., Queen's Medical Faculty, minutes, 1854–61; Kingston Town Council, proceedings, 1838–45. UNBL, MG H2, Penelope Winslow to Eliza Sampson, 25 Feb. 1817. *Argus; a Commercial, Agricultural, Political, and Literary Journal* (Kingston, [Ont.]), 5 Sept. 1848. *British American Journal Devoted to the Advancement of the Medical and Physical Sciences in the British-American Provinces* (Montreal), II (1861), 520–22. *British American Journal of Medical and Physical Science* (Montreal), III (1847–48), 53. Can., Prov. of, Legislative Assembly, *Journals*, 1849, III, app.B.B.B.B. *Chronicle & Gazette* (Kingston), 22 Aug. 1838–18 May 1844. *Chronicle and News* (Kingston), 31 Jan., 4 July 1849. *Daily British Whig* (Kingston), 3 May, 23 July 1844; 11 Nov. 1861. *Kingston Chronicle*, 25 April 1829, 12 March 1830, 17 Sept. 1831, 21 Jan. 1832. *Michigan Pioneer Coll.* (Lansing, Mich.), XV (1890), 635 (Sampson's claim for loss of articles on *Nancy*). G.B., WO, *Army list*, 1811–17. William Johnston, *Roll of commissioned officers in the medical service of the British army . . .* (Aberdeen, Scot., 1917). Canniff, *Medical profession in U.C.*, 610–11. Margaret [Sharp] Angus, *Kingston General Hospital, 1832–1972, a social and institutional history* (Montreal and London, 1973).

SASSEVILLE, FRANÇOIS, silversmith; b. 30 Jan. 1797 at Sainte-Anne-de-la-Pocatière (La Pocatière, Que.), son of Joseph Sasseville, a canteen-keeper there, and Geneviève Roy; d. 28 Feb. 1864 at Quebec.

On 13 Nov. 1819 François Sasseville signed an agreement with Étienne Lajoie, a navigator of Baie-Saint-Paul, concerning a piece of land in Gaspé county; he was described in it as "a young man of full age, an apprentice silversmith in this city of Quebec," but the word "apprentice" is crossed out, which might indicate he had just completed his time of service. Nothing else is known about him until 2 July 1839, when the descendants of silversmith Laurent Amiot* leased him the house of their father, who had died on 3 June. The lease stipulated that these descendants should "make over to the said Sieur Sasseville the whole shop as it had been left by their father, with any small quantity of silver that might remain, and including all ingredients and materials and articles peculiar to the silversmith's art." François Sasseville may have served his apprenticeship with his brother Joseph, who was seven years his senior and a silversmith at Quebec in 1811, but the lease of Laurent Amiot's silversmith's shop leaves no doubt as to the closeness of the ties he must have maintained with Amiot.

Several articles in Quebec newspapers during Sasseville's active period, from 1839 to 1864, bring out different aspects of his work and career. Heir to Amiot's clientele, Sasseville seems to have worked even more than did Amiot on religious objects. He had to compete therefore with French imports: in 1846, when he completed a storied ciborium, *Le Journal de Québec* mentioned that this was a work "which would do credit to the best European artists for the finished quality of the workmanship and the elegance of the form, and which is preferable by far to what usually comes to us from the other side of the Atlantic, because it is massive, durable, and honestly executed." In 1850 this paper again mentioned that Sasseville "will make you a chalice, a ciborium, or a monstrance as richly chiselled as you desire, and you will not have the sorrow of seeing it, under a heavy and forgetful hand, sink down on its base, and break," as did imported articles.

At the beginning of the 19th century mechanical devices such as the coining-press and the ram were introduced to silversmiths' workshops. It then became possible to strike silver coins in the cold state, and rapidly and cheaply to produce complete articles or medallions decorated with storied scenes. This kind of silver work imported

Saveuse

from France had found favour with the clergy and the parish councils. Sasseville produced works of simple decoration similar to those of Amiot, but also followed these French models. According to *Le Journal de Québec* of 17 Oct. 1850, he did not use mechanical processes; it is now known, however, that he did take advantage of these processes.

In October 1850 Sasseville and his nephew Pierre Lespérance, who had apprenticed under Laurence Amiot, won a prize for a chalice in the silver work section of the provincial industrial exhibition at Montreal. In *Le Journal de Québec* of 27 March 1858 a reporter mentions having seen "in the workshop of M. Sasseville, a Quebec silversmith, a superb monstrance of solid silver belonging to the cathedral, that M. Pierre Lespérance has just gilded by galvanoplasty." This process of gilding by electrochemical deposit had been invented simultaneously in France and England in 1839, and its use at Quebec shows that Sasseville and Lespérance kept up with the advances of the industrial revolution. It is difficult today to state precisely to what extent Lespérance managed to practise his craft independently of Sasseville before the latter's death in 1864.

In his will, Sasseville, a bachelor who had built up a small fortune, bequeathed the whole of his workshop to Pierre Lespérance, as well as 100 shares in the Banque du Peuple. He also bequeathed "to Ambroise Lafrance, if on the day of [his] death he was still [his] apprentice or employee . . . the sum of 100 piastres."

Since he succeeded Laurent Amiot, who no doubt trained him, François Sasseville inherited Amiot's clientele. It is therefore not surprising that several of his works scarcely differ in form or decoration from those of Amiot. The storied pieces, of which Sasseville was the proudest, were created to rival imports from France. All of his works, however, demonstrate the quality of his art. When he died, Pierre Lespérance continued the tradition, followed by Ambroise Lafrance, who died at the beginning of the 20th century and whose works again reflect the persistent influence of Laurent Amiot, and also that of François Sasseville.

JEAN TRUDEL

[Many of François Sasseville's works are held by the National Gallery of Canada (Ottawa), the Henry Birks Collection (Montreal), and by various parish councils. J.T.] ANQ-Q, État civil, Catholiques, Notre-Dame de Québec, 5 nov. 1811, 20 déc. 1819, 2 mars 1864; Greffe d'Étienne Boudreault, 13 nov. 1819; Greffe d'A.-Archange Parent, 20 juin 1836, 2 juill. 1839; Greffe d'A.-B. Sirois Duplessis, 30 nov. 1863, 14 mars 1864. Archives judiciaires, Kamouraska (Rivière-du-Loup, Qué.), Registre d'état civil, Sainte-Anne-de-la-Pocatière, 15 janv. 1788, 15 avril 1790, 30 janv. 1797. IBC, Centre de documentation, Fonds Morisset, Dossiers Joseph Sasseville; François Sasseville; Pierre Lespérance. *L'Ami de la religion et de la patrie* (Québec), 25 août 1848. *Le Journal de Québec*, 20 juin 1843; 10 oct. 1846; 17, 22, 26 oct. 1850; 7, 14 juin 1853; 28 mars 1858, 1er, 5, 17 mars 1864. Luc Lanel, *L'orfèvrerie* (3e éd., Paris, 1964). J. E. Langdon, *Canadian silversmiths, 1700–1900* (Toronto, 1966). Gérard Morisset, "Un chef-d'œuvre de François Sasseville," *Technique* (Montréal), XVII (1942), 526–30; "Nos orfèvres canadiens, Pierre Lespérance (1819–1882)," *Technique*, XXII (1947), 201–9; "L'orfèvre François Sasseville," *La Patrie* (Montréal), 4 juin 1950; "L'orfèvre François Sasseville," RSC *Trans.*, 3rd ser., XLIX (1955), sect.I, 51–54.

SAVEUSE DE BEAUJEU, GEORGES-RENÉ, Comte de Beaujeu, seigneur and member of the Legislative Council; b. 4 June 1810 at Montreal, son of Jacques-Philippe Saveuse de Beaujeu, lawyer and seigneur, and Catherine Chaussegros de Léry, daughter of Gaspard-Joseph Chaussegros* de Léry; d. 29 July 1865 at his manor-house, Coteau-du-Lac, Canada East.

Georges-Réne Saveuse de Beaujeu studied at the Collège de Montréal from 1820 to 1825. After his father's death in the terrible cholera epidemic of the summer of 1832, he inherited the fief of Nouvelle-Longueuil, which extended beyond the western limits of Lower Canada, and the seigneury of Soulanges. Georges-Réne Saveuse de Beaujeu was then 22 years old. On 20 Sept. 1832, at Saint-Jean-Port-Joli, he married Adélaïde, the younger daughter of Philippe-Joseph Aubert* de Gaspé, author of *Les anciens Canadiens*, and Susanne Allison. He settled down to a quiet life in the manor-house he built at Coteau-du-Lac, next to the old seigneurial dwelling at Les Cascades, in which his mother, who enjoyed the seigneurial income from Soulanges, lived until her death in 1845. At that time he added the dues and rents from the Soulanges seigneury to his income. In 1839 he had also obtained a grant of 821 acres of land in Newton Township.

In 1846, on the death of his paternal uncle Charles-François Liénard de Beaujeu, who had accompanied Jean-François de Galaup*, Comte de La Pérouse, to Hudson Bay, and whose only son had perished during the Russian campaign, Saveuse de Beaujeu took the title of Comte de Beaujeu. During the administration of Louis-Hippolyte LA FONTAINE and Robert Baldwin*, he was appointed in 1848 to the Legislative Council, of which his father had been a member from 1830 to 1832. The council became elective in 1856, and in the 1858 and 1862 elections Saveuse de Beaujeu was returned for the division of Rigaud. He was president of the Board of Agriculture of Lower Canada, lieutenant-colonel of the 8th battalion of Montreal militia, and in 1862 president of the Société Saint-Jean-Baptiste of Montreal. He was one of the founding members of the Société Historique de Montréal when it was formed in 1858.

The obituary notice in *La Minerve* the day after his death stressed that Saveuse de Beaujeu had devoted his leisure time to historical research and that his collection of documents was substantial. Nearly 30 years later a grandson, Monongahéla de Beaujeu, assistant secretary of the Antiquarian and Numismatic Society of Montreal, found material among them for two publications. The first, entitled *Documents inédits sur le colonel de Longueuil*, appeared in 1891 and is little more than a compilation of the numerous commissions received by Joseph-Dominique-Emmanuel Le Moyne* de Longueuil. The second, written from notes which had been collected by a former tutor of the family, Paul Stevens*, a Belgian, was published in 1892 under the title of *Le héros de la Monongahéla*. It is an elegantly turned eulogy, in the style of the period, and contains "speeches" after the manner of Livy; the subject is Saveuse's greatuncle Daniel-Hyacinthe-Marie Liénard* de Beaujeu, for whom the author claims the title of victorious commanding officer in the defence of Fort Duquesne.

According to *La Minerve*, over 3,000 persons, including several distinguished Montreal citizens, gathered at Saveuse de Beaujeu's funeral at Coteau-du-Lac. As he died intestate, the apportionment of his estate was decided by the Superior Court of Montreal on 23 Nov. 1870. Of his numerous children, four daughters – three of whom became nuns – and two sons reached adulthood. The elder son, Philippe-Arthur-Quiquerand, died penniless after living extravagantly as lord of the manor; the younger, Raoul, represented Soulanges in parliaments in Quebec and in Ottawa and died prematurely at the age of 40.

JEAN-JACQUES LEFEBVRE

ANQ-Q, AP-P-130. Archives du collège Bourget (Rigaud, Qué.), Archives des de Beaujeu, IV. *Documents inédits sur le colonel de Longueuil*, Monongahéla de Beaujeu, édit. (Montréal, 1891). *L'Écho du cabinet de lecture paroissial*, 15 août 1865. *La Minerve*, 5 août 1865. G. Turcotte, *Cons. législatif de Québec*, 55, 107, 150. [François Daniel], *Histoire des grandes familles françaises du Canada . . .* (Montréal, 1867), 333; *Nos gloires nationales; ou, histoire des principales familles du Canada . . .* (2v., Montréal, 1867), I, 149. É.-Z. Massicotte, *Processions de la Saint-Jean-Baptiste en 1924 et 1925* (Montréal, 1926). Monongahéla de Beaujeu, *Le héros de la Monongahéla; esquisse historique* (Montréal, 1892). P.-G. Roy, *La famille Aubert de Gaspé* (Lévis, Qué., 1907), 141. Alphonse Gauthier, "La famille de Georges-René Saveuse de Beaujeu (1810–1865)," SGCF *Mémoires*, VI (1954–55), 197–208.

SAWYER, JOSEPH. *See* NAWAHJEGEZHEGWABE

SCALLON, ÉDOUARD, businessman; b. 1813 at Saint-David-d'Yamaska, Lower Canada, son of Mathew Scallon, an Irishman who immigrated to Canada in 1810; d. 15 March 1864 at Joliette, Canada East.

In 1837, at age 24, Édouard Scallon settled at L'Industrie (Joliette), and went into partnership with Barthélemy Joliette*, the local seigneur, and Joliette's brother-in-law Charles Peter Loedel, both of whom were contractors and lumber merchants. They exploited the forest on the banks of the Rivière L'Assomption, upstream from the village of L'Industrie. The partnership lasted ten years. During this period Scallon diversified his investments and in 1840 bought the distillery built by Barthélemy Joliette. Unfortunately it was gutted by fire the following year, and Scallon decided not to rebuild.

In 1847 the three partners and Gaspard Tarieu Taillant de Lanaudière had the St Lawrence and Industry Village Rail-road Company incorporated. This railway was to link the St Lawrence and L'Assomption rivers following the dividing line between the seigneuries of Lavaltrie and Lanoraie. On 15 July 1853 the Societé d'Exploitation Forestière Scallon et Leprohon was formed, which included, besides Scallon, the principal contractors of the region: Bernard-Henri Leprohon, Gaspard de Lanaudière, and his aunt Marie-Charlotte Tarieu Taillant de Lanaudière, Barthélemy Joliette's widow. The company worked a farm and more than 120 miles of forest. That year Scallon built a sawmill and a flour mill. Five years later he sold the sawmill to an American for $20,000.

Through the lumber business Édouard Scallon managed to amass a fortune evaluated at about $100,000 at the time of his death in 1864. He was involved in land speculation and was probably the largest money-lender in the district. He even lent sums to Marie-Charlotte de Lanaudière, the seigneur of Lavaltrie, at the extremely high rate

Scoble

of 12 per cent, and took back mortgages on ten of her properties, including the fief of Lavaltrie.

Short and unprepossessing, Scallon was a cultivated man who had many contacts in other countries, particularly the United States and England. In 1862 he took a ten-month rest cure in France. He was the founder and president of an affiliate at Joliette of the Institut Canadien of Montreal, namely the Institut d'Artisans et Association de Bibliothèque of L'Industrie, which was formed in 1858.

In his will Scallon bequeathed most of his fortune to the parish of Joliette for the construction of a trades school for the less privileged, and to the Sisters of Providence for the expansion of the hospital built on land he had already given them. The École Industrielle, which opened in 1884, became a kindergarten after 1905.

Édouard Scallon died suddenly on 15 March 1864 at age 51, when he was at one of his lumber camps. He was certainly one of the most important architects of the rapid growth of Joliette and the surrounding district. His marriage with Mathilde Ducondu, on 14 Sept. 1841, was childless, but he adopted a daughter, Hermine.

ROGER BARRETTE

Archives de l'évêché de Joliette (Joliette, Qué.), Dossier Édouard Scallon; Dossier succession Édouard Scallon. Archives de la Société historique de Joliette (Joliette, Qué.), Famille Scallon; Joliette économique; Joliette: industrie et commerce; Liquidation et partage de la communauté de biens entre dame Mathilde Ducondu et feu Édouard Scallon ainsi que la succession du dit défunt (copie manuscrite, 1864); J.-M. Robert, "Histoire du site appelé communément Moulins des sœurs" (texte dactylographié, 1942–43); Omer Valois, "Trois Édouard Scallon" (texte dactylographié, Joliette, 1964). *Le Messager de Joliette* (Joliette, [Qué.]), 1864. *La Minerve*, 19 mars 1864. *Joliette, 1864–1964* (Joliette, Qué., 1964). *Joliette illustré, numéro souvenir de ses noces d'or, 1843–1893* ([Joliette, Qué.], 1893]). J.-C. Robert, "L'activité économique de Barthélemy Joliette et la fondation du village d'Industrie (Joliette), 1822–1850" (thèse de MA, université de Montréal, 1971); "Un seigneur entrepreneur, Barthélemy Joliette, et la fondation du village d'Industrie (Joliette), 1822–1850," *RHAF*, XXVI (1972–73), 375–95. *L'Action populaire* (Joliette, Qué.), 15 mai 1930.

SCOBLE, JOHN, anti-slavery leader and politician; b. 16 Jan. 1799 at Kingsbridge, Devonshire, England; m. in 1827 Mary Anne Stainburn, and they had six children; last known to be living in 1867.

John Scoble was educated in Devon and London, and became a Congregational minister. In 1831 he was appointed one of the full-time lecturers for the Agency Committee of the Anti-Slavery Society; following the passage of the 1833 Emancipation Act, the committee separated from the Anti-Slavery Society to become the more radical Society for the Universal Abolition of Slavery and the Slave Trade, and Scoble became its secretary. Joseph Sturge, a wealthy corn merchant, was its patron, and in 1836 he organized an expedition to the West Indies to examine the apprenticeship system which had supplanted slavery. Scoble joined it and published one of the four pamphlets, *British Guiana*, which resulted from the mission. Scoble concluded that apprenticeship was bad in principle, and that the Emancipation Act was being continually and systematically violated. In 1838 the agitation of abolitionists bore fruit and the apprenticeship system was abolished. The Central Negro Emancipation Committee, formed in 1837 to fight the West Indian system, sent Scoble to the West Indies and the United States in 1839 to disseminate the findings of the West Indian mission.

American abolitionists welcomed Scoble's interesting, forceful, and authoritative lectures and recognized the value of this personal link with British anti-slavery activity. During the visit, however, Scoble witnessed the serious rift between William Lloyd Garrison and other abolitionists led by Lewis Tappan and James G. Birney. Garrison opposed the use of political action for ending slavery and alienated many abolitionists with his abusive language toward churches and with his strong support of the peace movement and of the women's rights movement. Scoble supported Tappan and Birney and in 1839 reported his impressions of the disagreement to the British and Foreign Anti-Slavery Society, of which he was a charter member. In organizing the World Anti-Slavery Convention of 1840, the BFASS ruled that women could attend as observers but not as delegates, a decision which offended Garrison's supporters and transferred the rift to Britain. Although supported by British and American moderates, Scoble's opposition to Garrison's anti-political and anti-Christian views was considered by Garrisonians as an attempt to downgrade the significance of American slavery. Their impression of Scoble's insincerity and racial prejudice was reinforced by his suggestion to the painter of the 1840 convention portrait that he not be placed next to a black abolitionist.

As secretary of the BFASS from 1842 until 1852, Scoble was involved in world anti-slavery and peace congresses in 1843, 1849, and 1850. He successfully reorganized the anti-slavery movement in France by creating permanent and decentralized associations which were not exclusively tied to legislative lobbying. His feud with the Garrisonians was, however, a factor in his resignation as secretary of the BFASS in September 1852.

Scoble was drawn to Canada by the affairs of the British American Institute of Science and Industry near Dresden in Dawn Township, Canada West. The institute had opened in December 1842 as an academic and vocational school for blacks, especially fugitive slaves, but it did not exclude whites and Indians. The sale of agricultural and timber products from its 300 acres, in addition to contributions, was expected to provide financial support. Interest in the institute was rekindled in 1851 by the visit to England of Josiah Henson*, a fugitive slave and manager of the institute. The success of Henson's visit seeking funds for the institute was hampered by charges made by Edward Mathews, a Baptist minister, Samuel J. May, and Hiram Wilson, both original trustees of the institute, that he did not speak for the trustees and that his financial management was faulty. Scoble visited Canada in 1851 on behalf of a London committee of anti-slavery philanthropists who shared membership in the BFASS to investigate the situation for them and find ways of helping Henson and the institute. The trustees in Canada agreed to surrender their trust to the London committee on the understanding that the committee would meet the institute's liabilities to $7,000 and pursue its educational aims. The committee requested Scoble, who moved to Canada, and John ROAF of Toronto, another of the original trustees, to act for them in settling most of the institute's heavy liabilities at the rate of 63 cents to the dollar. They accomplished this settlement by the end of 1853, and, despite rumours to the contrary, Scoble received no pecuniary advantage from the settlement of accounts. Attempts at incorporation of the institute in Canada to end the liability of individuals in the event of bankruptcy were frustrated by James C. Brown, a trustee who refused to surrender his trust to the London committee.

Further disputes between former and current trustees throughout the 1850s hampered Scoble's efforts to achieve financial stability for the institute and to erect buildings and provide schooling from primary to college levels. Despite his understanding that the school was racially integrated and supported by voluntary funds, Scoble learned in 1852 that it received government support as a coloured separate school. He paid the school taxes and did not interfere with its operation, though he was relieved when it moved to Dresden in 1855. He discouraged donations until there could be proper guarantees against any such misappropriation of funds as had occurred before 1851, and because he believed local financial support must come first. The property produced little revenue because of difficulties with tenants, previous poor management, and the expense of clearing and fencing the land; these problems were compounded by the petty obstructions of Brown and serious disagreements with Henson. The American Baptist Free Mission Society, tenants on the land from 1851 to 1853, resented Scoble's control and in 1853 its agents departed with everything portable. Unable to find a suitable tenant and faced with extensive repairs, Scoble himself farmed the property. Henson was the tenant from 1857 to 1860; disagreements between him and Scoble over rents, improvements to the property, and payment for services as manager resulted in a series of lawsuits between 1861 and 1863. Henson hoped to gain control of the property because he was convinced that Dawn could achieve its educational goals. Scoble had resigned his trusteeship in December 1861 and requested in 1863 that the court appoint a receiver and reimburse him for certain expenses and legal costs. The court accepted Scoble's suggestion, but the property under court management did not produce sufficient revenue. Interest in the institute among black settlers in the area waned, and when incorporation was granted in 1868 the institute and lands were sold, with the revenues from the sale intended to endow the Wilberforce Educational Institute, an integrated school in Chatham.

In the winter of 1860–61 Scoble had played a prominent role in preventing the extradition of John ANDERSON, a fugitive slave wanted for murder in Missouri. An active Reformer in politics, Scoble was the secretary of the Reform Convention of 1859, and in the 1861 election ran in Elgin West. He was not declared elected until 23 Feb. 1863, and in the same year won re-election. During the discussions leading to confederation he advocated a legislative union decentralized by a strong system of municipal government and by representation by population. He joined John A. Macdonald* and John Sandfield Macdonald* in opposing the recommendations of George Brown*'s "Parliamentary Reform Committee" in June 1864 but he supported the "Great Coalition" formed at the same time. He continued to support it from George Brown's resignation in December 1865 until 1867. Brown and others worked actively and with success to prevent Scoble's renomination in 1867, and even local Reformers who respected his talents were suspicious of someone who was "smooth as an iceberg." In a series of letters to the *London Free*

Scott

Press in June and July 1867 Scoble ably defended his course, opposed the Reform Convention of 1867, and argued that Reformers ought to have supported the "Liberal element in the Cabinet" of John A. Macdonald. Scoble was not elected in 1867 and no trace of him can be found beyond that year.

Scoble was a forceful and self-assured man, well known in both Canada and Britain. His son, Sir Andrew Richard Scoble, became a member of the Judicial Committee of the Privy Council in the 1890s and another son, Thomas Clarkson Scoble, was an early advocate of the Hudson Bay Railway in Manitoba.

ELWOOD H. JONES

John Scoble was the author of *British Guiana . . .* (London, 1838); *Texas: its claims to be recognized as an independent power, by Great Britain . . .* (London, 1839); *Hill coolies; a brief exposition of the deplorable condition of the hill coolies in British Guiana and Mauritius . . .* (London, 1840); and with G. W. Alexander, *Liberté immédiate et absolue, ou esclavage . . .* (Paris, 1844). He also wrote an introduction to Lewis Tappan, *Reply to charges brought against the American and Foreign Anti-Slavery Society* (London, 1852).

Boston Public Library, Anti-slavery coll. Rhodes House Library, University of Oxford, MSS Brit. Emp. s.16–24 (Anti-Slavery Soc., anti-slavery papers, 1820–1951), British and Foreign Anti-Slavery Soc. papers. University of London, University College Library, Lord Brougham papers. UWO, 255 (John Scoble papers); Middlesex County, Court of Chancery files, no.103. [J. G. Birney], *Letters of James Gillespie Birney, 1831–1857*, ed. D. L. Dumond (2v., New York and London, 1938). British and Foreign Anti-Slavery Soc., *Annual report* (London), 1852. Can., Prov. of, *Confederation debates. Four fugitive slave narratives*, ed. R. W. Winks *et al.* (Reading, Mass., 1969). *Globe*, 1852–53; Nov. 1860–Feb. 1861. *London Free Press*, 1860–61; June–July 1867. *Provincial Freeman* (Windsor; Toronto; Chatham), 1852–53. *A side-light on Anglo-American relations, 1839–1858, furnished by the correspondence of Lewis Tappan and others with the British and Foreign Anti-Slavery Society*, ed. A. H. Abel and F. J. Klingberg (Lancaster, Pa., 1927). *CPC*, 1863. Careless, *Brown*. Victor Lauriston, *Romantic Kent; more than three centuries of history, 1626–1952* (Chatham, Ont., 1952). A. L. Murray, "Canada and the Anglo-American anti-slavery movement: a study in international philanthropy" (unpublished PHD thesis, University of Pennsylvania, Philadelphia, 1960). W. H. and J. H. Pease, *Black Utopia; Negro communal experiments in America* (Madison, Wis., 1963). Howard Temperley, *British antislavery, 1833–1870* (London, 1972). Winks, *Blacks in Can.*

SCOTT, JOHN, surgeon; b. in Strabane, County Tyrone (Northern Ireland) in 1816; d. between June 1864 and May 1865.

John Scott apprenticed as an apothecary at the age of 15 and in 1835 received a medical certificate from the University of Edinburgh. On 24 May 1841 he became a member of the Royal College of Surgeons, London. Shortly thereafter he immigrated to Canada, and in 1844 married the daughter of John ROAF, a Congregationalist minister and a prominent commissioner of the Toronto Lunatic Asylum. Between 1844 and 1850 Scott established in Toronto a reputation as a competent medical practitioner of temperamental disposition. With the support of his father-in-law, he was appointed in 1850 medical superintendent of the new Provincial Lunatic Asylum in Toronto at a salary of £300 per annum.

The old Toronto asylum, established by William Rees* in 1841, had been struggling under chaotic administration for nine years and the appointment of Scott, who was untrained in diseases of the mind, met with strong opposition from the city's Reform press. The *Globe* implied that nepotism was involved and that Scott had "neither the temper, the experience, nor the enlarged mind" necessary for the post. In 1851 these objections were partially vindicated when the Legislative Assembly received a petition from an attendant at the asylum charging Scott with malpractice and maladministration. Although the subsequent investigation sustained Scott against the charges, he was found "wanting in kindness and consideration" and possessed of "a natural infirmity of temper." In November of the same year it was discovered that Scott had dissected a body and buried the parts in two separate coffins. Although dissection was becoming popular in mid century psychiatry, Scott's methods and attitudes caused an outcry in Toronto's daily press for his removal. He was censured severely by the asylum's board of commissioners and narrowly avoided dismissal.

By 1852 the provincial asylum under Scott's administration was suffering from an inordinately high death rate, overcrowding, and a deficit which the legislature was reluctant to assume. At this critical period Scott was forced to leave his duties as superintendent to consult with the Ordnance Department in Montreal and Quebec, probably regarding the asylum's need to acquire more land. In October 1852 further trouble erupted when Scott intercepted a defamatory letter from Malcolm Cameron*, a Clear Grit member of the assembly, to the clerk of the asylum. Scott took the letter to the premier, Francis Hincks*, for redress, but instead was indicted before a grand jury for tampering with the mails. Although a "true bill" was returned the government did not prosecute him.

A bill to reorganize the administration of the asylum was passed by the legislature in March 1853, and Scott was officially allowed to resign, effective 1 July 1853. It was clear that his position had become completely untenable: the managing board was racked with dissension, Roaf had lost his influence, and, with the proposed reorganization, the government clearly indicated it wanted a new superintendent. Soon after leaving the lunatic asylum Scott was appointed to the staff of the Toronto General Hospital. His tenure there was equally unsettled, although, as a junior staff member, he was less open to attack. He was associated at the hospital with a medical clique, including W. R. Beaumont* and E. M. Hodder*, that feuded with a rival faction led by John ROLPH. Scott and his colleagues were also charged with condoning "filth" and "cruelty" in the hospital wards.

In September 1855 Scott was appointed associate coroner for the city of Toronto by the ministry of Augustin-Norbert MORIN and Allan Napier MACNAB. The pathological work of a city coroner probably appealed to Scott and he served in this capacity until 1864 without serious incident. However, public objections that coroners were "using too much enthusiasm" in their medical examinations served as a reminder of Scott's earlier inclinations toward extensive autopsy. In December 1863 Scott briefly disappeared and Toronto police were unable to locate him. He returned to perform his last inquest in January 1864, only to vanish again.

It was not until the following year that the grisly details of his death were revealed. In May 1865, after the spring break-up, a hunter found Scott's decomposing body in a marsh near Ashbridge's Bay (now in Toronto). At the subsequent inquest, a witness testified to having seen Dr Scott sitting on the ground on the east side of River St sometime in June 1864; upon returning the same way he found Scott gone. It was presumed that the doctor, "who had been addicted to the excessive use of intoxicating drinks for a couple of years before," had fallen into the Don River and drowned. Only the contents of the pockets had enabled Scott's son William to identify his body. It was a macabre end to a macabre career.

A. W. RASPORICH and I. H. CLARKE

Can., Prov. of, Legislative Assembly, *Journals*, 1850–53. *Globe*, 1850–65. *Leader*, 1860–65. Canniff, *Medical profession in U.C. The institutional care of the insane in the United States and Canada*, ed. H. M. Hurd (4v., Baltimore, Md, 1916–17), IV.

SCOTT, THOMAS, adventurer; b. *c.*1842, probably at Clandeboye, County Down (Northern Ireland); d. 4 March 1870 at Red River (Man.).

Almost nothing is known of the early life of Thomas Scott, whose death during the Red River disturbance of 1869–70 provoked a storm of English-French hostility in central Canada. His youth was spent in Ireland. According to Lord Dufferin [Blackwood*], when governor general of Canada, Scott "came of very decent people – his parents are at this moment [1874] tenant farmers on my estate in the neighbourhood of Clandeboye – but he himself seems to have been a violent and boisterous man such as are often found in the North of Ireland."

About 1863 Scott turned up in Canada West, where he was probably a labourer. He was a Presbyterian, an active and zealous Orangeman, and a member of the 49th Hastings Battalion of Rifles at Stirling. In the summer of 1869 Scott arrived at Red River and found employment as a labourer on the "Dawson Road" project, a new wagon road connecting Red River to Lake Superior, under Superintendent John Allan Snow* [*see* Simon James Dawson*]. In August he led a strike against Snow, who wisely capitulated after Scott threatened to throw him into the Seine River near Red River. However, the disgruntled superintendent laid a charge of aggravated assault against Scott and three of his cohorts at the autumn session of the General Quarterly Court of Assiniboia. Scott was convicted and fined £4 in November. Now out of work, he drifted around Upper Fort Garry (Winnipeg) and fell under the influence of John Christian Schultz*, leader of the Canadian party, a small Anglophone group which promoted the annexation of Red River to Canada. From this point on, Thomas Scott was caught up in the struggle for the future of the Red River Settlement.

By allying himself with Schultz's group in the early winter of 1869–70, Scott may have found kindred spirits but he had chosen the losing side. Louis Riel* and the Métis were in effective control of the settlement. An abortive resistance by the Canadian party resulted in the capture on 7 December of Schultz, Scott, Charles Mair*, and 53 others and their incarceration in Upper Fort Garry. Scott was an unexceptional prisoner until the night of 9 Jan. 1870 when he, Mair, and several others managed to escape. Scott fled to the Canadian enclave at Portage la Prairie bearing lurid tales of the treatment meted out by his captors. During the next month he helped to organize a relief expedition of Canadians, ostensibly to secure the release of the remaining prisoners and with a secondary objective of attempting to capture Riel. The latter, meanwhile, had released all the prisoners, as he had promised Donald Alexander Smith*, the emissary from Ottawa.

Scott and the Portage party descended on the Red River Settlement in mid February and tried to enlist the aid of the Kildonan settlers, but without success. Except for the irreconcilables among the Canadians, the people of Red River were prepared to allow Riel's provisional government, which would be broadly representative, to effect a settlement with Ottawa. A concilatory message from Riel to the Kildonan settlers ended the threat and the opposition melted away.

With little alternative but to return to Portage, Scott and his group decided on a last defiant gesture, to pass through Winnipeg under the very walls of Upper Fort Garry where Riel and his Métis followers were established. Unaware that the challenge to the provisional government had dissipated, Riel himself probably ordered the capture of the Portage group, which was accomplished without violence on 18 Feb. 1870. Thomas Scott and 47 others, including Major Charles Arkoll Boulton*, their presumed leader, were confined in the fort. Almost immediately a Métis court martial decided to execute Boulton, but Riel was persuaded to spare his life in return for a promise from Smith that he would do all in his power to evoke support for the provisional government.

Outside the walls of Upper Fort Garry the emergency seemed to be over. But inside Thomas Scott was proving a difficult prisoner. Although the evidence is not completely conclusive, it seems clear that Scott did not disguise his contempt for the Métis. He so insulted and provoked his guards that on 28 February they dragged him outdoors and beat him. The incident marked a tragic turning point.

Though there was acquiescence, if not enthusiasm, among most of the inhabitants of Red River in allowing Riel and the incoming provisional government to negotiate entry into confederation with Ottawa, Riel's leadership depended in the end on the continuing support of the armed Métis. After months of tension and threatened attack by the Canadian party, they were excitable and unruly. The reprieve of Boulton could be interpreted as magnanimity based on strength. To ignore Scott's challenge might be seen as weakness. There was a growing spirit among the Métis that Scott must be punished. A Métis court martial, an *ad hoc* tribunal employed frequently on the prairie, met on the evening of 3 March; its members included Ambroise-Dydime* and Jean-Baptiste Lépine*, André Nault*, and Elzéar GOULET. Scott was tried on the

charge of insubordination. By majority vote the court martial convicted him and the death penalty was invoked. The following day he was shot by a Métis firing squad.

In the long run the execution of Scott was a blunder. It jeopardized the entry of the Hudson's Bay territory into the dominion, poisoned relations between English and French Canadians, condemned Riel to the same fate 15 years later, and bedevilled the future development of Manitoba. In justifying his action, Riel explained to Smith that "We must make Canada respect us." Such respect depended on his abilty to control the local situation and, moreover, to demonstrate that control. We may accurately describe the action as mistaken, but only from hindsight.

Scott, an obscure if volatile figure during his life, became a *cause célèbre* after death. To a degree quite unconnected with his own tragic fate, he came to symbolize one of the unresolved problems of the new confederation. Was the Northwest to be the patrimony of Ontario or was its settlement to be a joint venture of English and French Canadians? The more extreme reaction may be seen in a resolution of Toronto Orangemen carried by the *Globe* on 13 April 1870: "Whereas Brother Thomas Scott, a member of our Order was cruelly murdered by the enemies of our Queen, country and religion, therefore be it resolved that . . . we, the members of L.O.L. No. 404 call upon the Government to avenge his death, pledging ourselves to assist in rescuing Red River Territory from those who have turned it over to Popery, and bring to justice the murderers of our countrymen." Thomas Scott thus became a martyr in the cause of Ontario expansion westward, a sentiment implicit even in the pathetic letter of his brother, Hugh Scott, to Sir John Alexander Macdonald*: "my brother was a very quiet and inoffensive young man, but yet when principle and loyalty to his Queen and Country were at stake throughout a brave and loyal man."

J. E. REA

PAC, MG 26, A, 14, 102; MG 27, I, A4; MG 29, E34. PAM, MG 2, B4; C14, 412, 417, 446; MG 3, B17; D1, 616, 619, 629; MG 7, C12, p.7; MG 12, A; B, Ketcheson coll., correspondence, pp.55, 57, 116, 135; telegram book, no.1, 118; Lieutenant-governor's coll., letterbooks, M, 36, 40. PRO, CO 42/685 (mfm. at PAC). Begg, *Red River journal* (Morton). Can., House of Commons, *Report of the select committee on the causes of the difficulties in the North-West Territory in 1869–70* (Ottawa, 1874). *Dufferin-Carnarvon correspondence* (de Kiewiet and Underhill). "Letter of Louis Riel and Ambroise Lépine to Lieutenant-Governor Morris, January 3, 1873," trans. and ed. A.-H. de Trémaudan, *CHR*, VII (1926), 137–60.

Manitoba: the birth of a province, ed. W. L. Morton (Altona, Man., 1965). *Preliminary investigation and trial of Ambroise D. Lepine for the murder of Thomas Scott . . .* , comp. [G. B.] Elliott and [E. F. T.] Brokovski ([Montreal], 1874). [Louis Riel], ''The execution of Thomas Scott,'' ed. A.-H. de Trémaudan, *CHR*, VI (1925), 222–36. Alexander Begg, *The creation of Manitoba; or, a history of the Red River troubles* (Toronto, 1871). A. S. Morton, *History of the Canadian west.* W. L. Morton, *Man.: a history* (1957). J. H. O'Donnell, *Manitoba as I saw it from 1869 to date, with flash-lights on the first Riel rebellion* (Winnipeg and Toronto, 1909), 40. Stanley, *Louis Riel*.

SEAMAN, AMOS PECK, industrialist, merchant, and agriculturalist; b. 14 Jan. 1788 in Sackville, N.B., the son of Nathan Seaman and Zena (Zeniah) Thomas; m. on 12 May 1814 Jane Metcalf, and they had seven sons and four daughters; d. 14 Sept. 1864 at his home in Minudie, N.S.

Amos Peck Seaman, an astute, turbulent, warm-hearted son of pre-loyalist settlers, came to Minudie in Cumberland County in 1796, ''a barefooted runaway boy, in an old birch bark canoe with a hole in the bow.'' His mother had given him the rudiments of an education in their poor hut in the parish of Sackville. Not until he grew to manhood was he able, with his wife's help, to further his education in night school. Little is known about Seaman's early life. By 1810, with his brother Job as business partner, he began trading with Boston merchants. Taking advantage of the economic boom of the wartime period, he was soon carrying goods between Nova Scotia, New England, and the West Indies in vessels built in his own small shipyards.

In 1823 Seaman became a tenant on the Minudie estate which had been granted to Joseph Frederic Wallet DesBarres*, in 1765. Acting as agent for the DesBarres family, Seaman collected rents for the lands during 1825 and 1826. On the property, in addition to rich, fertile marshlands called the Elysian Fields, were excellent sandstone deposits for the production of grindstones; between 1826 and 1834 Seaman and his partner, William Fowler, leased all the quarries on the estate. However, the squatters, tenants, and trespassers on this land were used to the old, erratic ways of the absentee proprietor DesBarres. Hostility from rivals and tenants did not end when Seaman purchased the 7,000-acre estate in 1834, and he was involved in legal and extra-legal wrangles for many years. The principal point at issue was Seaman's claim to the valuable grindstone deposits on Ragged Reef, below the highwater mark. Shrewd and obstinate, he appealed his case to the highest authorities. Eventually the

intervention of the colonial secretary, Lord Glenelg, in 1838 led to the confirmation of Seaman's claim.

Every year thousands of high-priced stones were shipped to American markets by Seaman's Atlantic Grindstone Company, and by other producers who leased quarry lots from him. By 1843 more than 100 men were employed in his quarries and stone factory alone, in addition to those in his ships and mills. In 1843 he built at Minudie the first steam-powered grist mill in Nova Scotia. Early in the 1840s coal mining also began on the Seaman estate. In 1847 Seaman boasted in his remarkable diary that he also had a ''steam saw mill in full operation cutting 150 logs a day.'' Through the purchase of more land, as well as the reclamation of some 1,500 acres from the sea with dikes, he amassed what may have been the largest estate in the province.

From his mansion, Seaman watched over the largely Acadian community with the paternalistic eye of a semi-feudal lord, winning for himself the title of ''king'' of Minudie. He held numerous posts in local government, constructed a schoolhouse and two churches, one Protestant, one Catholic, for the Minudie people, and helped establish the first freemason's lodge in Cumberland County. In 1850, reporting to a commission of inquiry into the state of the Bay of Fundy fisheries, he called for the early completion of a railroad to the Canadas to make accessible the market ''now shut to us by circuitous navigation.''

It seems only a little arrogant for Seaman to have dropped his middle name, Peck, as being too small a measure for his capacities. Increased wealth and leisure made it possible for him to travel in Great Britain and the United States. His children, after home tutoring, were sent to King's College in Windsor or to English schools. Three of Seaman's children – one a lawyer and secretary to Charles Tupper* – predeceased him. Saddened by their loss, and by the apparent greed of other members of his family, Seaman complained in 1864:

> I am Striving hard to Save the Ship
> abandend by more than half my Crew.
> . . . the Stores I leve to others may do them harm
> for as the[y] fall out by the way
> what the End may be its hard to Say.

Within a few months the old ''king'' was dead. He left behind him a fiendishly complicated will. Designed to assure a fair and equitable division of his property, it caused a long succession of lawsuits which contributed to the decline of his business empire and of the Minudie community.

A. A. MacKenzie

In re Seaman estate (n.p., 1866) (copy in N.S. Legislative Library, Halifax). M. H. Perley, *Report upon the fisheries of the Bay of Fundy* (Fredericton, 1851). G. N. D. Evans, *Uncommon obdurate: the several public careers of J. F. W. DesBarres* (Salem, Mass., and Toronto, 1969). C. B. Fergusson, *"The old king is back": Amos "King" Seaman and his diary* (PANS Bull., 23, Halifax, 1972). "The grindstone king," *Amherst Daily News* (Amherst, N.S.), 1 May 1963. "Smokestack on Ragged Reef," *Family Herald and Weekly Star* (Montreal), 23 March 1961.

SEATON, JOHN COLBORNE, Baron. *See* Colborne

SECORD, LAURA. *See* Ingersoll

SEELY (Seeley, Seelye), CALEB, sea captain, privateer, shipowner, and merchant; b. 31 Aug. 1787 at Saint John, N.B., son of Ebenezer and Hipzabeth Seely; d. 14 Feb. 1869 in Liverpool, N.S.

Caleb Seely's father, and probably his mother, arrived in Saint John from Connecticut as loyalists in 1783. Caleb was one of at least four children. In 1813, during the war with the United States, he became commander of the privateering schooner *Star* of Saint John, and by late summer had sent two sloops and a pinky to the prize courts.

With his earnings from the *Star* Seely joined Enos Collins* and Joseph Allison*, Halifax businessmen, and Joseph Freeman*, of Liverpool, N.S., as shareholder of the famous 67-ton, five-gun privateer, *Liverpool Packet*. A fast boat, originally designed and used as a tender to an African slaver, it had already gained a formidable privateering reputation under its former commander, Joseph Barss* of Liverpool. Seely was named the new commander and his letter of marque was issued on 19 Nov. 1813.

By Christmas 1813, when Seely returned from his first cruise on the New England coast, he had sent three sloops to the prize courts. Between January and October 1814 he made frequent return forays. American newspapers spoke highly of his treatment of the ships he boarded, and those he found not worth his trouble were released intact. Probably several of his prizes never reached the courts, having been blown ashore in storms or recaptured. By October, 14 more of his prizes had been lawfully condemned by the Court of Vice-Admiralty, and the shareholders of the *Liverpool Packet* had amassed considerable capital. Seely then handed over the command of the privateer to Lewis Knaut.

On 21 Jan. 1815 Seely married Phoebe Collins, sister of his business partner and daughter of a wealthy Liverpool shipowner and merchant, Hallet Collins. Seely settled in Liverpool and engaged in exporting timber, fish, and seal skins to Newfoundland, New England, and Great Britain, and importing manufactured goods and food. The trade was carried on in vessels owned by Seely and his partners, and they frequently travelled with the goods to transact business. At first Seely may have continued his partnership with Enos Collins. By 1827 and until 1833 he was in partnership with Patrick Gough. Afterwards he conducted business independently.

Seely's life in the post-war years followed a quiet course. He was an active layman in the Church of England, and in 1822 bought Simeon Perkins*' former house. From 1838 until his death he was a judge of the Inferior Court of Common Pleas. In the 1830 assembly elections he opposed James Ratchford DeWolf for Queens County, probably because DeWolf had insulted his business partner, Patrick Gough, during the 1829 debates over MHA John Alexander Barry*'s defiance of the assembly. Seely was roundly defeated.

Toward the end of his life Seely became embroiled in two controversies which shed some light on his personality. An 1857 letter to the *Liverpool Transcript* over irregularities in county financial matters reveals his strong sense of right and lack of fear in naming names to correct the situation. Later the same year, in a virulent public correspondence with a debtor whom he had had imprisoned for attacking him, he defended himself fiercely and somewhat intemperately.

Phoebe Seely died on 3 June 1847, having borne three sons and two daughters. Six months later Seely married Desire Grieve, *née* Parker, widow of a local doctor. After her death in 1855 he soon married Jane Sancton, who died in 1865.

Catherine Pross

PANS, Mfm. coll., Places, Liverpool, Business records, letterbook of the firm of Seely and Gough, 1827–33; MG 1, 818, 825, 854; Vertical mss file, Privateering, Liverpool, J. E. Mullins, "Liverpool privateering notes" (1812–25), pp.22–34. C.H.J. Snider, *Under the red jack; privateers of the Maritime provinces of Canada in the War of 1812* (London, 1928), 48–52, 240.

SELLAR, THOMAS, journalist; b. 20 Aug. 1828 at Elgin, Scotland, fourth of ten children born to

Alexander Sellar, notary, and Isabella Grant; d. 27 Oct. 1867 in Montreal.

Educated in Scotland, Thomas Sellar immigrated to Canada in July 1853. He found employment at the Toronto *Globe*, where he ran the counting room and became a lifelong confidant of George Brown*. A Protestant of staunch voluntaryist principles, he contributed articles on politico-religious subjects and was promoted to the post of sub-editor. With Brown's backing he acquired the Brampton *Weekly Times* in Peel County, Canada West, dedicating his opening number of 6 March 1857 to the Grit platform, but the paper floundered within the year and was sold to George Tye. In January 1858 Sellar invested in part-ownership of the Toronto *Echo and Protestant Episcopal Recorder*, the anti-Romanist voice of the evangelical branch of the Church of England in Canada. Primarily a political writer, Sellar left editorial policy on church matters in the hands of prominent Anglican clergymen through whose efforts the struggling journal was periodically subsidized. By 1860 he was sole owner of the *Echo*, and in 1861 moved its office from Toronto to the premises of the *Montreal Herald*.

Sellar continued his association with the *Globe* by acting as its Montreal correspondent – an assignment that enabled him, by 1866, to work off a debt of $1,000 due George Brown. Hounded by creditors, he sought to augment his meagre income by contributing Canadian newsletters to British journals. In 1863 he induced his younger brother, Robert*, to found the *Canadian Gleaner* for Brown's supporters in Huntingdon County, Canada East. Thomas was to receive a percentage of profits for writing the political editorials, but the *Gleaner* lost money and his connection with it was soon confined to its Montreal newsletter. He was, however, rewarded for these services to the Reformers with a welcome government appointment in October 1863 to issue marriage licences in Montreal.

Despite his straitened circumstances, Sellar was active in the literary and social life of the city. In 1865 he was president of the Mercantile Literary Society, secretary of the Mercantile Library Association, and vice-president of the Caledonian Society, and in 1866 was admitted to the Victoria Masonic Lodge. He would seem to have enjoyed the esteem of his professional colleagues as well. He was a founding member of the Canadian Press Association in 1859, and served as secretary-treasurer until 1864, vice-president until 1866, and president from August 1866 until August 1867. Politically, he never deviated from the Grit ideals of representation by population

and complete separation of church and state, and he opposed confederation as inimical to the interests of the British-Protestant minority of Canada East. His diary reveals him to have been a pious man of typically Victorian morality, constantly seeking God's aid in a losing struggle to overcome such "besetting sins" as his unfortunate susceptibility to strong drink. He was in and out of love several times, but ultimately married Louisa Nichols (also written Nicolls in his diary), his faithful fiancée of seven years, at Jarvis, Canada West, on 6 July 1866. During that summer he contracted inflammation of the lungs, yet insisted on attending the annual convention of the Canadian Press Association at Goderich, Canada West, and the diocesan synod of the Church of England at Kingston. He died at the age of 39 shortly after his return to Montreal. The *Echo*, with a "very unsatisfactory" circulation of 1,200 scattered throughout the Province of Canada in 1866, was not continued after his death.

ROBERT ANDREW HILL

PAC, MG 29, C86. Private Archives, Mr Keith Howden (Huntingdon, Que.), diary of Robert Sellar, 1858–78. *Canadian Gleaner* (Huntingdon, Que.), 1863–67. *Echo and Protestant Episcopal Recorder* (Toronto; Montreal), 1858–67. *Gazette* (Montreal), 28 Oct. 1867. *Globe*, 1861–67. *Early Toronto newspapers* (Firth). Morgan, *Bibliotheca Canadensis*. *A history of Canadian journalism* . . . (2v., Toronto, 1908–59), I. R. A. Hill, "Robert Sellar and the Huntingdon *Gleaner*: the conscience of rural Protestant Quebec, 1863–1919" (unpublished PHD thesis, McGill University, Montreal, 1970).

SEYMOUR, FREDERICK, colonial administrator; b. 6 Sept. 1820 at Belfast (Northern Ireland), fourth and youngest son of Henry Augustus Seymour and Margaret Williams; d. 10 June 1869 at Bella Coola, B.C.

Henry Augustus Seymour, the natural son of the 2nd Marquis of Hertford, was deprived of family properties in Ireland, a private income, and a position in the customs service on the succession of the 3rd Marquis of Hertford in 1822, and was forced to take his family to Brussels to reside. Because of the failure of his father's fortunes Frederick, unlike his three brothers, was given neither a good education nor an inheritance. Prince Albert, with whom his eldest brother had developed a friendship, intervened on Frederick's behalf in 1842 to obtain a junior appointment for him in the colonial service.

This appointment, as assistant colonial secretary of Van Diemen's Land (Tasmania), marked the beginning of a lifetime spent in colonies torn

Seymour

by political strife and encumbered with serious economic problems. After upheaval in Van Diemen's Land caused certain offices, including Frederick's own, to be abolished, he was appointed in 1848 special magistrate at Antigua in the Leeward Islands. In 1853 he was named president of Nevis, and was rewarded for good service in 1857 when he was made superintendent of British Honduras (Belize) and lieutenant governor of the Bay Islands. In 1862 he became lieutenant governor of British Honduras.

Early in 1863 Seymour spent some time in England, probably to recuperate from "Panama Fever." On his return to British Honduras the Duke of Newcastle, then colonial secretary, offered him the governorship of British Columbia. Newcastle had already informed Sir James Douglas* that he had recommended Seymour as "a man of much ability and energy who has shown considerable aptitude for the management of savage tribes." Pleased at the "prospect of a change from the swamps of Honduras to a fine country" Seymour accepted with alacrity. He returned to England for a brief visit, and then left for British Columbia accompanied by Arthur Nonus Birch*, a junior clerk in the Colonial Office, who was to act as his colonial secretary.

Newcastle had hoped to create a maritime regional union, similar to that being planned on the Atlantic seaboard, on the retirement of Douglas as governor of Vancouver Island and of British Columbia in 1864. But so intense was the rivalry between the two colonies that he set up separate establishments, appointing Arthur Edward Kennedy* as governor of Vancouver Island (which retained its House of Assembly) on 11 Dec. 1863, and Seymour as governor of the mainland colony on 11 Jan. 1864. The provision of a separate governor and legislative council for the gold colony involved additional expense, but it had always been understood at Whitehall that British Columbia, because of its great potential wealth, should be self-supporting; in 1863 the reports of gold production were encouraging and, to Douglas' amazement, Newcastle promised Seymour a salary of £3,000 and a government house to be built at the colony's expense.

The agitation for a separate administration on the mainland had been intense in New Westminster, and for the swearing in of "our first governor" on 21 April 1864, one day after his arrival in the colony, the little capital was en fête. The enthusiasm of the colonists offset any dismay that Seymour felt on first seeing New Westminster. Ambitious plans for a capital city had been drawn up by Colonel Richard Clement Moody* of the Royal Engineers, but only a few streets had

been laid out when the Royal Engineers departed in November 1863. Seymour later reported to Lord Cardwell, Newcastle's successor, that although "there was a display of energy wanting in the tropics, and thousands of trees . . . had been felled to make way for the great city expected to rise . . . Westminster appeared, to use the miners' expression, 'played out.'"

From the first the new governor had cordial relations with his colonists, and he soon found congenial companions among his officials. He quickly absorbed the local prejudice against Victoria and soon decided that Douglas' policies had been devised to concentrate control of the Cariboo trade in the hands of the merchants, bankers, and speculators of Vancouver Island. By 1866 he was convinced that the interests of the mainland colony had been neglected from the beginning.

Anxious to be accommodating, Seymour assured the Legislative Council, which was in its first session when he arrived, that he would complete Douglas' great highway to the interior mines. The 120-mile section of the Cariboo Road from Alexandria to Williams Creek was still to be surveyed; by the end of 1864 the survey was completed and one-third of its length constructed. The colony's finances, however, were worrisome. The sum of £10,000 was still owing for work done on the Cariboo Road in 1863, and the loans of £100,000 which Douglas had authorized in 1862 and 1863 were expended. Before Seymour's arrival, Douglas had authorized a further loan of £100,000; there was to be a delay in raising it and from its proceeds the imperial government deducted the cost of what Birch termed "some useless military huts." This decision Seymour protested vigorously.

The colony's financial problems were further worsened by an Indian insurrection, which occurred at Bute Inlet within a fortnight of Seymour's arrival in the colony and cost £18,000 to put down. Governor Kennedy, who first heard the news on 11 May that Indians had killed a ferryman and a road party employed by Alfred P. Waddington* in building a route from Bute Inlet to the Cariboo mines [see KLATSASSIN], was slow in informing Seymour. Seymour, in contrast to Kennedy, acted with dispatch. He did not declare martial law, but immediately ordered gold commissioner W. G. Cox* to proceed overland from Cariboo and chief inspector of police Chartres BREW to go by ship from New Westminster with volunteer forces. Meanwhile, the governor went ahead with his plan to have the Fraser River Indians gather at New Westminster for a week-long celebration of the queen's birthday. Some

3,500 Indians came, and at the end Seymour felt that he had established some of the same rapport that Douglas had enjoyed. Hardly had the gathering dispersed than Brew returned to report his failure to penetrate inland. Seymour assisted Brew in raising more men and decided to accompany him; "My great object," he later reported, "was to obtain moderation from the white men in the treatment of Indians."

Every difficulty was experienced by Brew's expedition: Seymour was astounded by the forbidding nature of the coastal range. On the Chilcotin Plateau many of the men became ill with dysentery and the health of both Brew and Seymour was affected. But there were exhilarating moments, such as when Alexis, one of the most powerful Chilcotin chiefs, was persuaded by the governor to assist in the hunt. Some of the leaders of the insurrection eventually surrendered to Cox. Seymour himself took personal satisfaction from the fact that he had assisted in taking eight Indian prisoners for trial.

On emerging at Alexandria, Seymour decided to inspect the Cariboo mines. The miners at Williams Creek and Richfield received him warmly, and the Indians on his trip down the Cariboo Road no less so. These adventures, however, had occupied three vital months when there were pressing problems awaiting the governor's attention. As it became increasingly clear that only £60,000 would be realized from the 1864 loan, Seymour recommended to his council in December the imposition in 1865 of a gold export tax and the raising of the level of customs duties to $12^{1/2}$ per cent.

Though the governor's faith in the prosperity of the colony had been reinforced by his visit to the Cariboo, news of the failure in November 1864 of Macdonald's Bank, a private bank doing business at the mines, gave cause for worry. But it was not until the spring of 1865 when the usual rush of miners from San Francisco failed to materialize that there were doubts about the colony's prospects. Even so, Seymour permitted the extension and the improvement of the Cariboo and Dewdney roads and, when a new mining area opened on the Big Bend of the Columbia River, the building of a road along the Thompson River to Kamloops and the provision of steam navigation on both Kamloops and Shuswap lakes. These works involved an expenditure of $1,342,000. Throughout 1865 business faltered in Victoria, where large supplies of goods had been stored in anticipation of a miners' rush, and in the small communities on the upper Fraser River. These reverses focussed attention on the need for retrenchment, and in Victoria the agita-tion for amalgamation of the colonies developed strength.

The Colonial Office required first-hand information and this it looked forward to obtaining from Seymour who left for England in September 1865. In his dispatches Seymour had deplored "the extreme inconvenience to myself of the position of two Governors of equal authority close to each other yet far from home," but stoutly opposed either the federation or the legislative union of the colonies as recommended by Kennedy and the assembly of Vancouver Island. In London, however, he found the London Committee for Watching the Affairs of British Columbia (a well-organized lobby representing the interests of the Hudson's Bay Company, the Bank of British Columbia, and investors in British Columbia bonds), the Colonial Office, the Treasury, the Foreign Office, and the Admiralty all recommending union. Seymour yielded to the inevitable, but insisted that British Columbia be dominant.

While he was in England Seymour married on 27 Jan. 1866 Florence Maria Stapleton. A few days later he sent a jubilant note to his attorney general: "We shall be in a position to dictate our own terms. The constitution will be that of British Columbia – with some alterations . . . Capital N. Westminster." On 17 February he composed in Paris a dispatch to Cardwell, explaining the opposition of his council to union and the necessity of obtaining its consent, and the importance of having the act of union proclaimed by the governor of British Columbia. He recommended making New Westminster the capital; using the constitution of British Columbia as a model but with the infusion of a larger popular element as a model for the new government; and retaining British Columbia's tariff acts.

Most of Seymour's suggestions were accepted, and the act of union was rushed through parliament at the end of the session of 1866. Royal assent came on 6 August. He then had an interview with Lord Carnarvon, now colonial secretary, who cancelled Kennedy's appointment and agreed to grant Seymour a salary of £4,000 as governor of the united colony. He was also assured by the Colonial Office that "It is understood that New Westminster should be the Capital. . . ."

It was an ailing Seymour who arrived in Victoria on 7 Nov. 1866, where he was received coldly. His reception in New Westminster, however, was gratifying. On 19 November, at New Westminster and Victoria, he issued simultaneously the proclamation of the union of the colonies. "There was no enthusiasm or excitement

Seymour

shown in either town," he admitted to Carnarvon. Seymour paid a month's visit to Victoria to allay the ire of the politicians at the abolition of their House of Assembly and of the merchants at the loss of their free port. "Matters are settling down," he wrote to the Colonial Office, "I believe that personally I am not extremely unpopular." But he deluded himself. "If he only knew the general opinion," wrote John Sebastian Helmcken*, "he would blush."

Depression was upon the whole country when the enlarged Legislative Council convened at New Westminster in January 1867. There was now an exodus of miners and the abandonment of the Collins Telegraph line to connect Russian and American territory had left 500 men unemployed. The gold export tax yielded a disappointingly small sum, and there was an unexpected deficit in the customs receipts caused by the heavy importation of tobacco and liquor by Victoria merchants before the extension of the mainland tariff. The united colony, with a population of 15,000, had a debt of $1,300,000. Not until 27 March 1867 did Seymour raise the bitterly contentious issue of the location of the capital.

The decision on the capital could have been his alone. But the initiative taken in his Paris dispatch had aroused resentment in both sections of the colony, and, since he was opposed to "any appearance of straining the vast power which the Governor possesses," he was disinclined to exert executive authority. His dilatoriness, combined with his decision to seek advice, proved disastrous for his own preference for New Westminster. By a vote of 13 to 8 the council on 29 March recommended Victoria. Seymour was dismayed and sought advice from the Colonial Office. The Duke of Buckingham and Chandos informed him in October 1867 that if he selected Victoria he would have the support of the home government.

In July 1867 Birch, who had administered the mainland colony not too economically during Seymour's 14-month absence, returned to London. Though there was no other official with Birch's experience, Seymour turned over affairs to his assistants and embarked on a northern voyage to investigate Indian disturbances. In August 1867 he travelled to Grouse Creek in Cariboo to intervene in a dispute between two mining companies, and in September he returned to the northern coast to visit William Duncan*'s Indian community at Metlakatla. The Colonial Office heard only spasmodically from him during these months. Then in December Seymour telegraphed requesting a loan for $50,000 and wrote describing the now critical financial position of his government. After another period of silence,

Birch inquired of an official in British Columbia in February 1868, "What in the world has become of you all?" If the governor had proved irresolute in selecting the capital, he now created the impression of being negligent of his duty. In the colony, Douglas confided to Alexander Grant Dallas* that "The whole machine is in a strange incomprehensible muddle – wanting a firm and experienced hand to bring it into good working order."

The possibility of securing relief from the colony's financial plight through entry into the proposed Canadian federation, rather than by annexation to the United States, as some citizens of Victoria advocated, had led Amor De Cosmos* to raise the matter of union with Canada in the Legislative Council on 10 March 1867. Seymour had agreed to telegraph London to ask if provision could be made in the confederation bill then before parliament for the ultimate admission of the colony. He also promised, after the council approved unanimously of the principle of union on 18 March, to communicate with the colonial secretary, the governor of Canada, and the governor of the HBC. But having received no reply to his telegram to London, and knowing that Canada still had to acquire possession of the territory between it and the seaboard colony, he considered an overture to Canada by himself to be improper and premature. Six months elapsed before he forwarded the union resolution to the Colonial Office on 24 Sept. 1867. The arrival of this dispatch caused a flurry of excitement at the Colonial Office, where Seymour's March telegram had been set aside during the Duke of Buckingham's first days in office. There was some exasperation with Seymour for his delay in sending the council resolution, but because the HBC's territory was not yet in Canada's possession, Buckingham informed Seymour that consideration of confederation would have to wait.

There the matter might have rested had not Samuel Leonard Tilley* of the Canadian government telegraphed Victoria in January 1868 that no approach had been made to it by Seymour. At a large public meeting De Cosmos charged the governor with bad faith, and two days later, on 1 Feb. 1868, a memorial was sent from Victoria to the governor general of Canada, Lord Monck*, asking that immediate steps be taken to bring the colony into confederation and tentatively suggesting terms of union. The Canadian cabinet then passed an order-in-council advocating British Columbia's admission.

A second telegram from Tilley, urging the preparation of an address to the queen, was re-

714

ceived by a Victoria journalist on 22 March while the Legislative Council was in session. De Cosmos demanded that the governor's correspondence, "if any," be brought down. Fortunately for Seymour the council turned to the capital question. On 2 April it reaffirmed its choice and named 25 May as the date of removal to Victoria. With their mainland capital lost, some residents of New Westminster so despaired of their own future as colonists that they signed a memorial advocating union with Canada. But the Legislative Council was opposed to taking precipitate action.

Seymour was ill in December 1867 and was slow in recovering his strength. Yet he had felt it incumbent on him to entertain the citizens of New Westminster as he had the people of Victoria. Then there had been the strain of the legislative session, of the transfer of the government offices to Victoria, and of the need to make additional dismissals. In November 1868 he was too ill to attend to business and a petition was got up in Victoria to ask for his recall and the appointment of Douglas as administrator. He rallied his strength to protest violently when Buckingham appointed as colonial secretary Philip J. Hankin, RN, whom Seymour had dismissed in 1867. Depressed also by the charged atmosphere in Victoria on the eve of another legislative session, Seymour confessed "to feeling rather worn out."

What the colony needed, said De Cosmos, was not a change of governor, but a change of government. Constitutional reform had been Seymour's aim from the beginning, but other matters had got in its way. He had always regarded Newcastle's modelling of the constitution of the mainland colony on that of Ceylon as a mistake, and from the first he had treated its Legislative Council as if it had been a legislative assembly. Considering the circumstances, Seymour was surprised at how well the first legislative session of the united colony had gone. In preparation for the elections in 1868, he liberalized the franchise on Vancouver Island, and before calling the session into being he included in the nominated magisterial positions two elected members. But to former members of the Vancouver Island assembly, these changes were far too modest.

The confederation movement, which gained strength during the year, drew some of its support from the desire for constitutional reform. A league of confederationists formed in Victoria in May 1868 agitated not only for admission to the Canadian federation but also for representative and responsible government. But since he was given no instructions in the matter of federation

with Canada, and the negotiations over the HBC's territory were still under way, Seymour advised the Legislative Council, when it met in Victoria on 17 Dec. 1868, to postpone consideration of the matter. Though it contained John Robson* and three other confederationists elected on the mainland, it agreed to a postponement in a vote on 17 Feb. 1869.

On hearing of this disappointing development, Sir John A. Macdonald* felt that no time should be lost in putting the screws on Vancouver Island. He wrote to Anthony Musgrave*, whose term as governor of Newfoundland had nearly ended, stating that Seymour should be recalled "as being perfectly unfit for his present position, under present circumstances. From all I hear he was never fit for it."

His colonists and their representatives, however, were in better temper in 1869 than Seymour had seen them for some time. On Seymour's recommendation a public school system was established, the system of courts improved, public health regulations drawn up, the mining of silver, lead, copper, and coal regulated, and a commission established to examine the Indian reserve system. In public finance the corner had been turned. Seymour had recently reduced the debt and made the final payment for military expenses incurred in Douglas' day. His original revenue measures were now yielding sufficient returns for him to improve the road system, and he was able to announce that the Admiralty would lend money to an English company to construct a graving dock at Esquimalt. In the interior, settlement was superseding gold-mining and farming was becoming established.

The end of this productive legislative session found Seymour suffering from extreme debility. He set to work to put his private and public affairs in order. On 3 April 1869 he signed his will. Five days later he at last swore in Hankin. These matters settled, Seymour prepared to sail to the northern coast where a prolonged, murderous quarrel between the Nass and the Tsimshian tribes was interfering with the spring fishery on the Nass River.

The welfare of the Indians had always been of major concern to Seymour, and he had been successful in establishing good relations with them. He had, however, just received from Colonial Secretary Granville a sharp reprimand for his "unsatisfactory" report on the northern disturbances resulting from the liquor traffic on the seacoast. Accompanied by Joseph Trutch*, commissioner of lands and works, Seymour boarded at Esquimalt on 17 May the HMS *Sparrowhawk*, which he had already twice sent to the northern coast to investigate disturbances. En route he picked up Duncan to serve as his interpreter. At the Nass River, the Nass chiefs were asked to accompany the governor, and at Fort Simpson the Tsimshian chiefs. On 2 June Seymour reached agreement with the warring chiefs on the amount of compensation to be paid each tribe, induced them to sign a peace treaty, and put them under the operation of the law. The ending of the inter-tribal war, Trutch reported, was "fully and satisfactorily accomplished," and this, the governor's last official act, was "creditable to his Administrative ability . . . and entirely in consonance with [his] kindliness of heart. . . ."

Seymour also intended to investigate complaints of white settlers about the Indians. But he became ill with dysentery and after the gunboat dropped anchor at Bella Coola his condition became serious. On the morning of 10 June he died. His body was taken to Esquimalt. There, on 16 June, with full honours, and with Douglas as pall-bearer, he was buried in the naval cemetery.

The Victoria *Daily British Colonist*, which had castigated his administration as energetically as it had earlier condemned Douglas', conceded that Seymour's faults were atoned for by his evident desire to conciliate everyone. To govern the gold colony with its motley mining population, and its still larger and apprehensive Indian population, Newcastle, probably because of royal intervention, had chosen a man with a frail constitution who lacked the strength of character and the impressive mien of his predecessor. Yet Seymour, by his initiative and his display of great physical courage, had won in his first 18 months in office the respect of the mainland population.

Newcastle, Cardwell, and Carnarvon were satisfied with his performance. It was after the Derby government took office in 1866 that difficulties developed. Seymour's advice that the mainland colony's consent to maritime union be obtained was disregarded, and the promise to locate the capital on the mainland was retracted. After the recall of Birch, a growing chilliness developed in the dispatches sent from London. Seymour's neglect of his correspondence, as well as his timidity in the capital question, damaged his reputation at the Colonial Office.

The rivalry between island and mainland was an established fact, and anger was bound to be vented on the man who permitted union of the colonies to take effect. In addition, the "exuberantly free press" had long cultivated a tradition of political agitation. As the mouthpiece of the small professional and mercantile class which sought preferment over the English officials, the press yielded no quarter in battle. Already it had emblazoned on its banner two victories over colonial governors – Douglas and Kennedy; a third was within its grasp.

Though he once admitted that much of the odium attached to Seymour's administration of the united colony was "a natural consequence of the acts of omission and commission of the administration of Sir James Douglas," De Cosmos could not forgive Seymour for not seizing the initiative in the confederation movement. Seymour was condemned by De Cosmos and by Canadian editors, and his reputation did not outlive this charge. Yet Seymour realized that as yet union with Canada was desired only by a vocal minority, hoping to achieve economic relief and governmental reform, neither of which were likely under the existing imperial auspices. Only after a change of government in England and the transfer of the territorial claims of the HBC was the nod given to Musgrave to promote union with Canada. Seymour, despite his accomplishments, then passed into history as British Columbia's forgotten governor.

MARGARET A. ORMSBY

PABC, B.C., Colonial Secretary, correspondence outward, January 1867–December 1870 (letterbook); Governor, despatches to London, 14 Sept. 1863–31 Dec. 1867; 11 Jan. 1868–24 July 1871 (letterbooks); Crease coll., Henry Pering Pellew Crease, correspondence inward, 1864–69; Florence Maria (Stapleton) Seymour letters; James Douglas, correspondence outward, private, 22 May 1867–11 Oct. 1870 (letterbook); Miscellaneous papers relating to Governor Frederick Seymour; O'Reilly coll., Florence Maria (Stapleton) Seymour letters; Frederick Seymour letters; Vancouver Island, Governor, despatches to London, 25 March 1864–19 Nov. 1966 (letterbook). PAC, MG 26, A; RG 7, G1, 166–88. PRO, CO 60. University of British Columbia Library, Special Collections Division (Vancouver), Trutch papers. University of Nottingham Library (Nottingham, Eng.), Newcastle MSS, letterbooks, 1859–64 (mfm. at PAC).

B.C., Legislative Council, *Journals*, 1864–69. G. B., Parl., Command paper, 1866, XLIX, [3667], pp.119–64, *Papers relative to the proposed union of British Columbia and Vancouver Island*; [3694], pp.165–68, *A further despatch relative to the proposed union of British Columbia and Vancouver Island . . . *; 1867, XLVIII, [3852], pp. 281–332, *Further papers relative to the union of British Columbia and Vancouver Island . . . *; House of Commons paper, 1867–68, XLVIII, 483, pp.337–50, *Copy or extracts of correspondence between Governor Kennedy of Vancouver Island, Governor Seymour of British Columbia, and the Colonial Office, on the subject of a site for the capital of British Columbia*; 1868–69, XLIII, 390, pp.341–72, *Papers on the union of British Columbia with the dominion of Canada. Minutes of a preliminary meeting of the delegates elected by the various districts of British Colum-*

bia, convened at Yale, pursuant to the following call: "Yale Convention" (New Westminster, B.C., 1868).

H. H. Bancroft, *History of British Columbia, 1792–1887* (San Francisco, 1890). *British Columbia and confederation*, ed. W. G. Shelton (Victoria, 1967). F. W. Howay and E. O. S. Scholefield, *British Columbia from the earliest times to the present* (4v., Vancouver, 1914). F. W. Howay *et al.*, *British Columbia and the United States: the north Pacific slope from fur trade to aviation*, ed. H. F. Angus (Toronto, 1942). Ormsby, *British Columbia*. F. W. Howay, "The attitude of Governor Seymour towards confederation," RSC *Trans.*, 3rd ser., XIV (1920), sect.II, 31–49. M. A. Ormsby, "Frederick Seymour, the forgotten governor," *BC Studies*, 22 (summer 1974), 3–25. W. N. Sage, "The critical period of British Columbia history, 1866–1871," *Pacific Hist. Rev.* (Glendale, Calif.), I (1932), 424–43; "From colony to province; the introduction of responsible government in British Columbia," *BCHQ*, III (1939), 1–14.

SHADE, ABSALOM, businessman and politician; b. *c.* 1793 in Wyoming County, Pa, reputed to be the youngest son of a farmer; d. 15 March 1862 at Galt (first called Shade's Mills, now part of Cambridge), Canada West. He married first, Mrs Andrews of Canandaigua, N.Y., and secondly, Isabella Davidson of Galt; there were no children by either marriage.

Absalom Shade trained as a carpenter in his youth and followed that trade in Buffalo, N.Y., until 1816. In that year he submitted a tender for the contract to build a court house and jail at Niagara-on-the-Lake, Upper Canada. Although Shade's tender was rejected, the young man so impressed William Dickson*, a member of the Legislative Council, that he hired Shade to manage and superintend the settlement of his lands in Dumfries Township, Gore District.

In July 1816 Shade and Dickson journeyed to Dumfries to examine the lands, and after an extensive survey chose the site of what became Galt as the nucleus of the projected settlement. Shade went to Buffalo to arrange his affairs, and returned that autumn with his wife and two step-children to take up permanent residence on the site. By winter Shade had repaired and completed for himself a combined saw and grist mill which had been abandoned by an earlier settler, and built a two-storey log house which served as both a dwelling and a shop.

Tradition has it that when Shade arrived in Dumfries Township he possessed only $100 and a chest of carpenter's tools. He soon amassed a large fortune. The key to his success was the monopoly he enjoyed over a wide spectrum of business activities. Cash was scarce, and with Dickson's financial backing Shade built up a large credit business at his store, where he charged a mark-up of 50 to 100 per cent on credit sales. When Dickson built the "Dumfries Mill" in 1818, Shade became its manager, ensuring a continuation of his control of milling. In 1820 Shade built a distillery adjacent to this mill and operated both businesses.

Because of Dickson's active campaigns to recruit settlers in Scotland and the United States, Shade's Mills expanded and prospered in spite of its distance from a good market for grain and the area's bad roads. As the population grew Shade's many businesses flourished. In 1824 he erected a large general store and grain handling depot on the banks of the Grand River. In 1827 when a post office was established at Shade's Mills, the village was renamed Galt. Shade became the postmaster and retained that position for 25 years.

In 1827 Shade bid for and received several large contracts to supply lumber, flour, pork, and other provisions to John Galt* and the Canada Company, then engaged in building roads through the Huron Tract. So profitable were these contracts that within a year Shade was able to purchase the Dumfries Mill from Dickson. As part of the transaction Shade received a guarantee that Dickson would not sell land to any other miller, distiller, merchant, or grain dealer who might compete with Shade. In 1832, Shade built a second store across the street from the first. At the original "Red Store" Shade conducted his credit business, while at the new "White Store" he dealt at somewhat lower prices for cash. His monopoly of Galt's mercantile trade secure, Shade now turned over the management of his many enterprises to James Fargis, his nephew, and James K. Andrews, his stepson. He then devoted his energies to public office, the promotion of transportation projects, and the management of numerous farming properties and a large mortgage and money-lending business.

Shade's many mercantile enterprises and his land dealings gave him a life-long interest in the improvement of transportation. In 1819, for example, he had initiated a subscription campaign to build a bridge across the Grand River at Shade's Mills. When subscriptions fell short, he underwrote much of the cost himself. In the early 1830s Shade undertook the daring experiment of building several large (18 × 16 ft) flat-bottom barges on the Grand River. In the spring, even though the high water was dangerous, he loaded the barges with barrels of flour, grain, pork, and other produce intended for export, and floated them down the Grand to Dunnville. The barges were then towed by horses via the Welland Canal to Port Dalhousie (St Catharines) where both the produce and the raft-timber were sold. As a natural outgrowth of this endeavour, Shade became an active promoter and one of the original incorporators of the Grand River Navigation Company, which was chartered in 1832 to improve navigation on the river, there being no good road from Galt to Dundas.

As Shade's fortunes grew and his business interests broadened, he became associated with the Hamilton business community in the founding of the Gore Bank in 1835. In 1852, in company with his Hamilton associates, he became an incorporator and shareholder in the Galt and Guelph Railway. He was also an active promoter of both the Preston and Berlin Railway and the Berlin and Stratford Gravel Road Company.

Always a strong Tory in politics, Shade served two terms in the House of Assembly. In 1831 one of the two sitting members for Halton County, James Crooks*, was elevated to the Legislative Council. Shade was elected to the assembly in Crooks' place and served out the term. In the election of 1834 Shade and his running mate, William Chisholm*, were defeated by James Durand and Caleb Hopkins*, but in the violent election of 1836 Shade and Chisholm were returned. Shade served without particular distinction until 1841 when he retired. Although he was frequently mentioned as a possible Tory candidate, he henceforth refused nomination. During the rebellion of 1837 he acted on the local commission of the peace to examine suspected rebels, and helped organize a detachment of militia for service on the Niagara frontier.

On the local political scene Shade held almost every nominated and elected municipal office over a 30-year period. After local government was organized in Dumfries Township in 1819, Shade frequently served as chairman of the township meetings, as well as holding such offices as pound keeper and assessor. In 1828 he was named a magistrate for Gore District and ably represented Dumfries' interests at the Gore District quarter sessions. When elective municipal government was established in 1841, Shade was elected a township councillor, and in 1852 was elected as the second reeve of the newly incorporated village of Galt.

In 1852 Shade retired from public life and devoted his time to managing his estate and numerous local charities. He died in 1862 after a short illness.

LEO A. JOHNSON

Cambridge Public Library (Galt, Ont.), Miscellaneous historical papers. PAC, MG 24, D16, Shade to Isaac Buchanan, 18 July 1854, 20 Feb. 1856; E1, Shade to Merritt, 14 March 1833, 25 July 1845, 17 March 1849; RG 1, L1, 18–39. PAO, Dickson (William) papers. *Correspondent and Advocate* (Toronto), 1836. *Dumfries Reformer and Western Counties Agricultural and Commercial Advertiser* (Galt), 19 March 1862. *Galt Reporter and Waterloo County Advertiser*, 21 March 1862, 1870–71. B. M. Dunham, *Grand River* (Toronto, 1945). R. S. Hamilton, *The early history of Galt, 1816–1866*, ed. A. W. Osborne and A. W. Taylor (Galt, Ont., 1956).

SHEPPARD, WILLIAM, businessman and member of the Executive Council of Lower Canada; b. 16 Aug. 1784 in England, son of William Sheppard and Sarai Maxfield; d. on the night of 1–2 July 1867 at Trois-Rivières, Que.

Little is known about the first 25 years of William Sheppard's life. He arrived in Canada with his father in 1792, and by 1809 was a merchant living in Montreal. On 28 September of that year he married at Quebec Harriet Campbell, daughter of the king's notary, Archibald CAMPBELL. Sheppard settled in Quebec and accumulated a fortune as a timber merchant. He also took an interest in shipbuilding, since in August 1826 he launched a brig and another vessel.

In 1816 Sheppard acquired at Sillery a magnificent villa surrounded by 100 acres of park and orchards. This estate had been created and named Samos by Bishop Pierre-Herman Dosquet* (Dosquet was bishop of Samos *in partibus*); Adam Mabane*, leader of the French party after the conquest, renamed it Woodfield. Sheppard installed there a library of 3,000 volumes, a picture gallery, and a small museum of natural history; he built aviaries and greenhouses, and took up gardening. Sheppard and his wife, who was a friend of the Countess of Dalhousie, were highly esteemed in Quebec intellectual and social circles. In 1824 he took part in the organization of the Literary and Historical Society of Quebec, as did the governor general, Lord Dalhousie [Ramsay*]. Sheppard was its president in 1833–34, 1841, 1843, and 1847. He and his wife read several papers to the society on natural history, applied sciences, and archaeology, in which he showed his interest in the plants of the region. From 1827 to 1829 Sheppard was also a member of the short-lived Société des Arts, whose members were mostly French Canadian.

On 22 Aug. 1837 he was appointed to the Executive Council of Lower Canada, of which he was a member until 1841; he seems however to have had little enthusiasm for the great game of politics. In 1847 Sheppard, who had invested the bulk of his fortune in the timber export trade, experienced a serious financial reverse. He had to get rid of Woodfield (which he had rebuilt after a fire in 1842), and he retired to his residence of Fairymead at Drummondville. He spent 20 years there, more or less forgotten by all but his old friends. Each year he returned to Sillery to collect rents from the villagers of Sheppardville, which he had founded and which the inhabitants later called Bergerville (now Sillery). Sir James MacPherson Le Moine*, who knew him, described Sheppard at this time as a tall, handsome old man with white hair, a pensive look, and hands full of flowers and ferns, a melancholy wanderer in the haunts of yesteryear.

Stricken by apoplexy while on his way to the Anglican synod at Quebec, Sheppard died on the Trois-Rivières dock around midnight on 1 July 1867. He left a large number of descendants.

PIERRE SAVARD

[For a complete list of the papers William Sheppard and his wife published in the Literary and Hist. Soc. of Quebec, *Trans.*, between 1829 and 1843, see *Index of the lectures, papers and historical documents published by the Literary and Historical Society of Quebec . . . 1829 to 1891*, comp. J. W. Strachan and F. C. Würtele, (Quebec, 1927). P.S.]
ANQ-Q, AP-G-239/94, Sheppard; État civil, Anglicans, Cathedral of the Holy Trinity (Quebec), 28 Sept. 1809. *Le Canadien*, 12 juill. 1867. P.-G. Roy, *Fils de Québec*, III, 18–20. George Gale, *Historic tales of old Quebec* (Quebec, 1923), 245. J. M. Le Moine, *L'album du touriste* . . . (2e éd., Québec, 1872), 80–85.

SHORTT, JONATHAN, Church of England clergyman and journalist; b. 15 Sept. 1809 at St Helier on the island of Jersey, son of Dr John Shortt and Harriet McCausland; m. first, Lucy Hartshorne (d. 1849), by whom he had two children, and m. in 1850 Isabel Harper, and they had three children; d. 24 Aug. 1867 at Port Hope, Ont.

Jonathan Shortt's father had served in the Peninsular War and was surgeon to the 79th Regiment in Canada from 1825 to 1835. Little is known about Jonathan's early life, but he was for some time a gentleman cadet at the Royal Military College at Sandhurst, England. He was in Montreal in 1829, when, instead of moving to Kingston with his father when the latter's regiment was transferred, he remained in Montreal to begin studies for the ministry of the Church of England under clergymen John Bethune* and Abraham Fuller Atkinson. At the same period he began lifelong friendships with Henry James Grasett*, later dean of St James' Cathedral, Toronto, and William Plenderleath* Christie, a prominent landowner and church builder. On 21 Oct. 1832, Shortt was ordained deacon at York

(Toronto) by Bishop Charles James Stewart*. He then assisted Archdeacon George J. MOUNTAIN at Quebec City until his appointment to Laprairie (La Prairie) near Montreal in August 1833. In 1834 he was ordained priest at Quebec and was stationed at the mission of Beckwith Township, Upper Canada. After three years at Beckwith Shortt was appointed rector of Port Hope, arriving in his new parish in September 1837. Here he remained for 30 years.

During his long ministry Port Hope increased in population and importance. Shortt was prominent in community affairs and became a well-known advocate of temperance, serving in 1859 as grand worthy patriarch of the Sons of Temperance in Canada West. He added to his meagre stipend by teaching school, as his predecessor, James Coghlan, had done. In November 1839 he advertised in the *Church* that he was prepared to instruct day pupils in French, Latin, history, geography, and elementary mathematics.

On behalf of a group of Anglican evangelicals he edited the *Echo and Protestant Episcopal Recorder* at Port Hope from its first issue of 14 Oct. 1851 until it moved to Toronto in 1854. The *Echo* accurately reflected Shortt's Irish background and his strongly Protestant, conservative churchmanship. The newspaper was not popular with all Canadian Anglicans. In 1853 an acidulous pen commented in the Hamilton *Gazette* on "that shallow, Jesuitical slip-slop carping against the distinctive doctrines of the Anglican Catholic Communion which characterises our semi-dissenting contemporary the Echo." Within the framework of his evangelical convictions, however, Shortt was essentially a moderate who gained the respect of his fellow Anglican clergy of different views. His obituary in 1867 stated that his editorials "were characterized by great clearness, logical acumen and bold faithfulness in the defence of truth," and that those he criticized "had never any reason to accuse his utterances of acerbity."

In 1857 when Shortt was to visit Ireland Bishop John STRACHAN of Toronto described him as one of his "senior and approved clergy" in a letter of introduction to Archbishop Richard Whately of Dublin. In that same year the archbishop of Canterbury, J. B. Sumner, granted Shortt the Lambeth degree of DD.

T. R. MILLMAN

Jonathan Shortt was the author of *"Peace in believing . . ."* (Toronto, 1847); *A sermon preached to the loyal Orange lodges, assembled in St. John's Church, Port Hope, July 12, 1853* (Montreal, 1853); and *Sea air in summer: a lecture* (Montreal, 1866). PAO, Strachan

Sibbald

(John) papers, letterbooks, 1839–43, 1844–49, 1852–66. QDA, 49 (B-3), p.122; 107 (G-1), 1, 1832–34. St Mark's Anglican Church (Port Hope, Ont.), Registers and vestry minutes of St John's Anglican Church, Port Hope. *Church*, 1837–56; especially 23 Sept., 4 Nov. 1837; 23, 30 June 1838; 5 Oct., 16 Nov. 1839; 8 May 1841; 14 July 1843; 13 June 1845; 16 July 1847; 22 Feb. 1849; 15 Aug. 1850. *Church Chronicle* (Toronto), October 1867. Church of England, Church Soc. of the Diocese of Toronto, *Annual report* (Cobourg; Toronto), 1843–67; Diocese of Toronto, *Journal of the Synod* (Toronto), 1865–67; *Proc. of the Synod* (Toronto), 1853–64. *Echo and Protestant Episcopal Recorder* (Port Hope; Toronto), 1851–54; 19 Jan., 9 March 1855; 1 May, 5 June 1857; 27 June, 10 Nov. 1859. Soc. for the Propagation of the Gospel in Foreign Parts, *Report* (London), 1841. *Historical records of the 79th Queen's Own Cameron Highlanders*, comp. T. A. Mackenzie *et al.* (London, 1887). W. A. Craick, *Port Hope historical sketches* (Port Hope, Ont., 1901). P. C. Moffatt, *Time was: the story of St. Mark's Anglican Church, Port Hope* (Cobourg, Ont., 1972).

SIBBALD, SUSAN. *See* MEIN

SIBLEY, JOSEPH, farmer and chairmaker; b. *c.* 1790, the son of Ezekiel Sibley and Mary West; m. Jane Woodworth, and they had ten children; d. 1 Feb. 1862 in St Andrew's (Wittenburg), N.S.

About 1812 Joseph Sibley, with his brothers and father, settled on the south branch of the St Andrews River in central Nova Scotia, where the small community of Wittenburg now stands. Probably the first settlers there, they cleared the land and established their farms. Joseph combined woodwork with farming and made, for local sale, various items needed in pioneer homes: buttertubs, spinning wheels, looms, and the like. In an era of home-made furniture he was particularly successful in producing chairs and selling them locally. He tried them in various styles before settling on the typical Sibley chair familiar to collectors, with slat backs and turned finials. The slats were usually made from birch or ash. The stretchers, hickory or ash, were dried; the uprights, usually maple, were green when the chairs were assembled, and as they dried they clamped the ends of the stretchers in a vise-like grip which made the chairs remarkably sturdy. Ash splits were woven to make the seats.

Joseph Sibley lived out his days in Wittenberg. Assisted by his sons, Michael (1833–1908) and Isaac, he farmed and made chairs and other items in slack seasons. The inventory of his estate shows "22 butter tubs, 16 sets chair rounds, 3 sets new chairs" on hand. As far as is known all Joseph's work was unsigned; he is notable not for examples of his workmanship but as the originator of the Sibley chairs. Michael took over

the business and expanded it to produce several kinds of furniture which reached a wider market. Therefore most of the Sibley chairs one sees date from the years the business was operated by Michael and by other members of the family who succeeded him.

ROSS GRAVES

Colchester County Registry of Deeds (Truro, N.S.), 7, p.390; 8, pp.351, 360; 9, pp.305, 518; 10, pp.122, 145, 157, 564; 11, p.484; 12, pp.442, 456, 468; 14, p.222; 16, p.17; 20, p.69; 21, p.178; 23, p.339; 24, p.402; 25, p.76; 27, p.414; 33, p.311; 36, p.257; 37, p.223; 40, p.66 (conveyances to which Joseph Sibley was a party). Colchester County Registry of Probate (Truro, N.S.), no.279, will of Joseph Sibley, docket 581 (papers re: estate of Joseph Sibley). Community Cemetery, Wittenberg, N.S. PANS, MG 4, no.18; RG 20, A, 28, 55 (Ezekiel Sibley, 1807, 1814); John Wright, "An attempt to gather up some of the history of St. Andrews, now Wittenberg, Colchester County, Nova Scotia, & its pioneers and their descendants, especially those of the Sibleys" (copy of MS in possession of Mrs Lois MacPhee, Stewiacke, N.S.). M. P. Burrows, *A history of Wittenburg (St. Andrews)* (mimeographed pamphlet, n.p., [1962]), 3–7, 35–37 (copy in PANS). George MacLaren, *Antique furniture by Nova Scotian craftsmen*, advisory ed. P. R. Blakeley (Toronto, [1961]), 57–61.

SIMMS, JAMES, lawyer, merchant, and public official; baptized 24 Feb. 1779 in Birmingham, England, the son of William and Mary Simms; d. 2 Jan. 1863 at Tulse Hill, Surrey, England.

From 1788 to 1792 James Simms attended school in West Bromwich, near Birmingham. He probably then studied law in Birmingham or London. In 1809 he came to Newfoundland, and by the last years of the Napoleonic wars was established in business in St John's. A sometime auctioneer, notary public, agent for trustees of insolvent estates, broker of codfish sales, and renter of wharfage and warehouse space, he was in a mercantile partnership with Joseph H. Costello in 1811–13. Simms traded in St John's and Twillingate, where his brother Joseph seems to have been established as a merchant. James Simms' varied experience enabled him to obtain a thorough knowledge of the legal and economic life of St John's and Newfoundland.

Simms was not, however, active as a businessman after 1825, when his official career began. In that year he was appointed acting attorney general of Newfoundland in the place of John William Molloy who vacated the office for a more lucrative seat on the Supreme Court. Simms' appointment, made permanent in October 1827, lasted until 1846.

The pre-eminent question throughout Simms'

term as attorney general was the form of government best suited to Newfoundland. Simms outlined his opposition to the proposed system of representative government in a written opinion requested by Governor Thomas John Cochrane* in 1831. Simms believed that the increased cost of this form of government would lead to further taxation of the fisheries, and that the additional burden would force fishermen to emigrate to the United States, to the great detriment of the industry. He asserted that, given the social and economic structure of Newfoundland, the new assembly would be filled with merchants resident in Newfoundland only during the short fishing season, whose participation in its work would consequently be restricted.

His alternative was an enlarged governor's council which he unrealistically believed would receive wide public approval. He felt the Newfoundland merchants, with their economic and social ties in Britain, could obtain favourable legislation for the fisheries through the British House of Commons.

Despite Simms' objections, Newfoundland was granted representative government in 1832 and Simms became a member of the Council under the new constitution. His appointment revealed one of the weaknesses of representative government: the Council under the new system, which exercised both executive and legislative functions, was filled with officials adamantly opposed to an elected assembly, who tried to thwart its actions whenever possible. Legislation passed by the assembly, such as the Revenue Bill of 1833, was repeatedly vetoed or amended by the Council. Simms was a leader of this group of conservatives and, according to a 19th century historian, "seems to have been their mouthpiece at all public meetings."

In April 1833 Simms was offered, but refused, a seat on the Supreme Court; however, in the same month he was made acting chief justice after the retirement of Richard Alexander TUCKER. Simms apparently expected to receive a permanent appointment to the chief justiceship, but in November 1833 Henry John BOULTON of Upper Canada was appointed. It is not surprising, therefore, that he and Boulton often clashed over legislation in the Council. Simms particularly objected to Boulton's advocacy of the more extensive application of English law in Newfoundland. The institution of the rigorous English law regarding insolvencies, for example, would disrupt the traditional ease with which Newfoundland firms were declared insolvent, an important consideration given the instability of the cod trade. In 1844 Simms served again as acting chief justice

for several months before the arrival of Thomas Norton.

Simms continued to serve in his offices through the early years of representative government and as an appointed member of the amalgamated legislature after 1842. He maintained a conservative outlook, opposing any extension of the powers of the assembly. Although he had refused an assistant judgeship in 1833, he did not object in 1846 when Governor Sir John Harvey* appointed him to fill a vacant seat on the Supreme Court, where he served for the next 12 years. His subsequent role in the colony's political life was relatively unimportant since at the time of this appointment he was removed from both the Executive and the Legislative councils. He was, however, involved in one controversy in 1849 when he was suspended for a time after a dispute with Governor John Gaspard Le Marchant*; the disagreement involved the provision of funds for circuit courts and in protest Simms had refused to take his turn on the circuit.

Simms' last years in the Supreme Court were marked by growing incapacity. The other assistant justice, Augustus Wallet DesBarres*, was also old and enfeebled. Only in 1858 were Simms and DesBarres pensioned off by a special act of the first assembly with responsible government, under the leadership of Philip Francis Little*. Simms retired to England, probably the same year, and died in 1863.

James Simms was one of those few public officials in Newfoundland whose public careers began with the introduction of colonial status in 1824, continued through representative government, and concluded in the period of responsible government after 1855. The relatively short time-span involved made appointed officials like Simms both unique and anachronistic in their own time.

DAVID J. DAVIS

PANL, GN 2/1, 1826–33; GN 2/2, 1826–33; GN 13, James Simms, "Observations on the propriety of instituting a local Legislative Assembly for Newfoundland" (c. 1831); P3/A/2 (James Simms correspondence, 1788, 1790, 1823). PRO, CO 199/20–25. Nfld., *Blue book*, 1828–58; House of Assembly, *Journal*, 1834–36, 1858. *Courier* (St John's), 12 May 1858. *Newfoundlander*, 27 Feb., 6 March 1834. *Newfoundland Mercantile Journal* (St John's), 1816. *Royal Gazette* (St John's), 3 Feb. 1863. Greene, "Influence of religion in the politics of Nfld., 1850–61." Marjorie Smith, "Newfoundland, 1815–1840: a study of a merchant-ocracy" (unpublished MA thesis, Memorial University of Newfoundland, St John's, 1968). E. A. Wells, "The struggle for responsible government in Newfoundland, 1846–1855" (unpublished MA thesis, Memorial University of Newfoundland, St John's, 1966).

Sinclair

SINCLAIR, WILLIAM, HBC chief factor; b. *c.* 1794 in Rupert's Land, eldest son of Chief Factor William Sinclair from the Orkney Islands, Scotland, and of Nahovway (otherwise Margaret, by family tradition a daughter of Chief Factor Moses Norton*, but possibly a Cree), and brother of James*, Colin, and Thomas Sinclair; m. 21 June 1823, Mary, daughter of fur-trader Alexander McKay*, and they had four daughters and four sons; d. 12 Oct. 1868 in Brockville, Ont.

An "active lad," five feet, five inches tall, dark, "peaceable and mild," William Sinclair entered the service of the Hudson's Bay Company in 1808 as an apprentice with a salary of £8 a year. He spent his first years at Oxford House, York Factory, Winnipeg River District, and Norway House before setting off for Britain in the company ship, *Prince of Wales*, in 1816. Turned back by ice, the ship wintered in James Bay. To relieve the resulting food shortage young Sinclair was dispatched with able-bodied passengers and letters to Fort Severn and the Capusco Goose Camp in the same region. In 1817 he was made clerk in Lesser Slave Lake District, where, on a journey stopped by ice, he resourcefully improvised a winter post for trading. His annual salary rose slowly to £100. Returning in 1819 from a year in England he served at Oxford House, Sandy Lake (Ont.), and Island Lake (Man.) before joining the Bow River expedition of 1822–23 led by Chief Factor Donald McKenzie* to the forks of the South Saskatchewan and Red Deer rivers; during this expedition Sinclair accompanied John Edward HARRIOTT on a seven-week, 850-mile journey over the little known southwestern plains to the Cypress Hills and Missouri country.

In 1824 began 20 years of service in the Winnipeg River and Rainy Lake districts (later combined), at first in outlying areas, collecting wild rice, hunting, gathering furs, heading off American competition along the border, or going with the annual boat brigade to York Factory. The "promising youth" of 1809–10 had become in the mid 1820s, in the opinion of Chief Factor John Dugald Cameron*, "a sober young man – careful and attentive," "very handy and industrious," though "rather of a sickly disposition." He was a good accountant but could not speak French, which was, according to Simon McGillivray Jr, "much against him in commanding Canadians." His first independent command was the Dalles post in 1831 where, after initial mistakes, he won Chief Factor John Stuart*'s approval; there were few to whom Stuart "would more willingly commit a charge." Stuart urged George Simpson* in 1831 to favour Sinclair since, though capable and "born in the service," he had "but little chance of being promoted." Nevertheless, in 1844 Sinclair was made chief trader.

Sinclair was transferred to Churchill in 1845 as the person best qualified to improve its trade, and was again appointed to Rainy Lake District in 1848; he became chief factor in 1850. He was assigned in 1854 to Fort Edmonton, in charge of the Saskatchewan District. There he attempted to make peace between the Crees and the Blackfoot Confederacy. In 1857 he was again in charge of the Rainy Lake District, going on in 1858 to command the key Norway House District. He went on retirement furlough in 1862. In 1854 he had "lands and a house in Red River," but in 1863 he settled near Brockville, Canada West, where he spent the remainder of his life.

Like other officers of the HBC, Sinclair was a prodigious traveller. He took on assignments such as re-establishing a grist mill, supplying birch bark and other canoe-building materials, apprehending a murderer, and collecting a musk-ox skin for John James Audubon. The "difficult and troublesome" service of organizing troop transport between York Factory and Red River in 1846, 1848, 1857, and 1861 he performed "in a highly satisfactory manner." From 1851 to at least 1863 he was a member of the council of the Northern Department.

William Sinclair was one of the country-born, mixed-blood sons of HBC officers to become commissioned officers in its service. George Simpson's estimate in 1832, in his confidential "Character Book," was critical: "a half breed of the Cree nation . . . Deficient in education – A good shot and tolerably active but possesses little judgement. A mean spirited low blackguard kind of fellow – Manages the business of a small outpost but moderately well and commands little respect among servants or Indians – ." By 1845 his opinion had changed. His official letters to Sinclair commend him as "an active intelligent officer" on whose "excellent management" and "usual great ability" he counted, though with occasional disappointments. The turning point in Sinclair's career seems to have been his satisfactory service with Chief Factor John Stuart.

IRENE M. SPRY

HBC Arch., A.16/64, p.207; A.30/11–14; A.34/2; A.36/12; B.4/b/1, 6, 10, 23 Oct., 14 Dec. 1829, 7 Feb. 1830, 26 May 1831; B.34/a/4, p.48; B.34/d/1, p.45; B.60/a/29b, 17 Sept. 1856, 11 March, 15 May 1857; B.105/a/10–14, 17, 19–20; B.115/a/1; B.115/d/2; B.134/b/22, 24, 26–28; B.135/a/1139; B.154/a/59, 65; B.239/a/132, 1 Aug. 1824; B.239/d/143, 147, 152, 170, 175, 195; B.239/1/8–15; B.239/k/1–3; C.1/785, 787–88; D.4/22, 6 July 1836; D.4/24, 28 Feb. 1838; D.4/57, 10

June 1845; D.4/65, 8 June 1844; D.4/67, 10 June, 22 Nov. 1845; D.4/69, 30 June, 18 Dec. 1847; D.4/70, 2 June, 9 July, 15 Nov. 1848, 19 Nov. 1849; D.4/71, 11 July, 18 Dec. 1850; D.4/75, 28 Jan. 1855, 19 Jan. 1856; D.4/76a, 6 Dec. 1856. [Particular thanks are due to the archivist of the Hudson's Bay Company and her colleagues for tracing much of the widely scattered material used in the biography that would otherwise have escaped notice. I.M.S.]

PAC, MG 19, D7, ser.2. United Counties of Leeds and Grenville Surrogate Court (Brockville, Ont.), register 2, pp.678–83. *Canadian North-West* (Oliver), I, 648, 664, 671, 681–82; II, 697, 706, 716, 732, 738, 765, 770, 791, 805, 822, 830, 842, 858, 865. HBRS, III (Fleming). D. G. Lent, *West of the mountains: James Sinclair and the Hudson's Bay Company* (Seattle, Wash., 1963), 19, 21, 23, 31–32, 42, 155, 201, 293, 295–96. E. W. Marwick, "A Harrayman in Hudson Bay," *Orcadian* (Kirkwall, Scot.), 18, 25 March 1965.

SLEIGH, BURROWS WILLCOCKS ARTHUR, soldier and author; b. in 1821 in Lower Canada, son of William Willcocks Sleigh MD and Sarah Campbell; m. twice (his first wife was a Miss Franklin, daughter of a member of the Royal Academy in London) and there were children by both marriages; d. 22 March 1869 at Chelsea, England.

Burrows Willcocks Arthur Sleigh was educated first in England, to which his parents had returned, and after 1834 in Lower Canada. In 1842 he enrolled as ensign in the 2nd West India Regiment and he obtained his lieutenancy by purchase in Jamaica in November 1844. In 1845 the 77th Foot arrived in Jamaica and Sleigh transferred to this regiment by purchase. The 77th was moved to Halifax, N.S., in the spring of 1846 and a few months later to Quebec; on 25 June 1848 it was gazetted as having returned to England. Although Sleigh also returned to England he probably sold his lieutenant's commission at this time thus ending his connection with the army.

While in England Sleigh bought from an absentee proprietor 100,000 acres of land in Kings County, in eastern Prince Edward Island, for £20,000, and about 1850 he returned to North America as an independent gentleman. He soon acquired some of the usual appurtenances of a landed proprietor, becoming a justice of the peace and a lieutenant-colonel in one of the Island militia regiments. But he did not, apparently, live much in Prince Edward Island; he preferred Halifax, which, as he put it, "from its resident gentry, the general tone of its society, the delightful environs . . . is one of the pleasantest places of residence in the Lower Provinces." He spent some time in 1851 travelling in the United States, and although he had a poor opinion of

that country he still preferred it to Prince Edward Island. Charlottetown's legal luminaries he designated "the forty thieves," and responsible government in the Island he considered a mockery stating that when the premier is seen "emerging from his tavern . . . the illusion vanishes," as it did also when "an Honourable Executive Councillor . . . descends from his bundles of dried cod-fish" to attend the council. Sleigh had equally caustic opinions about the Island tenants who, he believed, were animated largely by general knavery and animal cunning.

Sleigh tried in 1852 to establish a steamship service from New York to Quebec, via Halifax, Charlottetown, and Newcastle, N.B., using the 1,100-ton *Albatross*. The enterprise, which was greeted with some *éclat* by newspapers, received help from provincial legislatures, and had the possibility of commercial success. But owing to the lack of lighthouses and to the navigational difficulties in the Gulf of St Lawrence and on the river itself, the cost of marine insurance was ruinous; the scheme was abandoned and the *Albatross* sold probably in late 1852. It would seem to be at this point too that Sleigh returned to England and sold his Prince Edward Island estate.

In May 1853 Sleigh published in London his book, *Pine forests and hacmatack clearings*. About this time he also began to publish the *British Army Dispatch*, a newspaper which seems to have had some success and which he shortly afterwards sold for £900. He lived on this income for a time, then, with three partners, began the *Daily Telegraph*, the first of the twopenny dailies in London. The first issue appeared on 29 June 1855. Within a short time Sleigh, who had bought out his partners' interests for £450, was £2,400 in debt for machinery and paper, and he sold the *Telegraph*. He was no more successful in three attempts at election to the House of Commons. By 1857 he was in bankruptcy court, having been living by his own admission at the rate of £1,000 a year. His assets were not £50, and he owed £523. Nothing is known of his activities during the last 12 years of his life.

Ambitious, energetic, and improvident, Sleigh is one of the many examples of a man whose ideas outran his income. His connection with Canada is chiefly remembered in the book *Pine forests* which reflects his temperament in its vigorous, indeed exhilarating account of life in the North American colonies, with numerous salty and irreverent sketches of colonial politicians. His views about the seaminess of colonial politics have, alas, an air of verisimilitude. Joseph Howe*'s victory in Cumberland County, N.S., in the provincial election of 1851 was carried, according to Sleigh, mainly by rum. The day before the election Sleigh travelled to Amherst in the same stagecoach that carried barrels of rum, consigned to Howe.

P. B. WAITE

[There are no known collections of Sleigh papers on this side of the Atlantic, and it has not been possible to investigate English sources, which might have filled in some of the gaps. There is a stern account of his financial affairs in the *Law Times* of London, Eng., for 26 Dec. 1857. Sleigh is also mentioned briefly in accounts of the history of British newspapers; for his connection with the *Daily Telegraph* in 1855 *see* [E. F. Lawson], *Peterborough court; the story of the "Daily Telegraph"* (London, 1955), 1, 4. An abridged version of his fascinating adventure by iceboat is presented by P. B. Waite in the *Dal. Rev.*, XLII (1962–63), 55–67, as "Crossing Northumberland straits in March, 1852." P.B.W.]

B. W. A. Sleigh, *Pine forests and hacmatack clearings; or, travel, life, and adventure, in the British North American provinces* (London, 1853). Boase, *Modern English biog.*, III, 604–5. *Hart's army list*, 1842–48.

SMALL, JAMES EDWARD, lawyer, politician, and judge; b. February 1798 at York (Toronto), the son of John Small* and Eliza Goldsmith; d. 27 May 1869 at London, Ont.

James Edward Small was a member of one of the founding families of Upper Canada and an Anglican, but his career, like those of Robert Baldwin* and George Ridout*, was to be an atypical one, considering his social position. Small allied himself with Reformers rather than with the official class or Family Compact.

After 1807 he and Baldwin attended the Reverend George Okill STUART's Home District Grammar School, a fact unlikely to give them useful political connections with John STRACHAN when he wielded power. Small served as a midshipman on the *St. Lawrence* during the War of 1812, articled in law with William Warren Baldwin*, and was admitted to the bar in January 1821. The following May he married Frances Elizabeth, the daughter of Surveyor General Thomas Ridout*. They had four sons, all of whom attended Upper Canada College.

On 12 July 1817 Small had been the second for John Ridout, who was killed in a duel with Samuel Peters Jarvis*. Jarvis only was charged with murder and acquitted at that time, but in 1827 Small and Henry John BOULTON, who had seconded Jarvis, were charged by the radical editor Francis Collins* as accessories to the murder of Ridout. Both were acquitted by Judge John Walpole Willis*. The year before, Small,

Alexander Stewart of Niagara, and Marshall Spring Bidwell* were counsel for William Lyon MACKENZIE in his successful suit for compensation against the young Tories who had destroyed his printing shop.

Socially and professionally Small played a prominent role. He was frequently elected a bencher of the Law Society of Upper Canada, beginning in 1829. In 1830–31 he was a member of the committee which formulated new rules for admission to the bar, and in 1833 he was commissioned a magistrate. He was also a vice-president of the York Auxiliary (later Upper Canada) Bible and Tract Society from its establishment in 1828 until 1846. He was not successful, however, in obtaining the clerkship of the Executive Council in succession to his father.

Small, a moderate Reformer, began his complex political career in 1828 when he and Robert Baldwin were defeated in the elections for the House of Assembly in the two-member riding of York County by Mackenzie and Jesse KETCHUM. The following year Small, presenting himself as an independent but branded a Tory government supporter by Mackenzie, whom he later unsuccessfully sued for libel, lost to Baldwin in the town of York by-election. In January 1832 he again opposed Mackenzie in a by-election, after the latter's first expulsion from the assembly, but was decisively defeated. Victory finally came in the general election of October 1834, which resulted in a Reform landslide; he narrowly defeated Sheriff William Botsford JARVIS in Toronto. He proved an ineffectual legislator, and was easily defeated by William Henry Draper* in 1836. After the election Small, William Warren Baldwin, and George Ridout, who had all attacked Lieutenant Governor Sir Francis Bond Head* at a meeting of the Constitutional Reform Association, were dismissed from their various government offices. Small lost the post of commissioner of the Court of Requests. Meanwhile, he had been elected an alderman for St David's ward in 1836, but was not re-elected in 1837.

Undaunted, in 1839 he successfully contested the 3rd riding of York (later York East) when the sitting member, Thomas David Morrison*, was unseated for his part in the rebellion of 1837. In 1841 he held his seat, defeating John Simcoe Macaulay* in spite of Tory and radical opposition. He was, however, again defeated as alderman for St David's.

In the legislature Small supported Robert Baldwin and his call for responsible government. John Charles Dent* stated that although "his voice was weak, and his constitution delicate" his infrequent speeches were treated with respect. When Baldwin, Louis-Hippolyte LA FONTAINE, and their supporters were brought into the government by Sir Charles Bagot* in September 1842, Small succeeded Tory Henry Sherwood* as solicitor general for Canada West. He again defeated Macaulay in the by-election required when he joined the Executive Council. He held office only until November 1843 when the entire council, except Dominick DALY, resigned in a disagreement over patronage with Bagot's successor, Sir Charles Metcalfe*. In the election of 1844 Small defeated George Monro*, but was unseated by a legislative committee with a Tory majority because his qualifications were defective. He declined to stand for election in 1847.

In 1839 Small had formed a legal partnership with his former student, James Robert Gowan*, which lasted until January 1843, when he arranged Gowan's appointment as judge of the newly created Simcoe District. During the 1840s Small received his highest legal honours: he was solicitor for King's College from 1841 to 1849, became a QC in 1842, and was elected treasurer of the Law Society of Upper Canada in 1849.

Late that same year he was appointed judge of Middlesex County by Baldwin; when he accepted he asked that it not be a bar to something better. Judge David J. Hughes, in his vitriolic history of the bar in Middlesex, was to describe Small as "a man who was a better judge of a good dinner than he was of law. . . ." Hughes further asserted that Small boasted of never having read the Common Law Procedure Act, and accused him of maladministration of the division courts. A contemporary newspaper referred more kindly to his "advancing years and accumulating infirmities" in judging his administration. With the retirement of Baldwin in 1849 Small never obtained a better post, and his pleas for an assistant were only granted by John A. Macdonald*'s Conservative government shortly before he died.

Small owed his successes in life as much to his background as to any innate abilities, for he was not a man of forceful personality and he suffered from ill health. He was, however, like Baldwin, one of those who took a direction different from others of their class. Never at the centre of the stage, his loyalty to Baldwin and his political moderation were assets that helped in the transition to responsible government.

FREDERICK H. ARMSTRONG

MTCL, Robert Baldwin papers, J. E. Small to Baldwin, 31 March 1847; 23 March, 24 Aug., 29 Oct., 15 Dec. 1849. PAO, Small (James Edward) and Gowan (James Robert) papers. *Arthur papers* (Sanderson). Can., Prov. of, Legislative Assembly, *Journals*, 1844–45. *Journal of Education for Ont.*, XXII (1869), 87. *London Free Press* (London, Ont.), 27, 29 May 1869. Scadding, *Toronto of old* (1873), 84, 185, 396. *Town of York, 1815–34* (Firth). Armstrong, *Handbook of Upper Canadian chronology*, 103, 114, 121, 124, 133, 173. *Commemorative biographical record, county York*, 31–32. *Political appointments, 1841–65* (J.-O. Coté). *Political appointments and judicial bench* (N.-O. Coté). *The roll of pupils of Upper Canada College, Toronto, January, 1830, to June, 1916*, ed. A. H. Young (Kingston, Ont., 1917). R. M. and Joyce Baldwin, *The Baldwins and the great experiment* (Don Mills, Ont., 1969). Careless, *Union of the Canadas*. Cornell, *Alignment of political groups*. Dent, *Last forty years*, I, 103–4, 122, 137–38, 241, 249, 379; *Upper Canadian rebellion*, I, 135, 198–200, 228–29, 339–40. *History of Toronto and county of York*, II, 145–46. D. J. Hughes and T. H. Purdom, *History of the bar of the county of Middlesex . . .* ([London, Ont., 1912]). W. R. Riddell, *The legal profession in Upper Canada in its early periods* (Toronto, 1916), 29, 70, 88, 103, 141. G. E. Wilson, *The life of Robert Baldwin; a study in the struggle for responsible government* (Toronto, 1933).

SMITH, Sir HENRY, politician, lawyer, and land speculator; b. 23 April 1812 in London, England, the son of Henry Smith; m. Mary Talbot of Kingston, Upper Canada; d. 18 Sept. 1868 at Kingston.

Henry Smith immigrated to Canada with his parents before 1818. The family settled in Montreal where Henry attended Benjamin Workman's private school, and, after they moved to Kingston in the early 1820s, he completed his education at the Midland District Grammar School. He then studied law under Christopher Hagerman* and Thomas KIRKPATRICK, gaining admittance to the bar in 1834. Smith was "noted for his ability in addressing a jury" and was appointed a QC in 1846; in 1853 he became the lawyer for the Grand Trunk Railway in Kingston. He also speculated extensively and successfully in land throughout the Midland District. Richard William Scott* described Smith's technique: he "acquired a good deal of property as a Trustee as well as for his own behalf. . . . For example, he took out Patents for a number of his constituents, and, having in many instances, advanced part of the money for the purpose, occasionally took the Patents in his own name."

Smith, an Anglican, was a trustee and secretary of the Midland District Grammar School. He and John A. Macdonald* were intimate friends and political allies throughout the 1840s and most of the 1850s. They worked together on legal cases, and with several other Kingstonians founded the Cataraqui Club "for the cultivation

Smith

of literature." Smith, in the words of Macdonald, was a "confidential man" who could be trusted with highly sensitive information relating to ministerial personalities, public policy, party management, local concerns, and even an affair of honour in 1856 concerning Arthur Rankin, MLA for Essex.

In 1841 Smith was elected to the Legislative Assembly for Frontenac and held the seat until 1861. Through these years he was a moderate Conservative, a supporter of Governor General Sydenham [Thomson*], William Henry Draper*, and John A. Macdonald, and an effective though not a prominent parliamentarian.

Henry Smith's name became well known throughout Canada West because of his father, who had been appointed first warden of the provincial penitentiary near Kingston in 1835. In 1848–49 a commission of which George Brown* was secretary investigated charges of maladministration, corruption, and brutality towards inmates at the prison. A series of dramatic revelations about conditions there produced much unpleasant publicity for the Smiths and led to the warden's dismissal. For years Henry Smith Jr had worked on his father's behalf in the assembly, and throughout the inquiry Macdonald also supported Henry Smith Sr. The incident added greatly to the bitterness that poisoned relations between Reform and Conservative leaders.

By 1854 Smith was a senior Conservative and was appointed solicitor general for Canada West when Sir Allan Napier MACNAB and Augustin-Norbert MORIN formed a coalition government. His performance from September 1854 to February 1858 was undistinguished. When the government was reorganized in 1858 Smith was demoted to speaker of the house. His election as speaker was highly controversial; the Toronto Globe described him as "a rash, hot-headed partizan . . . [who] would not command the respect even of his own side of the Assembly." A majority of members from Canada West voted against him, and his tenure, which lasted until June 1861, was marred by controversy with the press, disputes with legislative councillors, and conflict with the Reform opposition.

In 1859 Smith carried to London an assembly address asking Queen Victoria to visit Canada to open the Victoria Bridge at Montreal. He also expected to receive a knighthood while in London, but failed to obtain his government's support. Both Reform and Conservative politicians publicly derided Smith's pretensions, causing him acute embarrassment and considerable humiliation. A serious rift developed between Smith and Macdonald over the matter. Ironi-

cally, the Prince of Wales, who came to Canada in the queen's place, unexpectedly knighted Smith at Quebec City on 21 Aug. 1860.

Several factors impelled Smith to leave the Conservative party in 1861. He faced the prospect of returning to the back benches, and he had incurred Macdonald's displeasure by supporting, with several other Conservatives, representation by population. Moreover, he may well have suspected that the Liberal-Conservative coalition was finished as an effective political instrument. Still smarting over his humiliation about the knighthood, he offered to work with the Reformers, published an address that was strongly critical of the government, and in the general election tried to take Frontenac out of the Conservative camp. The Reformers held him at arm's length, and his defection was bitterly resented by his former friends. After a protracted and sordid campaign, Smith was defeated by James MORTON. He was again defeated in Frontenac in 1863 by William Ferguson and Macdonald's powerful district organization.

Smith was able to win the provincial seat of Frontenac in 1867 as a Conservative supporting John Sandfield Macdonald*'s coalition government, but he became ill early in 1868 and died in September. He left "a considerable fortune" to his wife and eight surviving children.

DONALD SWAINSON

PAC, MG 24, B40, 4; C31; MG 26, A, 188, 297, 336, 341, 359, 504, 510, 537; MG 29, D61. PAO, Mackenzie-Lindsey papers; Smith (Sir Henry) papers. Can., Prov. of, Legislative Assembly, Journals, 1857. Canadian Mirror of Parl. (Kingston, [Ont.]), 1841. Debates of the Legislative Assembly of United Canada, I–IV. Macdonald, Letters (Johnson and Stelmack). Mirror of Parl. of the Prov. of Can. (Montreal), 1846. [H. J. Morgan], The tour of H.R.H. the Prince of Wales through British America and the United States (Montreal, 1860). Ont., Statutes, 1869; Legislative Assembly, Journals, 1868–69. "Parliamentary debates" (Canadian Library Assoc. mfm. project of the debates in the legislature of the Province of Canada and the parliament of Canada for 1846–74), 1846–61. Thompson's Mirror of Parl. . . . (Quebec), 1860. Canadian News, New Brunswick Herald, and British Columbian Intelligencer (London), 27 April 1859. Daily News (Kingston, Ont.), 18 Sept. 1868. Globe, 1858, 1861, 1867–69. Picton Gazette (Picton, [Ont.]), 1861. Pilot (Montreal), 1861. Morgan, Sketches of celebrated Canadians. Political appointments, 1841–65 (J.-O. Coté). Careless, Brown. Cornell, Alignment of political groups. Creighton, Macdonald, young politician. Joseph Pope, Memoirs of the Right Honourable John Alexander Macdonald, G.C.B., first prime minister of the dominion of Canada (2v., Ottawa, [1894]). Margaret [Sharp] Angus, The old stones of

Kingston: its buildings before 1867 ([Toronto], 1966). D. [W.] Swainson, "Sir Henry Smith and the politics of the union," *OH*, LXVI (1974), 161–79.

SMITH, HOLLIS, businessman and politician; b. 24 June 1800 at Plainfield, N.H., son of Levi Smith and Sally Wright; d. 29 March 1863 at Sherbrooke, Canada East.

"Born of the old pioneer stock" from the northern frontier of New England, Hollis Smith spent the early part of his life in Hatley Township (erected in 1803), south of Sherbrooke. Raised a Baptist, he attended local common schools, became a successful farmer, held office in agricultural societies, and moved to Compton. A "yeoman" and "trader," by 1831 he was living on a farm near Lennoxville, in Ascot Township, and operating general stores in Compton, Lennoxville, and Eaton. In 1832 he formed "a connection in trade" at Lennoxville with Samuel Brooks, and at Compton with Alder W. Kendrick "to keep a general assortment of such goods as are usually called for in a country store."

Smith gradually acquired land in many of the Eastern Townships and in the town of Sherbrooke. The British American Land Company, incorporated in England in 1834, sent Alexander Tilloch Galt* to Sherbrooke, and in 1835 Brooks, as their agent, contracted with his partner, Smith, to open 24 miles of "King's highway" north from Sherbrooke across Stoke Township. In 1841 Smith was one of the subscribers towards the erection of Bishop's College at Lennoxville, and in 1845 he was appointed one of its original trustees [*see* Lucius DOOLITTLE; Jasper Hume Nicolls*]. With Kendrick and Galt he was a member of the St Lawrence and Atlantic Railroad Company, and with Galt of the Sherbrooke Cotton Factory, both incorporated in 1845. In 1849 Kendrick, Smith, and Galt publicly agreed with the Montreal Annexation Manifesto.

Hollis Smith, though retaining his farm in Ascot, had moved by 1856 to Sherbrooke where for the rest of his life he was secretary of the Mutual Fire Insurance Company and, with his family, part of the "Episcopalian" (Anglican) élite. With the introduction in 1856 of elective seats in the Legislative Council, Smith was nominated for the Liberal opposition in the new Wellington division by John Sewell Sanborn*, also from New Hampshire, and John McConnell of Hatley, and supported by Antoine-Aimé* and Jean-Baptiste-Éric DORION. In effect he was the candidate of former annexationists. The Conservative government candidate was William Hoste Webb*, an "Englishman," nominated by Sanborn's relentless Tory opponent, John Henry Pope*, and vigorously supported by the provincial secretary, Timothy Lee Terrill*. Smith's roots among the American settlers in the southern part of the constituency, combined with his more recent business and Anglican connections, enabled him to win with 58 per cent of the poll in Wellington as a whole, and 82 per cent in the town of Sherbrooke. He took his seat in the Legislative Council on 19 March 1857 and immediately joined other Liberals in advocating such American-type reforms as the election of the speaker of the Legislative Council.

In the assembly elections of 1857, the Conservatives won every seat in the Wellington division except Sherbrooke, and even there Galt suddenly changed from Liberal to independent. In the upper house Smith did the same. On 2 Aug. 1858 he joined two other members in stating that the new Liberal government of George Brown* and Antoine-Aimé Dorion had "not sufficiently defined their policy" and that "only one Minister of the Crown in the Legislative Council is insufficient to carry on efficiently the legislation of the Government in this branch of the Legislature." Nevertheless he voted against the want of confidence motion which was carried by the Conservative majority. In the assembly, however, the motion was supported by all the members from Wellington: Christopher Dunkin*, Galt, Pope, Terrill, and Webb. Four days later Galt entered the new Conservative cabinet.

Smith too now became a Conservative. In 1859 he supported the decision to remove the seat of government from Toronto to Quebec, and in 1862, the speakership of the Legislative Council having become elective, he voted for the Conservative, Sir Allan Napier MACNAB. On 19 March 1863, in vigorous health, he left the legislature for the Easter recess, but on his arrival home the next day he was "attacked by apoplexy" and died nine days later.

The *Quebec Mercury* remarked that he "was free from violent partisanship" and that he acted "with entire indifference to the sectionalism which is the great bane of Canadian politics." A self-made businessman and a typical product of the peculiar society of the Eastern Townships, where the northern frontier of New England mingled with the southern frontier of British settlement, Hollis Smith was able to move all the way from the Baptist liberalism of the American pioneer farmers to the Anglican conservatism of the Canadian establishment. Bishop's University, of which he remained a trustee until his death, had a claim upon his estate. His wife, Dianna Harriet Kendrick, also American-born, died at Sherbrooke on 3 March 1882. They had

Smith

one son and two daughters. Frances Louisa married Edward Dagge Worthington*, MD, and Susan Selina, Alexander Manning*, mayor of Toronto for two terms.

GORDON O. ROTHNEY

Bishop's University Library (Lennoxville, Que.), Minutes of the corporation, 1845–64, pp.3, 7, 20; Trustees minutes, 1857–68, pp.3, 139, 141. PAC, RG 1, L3ᴸ, 183; RG 4, B15, 3, ff.771–72, 855–56; RG 31, 1831 census, Ascot Township; 1851 census, Sherbrooke Town. St Peter's Anglican Church (Sherbrooke, Que.), registers of baptisms, marriages, and burials, 19 Oct. 1857; 1 Aug. 1861; 1 April, 2 Sept. 1863. Can., Prov. of, Sessional papers, 1863, V, no. 48; Statutes, 1844–45, c.25, c.91; Legislative Council, Journals, 1857–63. Globe, 1 March 1893. Montreal Transcript, 23 Sept., 1 Oct. 1856. Quebec Daily Mercury, 1, 11 April 1863. St. Francis Courier and Sherbrooke Gazette, (Sherbrooke, [Que.]), 3 Jan., 22 May 1832. Sherbrooke Gazette (Sherbrooke, [Que.]), 10 Nov. 1849; 8 Feb. 1851; 22 June, 3 Aug. 1861; 5 Sept. 1863. Stanstead Journal (Rock Island, [Que.]), 18, 25 Sept. 1856. L.-P. Demers, Sherbrooke, découvertes, légendes, documents, nos rues et leurs symboles ([Sherbrooke, Qué., 1969]), 122, 125.

SMITH, JAMES, politician and judge; b. 16 May 1806 at Montreal, Lower Canada, son of James Smith and Susanna McClement; d. 29 Nov. 1868 in the same place.

James Smith received his primary education from John Doty*, the Anglican minister at Trois-Rivières. In 1816 he went to Scotland to complete his secondary studies. He returned to Canada in 1823 and settled in Montreal, where he studied law under Benjamin Beaubien and the future judge Samuel GALE. Called to the bar on 20 May 1828, he practised in Montreal in partnership with Duncan Fisher. In 1841 Governor Sir Charles Bagot appointed him, with Alexander Buchanan* and Joseph-André TASCHEREAU, to a commission for the study of the seigneurial system in Lower Canada. In March 1843, despite the commission's restricted powers, it presented a substantial report which declared the system obsolete and recommended its abolition.

On 2 Sept. 1844 James Smith entered the ministry of William Henry Draper* and Denis-Benjamin VIGER as a member of the Executive Council and attorney general for Lower Canada, a portfolio he also held in the ministry of Draper and Denis-Benjamin Papineau* until 22 April 1847. When Smith became a minister, Governor Charles Theophilus Metcalfe* was experiencing serious difficulty in replacing Louis-Hippolyte LA FONTAINE and Robert Baldwin*, who had just resigned. Refusing to accept a truly responsible government, he had vainly offered the post of attorney general for Lower Canada, La Fontaine's portfolio, to four French Canadians and two English Canadians. After all refused, Smith accepted the position, which he filled without much distinction. On 12 Nov. 1844 he had been elected MLA for Missisquoi; he represented it until 1847 when he became a judge of the Court of Queen's Bench. In 1849 he became a judge of the Superior Court of the district of Montreal, and in 1854 was appointed to the extraordinary court created by the act for the abolition of seigneurial tenure to study the legal questions raised by this measure.

In March 1865 Judge Smith was called upon to give a verdict on the extradition of the American Confederate soldiers who had raided the little village of St Albans in Vermont the preceding autumn and then taken refuge in Canada. They had already been set free by magistrate Charles-Joseph Coursol*, but were arrested again and tried by Smith, who refused to allow them to be extradited, because in his view the articles of the Webster-Ashburton Treaty made no provision for the offence they had committed. He retired on 25 Aug. 1868 and died on 29 November at Montreal.

J.-C. BONENFANT

Gazette (Montreal), 1 Dec. 1868. Morgan, Sketches of celebrated Canadians, 447–48. P.-G. Roy, Les juges de la prov. de Québec, 507. L. B. Shippee, Canadian-American relations, 1849–1874 (New Haven, N.Y., and Toronto, 1939), 154.

SMITH, PHILANDER, Methodist Episcopal clergyman and bishop; b. 27 April 1796 in Schoharie County, N.Y.; m. twice, the second time to Mrs Harriet Cadman on 18 Aug. 1850, at Brooklin, Canada West; he had at least one son, also a Methodist Episcopal minister; d. 28 March 1870 at Brooklin.

Philander Smith, the son of Presbyterian parents, lived in Delaware County, N.Y., as a child. He came to Upper Canada in 1815 and found employment near the village of Lyn. The Genesee conference of the Methodist Episcopal Church met at Elizabethtown (Brockville) in 1817, and Smith joined the church during the revival that began there. He became a supply preacher on the Hallowell (Picton) circuit in 1819 and was formally received on trial for the ministry in the following year.

His first appointment was to Smith's Creek circuit (Port Hope and Durham County). In 1821 he was on the Cornwall circuit and 1822–23 found him stationed in Kingston. He was ordained deacon in 1822 and elder in 1824, and was then sent to Augusta. Kingston and Bay of Quinte became his circuit in 1825. From 1826 to 1829 he was presiding elder of the Augusta district, which extended from Cornwall to Kingston and included the Ottawa valley and Perth.

In 1828 the Canadian branch of the church had become independent of the American parent organization. Smith requested superannuation for reasons of health in 1830 and held no appointment in the church during 1830 and 1831. At this time, however, he was reputed to be rich and to be carrying on a business. In 1832 he was appointed to Prescott as minister, but apparently because his endeavour to wind up his commercial activities involved an attempt to collect debts owed him by other Methodists he encountered hostility and criticism within the church. He was listed as a member of the York (Toronto) general conference of 1833, which voted to merge with the British Wesleyan Methodists. No appointment was listed for Smith that year and he was superannuated from 1834 to 1836. The minutes of 1837 list him with the Augusta circuit, but he requested a transfer to the Black River Conference of the Methodist Episcopal Church in New York State.

Smith did not make this transfer, but decided to leave the Wesleyan Methodist Church to join the continuing Methodist Episcopal Church, which dissenters from the 1833 merger had begun organizing in 1834. By 1835 the revived Methodist Episcopal Church numbered 1,243 members and 21 preachers and had elected its first bishop, John Reynolds. Smith was listed in its 1837 minutes as an elder and a conference missionary in the Bay of Quinte district. Still an elder, but a supernumerary, in 1838, he was then also vice-president of the church's missionary society for forming new congregations. Appointed to Brockville, 1841, and Elizabethtown, 1842–43, he was an elder on the new Augusta charge in 1844–45. He chaired the committee to examine preachers on trial in their knowledge of divinity, church history, English grammar, and geography. The committee reported that the candidates' chief claim to education was based on their knowledge of the Bible.

Smith served on numerous committees of both the general conference and the Bay of Quinte conference during the 1840s. In 1844 he was one of the deputation of three sent to the American general conference of the Methodist Episcopal Church to seek recognition of the status and continuing communion of the Canadian Methodist Episcopal Church; although they had been assured by many influential Americans that they would be welcomed, recognition was not granted because of objections raised by John Ryerson* who represented the dominant Methodist conference in Canada West. A long controversy simmered between the two Canadian groups of Wesleyan and Episcopal Methodists and recognition of the Canadian Methodist Episcopal Church by the American church was delayed until 1860.

Smith was one of the three who ordained the American John Alley to the post of general superintendent and bishop in the Canadian church in 1845. When Alley died, Smith was elected in 1847 co-superintendent and bishop, in association with John Reynolds. From then on he was co-signer of their annual pastoral letters and his name appears under reports of book committees, missionary committees, and the judgements of numerous disciplinary committees that heard grievances and disputes among the clergy and laity.

Smith was firmly attached to the strict Methodist discipline which he believed "next to the Bible, should regulate our conduct." He told his people that "Personal piety, communion with God, and benevolence to man being of paramount importance, demand your first and most vigilant attention," and insisted that "to be a strong church we must be a holy church." His emphasis on spiritual life was matched by a measure of puritanism. Methodists, in his view, should shun popular amusements such as plays, circuses, balls, and gaming as these were "ruinous to religion." He sought their support for the movement for Sabbath observance, and signed their petition to the Legislative Assembly in 1858 for its enforcement. He strongly promoted temperance societies and the conferences repeatedly memorialized the government to prohibit the manufacture and sale of alcohol.

Smith was also deeply interested in the cause of education. In 1853, under his chairmanship, the Bay of Quinte conference took the initial steps towards establishing the Belleville Seminary, later known as Albert College, their academy for secondary education and eventually for the training of ministers at university level. The Methodist Episcopal Church subscribed to the principle of voluntaryism and agents were appointed to collect contributions for the school. These voluntarist principles were tested in 1855–56, and again in 1859, by the availability of a government grant when desperate financial needs faced the school. The first board of managers, of which Smith was a member, in August 1855 rejected such grants as they would "render the Institutions which received them dependent on the Government of the day," and were a

Smith

"dangerous exercise of patronage." This issue aroused much controversy within the church. A special general conference in 1856 directed the return of a grant to the government, and the voluntary principle was backed with new measures in 1859. Smith always urged the faithful to give generously to the school and he served as chairman of its senate.

When Smith was elected bishop in 1847 the Methodist Episcopal Church had 7,493 members and 92 preachers. After a few years of slow growth, it expanded swiftly until by 1864 there were 21,468 members and 216 preachers. Preliminary steps towards a union of various Methodist bodies began to be discussed in the Methodist Episcopal Church in 1866. However desirable this object, Smith and James Richardson* maintained that past experience with the more conservative Wesleyan Methodists "prompts us to a cautious approach" so that union would take place only according to "constitutional and scriptural principles." No real negotiations or progress occurred in the 1860s.

Bishop Smith made his home in the village of Brooklin, north of Whitby, at least from 1850 on. There he bought a 40-acre farm. At his death the *Canada Christian Advocate* asserted that he was "the oldest effective minister in the Methodist church, if not the oldest of any denomination in the Province," and it paid tribute to "the unwavering nature of his faith," to his forcible and eloquent preaching, and to his administrative talents, noting that "as a presiding officer he has few if any superiors."

W. E. L. SMITH

UCA, Methodist Episcopal Church in Can., General Conference addresses, correspondence, reports of committees; General Conference journal, 1835–70. *Canada Christian Advocate* (Cobourg; Hamilton, Ont.), 6 Nov. 1845, 16 May 1848, 20 Aug. 1850, 6 April 1870. Methodist Episcopal Church in Can., *Minutes of the annual conference*, 1836–71. Wesleyan Methodist Church in Can., *Minutes of the annual conferences from 1824 to 1845* . . . (Toronto, 1846). Cornish, *Cyclopaedia of Methodism*, I, 48, 140. Carroll, *Case and his cotemporaries*, III, IV. W. E. L. Smith, *Albert College, 1857–1957* ([Belleville, Ont., 1957]). Thomas Webster, *History of the Methodist Episcopal Church in Canada* (Hamilton, Ont., 1870).

SMITH, RICHARD, mining engineer and administrator, industrialist, and politician; b. 30 Jan. 1783 at Tipton, Staffordshire, England, son of Thomas Smith and Mary Morris; d. 21 July 1868 near Lichfield, Staffordshire.

Son of a south Staffordshire coal operator, Richard Smith studied at the Royal School of Mines and was knowledgeable about coal mines "from my youth upwards." On 12 June 1811 he married Elizabeth Fereday, daughter of Samuel Fereday, an important Black Country coal and iron master. Smith's future dimmed, however, when he and Fereday suffered financial disaster in the collapse of the coal and iron boom at the end of the Napoleonic wars. An experienced practical expert on coal mining by this time, Smith re-established himself in London, and also managed coal operations in Wales and Portugal during this period.

In 1826 George IV by royal prerogative gave his brother, the Duke of York, a 60-year lease on all the unworked mineral resources in Nova Scotia and the duke sublet the rights to his creditors, the London jewellers Rundell, Bridge, and Rundell. On the advice of the British cabinet the General Mining Association, the jewellery firm's mining arm, hired Richard Smith to establish their coal mining operations in Nova Scotia.

On his arrival at Pictou in the early summer of 1827 Smith settled his large colony of men and machinery at a site seven miles up the East River which he named Albion Mines (now Stellarton) where small-scale coal operations had existed for about 20 years. The nearby leaseholders agreed to sell to the GMA, and under Smith's supervision brickworks, buildings, wharves, coke ovens, a sawmill, and a foundry were built, and track was laid for a horse-drawn railway. Though Smith found the gas in the ground "abundant, almost beyond precedent, and the water exceedingly troublesome," by September the GMA's first coal was raised from a newly opened, 212-ft pit. On 7 December a 20-horsepower steam engine, probably the first in Canada, started to pump water and hoist coal at the mine; its 75-ft stack became a local landmark. Equally ostentatious was Smith's impressive brick mansion, Mount Rundell, on a landscaped estate overlooking the industrial operations. Soon a steady stream of visitors viewed the curiosities of the coal mines and enjoyed the gay social life led by the GMA envoy and his wife at Mount Rundell.

In 1830 Smith turned to the important coal resources of Cape Breton Island, where GMA activities had been supervised since 1826 by the young mining engineer Richard Brown, later a chief agent for the GMA. Here too, after some confusion over the terms of the company's grant, the GMA had taken over the existing lease from small-scale operators, completing its monopoly of the colony's coal resources. A growing community of men, machinery, and buildings was established at Sydney Mines, where coal had been mined since 1785. Under the supervision of

Smith and Brown a new shaft was sunk on the main seam there and steam-powered engines installed, but progress was delayed for two years by problems with the pumping machinery and heavy water flow in the mine. Smaller mines were also opened at Bridgeport and Little Bras d'Or. By 1833 more than 900 men were employed by the GMA in Nova Scotia and coal production had tripled to more than 50,000 tons.

Smith had also plunged energetically into the political life of the colony. On behalf of the GMA he lobbied the assembly for a special clause to specify the GMA's mineral rights in all land grants, resisted the idea of an export tax on coal favoured by some assemblymen, secured stricter patrol of coal smuggling on the Cape Breton coast, demanded stiff punishment of alleged arsonists when a fire erupted at Albion Mines in 1832, and generally safeguarded the company's interests. The GMA's liberal outlay of capital won local acclaim, as did Smith's personal skill and energy in developing the coal operations. However, Smith also met growing criticism of the monopoly control and generous lease provisions the GMA enjoyed. Indeed Smith's insistence on strict enforcement of these tarnished his image as a benefactor of the colony. The assembly frowned most on the low rents and royalties, for the coal mines promised to be a major source of colonial revenue. By 1837 Reformers like Joseph Howe* had become staunch opponents of the GMA, but only in 1857 were mineral rights finally repatriated and the GMA's monopoly restricted.

Bitterness peaked in 1832 when Smith contested a new assembly seat in Cape Breton County against William Young*, an ally of the nascent Reform group [see DOYLE]. On the hustings the contest between "monopolist" and "patriot" was violent: at Sydney, Smith's supporters armed themselves with bludgeons, and in the rural sectors Young's backers seized the polls. Young was declared elected, but on Smith's request the assembly investigated his charges of intimidation and irregularities, unseated Young, and installed Smith. The latter served part of the 1833 and 1834 sessions, but returned to England in May 1834.

On his departure Smith probably had few regrets. He had disliked the rigours of life in Nova Scotia. Aggressive and overbearing, Smith left behind "some enemies as well as some friends," according to the *Novascotian*, and even Joseph Smith, who succeeded his uncle at the mines, thought it wise to rename one of the company's steamboats, then known as the *Richard Smith*. Yet Smith also took with him many tributes. The Halifax Mechanics' Institute voted him an honorary member; and Howe noted that Smith had "in very trying and difficult circumstances displayed intelligence, activity and a copiousness of scientific resource, very rarely combined in the same individual – and that have seldom, if ever, been witnessed in Nova Scotia."

In England Smith resumed his career as one of the "professional gentlemen" who supervised domestic industrial expansion. From 1836 to 1864 he managed the Earl of Dudley's coal, iron, and limestone holdings near Birmingham, developing an extensive network of mines, canals, railways, and ironworks. In 1857 he opened the Round Oak Ironworks, a model enterprise which earned an international reputation. He also served for a time as justice of the peace and as deputy lord lieutenant for Staffordshire. He retired at about the age of 81.

On the whole the record of Smith's stint in Nova Scotia was a laudable one. He left the coal industry with a production capacity far ahead of demand: despite Smith's efforts and to the disappointment of the GMA, Nova Scotia coal made slow headway in American markets. Smith claimed to have started coal mining on an "enlarged and scientific footing," and in this way inaugurated the industrial revolution in Nova Scotia. For this achievement, though, Smith must share the credit with his able deputies, mining engineers Joseph Smith at Albion Mines and Richard Brown at Sydney Mines, and with the hundreds of nameless "Miners, Colliers, Engineers and Mechanics" also dispatched by the GMA. Without the Duke of York and his jewellers, Nova Scotia might have supplied the capital and entrepreneurship to develop the coal mines, a project Samuel CUNARD had in mind before the arrival of the GMA. But the colony could not supply men with the practical experience and knowledge of Smith and his subordinates.

DAVID FRANK

PANS, MG 1, 89 (S. G. W. Archibald papers, correspondence, 1813–35); 151–59 (Richard Brown papers, documents, 1859–1914); RG 1, 194–96; 458–64; RG 5, R, 18, 1833; RG 21, A, 2–3; M, 17–20. PRO, CO 217/146–57. Richard Brown, *The coal fields and coal trade of the island of Cape Breton* (London, 1871; repr. Stellarton, N.S., 1899). G. B., Parl., House of Commons paper, 1835, V, 603, pp.1–360, *Report from the select committee on accidents in mines, together with the minutes of evidence, and index*, pp.223–36, 249–52. N.S., House of Assembly, *Journal and proc.*, 1824–36, 1857–58. *Acadian Recorder*, 1827–34. *Colonial Patriot* (Pictou, N.S.), 1827–34. *Mechanic and Farmer* (Pictou, N.S.), 1839. *Novascotian*, 1827–34. *Pictou Observer* (Pictou, N.S.), 1831–34. *Times* (London), 1825–34, 1868. *Directory of N.S. MLAs*. J. M. Came-

Smithurst

ron, *The Pictonian colliers* (Halifax, 1974). C. O. Macdonald, *The coal and iron industries of Nova Scotia* (Halifax, 1909). George Patterson, *A history of the county of Pictou, Nova Scotia* (Montreal, 1877). R. P. Fereday, "The career of Richard Smith," *Acorn* [house magazine of Round Oak Steel Works Limited, Brierley Hill, West Midlands, Eng.], 1966–67. H. B. Jefferson, "Mount Rundell, Stellarton, and the Albion Railway of 1839," N.S. Hist. Soc., *Coll.*, XXXIV (1963), 79–120. J. S. Martell, "Early coal mining in Nova Scotia," *Dal. Rev.*, XXV (1945–46), 156–72.

SMITHURST, JOHN, Church of England clergyman; b. 9 Sept. 1807 at Lea, Derbyshire, England, son of William and Christiana Smithurst; d. Sept. 1867 at Elora, Ont.

Nothing is known of John Smithurst's childhood and youth. On 10 Sept. 1836 he was accepted by the Church Missionary Society of England as a probationary candidate and placed in their college at Islington (now part of London). Like most missionary candidates of this period, many of them country-bred and influenced by evangelical vicars, Smithurst was deficient in education but strong in practical skills and spiritual conviction.

The society's committee appointed Smithurst to their North West America mission, and on 23 Dec. 1838 he was made a deacon by the bishop of London under whose jurisdiction the territories of the Hudson's Bay Company fell. The latter appointed him a company chaplain at Red River Settlement at a salary of £100 a year. Because the company was concerned about the influx of Indians into Red River, it intended to send Smithurst to Cumberland House to establish a settlement and school there. On 26 May 1839 he was ordained priest and arrived in Rupert's Land the following September.

In February 1840 the company agreed to Smithurst's being permanently located at the Indian Settlement already established at Netley Creek where it enters the Red River some 12 miles below Grand Rapids (St Andrew's). There had been an understanding with the company that missionaries might be sent to Cumberland, but a dispute about a bequest by James Leith*, former chief factor of Cumberland House, for the propagation of the "Christian Protestant Religion" among the natives of Rupert's Land, caused this change in arrangements. Smithurst's appointment as chaplain to the company ceased on 1 June 1840 and he served solely as a missionary of the society. He also took services at Grand Rapids. In October 1840 he officiated at the marriage of the important Saulteaux chief, PEGUIS.

Smithurst was the first Anglican missionary in Rupert's Land to attempt to learn an Indian language. By March 1842 he had completed his translation of the service of Evening Prayer in the *Prayer book* and then turned to the marriage service. He used the Roman alphabet, claiming that the syllabic system of the Reverend James Evans* was too imprecise. He admitted, however, that the Indians found it as easy to learn English; hence he decided to produce a Cree-English dictionary. None of Smithurst's linguistic work was published, and Bishop David Anderson* decided eventually to adopt Evans' syllabic system. Two mission extensions under Indian catechists came under Smithurst's care, that of Henry Budd* at W'passkwayaw (The Pas) and that of James Settee* at Beaver Creek; to both of these missions Smithurst paid visits, in 1842 and 1843 respectively.

In March and April 1842 Smithurst was involved in what came to be known as the colonial ordination controversy, after Recorder Adam Thom*, a rather inflexible individual, had published an *Essay* in which he questioned the authority of the Anglican bishop of Montreal to officiate in Rupert's Land. Bishop George Jehoshaphat MOUNTAIN, with a warm welcome from William COCKRAN and Smithurst and the approval of the bishop of London, was to make the long trip west for an episcopal visitation in the summer of 1844. The possibility of such a visitation had been discussed in 1840, and Smithurst thought he saw in Thom's *Essay* a fresh attack upon the privileges of the Church of England in Rupert's Land. The HBC had admitted some Wesleyan chaplains in 1840 and the evangelicals within the Church of England were concerned about themselves as members within the "Established Church." Smithurst informed the company that if Thom's thesis were correct and those whom the bishop of Montreal ordained were laid under civil disabilities, they would nevertheless be "clergymen appointed by Apostolic authority" whereas the Wesleyan ministers were "only lay teachers being possessed of no valid or legal ordination whatever." In the end, Smithurst was rebuked by both the company and the CMS for his share in the controversy. His lack of charity bore out an early description of him in his college days as "able to state the truth learnedly, but doing it without love. . . ."

During 1846–47 Smithurst voluntarily conducted garrison services for the 6th Regiment of Foot, about half of whom were quartered at Lower Fort Garry. In June 1849 he was appointed to the Council of Assiniboia. That same year he became involved in the dispute over freedom in the fur trade. By supplying Governor William Bletterman Caldwell* with information favourable to the HBC, he aroused the wrath of the Métis who succeeded in alienating the loyalties of a large part of his Indian flock. Smithurst's remaining two years in Red River were unhappy and, suffering from acute rheumatism, he resigned in 1851 and returned to England.

Smithurst immigrated to Canada West in 1852 and ended his days in Elora. For a time he was minister of St John's Church there, then he took up a bush farm in the township of Minto which he named Lea Hurst after his birth place. He never married. Lea in Derbyshire had also been the home of Florence Nightingale and it has been suggested that she and Smithurst were first cousins who would have married but for parental disapproval. This story, encouraged by Miss Nightingale's donation of a communion service to the church at Elora through Smithurst, her "dear friend," seems to have no basis in fact.

Smithurst was a conscientous missionary. During his 12 years in Red River he performed 323 baptisms at the Indian Settlement. He was also a man of great practical ability, whose mission had "the best arranged house and garden in the Red River Settlement." He was a churchman who held to evangelical standards. In August 1845 he told the CMS that he differed with his colleague Cockran over the latter's "irregularities in the reading of the Liturgy" and he was unsympathetic to Presbyterian scruples among the Kildonan settlers. His Tractarian churchmanship worried the society because he taught his Indians how to establish the dates of movable feasts, so that those away on winter traplines could return for Easter communion, but he declared he attached "no importance to ritual observance except as auxiliaries to devotion."

Smithurst bequeathed his books to the bishop of Toronto, John STRACHAN, for use by the University of Trinity College and also left money in trust for the building of a church. His residence went to the CMS.

A. N. THOMPSON

CMS Arch., Committee minutes, XV–XVIII, XXVIII; North West America mission, correspondence: colonial ordination, 1842; London correspondence outwards, 1821–60; Letters and journals of William Cockran, 1825–65; Letters and journals of John Smithurst, 1839–51; Letters of David Anderson, 1849–64; Letters of Robert James, 1846–51; Letters to home secretaries, 1822–74. HBC Arch. A.5/12, f.281; A.6/25, ff.114–15, 137; A.6/26, ff.88–89; A.36/12, f.219; D.4/39, ff.109d.–10; D.5/7, 157d.–58, 186–86d., 192–92d.; D.5/12, 335d.; D.5/24, ff.435d.–36; D.5/25, ff.225–26, 581–82. Methodist Missionary Soc. Archives (London), Correspondence, Canada, 1838–53 (mfm. at PAC). PABC, Donald Ross papers, letters of John Smithurst to Donald Ross, 1844–51.

Canadian North-West (Oliver), I, 354. Church Missionary Soc., *Proc. for Africa and the East* (London), 1838–52 (includes reports for North America). G.B., Parl., House of Commons paper, 1857, *Report from the select committee on the HBC*. HBRS, XIX (Rich and Johnson). Mactavish, *Letters of Letitia Hargrave* (MacLeod). [G. J. Mountain], *The journal of the bishop of Montreal, during a visit to the Church Missionary Society's north-west America mission . . .* (London, 1845). I. [G. Simpson] Finlayson, "York Boat journal," ed. A. M. Johnson, *Beaver*, outfit 282 (December 1951), 32–37. R. M. Ballantyne, *Hudson's Bay; or, every-day life in the wilds of North America, during six years residence in the territories of the honourable Hudson's Bay Company* (2nd ed., Edinburgh, 1848), 91. Boon, *Anglican Church.* Sarah Tucker, *The rainbow in the north: a short account of the first establishment of Christianity in Rupert's Land by the Church Missionary Society* (London, 1851). M. A. MacLeod, "The lamp shines in Red River," *Beaver*, outfit 267 (September 1936), 41–45.

SONEGO. *See* BUNCH SONEGO

SPARKS, NICHOLAS, landowner and timberer; b. 1794 in Darrah parish, County Wexford (Republic of Ireland); d. 27 Feb. 1862 in Ottawa, Canada West.

Nicholas Sparks was far more important for what he owned than for what he did. Indistinguishable from hundreds of other sharp businessmen in most ways, Sparks is remembered because he owned most of what became downtown Ottawa.

He immigrated to Lower Canada in 1816 and entered the service of the pioneer patriarch of the Ottawa valley, Philemon Wright*, at Hull. Sparks early demonstrated an aptitude for business. By 1819 he was travelling to Montreal and Quebec, purchasing supplies for Wright. He soon accumulated some capital and struck out on his own. In 1821 Sparks was living across the Ottawa River in Nepean Township, Carleton County, Upper Canada, and describing himself as a farmer. He purchased a lot on 25 September of that year from John Burrows Honey (later known as John Burrows), a surveyor. For a payment of £95, Sparks received 200 acres of land along with some food and chattels. The land was lot C, concession C, Nepean Township.

Lot C would become Sparks' life, the basis of his fortune and status. Defending his right to the property would preoccupy him for much of his career. Indeed Sparks' difficulties over the lot began immediately. Burrows Honey, it appears, had sold land he did not own. Although the original sale took place on 25 Sept. 1821, Burrows

Sparks

Honey did not receive clear title until 1823 for the south half and 1824 for the north half. The sale to Sparks, therefore, was not recorded at the county registry office until 20 June 1824. The confusion, which has led to considerable controversy among local historians over the purchase date, did not end there. Burrows Honey's title remained in doubt. As a result, Sparks repurchased the south 100 acres on 20 June 1826. Still there were doubts; Sparks made token payments of 5s. to John Burrows Honey and to his wife for title to the full 200 acres on 6 May and 10 July 1830 respectively. Out of this tangle it appears the famous purchase was not made on the usually accepted date of 20 June 1826 but rather nearly five years earlier on 25 Sept. 1821, although the legal technicalities were not resolved until 1830.

The 1826 date, however, has a fine touch of drama about it. Late in 1826 the decision was made to build the Rideau Canal through lot C. As the village of Bytown (Ottawa) sprang up around the canal terminus, Sparks became landlord for a whole community. Those months also saw Sparks cement the other foundation of his fortune. On 2 Nov. 1826 a marriage licence was issued to Sparks and Sally Olmstead, widow of Philemon Wright Jr. The marriage solidified Sparks' link with the leadership of the Ottawa timber trade.

Sparks was an important middle-rank figure in timbering on the Ottawa River for many years. His own substantial timber interests were supplemented by loose partnerships in the 1830s with the Wrights, William and John Thomson, and Peter White, and in the 1840s with the Quebec house of Anderson and Paradis. In timber, as in land, Sparks was a sharp businessman. He was chronically late in settling debts. In 1834 he was successfully sued for goods delivered but not paid for; three years later his creditor was still attempting to collect the £2,803.

It was in land that Sparks reaped the greatest dividends. He began to sell portions of lot C as early as 18 Dec. 1826 when he sold land west of the canal mouth for £200 an acre, the same land he had bought for 9s. 6d. an acre. Land sales and leases quickly made Sparks wealthy. As one of the few people with ready cash he also became Bytown's leading moneylender and often enough was able to regain land he had sold. For example, in January 1832 he accepted a lot in payment of a debt of £75. In May 1832 Sparks sold an adjacent lot for £600. The nicest irony in all of Sparks' complex dealings came in July 1844 when he leased part of a town lot, 66 ft by 99 ft, for £200 to John Burrows.

Lot C continued to have a complicated legal

career, however. On 17 Nov. 1826 Sparks had authorized Lieutenant Colonel John By*, commander of the canal works, to take land necessary for the construction. The agreement provided that not more than 200 ft on either side of the canal would be taken and "that such parts as may not be required for His Majesty's service shall be restored when the canal is completed." By took the necessary land, some 88 acres. In 1827 he attempted to purchase more, the high land which would be known as Barracks Hill until the parliament buildings were constructed on the site. Sparks demanded £500, a price By thought was too high. The colonel seized the property under the terms of the Rideau Canal Act of 1827, which allowed land to be taken for canal purposes.

Sparks began a 20-year campaign to recover his property. He sued By for trespass; he brought suit against the officers of the Ordnance Department who occupied the land; he organized petition campaigns; he pressed local members to raise the issue in the legislature. And, indeed, however ruthlessly Sparks dealt with his own clients, he had received similar treatment from the military. By and the Ordnance stretched the terms of the agreement and of the act beyond reason. The land taken for "canal purposes" was used for barracks, parade grounds, homes of officers, even pasture for horses.

In 1843 and 1845, Sparks' friends in the legislature attempted to regain his land for him by legislation. The imperial government was forced to give way. Although the Ordnance insisted it required the land for defence purposes, it accepted the principle of compensation. In September 1846 a board of arbitration met to determine that compensation. Thanks to political pressure in the Legislative Assembly, the board was weighted to Sparks' advantage. The queen's printer and former MLA for Bytown, Stewart DERBISHIRE, combined with the staunch defender of property rights, John A. Macdonald*, to overwhelm the Ordnance appointee, James Sutton Elliott. They awarded Sparks £27,000.

His victory over the military confirmed Sparks' position as the patriarch of Bytown. He was, however, a very private patriarch. He made some gifts to his community but surprisingly few given his resources. In 1828 he donated a lot for St Andrew's Presbyterian Church and four years later gave the site for the Anglican Christ Church. His last major donation was land for a jail and court-house in 1839. More typical was his role as a founding shareholder in Her Majesty's Theatre, an ambitious cultural venture on Wellington St. When the promoters were unable to meet his note in 1856, the patriarch would listen to no cultural arguments. He had his lawyer press for payment.

Sparks had few political ambitions, despite his prominence. He never stood for provincial office. Perhaps to protect his property, he was involved occasionally in municipal affairs, serving on the Bytown Council from 1847 to 1849 and the Ottawa City Council from 1855 to 1857, and in 1860.

Nicholas Sparks died on 27 Feb. 1862, aged 68. His wife and his three children – Nicholas, Mary, who married lumberman Alonzo Wright*, and Esther, who married James Dyson Slater – received a handsome inheritance. Some 78 debtors owed Sparks over $19,000. The estate included 440 lots in Ottawa, conservatively evaluated at $80,686, as well as property in surrounding townships, and a large home on Sparks St. It was an impressive demonstration of the fruits which could reward tenacity, shrewdness, and good luck in pioneer Canada.

MICHAEL S. CROSS

Christ Church (Anglican) (Ottawa), records of the parish (mfm. at PAC). PAC, MG 24, D8, 10, p.3121; 18, pp.6755–56; 30, pp.12646–48; 34, p.15291; 35, pp.16046–54; I9, 10, p.3040; 20, p.5137; 21, p.5536; 140; RG 1, E3, 54, pp.68–77; L1, 41, pp.551–53; L3, 472, bundle 20, nos.40–40e. PRO, WO 1/552, pp.95–122; 1/553, pp.591–871; 44/30, pp.21–64 (copies at PAC). *Bytown Gazette* ([Ottawa]), 1836–48. *Ottawa Citizen*, 1851–62. *Illustrated historical atlas of the county of Carleton (including city of Ottawa), Ont.* (Toronto, 1879; repr. Port Elgin, Ont., 1971), xviii–xxix. Lucien Brault, *Ottawa old & new* (Ottawa, 1946), 50, 52, 86, 119, 131–32, 218, 222. Davin, *Irishman in Can.*, 322–23. H. P. Hill, *History of Christ Church Cathedral, Ottawa, 1832–1932* (Ottawa, 1932), 8–9, 32–35, 113.

SPENCE, ROBERT, teacher, journalist, and politician; b. 1811 at Dublin (Republic of Ireland); d. unmarried on 25 Feb. 1868 at Toronto, Ont.

Robert Spence immigrated to Upper Canada in 1836 and taught school at Dundas, where public education began with his contract with the village authorities in 1840 to teach for a wage of 2s. a month per pupil. To augment his income he was at various times a worker in the paper mill at Crook's Hollow near Dundas, a commission merchant, and an auctioneer.

With the launching of the *Dundas Warder and Halton County General Advertiser* on 24 April 1846 Spence embarked on a new career as a newspaper owner and editor. The paper reflected Spence's enthusiasm for liberal principles and reform, and was a principal instrument in furthering his public career. It remained under his control until 1859, except for the period 1849 to 1853, when it was sold to Samuel I. Jones.

An editorial campaign begun in 1846 advocating the incorporation of Dundas as a town was successful, with elections first held on 18 April 1848. Spence was actively involved in the movement and was elected a ward councillor. By 17 Nov. 1848, however, he was striking out in editorials against his fellow councillors, dubbing them "despots" and accusing them of "jobbing."

In 1850 Spence was elected the first warden of the united counties of Wentworth and Halton. During his two-year term of office he became more widely known and was well regarded. James Durand, a former member of the assembly, reported to Robert Baldwin* in February 1850 that "Mr. Spence our Warden . . . made the speech of the day, it was well timed and tempered, and I am sure made a favourable impression on all who heard it. . . ." Spence ran in the 1854 election for the legislature as an independent in Wentworth North and defeated another Reformer by 506 votes to 339.

Spence entered the legislature at a watershed in the evolution of Canadian political parties. He nominated George-Étienne Cartier* as speaker of the assembly, thus demonstrating his support of the government of Augustin-Norbert MORIN and Francis Hincks*, whose fortunes were about to be eclipsed, and his opposition to the Clear Grits and more advanced Reformers. The Hincks–Morin administration fell a few days after the legislature convened in September 1854 and a new government was formed by Sir Allan MacNab, an arch-Tory, in alliance with Morin. Their coalition government had considerable support from moderate Reformers, including Spence, who was appointed postmaster general and considered a representative of a moderate political outlook in the cabinet.

The *Hamilton Spectator* in October 1854 described Spence's acceptance of office as "shameful recreancy" and cried that "the riding is betrayed." It appeared that an independent Reformer who had marched with Reformers for a decade or more had turned coat to accept office under a Compact Tory. Yet Spence could claim, quite credibly, that he had campaigned for good measures and not for party loyalty, that he had supported people who would achieve these good measures in legislation, and that he had at all times voted with a majority of his fellow Reformers, splintered though the movement was among moderates who supported the government and the Clear Grits and supporters of George Brown* who opposed it. At the by-election in early October 1854 necessitated by his accepting office, Spence defeated William McDougall*, the Clear Grit editor of the *North American*, by 542 to 207 votes.

As postmaster general Spence appears to have been a competent administrator who made a contribution to the reorganization of the civil service. He continued James MORRIS' policy of providing post offices for every hamlet; he abolished heavy postage on newspapers, and improved the handling of money orders and registered mail. His alignment with the coalition ministry in 1854 had, however, earned the lasting enmity of the Clear Grits, whose power was increasing, and in 1855 they launched the *Dundas Tribune and Wentworth Chronicle* to work against him. His political career was ended in 1857 when he was defeated by William Notman*, a Clear Grit. Within a few months of his defeat Spence was appointed collector of customs at Toronto. He continued in that office until his death.

P. G. CORNELL

MTCL, Robert Baldwin papers, James Durand to Baldwin, 28 Feb. 1850. *Dundas Warder and Halton County General Advertiser* (Dundas, [Ont.]), 3, 31 July 1857. *Hamilton Gazette*, (Hamilton, [Ont.]), 29 June–12 Oct. 1854. *Hamilton Spectator*, 26 July, 4 Aug., 11, 12 Sept. 1854; 3 Dec. 1857. Cornell, *Alignment of political groups*. Dent, *Last forty years*. *The history of the town of Dundas*, comp. T. R. Woodhouse (3v., [Dundas, Ont.], 1965–68).

SPENCER, JAMES, Methodist minister and journalist; b. 7 Feb. 1812 in Stamford Township, Upper Canada; m. in 1843 Sarah Lafferty of West Flamborough Township, and they had nine children; d. 9 Oct. 1863 at Paris, Canada West.

James Spencer was raised in a Methodist household and was converted under the ministry of Ephraim Evans* in 1830. Spencer concluded that he should enter the Methodist itinerancy, but, because of a deep sense of personal unworthiness, he resisted his conviction. Following studies in 1836 at the newly opened Upper Canada Academy where "his exemplary conduct and great laboriousness" earned him the sobriquet of "Bishop," he became a ministerial candidate in 1838. This decision intensified his inner distress. "I am sometimes at my wits end what to do. I am becoming more and more of the opinion that I am not in the proper employment for me." To his patron, the Reverend John Carroll*, he confided his doubts, and in 1841, when he had to change circuits, he wrote: "I am almost resolved at once and forever to leave the work of the ministry...."

The opportunity to change his vocation came in 1842 when Spencer was given leave to become a tutor in the new Victoria College at Cobourg. Unfortunately, his aspirations and his personality defeated his purpose. He was asked to teach English; he wished to teach science. Principal Egerton Ryerson* gave him leave to attend Wesleyan University in Middletown, Conn., to study natural science, and on his return offered him a probationary appointment; Spencer's angry refusal terminated his academic career. This episode was probably one source of the hostility which characterized his later relations with Ryerson.

Spencer returned to regular circuit duties. Between 1843 and 1851 he was stationed on the Dundas, Toronto, Nelson, and Guelph circuits, and he wrote letters to the Methodist newspaper in Toronto, the *Christian Guardian*, attacking the pretensions of the Church of England and the doctrine of apostolic succession. This polemic secured him a measure of notoriety among his brethren, which led to his being nominated as editor of the *Guardian*. Unsuccessful in 1849 and 1850, he was finally elected in 1851 to succeed the Reverend George R. Sanderson*. Spencer was re-elected annually until 1860, when he was succeeded by the Reverend Wellington Jeffers*.

Spencer's relatively long term as *Guardian* editor indicated that his ministerial colleagues were impressed by his skill, and, more important, that he embodied much of the mood of the Methodist conference in the 1850s. He assumed a combative and rather self-righteous posture which came naturally to a man who was personally insecure but convinced of the rectitude of his version of the Methodist cause. His controversialism reflected as well the fact that the conference was beset by the need for institutional consolidation, by its unwillingness to recognize that the evangelical imperative had to be reinterpreted and that the role of the laity deserved greater recognition, and by its determination to avoid direct involvement in political controversy, unless Methodist interests were at stake.

As editor Spencer played a rather equivocating role in the final settlement of the clergy reserves. He stood for equality of treatment by the state of all churches, but preferred that they be independent. In 1854, aware of the differences of opinion in the Methodist Church, he argued that the Methodist conference had "no authority to say that the people shall not receive aid from that source [the reserves] in supporting their religious institutions." At the same time he contended vigorously against the extension of separate schools and for the rights of the denominational universities. Committed as unequivocally as were the Clear Grits to the separation of church and state in the elementary schools, he assailed the efforts of Roman Catholics and Anglicans such as Bishop John STRACHAN to promote and strengthen separate schools. Those who preferred "bigoted sectarianism" to "the noble aims of national improvement" would be traitors "to the best interests of posterity" and would lend themselves to "the entire destruction of both civil and religious liberty." Conversely, he argued that in the area of university education, because of the contentious attitudes of the churches, one provincial university would be a failure. It made more sense to afford aid to the separate denominational colleges than to sink all funds "in the dead sea of one great university . . . ," a position to which his church would cling throughout the long discussion of the "university question."

Within the Methodist community, Spencer was a conspicuous defender of ministerial authority and of traditional religious practices. Since Methodists believed that religious life had to be nurtured and developed by spiritual discipline, great importance was attached to class meetings, weekly gatherings in small groups in which members recounted their experiences and took counsel with one another. Membership and participation in a class was a prerequisite for membership in the Methodist Church. To Egerton Ryerson, however, enforcement of this rule discouraged those baptized in the church from growing into membership and forced ministers either to impose a condition not required by Scriptures or to connive at its neglect. When his proposal to the 1854 conference that this requirement be dropped was rejected, Ryerson resigned from the conference, a move designed to emphasize his concern for the rights of the laity in the church.

Spencer's initial reaction was to suppress comment on the resignation in the *Guardian*. At the ensuing conference, Ryerson rejoined his colleagues. Spencer reported this event in a form Ryerson considered offensive and inaccurate. Spencer's reply stressed that Ryerson's version of events was incorrect and that the "Wesleyan Conference and the Church in Canada are not yet disposed to give up an essential good to remedy an imaginary evil, which if it exists, is the result of unfaithful practice and not from any radical defect in the system. . . ." The controversy was concluded in a bitter, sometimes personal, debate in the 1856 session. Enoch Wood* asserted that "this worthless matter [was] all brought about for electioneering purposes by the editor of the *Guardian*," but the controversy did illustrate clearly the growing cleavage between those such

as Spencer who upheld the authority of the conference and the existing pattern of discipline, and those such as Ryerson who believed that ministerial authority should be exercised tolerantly and that individuals should be encouraged to act responsibly.

Spencer was not re-elected as editor in 1860, an event which drew from John A. Macdonald* the comment that he was "truly glad to learn that Spencer ha[d] been ousted from the Editorial Chair," since Spencer had "played [George Brown*'s] game as much as he dared to do." Spencer was appointed to the Brampton and subsequently to the Paris circuit. Significantly, his successor as editor, Jeffers, had been one of his supporters in the dispute with Ryerson. Spencer's brethren also demonstrated their respect for him by appointing him their representative to the British Wesleyan conference in London in 1860 and in awarding him an honorary MA from Victoria College in 1863, but his career was cut short in that year by a severe attack of erysipelas. His funeral, attended by 30 ministers and a large congregation, was conducted by Anson Green*, president of the conference, and by Enoch Wood, superintendent of missions.

As his published sermons and editorials indicate, Spencer's religion was austere and rigid, yet deeply emotional. He was persuaded that Methodism as a system of belief and the Methodist Church as an institution were the very embodiment of evangelical Christianity. He was committed to the preservation of a society in which Christian doctrine would continue to be the ultimate foundation, but he was equally certain that this relationship could be maintained without the perpetuation of formal ties between the churches and the state. Rather it should be fostered by the preaching of conversion, by disciplined religious life, and by vigorous opposition to such social evils as intemperance and political corruption. As a man and a minister he was distinguished by "fearless integrity," "independence of spirit," and an "almost unmerciful" attitude "towards human iniquity." He was "ungenial and unsocial" in public, and genial in private. His sermons were "entirely free from display" for he sought to avoid "a wicked trifling with the sacred and solemn questions at issue between man and his Maker." In short he was a stern and impassioned but not a "shouting" Methodist.

G. S. FRENCH

James Spencer was the author of *Sermons by the Rev. James Spencer, M.A., of the Wesleyan Conference, Canada* (Toronto, 1864). [J. S. Carroll], *Past and present, or a description of persons and events connected*

Sprott

with Canadian Methodism for the last forty years (Toronto, 1860). *Christian Guardian*, 1851–60. Anson Green, *The life and times of the Rev. Anson Green, D.D....* (Toronto, 1877). Wesleyan Methodist Church in Can., *Minutes* (Toronto), 1864. Carroll, *Case and his cotemporaries. The chronicle of a century, 1829–1929: the record of one hundred years of progress in the publishing concerns of the Methodist, Presbyterian and Congregational churches in Canada*, ed. L. [A.] Pierce (Toronto, 1929). C. B. Sissons, *A history of Victoria University* (Toronto, 1952); *Ryerson*.

SPROTT (Sproat), JOHN, Presbyterian clergyman; b. 3 Feb. 1780 at Caldon Park, Stoneykirk, Wigtownshire, Scotland, the son of James Sproat, a farmer, and Margaret Hannay; d. 15 Sept. 1869 at Middle Musquodoboit, N.S.

John Sprott began studies for the ministry at age 18 with two years of preparatory work followed by four years at the University of Edinburgh. Connecting himself with the Relief Presbyterians, he studied at their Divinity Hall and was licensed as a preacher in 1809. He then did some pastoral work in Scotland before emigrating in 1818. Landing at Saint John, N.B., he later moved to Nova Scotia where he was associated with the Synod of Nova Scotia. His first years were spent ministering to the people around Windsor, Newport, and Rawdon; in 1825 he was admitted to the pastoral charge of the Musquodoboit Valley where he remained until 1849 when he resigned over some differences of opinion with his congregation. After that date he retired to his farm at Middle Musquodoboit, though he often preached where his services were needed, usually in the more remote rural areas of Nova Scotia. He claimed that "his horse had been in every stable in the province." He paid a short visit to the United States in 1850 and served as pastor of St Andrew's Church in St John's, Nfld, in 1854.

Possessing a good mind and a powerful imagination, Sprott read widely and carried on an extensive correspondence with newspapers in Nova Scotia and Scotland and with local figures of prominence such as Thomas McCulloch*, as well as with the bereaved and afflicted. Not much concerned with ecclesiastical differences, he wished for more unity among Christians. Respected by all, his frankness about matters occasionally annoyed people for he spoke out boldly, and his well-prepared sermons were "noted for short, pithy, sententious, and in some cases, eccentric remarks. . . ."

Sprott was married three times. His first two wives, Sarah Clarke and Charlotte Leslie, died at an early age. John Sprott had five children by his third wife, Jane Neilson of Wigtownshire, Scotland.

R. MacLean

PANS, RG 14, 25 (Halifax County), 1846. Presbyterian Church of the Lower Provinces of British North America, *Synod minutes* (Halifax), 1870. [John Sprott], *Memorials of the Rev. John Sprott*, ed. G. W. Sprott (Edinburgh, 1906). *Halifax Evening Reporter*, 21 Sept. 1869. *Novascotian*, 28 Sept. 1825. *Presbyterian Witness*, 25 Sept., 2 Oct. 1869. M. G. Burris, *My pioneer ancestors: an account of the Burris and Dean families of Musquodoboit, Nova Scotia, their origins, experiences, and surroinings . . .* (n.p., [1950?]). J. E. Rutledge, *Sheet Harbour, a local history* (Halifax, 1954). *Truro Daily News* (Truro, N.S.), 2 May 1916.

STAIRS, WILLIAM MACHIN, merchant, banker, and politician; b. 21 Jan. 1789 at Halifax, N.S., youngest son of John Stairs and Joanna Stayner; m. in 1814 Margaret Wiseman, and they had three sons and six daughters; d. 28 Nov. 1865 at Halifax.

Shortly after William Machin Stairs' birth, his father failed in business and, after being freed from debtors' prison by friends, departed for Philadelphia where he obtained a post in the United States Customs Department. In 1793 Joanna Stairs died during a yellow fever epidemic, and her husband sent the five children back to Halifax to be cared for by their uncle, John Stayner. William never again saw his father, but his uncle, a tanner, treated him with consideration and gave him a basic education at the Halifax Grammar School. When seasickness abruptly ended a projected career at sea, William took employment as a clerk in the counting-house of a Scottish-born Halifax merchant, William Kidston.

On reaching maturity Stairs went into business for himself as a small-scale general merchant on the local waterfront. In 1813 he formed a partnership with Henry Austen, and the two appear to have done reasonably well during the boom years of the War of 1812. A postwar recession brought the firm to the brink of bankruptcy, however, and only the backing of their chief creditor, Kidston, now a Glasgow merchant-banker, kept Austen and Stairs out of debtors' prison. Their partnership broke up about 1818, and for the next few years Stairs scrounged for business in relative obscurity. Spring and autumn found him advertising British manufactures and East Indian goods imported from Greenock, Scotland, and custom-house records indicate that by the early 1820s Stairs was involved in the shipment of timber from the Miramichi to Britain.

After a brief renewal of the connection with Austen about 1822–23, Stairs again struck out on his own and in 1824, encouraged by improving business conditions, bought Kidston's old premises for £1,680. His family lived over the shop for the next nine years while Stairs built up a substantial business with the outports along Nova Scotia's Atlantic coast and the shores of the Gulf of St Lawrence. By 1827 he possessed his own private signal, a "white flag, pierced blue," and his advertisements in the Halifax press offered, wholesale and retail, everything from black pepper to window glass. Although still a general merchant, by the late 1820s Stairs had begun to specialize in hardware, emphasizing such items as bolt and bar iron, ploughs, wire, sheet iron, and spikes.

Buoyed up by the continued economic expansion of the early 1830s, Stairs steadily enlarged the scope of his business. In Dartmouth he built facilities for storing timber, along with a paint and putty factory. As well, he ventured into shipbuilding. The success of these activities allowed Stairs to begin work on an impressive residence on Hollis St, then a prestigious address in Halifax. He also sent his eldest son, William James*, to Horton Academy for an education befitting the heir of an aspiring merchant gentleman.

Despite his accomplishments William Stairs lacked the wealth and family connections required to assure him a secure place within the ranks of the Halifax oligarchy. His identification with religious dissent, indicated by the decision to educate his son at a Baptist rather than Anglican institution, and subsequently confirmed by his desertion of the established Church of Scotland for the Free Church, rendered Stairs suspect in the eyes of the social establishment. His alienation did not become politically overt, however, until the mid 1830s when a business crisis, precipitated by squabbling among local bankers, threatened Stairs with commercial ruin. Personal insecurity and resentment against the machinations of vested interests combined to make Stairs one of the few supporters of reform within the Halifax merchant community. His commitment to change had its limits, however. He opposed abolition of debtor imprisonment and incorporation for Halifax on the grounds that both measures jeopardized property rights.

Joseph Howe* nevertheless valued Stairs as a personal friend and political ally and helped him win an assembly seat in 1841. Stairs began his legislative career as a supporter of the hybrid coalition of Tories and Reformers organized in 1840. When that coalition collapsed three years later, Stairs aligned himself with Howe and the more advanced Reformers who urged the estab

lishment of one-party cabinet government on the British model. Although defeated in the 1843 general election because of infighting between Protestant and Roman Catholic Reformers in Halifax [see DOYLE], Stairs remained politically active. He won election to the Halifax City Council in the late 1840s and served as mayor in 1847 and 1848. When the Liberal party came to power in 1848, Stairs was rewarded with a seat on the Legislative Council.

Stairs' enthusiasm for responsible government quickly faded once the new order established itself in power. Introduction of the spoils system offended Stairs' sensibilities and as he later told his cousin, Thomas Allen STAYNER, "Men trying to obtain Political power . . . do many shabby acts." In 1851, fearing that Howe's advocacy of government construction of railways would bankrupt Nova Scotia, Stairs protested by resigning from the upper house and at this point abandoned politics for the full-time pursuit of business.

During the 1840s Stairs had specialized in hardware and ship chandlery, doing enough business to warrant the purchase in 1844 of additional waterfront real estate valued at £2,500. As the firm expanded Stairs brought in two of his sons, William J. and John, the latter being replaced by a son-in-law, Robert Morrow, in 1854. Stairs also involved himself in a variety of corporate ventures, becoming a director of such enterprises as the Halifax Whaling Company, the Nova Scotia Electric Telegraph Company, the Union Marine Insurance Company, the Merchants' Exchange, the Halifax-Dartmouth Steamboat Company, and the Inland Navigation Company (this company embodied an attempt to revive the Shubenacadie Canal). In 1856 he played a leading role in the establishment of the Union Bank of Halifax and served as its president until his death.

By the 1850s William Stairs enjoyed unquestioned prominence within Halifax's commercial élite. His £4,000 mansion on Tobin St symbolized respectability acquired through material gain. Crippled by rheumatism, he travelled rarely and his correspondence suggests that old age made him increasingly intolerant and suspicious of change. The denominational quarrelling which erupted in Nova Scotia during the mid 1850s intensified Stairs' dislike of Irish Roman Catholics, whom he denounced in his correspondence as "Devils incarnate" not fit for public office because of their alleged lack of moral scruples. Railways also aroused Stairs' ire, and, influenced perhaps by his canal investments, he repeatedly denounced the scheme to build a line from Halifax to Quebec as "humbug," which would

Standing Buffalo

result in increased debt, higher taxes, and more political corruption.

When the Civil War broke out, Stairs immediately identified with the South, reasoning that "the arrogance and boasting of the Northern People require humbling." The crisis in British North American affairs occasioned by the South's eventual military collapse failed to inspire Stairs with enthusiasm for colonial union. Britain would not abandon the colonies, he assured T. A. Stayner. Furthermore, "Nova Scotia is too well off to have any desire to be joined to Canada, her credit is good – Coal Mines and Gold Mines [are] opening in every direction."

When William Stairs died, the local press praised him as a "highly esteemed resident" who had always displayed "liberality in character as a business man." Though platitudinous, these comments indicate that the deceased's career fitted the mid Victorian image of the ideal merchant whose success derived from industry and thrift. Stairs' one failing lay in the area of philanthropy; his entire estate, valued at $248,000, went only to members of his family.

DAVID A. SUTHERLAND

Halifax County Court of Probate (Halifax), no.1330, will of William Machin Stairs (mfm. at PANS). PANS, MG 1, 880–84 (William Stairs papers, 1771–1865); RG 1, 229, no.23; 314, no.26; 451, census of Halifax, 1851; RG 31, Revenue papers, quarterly returns, Port of Halifax, 1810–30; H. G. Stairs, "The Stairs of Halifax" (typescript, 1962). [*Charter of the Shubenacadie Canal Company with list of shareholders and act of incorporation* (Halifax, 1826)]. N.S., General Assembly, *Statutes*, 1845–65; Legislative Council, *Journal of the proc.*, 1848–51. *Acadian Recorder*, 28 May 1814, 29 Nov. 1865. *Halifax Citizen*, 28 Nov. 1865. *Halifax Journal*, 1816–31. *Morning Chronicle* (Halifax), 28 Nov. 1865. *Novascotian*, 1826–65. *Nova Scotia Royal Gazette* (Halifax), 28 Oct. 1812, 1 Jan. 1815. *Sun* (Halifax), 23 Feb. 1848. *Times* (Halifax), 30 Nov. 1841, 14 Nov. 1843. *Weekly Chronicle* (Halifax), 21 June 1811. *Belcher's farmer's almanack*, 1824–65. *Directory of N.S. MLAs. Halifax and its business: containing historical sketch and description of the city and its institutions* . . . (Halifax, 1876). *Halifax, N.S., business directory, for 1863* . . . , comp. Luke Hutchinson (Halifax, 1863). J. P. Martin, *The story of Dartmouth* (Dartmouth, N.S., 1957). W. J. Stairs, *Family history, Stairs, Morrow; including letters, diaries, essays, poems, etc.* (Halifax, 1906). C. St C. Stayner, "The Sandemanian loyalists," N.S. Hist. Soc., *Coll.*, XXIX (1951), 62–123.

STANDING BUFFALO. *See* TATANKA-NAJIN

STANTON, ROBERT, businessman, public servant, and publisher; b. 6 June 1794 at Dorchester (Saint-Jean), Lower Canada, eldest son of William Stanton of the Royal Navy and Margaret Stanton; d. 24 Feb. 1866 in Toronto, Canada West.

In 1805 Robert Stanton's father moved to York (Toronto), Upper Canada, with his large family to become sergeant-at-arms to the House of Assembly. Robert attended John STRACHAN's school at Cornwall in 1806, and enrolled in the Home District Grammar School, where Robert Baldwin* was a fellow pupil, when it opened at York in 1807. In 1810 he entered the office of the lieutenant governor, was transferred to the surveyor general's office in 1811, and in 1812 was a copying clerk to the assembly. Commissioned lieutenant in the militia, he saw action at Queenston Heights and in April 1813 was captured at York. He was commissioned lieutenant colonel on 2 April 1827, and colonel on 16 July 1835, in the 1st West York Regiment. A Tory, he helped defend Toronto against the rebels in 1837 along with five of his brothers.

Stanton had moved to Kingston as a clerk in the Commissariat Department after the War of 1812. There on 2 Sept. 1816 he married Frances D. Spafford and they had at least ten children. She died in 1844, and on 14 April 1845 he married Anna Louisa Newbigging, *née* Hagerman, niece of Christopher Hagerman*.

In Kingston Stanton was secretary in 1817–18 of the Lancastrian School Society which operated the Midland District Grammar School. In 1818 he was selling hardware at H. C. Thomson*'s shop; he opened his own in 1820. He was elected assessor for Kingston in 1819 and commissioned magistrate for the Midland District in 1821 and notary public in 1823. His skill in accounting led to his appointment to a committee to investigate the affairs of the "pretended" Bank of Upper Canada in February 1823. That year, as a returning officer for the counties of Lennox and Addington, he closed a poll on Good Friday to the detriment of candidate Marshall Spring Bidwell*; the election was declared null and void by the House of Assembly. Stanton's action was deemed illegal but not "corrupt and malicious." Nevertheless, his first encounter with a Reformer was not auspicious.

In 1826 Sir Peregrine Maitland* unexpectedly appointed Stanton king's printer. He sold his Kingston business, moved to York, and set up shop with Robert Watson as his foreman. Apart from his official duties as king's printer and as publisher of the *Upper Canada Gazette*, Stanton engaged in other ventures: he sold stationery and supplies, did job ruling (of paper) and book binding, and sold insurance for Phoenix of London. In

1834 he was a founder of the British America Assurance Company, and later was manager in Toronto of the Western Assurance Company. Stanton was the first printer to recognize the local trade union, the York Typographical Society, founded in 1832. Stanton also published, largely at his own expense, books, almanacs, and newspapers, some in conjunction with Watson. His most significant publication was the *U.E. Loyalist*, issued as a companion to the *Upper Canada Gazette* from 3 June 1826 to 24 May 1828 and then separately as the *Loyalist* for one year.

Stanton, as journalist, was a spokesman for the Family Compact, intending the *U.E. Loyalist* to have "a just degree of influence in matters in which the Government may have felt an interest." When the *Loyalist* degenerated into scathing editorials against anything related to Reform, Lieutenant Governor Sir John COLBORNE suggested that "the King's Printer should be more exclusively devoted to the performance of duties strictly official." Stanton complied with the suggestion, but not before he had earned the disapprobation of some of the Reformers.

Stanton was commissioned magistrate of the Home District on 12 June 1827, and served on the Board of Health in 1832 when cholera first reached York. He was a member of the rebellion losses commission in 1838. In 1841 he was defeated in the Toronto city elections by George GURNETT during an attempt to get moderates on the council. He held various offices in St James' (Church of England), was a member of the St George's Society, and accountant to the Toronto Turf Club.

The union of the two Canadas left Stanton's position as queen's printer in doubt. As Lord Sydenham [Thomson*] assured him he would be considered, Stanton opened an office in Kingston, the new capital. However, Sydenham died in September 1841, and that month Sir Richard Jackson*, the administrator, commissioned Stewart DERBISHIRE and George-Paschal DESBARATS as joint queen's printers. Stanton was justifiably upset, especially when informed that the appointment had been arranged prior to Sydenham's death. On Jackson's advice, Stanton memorialized Lord Stanley, as well as all the governors of Upper Canada whom he had known. The new governor, Sir Charles Bagot*, offered him the position of sheriff of the Midland District, but Stanton refused because of the large bond required. Finally, at Stanley's direction, Stanton was appointed a Home District commissioner of customs on 12 Aug. 1842 and collector of customs for the port of Toronto on 8 Aug. 1843.

The announcement of his appointment created an outcry among Reformers who protested to Baldwin that giving so lucrative a post to so staunch a Tory was a curious method of carrying out the principles of responsible government. Francis Hincks* threatened to resign as inspector general, but the Tory *Toronto Patriot* termed the appointment "the only honorable act of . . . [the government's] ten months of power."

Six years later Hincks, again inspector general, investigated Stanton's administration of the Toronto customs house. The ensuing report alleged falsification of customs records. Stanton pleaded innocent, but he and two assistants were dismissed in November 1849 and W. F. Meudell, the investigator, was appointed collector. Stanton was immediately appointed clerk of process at Osgoode Hall, a position he held until his death in 1866.

Stanton was a loyal servant to the crown and to the Tory principles of the Family Compact. A frequent casualty of the rise of Reform politics and government, at the same time he possessed sufficient tenacity to survive contrary winds of fortune without compromising his decidedly colonial world view.

HILARY BATES NEARY

PAC, RG 16, A5, 3, 24 Nov. 1849. PAO, Macaulay (John) papers. UTL-TF, [Robert Stanton], "Narrative memoranda connected with my memorial to Lord Stanley," [1841–43]. *Examiner* (Toronto), 2 Aug. 1843; 24 Oct., 14 Nov., 5 Dec. 1849. *Kingston Chronicle*, 22 Jan. 1819, 25 Feb. 1820. *Kingston Gazette*, 7 Sept. 1816, 11 Nov. 1817, 22 Dec. 1818. *Toronto Patriot*, 26 Feb., 14 March 1834; 13 Feb., 1 March, 5 June 1838; 1, 8 Aug. 1843. *Toronto Star Weekly*, 27 Oct. 1923. *Town of York, 1793–1815* (Firth). *Town of York, 1815–34* (Firth). *Upper Canada Gazette* (Toronto), 14 May, 27, 31 Aug., 3 Sept. 1835; 14 July 1836. Armstrong, *Handbook of Upper Canadian chronology*. *Early Toronto newspapers* (Firth). *Robertson's landmarks of Toronto*, III, 354, 372. W. R. Riddell, "The Bidwell elections: a political episode in Upper Canada a century ago," *OH*, XXI (1924), 236–44.

STARK, MARK YOUNG, Presbyterian minister; b. 9 Nov. 1799 at Dunfermline, Fife County, Scotland, son of Robert Stark and Elizabeth Young; m. 22 June 1835 Agatha Georgiana Street, and they had three sons and two daughters; d. 24 Jan. 1866 at Dundas, Canada West.

Mark Young Stark's mother having died in his infancy, he was raised by his stepmother, Mary Bannatyne, member of a prominent Glasgow family. After private tutelage in Essex, England, he matriculated at the University of Glasgow, graduating MA in classics in 1821. He completed theological studies at Glasgow in 1824 and was licensed to preach by the Glasgow presbytery of the Church of Scotland.

Stark was unable to secure a call under the oppressive patronage system that existed in the Church of Scotland, in spite of illustrious support from Professor Dugald Stewart and Sir George Napier. He travelled extensively on the Continent, becoming proficient in French, German, and Italian. His cultural interests also encompassed the areas of art and botany; after immigration to Canada he corresponded with the noted British botanist, Sir William Hooker, and hunted out rare specimens at his request.

Despairing of an ecclesiastical settlement in Scotland, Stark offered his services to the Glasgow Colonial Society, then directed by the Reverend Robert BURNS. Stark was appointed to Upper Canada on 19 Feb. 1833, but without the financial support usually provided by the society. Prior to leaving for Canada he was offered a living in the Church of England but refused it, preferring service within the Church of Scotland. He was called to Ancaster and Dundas and was ordained 26 Sept. 1833.

Stark was elected moderator of the Synod of the Presbyterian Church of Canada in Connexion with the Church of Scotland and so presided over the famous "Disruption Synod" held in Kingston in July 1844. In spite of sympathy for the Free Church cause in Scotland Stark at first saw no reason for a similar division within his own synod. When the division became inevitable, however, he identified himself wholeheartedly with men like Alexander Gale* of Hamilton, John Bayne* of Galt and George Brown* of the *Globe*, and helped form the Synod of the Presbyterian Church of Canada (Free Church). He was elected the first moderator of the new synod and wrote a lengthy and spirited defence of the secession in Canada for the first issue of the *Ecclesiastical and Missionary Record* in August 1844.

Stark was not fully supported by his congregations at Dundas and Ancaster (four of the six elders at Dundas refused to follow him) and he was eventually forced to leave church buildings at both places. Free Church supporters built Knox Church at Dundas and accommodation for services was arranged at Ancaster. Stark's work prospered, particularly at Dundas, under his gentle and conscientious leadership. In 1854 the Knox congregation separated from that at Ancaster, with permission of the Hamilton presbytery, and Stark remained as minister at Knox.

He served as the clerk of the Hamilton presbytery from 1841 to 1844 in the undivided church and from 1844 to 1857 in the Free Church. Throughout most of his ministerial career he was deeply involved in the finding and settlement of ministers. Because of his considerable intellectual abilities he was invited to serve on the College Committee charged with the development of Knox College founded in Toronto in 1844.

In 1861 the United Presbyterian Church and the Synod of the Presbyterian Church of Canada (Free Church) united. Stark had been at first apprehensive of the sectarianism implicit in the voluntaryism of the former, but he rejoiced nevertheless at the union. Locally he facilitated the reception of the United Presbyterian congregation in Dundas into Knox Church.

In failing health, Stark resigned his charge in 1863. His name, however, was kept on the roll of synod by special resolution, and he continued to provide ministerial assistance when requested until his successor, the Reverend John McColl, was inducted.

ALLAN L. FARRIS

Presbyterian Church in Can. Archives (Toronto), Stark (Mark Young) papers. Knox Presbyterian Church (Dundas, Ont.), Church session of the congregations at Dundas and Ancaster, in connection with the Synod of the Presbyterian Church of Can., records. UCA, Can. Presbyterian Church, minutes of the Synod, 1861–66; Glasgow Colonial Soc., correspondence; Presbyterian Church of Can. in Connexion with the Church of Scot., minutes of the Synod, 1833–44. Presbyterian Church of Can., minutes of the Synod, 1844–61; Stark (Mark Young) papers. Can. Presbyterian Church, *Home and Foreign Record* (Toronto), V, (1865–66), 147–51. Presbyterian Church of Can., *Ecclesiastical and Missionary Record* (Hamilton, [Ont.]), I (1844–45), 69. [M. Y. Stark], *Sermons by the late Rev. Mark Y. Stark, A.M., formerly minister of Knox's Church, Dundas*, ed. William Reid (Toronto, 1871). I. S. Rennie, "The Free Church and the relations of church and state in Canada, 1844–54" (unpublished MA thesis, University of Toronto, 1954). G. Smellie, *Memoir of the Rev. John Bayne, D.D., of Galt* (Toronto, 1871).

STAYNER, THOMAS ALLEN, soldier and postmaster general; b. 16 Dec. 1788 at Halifax, son of John Stayner and Mary Allen; d. 23 June 1868 at Toronto, Ont.

Thomas Allen Stayner, a descendant of a New England Puritan family, joined the British army and in 1808 was working as a clerk to the military secretary at Halifax. During the War of 1812 he was in Montreal. On 15 May 1817, at Champlain, N.Y., he married Louisa, younger daughter of Daniel Sutherland*; they were to have 16 children. Stayner remained in the regular army probably until 1823. The following year he was appointed postmaster at Quebec.

In 1827 Stayner succeeded his father-in-law as postmaster general of Upper and Lower Canada, where there were then more than 80 post offices. Since 1821 the Houses of Assembly of the two provinces had been challenging London's right to control postal services, fix rates, and have the benefit of the receipts. They regularly asked that this right be yielded to them. The real struggle began under Stayner. A few months after taking office, Stayner increased the number of post offices and added numerous couriers in recently settled regions. However, he acted without the authorization of his immediate superior, the British postmaster general, who criticized him for these excessive expenditures.

Stayner also incurred the wrath of the assemblies of the two Canadas and then of the Province of Canada, both at that time and until 1851. They denounced as illicit the profits he obtained by fixing the rates on Canadian newspapers; the postmaster general was allowed to keep revenue from that source, and Stayner thus received almost as large a salary as the governor general. The commissions of inquiry regularly set up by the assemblies recommended provincial post offices be established under the assemblies' control so that the postal revenues would be paid to Canada rather than to England.

Stayner also became the target for businessmen and for newspapers such as the *Colonial Advocate* of York (Toronto) and the *Montreal Gazette*. He was blamed for high rates, slow service, and dispatch of receipts to England. For some time he could count on the support of London and of political friends who held the executive power in Canada. Eventually, however, he could no longer satisfy both the British minister and the Canadian Houses of Assembly. Consequently, he gradually lost his prerogatives. In 1844 the right of the postmaster to retain the proceeds from the newspaper rates was abolished; as compensation, London granted Stayner an annual income of £2,500, although his successors were to receive only £1,500. That same year the central office was moved to Montreal, and the governor assumed the right to appoint and dismiss postmasters and to fix rates. Finally, on 6 April 1851, the assembly of the Province of Canada acquired full power over postal services [*see* James MORRIS]. The services had improved under Stayner's direction: between 1845 and 1851 the speed of service had increased and hundreds of post offices had been opened so that by 1851 there were 853. Stayner knew how to win the esteem of his British

superiors but he lost his popularity in Canada. Hence in 1851 he retired disappointed, but not poor.

In addition to his duties as postmaster general, Stayner was appointed a member of the Royal Institution for the Advancement of Learning in 1834, justice of the peace for Quebec district in 1838, and justice of the peace for Trois-Rivières district in 1839. Little is known about the last years of his life. After having lived in Montreal from 1844 until at least 1851, Stayner settled in Toronto and apparently became a director of the Bank of Upper Canada, and its vice-president in 1860.

ANDRÉ MARTINEAU

PAC, RG 3, 1, 1–14; 9, 5; RG 8, I (C series), 117, 122, 131, 226, 1169, 1203¹/₂ E and F. PANS, Vertical MSS file, "Allen family of Dartmouth, N.S.," comp. C. St C. Stayner. PRO, CO 42/441 (mfm. at PAC). *Colonial Advocate*, 19 Sept. 1833, 2 Oct. 1834. *Globe*, 25 June 1868. *Pilot and Journal of Commerce* (Montreal), 2 Aug. 1844. *Quebec Gazette*, 5 June 1817. William Smith, *The history of the Post Office in British North America* (Cambridge, Eng., 1920), 153–273.

STEELE, ELMES YELVERTON, naval officer, farmer, politician, and public servant; b. 6 Feb. 1781 at Colford (Coleford), Gloucestershire, England, one of ten children of Elmes Steele, MD, and Mary Benfield; m. first, in 1809, Elizabeth Seeley Coucher, by whom he had six children, and secondly, in 1847, Anne MacIan Macdonald, by whom he had six children; d. 6 Aug. 1865 in Medonte Township, Canada West.

Military careers were common in the Steele family. Five of Elmes' six brothers entered the army or navy and his uncle, Samuel, had served in Canada with Jeffery Amherst* in 1760. Not unnaturally, Elmes chose a career in the Royal Navy, entering as an officer cadet in 1798. He served with distinction on several ships during the Napoleonic wars and rose to the rank of captain. He was mentioned in dispatches for his part in a raid on the Spanish coast, escorted a convoy to Quebec in 1805 as lieutenant of the *Mercury*, and served as gunnery officer on board the *Leopard* when she fired on the United States ship *Chesapeake* in June 1807.

After Waterloo Steele went on half pay and settled with his family in France. In 1830, while he was in England exercising his right (granted in 1812) to vote as a freeman of the city of Gloucester, revolution erupted in Paris and his family joined him in England. In 1832 Steele came to Canada with his son John to claim land which had been offered to British officers. He selected a

1,000 acre site in Medonte Township north of Lake Simcoe and was joined by the rest of his family in 1833.

In 1837 Steele mustered volunteers in Medonte to help suppress the rebellion led by William Lyon MACKENZIE. All those who could bear arms marched to Barrie, where guns were issued, and then to Newmarket, where news of the rebels' defeat reached them. Steele and a friend continued to Toronto on business, passing the smouldering ruins of John Montgomery*'s tavern on the way. Steele retired from the navy with the rank of commander in 1838 and, although he was a lieutenant-colonel of the Simcoe County militia for two decades, he concentrated on civilian matters.

Appointed magistrate in 1833, he was also particularly active in promoting public works. In an 1839 petition Steele and others argued that a water route connecting Lake Huron and the Bay of Quinte by way of the Severn River, Lake Simcoe, and the Trent River would open up lands for settlement and increase the value of grain production and export. It would also provide a shorter, cheaper route for trade between Lower Canada, Upper Canada, and the rapidly developing western states of the United States, provide construction jobs for immigrant labourers, and create a secure communications route between the Canadian Great Lakes in the event of war with the United States.

On 15 Oct. 1839 Steele was elected chairman of a meeting at Finch's Tavern on Yonge St at which Reformers approved the recommendation for responsible government made by Lord Durham [Lambton*]. A Tory mob led by the sheriff of the Home District, William Botsford JARVIS, broke up the meeting. The death of at least one unarmed Reformer caused a scandal in the province and Steele gained a reputation as a staunch Reformer, although he had taken no part in provincial politics until that time. As a result, Reformers strongly supported Steele's candidacy in Simcoe in the election of 1841. He promised to further local interests such as roads and pensions, of particular interest to settlers many of whom were like himself former military men. His Tory opponent, William Benjamin Robinson*, he had also denounced in 1839 as an intimate of the Family Compact whose "misdeeds" he listed: "prodigality terminating in the bankruptcy of the province . . . arbitrary proceedings . . . insufferable pride and presumption. . . ." Steele defended the yeomanry who had been branded "with the stigma of rebel," and supported the union of the Canadas because it would "reduce to their proper level in the social circle every member of

the dominant faction." In the assembly Steele worked successfully for a good road from Toronto to Orillia, and campaigned for the restoration of pensions which army and navy veterans had commuted to get a start in Canada. He did not run in the election of 1844, having been branded by local interests as a follower of Lord Sydenham [Thomson*] rather than of Robert Baldwin*. Instead he restricted his efforts to his work as JP, to the promotion of non-political local projects, and support of the Anglican church he had endowed in Medonte. In his later years he lived for a time on what was to be the site of Orillia.

Steele's sons, especially Major-General Sir Samuel Benfield Steele*, maintained the family's tradition of distinguished military and civilian service.

RONALD J. STAGG

A collection of materials supplied by Harwood Steele to the DCB has been useful in the preparation of this biography. It consists of notes on and typed copies of manuscript sources, and photocopies of relevant secondary sources, including Katherine Day, "The letters of Capt. Steele's daughters" (unpublished paper delivered to the Orillia Hist. Soc., 19 March 1953). *Mirror* (Toronto), 26 Feb. 1841. Elmes Steele, *To W. B. Robinson, esq., M.P.P.* (broadsheet, 30 Oct. 1839). *The Toronto almanac and royal calendar, of Upper Canada . . .* (Toronto), 1839. A. F. Hunter, *A history of Simcoe County* (2v., Barrie, Ont., 1909; repr. 1v. in 2 pts., 1948). Elmes Henderson, "The public services, &c., of Commander Elmes Steele, R.N.," *OH*, XXIV (1927), 373–80. *Orillia Packet* (Orillia, Ont.), 26 March 1908. J. C. Steele, "Reminiscences of a pioneer," Simcoe County Pioneer and Hist. Soc., *Pioneer Papers* (Barrie, Ont.), no.4 (1911). M. E. Wilson, "The Steele family," *OH*, XXXIV (1942), 117–20.

STEPHENSON, ELEAZER WILLIAMS, stagecoach line operator and hotel proprietor; b. 1798 at Springfield, Mass.; m. in 1826 or 1827 Clarissa Chapin of Buffalo, N.Y., and they had one daughter; d. 28 April 1867 at St Catharines, Canada West.

Eleazer Williams Stephenson immigrated to St Catharines in April 1826, and opened a livery stable connected with Luther Dyer's hotel, the St Catharines House, previously William Hamilton MERRITT's residence. The following year his place of business was the Mechanics' Exchange building. Stephenson soon expanded his commercial interests. In May 1828 he joined four other businessmen from the Buffalo and Niagara River area in advertising daily stages connecting Buffalo and Niagara via Niagara Falls, with branch lines to St Catharines and Lockport, N.Y. In July 1828 Stephenson, John Burtis of Sandwich (Windsor, Ont.), and others advertised the first line of mail and passenger stages, to run three times a week, between Niagara and Sandwich via St Catharines, Ancaster, and Brantford. Connections were guaranteed with the Niagara-Buffalo line and with a line from Buffalo to Rochester, and a travelling time of five days between Rochester and Detroit was claimed. Passengers from Buffalo crossed the Niagara River by ferry linking Black Rock, N.Y., and Waterloo, a hamlet near Fort Erie. Rochester passengers crossed at Lewiston-Queenston. In June 1829 Stephenson and others advertised a semi-weekly stage between York (Toronto) and Niagara which completed the distance in 24 hours. Stephenson inaugurated a daily line of mail stages between Niagara and Hamilton in 1831 and made available livery service.

When railways made all but local stage lines obsolete in the early 1850s, Stephenson turned to the hotel business. For a time he ran the St Catharines House, where he had started in business. He acquired the St Catharines salt wells, first developed by W. H. Merritt, with the idea of establishing a health spa; he built the Stephenson House Hotel, opened in 1855, and in association with Dr Theophilus Mack* also built the Springbank Sanitarium in the mid 1850s. This health and resort complex became well known throughout Canada and the United States.

In January 1851 Stephenson had been elected to represent St Thomas ward on the town council and it then elected him mayor. He did not run in 1852. He belonged to many St Catharines societies, being steward of the St Andrew's Society in 1836, and was a member of the Independent Order of Foresters and the St George's Masonic Lodge. Though he was called "colonel" in many contemporary sources no evidence has been found to suggest that it was more than the customary title of stage-coach proprietors. Nineteenth century biographical works have associated him with the Welland Canal, but there is no evidence that he was involved with the company.

A contemporary wrote of Stephenson in 1856 that he "stands to-day as one of our most promising fellow-townsmen, enterprising citizens, and successful business men." He died in 1867 as a result of injuries received when a fractious team ran away with the carriage in which he was driving his nephew, Rufus Stephenson, mayor of Chatham, and a St Catharines municipal official.

J. J. TALMAN

Evening Journal (St Catharines, [Ont.]), 29–30 April, 2 May 1867. *Farmer's Journal and Welland Canal Intelligencer* (St Catharines, [Ont.]), 21 May, 9, 30 July, 6 Aug. 1828. Junius [Seymour Phelps], *St. Catharines A to Z by Junius, 1856* ([St Catharines, Ont.], 1967). (This volume reprints articles published in the *St. Catharines Journal* during 1856 under the title "A walk around town" by Junius.) *Canadian biographical dictionary*, I, 189. *Cyclopaedia of Canadian biog.* (Rose, 1886), 645. J. P. Merritt, *Biography of the Hon. W. H. Merritt . . .* (St Catharines, Ont., 1875).

STEVEN, ANDREW, merchant and banker; baptized 12 March 1789 in Girvan, Ayrshire, Scotland, son of James Steven and Mary Lees; d. 12 Dec. 1861 at Hamilton, Canada West, survived by his wife Laura and five children.

Andrew Steven immigrated in 1819 to York (Toronto) where he found employment with the merchant firm of D'Arcy Boulton* Jr and William PROUDFOOT. In 1822 he moved to Dundas, perhaps as an agent for the large trading company of John Spread Baldwin* and Jules-Maurice Quesnel*, and five years later started his own grocery business in Dundas. In 1832 Steven moved to Hamilton as manager of the new agency of the Bank of Upper Canada, but when the Gore Bank opened on 2 May 1836 he became its cashier, at a salary of £400 per annum. In this post he managed the bank's daily affairs and its correspondence and made policy recommendations to the president and board of directors. Economic crises in 1837 and 1857 impressed him with the importance of not overextending the bank's resources. He was consequently regarded by some "as being too cautious for the times."

A problem for the bank was the instability in direction caused by its charter, which stipulated that four of the ten directors, excluding the president, could not be re-elected except after the lapse of one year. In face of these yearly changes, much of the responsibility for the continuity of management fell upon Steven. Finally in 1860 he obtained an amended charter from the Legislative Assembly through Thomas Clark Street* and Isaac Buchanan*, both directors of the bank and members of the assembly. The number of directors was reduced to seven, all eligible for immediate re-election.

The Gore Bank had been promoted by Allan Napier MacNab and Absalom SHADE, prominent Tories in the western section of the province. In 1839 rumours spread that MacNab owed the bank £25,000, and that his supporters on the board of directors, his brother David, his law partner John Oglivy Hatt, and the bank's president James Matthew Whyte*, were similarly indebted. Their refusal to reveal debts raised suspicions that the Gore Bank was, as

Stewart

William Lyon MACKENZIE had charged in 1835, "a machine got up by Mr. Allan Napier MacNab and a few of his cronies" to enable them to draw on its resources. The disturbed stockholders, led by directors Edmund Ritchie and Colin Campbell Ferrie and supported and advised by Steven, challenged the leadership of Whyte and the MacNab group. Steven also tried to frustrate MacNab's financial transactions. As a result MacNab found Steven "personally obnoxious" and tried to have him dismissed in 1839. His position was affirmed, however, at the annual meeting that year, and Ferrie was elected the new president.

The Gore Bank acted as a clearing-house for business transactions, extending credit and discounting notes. To much of the public, association with a bank during this period simply permitted one to draw on it to pay debts and finance speculations, regardless of personal assets or even of the bank's real assets. Unsound assets and the scarcity of currency often created difficulties. In times of severe inflation or depression Upper Canadian banks suspended specie payments in order to avoid collapse.

Steven established the British connections of the Gore Bank, essential in an age of close financial ties between Canada and Britain. In 1847 the failure of the bank's London agent, Reid, Irving, and Company, shook the confidence held in the Gore Bank by its customers and the financial community in general. Immediately Steven was sent to England with funds to meet the obligations assumed in the bank's name and to restore confidence on that side of the Atlantic. At the same time he made arrangements for Glyn, Mills, and Company to become the bank's new agent. In 1847 also the negotiations concerning a merger of the Gore Bank and the larger Bank of Upper Canada, which had been assisted by Steven's friendship with its cashier, Thomas Gibbs RIDOUT, and the varied associations of the two banks, were discontinued because the Reid, Irving collapse and a consequent run on the Gore Bank dampened the Toronto-based bank's enthusiasm.

Little is known of Steven's private life, but he was a member of the committee which founded the Hamilton Mechanics' Institute in 1839. He was a founder of St Andrew's Presbyterian Church and an elder from 1833 to 1843. By 1851, however, he had become an Anglican, perhaps as a result of the Free Church disruption of 1844. Towards the end of his career with the Gore Bank, in November 1856, Steven became its president, and continued to exercise his charac-teristic restraint and moderation in conducting its affairs.

DAVID G. BURLEY

HPL, Ferrie papers; Hamilton biography, Andrew Steven. PAC, MG 24, D16, 57; D18. PAO, Street (Samuel) papers. M. F. Campbell, *A mountain and a city, the story of Hamilton* (Toronto, 1966), 93, 122, 134–35. Johnston, *Head of the lake* (1958), 216. Ross and Trigge, *History of the Canadian Bank of Commerce*, I, 163–248.

STEWART, ALEXANDER, lawyer, politician, and judge; b. 30 Jan. 1794 in Halifax, N.S., eldest of three children of James Stewart and Elizabeth Bremner; m. 26 June 1816 at Halifax Sarah Morse (d. February 1893), and they had seven children; d. 1 Jan. 1865 in Halifax.

Alexander Stewart's father died when the boy was only five years old. Although there is some suggestion that the family was in needy circumstances, Stewart was able to attend the Halifax Grammar School. He served briefly as a clerk in the Ordnance Department before entering the commission and auction business of John Moody, in which he became a partner in November 1814 at age 20. After only a year and a half with Moody Stewart had acquired the wherewithal to undertake a legal apprenticeship, first in Halifax, and later in Amherst in the office of his brother-in-law, James Shannon Morse. When Moody's firm failed in 1817, he became liable for its debts through not having taken the proper steps to make known his severance, and was compelled to surrender everything he possessed. Nonetheless, he was able to finish his legal training, becoming an attorney on 14 July 1821 and a barrister in 1822. Opening an office at Amherst with barely "tenpence in [his] pocket," he quickly established a flourishing practice in Cumberland County and in neighbouring Westmorland County, N.B. In 1834 he moved to Halifax and entered into partnership with his brother James.

Stewart's political career had begun in 1826 when he was elected to the assembly for Cumberland; he was re-elected in 1830. He soon established a reputation as a liberal in the assembly. During the late 1820s he insisted that the British government surrender without compensation its right to collect quitrents. He also advocated the removal of disabilities suffered by the province's Roman Catholics and supported strong financial aid for common schools. He demanded, further-more, that full responsibility for the custom house establishment be transferred to the assembly. After the Brandy Election of 1830, he took the lead in resisting the council's attempt to assume powers in dealing with money bills that the House of Lords had abandoned and winning the council's acceptance of the additional tax on brandy [see Enos Collins*]. On 27 March 1833 Stewart prepared an address to the crown calling for the transfer of all its casual and territorial revenues to the assembly, in return for a guaranteed and adequate civil list.

In 1834 Stewart condemned the multifarious duties of the council and initiated resolutions calling for its reform: he wanted the deliberations of the council opened to the public; he argued strongly that two councils should be created to separate the legislative and judicial functions; and he wanted councillors to be selected from the province generally, rather than exclusively from Halifax. Strongly in favour of the liberalization of trade, he presented the assembly's case for the establishment of free ports in the province to the British government in the summer of 1834, and won accolades from Nova Scotians for his efforts.

The Whiggish Stewart was becoming uneasy, however, about the beginnings of the popular movement for reform. In November 1834 he reacted strongly against the formation of a political union in Cumberland County, designed to "instruct [the people] how to bring their wishes, and their opinions, to bear upon their rulers." In December all Stewart's pent-up resentment burst into the open when in the pages of the *Novascotian* Joseph Howe* opposed Stewart's proposal for the commutation of quitrents in return for an annual grant of £2,000 by the province towards the lieutenant governor's salary. Stewart told the assembly that no matter what it did it would be "inconsiderately attacked by its natural protectors and supporters," the press, and that its constituents, "the madmen," would heap contumely upon it. Howe's reply was that if the assemblymen were degraded, the causes were to be found not in the misrepresentations of the press or in the madness of the people but "in their own acts and sentiments." Despite this exchange, Stewart was among the first to congratulate Howe for his "splendid defence" against a charge of libel in March 1835.

In the elections for the assembly in 1836 Stewart was opposed by Gaius Lewis and Andrew McKim, who advocated reforms such as an elective council that were anathema to him. He won the second seat in Cumberland by such a narrow margin that he had to face a controverted election trial which was not decided during the

session of 1837 and which he ultimately lost in February 1838 to McKim. In the interim, Stewart found his position altogether uncongenial in an assembly that contained Howe and a majority of members anxious to carry reform to a point he considered undesirable. The Whiggish liberalism that had made him a leader in one assembly had become anachronistic in the next. In the divisions on Howe's twelve resolutions in 1837 he was generally in opposition, especially on the question of an elective council, expressing his abhorrence at the introduction of anything that savoured of American republicanism, and declaring his determination to adhere to the British model. Stewart decided not to remain in a house in which he had lost his standing and the retention of his own seat was uncertain, despite Howe's hope that the assembly would continue to have the benefit of his powerful mind "whether he stands beside me, or fights in the ranks of the opposition." Stewart probably greeted his own appointment to the newly established Legislative Council on 16 Jan. 1838 with relief.

Stewart's political conduct now began to evoke bitterness. Having failed in its constitutional demands, the assembly chose William Young* and Herbert Huntington* to go to London following the session of 1839 to press its case; the Legislative Council left the appointment of its delegates to the lieutenant governor, Sir Colin Campbell*, who selected none other than Stewart. The outcome was that the Reformers meted out the penalty that often befalls an alleged turncoat and traitor, and made Stewart their *bête noire*, all the more so because Young and Huntington had minimal success in London. Perhaps his move from Presbyterianism to Anglicanism sometime during this period reinforced their suspicions. On 4 June 1840 Stewart became an executive councillor, despite a resolution passed by the assembly the previous March, on the motion of Howe, that "there are few men in Nova-Scotia, who enjoy so little of their confidence, and . . . they should regard his appointment as a direct insult to this House."

Surprisingly, in the face of the scorn of the Tories and the criticism of Reformers like Huntington, Howe joined Stewart in the coalition government arranged by Lord Sydenham [Thomson*] and formed in October 1840 by the new governor, Lord Falkland [Cary*]. Howe's Reform colleagues proved to be right, for Stewart did more than anyone to destroy the coalition. In 1841, even as Howe was rejoicing in the assembly in the substantial advance towards full responsibility under the coalition, Stewart was informing the Legislative Council that "Responsible Government, in a Colony, was responsible nonsense, – it was independence." These differences were patched up without damage to the administration; more serious was Stewart's statement to the Legislative Council in 1843 that, according to "the true principle of Colonial Government," the governor was responsible for the acts of his government to the queen, and his executive councillors were responsible to him. "Any other responsibility," he said, was "inconsistent with the relation of a colony to the Mother Country." The coalition ministry proceeded to hammer out a compromise initiated by E. M. Dodd* and acceptable to all its members, which declared that the council was responsible to both the governor and the assembly. From now on, however, the ministry barely staggered along.

Meanwhile Stewart had dealt the coalition another blow. Late in 1842, when the differences between Howe and James William Johnston* on the granting of aid to denominational colleges had come into the open, Stewart allegedly urged James Boyle Uniacke*, a Reformer but one-time Tory, to "embark in the same boat with himself and Mr. Johnston, form a junction between the Tories and Baptists . . . and throw Howe overboard." Because Stewart made no public denial until February 1844, the story circulated widely throughout 1843, reinforcing the general belief that the executive councillors were lacking in good faith towards one another. Hence there was no surprise when the coalition collapsed in December 1843.

Stewart remained in Johnston's succeeding Tory administration until early June 1846, when he was sworn in as the fourth and last master of the rolls and as judge of the Court of Vice-Admiralty. About a year earlier, on the initiative of Falkland, he had become a QC. As master of the rolls, Stewart undertook what his two predecessors had failed to do, using his powers under an act of 1833 to simplify the procedures of the Court of Chancery. The result was to eliminate a heavy backlog of cases and inordinate delays, but it was beyond Stewart's legal powers to deal effectively with the heavy fees and costs of the court.

It was only natural, when the Reformers came into office in 1848, that they would act against what they had long described as "the abominable, heart-breaking, pocket-picking system" of the Court of Chancery. Clearly some of them were also determined to settle old scores with Stewart. It was not until 1855, however, that they managed to have the court abolished and its equity jurisdiction transferred to the Supreme Court. As was usual, the British authorities insisted that provision be made for Stewart and he was offered a vacancy in the Supreme Court. But since his precedence was not to date back to his appointment as master of the rolls, the always proud Stewart accepted instead a pension smaller than the salary of a Supreme Court judge. Learning that he might be accorded some honour by the British government for his services, the Liberal Executive Council – still possessed of an intense dislike for Stewart – protested that other public men had much stronger claims than he. Nonetheless, he was invested with the CB at Buckingham Palace on 22 Feb. 1856. Stewart argued that in abolishing the Court of Chancery the legislature had not grasped the basis on which the fusion of law and equity could be effected, and that the result was a muddle in the administration of justice. But when the legislature restored a form of equity jurisdiction in the Supreme Court in 1864, it was partly to provide a place for the Conservative leader and premier, J. W. Johnston, and Stewart was not asked to resume his former function. He did, however, preside over the occasional cases in the Court of Vice-Admiralty until his death.

Able, formidable in debate, and vigorous in his own defence, Alexander Stewart attained high office and yet remained something of a tragic figure. Whiggish in political sentiment and more liberal in many respects than some Reformers, he came to be regarded as the most implacable of Tories. Altogether inflexible, he bluntly rejected the idea of responsible government in a colony. Insensitive to the reaction of others, he created the impression of having traitorously abandoned his earlier political views. The outcome was to make him one of the most detested of all Nova Scotian politicians.

J. MURRAY BECK

PANS, Vertical MSS file, "The Stewart family of Halifax and Amherst, N.S.," comp. C. St C. Stayner. Beck, *Government of N.S.*, 32–34, 130–31. C. J. Townshend, "Life of Honorable Alexander Stewart, C.B.," N.S. Hist. Soc., *Coll.*, XV (1911), 1–114.

STIMSON, ELAM, physician; b. 4 Oct. 1792 at Tolland, Connecticut; m. first, in 1819, Mary Anne Frances Bolles, by whom he had five children, and secondly, in 1832, Susan Bolles, by whom he had four children; d. 1 Jan. 1869 at St George, Ont.

Elam Stimson was the youngest in a poor family of 12 children, and as an adolescent he worked to support his family. He served as a sergeant in the United States Army for a year during the War of 1812, a time he considered "all but lost to me as regards usefulness. . . ." Following his service he returned to Tolland, taught school, and worked as a farm labourer while studying medicine with the village physician. In 1817–18 he attended lectures at the Medical Institute of Yale College, and in the fall of the latter year attended the New Hampshire Medical Institution at Dartmouth College. He was granted the degree of MD in April 1819 and returned to Tolland to practise.

In 1823 Stimson moved with his family to St Catharines, Upper Canada, and was licensed to practise by the Medical Board of Upper Canada on 7 July. He moved to Galt (Cambridge) in 1824 whence he travelled on horseback to patients in neighbouring townships. In 1831 he moved to London, where he formed a partnership with Dr James Corbin and was appointed a coroner and physician to the jail. In 1832 immigrants infected with cholera spread an epidemic from Quebec to western Upper Canada, and all cholera victims were quarantined upon entering the London District.

In a pamphlet published in 1835 Stimson vividly described cholera symptoms: "Spasms are . . . severe, attacking the legs, thighs and body. The fingers and toes are shrivelled and purple or black. The veins . . . are only flat black lines . . . and to the feel the skin is like a cold wet hide. . . ." Stimson considered the "remote cause of cholera to be some Atmospheric Impurity and the Proximate Cause an Imperfection in the Performance of the Chemical Functions of the Lungs." His treatment was massive doses of calomel with ginger tea and alcohol, and copious bleeding of the patient. Many of Stimson's patients, including his wife and a son, died.

In the fall of 1832 Stimson went to Connecticut where he married a younger sister of his first wife. The next year he returned to Upper Canada and settled at St George, where he practised until his death in 1869. One of his sons, Elam Rush, became a Church of England clergyman and was editor of the *Church Herald* (Toronto) and author of *History of the separation of church and state in Canada* (Toronto, 1887).

C. M. GODFREY

Elam Stimson was the author of *The cholera beacon, being a treatise on the epidemic cholera as it appeared in Upper Canada in 1832–4* . . . (Dundas, [Ont.], 1835). C. T. Campbell, *Pioneer days in London; some account of men and things in London before it became a city* (London, Ont., 1921). Canniff, *Medical profession in U.C.* Edwin Seaborn, "The Asiatic cholera in 1832 in the London District," *RSC Trans.*, 3rd ser., XXXI (1937), sect.II, 153–69; *The march of medicine in western Ontario* (Toronto, [1944]).

STINSON, JOSEPH, Methodist minister; baptized 1 March 1802 in Castle Donington, Leicestershire, son of William Stinson and Mary Cheatle; m. the daughter of the Reverend John Chettle in 1829; d. 26 Aug. 1862 at Toronto, Canada West.

Joseph Stinson, a well-educated member of a Methodist family, was recruited as a missionary by the Wesleyan Methodist Missionary Society and in 1823 was stationed in Melbourne, Lower Canada. From 1823 until his death, with some intervals, Stinson was an active and influential participant in the development of Methodism in Upper and Lower Canada, deeply involved in the shaping of the complex relationship between the English and Canadian Methodist bodies.

The growth of Methodism in Upper Canada was initiated and directed by the Methodist Episcopal Church in the United States. The societies in Lower Canada, however, had been given over in 1821 to the supervision of the English conference and its agency, the Missionary Society, in order to end the rivalry in the same fields between the English and American conferences. In 1828, in keeping with the emergence of Canadian self-awareness, the conference in Upper Canada became independent of the American church. Nevertheless a conflict developed in Upper Canada as a result of persistent efforts by the English conference to secure effective control over the Canadian Methodist societies. There were differences in church organization that caused conflict, the English Wesleyan conference being essentially a clerical oligarchy, whereas the Methodist Church in the United States was governed through its conferences, with the executive authority resting with its bishops and elders. The strongest issue was the British conference's attempt to disseminate Methodism as a means of promoting and cementing loyalty to the empire, the crown, and church establishment. The British missionaries and many English immigrants considered native Canadians to be Americans and therefore of doubtful loyalty. Stinson thought the Canadians' "political character" was "extremely objectionable." Canadian Methodist leaders such as James Richardson*, in contrast, conceived that they were loyal to their British heritage, but that it was essential to interpret and adapt this tradition in the light of Upper Canadian needs and interests.

In an effort to collaborate harmoniously with each other, and at the urging of the Colonial Office, the English and Canadian conferences united in 1833 [*see* John Ryerson*]. Stinson was appointed superintendent of missions in Upper

Stinson

Canada, an office he held until the union was dissolved in 1840. During these years, Stinson was actively engaged in the development of Indian missions and, as the permanent representative of the English conference, played a key role in the strained relations between the two conferences.

The English, American, and Canadian conferences were agreed on the importance of Christianizing and civilizing native peoples. The Canadian conference, spurred especially by William Case*, had by 1833 laid the foundations of extensive missionary activity to the scattered Indian tribes in what became southern and northern Ontario. Its work, funded in part after 1833 by government grants, was characterized by intensive efforts to convert the Indians to Methodist doctrines and practices, and, wherever possible, to establish model settlements in which, through education and example, they were encouraged to make permanent homes, practise agriculture, and permit their children to acquire certain skills and the rudiments of literacy. In so doing, the Methodists were brought into active and sometimes abrasive contact with the imperial and colonial governments, which were wrestling with the pressures exerted by humanitarian groups to give Indians clear title to their lands and by the advance of settlement in the colony which threatened Indian communities.

As superintendent of missions, Stinson visited Indian missions and recruited missionaries from England; he brought to his work indefatigable energy, a measure of realism, and scrupulous attention to detail. The information he accumulated about the Indian settlements justified the continuance of Wesleyan financial support for the missions and was used by the Missionary Society and the Aborigines' Protection Society, an interdenominational humanitarian organization, in their efforts to ensure equitable treatment for the Indians in the face of settlers' avarice and the resettlement plans sponsored by Sir Francis Bond Head* [see Jean-Baptiste ASSIGINACK]. The advance of settlement was not halted, but the missions were separated from regular circuits and consolidated. The Missionary Society was encouraged by the Hudson's Bay Company to extend its operations to the territories controlled by the company. With James Evans* as superintendent and with Stinson's encouragement, these missionary efforts were pursued by the Wesleyan Methodist Church of Canada after 1847. Appropriately, the last address Stinson gave in 1862 was entitled "The Aborigines of Canada."

From the outset, however, Stinson was concerned not simply with missions but with the wider task of establishing an effective working relationship between the English and Canadian conferences and the types of Methodism which they respectively represented. In large measure, he shared the conviction of his English brethren that "it would be a noble object to get the whole of Methodism in the British Empire *really under the control of the British Conference & one with it in spirit & in interest.*" To achieve this objective it was necessary that the Canadian Methodists accept the jurisdiction of the English and, more important, the principle of church establishment. The Canadians should avoid intervention in politics, and take a firm stand against republicanism, by which was meant opposition to or criticism of the existing political order in Upper Canada. Stinson considered the uprising in December 1837 "the most rascally unprincipled rebellion that ever disgraced a country." In the immediate post-rebellion period, when Egerton Ryerson* criticized the Church of England's claims to establishment and ownership of the clergy reserves, Stinson warned him of the danger implicit in his complaints and insisted that a majority of the population "would rather have [an established church] and connexion with Great Britain than republicanism. . . ."

As missions superintendent and president of the Canadian conference in 1839 and 1840, Stinson mediated between the proponents of the Canadian and Wesleyan positions, but he grew "sick" of the controversy. The dissolution of the union between the two conferences in 1840 marked a temporary frustration of his hopes for unity. He stayed in Canada until June 1842 as chairman of the British conference's Canada Western District, but he sought privately to persuade his English colleagues that they had "been too thin-skinned about Canadian Wigism." He also believed that conflict between Methodists was unseemly and dangerous, particularly at a time when the Roman Catholic Church was experiencing a revival and the Oxford movement was having a profound effect on the Church of England. His conciliatory efforts and those of Canadians like Anson Green* were rewarded with the reunion of the two conferences in 1847; the union continued amicably until the formation of the Methodist Church of Canada in 1874.

In England after 1842 Stinson was stationed on regular circuits, but he kept in touch with the situation in Canada West. As one who stood high in the esteem of the Canadian brethren, he was appointed president of their conference in 1858. He willingly left England that he might "live and die in Canada." From 1858 to 1861, when his health began to fail, he was continually on the move, delivering sermons and addresses in support of missions and the general advancement of Methodism. In this capacity he was "universally beloved by the members of the Conference."

Stinson left no written works of consequence and was not identified with any great ecclesiastical accomplishments. Methodists would remember him as a warm, generous, and tolerant representative of the Wesleyan strain in the ongoing development of Canadian Methodism – one who was able to ease the tension between the English and Canadian bodies. The eventual amalgamation of the two groups left the Canadian conference more open to transatlantic influences and hastened its consolidation as an institution. Hence, in the latter half of the 19th century, Canadian Methodism was a less abrasive force in society than it might have been. Apart from that, Stinson deserves recognition for his reorganization of Methodist missions to the Indians at a critical juncture in their development. Methodist concern for the welfare of the native peoples helped keep alive political interest in the formidable issue of their assimilation to the white man's culture.

G. S. FRENCH

Methodist Missionary Soc. Archives (London), Wesleyan Methodist Missionary Soc. correspondence (copies at UCA). *Christian Guardian*, 1833–40; 3 Sept. 1862. Anson Green, *The life and times of the Rev. Anson Green, D.D. . . .* (Toronto, 1877). Wesleyan Methodist Church, *Minutes of the conferences* (London), 1819–24. Wesleyan Methodist Church in Can., *Minutes* (Toronto), 1863. Carroll, *Case and his contemporaries.* G. G. Findlay and W. W. Holdsworth, *History of the Wesleyan Methodist Missionary Society* (5v., London, 1921–24), I. Sissons, *Ryerson.*

STRACHAN, JAMES McGILL, soldier, lawyer, politician, and businessman; b. 1 July 1808 at Cornwall, Upper Canada, son of John STRACHAN and Ann McGill, *née* Wood; m. in 1844 Augusta Anne, daughter of John Beverley ROBINSON; they had no children; d. 22 Jan. 1870 at Toronto, Ont.

James McGill Strachan was the eldest and most favoured of the Strachan children. He was born to privilege and cultivated its advantages with zeal in pursuing a multi-faceted career. Educated largely at home, Strachan, with his father's reluctant support, purchased a commission in the 68th Foot in 1826. He studied further at the Royal Military College at Sandhurst, England, and, on numerous leaves and assignments, travelled throughout Europe. In 1833 he purchased a cap-

taincy for £1,600 but resigned the commission in 1836 and returned to Canada to begin what he had once called the "detested" study of law. During the rebellion in Upper Canada in 1837–38 he served as military secretary to Lieutenant Governor Sir Francis Bond Head*, maintaining links between Head and militia troops in the field.

He was admitted to the bar on 16 Feb. 1838 and went into partnership with John Hillyard Cameron* in Toronto. Handsome, eloquent, and quick-witted, Strachan was a formidable figure. His firm was the legal representative of many substantial businesses, notably the Canada Company, a British-based land and colonization company.

Strachan contested Huron County's seat in the election of 1841, during which he was closely identified with the Family Compact and the Canada Company by his opponent, Dr William "Tiger" Dunlop*, who was supported by the prosperous settlers of Colborne Township. Strachan's spirited campaign was managed by his brother-in-law, Thomas Mercer JONES, and despite the *British Colonist*'s assertion that he had "no more chance, than a stump-tailed ox in fly time," he was elected. Dunlop unseated him, however, in a subsequent recount, and Strachan's only other political activity was as a Toronto alderman in 1842 and 1852.

Strachan was an inveterate speculator who launched himself with vigour and no small outlay of cash into abortive railway projects involving the Lake Huron and Toronto Railroad from 1836 to 1841 and the Toronto, Simcoe, and Huron Railway in 1850, as well as an unsuccessful land deal at Elora in 1851. During the recession of 1847 he had apparently become bankrupt as a result of land speculation in Toronto; at the same time his partnership with Cameron failed and the lucrative Canada Company account was lost. By 1853 he had regained enough credit to purchase a tract of land west of Toronto's centre and its superintendence, together with leisurely sportsman's pursuits, occupied the rest of his life.

ROGER D. HALL

PAO, Jarvis-Powell papers; Macaulay (John) papers; Maps Division, J. M. Strachan and W. J. FitzGerald, "Crookshank Estate" (1853); Strachan (John) papers, letterbooks. *British Colonist* (Toronto), 10 March 1841. G.B., WO, *Army list*, 1827, 1836. I. A. Stewart, "The 1841 election of Dr. William Dunlop as member of parliament for Huron County," *OH*, XXXIX (1947), 51–62.

STRACHAN, JOHN, teacher, clergyman, officeholder, and bishop; b. 12 April 1778 at Aber-

Strachan

deen, Scotland, son of John Strachan and Elizabeth Findlayson; d. 1 Nov. 1867 at Toronto, Ont.

In the course of his voluminous writings over a very long life John Strachan frequently referred to his childhood and adolescence, most fully in his manuscript autobiography written in 1799. His parents, who were "not rich but respectable," had six children of whom John was the youngest. His mother, who wanted one of her sons to become a minister, decided that "John the favourite must be made a gentleman," and receive a "liberal education." His father, an overseer in a granite quarry, reluctantly agreed to send him to the Aberdeen Grammar School where, after a slow start, he did well enough to obtain a bursary at King's College, Aberdeen.

After one session, 1793–94, Strachan's academic career nearly ended with the death of his father in an accident, for now he was without resources from his family. But in the fashion of penniless students at Scottish universities he turned to teaching, the first summer in the house of Lady Harriet Gordon at Banff and the second in a village school at Cannonside, 50 miles from home. Neither post was agreeable, but from them Strachan learned how to teach and assess strengths and weaknesses in human character; he also became more determined than ever to achieve his academic ambitions and to enter the world of gentlemen with literary tastes. In 1796, under more pleasant circumstances, he taught at a school near Denino (Dunino) in Fifeshire, not far from St Andrews, and attended the university as a part-time student. He took classes in divinity and was befriended by Thomas Duncan, later a professor, Thomas Chalmers, later the leader in the Free Church secession in the 1840s, and Dr James Brown, soon to be a professor at the University of Glasgow. The intellectual companionship at Denino and St Andrews was long a powerful inspiration for Strachan.

In the fall of 1796 Strachan returned to Aberdeen and was graduated AM in March 1797. He then returned to Denino and again enrolled at St Andrews. But now a complication arose: he fell desperately in love with a local girl, could not keep his mind on his studies, and his lack of funds put marriage out of the question. The only course was to leave Denino, and he was fortunate to acquire a school at Kettle, 20 miles distant, where the "emoluments" were twice as large. But he was now too far away to attend St Andrews, and the chances of rising above the station of parish school teacher must have seemed slight. Hence, he was receptive to an offer which came to him in March 1799 via Dr Brown, "to go to Upper Canada to teach." He sailed from Greenock on 26 Aug. 1799, travelling by way of New York. He hoped to secure a position there, "in case my situation should prove disagreeable." Strachan's passionate commitment to Upper Canada was yet to be acquired.

The youthful schoolmaster reached his new home at Kingston on the last day of 1799. His task, at an annual salary of £80, was to tutor the children of Richard Cartwright* and of a few other prominent people of the town, including those of the Church of England clergyman, John Stuart*. He had also been promised that an "Academy" would be established and that he would be mathematics teacher. He lived in the house of Cartwright, a well-read loyalist from New York who had once planned to take holy orders, a member of the Legislative Council, and a well-connected merchant. He continued his studies with Stuart, also a loyalist from New York and a man who had once been a Presbyterian. Three years in the intimate company of these two men, combined with the generally conservative atmosphere of Kingston, helped to set Strachan's outlook on the affairs of Upper Canada. In these years he also established contacts with leading merchants in Montreal.

It was soon apparent to Strachan, however, that there was no early prospect of the establishment of an academy. He would have to make his own way if he were to secure advancement, and so he came back to his mother's ambition that he become a clergyman. In 1802, probably with Cartwright's approval, he made a private inquiry through a friend concerning a vacancy at the St Gabriel Street Presbyterian Church in Montreal. (It turned out that the vacancy had been filled, but the "friend" kept the letter for 25 years and then published it when it would cause Archdeacon Strachan the most embarrassment.) In the next year, armed with a letter of reference from Cartwright, Strachan presented himself to Bishop Jacob Mountain* for ordination in the Church of England. The letter informed Mountain that Lieutenant Governor Peter Hunter* intended to appoint Strachan to the mission at Cornwall. On 22 May 1803 he was ordained deacon and on 3 June 1804 priest.

Since Strachan's taking orders in the Church of England later became the subject of intense controversy, it is as well to review the matter briefly. To his enemies the case was clear. He had been brought up a Presbyterian; he had been ready as recently as 1802 to take a Presbyterian church; he had soon realized, however, that his own career and ambitions would be best furthered by joining the Church of England, and so he had "turned his coat." On the other hand, his father had been a

752

non-juror and had often taken him to St John's Episcopal Church, Aberdeen, where they had heard the eminent Bishop John Skinner, and his mother belonged to a Presbyterian group that had seceded from the Church of Scotland. Strachan explained that on basic questions of theology he did not see fundamental differences between the Church of England and the Presbyterians, and that his decision in 1803 owed much to the personal example and influence of John Stuart.

Strachan began his new life at Cornwall in the summer of 1803, and at first he found little to encourage him. A letter in October of that year to Dr Brown reflected his mood and also touched on themes that would figure prominently in his later career. He considered Cornwall society "very indifferent," with few "independent or respectable" and few educated persons. The common people, "almost all Americans," had "little or no religion" and minds "prone to low cunning." Methodists, Lutherans, Catholics, and Presbyterians greatly outnumbered his flock, and he faced much work in building parishes. Strachan intended to "attack and expose" the Methodist notion of "sudden inspirations," and added, "I need hardly tell you that I am not popular. . . ." Despite his early opinion of the town, where he lived until 1812, it was at Cornwall that he laid the basis for all his later achievements in Canada. He soon acquired a reputation as an industrious and highly successful parish priest, and was making himself known to clergymen elsewhere in the British provinces. He established ties of marriage, of friendship, and of influence that bound him irrevocably to Canada. Finally, and in some ways most important, he quickly emerged as the most outstanding classroom teacher in the province.

Within a few weeks of his settling in Cornwall, Strachan was in touch with the parents of some of the boys whom he had been teaching in Kingston to suggest that they be sent to him to continue their schooling. Among those who came were John* and William Macaulay*. Another was a fatherless 12-year-old lad, John Beverley ROBINSON, recently in the household of John Stuart, soon to be almost an adopted son of Strachan, and later to be his closest and dearest friend. In 1804 Strachan had more than 20 students and by 1808 about 40, a figure that remained fairly constant down to 1812. The boys came from all parts of the province, and were the sons of leading figures in government, business, and the professions. Strachan deliberately set out to train them as potential rulers of the next generation.

At Kingston Strachan had been little more than a family tutor; now he had his own school and freedom to develop his own techniques and methods. Not surprisingly he borrowed heavily from his Scottish background, but he also adapted his curriculum to the needs of Upper Canadian society. When he could not find a textbook to suit local needs, he prepared one himself, *A concise introduction to practical arithmetic; for the use of schools* (Montreal, 1809). Although not neglecting the classics, he stressed the teaching of natural science and managed, through friends in the legislature, to secure an appropriation of £400 for the purchase of scientific apparatus. In short, the academic curriculum of the Cornwall Grammar School was up to date, varied, and of a high standard. Moreover, Strachan, who used corporal punishment less than was usual, devised intricate systems of rewards and competitions to a considerable extent operated by the boys themselves, which were calculated to interest them in their studies and make them extend themselves fully. Strachan also never saw the acquisition of knowledge as an end in itself. The boys were at school to learn to become British patriots and Christian gentlemen. Love of country, respect for the constitution, and the importance of performing civic duties were systematically inculcated. Prayers were said each day, Church of England students (who were in the majority) were taught the church catechism, and on Saturday morning Strachan delivered a religious and moral lecture on which the boys were quizzed during the following week. It was his confident hope that boys who had received this kind of training would do much to raise the tone of Upper Canadian society.

When his highly reputed school began receiving government support following the Grammar School Act of 1807, Strachan received an annual stipend of £100. In the spring of 1807 he married Ann Wood McGill, the daughter of a Cornwall physician and widow of Andrew McGill* of the prominent Montreal mercantile family. Strachan, who always found himself "happy in the connexion," wrote Brown that she had "a great share of beauty" and "an annuity of three hundred a year during her life." While they were at Cornwall, JAMES McGILL was born in 1808, Elizabeth in 1810 (d. 1812), and George Cartwright in 1812. Later, at York (Toronto), were born Elizabeth Mary (1814), who subsequently married Thomas Mercer JONES, John (1815), and Alexander Wood (1817). Two other daughters, born in 1821 and 1824, died as infants, and a third, Agnes (b. 1822), died before reaching her 17th birthday.

Strachan had married well and had built a good church, parsonage, and school. In 1811, after he

Strachan

suggested to Dr Brown that "a degree might in some measure increase my influence," Strachan received from the University of Aberdeen the honorary degree of Doctor of Divinity. He was clearly a success, but it is doubtful whether he saw Cornwall as a large enough stage for his talents and energies. In 1811 his long-standing ambition to found a university received some encouragement from a conversation with the elderly James McGill*. Without close relatives, McGill wondered how to dispose of his extensive property, and Strachan suggested that it should be left for the encouragement of education. In consequence McGill made a will leaving the bulk of his estate to four trustees, one of them Strachan, who were to turn it over to the Royal Institution for the Advancement of Learning if the latter established a college within ten years. McGill, who died in 1813, clearly contemplated that Strachan would be its principal. For various reasons he never was, but Strachan can be reckoned among the founders of McGill University.

Another event of 1811, the death of his old friend and mentor John Stuart, was more decisive for Strachan's future. He hoped to succeed Stuart at Kingston, but at the widow's request Bishop Mountain selected her son, George Okill STUART, then rector of York, to be bishop's commissary and rector at Kingston. Strachan's bitter disappointment was not assuaged by the offer of the post as rector at York, but when the administrator of the province, General Isaac Brock*, increased the income by offering him the chaplaincy of the garrison and of the Legislative Council, he accepted. He and his family arrived in the provincial capital in June 1812, at about the time that the United States Congress was declaring war on Great Britain.

Strachan had no very high opinion of little York and its petty politics. After the election of 1808 he had written that the new House of Assembly would "be composed of ignorant clowns, for the spirit of levelling seems to pervade the province." The one hope on the horizon was that "By an bye, my pupils will be getting forward, some of them perhaps into the House & then I shall have more in my power." He was also alarmed by the danger to the province arising from its proximity to the United States. In 1809 he had written that "the ruling party in that country [had] been hostile to Britain these eight years, and [had] been prevented from going to war only by their avarice, and the fear of rebellion in the Northern section of the Union. . . ." In 1810 he had sought to arouse patriotism and loyalty to king and constitution by composing and publishing *A discourse on the character of King George*

the Third. In August 1812 he delivered and subsequently published a sermon in which he denounced the United States for joining "the most cruel tyrant that has ever appeared . . . in fighting against the last pillar of freedom and happiness in the world." He saw Upper Canada as "environed almost with our enemies, and mixed with doubtful characters and secret Traitors"; it would be necessary "to arm the Government" with strong powers to combat both the invaders and internal disaffection. But he assured the people of Upper Canada that they had "nothing to fear" if they fixed their "attention upon God, and put on the grace of the Christian Soldier. . . ."

Strachan was as good as his word in performing his own duty. He took a strong interest in military strategy, praised Brock for taking the offensive, and criticized Sir George Prevost* and others who adopted a defensive policy. In December 1812 he joined with other "principal Inhabitants of the town of York" to form the Loyal and Patriotic Society of Upper Canada, of which he became president and later treasurer; a principal purpose of the society was to raise funds "to afford relief and aid to disabled militiamen and their families." He was indefatigable in ministering to the sick, the wounded, and the homeless throughout the war years. Above all, however, he achieved lasting fame in the annals of Upper Canada by his conduct during the two American invasions of York in the spring and summer of 1813. On the first occasion General Roger Hale Sheaffe* withdrew his small defending force, and it was left to certain leading residents to make terms with the enemy. Strachan was quickly to the forefront, helping to write the terms of capitulation, complaining when they were not enforced, seeking to prevent looting, and generally protecting the interests of his parishioners. He performed the same role when the Americans came back at the end of July, even extracting from Commodore Isaac Chauncey* a promise of the return of some books taken by American soldiers on the earlier occasion. Strachan's courage and activity in the face of the enemy were never forgotten by his fellow townsmen. The war also had a lasting effect on Strachan's own outlook: he was now completely and irrevocably an Upper Canadian. He believed that the province had been saved by "the astonishing exertions of the Militia," and with the return of peace he redoubled his efforts to ensure that Upper Canada would be made worthy of the heroes who had resisted the invader.

As before, Strachan's central concerns were in the sphere of religion and education, but with the close of the war he concluded that he could not achieve his objectives without playing a leading role on the provincial political stage. In 1814 he had already been considered by General Francis de Rottenburg* for appointment to the Executive Council, and in September of the next year he was made an honorary member of that body. He was a regular member from 1817 to 1836. Although his main fields of interest on the council related to religion and education, he quickly demonstrated an outstanding talent for administrative business, and during the 1820s at least he was one of the most important and influential members of the provincial government.

Strachan's early experience in the government soon convinced him that he must also seek a seat on the Legislative Council. In a letter to the retiring lieutenant governor, Francis Gore*, on 22 May 1817, he argued that the interests of the "established Church" were suffering because Presbyterians were in a majority on the Legislative Council, and he asserted that it was his "duty to offer [his] services." He admitted that his "motives [were] not altogether disinterested." He would be able to influence at least two members of the Council and "combat with success the probable opposition." Furthermore, "With the Lower House I shall by means of my pupils possess a growing influence. . . ." The appointment finally came in 1820, and Strachan remained in the upper house until the union of the Canadas in 1841.

As Strachan was acquiring political office, conducting the Home District Grammar School, serving his extensive parish (including preaching monthly at York Mills, seven miles north of the town), and building a large house (to be known as The Palace), he was also interesting himself in numerous incidents and issues in the life of York. In 1815 he was so outraged at the Earl of Selkirk [Douglas*]'s proposed settlement on the Red River that he wrote *A letter to the . . . Earl of Selkirk . . .* (London, 1816), denouncing the scheme as both impracticable and harmful to the interests of Upper Canada. Most notorious of all was his opposition to Robert GOURLAY. Indeed, at first he was alone in official circles in disapproving of Gourlay's "Address to the resident landowners of Upper Canada" (October 1817), and he stated that Gourlay became "exceedingly enraged against me as my opinions had by some strange breach of confidence been communicated to him." When Gourlay's plans were subsequently thwarted, "he began to write in the newspapers and giving me credit for all his disappointments. I became the particular object of his attack. His abuse and ravings I little regarded. . . ." Some months later Strachan wrote to Dr

Brown that "All my pupils now the leading characters in many parts of the Province opposed him sternly. A character like Mr. Gourlay in a quiet Colony like this where there is little or no spirit of inquiry & very little knowledge may do much harm . . . by exciting uneasiness irritation & . . . unreasonable hopes. I tried to infuse some energy into the administration but it was too feeble till [Sir Peregrine Maitland*] came out." Gourlay's writings and activities inspired Strachan to take up his own pen in defence of "the measures of Govt" and to counteract the "sullen discontent" that had "been infused into the minds of the people." He wrote to John Macaulay, proposing to prepare anonymous letters to be published in the *Kingston Gazette*. In 1819–20 he also published a religious newspaper, the *Christian Recorder*. As well, he prepared a book for the British public, aimed at convincing prospective settlers to come to Upper Canada rather than the United States. All were welcome except "levellers and democrats" who would find "no kindred spirits there." Strachan used the occasion of a visit from his brother James to have the book, *A visit to the province of Upper Canada in 1819* (Aberdeen, 1820), published under the latter's name, ostensibly as one of the emigrant guide–travel books of the period.

But for all these various activities Strachan's main interests continued to be education and religion. In February 1815, as news of the formal end of the war was arriving, Strachan prepared two reports setting out his ideas and proposals for improving the educational systems of the two Canadas. The first of these, sent to gentlemen in Lower Canada, was an appeal to the legislature of that province to set up a college in Montreal, its "Principal to be of the Church of England," in order to take advantage of James McGill's bequest. The college should be "on the Model of the Scotch or German Universities" and should be open to "young men of all denominations of Christians." He also called for the establishment of two grammar schools, at Quebec and Montreal, "to be appendages to and Nurseries for" the university. In effect, Strachan wished to set up an English-language structure of higher education to parallel the already existing French-language institutions. But as an earlier letter to "The Great Dugald Stewart" had indicated, he saw the proposed "College or University" as a place where "young men both French & English" would mix together and "the language of the Conquerors would gradually obtain the ascendency & the country become what alone can render it really valuable to the Crown an English colony."

755

Strachan

The second report, addressed to General Gordon Drummond*, the administrator, was a terse but comprehensive survey of the changes needed to improve Upper Canada's educational system. First, a university must be established as soon as possible to make it unnecessary to send "young men out of the Province to finish their education"; Great Britain was too far away and too expensive and "those sent to the United States commonly learn little beyond anarchy in Politics & infidelity in religion." The university should be open to "the youth of all denominations." Second, the existing system of district grammar schools should be continued and improved; he called for annual reports from the trustees, public examinations, free tuition "in order to open the way to the poorer Inhabitants to a liberal Education for their promising Children," and the careful selection of teachers ("That no person who is not a natural born subject of the King and fully qualified to teach . . . shall be capable of becoming [a] Master"). Third, he called for government support for a system of elementary (or "common") schools. Finally, he asked that a provincial "board of education" be set up to supervise the system at all levels. Strachan would devote much of the rest of his career to attempts to implement this wide-ranging plan.

The most immediate need was for support of common schools. In 1816 Lieutenant Governor Gore endorsed Strachan's proposals and later that year the legislature passed a Common School Act, which apparently had been largely drafted by Strachan. With two amendments in 1820 and 1824 this act remained the basis of Upper Canada's elementary school system until 1841. In 1819 a revised Grammar School Act also adopted some of his suggestions, but failed to provide for free education; the most that was thought to be financially feasible was free tuition for ten poor students in each district. Lack of money also prevented any start on a university in the decade after 1815.

Strachan's efforts to establish a board of education involved him in much more controversy than did his work in promoting school legislation. In December 1817 he wrote to the administrator, Samuel Smith*, that the colony needed "an Inspector or Superintendant of Schools in order to produce uniformity of System," and "To discharge the duties of this Office . . . I respectfully offer myself a Candidate." Delays followed but finally, in 1822, the Executive Council approved the appointment of a General Board of Education, with Strachan as president, at an annual stipend of £300. With the assent of the Colonial Office in 1823, the board began to function, and

Strachan relinquished his post as headmaster of the York grammar school, thus ending some 30 years of classroom teaching. The fact that the members of the board all belonged to the Church of England and that they were given power to supervise the school lands that had been reserved in Governor John Graves Simcoe*'s time was a source of alarm to the emerging reform movement, for it was increasingly believed that the school system was falling under Tory and Church of England control. With his numerous offices Strachan was also coming to be seen in reform circles as a political priest who was seeking to rule Upper Canada in defiance of public opinion. The board and its president were subjected to mounting criticism until it was abolished in 1833.

As Strachan surveyed "the State of Religion in Upper Canada" in 1815 he sounded themes which would recur throughout his long career. Since there were fewer than a dozen clergymen of the "established church" in the entire province, increased government assistance was a desperate need. To be sure, there were the clergy reserves, but since these could only be leased, not sold, they brought in little revenue in a province where land could be easily acquired in fee simple. Strachan did not rule out recruiting new clergymen in England, but on the whole he did not think that English born and trained clergymen would fit into the primitive conditions in Upper Canada. Strachan had earlier trained ("gratis") John Bethune* Jr, who had been admitted to holy orders, and was prepared to train other aspirants. He was already looking to the establishment of a theological seminary, and in 1816 and 1817 unsuccessfully sought support for one from the Upper Canadian legislature. As for other denominations in the province Strachan referred sympathetically to Roman Catholic and Church of Scotland clergymen as deserving government aid, but Methodists and Congregationalists "cannot expect the countenance of Govt and the people that follow them would immediately join the Church of England if Clergymen were supplied."

The need to strengthen the position of the Church of England in Upper Canada was further brought home to Strachan by the introduction in the assembly in 1817 of resolutions attacking the clergy reserves as "an appropriation beyond all precedent lavish"; the resolutions ("pregnant [with] revolutionary spirit," according to Strachan) only failed of adoption because of an abrupt prorogation of the legislature by the lieutenant governor. In the next year Gourlay's questionnaire also revealed some popular discontent with the reserves. Strachan's response was

756

not only to seek a seat on the Legislative Council, as already mentioned, but also to propose a corporation for superintending the reserves in order to place them firmly under the clergy's control and also, it was hoped, to initiate a more active leasing policy. After some delay the Upper Canada Clergy Corporation was constituted in 1819, to consist of the bishop of Quebec, the clergy of the Church of England in Upper Canada, and the inspector general and surveyor general of the province. A quorum consisted of three, and over the next several years the corporation was in fact run by Strachan, acting as chairman, and the two public officers. Of 37 meetings held by the end of 1827, Strachan missed only three.

But long before 1827 Strachan had concluded that a leasing policy was inadequate. Popular opposition to the clergy reserves was increasing in the early 1820s, and Strachan and Lieutenant Governor Maitland concluded that the only way to deflect it was to sell a portion of these lands, thus opening them to settlement and, it was hoped, increasing the revenues of the church. It was agreed that Strachan should go to London as an official delegate from the government of Upper Canada to put this policy to the British government, and he reached England at the end of March 1824. He found that the colonial secretary, Lord Bathurst, and the under secretary, Robert John Wilmot-Horton, were sympathetic to selling, but they were also deep in discussions with John Galt* and the officials of the Canada Company, looking to the sale of a much larger amount of crown land to that company. Strachan was asked to negotiate with Galt to see whether the company might buy the clergy reserves as well; Strachan was agreeable in principle but insisted that only about a third of the reserves should be sold, and on better terms than were initially offered so that the proceeds would ensure the security and growth of the Church of England in Upper Canada. Thinking that the company would modify its terms, he indicated in July 1824 "that the arrangement, as it would then stand, would be as fair as could be expected." He then went off to Scotland to visit friends and relatives, after a quarter century's absence. On his way back to Canada in September 1824, he discovered that the terms of sale had not been modified. It then became his duty, as he saw it, to oppose the Canada Company's proposals, and no sale occurred.

One other large question of public policy engaged Strachan's energies during his 1824 stay in Great Britain – the respective merits of union of Upper and Lower Canada or of union of all the British North American provinces. It was not a new interest for him. Almost as soon as he had heard of the Union Bill in 1822 he had sent off a series of objections to the Colonial Office, arguing that union of the two provinces would "make both Provinces discontented perhaps rebellious," and that it would in effect mean French rule because the anti-government minority in Upper Canada would combine with a solid *bloc* of French Canadians to dominate a united legislature. He had also been in correspondence with Attorney General John Beverley Robinson, who, from his arrival in London in 1822 to seek imperial intervention in a trade dispute between Upper and Lower Canada, had been immediately involved in the union question. Asked for his views by the Colonial Office, Strachan submitted a report in which he argued that the projected union would be harmful to British interests in general and to the Church of England in particular. Indeed, rather than a dual union Strachan endorsed Robinson's plan for a "General Legislative Union of the British Provinces in North America." Among its advantages, such a union "would become a great barrier against encroachments from the United States," and "In regard to . . . Lower Canada, the feelings and apprehensions which at present distract its peace would gradually subside. . . . The Canadian character would by degrees sink into the English without irritation."

Strachan was concerned with still another subject in 1824: his own future in the church. For several years he had been hoping that the elderly bishop of Quebec, Jacob Mountain, would retire, and that the occasion would be used to divide the large and unwieldy diocese. In 1819 he had asserted that Mountain's "habits and manners were calculated rather for an English Bishop than the Missionary Bishop of Canada. We want a primitive Bishop who will go round the Country & preach the Gospel. . . . We want a Bishop that will encourage his Clergy by frequent & liberal communications . . . & give them an example of attention to duty combined with learning and moderation." In 1824 Strachan put his case directly to the Colonial Office, asked that the diocese be divided, and that he be appointed bishop in Upper Canada, "an office to which no other Clergyman in either of the Canadas can with equal justice aspire." The Colonial Office refused, largely for financial reasons, and Strachan was fated to wait 15 more years for his mitre, always under the hazard that another might be appointed. For the time being he had to be satisfied with the promise of appointment as archdeacon of York. Even this honour was slow in coming; the letters patent were not issued until 1827.

In the autumn of 1824 Strachan returned from London to an Upper Canada that was rapidly changing, and in ways that were highly disquieting to him. William Lyon MACKENZIE was assailing the Family Compact in the *Colonial Advocate*. Anti-government (or "reform") men were gaining control of the assembly. Attacks on the clergy reserves were increasing. The "alien question" was sharpening political debate [*see* ROLPH]. The whole tone of society seemed to be turning more "Yankee" and democratic. Strachan was as convinced as ever that the province was essentially sound, but also that vigorous measures were needed to keep it on the right path. The British government must support loyal men and not countenance agitators. It must publicly declare that the Church of England was the established church in Upper Canada and that the church was entitled to all the proceeds of the clergy reserves. The educational system must be strengthened to encourage loyalty and social order. With his usual combativeness and energy Strachan resolved to fight for the right, as he saw it.

In the spring of 1826 Strachan returned to England, authorized by the provincial government to seek a university charter. This time he would be overseas for well over a year. By March 1827 the terms of the royal charter for the University of King's College had been announced. For the most part the charter represented Strachan's handiwork, but not in every respect. He had proposed that the president must be a member of the Church of England, but the charter more narrowly stipulated that the archdeacon of York must be president, a provision Strachan thought both unnecessary and unwise. It also provided that the governing body, the college council, must subscribe to the 39 Articles, which Strachan had not asked for. Nevertheless Strachan defended the charter, then and later, as the most liberal ever granted under the royal seal – more liberal than was thought wise by leading English churchmen. To be sure, the university would be firmly under church control, but there were to be no religious tests for students. It was to receive a handsome land endowment and annual payments from the Canada Company. The grant of the charter fulfilled Strachan's deepest ambition. He felt that he deserved well of the province, and he was to be astounded at the torrent of opposition that later assailed him. In fact, however, he did much to provoke this opposition by writing and publishing in England *An appeal to the friends of religion and literature, in behalf of the University*

of Upper Canada (London, 1827). In this appeal directed to church people, he unwisely described the university as "a missionary college," intended mainly to train Church of England clergymen, thus undercutting much of his emphasis on the liberal features of the charter.

In the summer of 1826 Strachan also resumed his discussions with the Canada Company regarding the sale of the clergy reserves, and when no agreement could be reached, the company agreed to buy, instead of all or part of the reserves, a block of some one million acres bordering on Lake Huron. Strachan thereupon renewed his application to the government for authority to sell the reserves. While the matter was before parliament, certain Scottish MPs, acting as spokesmen of the Kirk, made charges against the Church of England and called for a general inquiry into church affairs in Upper Canada. Asked by Wilmot-Horton for further information, Strachan "hastily drew up [a] letter to that Gentleman," to which he attached an "Ecclesiastical Chart." The letter declared that "the tendency of the population is towards the Church of England, and nothing but the want of moderate support prevents her from spreading over the whole province." He dismissed the "teachers of the different denominations," with a few exceptions, as coming "from the United States, where they gather their knowledge and form their sentiments." This hurried and provocative letter, with its inaccurate chart, seriously damaged Strachan and his cause for years to come.

Nevertheless, before his return to Canada in the summer of 1827 the imperial parliament passed an act authorizing the sale of one-quarter of the reserves, with sales not to exceed 100,000 acres in any one year. The act coincided with the adoption of a general sales policy for all crown lands and the appointment of a commissioner of crown lands (Peter Robinson*, John's older brother). The new system had both advantages and disadvantages as far as Strachan was concerned. In effect, the reserves were now administered by the government instead of the Clergy Corporation. But that administration was friendly to the church, and it was clearly understood that the proceeds from sales were to go to the support of a Protestant clergy, which the government of Upper Canada interpreted to mean the Church of England. Moreover, with a vigorous sales policy, the reserves should soon cease to be obstacles to settlement and they should produce revenues needed to encourage the growth of the church.

Strachan came home in 1827 with high hopes of achieving his goals in education and religion, but in fact he suffered bitter frustration and disappointment in the following years. The Reformers, who gained a majority in the assembly in 1828, were now not only opposed to the Church of England's exclusive claims to the clergy reserves but they were even coming to deny the very concept of an established church and to reject any government support for religious denominations. The majority also attacked the "exclusive" terms of the university charter and insisted that it be amended to eliminate Church of England control. Strachan's response to mounting popular criticism was to insist that government, both in Upper Canada and in London, stand firm in defence of the rights vested in the Church of England. The reserves had been granted by King George III; the grant had been confirmed by imperial statute; the university charter had been granted by George IV. These were grants that a colonial legislature could not touch. If government firmly resisted the clamour of demagogues the furore would die down, and the church would grow rapidly with the influx of British immigrants.

But, to Strachan's mounting dismay, government did not stand firm, either in Upper Canada or in Great Britain. In 1828 Sir John COLBORNE replaced Maitland as lieutenant governor. Strachan never developed the same bond of trust with Colborne that he had enjoyed with Maitland. To be sure, Colborne was a staunch Anglican, but he was determined to remain somewhat aloof from the advisers who had surrounded Maitland and to ensure that "public opinion [was] more consulted than it has been." Strachan found himself without his accustomed influence. More serious was the fact that Colborne thought that starting the university was premature, and that Upper Canada's first need was a good preparatory grammar school conceived on English lines. In 1829 he was instrumental in founding Upper Canada College. Strachan could not openly oppose this step, but he felt that delay in starting the university would be harmful to both church and state.

Nor was the political scene any brighter in the mother country. With the end of the Liverpool government, Great Britain seemed to be given over to a "false liberality"; the cry of reform now "stun[s] our ears." Strachan was particularly angry at the report of a select committee of the House of Commons issued in 1828. He believed that the committee made no real effort to ascertain the true state of affairs in the Canadas and that its report would "do great mischief in all the Colonies – its tendency is to prostrate everything British – to nourish discontent – to depress the

Friends of Good Govt and to strengthen Levellers and Democrats." The rise of British reform in the late 1820s and in the 1830s was a source of deep disillusionment to Canadian Tories. By 1833 Strachan lamented to a correspondent in England: "Here the movement party chime in with that of Great Britain and the Imperial Govt cherish all attacks on Constitutional bulwarks. . . . My Tory Friends as well as myself . . . believe the Revolution to have virtually commenced. . . ."

The times were out of joint, but Strachan refused to give way "to idle clamour founded upon misstatement and ignorance." He believed that "by losing control of the University the Church loses her right arm and her right eye," and he told Colborne that he "would perish on the Scaffold rather than give up the Reserves or College Charter." Despite the "torrents of Calumny" with which he had been "assailed," he had "a fearless elasticity which nothing has as yet moved. I am conscious of having done more for the Church in this Province than any other person ever has or perhaps ever can do. . . ." Strachan was quite aware that Bishop Charles James Stewart*, Mountain's successor, and perhaps other church leaders thought him too outspoken and unbending in a stubborn Scotch way; he thought they lacked political skill and toughness.

As Strachan's political role waned somewhat, he pursued his clerical duties with redoubled energy. He trained young men for the priesthood, and as archdeacon of York set out on long visitations of the province, travelling many hundreds of miles over primitive roads. He supervised the rebuilding of St James Church. In 1832 he made two notable pronouncements which illustrated his conception of the church. One of these, published in New York, was in the form of *A letter to the Rev. Thomas Chalmers . . . on the life and character of . . . Dr. Hobart, bishop of New-York . . .*, who had died in 1830. Strachan had known and deeply admired him since 1816 for at least two reasons: by his unceasing efforts Hobart had brought the Protestant Episcopal Church in New York to a flourishing condition, and by his readiness to engage in controversy he had fearlessly contended with error in his diocese. The second statement was in a sermon preached at the visitation of Bishop Stewart. Since the church was about to lose support which it had long received from the Society for the Propagation of the Gospel [*see* HAWKINS], it must, he argued, "in future . . . depend more upon [its] own resources and exertions than has been hitherto required." In calling for a return to the primitive usage of holding synods, Strachan was already anticipating the self-governing church that he would later bring into being.

But 1832 was most memorable for another event, the terrible cholera epidemic which caused the death of about one-twelfth of the population of York. Strachan was untiringly active in ministering to the sick, arranging for burials, and seeking to prevent panic. He took the leading role in a "Society for the Relief of the Orphan, Widow, and the Fatherless" and successfully appealed to the public for assistance in providing for the destitute. In 1834, when cholera returned, he again attended the stricken "without regard to considerations of personal danger or fatigue." Strachan's activities so impressed the citizens of Toronto that they presented him with a silver vase worth £100. In 1833 another recognition had come when his former pupils in Cornwall had presented him with a silver epergne worth 230 guineas. These ceremonies afforded brief respite from the controversies that were a regular part of Strachan's life.

Strachan's continued firm stand regarding the clergy reserves and the university increasingly focused criticism on his membership in the executive and legislative councils. Already, in 1832, the colonial secretary had indicated that both the Roman Catholic bishop, Alexander Macdonell*, and Strachan might be well advised to resign from the Legislative Council. In 1835 the colonial secretary indicated that he considered it inappropriate for Strachan to attend the Executive Council, and Strachan at once sent in his resignation, effective 1 Jan. 1836. He wrote to Alexander Neil Bethune* that "the situation [had] been for many years . . . irksome and with such Ministers at home more than irksome – besides the radicals hate the Clergy and I was daily exposed to insult," without being able to accomplish anything effective. Besides, he could see "responsible government" on the horizon; it was better to retire than to be dismissed.

The Legislative Council was another matter, and here he refused to budge. On 5 Feb. 1836 the Reform majority in the assembly adopted an address which declared that Macdonell and Strachan were "devoting their time and talents to political strife and secular measures. . . ." But Strachan had no intention of being "driven by violence and menace from the seat to which my Sovereign has appointed me. . . . I can perceive no honourable alternative but respectfully and firmly to maintain my post." In fact, however, Strachan no longer played an important political role, except where church and church-related matters were concerned. It was as well for him during the tempestuous months to follow. He was

of course associated with the Tory side on such issues as Colborne's endowment of the rectories, Sir Francis Bond Head*'s "bread and butter" election, and in the events leading to the rebellion of 1837, but he was not involved in policy-making or in political debate relating to these questions.

Instead, Strachan's central concern from 1835 to 1839, apart from the ever present and closely connected matters of the clergy reserves and the university, was the future of the diocese. He had long believed that it should be divided, and that he had earned the right to be appointed bishop in Upper Canada, but Bishop Stewart was not disposed to support Strachan's claims. When Stewart became dangerously ill, it was arranged that Archdeacon George Jehoshaphat MOUNTAIN (son of the former bishop) should go to England to be consecrated as coadjutor; he succeeded Stewart at the latter's death in 1837. Thus the diocese remained undivided, and again Strachan had been passed over. He made no attempt to hide his bitter disappointment. The clergy of Upper Canada also petitioned the imperial government for a division of the diocese. By 1838 the Colonial Office had made it clear that it was agreeable to division but that it could not provide the bishop with a salary. In May of that year Strachan indicated that the salary question could be postponed: "It would be deeply mortifying for me to be superseded by a stranger; for the best men like to rise in their own profession, and he that is disappointed at my age can scarcely console himself with the hope of future promotion." Early in 1839, at age 61, Strachan learned that he was to be appointed bishop, without a stipend, and that he would have to pay the £250 fee for the patent. (He had to borrow £350 sterling to cover this and other expenses.) It would be necessary for him to continue as archdeacon and as rector to find sufficient income. He set off for England to be consecrated and was back in Toronto before the end of the year to be enthroned in the newly rebuilt St James Cathedral, as it now was (it had burned in January 1839). The recognition, however grudging and long delayed, had come, and the era of "John Toronto," to last more than a quarter century, had begun.

Many matters occupied Strachan's attention in these years, including the founding of the *Church* newspaper in 1837 (published at Cobourg under the editorship of A. N. Bethune) and Lord Durham [Lambton*]'s mission. He attended his "first political meeting" to express confidence in Durham, but later, predictably, strongly opposed union of the Canadas and of course had contempt for the concept of responsible government. But the two most important questions, apart from the bishopric, continued to be the university and the clergy reserves.

When Strachan had returned from England in 1827 with the charter and a large endowment for the university, he had hoped that it could be in operation within a year or so. A college council and administrative officers had been quickly chosen. A highly desirable site just north of the town was secured. But as opposition to the charter mounted, the colonial secretary ordered that its operation be suspended until the legislature of Upper Canada had an opportunity to consider and propose amendments. From 1829 to 1836 Strachan and the members of the college council were sufficiently strong in the Legislative Council to turn back all amendments proposed by the assembly. On several occasions Strachan indicated he was not averse to amendments that did not change the basic character of the institution. With the victory of the conservative assembly in 1836, agreement between the two houses became possible, and the charter was amended in 1837 to reduce considerably the visible or explicit aspects of Church of England control over the university.

It might have seemed that progress toward opening the university could now have been made and, in fact, after the inevitable delay occasioned by the rebellion, tenders for the construction of buildings were called for in 1838. But another complication arose. The new lieutenant governor, Sir George Arthur*, took a close look at the accounts kept by the bursar, Colonel Joseph Wells*, and found them to be hopelessly muddled. Among other irregularities, he discovered that Wells, on his own responsibility, had lent considerable sums of money to various persons, including Strachan, without requiring adequate security. Although Strachan returned the money, the revelation was highly embarrassing to him and to the college council. This episode, and the impending union of the Canadas, were further causes of delay in the opening of the university. Only with the arrival of Governor General Sir Charles Bagot* in 1842 were obstacles removed; in April Bagot, as chancellor, laid the foundation stone of King's College, and President Strachan gave the blessing. The official opening took place on 8 June 1843, marked by a speech in which Strachan reviewed the vicissitudes of the university over the previous 16 years. They were far from over, as events would soon show, and the appearance of victory would be turned to defeat within a half dozen years.

Meanwhile, Strachan had been fighting an equally stubborn campaign over the clergy reserves, one also destined to end in failure. Irritation over the reserves was widely considered to be the most pressing problem facing Upper Canada in the late 1830s – a "Pandora's Box" as it was called. Sir George Arthur tried, early in 1839, to secure the passage of a bill to sell the reserves and use the proceeds "for religious purposes." Since this bill ignored the principle of an established church, which was "part and parcel of the Constitution of Great Britain," Strachan and John Macaulay voted against it in the Legislative Council, asserting that it promoted and encouraged "Error, Schism and Dissent against which all Christians are bound to pray." While he was in England that summer to be consecrated Strachan lobbied against the bill, which in fact was disallowed on a technicality. Governor General Charles Poulett Thomson* now tried his hand and early in 1840 obtained passage of a bill giving the Church of England and the Church of Scotland each a quarter of the proceeds with the remaining half to go to other denominations. Again, Strachan bitterly attacked the bill and again set out to build up pressure against it in England. And again the bill was disallowed, on the ground that its provisions were beyond the powers of the Upper Canada legislature. Only the imperial parliament could act, which it did in a bill passed in August 1840. Its terms were far from satisfactory to Strachan, but they were much better than he could ever have hoped for from a Canadian legislature. By a rather complicated formula of division, the Church of England, with about one-fifth of the population, would receive some five-twelfths of the proceeds from the sale of the reserves. At least the settlement promised to be a final one, and Strachan set out to realize as good a return on the sale of the church's five-twelfths as could be obtained. That quest led him into many further sharp controversies during the 1840s.

In the midst of these struggles Strachan was striving to provide leadership to his new diocese. He spent most of the spring, summer, and autumn of 1840 in lengthy and laborious travels across the province "in order to confirm the youth of our congregations and to consecrate such churches as may be ready." In September 1841 the primary visitation of the clergy was held in St James Cathedral when Strachan delivered his first charge. In it he sketched the history of the church in Upper Canada and of the clergy reserves controversy, warning that since the church had lost more than half of the reserves, the "parishes and congregations" would henceforth have to make greater efforts to support "their respective ministers." He also set forth his

Strachan

conception of the Church of England: apostolic and primitive, avoiding "Romish tyranny and corruption" on the one hand and "the reckless and deadly innovations of modern Dissenters" on the other. He recommended the writings of John Henry Newman and others of the Oxford movement, but warned that in avoiding "one error they have not always steered sufficiently clear of another." In 1839 and 1840 he had written to Newman thanking him for his "able defense of the true Church," but his reservations grew as Newman moved toward Rome. In 1845 he wrote of "Mr Newman and his party" that "we are well rid of such men."

In 1842 Strachan initiated two important projects. The first was the establishment of the Diocesan Theological Institution at Cobourg for the training of clergymen for the church. He had hoped, of course, that King's College would perform this function, but repeated delays in opening that institution, and then actual and threatened changes in its charter, convinced Strachan that the church must set up its own divinity school. Headed by Strachan's protégé and future successor, A. N. Bethune, the theological institute existed for nine years, until it was absorbed into Trinity College in 1852. The institute became an object of suspicion among evangelical and low church elements in the diocese, as Trinity continued to be in the next decade.

Strachan's second project was the establishment of the Church Society in April 1842. It replaced several existing smaller societies and provided a framework in which clergy and laity could work closely together to defend and advance the interests of the church. Its main tasks were to watch over the church's finances, to raise money for missionary activities, and to provide pensions for retired clergymen. The society made a determined, although ultimately unsuccessful, attempt to gain complete administrative control over the church's five-twelfths' share of the clergy reserves.

In the midst of his arduous diocesan duties Strachan was plagued by financial embarrassments, which indeed were of long standing and to some extent self-inflicted. There had always been heavy claims on his fair-sized income. He liked to "live well," as he once put it: a large house, carriage, servants, a good table. He wished to provide adequately for his several children, and he was generous (and unlucky) in lending money to relatives. He of course had to subscribe to innumerable charities and good works. Like most Upper Canadians he had dreams of achieving financial security by speculating in land and stocks, and, like most, his speculations proved to

be disappointments. In the 1830s his salary began to shrink as he gave up various offices and then became bishop without a stipend. He was now chronically in debt. He bombarded the British government with complaints that the diocese of Toronto (as large as the whole of England) was the only one ever established by the crown not to be provided with an endowment: "The Church of England stands here, as in Ireland, the only effectual barrier to separation from the Parent State. But she cannot so stand for any length of time under the frown of the Imperial Government." Finally, in 1846, it was agreed that there was sufficient money in the clergy reserves fund to grant him an annual salary of £1,250, provided he relinquished his posts as rector and archdeacon, which he did in 1847. But financial embarrassment continued to dog Strachan for the rest of his life.

The opening of King's College in 1843 meant no cessation of the attacks upon the institution. In that very year Robert Baldwin* introduced a bill to establish a "University of Toronto," in effect a federation of King's, Queen's, Victoria, and Regiopolis colleges, which would control the King's College endowment. This threat ended with Baldwin's resignation in 1843, but in 1844–45 a more serious challenge came in a similar bill for a "University of Upper Canada" introduced by a Conservative government headed by William Henry Draper*, and supported by many moderate Anglicans. It was particularly galling to Strachan to find that "our greatest enemies are among ourselves"; he bluntly informed one Conservative member that he could not "consider anyone who [supported the bill] in any other light than an enemy or a Traitor to our Holy Catholic Church." In the end the ultra-Tories forced Draper to withdraw the bill. University bills also failed in 1846 and 1847. Meanwhile, King's College continued in successful operation with high academic standards and a distinct Church of England atmosphere. Satisfied that it was functioning effectively, Strachan resigned as president early in 1848.

It was just at that time that an election returned to power the Reform party under Baldwin and Louis-Hippolyte LA FONTAINE, and again the former addressed himself to the university question. His bill, passed in 1849, completely secularized King's College and brought it under government control. (It was a painful spring for Strachan: St James Cathedral burned in April.) Again Strachan fought back with every ounce of his still considerable energy. He sent a petition to the assembly denouncing the "revolutionary character" of the bill and resolved to seek its disallowance in England. But as it became obvious that the British authorities did not intend to interfere, and after the "godless" University of Toronto came into being on 1 Jan. 1850, Strachan combined positive action with his continuing fulminations. On 7 Feb. 1850 he addressed a *Pastoral letter to the clergy and laity of the diocese of Toronto*, which even John Macaulay thought was strongly worded. After denouncing the "three leading features" of the "wicked and inconsistent measure" – "contempt for the people, enmity to religion and disloyalty to the Sovereign" – and noting that "the Church found the chief enemies of King's College among her own professing adherents," the bishop stated that if an appeal to queen and parliament for restitution of the endowment should fail, then he and the clergy and laity must find the funds "to restore the College, under a holier and more perfect form" – to found a church university. He would go to England to raise money, and he also appealed for donations within the diocese. He headed the subscription list with a gift of £1,000: "I shall have completed my seventy-second year before I can reach London, of which more than fifty years have been spent in Upper Canada; and one of my chief objects during all that time, was to bring King's College into active operation; and now, after more than six years of increasing prosperity, to see it destroyed by stolid ignorance and presumption, and the voice of prayer and praise banished from its halls, is a calamity not easy to bear."

In April 1850 Strachan set out for England to secure a charter and to raise money for the projected church university. When he returned in the autumn he had, after strenuous efforts, achieved a high degree of success. On 30 April 1851 the cornerstone of the University of Trinity College was laid, and classes began in January 1852.

After the destruction of King's College Strachan was more than ever convinced that the church must organize effectively to protect its interests. It was clear that the imperial authorities would no longer intervene on the church's behalf. Within Canada the church was almost without political power, because, as Strachan saw it, government under the union was dominated by an alliance of Roman Catholics and Dissenters. In an era of Canadian self-government the church itself must become self-governing as a sheer matter of survival. It was time to move toward the establishment of diocesan synods, which Strachan had long seen as one of the great strengths of the Protestant Episcopal Church in the United States.

Early in 1851, when there were strong indications that the government would seek to secularize the clergy reserves, Strachan sent out a summons for his triennial visitation requesting that "every Clergyman . . . invite the members of his mission or congregation . . . to select one or two of their number to accompany him to the Visitation." In his charge he asserted that "our meeting and proceedings will begin a new era in the history of the colonial church and may be the prelude not only of Diocesan Synods, but of the ultimate union of all the British North American Bishoprics, to convene at stated times in general Synods or Convocations." The next visitation, in 1853, openly declared itself to be a synod, even though it lacked the constitutional authority to do so. Another synod was held in 1856 and finally, after the legislature had passed an enabling act, the first fully constitutional synod was held in 1857. In the words of J. L. H. Henderson, "John Strachan was now the head of an autonomous church."

In 1857 a start was also made in solving the problem of the size of the rapidly growing diocese. In 1853 Strachan had written to the archbishop of Canterbury noting that "it is rather too much for a Bishop who will pass his 75th birthday in a few short weeks to be obliged to travel continuously three or four months over very rough roads every Summer often with very poor accommodation." Financial problems delayed the division, but in 1857 an election was held for the new western diocese of Huron and to Strachan's chagrin Bethune was passed over in favour of the low churchman, Benjamin Cronyn*, who had been opposing Strachan on various issues for several years. In 1861 the eastern portion was split off to form the diocese of Ontario and again Bethune was passed over by the church electors in favour of John Travers Lewis*.

By this time Strachan had fought his last great battle over the clergy reserves. In 1854 the legislature passed a bill secularizing the reserves (Strachan called it "the most atrocious specimen of oppressive legislation that has appeared since the days of the French Convention"), after long and complicated manœuvring in both England and Canada, and despite all of Strachan's efforts in opposition. His cherished ideal of a union between church and state had been formally and finally repudiated. But with his usual tenacity Strachan seized on one feature of the bill which stated that clergy stipends then being paid were not to be disturbed and, second, that these life interests might be commuted to form a fund to be administered by the Church Society. The bishop at once set out to convince his clergy to surrender

Strachan

their stipends and after arduous effort he succeeded in nearly every case. He had lost the battle over the reserves, and yet he had salvaged a sum from which to provide income to his clergy for years to come.

It was not until he was well into his 80s that Strachan's usual good health began to falter. In 1863 he received a severe blow in the death of Sir John Beverley Robinson. With the somewhat faulty memory of an old man, he wrote his daughter-in-law that "there never was an unpleasant word between us during his whole life." In the following January he wrote that he was "both deaf & blind to a very inconvenient degree," and "were I out of debt I would retire on two thirds of my salary or income but even that would put me to serious inconvenience." In July he reported that his sight was "somewhat better" and that he expected to undertake his "usual confirmation journies"; he had "a strong antipathy to the word resignation." In October 1865 came another heavy loss with the death of his wife Ann, his partner of 57 years; for some time she had been a recluse, grieving over the deaths of all but one of her children. At long last, in September 1866, Strachan acceded to pressures from the synod for the election of a coadjutor, and Bethune was elected on the ninth ballot. After the latter's consecration by Strachan in January 1867, the old bishop was relieved of most of his "more onerous duties," as he put it. He preached in the cathedral only once that year, and died on All Saints' Day, in his 90th year. He was given an impressive state funeral in Toronto.

Strachan has been correctly remembered as the Canadian arch tory of his era. Although he had shown some liberal or even radical tendencies as a student in Scotland, the course of the French Revolution and the circumstances of Upper Canada's position in North America turned him into a firm and unyielding defender of inherited tradition. He believed in an ordered society, an established church, the prerogative of the crown, and prescriptive rights; he did not believe that the voice of the people was the voice of God. No man could have fought harder or more persistently for what he understood to be right, but the liberal, secular, and nationalistic trends of the time were bound to bear him down. Yet it is remarkable what he did manage, with the help of others, to save and to fend off, for his time and many years afterward. The tie with the mother country remained close. Canadian politics and society were less obviously "democratic" than in the United States. Neither in the schools nor in the colleges did education become completely secular. Strachan even salvaged

something from the secularization of the clergy reserves.

Strachan's kind of toryism was so out of fashion in his day, and increasingly since, that there is some danger of its being misunderstood. It was not synonymous with religious intolerance. Strachan had good personal relations with men of other denominations and respected the historic Christian churches. He did believe that in every well-ordered state there should be an established church to perform certain special functions. This role meant no limitation on complete freedom of worship. His toryism was not synonymous with obscurantism. He believed in rational religion, opposed "enthusiasm" and superstition, and devoted much of his life to the encouragement of education at all levels. Nor was it synonymous with colonial subserviency or with rural conservatism. Strachan strongly resented uninformed interference in Canadian affairs by the British parliament or by Downing St bureaucrats. He was a vigorous advocate of such projects as canals and banks, and sought generally to advance the economic improvement of British North America.

Moreover, because Strachan fought so hard, so long, and at times so bitterly, he may be remembered as a harsh, narrow autocrat, devoid of human qualities. Lord Elgin [BRUCE] called him "the most dangerous and spiteful man in Upper Canada," and dozens of similar assessments could be quoted. But a close look at his long career reveals a more complex and also more appealing figure. From his school and college background in Scotland he acquired a love of controversy and a certain disputatiousness which over the years landed him in difficult situations that a more prudent man would easily have avoided. This warmth in his nature also led him to develop a large number of friendships that endured over the decades. His letters to his wife and family and his copious diocesan correspondence disclose his capacity for affection and his constant concern for the needs and problems of others. As he grew old and suffered the long series of losses and defeats, he did not become bitter but remained sanguine, and his native wit and humour took on a certain mellowness.

Amidst the defeats and the holding actions, his restless energies had yielded much positive accomplishment. The educational system, although it eventually departed from his conception in important respects, had received much of its original stimulus from him. He had personally trained many of the most capable Canadian leaders of the second quarter of the 19th century. Above all, he was a great church statesman, in some ways in spite of himself. In his long and losing fight to preserve the connection between church and state and the status of the Church of England, he turned that church into a vital Canadian institution, with its roots deep in native soil.

G. M. CRAIG

[John Strachan's writings, both in manuscript and in print, were extremely extensive, and for the most part have been preserved. The largest collection of his correspondence, including his letter books, is at the PAO. Strachan papers are also in the Trinity College Archives (Toronto), USPG (C/CAN/Strachan), MTCL, and PAC (MG 24, J1). Among other important collections containing material by him or relating to him are PAO: Bethune (Alexander Neil) papers, Boulton (Henry John) papers, Macaulay (John) papers, Osler family papers, Ridout papers, Robinson (John Beverley) papers; Trinity College Archives: Young (A. H.) papers; MTCL: Robert Baldwin papers, William Dummer Powell papers, Henry Scadding papers, Alexander Wood papers; PAC: Bagot papers (MG 24, A13), Colborne papers (MG 24, A40), Elgin papers (MG 24, A16); and QUA: Richard Cartwright papers, William Morris papers. This list is far from exhaustive. Many of Strachan's letters and statements are in a large number of collections of government documents, stretching from the War of 1812 to confederation, and are to be found at the PRO (especially CO 42) and the PAC (especially RG 1, E3; RG 5, A1; and RG 7, G).

One letterbook has been printed: *The John Strachan letter book, 1812–1834*, ed. G. W. Spragge (Toronto, 1946), and another has been transcribed, "Letter book of John Strachan, 1827–1834," ed. R. C. Good (unpublished MA thesis, University of Toronto, 1940). A vast amount of material by and relating to Strachan was printed in *Documentary history of education in U.C.* (Hodgins). A convenient introduction to his writings is *John Strachan: documents and opinions; a selection*, ed. J. L. H. Henderson (Toronto and Montreal, 1969). G.M.C.]

Many of Strachan's printed works are listed in *Bibliography of Canadiana* (Staton and Tremaine) and its *First supplement* (Boyle and Colbeck). Other important works by Strachan are: [ ], *An address to the members of the Church of England, from the bishop of Toronto, in behalf of the Upper Canada Church University* (London, 1850); *Canada church establishment: copy of a letter addressed to R. J. Wilmot Horton . . . respecting the state of the church in that province* ([London], 1827; also published as an appendix in U.C., House of Assembly, *Journal*, 1828); [ ], *Church university of Upper Canada: pastoral letter from the lord bishop of Toronto to the clergy and laity of the diocese of Toronto* (Toronto, 1850); [ ], *Circular letter from the bishop of Toronto, addressed to the clergy and laity of the bishopric and see of Toronto, 15th January, 1840, on the subject of the clergy reserves* ([Toronto, 1840]); *A discourse on the character of King George the Third, addressed to the inhabitants of British America* (Montreal, 1810); [ ], *Journal of the visitation of the diocese of Toronto (Upper Canada) in the summer of*

1840 . . . (London, 1841); [ ], *Pastoral letter to the clergy and laity of the diocese of Toronto, on the subject of the university . . .* (Toronto, 1850); *A pastoral letter to the laity of the diocese of Toronto* ([Toronto, 1861]); [ ], *The petition of John, by divine permission bishop of Toronto, to the honourable the Legislative Assembly of Canada, April 13th, 1849* (Toronto, 1849); [ ], *The report of the bishop of Toronto, to the Most Hon. the Duke of Newcastle, her majesty's secretary of state for the colonies, on the subject of the colonial church* (Toronto, 1853); *A sermon, on the death of the Rev. John Stuart, D.D., preached at Kingston, 25th August, 1811* (Kingston, [Ont.], 1811); *A sermon, preached at York before the Legislative Council and House of Assembly, August 2nd, 1812* (York [Toronto], [1812]).

For other writings by Strachan see also: *The Cornwall tribute: a piece of plate, presented to the Honourable and Venerable John Strachan, D.D., archdeacon of York, by forty-two of his former pupils, educated by him at Cornwall, presented second July, MDCCCXXXIII* (York [Toronto], 1833). "The correspondence of Bishop Strachan and John Henry Newman," ed. J. S. Moir, *Canadian Journal of Theology; a Quarterly of Christian Thought* (Toronto), III (1957), 219–25. [John Strachan], "John Strachan's journey from Montreal to Kingston in December 1799," ed. T. A. Reed, *OH*, XLII (1950), 213–17. U.C., House of Assembly, *Journal*, 1829, app., "Report from the president of the General Board of Education."

Church and state in Canada, 1627–1867: basic documents, ed. J. S. Moir (Toronto, 1967). [J. H. Harris], *A letter to the Hon. & Ven. Archdeacon Strachan . . . respecting the principles and effects of the Bible Society* (York [Toronto], 1833). Ernest Hawkins, *Annals of the diocese of Toronto* (London, 1848). Charles Lindsey, *The clergy reserves: their history and present position, showing the systematic attempts that have been made to establish in connection with the state, a dominant church in Canada . . .* (Toronto, 1851). William Morris, *Reply . . . to six letters, addressed to him by John Strachan, D.D., archdeacon of York* (Toronto, 1838). [A.] E. Ryerson, *Letters from the Reverend Egerton Ryerson to the Hon. and Reverend Doctor Strachan, published originally, in the "Upper Canada Herald"* (Kingston, [Ont.], 1828). Scadding, *Toronto of old* (1873). *Town of York, 1793–1815* (Firth). *Town of York, 1815–34* (Firth).

A. N. Bethune, *Memoir of the Right Reverend John Strachan, D.D., LL.D., first bishop of Toronto* (Toronto and London, 1870). Sylvia Boorman, *John Toronto: a biography of Bishop Strachan* (Toronto and Vancouver, 1969). W. P. Bull, *From Strachan to Owen: how the Church of England was planted and tended in British North America* (Toronto, 1937). David Flint, *John Strachan, pastor and politician* (Toronto, 1971). J. L. H. Henderson, "John Strachan as bishop, 1839–1867" (unpublished DD thesis, General Synod of Canada, Anglican Church of Canada, 1955); *John Strachan, 1778–1867* ([Toronto], 1969). J. D. Purdy, "John Strachan and education in Canada, 1800–1851" (unpublished PHD thesis, University of Toronto, 1962). T. B. Robertson, *The fighting bishop: John Strachan,*

Street

the first bishop of Toronto, and other essays in his times (Ottawa, 1926). Henry Scadding, *The first bishop of Toronto: a review and a study* (Toronto, 1868). [J.] F. Taylor, *The last three bishops, appointed by the crown for the Anglican Church of Canada* (Montreal, 1869; London and New York, 1870).

C. F. Headon, "The influence of the Oxford movement upon the Church of England in eastern and central Canada, 1840–1900" (unpublished PHD thesis, McGill University, Montreal, 1974). Moir, *Church and state in Canada West.* T. A. Reed, *A history of the University of Trinity College, Toronto, 1852–1952* ([Toronto], 1952). Sissons, *Ryerson.* W. S. Wallace, *A history of the University of Toronto, 1827–1927* (Toronto, 1927). Wilson, *Clergy reserves of U.C.* G. M. Craig, "Two contrasting Upper Canadian figures: John Rolph and John Strachan," RSC *Trans.*, 4th ser., XII (1974), sect.II, 237–48.

J. L. H. Henderson, "The abominable incubus: the church as by law established," Canadian Church Hist. Soc., *Journal*, XI (1969), 58–66. W. C. MacVean, "The 'Erastianism' of John Strachan," *Canadian Journal of Theology; a Quarterly of Christian Thought* (Toronto), XIII (1967), 189–204. O. R. Osmond, "The churchmanship of John Strachan," Canadian Church Hist. Soc., *Journal*, XVI (1974), 46–59. J. D. Purdy, "John Strachan and the Diocesan Theological Institute at Cobourg, 1842–1852," *OH*, LXV (1973), 113–23; "John Strachan's educational policies, 1815–1841," *OH*, LXIV (1972), 45–64. Alison Smith, "John Strachan and early Upper Canada, 1799–1814," *OH*, LII (1960), 159–73. G. W. Spragge, "The Cornwall Grammar School under John Strachan, 1803–1812," *OH*, XXXIV (1942), 63–84; "Dr. Strachan's motives for becoming a legislative councillor," *CHR*, XIX (1938), 397–402; "Elementary education in Upper Canada, 1820–1840," *OH*, XLIII (1951), 107–22; "John Strachan's contribution to education, 1800–1823," *CHR*, XXII (1941), 147–58. J. J. Talman, "The position of the Church of England in Upper Canada, 1791–1840," *CHR*, XV (1934), 361–75. A. H. Young, "John Strachan, 1778–1867," *Queen's Quarterly* (Kingston, Ont.), XXXV (1927–28), 386–407; "The mission of Cornwall, 1784–1812," *OH*, XXV (1929), 481–97.

STREET, JOHN AMBROSE, lawyer, politician, and office-holder; b. 22 Sept. 1795 at Burton, Sunbury County, N.B., of loyalist ancestry, son of Samuel Denny Street* and Abigail Freeman, and brother of George Frederick Street*; m. April 1823 Jane Isabella Hubbard, and they had 11 children; d. 5 May 1865 at Saint John, N.B.

John Ambrose Street was educated at Burton and Fredericton, N.B. He studied law in his father's office, and was admitted to the bar as an attorney on 22 Feb. 1817 and as a barrister on 4 Oct. 1819. In 1823 Street moved to Newcastle (where he resided until 1845) and that year was appointed registrar of wills and deeds for Northumberland County. For several years he served on Northumberland's Board of Health. He be-

came one of the county's leading lawyers and for a number of years represented the interests of Joseph CUNARD.

Street had been raised in an atmosphere of political activity: his father had been an MHA for York County and a member of the Council from 1819 to 1830. His father-in-law, William Hubbard, had sat as MHA for Sunbury County from 1785 to 1792. In 1833, when Cunard resigned as MHA for Northumberland County, Street was elected to succeed him, and re-elected in 1834 and 1837. In the latter year he was appointed QC, and in 1840 was appointed clerk of the crown in the Supreme Court. The following year he was a member of a commission with Judge Robert PARKER and Edward Barron Chandler* to revise the ordinance of fees and to consider the propriety of introducing new rules of pleading in the Supreme Court.

Street was an aggressive and skilled debater. Sometime before 1842 he quarrelled with Cunard, who subsequently backed Street's opponent, John Thomas Williston, in the "fighting elections" of 1842–43. Their only issue was whether or not the second MHA from Northumberland County should be elected from the north or the south side of the Miramichi River. In the first election, in December 1842, Alexander Rankin*, Cunard's business rival, who represented the north side, easily won a seat. In the contest for the second seat Street was supported by Rankin and most of the inhabitants of Newcastle and Douglastown, but was defeated by Williston, who was popular in Chatham. Street and his supporters protested in petitions sent to the assembly pointing out irregularities in the election; the assembly unseated Williston and called for new elections in January 1843. Street and Williston then launched inflammatory speaking campaigns. During the elections there were fights in Newcastle and Chatham involving 500 to 1,000 men, with rival groups attempting to keep their opponents from the polls. Street had urged the lieutenant governor, Sir William COLEBROOKE, to dispatch troops to keep order, and declared his own life to be in danger. Troops were not sent until one man had died as a result of these riots and it was reported that people unconnected with either faction were unable to travel between Newcastle and Chatham in safety. In letters to the *Gleaner and Northumberland Schediasma* and to Colebrooke, Street blamed the riots on the latter's failure to act sooner; Colebrooke accused Street of making provocative speeches designed to create disturbances. An inquiry into the riots and the conduct of the local magistrates during the election, carried out by John Allen, John M. Robinson, and William Wright*, was completed in August 1843 and Street was declared elected. Two years later he left Newcastle to reside in Fredericton. However, owing to Rankin's influence, he continued to represent Northumberland County in the assembly, and was re-elected in 1846 and 1850.

For many years a conservative in politics, Street opposed responsible government until it was achieved. He was one of those who in 1845 attacked the administration of King's College, claiming that instead of providing a liberal education the college taught only "the dead languages." He voted to amend its charter so as to reduce the influence of the Church of England in the administration of the college [see Edwin Jacob]. In the same year Street unsuccessfully introduced a bill calling for the registration of voters at elections. He also opposed the appointment of Alfred Reade, Governor Colebrooke's son-in-law, to the office of provincial secretary. Street declared that "the sooner Her Most Gracious Majesty was pleased to recall His Excellency from the Government of the Province, the better for the interests of the Country." In 1846 he led the attack on Colebrooke's use of £3,000 of public funds for surveying the crown lands in Madawaska without the assembly's authorization.

Between 1848 and 1850 Street bitterly criticized the government for its failure to act on Professor James F. W. Johnston*'s report on the agricultural capabilities of the province, John Wilkinson*'s report on the railway from Saint John to Shediac, and Moses Henry Perley's report on the fisheries; he also criticized its failure to develop the coal fields of the province and to introduce a new school act. It was, therefore, a great surprise when in 1851 Street joined the Executive Council to replace Lemuel Allan Wilmot* as attorney general. Lieutenant Governor Sir Edmund Walker Head had chosen Street to head the government on the advice of John R. Partelow and E. B. Chandler. A skilled debater and new leadership were needed. Street now headed a government composed of many of the men he had recently been attacking.

Street introduced considerable new legislation: a bill for an elected Legislative Council was adopted by the assembly, but rejected by the Legislative Council in 1851; a Municipal Corporation Act was passed in 1852 after many amendments; and bills for the construction of the Saint John–Shediac Railway and the St Andrews and Quebec Railway were passed in 1852. In that year also a school act was passed, and a law reform commission set up, which prepared a three-volume compendium of all unrepealed pro-

vincial acts (published in 1854) [see William Boyd Kinnear]. In 1852 Street introduced resolutions in favour of the construction of the Intercolonial Railway by the three Maritime provinces. These were passed in the assembly, but were opposed in Northumberland County and many voters called upon Street to resign. He chose to ignore the protests and his conduct was vindicated by his re-election in 1854.

Since 1851 Street had led the government in defending the method of appointing the chief justice and opposing attempts to reduce judges' fees and the salaries of office-holders, whom Street believed should be properly compensated for their services. As the spokesman for those resisting changes, he earned the ire of the liberals who were calling for reform. In October 1854 the government was forced to resign following defeat in the assembly – the first time in New Brunswick's history that such a resignation had occurred [see Charles Fisher*]. Responsible government had come to New Brunswick.

Street continued to sit as a member until his defeat at the polls in 1856. He was nominated again in 1857 but retired before election day. In 1861 and 1865 he unsuccessfully ran for a seat in York County. Before his death in 1865 he had become a supporter of confederation.

W. A. Spray

N.B. Museum, Street family papers. PANB, J. C. and H. B. Graves, "New Brunswick political biography," XI, p.80; REX/le/l–g, Manners-Sutton, letterbooks, 1854–58; REX/mi/ex, duplicate minutes, 4, p.29; 5, pp.56, 99–100; REX/pa/Register of appointments and commissions, 1785–1840, p.59; 1840–57, p.3; REX/px, 20, pp.1922–25; 115, p.201; 123, pp.48–59; RLE/S56/Pe/15, 55–60, 115, 140, 222; RLE/S56/re/6 (Report of the committee investigating the north county elections, 24 March 1843); RPS, letterbook, 1842–45, p.359; 1847–50, p.290. Fenety, *Political notes and observations*, 96, 98–99, 107–8, 123, 128, 135–36, 141–44, 167, 177–78, 186–89, 214, 247, 256–57, 277, 309, 333, 347–48, 364–476. N.B., House of Assembly, *Journals*, 1851–54; 1868, 58. *Gleaner* (Chatham, N.B.), 6 May 1865. *Head Quarters*, 10 May 1865. Hannay, *History of N.B.*, II, 12, 144–45. MacNutt, *New Brunswick*, 343–44, 354–56, 369.

STRICKLAND, SAMUEL, landowner, Canada Company official, and author; b. 6 Nov. 1804 at Stow House, Bungay, Suffolk, England, one of two sons and six daughters of Thomas Strickland and Elizabeth Homer; d. 3 Jan. 1867 at Lakefield, Canada West.

Thomas Strickland and his wife were both progressive and practical in their educational theories – their children, including Samuel,

Strickland

Susanna*, and Catharine*, were educated at home and every detail of their learning was supervised by their parents. Reminiscing about their early years, Catharine remembered their regimen as strict, but also broadly based, with an emphasis on the learning of skills which served them well when they later immigrated to Canada.

In 1818 Thomas Strickland suffered a financial disaster and died shortly after. Colonel Black, a friend of the family who had immigrated to Upper Canada, offered to sponsor and instruct Samuel in pioneer life. Strickland eagerly accepted the offer, sailed for Canada in 1825, and joined the Black family at Darlington (Durham County). After a few months of pioneer apprenticeship Strickland married his sponsor's daughter, Emma.

With a wife and prospects of a family, Strickland sought land of his own. In May 1826 he bought 200 acres of land in Douro Township near Peterborough, where Thomas Alexander Stewart and Robert Reid had established their families. Before the end of the summer, Emma Strickland had died in childbirth, leaving a son who also died at the age of three. Samuel stayed with the Reid family while clearing and cropping his own land, and in 1827 married Robert Reid's daughter, Mary.

In 1828 John Galt* employed Strickland as a Canada Company "engineer" and involved him in the development of Guelph, where he managed the company's stores, kept the labour rolls, and superintended the building of roads and bridges. Strickland, William Dunlop*, and Charles Prior supported Galt's policies in the Huron Tract, but after Galt was dismissed in 1829 Strickland did not find favour with the new administrator, Thomas Mercer JONES. Strickland actively built up Goderich, the chief town in the Huron Tract, and enthusiastically promoted the opening up of the entire district. But there was obviously no future possible for him as a Canada Company official, and in 1832 he moved back to the Douro district. With his small accumulation of capital he bought land eight miles farther north into the bush than his first farm. His sisters Catharine Parr Traill and Susanna Moodie had also emigrated from England and settled in the same area in the early 1830s.

For the next two decades Strickland engaged in all the activities of a hard-working farmer, an enthusiastic sportsman, and a leading citizen of the growing community of Lakefield. He was a justice of the peace, president of the Court of Requests, and a captain in the 4th Northumberland militia. He supported the construction of Lakefield's first mill, its bridge over the Otonabee

River, and its first passable road. He also established an agricultural school where, for a fee, young men were trained in the skills necessary to land-holding and farming in Upper Canada.

In 1852 Mary Strickland died giving birth to her 13th child, and Samuel, with one of his daughters, visited his sisters in England. There Agnes, now famous as a writer of historical novels and biographies, persuaded her brother to write down the story of his life and times in Canada. *Twenty-seven years in Canada West* (1853) is distinguished by the candour and practicality of its tone – as Strickland remarks in his preface, he had experienced "all the gradations of colonial experience" that a gentleman-farmer such as himself would be likely to find in Canada. Through optimistic argument Strickland attempts to persuade settlers of all degrees to settle in Canada, and to demonstrate to them that vigour and energy, willingness to adapt and, above all, to work hard, will bring them success. He writes in an eminently plain style, blending chronological factual data and anecdote, without emotional overtones, and with no romanticizing of his experiences. The book is a man's companion piece to his sister Catharine's *The backwoods of Canada . . .* (London, 1836) and *The Canadian settler's guide* (Toronto, 1855).

While in England Strickland became engaged to Katherine Rackham, whom he married in 1855. They returned to Canada, where his energy and optimism, the benevolent paternalism of his squirarchical attitudes, and his mild eccentricity made him a legend in the Lakefield district. In his middle and later years he was an impressive man, tall, portly, and white-haired, and he had a presence that commanded respect. The traveller Charles Weld draws an engaging picture of Strickland among his many children and the red-shirted young apprentice-farmers at his school. If, as some sceptics implied, the school was a bit of a "sell" and the boys learned more about hunting, fishing, and carrying their liquor like gentlemen than they learned about farming, they must certainly have also imbibed the generous spirit and abounding enthusiasm of their teacher.

Samuel Strickland's book, a document of almost three decades of pioneer experience, is witness to a life lived and recalled with a constant, positive energy, as a tough, challenging, but ultimately satisfying adventure.

CLARA MCCANDLESS THOMAS

Samuel Strickland, *Twenty-seven years in Canada West* (London, 1853; repr. Edmonton, 1970). Ipswich and East Suffolk Record Office (Ipswich, Eng.), Bungay St Mary baptismal register. *DNB*. A. Y. Morris,

Gentle pioneers; five nineteenth-century Canadians (Toronto and London, 1968). U. C. Pope-Hennessy, *Agnes Strickland, biographer of the queens of England, 1796–1874* (London, 1940). C. P. [Strickland] Traill, *Pearls and pebbles . . .* (Victoria, 1894). J. M. Strickland, *Life of Agnes Strickland* (Edinburgh, 1887).

STUART, CHARLES, soldier, magistrate, and pamphleteer; b. 1783 in Jamaica, of Scottish parents; d. 26 May 1865 at Lora Bay, Collingwood Township, Canada West.

Charles Stuart was educated in Belfast, Ireland, and at age 18 received a commission in the military service of the East India Company. He rose to the rank of captain of the 1st battalion of the 27th Regiment, but resigned in 1815, likely because of his superior officers' uneasiness about his uncompromising position on numerous social and military matters. Stuart's parents were Presbyterians of an extreme Calvinistic type and they deeply influenced his character.

In 1817, seeking a new life, Stuart immigrated to Upper Canada, and settled in Amherstburg. He corresponded regularly with Lieutenant Governor Sir Peregrine Maitland*, offering advice on how to govern the province better and expressing a desire to be ordained in the Church of England. By the fall of 1819, however, he was in England where he published *The emigrant's guide to Upper Canada*, a strange mixture of geography, politics, and moral sermonizing, which Edward Allen Talbot* said should be more aptly titled "The Pilgrim's Guide to the Celestial Regions." Talbot felt the book provided some useful information about Upper Canada, but that it also contained "a confused medley of polemical theology, whining cant and complimentary bombast. . . ." Returning to Amherstburg in 1820 Stuart renewed his efforts to uplift the moral life of the colony through his new position as magistrate. His religious eccentricities and a propensity to meddle in the personal affairs of others led him into a heated clash with the officers of the Fort Malden garrison concerning the extent of his jurisdiction over soldiers charged with civil offences. Calm was restored only when he resigned as magistrate in 1821.

Stuart eventually found an outlet for his religious and humanitarian zeal among the black refugees who were beginning to enter the area from the United States. He set up a small black colony near Amherstburg and helped the refugees establish themselves as farmers; he was described by the British physician John Jeremiah Bigsby* as "a working Christian . . . waging successful war with the Negro slavery of the United States." In 1822 he moved on to a new challenge as principal of Utica Academy in New York State. Here he began his life-long friendship with 15-year-old Theodore Dwight Weld who was to become one of the leading figures in the anti-slavery cause. During the late 1820s the two men were converted by revivalist Charles Grandison Finney; they joined his "Holy Band" and toured the country preaching and exhorting. In 1829 Stuart returned to England and enlisted as an agent and pamphleteer for the growing Anti-Slavery Society of the United Kingdom; he lectured incessantly and wrote some of the finest anti-slavery pamphlets of the time. English abolitionists described him as "a persevering, uncompromising friend of the cause." In his pamphlets Stuart attacked the American Colonization Society which was encouraging the settlement of black fugitives on the West African coast, and he presented as an alternative the Wilberforce colony near London, Upper Canada. If blacks were leaving the United States, he urged them to enjoy the hospitable setting in Canada.

Stuart's writings influenced the growth in the 1820s and early 1830s of the anti-slavery movement in the United States, and in 1834 he moved there to work again with Weld. During lecture tours in Vermont, New York, and Ohio, he was frequently the object of mob violence. A return to England in 1837 lengthened into 13 years of residence broken only by visits to the West Indies to view the results of emancipation achieved by anti-slavery forces in 1833. Stuart remained active in anti-slavery circles and in 1846–47 worked also on famine relief for Ireland. In 1840 he had been made an honorary life member of the British and Foreign Anti-Slavery Society; he also received a promotion from the rank of retired captain to retired major and an increase in his $800 annual pension.

Back in Canada in 1850, he assisted in the formation of the Anti-Slavery Society of Canada at Toronto in February 1851, serving as its first corresponding secretary and assisting the society through his connections with abolitionists such as John SCOBLE in England and Lewis Tappan in the United States. However, he served for only one year before moving into semi-retirement with his new bride, a distant relative, at Lora Bay in Collingwood Township. Over the next ten years he attended a few abolitionist conventions in the United States and in 1855 and 1858 he met with John Brown, who led the abolitionist attack on Harper's Ferry, Virginia, in 1859. However, more and more he concentrated on church work and the temperance cause in his own community near Thornbury, Canada West. By the end of the 1850s his work as an international abolitionist was over, although he continued to correspond with those active in the movement.

The first half of the 19th century saw a surge of interest in humanitarian projects throughout the English speaking world and although one could hardly expect the struggling pioneer settlers in Upper Canada to display a lively interest in such ventures, humanitarian impulses were not lacking. The outlet for these impulses was quite often to be found in societies to aid escaped slaves and other black immigrants. These Canadian societies were nurtured by the writings and speeches of abolitionists in the United States and England and in fact they were part of an international philanthropic movement, of which Charles Stuart was a tireless crusader.

DONALD G. SIMPSON

Charles Stuart was the author of *The emigrant's guide to Upper Canada; or, sketches of the present state of that province, collected from a residence therein during the years 1817, 1818, 1819, interspersed with reflections* (London, 1820); *Is slavery defensible from Scripture? To the Rev. Dr. Hincks, Killileagh* (Belfast, 1831); *Remarks on the colony of Liberia and the American Colonization Society, with some account of the settlement of coloured people at Wilberforce, Upper Canada* (London, 1832); and *The West India question . . .* (London, 1832; repr. New Haven, Conn., 1833).

William L. Clements Library, University of Michigan (Ann Arbor), Weld-Grimké papers. J. J. Bigsby, *The shoe and canoe, or, pictures of travel in the Canadas . . . with facts and opinions on emigration, state policy, and other points of public interest* (2v., London, 1850), I, 263–66. *Globe*, 9 June 1865. *Letters of Theodore Dwight Weld, Angelina Grimké Weld and Sarah Grimké, 1822–1844*, ed. G. H. Barnes and D. L. Dumond (2v., New York, 1934; repr. Gloucester, Mass., 1965), II, 589. D. G. Simpson, "Negroes in Ontario from early times to 1870" (2v., unpublished PHD thesis, University of Western Ontario, London, Ont., 1971). Fred Landon, "Captain Charles Stuart, abolitionist," *Western Ontario History Nuggets* (London, Ont.), 24 (1956), 1–19.

STUART, GEORGE OKILL, Church of England clergyman; b. 29 June 1776 at Fort Hunter (near Amsterdam, N.Y.), eldest of the eight children of the Reverend John Stuart* and Jane Okill; d. 5 Oct. 1862 at Kingston, Canada West.

George Okill Stuart's family came to Canada as loyalists in 1781 and settled in Montreal. His education probably began in his father's school. John Stuart moved to Kingston as a missionary in 1785 and established another school, where George's education continued for a few years. George entered Union College in Schenectady, N.Y., in 1789 or 1790, then attended King's College at Windsor, N.S. Bishop Charles Inglis*, founder of the college in 1789, regarded Stuart as a diligent student. For financial reasons Stuart's stay at King's College was brief, and he left in 1794 to become an usher in a Quebec City grammar school. In 1795 he returned to Kingston where he opened a school in August of that year. His desire for further education had been sharpened and in 1798 he went to Harvard College, which granted him an AB in 1801.

Stuart actually left Harvard in 1800 to be ordained deacon by the bishop of Quebec, Jacob Mountain*, on 7 June, and he was ordained priest on 22 Aug. 1801. His first appointment was to York (Toronto) in 1801 as a missionary of the Society for the Propagation of the Gospel. He also represented his father as chaplain to the Legislative Council before being appointed to that office in his own right. In 1807 he began holding services in a new frame church at York which was finally completed in 1809. Already acquainted with the problem of establishing schools with little government assistance, Stuart had opened a school at York; when it became the Home District Grammar School in 1807 he was its first master and received a small salary from the government. Stuart was an exponent of Joseph Lancaster's school system, in which monitors – older scholars – were employed in the instruction of younger pupils. In this system the number of pupils was limited only by the ability and desire of the applicants, and the method of instruction resulted in inexpensive schooling.

In 1812 Stuart left York, to succeed his father as incumbent at Kingston. He was himself succeeded as incumbent at York and master of the grammar school by John STRACHAN, who had hoped at first to take over at Kingston instead. When Stuart was appointed to Kingston he also became bishop's official in Upper Canada, and thus could act on the bishop's behalf and, when requested, as his legal representative. In 1821 he became archdeacon of York; when the archdeaconry was divided in 1827 he was named archdeacon of Kingston and Strachan was made archdeacon of York. Stuart continued as archdeacon of Kingston after the diocese of Toronto was created in 1839. King's College, Windsor, conferred on him an honorary DCL in 1827.

Stuart's archdeaconry extended from Newcastle in the west to the eastern borders of the province, and his incumbency at Kingston included for some time the chaplaincy to the Mohawk Indians at Tyendinaga. He also assisted in setting up parishes in eastern Upper Canada, such as Brockville, Augusta, and Prescott, as well as in his home centre. At Kingston he oversaw the building of the second St George's

Church which was consecrated by Bishop Charles James Stewart* in 1828. Stuart encouraged and helped train a number of candidates for holy orders. He looked mainly for men born in Canada at a time when many more clergymen were sorely needed for new parishes. He remained a missionary of the SPG until 1857 and was active in the Church Society of the diocese of Toronto and in synod affairs. He was also one of the original members of the council of Trinity College in 1851.

In his private life Stuart was a quiet man, but could be roused to determined action. To John Strachan, his bishop after 1839, he was a person who had to be "treated with honor and delicacy." In 1845 Strachan was urging him to leave more of his parochial duties to his assistant, William Macaulay Herchmer, and to consider "the propriety of doing as the Archdeacons do in [England] and visit from time to time one or more of the Districts which constitute your Archdeaconry." When the diocese of Ontario was created in 1862 Stuart was appointed its first dean by Bishop John Travers Lewis*. Stuart died in October of the same year at age 86.

In 1803 he had married Lucy Brooks, only daughter of John Brooks of Bedford, Mass., later governor of Massachusetts, and they had two boys and two girls. Only the eldest son, also George Okill Stuart*, lived to maturity; he became mayor of Quebec City and judge in the Vice-Admiralty Court there. Lucy died in 1813 and Stuart remarried in 1816 Ann Ellice Robison (or Robinson) of Portland, Maine, who died in 1856. There were no children by this marriage.

A. J. ANDERSON

Anglican Church of Can., Diocese of Ontario, Synod Archives (Kingston, Ont.), George Okill Stuart letters, 1789–1862. MTCL, G. O. Stuart, Account-book recording names of pupils and fees received at the Home District Grammar School at York, 1807–11. PAO, Strachan (John), papers. "Rev. G. O'Kill Stuart's register at St. John's," OH, I (1899), 18. Town of York, 1793–1815 (Firth). A. J. Anderson, The Anglican churches of Kingston (Kingston, Ont., 1963). A. N. Bethune, Memoir of the Right Reverend John Strachan, D.D., LL.D., first bishop of Toronto (Toronto and London, 1870). J. K. McMorine, "Early history of the Anglican Church in Kingston," OH, VIII (1907), 90–102. A. H. Young, "The Rev'd George Okill Stuart, M.A., LL.D. (second rector of York and Kingston)," OH, XXIV (1927), 512–34.

SUTTON, CATHERINE. *See* NAHNEBAHWE-QUAY

SUZANNE. *See* CONNOLLY

SUZOR, LOUIS-TIMOTHÉE, soldier and author; b. 24 Aug. 1834 at Cap-Santé, Lower Canada, son of Hippolyte Suzor, merchant, and Anne-Marie-Angélique Defoy; m. 1 June 1858, at Quebec, Sophie Évanturel, sister of François Évanturel*, lawyer and politician; d. 18 Aug. 1866 at Quebec.

Louis-Timothée Suzor's grandfather, François-Timothée, a surgeon in the army of the Marquis de La Fayette, came to the United States at the time of the American revolution. We do not know, however, when the Suzor family settled in Canada. Louis-Timothée studied for three years at the Séminaire de Québec (1844–47), then worked for various merchants, all of whom acknowledged his aptitude for business and figures. In 1852, overcome by the thirst for gold, he set out for Australia; he returned three years later with a fortune.

From 1855 to 1860 Suzor worked for a Quebec City business firm, while serving after 1856 as a private in the recently organized volunteer militia. He soon showed a special interest in a military career; he trained and attended courses at the army riding school on Rue Saint-Louis. As there was no manual of military training in French, Suzor, who was fully bilingual, undertook in 1857 to translate an English one.

On 3 May 1860 Suzor was promoted captain, on the recommendation of Melchior-Alphonse de SALABERRY, the deputy adjutant-general of Canada East, whose protégé he was. Suzor received command of a company of volunteer militiamen which was to form the nucleus of the later Voltigeurs de Québec. No political appointment was ever to prove as important for the militia in general and French Canadian soldiers in particular. Suzor devoted all his energies to military matters, giving freely of his time and money to the Canadian militia. Thanks to his dynamism, his competence, and the excitement produced by the American Civil War, which induced heads of firms to sacrifice one hour of work so that their employees could take military training, the number of Francophone corps in Quebec City grew from two to 16. Since the militia instructors were British regular soldiers who did not speak French, Suzor trained, in addition to his company of volunteers, the students of Université Laval, the École Normale Laval, the Séminaire de Québec, and the cadets of the military school at the Citadel. He paid for the clothing, equipment, and maintenance of the less privileged French Canadian volunteers from Lower Town; the government provided for the needs of the upper class which were Anglophone. Suzor also helped finance the Monument aux Braves de

1760, erected by the Société Saint-Jean-Baptiste of Quebec and unveiled on 19 Oct. 1863.

Suzor progressed rapidly in his career as a consequence, although at each promotion influential people also intervened on his behalf. On 28 March 1862 he was appointed adjutant of the 9th battalion of the newly formed Voltigeurs de Québec, which was commanded by Charles-René-Léonidas d'Irumberry* de Salaberry. On 21 November of that year he became brigade major of the 7th Military District (eastern part of Canada East). He was promoted lieutenant-colonel on 7 Oct. 1864, and was attached to the military school at Quebec City as an instructor; in 1865 he became commandant of the school, as a result of public pressure against the discrimination to which Francophone soldiers were subject. Finally, on 15 Nov. 1865, Suzor became assistant to the deputy adjutant-general, Salaberry. In describing Suzor as "fully endowed with intelligence, zeal, and capability," Sir Étienne-Paschal TACHÉ could have found no better words.

While training volunteer companies from 1862 to 1865, Suzor published no less than nine military works. Except for the *Traité d'art et d'histoire militaires*, these volumes, published at Suzor's own expense, are principally translations and adaptations of military manuals then in use. Nevertheless they represent a considerable body of work, amounting to about 3,000 pages of text. Published for instructional purposes and to assist Francophone volunteers, some of the volumes remained in use in Quebec for generations, for want of more modern manuals in French. As for the *Traité*, the only book Suzor really wrote, he expresses nothing personal or original in it. It is, rather, a synthesis of the different theories of the celebrated military writers in his day. Certain of these authors are now totally forgotten, but others such as Vegetius, Machiavelli, Étienne Bardin, François-Apollini Guibert, Karl von Clausewitz, Antoine-Henri Jomini, and Auguste-Frédéric-Louis Viesse de Marmont still must be read to trace the art of war through the centuries. Like Suzor's other volumes, the *Traité* was written for instructional purposes. After a discussion of army organization, the author turned to tactics, then strategy. The book remains important as one of the rare military treatises produced in Canada in the 19th century.

Stricken with cancer, Louis-Timothée Suzor learned at age 31 that his death was near. He was in the process of translating the important work of Colonel Patrick Leonard MacDougall*, *Modern warfare as influenced by modern artillery*, published in London in 1864, but he died with his task uncompleted. On his tomb was placed a superb marble monument, the work of Montreal sculptor Paul Ceredo.

Conscious that French Canadians were under-represented in the Canadian military system, Colonel Suzor worked unremittingly to interest his compatriots in the militia. He was above all a military educator, intensely enthusiastic about foreign teaching experiments and education in general. Moreover, his ten manuals illustrate his desire to instruct and his concern to form good citizens. According to his contemporaries, Louis-Timothée Suzor was a high-spirited, generous man, and above all a tireless worker.

JEAN-YVES GRAVEL

[Louis-Timothée Suzor is the author of *Traité d'art et d'histoire militaires suivi d'un traité de fortifications de campagne* (Québec, 1865); he also translated, compiled, or adapted the following works: *Aide-mémoire d'un caribinier volontaire, comprenant une compilation des termes de commandement usités dans l'armée anglaise, avec quelques notes explicatives – aussi: – Le manuel du sergent et la manière de se perfectionner dans l'art du tir, précédés d'un historique des armes* (Québec, 1862); *Boîte de théorie militaire avec tableaux* (Québec, 1864); *Code militaire* (Québec, 1864); *Exercices et évolutions d'infanterie tels que révisés par ordre de sa Majesté, 1862* (Québec, 1863); *Guide théorique et pratique des manœuvres de l'infanterie, précédé d'un historique de l'origine, de la composition et de l'administration, etc., etc., de l'armée anglaise telle qu'elle est constituée de nos jours, enrichi d'un grand nombre de planches et accompagné d'une boîte de théorie avec laquelle on peut exécuter toutes les évolutions d'une compagnie et d'un bataillon* (Québec, 1865); *Maximes, conseils et instructions sur l'art de la guerre* (Québec, 1865); *Tableau synoptique des évolutions d'un bataillon, accompagné de planches* (Québec, 1862); *Tableau synoptique des mouvements d'une compagnie* (Québec, 1863). J.-Y.G.]

ANQ-Q, État civil, Catholiques, Notre-Dame de Québec, 1er juin 1858, 18 août 1866. PAC, RG 9, I, C1, 132–66. Archives paroissiales, Sainte-Famille-du-Cap-Santé (Cap-Santé, Qué.), Registres des baptêmes, mariages et sépultures, 24 août 1834. *Le Canadien*, 27 mai 1867. *Le Courrier du Canada*, 20 août 1866. J.-Y. Gravel, "Les Voltigeurs de Québec dans la milice canadienne (1862–1898)" (thèse de D. ès L., université Laval, Québec, 1971). "Les disparus," *BRH*, XXXIII (1927), 372–73.

SYMES, GEORGE BURNS, merchant; b. 20 Jan. 1803 at Quebec, one of at least three sons of George Symes and Angélique-G. Cuvillier; d. 12 June 1863 at Montreal.

George Burns Symes' father, a native of Tenby, Wales, immigrated to Quebec City and by 1801 had established his own forwarding business, George Symes and Company, dealing in wheat, rum, furs, and timber, and in passenger traffic. George Symes built up contacts with Montreal financiers such as Augustin Cuvillier* and by the 1820s the Symes Wharf at the foot of Cap Diamant was one of Quebec City's busiest. Between 1818 and 1824 he served as master of Trinity House, which administered the Quebec harbour, regulated shipping, and arbitrated disputes between merchants. He was also a founding member in 1816 of the Quebec Exchange; it offered a reading room and the conviviality of a location in the basement of the Neptune Inn, but its primary purpose was to bring together merchants and ship captains: notices could be posted offering freight and charters and captains seeking a cargo made the Exchange their first stop.

Nothing is known of the early life of George Burns Symes. By the 1820s he was active in his father's business and represented the company on the Quebec City Committee of Trade. After his father's death in 1833 the firm was renamed G.B. Symes and Company; by the 1840s Symes had taken in a new partner, David Douglas Young, president of the Quebec Bank. After George Burns Symes' death the company continued as D.D. Young and Company and subsequently as A.F.A. Knight and Company until it went out of business around 1880. Symes' brother Robert was a Quebec retail merchant who specialized in furs, but also sold watch-guards, shoes, wheat, furniture, Welsh flannels, lambs-wool gloves, and "parisian negligées."

As a general merchant George Burns Symes traded in commodities as diverse as pig-iron and lobsters. An 1847 advertisement showed imports of sail twine, carpeting, glass, paint, tea, soap, and cod oil. He exported, primarily to England, such goods as flour, beef, pork, candles, oatmeal, moccasins, and timber. In the early years he advertised passage on sailing vessels making the return voyage to Liverpool or Hull, England. In 1854 Symes, along with such prominent Montrealers as Hugh Allan*, Sir George Simpson*, and William Dow, became a founding director of the Montreal Ocean Steamship Company. As Quebec City agent for the steamship line, Symes offered first-class passage to Liverpool for $80. Symes was a shipowner of some significance. He and Young were owners or part owners of at least 16 vessels in the period 1841–63, including the 889-ton *Clara Symes*. He also invested in the Quebec and Richmond Railway and was a director of the St Lawrence Navigation Company. Banks were a crucial part of the commercial process for timber merchants, since their businesses required extensive credit advances to the

timber-cutting companies. In 1844 Symes was a director of the Quebec branch of the Bank of Montreal and in 1861 a local director of the Bank of British North America.

G.B. Symes and Company, along with Peter Patterson*, Charles Aylwin, and Allan Gilmour*, took an early interest in the timber trade. The Symes' timber cove was located at Spencer Cove (Anse au Foulon) next to the Allan Gilmour property. During the spring season, rafts arrived at the coves from upcountry. Once in booms the square timber was classed, although most of Symes' timber was sold without culling. By May the coves were jammed with ships taking on their cargoes of oak and pine; in July 1851 three timber ships left the Symes' cove on the same day. If the rafts were delayed, ships had to wait, stevedores became restless, and contracts went unfilled. In June 1850 a Liverpool merchant took suit against Symes for a two-week delay in loading.

Like his father, Symes served as a warden of Trinity House and as a member of the managing committee of the Quebec Exchange (1860). He was a member of the Board of Trade and his business partner, Young, served as chairman of the Board of Arbitrators (1851). Symes was also an active participant in the social, cultural, and religious activities of Quebec's English speaking community. He was a founding director of the Stadacona Club (1861) and a member of the St George's Society (1848). Symes loved horses and was president of the Quebec Turf Club (1844) and vice-president of the Quebec Races (1847) which were held every August at Ancienne-Lorette. He was also a keen participant in the Quebec Tandem Club. During the winter members gathered once a week at Place d'Armes to ride through the city and out to Sainte-Foy, Charlesbourg, or Montmorency. One Quebec City resident dismissed these Sunday excursions by members of the city's élite as "a dull routine of driving up one street and down another, overturning pigs and frightening old ladies out of their propriety." Symes' brother Robert was also active in Quebec's social life. A member of the Quebec Horticultural Society and paymaster of the 6th battalion of the Quebec City militia, he was a lifelong supporter of the Literary and Historical Society of Quebec, a founding member of the Quebec Temperance Hall Association, and the first treasurer of the St George's Society, founded in 1835 to give financial assistance to English and Welsh immigrants and to help them "venerate the land of their forefathers."

Little is known of the family life of George Burns Symes. For many years he lived in a fashionable house on Mont-Carmel St in the upper town. He retired from business in 1862 and after a short illness died in Montreal of "inflammation." His body was brought to Quebec City by the Grand Trunk Railway. Obituaries referred to Symes as "the Merchant Prince" and speculated that his estate had a value of $500,000. His funeral service was held on 15 June 1863 in the Anglican cathedral and his pallbearers included Justice René-Édouard Caron*, Louis Panet*, James Bell FORSYTH, and William PRICE. His remains lie in Quebec City's Mount Hermon Cemetery.

BRIAN J. YOUNG

ANQ-Q, AP-G-278/1; Greffe de J. G. Clapham, 12 juin 1850. ASQ, Polygraphie, XXXV, 14. Can., Prov. of, *Statutes*, 1852–53, c.62; 1854–55, c.44. *Le Canadien*, 15 juin 1863. *Le Journal de Québec*, 13 juin 1863. *Morning Chronicle* (Quebec), 31 Dec. 1847; 5 March 1852; 30 June, 29 July 1856; 16 June 1863. *Quebec Gazette*, 20 Nov. 1833. J. E. Defebaugh, *History of the lumber industry of America* (2v., Chicago, 1906–7), I, 139. George Gale, *Historic tales of old Quebec* (Quebec, 1923), 165; *Quebec twixt old . . . and . . . new* (Quebec, 1915), 55. A. R. M. Lower, *Great Britain's woodyard; British America and the timber trade, 1763–1867* (Montreal and London, Ont., 1973), 220.

T

TACHÉ, Sir ÉTIENNE-PASCHAL, doctor, politician, and deputy adjutant-general of the militia; b. 5 Sept. 1795 at Saint-Thomas (Montmagny, Que.), son of Charles Taché and Geneviève Michon; d. 30 July 1865 in the town of his birth.

Étienne-Paschal Taché belonged to one of the wealthy families of New France who were completely ruined by the Seven Years' War and particularly the siege of Quebec, but who remained in the country and constituted the nucleus of the French Canadian bourgeoisie that developed in the early 19th century. His grandfather Jean Taché*, a Paris merchant, had settled at Quebec in 1730. He became one of the principal businessmen in the colony and the largest ship-owner in the port of Quebec; his marriage to Marie-Anne Jolliet de Mingan, the granddaughter of Louis Jolliet*, contributed substantially to his prosperity. After the Conquest, he found favour with General James Murray* and received a commission to practise as a notary anywhere in the province. Two of his ten children founded families in Canada and became co-seigneurs of Mingan. Étienne-Paschal was to belong to the elder branch, which was by far the most important, but also the poorer. Jean's younger son, Paschal-Jacques, improved his position through marrying the seigneuress of Kamouraska (and had only one son), whereas the elder, Charles, married Geneviève Michon, settled at Saint-Thomas (Montmagny), and raised a family of ten children with the inadequate income brought in by leasing the Chicoutimi trading post. We can understand why Philippe-Joseph Aubert* de Gaspé, knowing personally the different situations of the two families, considered Étienne-

Paschal a self made man, and why Pierre-Joseph-Olivier Chauveau* wrote in describing his character: "Sir Étienne had only received an incomplete education in his youth; he owed his advancement to his native talents, the studies he was capable enough to undertake by himself, his energy, and the fortunate combination of qualities that made up his active and courageous, but prudent and persevering personality."

Étienne-Paschal was precocious. When the War of 1812 broke out he was still an adolescent but he abandoned his studies at the Séminaire de Québec and joined the 5th battalion of the incorporated militia as an ensign. He became a lieutenant in the Chasseurs Canadiens and took part in several engagements, including Plattsburgh and Châteauguay. This military service marked the beginning of a career which had two distinct phases: from 1812 to 1841, Taché devoted himself particularly to medicine; and from 1841 to 1865, he was active in the political life of Canada.

During the War of 1812, in his off-duty moments in military camp, Taché began the medical studies he continued after the war under Pierre Fabre*, *dit* Laterrière, a Quebec doctor. The practice of medicine, surgery, and obstetrics in Lower Canada was at that time regulated by the rigorous legislation of 1788. It was subject to control by the governor and was not too effective; complete training in a school of medicine became possible only in 1823 with the founding of the Montreal Medical Institution. Taché therefore went to Philadelphia to finish his studies. He then obtained his licence from the medical board of Lower Canada on 18 March 1819. He took up residence in his native parish, where the following year he married Sophie Baucher, *dit* Morency, of Beaumont; they were to have 15 children. He practised medicine in Montmagny and the neighbouring parishes continuously for 22 years. In serving a vast territory on the south shore, he acquired the social prestige that had been passing from seigneurs to members of the professions since the introduction of the Canadian parliamentary system. He was by that very fact called upon to take an active part in the events of his day.

He was a member of the Quebec Medical Society when in 1831 it obtained the right to elect the members of the two boards of examiners of Quebec and Montreal; this event ended the English monopoly, through the Montreal Medical Institution, of admission to the practice of medicine in Lower Canada. Taché was a member of the Quebec board elected on 11 July 1831, which for the first time included a large majority of French Canadians.

At the time of the rebellion, Taché was not able to remain aloof from the subversive movement that, in the Montmagny region, echoed the revolutionary struggles in the districts of Montreal and Quebec. He became the heart of the nationalist movement in his region, and in 1836 attended the convention at Trois-Rivières where the Patriotes revealed their impatience; he organized a large meeting on 29 June 1837 at Montmagny, to which Louis-Joseph Papineau*, with Louis-Hippolyte LA FONTAINE, Jean-Joseph Girouard*, and Augustin-Norbert MORIN, came "to fire the zeal of his supporters"; Taché gave asylum to the fugitive Morin when he was being pursued after attempting in vain to regroup Papineau's revolutionary forces at Quebec against Elzéar Bédard*. Informed of Taché's activities, the English authorities were suspicious and in January 1839 issued a search warrant against him with orders for his arrest if the slightest piece of evidence could be found. Taché was absent when the search took place, and his house contained no firearms; this fruitless operation therefore did not lead to an arrest. Although he was not a supporter of armed rebellion, Taché did not reject such resistance as a "frightful catastrophe," as some did, and the rebels were in his eyes only "a few hundred men . . . driven to despair by administrations which were stigmatized and condemned even by leading men in England." Taché was therefore a Patriote, who at the time of the union became willing to compromise, as did Morin, La Fontaine, and George-Étienne Cartier*. He believed now in an alliance with the Upper Canadian Reformers and the possibility of deriving benefit from the union

of the Canadas. With that end in view he entered public life.

Taché officially began his active political career in the first elections held under the union. His candidacy seems to indicate a firm intention to make a career in parliament, since he then gave up the practice of medicine. On 8 April 1841 he was elected to the new Legislative Assembly as representative for the county of L'Islet, and his mandate was renewed in the autumn of 1844. During these first years of parliamentary life (1841–46), Taché shared the policies and the principles of the Reformers: under Sydenham [Thomson*], he repudiated the political structure of union and denounced the despotism of the governor and the repeated intrigues of the Tories; under Sir Charles Bagot*, he supported La Fontaine who, when called to power with Robert Baldwin*, undertook to see that the grievances common to the two Canadas or peculiar to Canada East were redressed; under Sir Charles Theophilus Metcalfe*, he remained a firm supporter of responsible government when the new governor took upon himself the right to exercise the royal prerogative without consulting the accountable ministers and brought about the resignation of the La Fontaine–Baldwin ministry, a return to absolute government, and then the formation of a ministry that lacked the confidence of the French Canadian Reform majority.

During this period of decisive constitutional and political struggles, Taché remained a politician in the second rank. Lacking the gift of eloquence, he spoke seldom in the assembly. In his occasional interventions he denounced above all the policy of the government which neglected the interests of Canada East, especially the Quebec and Gaspé regions, and favoured Canada West. Referring to one of his speeches, Sir Thomas Chapais* stated that Taché proved himself to be "forceful and well documented," thus establishing "the reputation of the representative for Montmagny."

But it was his speech on 24 April 1846, on a new militia bill, that created the greatest stir. At a time when relations were strained between England and the United States over the Oregon boundary issue, Taché – now a colonel – demanded that the Lower Canadian militia, virtually non-existent since the disturbance of 1837–38, be reorganized. Wishing to terminate a debate that turned into an attack on the loyalty of his compatriots rather than an examination of the bill, Taché described the French Canadians in strong terms: "Our Loyalty is not one of speculation, of pounds, shillings, and pence; we do not carry it on our lips, we do not make a traffic of it. But we are in

Taché

our habits, by our laws, and by our religion . . . monarchists and conservatives.'' To support his statement he recalled the part played by French Canadians in the wars of 1775 and 1812, then made the following prophecy, which was to remain attached to his name: ''. . . the last cannon which is shot on this continent in defence of Great Britain will be fired by the hand of a French Canadian.'' Taken out of context, the best known portions of his speech have aroused doubts about Taché's attachment to his own people; the speech is, however, an excellent expression of French Canadian nationalism of the time, which fought the dominance of the British in America without questioning the colonial tie. On 1 July 1846, shortly after this speech, Taché was appointed deputy adjutant-general of the militia for Canada East by the ministry of William Henry Draper* and Denis-Benjamin Papineau*, a government he nevertheless energetically opposed. He undertook to make the recently passed Militia Act acceptable to his compatriots, and he was made responsible for reorganizing the province's armed forces according to its provisions. Taché had therefore to give up his seat in parliament. It seems that in this way he spared himself defeat in the 1847 elections, for his programme in favour of municipal institutions, public elementary education, and consequently local taxation, had made him unpopular in his constituency. There is evidence in the small majority he had obtained in the preceding elections, and in a letter to La Fontaine in which he mentions his bitter struggle against the *éteignoirs* over education and rejoices that ''the well informed and honourable part of the county'' has prevailed over ''ignorance and bad faith.''

Taché's acceptance of an appointment from a Tory ministry aroused further doubts as to his nationalism. But his gesture was only one of numerous compromises to which Reformers had agreed after 1840, conciliation having shown itself to be the only effective policy against the repressive régime of the union. And on 11 March 1848, having retained the support of the Reform leaders, Taché was appointed a member of the Executive Council and commissioner of public works in the new La Fontaine–Baldwin ministry. On 23 May he was also made a legislative councillor. It was in the Executive Council that the second portion of his political life unfolded. Here he took part in the Reformers' last battle for ministerial responsibility. Tradition even has it that it was he who killed William Mason, one of those who attacked La Fontaine's house during the riot that followed the passage of the Rebellion Losses Bill. He had written his wife: ''I have fortified and stocked La Fontaine's house so as to sustain a siege; if the Tory loyalists present themselves, they will eat something indigestible,'' but the inquiry that followed the incident did not succeed in proving his responsibility.

Following the agitation that consumed Tory hopes at the same time as the parliament buildings, to quote the colourful but accurate remark of Bartholomew Conrad Augustus Gugy*, an era of profound political, economic, and social change began. It was then that Taché became a figure in the forefront of history. Up to 1857, he participated in all governments; he held in succession the offices of commissioner of public works until 26 Nov. 1849, receiver general from 27 Nov. 1849 to 23 May 1856, speaker of the Legislative Council from 19 April 1856 to 25 Nov. 1857, and commissioner of crown lands from 16 June to 25 Nov. 1857, while also being leader of the Lower Canadian section from 27 Jan. 1855 to 24 Nov. 1857. In association with La Fontaine, then with Morin, he led the struggle against the radical Rouge wing which, under Papineau's flag, flaunted ultra-democratic principles, inclined towards annexation to the United States, and was destroying the Reform party from within. In 1854, a significant year in the history of Canadian political parties, he was one of the chief architects of the coalition between Allan Napier MacNab and Morin. The purpose of this coalition was to set up a viable government to counter the radicalism of George Brown* who had split the Upper Canadian Reformers and brought defeat to the supporters of Francis Hincks*. Taché wrote a long letter on this 1854 crisis to Jean-Charles Chapais*, and although it is already well known to historians it contains so detailed an analysis that it cannot be ignored here. In it Taché considers all the possible political alliances and measures their chances of success. The Tories, if called to office, would not know how to stay there, even allied to the Quebec Conservative Joseph-Édouard Cauchon*. As for the Reformers, they could seek allies, but Cauchon would cause more supporters to defect than he would bring in reinforcements; Louis-Victor Sicotte*, without Cauchon, would add too little to the strength of the Reformers, and Antoine-Aimé Dorion* was ideologically incompatible. For Taché only one alliance remained possible, that of the Reformers with the Conservatives. Consequently he supported the MacNab–Morin ministry, which was shaping a new political party: guidance of that party was shortly to be entrusted to him.

For health reasons Morin relinquished the direction of the Lower Canadian section of the cabinet during an adjournment of the 1854–55 session. Taché was called upon to replace him, and the new MacNab–Taché ministry was formed on 27 Jan. 1855. In the course of the two sessions during which it was in office, the most important measures adopted concerned the Lower Canadian municipal system (18 Vict., c.100), the militia (18 Vict., c.77), the schools of Upper Canada (18 Vict., c.131), the election of the Legislative Council (19–20 Vict., c.140), and the setting up of a Council of Public Instruction for Lower Canada (19 Vict., c.14).

From a constitutional point of view, the double majority was a critical issue for the MacNab–Taché ministry. Deserted in the assembly by the Upper Canadian majority on a vote of non-confidence over the seat of the capital, Mac-Nab declared his willingness to continue with the support of a majority of all the members. His colleagues, however, refused to continue to hold power without the support of a majority in each section of the country. Faced with constitutional deadlock, MacNab was obliged to resign in May 1856, and, already in bad health, he temporarily retired from politics. To reconstruct the ministry, the governor, Sir Edmund Walker HEAD, called on Taché. In doing so he followed the advice of all the ministers except MacNab, and made due allowance for seniority, a criterion of political advancement at that period.

The new prime minister chose as his associate John Alexander Macdonald*, who had been aspiring for some time to the leadership of the Upper Canadian section, and who had had some part in MacNab's fall. Then he formed a ministry whose members, for the first time since 1854, agreed to enter the government as a single and new party, and not as a coalition ministry. It was therefore this Taché–Macdonald ministry that scaled the alliance of the Conservatives and Reformers, and that was the first to have the advantage of governing as a unified party. But the double majority question was not settled; it was a sword of Damocles for the Taché–Macdonald government, as it was to be for all subsequent ministries up to confederation. The record of the 1857 session was nevertheless a positive one: the re-shaping of the common law of Lower Canada (20 Vict., c.43), the decentralization of the court system (20 Vict., c.44), and the aid granted to the Grand Trunk Railway (20 Vict., c.11).

Although his government came out of the session stronger than it went in, Taché recommended dissolution of the houses to the governor, and took advantage of it to resign on 25 Nov. 1857. According to his personal correspondence, he had decided in the previous March to give up the government of the country and active politics. In reality his was no more than a semi-retirement, since he was a legislative councillor for life. But he was tired, and for three years he had been yearning for the rest and calm of private life, as is shown by these words to La Fontaine: "Public life, at the present time, whatever the position of the luckless mortal who is involved in it, is absolutely untenable. . . . my distaste is such that I pray God, with all the fervour I can muster, that we be defeated at the opening of the Houses." Hence in June 1858 he refused the post of adjutant-general offered him by the governor. In 1860, however, he accepted the presidency of the Council of Public Instruction and the post of aide-de-camp to the Prince of Wales during his stay in Canada, two positions that left him free of ministerial responsibilities.

But a group of political friends soon sought his assistance. In 1864 Canada was passing through another political crisis. The Liberal government of John Sandfield Macdonald* and Dorion, struggling with the same difficulties as the Conservative governments that had preceded it, was in constant danger of collapsing for want of a sufficient majority. Sandfield Macdonald then began negotiations with a view to a coalition. He sounded out Cartier, who declined, and then Taché, who refused in his turn, for he was not disposed to give up retirement to help his opponents. The prime minister therefore was forced to resign on 29 March 1864. Governor Monck* called on Cartier, who declined in favour of Taché, asserting that Upper Canadians were not prejudiced against him. Consequently Taché was invited to form a ministry based on agreement between parties. He was, in his own words, "thrown despite himself into a hornets' nest," having agreed "to lend a hand to friends" who were "very weak." After having no success with the Upper Canadian Liberals, Taché formed, with John A. Macdonald, an entirely Conservative ministry, which adopted a fine ministerial programme but survived only one month: Alexander Tilloch Galt* suffered a vote of censure, and his fall brought down the government as well. The defeat of the third government in two years was an obvious proof that any homogeneous ministry was doomed to impotence in parliament. Once again, coalition proved essential. Sandfield Macdonald, Monck, and Taché had already thought so, and now John A. Macdonald, Cartier, Galt, and even the impetuous and fanatical George Brown admitted as much. It was the latter, indeed, who had been the most intractable; if he was now converted to the idea of a coalition, it was because the two conditions he laid down

Taché

were realized. Taché, who was desired as prime minister, was the head of none of the three parties that eventually formed the coalition; he had remained outside the violent political struggles of recent years, and enjoyed the prestige of being a legislative councillor. Furthermore, all political parties except the Rouges of Lower Canada agreed to study the principle of a federal union of the British provinces.

On 22 June 1864 Taché therefore formed the coalition ministry from which Canadian confederation would originate. Once he had thus given new life to the administration of the country, Taché considered himself less necessary to the coalition government. The future was to prove, however, that when the time came to find a successor, he was the prime minister of the hour. Indeed, the coalition managed to continue only under the direction of Narcisse-Fortunat Belleau*, whose leadership closely resembled that of Taché.

Taché remained in the ministry only because he felt he had a mission: aware on one hand of the insidious evil that confederation might involve, and on the other of the influence he had on his colleagues, he made it his duty to watch over the direction of the project, to protect the interests of Lower Canada. With a vanity that was justified by the pressures he had faced the previous March, he wrote: "I wish to take my share of responsibility in the proposal that we are considering for the union of the provinces. Is this plan possible without sacrificing Lower Canada? That is what we shall have to see; for me it is an important matter, and as I hold the key of the shop I can always close it if I perceive that no good can be achieved." Thus Taché attributed to himself, almost exclusively, the fatherhood of confederation. In his capacity as prime minister, he did indeed preside over the important Quebec conference in 1864; he then undertook to defend before the Legislative Council the 72 resolutions that would determine the primary and secondary lines to be followed by confederation, and Macdonald was to take a similar role in the assembly.

But already during the session, on 16 Feb. 1865, Taché suffered a slight attack of paralysis which presaged his coming death. He died on 30 July, at the age of 69. On 2 August, after a state funeral, he was buried at Montmagny. Taché's premature death explains why too often his name is not linked with Canadian confederation, and he is thus denied the honour in favour of those who shared in all stages of the project and who witnessed its full realization. However, we unhesitatingly assert that Monck's description of Brown, as "*the* man whose conduct in 1864 had rendered the project of union feasible," applies equally to Taché (although Taché worked less obtrusively).

A fair evaluation of Taché's whole career requires the setting aside of usual standards of assessment and a realization that the strength that makes compromise possible may be as great as the strength behind creativity or resistance. Taché was a conciliator, known as "a moderate and safe man." A part of all political events during the union, from the first elections of 1841 to the adoption of the Quebec resolutions in June 1865, he deserves to be styled a great statesman, the more so because he did not let himself be submerged by politics. Perhaps he was first drawn to politics by inclination, but, as his private correspondence attests, it was through a sense of patriotic duty that he continued and consented to return to political life.

ANDRÉE DÉSILETS

ANQ-Q, AP-G-134; AP-G-242. BUM, Coll. Baby. PAC, MG 24, B1, B14, B40, B125, C19, C24, D16, E1. P.[-J.] Aubert de Gaspé, *Mémoires* (Ottawa, 1866). Can., prov. du, *Débats parlementaires sur la Confédération*; *Statuts*, 1854–55, c.77, c.100, c.131; 1856, c.14, c.140; 1857, c.11, c.44; Assemblée législative, *Journaux*, 1841–65. *JIP*, juillet–août 1856. *L'Aurore des Canadas*, 1841–46. *L'Avenir*, 1847–57. *Le Canadien*, 1841–49. *Le Courrier du Canada*, 1862–65. *Le Journal de Québec*, 1842–65. *La Minerve*, 1841–65. *Le Pays*, 1852–65. G. Turcotte, *Cons. législatif de Québec*.

Bernard, *Les Rouges*. J.-C. Bonenfant, *La naissance de la Confédération* (Montréal, 1969). Éveline Bossé, *Joseph-Charles Taché (1820–1894), un représentant de l'élite canadienne-française* (Québec, 1971). Careless, *Brown*; *Union of the Canadas*. Chapais, *Hist. du Canada*, VII, 79, 285–771 Cornell, *Alignment of political groups*. Creighton, *Macdonald, young politician*; *Road to confederation*. L.-O. David, *L'Union des deux Canadas, 1841–1867* (Montréal, 1898). Andrée Désilets, *Hector-Louis Langevin, un père de la Confédération canadienne (1826–1906)* (Québec, 1969). Alfred Duclos de Celles, *Cartier et son temps* (Montréal, 1913). Gérard Filteau, *Histoire des Patriotes* (3v., Montréal, 1938–39). Antoine Gérin-Lajoie, *Dix ans au Canada de 1840 à 1850: histoire de l'établissement du gouvernement responsable* (Québec, 1888). M. O. Hammond, *Confederation and its leaders* (Toronto, 1917). Monet, *Last cannon shot*. Joseph Pope, *Memoirs of the Right Honourable John Alexander Macdonald, G.C.B., first prime minister of the dominion of Canada* (2v., Ottawa, [1894]), I. P.-G. Roy, *A travers les "Anciens Canadiens" de Philippe Aubert de Gaspé* (Montréal, 1943), 266ff.; *La famille Taché* (Lévis, Qué., 1904). Robert Rumilly, *Papineau* (Montréal, [1944]). L.-P. Turcotte, *Canada sous l'Union*. L.-P. Audet, "La surintendance de l'éducation et la loi scolaire de 1841," *Cahiers des Dix*, 25 (1960);

147–69. Sylvio Leblond, "La médecine dans la province de Québec avant 1847," *Cahiers des Dix*, 35 (1970), 69–95. Antoine Roy, "Les Patriotes de la région de Québec pendant la rébellion de 1837–1838," *Cahiers des Dix*, 24 (1959), 253.

TASCHEREAU, JOSEPH-ANDRÉ, lawyer, politician, and judge; b. 30 Nov. 1806 at Sainte-Marie-de-la-Nouvelle-Beauce (Sainte-Marie, Que.), son of Thomas-Pierre-Joseph Taschereau and Françoise Boucher de La Bruère de Montarville; d. 30 March 1867 at Kamouraska, Canada East.

Joseph-André Taschereau, a timid and withdrawn child of the celebrated seigneurial family, was educated at home by such tutors as Abbé Édouard Quertier*. He early developed his passion for the law, described as "the only love in his life," and articled with Charles Panet, Judge George Van Felson*, and Judge William Power*. On 15 Feb. 1828 he was admitted to the Lower Canadian bar in company with his elder brother Pierre-Elzéar.

After less than a year of joint practice in Quebec City, Pierre-Elzéar, who in 1826 had inherited his father's seigneury, returned to the manor at Sainte-Marie-de-la-Nouvelle-Beauce. Joseph-André continued his practice from 1830 to 1835 while Pierre-Elzéar represented Beauce County as a radical Reformer in the assembly. After the latter resigned in November 1835, Joseph-André immediately contested and won the seat. During the crucial years between 1835 and 1837, Taschereau was one of the few French Canadians to desert the Patriote party's ranks, often voting with the largely English Conservative minority. In the 1841 general elections in Dorchester County (which now included Beauce County) after the union he was soundly defeated by his uncle Antoine-Charles Taschereau, the Reform candidate.

In 1842 Taschereau was named one of three commissioners inquiring into seigneurial tenure. A year later they submitted to parliament an elaborate report, with detailed descriptions of tenure as practised in Lower Canada and with a generally pro-seigneur tone. On 13 April 1843 Taschereau gave up his law practice to become inspector and superintendent of police for Quebec City. Though technically this public office made him ineligible, he contested Montmorency in the next year's general elections against the Reformer Joseph-Édouard Cauchon*, a supporter of Louis-Hippolyte LA FONTAINE; he was defeated. On 21 Aug. 1845 Taschereau relinquished his duties as superintendent of police and accepted the non cabinet position of solicitor general for Canada East in the administration of William Henry Draper* and of his friend Denis-Benjamin VIGER.

This appointment was made less than a month after the death of his brother Pierre-Elzéar, whose Dorchester seat Joseph-André won on 15 September defeating Horatio Patton, a local figure. The election in Canada East's largest constituency became a political *cause célèbre* which tested the relative strength of the rival factions under Montrealer Louis-Hippolyte La Fontaine and "reactionist" Quebec mayor René-Édouard Caron*. Using all his influence, including the support of his cousin, seigneur of Sainte-Marie, "reactionist" Taschereau campaigned as a man whose principles were as "liberal as it is possible for them to be under a monarchical constitution," and as a French Canadian nationalist with the motto: "My country before all." Asked about his deceased brother's different political principles, he replied merely that one must speak justly of the dead.

Taschereau had almost two disillusioning years in office, and was passed over in favour of William Badgley* as a successor for Attorney General James SMITH in Canada East; he resigned as solicitor general. He also announced his intention of joining the opposition, a contingency the ministry avoided by appointing him circuit judge on 22 May 1847. On 25 Nov. 1857 he was named judge of the Superior Court for the District of Kamouraska, where he had gone to live in 1852. He died in Kamouraska on 30 March 1867, still a bachelor, still in harness, of a disease of the nervous system.

Joseph-André Taschereau, younger brother of the seigneur and nephew of the regional political leader, was a maverick in the Taschereau clan. When both his brother and his uncle were confirmed Reformers, Joseph-André gravitated towards the Conservatives. His final political act was to join the administration to which his dead brother had been opposed. His holding of office and his political contest with his uncle suggest more family feuding and personal rebellion than genuine expressions of political conviction. His bachelorhood, his preference for books over friends, and his hermit-like existence, also indicate a certain bleakness in his personal life. As a lawyer, however, Taschereau excelled, and in his erudition, impartiality in rendering decisions, and intellectual capacity he achieved as much as any other member of his dynamic clan.

ELIZABETH GIBBS

Le Courrier du Canada, 1er, 3 avril 1867. *Le Journal de Québec*, 2 avril 1867. *Morning Chronicle* (Quebec), 1

Tatanka-najin

April 1867. Le Jeune, *Dictionnaire. Political appointments, 1841–65* (J.-O. Coté), 5. P.-G. Roy, *Les juges de la prov. de Québec*, 535. [M.] E. [Abbott] Nish, "Double majority: concept, practice and negotiations, 1840–1848" (unpublished MA thesis, McGill University, Montreal, 1966). Cornell, *Alignment of political groups*. Dent, *Last forty years*, II, 89–90. Maurice Grenier, "La chambre d'Assemblée du Bas-Canada, 1815–1837" (thèse de MA, université de Montréal, 1966). Monet, *Last cannon shot*, 190–91. Honorius Provost, *Sainte-Marie de la Nouvelle-Beauce: histoire religieuse* (Québec, 1967). P.-G. Roy, *La famille Taschereau* (Lévis, Qué., 1901); "Le docteur John Buchanan," *BRH*, XVII (1911), 102–3; "Les juges Taschereau," *BRH*, III (1897), 31. Régis Roy, "Les armes de la famille Taschereau," *BRH*, XXVIII (1922), 24–27.

TATANKA-NAJIN (known as **Standing Buffalo**), hereditary chief of the Sisseton-Santee Dakotas; b. *c.* 1820 at Otter Tail (Minn.); d. 1870 at Wolf Point, Montana.

Following the Traverse-des-Sioux treaty (1851) with the United States government, the Santee division of the Dakotas (also known as Sioux), comprising four bands, were allotted reservations along the upper Minnesota River in a rich land that settlers soon found attractive. Two of the bands, the Sisseton and Wahpeton, were in the 1860s living and hunting in the area around the Upper Agency (Granite Falls, Minn.); the Wakantonwan and Mdewakantonwan bands were largely in the area around the Lower Agency (near Redwood Falls, Minn.). The outbreak of the American Civil War interrupted the payment of treaty money; in 1862 no payment was received. In August of that year some of Standing Buffalo's band seized supplies but then withdrew from the agency area. However, later that month the Lower Agency Santees, hungry and defiant, broke into government stores, and killed many settlers, taking food and supplies. Standing Buffalo refused to join forces with these bands, upbraiding their chiefs such as Taoyateduta (Little Crow); he forbade them access to his reservation and protected settlers against further attacks where possible.

General Henry Hastings Sibley, sent by the United States government to quell the Indians, for the next few years pursued both those who had fought and those who had remained neutral. Standing Buffalo narrowly rescued his band from a battle at Big Mound, Iowa, in 1863. The bands took refuge in the Dakota territory; in the years 1862–64 numbers appeared in British territory around Red River, often starving. Standing Buffalo, who had made a peace agreement with the Saulteaux on the Souris River (Man.), seems not to have been uneasy about crossing the boundary into British territory in the spring of 1864, leading some 500 refugees to Upper Fort Garry (Winnipeg). The hope of all the Sioux was that the British would honour a pledge of assistance made in 1778 at Montreal, when several Dakota chiefs, including Sissetons, were given King George III silver medals in recognition of assistance during the American revolution. The Dakotas claimed also to have favoured the British side in the War of 1812.

Governor William MACTAVISH of Assiniboia urged Standing Buffalo to return peacefully to the United States. His reluctance to render aid can be explained by caution because of lack of supplies, unwillingness to take sides in an American conflict, and also the long record of clashes between Dakotas and the Saulteaux of the Red River country. These Indians had been hereditary enemies from the days when the latter had driven the Dakotas south and west to the plains; in the mid 1840s this enmity had been given a temporary lull only in a peace arranged by the Métis leader, Cuthbert James Grant*; in 1851 and 1853 there were fierce battles between the Dakotas and Métis buffalo hunters.

Having wintered in the Dakota territory after his lack of success in Red River, Standing Buffalo and his band returned to Upper Fort Garry again in the spring of 1866. Again they were sent away without the food, guns, and ammunition they requested. Hunting the buffalo in Assiniboia, they were attacked by Saulteaux, and moved west to the Wood Mountain area (Sask.). While they were camping on the Souris River in 1869 most of Standing Buffalo's family died of smallpox. In despair he joined a Dakota war party in Montana, where he was slain the next year by enemies.

Standing Buffalo's son Matokinajin became leader of the band in 1878 and obtained a reserve near what is now Fort Qu'Appelle, Sask. Descendants of Santee refugees live today on several reserves in Manitoba and Saskatchewan. The experience of these groups of dispossessed and wandering Dakotas was to be repeated when in the next decade Sitting Bull* fled to Canada.

GONTRAN LAVIOLETTE

PAC, RG 10, vol. 766. Private archives, Gontran Laviolette (Winnipeg), letters from S. J. Brown, 16 April 1923; G. C. Allanson, 8 Feb. 1934; and W. G. Benson, 15 July 1938; testimonies of Julius Standing-Buffalo (grandson of Tatanka-najin), Louis Tawiyaka, Alfred Goodvoice, Harry Goodpipe, William Isnana, Wojahunta, Wacinhowaste, Padani *et al.*, of Standing-Buffalo Indian Reserve, Fort Qu'Appelle, Sask., 1935–44. *Indian affairs; laws and treaties*, ed. C. J. Kappler (2v., Washington, 1903). *Nor'Wester*, 1861–

64. R. K. Andrist, *The long death: the last days of the Plains Indian* (New York, 1964), 27–68. Donald Gunn and C. R. Tuttle, *History of Manitoba from the earliest settlement to 1835 . . . and from the admission of the province into the dominion* (Ottawa, 1880). I. V. D. Heard, *History of the Sioux war and massacres of 1862 and 1863* (New York, 1863), 159–65. M. A. Jamieson, *Medals awarded to North American Indian chiefs, 1717–1922, and to loyal African and other chiefs in various territories within the British empire* (London, 1936). Gontran Laviolette, *The Sioux Indians in Canada* (Regina, 1944), 60–68. M. A. MacLeod and W. L. Morton, *Cuthbert Grant of Grantown: warden of the plains of Red River* (Toronto, 1963). R. W. Meyer, *History of the Santee Sioux; United States Indian policy on trial* (Lincoln, Nebr., 1967). Doane Robinson, *A history of the Dakota or Sioux Indians from their earliest traditions and first contact with white men . . .* (Aberdeen, S.D., 1904; repr. Minneapolis, Minn., 1967), 253–337.

TELLIER, RÉMI-JOSEPH, Jesuit priest; b. 9 Oct. 1796 at Tavaux (dept of Aisne), France; d. 7 Jan. 1866 at Montreal, Canada East.

Rémi-Joseph Tellier entered the noviciate of the Society of Jesus at Rome in October 1818. Before his ordination in 1831, he taught at various colleges of the society in France and Italy. From 1833 to 1837 he was rector of the Collège de Chambéry in Savoy, and held the same office at the Collège d'Aoste in Italy until 1840. In 1842 he was one of nine Jesuits to respond to an appeal of Bishop Ignace Bourget*, who wanted to re-establish the Jesuits in Canada. He reached Montreal on 31 May and on 2 July settled into the presbytery at Laprairie (La Prairie), the Jesuits' temporary residence.

The Jesuits had been the first officiating priests and the seigneurs of Prairie-de-la-Madeleine in the 17th and 18th centuries, and at Laprairie the society began its second career on Canadian soil. On 30 Jan. 1844, in a letter to Father Clément BOULANGER, his superior in France, Father Tellier expressed some hasty and pessimistic judgements on the future of Canada. "According to all appearances," he wrote, "the tottering French Canadian nation will soon sink down and expire; but catholicism will unite with England and so everything will be saved. At least such is the hope with which we like to beguile ourselves." Nevertheless, these views did not prevent him from devoting himself heart and soul to his parish which included 4,036 Catholics and 45 Protestant families. He was one of the country priests who in the autumn of 1847 went selflessly to aid the Irish victims of typhus in the sheds at Pointe-Saint-Charles (Montreal Island). Tellier, an experienced educator, was assigned in 1849 to Bishop Rémi Gaulin* of Kingston as director of Re-giopolis College. From 1850 to 1852 he lived at Toronto, where he gave valuable service to Bishop de Charbonnel*. He tried, unsuccessfully, to establish a college of the society there.

In 1846 the Jesuits of Canada, through Father Boulanger who was then the visitor to the French missions in America, had agreed to devote their energies to education in the diocese of New York. In that year New York and Canada had been combined into a single mission, which was answerable to Paris but had a superior general in America. From 1853 Father Tellier lived and worked at New York. He was in turn prefect of studies at St Francis Xavier College at New York and rector of St John's College at Fordham, and finally, in 1859, was appointed superior general of the New York–Canada mission. In this capacity he was in constant touch with his *confrères* in Canada. Each year he paid a canonical visit to the charitable organizations and houses of the society, and tried to improve the work of those under him. A contemporary wrote of Tellier in *L'Écho du cabinet de lecture paroissial*: "In the midst of a population that was foreign by nationality and religion, he was able through his activity, zeal, prudence, and firmness to win widespread esteem and approval for the Society he directed so worthily in this part of America." He also showed breadth and boldness in his thinking: Le Gesù, a church adjoining the Collège Sainte-Marie at Montreal, was an example. In addition to the Sulpicians, who looked disapprovingly upon the erection of a large church in the neighbourhood of Notre-Dame, the Jesuits of the college themselves had reservations about such a project. The building of Le Gesù, the cost of which they would have to meet, would only aggravate an already trying financial situation. Thanks to his tact and sensitivity, the superior general managed to get the daring plan accepted.

Confined by illness to the Hôtel-Dieu, Father Tellier was not able to attend the inaugural ceremony at Le Gesù in December 1865. On 7 Jan. 1866 he died peacefully at the Collège Sainte-Marie. His funeral took place two days later at Le Gesù, the first to be held in this church.

LÉON POULIOT

[Some of Rémi-Joseph Tellier's sermons and addresses were printed in contemporary newspapers, in particular in the *Mélanges religieux*, 28 June 1844, and in the *Toronto Mirror*, 6 Dec. 1851. In addition, the *Discours prononcé à la cathédrale de Toronto, par le révérend père R. J. Tellier, de la Compagnie de Jésus, le 24 juin 1851, jour de la fête, et en présence de l'association de St. Jean-Baptiste* was published at Toronto in 1851. The French text is accompanied by an English translation by Father Tellier. L.P.]

Testard

ASJCF, Lettres des nouvelles missions du Canada, 1843–52, 1re partie, 41–67, 391–97. *L'Écho du cabinet de lecture paroissial*, 15 janv. 1866. *La Minerve*, 8 janv. 1866. *True Witness and Catholic Chronicle* (Montreal), 8 Jan. 1866. P.-G. Roy, *Inv. concessions*, I, 227–30. *Les établissements des jésuites en France depuis quatre siècles . . .* , Pierre Delattre, édit. (5v., Enghien et Wetteren, Belgique, 1949–57), I, 1264–65. Édouard Lecompte, *Les jésuites du Canada au XIXe siècle* (Montréal, 1920), 50, 65–66, 73–74, 246–47, 250–51. L. K. Shook, "St Michael's College; the formative years, 1850–1853," CCHA *Report*, XVII (1950), 41–46.

TESTARD DE MONTIGNY, CASIMIR-AM-ABLE (he usually signed **C.T. de Montigny**), businessman, colonizer, and politician; b. 2 June 1787 at Montreal, son of Louis-Étienne Testard de Montigny, a lawyer, and Louise-Archange Gamelin, *dit* Gaucher, and great-grandson of Jacques Testard* de Montigny; m. first 9 Jan. 1815, at Sainte-Anne-de-Mascouche (La Plaine), Marthe Godon, and secondly, 30 Jan. 1855, at Saint-Jérôme, Marie-Louise Allaire; d. 10 Jan. 1863 at Saint-Jérôme, Canada East.

Casimir-Amable Testard de Montigny spent his youth in Montreal and completed his studies under the Sulpicians, for the first year at the Séminaire de Notre-Dame, then at the newly built Petit Séminaire from 1806 to 1808. Apparently he then took up trading in furs with the Indians of Lac-des-Deux-Montagnes, working from a small trading post on the Rivière du Nord, some 30 miles north of Montreal; around 1814 he established himself there permanently, thus creating a small centre of settlement. Around the 1830s, this settlement moved north to the present site of Saint-Jérôme. Testard de Montigny took an active part in all the events connected with the beginnings of Saint-Jérôme, the starting-point of the great colonization movement to be directed by the parish priest François-Xavier-Antoine Labelle* in the 1870s.

There are few documents through which we can determine the salient points of Testard de Montigny's career. He was the representative for the county of Effingham in the assembly of Lower Canada from 28 Aug. 1824 to 5 July 1827, but he initiated nothing worthy of mention in the political records of that period. Some ten years later, his hostility towards the Patriotes gave him cause for anxiety on more than one score. A major in the militia, member of the local élite, and firm supporter of the government, he was appointed commissioner of small causes for Saint-Jérôme on 5 April 1837. His attitude was particularly displeasing to several of his fellow citizens, who supported the claims of the Pat-riotes. Early in December 1837 Testard de Montigny went so far as to hold a public meeting at his house to persuade his compatriots to abstain from taking part in the rebellion movement; on that occasion "the address of the Magistrates of the City of Montreal," recommending the maintenance of peace and respect for law and order, was read to the gathering. A few days later, on 9 December, Testard de Montigny had to flee, since a number of Patriotes had decided to arrest him. They caught up with him a few miles north of Saint-Jérôme. He offered a ransom for his liberty, but the Patriotes demanded that he invite the villagers publicly to join the rebellion. The commissioner of small causes refused and was taken a prisoner to the camp at Saint-Eustache. Set free a few days later, he nonetheless continued to receive statements of witnesses denouncing friends and neighbours who had publicly uttered threats against the government or risen against the British army. He himself incriminated several fellow citizens, including Dr Léandre Dumouchel, and especially those who had initiated his arrest. His support of the government enabled him to keep his position as commissioner of small causes during these months of disturbances, even though his son-in-law, the notary André Bouchard, *dit* Lavallée, was arrested as a Patriote on 8 Feb. 1838 and imprisoned at Montreal; Montigny's commission was renewed on 22 Dec. 1838.

The rebellion over, Testard de Montigny continued his agricultural, commercial, and political activities. In 1846 and 1847 he managed to obtain grants of more than 400 acres of land in the township of Abercromby, and for two years, from 1849 to 1851, he represented the village of Saint-Jérôme, which then numbered 500, on the municipal council of Terrebonne County. During these years he made numerous financial transactions, particularly loans or the purchase, sale, or exchange of small pieces of land. Moreover, from 1820 on his name regularly appeared at the bottom of petitions about the development of Saint-Jérôme which were addressed either to civil or to religious authorities.

Casimir-Amable Testard de Montigny, considered the founder of Saint-Jérôme, withdrew from active life in 1859. Having already made ample provision for his other children he now made over the remainder of his assets to his son Benjamin-Antoine*, who thus received three pieces of land under cultivation, four houses, and three barns, the contents of these buildings, as well as his accounts receivable and payable, notes and mortgages. Testard de Montigny, his second wife, and the children born of this marriage, were from then on supported by Benjamin-Antoine. Casimir-Amable died four years later, on 10 Jan. 1863, at Saint-Jérôme.

MICHEL PAQUIN

ANQ-M, État civil, Catholiques, Notre-Dame (Montréal), 3 juin 1787. ANQ-Q, QBC 9, 27, f.33; 28, f.167; 29, ff.8, 47, 72, 112; QBC 25, Événements de 1837–1838, nos.562, 567, 574–75, 636. Archives judiciaires, Terrebonne (Saint-Jérôme, Qué.), Greffe d'André Bouchard, dit Lavallée, 1834–78; Greffe de J.-A. Hervieux, 1856–82; Greffe de Melchior Prévost, 1840–97; Greffe de J.-B.-L. Villemure, 1851–84 [The most important legal document is found in the *greffe* of J.-A. Hervieux: Testard de Montigny's deed of gift to his son. The deed, however, does not contain the details of Testard de Montigny's fortune, for Hervieux gave the donee the donor's schedule of notes and mortgages; that document has not been found. M.P.]; Registre d'état civil, Sainte-Anne de Mascouche, 9, 30 janv., 7 juin 1815, 28 avril, 28 août 1817, 1ᵉʳ févr. 1821, 18 août 1823, 8 janv., 8 nov. 1824, 10 juin 1826, 5 janv. 1829, 17 oct. 1835; Registre d'état civil, Saint-Jérôme, 27 oct. 1838, 25 nov. 1854, 30 mai 1855, 13 juin 1856, 26 janv., 20 juin 1857, 19 juin 1859. *Almanac de Québec . . .*, 1820, 95. Ivanhoë Caron, "Inventaire des documents relatifs aux événements de 1837 et 1838, conservés aux Archives de la province de Québec," ANQ *Rapport*, 1925–26, 176, 179. Desjardins, *Guide parlementaire*, 129. Fauteux, *Patriotes*, 290. Langelier, *List of lands granted*. Tanguay, *Dictionnaire*, VII, 285. É.-J. [-A.] Auclair, *Saint-Jérôme de Terrebonne* (Saint-Jérôme, Qué., 1934) (a portrait of Testard de Montigny is reproduced in this work but the original has not been located). Olivier Maurault, *Le collège de Montréal, 1767–1967*, Antonio Dansereau, édit. (2ᵉ éd., Montréal, 1967), 150–51, 202. [B.-A.] Testard de Montigny, *La colonisation, le nord de Montréal ou la région de Labelle* (Montréal, 1895), 46–78.

TÊTU, CHARLES-HILAIRE, merchant and postmaster; b. 22 June 1802 at Saint-Thomas-de-Montmagny (Montmagny, Que.), son of François Têtu and Charlotte Bonenfant; d. 9 Dec. 1863 at Rivière-Ouelle, Canada East.

Heir to the Têtu and Bonenfant families, François Têtu constantly enlarged his estates. He became seigneur of the Saint-Luc fief in the seigneury of Rivière-du-Sud, and a lieutenant-colonel in the militia. His wealth enabled him to educate and find suitable positions in society for his numerous children, who included a priest, a notary, a doctor, five merchants, and four farmers. Charles-Hilaire was the fifth of 18 children. He was not drawn to study, and at an early age went into business. In partnership with his first cousin Pierre-Thomas Casgrain, seigneur of Rivière-Ouelle, he ran a store in that village where "he sold something of everything." He was also a large shareholder in a local porpoise

fishing enterprise. He took an active interest in the business: with his son David he searched for the best fishing stations, he invented an ingenious system of nets to catch the porpoises, and he perfected a procedure for tanning and dressing the skins. He had this procedure patented, and won awards for it at the universal exhibitions in London in 1851 and Paris in 1855. From 1842 until his death he was also postmaster at Rivière-Ouelle.

The time and money devoted to fishing caused Têtu to neglect his business, and his financial difficulties were increased by the failure of some high risk ventures, for example several schooners purchased for the timber trade which were lost at sea. Pierre-Thomas Casgrain withdrew from the partnership, but, because he did not have the dissolution legally recorded, he was obliged to pay part of Têtu's debts. Although he was a man "of Herculean build," Têtu's health collapsed: chronic dyspepsia, induced or intensified by his fondness for pantagruelian meals, brought him to his grave.

As a member of the Bonenfant and Casgrain clans, Charles-Hilaire Têtu had participated in the social life that centred on the seigneurial manor-house at Rivière-Ouelle, the residence of Pierre and later of Pierre-Thomas Casgrain, and the meeting-place for the established local bourgeoisie, for the Casgrains and Têtus, and for the Letellier, Dionne, Chapais, and Gagnon families, all related through a complex network of marriages. Their relationship did not prevent vigorous confrontations at election time, with one group supporting the Letelliers of the Rouge party, another swearing by the Chapais of the Bleus. Têtu sided with the moderate Liberals, but still incurred the wrath of parish priest Charles Bégin, whose management of financial matters Têtu had criticized. But he still continued to be one of the most regular churchgoers in the parish.

By his first marriage, on 16 May 1826 with Marie-Thérèse Pâquet of Quebec, Charles-Hilaire Têtu had three children; one of them, Justine, married Hector-Louis Langevin* in 1854. Widowed in 1836, Têtu remarried on 19 Sept. 1837. His second wife was Elizabeth O'Brien, widow of François Laurent, a Quebec merchant, and they had three boys and four girls.

Charles-Hilaire Têtu died on 9 Dec. 1863 at Rivière-Ouelle; his wife went to Ottawa to live with her children and died there on 8 Jan. 1881.

NIVE VOISINE

ANQ-Q, AP-G-327. Mme E. Croff [M.-E. Perrault], *Nos ancêtres à l'œuvre à la Rivière-Ouelle* (Montréal,

Thomas

1931). P.-H. Hudon, *Rivière-Ouelle de la Bouteillerie, 3 siècles de vie* ([Rivière-Ouelle], Qué., 1972), 232–33, 272. Henri Têtu, *Histoire des familles Têtu, Bonenfant, Dionne et Perrault* (Québec, 1898), 91–96, 144–46. [Henri Têtu et H.-R. Casgrain], *David Têtu et les raiders de Saint-Alban; épisode de la guerre américaine, 1864–1865* (2e éd., Québec, 1891), 38–40.

THOMAS, SOPHIA (Mason), translator and editor; b. 15 Nov. 1822 at Red River, youngest daughter of Dr Thomas Thomas*, HBC chief factor and governor of the Northern Department, and an Indian woman; d. 10 Oct. 1861 in London, England.

When Dr Thomas died in 1828 he left each of his six daughters £1,000 in 3 per cent consolidated Bank of England annuities. Sophia had the benefit of a good upbringing, first in the home of the Reverend David Thomas Jones*, in whose trust she had been placed by her father, and, after Jones' death, in the home of the Reverend William COCKRAN. She received a sound education at the Red River Academy under the direction of John Macallum. An indication of her scholastic ability was the offer made to her in 1843 to be a governess in the ladies' section of the academy. She declined in order to marry at Red River a young Wesleyan Methodist missionary, the Reverend William Mason*.

The newly married couple set off on 11 Aug. 1843 by York boat for the Rossville mission, north of Lake Winnipeg, which was to be the centre of their missionary endeavour for 11 years. At that time Rossville mission was in the charge of the Reverend James Evans*, inventor of the syllabic system of writing the Cree language. Evans issued some religious literature but his efforts were hampered by the lack of a proper printing press. In the summer of 1845 he left with his family because of ill health, and that autumn the long-desired hand press arrived from England. It thus fell to William Mason to propagate the Gospel among the Indians by means of the printed word.

Sophia Mason had important qualities to offer in the missionary life, for in addition to a natural piety she was familiar with the ways of the Indians and had learned the Cree language at her mother's knee. Of the life of a missionary wife, her husband was to write: "Most people deem the cares of a family quite enough to employ the time of a female; but the labours of Sophia, notwithstanding her feeble and delicate constitution, were augmented by the Indian day school, visits to the Indian tents, and daily translations, besides having to attend to the wants of a large family, which she laboured to bring up in the fear and nurture of the Lord, and that in the wilderness, where, in time of sickness, no medical assistance could be procured."

In 1854 Mason left the Methodist Church, joined the Church of England, and moved to York Factory. Four years later the Masons sailed to England to superintend the printing of the New Testament in Cree syllabics; when this was completed in 1859, they remained to see the Old Testament through the press.

Unfortunately, when the two sections of the Bible were published, the title pages bore only the name of William Mason as translator. At Rossville mission the Masons' former native co-workers, John Sinclair and the Reverend Henry Bird Steinhauer*, maintained that much of the translation had been the result of their effort over several years. William Mason's own statements would suggest that the Rossville group prepared a rough draft, but that the final translation was his wife's. He wrote that "her sanction would decide generally any difficulty with respect to the most correct rendering of the passage into Cree," that "her perfect command and knowledge of the Indian language was invaluable," and that in London "she laboured night and day to finish the final revision of the Old Testament, having completed the New in 1859."

Shortly after her arrival in England in 1858 Sophia suffered a severe attack of pleurisy, and she continued to have pulmonary afflictions. Her translating was frequently interrupted by seizures of pain. In July 1861 she gave birth to her ninth child. She continued her work, and three months later was dead. The last of the Old Testament books, Malachi, had just come off the press.

BRUCE PEEL

HBC Arch. A.36/13, will of Thomas Thomas, 30 Nov. 1827. CMS Arch. (London), Journal of the Reverend William Mason, 10 Sept. 1854–28 Aug. 1858 (copy at University of Alberta Library, Edmonton). Nathaniel Burwash, "The gift to a nation of written language," RSC *Trans.*, 3rd ser., V (1911), sect.II, 3–21. [William Mason], "A short sketch of the life and missionary labours and happy death of Sophia Mason," *Church Missionary Gleaner* (London), new ser., XI (1861), 135–40.

THOMPSON, DAVID, soldier, teacher, and author; b. in Scotland, perhaps in 1790 but more probably in 1795 or 1796; buried 3 June 1868 at Niagara (Niagara-on-the-Lake), Ont. There is no evidence that he married.

David Thompson enlisted in the 1st Foot, 3rd battalion, of the British army in 1808 or 1809, and saw action in Europe in the Walcheren expedition and the Peninsular War before arriving in Upper Canada in 1812 and serving at Moraviantown, Lundy's Lane, and Fort Erie. In 1812 he was raised to the rank of corporal in the 1st battalion.

When he was discharged in 1815 Thompson, like so many other British soldiers stationed in the Canadas, chose not to return home. He settled at Niagara where, except for one short period, he lived the rest of his life. War wounds apparently prevented Thompson from farming extensively; from 1815 until 1855 he taught at common schools in and around the town of Niagara, and for a brief time in Frontenac County. In 1842 and 1843 he may have served as clerk of the town and township of Niagara. He was also first captain of the Niagara Independent Artillery Company from 1838 until at least 1855.

In 1832 Thompson wrote a *History of the late war between Great Britain and the United States*, which was printed by Thomas Sewell. The book had two purposes: to defend Britain's conduct against American accounts and to arouse the patriotism of the young by reminding them of the heroism of their forefathers. It is a partisan book, but not a mere polemic, for Thompson researched his subject well. More than a third of the text is devoted to the causes of the war: he concludes that France and the United States must share guilt equally and that Britain's only fault lay in failing to attack the United States before the Americans had time to prepare for war. The book contains some vivid descriptions of those battles in which Thompson took part, and he gives substantial credit to the Canadian militia in the defence of the country against invasion.

At the time of its publication the book was favourably noticed in several Upper Canadian newspapers. One 20th century authority has called it "the first important book published in Upper Canada," but it would, perhaps, be more accurate to say that it was the first important historical work published in that colony. Whatever its merits, it did not, apparently, sell well: a year after its publication Sewell brought suit against Thompson because the latter could not pay for the paper it had been printed on. It does not appear that he was convicted, but it seems that he was unable to raise bail before his trial and spent some time in jail.

Thompson was remembered in the community as a good teacher and useful citizen. And he remained throughout his life the old soldier and British American patriot: in 1854, when the Crimean War began, he was eager to raise a company of Canadian riflemen – "no country in the world," he wrote, "can produce better material for soldiers."

R. D. GIDNEY

David Thompson, *History of the late war between Great Britain and the United States of America; with a retrospective view of the causes from whence it originated . . .* (Niagara, [Ont.], 1832; repr. Toronto, 1845; [New York], 1966). PAC, RG 1, L3, 498, no.118; RG 8, I (C series), 36, pp.325–29; 199, pp.68–69. St Mark's Anglican Church (Niagara-on-the-Lake, Ont.), burial register. Can., Prov. of, Legislative Assembly, *Journals*, 1854–55, III, app.B, table L. *Niagara Gleaner* (Niagara, [Ont.]), 1818–37. *Niagara Mail* (Niagara, Ont.), 3 June 1868. *Literary history of Can.* (Klinck *et al.*), 214.

THOMPSON, JOHN SPARROW, editor, teacher, and writer; b. 1795 at Waterford (Republic of Ireland); m. 24 March 1829, in Halifax, N.S., Charlotte Pottinger, and they had seven children, two of whom seem to have died in infancy; d. 21 Oct. 1867 at Halifax.

John Sparrow Thompson's parents are almost unknown. His father died before Thompson was 24 and his mother, Mary (Sparrow?) Thompson, in 1832. Both were Methodists, reflecting, no doubt, John Wesley's mission to Waterford, 1747–53. About 1818 Thompson left Waterford for London. His life there may not have been altogether satisfactory; as early as 1819 his mother was writing that work could apparently be found in America. He may have been a shoemaker but does not seem to have had ambitions in a trade. He liked writing and became proficient at it. A friend wrote to him in 1826: ". . . what you feel you write in good style but you are deficient in the *language* of strong emotion, perhaps because you [think] . . . such language would be bombast. . . ." By this time Thompson had made up his mind. After a visit to Waterford, he sailed from England early in 1827 in the *Osprey* for Halifax.

In 1828 he started a private school. Halifax's score of private schools often provided a thin enough living for their instructors. Thompson had some real talent for teaching, having knowledge of mathematics and astronomy, and being well read in English literature and history. He was also an excellent shorthand writer, a subject his school taught. Advertisements for his school appear in the *Novascotian* in 1835–36 and 1844, and in the *Royal Gazette* in 1857. In the early 1850s he was a Halifax school commissioner, along with Alexander FORRESTER.

Thompson's teaching career was at times concurrent with, at others consecutive to, his editorial pursuits. In 1830 he became editor of the *Halifax Monthly Magazine*, a position he held until 1833. His facility in shorthand also brought him substantial extra income. It was Thompson who reported Joseph Howe*'s speech at his libel trial of 1835. Shortly after this Thompson founded the *Acadian Telegraph*, a newspaper whose first number included the beginning of his "Compendious history of Nova Scotia. . . ." This history, characteristically perhaps, he never finished. The newspaper lasted from August 1836 until February 1838. Thompson then became editor of Howe's *Novascotian* while Howe was in England from April to October 1838. In 1839 Thompson became editor of the *Pearl*, a literary weekly begun in 1837 and purchased by Howe in June 1839, which folded in August 1840. Thompson then became assistant editor, and subsequently editor, of the *Novascotian* until June 1842.

John Sparrow Thompson was more than a Reformer: he was a radical. He hated class privilege and believed in equal rights and opportunities for all men. On these grounds alone he could never be indifferent to politics; but aside from that, a man's duty as citizen enjoined his participation. Thompson had a strong sense of independence that scorned sycophancy or even trimming. When he wanted to commit the *Pearl* unequivocally to the temperance cause, Howe felt compelled to rein him in: "you . . . are about to rush headlong into a warfare with the whole state of society around you, for no sufficient reason, and with the certainty of sacrificing the very means in your hands of promoting the cause you espouse."

Thompson felt he owed a great deal to Howe. "I have long considered myself in several ways your debtor," Thompson wrote to him in 1836. And not infrequently Howe's letters of the later 1830s have remarks on delightful rides with Thompson about Halifax and the province. Howe was as passionate and impulsive personally as was Thompson politically; Thompson had a more controlled and purposeful nature, and a keener, if less ductile, mind. Thompson was also quite unambitious, and, given his penchant for uttering unpalatable truths, was probably unsuited for public life. Nor was he well suited for business. The failure of the *Acadian Telegraph* might owe something to the times and the number of other papers, but also to Thompson's unwillingness to sell himself or his paper. A friend wrote him in 1855 about the *Athenaeum*, with which Thompson was also associated: ". . . there must be business tact and energy. Especially there must be continuous personal application for

Advertisements. . . ." These Thompson could not give. He neither sought money nor worried too much about the making of it. In this, at least, he and Howe resembled each other. They remained close friends for life. It was said Howe would rarely write anything of importance that he did not first submit to Thompson's judgement.

It was owing to Howe that Thompson was appointed queen's printer in February 1843 during the coalition government. When Howe quarrelled with the governor, Lord Falkland [Lucius Bentinck Cary*], and resigned from the government in December 1843, Thompson's position was weakened. Falkland charged him with writing partisan reports against the government. These charges Thompson denied, but he resigned in February 1844. He may even have refused to write articles defending Lord Falkland. Resignation was not easy for Thompson; he was now nearing 50, with a family of at least four young children. His brother Joseph wrote consolingly from Ireland: "Yes, better to leave the field honourable in the estimation of friend and partisan rather than wage war (no matter how great the spoils) at the expense of the faintest reproach of conscience. . . ." There indeed spoke the Methodist conscience! How difficult life was for Thompson is suggested by his request to Howe for a loan in August 1846. Howe, in "exile" at Musquodoboit, could only send a blank promissory note with his endorsement; Thompson should "get some friend whose credit is good to put his name under mine. *Without that it will be useless to try*."

When Howe returned to office in 1848, in James Boyle Uniacke*'s Reform government, Thompson was reappointed queen's printer and served until April 1854. He was then replaced by William Annand*, who accepted the office on condition that provision be made for Thompson. Apparently it was not, for Thompson went back to teaching and newspaper work. A Conservative government between 1857 and 1860 prevented any official appointment, but in 1860, on Howe's return to power, Thompson was made chief official reporter for the assembly, which he remained until the electoral defeat of Howe's government in 1863. He was also appointed in 1861 chief of the money order department of the Nova Scotia Post Office, a position he held until just before his death.

Thompson had a strong belief in the virtues of local initiative. He was a firm supporter and for many years secretary of the Halifax Mechanics' Institute, founded in 1831. In later times he loved to gather a few friends to read a paper of his own or to hear another's. His sense of relevance and his sharp mind showed often to advantage, and he frequently carried a meeting by his cogent good sense. He had a strong dislike of affectation and sentimentality. Associated with Thompson's Methodism was his belief in temperance. At the opening of the new Temperance Hall in 1850, he described how the Sons of Temperance had met heretofore in the Mason's Hall: "although courtesy from the proprietors was invariably experienced, bacchanalian strains, frequently mingled with the Temperance Hymn and Address. . . ."

His chief literary work was a labour of love, a collected edition of the poetry of John McPherson* published in 1862. The extensive introduction suggests something of Thompson's own viewpoint: "Much of a country's wealth consists in her better minds. To allow the memory of such to disappear, may be considered about as inappropriate and injudicious, as would be the interring of money wealth. . . . Nova Scotia cannot afford to lose such property. . . ." McPherson, too, had had to teach, and his love of meditative peace was "sadly out of keeping with the noise, and roughness, and fagging, and poor pecuniary remuneration. . . ." There spoke Thompson's experience, too. But he was of tougher metal: an unsparing, yet modest critic whose earnestness was enlivened with an Irish wit, and an Irish accent, which he retained to the end of his life. Irishman that he was, he loved debate and argument. Yet Thompson was a man of charity, unlike many tough-minded reformers. He would burst out against some wrongdoer in high places and afterwards express, as a friend put it, "sympathy for the wicked fool, notwithstanding his offences." Thompson's philosophy can be summed up in a sentence from the edition of McPherson: "The mind is the true kingdom of man. . . ." This great gift, together with his integrity, firmness, and spirit, were to be passed on to his more famous son, Sir John Thompson*.

P. B. WAITE

[An attractive, indeed haunting, portrait of J. S. Thompson by William Valentine* hangs in the PANS. There is a useful collection of letters including some from Howe and McPherson in the J. S. Thompson papers at PAC (MG 24, C4). There are also a few Thompson letters in the Howe papers (PAC, MG 24, B29). Primary sources should also include the newspapers he edited and the journals to which he contributed. In addition, there are at least two pamphlets: *The building and its objects: an essay, read, – January 10, 1850, at the first public meeting of the Sons of Temperance in the new Temperance Hall, Poplar Grove, Halifax* (Halifax, 1850); *The eastern shore: report, to a committee of the Grand Division, S. of T., of Nova Scotia, concerning a temperance and educa-*

tional mission to the eastern shore of Halifax County (Halifax, 1860). His book on McPherson is: *Poems, descriptive and moral . . .* (Halifax, 1862).

There is a memoir on Thompson in vol. 293, ff.001804-10 of the Sir John Thompson papers (PAC, MG 26, D), written by William A. Hendry of Halifax for Lady Thompson. The information in that memoir was not available to Sir Joseph Andrew Chisholm* for his paper, "John Sparrow Thompson," N.S. Hist. Soc., *Coll.*, XXVI (1945), 1–31, which has considerable material on Thompson's newspaper activity. There is also a short article by "Occasional," in the *Acadian Recorder* (Halifax), 11 Jan. 1930. P.B.W.]

THOMPSON, THOMAS, schoolmaster and merchant; b. 1803 in Yorkshire, England, son of Thomas Thompson (who also came to Canada about 1830 but of whom no more is known); m. Rebecca Boyce, and they had three children; d. 12 Oct. 1868 in Toronto, Ont.

Thomas Thompson, who had taught school in England, arrived in York (Toronto) in 1830 and opened a private school. Soon after, he offered the premises as a meeting house to the Primitive Methodists who were struggling to establish themselves. Unlike many others, the school prospered and was later sold to immigrants who wished to establish themselves in the same way. Throughout his life Thompson's educational activities proved to be more financial than pedagogic; at the time of his death he held the mortgage of Joseph Day's Commercial College.

By 1833 business opportunities in a growing community about to be incorporated drew Thompson into retail trade. He is credited with opening the first boot and shoe store in the city; known to patrons as "cheap Thos. Thompson's shoe warehouse," he advertised his business as "Thomas Thompson's Cheap Shoe Store." He was undoubtedly one of the first merchants to market goods on the basis of a large stock, high volume of sales, low mark-up, and extensive advertising.

His tactics worked well and in a few years Thompson expanded into general merchandise, particularly dry goods, clothing, and millinery. The location of the business changed several times but always remained near the St Lawrence Market. He suffered heavy losses in the Toronto fire of 1849 but reopened "The Mammoth House," as the business had become known, within a year. "A lean man with resolute features, deep-set eyes, a drift of side-whisker, and a high black stock," Thompson developed a reputation for integrity and subtle ingenuity in business by concluding his advertisements for staple and fancy dry goods with a condemnation of

Thomson

other advertisers and an appeal to the wisdom of potential customers: "As the subscriber is much opposed to the system of puffing, now so common, he would merely request the public to call and examine for themselves." His son Thomas became a business partner in 1864 and took over the Mammoth House on his father's death.

Thompson should not be confused with Thomas Thompson, a saddler and harnessmaker, who was councilman and alderman for St Lawrence ward from 1861 to 1868.

HUGH A. STEVENSON

York County Surrogate Court (Toronto), will of Thomas Thompson, no.1079, 1868. *U.C. Land, Mercantile, and General Advertiser* (Toronto), January 1835. *Commemorative biographical record, county York*, 97. *Cyclopaedia of Canadian biog.* (Rose, 1886), 804–5. Middleton, *Municipality of Toronto*, III. *Robertson's landmarks of Toronto*, I.

THOMSON (Thompson), EDWARD WILLIAM, farmer, militia officer, and politician; b. January 1794 at Kingston, Upper Canada, son of loyalists Archibald Thomson, a carpenter, and Elizabeth McKay; d. 20 April 1865 in York Township, Canada West. Thomson married first in 1815 Sarah Maria Terry of Scarborough Township, by whom he had three sons and four daughters; secondly, in 1829 Mary (d. 1832), daughter of Jesse KETCHUM, by whom he had two children; and thirdly, in 1834, Selina Lee, widow of Dr Archibald Chisholm, the first physician to practise in London, Upper Canada, by whom he had one daughter.

Edward William Thomson moved with his family to Newark (Niagara-on-the-Lake) in 1795, to York (Toronto) in 1796, and to Scarborough Township in 1808. During the War of 1812 he served in Captain Duncan Cameron*'s flank company of the 3rd Regiment of York militia. He was present at the capture of Detroit by Isaac Brock*, was decorated for valiant services at Queenston Heights, and received a militia land grant. He was among those paroled after the American capture of York in 1813. Thomson maintained his military connections over a long period. He was promoted captain in the 1st West York Regiment in 1822, and transferred to the 3rd West York militia in 1827. He served during the rebellion of 1837–38 and became lieutenant-colonel of the 7th Regiment of North York militia in 1839. He transferred to the 7th battalion of York militia in 1846, and in 1856 was named commander of the 5th Militia District of Canada West.

During the 1820s Thomson moved to the Johns-town District and became involved, in association with George CRAWFORD, in the construction of locks on the St Lawrence and Rideau canals. In 1830 he moved from Maitland Rapids (Kilmarnock), Grenville County, to York. Two years later he transferred his contract to Crawford and moved to land in Toronto Township. He subsequently purchased and farmed a number of properties in the area which now forms part of Toronto. He was also a contractor on the Welland Canal, possibly in the 1840s when the wooden locks were replaced by larger stone structures. In 1847 the editor of the *British American Cultivator* described Thomson as a "native Canadian Farmer, who has passed through the various stages of hardships and trials, incident to a backwoodsman's life and withal a self-educated man."

Thomson was an elder in St Andrew's Presbyterian Church, Toronto, and a conservative in politics. Defeated for the assembly by William Lyon MACKENZIE in the 2nd Riding of the county of York in 1834, he was successful against him in 1836, a triumph probably more attributable to the election campaign of Sir Francis Bond Head* than to his own abilities as a politician. Charles Lindsey* claimed that Thomson tended to support the Family Compact in the assembly, but Sir Francis Hincks*' *Examiner* praised him for voting on several occasions to appropriate the Clergy Reserves for educational purposes, and for opposing any measures leading to political monopoly or exclusiveness. He was unsuccessful in 1851 against Amos Wright* in York East, and in 1863 against William Pearce Howland* in York West.

Thomson made his greatest contribution in the field of agriculture, first as a founder in 1830 and president of the Home District Agricultural Society, and later as the first president of the Provincial Agricultural Association, established in 1846, and of the York County Agricultural Society, founded in 1850. Thomson advocated the improvement of farm stock and produce, and he imported and bred pure livestock on his own farm. He also supported the domestic manufacture of agricultural implements, and the establishment of a model farm and agricultural museum. He was a Canadian representative at the exhibitions of 1851 and 1862 in London.

Thomson was, at various times, a magistrate, warden of the Home District, a founder and trustee of Queen's College at Kingston, and vice-president of the Upper Canada Bible Society. He was also president of the Farmers' Mutual Fire Insurance Company, and a director of the Farmers' Joint Stock Banking Company and of the Canada Landed Credit Company. He died on 20 April 1865 while walking to Toronto from his farm for a meeting of the council of the Provincial Agricultural Association.

ANN MACKENZIE

London Public Library and Art Museum (London, Ont.), Edwin Seaborn coll. MTCL, Humber Valley archives, E. W. Thomson file. PAC, RG 1, L3; RG 68, 1, General index, 1651–1841. PAO, Bull (William Perkins) coll.; "Data on United Empire Loyalists," comp. W. E. Reid (typescript); RG 8, I-6-A, 8,100. "The Proudfoot papers," ed. M. A. Garland, *OH*, XXVII (1931), 435–96. *Canada Farmer; a Fortnightly Journal of Agriculture, Horticulture, and Rural Affairs* (Toronto), 1 May 1865. *Examiner* (Toronto), 29 Dec. 1841. *Globe*, 21 April 1865. *Journal of Education for U.C.*, XVIII (1865), 62. *Illustrated historical atlas of the county of York . . .* (Toronto, 1878; repr. 1969).
W. P. Bull, *From Brock to Currie, the military developments and exploits of Canadians in general and of the men of Peel in particular, 1791 to 1930* (Toronto, [1936]). Dent, *Upper Canadian rebellion. Fourteen generations in North America*, comp. J. H. R. Thomson (Calgary, [1967?]). *A history of Upper Canada College, 1829–1892; with contributions by old Upper Canada College boys, lists of head-boys, exhibitioners, university scholars and medallists, and a roll of the school*, comp. George Dickson and G. M. Adam (Toronto, 1893). Lindsey, *Life and times of Mackenzie. Robertson's landmarks of Toronto*, II. Edwin Seaborn, *The march of medicine in western Ontario* (Toronto [1944]).

TILLSON, GEORGE, pioneer industrialist, entrepreneur, and community planner; b. 25 Nov. 1782 at Enfield (now covered by the Quabbin Reservoir), Mass., seventh of the nine children of Hopestill Shaw and Stephen Tillson, a descendant of a settler in the Plymouth plantation in 1639; d. 15 March 1864 at Tillsonburg, Canada West.

In 1804 George Tillson took up land at Blaisdell (Exeter, Maine), and in 1808 married Nancy Barker, daughter of one of the original proprietors in the area. He returned to Massachusetts about 1813, but speedily joined the general westward migration from New England. He farmed in Herkimer and Otsego counties, N.Y., and, according to tradition, was also employed at Canandaigua, N.Y., as an iron-moulder and pattern-maker; his father had worked in iron, while his mother managed the family farm at Enfield. Tillson is said to have joined Joseph Van Norman* and Hiram Capron, established iron manufacturers at Manchester (Niagara Falls, N.Y.). In 1822, with Van Norman and Capron, he became part-owner of the iron works at Normandale, Norfolk County, Upper Canada. Tillson

was described as "the principal and most experienced Engineer in the Furnace" and was credited with devising the system of flues that made the Normandale stove such a prized possession of pioneer households.

On the dissolution of the Normandale partnership in 1824, Tillson moved westward to Dereham Township. The abundance of bog iron in nearby Houghton and Middleton townships and the great stands of pine and hardwood were promising for industrial purposes, as was the water-power generated by the "rapids" in the Big Otter Creek. In 1824 Tillson "bargained" with William Warren Baldwin*, trustee for Maria Willcocks, for lots in Dereham Township containing about 600 acres of prime forest and including both banks of the Big Otter and of its confluents, Stoney and Clear creeks. Dereham was Tillson's final move. In 1829 he took the oath of allegiance.

Although the deeds for the property (which cost £300) came into Tillson's possession only in 1834, he had begun laying out his industrial complex along the Big Otter in 1825: a dam to harness the water-power, a blast furnace to refine bog ore, and a forge to produce simple iron objects. He also constructed a lock, probably to carry timber rafts past the dam. The resulting community, composed of his workmen and those of his son-in-law Benjamin Van Norman, who set up an axe factory, was first known as Dereham Forge. Tillson's qualified success in iron production forced him into an entrepreneurial role. He advanced capital, chiefly in land but also in money, to Van Norman for the axe factory and for a saw mill, and to E. W. Hyman* for a tannery, to instance only the earliest transactions. Real estate development followed. In 1837 Tillson surveyed his property and laid out streets to encourage the occupation of the high ground north of the river. A striking feature was the 100-foot width assigned to Broadway, the main street; it still imparts a pleasing spaciousness to downtown Tillsonburg, a designation in use as early as 1834 (spelled Tilsonburg, 1865–1902).

Communications absorbed much of Tillson's energy. From 1831, when he had been named commissioner of roads and bridges, he petitioned the courts of quarter sessions and later the district councils for local improvements. He desired the opening for timber rafts of the Big Otter Creek southward to Port Burwell (an unrealized dream), the construction of roads west and east to intersect the Talbot Road (these now form the highway between Aylmer and Courtland), and a road north to meet Governor's Road (which connected Woodstock and London). The western connection with the Talbot Road was undertaken in 1845 and the Ingersoll and Port Burwell Plank and Gravel Road Company was formed in 1849 to give outlets to the north and south. Tillson, his two sons, George Barker and Edwin Delevan, and his son-in-law were large stockholders in the company; as the remainder of the stock was generally held in small lots, Van Norman and the Tillsons must have enjoyed substantial influence in its direction. George Tillson secured such lucrative contracts for construction that he and his son Edwin were able to greatly enlarge their saw mills. The company also enhanced the value of real estate and its success encouraged Tillson to construct the first large-scale buildings in Tillsonburg, which he leased to timber-cutters from the United States. It was while engaged in 1864 on surveys for the road going east to Courtland that Tillson contracted the pneumonia that proved fatal. He was survived by his widow and three of his nine children.

Tillson's two sons were established mill operators during their father's lifetime. The younger, Edwin, fully developed the water potential of the Otter for grist, flour, and saw mills. The waterpower that made these industries possible declined with the clearing of Dereham's forests in the 1880s, and steam power was substituted.

Two phases of Tillson's career are obscure. The details of the preliminary agreement with Baldwin cannot be traced, but it must have been sufficiently iron-clad to allow him to build extensively before he received the deeds. Nor can the story of Tillson's arrest and trial at London during the rebellion of 1837 be substantiated. It was told many years later by his son, a boy of 12 when the incident supposedly took place; possibly Tillson was subjected to an informal interrogation.

George Tillson's career illustrates the advantages that accrued to the newcomer possessed of skill and capital. He was one of many immigrants from the United States who prompted Sir John COLBORNE to speak of "the influence of Yankeeism so prevalent about St. Thomas and along the lake shore." Membership in the then fashionable large family enabled Tillson to call upon a relative for every emergency; his nephew Harvey Tillson, the first clerk of Dereham Township, and his son-in-law Van Norman, who sat on the Brock District Council from 1842 and became in 1850 the first warden of Oxford County, were most notable. The ideal of the good citizen, carefully laying out his patrimony, was exemplified by George Tillson much as it was by his neighbour and old-time associate "King" Hiram Capron of Paris.

JOHN IRWIN COOPER

An account of a trip to Dereham Township in March 1825 by George Tillson is in the possession of Mr George Tillson, Shortsville, N.Y., and T. W. Dobbie, "Plan of the village of Tillsonburg . . . May, 1865," is in the possession of the law firm of Tillson and Tillson, Tillsonburg, Ont.

Land Registry Office (Woodstock, Ont.), J. P. Ball, "Plan of the village of Tillsonburg . . . 1 Sept. 1854" (fragment); will no.30620, will of George Tillson, 24 Jan. 1856. MTCL, William Warren Baldwin papers, Peter Lossing to W. W. Baldwin, 22 Nov. 1824. Oxford County Clerk's Office (Woodstock, Ont.), Minutes of the Municipal Council of the District of Brock, 1842–49. PAC, National Map Coll., George de Rottenburg, "Map of the principal communications in Canada West" (c. 1855–56). UWO, Norfolk County, Ont., Registrar, naturalization records, I. F. H. Baddeley, "An essay on the localities of metallic minerals in the Canadas, with some notices of their geological associations and situation . . . ," Literary and Hist. Soc. of Quebec, *Trans.*, II (1830), 332–426. Ont., Dept. of Planning and Development, *Otter valley conservation report, 1957* (Toronto, 1957). *Tillsonburg Observer* (Tillsonburg, [Ont.]), March 1864, December 1865. *The Oxford gazetteer; containing a complete history of the county of Oxford, from its first settlement; together, with a full abstract of each census . . .* , comp. T. S. Shenston (Hamilton, [Ont.], 1852). E. D. Tillson, *Record of George and Nancy Tillson's family, chronological history of the ancestry and posterity of Edwin D. Tillson of Tilsonburg . . . from A.D. 1670 to 1888* (Tillsonburg, Ont., n.d.). *Topographical and historical atlas of the county of Oxford, Ontario* (Toronto, [1876]). Craig, *Upper Canada*, 106–23. D. J. Hall, "Economic development in Elgin County, 1850–1880" (MA thesis, University of Guelph, Guelph, Ont., 1971; published, Petrolia, Ont., 1972). Fred Landon, *Western Ontario and the American frontier* (Toronto, 1941), 41–61, 170–85, 230–50; "The evolution of local government in Ontario," *OH*, XLII (1950), 1–5.

TOBIN, JOHN, merchant and politician; b. 1810 in Gowran, County Kilkenny (Republic of Ireland); m. 12 Jan. 1841 Catherine Walsh, and they had three boys and three girls; d. 9 June 1869 in Halifax, N.S.

Little is known about the early years of John Tobin's life. He was later considered to be a self-made man, and it is unlikely that he received much formal education. Immigrating to North America in the 1820s, he spent a few years in Newfoundland, and probably moved to Halifax around 1840. By the early 1850s he had established a wholesale-retail firm, John Tobin and Company, which dealt in general merchandise. His investments also came to include shares in Nova Scotian banks and trust companies.

Having reached a stage of financial stability by 1855, Tobin made a first, successful foray into politics and was elected a member of the assembly for Halifax Township. He seems to have responded to a draft from the Halifax Catholics to replace Laurence O'Connor DOYLE as the Catholic member on the Reform ticket for the Halifax constituencies. He soon became the acknowledged spokesman for the substantial Irish Catholic community in the Halifax area. He was re-elected in the two subsequent elections of 1859 and 1863. As a member of the assembly he took a keen interest in commercial affairs, usually serving on the committee dealing with trade, manufactures, and railways.

The late 1850s saw a great deal of religious and political turmoil in Nova Scotia. Joseph Howe*'s trip to the United States in the spring of 1855 to recruit soldiers for the British military effort in the Crimea was a source of community tension for the Irish Catholics in Halifax, as was the Gourley Shanty riot in May 1856, in which a group of Irish Catholic railway workers burned down the house of a Protestant worker claiming he had made disparaging remarks about the Roman Catholic Church. Howe's apparently anti-Catholic posturing during this period made the position of Tobin and other Catholics within the Reform party untenable. The climax came in February 1857, when Tobin and six other Catholic Reformers voted with the Conservatives in support of a non-confidence motion that toppled the government of William Young*. For the next three years Tobin bore the brunt of Reform attacks on the Catholic dissidents and was called upon time and again to come to the defence of his co-religionists.

In 1856 Tobin supported William Young's education bill which would have provided public support for denominational schools in Nova Scotia. He felt that such schools had for some time been a right safeguarded under the British constitution and that it was "a principle which has a foundation in nature, is inherent in the human race, and cannot be disturbed without violence to society." Unfortunately for Tobin, the bill was withdrawn when it became evident that it would have no chance of passing the assembly. Eight years later, Tobin supported amendments to Charles Tupper*'s education act ensuring that there would be separate schools for all religious denominations at public expense. When Tupper indicated his opposition to these amendments, Tobin acquiesced in his compromise solution which resulted in the creation of separate schools for Catholics in most parts of the province at public expense but placed them, along with all the other "public" schools, under one Council of Public Instruction – separate schools in practice if not by law.

Tobin's final foray into politics occurred in September 1867 when he sought election as a pro-confederation candidate in the federal constituency of Halifax. Touted as the "nominee of the Catholic people of Halifax" he loyally supported Tupper's position on confederation and campaigned actively along with Thomas L. Connolly*, the Roman Catholic archbishop of Halifax, to convince Catholics to support confederation. Despite his effort he was defeated in the anti-confederation backlash which swept Nova Scotia in the federal and provincial elections of 1867.

Tobin apparently committed suicide on 9 June 1869 after a period of emotional disturbance; the coroner's inquest, however, referred to "the accidental discharge of a rifle in his hand while he was labouring under mental aberration," and he was buried in Holy Cross Cemetery in Halifax, perhaps through the influence of his friend Archbishop Connolly.

DAVID B. FLEMMING

Halifax County Court of Probate (Halifax), no.1664, will of John Tobin (mfm. at PANS). PAC, MG 24, B29; MG 26, A; F; RG 31, 1861 census, Halifax County. PANS, RG 32, 37. N.S., House of Assembly, *Debates and proc.*, 1861, 1864, 1865, 1867. *Acadian Recorder*, 1856, 1859. *British Colonist* (Halifax), 1855. *Evening Express* (Halifax), 1858, 1867, 1869. *Morning Chronicle* (Halifax), 1869. *Novascotian*, 1841, 1853, 1855. *Directory of N.S. MLAs*. Beck, *Government of N.S.* P. R. Blakeley, *Glimpses of Halifax, 1867–1900* (Halifax, 1949). C. B. Fergusson, *The inauguration of the free school system in Nova Scotia* (PANS, *Bull.*, 21, Halifax, 1964). Nicholas Meagher, *The religious warfare in Nova Scotia, 1855–1860; its political aspect, the Honorable Joseph Howe's part in it, and the attitude of Catholics* ([Halifax, 1927]). W. L. Morton, *Critical years.*

TODD, ROBERT CLOW, artist and decorative painter; b. perhaps in 1809 at Berwick-upon-Tweed (Northumberland County, England); he was probably the son of John Todd and Alice (Alison) Clow; d. 7 May 1866 at Toronto, Canada West.

Robert Clow Todd spent his youth as a painter of arms on carriages in Edinburgh and London before immigrating to Lower Canada about 1834. He lived in Quebec City and in suburban Montmorency before moving to Toronto in 1853 where he spent the rest of his life. Todd advertised himself during his stay at Quebec as a painter of signs, carriage insignia, and ornamental work, and in Toronto as a "Banner, Herald, Sign, and Ornamental Painter." He may also have carved

Tonnancour

and gilded figures in wood. One assumes that his Toronto business was not profitable since he noted on his 1861 census return that the city was too new and too poor to support an ornamental artist.

Todd is remembered mainly for his oil paintings dating from his Quebec years. These are principally portraits of horses commissioned by local sportsmen. Some picture horses and sleighs posed with their owners before the Montmorency Falls in winter. Typical is "The ice cone, Montmorency Falls," now in the National Gallery of Canada in Ottawa. All these paintings are characterized by a vibrant linear quality and overtones reflecting an interest in genre. This same interest is found in works of such contemporaries as Cornelius Krieghoff* and James Duncan*. Other known Todd paintings give views of the Quebec lumber docks and Montmorency Falls in summer. One copy of an English print has been located. Allegedly he executed murals in at least one civic building in Toronto. Antoine-Sébastien Falardeau*, the artist, worked as an apprentice sign-painter in his shop during 1841, and Todd taught students both at the Séminaire de Québec and at Loretto Convent (Loretto Abbey) in Toronto. Todd was also interested in music.

The artist married Irish-born Mary Anne Boyle and had five sons. A grandson, Valent Ellison Todd, was a staff artist working for the Toronto *Evening Telegram* and the Montreal *Evening Star*.

J. RUSSELL HARPER

Information received from Sir John Gilmour and Mrs Mary Todd Peate. PAC, RG 31, 1861 census, Toronto, St Andrew's Ward, p.203. UTL-TF, MSS 144, March 1866. *Leader*, 24 Jan. 1854. *Quebec Gazette*, 8 Jan. 1834, 11 Jan. 1841. *Canada directory*, 1857–58. *City of Toronto illustrated business directory for 1865 . . .* (Toronto, 1865). Harper, *Early painters and engravers.* National Gallery of Can., *Catalogue of paintings and sculpture*, ed. R. H. Hubbard *et al.* (4v., Ottawa and Toronto, 1959–65), III: *Canadian school*, 313. *Quebec business directory*, 1854. H.-R. Casgrain, *A. S. Falardeau et A. E. Aubry* (Montréal, 1912), 21. Émile Falardeau, *Un maître de la peinture: Antoine-Sébastien Falardeau* (Montréal, 1936), 38–39. Gérard Morisset, *La peinture traditionnelle au Canada français* (Ottawa, 1960), 138.

TONNANCOUR, LÉONARD GODEFROY DE.
See GODEFROY

TORRANCE, JOHN, merchant, shipper, and entrepreneur; b. 8 June 1786, probably at Larkhall in Lanark County, Scotland, son of Thomas Torrance; d. 20 Jan. 1870 at Montreal.

The five brothers of the Torrance family came from the Galloway area of Scotland to the Canadas via New York shortly after 1800. Thomas* established himself as a general merchant in Montreal. John, aged 21 when he came to Montreal, was residing in Quebec City, probably as Thomas' representative, when he married Elizabeth Fisher (1794–1862), daughter of Duncan Fisher*, a Montreal merchant, at Montreal on 28 May 1811. Their marriage contract allowed her £1,000 should she outlive him, an indication that he was already prospering. They were to have 15 children, all of whom lived to adulthood; among their sons-in-law were Liverpool merchants and Alexander Tilloch Galt*.

John had returned to Montreal by 1814 and opened his own general store on Saint-Paul Street, near that of Thomas. By 1826 David Torrance*, a son of John's brother James of Kingston, had become a clerk in John's business, and in 1832 he married John's eldest daughter; they were business partners from 1833 until John retired in 1853. Their association may explain why one of John's sons, James, opened a rival firm.

John Torrance and Company dealt in a wide variety of goods, but specialized in groceries, spirits, and particularly tea. In the late 1820s, by importing tea directly from China and India, it was the first to rival the East India Company monopoly controlled by Forsyth, Richardson, and Company. From their own bonded warehouse the Torrances supplied and made loans to Upper Canadian merchants such as Jacob Keefer*. Communications being of the greatest importance to their business, they developed the Montreal and Quebec Steamboat Company, which first competed with and afterwards became allied with the Molson interests. With the exception of the Molsons, the Torrances probably did more than any other group to establish the St Lawrence steamboat services [*see* David Torrance*].

The Torrances were equally interested in railway development. As early as 1832 they were among the incorporators of the Champlain and St Lawrence Railroad. By 1847 their firm had invested £1,000 in the St Lawrence and Atlantic Railroad, a scheme promoted by John Alfred Poor* to link Montreal with the year-round port of Portland, Maine. John was a director from 1847 until the line became the Portland division of the Grand Trunk Railway in 1853. The president was Galt, and the directors included William Molson*, who was closely associated in John's other railway speculations. These involved a complex chain of railway incorporations to link

Montreal with its western hinterland and New York State. In 1846 Torrance was an incorporator of the Montreal and Lachine Railroad Company, of which he was later a director; when it became part of the Montreal and New York Railroad Company in 1850, Torrance had £500 invested and was again a director. He was also a director of the St Lawrence and Ottawa Grand Junction Railroad Company, chartered in 1850, to extend the Montreal and Lachine to Prescott, Canada West. Torrance developed close connections with American entrepreneurs, including Poor and Commodore Cornelius Vanderbilt of New York; in 1846 John's son Daniel married the commodore's daughter and later became vice-president of Vanderbilt's New York Central Railway.

John Torrance's financial activities complemented his commercial interests. He was a stockholder in the short-lived Bank of Canada in Montreal, and was elected a director of the Bank of Montreal in 1826, after the death of his brother Thomas, one of the early directors. John retired in 1857.

Through the 1840s John was a director of the Montreal Provident and Savings Bank (established 1841) and at one time had £2,000 invested in the City Bank. Insurance connections were also necessary to his shiping interests. From its establishment in 1840, until at least 1854, he was a director of the Montreal Fire, Life, and Inland Navigation Assurance Company, of which James Ferrier* was president and William Dow another director. By the 1850s Torrance was the Montreal director for the Equitable Fire Insurance Company of London, England. He further invested in a variety of land speculations and mortgages.

Although interested in political movements only as they affected commerce, Torrance was active in the development of Montreal. A founder of the Committee of Trade in 1822 and a petitioner for municipal incorporation in 1828, he was one of the first elected city councillors in 1833. Like most Montreal businessmen he joined the city's militia, being commissioned lieutenant in 1821, captain in 1830, and major in 1845. His most important foray into national politics came in 1849, when his was the first of the initial 325 signatures to the Annexation Manifesto, protesting against Britain's free trade and policies on responsible government. Torrance was elected one of the vice-presidents of the Montreal Annexation Association. The movement soon died but because of it Torrance was dismissed from the militia in January 1850.

Originally a member of the St Gabriel Street Presbyterian Church, Torrance, like his nephew David, became a Methodist and a strong supporter of St James Street Methodist Church, and assisted Dorchester Street Church in 1864. A supporter of various literary and educational associations, he was a life governor of the Montreal General Hospital and a founder and trustee of the Mount Royal Cemetery. He made gifts to McGill University including a fund for a gold medal in law as a memorial to his wife. His son Judge Frederick William Torrance was closely connected with this institution. John Torrance's hobby was gardening, and he was an incorporator of the Horticultural Society of Montreal in 1849. His 42-room mansion on then fashionable Saint-Antoine Street was renowned for its acres of gardens, greenhouses, vineries, and orchards. The estate was also famous for its high brick walls and great gate which according to family tradition closed firmly at 10 p.m.

When John Torrance died, he was not only a patriarch of Montreal, but also, as the *Gazette* commented, "one of our wealthiest citizens." His fortune was divided among his many children and his business was ably carried on by David, whose career closely paralleled his own. Today Torrance and his family are virtually forgotten. They were not active in politics, except for Galt, nor did they leave their name to surviving corporations or endowed institutions, as did the Molsons and the Redpaths. Yet the role played by John, his brother Thomas, and his nephew David in the evolution of what Donald Grant Creighton has called the "commercial empire of the St. Lawrence" was important. John Torrance may have chosen the right location and come at the right time, but his industry, astuteness, and intelligence did much to build up his city as well as his own fortune.

FREDERICK H. ARMSTRONG

ANQ-M, État civil, Presbytériens, St Gabriel, 28 May 1811; Testaments, Testaments olographes, John Torrance, 26 July 1861. PAC, MG 27, I, D8, 9, marriage contract of John Torrance and Elizabeth Fisher, 28 May 1811; RG 9, I, A3, 12, p.2316; C4, 5, p.126. Can., Prov. of, *Statutes*, 1846, c.82; 1847, c.67; 1849, c.153. L.C., *Statutes*, 1832, c.58. *Gazette* (Montreal), 20, 21 Jan. 1870. *Montreal Herald*, 15 Oct. 1849, 21 Jan. 1870. *Montreal Witness*, 11 March 1862, 20 Jan. 1870, 31 Jan. 1876. *Quebec Gazette*, 24 May 1821. *Alphabetical list of merchants, traders, and housekeepers in Montreal* (Doige). *Montreal directory*, 1842–67.

Atherton, *Montreal*, II, 531, 574, 577. Campbell, *History of Scotch Presbyterian Church*, 72–75, 313–16. James Croil, *Steam navigation in Canada and its relation to the commerce of Canada and the United States* (Toronto, 1898), 308–9, 313–15. Merrill Denison, *The*

Truillier

barley and the stream; the Molson story; a footnote to Canadian history (Toronto, 1955), 90, 92, 95, 148, 152, 159; *Canada's first bank*, I, 144, 228–29, 232–34, 243, 293; II, 30, 577. Rumilly, *Hist. de Montréal*, II, 152, 191, 277, 328. E. C. Springett, *For my children's children* (Montreal, 1937), 10–13.

TRUILLIER, *dit* **LACOMBE, PATRICE.** *See* LACOMBE

TUCKER, RICHARD ALEXANDER, lawyer, judge, and office-holder; b. 1784 in Bermuda, the son of Henry Tucker, president of the Council of Bermuda, and Frances Bruere, daughter of that island's governor; m. his cousin, Mary Todd Bruere, and they had two sons and two daughters; d. 11 Dec. 1868 at Clapton, Middlesex, England.

After schooling in Bermuda, Richard Alexander Tucker enrolled on 20 Oct. 1802 at Jesus College, Cambridge, and, beginning 16 July 1802, studied law at the Inner Temple. Upon receiving his MA in 1818 he joined the imperial service and was for a period deputy paymaster-general of British forces in British North America.

On 1 Oct. 1822 Tucker was appointed chief justice of Newfoundland and served as the sole judge in the colony until 1825, when imperial legislation established the Supreme Court of Newfoundland, adding two assistant judges. On 2 Jan. 1826 the new court opened with John William Molloy and Augustus Wallet DesBarres as assistants. Thereafter Tucker presided as chief justice of the court, as president of the Council, and as administrator of the colony in the governor's absence; he filled this latter role from October 1827 to August 1828 and during the winter of 1831–32.

Tucker bitterly and publicly opposed the granting of representative government to Newfoundland in 1832 and after its inauguration attempted, through his position in the Council, to destroy it by denying the assembly the power to raise revenues. The colony's first revenue bill of January 1833 sought to impose a tax upon wine and spirits. After the bill had passed the assembly, Tucker opposed it in the Council on the grounds that a colony had not the legal power to tax an item that was already taxed by the imperial government, and that even if such a power existed the assembly had no moral right to impose taxes upon people who could not afford to pay them. In short, it was Tucker's position that the Newfoundland people should admit that the new form of government "had been foolishly requested and unfortunately granted" and that they should throw themselves upon the mercy of the imperial government for support and sustenance.

Tucker was able to persuade the attorney general, James SIMMS, to vote with him and thus prevented passage of the bill through the four-member Council where a three-fourths majority was necessary. This obstructive action incensed Governor Thomas John Cochrane*, but even when James Stephen, legal adviser to the Colonial Office, overruled the chief justice, Tucker remained adamant in his stand. As an expedient, he suggested that he go on leave and allow the bill to be passed in his absence; he threatened, however, that if a test case subsequently came before him on the bench he would declare the law to be *ultra vires*. This solution was clearly unacceptable to Cochrane. Declaring his "unalterable purpose never to return to my office of Chief Justice . . . if it shall appear to His Majesty's Government that the grounds upon which I opposed the bill did not abundantly justify me in doing so," Tucker sailed for England in March 1833. Nor did he return to Newfoundland, for the British colonial secretary accepted his resignation.

After a brief residence in New York City, Tucker moved with his family to Kingston, Upper Canada, where in 1838 Lieutenant Governor Sir George Arthur* learned that he was living in obscurity and poverty. When approached about an appointment in the colony Tucker was still "resolved never to solicit office or accept it unless not only my conduct while in office [in Newfoundland] but also my propriety in leaving it" were recognized. Tucker had refused several lucrative legal offices in India offered him through the influence of his eldest brother who was in the East India Company. Arthur learned from Lord Glenelg in July 1838 that the "difficulty" of "some scruple of punctilious honor" was now removed as far as Tucker was concerned and the British government was favourable to an appointment for Tucker.

From 1 Oct. 1838 until the creation of the united province in February 1841 Tucker was provincial secretary of Upper Canada. In that office he supervised the recording, filing, and copying of many of the formal documents of government and reported provincial statistics. His experience of administration in Newfoundland contributed to the reorganization and enlarging of the provincial secretary's responsibilities. He also served as registrar of Upper Canada with duties complementing those of provincial secretary; he was appointed a member of the Heir and Devisee Commission, a commissioner of the peace in the Western, Brock, and Johnstown districts, and in 1839 a commissioner to inquire into the state of government departments. He was appointed registrar of the Province of Canada in 1841 and continued in that office till his retirement in January 1851, when he probably returned to England.

Though he held office, Tucker from 1838 took little part in official and political society. He felt that Lord Sydenham [Thomson*] had "left an almost impracticable system of Government to his successor." A devoted member of the Church of England, he maintained his Tory criticisms of responsible government and of French Canadian and Reform participation in the government of the union.

LESLIE HARRIS and P. G. CORNELL

National Library of Scotland (Edinburgh), MSS 2568–608 (Cochrane papers) (copies at PANL). PAC, RG 68, 1, General index, 1651–1841; 1841–67. PANL, GN 1/2, 1832–41. PAO, Macaulay (John) papers, R. A. Tucker to J. Macaulay, 28 March 1846, 15 Feb. 1847. PRO, CO 194/85–86. *Arthur papers* (Sanderson). Nfld., House of Assembly, *Journal*, 1833; Legislative Council, *Journals*, 1833. *Newfoundlander*, 1832–33. *Public Ledger*, 1832–33. *Royal Gazette* (St John's), 1832–33. *Alumni Cantabrigienses . . .* , comp. John and J. A. Venn (2 pts. in 10 v., Cambridge, 1922–54), pt.II, VI, 240. Armstrong, *Handbook of Upper Canadian chronology*. H. C. Wilkinson, *Bermuda from sail to steam; the history of the island from 1784 to 1901* (2v., London, 1973), I, 178–79; II, 444, 518–20.

TURCOTTE, JOSEPH-ÉDOUARD, lawyer, politician, and entrepreneur; b. 10 Oct. 1808 at Gentilly, Lower Canada, son of Joseph Turcot, a merchant, and Marguerite Marchildon; d. 20 Dec. 1864 at Trois-Rivières, Canada East.

Four Turcot (or Turcault) families were established in Canada. Abel Turcot, Joseph-Édouard's ancestor, was a native of Mouilleron-en-Pareds, in Vendée. He immigrated to Château-Richer, then settled at Sainte-Famille, on Île d'Orléans. Augustin Turcot, Joseph-Édouard's grandfather, lived at Trois-Rivières, and his son Joseph set up as a merchant at Gentilly, where he raised a large family.

Joseph-Édouard pursued his classical studies at the Séminaire de Nicolet from 1821 to 1829, then decided in favour of the priesthood. In 1831 he lost his right arm in an accident. This loss coincided with a change in his career, but no document permits us to establish a relationship of cause and effect between the two events. He turned to the legal profession and entered the office of Elzéar Bédard* at Quebec. Turcotte became involved in the political agitation of the day, writing liberal and revolutionary pieces inspired by the French *philosophes* and liberals. Then he joined the supporters of Louis-Joseph Papineau* and became a radical Patriote. As such, he attempted in the Nicolet by-election in the spring of 1835 to inherit the support given to the Patriote Louis Bourdages* but was defeated by Major Jean-Baptiste Hébert, an influential farmer in the Nicolet area. Called to the bar on 6 May 1836, Joseph-Édouard Turcotte practised his profession at Quebec and pursued his Patriote activities. In the June 1837 election he used his influence to assist Michael Connolly, candidate for the lower town of Quebec against John Munn*, and he joined the Comité permanent de Québec which was constituted in September of that year. He was left free at the time of the arrests in November 1837 and November 1838, and through speeches continued to serve the Patriote cause. He obtained from Judge Joseph-Rémi Vallières* de Saint-Réal a writ of habeas corpus for, among others, Célestin Houde, a farmer from Rivière-du-Loup (Louiseville), accused of seditious activities; despite the suspension of this right in Lower Canada [*see* Jean-Roch ROLLAND], Vallières was continuing to grant it. Like Augustin-Norbert MORIN, Louis-Hippolyte LA FONTAINE, and George-Étienne Cartier*, Turcotte thus distinguished himself as a Patriote, a fact not previously made known in Canadian historical studies.

Without abandoning the practice of law, Turcotte from now on devoted the greater part of his energies to politics. Having moved to Trois-Rivières in 1839, he stood as an anti-unionist candidate in Saint-Maurice in April 1841, and defeated the redoutable Colonel Bartholomew Conrad Augustus Gugy*. His political conduct, however, brought strong opposition. Because Turcotte had accepted two paid governmental posts, translator of laws in December 1841 and secretary of the commission on seigneurial tenure in April 1842 [*see* Joseph-André TASCHEREAU], he was the object of a campaign to force him to give up his seat in the Legislative Assembly. But the electors themselves were called upon to settle the question, and they re-elected him in July 1842. At that time political parties were only in the process of formation, and a great deal of freedom was left to representatives when votes were taken in the assembly. Turcotte, first known as a Reformer, associated himself temporarily with the Tories from both sections of the province in support of Governor Charles Theophilus Metcalfe* against the Executive Council in December 1843. This vote, for which he was later to be fiercely reproached, did not prevent him from campaigning as a Reformer in October 1844 and assisting other candidates who supported La Fontaine. According to *Le*

Turcotte

Canadien, his defeat in Saint-Maurice was occasioned not by his betrayal but by the fact that his supporters believed they had been neglected.

In the autumn of 1847 Turcotte caused another outcry. His sympathies went at first to the *éteignoirs* [*see* Jean-Baptiste Meilleur*] in their opposition to the school tax, then in December he accepted the post of solicitor general in the ministry of Henry Sherwood*. Once again he was charged with opportunism, and was called the "tool" of governors Sydenham [Thomson*], Bagot*, and Metcalfe, and of Dominick DALY. In the elections that followed he was defeated by Louis GUILLET in Champlain and by Louis-Joseph Papineau in Saint-Maurice, so that he was obliged to resign as solicitor general in March 1848. But Turcotte returned to the assembly in 1851 as member for Saint-Maurice, despite the persistent attacks of *La Minerve* and the *Journal de Québec*. During his two subsequent terms he made his greatest mark as a parliamentarian. He gave impassioned and eloquent speeches in the great debates of the day: the financing of schools, the abolition of seigneurial tenure, the choice before the government for a north shore railway in Quebec and the provincial guaranty required. From this time on he was identified with the Bleu party, although he sometimes opposed it in the house.

While pursuing a parliamentary career, Turcotte also engaged his energies and his capital in the development of the town and region of Trois-Rivières. He was mayor of Trois-Rivières from 1857 to 1863. The operation of the Radnor ironworks in the parish of Saint-Maurice, the building of a huge hotel at Shawinigan Falls, the founding of the Collège de Trois-Rivières in 1860, the extension of the town wharf, the promotion and construction of a branch line of the Grand Trunk linking Arthabaska to Trois-Rivières, the project of a railway branch line between Grandes-Piles and Trois-Rivières: these are some of the achievements that cost him his fortune and health, although they won him fame in the Trois-Rivières region. From 1847 to 1853 he was also owner and editor of the *Journal des Trois-Rivières*.

Turcotte was praised by most people for his enterprising spirit, and he was applauded universally for his talents as a speaker. He has been compared to Danton; Benjamin Sulte* dubbed him a Mirabeau. "Although a plain member," Sulte said, "he was listened to as if he were a minister." In fact, he enjoyed more prestige than many politicians of that period: he was asked at least twice to hold a portfolio, first in April 1847 when the government considered assigning three portfolios to Lower Canadian members [*see* Caron*; Draper*], and in March 1864 when Étienne-Paschal TACHÉ tried to form a coalition cabinet. In the 1850s, after the successive resignations of Robert Baldwin*, La Fontaine, and Morin, Turcotte stood out as a veteran mainstay of the Lower Canadian group in parliament. From March 1862 to May 1863 he held the position of speaker of the Legislative Assembly of United Canada. He died at Trois-Rivières on 20 Dec. 1864.

On 15 Nov. 1842 Joseph-Édouard Turcotte had married Flore Buteau, daughter of François Buteau of Quebec. Six daughters and four boys were born of their marriage; one son, Henri-René-Arthur, was to represent Trois-Rivières in the provincial parliament, and another, Gustave-Adolphe-Narcisse, represented Nicolet in the House of Commons.

LOUISETTE POTHIER

AAQ, 12A, K, 99. AJTR, Cour du banc de la reine, 1838–39. ANQ-Q, État civil, Catholiques, Notre-Dame de Québec, 15 nov. 1842. ANQ-TR, État civil, Catholiques, Immaculée-Conception (Trois-Rivières), 23 déc. 1864. Archives de la ville de Trois-Rivières, Registres des délibérations du conseil, 6 sept., 3 nov. 1858; 8 juin, 9 sept. 1859. Archives judiciaires, Nicolet (Nicolet, Qué.), Registre d'état civil, Saint-Édouard (Gentilly), 1808. ASQ, Polygraphie, XXXVIII, 16f. ASTR, Archives du séminaire, M 1, F53; Trifluviens du 19ᵉ et du 20ᵉ siècle, C 3, M80A. Private archives, Mme Camille Marchildon-Carette (Trois-Rivières), généalogie des Turcotte. *Le Canadien*, 11 juill. 1834, 1ᵉʳ, 6 avril 1835, 28 juin 1837, 20 déc. 1841, janv.–août 1842. *Le Courrier du Canada*, 28, 30 déc. 1864. *L'Écho du cabinet de lecture paroissial*, 1ᵉʳ janv. 1865. *L'Écho du St-Maurice* (Trois-Rivières), 27 août, 22 oct. 1858. *L'Ère nouvelle* (Trois-Rivières), 1ᵉʳ mars, 11 oct. 1854, 30 août 1858. *Le Journal de Québec*, 26 oct. 1844, 22 déc. 1864. *Journal des Trois-Rivières*, 1847–1853. *Le Libéral* (Québec), 19 sept. 1837. *La Minerve*, 30 déc. 1833; 26 mai, 24 juill., 20 oct. 1834; 12 févr. 1835; 4 avril 1836; 8, 15 nov. 1847. *L'Opinion publique*, 11 déc. 1873. *Quebec Gazette*, 26 March 1835, 4 May 1842. *La Voix du peuple* (Québec), 20 janv. 1852.

F.-J. Audet, *Les députés de la région des Trois-Rivières (1841–1867)* (Trois-Rivières, 1934), 26–41. Fauteux, *Patriotes*, 269. *Political appointments, 1841–65* (J.-O. Coté), 5. Chapais, *Hist. du Canada*, VI, 11–13. Cornell, *Alignment of political groups*, 15–17, 39, 66, 68, 88. J.-A.-I. Douville, *Histoire du collège-séminaire de Nicolet, 1803–1903, avec les listes complètes des directeurs, professeurs et élèves de l'institution* (2v., Montréal, 1903), II, 23, 141. Antoine Gérin-Lajoie, *Dix ans au Canada de 1840 à 1850: histoire de l'établissement du gouvernement responsable* (Québec, 1888), 414–15, 469. Louisette Pothier, "Joseph-Édouard Turcotte; ses débuts politiques (1808–1840)" (thèse de MA, université de Sherbrooke,

Sherbrooke, Qué., 1973). *Le répertoire national, ou recueil de littérature canadienne*, James Huston, édit. (4v., Montréal, 1848–50), I, 239, 241–330, 342. Louis Richard, *Histoire du collège des Trois-Rivières; première période, de 1860 à 1874* (Trois-Rivières, 1885), app., 103–4. Benjamin Sulte, "Trois-Rivières d'autrefois," *Mélanges historiques*, Gérard Malchelosse, édit. (21v., Montréal, 1918–34), XX, 54. Albert Tessier, "Un chemin montant, malaisé . . . ," *Cahiers des Dix*, 20 (1955), 115.

TURGEON, PIERRE-FLAVIEN, priest, educator, archbishop; b. 12 Nov. 1787 at Quebec, son of Louis Turgeon, a merchant, and his second wife, Louise-Élisabeth Dumont; d. 25 Aug. 1867 in the same city.

Pierre-Flavien Turgeon belonged to the sixth generation of a family from the department of Perche whose ancestor settled at Beauport, near Quebec, in the summer of 1662. His half-brother, Louis Turgeon, who was the first of three descendants to sit on the Legislative Council, acted as his guardian after his father's death in 1800. Pierre-Flavien had been admitted into the Séminaire de Québec the preceding year. As a youth he attracted attention by his unusual intellectual and moral precociousness. In 1806, before his year of rhetoric was completed, Joseph-Octave Plessis*, who had become bishop of Quebec in January, noticed him and appointed him his secretary. While acting in this capacity Turgeon was obliged to take philosophy and to pursue the regular ecclesiastical studies before being ordained a priest on 29 April 1810, the age limit having been waived. The Séminaire de Québec claimed his services, although he did not give up his post as the bishop's close assistant in the administration of the diocese.

At the Séminaire de Québec, where he was to stay for 22 years, Turgeon soon undertook various duties. He was fully qualified to teach by the autumn of 1811, professor of philosophy (1812–15), director of the Grand Séminaire (1815–18) and of the Petit Séminaire (1820–24). His intellectual capacity, special gift in psychology, and never-failing kindness made him a master revered by his pupils and a counsellor valued by many ecclesiastics. In the conduct of diocesan affairs he enjoyed the bishop's complete confidence. Between these two very different men a friendship was created that death alone would sever. Bishop Plessis clearly was preparing Turgeon to succeed him. The intense activity Turgeon was involved in proved too exacting, however, and illness, from which he was to suffer all his life, forced him to take periods of rest. Acting on this need he accompanied Bishop Plessis to Europe in 1819, his only voyage overseas. In the summer of 1822 he went to the diocese of Boston for another rest cure. His health did not permit him to resume teaching, and he was appointed bursar of the Séminaire de Québec in 1824. During his nine years of management, he inaugurated administrative reforms that improved the temporal affairs of the seminary which had been in a precarious state since the Conquest.

In 1825 Bishop Plessis was preparing to call Turgeon to the episcopate, to succeed Bishop Bernard-Claude Panet*, who wanted to give up the office of coadjutor because of his advanced age. But Plessis died before he did so. Turgeon was barely 38. Panet, who had become titular bishop, urged him to accept the mitre, reinforcing his request with a laudatory letter from the governor, Lord Dalhousie [Ramsay*]. From the Hôpital Général where he was confined by illness, Turgeon firmly declined in favour of Joseph Signay*, parish priest of Quebec. His action saddened his friend and travelling companion in Europe, Bishop Jean-Jacques Lartigue*, who at that time was assistant to the bishop of Quebec in the district of Montreal.

When Bishop Panet died in 1833, Turgeon could not continue to resist the pleas of the clergy. Signay, the new bishop, succeeded in having him elected as coadjutor and the election recognized by the civil government early in 1833 in spite of the insidious opposition at Rome of the Séminaire de Montréal. The French faction of the latter was trying to obtain the appointment of bishops who were firm supporters of their cause, favourable to recruiting French personnel, and prepared to negotiate with the government to obtain compensation for the Sulpicians' seigneurial rights. As a result of this faction's intrigues in Rome, Jean-Baptiste SAINT-GERMAIN, a great friend of the Sulpicians and parish priest of Saint-Laurent near Montreal, was selected by the Propaganda to be Bishop Signay's coadjutor. But as Pope Gregory XVI delayed approving this choice, Bishop Signay sent Abbé Thomas Maguire* from Quebec to offset the influence of the Sulpician Jean-Baptiste Thavenet* at Rome; Thavenet had described Turgeon as a personal enemy of the Sulpicians, and maintained that he had not been approved by Rome but had been appointed coadjutor by the governor. Maguire's mission secured the appointment of Turgeon. Gregory XVI in the end decided in his favour, and by a brief dated 28 Feb. 1834 appointed him bishop *in partibus* of Sidyme and coadjutor to Bishop Signay, with right of succession. Bishop Signay had already announced his election as coadjutor on 25 Feb. 1833 in his pastoral letter of installation. This move had been thought ill timed by Bishop Lartigue, who did not know that, in accordance with directives from Rome concerning the method of election of bishops, Turgeon had been recognized as early as 1829 as one of three priests worthy of elevation to the episcopate. Because of this action, which had been kept secret out of fear of antagonizing a Protestant government, Turgeon was actually the first Canadian bishop whose selection was approved by Rome and then by the civil government.

On 11 June 1834 Pierre-Flavien Turgeon received episcopal consecration from Bishop Signay, assisted by Bishop Lartigue and Bishop Rémi Gaulin*, coadjutor to the bishop of Kingston. Bishop Turgeon began his duties when the diocese of Quebec was struggling to recover from the confusion that followed the unexpected death of Bishop Plessis. During the 16 years of authority shared with Bishop Signay, he worked with fervour and zeal to consolidate the work Bishop Plessis had begun for the maintenenance of the faith and the advancement of the church. He gave of himself unsparingly, despite the illnesses that were to put a premature end to his career.

Bishop Turgeon was responsible for directing religious communities, particularly the Ursulines of which he was the ecclesiastical superior for 19 years; he also was entrusted with much of the temporal administration of the church: the incorporation of parishes, building and repair of churches, and work with the government on legislation relating to religious matters. He won his case with the Propaganda in 1844 in the dispute concerning the accounts for the income of religious communities in Canada which Thavenet had rendered. He was conscious of the role of the church in public life and believed it should intervene in the solution of any problems facing the country where, in his view, the interests of religion were at stake. Thus in February 1838, in a petition he had the clergy sign, which was presented to the imperial parliament, he emphatically objected to the projected union of the two Canadas and asked that the constitution of 1791 be maintained. When the anti-union movement was organized at Quebec in January 1840, under the presidency of John Neilson* [see René-Édouard Caron*], he jcined the clergy in signing a new petition, and personally canvassed for money to meet the expenses incurred in London by Vital Têtu, the bearer of the citizens' address.

The bishop made the spiritual renewal of the diocese the cornerstone of his work as an apostle. He played a large part in establishing pastoral retreats and developing popular retreats by bringing Bishop Charles-Auguste-Marie-Joseph de Forbin-Janson* to Quebec in 1840. In his determined struggle against intemperance, he applied himself to promoting campaigns in the diocese and temperance associations in each parish. In 1844, following his pastoral visits to the missions in the Gulf of St Lawrence, the Oblates of Mary Immaculate were brought into the diocese, to assume responsibility for preaching the gospel in the Saguenay missions and at the king's posts as far as Labrador. In 1849, to assist the clergy of the episcopal city, he obtained permission for the Jesuits to return to Quebec.

Bishop Turgeon was primarily a priest devoted to social causes. Throughout his whole career he took an interest in education. For many years he was special procurator and member of the corporations of the Séminaire de Nicolet and the Collège de Sainte-Anne-de-la-Pocatière in order to place these educational establishments on a sound footing. He supported the parish council schools, and in 1842, through Bishop Forbin-Janson, he introduced the Brothers of the Christian Schools into the diocese. He actively assisted Bishop Signay in setting up the Ladies of the Congregation of Notre-Dame in the *faubourg* Saint-Roch at Quebec [*see* Marie-Louise DORVAL]. He urged that the income from the Jesuit estates be devoted to the work of Catholic education and strenuously fought the system of non-denominational education proposed by Lord Durham [Lambton*] and defined by Arthur William BULLER. Impelled by both religious and patriotic motives, he strongly favoured encouraging colonization, and for a time (from August 1848) was president of an association in the district of Quebec which encouraged settlement in the Eastern Townships. His pastoral letter of 11 Aug. 1848 earnestly recommended this work to the clergy as the most effective means of curbing emigration to the towns and to the United States.

His concern for the poor and underprivileged was so great that he rightly acquired the reputation of being an apostle of charity. After the cholera epidemics in 1832 and 1834, Quebec was laid waste by two conflagrations that levelled the *faubourgs* Saint-Roch and Saint-Jean. In 1847 typhus brought heavy casualties, then a new cholera epidemic struck in 1849. The bishop spared neither energy nor money in the effort to meet the immense needs of the destitute and the orphans. His urgent appeals for charity never went unheeded. He was anxious also to provide the diocese with charitable organizations. Thus he supported in 1846 the timely initiative of Dr Joseph Painchaud*, founder of the Society of Saint-Vincent-de-Paul. He also helped to establish two religious communities. In 1849 he recruited the Sisters of Charity of the Hôpital Général de Montréal, who under the direction of Sister Marie-Anne-Marcelle Mallet* came to open a house for the care of orphans and the education of poor children. In 1850, with the assistance of Marie Fisbach*, he founded the Asile du Bon-Pasteur for the moral reformation of young girls.

When he had agreed to be coadjutor to Bishop Signay, Turgeon had taken on a post requiring tact. As assistant to a zealous but autocratic and aloof bishop, who through excessive prudence resisted both innovations and easy sharing of responsibilities, Bishop Turgeon managed to control numerous vexatious situations in the immediate *entourage* of the head of the diocese. Since his concern for preserving the bonds of solidarity between the local churches was well known, Bishop Lartigue and Bishop Ignace Bourget* left to him the task of pleading their case before Bishop Signay. By his patience he was instrumental in protecting unity in church government in a period when the district of Montreal was at the height of its development and relations between the heads of the two dioceses were often strained. It was largely his courageous intervention that brought to a successful conclusion in 1844 a long debated project, the establishment of the first ecclesiastical province with a metropolitan see at Quebec. Bishop Signay had long been opposed, alleging among other reasons that without a bishop's palace he would not have a place in which to assemble the suffragans. Bishop Turgeon volunteered to assume all responsibility for building a palace, and urged his superior to seek incorporation of the bishopric of Quebec; this was granted in January 1845. Construction, which was begun in the spring of 1844 following the plans of the architect Thomas Baillairgé*, was interrupted by the 1845 fire at Quebec and by lack of resources. In November 1847, however, the edifice, which still stands, was finally ready for inauguration; Bishop Turgeon had himself directed its construction.

In the autumn of 1846, Bishop Bourget went to Rome to ask for the resignation of Bishop Signay, who in his opinion had totally failed to take up the duties of a metropolitan. Bishop Turgeon thought he could discern in the sharp reactions of Bishop Signay a suspicion of intrigue, which dismayed him so much that he sent a telegram to Bishop Bourget, urging him to ask Rome to accept his own resignation as coadjutor. There were no results from Bishop Bourget's agitation.

On 10 Nov. 1849 Bishop Signay, increasingly in ill health, entrusted the administration of the archdiocese to his coadjutor, who was then 61. An essential difference between Bishop Turgeon's approach and the archbishop's quickly became apparent. The ecclesiastical province had existed for five years, and Turgeon was too devoted to the interests of the church in Canada to postpone further bringing the suffragans together. Although he was only an administrator he obtained authorization from Rome to convoke the first provincial council to be held in Canada. To spare Bishop Signay's feelings, he presided over a preliminary assembly of bishops at Montreal, which fixed 15 Aug. 1851 as the opening date of the council. But on 3 Oct. 1850 Bishop Signay died. Five days later Bishop Turgeon assumed the authority of the metropolitan see of Quebec. He obtained as his coadjutor Charles-François BAILLARGEON, then agent for the bishops of the ecclesiastical province of Quebec in Rome. After the first provincial council, which marked an important stage in the organization of the church in Canada, Bishop Turgeon called a second council in 1854.

Bishop Turgeon's name has remained closely linked with the founding of Université Laval, in which he played a decisive part. His predecessors and Bishop Bourget had wanted to found a Catholic university earlier, and the aim had been expressed at the first provincial council. The negotiations initiated by Bishop Turgeon at the end of 1851 with the Séminaire de Québec and Bishop Bourget were brought to a successful conclusion with remarkable dispatch. In its plan Montreal proposed a provincial university under the jurisdiction of the bishops; Turgeon countered with the more realistic project of a diocesan university under the authority of the archbishop of Quebec, with affiliation open to the other colleges of the ecclesiastical province. His plan was accepted. Bishop Bourget advocated only papal recognition of the establishment, but Turgeon had already secured civil recognition in the summer of 1852 [see Louis-Jacques CASAULT]. The archbishop's pastoral letter announcing the creation of Université Laval shows the fundamental importance he attributed to this undertaking, and the lofty conception he had of classical and university studies.

Turgeon's career as an archbishop lasted barely five years, but the stimulus he was able to give to his diocese made it significant. In order to reorganize the upper level of the administration, he created a special council of seven members and a general council of 13, displaying by the thrust of these structures of consultation and coordination an unprecedented example of collegiality in the church in Canada. The formation of the dioceses of Trois-Rivières and Saint-Hyacinthe in 1852 apparently lightened his pastoral task, but the rapid growth of the population and the attachment of the Labrador coast to Quebec in February 1853 added to his cares. As well as the six vicars general already in office, he was able to add two excellent men to his staff: Charles-Félix Cazeau*, his vicar general, and Jean-Baptiste-Antoine FERLAND.

In addition to ensuring that regular pastoral visits were conducted, Bishop Turgeon created ten new parishes and founded several missions. He continued also to promote charitable works and gave particular attention to the spiritual renewal of his clergy, by maintaining pastoral retreats and re-establishing ecclesiastical conferences. The archbishop carried out enlightened revision of theological studies and the training of ecclesiastics, and for the first time in the Canadian church he sent priests to Rome and Paris to pursue advanced studies. He promulgated and immediately put into effect the prescriptions of the provincial councils, chiefly its decrees concerning discipline, the catechism, and ritual.

His written work includes pastoral letters and instructions that reveal the extent of his doctrinal and pastoral concerns. It also contains notes, never published, evaluating Bishop Plessis. He drew up these notes in October 1849, at the request of Édouard-Gabriel Plante, the vicar at Quebec, apparently to end slander circulating about the bishop. The document provides a portrayal of the personality of Bishop Plessis unmatched anywhere, and makes one regret that Turgeon, at the death of the archbishop, declined the invitation of his friend Jacques Viger* to draft a biographical notice for *La Bibliothèque canadienne*.

At the time when Bishop Turgeon was exerting himself to the utmost, illness and exhaustion prevailed over his aptitude for hard work and his extraordinary apostolic spirit. On 19 Feb. 1855 he suffered an attack of hemiplegia. As the disease proved incurable, he handed over the administration of the diocese to his coadjutor, Bishop Baillargeon, on 11 April. He lived some 12 years longer, partly deprived of the faculty of speech. He died on 25 Aug. 1867.

Tall, with an expressive face, Bishop Turgeon was remembered as a remarkable man who, "by his keen intelligence, his affable behaviour, his gentle and likeable character, had won the esteem even of those who did not share his beliefs." Those who knew him regretted, with Bishop Lartigue, that he had not accepted the episcopate immediately after the death of Bishop Plessis in 1825 so that he could have presided over the destinies of the church in Canada at the time when, after gaining her autonomy, she was entering a decisive phase of expansion and development. In his pastoral letter of 18 Dec. 1843 to his diocesans, Bishop Turgeon proudly stressed their zeal for "the relief of suffering humanity, [and] the furtherance of religion and education in this country." These words sum up both his ideal of ministry and the most outstanding achievements of his episcopate.

ARMAND GAGNÉ

[The most important of Bishop Turgeon's papers are preserved in the AAQ. A partial inventory for the period 1833–40 was published in the ANQ *Rapport*, 1936–37, 1937–38, 1938–39. For the years 1833–50, the ACAM holds more than 375 of Turgeon's letters; a small number of copies are in the AAQ. In addition to the Verreau and Université Laval collections, the ASQ holds numerous documents relating to Turgeon. The Canadian material in the Archives de la Compagnie de Saint-Sulpice in Paris, which was inventoried in ANQ *Rapport*, 1969, contains interesting information.

There are only short biographical sketches of Bishop Turgeon; among the least imperfect is the one by Mgr Henri Têtu* in his *Notices biographiques: les évêques de Québec* (Québec, 1889), 583–616, and the opuscule *Souvenir consacré à la mémoire vénérée de Mgr P.-F. Turgeon, archevêque de Québec et premier visiteur de l'université Laval* (Québec, 1867), which contains the prelate's funeral eulogy by Abbé Benjamin Paquet* and a biographical notice by Abbé Cyrille-Étienne Légaré. For the period 1833–44, Lucien Lemieux's study, *L'établissement de la première prov. eccl.*, 299–402, is useful. This work, one of the first in Canadian Catholic history to be based on a parallel examination of both European and Canadian archives, gives a good outline of Turgeon's activity during ten years of the life of the church in Canada, and affords the best synthesis of the opposition that marked his appointment to the episcopate. A.G.]

J.-B.-A. Ferland, "Journal d'un voyage sur les côtes de la Gaspésie," *Les Soirées canadiennes; recueil de littérature nationale* (Québec), 1 (1861), 301–476. *Mandements des évêques de Québec* (Têtu et Gagnon), III, IV. [J.-O. Plessis], *Journal d'un voyage en Europe par Mgr Joseph-Octave Plessis, 1819–1820*, Henri Têtu, édit. (Québec, 1903). [H.-R. Casgrain], *L'asile du Bon-Pasteur de Québec d'après les annales de cet institut* (Québec, 1896), 43–185. *Une fondatrice et son œuvre: mère Mallet (1805–1871) et l'Institut des sœurs de la Charité de Québec, fondé en 1849* (Québec, 1939), 93–275, 425–30. P. B. Gams, *Series episcoporum ecclesiae catholicae, quotquot innotuerunt a beato Petro apostolo* (3 pts., Ratisbon, Germ., 1873–86), pt.I, 177. Jacques Grisé, "Le premier concile provincial de Québec, 1851" (mémoire de DES, université de Montréal, 1969). *L'œuvre d'un siècle; les Frères des écoles chrétiennes au Canada* (Montréal, 1937), 80–84, 302. Henri Têtu, *Histoire du palais épiscopal de Québec* (Québec, 1896), 105–80. René Bélanger, "Visite de Mgr Turgeon aux Ilets-de-Jérémie en juillet 1846," *Saguenayensia* (Chicoutimi, Qué.), 9 (1967), 38–39. Philippe Sylvain, "Les difficiles débuts de l'université Laval," *Cahier des Dix*, 36 (1971), 211–34.

U

UNIACKE, ROBERT FITZGERALD, evangelical clergyman of the Church of England and social activist; baptized 24 Dec. 1797 in Halifax, N.S., fourth son of Attorney General Richard John Uniacke* and Martha Maria Delesdernier; m. 1830 Elizabeth Gould Francklin, granddaughter of Michael Francklin*; d. 1 June 1870 at Halifax without offspring.

Robert Fitzgerald Uniacke was educated at the Halifax Grammar School, King's Collegiate School, and King's College, Windsor. He was articled in his father's Halifax law firm until he decided to enter holy orders after he experienced a religious conversion influenced by the preaching of Isaac Temple, tutor to the sons of Lieutenant Governor Dalhousie [Ramsay*]. Because Bishop Robert Stanser* was not in residence, Uniacke was ordained in England by the bishops of London and Chester (2 June 1822 and 23 March 1823). He served as a curate in the diocese of Chichester at Fishbourne (1822–24), and officiated at Mid Lavant.

In 1825 Uniacke returned to Nova Scotia as a missionary of the Society for the Propagation of the Gospel to be rector at St George's Church in Halifax. He arrived in the midst of the controversy at St Paul's Church over the right of the crown to name a rector to succeed John Inglis*, and attracted many Pauline dissentients to St George's. It became independent of St Paul's when a separate parish was created in 1827. With the assistance of curates after 1847, Uniacke remained rector until his death; his only absence was in 1838–39 when he successfully sought in Britain a cure for a serious throat infection.

Uniacke attended to both the spiritual and the temporal needs of his parishioners, mostly "Persons of limited Incomes." Because his parish comprised one-third of Halifax and extended eight miles into the country, he undertook a campaign of church building that resulted in the erection of St John's Chapel of Ease, Three Mile House (Fairview), and St Mark's Chapel, Richmond (northeast Halifax). He was also largely responsible for the construction of a church at Lakeland in Hants County near the Uniackes' fine country home, Mount Uniacke. He inherited this property in 1835 after agreeing to comply with the terms of his father's will that the sole recipient of the property give up all other claims on the estate.

Another major enthusiasm was education; besides Sunday Schools and evening classes Uniacke established at St George's and Three Mile House charity schools which were highly regarded as elementary schools open to poor children of all persuasions. The courage and physical exertions of both Uniacke and his wife during the cholera epidemic of 1834 endeared them to Haligonians. They were constant contributors to every good cause and active in parish relief, as well as in the establishment of homes for orphans and the aged.

Uniacke's evangelical fervour and low church predilections can best be illustrated by his relations with the exclusivist Bishop John Inglis and his Tractarian successor, Bishop Hibbert Binney*. Uniacke defied Inglis by supporting, joining, and actively directing evangelical Anglican organizations, especially the Colonial Church Society (subsequently the Colonial and Continental Church Society) and such interdenominational associations as the British and Foreign Bible Society. Binney felt the weight of Uniacke's opposition and influence over the junior clergy in Halifax, when the crusty, pious old rector stubbornly refused to join the diocesan synod on the ground that it would give too much power to the bishop, and an Anglo-Catholic bishop at that. Uniacke died noted for his good works but as steadfastly opposed to change as he had been a force for change in his youth.

JUDITH FINGARD

Halifax County Court of Probate (Halifax), no.1739, will of R. F. Uniacke; no.2201, will of E. G. Uniacke (mfm. at PANS). PANS, MG 1, 926B (Richard John Uniacke Sr papers), R. J. Uniacke's will; RG 5, P, 69–74, education. USPG, C/CAN/NS 8, ff.69, 405–25; 11, ff.26, 243, 248–49, 251–52, 255, 274, 356–56a; D 27, 489–91; E/PRE/B (1846), pp.313–15; E/PRE/C (1852–58), pp.1409–10, 1413–16; E, 6 (1859), p.279; E, 22 (1867), pp.1009–11; E, 24 (1868–69), pp.611–13. Hibbert Binney, *Remarks on diocesan synods, addressed to the clergy and laity of his diocese* (Halifax, 1864). Church of England, Diocese of Nova Scotia, *Journal of the Synod* (Halifax), 1866. Colonial and Continental Church Soc. (Halifax Branch), *Report*, 1848–71. *Formation and proceedings of the Halifax Association in Aid of the Colonial Church Society, 1847* (Halifax, 1847). G. W. Hill, *In memory of Robert Fitzgerald Uniacke, rector of St. George's, Halifax . . .* ([Halifax, 1870]). N.S., House of Assembly, *Journal and proc.*, 1839, 1845. N.S. Bible Soc., *Report* (Halifax), 1832–70. St George's District Visiting Soc., *Annual report* (Halifax), 1841–71. *Acadian Recorder*, 4 July 1818, 30 July 1831, 30 Aug. 1834, 1 June 1870. *Church Times* (Halifax), 1848–58. *Guardian* (Halifax), 1 July 1840; 12 April, 26 Nov. 1847. *Novascotian*, 6 June 1870.

V

VALADE, MARIE-LOUISE, known as **Mother Valade**, Sister of Charity of the Hôpital Général of Montreal, founder and superior of the Sisters of Charity at the Red River mission; b. 26 Dec. 1808 at Sainte-Anne-des-Plaines, Lower Canada, eldest daughter of a farmer, François Valade, and Marie-Charlotte Cadotte (Cadot); d. 13 May 1861 at Saint-Boniface (Man.).

Marie-Louise Valade entered the Hôpital Général of Montreal on 18 Sept. 1826, and took her vows on 21 Oct. 1828. On 21 April 1838 she became one of the 12 administrators, and in October 1843 she was elected a depositary. That year, in response to Bishop Joseph-Norbert Provencher*, who sought to "obtain the services of nuns to give persons of the female sex a sound grounding in religion and those other subjects which might make them good mothers," the Grey Nuns agreed to found an establishment at Red River. Mother Valade was given responsibility for it.

On 21 June 1844, after a long and arduous journey of 58 days in a bark canoe, Mother Valade and three other nuns reached Saint-Boniface. Twenty days later she started two classes, and entrusted her assistant, Sister Eulalie Lagrave, with the task of visiting the poor and the sick at home. She had a three-storey house built in which on 31 Dec. 1847 she set up her community. The house rapidly became a refuge for orphans, the aged, and the infirm.

The hard-working Mother Valade realized that in mission country self-sufficiency was necessary. She cultivated the land, thus improving the daily menu of dried meat; she manufactured material for clothes, and bought a carding machine, which she had adapted to Louis RIEL's "water power." She even attempted to extract sugar from local beetroot and maples.

In 1849, because the west was not developed enough to ensure a sufficient number of religious vocations, Mother Valade undertook the long journey to Montreal for reinforcements. Three novices and one nun responded to her appeal, and in 1850 she was able to open a school at Saint-François-Xavier. Until this time all the houses of the Grey Nuns throughout Canada formed a single community. But in 1851 the first provincial council of the bishops of Quebec proposed that those in each diocese should form an independent community, and the second provincial council of Quebec, in June 1854, confirmed this decision, In Mother Valade's eyes, this decree meant the death of the Red River house, whose members were recruited at the mother house in Montreal. She therefore supported Bishop Alexandre-Antonin Taché* in his efforts to check the disastrous effects of this decree. Finally, in 1858, with the help of Bishop Ignace Bourget*, they succeeded in re-establishing the union of the Red River and Montreal houses. Mother Valade, who had been invited to Montreal on this occasion, returned accompanied by three nuns. These fresh reinforcements made it possible to open a school at Saint-Norbert.

Mother Valade was the guiding spirit of her house. Of commanding stature, she possessed both a dignity of bearing, and a great kindliness that won the hearts of all. Worn out much more by illness, fatigue, and worries than by age, she died in her 53rd year. She left a well-organized house, three schools, including that of Saint-Vital, founded in 1860, and a staff of 21 nuns in charge of three infirm old men, 31 orphans, 21 resident and 43 non-resident pupils.

ÉLISABETH DE MOISSAC

ANQ-M, État civil, Catholiques, Saint-Martin (Laval, Qué.), 16 févr. 1808. Archives des Sœurs grises (Montréal), Correspondance de Saint-Boniface; Minutes du Conseil général, I, ff.28v, 31, 42v, 53v–55, 57v–60v. Archives paroissiales, Sainte-Anne-des-Plaines (Sainte-Anne-des-Plaines, Qué.), Registres des baptêmes, mariages et sépultures, 27 déc. 1808. [J.-N. Provencher] "Lettres de Mgr Provencher à Mgr Ignace Bourget," *Les Cloches de Saint-Boniface* (Saint-Boniface, Man.), XVIII (1919), 243–45, 263–65, 298; XIX (1920), 194–95, 219; XX (1921), 71–72, 114–15, 133, 150–52. Morice, *Dict. historique des Canadiens et Métis*, 307–9. Georges Dugas, *Monseigneur Provencher et les missions de la Rivière-Rouge* (Montréal, 1889), 209–10, 223–26, 269, 279. *L'Hôpital Général des Sœurs de la Charité (sœurs grises) depuis sa fondation jusqu'à nos jours* (3v. parus, Montréal, 1916–   ), II, 203–36, 341, 380–81, 432–34; III, 24, 59–62, 86–90.

VALLELY, PETER. *See* AYLEN

VALOIS, MICHEL-FRANÇOIS, physician, Patriote, and politician; b. 20 Aug. 1801 at Pointe-Claire, near Montreal, son of Pierre Valois, farmer, and Marie-Catherine Lefebvre; m. 28 July 1835 Marie-Louise-Florence-Eudoxie Godin, and they had 17 children; d. 24 May 1869 at Pointe-Claire, Que.

Michel-François Valois studied at the Collège

de Montréal from 1816 to 1821, and like the young men of the period who attended classical colleges he faced a relatively limited choice of careers: the priesthood and the liberal professions. He decided upon medicine, and on 10 May 1826 was licensed to practise his profession.

At that time a tense atmosphere prevailed in Montreal. Turbulent meetings and fiery speeches were becoming more frequent on the Champ de Mars. Those chiefly singled out for attack were the high officials and the English merchants, who were using their influence in various councils of Lower Canada to exercise more control over the management of public funds and to organize political patronage on a large scale. The 1822 plan of union added still further to the disquiet [see Louis-Joseph Papineau*]. Within this social context Valois awakened to nationalism, and, developing an interest in the European thinkers of the 18th century, began to be attracted to the ideas of liberty, individualism, democracy, and popular sovereignty.

Dr Valois rapidly became identified with the liberal cause in the parish in which he was born and now chose to live, and he soon came into conflict with the parish priest. In 1830 he was elected a trustee, by virtue of the assembly's schools act which placed the building and administration of schools directly in the hands of trustees in each parish; he then tried by every conceivable means to get a school built without the collaboration of his parish priest. By this move, he assumed a role of prime importance in education at the local level. But his struggle against the parish priest did not stop there: he also wanted to assert himself in the administration of the parish council. No doubt influenced by the proposed "notables bill," which directly threatened the status of the parish priest and his control over the management of the property and revenues of the church, the Pointe-Claire doctor openly stated that the parish council's money belonged to the parishioners. Hence his parish priest dreaded his being elected a churchwarden.

Valois attacked even more violently the English merchants who were the most powerful element in the government councils and who controlled a large proportion of the land in his area. Following the example of the French Canadian members of the assembly, he tried to conduct a struggle on a provincial scale. He was not content with verbally attacking the power of the English. From 1836 on, he took an active part in setting up local organizations in his region. It was not unusual to see him haranguing his fellow citizens from the church steps after Sunday mass. His house became a meeting ground which enabled

him to maintain direct and continuous contact with his own kind. It is not suprising therefore that Valois played a major role in the historic rally at Saint-Laurent on 15 May 1837. Although he exerted a major influence in his region, he does not seem to have entered into direct relationship with the Patriote leaders. The English government none the less placed him at the head of its list of most wanted men. Valois was pursued by a squad of soldiers detailed to round him up at Pointe-Claire but he managed to flee. However, he was captured after covering a few miles, and was taken to prison in Montreal in December 1837. He was later released, and is thought to have stayed for a while in the United States before going back to his native parish.

After the rebellion Dr Valois returned to private life. He still continued to take an interest in politics, but this time he seems to have been much more disposed to collaborate with the government. Valois was elected to the assembly in 1851 in the county of Montreal on the Rouge ticket, and in 1854 he was successful in Montreal in Jacques-Cartier, which he represented until 28 Nov. 1857. On 24 May 1869 he died at Pointe-Claire.

RICHARD CHABOT

ACAM, 355.110, 834–1. ANQ-M, Greffe de P.-C. Valois, 3 août 1840, 28 avril 1843, 18 janv. 1845, 25 mai 1848. ANQ-Q, QBC 25, Événements de 1837–38, nos.166–69. F.-J. Audet, *Les députés de Montréal*, 424–26. R.-L. Séguin, "Le docteur Valois, un patriote ignoré," *BRH*, LX (1954), 85–91.

VANKOUGHNET (Vankoughnet), **PHILIP MICHAEL MATTHEW SCOTT**, politician and judge; b. 21 Jan. 1822 at Cornwall, Upper Canada, son of Philip VanKoughnet* and Harriet Sophia Scott; m. Elizabeth, daughter of Colonel Charles Barker Turner*, and they had two sons; d. 7 Nov. 1869 at Toronto, Ont.

Philip Michael VanKoughnet studied under Hugh Urquhart at the Eastern District Grammar School, and was destined for the priesthood of the Church of England. In the rebellion of 1837–38 he served in his father's battalion of militia which saw action at the battle of the Windmill. Perhaps influenced by that experience and by a strongly loyalist and anti-rebellion speech of Christopher Alexander Hagerman*, attorney general of Upper Canada from 1837 to 1840, he chose to study law. In the fall of 1838 he entered the office of George Stephen Benjamin Jarvis* of Cornwall. A hard worker and a brilliant student, he moved to Toronto and the firm of

Vattemare

John Shuter Smith and Robert P. Crooks, and in 1843 was admitted to the bar of Upper Canada. He then joined the firm of Robert Easton Burns and Oliver Mowat*. VanKoughnet specialized in equity law, although he also took cases at common law, one of the few lawyers in Upper Canada to practise in both branches. So outstanding a reputation did he win that in 1850 the government of Louis-Hippolyte La Fontaine and Robert Baldwin* recommended him to be queen's counsel, despite the difference in political conviction between VanKoughnet and the ministry. He served on the council of the University of Trinity College and lectured there on equity jurisprudence.

In 1856, at the urging of his friend John A. Macdonald*, whom he had known at least since the meeting of the British American League in 1849, VanKoughnet accepted the posts of president of the Executive Council and minister of agriculture in the Étienne-Paschal Taché–Macdonald government. He successfully contested Rideau District, the first elective seat to be opened in the Legislative Council, in the same year. As minister of agriculture he turned what had been considered a sinecure into an active department. For instance, he offered $500 for the best essay on the control of the weevil, Hessian fly, and other crop-damaging insects. Henry Youle Hind* won the prize and his paper provided useful knowledge to farmers.

After passing through the "double shuffle" in 1858, VanKoughnet was appointed commissioner of crown lands and became chief superintendent of Indian affairs in 1860 when the department was transferred from imperial control [see R. T. Pennefather]. He had some success in settling long-standing land claims. He initiated a system of selling townships *en bloc* and established a price of 50¢ per acre paid in a combination of cash and credit. These actions led to a rapid opening of some of the colonization roads. He warned lumbermen of the wastage caused by fire and suggested the possibility of legislation to prevent it. VanKoughnet also tried, unsuccessfully, to have parliament adopt a contributory pension fund for civil servants.

In his 1856 election campaign VanKoughnet had suggested that the charter of the Hudson's Bay Company was invalid and that Canada should claim the northwest. It also fell to him as commissioner of crown lands to arrange the western exploring expeditions of Simon James Dawson* and Henry Youle Hind. He joined other expansionists such as William McMaster*, William P. Howland*, John McMurrich*, and Sandford Fleming* to petition in 1858 for the incorporation of the North-West Transportation, Navigation, and Railway Company. In a related attempt at expansion, he represented the Canadian government in London in 1861 seeking imperial financial support for the building of the Intercolonial Railway by Nova Scotia, New Brunswick, and Canada.

In March 1862 VanKoughnet was appointed chancellor of the Court of Chancery of Upper Canada, and distinguished himself in this office by the clarity, terseness, and humanity of his judgements. He became chancellor of Ontario in 1867. On 7 Nov. 1869 he died after a short illness, survived by his widow and two sons.

W. L. Morton

Chadwick, *Ontarian families*, I, 60–62. Dent, *Canadian portrait gallery*, IV, 127–29. *DNB*. Morgan, *Sketches of celebrated Canadians*. Read, *Lives of judges*. Hodgetts, *Pioneer public service*. R. S. Lambert, *Renewing nature's wealth; a centennial history of the public management of lands, forests & wildlife in Ontario, 1763–1967* ([Toronto], 1967). W. L. Morton, *Critical years*.

VATTEMARE, NICOLAS-MARIE-ALEXANDRE, ventriloquist, philanthropist, and promoter of cultural exchanges; b. 7 Nov. 1796 in Paris on the Île Saint-Louis; d. 7 April 1864 in Paris.

Nicolas-Marie-Alexandre Vattemare was the son of a Parisian lawyer who deemed it prudent to retire to his Normandy estate during the Revolution. Alexandre grew up at Lisieux, where his mother sent him to the seminary, as befitted the son of a good family. His gifts as a ventriloquist, which he discovered between the ages of seven and ten, caused the authorities of the seminary to expel him, just as some years later his ability shortened his medical studies in Paris. In 1815 he was invited to accompany a group of wounded Germans to Brandenburg as a nurse, and he amused them so well that some Berlin doctors advised him to make a career in ventriloquism. Immediate success in Berlin was repeated in the great cities of Europe. Fortune having smiled on him, he gave liberally to the charitable organizations of the towns through which he passed. He visited museums and libraries in these towns, and conceived a plan by which many people could share the large numbers of duplicates in books and other objects lying unused in collections. The ventriloquist-philanthropist became the "missionary of exchanges" among the princes and public figures of Europe. Only the French government was hesitant about his system, which he got into action in 1825 on a private basis by means of his Agence Européenne des Échanges. Faced with the reluctance of the French ministries, Vattemare decided to develop his system in America, as La Fayette and General Lewis Cass had suggested. He sailed in September 1839.

The ventriloquist "Mr Alexandre" prepared the way. But as soon as crowds had gathered, it was Vattemare who took over, and his idea was accepted warmly by the Americans. His plan of exchanges first interested Congress and an understanding was reached which allowed him to go to the principal American cities, from New York to New Orleans and Burlington. The states and cities received him cordially and supplied him with money, books, works of art, and natural history specimens for exchange.

In October 1840 he was at Montreal, where, if he had not already been informed, he showed himself to be an astute observer of the political situation. Instead of immediately presenting "Mr Alexandre", he made contact with civil and religious leaders and journalists, such as Bishop Ignace Bourget*, Governor Sydenham [Thomson*], Denis-Benjamin VIGER, "his Canadian host," and Joseph-Guillaume Barthe* of *L'Aurore des Canadas*. At the same time he communicated with the public through the newspapers, announcing his plan of exchange and urging the need to bring together people of different beliefs and political opinions. In mid December, having thus announced his intentions, Vattemare launched the idea of an institute that would combine the three principal Montreal societies (the Natural History Society, the Mechanics' Institute, the Montreal Library) under one roof, also to house the city hall, the stock exchange, and the post office. Enthusiastic, the Board of Trade won the support of the town council, which in turn asked the Special Council, through Lord Sydenham, for permission to borrow £50,000 for a building. These events occurred in January 1841, while "Mr Alexandre" was presenting his ventriloquist's shows and Vattemare was holding meetings with adult Anglophones and Francophones and with young people.

At the beginning of February, the Vattemare institute seemed settled, and its promoter set off for Quebec. His activity at Montreal had had wide coverage in the newspapers. "Mr Alexandre" and Vattemare again joined forces. The owner and editor of *Le Fantasque*, Napoléon Aubin*, gave full support to the establishment of a Vattemare institute, grouping the three societies of Quebec (the Literary and Historical Society, the Mechanics' Institute, the Quebec Library). The old Jesuit college would provide a roof for it. This institute, Aubin insisted, would

serve the whole population; a library, a natural history museum, and exhibition halls would meet the needs of popular instruction, and meanwhile chairs would be created for students in law and medicine. The exchange system would play a large part in the development of collections. Vattemare received the entire support of the press, with the *Quebec Gazette* stressing the opportunity for a *rapprochement* of races. Funds would come from a loan from the town council and a public subscription. The town council appeared to favour the scheme and appointed some of its members to study the question. A report was submitted on 10 March, but was never acted on. On 5 March Vattemare had already left Quebec for Boston.

The Vattemare institutes at Montreal and Quebec did not materialize, the Special Council disappeared with the union of the Canadas, and the whole scheme was rapidly forgotten with the elections. But three years later, in 1844, the young intellectuals of Montreal set up the Institut Canadien, much on the model of Vattemare's institute. The Institut Canadien, moreover, was to have numerous branches in the cities of Canada East. As early as 1847, at the time of Vattemare's second journey to the United States, *La Minerve* recognized the debt the Institut Canadien owed Vattemare, as did several others, including Pierre-Joseph-Olivier Chauveau* and Adolphe de Puibusque. In 1849 a number of books donated by Vattemare in 1847 to the parliament were destroyed in the burning of its buildings.

The visits of this extraordinary man, whose charm and talents were equalled only by his generosity, were as fruitful a contribution on the cultural level as that of Bishop Forbin-Janson*, made at the same moment, on the religious side. Alexandre Vattemare worked to the last to organize his exchange system through European governments. Three years after his death, on 7 April 1864, it would be accepted with the signing of the Convention des Princes.

CLAUDE GALARNEAU

ACAM, RLB, 2, p.249. ANQ-M, M-72-141. ANQ-Q, AP-G-76/1, lettre à Adolphe de Puibusque, 15 janv. 1847; lettre d'Adolphe de Puibusque à Faribault, 5 oct. 1847. Archives nationales (Paris), F[161], 160, 26 (dossier Puibusque), lettre à Salvandy, 12 mars 1849. AVM, Rapports et dossiers du conseil municipal, 1841, 2, 1re sér. AVQ, Procès-verbaux du conseil, 1840–42, 87–88, 92, 97. Bibliothèque de l'Arsenal (Paris), Rt 5560, 11162 (découpures de journaux du 30 janv. 1828 et du 5 avril 1883). Bibliothèque de l'Institute (Paris), Fonds Vattemare, M 61F4, 14–15.

Bas Canada, Conseil spécial, *Ordonnances*, 1840–

Vavasour

41, c.27. *Lettres à Pierre Margry de 1844 à 1886 (Papineau, Lafontaine, Faillon, Leprohon et autres)*, L.-P. Cormier, édit. (Québec, 1968), 134–36. *L'Aurore des Canadas*, 10 nov. 1840–29 janv. 1841. *L'Avenir*, 27 nov. 1847. *Le Canadien*, janv.–mars 1841, 8 sept. 1841, 3 août 1855. *Le Fantasque* (Québec), janv.–mars 1841. *L'Institut ou Journal des étudiants* (Québec), janv.–mars 1841. *Montreal Herald*, Jan. 1841. *Morning Chronicle* (Quebec), 4 May 1853. *Quebec Gazette*, January–March 1841.

Ægidius Fauteux, *Les bibliothèques canadiennes; étude historique* (Montréal, 1916), 34–42. Claude Galarneau, "Le philanthrope Vattemare, le rapprochement des 'races' et des classes au Canada: 1840–1855," *Shield of Achilles* (Morton), 94–110. Garneau, *Hist. du Canada* (1882–83), IV, lii–liii. Olivier Maurault, *Marges d'histoire* (3v., Montréal, 1929–30), III, 58, 71. Jean Ménard, *Xavier Marmier et le Canada, avec des documents inédits; relations franco-canadiennes au XIXᵉ siècle* (Québec, 1967), 63–64. J.-L. Dargent, "Alexandre Vattemare, 7 novembre 1796–7 avril 1864; fondateur de l'Agence européenne des échanges," *Bull. des bibliothèques de France* (Paris), A, IX (1964), 333–39. Olivier Maurault, "Souvenirs canadiens; album de Jacques Viger," *Cahiers des Dix*, 9 (1944), 92. Élisabeth Revai, "Le voyage d'Alexandre Vattemare au Canada: 1840–1841; un aperçu des relations culturelles franco-canadiennes: 1840–1857," *RHAF*, XXII (1968–69), 257–99. E. M. Richards, "Alexandre Vattemare and his system of international exchanges," Medical Library Assoc., *Bull.* (Chicago), XXXII (1944), 413–48.

VAVASOUR, MERVIN, soldier; b. probably at Fort George (Niagara-on-the-Lake), Upper Canada, in 1821, son of Captain Henry William Vavasour of the Royal Engineers and Louisa Dunbar, daughter of Sir George Dunbar; m. 23 Oct. 1860 Frances Elizabeth Hartwell Dickson in Manchester, England, and they had at least two daughters; after her death in 1863 m. Georgiana Oakes on 12 Jan. 1866; d. 27 March 1866 at Niagara Cottage, Henley on Thames, England.

Mervin Vavasour entered the Royal Military Academy, Woolwich, England, as a gentleman cadet in February 1837, and was commissioned into the Royal Engineers as a 2nd lieutenant on 19 March 1839. From 1839 to 1841 he attended the Royal Engineer Establishment (School of Military Engineering) at Chatham for instruction in field engineering and related subjects. He was posted to Canada and arrived at Montreal on 18 Sept. 1841.

Vavasour was first stationed at Kingston, and in 1842 was promoted lieutenant. From August 1843 to 13 Oct. 1846 he worked on the Ottawa and Rideau canals, with the exception of the period from 5 May 1845 to 20 July 1846 when he was on special service, participating in a military reconnaissance mission to the Oregon Territory with Henry James Warre*.

The political status of the territory west of the Rocky Mountains had been left unresolved since 1827 when Great Britain and the United States agreed to occupy it jointly. By 1845 British-American relations were strained. On 29 March Sir George Simpson* prepared a memorandum recommending the strengthening of British military and naval forces in Red River and Oregon and on the Pacific coast to provide more protection to British and Hudson's Bay Company interests. Soon after, Sir Richard Jackson*, commander of the forces in Canada, on instruction from Lord Aberdeen, selected Warre and Vavasour to go to the Oregon Territory disguised as travellers to examine how British territory on the Pacific coast might be defended in case of war with the United States. They arrived at Fort Vancouver (Vancouver, Wash.) on 25 Aug. 1845 and proceeded to reconnoitre much of the country from the Willamette valley to Fort Victoria. In September 1845 they conferred with Lieutenant William Peel, son of Sir Robert Peel, and Captain John GORDON of hms *America*. Gordon's ship had come to give support to the HBC and he had sent Peel to report on American settlement. Peel then went to London with his own, Gordon's, and John McLoughlin*'s reports on the situation in Oregon in February 1846. The arguments Peel presented to the British authorities for the retention of Vancouver Island if the 49th parallel were adopted as the boundary came at a critical time in the negotiations leading up to the Oregon Treaty signed by Great Britain and the United States on 15 June 1846. It is probable that the reports Peel transmitted strengthened the British approach towards the treaty, which did in effect divide British and American territory at the 49th parallel and reserve Vancouver Island as British territory.

Although neither Peel nor Gordon acknowledged the conversations they had with Warre and Vavasour, the views expressed by Warre and Vavasour on Oregon in their reports on the west coast (which arrived in London in July 1846, after the signing of the treaty) were similar. Warre and Vavasour were not encouraging about the defence of the area. They pointed out the deficiencies in the British military position in Oregon, stressed the impracticality of using overland routes for troops, who moreover would be dependent on inadequately provisioned posts, and commented on the shortcoming of Victoria as a port. They also wrote that HBC policies had encouraged American immigration to Oregon, a criticism which McLoughlin interpreted as "character assasinated in the dark."

Warre and Vavasour had left Oregon for Montreal on 25 March 1846. Vavasour embarked for England in October. He joined the Ordnance Survey of Ireland on 1 Jan. 1847 and served briefly on the Trigonometrical Survey of Great Britain in 1848. He then returned to the Survey of Ireland and was promoted 2nd captain in 1849. He went on sick leave in 1850, but recovered to serve in the West Indies in 1851–52. In 1853 he went on half pay, and died in 1866.

FRANCES WOODWARD

Institution of Royal Engineers (Chatham, Eng.), Conolly papers, index and notitia historica, 10, p.2. PAC, MG 24, F71. PRO, FO 5/440; 5/442; 5/457 (copies at PABC); WO 54/250–59. Royal Military Academy (Woolwich, Eng.), Register of cadets, 1837–39. P. J. De Smet, *Oregon missions and travels over the Rocky Mountains, in 1845–46* (New York, 1847). "Documents relative to Warre and Vavasour's military reconnoissance in Oregon, 1845–6," ed. Joseph Schafer, Oreg. Hist. Soc., *Quarterly* (Salem and Portland), X (1909), 1–99. HBRS, VII (Rich). [John McLoughlin], "McLoughlin's answer to Warre report," ed. H. A. Leader, *Oregon Hist. Quarterly* (Salem), XXXIII (1932), 214–29. [William Peel], "Report of Lieutenant Peel on Oregon in 1845–46," ed. L. M. Scott, Oreg. Hist. Soc., *Quarterly* (Eugene), XXIX (1928), 51–76. "Secret mission of Warre and Vavasour," *Washington Hist. Quarterly* (Seattle), III (1908–12), 131–53. H. [J.] Warre, *Sketches in North America and the Oregon Territory* ([London, 1848?]; repr. Barre, Mass., 1970).

Roll of officers of the Corps of Royal Engineers from 1660 to 1898, compiled from the ms. rolls of the late Captain T. W. J. Conolly, R.E. . . ., ed. R. F. Edwards (Chatham, Eng., 1898). B. M. Gough, *The Royal Navy and the northwest coast of North America, 1810–1914: a study of British maritime ascendancy* (Vancouver, 1971), 68–75; "H.M.S. *America* on the north Pacific coast," *Oregon Hist. Quarterly* (Portland), LXX (1969), 293–311. F. M. Woodward, "The influence of the Royal Engineers on the development of British Columbia," *BC Studies*, 24 (winter 1974–75), 3–51.

VIGER, DENIS-BENJAMIN, lawyer, journalist, essayist, and politician; b. 19 Aug. 1774 at Montreal, son of Denis Viger, a businessman and MHA, and Périne-Charles Cherrier, daughter of François-Pierre Cherrier; d. 13 Feb. 1861 in the same city.

Denis-Benjamin Viger belonged to a family that, like others of the period, was moving up in the social scale and ultimately played a decisive social and political role. His father Denis, a carpenter, became a building contractor and also engaged in the making of potash, exporting it to England. Like many French Canadian and Anglophone merchants, Denis Viger was attracted to politics, and from 1796 to 1800 he represented the county of Montreal East in the House of Assembly of Lower Canada. Through his mother, a Cherrier of Saint-Denis-sur-Richelieu, Denis-

Benjamin Viger was related to the Papineaus. He was also a cousin of Jacques Viger*, who became the first mayor of Montreal, and of lawyer Louis-Michel Viger*, a founder of the Banque du Peuple and eventually its president.

Viger came from a small family; his only sister, Périne, died unmarried in 1820 at the age of 40. He might have followed his father into contracting on a small scale, but in 1782 the latter sent him to the Sulpicians for a secondary education. He completed his studies at the Collège de Montréal without difficulty, and then decided to enter the much sought after profession of law. From 1794 to 1799 Viger received his legal training under Louis-Charles Foucher*, who was appointed solicitor general of the province in 1795, then under Joseph Bédard, a Montreal lawyer and brother of Pierre-Stanislas Bédard*, and finally under Jean-Antoine Panet*, at that time speaker of the assembly. When he was called to the bar on 9 March 1799 he had not only learned law but had acquired a taste for politics. He also had become imbued with a desire to be of service.

Viger was a serious young lawyer, intellectually inclined, idealistic, retiring, and often regarded as boring and awkward. Unlike Pierre-Stanislas Bédard, with whom he had characteristics in common, he was not without a flair for business. After 11 years of practising law, he was said to be "in easy financial circumstances." But it is doubtful whether the extent of his clientele in fact accounted for his comfortable state. He had been able to count on his father's assistance in establishing himself, and in 1808 he had married Marie-Amable Foretier, the 30-year-old daughter of Pierre Foretier*, a seigneur and former fur-trader. The Vigers were to have only one child, a daughter who died in 1814 at the age of eight months. Mme Viger was one of the legatees of Pierre Foretier's estate, which was administered by Jean-Baptiste-Toussaint Pothier*, and from 1816 to 1842 was the subject of an interminable lawsuit complicated by Pothier's bankruptcy. In 1842 Mme Viger finally was able to take possession of the Île Bizard seigneury, her father's property. On his mother's death in 1823, Viger inherited the family fortune, which included five houses and 47 acres of land in the *faubourg* Saint-Louis. From then on Viger was one of the most important landed proprietors in the town of Montreal. When he gave land for the establishment of his cousin, Bishop Jean-Jacques Lartigue*, some malicious persons cast doubt upon Viger's disinterestedness with the rumour that this generous gesture was aimed at increasing the value of sites he owned nearby. Viger carefully administered and enlarged his fortune, which seems to have been based on landed property and to have depended less and less on his earnings as a lawyer. This love of landed property brought tangible rewards, and gave him resources not available to most of the other Patriote leaders, though they were equally enamoured of land. Although he might later confuse his own interests and those of the group around him with the interests of the nation, Viger's career cannot nevertheless be reduced to the simple acquisition of dollars and cents. He was a bourgeois who had certain ideas and aspirations in common with the aristocracy, although he condemned it.

Viger was furthermore a young lawyer who liked to explore ideas and theories and to express them in writing, and he was ambitious in his intellectual pursuits. He bought books – at the end of his life his library contained more than 3,000 volumes – and he also read avidly. But he certainly would not have been able to find full satisfaction as a man of culture and independent means. Viger's intellectual activity was soon dominated by his interest in political issues. His first writings, published in the *Gazette de Montréal*, then a bilingual newspaper, date from 1792. His publications, his association with numerous newspapers and the financial support he gave them even when he was not the owner, are evidence that his thinking and activity centred on politics and national questions. The publication in 1809 of his *Considérations* clearly indicated his political concerns and the degree of his commitment. Viger had not waited for professional and business success to launch himself into politics. In 1804 he ran unsuccessfully for a seat in the assembly, but he did not give up and four years later he was returned in the western district of Montreal. He entered the assembly at the same time as his cousin Louis-Joseph Papineau*. Viger then began a long political career that did not end until 1858. He was among the first of the career politicians.

A member of the rising liberal professions, Viger entered political life when a nationalist ideology and political parties were beginning to take shape in Lower Canada. Like Pierre-Stanislas Bédard, he was a fervent admirer of English parliamentary institutions and of the felicitous balance within them between the three traditional principles of government: the monarchist, the aristocratic, and the democratic. His admiration for British institutions and for Great Britain was a consequence of theoretical considerations, of hostility to the excesses of the French revolution, and of aversion for Americans and their institutions, but it was also inspired by other factors. Like Bédard, he felt that the French Canadian nation was threatened by the activity of

English speaking merchants and by American immigration, and that these circumstances, as well as military tensions, gave Great Britain and British institutions a more significant role as a protective framework for the French Canadian nation. In his view, British institutions favoured the development of French Canadian culture, its fate being linked with the preservation of the old régime and the advancement of the French élite. When the War of 1812 broke out, Viger joined the French and English middle class and élite in the movement of national and imperial solidarity against the American invader. Viger had been appointed a lieutenant of militia in 1803 and was promoted captain at the time of the War of 1812. He was later raised to the rank of major, and finally retired from the militia in 1824 for reasons of health.

The Parti Canadien that Viger joined was a political group whose centre of decision-making was initially at Quebec, and whose leadership came from that city. At this period, the factors encouraging the growth of nationalism were operating with the greatest force in the Quebec region, among both the French Canadian middle class and peasants. Radical thinking and action were also most in evidence there. In this respect, Montrealers seemed behind the times. It must be noted too that the formation of the Parti Canadien was complicated by Quebec-Montreal rivalry. Viger belonged to a group of Montreal politicians who not only were aggrieved by the Quebecers' supremacy, but deplored the extremist tendencies of Bédard and those around him. The imprisonment of Bédard and the other editors of *Le Canadien* in 1810 aroused violent anger against Governor Sir James Henry Craig*, but does not seem to have horrified this Montreal group as much as has been thought today, or as they were willing to imply. Bédard's withdrawal from politics set in motion a long and bitter struggle for the leadership of the Parti Canadien, lasting until 1827, from which Montrealers emerged the winners. Papineau's victory was not assured until that date.

There were many candidates to succeed Bédard, particularly in the Quebec region. Although Governor Sir George Prevost* managed to persuade the Parti Candien to support the war effort, the battle for the party's leadership still went on, under the surface or openly, according to circumstances. A first successor emerged from Bédard's immediate circle, among his English speaking friends who were considered almost "true Canadiens" by the Quebec leader. Bédard maintained close relations with John Neilson* and Andrew* and James Stuart*. The latter, a brilliant lawyer, outstanding speaker, and ambitious man whose desire for rapid advancement had been frustrated by Governor Craig, adopted Bédard's policy, but used a different strategy. Instead of raising the question of ministerial responsibility from a broad constitutional point of view, as his predecessor had done, he made use of the technique of impeachment against judges Jonathan Sewell* and James Monk*, accusing them of usurping legislative authority and abusing their office and stressing Sewell's misdeeds as adviser to Craig. But although Stuart lived in Montreal and had considerable local support, he did not really succeed in winning recognition as a party leader. The Montrealers were not willing to see their party, a nationalist party, led by an Anglophone and a radical.

Did Viger contemplate leadership of the party during this period? It would not be surprising if he did so, for he was not without ambition. Yet Viger, whom political opponents characterized as having "long speech and long nose," lacked colour and self-confidence though he was respected. To his friends, he was not impressive when compared with the young and arrogant Papineau. The swing towards Papineau first became evident at a time when the instability of the party and the prevailing situation made a radical policy appear dangerous. The party did not have the strength to confront, as it had in 1810, the government, the merchant faction, the clergy, and the nobility. A policy of conciliation towards the French Canadian ruling classes was indispensable. Moreover the clergy increasingly felt the need to diversify its support. The Parti Canadien's objective of rallying all the groups which its leaders considered part of the nation did not, however, exclude a search for support among Anglophones. For from 1815 on the rapid increase of the English speaking population in the towns through immigration threatened to deprive the Parti Canadien of its urban roots and to make it appear to be a party with an exclusively rural base and ideology. Although Papineau belonged to the Montreal section of the party which became more influential as the centre of socioeconomic and ethnic conflict moved towards that city, he was obliged to take all these variables into account to command attention. His initial success was no doubt due to his personal gifts, and the particular circumstances that gained him the support of certain governors – in 1815 he was elected speaker of the House of Assembly, and three years later he began to emerge as Bédard's moderate and reform successor – but he also seems to have had a remarkable sense of timing and of the process of change. Ministerial respon-

sibility was temporarily set aside as an avowed political objective, and replaced by the issue of supply bills, which became a polarizing force for political action. To attract the votes of Irish Catholics and liberal Anglophones, and to win the support of Quebecers, he formed a close association with John Neilson, who became Papineau's lieutenant in the Quebec region. How can Viger's role at this time be defined, except in relation to the leadership question in the Montreal region?

Beyond any doubt, Viger was one of the principal leaders of the Parti Canadien. He had a major share in shaping its ideology, perhaps for some years, and he undoubtedly was instrumental in planning for parliamentary sessions and electoral campaigns. In this connection, Viger had realized that newspapers played a vital part in the diffusion of ideas, programmes, and slogans. In the House of Assembly he was active in debates – at the risk of sending his audience to sleep – or, more often, in house committees. Viger made his presence felt when it was necessary to defend the institutions of the old régime: the seigneurial system, the customary law of Paris, or the rights and privileges of the church. His hostility to any basic reform in these areas, and in particular to the establishment of registry offices, was not exceeded in vigour. During the quarrel over the establishment of the diocese of Montreal, a conflict which set Bishop Lartigue, the successive bishops of Quebec, and the French Canadian clergy against the Sulpicians, who tended to support the government, Viger became one of the chief proponents of the myth of the good national clergy. He not only upheld Lartigue's cause, but acted as liaison between the bishop of Montreal and the leaders of the Parti Canadien. He continued to serve as intermediary between his two cousins even after 1830, when relations between the clergy and the party deteriorated.

After 1815 the influence of the Montreal section of the Parti Canadien, for which Viger was one of the most active fieldworkers, increased steadily, but it does not follow that the Quebecers had lost hope of resuming the leadership. This possibility became apparent at the time of the 1822 union crisis. If there was one event that crystallized opinion, it was surely this one. French Canadian nationalists and defenders of the society of the old régime (seigneurs, clerics, professional people), liberal Anglophones, and Irish Catholics — all joined in a movement of intense opposition to the plan for union of the Canadas. Committees were set up in each district to mobilize the population, draft addresses, get

Viger

petitions signed, and choose delegates. Viger was the most prominent leader after Papineau; indeed the advocates of the union proposal gave the name of Vigerie to the opposition movement. Viger fought with pen and oratory. He helped Dr Jocelyn Waller* launch the *Canadian Spectator* in October 1822, as a means of organizing the opposition, and on 7 October, on the Champ de Mars, he made an anti-union speech which aroused his audience. But although the situation was acknowledged to be critical, unanimity was only achieved with great difficulty when it came to choosing delegates who would take the petitions to England. The Quebecers did not want decisions to be imposed by the Papineaus and the Vigers. Finally John Neilson, who was "a good Englishman" to quote Papineau, Pierre-Stanislas Bédard, then a judge (who in the event would be unable to obtain leave), and Louis-Joseph Papineau won the votes of the various local factions.

The departure of Papineau, the speaker of the assembly and leader of the party, led to a resurgence of the Quebec-Montreal rivalry. The Quebecers were determined to use his absence to recover their control of the party. Viger would have liked to become speaker and perhaps emerge as an eventual leader. But he came into conflict with another Montreal group, directed by Louis Bourdages*, so that Joseph-Rémi Vallières* de Saint-Réal, a Quebecer, was elected speaker of the house, while Andrew Stuart seems to have acted as interim leader. When the latter left for Europe, Vallières de Saint-Réal took over both offices, and proposed to hold them as long as possible. All Papineau could do when he returned was to note that the Quebecers were masters of the political scene. He even thought of withdrawing from public life. But the union crisis had helped to increase the prestige of Neilson and Papineau, and the latter had no difficulty, when the right moment came, in resuming the role of leader. His position was even strengthened. Like Bédard, Vallières de Saint-Réal accepted an appointment as judge.

During the governorship of Dalhousie [Ramsay*], the struggle intensified around the question of supply; other Montreal leaders became prominent and surpassed Viger in influence in some respects. Augustin Cuvillier*, an auctioneer, businessman, and owner of substantial property, became the financial expert of the Parti Canadien. Cuvillier was ambitious, and prompted by success he set his sights high. His disappointment would be intense when the supply question ceased to have any real significance, but meanwhile he was making his presence felt.

After the great electoral success in 1827, Papineau decided to make a determined effort against Governor Dalhousie, and revived the scenario of 1822: the formation of regional committees, signing of petitions in all areas, and appointment by these committees of delegates to express and defend the party's point of view in England. Neilson was again chosen, and Cuvillier and Viger were appointed his assistants. Significantly, the final choice of these three delegates took place in Montreal, at a meeting on 24 Jan. 1828. This mission arrived in England in March, under exceptionally favourable circumstances. The idea of reform was in the air, and during an interview the colonial secretary, William Huskisson, announced to the three delegates the setting up of a House of Commons committee which was to meet between 8 May and 15 July, to investigate Canadian problems and propose solutions. The three were summoned in turn to appear before this committee of 21 MPs. Viger was heard on 7 and 10 June. In his lengthy statement, he asserted that the old French law and the seigneurial system should be retained, asked that changes be made to allow French Canadians easier access to lands in the Eastern Townships, and suggested a reform of the Legislative Council to make it more representative.

On 22 July the committee presented its report, and on most points recognized the validity of the claims of the majority that controlled the House of Assembly of Lower Canada. On the question of supply, the Patriote party's victory was almost complete. His task completed, Viger travelled in France and Holland, and returned with the idea for a work which was published in 1831 under the title of *Considérations relatives à la dernière révolution de la Belgique*. In London Viger had projected the image of a moderate, "reasonable" man, according to Tory MP Thomas Wallace. Did this image induce Sir James Kempt*, the administrator of Canada, to offer him a seat on the Legislative Council as soon as he returned, in order to show the government's impartiality, improve relations between the houses, and doubtless weaken the Patriote party? We do not know, just as we do not know why Viger accepted. On his return to Quebec in December 1828, did Viger believe in the good faith of Great Britain, did he think he would be more useful if he agreed to be a member of the Legislative Council, or again, did he suppose that his future prospects would be better in the upper house than in the assembly? We do not know. In any case in August 1829 he accepted Kempt's offer. Viger took his seat in the Legislative Council in January 1831, but did not hold it long, as we shall see. He only had time to win a verbal battle with John Richardson*, who was opposed to the popular election of municipal officers. His diatribe against absolute power earned him the nicknames of Marat and Robespierre in the English press, nicknames out of keeping with his conciliatory spirit and moderation. The radicalizing of the Patriote movement, in process for some years, had come to involve a fundamental re-assessment of the Legislative Council.

The struggle for the control of supply was in reality only one stage of a long confrontation in which the assumption of power by the French Canadian middle class was at stake. Bédard had initially conceived his strategy within this overall perspective. Subsequently, circumstances had made it necessary to pursue more limited objectives, centred on the effort to gain participation in power. But as soon as London supported the Patriote party on the question of supply and proposed a solution that would safeguard the aspirations of all sides, Papineau declared that control of finance was no longer a priority for his party and did not respond to the English government's offer. From then on he adopted a new strategy, which involved radicalizing the Patriote party's action and ideology. Although there was still a concern to retain traditional Anglophone bases of support this strategy aimed at putting power into the hands of the French Canadian middle class, and pointed towards independence. The assurance and justification of such a victory lay in the application of the elective principle at all levels where power was exercised. It therefore became a primary objective to make legislative councillors subject to election. But in 1828 Papineau was not in a position to take this drastic step. This radical orientation implied a major constitutional change, whereas the Parti Canadien had always objected to any alteration of the 1791 constitution, and the Patriote party quite recently had proclaimed its inviolability. He also had to convince the other leaders of the party of the necessity for this redirection, and to make the electorate aware of the issue of an "elective Legislative Council." The effort was launched through a series of bills concerning schools, parish councils, urban municipalities, and local institutions, which all stipulated the election of officers by property owners. Then, in a second phase, while frequently repeating republican professions of faith and paying homage to American institutions, Papineau started a campaign of systematic disparagement of the councils of the government, and in particular the Legislative Council. An elective status for its members was then put forward as the only solution to the problems of Lower Canada. The Legislative Council was the symbol of English exploitation, but, if elective, it would become the symbol of justice and of French Canadian power. The "elective Legislative Council" was the slogan that dominated the general election of 1834, and gave Papineau and his party an extraordinary success.

This change of strategy, with its harder line of action, was helped by deteriorating economic conditions, the demographic context, and the sharpening of disparities between ethnic groups in both town and countryside. It also reflected major changes in the leaders of the Patriote party, and aroused aggressive reactions from the opposition. The restless atmosphere in the province stimulated the former leaders to more vigorous action, and produced new ones, nationalist, liberal, or radical, who sought an all-out clash with Great Britain. Revolution was talked of. It is indisputable that Papineau was increasingly influenced by men such as Ludger Duvernay*, Augustin-Norbert MORIN, Louis-Hippolyte LA FONTAINE, Charles-Séraphin Rodier*, or Amury Girod*, rather than by older men such as Viger. Papineau tried, but it was in vain, to keep the support of the liberal Anglophones, the Irish Catholics, and the American settlers in the townships. He established a closer relationship with Robert* and Wolfred NELSON. The Irishman E. B. O'Callaghan* even became his right-hand man. Obviously, this radicalization of the Patriote movement also meant ruptures and defections. The long association of Papineau and John Neilson was broken. Andrew Stuart was the first to pass to the other camp; Cuvillier and Frédéric-Auguste QUESNEL followed. But the strongest reactions came from the clergy and the British government, and even from the English supporters of the Patriote party. Once again, what was Viger's role in all this?

On 28 Feb. 1831, one month after Viger took up his duties as a legislative councillor, Louis Bourdages, probably at Papineau's instigation, proposed to the assembly that Viger should be appointed its agent in England. On 28 March the assembly, dispensing with the Legislative Council's assent, made the appointment by a resolution; its action led Lord Aylmer [Whitworth Aylmer*] to refuse Viger a letter of introduction to Lord Goderich. On 13 June Viger was in England, and secured François-Xavier GARNEAU as his secretary. The circumstances of his stay in London were in marked contrast to those of 1828, when the British authorities had been receptive. In 1831 they were convinced that the reason the Patriote party was rejecting the reforms it had offered and instead formulating unacceptable claims was that the party was about to collapse. Hence the radicalization of the Patriote movement was interpreted as a desperate reaction to safeguard the prestige of a few ambitious leading figures. As a consequence, although the British were preoccupied with their own parliamentary reform, Viger was able to communicate fairly easily with Lord Goderich. He met former administrators such as Sir Francis Nathaniel Burton* and Sir James Kempt. He kept in contact with the Radicals, who were seeking to take advantage of the discontent of the Canadas. But as English official circles became convinced that the Patriote movement was above all a nationalist movement, seeking power for a particular ethnic group and a particular social class, and aiming at political independence and the subjugation of the English minority, Viger's position became increasingly difficult. In 1833 E. G. G. Stanley, the secretary of state for the colonies, gave Viger to understand that he had nothing more to learn from him. The arrival in the spring of 1834 of Augustin-Norbert Morin, who brought the petitions inspired by the assembly's 92 Resolutions, in no way modified the British government's attitude. Between 12 May and 13 June 1834 Morin was called to testify before a commons committee on six occasions. Unable to count on the point of view of a "good Englishman" like John Neilson, who was now associated with the defenders of the constitution, Viger could not move the government. Disappointed by the turn of events, Viger returned to Canada on 1 November, in the middle of an election campaign. The warm welcome he received from an enthusiastic Montreal crowd was not enough to prevent him and Papineau from realizing that his mission had failed. In 1835 the radical John Arthur Roebuck*, much more aggressive than Viger, was instructed by the assembly to defend the interests of Lower Canada in England.

Despite his 60 years and his failure in London, Viger did not retire. Perhaps he was exhilarated by the great electoral victory of 1834. The confrontation between the British government and the Patriote party was taking a much more serious turn. The idea of acquiring independence by revolutionary means was spreading among militant Patriotes. It is certain that at this period Viger was not in retirement, and was following events closely. In 1834 he was active in the correspondence committee in Montreal. As part of the grand campaign designed to bring down the English business bourgeoisie, Viger published his *Observations*, which recommended boycott

of imported products subject to tax, development of local industry, and the practice of "purchase at home." The founding of the Banque du Peuple, a symbol of the economic regeneration of French Canadians and an instrument for the economic and political ambitions of a small group of well-endowed Patriotes, did not escape Viger's notice. Its ten-dollar bills were even printed bearing the effigies of Mercury, the god of trade, and of Viger. Moreover, in 1835 Viger replaced his cousin Jacques as president of the Société Saint-Jean-Baptiste, and presided at its annual banquet until 1837 [*see* Jean-François-Marie-Joseph MacDonell]. In 1835 he had been appointed president of the Union Patriotique, which sought responsible government, the election of legislative councillors, and the abolition of monopolies, particularly that of the British American Land Company.

The British parliament's adoption in March 1837 of the Russell Resolutions, which allowed the governor to draw upon public funds without the assembly's assent and categorically refused the reforms sought by the Patriote party, forced the leaders of that party to take up a revolutionary strategy. The extremists, the radicals, and others were ready to move immediately, and to undertake to overthrow the government. But more realistic minds prevailed. They knew that the mass of the people needed to be mobilized skilfully for new and more demanding objectives. To expect a spontaneous popular uprising did not seem useful in the circumstances. Preparing the people psychologically for any eventuality had to have as accompaniment the creation of revolutionary cadres, and of an organization for *matériel*. Equally serious problems existed at the leadership level. Since 1835 the chief Patriotes of the city of Quebec had not only held themselves aloof but had expressed their dissent. It was therefore necessary to reconstitute the leadership in the Quebec region and this was to be Morin's responsibility. The Patriote leaders then rallied around a plan which set a revolutionary process in motion but left the door open to possible capitulation by the British government. In this perspective, large meetings are only a stage in the advance of a revolutionary movement. Viger must have been involved in all these discussions and must have shared in one way or another in all the decisions. He was too close to the top level of the party, the permanent central committee, for these proceedings to have escaped his notice. He was one of those who called the Saint-Laurent meeting of 15 May 1837. But generally speaking, perhaps because of his age as well as for other reasons, Viger like many others stayed in the background. Nevertheless he too was compromised.

As public meetings continued to be held, so-called legal opposition quickly became a fiction. The extremists did not worry about precautions, and openly advocated recourse to arms. The radicals went further, and called for the abolition of tithes, of the seigneurial régime, and of the customary law of Paris. Thus the drive towards revolution progressed much more rapidly than had been foreseen, and took a turn which could be menacing for the nationalist élite, among them some of the directors of the Banque du Peuple, who thought solely of political independence for the benefit of the French Canadian middle class. Papineau and Viger were doubtless somewhat worried by these social tendencies, but the acceleration of the revolutionary movement also served their ends. *La Minerve*, a paper financed by Viger, not only did nothing to slow the process or to urge the radicals to be prudent but actively stirred up discontent. Hence the meeting at Saint-Charles on 23 Oct. 1837, where the Patriote leaders agreed to hold a great rally on 4 December, "after the freeze-up," occasioned no clash between radicals and nationalists over tithes or the seigneurial régime. When, following this meeting, the bishop of Montreal issued a pastoral letter condemning the revolutionary designs and the ideology of the Patriotes, it was Viger who undertook to reply. Annoyed by the defection of the "good national clergy," he entitled his article in *La Minerve* on 17 Aug. 1837: "Deuxième édition de la proclamation Gosford sous forme d'un mandement de l'évêque de Montréal." He discussed the implications of the pastoral letter, drew attention to the clergy's inconsistency and its links with the government, and concluded with a story suggesting that "A day will perhaps come when His Excellency will be the first to intone the *Domine Salvum Fac le gouvernement provisoire*." Viger did not attend the Saint-Charles meeting; nor was he a member of the Association des Fils de la Liberté. The latter nevertheless used some of his land for their military exercises.

For a long time the government had tended to interpret the activities of the Patriotes as blackmail intended to frighten it. In fact the British authorities, less clear-sighted than the clergy and the local English speaking minority, had believed that the Patriotes were incapable of a revolutionary adventure. But from the beginning of November 1837, and particularly after the riot of 6 November, it was no longer possible to ignore the real intentions of the Patriote leaders. At this point the government's reaction, which Étienne Parent*, the editor of *Le Canadien* of Quebec had predicted, began to take shape. The rumour, then the certainty, that the principal leaders would soon be arrested quickened and changed the tempo of events. All this activity enables us to understand the excitement in Montreal, and particularly the relations between Viger and the revolutionary movement.

There were earnest consultations between Papineau and the chief figures in the party. The testimony given by Angélique Labadie, *dit* Saint Pierre, a servant in Viger's household, not only agrees with what we know from other sources but also sheds a curious light on these critical moments. The first conversation she mentions, between Papineau, Viger, and Côme-Séraphin Cherrier* – which no doubt took place shortly after the Saint-Charles meeting – reveals the economic and political ambitions of this "family compact," and shows how persistent was the hope that the British government would capitulate before things went too far. The second conversation reported, between Papineau and Viger, enables us to grasp better Papineau's personal ambitions and the existence of a plan for revolution whose dénouement was to occur after the freeze-up. Viger is said to have stated "that it was necessary to proceed more quietly and to wait for the freeze-up, that at that time the blast of a whistle would rally large numbers of habitants and thousands of Americans to their cause, and that they would soon be masters of the country." The third conversation took place in more tragic circumstances, when Viger informed Papineau that a warrant of arrest was about to be issued against him, and advised him to leave the city. Viger may well have said on this occasion "that the sun shone for everybody and that it would shine again for them, and that perhaps he would see the day when they would be victorious; . . . that they must call upon the Supreme Being to sustain them in their cause; . . . that he would not be worried if he saw the streets stained with the blood of those who did not share their political views, and who were . . . nothing but reprobates." Such exchanges are frequent at times when events seem to be moving fast. Papineau, moreover, did not talk solely with his intimate friends and the Patriote leaders; he also had discussions during the few days preceding his departure from Montreal with an envoy of William Lyon MACKENZIE. One day Jesse Lloyd* arrived with the greatest secrecy in Montreal and went to Papineau's house; the latter hastily summoned Wolfred Nelson and E. B. O'Callaghan. Papineau is said to have asked his son, once Lloyd had left, never to utter a word about the visit. In a letter of September 1844 addressed to O'Callaghan, Mackenzie alluded to the results of this meeting: "When yourself and friends sent up [an emissary] to Toronto in Nov. 1837 to urge us to rise ag^t. the British Gov^t. it would certainly not have come to my thoughts that the men who did that would in the event of failure make a treaty with Eng^d. for the patronage of Canada to themselves and to our tory enemies. . . ." In this letter Mackenzie clearly associated the name of Viger with that of Papineau: "the *loyal* Papineaus, Vigers, Bruneaus."

Viger's role in the subsequent revolutionary events remains to a great extent obscure. We do not know the nature of his relations with the directors of the Banque du Peuple, which may be assumed to have been close, nor do we have exact information about the connection between the Banque du Peuple and the revolutionary movement. The only really explicit testimony is that of Abbé Étienne Chartier*, who denounced the treason of the directors of this institution. Chartier accused them in particular of having refused at the last moment to finance the insurrection. Might the intervention of English troops before the anticipated moment, or the fear of seeing an anti-feudal movement develop, underlie the withdrawal of the Banque du Peuple, as Chartier contended? What was the link between the arrest of bank president Louis-Michel Viger, the lightning trip of Édouard-Raymond Fabre* to Saint-Denis, and the flight of Papineau and O'Callaghan at the start of the battle?

In any case, Viger did not remain inactive. After *La Minerve* ceased publication in November 1837, François Lemaître published two papers in Montreal: *La Quotidienne*, from 30 Nov. 1837 to 3 Nov. 1838, and *Le Temps*, from 21 August to 30 Oct. 1838. These papers, which were accused of spreading discontent and diffusing ideas concerning independence, were said to be Viger's property. Lemaître occupied a house belonging to Viger and was active in the Association des Frères-Chasseurs, which was planning the second insurrection under the direction of Robert Nelson and Dr Cyrille-Hector-Octave Côté*. Were mere coincidences used by political opponents to incriminate Viger? The absence of direct evidence against him does not mean that he was completely innocent. It is certainly possible that he had used tactics similar to those of Papineau, who let the radicals use his name in 1838 as a symbol of the revolution and who, though he kept apart, maintained relations with certain revolutionary groups, out of fear that the movement might slip from his control completely. For it must not be thought that the second insurrection mobilized only radicals. Many – in fact the great majority – did not accept the radical ideology but joined the revolutionary adventure, telling themselves that the ideological differences would be settled after victory. In 1838, as in the preceding year, the Patriote movement was in essence nationalist, and the radicals had no greater success in getting their social message across. Viger, whose house had been searched on 18 Nov. 1837 but who had not been bothered subsequently – and who had indeed been visited frequently by Stewart DERBISHIRE in May 1838 and had received Charles Buller* and Edward Ellice Jr to dinner on 23 June – was thrown into prison on 4 Nov. 1838 when Sir John COLBORNE proclaimed martial law again. The *Herald* denounced him as the owner of seditious newspapers. On 18 December the superintendent of police, Pierre-Édouard LECLÈRE, offered to have him released on bail, with a promise of good conduct. Viger reacted as Bédard had in Craig's time, and demanded a trial. He remained in prison until 16 May 1840. During the first two months of his detention, Viger was not permitted to see anybody. He was not allowed to play the flageolet, his sole form of amusement. In August 1839 he was forbidden to exercise in the prison yard, despite the presence of soldiers. He could not have paper, pen, or newspapers.

The failure and disintegration of the revolutionary movement allowed the British government to enforce a solution which had been envisaged as early as 1810 by Anglophone businessmen and was now proposed by Lord Durham [Lambton*]: the political union of the Canadas. The mere notion of union evoked a series of tragic images. To the clergy, union meant the Protestant peril, threat to the culture, and destruction of the society of the old régime. The seigneurs shared these fears, but the lay élite, whether they favoured the institutions of the old régime or not, thought first of the cultural threat. When the union of the Canadas was finally decided upon in 1840, the French Canadian population had already begun to redefine itself in terms of this event which was so charged with symbolism. Although the union might eventually prove to be a poor method of cultural assimilation, it inaugurated a period of economic, institutional, and political change in which the different strata of the population of the two Canadas would share in one way or another.

Did Viger, his health impaired by his long detention, think of leaving politics when he came out of prison? If he did, the plan of union, a plan he had bitterly fought for 20 years, had only to appear again to give fresh impetus to this tenacious man. He quickly published statements in 1840 to clear his reputation and to cast upon his enemies sole responsibility for illegal acts committed under the impulse of the moment and as a result of much injustice. From 1840 on, with the support of *L'Aurore des Canadas*, then the only French newspaper in Montreal, he attacked the Special Council for pursuing a tyrannical policy, and prepared to come back into politics. One can understand why political veterans like John Neilson and Viger, who had long been companions in battle, and for nearly ten years opponents, appeared at first unable to accept the *fait accompli*, and found themselves side by side in their denunciation of the union and of the reasons behind its establishment. Their social conservatism prevented their contemplating annexation to the United States, or cooperating with the Upper Canadian Reformers to obtain ministerial responsibility. La Fontaine, who in 1837 had thought of supplanting Papineau and who later had continued to scheme in order to emerge as national leader, did not however have the same reasons as his elders or the diehard republicans to be inflexible. He favoured the abolition of the seigneurial régime and was able to look upon the union with more optimism. Like the Reformers of Upper Canada with whom he wanted to ally himself, he felt that the old colonial system was about to collapse, and that the philosophy of free trade, once accepted, necessitated the political autonomy of the colonies. In his mind, responsible government implied not only a certain autonomy in relation to Great Britain but a sharing of power between ethnic groups. In fact La Fontaine, unlike Neilson and Viger, acted in accordance with a political concept and strategy.

In the 1841 election the anti-unionists and the reformers of Canada East combined against the Tories, and managed to elect 20 of 42 representatives; Viger was returned in the county of Richelieu. The group was dominated by John Neilson and Viger and included few supporters of La Fontaine, himself defeated. Viger gave the impression of being a leader. He denounced the union because it did not respect proportional representation and restricted the use of French. He compared Canada East's situation to that of Belgium which, upon union with Holland before 1830, had had to discharge part of the latter's debt. On 3 Sept. 1841 he also supported Robert Baldwin*'s resolutions defining responsible government. However, the situation did not work out to Viger's advantage but to that of La Fon-

taine, whose Upper Canadian friends had him elected in York County. After the arrival of the new governor, Sir Charles Bagot*, in 1842, the Reformers' position improved, and the principle of ministerial responsibility, although not formally recognized, shaped the relations between the ministry and the governor. From the first Bagot helped undermine the influence of Viger and Neilson through appointments of French Canadians to office. But this rapid evolution of the political system was peculiarly fragile because it depended on the personality of the king's representative and his grasp of the Canadian context. Consequently it came almost abruptly to a halt under Bagot's successor, for Sir Charles Theophilus Metcalfe*, instructed by Lord Stanley, proposed to govern and to retain the privilege of distributing political favours. In November 1843 La Fontaine and Baldwin resigned. Viger's behaviour on that occasion finally led to his emergence as a political leader.

Viger decided to accept on 7 Dec. 1843 the offer of Metcalfe, "an enlightened despot," and form a ministry with the moderate Conservative William Henry Draper*: a baffling decision. Until 1830 Viger had shared Neilson's political ideas; subsequently he had favoured responsible government and had nibbled at republicanism. With such antecedents, Viger could have done battle in any group, except the one directed by Metcalfe. There were many French Canadians who cried treason. William Lyon Mackenzie was as hard on Viger as on Papineau, claiming "now we see his friends and family monopolizing the patronage of Canada under absolutism." When Viger was forced to explain his political ideas, he spoke of his admiration for American institutions but rejected annexation. He accepted the theory of responsible government but finally reverted to Neilson's ideas on the British constitution. In the end Viger put his trust in the idea of a benevolent and open-minded governor who, in his opinion, would take into account the majorities in both sections of the province. Ambition, social conservatism, and hostility to La Fontaine apparently explained the readjustment of his political thought to the circumstances of the moment.

The task undertaken by Viger was considerable, even if he enjoyed the governor's confidence. While trying to convince the public of the validity of his thesis through his actions, he also had to rally influential people around him. He even thought of repatriating Papineau, and started negotiations to get him the £4,500 of arrears in his salary as speaker of the assembly. The former Patriote leader was not averse to collecting the arrears but refused to accept the role offered him. On 15 June 1844 *Le Fantasque* wrote: "God created the world in six days; for nearly nine months now M. Viger has been trying to create a ministry – he is doing it no doubt in his own image: without end." Viger finally chose Denis-Benjamin Papineau* to become commissioner of crown lands on 2 Sept. 1844.

The difficulties Viger encountered in creating a dynamic and representative entourage were increased by the results of the elections of October 1844. Of his party's candidates, only Papineau succeeded in getting elected. Viger himself was defeated in Richelieu, and could not sit in the house until July 1845, after being elected at Trois-Rivières. It is true that the Tories had obtained a majority in Canada West but it is hard to believe that the results in Canada East could have strengthened the argument for double majority. Viger's system was based entirely on the good faith of the queen's representative. Whatever assessment one may make of the Metcalfe administration, it is impossible not to recognize the precarious and uncomfortable situation in which the two cousins found themselves. On 17 June 1846 Viger resigned, succumbing to the pressure of the majority. *L'Aurore des Canadas*, a newspaper which supported him, was falling into discredit. For some years *La Minerve* (revived in 1841) had been applauding La Fontaine's growing success.

On 25 Feb. 1848 Viger was again appointed a legislative councillor. He would be 74 in August. He lived on Rue Notre-Dame, a little east of Rue Bonsecours, in a two-storey stone house he had bought in 1836 for £2,800. Tired of political struggles – he did not attend the sessions of the council from 1849 to 1858, when his seat was proclaimed vacant – he wanted to enjoy the pleasures of a peaceful retirement with his wife. The latter continued to devote herself to charitable works: one of six founders of the Institution pour les Filles Repenties, and president of the Orphelinat Catholique de Montréal (1841–54), she cared about the welfare of the needy. Viger himself gave less and less attention to politics. On 15 March 1849 he spoke for the last time in the council, against the Rebellion Losses Bill contending that the province was already too burdened with debt. He intervened again, in the newspapers, to denounce annexation to the United States, then in 1851 to oppose the suppression of rent payments to the seigneurs, which he likened to an act of pillage. Fatigue, illness, and infirmity caused him to draw farther and farther away from politics. He read, and perhaps still played the flageolet. Louis-Joseph-Amédée Papineau*, in 1852, considered his library and picture gallery two of the finest collections in Canada, and allowed that his wine cellars were famous. In retirement this theorist and politician remained a man of culture, a lover of art and good living, and, as Papineau had noted in 1835, a man with a conciliatory and moderate spirit but also a man of tenacity and ambition. He did not read novels, for which he had little liking, but was deeply interested in history and law, two disciplines which had shaped him.

The death of his wife from cholera on 22 July 1854 saddened his old age. His last public act was to participate in the financing of *L'Ordre*, a newspaper founded by Cyrille BOUCHER and Joseph Royal*. Perhaps by this gesture he wanted to emphasize the importance he had attached all his life to the written word as an instrument of education and propaganda. It is possible, however, that this tenacious man, by sharing at the age of 84 in the creation of a newspaper that was Catholic, moderate, nationalist, and respectful of established authority, landed property, and agriculture, wished to ensure his work would continue and that the values for which he had fought would triumph. Viger passed away quietly on 13 Feb. 1861, at the age of 86 years and six months. He left his fortune to his cousin Côme-Séraphin Cherrier and his library to the Séminaire de Saint-Hyacinthe. Shortly after his death the *Montreal Gazette* expressed the opinion that the essence and the justification of his political activity were to be found in "a desire to secure the blessings of free government for his fellow countrymen."

FERNAND OUELLET and ANDRÉ LEFORT

Denis-Benjamin Viger rarely signed his works, but he sometimes used the pseudonym "Un Canadien." His works include: *Analyse d'un entretien sur la conservation des établissements du Bas-Canada, des lois, des usages, &c., de ses habitans* (Montréal, 1826); *Considérations relatives à la dernière révolution de la Belgique* ([Montréal], 1831; 2e éd., 1842); *Considérations sur les effets qu'ont produit en Canada, la conservation des établissemens du pays, les mœurs, l'éducation, etc. de ses habitans; et les conséquences qu'entraîneroient leur décadence par rapport aux intérêts de la Grande Bretagne* (Montréal, 1809); *La crise ministérielle et Mr. Denis Benjamin Viger . . .* (Kingston, Ont., 1844); *Mémoires relatifs à l'emprisonnement de l'honorable D. B. Viger* (Montréal, 1840); *Observations de l'hon. D. B. Viger, contre la proposition faite dans le Conseil législatif, le 4 mars, 1835, de rejeter le bill de l'Assemblée, pour la nomination d'un agent de la province* (Montréal, 1835); *Observations sur la réponse de Mathieu, lord Aylmer, à la députation du Tattersall . . . sur les affaires du Canada, le 15 avril, 1834* (Montréal, 1834).

[The major Quebec archives and the PAC hold numerous documents concerning the career of Denis-

Benjamin Viger. The following papers of pre-confederation politicians at the PAC (MG 24) were particularly helpful: the Viger papers (MG 24, B6), the Papineau papers (B2), the Neilson papers (B1), and the Cherrier papers (B46). The Papineau and Bourassa collections at the ANQ-Q include newspaper articles written by Viger. Also important are the Fonds Viger-Verreau at the ASQ and Viger's correspondence with Bishop Lartigue at the ACAM. A.L. and F.O.]

Bas-Canada, chambre d'Assemblée, *Journaux*, *1832–35. Siège de Québec en 1759, copie d'après un manuscrit apporté de Londres, par l'honorable D. B. Viger, lors de son retour en Canada, en septembre 1834–mai 1835* (Québec, 1836). [Ross Cuthbert], *An apology for Great Britain, in allusion to a pamphlet, intituled, "Considérations, &c. par un Canadien, M.P.P."* (Quebec, 1809). F.-X. Garneau, *Voyage en Angleterre et en France dans les années 1831, 1832 et 1833*, Paul Wyczynski, édit. (Ottawa, 1968). [Sir Francis Hincks], *The ministerial crisis: Mr. D. B. Viger, and his position, being a review of the Hon. Mr. Viger's pamphlet entitled "La crise ministérielle et Mr. Denis Benjamin Viger, etc. en deux parties"* (Kingston, [Ont.], 1844). Monet, *Last cannon shot*. Fernand Ouellet, *Éléments d'histoire sociale du Bas-Canada* (Montréal, 1972). É.-Z. Massicotte, "Les demeures de Denis-Benjamin Viger," *BRH*, XLVII (1941), 269–75. Fernand Ouellet, "Denis-Benjamin Viger et le problème de l'annexation," *BRH*, LVII (1951), 195–205; "Le mandement de Mgr Lartigue de 1837 et la réaction libérale," *BRH*, LVIII (1952), 97–104; "Papineau et la rivalité Québec-Montréal (1820–1840)," *RHAF*, XIII (1959–60), 311–27.

VON BUNNING. *See* BUNNING

W

WAISOWINDEBAY. *See* MUSQUAKIE

WAKEFIELD, EDWARD GIBBON, author and politician; b. 20 March 1796 in London, England, eldest son of Edward Wakefield, statistician, and Susanna Crash; d. 16 May 1862 in Wellington, New Zealand.

Edward Gibbon Wakefield's father, a man of radical and humanitarian views, was the author of a respected work on Ireland and a close friend of the noted Benthamites, James Mill and Francis Place. As a boy Edward Gibbon was apparently obstinate and wilful, produced by the unstable, financially pressed, early years of his parents' marriage. His troubled education at Tottenham, Westminster School (1807–9), and finally Edinburgh High School ended with his expulsion in 1810. From 1814 to 1820 Wakefield was connected with the British legation at Turin. While in England in 1816 he eloped with Eliza Susan Pattle, a 16-year-old ward in chancery and heiress to a Canton merchant; she bore him two children before her death in 1820. Wakefield was left with the interest from a trust fund of £70,000.

From 1820 to 1825 Wakefield was a member of the British legation at Paris. Seeking further means so as to secure a seat in the House of Commons, Wakefield in 1826 abducted 15-year-old Ellen Turner, daughter of a Cheshire silk manufacturer, and persuaded her to marry him. The marriage was not consummated, and Wakefield, along with his brother William Hayward, his accomplice, was tried amid considerable publicity. He was sentenced to three years imprisonment from May 1827.

While in prison Wakefield read everything he could about the colonies and developed a theory of "systematic colonization." His ideas were first advanced in *A letter from Sydney*, published anonymously in 1829. The heart of his argument was that colonial development languished because land was too easy to acquire and labour insufficient for development. Canada appears as an illustration of the effects of bad policy, on the evidence largely of Robert GOURLAY's *Statistical account of Upper Canada . . .* (1822). Gourlay had written that dispersed settlement in Upper Canada produced a people "who retrograded in civilization and moral worth." Wakefield now stated that an abundance of land produced "a people like what the Canadians will be and in the United States Americans are – a people who, though they increase in number make no progress in the art of living." Hence his solution: concentrated settlement achieved through the sale of land at a sufficient price. He explained, however, that the system would not work in Canada because an increased price for land would simply divert settlement to the United States.

Wakefield's argument, masterfully presented, won converts in John Stuart Mill and other prominent economists and public figures. His authorship was acknowledged after his release from prison in 1830, and he kept up his interest in colonization. In 1834 his views inspired the South Australian Association, and its apparent early

Wakefield

success gave a boost to Wakefield's adherents, although Wakefield separated himself from the enterprise in 1836. He then threw his energy into the New Zealand Association, formed in 1837.

It was as a subscriber to his colonization theory and an associate in the New Zealand Association that Lord Durham [Lambton*] became acquainted with Wakefield. Expecting to be commissioner of crown lands, Wakefield followed Durham to Canada in May 1838. However, the notoriety of the Turner abduction made this appointment impossible. Charles Buller*, who had come with Durham also, was appointed commissioner and, although Wakefield did the work, he was unpaid and officially unrecognized.

Before he left Canada on 20 Oct. 1838 Wakefield completed the report on public lands and emigration subsequently attached as appendix B to Durham's *Report*. He attempted here what he earlier had said could not be done: to fit his system to British North America. Past policy had alienated vast tracts without any comparable advance in settlement, thus undermining the market whatever the price of crown lands. Wakefield's answer was a tax of 2d. an acre on wild lands, and a programme of public works financed from the proceeds. He believed crown lands could be sold at $2.00 an acre although American lands were available at $1.25. Reform of the old system, he argued, should be the responsibility of the British parliament, the imperial government having created the problem. His recommendations bore no fruit.

While in Canada Wakefield established contact with French Canadian Patriote leaders. He had conversations with Louis-Hippolyte LA FONTAINE, and made a secret trip to Saratoga Springs, N.Y., where he failed to see Louis-Joseph Papineau*. His purpose remains ambiguous. He later claimed that he had no mission from Durham and that he did not report the conversations to anyone. La Fontaine understood the opposite. Like Durham, Wakefield professed to see little future for French Canada except in assimilation. La Fontaine and his friends, Wakefield wrote, were "profoundly ignorant of their own position and thoroughly devoid of judgment. . . ."

Wakefield's departure from Canada was a consequence of Durham's decision, against the advice of both himself and Buller, to resign. Arriving at Liverpool ten days before Durham landed at Plymouth, Wakefield promoted Durham's cause in Radical circles and wrote to Durham advising him to break with the government, advice that again Durham did not take. Durham's *Report* was completed in January 1839; according to Lord Henry Peter Brougham, Durham's

great antagonist, "Wakefield thought it, Buller wrote it, Durham signed it." Except for the ideas on colonization Wakefield's influence cannot be demonstrated, but a rumour that he was the individual who leaked the *Report* to the *Times* is more plausible.

From 1839 to 1846 Wakefield became principal director in London of the New Zealand Colonization Company, which planted settlements in New Zealand. But his interest in Canada did not lapse. In 1838 he had visited the Beauharnois seigneury of Edward ELLICE, the Whig politician and father of Durham's private secretary, and in 1839 he negotiated its sale as agent for the North American Colonial Association of Ireland, a joint stock company. His connection with this company brought Wakefield to Canada briefly in 1841 to lobby for Beauharnois as the site of the next section of the St Lawrence canal system. In July he saw Lord Sydenham [Thomson*], who was wary of anyone of Wakefield's reputation, but who adopted a favourable view of the association almost in spite of its agent. Sydenham died before the canal question was settled and in January 1842 Wakefield returned to Canada seeking to influence a new governor, Sir Charles Bagot*, and an assembly in which there was strong opposition to the Beauharnois route.

Wakefield now emerged as a champion of the French Canadians, cultivating the friendship of Denis-Benjamin VIGER and Jean-Joseph Girouard*, and agitating for equal justice for French Canadians in a series of letters to the London weekly, *Colonial Gazette*. In June the Beauharnois route was approved by the Executive Council, but Wakefield's activity had become an end in itself. He applauded Bagot's conciliatory moves towards the French Canadians and castigated the negative attitude of the Colonial Office. Most remarkable in his letters, appearing in July and August, was his evident access to inside information about Bagot's appointments. For example, his eighth letter, written on 10 August, correctly predicted that Bagot would bring La Fontaine into office within a month. There were embarrassing rumours that Wakefield was behind Bagot's policy, although Bagot claimed he saw Wakefield on two or three formal occasions only. Wakefield had access to Dominick DALY, the provincial secretary, and to Thomas William Clinton Murdoch, the civil secretary, but they can be ruled out as sources. The likely explanation is that Wakefield was paying a minor official to leak documents to him.

In November 1842 Wakefield won a by-election in Beauharnois as a La Fontaine candidate on the strength of the French parishes in the riding. Wakefield then left for England and returned only for the session in September 1843. He then sought legislation to enable the North American Colonial Association of Ireland to operate as a mortgage and trust company in Canada and he tried to advance a major scheme of colonization. The ministry did not support him and he turned against them. When Robert Baldwin* and La Fontaine resigned over the patronage issue on 26 November, Wakefield threw himself in with Viger and Daly on Sir Charles Theophilus Metcalfe*'s side. In the ensuing constitutional debate he insisted that the principle of responsible government was not at stake, as Baldwin and La Fontaine claimed, and that they had deliberately forced a rupture because they had lost popularity and were afraid of being turned out by the assembly.

Wakefield wrote a pamphlet and an article on Metcalfe after he had left Canada for the last time in 1844. In his desire to show himself consistent in the Metcalfe crisis, Wakefield defined responsible government as narrowly as possible and asserted that, because a colonial governor was answerable to the imperial parliament, it was necessary for him "to take a far more active part in public affairs than the Sovereign." He described Baldwin's views as "peculiar," but it was Wakefield who had misread the immediate future of colonial government in Canada.

Wakefield's activity in Canada had embarrassed some and antagonized others, but it had produced a tidy income for himself: between 1841 and 1844 his agency on behalf of the North American Colonial Association of Ireland had earned him £20,000. In all his colonization ventures Wakefield was essentially a promoter and lobbyist and his theory a justification for schemes of speculation in colonial lands. His reputation among Canadians was no higher when he left than it had been when he first came.

During a serious illness in 1846, following increased work for the New Zealand Colonization Company, Wakefield was edged out of its management. He took up the project of an Anglican colony in New Zealand, based once again on his theories. In 1853 he emigrated to New Zealand where he spent his last eight years in complete retirement.

H. J. M. JOHNSTON

[E. G. Wakefield's *A letter from Sydney, the principal town of Australia*, ed. Robert Gouger (London, 1829), *England and America; a comparison of the social and political state of both nations* (2v., London, 1833; 2nd ed., New York, 1834), *A view of Sir Charles Metcalfe's government of Canada, by a member of the provincial government* (London, 1844), and *A view of the art of colonization, with present reference to the British empire; in letters between a statesman and a colonist* (London, 1849; 2nd ed., Oxford, 1914) are included in *The collected works of Edward Gibbon Wakefield*, comp. M. F. L. Pritchard (Glasgow and London, 1968), which also contains a good representation of Wakefield's work on colonization. His article, "Sir Charles Metcalfe in Canada," *Fisher's Colonial Magazine and Commercial Maritime Journal* (London), new ser., I (1844), is reprinted in [Charles Buller and E. G. Wakefield], *Charles Buller and responsible government . . .*, ed. E. M. Wrong (n.p., 1926). Biographies of Wakefield include Richard Garnett, *Edward Gibbon Wakefield; the colonization of South Australia and New Zealand* ([London], 1898); A. J. Harrop, *The amazing career of Edward Gibbon Wakefield* (London, 1928); Irma O'Connor, *Edward Gibbon Wakefield: the man himself* (London, [1929]; and Paul Bloomfield, *Edward Gibbon Wakefield, builder of the British Commonwealth* ([London, 1961]). H.J.M.J.]

Colonial Gazette (London), 1842. *Debates of the Legislative Assembly of United Canada*, I–IV. Hincks, *Reminiscences*. [J. G. Lambton], *Lord Durham's report on the affairs of British North America*, ed. C. P. Lucas (3v., Oxford, 1912). [E. G. Wakefield], "Edward Gibbon Wakefield and the Beauharnois canal," ed. A. R. M. Lower, *CHR*, XIII (1932), 37–44. *DNB*. Dent, *Last forty years*, I. Gates, *Land policies of U.C.* C. D. W. Goodwin, *Canadian economic thought: the political economy of a developing nation, 1814–1914* (Durham, N.C., and London, 1961). U. N. MacDonnell, *Gibbon Wakefield and Canada subsequent to the Durham mission, 1839–42* (Kingston, Ont., 1925). Monet, *Last cannon shot*. C. W. New, *Lord Durham; a biography of John George Lambton, first Earl of Durham* (Oxford, 1929). Helen Taft Manning, "E. G. Wakefield and the Beauharnois canal," *CHR*, XLVIII (1967), 1–25.

WALSH, KYRAN, Roman Catholic priest; b. *c* 1808 in County Kilkenny (Republic of Ireland); d. 4 Sept. 1868 at Harbour Main, Nfld.

Educated at St John's College, Waterford (Republic of Ireland), Kyran Walsh came to Newfoundland about 1839 at the invitation of Roman Catholic Bishop Michael Anthony Fleming*, who ordained him sometime prior to 1841. During his service as parish priest at St Mary's on the southern coast, Walsh was intrumental in the building of a church, a school, and a presbytery. Because of his business ability, he was recalled to St John's by Bishop Fleming to assist in raising funds for the new Cathedral of St John the Baptist and was present at the laying of the foundation stone on 20 May 1841. He served in St John's until about 1857 when he was appointed parish priest at Harbour Main and vicar general of the diocese of St John's by Bishop John Thomas MULLOCK, positions he held until his death.

Ward

Like many of his contemporaries in Ireland, Walsh was a devoted disciple of Father Theobald Mathew, the renowned advocate of temperance. Shortly after his ordination he established a temperance society in St John's and he continued, by his zeal and example, to support the cause in Newfoundland.

Father Walsh was considered by some contemporaries as "the head and centre of the liberal party" after Philip Francis Little*'s retirement as premier in 1858. His influence was certainly not as great as that of the actual party leader, John Kent*, in the late 1850s and early 1860s, but at the local level he exerted formidable pressure which was acknowledged by both political candidates and voters. In the turbulent election contest of May 1861 [see Alexander BANNERMAN], George James HOGSETT, the Catholic Liberal candidate for Harbour Main, admitted that "Father Walsh was one of my most influential supporters," and voter David Kenny of Cat's Cove, an erstwhile Conservative supporter, testified that he had voted for the Liberal candidates on the advice of Walsh. During the assembly's inquiry into the riots at Harbour Main in this election, Walsh himself admitted that he had openly canvassed for Hogsett and Charles Furey, and that on election day he had led a crowd of some 250–300 men from Harbour Main and Salmon Cove to Cat's Cove as support for Liberal voters from Salmon Cove who feared interference with the poll. The ensuing collision with the people of Cat's Cove had resulted in one killed and ten wounded. Several weeks after the Cat's Cove incident a crowd that had attacked the property of the returning officer at Harbour Main, Patrick Strapp, was not persuaded to disperse until Walsh's return from St John's, although one witness described him as "an unprotesting spectator" while Strapp's seven buildings were razed.

At his death only the Protestant Liberal newspaper, the *Morning Chronicle*, spoke at length of Father Walsh's work in Newfoundland. The brief notes in other St John's newspapers and the complete lack of reference to Walsh in subsequent histories of the Roman Catholic Church in Newfoundland perhaps indicate that his partisan political activities had caused displeasure inside as well as outside the church.

ELINOR SENIOR

Nfld., House of Assembly, *Journal*, 1861, app., "Harbor Main election; evidence taken before the select committee appointed to inquire into the contested election for the district of Harbor Main," 58–92; 1863, app., "Election riots, 1861; commissioner's report, no 2, district of Harbor Main," 790. *Morning Chronicle* (St John's), 8 Sept. 1868. *Newfoundlander*, 8 Sept. 1868. *Patriot* (St John's), 12 Sept. 1868. Gunn, *Political history of Nfld*. Elinor Senior, "The origin and political activities of the Orange Order in Newfoundland, 1863–1890" (unpublished MA thesis, Memorial University of Newfoundland, St John's, 1959), 25, 28.

WARD, SAMUEL RINGGOLD, abolitionist, journalist, and lecturer; b. 17 Oct. 1817 in Maryland, son of slave parents, Anne (Harper?) and William Ward; d. probably in 1866 in Jamaica.

Samuel Ringgold Ward's parents escaped to Greenwich, N.J., in 1820 and in 1826 moved to New York where Samuel was educated by Quakers and became a teacher in black schools. In January 1838 he married a Miss Reynolds while he was teaching in Newark, N.J.; they were to have one son. Ward was licensed to preach in May 1839 by the New York Congregational (General) Association, and he held two white pastorates in New York State from 1841 to 1851. Between the two ministries, in 1843–46, he studied medicine and law. He had already come to the attention of Lewis Tappan, a leading New York abolitionist, and had been appointed an agent of the American Anti-Slavery Society in 1839. He had joined the Liberty party and in 1844 set out on his first lecture tour to abolition, temperance, and peace societies. From 1845 to 1848 Ward edited the *True American and Religious Examiner* in Cortlandville Township, N.Y., and in 1849 he went to Syracuse, N.Y., to edit the *Impartial Citizen*, which he took to Boston in 1850. In October 1851 he was active in aiding the escape of William Henry, a principal in the "Jerry" fugitive slave rescue case. To avoid arrest Ward fled to Toronto.

Ward quickly attracted the attention of the new Anti-Slavery Society of Canada and was appointed to the executive committee late in 1851. The following year, acting upon the suggestion of American abolitionist Samuel J. May Jr, the president of the society, Michael Willis*, sent Ward on a speaking tour of Canada West, during which Ward organized (with the help of the secretary of the society, Thomas Henning) branches in Grey County, Hamilton, Kingston, and Windsor. In April 1853 the society sent Ward to England to seek funds to help the fugitive slaves then pouring into Canada West, and within ten months he was able to raise £1,200. Ward remained in Britain addressing the 1853 and 1854 meetings of the British and Foreign Anti-Slavery Society, writing his *Autobiography of a fugitive Negro*, and inspiring Mary Jane Kinnaird, wife of an Anglican philanthropist, to found a mission school for the free coloured population of Canada.

According to Ward, an English Quaker friend, John Candler, offered him 50 acres of land in Jamaica, and Ward left for Kingston late in 1855 with his son to relieve his family "from a position of dependence." He also apparently left without paying debts to a London tradesman and to the Canadian Anti-Slavery Society. At first Ward served as pastor and political adviser to a group of Baptists in Kingston, but in 1860 he moved onto his land, wanting to "hasten back to what my father first taught me ... the tilling of the soil. . . ." He published in 1866 a vigorous defence of the Jamaican governor's suppression of the rebellion which broke out at Morant Bay in October 1865. Ward's defence of the savage reprisals against the rebels shows him to have been fully on the side of the government, although he did comment on the tendency of whites to stigmatize all blacks for the acts of a few. In 1866, or soon after, he died, apparently in poverty.

Ward was and is an enigma. A militant black well ahead of his fellow fugitives in his awareness of the necessity to win the full respect of the Canadian communities into which they moved, he was opposed to all self-segregated, utopian black settlements such as William King*'s Elgin settlement. He argued against the "begging system" prevalent in Canada West in the 1850s, by which roving black ministers sought funds and clothing for the fugitives, and yet himself undertook a begging mission to Britain. He was nominally editor and part-proprietor of the militant *Provincial Freeman*, a fugitive newspaper founded in Windsor in 1853 and under the real editorship of Mary Ann Shadd* who, with Ward, was the most outspoken black voice for the fugitive slaves in Canada. He insisted that Negroes arriving in Canada must speak with one voice in demanding their rights which, he concluded, were as little respected here as in the United States. Yet he was unpopular with many of the escaped slaves, clashing with Henry Bibb* of the rival *Voice of the Fugitive* and with the Refugee Home Society; and although he was regarded as an exceptionally fair and articulate lecturer, he directed his "belligerent spirit" against the officers of the British and Foreign Anti-Slavery Society, who found him to be an immediatist on the slavery issue. His superb presence on the platform (he was ranked next to Frederick Douglass as a speaker) placed him ahead of most white orators of the time. Ward nonetheless bowed to those he regarded as his British superiors and obviously enjoyed the company of the great. He also concluded that only the spread of Christianity and British civilization would lift Africa and blacks in general from their lowly status.

Contradictions aside, Ward was clear on the basic issue of the time: that slavery and racism, although related, were different, and that while slavery must be ended, and at once, the long battle against racism would stretch far into the future. In concluding that the Canadian abolitionists were too mild in their vision of that future, and too patronizing to the fugitives, Ward stood ahead of his time.

ROBIN W. WINKS

[S. R. Ward is an elusive figure, and even his *Autobiography of a fugitive Negro: his anti slavery labours in the United States, Canada, & England* (London, 1855; repr. New York, 1968; repr. Chicago, 1970) does not reveal much. The only known copy, possibly a reprint, of his *Reflections upon the Gordon rebellion* (1866) may be found at the University of Michigan (Ann Arbor), Dept. of Rare Books and Special Coll. The *Provincial Freeman* (Windsor; Toronto; Chatham), 1853–56, the *Liberator* (Boston), 1831–65, the *Voice of the Fugitive* (Sandwich; Windsor, [Ont.]), 1851–53, and the *Frederick Douglass' Paper* (Boston), 1847–63, make frequent reference to Ward; the *Anti-Slavery Reporter* (London), 1853–55, provides accounts of Ward's visit to England. Issues of the *Impartial Citizen* (Syracuse, N.Y.; Boston) for February 1849–June 1850 and September–December 1850 are held by the American Antiquarian Soc., Worcester, Mass. The Anti-Slavery Soc., anti-slavery papers, 1820–1951 (MSS Brit. Emp. s.16–24), at the Rhodes House Library, University of Oxford, contain many references to Ward between 1853 and 1855, as does the Anti-Slavery Soc. of Can., *Annual report* (Toronto), for 1852–57. R.W.W.]

Autographs for freedom, [ed. Julia Griffiths] (Boston, 1853). *DAB*. *The antislavery vanguard: new essays on the abolitionists*, ed. M. B. Duberman (Princeton, N.J., 1965). B. [L.] Fladeland, *Men & brothers: Anglo-American antislavery cooperation* (Urbana, Ill., 1972). Winks, *Blacks in Can*. R. K. Burke, "The Impartial Citizen of Samuel Ringgold Ward," *Journalism Quarterly* (Minneapolis, Minn.), [49] (1972), 759–60.

WARK. *See* WORK

WATERMAN, ZENAS, farmer, lumberman, justice of the peace, and politician; b. 1 Dec. 1789 at Liverpool, N.S., second child of Zenas Waterman and Eunice Dean; m. first on 20 Nov. 1811 Experience Freeman (1790–1853) and they had nine children, and secondly, on 1 Sept. 1853, Patience Freeman, who survived him without issue; d. 3 Aug. 1869 at Pleasant River, N.S.

Zenas Waterman spent his youth in Liverpool where his father kept a blacksmith shop and taught music. In 1802 his mother, not wanting her sons to join the privateers fighting against France and Spain or to be "pressed" into the Royal

Watson

Navy, persuaded her husband to pioneer a farm in the newly opened northern district of Queens County. At Pleasant River the Waterman family chopped their home out of the wilderness, sowed their crops, and planted an orchard, doing some of the first grafting in that district.

Shortly after his first marriage Zenas Waterman moved to the Twelve Mile (Middlefield), where, in partnership with James Morton, his wife's brother-in-law, he established an inn and built up a considerable lumbering business, owning and operating a mill at Bangs Falls on the Medway River. He is said to have shipped lumber to England, largely, if not entirely, in ships owned and commanded by Captain George Allen of Yarmouth. After 1840, in well-to-do middle age, Waterman returned to Pleasant River and the life of a farmer. His impressive residence, Brighton Farm, boasted 17 windows facing the road. In 1846 Waterman was instrumental in establishing a new Congregational Church in his community and held offices in it.

Throughout his life Zenas Waterman had a keen interest in public affairs. An 1837 by-election chose him to represent Queens County in the assembly, and on 25 Jan. 1838 he took his seat. He quickly proved his reputation as an exponent of reform principles, supporting Joseph Howe* on several contentious issues. In 1840 he was defeated, according to the *Novascotian*, by a "combination of the two parties in the town of Liverpool, who, though they have no love for each other, would rather divide power between them, than share it with the farmers in the northern district." Waterman remained a loyal Reformer, often taking to the hustings in support of his party's candidate. In 1848, following the advent of responsible government, Waterman was appointed a justice of the peace, a commission he held until his death.

In or out of public office, Zenas Waterman was best known for his efforts in the building of roads. A writer to the *Liverpool Transcript* of 10 Jan. 1861 lauds him as "the father of nearly all the improved lines of road," especially those connecting his northern district with the markets of Liverpool and other large centres.

Zenas Waterman, a stern, strong-willed man, was no doubt well beloved by his friends and equally disliked by those who opposed him. An advocate of temperance and reform, he forced his points home not by fluent speeches but by the sheer force of his personality.

JOHN N. GRANT

PANS, MG 1, 859; 933–35 (Waterman family papers, *c.* 1780–1913); RG 1, 175–76; 214¹/₂, 1846–51; RG 7, 219 [Provincial Secretary's papers]; RG 12, Census of Nova Scotia, 1860–61, 18; RG 34–319, A1–A2, 1842–63 [Queens County miscellaneous assessments]. Private archives, Mr Seth Bartling (Liverpool, N.S.), R. J. Long, "The annals of Liverpool and Queen's County, 1760–1867" (1926) (typescript at Dalhousie University Library, Halifax; mfm. at PANS). Queens County Hist. Soc. (Liverpool, N.S.), Queens County Total Abstinence Soc., minutes, 1838–64 (mfm. at PANS). N.S., House of Assembly, *Journal and proc.*, 1837–40. *Novascotian*, 1837–40, 1869. *Belcher's farmer's almanack*, 1849–69. *Epitaphs from the old cemeteries of Liverpool, Nova Scotia*, comp. Charles Warman (Boston, [1910]). J. F. More, *The history of Queens County, N.S.* (Halifax, 1873; repr. Belleville, Ont., 1972). E. F. Waterman, *The Waterman family*, ed. D. L. Jacobus (2v., New Haven, Conn., 1939–42). D. R. Jack, "Queens County, Nova Scotia," *Acadiensis* (Saint John, N.B.), IV (1904), 93–95. R. R. McLeod, "Old times in Liverpool, N.S.," and "The Northern District of Queens, N.S.," *Acadiensis* (Saint John, N.B.), IV (1904), 96–118 and 140–57, respectively; "Notes historical and otherwise of the Northern District of Queens County," N.S. Hist. Soc., *Coll.*, XVI (1912), 93–135.

WATSON, WILLIAM, miller, businessman, and municipal politician; b. in Bannockburn, Scotland, son of John Watson, a miller in Bannockburn, and Helen Walker; d. 8 April 1867 at Montreal.

John Watson immigrated to Montreal in 1801 with his wife and five children. He established himself as a miller in the Recollets *faubourg* where water power was available from the Îles des Sœurs channel, and ground wheat and other grains for the local market and for export. Alexander Ogilvie, a relative of John, was brought into partnership in 1811, and the ties between the Ogilvie and Watson families were further strengthened when Ogilvie married John's daughter Helen.

William Watson was brought into the firm at an early age, and when his father died in 1819 continued the partnership with Ogilvie. The business appears to have prospered in the 1810s and 1820s which was a period of general expansion for the export trade in Canadian cereals. In 1837 the mill was moved to the St Gabriel lock on the Lachine Canal, making it one of the first industries in Montreal to use the hydraulic power available from the Lachine rapids.

The Canada Corn Act of 1843 admitted flour produced in Canada into Great Britain at a nominal duty and as a consequence the Canadian milling industry expanded greatly. New mills were built all along the St Lawrence–Great Lakes system, many of them on the canals which were part of the system. The Lachine Canal enlargement of

1846 added an inducement to industrialists to select Montreal, and one of the largest mills to locate on the enlarged canal was that of Ira Gould in 1847. Gould, in partnership with John Young*, became a major Montreal manufacturer almost overnight.

Manufacturers such as Watson, Ogilvie, and Gould who had the capital to erect large, well-equipped, and heavily mechanized mills were able to withstand the transformations which were taking place in the industry in the late 1840s and early 1850s. Imperial policy no longer offered advantages to Canadian millers, but the domestic market for grains was expanding. Wheat yields in the Lower Canadian seigneuries were decreasing and millers such as Watson purchased wheat in the United States to satisfy the Lower Canadian market for flour. Upper Canadian wheat, which fetched higher prices, was milled for American consumers, while cheaper grades of wheat were reserved for the Maritime colonies. The Watson-Ogilvie mill provided a large share of the flour produced in Canada for these markets.

So prosperous had flour milling become during the early 1850s that Watson and Alexander Ogilvie greatly expanded their operations. In 1852 they erected the new Glenora Mill at their St Gabriel lock site. They took into partnership Alexander's eldest son, Alexander Walker Ogilvie*, and, temporarily, James Goudie, Alexander's brother-in-law. The new mill made flour, and also undertook custom work for a fee (normally 10 per cent) on other grains such as barley and peas. The Crimean War expanded demand for North American grain and flour in Britain and further opportunities for high profits were created by the Reciprocity Treaty of 1854 and the American Civil War in 1861. In fact, an adequate supply of suitable wheat was a growing problem for Montreal millers. When the productive capacity at the Glenora Mill was increased during the 1850s (by installing more millstones and renting more storage space) more agents had to be sent to Canada West to buy wheat. Another of Alexander Ogilvie's sons, John, entered the business in 1855, and he devoted much of his time to scouting western Upper Canada for supplies of wheat.

Alexander Ogilvie died in 1858. The firm, which had become in fact an Ogilvie enterprise as William Watson, now an elderly man, had allowed his young, aggressive nephews to take over, became one in name as well, as A. W. Ogilvie and Company. Watson remained a partner of the company, but the direction of its affairs had passed to younger hands. In addition, he had given up in 1857 the post of inspector of flour for

Montreal, in which he had succeeded his older brother Robert in 1827.

Except for serving three terms as a Montreal City Council member (1843–45), Watson devoted himself mainly to business. Like most of his fellow Montreal businessmen, he had widely diversified financial interests. The inventory of his estate prepared after he died in 1867 provides an invaluable indication of how the typical mid 19th century Montreal bourgeois was involved in several different facets of the city's expanding economy. It reveals that in addition to his interest in the flour mill, Watson possessed mortgages on real estate throughout the city, lots and rental properties for speculation, shares in an iron mine, intercity and street railways, and the Montreal Stock Exchange, and more than $18,000 in accounts receivable, most of it uncollectable. His holdings in real estate alone were immense; they included two farms on Montreal Island, one at Lachine and the other at Hochelaga, 13 farms in the Eastern Townships, eight lots in Montreal owned jointly with brewer William Dow, and 61 other lots on Montreal Island. He also owned 32 rent-paying properties in the city, which by 1867 were bringing him an annual revenue of nearly $10,000.

Aside from bequests to the Montreal General Hospital, the Montreal Ladies Benevolent Society, and Protestant Orphan Asylum, Watson, a bachelor, left his estate, including his share of the business, to the Ogilvies. At his death flour milling, which he had helped to establish in Montreal, was one of the city's major industries, and the firm with which he had been associated was on the verge of large-scale expansion.

GERALD TULCHINSKY

Private archives, Watson Ogilvie (Beaconsfield, Que.), Resources of the estate Watson, 1867–70. *Elgin Grey papers* (Doughty), II, 472; III, 1193, 1198. *Select documents in Canadian economic history*, ed. H. A. Innis and A. R. M. Lower (2v., Toronto, 1929–33), II, 267, 284–85, 353–54. J. G. Clark, *The grain trade in the old northwest* (Urbana, Ill., 1966). Jean Delage, "L'industrie manufacturière," *Montréal économique*, Esdras Minville, édit. (Montréal, 1943), 217. P. W. Gates, *The farmer's age: agriculture, 1815–1860* (New York, 1960). *Hist. de la corporation de la cité de Montréal* (Lamothe et al.), 205–6. R. L. Jones, *History of agriculture in Ontario, 1613–1880* (Toronto, 1946), 135, 192, 216. C. B. Kuhlmann, *The development of the flour milling industry in the United States with special reference to the industry in Minneapolis* (Boston, 1929), 60–64. D. A. MacGibbon, *The Canadian grain trade* (Toronto, 1932), 10–22. D. C. Masters, *The reciprocity treaty of 1854: its history, its relation to British colonial and foreign policy and to the development of*

Webster

Canadian fiscal autonomy (London and Toronto, 1936), 110–11. *Montreal in 1856; a sketch prepared for the celebration of the opening of the Grand Trunk Railway of Canada* (Montreal, 1856). *The Ogilvies of Montreal, with a genealogical account of the descendants of their grandfather, Archibald Ogilvie, with portraits and views* (Montreal, 1904). G. R. Stevens, *Ogilvie in Canada, pioneer millers, 1801–1951* (Montreal, n.d.). ''The development of the flour and grist milling industry in Canada,'' Canadian Bankers' Assoc., *Journal* (Toronto), 30 (1923), 488–95. [P.]D.[W.] McCalla, ''The Canadian grain trade in the 1840's, the Buchanans' case,'' CHA *Historical Papers*, 1974, 95–114.

WEBSTER, JOSEPH HARDING, educator; b. 1833 or 1834 at Cambridge, Kings County, N.S.; d. 21 April 1868 in Charlottetown, P.E.I.

After being educated in Nova Scotia, Joseph Harding Webster taught for three years in the model school at Truro. He accepted appointment in November 1859 as master of the Normal School in Charlottetown, P.E.I. Although this institution had been the centre of intense controversy between Protestants and Roman Catholics since its opening in 1856 [*see* George Coles*], Webster was able to reform and expand its operations. The term was increased from three to five months, and two additional teachers were hired for the associated model school. In early 1862 Webster could announce that the number of trainees attending the Normal School had grown from the six he found on arrival to 45. In his periodic reports he continued to express pleasure at the development of the institution, and the Board of Education appears to have been satisfied that the Normal School was fulfilling its purposes.

Webster nevertheless became a frequent target for virulent abuse in the Liberal and Roman Catholic press. His harshest critic was the editor of the ultramontane *Vindicator*, who was widely believed to be Father Angus MacDonald*, rector of the rival St Dunstan's College. The newspaper condemned the Normal School as ''essentially a Protestant Institution'' and Webster himself as a ''foreign educational humbug''; the co-educational classes meant that the Normal School provided ''little else than rendezvous for flirtation and courtship.'' When the *Vindicator* also insinuated that Webster, then a bachelor, had improper relations with female students and that he had driven a female colleague to an early grave, Webster initiated a libel suit against the publisher, Edward Reilly*. The matter ended on 5 Oct. 1864 with a complete retraction by Reilly, but not before this libel case had become probably the most sensational news item in Prince Ed-ward Island in the year of the Charlottetown conference.

In succeeding years Webster attracted little public attention and he appears to have performed his duties efficiently. On 9 March 1868 he retired as master of the Normal School for reasons of ill health. In the following month he died of ''pulmonary consumption'' at age 34, leaving a wife and one young child. He had played a decisive role in establishing the Normal School as a central institution in the Island's educational system during its formative years.

IAN ROSS ROBERTSON

PAPEI, P.E.I., Executive Council, Minutes, 10 March 1868. P.E.I., House of Assembly, *Journal*, 1860, app.J; 1861, app.W; 1862, app.DD; 1864, app.N; Legislative Council, *Debates and proc.*, 1879 (2nd session), 152. *Examiner* (Charlottetown), 3, 24 Dec. 1860; 26 Oct. 1863; 9 May 1864; 23 March, 27 April 1868. *Islander*, 13 March, 24 April 1868. *Patriot* (Charlottetown), 12 March, 23 April, 11 June 1868. *Protestant and Evangelical Witness* (Charlottetown), 26 Nov. 1859; 31 Jan. 1863; 9 Jan., 14 May, 17 Sept. 1864. *Ross's Weekly* (Charlottetown), 30 Nov. 1859. *Summerside Journal* (Summerside, P.E.I.), 26 March, 23 April 1868. *Vindicator* (Charlottetown), 21 Oct., 4, 11, 25 Nov. 1863; 6, 27 Jan., 2 March, 15 June, 13, 27 July, 5 Oct. 1864. Robertson, ''Religion, politics, and education in P.E.I.,'' chaps.1–7.

WEBSTER, WILLIAM BENNETT, doctor, geologist, and politican; b. 18 Jan. 1798 at Kentville, N.S., eldest of three sons of Dr Isaac Webster and Prudence Bentley; m. on 11 Sept. 1826 Wilhelmina Moore, and they had four children; d. 4 April 1861 at Halifax, N.S.

After early schooling in the Cornwallis area, William Bennett Webster went to Scotland, where he studied medicine at the University of Edinburgh. After graduation he travelled widely on the Continent and visited several clinics. About 1822 he returned to Nova Scotia to settle in Kentville. He followed his father in his profession, his Presbyterianism, and his inventiveness. He inherited considerable property and in his turn acquired more. In 1855 he was elected to the assembly for King's County and held the post until 1859 when the constituency was divided. He was then elected to represent Kings County, Southern Division, a seat he held until his death.

Webster was an energetic man of wide interests. He was considered by his fellow doctors to be highly capable and in 1836 he performed the first successful operation in the province for the removal of a cataract. He was active as a founder of the Nova Scotia Medical Society in 1854, and in 1858, as a member of the legislature, he helped draft a bill to legalize dissection. But he found time to indulge in many hobbies, one of which brought him as wide a reputation as did his profession. An amateur geologist, he studied the minerals of the Blomidon area in company with Abraham GESNER, his brother-in-law, and formed an outstanding geological collection which was eventually presented by his widow to the Provincial Museum. He discovered an interesting fossil which was named *Dictyonema Websteri* in his honour. He was also remembered as a man who invented "mechanical contrivances." An interest in town planning prompted him to lay out the main streets of Kentville, which a century later remain as he drew them.

MINERVA TRACY

Novascotian, 8 April 1861. *Directory of N.S. MLAs*, 358–59. David Allison, *History of Nova Scotia* (3v., Halifax, 1916), III, 581. A. W. H. Eaton, *The history of Kings County, Nova Scotia . . .* (Salem, Mass., 1910), 125, 510, 528–29, 857–60. K. A. MacKenzie, "Doctor Isaac Webster, 1766–1851," and "Founders of the Medical Society of Nova Scotia," in *Nova Scotia Medical Bull.* (Halifax), XXXIII (1954), 216, and XXXII (1953), 240, respectively. Harry Piers, "A brief historical account of the Nova Scotian Institute of Science, and the events leading up to its formation; with biographical sketches of its deceased presidents and other prominent members," N.S. Institute of Science, *Proc. and Trans.* (Halifax), XIII (1910–14), lvi–lvii.

WELLER, WILLIAM, entrepreneur and office-holder; b. 13 May 1799 in Vermont; d. 21 Sept. 1863 at Cobourg, Canada West.

William Weller came from northern New York with his father to settle in Upper Canada. In 1829 he and a partner, Hiram Norton of Prescott, purchased the existing York (Toronto) to Kingston stage coach line from Jonathan Ogden. In the summer of 1830 Weller was operating coaches twice a week between York and Carrying Place on the Bay of Quinte, where there was a connection with steamers to Prescott. He bought out Norton in 1830, and in the winter of that year was cooperating with H. Dickinson of Montreal and again with Norton to provide service from York to Montreal five times a week. In 1832 Weller purchased from George Playter the stage line running north on Yonge St from York to Holland Landing, and by 1835 he was offering winter service between Toronto and Hamilton with a branch line from Dundas to Niagara. In the same year he instituted tri-weekly service between Cobourg, Port Hope, and Peterborough and in 1844 began operating the steamer *Forester* on Rice Lake. By 1837 Weller was the acknowl-

edged king of land transport whose well-established fleet of brightly coloured Royal Mail Line coaches ran from Niagara to Montreal. At his Cobourg base he also operated repair shops and a carriage factory.

Travellers' accounts and the petitions of local settlers describe the appalling conditions of Upper Canada's roads in the first half of the 19th century. The crude corduroy roads built by statute labour were infrequently levelled or drained and were often pitted with holes; bridges might be washed out by spring floods or destroyed by fire. Water routes were used extensively because road travel was often impossible except in the dry summer and in winter when sleighs were possible. The trip from York to Montreal took five or six days, and when Weller himself drove Governor General Charles Poulett Thomson* between those two towns in 35 hours and 40 minutes in February 1840, the feat was widely praised and Weller won £1,000 in bets. Success in his enterprises enabled him in 1850 to reduce the stage fare between Toronto and Montreal from $20 to $16. Weller received a regular income from mail contracts, most for year-round service, but some for winter only. Between 1838 and 1852 he had 12 yearly contracts to deliver mail between Kingston and Montreal for which he received £2,625 annually.

Weller was a member of the Cobourg Board of Police from 1837 to 1844 and again in 1847, serving as its president in 1838, 1843, and 1844. Because of his interest in road improvements he became in 1847 a stockholder in the Cobourg and Port Hope Road Company and president of the Cobourg and Rice Lake Plank Road and Ferry Company. During the 1840s and 1850s Cobourg and Port Hope were competing as ports of outlet for the trade of the townships inland from the lake, with roads and railways as determining factors. As mayor of Cobourg in 1850, 1851, and 1863, and as a town councillor from 1852 to 1855 and again in 1857, Weller was deeply involved in Cobourg's attempt to establish its supremacy. The town was to accumulate a debt of $800,000 by 1860 in contrast to one of $2,000 in 1845. Council borrowed $12,000 in 1848 to build Victoria Hall, the town hall, purchased in 1850 the Port Hope to Rice Lake road for $14,400, allotting $6,000 for improvements, purchased the Cobourg Harbour Company for $40,000 and voted $24,000 for its completion, and between 1852 and 1858 bought shares in and made loans to the Cobourg and Peterborough Railway Company in the amount of $671,775. The railway was plagued by construction difficulties and was abandoned in 1860.

Wetherall

Weller himself had been a director in the late 1840s and early 1850s of two railway companies, and the increasing use of railways made his stage routes obsolete by the late 1850s. At the end of his career he owned a 65-acre land grant in Hamilton Township and valuable town lots in Cobourg, one of which was sold to the Grand Trunk Railway.

William Weller was a colourful character, robust, generous, and good-natured, and with a lively sense of humour. He probably had 22 children, 11 by his first wife, Mercy Willcox (Wilcox) who died in 1843, and 11 by his second wife, Margaret McKechin (Mackechnie). His youngest child, John Laing Weller*, was engineer in charge of constructing the Welland Ship Canal beginning in 1900.

MADELEIN MUNTZ

A scrapbook of Madelein Marcia Weller, daughter-in-law of William Weller, in the possession of the author, has been useful in preparing this biography. PAC, RG 1, L3, 538a, bundle 3, no.37; RG 11, ser.2, 411, file 153. United Counties of Northumberland and Durham Surrogate Court (Cobourg, Ont.), will of William Weller, 22 Feb. 1864. Can., Prov. of, Legislative Assembly, *Journals*, 1846, I, app.F; *Statutes*, 1846, c.80; 1847, c.87, c.94; 1852–53, c.40, c.242. *Christian Guardian*, 12 June 1830. *Church*, 26 Dec. 1850. *Cobourg Star* (Cobourg, [Ont.]), 11 Jan. 1831, 22 Jan. 1840, 23 Aug. 1843. Thomas Fowler, *Journal of a tour through British North America to the falls of Niagara . . .* (Aberdeen, Scot., 1832). *Globe*, 23 Sept. 1863. [A. B. Murphy] Jameson, *Winter studies and summer rambles in Canada*, ed. J. J. Talman and E. M. Murray (Toronto, 1943). *Town of York, 1815–34* (Firth). U.C., *Statutes*, 1834, c.28; 1836, c.19; 1837, c.74. *Valley of the Trent* (Guillet). *Heritage Kingston*, ed. J. D. Stewart and I. E. Wilson ([Kingston, Ont., 1973]). Craig, *Upper Canada*. E. C. Guillet, *Cobourg, 1798–1948* (Oshawa, Ont., 1948); *The lives and times of the Patriots: an account of the rebellion in Upper Canada, 1837–1838, and the Patriot agitation in the United States, 1837–1842* (Toronto, 1838; repr. 1968); *The pioneer farmer and backwoodsman* (2v., Toronto, 1963). Middleton, *Municipality of Toronto*, I, 225. D. E. Wattie, "Cobourg, 1784–1867" (unpublished MA thesis, University of Toronto, 1949). Howard Pammett, "The steamboat era on the Trent–Otonabee waterway, 1830–1950," *OH*, LVI (1964), 67–104.

WETHERALL, Sir GEORGE AUGUSTUS, soldier; b. in 1788 at Penton, Hampshire, England, only son of General Sir Frederick Augustus Wetherall, and his first wife, Elizabeth Mytton; m. Frances Diana Denton in 1812; d. 8 April 1868 at Sandhurst, England.

George Augustus Wetherall attended Hyde Abbey School, Winchester, and the military college at Farnham. At age seven he was already an officer, having been provided on 29 July 1795 with a lieutenant's commission in the 7th Fusiliers. His active service began in Halifax in 1803 when he joined his father's newly raised Nova Scotia Regiment of Fencible Infantry. Promoted captain on 13 May 1805, he exchanged to the 1st Foot (the Royals), then serving in the West Indies, on 27 Nov. 1806.

Captain Wetherall joined his father's staff as brigade-major at the Cape of Good Hope in 1809. He served his father as aide-de-camp during the conquest of Java in 1811, and became a major in his regiment in December 1819. From 1822 to 1826 he was military secretary to the governor of Madras, then became deputy judge advocate general for India. On 7 Aug. 1828, he was promoted lieutenant-colonel in the Royals. He commanded the Royals' 2nd battalion in Madras until 1831, then in the United Kingdom, 1831–36, and in Canada, 1836–43.

During the early autumn of 1837 Wetherall was in command of the Montreal garrison but returned to regimental duty on 1 November. The city was already tense as increasing bitterness between the adherents of Louis-Joseph Papineau* and his Patriote movement and the supporters of the government threatened open strife. On the 16th warrants were issued against Papineau and 25 of his leading supporters including Dr Wolfred NELSON. Most had fled the city, but the military could now act legally in support of the civil power. When, that night, a troop of Royal Montreal Cavalry with Patriote prisoners was set upon near Longueuil by armed men, political defiance had, in the eyes of many, become rebellion.

Wetherall was one of the first senior officers affected. Early on the 18th, with four companies of his own battalion, a detachment of artillery with two guns, some troopers of the Royal Montreal Cavalry, representatives of the magistrates, and a volunteer, Major Bartholomew-Conrad-Augustus Gugy*, provincial assistant quartermaster-general, he left Montreal with instructions to proceed to Fort Chambly on the left bank of the Richelieu. Meanwhile the commander of the forces, Sir John COLBORNE, was completing plans for a pincer movement against Saint-Denis and Saint-Charles. These villages were, respectively, the headquarters of Nelson, one of Papineau's ablest lieutenants, and of Thomas Storrow Brown*, the "general" recently appointed by Montreal's Patriote club, the Fils de la Liberté. Colonel Charles Stephen GORE, the deputy quartermaster-general for British North America, was to command the expedition, attacking south from Sorel against Saint-Denis, while Wetherall marched north against Saint-Charles. Violent weather and the vigilance of Patriote scouts seriously hampered Colborne's communications with his field commanders. The two forces, however, did set off for this concerted attack as planned.

The road which Wetherall, who was now reinforced by a company of the 66th, proceeded to take to Saint-Charles had been reduced to a treacherous morass by the first heavy rains of the winter and bridges had been cut; Wetherall's column had only marched half way, to Saint-Hilaire (Mont-Saint-Hilaire), by daybreak on the 23rd. Word of Gore's defeat reached Saint-Hilaire near midnight, leading Wetherall to believe he might have to face as many as 3,000 Patriotes at Saint-Charles. No orders came to him. Early on the 25th his force, now some 350 strong with the addition of a reserve company of the Royals, was en route to Saint-Charles.

Thomas Storrow Brown, who had spent the preceding week terrorizing loyalists and confiscating grain, cattle, and weapons, had grossly neglected the defences of his stronghold in the village. Moreover, Brown's force had melted away, and he was left with perhaps 100 muskets and a few score of men armed with the most primitive weapons. Wetherall halted out of range of the barricade Brown had erected and sent a prisoner forward with a message stating that government forces were en route to Saint-Denis and that there would be no injuries or reprisals if they were given peaceful passage through Saint-Charles. Brown, now both desperate and confused, finally replied that free passage would be granted if the British laid their arms along the roadside. Meanwhile Wetherall, his patience exhausted, had advanced to the barricade hoping for the appearance of either a white flag or a messenger. He was greeted with a fusillade. His guns now tore great holes in the barricade and he ordered a charge; the Patriotes fought bravely, but the affair was over within the hour. Brown fled north towards Saint-Denis early in the action. The British, with three dead and 18 wounded, counted 56 Patriote bodies, and suspected that many others had been killed.

Mopping up continued throughout the 26th. Many houses had been fired during the battle, and those that had sheltered sharpshooters, whether owned by Patriotes or loyalists who had fled, were burned the following day. On the 30th Wetherall entered Montreal in triumph with 30 prisoners and the Liberty Pole of Saint-Charles, complete with its red cap.

With the Richelieu district under control, Col-

borne turned his attention to Saint-Eustache, some 18 miles northwest of Montreal, from which the Patriote leaders Amury Girod* and Dr Jean-Olivier Chénier* controlled much of the rich farming country north of Lac-des-Deux-Montagnes. Colborne set out from Montreal on 13 December with nearly 2,000 men in two brigades commanded by lieutenant-colonels John Maitland of the 32nd and Wetherall of the Royals, a strong detachment of artillery, and some volunteer cavalry, and the Montreal Volunteer Rifle Corps. They reached Saint-Eustache before noon on the 14th. Colborne first directed his guns against a group of large stone houses. Wetherall, not long after, was ordered to advance down the main street and attack the Patriote citadel: the church, presbytery, and convent.

Chénier's position (Girod had fled early in the action) was desperate; although some 1,000 Patriotes had paraded on the 13th, he had now only 200 or so effectives, 70 or 80 of whom garrisoned the church. Wetherall's guns had little impact on the church, and the British infantry was hampered by the Patriotes' deadly fire. Finally Colonel Wetherall's son, Lieutenant Edward Robert Wetherall of the Royals, broke into and fired the presbytery, then the church; the convent had been earlier put to the torch.

It was now killing time. Desperate men fleeing from the church had little chance to save themselves. By 5 p.m. Dr Chénier and 70 of his men had been killed, and 118 were taken prisoner. The British and volunteer losses were negligible: one killed, nine wounded. That night the lootings and burnings of Saint-Denis and Saint-Charles were repeated, but on a larger scale. The troops, especially those of the 32nd, were bent on avenging the death of their comrade, Lieutenant George Weir, murdered at Saint-Denis on 23 November [see Gore], and the volunteers had many a score to settle with the Patriotes. Some 60 to 70 houses in addition to the religious buildings were destroyed. There is no evidence that Wetherall played any part in this aftermath and on the 17th he returned to Montreal with Colborne, who was satisfied that at Saint-Eustache the back of the rebellion had been broken.

On 13 June 1838 Wetherall received the CB and on 28 June a brevet-colonelcy in recognition of his services. Four years later he was appointed ADC to the Queen. Wetherall commanded the garrison in Canada West at London from 1840 to mid 1843, when he returned to Montreal as deputy adjutant-general. In June 1850 he was recalled to England to become deputy assistant quartermaster-general at the War Office. Promoted major-general in 1851, Wetherall became

Whelan

adjutant-general in December 1854, and general in October 1863. He received a KCB in 1856, and the GCB in 1865. From 1860 to 1865 he commanded the Northern District of Britain's Home Command. His last appointment, in 1866, was to the governorship of the Royal Military College, Sandhurst.

Sir George Augustus Wetherall was unquestionably a soldier of outstanding merit, one of the few British officers who served in North America to achieve a dominant post in the upper echelon of control at the War Office. As an individual he was both popular and respected.

JOHN W. SPURR

PRO, WO 17/1540–54 (mfm. at PAC). *Gentleman's Magazine*, CCXXIV (January–May 1868), 690. *Montreal Gazette*, 28 Nov.–16 Dec. 1837. Boase, *Modern English biog.*, III, 1291. *DNB*. G.B., WO, *Army list*, 1795–1839. *Hart's army list*, 1840–68. *The regimental records of the Royal Scots*, comp. J. C. Leask and H. M. McCance (Dublin, 1915), 421–26. L.-N. Carrier, *Les événements de 1837–1838* (Québec, 1877), 78–82, 91–92. Christie, *History of L.C.*, V, 2–9. [C.-A.-M. Globensky], *La rébellion de 1837 à Saint-Eustache précédé d'un exposé de la situation politique du Bas-Canada depuis la cession* (Québec, 1883). Joseph Schull, *Rebellion: the rising in French Canada, 1837* (Toronto, 1971), 63–64, 78–84, 113–23. J. H. Stocqueler [J. H. Siddons], *A personal history of the Horse-Guards, from 1750 to 1872* (London, 1873), 251–52. H. S. Thomas, *The story of Sandhurst* (London, 1961), 119.

WHELAN, EDWARD, journalist and politician; b. 1824 at Ballina, County Mayo (Republic of Ireland), son of a soldier in the British infantry; d. 10 Dec. 1867 in Charlottetown, P.E.I.

More than that of any other major figure in Prince Edward Island history, the early life of Edward Whelan is shrouded in romantic legend. He appears to have received a rudimentary education in Ballina and in Scotland before immigrating with his mother (who may have been widowed) to Halifax, N.S. In reply to insinuations by political enemies that they had arrived destitute, and that he had had to beg for his bread, Whelan wrote in 1855 that "enjoying in his mother's right the fruits of no small amount of property, he was never placed in [an] abject condition." According to the most precise account he has left, the year of their immigration was 1831, and he immediately enrolled in St Mary's school. In the following year he was apprenticed in the printing office of Joseph Howe*, who encouraged him to continue his education through reading, as he himself had done. Thus Whelan spent his formative years at the intellectual centre of English speaking British North America: the Halifax of Howe, Thomas McCulloch*, Thomas Chandler HALIBURTON, and "The Club." He eventually attended St Mary's Seminary, and studied directly under its first superior, Father Richard Baptist O'Brien, a dynamic Irish priest, who commenced classes in January 1840. Both O'Brien and Howe profoundly influenced the precocious youth. In early 1842, against Howe's wishes, Whelan left his office, where he had apparently remained during his studies at the seminary, and was ready, at age 18, to become an editor. Active in various Irish societies in Halifax, he succeeded O'Brien in directing the *Register*, an Irish Roman Catholic and Liberal newspaper strongly committed to repeal of the union between Ireland and England [*see* Laurence O'Connor DOYLE]. While yet in his teens, he also became known as a speaker at the mechanics' institute and at the Young Men's Catholic Institute, an organization established by O'Brien, a teacher of elocution and a well-known platform orator in his own right. One of Whelan's later associates wrote that as an orator he was "brilliant, impassioned, exciting. He had the faculty of seizing at once upon the minds of his hearers, and carrying them along with him. . . . His language was always correct, well chosen, and gracefully delivered." Writing several years after Whelan's death, James Hayden Fletcher*, himself an accomplished public lecturer, stated that "As a popular orator, we doubt if the Island has ever witnessed his equal."

In early 1843 Whelan left the *Register*, hoping to start a new Liberal semi-weekly in Halifax. The prospectus he issued for the *Spectator* did not avow any specific ethnic or religious commitment. But the project miscarried, and that summer Whelan left Halifax for Charlottetown. Accounts by Peter McCourt, William Lawson Cotton, D. C. Harvey*, Emmet J. Mullally, and Wayne E. MacKinnon, appearing many years after Whelan's death, assert that Island Reformers had consulted Howe on the choice of a journalist to found a newspaper independent of the local family compact, and that Howe had recommended the 19-year-old Irishman. This story, like so many others surrounding Whelan, appears to be apocryphal, for in 1855 he emphatically denied that he had come to the Island "under the auspices" of Howe. In any event, by mid June 1843 he was circulating a prospectus for the *Palladium*, a semi-weekly, in which he declared that his object would be "to investigate and assail, if not remedy, the evils which have grown out of the Landocracy System, a system whose principle is 'monopoly,' whose effect is oppression.'' In his first number, on 4 Sept. 1843, he also pledged "not to outstep the line of demarcation prescribed by the constitution." Edited with great gusto, the *Palladium* was a self-conscious advocate of local reform. Island Reformers had suffered defeat at the polls in 1842 following their failure to gain the acquiescence of the imperial government in their policy of escheat [*see* William COOPER]. The ideology of escheat was certain to come into question in this period of regrouping, and, while agreeing that the system of land tenure was pernicious, Whelan carefully avoided either becoming identified with escheat as a solution, or condemning it outright. He allowed Escheators access to his columns and admitted the justice of at least a partial escheat, but claimed that advocacy of a general escheat was impractical until responsible government had been obtained. This monumental reform, he argued, would provide the necessary leverage to force an end to leasehold tenure. Thus, from the beginning, Whelan tried to unify Island Reformers around the constitutional issue; although accepting the prevailing assumption that the root of the Island's problems lay in the land system, he would not commit himself firmly on local matters over which Reformers might disagree, such as escheat or annexation to Nova Scotia as solutions to the land question.

Whelan later wrote that although he had not wished to make the *Palladium* "peculiarly Irish or Catholic in its tone," a majority of his subscribers had been Irish Roman Catholics. This can probably be attributed to his vigorous advocacy of repeal. "Ireland *will be* a nation again. And where is the obstacle to prevent the accomplishment of her Nationality? English hatred and English jealousy." References to "Saxon villainy and perfidy" may have restricted his readership, but Whelan adduced different causes for discontinuing the *Palladium* in May 1845. He expressed bitterness at the failure of Island Liberals to make good their promises of financial support, despite a steadily increasing subscription list. Nineteen months of publication had left him with some £400 in bad debts. Deeply disillusioned, Whelan decided to leave the Island, and indeed there was a discernible slackening of interest in local news throughout the last months of the *Palladium*. He devoted the rest of 1845 to winding up its affairs, but, because of unforeseen circumstances, he remained on the Island several more months. To the surprise of many, he was named editor of the previously Tory *Morning News* in May 1846. The reasons for his appointment are not known with certainty, but it was probably linked to a growing rift between the local oligarchy and Lieutenant Governor Sir Henry Vere HUNTLEY. The publisher of the *News*, E. A. Moody, leaned towards Huntley; Whelan, for his part, believed the Reformers could exploit the feud for their own benefit. Consequently the *Morning News* became the organ of liberal reform on the Island until Moody's death in October. Apparently alarmed at the success of the *News*, which then had the largest circulation of any Island newspaper, the compact seems to have bought the press, thus depriving Whelan of his new editorial chair.

Yet in August 1846 Whelan had cemented his connection with the Island by gaining election as an assemblyman for St Peters in Kings County, at age 22. In his nomination speech at Grand River he stated that "the numerous slanders" of "my Charlottetown enemies" had been an important factor in his decision to contest the election. He was, in the words of one contemporary, "hated and sneered at by his opponents . . . [and] also feared. . . . In fact, like [Daniel O'Connell] he was the best abused man of his day." More than once over the years Whelan would return to this theme: "the desire for retaliation has given us more than anything else a personal interest in the struggle, from gratifying which no sacrifice or inconvenience will deter us." It was this fighting spirit which made his newspapers such effective *journaux de combat*; it also brought him before the courts several times, on charges of trespass, "riot and assault," and both civil and criminal libel. At least once, in 1850, he was a successful plaintiff in an assault case. Although he remained an assemblyman until the last year of his life, he never developed into a great parliamentarian. His attendance was sporadic, his interventions in most years were infrequent, and the debates never seemed to awaken in him the genius and passion apparent in his printed work. Perhaps this lack is a reflection of the fact that Whelan was always more artist than logician. In any event, the press remained his primary forum. Over the years in Charlottetown, Whelan was also a leading member of such community organizations as the mechanics' institute, the Charlottetown Repeal Association, the Benevolent Irish Society, and the Catholic Young Men's Literary Institute.

Even before Moody died, Whelan had decided to establish a new publication, one he would fully control and which would guarantee his security of tenure. He circulated a prospectus for a weekly, the *Examiner*, in the autumn of 1846, but was, according to Huntley, refused access to the existing presses "upon any terms; the Compact forbade it." The plant he purchased in Boston did not arrive before the close of navigation, and hence the first number of the *Examiner* did not appear until 7 Aug. 1847. The biting wit and brilliant writing of the *Palladium* remained, but two differences were immediately apparent: a general moderation in tone and a lack of concentration on Ireland. Indeed there was no editorial commentary on Ireland, apparently the result of a calculated decision to broaden the audience to which he appealed. The sensitivity of the Irish question became apparent when, on 16 Oct. 1848, with Ireland in a state of semi-insurrection and state trials being held, Whelan finally broke his silence. Although criticizing the rebel leaders for incapacity and bad judgement, he declared his faith in the justice of their cause. Their fault was that they had blundered into "beginning a war of independence, which they had neither men nor money to sustain . . . *we* cannot but regret, that such men ever espoused such a cause, or having espoused it, they did not succeed." He expected them to be convicted of high treason, given that they were being tried by "partizan judges . . . and a partizan jury." These were strong words, and the editorial was gleefully reprinted by the Tory *Islander* and *Royal Gazette*. Such leading local Liberals as William Swabey* (who was rumoured to have paid for the purchase and importation of the *Examiner*'s press) and Alexander Rae* quickly dissociated themselves from Whelan's sentiments. The controversy over his brief resumption of commentary on Ireland may have been a cause of the *Examiner*'s suspension of publication between February 1849 and January 1850; the ostensible reason was once again the failure of subscribers to pay.

Whelan's moderating of his tone was of a piece with the orientation of the Reform forces in P.E.I. in the late 1840s. With George Coles* firmly in command, moderation took control. Indeed in the third number of the *Examiner* Whelan drew an explicit distinction between "the Liberal Party, as now constituted," and "the old Escheat party." The break was more than a matter of semantics. In the columns of the *Examiner* responsible government replaced the land question as the focus of agitation. Constitutional change was often presented as a goal for its own sake or as a general panacea, rather than as a prerequisite to solution of the land question. In emphasizing this lowest common denominator of reform, Whelan was probably drawing upon his first-hand knowledge of the recent history of Nova Scotia, where Reformers had been slow to find a common platform. It was the peculiar virtue of Whelan as a strategist that he recognized the need, if the Reformers were to gain power by

parliamentary means, to focus on an issue which would bring together the diverse Reform constituencies of the colony. In this respect, he and Coles displayed greater political acumen and resolution than Howe. Part of the reason must have been that Whelan, as an Irish Roman Catholic immigrant, had fewer inhibitions about challenging the *status quo* than did Howe, the reverent son of a loyalist.

The struggle for responsible government grew in intensity in 1850, particularly after the electoral victory of the Reformers in February, and the subsequent refusal of the lieutenant governor, Sir Donald Campbell*, to accede to their demands. Throughout the year Whelan relentlessly hammered away at the issue. He spoke at numerous public meetings, and in late February decided to publish on a semi-weekly schedule in order to reach the public more frequently. In this highly charged atmosphere of confrontation, the *Examiner* was indispensable to the Reform cause in explaining and popularizing the idea of responsible government. By the time it was attained, Whelan's stature in the Reform movement was second only to that of Coles. Hence it was no surprise that in April 1851 the 27-year-old journalist was named to the first Executive Council formed on the principle of responsible government. In July he was also appointed queen's printer, despite intense indignation on the part of the incumbent of 21 years' standing, James Douglas Haszard*. Whelan held the position until 1859 (with the exception of several months in 1854) and again in 1867. He discontinued publication of the *Examiner* and made the hitherto rather staid *Royal Gazette* into something much more than a vehicle for official notices and proclamations. "Of all papers the *Gazette* should, in our estimation, be *the* political paper." The *Gazette* was to be the defender of the Liberal government *par excellence*, and thus was in every sense the successor of the *Examiner*, which was not resurrected until early 1854.

Whelan played a leading role in explaining and defending the major Liberal reforms of the 1850s: the Free Education Act, extension of the franchise, and the Land Purchase Act. As a good 19th century liberal he believed that these measures, through increasing the common Islander's educational attainments, political rights, and chances of becoming a freeholder, would enhance the political development, social stability, and economic prosperity of the community as a whole. Yet when the land reform programme of the Liberals proved inadequate for the task confronting it, Whelan shared Coles' reluctance to advocate more drastic measures. Indeed in the mid 1850s he polemicized at length with the old Escheators, who were growing restless. The other serious problem for the Liberals in the late 1850s was the dispute over the proper place of the Bible in the educational system. Whelan, always acutely aware of the dangers of religious squabbling in a mixed community, was appalled by the tenor of the campaign waged by Protestant militants for legal authorization of Bible reading in the district schools. He responded with a barrage of ridicule and invective in the *Examiner*, at one point portraying their organ, the *Protector and Christian Witness*, as rushing about with "a Bible in one hand and a bludgeon in the other . . . like a big bully . . . [who] while breaking the bones of his victims with the one, pretends to be very desirous of healing the wounds of the spirit with the other." Yet despite Whelan's wit and Coles' hard campaigning, the Bible question brought down the Liberal government in 1859.

The Liberals did not adapt quickly to their return to opposition. In the autumn of 1859 Whelan wrote that the party "appears to be without a leader, has lost heart, and is thoroughly cowed." Whelan himself provided little leadership: he was absent from the assembly much of the time, and in 1861 self-consciously commented: "I seldom trouble the House with my remarks." Yet as the politico-religious polemics between William Henry Pope* and David Laird* on the one side, and Father Angus MacDonald* on the other, rekindled the political atmosphere in 1861–62, Whelan became actively involved in the defence of MacDonald and Bishop Peter MacIntyre*, and attacked "Pope's Epistles Against the Romans." In the course of the controversies, the *Vindicator*, an ultramontane newspaper, was founded in Charlottetown, published by Edward Reilly*, a former employee of Whelan, and reputedly edited by MacDonald. In its first number, although conceding that Whelan was a Roman Catholic and had opened his columns to Catholic arguments, it stated rather ominously that "the *Examiner* is not a Catholic newspaper." The religious polarization of this period provided the basis for the successful Conservative campaign of 1863.

After the election, religious issues receded in importance. When union of the British North American colonies arose as a question of the day, the Tory government became hopelessly divided between supporters and opponents of confederation. The Liberals were in a position to profit from this situation, for they reflected the distaste of Islanders as a whole for confederation. The sole notable exception in their ranks was Whelan. Immediately prior to the Charlottetown confer-

ence he had expressed scepticism about the prospects for union, especially if it involved abolition of local legislatures. But by 5 September he was enthusiastic about the project, particularly because "a union will relieve us from the provoking intermeddling of the Colonial Office in our local legislation. . . . And what is still more gratifying to contemplate, proprietary influence at the Colonial Office would be . . . driven to the wall." Whelan was selected to be one of the delegates to the Quebec conference. Although not satisfied with the provisions for representation of the Island in federal legislative bodies, he remained an advocate of union, and vigorously promoted it in the columns of the *Examiner*. He also began to compile a collection of banquet speeches given in connection with both conferences, which he published in 1865. But as it became apparent that his advocacy was having little effect, Whelan grew increasingly disenchanted with "the petulance of this little place." When the Quebec resolutions were debated in the assembly, Coles pointedly remarked, referring to his long-time colleague, that "There are fewer old party ties to bind us now than formerly." During the debate on James Colledge Pope*'s "no terms" resolutions of 1866, Whelan complained that "I never, in the course of my parliamentary experience of 20 years, was made the subject of so much calumny – so many false accusations, as in reference to this question."

The other major issue which dominated the mid 1860s was once again the land question. With the failure of the Tories to make significant progress towards abolition of leasehold tenure, the Tenant League, a society sworn to withhold rents, arose. In the summer of 1865 the Tory government was sufficiently alarmed by the activities of the league, and the inability of the local authorities to deal effectively with it, that they summoned troops from Halifax. They also systematically purged the ranks of district teachers and magistrates of league sympathizers. Whelan's attitude towards such an organization had gone through several stages, reflecting the ever-present tension within him between the British liberal and the Irish radical. When an abortive tenant league had emerged in 1850–51, inspired by a tenants' movement in contemporary Ireland, Whelan refused to condemn it categorically, and had simply labelled it "premature"; writing hypothetically in 1855, he had emphatically denied that the government should raise or call upon special forces to assist civil authorities in the collection of rents; and as late as the autumn of 1860, when land agents were collecting rents at harvest-time with unusual zeal

Whelan

and the tenants were exhibiting acute restlessness, Whelan, while not counselling nonpayment, nonetheless advised the tenantry to organize, on democratic principles, centrally directed "Mutual Protection Societies, or Tenant Leagues" which would be necessary if they were "to be prepared, as a united people, for any emergency that may arise." He reminded his readers that what "was criminal on the part of the few poor devils who were too weak to carry their point, becomes praiseworthy and heroical with the many who are strong enough to bear down all opposition." But by the time serious disturbances arose in the mid 1860s Whelan had cut himself off from the tenants' movement, and was firmly committed to parliamentary means. He vigorously attacked the league, defended the use of troops, and indeed argued that the government should have suppressed it upon the publication in 1864 of its "dishonest and seditious pledge" in *Ross's Weekly*. Consequently, he became detested by the Leaguers, who no doubt remembered his earlier views, and whose leaders, such as George F. Adams, urged them to withdraw their subscriptions from the *Examiner*. Together, the land question and confederation ensured the defeat of the Conservatives in 1867. The Liberals, with one significant exception, had opposed confederation, and although not Leaguers, neither were they proprietors nor their agents. These two issues had also left Whelan largely isolated within his own party.

Although the Liberals had won decisively in 1867, victory brought its own problems. The question of the Tenant League, whose withholding of rents Coles had also opposed, had created a deep fissure between radicals and "Old Liberals." Whelan especially had suffered from this division, and the radical Liberal members were not disposed to return the queen's printership to him. Nonetheless, after a caucus debate which lasted two days, the "Old Liberals" won this test of strength, and Whelan was restored to his former office. The difficulty was that its acceptance obliged him to resign his seat in the assembly and to contest it again. Although he had won every previous election over a period of 21 years, he lost the by-election to Reilly, who was then editor of the Charlottetown *Herald*. He nevertheless remained queen's printer, for Reilly refused to accept the post on the condition of running for re-election.

There is no single cause or explanation for Whelan's defeat. His denunciations of the Tenant League and Fenianism (which he called an "infamous conspiracy") had cost him support among his traditional followers, i.e. leaseholders and Irish Roman Catholics. His advocacy of confederation was equally damaging. In 1867, anti-confederacy was a virtual test of fitness for the local legislature, and Whelan was the only prominent heretic in a party which was sound. On each of these three issues Reilly had the advantage: he had espoused the tenants' cause with single-minded vigour, was non-committal on Fenianism, and was unequivocally opposed to confederation, over which he had polemicized with Whelan since 1864.

But, for Whelan, the decisive cause of his defeat was to be found elsewhere. Two days before the election he wrote that "there would not be the shadow of a doubt about the matter if the Catholic electors, who are the majority of the voters, were not subjected to unseen influences that cannot be easily met and overcome." After his loss he charged that Reilly had "had a most unscrupulous person of a certain clerical 'order' to canvas for him incessantly." He was undoubtedly referring to Father William Phelan, recently arrived from Ireland, a friend and partisan of Reilly, who had just displaced Father Ronald Bernard MacDonald in St Peters parish. According to the Roman Catholic historian Father John C. Macmillan*, MacDonald "was well known to be a personal friend of Mr Whelan," and many believed that his timely removal after only a few months' service at St Peters was a sign of Bishop MacIntyre's displeasure with the queen's printer.

The reasons for the bishop's disapproval are obscure but nonetheless important. In the first place, Whelan's advocacy of confederation had made him an ally of William Pope, the most tenacious Island confederate and the *bête noire* of Island Catholicism. Secondly, Bishop MacIntyre was a crusader for total abstinence from alcoholic beverages, and Whelan, the leading Roman Catholic public man in the colony, was something less than an exemplar for the masses in this respect. One of his former reporters, Thomas Kirwan, would write in an obituary article that "he was a fast liver, and fast livers do not generally attain to patriarchal age." But perhaps most important was a factor noted by Macmillan: "A rumor . . . was in the air, that Mr. Whelan had grown somewhat indifferent in matters of faith, and had been for a time utterly neglectful with regard to the practices of his religion." Rumours of this nature concerning Whelan had been circulating for many years, fuelled on at least one occasion by his own remarks in the assembly. At this remove it is impossible to determine the truth with any precision; yet some lack of orthodoxy may be inferred from the fact that his second marriage, on 21 Oct. 1850 to Miss Mary Major Hughes, was performed by a clergyman of the Church of England. Thus, for a number of reasons, it seems likely that relations between Whelan and the bishop were strained. Indeed, the *Vindicator*, which appears to have been the organ of the Roman Catholic clergy, had been a conscious rival of Whelan for the attention of Island Catholics. In 1867 Bishop MacIntyre, an ardent and energetic ultramontane with little patience for dissenting views, was in all probability mobilizing his forces in order to gain public financial support for his educational institutions. In early 1868 he would present a memorial to the Coles government for such assistance. Whether Whelan would have supported anything more than a grant to St Dunstan's College is dubious, since he was an initiator of the secular Free Education Act, had publicly denied that Catholics were bound to accept political direction from ecclesiastics, and in 1860 had declared that "clergymen are generally the most incompetent persons in the world to have anything to do with the administration of secular affairs." It is true that in 1851 he had advocated public assistance for a Roman Catholic school in Charlottetown, but it had then become subject to the standard district school regulations; and throughout the succeeding years Whelan had repeatedly expressed his belief that separate schools would only entrench religious and national prejudices.

In any event, Whelan was convinced that his defeat had been owing to undue clerical influence. In September he noted with evident satisfaction the failure of Archbishop Thomas Connolly*'s manifesto in favour of confederation. "We hope this complete overthrow of his Grace's influence in the political world will be warning to all ecclesiastics everywhere not to meddle too much in political affairs." Apparently he never recovered from the bitterness of the defeat, which was the culmination of several unpleasant turns in his political career. Over the summer and autumn of 1867 his health slowly deteriorated. On 10 December he died at age 43, a broken man. The cause of death was given as dropsy. His obituary in the *Examiner* said that his "mantle, we fear, falls on no man." This was true in two respects: Prince Edward Island was never to know a more talented journalist, and the Roman Catholic laity did not for many years find another leader of his stature.

Whelan has become known as a romantic, even tragic figure, and deservedly so. Not only did he die before his time, a disappointed man, but, some five months after their marriage, his first wife, Mrs Mary Weymouth, a widow 11 years his

senior, had died on 15 Oct. 1845 following the birth of a boy who also appears to have died shortly afterwards; his two daughters by his second marriage predeceased him; and his son Edward, the only child to survive him, later perished in a drowning accident on Dominion Day, 1875, at age 20, on the threshold of a promising career in journalism. On the day before his death he had been awarded a prize for English composition at St Dunstan's College. The *Island Argus* reported that the son's funeral was "one of the very largest ever witnessed in Charlottetown. The name of the Hon. Edward Whelan is still cherished by the people." In 1900 the same writer, J. H. Fletcher, would recall that, growing up a Liberal in Prince Edward Island, he had read every word of every number of the *Examiner* and had come to believe "that its editor was the greatest man that lived on the Island. And I am still of the same opinion."

Edward Whelan's historical reputation has rested primarily on his contribution to the struggle for responsible government, and on his advocacy of confederation at a time and in a place where that cause was intensely unpopular. His role in each case reflects well on his political courage and tenacity, but it was undoubtedly in the former that he was more effective, and his behaviour in it deserves the more careful analysis, both in terms of Island history and for an understanding of his career as a whole. In the 1840s he had come to Prince Edward Island as a remarkably precocious young man, and effectively mobilized the newly settled Irish tenantry behind the Reform cause. At the same time he played what was probably a decisive part in moderating the demands of Island Reformers, suppressing points of difference, and creating the unified movement of which George Coles would assume leadership. Although no one was more aware than Whelan, the Irish immigrant, of the land question's importance, his strategy was "responsible government first." Yet after constitutional reform had been won, the land question continued to bedevil the colony, and since gradualism seemed to have exhausted its potential, Whelan's constituency began to drift towards radical solutions and direct action in the countryside, which he ultimately rejected. Contemporaneously, Irish nationalists, particularly in the exile communities, were becoming more willing to countenance violent methods. Whelan, who had begun his journalistic career in Nova Scotia and Prince Edward Island by appealing primarily to Irishmen, and whose strength had been his uneasy synthesis of British liberalism and Irish radicalism, suffered from this split in the Irish movement. He became more and more of a

Whelan

liberal constitutionalist in his later years, and grew increasingly impatient with radicalism whether at home or abroad. This isolation from the original sources of his strength in public life, when combined with his adherence to the confederate cause and his problems with the Roman Catholic clergy, led to his political downfall and hastened his death.

IAN ROSS ROBERTSON

[Edward Whelan's private papers perished in a fire at his former residence in 1876. But his newspapers and the records of proceedings in the Island assembly provide a comprehensive and detailed picture of his views. For the assembly debates see: *Royal Gazette* (Charlottetown), 1847–53; *Islander*, 1854; and P.E.I., House of Assembly, *Debates and proc.*, 1855–66. The following years of his newspapers have survived to a greater or less degree: *Register* (Halifax), 1843; *Palladium* (Charlottetown), 1843–45; *Morning News* (Charlottetown), 1846; *Examiner* (Charlottetown), 1847–51, 1855–67; and *Royal Gazette*, 1851–59, 1867. From August 1854 on his *Royal Gazette* resumed a traditional character. The author believes that Peter McCourt, in his *Biographical sketch of the Honorable Edward Whelan, together with a compilation of his principal speeches; also interesting and instructive addresses to the electors . . .* (Charlottetown, 1888), 10, and D. C. Harvey, *The centenary of Edward Whelan: lecture delivered in Strand Theatre, Charlottetown, Prince Edward Island, August 9, 1926* (n.p., n.d.; republished and more accessible in *Historical essays on the Atlantic provinces*, ed. G. A. Rawlyk, (Toronto, 1967)), 214, were wrong in stating that Whelan published the short-lived *Reporter* (Charlottetown) of 1847; nonetheless, it appears that he may have been its editor. There is no evidence to sustain the story Thomas Kirwan repeated in an otherwise excellent obituary article in the *Summerside Progress* (Summerside, P.E.I.), 16 Dec. 1867, that "Mr. W.'s first essay in publishing was made in one of the western towns of Nova Scotia." Important articles and letters from the *Morning News* (Charlottetown) of 16, 20, 23, 27 May 1846 will be found in McCourt, *Biographical sketch . . .*, 5–10, and in PRO, CO 226/69, 345–51.

The following individual numbers of newspapers are particularly useful for a study of Whelan's career: *Colonial Herald* (Charlottetown), 17 June 1843. *Constitutionalist* (Charlottetown), 9, 23 May, 6 June, 5 Sept., 3, 10 Oct. 1846. *Examiner*, 7, 14, 21 Aug., 18 Dec. 1847; 26 June, 31 July, 14 Aug., 11, 18 Sept., 16, 23, 30 Oct., 13 Nov. 1848; 1 Jan., 12 Feb. 1849; 12 Jan., 23 Feb., 2, 13 March, 3 Aug., 23; 30 Oct., 6, 9, 20 Nov., 11 Dec. 1850; 8, 11 Jan., 14, 28 April, 13 May, 7 July 1851; 18 June, 10 Dec. 1855; 14 July, 8 Dec. 1856; 19, 26 Jan., 2, 9 Feb., 13 July 1857; 7, 28 June, 19 July 1858; 12, 26 Sept., 3 Oct., 26 Dec. 1859; 11 Sept., 23 Oct., 5, 12 Nov., 17 Dec. 1860; 7, 14 Jan., 4 Feb., 20 May, 10, 24 June, 22 July, 5, 26 Aug., 16, 23 Sept. 1861; 17 March, 23, 30 June, 22 Sept., 10 Nov. 1862; 19 Jan., 9 Feb., 23 March, 24, 31 Aug., 16 Nov., 14 Dec. 1863; 4, 11, 25 Jan., 1 Feb., 2, 23, 30 May, 5 Sept., 17 Oct., 21 Nov., 26 Dec. 1864; 24 April, 12, 19, 26 June, 10, 24 July, 7, 21 Aug., 16 Oct., 13 Nov., 18 Dec. 1865; 12 March, 4 June, 16 July, 1 Oct., 10 Dec. 1866; 4 Feb., 18 March, 15, 29 April, 6 May, 16, 23 Sept., 16 Dec. (obit.), 30 Dec. 1867; 5 July 1875. *Express and Commercial Advertiser* (Charlottetown), 9 Nov. 1850. *Herald* (Charlottetown), 28 Dec. 1864; 24 April, 18 Dec. (obit.), 25 Dec. 1867; 8 Jan. 1868. *Island Argus* (Charlottetown), 6, 13 July, 21 Sept. 1875. *Islander*, 8 Sept. 1843; 18 Oct. 1845; 20 March 1847; 6, 20 Oct. 1848; 12 July, 8 Nov. 1850; 30 April 1852; 8 June 1855; 4 Jan., 3 Oct. 1856; 6 Jan. 1860; 23 Aug. 1861; 15 Jan. 1864; 26 April, 3 May, 13 Dec. (obit.) 1867; 15 Jan. 1869. *Morning News* (Charlottetown), 11, 15, 22, 29 April, 3, 10 June, 26 Sept., 3 Oct. 1846. *Palladium* (Charlottetown), 4, 7, 11, 14, 25 Sept., 16, 30 Nov., 14, 28 Dec. 1843; 4 Jan., 29 Feb., 21 March, 11, 25 April, 23 May, 27 June, 4, 11 July, 3, 10 Oct., 16 Nov., 21 Dec. 1844; 29 March, 19 April, 3 May 1845. *Patriot* (Charlottetown), 12 Dec. 1867 (obit.); 3, 8, 15 July 1875. *Protestant and Evangelical Witness* (Charlottetown), 12 Nov. 1864. *Register* (Halifax), 10 Jan., 25 April, 2 May 1843. *Royal Gazette* (Charlottetown), 5 Sept. 1843; 6, 13 May, 21 Oct. 1845; 24 Oct. 1848; 16 July 1850; 11 March, 14 July 1851; 23 Feb., 15 March, 26 April, 3, 24 May 1852; 24 Oct., 7 Nov., 26 Dec. 1853; 1 Aug. 1854; 22 March 1855; 26 Dec. 1867. *Summerside Journal* (Summerside, P.E.I.), 12 Dec. 1867 (obit.). *Summerside Progress* (Summerside, P.E.I.), 25 March, 23 Dec. 1867. *Vindicator* (Charlottetown), 17 Oct. 1862.

For some of Whelan's more important contributions to debates in the assembly, see *Royal Gazette*, 2, 16 March, 13 April 1847; 22 April 1851; 29 Jan. 1852; 7 March 1853. *Islander*, 28 Feb. 1854. P.E.I., House of Assembly, *Debates and proc.*, 1855, 35–38, 66; 1856, 27; 1857, 61–63; 1859, 63, 82, 86–88; 1860, 15; 1861, 16, 40–41, 135; 1862, 16; 1863, 44–45; 1864, 56–59; 1865, 7; 1866, 42, 107, 120; also see 1868, 147.

Whelan's compilation of speeches surrounding the Charlottetown and Quebec conferences appeared under the title *The union of the British provinces: a brief account of the several conferences held in the Maritime provinces and in Canada, in September and October, 1864, on the proposed confederation of the provinces, together with a report of the speeches delivered by the delegates from the provinces, on important public occasions* (Charlottetown, 1865; repr. Summerside, P.E.I., 1949). Several of Whelan's addresses, both in and out of the assembly, are reproduced in McCourt, *Biographical sketch. . . .* McCourt's collection contains an account of Whelan's life. Whelan has been the subject of two shorter studies: Harvey, *The centenary of Edward Whelan*, and E. J. Mullally, "The Hon. Edward Whelan, a father of confederation from Prince Edward Island, one of Ireland's gifts to Canada," CCHA *Report*, 1938–39, 67–84. Neither is fully reliable, and even the better, by Harvey, leans too heavily on McCourt, particularly concerning Whelan's early years, and consequently reproduces his factual errors.

See also: PAPEI, P.E.I., Land Registry Office, Land Conveyance Registers, liber 54, f.390. P.E.I., Supreme Court, Estates Division, liber 7, f.399 (will of Edward Whelan, 7 Dec. 1867) (mfm. at PAPEI). PAC, MG 26, A, 338, pp.154610–16. PANS, MG 20, 67. PRO, CO

226/69, 324–35; 226/71, 67–76; 226/72, 109–10; 226/75, 17–21; 226/100, 231–32. C. T. Bagnall, "A name which sends our thoughts back to the old time," *Prince Edward Island Magazine* (Charlottetown), 4 (1902–3), 351–53. F. W. P. Bolger, *Prince Edward Island and confederation, 1863–1873* (Charlottetown, 1964), chaps. 1–8. W. L. Cotton, "The press in Prince Edward Island," *Past and present in Prince Edward Island . . .*, ed. D. A. MacKinnon and A. B. Warburton (Charlottetown, [1906]), 116. J. H. Fletcher, "Newspaper life and newspaper men," *Prince Edward Island Magazine* (Charlottetown), 2 (1900–1), 69–70. A. A. Johnston, *A history of the Catholic Church in eastern Nova Scotia* (2v., Antigonish, N.S., 1960–71), II, 160, 166–67, 179–80, 215. W. E. MacKinnon, *The life of the party: a history of the Liberal party in Prince Edward Island* (Summerside, P.E.I., 1973), chaps. 2–4. J. C. Macmillan, *The history of the Catholic Church in Prince Edward Island from 1835 till 1891* (Quebec, 1913), chaps. 9, 11, 14, 16–17, 19–20. Robertson, "Religion, politics, and education in P.E.I.," chaps. 1–7, and pp.315–16. [Edward Whelan], "Edward Whelan reports from the Quebec conference," ed. P. B. Waite, *CHR*, XLII (1961), 23–45. I.R.R.]

WHELAN, PATRICK JAMES, tailor, convicted of the murder of Thomas D'Arcy McGEE; b. *c.* 1840 in Ireland, younger son of William Whelan and Mary Sullivan of Galway; m. 13 Feb. 1867 at St Patrick's Church, Montreal, Bridget Boyle, daughter of Donald Boyle and Catherine Twite of Kerry (Republic of Ireland), and they had no children; publicly hanged in Ottawa, 11 Feb. 1869.

Patrick James Whelan was apprenticed to a tailor at age 14. About 1865 he came to Canada and worked for Vallin, a tailor in Quebec City. He also joined the cavalry volunteers. He was later employed as a tailor by Gibb and Company in Montreal, and after November 1867 by Peter Eagleson, a tailor in Ottawa. He was skilled at his trade, and fond of horses, shooting, dancing, and drink.

When Thomas D'Arcy McGee was killed in Ottawa by a .32 calibre bullet on 7 April 1868, the assassin was immediately assumed to be a Fenian. Rumours of further Fenian terrorism became rampant, and the Habeas Corpus Act was suspended. Within 20 hours of the murder Whelan was arrested. In his pocket police found a fully loaded .32 calibre Smith and Wesson revolver. More than 40 other suspects were jailed, including Patrick Buckley, Sir John Alexander Macdonald*'s cabman. On 9 April Whelan was charged with the murder.

His jury trial in the Court of Common Pleas was held in Ottawa in September. It lasted 8 days and received international publicity. John Hillyard Cameron*, grand master of the Orange Order, defended Whelan and James O'Reilly* was the prosecutor. Chief Justice William Buell Richards* presided; beside him, unconcerned with the constitutional separation of powers, sat Prime Minister Sir John A. Macdonald. Everything about "the tailor with the red whiskers" was noted by the newspapers. He first appeared in court wearing a small green rosette, a white vest, and garnet cuff links. On the final day, however, he came dressed in black, and upon hearing the dreaded verdict of guilty said from the dock: "Now I am held to be a black assassin. And my blood runs cold. But I am innocent. I never took that man's blood."

An appeal was made to the Court of Queen's Bench of Ontario. Richards, who had in the meantime been named chief justice of the court, cast the deciding vote in the court's two to one decision against the appeal in December. The case was carried further, and in January 1869 Richards again cast the decisive vote when the Ontario Court of Appeal, which included the three justices of the Court of Queen's Bench, rejected the appeal by six to four. On 11 February, Whelan spoke from the scaffold to more than 5,000 spectators. He met his death with manliness and faith. Within five months the law was changed to ban public hangings in Canada.

The other suspects were all released or speedily acquitted, including Buckley who returned to Macdonald's employ. No proof was ever found that Whelan was a Fenian or that he had had an accomplice.

In October 1973 Whelan's revolver was located after being lost for a century. Tests were conducted by ballistics experts but with inconclusive results. There is room for doubt that Whelan was actually the assassin. The identification made of him at the scene of the crime can be discredited, and his trial and the rejections of his appeals were marred by bad procedure. He always denied that he had fired the shot but he admitted just before he was hanged that he did "know the man who shot Mr. McGee." The case is still shrouded in mystery.

T. P. SLATTERY

[Manuscripts, records, reports, newspapers, articles, and books are fully listed in the bibliography of the author's study of Whelan's trial, where there is also an appraisal of the sources: *"They got to find mee guilty yet"* (Toronto and Garden City, N.Y., 1972); and in his two articles on the recent ballistic tests in the *Gazette* (Montreal), 3 Nov. 1973, and the *Ottawa Journal*, 22 June 1974. T.P.S.]

George Spaight, *Trial of Patrick J. Whelan for the murder of the Hon. Thos. D'Arcy McGee . . .* (Ottawa, 1868).

White

WHITE, JOSEPH, potter; b. 28 Dec. 1799 in Bristol, England, son of Joseph White and Charlotte Somers; m. in England Elizabeth Wilkey, and they had seven children; d. 15 Jan. 1870 in Saint John, N.B.

A potter's son, Joseph White Jr established a pottery in Bristol with his brother James in 1828. The Whites' staples were stoneware dipped in a liquid glaze (a process that superseded salt-glazing in Bristol in the 1830s) and dark-bodied earthenware. Their stoneware glaze was of such quality that it was purchased by leading English potteries, including, it is said, Doultons. Joseph White later brought to Canada the formula for this glaze, superior for utilitarian stoneware to the old salt-glaze widely used in North America.

In 1855 White retired, leaving his son Joseph Augustus to manage the Bristol business. Another son, Frederick James, had been attracted to the gold mines of Nova Scotia but returned to England after a visit to Saint John with the news that a pottery owned by William Warwick in Crouchville (East Saint John), N.B., on Courtenay Bay was for sale. Joseph White was then persuaded to emerge from retirement to emigrate to New Brunswick. On 3 Sept. 1864 White, with his sons Frederick and James Alfred, arrived in the province, took possession of the Crouchville pottery, and began a bold attempt to produce in British North America wares that had made them prosperous at home. Joseph White came not as a journeyman looking for employment, but as a master potter, ready to take over an existing business and to introduce into New Brunswick improved potting methods and techniques.

Five weeks after their arrival they had an impressive showing of earthenware, "plain and ornamental," at that year's provincial fair in Fredericton. A circular handed out at the fair promised that from an enlarged Crouchville plant would be coming "better descriptions of Ware, as made . . . in England." Dark-bodied earthenware of "latest English Designs" and "superior" stoneware coated with a glaze "impervious to acids" were advertised in succeeding years. But potting in British North America was beset by difficulties: basic materials for anything but rough earthenware had to be imported; and British ware of all kinds poured into the country, usually underselling what could be made locally, particularly in port areas. The White pottery was struggling when Joseph White died in 1870. Though it survived in one form or another for nearly 20 years longer, finding customers as far away as Montreal for its tobacco pipes, stoneware, and black teapots, bankruptcy finally closed it.

Joseph White's influence, however, endured. He had brought from overseas the spirit of a more advanced industry, and despite the fact that the Crouchville pottery never knew significant financial success, White established a potting tradition that lived on in Canada. A grandson, James William Foley, founded his own pottery with Samuel Poole as partner; their wares made a good display at the Dominion Exhibition held in Saint John in 1883. The Foleys potted in Saint John until 1964, when fire gutted the plant; the firm, headed at that time by Joseph White's great-great-grandson, then moved to Labelle, Que.

ELIZABETH COLLARD

The White family papers, in the possession of Fenwick D. Foley, Saint John, N.B., were used in the preparation of the biography. N.B. Museum, White pottery, account book. St James Church (Bristol, Eng.), baptismal register, 1799–1800. *Daily Sun* (Saint John, N.B.), 3 Oct. 1883. *Morning News* (Saint John, N.B.), 7 Oct. 1864. *Morning Telegraph* (Saint John, N.B.), 8 Oct. 1864. *New Brunswick Courier*, 8 Oct. 1864. *St. John Daily Telegraph and Morning Journal* (Saint John, N.B.), 18 Jan. 1870. *Hutchinson's New Brunswick directory, for 1867–68* . . . , comp. Thomas Hutchinson (Montreal, [1867]), 33. *McAlpine's Nova Scotia directory, for 1868–69, containing directories of each place in the province* . . . (Halifax, [1868]), 47. Elizabeth Collard, *Nineteenth-century pottery and porcelain in Canada* (Montreal, 1967). W. J. Pountney, *Old Bristol potteries* (Bristol, Eng., 1920).

WIDDER, FREDERICK, Canada Company official; b. 1801 in England; d. 1 Feb. 1865 in Montreal, Canada East.

Frederick Widder's father, Charles Ignatius, was a London director of the British land and colonizing venture, the Canada Company. When Frederick Widder was sent to Upper Canada in 1839 to join the company's resident co-commissioners, William Allan* and Thomas Mercer JONES, he was probably being groomed to replace Allan, whose advancing years and Family Compact connections had become liabilities. Jones was only relatively less vulnerable to the criticism of Reformers, as Archdeacon John STRACHAN's son-in-law, and because of his baronial social and business style at Goderich, where he conducted the administration of the company's million-acre Huron Tract. During the 1830s William Allan, based in Toronto, had given waning attention to the company's other immense holdings, the former crown reserves scattered throughout Upper Canada. It was evident to Widder that the Huron Tract and crown reserves operations demanded co-ordination. General outcries against the provincial government's administration, especially of lands, forced the company to anticipate its own share of criticism, and to set its house in order.

Frederick Widder possessed those qualities of enterprise, efficiency, and moderation so much encouraged by another newcomer to Canada in 1839, Governor General Charles Poulett Thomson*, later Lord Sydenham. Although Widder would remain free of political or government attachments, he applauded the business-like atmosphere of Sydenham's regime. Displaying marked administrative talents, counselling with moderate men, and building a reputation for amiability and hospitality, he steadily gained respect among business and government leaders. Entrepreneurs such as William Hamilton MERRITT, governors such as Sydenham and Sir Charles Metcalfe*, and senior Crown Lands Office officials admired his enterprise and envied his success in selling company lands. He was active in the St George's Society and as lay vice-president of the Anglican diocesan Church Society concerned himself with his church's endowments. In the process of arriving at such prominence, Widder soon displaced Allan and eclipsed Jones who got entangled in local politics in the Goderich area. Widder's methods recommended themselves more favourably to the company's court of directors.

Largely through Widder's efforts, the company escaped censure in the general examination of the public administration begun by Sir George Arthur* and continued by Thomson. By 1841 Allan had been eased out, and Widder began to move as boldly as John Galt*, the company's first commissioner – even restoring some of Galt's tactics. In many ways, too, Widder anticipated Clifford Sifton*'s efforts to publicize Canada and lure immigrants. He revived the company's printed prospectus distributed throughout Canada and Britain. Books and pamphlets were widely circulated free or at cost, among them reissues of Dr William "Tiger" Dunlop*'s 1832 *Statistical sketches of Upper Canada* . . . and three pamphlets of the 1840s by J. J. E. LINTON of Stratford. Company agencies were established through prominent commercial and shipping firms at 27 British ports and agricultural centres.

Widder departed, however, from Galt's earlier insistence that the industrial poor should be ignored in preference for "persons of substance and respectability" from Britain's agricultural areas. Seeking sales to offset charges of unwarranted speculation, and anxious to discourage new local cliques like that of the prosperous gentlemen farmers in Colborne Township near Goderich, Widder would accept settlers with less literacy or farming experience. He also recruited

settlers already established in Canada. In 1842 every provincial postmaster received the company's prospectus for distribution, posters went to seigneuries in Canada East, and agents were contacted among the Maritimes' Scots. By the 1850s, with land sales booming, Widder's emphasis on experienced Canadian settlers supplanted the older appeals to British emigrants.

In 1843 Widder visited New York's German community and was impressed by their agricultural skills and capital resources. The company's directors agreed to employ an agent, William Rischmuller, to persuade Germans in the United States and Germany to come to the Huron Tract. In addition, Widder appointed James Buchanan as the company's resident agent at New York, and commissioned British consulates in Europe and shipping agencies at Bremen (Federal Republic of Germany) and Le Havre (France) to attract continental immigrants. Although Rischmuller defaulted, Widder persisted in the effort and established a German immigrant agency at Quebec in 1850 on the eve of a large-scale German migration. A growing German community in the Huron Tract was proof of his initiative. Indeed, throughout the 1840s and 1850s the court of directors exercised less supervision of its Canadian operations than formerly, generally acquiescing in Widder's strategies and approving his tactics.

Widder also won several major departures in financial operations. In 1842 he argued that most settlers were more interested in good initial terms to purchase or lease land than they were in obtaining favourable sites. Accordingly, he introduced in the Huron Tract a policy of deferring payments for a longer time, and he gave settlers an option to lease initially. In fixing prices for company lands, Widder carefully reviewed earlier surveys and turnover records, as well as soliciting advice from "long established, well informed settlers." He achieved a reduction in inspection and evaluation costs and complemented it by an imaginative attack on the delicate problem of collections. Widder devised an elaborate schedule correlating international grain prices as an index of Canada's economic condition: collections would only be pushed under favourable market conditions, thus avoiding adverse criticism in periods of general hardship. The results of this experiment were so gratifying in the Huron Tract that in 1843 the policy was extended to the company's other lands.

Another of Widder's important innovations in 1842 was the Settlers Provident Savings Bank, offering highly competitive terms and more accessible banking services. To woo prosperous emigrants, company settlers were enabled to enjoy free exchange and remittance facilities to Britain – and after 1850, through Rothschilds at Quebec, to Germany. Many of these facilities were centred on the Huron Tract, and despite the estrangement between himself and Jones, Widder could depend upon the cooperation of a new company servant in the Huron Tract, his younger brother Charles.

By 1844 Widder ambitiously proposed to Governor Metcalfe that the Canada Company should undertake on commission the administration of the province's public lands, beginning with the clergy reserves. Bishop Strachan, who had been demanding that the government grant the Church of England the management of its share of the clergy reserves, seized the opportunity offered by Widder's proposal to discredit the company and Widder and to bolster Jones' position with the directors. In a bitter and anonymous series of open letters, Strachan rebuked Widder and condemned his whole career as a company official. Widder's bold proposals were rejected by Governor Metcalfe as "noteworthy" but open to "insurmountable objections." From such visions, Widder turned to railway promotion. With his assurance of increased land sales, the court of directors readily agreed to become the British agent to sell stock in a railway from Toronto to Goderich. Widder successfully fought opposition from a league of Jones, the Colborne Clique, and American promoters who supported a rival line from Buffalo, N.Y., to Goderich. With Jones' dismissal in 1852 over the railway issue, Widder's attempt to bring the company's province-wide operations under his control in Toronto was finally successful. The company would participate in and profit directly by the expansive railway ventures of the 1850s.

Widder's success was reflected in his personal style of life. The drawing room of his stately residence on Front St, Lyndhurst, glittered, as John Ross Robertson* observed, as "the centre of social attraction from the mid-forties till the early sixties." The Widders' two daughters married distinguished Prussian and English military officers. A son and another daughter had both died in 1849.

Perhaps labours and successes had come too regularly to Frederick Widder. By the early 1860s his health, and that of his wife, Elizabeth Jane, were broken. Moreover, his authoritative conduct of the company's affairs was coming into question. In 1864 his resignation for reasons of health was accepted. Lyndhurst was sold to become the mother house of the Loretto Abbey. During their journey home to retirement in England, Mrs Widder died in Montreal in November

1864. Some two months later the effects of a paralytic stroke claimed her husband.

ALAN WILSON

PAO, Canada Company papers; Merritt (William Hamilton) papers; Strachan (John) papers. Aliquis [John Strachan], *Observations on the history and recent proceedings of the Canada Company; addressed in four letters to Frederick Widder, esq., one of the commissioners* (Hamilton, [Ont.], 1845). Gates, *Land policies of U.C.* H. J. M. Johnston, "Transportation and the development of the eastern section of the Huron Tract, 1828–1858" (unpublished MA thesis, University of Western Ontario, London, Ont., 1965). C. G. Karr, "The foundations of the Canada Land Company, 1823–1843" (unpublished MA thesis, University of Western Ontario, London, Ont., 1966). Robina and K. M. Lizars, *In the days of the Canada Company: the story of the settlement of the Huron Tract and a view of the social life of the period, 1825–1850* (Toronto and Montreal, 1896). *Robertson's landmarks of Toronto*, V. Wilson, *Clergy reserves of U.C.* G. C. Patterson, "Land settlement in Upper Canada, 1783–1840," Ont., Dept. of Archives, *Report* (Toronto), 1920.

WIER, BENJAMIN, entrepreneur and politician; b. 9 Aug. 1805 in. Newport Township, Hants County, N.S., the son of Benjamin and Phebe Wier; d. 14 April 1868 at Ottawa, Ont.

The Wier family migrated to Nova Scotia in the early 1760s as part of a band of Ulstermen brought out by the land speculator, Colonel Alexander McNutt*. Succeeding generations provided Anglican vestrymen, justices of the peace, and members of the provincial assembly. When Benjamin Wier's father died about 1827, however, his family was forced to auction off his property in order to satisfy his creditors.

By this time young Benjamin had married a cousin, Phoebe Wier, and had gone into business as a country storekeeper a few miles outside Windsor. Attracted by Halifax's commercial bustle in the prosperity of the late 1820s, Wier moved to the capital in 1830 and attempted to establish himself as a member of the Water St commercial gentry. His expectations suffered a severe blow, however, when Halifax's commercial boom collapsed in the mid 1830s. Deprived of his waterfront property by relentless creditors and reduced from the status of merchant to that of retail grocer, Wier nevertheless remained in Halifax. When trade revived in 1838 he formed a partnership with John Bowles Woodworth and moved back to the waterfront to conduct a modest wholesale-retail trade in everything from herring to shingles. The partnership collapsed, however, amidst a new trade recession in 1841, and

Woodworth's subsequent bankruptcy placed Wier's credit in jeopardy.

During these difficult years Benjamin Wier acquired the reputation of being an unmannered malcontent. In 1836, for example, he received a 10s. fine for assault and a £10 fine for selling liquor without a licence. Wier also became known as a political agitator. His name appeared on various petitions drawn up by Halifax shopkeepers demanding reform of the municipal administration and its allegedly discriminatory tax structure. In the mid 1830s, when warfare between the Halifax Banking Company and its new rival, the Bank of Nova Scotia, disrupted credit and spawned numerous business failures, Wier attended protest meetings and signed petitions which denounced Halifax's moneyed élite as being dangerously irresponsible. By the end of the 1830s he had become identified with the campaign against oligarchy led by Joseph Howe*. Like many other small property owners in Halifax, Wier saw reform as a means of achieving municipal incorporation under a democratic charter which would enable them to oust the traditional merchants from their position of dominance in civic affairs. Confronted with Howe's relative moderation on the issue of municipal reform, Wier did not see his ambitions fulfilled until the latter half of the 1840s when he helped democratize the 1841 city charter through a lowering of the property qualifications for councillors and electors. In 1851, after brief service in the new city council which gave him the reputation of being a Liberal partisan and advocate of the spoils system, Wier secured election to the provincial assembly for Halifax Township.

By this time Wier had finally established himself as a successful businessman. About 1845 he moved into the wholesale trade and began specializing in commerce with New England, shipping out fish in exchange for American foodstuffs, tobacco, tar, and other staple commodities. In 1847 he put two small sailing vessels on a regular packet run between Halifax and Boston. The service proved profitable and was continued until 1860 when steam replaced sail. During the 1850s Wier acquired a fleet of schooners which traded throughout the Gulf of St Lawrence, supplying the outports from Halifax and bringing back fish, oil, and timber for trans-shipment to New England.

As business expanded, Wier began taking in partners: Reuben Ingram Hart in 1850, followed by his son-in-law John Thomas Wylde, Levi Hart, and Charles James Wylde. Benjamin Wier and Company's premises on Lower Water St were valued at £12,000 in 1851, a considerable improvement over the £200 credited to Wier by municipal assessors in 1834. Wier had also purchased in 1849 a £1,400 residence amongst the Hollis St urban gentry. Before long the joint-stock companies spawned by mid Victorian prosperity had made these neighbours Wier's business associates. By 1860 he sat on the board of directors of such varied enterprises as the Halifax Marine Railway, the Grand Lake Land Company, the Chebucto Marine Insurance Company, the Union Marine Insurance Company, the Union Bank of Halifax, and the Acadian Iron and Steel Company, firms whose capital investment totalled around $2,800,000. As a mark of honour Wier was asked to assume stewardship responsibilities, such as serving on the directorate of the Halifax Visiting Dispensary. Wier's new respectability was further secured when he joined the masons, the Oddfellows, and the Halifax Yacht Club. In 1852 he was initiated into the Charitable Irish Society, the most influential lay organization within the local Irish community, and four years later became its president.

Wier's rise in society had a profound impact on his political views. Although his early assembly speeches argued for manhood suffrage and the ballot, by the mid 1850s his business, social, and political career had changed his attitude. He abandoned the pursuit of extended democracy and eventually began attacking those who dared question the institutional *status quo*. By now his political principles had been reduced to a few basic convictions: the construction of railways through state enterprise, free trade with the United States, retention of liberal liquor laws in the face of temperance agitation, and, above all, retention of power by the Liberal party.

Although "without education except what he has picked up for himself," Wier constituted a powerful presence on the floor of the legislature. A tall, large-framed man, with "a great massive face . . . and a harsh expression of countenance which he improves the wrong way by scowling," Wier possessed the energy and adroitness needed to bluster his way successfully through debate. Personifying the new breed of shrewdly ambitious businessmen-politicians emerging in mid Victorian society, Wier did not go unnoticed. In 1856 he was appointed to the Executive Council by Premier William Young*. The promotion came at a time when the Liberal party had begun to disintegrate as Irish Roman Catholics and Protestants divided over the issues of separate schools and volunteer enlistments for Britain's Crimean War. Despite the prestige he enjoyed as president of the Charitable Irish Society, Wier proved unable to reconcile the opposing factions,

Wier

and the Young government fell early in 1857 [*see* Joseph Howe]. Wier's only accomplishment while in power had been allegedly to promote implementation of the spoils system within the provincial civil service.

During the late 1850s Wier and Charles Tupper*, the Conservative leader, became bitter political foes, and their exchanges in the assembly frequently deteriorated into vicious name-calling. This rivalry was at full strength after the Liberals returned to power in the early 1860s. The new government found itself caught up in the frenzy of a Nova Scotian gold-rush, and although Premier Howe personally avoided the temptations of illicit profit, some of his colleagues proved less virtuous. Financial Secretary William Annand* and Benjamin Wier became the focal point of a major controversy in 1862–63 when Tupper discovered they had used privileged information available to them as cabinet members to speculate in gold mine property and also try to sell worthless real estate to unsuspecting British investors. Both men survived an inquiry by the lieutenant governor, but the scandal contributed to the government's and Wier's personal political downfall in the 1863 provincial election.

Loss of his seat proved to be of little consequence to Wier's personal well-being, since his business interests were expanding. In addition to large blocks of real estate in the province's gold fields, he acquired another $50,000 worth of Halifax waterfront property and some new corporate stock; he became a director of several additional enterprises such as the Nova Scotia Electric Telegraph Company, the Nova Scotia Permanent Benefit Building Society and Savings Fund, the Acadian Fire Insurance Company, the People's Bank of Halifax, the North Sydney Marine Railway Company, and the Sea Bay Coal Mining Company. A number of new social distinctions came his way, including a seat on the Halifax Chamber of Commerce and the commodoreship of the Halifax Yacht Squadron. His philanthropic donations increased, and he took an active interest in an Anglican chapel in the city where the poor could worship without paying pew rent.

Wier's most famous, or infamous, business venture in this period consisted of acting as Halifax agent for many of the Confederate blockade runners active during the Civil War. Profit rather than patriotism probably motivated this activity. In return for ship repair facilities in Halifax, the Confederates could supply him with valuable cotton for re-export to Britain, a lucrative but hazardous course for Wier which re-quired severing his business connections with New England. By late 1864, faced with the imminent collapse of the Confederacy, Wier found himself in an awkward position. Although he ultimately did re-establish trade with the north and become agent for a steamer service linking Halifax with the Grand Trunk terminus at Portland, Maine, he remained *persona non grata* in the eyes of the American government and could not get a visa to visit American territory. Therefore, despite his dislike of Tupper, Wier embraced the cause of British North American union as a solution to his own difficulties as well as to the problems of Nova Scotia when faced by a hostile United States. Furthermore, at meetings held to debate the union issue, Wier forcefully argued that construction of a Halifax to Quebec railway, something he had urged 20 years earlier, would give Nova Scotia a new future as a base for manufacturing. In other words, Wier had already perceived the dry rot of technological obsolescence in Nova Scotia's "Golden Age." Although he could not persuade many of his Halifax business colleagues to commit themselves to an urban-industrial future, his efforts obtained for him the reward of a seat in the Canadian Senate in 1867.

Wier's death in Ottawa early in 1868 abruptly ended his career just as it reached its peak. The anti-confederate *Morning Chronicle* admitted that the province had lost its "most enterprizing" merchant. The truth of this assertion was demonstrated by Wier's estate inventory which listed assets in excess of $200,000. Obituaries suggest Wier had inspired not affection but grudging admiration, and the dozens of Haligonians who turned out for his funeral did so in commemoration of one whose career had embodied a successful application of the contemporary gospel of self-help.

DAVID A. SUTHERLAND

Halifax County Court of Probate (Halifax), no.1544, will of Benjamin Wier (mfm. at PANS). National Archives (Washington), RG 59, U.S.A., Dept. of State, Dispatches of U.S. consuls in Halifax, N.S., 1860–65 (mfm. at PANS). PANS, MG 20, nos.68–69, 1850–83; RG 1, 291, no.157; 312, no.3; 313, no.115; 414, no.97; 451; RG 5, GP, 2, 1856; P, 122–23; RG 35, A, 3, Halifax assessments, 1833–41; Vertical MSS file, Benjamin Wier papers. St James Anglican Church (Newport and Walton, N.S.), register of baptisms (mfm. at PANS). Halifax Ragged and Industrial Schools, *Annual report*, 1864. N.S., General Assembly, *Statutes*, 1845–68; House of Assembly, *Debates and proc.*, 1855–63; *Journal and proc.*, 1838, app.44. *Acadian Recorder*, 23 Feb., 15 March, 31 May 1856. *British Colonist* (Halifax), 19 Aug. 1851; 4 Dec. 1858; December 1862;

January 1863; 16, 21 April 1868. *Evening Express* (Halifax), 15 April 1868. *Halifax Carnival Echo*, midsummer 1889. *Halifax Journal*, 31 March 1834, 1 Jan. 1838, 1 March 1841. *Halifax Morning Post*, 2 March 1841, 10 Feb. 1842. *Halifax Reporter*, 14 April 1868. *Morning Chronicle* (Halifax), December 1862, January 1863, 15 April 1868. *Novascotian*, 1830–68. *Presbyterian Witness*, 18 April 1868. *Sun* (Halifax), 28 Jan. 1847, 25 Feb. 1848, 6 May 1852, 1 Jan. 1856. *Times* (Halifax), 14 Nov. 1843. *Belcher's farmer's almanack*, 1830–68. *Canadian directory of parl.* (Johnson). *Directory of N.S. MLAs. Halifax, N.S., business directory, for 1863 . . .*, comp. Luke Hutchinson (Halifax, 1863). *McAlpine's Nova Scotia directory, for 1868–69, containing directories of each place in the province . . .* (Halifax, [1868]). *Nova Scotia registry of shipping: with standard rules for construction and classification*, comp. T. R. DeWolf (Halifax, 1866). F. W. Thirkell, *The first two hundred years; the story of the parish of Newport and Walton* ([Newport, N.S., 1959?]).

WILLIS, ROBERT, Church of England clergyman; b. 6 Aug. 1785 at Stillington, County Durham, England, son of John and Mary Willis; m. 19 Oct. 1819 at Halifax, N.S., Ann Maria Heaviside (d. 1821), and they had three daughters; secondly, on 12 July 1825 at Saint John, N.B., Mary Billopp, and they had four sons; d. 21 April 1865 in Halifax.

Robert Willis entered Lincoln College, Oxford, in 1804 and graduated BA in 1808. He was ordained a deacon of the Church of England and appointed curate of Richmond, Yorkshire, on 25 September of that year, then ordained a priest by the bishop of Chester on 10 Sept. 1809. In May 1812 Willis joined the Royal Navy chaplaincy service; he was posted to HMS *Queen* (1812–13), *Bulwark* (1813–15), *Akbar* (1815–16), and *Forth* (1816–17). He resigned from the navy to enter the service of the Society for the Propagation of the Gospel in July 1817. Shortly thereafter he was sent to Trinity Church, Saint John, N.B., to assist the Reverend George Pidgeon, whom he succeeded as rector on 13 Nov. 1818. Willis was appointed ecclesiastical commissary in New Brunswick for Bishop Robert Stanser* on 2 April 1821.

On the appointment of John Inglis* to the see of Nova Scotia, Willis was named his successor as rector of St Paul's, Halifax, on 11 Oct. 1824. This nomination raised a storm of opposition since the majority of the congregation favoured their more evangelical curate, John Thomas Twining*, for the position. The parish was torn asunder and almost two-thirds of its members left St Paul's. Some of the most influential and wealthy, including James W. Johnston*, established an independent chapel, which later joined the Baptist church, giving the latter a tremendous impetus in Nova Scotia. Many of the others went to St George's Church where Robert Fitzgerald UNIACKE became rector.

Willis' ministry at St Paul's was exceedingly difficult at first, but his conciliatory spirit eventually earned him the goodwill of his congregation. He was appointed archdeacon of Nova Scotia and Prince Edward Island in 1825, and in April of the same year, chaplain to the Nova Scotia Legislative Council, a post he held until his death. In 1826 he was admitted a Lambeth DD by the archbishop of Canterbury, and in 1848 King's College, Windsor, granted him a DCL in recognition of his services to Nova Scotia. The 40 years which Willis spent as rector of St Paul's saw a great many changes in the church and the parish; however, his particular gift was his ability to react to the events without causing controversy and to help his church adjust to the changes.

C. E. THOMAS

Church of England, Diocese of Chester Archives (Chester, Eng.), EDA I/9–I/10 (Bishop of Chester's Act Book, 25 Sept. 1808, 10 Sept. 1809). Durham County Records Office (Durham, Eng.), Redmarshall parish registers. Lambeth Palace Library (London), Faculty Office records, FI/Y, ff.121v–22. N.B. Museum, Marriage register A (1812–28). PRO, WO 7/67, 1812. St Paul's Anglican Church (Halifax), marriage register, 1816–22; burial register, 1855–1902 (mfm. at PANS). Trinity Anglican Church (Saint John, N.B.), papers, 1790–1860. USPG, Journal of SPG, 31, p.285 (19 Dec. 1817); 35, p.43 (11 Oct. 1824); 36, pp.135–37 (19 Dec. 1825). *Alumni Oxonienses: the members of the University of Oxford, 1715–1886 . . .*, ed. Joseph Foster (4v., Oxford and London, [1888]). University of King's College, *Calendar* (Windsor, N.S.), 1872–73, 56. G. H. Lee, *An historical sketch of the first fifty years of the Church of England in the province of New Brunswick (1783–1833)* (Saint John, N.B., 1880).

WILLSON (Wilson), DAVID, visionary, religious leader, author, and hymn writer; b. 7 June 1778 in Dutchess County, N.Y., son of "poor but pious Presbyterian parents," John and Catherine Willson; m. Phebe (Phoebe) Titus and they had three sons and two daughters; d. 16 Jan. 1866 in Sharon, East Gwillimbury Township, Canada West.

From Ireland John Willson came to America in 1770 and found that in the patroon country where he settled, near Poughkeepsie on the Hudson River, land could only be rented. His son's earliest "occupation was hard labor in cultivating the soil, till . . . left an orphan . . . at the age of fourteen . . . I inclined to mechanical business in joining timber one part unto another." He also became a sailor on *The Farmer*, a ship owned by relatives; on its trading voyages between New York and the West Indies the crew had to defend themselves from pirate attacks. When, not long before 1800, Willson married a Quaker girl from his home county she urged him to leave such unpeaceful expeditions and in 1801 they journeyed to Upper Canada where other Quakers were settling and land was easily attainable. Shipwrecked in Lake Ontario, Willson kicked the wheel of a spinning wheel overboard, lashed his two boys to it ''and the parents floated them to shore between them . . . having lost all their possessions in the wreck, and in order to save what money they had, they walked from York to their location in Sharon [then called Hope] carrying the boys . . . on their backs.''

By 1805 Willson owned his land, but not contentment; ''I have been separated from all flesh, religious and profane by the moving of a Spirit . . . often seeking lonely places wherein to retire and worship the Spirit that had received my soul in trust, to which I gave full credence and did obey. . . . I gained admittance [6 Feb. 1805] . . . into the society of the people called Quakers, after many years of tribulation and a rising and falling of the mind.'' At the end of seven years of prominent and respected, but silent, membership in the Yonge Street Meeting Willson's ''Spirit'' ''required him publicly to testify of the being of a God.'' ''I had thought they were as I knew I was, – feeling the movings of a Spirit on the mind.'' Not long before he was formally expelled from the Yonge Street Meeting on 15 Oct. 1812, Willson must have discovered that for the most part his contemporary Friends, pious, plain, reserved, austere, spiritually unadventurous, and distrustful of worship through music and art, were certainly not as he was. ''I appeared to the Elders and ministers of the church as a wild man from the desert . . . I wept bitterly . . . I was commanded . . . to sit in silence. . . .'' ''He then retired peaceably to his own house; some few followed him, who were anxious to obtain better information. These patiently heard, weighed the subjects and found full unity and friendship with him.'' ''Therefore we became a separate people . . . as our discipline led to peace with all people more than any one in our knowledge, we called ourselves Children of Peace, because we were but young therein.''

Now according to Willson's thinking, as revealed in a long list of publications, manuscripts, hundreds of hymns, and even in the symbolism of the buildings he designed, ''God is peace'' and lies at the ''centre'' of the divine-human soul or mind; ''The mind hath as many parts in it as there are in the creation, and the centre of it we wish to find.'' The guide to this peaceful centre in which innocence and experience, joy and misery, heaven and hell are joined is light or wisdom. Willson's passion for light, both inner and outer, can still be seen in the temple he designed as early as 1822, which the Children of Peace, led by master builder Ebenezer Doan, completed and opened 29 Oct. 1831; it ''contains 2952 panes of glass and is lighted once a-year with 116 candles'' on the eve of the September Harvest Feast, one of three instituted by Willson as festivals of neighbourhood unity. Like his monthly sacrifices for charity, when the congregation came by itself to the temple with their alms offerings, these feasts were accompanied by processions of women in white singing beneath marching banners, by a band of well-trained musicians, by music from pipe organs built by Robert COATES, chanted poems, meditations spoken by Willson, and all proving his belief that ''It is right to be delighted with the things of God.'' Led unofficially by Willson, the ''few hundreds'' that gathered about him in Sharon followed towards the ''centre'' so well that without detailed or rigid doctrinal frameworks they were able to worship God practically with the fullest development of such diverse talents as music and cooking, economic cooperation (''a fund for the mutual benefit of each other''), and supporting a domestic science school for girls. One of the loveliest examples of their architecture is a study they built for Willson ''composed entirely of glass'' where at his writing desk he kept proving his belief that ''Eden consists [not] of a certain tract of land; but . . . is known by a certain condition of the mind''; ''. . . there were no poor in Sharon.''

Music had been one of the reasons Willson originally quarrelled with the Quakers; the political implications of his communal experiment were, in 1837, very nearly the cause of the temple's destruction. Sharon was well known to the authorities (the Family Compact) since Willson made publicly announced expeditions down to York (Toronto) with choir and band where he once preached ''that there ought neither to be masters nor servants; that all mankind are equal.'' Scorned, threatened with jail, or worse, in the early days of the Children, Willson later met such jibes as ''village of Priapus,'' ''Orgies,'' ''superstition and idolatry,'' and ''Children of Wrath.'' But when in 1837 he would not approve William Lyon MACKENZIE's policy of violence, some of his own people called him ''Tory''! And some of the Children, including two of his sons, joined Mackenzie's rebels, were arrested and imprisoned for several months; ''it was with difficulty that the militia could be restrained from destroying their temple." But by 1842 this difficult turn on the road to "Peace" had been smoothed out. Willson's guidance was once more accepted and until his death Sharon flourished as never before.

There was one more turn through which one can sense Willson negotiating in his last writings: how, in such an informal organization, do you ensure that the listening to "His Spirit" continues to guide after the original listener has disappeared? His oldest son "read his father's sermons," but no new writer appeared; dark moments were the legal quarrels about the ownership of the buildings between Willson's heirs and representatives of his followers. The last illumination in the 19th century took place in September 1888. On 2 Sept. 1890 a grandson sold the temple to a stranger. Reopened, however, in 1918 as a museum, the temple still stands, well cared for, much visited and loved, a symbol of the power Willson's imagination is eventually seen as possessing, a power to bring people together towards "Peace" and to "An altar to all nations/ With forty-eight bright windows" placed – as he once wrote in 1822 – "on Ararat."

JAMES REANEY

PAO, Davidite record books, 1831–71; Misc. 1803, Families of Friends (Quakers) who settled on Yonge St., 1803. UWO, Archives of the Religious Soc. of Friends (Quakers) in Can., H-7-2 (Pelham Monthly Meeting of Friends, 1799–1806), f.135; 0-11-6 (Yonge Street Monthly Meeting, 1806–18), f.150. York Pioneer and Hist. Soc. Archives (Sharon, Ont.), L 24 (notebook containing miscellaneous prose and poetry by David Willson, 1815); L 1230 (38 copies of memorial and funeral verses by David Willson, printed as broadsides); Account book containing miscellaneous prose and poetry by David Willson, including a "Memorial of David Willson – 27 Dec. 1838"; Collection of 42 loose sheets of handwritten sermons and poetry by David Willson. There is also a copy at the York Pioneer and Hist. Soc. Archives of David Willson, *The Lord's celebration* (broadside, 1822). David Willson, *Hymns and prayers for the Children of Sharon: to be sung in worship on sabbath days* (Newmarket, [Ont.], 1846); *The impressions of the mind: to which are added some remarks on church and state discipline, and the acting principles of life* (Toronto, 1835); *The practical life of the author, from the year 1801 to 1860* (Newmarket, [Ont.], 1860); *The rights of Christ, according to the principles and doctrines of the Children of Peace* (Philadelphia, 1815), a pamphlet which also contains *Address to the crown of England* and *The pattern of Peace, or Babylon overthrown.* Other writings by David Willson may be found at the MTCL and at the York Pioneer and Hist. Soc. Archives; the latter also holds other manuscript material by and relating to David Willson. In addition, a letter from Carolyn Mann to the author, 1 Feb. 1973, was very helpful. A. G. Dorland, *A history of the Society of Friends (Quakers) in Canada* (Toronto, 1927), repub. as *The Quakers in Canada; a history* ([Toronto, 1968]). Helmut Kallmann, *A history of music in Canada, 1534–1914* (Toronto and London, 1960). C. E. McFaddin, "A study of the buildings of the Children of Peace, Sharon, Ontario" (unpublished MA thesis, 2v., University of Toronto, 1953). E. W. Trewhella, "The story of Sharon," *Newmarket Era* (Newmarket, Ont.) 14 June 1951–27 March 1952.

WILSON, JOHN, lawyer, politician, and judge; b. 5 Feb. 1807 at Paisley, Renfrewshire, Scotland, eldest son of Ebenezer Wilson and Jean Adam; d. 3 June 1869 in Westminster Township, Ont.

John Wilson's family, having first gone to Halifax, Nova Scotia, from Scotland, settled near Perth, Upper Canada, about 1823. John attended district common and grammar schools, then taught school himself before beginning the study of law at Perth in 1830 in the office of James Boulton. On 13 June 1830 he shot and killed fellow law student Robert Lyon in what was, reportedly, the province's last duel. Wilson, who despised "unchaste conversation," had informed Lyon's *fiancée* of some insulting remarks Lyon had made about her. She disavowed Lyon, and he blamed Wilson; a fist fight followed, then the fatal duel. Wilson and his second, Simon Robinson, surrendered, were tried for murder, and were acquitted.

Admitted a lawyer in 1835, Wilson assumed responsibility for Boulton's office at Niagara (Niagara-on-the-Lake), then moved to London to establish his own practice. He married Joanna Hughes on 20 May 1835 at St Thomas; the couple were to have eight children. Wilson quickly established himself in London; at one time he was in partnership with his brother-in-law, D. J. Hughes. In 1836 Wilson was a commissioner of the Court of Requests and a returning officer for London in the elections for the assembly. It was said that he abetted Tory attempts to intimidate Reformers at the poll, charges which he rejected. During the rebellion, Wilson helped disarm the local radicals, participated in the organization of a force to defend London from an expected attack, and joined other London volunteers to subdue suspected traitors of the St Thomas area. He was commissioned a militia captain in 1838 and served against the Patriots until January 1839, yet at the same time acted on behalf of people accused of treason.

Wilson was warden of the London District from February 1842 to November 1844, and in 1843 became a district superintendent of education; he held a succession of offices until 1863,

Windham

including that of solicitor for London from 1845 to 1849. Noted as an able lawyer and a generous man, he was affectionately nicknamed "Honest John Wilson." His great popularity led to his election to the Legislative Assembly as a Conservative for the town of London in 1847 and 1848. Although opposed to responsible government and the Rebellion Losses Bill, he denounced the Tory violence that greeted both. In 1849, declaring that if annexationist sentiment constituted treason in 1837 it did so in 1849 as well and damning the "ultra part of the Conservative Party," he felt obliged to offer himself for re-election, probably as an independent. He was successful, but in the 1851 election T. C. Dixon, whom he had defeated in 1849, bested him.

Re-elected in 1854 as an independent Conservative, Wilson found himself allied with Francis Hincks* and his Reformers. When Hincks' government resigned in September 1854, Hincks was prepared to instal Wilson as leader of his faction, but eventually decided to stay on and agreed to take his supporters into the coalition formed by Allan MacNab and A.-N. Morin. Wilson declared that he was "happy" at thus avoiding the leadership but he would not support the new government, perhaps because it encompassed the "ultras" of 1849, and in 1857 he refused to stand for re-election. Although he had previously asserted that he had forsaken politics, he secured election to the Legislative Council in May 1863. He never took his seat, for on 22 July he was appointed a judge of the Court of Common Pleas (he had become queen's counsel in 1856). He moved to Toronto, but retained his Westminster home. In the fall and winter of 1866–67 he presided over the trial of 16 of the Fenians captured after the invasion of Canada West the previous summer; eight were found guilty. Wilson sentenced seven of them to death, but all these sentences were commuted. Although his life was threatened at the time, it was reported in January 1867 that Wilson had travelled through the northern states "to show the Fenians that he is not afraid of them." Ironically, however, the strain of the trials apparently hastened his death.

Colin Read

London Public Library and Art Museum (London, Ont.), City of London scrapbooks, 35. PAO, Inderwick coll. *Daily Advertiser* (London), 3, 4 June 1869. *Documents relating to the resignation of the Canadian ministry in September, 1854* (Quebec, 1854), 21–27. *Trials of the Fenian prisoners at Toronto, who were captured at Fort Erie, C.W., in June, 1866*, reporters G. R. Gregg and E. P. Roden (Toronto, 1867). Read, *Lives of judges*, 337–45. *History of the county of Middlesex* (Brock), 133–35. Fred Williams, "A notable election in London, C.W., 1850," *Globe and Mail*, 18 Jan. 1939.

WINDHAM, Sir CHARLES ASH, soldier; b. 10 Oct. 1810 at Felbrigg, Norfolk, England, son of Vice-Admiral William Windham and Ann Thellusson; m. first in 1849 Marianne Catherine Emily Beresford, and they had five children, and secondly in 1866 Charlotte Jane Des Vœux; d. 2 Feb. 1870 at Jacksonville, Fla.

Charles Ash Windham was educated at the Royal Military College, Sandhurst, and commissioned in the Coldstream Guards as an ensign on 30 Dec. 1826. He was promoted lieutenant and captain on 31 May 1833, major in November 1846, and lieutenant-colonel on 29 Dec. 1846, in each case by purchase. In May 1838 he had been sent to Quebec with the 2nd battalion of the Coldstreams. In November, when the rebelling forces invaded Upper Canada at Prescott and also gathered in Napierville in Lower Canada, the battalion moved to Montreal, and the following month sent a detachment to Laprairie (La Prairie), but the battalion itself was not engaged. Before the risings the British garrison in North America had consisted of only eight weak battalions; as a result of them the militia was strengthened, some units were put on a semi-permanent basis, and a regular regiment of the Royal Canadian Rifles was authorized on the British establishment for permanent service in North America. The Coldstreams returned to Quebec in April 1840 and to England in 1842.

Promoted colonel on 20 June 1854, Windham was assistant quartermaster-general of the 4th Division in Crimea and was present, but saw little action, at the battles of Alma River, Balaklava, and Inkerman. He was outspoken in his criticism of laggard British military leadership in the Crimea. Given command of the assault on the Great Redan at Sevastopol on 8 Sept. 1855, he personally rode back to ask for reinforcements after suffering heavy losses, but a retreat had been ordered. He was criticized by soldiers for his conduct but made a popular hero by William Howard Russell, correspondent of the *Times*, for having "saved the honour of the army." "Redan Windham" became chief of staff later in the war and did much for the troops' welfare. On 6 April 1857 he became a Liberal MP for Norfolk.

Windham returned to service in 1857 during the Indian Mutiny. In November at Cawnpore (Kampur), in his first independent command, he made an attack on his own initiative despite orders to play a defensive role assisting in Sir Colin Campbell's advance to relieve Lucknow. He was forced to fall back. Though exonerated by the commander-in-chief, the Duke of Cambridge, in the House of Lords, Windham's action was debated for many years, and even led to a book in his defence. He received no other command in the field.

On 17 June 1861 Windham was made colonel of the 46th Foot and on 5 Feb. 1866 he became a lieutenant-general. On 3 Oct. 1867 he succeeded Sir John Michel* in the command of British forces in Canada, and from 14 to 30 Nov. 1868 he was administrator of Canada. As lieutenant-general commanding in North America, Windham continued to be responsible for the defence of Canada after Sir George-Étienne Cartier*, the minister of militia, had enacted legislation in 1868 to establish a volunteer force for the dominion. Cartier's soundness on defence was suspect in Britain because he showed little inclination to carry out the terms of the defence agreement of 1865 which had provided for a guaranteed loan for fortifications built by Canada in Montreal and farther west. Windham's relations with the minister deteriorated when an attempt by the Canadian government to evade paying for damage to Enfield rifles that the War Office had lent Canada during the American Civil War was frustrated by Windham's report that there had been neglect.

Though they had not exploited their victory at Ridgeway, Canada West, in June 1866 [see Alfred Booker*; John O'Neill*], Fenians in the United States continued uttering threats against Canada. Windham's ability to counter possible trouble, however, was hamstrung because the dominion government controlled the best sources of intelligence and refused to call out the militia at his behest. War in North America seemed closer when Senator Charles Sumner, on 13 April 1869, hinted at the annexation of Canada as compensation for the *Alabama* claim, and there was talk of the United States demanding astronomical reparations for the damage caused by Confederate raiding from Canada. Governor General Sir John Young* warned Windham that even if the dominion did call out its militia, by law it could not be put under his command until an invasion had actually occurred.

Windham's difficulties increased when Colonial Secretary Granville informed Young in a dispatch on 14 April that Edward Cardwell's policy of withdrawing garrisons from self-governing colonies would be applied in Canada; ultimately British garrisons would be kept only in imperial fortresses, and the garrison in Quebec and Ontario was to be reduced to 4,000 men immediately. The Canadian public was disturbed and their government tried to get the decision reversed, or its implementation delayed. Al-

though the Canadian government had constantly urged the importance of the gunboat service on the Great Lakes, when Lord Granville insisted that Canada should pay all the cost it laid up the last two ships without crews. Later, when it reluctantly decided to recommission them, Windham learned of the decision only from newspaper reports.

As his forces declined in number, Windham became increasingly concerned for their safety. In 1869, when he was refused 3,000 volunteer militia for Ontario and Quebec, he let it be known that he would carry out the colonial secretary's advice that the regulars should withdraw immediately from Toronto. Sir John A. Macdonald* assured him that if "more serious" information was received militia reinforcements would be forthcoming. Windham then persuaded the colonial secretary of the political necessity of leaving the troops temporarily in Toronto; he used this concession to win a promise from the Canadian government that he would not be ignored in future defence planning.

At the end of 1869, troubled by a heart condition, Windham went to the United States to convalesce. During a fire in February 1870 in a Florida sanitarium he was carried outside, and perhaps as a result he died the next day. His body was interred temporarily in Montreal and finally buried in Hanwell cemetery, Middlesex, England. Windham was succeeded in the command of British forces in North America by Major-General Sir Charles Hastings Doyle*, but Lieutenant-General James Alexander Lindsay* was charged with completing the withdrawal of the troops in central Canada.

Sir John A. Macdonald wrote of Windham that "his amiability and kindness made him a great favorite." William Howard Russell reported that Windham was "full of ideas, very keen, but . . . rather inclined to take the bit in his teeth." Windham was unfortunate in arriving in Canada at the height of disputes arising over the British government's wish to remove its troops and the Canadian government's reluctance to assume the costs of defence or to cooperate in measures to meet current threats. But the appointment in Canada at such a time had needed something more than a gracious old fire-eater.

RICHARD A. PRESTON

C. A. Windham, *The Crimean diary and letters of Lieut.-General Sir C. A. Windham, K.C.B., with observations upon his services during the Indian mutiny, and an introduction by W. H. Russell*, ed. H. [W.] Pearse (London, 1897).

PAC, MG 30, D62, 30, pp.856–64; RG 8, I (C series),

Winton

39, pp.127, 194, 201; 194, p.82. *Gazette* (Montreal), 4 Feb. 1870. *Illustrated London News*, 19 Feb. 1870. *Montreal Herald*, 4 Feb. 1870. Boase, *Modern English biog.*, III, 1536–37. *DNB*. J. M. Adye, *The defence of Cawnpore by the troops under the orders of Major General Charles A. Windham, C.B., in Nov. 1857* (London, 1858). F. S. Roberts, *Forty-one years in India, from subaltern to commander-in-chief* (2v., London, 1897), I, 361–64, 369, 377–80. C. P. Stacey, *Canada and the British army, 1846–1871; a study in the practice of responsible government* (2nd ed., Toronto, 1963), 219–22; "The garrison of Fort Wellington: a military dispute during the Fenian troubles," *CHR*, XIV (1933), 161–76.

WINTON, HENRY, editor and publisher; b. 21 Feb. 1817 at Dartmouth, Devon, England, eldest son of publisher Henry David* and Elizabeth Winton, and brother of Robert and Francis, later publishers of the St John's *Daily News* and the *St John's Day Book* (later the *Morning Chronicle*) respectively; m. Elizabeth Brown; d. 30 March 1866 in St John's, Nfld, after a lengthy illness.

Nothing is known of Henry Winton's early life, though he probably learned the publishing trade in his father's shop. By the 1850s the family was in St John's where Henry was a member of the Sons of Temperance, and in 1851 founded the *Banner of Temperance*, a semi-monthly which apparently ceased publication the same year. He was also a member of the St George's Society and a Congregationalist.

In 1855, after his father's death, Winton became editor, printer, and publisher of the *Public Ledger and Newfoundland General Advertiser*, though his mother remained proprietor until 1860 when Winton himself took over ownership. Despite the paper's motto, "Open to all parties – Influenced by none," he showed consistent support for the Conservatives and vigorously attacked the Liberal administrations of Philip Francis Little* and John Kent* between 1855 and 1861. He particularly criticized the influence of the Roman Catholic clergy on the Liberal government, especially the role of Bishop John Thomas MULLOCK. He also charged the Liberals with squandering public funds through patronage and high government salaries, and thereby swelling the public debt. In 1861 Winton was sued for libel by Patrick Jordan, a St John's merchant and Liberal supporter, who objected to a letter in the *Public Ledger* signed by "Quiz" accusing Jordan of embezzling £2,000 in filling contracts with the Board of Works to supply food to the St John's Hospital and the Lunatic Asylum. The case, however, was settled out of court.

Early in 1861 Winton stepped up his attacks when he began to publish the *Daily Sessional*, which appeared regularly for some months before the May election of that year; frequently referred to in the *Public Ledger*, it was abandoned that spring, "its mission having been accomplished with the close of the Session." In the bitter political and religious controversies of 1860–61 Winton was a staunch supporter of Governor Sir Alexander BANNERMAN, particularly when a petition was circulated by George James HOGSETT and others with Bishop Mullock's approval advocating the governor's removal after the 1861 elections. With a Conservative government under Hugh William Hoyles* in power, Winton's political journalism was more restrained. In 1865, however, he strongly opposed the coalition government which the Conservative leader, Frederic Bowker Terrington Carter*, formed with such Liberals as Ambrose Shea*, because of the record of past Liberal administrations. In the same year, after some initial hesitation, Winton's paper editorialized against entry by Newfoundland into the proposed confederation of the British North American colonies, which he feared would be a sacrifice of Newfoundland's interests.

CALVIN D. EVANS

Henry Winton was the author of a series of pamphlets on "The history of responsible government in Newfoundland . . . ," one of which has survived: *A chapter in the history of Newfoundland for the year 1861* (St John's, 1861). *Courier* (St John's), 31 March 1866. *Public Ledger*, 16 Jan. 1855; 8, 26 March, 26 April, 7 May, 17 Sept., 25 Oct. 1861; 6 April 1866. *Royal Gazette* (St John's), 3 April 1866. *Hutchinson's Newfoundland directory for 1864–65 . . .* , comp. T. Hutchinson (St John's, 1864). Gunn, *Political history of Nfld*. E. C. Moulton, "The political history of Newfoundland, 1861–1869" (unpublished MA thesis, Memorial University of Newfoundland, St John's, 1960). A. B. Perlin, "Continuing stories of old newspapers," *Daily News* (St John's), 18 Feb. 1955.

WIX, EDWARD, Church of England clergyman, missionary, and author; b. 1 Feb. 1802 in Faulkbourne, Essex, England, eldest son of the Reverend Samuel Wix and E. Walford; m. in 1828 a Miss Browne of Lowestoft, England, and they had two daughters and one son; d. 24 Nov. 1866 at Swanmore, Isle of Wight, England.

Edward Wix was educated at Merchant Taylors' School in London and Trinity College, Oxford. He graduated BA in 1824. In 1825 he was ordained and licensed as curate to his father, a well-known, controversial writer on behalf of the high church party, president of Sion College, London, and rector of Inworth, Essex. The following year he moved to Halifax as a missionary in the diocese of Nova Scotia whose bishop, John Inglis*, was a friend of his father. After an attack of typhus in 1828 he went to England where he quickly recovered. He took his MA at Oxford and married before returning to Nova Scotia. Almost at once he was transferred to Newfoundland, where he served first at Bonavista and then, on succeeding George Coster* as archdeacon in 1830, in St John's. There he began eight years of organizing, preaching, travelling, and fund-raising.

In 1830 he visited settlements in Trinity Bay and near St John's. In 1835 he spent six months on a missionary tour of the eastern, southern, and western coasts, during which he kept a journal, published in London in 1836 as *Six months of a Newfoundland missionary's journal*. Aimed at possible supporters of the mission to Newfoundland, it contained many interesting comments on contemporary life. He was critical of the Roman Catholics of St John's, "who are excited to frequent breaches of the peace by the most seditious Romish priesthood" and contrasted their behaviour with that of the friendly Roman Catholics of Placentia. He lamented the state of communications, asserting that it cost 25s. to convey a letter from Trinity to St John's. He was shocked by the material, moral, and spiritual destitution which he encountered. On the Isle of Valen he found females dirty and almost naked, and performed baptisms in private houses because the mothers lacked clothes for churchgoing. One man in Fortune Bay had not seen a clergyman for 56 years. Always he had to compete with "grog ships." In the Bay of Islands he found profligacy, drunken orgies, and incest, and stated that "profanity is the dialect." His journal's appeal for help to save Newfoundland from sinking into heathendom did much to convince the Church of England that a bishop was needed.

Wix was active in St John's as a member of the committee of the Society for Promoting Christian Knowledge, distributing prayer books, Bibles, and tracts, and as an agent of a newly formed branch of the British and Foreign Bible Society, established in 1835. He helped organize a temperance society which met almost every month between 1833 and 1838 and published the *Newfoundland Temperance Journal*. He was appointed to the Board of Education for St John's in 1836, and a commissioner of roads and bridges shortly before his departure. He was also the first vice-president of the Church Society of the archdeaconry of Newfoundland, which he helped to organize in March 1837. Most of his effort, however, was put into raising money. He felt that

one church was insufficient for the rapidly rising population of St John's, and during a trip to England late in 1833 obtained the necessary funds from church collections. With the aid of a grant of land from the British government, St Thomas' Church was built, and opened in 1836 as a 700-seat chapel of ease to the parish church, St John the Baptist. Services in St Thomas' were held three times on Sunday, and in the evening on Fridays and all saints' days. It was clearly intended to be a preaching house. The high church *Ecclesiologist* commented scathingly in 1848 that "the intention was certainly better than the effect" but mentioned that the marble altar and font Wix had obtained from Italy were "the only attempts at ritual solemnity – nay, decency – which the whole island, till a very recent period, possessed."

In October 1838 Wix left Newfoundland secretly and hurriedly, in a manner which, according to the Reverend Thomas Finch Hobday Bridge*, "both surprised and appalled the members of the Church." He left in poor health and in debt to the amount of £1,300, and after having been seen in the company of a prostitute. For the next five years he rested in England until in 1843 he took a curacy at St Leonard's, Shoreditch, Middlesex. He moved in 1847 to All Saints, Poplar, Middlesex, but had to resign after three years because of ill health. He spent the next 14 years nursing his health in Madeira, Italy, the Riviera, Algiers, and Malta, while occasionally contributing to the *Gentleman's Magazine* and the *Church Review*. He returned to England in 1864 and settled in 1866 in his son's parish at Swanmore, Isle of Wight.

A man of considerable ability, Wix did much to publicize the Newfoundland mission in England both through his book and by frequent letters in the reports of the Society for the Propagation of the Gospel and the SPCK. By his missionary work, his organizing, and his church building, he prepared the way for the first Church of England bishop of Newfoundland, Aubrey George Spencer*.

FREDERICK JONES

Edward Wix was the author of *An address delivered at an examination of the St. John's Church Sunday schools, June 15, 1832* (St John's, 1832); *Divine visitations: a sermon* (St John's, 1832); *The guilt of a denial of God's providence; a sermon on Zephaniah I.12* (St John's, 1832); *A retrospect of the operations of the Society for the Propagation of the Gospel in North America; a sermon preached Sunday, March 31, MDCCCXXXIII, at St. John's Church, Newfoundland* (St John's, 1833); *A sermon* (St John's, 1831); and *Six months of a Newfoundland missionary's journal, from*

Wood

February to August, 1835 (London, 1836). PRO, CO 194/140, K. B. Hamilton to Newcastle, 31 Oct. 1853. USPG, C/CAN/Nfl 5, f.268, T. F. H. Bridge to Campbell, 26 Oct. 1838. Soc. for Promoting Christian Knowledge, *Annual report* (London), 1830–39. Soc. for the Propagation of the Gospel in Foreign Parts, *Report* (London), 1830–39. *Times and General Commercial Gazette* (St John's), 30 Jan. 1867. *Alumni Oxonienses: the members of the University of Oxford, 1715–1886* . . . , ed. Joseph Foster (4v., Oxford and London, [1888]). *DNB.* H. W. LeMessurier, *The Church of Saint Thomas and its rectors, 1836–1928* (St John's, [1928]). "Colonial church architecture," *Ecclesiologist* (London), VIII (1847–48), 274–79.

WOOD, SAMUEL SIMPSON, Church of England minister and educator; b. 21 Feb. 1795 in Bideford, England, son of Captain Samuel Wood; d. 25 March 1868 in Upper Durham (Kirkdale), Que.

Samuel Simpson Wood was educated at James Tate's Richmond Grammar School before taking his BA in 1818 at Corpus Christi College, Cambridge. In 1819 Jacob Mountain*, first Church of England bishop of Quebec, engaged him as missionary of the Society for the Propagation of the Gospel and on 8 Nov. 1819 appointed him to Drummondville, where he established a church. He was appointed rector of St James' Church at Trois-Rivières in 1827 but was not inducted until January 1829. He remained in this parish until 1856, when he returned to the Drummondville area at Upper Durham (1856–68). From 1857 to 1863 he was also rural dean for much of the southeastern region of Canada East. In 1834 Wood had married Margaret Mary Hallowell, a cousin of John* and Alexander Neil Bethune*; eight of Wood's 12 children survived him.

In 1827–28, Wood was in England and took his MA at Cambridge. He also published *An apology for the colonial clergy of Great Britain: specially for those of Lower and Upper Canada*, an attack on the Colonial Clergy Act of 1819 which prevented clergymen ordained by colonial bishops from discharging the duties of priest in an ecclesiastical province in England except with the special permission of the archbishop of that province. The work briefly describes the problems Church of England clergymen faced in Canada, particularly respecting Catholics and Dissenters. It also treats such questions as the clergy reserves and the necessity for professors of the University of King's College at York (Toronto) to be clergy of the Church of England. The pamphlet is interesting as a reflection of a conservative Anglican mind. Wood returned to England in 1834 charged by Bishop Charles James Stewart* with arguing the case for stopping the sale of clergy reserves land and placing their management in the hands of the Church of England instead of a government board. Wood was also charged with directing a fund-raising campaign for Upper Canadian missions, getting the appointment of a suffragan bishop for Lower Canada, and securing amendments to the charter of McGill University permitting it to expand at will. In all these efforts he failed, although he did get the SPG to establish the basis of an episcopal library for the diocese of Quebec, which at that time included Upper Canada.

As a participant in the clergy reserves controversy and in the formation of the first Synod of the Diocese of Quebec (1859) and as one of the founders of the Church Society (1842), Wood shared in the difficult transition of the Church of England from an English state-supported institution to a more indigenous, voluntary church. He was among the vice-presidents of the Church Society from 1845 to his death. In 1858–59 he defended George Jehoshaphat MOUNTAIN in a controversy with evangelical churchmen over the voting system in the diocesan synod, in which the bishop tried to ensure that clergymen would have a predominant voice over lay members.

Wood was particularly eminent as an educator. He complained of the American influence on education exerted through American textbooks used even in government schools, and urged the establishment of "National Schools." In Trois-Rivières and Drummondville he established grammar schools, whose curriculum indicated the profound influence of Tate; they were to educate a colonial élite, and they tutored, among others, the sons of Chief Justice Sir James Stuart* and Sir John COLBORNE. In 1833 Wood was offered the principalship of McGill University, but declined because of its public duties. Having long tutored theology students, he was asked in 1840 to be principal of Bishop's College at Trois-Rivières but again declined when in 1843 it was established instead at Lennoxville. A contemporary described Wood as having "the true notion of education; a devout Christian, a consistent Churchman, and a genuine English gentleman himself, he aimed at making his pupils the same."

Well balanced, possessed of above average intelligence and a sense of humour, Wood was a persuasive and popular minister. Through his friendships with Charles James Stewart and particularly George Jehoshaphat Mountain, who shared his tastes and ideas, Wood's opinion, though rarely publicized, was well respected in the church, but his fear of publicity prevented his fulfilling their expectations. Himself a forgotten notable, his life and thought remain representative of the Anglican clergy of his time.

JAMES H. LAMBERT

S. S. Wood, *An apology for the colonial clergy of Great Britain: specially for those of Lower and Upper Canada* (London, 1828). Anglican Church of Canada, Diocese of Montreal, Synod Archives (Montreal), Letters and papers of George Jehoshaphat Mountain, 19, 23 Dec. 1833; 2 Jan., 26 Feb. 1834; 8 Aug. 1835. Church House Archives (Quebec), Diocese of Quebec, Minutes of the meetings of the Central Board of the Church Society of the diocese of Quebec, 1854–68. McGill University Archives (Montreal), Bills, invoices, and miscellaneous documents, 1821–39, 9 May, 2 July 1834; 20, 22 July, 8 Aug., 18 Nov. 1835. PAC, MG 24, A40, 1, p.208. PRO, CO 42/260, pp.711–12 (mfm. at PAC). QDA, 50 (B-4), pp.2–29, 42; 70 (B-24), pp.46–47, 49–50, 66–106, 108–9; 81 (C-10), p.65; 94 (D-13), 6, 30 Aug. 1834; 30 Jan., 2 Feb., 19 May, 28 Dec. 1835; 97 (D-16), 7, 22 April, 28 Aug. 1841; 16 Feb., 27 May, 26 July 1842; 114 (G-8), pp.18–28; 122 (G-16), p.25; 124, case 2, folder 13, p.3. USPG, C/CAN/Que., IV, 31, f.368; 33, f.370; 34, ff.370, 375; Journal of SPG, 32, pp.73, 110, 326 (mfm. at PAC).

"Address to the Rev. S. S. Wood, from the inhabitants of Drummondville and its vicinity," *Christian Sentinel, and Anglo-Canadian Churchman's Magazine* (Montreal), I (1827), 48–50. Church of England, Diocese of Quebec, *Proc. of the Diocesan Assembly* (Quebec), 1854, 4; *Report of the proceedings of the meetings of the bishop, clergy and laity . . . 24th June, 1858 . . .* (Quebec, 1859), 7–8, 11. *Berean* (Quebec), 3 July 1845, 9 July 1846, 8 July 1847, 13 July 1848. *Canadian Ecclesiastical Gazette* (Quebec), 18 July 1850; 14 Aug., 11 Sept. 1851; 1 March 1853. A. E. E. Legge, *The Anglican Church in Three Rivers, Quebec, 1768–1956* ([Russell, Ont.], 1956). Millman, *Life of Charles James Stewart.* "The late Rev. S. S. Wood," *Lennoxville Magazine* (Montreal), I (1868), 204–11. D. C. Masters, "G. J. Mountain," *CHA Report*, 1963, 89–101. A. J. Oakley, "Centenary biography: the Reverend Samuel Simpson Wood," *Quebec Diocesan Gazette*, XLIX (1942), 26–29. "A pioneer clergyman of Quebec diocese," *Canadian Church Magazine and Mission News* (Hamilton, Ont.), IV (1890), 80.

WOOLFORD, JOHN ELLIOTT, artist, topographical draughtsman, and architect; b. 1778 in London, England; d. 1866 at Fredericton, N.B.

John Elliott Woolford evidently spent some years studying drawing, probably as an apprentice in the Drawing Room of the Board of Ordnance in the Tower of London. He may also have studied under Paul Sandby, professor of drawing at the Royal Military Academy, Woolwich, who had perfected a method of etching called aquatint, in which Woolford became skilful. His experience at the Board of Ordnance may have

gained him a commission in the Royal Artillery or the Royal Engineers since there are consistent references to him as Major Woolford. He had entered the army as a young man and served in the Napoleonic wars, participating in the victorious campaign against Napoleon Bonaparte's army in Egypt, where his merits as a landscape artist and sketcher attracted the attention of the Earl of Dalhousie [Ramsay*]. Under Lord Dalhousie's patronage he settled in Scotland as an artist about 1807 after retiring from the army on half pay. While in Scotland he married Margaret Erskine, who was related to Anne Dundas, wife of Sir Howard DOUGLAS, later lieutenant governor of New Brunswick from 1823 to 1831.

When Lord Dalhousie arrived in Nova Scotia in October 1816 as the new lieutenant governor and commander-in-chief, Woolford was in his *entourage* as official draughtsman. In the *Acadian Recorder* of 26 June 1819 Woolford advertised engravings of two views of Dalhousie Castle, and described himself as "landscape and portrait painter and Draughtsman to His Excellency," under whose patronage the plates were offered. He also announced the first collection in "A Series of Picturesque Views of Nova Scotia," drawn and engraved by himself and printed in aquatint; it consisted of two views of Government House, a "perspective" view, and an elevation of the newly opened Province House. Accompanying Lord Dalhousie on his extensive travels through the colony, Woolford recorded his impressions of the towns and villages, the topography of the land, its forests, waterways, and historic sites in precise but vigorous line-and-wash drawings in sepia, suitable for future translation to aquatint prints.

Dated drawings indicate that when Lord Dalhousie left for Quebec in June 1820 to assume his new appointment as governor general of Canada, Woolford remained in Halifax. He was there until 1821, probably to supervise the construction of Dalhousie College. Lord Dalhousie had endowed the college and Woolford is said to have designed the new building, of which he painted a water-colour in 1822. In 1821, when Lord Dalhousie made a tour of Lower and Upper Canada as far as Lake Superior, Woolford was summoned to attend him as official draughtsman, and sketched the principal places and significant scenery on their route.

In 1823, through the earl's influence, Woolford was appointed assistant barrack-master at Saint John, N.B., and then barrack-master general at headquarters in Fredericton, an appointment he held for 36 years. His talents as an architect were employed by the army, and the design for the

Work

officers' quarters, completed in 1839, is attributed to him, although the only signature on the plan and elevation is Lieutenant Henry Wentworth's endorsement as garrison engineer officer.

Woolford's most notable achievements as an architect in Fredericton included his design for the new government house after the wooden mansion built by Governor Thomas Carleton*'s had been destroyed by fire in 1825. In 1828 he designed the building for King's College (University of New Brunswick) on the hill overlooking Fredericton, which was completed the following year, and in 1830 the stone county jail; both buildings were still standing in 1976.

During his career in the Fredericton garrison Woolford continued his sketching and painting and was associated with many capable amateur artists among the officers stationed there, including Colonel Alexander Cavalié MERCER, Robert Petley, Edward Thomas Coke, H. Pooley, and John Campbell. Between 1824 and 1831, when the Woolfords first came to Fredericton, Mrs Woolford's cousin, Lady Douglas, and Sir Howard were in residence, both active water-colour painters. In the 1830s John James Audubon, William Henry Bartlett*, and Albert Gallatin Hoit were also visiting and painting in the New Brunswick capital. In August 1842 Woolford and several other Fredericton artists exhibited paintings in the first New Brunswick Art Exhibition at the mechanics' institute in Saint John. In 1847 he made a number of drawings to illustrate Abraham GESNER's *New Brunswick, with notes for emigrants*, which were, however, poorly engraved on wood when the book was published in London that year. Later, in 1852, Woolford showed architectural models as well as drawings and paintings at the provincial exhibition in Saint John.

John Elliott Woolford retired from his post of barrack-master general in 1859, but remained in Fredericton until his death.

DONALD C. MACKAY

[Representative examples of J. E. Woolford's work are now in the Sigmund Samuel coll. of the Royal Ontario Museum (Toronto); the John Ross Robertson coll. of the MTCL; and the William Inglis Morse coll. of Dalhousie University (Halifax). The N.B. Museum, the York-Sunbury Hist. Museum (Fredericton), and Acadia University (Wolfville, N.S.) also have paintings by Woolford. D.C.M.]

PANS, Map coll., "Plans, elevations, and sections of the officers' new barrack and mess establishment . . . at Fredericton, New Brunswick" (1842). York County Court of Probate (Fredericton), Probate records, III, 597–98. Abraham Gesner, *New Brunswick, with notes for emigrants: comprehending the early history, an account of the Indians, settlement, topography, statistics, commerce, timber, manufactures, agriculture, fisheries, geology, natural history, social and political state, immigrants, and contemplated railways of that province* (London, 1847). *Head Quarters*, 17 Jan. 1866. J. R. Harper, *Early painters and engravers; Painting in Canada, a history* (Toronto, 1966). I. L. Hill, *Fredericton, New Brunswick, British North America* ([Fredericton, 1968]). *200 years of art in Halifax . . .* , comp. D. C. Mackay et al. ([Halifax, 1949]). G. [B.] MacBeath, "Artists in New Brunswick's past," *Arts in New Brunswick*, ed. R. A. Tweedie et al. (Fredericton, 1967), 121–48. D. C. Mackay, "Artists and their pictures," *Canadian Antiques Collector* (Toronto), 7 (February 1973), 81–86.

WORK, JOHN (originally **Wark**, but it was anglicized on his contract with the HBC, and he and a brother adopted that version permanently), HBC officer, legislative councillor of British Columbia; b. *c.* 1792 in Taughboyne parish, St Johnstown (near Londonderry) in County Donegal (Republic of Ireland), eldest of six children of Henry Wark; d. 22 Dec. 1861 at his farm, Hillside (now in Victoria, B.C.).

Nothing is known for certain of John Work's life before he joined the Hudson's Bay Company, but it was said later that he was "bred an operative farmer" and his not writing a "good hand" was taken as a sign of a deficient early education. Work, who may have run away from home, joined the HBC as a "writer" on 15 June 1814 at Stromness in the Orkney Islands. He served in two posts on Hudson Bay, as a steward at York Factory during 1814–15, then as second trader at Severn House. He became district master in 1818–19. He survived the paring of staff after the union of the HBC and the North West Company in 1821 to become a first class clerk in the Severn District. For 1822–23, he had charge of the Island Lake District.

Work, a "Highly meritorious active man tolerable clerk & excellent Trader," was assigned to the Columbia District in July 1823. He left York Factory on 18 July with two canoes and eight men in the charge of Peter Skene Ogden*. On this trip, Work began the series of 15 remarkably observant and informative journals of his field trips from July 1823 to October 1835. Crossing to the Columbia via the Athabasca River and Athabasca Pass, the party reached Boat Encampment at the big bend of the Columbia River on 13 October. Proceeding down the Columbia with the brigade that had been sent to meet them, they reached the mouth of the Spokane River on the 21st; Ogden and Work then rode overland with

William Kittson to their winter quarters at Spokane House (Wash.).

Work entered the familiar pattern of trade on the lower Columbia, determined by the arrival of the supply ship in the spring and the departure and arrival of the York Factory expresses in the spring and fall. During his first season, 1823–24, Work helped Finan McDonald extend the trade into the Flathead country (Mont.); and when the express arrived in late October 1824 Work went with Governor George Simpson* and Chief Factor John McLoughlin* down the Columbia to the headquarters of the district at Fort George (Astoria, Oreg.). In November Work accompanied an expedition under Chief Trader James McMillan* which Governor Simpson sent to explore the lower reaches of the Fraser River for the purpose of locating a site for a major post, since Simpson was convinced that the British could not retain the south bank of the Columbia. On the return trip in December, McMillan and Work discovered the Cowlitz Portage, which became an important link between the Columbia River and the head of Puget Sound (Wash.). In the spring of 1825 Work helped move the headquarters from Fort George to the newly established Fort Vancouver (Vancouver, Wash.) on the north bank of the river.

Finan McDonald retired from the HBC service that year, and Simpson assigned Work to the charge of Spokane House with instructions to establish a new and better located post on the Columbia at Kettle Falls. This Simpson named Fort Colvile. Work spent the 1825–26 season trading into the Flathead country (where he re-established Flathead House), and supervising the construction of Fort Colvile, which was to make the 60-mile pack train route from the Columbia to Spokane House unnecessary. Work closed Spokane House in April 1826, and from then until the summer of 1829 he was in charge of Fort Colvile. He took pride in the success of the post farm which helped to make the district independent of expensive imported provisions. During these years he was often away on short trading expeditions or procuring horses along the Snake River for the New Caledonia (British Columbia) brigades and the Fort Vancouver herds, and he sometimes accompanied the fur returns from New Caledonia and his own district to the lower Columbia. In 1829 the eye trouble that was to distress Work for the rest of his career, sometimes to the point of near blindness, began. For the winter of 1829–30, Work took charge of the Colvile District from John Warren Dease who was fatally ill, and moved his headquarters to the Flathead post where he was "rid of the farm and

pigs [at Fort Colvile] a circumstance I by no means regret. . . ."

In August 1830 Work was appointed successor to Peter Skene Ogden in charge of the Snake country brigade. Between that month and 18 July 1831 he travelled some 2,000 miles into what is now eastern Idaho, northwestern Utah, and along the Humboldt River (Nev.), a region thoroughly explored by Ogden. The returns of the expedition were profitable but still disappointing, and Work recommended a cessation of the annual Snake country brigades. One more brigade was sent by McLoughlin: Work went into the Salmon River (Idaho) and Flathead country in 1831–32. The rugged terrain and marauding Blackfeet made the expedition difficult, and the returns were not great, partly because of active competition from the Americans. In his report for 1832, Simpson recommended that the company withdraw from the Snake country. But on his return to the Columbia in July 1831 Work had received his commission as chief trader, dated 3 Nov. 1830, and thus the promotion of which he had despaired.

In early September 1832 Work went to the Bonaventura (Sacramento) valley of Mexican California which had first been penetrated for the HBC by Alexander Roderick McLeod* in 1829–30 and by Ogden in 1830. Trapping in the valley was not favourable because of an American party and an HBC brigade led by Michel Laframboise. Indian hostility forced Work and Laframboise to join forces in an exploration of the coast from San Francisco to Cape Mendocino. Work returned to Fort Vancouver in October 1833, disappointed in the hunt though McLoughlin estimated the 1,023 beaver and otter skins realized a profit of £627.

In December 1834 Work succeeded Ogden in charge of the coasting trade at Fort Simpson (Port Simpson, B.C.) on McLoughlin Bay. He sailed north on the HBC brig *Lama* that month, and during the next ten months supervised the construction of Fort Simpson, which had been relocated from the Nass River in 1833. He also traded along the northern coast of New Caledonia, on northern Vancouver Island, and among the Queen Charlotte Islands, always with keen competition from American coastal traders. In January 1836 he was back in Fort Simpson, his permanent residence until 1846; he found it inhospitable and the natives were "numerous, treacherous . . . and ferocious in the extreme." He was, however, frequently away supervising the trade and up to 1840 he usually accompanied the returns to the Columbia in the fall. To economize on imported foostuffs, Work estab-

Work

lished a garden at Fort Simpson, and in 1839 he assisted in surveying Cowlitz Farm for the Puget's Sound Agricultural Company, a subsidiary of the HBC charged with supplying provisions to the Russians at Sitka (Alaska).

Work's independence of action at Fort Simpson had begun to be curtailed in 1836 when the steamer *Beaver* arrived. With better communications assured, Chief Factor Duncan FINLAYSON assumed the management of coastal shipping from Fort Vancouver; and upon his departure a year later, James Douglas* assumed much the same duties as superintendent. McLoughlin himself had the responsibility for over-all supervision, and Work's position was restricted to that of field manager during the ten years he spent at Fort Simpson, where he felt isolated and purposefully disregarded. From this post, Work directed the trading operations of the *Beaver*, whose presence and expense were a source of continuous grumbling from McLoughlin. In January 1838 mutiny broke out on the ship then lying at the fort; when order was restored, Work assumed command and took the vessel to Fort Nisqually (Wash.). Its captain, William Henry McNeill*, was promoted chief trader in 1839, to Work's resentment, although it appears Work lacked decisiveness in quelling the disturbance.

Work strenuously sought to increase trade and effect economies, but he always felt his efforts were unrecognized. In his annual letters to Edward Ermatinger*, there is from 1829 on a repeated complaint about "the cursed country," his lack of advancement, and his desire to return to Ireland or join Ermatinger in Upper Canada. At Fort Simpson Work grew increasingly restive. One of his most bitter complaints to Ermatinger came in 1841: "Here I fill, with the exception of the Depots, one of the most important situations in the country, before I came to it it had created a heavy loss since then it has realised a handsome gain. Notwithstanding the opposition and other difficulties we had to contend with yet this it seems did not give satisfaction. . . ." James Douglas had been promoted chief factor in 1839; and, continued Work, "I find no fault with Mr. D he is a clever man but those that made the appointment lost sight of my exertions and the signal success attending them."

In the autumn of 1841 Governor Sir George Simpson paid two visits to Fort Simpson, where he conferred with James Douglas, Captain McNeill, and Work. He decided to close all the coastal posts except Fort Simpson and to rely on the *Beaver* for the coastal trade, since with the virtual disappearance of American competition and the accord with the Russian American Company a strong company presence was no longer needed on the coast. McLoughlin did not agree, and he deeply resented the fact that he had not been consulted; Simpson consented that Fort Stikine be maintained.

Work had injured himself seriously by falls in the summer of 1840 and in 1841 Simpson transferred John McLoughlin Jr's clerk, Roderick Finlayson*, from Fort Stikine to Fort Simpson to help Work, leaving McLoughlin alone with 20 unruly men. Young McLoughlin was murdered in April 1842, and the grieving father ever after blamed the transfer of Finlayson for leaving his son defenceless. He argued too that Work had not really needed Finlayson for he already had competent help. In 1844 Work sent three men involved in the murder south on the *Beaver* with instructions to hasten their arrival at Fort Vancouver. But there was a long delay, for which McLoughlin blamed Work. McLoughlin also criticized him for his lack of initiative in taking a deposition from Finlayson and in forwarding young McLoughlin's correspondence and other documents to Fort Vancouver. Work's relations with McLoughlin were further strained when McLoughlin sent a "severe reproof" for the manner in which Work employed the *Beaver* to compete with American interlopers in the trade with the northern Indians during the winter of 1842–43. McLoughlin sent detailed instructions for the operations of the *Beaver*, and Work felt he was being treated with condescension and "undeserved reprehension."

Work's health had become even more worrisome, for in 1843 he developed a lip-sore, possibly as a result of his constant pipe smoking. In September 1844 the sloop *Modeste* arrived at Fort Simpson, and the two ship's doctors removed about half of his upper lip. It required three more operations before the growth was totally excised.

Work's years of isolation and deprivation were coming to an end, for McLoughlin resigned from the company in March 1846, and coincidentally that same month Work was commissioned a chief factor. The Council of the Northern Department resolved in 1845 to place the Columbia Department in the hands of three chief factors; and in 1846 it appointed Douglas, Ogden, and Work to the board of management of the department, Work being placed in charge of the coastal area (including forts Simpson, Stikine, and Langley) and the *Beaver*. London, however, did not concur in Work's appointment until 1849.

Once again Work began extensive coastal travels. In 1849 he abandoned Fort Stikine and established Fort Rupert to exploit the coal beds of northern Vancouver Island. In 1850, when the miners and employees there went on strike for double pay, Work came by canoe from Fort Simpson, went to Fort Victoria (Victoria) to consult with Douglas, and then returned, also by canoe, to put down the "mutiny" by persuasion: some 1,500 miles of travel. Reports of the discovery of gold on the Queen Charlotte Islands reached him at Fort Simpson in 1850. His investigating party found no gold, but they did discover that the Queen Charlottes consisted of two large islands instead of one. Work himself crossed from Fort Simpson in 1851 and discovered gold. News of the discoveries inevitably reached California and set off a minor rush in 1852. When natives boarded the *Susan Sturgis*, Work was able to ransom the crew but not before the ship had been looted and burned. He continued to make Fort Simpson his headquarters until November 1851, when he and Dr William Fraser Tolmie* went to Fort Nisqually at the head of Puget Sound, where the *Beaver* and the sailing vessel *Mary Dare* landed passengers before going to Olympia (Wash.) to clear customs. The vessels were seized because of customs irregularities and it was not until February that Work was able to return to Fort Victoria.

Work spent his last summer at Fort Simpson in 1852, but his life increasingly centred on Fort Victoria where he had settled his large family in 1849 in order to obtain an education for his younger children. In April 1825, Governor Simpson had advised McLoughlin that Work should marry the daughter of a chief of the Cayuse Indians, to secure protection for the company's brigades on the Columbia River. Work did not marry a Cayuse, but during the winter of 1826 he made the first mention of his wife *à la façon du Nord*, Josette Legacé, a Spokane woman of mixed blood to whom he referred as his "Little Rib." She often accompanied Work on his expeditions. In December 1836 she and two of their four daughters had joined Work at Fort Simpson; the two older girls attended the Fort Vancouver school, then the Methodist mission on the Willamette River (Oreg.), and in 1841 came to Fort Simpson. There Work taught his children, who numbered ten (there were three sons); after the family moved to Fort Victoria, the youngest was born there in 1854. At Fort Victoria the children were placed in the school run by the Reverend Robert John* and Mrs Staines, and on 6 Nov. 1849 Work and Josette were married by Staines. Work became the father-in-law of several well-known company men: Dr William Fraser Tolmie, Roderick Finlayson, Edward Huggins, and James Allan Grahame*.

Although Work had often expressed his desire to find a "corner of the Civilized World in quietness," concern for the cultural duality of his family led him to settle permanently at Fort Victoria. In August 1852 he purchased 823 acres of farmland on its northern outskirts and built a mansion, Hillside. By 1859 he owned over 1,800 acres. In 1853 Governor James Douglas appointed Work, "a gentleman of probity and respectable character and the largest land holder on Vancouver's Island," to the Legislative Council of Vancouver Island. He was an active and faithful member, who supported Douglas in the controversy surrounding the appointment of David Cameron* as chief justice of Vancouver Island. His associations with the HBC inevitably linked him with the "Family-Company Compact." He opposed the establishment of an assembly for the colony in 1856 because there were "so few people to govern" and "nobody to pay taxes to cover expenses." During May and June 1861 Work acted for the governor in Douglas' absence, and he was a member of the council until his death.

Work continued his duties as chief factor of the HBC, and he and Douglas acted as trustees for its Fur Trade Branch which, in 1856, purchased land for the purpose of attracting *bona fide* settlers who could not afford the required minimum 20-acre lots at £1 per acre. Following Douglas' resignation from the company in 1858 to become governor of both Vancouver Island and British Columbia, a new board of management for the company's affairs was constituted, with Alexander Grant Dallas*, Dugald Mactavish*, and John Work as members. The creation of the crown colony of British Columbia had made the company's possessory rights there uncertain, and Work and Mactavish prepared a report on the company's claims to 14 interior posts.

In 1861 the debilitating fever with which Work had returned from California in 1833 evidently returned. After two months of suffering and increasing weakness, he died at Hillside on 22 December. Work's funeral was attended by all the leaders of the colony, chief factors of the HBC, and naval officers, and he was buried in what is now Pioneer Square next to Christ Church Cathedral, where his ivy-covered tomb is today a prominent landmark.

John Work, who came to be known in the HBC as the "Old Gentleman," was a conscientious, if somewhat unimaginative, servant of the company. A good leader of men, yet he followed with care the precedents and instructions of others, although he could show his pique at what he considered to be unjust treatment. John Tod*, who was one of Work's closest friends, described

Wugk

him in his late 40s as "a queer looking old chap – of his hair there remains but three small elf locks which protrude, far between over his Coat neck and the point of his nose is actually coming in contact with that of his chin. . . . Poor Work is always complaining and I doubt not he has some cause, but bating [barring?] his delicate state of health which give me much anxiety at times, I am inclined to believe that not a few of the evils of which he complains are merely imaginary." Governor Simpson in his famous "Character Book" described Work as: "A very steady pains taking Man, regular, oeconomical and attentive in business, and bears a fair private character . . . A queer looking fellow, of Clownish Manners and address, indeed there is a good deal of simplicity approaching to idiocy in his appearance, he is nevertheless a Shrewd Sensible Man, and not deficient in firmness when necessary. . . ."

Something of Work's elusive character emerges from his and John Tod's correspondence with Edward Ermatinger. He was a devoted family man whose constant concern was the well-being and happiness of his wife and children. He was deeply religious, emphasizing "the genuine Religion of the heart which is practical" and objecting to "mere professional Religion" which he considered to be "too much show and parade." Evidently not given to speculative thought, he could be harshly critical of those who were. He was often dogmatic and in his political views he was conservative and totally pro-British. His professional career can be better ascertained through the vividly descriptive journals which he so meticulously kept and through his matter-of-fact business correspondence. His career on the Pacific coast was long and honourable; of the four major company officials on the coast (McLoughlin, Douglas, Ogden, and Work), only Ogden had been there as early as had John Work. He lacked the forceful administrative and diplomatic skills of McLoughlin and Douglas, or the enterprise and spirit of adventure of Ogden, but his career spanned the history of the Pacific northwest from the land and coastal fur trade to the gold rush and settlement, and in that history Work had an important, if not commanding, role.

WILLIAM R. SAMPSON

[John Work], *Fur brigade to the Bonaventura; John Work's California expedition, 1832–1833, for the Hudson's Bay Company*, ed. A. B. Maloney ([San Francisco], 1945); *The journal of John Work, a chief-trader of the Hudson's Bay Co., during his expedition from Vancouver to the Flatheads and Blackfeet of the Pacific northwest*, ed. W. S. Lewis and P. C. Phillips (Cleveland, Ohio, 1923); *The journal of John Work,*

January to October, 1835, ed. H. D. Dee (Victoria, 1945); *The Snake country expedition of 1830–1831; John Work's field journal*, ed. F. D. Haines (Norman, Okla., [1971]).

HBC Arch. A.34/2, ff.18d.–19. PABC, Isaac Burpee, "The story of John Work of the Hudson's Bay Company, June 15th, 1814, to December 22nd, 1861" (typescript, 1943); Edward Ermatinger, Correspondence inward, 1828–56 (copies); Edward Ermatinger papers, 1826–43; John Work, Correspondence outward, 1828–49, 1850–58; "Journal of a journey, York Factory to Spokane House, 18 July – 28 October 1823"; "Journal of trading in Columbia valley, 15 April – 17 November 1824." HBRS, III (Fleming); IV (Rich); VI (Rich); VII (Rich); XXX (Williams), R. H. Dillon, *Siskiyou trail: the Hudson's Bay Company route to California* (New York, [1975]), 180–213, 222.

WUGK, CHARLES-DÉSIRÉ-JOSEPH (also known as **Charles Sabatier**), pianist and composer; b. 1 Dec. 1819 in Tourcoing, dept of Nord, France, son of Charles-Théophile Wugk, an immigrant from Saxony (German Democratic Republic), and Sophie-Joseph Vercambre of Tourcoing; d. 22 Aug. 1862 in Montreal, Canada East.

From 1838 to 1840 Charles-Désiré-Joseph Wugk was enrolled intermittently at the Conservatoire in Paris, studying elementary counterpoint and clarinet. The claims, made on the occasion of a Toronto appearance in 1856, that he had won a first prize in harmony and piano at the Conservatoire and been conductor at the grand opera in Brussels, cannot be confirmed. The assertion that he had been pianist to Marie-Louise de Bourbon, Duchesse de Montpensier, is more credible.

The young musician may have arrived in Quebec City as a sailor and gone to Montreal as early as 1848; it is certain only that he lived in Quebec from about 1854 and that his reputation as a virtuoso pianist had preceded him there. Sabatier, the surname he had now assumed, stayed in Quebec for four or five years, teaching, performing both in public and in private salons, and occasionally playing church organs. His guest appearance at St Lawrence Hall in Toronto in 1856 is evidence that his activity was not restricted to one city. From Quebec Sabatier moved to Saint-Jean-Chrysostôme not far from Lévis and for a brief time was church organist at Saint-Gervais-et-Protais (Saint-Gervais) where he joined a congenial circle of local élite who had gathered around the Abbé Paschal Pouliot. He then became music teacher at a convent in Chambly and finally settled in Montreal. Together with Paul Stevens* and Édouard Sempé he founded *L'Artiste*, "a journal of religion, criticism, literature, industrial arts and music," of which only two issues appeared, both in May 1860. With Sempé as librettist, he composed a *Cantate en l'honneur de Son Altesse royale le prince de Galles à l'occasion de son voyage au Canada.* The work was performed at a gala concert on 24 Aug. 1860 in the presence of the Prince of Wales who was "loud and frequent" in his applause and who asked to see Sabatier's score. The composer himself led the 250 singers of the Union musicale de Montréal, an orchestra, and a group of soloists, which included 16-year-old Adelina Patti who was to become internationally known. The libretto was published in the same year, and included an English translation by Rosanna Eleanora Leprohon [Mullins*], but of the ten musical numbers only a few appeared in print. A year or two later Sabatier went to the Hôtel-Dieu of Montreal to be cured of his drinking habits. He had a relapse and shortly after suffered a fatal stroke.

To his unsophisticated Canadian audience, Sabatier must have appeared as the incarnation of a romantic artist. It is more than likely that he was enough of a showman to cultivate this role deliberately. People admired his tall and handsome appearance and his pianistic prowess; they frowned on his bohemian life style and immoderate drinking; "A horrible example of a successful career wrecked for ever by a brutal and tyrannical passion," moralized the obituary in the *Journal de l'Instruction publique.* His nervous temperament and his impetuousness are reflected in a typical story that when, during a welcoming reception at the Hôtel Blanchard in Quebec, Sabatier spotted a porcelain bust of Napoleon III, he hurled it out of the window onto the pavement of the square Notre-Dame-des-Victoires, cursing the tyrant. Indeed his coming to Canada may have had something to do with the events of 1848, but possibly also with a broken marriage (he left two daughters in France). But as a musician he won the sincere respect of his musical colleagues in Canada, both as a brilliant pianist and as a teacher; Calixa Lavallée* and Dominique Ducharme were briefly among his pupils.

Besides the *Cantate,* Sabatier wrote original piano pieces, fantasias on operatic tunes by other composers (also for the piano), band music, and songs. About 30 pieces are known by title, and 12 survive in print. Sabatier probably composed many more, since one of his works, a "Mazurka caprice," bears the opus number 190. His music appears to be vivacious, brilliant, and superficial. A few typical titles are "Marche aux flambeaux," "La prière des anges," and "Mes derniers quadrilles" for piano, a "Grande marche canadienne" for band, and "L'Alouette" and "La Montréalaise" for voice. His special claim to fame rests on the patriotic song "Le drapeau de Carillon" to words by Octave Crémazie*, performed first by Édouard Gingras and the composer in Quebec on 15 May 1858, and later widely known among French Canadians.

HELMUT KALLMANN

Archives nationales (Paris), AJ^{37} 352^x 2, p.110. *JIP*, septembre 1862. *Globe*, 25 Sept. 1856. *La Minerve*, 9 Aug. 1860, 26 Aug. 1862. *Catalogue of Canadian composers*, ed. Helmut Kallmann (rev. ed., Toronto, 1952). *Dictionnaire biographique des musiciens canadiens* (2e éd., Lachine, Qué., 1935). Helmut Kallmann, *A history of music in Canada, 1534–1914* (Toronto and London, 1960). D. J. Sale, "Toronto's pre-confederation music societies, 1845–1867" (unpublished MA thesis, University of Toronto, 1968). N. A. Woods, *The Prince of Wales in Canada and the United States* (London, 1861). Arthur Letondal, "Un musicien oublié (Charles Waugk Sabatier)," *L'Action nationale* (Montréal), II (1933), 126–35. Nazaire Levasseur, "Musique et musiciens à Québec; souvenirs d'un amateur," *La Musique* (Québec), 2 (1920), 172–73, 185–87, 202–3. Léo Roy, "La vérité sur Sabatier," *L'Action nationale*, LVII (1967–68), 707–9. Henri Têtu, "Impressions musicales," *L'Action sociale catholique* (Québec), 13 mars 1915.

Y

YELLOWHEAD, WILLIAM. *See* MUSQUAKIE

YEO, JAMES, shipbuilder and owner, merchant, landowner, and farmer; b. 1789 (baptized 13 Feb. 1790) at Kilkhampton, Cornwall, England, eldest son of James Yeo and Ann Orsborn; m. first in 1812 Mary Francis, by whom he had three children, and secondly in 1819, Damaris Sargent of Kilkhampton, by whom he had five daughters and two sons; d. 25 Aug. 1868 at Port Hill, P.E.I.

James Yeo, the son of a shoemaker, was a labourer until 1814 or 1815 when he set up as a carter between Kilkhampton and Bideford, Devon. After his first wife's death in 1818 this business failed, partly as a result of Yeo's drunkenness. In May 1819 he married again and the couple probably immigrated the same year to Port Hill, Prince County, Prince Edward Island. There Yeo worked as superintendent of the lumbering gangs and helped with the management of the stores in the lumbering, shipbuilding, and mercantile business established by Thomas Burnard in 1818 and at that time managed by Thomas Burnard Chanter*. In 1826, after Burnard's death, Chanter disposed of the business at Port Hill to William Ellis*, a master shipbuilder who had also emigrated from the Bideford district. The business had a large number of outstanding accounts, many of which Yeo collected in the name of the Burnard family, with whom he was known to be associated; he then retained the proceeds, though they were in fact the legal property of Ellis. In this way Yeo acquired capital to set up on a small scale as a lumber dealer, storekeeper, and owner and master of the 35-foot merchant schooner *Mary Ann*, which he sailed from 1829 to 1832.

Possessed of enormous physical and mental energy and business acumen, Yeo greatly prospered. By the mid 1830s he already exercised considerable influence in Prince County, having bought the original business at Port Hill from Ellis in circumstances which generated legends of an Esau-like misappropriation of Ellis' inheritance persisting on the Island to this day.

In 1840 Yeo began shipbuilding on a large scale and soon became the greatest of the Island's shipbuilders. As such he played a vital part in the colony's economic development in the middle years of the century, when new ships built for sale in Britain were by far the most important Prince Edward Island export. He was responsible for the construction of at least 155 ships, from the *Marina* (1833) to the *Magdala* (completed three days before his death in 1868). Of these, several, especially *James Yeo*, *Palmyra*, and *William Yeo*, were among the largest ships ever built in Prince Edward Island. Yeo's youngest sons, James and John*, and his sons-in-law and their associates built at least another 200 vessels. Many of these ships, launched from sites all around the shores of the Island, were sailed unfinished to Britain for completion at a shipyard established in Appledore near Bideford by James Yeo's eldest son, William, who returned to Britain in 1843 to act as his father's principal agent. William Yeo's position in England was of great importance to his father's success in shipbuilding; both were also at any one time usually the owners of up to 20 ships sailing with cargoes bound for ports all over the world.

James Yeo had many other business interests, through which his wife and children and brothers and sisters were incorporated into the management of his affairs. He took advantage of the uncertainty of many of the settlers' titles to send his men to cut timber as long as it lasted; in this way he built up a sizeable export business. Moreover, his stores at Port Hill, ably managed by his wife Damaris, were the largest in the western part of the Island and were operated on a credit basis. Many settlers became indebted to him and through the resulting "power of the Ledger" he was able to exploit their labour and timber. He was also *de facto* land agent for Sir George Seymour's holdings in Lot 13, a position that was formalized in 1846, and in 1857 he purchased Seymour's 16,000 acres, which together with extensive properties already acquired elsewhere in the Island he held for many years.

Yeo also became a large-scale exporter of agricultural products, including oats, potatoes, and livestock, and by the late 1840s was loading ten ships a year for Britain as well as 40 schooners for the neighbouring provinces. A decade later, 11 of his ships, laden with cargoes of lumber and agricultural produce, arrived in British ports within one month. In the 1830s and 1840s relatively little money was in circulation in the colony and it was said that in this period Yeo was the only man in Prince County from whom settlers could obtain cash. He built up a role as financier until by the 1860s he was making large loans to the government. At that time the *Islander* claimed that his wage bill to his numerous employees alone exceeded the total government revenue. For the last ten years of his life he was frequently referred to in the Island newspapers as the richest man in the colony.

Yeo's great success was achieved by unflagging energy and ability. He could total figures quickly, and was able to make rapid assessments of the value of timber stands, crops, ships and their cargoes, and business enterprises. He personally supervised his operations, riding on horseback all over the Island and often sleeping in the saddle. A contemporary American visitor once said that "for six months he's never go to bed." He was spoken of, even by his admirers, however, as a hard man who retained the rough manners of his youth to the end of his life.

Yeo was first elected to the Island assembly in 1839 as a Conservative member for the first electoral district of Prince County. He remained a member until 1846 when he stood aside to allow the election of James Warburton*, later one of his bitterest opponents. About this time he was appointed a justice of the peace. In 1848 he was elected again and sat until he was defeated by 50 votes in 1863. After the election of 1859, when the Conservatives held power by a majority of four, Yeo held a position of particular advantage in the assembly, with control over the votes of his son John and of David Ramsay, a close associate. He undoubtedly used his position to his direct advantage in such matters as the appointment of relatives and associates to offices of influence in local administration. A month after his defeat he was elected to the Legislative Council on which he served until 1867. He was also a member of the Executive Council from 1859 to 1867. During much of his time as a member of the assembly Yeo wielded great influence in Island politics because of his wealth and the power this brought him with his numerous debtors. Contemporaries consequently nicknamed him the "Ledger Baron of Port Hill" and the "Driver of the Government."

Throughout his long political career, Yeo was concerned principally with practical issues of local administration. In the 1830s he confined himself to such questions as road-building, the issuing of treasury warrants, ferry service, and a custom house at Cascumpec. Lieutenant Governor Charles Augustus FitzRoy* noted that Yeo tended to follow Joseph Pope*'s lead in politics. He could operate his business best under the existing proprietorial system of land ownership, and it is no surprise that his politics were conservative; he was bitterly opposed to the land reforms espoused by William COOPER and the Escheat party, whom Yeo branded "Malignants," and to the granting of responsible government, as advocated by George Coles* and the Liberals.

James Yeo's part in the development of ship-building, shipping, and the export business in Prince Edward Island in the mid 19th century was unique both in scale and in the breadth and complexity of his operations. For all his ruthlessness he made a material contribution to the economic development of the province and indeed to the merchant shipping industry both in British North America and in Britain at the same period.

After his death in 1868 Yeo's fortune was split between a number of descendants. His eldest son, William, probably the largest single beneficiary, died four years later without a male heir, and his assets passed into other hands. John Yeo continued his father's business in P.E.I. with considerable success and enjoyed a long career in the provincial and federal governments, dying a senator in 1924.

BASIL GREENHILL

[Kilkhampton, Cornwall, Eng., Parish registers, 1790–1819, contain unusually complete records of the births, marriages, and deaths in James Yeo's complex family. His early career in Prince Edward Island is traceable through PAPEI, P.E.I., Supreme Court records, 1770–1900, and to a small extent through PAPEI, Port Hill papers. His career as shipbuilder and ship-owner can be followed in great detail through PAC, RG 42, I, 150–69, 391–93, and National Maritime Museum (London), Reports of Lloyds surveyors of the port of Bideford (mfm. at PAC). His career as a landed proprietor can be followed in PAPEI, P.E.I., Land Registry Office, Land conveyance registers, and there are a number of references to him in Warwick County Record Office (Warwick, Eng.), CR 114A (Seymour of Ragley papers). The activities of his son and agent in Britain, William Yeo, are the subject of numerous references in the North Devon press, notably the *North Devon Journal* (Barnstable, Eng.), 1840–72. There are also some useful references in Devon County Record Office (Exeter, Eng.), Northam parish registers, 1792–1820. James Yeo's political life was reported in the Prince Edward Island press, notably the *Islander*, 1830–68, especially September 1868. Greenhill and Giffard, *Westcountrymen in P.E.I.*, gives a detailed account of Yeo's career. B.G.]

YOUNG, PLOMER, army officer; b. 1787; d. 8 March 1863 at Kingston Villa, Trowbridge, England. He married, but the name of his wife is not known; a daughter married John Macaulay*, legislative councillor for Upper Canada and the Province of Canada.

Plomer Young entered the British army in 1805 and in 1806 became a lieutenant. In 1810 he participated in the capture of Île-de-France (Mauritius) and in the next few years served in the East Indies under Sir Robert Gillespie. Later he served in the 1st Anglo-Burmese War of 1824–26. He went on half pay as a major in the 32nd Regiment in 1828.

Returning to active duty on 1 Jan. 1838, Young was one of a group of 16 officers sent on "particular service" to Canada at Sir John COLBORNE's request to take charge of the defence of the Canadian border in the aftermath of the rebellions. He received the local rank of colonel and was assigned in March to Prescott, Upper Canada, where Fort Wellington was being renovated. On 11 Nov. 1838 Young learned that a force of Hunters, adherents in the United States to the cause of a republican Canada, had assembled and was crossing the St Lawrence. The force, under the command of Nils von Schoultz*, landed near Prescott and entrenched itself in a large 80-foot high stone windmill with strong, thick walls to which Young had not given any attention and which he had left undefended. Assisted by three armed vessels, some 70 marines and regulars sent from Kingston, and militia units brought to Prescott by George Macdonnell, Ogle Robert

Young

Gowan*, and John Pliny Crysler, Young kept the invaders confined to the vicinity of the windmill until the arrival on the 16th of Colonel Henry Dundas with four companies of the 83rd Regiment. That night, the fewer than 150 Hunters surrendered to the combined force of some 5,000 men.

Young's success in attacking the enemy and holding them down until the arrival of reinforcements was widely praised, and even the Duke of Wellington commended Young's action. Sir George Arthur* wrote to Dundas that Young "ought to gain a step for having so promptly met these Robbers & Murderers''; Young became lieutenant-colonel on 29 March 1839. Two months later he was appointed deputy adjutant-general of Lower Canada. He moved to Montreal to assume his new duties in which he was assisted by Louis Guy and Édouard-Louis-Antoine-Charles Juchereau Duchesnay. Young retained the post until 11 July 1841, then joined the staff of the commander of the forces, Sir Richard Jackson*. In 1843, when the bulk of the incorporated militia was disbanded, he succeeded Colonel Colley Lyons Lucas Foster* as assistant deputy adjutant-general of Canada West.

The militia continued to operate under acts passed before the union of Upper and Lower Canada until 1846 when, in response to the War Office which had been urging the creation of an effective militia force of 35,000 men, a new act was passed. The imperial government had declared itself prepared to pay if necessary for the arms and accoutrements of the proposed force and wanted an efficient and effective adjutant-general for it. As early as 1842 Sir Allan Napier MacNab had been assured of the post, and in 1846 was named to it. But after one day in office he resigned when political difficulties developed over the appointment of a deputy for Canada West. The post went to Young and he was gazetted on 1 Aug. 1846. He and his two deputies,

Étienne-Paschal Taché in Canada East and Donald Macdonell in Canada West, were charged with undertaking the reorganization of the militia as contemplated by the War Office. The Militia Act of 1846, however, did not mark the start of a new era. The War Office was by then less enthusiastic over the prospect of increased expenditure and decided that the existing obsolescent flintlocks would be used to arm the militia; moreover, the Canadian legislature allowed only one day's training per year. This legislature did not foresee any difficulties arising with the United States and, under less pressure from the War Office, did not replace Young when he ceased to be adjutant-general on 26 July 1847.

Young reverted to half pay in 1847, but in 1849 was appointed assistant adjutant-general commanding the Kingston garrison. He retained the post until 1855. He probably returned to England soon after this date, and died in 1863. He had been awarded a KH in 1836 and was promoted major-general in 1857.

George Mainer

PAC, RG 7, G1, 87, pp.78–79; 90, pp.170–71; 111, pp.204–5; 117, pp.298–303; RG 8, I (C series), 611–15. PAO, Jessup (Edward) papers. PRO, CO 42/514, p.258; WO 1/555, Byham to Stephen, 31 Jan., 13 Feb. 1846; 1/558, Byham to Stephen, 19 March 1847; Grey's minute dated 23 March 1847; 55/1551, pp.75–79, 119–21, 144–45, 160–61; 80/11. *Arthur papers* (Sanderson). *British Colonist* (Toronto), 22, 29 Nov. 1838. *Canada Gazette* (Montreal), 4, 11 July, 1 Aug. 1846. *Quebec Mercury*, 1838–39. Boase, *Modern English biog.*, III, 1578. Morgan, *Sketches of celebrated Canadians*, 346. E. C. Guillet, *The lives and times of the Patriots: an account of the rebellion in Upper Canada, 1837–1838, and the Patriot agitation in the United States, 1837–1842* (Toronto, 1938; repr. 1968). P. H. [Stanhope], Earl of Stanhope, *Notes of conversations with the Duke of Wellington, 1831–1851* (3rd ed., London, 1889), 131–32. G. F. G. Stanley, "Invasion: 1838," *OH*, LIV (1962), 237–52.

GENERAL BIBLIOGRAPHY AND
LIST OF ABBREVIATIONS

List of Abbreviations

AAQ   Archives de l'archidiocèse de Québec
ACAM   Archives de la chancellerie de l'arche-
         vêché de Montréal
ACFAS   Association canadienne-française
         pour l'avancement des sciences
ADB   *Australian Dictionary of Biography*
AHO   Archives historiques oblates
AJM   Archives judiciaires de Montréal
AJQ   Archives judiciaires de Québec
AJTR   Archives judiciaires de Trois-Rivières
ANQ   Archives nationales du Québec
ANQ-M   Archives nationales du Québec, dépôt
         de Montréal
ANQ-Q   Archives nationales du Québec, dépôt
         de Québec
ANQ-TR   Archives nationales du Québec, dépôt
         de Trois-Rivières
ASJCF   Archives de la Compagnie de Jésus,
         province du Canada français
ASQ   Archives du séminaire de Québec
ASSH   Archives du séminaire de Saint-
         Hyacinthe
ASSM   Archives du séminaire de Saint-
         Sulpice, Montréal
ASTR   Archives du séminaire de Trois-
         Rivières
AVM   Archives de la ville de Montréal
AVQ   Archives de la ville de Québec
BCHQ   *British Columbia Historical Quarterly*
BCHS   Brome County Historical Society
BNQ   Bibliothèque nationale du Québec
BRH   *Bulletin des recherches historiques*
BUM   Bibliothèques de l'université de
         Montréal
CCHA   Canadian Catholic Historical Associa-
         tion
CHA   Canadian Historical Association
CHR   *Canadian Historical Review*
CMS   Church Missionary Society
CPC   *Canadian parliamentary companion*
DAB   *Dictionary of American Biography*

DCB   *Dictionary of Canadian Biography*
DNB   *Dictionary of National Biography*
HBC   Hudson's Bay Company
HBRS   *Hudson's Bay Record Society*
HPL   Hamilton Public Library
HSSM   Historical and Scientific Society of
         Manitoba
IBC   Inventaire des biens culturels
JIP   *Journal de l'Instruction publique*
MTCL   Metropolitan Toronto Central Library
NWC   North West Company
OH   *Ontario History*
PABC   Provincial Archives of British Colum-
         bia
PAC   Public Archives of Canada
PAM   Provincial Archives of Manitoba
PANB   Provincial Archives of New
         Brunswick
PANL   Provincial Archives of Newfoundland
         and Labrador
PANS   Public Archives of Nova Scotia
PAO   Archives of Ontario
PAPEI   Public Archives of Prince Edward
         Island
PRO   Public Record Office
QDA   Quebec Diocesan Archives
QUA   Queen's University Archives
RHAF   *Revue d'histoire de l'Amérique*
         française
RSC   Royal Society of Canada
SCHÉC   Société canadienne d'histoire de
         l'Église catholique
SGCF   Société généalogique canadienne-
         française
UCA   United Church Archives
UNBL   University of New Brunswick Library
USPG   United Society for the Propagation of
         the Gospel
UTL-TF   University of Toronto, Thomas
         Fisher Rare Book Library
UWO   University of Western Ontario Library

General Bibliography

The General Bibliography is based on the sources most frequently cited in the individual bibliographies of volume IX. It should not be regarded as providing a complete list of background materials for the history of Canada in the 19th century.

Section I describes the principal archival sources and is arranged by country. Section II is divided into two parts. Part A contains printed primary sources including documents published by the various colonial, provincial, and federal governments. Part B provides a listing of the contemporary newspapers most frequently cited by contributors to the volume. Section III includes dictionaries, nominal lists, indexes, inventories, almanacs, and directories. Section IV contains secondary works of the 19th and 20th centuries, including a number of general histories and theses. Section V describes the principal journals and the publications of various societies consulted.

I. ARCHIVES AND MANUSCRIPT SOURCES

CANADA

ARCHIVES DE LA CHANCELLERIE DE L'ARCHE-VÊCHÉ DE MONTRÉAL. This archives holds about 900 photographs, 500 maps and plans, 634 registers divided into 17 series (mainly the correspondence of the bishops of Montreal), and some 500,000 files containing separate items on the dioceses, clergy, laity, institutions, missions, religious communities, etcetera. Pre-1896 documents are open to researchers. For a more complete description of the archives, see: *RHAF*, XIX (1965–66), 652–55; SCHÉC *Rapport*, 33 (1963), 69–70. A detailed inventory of several registers and files appears in *RHAF*, XIX (1965–66), 655–64; XX (1966–67), 146–66, 669–700; XXIV (1970–71), 111–42.

The following were used in the preparation of volume IX:
Dossiers
295: Diocèses du Québec
.099: Québec
.101: Québec
355: Paroisses
.105: Saint-Laurent
.110: Saint-Joachim (Pointe-Claire)
.114: L'Assomption
420: Clergé
.013: Saint-Germain, Jean-Baptiste
.080: Manseau, Antoine
465: Religieux pères
.101: Compagnie de Saint-Sulpice
.105: Clercs de Saint-Viateur

901: Fonds Lartigue-Bourget
.009: Signatures de la pétition du clergé
RL: Registres de lettres
RLB: Registres des lettres de Mgr Bourget, 1837–80. 25 vols. An analytical inventory of Mgr Bourget*'s correspondence from 1837 to 1850 was published in ANQ *Rapport*, 1945–46, 137–224; 1946–47, 81–175; 1948–49, 343–477; 1955–57, 177–221; 1961–64, 9–68; 1965, 87–132; 1966, 191–252; 1967, 123–70; 1969, 3–146.
RLL: Registres des lettres de Mgr Lartigue, 1819–40. 9 vols. An inventory of Mgr Lartigue*'s correspondence from 1819 to 1840 appears in ANQ *Rapport*, 1941–42, 345–496; 1942–43, 1–174; 1943–44, 207–334; 1944–45, 173–266; 1945–46, 39–134.

ARCHIVES DE LA COMPAGNIE DE JÉSUS, PROVINCE DU CANADA FRANÇAIS, Saint-Jérôme. Founded in 1844 by Father Félix Martin*, first rector of the Collège Sainte-Marie in Montreal, this archives was first known as the Archives du collège Sainte-Marie [see *DCB*, I, 686]. It was moved to Saint-Jérôme in 1968 and forms only a part of the ASJCF. In the year of its founding this archives received a valuable gift from the nuns of the Hôtel-Dieu in Quebec who had preserved a few of the papers of the old Collèges des Jésuites in Québec (1635–1800).

The collection includes thousands of photographs, miniature paintings, and 500 maps and plans (not yet numbered). The ASJCF holds numerous original documents (256 dated prior to 1800) and certified copies relating to the history of the missions of the Society of Jesus in Acadia, New France, Canada, and the United States, from 1608 to about 1930 (when French speaking Jesuits turned over to English speaking Jesuits their missions to the Indians around the Great Lakes and in Ontario) and documents relating to the history of the Roman Catholic Church in Canada in the 19th century. Much of the material for the period before 1800 has been published. See *DCB*, I, 698, *The Jesuit relations*. . . .

The ASJCF has papers previously held by other archives; all organization completed by these repositories has been maintained. The collection includes, first, a Fonds général, numbered from 1 to 6,828 (54 ft), containing the former archives of the Collège Sainte-Marie, some dating from the 17th and 18th centuries; numerous documents on the political and religious conflicts of the 19th century in Quebec, including the Jesuits' estates and the university issue; part of the Fonds Léon Gérin (4 ft); the Fonds Prud'homme (1 ft) and the Fonds Bernier (1 ft), relating to educational matters in western Canada; the correspondence of notary Cyrille Tessier, etcetera.

Series A and B concern the history of the Canadian Jesuits, 1841–1924. Series A comprises the archives of various mission residences and outposts, houses, and colleges including the chronicles of missions in the Great Lakes region, annual reports and correspondence of missionaries, such as the *Lettres des nouvelles missions du Canada, 1843–1852*, Lorenzo Cadieux, édit. (Montréal et Paris, 1973); documents relating to the colonizing venture at Nominingue, 1882–86. The Fonds Baraga is also in Series A. Series B includes documents concerning the residences and institutions outside Quebec, and material relating to the canonization of Canadian martyrs.

The Fonds Immaculée-Conception (5 ft) includes the correspondence between Abbé Louis-Édouard Bois* and Jean-Baptiste Meilleur*, the correspondence of Jules-Paul Tardivel*, etcetera. Series BO contains the papers left by the Jesuit fathers (90 boxes, not inventoried). The papers of Father Paul Desjardins are also included in this series. The ASJCF also holds other uninventoried papers of Jesuits who served in Canada, including the papers of Joseph-Papin Archambault*, those of the École sociale populaire, and a part of the academic and administrative records of the colleges of Edmonton, Saint-Boniface, Sainte-Marie, and Gaspé, which have recently been closed.

ARCHIVES DE L'ARCHIDIOCÈSE DE QUÉBEC. Contains some 1,200 ft of documents dating from 1638, about 5,000 photographs (1855 to the present), 400 maps and plans dating from the 18th century, an analytical card file for all pre-1930 documents, and a Répertoire général des registres officiels de l'archevêché in 6 vols., from 1659. A guide to the archives is found in SCHÉC *Rapport*, 2 (1934–35), 65–73.

Series cited in volume IX:
A: Évêques et archevêques de Québec
   12 A: Registres des insinuations ecclésiastiques
   20 A: Lettres manuscrites des évêques de Québec
  210 A: Registres des lettres expédiées. The correspondence of a number of bishops and archbishops of Quebec is inventoried in the ANQ *Rapport*. That of Mgr J.-O. Plessis* for 1797 to 1825 is found in 1927–28, 215–316, and 1928–29, 87–208; that of Mgr B.-C. Panet* covering the period 1806 to 1833 in 1933–34, 233–421; 1934–35, 319–420; 1935–36, 155–272; that of Mgr Joseph Signay* covering 1825 to 1846 in 1936–37, 125–330; 1937–38, 21–146 (which also includes the correspondence of Mgr P.-F. TURGEON as coadjutor to the Quebec see); 1938–39, 180–357.
C: Secrétairerie et chancellerie
   CB: Structures de direction
  1 CB: Vicaires généraux
   CD: Discipline diocésaine
 303 CD: Titres cléricaux
 515 CD: Séminaire de Nicolet
  61 CD: Paroisses
  71 CD: Oblats de Marie-Immaculée
Diocèse de Québec (being reclassified)
   CM: Église universelle
 101 CM: Cahier Signay
   CN: Église canadienne
 301 CN: Îles-de-la-Madeleine
 311 CN: Nouveau-Brunswick
 312 CN: Nouvelle-Écosse
 320 CN: Haut-Canada
 330 CN: Rivière-Rouge
   CP: Église du Québec
  26 CP: District et diocèse de Montréal
T: Papiers privés
  Papiers J.-B.-A. Ferland

ARCHIVES DE LA VILLE DE MONTRÉAL. The archives division of the city clerk's office of

Montreal was created in 1913 to hold the city's administrative records. At present the AVM holds slightly more than 15,500 ft of documents, classified in files or volumes, about 50,000 plans and maps dating from 1796, and some 200 ft of photographs from 1900. The section Documents administratifs is composed of all official papers dating from 1796. The section Documentation contains extracts from articles in newspapers, periodicals, and other printed matter referring to numerous subjects or individuals connected with the administration and history of Montreal. This last section contains the correspondence (originals and copies) of several mayors. The AVM also holds copies of material from other archives including the *terrier* of the Sulpicians. Indexes are available to facilitate research.

Cited in volume IX are:

Documentation, 1796–1976
Biographies autres que celles des maires et conseillers
Documents administratifs, 1796–1976
Procès-verbaux du conseil municipal, des comités et commissions
Rapports et dossiers du conseil municipal, des comités et commissions
Rôles d'évaluation

ARCHIVES DE LA VILLE DE QUÉBEC. The archives department of Quebec City was organized in 1925 under the direction of Valère Desjardins. Its most important records are those of the municipal administration, which date from the incorporation of Quebec in 1833. The archives contains 1,500 photographs, 1,500 maps and plans, and about 2,000 ft of documents. The documents date from 1692, but complete series begin in 1814. The AVQ also holds the Fonds Baillairgé which includes 494 plans and drawings of buildings in Quebec by Charles Baillairgé*. Further information can be found in the *Guide de consultation* (typescript, 2ᵉ éd., Québec, 1971).

The following were used in volume IX:
Procès-verbaux du conseil, 1833–36, 1840–1973. 64 registers.
Rôles d'évaluation et d'imposition, 1821–1970. Microfilms.

ARCHIVES DU SÉMINAIRE DE QUÉBEC. One of the more important collections of documents in North America, the archives dates from the founding of the seminary in 1663, but Mgr Thomas-Étienne Hamel*, and Mgr Amédée Gosselin* may be considered to have founded the ASQ at the end of the 19th and the beginning of the 20th century. It contains some 1,172 ft of documents, which include seminary papers and private papers dating from 1636 but the majority from 1675 to 1950, 2,800 maps and plans, and 5,000 engravings and photographs.

For volume IX, the following were used:
Évêques de Québec. 2 cartons.
Fonds H.-R. Casgrain
Fonds É.-G. Plante
Fonds Viger-Verreau. Collections of Abbé H.-A.-J.-B. Verreau* and Jacques Viger* including about 100 boxes, numerous notebooks, and a series of volumes by Viger entitled "Ma Saberdache" (*see* Fernand Ouellet, "Inventaire de la Saberdache de Jacques Viger," ANQ *Rapport*, 1955–57, 31–176).
Journal du séminaire, 1849–1970
Livres de comptes
C 44, 1850–57
C 51, 1855–59
Manuscrits
626, Journal de H. Laverdière, 16 sept. 1858– 9 juin 1861
676–77, Journal de C.-É. Légaré, 25 mars 1865–17 avril 1873
Plumitif, 1766–1950. 5 vols.
Polygraphie. 324 cartons.
Seigneuries. 70 cartons.
Séminaire. 256 cartons.
Université. 368 cartons.

ARCHIVES DU SÉMINAIRE DE SAINT-HYACINTHE, Saint-Hyacinthe, Que. Contains 230 ft of manuscripts dating from 1693, about 10,000 photographs and postcards, and 25 maps and plans (1873–1920). The manuscript collection contains material relating to the seminary, the papers of some of the seminary's superiors and professors, as well as those of some 50 political and religious leaders. The collection also includes lists of pupils and staff (from 1811 to the present), the early catalogues of the seminary library and of a number of private libraries, and a substantial number of miscellaneous documents.

The following were used in volume IX:
Section A: Séminaire
F: Fonds particuliers
Chroniques de l'abbé Tétreau, 1849–97
Fonds Pierre-Édouard Leclère, 1737–1938
Grands cahiers, 1821–1905. 8 cahiers.
G: Personnel du séminaire
Correspondance des supérieurs, 1811– 1976
Fonds Isaac Désaulniers, 1822–1972
M: Administration
Lettres d'affaires, 1810–1976

Archives du séminaire de Saint-Sulpice, Montreal. An important repository for the history of the Montreal region during the French régime, it contains the greater part of the papers dating from 1642 of Paul de Chomedey* de Maisonneuve which he left behind on his departure in 1665. The archives, divided into 58 sections, contains 500 ft of documents for the years 1586–1975, and almost 1,200 maps and plans, and 500 photographs.

The following were used in volume IX:

Section 8: Seigneuries, fiefs, arrière-fiefs, domaines, 1717–1930
   A: Seigneurie du Lac-des-Deux-Montagnes
Section 11: Enseignement, 1654–1960
Section 21: Correspondance générale, 1670–1920
Section 24: Histoire et géographie, biographies, divers, 1600–1920
   2: Biographies, 1642–1850
Section 25: Le séminaire de Saint-Sulpice, 1657–1960
   1: Règlements, visites, comptes rendus des assemblées, 1657–1900
   3: Lettres des supérieurs généraux, 1789–1959
Section 27: Le séminaire, les évêchés et les paroisses, 1654–1938
Section 36: Missions, 1668–1975

Archives du séminaire de Trois-Rivières. In 1934 the authorities of the seminary gave Abbé Albert Tessier* the task of arranging the archives of the institution. That year, important manuscripts were donated to the archives including the Pierre Boucher collection and the Hart collection. The latter contains thousands of accounts, notes, and letters on Canadian economic life in the 19th century. The ASTR is also an important documentary source for the political, religious, and economic history of the region. It holds about 100 ft of manuscripts dating from 1651, several thousand photographs, hundreds of maps and original plans, and the most important Trois-Rivières newspapers for the period 1865–1963. For a more complete description of the ASTR, see Yvon Thériault, "Inventaire sommaire des Archives du séminaire des Trois-Rivières," ANQ Rapport, 1961–64, 69–134.

Documents from the following sections were used in volume IX:

Fonds et papiers
  Archives de la famille Boucher
  Correspondance Taché
  Papiers J.-Napoléon Bureau
  Papiers Mgr Albert Tessier

Trifluviana
  Trifluviens du 19e et du 20e siècle

Archives historiques oblates, Ottawa. An important repository for the history of the Oblates of Mary Immaculate from the time of their arrival in Canada in 1841. Even before 1930, Father Jean-Marie-Rodrigue Villeneuve* had begun to collect a large number of documents relating to the Oblates. In 1933, Father Léo Deschâtelets obtained copies from Rome of the writings of the order's founder, minutes of general and executive meetings, and letters from the first Oblates in Canada.

The AHO holds many original papers pertaining to the Oblates as well as personal papers, including the manuscript of Father Louis-Marie Le Jeune*'s Dictionnaire and the notes of Father Louis Babel*'s trip to Labrador. There are also many manuscripts in Inuit and Indian languages, some written by Oblates (see Gaston Carrière, "Catalogue des manuscrits en langues indiennes [et esquimaudes] conservés aux Archives oblates, Ottawa," Anthropologica (Ottawa), XII (1970), 151–79).

The AHO holds 500 ft of original documents and 75 ft of photographs, but its most valuable possession is its large number of copies (typescripts, photocopies, or microfilm) which enable the researcher to find almost all the documents relating to the Oblates in Canada. The microfilm section, set up in 1941, comprises more than 500,000 pages and a descriptive file of about 250,000 cards. There are several indexes and also a photograph collection and library of some 10,000 volumes. The library includes a few works printed in Indian languages and a large collection of Oblate publications, in particular Missions des O.M.I., which are to the Oblates what the Relations were to the Jesuits.

Material consulted for volume IX includes:

Fonds manuscrits
  Auguste Brunet, "Le guide des voyageurs . . ."
  Nérée Gingras, "Mémoire du procès du père Brunet, oblat, de sa condamnation, de son emprisonnement, de son évasion de la prison de Kankakee . . ."
Copies from the following repositories were used:
Archives de l'archevêché de Saint-Boniface, Manitoba
  Correspondance de l'archevêché
  Alexandre Taché, "Notes sur l'établissement de la mission d'Athabaska"
Archives générales des Oblats de Marie-Immaculée, Rome

Correspondance Jean-Baptiste Honorat,
1841–52
Dossier Pierre-Henri Grollier
Histoire de la mission de Notre-Dame-des-
Sept-Douleurs établie au fond du lac
Athabasca
Archives provinciales des Oblats de Marie-
Immaculée, Montréal
Dossier Grollier
Archives provinciales des Oblats de Marie-
Immaculée, Edmonton
Codex historicus

ARCHIVES JUDICIAIRES. Judicial archives are located in the administrative centres of the judicial
districts of Quebec. The repositories hold the
registers of births, marriages, and deaths and
documents relating to the judicial affairs of the
district, notaries' *greffes* (minute books), and
records of surveyors.

Records held in the following districts were
used:
Bonaventure (New Carlisle)
Registre d'état civil
Saint-Joseph-de-Carleton
Kamouraska (Rivière-du-Loup)
Registre d'état civil
Sainte-Anne-de-la-Pocatière (La Pocatière)
Montréal (for pre-1875 documents *see* ANQ,
Montréal)
Registre d'état civil
Cimetière Notre-Dame-des-Anges
Nicolet
Registre d'état civil
Saint-Édouard (Gentilly)
Québec (for pre-1875 documents *see* ANQ,
Québec)
Greffes
Philippe Huot, 1848–1906
C.-A. Lemay, 1850–1911
Richelieu (Sorel)
Greffe de Paul Payan, 1850–85
Registre d'état civil
Saint-Pierre (Sorel)
Saint-François (Sherbrooke)
Greffe de G.-H. Napier, 1848–67
Saint-Hyacinthe
Greffe de P.-P. Dutalmé, 1798–1821
Terrebonne (Saint-Jérôme)
Greffes
André Bouchard, dit Lavallée, 1834–78
J.-A. Hervieux, 1856–82
Melchior Prévost, 1840–97
J.-B.-L. Villemure, 1851–84
Registre d'état civil
Lac-des-Deux-Montagnes
Sainte-Anne-de-Mascouche

Saint-Jérôme
Trois-Rivières (for pre-1875 documents *see*
ANQ, Trois-Rivières)
Documents judiciaires
Cour du banc de la reine
Greffe de la paix
Registre d'état civil
St Andrews (presbytérien)

ARCHIVES NATIONALES DU QUÉBEC. At the conquest, articles 43, 44, and 45 of the capitulation of
Montreal – contrary to the custom of international law at that time – permitted the administrators of New France to take the documents
concerning the government of the colony back to
France. Only records having a legal value for
individuals were to remain in the country, and
these suffered many misfortunes before the office
of the Archives de la province de Québec – now
the Archives nationales du Québec – was set up in
1920. (*See* Gilles Héon, ''Bref historique des
Archives du Québec,'' ANQ *Rapport*, 1970,
13–25.) In 1971, the ANQ began establishing regional repositories in each of the administrative
districts of Quebec. In addition to the repository
at Quebec, there is now a fully organized one in
Montreal, and another in the process of being set
up in Trois-Rivières. These new archives hold
pre-1875 records previously stored in the court-
houses in each of the administrative districts (*see*
Section I, Archives judiciaires). Notaries' minute
books, surveyors' records, and the registers of
births, marriages, and deaths for the parishes of
all denominations will be placed in the new repositories of the ANQ as they are created. The
judicial archives will also be kept here, and in the
Montreal and Trois-Rivières repositories these
include the documents of the French régime formerly held at ANQ-Q.

MONTRÉAL
Further information on the records and papers
held in this repository can be found in ''État
sommaire des Archives nationales du Québec à
Montréal,'' ANQ *Rapport*, 1972, 1–29.

The following were used in volume IX:
Documents judiciaires
Contrats de shérif, 1767–1889
État civil
Anglicans
Christ Church, 1766–1875
Garrison, 1760–64, 1814–50
Catholiques
Notre-Dame-de-Grâce (Montréal), 1856–74
Notre-Dame-de Montréal, 1643–1915
Saint-Antoine (Longueuil), 1669–1845

Saint-François-Xavier-de-Verchères,
1723–1846
Saint-Joseph (Chambly), 1706–1848
Saint-Martin (Laval), 1774–1849
Saint-Vincent-de-Paul (Laval), 1834–38,
1851–73
Méthodistes
St James, 1818–46, 1851–75
New Connection, 1839
Presbytériens
St Andrew (Montréal), 1815–75
St Gabriel, 1779–1845
Spanish-Portuguese Jewish Congregation,
1840–62
Greffes
J.-O. Bastien, fils, 1834–64
Joseph Belle, 1830–69
J.-O. Bureau, 1843–83
J.-M. Cadieux, 1805–27
J.-B. Constantin, 1805–69
T.-B. Doucet, 1838–67
I. J. Gibb, 1835–67
Henry Griffin, 1812–47
J. C. Griffin, 1844–92
Patrice Lacombe, 1831–63
Peter Lukin, fils, 1819–37
J.-M. Mondelet, 1794–1842
James Smith, 1848–75
P.-C. Valois, 1835–78
M: Archives privées
72: Fonds Romuald Trudeau, Mes tablettes,
1820–50
Testaments
Register of wills probated, 1780–1882
Testaments olographes, 1658–1875

QUÉBEC
Further information on the records and papers
held in this repository can be found in *État
général des archives publiques et privées*
(Québec, 1968). It should be noted that the registers of births, marriages, and deaths are held in
the Section de Généalogie, 1180 Rue Berthelot;
post-1867 records, maps, plans, and illustrations,
are at 115 Côte de la Montagne; pre-1867 records
and the collection of private archives are at Parc
des Champs de Bataille.
The following were used in volume IX:
AP: Archives privées
 G: Grandes collections
 40: Chaussegros de Léry, famille, 1682–1934
 68: Duvernay, Ludger, 1805–48
 69: Fabre, Édouard-Raymond, 1806–51
 76: Faribault, G.-B., 1814–61
 79: Fiset, Louis, 1724–1859
 85: Frémont, famille, 1788–1902

134: Langevin, famille Hector, 1765–1940
196: Ogden, Charles-Richard, 1788–1836
203: Penney, Hon. Edward Goff, 1849–67
219: Quebec Board of Trade, 1832–1958
239: Roy, Pierre-Georges
242: Taché, famille, 1680–1946
278: Trinity House of Quebec, 1805–78
327: Casgrain, abbé Alphonse, 1913
336: Baby, famille, 1765–1888
417: Papineau, famille, 1801–1902
418: Bourassa, Napoléon et famille, 1865–1929
 P: Petites collections
130: Beaujeu, famille de, 1863–68
184: Berthelot, Amable, 1834
931: Hale, famille, 1842, 1847, 1930
État civil
Anglicans
Cathedral of the Holy Trinity (Québec),
1768–1875
Catholiques
Hôpital Général de Québec, 1783–1813,
1815–1875
Notre-Dame-de-Foy (Sainte-Foy),
1679–1781 (incomplete collection),
1782–1827, 1829–75
Notre-Dame de Lévis, 1851–75
Notre-Dame de Québec, 1621–1714,
1721–1875
Saint-Roch (Québec), 1829–75
Presbytériens
St Andrews (Québec), 1770–1875
Greffes
Joseph Bernard, 1826–77
Henri Bolduc, 1847–85
É.-T. Boudreault, 1817–25
N. H. Bowen, 1850–72
Archibald Campbell, 1812–61
W. D. Campbell, 1852–85
John Childs, 1834–73
Charles Cinq-Mars, 1842–86
J. G. Clapham, 1839–89
J.-B. Couillard, 1823–70
C.-M. Defoy, 1822–58
William De Léry, 1824–42
F.-L. Gauvreau, 1844–87
S.-I. Glackmeyer, 1852–83
F.-M. Guay, père, 1832–78
James Haney, 1869–71
E. B. Lindsay, 1823–75
L. T. McPherson, 1816–70
Louis Panet, 1819–79
A.-Archange Parent, 1814–60
Joseph Petitclerc, 1831–66
A.-B. Sirois Duplessis, 1831–76
QBC: Québec et Bas-Canada
9: Licences, 1818–67
16: Seigneuries, 1766–1862

25: Procureur général, 1763–1852
   Événements de 1837–38
27: Instruction publique, 1842–99

TROIS-RIVIÈRES
Opened in 1976, this repository is in the process
of being organized.
   The following materials were used:
État civil
   Catholiques
      Immaculée-Conception (Trois-Rivières),
         1679–1875
   Presbytériens
      St Andrew's Church, 1846–75
Greffes
   R.-Honoré Dufresne, 1865–1920
   Petrus Hubert, 1834–76
   F.-L. Lottinville, 1840–95

ARCHIVES OF ONTARIO, Toronto. The archives
was established in 1903 and at present is an
agency of the Ministry of Culture and Recreation.
It is authorized to acquire, preserve, and analyse
all records of significance of the Ontario government. It also acquires from other sources,
through donation or purchase, manuscripts,
maps, photographs, pictures, posters, and early
newspapers relating to the history of the pro-
vince. Unpublished inventories, calendars,
catalogue entries, guides, and other finding aids
are available in the archives.
   The materials used in volume IX include:
Boulton (Henry John) papers
Canada Company papers
Cartwright (John Solomon) papers
Clarke (Colonel Charles) papers
Jarvis-Powell papers
Macaulay (John) papers
Mackenzie-Lindsey papers
Merritt (William Hamilton) papers
Robinson (Sir John Beverley) papers
Strachan (John) papers
Street (Samuel) papers
Toronto City Council papers
RG 1: Records of the Ministry of Natural
       Resources
   A: Offices of surveyor general and commis-
      sioner of crown lands
      I: Correspondence
      4: Commissioner's letterbooks, 1828–74
      6: Letters received, surveyor general
         and commissioner
      II: Reports and statements
      6: Statements, 1811–1907
   B: Accounts Branch
      IV: Survey accounts, 1796–1915

CB-1: Survey diaries, field notes, and reports
   C: Lands Branch
      IV: Township papers
RG 2: Records of the Ministry of Education
   B: General Board of Education (second)
      and Council of Public Instruction
      3: Minutes, Council of Public Instruc-
         tion, 1859–75
RG 8: Records of the Department of the Pro-
       vincial Secretary
   I-6: Office of the Registrar General
      A: District marriage registers, 1801–58
   I-7: Office of the clerk of the Legislative As-
        sembly
      F-2: Petitions, 1875–1933
RG 22: Court records
   6-2: Records of (local) surrogate courts,
        1793–1875
   7: Courts of General Quarter Sessions

ARCHIVES PAROISSIALES. Specific holdings in-
clude the registers of baptisms, marriages, and
burials (with copies held in the district judicial
archives), and parish account books and vestry
records.
   The following were used in volume IX:
L'Immaculée-Conception (Saint-Ours, Qué.)
   Livres de comptes
La Nativité-de-Notre-Dame-de-Bécancour
   (Bécancour, Qué.)
   Livres de comptes
Notre-Dame-de-Foy (Sainte-Foy, Qué.)
   Livres de comptes
Notre-Dame-de-L'Assomption (Arichat, N.-É.)
   Registres des baptêmes, mariages et sépultures
Notre-Dame de Québec
   Livres de comptes et délibérations
Saint-Antoine-de-la-Baie-du-Febvre (Baieville,
   Qué.)
   Livres de comptes
   Registres des baptêmes, mariages et sépultures
Saint-Casimir (Qué.)
   Livres de comptes et délibérations
Saint-Charles-de-Bellechasse (Saint-Charles,
   Qué.)
   Registres de la fabrique
Saint-Charles-des-Grondines (Grondines, Qué.)
   Livres de la fabrique
Saint-Denis-sur-Richelieu (Qué.)
   Registres des baptêmes, mariages et sépultures
Sainte-Anne-des-Plaines (Qué.)
   Registres des baptêmes, mariages et sépultures
Sainte-Anne-d'Yamachiche (Yamachiche, Qué.)
   Livres de comptes
Sainte-Famille-du-Cap-Santé (Cap-Santé, Qué.)
   Registres des baptêmes, mariages et sépultures

Sainte-Geneviève-de-Berthier (Berthierville, Qué.)
  Livres de comptes
  Registres des baptêmes, mariages et sépultures
Saint-François-du-Lac (Qué.)
  Livres de comptes
Saint-Jean-Baptiste (Deschaillons, Qué.)
  Livres de comptes
Saint-Laurent (île d'Orléans)
  Livres de comptes
Saint-Marc (Qué.)
  Registres des baptêmes, mariages et sépultures
Saint-Michel-de-Vaudreuil (Vaudreuil, Qué.)
  Registres des baptêmes, mariages et sépultures
Saint-Michel-d'Yamaska (Yamaska, Qué.)
  Livres de comptes
Saint-Pierre (Les Becquets, Qué.)
  Livres de comptes et délibérations
Saint-Roch (Québec)
  Livres de comptes et délibérations
Saint-Roch-de-l'Achigan (Qué.)
  Registres des baptêmes, mariages et sépultures

BIBLIOTHÈQUE NATIONALE DU QUÉBEC, DÉPARTEMENT DES MANUSCRITS, Montreal. In 1965, the Bibliothèque Saint-Sulpice (since 1967, the Bibliothèque nationale du Québec) owned enough archival material to create a separate manuscript department. No specific collection of papers occasioned its establishment; the Sulpicians began the collection of documents, and material is added every year. The repository at present holds 45,347 linear cm., consisting mainly of literary manuscripts of the late 19th and 20th centuries, but including also a number of private papers from the latter half of the 19th century and from the 20th century. The department also holds several hundred posters, more than 30,000 photographs, theatre programmes and other miscellaneous documents.

In 1970, the Société historique de Montréal deposited at the BNQ its complete collection of manuscripts, archives, documents and books (14,580 linear cm.), including the Collection La Fontaine. For a complete inventory of this collection see *Inventaire de la collection Lafontaine*, Elizabeth Nish [Gibbs], compil. (Publ. du Centre d'étude du Québec, Montréal, 1967).

BIBLIOTHÈQUES DE L'UNIVERSITÉ DE MONTRÉAL. In April 1971, the libraries of the Université de Montréal set up the Service des collections particulières to give researchers access to the numerous valuable documents acquired by the university through purchase and donation. At the same time the service initiated a series of publications.

The following collection was used:
Collection Baby. A large collection of original material, gathered by François-Louis-Georges Baby*, who bequeathed it to the Université de Montréal, it includes more than 20,000 items covering almost every subject of Canadian history from 1602 to 1905. In 1942, M. Camille Bertrand began to inventory this collection arranging the material in two large sections: Documents divers and Correspondance générale. Documents divers, mainly individual items, are catalogued under 20 general titles labelled A to S. The Correspondance générale, arranged alphabetically by the name of the signer of the letters, contains about 12,000 original letters kept in 120 boxes. The collection is too large and varied to be fully described here, but the researcher may consult the repository's 20,000 manuscript index cards or the *Catalogue de la collection François-Louis-Georges Baby*, prepared by Camille Bertrand, with preface by Paul Baby and introduction by Lucien Campeau (2v., Montréal, 1971). Handwritten copies of most items in the Baby Collection are held by the PAC.

BROME COUNTY HISTORICAL SOCIETY ARCHIVES, Knowlton, Que. This repository contains about 250 ft of original documents, covering the period dating from 1755. It holds the BCHS archives, the papers of individuals, families, and societies of various townships, and documents related to a number of New England states. There are also 1,000 photographs, 50 daguerreotypes, and a collection of local newspapers. Organized in 1897 and incorporated in 1898, the BCHS published *Transactions* from 1897 to 1938, and, in 1937, a *Catalogue of documents* with a bibliography of materials on the Eastern Townships. For a further description of the BCHS Archives see *Collections of the Brome County Historical Society, preliminary inventory* ([Ottawa and Knowlton], 1954) compiled by the PAC and the society.

Materials used in volume IX include:
W. F. Beattie, "The time of Marcus Child" (manuscript)
VII: Knowlton family papers
  Paul Holland Knowlton
VIII: Miscellaneous family papers
  Stephen Sewell Foster

HAMILTON PUBLIC LIBRARY, Hamilton, Ont. The HPL, established in 1890, has always emphasized the collection of Canadian materials. In 1914, a separate Canadiana collection was organized and has grown steadily. It includes a large local history collection, and picture and manuscript holdings have recently greatly expanded. Newspaper clippings, scrapbooks, pamphlets, and local periodicals have been indexed in detail.

Materials used in the preparation of volume IX include:

Ferrie papers

Hamilton biography

   William Paterson McLaren

   Sir Allan Napier MacNab

   Andrew Steven

Index to census and assessment rolls, 1835–

Land family papers

Land papers

HUDSON'S BAY COMPANY ARCHIVES, Winnipeg. In 1974, the HBC archives was transferred from London to Winnipeg and deposited in the PAM [see *DCB*, X, 747]. Dating from 1670, the records measure about 5,000 linear ft, and consist of correspondence, journals, account books, ships' logs, and maps. The archives as constituted at present was established in 1932, and the work of organization proceeded thereafter [see R. H. G. Leveson Gower, "The archives of the Hudson's Bay Company," *Beaver*, outfit 264 (December 1933), 40–42, 64; Joan Craig, "Three hundred years of records," *Beaver*, outfit 301 (autumn 1970), 65–70; "HBC archives to come to Manitoba," *Beaver*, outfit 304 (autumn 1973), 32–33]. In 1938, a publishing programme was undertaken by the Hudson's Bay Record Society [see section II], and in 1949, the HBC and PAC arranged jointly to microfilm the archives from 1670 to 1870. Information on the PAC copies is found in PAC *Report*, 1950, 13–14; 1952, 16–18; 1953–54, 21–22; 1955–58, 44–46.

The following were used in the preparation of volume IX:

Section A: London office records

A.1/: London minute books

A.5/: London correspondence outwards – general

A.6/: London correspondence outwards – official

A.10/: London inward correspondence – general

A.11/: London inward correspondence from HBC posts

A.12/: London inward correspondence from governors of HBC territories

A.16/: Officers' and servants' ledgers and account books

A.30/: Lists of servants in Hudson's Bay

A.31/: Lists of commissioned officers

A.33/: Commissioned officers' indentures and agreements

A.34/: Servants' characters and staff records

A.36/: Officers' and servants' wills

A.44/: Register books of wills and administrators of proprietors, etc.

Section B: North America trading post records

B.4/b: Fort Alexander outward correspondence

B.20/a: Bolsover House journals

B.34/a: Chesterfield House (Bow River) journal

B.34/d: Chesterfield House (Bow River) account books

B.34/e: Chesterfield House (Bow River) reports on district

B.39/a: Fort Chipewyan post journal

B.39/z: Fort Chipewyan, miscellaneous papers

B.60/a: Edmonton House journals

B.60/d: Edmonton House account books

B.80/a: Fort Good Hope journal

B.89/a: Île à la Crosse journals

B.105/a: Lac La Pluie journals

B.115/a: Lesser Slave Lake journals

B.115/d: Lesser Slave Lake account books

B.134/b: Montreal outward correspondence books

B.134/c: Montreal inward correspondence books

B.135/a: Moose Factory journals

B.135/c: Moose Factory inward correspondence

B.154/a: Norway House journals

B.154/b: Norway House outward correspondence

B.157/a: Peel River journals

B.159/a: Fort Pelly journals

B.181/a: Fort Resolution journals

B.188/e: Fort St James reports on district

B.200/a: Fort Simpson journals

B.200/b: Fort Simpson outward correspondence

B.200/d: Fort Simpson account books

B.226/b: Fort Victoria correspondence books

B.235/a: Winnipeg journals

B.239/a: York Factory journals

B.239/b: York Factory outward correspondence books

B.239/c: York Factory inward correspondence

B.239/d: York Factory account books

B.239/f: Lists of servants

B.239/g: Abstracts of servants' accounts

B.239/k: Minutes of Council

B.239/l: Northern Department district statement

B.239/u: Northern Department servants' engagement register

B.239/x: Northern Department servants' ledgers

Section C: Records of ships owned or chartered by the HBC

C.1/: Ships' logs

Section D: Journals and correspondence books, etc., of governors-in-chief of Rupert's Land, commissioners, etc.

D.4/: Governor George Simpson, correspondence outward

D.5/: Governor George Simpson, correspondence inward

D.6/1: Governor George Simpson – draft will, family letters, etc.

D.6/2: Governor George Simpson – passport

D.6/3: Governor George Simpson – minutes and correspondence concerning will

D.9/: William Mactavish, correspondence outward

D.10/: William Mactavish, correspondence inward

Section E: Miscellaneous

E.4/: Red River Settlement church registers

E.5/: Red River Settlement census returns

E.11/: Nicholas Garry papers – correspondence and miscellaneous papers

E.12/: Duncan Finlayson – draft and copy of marriage settlement with Isobel G. Simpson

Section F: Records relating to companies connected with or subsidiary to the HBC

F.4/: North West Company account books

INVENTAIRE DES BIENS CULTURELS, Quebec. When Gérard Morisset* established the Service de l'Inventaire des œuvres d'art in 1940, he succeeded in gaining government recognition for a project of recording and locating works of art which he had conducted personally for more than ten years. Aided by a staff which he himself had trained, Morisset until 1967 photographed articles of silver, works of architecture, and paintings, searched parish account books, newspapers, and notarial registers, and accumulated many thousands of documents on artisans and their work. This impressive collection (about 70,000 photographs, 40,000 biographical cards, 20,000 slides, 5,000 old photographs) had already acquired a special value as the result of the disappearance of a number of the works of art. The Inventaire des œuvres d'art, now known as the Fonds Morisset, is open to all researchers upon application to the Ministère des Affaires culturelles.

The two principal sections of the Morisset collection, the files concerning artists and craftsmen of Quebec (section 2), and those containing documents on architecture and works of art listed by area (section 5), contain useful material. There are also numerous files on architecture, works of art, and ethnography in Quebec in section 3. The slides have been individually described and classified to assist the researcher.

The material has all been systematically organized and there is a card index at the Centre de documentation, Service de l'Inventaire des biens culturels, 6 Rue de l'Université, Quebec.

MCCORD MUSEUM, Montreal. A large portion of the McCord Museum archives consists of documents collected between 1860 and 1919 by David Ross McCord. The documents – about 160 linear ft – cover the period from 1682 to the present. In addition, the McCord Museum holds a photograph collection which includes the famous Notman Photographic Archives – about 400,000 prints and negatives – a most important source for research on 19th and 20th century Canada and Canadians. For further information about the archives, *see* John Andreassen, *A preliminary guide to the manuscript collection, McGill University* (Montreal, 1969), 9–19.

The following material was used:
Antiquarian autographs
The Brothers in Law minute book, 1827–33
Hale family papers, 1829–1913
Library file
McCord papers, 1750–1930
McDonald, A. de Lery, family papers
Military papers
North West Company papers, 1783–1821
Notman Photographic Archives, 1856–1915

MCGILL UNIVERSITY LIBRARIES, DEPARTMENT OF RARE BOOKS AND SPECIAL COLLECTIONS, MANUSCRIPTS COLLECTION, Montreal. This repository, founded in 1965, holds 350 ft of Canadian documents dating from 1664 to the present, 4,654 photographs (1870–1945) and some 1,900 maps and plans. The collection includes documents relating to McGill University and a large selection of papers of scientists and explorers, scholars and authors, businessmen, other notable figures, various families, associations and institutions. In addition to Canadian documents, McGill University Libraries holds an important collection of European manuscripts (dating from the 9th century) and a collection of American manuscripts. For a more complete description, *see*: Richard Pennington, *McGill University Library, special collections: European and American manuscripts* (Montreal, 1962); John Andreassen, *A preliminary guide to the manuscript collection, McGill University* (Montreal, 1969).

The following were cited in volume IX:
Corse family papers
Frederick Griffin papers
James Hargrave diary
Robert Unwin Harwood papers
John McDonald of Garth papers
Ottawa and Rideau Forwarding Company

METROPOLITAN TORONTO CENTRAL LIBRARY, Toronto. The manuscript collection of MTCL contains approximately 650 ft of Canadian documents. There are several large collections of personal papers and business records and many single pieces: diaries, account books, letterbooks, etcetera. Most of the material is from the 19th century with the emphasis on pre-1850 politics. For further information on the library's holdings see: *Guide to the manuscript collection in the Toronto Public Libraries* (Toronto, 1954).

The materials used in the preparation of volume IX include:
William Allan (1770–1853), papers, 1793–[c. 1892]
Robert Baldwin (1804–58), papers, 1819–58
William Warren Baldwin (1775–1844), papers, 1794–1850
Samuel Peters Jarvis (1792–1857), papers, 1763–1875
William Dummer Powell (1755–1834), papers, 1735–1847
John Strachan (1778–1867), papers, 1796–1839
Alexander Wood (1772?–1844), papers, 1798–1837

NEW BRUNSWICK MUSEUM, Saint John, N.B. Established in 1930, the N.B. Museum became a provincial institution in 1942. Parent organizations, such as the Natural History Society of New Brunswick, had been acquiring manuscripts for nearly a century; these materials were transferred to the museum's Department of Canadian History in 1932 and formed the nucleus of the archives. For further information *see* W. A. Squires, *The history and development of the New Brunswick Museum (1842–1945)* (N.B. Museum pub., Administrative series, 2, Saint John, N.B., 1945). For a further description of the holdings *see* New Brunswick Museum, Department of Canadian History, Archives Division, *Inventory of manuscripts, 1967.*

The following were consulted for volume IX:
Brown, Hon. James (1790–1870), journal. Photocopy, 1844–70.
Chandler, Edward Barron (1800–80), papers, 1821–70

Ganong manuscript collection, 1686–1941
Jack, David Russell, scrapbooks, 1840–1912
New Brunswick Historical Society, papers, 1811–75
Perley, Moses Henry (1804–62), papers, 1837–57
Register of marriages for the city and county of Saint John, 1812–80, in 10 vols., with an index
Tilley family, papers, 1845–1931
Ward family, papers, 1775–1850
Webster manuscript collection, 1610–1956

PROVINCIAL ARCHIVES OF BRITISH COLUMBIA, Victoria. Established in 1893, this is the oldest archival institution in western Canada. Its manuscript collection is rich in material on the exploration of the Pacific northwest by land and sea and in material for the fur trade period. The official records for the colonial period (1849–71) are remarkably complete; records for the provincial period are also held. Substantial collections of private papers, some business records, and a large number of maps, including many of early cartographic interest, are held. There is an extensive collection of visual records – photographs, paintings, and lithographs. Integral to PABC's holdings is an extensive and valuable collection of some 50,000 volumes of books and pamphlets as well as printed ephemera relating to the Pacific northwest. The archives holds almost complete files of newspapers for the colonial period and selected titles for later years.

The materials used most frequently were:
Henry Maynard Ball, Journal, 18 Aug. 1864–22 Oct. 1865
British Columbia, Colonial secretary, Correspondence outward, May 1859–December 1870. 8 vols. Letterbook copies.
British Columbia, Governor, Despatches to London, 14 Sept. 1863–31 Dec. 1867; 11 Jan. 1868–24 July 1871. Letterbook copies.
Colonial correspondence. An artificial series created from the letters inward to departments of the colonial governments of British Columbia and Vancouver Island from both individuals and other government departments. The letters are filed under the names of the senders.
Crease collection
John Sebastian Helmcken, "Reminiscences." 5 vols., typescript, 1892.
Donald Ross papers
Vancouver Island, Governor, Despatches to London, 8 June 1859–28 Dec. 1861, 12 Jan. 1862–12 March 1864, 25 March 1864–19 Nov. 1866. Letterbook copies.

PROVINCIAL ARCHIVES OF MANITOBA, Winnipeg. In 1884, the librarian of the Legislative Library of Manitoba began to assemble documents relating to the Red River Settlement and to the Council of Assiniboia. The archives developed slowly as a special collection of the library until the end of the 1940s. In 1952 the government appointed an official archivist and a 1955 law made it an official repository, which became completely autonomous in 1970. In 1974, the archives of the Hudson's Bay Company (*q.v.*) held in London was transferred to Winnipeg and deposited in the PAM. Both archival collections can be consulted in the new Manitoba Archives Building. In addition to manuscript and government records the PAM holds more than 65,000 classified photographs, a small number of paintings and drawings, and an outstanding collection of maps. In 1974, all private papers were completely reorganized. There is a central card index and unpublished preliminary and analytical inventories of the private papers, to facilitate research.

The following were used in volume IX:

MG 1: Indians, exploration and fur trade
    D: Fur trade, individuals
        2: William Mactavish, 1847–64
        8: Robert Campbell, 1835–94
        14: Simon McTavish, 1792–94
MG 2: Red River Settlement
    A: Selkirk period, 1811–35
        5: Robert Parker Pelly, 1816–24
    B: Council of Assiniboia, 1835–69
        4: District of Assiniboia: General Quarterly Court, 1844–72
        5: Red River Settlement papers: Red River correspondence, 1845–47
    C: Individuals and settlement
        3: George Marcus Cary, 1836–60
        14: Alexander Ross family collection, 1810–1903
        21: Donald Ross, 1848
        23: Robert Logan family papers, 1819–1934
MG 3: Red River disturbance, Northwest rebellion and related papers
    B: Individuals *re* Red River disturbance and Red River expedition
        17: William S. volume, 1914
    D: Louis Riel
        1: Correspondence and papers, 1860–1926
MG 5: United States
    B: Individuals
        2: James Wickes Taylor, 1852–93
MG 7: Church records and religious figures
    B: Church of England (Anglican)
        4: St Andrew's Church
            Register of marriages, 1835–83

        7: St John's Church
            Register of baptisms, 1813–79
            Register of marriages, 1820–82
            Register of burials, 1821–75
    C: Presbyterian
        12: John Black, 1846–81
MG 9: Literary manuscripts and theses
    A: Manuscripts and related papers
        76: Margaret Arnett MacLeod, 1930–64
MG 12: Lieutenant governors
    A: Adams George Archibald, 1870–72
    B: Alexander Morris
        Ketcheson collection
            Correspondence, 1845–99
            Telegram book, 1873–77
        Lieutenant governors' collection
            Letterbooks, 1873–77
MG 14: Public life
    C: Individuals
        23: Charles Napier Bell (collector), 1784–1936

PROVINCIAL ARCHIVES OF NEW BRUNSWICK, Fredericton. Established in 1968, the PANB contains government records series from 1785 as well as several private manuscript collections, including that of the York-Sunbury Historical Society. Records and manuscripts formerly with the New Brunswick Legislative Library have also been transferred to the archives.

Materials used in the preparation of volume IX include:

J. C. and H. B. Graves, "New Brunswick political biography." 11 vols., typescript.
RED: Records of the Education Department
    be: Board of Education
        5: Inspection papers for provincial schools, 1844–45
REX: New Brunswick Executive Council records
    le/l–g: Lieutenant governors' letterbooks
        Colebrooke, 1841–48
        Head, 1848–54
        Manners-Sutton, 1854–61
    mi/ex: Minutes of the Executive Council
        Minute books and draft minutes, 1824–61
    pa: Papers of the Executive Council, New Brunswick series
        Registers of appointments and commissions, 1785–1857
        Education papers, University of New Brunswick, 1815–90
        Surveyor general's correspondence, 1842–44
    px: Papers of the Executive Council, Ottawa series
        7–8: Draft minutes, 1824–30

16–27: Crown lands and forests, 1784–1858
31–32: Emigration, 1819–60
33: Fisheries
40: Indians, 1809–54
41–43: Militia and military, 1812–58
56–85: Finance, 1816–61
96–109: Public officials, 1784–1867
115–18: Health and welfare, 1823–67
RLE: New Brunswick Legislative Assembly papers
S55, 19 Jan. 1842–4 April 1842
S56, 31 Jan. 1843–11 April 1843
S63, 7 Feb. 1850–26 April 1850
RNA: Crown Land Office papers, Department of Natural Resources
c/3: Surveyor general's letterbooks, 1785–1897
c/9: Return books for land and timber petitions, 1839–61
RPS: New Brunswick Provincial Secretary's Office
Departmental letterbooks, 1842–60
RJU: Records of the Justice Department
S: Supreme Court

Provincial Archives of Newfoundland and Labrador, St John's. Created by an act of the Newfoundland House of Assembly in 1959, the provincial archives took over the collection and preservation of existing public archives from Memorial University of Newfoundland, which had performed the task in the previous three years. Before 1956 government records were scattered through departmental offices.

Materials used in the preparation of volume IX include:

Government records – Newfoundland
GN 1: Governor's Office
1: Dispatches to the Colonial Office, 1818, 1823–1949
2: Dispatches from the Colonial Office, 1825–1949
3A: Incoming correspondence, 1850–1950
3B: Letterbooks, outgoing correspondence, 1855–58, 1868–95
GN 2: Department of the Colonial Secretary
1: Outgoing correspondence, 1749–1864, 1867–1934
2: Incoming correspondence, 1825–59, 1863–64, 1866–68, 1870, 1875, 1878–90
GN 9: Executive Council
Minutes, 1825–1900, 1915–34
GN 13: Department of Attorney General
P: Private records

Public Archives of Canada, Ottawa. In 1873 the government of Canada commissioned Douglas Brymner* and Abbé H.-A.-J.-B. Verreau* to investigate the holdings of English and French archives with a view to copying documents concerning the early history of Canada. The work of transcribing and microfilming such manuscripts, and of collecting original materials, including the records of the government of Canada, has proceeded since that time.

The following *General inventories* and *Preliminary inventories* to material used in the preparation of volume IX have been published by the Manuscript Division or the Public Records Division:

General inventory, manuscripts, 1: MG 1-MG 10 (1971).
General inventory, manuscripts, 3: MG 17-MG 21 (1974).
General inventory, manuscripts, 4: MG 22-MG 25 (1972).
General inventory, manuscripts, 5: MG 26-MG 27 (1972).
General inventory, manuscripts, 7: MG 29 (1975).
General inventory series, no. 1: records relating to Indian affairs (RG 10) (1975).

Other inventories, some of them largely superseded by unpublished inventories available at the PAC, are the following:

Manuscript Group 30, twentieth century manuscripts (1966).
Record Group 1, Executive Council, Canada, 1764–1867 (1953).
Record Group 2, Privy Council Office; Record Group 3, Post Office Department (1960).
Record Group 4, civil and provincial secretaries' offices, Canada East, 1760–1867; Record Group 5, civil and provincial secretaries' offices, Canada West, 1788–1867 (1953).
Record Group 7, Governor General's Office (1953).
Record Group 8, British military and naval records (1954).
Record Group 9, Department of Militia and Defence, 1776–1922 ([1957]).
Record Group 11, Department of Public Works; Record Group 12, Department of Transport (marine; railways and canals) (1951).
Record groups, no. 14: Records of parliament, 1775–1915; no. 15: Department of the Interior; no. 16: Department of National Revenue (1957).
Record Group 19, Department of Finance (1954).

Unpublished addenda for the above inventories

and unpublished inventories of other manuscripts and record groups, as well as finding aids to individual collections, are available for consultation at the PAC.

The following were found useful in the preparation of volume IX:

MG 8: Documents relatifs à la Nouvelle-France et au Québec (XVIIᵉ–XXᵉ siècles)
  A: Documents généraux
    1: Correspondance officielle. Transcriptions, 1614–1778.
  G: Archives paroissiales
    19: Montréal. Original, 1862–69; photocopies, 1770–80; transcriptions, 1642–1838.
    29: Saint-Eustache de la rivière du Chêne (église catholique). Transcriptions, 1769–1850.
MG 9: Provincial, local, and territorial records
  A: New Brunswick
    1: Executive Council. Microfilm, 1784–1867.
    10: Reports on archives and local records. Originals, 1907–8.
  E: Manitoba
    3: Census returns. Originals, 1831–70; photocopies, 1832–56.
MG 17: Ecclesiastical archives
  A: Roman Catholic Church
    7–2: Séminaire de Saint-Sulpice, Montréal. Original, 1828; transcriptions, 1635–1899; microfilm, 1556–1945.
MG 19: Fur trade and Indians
  A: Fur trade, general
    2: Ermatinger estate. Originals, 1758–1874; photocopies, 1766–1966.
    9: Fraser, Simon. Originals, 1840; photocopies, 1803–46.
    17: Macdonald of Garth, John. Photocopy, 1859.
    18: Larocque, François-Antoine. Originals, 1829–56.
    29: Anderson, James. Transcripts, 1849–63.
  B: Fur trade, companies and associations
    1: North West Company. Originals, 1798–1802, 1811; photocopies, 1801–11.
    2: American Fur Company. Originals, 1817–34; microfilm, 1803–55.
  D: Fur trade, post records and journals
    7: Norway House. Originals, 1830–65.
  E: Red River Settlement
    1: Selkirk, Thomas Douglas, 5th Earl of. Originals, 1803–8; microfilm, 1811–36, 1863; photocopies, c. 1811, 1816–18; transcripts, 1769–1870.

    3: Logan, Robert. Transcripts, 1819–50.
MG 23: Late eighteenth century papers
  C: Nova Scotia
    6: Inglis family. Originals, 1827–46; microfilm, 1755–1849; transcripts, 1759–1849.
  GII: Quebec and Lower Canada: political figures
    10: Sewell, Jonathan. Originals, 1650–1911.
    18: Hale family. Originals, 1799–1907.
  GIII: Quebec and Lower Canada: merchants and settlers
    3: Ruiter (Ruyter) family papers. Originals, 1776–1867.
  HI: Upper Canada: political figures
    4: Powell, William Dummer, and family. Originals, 1714–1924; photocopies, 1812; typescripts, n.d., 1805–7; transcripts, n.d., 1891.
  L: Miscellaneous
    4: Hamilton, Alexander. Original, 1796.
MG 24: Nineteenth century pre-confederation papers
  A: British officials and political figures
    3: Douglas, Sir Howard, and family. Originals, 1776–1859; photocopies, 1795.
    13: Bagot, Sir Charles. Originals, 1838–43; transcripts, 1816–43.
    14: Richmond and Lennox, Charles Lennox, 3rd and 4th Dukes of. Transcripts, 1819; microfilm, 1764–66.
    15: Derby, Edward George Geoffrey Smith Stanley, 14th Earl of. Microfilm, 1841–52.
    16: Elgin, James Bruce, 8th Earl of. Originals, 1847–48; microfilm, 1823–58.
    17: Harvey, Sir John. Originals, 1825–41; transcripts, 1813–41.
    25: Head, Sir Francis Bond, and family. Originals, 1836–38; photocopies, 1827–41; microfilm, 1827–40.
    27: Durham, John George Lambton, 1st Earl of. Originals, 1817–42; transcripts, 1838; typescripts, 1837, n.d.
    40: Colborne, Sir John, 1st Baron Seaton. Originals, 1828–39; photocopies, 1821–63; microfilm, 1821–63.
  B: North American political figures and events
    1: Neilson collection. Originals, 1666–1912; transcripts, 1804–37;

photocopies, 1763–68, 1821–34.

2: Papineau, famille. Originaux, 1766–1915; transcriptions, 1542–1915; photocopies, 1805–1915.

3: Ryland, Herman Witsius, and family. Originals, 1685–1877; photocopies, 1798–1836; transcripts, 1789–1833.

4: Young family. Originals, 1788–1853; transcripts, 1794–99.

6: Viger, Denis-Benjamin. Originaux, 1667–1858; photocopies, 1797–1845.

11: Baldwin, William Warren and Robert. Transcripts, 1807–55; photocopies, 1835–50; microfilm, 1791–1881.

14: La Fontaine, Louis-Hippolyte. Originaux, 1855, 1859–61; transcriptions, 1638–1908.

15: Gibson, William. Originals, 1827–46.

17: MacNab, Sir Allan Napier. Originals, 1839–46; photocopies, 1832, 1854; microfilm, 1818–84.

18: Mackenzie, William Lyon. Originals, 1766–1878; photostats, 1794–1851; photocopies, 1822, 1860; typescripts, 1835–61; transcripts, n.d., 1832; microfilm, 1818–68.

24: Rolph, John. Originals, 1810–85.

29: Howe, Joseph. Originals, 1830–73; photocopies, 1847, 1863–65.

30: Macdonald, John Sandfield. Originals, 1831–1926; photocopies, 1862–71; transcripts, 1871.

31: Chapman, Henry S. Originals, 1832–53.

33: Gourlay, Robert Fleming. Originals, 1834–51.

34: Nelson, Wolfred. Originals, 1819–85; transcripts, 1834–59; typescript, 1906.

37: Perrault, Charles-Ovide, et famille. Photocopies, 1835–39.

38: Duncombe, Charles. Originals, 1839–75, 1945; photocopies, 1835; transcripts, 1465–1903.

40: Brown, George. Originals, 1837, 1848–80.

46: Cherrier, Côme-Séraphin. Originaux, 1775–1914; photocopie, vers 1865.

51: Little, Philip Francis. Microfilm, 1840–58, 1890.

55: Bytown. Originals, 1849.

59: Dessaulles, Louis-Antoine. Original, 1852–74; photocopie, 1855; transcriptions, 1871.

75: Buell, William. Originals, 1833–34; transcripts, 1781–1906; typescripts, 1833–40.

82: Rébellion de 1837. Originaux, 1837; transcription, 1837.

125: Coursol, Charles-Joseph. Originaux, 1846–83.

126: Quesnel, Frédéric-Auguste. Originals, 1782–1856.

C: Correspondents of political figures

4: Thompson, Sir John Sparrow. Originals, 1819–67.

10: Graham, Christopher H. Originals, 1834, 1837–39.

16: Sadlier, James. Originals, 1855–68.

19: Ogden, Charles S. Originals, 1861–68.

24: Têtu, Félix. Original, 1850.

31: Smith, Sir Henry. Photocopy, 1857.

34: Benjamin, George. Photocopies, 1858–61.

D: Industry, commerce, and finance

8: Wright family. Originals, 1792–1864; photocopies, 1834–35; transcripts, 1837–76; typescripts, 1806; microfilm, 1816–62.

11: Phoenix Assurance Company. Photocopies, 1808–46.

16: Buchanan, Isaac, and family. Originals, 1813–83; microfilm, 1697–1896.

18: Whyte, James Matthew. Originals, 1817–42, 1918–21.

24: Bethune, Donald. Originals, 1821–53.

36: Glyn Mills and Company. Originals, 1838–81; transcripts, 1851–66; microfilm, 1838–74.

E: Transportation

1: Merritt, William Hamilton, and family. Originals, 1775–1897; microfilm, 1780–1873.

F: Military and naval figures

29: Communications and settlement. Originals, 1819–22.

71: Warre, Henry James. Originals, 1819–57.

87: Townshend, Henry Dives. Originals, 1654–1920.

G: Militia

20: Gourlay, William. Originals, 1795–1904.

33: Askin, John B. Originals, 1838, 1840.

45: Salaberry, famille de. Originaux, 1737–1880; transcriptions, 1775–1819; photocopies, 1748–58.

I: Immigration, land, and settlement

9: Hill collection. Originals, 1798–1942.

25: Gilkison family. Originals, 1808–57, 1906.

26: Hamilton, Alexander. Originals, 1792, 1802–44; transcripts, 1809, 1858, 1927, n.d.

40: Sparks, Nicholas, and family. Photocopies, 1844, 1849; microfilm, 1821–92.

47: Jarvis, William Botsford. Originals, 1826–51; transcripts, 1832–36.

69: Stikeman, Alfred. Originals, 1837–38.

75: Secord, Laura. Original, [1840].

107: O'Connor, Daniel. Originals, 1824–1901.

119: Joly, Pierre-Gustave. Microfilm, 1804–65.

J: Religious figures
    1: Strachan, John. Originals, 1820–38; transcripts, 1812; typescript, 1861; microfilm, 1794–1891.
    14: King, William. Originals, 1836–95; microfilm, 1849–95.

K: Education and cultural development
    2: Coventry, George. Originals, 1783–1884; transcripts, 1759–1862.
    11: Ogden, Charles Richard. Originals, c. 1830.

MG 26: Papers of the prime ministers
A: Macdonald, Sir John Alexander. Originals, 1809–1914; photocopy, 1969; typescripts, 1967.
D: Thompson, Sir John Sparrow David. Originals, 1867–95.
F: Tupper, Sir Charles. Originals, 1821–1919, 1958.

MG 27: Political figures, 1867–1950
I: 1867–96
A: Secretaries of state for the colonies
    4: Kimberley, John Wodehouse, 1st Earl. Microfilm, 1865–92.
D: Cabinet ministers
    15: Tilley, Sir Samuel Leonard. Originals, 1801–95; photocopies, 1864–65.
E: Members of the House of Commons and the Senate
    9: McGee, Thomas D'Arcy. Originals, 1862–1954; microfilm, 1841–73; transcripts, 1865.
    10A: Murphy, Edward. Originals, 1880–91.
    12: O'Donohoe, John. Originals, n.d., 1859–85; transcripts, n.d., 1859–61.
    32: Kierzkowski, Alexandre-Édouard. Originaux, 1823–1958.
H: Consuls

1: Archibald, Sir Edward Mortimer. Originals, 1800–1923; photocopies, 1865–66; transcripts, 1830–80.
II: 1896–1921
D: Cabinet ministers
    10: Lemieux, Rodolphe. Originaux, 1874–1974.
III: 1921–50
B: Cabinet ministers
    8: Murphy, Charles. Originals, 1863–1935; photocopy, 1869; transcripts, 1857–69.

MG 29: Nineteenth century post-confederation manuscripts
C: Social
    86: Sellar family. Originals, 1863–1911; photocopies, 1863–1947.
D: Cultural
    15: Moylan, James. Originals, 1857–91; photocopies, 1896–1931.
    61: Morgan, Henry James. Originals, 1855–1935; photocopies, 1855–95.
E: Professional and public life
    29: Denison, George Taylor III. Originals, 1847–1928, 1936, 1947.
    34: Kerr, John Andrew. Originals, 1869–1940.

MG 30: Twentieth century manuscripts
D: Education and cultural development
    58: Roy, Pierre-Georges. Originaux, c. 1915–23; photocopie, 1917.
    62: Audet, Francis-Joseph. Originaux, 1907–42.
    111: Underhill, Frank Hawkins. Originals, 1896–1971.
    159: Tweed, Tommy. Originals, 1885–1971.

RG 1: Executive Council, Canada, 1764–1867
E: State records
    1: Minute books (state matters). Originals, 1764–1867; certified typed copies, 1764–91.
    3: Upper Canada state papers. Originals, 1791–1841.
    7: Submissions to council. Originals, 1841–67.
L: Land records
    1: Minute books (land matters). Originals, 1787–1867.
    3: Upper Canada and Canada, petitions. Originals, 1791–1867.
    3^L: Quebec and Lower Canada, petitions. Originals, 1764–1842.

RG 3: Post Office Department
    1: Deputy Postmaster General T. A. Stayner's correspondence, 1841–51
    9: Miscellaneous records, 1807–1921

RG 4: Civil and provincial secretaries' offices, Quebec, Lower Canada, and Canada East
  A: Civil secretary's correspondence, 1760–1841
    1: Series. Originals, 1760–1840.
  B: Office records, 1763–1867
    8: Petitions for notaries' and advocates' commissions. Originals, 1760–1841.
    12: Lists of executive and legislative councillors, 1829–32
    15: Land records, 1831–64
    28: Bonds, licences, and certificates, 1763–1867
    30: School records, 1768–1856
    46: Miscellaneous records relating to Lord Selkirk's colony and the Red River disturbances, 1815–21
    72: Election records, Lower Canada and Canada East, 1792–1866
  C: Provincial secretary's correspondence, 1765–1867
    1: Numbered correspondence files, 1839–67
    2: Letterbooks, Quebec, Lower Canada, 1765–71, 1812–19, 1828–65
RG 5: Civil and provincial secretaries' offices, Upper Canada and Canada West
  A: Civil secretary's office, 1791–1840
    1: Upper Canada sundries, 1766–1840
  B: Miscellaneous records, 1788–1866
    9: Bonds, licences, and certificates, 1803–67
    30: Records of the commission of inquiry into the state of the public departments, 1839–40
    36: Records of the London District magistrates relating to the treason hearings, 1837–38
    41: Court martial proceedings, Fort Henry, U.C., 1838–39
  C: Provincial secretary's correspondence, 1821–67
    1: Numbered correspondence files, 1821–67
    4: Miscellaneous correspondence, 1840–59
RG 7: Governor general's office
  G1: Dispatches from the Colonial Office, 1784–1909
  G6: Dispatches from the British minister at Washington, 1815–1909
  G8: Records from the lieutenant governors' offices, 1771–1873
    B: New Brunswick, 1784–1867
    C: British Columbia, 1849–72

G9: Drafts of dispatches to the Colonial Office, 1792–1909
  A: Enclosures in dispatches to the Colonial Office, 1838–41, 1861–69
G16: Letterbooks, Upper Canada, 1793–1841
  A: Lieutenant governor's internal letterbooks, 1805–6, 1818–41
  B: Correspondence with the British Treasury, 1793–1834
  C: Civil secretary's letterbooks, 1799–1840
G20: Civil secretary's correspondence, 1841–1909
G23: Miscellaneous records relating to royal visits and vice-regal tours, 1860–1959
RG 8: British military and naval records
  I: C series (British military records)
  IV: Records of the Court of Vice-Admiralty, Halifax, 1784–1818
RG 9: Department of Militia and Defence, 1776–1922
  I: Pre-confederation records
  A: Adjutant general's office, Lower Canada, 1776–1847
    1: Correspondance, 1777–1847
    3: Ordres généraux, 1805–46
    5: Registres des officiers, 1808–46
    7: Rôles d'engagement et listes de paye de la milice incorporée pour la guerre de 1812, 1812–15
  B: Adjutant general's office, Upper Canada, 1795–1846
    1: Correspondence, 1802–47
    3: General orders, 1809–52
    5: Registers of officers, 1824–47
    7: War of 1812 records, 1812–15
  C: Adjutant general's office, United Canada, 1846–69
    1: Correspondence, 1846–69
    2: Returns, 1846–69
    4: General orders, 1846–68
    6: Register of officers, 1846–69
RG 10: Indian affairs
  A: Administrative records of the imperial government
  1: Records of the governor general and lieutenant governors
    789–92: General administration records, 1787–1836
  2: Records of the superintendent's office
    22–25: Chief superintendent's office correspondence, 1828–1930
    568, 586: Deputy superintendent general's office, letterbooks, 1789–1830
  3: Records of the military
    78–82, 141, 590–610, 655–55a: Secretary and resident agent, Montreal, 1820–57

83–102: Secretary of Indian affairs, Quebec, 1831–41

4: Records of the chief superintendent's office, Upper Canada
124–39: Jarvis correspondence, 1837–45
498–509: Letterbooks, 1829–45

5: Records of the civil secretary's office
263–72: General administration records, 1845–61
510–20: Letterbooks, 1844–61
752–60: Correspondence, 1844–61, abstracts of letters received

6: General office files
116–18: Departmental organization, 1809–60

B: Ministerial administration records
2: Deputy superintendent general's office
273–399: Correspondence, 1862–74
521–27: Letterbooks, 1862–67
722–24: Reports and statements, 1862–74

C: Field office records
I: Superintendency records
1: Central (Toronto) superintendency
405–35: Correspondence, 1845–79
532–66: Letterbooks, 1845–83

3: Northern (Manitowaning) superintendency
572–79: Letterbooks, 1846–77
612–19: Correspondence, 1822–96
620–21a: General administration files, 1846–72
691: Accounts, 1837–45

RG 11: Department of Public Works
(This record group has been reorganized and parts transferred to other record groups. Conversion lists for all references are available at the PAC.)

RG 16: Department of National Revenue
A: Customs
1: Correspondence and returns, Upper Canada, 1790–1841
4: Miscellaneous records, 1843–1934
5: Port records, 1795–1956

RG 17: Department of Agriculture
A: To 1920
I: Records of the minister, deputy minister, and secretary
1: Numbered correspondence
2: General letterbooks
III: Immigration Branch
1: Unnumbered correspondence and subject files

RG 19: Department of Finance
E: Departmental correspondence, 1840–1969

5: Records relating to committees, commissions, etc.
3769–4004: Rebellion losses, 1839–54

RG 30: Canadian National Railways
1–17: Great Western Railway, its predecessors, subsidiaries, and properties, Minutes, 1853–74
18–22: Great Western Railway, its predecessors, subsidiaries, and properties, Capital stock records, 1837–53
388–90: Lake St-Louis and Province Line Railway Company, Capital stock records, 1851–54

RG 31: Statistics Canada
A: Census Division
1: Census records, 1825–71

RG 42: Department of Marine
I: Shipping registers, 1787–1966

RG 68: Department of the Registrar General
1: Registration of proclamations, commissions, letters patent, warrants, and other instruments issued under the great seal of Canada
General index, 1651–1841
General index, 1841–67
4: Originals of registered documents, 1764–1975
A: Documents registered

PUBLIC ARCHIVES OF NOVA SCOTIA, Halifax. Founded in 1857 by the Nova Scotian government in order to preserve and arrange "the ancient records and documents illustrative of the History and progress of Society in this province," the PANS is the oldest provincial archives in Canada. The present fireproof building was officially opened on 14 Jan. 1931, and records were transferred from various government departments. The archives also contains court papers, municipal records, family and business papers, collections of societies such as the Nova Scotia Historical Society, community and church records, microfilm copies of deeds and wills from county registries and courts of probate, and a collection of Nova Scotian newspapers. For further information *see* C. B. Fergusson, *The Public Archives of Nova Scotia* (PANS *Bull.*, 19, Halifax, 1963). For a further description of the collections see *Catalogue or list of manuscript documents, arranged, bound and catalogued under the direction of the commissioner of public records . . .* (Halifax, 1877; 2nd ed., 1886). *Inventory of manuscripts in the Public Archives of Nova Scotia* was published in 1976.
Materials used include:

MG 1: Papers of families and individuals
817–63: Thomas Brenton Smith papers
MG 2: Political figures
724–25: George R. Young
731–82: Sir William Young papers. Business, politics, legal documents, 1814–86.
MG 3: Business papers
154: Halifax Fire Insurance Company papers
MG 4: Churches and communities
18: Cornwallis Township records
MG 5: Cemeteries
MG 12: Great Britain – Army
HQ: Headquarters Halifax
24–43: General orders, 1823–52
MG 20: Societies
61–70: Charitable Irish Society, Halifax. Minutes, accounts, miscellaneous, 1786–1944.
98: Guysborough Temperance and Total Abstinence Society. Minutes and list of members, 1843–60.
179/1: Halifax Visiting Dispensary. Minutes, 1855–87.
181: Halifax Medical Society. Minutes, 1853–61, 1861–68.
RG 1: Miscellaneous government documents which had been arranged in bound volumes
60–110: Dispatches from the secretary of state to the governors of Nova Scotia. Originals, 1800–67.
111–28: Dispatches from the governors of Nova Scotia to the secretary of state. Letterbook copies, 1808–67.
175–76: Commission books. July 1835–December 1853.
186–203: Executive Council. Minutes. Originals, 1749–1916.
209–14½: Executive Council. Minutes. Transcripts, 1749–1867.
224–65: Miscellaneous. January 1788–August 1855.
286–98: Legislative Council. Petitions, reports, resolutions, and miscellaneous papers. Originals, 1760–1833.
301–14: House of Assembly. Papers. Originals, 1758–1841.
414: City of Halifax. Miscellaneous records, 1790–1866.
449: Census of Nova Scotia, 1838
451: Census of Halifax County, 1851
455–57½: Nova Scotia railways, 1835–67
458–65½: Miscellaneous material on coal, gold, and iron in Nova Scotia and Cape Breton. Transcripts, 1800–68.

501A: Vice-Admiralty Court, Halifax. List of vessels captured, 1814–18.
RG 5: Records of the Legislative Assembly of Nova Scotia
GP: Governor's petitions, 1780–1891
P: Petitions, 1816–1926
R: Reports and resolutions, 1816–96
RG 7: Provincial secretary's papers
1–140: Letters received, 1804–1920
RG 14: Education and schools
RG 20: Lands and Forests
A: Land grants and petitions
B: Cape Breton
C: Land papers
RG 21: Mines and mining in Nova Scotia
A: Coal mines, gold mines, iron mines. General correspondence, reports and returns, petitions, leases and miscellaneous. 1795–1913.
M: Mines, mining, and mineral resources. Miscellaneous. Microfilm, 1827–1966.
RG 31: Treasury, finance, and economics
RG 32: Vital statistics
RG 34: General Sessions of the Peace
RG 35: Municipalities
A: Assessment records
RG 39: Supreme Court
J: Judgement books
7–80: 1784–1865

PUBLIC ARCHIVES OF PRINCE EDWARD ISLAND, Charlottetown. The PAPEI was created by an act of the Legislative Assembly which received royal assent in 1964, and is located in the Confederation Centre of the Arts, Charlottetown. Records received from various government offices and material that had been stored in Province House formed the nucleus of the collection. Funds for the operation of the archives are provided by an annual vote of the Legislature, the archives being a division of the Department of the Provincial Secretary.

Materials used in the preparation of volume IX include:
Central Academy, Minute book, 1834–56
Port Hill papers, 1822–47
Prince Edward Island
RG 1: Lieutenant governor, Commission books, 1790–1955
RG 5: Executive Council, Minutes, 1770–1959
RG 6.1: Courts, Supreme Court, 1778–1938
RG 6.2: Courts, Probate Court, 1806–1900. Microfilm.
RG 9: Collector of customs, Shipping registers, 1815–50. Microfilm.
RG 15: Commissioners of crown and public

lands, T. H. Haviland rent books, 1845–69

RG 16: Registry Office, Land registry records, 1767–1900

QUEBEC DIOCESAN ARCHIVES, Quebec. The collection and organization of the documents in this archives was begun by the Reverend H. C. Stuart early in the 20th century and continued from 1930 to 1940 by the Reverend A. R. Kelley. The ANQ-Q and the Church Society of the diocese of Quebec now each hold a part of this material. The archives contains documents concerning the history of the Anglican diocese of Quebec, dating from its creation in 1793, including letters patent, consecration records and papers of the bishops, correspondence relating to parishes and various associations and institutions of the diocese, and a considerable number of miscellaneous individual documents. The archives also has copies of letters and documents concerning the diocese (1759–1864) which are in England, and two important sections of printed material. For a fuller description of the archives *see*: A. R. Kelley, "The Quebec Diocesan Archives; a description of the collection of historical records of the Church of England in the Diocese of Quebec," ANQ *Rapport*, 1946–47, 181–298; A. M. Awcock, "Catalogue of the Quebec Diocesan Archives" (roneo copy at the archives, Shawinigan, Que., 1973).

The following were used in the preparation of volume IX:

Section A: Letters patent and records of consecration of bishops, 1793–1935

Section B: Parishes of the Diocese of Quebec, 1793–1885
50 (B-4), Drummondville
53 (B-7), Hatley
56 (B-10), Levis
68 (B-22), Sherbrooke
70 (B-24), Three Rivers

Section C: Correspondence of Right Reverend Jacob Mountain, 1792–1845
80 (C-9), 1818–21
81 (C-10), 1822–45

Section D: Copies of letters and papers referring to Diocese of Quebec, 1759–1864
91 (D-10), 1826–28
92 (D-11), 1829–30
94 (D-13), 1833–35
96 (D-15), 1838–40
97 (D-16), 1841–42
100 (D-20), 1846

Section G: Institutions of the diocese, 16 vols., 1800–73
114 (G-8), Travelling missionaries

118 (G-12), Education
119 (G-13), Red River
120 (G-14), Church Society
121 (G-15), List of deeds, acts, synods and other papers
122 (G-16), Synod of the Diocese of Quebec

Section Unbound manuscripts, 3 cases, 23 folders, 1798–1905
Case 2, folder 13: Mountain papers

QUEEN'S UNIVERSITY ARCHIVES, Kingston, Ont. During the past century the QUA has developed as a non-governmental repository with collections of private papers and records of national significance. Its holdings include the records of Queen's University from its founding in 1841, the personal papers of noted faculty members and of Canadians prominent in literature, politics, journalism, and business, and many family and business records pertaining to eastern Ontario. The official archives of the City of Kingston are also housed in this repository.

Materials used in the preparation of volume IX include:

John Solomon Cartwright papers, 1822–64
Kingston Town Council proceedings, 1838–45
Kingston City Council Proceedings, 1846–66
Thomas Kirkpatrick papers
Kirkpatrick-Nickle legal records
William Morris papers, 1823–53
Queen's records
A: Founding material
3: Doomsday book
B: Queen's letters
D: Board of Trustees
1: Minutes of the Board of Trustees
6: Accounts

UNITED CHURCH ARCHIVES, Toronto. During the 19th century, archival collections were assembled by the various Canadian Methodist and Presbyterian bodies, usually in the libraries of their colleges. Materials were also gathered at the Methodist Publishing House, and some foreign mission correspondence was collected at the Presbyterian Foreign Mission Office. Most of this material is now part of the United Church Archives. The largest part of this collection is at the Central Archives of the United Church, Victoria University, Toronto.

The Central Archives collection is national in scope and contains the official records of the boards and departments of the various denominations now merged into the United Church of Canada; copies of denominational publications; monographs and pamphlets published by the various denominations (or relating to them); papers of prominent ministers; some parish records; pictures of ministers, churches, home and foreign missions; tapes of oral history interviews; published parish histories and minutes of the various boards and administrative courts of the denominations concerned. Material of local interest and official records of the Conferences concerned are housed in regional Conference Archives.

Materials used in volume IX include:

Robert Burns papers

Canada Presbyterian Church, Minutes of the Synod, 1861–66

Glasgow Colonial Society, correspondence, 1825–40

Methodist Episcopal Church in Canada, General Conference, addresses, correspondence and reports, 1848–83; journals, 1835–83

Mission register for the Credit River Mission, 1836–67

Presbyterian Church of Canada, Minutes of the Synod, 1844–61

Presbyterian Church of Canada in connexion with the Church of Scotland, Minutes of the Synod, 1833–44

UNIVERSITY OF NEW BRUNSWICK LIBRARY, ARCHIVES AND SPECIAL COLLECTIONS DEPARTMENT, Fredericton. The department was established in 1939 by Dr A. G. Bailey, head of the History Department. At that time there was no provincial archives and he was embarking on a programme of research into the history of the Maritime provinces. He obtained a Rockefeller Grant in 1943 to aid in the purchase of relevant books, papers, and manuscripts; these materials, along with what university records were retrievable, constituted the nucleus from which the holdings of the department have grown.

Materials used in volume IX include:

BC-MS: Beaverbrook Collection
  Douglas, Sir Howard (1776–1861), letterbooks, 1812–41
MG H: Historical
  H 2: Winslow family papers, 1695–1815
  H 9: Maxwell, Lillian Mary Beckwith (1877–1956), papers, 1784–1951
  H10: Tilley, Sir Samuel Leonard (1818–96), correspondence and papers, 1852–70
  H12a: Gordon, Sir Arthur Hamilton, 1st Baron Stanmore (1829–1912), papers, 1861–66
UA: University Archives
  RG62: Robb, James, correspondence, 1837–64
  King's College, College Council, minute books, 1829–51

UNIVERSITY OF TORONTO, THOMAS FISHER RARE BOOK LIBRARY, RARE BOOKS AND SPE-

CIAL COLLECTIONS DEPARTMENT. The Rare Books and Special Collections Department was established late in 1955 and in 1973 was housed in the new Thomas Fisher Rare Book Library building. In addition to printed material, it has from the beginning held manuscript collections as well as individual manuscripts. Although the major collections are private papers of Canadian origin, there are manuscripts of European origin from documents of the 4th century to authors' corrected typescripts of the 20th century. For a more extensive description of holdings see *The Thomas Fisher Rare Book Library: a brief guide to the collections* ([Toronto], 1974).

Materials consulted in the preparation of volume IX include:

MS coll. 56: MacNab, Sir Allan Napier (1798–1862), papers
MS coll. 78: Elmsley, John (1801–63), papers
  MSS 144: Pearson, William Henry (1831–1920), holograph necrology, 1853–1920

UNIVERSITY OF WESTERN ONTARIO, D. B. WELDON LIBRARY, London, Ont. The library is the official depository for the Archives of the Society of Friends in Canada. The deposit of their papers began in 1926 and constituted the first major set of papers in the collection founded by Dr Fred Landon* and continued by Dr J. J. Talman and Dr Robert Lee. The Regional History Department was formally organized in 1942 with Elsie McL. Murray (Mrs W. W. Jury) as head. It is now called the Regional Collection and it has formed a comprehensive archives on southwestern Ontario. Major holdings include court, educational, and municipal records for several counties centring on London; records of business firms; records of societies and organizations; and personal, political, or literary papers of local personalities.

Major collections used in the preparation of volume IX include:

128: George J. Goodhue papers
Archives of the Religious Society of Friends (Quakers) in Canada
  H–7–2: Pelham Monthly Meeting of Friends, 1799–1806
  0–11–6: Yonge Street Monthly Meeting, 1806–18

GREAT BRITAIN

CHURCH MISSIONARY SOCIETY ARCHIVES, London. The CMS, founded in 1799, was first active in Canada in 1820 when it provided financial support for a minister in the Red River Settlement; thereafter its activities in the west expanded until they reached the Pacific in 1857. As the Anglican church in Canada grew and developed its own missionary activity the society gradually relinquished its control, and by 1920 all branches of CMS work had been merged with the Canadian missionary society. For copies of materials in the PAC see *General inventory, manuscripts, 3: MG 17–MG 21* (Ottawa, 1974).

The following were consulted in the preparation of volume IX:
Committee minutes
North-West America mission
  Colonial ordination
  Letters to home secretaries, 1822–74
  London correspondence outwards, 1821–60
  Letters of David Anderson, 1849–64
  Letters and journals of William Cockran, 1825–65
  Letters of Robert James, 1846–51
  Journal of the Reverend William Mason, 10 Sept. 1854–28 Aug. 1858
  Letters and journals of John Smithurst, 1839–51

PUBLIC RECORD OFFICE, London. For an introduction to the contents and arrangement of this archives see *Guide to the contents of the Public Record Office* (3v., London, 1963–68). For copies of Colonial Office documents available at the PAC see *Preliminary inventory, manuscript group 11* . . . (Ottawa, 1961).

Materials cited in volume IX include:
Admiralty
  Accounting departments
    Ships' musters
      Adm. 36: Series I (1688–1808)
      Adm. 37: Series II (1804–42)
    Admiralty and Secretariat
      Adm. 1: Papers (1660–1962)
    Registers, returns, and certificates
      Adm. 8: List books (1673–1893)
      Adm. 9: Returns of officers' services (1817–1822 and 1846)
Colonial Office. [*See* R. B. Pugh, *The records of the Colonial and Dominions offices* (PRO handbooks, 3, London, 1964).]
  British Columbia
    CO 60: Original correspondence (1858–71)
  Canada
    CO 42: Original correspondence (1700–1922)
    CO 43: Entry books (1763–1872)
    CO 537: Original correspondence, supplementary (1842–98)

New Brunswick
  CO 188: Original correspondence (1784–1867)
  CO 189: Entry books (1769–1867)
  CO 193: Miscellanea (1786–1865)
Newfoundland
  CO 194: Original correspondence (1696–1922)
  CO 195: Entry books (1623–1867)
  CO 199: Miscellanea (1677–1903)
Nova Scotia and Cape Breton
  CO 217: Original correspondence (1710–1867)
Prince Edward Island
  CO 226: Original correspondence (1769–1873)
  CO 227: Entry books (1769–1872)
  CO 231: Miscellanea (1807–71)
Vancouver Island
  CO 305: Original correspondence (1846–67)
Confidential print
  CO 880: North America ([1677]–1913)
Exchequer and Audit Department
  AO 2: Declared and passed accounts (In books) (1803–48)
Foreign Office. [See *Records of the Foreign Office, 1782–1939* (PRO handbooks, 13, 1969).]
  General correspondence
    FO 5: America, United States of. Series II (1793–1905).
Public Record Office
  Documents acquired by gift, deposit, or purchase
    PRO 30/22: Russell papers
Board of Trade
  Records of the registrar general of shipping and seamen
    BT 107: Transcripts and transactions, series I
    BT 108: Transcripts and transactions, series II: transcripts
    BT 109: Transcripts and transactions, series III: transactions
Treasury
  Out-letters
    T 28: Various (1763–1885)
War Office
  Correspondence
    WO 1: In-letters (1732–1868)
    WO 7: Out-letters: departmental (1715–1862)
  Returns
    WO 12: Muster books and pay lists: general (1732–1878)
    WO 17: Monthly returns (1759–1865)
    WO 25: Registers, various (1660–1938)

882

WO 42: Certificates of birth, etc.
(1755–1908)
WO 76: Officers' services, records of
(1755–1954)
Private collections
WO 80: Murray papers (1804–59)
Ordnance Office
WO 44: In-letters (1682–1873)
WO 54: Registers (1594–1871)
WO 55: Miscellanea (1568–1923)
Commissariat Department
WO 61: Registers (1791–1889)

UNITED SOCIETY FOR THE PROPAGATION OF THE GOSPEL, London. Formed in 1965 the USPG is responsible for continuing work formerly carried on by the Society for the Propagation of the Gospel in Foreign Parts (incorporated by royal charter, 1701) and the Universities' Mission to Central Africa (founded 1857). The archives is in the process of reorganizing and reclassifying some material. Thus classifications used by Canadian archives holding USPG microfilm do not always correspond to those of the archives itself. Indexes are available at USPG, however, and most dated references are easily transferred. For copies of USPG archives documents in the PAC see *General inventory, manuscripts, 3: MG 17–MG 21* (Ottawa, 1974).

The following were consulted:

Journal of proceedings of the Society for the Propagation of the Gospel. Comprises bound and indexed volumes of the proceedings of the general meetings held in London from 1701, and four appendices, A, B, C, D (1701–1860).

C/CAN: Unbound letters from Canada, 1752–1860. Letters from Newfoundland, Nova Scotia, Quebec, and Toronto groupings were used. Nominal card index is available at USPG.

D: Original letters received from 1850, bound in volumes. Handlist of writers and places, not alphabetical, available at USPG.

E: Reports from SPG missionaries from 1856, bound in volumes. Handlist available at USPG.

II. PRINTED PRIMARY SOURCES

A. OFFICIAL PUBLICATIONS AND CONTEMPORARY WORKS

ARCHIVES DU SÉMINAIRE DE QUÉBEC, Québec.
PUBLICATIONS
II: *Le séminaire de Québec* (Provost).
ARCHIVES NATIONALES DU QUÉBEC.
PUBLICATIONS [*See also* section III.]
Rapport. Documents and inventories from the ANQ – as well as from other archives – have been published in the *Rapport.* Volumes correspond to the fiscal years for 1920–21 to 1948–49 and 1959–60; those for the years 1949–51 to 1957–59 include two years; no volumes were published for 1961 or 1962, but publication was resumed in 1963. There is an index to the contents of the first 42 volumes: *Table des matières des rapports des Archives du Québec, tomes 1 à 42 (1920–1964)* (1965).
The Arthur papers; being the Canadian papers mainly confidential, private, and demi-official of Sir George Arthur, K.C.H., last lieutenant-governor of Upper Canada, in the manuscript collection of the Toronto Public Libraries. Edited by Charles Rupert Sanderson. 3 vols. Toronto, 1957–59.
BAS-CANADA. *See* LOWER CANADA
[BEGG, ALEXANDER.] *Alexander Begg's Red River journal and other papers relative to the Red River resistance of 1869–1870.* Edited with an introduction by William Lewis Morton. (Champlain Society publications, XXXIV.) Toronto, 1956.

CANADA
HOUSE OF COMMONS/CHAMBRE DES COMMUNES
House of Commons debates/Débats de la chambre des Communes, used for 1867–70.
Journals of the House of Commons of the Dominion of Canada . . ./Journaux de la chambre des Communes de la puissance du Canada . . . , 1867–70.
PARLIAMENT/PARLEMENT
Sessional papers . . . of the dominion of Canada/Documents de la session . . . de la puissance du Canada, from 1867–68 to 1872, and 1911.

CANADA, PROVINCE OF
LEGISLATIVE ASSEMBLY/ASSEMBLÉE LÉGISLATIVE
Journals of the Legislative Assembly of the Province of Canada/Journaux de l'Assemblée législative de la province du Canada, 1841–66.

General index to the "Journals of the Legislative Assembly" of Canada; in the 1st, 2nd, and 3rd parliaments, 1841–1851. Compiled by Alfred Todd. Montreal, 1855; reprinted, Washington, 1972.

General index to the "Journals of the Legislative Assembly" of Canada; in the 4th, 5th, 6th, 7th and 8th parliaments, 1852–1866. Compiled by Alfred Todd. Ottawa, 1867; reprinted, Washington, 1972. For the debates of the Legislative Assembly for the union period, see *Debates of the Legislative Assembly of United Canada* (Gibbs *et al.*).

LEGISLATIVE COUNCIL/CONSEIL LÉGISLATIF

Journals of the Legislative Council of the Province of Canada/Journaux du Conseil législatif de la province du Canada, 1841–66.

PARLIAMENT/PARLEMENT

Parliamentary debates on the subject of the confederation of the British North American provinces, 3rd session, 8th provincial parliament of Canada/Débats parlementaires sur la question de la confédération des provinces de l'Amérique britannique du Nord, 3e session, 8e parlement provincial du Canada. Quebec, 1865; the *Parliamentary debates* were reprinted at Ottawa in 1951.

Sessional papers . . . of the Province of Canada/Documents de la session . . . de la province du Canada, from XVIII (1860) to XXVI (1866). Volumes I (1841) to XVII (1859) were published as appendices to the *Journals* of the Legislative Assembly and Legislative Council of the Province of Canada. For the parliamentary debates from 1846 to 1874, *see* "Parliamentary debates."

Statutes of the Province of Canada . . . /Statuts de la province du Canada . . . , 1841–66.

PUBLICATIONS

For a complete, critical bibliography of the publications of the Province of Canada, *see* section IV: Bishop, *Pubs. of the government of the Prov. of Can.*

Canada Gazette. Kingston, Montreal, Toronto, Quebec, and Ottawa. Official publication of the government of the Province of Canada published weekly from 2 Oct. 1841 to 26 June 1869. The journal moved to follow the seat of government.

The Canadian North-West, its early development and legislative records; minutes of the councils of the Red River colony and the Northern Department of Rupert's Land. Edited by Edmund Henry Oliver. (PAC publications, 9.) 2 vols. Ottawa, 1914–15.

CHAMPLAIN SOCIETY. "Founded in 1905, with headquarters in Toronto, for the purpose of publishing rare and inaccessible materials relating to the history of Canada. Its publications are issued only to elected members, limited in number. . . ." [*See also* HUDSON'S BAY RECORD SOCIETY.]

PUBLICATIONS

XII: Thompson, *Narrative* (Tyrrell).

XIII–XV, XVII: *Select British documents of the Canadian War of 1812* (Wood).

XXII: *Documents relating to NWC* (Wallace).

XXIV: *Hargrave correspondence* (Glazebrook).

XXVIII: Mactavish, *Letters of Letitia Hargrave* (MacLeod).

XXXIII: *Dufferin-Carnarvon correspondence* (de Kiewiet and Underhill).

XXXIV: Begg, *Red River journal* (Morton).

XL: Thompson, *Narrative* (Glover).

XLIV: *Papers of Palliser expedition* (Spry).

XLV: Franchère, *Journal of a voyage* (Lamb).

CHAMPLAIN SOCIETY. ONTARIO SERIES. The Champlain Society was invited by the Ontario government to prepare and publish a series of documentary volumes "to preserve in printed form . . . a representative selection of the more interesting and significant records of the past . . . ." This series is sold through normal publishing channels.

PUBLICATIONS

I: *Valley of the Trent* (Guillet).

V: *Town of York, 1793–1815* (Firth).

VI: *Muskoka and Haliburton* (Murray).

VIII: *Town of York, 1815–1834* (Firth).

Debates of the Legislative Assembly of United Canada. Elizabeth Gibbs *et al.* 6 vols. in 8 to date. Montreal, 1970– . In progress.

Documentary history of education in Upper Canada from the passing of the Constitutional Act of 1791 to the close of Rev. Dr. Ryerson's administration of the Education Department in 1876. Edited by John George Hodgins. 28 vols. Toronto, 1894–1910.

Documents relating to the constitutional history of Canada. . . . Selected and edited with notes by Adam Shortt *et al.* (PAC publication.) 3 vols. Ottawa, 1907–35.

[II]: *1791–1818.* Edited by Arthur George Doughty and Duncan A. McArthur.

[III]: *1819–1828.* Edited by Arthur George Doughty and Norah Story.

Documents relating to the North West Company.

Edited with introduction, notes, and appendices by William Stewart Wallace. (Champlain Society publications, XXII.) Toronto, 1934.

Dufferin-Carnarvon correspondence, 1874–1878. Edited by Cornelis Willem de Kiewiet and Frank Hawkins Underhill. (Champlain Society publications, XXXIII.) Toronto, 1955.

The Elgin-Grey papers, 1846–1852. Edited with notes and appendices by Arthur George Doughty. (PAC publication.) 4 vols. Ottawa, 1937.

FENETY, GEORGE EDWARD. *Political notes and observations; or, a glance at the leading measures that have been introduced and discussed in the House of Assembly of New Brunswick. . . .* Fredericton, 1867.

FRANCHÈRE, GABRIEL. *Journal of a voyage on the north west coast of North America during the years 1811, 1812, 1813 and 1814.* Transcribed and translated by Wessie Tipping Lamp; edited with an introduction and notes by William Kaye Lamb. (Champlain Society publications, XLV.) Toronto, 1969.

Gentleman's Magazine, London. Published from January 1731 to September 1907. Monthly. Title varies. Volume numbering irregular.

GREAT BRITAIN, PARLIAMENT, HOUSE OF COMMONS PAPER, 1857 (session II) XV, 224, 260 (whole volume). *Report from the select committee on the Hudson's Bay Company; together with the proceedings of the committee, minutes of evidence, appendix and index.*

HARGRAVE, LETITIA. *See* MACTAVISH

The Hargrave correspondence, 1821–1843. Edited with introduction and notes by George Parkin de Twenebrokes Glazebrook. (Champlain Society publications, XXIV.) Toronto, 1938.

HINCKS, FRANCIS. *Reminiscences of his public life*. Montreal, 1884.

[HOWE, JOSEPH.] *The speeches and public letters of Joseph Howe (based upon Mr. Annand's edition of 1858)*. Revised and edited by Joseph Andrew Chisholm. 2 vols. Halifax, 1909.

HUDSON'S BAY RECORD SOCIETY. Initiated in 1938 by the Hudson's Bay Company after classification of its London archives (now in Winnipeg), which was begun in 1932, had progressed to the point where publication was feasible. Membership in the society is limited.

PUBLICATIONS

General editor for vols. I–XXII, Edwin Ernest Rich; for vols. XXIII–XXV, Kenneth Gordon Davies; for vols. XXVI–XXX, Glyndwr Williams. 30 vols. to date. Vols. I–XII were issued in association with the Champlain Society, Toronto, and reprinted in 1968 at Nendeln, Liechtenstein.

I: [Simpson, George.] *Journal of occurrences in the Athabasca Department by George Simpson, 1820 and 1821, and report*. Edited by Edwin Ernest Rich, with an introduction by Chester [Bailey] Martin. Toronto, 1938.

II: [Robertson, Colin.] *Colin Robertson's correspondence book, September 1817 to September 1822*. Edited with an introduction by Edwin Ernest Rich, assisted by R. Harvey Fleming. Toronto, 1939.

III: *Minutes of Council, Northern Department of Rupert Land, 1821–31*. Edited by R. Harvey Fleming, with an introduction by Harold Adams Innis. Toronto, 1940.

IV: [McLoughlin, John.] *The letters of John McLoughlin from Fort Vancouver to the governor and committee, first series, 1825–38*. Edited by Edwin Ernest Rich, with an introduction by William Kaye Lamb. London, 1941.

VI: [McLoughlin, John.] *The letters of John McLoughlin from Fort Vancouver to the governor and committee, second series, 1839–44*. Edited by Edwin Ernest Rich, with an introduction by William Kaye Lamb. London, 1943.

VII: [McLoughlin, John.] *The letters of John McLoughlin from Fort Vancouver to the governor and committee, third series, 1844–46*. Edited by Edwin Ernest Rich, with an introduction by William Kaye Lamb. London, 1944.

XIX: [Colvile, Eden.] *London correspondence inward from Eden Colvile, 1849–1852*. Edited by Edwin Ernest Rich, assisted by Alice Margaret Johnson, with an introduction by William Lewis Morton. London, 1956.

XXI–XXII: Rich, *History of HBC*. [*See* section IV.]

XXIV: *Northern Quebec and Labrador journals and correspondence, 1819–35*. Edited by Kenneth Gordon Davies, assisted by Alice Margaret Johnson, with an introduction by Glyndwr Williams. London, 1963.

XXVI: *Saskatchewan journals and correspondence; Edmonton House, 1795–1800, Chesterfield House, 1800–1802*. Edited with an introduction by Alice Margaret Johnson. London, 1967.

XXX: *Hudson's Bay miscellany, 1670–1870*. Edited with introductions by Glyndwr Williams. Winnipeg, 1975.

Journal de l'Instruction publique, Quebec and Montreal. Monthly. I (1857) – XXIII (1879).

Official publication of the Department of Public Instruction, published variously at Quebec and Montreal. It must not be confused with the *Journal of Education for Lower Canada* which is also an official publication of the same department. They were completely independent journals, and neither was a translation of the other.

Journal of Education for Ontario, Toronto. Monthly. I (January 1848) – XXX (1877). Official publication of the province's Department of Education, it began as the *Journal of Education for Upper Canada*. Title changed in 1867.

LOWER CANADA/BAS CANADA

HOUSE OF ASSEMBLY/CHAMBRE D'ASSEMBLÉE
Journals of the House of Assembly of Lower-Canada/Journaux de la chambre d'Assemblée du Bas-Canada, 1792–1837.

SPECIAL COUNCIL/CONSEIL SPÉCIAL
Journals of the Special Council of the province of Lower-Canada/Journaux du Conseil spécial de la province du Bas-Canada, 1838–41.

Ordinances made and passed by the administrator of the government and Special Council for the affairs of the province of Lower-Canada/Ordonnances faites et passées par son Excellence le gouverneur général et le Conseil spécial pour les affaires de la province du Bas-Canada, 1838–41.

The provincial statutes of Lower-Canada . . . /Status provinciaux du Bas-Canada . . ., 1792–1836.

[MACDONALD, JOHN ALEXANDER.] *The letters of Sir John A. Macdonald, 1836–1857*. Edited by James Keith Johnson. . . . *1858–1861*. Edited by James Keith Johnson and Carole B. Stelmack. (PAC publications, The papers of the prime ministers series, I–II.) Ottawa, 1968–69.

[MACTAVISH, LETITIA.] *The letters of Letitia Hargrave*. Edited with an introduction and notes by Margaret Arnett MacLeod. (Champlain Society publications, XXVIII.) Toronto, 1947.

Mandements, lettres pastorales et circulaires des évêques de Québec. 18 vols. to date. Québec, 1887–   . The first six volumes were edited by Henri Têtu and Charles-Octave Gagnon; no editors are given for later volumes. Volume numbering is peculiar: [1re série], I–IV; nouvelle série [2e série], I–V; nouvelle série [3e série], I–III; a second set of cumulative volume numbers begins with vol. V of the nouvelle série [2e série].

MORRIS, ALEXANDER. *The treaties of Canada with the Indians of Manitoba and the North-West Territories*. . . . Toronto, 1880; reprinted [n.p., 1971].

Muskoka and Haliburton, 1615–1875; a collection of documents. Edited with an introduction by Florence Beatrice Murray. (Champlain Society publications, Ontario series, VI.) Toronto, 1963.

NEW BRUNSWICK

HOUSE OF ASSEMBLY
Journals of the House of Assembly of the province of New Brunswick . . ., used for 1823–68.

NEWFOUNDLAND
Blue books, used for 1828–58.

HOUSE OF ASSEMBLY
Journal of the House of Assembly of Newfoundland . . ., used for 1833–68.

NOVA SCOTIA

GENERAL ASSEMBLY
The Statutes of Nova Scotia, passed in the . . . session of the General Assembly. . . . First called *Acts of the General Assembly of the province of Nova Scotia*. Used for 1845–68.

HOUSE OF ASSEMBLY
Debates and proceedings of the House of Assembly . . . of the province of Nova Scotia, used for 1848–67.

Journal and proceedings of the House of Assembly of the province of Nova Scotia, used for 1824–70.

LEGISLATIVE COUNCIL
Journal of the proceedings of Her Majesty's Legislative Council of the province of Nova Scotia, used for 1848–51.

ONTARIO

LEGISLATIVE ASSEMBLY
Journals of the Legislative Assembly of the province of Ontario . . ., used for 1868–69.
Statutes of the province of Ontario . . ., used for 1869.

The papers of the Palliser expedition, 1857–1860. Edited with an introduction and notes by Irene Mary Spry. (Champlain Society publications, XLIV.) Toronto, 1968.

"Parliamentary debates." Canadian Library Association project to microfilm the debates in the legislature of the Province of Canada and the parliament of Canada for the period 1846–74.

PRINCE EDWARD ISLAND
HOUSE OF ASSEMBLY
Debates and proceedings of the House of Assembly of Prince Edward Island, used for 1855–68.
Journal of the House of Assembly of Prince Edward Island, used for 1830–64.
LEGISLATIVE COUNCIL
Debates and proceedings of the Legislative Council of Prince Edward Island, used for 1859–63.
Debates and proceedings of the Legislative Council of the province of Prince Edward Island, used for 1879.
Journal of the Legislative Council of Prince Edward Island, used for 1839–63.

PUBLIC ARCHIVES OF CANADA, Ottawa.
BOARD OF HISTORICAL PUBLICATIONS
Documents relating to constitutional history, 1791–1818 (Doughty and McArthur).
Documents relating to constitutional history, 1819–28 (Doughty and Story).
NUMBERED PUBLICATIONS [*See also* section III.]
9: *Canadian North-West* (Oliver).
OTHER PUBLICATIONS [*See also* section III.]
Elgin-Grey papers. (Doughty).
THE PAPERS OF THE PRIME MINISTERS SERIES
I: Macdonald, *Letters* (Johnson).
II: Macdonald, *Letters* (Johnson and Stelmack).
Report and *Rapport*. 1881– . Published annually until 1952; irregularly thereafter.

QUEBEC
LEGISLATIVE ASSEMBLY/ASSEMBLÉE LÉGISLATIVE
Journals of the Legislative Assembly of the Province of Quebec/Journaux de l'Assemblée législative de la province de Québec, used for 1867–68 to 1870.
LEGISLATIVE COUNCIL/CONSEIL LÉGISLATIF
Journals of the Legislative Council of the Province of Quebec/Journaux du Conseil législatif de la province de Québec, used for 1868 to 1870.
PUBLICATIONS
For a complete critical bibliography of the publications of the Quebec government, *see* section III: *Répertoire des publ. du Québec* (Beaulieu *et al*.).
DEPARTMENT OF CROWN LANDS/DÉPARTEMENT DES TERRES DE LA COURONNE

LANGELIER, *List of lands granted*. [*See* section III.]
DEPARTMENT OF PUBLIC INSTRUCTION/DÉPARTEMENT DE L'INSTRUCTION PUBLIQUE
JIP.

SCADDING, HENRY. *Toronto of old: collections and recollections illustrative of the early settlement and social life of the capital of Ontario*. Toronto, 1873. Republished as *Toronto of old*. Abridged and edited by Frederick Henry Armstrong. Toronto, 1966.
Select British documents of the Canadian War of 1812. Edited with an introduction by William [Charles Henry] Wood. (Champlain Society publications, XIII–XV, XVII.) 3 vols. in 4. Toronto, 1920–28.
Le séminaire de Québec: documents et biographies. Honorius Provost, éditeur. (ASQ publications, II.) Québec, 1964.
THOMPSON, DAVID. *David Thompson's narrative of his explorations in Western America, 1784–1812*. Edited by Joseph Burr Tyrrell. (Champlain Society publications, XII.) Toronto, 1916; new edition entitled *David Thompson's narrative, 1784–1812*, edited with an introduction and notes by Richard [Gilchrist] Glover. (Champlain Society publications, XL.) Toronto, 1962.
The town of York, 1793–1815: a collection of documents of early Toronto. Edited with an introduction by Edith Grace Firth. (Champlain Society publications, Ontario series, V.) Toronto, 1962.
The town of York, 1815–1834: a further collection of documents of early Toronto. Edited with an introduction by Edith Grace Firth. (Champlain Society publications, Ontario series, VIII.) Toronto, 1966.

UPPER CANADA
HOUSE OF ASSEMBLY
Journal of the House of Assembly of Upper Canada . . . , used for 1820–40.

The valley of the Trent. Edited with an introduction and notes by Edwin Clarence Guillet. (Champlain Society publications, Ontario series, I.) Toronto, 1957.

B. NEWSPAPERS

Numerous sources have been used to determine the various titles of newspapers and their dates of publication. The printed sources include, for all areas of the country: Canadian Library Association, *Canadian newspapers on microfilm*, *catalogue* (2 pts. in 3, Ottawa, 1959–   ); for New Brunswick: J. R. Harper, *Historical directory of New Brunswick newspapers and periodicals* (Fredericton, 1961); for Newfoundland: "Chronological list of Newfoundland newspapers in the public collections at the Gosling Memorial Library and Provincial Archives," comp. Ian McDonald (copy deposited in the Reference Library, Arts and Culture Centre, St John's); for Nova Scotia: D. C. Harvey, "Newspapers of Nova Scotia, 1840–1867," *CHR*, XXVI (1945), 279–301; G. E. N. Tratt, "A survey and listing of Nova Scotian newspapers with particular reference to the period before 1867" (unpublished MA thesis, Mount Allison University, Sackville, N.B., 1957 (copy in PANS)); for Ontario: *Catalogue of Canadian newspapers in the Douglas Library, Queen's University*, comp. L. C. Ellison *et al.* (Kingston, 1969); *Early Toronto newspapers, 1793–1867: a catalogue of newspapers published in the town of York and the city of Toronto from the beginning to confederation*, ed. E. G. Firth (Toronto, 1961); W. S. Wallace, "The periodical literature of Upper Canada," *CHR*, XII (1931), 4–22; for Prince Edward Island: W. L. Cotton, "The press in Prince Edward Island," *Past and present of Prince Edward Island . . .* , ed. D. A. MacKinnon and A. B. Warburton (Charlottetown, [1906]), 112–21; R. L. Cotton, "Early press," *Historic highlights of Prince Edward Island*, ed. M. C. Brehaut (Charlottetown, 1955), 40–45; for Quebec: Beaulieu et Hamelin, *Journaux du Québec* and *La presse québécoise*; and for Manitoba: J. W. Dafoe, "Early Winnipeg Newspapers," HSSM *Papers*, 3rd ser., no. 3 (1947), 14–24.

Acadian Recorder, Halifax. Published from 16 Jan. 1813 until 10 May 1930. The paper was a weekly from 1813 until 27 Aug. 1863, a tri-weekly from 5 Sept. 1863 until 1930, and a daily from 1868 until 1930.

L'Aurore des Canadas, Montréal. Published from 15 Jan. 1839 to 23 March 1849.

L'Avenir, Montréal. Published from 24 June 1847 to 22 Dec. 1857.

British Colonist, Halifax. Its full title initially was *British Colonist: A Literary, Political and Commercial Journal*. Published from 25 July 1848 until 31 Dec. 1874 as a tri-weekly; a weekly was added in January 1849 and a daily edition later. From 11 Sept. 1851 until January 1855, the title was *British Colonist and North American Railway Journal*.

British Colonist, Victoria. See *Colonist*

British Whig, Kingston, Ont. Published from January 1834 to 30 Nov. 1926. Its full title was the *British Whig and General Advertiser for Canada West*, and it was published semi-weekly from 1834 to 1849. On 1 Jan. 1849 it became the *Daily British Whig*, but the semi-weekly continued to 1908.

Canadian Free Press, London, Ont. See *London Free Press*

Le Canadien, Québec. Published from 22 Nov. 1806 to 11 Feb. 1893.

Christian Guardian, Toronto. Published as a weekly at York (Toronto) from 21 Nov. 1829 until 10 June 1925 when it was superseded by the *New Outlook* which ceased publication on 24 Feb. 1939 to be succeeded by the *United Church Observer* on 1 March. A general index of the *Christian Guardian* for the years 1829–67 is available at the United Church Archives, Toronto. A selective index of church news and general historical information is in progress for the period after 1867 and some ten selected years have been completed.

Chronicle & Gazette, Kingston, Ont. Published from 1833 to 1847 as a semi-weekly. Its full name was *Chronicle & Gazette and Kingston Commercial Advertiser* in 1840 when the subtitle was dropped. The newspaper's predecessors were the *Kingston Gazette* (1810–18) and the *Kingston Chronicle* (1819–33), and it was continued after 1847 as the *Chronicle and News*.

Chronicle and News, Kingston, Ont. See *Chronicle & Gazette*; *Daily News*

Chronicle Telegraph. See *Quebec Chronicle Telegraph*

Church, Cobourg, Toronto, and Hamilton, Ont. Published as a weekly from 6 May 1837 to 25 July 1856. Began publication in Cobourg, then moved to Toronto from 11 July 1840 to 14 July 1843 when it returned to Cobourg only to move again to Toronto on 17 July 1846. Between 5 Aug. 1852 and 16 June 1853 the title was the *Canadian Churchman*. Between 3 Aug. 1855 and 25 July 1856 the *Church* was published in Hamilton.

Colonial Advocate, York (Toronto). A weekly, published from 1824 to 1834. Founded at Queenston on 18 May 1824 it moved to York in November. In December 1833 it became the *Advocate* and it amalgamated with the *Canadian Correspondent* to form the *Correspondent and Advocate* in 1834.

Colonist, Victoria. Published under various titles from 11 Dec. 1858 to the present. Until 28 July 1860 the full name was the *British Colonist*; from 31 July 1860 to 23 June 1866, the *Daily British Colonist*; from 25 June 1866 to 31 Dec. 1886, the *Daily British Colonist and Victoria*

Chronicle; and from 1 Jan. 1887 to the present, the *Daily Colonist*. The paper began as a weekly, then on 16 May 1859 a tri-weekly issue was begun. The weekly continued to 1888 as the *Weekly British Colonist*. The paper published five issues per week beginning on 31 July 1860, and after 16 Feb. 1861 became a full-scale daily.

Correspondent and Advocate, Toronto. See *Colonial Advocate*

Courier, St John's. Began publication as a semi-weekly in 1844 under the title *Morning Courier and General Advertiser*. In 1856 it became the *Courier* and it ceased publication in 1878.

Le Courrier de Saint-Hyacinthe, Saint-Hyacinthe, Qué. Began publication on 24 Feb. 1853.

Le Courrier du Canada, Québec. Published from 2 Feb. 1857 to 11 April 1901.

Daily Advertiser, London, Ont. A daily, begun 27 Oct. 1863 as the *London Evening Advertiser and Family Newspaper*, its name changed to the *London Evening Advertiser* on 23 May 1865 and to *Daily Advertiser* in the spring of 1869. On 4 Dec. 1880 its name became the *London Advertiser*. The *Weekly Advertiser* was begun in 1864, and its name had changed to *Western Advertiser* by 1873; in 1875 it combined with the *Weekly Liberal* (Toronto) to become the *Western Advertiser & Weekly Liberal* (London and Toronto), but by 1884 the title was again *Western Advertiser*.

Daily British Colonist, Victoria. See *Colonist*

Daily British Colonist and Victoria Chronicle. See *Colonist*

Daily British Whig, Kingston, Ont. See *British Whig*

Daily Colonist, Victoria. See *Colonist*

Daily Evening Mercury, Quebec. See *Quebec Daily Mercury*

Daily Morning News, Saint John, N.B. See *Morning News*

Daily News, Kingston, Ont. Published from 1851 to 1908, it sometimes appears as the *Kingston Daily News* and the *Kingston News*. It was the daily edition of the *Chronicle and News*, established in 1847 and published until the 1890s.

Daily Spectator, Hamilton, Ont. See *Hamilton Spectator*

Daily Telegraph, Saint John, N.B. See *Telegraph*

L'Écho du cabinet de lecture paroissial, Montréal. Published from 1 Jan. 1859 to 1875.

Evening Express, Halifax. A tri-weekly published from 1858 to 1876. Its full title was the *Evening Express and Commercial Record*.

Examiner, Charlottetown. Published from 7 Aug. 1847 until 1919 or 1920 when it was absorbed by the *Guardian* (Charlottetown). The *Examiner* was a weekly from 1847 until May 1877 when it became a daily only. A few months later the weekly edition was revived and both editions continued.

Examiner, Toronto. Published as a weekly from 3 July 1838 until 29 Aug. 1855 when it merged with the *Globe*.

Farmer's Advocate and Townships Gazette, Sherbrooke, Que. See *Sherbrooke Gazette*

Farmers' & Mechanics' Journal and St. Francis Gazette, Sherbrooke, Que. See *Sherbrooke Gazette*

Gazette, Montreal. Began publication on 3 June 1778.

La Gazette de Montréal. See *Gazette*

La Gazette de Québec. See *Quebec Gazette*

La Gazette du commerce et littéraire, pour la ville et district de Montréal. See *Gazette*

La Gazette littéraire pour la ville et district de Montréal. See *Gazette*

Gleaner, Chatham, N.B. Published from 1829 to 1880, it superseded the *Miramichi Mercury* which was founded in 1826. Its full title was the *Gleaner and Northumberland Schediasma*.

Globe, Toronto. Began as a weekly on 5 March 1844, became a semi-weekly 4 Nov. 1846, a tri-weekly 3 July 1849, and a daily 1 Oct. 1853. A second weekly series began 6 July 1849 and continued to 28 Jan. 1914; its title changed to *Weekly Globe and Canadian Farmer* on 5 Jan. 1877. A second semi-weekly series was published from 19 Oct. 1853 to 2 July 1855 when it became a tri-weekly which lasted until 1864. There was a second daily, the *Evening Globe*, from 19 Dec. 1861 to 20 July 1908. The *Western Globe*, published weekly in Toronto but issued from London, lasted from 16 Oct. 1845 until at least 1851. Title became the *Globe and Mail* when it merged with the *Daily Mail and Empire* (Toronto) on 23 Nov. 1936 and publication continued under this title in 1976.

Halifax Journal. Began publication on 5 Jan. 1781 as a weekly. In April 1854 it became a tri-weekly and the name was changed to *Morning Journal*. In June 1856 it was renamed the *Morning Journal and Commercial Advertiser*, and on 16 Jan. 1865 the *Unionist and Halifax Journal*.

Hamilton Spectator, Hamilton, Ont. Began publication on 15 July 1846 as a semi-weekly named the *Spectator and Journal of Commerce*. It was published as a weekly and a daily at different periods.

Head Quarters, Fredericton. A weekly, published from 1842(?) to 1875(?). Title varies. Its full title in 1844 was *The head Quarters, or*

Literary, Commercial and Agricultural Journal.

Herald, Montreal. Published from 19 Oct. 1811 to 18 Oct. 1957.

Islander, Charlottetown. Its full title was the *Islander, or Prince Edward Weekly Intelligencer and Advertiser* until 21 Jan. 1853 when it became the *Islander, or Prince Edward Island Weekly Intelligencer and Advertiser*. It was published from 2 Dec. 1842 until 1874 as a weekly. A new owner changed its title in 1872 to *Prince Edward Islander: A Weekly Newspaper of General Intelligence*. It was absorbed by the *Patriot* in 1874.

Le Journal de Québec, Québec. Published from 1 Dec. 1842 to 1 Oct. 1889.

Le Journal des Trois-Rivières. Published from 19 May 1865 to 19 March 1891. The less significant *Journal des Trois-Rivières* was published from 29 Aug. 1847 to 31 Dec. 1853.

Kingston Chronicle, Kingston, Ont. See *Chronicle & Gazette*

Kingston Gazette, Kingston, Ont. See *Chronicle & Gazette*

Leader, Toronto. Began publication as a semi-weekly on 1 July 1852 and as a weekly on 7 July. A daily edition was added on 11 July 1853. The semi-weekly ceased publication in 1864 but the daily and weekly editions continued to 1878.

London Advertiser, London, Ont. See *Daily Advertiser*

London Evening Advertiser, London, Ont. See *Daily Advertiser*

London Free Press, London, Ont. Began publication as a weekly on 2 Jan. 1849 as the *Canadian Free Press*. A daily edition, the *London Free Press and Daily Western Advertiser*, began on 5 May 1855 and, except for a brief interruption in the late 1850s, continued in 1976. The *Canadian Free Press* continued as a weekly, probably until 6 March 1868.

Mélanges religieux, Montréal. Published from 14 Dec. 1840 to 6 July 1852.

La Minerve, Montréal. Published from 9 Nov. 1826 to 27 May 1899.

Montreal Daily Herald. See *Herald*

Montreal Daily Transcript. See *Montreal Transcript*

Montreal Gazette. See *Gazette*

Morning Chronicle, Halifax. Published under various titles from 24 Jan. 1844 to the present. It began as a tri-weekly, then expanded in 1877 to a daily; it was also printed as a weekly from 1844 until 1912. The name changed to the *Halifax Chronicle* on 22 Jan. 1927; on 1 Jan. 1949 the paper merged with the *Herald* and its name became the *Halifax Chronicle-Herald*, which was shortened to the *Chronicle-Herald* on 26 Dec. 1959.

Morning Chronicle, Quebec. See *Quebec Chronicle Telegraph*

Morning Courier and General Advertiser, St John's. See *Courier*

Morning Freeman, Saint John, N.B. This paper began in 1849 as a weekly under the title *St. John Weekly Freeman*. The *Morning Freeman* was added in 1851 as a tri-weekly and lasted until 1878. The weekly continued until the year 1884.

Morning Journal, Halifax. See *Halifax Journal*

Morning News, Saint John, N.B. Published from 1839 until 1884 under a great variety of titles beginning with *Commercial News and General Advertiser*. At different times the paper was a weekly, a tri-weekly, and a daily. Used in this volume were the *Morning News* and the *Daily Morning News*.

Morning Telegraph, Saint John, N.B. See *Telegraph*

New Brunswick Courier, Saint John, N.B. A weekly, it began publication on 2 May 1811 and continued to 1865. The tri-weekly *Morning Courier (St. John Morning Courier)* was published briefly in 1855–56.

Newfoundlander, St. John's. Published from 1806 until 1884 although issues are only available from 1827. The paper was a weekly, then a semi-weekly.

Newfoundland Mercantile Journal, St John's. A weekly, published from 1816 to 1827.

Newfoundland Patriot, St John's. See *Patriot*

Nor'Wester, Winnipeg. The first newspaper published in the Red River Settlement, it was founded "in opposition to the existing order." It was published from 28 Dec. 1859 to 24 Nov. 1869.

Novascotian, Halifax. A weekly, published under various titles from 1824 until 1925. From 1824 until 1892 the full name was *Novascotian and Colonial Herald*, then in 1892 it became the *Nova Scotian and Weekly Chronicle* which lasted until 13 Oct. 1922. At that time the format changed and it became the *Nova Scotian: Nova Scotia's Farm and Home Journal* until it ceased publication.

Nova Scotia Royal Gazette, Halifax. See *Royal Gazette*

L'Opinion publique, Montréal. Published from 1 Jan. 1870 to 27 Dec. 1883.

Patriot, Charlottetown. Published from 8 July 1865 until the present. The *Patriot* began as a weekly and became a semi-weekly in 1867; in mid-1874 it reverted to being a weekly and in

1875 began also to feature a semi-weekly. Later it became a daily. This paper is sometimes said to have begun publication on 5 July 1859 because it was numbered consecutively from the *Protestant and Evangelical Witness* [*q.v.*]. For various reasons, including religious affiliation and financial support, it is not strictly correct to assume that the *Patriot* was a continuation of the *Protestant*.

Patriot, Kingston and Toronto. Began publication as a weekly in Kingston in 1828 as the *Patriot and Farmer's Monitor*. Moved to York (Toronto) on 7 Dec. 1832. A semi-weekly edition began in November 1833 and continued to April 1852; in March 1834 the title was changed to the *Patriot*, and in 1839 to the *Toronto Patriot*. In April 1850 a daily edition was added, entitled the *Toronto Daily Patriot and Express*; it continued to 1855 and was absorbed, for a time, by the *Leader* (Toronto). The weekly ceased publication in 1878.

Patriot, St John's. Published from 1834 to 1878 as a weekly, although issues are available only from 1854. In 1842 the name was changed from the *Newfoundland Patriot* to the *Patriot & Terra Nova Herald*; in 1877 it became the *Patriot and Catholic Herald* for four issues only. In 1878 it was the *Patriot and Terra Nova Advocate*.

Le Pays, Montréal. Published from 15 Jan. 1852 to 26 Dec. 1871.

Pilot, Montreal. Published from 5 March 1844 to 25 March 1862.

Pilot and Evening Journal of Commerce, Montreal. See *Pilot*

Pilot and Journal of Commerce, Montreal. See *Pilot*

Presbyterian Witness, Halifax and Toronto. A weekly, it was published from 1848 to 1925. Its full title until the end of 1897 was *Presbyterian Witness and Evangelical Advocate*. In 1920 it superseded the *Presbyterian and Westminster* of Toronto and moved to that city; it was published in London for a few months in 1921. In 1925 it united with the *Canadian Congregationalist* and the *Christian Guardian* [*q.v.*] to form the *New Outlook*.

Protestant and Evangelical Witness, Charlottetown. Published from 5 July 1859 until 1 July 1865. See also *Patriot*

Public Ledger, St John's. Published from 1820 to 1882 first as a semi-weekly, then as a tri-weekly, and finally as a daily. Its full title was the *Public Ledger and Newfoundland General Advertiser*.

Quebec Chronicle. See *Quebec Chronicle Telegraph*

Quebec Chronicle and Quebec Gazette. See *Quebec Chronicle Telegraph*

Quebec Chronicle Telegraph, Québec. Began publication on 18 May 1847.

Quebec Daily Evening Mercury. See *Quebec Daily Mercury*

Quebec Daily Mercury, Quebec. Published from 5 Jan. 1805 to 17 Oct. 1903.

Quebec Gazette, Quebec. Published from 21 June 1764 to 30 Oct. 1874.

Quebec Mercury. See *Quebec Daily Mercury*

Quebec Morning Chronicle. See *Quebec Chronicle Telegraph*

Royal Gazette, Charlottetown. Published from 1791 to the present. This paper began as a semi-monthly entitled *Royal Gazette, and Miscellany of the Island of Saint John* published by the king's or queen's printer. Subsequently it became a weekly.

Royal Gazette, Halifax. A weekly, it began publication as the *Halifax Gazette* on 23 March 1752, and after several changes in title it became the *Nova Scotia Royal Gazette* in 1801. On 16 Feb. 1843 its title changed to the *Royal Gazette*, its present name.

Royal Gazette, St John's. Published as a weekly from 1807 to 1924, although issues are available only from 1810. Its full title was the *Royal Gazette and Newfoundland Advertiser*. In 1926 the paper became the *Newfoundland Gazette* which continues to the present.

St. Francis Courier and Sherbrooke Gazette, Sherbrooke, Que. See *Sherbrooke Gazette*

St. John Daily Telegraph and Morning Journal. See *Telegraph*

St. John Morning Telegraph. See *Telegraph*

Le Sauvage. See *L'Avenir*

Sherbrooke Gazette, Sherbrooke, Que. Published from 1831 to 1908.

Sherbrooke Gazette and Eastern Townships Advertiser, Sherbrooke, Que. See *Sherbrooke Gazette*

Sherbrooke Gazette and Townships Advertiser, Sherbrooke, Que. See *Sherbrooke Gazette*

Spectator and Journal of Commerce, Hamilton, Ont. See *Hamilton Spectator*

Telegraph, Saint John, N.B. This paper, begun as the *Weekly Telegraph*, was published from 27 Sept. 1862 until July 1923, when it became the *Telegraph-Journal* which still exists as a daily. It was published at various times as a weekly, a semi-weekly, and a daily under a great many titles. The titles appearing in this volume include the *Morning Telegraph*, *St. John Morning Telegraph*, *St. John Daily Telegraph and Morning Journal*, *Daily Telegraph*, and *Telegraph-Journal*.

Telegraph-Journal, Saint John, N.B. See *Telegraph*

Times and General Commercial Gazette, St John's. Published from 29 Aug. 1832 until 23 March 1895 mainly as a semi-weekly but at times as a weekly.

Toronto Patriot. See *Patriot*

Weekly Globe, Toronto. See *Globe*

III. REFERENCE WORKS

ALLAIRE, JEAN-BAPTISTE-ARTHUR. *Dictionnaire biographique du clergé canadien-français*. 6 vols. Montréal et Saint-Hyacinthe, Qué., 1908–34.
  [I]: *Les anciens*. Montréal, 1910.
  [II]: *Les contemporains*. Saint-Hyacinthe, 1908.
  [III]: *Premier supplément*. Montréal, 1910.
  [IV]: *Le clergé canadien-français; revue mensuelle* (Montréal), I (1919). Only one issue of this journal was published.
  [V]: *Compléments, I*. Montréal, 1928.
  [VI]: [untitled.] Saint-Hyacinthe, 1934.

ALMANACS. Because titles within series vary and publishers or editors often change, the almanacs most frequently used in the preparation of volume IX have been listed below under a general title. The information in square brackets is given as a guide and may not be completely accurate.
Belcher's farmer's almanack ..., [1824–1930]. Halifax. Edited by Clement Horton Belcher from 1824 to 1870 when it was taken over by the firm of McAlpine and Barnes; it was later issued by the McAlpine Publishing Company. The issues for 1824 to 1831 were titled *The farmer's almanack ...*; in 1832 it became *Belcher's farmer's almanack ...*, a title it retained with minor variations until its disappearance.
Montreal almanack, [1829–72]. Published by Robert Armour, 1829–31; H. C. McLeod, 1839–42; Starke's, 1867–72. Its title varies: *Montreal almanack or Lower Canada register ...*, 1829–31; *Montreal almanack ...*, 1833–72.
The Montreal pocket almanack ..., [1842–91]. Published by Jos. Starke and Company, 1842–79; J. Theo. Robinson, 1880–91. Title varies: *The Montreal pocket almanack, and general register ...*, 1842–54, 1856; *The Montreal pocket almanack ...*, 1855, 1857, 1859; *Starke's pocket almanac and general register ...*, 1858, 1860, 1861, 1864–72, 1880–91; *Starke's pocket almanack ...*, 1862–63; *Starke's pocket almanac, advertiser and general register ...*, 1873–79.

New-Brunswick almanac. ... Saint John, N.B. Published from at least 1825 by Henry Chubb and Company. In 1828 its title was *An almanack ...*, but by 1832 it had become *The New-Brunswick almanack. ...* In 1849 it became *The New-Brunswick almanac, and register ... prepared by the Fredericton Athenæum*. Issues for the period 1825–66 were used in the preparation of volume IX.
The Quebec almanac ... / Almanach de Québec ..., [published from 1780 to 1841, except for 1781, 1790, and 1793]. Publishers included: Guillaume Brown, 1788; Samuel Neilson, 1791; John Neilson, 1794–1823; Neilson and Cowan, 1824–36; S. Neilson, 1837; W. Neilson, 1838–41. Its title varies: *Almanach de Québec ...*, 1780–91; *Almanac de Québec ...*, 1794–96; *Almanac de Québec ... / The Quebec almanac ...*, 1797–98; *Almanach de Québec ... / The Quebec almanac ...*, 1799–1802; *Almanach de Québec, et état civil et militaire de l'Amérique-britannique ... / The Quebec almanac, and British American royal kalendar ...*, 1803–12; *The Quebec almanac, and British American royal kalendar ...*, 1813–41.
Quebec pocket almanac and general register ..., [1849–53]. Published by Gilbert Stanley, 1849–53.

An alphabetical list of the merchants, traders, and housekeepers, residing in Montreal; to which is prefixed, a descriptive sketch of the town. Compiled by Thomas Doige. Montreal, 1819.

ARCHIVES NATIONALES DU QUÉBEC PUBLICATIONS [*See also* section II.]
  P.-G. Roy, *Inv. concessions*.
  —— *Les juges de la prov. de Québec*.

ARMSTRONG, FREDERICK HENRY. *Handbook of Upper Canadian chronology and territorial legislation*. London, Ont., 1967.

AUDET, FRANCIS-JOSEPH. *Les députés de la région des Trois-Rivières (1841–1867)*. (Pages Trifluviennes, sér. A, 13.) Trois-Rivières, 1934.
  —— *Les députés de Montréal (ville et comtés),*

1792–1867. Montréal, 1943.

———— *Les députés de Saint-Maurice (1808–1838) et de Champlain (1830–1838).* (Pages Trifluviennes, sér. A, 12.) Trois-Rivières, 1934.

———— *Les députés des Trois-Rivières (1808–1838).* (Pages Trifluviennes, sér. A, 11.) Trois-Rivières, 1934.

AUDET, FRANCIS-JOSEPH, et ÉDOUARD FABRE SURVEYER. *Les députés de Saint-Maurice et de Buckinghamshire, 1792–1808.* (Pages Trifluviennes, sér. A, 9a.) Trois-Rivières, 1934.

Australian dictionary of biography. General editor, Douglas Pike. 5 vols. to date. Melbourne, 1966– . In progress.

BEAULIEU, ANDRÉ, et al. *Guide d'histoire du Canada.* (Les cahiers de l'Institut d'histoire, 13.) Québec, 1969.

BEAULIEU, ANDRÉ, et JEAN HAMELIN. *La presse québécoise des origines à nos jours.* 2 vols. to date. Québec, 1973– . In progress.
I: *1764–1859.* 1973.
II: *1860–1879.* 1975.

———— *Les journaux du Québec de 1764 à 1964.* (Les cahiers de l'Institut d'histoire, 6.) Québec et Paris, 1965.

BEAULIEU, ANDRÉ, et WILLIAM FELIX EDMUND MORLEY. *La province de Québec.* (Histoires locales et régionales canadiennes des origines à 1950, William Felix Edmund Morley, éditeur, II.) Toronto et Buffalo, N.Y., 1971.

Belcher's farmer's almanack. See ALMANACS

BIBAUD, [FRANÇOIS-MARIE-UNCAS-]MAXIMILIEN. *Le panthéon canadien; choix de biographies, dans lequel on a introduit les hommes les plus célèbres des autres colonies britanniques.* Montréal, 1858; 2e édition, 1891.

A bibliography of Canadiana, being items in the Public Library of Toronto, Canada, relating to the early history and development of Canada. Edited by Frances Maria Staton and Marie Tremaine, with an introduction by George Herbert Locke. Toronto, 1934; reprinted, 1965. *A bibliography of Canadiana: first supplement. . . .* Edited by Gertrude Mabel Boyle, assisted by Marjorie Colbeck. Toronto, 1959; reprinted, 1969.

A bibliography of the Prairie provinces to 1953 with biographical index. Compiled by Bruce Braden Peel. Toronto, 1956. *. . . supplement.* Compiled by Bruce Braden Peel. Toronto, 1963. 2nd edition, Toronto and Buffalo, N.Y., 1973.

BISHOP, OLGA BERNICE. *Publications of the government of the Province of Canada, 1841–1867.* (National Library of Canada publication.) Ottawa, 1963.

———— *Publications of the governments of Nova Scotia, Prince Edward Island, New Brunswick, 1758–1952.* (National Library of Canada publication.) Ottawa, 1957.

BOASE, FREDERIC. *Modern English biography . . . with an index of the most interesting matter.* 3 vols. and 3 supplements. Privately printed in England, 1892–1921; reprinted [London], 1965. Contains memoirs of persons who died between 1851 and 1900.

BOIVIN, AURÉLIEN. *Le conte littéraire québécois au XIXe siècle; essai de bibliographie critique et analytique.* Montréal, 1975.

BORTHWICK, JOHN DOUGLAS. *History and biographical gazetteer of Montreal to the year 1892.* Montreal, 1892.

———— *Montreal, its history, to which is added biographical sketches, with photographs, of many of its principal citizens.* Montreal, 1875.

British Museum general catalogue of printed books. (Photolithographic edition to 1955.) 263 vols. London, 1961–66.

BURKE, JOHN. *A general and heraldic dictionary of the peerage and baronetage of the United Kingdom.* London, 1826. 105th edition, revised and enlarged. Edited by Peter Townend, 1970.

Canada, an encyclopædia of the country: the Canadian dominion considered in its historic relations, its natural resources, its material progress, and its national development. Edited by John Castell Hopkins. 6 vols. Toronto, 1898–1900. Also, *Index topical and personal to "Canada, an encyclopædia of the country. . . ."* Toronto and London, 1900.

Canada directory. See DIRECTORIES.

The Canadian biographical dictionary and portrait gallery of eminent and self-made men. 2 vols. Toronto, 1880–81.

The Canadian directory of parliament, 1867–1967. Edited by James Keith Johnson. (PAC publication.) Ottawa, 1968.

The Canadian parliamentary companion. Published in Quebec, 1862 and 1863, in Montreal from 1864 to 1874, and in Ottawa from 1875. Appeared irregularly from 1862, then annually from 1871. Became the *Canadian parliamentary guide . . .* early in the 20th century. Editor during the period of vol. IX of the *DCB* was Henry James Morgan.

CANADIAN RELIGIOUS CONFERENCE. *Abridged guide to the archives of religious communities in Canada.* Ottawa, 1974.

CARON-HOULE, FRANÇOISE. *Guide des rapports des Archives publiques du Canada, 1872–1972.* (PAC publication.) Ottawa, 1975.

Catalogue of pamphlets in the Public Archives of Canada. [1493–1931.] Compiled by Magdalen Casey. (PAC publications, 13.) 2 vols. Ottawa, 1931–32.

CENTRE D'ÉTUDES ACADIENNES, UNIVERSITÉ DE MONCTON. *Inventaire général des sources documentaires sur les Acadiens*. 1 vol. paru. Moncton, 1975– .

CHADWICK, EDWARD MARION. *Ontarian families; genealogies of United-Empire-Loyalist and other pioneer families of Upper Canada*. 2 vols. in 1. Toronto, 1894; reprinted with an introduction by William Felix Edmund Morley, Belleville, Ont., 1972. Another edition, 2 vols., Toronto, 1895–98; reprinted Lambertville, N.J., 1970.

Commemorative biographical record of the county of York, Ontario; containing biographical sketches of prominent and representative citizens and many of the early settled families. Toronto, 1907.

CORNISH, GEORGE HENRY. *Cyclopædia of Methodism in Canada, containing historical, educational, and statistical information*. . . . 2 vols. Toronto and Halifax, 1881–1903.

A cyclopædia of Canadian biography, being chiefly men of the time. . . . Edited by George MacLean Rose. (Rose's national biographical series, I–II.) 2 vols. Toronto, 1886–88.

DECHÊNE, LOUISE. "Inventaire des documents relatifs à l'histoire du Canada conservés dans les archives de la Compagnie de Saint-Sulpice à Paris," ANQ *Rapport*, 1969, 147–288.

DENT, JOHN CHARLES. *The Canadian portrait gallery*. 4 vols. Toronto, 1880–81.

DESJARDINS, JOSEPH. *Guide parlementaire historique de la province de Québec, 1792 à 1902*. Québec, 1902.

Dictionary of American biography [to 1928]. Edited by Allen Johnson and Dumas Malone. 20 vols. and index. New York, 1928–37. 3 supplements [to 1945]. New York, 1944–[73]. New edition, 22 vols. in 11. New York, [1959]. *Concise DAB*. New York, 1964. In progress.

Dictionary of national biography [to 1900]. Edited by Leslie Stephen and Sidney Lee. 63 vols.; supplement, 3 vols.; index and epitome. London, 1885–1903. 6 supplements [to 1960]. London, 1912–71. *Concise DNB*. 2 vols. London, 1952–61. *Corrections and additions to the "Dictionary of national biography"*. . . . (University of London, Institute of Historical Research publication.) Boston, Mass., 1966.

DIRECTORIES. Issued originally on an individual basis, these publications became regular, usually annual, in the 19th century. Because titles within series vary greatly and editors or compilers frequently changed, the directories most often used in the preparation of volume IX have been listed below by region and under a general title. The information in square brackets is given as a guide and may not be completely accurate.

Canada directory, [1851–66]. Used in volume IX were: *The Canada directory* . . . , ed. R. W. S. Mackay (Montreal, 1851); *The Canada directory for 1857–58* . . . (Montreal, [1857]); *Mitchell's Canada gazetteer and business directory for 1864–65* (Toronto, 1864); *Mitchell & Co.'s Canada classified directory for 1865–66* (Toronto, [1865]).

Montreal directory, [1842 to 1870 (last volume used in the preparation of volume IX)]. Montreal. Edited by Robert Walter Stuart Mackay, 1842–55; Mrs R. W. S. Mackay, 1856–63; John Lovell, 1863–[93]. Its title varies: *The Montreal directory* . . . , 1842 to 1855–56; *Mackay's Montreal directory*, 1856–70.

Quebec directory, [1844 to 1870 (last issue used in the preparation of volume IX)]. Quebec. Edited by Alfred Hawkins, 1844–48; Robert Walter Stuart Mackay, 1848–52; Samuel McLaughlin, 1854–58; Georges-Hippolyte Cherrier, 1858–72. Its title varies: *Quebec directory and stranger's guide to the city* . . . , 1844–45; *The Quebec directory and city and commercial register* . . . , 1847–48, which was in fact published at Montreal; *Mackay's Quebec directory* . . . , 1848–49; *Quebec business directory* . . . , 1850–54; *McLaughlin's Quebec directory* . . . , 1855–58; *The Quebec directory* . . . , 1858–71.

Toronto directory. The following issues are cited in volume IX: *York commercial directory, street guide, and register, 1833–4* . . . , comp. George Walton (York [Toronto], [1833]); *The city of Toronto and the Home District commercial directory and register with almanack and calendar for 1837* . . . , comp. George Walton (Toronto, [1837]); *The Toronto directory and street guide, for 1843–4*, comp. Francis Lewis (Toronto, 1843); *Brown's Toronto City and Home District directory, 1846–7* . . . (Toronto, 1846); *Rowsell's city of Toronto and county of York directory, for 1850–51* . . . , ed. J. Armstrong (Toronto, 1850); *Brown's Toronto general directory, 1856* . . . (Toronto, [1856]), also issued for 1861; *Caverhill's Toronto city directory, for 1859–60* . . . , comp. W. C. F. Caverhill (Toronto, [1859]); *Hutchinson's Toronto directory, 1862–63* . . . , comp.

Thomas Hutchinson (Toronto, n.d.); *Mitchell's Toronto directory, for 1864–5 . . .* (Toronto, 1864); *City of Toronto illustrated business directory for 1865 . . .* (Toronto, 1865); *Mitchell & Co.'s general directory for the city of Toronto, and gazetteer of the counties of York and Peel, for 1866* (Toronto, 1866).

A directory of the members of the Legislative Assembly of Nova Scotia, 1758–1958. With an introduction by Charles Bruce Fergusson. (PANS publications, Nova Scotia series, II.) Halifax, 1958.

Early Toronto newspapers, 1793–1867: a catalogue of newspapers published in the town of York and the city of Toronto from the beginning to confederation. Edited by Edith Grace Firth, with an introduction by Henry Cummings Campbell. Toronto, 1961.

Encyclopædia Britannica. 23 vols. Index and atlas in 1 vol. Chicago, 1966.

Encyclopedia Canadiana. John Everett Robbins, editor-in-chief. 10 vols. Ottawa, 1957–58; revised edition, 1966.

FAUTEUX, ÆGIDIUS. *Patriotes de 1837–1838.* Montréal, 1950.

GREAT BRITAIN, ADMIRALTY. *The commissioned sea officers of the Royal Navy, 1660–1815.* Editing begun by David B. Smith; project continued by the Royal Naval College in cooperation with the National Maritime Museum. 3 vols. [n.p., 1954?]

—— *The navy list. . . .* London, 1815–70.

Great Britain, War Office. *A list of the general and field officers as they rank in the army. . . .* [London, 1754–1868.]

—— *A list of the officers of the army and of the Corps of Royal Marines on full, retired, and half pay. . . .* London, 1849–64. *The army list.* London, 1798–1940. *See also* HART, HENRY GEORGE. *The new annual army list. . . .*

Guide des sources d'archives sur le Canada français, au Canada. (PAC publication.) Ottawa, 1975.

HARPER, JOHN RUSSELL. *Early painters and engravers in Canada.* Toronto, 1971.

—— *Historical directory of New Brunswick newspapers and periodicals.* Fredericton, 1961.

HART, HENRY GEORGE. *The new annual army list. . . .* London, 1840–1916. The title on the cover is *Hart's army list.*

HAYNE, DAVID MACKNESS, et MARCEL TIROL. *Bibliographie critique du roman canadien-français, 1837–1900.* [Québec et Toronto], 1968.

Landmarks of Canada; what art has done for Canadian history; a guide to the J. Ross Robertson historical collection in the Public Reference Library, Toronto, Canada. 2 vols. Toronto, 1917–21. New edition in 1 vol. Toronto, 1967.

[LANGELIER, JEAN-CHRYSOSTOME.]*List of lands granted by the crown in the province of Quebec from 1763 to 31st December 1890.* (Quebec, Department of Crown Lands publication.) Quebec, 1891.

LEBŒUF, JOSEPH-AIMÉ-ARTHUR. *Complément au dictionnaire généalogique Tanquay.* (SGCF publication, 2, 4, 6.) 3 series [3 vols.] Montréal, 1957–64.

The Legislative Assembly of the Province of Canada: an index to journal appendices and sessional papers, 1841–1866. Compiled by Patricia A. Damphouse. London, Ont., 1974.

LE JEUNE, LOUIS[-MARIE]. *Dictionnaire général de biographie, histoire, littérature, agriculture, commerce, industrie et des arts, sciences, mœurs, coutumes, institutions politiques et religieuses du Canada.* 2 vols. Ottawa, 1931.

Mackay's Montreal directory. See DIRECTORIES

McLaughlin's Quebec directory. See DIRECTORIES

MANITOBA LIBRARY ASSOCIATION. *Pioneers and early citizens of Manitoba; a dictionary of Manitoba biography from the earliest times to 1920.* [Compiled by Marjorie Morley *et al.*] Winnipeg, [1971].

Montreal almanack. See ALMANACS

Montreal directory. See DIRECTORIES

The Montreal pocket almanack. See ALMANACS

MORGAN, HENRY JAMES. *Bibliotheca Canadensis: or, a manual of Canadian literature.* Ottawa, 1867; reprinted Detroit, 1968.

—— *Sketches of celebrated Canadians, and persons connected with Canada, from the earliest period in the history of the province down to the present time.* Quebec and London, 1862.

MORICE, ADRIEN-GABRIEL. *Dictionnaire historique des Canadiens et des Métis français de l'Ouest.* Québec, 1908; Kamloops, B.C., 1908.

New-Brunswick almanac. See ALMANACS

New Brunswick history: a checklist of secondary sources. Compiled by Hugh A. Taylor. (PANB publication.) Fredericton, 1971. *. . . first supplement.* Compiled by Eric L. Swanick. (New Brunswick, Legislative Library publication.) Fredericton, 1974.

Notices nécrologiques des membres de la Congrégation des Oblats de Marie-Immaculée. 8 vols. Paris, 1868–1939.

NOTMAN, WILLIAM, and [JOHN] FENNINGS

TAYLOR. *Portraits of British Americans, with biographical sketches.* 3 vols. Montreal, 1865–68.

O'BYRNE, WILLIAM RICHARD. *A naval biographical dictionary; comprising the life and services of every living officer in her majesty's navy, from the rank of admiral of the fleet to that of lieutenant, inclusive. . . .* London, 1849. New and enlarged edition, 1 volume published and 4 parts of a second, London, 1861, [1859–62].

PAGES TRIFLUVIENNES. 25 vols. Trois-Rivières, 1932–39.
Série A
   2: Brouillette, *Le développement industriel.* [*See* section IV.]
   9a: F.-J. Audet et Fabre Surveyer. *Les députés de Saint-Maurice et de Buckinghamshire.*
   11: F.-J. Audet, *Les députés des Trois-Rivières (1808–1838).*
   12: F.-J. Audet, *Les députés de Saint-Maurice et de Champlain.*
   13: F.-J. Audet, *Les députés des Trois-Rivières (1841–1867).*

Place-names and places of Nova Scotia. With an introduction by Charles Bruce Fergusson. (PANS publications, Nova Scotia series, III.) Halifax, 1967.

Political appointments and elections in the Province of Canada from 1841 to 1860. Compiled by Joseph-Olivier Côté. Quebec, 1860. *. . . from 1841 to 1865.* 2nd edition, Ottawa, 1866. *. . . and appendix from 1st January, 1866, to 30th June, 1867, and index.* Edited by Narcisse-Omer Côté. Ottawa, 1918.

Political appointments, parliaments and the judicial bench in the dominion of Canada, 1867 to 1895. Edited by Narcisse-Omer Côté. Ottawa, 1896.

PUBLIC ARCHIVES OF CANADA
   NUMBERED PUBLICATIONS [*See also* section II.]
   13: *Catalogue of pamphlets in the PAC* (Casey).
   OTHER PUBLICATIONS [*See also* section II.]
   Canadian directory of parliament (Johnson).
   Caron-Houle, *Guide des rapports des APC.*
   Guide des sources d'archives.
   Union list of manuscripts (Gordon *et al.*; Maurice).

PUBLIC ARCHIVES OF NOVA SCOTIA
   PUBLICATIONS, Nova Scotia series
   II: *Directory of N.S. MLAs.*
   III: *Place-names of N.S.*

The Quebec almanac. See ALMANACS

Quebec directory. See DIRECTORIES

Quebec pocket almanac and general register. See ALMANACS

READ, DAVID BREAKENRIDGE. *The lives of the judges of Upper Canada and Ontario, from 1791 to the present time.* Toronto, 1888.

A register of the regiments and corps of the British army; the ancestry of the regiments and corps of the regular establishment. Edited by Arthur Swinson. London, 1972.

Répertoire des publications gouvernementales du Québec de 1867 à 1964. André Beaulieu *et al.*, compilateurs. Québec, 1968.

ROY, PIERRE-GEORGES. *Les avocats de la région de Québec.* Lévis, Qué., 1936.
—— *Fils de Québec.* 4 vols. Lévis, Qué., 1933.
—— *Inventaire des concessions en fief et seigneurie, fois et hommages et aveux et dénombrements, conservés aux Archives de la province de Québec.* (ANQ publication.) 6 vols. Beauceville, Qué., 1927–29.
—— *Les juges de la province de Québec.* (ANQ publication.) Québec, 1933.

STORY, NORAH. *The Oxford companion to Canadian history and literature.* Toronto, 1967.

TANGUAY, CYPRIEN. *Dictionnaire généalogique des familles canadiennes depuis la fondation de la colonie jusqu'à nos jours.* 7 vols. [Montréal], 1871–90. *Complément . . .* , by J.-A.-A. Lebœuf [*q.v.*].

TASSÉ, JOSEPH. *Les Canadiens de l'Ouest.* 2 vols. Montréal, 1878; 4ᵉ édition, 1882.

Toronto directory. See DIRECTORIES

TURCOTTE, GUSTAVE. *Le Conseil législatif de Québec, 1774–1933.* Beauceville, Qué., 1933.

Union list of manuscripts in Canadian repositories. Edited by Robert Stanyslaw Gordon *et al.* (PAC publication.) Ottawa, 1968; 2nd edition, edited by E. Grace Maurice, 2 vols., Ottawa, 1975.

WALBRAN, JOHN THOMAS. *British Columbia coast names, 1592–1906, to which are added a few names in adjacent United States territory, their origin and history with map and illustrations.* Ottawa, 1909; reprinted with an introduction by George Philip Vernon Akrigg, Vancouver, 1971.

WALLACE, WILLIAM STEWART. *The Macmillan dictionary of Canadian biography.* 3rd edition, revised and enlarged, London, 1963; reprinted, 1973. First published in Toronto in 1926 as *The dictionary of Canadian biography.* New edition in preparation.

WATTERS, REGINALD EYRE, and INGLIS FREEMAN BELL. *On Canadian literature, 1806–1960: a check-list of articles, books, and theses on English-Canadian literature, its authors, and language.* Toronto, 1966.

IV. STUDIES (BOOKS AND THESES)

ABBOTT, MAUDE ELIZABETH. *History of medicine in the province of Quebec*. Toronto, 1931; 2nd edition (McGill University publications, VIII, no. 63), Montreal, 1932.

ATHERTON, WILLIAM HENRY. *Montreal, 1535–1914*. 3 vols. Montreal and Vancouver, 1914.
   I: *Under the French régime, 1535–1760*.
   II: *Under British rule, 1760–1914*.
   III: *Biographical*.

AUDET, LOUIS-PHILIPPE. *Histoire de l'enseignement au Québec*. . . . [1608–1971.] 2 vols. Montréal et Toronto, 1971.

—— *Le système scolaire de la province de Québec*. 6 vols. parus. Québec, 1950– .
   I: *Aperçu général*. 1950.
   II: *L'instruction publique de 1635 à 1800*. 1951.
   III: *L'Institution royale; les débuts: 1801–1825*. 1952.
   IV: *L'Institution royale; le déclin: 1825–1846*. 1952.
   V: *Les écoles élémentaires dans le Bas-Canada, 1800–1836*. 1955.
   VI: *La situation scolaire à la veille de l'Union, 1836–1840*. 1956.

BECK, JAMES MURRAY. *The government of Nova Scotia*. (Canadian government series, 8.) Toronto, 1957.

BELISLE, ALEXANDRE. *Histoire de la presse franco-américaine; comprenant l'historique de l'émigration des Canadiens-français aux États-Unis, leur développement, et leurs progrès*. Worcester, Mass., 1911.

BERNARD, JEAN-PAUL. *Les Rouges; libéralisme, nationalisme et anticléricalisme au milieu du XIXᵉ siècle*. Montréal, 1971.

BOON, THOMAS CHARLES BOUCHER. *The Anglican Church from the Bay to the Rockies; a history of the ecclesiastical province of Rupert's Land and its dioceses from 1820 to 1950*. Toronto, 1962.

BROUILLETTE, BENOÎT. *Le développement industriel de la vallée du St-Maurice*. (Pages Trifluviennes, sér.A, no.2.) Trois-Rivières, 1932.

CAMPBELL, ROBERT. *A history of the Scotch Presbyterian Church, St. Gabriel Street, Montreal*. Montreal, 1887.

Canada and its provinces; a history of the Canadian people and their institutions. . . . Edited by Adam Shortt and Arthur George Doughty. 23 vols. Toronto, 1913–17.

Canada's smallest province: a history of P.E.I. Edited by Francis William Pius Bolger. Charlottetown, 1973.

Canadian business history; selected studies, 1497–1971. Edited by David Stirling Macmillan. Toronto, 1972.

CANADIAN CENTENARY SERIES. William Lewis Morton, executive editor; Donald Grant Creighton, advisory editor.
   7: Craig, *Upper Canada*.
   9: MacNutt, *Atlantic provinces*.
   10: Careless, *Union of the Canadas*.
   12: W. L. Morton, *Critical years*.

Canadian education: a history. Edited by John Donald Wilson *et al*. Scarborough, Ont., 1970.

CANADIAN GOVERNMENT SERIES. General editors, Robert MacGregor Dawson, 1946–58; James Alexander Corry, 1958–61; Crawford Brough Macpherson, 1961–75; Sidney John Roderick, 1975– .
   5: MacKinnon, *Government of P.E.I.*
   7: Hodgetts, *Pioneer public service*.
   8: Beck, *Government of N.S.*

CANADIAN STUDIES IN HISTORY AND GOVERNMENT SERIES. Editors, James Maurice Stockford Careless, 1958–60; Kenneth William Kirkpatrick McNaught, 1960–65; Goldwin Sylvester French, 1965– .
   1: Moir, *Church and state in Canada West*.
   2: Thompson, *French shore problem in Nfld*.
   3: Cornell, *Alignment of political groups*.
   7: Gunn, *Political history of Nfld*.
   8: Wilson, *Clergy reserves of U.C.*
   9: Gates, *Land policies of U.C.*

CANNIFF, WILLIAM. *The medical profession in Upper Canada, 1783–1850: an historical narrative, with original documents relating to the profession, including some brief biographies*. Toronto, 1894.

CARELESS, JAMES MAURICE STOCKFORD. *Brown of "The Globe."* 2 vols. Toronto, 1959–63.
   I: *The voice of Upper Canada, 1818–1859*. 1959; reprinted 1966.
   II: *Statesman of confederation, 1860–1880*. 1963.

—— *The union of the Canadas: the growth of Canadian institutions, 1841–1857*. (Canadian centenary series, 10.) Toronto, 1967.

CARRIÈRE, GASTON. *Histoire documentaire de la Congrégation des Missionnaires Oblats de Marie-Immaculée dans l'Est du Canada*. 11 vols. parus. Ottawa, 1957– .

CARROLL, JOHN [SALTKILL]. *Case and his cotemporaries; or, the Canadian itinerants' memorial: constituting a biographical history of Methodism in Canada, from its introduction into the province, till the death of the Rev. W. Case in 1855.* 5 vols. Toronto, 1867–77.

CHAPAIS, THOMAS. *Cours d'histoire du Canada.* 8 vols. Québec et Montréal, 1919–34; réimprimé Trois-Rivières, 1972.

CHOQUETTE, CHARLES-PHILIPPE. *Histoire de la ville de Saint-Hyacinthe.* Saint-Hyacinthe, Qué., 1930.

—— *Histoire du séminaire de Saint-Hyacinthe depuis sa fondation jusqu'à nos jours.* 2 vols. Montréal, 1911–12.

CHOUINARD, FRANÇOIS-XAVIER, et ANTONIO DROLET. *La ville de Québec, histoire municipale.* (Cahiers d'histoire, 15, 17, 19.) 3 vols. Québec, 1963–67.
   I: Chouinard, *Régime français.* 1963.
   II: Drolet, *Régime anglais jusqu'à l'incorporation (1759–1833).* 1965.
   III: Drolet, *De l'incorporation à la Confédération (1833–1867).* 1967.

CHRISTIE, ROBERT. *A history of the late province of Lower Canada, parliamentary and political, from the commencement to the close of its existence as a separate province. . . .* 6 vols. Quebec and Montreal, 1848–55.

CLARK, ANDREW HILL. *Three centuries and the Island, a historical geography of settlement and agriculture in Prince Edward Island, Canada.* Toronto, 1959.

CORNELL, PAUL GRANT. *The alignment of political groups in Canada, 1841–1867.* (Canadian studies in history and government series, 3.) Toronto, 1962.

COWAN, HELEN I. *British emigration to British North America, 1783–1837.* [Toronto], 1928. *. . . the first hundred years.* 2nd edition, [Toronto], 1961; reprinted 1967.

CRAIG, GERALD MARQUIS. *Upper Canada: the formative years, 1784–1841.* (Canadian centenary series, 7.) Toronto, 1963.

CREIGHTON, DONALD [GRANT]. *John A. Macdonald, the young politician.* Toronto, 1952; reprinted 1965.

—— *John A. Macdonald, the old chieftain.* Toronto, 1955; reprinted 1965.

—— *The road to confederation; the emergence of Canada: 1863–1867.* Toronto, 1964.

DAVID, LAURENT-OLIVIER. *Les patriotes de 1837–1838.* Montréal, [1884]; réimprimé [1937].

DAVIN, NICHOLAS FLOOD. *The Irishman in Canada.* London and Toronto, 1877; reprinted Shannon, 1969.

DAY, CATHERINE MATHILDA. *History of the Eastern Townships, province of Quebec,*

dominion of Canada, civil and descriptive, etc. Montreal, 1869.

DENISON, MERRILL. *Canada's first bank; a history of the Bank of Montreal.* 2 vols. Toronto and Montreal, 1966–67. Translated into French by Paul A. Horguelin and Jean-Paul Vinay as *La première banque au Canada; histoire de la Banque de Montréal.*

DENT, JOHN CHARLES. *The last forty years: Canada since the union of 1841.* 2 vols. Toronto, 1881. An abridged edition edited by Donald Swainson, was published at Toronto in 1972 as *The last forty years: the union of 1841 to confederation* (Carleton Library, 62).

—— *The story of the Upper Canadian rebellion; largely derived from original sources and documents.* 2 vols. Toronto, 1885.

DOUVILLE, JOSEPH-ANTOINE-IRENÉE. *Histoire du collège-séminaire de Nicolet, 1803–1903, avec les listes complètes des directeurs, professeurs et élèves de l'institution.* 2 vols. Montréal, 1903.

DROLET, *Ville de Québec.* See CHOUINARD, FRANÇOIS-XAVIER, et ANTONIO DROLET

FRENCH, GOLDWIN [SYLVESTER]. *Parsons & politics: the rôle of the Wesleyan Methodists in Upper Canada and the Maritimes from 1780 to 1855.* Toronto, 1962.

GARNEAU, FRANÇOIS-XAVIER. *Histoire du Canada depuis sa découverte jusqu'à nos jours.* 3 vols. Québec et Montréal, 1845–48, et un supplément en 1852; 8ᵉ édition, 9 vols., Montréal, 1944–46.

GARON, ANDRÉ. "La question du Conseil législatif électif sous l'Union des Canadas, 1840–1856." Thèse de DES, université Laval, Québec, 1969.

GATES, LILLIAN FRANCES. *Land policies of Upper Canada.* (Canadian studies in history and government series, 9.) Toronto, 1968.

GIRAUD, MARCEL. *Le Métis canadien: son rôle dans l'histoire des provinces de l'Ouest.* (Travaux et mémoires de l'Institut d'ethnologie, XLIV.) Paris, 1945.

GREENE, JOHN P. "The influence of religion in the politics of Newfoundland, 1850–1861." Unpublished MA thesis, Memorial University of Newfoundland, St John's, 1970.

GREENHILL, BASIL, and ANN GIFFARD. *Westcountrymen in Prince Edward's Isle: a fragment of the great migration.* London and Toronto, 1967.

GROULX, LIONEL. *L'enseignement français au Canada.* 2 vols. Montréal, 1931–33.
   I: *Dans le Québec.* 1931.
   II: *Les écoles des minorités.* 1933.

———— *Histoire du Canada français depuis la découverte.* 4 vols. Montréal, 1950; 4ᵉ édition, 2 vols. (Collection Fleur de Lys, Guy Frégault *et al.*, éditeurs), Montréal et Paris, 1960; réimprimé 1962.

GUNN, GERTRUDE E. *The political history of Newfoundland, 1832–1864.* (Canadian studies in history and government series, 7.) Toronto, 1966.

HAMELIN, JEAN, et YVES ROBY. *Histoire économique du Québec, 1851–1896.* (Histoire économique et sociale du Canada français.) Montréal, 1971.

HANNAY, JAMES. *History of New Brunswick.* 2 vols. Saint John, N.B., 1909.

HARPER, JOHN RUSSELL. *Painting in Canada, a history.* Toronto, 1966.

HARRIS, REGINALD V. *The Church of Saint Paul in Halifax, Nova Scotia: 1749–1949.* Toronto, 1949.

HEAGERTY, JOHN JOSEPH. *Four centuries of medical history in Canada and a sketch of the medical history of Newfoundland.* 2 vols. Toronto, 1928.

Histoire de la corporation de la cité de Montréal depuis son origine jusqu'à nos jours . . . . Joseph-Cléophas Lamothe *et al.*, éditeurs. Montréal, 1903.

Histoire de la littérature française du Québec. Pierre de Grandpré, éditeur. 4 vols. Montréal, 1967–69; réimprimé 1971–73.

HISTOIRE ÉCONOMIQUE ET SOCIALE DU CANADA FRANÇAIS. A collection published under the direction of the Centre de recherche en histoire économique du Canada français, Montreal.
Hamelin et Roby, *Hist. économique.*
Ouellet, *Hist. économique.*

HISTOIRE RELIGIEUSE DU CANADA. A collection published under the direction of the Research Centre in the Religious History of Canada, Ottawa.
Lemieux, *L'établissement de la première prov. eccl.*

History of the county of Middlesex, Canada, from the earliest time to the present; containing an authentic account of many important matters relating to the settlement, progress and general history of the county; and including a department devoted to the preservation of personal and private records, etc. Toronto and London, Ont., 1889; reprinted with introduction and corrections by Daniel James Brock, Belleville, Ont., 1972.

History of Toronto and county of York, Ontario; containing an outline of the history of the dominion of Canada; a history of the city of Toronto and the county of York, with the townships, towns, villages, churches, schools; general and local statistics; biographical sketches, etc., etc. 2 vols. Toronto, 1885.

HODGETTS, JOHN EDWIN. *The Canadian public service; a physiology of government, 1867–1970.* (Studies in the structure of power decision-making in Canada, edited by John Meisel, 7.) Toronto, 1973.

———— *Pioneer public service; an administrative history of the united Canadas, 1841–1867.* (Canadian government series, 7.) Toronto, 1955.

JOHNSTON, CHARLES MURRAY. *The head of the lake: a history of Wentworth County.* Hamilton, Ont., 1958; 2nd edition, 1967.

LAREAU, EDMOND. *Histoire de la littérature canadienne.* Montréal, 1874.

[LAWRENCE, JOSEPH WILSON.] *The judges of New Brunswick and their times.* Edited by Alfred Augustus Stockton. [Saint John, N.B., 1907.]

LEMIEUX, LUCIEN. *L'établissement de la première province ecclésiastique au Canada, 1783–1844.* (Histoire religieuse du Canada publication.) Montréal et Paris, 1968.

[LEMIRE-MARSOLET, DARIE-AURÉLIE, DITE SAINTE-HENRIETTE], et THÉRÈSE LAMBERT, DITE SAINTE-MARIE-MÉDIATRICE. *Histoire de la Congrégation de Notre-Dame de Montréal.* 13 vols. (numbered I–XI) and an index to date. Montréal, 1910– . Before her death in 1917 Sister Sainte-Henriette had completed nine volumes of her history as well as an index; only two volumes were published, in 1910. In 1941 her complete work was published and the first two volumes reissued. The index for the first nine volumes, prepared by Sister Sainte-Henriette, was published in 1969.

LÉTOURNEAU, FIRMIN. *Histoire de l'agriculture (Canada français).* s.l., 1950; 2ᵉ édition, [Montréal], 1952; réimprimé 1959; 3ᵉ édition, s.l., 1968.

LINDSEY, CHARLES. *The life and times of Wm. Lyon Mackenzie; with an account of the Canadian rebellion of 1837, and the subsequent frontier disturbances, chiefly from unpublished documents.* 2 vols. Toronto, 1862; reprinted 1971.

Literary history of Canada: Canadian literature in English. Edited by Carl Frederick Klinck *et al.* Toronto, 1965; new edition, 3 vols., 1976. Translated by Maurice Lebel as *Histoire littéraire du Canada: littérature canadienne de langue anglaise.* Québec, 1970.

MACKINNON, FRANK [FRANCIS PERLEY

TAYLOR]. *The government of Prince Edward Island.* (Canadian government series, 5.) Toronto, 1951.

MACMILLAN, JOHN C. *The history of the Catholic church in Prince Edward Island from 1835 till 1891.* Quebec, 1913.

MACNUTT, WILLIAM STEWART. *The Atlantic provinces: the emergence of colonial society, 1712–1857.* (Canadian centenary series, 9.) Toronto, 1965.

—— *New Brunswick, a history: 1784–1867.* Toronto, 1963.

MASTERS, DONALD C. *Protestant church colleges in Canada: a history.* (Studies in the history of higher education in Canada, 4.) Toronto, 1966.

MAURAULT, OLIVIER. *Le collège de Montréal, 1767–1967.* Antonio Dansereau, éditeur. 2e édition. Montréal, 1967. The first edition was published in Montreal in 1918 under the title *Le petit séminaire de Montréal.*

MIDDLETON, JESSE EDGAR. *The municipality of Toronto, a history.* 3 vols. Toronto and New York, 1923.

MILLMAN, THOMAS REAGH. *Jacob Mountain, first lord bishop of Quebec, a study in church and state, 1793–1825.* (University of Toronto studies, History and economics series, X.) Toronto, 1947.

—— *The life of the Right Reverend, the Honourable Charles James Stewart, D.D., Oxon., second Anglican bishop of Quebec.* London, Ont., 1953.

MOIR, JOHN SARGENT. *Church and state in Canada West: three studies in the relation of denominationalism and nationalism, 1841–1867.* (Canadian studies in history and government series, 1.) Toronto, 1959.

MONET, JACQUES. *The last cannon shot; a study of French-Canadian nationalism, 1837–1850.* Toronto, 1969.

MONRO, ALEXANDER. *New Brunswick; with a brief outline of Nova Scotia, and Prince Edward Island; their history, civil divisions, geography and productions.* . . . Halifax, 1855; reprinted Belleville, Ont., 1972.

MORICE, ADRIEN-GABRIEL. *A critical history of the Red River insurrection after official documents and non-Catholic sources.* Winnipeg, 1935.

—— *Histoire de l'Église catholique dans l'Ouest canadien, du lac Supérieur au Pacifique (1659–1915).* 3e édition, 4 vols., Saint-Boniface, Man., et Montréal, 1921–23. The first and second editions, in three volumes, cover from 1659 to 1915 and were published at Winnipeg and Montreal in 1912 and at Saint-Boniface and Montreal in 1915 respectively. The first edition was translated into English as *History of the Catholic church from Lake Superior to the Pacific (1659–1895).* 2 vols. Toronto, 1910.

MORTON, ARTHUR SILVER. *A history of the Canadian west to 1870–71; being a history of Rupert's Land (the Hudson's Bay Company's territory) and of the North-West Territory (including the Pacific slope).* London, [1939]; 2nd edition, edited by Lewis Gwynne Thomas, Toronto and Buffalo, N.Y., 1973.

MORTON, WILLIAM LEWIS. *The critical years: the union of British North America, 1857–1873.* (Canadian centenary series, 12.) Toronto, 1964.

—— *Manitoba: a history.* Toronto, 1957; 2nd edition, 1967.

ORMSBY, MARGARET ANCHORETTA. *British Columbia: a history.* Toronto, 1958; revised edition, 1971.

OUELLET, FERNAND. *Histoire économique et sociale du Québec, 1760–1850, structures et conjoncture.* (Histoire économique et sociale du Canada français.) Montréal et Paris, 1966.

PERRON, MARC-ANDRÉ. *Un grand éducateur agricole: Édouard-A. Barnard, 1835–1898; essai historique sur l'agriculture de 1760 à 1900.* [Montréal], 1955.

POULIOT, LÉON. *Monseigneur Bourget et son temps.* 4 vols. Montréal, 1955–76.

PROWSE, DANIEL WOODLEY. *A history of Newfoundland from the English, colonial, and foreign records.* London and New York, 1895; 2nd edition, London, 1896; 3rd edition, St John's, 1971; reprint of 1st edition, Belleville, Ont., 1972.

Le répertoire national, ou recueil de littérature canadienne. James Huston, compilateur. Montréal, 1848–50; 2e édition, 4 vols., 1893.

RICH, EDWIN ERNEST. *The history of the Hudson's Bay Company, 1760–1870.* (HBRS publications, XXI–XXII.) 2 vols. London, 1958–59; another edition, 3 vols., Toronto, 1960. A copy of this work available in the PAC contains notes and bibliographical material omitted from the printed version.

ROBERTSON, IAN ROSS. "Religion, politics and education in Prince Edward Island from 1856 to 1877." Unpublished MA thesis, McGill University, Montreal, 1968.

Robertson's landmarks of Toronto; a collection of historical sketches of the old town of York from 1792 until 1833, and of Toronto from 1834 to [1914]. Edited by John Ross Robertson. 6 series [6 vols.]. Toronto, 1894–1914; vols. 1 and 3 reprinted Belleville, Ont., 1976, 1974.

Ross, Alexander. *The Red River Settlement: its rise, progress and present state; with some account of the native races and its general history, to the present day.* London, 1856; reprinted Minneapolis, 1957, and Edmonton, 1972.

Ross, Victor, and Arthur St L. Trigge. *A history of the Canadian Bank of Commerce, with an account of the other banks which now form part of its organization.* 3 vols. Toronto, 1920–34.

Roy, Joseph-Edmond. *Histoire du notariat au Canada depuis la fondation de la colonie jusqu'à nos jours.* 4 vols. Lévis, Qué., 1899–1902.

Rumilly, Robert. *Histoire de la province de Québec.* 41 vols. parus. Montréal, [1940] – . 2ᵉ édition pour les vol. I à IX, s.d.; 3ᵉ édition pour les vol. I à VI, s.d.; réimpression en cours de la 1ʳᵉ édition, 7 vols. parus, Montréal, 1971– .

—— *Histoire de la Société Saint-Jean-Baptiste de Montréal; des Patriotes au fleurdelisé, 1834–1948.* Montréal, 1975.

—— *Histoire de Montréal.* 5 vols. Montréal, 1970–74.

The shield of Achilles: aspects of Canada in the Victorian age/Le bouclier d'Achille: regards sur le Canada de l'ère victorienne. Edited by William Lewis Morton. Toronto and Montreal, 1968.

Shook, Laurence Kennedy. *Catholic post-secondary education in English-speaking Canada: a history.* (Studies in the history of higher education in Canada, 6.) Toronto and Buffalo, N.Y., 1971.

Sissons, Charles Bruce. *Egerton Ryerson: his life and letters.* 2 vols. Toronto, 1937–47.

Stanley, George Francis Gilman. *Canada's soldiers; the military history of an unmilitary people.* Toronto, 1954; 2nd edition, 1960.

—— *Louis Riel.* Toronto, 1963.

The storied province of Quebec; past and present. Edited by William Wood *et al.* 5 vols. Toronto, 1931–32.

Studies in the history of higher education in Canada
4: Masters, *Protestant church colleges.*
6: Shook, *Catholic post-secondary education.*

Sylvain, Philippe. "Libéralisme et ultramontanisme au Canada français; affrontement idéologique et doctrinal (1840–1865), *Le bouclier d'Achille* (W. L. Morton), 111–38, 220–55.

Thompson, Frederic Fraser. *The French shore problem in Newfoundland: an imperial study.* (Canadian studies in history and government series, 2.) Toronto, 1961.

Tratt, Gertrude Ella Naomi. "A survey and listing of Nova Scotian newspapers with particular reference to the period before 1867." Unpublished MA thesis, Mount Allison University, Sackville, N.B., 1957.

Tremblay, Victor. *Histoire du Saguenay depuis les origines jusqu'à 1870.* (Société historique du Saguenay publication, 21.) 2ᵉ édition, Chicoutimi, Qué., 1968. A first edition, prepared by Victor Tremblay *et al.*, was published in 1938 at Chicoutimi as *L'histoire du Saguenay depuis l'origine jusqu'à 1870.*

Turcotte, Louis-Philippe. *Le Canada sous l'Union, 1841–1867.* 2 vols. Québec, 1871–72; 2ᵉ édition, 1882.

Wade, Mason. *French Canada; a history, 1760–1945.* Toronto, 1954. A second edition in 2 vols. was published in Toronto in 1968 as *The French Canadians, 1760–1967* and translated into French by Adrien Venne and Francis Dufau-Labeyrie as *Les Canadiens français de 1760 à nos jours.* Ottawa, 1963.

Wallace, Frederick William. *Wooden ships and iron men: the story of the square-rigged merchant marine of British North America, the ships, their builders and owners, and the men who sailed them.* London and Toronto, 1924; New York, 1925; Boston, 1937; 1937 edition reprinted Belleville, Ont., 1973.

Weale, David, and Harry Baglole. *The Island and confederation: the end of an era.* n.p., 1973.

Wilson, [George] Alan. *The clergy reserves of Upper Canada, a Canadian mortmain.* (Canadian studies in history and government series, 8.) Toronto, 1968.

Winks, Robin William. *The blacks in Canada: a history.* Montreal, 1971.

Young, James. *Public men and public life in Canada, being recollections of parliament and the press, and embracing a succinct account of the stirring events which led to the confederation of British North America into the dominion of Canada.* Toronto, 1902; reprinted with a second vol. entitled *Public men and public life in Canada . . . which followed the confederation . . . ,* 1912.

V. JOURNALS

Acadiensis: Journal of the History of the Atlantic Region/Revue de l'histoire de la région atlantique. Fredericton. I (1971–72)– . Published semi-annually by the Department of History of the University of New Brunswick.

Archives. Québec. I (1969)– . Published semi-annually until 1975, then quarterly, by the Association des archivistes du Québec.

BC Studies. Vancouver. Quarterly, 1 (winter 1968–69)– .

Beaver. Winnipeg. Publication of the HBC. Monthly until March 1925; thereafter quarterly. I (outfit 250, 1920)– . Index for I (outfit 250, 1920) – outfit 284 (March 1954) published [1955?].

British Columbia Historical Quarterly. Victoria. Quarterly, I (1937)–XII (1948); three times a year, XIII (1949)–XIV (1950), then semi-annually to XXI (1957–58), which is the last volume to date. Published by the Provincial Archives of British Columbia in cooperation with the British Columbia Historical Association.

Le Bulletin des recherches historiques. Published usually in Lévis, Qué. Journal of archaeology, history, biography, bibliography, numismatology, etc. Founded by Pierre-Georges Roy* as the organ of the Société des études historiques, the *BRH* became the journal of the Archives de la province de Québec (now the ANQ) in March 1923. Published monthly from 1895, it became a quarterly in 1949. In 1968 it ceased publication. I (1895)–LXX (1968). *Index*: I (1895)–XXXI (1925). 4 vols. Beauceville, Qué., 1925–26. For subsequent years see the manuscript index in the ANQ.

Les Cahiers des Dix. Montréal et Québec. I (1936)– . Annual review published by "Les Dix."

CANADIAN CATHOLIC HISTORICAL ASSOCIATION/SOCIÉTÉ CANADIENNE D'HISTOIRE DE L'ÉGLISE CATHOLIQUE, Ottawa. A bilingual society, founded 3 June 1933, it has published simultaneously each year (except for 1933–34) a *Rapport* in French and a *Report* in English, of which the contents are entirely different. 1933–34– . *Index*: 1933-34–1958. Title varies: *Study Sessions/Sessions d'étude* from 1966.

CANADIAN HISTORICAL ASSOCIATION/SOCIÉTÉ HISTORIQUE DU CANADA, Ottawa. The association, founded in 1922, continues the work of the Historic Landmarks Association of Canada (1915–21). Its aims are "to encourage historical research and public interest in history; to promote the preservation of historic sites and buildings, documents, relics, and other significant heirlooms of the past; to publish historical studies and documents as circumstances may permit." Publications include *Annual Report*, 1922– (title varies: *Historical Papers/ Communications historiques* from 1966), and historical booklets, issued irregularly. *Index* to annual reports: 1922–51; 1952–68.

Canadian Historical Review. Toronto. Quar-

terly. I (1920)– . *Index*: I (1920)–X (1929); XI (1930)–XX (1939); XXI (1940)–XXX (1949); XXXI (1950)–LI (1970). Université Laval has also published an index: *Canadian Historical Review, 1950–1964: index des articles et des comptes rendus de volumes*, René Hardy, comp. (Québec, 1969). Each issue includes a current bibliography of publications in English and French, a continuation of the annual *Review of Historical Publications relating to Canada* (I (for 1895–96)–XXII (for 1917–18); *Index*: I–X; XI–XX).

Canadian Journal. Toronto. Publication of the Canadian Institute which became the Royal Canadian Institute in 1914. Began as the *Canadian Journal: a repertory of industry, science and art; and a record of the proceedings of the Canadian Institute*, I (1852–53)–III (1854–55). Title was modified to the *Canadian Journal of Industry, Science and Art*, new series, I (1856)–IX (1866–67) and to the *Canadian Journal of Science, Literature and History*, XII (1868–70)–XV (1876–77). Superseded by the *Proceedings of the Canadian Institute, Toronto, being a continuation of "The Canadian Journal of Science, Literature and History,"* third series, I (1879–83)–VII (1888–89). Merged for a few years with the Canadian Institute, *Transactions*, then published irregularly for a time as Canadian Institute, *Proceedings*, new series, I (1895–98). Published as Royal Canadian Institute, *Proceedings*, third series or series IIIa, I (1935–36)– .

Dalhousie Review. Halifax. Quarterly publication of Dalhousie University. I (1921–22)– .

HISTORICAL AND SCIENTIFIC SOCIETY OF MANITOBA. Winnipeg. Incorporated in 1879, the society was founded by historians and businessmen to encourage science and to make Manitoba known. Since its founding the society has had numerous publications. These include: *Report*, I (1880)–XXVII (1906); several series known as *Transactions*, 1 (Oct. 1882)–72 (Nov. 1906); new series, 1 (Nov. 1924)–5 (July 1930); 3rd series, 1 (1944–45)– (the title of these transactions varies: *Publication*, 1–2, 4–6; *Transactions*, 3, 7–72; new series, 1–5; *Papers*, 3rd series); *Manitoba History*, I (March 1946)– . HSSM also published *Manitoba historical atlas; a selection of facsimile maps, plans, and sketches from 1612 to 1969*. Edited by John Warkentin and Richard I. Ruggles. Winnipeg, 1970.

NOVA SCOTIA HISTORICAL SOCIETY, Halifax. Publishes *Collections*. Issued irregularly. I (1878)– . The title *Report and Collections* was used in 1878 and 1882–83.

Ontario History. Toronto. Originally published

annually as Ontario Historical Society, *Papers and Records*, I (1899)–XXXVIII (1946). The title was changed to *Ontario History* with XXXIX (1947). Quarterly publication began with XLI (1949) and continues to the present. An index for volumes I (1899) to LXIV (1972) has been included in *Index to the publications of the Ontario Historical Society, 1899–1972* (Toronto, 1974).

Revue d'histoire de l'Amérique française. Montréal. Quarterly publication of the Institut d'histoire de l'Amérique française. Founded by Canon Lionel Groulx*, I (1947–48)– . Beginning with XXI (1967–68), each issue includes a bibliography of books recently published in French or English.

ROYAL SOCIETY OF CANADA/SOCIÉTÉ ROYALE DU CANADA, Ottawa. Under the patronage of the Marquess of Lorne [John Douglas Sutherland Campbell*], the society was formed in 1882 for the encouragement of literature and science in Canada. Originally it was composed of four sections, two for literature and two for sciences. Publishes *Proceedings and Transactions/Mémoires et comptes rendus*, of which sections I and II include historical articles. Annual. First series: I (1882–83)–XII (1894). Second series: I (1895)–XII (1906). Third series: I (1907)–LVI (1962). Fourth series: I (1963)– . Indexes.

SOCIÉTÉ GÉNÉALOGIQUE CANADIENNE-FRANÇAISE, Montréal. Founded on the initiative of Father Archange Godbout*, 3 Sept. 1943. Publishes *Mémoires*. Originally published semi-annually, now quarterly. I (1944–45)– .

Social History, a Canadian Review/Histoire sociale, revue canadienne. Ottawa. 1 (April 1968)– . Published semi-annually, under the direction of an interdisciplinary committee from various Canadian universities.

Contributors

ACHESON, THOMAS WILLIAM. Associate professor of history, University of New Brunswick, Fredericton, New Brunswick.
William Black. William Parks [in collaboration with J. R. Rice].

AKRIGG, HELEN B. Writer, Vancouver, British Columbia.
John James Cochrane.

ANDERSON, A. J. Secretary of Synod, Diocese of Ontario, Anglican Church of Canada, Kingston, Ontario.
George Okill Stuart.

ANGUS, MARGARET SHARP. Writer, Kingston, Ontario.
John Counter. William Coverdale. John C. Fox. Overton Smith Gildersleeve. James Sampson.

ANICK, NORMAN. Historian, National Historic Parks and Sites Branch, Parks Canada, Department of Indian Affairs and Northern Development, Ottawa, Ontario.
John McDonald [in collaboration with C. M. Livermore].

ARMSTRONG, FREDERICK H. Associate professor of history, University of Western Ontario, London, Ontario.
Augustus Warren Baldwin. George Jervis Goodhue. George Gurnett. John Kinder Labatt. George Macbeth. William Lyon Mackenzie [in collaboration with R. J. Stagg]. *Alexander Mathieson. Lucius James O'Brien. Frédéric-Auguste Quesnel. Hugh Richardson. James Edward Small. John Torrance.*

ARTHUR, M. ELIZABETH. Professor of history, Lakehead University, Thunder Bay, Ontario.
Cuthbert Cumming. Robert McVicar.

AUDET, LOUIS-PHILIPPE. Professeur à la retraite, Sillery, Québec.
John Bruce. Sir Arthur William Buller. Louis Guillet.

BAGLOLE, HARRY. Writer, Belfast, Prince Edward Island.
William Cooper.

BAILEY, ALFRED GOLDSWORTHY. Professor emeritus of history, University of New Brunswick, Fredericton, New Brunswick.
Julia Catherine Beckwith (Hart). James Robb.

BALF, MARY. Curator and archivist, Kamloops Museum Association, Kamloops, British Columbia.
Jean-Baptiste Lolo. Donald McLean.

BALLSTADT, CARL P. A. Associate professor of English, McMaster University, Hamilton, Ontario.
John Wedderburn Dunbar Moodie.

BARRETTE, ROGER. Chef de division, Service de l'hébergement, Ministère des Affaires sociales du Québec, Québec.
Pierre-Louis Panet. Édouard Scallon.

BASKERVILLE, PETER. Assistant professor of history,

University of Vermont, Burlington, Vermont, U.S.A.
Donald Bethune. William Paterson McLaren. Sir Allan Napier MacNab.

BECK, J. MURRAY. Professor of political science, Dalhousie University, Halifax, Nova Scotia.
Alexander Stewart.

BÉLANGER, RENÉ, P.D. Écrivain, Québec, Québec.
Alexis Belanger.

BELL, MICHAEL. Director, Agnes Etherington Art Centre, Queen's University, Kingston, Ontario.
Alexander Cavalié Mercer.

BELLAVANCE, MARCEL. Historien, Direction des lieux et des parcs historiques nationaux, Ministère des Affaires indiennes et du Nord, Québec, Québec.
François-Xavier Desjardins [in collaboration with G. Goyer].

BENSLEY, EDWARD HORTON. Research associate, Department of the history of medicine, McGill University, Montreal, Quebec.
Archibald Hall.

BERNARD, JEAN-PAUL. Professeur d'histoire, Université du Québec à Montréal, Québec.
Thomas Boutillier. P.-J. Guitté. Joseph Papin.

BEYEA, MARION. Archivist, Anglican Church of Canada, Toronto, Ontario.
James Scott Howard.

BILAS, IRENE. Formerly assistant research director, Centre d'étude du Québec, Concordia University, Montreal, Quebec.
Dunbar Ross.

BLAKELEY, PHYLLIS R. Assistant provincial archivist, Public Archives of Nova Scotia, Halifax, Nova Scotia.
John Charles Beckwith. Sir Samuel Cunard. Angus McAskill. Frederick William Morris.

BLAKEY SMITH, DOROTHY. Formerly archivist, Provincial Archives of British Columbia, Victoria, British Columbia.
John Boles Gaggin. Edward Mallcott Richardson.

BOISSONNAULT, CHARLES-MARIE. Écrivain, Québec, Québec.
Charles-Jacques Frémont. Joseph Morrin.

BONENFANT, JEAN-CHARLES. Professeur de droit, Université Laval, Québec, Québec.
Samuel Gale. James Smith.

BOULIANNE, RÉAL G. Associate dean (extension), Faculty of Education, McGill University, Montreal, Quebec.
Robert Raby Burrage.

BOWSFIELD, HARTWELL. Assistant professor of history, York University, Downsview, Ontario.
Norbert Parisien.

BRIDGMAN, HARRY JOHN. Lecturer in history, University of Victoria, British Columbia.

Robert Burns.

BROCK, DANIEL JAMES. Teacher of history, London and Middlesex County Roman Catholic Separate School Board, London, Ontario.
Dennis O'Brien. Thomas Parke.

BROOKS, WILLIAM HOWARD. Assistant professor of history, St Paul's College, University of Manitoba, Winnipeg, Manitoba.
John Peter Pruden.

BRUN, RÉGIS. Ex-archiviste, Centre d'études acadiennes, Université de Moncton, Nouveau-Brunswick.
Joseph-Marie Paquet.

BUCKNER, PHILLIP A. Associate professor of history, University of New Brunswick, Fredericton, New Brunswick.
Sir William MacBean George Colebrooke. Neville Parker. Robert Parker.

BUGGEY, SUSAN. Head, Priority Sites, Research Division, National Historic Parks and Sites Branch, Parks Canada, Department of Indian Affairs and Northern Development, Ottawa, Ontario.
John Bazalgette. Martin Gay Black. William Rufus Blake. John Esson.

BURLEY, DAVID G. Graduate student of history, McMaster University, Hamilton, Ontario.
Andrew Steven.

BURNS, FLORA HAMILTON. Writer, Victoria, British Columbia.
James Murray Reid.

BURNS, ROBERT JOSEPH. Historian, National Historic Parks and Sites Branch, Parks Canada, Department of Indian Affairs and Northern Development, Cornwall, Ontario.
James Grant Chewett. William Botsford Jarvis. George Herchmer Markland. Thomas Gibbs Ridout.

BURNS, ROBIN B. Associate professor of history, Concordia University, Montreal, Quebec.
Thomas D'Arcy McGee.

BURNSIDE, ALBERT. United Church minister, Edith Rankin Memorial Church, Kingston, Ontario.
James Brennan.

CAMERON, WENDY. Toronto, Ontario.
Alexander McDonell.

CARELESS, J. M. S. Professor of history, University of Toronto, Ontario.
Peter Brown. John Roaf.

CARRIÈRE, GASTON, O.M.I. Archiviste, Archives historiques oblates, Ottawa, Ontario.
Jean-Claude-Léonard Baveux. Alexandre-Auguste Brunet. Pierre-Henri Grollier.

CARROLL, E. G. Vancouver, British Columbia.
Paul Mabey.

CAUCHON, MICHEL. Directeur, Service de l'inventaire des biens culturels, Direction générale du patrimoine, Ministère des Affaires culturelles du Québec, Québec.
Alexis Milette.

CHABOT, RICHARD. Assistant professeur d'histoire, Université du Québec à Montréal, Québec.
Léonard Godefroy de Tonnancour. Michel-François Valois.

†CHARLAND, THOMAS-M., O.P. Bibliothécaire et archiviste, Couvent des Dominicains, Montréal, Québec.
Ignace Gill. Joseph-Pierre-Anselme Maurault.

CLARKE, IAN H. Graduate student in history, University of Manitoba, Winnipeg, Manitoba.
John Palmer Litchfield [in collaboration with A. W. Rasporich]. *John Scott* [with A. W. Rasporich].

COGSWELL, FREDERICK WILLIAM. Professor of English, University of New Brunswick, Fredericton, New Brunswick.
Thomas Chandler Haliburton.

COLLARD, ELIZABETH. Writer, Montreal, Quebec.
John Hilton. Joseph White.

COLTHART, JAMES M. Academic relations officer, Canadian Embassy, Washington, District of Columbia, U.S.A.
Edward Ellice.

COOKE, W. M. E. Ottawa, Ontario.
Samuel Gurney Cresswell.

COOPER, JOHN IRWIN. Professor emeritus of history, McGill University, Montreal, Quebec.
Francis Fulford. Hubert Paré. George Tillson.

CORNELL, PAUL GRANT. Professor of history, University of Waterloo, Ontario.
James Morris. Robert Spence. Richard Alexander Tucker [in collaboration with L. Harris].

CRAIG, G. M. Professor of history, University of Toronto, Ontario.
John Rolph. John Strachan.

CRAIG, JOAN. Formerly archivist, Hudson's Bay Company, London, England.
John Bell. James Robert Clare.

CREIGHTON, PHYLLIS. Translations editor, *Dictionary of Canadian Biography/Dictionnaire biographique du Canada*, University of Toronto Press, Ontario.
Mary Heaviside (Lady Love).

CROSS, MICHAEL S. Professor of history, Dalhousie University, Halifax, Nova Scotia.
Peter Aylen. Stewart Derbishire. Charles Duncombe. Henry James Friel. Nicholas Sparks.

CULLEN, MARY K. Historian, National Historic Parks and Sites Branch, Parks Canada, Department of Indian Affairs and Northern Development, Ottawa, Ontario.
John Myrie Holl. Robert Hutchinson.

DANSEREAU, ANTONIO, P.S.S. Archiviste, Collège de Montréal, Québec.
Pierre-Louis Billaudèle. Nicolas Dufresne.

DAVIS, DAVID J. Archivist, Provincial Archives of Newfoundland and Labrador, St John's, Newfoundland.
James Crowdy. Laurence O'Brien. John Rochfort. William Bickford Row. James Simms.

DECHÊNE, LOUISE. Professeur agrégé d'histoire, Université de Montréal, Québec.
William Price.

DE LAGRAVE, FRANÇOIS. Professeur d'histoire, Polyvalente de Chavigny, Trois-Rivières-Ouest, Québec.
Louis Roblot, known as *Brother Aidant.*

DEMPSEY, HUGH A. Director of history, Glenbow-Alberta Institute, Calgary, Alberta.

Maskepetoon. Peenaquim. Peguis.

DESBARATS, AILEEN ANNE. Formerly librarian, Lande Collection of Canadiana, Department of Rare Books, Special Collections, McLennan Library, McGill University, Montreal, Quebec.
George-Paschal Desbarats.

DÉSILETS, ANDRÉE. Professeur titulaire d'histoire, Université de Sherbrooke, Québec.
Marie-Rosalie Cadron, dite de la Nativité (Jetté). Charles de Cazes. Marie-Louise Dorval, dite Sainte-Élisabeth. Marie-Catherine Huot, dite Sainte-Madeleine. Charles-Irénée Lagorce. François-Xavier Lemieux. Sir Étienne-Paschal Taché.

DESJARDINS, ÉDOUARD, M.D. Rédacteur en chef, *l'Union médicale du Canada*, Montréal, Québec.
Francis Badgley.

DEVEAU, J.-ALPHONSE. Directeur du Centre acadien, Collège Sainte-Anne, Church Point, Nouvelle-Écosse.
Anselm-François Comeau.

DODGE, ERNEST S. Director, Peabody Museum, Salem, Massachusetts, U.S.A.
Sir James Clark Ross.

DONNELLY, JOSEPH P., S.J. St Louis, Missouri, U.S.A.
Nicolas Point.

DORGE, LIONEL. Secrétaire-archiviste, Société historique de Saint-Boniface, Manitoba.
François-Jacques Bruneau.

DOUGLAS, BRONWEN. Lecturer, La Trobe University, Bundoora, Victoria, Australia.
George Nicol Gordon [in collaboration with B. W. Hodgins].

DOUGLAS, GEORGE L. Formerly librarian, Knox College, University of Toronto, Ontario.
Daniel Ward Eastman.

DOUGLAS, R. ALAN. Curator, Hiram Walker Historical Museum, Windsor, Ontario.
John Prince.

DUBUC, ALFRED. Professeur titulaire d'histoire, Université du Québec à Montréal, Québec.
Thomas Molson.

DUNLOP, ALLAN C. Research assistant, Public Archives of Nova Scotia, Halifax, Nova Scotia.
James Daniel Bain Fraser.

DYSTER, BARRIE. Lecturer in history, University of New South Wales, Kensington, New South Wales, Australia.
William Proudfoot.

EADIE, JAMES ALBERT. Head, Department of history, Napanee District Secondary School, Napanee, Ontario; secretary, Lennox and Addington Historical Society, Napanee, Ontario.
David Roblin.

EDDY, BARBARA J. Education librarian, Education Library, Memorial University of Newfoundland, St John's, Newfoundland.
Belinda Molony, known as Mary Xavier.

EDDY, EARL B. Formerly minister, St Paul's United Church, Windsor, Ontario.
Adam Lillie.

EDWARDS, MURRAY D. Producer, Ontario Educational Communications Authority, Toronto, Ontario.
John Nickinson.

ELLIOTT, SHIRLEY B. Legislative librarian, Legislative Library, Halifax, Nova Scotia.
Clement Horton Belcher.

EVANS, CALVIN D. Head, Humanities and Social Science Division, McLaughlin Library, University of Guelph, Ontario.
Henry Winton.

FARRIS, ALLAN L. Principal, Knox College, University of Toronto, Ontario.
Mark Young Stark.

FERGUSSON, CHARLES BRUCE. Archivist, Public Archives of Nova Scotia, Halifax, Nova Scotia; associate professor of history, Dalhousie University, Halifax, Nova Scotia.
Laurence O'Connor Doyle. Thomas Horace Fuller.

FILTEAU, HUGUETTE. Adjoint au directeur des recherches, *Dictionnaire biographique du Canada/Dictionary of Canadian Biography*, Les Presses de l'université Laval, Québec, Québec.
Ludger Labelle [in collaboration with J. Hamelin].

FINGARD, JUDITH. Associate professor of history, Dalhousie University, Halifax, Nova Scotia.
Alexander Forrester. Robert Fitzgerald Uniacke.

FLEMMING, DAVID B. Historian, National Historic Parks and Sites Branch, Parks Canada, Department of Indian Affairs and Northern Development, Halifax, Nova Scotia.
John Joseph Quinan. John Tobin.

FOSTER, JOHN E. Assistant professor of history, University of Alberta, Edmonton, Alberta.
William Cockran.

FOWLER, MARIAN E. Course director, Department of humanities, Atkinson College, York University, Toronto, Ontario.
Susan Mein (Sibbald).

FRANCIS D'ASSISI, REVEREND SISTER. Formerly president, Mount Saint Vincent University, Halifax, Nova Scotia.
Rosanna McCann, named Mary Basilia.

FRANK, DAVID ALEXANDER. Graduate student in history, Dalhousie University, Halifax, Nova Scotia.
Richard Smith.

FRASER, JAMES ANDREW. Formerly research assistant, Provincial Archives of New Brunswick, Fredericton, New Brunswick.
John Mercer Johnson [in collaboration with C. M. Wallace].

FRENCH, GOLDWIN SYLVESTER. President, Victoria University, Toronto, Ontario.
Nathan Bangs. George Frederick Playter. James Spencer. Joseph Stinson.

FRIESEN, GERALD. Assistant professor of history, University of Manitoba, Winnipeg, Manitoba.
Duncan Finlayson. Gabriel Franchère.

GAGNÉ, ARMAND. Directeur, Archives de l'archidiocèse de Québec, Québec.
Pierre-Flavien Turgeon.

GAGNON, JEAN-PIERRE. Historien, Service historique, Ministère de la Défense nationale, Ottawa, Ontario.

907

Maximilien Globensky. Louis-Joseph Massue. Melchior-Alphonse de Salaberry.

GAGNON, SERGE. Professeur d'histoire, Université d'Ottawa, Ontario.
Étienne-Michel Faillon. Jean-Baptiste-Antoine Ferland.

GALARNEAU, CLAUDE. Professeur titulaire d'histoire, Université Laval, Québec, Québec.
Hyacinthe-Poirier Leblanc de Marconnay. Nicolas-Marie-Alexandre Vattemare.

GARON, ANDRÉ. Professeur adjoint d'histoire, Université Laval, Québec, Québec.
Charles-François-Xavier Baby.

GARON, ROBERT. Archiviste, Ministère des Affaires intergouvernementales du Québec, Québec.
Jeffery Hale.

GATES, LILLIAN FRANCIS. Ithaca, New York, U.S.A.
Jesse Ketchum.

GIBBON, A. D., M.D. Paediatrician, Saint John, New Brunswick.
Robert Bayard.

GIBBS, ELIZABETH. Research director, Centre d'étude du Québec, Concordia University, Montreal, Quebec.
Sir Dominick Daly. Sewell Foster. Dominique Mondelet. Joseph-André Taschereau.

GIBSON, JAMES ALEXANDER. Professor emeritus of history, Brock University, St Catharines, Ontario.
Sir Edmund Walker Head.

GIDNEY, R. D. Associate professor of history and comparative education, University of Western Ontario, London, Ontario.
David Thompson.

GIGUÈRE, GEORGES-ÉMILE. Historien, Montréal, Québec.
Clément Boulanger.

GILLIS, ROBERT PETER. Archivist, Natural Resource Section, Public Records Division, Public Archives of Canada, Ottawa, Ontario.
Samuel Dickson.

GNAROWSKI, MICHAEL. Professor of English, Carleton University, Ottawa, Ontario.
Oliver Goldsmith.

GODFREY, CHARLES M. Professor of rehabilitative medicine, University of Toronto, Ontario.
Elam Stimson.

GOOSSEN, N. JAYE. Research historian, Historic Resources Branch, Department of Tourism, Recreation, and Cultural Affairs, Winnipeg, Manitoba.
William Mactavish.

GOUGH, BARRY MORTON. Associate professor of history, Wilfrid Laurier University, Waterloo, Ontario.
Sir Robert Lambert Baynes. John Gordon. Walter Colquhoun Grant.

GOYER, GÉRARD. Chargé de recherche, *Dictionnaire biographique du Canada/Dictionary of Canadian Biography*, Les Presses de l'université Laval, Québec, Québec.
François-Xavier Desjardins [in collaboration with M. Bellavance]. *Charles-Marie Labillois. Joseph Montferrand*, dit *Favre* [in collaboration with J. Hamelin].

GRANT, JOHN NORMAN. Teacher of history, Sackville High School, Halifax County, Nova Scotia.
William Francis Cook. Zenas Waterman.

GRAVEL, JEAN-YVES. Adjoint au président, Agence canadienne de développement international, Ottawa, Ontario.
Louis-Théodore Besserer. Louis-Timothée Suzor.

GRAVES, ROSS. Teacher of history, South Colchester High School, Brookfield, Nova Scotia.
Joseph Sibley.

GREENE, JOHN P. High school teacher, St John's, Newfoundland.
Clement Pitt Benning.

GREENFIELD, KATHARINE. Head, Special collections, Hamilton Public Library, Ontario.
William Craigie.

GREENHILL, BASIL. Director, National Maritime Museum, Greenwich, London, England.
James Yeo.

GRIFFITHS, NAOMI. Associate professor of history, Carleton University, Ottawa, Ontario.
François-Xavier-Stanislas Lafrance.

GUAY, MICHÈLE. Chargée de cours, Centre d'études canadiennes-françaises, McGill University, Montréal, Québec.
Jean-François-Marie-Joseph MacDonell.

GUNDY, H. PEARSON. Professor emeritus of English language and literature, Queen's University, Kingston, Ontario.
James George. Stephen Miles.

HALL, ROGER D. Assistant professor of history, University of Western Ontario, London, Ontario.
Thomas Mercer Jones. James McGill Strachan.

HAMELIN, JEAN. Directeur général adjoint, *Dictionnaire biographique du Canada/Dictionary of Canadian Biography*, Les Presses de l'université Laval; professeur d'histoire, Université Laval, Québec, Québec.
Ludger Labelle [in collaboration with H. Filteau]. *Joseph Montferrand*, dit *Favre* [in collaboration with G. Goyer].

HAMEL-MINH, LOUISE. Archiviste responsable, Section iconothèque, Archives nationales du Québec, Québec.
Jules-Isaïe Benoît, dit *Livernois*.

HAMILTON, WILLIAM B. Director, Atlantic Institute of Education, Halifax, Nova Scotia.
Charles Dickson Archibald.

HARDY, RENÉ. Professeur d'histoire, Université du Québec à Trois-Rivières, Québec.
Henriette Odin (Feller).

HARE, JOHN E. Professeur agrégé d'histoire, Université d'Ottawa, Ontario.
Olivier-Arthur Cassegrain. Joseph Lenoir, dit *Rolland.*

HARPER, JOHN RUSSELL. Visiting professor of fine arts, Concordia University, Montreal, Quebec.
Robert Clow Todd.

HARRIS, LESLIE. Vice-president (academic), Memorial University of Newfoundland, St John's, Newfoundland.
Richard Alexander Tucker [in collaboration with P. G. Cornell].

HEADON, CHRISTOPHER FERGUS. Dean and registrar,

College of Thorneloe University; assistant professor of church history, Laurentian University, Sudbury, Ontario.

Edward Henry Dewar.

†HENDERSON, JOHN LANCELEY HODGE. Professor of history; librarian, Huron College, London, Ontario.

Ernest Hawkins [in collaboration with T. R. Millman].

HENDRICKSON, JAMES E. Associate professor of history, University of Victoria, British Columbia.

George Hunter Cary.

HETT, ROBERT RALPH. Associate professor of history, University of Alberta, Edmonton, Alberta.

James Christie Palmer Esten.

HEWLETT, EDWARD SLEIGH. Vice-principal, Port Kells School, Surrey, British Columbia.

Klatsassin.

HILL, ROBERT ANDREW. Chairman, Department of history, economics, and political science, John Abbott College, Sainte-Anne-de-Bellevue, Quebec.

Thomas Sellar.

HODGINS, BRUCE W. Professor of history, Trent University, Peterborough, Ontario.

Adam Johnston Fergusson Blair. Michael Hamilton Foley. George Nicol Gordon [in collaboration with B. Douglas]. *Archibald McLean.*

HOLLAND, CLIVE A. Assistant librarian and curator, Scott Polar Research Institute, Cambridge, England.

Sir Horatio Thomas Austin. John Hepburn.

HOLMAN, HARRY TINSON. Assistant archivist, Public Archives of Prince Edward Island, Charlottetown, Prince Edward Island.

William Douse.

HOPWOOD, VICTOR G. Professor of English, University of British Columbia, Vancouver, British Columbia.

Thomas McMicking.

HOVIUS, JOHN. Lawyer, Hamilton, Ontario.

Henry Eccles.

HUGHES, RICHARD DAVID. Instructor of geology, Department of physical and life sciences, Cariboo College, Kamloops, British Columbia.

Joseph Beete Jukes.

INGERSOLL, L. K. Director, Museums Branch, Historical Resources Administration, Fredericton, New Brunswick.

Wilford Fisher.

JACKSON, JAMES A. Chairman of social studies, Technical-Vocational High School, Winnipeg; associate professor of history, University of Manitoba, Winnipeg, Manitoba.

Elzéar Goulet.

JAIN, GENEVIÈVE LALOUX. Saint John, New Brunswick.

John William Dering Gray.

JOHNSON, J. K. Professor of history, Carleton University, Ottawa, Ontario.

William Johnston. Donald Macdonell.

JOHNSON, KENNETH W. Archivist, Trent University Archives, Peterborough, Ontario.

Wilson Seymour Conger.

JOHNSON, LEO A. Associate professor of history and sociology, University of Waterloo, Ontario.

Absalom Shade.

JOHNSON, ROBERT E. Professor of biology, Knox College, Galesburg, Illinois, U.S.A.

Sir John Richardson.

JOHNSTON, HUGH J. M. Associate professor of history, Simon Fraser University, Burnaby, British Columbia.

Thomas McQueen. Edward Gibbon Wakefield.

JONES, ELWOOD H. Associate professor of history, Trent University, Peterborough, Ontario.

Rowland Burr. Adam Fergusson. Daniel Morrison. John Scoble.

JONES, FREDERICK. Senior lecturer in history, Bournemouth College of Technology, England.

Wellmein William Le Gallais. Henry Lind. John Thomas Mullock. Edward Wix.

KALLMANN, HELMUT. Chief, Music Division, National Library of Canada, Ottawa, Ontario.

Richard Coates. Abraham Nordheimer. Joseph-Julien Perrault. Charles-Désiré-Joseph Wugk, also known as *Charles Sabatier.*

KERNAGHAN, LOIS KATHLEEN. Research assistant, Public Archives of Nova Scotia, Halifax, Nova Scotia.

Hugh William Blackadar. Andrew MacKinlay.

KIDD, KENNETH E. Professor emeritus of anthropology, Trent University, Peterborough, Ontario.

Sir Joshua Jebb.

KLASSEN, HENRY C. Associate professor of history, University of Calgary, Alberta.

John Bunn. Thomas Kay.

KOS-RABCEWICZ-ZUBKOWSKI, LUDWIK. Professeur de criminologie, Université d'Ottawa, Ontario.

Alexandre-Édouard Kierzkowski.

LAMALICE, ANDRÉ L. J. Chargé des publications françaises, Archives publiques du Canada, Ottawa, Ontario.

François-Antoine Larocque.

LAMB, WILLIAM KAYE. Formerly dominion archivist, Vancouver, British Columbia.

Simon Fraser.

LAMBERT, JAMES H. Formerly co-ordinator, Ecclesiastical archives, Public Archives of Canada, Ottawa, Ontario.

Samuel Simpson Wood.

LAMONDE, YVAN. Professeur d'histoire, Centre d'études canadiennes-françaises, McGill University, Montréal, Québec.

Georges-Barthélemi Faribault. Isaac-Stanislas Lesieur-Désaulniers.

LAND, R. BRIAN. Professor of library science, University of Toronto, Ontario.

Robert Land.

LA TERREUR, MARC. Directeur, Département d'histoire, Université Laval, Québec, Québec.

Thomas Cary.

LAVIOLETTE, GONTRAN, O.M.I. Winnipeg, Manitoba.

Tatanka-najin.

LEBLOND, SYLVIO. Professeur émérite, Université Laval, Québec, Québec.

George Mellis Douglas.

LEFEBVRE, JEAN-JACQUES. Ex-archiviste en chef,

909

Cour supérieure, Palais de justice, Montréal, Québec.
Georges-René Saveuse de Beaujeu.

LEFORT, ANDRÉ. Professeur d'histoire, Bishop's University, Lennoxville, Québec.
Denis-Benjamin Viger [in collaboration with F. Ouellet].

LEIGHTON, DOUGLAS. Assistant professor of history, Huron College, London, Ontario.
Jean-Baptiste Assiginack. Francis Assikinack. George Ironside. Duncan Campbell Napier. Richard Theodore Pennefather.

LEMIEUX, LUCIEN. Professeur agrégé de théologie, Université de Montréal, Québec.
Charles-François Baillargeon. Pierre-Marie Mignault.

LEMIRE, MAURICE. Professeur titulaire de littérature, Université Laval, Québec, Québec.
Patrice Lacombe.

LÉVESQUE, BENOÎT. Professeur de sociologie, Université du Québec à Rimouski, Québec.
Antoine Manseau.

LIVERMORE, CAROL M. Historian, National Historic Parks and Sites Branch, Parks Canada, Department of Indian Affairs and Northern Development, Ottawa, Ontario.
John McDonald [in collaboration with N. Anick].

LORTIE, LÉON. Retraité; historiographe de l'université de Montréal, Québec.
Augustin De Lisle.

McCALLA, DOUGLAS. Associate professor of history, Trent University, Peterborough, Ontario.
Robert William Harris.

McGIVERN, JAMES SABINE, S.J. Archivist, Archdiocese of Toronto, Ontario.
Frederic Baraga. Edward John Gordon.

MACKAY, DONALD CAMERON. Formerly principal, Nova Scotia College of Art and Design, Halifax, Nova Scotia.
Peter Nordbeck. John Elliott Woolford.

McKENNA, ED. Historian, Ontario Ministry of Culture and Recreation, Toronto, Ontario.
Sir Francis Cockburn.

MACKENZIE, ANN. Graduate student in history, University of Guelph, Ontario.
Edward William Thomson.

MACKENZIE, ANTHONY A. Assistant professor of history, St Francis Xavier University, Antigonish, Nova Scotia.
Alexander McGillivray. John Joseph Marshall. Amos Peck Seaman.

MCKENZIE, RUTH. Writer, Ottawa, Ontario.
James FitzGibbon. Laura Ingersoll (Secord).

MACKINNON, CHARLES F. Archivist, Public Archives of Canada, Ottawa, Ontario.
Robert Foulis.

MACKINNON, CLARENCE STUART. Assistant professor of history, University of Alberta, Edmonton, Alberta.
James Anderson.

MACLEAN, RAYMOND A. Professor of history, St Francis Xavier University, Antigonish, Nova Scotia.
Peter MacLean. Norman McLeod. John Sprott.

MACMILLAN, DAVID STIRLING. Professor of history, Trent University, Peterborough, Ontario.
Robert Rankin.

†MACNUTT, WILLIAM STEWART. Professor emeritus of history, University of New Brunswick, Fredericton, New Brunswick.
Thomas Baillie. John Hooper. John Richard Partelow.

MACPHERSON, IAN. Associate professor of history, University of Winnipeg, Manitoba.
William Buell.

†MAGILL, MAXWELL LEROY. Toronto, Ontario.
Thomas Kirkpatrick. James Morton.

MAINER, GEORGE GRAHAM. Teacher, York County Board of Education, Ontario.
Hugh Plunkett Bourchier. Plomer Young.

MARSTON, MONICA. Teacher of history, Eastern Quebec Regional School Board, Sillery, Quebec.
George Jehoshaphat Mountain.

MARTINEAU, ANDRÉ. Chef, Section des archives du commerce et des communications, Archives publiques du Canada, Ottawa, Ontario.
Thomas Allen Stayner.

MASSEY, GEORGES. Professeur d'histoire, Université du Québec à Trois-Rivières, Québec.
John McDougall.

MATTHEWS, KEITH. Chairman, Maritime history group, Memorial University of Newfoundland, St John's, Newfoundland.
Thomas Holdsworth Brooking.

MEIKLEHAM, MARGET H. C. Formerly archivist and librarian, Canadian Baptist Archives, McMaster Divinity College, Hamilton, Ontario.
Thomas Ford Caldicott.

METCALF, GEORGE. Associate professor of history, University of Western Ontario, London, Ontario.
Samuel Bealey Harrison.

MILLER, CARMAN. Assistant professor of history, McGill University, Montreal, Quebec.
Joseph Abbott. John Boston. Moses Judah Hayes.

MILLMAN, THOMAS R. Formerly archivist, Anglican Church of Canada, Toronto, Ontario.
Lucius Doolittle. Ernest Hawkins [in collaboration with J. L. H. Henderson]. *Jonathan Shortt.*

MOISSAC, ÉLISABETH DE, S.G.M. Bibliothécaire, Maison provinciale des Sœurs Grises, Saint-Boniface, Manitoba.
Marie-Louise Valade, known as *Mother Valade.*

MONET, JACQUES, S.J. Directeur, Département d'histoire, Université d'Ottawa, Ontario.
Sir Louis-Hippolyte La Fontaine.

MOODY, BARRY M. Assistant professor of history, Acadia University, Wolfville, Nova Scotia.
William Henry Chipman.

MORLEY, WILLIAM F. E. Curator of Special Collections, Douglas Library, Queen's University, Kingston, Ontario.
Andrew Bell.

MORRISON, BRIAN H. Toronto, Ontario.
Robert Easton Burns.

MORTON, WILLIAM LEWIS. Visiting professor of history, University of Manitoba, Winnipeg, Manitoba.
William Agar Adamson. James Bruce. George

910

Gladman. Louis Riel. Philip Michael Matthew Scott VanKoughnet.

MOULTON, EDWARD C. Associate professor of history, University College, University of Manitoba, Winnipeg, Manitoba.
Sir Alexander Bannerman [in collaboration with I. R. Robertson].

MUNTZ, MADELEIN. Teacher of history, Parry Sound High School, Ontario.
William Weller.

MURRAY, FLORENCE BEATRICE. Professor emeritus of library science, University of Toronto, Ontario.
Edward Madan Miles.

NEARY, HILARY BATES. Public services librarian, Fanshawe College, London, Ontario.
Robert Stanton.

†NEATBY, HILDA. Professor of history, Queen's University, Kingston, Ontario.
William Leitch. John Machar.

NEATBY, LESLIE HAMILTON. Formerly professor of classics, University of Saskatchewan, Saskatoon, Saskatchewan.
Edwin Jesse De Haven.

NEIDHARDT, W. S. History instructor, Northview Heights Secondary School, Willowdale, Ontario.
Michael Murphy.

NEWELL, DIANNE. Graduate student in history, University of Western Ontario, London, Ontario.
Thomas Helliwell.

NOPPEN, LUC. Professeur d'histoire de l'art, Université Laval, Québec, Québec.
Vincent Chartrand. André-Raphaël Giroux.

O'DEA, FABIAN. Barrister, St John's, Newfoundland.
Patrick Kough.

O'FARRELL, JOHN K. A. Professor of history, University of Windsor, Ontario.
Henry Edward Dormer.

O'GALLAGHER, MARIANNA, S.C.H. Teacher of history, St Patrick High School, Quebec, Quebec.
John B. Ryan.

OGDEN, R. LYNN. Regional director, Prairie Conservation Centre, National Museums of Canada, Ottawa, Ontario.
George Skeffington Connor.

ORMSBY, MARGARET A. Professor emeritus of history, University of British Columbia, Vancouver, British Columbia.
Chartres Brew. Frederick Seymour.

ORMSBY, WILLIAM G. Professor of history, Brock University, St Catharines, Ontario.
John George Bowes.

OUELLET, FERNAND. Professeur titulaire d'histoire, Université d'Ottawa, Ontario.
Denis-Benjamin Viger [in collaboration with A. Lefort].

PAQUIN, MICHEL. Adjoint au directeur des recherches. *Dictionnaire biographique du Canada/ Dictionary of Canadian Biography*, Les Presses de l'université Laval, Québec, Québec.
Casimir-Amable Testard de Montigny.

PARADIS, JEAN-MARC. Professeur d'histoire, Université du Québec à Trois-Rivières, Québec.
Augustin-Norbert Morin.

PAUTLER, MARY ROSE, C.S.J. Communications coordinator and archivist, St Joseph's Convent, Hamilton, Ontario.
Maria Bunning, named *Sister Mary Martha.*

PEEL, BRUCE BRADEN. Librarian, University of Alberta, Edmonton, Alberta.
Suzanne Connolly. Sophia Thomas (Mason).

PERRON, MARC-ANDRÉ. Réalisateur, Société Radio-Canada, Montréal, Québec.
Frédéric-M.-F. Ossaye.

PETTIT, SYDNEY G. Professor emeritus of history, University of Victoria, British Columbia.
Edward Hammond King.

PHELPS, MARION L. Curator and archivist, Brome County Historical Museum and Archives, Knowlton, Quebec.
Moses French Colby. Paul Holland Knowlton. John Robert Lambly.

PILON, HENRI. Supervisory editor, *Dictionary of Canadian Biography/Dictionnaire biographique du Canada*, University of Toronto Press; archivist, Trinity College, University of Toronto, Ontario.
John Elmsley.

PINCOMBE, C. ALEXANDER. Director, Moncton Museum, Moncton, New Brunswick.
William Botsford. Michael Spurr Harris.

POTHIER, LOUISETTE. Professeur d'histoire, Séminaire de Sherbrooke, Québec.
Joseph-Édouard Turcotte.

POULIOT, LÉON, S.J. Assistant archiviste de la Compagnie de Jésus, Saint-Jérôme, Québec.
Rémi-Joseph Tellier.

PRESTON, RICHARD ARTHUR. W. K. Boyd professor of history, Duke University, Durham, North Carolina, U.S.A.
Sir Charles Ash Windham.

PRICE, BRIAN J. Associate pastor, St John's Church, Perth, Ontario; archdiocesan archivist, Archives of the Archdiocese of Kingston, Ontario.
Patrick Dollard.

PROSS, CATHERINE A. Librarian, Public Archives of Nova Scotia, Halifax, Nova Scotia.
Matthew McClearn. Caleb Seely.

PROVOST, HONORIUS, PTRE. Archiviste, Séminaire de Québec, Québec.
Charles-Joseph Chaussegros de Léry. Louis Gingras.

PRYKE, KENNETH GEORGE. Professor of history, University of Windsor, Ontario.
Stephen Fulton. Thomas Killam. William Murdoch.

RALSTON, H. KEITH. Senior instructor of history, University of British Columbia, Vancouver, British Columbia.
Leonard McClure.

RASPORICH, ANTHONY W. Associate professor of history and head, Department of history, University of Calgary, Alberta.
John Palmer Litchfield [in collaboration with I. H. Clarke]. *John Scott* [with I. H. Clarke].

REA, J. E. Associate professor of history, University of Manitoba, Winnipeg, Manitoba.
Robert Logan. Thomas Scott.

READ, COLIN FREDERICK. Assistant professor of history, Huron College, London, Ontario.
Samuel Chandler. John Wilson.

REANEY, JAMES. Professor of English, University of Western Ontario, London, Ontario.
David Willson.

REINDERS, ROBERT C. Senior lecturer, Department of American studies, University of Nottingham, England.
John Anderson.

RICE, JAMES RICHARD. Lecturer in history, McGill University, Montreal, Quebec.
George King. William Parks [in collaboration with T. W. Acheson].

RICH, EDWIN ERNEST. Emeritus Vere Harmsworth professor of imperial and naval history, University of Cambridge, England.
Joseph Larocque.

RIOUX, JEAN-ROCH. Professeur d'histoire, Séminaire Saint-Augustin, Cap-Rouge, Québec.
Joseph Guibord.

ROBERT, JEAN-CLAUDE. Professeur d'histoire, Université du Québec à Montréal, Québec.
Joshua Bell. Louis Boyer.

ROBERTSON, IAN ROSS. Assistant professor of history, University of Toronto, Ontario.
Sir Alexander Bannerman [in collaboration with E. C. Moulton]. *Thomas Heath Haviland. Sir Henry Vere Huntley. Joseph Harding Webster. Edward Whelan.*

ROLAND, CHARLES G. Associate professor of the history of medicine, Mayo Clinic, Rochester, Minnesota, U.S.A.
James Barry. Gerald O'Reilly.

ROTHNEY, GORDON OLIVER. Professor of Canadian history, University of Manitoba, Winnipeg, Manitoba.
Hollis Smith.

ROUSSEAU, LOUIS. Professeur de sciences religieuses, Université du Québec à Montréal, Québec.
Jean-Baptiste Saint-Germain.

ROY, JEAN-LOUIS. Professeur d'histoire, Centre d'études canadiennes-françaises, McGill University, Montréal, Québec.
Pierre-Édouard Leclère. Louis Perrault.

RUDKIN, DAVID WILLIAM. University archivist, University of Toronto Archives, Ontario.
Henry Boys.

RUSSELL, LORIS S. Curator emeritus, Royal Ontario Museum, Toronto, Ontario; professor emeritus of geology, University of Toronto, Ontario.
Abraham Gesner.

RYAN, SHANNON. Assistant professor of history, Memorial University of Newfoundland, St John's, Newfoundland.
John Dalton.

STE. CROIX, LORNE J. Graduate student of history, University of Toronto, Ontario.
James Moir Ferres. Benjamin Holmes. Charles Richard Ogden.

SAMPSON, WILLIAM R. Assistant professor of history, University of Alberta, Edmonton, Alberta.

Peter Warren Dease. Henry Newsham Peers. John Work.

SAUNDERS, ROBERT E. Superintendent of schools, Lennox and Addington County Board of Education, Napanee, Ontario.
Sir John Beverley Robinson.

SAVARD, PIERRE. Professeur titulaire d'histoire; directeur, Centre de recherche en civilisation canadienne-française, Université d'Ottawa, Ontario.
Pierre-Martial Bardy. Archibald Campbell. François-Xavier Garneau [in collaboration with P. Wyczynski]. *William Sheppard.*

SÉGUIN, NORMAND. Professeur d'histoire, Université du Québec à Chicoutimi, Québec.
Jean-Baptiste Honorat.

SENIOR, ELINOR. Lecturer, Marianopolis College, Montreal, Quebec.
Henry John Boulton [in collaboration with H. Senior]. *Frederick William Ermatinger. George James Hogsett. Kyran Walsh.*

SENIOR, HEREWARD. Professor of history, McGill University, Montreal, Quebec.
George Benjamin. George Strange Boulton. Henry John Boulton [in collaboration with E. Senior].

SIMPSON, DONALD G. Professor of history of education, Althouse College of Education, University of Western Ontario, London, Ontario.
Charles Stuart.

SLATTERY, TIMOTHY PATRICK. Lawyer, Montreal, Quebec.
Patrick James Whelan.

SMITH, DONALD B. Assistant professor of history, University of Calgary, Alberta.
Kahgegagahbowh. Nahnebahwequay (Catherine Sutton). Nawahjegezhegwabe.

SMITH, WALDO EDWARD LOVEL. Formerly professor of church history, Queen's Theological College, Kingston, Ontario.
Philander Smith.

SPRAY, WILLIAM ARTHUR. Associate professor of history, St Thomas University, Fredericton, New Brunswick.
Joseph Cunard. Moses Henry Perley. John Ambrose Street.

SPRY, IRENE M. Professor emeritus of economics, University of Ottawa, Ontario.
William Sinclair.

SPURR, JOHN WHEELOCK. Chief librarian, Royal Military College of Canada, Kingston, Ontario.
Thomas Evans. William Newton Fowell. Sir Charles Stephen Gore. Sir George Augustus Wetherall.

STAGG, RONALD J. Teacher of history, Ryerson Polytechnical Institute, Toronto, Ontario.
Connell James Baldwin. David Gibson. William Lyon Mackenzie [in collaboration with F. H. Armstrong]. *Elmes Yelverton Steele.*

STEVENSON, HUGH A. Associate professor of history and comparative education, Althouse College of Education, University of Western Ontario, London, Ontario.
Thomas Thompson.

STORY, G. M. Professor of English, Memorial Uni-

versity of Newfoundland, St John's, Newfoundland.
William Eppes Cormack.

SUTHERLAND, DAVID ALEXANDER. Assistant professor of history, Dalhousie University, Halifax, Nova Scotia.
William Machin Stairs. Benjamin Wier.

SWAINSON, DONALD. Associate professor of history, Queen's University, Kingston, Ontario.
William Hume Blake. George Crawford. Sir Henry Smith.

SWIFT, MICHAEL. Provincial archivist, Provincial Archives of New Brunswick, Fredericton, New Brunswick.
James Brown.

SYLVAIN, PHILIPPE. Professeur titulaire d'histoire; directeur, Laboratoire d'histoire religieuse, Université Laval, Québec, Québec.
Cyrille Boucher. Louis-Jacques Casault. Charles Daoust. Jean-Baptiste-Éric Dorion.

TALMAN, JAMES JOHN. Professor of history, University of Western Ontario, London, Ontario.
John Baptist Askin. George Coventry. William Hamilton Merritt. Eleazer Williams Stephenson.

THOMAS, CHRISTMAS EDWARD. Research assistant, Public Archives of Nova Scotia, Halifax, Nova Scotia.
Robert Willis.

THOMAS, CLARA MCCANDLESS. Professor of English, York University, Downsview, Ontario.
Samuel Strickland.

THOMAS, LEWIS GWYNNE. Formerly professor of history, University of Alberta, Edmonton, Alberta.
John Edward Harriott.

THOMAS, LEWIS HERBERT. Professor of history, University of Alberta, Edmonton, Alberta.
Eugene Francis O'Beirne.

THOMPSON, ARTHUR NEWEY. Rector, St George's Anglican Church, Winnipeg, Manitoba.
John Smithurst.

THOMPSON, FREDERIC FRASER. Professor and head, Department of history, Royal Military College of Canada, Kingston, Ontario.
Sir Charles Henry Darling.

THOMPSON, JOHN BESWARICK. Formerly historian, National Historic Parks and Sites Branch, Department of Indian Affairs and Northern Development, Ottawa, Ontario.
Charles John Forbes. Robert Unwin Harwood. John Augustus Mathison. Wolfred Nelson.

THORPE, WENDY L. Research assistant, Public Archives of Nova Scotia, Halifax, Nova Scotia.
James Walton Nutting.

TONER, P. M. Saint John, New Brunswick.
Robert Cooney. William Boyd Kinnear. Francis McPhelim.

TRACY, MINERVA. Port Maitland, Nova Scotia.
Andrew Henderson. William Charles McKinnon. William Bennett Webster.

TRATT, GERTRUDE E. N. Teacher, Halifax, Nova Scotia.
William Cunnabell.

TRUDEL, JEAN. Conservateur de l'art canadien ancien, Galerie nationale du Canada, Musées nationaux du Canada, Ottawa, Ontario.
François Sasseville.

TULCHINSKY, GERALD. Associate professor of history, Queen's University, Kingston, Ontario.
William Dow. Adam Ferrie. John Frothingham. Robert Gillespie. Frederick Warren Harris. George Moffatt. John Redpath. William Watson.

TURNER, WESLEY B. Assistant professor of history, Brock University, St Catharines, Ontario.
Alexander Carlisle Buchanan. Anthony Bewden Hawke. William Hutton.

VACHON, CLAUDE. Documentaliste, Fédération des commissions scolaires catholiques du Québec, Sainte-Foy, Québec.
Louis Fiset. Jean-Roch Rolland.

VALLIÈRES, MARC. Professeur d'histoire, Université Laval, Québec, Québec.
Julien Chabot. Henry LeMesurier. Henry John Noad.

VAN KIRK, SYLVIA. Assistant professor of history, University of Toronto, Ontario.
James Hargrave.

VÉZINA, RAYMOND. Chef, Section de peintures, gravures et dessins, Archives publiques du Canada, Ottawa, Ontario.
Théophile Hamel.

VOISINE, NIVE. Directeur des études avancées, Département d'histoire, Université Laval, Québec, Québec.
Louis-Charles Boucher de Niverville. Thomas Cooke. Thomas-Ferruce Picard Destroismaisons. Charles-Hilaire Têtu.

WAITE, PETER B. Professor of history, Dalhousie University, Halifax, Nova Scotia.
Burrows Willcocks Arthur Sleigh. John Sparrow Thompson.

WALLACE, CARL MURRAY. Associate professor of history, Laurentian University, Sudbury, Ontario.
James Hogg. Robert Jardine. John Mercer Johnson [in collaboration with J. A. Fraser]. Ezekiel McLeod.

WALLOT, JEAN-PIERRE. Vice-doyen aux études, Faculté des arts et des sciences, Université de Montréal, Québec.
Edward Bowen. Ross Cuthbert.

WATERSTON, ELIZABETH. Professor and chairman, Department of English, University of Guelph, Ontario.
William Bristow. David Kinnear.

WEALE, DAVID. Lecturer, University of Prince Edward Island, Charlottetown, Prince Edward Island.
Donald McDonald.

WHALEN, JAMES M. Historical research officer, Public Archives of Canada, Ottawa, Ontario.
James Watson Chandler. Calvin Luther Hatheway. John Montgomery.

WHITELEY, WILLIAM HENRY. Associate professor of history, Memorial University of Newfoundland, St John's, Newfoundland.
Edward Chappell.

WHITFIELD, CAROL M. Head, Military History, Research Division, National Historic Parks and Sites

Branch, Parks Canada, Department of Indian Affairs and Northern Development, Ottawa, Ontario.

George Richard John Macdonell. William Scarth Moorsom.

WILBUR, RICHARD. Professor of history, Concordia University, Montreal, Quebec.

John Gregory. Edwin Jacob.

WILSON, ALAN. Professor of history; chairman, Canadian Studies Programme, Trent University, Peterborough, Ontario.

John Colborne. Frederick Widder.

WILSON, J. DONALD. Associate professor of history of education, University of British Columbia, Vancouver, British Columbia.

Thomas Jaffray Robertson.

WINKS, ROBIN W. Professor of history, Yale University, New Haven, Connecticut, U.S.A.

John James Edmonstoune Linton. Samuel Ringgold Ward.

WISE, SYDNEY FRANCIS. Professor of history, Carleton University, Ottawa, Ontario.

Robert Fleming Gourlay.

WOLFENDEN, MADGE. Formerly assistant provincial archivist, Provincial Archives of British Columbia, Victoria, British Columbia.

Horace Douglas Lascelles.

WOOD, JOHN S. Formerly Gooderham professor of French, Victoria College, University of Toronto; translator into English of biographies in French, *Dictionary of Canadian Biography/Dictionnaire biographique du Canada*, University of Toronto Press, Ontario.

WOODWARD, FRANCES M. Reference librarian, Special Collections Division, University of British Columbia, Vancouver, British Columbia.

Mervin Vavasour.

WRIGHT, C. P. Wolfville, Nova Scotia.

Charles Porter.

WYCZYNSKI, PAUL. Titulaire de recherche, Centre de recherche en civilisation canadienne-française, Université d'Ottawa, Ontario.

François-Xavier Garneau [in collaboration with P. Savard].

YOUNG, BRIAN J. Assistant professor of history, McGill University, Montreal, Quebec.

John Anthony Donegani. James Bell Forsyth. George Burns Symes.

YOUNG, D. MURRAY. Professor and chairman, Department of history, University of New Brunswick, Fredericton, New Brunswick.

Sir Howard Douglas.

Index

Included in the index are the names of persons mentioned in volume IX. They are listed by their family names, with titles and first names following. Wives are entered under their maiden names with their married names in parentheses. Persons who appear in incomplete citations in the text are fully identified when possible. An asterisk indicates that the person has received a biography in a volume already published, or will probably receive one in a subsequent volume. A death date or last floruit date refers the reader to the volume in which the biography will be found. Numerals in bold face indicate the pages on which a biography appears. Titles, nicknames, variant spellings, married and religious names are fully cross-referenced.

947